Statistical Record of Native North Americans

Marlita A. Reddy, Editor

Gale Research Inc. • DETROIT • WASHINGTON, D.C. • LONDON

Marlita A. Reddy, *Editor*

Editorial Code and Data, Inc. Staff

Gary Alampi, *Associate Editor*
Arsen J. Darnay, *Senior Editor*
Nancy Ratliff and Sherae R. Fowler, *Data Entry Associates*

Gale Research, Inc. Staff

Carol DeKane Nagel, *Developmental Editor*
Lawrence W. Baker, *Senior Developmental Editor*

Mary Beth Trimper, *Production Director*
Shanna Heilveil, *Production Assistant*
Cynthia Baldwin, *Art Director*
Arthur Chartow, *Technical Design Services Manager*
Bernadette M. Gornie, *Cover Design*

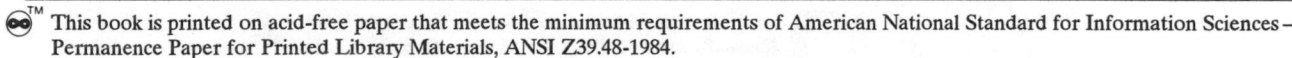
ISBN 0-8103-8963-0
Printed in the United States of America

Published simultaneously in the United Kingdom
by Gale Research International Limited
(An affiliated company of Gale Research Inc.)

I(T)P™

The trademark **ITP** is used under license.

TABLE OF CONTENTS

CHAPTER 1 - HISTORY continued:

CHAPTER 1 - HISTORY continued:

CHAPTER 1 - HISTORY continued:

CHAPTER 2 - DEMOGRAPHICS continued:

CHAPTER 2 - DEMOGRAPHICS continued:

CHAPTER 2 - DEMOGRAPHICS continued:

CHAPTER 4 - EDUCATION continued:

CHAPTER 4 - EDUCATION continued:

CHAPTER 4 - EDUCATION continued:

CHAPTER 6 - HEALTH AND HEALTH CARE continued:

CHAPTER 7 - SOCIAL AND ECONOMIC CONDITIONS continued:

CHAPTER 7 - SOCIAL AND ECONOMIC CONDITIONS continued:

CHAPTER 8 - BUSINESS AND INDUSTRY continued:

CHAPTER 12 - CANADA continued:

CHAPTER 12 - CANADA continued:

CHAPTER 12 - CANADA continued:

CHAPTER 12 - CANADA continued:

INTRODUCTION

Statistical Record of Native North Americans (*SRNNA*) is a compilation of statistical data on the indigenous population of North America. The information compiled in this book exists only scattered among many federal and state agencies, tribal governments, associations, and other organizations. Much of the information is not available in published format. The goal in producing this book is to provide a tool which makes these diverse data accessible to the public while providing full citations of the original sources so that the researcher can do additional work using the sources, if so desired.

Who are the Native North Americans?

There is no widely accepted name for the diversity of peoples who, together, form the indigenous nations of North America. These Native inhabitants have been referred to as "Indians," "Native Americans," "First Peoples," "Aboriginal Peoples," and "Indigenous Peoples." In *SRNNA* we have used the term **Native North Americans**. The term includes the Native populations of the United States (including Alaska) and Canada. Since *SRNNA* reports on statistical data from a wide range of sources, the names used in each source have been left unchanged.

There are also many definitions of the term "American Indian." Government agencies and tribes use different criteria to determine tribal membership. Thus data from different sources are not always directly comparable. The two largest sources of statistical information are the

Bureau of Indian Affairs (BIA) and the Bureau of the Census. The BIA generally regards someone as an Indian if that person is a member of one of the 510 federally recognized tribes and, in order to qualify for certain BIA services, derives from at least one-quarter Indian ancestry. The Census Bureau recognizes a person as Indian if he/she claims to be such on the Census questionnaire.[1]

Sources

Data for *SRNNA* were obtained through an extensive library search and contacts with federal agencies and national organizations and associations. Scores of agencies and organizations were consulted as well as the works of a number of recognized historians.

The source for each table is shown with the table. The source block will in many instances contain citation of a *primary* source — the source used by the author of the table.

A more detailed discussion of sources is presented in the next section, *Guide to Chapters and Contents*.

Scope and Coverage

Statistical Record of Native North Americans includes statistics on:

- Native North Americans as compared with other racial/ethnic groups under many specific subject headings.

- Native North Americans as compared with one another (e.g., by reservation, by tribe, by sex, by age, etc.)

- Individual tribal data under rare circumstances (e.g., historical data on the Yani tribe).

---

1 For one discussion of the political ramifications of Indian identification the reader may refer to Jaimes, M. Annette, "Federal Indian Identification Policy: A Usurpation of Indigenous Sovereignty in North America," in Jaimes, M. Annette (ed.), *The State of Native America: Genocide, Colonization, and Resistance*, Boston: South End Press, 1992.

Historical and Current Data

The period covered in *SRNNA* extends from 20th century estimates of pre-European contact populations to population projections for 2040. Data about the original Native North American population are, by and large, estimates by specialists drawing on early accounts of explorers, traders, artists, adventurers, missionaries, and military people—some of whom had reasons for either minimizing or exaggerating their estimates of population. There is, not surprisingly, neither scholarly nor general agreement about the validity of these early estimates. In fact, the subject is embroiled in controversy. Historical data are nonetheless presented—and in all of their diversity—to make these estimates available alongside the later and more systematically collected data. The first census data came from the 1890 census.

1980 versus 1990 Census

SRNNA presents the most recently published Census data available on Native North Americans. Significant amounts of information from the 1980 Census are presented—despite the fact that the 1990 Census has already been held. The reasons for this are that major portions of the 1990 Census are not yet available—and *will **not** be available for some years to come.* For example, the detailed data on tribes published in *SRNNA*, although **collected** in 1980, was not **published** until 1989.

SRNNA, therefore, presents the most recent data available on specific Native North American **tribes** taken from the 1980 Census. The most recent data on **reservations** and other statistical areas were compiled from the 1990 Census and have been included in this volume.

Indigenous Peoples of Canada

Statistical Record of Native North Americans includes in its coverage tabular data on the First Nations within Canada. These data come from the Canadian Census of 1986 (which are the most recent data available at press time). The data come from Statistics Canada, the Department of Secretary of State, Canada, and the Department of Indian and Northern Development. The data provide information on both on-reserve and off-reserve populations.

Canadian data are presented in a separate chapter and use the chapter headings from the rest of the book as subtopics within the chapter to provide an arrangement format parallel to the book as a whole. This was done because the designations used within the Canadian statistical bureaus do not always directly correspond to those of the U.S. Census Bureau and the BIA and, furthermore, governmental and monetary system differences between the two countries do not allow direct comparison of the data involved. For further background information on Canadian data, please consult the corresponding chapter overview below.

Arrangement of the Data

SRNNA is organized by chapter and topic. There are twelve chapters on broad topics such as History, Demographics, and The Family. Within these chapters, data are organized by topics. In the chapter on Demographics, for instance, topics are Population, Tribal Enrollment, Population Trends, Geographic Mobility, and Housing and Household Characteristics. These topics are arranged in order from broad to narrow coverage of data.

Tables under each topic are arranged in order of the scope of coverage. Data that compare Native Peoples to other groups come first. Next are tables comparing Native Peoples to each other. Finally, data on individual tribes or reservations (where available) are presented.

Canadian data are shown in a separate chapter, as explained above. Historical data are presented within a separate chapter when the data are chronologically historical in nature — that is to say, if the data presented cover the years 1910 or 1930 but do not include current data, the information has been placed in the Treaties/History chapter. If, however, the data are anthropological/historical in nature but make a comparison to available current data (e.g., *Huron Indian Population, Early 1600's to 1980*), they will be found in the appropriate chapter under the appropriate topic (in this case, *Demographics* and *Population Trends*).

Keyword Index

SRNNA has a single *Keyword Index* which refers to subjects, concepts, institutions and organizations. More than 3,000 terms will be found in the index.

Acknowledgements

The editors would like to express their thanks to Mr. George Russell of Thunderbird Enterprises and Professors Gordon Henry of the Department of Languages and Literature and Patrick LeBeau of the Department of History at Ferris State University. All three consented to serve the editorial staff in an advisory capacity and spent liberally of their time and attention. While their ideas and suggestions have been invaluable — and thus they have a large share in the merits of this book — they are in no way responsible for any shortcomings of *SRNNA*.

The editors would like to express thanks to the many individuals in the federal government, associations, and publishers who helped in the creation of *SRNNA* by providing reports, data, references, and permissions, especially Americans for Indian Opportunity, the National Indian Gaming Association, and the Senate Subcommittee on Indian Affairs.

Management of research was ably carried out by Gary Alampi, Editorial Code & Data, Inc. Nancy Ratliff and Sherae Fowler struggled valiantly with the mass and complexity of the data presented in the book in rendering many different kinds of materials into machine-readable format. Carol Nagel, coordinating editor for Gale Research, deserves a note of appreciation for her encouragement and ready help throughout the compilation and refinement of this material.

Comments and Suggestions

The editors welcome comments and suggestions for improving *SRNNA* in its future editions. Please write to:

> The Editors
>
> *Statistical Record of Native North Americans*
>
> Gale Research Inc.
>
> 835 Penobscot Building
>
> Detroit, MI 48226-4094

GUIDE TO CHAPTERS AND CONTENTS

This section presents a discussion of *SRNNA*'s twelve chapters. The intention is to provide some comment on the main sources consulted, to highlight issues and controversies that surround the data presented, and to provide a brief summary of the more important contents of each chapter. After the chapter summaries, a section entitled *References* provides a listing of additional sources. The listing is not — and is not intended to be — exhaustive.

Chapter 1 - History

The information presented in this chapter has been included because of reader interest in the subject. The data are from a variety of sources, including the U.S. Census Bureau, the Bureau of Indian Affairs, and various scholars in the fields of history and anthropology.

The data estimates presented range from pre-Columbian contact to the Census of 1963. As explained in the *Introduction*, if estimates were juxtaposed with comparable current data, the tables were placed in chapters according to subject matter. Any information referring to years prior to 1980, which was the most current *complete* Census release, are found in this chapter.

Some consider historical data questionable and objectionable, especially (but not exclusively) data collected before 1890; 1890 data are considered to be the first complete data on

American Indians compiled by the federal government. The question of population counts are a prime example of this controversy, as illustrated in the table entitled "20th Century Estimates of the Population of Aboriginal North America Before 1492." Such estimates range from as few as 900,000 persons to as many as 12,250,000. Even an estimate of 2,000,000 would indicate a population decline and a loss of some 6.1 million indigenous persons (about 81% of the indigenous population) by the 1890 Census. This population decline has been attributed by various scholars to genocide through the introduction of diseases, alcohol, and firearms — as well as intentional violence in the westward expansion of the European settlers.[1]

By including the historical data, the editors in no way mean to imply that they are either accurate or inaccurate. The intention is to provide a sampling of information for reader reference and resources for following up such data by way of full citations below each table. Further suggestions for historical background are also presented below.

The terminology and designations of tribes by different sources throughout this chapter have been reproduced with their original spellings. Names of tribes and languages may vary in appearance, depending on the time of data compilation and the source of the information.

Chapter 2 - Demographics

Data for this chapter were drawn from the most recent 1990 Census of Population (not fully released by the government), the 1980 Census (of which some portions dealing with Native Americans became available as late as 1989), and historical data not shown in the chapter *History*.

Population Trends

This section contains population estimates of the indigenous peoples of the United States from pre-European contact until 1980. While there is historical/anthropological content in

---

1   For two discussions of such a viewpoint, the reader is referred to Stiffarm, Lenore A. and Lane, Phil Jr., "The Demography of North America: A Question of American Indian Survival," in Jaimes, M. Annette (ed.), *The State of Native America: Genocide, Colonization, and Resistance*, Boston: South End Press, 1992; and Thornton, Russell, *American Indian Holocaust and Survival: A Population History Since 1492*, Norman, OK: University of Oklahoma Press, 1987.

the data, these particular tables show a trend toward the 1980 Census (which is the most recent completely released data), and were therefore included in the Demographics chapter.

Even in the most current U.S. Censuses, there has been some question about the accuracy of minority data and the validity of representation of these groups in the population.[2] Even more controversy surrounds the period before 1890. Since the turn of the 20th century, estimates of the pre-1492 North American indigenous population have varied from 1.2 million to 18.0 million. The higher the estimate taken as the base, the more likely the contention that European arrivals engaged in involuntary or intentional genocide.[3]

SRNNA presents but does not interpret these data. Rather, the editors have tried to present a sampling of relevant materials in this chapter as well as in the chapter titled *History*. *History* shows data that are not directly juxtaposed with current data.

Population

This section contains current population data on the indigenous population (including American Indians, Eskimos, and Aleuts) from the 1990 Census. Because the 1990 Census has yet to be released in its complete form, data from the 1980 Census were used as well—especially for data by tribe, first released in 1989. Please note that the designation "Indian" by the Census Bureau is entirely dependent on the individual responses of U.S. residents and does not necessarily ensure recognition by the tribe.

Population by Area. The Census Bureau estimates that in 1990 there were 1.959 million Native persons living in the United States, including 57,000 Eskimos and 24,000 Aleuts, representing about 1% of the total U.S. population. This represents an increase of about 600,000 for the group since 1980. The majority of the population resided in the West (47%) and in the South (28%). The most populous states were Oklahoma, California, and Arizona, which were the only states to exceed a population of 200,000. Among the largest 70 major U.S. metropolitan areas, the densest Native population were in Tulsa (6.8%), Tucson (3.0), Phoenix (1.8), Bakersfield (1.3), Fresno (1.1), and Sacramento (1.1). The remaining 65 metro areas had less than 1% Native populations. The section also provides data for Alaska Native Regional

2   Stiffarm, *op. cit.*

3   Thornton, *op. cit.*

Corporations; these are are corporate entities organized to conduct business for profit and, as such, have legally established boundaries.

Population by Tribe. The largest tribes responding to the census were Cherokee, Navajo, Chippewa, and Sioux; these were the only tribes whose populations exceeded 100,000. Detailed population estimates for all tribes responding to the 1980 Census, by age, by state, and by U.S. Census region are presented in this section. Again, please keep in mind that these data were compiled from the responses of individuals who identified themselves as American Indians or Native Alaskans on their census forms. Tribal enrollment status data can be found under the subtopic *Population on Reservations*.

Population on Reservations. This section contains population data from the 1990 Census for reservations across the United States. There were 807,817 persons living in American Indian and Alaska Native Areas. About 54% of these persons were Native North Americans, constituting about 22% of the Native population. Data are presented by age, sex, and tribal enrollment status of persons residing on reservations.

Chapter 3 - The Family

About 71% of the 300,000 American Indian and Native Alaskan families in the United States were married couples; the comparable figure for the total population was 82%. Twenty-three percent of families were headed by a female householder with no husband present (14% for the general population). Detailed family characteristics are presented in this chapter by major tribal group.

Native families in reservation states tended to be larger than those of the general population, with an average of 4.6 persons per family for American Indians and Alaska Natives versus 3.8 persons for the average family in the United States (all races).

Family income tended to be lower than that of the general population. Median income for Native families was $13,700 versus $19,900 for all races. Average income for Native families was $16,500 versus $23,100. (These figures differ from those provided in the chapter *Social and Economic Conditions* because they measure only Native persons in 33 reservation states, rather than the entire Census population. The trends, however, remain the same.)

A study of nearly 14,000 Native American adolescents in 50 tribes showed that family size affected the emotional welfare of teens; teens worried about parental abuse, domestic violence, and poverty.[4] Statistics on the impact of social, economic, and health conditions on Native American children and adolescents are presented in this chapter. Additional data can be found in the chapters entitled *Education* and *Health and Health Care*.

Chapter 4 - Education

The most recent detailed data on education of the Native population of the United States come from the 1980 Census. According to this information, 56% of American Indians and Alaska Natives have completed high school; in the United States as a whole, the result was 67%. About 8% of Native persons have completed four or more years of college (16% of all U.S. residents). Completion rates by tribe and by reservation are presented in detail for 1980 (the most current available data) in the *Educational Progress* section.

Schools

Elementary Schools. Of the 69,903 children enrolled in elementary schools on reservations in 1980 (most recently extrapolated data), the majority (61%) went to public schools. About 22% attended BIA schools (including both day and boarding institutions), 5% attended private schools, and 3.5% went to tribal schools. About 9% of those enrolled did not report type of school.

High Schools. 29,597 persons were enrolled in high schools on reservations in 1980. The majority (66%) attended public schools, 16.5% went to BIA schools (day and boarding schools), about 4% to private schools, and 4.5% to tribal high schools; 9.5% of those enrolled in high schools did not report type of school. Among persons between the ages of 16 and 19 on reservations, the dropout rate was about 27%.

---

4   Indian Health Service, Maternal and Child Health Service, Robert Wood Johnson Foundation, *The State of Native American Youth*, February, 1992.

Higher Education

According to the National Advisory Council on Indian Education, there were an estimated 97,657 American Indian and Alaska Native students enrolled in higher education institutions in 1990. This represented less than 1% of the total student population. Of these Native students, about 55% were in 2-year colleges. There has been an overall increase in higher education enrollment by Native students since 1980, when there were 84,000 enrollees. Of undergraduate degrees awarded, the greatest number were in Business and Management (24% of associate's degrees and 20% of bachelor's degrees in the 1988-89 academic year).

American Indians and Native Alaskans constituted only 0.4% of the 309,000 master's degrees conferred in the 1988-89 academic year, with the greatest number being in Education (34%). Eighty-four Native students received doctorates in the same year, which represented 0.2% of all doctoral degrees. This also represented a decline since the 1980-81 academic year, when there were 130 doctorates awarded to Native students (0.4% of all doctorates). The majority of masters and doctors degrees were in education (42%).

As of 1987, American Indians and Alaska Natives made up about 1% of faculty in higher education institutions. This figure did not vary greatly across academic disciplines or by type of institution, except in the case of 2-year colleges; these had approximately 2% Native faculty.

Educational Progress

Figures from the U.S. Department of Education show that, as of 1986, American Indian and Alaska Native students had the lowest high school completion rates among all race/ethnicities. Detailed statistics on completion rates for 1980 are presented in this section.

For Native high school students taking the Scholastic Aptitude Test (SAT) in 1992, the average score was 837, the second highest among all minority groups (the highest average was 945 for Asian Americans). Native students also showed the second highest 5-year improvement (up 12% since 1987) among all races and ethnicities. This section presents achievement scores and trends for a variety of disciplines, as well as statistics on risks to minority students' educational progress. For additional data on these risk factors, the reader should consult the section in this chapter entitled *School Environment* and the chapter entitled *The Family*.

Chapter 5 - Culture

While cultural issues are not generally quantifiable, this chapter has been included to present statistical information on the areas of language and employment in traditional occupations.

Language

Of an estimated 413,614 children between the ages of 5 and 7 surveyed by the Census Bureau in 1980, about 77% spoke only English at home. Of the reminder, 83% spoke some American Indian or Native Alaskan language at home.

Of the estimated 915,707 persons surveyed who were 18 years or older, about 73% spoke only English at home, with 77% of the remaining persons speaking an American Indian or Alaska Native language at home. Detailed information is presented, by major tribal groups in the United States and for selected areas of Oklahoma.

Traditional Occupations

Of an estimated 4,120 employed in traditional occupations on reservations across the United States, the largest number were employed in handworking occupations (33%). The next most reported occupations were in jewelry-related occupations and positions in tribal government. Detailed information is presented in this chapter, by major tribal groups in the United States and for selected areas of Oklahoma.

Chapter 6 - Health and Health Care

It is the administrative responsibility of the Department of Health and Human Services to provide federal health services to American Indians and Alaska Natives. Since 1954, pursuant to passage of a public law (P.L. 83-568), it has provided these services through the Indian Health Service (IHS), which is part of Public Health Service.

Births

The birth rate for Native peoples has exceeded that of the general U.S. population and has exceeded the birth rate of all other minorities since at least 1955. In 1987 (the most recent year available), the birth rate for all Indians and Alaska Natives was 28.0 per 1,000 persons (27.5 per 1,000 for Indians and 36.0 for Alaska Natives), as compared to 15.6 per 1,000 for all races and 21.4 for all minorities.

Native births were shown to be less likely to be low weight (6.2% of all Native births versus 6.9% of all births) and more likely to be preterm (11.7% of all Native births versus 10.2% of all births).

Native mothers tended to give birth at an earlier age than the total U.S. population, with 42% of Native mothers giving birth below age 20 (for all U.S., the percentage of mothers under age 20 was 23%).

In spite of the fact that, as with the general population, the Native maternal death rate decreased overall since 1958, as late as 1986 the maternal mortality rate exceeded that of the White population by as much as 50%.[5]

Deaths

Life expectancy of both sexes among the indigenous population has increased from 51.0 years in 1940 to 71.1 years in 1980, which is still lower than that of the U.S. White population. Whites had a life expectancy of 74.4 years. In 1988 the overall age-adjusted mortality rate for American Indians and Alaska Natives was 574.3 per 100,00 persons. This was greater than the U.S. figure of 535.5 per 100,000 persons. The rate difference was most pronounced in infancy and between the ages of 25 and 44. Overall, Native persons were much more likely than the general population to die from accidents (both motor vehicle-related and other), chronic liver disease and cirrhosis, diabetes, pneumonia or influenza, suicide or homicide, and tuberculosis. They were less likely to die from cardiovascular disease (any type), tumors, and chronic obstructive lung diseases. In 1987 the infant mortality rate for Native peoples was shown to be just slightly lower than that of the U.S. population (9.7 per 1,000 versus 10.1 per 1,000 for all of the United States.). Please note, however, that some studies have shown undercounting of American Indians and Alaska Natives by as much as 26% in these statistics.[6]

---

5   U.S. Department of Health and Human Services, *Health Status of Minorities and Low-Income Groups: Third Edition*, p. 87.

6   *Ibid*, p. 89

Health Concerns

Despite the fact that among the IHS population health problems have decreased anywhere from 56% to 91% since 1955, numerous health concerns remain. The leading causes of hospitalization in 1989 were births and delivery complications, injuries and poisonings, and digestive system disorders. Leading causes for outpatient care were upper respiratory infections and colds, ear infections, and diabetes. Substance abuse, especially alcohol abuse, is a major health concern for Native Americans; and while alcohol-related mortality declined steadily from the early 1970s to 1985, it rose from 24.6 deaths per 100,000 in 1986 to 33.9 in 1988. This most recent rate compares to a rate of only 6.2 per 100,000 for all races. Contacts for treatment at IHS facilities were twice as likely to be male than female and tended to be in the 15 to 24 age range.

Chapter 7 - Social and Economic Conditions

Employment

Of the 580,000 American Indians and Alaska Natives participating in the U.S. civilian labor force in 1980, 13% were unemployed. Of all tribes reporting having unemployment, the Kalispel tribe showed the highest unemployment rate (44.6%); the Chickahominy reported the lowest rate (1.6%). The Hitchiti, Long Island, and Rappahannock tribes reported no unemployment, but together these tribes represented less than 0.1% of the American Indian labor force. The unemployment rate on the largest reservations, which is more recent and perhaps more indicative of the state of the labor force, shows that the unemployment rate varies from 13.8% for the Zuni Pueblo to 35.3% for Fort Apache.

Of an estimated 493,000 Native persons age 16 and older who were employed as of the 1980 Census, the largest percentage worked in the service industries (about 20%). The smallest percentage worked in finance, insurance, and real estate (slightly more than 3% of all employed Native persons). Detailed data are presented for all U.S. industries by reservation and by major tribal group.

Income and Poverty

The median annual income for American Indians and Alaska Natives dropped from $20,541 in 1980 (adjusted for inflation) to $20,025 in 1990. It was the only decrease in income among all race/ethnicities. The percentage of Native persons living below the poverty line increased from 27.5% in 1980 to 30.9% in 1990; for children the percentage went from 32.5% to 37.6%.

Housing Characteristics

In 1980, there were about 81,000 housing units on reservations. Of these, nearly one-quarter lacked complete plumbing facilities, with about 20% having no indoor toilet. More than 50% had no telephone and 16% had no electric lighting. Detailed information is presented on these, as well as other housing characteristics, for reservations and for selected areas of Oklahoma. Additional information on sanitation can also be found in the *Environment* section of the chapter entitled *Land and Water Management*.

Chapter 8 - Business and Industry

The data in this section come from the U.S. Department of Commerce, the Department of Energy, the Department of the Interior Minerals Management Service, the U.S. Senate Subcommittee on Indian Affairs, and the National Indian Gaming Association.

Minority-Owned and Native-Owned Firms

In 1987 there were more than 1.2 million minority-owned firms in the United States. These firms constituted 8.9% of all U.S. firms and 3.9% of all sales and receipts for U.S. firms. Native-owned firms represented 1.8% of minority firms and 1.2% of those sales and receipts. With average sales and receipts of $43,000, Native American and Alaska Native-owned firms were below average as compared to all minority firms ($64,000) and well below average for all U.S. firms ($145,000). Businesses owned by Native women had the lowest average receipts per firm in the United States ($32,000).

In terms of growth, Native-owned businesses have shown a 57% increase in number of firms since 1982 (64% for all minority firms) and an 84% increase in receipts (126% for all minority firms).

Like all firms in the United States, the largest concentration of minority firms is in the service industries and the largest concentration of sales and receipts is in the retail industry. Native-owned firms follow the same pattern. But while the largest *minority* share of U.S. firms was in the transportation and utilities industries, the largest Native owned share was in agriculture, fishing, and forestry; the Native North American companies, however, were only 1% of this sector's total firms and only 0.5% of the sector's sales and receipts.

Overall, minority-owned firms tend to be concentrated in a few States; California, Texas, New York, and Florida are home to more than one-half of all minority firms in the United States and account for about 59% of minority firm receipts. Similarly, more than one-half of Native-owned firms are located in four States—Alaska, California, Oklahoma, and North Carolina—which account for about 46% of Native firm receipts.

Like most minority-owned businesses, Native-owned firms tend to be proprietorships rather than partnerships or corporations. Among minority firms, Native-owned firms are the least likely to incorporate—2% of all Native-owned firms are corporations as compared with 3% for all minority-owned firms and 7% for all U.S. firms.

Minerals Leasing

While Native-owned firms constitute less than 0.1% of the mining industry in number of firms and receipts, Indian land holds significant resources, including oil, gas, and coal as well other minerals such as phosphate, quartz crystal, sand and gravel, potash, and sodium.

Actual and potential oil- and gas-producing Native American lands in 1990 measured more than 1.6 million acres—8% of all federal and Indian on-shore production-capable lands. Coal-bearing land measured more than 115,000 acres in 1990, which made up more than 30% of all federal and Indian coal-leased land.

SRNNA provides revenue data for these minerals leases; please note, however, that these revenues are part of an estimated $2.0 billion held in trust by the Bureau of Indian Affairs in Tribal and Individual Indian Money (IIM) accounts. The accounting of these trust funds has been under investigation over the past six years by The Environment, Energy, and Natural Resources House Subcommittee of the Congress. For an explanation of the process of lease revenue management please consult, "Indians are sold out by the U.S.; honor system license to loot; U.S. fails to protect oil on Indian, federal lands," in *The Arizona Republic*, October 4, 1987. For further discussion of the investigation, consult *Misplaced Trust: The Bureau of Indian Affairs' Mismanagement of the Indian Trust Fund*, Subcommittee on Environment, Energy, and Natural Resources, March 18, 1992.

Tribal Casinos and Gaming

Since the passage of the Indian Gaming Regulatory Act by Congress in 1988, revenues from tribal gaming have reached $5.0 billion annually.[7] There has been a great deal of controversy over this industry; some state governments are opposed to provisions of the federal statute in order to protect the gaming industry because gaming is opposed in the state and for other reasons.

The data in this section come from the Senate Subcommittee on Indian Affairs, *USA TODAY*, and the National Indian Gaming Association (NIGA). NIGA is an organization founded "to protect and preserve the general welfare of tribes striving for self-sufficiency through gaming enterprises in Indian country." It distributes a packet of information which provides background about issues surrounding the development of Indian gaming in the United States and is cited below under *References*.

Chapter 9 - Land and Water Management

Certain subjects do not lend themselves well to quantification, and a number of issues in the forefront of the Native community are cultural in nature. An example of such an issue is religious freedom, which is the basis of a great many land claim suits brought to court by members of the indigenous population. While the editors are aware that this is an issue of great consequence, both politically and culturally, statistical data are not readily available in this context. For discussions of the issue of religious freedom, please see *References* below.

Information in this chapter includes quantitative data on land ownership, land use, BIA jurisdiction of lands, and condition of the environment on reservation lands. For additional information on minerals leasing, see the chapter entitled *Business and Industry*. Data on water rights were not available in time for publication, but suggestions for obtaining such information are provided below.

---

7   Holstrom, David, "Indian Gaming Booms Nationwide," *The Christian Science Monitor*, November 10, 1992.

Land Ownership

This section provides data on land ownership and BIA jurisdiction and record management for these land tracts. The Department of the Interior, through the BIA, is responsible for "maintaining land ownership records and title documents, negotiating and awarding leases and permits for use of the land, and distributing to the Indian land owners the income generated by leases and permits."[8] In a study of 12 reservations, the General Accounting Office found that more than 50% of the 83,000 land tracts were owned in their entirety by either the tribe or an Indian individual. Twenty percent of these tracts, however, had at least one ownership interest of less than 2%. These small ownership interests constituted about 60% of the 1.1 million ownership records that the BIA is required to maintain. Detailed information in presented by reservation, by ownership type, and by land type. Additional information on ownership can be found in the section entitled *Land Use*.

Land Use

As of 1989, a total of 54,246,537 acres of land were under BIA jurisdiction. Land designated for Indian use constituted 5,568,008 acres of this land. The largest portion of Indian-use land was designated for forest grazing (9,469,490 acres); the smallest portion was designated for commercial forestlands (8,803 acres). Detailed information is presented in this section, by state, and by type of land use.

Environmental Issues

This section presents most recent data available (1986) on the environmental conditions of selected reservations in the United States. Major environmental problems reported by tribes include water quality, solid waste management and disposal, hazardous waste and disposal, and sewage treatment. Information on these topics is provided for selected states and for selected tribes and reservations.

---

8   U.S. General Accounting Office, *Land Ownership at Indian Reservations*, GAO/RCED- 92-96BR.

Chapter 10 - Government Relations

While tabular data on tribal government systems were not available at time of publication, the reader is advised to contact Americans for Indian Opportunity (address given below), which distributes a number of publications that provide background on this subject. Other suggestions for further information are also provided.

Federal Assistance Programs

This section provides budgets and expenditures for assistance programs available to Native Americans in the United States. Data are shown for fiscal years 1987 through 1989 and are arranged by federal department. Related information can also be found in the chapters entitled *Education* and *Social and Economic Conditions*.

Government Representation

This section provides statistics on Native American representation in the United States government at the federal, state, and local levels. "Local government" in this context does not refer to indigenous self-government but to employment in or appointment to U.S. city or county positions.

In 1990 there were 28,728 American Indians and Alaska Natives employed as full-time state and local government employees. This represented 0.5% of all employees in that year. The median income was $22,507 per year, as compared to $24,499 for all employees of the same category. This section provides detailed data, by type of occupation and for part-time as well as full-time employees.

Chapter 11 - Law and Law Enforcement

At the time of this writing, the BIA did not have compiled statistics available on law enforcement on reservation lands. Major compilations of statistical data for the United States, published by the Department of Justice, did not report Native Americans as a separate group except in the cases that have been included in this chapter. This does not necessarily mean that such statistics do not exist at all, only that we were unable to locate such data before publication. Other references to available information are listed below under *References*.

Statistics presented in this section provide tabular data on arrest rates, crime rates, and law enforcement representation.

In 1989, for all ages, the proportion of arrests that were American Indians and Alaska Natives was 1% or less of all persons arrested. These figures do not change drastically when considering the populations above and below the age of 18. Variation occurs when measuring arrests in urban versus rural areas, with Native representation being twice as high in rural areas (2.2% versus 1.0%).

The limited law enforcement data the editors were able to locate show low representation of Native Americans in this field. Because tables that only reported Native Americans as part of the category "Other" were not included in *SRNNA*, available information is so scant that it is impossible to draw any conclusions about the field as a whole from the data presented.

Chapter 12 - Canada

Data in this chapter are from the 1986 Canadian Census (the most recent) and from the Department of Indian and Northern Development (DIAND). Please note, however, that 139 reserves, with a population of about 45,000, were incompletely enumerated in the 1986 census. This represented approximately 6% of the total population claiming indigenous origin. In the discussion that follows, references to dollars are to Canadian dollars.

Indigenous peoples of Canada are generally designated by Statistics Canada as belonging to three classifications. These are Indians, Inuits, and Métis. Within the designation **Indian**, there are three classifications: Status Indians – those registered as Indians with the federal government in the *Indian Act*; non-Status Indians – those affiliated with an Indian band ancestrally or culturally but not registered with the Canadian federal government as such; and Treaty Indians – those who can prove descent from a band having a treaty with the federal government (these persons may also be Status Indians). Persons classified as **Inuits** are those persons descended from Native inhabitants of the northernmost provinces in Canada. Persons classified as **Métis** are persons of mixed Indian and European descent, through lineage from earlier Métis persons, self-proclaimed as Métis, and/or accepted as such by the Métis community.

Population

According to Statistics Canada, there are 598 Indian bands on 2,284 reserves and Crown lands. A total of 711,725 persons designated themselves as having Aboriginal origin. This included 263,245 registered Indians and 33,460 Inuits; the remainder were either non-Status Indians or Métis. Together, the group represented about 3% of the total Canadian population. Most of the Native population (about 86%) resides in the provinces west of Quebec. The largest Native population was in Ontario (167,375), followed by British Columbia (126,625) and Alberta (103,930) respectively. The most concentrated Native populations resided in the Northwest Territories (58.7% of the total population), the Yukon Territory (21.4%), and Manitoba (8.1%). Slightly more than 60% of the registered Indian population resides on reserves, the largest percentage in Quebec (81.5%) and the smallest in the Yukon Territory (45.0%).

Families of registered Indians in Canada tend, on the whole, to be larger than those of the general population. The average number of persons per family for on-reserve populations was 4.2, for off-reserve families, 3.4, and for families near reserves, 3.3. The national average was 3.1 persons per family. The largest average family size was 4.3 persons for all registered Indians in the Northwest Territories and 3.8 for all Census families in the same area.

Education

Native persons living on reserves are far more likely than the general population to have less than a 9th grade education. In 1986, 44.7% of the on-reserve population age 15 years and older had less than a 9th grade education; the value for all other Canadians was 17.1%. About 22% of the reserve population had completed at least high school (compared with 56% of all other Canadians). Please note that 139 reserves were not included in the Census and this could affect results of such a survey in either direction depending on the academic achievement of the 45,000 indigenous persons left uncounted.

Employment

Slightly more than 30% of the enumerated registered Indian population over the age of 15 was employed in 1986. This compares with a figure of 60% employed for the rest of the Canadian population. The population residing near reserves had an employment figure closer to the general population (52%). The figures do not imply that the remainder of any of these groups is to be automatically considered unemployed; they may be employed but are not

Jaimes, M. Annette (ed.). *The State of Native America: Genocide, Colonization, and Resistance*, Boston: South End Press, 1992.

National Center for American Indian Enterprise Development, 953 E. Juanita Ave., Mesa, AZ 85204.

Northwest Indian Fisheries Commission, *Annual Report FY1988*.

O'Brien, Sharon. *American Indian Tribal Governments*, Norman: University of Oklahoma, 1990.

Prucha, Francis Paul. *Documents of United States Indian Policy*, Lincoln: University of Nebraska Press, 1990.

Prucha, Francis Paul. *Indian-White Relations in the United States: A Bibliography of Works Published 1975-1980*, Lincoln: University of Nebraska Press, 1982.

Ruoff, A. LaVonne. "History in *Winter in the Blood*: Background and Bibliography," *American Indian Quarterly* 4 (No. 2, 1978): 169-172.

Ruoff, A. LaVonne. *American Indian Literature: An Introduction, Bibliographic Review and Selected Bibliography*, Modern Lang., 1990.

Russell, George. *The American Indian Digest Handbook*, Phoenix: Thunderbird Enterprises, 1993.

Statistics Canada. *1991 Catalogue of Products and Services*, Ottawa: Minister of Supply and Services, 1992. [Available from Publications Sales and Services, Statistics Canada, Ottawa, ON K1A OT6]

Thornton, Russell. *American Holocaust and Survival: A Population History Since 1492*, Norman, OK: University of Oklahoma Press, 1987.

U.S. Department of the Interior, Bureau of Indian Affairs. *American Indians Today: Answers to Your Questions: Third Edition*, Washington, D.C., 1991.

U.S. Department of the Interior, Bureau of Indian Affairs. *Federal Register of Recognized Tribes*, Washington, D.C., 1991.

U.S. Department of the Interior, Bureau of Indian Affairs, *Indian Land Areas - 1989* (map), Washington, D.C., 1989.

U.S. Department of the Interior, Bureau of Indian Affairs, Branch of Acknowledgement and Research. *List of Tribal Petitioners by State*, Washington, D.C., 1991.

U.S. Department of the Interior, Bureau of Indian Affairs, Division of Tribal Government Services, Office of Public Information. *Tribal Leaders List*, Washington, D.C., 1991.

U.S. Department of Labor, Bureau of Labor Statistics. *Indian Labor Force*. Washington, D.C., 1991.

Vecsey, Christopher (ed.). *Handbook of American Indian Religious Freedom*, New York: The Crossroad Publishing Co., 1991.

Chapter 1
HISTORY

Population

★ 1 ★

20th Century Estimates of the Population of Aboriginal North America Before 1492

Numbers are shown in thousands.

Scholar (date)	North America (000)	Conterminous United States (000)
Mooney (1910)	1,148	846
Rivet (1924)	1,148	-
Sapper (1924)	2,000-3,500	-
Mooney (1928)	1,153	849
Wilcox (1931)	1,002	-
Kroeber (1939)	900	720
Rosenblat (1945)	1,000	-
Steward (1945)	1,000	-
Ashburn (1947)	2,000-2,500	-
Steward (1949)	1,001	-
Aschmann (1959)	2,240	-
Driver (1961)	1,000-2,000	-
Dobyns (1966)	9,800-12,250	-
Driver (1969)	3,500	2,500
Ubelaker (1976)	2,171	-
Denevan (1976)	4,400	-
Thornton and Marsh-Thornton (1981)	-	1,845
Dobyns(1983)	18,000[1]	-

Source: Russell Thornton, *American Indian Holocaust and Survival: A Population History Since 1492,* University of Oklahoma Press, 1987, p. 26. Published by permission. *Notes:* A dash (-) indicates no data was given. 1. North of Mesoamerica.

★ 2 ★

20th Century Estimates of Western Hemisphere Total Aboriginal Population Before 1492

Numbers are shown in thousands.

Scholar/date	Estimate (000)
Rivet (1924)	40,000-50,000
Sapper (1924)	40,000-50,000
Spinden (1928)	50,000-75,000[1]
Wilcox (1931)	13,101
Kroeber (1939)	8,400
Rosenblat (1945)	13,385
Steward (1945)	13,170
Sapper (1948)	31,000
Steward (1949)	15,491
Rivet (1952)	15,500
Borah (1964)	100,000
Dobyns (1966)	90,043-112,554
Morner (1967)	33,300
Driver (1969)	30,000
Denevan (1976)	57,300 (43,000-72,000)

Source: Russell Thornton, *American Indian Holocaust and Survival: A Population History Since 1492*, University of Oklahoma Press, 1987, p. 23. Published by permission. *Note:* 1. Circa A.D. 1200.

★ 3 ★

Denevan's Population Estimates for the Western Hemisphere in 1492

Numbers are shown in thousands.

Area	Population (000)
North America	4,400
Mexico	21,400
Central America	5,650
Caribbean	5,850
Andes	11,500
Lowland South America	8,500
Western Hemisphere	57,300

Source: Russell Thornton, *American Indian Holocaust and Survival: A Population History Since 1492*, University of Oklahoma Press, 1987, p. 25. Published by permission. Primary source: Denevan, "Epilogue," pp. 289-292 in William M. Denevan, ed., *The Native Population of the Americas in 1492*. Madison: University of Wisconsin Press, 1976, p. 291.

★4★

Dobyns's Population Estimates for the Western Hemisphere in 1492

Numbers are shown in thousands.

Area	Population (000)
North America	9,800-12,250
Mexican Civilization	30,000-37,500
Central America	10,800-13,500
Caribbean Islands	443-554
Andean Civilization	30,000-37,500
Marginal South America	9,000-11,250
Western Hemisphere	90,043-112,554

Source: Russell Thornton, *American Indian Holocaust and Survival: A Population History Since 1492*, University of Oklahoma Press, 1987, p. 24. Published by permission. Primary source: Dobyns, "Estimating Aboriginal American Population: An Appraisal of Techniques with a New Hemisphere Estimate," *Current Anthropology*, 1966, p. 415.

★5★

Kroeber's American Indian Population Estimates for the Western Hemisphere in 1500

Numbers are shown in thousands.

Area	Population (000)
North of the Rio Grande River	900
Northwest Mexico	100
Northeast Mexico	100
Central and Southern Mexico, Guatemala, El Salvador	3,000
Honduras, Nicaragua	100
Native North America	4,200
Inca Empire	3,000
Rest of South America	1,000
West Indies	200
Native South America	4,200
Western hemisphere	8,400

Source: Russell Thornton, *American Indian Holocaust and Survival: A Population History Since 1492*, University of Oklahoma Press, 1987, p. 24. Published by permission. Primary source: Kroeber, "Cultural and Natural Areas of Native North America," *University of California Publications in American Archaeology and Ethnology*, 1939, p. 166.

★ 6 ★

Mooney's Population Estimates for Aboriginal North America With European Contact Dates

Area	European contact date	Population
North Atlantic States	1600	55,600
South Atlantic States	1600	52,200
Gulf States	1650	114,400
Central States	1650	75,300
Northern Plains	1780	100,800
Southern Plains	1690	41,000
Columbia Region	1780	88,800
California	1769	260,000
Central Mountain Region	1845	19,300
New Mexico and Arizona	1680	72,000
Greenland	1721	10,000
Eastern Canada	1600	54,200
Central Canada	1670	50,950
British Columbia	1780	85,800
Alaska	1740	72,600
North America		1,152,950

Source: Russell Thornton, *American Indian Holocaust and Survival: A Population History Since 1492*, University of Oklahoma Press, 1987, p. 27. Published by permission. Primary source: Mooney, "The Aboriginal Population of America North of Mexico," pp. 1-40 in John R. Swanton, ed., *Smithsonian Miscellaneous Collections*, vol. 80.

★ 7 ★

Mooney's Population Estimates for Aboriginal North America With Ubelaker's Revised Estimates

In 1976, Douglas H. Ubelaker revised James Mooney's population estimates, which were originally published in 1929.

Area	Mooney's population	Revised estimate
North Atlantic States	55,600	157,348
South Atlantic States	52,200	92,916
Gulf States	114,400	473,616
Central States	75,300	167,919
Northern Plains	100,800	140,112
Southern Plains	41,000	264,040
Columbia Region	88,800	111,000
California	260,000	310,000
Central Mountain and Region	19,300	19,300
New Mexico and Arizona	72,000	113,760

[Continued]

★7★

Mooney's Population Estimates for Aboriginal North America With Ubelaker's Revised Estimates

[Continued]

Area	Mooney's population	Revised estimate
Conterminous United States	879,400	1,850,011
Greenland	10,000	10,000
Eastern Canada	54,200	81,842
Central Canada	50,950	36,684
British Columbia	85,800	119,262
Alaska	72,600	73,326
Other areas	273,550	321,114
North America	1,152,950	2,171,125

Source: Russell Thornton, *American Indian Holocaust and Survival: A Population History Since 1492,* University of Oklahoma Press, 1987, p. 29. Published by permission. Primary source: Ubelaker, "Prehistoric New World Population Size: Historical Review and Current Appraisal of North American Estimates," *American Journal of Physical Anthropology,* 1976, p. 664; Mooney, "The Aboriginal Population of America North of Mexico," pp. 1-40 in John R. Swanton, ed., *Smithsonian Miscellaneous Collections,* vol. 80.

★8★

Questions Asked of American Indians in Supplemental Schedules of U.S. Census Enumerations, 1880-1970

An (X) indicates that the questions was asked; a dash (-) indicates that the question was not asked.

Question	1880	1890	1900	1910	1920	1930	1940	1950	1960	1970
Whether a chief	X	-	-	-	-	-	-	-	-	-
By what authority	X	-	-	-	-	-	-	-	-	-
Whether a war chief	X	-	-	-	-	-	-	-	-	-
Length of time on reservation	X	-	-	-	-	-	-	-	-	-
Length of time person has worn citizen's dress	X	-	-	-	-	-	-	-	-	-
Number of persons who wear citizen's dress, wholly and in part	-	X	-	-	-	-	-	-	-	-
Total population of agency, by tribe	-	X	-	-	-	-	-	-	-	-
Total population of tribe and what Indian language is spoken	-	X	-	-	-	-	-	-	-	-
Whether tribe is increasing or decreasing	-	X	-	-	-	-	-	-	-	-
Number of Negroes, mulattos, quadroons, ocoroons with the tribe	-	X	-	-	-	-	-	-	-	-
Number of persons in this family	-	X	-	-	-	-	-	-	-	-
Probable wealth and wages earned	-	X	-	-	-	-	-	-	-	-
Tribe or clan (of individual)	X	X	X	X	-	-	-	X	-	-
Tribe(s) of parents	-	-	X	X	-	-	-	-	-	-
Proportions of Indian or other blood	X	X	X	X	-	-	-	X	-	-

[Continued]

★8★

Questions Asked of American Indians in Supplemental Schedules of U.S. Census Enumerations, 1880-1970
[Continued]

Question	1880	1890	1900	1910	1920	1930	1940	1950	1960	1970
Number of times married	-	-	-	X	-	-	-	-	-	-
Now living in polygamy (1890, number of wives)	-	X	X	-	-	-	-	-	-	-
If living in polygamy, whether wives are sisters	-	X	-	X	-	-	-	-	-	-
Vaccinated	X	-	-	-	-	-	-	-	-	-
Persons property:										
Number and value of horses owned	X	-	-	-	-	-	-	-	-	-
Number and value of cattle, oxen, milch cows owned	X	-	-	-	-	-	-	-	-	-
Number and value of sheep owned	X	-	-	-	-	-	-	-	-	-
Number and value of swine owned	X	-	-	-	-	-	-	-	-	-
Number and value of mules and asses owned	X	-	-	-	-	-	-	-	-	-
Number and value of domestic fowls owned	X	-	-	-	-	-	-	-	-	-
Pounds and value of wool owned	X	-	-	-	-	-	-	-	-	-
Number of dogs owned	X	-	-	-	-	-	-	-	-	-
Number and kinds of firearms owned	X	-	-	-	-	-	-	-	-	-
Land in severalty:										
Received land allotment (give year)	-	-	-	X	-	-	-	-	-	-
Number acres held by patent	X	-	-	-	-	-	-	-	-	-
Number acres held by allotment without patent	X	-	-	-	-	-	-	-	-	-
Number acres held by tribal regulation	X	-	-	-	-	-	-	-	-	-
Number of families actually living on and cultivating lands allotted in severalty	-	X	-	-	-	-	-	-	-	-
Number of other families engaged in agriculture or other civilized pursuits	-	X	-	-	-	-	-	-	-	-
How supported (wholly or fractional):										
Self-supporting, for how many years	X	-	-	-	-	-	-	-	-	-
By family	X	-	-	-	-	-	-	-	-	-
By civilized industries	X	X	-	-	-	-	-	-	-	-
By government	X	X	-	-	-	-	-	-	-	-
By hunting	X	X	-	-	-	-	-	-	-	-
By fishing	X	X	-	-	-	-	-	-	-	-
By natural products of soil, such as roots, berries, etc.	X	X	-	-	-	-	-	-	-	-
Number of Indian children of school age	-	X	-	-	-	-	-	-	-	-
Number of Indian children for whom school accommodations are provided	-	X	-	-	-	-	-	-	-	-
Number of Indian apprentices who have been learning trades during year, and trade	-	X	-	-	-	-	-	-	-	-
Number of missionaries, by sex and denomination	-	X	-	-	-	-	-	-	-	-
Number of church members, by denomination	-	X	-	-	-	-	-	-	-	-
Ability to read English	X[1]	X[1]	-	-	-	-	-	X	-	-
Ability to write English	X[1]	X[1]	-	-	-	-	-	X	-	-
Ability to speak English	X[1]	X[1]	-	X	-	-	-	X	-	-
Ability to read or write native language	X[1]	-	-	-	-	-	-	-	-	-
Ability to read any language other than English	-	-	-	-	-	-	-	X	-	-

[Continued]

★8★

Questions Asked of American Indians in Supplemental Schedules of U.S. Census Enumerations, 1880-1970
[Continued]

Question	1880	1890	1900	1910	1920	1930	1940	1950	1960	1970
Ability to write any language other than English	-	-	-	-	-	-	-	X	-	-
Ability to speak any other foreign language	X[1]	-	-	-	-	-	-	X	-	-
Graduated from educational institution (name and location)	-	-	-	X	-	-	-	-	-	-
In 1949, whether he attended or participated in any native Indian ceremonies	-	-	-	-	-	-	-	X	-	-
Military service, with time and organization	-	X	-	-	-	-	-	-	-	-
Taxed and not taxed	-	X	X	X	-	-	-	-	-	-
Number of white persons killed by Indians, according to sex	-	X	-	-	-	-	-	-	-	-
Number and kind of crimes against Indians committed by whites	-	X	-	-	-	-	-	-	-	-
Number of whites punished for above crimes	-	X	-	-	-	-	-	-	-	-
Number of whiskey sellers prosecuted, and kind and extent of punishment of each	X	-	-	-	-	-	-	-	-	-
Number of whites unlawfully on reservation	-	X	-	-	-	-	-	-	-	-
Occupation; area occupied, quality	-	X	-	-	-	-	-	-	-	-
Number of Indian criminals punished:										
By courts of Indian offenses	-	X	-	-	-	-	-	-	-	-
By other methods (civil, military, or tribal authority)	-	X	-	-	-	-	-	-	-	-
Number of Indians killed by Indians of same tribe, hostile Indians, by U.S. soldiers, by citizens	-	X	-	-	-	-	-	-	-	-
Indian deaths during year	X	X	-	-	-	-	-	-	-	-

Housing questions

	1880	1890	1900	1910	1920	1930	1940	1950	1960	1970
House, pueblo, or lodge	X	-	-	X	-	-	-	-	-	-
Construction material, if a house	X	X	-	-	-	-	-	-	-	-
Type of floor construction	-	-	-	-	-	-	-	X	-	-
Number of houses owned by Indians	-	X	-	-	-	-	-	-	-	-
Number of houses built for Indians by government and cost of same	-	X	-	-	-	-	-	-	-	-
Number of houses occupied by Indians	-	X	-	-	-	-	-	-	-	-
If occupied by Indian, fixed or movable dwelling	-	-	X	-	-	-	-	-	-	-
Number of families in dwelling	-	X	-	-	-	-	-	-	-	-
Number of persons in dwelling	-	X	-	-	-	-	-	-	-	-
Owned or rented	-	X	-	-	-	-	-	-	-	-
If owned, whether mortgaged	-	X	-	-	-	-	-	-	-	-
Residing on own lands	-	-	-	X	-	-	-	-	-	-

Source: Russell Thornton, *American Indian Holocaust and Survival: A Population History Since 1492*, University of Oklahoma Press, 1987, pp. 217-219. Published by permission. Primary source: U.S. Bureau of the Census, *Population and Housing Inquiries in U.S. Decennial Censuses*, 1790-1970. U.S. Department of Commerce Working Paper 39. Washington, D.C.: U.S. Government Printing Office, 1973, pp. 27-31 and 38. *Note:* 1. Asked of adults only.

★9★

Selected Population Characteristics Reported in 1872

This table shows opinions expressed by the Commissioner of Indian Affairs (or his agents) in 1872.

Characteristic	Population
Means of support	
"Supporting themselves on reservations, receiving nothing from government except interest on their own funds or annuities pursuant to treaties"	130,000
"Entirely subsisted by the government"	31,000
"In part subsisted by the government"	84,000
"Subsisting by hunting, fishing, roots, berries; begging or stealing"	55,000
Connection with the government	
"On reservations under complete control of agents"	150,000
"Visited agency at times for food or gossip, but generally roaming on or off their reservations, engaged in hunting or fishing"	95,000
"Never visited agency, and over whom government exercised practically no control, but most of whom were inoffensive"	55,000
Treaties and reservations	
"Had treaties with the government, 92 reservations"	180,000
"No treaties, but 15 reservations with agents in charge"	40,000
"No treaties, no reservations, but were more or less under the control of agents appointed for them and received more or less subsistence"	25,000
"No treaties, no reservations, practically no government control"	55,000
Degree of "Civilization" (with no degree of assurance)	
"Civilized"	97,000
"Semi-Civilized"	125,000
"Wholly barbarous"	78,000

Source: *Fact Book*, Albuquerque Area Office, Division of Administration, February 1989, U.S. Department of the Interior, p. 3. Primary source: Commissioner of Indian Affairs, Annual Report (Washington, D.C.: Government Printing Office, 1872, pp. 15, 84).

★ 10 ★

United States American Indian Population, 1870-1910

Year	Indian population		Alaska Census returns
	United States		
	Census returns	Reports of the Commissioner of Indian Affairs[1]	
1910	265,683	279,023	25,331
1900	237,196	250,000	29,536
1890	248,253	228,000	25,354
1880	-	244,000	32,996[2]
1870	-	278,000	-

Source: U.S. Bureau of the Census, *Indian Population in the United States and Alaska, 1910*, United States Government Printing Office, Washington, D.C., 1915, p. 10. *Notes:* A dash (-) indicates data were not available. 1. Figures are exclusive of freedmen and intermarried whites as follows: 1910, 25,927; 1900, 20,000 (estimate); 1880, 12,000 (estimate); and 1870, 10,000 (estimate.) 2. Partly estimated.

★ 11 ★

Attrition of American Indian Tribes in U.S. Regions

Region	Characteristics at European contact				Characteristics in 1907						
	Date	Population	Number of tribes	Mean size	Contact size, %	Population	Number of tribes	Mean size	Tribes extinct	Tribes nearing extinction	Tribes extinct or near extinction, %
North Atlantic	1600	55,600	24	2,317	39.4	21,900	10	2,190	14	6	83.3
South Atlantic	1600	52,200	35	1,491	4.2	2,170	15	145	20	14	97.1
Gulf States	1650	114,400	39	2,933	54.8	62,700	12	5,225	27	4	79.5
Central States	1650	75,300	12	6,275	61.3	46,126	10	4,613	2	1	25.0
Northern Plains	1780	100,800	20	5,040	50.1	50,477	19	2,804	1	1	10.0
Southern Plains	1690	41,000	12	3,417	7.0	2,861	7	409	5	0	41.7
Columbia Region	1780	88,800	95	935	17.4	15,431	83	211	12	40	54.7
Central Mountains	1845	19,300	6	3,217	59.8	11,544	6	1,924	0	0	0
New Mexico and Arizona	1680	72,000	25	2,880	74.8	53,832	19	2,833	6	1	28.0
California	1769	260,000	45	5,778	7.2	18,797	36	696	9	9	40.0
Total		849,000	313			285,838	217		96	66	
Average	1704			2,712	66.3			1,470			57.5

Source: Russell Thornton, *We Shall Live Again: The 1870 and 1890 Ghost Dance Movements as Demographic Revitalization*, Cambridge University Press, 1986, P. 22. Published by permission. *Notes:* Information on which this table is based was obtained from Mooney (1928), Smith (1928), and Kroeber (1957).

★ 12 ★

American Indian Population and Percent Distribution, by Age Group, 1900-1930

Age group	1900	1910	1920	1930
All ages	237,196	265,683	244,437	332,397
Under 20 years	117,779	136,804	123,102	169,091
20 to 49 years	83,819	91,906	86,151	118,090
50 years and over	30,964	36,024	34,393	44,767
Age unknown	4,634	949	791	449
Percent	100.0	100.0	100.0	100.0
Under 20 years	49.7	51.5	50.4	50.9
20 to 49 years	35.3	34.6	35.2	35.5
50 years and over	13.1	13.6	14.1	13.5
Age unknown	2.0	0.4	0.3	0.1

Source: Dr. Leon E. Truesdell, U.S. Department of Commerce, Bureau of the Census, Fifteenth Census of the United States: 1930, *The Indian Population of the United States and Alaska*, U.S. Government Printing Office, 1937, p. 86.

★ 13 ★

American Indian Population Distribution and Population per 10,000 Persons, 1910 and 1930

The Indian population of the United States per 100 square miles of land was 11.2 in 1930, as compared with 8.9 in 1910. Only in the state of Oklahoma was the Indian population in excess of one person per single square mile. Of the states not shown in this table, Rhode Island and Massachusetts ranked high in the number of Indians person 100 square miles.

State	1910				1930			
	Total population	Indian population	Percent distribution of Indian population	Indians per 10,000 total population	Total population	Indian population	Percent distribution of Indian population	Indians per 10,000 total population
United States	91,972,266	265,683	100.0	28.9	122,775,046	332,397	100.0	27.1
Oklahoma	1,657,155	74,825	28.2	451.5	2,396,040	92,725	27.9	387.0
Arizona	204,354	29,201	11.0	1,428.9	435,573	43,726	13.2	1,003.9
New Mexico	327,301	20,573	7.7	628.6	423,317	28,941	8.7	683.7
South Dakota	583,888	19,137	7.2	327.8	692,849	21,833	6.6	315.1
California	2,377,549	16,371	6.2	68.9	5,677,251	19,212	5.8	33.8
North Carolina	2,206,287	7,851	3.0	35.6	3,170,276	16,579	5.0	52.3
Montana	376,053	10,745	4.0	285.7	537,606	14,798	4.5	275.3
Wisconsin	2,333,860	10,142	3.8	43.5	2,939,006	11,548	3.5	39.3
Washington	1,141,990	10,997	4.1	96.3	1,563,396	11,253	3.4	72.0
Minnesota	2,075,708	9,053	3.4	43.6	2,563,953	11,077	3.3	43.2
North Dakota	577,056	6,486	2.4	112.4	680,845	8,387	2.5	123.2

[Continued]

★ 13 ★

American Indian Population Distribution and Population per 10,000 Persons, 1910 and 1930
[Continued]

State	1910				1930			
	Total population	Indian population	Percent distribution of Indian population	Indians per 10,000 total population	Total population	Indian population	Percent distribution of Indian population	Indians per 10,000 total population
Michigan	2,810,173	7,519	2.8	26.8	4,842,325	7,080	2.1	14.6
New York	9,113,614	6,046	2.3	6.6	12,588,066	6,973	2.1	5.5
Nevada	81,875	5,240	2.0	640.0	91,058	4,871	1.5	534.9
Oregon	672,765	5,090	1.9	75.7	953,786	4,776	1.4	50.1
Idaho	325,594	3,488	1.3	107.1	445,032	3,638	1.1	81.7
Nebraska	1,192,214	3,502	1.3	29.4	1,377,963	3,256	1.0	23.6
Utah	373,351	3,123	1.2	83.6	507,847	2,869	0.9	56.5
Kansas	1,690,949	2,444	0.9	14.5	1,880,999	2,454	0.7	13.0
Wyoming	145,965	1,486	0.6	101.8	225,565	1,845	0.6	81.8
All other States	61,704,565	12,364	4.7	2.0	78,782,293	14,556	4.4	1.8

Source: Dr. Leon E. Truesdell, U.S. Department of Commerce, Bureau of the Census, Fifteenth Census of the United States: 1930, *The Indian Population of the United States and Alaska*, U.S. Government Printing Office, 1937, p.5.

★ 14 ★

American Indian Population Distribution, by Selected State and Full/Mixed Blood Status, 1910 and 1930

State	1910			1930		
	Full blood	Mixed blood	Not reported	Full blood	Mixed blood	Not reported
Arizona	94.2	1.4	4.3	86.4	2.2	11.3
California	70.0	28.1	1.9	39.2	36.8	24.0
Idaho	83.6	15.0	1.4	66.1	30.9	3.0
Kansas	36.5	62.9	0.6	14.2	60.6	25.1
Michigan	52.2	47.6	0.2	17.1	35.2	47.7
Minnesota	44.1	55.8	0.1	23.0	67.4	9.6
Montana	59.7	37.5	2.8	37.0	60.1	2.9
Nebraska	69.3	28.4	2.4	45.9	33.2	20.9
Nevada	86.6	10.3	3.1	72.6	26.7	0.7
New Mexico	99.0	0.9	0.1	89.7	2.1	8.2
New York	54.7	38.9	6.4	24.9	44.6	30.5
North Carolina	19.1	80.3	0.5	37.9	54.8	7.3
North Dakota	40.5	57.7	1.8	27.0	65.9	7.1
Oklahoma	36.6	62.6	0.8	28.1	66.3	5.6
Oregon	63.3	36.4	0.2	45.1	48.3	6.6
South Dakota	70.4	28.7	0.9	52.3	46.1	1.6

[Continued]

11

★ 14 ★

American Indian Population Distribution, by Selected State and Full/Mixed Blood Status, 1910 and 1930
[Continued]

State	1910			1930		
	Full blood	Mixed blood	Not reported	Full blood	Mixed blood	Not reported
Utah	95.1	3.4	1.5	77.1	10.1	12.8
Washington	68.7	30.6	0.6	46.0	43.6	10.4
Wisconsin	54.7	45.1	0.2	35.1	55.2	9.6
Wyoming	80.5	19.5	-	60.5	35.3	4.2

Source: Dr. Leon E. Truesdell, U.S. Department of Commerce, Bureau of the Census, Fifteenth Census of the United States: 1930, *The Indian Population of the United States and Alaska,* U.S. Government Printing Office, 1937, p. 71. *Note:* A dash (-) represents zero.

★ 15 ★

American Indian Population in the United States, 1800-1910

Date	Population
1800	600,000[1]
1820	471,000[2]
1847	383,000[3]
1857	313,000[4]
1870	278,000[5]
1880	244,000[5]
1890	228,000[5]
1900	250,000[5]
1910	279,000[5]

Source: Russell Thornton, *We Shall Live Again: The 1870 and 1890 Ghost Dance Movements as Demographic Revitalization,* Cambridge University Press, 1986, P. 24. Published by permission. *Notes:* 1. From U.S. Bureau of Indian Affairs (1943), as cited by Hadley (1957:24). 2. From Morse (1970[1822]:375). 3. From Schoolcraft (1851-57), as cited by Mallery (1877:341). 4. From Schoolcraft (1851-57), as cited by Dobyns (1976:55). 5. From U.S. Bureau of the Census (1915:10).

★ 16 ★

American Indian Population in Urban and Rural Areas, by Geographic Division, 1910-1930

Geographic division	1910			1920			1930		
	Urban	Rural	Percent urban	Urban	Rural	Percent urban	Urban	Rural	Percent urban
United States	11,925	253,758	4.5	15,219	229,218	6.2	32,816	299,581	9.9
New England	800	1,276	38.5	766	949	44.7	1,041	1,425	42.2
Middle Atlantic	825	6,892	10.7	906	5,034	15.3	2,181	5,528	28.3
East North Central	1,319	16,936	7.2	1,634	14,061	10.4	3,822	15,995	19.3
West North Central	1,629	39,777	3.9	1,815	35,448	4.9	3,497	44,748	7.2
South Atlantic	131	8,923	1.4	196	13,477	1.4	218	18,842	1.1
East South Central	137	2,475	5.2	51	1,572	3.1	99	2,007	4.7
West South Central	4,589	72,178	6.0	5,352	55,266	8.8	15,108	80,562	15.8
Mountain	1,272	74,066	1.7	1,772	75,127	2.3	2,677	99,406	2.6
Pacific	1,223	31,235	3.8	2,727	28,284	8.8	4,173	31,068	11.8

Source: Dr. Leon E. Truesdell, U.S. Department of Commerce, Bureau of the Census, Fifteenth Census of the United States: 1930, *The Indian Population of the United States and Alaska*, U.S. Government Printing Office, 1937, p.6.

★ 17 ★

American Indian Population of the United States and Alaska, 1890-1930

For cautionary explanation, see notes.

Year	Continental United States	Alaska
1890	248,253	25,354
1900	237,196	29,536
1910	265,683	25,331
1920	244,437	26,558
1930	332,397	29,983

Source: Dr. Leon E. Truesdell, U.S. Department of Commerce, Bureau of the Census, Fifteenth Census of the United States: 1930, *The Indian Population of the United States and Alaska*, U.S. Government Printing Office, 1937, p.2. *Notes:* Effect of changes in the method of enumeration - In the case of the Indian population, rates of increase or decrease are of little significance, as the size of the Indian population depends entirely upon the attention paid to the enumeration of mixed bloods, and the interpretation of the term "Indian" in the instructions to enumerators. It is not without significance that the two censuses in which specific questions were asked as to tribe and blood, the number of Indians should have been much larger than at censuses in which these questions were not asked. If the definition of the Indian population were limited to Indians maintaining tribal relations, the enumeration of the Bureau of Indian Affairs is probably more nearly accurate than that of the census. This enumeration in 1932 showed a total of 228,381. On the other hand, if all persons having even a trace of Indian blood were returned as Indians, the number would far exceed even the total returned at the census of 1930.

★ 18 ★

American Indian Population per 10,000 Total Population for Selected States, 1890-1910

State	1910			1900			1890		
	Total population	Indian population		Total population	Indian population		Total population	Indian population	
		Number	Per 10,000 of the total population		Number	Per 10,000 of the total population		Number	Per 10,000 of the total population
United States	91,972,266	265,683	28.9	75,994,575	237,196	31.2	62,947,714	248,253	39.4
Arizona	204,354	29,201	1,428.9	122,931	26,480	2,154.1	88,243	29,981	3,397.5
California	2,377,549	16,371	68.9	1,485,053	15,377	103.5	1,213,398	16,624	137.0
Colorado	799,024	1,482	18.5	539,700	1,437	26.6	413,249	1,092	26.4
Idaho	325,594	3,488	107.1	161,772	4,226	261.2	88,548	4,223	476.9
Kansas	1,690,949	2,444	14.5	1,470,495	2,130	14.5	1,428,108	1,682	11.8
Michigan	2,810,173	7,519	26.8	2,420,982	6,354	26.2	2,093,890	5,625	26.9
Minnesota	2,075,708	9,053	43.6	1,751,394	9,182	52.4	1,310,283	10,096	77.1
Mississippi	1,797,114	1,253	7.0	1,551,270	2,203	14.2	1,289,600	2,036	15.8
Montana	376,053	10,745	285.7	243,329	11,343	466.2	142,924	11,206	784.1
Nebraska	1,192,214	3,502	29.4	1,066,300	3,322	31.2	1,062,656	6,431	60.5
Nevada	81,875	5,240	640.0	42,335	5,216	1,232.1	47,355	5,156	1,088.8
New Mexico	327,301	20,573	628.6	195,310	13,144	673.0	160,282	160,282	938.6
New York	9,113,614	6,046	6.6	7,268,894	5,257	7.2	6,003,174	6,044	10.1
North Carolina	2,206,287	7,851	35.6	1,893,810	5,687	30.0	1,617,949	1,516	9.4
North Dakota	577,056	6,486	112.4	319,146	6,968	218.3	190,983	8,174	428.0
Oklahoma[1]	1,657,155	74,825	451.5	790,391	64,445	815.4	258,657	64,456	2,491.9
Oregon	672,765	5,090	75.7	413,536	4,951	119.7	317,704	4,971	156.5
South Dakota	583,888	19,137	327.8	401,570	20,225	503.6	348,600	19,854	569.5
Utah	373,351	3,123	83.6	276,749	2,623	94.8	210,779	3,456	164.0
Washington	1,141,990	10,997	96.3	518,103	10,039	193.8	357,232	11,181	313.0
Wisconsin	2,333,860	10,142	43.5	2,069,042	8,372	40.5	1,693,330	9,930	58.6
Wyoming	145,965	1,486	101.8	92,531	1,686	182.2	62,555	1,844	294.8
Total for 22 states	32,863,839	256,054	77.9	25,094,643	230,667	91.9	20,399,499	240,622	118.0
All other states	59,108,427	9,629	1.6	50,899,932	6,529	1.3	42,548,215	7,631	1.8

Source: U.S. Bureau of the Census, *Indian Population in the United States and Alaska, 1910,* United States Government Printing Office, Washington, D.C., 1915, p. 13. *Note:* 1. Includes population of Indian Territory for 1900 and 1890.

★ 19 ★

American Indian Population per 100 Square Miles for Selected States in 1910

State	Land area in square miles	Indian population: 1910	
		Total	Per 100 square miles
United States	2,973,890	265,683	8.9
Oklahoma	69,414	74,825	107.8
Arizona	113,810	29,201	25.7
South Dakota	76,868	19,137	24.9
Wisconsin	55,256	10,142	18.4
New Mexico	122,503	20,573	16.8
Washington	66,836	10,997	16.5
North Carolina	48,740	7,851	16.1
Michigan	57,480	7,519	13.1
New York	47,654	6,046	12.7
Minnesota	80,858	9,053	11.2
California	155,652	16,371	10.5
North Dakota	70,183	6,486	9.2
Montana	146,201	10,745	7.3
Oregon	95,607	5,090	5.3
Nevada	109,821	5,240	4.8
Nebraska	76,808	3,502	4.6
Idaho	83,354	3,488	4.2
Utah	82,184	3,123	3.8
Mississippi	46,362	1,253	2.7
Kansas[1]	81,774	1,853	2.3
Wyoming	97,594	1,486	1.5
Colorado	103,658	1,482	1.4
Total for 22 states	1,888,617	255,463	13.5
All other states	1,085,273	10,220	0.9

Source: U.S. Bureau of the Census, *Indian Population in the United States and Alaska, 1910,* United States Government Printing Office, Washington, D.C., 1915, p. 14. *Notes:* 1. Exclusive of 591 Indians in Haskell Institute, who are included in the total for "All other states."

★ 20 ★

American Indian Population, by Geographic Division and State, 1890-1930

Geographic division and state	1890	1900	1910	1920	1930
United States	248,253	237,196	265,683	244,437	332,397
Geographic Divisions:					
New England	1,445	1,600	2,076	1,716	2,466
Middle Atlantic	7,209	6,959	7,717	5,940	7,709
East North Central	16,202	15,027	18,255	15,695	19,817
West North Central	46,822	42,339	41,406	37,263	48,245
South Atlantic	2,359	6,585	9,054	13,673	19,060
East South Central	3,396	2,590	2,612	1,623	2,106
West South Central	66,042	65,574	76,767	60,618	95,670
Mountain	72,002	66,155	75,338	76,899	102,083
Pacific	32,776	30,367	32,458	31,011	35,241
New England:					
Maine	559	798	692	839	1,012
New Hampshire	16	22	34	28	64
Vermont	34	5	26	24	36
Massachusetts	428	587	688	555	874
Rhode Island	180	35	284	110	318
Connecticut	228	153	152	159	152
Middle Atlantic:					
New York	6,044	5,257	6,046	5,503	6,973
New Jersey	84	63	165	100	213
Pennsylvania	1,081	1,639	1,503	337	523
East North Central:					
Ohio	206	42	127	151	435
Indiana	343	243	279	125	285
Illinois	98	16	188	194	469
Michigan	5,625	6,354	7,519	5,614	7,080
Wisconsin	9,930	8,372	10,142	9,611	11,548
West North Central:					
Minnesota	10,096	9,162	9,053	8,761	11,077
Iowa	457	382	471	529	660
Missouri	128	130	313	171	576
North Dakota	8,174	6,968	6,486	6,254	8,387
South Dakota	19,854	20,225	19,137	16,384	21,833
Nebraska	6,431	3,322	3,502	2,888	3,256
Kansas	1,682	2,130	2,444	2,276	2,454
South Atlantic:					
Delaware	4	9	5	2	5
Maryland	44	3	55	32	50
District of Columbia	25	22	68	37	40

[Continued]

★ 20 ★

American Indian Population, by Geographic Division and State, 1890-1930

[Continued]

Geographic division and state	1890	1900	1910	1920	1930
Virginia	349	354	539	824	779
West Virginia	9	12	36	7	18
North Carolina	1,516	5,687	7,851	11,824	16,579
South Carolina	173	121	331	304	959
Georgia	68	19	95	125	43
Florida	171	358	74	518	587
East South Central:					
Kentucky	71	102	234	57	22
Tennessee	146	108	216	56	161
Alabama	1,143	177	909	405	465
Mississippi	2,036	2,203	1,253	1,105	1,458
West South Central:					
Arkansas	250	66	460	106	408
Louisiana	628	593	780	1,066	1,536
Oklahoma	64,456	64,445	74,825	57,337	92,725
Texas	708	470	702	2,109	1,001
Mountain:					
Montana	11,206	11,343	10,745	10,956	14,798
Idaho	4,283	4,226	3,488	3,098	3,638
Wyoming	1,844	1,686	1,486	1,343	1,845
Colorado	1,092	1,437	1,482	1,383	1,395
New Mexico	15,044	13,144	20,573	19,512	28,941
Arizona	29,981	26,480	29,201	32,989	43,726
Utah	3,456	2,623	3,123	2,711	2,869
Nevada	5,156	5,216	5,240	4,907	4,871
Pacific:					
Washington	11,181	10,039	10,997	9,061	11,253
Oregon	4,971	4,951	5,090	4,590	4,776
California	16,624	15,377	16,371	17,360	19,212

Source: Dr. Leon E. Truesdell, U.S. Department of Commerce, Bureau of the Census, Fifteenth Census of the United States: 1930, *The Indian Population of the United States and Alaska*, U.S. Government Printing Office, 1937, p. 3.

★ 21 ★

California Indian Population, Prehistory to 1900

Date	Population
Prehistory	310,000+
1800	260,000
1834	210,000
1849	100,000
1852	85,000
1856	50,000
1860	35,000
1870	30,000
1880	20,500
1890	18,000
1900	15,500[1]
1907	18,797

Source: Russell Thornton, *We Shall Live Again: The 1870 and 1890 Ghost Dance Movements as Demographic Revitalization,* Cambridge University Press, 1986, P. 25. Published by permission. *Notes:* Information on which this table was based was obtained from Merriam (1905), Mooney (1928), Cook (1976a), and Thornton (1980). 1. Cook (1976a) disagrees with the nadir figure reported here (from Merriam, 1905), arguing that the actual nadir was between some 20,000 and 25,000 and occurred during the decade 1890-1900.

★ 22 ★

Population History of Indians in Texas, 1690-1890

Tribe or group	1690 population	1890 population	Reduction (%)
Karankawan	2,800	Extinct	100
Akokisa	500	Extinct	100
Bidui	500	Extinct	100
Coahuiltecan	7,500	Extinct	100
Tonkawan	1,600	56	97
Caddo (of Texas)	8,500	536	94
Wichita (of Texas)	3,200	358	89
Kichai	500	66	87
Lipan Apache	500	60	88
Mescalero Apache	700	473	32
Kiowa-Apache	300+(1780)	326	+9
Comanche	7,000	1,598	77
Kiowa	2,000 (1780)	1,140	43

[Continued]

★ 22 ★

Population History of Indians in Texas, 1690-1890
[Continued]

Tribe or group	1690 population	1890 population	Reduction (%)
Arapaho	3,000 (1780)	5,630	13
Cheyenne	3,500+ (1780)	5,630	13

Source: Russell Thornton, *American Indian Holocaust and Survival: A Population History Since 1492*, University of Oklahoma, Press, 1987, p. 131. Published by permission. Primary source: Ewers, "The Influence of Epidemics on the Indian Populations and Cultures of Texas," *Plains Anthropologist*, 1973, p. 106.

★ 23 ★

American Indian Population Decline on Martha's Vineyard and Nantucket Islands, 1642-1792

Date	Population	
	From	To
Martha's Vineyard		
1642-1674	3,000	1,500
1674-1698	1,500	1,000
1698-1720	1,000	800
1720-1764	800	313
Nantucket		
1659-1674	3,000	1,500
1674-1698	1,500	1,000
1698-1763	1,000	348
1763-1792	348	20

Source: Russell Thornton, *American Indian Holocaust and Survival: A Population History Since 1492*, University of Oklahoma Press, 1987, 83. Published by permission. Primary source: Cook, "The Significance of Disease in the Extinction of the New England Indians," *Human Biology*, 1973, pp. 502-503.

★24★

Alaskan Indian Population, by Linguistic Stock, Tribe, Sex, and Age Group, and Mixture of Blood, 1910 - I

Tribe and mixture of blood	Both sexes	Male				Female			
		Total[1]	Under 20 yrs.	20 to 50 yrs.	51 yrs. and over	Total[1]	Under 20 yrs.	20 to 50 yrs.	51 yrs. and over
Algonquian stock									
Total	3	2	-	2	-	1	1	-	-
Full blood	1	1	-	1	-	-	-	-	-
Mixed blood (white and Indian)	2	1	-	1	-	1	1	-	-
Athapaskan stock									
Total	3,916	2,009	902	948	159	1,907	893	884	130
Full blood	3,642	1,875	797	921	157	1,767	777	861	129
Mixed blood	274	134	105	27	2	140	116	23	1
White and Indian	273	134	105	27	2	139	115	23	1
Other races and Indian (Japanese)	1	-	-	-	-	1	1	-	-
Ahtena	297	161	66	75	20	136	59	66	11
Full blood	293	158	64	74	20	135	58	66	11
Mixed blood (white and Indian)	4	3	2	1	-	1	1	-	-
Hankutchin	127	79	37	31	11	48	24	23	1
Full blood	127	79	37	31	11	48	24	23	1
Kaiyuhkhotana	160	78	26	46	6	82	33	43	6
Full blood	155	75	23	46	6	80	31	43	6
Mixed blood (white and Indian)	5	3	3	-	-	2	2	-	-
Knaiakhotana	697	380	178	169	33	317	158	138	21
Full blood	672	364	165	166	33	308	151	136	21
Mixed blood (white and Indian)	25	16	13	3	-	9	7	2	-
Kutchin	359	188	83	86	19	171	80	78	13
Full blood	349	184	80	85	19	165	74	78	13
Mixed blood (white and Indian)	10	4	3	1	-	6	6	-	-
Nahane	8	5	3	2	-	3	2	1	-
Full blood	2	1	-	1	-	1	-	1	-
Mixed blood (white and Indian)	6	4	3	1	-	2	2	-	-
Natsitkutchin	177	96	39	45	12	81	35	35	11
Full blood	176	96	39	45	12	80	34	35	11
Mixed blood (Japanese and Indian)	1	-	-	-	-	1	1	-	-
Tenankutchin	415	216	97	98	21	199	89	97	13
Full blood	396	204	87	96	21	192	83	96	13
Mixed blood (white and Indian)	19	12	10	2	-	7	6	1	-

[Continued]

★ 24 ★

Alaskan Indian Population, by Linguistic Stock, Tribe, Sex, and Age Group, and Mixture of Blood, 1910 - I

[Continued]

Tribe and mixture of blood	Both sexes	Male				Female			
		Total[1]	Under 20 yrs.	20 to 50 yrs.	51 yrs. and over	Total[1]	Under 20 yrs.	20 to 50 yrs.	51 yrs. and over
Tukkuthkutchin	6	1	1	-	-	5	2	3	-
Full blood	3	-	-	-	-	3	-	3	-
Mixed blood (white and Indian)	3	1	1	-	-	2	2	-	-
Unakhotana	193	98	37	56	5	95	50	41	4
Full blood	170	89	30	54	5	81	36	41	4
Mixed blood (white and Indian)	23	9	7	2	-	14	14	-	-
Vuntakutchin	5	2	-	2	-	3	-	3	-
Full blood	5	2	-	2	-	3	-	3	-
Tribe not reported	1,472	705	335	338	32	767	361	356	50
Full blood	1,294	623	272	321	30	671	286	336	49
Mixed blood (white and Indian)	178	82	63	17	2	96	75	20	1
Eskimauan stock									
Total	14,087	7,310	3,505	3,176	557	6,777	3,135	3,019	547
Full blood	12,859	6,666	3,007	3,049	543	6,193	2,691	2,890	540
Mixed blood	1,228	644	498	127	14	584	444	129	7
White and Indian	1,209	637	491	127	14	572	433	128	7
Other races and Indian	19	7	7	-	-	12	11	1	-
Chinese	5	2	2	-	-	3	3	-	-
Japanese	14	5	5	-	-	9	8	1	-
Aleut	1,451	758	404	288	61	693	353	287	50
Full blood	999	523	249	221	52	476	207	225	44
Mixed blood	452	235	155	67	9	217	146	62	6
White and Indian	449	234	154	67	9	215	144	62	6
Other races and Indian (Japanese)	3	1	1	-	-	2	2	-	-
Chnagmiut	326	180	100	66	14	146	69	65	12
Full blood	299	165	85	66	14	134	57	65	12
Mixed blood (white and Indian)	27	15	15	-	-	12	12	-	-
Ikogmiut	782	374	172	173	29	408	186	194	28
Full blood	768	366	165	172	29	402	180	194	28
Mixed blood (white and Indian)	14	8	7	1	-	6	6	-	-
Imaklimiut	2	1	-	1	-	1	1	-	-
Full blood	2	1	-	1	-	1	1	-	-
Iprackmiut	4	3	2	1	-	1	-	1	-

[Continued]

★ 24 ★

Alaskan Indian Population, by Linguistic Stock, Tribe, Sex, and Age Group, and Mixture of Blood, 1910 - I

[Continued]

Tribe and mixture of blood	Both sexes	Male				Female			
		Total[1]	Under 20 yrs.	20 to 50 yrs.	51 yrs. and over	Total[1]	Under 20 yrs.	20 to 50 yrs.	51 yrs. and over
Full blood	4	3	2	1	-	1	-	1	-
Kaialigmiut	192	98	49	37	12	94	37	47	10
Full blood	191	98	49	37	12	93	36	47	10
Mixed blood (white and Indian)	1	-	-	-	-	1	1	-	-
Kakuakamiut	22	10	6	3	1	12	6	4	2
Full blood	22	10	6	3	1	12	6	4	2
Kangmaligmiut	1	-	-	-	-	1	1	-	-
Full blood	1	-	-	-	-	1	1	-	-
Kaviagmiut	238	120	66	48	6	118	55	51	12
Full blood	209	109	55	48	6	100	37	51	12
Mixed blood (white and Indian)	29	11	11	-	-	18	18	-	-
Kekchabukmiut	32	16	6	9	1	16	5	10	1
Full blood	32	16	6	9	1	16	5	10	1
Kinugumiut	594	330	156	148	26	264	118	120	26
Full blood	576	322	148	148	26	254	108	120	26
Mixed blood (white and Indian)	18	8	8	-	-	10	10	-	-
Kopagmiut	9	3	2	1	-	6	-	6	-
Full blood	9	3	2	1	-	6	-	6	-
Kowagmiut	561	301	141	141	19	260	114	125	21
Full blood	546	293	133	141	19	253	107	125	21
Mixed blood (white and Indian)	15	8	8	-	-	7	7	-	-

Source: U.S. Bureau of the Census, *Indian Population in the United States and Alaska, 1910,* United States Government Printing Office, Washington, D.C., 1915, pp. 154-156.
Notes: A dash (-) represents zero. 1. Totals include persons of unknown age.

★ 25 ★

Alaskan Indian Population, by Linguistic Stock, Tribe, Sex, and Age Group, and Mixture of Blood, 1910 - II

Tribe and mixture of blood	Both sexes	Male				Female			
		Total[1]	Under 20 yrs.	20 to 50 yrs.	51 yrs. and over	Total[1]	Under 20 yrs.	20 to 50 yrs.	51 yrs. and over
Eskimauan stock (cont.)									
Kukpaurungmiut	6	4	3	1	-	2	-	1	1
Full blood	6	4	3	1	-	2	-	1	1
Kunmiut	77	43	21	20	2	34	12	19	3
Full blood	77	43	21	20	2	34	12	19	3
Kusetrinmiut	133	82	47	32	3	51	21	25	5
Full blood	125	77	42	32	3	48	18	25	5
Mixed blood (white and Indian)	8	5	5	-	-	3	3	-	-
Kuskovakmiut	370	212	135	67	10	158	82	67	9
Full blood	361	206	130	66	10	155	79	67	9
Mixed blood (white and Indian)	9	6	5	1	-	3	3	-	-
Kuskowik	37	18	11	5	2	19	7	10	2
Full blood	36	17	10	5	2	19	7	10	2
Mixed blood (white and Indian)	1	1	1	-	-	-	-	-	-
Kuskwogmiut	1,480	741	344	342	55	739	337	348	54
Full blood	1,447	723	326	342	55	724	322	348	54
Mixed blood (white and Indian)	33	18	18	-	-	15	15	-	-
Magemiut	376	176	85	79	12	200	103	80	17
Full blood	376	176	85	79	12	200	103	80	17
Malemiut	563	292	149	118	21	271	136	110	19
Full blood	546	282	139	118	21	264	129	110	19
Mixed blood	17	10	10	-	-	7	7	-	-
White and Indian	14	8	8	-	-	6	6	-	-
Other races and Indian (Chinese)	3	2	2	-	-	1	1	-	-
Naparktoo	9	8	1	6	1	1	-	1	-
Full blood	9	8	1	6	1	1	-	1	-
Neechuktamiut	25	12	5	6	1	13	6	5	2
Full blood	25	12	5	6	1	13	6	5	2
Nunatogmiut	285	158	56	83	16	127	50	60	11
Full blood	277	153	52	82	16	124	47	60	11
Mixed blood (white and Indian)	8	5	4	1	-	3	3	-	-
Nunivagmiut	301	161	69	80	12	140	54	75	11

[Continued]

★ 25 ★

Alaskan Indian Population, by Linguistic Stock, Tribe, Sex, and Age Group, and Mixture of Blood, 1910 - II

[Continued]

Tribe and mixture of blood	Both sexes	Male				Female			
		Total[1]	Under 20 yrs.	20 to 50 yrs.	51 yrs. and over	Total[1]	Under 20 yrs.	20 to 50 yrs.	51 yrs. and over
Full blood	299	160	68	80	12	139	53	75	11
Mixed blood (white and Indian)	2	1	1	-	-	1	1	-	-
Nunochogmiut	158	73	32	38	3	85	36	39	10
Full blood	158	73	32	38	3	85	36	39	10
Nushagagmiut	31	20	7	8	5	11	6	4	1
Full blood	24	16	3	8	5	8	3	4	1
Mixed blood (white and Indian)	7	4	4	-	-	3	3	-	-
Nuwukmiut	81	40	16	20	4	41	17	23	1
Full blood	71	34	12	18	4	37	16	20	1
Mixed blood (white and Indian)	10	6	4	2	-	4	1	3	-
Pitukmiut	4	3	-	1	1	1	-	-	-
Full blood	4	3	-	1	1	1	-	-	-
Polazramiut	14	8	6	2	-	6	4	2	-
Full blood	14	8	6	2	-	6	4	2	-
Selawigmiut	258	140	54	79	7	118	43	65	10
Full blood	258	140	54	79	7	118	43	65	10
Sidarumiut	5	3	1	2	-	2	-	1	1
Full blood	4	2	-	2	-	2	-	1	1
Mixed blood (white and Indian)	1	1	1	-	-	-	-	-	-
Tikeramiut	320	159	60	83	15	161	67	70	23
Full blood	300	153	54	83	15	147	53	70	23
Mixed blood (white and Indian)	20	6	6	-	-	14	14	-	-
Togiagmiut	93	52	26	18	8	41	13	23	5
Full blood	89	48	22	18	8	41	13	23	5
Mixed blood (white and Indian)	4	4	4	-	-	-	-	-	-
Ukivokmiut	140	77	38	37	2	63	26	36	1
Full blood	140	77	38	37	2	63	26	36	1
Unaligmiut	441	221	131	74	16	220	101	102	17
Full blood	421	211	121	74	16	210	91	102	17
Mixed blood (white and Indian)	20	10	10	-	-	10	10	-	-
Utkiavinmiut	123	63	30	30	3	60	23	36	1

[Continued]

★ 25 ★

Alaskan Indian Population, by Linguistic Stock, Tribe, Sex, and Age Group, and Mixture of Blood, 1910 - II

[Continued]

Tribe and mixture of blood	Both sexes	Male				Female			
		Total[1]	Under 20 yrs.	20 to 50 yrs.	51 yrs. and over	Total[1]	Under 20 yrs.	20 to 50 yrs.	51 yrs. and over
Full blood	119	62	30	29	3	57	21	35	1
Mixed blood (white and Indian)	4	1	-	1	-	3	2	1	-
Utukamiut	127	65	26	34	5	62	22	32	8
Full blood	116	57	18	34	5	59	19	32	8
Mixed blood (white and Indian)	11	8	8	-	-	3	3	-	-
Yuit	292	149	61	71	17	143	55	63	25
Full blood	290	148	60	71	17	142	54	63	25
Mixed blood (white and Indian)	2	1	1	-	-	1	1	-	-
Southern Eskimo	3,650	1,899	875	861	155	1,751	857	745	135
Full blood	3,186	1,645	678	809	150	1,541	708	686	134
Mixed blood	464	254	197	52	5	210	149	59	1
White and Indian	454	250	193	52	5	204	144	58	1
Other races and Indian (Japanese)	10	4	4	-	-	6	5	1	-
Tribe not reported	474	237	112	63	12	237	112	67	13
Full blood	423	219	97	61	12	204	83	63	13
Mixed blood	51	18	15	2	-	33	29	4	-
White and Indian	48	18	2	-	30	26	4	-	
Other races and Indian	3	-	-	-	-	3	3	-	-
Chinese	2	-	-	-	-	2	2	-	-
Japanese	1	-	-	-	-	1	1	-	-

Source: U.S. Bureau of the Census, *Indian Population in the United States and Alaska, 1910,* United States Government Printing Office, Washington, D.C., 1915, pp. 154-156.
Notes: A dash (-) represents zero. 1. Totals include persons of unknown age.

★ 26 ★

Alaskan Indian Population, by Linguistic Stock, Tribe, Sex, and Age Group, and Mixture of Blood, 1910 - III

Tribe and mixture of blood	Both sexes	Male				Female			
		Total[1]	Under 20 yrs.	20 to 50 yrs.	51 yrs. and over	Total[1]	Under 20 yrs.	20 to 50 yrs.	51 yrs. and over
Hadian stock									
Total	530	281	143	106	29	249	130	95	23
Full blood	377	201	88	83	29	176	81	72	22
Mixed blood (white and Indian)	153	80	55	23	-	73	49	23	1

[Continued]

★ 26 ★

Alaskan Indian Population, by Linguistic Stock, Tribe, Sex, and Age Group, and Mixture of Blood, 1910 - III

[Continued]

Tribe and mixture of blood	Both sexes	Male				Female			
		Total[1]	Under 20 yrs.	20 to 50 yrs.	51 yrs. and over	Total[1]	Under 20 yrs.	20 to 50 yrs.	51 yrs. and over
Tlingit stock									
Total	4,426	2,223	995	949	278	2,203	1,004	934	263
Full blood	3,890	1,945	791	879	274	1,945	792	896	255
Mixed blood	536	278	204	70	4	258	212	38	8
White and Indian	522	271	197	70	4	251	205	38	8
Other races and Indian	13	6	6	-	-	7	7	-	-
Chinese	2	1	1	-	-	1	1	-	-
Japanese	11	5	5	-	-	6	6	-	-
Mixture unknown	1	1	1	-	-	-	-	-	-
Auk	267	143	47	82	14	124	55	61	8
Full blood	242	132	37	81	14	110	43	60	7
Mixed blood (white and Indian)	25	11	10	1	-	14	12	1	1
Chilkat	690	350	140	167	43	340	144	151	45
Full blood	629	318	112	163	43	311	119	148	44
Mixed blood (white and Indian)	61	32	28	4	-	29	25	3	1
Henya	214	114	50	49	15	100	52	39	9
Full blood	192	101	41	45	15	91	44	38	9
Mixed blood (white and Indian)	22	13	9	4	-	9	8	1	-
Huna	625	303	141	125	36	322	136	143	43
Full blood	590	286	127	122	36	304	120	141	43
Mixed blood (white and Indian)	35	17	14	3	-	18	16	2	-
Hutsnuwu	536	268	131	101	36	268	123	109	36
Full blood	498	247	111	100	36	251	107	108	36
Mixed blood	38	21	20	1	-	17	16	1	-
White and Indian	31	18	17	1	-	13	12	1	-
Other races and Indian	7	3	3	-	-	4	4	-	-
Chinese	1	-	-	-	-	1	1	-	-
Japanese	6	3	3	-	-	3	3	-	-
Kake	322	163	80	52	31	159	73	65	21
Full blood	276	141	63	47	31	135	54	61	20
Mixed blood	46	22	17	5	-	24	19	4	1
White and Indian	45	22	17	5	-	23	18	4	1
Other races and Indian (Japanese)	1	-	-	-	-	1	1	-	-
Kuyu	29	17	4	10	3	12	6	4	2
Full blood	29	17	4	10	3	12	6	4	2

[Continued]

★ 26 ★

Alaskan Indian Population, by Linguistic Stock, Tribe, Sex, and Age Group, and Mixture of Blood, 1910 - III
[Continued]

Tribe and mixture of blood	Both sexes	Male				Female			
		Total[1]	Under 20 yrs.	20 to 50 yrs.	51 yrs. and over	Total[1]	Under 20 yrs.	20 to 50 yrs.	51 yrs. and over
Sitka	608	295	131	115	49	313	144	117	51
Full blood	527	248	97	104	47	279	118	109	51
Mixed blood	81	47	34	11	2	34	26	8	-
White and Indian	80	46	33	11	2	34	26	8	-
Mixture unknown	1	1	1	-	-	-	-	-	-
Stikine	189	96	35	49	12	93	44	34	15
Full blood	150	72	27	33	12	78	30	34	14
Mixed blood (white and Indian)	39	24	8	16	-	15	14	-	1
Taku	142	70	31	31	8	72	27	38	6
Full blood	128	62	23	31	8	66	22	37	6
Mixed blood	14	8	8	-	-	6	5	1	-
White and Indian	13	7	7	-	-	6	5	1	-
Other races and Indian (Chinese)	1	1	1	-	-	-	-	-	-
Tongas	184	88	42	38	8	96	52	35	9
Full blood	156	76	33	35	8	80	40	31	9
Mixed blood (white and Indian)	28	12	9	3	-	16	12	4	-
Yakutat	307	143	70	65	8	164	78	77	9
Full blood	276	131	59	64	8	145	59	77	9
Mixed blood	31	12	11	1	-	19	19	-	-
White and Indian	30	12	11	1	-	18	18	-	-
Other races and Indian (Japanese)	1	-	-	-	-	1	1	-	-
Tribe not reported	313	173	93	65	15	140	70	61	9
Full blood	197	114	57	44	13	83	30	48	5
Mixed blood	116	59	36	21	2	57	40	13	4
White and Indian	113	57	34	21	2	56	39	13	4
Other races and Indian (Japanese)	3	2	2	-	-	1	1	-	-
Tsimshian stock									
Total	729	384	187	143	54	345	178	119	48
Full blood	615	333	151	131	51	282	138	96	48
Mixed blood (white and Indian)	114	51	36	12	3	63	40	23	-

Source: U.S. Bureau of the Census, *Indian Population in the United States and Alaska, 1910*, United States Government Printing Office, Washington, D.C., 1915, pp. 154-156.
Notes: A dash (-) represents zero. 1. Totals include persons of unknown age.

★ 27 ★

American Indian Population, by Linguistic Stock, Tribe, and State, 1910 and 1930 - I

Population is shown for states which have five or more Indians of the specified tribe in either 1910 or 1930. Linguistic Stocks appear in boldened letters.

Linguistic stock, tribe and state	Number	
	1910	1930
Algonquian	39,926	40,670
Arapaho	1,419	1,241
Wyoming	703	863
Oklahoma	685	360
Montana	18	4
Kansas	6	3
Other states	7	11
Blackfeet	2,367	3,145
Montana	2,254	3,033
Washington	-	16
Ohio	-	14
Nebraska	33	12
Oklahoma	15	11
South Dakota	1	11
Idaho	3	7
California	1	6
Pennsylvania	12	6
Oregon	6	6
North Dakota	35	1
Other states	7	22
Cheyenne	3,055	2,695
Montana	1,346	1,408
Oklahoma	1,522	1,220
South Dakota	133	27
Kansas	5	9
Washington	-	8
Arizona	-	6
California	-	5
Pennsylvania	33	-
Colorado	6	-
Other states	10	12
Chippewa	20,214	21,549
Minnesota	8,234	9,495
Wisconsin	4,299	4,437
North Dakota	2,966	3,827
Michigan	3,725	1,685
Montana	486	1,549
South Dakota	73	280
Oklahoma	64	56
Oregon	48	48

[Continued]

★ 27 ★

American Indian Population, by Linguistic Stock, Tribe, and State, 1910 and 1930 - I
[Continued]

Linguistic stock, tribe and state	Number	
	1910	1930
Kansas	92	33
Washington	6	28
Idaho	-	18
Arizona	1	14
New Mexico	-	12
California	6	10
Illinois	-	10
Ohio	3	8
Colorado	-	7
Nebraska	64	7
Missouri	1	6
Nevada	-	6
Pennsylvania	134	2
Other states	12	11
Delaware	985	971
Oklahoma	895	874
Kansas	55	45
Arizona	-	12
New York	7	10
Minnesota	-	8
Arkansas	-	5
Pennsylvania	9	1
Other states	19	16
Gros Ventres (Atsina)	510	631
Montana	503	615
Wyoming	1	6
Other states	6	10
Kickapoo	348	523
Kansas	211	278
Oklahoma	135	219
Nebraska	1	8
Washington	-	8
Other states	1	10
Menominee	1,422	1,969
Wisconsin	1,350	1,950
South Dakota	3	7
Michigan	34	5
Minnesota	13	1
Oklahoma	7	1
Pennsylvania	9	-

[Continued]

★ 27 ★

American Indian Population, by Linguistic Stock, Tribe, and State, 1910 and 1930 - I
[Continued]

Linguistic stock, tribe and state	Number	
	1910	1930
Other states	6	5
Miami and Illinois	360	284
Oklahoma	241	222
Indiana	92	47
Kansas	11	7
Colorado	-	5
Missouri	6	-
Other states	10	3
Ottawa	2,717	1,745
Michigan	2,454	1,469
Oklahoma	170	167
Wisconsin	50	84
California	-	6
Illinois	-	5
Minnesota	-	5
Nebraska	23	3
Kansas	14	-
Pennsylvania	6	-
Other states	-	6
Potawatomi	2,440	1,854
Kansas	819	654
Oklahoma	866	636
Wisconsin	245	425
Michigan	461	89
Nebraska	21	14
Minnesota	1	7
Arizona	3	5
Utah	-	5
South Dakota	10	4
Iowa	6	1
Other states	8	14

Source: Dr. Leon E. Truesdell, U.S. Department of Commerce, Bureau of the Census, Fifteenth Census of the United States: 1930, *The Indian Population of the United States and Alaska*, U.S. Government Printing Office, 1937, pp. 56-68. *Note:* A dash (-) indicates 5 or less Indians were counted.

★ 28 ★

American Indian Population, by Linguistic Stock, Tribe, and State, 1910 and 1930 - II

Population is shown for states which have five or more Indians of the specified tribe in either 1910 or 1930. Linguistic Stocks appear in boldened letters.

Linguistic stock, tribe and state	Number	
	1910	1930
Algonquian (cont.)		
Sauk and Fox	724	887
Oklahoma	347	478
Iowa	257	344
Kansas	69	23
Nebraska	13	20
Michigan	1	5
Missouri	5	3
Washington	8	2
Pennsylvania	14	1
Tennessee	6	-
Other states	4	11
Shawnee	1,338	1,161
Oklahoma	1,300	1,107
Colorado	-	13
Texas	-	6
New Mexico	-	6
Kansas	14	4
Missouri	14	3
Other states	10	22
Eastern Algonquians	2,027	2,015
Wisconsin	693	813
Maine	634	761
New York	191	194
Rhode Island	-	130
Massachusetts	372	54
Connecticut	77	25
Minnesota	8	14
Oklahoma	9	10
Illinois	-	6
Pennsylvania	25	-
Other states	19	8
Virginia-Carolina Indians	5,195	12,975
North Carolina	5,865	12,402
South Carolina	-	352
Virginia	330	203
Oklahoma	-	8
Arizona	-	6
Other states	-	4

[Continued]

★ 28 ★

American Indian Population, by Linguistic Stock, Tribe, and State, 1910 and 1930 - II
[Continued]

Linguistic stock, tribe and state	Number	
	1910	1930
Athapaskan	30,402	47,418
Apache	6,119	6,537
Arizona	4,652	5,113
New Mexico	1,155	1,284
Oklahoma	282	99
California	4	14
Washington	-	7
Colorado	1	5
Kansas	13	-
Other states	12	15
Kiowa Apache	139	164
Oklahoma	139	183
Illinois	-	1
Navaho	22,455	39,064
Arizona	11,001	20,707
New Mexico	10,354	16,971
Utah	1,039	1,109
Colorado	8	185
California	20	42
South Dakota	4	12
Nevada	-	8
Washington	-	7
Oklahoma	4	5
Missouri	-	5
Pennsylvania	13	1
Kansas	8	1
Other states	4	11
Oregon Athapaskans	656	504
Oregon	499	489
California	129	7
Washington	23	6
Other states	5	2
California Athapaskans	1,033	1,129
California	999	1,115
Washington	15	5
Oregon	8	4
Arizona	6	2
Kansas	5	-
Other states	-	3

[Continued]

★ 28 ★

American Indian Population, by Linguistic Stock, Tribe, and State, 1910 and 1930 - II

[Continued]

Linguistic stock, tribe and state	Number	
	1910	1930
Caddoan	1,863	2,115
Arikara	444	420
North Dakota	425	412
New York	6	-
Other states	13	8
Caddo	452	625
Oklahoma	436	615
Kansas	5	5
Pennsylvania	8	-
Other states	3	5
Pawnee	633	770
Oklahoma	573	729
Arizona	19	12
Kansas	14	11
California	-	7
Pennsylvania	18	-
South Dakota	5	-
Other states	4	11
Wichita and Kichai	334	300
Oklahoma	295	292
South Dakota	20	2
Pennsylvania	15	-
Other states		
Chimakuan	306	375
Washington	306	371
Other states	-	4
Chinookan	897	561
Oregon	352	447
Washington	524	104
Oklahoma	4	8
Montana	12	1
Other states	5	1
Chitimachan	69	51
Louisiana	50	51
Pennsylvania	19	-

[Continued]

33

★ 28 ★

American Indian Population, by Linguistic Stock, Tribe, and State, 1910 and 1930 - II

[Continued]

Linguistic stock, tribe and state	Number	
	1910	1930
Chumashan	38	14
California	38	13
Arizona	-	1

Source: Dr. Leon E. Truesdell, U.S. Department of Commerce, Bureau of the Census, Fifteenth Census of the United States: 1930, *The Indian Population of the United States and Alaska*, U.S. Government Printing Office, 1937, pp. 56-68. *Note:* A dash (-) indicates 5 or less Indians were counted.

★ 29 ★

American Indian Population, by Linguistic Stock, Tribe, and State, 1910 and 1930 - III

Population is shown for states which have five or more Indians of the specified tribe in either 1910 or 1930. Linguistic Stocks appear in boldened letters.

Linguistic stock, tribe and state	Number	
	1910	1930
Costanoan (Santa Cruz)	17	-
California	17	-
Iroquoian	39,679	52,457
Iroquois	7,837[1]	6,866
New York	4,918	4,365
Wisconsin	2,122	1,732
Oklahoma	263	340
Pennsylvania	362	81
Michigan	17	78
Minnesota	8	45
California	6	30
South Dakota	10	29
Arizona	2	22
Colorado	-	17
Kansas	35	14
Illinois	1	12
Washington	-	10
North Dakota	1	9
Nebraska	5	8
Ohio	12	7
Montana	1	7
New Mexico	2	6
Arkansas	-	6
Indiana	-	6
Missouri	-	6

[Continued]

★ 29 ★

American Indian Population, by Linguistic Stock, Tribe, and State, 1910 and 1930 - III

[Continued]

Linguistic stock, tribe and state	Number	
	1910	1930
Nevada	-	5
Other states	11	31
Wyandot	353	353
Oklahoma	320	323
South Dakota	2	15
Kansas	21	4
California	5	1
Other states	5	10
Cherokee	31,489	45,238
Oklahoma	29,610	40,904
North Carolina	1,406	1,963
Alabama	9	287
Virginia	19	268
California	34	258
Kansas	71	191
Arkansas	-	180
Oregon	19	126
Texas	-	117
Arizona	4	101
Michigan	3	96
Missouri	13	88
Washington	8	82
Colorado	12	76
New Mexico	1	61
Illinois	-	51
Wisconsin	14	40
Tennessee	45	38
Idaho	8	36
Montana	12	31
Ohio	15	29
New York	5	26
Iowa	-	26
Nebraska	-	25
Pennsylvania	50	18
Georgia	-	15
South Dakota	7	13
Wyoming	-	13
Louisiana	1	12
Indiana	-	10
Nevada	-	9
Massachusetts	-	8
New Jersey	-	7

[Continued]

★ 29 ★

American Indian Population, by Linguistic Stock, Tribe, and State, 1910 and 1930 - III
[Continued]

Linguistic stock, tribe and state	Number	
	1910	1930
Mississippi	-	6
Minnesota	2	5
Florida	-	5
North Dakota	34	4
South Dakota	87	2
Other states	-	11
Kalapooian	106	45
Oregon	78	28
California	-	11
Washington	28	2
Other states	-	4
Karok (Orleans)	775	755
California	775	723
Oklahoma	-	18
Oregon	-	9
Other states	-	5
Keresan	4,027	4,134
New Mexico	3,996	4,092
Arizona	-	27
California	19	7
Oklahoma	4	6
Other states	8	2
Kiowan (Kiowa)	1,126	1,050
Oklahoma	1,107	1,046
Kansas	17	-
Other states	2	4
Kusan (Kusa)	93	107
Oregon	93	99
Other states	-	8

Source: Dr. Leon E. Truesdell, U.S. Department of Commerce, Bureau of the Census, Fifteenth Census of the United States: 1930, *The Indian Population of the United States and Alaska*, U.S. Government Printing Office, 1937, pp. 56-68. *Notes:* A dash (-) indicates 5 or less Indians were counted. 1. Includes 61 of returned as "Iroquois" but with tribe not reported. Not distributed by States.

★ 30 ★

American Indian Population, by Linguistic Stock, Tribe, and State, 1910 and 1930 - IV

Population is shown for states which have five or more Indians of the specified tribe in either 1910 or 1930. Linguistic Stocks appear in boldened letters.

Linguistic stock, tribe and state	Number	
	1910	1930
Kutenaian (Kutenai)	538	287
Montana	424	185
Idaho	107	101
Other states	7	1
Maidu	1,100	93
California	1,098	75
Wisconsin	-	11
Other states	2	7
Miwok	699	491
California	698	485
Other states	1	6
Muskhogean	29,191	33,633
Chickasaw	4,204	4,745
Oklahoma	4,191	4,685
California	-	14
Missouri	-	11
Louisiana	-	8
Colorado	-	8
Texas	-	5
Other states	13	14
Choctaw	15,917	17,757
Oklahoma	14,551	16,461
Mississippi	1,162	624
Louisiana	115	190
Texas	-	66
California	-	41
Arizona	-	40
Alabama	57	27
Kansas	11	24
Colorado	-	20
New Mexico	-	18
Michigan	-	14
Missouri	-	8
Oregon	1	7
Arkansas	-	7
Wyoming	-	7
South Dakota	8	1
Virginia	8	-
Other states	4	22

[Continued]

★ 30 ★

American Indian Population, by Linguistic Stock, Tribe, and State, 1910 and 1930 - IV
[Continued]

Linguistic stock, tribe and state	Number	
	1910	1930
Creek	7,341	9,083
Oklahoma	6,654	8,607
Texas	199	180
Louisiana	196	134
Kansas	33	43
Alabama	185	36
Oregon	1	24
Missouri	2	11
California	3	10
Arizona	-	9
New Mexico	-	7
Wisconsin	-	6
Arkansas	-	5
Montana	34	3
South Dakota	9	2
North Carolina	7	1
Mississippi	6	-
Other states	12	5
Seminole	1,729	2,048
Oklahoma	1,503	1,789
Florida	16	227
California	1	7
Arizona	-	6
Oregon	-	6
Michigan	-	5
Texas	200	2
Kansas	8	-
Other states	1	6
Piman	8,034	9,587
Papago	3,798	5,205
Arizona	3,785	5,163
California	6	29
Other states	7	13
Pima	4,236	4,382
Arizona	4,167	4,322
California	60	22
South Dakota	-	13
Oklahoma	-	10
Montana	-	5
Kansas	5	2
Other states	4	8

[Continued]

★ 30 ★

American Indian Population, by Linguistic Stock, Tribe, and State, 1910 and 1930 - IV
[Continued]

Linguistic stock, tribe and state	Number	
	1910	1930
Pomo	1,193	1,143
California	1,162	1,134
Kansas	6	-
Other states	5	9
Salinan (San Antonio)	16	-
California	16	-
Salishan	7,723	9,333
Washington Coast Salish	3,918	4,106
Oregon	57	26
Idaho	-	11
California	-	8
Pennsylvania	5	1
Other states	6	5

Source: Dr. Leon E. Truesdell, U.S. Department of Commerce, Bureau of the Census, Fifteenth Census of the United States: 1930, *The Indian Population of the United States and Alaska,* U.S. Government Printing Office, 1937, pp. 56-68. *Note:* A dash (·) indicates 5 or less Indians were counted.

★ 31 ★

American Indian Population, by Linguistic Stock, Tribe, and State, 1910 and 1930 - V

Population is shown for states which have five or more Indians of the specified tribe in either 1910 or 1930. Linguistic Stocks appear in boldened letters.

Linguistic stock, tribe and state	Number	
	1910	1930
Interior Salish	3,780	5,211
Washington	2,242	2,607
Montana	939	2,036
Idaho	419	480
Oregon	151	72
Nebraska	7	1
Pennsylvania	19	-
Other states	3	15
Tillamook	25	16
Oregon	18	9
Washington	6	2
Other states	1	5

[Continued]

★ 31 ★

American Indian Population, by Linguistic Stock, Tribe, and State, 1910 and 1930 - V

[Continued]

Linguistic stock, tribe and state	Number	
	1910	1930
Shapwailutan	5,698[1]	6,352
Klamath and Modoc	978	2,034
Oregon	858	1,057
California	36	922
Oklahoma	33	31
Washington	5	8
Nevada	-	8
Arizona	6	2
Pennsylvania	25	-
Missouri	10	-
Other states	5	6
Shahaptians	4,374	4,119
Washington	1,984	1,890
Idaho	1,074	1,091
Oregon	1,206	1,054
Montana	66	39
California	2	14
Nevada	-	8
Nebraska	-	6
Kansas	7	2
Pennsylvania	33	-
Other states	2	15
Cayuse and Molala	329	199
Oregon	302	193
Washington	11	1
South Dakota	5	-
Other states	11	5
Shastan	1,578	844
California	1,383	693
Oregon	177	138
Washington	2	5
Nevada	8	1
Oklahoma	7	1
Other states	1	6
Shoshonean	16,842	15,985
Bannock	413	415
Idaho	363	313
Oklahoma	-	66
Wyoming	9	11
Oregon	2	7

[Continued]

★ 31 ★

American Indian Population, by Linguistic Stock, Tribe, and State, 1910 and 1930 - V
[Continued]

Linguistic stock, tribe and state	Number	
	1910	1930
California	4	6
Utah	1	6
Montana	23	1
Pennsylvania	5	-
Other states	6	5
Comanche	1,171	1,423
Oklahoma	1,160	1,390
California	-	8
Kansas	7	6
Arizona	-	5
Other states	4	14
Hopi	2,009	2,752
Arizona	1,941	2,701
California	42	22
New Mexico	9	12
Nevada	-	7
Washington	-	7
Pennsylvania	13	-
Other states	4	3
Paiute-Mono-Paviotan	5,631	5,060
Nevada	2,782	2,660
California	1,968	1,531
Oregon	341	291
Arizona	97	249
Utah	238	193
Idaho	152	112
Montana	27	11
Oklahoma	-	5
Washington	7	4
Wyoming	8	-
Pennsylvania	5	-
Other states	6	4
Shoshoni	3,840	3,994
Nevada	1,555	1,633
Idaho	1,259	1,251
Wyoming	700	787
California	33	177
Utah	248	107
Arizona	4	9
Montana	10	8

[Continued]

★ 31 ★

American Indian Population, by Linguistic Stock, Tribe, and State, 1910 and 1930 - V

[Continued]

Linguistic stock, tribe and state	Number	
	1910	1930
Washington	-	6
Oregon	-	6
Pennsylvania	27	-
Other states	4	10
Ute	2,281	1,980
Utah	1,509	1,269
Colorado	725	669
Wyoming	6	18
New Mexico	-	5
Washington	-	5
Nevada	6	3
Oklahoma	14	2
Kansas	12	-
Other states	9	9
Southern California	1,497	361
California	1,493	350
Oklahoma	-	10
Other states	4	1

Source: Dr. Leon E. Truesdell, U.S. Department of Commerce, Bureau of the Census, Fifteenth Census of the United States: 1930, *The Indian Population of the United States and Alaska*, U.S. Government Printing Office, 1937, pp. 56-68. *Notes:* A dash (-) indicates 5 or less Indians were counted. 1. Includes 61 of Iroquois stock, 17 of Shapwailutan stock, and 13 of Tanoan stock included also in totals for stocks.

★ 32 ★

American Indian Population, by Linguistic Stock, Tribe, and State, 1910 and 1930 - VI

Population is shown for states which have five or more Indians of the specified tribe in either 1910 or 1930. Linguistic Stocks appear in boldened letters.

Linguistic stock, tribe and state	Number	
	1910	1930
Siouan	32,941	37,329
Catawba	124	166
South Carolina	99	159
Colorado	14	-
North Carolina	6	-
Other states	5	7

[Continued]

★ 32 ★

American Indian Population, by Linguistic Stock, Tribe, and State, 1910 and 1930 - VI
[Continued]

Linguistic stock, tribe and state	Number	
	1910	1930
Crow	1,799	1,674
Montana	1,698	1,625
Oklahoma	2	13
South Dakota	53	12
Indiana	-	6
Washington	-	5
Kansas	14	1
California	11	-
North Dakota	11	-
Pennsylvania	5	-
Other states	5	12
Hidatsa	547	528
North Dakota	520	519
South Dakota	1	9
Pennsylvania	10	-
Montana	9	-
Wyoming	6	-
Kansas	1	-
Iowa	244	176
Nebraska	38	83
Oklahoma	79	71
Kansas	124	19
Kansas	238	318
Oklahoma	252	313
Kansas	6	1
Other states	-	4
Mandan	209	271
North Dakota	197	258
Montana	5	12
South Dakota	5	1
District of Columbia	2	-
Oto and Missouri	345	627
Oklahoma	326	614
California	-	7
Nebraska	10	1
Kansas	6	1
Other states	3	4
Omaha	1,105	1,103

[Continued]

★ 32 ★

American Indian Population, by Linguistic Stock, Tribe, and State, 1910 and 1930 - VI
[Continued]

Linguistic stock, tribe and state	Number	
	1910	1930
Nebraska	1,075	1,027
Oklahoma	5	48
Colorado	-	12
South Dakota	-	6
Kansas	11	2
Pennsylvania	11	-
Other states	3	8
Osage	1,373	2,344
Oklahoma	1,345	2,106
Kansas	12	112
California	-	21
Oregon	-	20
Colorado	-	19
New Mexico	1	12
Arizona	2	8
Arkansas	-	7
Washington	-	7
Texas	-	6
Illinois	-	5
Pennsylvania	7	2
Other states	6	19
Ponca	875	939
Oklahoma	619	743
Nebraska	193	161
South Dakota	18	31
Kansas	42	-
Other states	3	4
Quapaw	231	222
Oklahoma	221	212
Kansas	6	10
Other states	4	-
Dakota	22,778	25,934
South Dakota	18,340	20,918
North Dakota	1,900	2,307
Montana	887	1,251
Nebraska	794	690
Minnesota	457	311
Oklahoma	56	144
California	3	49
Washington	6	28

[Continued]

★ 32 ★

American Indian Population, by Linguistic Stock, Tribe, and State, 1910 and 1930 - VI

[Continued]

Linguistic stock, tribe and state	Number	
	1910	1930
Idaho	-	26
Arizona	3	23
Wyoming	11	22
Kansas	93	21
Michigan	1	17
Pennsylvania	97	15
Colorado	-	14
Oregon	2	14
Illinois	8	13
Nevada	2	13
New Mexico	-	13
Wisconsin	33	9
New York	1	8
Missouri	11	6
Kentucky	-	6
Tennessee	-	5
Iowa	7	3
New Jersey	62	1
Other states	4	7
Assiniboin	1,253	1,581
Montana	1,229	1,467
North Dakota	8	94
Nevada	-	5
Kansas	6	1
Oregon	6	1
Other states	4	13

Source: Dr. Leon E. Truesdell, U.S. Department of Commerce, Bureau of the Census, Fifteenth Census of the United States: 1930, *The Indian Population of the United States and Alaska*, U.S. Government Printing Office, 1937, pp. 56-68. *Note:* A dash (-) indicates 5 or less Indians were counted.

★ 33 ★

American Indian Population, by Linguistic Stock, Tribe, and State, 1910 and 1930 - VII

Population is shown for states which have five or more Indians of the specified tribe in either 1910 or 1930. Linguistic Stocks appear in in boldened letters.

Linguistic group, tribe and state	Number	
	1910	1930
Winnebago	1,820	1,446
Wisconsin	735	937
Nebraska	1,007	423
Minnesota	8	15
Oklahoma	9	14
Kansas	5	14
South Dakota	2	12
Iowa	32	5
Illinois	-	5
Pennsylvania	17	3
Other states	5	18
Tanoan	3,140[1]	3,412
New Mexico	3,077	3,348
California	3	32
Arizona	8	9
Texas	34	-
Other states	5	23
Tonkawan (Tonkawa)	42	48
Oklahoma	42	46
Other states	-	2
Tunican (Tunica)	43	1
Louisiana	43	1
Washoan (Washo)	819	668
Nevada	536	389
California	273	275
Oregon	5	-
Other states	5	4
Wintun	710	512
California	703	508
Other states	7	4
Wiyot (Humboldt Bay)	152	236
California	152	230
Oregon	-	4
Nevada	-	2
Yakonan	55	9
Oregon	47	7

[Continued]

★ 33 ★

American Indian Population, by Linguistic Stock, Tribe, and State, 1910 and 1930 - VII
[Continued]

Linguistic group, tribe and state	Number	
	1910	1930
Washington	7	2
South Dakota	1	-
Yuman	39	9
California	39	9
Yokuts	533	1,145
California	530	1,085
Nevada	-	29
Oregon	-	13
Oklahoma	-	9
Arizona	2	6
Other states	1	3
Yuchaan	78	216
Oklahoma	74	1195
North Carolina	-	5
Other states	4	16
Yukian	198	177
California	194	150
Oregon	3	24
Other states	1	3
Yuman	4,267	4,537
Cocopa	245	99
Arizona	229	89
California	16	10
Diegueno	756	322
California	756	321
Nevada	-	1
Northern Yumans	988	646
Arizona	983	639
Other states	5	7
Maricopa	386	310
Arizona	382	295
California	4	5
Other states	-	10
Mohave	1,058	854
Arizona	667	574

[Continued]

★ 33 ★

American Indian Population, by Linguistic Stock, Tribe, and State, 1910 and 1930 - VII

[Continued]

Linguistic group, tribe and state	Number	
	1910	1930
California	389	277
Other states	2	3
Yuma	834	2,306
California	642	2,231
Arizona	191	69
Other states	1	6
Yurok	668	471
California	668	440
Nevada	-	26
Zunian (Zuni)	1,667	1,749
New Mexico	1,664	1,726
Arizona	1	10
Other states	2	13

Source: Dr. Leon E. Truesdell, U.S. Department of Commerce, Bureau of the Census, Fifteenth Census of the United States: 1930, *The Indian Population of the United States and Alaska,* U.S. Government Printing Office, 1937, pp. 56-68. *Notes:* A dash (-) indicates 5 or less Indians were counted. 1. Includes 13 of Tanoan stock not reported by tribe and not classified by state.

★ 34 ★

American Indian Population, by Linguistic Stock, Tribe, and State, 1910 and 1930 - VIII

Population is shown for states which have five or more Indians of the specified tribe in either 1910 or 1930. Linguistic Stocks appear in boldened letters.

Linguistic stock, tribe and state	Number	
	1910	1930
Other tribes of the Unites States, including stocks and tribes not reported	20,425[1]	35,150
California	1,856	5,578
Oklahoma	4,407	4,900
Michigan	790	3,291
North Carolina	565	2,197
New York	886	1,875
Arizona	498	1,345
New Mexico	313	1,267
Washington	1,343	1,173
Minnesota	314	1,090

[Continued]

★ 34 ★

American Indian Population, by Linguistic Stock, Tribe, and State, 1910 and 1930 - VIII

[Continued]

Linguistic stock, tribe and state	Number	
	1910	1930
Louisiana	375	1,089
Wisconsin	588	1,052
Kansas	500	894
Mississippi	82	824
Massachusetts	291	753
Nebraska	198	738
Texas	269	575
North Dakota	374	538
South Carolina	143	445
Montana	440	422
Missouri	246	407
Oregon	664	402
Florida	56	348
Pennsylvania	438	331
Ohio	92	323
South Dakota	372	322
Colorado	714	309
Virginia	178	301
Illinois	179	291
Iowa	169	263
Arkansas	460	194
Indiana	184	194
Rhode Island	284	184
New Jersey	106	170
Utah	85	161
Maine	87	144
Connecticut	75	121
Tennessee	155	113
Alabama	658	112
Idaho	87	104
Wyoming	29	84
Maryland	55	47
New Hampshire	31	35
District of Columbia	57	34
Nevada	336	27
Vermont	26	26
Georgia	95	25
Kentucky	234	15

[Continued]

★ 34 ★

American Indian Population, by Linguistic Stock, Tribe, and State, 1910 and 1930 - VIII
[Continued]

Linguistic stock, tribe and state	Number	
	1910	1930
West Virginia	36	14
Delaware	5	3

Source: Dr. Leon E. Truesdell, U.S. Department of Commerce, Bureau of the Census, Fifteenth Census of the United States: 1930, *The Indian Population of the United States and Alaska*, U.S. Government Printing Office, 1937, pp. 56-68. *Notes:* A dash (-) indicates 5 or less Indians were counted. 1. Includes 61 of Iroquois stock, 17 of Shapwailuton stock, and 13 of Tenoan stock included also in totals for these stocks.

★ 35 ★

American Indian Population, by Linguistic Stock, Tribe, and State, 1910 and 1930 - IX

Population is shown for states which have five or more Indians of the specified tribe in either 1910 or 1930. Linguistic Stocks appear in boldened letters.

Linguistic stock, tribe and state	Number	
	1910	1930
Alaskan and foreign tribes	1,781	6,253
Canadian and Mexican tribes	1,781	5,651
Arizona	534	2,097
Montana	309	1,043
Washington	596	522
New York	24	408
North Dakota	5	401
Michigan	28	289
Maine	168	106
California	38	99
Oklahoma	1	75
New Mexico	-	69
South Dakota	-	66
Minnesota	2	55
Massachusetts	24	44
Louisiana	-	44
Illinois	-	41
Idaho	2	37
Ohio	-	36
Pennsylvania	4	35
Wisconsin	2	29
New Hampshire	-	29
Oregon	42	24

[Continued]

★ 35 ★

American Indian Population, by Linguistic Stock, Tribe, and State, 1910 and 1930 - IX

[Continued]

Linguistic stock, tribe and state	Number	
	1910	1930
Texas	-	15
Colorado	-	13
Kansas	1	12
New Jersey	-	11
Wyoming	-	10
Connecticut	-	10
Vermont	-	6
Nebraska	1	5
Other states	-	20
Alaskan tribes	85	385
Washington	6	226
Oregon	79	90
Idaho	-	18
California	-	18
New York	-	8
Other states	-	25
Other foreign-born Indians	1[1]	217
New York	-	56
California	1[1]	35
New Jersey	1[1]	17
Pennsylvania	1[1]	16
Texas	1[1]	10
Missouri	1[1]	8
Louisiana	1[1]	7
Ohio	1[1]	6
Michigan	1[1]	6
Massachusetts	1[1]	5
Illinois	1[1]	5
Minnesota	1[1]	5
Washington	1[1]	5
Other states	1[1]	36

Source: Dr. Leon E. Truesdell, U.S. Department of Commerce, Bureau of the Census, Fifteenth Census of the United States: 1930, *The Indian Population of the United States and Alaska,* U.S. Government Printing Office, 1937, pp. 56-68. *Notes:* A dash (-) indicates 5 or less Indians were counted. 1. Not tabulated in 1910.

★ 36 ★

American Indian Population, by State and Tribe, 1910: Alabama - California

State and tribe	Number
Alabama	909
Cherokee	9
Choctaw	57
Creek	185
Not reported[1]	658
Arizona	29,201
Apache	4,652
Apache	2,344
Chiricahua Apache	24
Coyotero Apache	490
San Carlos Apache	1,087
Tonto Apache	655
White Mountain Apache	52
Chemehuevi	28
Cherokee	4
Chickasaw	1
Chippewa	1
Chuckhansi	2
Cocopa	229
Havasupai	174
Hopi	1,941
Hupa	6
Isleta	8
Kawia	1
Klamath	4
Little Lake	1
Maricopa	382
Mayo	40
Modoc	2
Mohave	667
Navajo	11,001
Oneida	1
Opata	5
Osage	2
Paiute	69
Papago	3,785
Pawnee	19
Piegan	3
Pima	4,167
Pomo	1
Potawatomi	3
Seneca	1
Serrano	1
Shawnee	3
Shoshoni	4

[Continued]

★ 36 ★

American Indian Population, by State and Tribe, 1910: Alabama - California
[Continued]

State and tribe	Number
Sioux	3
Ute	1
Walapai	496
Yaqui	489
Yavapai	289
Yuki	1
Yuma	191
Yuma Apache	24
Zuni	1
Not reported[1]	498
Arkansas	460
Not reported[1]	460
California	16,371
Apache	4
Arapaho	1
Bannock	4
Blackfeet	1
Cayuse	1
Chemehuevi	260
Cherokee	34
Chetco	1
Chimariko	31
Chippewa	6
Choinimni	18
Chookiminah	4
Chukchansi	142
Clear Lake	193
Coast Yuki	15
Cocopa	16
Creek	3
Crow	11
Delaware	3
Diegueno	756
Gabrieleno	11
Gynomehro	33
Hat Creek	240
Hopi	42
Humboldt Bay	152
Hupa	617
Isleta	3
Juaneno	16
Kai-Pomo	51
Kashowoo	4

[Continued]

★ 36 ★

American Indian Population, by State and Tribe, 1910:
Alabama - California
[Continued]

State and tribe	Number
Kawaiisu	23
Kawia	754
Kern River	105
Kiowa	1
Klamath	16
Laguna	19
Little Lake	84
Lower Lake	96
Maidu	1,098
Maricopa	4
Marin	22
Mattole	34
Miami	1
Middle Town	7
Miwok	669
Modoc	20
Mohave	389
Mono	1,388
Navajo	20

Source: U.S. Bureau of the Census, *Indian Population in the United States and Alaska, 1910*, United States Government Printing Office, Washington, D.C., 1915, pp. 22-24. *Notes:* 1. Under "Not reported" are included Indians enumerated on the general population schedule only for whom no inquiry as to stock or tribe was made, or Indians for whom special schedules were obtained but whose stock or tribe was not reported.

★ 37 ★

American Indian Population, by State and Tribe, 1910:
California - Georgia

State and tribe	Number
California - continued	
Nomelaki	122
Omaha	2
Orleans	775
Paiute	210
Panamint	9
Papago	6
Patwin	186
Paviotso	101
Peoria	1
Pima	60
Pit River	888

[Continued]

★ 37 ★

American Indian Population, by State and Tribe, 1910: California - Georgia
[Continued]

State and tribe	Number
Pomo	776
Potawatomi	1
Quapaw	1
Redwood-Huchnom	15
Redwood-Whilkut	74
Rogue River	9
Saiaz	6
San Antonio	16
San Luis Obispo	1
San Luiseno	467
Santa Barbareno	2
Santa Cruz	17
Santa Ynez	35
Seminole	1
Seneca	6
Serrano	115
Shasta	255
Shoshoni	33
Sioux	3
Tachi	27
Tehachapi	2
Tolowa	118
Umpqua	1
Wailaki	217
Walapai	2
Wappo	73
Wasco	1
Washo	273
Wechikhit	6
Weitspec	668
Wikchamni	24
Winnebago	1
Wintun	395
Wyandot	5
Yakima	2
Yana	39
Yaqui	38
Yukuts	302
Yowdanchi	3
Yuki	91
Yuma	642
Not reported[1]	1,825
Colorado	1,482
Apache	1

[Continued]

55

★ 37 ★

American Indian Population, by State and Tribe, 1910:
California - Georgia
[Continued]

State and tribe	Number
Catawba	14
Cherokee	12
Cheyenne	6
Creek	2
Navajo	8
Ute	725
Capote Ute	60
Moache Ute	155
Southern Ute	236
Ute	33
Wiminuchi Ute	241
Not reported[1]	714
Connecticut	152
Mohegan	22
Narraganset	5
Niantic	1
Pequot	49
Not reported[1]	75
Delaware	5
Not reported[1]	5
District of Columbia	68
Chippewa	4
Crow	1
Mandan	2
Yuchi	4
Not reported[1]	57
Florida	74
Mohawk	2
Seminole	16
Not reported[1]	56
Georgia	95
Not reported[1]	95

Source: U.S. Bureau of the Census, *Indian Population in the United States and Alaska, 1910,* United States Government Printing Office, Washington, D.C., 1915, pp. 22-24. *Notes:* 1. Under "Not reported" are included Indians enumerated on the general population schedule only for whom no inquiry as to stock or tribe was made, or Indians for whom special schedules were obtained but whose stock or tribe was not reported.

★ 38 ★

American Indian Population, by State and Tribe, 1910:
Idaho - Kansas

State and tribe	Number
Idaho	3,488
Bannock	363
Brotherton	2
Cayuse	4
Cherokee	8
Coeur d'Alene	284
Colville	17
Cree	2
Delaware	4
Flathead	6
Kalispel	15
Kutenai	107
Modoc	1
Mohawk	2
Nez Perces	1,035
Okinagan	1
Paviotso	152
Piegan	3
Shoshoni	1,259
Spokan	96
Umatilla	22
Wallawalla	1
Warm Springs	4
Wyandot	1
Yakima	12
Not reported[1]	87
Illinois	188
Tenton Sioux-Oglala Sioux	8
Tuscarora	1
Not reported[1]	179
Indiana	279
Delaware	2
Miami	90
Penobscot	1
Wea	2
Not reported[1]	184
Iowa	471
Potawatomi	6
Sauk and Fox	257
Sioux	7
Winnebago	32
Not reported[1]	169

[Continued]

★ 38 ★

American Indian Population, by State and Tribe, 1910: Idaho - Kansas
[Continued]

State and tribe	Number
Kansas	2,444
Apache	9
Arapaho	6
Arikara	1
Assiniboin	6
Caddo	5
Cayuga	1
Cayuse	1
Cherokee	71
Cheyenne	5
Chickasaw	4
Chippewa	92
Choctaw	11
Comanche	7
Cree	1
Creek	33
Crow	14
Delaware	14
Flathead	1
Gros Ventres	1
Hidatsa	1
Hopi	2
Hupa	5
Iowa	124
Isleta	1
Kalispel	2
Kansa	6
Kickapoo	211
Kiowa	17
Klamath	2
Little Lake	6
Menominee	4
Mescalero Apache	4
Miami	8
Modoc	1
Molala	1
Munsee	41
Navajo	8
Nez Perces	1
Omaha	11
Oneida	26
Osage	12
Oto	6
Ottawa	14
Paiute	2

[Continued]

★ 38 ★

American Indian Population, by State and Tribe, 1910:
Idaho - Kansas
[Continued]

State and tribe	Number
Papago	3
Pawnee	14
Peoria	3
Pima	5
Ponca	42
Potawatomi	819
Puyallup	3
Quapaw	6
Rogue River	3
Sauk and Fox	69
Seminole	8
Seneca	7
Shawnee	14
Shoshoni	1
Sioux	40
Sisseton Sioux	6
Stockbridges	1
Teton Sioux	34
Brule Sioux	4
Oglala Sioux	4
Sans Arc Sioux	2
Teton Sioux	

Source: U.S. Bureau of the Census, *Indian Population in the United States and Alaska, 1910,* United States Government Printing Office, Washington, D.C., 1915, pp. 22-24. *Notes:* 1. Under "Not reported" are included Indians enumerated on the general population schedule only for whom no inquiry as to stock or tribe was made, or Indians for whom special schedules were obtained but whose stock or tribe was not reported.

★ 39 ★

American Indian Population, by State and Tribe, 1910:
Kansas - Missouri

State and tribe	Number
Kansas - cont.	
Tillamook	1
Tuscarora	1
Ute	12
Southern Ute	1
Ute	11
Wasco	3
Washo	1
Wichita	4

[Continued]

★ 39 ★

American Indian Population, by State and Tribe, 1910: Kansas - Missouri
[Continued]

State and tribe	Number
Winnebago	5
Wyandot	21
Yakima	6
Yankton Sioux	11
Yanktonai Sioux	2
Not reported[1]	500
Kentucky	234
Not reported[1]	234
Louisiana	780
Alibamu	111
Cherokee	1
Chitimacha	50
Choctaw	115
Koasati	85
Tunica	43
Not reported[1]	375
Maine	892
Abenaki	7
Chippewa	1
Malecite	138
Micmac	23
Mohawk	1
Passamaquoddy	381
Penobscot	253
St. Regis	1
Not reported[1]	87
Maryland	55
Not reported[1]	55
Massachusetts	688
Blackfeet	1
Malecite	3
Mashpee	201
Micmac	21
Narraganset	2
Pequot	17
Wampanoag	152
Not reported[1]	291
Michigan	7,519
Brotherton	2

[Continued]

★ 39 ★

American Indian Population, by State and Tribe, 1910:
Kansas - Missouri
[Continued]

State and tribe	Number
Cherokee	3
Chippewa	3,725
Cree	28
Iowa	1
Menominee	34
Miami	2
Mohawk	5
Oneida	10
Onondaga	1
Ottawa	2,454
Potawatomi	461
Sauk and Fox	1
Sioux	1
Tuscarora	1
Not reported[1]	790
Minnesota	9,053
Brotherton	3
Cherokee	2
Chippewa	8,234
Cree	1
Creek	2
Crow	1
Laguna	3
Menominee	13
Micmac	1
Oneida	7
Onondaga	1
Potawatomi	1
Santee Sioux	232
Sioux	161
Sisseton Sioux	63
Stockbridges	5
Teton Sioux-Oglala Sioux	1
Winnebago	8
Not reported[1]	314
Mississippi	1,253
Chippewa	1
Choctaw	1,162
Creek	6
Ute	2
Not reported[1]	82

[Continued]

★ 39 ★

American Indian Population, by State and Tribe, 1910:
Kansas - Missouri
[Continued]

State and tribe	Number
Missouri	313
Apache	1
Cherokee	13
Cheyenne	2
Chippewa	1
Creek	2
Miami	1
Modoc	10
Paviotso	2
Peoria	5
Sauk and Fox	5
Shawnee	14
Sioux	11
Not reported[1]	246

Source: U.S. Bureau of the Census, *Indian Population in the United States and Alaska, 1910,* United States Government Printing Office, Washington, D.C., 1915, pp. 22-24. *Notes:* 1. Under "Not reported" are included Indians enumerated on the general population schedule only for whom no inquiry as to stock or tribe was made, or Indians for whom special schedules were obtained but whose stock or tribe was not reported.

★ 40 ★

American Indian Population, by State and Tribe, 1910:
Montana - New Hampshire

State and tribe	Number
Montana	10,745
Arapaho	18
Arikara	4
Assiniboine	1,229
Bannock	23
Blackfeet	33
Cayuse	2
Cherokee	12
Cheyenne	1,346
Chinook	12
Chippewa	486
Colville	17
Cree	309
Creek	34
Crow	1,698
Delaware	1
Flathead	400

[Continued]

★ 40 ★

American Indian Population, by State and Tribe, 1910: Montana - New Hampshire

[Continued]

State and tribe	Number
Gros Ventres	503
Hidatsa	9
Kalispel	386
Kiowa	1
Kutenai	424
Mandan	5
Nez Perces	54
Okinagan	2
Paiute	1
Paviotso	26
Pawnee	2
Piegan	2,221
Potawatomi	1
Santee Sioux	107
Seneca	1
Shawnee	1
Shoshoni	10
Sioux	86
Sisseton Sioux	255
Spokan	134
Teton Sioux	66
Oglala Sioux	26
Teton Sioux	40
Umatilla	10
Ute	1
Warm Springs	1
Yakima	1
Yankton Sioux	372
Yanktonai Sioux	1
Not reported[1]	440
Nebraska	3,502
Arikara	1
Bannock	1
Blackfeet	12
Cheyenne	4
Chippewa	64
Creek	1
Flathead	6
Iowa	38
Kalispel	1
Kickapoo	1
Koasati	2
Kutenai	1
Malecite	1

[Continued]

★ 40 ★

American Indian Population, by State and Tribe, 1910: Montana - New Hampshire
[Continued]

State and tribe	Number
Menominee	1
Omaha	1,075
Oneida	5
Oto	10
Ottawa	23
Passamaquoddy	3
Pawnee	1
Penobscot	1
Piegan	21
Ponca	193
Potawatomi	21
Quapaw	1
Santee Sioux	708
Sauk and Fox	13
Shoshoni	1
Sioux	62
Sisseton Sioux	15
Teton Sioux	3
Oglala Sioux	2
Teton Sioux	1
Winnebago	1,007
Wyandot	1
Yankton Sioux	6
Not reported[1]	198
Nevada	5,240
Apache-White Mountain Apache	3
Bannock	1
Chemehuevi	60
Creek	1
Maidu	1
Miwok	1
Mohave	1
Mono	60
Paiute	247
Panamint	1
Papago	3
Paviotso	2,414
Pit River	8
Shoshoni	1,555
Sisseton Sioux	1
Teton Sioux	1
Ute	6
Washo	536
Wintun	4

[Continued]

★ 40 ★

American Indian Population, by State and Tribe, 1910: Montana - New Hampshire

[Continued]

State and tribe	Number
Not reported[1]	336
New Hampshire	34
Penobscot	3
Not reported[1]	31

Source: U.S. Bureau of the Census, *Indian Population in the United States and Alaska, 1910,* United States Government Printing Office, Washington, D.C., 1915, pp. 22-24. *Notes:* 1. Under "Not reported" are included Indians enumerated on the general population schedule only for whom no inquiry as to stock or tribe was made, or Indians for whom special schedules were obtained but whose stock or tribe was not reported.

★ 41 ★

American Indian Population, by State and Tribe, 1910: New Jersey - Ohio

State and tribe	Number
New Jersey	168
Sioux	62
Not reported[1]	106
New Mexico	20,573
Acoma	691
Apache	25
Cherokee	1
Cochiti	237
Hopi	9
Isleta	910
Jemez	499
Jicarilla Apache	694
Laguna	1,441
Lipan Apache	20
Mescalero Apache	416
Nambe	88
Navajo	10,354
Osage	1
Pecos	9
Picuris	104
Pima	1
Pojoaque	16
San Felipe	490
San Ildefonso	123
San Juan	384

[Continued]

★ 41 ★

American Indian Population, by State and Tribe, 1910: New Jersey - Ohio

[Continued]

State and tribe	Number
Sandia	73
Santa Ana	211
Santa Clara	277
Santo Domingo	817
Seneca	2
Sia	109
Taos	517
Tesuque	77
Zuni	1,664
Not reported[1]	313
New York	6,046
Abenaki	24
Arikara	6
Brotherton	3
Cayuga	53
Cherokee	5
Chippewa	3
Clallam	1
Delaware	2
Mohawk	320
Montauk	6
Munsee	5
Oneida	211
Onondaga	327
Passamaquoddy	2
Pawnee	1
Penobscot	5
Poosepatuck	1
St. Regis	1,140
Seneca	2,485
Shinnecock	167
Sioux	1
Stockbridges	7
Tuscarora	382
Ute-White River Ute	1
Winnebago	1
Wyandot	1
Not reported[1]	886
North Carolina	7,851
Catawba	6
Cherokee	1,406
Chippewa	2
Creek	7

[Continued]

66

★ 41 ★

American Indian Population, by State and Tribe, 1910: New Jersey - Ohio

[Continued]

State and tribe	Number
Croatan	5,865
Not reported[1]	565
North Dakota	6,486
Arikara	425
Assiniboine	8
Blackfeet	35
Cherokee	34
Cheyenne	1
Chippewa	2,966
Cree	5
Creek	1
Crow	11
Gros Ventres	3
Hidatsa	520
Mandan	197
Munsee	1
Omaha	1
Oneida	1
Peoria	3
Santee Sioux	100
Sioux	99
Sisseton Sioux	621
Teton Sioux	370
Brule Sioux	4
Hunkpapa Sioux	142
Minniconjou Sioux	10
Oglala Sioux	6
Sans Arc Sioux	6
Sihasapa	137
Teton Sioux	60
Two Kettle Sioux	5
Yankton Sioux	159
Yanktonai Sioux	551
Not reported[1]	374
Ohio	127
Cherokee	15
Chippewa	3
Creek	1
Mohawk	12
Sauk and Fox	2

[Continued]

★ 41 ★

American Indian Population, by State and Tribe, 1910: New Jersey - Ohio
[Continued]

State and tribe	Number
Sioux	2
Not reported[1]	92

Source: U.S. Bureau of the Census, *Indian Population in the United States and Alaska, 1910*, United States Government Printing Office, Washington, D.C., 1915, pp. 22-24. *Notes:* 1. Under "Not reported" are included Indians enumerated on the general population schedule only for whom no inquiry as to stock or tribe was made, or Indians for whom special schedules were obtained but whose stock or tribe was not reported.

★ 42 ★

American Indian Population, by State and Tribe, 1910: Oklahoma - Oregon

State and tribe	Number
Oklahoma	74,825
Apache	271
Apache	30
Chiricahua	237
San Carlos	2
White Mountain	2
Arapaho	685
Arikara	1
Blackfeet	12
Caddo	436
Cayuga	17
Cherokee	29,610
Cheyenne	1,522
Chickasaw	4,191
Chinook	1
Chippewa	64
Choctaw	14,551
Clatsop	3
Comanche	1,160
Creek	6,654
Crow	2
Delaware	874
Iowa	79
Kansa	232
Kichai	10
Kickapoo	135
Kiowa	1,107
Kiowa Apache	139
Laguna	4

[Continued]

★ 42 ★

American Indian Population, by State and Tribe, 1910: Oklahoma - Oregon

[Continued]

State and tribe	Number
Lipan Apache	7
Menominee	7
Mescalero Apache	4
Miami	123
Missouri	12
Modoc	33
Mohawk	11
Montauk	2
Munsee	21
Navajo	4
Omaha	5
Oneida	18
Onondaga	1
Osage	1,345
Oto	314
Ottawa	170
Pawnee	573
Peoria	114
Piankashaw	2
Piegan	3
Pit River	7
Ponca	619
Potawatomi	866
Quapaw	221
St. Regis	1
Sauk and Fox	347
Seminole	1,503
Seneca	215
Shawnee	1,300
Sioux	53
Stockbridges	7
Tawakoni	1
Teton Sioux	3
Brule Sioux	1
Sans Arc Sioux	1
Sihasapa	1
Tonkawa	42
Ute	14
Waco	5
Wea	2
Wichita	279
Winnebago	9
Wyandot	320
Yaqui	1
Yuchi	74

[Continued]

★ 42 ★

American Indian Population, by State and Tribe, 1910: Oklahoma - Oregon
[Continued]

State and tribe	Number
Not reported[1]	4,407
Oregon	5,090
Ahtena	2
Aleut	40
Alsea	27
Apache	2
Assiniboine	6
Auk	2
Bannock	2
Blackfeet	4
Cayuse	277
Chastacosta	7
Chehalis	3
Cherokee	19
Chetco	7
Chickasaw	4
Chilkat	4
Chinook	125
Chippewa	48
Choctaw	1
Clackamas	39
Clallam	11
Clatsop	4
Coeur d'Alene	4
Columbia	52
Colville	25
Cow Creek	9
Cree	22
Creek	1
Crow	3
Delaware	2
Dwamish	1
Flathead	27
Haida	25
Kake	3
Kalapooia	5
Kalispel	3
Klamath	646
Klikitat	35
Kusa	93

[Continued]

★ 42 ★

American Indian Population, by State and Tribe, 1910: Oklahoma - Oregon

[Continued]

State and tribe	Number
Kutenai	2
Lakmiut	8

Source: U.S. Bureau of the Census, *Indian Population in the United States and Alaska, 1910*, United States Government Printing Office, Washington, D.C., 1915, pp. 22-24. *Notes:* 1. Under "Not reported" are included Indians enumerated on the general population schedule only for whom no inquiry as to stock or tribe was made, or Indians for whom special schedules were obtained but whose stock or tribe was not reported.

★ 43 ★

American Indian Population, by State and Tribe, 1910: Oregon - Pennsylvania

State and tribe	Number
Oregon - cont.	
Lummi	3
Maidu	1
Makah	6
Malemiut	2
Mary's River	24
Menominee	1
Modoc	212
Molala	25
Muckleshoot	3
Munsee	1
Nez Perces	58
Nisqualli	8
Okinagan	11
Oto	1
Paloos	7
Paviotso	341
Piegan	2
Pima	1
Pit River	81
Potawatomi	1
Puyallup	21
Quinaielt	1
Rogue River	368
Sanpoil	1
Santee Sioux	1
Santiam	9
Seneca	2
Shasta	96

[Continued]

★ 43 ★

American Indian Population, by State and Tribe, 1910: Oregon - Pennsylvania
[Continued]

State and tribe	Number
Sioux	1
Siuslaw	7
Skokomish	2
Snohomish	3
Spokan	28
Suquamish	1
Tenankutchin	1
Tillamook	18
Tolowa	3
Tsimshian	14
Umatilla	152
Umpqua	90
Upper Coquille	15
Wailaki	8
Wallawalla	390
Wapato	17
Warm Springs	502
Wasco	184
Washo	5
Winnebago	2
Yakima	62
Yamel	4
Yaquina	13
Yonkalla	11
Yuki	3
Zuni	2
Not reported[1]	664
Pennsylvania	1,503
Abenaki	4
Apache	3
Arapaho	3
Arikara	3
Assiniboine	1
Bannock	5
Caddo	8
Catawba	1
Cayuga	10
Cayuse	2
Cherokee	50
Chetco	1
Cheyenne	33
Chippewa	134
Chitimacha	19
Clallam	2

[Continued]

★ 43 ★

American Indian Population, by State and Tribe, 1910:
Oregon - Pennsylvania
[Continued]

State and tribe	Number
Coeur d'Alene	1
Colville	9
Comanche	4
Crow	5
Delaware	7
Hidatsa	10
Hopi	13
Iowa	1
Klamath	23
Lipan Apache	1
Little Lake	3
Lummi	2
Mashpee	5
Menominee	9
Miami	1
Modoc	2
Mohave	1
Mohawk	3
Munsee	2
Narraganset	1
Navajo	13
Nez Perces	31
Nomelaki	3
Okinagan	2
Omaha	11
Oneida	40
Onondaga	33
Osage	7
Ottawa	6
Paiute	5
Pawnee	18
Pecos	1
Penobscot	3
Peoria	1
Piegan	12
Pima	2
Pit River	
Ponca	3
Potawatomi	3
Puyallup	1
Quapaw	1
St. Regis	77
San Juan	1
Sanpoil	1

[Continued]

★ 43 ★

American Indian Population, by State and Tribe, 1910: Oregon - Pennsylvania
[Continued]

State and tribe	Number
Sauk and Fox	14
Seminole	1

Source: U.S. Bureau of the Census, *Indian Population in the United States and Alaska, 1910,* United States Government Printing Office, Washington, D.C., 1915, pp. 22-24. *Notes:* 1. Under "Not reported" are included Indians enumerated on the general population schedule only for whom no inquiry as to stock or tribe was made, or Indians for whom special schedules were obtained but whose stock or tribe was not reported.

★ 44 ★

American Indian Population, by State and Tribe, 1910: Pennsylvania - Utah

State and tribe	Number
Pennsylvania - cont.	
Seneca	184
Serrano	2
Shawnee	4
Shoshoni	27
Sioux	96
Spokan	6
Stockbridges	6
Teton Sioux-Sihasapa	1
Tuscarora	15
Umatilla	2
Umpqua	1
Wampanoag	10
Washo	3
Wichita	15
Winnebago	17
Wyandot	2
Yuma	1
Not reported[1]	438
Rhode Island	284
Not reported[1]	284
South Carolina	331
Catawba	99
Cherokee	87
Oneida	2
Not reported[1]	143

[Continued]

★ 44 ★

American Indian Population, by State and Tribe, 1910: Pennsylvania - Utah
[Continued]

State and tribe	Number
South Dakota	19,137
Alsea	1
Apache	1
Arapaho	3
Arikara	3
Assiniboine	3
Bannock	4
Blackfeet	1
Caddo	3
Cayuse	5
Cherokee	7
Cheyenne	133
Chickasaw	1
Chippewa	73
Choctaw	8
Clallam	1
Clatsop	1
Creek	9
Crow	53
Delaware	1
Gros Ventres	2
Hidatsa	1
Hopi	2
Kutenai	3
Laguna	4
Mandan	5
Menominee	3
Navajo	4
Nez Perces	1
Oneida	7
Onondaga	1
Osage	4
Paiute	2
Papago	1
Pawnee	5
Peoria	1
Ponca	18
Potawatomi	10
Quapaw	1
Santee Sioux	378
Sauk and Fox	1
Seneca	2
Shawnee	2
Shoshoni	2
Sioux	277

[Continued]

★ 44 ★

American Indian Population, by State and Tribe, 1910: Pennsylvania - Utah
[Continued]

State and tribe	Number
Sisseton Sioux	1,553
Stockbridges	3
Teton Sioux	13,795
Brule Sioux	795
Hunkpapa Sioux	930
Minniconjou Sioux	387
Oglala Sioux	5,998
Sans Arc Sioux	213
Sihasapa	346
Teton Sioux	4,838
Two Kettle Sioux	288
Umatilla	1
Ute	4
Wichita	20
Winnebago	2
Wyandot	2
Yankton Sioux	1,534
Yanktonai Sioux	803
Not reported[1]	372
Tennessee	216
Cherokee	45
Chickasaw	3
Choctaw	4
Creek	2
Osage	1
Sauk and Fox	6
Not reported[1]	155
Texas	702
Alibamu	187
Creek	1
Isleta	34
Koasati	11
Seminole	200
Not reported[1]	269

Source: U.S. Bureau of the Census, *Indian Population in the United States and Alaska, 1910,* United States Government Printing Office, Washington, D.C., 1915, pp. 22-24. *Notes:* 1. Under "Not reported" are included Indians enumerated on the general population schedule only for whom no inquiry as to stock or tribe was made, or Indians for whom special schedules were obtained but whose stock or tribe was not reported.

★ 45 ★

American Indian Population, by State and Tribe, 1910: Utah - Washington

State and tribe	Number
Utah	3,123
Bannock	1
Chippewa	1
Navajo	1,039
Pahvant	37
Paiute	238
Shoshoni	248
Sioux	2
Ute	1,472
Capote Ute	4
Grand River Ute	1
Moache Ute	1
Uinta Ute	373
Uncompahgre Ute	412
Ute	362
White River Ute	319
Not reported[1]	85
Vermont	26
Not reported[1]	26
Virginia	539
Catawba	4
Cherokee	19
Chickahominy	115
Choctaw	8
Mattapony	1
Pamunkey	83
Powhatan	131
Not reported[1]	178
Washington	10,997
Alsea	1
Bellacoola	2
Cayuse	6
Chehalis	279
Cherokee	8
Chimakum	3
Chinook	177
Chippewa	6
Clackamas	1
Clallam	383
Clatsop	18
Coeur d'Alene	4
Columbia	333
Colville	717

[Continued]

★ 45 ★

American Indian Population, by State and Tribe, 1910:
Utah - Washington
[Continued]

State and tribe	Number
Comox	1
Cowichan	62
Cowlitz	105
Cree	91
Dwamish	19
Flathead	46
Haida	6
Hoh	44
Hupa	11
Kalispel	157
Kitamat	1
Klamath	4
Klikitat	370
Kutenai	1
Kwakiutl	1
Laguna	1
Lummi	348
Makah	354
Methow	14
Missouri	1
Modoc	1
Molala	5
Muckleshoot	191
Nespelim	46
Nez Perces	79
Nisqualli	129
Nooksak	85
Nootka	15
Okinagan	256
Paiute	5
Paloos	75
Paviotso	2
Pisquow	52
Potawatomi	1
Puyallup	278
Quileute	259
Quinaielt	287
Redwood-Whilkut	2
Rogue River	3
San Juan	2
Sanpoil	238
Sauk and Fox	8
Shasta	2
Shuswap	9
Sioux	2

[Continued]

★ 45 ★

American Indian Population, by State and Tribe, 1910:
Utah - Washington

[Continued]

State and tribe	Number
Skagit	56
Skokomish	193
Snohomish	661
Snoqualmu	93
Songish	23
Spokan	379
Squaxon	44
Stockbridges	2
Suquamish	306
Swinomish	333
Takelma	1
Tillamook	6
Tlatskanai	3
Topinish	47
Tsimshian	37
Twana	60
Umatilla	85
Umpqua	17
Wailaki	2
Walapai	3
Wallawalla	6

Source: U.S. Bureau of the Census, *Indian Population in the United States and Alaska, 1910,* United States Government Printing Office, Washington, D.C., 1915, pp. 22-24. *Notes:* 1. Under "Not reported" are included Indians enumerated on the general population schedule only for whom no inquiry as to stock or tribe was made, or Indians for whom special schedules were obtained but whose stock or tribe was not reported.

★ 46 ★

American Indian Population, by State and Tribe, 1910:
Washington - Wyoming

State and tribe	Number
Washington - cont.	
Wapato	27
Warm Springs	43
Wasco	54
Washo	1
Wikchamni	1
Winnebago	1
Wishram	274
Yakima	1,279
Yamel	1

[Continued]

★ 46 ★

American Indian Population, by State and Tribe, 1910:
Washington - Wyoming
[Continued]

State and tribe	Number
Yankton Sioux	4
Yaquina	6
Not reported[1]	1,342
West Virgina	36
Not reported[1]	36
Wisconsin	10,142
Abenaki	2
Brotherton	162
Cherokee	14
Chippewa	4,299
Delaware	4
Iowa	1
Kickapoo	1
Klamath	1
Menominee	1,350
Mohawk	12
Montauk	21
Narraganset	8
Oneida	2,107
Onondaga	1
Osage	1
Oto	1
Ottawa	50
Potawatomi	245
Santee Sioux	13
Sauk and Fox	1
Seneca	2
Sioux	18
Stockbridges	502
Teton Sioux	
Brule Sioux	2
Twana	1
Winnebago	735
Not reported[1]	588
Wyoming	1,486
Apache	1
Arapaho	703
Bannock	9
Chemehuevi	7
Cheyenne	3
Gros Ventres	1
Hidatsa	6

[Continued]

★ 46 ★

American Indian Population, by State and Tribe, 1910:
Washington - Wyoming
[Continued]

State and tribe	Number
Navajo	4
Oneida	1
Paiute	1
Piegan	3
Potawatomi	1
Shoshoni	700
Sioux	9
Ute	6
Yankton Sioux	2
Not reported[1]	29

Source: U.S. Bureau of the Census, *Indian Population in the United States and Alaska, 1910*, United States Government Printing Office, Washington, D.C., 1915, pp. 22-24. *Notes:* 1. Under "Not reported" are included Indians enumerated on the general population schedule only for whom no inquiry as to stock or tribe was made, or Indians for whom special schedules were obtained but whose stock or tribe was not reported.

★ 47 ★

Indian Reservation Population and Land Areas for Selected States,
1962 and 1963

State & jurisdictional area	Population of reservations (land units, 1962)			Land area (acres, 1963)		
	Total	Within units	Adjacent to units	Tribal land	Allotted land	Gov't owned
State						
Alaska	38,332	1,012	37,320	87,636	9,723	4,064,502
Arizona	81,924	80,071	1,853	19,389,947	260,376	90,502
California	8,861	6,758	2,130	466,984	84,678	119
Colorado	1,411	1,303	108	746,290	5,021	573
Florida	1,003	739	264	79,014	-	-
Idaho	4,134	3,679	455	400,805	389,890	41,859
Iowa	531	490	41	4,105	-	-
Kansas	1,289	645	644	1,784	26,083	321
Louisiana	268	118	150	262	.16	-
Michigan	1,216	916	300	7,816	9,407	4,016
Minnesota	11,580	9,500	2,080	670,761	54,520	28,698
Mississippi	3,594	3,063	531	16,270	209	214
Missouri	-	-	-	-	373	-
Montana	20,566	18,963	1,603	1,627,839	3,617,089	128,263
Nebraska	2,196	2,078	118	14,239	52,775	322
Nevada	4,168	3,670	498	1,062,316	79,348	7,811
New Mexico	52,188	48,041	4,147	5,917,691	647,857	126,533

[Continued]

★ 47 ★

Indian Reservation Population and Land Areas for Selected States, 1962 and 1963
[Continued]

State & jurisdictional area	Population of reservations (land units, 1962)			Land area (acres, 1963)		
	Total	Within units	Adjacent to units	Tribal land	Allotted land	Gov't owned
North Carolina	5,500	5,470	30	56,437	-	136
North Dakota	11,490	8,247	3,243	131,202	729,734	6,737
Oklahoma	61,769	57,543	4,226	58,519	1,583,998	33,313
Oregon	2,305	2,138	167	496,242	194,589	1,254
South Dakota	27,669	25,397	2,272	1,937,706	2,873,429	136,639
Texas	-	-	-	-	11	-
Utah	4,885	4,474	411	2,047,997	67,843	439
Washington	11,220	8,733	2,487	1,833,750	708,333	90
Wisconsin	5,322	4,149	1,173	60,088	84,854	39,447
Wyoming	3,758	3,417	341	1,761,074	126,603	962
Total	367,179	300,614	66,565	38,876,774	11,606,743	4,712,750
Area						
Aberdeen	41,307	35,715	5,592	2,083,731	3,644,918	143,698
Anadarko	17,718	14,286	3,432	16,425	604,188	13,247
Billings	24,324	22,380	1,944	3,388,913	3,753,527	129,225
Gallup	109,132	104,598	4,534	16,731,758	760,739	78,886
Juneau	38,332	1,012	37,320	87,636	9,723	4,064,502
Minneapolis	18,649	15,055	3,594	742,141	148,781	72,161
Muskogee	49,250	47,090	2,160	60,455	1,007,675	20,601
Phoenix	36,931	34,373	2,558	12,672,606	307,211	147,091
Portland	17,414	14,305	3,109	2,566,983	1,293,452	43,203
Sacramento	7,619	5,591	2,028	390,675	76,529	-
Central Office	6,503	6,209	294	135,451	-	136

Source: United States Department of Interior, Bureau of Indian Affairs, *U.S. Indian Population (1962) and Land (1963),* Government Printing Office, November 1963, p. 6. *Note:* A dash (-) represents zero.

★ 48 ★

Indian Reservation Population and Land Areas, 1962 and 1963: Alaska - I

State, Area office, jurisdiction and land unit	Principal tribe	Estimated Population June 30, 1962			Land Area (Acres) Reported June 30, 1963		
		Total	Within units	Adjacent to units	Tribal land	Allotted land	Gov't owned
Alaska total		38,332	1,012	37,320	87,636	9,723	4,064,502
Juneau Area Office		9,953	1,012	8,941	87,636	9,723	945
Angoon	Tlingit	395	-	395	-	-	-
Annette Island (Metlakatla)	Tsimshian	800	800	-	86,741	-	-
Chilkat Fishing Reserve (Haines)[1]	Tlingit	-	-	-	-	-	17
Craig	Haida	273	-	273	-	-	
Douglas-Juneau Area	Tlingit	1,062	-	1,062	-	-	-
Haines (Chilkoot Indian Association)	Tlingit	512	-	512	-	-	-
Hood Bay[2]	Tlingit	-	-	-	-	-	613
Hoonah	Tlingit	825	-	825	-	-	-
Hydaburg	Haida	251	-	251	-	-	
Kake	Tlingit	455	-	455	-	-	
Kasaan	Haida	47	-	47	-	-	
Ketchikan	Tlingit	500	-	500	-	-	
Klawock	Tlingit	351	-	351	-	-	
Klukwan (Chilkat Indian Village)	Tlingit	212	212	-	895	-	.20
Mt. Edgecumbe	(mixed)	300	-	300	-	-	
Petersburg	Tlingit	1,502	-	1,502	-	-	
Public Domain Allotments[3]		-	-	-	-	9,723	-
Saxman	Tlingit	153	-	153	-	-	-
Sitka	Tlingit	1,000	-	1,000	-	-	-
Wrangell	Tlingit	1,315	-	1,315	-	-	171
Yendistucky (Haines)[1]	Tlingit	-	-	-	-	-	144
Anchorage Area Field Office		6,114	-	6,114	-	-	137,975
Afognak	Eskimo	180	-	180	-	-	4
Akutan	Aleut	107	-	107	-	-	72,040
Alitak	Eskimo	105	-	105	-	-	1
Amaknak Island[4]	Aleut	-	-	-	-	-	110
Anchorage	(mixed)	1,800	-	1,800	-	-	-
Atka	Aleut	119	-	119	-	-	40
Belkofski	Aleut	57	-	57	-	-	-
Chenega (Chanega)	Eskimo	80	-	80	-	-	.30
Chignik (Anchorage Bay)	Eskimo	110	-	110	-	-	1
Chignik Lake[5]	Aleut	120	-	120	-	-	-
Chitina[6]	Athapascan	30	-	30	-	-	-
Circle[7]	Athapascan	50	-	50	-	-	1
Copper Center	Athapascan	150	-	150	-	-	1,041
Egegik	Eskimo	150	-	150	-	-	5
Eklutna	Athapascan	40	-	40	-	-	1,968
Ekwok (Ekwak)	Eskimo	105	-	105	-	-	6
English Bay	Eskimo	75	-	75	-	-	-

[Continued]

83

★ 48 ★

Indian Reservation Population and Land Areas, 1962 and 1963: Alaska - I
[Continued]

State, Area office, jurisdiction and land unit	Principal tribe	Estimated Population June 30, 1962			Land Area (Acres) Reported June 30, 1963		
		Total	Within units	Adjacent to units	Tribal land	Allotted land	Gov't owned
Kanatak	Eskimo	0	-	0	-	-	-
Karluk	Aleut	130	-	130	-	-	35,203
Koliganek	Eskimo	100	-	100	-	-	-
Levelock	Eskimo	90	-	90	-	-	11
Manokotak	Eskimo	150	-	150	-	-	-
Newhalen	Eskimo	110	-	110	-	-	30
New Stuyahok	Eskimo	140	-	140	-	-	-
Nikolski	Aleut	80	-	80	-	-	-
Nondalton	Eskimo	190	-	190	-	-	2
Old Harbor	Aleut	191	-	191	-	-	8
Ouzinkie	Aleut	180	-	180	-	-	6
Perryville	Aleut	90	-	90	-	-	-
Pilot Point	Aleut	50	-	50	-	-	13
Port Graham	Eskimo	130	-	130	-	-	-
Rampart[7]	Athapascan	50	-	50	-	-	5
St. George Island[8]	Aleut	250	-	250	-	-	-
St. Paul Island	Aleut	359	-	359	-	-	-
Sevenosky (Savonoski)[9]	Eskimo	25	-	25	-	-	-
Tatitlek	Eskimo	96	-	96	-	-	520
Togiak	Eskimo	240	-	240	-	-	40
Tyonek	Athapascan	185	-	185	-	-	26,920
Bethel Area Field Office		8,595	-	8,595	-	-	2,845
Akiachak	Eskimo	240	-	240	-	-	40
Akiak	Eskimo	175	-	175	-	-	1,373
Alakanuk	Eskimo	229	-	229	-	-	-
Bethel	Eskimo	1,250	-	1,250	-	-	4
Chaneliak	Eskimo	30	-	30	-	-	6
Chevak	Eskimo	343	-	343	-	-	2
Chifornak	Eskimo	135	-	135	-	-	-
Chowhoctolik[10]	Eskimo	69	-	69	-	-	-
Eek	Eskimo	207	-	207	-	-	4
Goodnews Bay	Eskimo	157	-	157	-	-	4
Holikachuk	Athapascan	116	-	116	-	-	7
Hooper Bay	Eskimo	482	-	482	-	-	6
Kalskag	Athapascan	125	-	125	-	-	4
Kasigluk	Eskimo	252	-	252	-	-	2
Kipnuk	Eskimo	254	-	254	-	-	13
Kotlik	Eskimo	116	-	116	-	-	-
Kwethluk	Eskimo	345	-	345	-	-	3
Kwigillingok	Eskimo	305	-	305	-	-	3
Emmonak[11]	Eskimo	378	-	378	-	-	-
Lower Kalskag	Athapascan	137	-	137	-	-	-

[Continued]

★ 48 ★

Indian Reservation Population and Land Areas, 1962 and 1963: Alaska - I
[Continued]

State, Area office, jurisdiction and land unit	Principal tribe	Estimated Population June 30, 1962			Land Area (Acres) Reported June 30, 1963		
		Total	Within units	Adjacent to units	Tribal land	Allotted land	Gov't owned
Mekoryuk	Eskimo	246	-	246	-	-	6
Mountain Village	Eskimo	323	-	323	-	-	1,280
Napakiak	Eskimo	241	-	241	-	-	4
Napaskiak	Eskimo	168	-	168	-	-	7
Newktok	Eskimo	157	-	157	-	-	-
Nightmute	Eskimo	254	-	254	-	-	-
Nunapitchuk	Eskimo	289	-	289	-	-	4
Nunivak (Nash Harbor)	Eskimo	0	-	0	-	-	3
Oscarville[9]	Eskimo	42	-	42	-	-	-
Pilot Station	Eskimo	245	-	245	-	-	4
Quinhagak (Kwinhagak)	Eskimo	236	-	236	-	-	-
Scammon Bay	Eskimo	152	-	152	-	-	4
Shageluk	Athapascan	161	-	161	-	-	3
Sheldons Point[9]	Eskimo	92	-	92	-	-	-
Sleetmute	Athapascan	145	-	145	-	-	40
Tanunak (Tununak)	Eskimo	199	-	199	-	-	19
Tuluksak	Eskimo	150	-	150	-	-	-
Tuntutuliak	Eskimo	150	-	150	-	-	-
Fairbanks Area Field Office		5,911	-	5,911	-	-	2,176,946
Anaktuvuk Pass	Eskimo	107	-	107	-	-	-
Arctic Village	Athapascan	89	-	89	-	-	-
Barrow	Eskimo	1,292	-	1,292	-	-	5
Barter Island	Eskimo	125	-	125	-	-	-
Beaver	Athapasan & Eskimo	102	-	102	-	-	2
Chalkyitsik	Athapascan	62	-	62	-	-	-
Eagle	Athapascan	58	-	58	-	-	40
Fairbanks[9]	(mixed)	1,392	-	1,392	-	-	-
Fort Yukon	Athapascan	650	-	650	-	-	115
Galena	Athapascan	174	-	174	-	-	7
Kaltag	Athapascan	172	-	172	-	-	2

Source: United States Department of the Interior, Bureau of Indian Affairs, *U.S. Indian Population (1962) and Land (1963)*, Government Printing Office, November 1963, pp. 7-11. *Notes:* A dash (-) represents zero. Only those communities are listed which have at least one of the following: trust or restricted land; Bureau School, operating, projected or contract; Bureau radio station; or organization under the Alaska Act. Exceptions are noted and explained. 1. No constant population. 2. Cannery town, people live in and are counted in Angoon. 3. Mostly unoccupied town lots. 4. Fishing reserve, no constant population. 5. Contract school. 6. Land reserve revoked 1961. 7. In Fairbanks area but administered by Anchorage. 8. School operated by State for Fish and Wildlife Service. 9. Projected school only. 10. School closed 1960; new school projected. 11. Formerly Kwiguk.

★ 49 ★

Indian Reservation Population and Land Areas, 1962 and 1963: Alaska - II

State, Area office, jurisdiction and land unit	Principal tribe	Estimated Population June 30, 1962			Land Area (Acres) Reported June 30, 1963		
		Total	Within units	Adjacent to units	Tribal land	Allotted land	Gov't owned
Fairbanks Area Field Office - continued							
Kokrines	Athapascan	25	-	25	-	-	4
Koyukuk[1]	Athapascan	124	-	124	-	-	-
Meade River[2]	Eskimo	20	-	20	-	-	-
Minto	Athapascan	178	-	178	-	-	11
Nenana	Athapascan	182	-	182	-	-	506
Northway	Athapascan	125	-	125	-	-	-
Point Lay	Eskimo	50	-	50	-	-	3
Stevens Village	Athapascan	90	-	90	-	-	1
Tanacross	Athapascan	106	-	106	-	-	2
Tanana	Athapascan	289	-	289	-	-	-
Tetlin	Athapascan	105	-	105	-	-	768,040
Venetie	Athapascan	120	-	120	-	-	1,408,000
Wainwright	Eskimo	274	-	274	-	-	208
Nome Area Field Office		7,759	-	7,759	-	-	1,745,791
Buckland	Eskimo	78	-	78	-	-	-
Cape Denbigh (reserve)[3]	Eskimo	0	-	0	-	-	48,000
Deering	Eskimo	65	-	65	-	-	1
Diomede Island	Eskimo	83	-	83	-	-	3,001
Elim	Eskimo	174	-	174	-	-	316,000
Gambell	Eskimo	353	-	353	-	-	1
Golovin	Eskimo	82	-	82	-	-	1
Kiana	Eskimo	216	-	216	-	-	8
Kings Island	Eskimo	43	-	43	-	-	1
Kivalina	Eskimo	138	-	138	-	-	5
Kotzebue	Eskimo	1,216	-	1,216	-	-	25
Koyuk	Eskimo	130	-	130	-	-	4
Lost River	Eskimo	2	-	2	-	-	-
Noatak	Eskimo	264	-	264	-	-	3
Nome	Eskimo	1,480	-	1,480	-	-	1
Noorvik	Eskimo	371	-	317	-	-	144,000
Point Hope	Eskimo	322	-	322	-	-	6,400
St. Lawrence Island[3] (see Gambell & Savoonga)	Eskimo	0	-	0	-	-	1,205,000
St. Michael	Eskimo	208	-	208	-	-	11
Savoonga	Eskimo	365	-	365	-	-	6
Selawik	Eskimo	353	-	353	-	-	3
Shaktoolik	Eskimo	171	-	171	-	-	2
Shishmaref	Eskimo	211	-	211	-	-	4
Shungnak	Eskimo	149	-	149	-	-	8
Soloman	Eskimo	2	-	2	-	-	3
Stebbins	Eskimo	147	-	147	-	-	4
Teller Reindeer Reserve	Eskimo	184	-	184	-	-	2

[Continued]

★ 49 ★

Indian Reservation Population and Land Areas, 1962 and 1963: Alaska - II

[Continued]

State, Area office, jurisdiction and land unit	Principal tribe	Estimated Population June 30, 1962			Land Area (Acres) Reported June 30, 1963		
		Total	Within units	Adjacent to units	Tribal land	Allotted land	Gov't owned
Teller Mission	Eskimo	97	-	97	-	-	12
Unalakleet	Eskimo	577	-	577	-	-	871
Wales	Eskimo	140	-	140	-	-	21,214
White Mountain	Eskimo	138	-	138	-	-	1,200

Source: United States Department of the Interior, Bureau of Indian Affairs, *U.S. Indian Population (1962) and Land (1963)*, Government Printing Office, November 1963, pp. 7-11. *Notes:* A dash (-) represents zero. Only those communities are listed which have at least one of the following: trust or restricted land, Bureau School, operating, projected or contract; Bureau radio station; or organization under the Alaska Act. Exceptions are noted and explained. 1. Land reserve revoked 1960. 2. Radio station closed 1960. 3. Reindeer reserve; no constant population.

★ 50 ★

Indian Reservation Population and Land Areas, 1962 and 1963: Arizona

State, Area office, jurisdiction and land unit	Principal tribe	Estimated Population June 30, 1962			Land Area (Acres) Reported June 30, 1963		
		Total	Within units	Adjacent to units	Tribal land	Allotted land	Gov't owned
Arizona total		81,924	80,071	1,853	19,389,947	260,376	90,502
Gallup Area Office							
Navajo Agency		84,300	79,916	4,384	12,626,876	662,779	75,856
(Also NM & UT)							
Navajo (AZ, NM & UT) Arizona only	Navajo	52,300	52,207	93	8,881,305	80,145	3
(Reservation totals:							
Within 79,916							
Adjacent 4,384)							
Subagencies							
Chinle			15,874	-			
Crownpoint			11,903	4,097			
Fort Defiance			21,024	101			
Shiprock			16,278	186			
Tuba City			14,837	-			
Navajo Public Domain							
Allotments (AZ & UT) Arizona only		-	-	-	-	7,378	-
Flagstaff Dormitory		-	-	-	-	-	25
Holbrook Dormitory		-	-	-	-	-	8
Snowflake Dormitory		-	-	-	-	-	3
Winslow Dormitory		-	-	-	-	-	11
Flagstaff Industrial Site		-	-	-	-	-	75
Muskogee Area Office							
Osage Agency (OK)							
(See LA, MO, NM, OK, SD & TX)							
Osage Off Reservation	Osage	-	-	-	-	3	-

[Continued]

★ 50 ★

Indian Reservation Population and Land Areas, 1962 and 1963: Arizona

[Continued]

State, Area office, jurisdiction and land unit	Principal tribe	Estimated Population June 30, 1962			Land Area (Acres) Reported June 30, 1963		
		Total	Within units	Adjacent to units	Tribal land	Allotted land	Gov't owned
Lands Arizona only							
Phoenix Area Office							
Colorado River Agency (Also CA & NV)		3,674	3,466	208	1,322,732	15,565	819
Big Sandy (Truxton Canyon)	Hualapai	12	12	-	60	650	-
Camp Verde	Yavapai-Apache	206	170	36	498	80	-
Cocopah	Cocopah	84	80	4	528	-	-
Colorado River (AZ & CZ) Arizona only	Mohave & Chemehuevi	1,431	1,368	63	219,790	6,046	-
(Reservation totals: Within 1,368, Adjacent 63)							
Colorado River Off Reservation Lands	Mohave	-	-	-	159	-	-
Fort Mohave (AZ, NV & CA) Arizona only	Mohave	-	-	-	23,669	-	-
(Reservation total: Within 277)							
Fort Yuma (AZ & CA) Arizona only	Yuma	30	-	30	-	480	-
(Reservation totals: Within 890, Adjacent 105)							
Havasupai	Havasupai	186	186	-	3,058	-	-
Hualapai	Hualapai	410	410	-	991,680	-	783
Yavapai	Yavapai	73	73	-	1,399	160	-
Fort Apache Agency		4,250	4,050	200	1,664,872	-	-
Fort Apache	Apache	4,250	4,050	200	1,664,872	-	-
Hopi Agency		5,311	4,365	946	2,592,629	-	-
Hopi	Hopi	5,176	4,270	906	2,472,216	-	-
Kaibab	Paiute	135	95	40	120,413	-	-
Papago Agency		4,985	4,945	40	2,814,049	41,683	30
Gila Bend	Papago	165	125	40	10,297	-	-
Papago (Sells)	Papago	4,400	4,400	-	2,7744,050	320	-
San Xavier	Papago	420	420	-	29,702	41,363	30
Phoenix School		-	-	-	-	-	104
Pima Agency		6,280	6,140	140	296,302	97,627	3
Ak Chin (Maricopa)	Papago	155	140	15	21,840	-	-
Gila River	Pima & Maricopa (no population)	6,125	6,000	125	274,462	97,467	3
Peeples Valley Public Domain Allotments		-	-	-	-	160	-
Salt River Agency		2,251	1,950	301	46,108	25,164	27
Fort McDowell	Mohave-Apache	315	300	15	24,680	-	-
Salt River	Pima & Maricopa	1,936	1,650	286	21,428	25,164	27
San Carlos Agency		4,115	4,115	-	1,853,841	960	22,415
San Carlos	Apache	4,115	4,115	-	1,853,841	960	22,415

[Continued]

★ 50 ★

Indian Reservation Population and Land Areas, 1962 and 1963: Arizona
[Continued]

State, Area office, jurisdiction and land unit	Principal tribe	Estimated Population June 30, 1962			Land Area (Acres) Reported June 30, 1963		
		Total	Within units	Adjacent to units	Tribal land	Allotted land	Gov't owned
San Carlos Irrigation Project (Also AZ & NM) Arizona only		- -	- -	- -	- -	- -	115,695 67,015

Source: United States Department of the Interior, Bureau of Indian Affairs, *U.S. Indian Population (1962) and Land (1963)*, Government Printing Office, November 1963, pp. 11-12. *Note:* A dash (-) represents zero.

★ 51 ★

Indian Reservation Population and Land Areas, 1962 and 1963: California - I

State, Area Office, jurisdiction and land unit	Principal tribe	Estimated Population June 30, 1962			Land Area (Acres) Reported June 30, 1963		
		Total	Within units	Adjacent to units	Tribal land	Allotted land	Gov't owned
California		8,861	6,758	2,103	466,984	84,678	119
Phoenix Area Office							
Colorado River Agency (AZ) Chemehuevi	(no population)	-	-	-	28,224	-	-
Colorado River (AZ & CA) (Reservation totals: Within 1,368 Adjacent 63)	Mohave & Chemehuevi	-	-	-	38,336	-	-
Fort Mohave (AZ, CA & NV) California only (Reservation total: Within 277)	Mohave	277	277	-	9,132	-	-
Fort Yuma (AZ & CA) California only (Reservation totals: Within 890 Adjacent 105)	Yuma	965	890	75	617	8,149	36
Sherman Institute	-	-	-	-	-	83	
Sacramento Area Office							
California Agency		3,947	2,488	1,459	87,188	24,326	-
Alturas	Pit River	9	9	-	20	-	-
Auburn[1,2]	Maidu	83	70	13	-	-	-
Berry Creek	(no population)	-	-	-	33	-	-
Big Band (Henderson)	Pit River	5	5	-	40	-	-
Big Pine	Paiute	56	36	20	279	-	-
Big Sandy (Auberry)[1,2]	Mono	100	80	20	285	-	-
Big Valley (Mission)[1,2]	Pomo	226	159	67	118	-	-
Bishop	Paiute	570	470	100	875	-	-

[Continued]

89

★ 51 ★

Indian Reservation Population and Land Areas, 1962 and 1963: California - I

[Continued]

State, Area Office, jurisdiction and land unit	Principal tribe	Estimated Population June 30, 1962			Land Area (Acres) Reported June 30, 1963		
		Total	Within units	Adjacent to units	Tribal land	Allotted land	Gov't owned
Cachil Dehe (Colusa)	Wintun	40	17	23	257	-	-
California Agency Public Domain Allotments	(mixed)	40	40	-	-	17,254	-
Cedarville	Paiute	13	12	1	17	-	-
Chico (Meechupta)[1,2]	(mixed)	113	15	98	12	-	-
Cloverdale[1,2]	Pomo	20	20	-	2	-	-
Cold Springs[1,2] (Sycamore)	Mono	28	25	3	160	-	-
Colfax	(no population)	-	-	-	40	-	-
Cortina	Me-Wuk	14	1	13	640	-	-
Dry Creek	Pomo	20	20	-	75	-	-
Enterprise	Maidu	8	8	-	81	-	-
Fort Bidwell	Paiute	104	84	20	3,335	-	-
Fort Independence	Paiute	32	32	-	236	121	-
Graton[1,2]	Pomo	1	1	-	15	-	-
Greenville[1,2]	Maidu	22	22	-	135	-	-
Grindstone Creek	Wintun	28	28	-	80	-	-
Guidiville[1,2]	Pomo	21	21	-	-	-	-
Hopland[1,2]	Pomo	106	81	25	2,070	-	-
Indian Rance[1,2]	Paiute	9	4	5	560	-	-
Jackson (Amador)	Me-Wuk	6	6	-	331	-	-
Laytonville	Kai-Pomo	50	50	-	200	-	-
Likely	(no population)	-	-	-	40	-	-
Lone Pine	Paiute & Shoshone	82	75	7	237	-	-
Lookout	Pit River	4	4	-	50	-	-
Manchester (Point Arena)	Pomo	92	72	20	363	-	-
Middletown[1,2]	Pomo	40	18	22	109	-	-
Montgomery Creek[1,2]	(no population)	-	-	-	72	-	-
Nevada City[1,2]	Maidu	2	2	-	-	-	-
Picayune[1,2]	Chukchansi	11	11	-	-	-	-
Pinoleville[1,2]	Pomo	67	67	-	8	-	-
Roaring Creek	Pit River	4	4	-	80	-	-
Robinson[1,2]	Pomo	76	67	9	11	-	-
Round Valley (Covelo)	Wailaki & Maidu	1,115	360	755	11,959	6,951	-

Source: United States Department of the Interior, Bureau of Indian Affairs, U.S. Indian Population (1962) and Land (1963), Government Printing Office, November 1963, pp. 11-15. Notes: A dash (-) represents zero. 1. Land trusteeship terminated prior to June 30, 1962. 2. Land units for which Federal land trusteeship has been terminated.

★ 52 ★

Indian Reservation Population and Land Areas, 1962 and 1963: California - II

State, Area Office, jurisdiction and land unit	Principal tribe	Estimated Population June 30, 1962			Land Area (Acres) Reported June 30, 1963		
		Total	Within units	Adjacent to units	Tribal land	Allotted land	Gov't owned
Sacramento Area Office (continued)							
California Agency (continued)							
Rumsey	Wintun	17	6	11	141	-	-
Santa Rosa	Tache	96	96	-	170	-	-
Sheep Ranch	Me-Wuk	3	3	-	2	-	-
Sherwood Valley	(mixed)	12	-	12	291	-	-
Shingle Springs	Me-Wuk	5	-	5	240	-	-
Stewart's Point	Pomo	66	54	12	40	-	-
Strathmore	(no population)	-	-	-	40	-	-
Sulphur Bank	Pomo	35	30	5	50	-	-
Susanville	(mixed)	32	27	5	30	-	-
Taylorsville	(no population)	-	-	-	160	-	-
Tule River	Tule River	325	172	153	54,116	-	-
Tuolume	Me-Wuk	46	36	10	323	-	-
Upper Lake[1,2]	Pomo	64	46	18	-	-	-
X L Ranch	Pit River	29	22	7	8,760	-	-
Hoopa Area Field Office		1,736	1,736	-	89,591	8,767	-
Big Lagoon	Yurok	6	6	-	9	-	-
Blue Lake[1,2]	Blue Lake	22	22	-	26	-	-
Coast Indian Community (Resighini)	Yurok	57	57	-	228	-	-
Elk Valley (Crescent City)[1,2]	Crescent City	30	30	-	-	-	-
Hoopa Public Domain Allotments	(mixed)	75	75	-	368	4,348	-
Hoopa Valley	Hoopa	992	992	-	84,632	1,436	-
Hoopa Valley Extension (Klamath Strip)	Yurok	360	360	-	3,485	2,983	-
Quartz Valley[1,2]	Shasta	36	36	-	604	-	-
Rohnerville[1,2]	Bear River	29	29	-	15	-	-
Smith River[1,2]	Smith River	102	102	-	164	-	-
Trinidad	Yurok	27	27	-	60	-	-
Palm Springs Office		78	74	4	2,056	26,507	Gov't owned
Agua Caliente (Palm Springs)	Coahuila	78	74	4	2,056	26,507	
Riverside Area Field Office		1,858	1,293	565	211,840	16,929	-
Augustine	Coahuila	2	-	2	369	160	-
Barona Ranch	Diegueno	123	103	20	5,005	-	-
Cabazon	Coahuila	11	2	9	1,153	621	-
Campo	Diegueno	53	22	31	15,010	-	-
Capitan Grande	(no population)	-	-	-	15,636	-	-
Cuyapaipe	Diegueno	1	-	1	4,080	-	-

[Continued]

★ 52 ★

Indian Reservation Population and Land Areas, 1962 and 1963: California - II
[Continued]

State, Area Office, jurisdiction and land unit	Principal tribe	Estimated Population June 30, 1962			Land Area (Acres) Reported June 30, 1963		
		Total	Within units	Adjacent to units	Tribal land	Allotted land	Gov't owned
Inaja & Cosmit	Diegueno	20	13	7	880	-	-
La Jolla	Luiseno	76	36	40	7,588	694	-
La Posta	(no population)	-	-	-	3,879	-	-
Los Coyotes	Luiseno	29	21	8	25,050	-	-
Manzanita	Diegueno	19	8	11	4,320	-	-
Mesa Grande	Luiseno	49	29	20	120	-	-
Mission Creek	Serrano	7	-	7	2,402	108	-
Mission Reserve	(no population)	-	-	-	9,480	-	-
Morongo	Serrano	257	187	70	30,927	1,343	-
Pala	Luiseno	215	160	55	6,512	1,286	-
Pauma & Yuima	Luiseno	55	40	15	250	-	-
Pechanga	Luiseno	17	7	10	2,861	1,264	-
Ramona	(no population)	-	-	-	560	-	-
Rincon	Luiseno	165	100	65	3,319	380	-
San Manuel	Serrano	37	29	8	653	-	-
San Pasqual	Luiseno	57	27	30	1,375	-	-
Santa Rosa	Coahuila	15	2	13	11,093	-	-
Santa Ynez	Chumash	50	20	30	99	-	-
Santa Ysabel	Diegueno	136	106	30	15,527	-	-
Soboba	Serrano	213	188	25	5,056	-	-
Sycuan	Diegueno	12	9	3	371	269	-
Torres-Martinez	Coahuila	75	63	12	18,223	8,141	-
Twenty-Nine Palms	(no population)	-	-	-	161	-	-
Viejas (Baron Long)	Diegueno	102	87	15	1,609	-	-
Riverside Public Domain Allotments	(no population)	-	-	-	-	2,663	-

Source: United States Department of the Interior, Bureau of Indian Affairs, *U.S. Indian Population (1962) and Land (1963),* Government Printing Office, November 1963, pp. 11-15. *Notes:* A dash (-) represents zero. 1. Land trusteeship terminated prior to June 30, 1962. 2. Land units for which Federal land trusteeship has been terminated.

★ 53 ★

Indian Reservation Population and Land Areas, 1962 and 1963: Colorado - Michigan

State, area office, jurisdiction and land unit	Principal tribe	Estimated Population June 30, 1962			Land Area (Acres) Reported June 30, 1963		
		Total	Within units	Adjacent to units	Tribal land	Allotted land	Gov't owned
Colorado		1,411	1,303	108	746,290	5,021	573
Gallup Area Office							
Consolidated Ute Agency		1,601	1,493	108	856,139	14,480	613
(Also N Mex & Utah)							
Southern Ute	Ute	679	616	63	298,261	5,021	573
Ute Mountain (Colorado, N Mex & Utah)							
Colorado only		732	687	45	448,029	-	-
(Reservation totals: Within 877 Adjacent 45)							
Florida		1,003	739	264	79,014	-	-
Central Office							
Seminole Agency		1,003	739	264	79,014	-	-
Big Cypress	Seminole	291	261	30	42,728	-	-
Brighton	Seminole	312	248	64	35,805	-	-
Dania	Seminole	272	230	42	481	-	-
Tamiami Trail	Miccosukee Seminole	128	-	128	-	-	-
Idaho		4,134	3,679	455	400,805	389,890	41,859
Portland Area Office							
Fort Hall Agency (Also Utah)		1,778	1,753	25	208,582	274,582	41,517
Fort Hall	Shoshone-Bannock	1,773	1,748	25	208,582	273,711	41,517
Northern Idaho Agency (Also Wash)		2,247	1,795	452	47,007	120,479	342
Coeur d' Alene	Coeur d'Alene	523	363	160	13,032	55,583	330
Kootenai	Kootenai	58	50	8	-	3,533	12
Nez Perce (Lapwai)	Nez Perce	1,530	1,268	262	33,646	57,063	-
Phoenix Area Office							
Nevada Agency (Nev)							
Duck Valley (Western Shosone) (Idaho & Nev) Idaho Only	Shoshone & Pauite	250	250	-	145,545	-	-
(Reservation total: Within 1,000)							
Iowa		531	490	41	4,105	-	-
Minneapolis Area Office							
Sac & Fox Area Field Office		531	490	41	3,476	-	-
Sac & Fox	Sac & Fox	531	490	41	3,476	-	-
Aberdeen Area Office							
Winnebago Agency (Nebr)							
Winnebago Off Reservation Lands (Iowa & Nebr) Iowa only	Winnebago	-	-	-	629		-
Kansas		1,289	645	644	1,784	26,083	321
Anadarko Area Office							
Potawatomi Area Field Office (Also Nebr)		1,337	652	685	1,829	26,628	1
Iowa (Kans & Nebr)							
Kansas only							
(Reservation totals: Within 51 Adjacent 60)	Iowa	70	45	25	714	254	-
Kickapoo	Kickapoo	255	160	95	980	4,050	1
Potawatomi	Potawatomi	956	436	520	90	21,596	-
Sac & Fox (Kans & Nebr) Kansas only							
(Reservation totals: Within 5 Adjacent 10)		8	4	4	-	69	-
Shawnee Public Domain Allotments	Shawnee	-	-	-	-	114	-
Haskell Institute	-	-	-	-	-	320	

[Continued]

★ 53 ★

Indian Reservation Population and Land Areas, 1962 and 1963: Colorado - Michigan

[Continued]

State, area office, jurisdiction and land unit	Principal tribe	Estimated Population June 30, 1962			Land Area (Acres) Reported June 30, 1963		
		Total	Within units	Adjacent to units	Tribal land	Allotted land	Gov't owned
Louisiana		268	118	150	262	.16	-
Muskogee Area Office							
Choctaw Agency (Miss)							
Chitimacha	Chitimacha	268	118	150	262	-	-
Osage Agency (Okla)							
(Also Ariz, Mo, N Mex, S Dak & Texas)							
Osage Off Reservation Lands Louisiana only	Osage	-	-	-	-	.16	-
Michigan		1,216	916	300	7,816	9,407	4,016
Minneapolis Area Office							
Great Lakes Agency (Wis)							
Bay Mills (Includes Sugar Island)	Chippewa	229	229	-	2,189	-	-
Hannahville	Potawatomi	134	134	-	3,539	-	-
Isabella (Saginaw)							
(Includes Sagining-Pinconing)	Chippewa	345	290	55	506	683	-
Keweenaw Bay (L'Anse	Chippewa	508	263	245	1,602	8,244	4,016
and Ontonagon)		-	-	-	160	160	-
Michigan Public Domain Allotments	(no population)	-	-	-	-	320	-

Source: United States Department of the Interior, Bureau of Indian Affairs, *U.S. Indian Population (1962) and Land (1963)*, Government Printing Office, November 1963, pp. 15-18. *Note:* A dash (-) represents zero.

★ 54 ★

Indian Reservation Population and Land Areas, 1962 and 1963: Minnesota - Montana

State, area office, jurisdiction and land unit	Principal tribe	Estimated Population June 30, 1962			Land Area (Acres) Reported June 30, 1963		
		Total	Within units	Adjacent to units	Tribal land	Allotted land	Gov't owned
Minnesota		11,580	9,500	2,080	670,761	54,520	28,698
Minneapolis Area Office							
Great Lakes Agency (Wis)							
Winnebago (Minn & Wis) Minnesota only	Winnebago	13	13	-	-	289	-
Houston County (Reservation total: Within 358)							
Minnesota Agency		11,567	9,487	2,080	670,761	54,231	28,698
Fond du Lac	Chippewa	850	650	200	3,932	17,582	-
Grand Portage (Pigeon River)	Chippewa	335	185	150	32,179	8,404	79
Leech Lake (Includes Chippewa of the Miss, White Oak Point or Winnibigoshish, Cass Lake and Leech Lake)	Chippewa	2,750	2,350	400	12,320	11,238	4
Mille Lac	Chippewa	820	520	300	3,247	132	-
Minnesota Public Domain Allotments	(no population)	-	-	-	81	483	-
Nett Lake (Bois Fort) (Includes Deer Creek & Vermillion)	Chippewa	665	465	200	25,976	14,221	5
Red Lake	Chippewa	3,200	2,900	300	564,363	102	-
Southern Minnesota	Sioux	397	267	130	-	-	-

[Continued]

★ 54 ★

Indian Reservation Population and Land Areas, 1962 and 1963: Minnesota - Montana
[Continued]

State, area office, jurisdiction and land unit	Principal tribe	Estimated Population June 30, 1962			Land Area (Acres) Reported June 30, 1963		
		Total	Within units	Adjacent to units	Tribal land	Allotted land	Gov't owned
Communities Includes:							
Lower Sioux (Morton)		-	142	50	1,743	-	-
Prairie Island (Red Wing)		-	46	40	534	-	-
Prior Lake (Shakopee)		-	22	-	258	-	-
Upper Sioux (Granite Falls)		-	57	40	746	-	-
White Earth	Chippewa	2,550	2,150	400	25,382	2,069	28,610
Mississippi		3,594	3,063	531	16,270	209	214
Muskegee Area Office							
Choctaw Agency (Also La)		3,862	3,181	681	16,532	209	214
Choctaw	Choctaw	3,594	3,063	531	16,270	209	214
Missouri		-	-	-	-	373	-
Muskogee Area Office							
Osage Agency (Okla)							
(See Ariz, La, N Mex, Okla, S Dak & Texas)							
Osage Off Reservation Lands Missouri only	Osage	-	-	-	-	373	-
Montana		20,566	18,963	1,603	1,617,839	3,617,089	128,263
Billings Area Office							
Blackfeet Agency		5,804	5,804	-	148,397	795,178	14,018
Blackfeet	Blackfeet	5,804	5,804	-	148,397	795,178	14,018
Crow Agency		3,526	3,126	400	266,408	1,307,985	1,097
Crow	Crow	3,526	3,126	400	266,408	1,307,985	1,097
Flathead Agency		2,881	2,528	353	531,574	86,098	2,222
Flathead	Salish & Kootenai	2,881	2,528	353	531,574	86,098	2,222
Fort Belknap Consolidated Agency		2,955	2,320	635	252,741	497,062	25,533
Fort Belknap	Gros Ventre & Assiniboine	2,050	1,420	630	145,230	451,522	25,533
Fort Belknap (Turtle Mountain Public Domain Allotments)	Chippewa	5	-	5	-	45,540	-
Rocky Boys	Chippewa & Cree	900	900	-	107,511	-	-
Fort Peck Agency (Also N Dak)		3,271	3,056	215	196,660	738,702	85,392
Fort Peck	Assiniboine & Sioux	3,071	3,056	15	196,660	701,247	85,392
Fort Peck (Turtle Mt. Public Domain Allotments) (Mont & N Dak) Montana only		200	-	200	-	27,620	-
Northern Cheyenne Agency		2,129	2,129	-	232,059	201,899	1
Northern Cheyenne (Tongue River)	Cheyenne	2,219	2,129	-	232,059	201,219	1
Northern Cheyenne (Tongue River) (Turtle Mountain Public Domain Allotments)	Chippewa	-	-	-	-	680	-

Source: United States Department of the Interior, Bureau of Indian Affairs, *U.S. Indian Population (1962) and Land (1963)*, Government Printing Office, November 1963, pp. 11-15. *Notes:* A dash (-) represents zero. 1. Land trusteeship terminated prior to June 30, 1962. 2. Land units for which Federal land trusteeship has been terminated.

★ 55 ★

Indian Reservation Population and Land Areas, 1962 and 1963: Nebraska - Nevada

State, area office, jurisdiction and land unit	Principal tribe	Estimated Population June 30, 1962			Land Area (Acres) Reported June 30, 1963		
		Total	Within units	Adjacent to units	Tribal land	Allotted land	Gov't owned
Nebraska		2,196	2,078	118	14,239	52,775	322
Aberdeen Area Office							
Winnebago Agency (Also Iowa)		2,148	2,071	77	14,426	52,230	167
Omaha	Omaha	1,169	1,137	32	6,698	21,004	-
Ponca[1,2]	Ponca	70	55	15	691	2,181	153
Santee	Santee Sioux	300	270	30	3,599	2,473	-
Winnebago	Winnebago	609	609	-	2,809	26,572	14
Winnebago Off Reservation Lands (Iowa & Nebr) Nebraska only		-	-	-	-	.16	-
Pine Ridge Agency (S Dak)							
Pine Ridge (Nebr & S Dak) Nebraska only (Reservation totals: Within 8,480 Adjacent 300)	Sioux	-	-	-	397	-	155
Anadarko Area Office							
Potawatomi Area Field Office (Kans)							
Iowa (Kans & Nebr) Nebraska only (Reservation totals: Within 51 Adjacent 60)	Iowa	41	6	35	-	496	-
Sac & Fox (Kans & Nebr) Sac & Fox Nebraska only (Reservation totals: Within 5 Adjacent 10)		7	1	6	-	49	-
Old Nemaha Reserve	Santee Sioux	-	-	-	45	-	-
Nevada		4,168	3,670	498	1,062,316	79,348	7,811
Phoenix Area Office							
Colorado River Agency (Ariz)							
Fort Mohave (Ariz, Nev, Mohave & Calif) Nevada only (Reservation total: Within 277)		-	-	-	5,582	-	-
Nevada Agency (Also Idaho, Ore, & Utah)		4,455	3,957	498	1,259,266	79,428	7,891
Colonies:							
Battle Mountain	Paiute & Shoshone	77	62	15	680	-	-
Carson	Washoe & Paiute	108	108	-	156	-	-
Elko	Shoshone	230	110	120	193	-	-
Ely	Paiute & Shoshone	85	25	60	10	-	-
Fallon	Shoshone & Paiute	74	59	15	60	-	-
Las Vegas	Paiute	43	43	-	10	-	-
Lovelock	Paiute	97	94	3	20	-	-
Reno-Sparks	Washoe & Paiute	418	418	-	28	-	-
Winnemucca	Paiute	42	42	-	340	-	-
Yerington	Paiute	192	127	65	10	-	-
Nevada Public Domain Allotments (Includes Pinenut Allotments)	Paiute	25	-	25	-	64,998	-
Reservations:							
Duck Valley (Western Shoshone) (Nev & Idaho) Nevada only (Reservation total: Within 1,000)	Shoshone & Paiute	750	750	-	144,274	-	-
Duckwater	Shoshone	50	50	-	3,785	-	-
Fallon (Paiute)	Shoshone & Paiute	130	119	11	830	4,650	-
Fort McDermitt (Nev & Ore) Nevada only (Reservation totals: Within 428 Adjacent 81)		509	428	81	16,236	145	-
Goshute (Nev & Utah) Nevada only (Reservation totals: Within 74 Adjacent 20)	Shoshone	57	37	20	71,554	-	-
Moapa River	Paiute	105	105	-	1,174	-	-

[Continued]

★ 55 ★

Indian Reservation Population and Land Areas, 1962 and 1963: Nebraska - Nevada

[Continued]

State, area office, jurisdiction and land unit	Principal tribe	Estimated Population June 30, 1962			Land Area (Acres) Reported June 30, 1963		
		Total	Within units	Adjacent to units	Tribal land	Allotted land	Gov't owned
Odgers Ranch	Paiute	3	3	-	1,987	-	-
Pyramid Lake	Paiute	408	338	70	475,086	-	-
Ruby Valley	Shoshone	15	15	-	80	-	-
South Fork (Te-Moak)	Shoshone	70	70	-	13,050	-	-
Summit Lake	Paiute	6	6	-	9,741	765	-
Walker River	Paiute	344	344	310,757	8,790	964	-
Washoe-Dresslerville:							
Dresslerville	Washoe	131	131		40	-	-
Washoe (Excluding Pinenut Allotments)							
Wildhorse Reservoir	(no population)	-	-	-	-	-	3,871
Yerington (Campbell Ranch)	Paiute	65	52	13	1,156	-	-
Yomba	Shoshone	134	134	-	4,682	-	-
Stewart School	(no population)	-	-	-	-	-	2,976

Source: United States Department of the Interior, Bureau of Indian Affairs, *U.S. Indian Population (1962) and Land (1963),* Government Printing Office, November 1963, pp. 20-21. *Notes:* A dash (-) represents zero. 1. Land trusteeship terminated prior to June 30, 1962. 2. Land units for which Federal land trusteeship has been terminated.

★ 56 ★

Indian Reservation Population and Land Areas, 1962 and 1963: New Mexico - North Dakota

State, area office, jurisdiction and land unit	Principal tribe	Estimated Population June 30, 1962			Land Area (Acres) Reported June 30, 1963		
		Total	Within units	Adjacent to units	Tribal land	Allotted land	Gov't owned
New Mexico		52,188	48,041	4,147	5,917,691	647,857	126,533
Gallup Area Office							
Consolidated Ute Agency (Colo)							
Ute Mountain (Colo, N Mex, & Utah) New Mexico only	Ute	-	-	-	107,520	-	-
(Reservation totals: Within 877 Adjacent 45)							
Jicarilla Agency		1,394	1,394	-	741,981	322	-
Jicarilla	Apache	1,394	1,394	-	741,981	322	-
Mescalero Agency		1,317	1,275	42	460,074	-	100
Mescalero	Apache	1,317	1,275	42	460,074	-	100
Navajo Agency (Ariz)							
Navajo Off Reservation Lands	Navajo	-	-	-	178,4113	564,376	75,699
Azrec Dormitory	(no population)	-	-	-	-	-	5
Gallup Indian Center	(no population)	-	-	-	-	-	1
Gallup Supply Center	(no population)	-	-	-	-	-	20
Navajo (Ariz, N Mex & Utah) New Mexico only	Navajo	28,957	24,852	4,105	2,383,015	-	-
(Reservation totals: Within 79,916 Adjacent 4,384)							
United Pueblos Agency		15,259	15,259	-	1,571,636	33,592	1,892
Acoma	Pueblo (Keresan)	1,674	1,674	-	245,801	320	9
Canoncito (Navajo Community)	Navajo	646	646	-	68,144	8,629	40

[Continued]

97

★ 56 ★

Indian Reservation Population and Land Areas, 1962 and 1963: New Mexico - North Dakota
[Continued]

State, area office, jurisdiction and land unit	Principal tribe	Estimated Population June 30, 1962			Land Area (Acres) Reported June 30, 1963		
		Total	Within units	Adjacent to units	Tribal land	Allotted land	Gov't owned
Cochiti	Pueblo (Keresan)	387	387	-	28,136	-	3
Isleta	Pueblo (Tano-Tigua)	1,974	1,974	-	210,937	-	11
Jemez	Pueblo (Tano-Jemez)	1,076	1,076	-	88,380	-	7
Laguna	Pueblo (Keresan)	2,956	2,956	-	409,978	4,158	1,017
Nambe	Pueblo (Tano-Tewa)	135	135	-	19,077	-	2
Picuris (San Lorenzo)	Pueblo (Tano-Tigua)	100	100	-	14,961	-	-
Pojoaque	Pueblo (Tano-Tewa)	41	41	-	11,599	-	-
Puertociot (Alamo Navajo Community) Sandia	Pueblo (Tano-Tigua)	124	124	-	22,884	-	1
San Felipe	Pueblo (Keresan)	1,060	1,060	-	48,853	71	6
San Ildefonso	Pueblo (Tano-Tewa)	224	224	-	26,191	-	1
San Juan	Pueblo (Tano-Tewa)	670	670	-	12,232	-	2
Santa Ana	Pueblo (Keresan)	366	366	-	42,082	-	3
Santa Clara	Pueblo (Tano-Tewa)	535	535	-	45,741	-	3
Santo Domingo	Pueblo (Keresan)	1,495	1,495	-	69,259	-	-
Taos	Pueblo (Tano-Tigua)	896	896	-	47,334	-	7
Tesuque	Pueblo (Tano-Tewa)	142	142	-	17,024	-	3
Zia	Pueblo (Keresan)	377	377	-	111,360	-	429
Albuquerque School	(no population)	-	-	-	-	-	259
Magdalena Dormitory	(no population)	-	-	-	-	-	9
Institute of American Indian Arts		-	-	-	-	-	111
Zuni Agency		5,261	5,261	-	475,052	49,566	25
Zuni	Pueblo (Zuni)	4,250	4,250	-	405,034	1,933	-
Ramah (Navajo Community)	Navajo	1,011	1,011	-	70,018	47,633	25
Muskogee Area Office Osage Agency (Okla) (See Ariz, La, Mo, Okla, S Dak & Texas) Osage Off Reservation Lands New Mexico only	Osage	-	-	-	-	1	-
Phoenix Area Office San Carlos Irrigation Project (Ariz) New Mexico only		-	-	-	-	-	48,680

[Continued]

★ 56 ★

Indian Reservation Population and Land Areas, 1962 and 1963: New Mexico - North Dakota

[Continued]

State, area office, jurisdiction and land unit	Principal tribe	Estimated Population June 30, 1962			Land Area (Acres) Reported June 30, 1963		
		Total	Within units	Adjacent to units	Tribal land	Allotted land	Gov't owned
North Carolina		5,500	5,470	30	56,437	-	136
Central Office							
Cherokee Agency		5,500	5,470	30	56,437	-	136
Qualla Boundary (Cherokee)	Eastern Cherokee	5,500	5,470	30	56,437	-	136
North Dakota		11,490	8,247	3,243	131,202	729,734	6,737
Aberdeen Area Office							
Fort Berthold Agency		2,254	1,815	439	39,744	384,927	174
Fort Berthold	Gros Ventre, Arikara & Mandan (no population)	2,254	1,815	439	39,744	382,047	174
Fort Berthold Public Domain Allotments		-	-	-	-	2,880	-
Standing Rock Agency (Also S Dak)		4,350	4,350	-	259,901	599,140	10,317
Standing Rock (N Dak & S Dak) North Dakota only (Reservation total: Within 4,350)	Sioux	2,050	2,050	-	55,766	248,250	3,898
Turtle Mountain Agency		7,186	4,382	2,804	35,692	83,169	2,613
Fort Totten (Devils Lake)	Sioux	1,476	1,426	50	120	48,118	2,080
Turtle Mountain	Chippewa	5,530	2,956	2,574	8,153	26,131	533
(See also Turtle Mountain Public Domain Allotments under Fort Peck, Northern Cheyenne (Tongue River) Agencies)							
Turtle Mountain Off Reservation Lands	Chippewa	180	-	180	27,419	8,920	-
Sisseton Agency (S Dak)							
Sisseton (N Dak & S Dak) North Dakota only (Reservation totals: Within 2,173 Adjacent 98)		-	-	-	-	3,553	-
Wahpeton School		-	-	-	-	-	52
Billings Area Office							
Fort Peck Agency (Mont)							
Fort Peck (Turtle Mountain Public Domain Allotments) (Mont & N Dak) North Dakota only		-	-	-	-	9,835	-
Pawnee Indian Agency		2,841	1,875	966	2,521	79,653	686
Kaw	Kaw	248	144	104	20	-	1
Otoe & Missouri	Otoe & Missouri	973	512	461	1,400	32,317	-

Source: United States Department of the Interior, Bureau of Indian Affairs, *U.S. Indian Population (1962) and Land (1963)*, Government Printing Office, November 1963, pp. 21-24. *Note:* A dash (-) represents zero.

★ 57 ★

Indian Reservation Population and Land Areas, 1962 and 1963: Oklahoma - Oregon

State, area office, jurisdiction and land unit	Principal tribe	Estimated Population June 30, 1962			Land Area (Acres) Reported June 30, 1963		
		Total	Within units	Adjacent to units	Tribal land	Allotted land	Gov't owned
Oklahoma		61,769	57,543	4,226	58,519	1,583,998	33,313
Anadarko Area Office							
Concho Indian Agency		3,640	3,165	475	5,873	111,680	319
Cheyenne & Arapaho	Cheyenne &						

[Continued]

★ 57 ★

Indian Reservation Population and Land Areas, 1962 and 1963: Oklahoma - Oregon
[Continued]

State, area office, jurisdiction and land unit	Principal tribe	Estimated Population June 30, 1962			Land Area (Acres) Reported June 30, 1963		
		Total	Within units	Adjacent to units	Tribal land	Allotted land	Gov't owned
Anadarko Indian Agency	Arapaho	3,640	3,165	475	5,873	111,680	319
Kiowa, Comanche & Apache		7,500	6,602	898	5,353	336,084	3,175
	Kiowa, Commanche & Apache						
Fort Still Apache	Fort Still Apache	5,566	4,898	668	3,047	262,442	2,791
Wichita		92	82	10	-	3,183	-
	Caddo, Dela- ware, Wichita	1,842	1,622	220	2,306	69,829	384
Caddo			890	112			
Delaware			360	52			
Wichita			372	56			
Pawnee Indian Agency		2,841	1,875	966	2,521	79,653	686
Kaw	Kaw	248	144	104	20	-	1
Otoe & Missouri	Otoe & Missouri	973	512	461	1,400	32,317	-
Pawnee	Pawnee	687	584	103	-	26,495	680
Ponca	Ponca	876	605	271	940	20,280	5
Tonkawa	Tonkawa	57	30	27	161	561	-
Shawnee Indian Agency		2,400	1,992	408	849	50,143	194
Iowa	Iowa	258	116	142	15	1,749	-
Kickapoo	Mexican Kickapoo	416	406	10	17	6,575	-
Potawatomi	Citizen Potawatomi	318	242	76	1	5,124	194
Sac & Fox	Sac & Fox	656	598	58	805	20,679	-
Shawnee	Absentee Shawnee	752	630	122	11	16,016	-
Chilocco School		-	-	-	-	-	8,552
Muskogee Area Office							
Five Civilized Tribes Agency		40,042	40,042	-	41,590	727,215	20,387
Members of Five Cilivized Tribes within former Indian Territory, Oklahoma, for whom Bureau assumes some responsibility. Cannot be identified by reservation boundaries.							
All are counted as "within or on reservation" because there are 768,805 acres of tribal and allotted land in this agency; and, at the current population-land ratio of Oklahoma, this acreage would contain 40,000 people.		-	-	-	41,590	727,215	20,387
Cherokee	Cherokee	13,215	13,215	-	-	-	-
United Keetoowah Band	Cherokee						
Chickasaw	Chickasaw	3,491	3,491	-	-	-	-
Choctaw[1,2]	Choctaw	7,729	7,729	-	-	-	-
Creek	Creek	13,254	13,264	-	-	-	-
Alabama-Quassarte	Creek						
Kialegee	Creek						

[Continued]

★ 57 ★

Indian Reservation Population and Land Areas, 1962 and 1963: Oklahoma - Oregon

[Continued]

State, area office, jurisdiction and land unit	Principal tribe	Estimated Population June 30, 1962			Land Area (Acres) Reported June 30, 1963		
		Total	Within units	Adjacent to units	Tribal land	Allotted land	Gov't owned
Thlopthlocco	Creek						
Seminole	Seminole	2,343	2,343	-	-	-	-
Osage Agency		2,872	2,179	693	645	261,146	-
(Also Ariz, La, Mo, N Mex, S Dak, & Texas)							
Osage	Osage	2,872	2,179	693	645	258,679	-
Osage Off Reservation Lands Oklahoma only	Osage	-	-	-	-	1,439	-
Quapaw Area Field Office		2,474	1,688	786	1,688	19,105	-
Eastern Shawnee	Shawnee	299	200	99	58	1,484	-
Miami	Miami	299	195	104	-	-	-
Quapaw	Quapaw	1,144	805	339	577	13,150	-
Seneca-Cayuga	Seneca-Cayuga	732	488	244	1,053	4,471	-
Oregon		2,305	2,138	167	496,242	194,589	1,254
Phoenix Area Office							
Nevada Agency (Nev)							
Fort McDermitt (Ore & Nev) Oregon only	Paiute	-	-	-	18,269	-	-
(Reservation totals: Within 428 Adjacent 81)							
Portland Area Office							
Klamath[1,2]	Klamath, Modoc & Snake	1,185	-	-	-	-	5
Warm Springs Agency		2,305	2,138	167	477,973	194,589	828
Burns-Paiute	Paiute	172	172	-	-	11,174	771
Celillo Village	Walla Walla	42	42	-	35	-	41
The Dalles Unit	Chinock	-	-	-	-	6,482	-
(Residents included in Warm Springs)							
Umatilla	Walla Walla & Cayuse	645	541	104	15,437	75,241	.22
Warm Springs	Walla Walla & Wasco	1,446	1,383	63	462,501	101,692	16
Chemawa School		-	-	-	-	-	421

Source: United States Department of the Interior, Bureau of Indian Affairs, *U.S. Indian Population (1962) and Land (1963)*, Government Printing Office, November 1963, pp. 24-26. *Notes:* A dash (-) represents zero. 1. Land trusteeship terminated prior to June 30, 1962. 2. Land units for which Federal land trusteeship has been terminated.

★ 58 ★

Indian Reservation Population and Land Areas, 1962 and 1963: South Dakota - Utah

State, area office, jurisdiction and land unit	Principal tribe	Estimated Population June 30, 1962			Land Area (Acres) Reported June 30, 1963		
		Total	Within units	Adjacent to units	Tribal land	Allotted land	Gov't owned
South Dakota		27,669	25,397	2,272	1,937,706	2,873,429	136,639
Aberdeen Area Office							
Cheyenne River Agency		3,734	3,734	-	894,321	570,076	4,417
Cheyenne River	Sioux	3,734	3,734	-	885,931	563,440	4,417
Cheyenne River Off Reservation Lands	Sioux	-	-	-	8,390	6,636	-
Flandreau School		283	46	237	2,100	-	256
Flandreau	Santee						

[Continued]

★ 58 ★

Indian Reservation Population and Land Areas, 1962 and 1963: South Dakota - Utah
[Continued]

State, area office, jurisdiction and land unit	Principal tribe	Estimated Population June 30, 1962			Land Area (Acres) Reported June 30, 1963		
		Total	Within units	Adjacent to units	Tribal land	Allotted land	Gov't owned
Flandreau School	Sioux (no population)	283	46	237	2,100	-	-
		-	-	-	-	-	256
Pierre Agency		1,567	1,330	237	65,666	134,434	32,468
Crow Creek	Sioux	1,058	902	156	20,322	90,849	18,976
Lower Brule	Sioux	509	428	81	45,344	43,585	13,285
Pierre School	(no population)						
		-	-	-	-	-	207
Pine Ridge Agency (Also Nebr)		8,780	8,480	300	366,740	1,152,792	53,768
Pine Ridge (S Dak & Nebr) South Dakota only		8,780	8,480	300	366,343	1,152,792	53,613
(Reservation totals: Within 8,480, Adjacent 300)							
Rosebud Agency		8,734	7,334	1,400	404,291	559,302	39,245
Rosebud	Sioux	7,201	5,844	1,357	398,923	528,344	39,245
Yankton	Sioux	1,533	1,490	43	5,368	30,958	-
Sisseton Agency (Also N Dak)		2,271	2,173	98	850	108,848	82
Sisseton (N Dak & S Dak) South Dakota only		2,271	2,273	98	850	105,295	82
(Reservation totals: Within 2,173, Adjacent 98)							
Standing Rock Agency (N Dak)							
Standing Rock (N Dak & S Dak) South Dakota only	Sioux	2,300	2,300	-	204,135	350,890	6,419
(Reservation total: Within 4,350)							
Sioux Sanatorium		-	-	-	-	-	139
Muskogee Area Office							
Osage Agency (Okla)							
(See Ariz, La, Mo, N Mex, Okla & Texas)							
Osage Off Reservation Lands South Dakota only	Osage	-	-	-	-	640	-
Texas		-	-	-	-	11	-
Muskogee Area Office							
(See Ariz, La, Mo, N Mex, Okla & S Dak)							
Osage Off Reservation Lands Texas only	Osage	-	-	-	-	11	-
Utah		4,885	4,474	411	2,047,997	67,843	439
Gallup Area Office							
Consolidated Ute Agency (Colo)							
Ute Mountain (Includes Allen Canyon Community) (Colo, N Mex, & Utah) Utah only	Ute	190	190	-	2,329	9,459	40
(Reservation totals: Within 877, Adjacent 45)							
Navajo Agency (Ariz)							
Navajo (Ariz, N Mex, & Utah) Utah only		3,043	2,587	186	1,184,143	10,720	-
(Reservation totals: Within 79,916, Adjacent 4,384)							
Navajo Public Domain Allotments (Ariz & Utah) Utah only	Navajo	-	-	-	-	160	-
Richfield Dormitory	(no population)						
		-	-	-	-	-	6
Intermountain School		-	-	-	-	-	289
Phoenix Area Office							
Nevada Agency (Nev)							
Goshute (Nev & Utah) Utah only (Includes Gandy & Ipabah)		37	37	-	38,718	80	80
(Reservation totals: Within 74, Adjacent 20)							
Uintah & Ouray Agency		1,610	1,385	225	822,807	46,784	24
Skull Valley	Goshute	45	15	30	17,284	480	-
Uintah & Ouray	Ute (Full Blood)	1,565	1,370	195	805,523	46,304	24

[Continued]

★ 58 ★

Indian Reservation Population and Land Areas, 1962 and 1963: South Dakota - Utah
[Continued]

State, area office, jurisdiction and land unit	Principal tribe	Estimated Population June 30, 1962			Land Area (Acres) Reported June 30, 1963		
		Total	Within units	Adjacent to units	Tribal land	Allotted land	Gov't owned
Portland Area Office Fort Hall Agency (Idaho) Washakie	Shoshone	5	5	-	-	640	-

Source: United States Department of the Interior, Bureau of Indian Affairs, *U.S. Indian Population (1962) and Land (1963)*, Government Printing Office, November 1963, pp. 26-28. *Note:* A dash (-) represents zero.

★ 59 ★

Indian Reservation Population and Land Areas, 1962 and 1963: Washington - Wyoming

State, area office, jurisdiction and land unit	Principal tribe	Estimated Population June 30, 1962			Land Area (Acres) Reported June 30, 1963		
		Total	Within units	Adjacent to units	Tribal land	Allotted land	Gov't owned
Washington		11,220	8,733	2,487	1,833,750	708,333	90
Portland Area Office							
Colville Agency		3,650	2,022	1,628	1,021,684	182,113	47
Colville	Colville	2,952	1,712	1,240	925,660	136,932	8
Colville Public Domain Allotments	Colville	81	-	81	-	2,456	-
Spokane	Spokane	617	310	307	96,024	42,725	39
Northern Idaho Agency (Idaho)							
Kalispel	Kalispel	136	114	22	329	4,300	-
Western Washington Agency		4,072	3,760	312	36,182	174,029	20
Chehalis	Chehalis	141	116	25	21	1,843	-
Hoh	Hoh	26	26	-	443	-	-
Lower Elwah	Clallam	134	134	-	372	-	-
Lummi	Lummi	660	600	60	12	7,720	-
Makah	Makah	558	558	-	24,499	2,517	-
Muckleshoot	Muckleshoot	306	271	35	.29	1,445	-
Nisqually	Nisqually	67	25	42	2	931	-
Ozette	(no population)	-	-	-	719	-	-
Port Gamble	Clallam	121	121	-	1,301	-	-
Port Madison	Suquamish	104	74	30	41	2,652	.41
Puyallup	Puyallup	-	-	-	33	-	-
Quileute	Quileute	154	154	-	584	10	-
Quinault	Quinault	594	574	20	3,872	134,471	18
Shoalwater	Shoalwater	12	12	-	335	-	-
Skokomish	Skokomish	143	143	-	16	2,942	-
Squaxon Island	Squaxon Island	6	6	-	-	918	2
Swinomish	Swinomish	367	320	47	247	4,080	-
Tulalip	Snohomish	429	376	53	3,685	7,716	-
Western Washington Public Domain Allotments: Clallam, Nooksack, Skagit, Snoqualmie, Duwamish & Jamestown	(mixed)						
Yakima Agency		3,362	2,837	525	775,555	347,894	23
Yakima	Yakima	3,207	2,837	370	775,371	321,116	23
Yakima Public Domain Allotments (Includes Vancouver Allotments)	Yakima	155	-	155	184	26,778	-

[Continued]

★ 59 ★

Indian Reservation Population and Land Areas, 1962 and 1963: Washington - Wyoming
[Continued]

State, area office, jurisdiction and land unit	Principal tribe	Estimated Population June 30, 1962			Land Area (Acres) Reported June 30, 1963		
		Total	Within units	Adjacent to units	Tribal land	Allotted land	Gov't owned
Wisconsin		5,322	4,149	1,173	60,088	84,854	39,447
Minneapolis Area Office							
Great Lakes Agency (Also Mich & Minn)		6,551	5,078	1,473	67,904	94,550	43,463
Bad River (La Pointe)	Chippewa	509	509	-	6,974	34,509	13,110
Chippewa Communities	Chippewa	272	207	65	1,698	-	-
(St. Croix, Clam Lake, Danbury, Round Lake, Sand Lake)							
Lac Courte Oreilles	Chippewa	950	856	94	3,029	27,454	13,185
Lac de Flambeau	Chippewa	910	910	-	26,142	15,249	40
Mole Lake (Sakoagon)	Chippewa	117	117	-	1,666	-	-
Oneida	Oneida	1,356	416	940	2,057	534	-
Potawatomi	Forest Potawatomi	234	234	-	11,146	600	-
Red Cliff	Chippewa	375	325	50	5,086	2,145	-
Stockbridge - Munsee	Stockbridge-Munsee	254	230	24	2,250	-	13,077
Winnebago (Minn & Wis)	Winnebago	345	345	-	40	3,848	35
Wisconsin only (Reservation total: Within 358)							
Wisconsin Public Domain Allotments	Chippewa	-	-	-	-	515	-
Wyoming		3,758	3,417	341	1,761,074	126,603	962
Billings Area Office							
Wind River Agency		3,758	3,417	341	1,761,074	126,603	962
Wind River	Arapaho (2,230) Shoshone (1,528)	3,758	3,417	341	1,761,074	126,603	962

Source: United States Department of the Interior, Bureau of Indian Affairs, *U.S. Indian Population (1962) and Land (1963)*, Government Printing Office, November 1963, pp. 29-31. *Note:* A dash (-) represents zero.

★ 60 ★

Cahuilla Population History from Aboriginal Times to 1980

Date	Population
Aboriginal times	2,500-10,000
1850	2,000-3,000
1890	1,100-1,200
1910	755

[Continued]

★ 60 ★

Cahuilla Population History from Aboriginal Times to 1980
[Continued]

Date	Population
1970	1,000
1980	?

Source: Russell Thornton, *American Indian Holocaust and Survival: A Population History Since 1492*, University of Oklahoma, Press, 1987, p. 126. Published by permission. Primary source: U.S. Bureau of the Census, *Indian Population of the United States and Alaska, 1910*. Washington, D.C.: U.S. Government Printing Office, 1915, p. 97; Harvey, "Population of the Cahuilla Indians: Decline and Its Causes," *Eugenics Quarterly*, p. 194; Bean, "Cults and Their Transformations," pp. 662-672 in Robert F. Heizer, ed., *California*, vol. 8 of *Handbook of North American Indians*. Washington, D.C.: Smithsonian Institution, 1978, p. 584.

★ 61 ★

California Indian Population History, Pre-European Contact to 1980

Date	Population
Pre-European	310,000?-705,000
1800	260,000
1834	210,000
1849	100,000
1852	85,000
1856	50,000
1860	35,000
1870	30,000
1880	20,500
1890	18,000
1900	15,000-20,000
1907	18,000
1980	198,275[1]

Source: Russell Thornton, *American Indian Holocaust and Survival: A Population History Since 1492*, University of Oklahoma, Press, 1987, p. 109. Published by permission. Primary source: Merriam, "The Indian Population of California," *American Anthropologist*, 1905, p. 60; Mooney, "The Aboriginal Population of America North of Mexico," pp. 1-40 in John R. Swanton, ed., *Smithsonian Miscellaneous Collections*, vol. 80, 1928, p. 19; Cook S., *The Population of the California Indians, 1669-1970*. Berkeley: University of California Press, 1976, pp. 69-71; Cook, N., *Demographic Collapse: Indian Peru, 1520- 1620*. Cambridge, England: Cambridge University Press, 1981, p. 91; Powers, *Tribes of California*. Contributions to North American Ethnology, vol. 3. Reprint. Washington, D.C.: U.S. Government Printing Office, 1976. Swagerty and Thornton, "Preliminary 1980 Census Counts for American Indians, Eskimos, and Aleuts," *American Indian Culture and Research Journal*, 1982, p. 92; U.S. Bureau of the Census, *1980 Census of Population, Supplementary Report. American Indian Areas and Alaska Native Villages: 1980*. PC80-S1-13. Washington, D.C.: U.S. Government Printing Office, 1984, p. 14. *Note:* 1. Includes recent immigrants to California.

★ 62 ★

Cherokee Population History, 1650-1980

Date	Population
1650	22,000
1808-1809	13,395
1826	17,713
1835	21,542
1851-1852	15,802
1866	15,566
1875	19,717
1880	21,920
1890	28,000
1900	32,376
1910	31,489
1970	66,150
1980	232,000 +

Source: Russell Thornton, *American Indian Holocaust and Survival: A Population History Since 1492,* University of Oklahoma, Press, 1987, p. 115. Published by permission. Primary source: U.S. Bureau of the Census, *Indian Population of the United States and Alaska, 1910.* Washington, D.C.: U.S. Government Printing Office, 1915, p. 83; *The Indian Population of the United States and Alaska.* Washington, D.C.: U.S. Government Printing Office, 1937, p. 188; Mooney, "The Aboriginal Population of America North of Mexico," pp. 1-40 in John R. Swanton, ed., *Smithsonian Miscellaneous Collections,* vol. 80, 1928, p. 8. Thornton, "Cherokee Population Losses During the Trail of Tears: A New Perspective and a New Estimate," *Ethnohistory,* 1984, pp. 295, 297.

★ 63 ★

Cheyenne Population History, 1780-1980

Date	Population
1780	3,500 +
1875	4,000
1880	3,767
1890	3,654
1900	3,446
1910	3,055
1930	2,695

[Continued]

★ 63 ★

Cheyenne Population History, 1780-1980
[Continued]

Date	Population
1970	6,872
1980	9,918

Source: Russell Thornton, *American Indian Holocaust and Survival: A Population History Since 1492*, University of Oklahoma, Press, 1987, p. 120. Published by permission. Primary source: U.S. Bureau of the Census, *Indian Population of the United States and Alaska, 1910*. Washington, D.C.: U.S. Government Printing Office, 1915, p. 73; *The Indian Population of the United States and Alaska*. Washington, D.C.: U.S. Government Printing Office, 1937, p. 37; *1970 Census of the Population Subject Report. American Indians*. Final Report PC(2)- 1F. Washington, D.C.: U.S. Government Printing Office, 1973, p. 188; Unpublished American Indian population data from 1980 census, 1981; Mooney, "The Aboriginal Population of America North of Mexico," pp. 1-40 in John R. Swanton, ed., *Smithsonian Miscellaneous Collections*, vol. 80, 1928, p. 13.

★ 64 ★

Huron Population History, Early 1600s to 1980

Date	Population
Huron of Huronia	
Early 1600s	20,000-35,000
1640	10,000
Wyandot	
Mid-1660s	500
1880	251
1890	288
1900	339
1910	353
1980	1,091
Huron of Lorette	
1966	979

Source: Russell Thornton, *American Indian Holocaust and Survival: A Population History Since 1492*, University of Oklahoma Press, 1987, p. 73. Published by permission. Primary source: U.S. Bureau of the Census, *Indian Population of the United States and Alaska*, 1910. Washington, D.C.: U.S. Government Printing Office, 1915, p. 85; Unpublished American Indian population data from 1980 census, 1981; Heidenreich, "Huron," pp. 368-388 in Bruce G. Trigger, ed., *Northeast*, vol. 15 of *Handbook of North American Indians*. Washington, D.C.: Smithsonian Institution, 1978 pp. 369-370; Morissonneau, "Huron of Lorette," pp. 389- 393 in Bruce G. Trigger, ed., *Northeast*, vol. 15 of *Handbook of North American Indians*. Washington, D.C.: Smithsonian Institution, 1978, p. 392; Tooker, "Wyandot," pp. 398-406 in Bruce G. Trigger, ed., *Northeast*, vol. 15 of *Handbook of North American Indians*. Washington, D.C.: Smithsonian Institution, 1978, pp. 403-404.

★ 65 ★

Illinois Indian Population History, 1670-1980

Date	Population
1670-80	10,500 +
1700	6,000
1736	2,500
1763	1,950
1800	500
1840	200
1910	130
1956	439
1980	645

Source: Russell Thornton, *American Indian Holocaust and Survival: A Population History Since 1492,* University of Oklahoma Press, 1987, p. 88. Published by permission. Primary source: U.S. Bureau of the Census, *Indian Population of the United States and Alaska,* 1910. Washington, D.C.: U.S. Government Printing Office, 1915, p. 75; Unpublished American Indian population data from 1980 census, 1981; Blasingham, "The Depopulation of the Illinois Indians," *Ethnohistory,* 1956, p. 372; Callender, "Illinois," pp. 673-80 in Bruce G. Trigger, ed., *Northeast,* vol. 15, of *Handbook of North American Indians.* Washington, D.C.: Smithsonian Institution, 1978, p. 697.

★ 66 ★

Kalapuya Population History, 1780-1980

Date	Population
1780	3,000
1910	106
1970	95
1980	65

Source: Russell Thornton, *American Indian Holocaust and Survival: A Population History Since 1492,* University of Oklahoma, Press, 1987, p. 125. Published by permission. Primary source: U.S. Bureau of the Census, *Indian Population of the United States and Alaska, 1910.* Washington, D.C.: U.S. Government Printing Office, 1915, p. 85; *1970 Census of the Population Subject Report. American Indians.* Final Report PC (2)- 1F. Washington, D.C.: U.S. Government Printing Office, 1973, p. 188; Unpublished American Indian population data from 1980 census, 1981; Mooney, "The Aboriginal Population of America North of Mexico," pp. 1-40 in John R. Swanton, ed., *Smithsonian Miscellaneous Collections,* vol. 80, 1928, p. 18.

★ 67 ★

Kansas Population History, From Early 1700s to 1980

Date	Size
Early 1700s	5,000
Late 1700s	3,000
Early 1800s	1,500
1861	866
1870	574
1880	397
1900	217
1910	238
1980	677

Source: Russell Thornton, *American Indian Holocaust and Survival: A Population History Since 1492*, University of Oklahoma, Press, 1987, p. 127. Published by permission. Primary source: U.S. Bureau of the Census, *Indian Population of the United States and Alaska, 1910.* Washington, D.C.: U.S. Government Printing Office, 1915, p. 100; Unpublished American Indian population data from 1980 census, 1981; Mooney, "The Aboriginal Population of America North of Mexico," pp. 1-40 in John R. Swanton, ed., *Smithsonian Miscellaneous Collections*, vol. 80, 1928, p. 13; Unrau, "The Depopulation of the Dheghia-Siouan Kansa Prior to Removal," *New Mexico Historical Review*, 1973, p. 316-321.

★ 68 ★

Kickapoo Population History, Late 1700s to 1980

Location	Population
Late 1700s	
United States	2,700
1832	
United States	2,000
1875	
United States	806
Kansas	380
Oklahoma	426
Mexico	350
1905	
United States	432
Kansas	185
Oklahoma	247
Mexico	400
1950s	
United States	722

[Continued]

109

★ 68 ★

Kickapoo Population History, Late 1700s to 1980
[Continued]

Location	Population
Kansas	343
Oklahoma	379
Mexico	387
United States	1,249
1980	
United States	2,355

Source: Russell Thornton, *American Indian Holocaust and Survival: A Population History Since 1492*, University of Oklahoma Press, 1987, p. 235. Published by permission. Primary source: U.S. Bureau of the Census, *Indian Population of the United States and Alaska*, 1910. Washington, D.C.: U.S. Government Printing Office, 1915, p. 74; 1970 *Census of the Population, Subject Report, American Indians* Final Report PC (2)- 1F. Washington, D.C.: U.S. Government Printing Office, 1973. p. 188; Unpublished American Indian population data from 1980 census, 1981. Latorre and Latorre, *The Mexican Kickapoo Indians*, Austin: University of Texas, Press; Laughlin, William S., Jorgen B. Jorgensen, and Bruno Frolich, 1976, p. 28; Callender, Pope, and Pope, "Kickapoo," pp. 656-672 in Bruce G. Trigger, ed., *Northeast*, vol. 15 of *Handbook of North American Indians*. Washington, D.C.: Smithsonian Institution, 1978, pp. 666-667.

★ 69 ★

Mandan Population History, 1738-1980

Date	Population
1738	15,000
1750	9,000
1780	3,600
1837 (June)	1,600-2,000
1837 (October)	138
1855	252
1866	400
1877	420
1890	251
1904	250
1910	209
1929	329
1937	355
1980	1,013

Source: Russell Thornton, *American Indian Holocaust and Survival: A Population History Since 1492*, University of Oklahoma Press, 1987, p. 96. Published by permission. Primary source: U.S. Bureau of the Census, *Indian Population of the United States and Alaska*, 1910. Washington, D.C.: U.S. Government Printing Office, 1915, p. 100; Unpublished American Indian population data from 1980 census, 1981; Mooney, "The Aboriginal Population of American North of Mexico," pp. 1-40 in John R. Swanton, ed., *Smithsonian Miscellaneous Collections*, vol. 80; Moore, John H., 1928, p. 13; Glassner, "Population Figures for Mandan Indians," *The Indian Historian*, 1974, pp. 45-46.

★ 70 ★

Omaha Indian Population History, Late 1700s to 1980

Date	Population
Late 1700s	3,000-3,500
1802	Less than 300
1876	1,076
1882	1,100
1884	1,179
1910	1,105
1930	1,103
1960	1,100 (approximately)
1975	2,600
1980	3,090

Source: Russell Thornton, *American Indian Holocaust and Survival: A Population History Since 1492*, University of Oklahoma, Press, 1987, p. 93. Published by permission. Primary source: "Omaha Sociology," *Third Annual Report of the Bureau of Ethnology.* Washington, D.C.: U.S. Government Printing Office, 1884, p. 214; Fletcher and LaFlesche, *The Omaha Tribe. Twenty-Seventh Annual Report of the Bureau of American Ethnology...1905-06.* Washington, D.C.: U.S. Government Printing Office, 1911, p. 33; U.S. Bureau of the Census, *Indian Population of the United States and Alaska*, 1910. Washington, D.C.: U.S. Government Printing Office, 1915. p. 101; Unpublished American Indian population data from 1980 census, 1981; Ross, "The Omaha People," *The Indian Historian*, 1970, p. 22; Liberty, "Population Trends Among Present-Day Omaha Indians." *Plains Anthropologist*, 1975, pp. 225, 227.

★ 71 ★

Tolowa Population History, Pre-European Contact to 1983

Date	Population
Pre-European	2,400+
1850	316
1870	200
1910	121-150
1950	154

[Continued]

★ 71 ★

Tolowa Population History, Pre-European Contact to 1983
[Continued]

Date	Population
1981	396
1983	400-450

Source: Russell Thornton, *American Indian Holocaust and Survival: A Population History Since 1492*, University of Oklahoma Press, 1987, p. 207. Published by permission. Primary source: U.S. Bureau of the Census, *Indian Population of the United States and Alaska*, 1990. Washington, D.C.: U.S. Government Printing Office, 1915, p. 79; Unpublished American Indian population data from 1980 census, 1981; Kroeber, *Handbook of the Indians of California*, Washington, D.C.: U.S. Government Printing Office, 1925, p. 883; Tax, *Map of the North American Indians: 1950 Distribution of Descendants of the Aboriginal Population of Alaska, Canada and the United States*. Chicago: Department of Anthropology, University of Chicago, 1960; Baumhoff, "Ecological Determinants of Aboriginal California Populations." *University of California Publications in American Archaeology and Ethnology*, 1963, p. 231; Cook, *The Population of the California Indians, 1769-1970*. Berkeley: University of California Press, 1976b, pp. 55-56; Heth, Unpublished recording of Yurok and Tolowa Indians. Department of Music and American Indian Studies Center, University of California, Los Angeles, 1976; Thornton, "Demographic Antecedents of a Revitalization Movement: Population Change, Population Size and the 1890 Ghost Dance." *American Sociological Review*, 1981, p. 703; Bommelyn, Personal communication, 1983.

★ 72 ★

Yana Population History, Pre-European Contact to 1980

Date	Population
Precontact	2,000-3,000
1848	1,900
1867	100
1864	35
1910	39
1928	12
1973	20
1980	0?

Source: Russell Thornton, *American Indian Holocaust and Survival: A Population History Since 1492*, University of Oklahoma, Press, 1987, p. 111. Published by permission. Primary source: U.S. Bureau of the Census, *Indian Population of the United States and Alaska, 1910*. Washington, D.C.: U.S. Government Printing Office, 1915, p. 108; Unpublished American Indian population data from 1980 census, 1981; Johnson, "Tribal Demography: The Hopi and Navajo Population as Seen Through Manuscripts from the 1900 U.S. Census," *Social Science History*, 1978, p. 362; Thornton, "Recent Estimates of the Prehistoric California Indian Population," *Current Anthropology*, 1980, p. 703.

★ 73 ★

Yuki Population History, Pre-European Contact to 1980

Date	Population
Pre-European	6,000-12,000 + [1]
1858	2,300 +
1864	600
1870	238
1880	168
1910	95
1973	32 +
1980	96

Source: Russell Thornton, *American Indian Holocaust and Survival: A Population History Since 1492*, University of Oklahoma Press, 1987, p. 203. Published by permission. Primary source: Miller, "Whatever Happened to the Yuki." *The Indian Historian*, 1975, p. 6; "Yuki, Huchnom, and Coast Yuki," pp. 249-255 in Robert F. Heizer, ed., *California*, vol. 8 of *Handbook of North American Indians*. Washington, D.C.: Smithsonian Institution, 1978, p. 250; U.S. Bureau of the Census, Unpublished American Indian population data from 1980 census, 1981. *Notes:* 1. Estimates of this population have ranged as high as 20,000 (see Miller, 1975, 1978, 1979).

Blood Status

★ 74 ★

Full-Blood and Mixed-Blood Indians in the United States and Alaska, 1910

Class	Indian population: 1910			
	United States		Alaska	
	Number	Percent of total	Number	Percent of total
Total	265,683	100.0	25,331	100.0
Full blood	150,053	56.5	21,444	84.7
Mixed blood	93,423	35.2	3,887	15.3
White and Indian[1]	88,030	33.1	3,843	15.2
Negro and Indian	2,255	0.8	-	-
White, Negro, and Indian	1,793	0.7	-	-
Other mixtures	80	[2]	43	0.2
Mixture unknown	1,265	0.5	1	[2]
Not reported	22,207	8.4	-	-

Source: U.S. Bureau of the Census, *Indian Population in the United States and Alaska, 1910*, United States Government Printing Office, Washington, D.C., 1915, p. 31. *Notes:* A dash (-) represents zero. 1. Includes Mexican and Indian. 2. Less than one-tenth of 1 percent.

★ 75 ★

Full-Blood and Mixed-Blood Indians, by State, 1910

| State | Indians reported on special schedule | | | | | | |
| | Number | | | | Percent of total | | |
	Total	Full-blood	Mixed-blood	Blood not reported	Full-blood	Mixed-blood	Blood not reported
United States	247,137	150,053	93,423	3,661	60.7	37.8	1.5
Arizona	28,748	27,087	414	1,247	94.2	1.4	4.3
California	14,994	10,493	4,217	284	70.0	28.1	1.9
Colorado	769	718	50	1	93.4	6.5	0.1
Idaho	3,426	2,864	514	48	83.6	15.0	1.4
Kansas	1,413[1]	516	889	8	36.5	62.9	0.6
Michigan	6,761	3,528	3,218	15	52.2	47.6	0.2
Minnesota	8,756	3,859	4,886	11	44.1	55.8	0.1
Mississippi	1,176	1,077	90	9	91.6	7.7	0.8
Montana	10,394	6,204	3,895	295	59.7	37.5	2.8
Nebraska	3,312	2,294	939	79	69.3	28.4	2.4
Nevada	4,949	4,287	508	154	86.6	10.3	3.1
New Mexico	20,279	20,085	175	19	99.0	0.9	0.1
New York	5,209	2,850	2,028	331	54.7	38.9	6.4
North Carolina	7,287	1,394	5,855	38	19.1	80.3	0.5
North Dakota	6,168	2,499	3,561	108	40.5	57.7	1.8
Oklahoma	70,744	25,887	44,288	599	36.6	62.6	0.8
Oregon	4,580	2,901	1,668	11	63.3	36.4	0.2
South Dakota	18,822	13,247	5,408	167	70.4	28.7	0.9
Utah	3,051	2,900	105	46	95.1	3.4	1.5
Washington	9,852	6,770	3,019	63	68.7	30.6	0.6
Wisconsin	9,597	5,249	4,330	18	54.7	45.1	0.2
Wyoming	1,458	1,174	284	-	80.5	19.5	-
Total for 22 states	241,775	147,883	90,341	3,551	61.2	37.4	1.75
All other states	5,362	2,170	3,082	110	40.5	57.5	2.1

Source: U.S. Bureau of the Census, *Indian Population in the United States and Alaska, 1910,* United States Government Printing Office, Washington, D.C., 1915, p. 32. *Notes:* A dash (-) represents zero. 1. Exclusive of 591 Indians in Haskell Institute, who are included in the total for "All other states."

★ 76 ★

Full-Blood and Mixed-Blood Indians, by Linguistic Stock, Tribe, and State, 1910: A - Mi

Data are shown for tribes having 200 or more members in 1910

Stock, tribe, and state	Indians reported on special schedule : 1910						
	Number				Percent of total		
	Total	Full blood	Mixed blood	Blood not reported	Full blood	Mixed blood	Blood not reported
UNITED STATES							
Algonquian stock	40,975	18,396	22,319	260	44.9	54.5	0.6
Arapaho	1,419	1,311	108	-	92.4	7.6	-
Oklahoma	685	621	64	-	90.7	9.3	-
Wyoming	703	661	42	-	94.0	6.0	-
Cheyenne	3,055	2,662	319	74	87.1	10.4	2.4
Montana	1,346	1,181	97	68	87.7	7.2	5.1
Oklahoma	1,522	1,379	139	4	90.6	9.1	0.3
South Dakota	133	74	57	2	55.6	42.9	1.5
Chippewa	20,214	6,970	13,138	106	34.5	65.0	0.5
Michigan	3,725	1,558	2,152	15	41.8	57.8	0.4
Minnesota	8,234	3,595	4,629	10	43.7	56.2	0.1
Montana	486	84	402	-	17.3	82.7	-
North Dakota	2,966	58	2,829	79	2.0	95.4	2.7
Pennsylvania	134	31	103	-	23.1	76.9	-
Wisconsin	4,299	1,601	2,696	2	37.2	62.7	[1]
Cree	459	40	418	1	8.7	91.1	0.2
Montana	309	35	273	1	11.3	88.3	0.3
Delaware	914	279	633	2	30.5	69.3	0.2
Gros Ventres	510	390	119	1	76.5	23.3	0.2
Kickapoo	348	240	107	1	69.0	30.7	0.3
Kansas	211	112	99	-	53.1	46.9	-
Oklahoma	135	126	8	1	93.3	5.9	0.7
Mashpee	206	1	205	-	0.5	99.5	-
Menominee	1,422	704	716	2	49.5	50.4	0.1
Miami	226	59	166	1	26.1	73.5	0.4
Oklahoma	123	22	100	1	17.9	81.3	0.8
Ottawa	2,717	1,720	997	-	63.3	36.7	-
Michigan	2,454	1,664	790	-	67.8	32.2	-
Oklahoma	170	12	158	-	7.1	92.9	-
Passamaquoddy	386	295	91	-	76.4	23.6	-
Penobscot	266	85	181	-	32.0	68.0	-
Piegan	2,268	1,214	1,053	1	53.5	46.4	[1]
Potawatomi	2,440	960	1,478	2	39.3	60.6	0.1
Kansas	819	319	500	-	38.9	61.1	-
Michigan	461	281	180	-	61.0	39.0	-
Oklahoma	866	115	749	2	13.3	86.5	0.2
Wisconsin	245	227	18	-	92.7	7.3	-
Sauk and Fox	724	547	171	6	75.6	23.6	0.8
Iowa	257	245	12	-	95.3	4.7	-
Oklahoma	347	260	81	6	74.9	23.3	1.7

[Continued]

115

★ 76 ★

Full-Blood and Mixed-Blood Indians, by Linguistic Stock, Tribe, and State, 1910: A - Mi
[Continued]

Stock, tribe, and state	Indians reported on special schedule : 1910						
	Number				Percent of total		
	Total	Full blood	Mixed blood	Blood not reported	Full blood	Mixed blood	Blood not reported
Shawnee	1,338	535	800	3	40.0	59.8	0.2
Stockbridges	533	184	340	9	34.5	63.8	1.7
Athabaskan stock	30,406	28,264	1,045	1,097	93.0	3.4	3.6
Apache	4,973	3,801	127	1,045	76.4	2.6	21.0
Arizona	4,652	3,491	116	1,045	75.0	2.5	22.5
Oklahoma	271	263	8	-	97.0	3.0	-
Hupa	639	345	294	-	54.0	46.0	-
Jicarilla Apache	694	694	-	-	100.0	-	-
Mescalero Apache	424	411	13	-	96.9	3.1	-
Navajo	22,455	22,304	99	52	99.3	0.4	0.2
Arizona	11,001	10,900	49	52	99.1	0.4	0.5
New Mexico	10,354	10,322	32	-	99.7	0.3	-
Utah	1,039	1,034	5	-	99.5	0.5	-
Rogue River	383	223	160	-	58.2	41.8	-
Wailaki	227	82	145	-	36.1	63.9	-
Caddoan stock	1,863	1,574	277	12	84.5	14.9	0.6
Arikara	444	372	72	-	83.8	16.2	-
Caddo	452	336	116	-	74.3	25.7	-
Pawnee	633	544	77	12	85.9	12.2	1.9
Wichita	318	308	10	-	96.9	3.1	-
Chimakuan stock	306	286	20	-	93.5	6.5	-
Quileute	259	240	19	-	92.7	7.3	-
Chinookan stock	897	459	436	2	51.2	48.6	0.2
Chinook	315	53	261	1	16.8	82.9	0.3
Oregon	125	12	112	1	9.6	89.6	0.8
Washington	177	41	136	-	23.2	76.8	-
Wasco	242	159	83	-	65.7	34.3	-
Oregon	184	134	50	-	72.8	27.2	-
Wishram	274	216	57	1	78.8	20.8	0.4
Croatan group	5,865	458	5,372	35	7.8	91.6	0.6
Croatan	5,865	458	5,372	35	7.8	91.6	0.6
Iroquoian stock	39,679	11,936	27,143	600	30.1	68.4	1.5
Cherokee	31,489	6,900	24,329	260	21.9	77.3	0.8
North Carolina	1,406	934	469	3	66.4	33.4	0.2
Oklahoma	29,610	5,919	23,440	251	20.0	79.2	0.8
Mohawk	368	63	304	1	17.1	82.6	0.3

[Continued]

Full-Blood and Mixed-Blood Indians, by Linguistic Stock, Tribe, and State, 1910: A - Mi
[Continued]

Stock, tribe, and state	Indians reported on special schedule : 1910						
	Number				Percent of total		
	Total	Full blood	Mixed blood	Blood not reported	Full blood	Mixed blood	Blood not reported
Oneida	2,436	2,098	333	5	86.1	13.7	0.2
New York	211	188	23	-	89.1	10.9	-
Wisconsin	2,107	1,854	248	5	88.0	11.8	0.2
Onondaga	365	299	64	2	81.9	17.5	0.5
St. Regis	1,219	133	1,086	-	10.9	89.1	-
Seneca	2,907	2,022	572	313	69.6	19.7	10.8
New York	2,485	1,858	314	313	74.8	12.6	12.6
Oklahoma	215	70	145	-	32.6	67.4	-
Pennsylvania	184	85	99	-	46.2	53.8	-
Tuscarora	400	305	83	12	76.3	20.8	3.0
Wyandot	353	34	318	1	9.6	90.1	0.3
Karok stock	775	364	411	-	47.0	53.0	-
Orleans	775	364	411	-	47.0	53.0	-
Keresan stock	4,027	3,976	33	18	98.7	0.8	0.4
Acoma	691	686	5	-	99.3	0.7	-
Cochiti	237	237	-	-	100.0	-	-
Laguna	1,472	1,427	27	18	96.9	1.8	1.2
San Felipe	490	489	1	-	99.8	0.2	-
Santa Ana	211	211	-	-	100.0	-	-
Santo Domingo	817	817	-	-	100.0	-	-
Kiowan stock	1,126	818	296	12	72.6	26.3	1.1
Kiowa	1,126	818	296	12	72.6	26.3	1.1
Kutenaian stock	538	255	283	-	47.4	52.6	-
Kutenai	538	255	283	-	47.4	52.6	-
Idaho	107	103	4	-	96.3	3.7	
Montana	424	148	276	-	34.9	65.1	-
Lutuamian stock	978	657	320	1	67.2	32.7	0.1
Klamath	696	459	236	1	65.9	33.9	0.1
Modoc	282	198	84	-	70.2	29.8	-
Oregon	212	168	44	-	79.2	20.8	-
Maidu stock	1,100	544	541	15	49.5	49.2	1.4
Maidu	1,100	544	541	49.5	49.2	1.4	

[Continued]

★ 76 ★

Full-Blood and Mixed-Blood Indians, by Linguistic Stock, Tribe, and State, 1910: A - Mi
[Continued]

| Stock, tribe, and state | Indians reported on special schedule : 1910 | | | | | | |
| | Number | | | Percent of total | | |
	Total	Full blood	Mixed blood	Blood not reported	Full blood	Mixed blood	Blood not reported
Miwok stock	699	343	355	1	49.1	50.8	0.1
Miwok	670	335	334	1	50.0	49.9	0.1

Source: U.S. Bureau of the Census, *Indian Population in the United States and Alaska, 1910,* United States Government Printing Office, Washington, D.C., 1915, pp. 32-34. *Notes:* A dash (-) represents zero. 1. Less than one-tenth of 1 percent.

★ 77 ★

Full-Blood and Mixed-Blood Indians, by Linguistic Stock, Tribe, and State, 1910: Mu - Si

Data are shown for tribes having 200 or more members in 1910.

| Stock, tribe, and state | Indians reported on special schedule : 1910 | | | | | | |
| | Number | | | Percent of total | | |
	Total	Full blood	Mixed blood	Blood not reported	Full blood	Mixed blood	Blood not reported
UNITED STATES (cont.)							
Muskhogean stock	29,191	13,625	15,321	245	46.7	52.5	0.8
Alibamu	298	288	6	4	96.6	2.0	1.3
Louisiana	111	101	6	4	91.0	5.4	3.6
Texas	187	187	-	-	100.0	-	-
Chickasaw	4,204	1,128	3,075	1	26.8	73.1	[1]
Choctaw	15,917	7,094	8,715	108	44.6	54.8	0.7
Louisiana	115	81	13	21	70.4	11.3	18.3
Mississippi	1,162	1,075	78	9	92.5	6.7	0.8
Oklahoma	14,551	5,934	8,539	78	40.8	58.7	0.5
Creek	6,945	3,730	3,131	84	53.7	45.1	1.2
Alabama	185	4	181	-	2.2	97.8	-
Oklahoma	6,654	3,702	2,872	80	55.6	43.2	1.2
Seminole	1,729	1,289	392	48	74.6	22.7	2.8
Oklahoma	1,503	1,227	228	48	81.6	15.2	3.2
Texas	200	38	162	-	19.0	81.0	-
Piman stock	8,607	8,344	167	96	96.9	1.9	1.1
Papago	3,798	3,703	55	40	97.5	1.4	1.1
Pima	4,236	4,175	19	42	98.6	0.4	1.0
Yaqui	528	426	88	14	80.7	16.7	2.7
Pomo stock	1,193	907	220	66	76.0	18.4	5.5

[Continued]

★ 77 ★

Full-Blood and Mixed-Blood Indians, by Linguistic Stock, Tribe, and State, 1910: Mu - Si
[Continued]

| Stock, tribe, and state | Indians reported on special schedule : 1910 | | | | | |
| | Number | | | Percent of total | | |
	Total	Full blood	Mixed blood	Blood not reported	Full blood	Mixed blood	Blood not reported
Pomo	777	607	117	53	78.1	15.1	6.8
Salishan stock	7,833	5,006	2,746	81	63.9	35.1	1.0
Chehalis	282	201	81	-	71.3	28.7	-
Clallam	398	252	146	-	63.3	36.7	-
Coeur d'Alene	293	236	34	23	80.5	11.6	7.8
Columbia	385	292	88	5	75.8	22.9	1.3
Colville	785	345	437	3	43.9	55.7	0.4
Flathead	486	206	280	-	42.4	57.6	-
Montana	400	180	220	-	45.0	55.0	-
Kalispel	564	361	202	1	64.0	35.8	0.2
Montana	386	226	160	-	58.5	41.5	-
Washington	157	127	30	-	80.9	19.1	-
Lummi	353	200	153	-	56.7	43.3	-
Okinagan	272	121	135	16	44.5	49.6	5.9
Puyallup	303	178	119	6	58.7	39.3	2.0
Quinaielt	288	219	69	-	76.0	24.0	-
Sanpoil	240	180	41	19	75.0	17.1	7.9
Snohomish	664	472	190	2	71.1	28.6	0.3
Spokan	643	409	233	1	63.6	36.2	0.2
Montana	134	53	81	-	39.6	60.4	-
Washington	379	281	98	-	74.1	25.9	-
Suquamish	307	177	130	-	57.7	42.3	-
Swinomish	333	279	54	-	83.8	16.2	-
Shahaptian stock	4,391	3,372	998	21	76.8	22.7	0.5
Klikitat	405	335	64	6	82.7	15.8	1.5
Nez Perces	1,259	970	276	13	77.0	21.9	1.0
Idaho	1,035	804	218	13	77.7	21.1	1.3
Umatilla	272	219	53	-	80.5	19.5	-
Oregon	152	131	21	-	86.2	13.8	-
Wallawalla	397	126	271	-	31.7	68.3	-
Warm Springs	550	538	12	-	97.8	2.2	-
Yakima	1,362	1,043	317	2	76.6	23.3	0.1
Shastan stock	1,578	1,162	413	3	73.6	26.2	0.2
Hat Creek	240	220	20	-	91.7	8.3	-
Pit River	985	841	144	-	85.4	14.6	-
Shasta	353	101	249	3	28.6	70.5	0.8
California	255	62	192	1	24.3	75.3	0.4
Shoshonean stock	16,842	14,672	1,928	242	87.1	11.4	1.4

[Continued]

119

★ 77 ★

Full-Blood and Mixed-Blood Indians, by Linguistic Stock, Tribe, and State, 1910: Mu - Si
[Continued]

| Stock, tribe, and state | Indians reported on special schedule : 1910 | | | | | | |
| | Number | | | | Percent of total | | |
	Total	Full blood	Mixed blood	Blood not reported	Full blood	Mixed blood	Blood not reported
Bannock	413	323	90	-	78.2	21.8	-
Chemehuevi	355	315	40	-	88.7	11.3	-
California	260	242	18	-	93.1	6.9	-
Comanche	1,171	736	407	28	62.9	34.8	2.4
Hopi	2,009	2,006	3	-	99.9	0.1	-
Kawia	755	702	52	1	93.0	6.9	0.7
Mono	1,448	1,215	223	10	83.9	15.4	0.7
Paiute	780	674	78	28	86.4	10.0	3.6
California	210	183	27	-	87.1	12.9	-
Nevada	247	229	18	-	92.7	7.3	-
Utah	238	198	13	27	83.2	5.5	11.3
Paviotso	3,038	2,664	227	147	87.7	7.5	4.8
California	101	80	20	1	79.2	19.8	1.0
Idaho	152	133	18	1	87.5	11.8	0.7
Nevada	2,414	2,113	156	145	87.5	6.5	6.0
Oregon	341	334	7	-	97.9	2.1	-
San Luiseno	467	351	115	1	75.2	24.6	0.2
Shoshoni	3,840	3,329	505	6	86.7	13.2	0.2
Idaho	1,259	1,153	101	5	91.6	8.0	0.4
Nevada	1,555	1,392	162	1	89.5	10.4	0.1
Utah	248	240	8	-	96.8	3.2	-
Wyoming	700	502	198	-	71.7	28.3	-
Ute	2,244	2,112	112	20	94.1	5.0	0.9
Colorado	725	707	18	-	97.5	2.5	-
Utah	1,472	1,382	71	19	93.9	4.8	1.3
Siouan stock	32,941	22,535	9,905	501	68.4	30.1	1.5
Assiniboine	1,253	793	447	13	63.3	35.7	1.0
Crow	1,799	1,242	396	161	69.0	22.0	8.9
Hidatsa	547	418	129	-	76.4	23.6	-
Iowa	244	59	185	-	24.2	75.8	-
Kansas	124	10	114	-	8.1	91.9	-
Kansa	238	71	167	-	29.8	70.2	-
Mandan	209	165	44	-	78.9	21.1	-
Omaha	1,105	885	144	76	80.1	13.0	6.9
Osage	1,373	591	779	3	43.0	56.7	0.2
Oto	332	211	121	-	63.6	36.4	-
Ponca	875	461	408	6	52.7	46.6	0.7
Nebraska	193	60	133	-	31.1	68.9	-
Oklahoma	619	374	239	6	60.4	38.6	1.0
Quapaw	231	63	118	50	27.3	51.1	21.6
Santee Sioux	1,539	799	740	-	51.9	48.1	-

[Continued]

★ 77 ★

Full-Blood and Mixed-Blood Indians, by Linguistic Stock, Tribe, and State, 1910: Mu - Si

[Continued]

Stock, tribe, and state	Indians reported on special schedule : 1910						
	Number				Percent of total		
	Total	Full blood	Mixed blood	Blood not reported	Full blood	Mixed blood	Blood not reported
Minnesota	232	100	132	-	43.1	56.9	-
Montana	107	78	29	-	72.9	27.1	-
Nebraska	708	410	298	-	57.9	42.1	-
North Dakota	100	66	34	-	66.0	34.0	-
South Dakota	378	145	233	-	38.4	61.6	-
Sioux	996	494	477	25	49.6	47.9	2.5
Minnesota	161	117	43	1	72.7	26.7	0.6
South Dakota	277	98	176	3	35.4	63.5	1.1
Sisseton Sioux	2,514	1,631	876	7	64.9	34.8	0.3
Montana	255	204	51	-	80.0	20.0	-
North Dakota	621	469	146	6	75.5	23.5	1.0
South Dakota	1,553	926	626	1	59.6	40.3	0.1
Teton Sioux	14,284	10,598	3,551	135	74.2	24.9	0.9
North Dakota	370	225	145	-	60.8	39.2	-
South Dakota	13,795	10,289	3,371	135	74.6	24.4	1.0

Source: U.S. Bureau of the Census, *Indian Population in the United States and Alaska, 1910,* United States Government Printing Office, Washington, D.C., 1915, pp. 32-34. *Notes:* A dash (-) represents zero. 1. Less than one-tenth of 1 percent.

★ 78 ★

Full-Blood and Mixed-Blood Indians, by Linguistic Stock, Tribe, and State, 1910: Si - Z and Alaska

Data are shown for tribes having 200 or more members in 1910.

Stock, tribe, and state	Indians reported on special schedule: 1910						
	Number				Percent of total		
	Total	Full blood	Mixed blood	Blood not reported	Full blood	Mixed blood	Blood not reported
UNITED STATES (cont.)							
Siouan stock continued							
Teton Sioux							
Brule Sioux	806	593	212	1	73.6	26.3	0.1
Hunkpapa Sioux	1,072	954	109	9	89.0	10.2	0.8
North Dakota	142	119	23	-	83.8	16.2	-
South Dakota	930	835	86	9	89.8	9.2	1.0
Minniconjou Sioux	397	353	33	11	88.9	8.3	2.8
Oglala Sioux	6,045	4,168	1,794	83	68.9	29.7	1.4
Sans Arc Sioux	222	64	152	6	28.8	68.5	2.7

[Continued]

★ 78 ★

Full-Blood and Mixed-Blood Indians, by Linguistic Stock, Tribe, and State, 1910: Si - Z and Alaska
[Continued]

Stock, tribe, and state	Indians reported on special schedule: 1910						
	Number				Percent of total		
	Total	Full blood	Mixed blood	Blood not reported	Full blood	Mixed blood	Blood not reported
Sihasapa	485	33	143	9	68.7	29.5	1.9
North Dakota	137	50	87	-	36.5	63.5	-
South Dakota	346	282	55	9	81.5	15.9	2.6
Two Kettle Sioux	293	143	146	4	48.8	49.8	1.4
Other Teton Sioux	4,964	3,990	962	12	80.4	19.4	0.2
Winnebago	1,820	1,543	277	-	84.8	15.2	-
Nebraska	1,007	865	142	-	85.9	14.1	-
Wisconsin	735	630	105	-	85.7	14.3	-
Yankton Sioux	2,088	1,348	718	22	64.6	34.4	1.1
Montana	372	279	92	1	75.0	24.7	0.3
North Dakota	159	156	3	-	98.1	1.9	-
South Dakota	1,534	910	603	21	59.3	39.3	1.4
Yanktonai Sioux	1,357	1,144	210	3	84.3	15.5	0.2
North Dakota	551	473	78	-	85.8	14.2	-
South Dakota	803	668	132	3	83.2	16.4	0.4
Tanoan stock	3,140	3,005	101	34	95.7	3.2	1.1
Isleta	956	894	28	34	93.5	2.9	3.6
Jemez	499	499	-	-	100.0	-	-
San Juan	387	382	5	-	98.7	1.3	-
Santa Clara	277	268	9	-	96.8	3.2	-
Taos	517	509	8	-	98.5	1.5	-
Wailatpuan stock	329	268	60	1	81.5	18.2	0.3
Cayuse	298	254	43	1	85.2	14.4	0.3
Wakashan stock	388	361	27	-	93.0	7.0	-
Makah	360	342	18	-	95.0	5.0	-
Washoan stock	819	643	170	6	78.5	20.8	0.7
Washo	819	643	170	6	78.5	20.8	0.7
California	273	228	45	-	83.5	16.5	-
Nevada	536	414	116	6	77.2	21.6	1.1
Wintun stock	710	282	373	55	39.7	52.5	7.7
Wintun	399	121	278	-	30.3	69.7	-

[Continued]

★ 78 ★

Full-Blood and Mixed-Blood Indians, by Linguistic Stock, Tribe, and State, 1910: Si - Z and Alaska

[Continued]

Stock, tribe, and state	Indians reported on special schedule: 1910						
	Number				Percent of total		
	Total	Full blood	Mixed blood	Blood not reported	Full blood	Mixed blood	Blood not reported
Yokuts stock	533	401	104	28	75.2	19.5	5.3
Yokuts	302	255	35	12	84.4	11.6	4.0
Yuman stock	4,279	4,000	221	58	93.5	5.2	1.4
Cocopa	245	243	2	-	99.2	0.8	-
Diegueno	756	585	171	-	77.4	22.6	-
Maricopa	386	367	2	17	95.1	0.5	4.4
Mohave	1,058	1,038	9	11	98.1	0.9	1.0
Arizona	667	651	5	11	97.6	0.7	1.6
California	389	385	4	-	99.0	1.0	-
Walapai	501	485	16	-	96.8	3.2	-
Yavapai	289	256	5	28	88.6	1.7	9.7
Yuma	834	816	16	2	97.8	1.9	0.2
Arizona	191	187	4	-	97.9	2.1	-
California	642	628	12	2	97.8	1.9	0.3
Yurok stock	668	528	140	-	79.0	21.0	-
Weitspec	668	528	140	-	79.0	21.0	-
Zunian stock	1,667	1,652	15	-	99.1	0.9	-
Zuni	1,667	1,652	15	-	99.1	0.9	-
ALASKA							
Athabaskan stock	3,916	3,642	274	-	93.0	7.0	-
Ahtena	297	293	4	-	98.7	1.3	-
Knajakhotana	697	672	25	-	96.4	3.6	-
Kutchin	359	349	10	-	97.2	2.8	-
Tenankutchin	415	396	19	-	95.4	4.6	-
Eskimauan stock	14,087	12,859	1,228	-	91.3	8.7	-
Aleut	1,451	999	452	-	68.8	31.2	-
Chnagmiut	326	299	27	-	91.7	8.3	-
Ikogmiut	782	768	14	-	98.2	1.8	-
Kaviagmiut	238	209	29	-	87.8	12.2	-
Kinugumiut	594	576	18	-	97.0	3.0	-
Kowagmiut	561	546	15	-	97.3	2.7	-
Kuskovakmiut	370	361	9	-	97.6	2.4	-

[Continued]

123

★ 78 ★

Full-Blood and Mixed-Blood Indians, by Linguistic Stock, Tribe, and State, 1910: Si - Z and Alaska
[Continued]

Stock, tribe, and state	Indians reported on special schedule: 1910						
	Number				Percent of total		
	Total	Full blood	Mixed blood	Blood not reported	Full blood	Mixed blood	Blood not reported
Kuskwogmiut	1,480	1,447	33	-	97.8	2.2	-
Magemiut	376	376	-	-	100.0	-	-
Malemiut	563	546	17	-	97.0	3.0	-
Nunatogmiut	285	277	8	-	97.2	2.8	-
Nunivagmiut	301	299	2	-	99.3	0.7	-
Selawigmiut	258	258	-	-	100.0	-	-
Tikeramiut	320	300	20	-	93.8	6.3	-
Unaligmiut	441	421	20	-	95.5	4.5	-
Yuit	292	290	2	-	99.3	0.7	-
Southern Eskimo	3,650	3,186	464	-	87.3	12.7	-
Hadian stock	530	377	153	-	71.1	28.9	-
Haida	530	377	153	-	71.1	28.9	
Tlingit stock	4,426	3,890	536	-	87.9	12.1	-
Auk	267	242	25	-	90.6	9.4	-
Chilkat	690	629	61	-	91.2	8.8	-
Henya	214	192	22	-	89.7	10.3	-
Huna	625	590	35	-	94.4	5.6	-
Hutsnuwu	536	498	38	-	92.9	7.1	-
Kake	322	276	46	-	85.7	14.3	-
Sitka	608	527	81	-	86.7	13.3	-
Yakutat	307	276	31	-	89.9	10.1	-
Tsimshian stock	729	615	114	-	84.4	15.6	-
Tsimshian	729	615	114	-	84.4	15.6	-

Source: U.S. Bureau of the Census, *Indian Population in the United States and Alaska, 1910,* United States Government Printing Office, Washington, D.C., 1915, pp. 32-34. *Notes:* A dash (-) represents zero. 1. Less than one-tenth of 1 percent.

★ 79 ★

Mixed-Tribal Status of Full-Blood Indians, by State, 1910

State	Full-blood Indians: 1910						
	Number				Percent of total		
	Total	Full-tribal blood	Mixed-tribal blood	Tribal blood of one parent unknown	Full-tribal blood	Mixed-tribal blood	Tribal blood of one parent unknown
United States	150,053	139,289	10,251	513	92.8	6.8	0.3
Arizona	27,087	26,519	563	5	97.9	2.1	[1]
California	10,493	9,633	791	69	91.8	7.5	0.7
Colorado	718	703	15	-	97.9	2.1	-
Idaho	2,864	2,676	176	12	93.4	6.1	0.4
Kansas[2]	516	411	101	4	79.7	19.6	0.8
Michigan	3,528	3,173	349	6	89.9	9.9	0.2
Minnesota	3,859	3,832	22	5	99.3	0.6	0.1
Mississippi	1,077	1,077	-	-	100.0	-	-
Montana	6,204	5,730	455	19	92.4	7.3	0.3
Nebraska	2,294	2,260	33	1	98.5	1.4	[1]
Nevada	4,287	4,183	102	2	97.6	2.4	[1]
New Mexico	20,085	19,726	352	7	98.2	1.8	[1]
New York	2,850	2,111	712	27	74.1	25.0	0.9
North Carolina	1,394	1,379	15	-	98.9	1.1	-
North Dakota	2,499	1,554	939	6	62.2	37.6	0.2
Oklahoma	25,8887	24,611	1,193	83	95.1	4.6	0.3
Oregon	2,901	2,219	662	20	76.5	22.8	0.7
South Dakota	13,247	11,034	2,108	105	83.3	15.9	0.8
Utah	2,900	2,800	91	9	96.6	3.1	0.3
Washington	6,770	5,444	1,227	99	80.4	18.1	1.5
Wisconsin	5,249	5,000	225	24	95.3	4.3	0.5
Wyoming	1,174	1,155	19	-	98.4	1.6	-
Total for 22 states	147,883	137,230	10,150	503	92.8	6.9	0.3
All other states	2,170	2,059	101	10	94.9	4.7	0.5

Source: U.S. Bureau of the Census, *Indian Population in the United States and Alaska, 1910,* United States Government Printing Office, Washington, D.C., 1915, p. 38. *Notes:* A dash (-) represents zero. 1. Less than one-tenth of 1 percent. 2. Exclusive of Indians in Haskell Institute, who are included in the total for "All other states."

★ 80 ★

Mixed-Tribal Blood Status of Full-Blooded Indians, by Linguistic Stock, Tribe, and State, 1910: A - Ke

Data are shown for tribes having 200 or more Indians in 1910.

| Tribe and state | Full-blood Indians: 1910 | | | | | | | Percent full tribal of all Indians |
| | Number | | | | Percent of total | | | |
	Total	Full-tribal blood	Mixed-tribal blood	Tribal blood of one parent unknown	Full-tribal blood	Mixed-tribal blood	Tribal blood of one parent unknown	
Algonquian stock								
Arapaho	1,311	1,269	42	-	96.8	3.2	-	89.4
Oklahoma	621	601	20	-	96.8	3.2	-	87.7
Wyoming	661	654	7	-	98.9	1.1	-	93.0
Cheyenne	2,662	2,507	139	16	94.2	5.2	0.6	82.1
Montana	1,181	1,103	64	14	93.4	5.4	1.2	81.9
Oklahoma	1,379	1,346	33	-	97.6	2.4	-	88.4
South Dakota	74	30	42	2	40.5	56.8	2.7	22.6
Chippewa	6,970	6,784	173	13	97.3	2.5	0.2	33.6
Michigan	1,558	1,433	122	3	92.0	7.8	0.2	38.5
Minnesota	3,595	3,575	15	5	99.4	0.4	0.1	43.4
Montana	84	78	6	-	92.9	7.1	-	16.0
North Dakota	58	57	1	-	98.3	1.7	-	1.9
Pennsylvania	31	31	-	-	-	-	-	23.1
Wisconsin	1,601	1,574	22	5	98.3	1.4	0.3	36.6
Cree	40	26	13	1	-	-	-	5.7
Montana	35	24	11	-	-	-	-	7.8
Delaware	279	213	66	-	76.3	23.7	-	23.3
Gros Ventres	390	357	33	-	91.5	8.5	-	70.0
Kickapoo	240	200	36	4	83.3	15.0	1.7	57.5
Kansas	112	79	29	4	70.5	25.9	3.6	37.4
Oklahoma	126	119	7	-	94.4	5.6	-	88.1
Mashpee	1	1	-	-	-	-	-	0.5
Menominee	704	665	33	6	94.5	4.7	0.9	46.8
Miami	59	47	12	-	79.7	20.3	-	20.8
Oklahoma	22	12	10	-	-	-	-	9.8
Ottawa	1,720	1,535	180	5	89.2	10.5	0.3	56.5
Michigan	1,664	1,496	167	1	89.9	10.0	0.1	61.0
Oklahoma	12	7	5	-	-	-	-	4.1
Passamaquoddy	295	289	6	-	98.0	2.0	-	74.9
Penobscot	85	60	25	-	70.6	29.4	-	22.6
Piegan	1,214	1,206	8	-	99.3	0.7	-	53.2
Potawatomi	960	795	164	1	82.8	17.1	0.1	32.6
Kansas	319	269	50	-	84.3	15.7	-	32.8
Michigan	281	226	55	-	80.4	19.6	-	49.0
Oklahoma	115	78	36	1	67.8	31.3	0.9	9.0
Wisconsin	227	211	16	-	93.0	7.0	-	86.1
Sauk and Fox	547	490	55	2	89.6	10.1	0.4	67.7
Iowa	245	218	27	-	89.0	11.0	-	84.8
Oklahoma	260	235	24	1	90.4	9.2	0.4	67.7

[Continued]

★ 80 ★

Mixed-Tribal Blood Status of Full-Blooded Indians, by Linguistic Stock, Tribe, and State, 1910: A - Ke

[Continued]

Tribe and state	Full-blood Indians: 1910							Percent full tribal of all Indians
	Number				Percent of total			
	Total	Full-tribal blood	Mixed-tribal blood	Tribal blood of one parent unknown	Full-tribal blood	Mixed-tribal blood	Tribal blood of one parent unknown	
Shawnee	535	467	68	-	87.3	12.7	-	34.9
Stockbridges	184	143	40	1	77.7	21.7	0.5	26.8
Athabaskan stock								
Apache	3,801	3,749	50	2	98.6	1.3	0.1	75.4
Arizona	3,491	3,469	21	1	99.4	0.6	[1]	74.6
Oklahoma	263	245	17	1	93.2	6.5	0.4	90.4
Hupa	345	325	20	-	94.2	5.8	-	50.9
Jicarilla Apache	694	692	2	-	99.7	0.3	-	99.7
Mescalero Apache	411	392	19	-	95.4	4.6	-	92.5
Navajo	22,304	22,241	63	-	99.7	0.3	-	99.0
Arizona	10,900	10,888	12	-	99.9	0.1	-	99.0
New Mexico	10,322	10,291	31	-	99.7	0.3	-	99.4
Utah	1,034	1,023	11	-	98.9	1.1	-	98.5
Rogue River	223	167	48	8	74.9	21.5	3.6	43.6
Wailaki	82	74	8	-	90.2	9.8	-	32.6
Caddoan stock								
Arikara	372	319	50	3	85.8	13.4	0.8	71.8
Caddo	336	299	37	-	89.0	11.0	-	66.2
Pawnee	544	530	14	-	97.4	2.6	-	83.7
Wichita	308	274	34	-	89.0	11.0	-	86.2
Chimakuan stock								
Quileute	240	206	33	1	85.8	13.8	0.4	79.5
Chinookan stock								
Chinook	53	31	20	2	58.5	37.7	3.8	9.8
Oregon	12	3	7	2	-	-	-	2.4
Washington	41	28	13	-	-	-	-	15.8
Wasco	159	95	64	-	59.7	40.3	-	39.3
Oregon	134	84	50	-	62.7	37.3	-	45.7
Wishram	216	154	56	6	71.3	25.9	2.8	56.2
Croatan group								
Croatan	458	457	1	-	99.8	0.2	-	7.8

[Continued]

★ 80 ★

Mixed-Tribal Blood Status of Full-Blooded Indians, by Linguistic Stock, Tribe, and State, 1910: A - Ke

[Continued]

Tribe and state	Full-blood Indians: 1910							Percent full tribal of all Indians
	Number				Percent of total			
	Total	Full-tribal blood	Mixed-tribal blood	Tribal blood of one parent unknown	Full-tribal blood	Mixed-tribal blood	Tribal blood of one parent unknown	
Iroquoian stock								
Cherokee	6,900	6,785	95	20	98.3	1.4	0.3	21.5
North Carolina	934	920	14	-	98.5	1.5	-	65.4
Oklahoma	5,919	5,827	72	20	98.4	1.2	0.3	19.7
Mohawk	63	38	19	6	60.3	30.2	9.5	10.3
Oneida	2,098	1,904	184	10	90.8	8.8	0.5	78.2
New York	188	89	98	1	47.3	52.1	0.5	42.2
Wisconsin	1,854	1,760	85	9	94.9	4.6	0.5	83.5
Onondaga	299	135	164	-	45.2	54.8	-	37.0
St. Regis	133	94	39	-	70.7	29.3	-	7.7
Seneca	2,022	1,738	271	13	86.0	13.4	0.6	59.8
New York	1,858	1,582	263	13	85.1	14.2	0.7	63.7
Oklahoma	70	63	7	-	90.0	10.0	-	29.3
Pennsylvania	85	85	-	-	100.0	-	-	46.2
Tuscarora	305	218	86	1	71.5	28.2	0.3	54.5
Wyandot	34	12	22	-	-	-	-	3.4
Karok stock								
Orleans	364	334	30	-	91.8	8.2	-	43.1
Keresan stock								
Acoma	686	685	1	-	99.9	0.1	-	99.1
Cochiti	237	235	2	-	99.2	0.8	-	99.2
Laguna	1,427	1,396	31	-	97.8	2.2	-	94.8
San Felipe	489	487	2	-	99.6	0.4	-	99.4
Santa Ana	211	206	5	-	97.6	2.4	-	97.6
Santo Domingo	817	811	6	-	99.3	0.7	-	99.3

Source: U.S. Bureau of the Census, *Indian Population in the United States and Alaska, 1910,* United States Government Printing Office, Washington, D.C., 1915, pp. 41-42. *Notes:* A dash (-) represents zero. 1. Less than one-tenth of 1 percent.

★ 81 ★

Mixed-Tribal Blood Status of Full-Blooded Indians, by Linguistic Stock, Tribe, and State, 1910: Ki - Sh

Data are shown for tribes having 200 or more Indians in 1910.

| Tribe and state | Full-blood Indians: 1910 | | | | | | | Percent full tribal of all Indians |
| | Number | | | Percent of total | | | |
	Total	Full-tribal blood	Mixed-tribal blood	Tribal blood of one parent unknown	Full-tribal blood	Mixed-tribal blood	Tribal blood of one parent unknown	
Kiowan stock								
Kiowa	818	766	48	4	93.6	5.9	0.5	68.0
Kutenaian stock								
Kutenai	255	246	9	-	96.5	3.5	-	45.7
Idaho	103	103	-	-	100.0	-	-	96.3
Montana	148	142	6	-	95.9	4.1	-	33.5
Lutuamian stock								
Klamath	459	380	79	-	82.8	17.2	-	54.6
Modoc	198	124	74	-	62.6	37.4	-	44.0
Oregon	168	98	70	-	58.3	41.7	-	46.2
Maidu stock								
Maidu	544	513	31	-	94.3	5.7	-	46.6
Miwok stock								
Miwok	335	308	22	5	91.9	6.6	1.5	46.0
Muskhogean stock								
Alibamu	288	287	1	-	99.7	0.3	-	96.3
Louisiana	101	101	-	-	100.0	-	-	91.0
Texas	187	186	1	-	99.5	0.5	-	99.5
Chickasaw	1,128	1,040	80	8	92.2	7.1	0.7	24.7
Choctaw	7,094	6,975	106	13	98.3	1.5	0.2	43.8
Louisiana	81	80	-	1	98.8	-	1.2	69.6
Mississippi	1,075	1,075	-	-	100.0	-	-	92.5
Oklahoma	5,934	5,817	105	12	98.0	1.8	0.2	40.0
Creek	3,730	3,531	192	7	94.7	5.1	0.2	50.8
Alabama	4	4	-	-	-	-	-	2.2
Oklahoma	3,702	3,516	179	7	95.0	4.8	0.2	52.8
Seminole	1,289	1,158	131	-	89.8	10.2	-	67.0
Oklahoma	1,227	1,098	129	-	89.5	10.5	-	73.1
Texas	38	38	-	-	-	-	-	19.0

[Continued]

★ 81 ★

Mixed-Tribal Blood Status of Full-Blooded Indians, by Linguistic Stock, Tribe, and State, 1910: Ki - Sh
[Continued]

Tribe and state	Full-blood Indians: 1910							
	Number				Percent of total			Percent full tribal of all Indians
	Total	Full-tribal blood	Mixed-tribal blood	Tribal blood of one parent unknown	Full-tribal blood	Mixed-tribal blood	Tribal blood of one parent unknown	
Piman stock								
Papago	3,703	3,638	62	3	98.2	1.7	0.1	95.8
Pima	4,175	4,039	136	-	96.7	3.3	-	95.3
Yaqui	426	401	25	-	94.1	5.9	-	75.9
Pomo stock								
Pomo	607	568	34	5	93.6	5.6	0.8	73.1
Salishan stock								
Chehalis	201	109	90	2	54.2	44.8	1.0	38.7
Clallam	252	214	35	3	84.9	13.9	1.2	53.8
Coeur d'Alene	236	199	30	7	84.3	12.7	3.0	67.9
Columbia	292	215	69	8	73.6	23.6	2.7	55.8
Colville	345	321	17	7	93.0	4.9	2.0	40.9
Flathead	206	168	37	1	81.6	18.0	0.5	34.6
Montana	180	152	28	-	84.4	15.6	-	38.0
Kalispel	361	319	40	2	88.4	11.1	0.6	56.6
Montana	226	191	33	2	84.5	14.6	0.9	49.5
Washington	127	124	3	-	97.6	2.4	-	79.0
Lummi	200	101	89	10	50.5	44.5	5.0	28.6
Okinagan	121	90	28	3	74.4	23.1	2.5	33.1
Puyallup	178	143	24	11	80.3	13.5	6.2	47.2
Quinaielt	219	198	21	-	90.4	9.6	-	68.8
Sanpoil	180	169	7	4	93.9	3.9	2.2	70.4
Snohomish	472	434	38	-	91.9	8.1	-	65.4
Spokan	409	356	51	2	87.0	12.5	0.5	55.4
Montana	53	41	12	-	77.4	22.6	-	30.6
Washington	281	261	20	-	92.9	7.1	-	68.9
Suquamish	177	145	27	5	81.9	15.3	2.8	47.2
Swinomish	279	270	6	3	96.8	2.2	1.1	8.11
Shahaptian stock								
Klikitat	335	252	80	3	75.2	23.9	0.9	62.2
Nez Perces	970	865	104	1	89.2	10.7	0.1	68.7
Idaho	804	756	47	1	94.0	5.8	0.1	73.0
Umatilla	219	158	61	-	72.1	27.9	-	58.1
Oregon	131	98	33	-	74.8	25.2	-	64.5

[Continued]

★ 81 ★

Mixed-Tribal Blood Status of Full-Blooded Indians, by Linguistic Stock, Tribe, and State, 1910: Ki - Sh
[Continued]

Tribe and state	Full-blood Indians: 1910							
	Number				Percent of total			Percent full tribal of all Indians
	Total	Full-tribal blood	Mixed-tribal blood	Tribal blood of one parent unknown	Full-tribal blood	Mixed-tribal blood	Tribal blood of one parent unknown	
Wallawalla	126	100	26	-	79.4	20.6	-	25.2
Warm Springs	538	470	68	-	87.4	12.6	-	85.5
Yakima	1,043	916	125	2	87.8	12.0	0.2	67.3
Shastan stock								
Hat Creek	220	174	46	-	79.1	20.9	-	72.5
Pit River	841	697	137	7	82.9	16.3	0.8	70.8
Shasta	101	75	26	-	74.3	25.7	-	21.2
California	62	53	9	-	85.5	14.5	-	20.8
Shoshonean stock								
Bannock	323	305	18	-	94.4	5.6	-	73.8
Chemehuevi	315	297	18	-	94.3	5.7	-	83.7
California	242	235	7	-	97.1	2.9	-	90.4
Comanche	736	690	24	22	93.8	3.3	3.0	58.9
Hopi	2,006	1,995	10	1	99.5	0.5	[1]	99.3
Kawia	702	652	45	5	92.9	6.4	0.7	86.4
Mono	1,215	1,155	56	4	95.1	4.6	0.3	79.8
Paiute	674	656	15	3	97.3	2.2	0.4	84.1
California	183	175	5	3	95.6	2.7	1.6	83.3
Nevada	229	222	7	-	96.9	3.1	-	89.9
Utah	198	196	2	-	99.0	1.0	-	82.4
Paviotso	2,664	2,598	65	1	97.5	2.4	[1]	85.5
California	80	64	16	-	80.0	20.0	-	63.4
Idaho	133	132	-	1	99.2	-	0.8	86.8
Nevada	2,113	2,089	24	-	98.9	1.1	-	86.5
Oregon	334	313	21	-	93.7	6.3	-	91.8
San Luiseno	351	339	7	5	96.6	2.0	1.4	72.6
Shoshoni	3,329	3,224	103	2	96.8	3.1	0.1	84.0
Idaho	1,153	1,113	40	-	96.5	3.5	-	88.4
Nevada	1,392	1,341	49	2	96.3	3.5	0.1	86.2
Utah	240	237	3	-	98.7	1.3	-	95.6
Wyoming	502	495	7	-	98.6	1.4	-	70.7
Ute	2,112	2,088	20	4	98.9	0.9	0.2	93.0
Colorado	707	707	-	-	100.0	-	-	97.5
Utah	1,382	1,366	12	4	98.8	0.9	0.3	92.8

Source: U.S. Bureau of the Census, *Indian Population in the United States and Alaska, 1910,* United States Government Printing Office, Washington, D.C., 1915, pp. 41-42. *Notes:* A dash (-) represents zero. 1. Less than one-tenth of 1 percent.

★ 82 ★

Mixed-Tribal Blood Status of Full-Blooded Indians, by Linguistic Stock, Tribe, and State, 1910: Si - Z

Data are shown for tribes having 200 or more Indians in 1910.

Tribe and state	Full-blood Indians: 1910							Percent full tribal of all Indians
	Number				Percent of total			
	Total	Full-tribal blood	Mixed-tribal blood	Tribal blood of one parent unknown	Full-tribal blood	Mixed-tribal blood	Tribal blood of one parent unknown	
Siouan stock								
Assiniboine	793	762	30	1	96.1	3.8	0.1	60.8
Crow	1,242	1,178	64	-	94.8	5.2	-	65.5
Hidatsa	418	235	182	1	56.2	43.5	0.2	43.0
Iowa	59	34	25	-	57.6	42.4	-	13.9
Kansas	10	5	5	-	-	-	-	4.0
Kansa	71	66	5	-	93.0	7.0	-	27.7
Mandan	165	79	86	-	47.9	52.1	-	37.8
Omaha	885	877	8	-	99.1	0.9	-	79.4
Osage	591	583	8	-	98.6	1.4	-	42.5
Oto	211	185	23	3	87.7	10.9	1.4	55.7
Ponca	461	455	6	-	98.7	1.3	-	52.0
Nebraska	60	58	2	-	96.7	3.3	-	30.1
Oklahoma	374	373	1	-	99.7	0.3	-	60.3
Quapaw	63	31	32	-	49.2	50.8	-	13.4
Santee Sioux	799	672	125	2	84.1	15.6	0.3	43.7
Minnesota	100	99	1	-	99.0	1.0	-	42.7
Montana	78	65	13	-	83.3	16.7	-	60.7
Nebraska	410	403	7	-	98.3	1.7	-	56.9
North Dakota	66	16	50	-	24.2	75.8	-	16.0
South Dakota	145	89	54	2	61.4	37.2	1.4	23.5
Sioux	494	441	50	3	89.3	10.1	0.6	44.3
Minnesota	117	115	2	-	98.3	1.7	-	71.4
South Dakota	98	92	5	1	93.9	5.1	1.0	33.2
Sisseton Sioux	1,631	1,394	228	9	85.5	14.0	0.6	55.4
Montana	204	162	42	-	79.4	20.6	-	63.5
North Dakota	469	424	45	-	90.4	9.6	-	68.3
South Dakota	926	786	131	9	84.9	14.1	1.0	50.6
Teton Sioux	10,598	9,747	772	79	92.0	7.3	0.7	68.2
North Dakota	225	129	96	-	57.3	42.7	-	34.9
South Dakota	10,289	9,560	650	79	92.9	6.3	0.8	69.3
Brule Sioux	593	441	145	7	74.4	24.5	1.2	54.7
Hunkpapa Sioux	954	453	469	32	47.5	49.2	3.4	42.3
North Dakota	119	25	94	-	21.0	79.0	-	17.6
South Dakota	835	428	375	32	51.3	44.9	3.8	46.0
Minniconjou Sioux	353	142	197	14	40.2	55.8	4.0	35.8
Oglala Sioux	4,168	3,744	405	19	89.8	9.7	0.5	61.9
Sans Arc Sioux	64	21	43	-	32.8	67.2	-	9.5
Sihasapa	333	122	206	5	36.6	61.9	1.5	25.2
North Dakota	50	24	26	-	48.0	52.0	-	17.5

[Continued]

★ 82 ★

Mixed-Tribal Blood Status of Full-Blooded Indians, by Linguistic Stock, Tribe, and State, 1910: Si - Z

[Continued]

| Tribe and state | Full-blood Indians: 1910 | | | | | | | Percent full tribal of all Indians |
| | Number | | | | Percent of total | | | |
	Total	Full-tribal blood	Mixed-tribal blood	Tribal blood of one parent unknown	Full-tribal blood	Mixed-tribal blood	Tribal blood of one parent unknown	
South Dakota	282	97	180	5	34.4	63.8	1.8	28.0
Two Kettle Sioux	143	55	87	1	38.5	60.8	0.7	18.8
Other Teton Sioux	3,990	3,928	61	1	98.4	1.5	[1]	79.1
Winnebago	1,543	1,530	13	-	99.2	0.8	-	84.1
Nebraska	865	860	5	-	99.4	0.6	-	85.4
Wisconsin	630	628	2	-	99.7	0.3	-	85.4
Yankton Sioux	1,348	1,026	317	5	76.1	23.5	0.4	49.1
Montana	279	220	58	1	78.9	20.8	0.4	59.1
North Dakota	156	40	116	-	25.6	74.4	-	25.2
South Dakota	910	763	143	4	83.8	15.7	0.4	49.7
Yanktonai Sioux	1,144	768	371	5	67.1	32.4	0.4	56.6
North Dakota	473	293	179	1	61.9	37.8	0.2	53.2
South Dakota	668	474	190	4	71.0	28.4	0.6	59.0
Tanoan stock								
Isleta	894	851	43	-	95.2	4.8	-	89.0
Jemez	499	418	81	-	83.8	16.2	-	83.8
San Juan	382	380	2	-	99.5	0.5	-	98.2
Santa Clara	268	251	17	-	93.7	6.3	-	90.6
Taos	509	505	4	-	99.2	0.8	-	97.7
Wailatpuan stock								
Cayuse	254	194	59	1	76.4	23.2	0.4	65.1
Wakashan stock								
Makah	342	252	88	2	73.7	25.7	0.6	70.0
Washoan stock								
Washo	643	620	23	-	96.4	3.6	-	75.7
California	228	209	19	-	91.7	8.3	-	76.6
Nevada	414	410	4	-	99.0	1.0	-	76.5
Wintun stock								
Wintun	121	108	13	-	89.3	10.7	-	27.1

[Continued]

★ 82 ★

Mixed-Tribal Blood Status of Full-Blooded Indians, by Linguistic Stock, Tribe, and State, 1910: Si - Z
[Continued]

Tribe and state	Full-blood Indians: 1910							
	Number				Percent of total			Percent full tribal of all Indians
	Total	Full-tribal blood	Mixed-tribal blood	Tribal blood of one parent unknown	Full-tribal blood	Mixed-tribal blood	Tribal blood of one parent unknown	
Yokuts stock								
Yokuts	255	241	12	2	94.5	4.7	0.8	79.8
Yuman stock								
Cocopa	243	242	1	-	99.6	0.4	-	98.8
Diegueno	585	568	14	3	97.1	2.4	0.5	75.1
Maricopa	367	339	27	1	92.4	7.4	0.3	87.8
Mohave	1,038	966	72	-	93.1	6.9	-	91.3
Arizona	651	584	67	-	89.7	10.3	-	87.6
California	385	381	4	-	99.0	1.0	-	97.9
Walapai	485	471	14	-	97.1	2.9	-	94.0
Yavapai	256	243	13	-	94.9	5.1	-	84.1
Yuma	816	784	29	3	96.1	3.6	0.4	94.0
Arizona	187	177	10	-	94.7	5.3	-	92.7
California	628	606	19	3	96.5	3.0	0.5	94.4
Yurok stock								
Weitspec	528	514	14	-	97.3	2.7	-	76.9
Zunian stock								
Zuni	1,652	1,641	11	-	99.3	0.7	-	98.4

Source: U.S. Bureau of the Census, *Indian Population in the United States and Alaska, 1910*, United States Government Printing Office, Washington, D.C., 1915, pp. 41-42. *Notes:* A dash (-) represents zero. 1. Less than one-tenth of 1 percent.

★ 83 ★

Indian and White Mixed-Bloods, by State and Degree of Mixture, 1910

State	Number					Percent of total			
	Total	Less than half White	Half White, half Indian	More than half White	Unknown proportions	Less than half White	Half White, half Indian	More than half White	Unknown proportions
United States	88,030	18,169	24,353	43,937	1,571	20.6	27.7	49.9	1.8
Arizona	393	74	115	30	174	18.8	29.3	7.6	44.3
California	4,069	1,044	2,189	651	185	25.7	53.8	16.0	4.5
Colorado	44	4	15	16	9	1	1	1	1

[Continued]

★ 83 ★

Indian and White Mixed-Bloods, by State and Degree of Mixture, 1910
[Continued]

State	Number					Percent of total			
	Total	Less than half White	Half White, half Indian	More than half White	Unknown proportions	Less than half White	Half White, half Indian	More than half White	Unknown proportions
Idaho	503	190	193	87	33	37.8	38.4	17.3	6.6
Kansas[2]	823	340	202	280	1	41.3	24.5	34.0	0.1
Michigan	3,138	1,454	726	925	33	46.3	23.1	29.5	1.1 [3]
Minnesota	4,799	1,393	1,427	1,978	1	29.0	29.7	41.2	
Mississippi	69	39	15	15	-	56.5	21.7	21.7	-
Montana	3,808	676	1,646	1,424	62	17.8	43.2	37.4	1.6
Nebraska	926	367	208	351	-	39.6	22.5	37.9	-
Nevada	503	176	292	21	14	35.0	58.1	4.2	2.8
New Mexico	163	63	36	1	63	38.7	22.1	0.6	38.7
New York	1,636	242	1,200	188	6	14.8	73.3	11.5	0.4
North Carolina	5,105	2,734	1,896	475	-	53.6	37.1	9.3	-
North Dakota	3,541	273	2,481	778	9	7.7	70.1	22.0	0.3
Oklahoma	41,856	4,120	5,451	31,542	743	9.8	13.0	75.4	1.8
Oregon	1,601	362	626	590	23	22.6	39.1	36.9	1.4
South Dakota	5,263	1,810	1,888	1,470	95	34.4	35.9	27.9	1.8
Utah	102	25	48	29	-	24.5	47.1	28.4	-
Washington	2,896	758	1,233	900	5	26.2	42.6	31.1	0.2
Wisconsin	4,136	1,306	1,517	1,271	42	31.6	36.7	30.7	1.0
Wyoming	283	64	87	95	37	22.6	30.7	33.6	13.1
Total for 22 states	85,657	17,514	23,491	43,117	1,535	20.4	27.4	50.3	1.8
All other states	2,373	655	862	820	36	27.6	36.3	34.6	1.5

Source: U.S. Bureau of the Census, *Indian Population in the United States and Alaska, 1910,* United States Government Printing Office, Washington, D.C., 1915, p. 35. *Notes:* A dash (-) represents zero. 1. Percent not shown where base is less than 50. 2. Exclusive of Indians in Haskell Institute, who are included in the total for "All other states." 3. Less than one-tenth of 1 percent.

★ 84 ★

Indian and White Mixed-Bloods, by Linguistic Stock, Tribe, State, and Degree of Mixture, 1910 - I

Stock, tribe, and state	Number					Percent of total			
	Total	Less than half white	Half white, half Indian	More than half white	Unknown proportions	Less than half white	Half white, half Indian	More than half white	Unknown proportions
Algonquian stock	21,318	5,565	7,780	7,804	169	26.1	36.5	36.6	0.8
Arapaho	101	53	30	10	8	52.5	29.7	9.9	7.9
Cheyenne	319	122	106	77	14	38.2	33.2	24.1	4.4
Oklahoma	139	78	38	17	6	56.1	27.3	12.2	4.3
Chippewa	13,031	3,051	5,516	4,388	76	23.4	42.3	33.7	0.6
Michigan	2,123	830	506	766	21	39.1	23.8	36.1	1.0
Minnesota	4,556	1,349	1,362	1,844	1	29.6	29.9	40.5	[1]
Montana	402	57	257	77	11	14.2	63.9	19.2	2.7
North Dakota	2,829	27	2,153	648	1	1.0	76.1	22.9	[1]
Pennsylvania	103	17	44	42	-	16.5	42.7	40.8	-
Wisconsin	2,693	714	1,121	816	42	26.5	41.6	30.3	1.6
Cree	413	10	196	204	3	2.4	47.5	49.4	0.7
Montana	273	9	177	84	3	3.3	64.8	30.8	1.1
Delaware	631	68	143	405	15	10.8	22.7	64.2	2.4
Gros Ventres	118	21	64	32	1	17.8	54.2	27.1	0.8
Kickapoo	103	61	31	10	1	59.2	30.1	9.7	1.0

[Continued]

135

★ 84 ★

Indian and White Mixed-Bloods, by Linguistic Stock, Tribe, State, and Degree of Mixture, 1910 - I

[Continued]

Stock, tribe, and state	Number					Percent of total			
	Total	Less than half white	Half white, half Indian	More than half white	Unknown proportions	Less than half white	Half white, half Indian	More than half white	Unknown proportions
Menominee	713	318	180	215	-	44.6	25.2	30.2	-
Miami	164	42	42	80	-	25.6	25.6	48.8	-
Oklahoma	100	18	4	78	-	18.0	4.0	78.0	-
Ottawa	966	523	213	221	9	54.1	22.0	22.9	0.9
Michigan	759	502	176	72	9	66.1	23.2	9.5	1.2
Oklahoma	158	8	17	133	-	5.1	10.8	84.2	-
Penobscot	181	115	59	7	-	63.5	32.6	3.9	-
Piegan	1,025	200	377	422	26	19.5	36.8	41.2	2.5
Potawatomi	1,461	418	212	828	3	28.6	14.5	56.7	0.2
Kansas	486	217	127	141	1	44.7	26.1	29.0	0.2
Michigan	177	118	19	38	2	66.7	10.7	21.5	1.1
Oklahoma	749	66	58	625	-	8.8	7.7	83.4	-
Sauk and Fox	154	52	45	57	-	33.8	29.2	37.0	-
Shawnee	776	139	101	527	9	17.9	13.0	67.9	1.2
Stockbridges	216	72	84	60	-	33.3	38.9	27.8	-
Athabaskan stock	1,015	235	562	142	76	23.2	55.4	14.0	7.5
Apache	122	34	52	14	22	27.9	42.6	11.5	18.0
Arizona	111	34	44	13	20	30.6	39.6	11.7	18.0
Hupa	292	22	217	53	-	7.5	74.3	18.2	-
Rogue River	159	40	72	37	10	25.2	45.3	23.3	6.3
Wailaki	143	18	106	19	-	12.6	74.1	13.3	-
Caddoan stock	261	94	84	77	6	36.0	32.2	29.5	2.3
Caddo	111	30	36	40	5	27.0	32.4	36.0	4.5
Chinookan stock	416	63	183	170	-	15.1	44.0	40.9	-
Chinook	261	18	122	121	-	6.9	46.7	46.4	-
Oregon	112	13	56	43	-	11.6	50.0	38.4	-
Washington	136	5	60	71	-	3.7	44.1	52.2	-
Croatan group	4,668	2,540	1,856	272	-	54.4	39.8	5.8	-
Croatan	4,668	2,540	1,856	272	-	54.4	39.8	5.8	-
Iroquoian stock	26,102	2,137	3,835	19,994	136	8.2	14.7	76.6	0.5
Cherokee	23,510	1,702	2,294	19,384	130	7.2	9.8	82.5	0.6
North Carolina	429	192	39	198	-	44.8	9.1	46.2	-
Oklahoma	22,722	1,429	2,172	18,997	124	6.3	9.6	83.6	0.5
Mohawk	293	14	252	27	-	4.8	86.0	9.2	-
Oneida	312	107	103	102	-	34.3	33.0	32.7	-
Wisconsin	227	78	75	74	-	34.4	33.0	32.6	-
St. Regis	1,005	44	848	107	6	4.4	84.4	10.6	0.6
Seneca	479	163	208	108	-	34.0	43.4	22.5	-
New York	221	108	59	54	-	48.9	26.7	24.4	-
Oklahoma	145	45	60	40	-	31.0	41.4	27.6	-
Wyandot	317	31	44	242	-	9.8	13.9	76.3	-

[Continued]

★ 84 ★

Indian and White Mixed-Bloods, by Linguistic Stock, Tribe, State, and Degree of Mixture, 1910 - I
[Continued]

Stock, tribe, and state	Number					Percent of total			
	Total	Less than half white	Half white, half Indian	More than half white	Unknown proportions	Less than half white	Half white, half Indian	More than half white	Unknown proportions
Karok stock	401	84	252	65	-	20.9	62.8	16.2	-
Orleans	401	84	252	65	-	20.9	62.8	16.2	-
Kiowan stock	296	103	39	1	153	34.8	13.2	0.3	51.7
Kiowa	296	103	39	1	153	34.8	13.2	0.3	51.7
Kutenaian stock	283	22	60	201	-	7.8	21.2	71.0	-
Kutenai	283	22	60	201	-	7.8	21.2	71.0	-
Montana	276	22	54	200	-	8.0	19.6	72.5	-
Lutuamian stock	294	79	148	67	-	26.9	50.3	22.8	-
Klamath	210	63	98	49	-	30.0	46.7	23.3	-
Maidu stock	525	161	290	71	3	30.7	55.2	13.5	0.6
Maidu	525	161	290	71	3	30.7	55.2	13.5	0.6
Miwok stock	354	87	169	76	22	24.6	47.7	21.5	6.2
Miwok	333	73	165	74	21	21.9	49.5	22.2	6.3
Muskhogean stock	13,723	1,648	2,336	9,586	153	12.0	17.0	69.9	1.1
Chickasaw	2,881	182	493	2,189	17	6.3	17.1	76.0	0.6
Choctaw	8,149	900	1,296	5,865	88	11.0	15.9	72.0	1.1
Oklahoma	7,995	838	1,273	5,831	53	10.5	15.9	72.9	0.7
Creek	2,527	503	490	1,497	37	19.9	19.4	59.2	1.5
Alabama	181	1	8	172	-	0.6	4.4	95.0	-
Oklahoma	2,301	498	456	1,310	37	21.6	19.8	56.9	1.6
Seminole	164	63	57	33	11	38.4	34.8	20.1	6.7
Oklahoma	157	63	53	30	11	40.1	33.8	19.1	7.0
Piman stock	166	23	19	3	121	13.9	11.4	1.8	72.9
Pomo stock	209	80	102	27	-	38.3	48.8	12.9	-
Pomo	109	43	45	21	-	39.4	41.3	19.3	-
Salishan stock	2,687	750	1,133	801	3	27.9	42.2	29.8	0.1
Clallam	132	43	54	35	-	32.6	40.9	26.5	-
Colville	428	52	215	160	1	12.1	50.2	37.4	0.2
Flathead	280	95	70	115	-	33.9	25.0	41.1	-
Montana	220	90	49	81	-	40.9	22.3	36.8	-
Kalispel	200	37	53	110	-	18.5	26.5	55.0	-
Montana	158	24	44	90	-	15.2	27.8	57.0	-
Lummi	141	73	46	22	-	51.8	32.6	15.6	-
Okinagan	132	18	64	50	-	13.6	48.5	37.9	-
Puyallup	119	50	45	24	-	42.0	37.8	20.2	-
Snohomish	190	57	96	37	-	30.0	50.5	19.5	-

[Continued]

137

★ 84 ★

Indian and White Mixed-Bloods, by Linguistic Stock, Tribe, State, and Degree of Mixture, 1910 - I

[Continued]

Stock, tribe, and state	Number					Percent of total			
	Total	Less than half white	Half white, half Indian	More than half white	Unknown proportions	Less than half white	Half white, half Indian	More than half white	Unknown proportions
Spokan	233	44	96	93	-	18.9	41.2	39.9	-
Suquamish	127	58	53	16	-	45.7	41.7	12.6	-

Source: U.S. Bureau of the Census, *Indian Population in the United States and Alaska, 1910,* United States Government Printing Office, Washington, D.C., 1915, pp. 36-37. *Notes:* A dash (-) represents zero. 1. Less than one-tenth of 1 percent.

★ 85 ★

Indian and White Mixed-Bloods, by Linguistic Stock, Tribe, State, and Degree of Mixture, 1910 - II

Stock, tribe, and state	Number					Percent of total			
	Total	Less than half white	Half white, half Indian	More than half white	Unknown proportions	Less than half white	Half white, half Indian	More than half white	Unknown proportions
Shahaptian stock	977	272	359	338	8	27.8	36.7	34.6	0.8
Nez Perces	276	120	101	55	-	43.5	36.6	19.9	-
Idaho	218	114	71	33	-	52.3	32.6	15.1	-
Wallawalla	266	20	100	146	-	7.5	37.6	54.9	-
Yakima	312	80	135	95	2	25.6	43.3	30.4	0.6
Shastan stock	393	103	196	94	-	26.2	49.9	23.9	-
Pit River	142	43	73	26	-	30.3	51.4	18.3	-
Shasta	231	49	115	67	-	21.2	49.8	29.0	-
California	174	29	94	51	-	16.7	54.0	29.3	-
Shoshonean stock	1,884	546	771	287	280	29.9	40.9	15.2	14.9
Comanche	399	119	85	48	147	29.8	21.3	12.0	36.8
Mono	223	62	144	9	8	27.8	64.6	4.0	3.6
Paviotso	215	85	110	18	2	39.5	51.2	8.4	0.9
Nevada	155	62	88	4	1	40.0	56.8	2.6	0.6
San Luiseno	115	44	30	6	35	38.3	26.1	5.2	30.4
Shoshoni	504	132	207	117	448	26.2	41.1	23.2	9.5
Idaho	101	21	36	24	20	20.8	35.6	23.8	19.8
Nevada	161	55	99	6	1	34.2	61.5	3.7	0.6
Wyoming	198	47	52	73	26	23.7	26.3	36.9	13.1
Siouan stock	9,672	3,022	3,114	3,320	216	31.2	32.2	34.3	2.2
Assiniboine	441	72	203	166	-	16.3	46.0	37.6	-
Crow	372	66	195	104	7	17.7	52.4	28.0	1.9
Hidatsa	129	65	43	21	-	50.4	33.3	16.3	-
Iowa	183	46	35	99	3	25.1	19.1	54.1	1.6
Kansas	114	20	14	80	-	17.5	12.3	70.2	-
Kansa	167	15	35	115	2	9.0	21.0	68.9	1.2
Omaha	144	38	32	74	-	26.4	22.2	51.4	-
Osage	759	39	84	632	4	5.1	11.1	83.3	0.5
Oto	114	76	16	22	-	66.7	14.0	19.3	-

[Continued]

★ 85 ★

Indian and White Mixed-Bloods, by Linguistic Stock, Tribe, State, and Degree of Mixture, 1910 - II
[Continued]

Stock, tribe, and state	Number					Percent of total			
	Total	Less than half white	Half white, half Indian	More than half white	Unknown proportions	Less than half white	Half white, half Indian	More than half white	Unknown proportions
Ponca	369	160	64	72	73	43.4	17.3	19.5	19.8
Nebraska	133	51	22	60	-	38.3	16.5	45.1	-
Oklahoma	200	92	30	5	73	46.0	15.0	2.5	36.5
Quapaw	116	4	22	81	9	3.4	19.0	69.8	7.8
Santee Sioux	714	286	160	268	-	40.1	22.4	37.5	-
Minnesota	126	24	27	75	-	19.0	21.4	59.5	-
Nebraska	293	158	66	69	-	53.9	22.5	23.5	-
South Dakota	218	84	55	79	-	38.5	25.2	36.2	-
Sioux	474	75	187	198	14	15.8	39.5	41.8	3.0
South Dakota	173	26	77	70	-	15.0	44.5	40.5	-
Sisseton Sioux	863	354	346	157	6	41.0	40.1	18.2	0.7
North Dakota	139	33	100	2	4	23.7	71.9	1.4	2.9
South Dakota	620	292	208	118	2	47.1	33.5	19.0	0.3
Teton Sioux	3,508	1,142	1,277	995	94	32.6	36.4	28.4	2.7
North Dakota	140	35	81	24	-	25.0	57.9	17.1	-
South Dakota	3,333	1,106	1,183	952	92	33.2	35.5	28.6	2.8
Brule Sioux	200	40	63	96	1	20.0	31.5	48.0	0.5
Hunkpapa Sioux	109	48	42	19	-	44.0	38.5	17.4	-
Minniconjou Sioux	33	10	11	12	-	-	-	-	-
Oglala Sioux	1,776	512	638	534	92	28.8	35.9	30.1	5.2
Sans Arc Sioux	152	22	44	86	-	14.5	28.9	56.6	-
Sihasapa	140	45	78	17	-	32.1	55.7	12.1	-
Two Kettle Sioux	145	55	61	29	-	37.9	42.1	20.0	-
Other Teton Sioux	953	410	340	202	1	43.0	35.7	21.2	0.1
Winnebago	276	197	39	40	-	71.4	14.1	14.5	-
Nebraska	141	92	22	27	-	65.2	15.6	19.1	-
Wisconsin	105	93	9	3	-	88.6	8.6	2.9	-
Yankton Sioux	683	187	295	200	1	27.4	43.2	29.3	0.1
South Dakota	568	167	244	157	-	29.4	43.0	27.6	-
Yanktonai Sioux	198	101	58	39	-	51.0	29.3	19.7	-
South Dakota	124	74	35	15	-	59.7	28.2	12.1	-
Tanoan stock	101	36	22	3	40	35.6	21.8	3.0	39.6
Washoan stock	168	60	92	15	1	35.7	54.8	8.9	0.6
Washo	168	60	92	15	1	35.7	54.8	8.9	0.6
Nevada	115	44	65	5	1	38.3	56.5	4.3	0.9
Wintun stock	362	73	181	104	4	20.2	50.0	28.7	1.1
Wintun	269	39	137	93	-	14.5	50.9	34.6	-
Yokuts stock	103	30	58	3	12	29.1	56.3	2.9	11.7
Yuman stock	216	86	70	9	51	39.8	32.4	4.2	23.6
Diegueno	171	74	51	3	43	43.3	29.8	1.8	25.1

[Continued]

139

★ 85 ★

Indian and White Mixed-Bloods, by Linguistic Stock, Tribe, State, and Degree of Mixture, 1910 - II

[Continued]

Stock, tribe, and state	Number					Percent of total			
	Total	Less than half white	Half white, half Indian	More than half white	Unknown proportions	Less than half white	Half white, half Indian	More than half white	Unknown proportions
Yurok stock	134	46	82	6	-	34.3	61.2	4.5	-
Weitspec	134	46	82	6	-	34.3	61.2	4.5	-

Source: U.S. Bureau of the Census, *Indian Population in the United States and Alaska, 1910*, United States Government Printing Office, Washington, D.C., 1915, pp. 36-37. *Notes:* A dash (-) represents zero. 1. Less than one-tenth of 1 percent.

★ 86 ★

Intermarriage Rates of Married American Indians, by Age Group, 1970

Age groups	Urban	Rural	Total
16 to 24 years			
Male	48	76	60
Female	47	76	59
24 to 44 years			
Male	49	80	65
Female	45	76	61
45 years and over			
Male	48	81	67
Female	44	77	63
Total			
Male	49	80	65
Female	45	77	62

Source: Russell Thornton, *American Indian Holocaust and Survival: A Population History Since 1492*, University of Oklahoma Press, 1987, p. 237. Published by permission. Primary source: U.S. Department of Health, Education, and Welfare, *A Study of Selected Socio-Economic Characteristics of Ethnic Minorities Based on the 1970 Census.* Vol. 3, *American Indians*, Washington, D.C., p. 36.

Education

★ 87 ★

School Enrollment of Persons 5 to 20 Years Old, 1900-1930

Data include primary schools and colleges.

Year	Total			Male			Female		
	Total number	Attending school		Total number	Attending school		Total number	Attending school	
		Number	Percent		Number	Percent		Number	Percent
1900	89,632	36,243	40.4	45,440	18,688	41.1	44,192	17,555	39.7
1910	102,163	51,877	50.8	51,964	26,820	51.6	50,199	25,057	49.9
1920	90,605	50,939	53.8	47,248	25,360	53.7	47,357	25,579	54.0
1930	129,145	77,806	60.2	64,945	39,945	60.2	64,200	38,722	60.3

Source: Dr. Leon E. Truesdell, U.S. Department of Commerce, Bureau of Census, Fifteenth Census of the United States: 1930, *The Indian Population of the United States and Alaska*, U.S. Government Printing Office, 1937, p. 131.

★ 88 ★

Percent of Persons 5 to 20 Years Old Attending School, by Race/Ethnicity, 1900-1930

Data include primary schools and colleges.

Race and ethnicity	1900	1910	1920	1930
All classes	50.5	59.2	64.3	69.9
Indian	40.4	50.8	53.8	60.2
White	53.6	61.3	65.7	71.2
Native	54.9	62.8	66.6	71.6
Foreign born	31.1	38.7	44.2	54.1
Negro	31.0	44.7	53.5	60.0
Chinese	25.4	45.5	62.8	75.6
Japanese	4.8	24.2	52.9	84.0

Source: Dr. Leon E. Truesdell, U.S. Department of Commerce, Bureau of Census, Fifteenth Census of the United States: 1930, *The Indian Population of the United States and Alaska*, U.S. Government Printing Office, 1937, p. 131.

★ 89 ★

School Attendance of American Indians 6 to 19 Years Old, by Linguistic Stock, Tribe, Principle State, and Sex, 1910: Al - Ch

Data are shown for tribes having 100 or more members in 1910.

Linguistic stock, tribe, and state	Indian males 6 to 19 years of age: 1910					Indian females 6 to 19 years of age: 1910				
	Total number	Attending school				Total number	Attending school			
		Total	6 to 9 years of age	10 to 14 years of age	15 to 19 years of age		Total	6 to 9 years of age	10 to 14 years of age	15 to 19 years of age
UNITED STATES										
Algonquian stock	7,040	4,539	1,210	2,118	1,211	6,724	4,336	1,247	1,965	1,124
Arapaho	184	139	31	63	45	187	133	46	54	33
Oklahoma	75	54	14	21	19	75	50	19	19	12
Wyoming	102	79	17	41	21	110	82	27	35	20
Brotherton	25	20	5	11	4	32	22	9	6	7
Wisconsin	25	20	5	11	4	30	21	8	6	7
Cheyenne	432	274	61	115	98	421	240	57	107	76
Montana	203	104	18	43	43	224	94	15	46	33
Oklahoma	189	141	41	65	35	164	122	37	55	30
South Dakota	22	12	1	6	5	21	13	3	3	7
Chickahominy (Virginia)	15	2	2	-	-	18	5	2	2	1
Chippewa	3,618	2,440	659	1,159	622	3,437	2,336	664	1,056	616
Kansas	20	20	1	5	14	32	30	1	4	25
Michigan	597	365	118	180	67	547	336	101	164	71
Minnesota	1,491	1,083	304	487	292	1,327	970	291	421	258
Montana	86	24	5	16	3	81	24	4	14	6
Nebraska	28	28	6	11	11	30	30	3	10	17
North Dakota	568	340	66	175	99	611	356	90	190	76
Oklahoma	13	7	3	4	-	7	3	2	1	-
Pennsylvania	42	42	1	6	35	43	43	-	4	39
South Dakota	9	6	4	1	1	13	7	2	3	2
Wisconsin	752	513	149	269	95	733	527	169	241	117
Cree	83	49	9	25	15	96	68	20	31	17
Montana	54	27	5	12	10	60	46	12	23	11
Washington	21	17	4	8	5	21	14	4	6	4
Delaware	189	149	43	60	46	175	133	39	68	26
Oklahoma	185	145	43	58	44	166	126	38	63	25
Gros Ventres	66	20	-	13	7	86	35	1	20	14
Montana	65	20	-	13	7	86	35	1	20	14
Kickapoo	54	33	6	17	10	38	23	5	13	5
Kansas	38	28	3	16	9	26	18	4	11	3
Oklahoma	16	5	3	1	1	11	4	1	2	1
Malecite	27	19	8	7	4	27	18	7	7	4
Maine	26	18	8	7	3	26	17	7	6	4
Mashpee	32	25	7	9	9	31	26	8	12	6
Massachusetts	29	22	7	9	6	30	25	8	12	5
Menominee	275	190	67	99	24	255	174	61	90	23
Wisconsin	262	178	62	94	22	244	166	60	86	20
Miami	44	34	11	17	6	45	35	10	16	9
Indiana	13	8	3	5	-	17	9	3	5	1
Oklahoma	27	22	8	11	3	26	24	7	10	7
Ottawa	450	291	84	135	72	385	250	71	112	67
Michigan	376	230	72	107	51	341	214	60	101	53
Oklahoma	30	21	6	10	5	31	23	10	7	6
Wisconsin	23	20	6	9	5	5	5	1	4	-
Passamaquoddy	49	36	10	13	13	56	36	12	15	9
Maine	47	34	10	13	11	55	35	12	14	9
Penobscot	44	26	8	16	2	43	23	9	9	5
Maine	42	24	8	15	1	39	19	9	6	4

[Continued]

★ 89 ★

School Attendance of American Indians 6 to 19 Years Old, by Linguistic Stock, Tribe, Principle State, and Sex, 1910: Al - Ch

[Continued]

Linguistic stock, tribe, and state	Indian males 6 to 19 years of age: 1910					Indian females 6 to 19 years of age: 1910				
	Total number	Attending school				Total number	Attending school			
		Total	6 to 9 years of age	10 to 14 years of age	15 to 19 years of age		Total	6 to 9 years of age	10 to 14 years of age	15 to 19 years of age
Peoria	22	20	6	8	6	29	22	7	7	8
Oklahoma	19	17	5	8	4	25	19	7	7	5
Piegan	399	84	20	41	23	390	108	25	50	33
Montana	385	71	20	39	12	379	97	25	46	26
Potawatomi	469	314	74	144	96	378	249	59	118	72
Kansas	161	117	17	57	43	120	88	12	50	26
Michigan	77	55	14	28	13	67	41	13	21	7
Oklahoma	174	124	39	50	35	149	112	31	46	35
Wisconsin	44	8	-	6	2	33	4	1	1	2
Powhatan (Virginia)	27	4	2	1	1	26	8	1	6	1
Sauk and Fox	124	83	19	34	30	115	62	17	31	14
Iowa	47	27	6	11	10	38	11	3	6	2
Kansas	20	18	2	4	12	19	15	2	8	5
Oklahoma	52	34	10	17	7	49	29	10	15	4
Shawnee	208	147	41	68	38	244	170	61	66	43
Oklahoma	200	139	40	66	33	230	156	58	65	33
Shinnecock (New York)	19	15	8	3	4	29	24	12	9	3
Stockbridges	75	51	13	27	11	77	62	24	30	8
Wisconsin	74	50	13	27	10	71	56	23	27	6
Wampanoag	29	23	3	13	7	19	13	3	8	2
Massachusetts	26	20	3	13	4	18	12	3	8	1
Athabaskan stock	5,557	1,094	208	504	382	5,235	796	210	336	250
Apache	793	352	51	171	130	650	244	39	101	104
Arizona	747	314	39	162	113	611	217	29	90	98
Oklahoma	37	32	12	8	12	34	23	8	11	4
Hupa	110	26	6	10	10	102	23	1	14	8
California	106	22	5	9	8	95	18	1	13	4
Jicarilla Apache (New Mexico)	105	66	16	32	18	93	62	27	8	27
Kiowa Apache (Oklahoma)	17	11	1	7	3	19	12	2	4	6
Mescalero Apache	53	45	19	17	9	71	53	18	26	9
New Mexico	51	43	19	17	7	70	52	18	26	8
Navajo	4,302	464	76	210	178	4,138	289	81	135	73
Arizona	2,180	259	53	126	80	2,093	176	63	79	34
New Mexico	1,910	171	20	75	76	1,896	103	17	52	34
Utah	179	4	1	2	1	146	7	-	2	5
Rogue River	75	60	13	33	14	58	37	12	21	4
Oregon	75	60	13	33	14	55	36	11	21	4
Tolowa (California)	20	16	8	5	3	13	8	2	2	4
Umpqua	18	10	5	1	4	14	10	3	6	1
Oregon	15	8	3	1	4	10	7	-	6	1
Wailaki	35	26	7	10	9	37	28	12	10	6
California	31	22	7	10	5	32	24	10	10	4
Caddoan stock	324	248	63	98	87	338	271	77	107	87
Arikara	76	59	10	23	26	82	68	16	29	23
North Dakota	71	57	9	23	25	82	68	16	29	23
Caddo	93	70	23	26	21	90	73	31	29	13
Oklahoma	89	67	23	26	18	88	71	31	29	11
Pawnee	96	70	16	31	23	98	75	13	32	30

[Continued]

★ 89 ★

School Attendance of American Indians 6 to 19 Years Old, by Linguistic Stock, Tribe, Principle State, and Sex, 1910: Al - Ch

[Continued]

Linguistic stock, tribe, and state	Indian males 6 to 19 years of age: 1910					Indian females 6 to 19 years of age: 1910				
	Total number	Attending school				Total number	Attending school			
		Total	6 to 9 years of age	10 to 14 years of age	15 to 19 years of age		Total	6 to 9 years of age	10 to 14 years of age	15 to 19 years of age
Oklahoma	82	57	16	24	17	84	61	13	26	22
Wichita	56	48	14	17	17	67	54	17	16	21
Oklahoma	45	39	14	16	9	59	48	17	15	16
Chimakuan stock	46	32	9	13	10	33	17	7	5	5
Quileute (Washington)	40	27	9	13	5	26	15	6	4	5
Chimarikan stock	5	5	1	4	-	6	6	4	2	-
Chinookan stock	155	110	29	55	26	122	88	27	40	21
Chinook	55	43	11	21	11	59	46	16	23	7
Oregon	32	26	3	16	7	29	24	6	12	6
Washington	21	15	8	4	3	30	22	10	11	1
Wasco	40	34	10	16	8	29	22	7	6	9
Oregon	29	24	6	13	5	21	16	6	3	7
Washington	10	9	4	2	3	8	6	1	3	2
Wishram (Washington)	42	20	3	13	4	28	16	4	8	4

Source: U.S. Bureau of the Census, *Indian Population in the United States and Alaska, 1910*, United States Government Printing Office, Washington, D.C., 1915, pp. 205-216. *Note:* A dash (-) represents zero.

★ 90 ★

School Attendance of American Indians 6 to 19 Years Old, by Linguistic Stock, Tribe, Principle State, and Sex, 1910: Ch - Sa

Data are shown for tribes having 100 or more members in 1910.

Linguistic stock, tribe, and state	Indian males 6 to 19 years of age: 1910					Indian females 6 to 19 years of age: 1910				
	Total number	Attending school				Total number	Attending school			
		Total	6 to 9 years of age	10 to 14 years of age	15 to 19 years of age		Total	6 to 9 years of age	10 to 14 years of age	15 to 19 years of age
UNITED STATES (cont.)										
Chitimachan stock	25	22	3	10	9	10	7	1	3	3
Chumashan stock	5	4	1	2	1	7	4	1	1	2
Costanoan stock	3	2	-	2	-	4	1	-	1	-
Croatan group	1,027	602	184	251	167	1,001	602	194	269	139
Croatan (North Carolina)	1,027	602	184	251	167	1,001	602	194	269	139

[Continued]

★ 90 ★

School Attendance of American Indians 6 to 19 Years Old, by Linguistic Stock, Tribe, Principle State, and Sex, 1910: Ch - Sa

[Continued]

Linguistic stock, tribe, and state	Indian males 6 to 19 years of age: 1910					Indian females 6 to 19 years of age: 1910				
	Total number	Attending school				Total number	Attending school			
		Total	6 to 9 years of age	10 to 14 years of age	15 to 19 years of age		Total	6 to 9 years of age	10 to 14 years of age	15 to 19 years of age
Eskimauan stock	19	19	2	12	5	22	22	3	10	9
Haidan stock	17	17	1	4	12	6	6	-	-	6
Iroquoian stock	7,318	5,004	1,480	2,178	1,346	7,139	4,917	1,532	2,235	1,150
Cherokee	5,989	4,095	1,236	1,788	1,071	5,767	3,941	1,258	1,810	873
Kansas	11	7	1	5	1	15	12	3	5	4
North Carolina	225	158	41	76	41	178	129	40	52	37
Oklahoma	5,664	3,867	1,180	1,682	1,005	5,511	3,764	1,205	1,740	819
Pennsylvania	17	17	-	-	17	6	6	-	1	5
South Carolina	16	7	-	4	3	13	2	-	1	1
Mohawk	56	32	10	17	5	50	36	11	20	5
New York	46	27	10	15	2	44	30	9	16	5
Oneida	381	251	90	103	58	351	222	70	101	51
New York	39	28	11	11	6	26	13	4	7	2
Wisconsin	316	198	75	88	35	303	188	64	92	32
Onondaga	54	38	10	17	11	69	53	16	24	13
New York	44	29	10	15	4	59	44	16	22	6
St. Regis	229	153	32	73	48	252	209	62	89	58
New York	200	124	32	66	26	222	179	62	83	34
Pennsylvania	29	29	-	7	22	30	30	-	6	24
Seneca	459	312	78	134	100	473	306	86	124	96
New York	359	226	69	112	45	382	233	75	104	54
Oklahoma	35	22	5	14	3	41	24	9	11	4
Pennsylvania	61	60	4	8	48	46	45	2	9	34
Tuscarora	58	50	10	13	27	66	56	11	25	20
New York	52	44	10	13	21	61	51	11	24	16
Wyandot	76	58	10	28	20	67	58	12	27	19
Oklahoma	62	45	9	23	13	58	49	12	24	13
Kalapooian stock	13	8	1	5	2	22	14	3	9	2
Karok stock	127	60	20	29	11	110	64	13	34	17
Orleans (California)	127	60	20	29	11	110	64	13	34	17
Keresan stock	659	323	92	159	72	596	275	90	126	59
Acoma (New Mexico)	117	32	-	23	9	100	32	-	24	8
Cochiti (New Mexico)	35	27	9	16	2	29	15	6	6	3
Laguna	252	174	63	67	44	232	164	62	63	39
New Mexico	237	159	63	65	31	226	158	60	62	36
San Felipe (New Mexico)	77	38	6	23	9	73	24	9	10	5
Santa Ana (New Mexico)	25	9	2	6	1	24	12	5	7	-
Santo Domingo (New Mexico)	130	29	8	15	6	123	17	6	9	2
Sia (New Mexico)	23	14	4	9	1	15	11	2	7	2
Kiowan stock	181	129	26	62	41	194	112	29	60	23
Kiowa	181	129	26	62	41	194	112	29	60	23
Oklahoma	169	117	26	61	30	192	110	29	59	22

[Continued]

145

★ 90 ★

School Attendance of American Indians 6 to 19 Years Old, by Linguistic Stock, Tribe, Principle State, and Sex, 1910: Ch - Sa

[Continued]

Linguistic stock, tribe, and state	Indian males 6 to 19 years of age: 1910					Indian females 6 to 19 years of age: 1910				
	Total number	Attending school				Total number	Attending school			
		Total	6 to 9 years of age	10 to 14 years of age	15 to 19 years of age		Total	6 to 9 years of age	10 to 14 years of age	15 to 19 years of age
Kusan stock	14	8	-	8	-	13	10	5	4	1
Kutenaian stock	88	38	7	21	10	71	41	9	24	8
Kutenai	88	38	7	21	10	71	41	9	24	8
Idaho	12	1	1	-	-	7	-	-	-	-
Montana	73	34	6	20	8	64	41	9	24	8
Lutuamian stock	138	110	26	45	39	145	120	42	41	37
Klamath	96	80	17	34	29	100	85	31	27	27
Oregon	86	71	17	32	22	87	72	31	27	14
Modoc	42	30	9	11	10	45	35	11	14	10
Oregon	25	18	3	7	8	35	27	9	12	6
Maidu stock	178	111	43	50	18	197	145	52	61	32
Maidu	178	111	43	50	18	197	145	52	61	32
California	178	111	43	50	18	196	144	52	60	32
Miwok stock	104	56	20	26	10	109	48	8	27	13
Miwok (California)	99	51	19	22	10	102	45	8	26	11
Muskhogean stock	5,277	3,307	987	1,432	888	5,151	3,065	999	1,319	747
Alibamu	58	18	1	9	8	64	11	-	6	5
Louisiana	28	6	1	3	2	31	3	-	1	2
Texas	30	12	-	6	6	33	8	-	5	3
Chickasaw (Oklahoma)	821	611	171	276	164	837	602	210	252	140
Choctaw	2,953	1,921	592	811	518	2,787	1,705	552	749	404
Alabama	8	-	-	-	-	12	-	-	-	-
Louisiana	17	-	-	-	-	15	-	-	-	-
Mississippi	205	59	16	25	18	182	30	12	12	6
Oklahoma	2,721	1,860	574	786	500	2,572	1,672	538	736	398
Creek	1,120	645	189	284	172	1,155	617	200	255	162
Alabama	25	15	5	7	3	37	22	8	8	6
Oklahoma	1,074	614	180	268	166	1,105	591	191	245	155
Seminole	308	112	34	52	26	281	128	37	57	34
Oklahoma	262	105	32	47	26	254	116	35	49	32
Texas	45	7	2	5	-	24	11	2	8	1
Piman stock	1,556	800	188	326	286	1,369	710	185	306	219
Papago	693	230	58	81	91	606	190	42	86	62
Arizona	686	223	58	81	84	606	190	42	86	62
Pima	763	528	118	225	185	672	493	134	206	153
Arizona	725	492	117	220	155	648	469	134	200	135
California	34	32	1	4	27	24	24	-	6	18
Yaqui	93	40	12	20	8	82	27	9	14	4
Arizona	86	33	9	16	8	76	21	7	12	2

[Continued]

★ 90 ★

School Attendance of American Indians 6 to 19 Years Old, by Linguistic Stock, Tribe, Principle State, and Sex, 1910: Ch - Sa
[Continued]

Linguistic stock, tribe, and state	Indian males 6 to 19 years of age: 1910					Indian females 6 to 19 years of age: 1910				
	Total number	Attending school				Total number	Attending school			
		Total	6 to 9 years of age	10 to 14 years of age	15 to 19 years of age		Total	6 to 9 years of age	10 to 14 years of age	15 to 19 years of age
Pomo stock	154	94	27	39	28	167	103	29	40	34
Clear Lake (California)	26	14	4	5	5	25	13	7	4	2
Pomo (California)	103	70	20	31	19	112	75	20	33	22
Salinan stock	2	2	-	1	1	1	-	-	-	-

Source: U.S. Bureau of the Census, *Indian Population in the United States and Alaska, 1910*, United States Government Printing Office, Washington, D.C., 1915, pp. 205-216. *Note:* A dash (-) represents zero.

★ 91 ★

School Attendance of American Indians 6 to 19 Years Old, by Linguistic Stock, Tribe, Principle State, and Sex, 1910: Sa - Sh

Data are shown for tribes having 100 or more members in 1910.

Linguistic stock, tribe, and state	Indian males 6 to 19 years of age: 1910					Indian females 6 to 19 years of age: 1910				
	Total number	Attending school				Total number	Attending school			
		Total	6 to 9 years of age	10 to 14 years of age	15 to 19 years of age		Total	6 to 9 years of age	10 to 14 years of age	15 to 19 years of age
UNITED STATES (cont.)										
Salishan stock	1,292	630	142	308	180	1,161	567	136	285	146
Chehalis	48	28	4	19	5	41	31	8	14	9
Washington	46	26	3	18	5	40	30	8	13	9
Clallam	75	47	18	19	10	69	49	12	30	7
Washington	67	39	17	15	7	68	48	12	29	7
Coeur d'Alene	48	15	1	-	7	35	11	2	7	2
Idaho	45	12	1	6	5	34	10	2	6	2
Columbia	57	33	9	15	9	49	28	10	12	6
Oregon	11	3	3	-	-	9	5	1	1	3
Washington	46	30	6	15	9	40	23	9	11	3
Colville	135	43	6	21	16	122	40	5	26	9
Washington	119	29	5	17	7	108	30	4	22	4
Cowlitz (Washington)	16	9	4	4	1	10	5	-	4	1
Flathead	82	50	7	30	13	95	55	18	24	13
Montana	60	33	3	23	7	73	36	13	16	7
Kalispel	85	33	5	17	11	73	30	4	14	12
Montana	57	26	5	13	8	46	23	3	10	10
Washington	21	4	-	3	1	23	6	1	4	1

[Continued]

★ 91 ★

School Attendance of American Indians 6 to 19 Years Old, by Linguistic Stock, Tribe, Principle State, and Sex, 1910: Sa - Sh

[Continued]

Linguistic stock, tribe, and state	Indian males 6 to 19 years of age: 1910					Indian females 6 to 19 years of age: 1910				
	Total number	Attending school				Total number	Attending school			
		Total	6 to 9 years of age	10 to 14 years of age	15 to 19 years of age		Total	6 to 9 years of age	10 to 14 years of age	15 to 19 years of age
Lummi	85	34	11	15	8	67	20	5	11	4
Washington	81	30	11	12	7	67	20	5	11	4
Muckleshoot	38	24	10	6	8	33	22	5	11	6
Washington	36	22	10	6	6	33	22	5	11	6
Nisqualli	17	12	2	2	8	16	9	1	6	2
Washington	14	9	2	1	6	13	7	1	5	1
Okinagan	43	23	2	13	8	39	21	3	9	9
Washington	38	18	2	11	5	34	16	3	9	4
Puyallup	51	42	9	15	18	50	32	10	10	12
Washington	40	31	8	13	10	42	24	9	9	6
Quinaielt	37	18	4	12	2	28	18	2	10	6
Washington	36	17	4	11	2	28	18	2	10	6
Sanpoil (Washington)	27	2	1	-	1	28	3	2	1	-
Skokomish	24	16	5	10	1	41	27	5	17	5
Washington	23	15	5	10	-	40	26	5	16	5
Snohomish	116	25	7	13	5	113	21	6	12	2
Washington	115	24	7	13	4	103	21	6	13	2
Spokan	91	47	2	33	12	95	49	3	28	18
Idaho	12	4	-	4	-	12	4	1	2	1
Montana	16	9	2	4	3	18	11	-	8	3
Washington	52	25	-	21	4	57	28	1	18	9
Suquamish (Washington)	56	30	10	13	7	45	26	9	11	6
Swinomish (Washington)	62	34	5	15	14	39	22	12	5	5
Shahaptian stock	559	326	93	127	106	590	364	110	162	92
Klikitat	51	28	6	12	10	53	30	5	12	13
Washington	44	22	5	9	8	47	24	5	10	9
Nez Perces	165	92	26	40	26	163	90	24	40	26
Idaho	128	66	21	30	15	132	69	19	32	18
Montana	7	4	-	4	-	8	6	2	4	-
Oregon	11	10	4	4	2	7	7	2	3	2
Washington	10	3	1	2	-	8	-	-	-	-
Umatilla	21	14	4	4	6	32	21	8	6	7
Oregon	13	12	3	3	6	18	16	6	6	4
Washington	6	1	1	-	-	8	2	2	-	-
Wallawalla (Oregon)	72	59	19	23	17	67	59	16	29	14
Warm Springs	61	39	15	16	8	71	45	14	25	6
Oregon	55	36	13	16	7	66	43	14	23	6
Yakima	175	86	21	29	36	186	111	41	45	25
Oregon	2	2	1	-	1	7	6	-	1	5

[Continued]

School Attendance of American Indians 6 to 19 Years Old, by Linguistic Stock, Tribe, Principle State, and Sex, 1910: Sa - Sh

[Continued]

Linguistic stock, tribe, and state	Indian males 6 to 19 years of age: 1910					Indian females 6 to 19 years of age: 1910				
	Total number	Attending school				Total number	Attending school			
		Total	6 to 9 years of age	10 to 14 years of age	15 to 19 years of age		Total	6 to 9 years of age	10 to 14 years of age	15 to 19 years of age
Washington	169	81	20	29	32	177	103	41	43	19
Shastan stock	253	142	34	72	36	291	140	32	58	50
Hat Creek (California)	37	22	8	10	4	29	10	3	3	4
Pit River	152	67	16	35	16	193	84	20	35	29
California	135	50	12	29	9	169	66	16	30	20
Oregon	13	13	4	5	4	16	12	3	4	5
Shasta	64	53	10	27	16	69	46	9	20	17
California	43	32	7	15	10	48	26	8	8	10
Oregon	21	21	3	12	6	21	20	1	12	7
Shoshonean stock	2,509	1,351	321	623	407	2,334	1,180	332	541	307
Bannock	59	42	10	10	22	47	28	5	11	12
Idaho	47	34	9	9	16	37	20	5	9	6
Chemehuevi	40	15	6	5	4	41	9	4	3	2
California	32	7	2	4	1	26	1	1	-	-
Nevada	7	7	4	-	3	9	6	3	2	1
Comanche	189	131	32	56	43	172	111	24	58	29
Oklahoma	182	124	32	54	38	168	107	24	57	26
Hopi	337	278	72	133	73	278	210	97	76	37
Arizona	304	246	72	115	59	266	199	97	69	33
Kawia (California)	130	95	27	37	31	121	97	29	41	27
Kern River (California)	20	4	1	2	1	20	5	1	3	1
Mono	209	99	27	51	21	237	111	16	62	33
California	203	99	27	51	21	227	109	16	61	32
Nevada	6	-	-	-	-	10	2	-	1	1
Paiute	114	62	18	22	22	111	39	13	17	9
Arizona	10	5	2	1	2	12	1	1	-	-
California	50	42	10	16	16	40	29	9	13	7
Nevada	21	10	6	3	1	24	5	2	3	-
Utah	32	4	-	2	2	34	3	1	1	1
Paviotso	407	271	65	137	69	396	227	58	119	50
California	11	4	2	1	1	5	1	-	1	-
Idaho	21	14	1	9	4	18	7	-	4	3
Nevada	334	225	54	114	57	335	195	53	100	42
Oregon	40	27	8	12	7	34	23	5	13	5
San Luiseno (California)	83	65	9	28	28	81	60	6	27	27
Serrano (California)	83	65	9	28	28	81	60	6	27	27
Shoshoni	546	204	39	94	71	507	200	47	92	61
Idaho	171	58	12	27	19	155	63	14	26	23

[Continued]

★91★

School Attendance of American Indians 6 to 19 Years Old, by Linguistic Stock, Tribe, Principle State, and Sex, 1910: Sa - Sh

[Continued]

Linguistic stock, tribe, and state	Indian males 6 to 19 years of age: 1910					Indian females 6 to 19 years of age: 1910				
	Total number	Attending school				Total number	Attending school			
		Total	6 to 9 years of age	10 to 14 years of age	15 to 19 years of age		Total	6 to 9 years of age	10 to 14 years of age	15 to 19 years of age
Nevada	223	52	13	20	19	211	52	17	19	16
Utah	28	20	4	14	2	31	20	4	12	4
Wyoming	103	58	10	30	18	98	56	12	34	10
Ute	338	71	11	40	20	290	62	24	23	15
Colorado	118	48	11	23	14	96	42	18	16	8
Utah	208	16	-	12	4	185	12	5	5	2

Source: U.S. Bureau of the Census, *Indian Population in the United States and Alaska, 1910,* United States Government Printing Office, Washington, D.C., 1915, pp. 205-216.
Note: A dash (-) represents zero.

★92★

School Attendance of American Indians 6 to 19 Years Old, by Linguistic Stock, Tribe, Principle State, and Sex, 1910: Si - Win

Data are shown for tribes having 100 or more members in 1910.

Linguistic stock, tribe, and state	Indian males 6 to 19 years of age: 1910					Indian females 6 to 19 years of age: 1910				
	Total number	Attending school				Total number	Attending school			
		Total	6 to 9 years of age	10 to 14 years of age	15 to 19 years of age		Total	6 to 9 years of age	10 to 14 years of age	15 to 19 years of age
UNITED STATES (cont.)										
Siouan stock	5,112	3,241	768	1,469	1,004	4,910	3,160	785	1,398	977
Assiniboine	183	110	35	44	31	156	93	28	39	26
Montana	177	105	35	44	26	154	92	27	39	26
Catawba	25	18	6	9	3	20	17	4	10	3
South Carolina	18	13	4	7	2	18	15	3	9	3
Crow	262	183	50	81	52	237	150	33	64	53
Montana	235	158	45	71	42	216	132	30	60	42
South Dakota	11	9	4	2	3	6	5	1	1	3
Hidatsa	122	86	19	32	35	99	65	20	22	23
North Dakota	119	83	19	31	33	90	56	20	19	17
Iowa	45	30	4	19	7	47	33	9	16	8
Kansas	26	18	3	11	4	25	19	3	9	7
Oklahoma	12	7	1	4	2	10	5	3	2	-
Kansa	41	26	6	9	11	49	35	17	14	4
Oklahoma	39	24	6	9	9	47	33	17	13	3
Mandan	35	17	3	10	4	30	21	5	5	11
North Dakota	33	17	3	10	4	30	21	5	5	11
Omaha	199	100	18	41	41	188	110	28	53	29
Nebraska	187	89	18	41	30	188	110	28	53	29
Osage	251	192	62	76	54	241	183	58	77	48
Oklahoma	245	186	62	74	50	231	173	58	76	39

[Continued]

★ 92 ★

School Attendance of American Indians 6 to 19 Years Old, by Linguistic Stock, Tribe, Principle State, and Sex, 1910: Si - Win

[Continued]

Linguistic stock, tribe, and state	Indian males 6 to 19 years of age: 1910					Indian females 6 to 19 years of age: 1910				
	Total number	Attending school				Total number	Attending school			
		Total	6 to 9 years of age	10 to 14 years of age	15 to 19 years of age		Total	6 to 9 years of age	10 to 14 years of age	15 to 19 years of age
Oto	73	59	19	22	18	47	36	14	14	8
Oklahoma	66	56	17	22	17	44	34	13	14	7
Ponca	148	112	35	39	38	184	154	36	65	53
Nebraska	38	23	4	13	6	37	24	7	14	3
Oklahoma	96	75	31	24	20	117	101	29	41	31
Quapaw	54	41	8	22	11	51	39	9	20	10
Oklahoma	50	37	8	22	7	48	36	9	18	9
Santee Sioux	243	150	36	82	32	236	147	32	67	48
Minnesota	39	31	12	17	2	46	30	13	12	5
Montana	16	11	4	6	1	13	8	3	-	5
Nebraska	111	55	3	32	20	117	68	9	35	24
North Dakota	11	7	4	2	1	10	5	1	3	1
South Dakota	64	44	12	25	7	45	32	4	16	12
Sioux	201	148	26	41	81	152	111	19	43	49
Minnesota	26	19	3	7	9	37	32	7	20	5
Montana	13	6	3	2	1	15	8	3	3	2
Nebraska	6	3	-	-	3	11	6	-	4	2
New Jersey	3	-	-	-	-	1	-	-	-	-
North Dakota	19	9	3	2	4	9	7	2	2	3
Oklahoma	7	4	1	2	1	6	5	1	2	2
Pennsylvania	37	37	-	2	35	17	17	-	2	15
South Dakota	68	50	14	20	16	33	16	3	2	11
Sisseton Sioux	380	226	67	97	62	359	228	71	103	54
Minnesota	10	7	3	3	1	9	5	2	3	-
Montana	37	28	9	12	7	32	22	9	7	6
North Dakota	83	51	18	20	13	102	67	20	34	13
South Dakota	243	134	36	60	38	215	133	40	58	35
Teton Sioux	2,117	1,264	252	624	388	2,020	1,248	273	551	424
Montana	11	7	2	3	2	6	6	4	-	2
North Dakota	56	44	11	14	19	59	45	8	20	17
South Dakota	2,044	1,207	239	607	361	1,940	1,183	260	527	396
Brule Sioux	107	79	24	30	25	99	74	28	22	24
South Dakota	106	78	24	30	24	97	72	28	22	22
Hunkpapa Sioux	132	87	19	40	28	154	104	28	42	34
North Dakota	14	8	1	2	5	22	12	2	7	3
South Dakota	118	79	18	38	23	132	92	26	35	31
Minniconjou Sioux (South Dakota)	48	16	1	10	5	47	18	4	5	9
Oglala Sioux	953	541	123	272	146	887	525	125	234	166
South Dakota	949	539	122	271	146	881	520	123	232	165
Sans Arc Sioux (South Dakota)	42	28	8	14	6	32	20	7	9	4
Sihasapa	60	43	11	15	17	60	35	7	15	13
North Dakota	21	18	8	7	3	23	19	5	7	7
South Dakota	39	25	3	8	14	37	16	2	8	6
Two Kettle Sioux (South Dakota)	43	19	3	8	8	41	18	4	10	4
Other Teton Sioux	732	451	63	235	153	700	454	70	214	170
North Dakota	20	17	2	4	11	14	14	1	6	7
South Dakota	699	423	60	228	135	673	427	66	206	155
Winnebago	296	199	47	96	56	291	176	47	78	51
Nebraska	155	98	29	43	26	123	67	20	28	19
Wisconsin	120	81	14	46	21	161	104	27	50	27
Yankton Sioux	273	163	45	68	50	315	174	52	77	45
Montana	53	38	11	11	16	54	41	12	16	13

[Continued]

★92★

School Attendance of American Indians 6 to 19 Years Old, by Linguistic Stock, Tribe, Principle State, and Sex, 1910: Si - Win

[Continued]

Linguistic stock, tribe, and state	Indian males 6 to 19 years of age: 1910					Indian females 6 to 19 years of age: 1910				
	Total number	Attending school				Total number	Attending school			
		Total	6 to 9 years of age	10 to 14 years of age	15 to 19 years of age		Total	6 to 9 years of age	10 to 14 years of age	15 to 19 years of age
North Dakota	15	9	2	5	2	15	10	4	3	3
South Dakota	199	110	32	49	29	238	116	35	54	27
Yanktonai Sioux	163	116	30	57	29	188	140	30	80	30
North Dakota	68	51	13	25	13	76	58	12	33	13
South Dakota	95	65	17	32	16	112	82	18	47	17
Tanoan stock	456	285	110	124	51	455	268	126	111	31
Isleta	110	72	32	25	15	105	74	38	29	7
New Mexico	102	69	31	25	13	98	71	37	27	7
Jemez (New Mexico)	77	56	12	39	5	72	45	16	24	5
Picuris (New Mexico)	15	13	8	3	2	13	8	2	5	1
San Ildefonso (New Mexico)	22	15	10	5	-	21	18	13	3	2
San Juan	71	51	17	26	8	67	45	24	16	5
New Mexico	70	50	17	26	7	65	45	24	16	5
Santa Clara (New Mexico)	34	21	11	5	5	47	23	3	12	8
Taos (New Mexico)	83	36	16	15	5	91	30	19	11	-
Tlingit stock	15	15	-	3	12	10	10	1	4	5
Tonkawan stock	5	4	1	3	-	3	2	-	1	1
Tsimshian stock	17	15	1	4	10	5	3	2	1	-
Tunican stock	11	3	2	1	-	8	1	1	-	-
Wailatpuan stock	57	46	18	16	12	52	47	17	21	9
Cayuse	52	43	15	16	12	51	47	17	21	9
Oregon	46	37	13	15	9	47	43	14	20	9
Wakashan stock	54	42	17	12	13	61	44	17	20	7
Makah	52	42	17	12	13	60	44	17	20	7
Washington	50	40	17	11	12	57	41	17	18	6
Washoan stock	112	37	9	12	16	95	25	5	12	8
Washo	112	37	9	12	16	95	25	5	12	8
California	36	10	1	4	5	32	3	1	2	-
Nevada	72	23	8	7	8	60	19	4	10	5
Wintun stock	106	45	7	29	9	99	48	14	19	15
Nomelaki	22	14	3	10	1	16	10	3	3	4
California	22	14	3	10	1	14	8	3	3	2
Patwin (California)	21	-	-	-	-	27	1	1	-	-
Wintun	63	31	4	19	8	56	37	10	16	11
California	62	30	4	18	8	53	34	10	16	8

Source: U.S. Bureau of the Census, *Indian Population in the United States and Alaska, 1910,* United States Government Printing Office, Washington, D.C., 1915, pp. 205-216. *Note:* A dash (-) represents zero.

★ 93 ★

School Attendance of American Indians 6 to 19 Years Old, by Linguistic Stock, Tribe, Principle State, and Sex, 1910: Wiy - Z and Alaska

Data are shown for tribes having 100 or more members in 1910.

Linguistic stock, tribe, and state	Indian males 6 to 19 years of age: 1910					Indian females 6 to 19 years of age: 1910				
	Total number	Attending school				Total number	Attending school			
		Total	6 to 9 years of age	10 to 14 years of age	15 to 19 years of age		Total	6 to 9 years of age	10 to 14 years of age	15 to 19 years of age
UNITED STATES (cont.)										
Wiyat stock	26	21	9	9	3	13	9	3	6	-
Humboldt Bay (California)	26	21	9	9	3	13	9	3	6	-
Yakonan stock	11	9	1	3	5	9	7	2	3	2
Yanan stock	8	4	-	2	2	6	2	1	1	-
Yokuts stock	71	32	4	15	13	78	31	7	15	9
Chuckhansi	17	11	1	5	5	31	16	2	6	8
California	17	11	1	5	5	29	14	2	6	6
Yokuts (California)	47	20	3	10	7	35	14	4	9	1
Yuchean stock	21	11	1	4	6	10	2	-	1	1
Yukian stock	22	16	8	4	4	25	13	2	3	8
Yuman stock	711	469	131	192	146	593	349	99	163	87
Cocopa	40	-	-	-	-	24	1	1	-	-
Arizona	39	-	-	-	-	22	-	-	-	-
Diegueno (California)	137	94	30	32	32	141	100	25	51	24
Havasupai (Arizona)	21	18	3	8	7	15	12	3	3	6
Maricopa (Arizona)	64	52	14	23	15	64	44	10	16	18
Mohave	173	123	35	54	34	117	76	19	44	13
Arizona	111	69	20	33	16	85	52	10	32	10
California	62	54	15	21	18	32	24	9	12	3
Walapai	113	79	26	30	23	78	37	13	21	3
Arizona	111	77	26	30	21	76	35	11	21	3
Yavapai (Arizona)	58	33	11	15	7	45	23	9	9	5
Yuma	102	69	12	29	28	106	56	19	19	18
Arizona	19	9	3	3	3	23	2	1	-	1
California	82	59	9	26	24	83	54	18	19	17
Yurok stock	107	58	24	25	9	93	55	16	24	15
Weitspec (California)	107	58	24	25	9	93	55	16	24	15
Zunian stock	214	64	18	32	14	222	53	19	25	9
Zuni	214	64	18	32	14	222	53	19	25	9
New Mexico	212	63	18	32	13	222	53	19	25	9
ALASKA										
Athabaskan stock	556	225	40	108	77	526	176	35	90	51
Ahtena	50	7	-	5	2	35	3	1	1	1
Hankutchin	23	15	4	9	2	12	7	5	-	2

[Continued]

153

★ 93 ★

School Attendance of American Indians 6 to 19 Years Old, by Linguistic Stock, Tribe, Principle State, and Sex, 1910: Wiy - Z and Alaska

[Continued]

Linguistic stock, tribe, and state	Indian males 6 to 19 years of age: 1910					Indian females 6 to 19 years of age: 1910				
	Total number	Attending school				Total number	Attending school			
		Total	6 to 9 years of age	10 to 14 years of age	15 to 19 years of age		Total	6 to 9 years of age	10 to 14 years of age	15 to 19 years of age
Kaiyuhkhotana	14	8	2	2	4	17	9	4	3	2
Knajakhotana	114	44	9	17	18	96	36	9	17	10
Kutchin	49	14	5	6	3	52	8	-	5	3
Natsitkutchin	34	3	-	2	1	27	1	-	-	1
Tenankutchin	56	15	4	7	4	58	12	6	4	2
Unakhotana	18	9	4	4	1	26	9	2	6	1
Eskimauan stock	2,039	707	205	315	187	1,775	513	154	240	119
Aleut	248	78	18	36	24	209	59	8	39	12
Chnagmiut	50	24	7	8	9	32	11	6	3	2
Ikogmiut	80	1	-	1	-	101	4	-	3	1
Kaialigmiut	25	2	2	-	-	22	1	1	-	-
Kaviagmiut	38	18	8	5	5	24	17	6	9	3
Kinugumiut	91	48	11	25	12	60	28	9	8	11
Kowagmiut	84	52	18	19	15	70	51	12	26	12
Kusetrinmiut	28	20	7	10	3	7	1	-	1	-
Kuskovakmiut	69	20	1	14	5	50	6	1	4	1
Kuskwogmiut	205	34	10	16	8	178	16	5	11	-
Magemiut	46	7	1	4	2	65	25	2	11	12
Malemiut	93	47	12	22	13	81	43	6	21	16
Nunatogmiut	39	7	2	4	1	30	4	1	2	1
Nunivagmiut	47	4	1	2	1	34	1	-	1	-
Nunochogmiut	8	-	-	-	-	20	-	-	-	-
Selawigmiut	21	14	5	7	2	12	5	5	-	-
Tikeramiut	37	14	3	8	3	38	7	1	3	3
Ukivokmiut	23	7	3	2	2	12	3	2	1	-
Unaligmiut	62	28	8	15	5	60	14	5	7	2
Utkiavinmiut	10	8	-	6	2	11	7	4	2	1
Utukamiut	10	8	1	5	2	10	8	3	4	1
Yuit	39	35	7	14	14	29	23	9	7	7
Southern Eskimo	560	165	61	64	40	512	131	51	56	24
Hadian stock	88	75	22	26	27	82	58	23	17	18
Haida	88	75	22	26	27	82	58	23	17	18
Tlingit stock	611	380	139	157	84	636	384	156	168	60
Auk	34	17	5	6	6	41	26	12	13	1
Chilkat	95	59	23	24	12	99	54	24	17	13
Henya	29	18	8	7	3	32	26	9	12	5
Huna	86	66	26	24	16	100	60	24	30	6
Hutsnuwu	68	37	11	23	3	76	40	21	16	3
Kake	47	37	16	11	10	46	33	14	13	6
Sitka	87	63	23	27	13	82	55	18	24	13
Stikine	21	12	3	6	3	28	18	9	9	-
Taku	19	7	1	3	3	15	9	2	7	-
Tongas	31	13	4	5	4	32	22	9	10	3
Yakutat	42	19	9	9	1	46	17	6	6	5

[Continued]

★ 93 ★

School Attendance of American Indians 6 to 19 Years Old, by Linguistic Stock, Tribe, Principle State, and Sex, 1910: Wiy - Z and Alaska
[Continued]

Linguistic stock, tribe, and state	Indian males 6 to 19 years of age: 1910					Indian females 6 to 19 years of age: 1910				
	Total number	Attending school				Total number	Attending school			
		Total	6 to 9 years of age	10 to 14 years of age	15 to 19 years of age		Total	6 to 9 years of age	10 to 14 years of age	15 to 19 years of age
Tsimshian stock	129	80	16	42	22	112	72	39	29	4
Tsimshian	129	80	16	42	22	112	72	39	29	4

Source: U.S. Bureau of the Census, *Indian Population in the United States and Alaska, 1910,* United States Government Printing Office, Washington, D.C., 1915, pp. 205-216. *Note:* A dash (-) represents zero.

★ 94 ★

School Attendance of Indians 6 to 19 Years Old, by Geographic Division, State, and Age Group, 1910

Division and state	Indians 6 to 19 years of age: 1910				
	Total number	Number attending school			
		Total	6 to 9 years of age	10 to 14 years of age	15 to 19 years of age
UNITED STATES	88,786	50,115	13,984	22,446	13,685
Geographic divisions					
New England	577	398	126	196	76
Middle Atlantic	2,746	2,040	409	715	916
East North Central	5,942	3,883	1,203	1,934	746
West North Central	13,361	8,728	2,066	3,938	2,724
South Atlantic	3,091	1,797	542	788	467
East South Central	907	261	77	126	58
West South Central	27,765	18,525	5,744	8,198	4,583
Mountain	24,321	8,516	2,231	3,879	2,406
Pacific	10,076	5,967	1,586	2,672	1,709
New England					
Maine	259	163	58	70	35
New Hampshire	9	8	3	4	1
Vermont	4	3	1	2	-
Massachusetts	191	149	45	75	29
Rhode Island	81	54	12	34	8
Connecticut	33	21	7	11	3
Middle Atlantic					
New York	1,855	1,239	390	574	275
New Jersey	54	25	1	9	15
Pennsylvania	837	776	18	132	626

[Continued]

★ 94 ★

School Attendance of Indians 6 to 19 Years Old, by Geographic Division, State, and Age Group, 1910
[Continued]

Division and state	Indians 6 to 19 years of age: 1910				
	Total number	Number attending school			
		Total	6 to 9 years of age	10 to 14 years of age	15 to 19 years of age
East North Central					
Ohio	40	26	5	17	4
Indiana	111	66	20	41	5
Illinois	44	32	8	12	12
Michigan	2,303	1,448	433	719	296
Wisconsin	3,444	2,311	737	1,145	429
West North Central					
Minnesota	3,094	2,259	661	1,003	595
Iowa	111	54	17	22	15
Missouri	100	68	20	37	11
North Dakota	2,258	1,421	347	669	405
South Dakota	5,543	3,326	765	1,554	1,007
Nebraska	1,224	754	154	343	257
Kansas	1,031	846	102	310	434
South Atlantic					
Delaware	4	4	-	2	2
Maryland	29	22	3	9	10
District of Columbia	18	14	2	10	2
Virginia	192	57	23	24	10
West Virginia	17	14	5	5	4
North Carolina	2,668	1,608	490	700	418
South Carolina	115	62	15	31	16
Georgia	29	11	2	6	3
Florida	19	5	2	1	2
East South Central					
Kentucky	92	16	5	9	2
Tennessee	76	35	10	18	7
Alabama	320	112	33	55	24
Mississippi	419	98	29	44	25
West South Central					
Arkansas	167	104	33	51	20
Louisiana	321	56	13	27	16
Oklahoma	27,060	18,288	5,689	8,072	4,527
Texas	217	77	9	48	20
Mountain					
Montana	3,292	1,519	363	723	433
Idaho	875	382	92	173	117

[Continued]

★ 94 ★

School Attendance of Indians 6 to 19 Years Old, by Geographic Division, State, and Age Group, 1910
[Continued]

Division and state	Indians 6 to 19 years of age: 1910				
	Total number	Number attending school			
		Total	6 to 9 years of age	10 to 14 years of age	15 to 19 years of age
Wyoming	437	289	68	146	75
Colorado	588	403	84	167	152
New Mexico	6,794	1,799	578	817	404
Arizona	10,039	3,366	855	1,481	1,030
Utah	870	101	19	59	23
Nevada	1,426	657	172	313	172
Pacific					
Washington	3,264	1,710	496	810	404
Oregon	1,714	1,349	332	580	437
California	5,098	2,908	758	1,282	868

Source: U.S. Bureau of the Census, *Indian Population in the United States and Alaska, 1910*, United States Printing Office, Washington, D.C., 1915, p. 199. *Note:* A dash (-) represents zero.

★ 95 ★

School Attendance, by Tribe, Tribal Group, Age Group, and Sex, 1930 - I

Tribe or stock	Indians 5 years old and over attending school			5 and 6 years		7 to 13 years	
	Total	Male	Female	Male	Female	Male	Female
Total	79,856	40,252	39,604	2,211	2,297	24,096	23,653
Arapaho	304	163	141	16	12	89	87
Blackfeet	865	460	405	22	13	282	258
Cheyenne	609	316	293	7	4	164	165
Chippewa	5,645	2,744	2,901	141	157	1,827	1,878
Delaware	308	166	142	12	7	100	86
Gros Ventres (Atsina)	162	73	89	3	1	41	55
Kickapoo	122	61	61	2	2	35	38
Menominee	577	301	276	19	15	166	174
Ottawa	438	247	191	23	24	147	114
Potawatomie	427	206	221	4	21	146	134
Sauk and Fox	212	96	116	7	6	52	53
Shawnee	321	161	160	13	9	91	96
Eastern Algonquians	513	243	270	21	30	157	170
Virginia-Carolina Indians	3,422	1,760	1,662	89	107	1,205	1,039

[Continued]

★ 95 ★

School Attendance, by Tribe, Tribal Group, Age Group, and Sex, 1930 - I
[Continued]

Tribe or stock	Indians 5 years old and over attending school			5 and 6 years		7 to 13 years	
	Total	Male	Female	Male	Female	Male	Female
Apache	1,280	662	618	11	13	431	432
Navaho	5,249	2,882	2,367	67	66	1,461	1,299
Oregon Athapaskans	132	74	58	3	6	43	34
California Athapaskans	266	129	137	7	18	83	82
Arikara	118	51	67	1	1	30	38
Caddo	157	78	79	3	3	46	43
Pawnee	276	146	130	11	5	78	85
Chinookan Stock	143	63	80	2	7	40	43
Iroquois	1,838	901	937	70	66	574	552
Wyandot	112	56	56	4	2	27	28
Cherokee	13,241	6,702	6,539	468	488	4,064	3,972
Karok Stock (Orleans)	199	86	113	4	8	50	67
Keresan Stock	1,058	527	531	21	30	304	281
Kiowan Stock (Kiowa)	291	141	150	9	5	75	90
Miwok Stock	127	57	70	4	4	40	44
Chickasaw	1,510	737	773	39	59	448	426
Choctaw	5,365	2,716	2,649	172	183	1,606	1,576
Creek	2,610	1,320	1,290	75	85	756	729
Seminole	530	296	234	12	18	178	122
Papago	775	391	384	20	27	227	204
Pima	1,075	538	537	23	22	284	274
Pomo Stock	234	108	126	6	5	70	88
Washington Coast Salish	939	452	487	21	20	291	328
Interior Salish	1,204	603	601	24	31	390	361
Klamath and Modoc	558	286	272	27	18	179	164
Shahaptians	946	453	493	16	21	279	291
Shastan Stock	160	84	76	6	4	63	46
Comanche	387	195	192	6	6	113	105
Hopi	857	416	441	38	33	212	223
Mono-Paviotso	117	49	68	7	4	21	39
Pauite	911	448	463	18	30	278	292
Shoshoni	796	392	404	25	23	247	235
Ute	430	218	212	10	10	127	122
Crow	437	215	222	7	9	143	137
Hidatsa	133	65	68	3	5	40	38
Oto and Missouri	251	116	135	7	4	81	97
Omaha	304	147	157	15	9	83	86
Osage	771	415	356	36	27	217	204

[Continued]

★ 95 ★

School Attendance, by Tribe, Tribal Group, Age Group, and Sex, 1930 - I
[Continued]

Tribe or stock	Indians 5 years old and over attending school			5 and 6 years		7 to 13 years	
	Total	Male	Female	Male	Female	Male	Female
Ponca	272	123	149	7	4	77	114
Dakota	6,377	3,249	3,128	116	127	1,877	1,815
Assiniboine	440	215	225	9	7	123	133
Winnebago	450	208	242	7	19	120	133
Tanoan Stock	869	454	415	29	20	245	243
Washoan Stock (Washo)	111	60	51	4	1	35	34
Wintun Stock	118	54	64	1	7	29	38
Yokuts Stock	288	157	131	9	9	101	83
Northern Yumans	125	55	70	2	3	32	45
Mohave	188	91	97	6	5	54	62
Yuma	525	266	259	9	19	162	155
Yurok Stock	125	56	69	3	5	55	43
Zunian Stock (Zuni)	420	246	174	10	7	120	86

Source: Dr. Leon E. Truesdell, U.S. Department of Commerce, Bureau of the Census, Fifteenth Census of the United States: 1930, *The Indian Population of the United States and Alaska,* U.S. Government Printing Office, 1937, pp. 140-141. *Notes:* A dash (-) represents zero. The statistics of school attendance obtained in the census of 1930 are based upon the answer to a question on the population schedule as to whether the person enumerated had attended school or college at any time between September 1, 1929, and the census date, April 1, 1930. The total number of persons returned as attending school is, therefore, larger than the number who were in attendance at any one time between these two dates.

★ 96 ★

School Attendance, by Tribe, Tribal Group, Age Group, and Sex, 1930 - II

Tribe or stock	14 and 15 years		16 and 17 years		18 to 20 years		21 years and over	
	Male	Female	Male	Female	Male	Female	Male	Female
Total	5,921	5,998	4,184	4,307	2,672	2,467	1,168	882
Arapaho	22	19	16	15	18	6	2	2
Blackfeet	70	65	46	44	28	20	12	5
Cheyenne	65	60	37	41	28	18	15	5
Chippewa	425	428	231	278	80	125	40	35
Delaware	22	24	21	14	7	9	4	2
Gros Ventres (Atsina)	8	13	11	12	8	6	2	2
Kickapoo	11	8	8	8	5	3	-	2
Menominee	47	43	50	27	17	16	2	1
Ottawa	37	32	23	15	13	3	4	3
Potawatomie	32	31	20	21	3	8	1	6

[Continued]

★ 96 ★

School Attendance, by Tribe, Tribal Group, Age Group, and Sex, 1930 - II
[Continued]

Tribe or stock	14 and 15 years		16 and 17 years		18 to 20 years		21 years and over	
	Male	Female	Male	Female	Male	Female	Male	Female
Sauk and Fox	12	29	14	16	8	8	3	4
Shawnee	18	28	21	16	16	8	2	3
Eastern Algonquians	38	43	20	21	2	3	5	3
Virginia-Carolina Indians	227	247	161	159	56	77	22	33
Apache	87	74	68	54	49	35	16	10
Navaho	438	350	369	308	369	250	178	94
Oregon Athapaskans	13	10	5	5	7	3	3	-
California Athapaskans	21	18	9	14	5	5	4	-
Arikara	8	12	2	8	8	5	2	3
Caddo	8	14	10	7	8	11	3	1
Pawnee	29	17	9	15	11	6	8	2
Chinookan Stock	8	14	6	11	3	5	4	-
Iroquois	122	174	79	87	40	50	16	8
Wyandot	8	8	7	12	7	5	3	1
Cherokee	942	951	697	679	394	363	137	126
Karok Stock (Orleans)	16	15	7	8	5	11	4	4
Keresan Stock	93	113	56	51	41	50	12	6
Kiowan Stock (Kiowa)	26	26	16	20	13	7	2	2
Miwok Stock	9	12	3	7	1	3	-	-
Chickasaw	97	114	83	98	51	50	19	26
Choctaw	348	369	298	262	198	175	94	84
Creek	191	185	132	172	130	89	36	30
Seminole	37	42	42	33	23	17	4	2
Papago	60	66	52	57	24	22	8	8
Pima	67	73	69	71	59	75	36	22
Pomo Stock	19	19	8	11	3	3	2	-
Washington Coast Salish	76	72	41	40	18	24	5	3
Interior Salish	86	105	67	54	25	42	11	8
Klamath and Modoc	32	41	26	28	18	20	4	1
Shahaptians	60	81	53	64	35	32	10	4
Shastan Stock	11	11	3	10	-	4	1	1
Comanche	32	35	24	30	16	11	4	5
Hopi	56	66	56	59	36	43	18	17
Mono-Paviotso	9	11	9	4	-	8	3	2
Pauite	79	66	42	47	23	22	8	6
Shoshoni	56	58	37	43	16	32	11	13
Ute	29	35	22	22	23	20	7	3
Crow	31	37	18	23	15	10	1	6
Hidatsa	7	9	6	7	8	8	1	1

[Continued]

★ 96 ★

School Attendance, by Tribe, Tribal Group, Age Group, and Sex, 1930 - II

[Continued]

Tribe or stock	14 and 15 years		16 and 17 years		18 to 20 years		21 years and over	
	Male	Female	Male	Female	Male	Female	Male	Female
Oto and Missouri	16	21	6	11	6	2	-	-
Omaha	22	29	14	17	4	9	9	7
Osage	72	50	44	39	38	26	8	10
Ponca	23	14	8	10	6	5	2	2
Dakota	512	493	375	364	254	242	115	87
Assiniboine	36	30	31	33	10	19	6	3
Winnebago	33	31	21	36	15	19	12	4
Tanoan Stock	82	75	43	54	43	20	12	3
Washoan Stock (Washo)	10	9	5	4	3	2	3	1
Wintun Stock	15	12	6	4	2	3	1	-
Yokuts Stock	28	19	8	14	5	4	6	2
Northern Yumans	10	5	1	8	8	5	2	4
Mohave	12	9	6	9	5	9	8	3
Yuma	38	37	26	30	22	10	9	8
Yurok Stock	14	10	4	10	2	1	-	-
Zunian Stock (Zuni)	52	34	33	34	19	10	12	3

Source: Dr. Leon E. Truesdell, U.S. Department of Commerce, Bureau of the Census, Fifteenth Census of the United States: 1930, *The Indian Population of the United States and Alaska*, U.S. Government Printing Office, 1937, pp. 140-141. *Notes:* A dash (-) represents zero. The statistics of school attendance obtained in the census of 1930 are based upon the answer to a question on the population schedule as to whether the person enumerated had attended school or college at any time between September 1, 1929, and the census date, April 1, 1930. The total number of persons returned as attending school is, therefore, larger than the number who were in attendance at any one time between these two dates.

★ 97 ★

Illiterate American Indians 10 Years Old and Older, by Linguistic Stock, Tribe, and Sex, 1910: A - K

Data are shown for linguistic stocks with 200 or more Indians and tribes with more than 100 members in 1910.

Linguistic stock and tribe	Indians 10 years of age and over: 1910			Indian males 10 years of age and over			Indian females 10 years of age and over		
	Total number	Illiterate		Total number	Illiterate		Total number	Illiterate	
		Number	Percent		Number	Percent		Number	Percent
UNITED STATES									
Algonquian stock	29,872	11,509	38.5	15,486	5,345	34.5	14,380	6,164	42.8
Arapaho	1,047	492	47.0	545	206	37.8	502	286	57.0
Brotherton	132	3	2.3	70	3	4.3	62	-	-
Cheyenne	2,427	1,404	57.8	1,176	598	50.9	1,251	806	64.4
Chickahominy	89	24	27.0	47	14	-	42	10	-
Chippewa	14,629	5,800	39.6	7,552	2,727	36.1	7,077	3,073	43.4
Cree	326	95	29.1	166	49	29.5	160	46	28.8

[Continued]

★97★

Illiterate American Indians 10 Years Old and Older, by Linguistic Stock, Tribe, and Sex, 1910: A - K
[Continued]

Linguistic stock and tribe	Indians 10 years of age and over: 1910			Indian males 10 years of age and over			Indian females 10 years of age and over		
	Total number	Illiterate		Total number	Illiterate		Total number	Illiterate	
		Number	Percent		Number	Percent		Number	Percent
Delaware	636	90	14.2	312	28	9.0	324	62	19.1
Gros Ventres	376	199	52.9	189	93	49.2	187	106	56.7
Kickapoo	251	131	52.2	139	68	48.9	112	63	56.3
Malecite	101	35	34.7	48	17	-	53	18	34.0
Mashpee	166	1	0.6	91	-	-	75	1	1.3
Menominee	1,029	381	37.0	571	198	34.7	458	183	40.0
Miami	171	17	9.9	94	8	8.5	77	9	11.7
Ottawa	2,034	664	32.6	1,083	297	27.4	951	367	38.6
Passamaquoddy	310	110	35.5	166	45	27.1	144	65	45.1
Penobscot	231	60	26.0	124	31	25.0	107	29	27.1
Peoria	83	10	12.0	40	1	-	43	9	-
Piegan	1,602	978	61.0	810	480	59.3	792	498	62.9
Potawatomi	1,697	527	31.1	968	284	29.3	729	243	33.3
Powhatan	91	19	20.9	45	14	-	46	5	-
Sauk and Fox	521	151	29.0	280	61	21.8	241	90	37.3
Shawnee	886	248	28.0	424	95	22.4	462	153	33.1
Shinnecock	121	-	-	59	-	-	62	-	-
Stockbridges	384	17	4.4	197	8	4.1	187	9	4.8
Wampanoag	133	3	2.3	79	3	3.8	54	-	-
All other tribes	399	50	12.5	211	17	8.1	188	33	17.6
Athabaskan stock	20,460	16,982	83.0	10,252	8,136	79.4	10,208	8,840	86.7
Apache	3,480	2,386	68.6	1,754	1,060	60.4	1,726	1,326	76.8
Hupa	497	204	41.0	241	95	39.4	256	109	42.6
Jicarilla Apache	486	378	77.8	252	183	72.6	234	195	83.3
Kiowa Apache	98	40	40.8	42	15	-	56	25	44.6
Mescalero Apache	312	164	52.6	129	52	40.3	183	112	61.2
Navajo	14,797	13,496	91.2	7,429	6,592	88.7	7,368	6,904	93.7
Rogue River	286	101	35.3	153	46	30.1	133	55	41.4
Tolowa	84	44	52.4	44	19	-	40	25	-
Umpqua	79	26	32.9	40	12	-	39	14	-
Wailaki	164	52	31.7	79	17	21.5	85	35	41.2
All other tribes	164	52	31.7	79	17	21.5	85	35	41.2
Caddoan stock	1,354	537	39.7	673	248	36.8	681	289	42.4
Arikara	336	190	56.5	163	92	56.4	173	98	56.6
Caddo	302	89	29.5	161	41	25.5	141	48	34.0
Pawnee	473	162	34.2	227	73	32.2	246	89	36.2
Wichita	229	92	40.2	114	39	34.2	115	53	46.1
All other tribes	14	4	-	8	3	-	6	1	-

[Continued]

★ 97 ★

Illiterate American Indians 10 Years Old and Older, by Linguistic Stock, Tribe, and Sex, 1910: A - K

[Continued]

Linguistic stock and tribe	Indians 10 years of age and over: 1910			Indian males 10 years of age and over			Indian females 10 years of age and over		
	Total number	Illiterate		Total number	Illiterate		Total number	Illiterate	
		Number	Percent		Number	Percent		Number	Percent
Chimakuan stock	228	123	53.9	113	52	46.0	115	71	61.7
Quileute	193	100	51.8	95	42	44.2	98	58	59.2
All other tribes	35	23	-	18	10	-	17	13	-
Chinookan stock	676	230	34.0	353	92	26.1	323	138	42.7
Chinook	224	40	17.9	123	20	16.3	101	20	19.8
Wasco	184	61	33.2	95	18	18.9	89	43	48.3
Wishram	222	116	52.3	112	52	46.4	110	64	58.2
All other tribes	46	13	-	23	2	-	23	11	-
Croatan group	3,943	1,932	49.0	1,954	869	44.5	1,989	1,063	53.4
Croatan	3,943	1,932	49.0	1,954	869	44.5	1,989	1,063	53.4
Iroquoian stock	26,201	5,689	21.7	13,490	2,771	20.5	12,711	2,918	23.0
Cherokee	20,154	3,999	19.8	10,319	1,883	18.2	9,835	2,116	21.5
Mohawk	291	139	47.8	136	58	42.6	155	81	52.3
Oneida	1,739	519	29.8	930	296	31.8	809	223	27.6
Onondaga	275	75	27.3	138	29	21.0	137	46	33.6
St. Regis	912	375	41.1	499	209	41.9	413	166	40.2
Seneca	2,155	501	23.2	1,109	256	23.1	1,046	245	23.4
Tuscarora	309	51	16.5	168	24	14.3	141	27	19.1
Wyandot	253	15	5.9	137	8	5.8	116	7	6.0
All other tribes	113	15	13.3	54	8	14.8	59	7	11.9
Karok stock	555	251	45.2	275	111	40.4	280	140	50.0
Orleans	555	251	45.2	275	111	40.4	280	140	50.0
Keresan stock	2,954	2,195	74.3	1,593	1,118	70.2	1,361	1,077	79.1
Acoma	518	423	81.7	257	198	77.0	261	225	86.2
Cochiti	183	109	59.6	103	54	52.4	80	55	68.8
Laguna	1,050	633	60.3	551	302	54.8	499	331	66.3
San Felipe	379	312	82.3	227	175	77.1	152	137	90.1
Santa Ana	155	135	87.1	98	87	88.8	57	48	84.2
Santo Domingo	581	518	89.2	310	268	86.5	271	250	92.3
Sia	88	65	73.9	47	34	-	41	31	-
Kiowan stock	750	330	44.0	361	140	38.8	389	190	48.8
Kiowa	750	330	44.0	361	140	38.8	389	190	48.8

[Continued]

★ 97 ★

Illiterate American Indians 10 Years Old and Older, by Linguistic Stock, Tribe, and Sex, 1910: A - K

[Continued]

Linguistic stock and tribe	Indians 10 years of age and over: 1910			Indian males 10 years of age and over			Indian females 10 years of age and over		
	Total number	Illiterate		Total number	Illiterate		Total number	Illiterate	
		Number	Percent		Number	Percent		Number	Percent
Kutenaian stock	395	215	54.4	210	111	52.9	185	104	56.2
Kutenai	395	215	54.4	210	111	52.9	185	104	56.2

Source: U.S. Bureau of the Census, *Indian Population in the United States and Alaska, 1910,* United States Government Printing Office, Washington, D.C., 1915, pp. 226-231. *Notes:* A dash (-) represents zero or a lack of 50 persons for a percentage base.

★ 98 ★

Illiterate American Indians 10 Years Old and Older, by Linguistic Stock, Tribe, and Sex, 1910: L - S

Data are shown for linguistic stocks with 200 or more Indians and tribes with more than 100 members in 1910.

Linguistic stock and tribe	Indians 10 years of age and over: 1910			Indian males 10 years of age and over			Indian females 10 years of age and over		
	Total number	Illiterate		Total number	Illiterate		Total number	Illiterate	
		Number	Percent		Number	Percent		Number	Percent
UNITED STATES (cont.)									
Lutuamian stock	727	260	35.8	347	99	28.5	380	161	42.4
Klamath	521	190	36.5	249	76	30.5	272	114	41.9
Modoc	206	70	34.0	98	23	23.5	108	47	43.5
Maidu stock	810	335	41.4	421	172	40.9	389	163	41.9
Maidu	810	335	41.4	421	172	40.9	389	163	41.9
Miwok stock	530	325	61.3	254	151	59.4	276	174	63.0
Miwok	505	318	63.0	238	147	61.8	267	171	64.0
All other tribes	25	7	-	16	4	-	9	3	-
Muskhogean stock	18,957	6,357	33.5	9,608	2,785	29.0	9,349	3,572	38.2
Alibamu	225	140	62.2	114	65	57.0	111	75	67.6
Chickasaw	2,563	379	14.8	1,268	128	10.1	1,295	251	19.4
Choctaw	10,185	3,168	31.1	5,202	1,375	26.4	4,983	1,793	36.0
Creek	4,697	1,942	41.3	2,349	869	37.0	2,348	1,073	45.7
Seminole	1,216	666	54.8	639	317	49.6	577	349	60.5
All other tribes (Koasati)	71	62	87.3	36	31	-	35	31	-
Piman stock	6,149	3,901	63.4	3,234	1,936	59.9	2,915	1,965	67.4
Papago	2,655	1,953	73.6	1,365	969	71.0	1,290	984	76.3
Pima	3,083	1,614	52.4	1,631	782	47.9	1,452	832	57.3

[Continued]

★ 98 ★

Illiterate American Indians 10 Years Old and Older, by Linguistic Stock, Tribe, and Sex, 1910: L - S
[Continued]

Linguistic stock and tribe	Indians 10 years of age and over: 1910			Indian males 10 years of age and over			Indian females 10 years of age and over		
	Total number	Illiterate		Total number	Illiterate		Total number	Illiterate	
		Number	Percent		Number	Percent		Number	Percent
Yaqui	378	307	81.2	222	175	78.8	156	132	84.6
All other tribes	33	27	-	16	10	-	17	17	-
Pomo stock	919	473	51.5	465	211	45.4	454	262	57.7
Clear Lake	141	57	40.4	73	27	37.0	68	30	44.1
Pomo	606	313	51.7	308	139	45.1	298	174	58.4
All other tribes	172	103	59.9	84	45	53.6	88	58	65.9
Salishan stock	5,759	2,703	46.9	2,993	1,244	41.6	2,766	1,459	52.7
Chehalis	199	73	36.7	114	36	31.6	85	37	43.5
Clallam	280	80	28.6	144	27	18.8	136	53	39.0
Coeur d'Alene	215	107	49.8	116	50	43.1	99	57	57.6
Columbia	288	200	69.4	156	102	65.4	132	98	74.2
Colville	589	341	57.9	310	180	58.1	279	161	57.7
Cowlitz	75	30	40.0	39	12	-	36	18	-
Flathead	343	140	40.8	177	61	34.5	166	79	47.6
Kalispel	430	284	66.0	216	138	63.9	214	146	68.2
Lummi	223	51	22.9	127	28	22.0	96	23	24.0
Muckleshoot	142	60	42.3	75	27	36.0	67	33	49.3
Nisqualli	112	53	47.3	56	21	37.5	56	32	57.1
Okinagan	206	105	51.0	103	48	46.6	103	57	55.3
Puyallup	231	54	23.4	118	21	17.8	113	33	29.2
Quinaielt	205	82	40.0	107	39	36.4	98	43	43.9
Sanpoil	184	169	91.8	87	79	90.8	97	90	92.8
Skokomish	141	51	36.2	62	21	33.9	79	30	38.0
Snohomish	478	203	42.5	251	89	35.5	227	114	50.2
Spokan	512	226	44.1	251	93	37.1	261	133	51.0
Suquamish	217	80	36.9	118	37	31.4	99	43	43.4
Swinomish	243	121	49.8	134	50	37.3	109	71	65.1
All other tribes	446	193	43.3	232	85	36.6	214	108	50.5
Shahaptian stock	3,372	1,771	52.5	1,567	728	46.5	1,805	1,043	57.8
Klikitat	325	179	55.1	148	70	47.3	177	109	61.6
Nez Perces	980	451	46.0	480	182	37.9	500	269	53.8
Umatilla	217	153	70.5	94	61	64.9	123	92	74.8
Wallawalla	290	119	41.0	143	51	35.7	147	68	46.3
Warm Springs	408	216	52.9	184	97	52.7	224	119	53.7
Yakima	1,028	563	54.8	463	228	49.2	565	335	59.3
All other tribes	124	90	72.6	55	39	70.9	69	51	73.9
Shastan stock	1,226	721	58.8	595	339	57.0	631	382	60.5
Hat Creek	190	138	72.6	100	71	71.0	90	67	74.4

[Continued]

★ 98 ★

Illiterate American Indians 10 Years Old and Older, by Linguistic Stock, Tribe, and Sex, 1910: L - S
[Continued]

Linguistic stock and tribe	Indians 10 years of age and over: 1910			Indian males 10 years of age and over			Indian females 10 years of age and over		
	Total number	Illiterate		Total number	Illiterate		Total number	Illiterate	
		Number	Percent		Number	Percent		Number	Percent
Pit River	767	508	66.2	369	243	65.9	398	265	66.6
Shasta	269	75	27.9	126	25	19.8	148	50	35.0
Shoshonean stock	12,894	8,411	65.2	6,645	4,055	61.0	6,249	4,356	69.7
Bannock	338	231	68.3	176	119	67.6	162	112	69.1
Chemehuevi	262	203	77.5	136	94	69.1	126	109	86.5
Comanche	876	455	51.9	427	192	45.0	449	263	58.6
Hopi	1,420	764	53.8	795	395	49.7	625	369	59.0
Kawia	605	310	51.2	333	159	47.7	272	151	55.5
Kern River	80	50	62.5	37	23	-	43	27	-
Mono	1,090	698	64.0	501	304	60.7	589	394	66.9
Paiute	585	447	76.4	313	221	70.6	272	226	83.1
Paviotso	2,480	1,653	66.7	1,209	754	62.4	1,271	899	70.7
San Luiseno	389	124	31.9	203	48	23.6	186	76	40.9
Serrano	91	33	36.3	49	16	-	42	17	-
Shoshoni	2,955	2,078	70.3	1,515	1,010	66.7	1,440	1,068	74.2
Ute	1,641	1,293	78.8	911	689	75.6	730	604	82.7
All other tribes	82	72	87.8	40	31	-	42	41	-
Siouan stock	24,598	10,784	43.8	12,350	4,670	37.8	12,248	6,114	49.9
Assiniboine	925	488	52.8	455	215	47.3			
Catawba	78	30	38.5	42	16	-	36	14	-
Crow	1,402	780	55.6	702	373	53.1	700	407	58.1
Hidatsa	394	162	41.1	208	72	34.6	186	90	48.4
Iowa	179	19	10.6	94	9	9.6	85	10	11.8
Kansa	138	24	17.4	88	16	18.2	50	8	16.0
Mandan	162	87	53.7	84	42	50.0	78	45	57.7
Omaha	791	366	46.3	407	164	40.3	384	202	52.6
Osage	898	198	22.0	465	87	18.7	433	111	25.6
Oto	245	59	24.1	135	26	19.3	110	33	30.0
Ponca	643	198	30.8	307	89	29.0	336	109	32.4
Quapaw	169	46	27.2	84	19	22.6	85	27	31.8
Santee Sioux	1,112	283	25.4	564	109	19.3	548	174	31.8
Sioux	790	223	28.2	449	103	22.9	341	120	35.2
Sisseton Sioux	1,888	761	40.3	957	313	32.7	931	448	48.1
Teton Sioux	10,739	5,129	47.8	5,349	2,214	41.4	5,390	2,915	54.1
Brule Sioux	591	265	44.8	301	110	36.5	290	155	53.4
Hunkpapa Sioux	813	417	51.3	403	184	45.7	410	233	56.8
Minniconjou Sioux	318	210	66.0	150	91	60.7	168	119	70.8
Oglala Sioux	4,486	2,060	45.9	2,242	901	40.2	2,244	1,159	51.6
Sans Arc Sioux	146	52	35.6	77	23	29.9	69	29	42.0
Sihasapa	372	163	43.8	191	70	36.6	181	93	51.4

[Continued]

★ 98 ★

Illiterate American Indians 10 Years Old and Older, by Linguistic Stock, Tribe, and Sex, 1910: L - S
[Continued]

Linguistic stock and tribe	Indians 10 years of age and over: 1910			Indian males 10 years of age and over			Indian females 10 years of age and over		
	Total number	Illiterate		Total number	Illiterate		Total number	Illiterate	
		Number	Percent		Number	Percent		Number	Percent
Two Kettle Sioux	216	102	47.2	125	48	38.4	91	54	59.3
Other Teton Sioux	3,797	1,860	49.0	1,860	787	42.3	1,937	1,073	55.4
Winnebago	1,406	633	45.0	714	257	36.0	692	376	54.3
Yankton Sioux	1,583	744	47.0	754	313	41.5	829	431	52.0
Yanktonai Sioux	1,045	551	52.7	486	232	47.7	559	319	57.1
All other tribes	11	3	-	6	1	-	5	2	-

Source: U.S. Bureau of the Census, *Indian Population in the United States and Alaska, 1910,* United States Government Printing Office, Washington, D.C., 1915, pp. 226-231. *Notes:* A dash (-) represents zero or a lack of 50 persons for a percentage base.

★ 99 ★

Illiterate American Indians 10 Years Old and Older, by Linguistic Stock, Tribe, and Sex, 1910: T - Z and Alaska

Data are shown for linguistic stocks with 200 or more Indians and tribes with more than 100 members in 1910.

Linguistic stock and tribe	Indians 10 years of age and over: 1910			Indian males 10 years of age and over			Indian females 10 years of age and over		
	Total number	Illiterate		Total number	Illiterate		Total number	Illiterate	
		Number	Percent		Number	Percent		Number	Percent
UNITED STATES (cont.)									
Tanoan stock	2,348	1,506	64.1	1,268	762	60.1	1,080	744	68.9
Isleta	717	531	74.1	381	280	73.5	336	251	74.7
Jemez	396	300	75.8	231	169	73.2	165	131	79.4
Picuris	76	47	61.8	37	20	-	39	27	-
San Ildefonso	85	51	60.0	41	21	-	44	30	-
San Juan	297	191	64.3	165	95	57.6	132	96	72.7
Santa Clara	199	111	55.8	103	56	54.4	96	55	57.3
Taos	371	169	45.6	198	66	33.3	173	103	59.5
All other tribes	207	106	51.2	112	55	49.1	95	51	53.7
Wailatpuan stock	247	127	51.4	118	55	46.6	129	72	55.8
Cayuse	225	123	54.7	105	54	51.4	120	69	57.5
All other tribes	22	4	-	13	1	-	9	3	-
Wakashan stock	279	116	41.6	142	52	36.6	137	64	46.7
Makah	256	104	40.6	134	52	38.8	122	52	42.6
All other tribes	23	12	-	8	-	-	15	12	-

[Continued]

167

★ 99 ★

Illiterate American Indians 10 Years Old and Older, by Linguistic Stock, Tribe, and Sex, 1910: T - Z and Alaska
[Continued]

Linguistic stock and tribe	Indians 10 years of age and over: 1910			Indian males 10 years of age and over			Indian females 10 years of age and over		
	Total number	Illiterate		Total number	Illiterate		Total number	Illiterate	
		Number	Percent		Number	Percent		Number	Percent
Washoan stock	650	478	73.5	334	220	65.9	316	258	81.6
Washo	650	478	73.5	334	220	65.9	316	258	81.6
Wintun stock	545	262	48.1	297	139	46.8	248	123	49.6
Nomelaki	101	43	42.6	52	20	38.5	49	23	-
Patwin	138	100	72.5	81	56	69.1	57	44	77.2
Wintun	306	119	38.9	164	63	38.4	142	56	39.4
Yokuts stock	407	252	61.9	218	122	56.0	189	130	68.8
Chuckhansi	112	57	50.9	56	21	37.5	56	36	64.3
Yokuts	231	145	62.8	133	78	58.6	98	67	68.4
All other tribes	64	50	78.1	29	23	-	35	27	-
Yuman stock	3,290	2,007	61.0	1,806	1,040	57.6	1,484	967	65.2
Cocopah	182	170	93.4	103	94	91.3	79	76	96.2
Diegueno	568	294	51.8	305	156	51.1	263	138	52.5
Havasupai	137	98	71.5	83	57	68.7	54	41	75.9
Maricopa	287	139	48.4	152	69	45.4	135	70	51.9
Mohave	822	422	51.3	460	227	49.3	362	195	53.9
Walapai	370	226	61.1	207	108	52.2	163	118	72.4
Yavapai	229	155	67.7	126	79	62.7	103	76	73.8
Yuma	667	480	72.0	355	239	67.3	312	241	77.2
All other tribes	28	23	-	15	11	-	13	12	-
Yurok stock	505	330	65.3	249	152	61.0	256	178	69.5
Weitspec	505	330	65.3	249	152	61.0	256	178	69.5
Zunian stock	1,202	1,046	87.0	631	539	85.4	571	507	88.8
Zuni	1,202	1,046	87.0	631	539	85.4	571	507	88.8
ALASKA									
Athabaskan stock	2,886	2,318	80.3	1,507	1,202	79.8	1,379	1,116	80.9
Ahtena	227	214	94.3	129	120	93.0	98	94	95.9
Hankutchin	86	63	73.3	58	41	70.7	28	22	-
Kaiyuhkhotana	125	99	79.2	64	51	79.7	61	48	78.7
Knajakhotana	516	395	76.6	283	216	76.3	233	179	76.8
Kutchin	276	233	84.4	140	117	83.6	136	116	85.3
Natsitkutchin	150	146	97.3	84	81	96.4	66	65	98.5
Tenankutchin	302	258	85.4	156	133	85.3	146	125	85.6
Unakhotana	136	118	86.8	72	63	87.5	64	55	85.9
All other tribes	1,068	792	74.2	521	380	72.9	547	412	75.3

[Continued]

★ 99 ★

Illiterate American Indians 10 Years Old and Older, by Linguistic Stock, Tribe, and Sex, 1910: T - Z and Alaska
[Continued]

Linguistic stock and tribe	Indians 10 years of age and over: 1910			Indian males 10 years of age and over			Indian females 10 years of age and over		
	Total number	Illiterate Number	Percent	Total number	Illiterate Number	Percent	Total number	Illiterate Number	Percent
Eskimauan stock	9,964	7,857	78.9	5,147	3,870	75.2	4,817	3,987	82.8
Aleut	1,001	650	64.9	516	305	59.1	485	345	71.1
Chnagmiut	202	167	82.7	110	87	79.1	92	80	87.0
Ikogmiut	529	499	94.3	247	233	94.3	282	266	94.3
Kaialigmiut	127	125	98.4	62	61	98.4	65	64	98.5
Kaviagmiut	163	91	55.8	81	46	56.8	82	45	54.9
Kinugumiut	424	311	73.3	236	160	67.8	188	151	80.3
Kowagmiut	410	320	78.0	214	171	79.9	196	149	76.0
Kusetrinmiut	90	63	70.0	56	35	62.5	34	28	-
Kuskovakmiut	232	199	85.8	121	97	80.2	111	102	91.9
Kuskwogmiut	1,068	996	93.3	544	502	92.3	524	494	94.3
Magemiut	262	227	86.6	118	108	91.5	144	119	82.6
Malemiut	407	225	55.3	210	114	54.3	197	111	56.3
Nunatogmiut	224	178	79.5	130	97	74.6	94	81	86.2
Nunivagmiut	236	224	94.9	127	122	96.1	109	102	93.6
Nunochogmiut	107	104	97.2	42	42	-	65	62	95.4
Selawigmiut	177	159	89.8	98	83	84.7	79	76	96.2
Tikeramiut	252	137	54.4	127	62	48.8	125	75	60.0
Ukivokmiut	94	82	87.2	50	41	82.0	44	41	-
Unaligmiut	274	188	68.6	126	73	57.9	148	115	77.7
Utkiavinmiut	86	66	76.7	43	30	-	43	36	-
Utukamiut	91	79	86.8	46	36	-	45	43	-
Yuit	226	155	68.6	119	66	55.5	107	89	83.2
Southern Eskimo	2,613	2,106	80.6	1,383	1,056	76.4	1,230	1,050	85.4
All other tribes	669	506	75.6	341	243	71.3	328	263	80.2
Hadian stock	369	123	33.3	198	58	29.3	171	65	38.0
Haida	369	123	33.3	198	58	29.3	171	65	38.0
Tlingit stock	3,240	2,021	62.4	1,634	949	58.1	1,606	1,072	66.7
Auk	213	138	64.8	120	74	61.7	93	64	68.8
Chilkat	536	339	63.2	270	158	58.5	266	181	68.0
Henya	146	90	61.6	78	47	60.3	68	43	63.2
Huna	470	338	71.9	221	144	65.2	249	194	77.9
Hutsnuwu	373	249	66.8	186	120	64.5	187	129	69.0
Kake	232	134	57.8	114	66	57.9	118	68	57.6
Sitka	446	249	55.8	225	114	50.7	221	135	61.1
Stikine	139	72	51.8	69	30	43.5	70	42	60.0
Taku	111	83	74.8	54	38	70.4	57	45	78.9
Tongas	129	60	46.5	65	27	41.5	64	33	51.6
Yakutat	211	162	76.8	96	76	79.2	115	86	74.8
All other tribes	234	107	45.7	136	55	40.4	98	52	53.1

[Continued]

★ 99 ★

Illiterate American Indians 10 Years Old and Older, by Linguistic Stock, Tribe, and Sex, 1910: T - Z and Alaska
[Continued]

Linguistic stock and tribe	Indians 10 years of age and over: 1910			Indian males 10 years of age and over			Indian females 10 years of age and over		
	Total number	Illiterate		Total number	Illiterate		Total number	Illiterate	
		Number	Percent		Number	Percent		Number	Percent
Tsimshian stock	520	117	22.5	294	45	15.3	226	72	31.9
Tsimshian	520	117	22.5	294	45	15.3	226	72	31.9

Source: U.S. Bureau of the Census, *Indian Population in the United States and Alaska, 1910,* United States Government Printing Office, Washington, D.C., 1915, pp. 226-231. *Notes:* A dash (-) represents zero or a lack of 50 persons for a percentage base.

★ 100 ★

Illiterate Persons 10 Years Old and Older in the U.S. and Alaska, by Race/Ethnicity and Sex, 1900 and 1910

Race/ethnicity and year	Males 10 years of age and older			Females 10 years of age and older		
	Total number	Illiterate		Total number	Illiterate	
		Number	Percent		Number	Percent
United States						
All groups: 1910	37,027,558	2,814,950	7.6	34,552,712	2,701,213	7.8
Indian	96,582	40,104	41.5	92,176	45,341	49.2
Chinese	65,479	9,849	15.0	3,445	1,042	30.2
Japanese	60,809	5,247	8.6	6,852	966	14.1
Negro	3,637,386	1,096,000	30.1	3,680,536	1,131,731	30.7
White	33,164,229	1,662,505	5.0	30,769,641	1,522,128	4.9
Native	25,843,033	796,055	3.1	25,146,308	738,217	2.9
Foreign born	7,321,196	866,450	11.8	5,623,333	783,911	13.9
All other	3,073	1,245	40.5	62	5	8.1
All groups: 1900	29,703,440	3,011,224	10.1	28,246,384	3,168,845	11.2
Indian	86,504	45,376	52.5	85,048	50,971	59.9
Chinese	84,141	23,052	27.4	3,541	2,344	66.2
Japanese	23,214	4,211	18.1	877	175	20.0
Negro	3,181,650	1,371,432	43.1	3,233,931	1,481,762	45.8
White	26,327,931	1,567,153	6.0	24,922,987	1,633,593	6.6
Native	20,912,940	955,517	4.6	20,323,722	958,094	4.7
Foreign born	5,414,991	611,636	11.3	4,599,265	675,499	14.7
Alaska						
All groups: 1910	41,108	7,867	19.1	13,859	6,683	48.2
Indian	9,300	6,311	67.9	8,744	6,571	75.1
Chinese	1,206	186	15.4	2	1	[1]

[Continued]

★ 100 ★

Illiterate Persons 10 Years Old and Older in the U.S. and Alaska, by Race/ Ethnicity and Sex, 1900 and 1910

[Continued]

Race/ethnicity and year	Males 10 years of age and older			Females 10 years of age and older		
	Total number	Illiterate		Total number	Illiterate	
		Number	Percent		Number	Percent
Japanese	884	58	6.6	25	4	[1]
Negro	141	16	11.3	62	5	8.1
White	29,285	1,234	4.2	5,025	102	2.0
Native	13,025	78	0.6	3,437	34	1.0
Foreign born	16,260	1,156	7.1	1,588	68	4.3
All other	292	62	21.2	1	-	-
All groups: 1900	41,968	13,124	31.3	14,013	10,187	72.7
Indian	11,717	9,980	85.2	11,340	10,035	88.5
Chinese	3,113	2,389	76.7	2	1	[1]
Japanese	267	124	46.4	12	11	[1]
Negro	151	6	4.0	14	-	-
White	26,720	625	2.3	2,645	140	5.3
Native	18,624	116	0.6	2,000	77	3.9
Foreign born	8,096	509	6.3	645	63	9.8

Source: U.S. Bureau of the Census, *Indian Population in the United States and Alaska, 1910*, United States Government Printing Office, Washington, D.C., 1915, p. 212. *Notes:* A dash (-) represents zero. 1. Percentages are not shown where base is less than 50.

★ 101 ★

Percent Illiterate in the Indian Population, for 20 Selected States, by Sex and Age Group, 1910 and 1930

State	1910				1930			
	10 years old and over		21 years old and over		10 years old and over		21 years old and over	
	Male	Female	Male	Female	Male	Female	Male	Female
United States	41.5	49.2	50.8	61.4	24.0	27.6	30.4	36.2
Arizona	68.4	77.8	78.0	87.8	49.9	57.2	58.7	68.6
California	45.4	52.7	57.2	67.4	18.5	23.7	23.2	32.8
Idaho	55.6	63.3	65.1	75.8	26.0	32.8	33.7	45.2
Kansas	18.7	18.7	28.9	35.6	9.3	9.4	12.7	13.6
Michigan	30.1	39.4	37.9	51.8	13.1	17.2	17.1	24.0
Minnesota	35.3	45.1	47.3	60.3	15.4	20.8	22.8	31.7
Montana	52.1	59.6	62.6	72.5	21.0	24.4	30.0	36.1
Nebraska	29.6	41.5	38.4	56.7	10.2	13.3	14.4	20.5
Nevada	67.2	76.3	76.8	86.4	37.7	46.1	48.9	61.2
New Mexico	78.5	85.0	86.4	92.9	53.9	61.4	65.4	74.1

[Continued]

★ 101 ★

Percent Illiterate in the Indian Population, for 20 Selected States, by Sex and Age Group, 1910 and 1930
[Continued]

State	1910				1930			
	10 years old and over		21 years old and over		10 years old and over		21 years old and over	
	Male	Female	Male	Female	Male	Female	Male	Female
New York	28.0	27.8	34.6	37.2	11.8	11.5	15.5	16.3
North Carolina	43.3	51.1	52.0	64.3	31.1	28.0	38.5	37.9
North Dakota	43.6	48.6	58.1	65.3	20.5	20.9	27.8	31.5
Oklahoma	22.0	28.4	28.1	38.1	10.4	12.0	14.2	17.2
Oregon	29.7	43.5	42.5	60.0	11.5	19.4	16.5	27.1
South Dakota	39.0	52.0	49.6	65.6	13.1	19.5	18.3	27.7
Utah	80.3	86.2	85.0	93.2	56.1	58.0	65.7	70.6
Washington	39.6	52.0	48.6	64.4	13.7	19.5	18.1	27.5
Wisconsin	31.2	36.4	40.6	49.7	12.6	14.5	18.1	22.5
Wyoming	45.4	57.6	57.9	74.9	23.2	25.9	30.6	37.3

Source: Dr. Leon E. Truesdell, U.S. Department of Commerce, Bureau of Census, Fifteenth Census of the United States: 1930, *The Indian Population of the United States and Alaska*, U.S. Government Printing Office, 1937, p. 145. *Notes:* The Census Bureau defines as illiterate any person 10 years old or over who is not able to read and write, either in English or in some other language. The Census Bureau has never prescribed any specific test of ability to read or write. At the Census of 1930, the enumerator was instructed to write "yes" or "no" in response to the question on the schedule, "whether able to read and write." The enumerator was, however, specifically instructed not to write "yes" (which would classify the person as literate) simply because the person was able to write his or her name.

★ 102 ★

Percent Illiterate in the Population, by Race/Ethnicity, 1900-1930

Data are shown for persons 10 years old and older.

Class	1900	1910	1920	1930
All classes	10.7	7.7	6.0	4.3
Indian	56.2	45.3	34.9	25.7
White	6.2	5.0	4.0	3.0
Native	4.6	3.0	2.0	1.6
Foreign born	12.9	12.7	13.1	10.8
Negro	44.5	30.4	22.9	16.3
All other races	26.6	13.1	14.5	12.3

Source: Dr. Leon E. Truesdell, U.S. Department of Commerce, Bureau of Census, Fifteenth Census of the United States: 1930, *The Indian Population of the United States and Alaska*, U.S. Government Printing Office, 1937, p. 143. *Notes:* The Census Bureau defines as illiterate any person 10 years old or over who is not able to read and write, either in English or in some other language. The Census Bureau has never prescribed any specific test of ability to read or write. At the Census of 1930, the enumerator was instructed to write "yes" or "no" in response to the question on the schedule, "whether able to read and write." The enumerator was, however, specifically instructed not to write "yes" (which would classify the person as literate) simply because the person was able to write his or her name.

Health Conditions

★ 103 ★

Epidemics Among Texas Indians, 1528-1892

Tribe/area	Date	Epidemic
Karankawan	1528	Cholera(?)
Coahuiltecan	1674-75	Smallpox
La Salle's Fort	1688-89	Smallpox
Caddo	1691	?
Coahuiltecan	1706	Smallpox
Caddo	1718	?
San Antonio missions	1739	Smallpox and measles
Tonkawa and Atakapan	Before 1746	Smallpox and measles
San Xavier missions; Tonkawa and Atakapan	1750	Smallpox
San Antonio missions	1751	?
San Xavier missions; Tonkawan and Atakapan	1753	Malaria or dysentery
East Texas	1759	Smallpox
San Antonio missions	1763	?
San Lorenzo de la Santa Cruz Mission; Lipan Apache	1763-64	Smallpox
Karankawan	1766	Smallpox or measles
Caddo, Wichita, Tonkawa, or Atakapan	1777-78	Cholera or plague
Texas	1778	Smallpox
Texas	1801-1802	Smallpox
Caddo	1803	Measles
Caddo, Wichita, Comanche, Kiowa, Kiowa-Apache	1816	Smallpox
Kiowa, Kiowa-Apache, Comanche	1839-40	Smallpox
Kiowa, Kiowa-Apache, Apache, Cheyenne, Comanche	1849	Cholera
Kiowa, Kiowa-Apache, Comanche, Cheyenne, and Arapaho	1861-62	Smallpox
Wichita, Caddo	1864	Smallpox
Wichita, Caddo	1867	Cholera
Mescalero Apache	1877	Smallpox
Kiowa, Kiowa-Apache, Cheyenne, Arapaho	1877	Measles and fever
Kiowa, Kiowa-Apache, Comanche, Arapaho	1889-90	Influenza
Comanche, Wichita, and Caddo	1892	Measles, influenza and whooping cough

Source: Russell Thornton, *American Indian Holocaust and Survival: A Population History Since 1492*, University of Oklahoma, Press, 1987, p. 130. Published by permission. Primary source: Ewers, "The Influence of Epidemics on the Indian Populations and Cultures of Texas," *Plains Anthropologist*, 1973, p. 108-109.

★ 104 ★

Life Expectancy of Selected American Indian and Non-Indian Populations

Population (date)	Life expectancy
American Indian	
Indian Knoll, Kentucky (3000 B.C.)	18.6-19.02?
Texas Indians (A.D. 850-1700)	30.5
Pecos Pueblo (A.D. 800-1700)	25.0-27.4-42.9?
Tidewater Potomac, I (A.D. 1500-1600)	20.9
Mississippian (A.D. 1050-1200)	33.0
Mississippian (A.D. 1200-1300)	24.3
Tidewater Potomac, II (A.D. 1500-1600)	22.9
Non-Indian	
Egypt (A.D. 1050-1600)	19.2
Ancient Greece (670 B.C.-A.D. 600)	23.0
England (11th century)	35.3
European ruling families (A.D. 1480-1579)	33.7

Source: Russell Thornton, *American Indian Holocaust and Survival: A Population History Since 1492*, University of Oklahoma Press, 1987, p. 39. Published by permission. Primary source: Goldstein, "Some Vital Statistics Based on Skeletal Material," *Human Biology*, 1953, p. 4; Ubelaker, "Reconstruction of Demographic Profiles from Ossuary Skeletal Samples: A Case Study from the Tidewater Potomac," *Smithsonian Contributions to Anthropology*, no. 18. Washington, D.C.: Smithsonian Institution Press, 1974, p. 64; Lallo and Rose, "Patterns of Stress, Disease and Mortality in Two Prehistoric Populations from North America," *Journal of Human Evolution*, 1979, p. 332; Ruff, "Reasessment of Demographic Estimates for Pecos Pueblo," *American Journal of Physical Anthropology*, 1981, p. 150; Storey, "An Estimate of Mortality in a Pre- Columbian Urban Population," *American Anthropologist*, 1985, p. 530.

★ 105 ★

Mortality from 19th Century Epidemics Among the Omaha Indians

Date	Epidemic	Mortality
1801-1802	Smallpox	75% over 1,500
1837	Smallpox	Over 300
1849	Cholera	Over 500
1874	Measles	76
1888	Measles	87
1889	Measles	50

Source: Russell Thornton, *American Indian Holocaust and Survival: A Population History Since 1492*, University of Oklahoma, Press, 1987, p. 94. Published by permission. Primary source: Liberty, "Population Trends Among Present-Day Omaha Indians," *Plains Anthropologist*, 1975, p. 228. *Note:* There were, in addition, known tuberculosis epidemics.

★ 106 ★

Probable Smallpox Epidemics Among North American Indians, 1520-1797

Date	Areas of outbreak
1520-1524	Total geographic area unknown; possibly from Chile across present United States
1592-1593	Central Mexico to Sinaloa; Southern New England; Eastern Great Lakes
1602	Sinola and Northward
1639	French and British Northeastern North America
1646-1648	New Spain North to Nuevo Leon, Western Sierra Madre to Florida
1649-1650	Northeastern United States, Florida
1655	Florida
1662-1663	Mid-Atlantic, Northeast, Canada
1665-1667	Florida to Virginia
1669-1670	United States and Canada
1674-1675	Texas, Northeastern New Spain
1677-1679	Northeast in New France and British Territory
1687-1691	Northeast in French and British Frontiers; Texas
1696-1699	Southeastern and Gulf Coast
1701-1703	Northeastern to Illinois
1706	Texas and Northeastern New Spain
1715-1721	Northeast to Texas
1729-1733	New England; California Tribes; Southeast
1738-1739	Southeast to Hudson Bay; Texas Peoples
1746	New York, New England; New Spain
1750-1752	Texas to Great Lakes
1755-1760	From Canada and New England and Great Lakes to Virginia, Carolinas, and Texas
1762-1766	From Central Mexico through Texas and the Southeast to Great Lakes; Northwest Coast
1779-1783	From Central Mexico across all of North America
1785-1787	Alaskan coast across northern Canada
1788	New Mexico Pueblos
1793-1797	New Spain

Source: C. Matthew Snipp, *American Indians: The First of This Land*, Russell Sage Foundation, p. 22. Published by permission. Primary source: Henry F. Dobyns, *Their Number Became Thinned: Native American Population Dynamics in Eastern North America*, Knoxville, TN: University of Tennessee Press, 1983, pp. 15-16.

Land Status

★ 107 ★

Extensions of the Trust or Restricted Status of Certain Indian Lands - I

This table contains citations of Executive orders (E.O.) and acts of Congress continuing the trust or restricted period of Indian Land, which would have otherwise expired within the several Indian reservations in the states named. A numeral "1" to the right of the name of a reservation indicates that the reservation is subject to the benefits of the Indian Reorganization Act of June 18, 1934 (48 Stat. 984; 25 U.S.C. 461-479), and the trust or restricted period of the land is extended indefinitely. Where the name of a reservation is *not* preceded by a "1", such a reservation is not subject to the Reorganization Act and is not subject to the benefits of indefinite trust or a restricted period extension. Such a reservation is dependent upon acts of Congress or Executive orders for extension of the trust or restricted period of the land. For the purpose of ensuring the continuation of the trust or restricted status of Indians allotments within Indian reservations not subject to the Reorganization Act, Congress, by the act of June 15, 1935 (49 Stat. 378), reimposed such restrictions as may have been expired between the dates of June 18, 1934, and December 31, 1936.

State	Reservation	Executive order number	Date	Period of extension
Arizona	Papago[1]	2066	Oct. 27, 1914	10 years
Do.	Do.	4464	June 28, 1926	Do.
California	Agua Caliente	3446	Apr. 30, 1921	Do.
Do.	Do.	5580	Mar. 16, 1931	Do.
Do.	Cabazon and Twenty-Nine Palms	3302	July 7, 1920	5 years
Do.	Do.	4159	Feb. 19, 1925	10 years
Do.	Capitan Grande[1]	3048	Feb. 27, 1919	5 years
Do.	Do.		Act. of Feb. 8, 1927 (44 Stat. 1061)	10 years.
Do.	Hoopa Valley (Klamath River)	2943	Aug. 23, 1918	1 year.
Do.	Do.		Sept. 23, 1919	Do.
Do.	Do.	3304	July 10, 1920	10 years.
Do.	Do.	3980	Mar. 26, 1924	15 years.
Do.	Do.	5416	Aug. 4, 1930	10 years.
	Mission Bands:			
Do.	Augustine	2795	Jan. 26, 1918	Do.
Do.	Campo	2795	Do.	Do.
Do.	Cuyapipe[1]	2795	Do.	Do.
Do.	Inaja	2795	Do.	Do.
Do.	Laguna[1]	2795	Do.	Do.
Do.	La Posta[1]	2795	Do.	Do.
Do.	Mazanita[1]	2795	Do.	Do.
Do.	Mesa Grande	2795	Do.	Do.
Do.	Pala	2795	Do.	Do.
Do.	Ramona	2795	Do.	Do.
Do.	Santa Ysabel	2795	Do.	Do.
Do.	Sycuan	2795	Do.	Do.
Do.	Do.	3383	Jan. 7, 1921	25 years.
Do.	San Manuel	2795	Jan. 26, 1918	10 years.

[Continued]

★ 107 ★

Extensions of the Trust or Restricted Status of Certain Indian Lands - I
[Continued]

State	Reservation	Executive order number	Date	Period of extension
Do.	Temecula	2795	Do.	Do.
Do.	All of above Mission Bands	4795	Nov. 23, 1927	Do.
Do.	Morongo	6341	Oct. 17, 1933	Do.
Do.	Pala	3383	Jan. 7, 1921	25 years.
Do.	Do.		Act of Feb. 11, 1936 (49 Stat. 1106)	10 years.
Do.	Potrero and Rincon	2684	Aug. 16, 1917	Do.
Do.	Do.	4687	July 11, 1927	Do.
Do.	Round Valley[1]	3223	Feb. 5, 1920	3 years.
Do.	Do.	3805	Mar. 5, 1923	10 years.
Do.	Do.	3995	Apr. 19, 1924	Do.
Do.	Do.	5953	Nov. 23, 1932	Do.
Do.	Temecula	3699	June 27, 1922	Do.
Do.	Do.	5768	Dec. 30, 1931	Do.
Do.	Torres-Martinez	7009	Apr. 10, 1935	Do.
Idaho	Nez Perce	3250	Mar. 24, 1920	Do.
Idaho Do.	Nez Perce Do.	4694	July 22, 1927	10 years.
Do.	Do.	5305	Mar. 18, 1930	Do.
Kansas and Nebraska	Iowa[1]	2966	Sept. 23, 1918	Do.
Do.	Do.	5023	Jan. 10, 1929	Do.
Do.	Sac and Fox[1]	2607	May 4, 1917	Do.
Do.	Do.	4571	Jan. 24, 1927	Do.
Do.	Do.	5768	Dec. 30, 1931	Do.
Do.	Kickapoo	3301	July 3, 1920	1 year.
Do.	Do.	3447	May 2, 1921	10 years.
Do.	Do.	5415	Aug. 4, 1930	Do.
Do.	Do.	5626	May 18, 1931	Do.
Do.	Potawatomi[1]	2747	Nov. 2, 1917	Do.
Do.	Do.	2927	July 30, 1918	Do.
Do.	Do.	3312	July 21, 1920	Do.
Do.	Do.	4688	July 11, 1927	Do.
Do.	Do.	4858	Apr. 16, 1928	Do.
Do.	Do.	5299	Mar. 10, 1930	Do.
Do.	Do.	5356	May 28, 1930	Do.
Do.	Do.	5556	Feb. 11, 1931	Do.
Minnesota	Fond du Lac[1]	3445	Apr. 30, 1921	Do.
Do.	Do.	5575	Mar. 12, 1931	Do.
Do.	Grand Portago[1]	3613	Jan. 12, 1922	Do.
Do.	Do.	5768	Dec. 30, 1931	Do.
Do.	Winnibigoshish[1]	3614	Jan 12, 1922	Do.
Do.	Do.	5466	Oct. 22, 1930	Do.
Do.	Do.	5768	Dec. 30, 1931	Do.
Do.	Deer Creek[1]	4154	Feb. 10, 1925	Do.
Do.	Bois Fort[1]	4233	May 26, 1925	Do.

[Continued]

★ 107 ★

Extensions of the Trust or Restricted Status of Certain Indian Lands - I
[Continued]

State	Reservation	Executive order number	Date	Period of extension
Do.	Leech Lake, Cass Lake[1] and White Oak Point	4298	Aug. 29, 1925	Do.
Do.	Do.	5466	Oct. 22, 1930	Do.
Do.	White Earth[1]	4642	May 5, 1927	Do.
Do.	Do.	5768	Dec. 30, 1931	Do.
Do.	Do.	5953	Nov. 23, 1932	Do.
Do.	Red Lake[1]	5383	June 26, 1930	Do.
Montana	Crow	5301	Mar. 12, 1930	Do.
Do.	Do.	5768	Dec. 30, 1931	Do.
Do.	Do.	7001	Apr. 5, 1935	Do.
Do.	Do.		Act of April 1940 (54 Stat.106)	To May 23, 1940.
Do.	Flathead[1]	5953	Nov. 23, 1932	Do.
Nebraska	Omaha[1]		July 3, 1909	Do.
Do.	Do.	3111	July 10, 1919	Do.
Do.	Do.	4145	Jan. 28, 1925	Do.
Do.	Do.	4548	Dec. 4, 1926	Do.
Do.	Do.	5148	July 3, 1929	Do.
Do.	Do.	5253	Dec. 31, 1929	Do.
Do.	Ponca[1]	2374	Apr. 29, 1916	Do.
Do.	Do.	4407	Mar. 30, 1926	Do.
Do.	Santee[1]		Dec. 12, 1910	Do.
Do.	Do.	3348	Nov. 5, 1920	Do.
Do.	Do.	3722	Aug. 12, 1922	Do.
Do.	Santee Sarah Jones[1] allotment.	4075	Sept. 17, 1924	Do.
Do.	Santee[1]	5474	Oct. 31, 1930	Do.
Do.	Do.	5768	Dec. 30, 1931	Do.
Do.	Do.	5953	Nov. 23, 1932	Do.
Do.	Winnebago[1]	2965	Sept. 20, 1918	Do.
Do.	Do.	4548	Dec. 4, 1926	Do.
Do.	Do.	4979	Oct. 16, 1928	Do.
Do.	Do.	4994	Nov. 14, 1928	Do.
Do.	Sac and Fox, William Banks allotment[1]	3878	July 27, 1923	1 year.
Nevada	Walker River[1]	5730	Oct. 8, 1931	10 years.
North Dakota	Devils Lake	2804	Feb. 11, 1918	Do.
Do.	Do.	3853	May 23, 1923	Do.
Do.	Do.	4775	Nov. 30, 1927	Do.
Do.	Do.	5303	Mar. 12, 1930	Do.
Do.	Do.	5768	Dec. 30, 1931	Do.
Do.	Do.	5953	Nov. 23, 1932	Do.
Do.	Fort Berthold[1]	4293	Aug. 25, 1925	Do.

[Continued]

★ 107 ★

Extensions of the Trust or Restricted Status of Certain Indian Lands - I
[Continued]

State	Reservation	Executive order number	Date	Period of extension
Do.	Standing Rock[1]	5768	Dec. 30, 1931	Do.
Do.	Do.	5953	Nov. 23, 1932	Do.

Source: Code of Federal Regulations: Indians, Title 25, Revised as of April 1, 1992, Office of the Federal Register National Archives and Records Administration, p. 722-723. *Notes:* Do. means ditto. 1. Trust or restricted period of land is extended indefinitely.

★ 108 ★

Extensions of the Trust or Restricted Status of Certain Indian Lands - II

This table contains citations of Executive orders (E.O.) and acts of Congress continuing the trust or restricted period of Indian Land, which would have otherwise expired within the several Indian reservations in the states named. A numeral "1" to the right of the name of a reservation indicates that the reservation is subject to the benefits of the Indian Reorganization Act of June 18, 1934 (48 Stat. 984; 25 U.S.C. 461-479), and the trust or restricted period of the land is extended indefinitely. Where the name of a reservation is *not* preceded by a "1", such a reservation is not subject to the Reorganization Act and is not subject to the benefits of indefinite trust or a restricted period extension. Such a reservation is dependent upon acts of Congress or Executive orders for extension of the trust or restricted period of the land. For the purpose of ensuring the continuation of the trust or restricted status of Indians allotments within Indian reservations not subject to the Reorganization Act, Congress, by the act of June 15, 1935 (49 Stat. 378), reimposed such restrictions as may have been expired between the dates of June 18, 1934, and December 31, 1936.

State	Reservation	Executive order number	Date	Period of extension
Oklahoma	Absentee Shawnee and Citizen Potawatomi.	5953	Nov. 23, 1932	Do.
Do.	Do.	2512	Jan. 15, 1917	Do.
Do.	Do.	4557	Dec. 23, 1926	Do.
Do.	Cheyenne and Arapaho	2580	Apr. 4, 1917	Do.
Do.	Do.	4587	Feb. 17, 1927	Do.
Do.	Eastern Shawnee	2317	Feb. 15, 1916	Do.
Do.	Do.	4384	Feb. 20, 1926	Do.
Do.	Do.	5768	Dec. 30, 1931	Do.
Do.	Mexican Kickapoo	3047	Feb. 27, 1919	5 years.
Do.	Do.	4029	June 19, 1924	10 years.
Do.	Do.		Act of Feb. 17, 1933 (47 Stat. 819)	Do.
Do.	Modoc	2453	Sept. 14, 1916	Do.
Do.	Do.	4470	July 1, 1926	Do.
Do.	Ottawa, Sonoca and Wyandotte	2591	Apr. 11, 1917	Do.
Do.	Do.	4588	Feb. 17, 1927	Do.
Do.	Pawnee	2816	Mar. 2, 1918	Do.
Do.	Do.	4898	May 29, 1928	Do.

[Continued]

★ 108 ★

Extensions of the Trust or Restricted Status of Certain Indian Lands - II
[Continued]

State	Reservation	Executive order number	Date	Period of extension
Do.	Ponca	3327	Sept. 19, 1920	1 year.
Do.	Do.	3363	Dec. 1, 1920	25 years.
Do.	Do.	5539	Jan. 23, 1931	10 years.
Do.	Sac and Fox, and Iowa		Mar. 27, 1896	Do.
Do.	Do.		July 23, 1906	Do.
Do.	Do.		Aug. 28, 1906	Do.
Do.	Do.	2432	Aug. 1, 1916	Do.
Do.	Do.	4435	Apr. 29, 1926	Do.
Do.	Tonkawa	2866	May 25, 1918	Do.
Do.	Tonkawa (Oakland)	4816	Feb. 25, 1928	Do.
Do.	Kaw		Act of March 1923 (42 Stat. 1561)	25 years.
Do.	Do.		Act of May 27, 1924 (43 Stat. 176)	20 years.
Do.	Otoe and Missouri	4281	Aug. 11, 1925	10 years.
Do.	Do.	5728	Sept. 29, 1931	Do.
Do.	Do.	5768	Dec. 30, 1931	Do.
Do.	Kiowa, Comanche, Apache, and Wichita.	4398	Mar. 18, 1926	Do.
Do.	Do.	5953	Nov. 23, 1932	Do.
Do.	Do.	5955	Nov. 30, 1932 (Gertrude Lamb)	Do.
Do.	Seneca	5306	Mar. 18, 1930	Do.
Do.	Quapaw		Act of Mar. 3, 1921 (41 Stat. 1248) as amended Nov. 18, 1921 (42 Stat. 1570)	25 years.
Do.	Do.		As supplemented or amended by the act of July 27, 1939 (53 Stat. 1127)	
Oregon	Grande Rande[1]	2376	Apr. 29, 1916	10 years.
Do.	Do.	4408	Mar. 30, 1926	Do.
Do.	Siletz	3110	July 10, 1919	Do.
Do.	Siletz (cont.)	5087	Apr. 1, 1929	Do.
Do.	Warm Springs[1]	3586	Dec. 7, 1921	Do.
Do.	Do.	5734	Oct. 17, 1931	Do.
Do.	Umatilla	4024	June 10, 1924	Do.
Do.	Do.	5516	Dec. 17, 1930	Do.
Do.	Klamath	6961	Feb. 4, 1935	Do.
Do.	Do.		Act of Dec. 24, 1942 (56 Stat. 1081)	25 years.
South Dakota	Crow Creek	3362	Nov. 30, 1920	Do.
Do.	Do.	5768	Dec. 30, 1931	10 years.

[Continued]

180

★ 108 ★

Extensions of the Trust or Restricted Status of Certain Indian Lands - II
[Continued]

State	Reservation	Executive order number	Date	Period of extension
Do.	Do.	6968	Feb. 9, 1935	Do.
Do.	Rosebud[1]	4417	Apr. 14, 1926	Do.
Do.	Do.	5028	Jan. 16, 1929	Do.
Do.	Do.	5302	Mar. 12, 1930	Do.
Do.	Do.	5768	Dec. 30, 1931	Do.
Do.	Sisseton and Wahpeton	1916	Apr. 16, 1914	Do.
Do.	Do.	3994	Apr. 19, 1924	15 years.
Do.	Yankton Sioux[1]	2363	Apr. 20, 1916	10 years.
Do.	Do.	4406	Mar. 30, 1926	Do.
	Crow Creek	5173	Aug. 9, 1929	10 years.
Do.	Lower Brule[1]	4981	Oct. 20, 1923	Do.
Do.	Pine Ridge[1]	5557	Feb. 13, 1931	Do.
Do.	Do.	5768	Dec. 30, 1931	Do.
Do.	Do.	5953	Nov. 23, 1932	Do.
Do.	Cheyenne River[1]	5546	Jan. 31, 1931	Do.
Do.	Do.	5766	Dec. 30, 1931	Do.
Utah	Uncompahgra, Uintah and White River Bands of Utes[1]	5357	May 26, 1930	Do.
Washington	Chief Moses Band	2109	Dec. 23, 1914	Do.
Do.	Do.	4382	Feb. 10, 1926	10 years from Mar. 8, 1926.
Do.	Colville	4157	Feb. 17, 1925	10 years.
Do.	Do.	6962	Feb. 4, 1935	Do.
Do.	Quinault[1]	5768	Dec. 30, 1931	Do.
Do.	Spokane	6939	Jan. 7, 1935	10 years.
Do.	Yakima	3630	Feb. 3, 1922	Do.
Do.	Do.	4168	Mar. 11, 1925	Do.
Do.	Do.	5746	Nov. 10, 1931	Do.
Do.	Do.	7036	May 8, 1935	Do.
Do.	Do.		Act of May 27, 1937 (50 Stat. 210)	To July 9, 1942
Wisconsin	Oneida[1]	2623	May 19, 1917	1 year.
Do.	Do.	2856	Mar. 4, 1918	9 years.
Do.	Do.	4600	Mar. 1, 1927	10 years.
Wyoming	Wind River	5768	Dec. 30, 1931	Do.
Do.	Do.	5953	Nov. 23, 1932	Do.

Source: Code of Federal Regulations: Indians, Title 25, Revised as of April 1, 1992, Office of the Federal Register National Archives and Records Administration, p. 722-723. *Notes:* Do. means ditto. 1. Trust or restricted period of land is extended indefinitely.

Language

★ 109 ★

Ability of American Indians 10 Years Old and Older to Speak English, by Geographic Division, State, Sex, and Age Group, 1910

Geographic division and state	Indian males 10 years of age and over: 1910				Indian females 10 years of age and over: 1910			
	Total number	Unable to speak English			Total number	Unable to speak English		
		Total	10 to 19 years of age	20 years of age and over		Total	10 to 19 years of age	20 years of age and over
UNITED STATES	96,582	26,705	5,011	21,694	92,176	32,350	5,230	27,120
Geographic divisions								
New England	869	5	1	4	791	12	1	11
Middle Atlantic	3,352	191	26	165	2,816	292	28	264
East North Central	7,157	890	183	707	6,405	1,434	155	1,279
West North Central	15,625	4,508	458	4,050	15,019	5,944	485	5,459
South Atlantic	3,155	222	23	199	3,036	219	16	203
East South Central	915	119	41	78	839	146	50	96
West South Central	25,297	3,603	707	2,896	24,991	4,691	780	3,911
Mountain	27,734	15,575	3,456	12,119	26,146	17,002	3,576	13,426
Pacific	12,478	1,592	116	1,476	12,133	2,610	139	2,471
New England								
Maine	386	4	1	3	332	12	1	11
New Hampshire	14	-	-	-	13	-	-	-
Vermont	11	1	-	1	8	-	-	-
Massachusetts	290	-	-	-	258	-	-	-
Rhode Island	108	-	-	-	119	-	-	-
Connecticut	60	-	-	-	61	-	-	-
Middle Atlantic								
New York	2,359	174	26	148	2,209	285	28	257
New Jersey	107	12	-	12	47	6	-	6
Pennsylvania	886	5	-	5	560	1	-	1
East North Central								
Ohio	59	-	-	-	49	-	-	-
Indiana	120	2	-	2	102	2	-	2
Illinois	84	-	-	-	80	1	-	1
Michigan	3,028	445	118	327	2,674	675	96	579
Wisconsin	3,806	443	65	378	3,500	756	59	697
West North Central								
Minnesota	3,290	729	123	606	3,218	1,014	100	914
Iowa	259	115	4	111	114	30	10	20
Missouri	116	3	-	3	122	2	-	2

[Continued]

★ 109 ★

Ability of American Indians 10 Years Old and Older to Speak English, by Geographic Division, State, Sex, and Age Group, 1910
[Continued]

Geographic division and state	Indian males 10 years of age and over: 1910				Indian females 10 years of age and over: 1910			
	Total number	Unable to speak English			Total number	Unable to speak English		
		Total	10 to 19 years of age	20 years of age and over		Total	10 to 19 years of age	20 years of age and over
North Dakota	2,366	941	156	785	2,288	1,110	180	930
South Dakota	7,166	2,422	144	2,278	7,179	3,327	157	3,170
Nebraska	1,317	201	25	176	1,283	386	31	355
Kansas	1,111	97	6	91	815	75	7	68
South Atlantic								
Delaware	4	-	-	-	1	-	-	-
Maryland	18	-	-	-	32	-	-	-
District of Columbia	35	1	-	1	26	-	-	-
Virginia	208	-	-	-	180	-	-	-
West Virginia	14	-	-	-	12	-	-	-
North Carolina	2,698	220	23	197	2,626	219	16	203
South Carolina	112	-	-	-	105	-	-	-
Georgia	33	-	-	-	33	-	-	-
Florida	33	1	-	1	21	-	-	-
East South Central								
Kentucky	85	1	-	1	70	-	-	-
Tennessee	73	-	-	-	86	-	-	-
Alabama	287	-	-	-	292	-	-	-
Mississippi	470	118	41	77	391	146	50	96
West South Central								
Arkansas	143	1	-	1	185	-	-	-
Louisiana	271	77	36	41	262	95	34	61
Oklahoma	24,580	3,457	660	2,797	24,306	4,523	724	3,799
Texas	303	68	11	57	238	73	22	51
Mountain								
Montana	3,978	1,588	191	1,397	3,961	1,908	189	1,719
Idaho	1,355	473	34	439	1,349	607	26	581
Wyoming	575	197	5	192	523	253	8	245
Colorado	609	232	46	186	461	252	43	209
New Mexico	7,240	5,414	1,314	4,100	6,861	5,562	1,403	4,159
Arizona	10,625	6,594	1,633	4,961	9,863	7,132	1,682	5,450
Utah	1,232	747	171	576	1,058	769	152	617
Nevada	2,120	330	62	268	2,070	519	73	446
Pacific								
Washington	4,066	668	48	620	4,035	1,086	49	1,037

[Continued]

★ 109 ★

Ability of American Indians 10 Years Old and Older to Speak English, by Geographic Division, State, Sex, and Age Group, 1910

[Continued]

Geographic division and state	Indian males 10 years of age and over: 1910				Indian females 10 years of age and over: 1910			
	Total number	Unable to speak English			Total number	Unable to speak English		
		Total	10 to 19 years of age	20 years of age and over		Total	10 to 19 years of age	20 years of age and over
Oregon	1,954	213	6	207	1,950	466	8	458
California	6,458	711	62	649	6,148	1,058	85	976

Source: U.S. Bureau of the Census, *Indian Population in the United States and Alaska, 1910*, United States Government Printing Office, Washington, D.C., 1915, p. 236.
Note: A dash (-) represents zero.

★ 110 ★

Ability of American Indians 10 Years Old and Older to Speak English, by Linguistic Stock, Tribe, and Sex, 1910: A - K

Data are shown for linguistic stocks with 200 or more Indians and tribes with more than 100 members in 1910.

Linguistic stock and tribe	Indians 10 years of age and over: 1910			Indian males 10 years of age and over			Indian females 10 years of age and over		
	Total number	Unable to speak English		Total number	Unable to speak English		Total number	Unable to speak English	
		Number	Percent		Number	Percent		Number	Percent
UNITED STATES									
Algonquian stock	29,872	7,716	25.8	15,486	3,306	21.3	14,386	4,410	30.7
Arapaho	1,047	399	38.1	545	154	28.3	502	245	48.8
Brotherton	132	-	-	70	-	-	62	-	-
Cheyenne	2,427	1,196	49.3	1,176	505	42.9	1,251	691	55.2
Chickahominy	89	-	-	47	-	-	42	-	-
Chippewa	14,629	3,875	26.5	7,552	1,692	22.4	7,077	2,183	30.8
Cree	326	25	7.7	166	6	3.6	160	19	11.9
Delaware	636	25	3.9	312	4	1.3	324	21	6.5
Gros Ventres	376	163	43.4	189	76	40.2	187	87	46.5
Kickapoo	251	81	32.3	139	37	26.6	112	44	39.3
Malecite	101	3	3.0	48	-	-	53	3	5.7
Mashpee	166	-	-	91	-	-	75	-	-
Menominee	1,029	202	19.6	571	84	14.7	458	118	25.8
Miami	171	4	2.3	94	2	2.1	77	2	2.6
Ottawa	2,034	395	19.4	139	139	12.8	951	256	26.9
Passamaquoddy	310	10	3.2	166	4	2.4	144	6	4.2
Penobscot	231	2	0.9	124	-	-	107	2	1.9
Peoria	83	2	2.4	40	1	-	43	1	-
Piegan	1,602	864	53.9	810	417	51.5	792	447	56.4
Potawatomi	1,697	241	14.2	968	111	11.5	729	130	17.8

[Continued]

★ 110 ★

Ability of American Indians 10 Years Old and Older to Speak English, by Linguistic Stock, Tribe, and Sex, 1910: A - K
[Continued]

Linguistic stock and tribe	Indians 10 years of age and over: 1910			Indian males 10 years of age and over			Indian females 10 years of age and over		
	Total number	Unable to speak English		Total number	Unable to speak English		Total number	Unable to speak English	
		Number	Percent		Number	Percent		Number	Percent
Powhatan	91	-	-	45	-	-	46	-	-
Sauk and Fox	521	68	13.1	280	21	7.5	241	47	19.5
Shawnee	886	137	15.5	424	44	10.4	462	93	20.1
Shinnecock	121	-	-	59	-	-	62	-	-
Stockbridges	384	1	0.3	197	-	-	187	1	0.5
Wampanoag	133	-	-	79	-	-	54	-	-
All other tribes	399	23	5.8	211	9	4.3	188	14	7.4
Athabaskan stock	20,460	15,791	77.2	10,252	7,549	73.6	10,208	8,242	80.7
Apache	3,480	2,149	61.8	1,754	922	52.6	1,726	1,227	71.1
Hupa	497	-	-	241	-	-	256	-	-
Jicarilla Apache	486	361	74.3	252	174	69.0	234	187	79.9
Kiowa Apache	98	21	21.4	42	5	-	56	16	28.6
Mescalero Apache	312	158	50.6	129	50	38.8	183	108	59.0
Navajo	14,797	13,048	88.2	7,429	6,384	85.9	7,368	6,664	90.4
Rogue River	286	17	5.9	153	2	1.3	133	15	11.3
Tolowa	84	1	1.2	44	1	-	40	-	-
Umpqua	79	14	17.7	40	5	-	39	9	-
Wailaki	164	3	1.8	79	-	-	85	3	3.5
All other tribes	177	19	10.7	89	6	6.7	88	13	14.8
Caddoan stock	1,354	321	23.7	673	154	22.9	681	167	24.5
Arikara	336	186	55.4	163	88	54.0	173	98	56.6
Caddo	302	58	19.2	161	28	17.4	141	30	21.3
Pawnee	473	42	8.9	227	22	9.7	246	20	8.1
Wichita	229	34	14.8	114	15	13.2	115	19	16.5
All other tribes	14	1	-	8	1	-	6	-	-
Chimakuan stock	228	104	45.6	113	41	36.3	115	63	54.8
Quileute	193	84	43.5	95	33	34.7	98	51	52.0
All other tribes	35	20	-	18	8	-	17	12	-
Chinookan stock	676	114	16.9	353	34	9.6	323	80	24.8
Chinook	224	8	3.6	123	1	0.8	101	7	6.9
Wasco	184	47	25.5	95	12	12.6	89	35	39.3
Wishram	222	54	24.3	112	21	18.8	110	33	30.0
All other tribes	46	5	-	23	-	-	23	5	-
Croatan group	3,943	-	-	1,954	-	-	1,989	-	-
Croatan	3,943	-	-	1,954	-	-	1,989	-	-

[Continued]

185

★ 110 ★

Ability of American Indians 10 Years Old and Older to Speak English, by Linguistic Stock, Tribe, and Sex, 1910: A - K

[Continued]

Linguistic stock and tribe	Indians 10 years of age and over: 1910			Indian males 10 years of age and over			Indian females 10 years of age and over		
	Total number	Unable to speak English		Total number	Unable to speak English		Total number	Unable to speak English	
		Number	Percent		Number	Percent		Number	Percent
Iroquoian stock	26,201	3,121	11.9	13,490	1,441	10.7	12,711	1,680	13.2
Cherokee	20,154	2,445	12.1	10,319	1,189	11.5	9,835	1,256	12.8
Mohawk	291	95	32.6	136	25	18.4	155	70	45.2
Oneida	1,739	198	11.4	930	77	8.3	809	121	15.0
Onondaga	275	3	1.1	138	1	0.7	137	2	1.5
St. Regis	912	207	22.7	499	86	17.2	413	121	29.3
Seneca	2,155	167	7.7	1,109	62	5.6	1,046	105	10.0
Tuscarora	309	1	0.3	168	-	-	141	1	0.7
Wyandot	253	3	1.2	137	-	-	116	3	2.6
All other tribes	113	2	1.8	54	1	1.9	59	1	1.7
Karok stock	555	63	11.4	275	24	8.7	280	39	13.9
Orleans	555	63	11.4	275	24	8.7	280	39	13.9
Keresan stock	2,954	2,070	70.1	1,593	1,041	65.3	1,361	1,029	75.6
Acoma	518	421	81.3	257	197	76.7	261	224	85.8
Cochiti	183	106	57.9	103	52	50.5	80	54	67.5
Laguna	1,050	577	55.0	551	274	49.7	499	303	60.7
San Felipe	379	284	74.9	227	158	69.6	152	126	82.9
Santa Ana	155	125	80.6	98	80	81.6	57	45	78.9
Santo Domingo	581	493	84.9	310	246	79.4	271	247	91.1
Sia	88	64	72.7	47	34	-	41	30	-
Kiowan stock	750	280	37.3	361	106	29.4	389	174	44.7
Kiowa	750	280	37.3	361	106	29.4	389	174	44.7
Kutenaian stock	395	74	18.7	210	37	17.6	185	37	20.0
Kutenai	395	74	18.7	210	37	17.6	185	37	20.0

Source: U.S. Bureau of the Census, *Indian Population in the United States and Alaska, 1910,* United States Government Printing Office, Washington, D.C., 1915, pp. 244-246. *Notes:* A dash (-) represents zero or a lack of 50 persons for a percentage base.

★ 111 ★

Ability of American Indians 10 Years Old and Older to Speak English, by Linguistic Stock, Tribe, and Sex, 1910: L - S

Data are shown for linguistic stocks with 200 or more Indians and tribes with more than 100 members in 1910.

Linguistic stock and tribe	Indians 10 years of age and over: 1910			Indian males 10 years of age and over			Indian females 10 years of age and over		
	Total number	Unable to speak English		Total number	Unable to speak English		Total number	Unable to speak English	
		Number	Percent		Number	Percent		Number	Percent
UNITED STATES (cont.)									
Lutuamian stock	727	140	19.3	347	44	12.7	380	96	25.3
Klamath	521	107	20.5	249	36	14.5	272	71	26.1
Modoc	206	33	16.0	98	8	8.2	108	25	23.1
Maidu stock	810	16	2.0	421	2	0.5	389	14	3.6
Maidu	810	16	2.0	421	2	0.5	389	14	3.6
Miwok stock	530	25	4.7	254	9	3.5	276	16	5.8
Miwok	505	24	4.8	238	8	3.4	267	16	6.0
All other tribes	25	1	-	16	1	-	9	-	-
Muskhogean stock	18,957	4,367	23.0	9,608	1,867	19.4	9,349	2,500	26.7
Alibamu	225	115	51.1	114	54	47.4	111	61	55.0
Chickasaw	2,563	160	6.2	1,268	38	3.0	1,295	122	9.4
Choctaw	10,185	2,184	21.4	5,202	929	17.9	4,983	1,255	25.2
Creek	4,697	1,304	27.8	2,349	560	23.8	2,348	744	31.7
Seminole	1,216	550	45.2	639	259	40.5	577	291	50.4
All other tribes (Koasati)	71	54	76.1	36	27	-	35	27	-
Piman stock	6,149	3,750	61.0	3,234	1,848	57.1	2,915	1,902	65.2
Papago	2,655	1,920	72.3	1,365	944	69.2	1,290	976	75.7
Pima	3,083	1,504	48.8	1,631	726	44.5	1,452	778	53.6
Yaqui	378	300	79.4	222	169	76.1	156	131	84.0
All other tribes	33	26	-	16	9	-	17	17	-
Pomo stock	919	27	2.9	465	5	1.1	454	22	4.8
Clear Lake	141	1	0.7	73	-	-	68	1	1.5
Pomo	606	18	3.0	308	2	0.6	298	16	5.4
All other tribes	172	8	4.7	84	3	3.6	88	5	5.7
Salishan stock	5,759	974	16.9	2,993	386	12.9	2,766	588	21.3
Chehalis	199	28	14.1	114	12	10.5	85	16	18.8
Clallam	280	16	5.7	144	4	2.8	136	12	8.8
Coeur d'Alene	215	2	0.9	116	2	1.7	99	-	-
Columbia	288	122	42.4	156	59	37.8	132	63	47.7
Colville	589	54	9.2	310	20	6.5	279	34	12.2
Cowlitz	75	11	14.7	39	2	-	36	9	-
Flathead	343	64	18.7	177	27	15.3	166	37	22.3
Kalispel	430	139	32.3	216	65	30.1	214	74	34.6

[Continued]

★ 111 ★

Ability of American Indians 10 Years Old and Older to Speak English, by Linguistic Stock, Tribe, and Sex, 1910: L - S
[Continued]

Linguistic stock and tribe	Indians 10 years of age and over: 1910			Indian males 10 years of age and over			Indian females 10 years of age and over		
	Total number	Unable to speak English		Total number	Unable to speak English		Total number	Unable to speak English	
		Number	Percent		Number	Percent		Number	Percent
Lummi	223	20	9.0	127	8	6.3	96	12	12.5
Muckleshoot	142	36	25.4	75	15	20.0	67	21	31.3
Nisqualli	112	18	16.1	56	6	10.7	56	12	21.4
Okinagan	206	46	22.3	103	19	18.4	103	27	26.2
Puyallup	231	27	11.7	118	10	8.5	113	17	15.0
Quinaielt	205	49	23.9	107	22	20.6	98	27	27.6
Sanpoil	184	61	33.2	87	22	25.3	97	39	40.2
Skokomish	141	17	12.1	62	5	8.1	79	12	15.2
Snohomish	478	46	9.6	251	16	6.4	227	30	13.2
Spokan	512	38	7.4	251	13	5.2	261	25	9.6
Suquamish	217	36	16.6	118	15	12.7	99	21	21.2
Swinomish	243	55	22.6	134	18	13.4	109	37	33.9
All other tribes	446	89	20.0	232	26	11.2	214	63	29.4
Shahaptian stock	3,372	1,098	32.6	1,567	378	24.1	1,805	720	39.9
Klikitat	325	95	29.2	148	30	20.3	177	65	36.7
Nez Perces	980	250	25.5	480	75	15.6	500	175	35.0
Umatilla	217	110	50.7	94	38	40.4	123	72	58.5
Wallawalla	290	70	24.1	143	27	18.9	147	43	29.3
Warm Springs	408	118	28.9	184	44	23.9	224	74	33.0
Yakima	1,028	377	36.7	463	136	29.4	565	241	42.7
All other tribes	124	78	62.9	55	28	50.9	69	50	72.5
Shastan stock	1,226	114	9.3	595	46	7.7	631	68	10.8
Hat Creek	190	1	0.5	100	-	-	90	1	1.1
Pit River	767	98	12.8	369	41	11.1	398	57	14.3
Shasta	269	15	5.6	126	5	4.0	143	10	7.0
Shoshonean stock	12,894	4,970	38.5	6,645	2,237	33.7	6,249	2,733	43.7
Bannock	338	214	63.3	176	106	60.2	162	108	66.7
Chemehuevi	262	134	51.1	136	44	32.4	126	90	71.4
Comanche	876	328	37.4	427	132	30.9	449	196	43.7
Hopi	1,420	714	50.3	795	370	46.5	625	344	55.0
Kawia	605	166	27.4	333	82	24.6	272	84	30.9
Kern River	80	5	6.3	37	1	-	43	4	-
Mono	1,090	235	21.6	501	67	13.4	589	168	28.5
Paiute	585	240	41.0	313	101	32.3	272	139	51.1
Paviotso	2,480	537	21.7	1,209	183	15.1	1,271	354	27.9
San Luiseno	389	89	22.9	203	33	16.3	186	56	30.1
Serrano	91	27	29.7	49	12	-	42	15	-
Shoshoni	2,955	1,246	42.2	1,515	586	38.7	1,440	660	45.8

[Continued]

★ 111 ★

Ability of American Indians 10 Years Old and Older to Speak English, by Linguistic Stock, Tribe, and Sex, 1910: L - S
[Continued]

Linguistic stock and tribe	Indians 10 years of age and over: 1910			Indian males 10 years of age and over			Indian females 10 years of age and over		
	Total number	Unable to speak English		Total number	Unable to speak English		Total number	Unable to speak English	
		Number	Percent		Number	Percent		Number	Percent
Ute	1,641	988	60.2	911	499	54.8	730	489	67.0
All other tribes	82	47	57.3	40	21	-	42	26	-
Siouan stock	24,598	8,963	36.4	12,350	3,733	30.2	12,248	5,230	42.7
Assiniboine	925	422	45.6	455	189	41.5	470	233	49.6
Catawba	78	-	-	42	-	-	36	-	-
Crow	1,402	723	51.6	7.2	345	49.1	700	378	54.0
Hidatsa	394	135	34.3	208	52	25.0	186	83	44.6
Iowa	179	7	3.9	94	4	4.3	85	3	3.5
Kansa	138	1	0.7	88	-	-	50	1	2.0
Mandan	162	77	47.5	84	33	39.3	78	44	56.4
Omaha	791	212	26.8	407	74	18.2	384	138	35.9
Osage	898	111	12.4	465	54	11.6	433	57	13.2
Oto	245	31	12.7	135	16	11.9	110	15	13.6
Ponca	643	136	21.2	307	56	18.2	336	80	23.8
Quapaw	169	5	3.0	84	-	-	85	5	5.9
Santee Sioux	1,112	193	17.4	564	61	10.8	548	132	24.1
Sioux	790	121	15.3	449	47	10.5	341	74	21.7
Sisseton Sioux	1,888	560	29.7	957	207	21.6	931	353	37.9
Teton Sioux	10,739	4,656	43.4	5,349	1,987	37.1	5,390	2,669	49.5
Brule Sioux	591	218	36.9	301	86	28.6	290	132	45.5
Hunkpapa Sioux	813	405	49.8	403	174	43.2	410	231	56.3
Minniconjou Sioux	318	195	61.3	150	77	51.3	168	118	70.2
Oglala Sioux	4,486	1,795	40.0	2,242	771	34.4	2,244	1,024	45.6
Sans Arc Sioux	146	39	26.7	77	13	16.9	69	26	37.7
Sihasapa	372	143	38.4	191	63	33.0	181	80	44.2
Two Kettle Sioux	216	77	35.6	125	37	29.6	91	40	44.0
Other Teton Sioux	3,797	1,784	47.0	1,860	766	41.2	1,937	1,018	52.6
Winnebago	1,406	406	28.9	714	126	17.6	692	280	40.5
Yankton Sioux	1,583	660	41.7	754	270	35.8	829	390	47.0
Yanktonai Sioux	1,045	505	48.3	486	211	43.4	559	294	52.6
All other tribes	11	2	-	6	1	-	5	1	-

Source: U.S. Bureau of the Census, *Indian Population in the United States and Alaska, 1910,* United States Government Printing Office, Washington, D.C., 1915, pp. 244-246. *Notes:* A dash (-) represents zero or a lack of 50 persons for a percentage base.

★ 112 ★

Ability of American Indians 10 Years Old and Older to Speak English, by Linguistic Stock, Tribe, and Sex, 1910: T - Z and Alaska

Data are shown for linguistic stocks with 200 or more Indians and tribes with more than 100 members in 1910.

Linguistic stock and tribe	Indians 10 years of age and over: 1910			Indian males 10 years of age and over			Indian females 10 years of age and over		
	Total number	Unable to speak English		Total number	Unable to speak English		Total number	Unable to speak English	
		Number	Percent		Number	Percent		Number	Percent
UNITED STATES (cont.)									
Tanoan stock	2,348	1,299	55.3	1,268	671	52.9	1,080	628	58.4
Isleta	717	492	68.6	381	249	65.4	336	243	72.3
Jemez	396	294	74.2	231	164	71.0	165	130	78.8
Picuris	76	44	57.9	37	20	-	39	24	-
San Ildefonso	85	41	48.2	41	16	-	44	25	-
San Juan	297	162	54.5	165	83	50.3	132	79	59.8
Santa Clara	199	92	46.2	103	46	44.7	96	46	47.9
Taos	371	92	24.8	198	50	25.3	173	42	24.3
All other tribes	207	82	39.6	112	43	38.4	95	39	41.1
Wailatpuan stock	247	77	31.2	118	26	22.0	129	51	39.5
Cayuse	225	77	34.2	105	26	24.8	120	51	42.5
All other tribes	22	--	-	13	-	-	9	-	-
Wakashan stock	279	102	36.6	142	44	31.0	137	58	42.3
Makah	256	92	35.9	134	44	32.8	122	48	39.3
All other tribes	23	10	-	8	-	-	15	10	-
Washoan stock	650	39	6.0	334	19	5.7	316	20	6.3
Washo	650	39	6.0	334	19	5.7	316	20	6.3
Wintun stock	545	28	5.1	297	14	4.7	248	14	5.6
Nomelaki	101	8	7.9	52	5	9.6	49	3	-
Patwin	138	2	1.4	81	-	-	57	2	3.5
Wintun	306	18	5.9	164	9	5.5	142	9	6.3
Yokuts stock	407	40	9.8	218	9	4.1	189	31	16.4
Chuckhansi	112	6	5.4	56	-	-	56	6	10.7
Yokuts	231	21	9.1	133	9	6.8	98	12	12.2
All other tribes	64	13	20.3	29	-	-	35	13	-
Yuman stock	3,290	1,229	37.4	1,806	573	31.7	1,484	656	44.2
Cocopah	182	125	68.7	103	59	57.3	79	66	83.5
Diegueno	568	187	32.9	305	83	27.2	263	104	39.5
Havasupai	137	7	5.1	83	3	3.6	54	4	7.4
Maricopa	287	130	45.3	152	64	42.1	135	66	48.9
Mohave	822	245	29.8	460	121	26.3	362	124	34.3
Walapai	370	113	30.5	207	47	22.7	163	66	40.5
Yavapai	229	112	48.9	126	53	42.1	103	59	57.3

[Continued]

Ability of American Indians 10 Years Old and Older to Speak English, by Linguistic Stock, Tribe, and Sex, 1910: T - Z and Alaska
[Continued]

Linguistic stock and tribe	Indians 10 years of age and over: 1910			Indian males 10 years of age and over			Indian females 10 years of age and over		
	Total number	Unable to speak English		Total number	Unable to speak English		Total number	Unable to speak English	
		Number	Percent		Number	Percent		Number	Percent
Yuma	667	289	43.3	355	133	37.5	312	156	50.0
All other tribes	28	21	-	15	10	-	13	11	-
Yurok stock	505	81	16.0	249	25	10.0	256	56	21.9
Weitspec	505	81	16.0	249	25	10.0	256	56	21.9
Zunian stock	1,202	979	81.4	631	505	80.0	571	474	83.0
Zuni	1,202	979	81.4	631	505	80.0	571	474	83.0
ALASKA									
Athabaskan stock	2,886	1,308	45.3	1,507	565	37.5	1,379	743	53.9
Ahtena	227	117	51.5	129	54	41.9	98	63	64.3
Hankutchin	86	19	22.1	58	11	10.0	28	8	-
Kaiyuhkhotana	125	68	54.4	64	29	45.3	61	39	63.9
Knajakhotana	516	291	56.4	283	132	46.6	233	159	68.2
Kutchin	276	211	76.4	140	104	74.3	136	107	78.7
Natsitkutchin	150	119	79.3	84	58	69.0	66	61	92.4
Tenankutchin	302	143	47.4	156	58	37.2	146	85	58.2
Unakhotana	136	80	58.8	72	37	51.4	64	43	67.2
All other tribes	1,068	260	24.3	521	82	15.7	547	178	32.5
Eskimauan stock	9,964	7,134	71.6	5,147	3,392	65.9	4,817	3,742	77.7
Aleut	1,001	616	61.5	516	305	59.1	485	311	64.1
Chnagmiut	202	132	65.3	110	58	52.7	92	74	80.4
Ikogmiut	529	486	91.9	247	223	90.3	282	263	93.3
Kaialigmiut	127	125	98.4	62	61	98.4	65	64	98.5
Kaviagmiut	163	66	40.5	81	30	37.0	82	36	43.9
Kinugumiut	424	298	70.3	236	149	63.1	188	149	79.3
Kowagmiut	410	231	56.3	214	101	47.2	196	130	66.3
Kusetrinmiut	90	28	31.1	56	22	39.3	34	6	-
Kuskovakmiut	232	190	81.5	121	91	75.2	111	99	89.2
Kuskwogmiut	1,068	994	93.1	544	502	92.3	524	492	93.9
Magemiut	262	219	83.6	118	102	86.4	144	117	81.3
Malemiut	407	168	41.3	210	79	37.6	197	89	45.2
Nunatogmiut	224	172	76.8	130	94	72.3	94	78	83.0
Nunivagmiut	236	224	94.9	127	122	96.1	109	102	93.6
Nunochogmiut	107	102	95.3	42	41	-	65	61	93.8
Selawigmiut	177	137	77.4	98	65	66.3	79	72	91.1
Tikeramiut	252	135	53.6	127	61	48.0	125	74	59.2
Ukivokmiut	94	80	85.1	50	39	78.0	44	41	-

[Continued]

★ 112 ★

Ability of American Indians 10 Years Old and Older to Speak English, by Linguistic Stock, Tribe, and Sex, 1910: T - Z and Alaska
[Continued]

Linguistic stock and tribe	Indians 10 years of age and over: 1910			Indian males 10 years of age and over			Indian females 10 years of age and over		
	Total number	Unable to speak English		Total number	Unable to speak English		Total number	Unable to speak English	
		Number	Percent		Number	Percent		Number	Percent
Unaligmiut	274	152	55.5	126	54	42.9	148	98	66.2
Utkiavinmiut	86	64	74.4	43	29	-	43	35	-
Utukamiut	91	74	81.3	46	35	-	45	39	-
Yuit	226	134	59.3	119	48	40.3	107	86	80.4
Southern Eskimo	2,613	1,856	71.0	1,383	868	62.8	1,230	988	80.3
All other tribes	669	451	67.4	341	213	62.5	328	238	72.6
Hadian stock	369	58	15.7	198	23	11.6	171	35	20.5
Haida	369	58	15.7	198	23	11.6	171	35	20.5
Tlingit stock	3,240	1,343	41.5	1,634	509	31.2	1,606	834	51.9
Auk	213	58	27.2	120	22	18.3	93	36	38.7
Chilkat	536	238	44.4	270	97	35.9	266	141	53.0
Henya	146	72	49.3	78	38	48.7	68	34	50.0
Huna	470	252	53.6	221	84	38.0	249	168	67.5
Hutsnuwu	373	167	44.8	186	57	30.6	187	110	58.8
Kake	232	95	40.9	114	41	36.0	118	54	45.8
Sitka	446	191	42.8	225	77	34.2	221	114	51.6
Stikine	139	48	34.5	69	18	26.1	70	30	42.9
Taku	111	38	34.2	54	9	16.7	57	29	50.9
Tongas	129	43	33.3	65	13	20.0	64	30	46.9
Yakutat	211	88	41.7	96	28	29.2	115	60	52.2
All other tribes	234	53	22.6	136	25	18.4	98	28	28.6
Tsimshian stock	520	94	18.1	294	30	10.2	226	64	28.3
Tsimshian	520	94	18.1	294	30	10.2	226	64	28.3

Source: U.S. Bureau of the Census, *Indian Population in the United States and Alaska, 1910,* United States Government Printing Office, Washington, D.C., 1915, pp. 244-246. *Notes:* A dash (-) represents zero or a lack of 50 persons for a percentage base.

★ 113 ★

American Indian Linguistic Stocks: Classifications by the U.S. Census Bureau in 1910 and 1930 - I

See the end of the table for original notes accompanying these data.

Classification in 1910	Classification in 1930
ALGONQUIAN STOCK	ALGONQUIAN STOCK
Arapaho	Arapaho
Blackfeet, Piegan	Blackfeet
Cheyenne	Cheyenne
Chippewa	Chippewa
Delaware, Munsee	Delaware
Gros Ventres (Atsina)	Gros Ventres (Atsina)
Kickapoo	Kickapoo
Menominee	Menominee
Miami, Peoria, Piankashaw, Wea	Miami and Illinois
Ottawa	Ottawa
Potawatomi	Potawatomi
Sauk and Fox	Sauk and Fox
Shawnee	Shawnee
Brotherton, Mashpee, Mohegan, Montauk, Narragansett, Niantic, Passamaquoddy Penobscot, Pequot, Poospatuck, Shinnecock, Stockbridges, Wampanoag	Eastern Algonquians
Croatan group, and Virginia Algonquians, Croaten, Chickahominy, Mattapony, Pamunkey, Powhaten	Virginia-Carolina Indians
ATHAPASKAN STOCK - Chiricahua Apache, Coyotero Apache, Jicarilla Apache, Lipan Apache, Mescalero Apache, San Carlos Apache, Tonto Apache, White Mountain Apache	ATHAPASKAN STOCK - Apache
Kiowa Apache Navaho	Kiowa Apache Navaho
Chastacosta, Chetco, Cow Creek, Rogue River, Tlatskanai, Tolowa, Umpqua, Upper Coquille	Oregon Athapaskans
Hupa, Kai-Pomo, Mattole, Redwood (Whilkut), Saiaz, Wailakki	California Athapaskans
CADDOAN STOCK	CADDOAN STOCK
Arikara	Arikara
Caddo	Caddo

[Continued]

★ 113 ★

American Indian Linguistic Stocks: Classifications by the U.S. Census Bureau in 1910 and 1930 - I

[Continued]

Classification in 1910	Classification in 1930
Pawnee Kichai, Tawakoni, Waco, Wichita	Pawnee Wichita and Kichai
CHIMAKUAN STOCK Chimakum, Hoh, Quileute	CHIMAKUAN STOCK
CHINOOKAN STOCK Chinook, Clackamas, Clatsop, Wasco, Wishram	CHINOOKAN STOCK
CHITIMACHAN STOCK Chitimacha	CHITIMACHAN STOCK Chitimacha
CHUMASHAN STOCK San Luis Obispo, Santa Barbareno, Santa Ynez	CHUMASHAN STOCK
COSTANOAN STOCK Santa Cruz	COSTANOAN STOCK Santa Cruz
IROQUOIAN STOCK Cayuga, Mohawk, Oneida, Onondaga, St. Regis, Seneca, Tuscarora Wyandot Cherokee	IROQUOIAN STOCK Iroquois Wyandot Cherokee
KALAPOOIAN STOCK Kalapooia, Lakmiut, Mary's River, Santiam, Wapato, Yamel, Yonkalla	KALAPOOIAN STOCK
KAROK STOCK Orleans	KAROK STOCK Orleans
KERESAN STOCK Acoma, Cochiti, Laguna, San Felipe, Santa Ana, Santa Domingo, Sia	KERESAN STOCK
KIOWAN STOCK Kiowa	KIOWAN STOCK Kiowa

[Continued]

★ 113 ★

American Indian Linguistic Stocks: Classifications by the U.S. Census Bureau in 1910 and 1930 - I
[Continued]

Classification in 1910	Classification in 1930
KUSAN STOCK Kusa	KUSAN STOCK
KUTENAIAN STOCK Kutenai	KUTENAIAN STOCK Kutenai
MAIDU STOCK Maidu	MAIDU STOCK Maidu
MIWOK STOCK Marin, Middletown, Miwok	MIWOK STOCK
MUSKHOGEAN STOCK Chickasaw Choctaw Alibamu, Creek, Koasati Seminole	MUSKHOGEAN STOCK Chickasaw Choctaw Creek Seminole
PIMAN STOCK Papago Pima	PIMAN STOCK Papago Pima
POMO STOCK Clear Lake, Gynomehro, Little Lake, Lower Lake, Pomo	POMO STOCK
SALINAN STOCK San Antonio	SALINAN STOCK San Antonio
SALISHAN STOCK Chehalis, Clallam, Cowlitz,	SALISHAN STOCK Washington Coast Salish

[Continued]

★ 113 ★

American Indian Linguistic Stocks: Classifications by the U.S. Census Bureau in 1910 and 1930 - I

[Continued]

Classification in 1910	Classification in 1930
Dwamish, Lummi, Muckelshoot, Nisqualli, Nooksak, Puyallup, Quinaielt, Skagit, Skokomish, Snohomish, Snoqualmu, Squaxon, Suquamish, Swinomish, Twana	

Source: Dr. Leon E. Truesdell, U.S. Department of Commerce, Bureau of the Census, Fifteenth Census of the United States: 1930, *The Indian Population of the United States and Alaska,* U.S. Government Printing Office, 1937, pp. 33-36. *Notes: Linguistic stocks.* - On the basis of resemblances between languages, the Indian tribes are grouped into linguistic stocks or families. These linguistic stocks are analogous to the Semitic and Indo-European stocks within the white race, while the languages of the tribes within a stock differ, just as German differs from Russian, or English from Greek. Tribes with related languages were probably at a remote "period" related by blood, although the prevalence of adoption and intermarriage with other tribes has weakened the tie of blood and also the bond of common ceremonial observances until there is often little resemblance between tribes of the same stock other than that of language. *Enumeration by stock and tribe, 1930 and 1910.* - Classification by stock and tribe, on the basis of a census enumeration, is very difficult, and the results are subject to a considerable margin or error. The popular local designations of Indian tribes do not always correspond with the scientific name, and the enumerator, who is rarely an ethnologist, could do no better than to give the name by which the tribe was locally known. If this name was not readily identified with one of the recognized tribes, the Indian was necessarily assigned to the miscellaneous group and lost to the tribal classification. No instructions were given as to the tribal allocation of Indians of mixed tribal blood. Such Indians are probably included in the tribes which they prefer to claim, or in which they have the reputation of membership. The tabulation by stock and tribe from the Census of 1910 differentiated 52 linguistic stocks, divided into 280 tribes. In 1930, for convenience of tabulation, many of the smaller tribes were thrown together into groups of tribes, reducing the number of tribes and groups to 100, and the number of linguistic stocks to 40.

★ 114 ★

American Indian Linguistic Stocks: Classifications by the U.S. Census Bureau in 1910 and 1930 - II

See the end of the table for original notes accompanying these data.

Classification in 1910	Classification in 1930
SALISHAN STOCK (cont.) Coeur d'Alene, Columbia, Colville, Flathead, Kalispel, Methow, Nespelim, Okinagan, Pend d'Oreilles, Pisquow, Sanpoil, Spokan	Interior Salish
Tillamook	Tillamook
LUTUAMIAN STOCK Klamath, Modoc	SHAPWAILUTAN STOCK Klamath and Modoc
SHAHAPTIAN STOCK	Shahaptians

[Continued]

★ 114 ★

American Indian Linguistic Stocks: Classifications by the U.S. Census Bureau in 1910 and 1930 - II
[Continued]

Classification in 1910	Classification in 1930
Klickitat, Nez Perces, Paloos, Topinish, Umatilla, Walla Walla, Warm Springs, Yakima	
WAIILATUPUAN STOCK Cayuse, Molala	Cayuse, Molala
SHASTAN STOCK Hat Creek Pit River Shasta	**SHASTAN STOCK**
SHOSHONEAN STOCK Bannock Comanche Hopi Mono, Panamint, Paviotso Chemehuevi, Paiute Shoshoni Pahvant, Ute Gabrieleno, Juaneno, Kawaiisu, Kawai, Kern River, Luiseno (San Luiseno), Serrano, Tehachapi	**SHOSHONEAN STOCK** Bannock Comanche Hopi Mono-Paviotso Paiute Shoshoni Ute Southern California
SIOUAN STOCK Catawba Crow Hidatsa Iowa Kensa Mandan Oto, Missouri Omaha Osage Ponca Quapaw Santee Sioux, Sioux, Sisseton Sioux, Teton Sioux, Yanktonai Sioux, Yankton Sioux, Assiniboin Winnebago	**SIOUAN STOCK** Catawba Crow Hidatsa Iowa Kensa Mandan Oto and Missouri Omaha Osage Ponca Quapaw Dakota Assiniboin Winnebago

[Continued]

★ 114 ★

American Indian Linguistic Stocks: Classifications by the U.S. Census Bureau in 1910 and 1930 - II

[Continued]

Classification in 1910	Classification in 1930
TANOAN STOCK Isleta, Jemez, Nambe, Pecos, Picuria, Pojoaque, San Ildefonso, San Juan, Sandia, Santa Clara, Taos, Tesuque	TANOAN STOCK
TONKAWAN STOCK Tonkawa	TONKAWAN STOCK Tonkawa
TUNICAN STOCK Tunica	TUNICAN STOCK Tunica
WASHOAN STOCK Washo	WASHOAN STOCK Washo
WINTUN STOCK Nomelaki, Patwin, Wintun	WINTUN STOCK
WIYOT STOCK Humboldt Bay	WIYOT STOCK Humboldt Bay
YANAN STOCK Yana	YANAN STOCK Yana
YOKUTS STOCK Choinimni, Chookiminah, Chukchansi, Kashowoo, Techi, Wechikhit, Wikchamni, Yokuts, Yowdanchi	YOKUTS STOCK
YUCHEAN STOCK Yuchi	YUCHEAN STOCK Yuchi
YUKIAN STOCK Coast Yuki, Redwood (Huchnom), Wappo, Yuki	YUKIAN STOCK
YUMAN STOCK Cocopa Diegueno Havasupai, Walapai, Yavapai, Yuma Apache Maricopa Mohave	YUMAN STOCK Cocopa Diegueno Northern Yumans Maricopa Mohave

[Continued]

★ 114 ★

American Indian Linguistic Stocks: Classifications by the U.S. Census Bureau in 1910 and 1930 - II
[Continued]

Classification in 1910	Classification in 1930
Yuma	Yuma
YUROK STOCK Weitspek	YUROK STOCK Weitspek
ZUNIAN STOCK Zuni	ZUNIAN STOCK Zuni
CHIMARIKAN STOCK Chimariko	Other tribes of the United States, including tribe
TAKELMAN STOCK Takelma Other tribes Tribes not reported	
ALGONQUIAN STOCK Abnaki, Cree, Malecite, Micmac	Canadian and Mexican tribes
PIMAN STOCK Mayo, Opata, Yaqui	
SALISHAN STOCK Bellacoola, Comox, Cowichan, Shuswap, Songish	
TSIMSHIAN STOCK Tsimshian	
WAKASHAN STOCK Kitamat, Kwakiutl, Makah, Nootka	
ATHAPASKAN STOCK	Alaskan tribes

[Continued]

★114★

American Indian Linguistic Stocks: Classifications by the U.S. Census Bureau in 1910 and 1930 - II
[Continued]

Classification in 1910	Classification in 1930
Ahtena, Tenankutchin Eskimauan stock Aleut, Malemiut	
HAIDEN STOCK Haida	
TLINGIT STOCK Auk, Chilkat, Kake No corresponding classification	Indians born in other foreign countries

Source: Dr. Leon E. Truesdell, U.S. Department of Commerce, Bureau of the Census, Fifteenth Census of the United States: 1930, *The Indian Population of the United States and Alaska*, U.S. Government Printing Office, 1937, pp. 33-36. *Notes: Linguistic stocks.* - On the basis of resemblances between languages, the Indian tribes are grouped into linguistic stocks or families. These linguistic stocks are analogous to the Semitic and Indo-European stocks within the white race, while the languages of the tribes within a stock differ just as German differs from Russian, or English from Greek. Tribes with related languages were probably at a remote "period" related by blood, although the prevalence of adoption and intermarriage with other tribes has weakened the tie of blood and also the bond of common ceremonial observances until there is often little resemblances between tribes of the same stock other than that of language. *Enumeration by stock and tribe, 1930 and 1910.* - Classification by stock and tribe, on the basis of a census enumeration, is very difficult, and the results are subject to a considerable margin or error. The popular local designations of Indian tribes do not always correspond with the scientific name, and the enumerator, who is rarely an ethnologist, could do no better than to give the name by which the tribe was locally known. If this name was not readily identified with one of the recognized tribes the Indian was necessarily assigned to the miscellaneous group and lost to the tribal classification. No instructions were given as to the tribal allocation of Indians of mixed tribal blood. Such Indians are probably included in the tribes which they prefer to claim, or in which they have the reputation of membership. The tabulation by stock and tribe from the Census of 1910 differentiated 52 linguistic stocks, divided into 280 tribes. In 1930, for convenience of tabulation, many of the smaller tribes were thrown together into groups of tribes, reducing the number of tribes and groups to 100, and the number of linguistic stocks to 40.

Marriage

★ 115 ★

Marital Status of American Indians 15 Years Old and Older, by Sex, 1900-1930

Sex and marital status	1900 Number	1900 Percent	1910 Number	1910 Percent	1920 Number	1920 Percent	1930 Number	1930 Percent
Male								
Total	72,076	100.0	80,383	100.0	76,321	100.0	103,441	100.0
Single	24,323	33.7	27,391	34.1	26,450	34.7	38,021	36.8
Married	41,067	57.0	46,154	57.4	43,095	56.5	56,382	54.5
Widowed	4,974	6.9	5,319	6.6	5,711	7.5	7,173	6.9
Divorced	418	0.6	679	0.8	680	0.8	1,646	1.6
Unknown	1,294	1.8	840	1.0	385	0.5	219	0.2
Female								
Total	71,497	100.0	76,982	100.0	70,431	100.0	96,084	100.0
Single	14,350	20.1	16,324	21.2	16,238	23.1	23,335	24.3
Married	43,906	61.4	49,095	63.8	43,923	62.4	59,168	61.6
Widowed	11,458	16.0	10,071	13.1	9,217	13.1	11,541	12.0
Divorced	870	1.2	959	1.2	826	1.1	1,876	2.0
Unknown	913	1.3	533	0.7	227	0.3	164	0.2

Source: Dr. Leon E. Truesdell, U.S. Department of Commerce, Bureau of the Census, Fifteenth Census of the United States: 1930, *The Indian Population of the United States and Alaska*, U.S. Government Printing Office, 1937, p. 121.

★ 116 ★

Marital Status of American Indians Age 15 Years Old and Older, by State and Sex, 1910 and 1930

Figures are shown in percent.

State	1910 Male Single	1910 Male Married	1910 Male Widowed	1910 Female Single	1910 Female Married	1910 Female Widowed	1930 Male Single	1930 Male Married	1930 Male Widowed	1930 Female Single	1930 Female Married	1930 Female Widowed
United States	34.1	57.4	6.6	21.2	63.8	13.1	36.8	54.5	6.9	24.3	61.6	12.0
Arizona	28.5	61.6	6.7	17.1	67.6	12.1	34.1	57.3	7.6	22.0	64.1	12.8
California	37.1	50.3	10.4	22.6	59.2	16.0	42.7	45.7	8.9	23.9	58.8	14.1
Idaho	24.3	64.3	6.6	12.2	68.6	16.0	28.9	57.5	9.3	16.0	63.8	16.7
Kansas	56.2	34.4	7.6	45.6	46.9	6.6	41.7	50.6	5.3	22.1	66.2	9.4
Michigan	40.0	49.8	9.2	23.8	61.0	14.0	42.3	45.8	9.8	22.3	61.9	14.0
Minnesota	34.6	56.1	6.7	19.6	62.1	14.5	39.6	50.6	7.7	25.0	60.5	11.9
Montana	29.7	64.6	4.5	15.7	69.7	13.3	33.6	56.1	7.3	19.3	67.8	10.5
Nebraska	33.2	60.3	6.0	22.0	65.5	11.9	33.3	56.3	8.3	27.6	58.9	11.2

[Continued]

★ 116 ★

Marital Status of American Indians Age 15 Years Old and Older, by State and Sex, 1910 and 1930
[Continued]

| State | 1910 | | | | | | 1930 | | | | | |
| | Male | | | Female | | | Male | | | Female | | |
	Single	Married	Widowed	Single	Married	Widowed	Single	Married	Widowed	Single	Married	Widowed
Nevada	26.8	61.9	7.4	14.4	67.1	14.8	36.7	52.9	7.8	21.7	58.0	17.5
New Mexico	13.0	60.5	7.6	17.7	66.1	13.7	34.5	56.2	8.4	24.4	61.0	13.1
New York	34.5	54.1	9.0	24.7	59.4	15.6	36.9	52.9	8.7	25.4	60.6	12.3
North Carolina	33.3	62.8	3.4	27.7	63.1	8.9	36.8	58.4	4.3	30.1	60.7	8.1
North Dakota	33.1	61.1	4.6	22.6	66.1	10.3	36.3	54.7	7.7	25.8	63.5	8.7
Oklahoma	34.9	58.4	5.3	23.0	63.7	11.9	37.9	55.7	4.6	26.8	59.4	11.3
Oregon	42.0	48.4	7.7	21.1	56.6	20.5	39.1	49.4	7.4	21.4	58.8	15.8
South Dakota	29.3	63.3	5.4	20.1	65.9	12.3	33.1	58.0	7.3	22.5	65.0	11.0
Utah	23.3	63.4	10.4	9.3	74.5	13.6	28.3	61.5	8.6	13.7	73.6	11.8
Washington	32.5	57.2	7.7	15.7	65.2	17.4	36.8	53.4	7.2	18.7	64.9	13.6
Wisconsin	35.4	55.2	7.5	23.2	63.1	12.0	41.0	49.2	7.8	26.6	60.0	11.2
Wyoming	22.9	60.3	9.4	9.1	66.6	17.5	29.4	59.3	9.2	16.5	71.7	10.8

Source: Dr. Leon E. Truesdell, U.S. Department of Commerce, Bureau of the Census, Fifteenth Census of the United States: 1930, *The Indian Population of the United States and Alaska*, U.S. Government Printing Office, 1937, p. 121.

★ 117 ★

Marital Status of American Indians Age 15 Years Old and Older, by Selected Tribe and Sex, 1910 and 1930

Figures are shown in percent.

| Tribe | 1910 | | | | | | 1930 | | | | | |
| | Male | | | Female | | | Male | | | Female | | |
	Single	Married	Widowed	Single	Married	Widowed	Single	Married	Widowed	Single	Married	Widowed
All tribes	34.1	57.4	6.6	21.2	63.8	13.1	36.8	54.5	6.9	24.3	61.6	12.0
Arapaho	20.0	67.9	5.3	7.6	72.1	14.9	26.0	69.4	4.3	18.6	74.2	6.4
Blackfeet	32.3	63.8	2.0	17.4	71.0	10.0	36.2	55.4	5.4	20.1	68.9	9.3
Cheyenne	25.7	68.0	5.5	16.9	68.5	12.2	26.8	62.0	8.9	19.1	69.0	8.8
Chippewa	37.2	54.2	6.9	23.2	62.1	12.7	40.4	50.4	7.7	25.3	61.8	10.8
Menominee	32.6	57.0	9.7	22.8	63.8	12.6	41.2	49.3	7.5	24.7	63.9	9.3
Ottawa	36.2	52.7	10.2	23.8	61.4	14.0	41.9	46.8	10.4	23.2	58.6	15.1
Potawatomi	40.0	48.3	10.4	24.2	64.2	10.8	38.9	52.1	8.4	24.8	66.1	7.6
Apache	24.2	63.4	8.2	13.9	62.3	20.2	30.7	59.1	8.7	16.7	67.8	14.2
Navaho	29.8	64.4	3.9	15.1	69.8	11.4	34.5	60.1	4.5	21.1	63.6	13.7
Iroquois	37.6	52.3	7.9	25.8	59.8	11.9	38.7	51.1	8.0	26.3	60.2	11.0
Cherokee	38.2	55.8	4.7	26.3	62.0	10.5	40.5	53.6	4.4	27.6	59.9	10.1
Keresans	35.9	53.6	10.4	22.8	63.5	13.5	39.3	47.4	12.8	30.5	59.5	9.6
Chickasaw	36.3	57.1	5.0	25.9	60.0	12.6	39.0	54.1	5.1	30.9	53.4	13.1
Choctaw	33.2	59.1	6.3	22.8	62.9	12.6	38.8	54.6	4.9	27.9	57.6	12.5
Creek	32.6	60.4	6.2	22.7	61.4	14.9	35.7	55.9	6.0	27.7	56.7	13.0
Seminole	32.7	58.5	6.9	22.1	62.8	13.8	35.6	58.9	5.1	27.3	57.0	14.2
Papago	30.7	60.7	5.4	23.5	66.2	7.6	36.7	52.4	10.3	30.7	56.3	12.3
Pima	30.2	59.3	10.1	19.6	66.2	13.9	32.7	56.4	10.3	25.2	62.7	11.3
Klamath and Modoc	38.6	51.3	9.1	19.9	52.4	26.5	43.6	44.7	9.1	20.8	57.9	17.5
Shahaptians	26.1	61.9	8.0	15.6	61.4	19.9	30.7	58.1	7.2	18.8	58.8	18.4

[Continued]

202

★ 117 ★

Marital Status of American Indians Age 15 Years Old and Older, by Selected Tribe and Sex, 1910 and 1930
[Continued]

Tribe	1910						1930					
	Male			Female			Male			Female		
	Single	Married	Widowed	Single	Married	Widowed	Single	Married	Widowed	Single	Married	Widowed
Comanche	23.4	68.5	7.8	14.3	65.1	19.3	28.5	65.4	4.3	25.9	61.0	11.6
Hopi	26.4	56.5	10.3	16.2	66.9	10.0	29.8	57.8	11.2	26.5	65.4	7.2
Shoshoni	24.9	63.4	8.4	12.6	68.8	15.9	31.8	54.4	11.4	18.8	62.5	16.3
Ute	25.3	59.0	12.5	9.3	73.0	14.8	27.1	60.0	11.1	15.0	72.0	12.2
Crow	21.7	67.9	9.2	13.6	69.0	16.8	25.2	63.4	6.9	18.1	68.8	10.2
Omaha	30.8	63.1	6.1	15.5	70.7	13.9	30.4	59.1	10.1	22.3	64.9	12.5
Osage	29.9	64.0	3.9	23.1	67.0	8.8	28.0	65.3	2.9	19.7	66.8	9.6
Dakota	29.8	63.4	5.1	19.9	66.0	12.5	32.6	58.3	7.4	22.1	65.1	11.1
Assiniboine	26.4	69.8	3.5	13.0	74.2	12.1	31.6	57.9	8.6	20.6	66.8	10.3
Winnebago	30.9	60.5	6.0	21.6	63.4	12.9	38.1	54.3	6.5	30.2	54.5	12.1
Tanoans	31.0	57.2	10.5	18.5	68.6	12.1	36.7	50.2	11.7	26.7	60.6	11.3
Yuma	30.6	57.4	9.0	26.4	58.5	11.3	40.4	48.1	10.5	23.0	60.9	13.6

Source: Dr. Leon E. Truesdell, U.S. Department of Commerce, Bureau of the Census, Fifteenth Census of the United States: 1930, *The Indian Population of the United States and Alaska*, U.S. Government Printing Office, 1937, p. 121.

★ 118 ★

Marital Status of American Indian Females 15 Years Old and Older, by Linguistic Stock and Tribe, 1910: A - Sa

Data are shown for tribes having 200 or more members.

Linguistic stock and tribe	Indian females 15 years of age and over: 1910								Marital condition not reported
	Total	Single		Married		Widowed		Divorced	
		Number	Percent	Number	Percent	Number	Percent		
Algonquian stock	11,974	2,653	22.2	7,570	63.2	1,530	12.8	140	81
Arapaho	437	33	7.6	315	72.1	65	14.9	1	23
Cheyenne	1,107	187	16.9	758	68.5	135	12.2	24	3
Chippewa	5,830	1,353	23.2	3,620	62.1	738	12.7	79	40
Cree	126	33	26.2	79	62.7	11	8.7	1	2
Delaware	252	64	25.4	142	56.3	42	16.7	4	-
Gros Ventres	154	26	16.9	108	70.1	18	11.7	2	-
Kickapoo	97	16	16.5	66	68.0	13	13.4	-	2
Mashpee	63	17	27.0	35	55.6	10	15.9	1	-
Menominee	356	81	22.8	227	63.8	45	12.6	3	-
Miami	60	23	38.3	27	45.0	10	16.7	-	-
Ottawa	821	195	23.8	504	61.4	115	14.0	6	1
Passamaquoddy	126	29	23.0	78	61.9	19	15.1	-	-
Penobscot	97	28	28.9	58	59.8	9	9.3	2	-
Piegan	649	113	17.4	461	71.0	65	10.0	3	7
Potawatomi	590	143	24.2	379	64.2	64	10.8	4	-
Sauk and Fox	199	42	21.1	128	64.3	28	14.1	-	1

[Continued]

★ 118 ★

Marital Status of American Indian Females 15 Years Old and Older, by Linguistic Stock and Tribe, 1910: A - Sa
[Continued]

Linguistic stock and tribe	Indian females 15 years of age and over: 1910								
	Total	Single		Married		Widowed		Divorced	Marital condition not reported
		Number	Percent	Number	Percent	Number	Percent		
Shawnee	386	98	25.4	227	58.8	56	14.5	5	-
Stockbridges	156	33	21.2	96	61.5	24	15.4	2	1
Athabaskan stock	8,446	1,297	15.4	5,692	67.4	1,165	13.8	237	55
Apache	1,529	189	12.4	987	64.6	300	19.6	43	10
Hupa	218	63	28.9	119	54.6	35	16.1	-	1
Jicarilla Apache	221	49	22.2	127	57.5	34	15.4	10	1
Mescalero Apache	157	27	17.2	75	47.8	52	33.1	3	-
Navajo	5,940	897	15.1	4,148	69.8	680	11.4	174	41
Rogue River	110	17	15.5	67	60.9	21	19.1	4	1
Wailaki	74	17	23.0	46	62.2	11	14.9	-	1
Caddoan stock	566	132	23.3	353	62.4	76	13.4	4	1
Arikara	140	38	27.1	90	64.3	10	7.1	1	1
Caddo	110	21	19.1	72	65.5	16	14.5	1	-
Pawnee	212	49	23.1	129	60.8	32	15.1	2	-
Wichita	99	24	24.2	57	57.6	18	18.2	-	-
Chimakuan stock	109	9	8.3	81	74.3	17	15.6	2	-
Quileute	93	8	8.6	71	76.3	14	15.1	-	-
Chinookan stock	275	48	17.5	176	64.0	50	18.2	-	1
Chinook	75	15	20.0	50	66.7	10	13.3	-	-
Wasco	82	16	19.5	46	56.1	20	24.4	-	-
Wishram	98	15	15.3	66	67.3	16	16.3	-	1
Croatan group	1,624	467	28.8	1,010	62.2	141	8.7	1	5
Croatan	1,624	467	28.8	1,010	62.2	141	8.7	1	5
Iroquoian stock	10,132	2,658	26.2	6,225	61.4	1,096	10.8	96	57
Cherokee	7,741	2,036	26.3	4,797	62.0	814	10.5	52	42
Mohawk	131	25	19.1	91	69.5	12	9.2	1	2
Oneida	682	155	22.7	444	65.1	67	9.8	15	1
Onondaga	113	34	30.1	58	51.3	21	18.6	-	-
St. Regis	319	105	32.0	181	56.7	28	8.8	-	5
Seneca	903	219	24.3	527	58.4	126	14.0	27	4
Tuscarora	114	36	31.6	62	54.4	15	13.2	1	-
Wyandot	87	28	32.2	51	58.6	8	9.2	-	-
Karok stock	233	51	21.9	141	60.5	38	16.3	2	1
Orleans	233	51	21.9	141	60.5	38	16.3	2	1

[Continued]

★ 118 ★

Marital Status of American Indian Females 15 Years Old and Older, by Linguistic Stock and Tribe, 1910: A - Sa

[Continued]

Linguistic stock and tribe	Indian females 15 years of age and over: 1910								Divorced	Marital condition not reported
	Total	Single		Married		Widowed				
		Number	Percent	Number	Percent	Number	Percent			
Keresan stock	1,154	263	22.8	733	63.5	156	13.5	2	-
Acoma	214	45	21.0	132	61.7	35	16.4	2	-
Cochiti	74	9	12.2	53	71.6	12	16.2	-	-
Laguna	418	109	26.1	254	60.8	55	13.2	-	-
San Felipe	135	29	21.5	85	63.0	21	15.6	-	-
Santa Ana	47	8	[1]	34	[1]	5	[1]	-	-
Santo Domingo	232	56	24.1	154	66.4	22	9.5	-	-
Kiowan stock	314	31	9.9	251	79.9	27	8.6	1	4
Kiowa	314	31	9.9	251	79.9	27	8.6	1	4
Kutenaian stock	154	18	11.7	116	75.3	20	13.0	-	-
Kutenai	154	18	11.7	116	75.3	20	13.0	-	-
Lutuamian stock	332	66	19.9	174	52.4	88	26.5	4	-
Klamath	240	50	20.8	130	54.2	60	25.0	-	-
Modoc	92	16	17.4	44	47.8	28	30.4	4	-
Maidu stock	316	62	19.6	195	61.7	56	17.7	1	2
Maidu	316	62	19.6	195	61.7	56	17.7	1	2
Miwok stock	236	51	21.6	130	55.1	50	21.2	2	3
Miwok	229	47	20.5	127	55.5	50	21.8	2	3
Muskhogean stock	7,606	1,761	23.2	4,721	62.1	1,013	13.3	70	41
Alibamu	85	26	30.6	46	54.1	13	15.3	-	-
Chickasaw	1,012	262	25.9	607	60.0	128	12.6	7	8
Choctaw	3,995	912	22.8	2,511	62.9	504	12.6	40	28
Creek	1,994	445	22.3	1,229	61.6	299	15.0	17	4
Seminole	494	109	22.1	310	62.8	68	13.8	6	1
Piman stock	2,440	515	21.1	1,633	66.9	259	10.6	6	27
Papago	1,087	255	23.5	720	66.2	83	7.6	2	27
Pima	1,212	238	19.6	802	66.2	168	13.9	4	-
Yaqui	129	19	14.7	103	79.8	7	5.4	-	-
Pomo stock	395	71	18.0	237	60.0	72	18.2	11	4
Pomo	260	46	17.7	154	59.2	48	18.5	10	2
Salishan stock	2,351	387	16.5	1,545	65.7	388	16.5	16	15
Chehalis	69	13	18.8	45	65.2	8	11.6	3	-

[Continued]

205

★ 118 ★

Marital Status of American Indian Females 15 Years Old and Older, by Linguistic Stock and Tribe, 1910: A - Sa
[Continued]

Linguistic stock and tribe	Indian females 15 years of age and over: 1910								
	Total	Single		Married		Widowed		Divorced	Marital condition not reported
		Number	Percent	Number	Percent	Number	Percent		
Clallam	102	15	14.7	76	74.5	8	7.8	2	1
Coeur d'Alene	85	11	12.9	64	75..3	10	11.8	-	-
Columbia	118	15	12.7	73	61.9	25	21.2	1	4
Colville	237	48	20.3	149	62.9	37	15.6	2	1
Flathead	134	24	17.9	90	67.2	19	14.2	1	-
Kalispel	189	24	12.7	127	67.2	37	19.6	1	-
Lummi	70	15	21.4	50	71.4	4	5.7	-	1
Okinagan	92	16	17.4	57	62.0	19	20.7	-	-
Puyallup	97	30	30.9	48	49.5	18	18.6	1	-
Quinaielt	86	9	10.5	65	75.6	12	14.0	-	-
Sanpoil	87	16	18.4	51	58.6	20	23.0	-	-
Snohomish	190	29	15.3	131	68.9	24	12.6	-	6
Spokan	228	45	19.7	146	64.0	35	15.4	1	1
Suquamish	83	15	18.1	54	65.1	12	14.5	2	-
Swinomish	102	12	11.8	69	67.6	21	20.6	-	-

Source: U.S. Bureau of the Census, *Indian Population in the United States and Alaska, 1910,* United States Government Printing Office, Washington, D.C., 1915, pp. 165-167. *Notes:* A dash (-) represents zero. 1. Percentages are not shown where base is less than 50.

★ 119 ★

Marital Status of American Indian Females 15 Years Old and Older, by Linguistic Stock and Tribe, 1910: Sh - Z

Data are shown for tribes having 200 or more members.

Linguistic stock and tribe	Indian females 15 years of age and over: 1910								
	Total	Single		Married		Widowed		Divorced	Marital condition not reported
		Number	Percent	Number	Percent	Number	Percent		
Shahaptian stock	1,594	248	15.6	978	61.4	318	19.9	30	20
Klikitat	162	31	19.1	96	59.3	29	17.9	2	4
Nez Perces	447	62	13.9	279	62.4	88	19.7	10	8
Umatilla	114	13	11.4	55	48.2	38	33.3	6	2
Wallawalla	116	24	20.7	75	64.7	13	11.2	4	-
Warm Springs	193	22	11.4	131	67.9	40	20.7	-	-
Yakima	501	87	17.4	308	61.5	93	18.6	8	5

[Continued]

★ 119 ★

Marital Status of American Indian Females 15 Years Old and Older, by Linguistic Stock and Tribe, 1910: Sh - Z
[Continued]

Linguistic stock and tribe	Indian females 15 years of age and over: 1910								Marital condition not reported
	Total	Single		Married		Widowed		Divorced	
		Number	Percent	Number	Percent	Number	Percent		
Shastan stock	537	123	22.9	311	57.9	92	17.1	6	5
Hat Creek	85	9	10.2	62	72.9	13	15.3	1	-
Pit River	337	75	22.3	206	61.1	47	13.9	4	5
Shasta	115	39	33.9	43	37.4	32	27.8	1	-
Shoshonean stock	5,440	806	14.8	3,598	66.1	852	15.7	94	90
Bannock	148	22	14.9	99	66.9	25	16.9	2	-
Chemehuevi	112	8	7.1	76	67.9	26	23.2	1	1
Comanche	384	55	14.3	250	65.1	74	19.3	4	1
Hopi	538	87	16.2	360	66.9	54	10.0	37	-
Kawia	226	49	21.7	142	62.8	29	12.8	1	5
Mono	505	90	17.8	299	59.2	94	18.6	14	8
Paiute	238	39	16.4	157	66.0	40	16.8	2	-
Paviotso	1,118	143	12.8	750	67.1	173	15.5	5	47
San Luiseno	155	66	42.6	65	41.9	22	14.2	2	-
Shoshoni	1,274	161	12.6	876	68.8	202	15.9	16	19
Ute	634	59	9.3	463	73.0	94	14.8	9	9
Siouan stock	10,509	2,062	19.6	6,976	66.4	1,315	12.5	99	57
Assiniboine	414	54	13.0	307	74.2	50	12.1	2	1
Crow	626	85	13.6	432	69.0	105	16.8	2	2
Hidatsa	153	42	27.5	91	59.5	18	11.8	-	2
Iowa	68	19	27.9	46	67.6	3	4.4	-	-
Kansa	33	8	[1]	23	[1]	2	[1]	-	-
Mandan	73	21	28.8	35	47.9	13	17.8	-	4
Omaha	317	49	15.5	224	70.7	44	13.9	-	-
Osage	351	81	23.1	235	67.0	31	8.8	4	-
Oto	96	12	12.5	74	77.1	9	9.4	1	-
Ponca	268	70	26.1	176	65.7	20	7.5	1	1
Quapaw	64	15	23.4	38	59.4	9	14.1	1	1
Santee Sioux	471	101	21.4	303	64.3	60	12.7	5	2
Sioux	295	92	31.2	169	57.3	27	9.2	2	5
Sisseton Sioux	800	140	17.5	535	66.9	114	14.3	8	3
Teton Sioux	4,673	935	20.0	3,073	65.8	591	12.6	52	22
Brule Sioux	260	39	15.0	178	68.5	31	11.9	10	2
Hunkpapa Sioux	364	65	17.9	245	67.3	49	13.5	3	2
Minniconjou Sioux	154	31	20.1	93	60.4	29	18.8	1	-
Oglala Sioux	1,930	394	20.4	1,294	67.0	227	11.8	12	3
Sans Arc Sioux	58	11	19.0	37	63.8	10	17.2	-	-
Sihasapa	161	26	16.1	116	72.0	16	9.9	3	-
Two Kettle Sioux	75	14	18.7	53	70.7	8	10.7	-	-

[Continued]

★119★

Marital Status of American Indian Females 15 Years Old and Older, by Linguistic Stock and Tribe, 1910: Sh - Z

[Continued]

Linguistic stock and tribe	Indian females 15 years of age and over: 1910								
	Total	Single		Married		Widowed		Divorced	Marital condition not reported
		Number	Percent	Number	Percent	Number	Percent		
Other Teton Sioux	1,671	355	21.2	1,057	63.3	221	13.2	23	15
Winnebago	588	127	21.6	373	63.4	76	12.9	9	3
Yankton Sioux	719	133	18.5	510	70.9	66	9.2	5	5
Yanktonai Sioux	470	75	16.0	312	66.4	72	15.3	6	5
Tanoan stock	932	172	18.5	639	68.6	113	12.1	5	3
Isleta	305	31	10.2	211	69.2	58	19.0	5	-
Jemez	139	26	18.7	100	71.9	11	7.9	-	2
San Juan	113	22	19.5	79	69.9	11	9.7	-	1
Santa Clara	79	29	36.7	43	54.4	7	8.9	-	-
Taos	139	30	21.6	101	72.7	8	5.8	-	-
Wailatpuan stock	107	12	11.2	52	48.6	36	33.6	7	-
Cayuse	99	11	11.1	46	46.5	36	36.4	6	-
Wakashan stock	117	15	12.8	83	70.9	19	16.2	-	-
Makah	102	14	13.7	71	69.6	17	16.7	-	-
Washoan stock	292	43	14.7	208	71.2	30	10.3	8	3
Washo	292	43	14.7	208	71.2	30	10.3	8	3
Wintun stock	217	34	15.7	157	72.4	24	11.1	2	-
Wintun	120	25	20.8	82	68.3	12	10.1	1	-
Yokuts stock	164	31	18.9	108	65.9	24	14.6	1	-
Yokuts	85	14	16.5	61	71.8	10	11.8	-	-
Yuman stock	1,272	205	16.1	850	66.8	185	14.5	17	15
Cocopa	78	18	23.1	45	57.7	14	17.9	-	1
Diegueno	209	42	20.1	127	60.8	30	14.4	1	9
Maricopa	118	21	17.8	82	69.5	15	12.7	-	-
Mohave	310	29	9.4	212	68.4	64	20.6	1	4
Walapai	123	6	4.9	103	83.7	14	11.4	-	-
Yavapai	88	10	11.4	63	71.6	10	11.4	5	-
Yuma	284	75	26.4	166	58.5	32	11.3	10	1
Yurok stock	224	35	15.6	137	61.2	51	22.8	1	-
Weitspec	224	35	15.6	137	61.2	51	22.8	1	-

[Continued]

★ 119 ★

Marital Status of American Indian Females 15 Years Old and Older, by Linguistic Stock and Tribe, 1910: Sh - Z
[Continued]

Linguistic stock and tribe	Indian females 15 years of age and over: 1910								
	Total	Single		Married		Widowed		Divorced	Marital condition not reported
		Number	Percent	Number	Percent	Number	Percent		
Zunian stock	504	61	12.1	349	69.2	63	12.5	31	-
Zuni	504	61	12.1	349	69.2	63	12.5	31	-

Source: U.S. Bureau of the Census, *Indian Population in the United States and Alaska, 1910*, United States Government Printing Office, Washington, D.C., 1915, pp. 165-167. *Notes:* A dash (-) represents zero. 1. Percentages are not shown where base is less than 50.

★ 120 ★

Marital Status of American Indian Males 15 Years Old and Older, by Linguistic Stock and Tribe, 1910: A - Sa

Data are shown for tribes having 200 or more members.

Linguistic stock and tribe	Indian males 15 years of age and over: 1910								
	Total	Single		Married		Widowed		Divorced	Marital condition not reported
		Number	Percent	Number	Percent	Number	Percent		
Algonquian stock	12,849	4,598	35.8	7,160	55.7	898	7.0	93	100
Arapaho	474	95	20.0	322	67.9	25	5.3	3	29
Cheyenne	1,020	262	25.7	694	68.0	56	5.5	5	3
Chippewa	6,180	2,297	37.2	3,352	54.2	426	6.9	56	49
Cree	132	63	47.7	64	48.5	5	3.8	-	-
Delaware	249	116	46.6	118	47.4	14	5.6	1	-
Gros Ventres	168	51	30.4	108	64.3	8	4.8	-	1
Kickapoo	117	27	23.1	73	62.4	16	13.7	-	1
Mashpee	81	38	46.9	34	42.0	6	7.4	3	-
Menominee	454	148	32.6	259	57.0	44	9.7	3	-
Miami	76	38	50.0	34	44.7	4	5.3	-	-
Ottawa	928	336	489	52.7	95	10.2	4	4	
Passamaquoddy	151	54	35.8	81	53.6	15	9.9	1	-
Penobscot	104	28	26.9	65	62.5	9	8.7	2	-
Piegan	639	212	33.2	408	63.8	13	2.0	2	4
Potawatomi	795	318	40.0	384	48.3	83	10.4	7	3
Sauk and Fox	245	85	34.7	139	56.7	18	7.3	-	3
Shawnee	347	133	38.3	193	55.6	20	5.8	-	1
Stockbridges	169	71	42.0	78	46.2	18	10.7	2	-
Athabaskan stock	8,258	2,393	28.9	5,270	63.6	423	5.1	79	120
Apache	1,472	349	23.7	940	63.9	118	8.0	17	48

[Continued]

209

★ 120 ★

Marital Status of American Indian Males 15 Years Old and Older, by Linguistic Stock and Tribe, 1910: A - Sa
[Continued]

Linguistic stock and tribe	Indian males 15 years of age and over: 1910								
	Total	Single		Married		Widowed		Divorced	Marital condition not reported
		Number	Percent	Number	Percent	Number	Percent		
Hupa	194	76	39.2	101	52.1	17	8.8	-	-
Jicarilla Apache	215	59	27.4	130	60.5	17	7.9	9	-
Mescalero Apache	112	28	25.0	70	62.5	13	11.6	1	-
Navajo	5,918	1,762	29.8	3,814	64.4	228	3.9	43	71
Rogue River	119	38	31.9	59	49.6	18	15.1	4	-
Wailaki	68	21	30.9	43	63.2	2	2.9	2	-
Caddoan stock	564	193	34.2	333	59.0	32	5.7	1	5
Arikara	136	40	29.4	81	59.6	10	7.4	1	4
Caddo	131	50	38.2	70	53.4	10	7.6	-	1
Pawnee	195	69	35.4	121	62.1	5	2.6	-	-
Wichita	95	32	33.7	57	60.0	6	6.3	-	-
Chimakuan stock	99	29	29.3	67	67.7	-	-	3	-
Quileute	81	23	28.4	55	67.9	-	-	3	-
Chinookan stock	289	103	35.6	161	55.7	24	8.3	-	1
Chinook	100	48	48.0	39	39.0	13	13.0	-	-
Wasco	78	21	26.9	55	70.5	1	1.3	-	1
Wishram	94	27	28.7	58	61.7	9	9.6	-	-
Croatan group	1,588	526	33.1	1,006	63.4	48	3.0	4	4
Croatan	1,588	526	33.1	1,006	63.4	48	3.0	4	4
Iroquoian stock	10,946	4,171	38.1	6,007	54.9	603	5.5	69	96
Cherokee	8,208	3,134	38.2	4,581	55.8	389	4.7	39	65
Mohawk	115	43	37.4	56	48.7	7	6.1	-	9
Oneida	805	299	37.1	443	55.0	47	5.8	16	-
Onondaga	121	51	42.1	60	49.6	10	8.3	-	-
St. Regis	420	173	41.2	207	49.4	28	6.7	-	12
Seneca	964	334	34.6	511	53.0	97	10.1	13	9
Tuscarora	155	72	46.5	72	46.5	11	7.1	-	-
Wyandot	109	49	45.0	52	47.7	6	5.5	1	1
Karok stock	229	100	43.7	108	47.2	20	8.7	1	-
Orleans	229	100	43.7	108	47.2	20	8.7	1	-
Keresan stock	1,340	481	35.9	718	53.6	140	10.4	1	-
Acoma	210	72	34.3	125	59.5	12	5.7	1	-
Cochiti	86	20	23.3	60	69.8	6	7.0	-	-
Laguna	462	165	35.7	254	55.0	43	9.3	-	-

[Continued]

★ 120 ★

Marital Status of American Indian Males 15 Years Old and Older, by Linguistic Stock and Tribe, 1910: A - Sa

[Continued]

Linguistic stock and tribe	Total	Indian males 15 years of age and over: 1910							Divorced	Marital condition not reported
		Single		Married		Widowed				
		Number	Percent	Number	Percent	Number	Percent			
San Felipe	198	86	43.4	80	40.4	32	16.2	-	-
Santa Ana	85	35	41.2	35	41.2	15	17.6	-	-
Santo Domingo	262	84	32.1	150	57.3	28	10.7	-	-
Kiowan stock	181	45	24.9	121	66.9	11	6.1	4	-
Kiowa	293	61	20.8	225	76.8	6	2.0	-	1
Kutenaian stock	181	45	24.9	121	66.9	11	6.1	4	-
Kutenai	181	45	24.9	121	66.9	11	6.1	4	-
Lutuamian stock	298	115	38.6	153	51.3	27	9.1	3	-
Klamath	213	86	40.4	108	50.7	17	8.0	2	-
Modoc	85	29	34.1	45	52.9	10	11.8	1	-
Maidu stock	364	130	35.7	179	49.2	45	12.4	7	3
Maidu	364	130	35.7	179	49.2	45	12.4	7	3
Miwok stock	220	72	32.7	117	53.2	24	10.9	2	5
Miwok	208	67	32.2	112	53.8	22	10.6	2	5
Muskhogean stock	7,745	2,587	33.4	4,582	59.2	478	6.2	41	57
Alibamu	93	39	41.9	46	49.5	8	8.6	-	-
Chickasaw	955	347	36.3	545	57.1	48	5.0	6	9
Choctaw	4,174	1,386	33.2	2,468	59.1	265	6.3	19	36
Creek	1,958	629	32.1	1,192	60.9	119	6.1	10	8
Seminole	535	175	32.7	313	58.5	37	6.9	6	4
Piman stock	2,715	843	31.0	1,622	59.7	208	7.7	8	34
Papago	1,143	351	30.7	694	60.7	62	5.4	2	34
Pima	1,369	413	30.2	812	59.3	138	10.1	6	-
Yaqui	189	71	37.6	111	58.7	7	3.7	-	-
Pomo stock	412	114	27.7	242	58.7	45	10.9	8	3
Pomo	269	73	27.1	162	60.2	23	8.6	8	3
Salishan stock	2,521	800	31.7	1,480	58.7	186	7.4	21	34
Chehalis	93	30	32.3	57	61.3	6	6.5	-	-
Clallam	121	42	34.7	74	61.2	3	2.5	2	-
Coeur d'Alene	102	29	28.4	70	68.6	2	2.0	1	-
Columbia	137	34	24.8	81	59.1	11	8.0	-	11
Colville	262	105	40.1	124	47.3	23	8.8	8	2

[Continued]

★ 120 ★

Marital Status of American Indian Males 15 Years Old and Older, by Linguistic Stock and Tribe, 1910: A - Sa

[Continued]

Linguistic stock and tribe	Indian males 15 years of age and over: 1910								
	Total	Single		Married		Widowed		Divorced	Marital condition not reported
		Number	Percent	Number	Percent	Number	Percent		
Flathead	144	54	37.5	81	56.3	8	5.6	1	-
Kalispel	191	58	30.4	119	62.3	12	6.3	2	-
Lummi	87	26	29.9	47	54.0	9	10.3	-	5
Okinagan	84	26	31.0	50	59.5	4	4.8	2	2
Puyallup	101	43	42.6	49	48.5	8	7.9	1	-
Quinaielt	92	22	23.9	62	67.4	7	7.6	1	-
Sanpoil	78	30	38.5	39	50.0	7	9.0	-	2
Snohomish	212	66	31.1	122	57.5	17	8.0	1	6
Spokan	207	52	25.1	133	64.3	21	10.1	-	1
Suquamish	95	32	33.7	58	61.1	4	4.2	1	-
Swinomish	110	29	26.4	74	67.3	5	4.5	-	2

Source: U.S. Bureau of the Census, *Indian Population in the United States and Alaska, 1910*, United States Government Printing Office, Washington, D.C., 1915, pp. 165-167. *Notes:* A dash (-) represents zero. 1. Percentages are not shown where base is less than 50.

★ 121 ★

Marital Status of American Indian Males 15 Years Old and Older, by Linguistic Stock and Tribe, 1910: Sh - Z

Data are shown for tribes having 200 or more members.

Linguistic stock and tribe	Indian males 15 years of age and over: 1910								
	Total	Single		Married		Widowed		Divorced	Marital condition not reported
		Number	Percent	Number	Percent	Number	Percent		
Shahaptian stock	1,392	363	26.1	861	61.9	112	8.0	33	23
Klikitat	131	35	26.7	84	64.1	5	3.8	6	1
Nez Perces	425	107	25.2	261	61.4	33	7.8	15	9
Umatilla	89	18	20.2	57	64.0	11	12.4	2	1
Wallawalla	119	45	37.8	65	54.6	8	6.7	1	-
Warm Springs	165	27	16.4	123	74.5	14	8.5	-	1
Yakima	411	120	29.2	236	57.4	39	9.5	8	8
Shastan stock	489	151	30.9	284	58.1	51	10.4	3	-
Hat Creek	86	18	20.9	58	67.4	10	11.6	-	-
Pit River	305	78	25.6	187	61.3	38	12.5	2	-
Shasta	98	55	56.1	39	39.8	3	3.1	1	-

[Continued]

★ 121 ★

Marital Status of American Indian Males 15 Years Old and Older, by Linguistic Stock and Tribe, 1910: Sh - Z
[Continued]

Linguistic stock and tribe	Indian males 15 years of age and over: 1910									
	Total	Single		Married		Widowed		Divorced	Marital condition not reported
		Number	Percent	Number	Percent	Number	Percent		
Shoshonean stock	5,696	1,542	27.1	3,406	59.8	541	9.5	87	120
Bannock	160	54	33.8	91	56.9	13	8.1	2	-
Chemehuevi	122	28	23.0	79	64.8	15	12.3	-	-
Comanche	359	84	23.4	246	68.5	28	7.8	1	-
Hopi	651	172	26.4	368	56.5	67	10.3	43	1
Kawia	291	95	32.6	147	50.5	40	13.7	-	9
Mono	422	123	29.1	245	58.1	42	10.0	9	3
Paiute	274	82	29.9	161	58.8	26	9.5	2	3
Paviotso	1,032	243	23.5	655	63.5	70	6.8	4	60
San Luiseno	173	88	50.9	63	36.4	20	11.6	2	-
Shoshoni	1,320	329	24.9	837	63.4	111	8.4	15	28
Ute	783	198	25.3	462	59.0	98	12.5	9	16
Siouan stock	10,517	3,107	29.5	6,692	63.6	546	5.2	91	81
Assiniboine	397	105	26.4	277	69.8	14	3.5	-	1
Crow	608	132	21.7	413	67.9	56	9.2	6	1
Hidatsa	169	69	40.8	93	55.0	3	1.8	-	4
Iowa	72	22	30.6	46	63.9	2	2.8	1	1
Kansa	77	23	29.9	50	64.9	2	2.6	-	33
Mandan	67	18	26.9	39	58.2	5	7.5	-	5
Omaha	344	106	30.8	217	63.1	21	6.1	-	-
Osage	381	114	29.9	244	64.0	15	3.9	3	5
Oto	111	32	28.8	76	68.5	2	1.8	1	-
Ponca	264	84	31.8	170	64.4	9	3.4	1	-
Quapaw	58	21	36.2	33	56.9	3	5.2	-	1
Santee Sioux	470	144	30.6	298	63.4	22	4.7	5	1
Sioux	396	191	48.2	186	47.0	12	3.0	2	5
Sisseton Sioux	832	246	29.6	529	63.6	38	4.6	8	11
Teton Sioux	4,551	1,341	29.5	2,884	63.4	249	5.5	45	32
Brule Sioux	268	66	24.6	183	68.3	13	4.9	3	3
Hunkpapa Sioux	354	102	28.8	236	66.7	16	4.5	-	-
Minniconjou Sioux	130	38	29.2	76	58.5	15	11.5	1	-
Oglala Sioux	1,866	575	30.8	1,187	63.6	89	4.8	5	10
Sans Arc Sioux	61	22	36.1	37	60.7	1	1.6	1	-
Sihasapa	173	53	30.6	109	63.0	9	5.2	2	-
Two Kettle Sioux	112	33	29.5	71	63.4	6	5.4	2	-
Other Teton Sioux	1,587	452	28.5	985	62.1	100	6.3	31	19
Winnebago	602	186	30.9	364	60.5	36	6.0	9	7
Yankton Sioux	660	162	24.5	458	69.4	35	5.3	2	3
Yanktonai Sioux	421	100	23.8	292	69.4	19	4.5	6	4

[Continued]

Marital Status of American Indian Males 15 Years Old and Older, by Linguistic Stock and Tribe, 1910: Sh - Z
[Continued]

Linguistic stock and tribe	Indian males 15 years of age and over: 1910								
	Total	Single		Married		Widowed		Divorced	Marital condition not reported
		Number	Percent	Number	Percent	Number	Percent		
Tanoan stock	1,120	347	31.0	641	57.2	118	10.5	7	7
Isleta	352	104	29.5	213	60.5	29	8.2	6	-
Jemez	189	55	29.1	105	55.6	23	12.2	-	6
San Juan	138	44	31.9	76	55.1	17	12.3	-	1
Santa Clara	97	39	40.2	47	48.5	10	10.3	1	-
Taos	169	44	26.0	106	62.7	19	11.2	-	-
Wailatpuan stock	99	23	23.2	61	61.6	12	12.1	3	-
Cayuse	87	20	23.0	56	64.4	8	9.2	3	-
Wakashan stock	130	28	21.5	94	72.3	8	6.2	-	-
Makah	122	27	22.1	87	71.3	8	6.6	-	-
Washoan stock	295	77	26.1	187	63.4	22	7.5	3	6
Washo	295	77	26.1	187	63.4	22	7.5	3	6
Wintun stock	261	86	33.0	130	49.8	43	16.5	2	-
Wintun	142	54	38.0	61	43.0	25	17.6	2	-
Yokuts stock	192	65	33.9	107	55.7	20	10.4	-	-
Yokuts	117	38	32.5	65	55.6	14	12.0	-	-
Yuman stock	1,561	455	29.1	875	56.1	160	10.2	16	55
Cocopa	94	35	37.2	40	42.6	13	13.8	-	6
Diegueno	267	98	36.7	131	49.1	26	9.7	2	10
Maricopa	127	33	26.0	75	59.1	18	14.2	-	1
Mohave	397	97	24.4	223	56.2	40	10.1	2	35
Walapai	165	49	29.7	101	61.2	13	7.9	1	1
Yavapai	99	22	22.2	67	67.7	9	9.1	1	-
Yuma	324	99	30.6	186	57.4	29	9.0	10	-
Yurok stock	213	68	31.9	115	54.0	30	14.1	-	-
Weitspec	213	68	31.9	115	54.0	30	14.1	-	-
Zunian stock	563	144	25.6	345	61.3	57	10.1	17	-
Zuni	563	144	25.6	345	61.3	57	10.1	17	-

Source: U.S. Bureau of the Census, *Indian Population in the United States and Alaska, 1910*, United States Government Printing Office, Washington, D.C., 1915, pp. 165-167. *Notes:* A dash (-) represents zero. 1. Percentages are not shown where base is less than 50.

U.S. Government

★ 122 ★

BIA Employees, 1852-1934

The total number of Bureau of Indian Affairs employees is shown for selected years.

Date	Number of employees
1852	108
1888	1,725
1911	6,000
1933	5,000
1934	12,000

Source: Fact Book, Albuquerque Area Office Division of Administration, February 1989, U.S. Department of the Interior, p. 2. Primary source: Theodore W. Taylor, "The Regional Organization of the Bureau of Indian Affairs." (Ph.D. dissertation, Harvard University), December 1959, p. 98.

★ 123 ★

Federal Restoration of Terminated American Indian Tribes

Tribe or band	State	Population	Acres	Termination statute	Date of act	Effective date	Current status
Menominee	Wisconsin	3,270	233,881	68 stat. 250	1954	1961	Restored
Klamath	Oregon	2,133	862,662	68 stat. 718	1954	1961	Restored
Western Oregon[1] (61 tribes and bands)	Oregon	2,081	3,158	68 stat. 724	1954	1956	Restored[2]
Alabama-Coushatta	Texas	450	3,200	68 stat. 768	1954	1955	Restored
Mixed blood Utes	Utah	490	211,430	68 stat. 868	1954	1961	Terminated
Southern Paiute	Utah	232	42,839	68 stat. 1099	1954	1957	Restored
Lower Lake Rancheria	California	unknown	unknown	70 stat. 58	1956	1956	Restored
Wyandotte	Oklahoma	1,157	94	70 stat. 893	1956	1959	Restored
Peoria	Oklahoma	640	unknown	70 stat. 937	1956	1959	Restored
Ottawa	Oklahoma	630	0	70 stat. 963	1957	1959	Restored
Coyote Valley Ranch	California	unknown	unknown	71 stat. 283	1957	1957	Restored
California Rancherias[1] (37-38 rancherias)	California	1,107	4,315	72 stat. 619	1958	1961-70	Restored[2]
Catawba	S. Carolina	631	3,388	73 stat. 502	1959	1962	Pending

[Continued]

215

★ 123 ★

Federal Restoration of Terminated American Indian Tribes
[Continued]

Tribe or band	State	Population	Acres	Termination statute	Date of act	Effective date	Current status
Ponca	Nebraska	442	834	76 stat. 429	1962	1966	Restored
Total		13,263	1,365,801				

Source: Elizabeth S. Grobsmith and Beth R. Ritter, "The Ponca Tribe of Nebraska: The Process of Restoration of a Federally Terminated Tribe," *Human Organization*, Vol. 51, No. 1, 1992, p. 4. Primary source: Prucha (1984:1048), Wilkinson & Biggs (1977:151), Mills (1989:4), Goodman (1990), Schmidt (1990): personal communication. *Notes:* 1. Figures are aggregates. 2. Those tribes seeking restoration have been restored.

★ 124 ★

House and Senate Committees: 1838-1920

Committees having jurisdiction over Indian affairs are shown by year.

Years	Senate	House
1938		Select Committee on Indian Fighters
1878	Joint Committee on Transfer of the Indian Bureau	
1879-1880	Select Committee to Examine into Removal of Northern Cheyennes	
1881	Select Committee to Examine into Circumstances Connected With Removal of Northern Cheyennes from the Sioux Reservation to the Indian Territory	
1836-1892	Select Committee on Indian Traders	Select Committee on Expenditures for the Indians and Yellowstone Park
1888-1892	Select Committee on Indian Traders Select Committee on the Five Civilized Tribes	Select Committee on Indian Depredation Claims (1888-1891)

[Continued]

★ 124 ★

House and Senate Committees: 1838-1920
[Continued]

Years	Senate	House
1893-1908	Select Committee to Investigate Trespassers on Indian (Cherokee) Lands	
	Select Committee on the Five Civilized Tribes	
	Standing Committee on Indian Depredations	
1909-1920	Standing Committee on Indian Depredations	
	Standing Committee on the Five Civilized Tribes	
	Standing Committee to Investigate Trespassers on Indian Lands	

Source: Richard Jones, *American Indian Policy: Background, Nature, History, Current Issues, Future Trends, Congressional Research Service Report No. 87227,* p. 80.

★ 125 ★

Land Units for Which Federal Trusteeship Had Been Terminated by Acts of Congress, 1963 - I

Land unit, jurisdiction	Principle Tribe		Public Law	Statute Ref.	Effective
	Name	Population			
California					
Sacramento Area Office					
Lower Lake	Pomo	8	84-443	(70 Stat. 58)	Mar 2, 1956
Coyote Valley	Pomo	30	85-91	(71 Stat. 283)	Jul 10, 1957
Laguna	Diegueno	0	80-335	(61 Stat. 731)	Feb 4, 1985
Buena Vista	Me-Wuk	5	85-671	(72 Stat. 619)	Apr 11, 1961
Cache Creek	Pomo	4	85-671	(72 Stat. 619)	do
Mark West	Pomo	0	85-671	(72 Stat. 619)	do
Paskenta	Wintun	6	85-671	(72 Stat. 619)	do
Ruffeys	Ruffy	0	85-671	(72 Stat. 619)	do
Strawberry Valley	Maidu	2	85-671	(72 Stat. 619)	do
Alexander Valley	Wappo	12	85-671	(72 Stat. 619)	Aug 1, 1961
Chicken Ranch	Me-Wuk	16	86-671	(72 Stat. 619)	do
Lytton	Pomo	33	85-671	(72 Stat. 619)	do

[Continued]

★ 125 ★

Land Units for Which Federal Trusteeship Had Been Terminated by Acts of Congress, 1963 - I
[Continued]

Land unit, jurisdiction	Principle Tribe		Public Law	Statute Ref.	Effective
	Name	Population			
Mooretown	Maidu	4	85-671	(72 Stat. 619)	do
Potter Valley	Pomo	11	85-671	(72 Stat. 619)	do
Redwood Valley	Pomo	27	85-671	(72 Stat. 619)	do
Table Bluff	Miami	48	85-671	(72 Stat. 619)	do
Redding	Clear Creek (mixed)	44	85-671	(72 Stat. 619)	Prior to
North Fork	Momo	1	85-671	(72 Stat. 619)	do
Scotts Valley	Pomo	45	85-671	(72 Stat. 619)	do
Table Mountain	Chukchansi	51	85-671	(72 Stat. 619)	do
Wilton	Me-Wuk	32	85-671	(72 Stat. 619)	do
Auburn	Maidu	83	85-671	(72 Stat. 619)	do
Guidiville	Pomo	21	85-671	(72 Stat. 619)	do
Nevada City	Maidu	2	85-671	(72 Stat. 619)	do
Picayunne	Chukchansi	11	85-671	(72 Stat. 619)	do
Upper Lake	Pomo	64	85-671	(72 Stat. 619)	do
Elk Valley	Cresent City	30	85-671	(72 Stat. 619)	do
Oklahoma Muskogee Area Office					
Wyandotte (also Kans)	Wyandotte[2]	423	84-887	(70 Stat. 893)	Aug 1, 1959
Peoria	Peoria[3]	230	84-921	(70 Stat. 937)	Aug 2, 1959
Ottawa	Ottawa	244	84-943	(70 Stat. 963)	Aug 13, 1961
Modoc (also Mo)	Modoc[4]	29	83-587	(68 Stat. 718)	Aug 13, 1961
Oregon Portland Area Office					
Grand Ronde & Siletz	Clackamas, Umpqua, Rogue River, and Klamath	2,100	83-588	(68 Stat. 724)	Aug 13, 1956
Western Oregon Public Domain Allotments (Includes Coos Bay)	Kusa, Rogue River, Klamath, and Umpqua	803	83-588	(68 Stat. 724)	Aug 13, 1956
Klamath	Klamath, Modoc, and Snake[4]	1,185	83-587 85-132 85-731	(68 Stat. 718) (71 Stat. 347) (72 Stat. 816)	Aug 13, 1961

[Continued]

★ 125 ★

Land Units for Which Federal Trusteeship Had Been Terminated by Acts of Congress, 1963 - I
[Continued]

Land unit, jurisdiction	Principle Tribe		Public Law	Statute Ref.	Effective
	Name	Population			
			86-247	(73 Stat. 477)	
South Carolina Central Office Catawba	Catawba Roll	353 631	86-322	(73 Stat. 592)	Jul 2, 1962
Texas Anadarko Area Office Alabama-Coushatta	Alabama-Coushatta[5]	385	83-627	(68 Stat. 768)	Jul 1, 1955
Utah Phoenix Area Office Cedar City	Paiute	28	83-762	(68 Stat. 1099)	Mar 1, 1957
Indian Peaks	Paiute	26	83-762	(68 Stat. 1099)	do
Kanosh	Paiute	42	83-762	(68 Stat. 1099)	do
Koosharem	Paiute	34	83-762	(68 Stat. 1099)	do
Shivwitz	Paiute	130	83-762	(68 Stat. 1099)	do
Uintah and Ouray	Ute (mixed blood only) (Affiliated Ute Citizens of Ouray)[6]	269	83-671	(68 Stat. 868)	Aug 27, 1961
Wisconsin Minneapolis Area Office Menominee	Menominee	2,221	83-399 84-715 84-718 85-488 86-733	(68 Stat. 250) (70 Stat. 544) (70 Stat. 549) (72 Stat. 290) (74 Stat. 867)	Apr 30, 1961

Source: United States Department of Interior, Bureau of Indian Affairs, *U.S. Indian Population (1962) and Land (1963)*, Government Printing Office, November 1963, pp. 31-33. *Notes:* 1. Land trusteeship terminated prior to June 30, 1962. Group termination effective on date of proclamation. Proclamation delayed to secure additions to sanitary facilities. 2. Termination of relations with tribal organization delayed by search for trustee to dispose of Wyandotte (Huron) Cemetery in Kansas City. 3. Termination of relations with tribal organization effective when claims pending before the Indian Claims Commission and the United States Court of Claims are settled. 4. Supervision over claims attorney contracts. 5. Tribal members are still eligible for Federal educational and medical aid. 6. Subject to distribution of unadjudicated and unliquidated claims and gas mineral rights.

★ 126 ★

Land Units for Which Federal Trusteeship Had Been Terminated by Acts of Congress, 1963 - II

Land unit	Public law	Statute ref.	Effective
California			
Big Sandy (Auberry)	85-671	(72 Stat. 619)	
Big Valley (Mission)	85-671	(72 Stat. 619)	
Blue Lake	85-671	(72 Stat. 619)	
Chico (Meechupta)	85-671	(72 Stat. 619)	
Cloverdale	85-671	(72 Stat. 619)	
Cold Springs	85-671	(72 Stat. 619)	
Graton	85-671	(72 Stat. 619)	
Greenville	85-671	(72 Stat. 619)	Not later than
Hopland	85-671	(72 Stat. 619)	three years
Indian Ranch	85-671	(72 Stat. 619)	after approval
			of each plan
Middletown	85-671	(72 Stat. 619)	
Pinoleville	85-671	(72 Stat. 619)	
Quartz Valley	85-671	(72 Stat. 619)	
Robinson	85-671	(72 Stat. 619)	
Rohnerville	85-671	(72 Stat. 619)	
Smith River	85-671	(72 Stat. 619)	
Nebraska			
Ponca	87-629[1]	(76 Stat. 429)	Sept 5, 1965
Oklahoma			
Choctaw	86-192	(72 Stat. 420)	Aug 25, 1962
(tribal land only)	87-609[2]	(76 Stat. 405)	Aug 25, 1962

Source: United States Department of Interior, Bureau of Indian Affairs, *U.S. Indian Population (1962) and Land (1963),* Government Printing Office, November 1963, pp. 36. *Notes:* 1. Act of Sept. 5, 1962. 2. Act of Aug. 24, 1962.

★ 127 ★

Land Units for Which Federal Trusteeship Had Been Terminated by Other Means Than an Act of Congress, 1963

Other means include transfers, expired of restrictions, or disposal by fee patent.

State, jurisdiction, land unit	Principal tribe		Page Reference House Report 2503, 82nd Congress	Other references
	Name	Population		
Arizona				
Phoenix Area Office				
City of Tucson (lots)	Papago	0	-	Reported F.Y. 1960
New York				
Central Office				
Allegany	Seneca	1,110	p. 688	[1]
Cattaraugus	Seneca & Cayuga	2,464	p. 690	Public Law 80-881
Oil Springs	Seneca	0	p. 703	(62 Stat. 1224)
Oneida	Oneida	369	p. 703	Jul 2, 1948 (Legal Jurisdiction)
Onondaga	Onondaga	744	p. 703	
St. Regis	Mohawk	1,865	p. 708	Public Law 81-690
Tonawanda	Seneca	688	p. 712	(64 Stat. 442)
Tuscarora	Tuscarora	452	p. 713	Aug 14, 1950 (Lease income)
				Public Law 81-785 (64 Stat. 845) Sept 13, 1950
Pennsylvania				
Central Office				
Cornplanter	Seneca[1]	30	p. 692	
Louisiana				
Muskogee Area Office				
Coushatta	Coushatta	200	p. 1,248	None
Michigan				
Minneapolis Area Office				
Scattered Ottawa and Chippewa (Beaver, Hog and Fox Islands, etc.)	Ottawa & Chippewa	3,895	p. 771 p. 1,175 p. 688 p. 695	None

[Continued]

★ 127 ★

Land Units for Which Federal Trusteeship Had Been Terminated by Other Means Than an Act of Congress, 1963
[Continued]

State, jurisdiction, land unit	Principal tribe		Page Reference House Report 2503, 82nd Congress	Other references
	Name	Population		
Minnesota				
Minneapolis Area Office				
Pipestone	Sioux	103	p. 705	None
Wabasha Community	Sioux	0	p. 714	None
			p. 983	
Nevada				
Phoenix Area Office				
Austin	Shoshone	139	p. 734	None
			p. 1,135	
Beowawe	Shoshone	61	p. 1,135	None
Carlin	Shoshone	13	p. 743	None
			p. 1,135	
Eureka	Shoshone	23	p. 804	None
			p. 1,135	
Wells	Shoshone	52	p. 968	None
			p. 1,017	
			p. 1,135	

Source: United States Department of Interior, Bureau of Indian Affairs, *U.S. Indian Population (1962) and Land (1963),* Government Printing Office, November 1963, pp. 34-35. *Notes:* A dash (-) means not applicable 1. Still subject to Acts of November 11, 1794 (Annual payment of $2,700 in cloth), and of February 19, 1831 (Annual cash payment of $6,000), and the provision of legal services.

Chapter 2
DEMOGRAPHICS

Population

★ 128 ★

U.S Population Distribution, by Race/Ethnicity, 1990

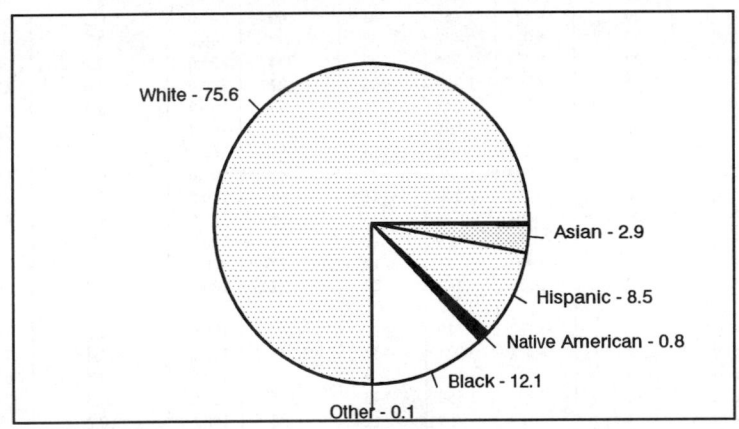

Race and ethnicity	Percent
White	75.6
Black	12.1
Hispanic[1]	8.5
Asian	2.9
Native American	0.8
Other	0.1

Source: USA TODAY, May 29, 1992, p. 7A. Primary source: U.S. Census Bureau. *Note:* 1. Persons of Hispanic origin may be of any race.

★ 129 ★

Population, by State, Geographic Region, and Race/Ethnicity, 1990

Numbers are in thousands.

Region, Division, and State	Number (1,000)						Percent distribution					
	Total[1]	American Indian, Eskimo, Aleut	White	Black	Asian, Pacific Islander	Hispanic origin[2]	Total[1]	American Indian, Eskimo, Aleut	White	Black	Asian Pacific Islander	Hispanic origin[2]
U.S.	248,710	1,959	199,686	29,986	7,274	22,354	100.0	0.8	80.3	12.1	2.9	9.0
Northeast	50,809	125	42,069	5,613	1,335	3,754	100.0	0.2	82.8	11.0	2.6	7.4
North East	13,207	33	12,033	628	232	568	100.0	0.2	91.1	4.8	1.8	4.3
Maine	1,228	6	1,208	5	7	7	100.0	0.5	98.4	0.4	0.5	0.6
New Hampshire	1,109	2	1,087	7	9	11	100.0	0.2	98.0	0.6	0.8	1.0
Vermont	563	2	555	2	3	4	100.0	0.3	98.6	0.3	0.6	0.7
Massachusetts	6,016	12	5,405	300	143	288	100.0	0.2	89.8	5.0	2.4	4.8
Rhode Island	1,003	4	917	39	18	46	100.0	0.4	91.4	3.9	1.8	4.6
Connecticut	3,287	7	2,859	274	51	213	100.0	0.2	87.0	8.3	1.5	6.5
Middle Atlantic	37,602	92	30,036	4,986	1,104	3,186	100.0	0.2	79.9	13.3	2.9	8.5
New York	17,990	63	13,385	2,859	694	2,214	100.0	0.3	74.4	15.9	3.9	12.3
New Jersey	7,730	15	6,130	1,037	273	740	100.0	0.2	79.3	13.4	3.5	9.6
Pennsylvania	11,882	15	10,520	1,090	137	232	100.0	0.1	88.5	9.2	1.2	2.0
Midwest	59,669	338	52,018	5,716	768	1,727	100.0	0.6	87.2	9.6	1.3	2.9
East North Central	42,009	150	35,764	4,817	573	1,438	100.0	0.4	85.1	11.5	1.4	3.4
Ohio	10,847	20	9,522	1,155	91	140	100.0	0.2	87.8	10.6	0.8	1.3
Indiana	5,544	13	5,021	432	38	99	100.0	0.2	90.6	7.8	0.7	1.8
Illinois	11,431	22	8,953	1,694	285	904	100.0	0.2	78.3	14.8	2.5	7.9
Michigan	9,295	56	7,756	1,292	105	202	100.0	0.6	83.4	13.9	1.1	2.2
Wisconsin	4,892	39	4,513	245	54	93	100.0	0.8	92.2	5.0	1.1	1.9
West North Central	17,660	188	16,254	899	195	289	100.0	1.1	92.0	5.1	1.1	1.6
Minnesota	4,375	50	4,130	95	78	54	100.0	1.1	94.4	2.2	1.8	1.2
Iowa	2,777	7	2,683	48	25	33	100.0	0.3	96.6	1.7	0.9	1.2
Missouri	5,117	20	4,486	548	41	62	100.0	0.4	87.7	10.7	0.8	1.2
North Dakota	639	26	604	4	3	5	100.0	4.1	94.6	0.6	0.5	0.7
South Dakota	696	51	638	3	3	5	100.0	7.3	91.6	0.5	0.4	0.8
Nebraska	1,578	12	1,481	57	12	37	100.0	0.8	93.8	3.6	0.8	2.3
Kansas	2,478	22	2,232	143	32	94	100.0	0.9	90.1	5.8	1.3	3.8
South	85,446	563	65,582	15,829	1,122	6,767	100.0	0.7	76.8	18.5	1.3	7.9
South Atlantic	45,567	172	33,391	8,924	631	2,133	100.0	0.4	76.6	20.5	1.4	4.9
Delaware	666	2	535	112	9	16	100.0	0.3	80.3	16.9	1.4	2.4
Maryland	4,781	13	3,394	1,190	140	125	100.0	0.3	71.0	24.9	2.9	2.6
District of Columbia	607	1	180	400	11	33	100.0	0.2	29.6	65.8	1.8	5.4
Virginia	6,187	15	4,792	1,163	159	160	100.0	0.2	77.4	18.8	2.6	2.6
West Virginia	1,793	2	1,726	56	7	8	100.0	0.1	96.2	3.1	0.4	0.5
North Carolina	6,629	80	5,008	1,456	52	77	100.0	1.2	75.6	22.0	0.8	1.2
South Carolina	3,487	8	2,407	1,040	22	31	100.0	0.2	69.0	29.8	0.6	0.9
Georgia	6,478	13	4,600	1,747	76	109	100.0	0.2	71.0	27.0	1.2	1.7
Florida	12,938	36	10,749	1,760	154	1,574	100.0	0.3	83.1	13.6	1.2	12.2
East South Central	15,176	41	12,049	2,977	84	95	100.0	0.3	79.4	19.6	0.6	0.6
Kentucky	3,685	6	3,392	263	18	22	100.0	0.2	92.0	7.1	0.5	0.6
Tennessee	4,877	10	4,048	778	32	33	100.0	0.2	83.0	16.0	0.7	0.7
Alabama	4,041	17	2,976	1,021	22	25	100.0	0.4	73.6	25.3	0.5	0.6
Mississippi	2,573	9	1,633	915	13	16	100.0	0.3	63.5	35.6	0.5	0.6
West South Central	26,703	350	20,142	3,929	407	4,539	100.0	1.3	75.4	14.7	1.5	17.0
Arkansas	2,351	13	1,945	374	13	20	100.0	0.5	82.7	15.9	0.5	0.8
Louisiana	4,220	19	2,839	1,299	41	93	100.0	0.4	67.3	30.8	1.0	2.2
Oklahoma	3,146	252	2,584	234	34	86	100.0	8.0	82.1	7.4	1.1	2.7
Texas	16,987	66	12,775	2,022	319	4,340	100.0	0.4	75.2	11.9	1.9	25.5
West	52,786	933	40,017	2,828	4,048	10,106	100.0	1.8	75.8	5.4	7.7	19.1
Mountain	13,659	481	11,762	374	217	1,992	100.0	3.5	86.1	2.7	1.6	14.6
Montana	799	48	741	2	4	12	100.0	6.0	92.7	0.3	0.5	1.5
Idaho	1,007	14	950	3	9	53	100.0	1.4	94.4	0.3	0.9	5.3
Wyoming	454	9	427	4	3	26	100.0	2.1	94.2	0.8	0.6	5.7
Colorado	3,294	28	2,905	133	60	424	100.0	0.8	88.2	4.0	1.8	12.9
New Mexico	1,515	134	1,146	30	14	579	100.0	8.9	75.6	2.0	0.9	38.2
Arizona	3,665	204	2,963	111	55	688	100.0	5.6	80.8	3.0	1.5	18.8
Utah	1,723	24	1,616	12	33	85	100.0	1.4	93.8	0.7	1.9	4.9
Nevada	1,202	20	1,013	79	38	124	100.0	1.6	84.3	6.6	3.2	10.4

[Continued]

★ 129 ★

Population, by State, Geographic Region, and Race/Ethnicity, 1990

[Continued]

Region, Division, and State	Number (1,000)						Percent distribution					
	Total[1]	American Indian, Eskimo, Aleut	White	Black	Asian, Pacific Islander	Hispanic origin[2]	Total[1]	American Indian, Eskimo, Aleut	White	Black	Asian Pacific Islander	Hispanic origin[2]
Pacific	39,127	453	28,255	2,454	3,831	8,114	100.0	1.2	72.2	6.3	9.8	20.7
Washinton	4,867	81	4,309	150	211	215	100.0	1.7	88.5	3.1	4.3	4.4
Oregon	2,842	38	2,637	46	69	113	100.0	1.4	92.8	1.6	2.4	4.0
California	29,760	242	20,524	2,209	2,846	7,688	100.0	0.8	69.0	7.4	9.6	25.8
Alaska	550	86	415	22	20	18	100.0	15.6	75.5	4.1	3.6	3.2
Hawaii	1,108	5	370	27	685	81	100.0	0.5	33.4	2.5	61.8	7.3

Source: "Resident Population, by Race and Hispanic Origin—States: 1990," *Statistical Abstract of the United States,* 1991, p. 22. Primary source: U.S. Bureau of the Census, press release CB91-100. 1990 Census note: The population counts set forth herein are subject to possible correction for undercount or overcount. The United States Department of Commerce is considering whether to correct these counts and will publish corrected counts, if any, not later than July 15, 1991. *Notes:* 1. Includes other races not shown separately. 2. Persons of Hispanic origin may be of any race.

★ 130 ★

Population Distribution, by Age

American Indians and Alaska Natives, Reservation States and U.S. all races, 1980 census data.

Age group	Percent			
	Indian and Alaska Native		U.S. all races	
	Number	Percent	Number	Percent
All ages	1,303,193	100.000	226,504,825	100.000
Under 5 years	140,111	10.751	16,344,407	7.216
5-9 years	136,989	10.512	16,697,134	7.372
10-14 years	145,673	11.178	18,240,919	8.053
15-19 years	157,612	12.094	21,161,667	9.343
20-24 years	135,587	10.404	21,312,557	9.409
25-29 years	113,271	8.692	19,517,672	8.617
30-34 years	96,621	7.414	17,557,957	7.752
35-39 years	75,710	5.810	13,963,008	6.165
40-44 years	62,363	4.785	11,668,239	5.151
45-49 years	52,496	4.029	11,088,383	4.895
50-54 years	46,654	3.580	11,708,984	5.169
55-59 years	40,604	3.116	11,614,054	5.128
60-64 years	30,928	2.373	10,085,711	4.453
65-69 years	25,981	1.994	8,780,844	3.877
70-74 years	18,204	1.397	6,796,742	3.001
75-79 years	12,577	0.965	4,792,597	2.116
80-84 years	6,427	0.493	2,934,229	1.295
85 years and over	5,385	0.413	2,239,721	0.989
Median age		22.6		30.0

Source: Trends in Indian Health, 1991, U.S. Department of Health and Human Services, Public Health Service, Indian Health Service, p. 21. *Note:* Percentages may not sum to totals due to rounding.

★ 131 ★

Median Ages for Selected Racial/Ethnic Groups, by Sex, 1920 and 1930

Color and Nativity	Total		Male		Female	
	1920	1930	1920	1930	1920	1930
All classes	25.2	26.4	25.8	26.7	24.7	26.1
Indian	19.7	19.6	20.4	20.0	19.0	19.1
White	25.6	26.9	26.1	27.1	25.1	26.6
Native white	22.4	23.7	22.4	23.6	22.3	23.8
Foreign-born white	40.0	43.9	40.1	44.1	29.9	43.7
Black	22.3	23.4	22.8	23.7	22.0	23.2
Chinese	40.2	32.3	42.7	35.1	19.4	17.3
Japanese	30.2	24.5	34.1	29.7	24.0	15.9

Source: Dr. Leon E. Truesdell, U.S. Department of Commerce, Bureau of the Census, Fifteenth Census of the United States: 1930, *The Indian Population of the United States and Alaska*, U.S. Government Printing Office, 1937, p. 88.

★ 132 ★

Minority Populations, by State, 1990

State	American Indian[1]	African American	Asian or Pacific Islander	Hispanic	Total combined Non-white Population[2]
Alabama	16,221	1,017,713	21,217	24,629	1,079,780
Alaska	84,594	21,799	18,730	17,803	142,926
Arizona	190,091	104,809	51,530	688,338	1,034,768
Arkansas	12,393	372,762	12,144	19,876	417,175
California	184,065	2,092,446	2,710,353	7,687,938	12,674,802
Colorado	22,068	128,057	56,773	424,302	631,200
Connecticut	5,950	260,840	49,114	213,116	529,020
Delaware	1,938	111,011	8,854	15,820	137,623
Dist. of Columbia	1,252	395,213	10,734	32,710	439,909
Florida	32,910	1,701,103	146,159	1,574,143	3,454,315
Georgia	12,621	1,737,165	73,725	108,922	1,932,433
Hawaii	4,001	25,916	646,404	81,390	757,711
Idaho	12,418	3,211	9,053	52,927	77,609
Illinois	18,213	1,673,703	275,568	904,446	2,871,930
Indiana	11,999	428,612	36,618	98,788	576,017
Iowa	6,765	47,493	24,926	32,647	111,831
Kansas	20,363	140,761	30,814	93,670	285,608
Kentucky	5,518	261,360	17,201	21,984	306,063
Louisiana	17,539	1,291,470	39,302	93,044	1,441,355
Maine	5,898	4,937	6,505	6,829	24,169

[Continued]

★ 132 ★

Minority Populations, by State, 1990
[Continued]

State	American Indian[1]	African American	Asian or Pacific Islander	Hispanic	Total combined Non-white Population[2]
Maryland	12,143	1,177,823	136,619	125,102	1,451,687
Massachusetts	10,545	274,464	140,338	287,549	712,896
Michigan	52,571	1,282,744	102,506	201,596	1,639,417
Minnesota	48,251	93,040	76,229	53,884	271,404
Mississippi	8,316	911,891	12,543	15,931	948,681
Missouri	18,873	545,527	40,087	61,702	666,189
Montana	46,475	2,242	4,123	12,174	65,014
Nebraska	11,719	56,711	12,026	36,969	117,425
Nevada	17,480	76,503	35,897	124,419	254,299
New Hampshire	2,042	6,749	9,197	11,333	29,321
New Jersey	12,490	984,845	264,341	739,861	2,001,537
New Mexico	128,068	27,642	12,587	579,224	747,521
New York	50,540	2,569,126	666,843	2,214,026	5,500,535
North Carolina	78,930	1,449,142	50,593	76,726	1,655,391
North Dakota	25,590	3,451	3,345	4,665	37,051
Ohio	19,137	1,147,440	89,195	139,696	1,395,468
Oklahoma	246,631	231,462	32,366	86,160	596,619
Oregon	35,749	44,982	67,422	112,707	260,860
Pennsylvania	13,505	1,072,459	134,056	232,262	1,452,282
Rhode Island	3,629	34,283	17,584	45,752	101,248
South Carolina	8,004	1,035,947	21,304	30,551	1,095,806
South Dakota	49,648	3,176	3,013	5,252	61,089
Tennessee	9,685	774,925	30,938	32,741	848,289
Texas	52,803	1,976,360	303,825	4,339,905	6,672,893
Utah	12,654	7,060	21,132	49,489	90,335
Vermont	1,651	1,868	3,159	3,661	10,339
Virginia	14,347	1,153,133	154,183	160,288	1,481,951
Washington	76,397	146,000	203,668	214,570	640,635
West Virginia	2,363	55,986	7,252	8,489	74,090
Wisconsin	37,769	241,697	52,284	93,194	424,944
Wyoming	8,857	3,426	2,622	25,751	40,656

Source: "Ranking of Total Combined Non-White Population of States, 1990," *Black Issues in Higher Education,* 8, August 29, 1991, p. 47. Primary source: *1990 Census of Population and Housing,* P.L. 94-171 Redistricting Data. Published by permission. *Notes:* 1. Includes Eskimo and Aleut Populations. 2. Excludes other (non-white) race populations. This "Other Race" category was excluded to enable comparisons to 1980 census compilations. Nationally, nearly 10 million persons listed their race as "Other."

★ 133 ★

Population in Major Metropolitan Areas, 1990

The number, in thousands, and the percent of total population for selected minorities are shown for the 70 largest U.S. metropolitan areas, for 1990[1].

Metropolitan area[1]	Total population (1,000)	Percent of total metropolitan population			
		American Indian, Eskimo, Aleut	Black	Asian and Pacific Islander	Hispanic origin[2]
New York- Northern New Jersey- Long Island, NY-NJ-CT CMSA	18,087	0.3	18.2	4.8	15.4
Los Angeles-Anaheim-Riverside, CA CMSA	14,532	0.6	8.5	9.2	32.9
Chicago-Gary-Lake County (IL), IL-IN-WI CMSA	8,066	0.2	19.2	3.2	11.1
San Francisco-Oakland-San Jose, CA CMSA	6,253	0.7	8.6	14.8	15.5
Philadelphia-Wilmington-Trenton, PA-NJ-DE-MD CMSA	5,899	0.2	18.7	2.1	3.8
Detroit-Ann Arbor, MI CMSA	4,665	0.4	20.9	1.5	1.9
Boston-Lawrence-Salem, MA-NH CMSA	4,172	0.2	5.7	2.9	4.6
Washington, DC-MD-VA MSA	3,924	0.3	26.6	5.2	5.7
Dallas-Fort Worth, TX CMSA	3,885	0.5	14.3	2.5	13.4
Houston-Galveston-Brazoria, TX CMSA	3,711	0.3	17.9	3.6	20.8
Miami-Fort Lauderdale, FL CMSA	3,193	0.2	18.5	1.4	33.3
Atlanta, GA MSA	2,834	0.2	26.0	1.8	2.0
Cleveland-Akron-Lorain, OH CMSA	2,760	0.2	16.0	1.0	1.9
Seattle-Tacoma, WA CMSA	2,559	1.3	4.8	6.4	3.0
San Diego, CA MSA	2,498	0.8	6.4	7.9	20.4
Minneapolis-St. Paul, MN-WI MSA	2,464	1.0	3.6	2.6	1.5
St. Louis, MO-IL MSA	2,444	0.2	17.3	1.0	1.1
Baltimore, MD MSA	2,382	0.3	25.9	1.8	1.3
Pittsburgh-Beaver Valley, PA CMSA	2,243	0.1	8.0	0.7	0.6
Phoenix, AZ MSA	2,122	1.8	3.5	1.7	16.3
Tampa-St. Petersburg-Clearwater, FL MSA	2,068	0.3	9.0	1.1	6.7
Denver-Boulder, CO CMSA	1,848	0.8	5.3	2.3	12.2
Cincinnati-Hamilton, OH-KY-IN CMSA	1,744	0.1	11.7	0.8	0.5
Milwaukee-Racine, WI CMSA	1,607	0.5	13.3	1.2	3.8
Kansas City, MO-KS MSA	1,566	0.5	12.8	1.1	2.9
Sacramento, CA MSA	1,481	1.1	6.9	7.7	11.6
Portland-Vancouver, OR-WA CMSA	1,478	0.9	2.8	3.5	3.4
Norfolk-Virginia Beach-Newport News, VA MSA	1,396	0.3	28.5	2.5	2.3
Columbus, OH MSA	1,377	0.2	12.0	1.5	0.8
San Antonio, TX MSA	1,302	0.4	6.8	1.2	47.6
Indianapolis, IN MSA	1,250	0.2	13.8	0.8	0.9
New Orleans, LA MSA	1,239	0.3	34.7	1.7	4.3
Buffalo-Niagara Falls, NY CMSA	1,189	0.6	10.3	0.9	2.0
Charlotte-Gastonia-Rock Hill, NC-SC MSA	1,162	0.4	19.9	1.0	0.9
Providence-Pawtucket-Fall River, RI-MA CMSA	1,142	0.3	3.3	1.8	4.2

[Continued]

★ 133 ★

Population in Major Metropolitan Areas, 1990
[Continued]

Metropolitan area[1]	Total population (1,000)	Percent of total metropolitan population			
		American Indian, Eskimo, Aleut	Black	Asian and Pacific Islander	Hispanic origin[2]
Hartford-New Britain-Middleton, CT CMSA	1,086	0.2	8.7	1.5	7.0
Orlando, FL MSA	1,073	0.3	12.4	1.9	9.0
Salt Lake City-Ogden, UT MSA	1,072	0.8	1.0	2.4	5.8
Rochester, NY MSA	1,002	0.3	9.4	1.4	3.1
Nashville, TN MSA	985	0.2	15.5	1.0	0.8
Memphis, TN-AR-MS MSA	982	0.2	40.6	0.8	0.8
Oklahoma City, OK MSA	959	4.8	10.5	1.9	3.6
Louisville, KY-IN MSA	953	0.2	13.1	0.6	0.6
Dayton-Springfield, OH MSA	951	0.2	13.3	1.0	0.8
Greensboro-Winston-Salem-High Point, NC MSA	942	0.3	19.3	0.7	0.8
Birmingham, AL MSA	908	0.2	27.1	0.4	0.4
Jacksonville, FL MSA	907	0.3	20.0	1.7	2.5
Albany-Schenectady-Troy, NY MSA	874	0.2	4.7	1.2	1.8
Richmond-Petersburg, VA MSA	866	0.3	29.2	1.4	1.1
West Palm Beach-Boca Raton-Delray Beach, FL MSA	864	0.1	12.5	1.0	7.7
Honolulu, HI MSA	836	0.4	3.1	63.0	6.8
Austin, TX MSA	782	0.4	9.2	2.4	20.5
Las Vegas, NV MSA	741	0.9	9.5	3.5	11.2
Raleigh-Durham, NC MSA	735	0.3	24.9	1.9	1.2
Scranton-Wilkes-Barre, PA MSA	734	0.1	1.0	0.5	0.8
Tulsa, OK MSA	709	6.8	8.2	0.9	2.1
Grand Rapids, MI MSA	688	0.5	6.0	1.1	3.3
Allentown-Bethlehem, PA-NJ MSA	687	0.1	2.0	1.1	4.2
Fresno, CA MSA	667	1.1	5.0	8.6	35.5
Tucson, AZ MSA	667	3.0	3.1	1.8	24.5
Syracuse, NY MSA	660	0.6	5.9	1.2	1.4
Greenville-Spartanburg, SC MSA	641	0.1	17.4	0.7	0.8
Omaha, NE-IA MSA	618	0.5	8.3	1.0	2.6
Toledo, OH MSA	614	0.2	11.4	1.0	3.3
Knoxville, TN MSA	605	0.2	6.0	0.8	0.5
El Paso, TX MSA	592	0.4	3.7	1.1	69.6
Harrisburg-Lebanon-Carlisle, PA MSA	588	0.1	6.7	1.1	1.7
Bakersfield, CA MSA	543	1.3	5.5	3.0	28.0

[Continued]

★ 133 ★

Population in Major Metropolitan Areas, 1990
[Continued]

Metropolitan area[1]	Total population (1,000)	Percent of total metropolitan population			
		American Indian, Eskimo, Aleut	Black	Asian and Pacific Islander	Hispanic origin[2]
New Haven-Meriden, CT MSA	530	0.2	12.1	1.6	6.2
Springfield, MA MSA	530	0.2	6.6	1.0	9.0

Source: "Largest Metropolitan Areas—Racial and Hispanic Origin Populations: 1990," Statistical Abstract of the United States, 1991, p. 33. Primary source: U.S. Bureau of the Census, press release CB91-66 and unpublished data. Notes: 1990 Census note: The population counts set forth herein are subject to possible correction for undercount or overcount. The United States Department of Commerce is considering whether to correct these counts and will publish corrected counts, if any, not later than July 15, 1991. 1. Metropolitan areas are shown in rank order of total population of consolidated metropolitan statistical areas (CMSA) and metropolitan statistical areas (MSA). 2. Persons of Hispanic origin may be of any race.

★ 134 ★

Mixed-Race Births, 1978 and 1989

Races	Number of births	
	1978	1989
Native American/White	12,860	21,088
Native American/Black	557	1,308
Native American/Asian	379	711

Source: USA TODAY, December 11, 1992, p. 7A. Primary source: The Population Reference Bureau, based on figures from the National Center for Health Statistics.

★ 135 ★

Estimated Populations of Indigenous Peoples for Selected Countries, 1992

Country	Indigenous population (million)	Share of national population (percent)
Papua New Guinea	3.0	77
Bolivia	5.6	70
Guatemala	4.6	47
Peru	9.0	40
Ecuador	3.8	38

[Continued]

★ 135 ★

Estimated Populations of Indigenous Peoples for Selected Countries, 1992

[Continued]

Country	Indigenous population (million)	Share of national population (percent)
Myanmar	14.0	33
Laos	1.3	30
Mexico	10.9	12
New Zealand	0.4	12
Chile	1.2	9
Phillipines	6.0	9
India	63.0	7
Malaysia	0.8	4
Canada	0.9	4
Australia	0.4	2
Brazil	1.5	1
Bangladesh	1.2	1
Thailand	0.5	1
United States	2.0	1
Former Soviet Union	1.4	<1

Source: Alan Thein Durning, *Guardians of the Land: Indigenous Peoples and the Health of the Earth,* Worldwatch Paper 112, Worldwatch Institute, 1992, p. 12. *Note:* 1. Generally excludes those of mixed ancestry.

★ 136 ★

Native American Populations in North and South America, by Country, 1991

Estimated populations are shown, by country, for 1991.

	Estimated Population	% of Total Population
Mexico	10,537,000	12.4
Peru	8,097,000	38.6
Guatemala	5,423,000	60.3
Bolivia	4,985,000	71.2
Ecuador	3,753,000	37.5
United States	1,959,000	0.8
Canada	892,000	3.4
Chile	767,000	5.9
Colombia	708,000	2.2
El Salvador	500,000	10.0

[Continued]

★ 136 ★

Native American Populations in North and South America, by Country, 1991

[Continued]

	Estimated Population	% of Total Population
Argentina	477,000	1.5
Brazil	325,000	0.2
Venezuela	290,000	1.5
Panama	194,000	8.0
Honduras	168,000	3.4
Paraguay	101,000	2.5
Nicaragua	66,000	1.7
Guyana	29,000	3.9
Costa Rica	19,000	0.6
Belize	15,000	9.1
Surinam	11,000	2.9
French Guyana	1,000	1.2
Uruguay	0	0.0
Total	39,317,000	5.8

Source: Report on the Americas, Volume XXV, No.3, December 1991, p.16. Computed from: Enrique Mayer & Elio Masferrer, "La Poblacion Indigena de America," America Indigena, Vol. 39, No. 2 (1979); World Bank, Informe sobre el desarrollo mundial 1991; U.S. and Canada census.

★ 137 ★

Population of American Indians and the Total United States Population, 1890-1980

Date	American Indian		Total United States	
	Size	Change from previous decade (%)	Size	Change from previous decade (%)
1890	248,253		62,947,714	
1900	237,196	-4.5	75,994,575	20.7
1910	276,927	16.8	91,972,266	21.0
1920	244,437	-11.7	105,710,620	14.9
1930	343,352	40.5	122,775,046	16.1
1940	345,252	0.6	131,669,275	7.2
1950	357,499	3.5	151,325,798	14.5
1960	523,591	46.5	179,323,175	18.5

[Continued]

★ 137 ★

Population of American Indians and the Total United States Population, 1890-1980

[Continued]

Date	American Indian		Total United States	
	Size	Change from previous decade (%)	Size	Change from previous decade (%)
1970	792,730	51.4	203,302,031	13.4
1980	1,366,676	72.4	226,545,805	11.4

Source: Russell Thornton, *American Indian Holocaust and Survival: A Population History Since 1492*, University of Oklahoma, Press, 1987, p. 160. Published by permission. Primary source: U.S. Bureau of the Census, *Indian Population of the United States and Alaska*, 1910. Washington, D.C.: U.S. Government Printing Office, 1915. p. 10; *1970 Census of the Population. Subject Report. American Indians.* Final Report PC (2)- 1F. Washington, D.C.: U.S. Government Printing Office, 1973, p. 11; *Statistical Abstract of the United States, 1982-1983.* Washington, D.C.: U.S. Government Printing Office, 1982-1983, p. 6; *1980 Census of the Population, Supplementary Report, American Indians Areas and Alaska Native Villages: 1980.* PC80-S1-13. Washington, D.C.: U.S. Government Printing Office, 1984, p. 14; Swagerty and Thornton, "Preliminary 1980 Census Counts for American Indians, Eskimos and Aleuts," *American Indian Culture and Research Journal*, 1982, p. 92.

★ 138 ★

Population of the Top 50 American Indian Tribes, 1990

Population is shown in thousands.

Tribe	Population
Cherokee	308,132
Navajo	219,198
Chippewa	103,826
Sioux	103,255
Choctaw	82,299
Pueblo	52,939
Apache	50,051
Iroquois	49,038
Lumbee	48,444
Creek	43,550
Blackfoot	32,234
Canadian/Latin American	22,379
Chickasaw	20,631
Potawatomi	16,763
Tohono O'Odham	16,041
Pima	14,431
Tlingit	13,925
Seminole	13,797
Athabaskans	13,738
Cheyenne	11,456
Comanche	11,322
Paiute	11,142

[Continued]

★ 138 ★

Population of the Top 50 American Indian Tribes, 1990
[Continued]

Tribe	Population
Salish	10,246
Yaqui	9,931
Osage	9,527
Kiowa	9,421
Delaware	9,321
Shoshone	9,215
Crow	8,588
Cree	8,290
Yakima	7,850
Houma	7,810
Menominee	7,543
Ottawa	7,522
Ute	7,273
Colville	7,140
Yuman	7,128
Winnebago	6,920
Arapaho	6,350
Shawnee	6,179
Assiniboine	5,274
Pomo	4,766
Sac and Fox	4,517
Miami	4,477
Salish	4,455
Yurok	4,296
Omaha	4,143
Nez Perce	4,113
Eastern tribes	3,928

Source: Indian Country Today, December 3, 1992, p. A1. Primary source: U.S. Census.

★ 139 ★

States With The Most Native Americans, 1990

| Oklahoma - 252,089 |
| California - 236,078 |
| Arizona - 203,009 |
| New Mexico - 134,097 |
| North Carolina - 79,825 |

State	Population
Oklahoma	252,089
California	236,078
Arizona	203,009
New Mexico	134,097
North Carolina	79,825

Source: USA TODAY, November 27, 1992, p. 1A. Primary source: U.S. Census Bureau.

★ 140 ★

American Indian, Eskimo, and Aleut Population, by Geographic Region and State, 1990

Region, division, and state	American Indians, Eskimo, and Aleut			
	Total	American Indian	Eskimo	Aleut
U.S.	1,959	1,878	57	24
Northeast	125	122	2	2
New England	33	32	(Z)	(Z)
Maine	6	6	(Z)	(Z)
New Hampshire	2	2	(Z)	(Z)
Vermont	2	2	(Z)	(Z)
Maine	12	12	(Z)	(Z)
Rhode Island	4	4	(Z)	(Z)
Connecticut	7	6	(Z)	(Z)
Midwest Atlantic	92	90	1	2
New York	63	61	1	1
New Jersey	15	15	(Z)	(Z)
Pennsylvania	15	14	(Z)	(Z)
Midwest	338	334	2	2
East North Central	150	147	1	1
Ohio	20	20	(Z)	(Z)

[Continued]

★ 140 ★

American Indian, Eskimo, and Aleut Population, by Geographic Region and State, 1990
[Continued]

Region, division, and state	American Indians, Eskimo, and Aleut			
	Total	American Indian	Eskimo	Aleut
Indiana	13	12	(Z)	(Z)
Illinois	22	21	(Z)	(Z)
Michigan	56	56	(Z)	(Z)
Wisconsin	39	39	(Z)	(Z)
West North Central	188	187	1	1
Minnesota	50	49	(Z)	(Z)
Iowa	7	7	(Z)	(Z)
Missouri	20	20	(Z)	(Z)
North Dakota	26	26	(Z)	(Z)
South Dakota	51	51	(Z)	(Z)
Nebraska	12	12	(Z)	(Z)
Kansas	22	22	(Z)	(Z)
South	563	557	3	3
South Atlantic	172	170	1	1
Delaware	2	2	(Z)	(Z)
Maryland	13	13	(Z)	(Z)
District of Colombia	1	1	(Z)	(Z)
Virginia	15	15	(Z)	(Z)
West Virginia	2	2	(Z)	(Z)
North Carolina	80	80	(Z)	(Z)
South Carolina	8	8	(Z)	(Z)
Georgia	13	13	(Z)	(Z)
Florida	36	35	(Z)	(Z)
East South Central	41	40	(Z)	(Z)
Kentucky	6	6	(Z)	(Z)
Tennessee	10	10	(Z)	(Z)
Alabama	17	16	(Z)	(Z)
Mississippi	9	8	(Z)	(Z)
West South Central	350	347	1	1
Arizona	13	13	(Z)	(Z)
Louisiana	19	18	(Z)	(Z)
Oklahoma	252	252	(Z)	(Z)
Texas	66	64	1	1
West	933	866	51	17
Mountain	481	478	1	1
Montana	48	48	(Z)	(Z)
Idaho	14	14	(Z)	(Z)
Wyoming	9	9	(Z)	(Z)
Colorado	28	27	(Z)	(Z)
New Mexico	134	134	(Z)	(Z)
Arizona	204	203	(Z)	(Z)

[Continued]

★ 140 ★

American Indian, Eskimo, and Aleut Population, by Geographic Region and State, 1990
[Continued]

Region, division, and state	American Indians, Eskimo, and Aleut			
	Total	American Indian	Eskimo	Aleut
Utah	24	24	(Z)	(Z)
Nevada	20	19	(Z)	(Z)
Pacific	453	387	49	16
Washington	81	78	2	2
Oregon	38	37	1	1
California	242	236	3	4
Alaska	86	31	44	10
Hawaii	5	5	(Z)	(Z)

Source: U.S. Bureau of the Census, *Statistical Abstract of the United States: 1992*, (112th edition). Washington, D.C., 1992, pp. 24-25. Primary source: U.S. Bureau of the Census, press release CB91-215. *Note:* A (Z) stands for less than 500.

★ 141 ★

American Indian Population in Urban and Rural Areas, by Geographic Division and State, 1930

Division and state	Total Indian population	Urban		Rural-farm		Rural-nonfarm	
		Number	Percent	Number	Percent	Number	Percent
United States	332,397	32,816	9.9	188,946	56.8	110,635	33.3
Geographic divisions:							
New England	2,466	1,041	42.2	98	4.0	1,327	53.8
Middle Atlantic	7,709	2,181	28.3	1,990	25.8	3,538	45.9
East North Central	19,817	3,822	19.3	4,423	22.3	11,572	58.4
West North Central	48,245	3,497	7.2	27,026	56.0	17,722	36.7
South Atlantic	19,060	218	1.1	16,437	86.2	2,405	12.6
East South Central	2,106	99	4.7	1,803	85.6	204	9.7
West South Central	95,670	15,108	15.8	56,874	59.4	23,688	24.8
Mountain	102,083	2,677	2.6	67,138	65.8	32,268	31.6
Pacific	35,241	4,173	11.9	13,157	37.3	17,911	50.8
New England:							
Maine	1,012	390	38.5	36	3.6	586	57.9
New Hampshire	64	24	-	18	-	22	-
Vermont	36	8	-	16	-	12	-
Massachusetts	874	285	32.6	3	0.3	586	67.0
Rhode Island	318	245	77.0	6	1.9	67	21.1
Connecticut	162	89	54.9	19	11.7	54	33.3

[Continued]

237

★ 141 ★

American Indian Population in Urban and Rural Areas, by Geographic Division and State, 1930
[Continued]

Division and state	Total Indian population	Urban		Rural-farm		Rural-nonfarm	
		Number	Percent	Number	Percent	Number	Percent
Middle Atlantic:							
New York	6,973	1,706	24.5	1,893	27.1	3,374	48.4
New Jersey	213	151	70.9	9	4.2	53	24.9
Pennsylvania	523	324	62.0	88	16.8	111	21.2
East North Central:							
Ohio	435	268	61.6	70	16.1	97	22.3
Indian	285	160	56.1	72	25.3	53	18.6
Illinois	469	368	78.5	24	5.1	77	16.4
Michigan	7,080	1,849	26.1	1,251	17.7	3,980	56.2
Wisconsin	11,548	1,177	10.2	3,006	26.0	7,365	63.8
West North Central:							
Minnesota	11,077	918	8.3	2,189	19.8	7,970	72.0
Iowa	660	251	38.0	204	30.9	205	31.1
Missouri	578	378	65.4	101	17.5	99	17.1
North Dakota	8,387	392	4.7	5,461	65.1	2,534	30.2
South Dakota	21,833	483	2.2	16,297	74.6	5,053	23.1
Nebraska	3,256	228	7.0	1,616	49.6	1,412	43.4
Kansas	2,454	847	34.5	1,158	47.2	449	18.3
South Atlantic:							
Delaware	5	4	-	-	-	1	-
Maryland	50	25	-	11	-	14	-
District of Columbia	40	40	-	-	-	-	-
Virginia	779	35	4.5	628	80.6	116	14.9
West Virginia	18	7	-	3	-	8	-
North Carolina	16,579	51	0.3	15,000	90.5	1,528	9.2
South Carolina	959	26	2.7	765	79.8	168	17.5
Georgia	43	16	-	6	-	21	-
Florida	587	14	2.4	24	4.1	549	93.5
East South Central:							
Kentucky	22	13	-	2	-	7	-
Tennessee	161	24	14.9	84	52.2	53	32.9
Alabama	465	26	5.6	320	68.8	119	25.6
Mississippi	1,458	36	2.5	1,397	95.8	25	1.7
West South Central:							
Arkansas	408	106	26.0	91	22.3	211	51.7
Louisiana	1,536	59	3.8	605	39.4	872	56.8
Oklahoma	92,725	14,593	15.7	55,820	60.2	22,312	24.1
Texas	1,001	350	35.0	358	35.8	293	29.3

[Continued]

★ 141 ★

American Indian Population in Urban and Rural Areas, by Geographic Division and State, 1930

[Continued]

Division and state	Total Indian population	Urban		Rural-farm		Rural-nonfarm	
		Number	Percent	Number	Percent	Number	Percent
Mountain:							
Montana	14,798	389	2.6	8,069	54.5	6,340	42.8
Idaho	3,638	135	3.7	2,508	68.9	995	27.4
Wyoming	1,845	65	3.5	1,150	62.3	630	34.1
Colorado	1,395	319	22.9	727	52.1	349	25.0
New Mexico	28,941	695	2.4	18,946	65.5	9,300	32.1
Arizona	43,726	734	1.7	31,626	72.3	11,366	26.0
Utah	2,869	91	3.2	2,097	73.1	681	23.7
Nevada	4,871	249	5.1	2,015	41.4	2,607	53.5
Pacific:							
Washington	11,253	1,053	9.4	4,685	41.6	5,515	49.0
Oregon	4,776	384	8.0	2,487	52.1	1,905	39.9
California	19,212	2,736	14.2	5,985	31.1	10,491	54.6

Source: Dr. Leon E. Truesdell, U.S. Department of Commerce, Bureau of the Census, Fifteenth Census of the United States: 1930, *The Indian Population of the United States and Alaska,* U.S. Government Printing Office, 1937, p.6.

★ 142 ★

Urban and Rural American Indian Population, by Major Tribal Group, 1980: Abenaki - Pamunkey

Data are estimates based on a sample and are the most recent available.

Major Tribal Group	Urban and Rural Population			
	Urban	Rural	Farm	Total persons
All American Indians	806,590	671,933	26,627	1,476,523
Abenaki (n.e.c)	478	351	43	829
Alabama Coushatta[1]	302	756	4	1,056
Alaska Native (n.e.c.)	432	155	6	587
Alaska Athabaskans	3,783	6,353	7	10,136
Aleut and Eskimo	458	203	-	661
Algonquian (n.e.c.)	1,296	413	23	1,709
Apache	19,277	16,584	401	35,861
Arapaho	1,655	2,768	41	4,423
Arikara	658	878	131	1,536
Assiniboine	1,480	2,508	70	3,986
Bannock	216	274	-	490
Blackfoot[1]	14,548	7,416	337	21,964

[Continued]

239

★ 142 ★

Urban and Rural American Indian Population, by Major Tribal Group, 1980: Abenaki - Pamunkey
[Continued]

Major Tribal Group	Urban and Rural Population			
	Urban	Rural	Farm	Total persons
Brotherton	104	69	3	173
Caddo	1,137	596	2	1,733
Cahuilla	730	510	-	1,240
California tribes (n.e.c.)	332	254	2	586
Canadian and Latin American	6,318	1,486	36	7,804
Catawba	313	1,187	-	1,500
Cayuse	46	111	-	157
Chehalis	139	120	-	259
Chemakuan	107	373	-	480
Chemehuevi	374	93	-	467
Cherokee	151,914	80,166	3,783	232,080
Cheyenne	5,225	4,693	80	9,918
Chickahominy	302	536	-	838
Chickasaw	6,559	3,758	237	10,317
Chinook	533	863	16	1,396
Chippewa	38,921	34,681	1,057	73,602
Chitimacha	174	172	-	346
Choctaw	28,370	21,850	969	50,220
Chumash[1]	1,270	188	19	1,458
Clallam	425	468	34	893
Coeur d'Alene	405	279	-	684
Coharie	44	464	50	508
Colorado River	202	752	-	654
Colville	1,648	3,808	124	5,456
Comanche	5,640	3,397	156	9,037
Coos	59	69	6	128
Costanoan	467	39	-	506
Cowlitz	482	467	11	949
Cree	3,794	2,817	375	6,611
Creek	18,667	9,611	598	28,278
Croatan	138	49	-	187
Crow	2,522	4,552	304	7,074
Cupeno	113	174	-	287
Delaware	3,722	1,659	142	5,381
Diegueno	660	734	-	1,394
Eastern tribes (n.e.c.)	883	1,754	68	2,637
Flathead	1,737	3,211	238	4,948
Fort Hall	215	235	7	450
Gabrieleno	1,686	123	-	1,610
Gros Ventres	911	1,210	81	2,121

[Continued]

★ 142 ★

Urban and Rural American Indian Population, by Major Tribal Group, 1980: Abenaki - Pamunkey
[Continued]

Major Tribal Group	Urban and Rural Population			
	Urban	Rural	Farm	Total persons
Haida	952	482	-	1,434
Haliwa	464	1,623	52	2,087
Hidatsa	370	1,179	136	1,549
Hitchiti	11	11	-	22
Hoopa	711	1,273	32	1,984
Houma	1,102	1,498	-	2,600
Iowa	649	298	20	947
Iroquois	24,353	13,865	489	38,218
Kalispel	104	77	-	181
Karok	1,065	874	-	1,959
Kaw	464	213	11	677
Kickapoo	1,464	891	60	2,355
Kiowa	4,598	2,789	115	7,396
Klamath	1,342	765	15	2,107
Konkow	208	129	-	337
Kootenai	190	196	38	365
Long Island	285	19	-	304
Luiseno	547	690	-	1,237
Lumbee[2]	6,560	22,071	2,407	28,631
Lummi[2]	1,308	2,792	84	4,100
Maidu	640	537	-	1,177
Makah	252	788	-	1,040
Maliseet	318	209	-	527
Mandan	463	550	31	1,013
Mattaponi	81	55	-	136
Menominee	2,712	3,332	19	6,044
Miami	1,647	683	38	2,330
Miccouskee[1]	46	16	-	62
Micmac[3]	815	328	24	1,143
Mission Indians	2,001	496	15	2,497
Miwok	1,305	837	12	2,142
Modoc	580	183	23	763
Mohegan	429	92	-	521
Mono	733	645	-	1,378
Nanticoke	379	604	67	983
Narragansett	1,691	381	6	2,072
Navajo	48,918	109,715	2,061	158,633
Nez Perce[1]	1,320	902	32	2,222
Nomalaki	150	78	-	228

[Continued]

241

★ 142 ★

Urban and Rural American Indian Population, by Major Tribal Group, 1980: Abenaki - Pamunkey
[Continued]

Major Tribal Group	Urban and Rural Population			
	Urban	Rural	Farm	Total persons
Northwest tribes (n.e.c.)	163	113	2	276
Omaha	1,632	1,458	54	3,090
Oregon Athabaskan	296	337	-	633
Osage	4,728	2,158	203	6,884
Oto	987	523	-	1,510
Ottawa	3,797	2,712	39	6,509
Pauite[1]	4,334	5,189	119	9,523
Pamunkey	254	81	-	335

Source: U.S. Bureau of the Census, *1980 Census of Population, Volume 2, Subject Reports, Characteristics of American Indians, by Tribes and Selected Areas: 1980*, PC80-2-1C, Section 1: Tables I-II, issued September 1989, U.S. Department of Commerce, U.S. Government Printing Office, Washington, D.C., pp. 150-202. *Notes:* (N.E.C.) stands for not elsewhere classified. A dash (-) represents zero or a percent which rounds to less than 0.1. 1. Reporting and/or processing problems may have affected the data for this tribe. 2. Miscoding of entries of "Lummee," "Lummi," "Lumbee," or "Lumbi" may have affected the data for this tribe. 3. Any entry with the spelling "Micmac" was miscoded to Cheyenne River Sioux.

★ 143 ★

Urban and Rural American Indian Population, by Major Tribal Group, 1980: Papago - Yurok

Data are estimates based on a sample and are the most recent available.

Major Tribal Group	Urban and Rural Population			
	Urban	Rural	Farm	Total persons
Papago	4,402	8,895	162	13,297
Passamaquoddy	612	1,156	2	1,768
Pawnee	1,567	887	15	2,454
Penobscot	683	707	7	1,390
Peoria	494	151	27	645
Pequot	336	99	-	435
Pima	3,483	8,239	62	11,722
Piscataway	155	323	-	478
Pit River	576	700	19	1,276
Pomo	2,037	1,117	34	3,154
Ponca	1,138	918	46	2,056
Potawatomi	6,195	3,520	273	9,715
Powhatan	268	52	-	320
Pueblo[1]	18,722	23,830	166	42,552
Puget Sound Salish	3,445	3,146	33	6,591
Quapaw	638	291	22	929
Quinault	610	1,049	6	1,659

[Continued]

★ 143 ★

Urban and Rural American Indian Population, by Major Tribal Group, 1980: Papago - Yurok

[Continued]

Major Tribal Group	Urban and Rural Population			
	Urban	Rural	Farm	Total persons
Rappahannock	32	234	21	266
Sac and Fox Mesquakie	1,980	1,401	137	1,980
Salinan	234	50	34	284
Schaghicoke	178	21	-	199
Seminole[1]	7,068	3,295	64	10,363
Serrano	126	80	-	206
Shasta	191	139	-	330
Shawnee	2,803	1,540	187	4,343
Shinnecock	963	77	-	1,040
Shoshone	4,767	5,063	337	9,830
Siletz	518	186	-	704
Sioux	35,715	42,893	3,057	78,608
Siuslaw	204	147	12	351
Spokane	653	1,100	2	1,753
Stockbridge	875	672	3	1,547
Tlingit	6,326	3,183	-	9,509
Tolowa	129	267	-	396
Tonkawa	100	142	-	242
Tsimshian	780	807	-	1,587
Umatilla	449	516	9	965
Ute	1,848	3,973	149	5,821
Wailaki[2]	251	332	4	583
Walla-Walla	83	179	-	262
Wampanoag	725	690	-	1,415
Warm Springs	225	1,111	51	1,336
Washo	974	440	-	1,414
Wichita	351	356	-	707
Winnebago	2,663	2,502	29	5,165
Wintu	1,354	690	24	2,044
Wiyot	145	98	8	243
Yakima	2,495	4,011	258	6,506
Yaqui	4,407	790	34	5,197
Yavapai Apache	137	12	-	149
Yokuts	854	910	100	1,764
Yuchi	148	97	7	245
Yuman	2,433	4,178	29	6,711
Yurok	1,645	1,349	-	2,994
Other specific tribes (n.e.c.)	172	287	-	459

[Continued]

★ 143 ★

Urban and Rural American Indian Population, by Major Tribal Group, 1980: Papago - Yurok
[Continued]

Major Tribal Group	Urban and Rural Population			
	Urban	Rural	Farm	Total persons
Tribe not specified	24,746	9,783	572	34,529
Tribe not reported	192,173	112,282	4,960	304,455

Source: U.S. Bureau of the Census, *1980 Census of Population, Volume 2, Subject Reports, Characteristics of American Indians, by Tribes and Selected Areas: 1980*, PC80-2-1C, Section 1: Tables I-II, issued September 1989, U.S. Department of Commerce, U.S. Government Printing Office, Washington, D.C., pp. 150-202. *Notes:* (N.E.C.) stands for not elsewhere classified. A dash (-) represents zero or a percent which rounds to less than 0.1. 1. Reporting and/or processing problems may have affected the data for this tribe. 2. Any Mohawk entry of "Ganienka" was miscoded to Wailaki.

★ 144 ★

Urban Indian Population of States With More Than 10,000 American Indians, 1970 and 1980

State	1970		1980		Percent increase
	Number	Percent	Number	Percent	
California	67,202	76.1	161,192	81.3	139.9
Oklahoma	47,623	49.2	83,936	49.6	76.3
Arizona	16,442	17.4	47,996	31.5	191.9
Washington	16,102	52.2	32,843	56.4	104.0
Texas	14,567	86.1	31,811	80.8	118.4
New Mexico	13,405	18.7	31,316	30.0	133.6
New York	17,161	67.1	27,035	69.4	57.5
Michigan	10,541	65.8	25,370	63.9	140.7
Minnesota	11,703	52.4	20,316	58.3	73.6
Oregon	6,976	52.8	15,439	58.1	121.3
North Carolina	6,194	14.0	14,261	22.1	130.2
Florida	4,275	66.9	13,975	73.9	226.9
Illinois	9,542	92.6	13,698	86.4	43.6
Wisconsin	7,439	39.6	13,625	46.5	83.2
Colorado	5,421	67.7	12,821	72.3	136.5
South Dakota	9,115	29.4	11,816	26.3	29.6
Kansas	6,130	74.2	10,794	70.8	76.1
Utah	3,689	35.0	10,301	53.8	179.2
Arkansas	4,696	29.2	9,971	45.6	112.3
Montana	5,070	19.2	9,748	26.2	92.3
Ohio	5,079	82.2	9,219	76.9	81.5
Nevada	2,832	37.9	8,006	60.6	182.7
Montana	3,617	74.0	7,804	64.3	115.8
Louisiana	1,543	34.1	5,981	50.0	287.6

[Continued]

★ 144 ★

Urban Indian Population of States With More Than 10,000 American Indians, 1970 and 1980

[Continued]

State	1970		1980		Percent increase
	Number	Percent	Number	Percent	
North Dakota	1,810	13.3	4,120	20.5	127.6
Idaho	1,990	30.0	3,403	32.7	71.0

Source: Russell Thornton, *American Indian Holocaust and Survival: A Population History Since 1492,* University of Oklahoma Press, 1987, p. 228. Published by permission. Primary source: U.S. Bureau of the Census, 1970 *Census of the Population, Subject Report, American Indians.* Final Report PC (2)- 1F. Washington, D.C.: U.S. Government Printing Office, 1973, p. 1. *General Population Characteristics: United States Summary.* PC80-1-B1, Pt. 1. Washington, D.C.: U.S. Government Printing Office, 1983, pp. 125, 128.

★ 145 ★

American Indian, Eskimo, and Aleut Population in Selected Metropolitan Areas as a Percentage of Total Population, 1990

Numbers are in thousands.

Metropolitan area	Number of specified group 1,000	Percent of total metro.
Los Angeles-Anaheim-Riverside, CA CMSA	87	0.6
Tulsa, OK MSA	48	6.8
New York-Northern New Jersey-Long Island, NY-NJ-CT CMSA	46	0.3
Oklahoma City, OK MSA	46	4.8
San Francisco-Oakland-San Jose, CA CMSA	41	0.7
Phoenix, AZ MSA	38	1.8
Seattle-Tacoma, WA CMSA	32	1.3
Minneapolis-St. Paul, MN-WI MSA	24	1.0
Tucson, AZ MSA	20	3.0
San Diego, CA MSA	20	0.8

Source: Metropolitan Areas With Large Numbers of Selected Racial Groups and of Hispanic Origin Population: 1990, *Statistical Abstract of the United States*, 1991, p. 32. Primary source: U.S. Bureau of the Census, unpublished data. *Notes:* 1990 Census note: The population counts set forth herein are subject to possible correction for undercount or overcount. The United States Department of commerce is considering whether to correct these courts an will publish corrected counts, if any, not later than July 15, 1991.

★ 146 ★

American Indian Population of Standard Metropolitan Statistical Areas With More Than 10,000 American Indians, 1970 and 1980

City (SMSA)[1]	1970 population	1980 population	Percentage increase, 1970-80
Los Angeles-Long Beach, California	23,908	47,234	97.6
Tulsa, Oklahoma	15,183	38,463	153.0
Phoenix, Arizona	10,127	22,788	125.0
Oklahoma City, Oklahoma	12,951	24,695	90.7
Albuquerque, New Mexico	5,822	20,721	255.9
San Francisco-Oakland, California	12,041	17,546	45.7
Riverside-San Bernadino-Ontario, California	5,941	17,107	187.9
Minneapolis-St. Paul, Minnesota	9,911	15,831	59.7
Seattle-Everett, Washington	8,814	15,162	72.0
Tucson, Arizona	8,704	14,880	71.0
San Diego, California	6,007	14,355	139.0
New York, New York	9,984	13,440	34.6
Anaheim-Santa Ana-Garden Grove, California	3,664	12,782	248.9
Detroit, Michigan	5,203	12,372	137.8
Dallas-Ft. Worth, Texas	5,500	11,076	101.4
Sacramento, California	3,548	10,944	208.5
Chicago, Illinois	8,203	10,415	27.0

Source: Russell Thornton, *American Indian Holocaust and Survival: A Population History Since 1492*, University of Oklahoma Press, 1987, p. 229. Published by permission. Primary source: U.S. Bureau of the Census, 1970 *Census of the Population, Subject Report, American Indians*. Final Report PC (2)- 1F. Washington, D.C.: U.S. Government Printing Office, 1973, pp. 138-141. *General Population Characteristics: United States Summary*, PC80-1-B1, Pt. 1. Washington, D.C.: U.S. Government Printing Office, 1983, pp. 201-211. *Note:* 1. SMSA stands for Standard Metropolitan Statistical Area.

★ 147 ★

Population of Native North Americans by MSA in 1990 - I: A-K

Metropolitan Statistical Areas	Total area popu- lation	American Indians, Eskimos, and Aleuts				
		Total	% of area's population	American Indians	Eskimos	Aleuts
Abilene, TX MSA	119,655	450	0.4	432	6	12
Albany, GA MSA	112,561	281	0.2	279	1	1
Albany--Schenectady--Troy, NY MSA	874,304	1,560	0.2	1,520	19	21
Albuquerque, NM MSA	480,577	16,296	3.4	16,201	64	31
Alexandria, LA MSA	131,556	564	0.4	558	3	3
Allentown--Bethlehem--Easton, PA--NJ MSA	686,688	688	0.1	643	21	24
Altoona, PA MSA	130,542	118	0.1	115	1	2

[Continued]

★ 147 ★

Population of Native North Americans by MSA in 1990 - I: A-K
[Continued]

Metropolitan Statistical Areas	Total area population	American Indians, Eskimos, and Aleuts				
		Total	% of area's population	American Indians	Eskimos	Aleuts
Amarillo, TX MSA	187,547	1,355	0.7	1,350	2	3
Anchorage, AK MSA	226,338	14,569	6.4	5,985	6,034	2,550
Anderson, IN MSA	130,669	299	0.2	284	11	4
Anderson, SC MSA	145,196	173	0.1	170	2	1
Anniston, AL MSA	116,034	296	0.3	293	3	
Appleton--Oshkosh--Neenah, WI MSA	315,121	2,796	0.9	2,752	18	26
Asheville, NC MSA	174,821	486	0.3	480	1	5
Athens, GA MSA	156,267	257	0.2	241	7	9
Atlanta, GA MSA	2,833,511	5,532	0.2	5,334	64	134
Atlantic City, NJ MSA	319,416	778	0.2	750	16	12
Augusta, GA--SC MSA	396,809	941	0.2	910	23	8
Austin, TX MSA	781,572	2,827	0.4	2,662	57	108
Bakersfield, CA MSA	543,477	7,026	1.3	6,947	44	35
Baltimore, MD MSA	2,382,172	6,444	0.3	6,264	89	91
Bangor, ME MSA	88,745	1,008	1.1	997	10	1
Baton Rouge, LA MSA	528,264	902	0.2	875	9	18
Battle Creek, MI MSA	135,982	696	0.5	687	1	8
Beaumont--Port Arthur, TX MSA	361,226	890	0.2	872	3	15
Bellingham, WA MSA	127,780	4,014	3.1	3,848	54	112
Benton Harbor, MI MSA	161,378	685	0.4	676	5	4
Billings, MT MSA	113,419	3,235	2.9	3,225	5	5
Biloxi--Gulfport, MS MSA	197,125	595	0.3	571	16	8
Binghamton, NY MSA	264,497	450	0.2	436	8	6
Birmingham, AL MSA	907,810	1,506	0.2	1,458	22	26
Bismarck, ND MSA	83,831	2,016	2.4	2,016		
Bloomington, IN MSA	108,978	216	0.2	212	4	
Bloomington--Normal, IL MSA	129,180	203	0.2	192	6	5
Boise City, ID MSA	205,775	1,382	0.7	1,354	17	11
Boston--Lawrence--Salem, MA--NH CMSA	4,171,643	7,542	0.2	7,261	145	136
Bradenton, FL MSA	211,707	501	0.2	470	6	25
Bremerton, WA MSA	189,731	3,211	1.7	3,068	59	84
Brownsville--Harlingen, TX MSA	260,120	413	0.2	406	7	
Bryan--College Station, TX MSA	121,862	274	0.2	264	7	3
Buffalo--Niagara Falls, NY CMSA	1,189,288	7,611	0.6	7,567	26	18
Burlington, NC MSA	108,213	303	0.3	299	4	
Burlington, VT MSA	131,439	299	0.2	291	6	2
Canton, OH MSA	394,106	1,015	0.3	994	9	12
Casper, WY MSA	61,226	404	0.7	396	7	1
Cedar Rapids, IA MSA	168,767	363	0.2	359	4	
Champaign--Urbana--Rantoul, IL MSA	173,025	331	0.2	319	5	7
Charleston, SC MSA	506,875	1,613	0.3	1,564	29	20
Charleston, WV MSA	250,454	292	0.1	276	7	9
Charlotte--Gastonia--Rock Hill, NC--SC MSA	1,162,093	4,107	0.4	4,032	17	58

[Continued]

★ 147 ★

Population of Native North Americans by MSA in 1990 - I: A-K
[Continued]

Metropolitan Statistical Areas	Total area popu-lation	American Indians, Eskimos, and Aleuts				
		Total	% of area's population	American Indians	Eskimos	Aleuts
Charlottesville, VA MSA	131,107	148	0.1	138	4	6
Chattanooga, TN--GA MSA	433,210	891	0.2	879	5	7
Cheyenne, WY MSA	73,142	528	0.7	518	7	3
Chicago--Gary--Lake County, IL--IN--WI CMSA	8,065,633	15,758	0.2	15,098	306	354
Chico, CA MSA	182,120	3,241	1.8	3,212	20	9
Cincinnati--Hamilton, OH--KY--IN CMSA	1,744,124	2,457	0.1	2,365	34	58
Clarksville--Hopkinsville, TN--KY MSA	169,439	688	0.4	674	13	1
Cleveland--Akron--Lorain, OH CMSA	2,759,823	5,133	0.2	4,994	78	61
Colorado Springs, CO MSA	397,014	3,242	0.8	3,158	59	25
Columbia, MO MSA	112,379	394	0.4	379	3	12
Columbia, SC MSA	453,331	1,013	0.2	968	24	21
Columbus, GA--AL MSA	243,072	765	0.3	689	69	7
Columbus, OH MSA	1,377,419	2,880	0.2	2,813	29	38
Corpus Christi, TX MSA	349,894	1,394	0.4	1,373	13	8
Cumberland, MD--WV MSA	101,643	71	0.1	67	4	
Dallas--Fort Worth, TX CMSA	3,885,415	18,972	0.5	18,608	174	190
Danville, VA MSA	108,711	117	0.1	117		
Davenport--Rock Island--Moline, IA--IL MSA	350,861	902	0.3	888	8	6
Dayton--Springfield, OH MSA	951,270	1,915	0.2	1,872	17	26
Daytona Beach, FL MSA	370,712	915	0.2	898	13	4
Decatur, AL MSA	131,556	2,434	1.9	2,431	2	1
Decatur, IL MSA	117,206	157	0.1	149	8	
Denver--Boulder, CO CMSA	1,848,319	13,884	0.8	13,600	159	125
Des Moines, IA MSA	392,928	1,015	0.3	977	7	31
Detroit--Ann Arbor, MI CMSA	4,665,236	17,961	0.4	17,731	78	152
Dothan, AL MSA	130,964	526	0.4	521	5	
Dubuque, IA MSA	86,403	77	0.1	73	3	1
Duluth, MN--WI MSA	239,971	4,487	1.9	4,452	14	21
Eau Claire, WI MSA	137,543	617	0.4	599	5	13
El Paso, TX MSA	591,610	2,590	0.4	2,542	22	26
Elkhart--Goshen, IN MSA	156,198	453	0.3	440	10	3
Elmira, NY MSA	95,195	211	0.2	203	2	6
Enid, OK MSA	56,735	1,234	2.2	1,227	1	6
Erie, PA MSA	275,572	438	0.2	428	6	4
Eugene--Springfield, OR MSA	282,912	3,207	1.1	3,123	45	39
Evansville, IN--KY MSA	278,990	477	0.2	471	5	1
Fargo--Moorhead, ND--MN MSA	153,296	1,497	1.0	1,489	8	
Fayetteville, NC MSA	274,566	4,425	1.6	4,397	13	15
Fayetteville--Springdale, AR MSA	113,409	1,486	1.3	1,478	2	6
Fitchburg--Leominster, MA MSA	102,797	196	0.2	185	7	4
Flint, MI MSA	430,459	3,132	0.7	3,109	11	12
Florence, AL MSA	131,327	302	0.2	300	1	1
Florence, SC MSA	114,344	145	0.1	140	1	4

[Continued]

★147★

Population of Native North Americans by MSA in 1990 - I: A-K
[Continued]

Metropolitan Statistical Areas	Total area popu- lation	American Indians, Eskimos, and Aleuts				
		Total	% of area's population	American Indians	Eskimos	Aleuts
Fort Collins--Loveland, CO MSA	186,136	1,063	0.6	1,040	9	14
Fort Myers--Cape CoraL, Fl MSA	335,113	672	0.2	665	4	3
Fort Pierce, FL MSA	251,071	526	0.2	509	13	4
Fort Smith, AR--OK MSA	175,911	9,054	5.1	9,044	4	6
Fort Walton Beach, FL MSA	143,776	776	0.5	751	17	8
Fort Wayne, IN MSA	363,811	1,056	0.3	1,043	6	7
Fresno, CA MSA	667,490	7,119	1.1	6,954	40	125
Gadsden, AL MSA	99,840	250	0.3	243	7	
Gainesville, FL MSA	204,111	443	0.2	429	10	4
Glens Falls, NY MSA	118,539	214	0.2	211	3	
Grand Forks, ND MSA	70,683	1,244	1.8	1,236	8	
Grand Rapids, MI MSA	688,399	3,394	0.5	3,373	12	9
Great Falls, MT MSA	77,691	3,072	4.0	3,053	14	5
Greeley, CO MSA	131,821	785	0.6	759	10	16
Green Bay, WI MSA	194,594	3,869	2.0	3,843	7	19
Greensboro--Winston-Salem--High Point, NC MSA	942,091	3,196	0.3	3,167	21	8
Greenville--Spartanburg, SC MSA	640,861	959	0.1	934	9	16
Hagerstown, MD MSA	121,393	241	0.2	238	3	
Harrisburg--Lebanon--Carlisle, PA MSA	587,986	737	0.1	713	11	13
Hartford--New Britain--Middletown, CT CMSA	1,085,837	1,826	0.2	1,769	26	31
Hickory--Morganton, NC MSA	221,700	417	0.2	399	18	
Honolulu, HI MSA	836,231	3,532	0.4	3,293	83	156
Houma--Thibodaux, LA MSA	182,842	6,814	3.7	6,809	5	
Houston--Galveston--Brazoria, TX CMSA	3,711,043	11,029	0.3	10,677	170	182
Huntington--Ashland, WV--KY--OH MSA	312,529	372	0.1	368	4	
Huntsville, AL MSA	238,912	1,601	0.7	1,583	12	6
Indianapolis, IN MSA	1,249,822	2,510	0.2	2,435	49	26
Iowa City, IA MSA	96,119	176	0.2	162	9	5
Jackson, MI MSA	149,756	655	0.4	646	5	4
Jackson, MS MSA	395,396	346	0.1	338	2	6
Jackson, TN MSA	77,982	66	0.1	64	1	1
Jacksonville, FL MSA	906,727	2,587	0.3	2,529	27	31
Jacksonville, NC MSA	149,838	939	0.6	919	16	4
Jamestown--Dunkirk, NY	141,895	558	0.4	556	1	1
Janesville--Beloit, WI MSA	139,510	369	0.3	368	1	
Johnson City--Kingsport--Bristol, TN--VA MSA	436,047	766	0.2	751	7	8
Johnstown, PA MSA	241,247	152	0.1	148	4	
Joplin, MO MSA	134,910	2,452	1.8	2,440	11	1
Kalamazoo, MI MSA	223,411	1,017	0.5	1,007	1	9
Kankakee, IL MSA	96,255	150	0.2	143	6	1
Kansas City, MO--KS MSA	1,566,280	7,631	0.5	7,503	68	60
Killeen--Temple, TX MSA	255,301	1,405	0.6	1,376	13	16

[Continued]

★ 147 ★

Population of Native North Americans by MSA in 1990 - I: A-K

[Continued]

Metropolitan Statistical Areas	Total area popu- lation	American Indians, Eskimos, and Aleuts				
		Total	% of area's population	American Indians	Eskimos	Aleuts
Knoxville, TN MSA	604,816	1,505	0.2	1,485	8	12
Kokomo, IN MSA	96,946	246	0.3	243	2	1

Source: Census of Population and Housing, 1990: Summary Tape File 1 on CD-ROM, U.S. Bureau of the Census, Washington, D.C. 1991.

★ 148 ★

Population of Native North Americans by MSA in 1990 - II: L-Y

Metropolitan Statistical Areas	Total area popu- lation	American Indians, Eskimos, and Aleuts				
		Total	% of area's population	American Indians	Eskimos	Aleuts
La Crosse, WI MSA	97,904	340	0.3	325	5	10
Lafayette, LA MSA	208,740	440	0.2	436	2	2
Lafayette--West Lafayette, IN MSA	130,598	320	0.2	311	8	1
Lake Charles, LA MSA	168,134	387	0.2	383	3	1
Lakeland--Winter Haven, FL MSA	405,382	1,158	0.3	1,119	27	12
Lancaster, PA MSA	422,822	484	0.1	469	5	10
Lansing--East Lansing, MI MSA	432,674	2,655	0.6	2,622	20	13
Laredo, TX MSA	133,239	201	0.2	185	3	13
Las Cruces, NM MSA	135,510	1,009	0.7	980	16	13
Las Vegas, NV MSA	741,459	6,416	0.9	6,292	67	57
Lawrence, KS MSA	81,798	2,161	2.6	2,134	21	6
Lawton, OK MSA	111,486	5,153	4.6	5,129	16	8
Lewiston--Auburn, ME MSA	88,141	197	0.2	195	2	
Lexington-Fayette, KY MSA	348,428	561	0.2	537	14	10
Lima, OH MSA	154,340	252	0.2	247	2	3
Lincoln, NE MSA	213,641	1,207	0.6	1,196	4	7
Little Rock--North Little Rock, AR MSA	513,117	1,870	0.4	1,828	27	15
Longview--Marshall, TX MSA	162,431	670	0.4	658	9	3
Los Angeles--Anaheim--Riverside, CA CMSA	14,531,529	87,487	0.6	85,004	1,036	1,447
Louisville, KY--IN MSA	952,662	1,576	0.2	1,546	13	17
Lubbock, TX MSA	222,636	686	0.3	675	5	6
Lynchburg, VA MSA	142,199	277	0.2	271	4	2
Macon--Warner Robins, GA MSA	281,103	571	0.2	558	7	6
Madison, WI MSA	367,085	1,201	0.3	1,151	23	27
Manchester, NH MSA	147,809	278	0.2	267	9	2
Mansfield, OH MSA	126,137	223	0.2	220	2	1
Mcallen--Edinburg--Mission, TX MSA	383,545	668	0.2	625	22	21
Medford, OR MSA	146,389	1,863	1.3	1,830	25	8

[Continued]

★ 148 ★

Population of Native North Americans by MSA in 1990 - II: L-Y
[Continued]

Metropolitan Statistical Areas	Total area population	American Indians, Eskimos, and Aleuts				
		Total	% of area's population	American Indians	Eskimos	Aleuts
Melbourne--Titusville--Palm Bay, FL MSA	398,978	1,369	0.3	1,341	18	10
Memphis, TN--AR--MS MSA	981,747	1,791	0.2	1,740	15	36
Merced, CA MSA	178,403	1,516	0.8	1,461	6	49
Miami--Fort Lauderdale, FL CMSA	3,192,582	5,700	0.2	5,486	79	135
Midland, TX MSA	106,611	414	0.4	412	1	1
Milwaukee--Racine, WI CMSA	1,607,183	8,522	0.5	8,430	35	57
Minneapolis--St. Paul, MN--WI MSA	2,464,124	23,956	1.0	23,621	110	225
Mobile, AL MSA	476,923	2,570	0.5	2,547	14	9
Modesto, CA MSA	370,522	4,039	1.1	3,965	27	47
Monroe, LA MSA	142,191	239	0.2	227	11	1
Montgomery, AL MSA	292,517	622	0.2	589	10	23
Muncie, IN MSA	119,659	274	0.2	268	6	
Muskegon, MI MSA	158,983	1,338	0.8	1,331	7	
Naples, FL MSA	152,099	428	0.3	424	2	2
Nashville, TN MSA	985,026	2,121	0.2	2,093	19	9
New Bedford, MA MSA	175,641	504	0.3	502	2	
New Haven--Meriden, CT MSA	530,180	947	0.2	925	10	12
New London--Norwich, CT--RI MSA	266,819	1,433	0.5	1,405	17	11
New Orleans, LA MSA	1,238,816	3,615	0.3	3,557	26	32
New York--Northern New Jersey--Long Island, NY--NJ--CT CMSA	18,087,251	46,191	0.3	44,337	726	1,128
Norfolk--Virginia Beach--Newport News, VA MSA	1,396,107	4,679	0.3	4,556	67	56
Ocala, FL MSA	194,833	638	0.3	634	4	
Odessa, TX MSA	118,934	647	0.5	641	4	2
Oklahoma City, OK MSA	958,839	45,720	4.8	45,623	58	39
Olympia, WA MSA	161,238	2,498	1.5	2,364	51	83
Omaha, NE--IA MSA	618,262	3,159	0.5	3,126	17	16
Orlando, FL MSA	1,072,748	3,199	0.3	3,109	37	53
Owensboro, KY MSA	87,189	101	0.1	100	1	
Panama City, FL MSA	126,994	949	0.7	933	1	15
Parkersburg--Marietta, WV--OH MSA	149,169	242	0.2	237	4	1
Pascagoula, MS MSA	115,243	254	0.2	248	3	3
Pensacola, FL MSA	344,406	3,347	1.0	3,326	15	6
Peoria, IL MSA	339,172	587	0.2	574	5	8
Philadelphia--Wilmington--Trenton, PA--NJ--DE--MD CMSA	5,899,345	11,307	0.2	10,962	159	186
Phoenix, AZ MSA	2,122,101	38,017	1.8	37,708	163	146
Pine Bluff, AR MSA	85,487	227	0.3	225	1	1
Pittsburgh--Beaver Valley, PA CMSA	2,242,798	2,257	0.1	2,187	42	28
Pittsfield, MA MSA	79,250	142	0.2	135	6	1
Portland, ME MSA	215,281	562	0.3	555	3	4
Portland--Vancouver, OR--WA CMSA	1,477,895	13,603	0.9	13,034	257	312
Portsmouth--Dover--Rochester, NH--ME MSA	223,578	414	0.2	400	11	3

[Continued]

251

★ 148 ★

Population of Native North Americans by MSA in 1990 - II: L-Y
[Continued]

Metropolitan Statistical Areas	Total area popu- lation	American Indians, Eskimos, and Aleuts				
		Total	% of area's population	American Indians	Eskimos	Aleuts
Poughkeepsie, NY MSA	259,462	374	0.1	360	6	8
Providence--Pawtucket--Fall River, RI--MA CMSA	1,141,510	3,782	0.3	3,694	44	44
Provo--Orem, UT MSA	263,590	1,913	0.7	1,883	11	19
Pueblo, CO MSA	123,051	991	0.8	979	8	4
Raleigh--Durham, NC MSA	735,480	1,933	0.3	1,896	16	21
Rapid City, SD MSA	81,343	5,835	7.2	5,804	27	4
Reading, PA MSA	336,523	333	0.1	318	10	5
Redding, CA MSA	147,036	3,954	2.7	3,885	26	43
Reno, NV MSA	254,667	4,921	1.9	4,832	53	36
Richland--Kennewick--Pasco, WA MSA	150,033	1,124	0.7	1,086	21	17
Richmond--Petersburg, VA MSA	865,640	2,705	0.3	2,681	15	9
Roanoke, VA MSA	224,477	281	0.1	277	4	
Rochester, MN MSA	106,470	295	0.3	286	8	1
Rochester, NY MSA	1,002,410	2,870	0.3	2,824	28	18
Rockford, IL MSA	283,719	697	0.2	665	19	13
Sacramento, CA MSA	1,481,102	17,021	1.1	16,650	165	206
Saginaw--Bay City--Midland, MI MSA	399,320	1,975	0.5	1,948	15	12
St. Cloud, MN MSA	190,921	637	0.3	625	9	3
St. Joseph, MO MSA	83,083	273	0.3	273		
St. Louis, MO--IL MSA	2,444,099	4,947	0.2	4,805	57	85
Salem, OR MSA	278,024	4,041	1.5	3,904	83	54
Salinas--Seaside--Monterey, CA MSA	355,660	3,017	0.8	2,944	46	27
Salt Lake City--Ogden, UT MSA	1,072,227	8,337	0.8	8,210	82	45
San Angelo, TX MSA	98,458	373	0.4	360	8	5
San Antonio, TX MSA	1,302,099	4,648	0.4	4,529	58	61
San Diego, CA MSA	2,498,016	20,066	0.8	19,564	193	309
San Francisco--Oakland--San Jose, CA CMSA	6,253,311	40,847	0.7	39,255	662	930
Santa Barbara--Santa Maria--Lompoc, CA MSA	369,608	3,351	0.9	3,279	42	30
Santa Fe, NM MSA	117,043	2,948	2.5	2,930	9	9
Sarasota, FL MSA	277,776	483	0.2	462	14	7
Savannah, GA MSA	242,622	515	0.2	489	21	5
Scranton--Wilkes-Barre, PA MSA	734,175	580	0.1	553	20	7
Seattle--Tacoma, WA CMSA	2,559,164	32,071	1.3	29,643	1,126	1,302
Sharon, PA MSA	121,003	115	0.1	111	3	1
Sheboygan, WI MSA	103,877	357	0.3	344	1	12
Sherman--Denison, TX MSA	95,021	1,046	1.1	1,028	1	17
Shreveport, LA MSA	334,341	865	0.3	849	9	7
Sioux City, IA--NE MSA	115,018	1,999	1.7	1,993	3	3
Sioux Falls, SD MSA	123,809	1,680	1.4	1,675	3	2
South Bend--Mishawaka, IN MSA	247,052	846	0.3	840	4	2
Spokane, WA MSA	361,364	5,539	1.5	5,390	95	54
Springfield, IL MSA	189,550	319	0.2	313	4	2
Springfield, MO MSA	240,593	1,471	0.6	1,450	11	10

[Continued]

★ 148 ★

Population of Native North Americans by MSA in 1990 - II: L-Y
[Continued]

Metropolitan Statistical Areas	Total area popu- lation	American Indians, Eskimos, and Aleuts				
		Total	% of area's population	American Indians	Eskimos	Aleuts
Springfield, MA MSA	529,519	864	0.2	835	13	16
State College, PA MSA	123,786	179	0.1	168	7	4
Steubenville--Weirton, OH--WV MSA	142,523	237	0.2	224	4	9
Stockton, CA MSA	480,628	5,085	1.1	4,999	38	48
Syracuse, NY MSA	659,864	3,948	0.6	3,915	18	15
Tallahassee, FL MSA	233,598	568	0.2	554	8	6
Tampa--St. Petersburg--Clearwater, FL MSA	2,067,959	5,467	0.3	5,331	76	60
Terre Haute, IN MSA	130,812	338	0.3	325	8	5
Texarkana, TX--Texarkana, AR MSA	120,132	560	0.5	554	2	4
Toledo, OH MSA	614,128	1,423	0.2	1,398	9	16
Topeka, KS MSA	160,976	1,836	1.1	1,827	4	5
Tucson, AZ MSA	666,880	20,330	3.0	20,231	56	43
Tulsa, OK MSA	708,954	48,196	6.8	48,116	45	35
Tuscaloosa, AL MSA	150,522	253	0.2	246	7	
Tyler, TX MSA	151,309	520	0.3	513	6	1
Utica--Rome, NY MSA	316,633	613	0.2	598	9	6
Victoria, TX MSA	74,361	208	0.3	194	4	10
Visalia--Tulare--Porterville, CA MSA	311,921	3,992	1.3	3,938	26	28
Waco, TX MSA	189,123	563	0.3	551	4	8
Washington, DC--MD--VA MSA	3,923,574	11,036	0.3	10,685	145	206
Waterbury, CT MSA	221,629	538	0.2	518	2	18
Waterloo--Cedar Falls, IA MSA	146,611	237	0.2	237		
Wausau, WI MSA	115,400	490	0.4	464	7	19
West Palm Beach--Boca Raton--Delray Beach, FL MSA	863,518	1,211	0.1	1,169	26	16
Wheeling, WV--OH MSA	159,301	145	0.1	143	2	
Wichita, KS MSA	485,270	5,160	1.1	5,132	13	15
Wichita Falls, TX MSA	122,378	903	0.7	876	6	21
Williamsport, PA MSA	118,710	219	0.2	216	1	2
Wilmington, NC MSA	120,284	435	0.4	433	2	
Worcester, MA MSA	436,905	891	0.2	876	11	4
Yakima, WA MSA	188,823	8,405	4.5	8,355	25	25
York, PA MSA	417,848	501	0.1	485	5	11
Youngstown--Warren, OH MSA	492,619	785	0.2	767	13	5
Yuba City, CA MSA	122,643	2,616	2.1	2,585	12	19
Yuma, AZ MSA	106,895	1,429	1.3	1,420	5	4

Source: *Census of Population and Housing, 1990: Summary Tape File 1 on CD-ROM*, U.S. Bureau of the Census, Washington, D.C. 1991.

★ 149 ★

Congressional Districts With the Most Native Americans as a Percentage of Total Population

State	Location	Congressional district number	American Indians, Eskimos, and Aleuts(%)
New Mexico	Santa Fe, NM	3	20.9
Alaska	At-large, AR	-	16.0
Arizona	Phoenix-Scottsdale, AZ	4	15.4
Oklahoma	Muskogee, OK	2	11.6
Oklahoma	Lawton, OK	3	7.6
North Carolina	Fayetteville, NC	7	7.6
Montana	Billings-Great Falls, MT	2	6.7
South Dakota	At-large, SD	-	6.5
Arizona	Phoenix-Yuma, AZ	2	5.2
Arizona	Phoenix-Flagstaff, AZ	3	5.1

Source: Linda F. Williams, *Congressional District Fact Book, Second Edition*, Joint Center for Political Studies, Inc., 1986, p. 22.

★ 150 ★

American Indian Population On and Off Reservations, by Selected Tribal Affiliation, 1991

The number of tribal members is shown, by residence status and tribal affiliation, for 1991.

Reservation	Tribal Affiliation	Residing on reservation	Residing off reservation	Total tribal membership
Blackfeet	Blackfeet	7,217	6,623	13,840
Cheyenne River	Cheyenne Sioux	3,690	5,970	9,660
Colville	Colville	4,170	3,475	7,645
Crow	Crow	6,210	2,382	8,592
Fort Berthold	Arikara, Mandan, Hidatsa	4,600	4,500	9,100
Fort Peck	Assiniboine-Sioux	5,146	4,485	9,631
Pine Ridge	Oglala Sioux	12,107	7,000	19,107
Rosebud	Rosebud Sioux	10,973	1,810	12,783
Standing Rock	Standing Rock-Sioux	4,799	8,611	13,410
Turtle Mountain	Chippewa	4,420	22,080	26,500
Wind River	Arapahoe,	5,003	2,278	7,281

[Continued]

★ 150 ★

American Indian Population On and Off Reservations, by Selected Tribal Affiliation, 1991

[Continued]

Reservation	Tribal Affiliation	Residing on reservation	Residing off reservation	Total tribal membership
Yakima	Shoshone Yakima	5,585	2,514	8,099
Total		73,920	71,728	145,648

Source: *Indian Programs: Profile of Land Ownership at 12 Reservations*, United States General Accounting Office, GAO/RCED-92-96BR, February 1992, p. 8.

★ 151 ★

American Indian Population, by Reservation and Non-Reservation States, 1960

Figures are based on BIA data[1].

State	Population 1960
States with Federal Reservations	
Alaska[2]	14,444
Arizona	83,387
California	39,014
Colorado	4,288
Florida	2,504
Idaho	5,231
Iowa	1,708
Kansas	5,069
Louisiana	3,587
Michigan	9,701
Minnesota	15,496
Mississippi	3,119
Montana	21,181
Nebraska	5,545
Nevada	6,681
New Mexico	56,255
North Carolina	38,129
North Dakota	11,736
Oklahoma	64,689
Oregon	8,026
South Dakota	25,794
Utah	6,961
Washington	21,076
Wisconsin	14,297
Wyoming	4,020

[Continued]

★ 151 ★

American Indian Population, by Reservation and Non-Reservation States, 1960

[Continued]

State	Population 1960
Total	471,938
States with no Federal Reservations	
Alabama	1,276
Arkansas	580
Connecticut	923
Delaware	597
Georgia	749
Hawaii	472
Illinois	4,704
Indiana	948
Kentucky	391
Maine	1,879
Maryland	1,538
Massachusetts	2,118
Missouri[3]	1,723
New Hampshire	135
New Jersey	1,699
New York	16,491
Ohio	1,910
Pennsylvania	2,122
Rhode Island	932
South Carolina	1,098
Tennesee	638
Texas[3]	5,750
Vermont	57
Virginia	2,155
West Virginia	181
District of Columbia	587
Total	51,653
Indians, Total	523,591

[Continued]

★ 151 ★

American Indian Population, by Reservation and Non-Reservation States, 1960

[Continued]

State	Population 1960
Eskimos and Aleuts (Alaska)[2]	28,078
Total	551,669

Source: United States Department of the Interior, Bureau of Indian Affairs, *U.S. Indian Population (1962) and Land (1963)*, Government Printing Office, November 1963, p. 5. *Notes:* In 1960 a little more than half of the total number of Indians, Eskimos, and Aleuts lived within Federal reservations, and about five-eighths of them lived within or adjacent to Federal reservations. The "adjacent to" group are Indians living nearby who have interests in the reservation, may be occasional residents, and may be getting Bureau services. A study of county data shows that there has been considerable movement away from the reservations; and that a large portion of the off-reservation Indian population (especially in the states without Federal reservations) is concentrating in the larger cities. 1. Differences between these figures and those which are presented elsewhere relate both to changes in population occurring since 1960 and to the fact that the Bureau's 1962 figures are only for persons living on trust or restricted land. 2. The figure of 28,078 officially released October 1963 represents the Alaskan native population (Aleuts 5,755, Eskimos 22,323) of Alaska. 3. These states are listed because they contain bits of off-reservation land, but they do not have any Federal Indian reservations.

★ 152 ★

Population and Tribal Enrollment Status on Reservations, by Tribal Affiliation, Age Group, and Sex, 1980: Acoma Pueblo - Burns

Data are the latest available.

Identified reservations; tribes of 30 or more American Indians	Total				Enrolled in tribe					Enrollment status not reported
				18 years and over	Both sexes			Under 18 years	18 Years and over	
	Both sexes	Female	Under 18 years		Total	Percent enrolled of total	Female			
Total persons	336,280	170,979	155,271	181,010	292,539	87.0	148,989	130,025	162,513	24,594
Acoma Pueblo, New Mexico	2,268	1,205	962	1,306	2,197	96.9	1,163	916	1,280	38
Pueblo	2,196	1,166	940	1,256	2,143	97.6	1,136	911	1,232	25
Acoma	2,106	1,129	896	1,209	2,070	98.3	1,105	876	1,194	25
Laguna	67	26	38	29	52	77.9	21	28	24	-
All other American Indians	72	39	21	51	53	74.1	28	5	48	13
Tribe not reported	24	14	13	11	13	55.4	9	2	11	10
Agua Caliente Reservation, California	-	-	-	-	-	-	-	-	-	-
Alabama-Coushatta Reservation, Texas	498	251	201	298	465	93.3	237	181	284	15
Alabama-Coushatta	481	243	191	290	451	93.8	230	174	277	11
All other American Indians	18	8	10	8	14	78.1	8	6	8	4
Tribe not reported	4	1	4	-	1	28.7	1	1	-	3
Alamo Reservation, New Mexico	1,066	555	536	530	636	59.6	323	314	322	423
Navajo	839	429	417	422	632	75.3	321	313	319	200
All other American Indians	227	126	119	108	4	1.8	2	1	3	223
Tribe not reported	225	124	119	106	3	1.3	1	1	2	222
Allegany Reservation, New York	920	467	364	556	791	86.0	406	288	503	51

[Continued]

257

★ 152 ★

Population and Tribal Enrollment Status on Reservations, by Tribal Affiliation, Age Group, and Sex, 1980: Acoma Pueblo - Burns
[Continued]

Identified reservations; tribes of 30 or more American Indians	Total				Enrolled in tribe					Enrollment status not reported
	Both sexes	Female	Under 18 years	18 years and over	Both sexes		Female	Under 18 years	18 Years and over	
					Total	Percent enrolled of total				
Iroquois	845	431	323	522	773	91.4	398	279	494	8
Seneca	805	411	310	494	744	92.5	384	272	472	5
All other American Indians	75	36	41	34	19	25.1	8	9	9	43
Tribe not reported	50	22	27	23	5	10.4	2	2	3	41
Alturas Rancheria, California	7	...	...	...	...	...	...	...	...	...
Annette Islands Reserve, Alaska	949	445	400	548	644	67.9	305	261	383	147
Tlingit	47	18	12	35	21	44.3	8	-	21	14
Tsimshian	747	345	330	417	581	77.9	272	241	340	92
All other American indians	155	82	59	97	42	26.8	25	20	22	40
Tribe not reported	38	18	12	26	13	33.3	8	8	5	19
Augustine Reservation, California	-	-	-	-	-	-	-	-	-	-
Bad River Reservation, Wisconsin	699	347	311	388	675	96.6	339	299	376	5
Chippewa	665	325	297	368	645	97.1	319	285	360	-
Bad River	217	108	89	128	210	97.0	106	82	128	-
Chippewa	427	211	207	220	419	98.3	207	201	218	-
All other American Indians	34	22	14	20	30	86.8	20	14	16	5
Tribe not reported	2	2	-	2	-	-	-	-	-	2
Barona Rancheria, California	222	105	96	126	182	81.9	90	67	115	6
Diegueno	182	88	85	97	152	83.6	76	61	92	4
All other American Indians	40	17	11	29	30	74.3	14	6	23	2
Tribe not reported	2	2	-	2	1	53.5	1	-	1	-
Bay Mills Reservation, Michigan	277	129	122	155	265	95.7	127	117	148	6
Chippewa	273	127	119	154	263	96.4	124	115	148	4
Bay Mills	227	106	101	126	219	96.6	104	98	121	4
Chippewa	39	19	16	22	37	94.8	19	15	21	-
All other American Indians	4	2	3	1	2	49.8	2	2	-	1
Tribe not reported	3	2	3	-	2	63.3	2	2	-	1
Benton Paiute Reservation, California	12	...	...	...	...	...	...	...	...	...
Berry Creek Rancheria, California	-	-	-	-	-	-	-	-	-	-
Big Bend Rancheria, California	8	...	...	...	...	...	...	...	...	...
Big Cypress Reservation, Florida	350	180	158	193	346	98.6	177	155	190	3
Seminole	340	176	158	182	336	98.9	173	155	181	3
All other American Indians	11	5	-	11	10	89.5	4	-	10	-
Tribe not reported	-	-	-	-	-	-	-	-	-	-
Big Lagoon Rancheria, California	8	...	...	...	...	...	...	...	...	...
Big Pine Rancheria, California	269	133	119	150	241	89.5	115	99	142	7
Paiute	240	115	112	128	218	90.9	103	93	125	2
All other American Indians	29	17	7	22	23	78.2	12	6	17	5
Tribe not reported	5	4	1	4	-	-	-	-	-	4

[Continued]

Population and Tribal Enrollment Status on Reservations, by Tribal Affiliation, Age Group, and Sex, 1980: Acoma Pueblo - Burns

[Continued]

Identified reservations; tribes of 30 or more American Indians	Total				Enrolled in tribe					Enrollment status not reported
					Both sexes					
	Both sexes	Female	Under 18 years	18 years and over	Total	Percent enrolled of total	Female	Under 18 years	18 Years and over	
Bishop Rancheria, California	782	392	324	458	688	88.0	345	267	422	31
Paiute	677	337	284	393	614	90.8	307	239	376	16
Shoshone	35	18	11	24	28	81.0	15	9	19	2
All other American Indians	70	38	29	42	46	65.1	23	19	27	13
Tribe not reported	11	6	3	7	1	11.7	1	1	-	9
Blackfeet Reservation, Montana	5,525	2,798	2,415	3,110	4,567	82.7	2,310	1,853	2,714	562
Blackfoot	4,853	2,440	2,148	2,705	4,272	88.0	2,144	1,743	2,529	333
Chippewa	57	30	33	24	24	42.4	12	17	7	10
Cree	167	79	46	121	63	37.8	28	16	47	28
Flathead	36	31	24	12	36	100.0	31	24	12	-
All other American Indians	412	218	164	248	170	41.4	94	52	118	191
Tribe not reported	203	101	85	117	24	11.7	10	10	14	170
Bois Forte Reservation (Nett Lake), Minnesota	407	201	201	206	364	89.4	180	169	195	7
Chippewa	387	187	189	198	352	91.0	172	160	192	2
Bois Forte	39	18	14	25	38	97.4	18	13	25	1
Chippewa	338	165	171	167	304	89.9	150	143	161	1
All other American Indians	20	14	12	8	12	60.0	8	9	3	5
Tribe not reported	6	3	4	2	3	50.0	1	2	1	2
Bridgeport Colony, California	51	32	21	30	47	91.2	29	17.2	29	-
Paiute	44	27	18	27	40	89.8	23	14	26	-
All other American Indians	7	6	3	4	7	100.0	6	3	4	-
Tribe not reported	-	-	-	-	-	-	-	-	-	-
Brighton Reservation, Florida	330	167	147	183	294	89.1	148	131	163	28
Seminole	317	160	143	174	288	90.9	143	131	158	24
All other American Indians	12	7	3	9	5	43.9	4	-	5	4
Tribe not reported	5	-	2	2	-	-	-	-	-	4
Burns Reservation, Oregon	160	74	64	96	148	92.5	69	55	93	4
Paiute	143	66	56	87	134	93.7	63	50	84	4
Burns Paiute	38	21	20	18	37	97.4	20	19	18	-
Paiute	104	45	36	68	96	92.3	43	31	65	4
All other American Indians	17	8	8	9	14	82.4	6	5	9	-
Tribe not reported	2	1	1	1	2	100.0	1	1	1	-

Source: U.S. Bureau of the Census, Subject Reports, PC80-2-1D, Part 1, *American Indians, Eskimos, and Aleuts on Identified Reservations and in the Historic Areas of Oklahoma (Excluding Urbanized Areas)*, U.S. Government Printing Office, Washington, D.C., 1986, pp. 16-31. *Notes:* Three dots (...) means not applicable, or that the data are being withheld to avoid disclosure of information for individuals. A dash (-) represents zero or a percent which rounds to less than 0.1. Also, a dash (-) is used because the number of supplementary questionnaires for the reservations was insufficient to produce reliable estimates.

★ 153 ★

Population and Tribal Enrollment Status on Reservations, by Tribal Affiliation, Age Group, and Sex, 1980: Cabazon - Cortina Rancheria

Data are the latest available.

Identified reservations; tribes of 30 or more American Indians	Total				Enrolled in tribe					Enrollment status not reported
	Both sexes	Female	Under 18 years	18 years and over	Both sexes		Female	Under 18 years	18 Years and over	
					Total	Percent enrolled of total				
Cabazon Reservation, California	8	...	...	...	...	...	...	...	...	...
Cachil Dehe Rancheria, California	17	...	...	...	...	...	...	...	...	...
Cahuilla Reservation, California	29	...	...	...	...	...	...	...	...	...
Campo Reservation, California	84	46	37	46	73	87.0	40	31	42	1
Diegueno	49	29	22	27	44	88.6	24	19	25	1
Mission Indians	32	15	14	18	27	83.6	13	11	16	-
All other American Indians	2	2	1	1	2	100.0	2	1	1	-
Tribe not reported	-	-	-	-	-	-	-	-	-	-
Camp Verde Reservation, Arizona	179	92	87	92	154	86.0	79	76	78	13
Yavapai apache	128	67	64	64	117	91.4	62	56	61	4
All other American Indians	51	25	23	28	37	72.5	17	20	17	9
Tribe not reported	10	6	4	6	1	10.0	1	1	-	9
Canoncito Reservation, New Mexico	968	487	472	496	927	95.7	467	451	476	23
Navajo	921	467	452	469	899	97.6	455	436	463	5
All other American Indians	48	20	20	27	28	59.5	12	16	13	18
Tribe not reported	18	9	5	13	1	6.2	1	-	1	17
Capitan Grande Reservation, California	-	-	-	-	-	-	-	-	-	-
Carson Colony, Nevada	213	116	82	131	197	92.3	105	68	129	1
Paiute	41	24	19	22	36	88.4	20	15	21	-
Washo	120	64	40	80	11	92.3	59	31	80	1
All other American Indians	52	28	23	29	49	95.2	26	21	28	-
Tribe not reported	4	-	-	4	4	100.0	-	-	4	-
Catawba Reservation, South Carolina	993	482	411	582	954	96.1	471	384	570	3
Catawba	982	481	410	573	953	97.0	471	384	569	-
All other American Indians	11	2	1	10	1	10.7	-	-	1	3
Tribe not reported	3	-	1	2	-	-	-	-	-	3
Cattaraugus Reservation, New York	1,844	954	738	1,107	1,626	88.1	847	662	964	151
Iroquois	1,712	892	688	1,024	1,606	93.8	840	652	954	49
Cayuga	66	33	18	49	42	63.3	18	7	35	1
Seneca	1,578	833	651	927	1,522	96.4	805	633	889	36
All other American Indians	132	62	50	83	20	14.8	7	10	10	102
Tribe not reported	112	56	42	71	16	14.5	6	8	8	95
Cedarville Rancheria, California	6	...	...	...	...	...	...	...	...	...
Chehalis Reservation, Washington	200	104	96	104	167	83.4	90	68	98	2
Chehalis	116	69	60	56	99	85.6	60	46	54	1
Quinault	37	15	17	20	31	83.2	13	10	20	-
All other American Indians	47	20	19	27	37	78.1	17	12	24	1
Tribe not reported	1	-	1	-	-	-	-	-	-	1
Chemehuevi Reservation, California	19	...	...	...	...	...	...	...	...	...

[Continued]

★ 153 ★

Population and Tribal Enrollment Status on Reservations, by Tribal Affiliation, Age Group, and Sex, 1980: Cabazon - Cortina Rancheria
[Continued]

Identified reservations; tribes of 30 or more American Indians	Total				Enrolled in tribe					Enrollment status not reported
					Both sexes					
	Both sexes	Female	Under 18 years	18 years and over	Total	Percent enrolled of total	Female	Under 18 years	18 Years and over	
Cheyenne River Reservation, South Dakota	1,520	738	768	752	1,384	91.1	673	656	728	51
Sioux	1,459	706	741	719	1,367	93.6	660	652	714	10
Cheyenne River Sioux	1,251	612	656	595	1,167	93.3	573	574	593	10
Dakota Sioux	116	50	51	65	114	98.1	50	49	65	-
Standing Rock Sioux	34	16	10	24	31	91.4	13	8	24	-
All other American Indians	61	32	28	33	17	28.8	12	4	13	41
Tribe not reported	32	15	13	19	8	25.7	6	3	5	24
Chitimacha Reservation, Los Angeles	185	92	87	98	167	90.3	85	77	90	15
Chitimacha	170	85	78	92	166	97.7	84	77	89	1
All other American Indians	15	7	9	6	1	8.8	1	-	1	14
Tribe not reported	14	5	9	5	-	-	-	-	-	14
Cochiti Pueblo, New Mexico	616	327	269	347	603	97.8	321	263	340	9
Pueblo	585	306	262	323	578	98.8	304	259	319	5
Cochiti	566	292	258	307	558	98/7	289	255	303	5
All other American Indians	31	21	6	24	25	80.3	17	4	21	4
Tribe not reported	5	2	2	2	-	-	-	-	-	2
Cocopah Reservation, Arizona	349	172	155	194	311	89.0	155	129	182	18
Yuman	328	159	143	185	295	89.8	145	119	176	14
Cocopah	318	155	141	177	285	89.8	141	118	167	14
All other American Indians	21	13	12	9	16	76.2	10	10	6	4
Tribe not reported	6	2	3	3	3	50.0	1	2	1	3
Coeur d'Alene Reservation, Idaho	563	298	263	300	472	83.9	253	222	250	43
Coeur d'Alene	340	191	159	181	307	90.2	174	143	164	24
Colville	53	27	33	21	46	87.1	26	30	17	-
Flathead	36	16	16	21	33	92.0	15	16	18	2
All other American Indians	133	64	56	78	85	64.2	38	34	51	16
Tribe not reported	12	8	7	5	1	8.9	-	1	-	11
Cold Springs Rancheria, California	63	33	28	35	60	95.0	32	25	35	3
Mono	58	30	25	33	56	96.5	29	23	33	2
All other American Indians	5	2	2	2	4	75.8	2	1	2	1
Tribe not reported	1	-	1	-	-	-	-	-	-	1
Colorado River Reservation, Arizona-California	1,967	981	898	1,070	1,533	77.9	768	673	860	325
Chemehuevi	66	34	37	29	25	38.4	8	15	10	27
Colorado River	1,251	602	566	685	1,179	94.2	569	525	654	58
Navajo	100	46	46	54	79	78.9	37	32	47	6
Pueblo	45	30	22	23	26	57.5	20	10	16	6
Hopi	39	27	18	21	25	63.8	19	10	15	1
Yuman	131	67	50	81	59	45.2	35	19	40	69
Mohave	99	48	39	60	29	29.5	18	8	21	67
All other American Indians	374	201	176	197	164	43.9	98	71	93	160
Tribe not reported	137	69	67	70	2	1.5	2	1	1	155
Colville Reservation, Washington	3,568	1,766	1,516	2,050	3,119	87.4	1,526	1,260	1,858	97
Colville	3,094	1,521	1,336	1,758	2,801	90.5	1,365	1,158	1,644	41
Yakima	47	30	23	24	42	89.2	27	21	21	1
All other American Indians	427	216	157	270	275	64.5	133	81	194	55

[Continued]

261

★ 153 ★

Population and Tribal Enrollment Status on Reservations, by Tribal Affiliation, Age Group, and Sex, 1980: Cabazon - Cortina Rancheria

[Continued]

Identified reservations; tribes of 30 or more American Indians	Total				Enrolled in tribe					Enrollment status not reported
	Both sexes	Female	Under 18 years	18 years and over	Both sexes		Female	Under 18 years	18 Years and over	
					Total	Percent enrolled of total				
Tribe not reported	41	25	21	20	9	22.6	5	4	5	21
Cortina Rancheria, California	2	...	...	...	...	...	...	...	...	...

Source: U.S. Bureau of the Census, Subject Reports, PC80-2-1D, Part 1, *American Indians, Eskimos, and Aleuts on Identified Reservations and in the Historic Areas of Oklahoma (Excluding Urbanized Areas)*, U.S. Government Printing Office, Washington, D.C., 1986, pp. 16-31. *Notes:* Three dots (...) means not applicable, or that the data are being withheld to avoid disclosure of information for individuals. A dash (-) represents zero or a percent which rounds to less than 0.1. Also, a dash (-) is used because the number of supplementary questionnaires for the reservations was insufficient to produce reliable estimates.

★ 154 ★

Population and Tribal Enrollment Status on Reservations, by Tribal Affiliation, Age Group, and Sex, 1980: Coushatta - Fort Apache

Data are the latest available.

Identified reservations; tribes of 30 or more American Indians	Total				Enrolled in tribe					Enrollment status not reported
	Both sexes	Female	Under 18 years	18 years and over	Both sexes		Female	Under 18 years	18 Years and over	
					Total	Percent enrolled of total				
Coushatta Reservation, Louisiana	18	...	...	...	...	...	...	...	...	...
Coyote Valley Rancheria, California	-	-	-	-	-	-	-	-	-	-
Crow Reservation, Montana	3,948	2,018	1,778	2,170	3,734	94.6	1,905	1,666	2,068	112
Cheyenne	39	18	13	26	36	90.8	17	13	23	2
Crow	3,628	1,858	1,676	1,953	3,499	96.4	1,786	1,601	1,898	74
Sioux	43	25	5	38	35	81.1	19	1	34	1
All other American Indians	238	118	84	154	166	69.6	83	512	114	35
Tribe not reported	33	14	19	14	7	20.3	1	7	-	25
Crow Creek Reservation, South Dakota	1,486	751	770	716	1,305	87.8	657	618	687	50
Sioux	1,417	721	735	682	1,271	89.7	648	607	664	25
Cheyenne River Sioux	34	19	22	12	32	92.4	19	19	12	-
Crow Creek Sioux	1,033	508	543	489	947	91.7	472	468	479	21
Lower Brule Sioux	85	58	47	38	75	88.6	50	37	38	-
Sioux	82	44	46	37	55	66.9	29	21	34	2
Sisseton Sioux	35	14	18	17	35	100.0	14	18	17	-
Standing Rock Sioux	37	24	22	16	36	95.6	24	20	16	-
Yankton Sioux	75	35	34	41	63	84.4	26	22	41	-
All other American Indians	69	30	35	34	34	49.4	9	11	23	25
Tribe not reported	36	22	22	14	8	20.6	3	4	4	19
Cuyapaipe Reservation, California	2	...	...	...	...	...	...	...	...	...
Deer Creek Reservation, Minnesota	4	...	...	...	...	...	...	...	...	...
Dresslerville Colony, Nevada	126	64	57	68	119	94.9	61	54	66	1
Washo	111	56	51	60	108	97.8	56	49	60	1

[Continued]

★ 154 ★

Population and Tribal Enrollment Status on Reservations, by Tribal Affiliation, Age Group, and Sex, 1980: Coushatta - Fort Apache

[Continued]

Identified reservations; tribes of 30 or more American Indians	Total				Enrolled in tribe					Enrollment status not reported
					Both sexes					
	Both sexes	Female	Under 18 years	18 years and over	Total	Percent enrolled of total	Female	Under 18 years	18 Years and over	
All other American Indians	15	8	6	9	11	72.9	5	5	6	-
Tribe not reported	-	-	-	-	-	-	-	-	-	-
Dry Creek Rancheria, California	43	23	19	24	31	72.1	18	17	14	2
Pomo	32	16	14	18	22	68.8	12	12	10	1
All other American Indians	11	7	5	6	9	81.8	6	5	4	1
Tribe not reported	1	1	1	-	1	100.0	1	1	-	-
Duck Valley Reservation, Idaho-Nevada	933	463	403	530	848	90.9	423	352	496	34
Paiute	162	70	64	97	148	91.3	67	57	91	3
Shoshone	693	351	312	380	660	95.2	336	287	372	10
All other American Indians	78	41	27	52	41	52.2	19	8	33	21
Tribe not reported	36	16	15	21	9	24.1	3	1	7	21
Duckwater Reservation, Nevada	103	53	37	66	103	100.0	53	37	66	-
Shoshone	96	49	33	63	96	100.0	49	33	63	-
All other American Indians	7	3	4	3	7	100.0	3	4	3	-
Tribe not reported	-	-	-	-	-	-	-	-	-	-
Eastern Cherokee Reservation, North Carolina	4,822	2,426	1,978	2,844	4,643	96.3	2,324	1,883	2,760	50
Cherokee	4,657	2,331	1,902	2,755	4,546	97.6	2,274	1,841	2,705	27
Cherokee	1,874	947	817	1,056	1,845	98.5	933	800	1,045	9
Eastern Cherokee	2,771	1,383	1,083	1,688	2,690	97.1	1,339	1,038	1,652	18
All other American Indians	165	95	76	89	97	58.9	50	42	55	23
Tribe not reported	60	31	31	29	37	61.7	19	19	18	19
Eastern Pequot Reservation, Connecticut	18	...	...	...	...	...	...	...	...	...
Ely Colony, Nevada	63	32	31	32	55	88.0	27	25	30	1
Shoshone	59	29	31	28	53	89.5	25	25	28	-
All other American Indians	4	3	-	4	2	64.5	1	-	2	1
Tribe not reported	1	1	-	1	-	-	-	-	-	1
Enterprise Rancheria, California	16	...	...	...	...	...	...	...	...	...
Fallon Colony, Nevada	46	23	14	32	46	100.0	23	14	32	-
Fallon Reservation, Nevada	258	135	96	162	228	88.3	120	77	150	6
Paiute	166	86	70	96	158	95.1	84	64	93	1
Shoshone	48	26	11	37	42	87.8	22	9	33	1
All other American Indians	45	23	15	30	28	63.4	14	4	24	3
Tribe not reported	5	2	3	2	3	59.8	1	2	1	1
Flandreau Reservation, South Dakota	158	82	75	83	142	89.8	75	62	80	3
Sioux	143	76	68	75	130	90.8	69	56	74	-
Flandreau Sioux	98	51	49	48	89	90.8	46	40	48	-
All other American Indians	15	6	7	8	12	80.0	6	6	6	3
Tribe not reported	3	-	1	2	-	-	-	-	-	3
Flathead Reservation, Montana	3,622	1,755	1,529	2,093	2,490	68.7	1,213	856	1,634	623
Assiniboine	30	19	13	17	19	64.0	12	4	15	3
Blackfoot	90	49	29	60	64	70.8	36	14	49	14

[Continued]

263

★ 154 ★

Population and Tribal Enrollment Status on Reservations, by Tribal Affiliation, Age Group, and Sex, 1980: Coushatta - Fort Apache
[Continued]

Identified reservations; tribes of 30 or more American Indians	Total				Enrolled in tribe					Enrollment status not reported
				18 years and over	Both sexes					
	Both sexes	Female	Under 18 years		Total	Percent enrolled of total	Female	Under 18 years	18 Years and over	
Chippewa	38	20	10	29	26	67.3	14	7	19	3
Cree	52	15	20	32	21	40.7	4	8	13	1
Flathead	2,490	1,193	1,003	1,487	1,895	76.1	919	612	1,283	270
Kootenai	270	129	115	156	217	80.3	103	80	137	33
Sioux	51	22	26	25	43	84.1	17	21	22	2
All other American Indians	601	307	313	287	205	34.2	107	110	95	298
Tribe not reported	304	149	142	161	19	6.2	15	10	9	268
Fond du Lac Reservation, Minnesota	511	252	229	282	433	84.8	212	164	269	11
Chippewa	491	237	224	267	426	86.8	208	164	262	6
Chippewa	426	209	193	233	367	86.2	182	138	229	5
Minnesota chippewa	41	19	23	18	36	88.6	17	19	17	-
All other American Indians	20	15	5	14	7	34.1	4	-	7	5
Tribe not reported	14	10	4	10	4	28.4	2	-	4	5
Fort Apache Reservation, Arizona	6,868	3,475	3,282	3,586	6,302	91.8	3,191	2,990	3,312	444
Apache	6,092	3,086	2,917	3,175	5,978	98.1	3,034	2,835	3,144	45
Apache (N.E.C.)	2,127	1,079	1,026	1,101	2,081	97.8	1,059	992	1,090	20
San Carlos Apache	96	49	34	62	85	88.7	42	28	57	-
White Mountain Apache	3,860	1,954	1,852	2,007	3,806	98.6	1,928	1,813	1,993	25
Navajo	176	75	77	99	154	87.5	70	70	84	5
Pueblo	54	24	22	31	45	83.7	20	19	26	1
All other American Indians	546	290	266	280	125	22.8	68	66	58	392
Tribe not reported	423	226	208	215	28	6.5	14	20	7	391

Source: U.S. Bureau of the Census, Subject Reports, PC80-2-1D, Part 1, *American Indians, Eskimos, and Aleuts on Identified Reservations and in the Historic Areas of Oklahoma (Excluding Urbanized Areas)*, U.S. Government Printing Office, Washington, D.C., 1986, pp. 16-31. *Notes:* Three dots (...) means not applicable, or that the data are being withheld to avoid disclosure of information for individuals. A dash (-) represents zero or a percent which rounds to less than 0.1. Also, a dash (-) is used because the number of supplementary questionnaires for the reservations was insufficient to produce reliable estimates.

★ 155 ★

Population and Tribal Enrollment Status on Reservations, by Tribal Affiliation, Age Group, and Sex, 1980: Fort Belknap - Grand Portage

Data are the latest available.

Identified reservations; tribes of 30 or more American Indians	Total				Enrolled in tribe					Enrollment status not reported
				18 years and over	Both sexes					
	Both sexes	Female	Under 18 years		Total	Percent enrolled of total	Female	Under 18 years	18 Years and over	
Fort Belknap Reservation, Montana	1,873	903	870	1,003	1,457	77.8	702	618	838	247
Assiniboine	716	334	313	403	577	80.6	265	227	350	78
Chippewa	67	29	18	49	45	66.5	19	8	37	8
Cree	36	12	16	21	20	54.3	5	8	12	9
Gros Ventres	850	427	412	438	708	83.3	357	320	388	83
Sioux	38	15	14	24	27	71.4	11	8	19	2
All other American Indians	165	86	97	68	80	48.4	45	48	32	67

[Continued]

Population and Tribal Enrollment Status on Reservations, by Tribal Affiliation, Age Group, and Sex, 1980: Fort Belknap - Grand Portage
[Continued]

Identified reservations; tribes of 30 or more American Indians	Total				Enrolled in tribe					Enrollment status not reported
					Both sexes					
	Both sexes	Female	Under 18 years	18 years and over	Total	Percent enrolled of total	Female	Under 18 years	18 Years and over	
Tribe not reported	64	29	40	24	6	9.9	3	4	2	52
Fort Berthold Reservation, North Dakota	2,615	1,324	1,239	1,376	2,357	90.2	1,214	1,082	1,276	165
Arikara	527	270	241	286	498	94.5	262	226	271	20
Chippewa	69	31	44	25	65	94.8	29	42	24	2
Gros Ventres	173	90	98	75	152	87.8	81	84	67	16
Mandan	411	192	209	203	388	94.3	180	189	199	3
Sioux	102	68	37	66	95	92.7	65	34	60	4
Other specified tribes	66	30	23	43	57	86.1	30	17	40	7
Fort Berthold	66	30	23	43	57	86.1	30	17	40	7
All other American Indians	1,266	643	588	679	1,103	87.1	567	489	614	114
Tribe not reported	108	56	53	55	16	15.1	12	7	9	87
Fort Bidwell Reservation, California	94	51	39	55	91	97.8	50	37	55	-
Paiute	70	39	30	41	68	97.0	38	28	41	-
All other American Indians	23	12	9	14	23	100.0	12	9	14	-
Tribe not reported	-	-	-	-	-	-	-	-	-	-
Fort Hall Reservation, Idaho	2,518	1,280	1,105	1,413	2,172	86.3	1,114	919	1,253	168
Bannock	139	68	42	97	127	91.4	62	36	92	3
Fort Hall	761	377	352	408	705	92.7	360	324	382	11
Navajo	49	23	26	23	44	88.6	21	20	23	-
Shoshone	1,301	668	558	743	1,130	86.9	579	471	659	88
All other American Indians	268	143	126	142	166	61.9	91	68	97	66
Tribe not reported	78	36	42	36	13	17.2	5	9	5	60
Fort Independence Reservation, California	32	13	5	27	26	81.9	12	3	24	2
Fort McDermitt Reservation, Nevada-Oregon	467	230	228	239	313	67.1	157	135	178	26
Paiute	402	197	195	207	283	70.3	144	118	165	22
All other American Indians	65	34	33	31	31	47.3	13	18	13	4
Tribe not reported	9	7	5	4	3	36.6	2	2	1	3
Fort McDowell Reservation, Arizona	349	161	134	215	303	86.8	140	110	193	24
Yuman	272	119	108	163	240	88.5	105	89	152	17
Yavapai	267	116	107	159	236	88.3	103	88	148	17
All other American Indians	77	42	25	52	62	80.9	35	21	42	7
Tribe not reported	3	1	1	2	1	35.3	1	-	1	2
Fort Mojave Reservation, Arizona-California-Nevada	128	69	64	64	104	81.3	57	54	50	22
Yuman	99	54	55	44	95	96.0	52	52	43	3
Mohave	97	52	55	42	93	95.9	50	52	41	3
All other American Indians	29	15	9	20	9	31.0	5	2	7	19
Tribe not reported	19	10	7	12	-	-	-	-	-	19
Fort Peck Reservation, Montana	4,246	2,156	1,980	2,265	3,534	83.2	1,817	1,502	2,032	196
Assiniboine	1,242	649	547	695	1,056	85.0	555	409	647	66
Chippewa	306	151	133	173	224	73.2	114	80	144	25
Cree	43	19	14	29	32	75.6	16	13	20	3
Gros Ventres	37	17	16	21	35	94.1	17	15	20	1
Sioux	2,356	1,188	1,130	1,226	2,055	87.2	1,051	922	1,132	115
Fort Peck	368	163	199	169	344	93.5	156	178	166	7

[Continued]

★ 155 ★

Population and Tribal Enrollment Status on Reservations, by Tribal Affiliation, Age Group, and Sex, 1980: Fort Belknap - Grand Portage
[Continued]

Identified reservations; tribes of 30 or more American Indians	Total				Enrolled in tribe					Enrollment status not reported
					Both sexes					
	Both sexes	Female	Under 18 years	18 years and over	Total	Percent enrolled of total	Female	Under 18 years	18 Years and over	
Sioux	1,956	1,002	922	1,034	1,685	86.1	875	740	945	106
All other American Indians	262	131	140	122	132	50.6	65	63	70	86
Tribe not reported	64	25	36	28	15	22.9	2	4	11	43
Fort Totten Reservation, North Dakota	2,217	1,108	1,165	1,052	2,034	91.8	1,008	1,022	1,013	50
Chippewa	225	111	101	124	174	77.6	83	57	118	4
Sioux	1,837	916	979	858	1,763	96.0	879	924	838	16
Devil's Lake Sioux	792	405	421	371	774	97.7	396	412	362	5
Sioux	950	474	502	447	897	94.4	446	460	437	9
Sisseton Sioux	32	11	25	7	32	100.0	11	25	7	-
Standing Rock Sioux	34	14	17	17	33	95.8	14	16	17	1
All other American Indians	155	80	85	71	97	62.6	47	41	57	30
Tribe not reported	61	29	44	17	18	30.1	6	9	9	25
Fort Yuma Reservation, Arizona-California	1,103	574	473	630	872	79.1	452	374	498	169
Yuman	935	502	411	524	782	83.6	415	334	448	112
Cocopah	82	41	32	49	62	75.8	30	22	39	14
Quechan	827	449	369	457	699	84.5	376	306	393	96
All other American Indians	168	71	62	106	90	53.6	36	39	51	57
Tribe not reported	19	8	4	16	4	21.9	2	1	3	15
Gila Bend Reservation, Arizona	-	-	-	-	-	-	-	-	-	-
Gila River Reservation, Arizona	6,903	3,497	3,055	3,848	5,983	86.7	3,066	2,387	3,596	112
Apache	57	36	26	31	48	84.1	31	19	29	-
Navajo	47	28	8	39	40	85.7	27	3	37	-
Papago	206	98	62	144	165	80.0	83	51	114	5
Pima	5,851	2,980	2,668	3,185	5,132	87.7	2,644	2,112	3,020	44
Pueblo	49	27	19	30	41	83.7	20	12	29	-
Hopi	36	21	14	23	31	85.4	16	10	22	-
Yuman	471	232	178	293	426	90.5	210	138	288	10
Maricopa	413	200	153	260	376	91.2	184	121	256	10
All other American Indians	222	96	94	128	132	59.3	52	53	79	53
Tribe not reported	99	49	60	39	48	48.9	20	30	18	36
Golden Hill Reservation, Connecticut	3	...	...	...	...	...	...	...	...	...
Goshute Reservation, Nevada-Utah	105	38	23	82	94	89.1	32	23	70	6
Shoshone	90	28	22	67	84	93.6	25	22	61	-
Goshute	90	28	22	67	84	93.6	25	22	61	-
All other American Indians	15	10	1	14	10	63.0	7	1	9	6
Tribe not reported	6	3	-	6	-	-	-	-	-	6
Grand Portage Reservation, Minnesota	184	88	57	127	138	74.9	71	20	118	7
Chippewa	173	82	57	116	135	78.0	69	20	115	-
All other American Indians	11	6	-	11	3	25.5	2	-	3	7
Tribe not reported	8	4	-	8	-	-	-	-	-	7

Source: U.S. Bureau of the Census, Subject Reports, PC80-2-1D, Part 1, *American Indians, Eskimos, and Aleuts on Identified Reservations and in the Historic Areas of Oklahoma (Excluding Urbanized Areas)*, U.S. Government Printing Office, Washington, D.C., 1986, pp. 16-31. *Notes:* Three dots (...) means not applicable, or that the data are being withheld to avoid disclosure of information for individuals. A dash (-) represents zero or a percent which rounds to less than 0.1. Also, a dash (-) is used because the number of supplementary questionnaires for the reservations was insufficient to produce reliable estimates.

★ 156 ★

Population and Tribal Enrollment Status on Reservations, by Tribal Affiliation, Age Group, and Sex, 1980: Grindstone Creek Rancheria - Jicarilla Apache

Data are the latest available.

Identified reservations; tribes of 30 or more American Indians	Total				Enrolled in tribe					Enrollment status not reported
					Both sexes					
	Both sexes	Female	Under 18 years	18 years and over	Total	Percent enrolled of total	Female	Under 18 years	18 Years and over	
Grindstone Creek Rancheria, California	72	36	33	39	62	86.5	32	26	36	1
Nomalaki	53	28	27	27	48	89.8	25	23	25	1
All other American Indians	19	8	6	12	14	77.0	7	3	11	-
Tribe not reported	-	-	-	-	-	-	-	-	-	-
Hannahville Community, Michigan	204	90	119	85	197	96.8	90	116	82	-
Potawatomi	158	75	89	69	155	97.8	75	85	69	-
All other American Indians	46	16	31	15	43	93.2	16	31	12	-
Tribe not reported	-	-	-	-	-	-	-	-	-	-
Hassanamisco Reservation, Massachusetts	1	...	...	...	...	...	...	...	...	...
Havasupai Reservation, Arizona	267	132	110	157	234	87.8	119	96	138	28
Yuman	260	130	104	155	234	90.3	119	96	138	20
Havasupai	260	130	104	155	234	90.3	119	96	138	20
All other American Indians	7	2	5	2	-	-	-	-	-	7
Tribe not reported	7	2	5	2	-	-	-	-	-	7
Hoh Reservation, Washington	44	24	20	24	36	80.6	18	15	21	2
Chemakuan	33	20	16	17	27	82.7	16	12	15	2
Hoh	33	20	16	17	27	82.7	16	12	15	2
All other American Indians	11	5	5	7	9	74.7	2	3	6	-
Tribe not reported	-	-	-	-	-	-	-	-	-	-
Hollywood Reservation, Florida	416	222	187	229	402	96.7	213	180	222	4
Seminole	374	192	175	199	364	97.4	187	168	196	1
Seminole Tribe of Florida	358	186	168	190	348	97.3	181	161	187	1
All other American Indians	42	30	12	30	38	90.6	26	12	26	3
Tribe not reported	2	1	-	2	1	46.4	-	-	1	1
Hoopa Valley Reservation, California	1,486	778	623	863	1,055	71.0	551	395	660	146
Hoopa	843	438	387	457	747	88.6	382	317	430	18
Karok	67	27	24	43	47	70.6	22	12	35	1
Yurok	281	165	109	172	151	53.7	93	39	112	15
All other American Indians	295	148	103	192	111	37.5	54	28	83	113
Tribe not reported	113	57	44	70	2	1.7	2	2	-	109
Hoopa Valley Extension Reservation, California	418	206	161	257	242	58.0	118	74	168	45
Yurok	304	148	114	191	204	67.1	99	59	146	8
All other American Indians	114	59	48	66	38	33.5	18	16	22	38
Tribe not reported	37	18	15	21	2	5.7	-	2	-	34
Hopi Reservation, Arizona	6,592	3,385	2,741	3,851	5,372	81.5	2,783	2,056	3,316	787
Apache	30	8	13	17	27	91.6	8	13	15	-
Navajo	1,763	890	768	995	1,688	95.7	850	728	959	25
Pueblo	3,965	2,099	1,613	2,352	3,555	89.6	1,877	1,267	2,287	52
Arizona Tewa	294	155	139	155	270	91.7	141	117	152	5
Hopi	3,515	1,861	1,429	2,086	3,138	89.3	1,653	1,109	2,028	43
Tewa	125	68	39	87	123	97.9	68	37	85	3
All other American Indians	834	388	347	487	103	12.3	48	48	55	709
Tribe not reported	669	319	281	388	23	3.5	15	14	9	637

[Continued]

267

★ 156 ★

Population and Tribal Enrollment Status on Reservations, by Tribal Affiliation, Age Group, and Sex, 1980: Grindstone Creek Rancheria - Jicarilla Apache
[Continued]

Identified reservations; tribes of 30 or more American Indians	Total				Enrolled in tribe					Enrollment status not reported
					Both sexes					
	Both sexes	Female	Under 18 years	18 years and over	Total	Percent enrolled of total	Female	Under 18 years	18 Years and over	
Hopland Rancheria, California	-	-	-	-	-	-	-	-	-	-
Hualapai Reservation, Arizona	810	396	354	456	653	80.6	324	275	377	119
Yuman	635	308	294	340	591	93.1	290	260	331	10
Havasupai	34	21	12	22	32	93.9	19	9	22	-
Hualapai	575	272	270	305	535	93.1	258	240	296	10
All other American Indians	175	88	60	116	62	35.1	34	15	46	109
Tribe not reported	113	53	44	68	4	3.7	1	2	2	108
Inaja-Cosmit Reservation, California	-	-	-	-	-	-	-	-	-	-
Indian Township Reservation, Maine	328	152	160	168	324	98.9	151	158	166	1
Passamaquoddy	317	146	158	159	316	99.6	146	157	159	-
All other American Indians	11	6	1	10	8	77.7	5	1	7	1
Tribe not reported	1	1	-	1	1	100.0	1	-	1	-
Iowa Reservation, Kansas-Nebraska	31	13	13	18	27	86.2	9	10	17	2
Isabella Reservation, Michigan	509	272	236	273	428	84.1	229	183	245	11
Chippewa	358	194	167	191	324	90.6	174	143	181	5
Chippewa	244	139	105	139	225	92.2	126	91	133	2
Saginaw Chippewa	109	53	60	49	98	90.0	47	51	46	3
Ottawa	76	43	31	45	55	73.1	31	19	36	-
Potawatomi	34	17	19	15	34	100.0	17	19	15	-
All other American Indians	41	18	20	22	14	34.7	8	2	12	7
Tribe not reported	8	2	6	2	1	16.2	-	1	-	4
Isleta Pueblo, New Mexico	2,289	1,165	897	1,392	2,190	95.7	1,103	844	1,346	45
Pueblo	2,197	1,110	869	1,328	2,133	97.1	1,071	830	1,303	20
Isleta	1,069	1,040	837	1,232	2,012	97.2	1,006	799	1,213	20
Laguna	59	36	15	44	56	95.9	35	15	42	-
All other American Indians	92	55	28	63	57	62.2	32	15	43	25
Tribe not reported	28	16	18	10	9	31.4	2	7	1	19
Jackson Rancheria, California	15	...	...	...	...	...	...	...	...	...
Jemez Pueblo, New Mexico	1,502	788	672	830	1,462	97.4	763	657	805	19
Pueblo	1,436	745	644	791	1,423	99.1	740	638	785	4
Jemez	1,380	709	626	753	1,369	99.3	705	620	750	4
All other American Indians	66	43	28	38	39	59.3	23	20	20	15
Tribe not reported	17	9	8	9	2	13.6	1	2	-	15
Jicarilla Apache Reservation, New Mexico	1,715	863	810	905	1,677	97.8	840	784	893	16
Apache	1,539	780	745	794	1,525	99.0	770	734	790	4
Jicarilla Apache	1,511	769	735	776	1,496	99.0	759	724	772	4
Navajo	81	41	23	59	79	96.6	41	21	58	1
Pueblo	46	19	16	31	46	100.0	19	16	31	-

[Continued]

★ 156 ★

Population and Tribal Enrollment Status on Reservations, by Tribal Affiliation, Age Group, and Sex, 1980: Grindstone Creek Rancheria - Jicarilla Apache
[Continued]

Identified reservations; tribes of 30 or more American Indians	Total				Enrolled in tribe					Enrollment status not reported
	Both sexes	Female	Under 18 years	18 years and over	Both sexes		Female	Under 18 years	18 Years and over	
					Total	Percent enrolled of total				
All other American Indians	48	22	26	22	27	56.6	9	13	14	12
Tribe not reported	14	7	10	4	6	42.1	1	3	2	8

Source: U.S. Bureau of the Census, Subject Reports, PC80-2-1D, Part 1, *American Indians, Eskimos, and Aleuts on Identified Reservations and in the Historic Areas of Oklahoma (Excluding Urbanized Areas)*, U.S. Government Printing Office, Washington, D.C., 1986, pp. 16-31. *Notes:* Three dots (...) means not applicable, or that the data are being withheld to avoid disclosure of information for individuals. A dash (-) represents zero or a percent which rounds to less than 0.1. Also, a dash (-) is used because the number of supplementary questionnaires for the reservations was insufficient to produce reliable estimates.

★ 157 ★

Population and Tribal Enrollment Status on Reservations, by Tribal Affiliation, Age Group, and Sex, 1980: Kaibab - Lower Elwah

Data are the latest available.

Identified reservations; tribes of 30 or more American Indians	Total				Enrolled in tribe					Enrollment status not reported
	Both sexes	Female	Under 18 years	18 years and over	Both sexes		Female	Under 18 years	18 Years and over	
					Total	Percent enrolled of total				
Kaibab Reservation, Arizona	93	51	38	55	92	98.9	50	37	55	-
Paiute	86	47	37	48	84	98.8	45	36	48	-
All other American Indians	7	4	1	6	7	100.0	4	1	6	-
Tribe not reported	-	-	-	-	-	-	-	-	-	-
Kalispel Reservation, Washington	99	45	49	50	97	98.0	44	48	49	-
Kalispel	52	26	22	30	51	98.1	25	21	30	-
All other American Indians	47	19	27	20	46	97.9	19	27	19	-
Tribe not reported	-	-	-	-	-	-	-	-	-	-
Kickapoo Reservation, Kansas	356	174	150	206	341	95.9	163	142	199	5
Kickapoo	229	117	99	130	223	97.3	111	93	130	-
Potawatomi	91	39	43	48	89	98.2	37	43	46	2
Prairie Band	91	39	43	48	89	98.2	37	43	46	2
All other American Indians	36	18	8	28	29	80.9	15	6	23	3
Tribe not reported	2	2	-	2	-	-	-	-	-	2
Kootenai Reservation, Idaho	-	-	-	-	-	-	-	-	-	-
Lac Courte Oreilles Reservation, Wisconsin	1,145	585	521	624	1,041	90.9	532	460	581	40
Chippewa	1,082	553	497	585	1,008	93.1	514	446	561	25
Chippewa	687	355	320	367	627	91.3	322	277	350	21
Lac Courte Oreilles	381	184	174	208	366	96.0	178	165	201	4
All other American Indians	63	32	24	39	34	53.6	18	14	19	15
Tribe not reported	19	13	7	12	5	25.2	3	3	2	14
Lac du Flambeau Reservation, Wisconsin	1,089	568	522	568	861	79.0	461	339	522	19
Blackfoot	332	159	159	172	253	76.3	131	94	159	-
Chippewa	693	389	339	354	565	81.6	316	232	334	5

[Continued]

269

★ 157 ★

Population and Tribal Enrollment Status on Reservations, by Tribal Affiliation, Age Group, and Sex, 1980: Kaibab - Lower Elwah

[Continued]

Identified reservations; tribes of 30 or more American Indians	Total				Enrolled in tribe					Enrollment status not reported
					Both sexes					
	Both sexes	Female	Under 18 years	18 years and over	Total	Percent enrolled of total	Female	Under 18 years	18 Years and over	
All other American Indians	64	19	23	41	42	65.9	14	12	30	14
Tribe not reported	10	2	9	1	1	13.9	-	-	1	9
Laguna Pueblo, New Mexico	3,565	1,866	1,456	2,109	3,242	90.9	1,694	1,223	2,019	78
Navajo	127	62	62	66	115	90.1	52	54	61	-
Pueblo	3,263	1,701	1,329	1,934	3,007	92.1	1,575	1,121	1,886	33
Acoma	76	37	11	65	71	93.4	36	11	60	2
Hopi	35	23	7	28	28	79.5	18	1	27	1
Laguna	3,072	1,590	1,300	1,771	2,839	92.4	1,477	1,099	1,740	28
All other American Indians	174	103	65	109	120	69.1	68	48	72	45
Tribe not reported	78	50	26	52	31	40.4	22	13	18	45
La Jolla Reservation, California	140	69	74	66	114	81.1	54	52	62	3
Luiseno	107	52	60	47	88	82.7	42	43	45	2
All other American Indians	33	16	13	29	25	76.0	13	9	16	1
Tribe not reported	-	-	-	-	-	-	-	-	-	-
L'anse Reservation, Michigan	564	279	275	289	512	90.8	253	231	281	3
Chippewa	540	272	267	272	490	90.8	247	224	266	3
All other American Indians	24	7	8	16	22	89.6	6	7	15	-
Tribe not reported	-	-	-	-	-	-	-	-	-	-
La Posta Reservation, California	1	...	...	...	...	...	...	...	...	...
Las Vegas Colony, Nevada	105	57	47	58	90	85.5	51	39	51	2
Paiute	70	42	30	40	60	85.9	38	23	37	2
All other American Indians	36	15	17	18	30	84.6	12	16	14	-
Tribe not reported	-	-	-	-	-	-	-	-	-	-
Laytonville Rancheria, California	105	54	45	60	80	76.2	38	31	49	1
California Tribes (N.E.C.)	74	37	32	42	66	89.2	31	28	38	1
Cahto	74	37	32	42	66	89.2	31	28	38	1
All other American Indians	31	17	13	18	14	45.2	7	3	11	-
Tribe not reported	-	-	-	-	-	-	-	-	-	-
Leech Lake Reservation, Minnesota	2,734	1,396	1,280	1,454	2,302	84.2	1,191	934	1,368	102
Chippewa	2,598	1,307	1,218	1,380	2,243	86.3	1,151	916	1,327	63
Chippewa	1,881	953	875	1,007	1,617	86.0	833	650	967	58
Leech Lake	35	12	17	18	32	90.2	12	16	16	2
Minnesota Chippewa	569	280	276	293	493	86.6	250	210	282	3
Red Lake Chippewa	37	19	22	15	33	90.2	17	18	15	-
White Earth	50	30	19	31	42	84.2	26	11	31	-
All other American Indians	136	89	62	73	59	43.8	40	19	41	39
Tribe not reported	48	26	22	26	11	23.4	7	5	7	32
Likely Rancheria, California	-	-	-	-	-	-	-	-	-	-
Lone Pine Rancheria, California	172	99	79	93	162	94.2	94	74	88	2
Paiute	87	52	50	37	86	98.6	51	50	36	1
Shoshone	73	39	28	44	66	91.2	37	23	43	1
All other American Indians	13	8	1	11	10	81.2	7	1	9	-
Tribe not reported	-	-	-	-	-	-	-	-	-	-

[Continued]

Population and Tribal Enrollment Status on Reservations, by Tribal Affiliation, Age Group, and Sex, 1980: Kaibab - Lower Elwah

[Continued]

Identified reservations; tribes of 30 or more American Indians	Total				Enrolled in tribe					Enrollment status not reported
	Both sexes	Female	Under 18 years	18 years and over	Both sexes		Female	Under 18 years	18 Years and over	
					Total	Percent enrolled of total				
Lookout Rancheria, California	12	...	...	...	...	...	...	...	...	...
Los Coyotes Reservation, California	44	21	16	28	37	83.6	19	15	22	-
Lovelock Colony, Nevada	112	55	52	60	106	94.1	53	48	57	5
Paiute	105	50	50	55	103	98.4	50	48	55	-
All other American Indians	7	4	2	5	2	32.6	2	-	2	5
Tribe not reported	5	2	2	3	-	-	-	-	-	5
Lower Brule Reservation, South Dakota	830	426	422	408	677	81.5	349	307	369	38
Sioux	778	402	395	383	655	84.3	339	300	355	13
Crow Creek Sioux	33	17	9	23	30	92.6	15	9	21	2
Lower Brule Sioux	609	314	324	285	519	85.2	273	254	266	11
Rosebud Sioux	62	36	30	32	36	57.7	20	9	26	-
All other American Indians	52	25	27	26	21	40.7	10	7	14	25
Tribe not reported	22	13	16	6	1	5.2	1	1	-	18
Lower Elwah Reservation, Washington	47	24	22	25	34	72.3	18	14	20	12
Clallam	35	18	16	19	32	91.4	16	13	19	2
Lower Elwah	33	18	16	17	30	90.9	16	13	17	2
All other American Indians	12	6	6	6	2	16.7	2	1	1	10
Tribe not reported	10	4	5	5	-	-	-	-	-	10

Source: U.S. Bureau of the Census, Subject Reports, PC80-2-1D, Part 1, *American Indians, Eskimos, and Aleuts on Identified Reservations and in the Historic Areas of Oklahoma (Excluding Urbanized Areas)*, U.S. Government Printing Office, Washington, D.C., 1986, pp. 16-31. *Notes:* Three dots (...) means not applicable, or that the data are being withheld to avoid disclosure of information for individuals. A dash (-) represents zero or a percent which rounds to less than 0.1. Also, a dash (-) is used because the number of supplementary questionnaires for the reservations was insufficient to produce reliable estimates.

Population and Tribal Enrollment Status on Reservations, by Tribal Affiliation, Age Group, and Sex, 1980: Lower Sioux - Navajo

Data are the latest available.

Identified reservations; tribes of 30 or more American Indians	Total				Enrolled in tribe					Enrollment status not reported
	Both sexes	Female	Under 18 years	18 years and over	Both sexes		Female	Under 18 years	18 Years and over	
					Total	Percent enrolled of total				
Lower Sioux Community, Minnesota	71	32	22	49	61	86.5	28	16	45	2
Sioux	69	31	22	47	61	88.6	28	16	45	2
Mdewakanton Sioux	57	21	19	38	52	90.2	21	13	38	-
All other American Indians	2	2	-	2	-	-	-	-	-	-
Tribe not reported	-	-	-	-	-	-	-	-	-	-
Lummi Reservation, Washington	1,259	603	592	667	1,120	89.0	532	493	627	49
Lummi	1,078	503	522	557	995	92.3	461	453	542	13
Puget Sound Salish	55	31	14	40	52	94.2	28	13	38	1

[Continued]

Population and Tribal Enrollment Status on Reservations, by Tribal Affiliation, Age Group, and Sex, 1980: Lower Sioux - Navajo

[Continued]

Identified reservations; tribes of 30 or more American Indians	Total				Enrolled in tribe					Enrollment status not reported
	Both sexes	Female	Under 18 years	18 years and over	Both sexes		Female	Under 18 years	18 Years and over	
					Total	Percent enrolled of total				
All other American Indians	126	69	56	70	73	58.5	43	27	46	34
Tribe not reported	15	6	10	5	2	14.2	-	2	-	13
Makah Reservation, Washington	798	396	383	415	737	92.3	370	354	382	37
Makah	706	344	344	362	687	97.3	337	337	350	8
All other American Indians	92	52	39	53	49	53.7	32	17	32	30
Tribe not reported	23	8	13	10	-	-	-	-	-	23
Manchester Rancheria, California	77	34	29	48	58	75.1	28	20	38	3
Pomo	71	31	28	43	56	78.0	26	20	36	3
All other American Indians	6	3	1	4	2	37.8	2	-	2	-
Tribe not reported	-	-	-	-	-	-	-	-	-	-
Manzanita Reservation, California	13	...	...	...	...	...	...	...	...	...
Maricopa Reservation, Arizona	371	186	163	208	301	81.1	146	135	166	24
Papago	260	133	111	149	229	88.2	112	95	134	10
Pima	96	49	48	48	69	71.4	33	40	29	7
All other American Indians	15	4	4	11	3	22.2	-	-	3	7
Tribe not reported	6	1	2	3	2	32.2	-	-	2	4
Mattaponi Reservation, Virginia	60	31	19	41	49	81.7	28	14	35	9
Mattaponi	48	24	16	32	44	91.7	24	14	30	4
All other American Indians	12	7	3	9	5	41.7	4	-	5	5
Tribe not reported	5	2	3	2	-	-	-	-	-	5
Menominee Reservation, Wisconsin	2,377	1,194	1,085	1,292	1,755	73.8	872	756	999	461
Iroquois	34	18	17	17	21	60.9	13	6	15	5
Menominee	2,039	997	921	1,118	1,679	82.3	829	738	941	219
All other American Indians	304	179	147	157	55	18.1	31	13	43	237
Tribe not reported	209	129	108	101	3	1.3	2	-	3	205
Mesa Grande Reservation, California	-	-	-	-	-	-	-	-	-	-
Mescalero Apache Reservation, New Mexico	1,924	1,002	987	937	673	35.0	356	338	334	1,237
Apache	1,144	589	613	532	624	54.5	333	322	302	508
Apache (N.E.C.)	87	48	59	28	24	27.0	13	12	11	61
Mescalero Apache	1,045	536	549	496	589	56.4	315	305	284	446
All other American Indians	780	413	374	405	48	6.2	23	16	32	729
Tribe not reported	688	370	347	341	6	0.9	3	4	2	681
Miccosukee Reservation, Florida	271	140	116	155	189	69.7	99	75	114	5
Miccosukee	225	119	97	128	168	74.7	89	67	101	1
Seminole	37	17	15	22	18	48.6	9	6	12	-
All other American Indians	9	4	4	5	3	33.3	1	2	1	4
Tribe not reported	3	2	3	-	2	66.7	1	2	-	-
Middletown Rancheria, California	38	16	17	21	29	76.3	8	9	20	1
Pomo	33	14	14	19	24	72.7	6	6	18	1
All other American Indians	5	2	3	2	5	100.0	2	3	2	-
Tribe not reported	1	-	-	1	1	100.0	-	-	1	-

[Continued]

★ 158 ★

Population and Tribal Enrollment Status on Reservations, by Tribal Affiliation, Age Group, and Sex, 1980: Lower Sioux - Navajo
[Continued]

Identified reservations; tribes of 30 or more American Indians	Total				Enrolled in tribe					Enrollment status not reported
					Both sexes					
	Both sexes	Female	Under 18 years	18 years and over	Total	Percent enrolled of total	Female	Under 18 years	18 Years and over	
Mille Lacs Reservation, Minnesota	-	-	-	-	-	-	-	-	-	-
Mississippi Choctaw Reservation	2,753	1,427	1,348	1,405	2,639	95.8	1,370	1,270	1,369	49
Choctaw	2,678	1,392	1,315	1,363	2,600	97.1	1,353	1,254	1,346	18
All other American Indians	75	35	33	42	38	51.0	17	16	23	32
Tribe not reported	41	19	21	20	11	26.3	4	7	4	30
Moapa River Reservation, Nevada	182	86	87	95	163	89.4	79	70	92	2
Paiute	166	77	79	87	150	90.4	72	65	85	2
All other American Indians	16	9	9	8	13	79.0	8	5	8	-
Tribe not reported	1	1	1	-	1	100.0	1	1	-	-
Montgomery Creek Rancheria, California	1	...	...	...	...	...	...	...	...	...
Morongo Reservation, California	313	149	133	180	272	87.0	135	105	168	6
Cahuilla	91	45	46	45	77	84.5	40	36	41	4
California Tribes (N.E.C.)	69	41	27	42	63	91.1	38	21	42	-
Morongo	69	41	27	42	63	91.9	38	21	42	-
Serrano	86	38	41	45	78	91.4	35	35	44	-
All other American Indians	67	24	19	48	54	80.7	22	13	41	2
Tribe not reported	4	2	1	3	2	49.6	-	-	2	2
Muckleshoot Reservation, Washington	364	167	189	175	284	77.9	136	137	147	57
Puget Sound Salish	271	128	140	131	245	90.4	118	122	123	9
Muckleshoot	241	114	130	110	215	89.2	104	112	102	9
All other American Indians	93	39	49	45	39	41.7	18	15	24	48
Tribe not reported	43	14	28	16	-	-	-	-	-	43
Nambe Pueblo, New Mexico	188	84	71	117	107	57.0	47	44	63	76
Pueblo	151	64	58	93	107	70.8	47	44	63	40
Nambe	109	44	47	62	81	74.1	34	38	43	27
All other American Indians	37	20	13	23	-	-	-	-	-	35
Tribe not reported	35	19	13	22	-	-	-	-	-	35
Navajo Reservation, Arizona-New Mexico-Utah	104,509	53,809	50,479	54,030	94,431	90.4	48,633	45,362	49,068	8,891
Apache	135	77	65	70	125	92.8	75	60	65	3
Cherokee	67	35	26	42	33	49.3	25	12	22	14
Cheyenne	30	13	16	14	27	91.2	11	16	11	-
Choctaw	34	16	10	24	20	58.8	9	4	16	3
Cowlitz	82	42	56	26	82	100.0	42	56	26	-
Creek	36	17	16	20	30	83.4	15	13	18	-
Kiowa	37	14	14	23	37	100.0	14	14	23	-
Navajo	95,674	49,293	46,293	49,381	92,511	96.7	47,652	44,540	47,971	2,151
Paiute	45	29	14	32	38	83.3	23	13	25	-
Pueblo	798	406	310	488	728	91.2	376	269	459	13
Hopi	576	294	247	330	529	91.8	273	213	316	8
Laguna	57	29	14	43	52	91.8	27	14	38	3
Zuni	57	31	29	28	52	91.4	28	26	26	2
Sioux	101	46	39	62	85	84.8	38	31	55	8

[Continued]

273

★ 158 ★

Population and Tribal Enrollment Status on Reservations, by Tribal Affiliation, Age Group, and Sex, 1980: Lower Sioux - Navajo
[Continued]

Identified reservations; tribes of 30 or more American Indians	Total				Enrolled in tribe					Enrollment status not reported
	Both sexes	Female	Under 18 years	18 years and over	Both sexes		Female	Under 18 years	18 Years and over	
					Total	Percent enrolled of total				
All other American Indians	7,469	3,821	3,619	3,850	714	9.6	354	336	378	6,699
Tribe not reported	6,995	3,589	3,441	3,554	368	5.3	174	205	163	6,612

Source: U.S. Bureau of the Census, Subject Reports, PC80-2-1D, Part 1, *American Indians, Eskimos, and Aleuts on Identified Reservations and in the Historic Areas of Oklahoma (Excluding Urbanized Areas)*, U.S. Government Printing Office, Washington, D.C., 1986, pp. 16-31. *Notes:* Three dots (...) means not applicable, or that the data are being withheld to avoid disclosure of information for individuals. A dash (-) represents zero or a percent which rounds to less than 0.1. Also, a dash (-) is used because the number of supplementary questionnaires for the reservations was insufficient to produce reliable estimates.

★ 159 ★

Population and Tribal Enrollment Status on Reservations, by Tribal Affiliation, Age Group, and Sex, 1980: Nez Perce - Picuris Pueblo

Data are the latest available.

Identified reservations; tribes of 30 or more American Indians	Total				Enrolled in tribe					Enrollment status not reported
	Both sexes	Female	Under 18 years	18 years and over	Both sexes		Female	Under 18 years	18 Years and over	
					Total	Percent enrolled of total				
Nez Perce Reservation, Idaho	1,499	764	660	838	1,287	85.9	668	525	761	63
Colville	35	19	11	24	33	94.3	19	10	23	1
Nez Perce	1,173	596	509	664	1,055	89.9	544	425	629	28
Yakima	39	22	26	13	39	100.0	22	26	13	-
All other American Indians	252	126	114	138	160	63.6	83	64	96	34
Tribe not reported	23	11	13	10	3	13.4	1	2	1	18
Nisqually Reservation, Washington	43	21	17	25	39	91.6	20	16	23	2
Puget Sound Salish	37	19	16	21	36	96.9	19	15	21	-
All other American Indians	6	2	1	5	3	57.5	1	1	2	2
Tribe not reported	-	-	-	-	-	-	-	-	-	-
Nooksack Reservation, Washington	-	-	-	-	-	-	-	-	-	-
Northern Cheyenne Reservation, Montana	3,066	1,549	1,526	1,540	2,862	93.3	1,450	1,397	1,465	105
Cheyenne	2,658	1,338	1,346	1,311	2,530	95.2	1,279	1,258	1,272	65
Cheyenne	185	93	88	97	164	88.8	82	80	84	17
Northern Cheyenne	2,441	1,231	1,248	1,193	2,336	95.7	1,184	1,167	1,169	48
Southern Cheyenne	32	14	11	22	30	93.2	13	11	19	-
Crow	90	36	50	39	87	97.4	36	49	38	1
Sioux	96	54	45	51	87	90.5	50	37	50	7
All other American Indians	223	121	84	139	157	70.5	85	52	105	32
Tribe not reported	23	14	17	6	9	38.4	5	8	1	13
Oil Springs Reservation, New York	-	-	-	-	-	-	-	-	-	-
Omaha Reservation, Iowa-Nebraska	1,241	639	590	651	536	43.2	293	210	326	621
Omaha	630	324	296	333	473	75.2	251	185	288	75
All other American Indians	612	315	294	318	63	10.3	41	25	38	546

[Continued]

★ 159 ★

Population and Tribal Enrollment Status on Reservations, by Tribal Affiliation, Age Group, and Sex, 1980: Nez Perce - Picuris Pueblo

[Continued]

Identified reservations; tribes of 30 or more American Indians	Total				Enrolled in tribe					Enrollment status not reported
				18	Both sexes					
	Both sexes	Female	Under 18 years	years and over	Total	Percent enrolled of total	Female	Under 18 years	18 Years and over	
Tribe not reported	558	277	272	286	15	2.7	8	6	9	543
Oneida Reservation, Wisconsin	1,792	913	736	1,056	1,447	80.8	755	485	962	113
Iroquois	1,604	822	655	949	1,369	85.3	718	459	909	46
Oneida	1,582	811	648	934	1,349	85.3	709	454	896	46
Menominee	42	21	23	19	36	85.6	17	19	17	-
All other American Indians	146	70	58	88	43	29.3	19	7	36	67
Tribe not reported	60	32	24	36	4	6.2	1	1	3	55
Onondaga Reservation, New York	-	-	-	-	-	-	-	-	-	-
Ontonagan Reservation, Michigan	-	-	-	-	-	-	-	-	-	-
Osage Reservation, Oklahoma	4,701	2,397	1,791	2,910	2,877	61.2	1,511	1,016	1,861	200
Cherokee	1,774	878	650	1,124	633	35.7	325	215	418	44
Chickasaw	30	17	5	25	18	58.6	10	4	14	2
Choctaw	122	55	52	70	52	42.2	26	22	29	8
Creek	204	111	80	124	128	62.6	68	41	87	6
Delaware	59	18	26	33	34	56.8	8	10	23	1
Iroquois	101	64	41	60	66	65.4	41	18	48	3
Seneca	66	39	29	38	45	68.1	26	14	31	2
Kaw	41	24	8	33	40	97.5	24	8	32	-
Osage	1,679	873	632	1,047	1,470	87.6	771	528	942	24
Pawnee	52	22	17	35	48	90.5	22	15	32	1
Ponca	52	29	26	26	46	87.5	25	20	26	-
Potawatomi	138	84	50	87	102	74.0	63	24	78	4
Shawnee	37	23	15	22	31	84.8	20	11	20	2
Sioux	41	21	15	26	28	68.6	14	9	19	-
All other American Indians	370	178	172	198	183	49.3	95	89	93	106
Tribe not reported	97	50	47	50	12	11.9	7	7	5	79
Ozette Reservation, Washington	2	...	...	...	...	...	...	...	...	...
Pala Reservation, California	433	228	177	256	378	87.4	194	146	233	4
Cupeno	212	121	91	121	195	92.1	107	80	115	-
Luiseno	84	42	29	55	76	90.4	39	24	52	-
Luiseno	45	23	14	31	39	87.1	20	11	28	-
Pala	38	18	13	25	37	97.2	18	13	24	-
All other American Indians	137	64	57	80	107	78.2	47	42	65	4
Tribe not reported	7	7	4	2	5	81.1	5	3	2	-
Pamunkey Reservation, Virginia	45	25	12	33	44	97.8	24	12	32	-
Pamunkey	45	25	12	33	44	97.8	24	12	32	-
Papago Reservation, Arizona	6,772	3,437	2,909	3,863	6,039	89.2	3,038	2,468	3,571	144
Papago	6,452	3,284	2,780	3,671	5,813	90.1	2,928	2,381	3,432	85
Pima	79	31	28	42	60	85.0	28	24	36	-
Pueblo	30	17	8	22	23	75.3	12	6	17	1
All other American Indians	220	105	92	128	143	65.3	70	58	86	58
Tribe not reported	99	45	51	48	43	43.9	16	21	22	53
Pascua Yaqui Reservation, Arizona	548	288	278	270	523	95.4	277	268	254	14

[Continued]

275

★ 159 ★

Population and Tribal Enrollment Status on Reservations, by Tribal Affiliation, Age Group, and Sex, 1980: Nez Perce - Picuris Pueblo
[Continued]

Identified reservations; tribes of 30 or more American Indians	Total				Enrolled in tribe					Enrollment status not reported
					Both sexes					
	Both sexes	Female	Under 18 years	18 years and over	Total	Percent enrolled of total	Female	Under 18 years	18 Years and over	
Yaqui	526	277	267	259	515	97.9	274	263	252	2
All other American Indians	22	11	11	11	8	34.9	3	5	2	12
Tribe not reported	10	6	5	4	-	-	-	-	-	10
Pauma Reservation, California	83	48	29	54	77	92.6	42	23	54	-
Luiseno	60	33	20	39	58	97.9	32	19	39	-
All other American Indians	23	15	9	15	18	79.0	10	4	15	-
Tribe not reported	-	-	-	-	-	-	-	-	-	-
Payson Community of Yavapai-Apache, Arizona	-	-	-	-	-	-	-	-	-	-
Pechanga Reservation, California	116	58	49	67	105	90.3	53	46	59	3
Cahuilla	30	15	13	17	29	96.7	14	13	16	1
Luiseno	66	35	34	33	62	93.8	33	31	30	1
All other American Indians	19	8	2	17	13	68.4	6	1	12	1
Tribe not reported	2	-	-	2	2	100.0	-	-	2	-
Penobscot Reservation, Maine	403	189	165	238	378	93.8	178	146	232	7
Penobscot	380	174	158	222	362	95.2	166	142	220	2
All other American Indians	23	15	7	16	16	69.6	12	4	12	5
Tribe not reported	3	1	2	1	2	66.7	1	1	1	1
Picuris Pueblo, New Mexico	136	61	52	84	122	89.7	56	44	78	3
Pueblo	112	53	39	73	105	93.8	49	36	68	-
Isleta	78	36	23	55	71	91.1	32	21	50	-
Picuris	34	17	16	19	34	100.0	17	16	19	-
All other American Indians	24	8	13	11	17	70.8	7	7	10	3
Tribe not reported	-	-	-	-	-	-	-	-	-	-

Source: U.S. Bureau of the Census, Subject Reports, PC80-2-1D, Part 1, *American Indians, Eskimos, and Aleuts on Identified Reservations and in the Historic Areas of Oklahoma (Excluding Urbanized Areas)*, U.S. Government Printing Office, Washington, D.C., 1986, pp. 16-31. *Notes:* Three dots (...) means not applicable, or that the data are being withheld to avoid disclosure of information for individuals. A dash (-) represents zero or a percent which rounds to less than 0.1. Also, a dash (-) is used because the number of supplementary questionnaires for the reservations was insufficient to produce reliable estimates.

★ 160 ★

Population and Tribal Enrollment Status on Reservations, by Tribal Affiliation, Age Group, and Sex, 1980: Pine Creek - Red Lake

Data are the latest available.

Identified reservations; tribes of 30 or more American Indians	Total				Enrolled in tribe					Enrollment status not reported
					Both sexes					
	Both sexes	Female	Under 18 years	18 years and over	Total	Percent enrolled of total	Female	Under 18 years	18 Years and over	
Pine Creek Reservation, Michigan	20	...	...	...	...	...	...	...	...	...
Pine Ridge Reservation, South Dakota	11,867	5,922	5,882	5,985	10,843	91.4	5,433	5,204	5,640	512
Sioux	11,530	5,755	5,730	5,801	10,668	92.5	5,338	5,131	5,537	386
Cheyenne River Sioux	87	37	44	43	79	90.2	34	36	43	2
Oglala Sioux	10,078	4,992	5,041	5,037	9,463	93.9	4,699	4,590	4,872	222
Pine Ridge Sioux	50	23	18	32	34	68.0	16	4	30	2
Rosebud Sioux	195	95	89	107	170	87.2	83	71	99	7
Sioux	1,008	546	487	520	828	82.1	453	391	437	138
All other American Indians	337	167	153	184	175	52.0	95	72	102	126
Tribe not reported	164	78	79	85	45	27.5	26	23	22	116
Pleasant Point Reservation, Maine	504	260	252	252	487	96.7	252	245	243	14
Passamaquoddy	485	253	242	243	478	98.5	249	239	239	6
All other American Indians	19	6	10	9	10	51.7	4	6	4	8
Tribe not reported	13	4	7	5	4	28.6	1	4	-	8
Pojoaque Pueblo, New Mexico	98	51	45	53	77	78.6	38	29	48	-
Pueblo	96	49	45	51	75	78.2	37	29	46	-
Pojoaque	63	35	26	36	49	77.6	26	17	31	-
All other American Indians	2	2	-	2	2	100.0	2	-	2	-
Tribe not reported	-	-	-	-	-	-	-	-	-	-
Poospatuck Reservation, New York	94	55	48	46	84	89.1	47	46	38	2
Long Island	83	49	41	42	77	93.1	44	40	37	1
Poospatuck	82	48	41	40	77	94.4	44	40	37	1
All other American Indians	11	6	7	4	7	59.7	3	6	1	1
Tribe not reported	7	4	5	2	4	63.8	2	3	1	1
Port Gamble Reservation, Washington	261	128	109	152	234	89.8	111	91	144	11
Clallam	232	112	99	133	216	93.3	102	86	131	1
Port Gamble Clallam	232	112	99	133	216	93.3	102	86	131	1
All other American Indians	29	16	10	19	18	61.9	9	5	13	10
Tribe not reported	9	5	5	3	-	-	-	-	-	9
Port Madison Reservation, Washington	150	66	55	95	115	76.4	48	35	80	11
Puget Sound Salish	68	30	22	46	59	86.3	25	15	44	-
Suquamish	46	23	12	34	43	92.1	19	10	33	-
All other American Indians	82	36	33	49	56	68.1	22	20	36	11
Tribe not reported	12	6	4	8	2	12.3	2	2	-	11
Potawatomi Reservation, Wisconsin	219	98	108	111	213	97.3	92	105	108	2
Potawatomi	203	88	104	99	200	98.5	85	102	98	-
All other American Indians	16	10	4	12	13	81.3	7	3	10	2
Tribe not reported	2	2	1	1	-	-	-	-	-	2
Potawatomi Reservation, Kansas	331	171	126	205	314	94.7	160	108	205	-
Potawatomi	273	144	94	179	256	93.6	133	76	179	-
Prairie Band	254	134	87	168	244	95.9	127	76	168	-
All other American Indians	58	27	32	26	58	100.0	27	32	26	-
Tribe not reported	3	1	-	3	3	100.0	1	-	3	-

[Continued]

277

★ 160 ★

Population and Tribal Enrollment Status on Reservations, by Tribal Affiliation, Age Group, and Sex, 1980: Pine Creek - Red Lake

[Continued]

Identified reservations; tribes of 30 or more American Indians	Total				Enrolled in tribe					Enrollment status not reported
	Both sexes	Female	Under 18 years	18 years and over	Both sexes		Female	Under 18 years	18 Years and over	
					Total	Percent enrolled of total				
Prairie Island Community, Minnesota	84	41	35	49	82	97.6	40	33	49	-
Sioux	78	40	31	47	78	100.0	40	31	47	-
All other American Indians	6	1	4	2	4	66.7	-	2	2	-
Tribe not reported	1	-	-	1	1	100.0	-	-	1	-
Puyallup Reservation, Washington	850	443	407	443	593	69.8	309	238	355	40
Blackfoot	53	35	31	23	39	73.5	27	20	19	-
Cherokee	66	43	39	27	16	25.0	9	11	6	-
Chippewa	54	31	26	28	33	61.1	20	7	25	2
Puget Sound Salish	280	133	128	152	262	93.5	127	112	150	1
Puyallup	183	78	93	90	172	94.4	75	83	90	1
Tulalip	30	22	13	18	29	94.7	22	11	18	-
Sioux	38	21	19	19	19	50.7	13	5	14	-
All other American Indians	359	180	165	194	224	62.3	113	81	142	37
Tribe not reported	36	21	21	15	5	14.2	5	1	4	25
Pyramid Lake Reservation, Nevada	720	352	300	420	648	90.0	310	247	401	14
Paiute	618	299	254	364	567	91.8	270	215	353	10
Paiute	63	30	27	36	43	68.7	17	13	30	6
Pyramid Lake	543	265	224	319	512	94.3	248	199	313	4
All other American Indians	102	53	46	56	81	79.4	40	32	49	4
Tribe not reported	5	2	2	3	2	32.4	3	-	2	2
Quileute Reservation, Washington	266	118	130	136	233	87.7	104	109	124	12
Chemakuan	219	92	111	109	204	93.2	85	99	105	4
Quileute	211	89	107	104	197	93.5	84	97	101	2
All other American Indians	47	26	19	28	29	62.2	19	10	19	9
Tribe not reported	14	4	9	5	1	7.5	-	1	-	9
Quinault Reservation, Washington	944	442	421	523	829	87.8	397	341	489	34
Puget Sound Salish	34	20	12	23	31	89.8	19	10	20	-
Quinault	766	366	352	414	698	91.1	334	298	400	21
All other American Indians	144	56	57	87	100	69.9	44	32	68	13
Tribe not reported	12	3	6	6	3	22.7	-	-	3	6
Ramah Community, New Mexico	1,133	616	480	653	1,080	95.3	591	465	615	37
Navajo	1,100	603	471	629	1,068	97.1	587	460	608	19
All other American Indians	22	11	5	16	3	14.8	1	1	2	18
Tribe not reported	22	11	5	16	3	14.8	1	1	2	18
Ramona Reservation, California	-	-	-	-	-	-	-	-	-	-
Red Cliff Reservation, Wisconsin	589	270	294	295	563	95.5	257	289	273	17
Chippewa	571	260	291	280	556	97.4	253	289	267	13
All other American Indians	18	10	4	14	6	35.8	3	-	6	4
Tribe not reported	6	4	-	6	1	26.1	1	-	1	4
Red Lake Reservation, Minnesota	2,826	1,390	1,372	1,454	2,544	90.0	1,236	1,147	1,397	58
Chippewa	2,752	1,352	1,331	1,420	2,497	90.7	1,216	1,125	1,372	47
Chippewa	2,146	1,037	1,048	1,097	1,938	90.3	928	883	1,056	41
Red Lake Chippewa	584	298	278	307	539	92.3	273	239	300	6

[Continued]

★ 160 ★

Population and Tribal Enrollment Status on Reservations, by Tribal Affiliation, Age Group, and Sex, 1980: Pine Creek - Red Lake
[Continued]

Identified reservations; tribes of 30 or more American Indians	Total				Enrolled in tribe					Enrollment status not reported
				18 years and over	Both sexes			Under 18 years	18 Years and over	
	Both sexes	Female	Under 18 years		Total	Percent enrolled of total	Female			
All other American Indians	74	38	41	33	47	63.3	19	22	25	11
Tribe not reported	24	15	18	6	12	48.0	7	7	5	7

Source: U.S. Bureau of the Census, Subject Reports, PC80-2-1D, Part 1, *American Indians, Eskimos, and Aleuts on Identified Reservations and in the Historic Areas of Oklahoma (Excluding Urbanized Areas)*, U.S. Government Printing Office, Washington, D.C., 1986, pp. 16-31. *Notes:* Three dots (...) means not applicable, or that the data are being withheld to avoid disclosure of information for individuals. A dash (-) represents zero or a percent which rounds to less than 0.1. Also, a dash (-) is used because the number of supplementary questionnaires for the reservations was insufficient to produce reliable estimates.

★ 161 ★

Population and Tribal Enrollment Status on Reservations, by Tribal Affiliation, Age Group, and Sex, 1980: Reno-Sparks - San Ildefonso Pueblo

Data are the latest available.

Identified reservations; tribes of 30 or more American Indians	Total				Enrolled in tribe					Enrollment status not reported
				18 years and over	Both sexes			Under 18 years	18 Years and over	
	Both sexes	Female	Under 18 years		Total	Percent enrolled of total	Female			
Reno-Sparks Colony, Nevada	454	237	180	274	356	78.5	174	132	224	11
Paiute	314	164	135	179	251	79.8	126	105	146	3
Shoshone	38	26	8	30	26	68.4	15	4	21	-
Washo	71	32	25	47	57	79.9	22	14	43	4
All other American Indians	30	15	12	18	22	73.4	11	8	14	4
Tribe not reported	4	2	2	3	-	-	-	-	-	4
Resighini Rancheria, California	20	...	...	...	...	...	...	...	...	...
Rincon Reservation, California	297	155	137	160	183	61.7	92	55	128	17
Luiseno	221	117	110	111	149	67.7	78	51	99	1
All other American Indians	76	38	27	49	34	44.4	15	5	29	16
Tribe not reported	3	1	-	3	-	-	-	-	-	3
Roaring Creek Rancheria, California	24	...	...	...	...	...	...	...	...	...
Rocky Boy's Reservation, Montana	1,544	784	782	763	1,404	90.9	7100	696	708	42
Assiniboine	40	27	17	23	38	94.5	25	15	23	-
Cree	1,261	621	644	617	1,183	93.8	581	604	579	16
All other American Indians	243	136	121	122	183	75.5	103	78	106	26
Tribe not reported	55	25	30	25	22	40.8	8	4	19	24
Rosebud Reservation, South Dakota	5,643	2,927	2,778	2,865	4,303	76.3	2,225	1,776	2,527	491
Sioux	5,349	2,764	2,631	2,718	4,167	77.9	2,143	1,724	2,442	390
Cheyenne River Sioux	45	13	27	18	43	95.9	13	27	16	2
Oglala Sioux	141	71	53	88	122	86.9	58	37	85	3
Pine Ridge Sioux	42	17	8	33	39	94.6	17	7	32	-
Rosebud Sioux	4,614	2,396	2,281	2,334	3,614	78.3	1,875	1,501	2,113	288
Sioux	333	182	184	148	194	58.4	103	91	103	92

[Continued]

279

★ 161 ★

Population and Tribal Enrollment Status on Reservations, by Tribal Affiliation, Age Group, and Sex, 1980: Reno-Sparks - San Ildefonso Pueblo

[Continued]

Identified reservations; tribes of 30 or more American Indians	Total				Enrolled in tribe					Enrollment status not reported
	Both sexes	Female	Under 18 years	18 years and over	Both sexes		Female	Under 18 years	18 Years and over	
					Total	Percent enrolled of total				
Standing Rock Sioux	35	14	17	17	35	100.0	14	17	17	-
Yankton Sioux	56	26	28	28	47	85.2	22	23	25	2
All other American Indians	294	163	147	147	137	46.6	82	52	84	101
Tribe not reported	129	66	75	54	31	24.5	19	16	16	78
Round Valley Reservation, California	528	273	239	289	466	88.3	246	198	268	13
California Tribes (N.E.C.)	89	47	50	40	77	86.1	39	38	39	-
Yuchi	88	46	50	39	76	86.0	38	38	38	-
Konkow	62	31	26	36	59	94.9	30	24	35	1
Nomalaki	82	42	36	46	74	91.1	41	30	45	1
Pomo	92	43	37	55	82	88.9	39	32	50	1
Wailaki	122	67	56	66	112	91.5	61	48	64	-
All other American Indians	81	45	35	46	63	77.3	36	27	36	10
Tribe not reported	18	11	8	10	11	61.8	7	6	5	5
Rumsey Rancheria, California	13	...	...	...	...	...	...	...	...	...
Sac and Fox Reservation, Iowa	490	244	239	251	410	83.7	204	179	231	13
Sac and Fox - Mesquakie	450	221	216	234	387	86.0	191	170	218	9
All other American Indians	40	23	23	17	23	57.1	14	9	14	5
Tribe not reported	4	2	1	2	-	-	-	-	-	4
Sac and Fox Reservation, Kansas-Nebraska	3	...	...	...	...	...	...	...	...	...
St. Croix Reservation, Wisconsin	409	200	183	226	319	78.0	154	130	188	23
Chippewa	389	192	178	211	310	79.6	150	128	182	14
Chippewa	205	102	96	109	148	72.5	69	60	88	14
Minnesota Chippewa	35	17	19	16	35	100.0	17	19	16	-
St. Croix Chippewa	134	63	62	73	112	83.5	54	47	65	-
All other American Indians	19	8	5	14	9	45.9	4	2	7	9
Tribe not reported	10	7	5	5	4	41.5	4	2	2	6
St. Regis Mohawk Reservation, New York	1,749	846	639	1,110	1,571	89.8	742	559	1,012	72
Iroquois	1,663	803	608	1,055	1,540	92.6	728	549	991	24
Mohawk	1,658	801	605	1,053	1,535	92.6	726	546	989	24
All other American Indians	86	43	31	55	31	36.1	15	10	21	48
Tribe not reported	31	17	8	23	7	24.0	6	2	6	22
Salt River Reservation, Arizona	2,604	1,324	1,173	1,431	2,212	84.9	1,123	895	1,317	49
Navajo	39	19	20	19	26	65.4	9	9	17	-
Papago	75	39	34	41	58	77.5	33	25	34	2
Pima	2,108	1,075	970	1,138	1,832	86.9	933	762	1,070	32
Yuman	233	116	94	139	199	85.4	99	67	132	3
Maricopa	207	106	85	122	174	84.1	90	59	115	3
All other American Indians	148	74	55	93	96	64.9	50	32	64	11
Tribe not reported	31	13	16	16	15	47.4	6	9	6	4
San Carlos Reservation, Arizona	5,795	2,955	2,710	3,085	5,031	86.8	2,578	2,274	2,757	644
Apache	5,173	2,651	2,413	2,759	4,852	93.8	2,494	2,215	2,637	229
Apache (N.E.C.)	416	221	201	215	337	81.1	186	156	182	75
San Carlos Apache	4,725	2,415	2,203	2,522	4,489	95.0	2,297	2,051	2,438	154
Navajo	58	21	16	42	44	75.8	15	9	34	2

[Continued]

★ 161 ★

Population and Tribal Enrollment Status on Reservations, by Tribal Affiliation, Age Group, and Sex, 1980: Reno-Sparks - San Ildefonso Pueblo
[Continued]

Identified reservations; tribes of 30 or more American Indians	Total				Enrolled in tribe					Enrollment status not reported
				18	Both sexes					
	Both sexes	Female	Under 18 years	years and over	Total	Percent enrolled of total	Female	Under 18 years	18 Years and over	
All other American Indians	564	283	281	284	134	23.8	69	49	85	413
Tribe not reported	432	212	228	204	21	5.0	8	7	14	411
Sandia Pueblo, New Mexico	227	119	94	133	185	81.6	103	81	105	32
Pueblo	184	103	81	104	180	97.8	101	80	101	-
Sandia	156	92	66	91	154	98.7	91	65	90	-
All other American Indians	43	16	13	29	5	11.8	2	1	4	32
Tribe not reported	32	12	10	21	-	-	-	-	-	32
Sandy Lake Reservation, Minnesota	-	-	-	-	-	-	-	-	-	-
San Felipe Pueblo, New Mexico	1,792	920	869	923	1,779	99.3	915	864	915	3
Pueblo	1,772	909	864	908	1,763	99.5	904	860	903	2
San Felipe	1,742	890	862	880	1,736	99.6	888	858	877	2
All other American Indians	20	12	5	15	16	83.3	12	4	13	1
Tribe not reported	6	3	5	1	5	81.9	3	4	1	1
San Idelfonso Pueblo, New Mexico	485	254	175	310	467	96.4	245	165	302	12
Pueblo	469	246	173	296	458	97.7	239	165	293	7
San Ildefonso	223	117	84	139	221	99.0	117	82	139	2
Tewa	214	109	82	132	205	95.9	102	76	130	4
All other American Indians	16	8	2	13	9	58.2	6	-	9	5
Tribe not reported	9	4	2	7	4	46.6	1	-	4	5

Source: U.S. Bureau of the Census, Subject Reports, PC80-2-1D, Part 1, *American Indians, Eskimos, and Aleuts on Identified Reservations and in the Historic Areas of Oklahoma (Excluding Urbanized Areas)*, U.S. Government Printing Office, Washington, D.C., 1986, pp. 16-31. *Notes:* Three dots (...) means not applicable, or that the data are being withheld to avoid disclosure of information for individuals. A dash (-) represents zero or a percent which rounds to less than 0.1. Also, a dash (-) is used because the number of supplementary questionnaires for the reservations was insufficient to produce reliable estimates.

★ 162 ★

Population and Tribal Enrollment Status on Reservations, by Tribal Affiliation, Age Group, and Sex, 1980: San Juan Pueblo - Skull Valley

Data are the latest available.

Identified reservations; tribes of 30 or more American Indians	Total				Enrolled in tribe					Enrollment status not reported
				18	Both sexes					
	Both sexes	Female	Under 18 years	years and over	Total	Percent enrolled of total	Female	Under 18 years	18 Years and over	
San Juan Pueblo, New Mexico	837	434	351	486	781	93.3	419	327	454	45
Pueblo	748	395	307	441	719	96.1	386	300	419	23
San Juan	171	93	57	114	166	97.2	91	56	111	2
Tewa	473	255	207	266	465	98.3	250	204	261	8
Tigua	43	24	22	21	42	96.9	22	21	21	-
All other American Indians	89	39	44	45	62	69.7	33	27	35	22
Tribe not reported	19	6	13	6	2	12.7	1	2	-	17

[Continued]

Population and Tribal Enrollment Status on Reservations, by Tribal Affiliation, Age Group, and Sex, 1980: San Juan Pueblo - Skull Valley

[Continued]

Identified reservations; tribes of 30 or more American Indians	Total				Enrolled in tribe					Enrollment status not reported
	Both sexes	Female	Under 18 years	18 years and over	Both sexes		Female	Under 18 years	18 Years and over	
					Total	Percent enrolled of total				
San Manuel Reservation, California	-	-	-	-	-	-	-	-	-	-
San Pasqual Reservation, California	123	61	52	71	56	45.7	31	8	48	23
Diegueno	109	54	49	60	49	44.7	27	8	41	18
All other American Indians	14	7	3	11	7	53.4	4	-	7	5
Tribe not reported	4	2	1	3	1	24.8	1	-	1	3
Santa Ana Pueblo, New Mexico	407	205	146	261	389	95.5	197	136	253	12
Pueblo	393	201	143	250	385	98.0	196	136	250	1
Santa Ana	367	185	137	229	360	98.3	182	131	229	1
All other American Indians	14	4	2	12	3	23.8	1	-	3	11
Tribe not reported	11	3	2	8	-	-	-	-	-	11
Santa Clara Pueblo, New Mexico	1,847	914	781	1,065	1,569	85.0	767	608	961	66
Apache	35	20	23	12	35	100.0	20	23	12	-
Navajo	64	29	29	35	59	92.0	24	29	30	3
Pueblo	1,532	751	609	924	1,360	88.7	665	499	861	10
San Juan	66	25	36	31	54	80.8	20	25	28	-
Santa Clara	1,000	503	379	621	878	87.8	435	305	573	3
Santa Domingo	33	23	15	18	33	100.0	23	15	18	-
Tewa	349	161	135	214	321	92.0	155	120	201	8
All other American Indians	215	115	121	94	116	53.8	59	57	59	54
Tribe not reported	89	46	59	31	36	40.0	18	20	15	46
Santa Rosa Rancheria, California	122	54	68	54	117	95.7	51	64	53	1
Yokuts	116	50	67	49	112	96.4	47	63	49	-
Tachi	111	46	67	44	107	96.3	44	63	44	-
All other American Indians	6	4	1	5	5	81.3	4	1	4	1
Tribe not reported	2	1	1	1	2	100.0	1	1	1	-
Santa Rosa Reservation, California	12	...	...	...	...	...	...	...	...	...
Santa Ynez Reservation, California	120	60	51	69	72	60.2	38	20	53	1
Chumash	111	56	49	62	72	64.8	38	20	53	-
All other American Indians	9	4	2	6	-	-	-	-	-	1
Tribe not reported	1	1	1	-	-	-	-	-	-	-
Santa Ysabel Reservation, California	181	88	68	113	118	65.3	56	25	93	8
Diegueno	137	65	59	78	93	68.1	44	24	69	7
Diegueno	63	32	31	32	43	67.7	24	15	27	5
Santa Ysabel	71	33	28	43	48	67.4	21	9	39	2
All other American Indians	44	22	9	35	25	56.7	11	1	24	1
Tribe not reported	1	-	-	1	1	100.0	-	-	1	-
Santee Reservation, Nebraska	407	195	193	214	167	41.0	73	69	98	229
Sioux	190	90	85	105	147	77.6	64	62	85	35
Santee Sioux	177	84	83	95	136	76.6	59	60	76	34
All other American Indians	218	105	190	109	20	9.1	8	7	1	191
Tribe not reported	192	93	97	96	1	0.5	-	-	1	191
Santo Domingo Pueblo, New Mexico	2,140	1,052	999	1,141	2,110	98.6	1,035	990	1,120	6
Pueblo	2,131	1,046	996	1,135	2,103	98.6	1,030	988	1,115	6

[Continued]

★ 162 ★

Population and Tribal Enrollment Status on Reservations, by Tribal Affiliation, Age Group, and Sex, 1980: San Juan Pueblo - Skull Valley

[Continued]

Identified reservations; tribes of 30 or more American Indians	Total				Enrolled in tribe					Enrollment status not reported
				18 years and over	Both sexes					
	Both sexes	Female	Under 18 years		Total	Percent enrolled of total	Female	Under 18 years	18 Years and over	
Santo Domingo	2,111	1,030	995	1,116	2,085	98.8	1,017	986	1,099	6
All other American Indians	9	6	3	6	7	86.8	5	3	5	-
Tribe not reported	4	3	1	2	4	100.0	3	1	2	-
San Xavier Reservation, Arizona	850	435	356	494	779	91.6	401	314	465	14
Papago	805	415	346	459	752	93.4	391	311	441	5
All other American Indians	45	20	10	35	27	60.4	10	4	24	9
Tribe not reported	10	6	5	6	4	35.2	2	2	1	5
Sauk-Suiattle Reservation, Washington	-	-	-	-	-	-	-	-	-	-
Sault Ste. Marie Reservation, Michigan	-	-	-	-	-	-	-	-	-	-
Schaghticoke Reservation, Connecticut	6	...	...	...	...	...	...	...	...	...
Shakopee Community, Minnesota	77	35	35	42	64	83.3	30	28	36	11
Sioux	62	30	28	34	62	100.0	30	28	34	-
Mdewakanton Sioux	51	22	23	28	51	100.0	22	23	28	-
All other American Indians	15	4	7	8	2	14.1	-	-	2	11
Tribe not reported	12	3	5	7	1	8.0	-	-	1	11
Sheep Ranch Rancheria, California	2	...	...	...	...	...	...	...	...	...
Sherwood Valley Rancheria, California	17	...	...	...	...	...	...	...	...	...
Shingle Springs Rancheria, California	-	-	-	-	-	-	-	-	-	-
Shinnecock Reservation, New York	194	105	60	134	161	82.7	82	46	115	29
Shinnecock	181	94	58	123	159	87.7	80	46	113	20
All other American Indians	13	11	2	11	2	14.5	2	-	2	9
Tribe not reported	9	8	2	7	2	20.3	2	-	2	7
Shoalwater Reservation, Washington	28	...	...	...	...	...	...	...	...	...
Sisseton Reservation, North Dakota-South Dakota	2,589	1,332	1,284	1,305	2,202	85.1	1,131	1,056	1,146	273
Sioux	2,454	1,255	1,200	1,254	2,144	87.4	1,096	1,026	1,118	214
Dakota Sioux	37	22	8	29	32	85.8	19	5	26	2
Sioux	956	491	470	486	858	89.8	439	415	443	49
Sisseton Sioux	1,403	714	699	704	1,213	86.5	619	592	621	153
All other American Indians	135	78	84	52	58	42.6	35	30	28	60
Tribe not reported	65	35	50	15	10	14.8	6	8	2	43
Skokomish Reservation, Washington	305	159	143	162	276	90.6	138	124	152	2
Puget Sound Salish	253	133	129	124	236	93.3	121	113	123	-
Skokomish	233	122	120	113	219	94.2	110	108	112	-
All other American Indians	52	26	14	38	40	77.2	17	11	29	2

[Continued]

★ 162 ★

Population and Tribal Enrollment Status on Reservations, by Tribal Affiliation, Age Group, and Sex, 1980: San Juan Pueblo - Skull Valley

[Continued]

Identified reservations; tribes of 30 or more American Indians	Total				Enrolled in tribe					Enrollment status not reported
					Both sexes					
	Both sexes	Female	Under 18 years	18 years and over	Total	Percent enrolled of total	Female	Under 18 years	18 Years and over	
Tribe not reported	4	3	1	3	-	-	-	-	-	2
Skull Valley Reservation, Utah	-	-	-	-	-	-	-	-	-	-

Source: U.S. Bureau of the Census, Subject Reports, PC80-2-1D, Part 1, *American Indians, Eskimos, and Aleuts on Identified Reservations and in the Historic Areas of Oklahoma (Excluding Urbanized Areas)*, U.S. Government Printing Office, Washington, D.C., 1986, pp. 16-31. *Notes:* Three dots (...) means not applicable, or that the data are being withheld to avoid disclosure of information for individuals. A dash (-) represents zero or a percent which rounds to less than 0.1. Also, a dash (-) is used because the number of supplementary questionnaires for the reservations was insufficient to produce reliable estimates.

★ 163 ★

Population and Tribal Enrollment Status on Reservations, by Tribal Affiliation, Age Group, and Sex, 1980: Soboba - Tesuque Pueblo

Data are the latest available.

Identified reservations; tribes of 30 or more American Indians	Total				Enrolled in tribe					Enrollment status not reported
					Both sexes					
	Both sexes	Female	Under 18 years	18 years and over	Total	Percent enrolled of total	Female	Under 18 years	18 Years and over	
Soboba Reservation, California	230	110	110	120	222	96.7	106	103	119	-
Cahuilla	192	96	97	95	185	96.6	92	92	94	-
Soboba	181	91	92	89	174	96.4	87	87	87	-
All other American Indians	38	14	13	25	37	97.0	14	12	25	-
Tribe not reported	1	-	-	1	1	100.0	-	-	1	-
Sokaogon Chippewa Community, Wisconsin	95	46	34	61	90	94.7	42	31	59	-
Chippewa	91	43	34	57	86	94.5	39	31	55	-
Sokaogon Chippewa	87	39	31	56	86	98.8	39	31	55	-
All other American Indians	4	3	-	4	4	100.0	3	-	4	-
Tribe not reported	-	-	-	-	-	-	-	-	-	-
Southern Paiute Reservation, Utah	185	105	89	96	184	99.1	103	88	96	-
Paiute	168	95	80	88	167	99.0	94	79	88	-
Paiute	93	53	38	54	91	98.3	51	37	54	-
Southern Paiute	76	43	42	34	76	100.0	43	42	34	-
All other American Indians	17	9	9	8	17	100.0	9	9	8	-
Tribe not reported	-	-	-	-	-	-	-	-	-	-
Southern Ute Reservation, Colorado	877	439	430	448	652	74.3	324	305	347	175
Navajo	40	20	17	22	35	87.3	17	16	18	3
Ute	667	337	337	330	557	83.5	279	260	297	74
Ute	614	309	306	308	514	83.9	257	236	279	67
Ute Mountain Ute	53	28	31	22	42	79.8	21	24	18	6
All other American Indians	171	83	76	96	61	35.4	28	28	33	98
Tribe not reported	94	46	43	52	5	5.6	4	4	1	89
Spokane Reservation, Washington	1,052	501	434	618	949	90.2	451	370	579	8

[Continued]

Population and Tribal Enrollment Status on Reservations, by Tribal Affiliation, Age Group, and Sex, 1980: Soboba - Tesuque Pueblo

[Continued]

Identified reservations; tribes of 30 or more American Indians	Total				Enrolled in tribe					Enrollment status not reported
					Both sexes					
	Both sexes	Female	Under 18 years	18 years and over	Total	Percent enrolled of total	Female	Under 18 years	18 Years and over	
Colville	64	36	34	30	58	90.6	33	31	27	1
Spokane	843	396	347	496	769	91.2	362	296	473	1
All other American Indians	145	68	53	92	122	84.0	55	43	79	6
Tribe not reported	6	4	3	3	-	-	-	-	-	5
Squaxin Island Reservation, Washington	32	16	16	16	23	71.9	13	10	13	1
Standing Rock Reservation, North Dakota-South Dakota	4,587	2,272	2,227	2,360	3,983	86.8	1,976	1,844	2,139	323
Cheyenne	54	24	21	33	48	88.6	24	19	29	-
Chippewa	42	19	17	25	31	73.5	13	9	21	-
Sioux	4,065	2,024	2,003	2,062	3,767	92.7	1,873	1,753	2,014	43
Cheyenne River Sioux	104	41	47	57	100	96.6	39	44	57	-
Oglala Sioux	44	22	24	20	37	83.7	18	18	18	-
Sioux	1,978	967	970	1,008	1,856	93.8	900	873	983	19
Standing Rock Sioux	1,866	962	934	932	1,701	91.2	884	790	910	24
Other specified tribes	35	12	20	15	35	100.0	12	20	15	-
Fort Berthold	34	11	20	13	34	100.0	11	20	13	-
All other American Indians	391	193	166	225	103	26.3	55	43	60	280
Tribe not reported	287	139	121	166	10	3.6	5	5	5	277
Stewart's Point Rancheria, California	73	30	28	45	55	75.0	21	21	33	12
Pomo	67	27	25	42	50	74.2	19	18	31	11
Kashaya	56	20	21	34	48	85.5	18	18	29	2
All other American Indians	6	3	3	3	5	83.3	2	3	2	1
Tribe not reported	-	-	-	-	-	-	-	-	-	-
Stockbridge Reservation, Wisconsin	582	297	231	351	431	74.1	211	124	307	37
Iroquois	64	24	25	39	62	96.7	22	23	39	-
Oneida	64	24	25	39	62	96.7	22	23	39	-
Menominee	65	24	24	40	36	56.2	10	13	24	2
Stockbridge	412	221	165	247	317	77.0	168	89	229	23
All other American Indians	41	28	17	24	15	37.7	10	-	15	12
Tribe not reported	5	4	5	-	-	-	-	-	-	5
Sulphur Bank Rancheria, California	115	54	58	57	111	96.8	54	56	56	2
Pomo	111	52	57	54	109	97.8	52	54	54	2
All other American Indians	4	1	1	2	3	66.9	1	1	1	-
Tribe not reported	1	-	1	-	1	100.0	-	1	-	-
Summit Lake Reservation, Nevada	15	...	...	...	...	...	...	...	...	...
Susanville Reservation, California	83	43	34	50	37	44.3	17	10	27	30
Paiute	39	23	19	20	22	57.3	12	7	16	7
All other American Indians	44	21	15	30	15	32.9	6	3	11	23
Tribe not reported	23	11	8	15	-	-	-	-	-	23
Swinomish Reservation, Washington	423	203	174	249	368	87.0	173	135	234	10
Puget Sound Salish	343	164	143	200	302	87.9	142	109	193	3
Swinomish	302	149	120	182	262	86.9	129	88	175	3
Upper Skagit	30	10	18	11	28	96.2	9	17	11	-
All other American Indians	80	39	31	49	67	83.4	31	26	41	7
Tribe not reported	2	1	1	1	-	-	-	-	-	2

[Continued]

★ 163 ★

Population and Tribal Enrollment Status on Reservations, by Tribal Affiliation, Age Group, and Sex, 1980: Soboba - Tesuque Pueblo
[Continued]

Identified reservations; tribes of 30 or more American Indians	Total				Enrolled in tribe					Enrollment status not reported
					Both sexes					
	Both sexes	Female	Under 18 years	18 years and over	Total	Percent enrolled of total	Female	Under 18 years	18 Years and over	
Sycuan Reservation, California	56	18	29	27	34	61.8	15	14	20	-
Diegueno	51	15	29	22	30	58.2	12	14	16	-
All other American Indians	5	3	-	5	5	100.0	3	-	5	-
Tribe not reported	-	-	-	-	-	-	-	-	-	-
Tama Reservation, Georgia	30	12	7	23	25	82.2	11	5	19	-
Taos Pueblo, New Mexico	1,049	513	368	681	1,007	96.0	493	344	663	24
Pueblo	985	485	342	644	968	98.3	474	330	639	24
Taos	957	469	335	621	941	98.4	458	325	616	8
All other American Indians	64	27	27	37	39	60.8	19	14	25	15
Tribe not reported	15	3	6	10	-	-	-	-	-	15
Te-Moak Reservation, Nevada	91	46	31	60	81	89.2	42	27	55	3
Shoshone	81	40	27	55	72	87.9	35	22	49	3
All other American Indians	10	6	4	5	10	100.0	6	4	5	-
Tribe not reported	-	-	-	-	-	-	-	-	-	-
Tesuque Pueblo, New Mexico	236	124	91	145	213	90.3	107	78	135	8
Pueblo	215	115	83	133	200	93.1	103	73	127	5
Tesuque	193	104	79	113	179	93.1	92	70	109	4
All other American Indians	21	9	8	12	12	60.7	4	4	8	2
Tribe not reported	7	4	3	4	-	-	-	-	-	2

Source: U.S. Bureau of the Census, Subject Reports, PC80-2-1D, Part 1, *American Indians, Eskimos, and Aleuts on Identified Reservations and in the Historic Areas of Oklahoma (Excluding Urbanized Areas)*, U.S. Government Printing Office, Washington, D.C., 1986, pp. 16-31. *Notes:* Three dots (...) means not applicable, or that the data are being withheld to avoid disclosure of information for individuals. A dash (-) represents zero or a percent which rounds to less than 0.1. Also, a dash (-) is used because the number of supplementary questionnaires for the reservations was insufficient to produce reliable estimates.

★ 164 ★

Population and Tribal Enrollment Status on Reservations, by Tribal Affiliation, Age Group, and Sex, 1980: Tigua - Warm Springs

Data are the latest available.

Identified reservations; tribes of 30 or more American Indians	Total				Enrolled in tribe					Enrollment status not reported
					Both sexes					
	Both sexes	Female	Under 18 years	18 years and over	Total	Percent enrolled of total	Female	Under 18 years	18 Years and over	
Tigua Reservation, Texas	366	188	203	163	345	94.3	171	195	150	5
Pueblo	358	180	203	155	343	95.8	169	195	148	3
Tigua	358	180	203	155	343	95.8	169	195	148	3
All other American Indians	8	8	-	8	2	25.0	2	-	2	2
Tribe not reported	-	-	-	-	-	-	-	-	-	-
Tonawanda Reservation, New York	438	235	1148	290	335	76.4	176	112	223	69
Iroquois	362	190	120	242	326	90.2	171	109	218	2

[Continued]

★ 164 ★

Population and Tribal Enrollment Status on Reservations, by Tribal Affiliation, Age Group, and Sex, 1980: Tigua - Warm Springs

[Continued]

Identified reservations; tribes of 30 or more American Indians	Total				Enrolled in tribe					Enrollment status not reported
					Both sexes					
	Both sexes	Female	Under 18 years	18 years and over	Total	Percent enrolled of total	Female	Under 18 years	18 Years and over	
Seneca	311	168	106	205	286	91.9	153	98	188	-
Seneca	85	41	28	57	60	70.4	26	20	40	-
Tonawanda Seneca	215	118	73	142	215	100.0	118	73	142	-
All other American Indians	76	45	28	48	8	10.9	5	3	5	66
Tribe not reported	69	43	23	46	3	3.8	3	-	3	66
Torres-Martinez Reservation, California	-	-	-	-	-	-	-	-	-	-
Trinidad Rancheria, California	46	21	15	31	31	68.3	15	9	22	4
Yurok	33	16	10	23	28	83.4	15	7	21	2
All other American Indians	12	6	5	8	3	27.6	-	2	1	2
Tribe not reported	2	1	-	2	-	-	-	-	-	2
Tulalip Reservation, Washington	763	395	353	410	684	89.7	359	305	380	16
Puget Sound Salish	622	320	292	330	586	94.2	302	267	320	10
Tulalip	537	280	262	275	513	95.5	267	240	273	9
All other American Indians	141	76	62	79	98	69.4	57	38	60	6
Tribe not reported	7	3	2	4	1	16.1	1	-	1	6
Tule River Reservation, California	424	205	223	201	377	88.9	188	205	172	13
Yokuts	385	188	210	176	355	92.0	174	195	160	7
Tule River	375	182	201	174	345	92.2	168	187	158	6
All other American Indians	39	17	14	25	22	57.1	13	10	12	6
Tribes not reported	8	4	6	2	2	27.0	2	2	-	4
Tunica-Biloxi Reservation, Louisiana	7	...	...	...	...	...	...	...	...	...
Tuolumne Rancheria, California	81	34	35	46	52	64.2	23	14	38	1
Miwok	74	29	35	39	49	66.2	20	14	35	-
All other American Indians	7	5	-	7	3	42.9	3	-	3	1
Tribe not reported	-	-	-	-	-	-	-	-	-	-
Turtle Mountain Reservation, North Dakota	4,011	2,028	1,939	2,072	3,717	92.7	1,865	1,715	2,002	72
Chippewa	3,887	1,955	1,873	2,013	3,660	94.2	1,830	1,687	1,974	39
Chippewa	3,397	1,704	1,630	1,768	3,218	94.7	1,603	1,487	1,731	32
Turtle Mountain	481	247	239	242	434	90.3	223	195	239	6
All other American Indians	124	73	66	59	56	45.2	35	29	28	34
Tribe not reported	43	21	21	21	14	32.9	8	5	9	15
Tuscarora Reservation, New York	-	-	-	-	-	-	-	-	-	-
Twenty-Nine Palms Reservation, California	-	-	-	-	-	-	-	-	-	-
Uintah and Ouray Reservation, Utah	2,189	1,136	1,023	1,166	1,392	63.6	741	528	865	428
Navajo	90	43	55	35	55	60.9	22	33	22	24
Shoshone	46	32	28	19	39	85.1	28	27	13	-
Ute	1,654	856	754	900	1,172	70.8	625	411	761	168
All other American Indians	398	206	186	213	126	31.6	66	57	69	236
Tribe not reported	189	94	75	114	3	1.7	1	3	-	173
Umatilla Reservation, Oregon	902	499	373	529	749	83.1	426	270	479	42
Cayuse	46	26	13	33	36	78.7	19	5	32	1

[Continued]

★ 164 ★

Population and Tribal Enrollment Status on Reservations, by Tribal Affiliation, Age Group, and Sex, 1980: Tigua - Warm Springs
[Continued]

Identified reservations; tribes of 30 or more American Indians	Total				Enrolled in tribe					Enrollment status not reported
	Both sexes	Female	Under 18 years	18 years and over	Both sexes		Female	Under 18 years	18 Years and over	
					Total	Percent enrolled of total				
Nez Perce	62	33	26	36	51	82.6	27	18	33	1
Umatilla	399	220	155	244	357	89.4	199	120	238	5
Walla-Walla	70	43	12	58	62	88.8	36	9	53	-
Yakima	155	103	79	76	148	95.1	101	73	75	-
All other American Indians	169	74	87	82	95	56.1	45	45	49	35
Tribe not reported	27	15	9	18	4	16.4	2	3	1	22
Upper Sioux Community, Minnesota	52	27	18	34	52	100.0	27	18	34	-
Sioux	44	25	14	30	44	100.0	25	14	30	-
Sisseton Sioux	42	23	14	28	42	100.0	23	14	28	-
All other American Indians	8	2	4	4	8	100.0	2	4	4	-
Tribe not reported	-	-	-	-	-	-	-	-	-	-
Upper Skagit Reservation, Washington	-	-	-	-	-	-	-	-	-	-
Ute Mountain Reservation, Colorado-New Mexico	1,101	550	448	654	659	59.8	344	262	397	432
Navajo	60	32	23	37	31	51.2	21	10	21	24
Ute	927	462	388	539	601	64.8	312	244	357	322
Ute	554	272	242	312	245	44.2	130	108	137	307
Ute Mountain Ute	374	191	147	227	356	95.2	182	136	220	16
All other American Indians	115	56	36	78	28	24.3	11	9	19	86
Tribe not reported	85	41	29	56	7	8.1	1	2	4	78
Vermillion Lake Reservation, Minnesota	104	49	43	61	96	92.1	48	37	59	2
Chippewa	100	47	43	57	94	93.6	46	37	57	-
Bois Forte	37	21	13	24	37	100.0	21	13	24	-
Chippewa	53	21	25	27	46	87.9	20	19	27	-
All other American Indians	4	2	-	4	2	49.1	2	-	2	2
Tribe not reported	2	-	-	2	-	-	-	-	-	2
Viejas Rancheria, California	145	68	60	86	123	84.5	61	49	74	3
Diegueno	106	53	43	63	92	86.6	47	34	58	3
All other American Indians	39	15	16	23	31	78.7	14	15	16	-
Tribe not reported	2	-	-	2	2	100.0	-	-	2	-
Walker River Reservation, Nevada	474	244	190	284	408	86.1	207	152	256	10
Paiute	400	200	171	229	352	88.0	174	139	213	1
All other American Indians	74	44	19	55	56	75.7	33	13	43	9
Tribe not reported	1	-	1	-	-	-	-	-	-	-
Wampanoag Reservation, Massachusetts	-	-	-	-	-	-	-	-	-	-
Warm Springs Reservation, Oregon	1,991	973	925	1,066	1,710	85.9	830	773	937	218
Chinook	285	135	129	157	273	95.6	128	120	153	3
Paiute	53	31	13	40	47	87.2	26	13	33	7
Warm Springs	1,151	576	592	560	1,087	94.4	541	548	540	51
Yakima	90	41	35	55	81	90.0	36	31	50	7

[Continued]

★ 164 ★

Population and Tribal Enrollment Status on Reservations, by Tribal Affiliation, Age Group, and Sex, 1980: Tigua - Warm Springs
[Continued]

Identified reservations; tribes of 30 or more American Indians	Total				Enrolled in tribe					Enrollment status not reported
					Both sexes					
	Both sexes	Female	Under 18 years	18 years and over	Total	Percent enrolled of total	Female	Under 18 years	18 Years and over	
All other American Indians	411	191	156	255	223	54.2	99	62	161	150
Tribe not reported	171	89	94	77	31	17.8	20	14	16	133

Source: U.S. Bureau of the Census, Subject Reports, PC80-2-1D, Part 1, *American Indians, Eskimos, and Aleuts on Identified Reservations and in the Historic Areas of Oklahoma (Excluding Urbanized Areas)*, U.S. Government Printing Office, Washington, D.C., 1986, pp. 16-31. *Notes:* Three dots (...) means not applicable, or that the data are being withheld to avoid disclosure of information for individuals. A dash (-) represents zero or a percent which rounds to less than 0.1. Also, a dash (-) is used because the number of supplementary questionnaires for the reservations was insufficient to produce reliable estimates.

★ 165 ★

Population and Tribal Enrollment Status on Reservations, by Tribal Affiliation, Age Group, and Sex, 1980: Washoe - Zuni Pueblo

Data are the latest available.

Identified reservations; tribes of 30 or more American Indians	Total				Enrolled in tribe					Enrollment status not reported
					Both sexes					
	Both sexes	Female	Under 18 years	18 years and over	Total	Percent enrolled of total	Female	Under 18 years	18 Years and over	
Washoe Reservation, Nevada	-	-	-	-	-	-	-	-	-	-
Western Pequot Reservation, Connecticut	16	...	...	...	...	...	...	...	...	...
White Earth Reservation, Minnesota	2,548	1,198	1,142	1,406	2,092	82.1	995	752	1,340	53
Chippewa	2,391	1,120	1,068	1,323	1,994	83.4	940	710	1,284	22
Chippewa	2,085	970	938	1,147	1,752	84.0	821	640	1,111	19
Mille Lac	59	27	23	35	49	83.7	21	14	35	3
Minnesota Chippewa	185	95	84	101	145	78.3	78	47	98	-
White Earth	49	19	23	26	35	70.9	11	9	26	-
Iroquois	37	21	20	17	34	92.2	21	18	16	-
Oneida	37	21	20	17	34	92.2	21	18	16	-
Sioux	49	25	19	30	45	91.1	25	16	29	-
All other American Indians	71	32	36	35	19	27.0	9	8	11	31
Tribe not reported	38	20	19	19	7	17.8	4	1	6	21
Wind River Reservation, Wyoming	4,147	2,104	1,900	2,247	3,251	78.4	1,656	1,331	1,920	331
Arapaho	2,241	1,168	1,062	1,178	1,860	83.0	977	775	1,085	55
Cheyenne	62	32	21	41	48	78.0	21	17	32	7
Navajo	35	13	21	14	24	67.2	9	14	10	3
Shoshone	1,212	613	498	714	1,030	85.0	5221	393	637	53
Sioux	102	44	57	45	82	81.0	33	40	42	4
All other American Indians	495	235	241	225	206	41.7	96	91	115	210
Tribe not reported	240	118	119	121	24	10.1	13	11	13	200
Winnebago Reservation, Nebraska	1,098	593	505	593	587	53.5	333	276	311	470
Omaha	58	36	26	32	50	84.9	32	19	30	3
Winnebago	527	296	260	267	480	91.1	272	229	251	26
All other American Indians	513	261	219	294	58	11.2	30	28	30	440

[Continued]

★ 165 ★

Population and Tribal Enrollment Status on Reservations, by Tribal Affiliation, Age Group, and Sex, 1980: Washoe - Zuni Pueblo

[Continued]

Identified reservations; tribes of 30 or more American Indians	Total				Enrolled in tribe					Enrollment status not reported
	Both sexes	Female	Under 18 years	18 years and over	Both sexes		Female	Under 18 years	18 Years and over	
					Total	Percent enrolled of total				
Tribe not reported	432	219	175	257	-	-	-	-	-	431
Winnemucca Colony, Nevada	34	18	16	18	32	95.2	18	15	18	-
Wisconsin Winnebago Reservation	352	188	180	172	229	64.9	125	101	127	102
Winnebago	249	139	126	123	202	81.1	116	88	114	26
All other American Indians	103	49	54	49	26	25.6	10	13	13	76
Tribe not reported	73	36	41	32	-	-	-	-	-	73
Woodfords Community, California	-	-	-	-	-	-	-	-	-	-
XL Ranch Reservation, California	24	...	...	...	...	...	...	...	...	...
Yakima Reservation, Washington	4,947	2,524	2,212	2,735	4,350	87.9	2,226	1,814	2,536	143
Arapaho	30	11	24	6	24	79.9	9	18	6	-
Blackfoot	95	39	43	53	80	83.9	35	30	50	2
Chippewa	40	21	17	23	33	80.9	15	13	19	1
Colville	169	88	82	87	153	90.4	79	68	85	-
Navajo	31	18	12	19	19	59.6	13	5	14	2
Nez Perce	91	56	37	54	69	75.8	46	17	52	-
Puget Sound Salish	76	46	30	45	63	83.2	40	19	44	-
Sioux	45	21	26	19	23	50.2	8	11	11	7
Umatilla	44	27	12	31	41	94.7	27	11	31	-
Warm Springs	83	40	46	38	77	92.5	38	40	37	-
Yakima	3,762	1,926	1,682	2,079	3,476	92.4	1,783	1,483	1,993	36
All other American Indians	480	232	201	279	292	60.9	132	99	194	95
Tribe not reported	82	50	25	56	25	30.5	15	7	18	49
Yankton Reservation, South Dakota	1,635	861	785	850	1,475	90.2	776	674	801	66
Sioux	1,564	829	757	806	1,429	91.4	753	656	773	53
Rosebud Sioux	52	29	16	36	42	81.0	22	16	26	4
Sioux	614	318	301	313	562	91.5	291	258	303	15
Yankton Sioux	834	443	429	405	768	92.1	408	377	391	31
All other American Indians	71	32	28	43	46	64.4	23	19	28	13
Tribe not reported	27	17	13	14	13	50.4	10	10	4	13
Yavapai Reservation, Arizona	66	37	25	41	58	87.9	34	20	38	2
Yuman	57	32	21	36	52	91.2	31	17	35	-
Yavapai	54	31	21	33	49	90.7	30	17	32	-
All other American Indians	9	5	4	5	6	66.7	3	3	3	2
Tribe not reported	1	1	-	1	-	-	-	-	1	
Yerington Reservation, Nevada	110	55	51	58	104	95.0	51	47	57	3
Paiute	92	48	46	47	88	95.2	43	41	47	2
All other American Indians	17	7	6	12	16	94.1	7	6	10	1
Tribe not reported	3	1	1	2	2	69.5	1	1	1	1
Yomba Reservation, Nevada	57	19	22	35	55	96.4	18	21	34	1
Shoshone	48	16	19	28	47	97.8	15	18	28	-
All other American Indians	9	3	3	6	8	89.2	3	3	5	1
Tribe not reported	1	-	-	1	-	-	-	-	-	1

[Continued]

★ 165 ★

Population and Tribal Enrollment Status on Reservations, by Tribal Affiliation, Age Group, and Sex, 1980: Washoe - Zuni Pueblo

[Continued]

Identified reservations; tribes of 30 or more American Indians	Total				Enrolled in tribe					Enrollment status not reported
				18	Both sexes					
	Both sexes	Female	Under 18 years	years and over	Total	Percent enrolled of total	Female	Under 18 years	18 Years and over	
Zia Pueblo, New Mexico	516	266	223	293	513	99.5	265	222	292	1
Pueblo	509	263	221	288	507	99.5	262	219	287	1
Zia	499	255	217	282	496	99.5	254	216	281	1
All other American Indians	7	3	2	5	7	100.0	3	2	5	-
Tribe not reported	-	-	-	-	-	-	-	-	-	-
Zuni Pueblo, New Mexico	5,973	3,089	2,808	3,165	5,682	95.1	2,938	2,651	3,031	81
Navajo	75	44	25	51	68	91.5	41	21	47	-
Pueblo	5,770	2,995	2,725	3,044	5,539	96.0	2,866	2,597	2,942	44
All other American Indians	129	50	60	69	74	57.8	30	33	41	36
Tribe not reported	75	28	40	35	40	52.6	15	22	17	30
San Felipe/Santa Ana Joint Area, New Mexico	-	-	-	-	-	-	-	-	-	-
San Felipe/Santo Domingo Joint Area, New Mexico	115	65	59	56	115	100.0	65	59	56	-
Pueblo	115	65	59	56	115	100.0	65	59	56	-
Santo Domingo	95	49	49	46	95	100.0	49	49	46	-
Other Reservation Lands in Montana	-	-	-	-	-	-	-	-	-	-

Source: U.S. Bureau of the Census, Subject Reports, PC80-2-1D, Part 1, *American Indians, Eskimos, and Aleuts on Identified Reservations and in the Historic Areas of Oklahoma (Excluding Urbanized Areas),* U.S. Government Printing Office, Washington, D.C., 1986, pp. 16-31. *Notes:* Three dots (...) means not applicable, or that the data are being withheld to avoid disclosure of information for individuals. A dash (-) represents zero or a percent which rounds to less than 0.1. Also, a dash (-) is used because the number of supplementary questionnaires for the reservations was insufficient to produce reliable estimates.

★ 166 ★

Population of Alaska Native Regional Corporation Areas, by Age and Sex: 1990 - I

American Indian/Alaska Native Area State	All persons	American Indian, Eskimo, or Aleut					
		Total	Female	Age			
				Under 5 years	16 years and over	18 years and over	18 to 20 years
Alaska Native Regional Corporation[1]							
Ahtna	3,089	592	292	81	388	371	22
Aleut	11,942	2,118	939	250	1,391	1,333	89
Arctic Slope	5,979	4,336	2,090	714	2,549	2,434	160
Bering Straits	8,288	6,148	2,936	879	3,808	3,576	267
Bristol Bay	7,028	4,639	2,278	714	2,875	2,737	170
Calista	19,447	16,775	8,184	2,676	10,089	9,459	785
Chugach	11,450	1,550	708	160	1,091	1,046	62
Cook Inlet	302,473	18,581	9,892	2,275	12,290	11,630	962
Dayon	91,936	10,793	5,406	1,387	6,798	6,412	506

[Continued]

★ 166 ★

Population of Alaska Native Regional Corporation Areas, by Age and Sex: 1990 - I
[Continued]

American Indian/Alaska Native Area State	All persons	American Indian, Eskimo, or Aleut						
		Total	Female	Age				
				Under 5 years	16 years and over	18 years and over	18 to 20 years
Koniag	13,309	2,126	1,033	264	1,414	1,324	102
Sealaska	67,520	11,622	5,809	1,478	7,487	7,106	542

Source: Summary Population and Housing Characteristics, United States Summary, United States Bureau of the Census, CP H-1, pp. 402-416. *Notes:* 1. Alaska Native Regional Corporations (ANRC's) are corporate entities established under the Alaska Native Claims Settlement Act of 1972 to conduct both business and nonprofit affairs of Alaska Natives. Alaska is divided into 12 ANRC's that cover the entire state, except for the Annette Islands Reserve. The boundaries of the 12 ANRC's were established by the Department of the Interior, in cooperation with Alaska Natives. Each ANRC was designed to include, as far as practicable, Alaska Natives with a common heritage and common interests. The ANRC boundaries for the 1990 census were identified by the Bureau of Land Management. A 13th region was established for Alaska Natives who are not permanent residents and who chose not to enroll in one of the 12 ANRC's; no census products were prepared for the 13th region. ANRC's were first identified for the 1980 census.

★ 167 ★

Population of Alaska Native Regional Corporation Areas, by Age and Sex: 1990 - II

American Indian/Alaska Native Area State	American Indian, Eskimo, or Aleut						Median age
	Age						
	21 to 24 years	25 to 44 years	45 to 54 years	55 to 59 years	60 to 64 years	65 years and over	
Alaska Native Regional Corporation[1]							
Ahtna	27	159	52	25	18	68	28.0
Aleut	128	715	161	84	53	103	26.2
Arctic Slope	267	1,287	303	144	93	180	22.8
Bering Straits	365	1,787	457	182	156	362	23.6
Bristol Bay	278	1,389	355	146	125	274	24.6
Calista	1,190	4,653	1,115	469	367	880	22.0
Chugach	95	574	134	57	53	71	28.4
Cook Inlet	1,298	6,412	1,551	515	324	568	25.2
Dayon	658	3,350	774	317	254	553	24.1
Koniag	128	649	189	81	59	116	25.9
Sealaska	753	3,536	972	391	282	630	25.0

Source: Summary Population and Housing Characteristics, United States Summary, United States Bureau of the Census, CP H-1, pp. 402-416. *Notes:* 1. Alaska Native Regional Corporations (ANRC's) are corporate entities established under the Alaska Native Claims Settlement Act of 1972 to conduct both business and nonprofit affairs of Alaska Natives. Alaska is divided into 12 ANRC's that cover the entire state, except for the Annette Islands Reserve. The boundries of the 12 ANRC's were established by the Department of the Interior, in cooperation with Alaska Natives. Each ANRC was designed to include, as far as practicable, Alaska Natives with a common heritage and common interests. The ANRC boundaries for the 1990 census were identified by the Bureau of Land Management. A 13th region was established for Alaska Natives who are not permanent residents and who chose not to enroll in one of the 12 ANRC's; no census products were prepared for the 13th region. ANRC's were first identified for the 1980 census.

★ 168 ★

Population of Alaska Native Village Statistical Areas, by Age and Sex: 1990, Akhiok-Kasaan - I

American Indian/Alaska Native Area State	All persons	American Indian, Eskimo, or Aleut					
		Total	Female	Age			
				Under 5 years	16 years and over	18 years and over	18 to 20 years
Alaska Native Village Statistical Area[1]							
All areas	77,700	47,244	22,650	7,113	28,696	27,026	1,991
Akhiok	77	72	32	11	40	37	-
Akiachak	483	459	229	61	282	264	26
Akiak	285	277	141	47	157	149	9
Akutan	589	80	30	11	55	54	2
Alakanuk	544	521	269	76	303	282	30
Alatna	31	29	12	1	18	17	1
Aleknagik	185	154	75	16	101	95	7
Alexander	40	10	7	-	9	9	1
Allakaket	138	131	54	17	85	83	4
Ambler	311	279	132	55	144	128	8
Anaktuvuk Pass	259	220	115	31	125	116	9
Andreafsky	410	346	162	47	213	198	11
Angoon	638	525	259	79	306	287	13
Aniak	540	382	200	55	206	197	13
Anvik	82	75	42	11	44	42	1
Arctic Villagae	96	90	49	20	53	50	4
Atka	98	91	42	5	66	61	5
Atkasook	216	201	91	26	128	121	12
Atmautluak	258	250	122	26	155	145	11
Barrow	2,763	1,771	890	308	1,035	983	72
Beaver	103	98	41	10	69	64	8
Belkofski	-	-	-	-	-	-	-
Bethel	4,674	2,986	1,534	449	1,875	1,775	143
Bill Moore's	-	-	-	-	-	-	-
Birch Creek	42	38	15	2	21	21	-
Brevig Mission	198	183	94	30	105	104	5
Buckland	318	302	135	52	160	145	11
Cantwell	147	33	16	5	23	22	-
Canyon Village	-	-	-	-	-	-	-
Chalkyitsik	90	83	37	5	54	50	2
Chefornak	320	312	155	62	178	167	22
Chenega	94	65	33	10	39	37	3
Chevak	598	556	249	123	299	280	23
Chignik	188	85	39	9	59	56	3
Chignik Lagoon	53	30	16	3	23	21	1
Chignik Lake	133	122	57	23	70	66	5

[Continued]

293

★ 168 ★

Population of Alaska Native Village Statistical Areas, by Age and Sex: 1990, Akhiok-Kasaan - I

[Continued]

American Indian/Alaska Native Area State	All persons	American Indian, Eskimo, or Aleut					
		Total	Female	Age			
				Under 5 years	16 years and over	18 years and over	18 to 20 years
Chilkat	129	112	51	12	70	64	4
Chilkoot	221	27	11	4	19	19	1
Chistochina	60	37	21	6	23	22	3
Chitina	49	23	8	2	16	15	-
Chuathbaluk	97	87	37	13	51	47	2
Chulloonawick	-	-	-	-	-	-	-
Circle	73	63	28	9	37	37	2
Clark's Point	60	53	26	6	34	33	1
Copper Center	449	155	77	24	101	98	6
Council	8	5	2	-	5	5	1
Craig	1,260	288	157	40	173	170	11
Crooked Creek	106	96	44	19	57	55	2
Deering	157	148	69	21	85	79	5
Dillingham	2,017	1,125	587	176	686	656	37
Dot Lake	53	31	13	3	20	18	1
Eagle	35	28	12	1	22	22	1
Eek	254	243	112	32	158	150	9
Egegik	122	86	37	12	57	56	1
Eklutna	381	48	26	5	27	27	1
Ekuk	3	2	2	-	2	2	-
Ekwok	77	67	33	10	46	46	4
Elim	264	242	106	43	138	132	10
Emmonak	642	591	279	107	360	340	42
English Bay	158	144	72	22	76	72	6
Evansville	69	27	16	2	18	16	1
Eyak	172	13	5	3	7	7	-
False Pass	68	52	24	5	32	30	-
Fort Yukon	580	493	226	58	313	299	21
Gakana	25	-	-	-	-	-	-
Galena	833	377	178	57	233	212	13
Gambell	525	505	212	73	315	299	24
Georgetown	-	-	-	-	-	-	-
Golavin	127	118	57	19	70	66	6
Goodnews Bay	241	231	108	37	153	146	8
Grayling	208	194	97	35	107	98	6
Grouse Creek Group	580	81	46	11	47	46	1
Gulkana	103	61	29	6	41	40	2
Hamilton	-	-	-	-	-	-	-

[Continued]

★ 168 ★

Population of Alaska Native Village Statistical Areas, by Age and Sex: 1990, Akhiok-Kasaan - I

[Continued]

American Indian/Alaska Native Area State	All persons	American Indian, Eskimo, or Aleut						
		Total	Female	Age				
				Under 5 years	16 years and over	18 years and over	18 to 20 years	
Healy Lake	47	40	20	1	22	22	1	
Holy Cross	-	-	-	-	-	-	-	
Hoonah	795	534	250	55	346	326	20	
Hooper Bay	845	811	397	169	444	420	33	
Hughes	54	50	23	3	36	34	2	
Huslia	207	188	91	24	116	109	6	
Hydaburg	384	342	148	32	221	209	15	
Igiugig	33	26	12	4	19	18	2	
Iliamna	94	62	33	10	37	37	1	
Inalik	178	167	74	26	95	94	10	
Ivanof Bay	35	33	13	5	19	17	1	
Kake	700	514	228	77	330	309	22	
Kaktovik	224	189	84	28	125	123	4	
Kalskag	172	146	71	21	88	82	2	
Kaltag	240	222	100	33	126	114	6	
Karluk	71	65	24	7	36	31	5	
Kasaan	54	29	17	4	20	20	3	

Source: Summary Population and Housing Characteristics, United States Summary, United States Bureau of the Census, CP H-1, pp. 402-416. *Notes:* A dash (-) indi cates that no data were given in the original source.1. Alaska Native villages (ANV's) constitute tribes, bands, clans, groups, villages, communities, or associations in Alaska that are recognized pursuant to the Alaska Native Claims Settlement Act of 1972, Public Law 92-203. Because ANV's do not have legally designated boundaries, the Census Bureau has established Alaska Native village statistical areas (ANVSA's) for statistical purposes. For the 1990 census, the Census Bureau cooperated with officials of the nonprofit corporation within each participating Alaska Native Regional Corporation (ANRC), as well as other knowledgeable officials, to delineate boundaries that encompass the settles area associated with each ANV.

★ 169 ★

Population of Alaska Native Village Statistical Areas, by Age and Sex: 1990, Akhiok-Kasaan - II

American Indian/Alaska Native Area State	American Indian, Eskimo, or Aleut						
	Age						Median age
	21 to 24 years	25 to 44 years	45 to 54 years	55 to 59 years	60 to 64 years	65 years and over	
Alaska Native Village Statistical Area[1]							
All areas	2,955	13,562	3,336	1,481	1,143	2,558	23.0
Akhiok	5	19	10	2	1	-	21.5
Akiachak	31	121	35	16	9	26	22.2

[Continued]

★ 169 ★

Population of Alaska Native Village Statistical Areas, by Age and Sex: 1990, Akhiok-Kasaan - II

[Continued]

American Indian/Alaska Native Area State	American Indian, Eskimo, or Aleut						
	Age						Median age
	21 to 24 years	25 to 44 years	45 to 54 years	55 to 59 years	60 to 64 years	65 years and over	
Akiak	12	76	18	8	7	19	21.4
Akutan	8	30	6	1	1	6	26.5
Alakanuk	41	120	30	26	16	19	19.8
Alatna	-	10	3	-	1	2	27.5
Aleknagik	6	44	10	9	7	12	27.1
Alexander	1	3	3	-	1	-	30.0
Allakaket	7	42	14	5	4	7	27.2
Ambler	25	59	17	3	5	11	16.5
Anaktuvuk Pass	12	55	20	10	5	5	20.0
Andreafsky	26	95	24	12	8	22	22.9
Angoon	30	151	44	12	8	29	22.8
Aniak	21	113	23	5	6	16	19.6
Anvik	1	21	5	3	4	7	26.4
Arctic Villagae	3	26	7	5	-	5	22.0
Atko	4	29	7	4	6	6	31.8
Atkasook	15	57	19	8	7	3	23.6
Atmautluak	15	74	21	4	6	14	23.0
Barrow	97	546	111	46	38	73	22.3
Beaver	2	35	8	3	1	7	27.8
Belkofski	-	-	-	-	-	-	-
Bethel	221	987	204	62	44	114	23.6
Bill Moore's	-	-	-	-	-	-	-
Birch Creek	2	11	3	1	2	2	25.0
Brevig Mission	11	62	10	5	2	9	23.5
Buckland	18	75	15	6	4	16	17.3
Cantwell	-	6	9	2	1	4	43.8
Canyon Village	-	-	-	-	-	-	-
Chalkyitsik	5	21	4	9	2	7	26.3
Chefornak	23	77	20	4	4	17	19.3
Chenega	5	18	6	2	1	2	22.4
Chevak	41	151	17	15	11	22	18.3
Chignik	5	34	4	4	1	5	27.1
Chignik Lagoon	2	8	2	3	1	4	30.0
Chignik Lake	12	30	9	1	2	7	21.0
Chilkat	4	35	7	4	2	8	25.0
Chilkoot	1	8	1	7	1	-	33.8
Chistochina	2	8	2	2	2	3	21.5
Chitina	-	9	3	-	-	3	35.8

[Continued]

★ 169 ★

Population of Alaska Native Village Statistical Areas, by Age and Sex: 1990, Akhiok-Kasaan - II

[Continued]

American Indian/Alaska Native Area State	American Indian, Eskimo, or Aleut						
	Age						Median age
	21 to 24 years	25 to 44 years	45 to 54 years	55 to 59 years	60 to 64 years	65 years and over	
Chuathbaluk	6	26	3	2	4	4	22.8
Chulloonawick	-	-	-	-	-	-	-
Circle	2	20	8	2	-	3	27.5
Clark's Point	3	21	-	3	2	3	27.1
Copper Center	10	40	7	9	3	23	26.6
Council	-	1	2	-	-	1	47.5
Craig	14	98	19	10	7	11	25.2
Crooked Creek	11	23	3	1	5	10	23.0
Deering	12	35	12	8	1	6	21.5
Dillingham	57	345	94	31	30	62	25.0
Dot Lake	-	6	3	3	1	4	28.8
Eagle	1	13	3	-	1	3	32.5
Eek	14	75	15	9	6	22	26.1
Egegik	4	30	8	5	3	5	29.4
Eklutna	-	13	9	-	2	2	28.3
Ekuk	-	-	1	-	-	1	62.5
Ekwok	3	21	7	1	4	6	30.8
Elim	9	73	13	10	4	13	21.5
Emmonak	59	128	50	19	14	28	21.2
English Bay	10	37	13	3	-	3	18.0
Evansville	-	9	-	1	2	3	28.8
Eyak	-	7	-	-	-	-	27.5
False Pass	-	21	3	1	-	5	31.7
Fort Yukon	27	162	34	13	16	26	25.4
Gakana	-	-	-	-	-	-	-
Galena	19	113	33	10	14	10	23.3
Gambell	39	152	34	17	14	19	23.4
Georgetown	-	-	-	-	-	-	-
Golavin	4	32	11	2	3	8	21.5
Goodnews Bay	26	59	20	10	3	20	24.5
Grayling	11	50	11	4	8	8	18.3
Grouse Creek Group	5	27	4	3	4	2	24.6
Gulkana	-	19	4	4	4	7	33.8
Hamilton	-	-	-	-	-	-	-
Healy Lake	3	12	4	-	-	2	22.0
Holy Cross	-	-	-	-	-	-	-
Hoonah	23	163	60	16	14	30	26.9
Hooper Bay	41	221	39	20	15	51	19.4

[Continued]

★ 169 ★

Population of Alaska Native Village Statistical Areas, by Age and Sex: 1990, Akhiok-Kasaan - II
[Continued]

American Indian/Alaska Native Area State	American Indian, Eskimo, or Aleut						
	Age						Median age
	21 to 24 years	25 to 44 years	45 to 54 years	55 to 59 years	60 to 64 years	65 years and over	
Hughes	5	15	3	1	2	6	28.3
Huslia	13	51	16	5	9	9	23.7
Hydaburg	17	97	31	17	6	26	26.1
Igiugig	1	5	5	4	-	1	30.0
Iliamna	3	17	11	-	2	3	26.1
Inalik	11	44	12	6	5	6	21.3
Ivanof Bay	2	12	-	-	-	2	18.5
Kake	30	149	45	20	15	28	25.0
Kaktovik	18	59	16	8	8	10	26.7
Kalskag	7	49	8	7	3	6	25.0
Kaltag	12	63	11	10	2	10	19.8
Karluk	4	15	4	-	1	2	17.3
Kasaan	-	10	3	3	-	1	31.9

Source: Summary Population and Housing Characteristics, United States Summary, United States Bureau of the Census, CP H-1, pp. 402-416. *Notes:* A dash (-) indi cates that no data were given in the original source.1. Alaska Native villages (ANV's) constitute tribes, bands, clans, groups, villages, communities, or associations in Alaska that are recognized pursuant to the Alaska Native Claims Settlement Act of 1972, Public Law 92-203. Because ANV's do not have legally designated boundaries, the Census Bureau has established Alaska Native village statistical areas (ANVSA's) for statistical purposes. For the 1990 census, the Census Bureau cooperated with officials of the nonprofit corporation within each participating Alaska Native Regional Corporation (ANRC), as well as other knowledgeable officials, to delineate boundaries that encompass the settles area associated with each ANV.

★ 170 ★

Population of Alaska Native Village Statistical Areas, by Age and Sex: 1990, Kasigluk-Tokotna - I

American Indian/ Alaska Native Area State	All persons	American Indian, Eskimo, or Aleut					
		Total	Female	Age			
				Under 5 years	16 years and over	18 years and over	18 to 20 years
Alaska Native Village Statistical Area[1]							
Kasigluk	425	405	212	63	233	213	19
Kiana	385	360	179	63	193	181	17
King Cove	451	177	78	19	116	110	7
King Salmon	696	108	51	12	71	64	8
Kipnuk	470	458	203	75	281	263	20
Kivalina	317	309	145	46	174	162	10
Klawack	722	392	179	45	265	246	25
Knik	272	31	14	2	21	20	2

[Continued]

★ 170 ★

Population of Alaska Native Village Statistical Areas, by Age and Sex: 1990, Kasigluk-Tokotna - I

[Continued]

American Indian/ Alaska Native Area State	All persons	American Indian, Eskimo, or Aleut					
		Total	Female	Age			
				Under 5 years	16 years and over	18 years and over	18 to 20 years
Kobuk	69	62	27	13	29	27	2
Kokhanok	152	137	69	19	83	77	1
Koliganek	181	174	92	35	102	97	4
Kongiganak	294	286	124	54	166	159	11
Kotlik	461	447	223	83	252	234	17
Kotzebue	2,751	2,067	1,068	357	1,225	1,159	103
Koyuk	231	219	100	33	135	128	13
Koyukuk	126	123	53	21	75	75	4
Kwethluk	558	538	256	70	331	316	26
Kwigillingok	278	264	124	35	181	171	14
Lake Minchumina	32	6	2	1	2	2	-
Larsen Bay	147	124	61	17	84	78	13
Levelock	105	87	36	12	58	55	3
Lime Village	42	40	19	5	25	24	1
Lower Kalskag	291	286	135	44	164	154	9
McGrath	528	248	133	31	147	125	8
Manley Hot Springs	96	14	6	2	9	9	-
Manokotak	385	368	175	62	218	210	19
Marshall	273	253	123	31	158	144	6
Mary's Igloo	-	-	-	-	-	-	-
Medfra	-	-	-	-	-	-	-
Mekoryuk	177	176	73	10	127	121	6
Mentasta Lake	96	70	32	9	44	41	3
Minto	218	212	94	25	133	129	6
Mountain Village	674	614	308	109	344	310	40
Naknek	575	236	121	36	142	135	5
Napaimute	3	3	2	-	3	3	1
Napakiak	318	300	144	39	182	177	15
Napaskiak	328	311	158	54	184	167	17
Nelson Lagoon	83	67	33	8	49	46	4
Nenana	393	188	84	26	118	111	9
Newhalen	160	151	73	24	84	81	9
New Stuyahok	391	375	177	67	229	214	16
Newtok	207	193	95	29	112	102	13
Nightmute	153	146	73	15	97	90	8
Nikolai	109	97	42	5	66	64	4
Nikolski	35	29	11	1	25	25	1
Ninilchik	10,523	455	232	48	288	270	12

[Continued]

Population of Alaska Native Village Statistical Areas, by Age and Sex: 1990, Kasigluk-Tokotna - I

[Continued]

American Indian/ Alaska Native Area State	All persons	American Indian, Eskimo, or Aleut					
		Total	Female	Age			
				Under 5 years	16 years and over	18 years and over	18 to 20 years
Noatak	333	322	143	47	204	190	20
Nondalton	178	159	76	28	91	88	3
Noorvik	531	498	231	85	286	266	20
Northway	113	107	47	14	60	55	5
Nuiqsut	354	328	152	63	182	174	7
Nulato	359	348	174	54	198	188	8
Nunapitchuk	378	367	171	54	237	224	20
Ohogamiut	-	-	-	-	-	-	-
Old Harbor	284	252	118	36	155	146	15
Oscarville	57	52	24	7	34	31	4
Ouzinkie	209	178	82	21	128	118	8
Paimiut	-	-	-	-	-	-	-
Pedro Bay	42	38	25	1	28	27	1
Pelican	222	65	34	6	43	42	7
Perryville	108	102	45	9	64	60	5
Pilot Point	53	45	22	7	29	28	3
Pilot Station	463	440	207	94	236	223	19
Pitkas Point	135	129	66	24	74	68	3
Platinum	64	59	24	8	39	34	1
Point Hope	639	587	261	108	303	287	19
Point Lay	139	113	47	15	79	73	10
Portage Creek	5	3	1	1	2	2	-
Port Graham	166	150	69	15	101	98	7
Port Heiden	119	86	36	13	55	54	-
Port Lions	222	150	65	21	97	93	8
Quinhagak	501	470	222	63	301	280	24
Rampart	68	64	26	10	40	38	1
Red Devil	53	27	15	4	17	16	1
Ruby	170	126	52	17	74	69	1
Russian Mission	246	233	110	43	119	106	6
St. George	138	131	70	17	78	77	1
St. Mary's	31	20	9	4	12	11	-
St. Michael	295	269	128	39	156	136	14
St. Paul	763	504	219	58	321	312	25
Salamatof	999	104	22	2	96	95	3
Sand Point	878	433	174	55	276	260	12
Savoonga	519	494	245	69	317	299	19
Saxman	369	284	132	33	187	180	13

[Continued]

Population of Alaska Native Village Statistical Areas, by Age and Sex: 1990, Kasigluk-Tokotna - I

[Continued]

American Indian/ Alaska Native Area State	All persons	American Indian, Eskimo, or Aleut					
		Total	Female	Age			
				Under 5 years	16 years and over	18 years and over	18 to 20 years
Scammon Bay	343	331	165	64	183	164	12
Selawik	596	569	258	106	308	287	18
Seldovia	316	48	19	4	39	38	3
Shageluk	139	132	58	23	78	77	1
Shaktoolik	178	168	78	30	100	94	9
Sheldon Point	109	101	48	23	58	52	4
Shishmaref	456	431	207	66	250	233	22
Shungnak	223	211	110	32	126	118	8
Slana	63	4	2	-	2	2	-
Sleetmute	106	92	50	10	66	63	5
Solomon	6	6	1	-	6	6	-
South Naknek	136	108	45	16	69	67	2
Stebbins	400	379	189	71	202	179	21
Stevens Village	102	93	37	8	62	57	2
Stony River	51	45	24	7	30	30	2
Tokotna	38	17	10	3	9	9	1

Source: Summary Population and Housing Characteristics, United States Summary, United States Bureau of the Census, CP H-1, pp. 402-416. *Notes:* A dash (-) indicates that no data were given in the original source. 1. Alaska Native villages (ANV's) constitute tribes, bands, clans, groups, villages, communities, or associations in Alaska that are recognized pursuant to the Alaska Native Claims Settlement Act of 1972, Public Law 92-203. Because ANV's do not have legally designated boundaries, the Census Bureau has established Alaska Native village statistical areas (ANVSA's) for statistical purposes. For the 1990 census, the Census Bureau cooperated with officials of the nonprofit corporation within each participating Alaska Native Regional Corporation (ANRC), as well as other knowledgeable officials, to delineate boundaries that encompass the settles area associated with each ANV.

Population of Alaska Native Village Statistical Areas, by Age and Sex: 1990, Kasigluk-Tokotna - II

American Indian/ Alaska Native Area State	American Indian, Eskimo, or Aleut						
	Age						Median age
	21 to 24 years	25 to 44 years	45 to 54 years	55 to 59 years	60 to 64 years	65 years and over	
Alaska Native Village Statistical Area[1]							
Kasigluk	23	108	25	10	3	25	19.7
Kiana	16	83	24	11	9	21	18.2
King Cove	12	48	23	11	3	6	25.8
King Salmon	8	35	5	2	3	3	21.5
Kipnuk	33	132	33	16	7	22	23.0

[Continued]

★ 171 ★

Population of Alaska Native Village Statistical Areas, by Age and Sex: 1990, Kasigluk-Tokotna - II

[Continued]

American Indian/ Alaska Native Area State	American Indian, Eskimo, or Aleut						
	Age						Median age
	21 to 24 years	25 to 44 years	45 to 54 years	55 to 59 years	60 to 64 years	65 years and over	
Kivalina	22	74	23	10	7	16	19.0
Klawack	28	113	39	13	10	18	24.7
Knik	3	9	4	-	-	2	24.5
Kobuk	2	14	2	1	-	6	14.5
Kokhanok	9	44	8	3	4	8	24.5
Koliganek	11	54	6	6	5	11	22.9
Kongiganak	23	79	18	7	3	18	22.3
Kotlik	29	120	29	11	8	20	19.9
Kotzebue	144	607	112	53	41	99	21.9
Koyuk	14	56	22	6	4	13	23.0
Koyukuk	4	48	6	4	1	8	26.7
Kwethluk	35	144	32	22	13	44	23.4
Kwigillingok	24	79	19	6	6	23	25.2
Lake Minchumina	-	1	-	1	-	-	8.3
Larsen Bay	10	31	7	5	4	8	22.4
Levelock	5	27	6	1	4	9	26.9
Lime Village	1	13	1	2	1	5	27.5
Lower Kalskag	20	78	19	8	4	16	21.5
McGrath	12	66	20	5	3	11	18.5
Manley Hot Springs	1	4	2	1	-	1	30.0
Manokotak	27	95	32	11	9	17	22.6
Marshall	13	81	16	10	4	14	24.5
Mary's Igloo	-	-	-	-	-	-	-
Medfra	-	-	-	-	-	-	-
Mekoryuk	10	57	17	3	12	16	29.5
Mentasta Lake	5	17	6	2	1	7	22.0
Minto	9	65	14	5	4	26	27.0
Mountain Village	45	135	39	15	15	21	18.3
Naknek	8	71	24	7	5	15	26.0
Napaimute	1	-	-	-	1	-	23.5
Napakiak	19	81	24	10	5	23	23.6
Napaskiak	16	80	17	9	12	16	19.8
Nelson Lagoon	7	24	6	-	-	5	25.7
Nenana	2	61	12	5	7	15	26.9
Newhalen	7	40	11	3	7	4	19.8
New Stuyahok	28	105	32	6	6	21	22.5
Newtok	13	50	11	5	3	7	19.3
Nightmute	13	39	8	6	6	10	23.5

[Continued]

★ 171 ★

Population of Alaska Native Village Statistical Areas, by Age and Sex: 1990, Kasigluk-Tokotna - II

[Continued]

American Indian/ Alaska Native Area State	American Indian, Eskimo, or Aleut						
	Age						Median age
	21 to 24 years	25 to 44 years	45 to 54 years	55 to 59 years	60 to 64 years	65 years and over	
Nikolai	7	30	7	8	1	7	27.2
Nikolski	-	3	5	3	3	10	57.5
Ninilchik	17	147	31	21	11	31	28.2
Noatak	27	84	22	15	8	14	22.4
Nondalton	9	40	11	10	5	10	22.9
Noorvik	37	121	26	18	20	24	20.4
Northway	3	22	8	4	3	10	18.8
Nuiqsut	27	83	28	13	2	14	21.8
Nulato	19	102	19	11	13	16	22.4
Nunapitchuk	24	108	31	7	12	22	24.4
Ohogamiut	-	-	-	-	-	-	-
Old Harbor	18	73	13	9	7	11	22.2
Oscarville	4	12	6	2	1	2	22.0
Ouzinkie	7	54	21	5	9	14	30.7
Paimiut	-	-	-	-	-	-	-
Pedro Bay	-	12	3	4	3	4	35.0
Pelican	6	21	2	5	-	1	22.9
Perryville	5	29	10	1	3	7	24.3
Pilot Point	3	15	3	-	-	4	24.5
Pilot Station	33	104	24	13	15	15	18.4
Pitkas Point	11	39	8	2	1	4	21.3
Platinum	4	15	7	4	1	2	24.5
Point Hope	25	162	34	21	7	19	16.8
Point Lay	10	30	14	3	2	4	23.5
Portage Creek	-	1	-	-	-	1	27.5
Port Graham	7	42	20	6	7	9	29.5
Port Heiden	6	32	8	2	4	2	27.5
Port Lions	6	43	13	9	3	11	26.7
Quinhagak	27	134	36	14	17	28	24.3
Rampart	7	16	8	2	2	2	23.8
Red Devil	1	9	1	1	1	2	26.3
Ruby	7	33	13	2	2	11	24.1
Russian Mission	16	52	10	4	4	14	16.3
St. George	3	48	3	7	6	9	28.1
St. Mary's	-	9	1	-	1	-	26.7
St. Michael	11	69	17	7	8	10	18.3
St. Paul	36	158	42	17	9	25	24.9
Salamatof	13	62	5	3	2	7	31.3

[Continued]

★ 171 ★

Population of Alaska Native Village Statistical Areas, by Age and Sex: 1990, Kasigluk-Tokotna - II
[Continued]

American Indian/ Alaska Native Area State	American Indian, Eskimo, or Aleut						
	Age						Median age
	21 to 24 years	25 to 44 years	45 to 54 years	55 to 59 years	60 to 64 years	65 years and over	
Sand Point	25	141	36	20	10	16	25.7
Savoonga	41	141	42	22	11	23	24.3
Saxman	14	92	31	10	4	16	27.4
Scammon Bay	22	78	22	7	2	21	17.7
Selawik	24	162	20	11	18	34	18.3
Seldovia	1	16	6	6	1	5	34.4
Shageluk	11	38	4	6	7	10	24.7
Shaktoolik	10	48	6	3	3	15	21.3
Sheldon Point	8	22	8	4	3	3	20.2
Shishmaref	32	107	31	14	14	13	20.4
Shungnak	16	57	7	7	10	13	22.7
Slana	-	1	-	-	1	-	27.0
Sleetmute	7	16	14	11	4	6	32.0
Solomon	-	2	-	-	1	3	63.5
South Naknek	9	33	7	7	-	9	26.1
Stebbins	23	87	14	5	9	20	17.1
Stevens Village	2	26	11	3	2	11	30.8
Stony River	4	19	2	-	1	2	25.9
Tokotna	-	4	3	-	1	-	20.5

Source: Summary Population and Housing Characteristics, United States Summary, United States Bureau of the Census, CP H-1, pp. 402-416. *Notes:* A dash (-) indicates that no data were given in the original source. 1. Alaska Native villages (ANV's) constitute tribes, bands, clans, groups, villages, communities, or associations in Alaska that are recognized pursuant to the Alaska Native Claims Settlement Act of 1972, Public Law 92-203. Because ANV's do not have legally designated boundaries, the Census Bureau has established Alaska Native village statistical areas (ANVSA's) for statistical purposes. For the 1990 census, the Census Bureau cooperated with officials of the nonprofit corporation within each participating Alaska Native Regional Corporation (ANRC), as well as other knowledgeable officials, to delineate boundaries that encompass the settles area associated with each ANV.

★ 172 ★

Population of Alaska Native Village Statistical Areas, by Age and Sex: 1990, Tanacross-Yokutat - I

American Indian/Alaska Native Area State	All persons	American Indian, Eskimo, or Aleut					
		Total	Female	Age			
				Under 5 years	16 years and over	18 years and over	18 to 20 years
Alaska Native Village Statistical Area[1]							
Tanacross	106	100	45	6	72	68	1
Tanana	345	270	129	31	175	164	10

[Continued]

Population of Alaska Native Village Statistical Areas, by Age and Sex: 1990, Tanacross-Yokutat - I

[Continued]

American Indian/Alaska Native Area State	All persons	American Indian, Eskimo, or Aleut					
		Total	Female	Age			
				Under 5 years	16 years and over	18 years and over	18 to 20 years
Tatitlek	119	103	54	15	68	64	7
Tazlina	247	57	29	8	33	32	2
Telida	11	10	2	1	4	4	-
Teller	151	131	58	23	74	69	1
Tenakee Springs	94	9	6	-	9	9	-
Tetlin	87	83	33	7	60	56	4
Togiak	613	535	267	84	340	318	25
Tok	935	117	63	17	69	65	3
Toksook Bay	420	401	197	62	257	241	33
Tulusak	358	342	170	54	196	187	14
Tuntutuliak	300	290	134	44	184	172	14
Tununak	316	304	142	45	190	178	13
Twin Hills	66	61	28	12	41	41	1
Tyonek	154	142	59	8	103	94	6
Ugashik	7	6	1	-	6	6	2
Ukivok	-	-	-	-	-	-	-
Unalakleet	714	584	279	80	356	330	16
Unalaska	3,089	259	109	31	186	175	11
Venetie	182	171	82	17	106	99	7
Wainwright	492	464	227	64	270	260	14
Wales	161	143	64	26	86	83	6
White Mountain	180	158	72	23	100	95	2
Wiseman	33	5	4	-	1	1	-
Yokutat	534	294	145	34	199	187	15

Source: *Summary Population and Housing Characteristics, United States Summary*, United States Bureau of the Census, CP H-1, pp. 402-416. *Notes:* A dash (-) indicates that no data were given in the original source. 1. Alaska Native villages (ANV's) constitute tribes, bands, clans, groups, villages, communities, or associations in Alaska that are recognized pursuant to the Alaska Native Claims Settlement Act of 1972, Public Law 92-203. Because ANV's do not have legally designated boundaries, the Census Bureau has established Alaska Native village statistical areas (ANVSA's) for statistical purposes. For the 1990 census, the Census Bureau cooperated with officials of the nonprofit corporation within each participating Alaska Native Regional Corporation (ANRC), as well as other knowledgeable officials, to delineate boundaries that encompass the settles area associated with each ANV.

★ 173 ★

Population of Alaska Native Village Statistical Areas, by Age and Sex: 1990, Tanacross-Yokutat - II

American Indian/Alaska Native Area State	American Indian, Eskimo, or Aleut						
	Age						Median age
	21 to 24 years	25 to 44 years	45 to 54 years	55 to 59 years	60 to 64 years	65 years and over	
Alaska Native Village Statistical Area[1]							
Tanacross	3	31	16	3	2	12	36.5
Tanana	11	80	17	11	10	25	27.7
Tatitlek	3	37	7	2	4	4	26.8
Tazlina	2	17	4	4	1	2	24.3
Telida	-	4	-	-	-	-	14.0
Teller	6	38	11	4	5	4	22.4
Tenakee Springs	-	1	-	2	1	5	67.5
Tetlin	5	22	7	5	3	10	28.9
Togiak	40	160	31	19	13	30	23.4
Tok	7	33	9	6	1	6	21.9
Toksook Bay	35	97	39	8	13	16	21.8
Tulusak	29	91	16	9	10	18	21.2
Tuntutuliak	27	78	22	7	10	14	23.1
Tununak	22	80	26	12	7	18	23.6
Twin Hills	4	20	5	3	1	7	28.9
Tyonek	12	43	15	7	2	9	27.3
Ugashik	1	1	-	-	1	1	30.0
Ukivok	-	-	-	-	-	-	-
Unalakleet	24	166	46	17	21	40	24.6
Unalaska	13	105	15	11	9	11	28.4
Venetie	7	57	7	8	2	11	24.7
Wainwright	28	133	32	21	14	18	23.2
Wales	4	47	6	4	4	12	25.6
White Mountain	6	53	12	5	3	14	29.0
Wiseman	-	1	-	-	-	-	8.5
Yokutat	19	91	22	5	13	22	26.4

Source: Summary Population and Housing Characteristics, United States Summary, United States Bureau of the Census, CP H-1, pp. 402-416. *Notes:* A dash (-) indicates that no data were given in the original source. 1. Alaska Native villages (ANV's) constitute tribes, bands, clans, groups, villages, communities, or associations in Alaska that are recognized pursuant to the Alaska Native Claims Settlement Act of 1972, Public Law 92-203. Because ANV's do not have legally designated boundaries, the Census Bureau has established Alaska Native village statistical areas (ANVSA's) for statistical purposes. For the 1990 census, the Census Bureau cooperated with officials of the nonprofit corporation within each participating Alaska Native Regional Corporation (ANRC), as well as other knowledgeable officials, to delineate boundaries that encompass the settles area associated with each ANV.

★ 174 ★

Population of American Indian and Alaska Native Areas, by Age and Sex: 1990, Acoma-Colville - I

American Indian/Alaska Native Area State	All persons	American Indian, Eskimo, or Aleut					
		Total	Female	Age			
				Under 5 years	16 years and over	18 years and over	18 to 20 years
American Indian reservation and Trust Lands[1,2]							
All areas	807,817	437,358	222,979	57,235	267,407	249,558	22,540
Acoma Pueblo and Trust Lands, NM	2,590	2,551	1,359	245	1,650	1,554	118
Acoma Trust Lands, NM	-	-	-	-	-	-	-
Agua Caliente Reservation, CA	20,206	117	62	7	97	94	6
Alabama and Caushatta Reservation, TX	478	477	224	32	336	311	24
Alamo Navajo Reservation, NM	1,271	1,228	669	131	761	697	86
Allegany Reservation, NY	7,315	1,062	541	117	717	682	53
Alturas Rancheria, CA	5	5	3	-	5	5	1
Annette Islands Reserve, AK	1,469	1,209	560	137	757	721	47
Augustine Reservation, CA	-	-	-	-	-	-	-
Bad River Reservation, WI	1,070	868	440	99	539	512	28
Barana Rancheria, CA	537	373	181	33	262	246	19
Bay Mills Reservation, MI	461	403	184	49	237	220	24
Benton Paiute Reservation, CA	63	52	23	5	34	32	3
Berry Creek Rancheria, CA	2	2	1	-	2	2	-
Big Bend Rancheria, CA	3	3	1	-	2	2	-
Big Cypress Reservation, FL	484	447	235	33	314	287	36
Big Lagoon Rancheria, CA	22	19	7	2	13	12	1
Big Pine Rancheria, CA	452	331	189	31	210	193	23
Big Sandy Rancheria, CA	51	38	23	4	28	28	1
Big Valley Rancheria, CA	108	90	53	6	65	61	3
Bishop Rancheria, CA	1,408	935	467	110	590	563	40

[Continued]

★ 174 ★

Population of American Indian and Alaska Native Areas, by Age and Sex: 1990, Acoma-Colville - I
[Continued]

American Indian/Alaska Native Area State	All persons	American Indian, Eskimo, or Aleut					
		Total	Female	Age			
				Under 5 years	16 years and over	18 years and over	18 to 20 years
Blackfeet Reservation, MT	8,549	7,025	3,556	918	4,228	3,960	289
Blue Lake Rancheria, CA	58	30	13	2	24	22	-
Bois Forte (Nett Lake) Reservation, MN	358	346	167	38	216	209	21
Bridgeport Colony, CA	49	37	23	7	21	20	-
Brighton Reservation, FL	524	402	215	33	254	239	15
Burns Paiute Reservation and Trust Lands, OR	163	151	79	20	99	96	7
Cabazon Reservation, CA	819	20	12	2	10	9	1
Cahuilla Reservation, CA	104	82	45	14	47	46	1
Campo Reservation, CA	281	143	78	20	91	87	5
Camp Verde Reservation, AZ	618	569	285	89	337	319	27
Canoncito Reservation, NM	1,189	1,177	617	168	720	669	57
Captain Grande Reservation, CA	-	-	-	-	-	-	-
Carson Colony, NV	248	235	133	26	160	149	9
Catawba Reservation (state), SC	174	124	63	15	78	74	8
Cataragus Reservation, NY	2,178	2,051	1,080	223	1,358	1,280	105
Cedarville Rancheria, CA	8	6	2	-	4	4	-
Chehalis Reservation, WA	491	308	150	54	170	164	14
Chemehuevi Reservation, CA	358	95	49	14	62	56	4
Cheyenne River Reservation, SD	7,743	5,100	2,652	731	2,884	2,657	235
Chicken Ranch Rancheria, CA	73	10	4	-	5	4	1
Chitimacha Reservation, LA	286	212	100	33	126	118	10
Cochiti Pueblo, NM	1,342	666	336	63	462	434	37

[Continued]

★ 174 ★

Population of American Indian and Alaska Native Areas, by Age and Sex: 1990, Acoma-Colville - I
[Continued]

American Indian/Alaska Native Area State	All persons	American Indian, Eskimo, or Aleut						
		Total	Female	Age				
				Under 5 years	16 years and over	18 years and over	18 to 20 years
Cacopah Reservation, AZ	515	436	230	49	267	252	26
Coer d'Alene Reservation and Trust Lands, ID	5,802	749	361	87	480	436	37
Coer d'Alene Reservation, ID	5,800	749	361	87	480	436	37
Coer d'Alene Trust Lands, ID	2	-	-	-	-	-	-
Cold Springs Rancheria, CA	192	159	83	34	85	81	4
Colorado River Reservation	7,865	2,345	1,221	277	1,430	1,340	120
Arizona	6,790	2,321	1,205	275	1,415	1,325	120
California	1,075	24	16	2	15	15	-
Calusa (Cachil Dehe) Rancheria, CA	22	19	10	-	11	11	-
Colville Reservation, WA	6,957	3,788	1,886	443	2,402	2,263	187

Source: Summary Population and Housing Characteristics, United States Summary, United States Bureau of the Census, CP H-1, pp. 402-416. *Notes:* A dash (-) indicates no data were given in the original source. 1. Federal American Indian reservations are areas with boundaries established by treaty, statute, and/or executive or court order, and recognized by the federal government as territory in which American Indian tribes have jurisdiction. State reservations are lands held in trust by state governments for the use and benefit of a given tribe. The reservations and their boundaries were identified for the 1990 census by the Bureau of Indian Affairs (BIA), Department of Interior (for federal reservations), and state governments (for state reservations). The names of American Indian reservations recognized by state governments, but not by the federal government, are followed by "state." Areas composed of reservation lands that are administered jointly and/or are claimed by two reservations, as identified by the BIA, are called "joint areas," and are treated as separate American Indian reservations for census purposes. Federal reservations may cross state boundaries, and federal and state reservations may cross county, county subdivision, and place boundaries. For reservations that cross state boundaries, only the portion of the reservations in a given state are shown in the data products for that state; the entire reservations are shown in data products for the United States. 2. Trust lands are property associated with a particular American Indian reservation or tribe, held in trust by the federal government. Trust lands may be held in trust either for a tribe (tribal trust lands) or for an individual member of a tribe (individual trust land). Trust lands recognized for the 1990 census comprised all tribal trust lands and inhabited individual trust lands located outside of a reservation boundary. As with other American Indian areas, trust lands may be located in more than one state. Only the trust lands in a given state are shown in the data products for that state; all trust lands associated with a reservation or tribe are shown in data products for the United States. The Census Bureau first reported data for tribal trust lands for the 1980 census.

★ 175 ★

Population of American Indian and Alaska Native Areas, by Age and Sex: 1990, Acoma-Colville - II

American Indian/Alaska Native Area State	American Indian, Eskimo, or Aleut						
	Age						Median age
	21 to 24 years	25 to 44 years	45 to 54 years	55 to 59 years	60 to 64 years	65 years and over	
American Indian reservation and Trust Lands[1,2]							
All areas	26,313	118,461	33,196	13,129	10,842	25,077	22.3
Acoma Pueblo and Trust Lands, NM	149	713	198	92	88	196	25.3
Acoma Trust Lands, NM	-	-	-	-	-	-	-

[Continued]

Population of American Indian and Alaska Native Areas, by Age and Sex: 1990, Acoma-Colville - II
[Continued]

American Indian/Alaska Native Area State	American Indian, Eskimo, or Aleut						
	Age						Median age
	21 to 24 years	25 to 44 years	45 to 54 years	55 to 59 years	60 to 64 years	65 years and over	
Agua Caliente Reservation, CA	5	42	12	7	4	18	37.3
Alabama and Caushatta Reservation, TX	26	123	56	19	19	44	28.0
Alamo Navajo Reservation, NM	83	335	82	34	18	59	20.9
Allegany Reservation, NY	70	284	90	51	27	107	26.5
Alturas Rancheria, CA	-	-	1	-	1	2	63.5
Annette Islands Reserve, AK	68	362	110	30	39	65	25.1
Augustine Reservation, CA	-	-	-	-	-	-	-
Bad River Reservation, WI	47	252	75	35	26	49	25.2
Barana Rancheria, CA	34	117	40	18	9	9	26.0
Bay Mills Reservation, MI	34	102	23	11	10	16	20.2
Benton Paiute Reservation, CA	2	7	7	2	2	9	30.0
Berry Creek Rancheria, CA	-	-	-	-	-	2	85.0
Big Bend Rancheria, CA	-	-	-	-	-	2	67.5
Big Cypress Reservation, FL	17	133	44	9	15	33	26.5
Big Lagoon Rancheria, CA	1	7	-	1	1	1	30.8
Big Pine Rancheria, CA	21	87	28	7	9	18	21.6
Big Sandy Rancheria, CA	4	7	4	1	2	9	35.0
Big Valley Rancheria, CA	5	24	9	4	4	12	34.2
Bishop Rancheria, CA	45	286	67	38	33	54	25.7
Blackfeet Reservation, MT	400	1,931	586	196	167	391	22.7
Blue Lake Rancheria, CA	1	9	1	3	2	6	38.3
Bois Forte (Nett Lake) Reservation, MN	20	99	25	11	10	23	23.6

[Continued]

Population of American Indian and Alaska Native Areas, by Age and Sex: 1990, Acoma-Colville - II

[Continued]

American Indian/Alaska Native Area State	American Indian, Eskimo, or Aleut						Median age
	Age						
	21 to 24 years	25 to 44 years	45 to 54 years	55 to 59 years	60 to 64 years	65 years and over	
Bridgeport Colony, CA	-	12	3	2	1	2	26.3
Brighton Reservation, FL	23	114	32	6	10	39	25.0
Burns Paiute Reservation and Trust Lands, OR	14	43	11	9	1	11	24.9
Cabazon Reservation, CA	-	2	3	2	1	-	16.5
Cahuilla Reservation, CA	3	27	5	2	3	5	25.6
Campo Reservation, CA	6	43	11	5	5	12	26.9
Camp Verde Reservation, AZ	31	157	46	11	12	35	21.6
Canoncito Reservation, NM	93	344	94	31	19	31	21.8
Captain Grande Reservation, CA	-	-	-	-	-	-	-
Carson Colony, NV	14	81	18	8	9	10	27.0
Catawba Reservation (state), SC	3	32	11	4	2	14	25.7
Cataragus Reservation, NY	116	577	162	87	63	170	26.0
Cedarville Rancheria, CA	-	2	-	-	1	1	35.0
Chehalis Reservation, WA	30	79	16	3	5	17	20.3
Chemehuevi Reservation, CA	5	32	4	1	3	7	24.7
Cheyenne River Reservation, SD	264	1,330	341	139	124	224	19.2
Chicken Ranch Rancheria, CA	1	-	2	-	-	-	16.0
Chitimacha Reservation, LA	9	61	11	5	3	19	21.7
Cochiti Pueblo, NM	43	178	61	44	20	51	27.1
Cacopah Reservation, AZ	21	128	32	9	10	26	21.8
Coer d'Alene Reservation and Trust Lands, ID	57	192	60	20	22	48	23.0
Coer d'Alene Reservation, ID	57	192	60	20	22	48	23.0
Coer d'Alene Trust Lands, ID	-	-	-	-	-	-	-

[Continued]

★ 175 ★

Population of American Indian and Alaska Native Areas, by Age and Sex: 1990, Acoma-Colville - II
[Continued]

American Indian/Alaska Native Area State	American Indian, Eskimo, or Aleut						
	Age						Median age
	21 to 24 years	25 to 44 years	45 to 54 years	55 to 59 years	60 to 64 years	65 years and over	
Cold Springs Rancheria, CA	15	31	12	10	1	8	18.8
Colorado River Reservation	128	685	169	50	60	128	22.5
Arizona	128	680	167	49	57	124	22.4
California	-	5	2	1	3	4	35.0
Calusa (Cachil Dehe) Rancheria, CA	-	8	1	-	-	2	32.5
Colville Reservation, WA	191	1,057	303	145	96	284	24.8

Source: Summary Population and Housing Characteristics, United States Summary, United States Bureau of the Census, CP H-1, pp. 402-416. Notes: A dash (-) indicates no data were given in the original source. 1. Federal American Indian reservations are areas with boundaries established by treaty, statute, and/or executive or court order, and recognized by the federal government as territory in which American Indian tribes have jurisdiction. State reservations are lands held in trust by state governments for the use and benefit of a given tribe. The reservations and their boundaries were identified for the 1990 census by the Bureau of Indian Affairs (BIA), Department of Interior (for federal reservations), and state governments (for state reservations). The names of American Indian reservations recognized by state governments, but not by the federal government, are followed by "state." Areas composed of reservation lands that are administered jointly and/or are claimed by two reservations, as identified by the BIA, are called "joint areas," and are treated as separate American Indian reservations for census purposes. Federal reservations may cross state boundaries, and federal and state reservations may cross county, county subdivision, and place boundaries. For reservations that cross state boundaries, only the portion of the reservations in a given state are shown in the data products for that state; the entire reservations are shown in data products for the United States. 2. Trust lands are property associated with a particular American Indian reservation or tribe, held in trust by the federal government. Trust lands may be held in trust either for a tribe (tribal trust lands) or for an individual member of a tribe (individual trust land). Trust lands recognized for the 1990 census comprised all tribal trust lands and inhabited individual trust lands located outside of a reservation boundary. As with other American Indian areas, trust lands may be located in more than one state. Only the trust lands in a given state are shown in the data products for that state; all trust lands associated with a reservation or tribe are shown in data products for the United States. The Census Bureau first reported data for tribal trust lands for the 1980 census.

★ 176 ★

Population of American Indian and Alaska Native Areas, by Age and Sex: 1990, Coos-Grindstone Creek - I

American Indian/Alaska Native Area State	All persons	American Indian, Eskimo, or Aleut					
		Total	Female	Age			
				Under 5 years	16 years and over	18 years and over	18 to 20 years
American Indian reservation and Trust Lands[1,2]							
Coos, Lower Umpaqua, and Siuslaw Reservation, OR	4	1	1	-	1	1	-
Cortina Rancherio, CA	30	22	9	2	17	16	1
Coushatta Reservation, LA	36	33	15	2	24	18	1
Cow Creek Reservation, OR	58	11	6	4	6	6	-
Coyote Valley Reservation, CA	135	122	60	20	65	60	6
Crow Reservation and Trust Lands, MT	6,370	4,724	2,392	585	2,837	2,645	225
Crow Reservation, MT	6,366	4,724	2,392	585	2,837	2,645	225
Crow Trust Lands, MT	4	-	-	-	-	-	-

[Continued]

★ 176 ★

Population of American Indian and Alaska Native Areas, by Age and Sex: 1990, Coos-Grindstone Creek - I

[Continued]

American Indian/Alaska Native Area State	All persons	American Indian, Eskimo, or Aleut					
		Total	Female	Age			
				Under 5 years	16 years and over	18 years and over	18 to 20 years
Crow Creek Reservation, SD	1,756	1,531	721	211	857	791	69
Cuyapaipe Reservation, CA	-	-	-	-	-	-	-
Deer Creek Reservation, MN	186	6	4	-	6	5	1
Devils Lake Sioux Reservation, ND	3,588	2,676	1,340	413	1,461	1,350	148
Dresslerville Colony, NV	152	144	78	23	93	90	6
Dry Creek Rancheria, CA	75	38	22	6	25	24	3
Duck Valley Reservation	1,101	1,022	501	109	655	615	45
Idaho	193	188	86	18	116	107	9
Nevada	908	834	415	91	539	508	36
Duckwater Reservation, NV	135	115	61	16	75	74	4
Eastern Cherokee Reservation, NC	6,527	5,388	2,681	554	3,614	3,400	300
Elk Valley Rancheria, CA	77	32	21	2	22	20	1
Ely Colony, NV	59	52	27	4	34	30	3
Enterprise Rancheria, CA	5	5	3	-	5	5	-
Fallon Colony, NV	165	150	92	26	90	82	5
Fallon Reservation, NV	381	356	195	27	247	238	12
Flanadreau Reservation, SD	279	249	126	29	150	142	13
Flathead Reservation, MT	21,259	5,130	2,476	591	3,347	3,139	357
Fond du Lac Reservation, MN	3,229	1,106	528	172	613	586	47
Fort Apache Reservation, AZ	10,394	9,825	5,044	1,539	5,734	5,372	471
Fort Belknap Reservation and Trust Lands, MT	2,508	2,338	1,164	337	1,390	1,390	1,292
Fort Berthold Reservation, ND	5,395	2,999	1,533	403	1,818	1,694	155
Fort Bidwell Reservation, CA	118	107	53	10	60	58	3
Fort Hall Reservation and Trust Lands, ID	5,114	3,035	1,548	376	1,942	1,819	177
Fort Hall Reservation, ID	5,060	3,035	1,548	376	1,942	1,819	177
Fort Hall Trust Lands, ID	54	-	-	-	-	-	-
Fort Independence Reservation, CA	69	38	19	1	30	30	2
Fort McDermitt Reservation, NV	396	387	178	43	260	241	26
Fort McDowell Reservation, AZ	640	560	281	88	326	313	27

[Continued]

★ 176 ★

Population of American Indian and Alaska Native Areas, by Age and Sex: 1990, Coos-Grindstone Creek - I

[Continued]

American Indian/Alaska Native Area State	All persons	American Indian, Eskimo, or Aleut					
		Total	Female	Age			
				Under 5 years	16 years and over	18 years and over	18 to 20 years
Fort Mojave Reservation and Trust Lands,AZ-CA-NV	758	592	350	99	347	325	26
Fort Mojave Reservation	496	340	211	74	180	166	15
Arizona	454	340	211	74	180	166	15
California	42	-	-	-	-	-	-
Nevada	-	-	-	-	-	-	-
Fort Mojave Trust Lands, CA	262	252	139	25	167	159	11
Fort Peck Reservation, MT	10,595	5,782	2,953	890	3,482	3,272	296
Fort Yuma (Quechan) Reservation	2,084	1,160	640	153	723	680	62
Arizona	16	-	-	-	-	-	-
California	2,068	1,160	640	153	723	680	62
Gila Bend Reservation and Trust Lands, AZ	-	-	-	-	-	-	-
Gila River Reservation, AZ	9,540	9,116	4,780	1,232	5,629	5,290	465
Golden Hill Reservation, CT (state)	10	2	-	-	2	2	2
Goshute Reservation	99	98	48	6	67	64	3
Nevada	23	23	11	2	12	12	1
Utah	76	75	37	4	55	52	2
Grand Portage Reservation, MN	306	207	111	25	143	139	5
Grand Ronde Reservation, OR	57	1	-	-	1	1	-
Grand Traverse Reservation and Trust Lands, MI	228	208	122	28	129	116	10
Grand Traverse Reservation, MI	12	11	8	2	8	8	-
Grand Traverse Trust Lands, MI	216	197	114	26	121	108	10
Greenville Rancheria, CA	24	7	5	-	7	7	-
Grindstone Creek Rancheria, CA	103	102	54	12	56	52	9

Source: Summary Population and Housing Characteristics, United States Summary, United States Bureau of the Census, CP H-1, pp. 402-416. *Notes:* A dash (-) indicates no data were given in the original source. 1. Federal American Indian reservations are areas with boundaries established by treaty, statute, and/or executive or court order, and recognized by the federal government as territory in which American Indian tribes have jurisdiction. State reservations are lands held in trust by state governments for the use and benefit of a given tribe. The reservations and their boundaries were identified for the 1990 census by the Bureau of Indian Affairs (BIA), Department of Interior (for federal reservations), and state governments (for state reservations). The names of American Indian reservations recognized by state governments, but not by the federal government, are followed by "state." Areas composed of reservation lands that are administered jointly and/or are claimed by two reservations, as identified by the BIA, are called "joint areas," and are treated as separate American Indian reservations for census purposes. Federal reservations may cross state boundaries, and federal and state reservations may cross county, county subdivision, and place boundaries. For reservations that cross state boundaries, only the portion of the reservations in a given state are shown in the data products for that state; the entire reservations are shown in data products for the United States. 2. Trust lands are property associated with a particular American Indian reservation or tribe, held in trust by the federal government. Trust lands may be held in trust either for a tribe (tribal trust lands) or for an individual member of a tribe (individual trust land). Trust lands recognized for the 1990 census comprised all tribal trust lands and inhabited individual trust lands located outside of a reservation boundary. As with other American Indian areas, trust lands may be located in more than one state. Only the trust lands in a given state are shown in the data products for that state; all trust lands associated with a reservation or tribe are shown in data products for the United States. The Census Bureau first reported data for tribal trust lands for the 1980 census.

★ 177 ★

Population of American Indian and Alaska Native Areas, by Age and Sex: 1990, Coos-Grindstone Creek - II

American Indian/Alaska Native Area State	American Indian, Eskimo, or Aleut						
	Age						Median age
	21 to 24 years	25 to 44 years	45 to 54 years	55 to 59 years	60 to 64 years	65 years and over	
American Indian reservation and Trust Lands[1,2]							
Coos, Lower Umpqua, and Siuslaw Reservation, OR	-	-	1	-	-	-	52.5
Cortina Rancherio, CA	-	9	1	-	2	3	37.5
Coushatta Reservation, LA	2	8	3	-	3	1	22.8
Cow Creek Reservation, OR	-	4	-	-	2	-	32.5
Coyote Valley Reservation, CA	10	33	2	1	2	6	17.5
Crow Reservation and Trust Lands, MT	272	1,355	386	143	99	165	21.8
Crow Reservation, MT	272	1,355	386	143	99	165	21.8
Crow Trust Lands, MT	-	-	-	-	-	-	-
Crow Creek Reservation, SD	93	373	118	31	30	77	18.9
Cuyapaipe Reservation, CA	-	-	-	-	-	-	-
Deer Creek Reservation, MN	-	1	1	-	-	2	40.0
Devils Lake Sioux Reservation, ND	169	652	173	72	42	94	18.2
Dresslerville Colony, NV	6	42	20	12	2	2	27.0
Dry Creek Rancheria, CA	6	11	3	-	-	1	23.0
Duck Valley Reservation	55	267	109	37	23	79	25.3
Idaho	10	54	11	6	6	11	23.0
Nevada	45	213	98	31	17	68	25.9
Duckwater Reservation, NV	3	34	10	8	3	12	29.7
Eastern Cherokee Reservation, NC	305	1,541	536	193	140	385	26.1
Elk Valley Rancheria, CA	1	7	5	3	1	2	28.3
Ely Colony, NV	1	12	7	1	-	6	23.5
Enterprise Rancheria, CA	-	4	-	-	-	1	29.2
Fallon Colony, NV	15	36	9	2	4	11	22.2
Fallon Reservation, NV	19	105	30	20	24	28	30.1
Flanadreau Reservation, SD	9	82	15	6	3	14	23.1
Flathead Reservation, MT	304	1,486	407	161	124	300	23.7
Fond du Lac Reservation, MN	62	311	92	22	13	39	20.1
Fort Apache Reservation, AZ	727	2,762	668	247	177	320	20.9

[Continued]

315

★ 177 ★

Population of American Indian and Alaska Native Areas, by Age and Sex: 1990, Coos-Grindstone Creek - II

[Continued]

American Indian/Alaska Native Area State	American Indian, Eskimo, or Aleut						
	Age						Median age
	21 to 24 years	25 to 44 years	45 to 54 years	55 to 59 years	60 to 64 years	65 years and over	
Fort Belknap Reservation and Trust Lands, MT	122	616	176	71	59	147	22.0
Fort Berthold Reservation, ND	164	809	239	103	83	141	21.9
Fort Bidwell Reservation, CA	3	28	3	5	8	8	22.8
Fort Hall Reservation and Trust Lands, ID	172	894	230	94	86	166	23.8
Fort Hall Reservation, ID	172	894	230	94	86	166	23.8
Fort Hall Trust Lands, ID	-	-	-	-	-	-	-
Fort Independence Reservation, CA	1	5	5	5	4	8	48.8
Fort McDermitt Reservation, NV	26	104	37	11	7	30	24.3
Fort McDowell Reservation, AZ	36	164	38	19	11	18	21.7
Fort Mojave Reservation and Trust Lands, AZ-CA-NV	43	152	43	19	13	29	21.3
Fort Mojave Reservation	29	86	13	5	6	12	17.6
Arizona	29	86	13	5	6	12	17.6
California	-	-	-	-	-	-	-
Nevada	-	-	-	-	-	-	-
Fort Mojave Trust Lands, CA	14	66	30	14	7	17	26.9
Fort Peck Reservation, MT	364	1,697	414	155	111	235	21.9
Fort Yuma (Quechan) Reservation	63	302	107	35	34	77	23.6
Arizona	-	-	-	-	-	-	-
California	63	302	107	35	34	77	23.6
Gila Bend Reservation and Trust Lands, AZ	-	-	-	-	-	-	-
Gila River Reservation, AZ	621	2,602	691	247	205	459	22.7
Golden Hill Reservation, CT (state)	-	-	-	-	-	-	20.0
Goshute Reservation	5	33	10	7	2	4	30.0
Nevada	1	6	2	1	1	-	18.5
Utah	4	27	8	6	1	4	31.3
Grand Portage Reservation, MN	7	73	28	7	7	12	31.8
Grand Ronde Reservation, OR	-	-	1	-	-	-	47.5
Grand Traverse Reservation and Trust Lands, MI	10	51	13	8	6	18	21.7
Grand Traverse Reservation, MI	1	4	-	1	1	1	32.5
Grand Traverse Trust Lands, MI	9	47	13	7	5	17	20.8

[Continued]

★ 177 ★

Population of American Indian and Alaska Native Areas, by Age and Sex: 1990, Coos-Grindstone Creek - II

[Continued]

American Indian/Alaska Native Area State	American Indian, Eskimo, or Aleut						
	Age						Median age
	21 to 24 years	25 to 44 years	45 to 54 years	55 to 59 years	60 to 64 years	65 years and over	
Greenville Rancheria, CA	-	1	3	-	-	3	52.5
Grindstone Creek Rancheria, CA	3	26	11	2	-	1	18.5

Source: Summary Population and Housing Characteristics, United States Summary, United States Bureau of the Census, CP H-1, pp. 402-416. *Notes:* A dash (-) indicates that no data were given in the original source. 1. Federal American Indian reservations are areas with boundaries established by treaty, statute, and/or executive or court order, and recognized by the federal government as territory in which American Indian tribes have jurisdiction. State reservations are lands held in trust by state governments for the use and benefit of a given tribe. The reservations and their boundaries were identified for the 1990 census by the Bureau of Indian Affairs (BIA), Department of Interior (for federal reservations), and state governments (for state reservations). The names of American Indian reservations recognized by state governments, but not by the federal government, are followed by "state." Areas composed of reservation lands that are administered jointly and/or are claimed by two reservations, as identified by the BIA, are called "joint areas," and are treated as separate American Indian reservations for census purposes. Federal reservations may cross state boundaries, and federal and state reservations may cross county, county subdivision, and place boundaries. For reservations that cross state boundaries, only the portion of the reservations in a given state are shown in the data products for that state; the entire reservations are shown in data products for the United States. 2. Trust lands are property associated with a particular American Indian reservation or tribe, held in trust by the federal government. Trust lands may be held in trust either for a tribe (tribal trust lands) or for an individual member of a tribe (individual trust land). Trust lands recognized for the 1990 census comprised all tribal trust lands and inhabited individual trust lands located outside of a reservation boundary. As with other American Indian areas, trust lands may be located in more than one state. Only the trust lands in a given state are shown in the data products for that state; all trust lands associated with a reservation or tribe are shown in data products for the United States. The Census Bureau first reported data for tribal trust lands for the 1980 census.

★ 178 ★

Population of American Indian and Alaska Native Areas, by Age and Sex: 1990, Hannahville-Lummi - I

American Indian/Alaska Native Area State	All persons	American Indian, Eskimo, or Aleut					
		Total	Female	Age			
				Under 5 years	16 years and over	18 years and over	18 to 20 years
American Indian reservation and trust Lands[1,2]							
Hannahville Community and Trust Lands, MI	181	173	83	23	101	95	15
Hannahville Community, MI	152	144	70	21	79	76	13
Hannahville Trust Lands, MI	29	29	13	2	22	19	2
Hassanamisco Reservation, MA (State)	1	1	1	-	1	1	-
Havasupai Reservation, AZ	423	400	199	58	242	233	9
Hoh Reservation, WA	96	74	36	10	44	42	7
Hollywood Reservation, FL	1,394	481	252	62	280	271	24
Hoopa Valley Reservation, CA	2,143	1,733	910	232	1,066	996	67
Hopi Reservation and Trust Lands, AZ	7,360	7,061	3,583	771	4,637	4,371	325
Hopland Rancheria, CA	189	142	82	19	77	70	5
Houlapai Reservation and Trust Lands, AZ	822	802	412	111	483	461	33

[Continued]

★ 178 ★

Population of American Indian and Alaska Native Areas, by Age and Sex: 1990, Hannahville-Lummi - I

[Continued]

American Indian/Alaska Native Area State	All persons	American Indian, Eskimo, or Aleut					
		Total	Female	Age			
				Under 5 years	16 years and over	18 years and over	18 to 20 years
Inaja-Cosmit Reservation, CA	-	-	-	-	-	-	-
Indian Township Reservation, ME	617	541	259	77	320	294	27
Iowa Reservation	172	83	36	13	47	45	1
Kansas	157	71	30	10	42	41	1
Nebraska	15	12	6	3	5	4	-
Isabella Reservation and Trust Lands, MI	22,944	795	405	99	500	476	46
Isabella Reservation, MI	22,870	740	377	95	457	439	41
Isabella Trust Lands, MI	74	55	28	4	43	37	5
Isleta Pueblo, NM	2,915	2,699	1,411	273	1,835	1,742	132
Jackson Rancheria, CA	21	13	5	1	10	9	-
Jamestown Klallam Reservation and Trust Lands, WA	22	4	1	-	2	2	-
Jamestown Klallam Reservation, WA	8	4	1	-	2	2	-
Jamestown Klallam Trust Lands, WA	14	-	-	-	-	-	-
Jamul Village, CA	-	-	-	-	-	-	-
Jemez, NM	1,750	1,738	897	191	1,121	1,068	85
Jircarilla Apache Reservation, NM	2,617	2,375	1,222	318	1,434	1,331	141
Kaibab Reservation, AZ	165	102	51	11	66	60	3
Kalispel Reservation, WA	100	91	45	17	61	56	6
Karok Reservation and Trust Lands, CA	421	33	21	6	12	12	1
Karok Reservation, CA	-	-	-	-	-	-	-
Korak Trust Lands, CA	421	33	21	6	12	12	1
Kickapoo Reservation, KS	478	370	193	62	220	207	22
Kootenai Reservation, ID	65	61	32	11	36	32	2
Lac Courte Oreilles Reservation and Trust Lands, WI	2,408	1,771	888	240	1,050	986	87
Lac du Flambeau Reservation, WI	2,434	1,432	712	201	894	850	80
Lac Vieux Desert Reservation, MI	124	119	60	22	74	67	5
Laguna Pueblo and Trust Lands, NM	3,731	3,634	1,914	304	2,481	2,356	153
La Jolla Reservation, CA	152	121	64	19	53	50	3
Lake Traverse (Sisseton) Reservation	10,733	2,821	1,438	432	1,646	1,524	156
North Dakota	237	1	-	-	1	1	-
South Dakota	10,496	2,820	1,438	432	1,645	1,523	156
L'Anse Reservation and Trust Lands, MI	3,293	724	379	88	462	435	43

[Continued]

★ 178 ★

Population of American Indian and Alaska Native Areas, by Age and Sex: 1990. Hannahville-Lummi - I

[Continued]

American Indian/Alaska Native Area State	All persons	American Indian, Eskimo, or Aleut					
		Total	Female	Age			
				Under 5 years	16 years and over	18 years and over	18 to 20 years
L'Anse Reservation, MI	3,273	717	376	88	458	431	43
L'Anse Trust Lands, MI	20	7	3	-	4	4	-
La Posta Reservation, CA	10	3	2	-	3	3	-
Las Vegas Colony, NV	80	72	27	8	47	44	3
Laytonville Rancheria, CA	142	129	67	13	89	84	9
Leech Lake Reservation, MN	8,669	3,390	1,740	474	1,974	1,857	144
Likely Rancheria, CA	-	-	-	-	-	-	-
Lone Pine Rancheria, CA	244	168	92	16	117	109	14
Lookout Rancheria, CA	17	12	5	2	8	7	1
Los Coyotes Reservation, CA	58	42	18	7	23	21	1
Lovelock Colony, NV	94	80	39	6	51	46	2
Lower Brule Reservation, SD	1,123	994	487	143	539	499	54
Lower Elwha Reservation and Trust Lands, WA	137	130	61	11	90	81	7
Lower Sioux Community, MN	259	225	109	40	126	122	17
Lummi Reservation, WA	3,147	1,594	740	212	991	916	94

Source: Summary Population and Housing Characteristics, United States Summary, United States Bureau of the Census, CP H-1, pp. 402-416. *Notes:* A dash (-) indicates that no data were given in the original source. 1. Federal American Indian reservations are areas with boundaries established by treaty, statute, and/or executive or court order, and recognized by the federal government as territory in which American Indian tribes have jurisdiction. State reservations are lands held in trust by state governments for the use and benefit of a given tribe. The reservations and their boundaries were identified for the 1990 census by the Bureau of Indian Affairs (BIA), Department of Interior (for federal reservations), and state governments (for state reservations). The names of American Indian reservations recognized by state governments, but not by the federal government, are followed by "state." Areas composed of reservation lands that are administered jointly and/or are claimed by two reservations, as identified by the BIA, are called "joint areas," and are treated as separate American Indian reservations for census purposes. Federal reservations may cross state boundaries, and federal and state reservations may cross county, county subdivision, and place boundaries. For reservations that cross state boundaries, only the portion of the reservations in a given state are shown in the data products for that state; the entire reservations are shown in data products for the United States. 2. Trust lands are property associated with a particular American Indian reservation or tribe, held in trust by the federal government. Trust lands may be held in trust either for a tribe (tribal trust lands) or for an individual member of a tribe (individual trust land). Trust lands recognized for the 1990 census comprised all tribal trust lands and inhabited individual trust lands located outside of a reservation boundary. As with other American Indian areas, trust lands may be located in more than one state. Only the trust lands in a given state are shown in the data products for that state; all trust lands associated with a reservation or tribe are shown in data products for the United States. The Census Bureau first reported data for tribal trust lands for the 1980 census.

Population of American Indian and Alaska Native Areas, by Age and Sex: 1990, Hannahville-Lummi - II

American Indian/Alaska Native Area State	American Indian, Eskimo, or Aleut						
	Age						Median age
	21 to 24 years	25 to 44 years	45 to 54 years	55 to 59 years	60 to 64 years	65 years and over	
American Indian reservation and Trust Lands[1,2]							
Hannahville Community and Trust Lands, MI	9	52	9	1	1	8	19.8
Hannahville Community, MI	7	42	6	1	1	6	19.2
Hannahville Trust Lands, MI	2	10	3	-	-	2	25.6
Hassanamisco Reservation, MA (State)	-	-	-	-	-	1	72.5
Havasupai Reservation, AZ	25	134	26	9	7	23	24.8
Hoh Reservation, WA	3	18	8	1	3	2	19.5
Hollywood Reservation, FL	34	139	36	6	9	23	21.9
Hoopa Valley Reservation, CA	95	465	152	50	43	124	23.5
Hopi Reservation and Trust Lands, AZ	367	2,087	554	226	202	610	26.3
Hopland Rancheria, CA	8	35	6	4	4	8	17.8
Houlapai Reservation and Trust Lands, AZ	47	256	45	16	21	43	23.6
Inaja-Cosmit Reservation, CA	-	-	-	-	-	-	-
Indian Township Reservation, ME	39	138	42	13	5	30	20.4
Iowa Reservation	3	31	2	3	1	4	24.5
Kansas	3	28	1	3	1	4	25.8
Nebraska	-	3	1	-	-	-	13.0
Isabella Reservation and Trust Lands, MI	56	225	56	21	26	46	23.2
Isabella Reservation, MI	52	210	49	19	24	44	22.9
Isabella Trust Lands, MI	4	15	7	2	2	2	25.8
Isleta Pueblo, NM	137	826	246	92	86	223	27.5
Jackson Rancheria, CA	2	5	1	-	-	1	30.8
Jamestown Klallam Reservation and Trust Lands, WA	-	2	-	-	-	-	25.0
Jamestown Klallam Reservation, WA	-	2	-	-	-	-	25.0
Jamestown Klallam Trust Lands, WA	-	-	-	-	-	-	-
Jamul Village, CA	-	-	-	-	-	-	-
Jemez, NM	112	543	138	38	40	112	25.1
Jircarilla Apache Reservation, NM	147	677	165	63	57	81	21.1
Kaibab Reservation, AZ	5	34	7	1	4	6	25.7
Kalispel Reservation, WA	3	26	6	2	6	7	25.7
Karok Reservation and Trust Lands, CA	1	10	-	-	-	-	11.3
Karok Reservation, CA	-	-	-	-	-	-	-

[Continued]

★ 179 ★

Population of American Indian and Alaska Native Areas, by Age and Sex: 1990, Hannahville-Lummi - II

[Continued]

American Indian/Alaska Native Area State	American Indian, Eskimo, or Aleut						
	Age						Median age
	21 to 24 years	25 to 44 years	45 to 54 years	55 to 59 years	60 to 64 years	65 years and over	
Korak Trust Lands, CA	1	10	-	-	-	-	11.3
Kickapoo Reservation, KS	18	83	27	17	13	27	21.0
Kootenai Reservation, ID	-	22	-	1	4	3	19.5
Lac Courte Oreilles Reservation and Trust Lands, WI	99	489	115	57	35	104	21.5
Lac Courte Oreilles Reservation, WI	99	489	115	57	35	104	21.5
Lac Courte Oreilles Trust Lands, WI	-	-	-	-	-	-	-
Lac du Flambeau Reservation, WI	92	391	121	58	39	69	23.4
Lac Vieux Desert Reservation, MI	10	31	12	5	-	4	21.4
Laguna Pueblo and Trust Lands, NM	195	1,020	344	129	135	380	28.2
La Jolla Reservation, CA	3	28	6	-	5	5	13.3
Lake Traverse (Sisseton) Reservation	161	652	238	83	65	169	20.2
North Dakota	-	1	-	-	-	-	32.5
South Dakota	161	651	238	83	65	169	20.2
L'Anse Reservation and Trust Lands, MI	53	202	56	22	18	41	23.3
L'Anse Reservation, MI	53	200	55	22	18	40	23.2
L'Anse Trust Lands, MI	-	2	1	-	-	1	32.5
La Posta Reservation, CA	-	2	-	1	-	-	32.5
Las Vegas Colony, NV	1	26	9	4	1	-	27.2
Laytonville Rancheria, CA	10	40	8	5	3	9	25.2
Leech Lake Reservation, MN	182	884	232	95	95	225	21.4
Likely Rancheria, CA	-	-	-	-	-	-	-
Lone Pine Rancheria, CA	9	50	10	6	7	13	25.9
Lookout Rancheria, CA	-	5	-	-	-	1	22.5
Los Coyotes Reservation, CA	1	11	4	-	1	3	18.5
Lovelock Colony, NV	4	14	6	3	6	11	25.0
Lower Brule Reservation, SD	62	247	61	19	20	36	18.1
Lower Elwha Reservation and Trust Lands, WA	8	37	13	5	3	8	25.6

[Continued]

★ 179 ★

Population of American Indian and Alaska Native Areas, by Age and Sex: 1990, Hannahville-Lummi - II
[Continued]

| American Indian/Alaska Native Area State | American Indian, Eskimo, or Aleut | | | | | | |
| | Age | | | | | | Median age |
	21 to 24 years	25 to 44 years	45 to 54 years	55 to 59 years	60 to 64 years	65 years and over	
Lower Sioux Community, MN	11	55	20	6	5	8	19.5
Lummi Reservation, WA	91	442	118	54	39	78	21.8

Source: Summary Population and Housing Characteristics, United States Summary, United States Bureau of the Census, CP H-1, pp. 402-416. *Notes:* A dash (-) indicates that no data were given in the original source. 1. Federal American Indian reservations are areas with boundaries established by treaty, statute, and/or executive or court order, and recognized by the federal government as territory in which American Indian tribes have jurisdiction. State reservations are lands held in trust by state governments for the use and benefit of a given tribe. The reservations and their boundaries were identified for the 1990 census by the Bureau of Indian Affairs (BIA), Department of Interior (for federal reservations), and state governments (for state reservations). The names of American Indian reservations recognized by state governments, but not by the federal government, are followed by "state." Areas composed of reservation lands that are administered jointly and/or are claimed by two reservations, as identified by the BIA, are called "joint areas," and are treated as separate American Indian reservations for census purposes. Federal reservations may cross state boundaries, and federal and state reservations may cross county, county subdivision, and place boundaries. For reservations that cross state boundaries, only the portion of the reservations in a given state are shown in the data products for that state; the entire reservations are shown in data products for the United States. 2. Trust lands are property associated with a particular American Indian reservation or tribe, held in trust by the federal government. Trust lands may be held in trust either for a tribe (tribal trust lands) or for an individual member of a tribe (individual trust land). Trust lands recognized for the 1990 census comprised all tribal trust lands and inhabited individual trust lands located outside of a reservation boundary. As with other American Indian areas, trust lands may be located in more than one state. Only the trust lands in a given state are shown in the data products for that state; all trust lands associated with a reservation or tribe are shown in data products for the United States. The Census Bureau first reported data for tribal trust lands for the 1980 census.

★ 180 ★

Population of American Indian and Alaska Native Areas, by Age and Sex: 1990, Makah-Papago - I

| American Indian/Alaska Native Area State | All persons | American Indian, Eskimo, or Aleut | | | | | |
| | | Total | Female | Age | | | |
				Under 5 years	16 years and over	18 years and over	18 to 20 years
American Indian reservations and Trust Lands[1,2]							
Makah Reservation, WA	1,214	940	454	118	574	555	46
Manchester (Point Arena) Rancheria, CA	200	178	91	27	101	98	2
Manzanita Reservation, CA	84	47	19	-	28	26	2
Maricopa (Ak-Chin) Reservation, AZ	446	405	211	47	256	242	26
Mashantucket Pequot Reservation, CT	83	55	26	9	34	31	-
Mattaponi Reservation, VA (state)	70	65	32	4	54	52	6
Menominee Reservation, WI	3,397	3,182	1,628	447	1,866	1,743	135
Mesa Grande Reservation, CA	96	72	34	8	49	44	3
Mescalero Apache Reservation, NM	2,695	2,516	1,306	362	1,430	1,344	129
Miccosukee Reservation, FL	94	94	50	22	53	49	8

[Continued]

★ 180 ★

Population of American Indian and Alaska Native Areas, by Age and Sex: 1990, Makah-Papago - I

[Continued]

American Indian/Alaska Native Area State	All persons	American Indian, Eskimo, or Aleut					
		Total	Female	Age			
				Under 5 years	16 years and over	18 years and over	18 to 20 years
Middletown Rancheria, CA	79	18	8	4	11	10	1
Mille Lacs Reservation, MN	470	428	220	58	267	251	27
Minnesota Chippewa Trust Lands, MN	43	28	11	-	21	19	2
Mississippi Choctaw Reservation and Trust Lands, MS	4,073	3,932	2,025	538	2,288	2,107	214
Mississippi Choctaw Reservation, MS	3,782	3,655	1,873	496	2,135	1,968	204
Mississippi Choctaw Trust Lands, MS	291	277	152	42	153	139	10
Maapa River Reservation, NV	375	190	99	16	133	125	15
Montgomery Creek Rancheria, CA	11	9	5	2	5	5	-
Morongo Reservation, CA	1,072	527	263	70	339	326	25
Muckleshoot Reservation and Trust Lands, WA	3,841	864	432	152	451	419	46
Nambe Pueblo and Trust Lands, NM	1,402	329	160	43	202	191	15
Narragansett Reservation, RI	31	17	10	2	10	10	-
Navajo Reservation and Trust Lands, AZ-NM-UT	148,451	143,405	73,676	18,938	87,349	81,078	7,698
Navajo Reservation	128,356	123,944	63,635	16,290	75,393	69,925	6,691
Arizona	90,942	87,577	44,759	11,763	52,990	49,153	4,727
New Mexico	31,914	31,115	16,174	3,793	19,270	17,899	1,644
Utah	5,500	5,252	2,702	734	3,133	2,873	320
Navajo Trust Lands	20,095	19,461	10,041	2,648	11,956	11,153	1,007
Arizona	22	13	9	1	6	5	2
New Mexico	20,073	19,448	10,032	2,647	11,950	11,148	1,005
Nez Perce Reservation, ID	16,160	1,863	953	201	1,222	1,139	92
Nisqually Reservation, WA	578	365	188	42	211	191	18
Nooksack Reservation and Trust Lands, WA	556	412	202	57	250	235	31
Nooksack Reservation, WA	19	12	7	2	9	9	-
Nooksack Trust Lands, WA	537	400	195	55	241	226	31
Northern Cheyenne Reservation and Trust Lands, MT - SD	3,923	3,542	1,768	519	2,044	1,891	188
North Fork Rancheria, CA	4	-	-	-	-	-	-
Northwestern Shoshoni Reservation, UT	-	-	-	-	-	-	-
Oil Springs Reservation, NY	5	-	-	-	-	-	-
Omaha Reservation, NE	5,227	1,908	972	326	1,047	985	95
Oneido (East) Reservation, NY	37	37	20	8	27	26	2
Oneido (West) Reservation, WI	18,033	2,447	1,240	319	1,536	1,424	105

[Continued]

★ 180 ★

Population of American Indian and Alaska Native Areas, by Age and Sex: 1990, Makah-Papago - I

[Continued]

American Indian/Alaska Native Area State	All persons	American Indian, Eskimo, or Aleut					
				Age			
		Total	Female	Under 5 years	16 years and over	18 years and over	18 to 20 years
Onondaga Reservation, NY	771	2	-	-	2	1	-
Ontonagon Reservation, MI	-	-	-	-	-	-	-
Osage Reservation, OK	41,299	6,088	3,129	627	3,997	3,750	240
Ozette Reservation, WA	12	-	-	-	-	-	-
Paiute of Utah Reservation, UT	645	323	179	58	180	171	20
Pala Reservation, CA	1,071	563	282	93	336	328	27
Pamunkey Reservation (state)	49	35	16	2	31	31	1
Papago Reservation, AZ	8,730	8,480	4,337	1,020	5,397	5,031	427

Source: Summary Population and Housing Characteristics, United States Summary, United States Bureau of the Census, CP H-1, pp. 402-416. *Notes:* A dash (-) indicates no data were given in the original source. 1. Federal American Indian reservations are areas with boundaries established by treaty, statute, and/or executive or court order, and recognized by the federal government as territory in which American Indian tribes have jurisdiction. State reservations are lands held in trust by state governments for the use and benefit of a given tribe. The reservations and their boundaries were identified for the 1990 census by the Bureau of Indian Affairs (BIA), Department of Interior (for federal reservations), and state governments (for state reservations). The names of American Indian reservations recognized by state governments, but not by the federal government, are followed by "state." Areas composed of reservation lands that are administered jointly and/or are claimed by two reservations, as identified by the BIA, are called "joint areas," and are treated as separate American Indian reservations for census purposes. Federal reservations may cross state boundaries, and federal and state reservations may cross county, county subdivision, and place boundaries. For reservations that cross state boundaries, only the portion of the reservations in a given state are shown in the data products for that state; the entire reservations are shown in data products for the United States. 2. Trust lands are property associated with a particular American Indian reservation or tribe, held in trust by the federal government. Trust lands may be held in trust either for a tribe (tribal trust lands) or for an individual member of a tribe (individual trust land). Trust lands recognized for the 1990 census comprised all tribal trust lands and inhabited individual trust lands located outside of a reservation boundary. As with other American Indian areas, trust lands may be located in more than one state. Only the trust lands in a given state are shown in the data products for that state; all trust lands associated with a reservation or tribe are shown in data products for the United States. The Census Bureau first reported data for tribal trust lands for the 1980 census.

★ 181 ★

Population of American Indian and Alaska Native Areas, by Age and Sex: 1990, Makah-Papago - II

American Indian/Alaska Native Area State	American Indian, Eskimo, or Aleut						
	Age						
	21 to 24 years	25 to 44 years	45 to 54 years	55 to 59 years	60 to 64 years	65 years and over	Median age
American Indian reservation and Trust Lands[1,2]							
Makah Reservation, WA	48	282	83	24	18	54	24.3
Manchester (Point Arena) Rancheria, CA	8	42	22	7	4	13	24.4
Manzanita Reservation, CA	1	17	2	2	1	1	21.5
Maricopa (Ak-Chin) Reservation, AZ	27	129	25	7	7	21	22.9

[Continued]

★ 181 ★

Population of American Indian and Alaska Native Areas, by Age and Sex: 1990, Makah-Papago - II

[Continued]

| American Indian/Alaska Native Area State | American Indian, Eskimo, or Aleut | | | | | | |
| | Age | | | | | | Median age |
	21 to 24 years	25 to 44 years	45 to 54 years	55 to 59 years	60 to 64 years	65 years and over	
Mashantucket Pequot Reservation, CT	2	20	3	2	2	2	25.9
Mattaponi Reservation, VA (state)	7	16	11	2	-	10	32.5
Menominee Reservation, WI	189	826	243	99	74	177	21.4
Mesa Grande Reservation, CA	-	17	8	4	2	10	33.8
Mescalero Apache Reservation, NM	190	727	140	44	43	71	19.8
Miccosukee Reservation, FL	9	20	6	5	-	1	18.5
Middletown Rancheria, CA	-	3	2	4	-	-	22.0
Mille Lacs Reservation, MN	29	94	25	21	12	43	21.9
Minnesota Chippewa Trust Lands, MN	3	6	4	-	-	4	25.0
Mississippi Choctaw Reservation and Trust Lands, MS	237	1,051	286	108	88	123	19.8
Mississippi Choctaw Reservation, MS	222	974	269	103	82	114	19.8
Mississippi Choctaw Trust Lands, MS	15	77	17	5	6	9	18.3
Maapa River Reservation, NV	15	51	18	13	3	10	25.0
Montgomery Creek Rancheria, CA	-	4	-	-	1	-	31.3
Morongo Reservation, CA	29	149	54	13	19	37	25.9
Muckleshoot Reservation and Trust Lands, WA	49	208	65	15	13	23	16.9
Nambe Pueblo and Trust Lands, NM	15	106	27	6	11	11	24.1
Narragansett Reservation, RI	1	4	4	-	-	1	27.5
Navajo Reservation and Trust Lands, AZ-NM-UT	8,751	37,265	10,648	4,405	3,711	8,600	21.8
Navajo Reservation	7,498	31,862	9,247	3,829	3,210	7,488	21.7
Arizona	5,329	22,355	6,497	2,715	2,268	5,262	21.5
New Mexico	1,856	8,334	2,373	972	778	1,942	22.5
Utah	313	1.273	377	142	164	284	20.2
Navajo Trust Lands	1,253	5,303	1,401	576	501	1,112	22.3
Arizona	-	2	1	-	-	-	15.5
New Mexico	1,253	5,301	1,400	576	501	1,112	22.3
Nez Perce Reservation, ID	105	562	157	73	43	107	25.4
Nisqually Reservation, WA	12	118	20	5	8	10	19.5
Nooksack Reservation and Trust Lands, WA	31	96	32	10	5	30	20.5
Nooksack Reservation, WA	-	4	-	1	1	3	37.5
Nooksack Trust Lands, WA	31	92	32	9	4	27	19.9
Northern Cheyenne Reservation and Trust Lands, MT - SD	234	947	233	90	65	134	19.8

[Continued]

★ 181 ★

Population of American Indian and Alaska Native Areas, by Age and Sex: 1990, Makah-Papago - II

[Continued]

American Indian/Alaska Native Area State	American Indian, Eskimo, or Aleut						
	Age						Median age
	21 to 24 years	25 to 44 years	45 to 54 years	55 to 59 years	60 to 64 years	65 years and over	
North Fork Rancheria, CA	-	-	-	-	-	-	-
Northwestern Shoshoni Reservation, UT	-	-	-	-	-	-	-
Oil Springs Reservation, NY	-	-	-	-	-	-	-
Omaha Reservation, NE	127	423	144	42	37	117	19.0
Oneido (East) Reservation, NY	11	10	1	-	2	-	22.6
Oneido (West) Reservation, WI	118	643	189	83	85	201	24.3
Onondaga Reservation, NY	-	1	-	-	-	-	23.5
Ontonagon Reservation, MI	-	-	-	-	-	-	-
Osage Reservation, OK	258	1,681	557	225	203	586	27.4
Ozette Reservation, WA	-	-	-	-	-	-	-
Paiute of Utah Reservation, UT	21	75	18	17	9	11	19.7
Pala Reservation, CA	36	142	46	23	16	38	23.3
Pamunkey Reservation (state)	3	4	2	5	4	12	58.5
Papago Reservation, AZ	546	2,229	733	310	216	570	23.7

Source: Summary Population and Housing Characteristics, United States Summary, United States Bureau of the Census, CP H-1, pp. 402-416. *Notes:* A dash (-) indicates that no data were given in the original source. 1. Federal American Indian reservations are areas with boundaries established by treaty, statute, and/or executive or court order, and recognized by the federal government as territory in which American Indian tribes have jurisdiction. State reservations are lands held in trust by state governments for the use and benefit of a given tribe. The reservations and their boundaries were identified for the 1990 census by the Bureau of Indian Affairs (BIA), Department of Interior (for federal reservations), and state governments (for state reservations). The names of American Indian reservations recognized by state governments, but not by the federal government, are followed by "state" Areas composed of reservation lands that are administered jointly and/or are claimed by two reservations, as identified by the BIA, are called "joint areas," and are treated as separate American Indian reservations for census purposes. Federal reservations may cross state boundaries, and federal and state reservations may cross county, county subdivision, and place boundaries. For reservations that cross state boundaries, only the portion of the reservations in a given state are shown in the data products for that state; the entire reservations are shown in data products for the United States. 2. Trust lands are property associated with a particular American Indian reservation or tribe, held in trust by the federal government. Trust lands may be held in trust either for a tribe (tribal trust lands) or for an individual member of a tribe (individual trust land). Trust lands recognized for the 1990 census comprised all tribal trust lands and inhabited individual trust lands located outside of a reservation boundary. As with other American Indian areas, trust lands may be located in more than one state. Only the trust lands in a given state are shown in the data products for that state; all trust lands associated with a reservation or tribe are shown in data products for the United States. The Census Bureau first reported data for tribal trust lands for the 1980 census.

★ 182 ★

Population of American Indian and Alaska Native Areas, by Age and Sex: 1990, Pascua-Rocky - I

American Indian/Alaska Native Area State	All persons	American Indian, Eskimo, or Aleut					
		Total	Female	Age			
				Under 5 years	16 years and over	18 years and over	18 to 20 years
American Indian reservation and Trust Lands[1,2]							
Pascua Yoqui Reservation, AZ	2,412	2,284	1,219	385	1,200	1,115	110
Passamaquaddy Trust Lands, ME	3	1	-	-	1	1	-
Paucatuck Eastern Peqquot Reservation, CT (state)	18	15	7	1	14	14	3
Pauma Reservation, CA	148	137	80	29	61	60	5
Payson (Yavapai-Apache) Community, AZ	102	97	43	13	64	60	7
Pechanga Reservation, CA	398	289	141	24	188	172	7
Penobscot Reservation and Trust Lands, ME	485	417	206	40	278	258	17
Penobscot Reservation, ME	476	417	206	40	278	258	17
Penobscot Trust Lands, ME	9	-	-	-	-	-	-
Picayune Rancheria, CA	32	15	6	1	8	8	-
Picuris Pueblo, NM	1,882	147	68	14	102	98	5
Pine Creek Reservation, MI (state)	24	20	12	-	18	17	1
Pine Ridge Reservation and Trust Lands, NE-SD	12,215	11,182	5,526	1,629	6,436	5,926	688
Pine Ridge Reservation, SD	11,385	10,455	5,162	1,530	6,050	5,571	642
Pine Ridge Trust Lands	830	727	364	99	386	355	46
Nebraska	26	16	10	2	9	9	-
South Dakota	804	711	354	97	377	346	46
Pinoleville Rancheria, CA	130	77	38	15	53	47	3
Pit River Trust Lands, CA	7	1	1	-	1	1	-
Pleasant Point Reservation, ME	572	523	271	61	322	306	25
Poarch Creek Reservation and Trust Lands, AL	212	149	77	20	98	94	9
Pojaaque Pueblo, NM	2,556	177	92	14	116	111	9
Poospatuck Reservation, NY (state)	136	95	45	11	65	63	8
Port Gamble Reservation, WA	552	377	195	55	226	207	19
Port Madison Reservation, WA	4,834	388	194	43	235	219	26
Potawatomi (Kansas) Reservation, KS	1,082	502	245	60	302	290	17
Potawatomi (Wisconsin) Reservation and Trust Lands, WI	279	266	121	36	153	144	16
Prarie Island Community, MN	60	56	28	6	37	37	2
Puyallup Reservation and Trust Lands, WA	32,406	937	480	111	595	559	42
Puyallup Reservation, WA	32,392	936	480	111	594	558	42

[Continued]

★ 182 ★

Population of American Indian and Alaska Native Areas, by Age and Sex: 1990, Pascua-Rocky - I
[Continued]

American Indian/Alaska Native Area State	All persons	American Indian, Eskimo, or Aleut					
		Total	Female	Age			
				Under 5 years	16 years and over	18 years and over	18 to 20 years
Puyallup Trust Lands, WA	14	1	-	-	1	1	-
Pyramid Lake Reservation, NV	1,388	959	484	128	578	553	41
Quartz Valley Rancheria, CA	124	19	9	2	16	14	-
Quileute Reservation, WA	381	303	144	38	193	184	19
Quinault Reservation, WA	1,216	943	428	120	601	566	41
Ramah Navajo Community, NM	194	191	95	25	120	111	13
Ramana Reservation, CA	-	-	-	-	-	-	-
Rankokus Reservation, NJ (state)	-	-	-	-	-	-	-
Red Cliff Reservation and Trust Lands, WI	857	727	362	85	466	433	40
Redding Rancheria, CA	101	79	38	6	57	49	5
Red Lake Reservation, MN	3,699	3,602	1,773	504	2,126	1,975	195
Redwood Valley Rancheria, CA	142	14	9	2	9	8	-
Reno-Sparks Colony, NV	264	262	143	19	184	173	15
Resighini Rancheria, CA	28	26	12	2	15	14	-
Rincon Reservation, CA	1,352	379	181	46	244	229	21
Roaring Creek Rancheria, CA	18	18	10	6	8	7	-
Robinson Rancheria, CA	139	113	61	20	57	53	8
Rocky Boy's Reservation and Trust Lands, MT	1,954	1,882	916	259	1,111	1,031	101
Rocky Boy's Reservation, MT	1,547	1,485	723	214	862	800	85
Rocky Boy's Trust Lands, MT	407	397	193	45	249	231	16

Source: Summary Population and Housing Characteristics, United States Summary, United States Bureau of the Census, CP H-1, pp. 402-416. *Notes:* A dash (-) indicates that no data were given in the original source. 1. Federal American Indian reservations are areas with boundaries established by treaty, statute, and/or executive or court order, and recognized by the federal government as territory in which American Indian tribes have jurisdiction. State reservations are lands held in trust by state governments for the use and benefit of a given tribe. The reservations and their boundaries were identified for the 1990 census by the Bureau of Indian Affairs (BIA), Department of Interior (for federal reservations), and state governments (for state reservations). The names of American Indian reservations recognized by state governments, but not by the federal government, are followed by "state." Areas composed of reservation lands that are administered jointly and/or are claimed by two reservations, as identified by the BIA, are called "joint areas," and are treated as separate American Indian reservations for census purposes. Federal reservations may cross state boundaries, and federal and state reservations may cross county, county subdivision, and place boundaries. For reservations that cross state boundaries, only the portion of the reservations in a given state are shown in the data products for that state; the entire reservations are shown in data products for the United States. 2. Trust lands are property associated with a particular American Indian reservation or tribe, held in trust by the federal government. Trust lands may be held in trust either for a tribe (tribal trust lands) or for an individual member of a tribe (individual trust land). Trust lands recognized for the 1990 census comprised all tribal trust lands and inhabited individual trust lands located outside of a reservation boundary. As with other American Indian areas, trust lands may be located in more than one state. Only the trust lands in a given state are shown in the data products for that state; all trust lands associated with a reservation or tribe are shown in data products for the United States. The Census Bureau first reported data for tribal trust lands for the 1980 census.

★ 183 ★

Population of American Indian and Alaska Native Areas, by Age and Sex: 1990, Pascua-Rocky - II

American Indian/Alaska Native Area State	American Indian, Eskimo, or Aleut						
	Age						Median age
	21 to 24 years	25 to 44 years	45 to 54 years	55 to 59 years	60 to 64 years	65 years and over	
American Indian reservation and Trust Lands[1,2]							
Pascua Yoqui Reservation, AZ	145	568	147	47	48	50	17.4
Passamaquaddy Trust Lands, ME	-	1	-	-	-	-	42.5
Paucatuck Eastern Peqquot Reservation, CT (state)	2	4	3	1	-	1	35.8
Pauma Reservation, CA	3	41	6	2	-	3	12.2
Payson (Yavapai-Apache) Community, AZ	5	31	8	5	3	1	24.6
Pechanga Reservation, CA	16	65	26	12	17	29	26.9
Penobscot Reservation and Trust Lands, ME	17	128	29	17	19	31	27.1
Penobscot Reservation, ME	17	128	29	17	19	31	27.1
Penobscot Trust Lands, ME	-	-	-	-	-	-	-
Picayune Rancheria, CA	-	7	-	-	1	-	26.3
Picuris Pueblo, NM	5	47	17	7	3	14	29.8
Pine Creek Reservation, MI (state)	1	7	1	1	2	4	40.0
Pine Ridge Reservation and Trust Lands, NE-SD	683	2,692	789	280	262	532	19.3
Pine Ridge Reservation, SD	644	2,520	753	263	245	504	19.4
Pine Ridge Trust Lands	39	172	36	17	17	28	17.4
Nebraska	2	5	1	-	1	-	21.5
South Dakota	37	167	35	17	16	28	17.3
Pinoleville Rancheria, CA	6	22	5	1	1	9	24.7
Pit River Trust Lands, CA	-	-	-	-	-	1	67.5
Pleasant Point Reservation, ME	25	154	33	20	13	36	24.1
Poarch Creek Reservation and Trust Lands, AL	10	37	7	4	4	23	25.2
Pojaaque Pueblo, NM	14	60	15	6	3	4	24.9
Poospatuck Reservation, NY (state)	5	29	8	2	3	8	26.6
Port Gamble Reservation, WA	14	105	25	20	9	15	20.9
Port Madison Reservation, WA	16	120	30	9	5	13	20.9
Potawatomi (Kansas) Reservation, KS	32	123	35	21	13	49	23.7
Potawatomi (Wisconsin) Reservation and Trust Lands, WI	16	57	20	11	13	11	19.7
Prarie Island Community, MN	7	15	6	1	1	5	25.0
Puyallup Reservation and Trust Lands, WA	57	273	77	33	22	55	24.4
Puyallup Reservation, WA	57	272	77	33	22	55	24.4

[Continued]

329

★ 183 ★

Population of American Indian and Alaska Native Areas, by Age and Sex: 1990, Pascua-Rocky - II

[Continued]

American Indian/Alaska Native Area State	American Indian, Eskimo, or Aleut						
	Age						Median age
	21 to 24 years	25 to 44 years	45 to 54 years	55 to 59 years	60 to 64 years	65 years and over	
Puyallup Trust Lands, WA	-	1	-	-	-	-	37.5
Pyramid Lake Reservation, NV	45	271	74	39	18	65	24.0
Quartz Valley Rancheria, CA	1	3	3	-	1	6	47.5
Quileute Reservation, WA	18	99	33	7	2	6	24.0
Quinault Reservation, WA	49	291	93	30	15	47	25.3
Ramah Navajo Community, NM	12	48	13	3	5	17	21.8
Ramana Reservation, CA	-	-	-	-	-	-	-
Rankokus Reservation, NJ (state)	-	-	-	-	-	-	-
Red Cliff Reservation and Trust Lands, WI	48	197	67	20	19	42	23.5
Redding Rancheria, CA	4	24	9	1	1	5	25.6
Red Lake Reservation, MN	210	946	217	125	102	180	20.7
Redwood Valley Rancheria, CA	-	3	2	1	1	1	35.0
Reno-Sparks Colony, NV	25	71	35	10	7	10	25.5
Resighini Rancheria, CA	-	13	-	1	-	-	27.5
Rincon Reservation, CA	26	97	29	16	10	30	23.7
Roaring Creek Rancheria, CA	2	3	1	-	1	-	12.0
Robinson Rancheria, CA	6	30	1	4	2	2	16.3
Rocky Boy's Reservation and Trust Lands, MT	119	522	139	43	33	74	20.7
Rocky Boy's Reservation, MT	104	393	106	29	27	56	20.2
Rocky Boy's Trust Lands, MT	15	129	33	14	6	18	25.2

Source: Summary Population and Housing Characteristics, United States Summary, United States Bureau of the Census, CP H-1, pp. 402-416. *Notes:* A dash (-) indicates that no data were given in the original source. 1. Federal American Indian reservations are areas with boundaries established by treaty, statute, and/or executive or court order, and recognized by the federal government as territory in which American Indian tribes have jurisdiction. State reservations are lands held in trust by state governments for the use and benefit of a given tribe. The reservations and their boundaries were identified for the 1990 census by the Bureau of Indian Affairs (BIA), Department of Interior (for federal reservations), and state governments (for state reservations). The names of American Indian reservations recognized by state governments, but not by the federal government, are followed by "state." Areas composed of reservation lands that are administered jointly and/or are claimed by two reservations, as identified by the BIA, are called "joint areas," and are treated as separate American Indian reservations for census purposes. Federal reservations may cross state boundaries, and federal and state reservations may cross county, county subdivision, and place boundaries. For reservations that cross state boundaries, only the portion of the reservations in a given state are shown in the data products for that state; the entire reservations are shown in data products for the United States. 2. Trust lands are property associated with a particular American Indian reservation or tribe, held in trust by the federal government. Trust lands may be held in trust either for a tribe (tribal trust lands) or for an individual member of a tribe (individual trust land). Trust lands recognized for the 1990 census comprised all tribal trust lands and inhabited individual trust lands located outside of a reservation boundary. As with other American Indian areas, trust lands may be located in more than one state. Only the trust lands in a given state are shown in the data products for that state; all trust lands associated with a reservation or tribe are shown in data products for the United States. The Census Bureau first reported data for tribal trust lands for the 1980 census.

★ 184 ★

Population of American Indian and Alaska Native Areas, by Age and Sex: 1990, Rohnerville-Sobaba - I

American Indian/Alaska Native Area State	All persons	American Indian, Eskimo, or Aleut					
		Total	Female	Age			
				Under 5 years	16 years and over	18 years and over	18 to 20 years
American Indian reservation and Trust Lands[1,2]							
Rohnerville Rancheria, CA	14	1	1	-	1	1	-
Rosebud Reservation and Trust Lands, SD	9,696	8,043	4,092	1,198	4,488	4,136	435
Rosebud Reservation, SD	8,352	6,883	3,520	1,041	3,846	3,539	375
Rosebud Trust Lands, SD	1,344	1,160	572	157	642	597	60
Round Valley Reservation and Trust Lands, CA	1,183	577	302	87	344	327	30
Rumsey Rancheria, CA	8	4	1	-	3	3	-
Sac and Fox (Iowa) Reservation, IA	577	564	277	63	345	323	32
Sac and Fox (KS-NE) Reservation and Trust Lands, KS-NE	210	49	31	11	30	27	3
Sac and Fox Reservation	209	48	30	11	29	26	3
Kansas	82	44	27	9	27	24	3
Nebraska	127	4	3	2	2	2	-
Sac and Fox (KS-NE) Trust Lands	1	1	1	-	1	1	-
Kansas	1	1	1	-	1	1	-
Nebraska	-	-	-	-	-	-	-
St. Croix Reservation, WI	505	462	229	61	285	268	31
St. Regis Mohawk Reservation, NY	1,978	1,923	992	221	1,351	1,282	107
Salt River Reservation, AZ	4,852	3,533	1,810	508	2,093	1,974	167
San Carlos Reservation, AZ	7,294	7,110	3,639	1,054	4,181	3,932	321
Sandia Pueblo, NM	3,971	358	183	42	247	235	23
Sandy Lake Reservation, MN	37	36	22	4	22	21	1
San Filipe Pueblo, NM	2,434	1,859	971	231	1,188	1,109	114
San Ildefonso Pueblo, NM	1,499	347	174	36	226	216	28
San Juan Pueblo, NM	5,209	1,276	642	119	918	858	46
San Manuel Reservation, CA	80	56	29	9	37	35	3
San Pasqual Reservation, CA	512	212	107	26	120	107	12
Santa Ana Pueblo, NM	593	481	256	60	320	309	20
Santa Clara Pueblo, NM	10,193	1,246	651	118	843	801	50
Santa Rosa Rancheria, CA	323	284	141	33	137	127	12
Santa Rosa Reservation, CA	50	37	22	8	20	20	1
Santa Ynez Reservation, CA	279	213	132	33	134	126	10

[Continued]

★ 184 ★

Population of American Indian and Alaska Native Areas, by Age and Sex: 1990, Rohnerville-Sobaba - I

[Continued]

American Indian/Alaska Native Area State	All persons	American Indian, Eskimo, or Aleut					
		Total	Female	Age			
				Under 5 years	16 years and over	18 years and over	18 to 20 years
Santa Ysabel Reservation, CA	169	150	74	10	108	98	11
Santee Reservation, NE	758	425	219	52	259	242	21
Santo Domingo Pueblo, NM	2,992	2,947	1,450	332	1,928	1,794	176
San Xavier Reservation, AZ	1,172	1,073	567	121	674	630	64
Saulk-Suiattle Reservation, WA	124	69	38	11	34	32	4
Sault Ste. Marie Reservation and Trust Lands, MI	768	554	289	92	271	242	20
Sault Ste. Marie Reservation, MI	385	315	169	52	148	130	12
Sault Ste. Marie Trust Lands, MI	383	239	120	40	123	112	8
Schaghticoke Reservation, CT (state)	10	7	2	-	7	7	-
Seminole Trust Lands, FL	114	93	51	24	54	48	6
Shakopee Community, MN	203	153	76	26	101	93	4
Sheep Ranch Rancheria, CA	-	-	-	-	-	-	-
Sherwood Valley Rancheria, CA	15	9	3	-	9	8	-
Shingle Springs Rancheria, CA	18	7	4	-	5	5	-
Shinnecock Reservation, NY (state)	375	339	164	25	245	238	13
Shoalwater Reservation, WA	131	66	32	13	42	39	5
Siletz Reservation, OR	5	-	-	-	-	-	-
Skokomish Reservation, WA	614	431	206	53	272	256	20
Skull Valley Reservation, UT	32	32	15	1	24	21	2
Smith River Rancheria, CA	104	72	33	5	47	40	2
Sobaba Reservation, CA	369	308	139	46	179	168	17

Source: Summary Population and Housing Characteristics, United States Summary, United States Bureau of the Census, CP H-1, pp. 402-416. *Notes:* A dash (-) indicates no data were given in the original source. 1. Federal American Indian reservations are areas with boundaries established by treaty, statute, and/ or executive or court order, and recognized by the federal government as territory in which American Indian tribes have jurisdiction. State reservations are lands held in trust by state governments for the use and benefit of a given tribe. The reservations and their boundaries were identified for the 1990 census by the Bureau of Indian Affairs (BIA), Department of Interior (for federal reservations), and state governments (for state reservations). The names of American Indian reservations recognized by state governments, but not by the federal government, are followed by "state." Areas composed of reservation lands that are administered jointly and/or are claimed by two reservations, as identified by the BIA, are called "joint areas," and are treated as separate American Indian reservations for census purposes. Federal reservations may cross state boundaries, and federal and state reservations may cross county, county subdivision, and place boundaries. For reservations that cross state boundaries, only the portion of the reservations in a given state are shown in the data products for that state; the entire reservations are shown in data products for the United States. 2. Trust lands are property associated with a particular American Indian reservation or tribe, held in trust by the federal government. Trust lands may be held in trust either for a tribe (tribal trust lands) or for an individual member of a tribe (individual trust land). Trust lands recognized for the 1990 census comprised all tribal trust lands and inhabited individual trust lands located outside of a reservation boundary. As with other American Indian areas, trust lands may be located in more than one state. Only the trust lands in a given state are shown in the data products for that state; all trust lands associated with a reservation or tribe are shown in data products for the United States. The Census Bureau first reported data for tribal trust lands for the 1980 census.

Population of American Indian and Alaska Native Areas, by Age and Sex: 1990, Rohnerville-Sobaba - II

American Indian/Alaska Native Area State	American Indian, Eskimo, or Aleut						
	Age						Median age
	21 to 24 years	25 to 44 years	45 to 54 years	55 to 59 years	60 to 64 years	65 years and over	
American Indian reservation and Trust Lands[1,2]							
Rohnerville Rancheria, CA	-	-	-	-	1	-	63.5
Rosebud Reservation and Trust Lands, SD	489	1,976	495	223	173	354	18.8
Rosebud Reservation, SD	427	1,679	417	186	149	306	18.8
Rosebud Trust Lands, SD	62	288	78	37	24	48	18.8
Round Valley Reservation and Trust Lands, CA	25	136	45	21	20	50	22.4
Rumsey Rancheria, CA	-	3	-	-	-	-	37.5
Sac and Fox (Iowa) Reservation, IA	26	134	49	22	25	35	22.6
Sac and Fox (KS-NE) Reservation and Trust Lands, KS-NE	-	14	6	2	-	2	19.5
Sac and Fox Reservation	-	14	6	2	-	1	19.0
Kansas	-	13	6	1	-	1	19.0
Nebraska	-	1	-	1	-	-	15.0
Sac and Fox (KS-NE) Trust Lands	-	-	-	-	-	1	77.5
Kansas	-	-	-	-	-	1	77.5
Nebraska	-	-	-	-	-	-	-
St. Croix Reservation, WI	29	115	38	20	11	24	22.0
St. Regis Mohawk Reservation, NY	121	553	199	71	52	179	28.0
Salt River Reservation, AZ	239	1,038	274	74	56	126	21.6
San Carlos Reservation, AZ	500	1,978	506	206	160	261	21.5
Sandia Pueblo, NM	22	112	29	12	11	26	27.6
Sandy Lake Reservation, MN	2	11	1	4	1	1	25.0
San Filipe Pueblo, NM	125	566	147	48	28	81	23.2
San Ildefonso Pueblo, NM	19	91	20	12	20	26	23.9
San Juan Pueblo, NM	94	413	119	51	32	103	28.3
San Manuel Reservation, CA	7	14	5	3	-	3	23.5
San Pasqual Reservation, CA	4	54	11	6	8	12	18.3
Santa Ana Pueblo, NM	25	158	42	12	18	34	27.9
Santa Clara Pueblo, NM	65	400	112	43	35	96	27.7
Santa Rosa Rancheria, CA	16	67	15	4	5	8	15.4
Santa Rosa Reservation, CA	5	7	2	-	3	2	21.2
Santa Ynez Reservation, CA	11	53	16	7	9	20	24.5

[Continued]

★ 185 ★

Population of American Indian and Alaska Native Areas, by Age and Sex: 1990, Rohnerville-Sobaba - II

[Continued]

American Indian/Alaska Native Area State	American Indian, Eskimo, or Aleut						
	Age						Median age
	21 to 24 years	25 to 44 years	45 to 54 years	55 to 59 years	60 to 64 years	65 years and over	
Santa Ysabel Reservation, CA	6	51	13	3	1	13	26.9
Santee Reservation, NE	26	109	36	13	7	30	21.9
Santo Domingo Pueblo, NM	226	905	215	63	58	151	23.6
San Xavier Reservation, AZ	58	342	73	35	13	45	22.8
Saulk-Suiattle Reservation, WA	2	21	2	-	1	2	15.8
Sault Ste. Marie Reservation and Trust Lands, MI	29	144	18	7	7	17	15.3
Sault Ste. Marie Reservation, MI	15	75	9	4	3	12	13.9
Sault Ste. Marie Trust Lands, MI	14	69	9	3	4	5	17.1
Schaghticoke Reservation, CT (state)	2	2	2	1	-	-	43.8
Seminole Trust Lands, FL	8	25	7	1	-	1	19.5
Shakopee Community, MN	9	44	13	5	6	12	26.3
Sheep Ranch Rancheria, CA	-	-	-	-	-	-	-
Sherwood Valley Rancheria, CA	-	3	2	2	-	1	47.5
Shingle Springs Rancheria, CA	-	2	-	-	1	2	37.5
Shinnecock Reservation, NY (state)	12	106	27	13	15	52	33.0
Shoalwater Reservation, WA	1	21	5	4	1	2	23.5
Siletz Reservation, OR	-	-	-	-	-	-	-
Skokomish Reservation, WA	31	128	43	12	8	14	23.7
Skull Valley Reservation, UT	5	9	2	-	2	1	22.0
Smith River Rancheria, CA	4	14	6	1	5	8	23.5
Sobaba Reservation, CA	18	95	11	11	6	10	20.5

Source: Summary Population and Housing Characteristics, United States Summary, United States Bureau of the Census, CP H-1, pp. 402-416. *Notes:* A dash (-) indicates no data were given in the original source. 1. Federal American Indian reservations are areas with boundaries established by treaty, statute, and/or executive or court order, and recognized by the federal government as territory in which American Indian tribes have jurisdiction. State reservations are lands held in trust by state governments for the use and benefit of a given tribe. The reservations and their boundaries were identified for the 1990 census by the Bureau of Indian Affairs (BIA), Department of Interior (for federal reservations), and state governments (for state reservations). The names of American Indian reservations recognized by state governments, but not by the federal government, are followed by "(State)." Areas composed of reservation lands that are administered jointly and/or are claimed by two reservations, as identified by the BIA, are called "joint areas," and are treated as separate American Indian reservations for census purposes. Federal reservations may cross state boundaries, and federal and state reservations may cross county, county subdivision, and place boundaries. For reservations that cross state boundaries, only the portion of the reservations in a given state are shown in the data products for that state; the entire reservations are shown in data products for the United States. 2. Trust lands are property associated with a particular American Indian reservation or tribe, held in trust by the federal government. Trust lands may be held in trust either for a tribe (tribal trust lands) or for an individual member of a tribe (individual trust land). Trust lands recognized for the 1990 census comprised all tribal trust lands and inhabited individual trust lands located outside of a reservation boundary. As with other American Indian areas, trust lands may be located in more than one state. Only the trust lands in a given state are shown in the data products for that state; all trust lands associated with a reservation or tribe are shown in data products for the United States. The Census Bureau first reported data for tribal trust lands for the 1980 census.

★ 186 ★

Population of American Indian and Alaska Native Areas, by Age and Sex: 1990, Sokaagon-Ute - I

American Indian/Alaska Native Area State	All persons	American Indian, Eskimo, or Aleut					
		Total	Female	Age			
				Under 5 years	16 years and over	18 years and over	18 to 20 years
American Indian reservation and Trust Lands[1,2]							
Sokaagon Chippewa Community and Trust Lands, WI	357	311	155	68	162	150	9
Sokaagon Chippewa Community, WI	266	230	115	53	117	108	8
Sokaagon Chippewa Trust Lands, WI	91	81	40	15	45	42	1
Southern Ute Reservation, CO	7,804	1,044	543	128	684	633	59
Spokane Reservation, WA	1,502	1,229	613	175	750	708	60
Squaxin Island Reservation and Trust Lands, WA	157	127	73	24	69	62	4
Standing Rock Reservation	7,956	4,870	2,417	710	2,713	2,501	227
Norh Dakota	3,761	2,836	1,404	399	1,590	1,466	141
South Dakota	4,195	2,034	1,013	311	1,123	1,035	86
Stewarts Point Rancheria, CA	91	86	41	10	58	56	3
Stillaguamish Reservation, WA	113	96	50	13	52	48	8
Stockbridge Reservation, WI	581	447	219	32	307	294	22
Sulphur Bank (El-Em) Rancheria, CA	93	90	42	13	56	47	8
Summit Lake Reservation, NV	7	6	2	-	5	5	1
Susanville Reservation, CA	454	154	76	22	89	88	6
Swinomish Reservation, WA	2,282	585	291	61	377	343	34
Sycuan Reservation, CA	4	-	-	-	-	-	-
Toble Bluff Rancheria, CA	48	43	18	1	27	27	3
Table Mountain Rancheria, CA	51	48	28	2	41	39	3
Tama Reservation , GA (state)	22	16	8	2	12	11	1
Taos Pueblo and Trust Lands, NM	4,745	1,212	599	107	883	846	52
Taos Pueblo, NM	4,681	1,211	598	106	883	846	52
Taos Trust Lands, NM	64	1	1	1	-	-	-
Te-Maak Reservation and Trust Lands, NV	949	831	417	98	550	516	44
Te-Maak Reservation, NV	918	800	405	94	525	491	44
Te-Maak Trust Lands, NV	31	31	12	4	25	25	-
Tesuque Pueblo and Trust Lands, NM	697	232	114	36	167	162	13
Tonawanda Reservation, NY	501	453	246	53	326	309	14
Torres-Martinez Reservation, CA	1,462	143	71	17	88	83	10
Trinidad Rancheria, CA	78	59	29	12	37	35	4

[Continued]

335

★ 186 ★

Population of American Indian and Alaska Native Areas, by Age and Sex: 1990, Sokaagon-Ute - I

[Continued]

American Indian/Alaska Native Area State	All persons	American Indian, Eskimo, or Aleut					
		Total	Female	Age			
				Under 5 years	16 years and over	18 years and over	18 to 20 years
Tulalip Reservation, WA	7,103	1,204	624	168	704	660	47
Tule River Reservation, CA	798	745	379	92	437	406	42
Tunica-Biloxi Reservation, LA	29	16	9	1	12	12	1
Tuolumne Rancheria, CA	135	107	49	8	77	73	6
Turtle Mountain Reservation and Trust Lands, ND-SD	7,106	6,772	3,415	909	4,021	3,743	368
Turtle Mountain Reservation, ND	4,987	4,746	2,399	596	2,920	2,728	266
Turtle Mountain Trust Lands, ND	2,119	2,026	1,016	313	1,101	1,015	102
Tuscarara Reservation, NY	772	310	156	52	215	215	28
Twenty-Nine Palms Reservation, CA	-	-	-	-	-	-	-
Unitah and Quray Reservation, UT	17,224	2,650	1,386	393	1,487	1,389	109
Umatilla Reservation, OR	2,502	1,029	539	108	681	642	52
Upper Lake Rancheria, CA	76	28	19	2	16	14	1
Upper Sioux Community, MN	49	43	26	2	30	30	3
Upper Skagit Reservation, WA	180	162	87	21	103	99	12
Ute Mountain Reservation and Trust Lands, CO-NM-UT	1,320	1,264	624	161	837	785	64
Ute Mountain Reservation	1,314	1,264	624	161	837	785	64
Colorado	1,069	1,019	498	126	686	646	57
New Mexico	-	-	-	-	-	-	-
Utah	245	245	126	35	151	139	7
Ute Mountain Trust Lands, UT	6	-	-	-	-	-	-

Source: Summary Population and Housing Characteristics, United States Summary, United States Bureau of the Census, CP H-1, pp. 402-416. *Notes:* A dash (-) indicates no data were given in the original source. 1. Federal American Indian reservations are areas with boundaries established by treaty, statute, and/or executive or court order, and recognized by the federal government as territory in which American Indian tribes have jurisdiction. State reservations are lands held in trust by state governments for the use and benefit of a given tribe. The reservations and their boundaries were identified for the 1990 census by the Bureau of Indian Affairs (BIA), Department of Interior (for federal reservations), and state governments (for state reservations). The names of American Indian reservations recognized by state governments, but not by the federal government, are followed by "state." Areas composed of reservation lands that are administered jointly and/or are claimed by two reservations, as identified by the BIA, are called "joint areas," and are treated as separate American Indian reservations for census purposes. Federal reservations may cross state boundaries, and federal and state reservations may cross county, county subdivision, and place boundaries. For reservations that cross state boundaries, only the portion of the reservations in a given state are shown in the data products for that state; the entire reservations are shown in data products for the United States. 2. Trust lands are property associated with a particular American Indian reservation or tribe, held in trust by the federal government. Trust lands may be held in trust either for a tribe (tribal trust lands) or for an individual member of a tribe (individual trust land). Trust lands recognized for the 1990 census comprised all tribal trust lands and inhabited individual trust lands located outside of a reservation boundary. As with other American Indian areas, trust lands may be located in more than one state. Only the trust lands in a given state are shown in the data products for that state; all trust lands associated with a reservation or tribe are shown in data products for the United States. The Census Bureau first reported data for tribal trust lands for the 1980 census.

★ 187 ★

Population of American Indian and Alaska Native Areas, by Age and Sex: 1990, Sokaagon-Ute - II

American Indian/Alaska Native Area State	American Indian, Eskimo, or Aleut						
	Age						Median age
	21 to 24 years	25 to 44 years	45 to 54 years	55 to 59 years	60 to 64 years	65 years and over	
American Indian reservation and Trust Lands[1,2]							
Sokaagon Chippewa Community and Trust Lands, WI	17	85	17	11	2	9	17.1
Sokaagon Chippewa Community, WI	11	60	12	8	2	7	16.5
Sokaagon Chippewa Trust Lands, WI	6	25	5	3	-	2	21.5
Southern Ute Reservation, CO	68	304	99	27	20	56	24.0
Spokane Reservation, WA	63	343	97	41	31	73	23.0
Squaxin Island Reservation and Trust Lands, WA	2	36	11	1	-	8	17.8
Standing Rock Reservation	265	1,223	360	123	102	201	18.8
Norh Dakota	154	756	198	69	52	96	18.9
South Dakota	111	467	162	54	50	105	18.6
Stewarts Point Rancheria, CA	8	18	6	7	3	11	26.7
Stillaguamish Reservation, WA	2	26	10	-	-	2	18.0
Stockbridge Reservation, WI	26	109	45	10	20	62	28.2
Sulphur Bank (El-Em) Rancheria, CA	1	22	6	3	3	4	19.3
Summit Lake Reservation, NV	-	3	-	-	1	-	31.7
Susanville Reservation, CA	9	50	4	4	8	7	23.5
Swinomish Reservation, WA	40	165	50	21	11	22	22.2
Sycuan Reservation, CA	-	-	-	-	-	-	-
Toble Bluff Rancheria, CA	1	10	5	3	3	2	30.5
Table Mountain Rancheria, CA	3	14	5	4	3	7	34.2
Tama Reservation , GA (state)	-	5	3	2	-	-	30.0
Taos Pueblo and Trust Lands, NM	76	356	121	54	35	152	30.9
Taos Pueblo, NM	76	356	121	54	35	152	31.0
Taos Trust Lands, NM	-	-	-	-	-	-	4.0
Te-Maak Reservation and Trust Lands, NV	44	261	70	26	23	48	25.8
Te-Maak Reservation, NV	44	255	64	20	21	43	25.2
Te-Maak Trust Lands, NV	-	6	6	6	2	5	50.8
Tesuque Pueblo and Trust Lands, NM	12	67	28	18	6	18	29.0
Tonawanda Reservation, NY	29	123	46	23	24	50	30.8
Torres-Martinez Reservation, CA	6	42	11	7	2	5	22.3
Trinidad Rancheria, CA	3	19	1	3	4	1	23.5

[Continued]

Population of American Indian and Alaska Native Areas, by Age and Sex: 1990, Sokaagon-Ute - II
[Continued]

American Indian/Alaska Native Area State	American Indian, Eskimo, or Aleut						
	Age						Median age
	21 to 24 years	25 to 44 years	45 to 54 years	55 to 59 years	60 to 64 years	65 years and over	
Tulalip Reservation, WA	58	365	99	28	24	39	22.2
Tule River Reservation, CA	49	222	37	14	18	24	20.4
Tunica-Biloxi Reservation, LA	2	2	2	-	2	3	27.5
Tuolumne Rancheria, CA	3	27	13	3	6	15	35.7
Turtle Mountain Reservation and Trust Lands, ND-SD	391	1,785	514	185	149	351	20.9
Turtle Mountain Reservation, ND	280	1,228	404	147	114	289	22.3
Turtle Mountain Trust Lands, ND	111	557	110	38	35	62	18.1
Tuscarara Reservation, NY	17	85	25	7	25	28	30.4
Twenty-Nine Palms Reservation, CA	-	-	-	-	-	-	-
Unitah and Quray Reservation, UT	165	704	189	62	41	119	19.6
Umatilla Reservation, OR	50	302	98	36	31	73	26.4
Upper Lake Rancheria, CA	2	7	-	1	-	3	18.5
Upper Sioux Community, MN	1	11	2	-	6	7	34.2
Upper Skagit Reservation, WA	15	49	9	3	4	7	22.8
Ute Mountain Reservation and Trust Lands, CO-NM-UT	111	385	105	39	26	55	24.3
Ute Mountain Reservation	111	385	105	39	26	55	24.3
Colorado	84	318	91	32	21	43	24.8
New Mexico	-	-	-	-	-	-	-
Utah	27	67	14	7	5	12	22.8
Ute Mountain Trust Lands, UT	-	-	-	-	-	-	-

Source: Summary Population and Housing Characteristics, United States Summary, United States Bureau of the Census, CP H-1, pp. 402-416. *Notes:* a dash (-) indicates no data were given in the original source. 1. Federal American Indian reservations are areas with boundaries established by treaty, statute, and/ or executive or court order, and recognized by the federal government as territory in which American Indian tribes have jurisdiction. State reservations are lands held in trust by state governments for the use and benefit of a given tribe. The reservations and their boundaries were identified for the 1990 census by the Bureau of Indian Affairs (BIA), Department of Interior (for federal reservations), and state governments (for state reservations). The names of American Indian reservations recognized by state governments, but not by the federal government, are followed by "state." Areas composed of reservation lands that are administered jointly and/or are claimed by two reservations, as identified by the BIA, are called "joint areas," and are treated as separate American Indian reservations for census purposes. Federal reservations may cross state boundaries, and federal and state reservations may cross county, county subdivision, and place boundaries. For reservations that cross state boundaries, only the portion of the reservations in a given state are shown in the data products for that state; the entire reservations are shown in data products for the United States. 2. Trust lands are property associated with a particular American Indian reservation or tribe, held in trust by the federal government. Trust lands may be held in trust either for a tribe (tribal trust lands) or for an individual member of a tribe (individual trust land). Trust lands recognized for the 1990 census comprised all tribal trust lands and inhabited individual trust lands located outside of a reservation boundary. As with other American Indian areas, trust lands may be located in more than one state. Only the trust lands in a given state are shown in the data products for that state; all trust lands associated with a reservation or tribe are shown in data products for the United States. The Census Bureau first reported data for tribal trust lands for the 1980 census.

★ 188 ★

Population of American Indian and Alaska Native Areas, by Age and Sex: 1990, Vermillion-Zuni - I

American Indian/Alaska Native Area State	All persons	American Indian, Eskimo, or Aleut					
		Total	Female	Age			
				Under 5 years	16 years and over	18 years and over	18 to 20 years
American Indian reservation and Trust Lands[1,2]							
Vermillion Lake Reservation, MN	91	87	41	13	49	43	-
Viejas Rancheria, CA	411	227	104	35	121	117	8
Walker River Reservation, NV	802	620	317	95	403	378	29
Warm Springs Reservation and Trust Lands, OR	3,076	2,820	1,404	434	1,627	1,514	142
Warm Springs Reservation, OR	3,076	2,820	1,404	434	1,627	1,514	142
Warm Springs Trust Lands, OR	-	-	-	-	-	-	-
Washoe Reservation, NV	157	65	39	5	47	44	8
White Earth Reservation, MN	8,727	2,759	1,364	320	1,686	1,583	99
Wind River Reservation, WY	21,851	5,676	2,835	730	3,384	3,150	292
Winnebago Reservation, NE	2,341	1,156	587	160	672	639	64
Winnemucca Colony, NV	67	61	30	6	43	43	2
Wisconsin Winnebago Reservation and Trust Lands, WI	700	570	282	73	346	316	36
Wisconsin Winnebago Reservation, WI	506	468	234	70	263	245	28
Wisconsin Winnebago Trust Lands, WI	194	102	48	3	83	71	8
Woodfords Community, CA	14	-	-	-	-	-	-
XL Ranch Reservation, CA	35	27	11	-	22	21	2
Yakima Reservation and Trust Lands, WA	27,668	6,307	3,235	830	3,849	3,592	324
Yakima Reservation, WA	27,522	6,176	3,157	811	3,770	3,521	321
Yakima Trust Lands, WA	146	131	78	19	79	71	3
Yakatan Reservation, SD	6,269	1,994	1,018	273	1,146	1,041	110
Yavapai Reservation, AZ	176	134	73	24	80	75	10
Yerington Reservation and Trust Lands, NV	428	324	179	48	205	196	15
Yerington Reservation, NV	275	186	99	25	126	119	12
Yerlington Trust Lands, NV	153	138	80	23	79	77	3
Yomba Reservation, NV	95	88	35	7	57	52	5
Ysleta Del Sur Pueblo, TX	292	211	102	18	138	121	12
Yurok Reservation, CA	1,357	463	242	63	285	266	11
Zia Pueblo and Trust Lands, NM	637	637	327	66	418	387	31
Zuni Pueblo	7,412	7,073	3,625	790	4,651	4,359	403
Arizona	7	-	-	-	-	-	-
New Mexico	7,405	7,073	3,625	790	4,651	4,359	403

[Continued]

★ 188 ★

Population of American Indian and Alaska Native Areas, by Age and Sex: 1990, Vermillion-Zuni - I

[Continued]

American Indian/Alaska Native Area State	All persons	American Indian, Eskimo, or Aleut						
		Total	Female	Age				
				Under 5 years	16 years and over	18 years and over	18 to 20 years
San Felipe/Santa Ana joint area, NM	-	-	-	-	-	-	-
San Felipe/Santa Domingo joint area, NM	-	-	-	-	-	-	-
Crow/Northern Cheyene Area, MT	7	1	-	-	1	1	-

Source: Summary Population and Housing Characteristics, United States Summary, United States Bureau of the Census, CP H-1, pp. 402-416. *Notes:* A dash (-) indicates no data were given in the original source. 1. Federal American Indian reservations are areas with boundaries established by treaty, statute, and/or executive or court order, and recognized by the federal government as territory in which American Indian tribes have jurisdiction. State reservations are lands held in trust by state governments for the use and benefit of a given tribe. The reservations and their boundaries were identified for the 1990 census by the Bureau of Indian Affairs (BIA), Department of Interior (for federal reservations), and state governments (for state reservations). The names of American Indian reservations recognized by state governments, but not by the federal government, are followed by "state." Areas composed of reservation lands that are administered jointly and/or are claimed by two reservations, as identified by the BIA, are called "joint areas," and are treated as separate American Indian reservations for census purposes. Federal reservations may cross state boundaries, and federal and state reservations may cross county, county subdivision, and place boundaries. For reservations that cross state boundaries, only the portion of the reservations in a given state are shown in the data products for that state; the entire reservations are shown in data products for the United States. 2. Trust lands are property associated with a particular American Indian reservation or tribe, held in trust by the federal government. Trust lands may be held in trust either for a tribe (tribal trust lands) or for an individual member of a tribe (individual trust land). Trust lands recognized for the 1990 census comprised all tribal trust lands and inhabited individual trust lands located outside of a reservation boundary. As with other American Indian areas, trust lands may be located in more than one state. Only the trust lands in a given state are shown in the data products for that state; all trust lands associated with a reservation or tribe are shown in data products for the United States. The Census Bureau first reported data for tribal trust lands for the 1980 census.

★ 189 ★

Population of American Indian and Alaska Native Areas, by Age and Sex: 1990, Vermillion-Zuni - II

American Indian/Alaska Native Area State	American Indian, Eskimo, or Aleut						
	Age						Median age
	21 to 24 years	25 to 44 years	45 to 54 years	55 to 59 years	60 to 64 years	65 years and over	
American Indian reservation and Trust Lands[1,2]							
Vermillion Lake Reservation,MN	3	22	7	1	8	2	17.9
Viejas Rancheria, CA	10	63	18	8	5	5	19.2
Walker River Reservation, NV	28	169	62	22	18	50	26.0
Warm Springs Reservation and Trust Lands, OR	163	824	181	75	49	80	20.2
Warm Springs Reservation, OR	163	824	181	75	49	80	20.2
Warm Springs Trust Lands, OR	-	-	-	-	-	-	-
Washoe Reservation, NV	3	22	3	1	3	4	26.3
White Earth Reservation, MN	120	753	218	81	88	224	24.5
Wind River Reservation, WY	350	1,533	450	160	111	254	21.2
Winnebago Reservation, NE	60	299	83	28	28	77	20.8

[Continued]

★ 189 ★

Population of American Indian and Alaska Native Areas, by Age and Sex: 1990, Vermillion-Zuni - II

[Continued]

American Indian/Alaska Native Area State	American Indian, Eskimo, or Aleut						
	Age						Median age
	21 to 24 years	25 to 44 years	45 to 54 years	55 to 59 years	60 to 64 years	65 years and over	
Winnemucca Colony, NV	6	23	7	1	3	1	27.8
Wisconsin Winnebago Reservation and Trust Lands, WI	29	137	32	23	21	38	20.5
Wisconsin Winnebago Reservation, WI	28	110	25	20	10	24	19.0
Wisconsin Winnebago Trust Lands, WI	1	27	7	3	11	14	33.3
Woodfords Community, CA	-	-	-	-	-	-	-
XL Ranch Reservation, CA	2	8	1	1	-	7	40.5
Yakima Reservation and Trust Lands, WA	338	1,786	485	186	150	323	22.4
Yakima Reservation, WA	324	1,756	471	181	148	320	22.4
Yakima Trust Lands, WA	14	30	14	5	2	3	21.8
Yakatan Reservation, SD	100	482	137	66	30	116	19.0
Yavapai Reservation, AZ	1	44	9	3	3	2	20.0
Yerington Reservation and Trust Lands, NV	16	95	26	11	11	22	25.4
Yerington Reservation, NV	6	56	15	7	10	13	26.7
Yerlington Trust Lands, NV	10	39	11	4	1	9	21.8
Yomba Reservation, NV	4	32	2	1	4	4	24.0
Ysleta Del Sur Pueblo, TX	19	51	20	6	4	9	21.7
Yurok Reservation, CA	24	114	38	19	25	35	24.9
Zia Pueblo and Trust Lands, NM	43	193	53	12	14	41	24.5
Zuni Pueblo	534	2,248	448	157	178	391	24.1
Arizona	-	-	-	-	-	-	-
New Mexico	534	2,248	448	157	178	391	24.1
San Felipe/Santa Ana joint area, NM	-	-	-	-	-	-	-
San Felipe/Santo Domingo joint area, NM	-	-	-	-	-	-	-
Crow/Northern Cheyene Area, MT	-	-	1	-	-	-	52.5

Source: *Summary Population and Housing Characteristics, United States Summary*, United States Bureau of the Census, CP H-1, pp. 402-416. Notes: A dash (-) indicates no data given in original source. 1. Federal American Indian reservations are areas with boundaries established by treaty, statute, and/or executive or court order, and recognized by the federal government as territory in which American Indian tribes have jurisdiction. State reservations are lands held in trust by state governments for the use and benefit of a given tribe. The reservations and their boundaries were identified for the 1990 census by the Bureau of Indian Affairs (BIA), Department of Interior (for federal reservations), and state governments (for state reservations). The names of American Indian reservations recognized by state governments, but not by the federal government, are followed by "state." Areas composed of reservation lands that are administered jointly and/or are claimed by two reservations, as identified by the BIA, are called "joint areas," and are treated as separate American Indian reservations for census purposes. Federal reservations may cross state boundaries, and federal and state reservations may cross county, county subdivision, and place boundaries. For reservations that cross state boundaries, only the portion of the reservations in a given state are shown in the data products for that state; the entire reservations are shown in data products for the United States. 2. Trust lands are property associated with a particular American Indian reservation or tribe, held in trust by the federal government. Trust lands may be held in trust either for a tribe (tribal trust lands) or for an individual member of a tribe (individual trust land). Trust lands recognized for the 1990 census comprised all tribal trust lands and inhabited individual trust lands located outside of a reservation boundary. As with other American Indian areas, trust lands may be located in more than one state. Only the trust lands in a given state are shown in the data products for that state; all trust lands associated with a reservation or tribe are shown in data products for the United States. The Census Bureau first reported data for tribal trust lands for the 1980 census.

★ 190 ★

Population of Tribal Designated Statistical Areas, by Age and Sex: 1990 - I

American Indian/Alaska Native Area State	All persons	American Indian, Eskimo, or Aleut					
		Total	Female	Age			
				Under 5 years	16 years and over	18 years and over	18 to 20 years
Tribal Designated Statistical Area[1]							
All areas	1,616,872	53,644	27,435	4,996	36,607	34,345	3,150
Apache Choctaw TDSA (state), LA	22,646	639	308	51	436	419	34
Chickahominy TDSA (state), VA	2,791	466	239	19	391	376	30
Clifton Choctaw TDSA (state), LA	411	153	80	6	127	119	4
Coharie TDSA (state), NC	116,053	1,306	659	96	926	886	51
Coquille Indian TDSA, OR	404,117	5,483	2,755	457	3,890	3,671	342
Delaware-Muncie TDSA (state), KS	265	10	4	-	9	8	2
Eastern Chickahominy TDSA (state), VA	99	30	15	-	27	24	3
Florida Tribe of Eastern Creek TDSA (state), FL	195	-	-	-	-	-	-
Haliwa-Saponi TDSA (state), NC	6,436	2,244	1,134	184	1,606	1,519	145
Jena Band of Chactow TDSA (state), LA	60,334	265	123	10	190	177	13
Klamath TDSA, OR	41,035	1,839	946	241	1,165	1,090	111
Lumbee TDSA (state), NC	50,039	28,863	14,996	2,666	19,858	18,577	1,748
Meherrin TDSA (state), NC	55,306	296	146	16	225	208	13
Mahegan TDSA (state), CT	24,636	219	121	21	163	159	11
Ponca TDSA (state), NE	8	-	-	-	-	-	-
Ramapough TDSA (state), NJ	809	273	138	27	198	179	15
United Houma Nation TDSA (state), LA	817,386	10,079	5,038	1,073	6,353	5,936	558
Waccamaw Siouan TDSA (state), NC	2,667	1,226	613	107	854	817	60
Wampanoog-Gay Head TDSA, MA	11,639	253	120	22	189	180	10

Source: Summary Population and Housing Characteristics, United States Summary, United States Bureau of the Census, CP H-1, pp. 402-416. *Notes:* A dash (-) indiacates that no data were given in the original source.1. Tribal designated statistical areas (TDSA's) are areas, delineated outside Oklahoma by federally- and state-recognized tribes without a land base or associated trust lands, to provide statistical areas for which the Census Bureau tabulates data. TDSA's represent areas generally containing the American Indian population over which federally- recognized tribes have jurisdiction and areas in which state tribes provide benefits and services to their members. The names of TDSA's delineated by state-recognized tribes are followed by "(state)." The Census Bureau did not recognize TDSA's before the 1990 census.

★ 191 ★

Population of Tribal Designated Statistical Areas, by Age and Sex: 1990 - II

American Indian/Alaska Native Area State	American Indian, Eskimo, or Aleut						Median age
	Age						
	21 to 24 years	25 to 44 years	45 to 54 years	55 to 59 years	60 to 64 years	65 years and over	
Tribal Designated Statistical Area[1]							
All areas	3,380	16,309	4,770	1,656	1,541	3,539	26.2
Apache Choctaw TDSA (state), LA	26	198	39	29	17	76	29.4
Chickahominy TDSA (state), VA	24	160	62	27	20	53	36.3
Clifton Choctaw TDSA (state), LA	8	45	24	12	8	18	38.8
Coharie TDSA (state), NC	73	413	126	49	43	131	30.2
Coquille Indian TDSA, OR	352	1,815	521	157	166	318	27.5
Delaware-Muncie TDSA (state), KS	1	2	1	1	1	-	23.5
Eastern Chickahominy TDSA (state), VA	-	7	6	-	1	7	43.3
Florida Tribe of Eastern Creek TDSA (state), FL	-	-	-	-	-	-	-
Haliwa-Saponi TDSA (state), NC	137	686	222	71	81	177	28.2
Jena Band of Chactow TDSA (state), LA	18	87	26	7	8	18	27.7
Klamath TDSA, OR	121	542	123	61	35	97	22.8
Lumbee TDSA (state), NC	1,777	8,750	2,581	875	858	1,988	26.4
Meherrin TDSA (state), NC	13	70	33	17	18	44	36.1
Mahegan TDSA (state), CT	15	78	22	7	11	15	29.7
Ponca TDSA (state), NE	-	-	-	-	-	-	-
Ramapough TDSA (state), NJ	17	82	26	13	6	20	27.5
United Houma Nation TDSA (state), LA	707	2,916	815	271	220	449	23.0
Waccamaw Siouan TDSA (state), NC	75	370	129	49	35	99	29.2
Wampanoog-Gay Head TDSA, MA	16	88	14	10	13	29	30.6

Source: Summary Population and Housing Characteristics, United States Summary, United States Bureau of the Census, CP H-1, pp. 402-416. *Notes:* A dash (-) indiacates that no data were given in the original source.1. Tribal designated statistical areas (TDSA's) are areas, delineated outside Oklahoma by federally- and state-recognized tribes without a land base or associated trust lands, to provide statistical areas for which the Census Bureau tabulates data. TDSA's represent areas generally containing the American Indian population over which federally- recognized tribes have jurisdiction and areas in which state tribes provide benefits and services to their members. The names of TDSA's delineated by state-recognized tribes are followed by "(state)." The Census Bureau did not recognize TDSA's before the 1990 census.

★ 192 ★

Population of Tribal Jurisdiction Statistical Areas, by Age and Sex: 1990 - I

American Indian/Alaska Native Area State	All persons	American Indian, Eskimo, or Aleut					
		Total	Female	Age			
				Under 5 years	16 years and over	18 years and over	18 to 20 years
Tribal Jurisdiction Statistical Area[1]							
All areas	2,082,377	200,789,	102,606	20,396	132,884	124,897	10,644
Absentee Shawnee-Citizens Band of Patawatomi TJSA, OK	91,166	6,457	3,192	540	4,256	3,975	344
Caddo-Witchita-Delaware TJSA, OK	8,195	545	272	74	340	315	27
Cherokee TJSA, OK	399,385	66,356	33,746	6,722	44,130	41,477	3,583
Cheyenne-Arapaho TJSA, OK	150,826	6,719	3,494	796	4,095	3,852	330
Chickasaw TJSA, OK	257,858	21,248	10,895	2,185	13,998	13,123	1,209
Choctow TJSA, OK	209,339	28,411	14,490	2,884	18,657	17,480	1,452
Creek TJSA, OK	635,250	44,964	23,136	4,395	30,476	28,785	2,301
Iowa TJSA, OK	3,979	239	122	23	159	148	12
Kow TJSA, OK	13,110	673	364	80	426	406	29
Kiowa-Comanche-Appache-Fort Aill Apache TJSA, OK	205,400	13,108	6,777	1,442	8,519	8,026	728
Otoe-Missouria TJSA, OK	2,775	478	253	56	294	283	29
Pawnee TJSA, OK	15,443	1,624	804	167	1,077	1,012	76
Sac and Fox TJSA, OK	51,042	4,704	2,407	490	3,081	2,864	250
Seminole TJSA, OK	22,964	3,786	1,947	396	2,440	2,280	188
Tonkawa TJSA, OK	12,289	920	444	88	564	522	59
Creek-Seminole Joint Area TJSA, OK	2,448	518	241	53	346	326	24
Iowa-Sac and Fox Joint Area TJSA, OK	908	39	22	5	26	23	3

Source: Summary Population and Housing Characteristics, United States Summary, United States Bureau of the Census, CP H-1, pp. 402-416. *Notes:* 1. Tribal jurisdiction statistical areas (TJSA's) are areas, delineated by federally recognized tribes in Oklahoma without a reservation, for which the Census Bureau tabulates data. TJSA's represent areas generally containing the American Indian population over which one or more tribal governments have jurisdiction. If tribal officials delineated adjacent TJSA's so that they include some duplicate territory, the overlap area is called a "joint use area," which is treated as a separate TJSA for census purposes.

★ 193 ★

Population of Tribal Jurisdiction Statistical Areas, by Age and Sex: 1990 - II

American Indian/Alaska Native Area State	American Indian, Eskimo, or Aleut						
	Age						Median age
	21 to 24 years	25 to 44 years	45 to 54 years	55 to 59 years	60 to 64 years	65 years and over	
Tribal Jurisdiction Statistical Area[1]							
All areas	11,232	55,164	17,251	6,930	6,375	17,301	25.9
Absentee Shawnee-Citizens Band of Patawatomi TJSA, OK	318	1,886	645	236	177	369	25.9
Caddo-Witchita-Delaware TJSA, OK	29	144	37	28	12	38	23.2
Cherokee TJSA, OK	3,756	17,882	5,880	2,344	2,142	5,890	26.0
Cheyenne-Arapaho TJSA, OK	381	1,962	516	197	158	308	22.7
Chickasaw TJSA, OK	1,132	5,631	1,734	677	717	2,023	25.5
Choctow TJSA, OK	1,472	7,337	2,305	991	971	2,952	25.9
Creek TJSA, OK	2,622	13,142	4,052	1,558	1,382	3,728	26.9
Iowa TJSA, OK	14	71	23	7	4	17	25.5
Kow TJSA, OK	30	177	62	23	22	63	26.1

[Continued]

Population of Tribal Juriodiction Statistical Areas, by Age and Sex: 1990 - II
[Continued]

American Indian/Alaska Native Area State	American Indian, Eskimo, or Aleut						Median age
	Age						
	21 to 24 years	25 to 44 years	45 to 54 years	55 to 59 years	60 to 64 years	65 years and over	
Kiowa-Comanche-Appache-Fort Aill Apache TJSA, OK	840	3,688	1,016	443	410	901	24.5
Otoe-Missouria TJSA, OK	25	117	33	18	14	47	23.3
Pawnee TJSA, OK	69	466	154	56	55	136	27.2
Sac and Fox TJSA, OK	263	1,305	375	160	148	363	25.0
Seminole TJSA, OK	219	948	298	147	129	351	24.6
Tonkawa TJSA, OK	46	262	69	25	17	44	21.2
Creek-Seminole Joint Area TJSA, OK	16	134	47	20	17	68	29.2
Iowa-Sac and Fox Joint Area TJSA, OK	-	12	5	-	-	3	25.5

Source: Summary Population and Housing Characteristics, United States Summary, United States Bureau of the Census, CP H-1, pp. 402-416. *Notes:* A dash (-) indiacates that no data were given in the original source. 1. Tribal jurisdiction statistical areas (TJSA's) are areas, delineated by federally recognized tribes in Oklahoma without a reservation, for which the Census Bureau tabulates data. TJSA's represent areas generally containing the American Indian population over which one or more tribal governments have jurisdiction. If tribal officials delineated adjacent TJSA's so that they include some duplicate territory, the overlap area is called a "joint use area," which is treated as a separate TJSA for census purposes.

American Indian Population, by Tribe and State, 1980: Midwest Region, Abenaki-Chinook

Data are estimates based on a sample and are the most recent available.

Tribe	Midwest Region											
	East North Central Division					West North Central Division						
	OH	IN	IL	MI	WI	MN	IA	MO	ND	SD	NE	KS
All American Indians	15,300	9,495	19,118	44,712	30,553	36,527	6,311	14,820	19,905	45,525	9,059	17,829
Abenaki (n.e.c)	2	3	-	7	-	-	-	-	-	-	-	18
Alabama Coushatta[1]	-	-	-	-	4	-	-	-	2	-	-	-
Alaska Native (n.e.c.)												
Total	-	-	4	-	24	-	-	-	-	2	-	-
Alaska Native	-	-	4	-	24	-	-	-	-	2	-	-
Sealaska	-	-	-	-	-	-	-	-	-	-	-	-
Alaska Athabaskans												
Total	36	10	42	56	29	-	9	15	-	15	10	3
Alaskan Athabaskans	36	10	18	6	25	7	9	15	-	-	5	2
Doyon	-	-	24	5	4	2	-	-	-	15	-	-
Taniana	-	-	-	45	-	5	-	-	-	-	5	1
Other Alaskan Athabaskans	-	-	-	-	-	-	-	-	-	-	-	-
Aleut and Eskimo												
Total	-	-	8	7	-	-	-	-	-	-	-	-
Akutan	-	-	-	7	-	-	-	-	-	-	-	-
Aleut	-	8	-	-	-	-	-	-	-	-	-	-
Calista	-	-	-	-	-	-	-	-	-	-	-	-
Chugach	-	-	-	-	-	-	-	-	-	-	-	-
Eskimo	-	-	-	-	-	-	-	-	-	-	-	-
Kotzebue Sound	-	-	-	-	-	-	-	-	-	-	-	-
Other Aleut and Eskimo	-	-	-	-	-	-	-	-	-	-	-	-
Algonquian (n.e.c.)	11	7	8	247	-	-	-	12	-	5	10	-
Apache												
Total	380	126	247	746	200	150	88	273	74	21	41	400

[Continued]

American Indian Population, by Tribe and State, 1980: Midwest Region, Abenaki-Chinook
[Continued]

Tribe	Midwest Region											
	East North Central Division					West North Central Division						
	OH	IN	IL	MI	WI	MN	IA	MO	ND	SD	NE	KS
Apache (n.e.c.)	361	120	237	715	179	139	86	247	61	19	41	355
Chiricahua	2	6	6	22	-	-	-	17	-	2	-	2
Fort Sill Apache	-	-	-	-	-	-	-	-	-	-	-	5
Jicarilla	-	-	-	-	13	-	-	-	-	-	-	5
Kiowa Apache	-	-	-	4	-	-	-	3	-	-	-	5
Mescalero Apache	17	-	4	5	5	11	2	-	13	-	-	12
Payson Apache	-	-	-	-	-	-	-	-	-	-	-	-
San Carlos Apache	-	-	-	-	-	-	-	6	-	-	-	8
White Mountain Apache	-	-	-	-	3	-	-	-	-	-	-	8
Other Apache	-	-	-	-	-	-	-	-	-	-	-	-
Arapaho	44	5	21	5	3	-	5	8	2	30	5	36
Arikara	7	-	6	1	12	-	2	32	880	32	-	5
Assiniboine	11	-	57	5	-	-	-	-	12	93	5	-
Bannock	-	-	-	8	51	-	-	-	-	-	-	-
Blackfoot[1]	605	282	494	832	159	179	96	456	37	18	52	283
Caddo	-	-	-	-	-	-	-	-	-	-	-	29
Cahuilla												
Total	-	-	7	-	-	-	-	6	-	-	-	-
Cahuilla	-	-	-	-	-	-	-	-	-	-	-	-
Soboba	-	-	-	-	-	-	-	-	-	-	-	-
Torres-Martinez	-	-	-	-	-	-	-	-	-	-	-	-
Other Cahuilla	-	-	7	-	-	-	-	6	-	-	-	-
California tribes (n.e.c.)												
Total	4	2	15	5	-	6	-	-	-	9	-	4
Cahto	-	-	-	-	-	-	-	-	-	9	-	-
Digger	-	-	-	-	-	-	-	-	-	-	-	-
Mattole	-	2	-	-	-	-	-	-	-	-	-	4
Morongo	2	-	-	-	-	-	-	-	-	-	-	-
Wappo	2	-	-	-	-	-	-	-	-	-	-	-
Yuki	-	-	6	-	-	6	-	-	-	-	-	-
Other California	-	-	9	5	-	-	-	-	-	-	-	-
Canadian and Latin American	105	68	281	469	73	119	25	25	17	4	-	54
Catawba	-	-	31	2	8	-	-	-	-	-	-	-
Cayuse	-	-	-	-	-	-	-	-	-	-	-	-
Chehalis	-	-	-	-	-	-	-	-	-	-	-	-
Chemakuan												
Total	-	2	-	-	-	-	-	-	-	-	-	-
Hoh	-	-	-	-	-	-	-	-	-	-	-	-
Quileute	-	2	-	-	-	-	-	-	-	-	-	-
Other Chemakuan	-	-	-	-	-	-	-	-	-	-	-	-
Chemehuevi	-	-	-	-	-	-	-	19	-	-	-	-
Cherokee												
Total	5,667	3,265	4,182	7,972	940	842	973	5,857	175	237	475	4,760
Cherokee	5,667	3,265	4,182	7,960	936	-	951	5,857	175	237	475	4,760
Eastern Cherokee	-	-	-	9	-	-	6	-	-	11	-	2
Etowah Cherokee	-	-	-	-	-	-	-	-	-	-	-	-
Tuscola	-	-	-	-	4	-	-	-	-	-	-	-
United Keetoowah	-	-	-	3	-	-	16	-	-	-	-	-
Western Cherokee	-	-	-	-	-	-	-	-	-	-	-	-
Other Cherokee	-	-	-	-	-	-	-	-	-	-	-	-
Cheyenne												
Total	69	85	57	121	34	48	68	73	13	294	67	155
Cheyenne	69	58	57	108	31	30	55	62	13	275	26	152
Northern Cheyenne	-	27	-	-	3	18	13	11	-	19	41	2

[Continued]

★ 194 ★

American Indian Population, by Tribe and State, 1980: Midwest Region, Abenaki-Chinook
[Continued]

Tribe	Midwest Region											
	East North Central Division					West North Central Division						
	OH	IN	IL	MI	WI	MN	IA	MO	ND	SD	NE	KS
Southern Cheyenne	-	-	-	13	-	-	-	-	-	-	-	1
Chickahominy	7	11	-	18	-	-	-	-	-	-	-	-
Chickasaw	96	12	73	62	5	9	27	129	1	-	23	106
Chinook												
Total	-	-	21	12	26	73	-	-	5	-	2	-
Chinook	-	-	21	12	26	73	-	-	5	-	2	-
Clatsop	-	-	-	-	-	-	-	-	-	-	-	-
Columbia River Chinook	-	-	-	-	-	-	-	-	-	-	-	-
Other Chinook	-	-	-	-	-	-	-	-	-	-	-	-

Source: U.S. Bureau of the Census, *1980 Census of Population, Volume 2, Subject Reports, Characteristics of American Indians, by Tribes and Selected Areas: 1980,* PC80-2-1C, Section 1: Tables I-II, issued September 1989, U.S. Department of Commerce, U.S. Government Printing Office, Washington, D.C., pp. 1-53. *Notes:* (N.E.C.) stands for not elsewhere classified. A dash (-) represents zero or a percent which rounds to less than 0.1. 1. Reporting and/or processing problems may have affected the data for this tribe.

★ 195 ★

American Indian Population, by Tribe and State, 1980: Midwest Region, Chippewa-Iowa

Data are estimates based on a sample and are the most recent available.

Tribe	Midwest Region											
	East North Central Division					West North Central Division						
	OH	IN	IL	MI	WI	MN	IA	MO	ND	SD	NE	KS
Chippewa												
Total	382	213	1,533	12,881	8,370	24,125	256	198	9,201	335	118	256
Bad River	-	-	7	-	190	29	-	-	-	-	-	-
Bay Mills Chippewa	-	-	-	291	2	16	-	-	-	-	-	-
Bois Forte	-	-	-	-	-	73	-	-	-	-	-	-
Chippewa	377	207	1,505	11,720	7,678	22,749	256	190	8,971	303	116	252
Lac Courte Oreilles	-	-	-	-	260	-	-	-	-	-	-	-
Lac du Flambeau	-	-	-	18	-	-	-	-	-	-	-	-
Lake Superior	-	-	-	-	-	58	-	-	-	-	-	-
Leech Lake	-	-	-	-	-	55	-	-	-	-	-	-
Leelanau	-	-	18	-	-	-	-	-	-	-	-	-
Mille Lac	-	-	-	-	2	45	-	-	-	-	-	-
Minnesota Chippewa	-	-	2	30	13	645	-	-	9	6	-	-
Ontonagon	-	7	-	48	-	-	-	-	-	-	-	-
Red Cliff Chippewa	-	-	-	9	13	21	-	-	-	-	-	-
Red Lake Chippewa	-	-	6	-	5	150	-	-	-	8	-	-
Saginaw Chippewa	-	6	-	229	1	33	-	-	-	-	-	-
St. Croix Chippewa	-	-	-	-	9	7	-	-	-	-	-	-
Sault Ste. Marie Chippewa	5	-	-	566	13	5	-	5	3	-	-	4
Sokoagon Chippewa	-	-	-	-	89	-	-	-	-	-	-	-
Turtle Mountain	-	-	-	12	17	47	-	-	186	18	2	-
White Earth	-	-	6	-	12	154	-	3	32	-	-	-

[Continued]

347

American Indian Population, by Tribe and State, 1980: Midwest Region, Chippewa-Iowa
[Continued]

| Tribe | Midwest Region | | | | | | | | | | | |
| | East North Central Division | | | | | West North Central Division | | | | | | |
	OH	IN	IL	MI	WI	MN	IA	MO	ND	SD	NE	KS
Other Chippewa	-	-	-	6	-	38	-	-	-	-	-	-
Chitimacha	-	-	-	-	-	-	-	-	-	-	-	-
Choctaw												
Total	141	86	669	318	35	73	79	401	2	7	39	625
Choctaw	139	86	669	316	35	69	79	401	2	7	39	625
Clifton Choctaw	2	-	-	2	-	4	-	-	-	-	-	-
Chumash[1]												
Total	-	-	11	-	-	6	-	8	-	-	-	-
Chumash	-	-	11	-	-	6	-	8	-	-	-	-
Other Chumash	-	-	-	-	-	-	-	-	-	-	-	-
Clallam												
Total	-	-	-	-	-	9	-	-	-	-	-	-
Clallam	-	-	-	-	-	9	-	-	-	-	-	-
Lower Elwah	-	-	-	-	-	-	-	-	-	-	-	-
Port Gamble Clallam	-	-	-	-	-	-	-	-	-	-	-	-
Other Clellam	-	-	-	-	-	-	-	-	-	-	-	-
Coeur d' Alene	-	-	-	-	-	-	-	-	-	-	-	-
Coharie	-	-	-	-	-	-	-	-	-	-	-	-
Colorado River	-	-	-	-	-	-	-	-	-	-	-	6
Colville	3	17	-	-	-	-	-	2	-	-	2	-
Comanche	131	46	83	54	53	28	14	67	11	-	7	114
Coos	-	-	-	-	-	-	-	-	-	-	-	-
Costanoan	-	7	-	-	-	-	-	4	-	-	5	-
Cowitz	-	-	-	-	-	-	-	-	-	-	-	-
Cree	35	5	79	142	51	168	13	50	132	24	24	4
Creek												
Total	85	37	154	93	73	27	11	373	-	20	27	594
Creek	73	37	154	93	73	27	11	373	-	20	27	594
Eastern Creek	12	-	-	-	-	-	-	-	-	-	-	-
Lower Muskogee	-	-	-	-	-	-	-	-	-	-	-	-
Muskogee	-	-	-	-	-	-	-	-	-	-	-	-
Thlopthlocco	-	-	-	-	-	-	-	-	-	-	-	-
Other Creek	-	-	-	-	-	-	-	-	-	-	-	-
Croatan	-	-	2	7	7	-	-	-	-	-	-	-
Crow	11	9	80	175	12	50	25	43	7	46	57	16
Cupeno												
Total	-	-	-	-	-	-	-	-	-	-	-	-
Agua Caliente	-	-	-	-	-	-	-	-	-	-	-	-
Cupeno	-	-	-	-	-	-	-	-	-	-	-	-
Delaware												
Total	74	11	64	87	20	23	24	69	-	-	-	174
Delaware	74	11	64	81	7	19	24	62	-	-	-	170
Munsee	-	-	-	6	13	4	-	7	-	-	-	4
Sand Hill	-	-	-	-	-	-	-	-	-	-	-	-

[Continued]

★ 195 ★

American Indian Population, by Tribe and State, 1980: Midwest Region, Chippewa-Iowa
[Continued]

| Tribe | Midwest Region | | | | | | | | | | | |
| | East North Central Division | | | | | West North Central Division | | | | | | |
	OH	IN	IL	MI	WI	MN	IA	MO	ND	SD	NE	KS
Diegueno												
Total	-	2	-	-	10	-	-	-	-	-	-	-
Diegueno	-	-	-	-	10	-	-	-	-	-	-	-
Manzanita	-	-	-	-	-	-	-	-	-	-	-	-
San Pascual	-	-	-	-	-	-	-	-	-	-	-	-
Santa Ysabel	-	-	-	-	-	-	-	-	-	-	-	-
Other Diegueno	-	2	-	-	-	-	-	-	-	-	-	-
Eastern tribes (n.e.c.)												
Total	29	36	75	1	7	-	2	-	-	-	-	8
Moor	-	-	-	-	-	-	-	-	-	-	-	-
Nansemond	-	-	-	-	-	-	-	-	-	-	-	-
Natchez	13	-	-	-	-	-	2	-	-	-	-	-
Nipmuc	-	-	-	-	-	-	-	-	-	-	-	-
Southeastern Indians	16	20	58	1	7	-	-	-	-	-	-	8
Tunica	-	-	17	-	-	-	-	-	-	-	-	-
Other Eastern	-	16	-	-	-	-	-	-	-	-	-	-
Flathead	-	7	-	5	13	-	-	4	6	35	-	22
Fort Hall	-	-	-	-	-	-	-	-	-	-	-	7
Gabrieleno	-	6	-	-	-	-	-	-	-	-	-	32
Gros Ventres												
Total	-	-	-	2	4	49	-	-	170	17	-	12
Atsina	-	-	-	2	-	-	-	-	57	-	-	-
Gros Ventres	-	-	-	-	4	49	-	-	113	17	-	12
Haida	-	-	-	2	-	11	6	-	-	-	-	-
Haliwa	-	-	-	-	-	-	-	-	-	-	-	-
Hidatsa	-	-	24	-	-	23	-	-	1,169	32	-	29
Hitchiti	-	-	-	-	-	-	-	-	-	-	-	-
Hoopa	-	-	-	21	-	-	-	-	-	-	-	11
Houma	-	-	15	-	-	2	-	-	-	1	-	-
Iowa	-	-	6	15	-	23	8	100	-	-	119	253

Source: U.S. Bureau of the Census, *1980 Census of Population, Volume 2, Subject Reports, Characteristics of American Indians, by Tribes and Selected Areas: 1980,* PC80-2-1C, Section 1: Tables I-II, issued September 1989, U.S. Department of Commerce, U.S. Government Printing Office, Washington, D.C., pp. 1-53. *Notes:* (N.E.C.) stands for not elsewhere classified. A dash (-) represents zero or a percent which rounds to less than 0.1. 1. Reporting and/or processing problems may have affected the data for this tribe.

★ 196 ★

American Indian Population, by Tribe and State, 1980: Midwest Region, Iroquois-Pomo

Data are estimates based on a sample and are the most recent available.

Tribe	Midwest Region											
	East North Central Division					West North Central Division						
	OH	IN	IL	MI	WI	MN	IA	MO	ND	SD	NE	KS
Iroquois												
Total	438	205	836	1,803	5,028	196	69	308	24	90	60	249
Cayuga	16	-	13	44	-	-	-	-	-	-	-	5
Iroquois (n.e.c.)	92	70	108	220	18	27	10	61	6	2	37	13
Mohawk[1]	130	70	77	895	22	55	43	67	2	15	9	35
Oneida	23	48	542	380	4,961	108	8	31	3	70	-	49
Onondaga	5	7	7	17	-	-	5	-	-	-	-	-
Seneca												
Total	98	6	62	111	9	-	3	55	5	3	4	67
Seneca	74	6	62	111	7	-	3	55	5	3	-	67
Seneca Nation	24	-	-	-	2	-	-	-	-	-	-	-
Tonawanda Seneca	-	-	-	-	-	-	-	-	-	-	4	-
Seneca-Cayuga	-	2	-	-	-	-	-	40	-	-	-	43
Tuscarora	27	2	-	62	10	2	-	-	8	-	10	-
Wyandot	47	-	27	74	8	4	-	54	-	-	-	37
Kalispel	-	-	-	-	-	-	-	-	-	-	-	-
Karok	-	-	6	-	-	-	-	-	-	-	1	-
Kaw	-	-	20	4	-	-	-	21	-	2	-	96
Kickapoo	2	3	48	-	-	-	-	107	-	2	12	658
Kiowa	21	9	15	10	29	22	45	16	23	34	22	167
Klamath	41	6	7	2	-	-	-	6	2	-	-	-
Konkow	-	-	-	-	-	-	-	-	-	-	-	-
Kootenai	-	-	6	-	-	-	-	-	2	-	-	-
Long Island												
Total	-	-	-	-	26	-	-	-	-	-	-	-
Matinecock	-	-	-	-	-	-	-	-	-	-	-	-
Montauk	-	-	-	-	26	-	-	-	-	-	-	-
Poosepatuck	-	-	-	-	-	-	-	-	-	-	-	-
Other Long Island	-	-	-	-	-	-	-	-	-	-	-	-
Luiseno												
Total	8	-	-	-	-	-	-	-	-	-	-	-
LaJolla	-	-	-	-	-	-	-	-	-	-	-	-
Luiseno	8	-	-	-	-	-	-	-	-	-	-	-
Pala	-	-	-	-	-	-	-	-	-	-	-	-
Pauma	-	-	-	-	-	-	-	-	-	-	-	-
Pechanga	-	-	-	-	-	-	-	-	-	-	-	-
Lumbee[2]	28	9	23	140	55	6	-	6	-	6	-	10
Lummi[2]	35	-	-	-	-	-	6	-	-	6	-	-
Maidu	-	-	-	-	-	-	22	-	-	-	-	-
Makah	-	-	-	7	-	-	-	7	-	-	-	-
Maliseet	1	-	-	-	-	-	-	-	-	-	-	-
Mandan	-	-	15	-	-	23	-	-	400	112	-	-
Mattaponi	9	-	-	-	6	-	-	-	-	-	-	-

[Continued]

★ 196 ★

American Indian Population, by Tribe and State, 1980: Midwest Region, Iroquois-Pomo
[Continued]

| Tribe | Midwest Region | | | | | | | | | | | |
| | East North Central Division | | | | | West North Central Division | | | | | | |
	OH	IN	IL	MI	WI	MN	IA	MO	ND	SD	NE	KS
Menominee	56	28	434	173	4,772	25	41	6	10	9	6	12
Miami	71	1,089	42	64	57	-	-	86	-	-	6	153
Miccosukee[3]	-	-	-	-	-	-	-	-	-	-	-	-
Micmac[4]	18	-	-	-	-	18	-	-	-	-	-	2
Mission Indians	-	-	16	-	11	-	8	5	1	-	-	6
Miwok	-	2	-	5	-	-	3	-	-	-	-	3
Modoc	-	-	5	-	-	-	-	2	-	-	-	-
Mohegan	-	-	-	5	-	-	-	-	-	-	-	-
Mono	12	-	-	-	-	-	-	-	-	-	-	7
Nanticoke	-	-	-	14	-	-	-	-	-	-	-	-
Narragansett	7	-	-	37	8	-	-	-	-	-	-	-
Navajo	227	60	194	169	85	82	29	152	56	74	15	465
Nez Perce[3]	6	12	30	37	-	-	-	9	-	-	19	-
Nomalaki	-	-	-	-	-	-	-	-	-	-	-	-
Northwest tribes (n.e.c)												
Total	-	-	-	1	-	-	-	-	-	-	-	-
Columbia Wenatchee	-	-	-	1	-	-	-	-	-	-	-	-
Kalapuya	-	-	-	-	-	-	-	-	-	-	-	-
Tillamook	-	-	-	-	-	-	-	-	-	-	-	-
Other Northwest	-	-	-	-	-	-	-	-	-	-	-	-
Omaha	-	11	-	-	2	14	220	40	-	18	2,118	46
Oregon Athabaskan	11	-	7	-	5	-	-	-	-	9	-	-
Osage	16	25	68	88	5	-	-	202	-	9	25	271
Oto	-	15	2	10	4	24	-	28	-	-	6	94
Ottawa	139	74	124	5,052	127	12	-	45	-	-	-	33
Paiute[3]												
Total	-	9	42	22	13	20	5	-	4	12	-	17
Burns Paiute	-	-	-	-	-	-	-	-	-	-	-	-
Northern Paiute	-	-	-	-	-	-	-	-	-	-	-	-
Paiute	-	9	42	22	13	20	5	-	4	12	-	17
Pyramind Lake	-	-	-	-	-	-	-	-	-	-	-	-
Southern Paiute	-	-	-	-	-	-	-	-	-	-	-	-
Walker River	-	-	-	-	-	-	-	-	-	-	-	-
Other Paiute	-	-	-	-	-	-	-	-	-	-	-	-
Pamunkey	-	-	-	-	-	-	-	-	-	-	-	-
Papago												
Total	27	7	5	-	5	-	-	-	-	17	-	75
Papago	27	7	5	-	-	-	-	-	-	17	-	75
Other Papago	-	-	-	-	5	-	-	-	-	-	-	-
Passamaquoddy												
Total	-	-	6	3	-	-	-	-	-	-	25	33
Passamaquoddy	-	-	6	3	-	-	-	-	-	-	25	33
Other Passamaquoddy	-	-	-	-	-	-	-	-	-	-	-	-

[Continued]

★ 196 ★

American Indian Population, by Tribe and State, 1980: Midwest Region, Iroquois-Pomo

[Continued]

Tribe	Midwest Region											
	East North Central Division					West North Central Division						
	OH	IN	IL	MI	WI	MN	IA	MO	ND	SD	NE	KS
Pawnee	15	16	-	28	1	3	9	51	4	9	18	93
Penobscot	12	5	-	8	4	-	-	-	3	-	-	-
Peoria	-	-	-	31	-	-	-	47	-	-	-	49
Pequot	-	-	-	-	-	-	-	-	-	-	-	-
Pima	16	12	4	-	-	-	2	37	-	16	-	7
Piscataway	-	-	-	-	-	-	-	-	-	-	-	-
Pit River	14	-	-	-	-	-	-	-	2	-	-	-
Pomo												
Total	-	-	-	-	-	32	-	-	-	-	-	8
Eastern Pomo	-	-	-	-	-	-	-	-	-	-	-	-
Kashaya	-	-	-	-	-	-	-	-	-	-	-	-
Northern Pomo	-	-	-	-	-	-	-	-	-	-	-	-
Pomo	-	-	-	-	-	32	-	-	-	-	-	8
Other Pomo	-	-	-	-	-	-	-	-	-	-	-	-

Source: U.S. Bureau of the Census, *1980 Census of Population, Volume 2, Subject Reports, Characteristics of American Indians, by Tribes and Selected Areas: 1980,* PC80-2-1C, Section 1: Tables I-II, issued September 1989, U.S. Department of Commerce, U.S. Government Printing Office, Washington, D.C., pp. 1-53. *Notes:* (N.E.C.) stands for not elsewhere classified. A dash (-) represents zero or a percent which rounds to less than 0.1. 1. Any Mohawk entry of "Ganienka" was miscoded to Wailaki. 2. Miscoding of entries of "Lummee," "Lummi," "Lumbee," or "Lumbi" may have affected the data for this tribe. 3. Reporting and/or processing may have affected the data for this tribe. 4. Any entry with the spelling "Micmac" was miscoded to Cheyenne River Sioux.

★ 197 ★

American Indian Population, by Tribe and State, 1980: Midwest Region, Ponca-Sioux

Data are estimates based on a sample and are the most recent available.

Tribe	Midwest Region											
	East North Central Division					West North Central Division						
	OH	IN	IL	MI	WI	MN	IA	MO	ND	SD	NE	KS
Ponca	10	-	4	6	8	-	21	7	-	41	84	160
Potawatomi												
Total	79	193	105	1,620	671	31	2	176	7	-	38	1,634
Citizen Band	-	8	-	16	2	-	-	9	-	-	-	36
Forest County	-	-	-	-	1	-	-	-	-	-	-	-
Huron Potawatomi	-	-	10	105	6	-	-	-	-	-	-	6
Potawatomie	79	181	88	1,469	588	31	-	167	7	-	38	1,331
Prairie Band	-	4	7	23	68	-	2	-	-	-	-	258
Other Potawatomi	-	-	-	7	6	-	-	-	-	-	-	3
Powhatan	-	-	3	6	5	-	-	22	-	-	-	-
Pueblo[1]												
Total	128	12	170	54	62	28	3	28	-	39	28	97
Acoma	-	-	-	-	-	-	-	-	-	-	-	10

[Continued]

★197★

American Indian Population, by Tribe and State, 1980: Midwest Region, Ponca-Sioux

[Continued]

Tribe	Midwest Region											
	East North Central Division					West North Central Division						
	OH	IN	IL	MI	WI	MN	IA	MO	ND	SD	NE	KS
Arizona Tewa	-	-	7	-	17	-	-	-	-	-	-	-
Cochiti	-	-	-	-	-	-	-	-	-	-	-	-
Hopi	5	-	11	7	11	14	-	19	-	6	-	20
Isleta	5	-	5	-	-	-	-	-	-	-	-	-
Jemez	-	-	41	-	-	-	-	-	-	-	-	-
Keres (n.e.c.)	-	-	-	-	-	-	-	-	-	-	-	-
Laguna	-	-	9	-	-	-	3	-	-	-	-	-
Nambe	-	-	7	-	-	-	-	-	-	-	-	-
Picuris	-	-	-	-	-	-	-	-	-	-	-	-
Pojoaque	-	-	-	-	-	-	-	-	-	-	-	-
Pueblo (n.e.c.)	76	12	52	36	13	-	-	-	-	8	26	28
Sandia	-	-	-	-	-	1	-	-	-	-	-	-
San Felipe	-	-	-	-	-	-	-	-	-	-	-	-
San Ildefonso	-	-	-	-	-	-	-	-	-	-	-	-
San Juan	-	-	-	-	-	-	-	-	-	-	-	-
Santa Ana	-	-	-	-	-	-	-	-	-	-	-	-
Santa Clara[1]	-	-	-	-	-	-	9	-	-	-	2	-
Santo Domingo	-	-	9	-	8	-	-	-	-	5	-	5
Taos	-	-	-	11	-	-	-	-	-	-	-	34
Tesuque	-	-	-	-	-	-	-	-	-	-	-	-
Tewa	42	-	21	-	-	6	-	-	-	16	-	-
Tigua[1]	-	-	-	-	-	-	-	-	-	-	-	-
Zia	-	-	-	-	-	-	-	-	-	-	-	-
Zuni	-	-	8	-	13	7	-	-	-	4	-	-
Puget Sound Salish												
Total	7	-	11	21	9	3	10	13	-	-	-	8
Duwamish	-	-	7	-	-	-	-	-	-	-	-	-
Muckleshoot	-	-	-	-	-	-	-	6	-	-	-	8
Nisqually	-	-	-	-	-	-	-	-	-	-	-	-
Nooksack	-	-	-	-	-	-	-	-	-	-	-	-
Puget Sound Salish (n.e.c.)	-	-	-	6	-	3	-	-	-	-	-	-
Puyallup	-	-	-	11	-	-	-	-	-	-	-	-
Samish	-	-	-	4	-	-	-	-	-	-	-	-
Sauk-Sauiatte	-	-	-	-	-	-	-	7	-	-	-	-
Skokomish	-	-	-	-	-	-	10	-	-	-	-	-
Skykomish	-	-	-	-	-	-	-	-	-	-	-	-
Snohomish	-	-	-	-	-	-	-	-	-	-	-	-
Snoqualmie	-	-	-	-	-	-	-	-	-	-	-	-
Squaxin Island	-	-	-	-	-	-	-	-	-	-	-	-
Steilacoom	-	-	-	-	-	-	-	-	-	-	-	-
Stillaguamish	-	-	-	-	-	-	-	-	-	-	-	-
Suquamish	-	-	4	-	-	-	-	-	-	-	-	-
Swinomish	-	-	-	-	-	-	-	-	-	-	-	-
Tulalip	-	-	-	-	9	-	-	-	-	-	-	-

[Continued]

★ 197 ★

American Indian Population, by Tribe and State, 1980: Midwest Region, Ponca-Sioux
[Continued]

| Tribe | Midwest Region | | | | | | | | | | | |
| | East North Central Division | | | | | West North Central Division | | | | | | |
	OH	IN	IL	MI	WI	MN	IA	MO	ND	SD	NE	KS
Upper Skagit	7	-	-	-	-	-	-	-	-	-	-	-
Quapaw	-	-	12	7	-	-	-	27	-	-	-	151
Quinault	6	-	9	-	-	-	2	-	-	-	-	-
Rappahannock	-	-	-	-	-	-	-	-	-	-	-	-
Sac and Fox Mesquakie	11	4	32	-	5	30	870	101	2	-	26	134
Salinan	-	-	-	-	-	-	-	-	-	-	-	-
Schaghticoke	-	-	-	-	-	-	-	-	-	-	-	-
Seminole[1]												
Total	153	84	67	264	11	36	24	53	-	14	6	139
Seminole	153	84	67	264	11	36	18	53	-	14	6	139
Seminole Nation of Oklahoma	-	-	-	-	-	-	-	-	-	-	-	-
Seminole Tribe of Florida	-	-	-	-	-	-	-	-	-	-	-	-
Other Seminole	-	-	-	-	-	-	6	-	-	-	-	-
Serrano	-	-	-	-	-	-	-	-	-	-	-	-
Shasta	-	-	-	-	-	-	-	16	-	-	-	10
Shawnee												
Total	113	92	68	129	31	22	18	188	2	13	6	133
Absentee Shawnee	-	-	5	-	-	-	-	-	-	-	-	8
Shawnee	113	92	63	129	31	22	18	188	2	13	6	125
Shinnecock	-	-	-	-	-	-	-	-	-	-	-	-
Shoshone												
Total	6	17	67	40	19	19	10	70	15	66	8	98
Goshute	-	8	-	-	-	-	-	-	-	-	-	-
Shoshone	6	9	14	35	19	12	10	70	15	33	8	98
Te-Moak Western Shoshone[1]	-	-	-	-	-	-	-	-	-	-	-	-
Yomba[1]	-	-	44	5	-	-	-	-	-	-	-	-
Other Shoshone	-	-	9	-	-	7	-	-	-	33	-	-
Siletz	-	6	-	-	-	-	-	-	-	-	-	-
Sioux												
Total	515	231	750	727	393	2,938	1,077	438	4,749	38,417	2,701	569
Blackfoot Sioux	-	-	-	31	-	27	-	5	8	3	-	-
Brule Sioux	-	-	-	-	2	-	-	2	-	25	-	-
Cheyenne River Sioux[2]	-	-	32	9	3	2	-	-	41	2,765	18	-
Crow River Sioux[2]	-	-	-	-	-	7	-	-	-	1,123	21	-
Dakota Sioux	-	-	6	6	2	102	-	-	82	889	65	-
Devil's Lake Sioux	-	-	-	-	-	4	-	-	77	15	11	-
Fladreau Santee	-	-	-	-	-	-	-	-	38	49	-	-
Fort Peck	-	-	-	-	-	-	-	-	-	-	-	-
Lower Brule Sioux	-	-	-	5	6	6	-	-	8	693	2	-
Mdewakanton Sioux	-	-	8	-	-	105	-	-	-	-	-	-
Oglala Sioux	12	6	38	8	14	149	24	37	48	10,335	445	96
Pine Ridge Sioux	-	-	-	-	-	-	-	8	-	71	10	-
Prior Lake Sioux	-	-	-	-	-	44	-	-	17	-	9	-
Rosebud Sioux	2	10	8	-	6	8	38	2	13	5,179	70	34

[Continued]

★ 197 ★

American Indian Population, by Tribe and State, 1980: Midwest Region, Ponca-Sioux
[Continued]

Tribe	Midwest Region											
	East North Central Division					West North Central Division						
	OH	IN	IL	MI	WI	MN	IA	MO	ND	SD	NE	KS
Santee Sioux	-	-	-	5	9	65	229	1	2	275	443	46
Sioux	451	209	620	658	331	2,195	721	379	4,192	13,084	1,461	354
Sisseton Sioux	-	-	-	-	9	133	28	2	4	715	23	-
Standing Rock Sioux	-	-	9	-	2	8	-	-	191	1,533	9	-
Teton Sioux	27	1	7	5	7	49	-	-	12	136	9	16
Wahpeton Sioux	-	-	-	-	-	7	-	-	-	30	-	-
Yankton Sioux	23	5	18	-	-	15	37	-	7	1,427	96	23
Yanktonai Sioux	-	-	-	-	-	-	-	-	9	66	-	-
Other Sioux	-	-	4	-	2	12	-	2	-	4	9	-

Source: U.S. Bureau of the Census, *1980 Census of Population, Volume 2, Subject Reports, Characteristics of American Indians, by Tribes and Selected Areas: 1980*, PC80-2-1C, Section 1: Tables I-II, issued September 1989, U.S. Department of Commerce, U.S. Government Printing Office, Washington, D.C., pp. 1-53. *Notes:* (N.E.C.) stands for not elsewhere classified. A dash (-) represents zero or a percent which rounds to less than 0.1. 1. Reporting and/or processing problems may have affected the data for this tribe. 2. Any entry with the spelling "Micmac" was miscoded to Cheyenne River Sioux.

★ 198 ★

American Indian Population, by Tribe and State, 1980: Midwest Region, Siuslaw-Yurok

Data are estimates based on a sample and are the most recent available.

Tribe	Midwest Region											
	East North Central Division					West North Central Division						
	OH	IN	IL	MI	WI	MN	IA	MO	ND	SD	NE	KS
Siuslaw	-	-	-	-	-	-	-	-	-	-	-	-
Spokane	-	-	-	-	-	-	-	-	-	-	-	-
Stockbridge	-	9	36	9	934	79	-	-	-	6	10	-
Tlingit	5	2	8	79	9	51	10	-	-	3	-	33
Tolowa	-	-	-	-	-	-	-	-	-	-	-	-
Tonkawa	-	-	6	-	-	-	-	-	-	-	-	-
Tsimishian	-	-	-	23	-	-	-	-	30	-	8	-
Umatilla	-	-	-	-	-	-	-	3	-	-	11	-
Ute												
Total	9	2	-	30	-	6	-	12	9	10	3	22
Uintah Ute	-	-	-	-	-	-	-	-	-	-	-	-
Ute	9	2	-	30	-	6	-	12	9	10	3	22
Ute Mountain Ute	-	-	-	-	-	-	-	-	-	-	-	-
Other Ute	-	-	-	-	-	-	-	-	-	-	-	-
Wailaki[1]	6	-	-	-	-	-	-	-	-	5	-	-
Walla-Walla	-	-	-	-	-	-	-	-	-	-	-	-
Wampanoag	-	-	43	-	8	-	-	13	-	-	-	-
Warm Springs	-	-	-	-	-	-	-	-	-	-	-	8
Washo												
Total	-	-	-	-	-	4	-	-	-	-	-	-

[Continued]

★ 198 ★

American Indian Population, by Tribe and State, 1980: Midwest Region, Siuslaw-Yurok
[Continued]

| Tribe | Midwest Region | | | | | | | | | | | |
| | East North Central Division | | | | | West North Central Division | | | | | | |
	OH	IN	IL	MI	WI	MN	IA	MO	ND	SD	NE	KS
Washo	-	-	-	-	-	4	-	-	-	-	-	-
Other Washo	-	-	-	-	-	-	-	-	-	-	-	-
Wichita	-	-	8	-	-	-	5	-	-	10	-	53
Winnebago	13	16	305	55	2,068	395	280	25	24	49	1,065	49
Wintu	-	-	-	-	-	-	7	-	-	-	2	-
Wiyot	-	-	-	-	-	-	-	-	5	-	-	-
Yakima	4	-	-	4	-	14	6	-	-	-	7	22
Yaqui												
Total	-	3	5	5	-	-	11	-	-	-	-	19
Barrio Libre	-	-	-	-	-	-	11	-	-	-	-	-
Yaqui	-	3	5	5	-	-	-	-	-	-	-	19
Other Yaqui	-	-	-	-	-	-	-	-	-	-	-	-
Yavapai Apache	-	-	7	-	-	-	2	-	-	-	-	-
Yokuts												
Total	8	-	-	-	18	-	-	6	-	-	-	-
Chuckhansi	-	-	-	-	-	-	-	6	-	-	-	-
Tachi	8	-	-	-	-	-	-	-	-	-	-	-
Tule River	-	-	-	-	-	-	-	-	-	-	-	-
Yokuts	-	-	-	-	18	-	-	-	-	-	-	-
Yuchi	-	-	-	-	-	-	-	-	-	-	-	23
Yuman												
Total	8	7	9	-	8	9	-	30	-	21	19	8
Cocopah	-	-	-	-	-	-	-	-	-	-	-	-
Havasupai	8	7	9	-	-	-	-	7	-	-	-	-
Hualapai	-	-	-	-	-	-	-	-	-	-	-	8
Maricopa	-	-	-	-	-	-	-	-	-	-	-	-
Mohave	-	-	-	-	8	7	-	-	-	21	19	-
Quechan	-	-	-	-	-	2	-	23	-	-	-	-
Yavapai	-	-	-	-	-	-	-	-	-	-	-	-
Yurok	2	-	-	-	-	11	-	4	38	-	-	2
Other specified tribes (n.e.c.)												
Total	-	-	-	-	3	-	-	-	6	4	-	7
Fort Berthold	-	-	-	-	-	-	-	-	-	4	-	-
Gila River	-	-	-	-	-	-	-	-	-	-	-	-
Grand Rhonde	-	-	-	-	-	-	-	-	-	-	-	-
Los Coyotes	-	-	-	-	-	-	-	-	-	-	-	-
Round Valley	-	-	-	-	-	-	-	-	6	-	-	-
Scotts Valley	-	-	-	-	-	-	-	-	-	-	-	-
Shoalwater	-	-	-	-	-	-	-	-	-	-	-	7
All other specified	-	-	-	-	3	-	-	-	-	-	-	-

[Continued]

★ 198 ★

American Indian Population, by Tribe and State, 1980: Midwest Region, Siuslaw-Yurok
[Continued]

Tribe	Midwest Region											
	East North Central Division					West North Central Division						
	OH	IN	IL	MI	WI	MN	IA	MO	ND	SD	NE	KS
Tribe not specified	703	282	768	1,128	727	564	156	375	191	872	140	576
Tribe not reported	4,349	2,578	6,310	8,414	4,981	5,707	1,607	3,825	2,361	4,253	1,476	3,293

Source: U.S. Bureau of the Census, *1980 Census of Population, Volume 2, Subject Reports, Characteristics of American Indians, by Tribes and Selected Areas: 1980,* PC80-2-1C, Section 1: Tables I-II, issued September 1989, U.S. Department of Commerce, U.S. Government Printing Office, Washington, D.C., pp. 1-53. *Notes:* (N.E.C.) stands for not elsewhere classified. A dash (-) represents zero or a percent which rounds to less than 0.1. 1. Any Mohawk entry of "Ganienka" was miscoded to Wailaki.

★ 199 ★

American Indian Population, by Tribe and State, 1980: Northeast Region, Abenaki-Chinook

Data are estimates based on a sample and are the most recent available.

Tribe	Northeast Region											
	Total Northeast Region	New England division						Mid Atlantic Division				
		Total New England	ME	NH	VT	MA	RI	Total Mid Atlantic	CT	NY	NJ	PA
All American Indians	88,211	23,747	4,360	1,342	1,041	8,996	3,186	64,464	4,822	43,508	10,028	10,928
Abenaki (n.e.c)	678	529	37	15	385	58	-	149	34	97	22	30
Alabama Coushatta[1]	19	-	-	-	-	-	-	19	-	19	-	-
Alaska Native (n.e.c.)												
Total	13	9	-	-	-	9	-	4	-	4	-	-
Alaska Native	4	-	-	-	-	-	-	4	-	4	-	-
Sealaska	9	9	-	-	-	9	-	-	-	-	-	-
Alaska Athabaskans												
Total	126	10	-	-	-	10	-	116	-	36	20	60
Alaskan Athabaskans	104	10	-	-	-	10	-	94	-	24	20	50
Doyon	4	-	-	-	-	-	-	4	-	4	-	-
Taniana	18	-	-	-	-	-	-	18	-	8	-	10
Other Alaskan Athabaskans	-	-	-	-	-	-	-	-	-	-	-	-
Aleut and Eskimo												
Total	63	32	-	12	-	-	-	31	20	-	-	31
Akutan	29	-	-	-	-	-	-	29	-	-	-	29
Aleut	2	-	-	-	-	-	-	2	-	-	-	2
Calista	-	-	-	-	-	-	-	2	-	-	-	2
Chugach	-	-	-	-	-	-	-	-	-	-	-	-
Eskimo	-	-	-	-	-	-	-	-	-	-	-	-
Kotzebue Sound	9	9	-	9	-	-	-	-	-	-	-	-
Other Aleut and Eskimo	23	23	-	3	-	-	-	-	20	-	-	-
Algonquian (n.e.c.)	730	271	11	16	43	162	-	459	39	405	17	37
Apache												
Total	1,169	298	23	16	-	208	6	871	45	505	131	235
Apache (n.e.c.)	960	218	23	9	-	149	6	742	31	431	113	198
Chiricahua	57	24	-	-	-	24	-	33	-	15	18	-
Fort Sill Apache	-	-	-	-	-	-	-	-	-	-	-	-
Jicarilla	10	-	-	-	-	-	-	10	-	10	-	-
Kiowa Apache	12	-	-	-	-	-	-	12	-	-	-	12
Mescalero	102	39	-	7	-	25	-	63	7	38	-	25
Payson Apache	-	-	-	-	-	-	-	-	-	-	-	-

[Continued]

357

American Indian Population, by Tribe and State, 1980: Northeast Region, Abenaki-Chinook
[Continued]

| Tribe | Total Northeast Region | Northeast Region | | | | | | | | | | |
| | | New England division | | | | | | Mid Atlantic Division | | | | |
		Total New England	ME	NH	VT	MA	RI	Total Mid Atlantic	CT	NY	NJ	PA
San Carlos Apache	10	10	-	-	-	-	10	-	-	-	-	-
White Mountain Apache												
Apache	18	7	-	-	-	-	-	11	7	11	-	-
Other Apache	-	-	-	-	-	-	-	-	7	-	-	-
Arapaho	58	42	13	-	-	29	-	16	-	7	-	9
Arikara	2	-	-	-	-	-	-	2	-	-	-	2
Assiniboine	-	-	-	-	-	-	-	-	-	-	-	-
Bannock	-	-	-	-	-	-	-	-	-	-	-	-
Blackfoot[1]	2,399	661	36	46	44	276	22	1,738	237	775	430	533
Caddo	16	-	-	-	-	-	-	16	-	16	-	-
Cahuilla												
Total	32	30	-	15	-	-	-	12	5	12	-	-
Cahuilla	27	15	-	15	-	-	-	12	-	12	-	-
Soboba	-	-	-	-	-	-	-	-	-	-	-	-
Torres-Martinez	-	-	-	-	-	-	-	-	-	-	-	-
Other Cahuilla	5	5	-	-	-	-	-	-	5	-	-	-
California tribes (n.e.c.)												
Total	30	24	-	-	2	17	-	6	5	-	6	-
Cahto	-	-	-	-	-	-	-	-	-	-	-	-
Digger	-	-	-	-	-	-	-	-	-	-	-	-
Mattole	5	5	-	-	-	-	-	-	5	-	-	-
Morongo	-	-	-	-	-	-	-	-	-	-	-	-
Wappo	-	-	-	-	-	-	-	-	-	-	-	-
Yuki	9	9	-	-	2	7	-	-	-	-	-	-
Other California	16	10	-	-	-	10	-	6	-	-	6	-
Canadian and Latin American	1,007	289	30	17	9	138	26	718	69	446	161	111
Catawba	5	-	-	-	-	-	-	5	-	-	-	5
Cayuse	13	-	-	-	-	-	-	13	-	6	-	7
Chehalis	-	-	-	-	-	-	-	-	-	-	-	-
Chemakuan												
Total	-	-	-	-	-	-	-	-	-	-	-	-
Hoh	-	-	-	-	-	-	-	-	-	-	-	-
Quileute	-	-	-	-	-	-	-	-	-	-	-	-
Other Chemakuan	-	-	-	-	-	-	-	-	-	-	-	-
Chemehuevi	5	-	-	-	-	-	-	5	-	5	-	-
Cherokee												
Total	11,951	2,503	201	112	77	1,105	309	9,448	699	4,587	2,053	2,808
Cherokee	11,865	2,503	201	112	77	1,105	309	9,362	699	4,521	2,033	2,808
Eastern Cherokee	20	-	-	-	-	-	-	20	-	12	8	-
Etowah Cherokee	8	-	-	-	-	-	-	8	-	8	-	-
Tuscola	46	-	-	-	-	-	-	46	-	46	-	-
United Keetoowah	-	-	-	-	-	-	-	-	-	46	-	-
Western Cherokee	12	-	-	-	-	-	-	12	-	-	12	-
Other Cherokee	-	-	-	-	-	-	-	-	-	-	-	-
Cheyenne												
Total	212	18	-	-	-	6	6	194	6	120	33	41
Cheyenne	212	18	-	-	-	6	6	194	6	12-	33	41
Northern Cheyenne	-	-	-	-	-	-	-	-	-	-	-	-
Southern Cheyenne	-	-	-	-	-	-	-	-	-	-	-	-
Chickahominy	166	14	-	-	-	14	-	152	-	152	-	-
Chickasaw	99	51	5	-	-	12	-	48	34	28	5	15
Chinook												
Total	39	-	-	-	-	-	-	39	-	6	-	33
Chinook	39	-	-	-	-	-	-	39	-	6	-	33
Clatsop	-	-	-	-	-	-	-	-	-	-	-	-

[Continued]

★ 199 ★

American Indian Population, by Tribe and State, 1980: Northeast Region, Abenaki-Chinook
[Continued]

Tribe	Northeast Region											
	Total Northeast Region	New England division						Mid Atlantic Division				
		Total New England	ME	NH	VT	MA	RI	Total Mid Atlantic	CT	NY	NJ	PA
Columbia River Chinook	-	-	-	-	-	-	-	-	-	-	-	-
Other Chinook	-	-	-	-	-	-	-	-	-	-	-	-

Source: U.S. Bureau of the Census, *1980 Census of Population, Volume 2, Subject Reports, Characteristics of American Indians, by Tribes and Selected Areas: 1980,* PC80-2-1C, Section 1: Tables I-II, issued September 1989, U.S. Department of Commerce, U.S. Government Printing Office, Washington, D.C., pp. 1-53. *Notes:* (N.E.C.) stands for not elsewhere classified. A dash (-) represents zero or a percent which rounds to less than 0.1. 1. Reporting and/or processing problems may have affected the data for this tribe.

★ 200 ★

American Indian Population, by Tribe and State, 1980: Northeast Region, Chippewa-Iowa

Data are estimates based on a sample and are the most recent available.

Tribe	Northeast Region											
	Total Northeast Region	New England Division						Mid Atlantic Division				
		Total New England	ME	NH	VT	MA	RI	Total Mid Atlantic	CT	NY	NJ	PA
Chippewa												
Total	1,154	399	40	44	9	164	92	755	50	505	120	130
Bad River	-	-	-	-	-	-	-	-	-	-	-	-
Bay Mills Chippewa	-	-	-	-	-	-	-	-	-	-	-	-
Bois Forte	-	-	-	-	-	-	-	-	-	-	-	-
Chippewa	1,038	361	40	44	9	126	92	677	50	446	101	130
Lac Courte Oreilles	-	-	-	-	-	-	-	-	-	-	-	-
Lac du Flambeau	19	-	-	-	-	-	-	19	-	-	19	-
Lake Superior	-	-	-	-	-	-	-	-	-	-	-	-
Leech Lake	-	-	-	-	-	-	-	-	-	-	-	-
Leetanau	-	-	-	-	-	-	-	-	-	-	-	-
Mille Lac	-	-	-	-	-	-	-	-	-	-	-	-
Minnesota Chippewa	-	-	-	-	-	-	-	-	-	-	-	-
Ontonagon	11	-	-	-	-	-	-	11	-	11	-	-
Red Cliff Chippewa	-	-	-	-	-	-	-	-	-	-	-	-
Red Lake Chippewa	8	-	-	-	-	-	-	8	-	8	-	-
Saginaw Chippewa	40	-	-	-	-	-	-	-	-	40	40	-
St. Croix Chippewa	-	-	-	-	-	-	-	-	-	-	-	-
Sault Ste. Marie Chippewa	32	32	-	-	-	32	-	-	-	-	-	-
Sokoagon Chippewa	-	-	-	-	-	-	-	-	-	-	-	-
Turtle Mountain	6	6	-	-	-	6	-	-	-	-	-	-
White Earth	-	-	-	-	-	-	-	-	-	-	-	-
Other Chippewa	-	-	-	-	-	-	-	-	-	-	-	-
Chitimacha	-	-	-	-	-	-	-	-	-	-	-	-
Choctaw												
Total	481	177	6	30	6	84	27	304	24	200	29	75
Choctaw	473	169	6	30	6	84	19	304	24	200	29	75

[Continued]

American Indian Population, by Tribe and State, 1980: Northeast Region, Chippewa-Iowa
[Continued]

Tribe	Total Northeast Region	Northeast Region										
		New England Division						Mid Atlantic Division				
		Total New England	ME	NH	VT	MA	RI	Total Mid Atlantic	CT	NY	NJ	PA
Clifton Choctaw	8	8	-	-	-	-	8	-	-	-	-	-
Chumash[1]												
Total	-	-	-	-	-	-	-	-	-	-	-	-
Chumash	-	-	-	-	-	-	-	-	-	-	-	-
Other Chumash	-	-	-	-	-	-	-	-	-	-	-	-
Clallam												
Total	-	-	-	-	-	-	-	-	-	-	-	-
Clallam	-	-	-	-	-	-	-	-	-	-	-	-
Lower Elwah	-	-	-	-	-	-	-	-	-	-	-	-
Port Gamble Clallam	-	-	-	-	-	-	-	-	-	-	-	-
Other Clellam	-	-	-	-	-	-	-	-	-	-	-	-
Coeur d' Alene	-	-	-	-	-	-	-	-	-	-	-	-
Coharie		-	-	-	-	-	-	-	-	-	-	-
Colorado River	16	-	-	-	-	-	-	16	-	9	7	-
Colville	9	9	-	-	2	-	-	-	7	-	-	-
Comanche	206	48	-	19	1	22	-	158	6	85	42	31
Coos	-	-	-	-	-	-	-	-	-	-	-	-
Costanoan	2	-	-	-	-	-	-	2	-	-	-	2
Cowitz	-	-	-	-	-	-	-	-	-	-	-	-
Cree	358	103	4	-	16	19	8	255	56	101	58	96
Creek												
Total	534	105	6	5	13	81	-	429	-	208	98	123
Creek	496	105	6	5	13	81	-	391	-	208	91	92
Eastern Creek	31	-	-	-	-	-	-	31	-	-	-	31
Lower Muskogee	-	-	-	-	-	-	-	-	-	-	-	-
Muskogee	-	-	-	-	-	-	-	-	-	-	-	-
Thiopthiocco	-	-	-	-	-	-	-	-	-	-	-	-
Other Creek	7	-	-	-	-	-	-	7	-	-	7	-
Croatan	8	8	8	-	-	-	-	-	-	-	-	-
Crow	165	89	3	17	6	63	-	76	-	-	30	46
Cupeno												
Total	9	-	-	-	-	-	-	9	-	-	9	-
Agua Caliente	9	-	-	-	-	-	-	9	-	-	9	-
Cupeno	-	-	-	-	-	-	-	-	-	-	-	-
Delaware												
Total	1,507	79	8	6	1	43	-	1,428	21	438	740	250
Delaware	933	68	8	6	1	32	-	865	21	143	472	250
Munsee	26	-	-	-	-	-	-	26	-	21	5	-
Sand Hill	548	11	-	-	-	11	-	537	-	274	263	-
Diegueno												
Total	-	-	-	-	-	-	-	-	-	-	-	-
Diegueno	-	-	-	-	-	-	-	-	-	-	-	-
Manzanita	-	-	-	-	-	-	-	-	-	-	-	-

[Continued]

★ 200 ★

American Indian Population, by Tribe and State, 1980: Northeast Region, Chippewa-Iowa

[Continued]

Tribe	Total Northeast Region	Northeast Region										
		New England Division						Mid Atlantic Division				
		Total New England	ME	NH	VT	MA	RI	Total Mid Atlantic	CT	NY	NJ	PA
San Pascual	-	-	-	-	-	-	-	-	-	-	-	-
Santa Ysabel	-	-	-	-	-	-	-	-	-	-	-	-
Other Diegueno	-	-	-	-	-	-	-	-	-	-	-	-
Eastern tribes (n.e.c.)												
Total	206	99	5	-	3	61	-	107	30	35	46	26
Moor	59	-	-	-	-	-	-	59	-	-	35	24
Nansemond	-	-	-	-	-	-	-	-	-	-	-	-
Natchez	8	6	-	-	-	-	-	2	6	-	-	2
Nipmuc	60	60	-	-	3	57	-	-	-	-	-	-
Southeastern Indians	65	19	2	-	-	4	-	46	13	35	11	-
Tunica	-	-	-	-	-	-	-	-	-	-	-	-
Other Eastern	14	14	3	-	-	-	-	-	11	-	-	-
Flathead	7	-	-	-	-	-	-	7	-	-	-	7
Fort Hall	23	-	-	-	-	-	-	23	-	23	-	-
Gabrieleno	3	-	-	-	-	-	-	3	-	-	3	
Gros Ventres												
Total	9	-	-	-	-	-	-	9	-	9	-	-
Atsina	5	-	-	-	-	-	-	5	-	5	-	-
Gros Ventres	4	-	-	-	-	-	-	4	-	4	-	-
Haida	12	12	-	-	-	12	-	-	-	-	-	-
Haliwa	151	-	-	-	-	-	-	151	-	-	34	117
Hidatsa	8	8	8	-	-	-	-	-	-	-	-	-
Hitchiti	-	-	-	-	-	-	-	-	-	-	-	-
Hoopa	8	-	-	-	-	-	-	8	-	8	-	-
Houma	21	-	-	-	-	-	-	21	-	15	-	6
Iowa	2	2	2	-	-	-	-	-	-	-	-	-

Source: U.S. Bureau of the Census, *1980 Census of Population, Volume 2, Subject Reports, Characteristics of American Indians, by Tribes and Selected Areas: 1980,* PC80-2-1C, Section 1: Tables I-II, issued September 1989, U.S. Department of Commerce, U.S. Government Printing Office, Washington, D.C., pp. 1-53. *Notes:* (N.E.C.) stands for not elsewhere classified. A dash (-) represents zero or a percent which rounds to less than 0.1. 1. Reporting and/or processing problems may have affected the data for this tribe.

★ 201 ★

American Indian Population, by Tribe and State, 1980: Northeast Region, Iroquois-Pomo

Data are estimates based on a sample and are the most recent available.

Tribe	Total Northeast Region	Northeast Region										
		New England Division						Mid Atlantic Division				
		Total New England	ME	NH	VT	MA	RI	Total Mid Atlantic	CT	NY	NJ	PA
Iroquois												
Total	19,270	1,561	114	86	73	929	35	17,709	324	16,265	599	845
Cayuga	565	9	-	-	2	7	-	556	-	548	8	-
Iroquois (n.e.c.)	1.498	342	45	25	35	188	7	1,156	42	897	106	153
Mohawk[1]	9,422	917	13	48	29	574	28	8,505	225	7,919	335	251
Oneida	959	51	-	-	-	44	-	908	7	865	19	24
Onondaga	721	16	9	0	7	-	-	705	-	687	-	18
Seneca												
Total	5,075	173	30	13	-	87	-	4,902	43	4,507	505	345
Seneca	4,815	159	30	13	-	73	-	4,656	43	4,266	50	340
Seneca Nation	64	14	-	-	-	14	-	50	-	45	-	5
Tonawanda Seneca	196	-	-	-	-	-	-	196	-	196	-	-
Seneca-Cayuga	-	-	-	-	-	-	-	-	-	-	-	-
Tuscarora	970	35	6	-	-	22	-	935	7	826	55	54
Wyandot	60	18	11	-	-	7	-	42	-	16	26	-
Kalispel	-	-	-	-	-	-	-	-	-	-	-	-
Karok	4	3	-	3	-	-	-	1	-	1	-	-
Kaw	13	-	-	-	-	-	-	13	-	13	-	-
Kickapoo	27	13	-	-	-	13	-	14	-	-	-	14
Kiowa	32	12	-	-	-	6	-	20	6	6	6	8
Klamath	-	-	-	-	-	-	-	-	-	-	-	-
Konkow	8	-	-	-	-	-	-	8	-	8	-	-
Kootenai	-	-	-	-	-	-	-	-	-	-	-	-
Long Island												
Total	191	18	-	-	-	13	-	173	5	173	-	-
Matinecock	109	-	-	-	-	-	-	109	-	109	-	-
Montauk	55	13	-	-	-	13	-	42	-	42	-	-
Poosepatuck	27	5	-	-	-	-	-	22	5	22	-	-
Other Long Island	-	-	-	-	-	-	-	-	-	-	-	-
Luiseno												
Total	6	-	-	-	-	-	-	6	-	-	6	-
LaJolla	-	-	-	-	-	-	-	-	-	-	-	-
Luiseno	6	-	-	-	-	-	-	6	-	-	6	-
Pala	-	-	-	-	-	-	-	-	-	-	-	-
Pauma	-	-	-	-	-	-	-	-	-	-	-	-
Pechanga	-	-	-	-	-	-	-	-	-	-	-	-
Lumbee[2]	228	59	29	-	-	-	9	169	21	22	38	109
Lummi[2]	-	-	-	-	-	-	-	-	-	-	-	-
Maidu	22	11	-	-	-	-	-	11	11	-	11	-
Makah	-	-	-	-	-	-	-	-	-	-	-	-
Maliseet	502	502	446	31	-	12	-	-	13	-	-	-
Mandan	6	-	-	-	-	-	-	6	-	6	-	-
Mattaponi	11	-	-	-	-	-	-	11	-	6	-	5

[Continued]

★ 201 ★

American Indian Population, by Tribe and State, 1980: Northeast Region, Iroquois-Pomo
[Continued]

| Tribe | Total Northeast Region | Northeast Region | | | | | | | | | | |
| | | New England Division | | | | | | Mid Atlantic Division | | | | |
		Total New England	ME	NH	VT	MA	RI	Total Mid Atlantic	CT	NY	NJ	PA
Menominee	53	22	-	-	2	20	-	31	-	22	7	2
Miami	15	7	-	-	-	7	-	8	-	-	-	8
Miccosukee[3]	11	-	-	-	-	-	-	11	-	11	-	-
Micmac[4]	990	943	317	65	19	452	-	47	90	35	6	6
Mission Indians	45	24	-	24	-	-	-	21	-	-	13	8
Miwok	26	10	-	-	-	10	-	16	-	-	-	16
Modoc	15	3	3	-	-	-	-	12	-	-	12	-
Mohegan	419	360	12	2	-	35	43	59	268	46	7	6
Mono	59	49	-	-	-	42	7	10	-	-	8	2
Nanticoke	501	-	-	-	-	-	-	501	-	7	453	41
Narragansett	1,948	1,838	-	-	-	221	1,512	110	105	105	5	-
Navajo	493	219	26	27	4	145	-	274	17	82	54	138
Nez Perce[3]	19	5	-	-	-	5	-	14	-	8	-	6
Nomalaki	-	-	-	-	-	-	-	-	-	-	-	-
Northwest tribes (n.e.c)												
Total	46	23	-	-	-	-	23	23	-	16	-	7
Columbia Wenatchee	30	23	-	-	-	-	23	7	-	-	-	7
Kalapuya	-	-	-	-	-	-	-	-	-	-	-	-
Tillamook	-	-	-	-	-	-	-	-	-	-	-	-
Other Northwest	16	-	-	-	-	-	-	16	-	16	-	-
Omaha	33	16	-	6	-	-	-	17	10	8	-	9
Oregon Athabaskan	43	-	-	-	-	-	-	43	-	43	-	-
Osage	115	19	-	-	-	19	-	96	-	32	49	15
Oto	34	2	-	2	-	-	-	32	-	22	-	10
Ottawa	39	-	-	-	-	-	-	39	-	17	15	7
Paiute[3]												
Total	46	-	-	-	-	-	-	46	-	27	8	11
Burns Paiute	-	-	-	-	-	-	-	-	-	-	-	-
Northern Paiute	-	-	-	-	-	-	-	-	-	-	-	-
Paiute	46	-	-	-	-	-	-	46	-	27	8	11
Pyramind Lake	-	-	-	-	-	-	-	-	-	-	-	-
Southern Paiute	-	-	-	-	-	-	-	-	-	-	-	-
Walker River	-	-	-	-	-	-	-	-	-	-	-	-
Other Paiute	-	-	-	-	-	-	-	-	-	-	-	-
Pamunkey	164	-	-	-	-	-	-	164	-	-	79	85
Papago												
Total	51	22	-	-	2	7	-	29	13	17	-	12
Papago	51	22	-	-	2	7	-	29	13	17	-	12
Other Papago	-	-	-	-	-	-	-	-	-	-	-	-
Passamaquoddy												
Total	1,579	1,542	1,240	35	2	142	20	37	103	29	-	8
Passamaquoddy	1,579	1,542	1,240	35	2	142	20	37	103	29	-	8
Other Passamaquoddy	-	-	-	-	-	-	-	-	-	-	-	-

[Continued]

★ 201 ★

American Indian Population, by Tribe and State, 1980: Northeast Region, Iroquois-Pomo
[Continued]

Tribe	Total Northeast Region	Northeast Region										
		New England Division						Mid Atlantic Division				
		Total New England	ME	NH	VT	MA	RI	Total Mid Atlantic	CT	NY	NJ	PA
Pawnee	60	16	-	1	-	-	-	44	15	33	9	2
Penobscot	1,095	1,030	752	69	11	135	-	65	63	43	16	6
Peoria	30	7	-	7	-	-	-	23	-	23	-	-
Pequot	359	325	-	2	-	15	52	34	256	26	-	8
Pima	42	7	-	-	-	7	-	35	-	23	12	-
Piscataway	-	-	-	-	-	-	-	-	-	-	-	-
Pit River	-	-	-	-	-	-	-	-	-	-	-	-
Pomo												
Total	-	-	-	-	-	-	-	-	-	-	-	-
Eastern Pomo	-	-	-	-	-	-	-	-	-	-	-	-
Kashaya	-	-	-	-	-	-	-	-	-	-	-	-
Northern Pomo	-	-	-	-	-	-	-	-	-	-	-	-
Pomo	-	-	-	-	-	-	-	-	-	-	-	-
Other Pomo	-	-	-	-	-	-	-	-	-	-	-	-

Source: U.S. Bureau of the Census, *1980 Census of Population, Volume 2, Subject Reports, Characteristics of American Indians, by Tribes and Selected Areas: 1980,* PC80-2-1C, Section 1: Tables I-II, issued September 1989, U.S. Department of Commerce, U.S. Government Printing Office, Washington, D.C., pp. 1-53. *Notes:* (N.E.C.) stands for not elsewhere classified. A dash (-) represents zero or a percent which rounds to less than 0.1. 1. Any Mohawk entry of "Ganienka" was miscoded to Wailaki. 2. Miscoding of entries of "Lummee," "Lummi," "Lumbee," or "Lumbi" may have affected the data for this tribe. 3. Reporting and/or processing may have affected the data for this tribe. 4. Any entry with the spelling "Micmac" was miscoded to Cheyenne River Sioux.

★ 202 ★

American Indian Population, by Tribe and State, 1980: Northeast Region, Ponca-Sioux

Data are estimates based on a sample and are the most recent available.

Tribe	Total Northeast Region	Northeast Region										
		New England Division						Mid Atlantic Division				
		Total New England	ME	NH	VT	MA	RI	Total Mid Atlantic	CT	NY	NJ	PA
Ponca	17	4	-	-	-	4	-	13	-	10	-	3
Potawatomi												
Total	124	19	-	-	-	9	10	105	-	57	9	39
Citizen Band	14	-	-	-	-	-	-	14	-	-	7	7
Forest County	-	-	-	-	-	-	-	-	-	-	-	-
Huron Potawatomi	-	-	-	-	-	-	-	-	-	-	-	-
Potawatomie	110	19	-	-	-	9	10	91	-	57	2	32
Prairie Band	-	-	-	-	-	-	-	-	-	-	-	-
Other Potawatomi	-	-	-	-	-	-	-	-	-	-	-	-
Powhatan	130	15	9	-	-	6	-	115	-	40	38	37
Pueblo[1]												
Total	169	39	-	-	3	13	-	130	23	67	34	29
Acoma	-	-	-	-	-	-	-	-	-	-	-	-
Arizona Tewa	-	-	-	-	-	-	-	-	-	-	-	-
Cochiti	4	4	-	-	-	4	-	-	-	-	-	-

[Continued]

★ 202 ★

American Indian Population, by Tribe and State, 1980: Northeast Region, Ponca-Sioux
[Continued]

Tribe	Total Northeast Region	Northeast Region										
		New England Division						Mid Atlantic Division				
		Total New England	ME	NH	VT	MA	RI	Total Mid Atlantic	CT	NY	NJ	PA
Hopi	60	20	-	-	3	-	-	40	17	-	-	-
Isleta	-	-	-	-	-	-	-	-	-	-	-	-
Jemez	-	-	-	-	-	-	-	-	-	-	-	-
Keres (n.e.c.)	-	-	-	-	-	-	-	-	-	-	-	-
Laguna	5	-	-	-	-	-	-	5	-	-	-	5
Nambe	-	-	-	-	-	-	-	-	-	-	-	-
Picuris	-	-	-	-	-	-	-	-	-	-	-	-
Pojoaque	-	-	-	-	-	-	-	-	-	-	-	-
Pueblo (n.e.c.)	29	9	-	-	-	9	-	20	-	-	12	8
Sandia	6	6	-	-	-	-	-	-	6	-	-	-
San Felipe	-	-	-	-	-	-	-	-	-	-	-	-
San Ildefonso	-	-	-	-	-	-	-	-	-	-	-	-
San Juan	-	-	-	-	-	-	-	-	-	-	-	-
Santa Ana	-	-	-	-	-	-	-	-	-	-	-	-
Santa Clara[1]	-	-	-	-	-	-	-	-	-	-	-	-
Santo Domingo	43	-	-	-	-	-	-	43	-	43	-	-
Taos	15	-	-	-	-	-	-	15	-	15	-	-
Tesuque	-	-	-	-	-	-	-	-	-	-	-	-
Tewa	-	-	-	-	-	-	-	-	-	-	-	-
Tigua[1]	2	-	-	-	-	-	-	2	-	2	-	-
Zia	-	-	-	-	-	-	-	-	-	-	-	-
Zuni	5	-	-	-	-	-	-	5	-	-	-	5
Puget Sound Salish												
Total	13	-	-	-	-	-	-	13	-	-	-	13
Duwamish	11	-	-	-	-	-	-	11	-	-	-	11
Muckleshoot	-	-	-	-	-	-	-	-	-	-	-	-
Nisqually	-	-	-	-	-	-	-	-	-	-	-	-
Nooksack	-	-	-	-	-	-	-	-	-	-	-	-
Puget Sound Salish (n.e.c.)	-	-	-	-	-	-	-	-	-	-	-	-
Puyallup	-	-	-	-	-	-	-	-	-	-	-	-
Samish	-	-	-	-	-	-	-	-	-	-	-	-
Sauk-Sauiatte	-	-	-	-	-	-	-	-	-	-	-	-
Skokomish	-	-	-	-	-	-	-	-	-	-	-	-
Skykomish	-	-	-	-	-	-	-	-	-	-	-	-
Snohomish	-	-	-	-	-	-	-	-	-	-	-	-
Snoqualmie	2	-	-	-	-	-	-	2	-	-	-	2
Squaxin Island	-	-	-	-	-	-	-	-	-	-	-	-
Steilacoom	-	-	-	-	-	-	-	-	-	-	-	-
Stillaguamish	-	-	-	-	-	-	-	-	-	-	-	-
Suquamish	-	-	-	-	-	-	-	-	-	-	-	-
Swinomish	-	-	-	-	-	-	-	-	-	-	-	-
Tulalip	-	-	-	-	-	-	-	-	-	-	-	-
Upper Skagit	-	-	-	-	-	-	-	-	-	-	-	-
Quapaw	5	-	-	-	-	-	-	5	-	5	-	-
Quinault	-	-	-	-	-	-	-	-	-	-	-	-
Rappahannock	25	7	-	-	-	7	-	18	-	-	18	-
San and Fox Mesquakie	36	6	-	-	-	-	-	30	6	15	13	2
Salinan	6	6	-	-	-	6	-	-	-	-	-	-
Schaghticoke	194	184	-	-	-	-	-	10	184	10	-	-
Seminole[1]												
Total	728	135	2	23	2	60	10	593	38	326	168	99
Seminole	715	135	2	23	2	60	10	580	38	313	168	99
Seminole Nation of Oklahoma	-	-	-	-	-	-	-	-	-	-	-	-

[Continued]

★ 202 ★

American Indian Population, by Tribe and State, 1980: Northeast Region, Ponca-Sioux

[Continued]

Tribe	Total Northeast Region	Northeast Region										
		New England Division						Mid Atlantic Division				
		Total New England	ME	NH	VT	MA	RI	Total Mid Atlantic	CT	NY	NJ	PA
Seminole Tribe of Florida	13	-	-	-	-	-	-	13	-	13	-	-
Other Seminole	-	-	-	-	-	-	-	-	-	-	-	-
Serrano	-	-	-	-	-	-	-	-	-	-	-	-
Shasta	-	-	-	-	-	-	-	-	-	-	-	-
Shawnee												
Total	222	114	47	13	-	34	-	108	20	16	32	60
Absentee Shawnee	-	-	-	-	-	-	-	-	-	-	-	-
Shawnee	222	114	47	13	-	34	-	108	20	16	32	60
Shinnecock	965	76	-	13	-	-	30	889	33	781	61	47
Shoshone												
Total	118	25	-	6	-	5	-	93	14	22	36	35
Goshute	-	-	-	-	-	-	-	-	-	-	-	-
Shoshone	104	11	-	6	-	5	-	93	-	22	36	35
Te-Moak Western Shoshone[1]	-	-	-	-	-	-	-	-	-	-	-	-
Yomba[1]	-	-	-	-	-	-	-	-	-	-	-	-
Other Shoshone	14	14	-	-	-	-	-	-	14	-	-	-
Siletz	-	-	-	-	-	-	-	-	-	-	-	-
Sioux												
Total	2,220	1,004	277	43	21	424	40	1,216	199	598	239	379
Blackfoot Sioux	43	5	-	-	-	5	-	38	-	36	-	2
Brule Sioux	22	22	-	22	-	-	-	-	-	12	5	-
Cheyenne River Sioux[2]	500	483	187	6	-	220	21	17	49	12	5	-
Crow River Sioux[2]	-	-	-	-	-	-	-	-	-	-	-	-
Dakota Sioux	35	7	-	-	-	-	-	28	7	4	14	10
Devil's Lake Sioux	-	-	-	-	-	-	-	-	-	-	-	-
Fladreau Santee	-	-	-	-	-	-	-	-	-	-	-	-
Fort Peck	-	-	-	-	-	-	-	-	-	-	-	-
Lower Brule Sioux	-	-	-	-	-	-	-	-	-	-	-	-
Mdewakanton Sioux	5	5	-	-	-	5	-	-	-	-	-	-
Oglala Sioux	92	30	6	-	-	11	6	62	7	32	9	21
Pine Ridge Sioux	-	-	-	-	-	-	-	-	-	-	-	-
Prior Lake Sioux	-	-	-	-	-	-	-	-	-	-	-	-
Rosebud Sioux	3	-	-	-	-	-	-	3	-	3	-	-
Santee Sioux	-	-	-	-	-	-	-	-	-	-	-	-
Sioux	1,451	432	81	15	21	172	7	1,019	136	506	192	321
Sisseton Sioux	11	11	-	-	-	11	-	-	-	-	-	-
Standing Rock Sioux	-	-	-	-	-	-	-	-	-	-	-	-
Teton Sioux	42	6	-	-	-	-	6	36	-	5	11	20
Wahpeton Sioux	-	-	-	-	-	-	-	-	-	-	-	-
Yankton Sioux	13	-	-	-	-	-	-	13	-	-	8	5
Yanktonai Sioux	3	3	3	-	-	-	-	-	-	-	-	-
Other Sioux	-	-	-	-	-	-	-	-	-	-	-	-

Source: U.S. Bureau of the Census, *1980 Census of Population, Volume 2, Subject Reports, Characteristics of American Indians, by Tribes and Selected Areas: 1980*, PC80-2-1C, Section 1: Tables I-II, issued September 1989, U.S. Department of Commerce, U.S. Government Printing Office, Washington, D.C., pp. 1-53. *Notes:* (N.E.C.) stands for not elsewhere classified. A dash (-) represents zero or a percent which rounds to less than 0.1. 1. Reporting and/or processing problems may have affected the data for this tribe. 2. Any entry with the spelling "Micmac" was miscoded to Cheyenne River Sioux.

★ 203 ★

American Indian Population, by Tribe and State, 1980: Northeast Region, Siuslaw-Yurok

Data are estimates based on a sample and are the most recent available.

Tribe	Total Northeast Region	Northeast Region										
		New England Division						Mid Atlantic Division				
		Total New England	ME	NH	VT	MA	RI	Total Mid Atlantic	CT	NY	NJ	PA
Siuslaw	-	-	-	-	-	-	-	-	-	-	-	-
Spokane	-	-	-	-	-	24	-	-	-	-	28	-
Stockbridge	155	51	-	3	-	24	-	104	24	67	28	9
Tlingit	73	39	-	-	-	22	12	34	5	14	-	20
Tolowa	2	2	-	-	2	-	-	-	-	-	-	-
Tonkawa	-	-	-	-	-	-	-	-	-	-	-	-
Tsimishian	-	-	-	-	-	-	-	-	-	-	-	-
Umatilla	11	-	-	-	-	-	-	11	-	6	-	5
Ute												
Total	34	22	2	-	-	6	14	12	-	-	7	5
Uintah Ute	-	-	-	-	-	-	-	-	-	-	-	-
Ute	34	22	2	-	-	6	14	12	-	-	7	5
Ute Mountain Ute	-	-	-	-	-	-	-	-	-	-	-	-
Other Ute	-	-	-	-	-	-	-	-	-	-	-	-
Wailaki[2]	-	-	-	-	-	-	-	-	-	-	-	-
Walla-Walla	-	-	-	-	-	-	-	-	-	-	-	-
Wampanoag	1,206	1,084	2	10	-	988	32	122	52	94	22	6
Warm Springs	5	-	-	-	-	-	-	5	-	5	-	-
Washo												
Total	2	2	-	-	-	-	-	-	2	-	-	-
Washo	2	2	-	-	-	-	-	-	2	-	-	-
Other Washo	-	-	-	-	-	-	-	-	-	-	-	-
Wichita	10	-	-	-	-	-	-	-	-	-	-	-
Winnebago	48	24	5	19	-	-	-	24	-	7	10	7
Wintu	-	-	-	-	-	-	-	-	-	-	-	-
Wiyot	-	-	-	-	-	-	-	-	-	-	-	-
Yakima	42	31	4	-	-	7	-	11	20	11	-	-
Yaqui												
Total	34	9	7	-	2	-	-	25	-	23	-	2
Barrio Libre	22	9	7	-	2	-	-	13	-	11	-	2
Yaqui	12	-	-	-	-	-	-	12	-	12	-	-
Other Yaqui	-	-	-	-	-	-	-	-	-	-	-	-
Yavapai Apache	13	13	-	-	-	13	-	-	-	-	-	-
Yokuts												
Total	-	-	-	-	-	-	-	-	-	-	-	-
Chuckhansi	-	-	-	-	-	-	-	-	-	-	-	-
Tachi	-	-	-	-	-	-	-	-	-	-	-	-
Tule River	-	-	-	-	-	-	-	-	-	-	-	-
Yokuts	-	-	-	-	-	-	-	-	-	-	-	-
Yuchi	6	6	-	-	-	6	-	-	-	-	-	-
Yuman												
Total	60	25	-	-	-	25	-	35	-	28	-	7
Cocopah	39	25	-	-	-	25	-	14	-	14	-	-
Havasupai	-	-	-	-	-	-	-	-	-	-	-	-
Hualapai	-	-	-	-	-	-	-	-	-	-	-	-
Maricopa	14	-	-	-	-	-	-	14	-	14	-	-
Mohave	7	-	-	-	-	-	-	7	-	-	-	7
Quechan	-	-	-	-	-	-	-	-	-	-	-	-
Yavapai	-	-	-	-	-	-	-	-	-	-	-	-
Yurok	29	-	-	-	-	-	-	29	-	15	-	14
Other specified tribes (n.e.c.)												
Total	20	4	-	-	-	-	4	16	-	12	-	4
Fort Berthold	-	-	-	-	-	-	-	-	-	-	-	-

[Continued]

367

★ 203 ★

American Indian Population, by Tribe and State, 1980: Northeast Region, Siuslaw-Yurok

[Continued]

Tribe	Total Northeast Region	Northeast Region										
		New England Division						Mid Atlantic Division				
		Total New England	ME	NH	VT	MA	RI	Total Mid Atlantic	CT	NY	NJ	PA
Gila River	-	-	-	-	-	-	-	-	-	-	-	-
Grand Rhode	-	-	-	-	-	-	-	-	-	-	-	-
Los Coyotes	-	-	-	-	-	-	-	-	-	-	-	-
Round Valley	-	-	-	-	-	-	-	-	-	-	-	-
Scotts Valley	-	-	-	-	-	-	-	-	-	-	-	-
Shoalwater	4	4	-	-	-	-	4	-	-	-	-	-
All other specified	16	-	-	-	-	-	-	16	-	12	-	4
Tribe not specified	4,493	812	65	100	16	328	115	3,681	188	2,356	749	576
Tribe not reported	24,608	5,405	555	382	265	2,174	722	19,203	1,307	12,876	3,057	3,270

Source: U.S. Bureau of the Census, *1980 Census of Population, Volume 2, Subject Reports, Characteristics of American Indians, by Tribes and Selected Areas: 1980*, PC80-2-1C, Section 1: Tables I-II, issued September 1989, U.S. Department of Commerce, U.S. Government Printing Office, Washington, D.C., pp. 1-53. *Notes:* (N.E.C.) stands for not elsewhere classified. A dash (-) represents zero or a percent which rounds to less than 0.1. 1. Reporting and/ or processing problems may have affected the data for this tribe. 2. Any Mohawk entry of "Ganienka" was miscoded to Wailaki. 3. Miscoding of entries of "Lummee," "Lummi," or "Lumbi" may have affected the data for this tribe. 4. Any entry with the spelling "Micmac" was miscoded to Cheyenne River Sioux.

★ 204 ★

American Indian Population, by Tribe and State, 1980: South Region, Abenaki-Chinook - I

Data are estimates based on a sample and are the most recent available.

Tribe	Total South Region	South Region									
		South Atlantic Division									
		Total South Atlantic	DE	MD	DC	VA	WV	NC	SC	GA	FL
All American Indians	405,009	130,549	1,380	8,946	986	9,867	2,317	65,808	6,655	9,876	24,714
Abenaki (n.e.c)	59	26	-	15	-	6	-	5	-	-	-
Alabama Coushatta[1]	1,007	10	-	-	-	-	-	1	-	-	9
Alaska Native (n.e.c.)											
Total	28	12	-	-	-	-	-	-	-	-	12
Alaska Native	16	-	-	-	-	-	-	-	-	-	-
Sealaska	12	12	-	-	-	-	-	-	-	-	12
Alaska Athabaskans											
Total	214	83	-	15	-	8	7	22	-	9	22
Alaskan Athabaskans	107	68	-	15	-	8	-	22	-	7	16
Doyon	92	-	-	-	-	-	-	-	-	-	-
Taniana	15	15	-	-	-	-	7	-	-	2	6
Other Alaskan Athabaskans	-	-	-	-	-	-	-	-	-	-	-
Aleut and Eskimo											
Total	50	36	-	-	-	-	-	24	-	-	12
Akutan	-	-	-	-	-	-	-	-	-	-	-

[Continued]

American Indian Population, by Tribe and State, 1980: South Region, Abenaki-Chinook - I
[Continued]

Tribe	Total South Region	South Region — South Atlantic Division									
		Total South Atlantic	DE	MD	DC	VA	WV	NC	SC	GA	FL
Aleut	10	-	-	-	-	-	-	-	-	-	-
Calista	8	8	-	-	-	-	-	8	-	-	-
Chugach	-	-	-	-	-	-	-	-	-	-	-
Eskimo	14	14	-	-	-	-	-	14	-	-	-
Kotzebue Sound	4	-	-	-	-	-	-	-	-	-	-
Other Aleut and Eskimo	14	14	-	-	-	-	-	2	-	-	12
Algonquian (n.e.c.)	114	56	-	-	-	5	-	10	-	19	22
Apache											
Total	4,292	976	14	117	-	196	37	175	27	70	340
Apache (n.e.c.)	3,777	932	14	117	-	185	30	175	27	62	322
Chiricahua	117	28	-	-	-	5	7	-	-	-	16
Fort Sill Apache	59	-	-	-	-	-	-	-	-	-	-
Jicarilla	11	6	-	-	-	6	-	-	-	-	-
Kiowa Apache	155	-	-	-	-	-	-	-	-	-	-
Mescalero	114	2	-	-	-	-	-	-	-	-	2
Payson Apache	-	-	-	-	-	-	-	-	-	-	-
San Carlos Apache	29	-	-	-	-	-	-	-	-	-	-
White Mountain Apache	22	8	-	-	-	-	-	-	-	8	-
Other Apache	8	-	-	-	-	-	-	-	-	-	-
Arapaho	1,033	41	-	9	-	6	11	2	-	6	7
Arikara	138	78	-	72	-	-	-	-	-	6	-
Assiniboine	107	29	-	-	-	-	-	7	-	-	22
Bannock	47	23	-	-	-	9	-	-	-	-	14
Blackfoot[1]	2,634	1,188	21	119	12	120	58	186	71	112	489
Caddo	1,393	19	-	6	-	6	-	-	-	-	7
Cahuilla											
Total	49	-	-	-	-	-	-	-	-	-	-
Cahuilla	42	-	-	-	-	-	-	-	-	-	-
Soboba	7	-	-	-	-	-	-	-	-	-	-
Torres-Martinez	-	-	-	-	-	-	-	-	-	-	-
Other Cahuilla	-	-	-	-	-	-	-	-	-	-	-
California tribes (n.e.c.)											
Total	33	15	-	6	-	-	-	-	-	-	9
Cahto	-	-	-	-	-	-	-	-	-	-	-
Digger	14	6	-	6	-	-	-	-	-	-	-
Mattole	9	9	-	-	-	-	-	-	-	-	9
Morongo	-	-	-	-	-	-	-	-	-	-	-
Wappo	10	-	-	-	-	-	-	-	-	-	-
Yuki	-	-	-	-	-	-	-	-	-	-	-
Other California	-	-	-	-	-	-	-	-	-	-	-
Canadian and Latin American	1,271	500	16	71	10	38	29	57	22	37	220
Catawba	1,356	1,266	-	-	-	5	-	128	1,116	17	-
Cayuse	-	-	-	-	-	-	-	-	-	-	-

[Continued]

★ 204 ★

American Indian Population, by Tribe and State, 1980: South Region, Abenaki-Chinook - I
[Continued]

Tribe	Total South Region	South Region										
		South Atlantic Division										
		Total South Atlantic	DE	MD	DC	VA	WV	NC	SC	GA	FL
Chehalis	-	-	-	-	-	-	-	-	-	-	-
Chemakuan											
Total	-	-	-	-	-	-	-	-	-	-	-
Hoh	-	-	-	-	-	-	-	-	-	-	-
Quileute	-	-	-	-	-	-	-	-	-	-	-
Other Chemakuan	-	-	-	-	-	-	-	-	-	-	-
Chemehuevi	14	5	-	-	-	-	-	5	-	-	-
Cherokee											
Total	109,419	21,367	215	1,852	208	1,836	579	7,688	1,092	2,855	5,042
Cherokee	108,433	20,467	215	1,852	195	1,836	573	6,815	1,092	2,855	5,034
Eastern Cherokee	888	845	-	-	-	-	-	845	-	-	-
Etowah Cherokee	13	7	-	-	-	-	-	7	-	-	-
Tuscola	28	14	-	-	-	-	-	14	-	-	-
United Keetoowah	36	13	-	-	13	-	-	-	-	-	-
Western Cherokee	21	21	-	-	-	-	6	7	-	-	8
Other Cherokee	-	-	-	-	-	-	-	-	-	-	-
Cheyenne											
Total	3,803	167	6	5	27	26	42	2	-	-	59
Cheyenne	3,696	144	6	5	4	26	42	2	-	-	59
Northern Cheyenne	65	-	-	-	-	-	-	-	-	-	-
Southern Cheyenne	42	23	-	-	23	-	-	-	-	-	-
Chickahominy	610	552	-	5	-	547	-	-	-	-	-
Chickasaw	7,394	134	-	13	6	14	19	24	-	17	41
Chinook											
Total	6	5	-	-	-	5	-	-	-	-	-
Chinook	1	-	-	-	-	-	-	-	-	-	-
Clatsop	-	-	-	-	-	-	-	-	-	-	-
Columbia River Chinook	-	-	-	-	-	-	-	-	-	-	-
Other Chinook	5	5	-	-	-	5	-	-	-	-	-

Source: U.S. Bureau of the Census, *1980 Census of Population, Volume 2, Subject Reports, Characteristics of American Indians, by Tribes and Selected Areas: 1980,* PC80-2-1C, Section 1: Tables I-II, issued September 1989, U.S. Department of Commerce, U.S. Government Printing Office, Washington, D.C., pp. 1-53. *Notes:* (N.E.C.) stands for not elsewhere classified. A dash (-) represents zero or a percent which rounds to less than 0.1. 1. Reporting and/or processing problems may have affected the data for this tribe.

American Indian Population, by Tribe and State, 1980: South Region, Abenaki-Chinook - II

Data are estimates based on a sample and are the most recent available.

Tribe	Total South Region	South Region (cont.)									
		East South Central Division					West South Central Division				
		Total East South Central	KY	TN	AL	MS	West South Central Total	AR	LA	OK	TX
All American Indians	405,009	27,518	4,497	6,946	9,239	6,836	246,942	12,713	12,841	171,092	50,296
Abenaki (n.e.c)	59	12	12	-	-	-	21	-	-	-	21
Alabama Coushatta[1]	1,007	-	-	-	-	-	997	-	135	49	813
Alaska Native (n.e.c.)											
Total	28	-	-	-	-	-	16	-	10	-	6
Alaska Native	16	-	-	-	-	-	16	-	10	-	6
Sealaska	12	-	-	-	-	-	-	-	-	-	-
Alaska Athabaskans											
Total	214	64	5	8	51	-	67	9	-	50	8
Alaskan Athabaskans	107	5	5	-	-	-	34	9	-	17	8
Doyon	92	59	-	8	51	-	33	-	-	33	-
Taniana	15	-	-	-	-	-	-	-	-	-	-
Other Alaskan Athabaskans	-	-	-	-	-	-	-	-	-	-	-
Aleut and Eskimo											
Total	50	-	-	-	-	-	14	-	-	14	-
Akutan	-	-	-	-	-	-	-	-	-	-	-
Aleut	10	*	*	*	*	*	10	*	*	10	*
Calista	8	-	-	-	-	-	-	-	-	-	-
Chugach	-	-	-	-	-	-	-	-	-	-	-
Eskimo	14	-	-	-	-	-	-	-	-	-	-
Kotzebue Sound	4	-	-	-	-	-	4	-	-	4	-
Other Aleut and Eskimo	14	-	-	-	-	-	-	-	-	-	-
Algonquian (n.e.c.)	114	14	-	-	14	-	44	19	6	19	-
Apache											
Total	4,292	332	127	70	115	20	2,984	237	133	1,097	1,517
Apache (n.e.c.)	3,777	299	127	63	89	20	2,546	228	114	861	1,343
Chiricahua	117	19	-	-	19	-	70	9	19	22	20
Fort Sill Apache	59	-	-	-	-	-	59	-	-	59	-
Jicarilla	11	-	-	-	-	-	5	-	-	-	5
Kiowa Apache	155	-	-	-	-	-	155	-	-	119	36
Mescalero	114	7	-	7	-	-	105	-	-	24	81
Payson	-	-	-	-	-	-	-	-	-	-	-
San Carlos	29	7	-	-	7	-	22	-	-	9	13
White Mountain Apache	22	-	-	-	-	-	14	-	-	3	11
Other Apache	8	-	-	-	-	-	8	-	-	-	8
Arapaho	1,033	2	2	-	-	-	990	2	-	886	102
Arikara	138	-	-	-	-	-	60	-	-	36	24
Assiniboine	107	-	-	-	-	-	78	27	-	33	18
Bannock	47	-	-	-	-	-	24	-	-	-	24
Blackfoot[1]	2,634	297	123	73	49	52	1,149	158	93	223	675
Caddo	1,393	11	-	-	11	-	1,363	14	-	1,231	118
Cahuilla											
Total	49	-	-	-	-	-	49	-	35	-	14
Cahuilla	42	-	-	-	-	-	42	-	35	-	7
Soboba	7	-	-	-	-	-	7	-	-	-	7
Torres-Martinez	-	-	-	-	-	-	-	-	-	-	-
Other Cahuilla	-	-	-	-	-	-	-	-	-	-	-
California tribes (n.e.c.)											
Total	33	18	8	10	-	-	-	-	-	-	-
Cahto	-	-	-	-	-	-	-	-	-	-	-

[Continued]

371

American Indian Population, by Tribe and State, 1980: South Region, Abenaki-Chinook - II
[Continued]

Tribe	Total South Region	South Region (cont.)									
		East South Central Division					West South Central Division				
		Total East South Central	KY	TN	AL	MS	West South Central Total	AR	LA	OK	TX
Digger	14	8	8	-	-	-	-	-	-	-	-
Mattole	9	-	-	-	-	-	-	-	-	-	-
Morongo	-	-	-	-	-	-	-	-	-	-	-
Wappo	10	-	-	10	-	-	-	-	-	-	-
Yuki	-	-	-	-	-	-	-	-	-	-	-
Other California	-	-	-	-	-	-	-	-	-	-	-
Canadian and Latin American	1,271	49	7	36	-	6	722	7	60	142	513
Catawba	1,356	-	-	-	-	-	90	38	-	-	52
Cayuse	-	-	-	-	-	-	-	-	-	-	-
Chehalis	-	-	-	-	-	-	-	-	-	-	-
Chemakuan											
Total	-	-	-	-	-	-	-	-	-	-	-
Hoh	-	-	-	-	-	-	-	-	-	-	-
Quileute	-	-	-	-	-	-	-	-	-	-	-
Other Chemakuan	-	-	-	-	-	-	-	-	-	-	-
Chemehuevi	14	-	-	-	-	-	9	-	-	9	-
Cherokee											
Total	109,419	6,855	1,801	2,318	2,033	703	81,197	6,385	1,631	59,270	13,911
Cherokee	108,433	6,848	1,801	2,318	2,026	703	81,118	6,385	1,631	59,229	13,873
Eastern Cherokee	888	7	-	-	7	-	36	-	-	5	31
Etowah Cherokee	13	-	-	-	-	-	6	-	-	6	-
Tuscola	28	-	-	-	-	-	14	-	-	7	7
United Keetoowah	36	-	-	-	-	-	23	-	-	23	-
Western Cherokee	21	-	-	-	-	-	-	-	-	-	-
Other Cherokee	-	-	-	-	-	-	-	-	-	-	-
Cheyenne											
Total	3,803	41	13	28	-	-	3,595	20	-	3,364	211
Cheyenne	3,696	41	13	28	-	-	3,511	20	-	3,302	189
Northern Cheyenne	65	-	-	-	-	-	65	-	-	43	22
Southern Cheyenne	42	-	-	-	-	-	19	-	-	19	-
Chickahominy	610	-	-	-	-	-	58	-	-	26	32
Chickasaw	7,394	77	21	51	5	-	7,183	59	23	6,027	1,074
Chinook											
Total	6	-	-	-	-	-	1	-	-	1	-
Chinook	1	-	-	-	-	-	1	-	-	1	-
Clatsop	-	-	-	-	-	-	-	-	-	-	-
Columbia River Chinook	-	-	-	-	-	-	-	-	-	-	-
Other Chinook	5	-	-	-	-	-	-	-	-	-	-

Source: U.S. Bureau of the Census, *1980 Census of Population, Volume 2, Subject Reports, Characteristics of American Indians, by Tribes and Selected Areas: 1980,* PC80-2-1C, Section 1: Tables I-II, issued September 1989, U.S. Department of Commerce, U.S. Government Printing Office, Washington, D.C., pp. 1-53. *Notes:* (N.E.C.) stands for not elsewhere classified. A dash (-) represents zero or a percent which rounds to less than 0.1. 1. Reporting and/or processing problems may have affected the data for this tribe.

★ 206 ★

American Indian Population, by Tribe and State, 1980: South Region, Chippewa-Iowa - 1

Data are estimates based on a sample and are the most recent available.

Tribe	Total South Region	South Region									
		South Atlantic Division									
		Total South Atlantic	DE	MD	DC	VA	WV	NC	SC	GA	FL
Chippewa											
Total	2,133	820	12	101	22	111	28	55	30	117	344
Bad River	-	-	-	-	-	-	-	-	-	-	-
Bay Mills Chippewa	36	-	-	-	-	-	-	-	-	-	-
Bois Forte	-	-	-	-	-	-	-	-	-	-	-
Chippewa	1,950	742	12	89	22	68	28	55	30	108	330
Lac Courte Oreilles	-	-	-	-	-	-	-	-	-	-	-
Lac du Flambeau	-	-	-	-	-	-	-	-	-	-	-
Lake Superior	-	-	-	-	-	-	-	-	-	-	-
Leech Lake	-	-	-	-	-	-	-	-	-	-	-
Leelanau	-	-	-	-	-	-	-	-	-	-	-
Mille Lac	12	12	-	12	-	-	-	-	-	-	-
Minnesota Chippewa	-	-	-	-	-	-	-	-	-	-	-
Ontonagon	18	-	-	-	-	-	-	-	-	-	-
Red Cliff Chippewa	-	-	-	-	-	-	-	-	-	-	-
Red Lake Chippewa	9	9	-	-	-	-	-	-	-	9	-
Saginaw Chippewa	7	-	-	-	-	-	-	-	-	-	-
St. Croix Chippewa	-	-	-	-	-	-	-	-	-	-	-
Sault Ste. Marie Chippewa	29	-	-	-	-	-	-	-	-	-	-
Sokoagon Chippewa	-	-	-	-	-	-	-	-	-	-	-
Turtle Mountain	24	24	-	-	-	-	-	-	-	-	14
White Earth	48	43	-	-	-	43	-	-	-	-	-
Other Chippewa	-	-	-	-	-	-	-	-	-	-	-
Chitimacha	304	-	-	-	-	-	-	-	-	-	-
Choctaw											
Total	36,023	694	-	24	9	111	-	84	25	94	347
Choctaw	35,831	694	-	24	9	111	-	84	25	94	347
Clifton Choctaw	192	-	-	-	-	-	-	-	-	-	-
Chumash[1]											
Total	7	-	-	-	-	-	-	-	-	-	-
Chumash	7	-	-	-	-	-	-	-	-	-	-
Other Chumash	-	-	-	-	-	-	-	-	-	-	-
Clallam											
Total	26	5	-	5	-	-	-	-	-	-	-
Clallam	5	5	-	5	-	-	-	-	-	-	-
Lower Elwah	-	-	-	-	-	-	-	-	-	-	-
Port Gamble Clallam	21	-	-	-	-	-	-	-	-	-	-
Other Clellam	-	-	-	-	-	-	-	-	-	-	-
Coeur d' Alene	-	-	-	-	-	-	-	-	-	-	-
Coharie	491	491	-	-	-	-	-	491	-	-	-
Colorado River	-	-	-	-	-	-	-	-	-	-	-
Colville	130	8	-	2	-	6	-	-	-	-	-

[Continued]

★ 206 ★

American Indian Population, by Tribe and State, 1980: South Region, Chippewa-Iowa - I

[Continued]

| Tribe | Total South Region | South Region | | | | | | | | | |
| | | South Atlantic Division | | | | | | | | | |
		Total South Atlantic	DE	MD	DC	VA	WV	NC	SC	GA	FL
Comanche	5,751	241	-	12	-	47	-	73	-	40	69
Coos	-	-	-	-	-	-	-	-	-	-	-
Costanoan	15	-	-	-	-	-	-	-	-	-	-
Cowitz	13	-	-	-	-	-	-	-	-	-	-
Cree	303	166	-	60	-	14	13	9	11	7	52
Creek											
Total	21,587	2,724	-	49	18	62	-	77	10	315	2,193
Creek	21,315	2,537	-	49	18	62	-	77	10	283	2,038
Eastern Creek	39	25	-	-	-	-	-	-	-	-	25
Lower Muskogee	176	162	-	-	-	-	-	-	-	32	130
Muskogee	-	-	-	-	-	-	-	-	-	-	-
Thlopthlocco	42	-	-	-	-	-	-	-	-	-	-
Other Creek	13	-	-	-	-	-	-	-	-	-	-
Croatan	105	83	-	-	-	12	-	56	-	-	15
Crow	223	24	-	-	-	-	-	7	7	-	10
Cupeno											
Total	11	4	-	-	-	-	-	4	-	-	-
Agua Caliente	11	4	-	-	-	-	-	4	-	-	-
Cupeno	-	-	-	-	-	-	-	-	-	-	-
Delaware											
Total	2,194	190	15	24	9	18	18	-	39	-	67
Delaware	2,177	183	15	24	9	18	18	-	39	-	60
Munsee	-	-	-	-	-	-	-	-	-	-	-
Sand Hill	17	7	-	-	-	-	-	-	-	-	-
Diegueno											
Total	6	-	-	-	-	-	-	-	-	-	-
Diegueno	6	-	-	-	-	-	-	-	-	-	-
Manzanita	-	-	-	-	-	-	-	-	-	-	-
San Pascual	-	-	-	-	-	-	-	-	-	-	-
Santa Ysabel	-	-	-	-	-	-	-	-	-	-	-
Other Diegueno	-	-	-	-	-	-	-	-	-	-	-
Eastern tribes (n.e.c.)											
Total	1,986	1,906	35	6	-	10	-	1,440	334	48	33
Moor	26	17	11	6	-	-	-	-	-	-	-
Nansemond	26	26	24	-	-	-	-	2	-	-	-
Natchez	10	-	-	-	-	-	-	-	-	-	-
Nipmuc	6	-	-	-	-	-	-	-	-	-	-
Southeastern Indians	1,871	1,824	-	-	-	10	-	1,412	328	41	33
Tunica	34	26	-	-	-	-	-	26	-	-	-
Other Eastern	13	13	-	-	-	-	-	-	6	7	-
Flathead	61	22	-	-	-	8	-	-	-	-	14
Fort Hall	7	-	-	-	-	-	-	-	-	-	-

[Continued]

★ 206 ★

American Indian Population, by Tribe and State, 1980: South Region, Chippewa-Iowa - I
[Continued]

Tribe	Total South Region	South Region									
		South Atlantic Division									
		Total South Atlantic	DE	MD	DC	VA	WV	NC	SC	GA	FL
Gabrieleno	7	7	-	-	-	-	-	-	7	-	-
Gros Ventres											
Total	47	-	-	-	-	-	-	-	-	-	-
Atsina	-	-	-	-	-	-	-	-	-	-	-
Gros Ventres	47	-	-	-	-	-	-	-	-	-	-
Haida	10	10	-	-	-	-	-	-	-	10	-
Haliwa	1,919	1,919	-	176	-	106	-	1,637	-	-	-
Hidatsa	17	-	-	-	-	-	-	-	-	-	-
Hitchiti	15	11	-	-	-	-	-	-	-	-	11
Hoopa	37	30	-	-	-	6	-	-	-	-	24
Houma	2,490	50	-	5	-	7	-	-	-	-	38
Iowa	258	13	-	13	-	-	-	-	-	-	-

Source: U.S. Bureau of the Census, *1980 Census of Population, Volume 2, Subject Reports, Characteristics of American Indians, by Tribes and Selected Areas: 1980,* PC80-2-1C, Section 1. Tables I-II, Issued September 1989, U.S. Department of Commerce, U.S. Government Printing Office, Washington, D.C., pp. 1-53. *Notes:* (N.E.C.) stands for not elsewhere classified. A dash (-) represents zero or a percent which rounds to less than 0.1.
1. Reporting and/or processing problems may have affected the data for this tribe.

★ 207 ★

American Indian Population, by Tribe and State, 1980: South Region, Chippewa-Iowa - II

Data are estimates based on a sample and are the most recent available.

Tribe	Total South Region	South Region (cont.)									
		East South Central Division					West South Central Division				
		Total East South Central	KY	TN	AL	MS	West South Central Total	AR	LA	OK	TX
Chippewa											
Total	2,133	302	115	115	40	32	1,011	107	40	322	542
Bad River	-	-	-	-	-	-	-	-	-	-	-
Bay Mills Chippewa	36	-	36	-	-	-	-	-	-	-	-
Bois Forte	-	-	-	-	-	-	-	-	-	-	-
Chippewa	1,950	243	56	115	40	32	965	85	35	314	531
Lac Courte Oreilles	-	-	-	-	-	-	-	-	-	-	-
Lac du Flambeau	-	-	-	-	-	-	-	-	-	-	-
Lake Superior	-	-	-	-	-	-	-	-	-	-	-
Leech Lake	-	-	-	-	-	-	-	-	-	-	-
Leelanau	-	-	-	-	-	-	-	-	-	-	-
Mille Lac	12	-	-	-	-	-	-	-	-	-	-
Minnesota Chippewa	-	-	-	-	-	-	-	-	-	-	-
Ontonagon	18	-	-	-	-	-	18	18	-	-	-
Red Cliff Chippewa	-	-	-	-	-	-	-	-	-	-	-
Red Lake Chippewa	9	-	-	-	-	-	-	-	-	-	-

[Continued]

★ 207 ★

American Indian Population, by Tribe and State, 1980: South Region, Chippewa-Iowa - II

[Continued]

| Tribe | Total South Region | South Region (cont.) | | | | | | | | | |
| | | East South Central Division | | | | | West South Central Division | | | | |
		Total East South Central	KY	TN	AL	MS	West South Central Total	AR	LA	OK	TX
Saginaw Chippewa	7	2	2	-	-	-	5	-	-	-	5
St. Croix Chippewa	-	-	-	-	-	-	-	-	-	-	-
Sault Ste. Marie Chippewa	29	21	21	-	-	-	8	-	-	8	-
Sokoagon Chippewa	-	-	-	-	-	-	-	-	-	-	-
Turtle Mountain	24	-	-	-	-	-	10	4	-	-	6
White Earth	48	-	-	-	-	-	5	-	5	-	-
Other Chippewa	-	-	-	-	-	-	-	-	-	-	-
Chitimacha	304	6	-	-	-	6	298	-	291	-	7
Choctaw											
Total	36,023	4,248	99	215	934	3,000	31,081	1,064	1,221	24,162	4,634
Choctaw	35,831	4,248	99	215	934	3,000	30,889	1,059	1,221	24,001	4,608
Clifton Choctaw	192	-	-	-	-	-	192	5	-	161	26
Chumash[1]											
Total	7	7	-	-	7	-	-	-	-	-	-
Chumash	7	7	-	-	7	-	-	-	-	-	-
Other Chumash	-	-	-	-	-	-	-	-	-	-	-
Clallam											
Total	26	-	-	-	-	-	21	-	-	21	-
Clallam	5	-	-	-	-	-	-	-	-	-	-
Lower Elwah	-	-	-	-	-	-	-	-	-	-	-
Port Gamble Clallam	21	-	-	-	-	-	21	-	-	21	-
Other Clellam	-	-	-	-	-	-	-	-	-	-	-
Coeur d' Alene	-	-	-	-	-	-	-	-	-	-	-
Coharie	491	-	-	-	-	-	-	-	-	-	-
Colorado River	-	-	-	-	-	-	-	-	-	-	-
Colville	130	14	-	-	14	-	108	9	-	91	8
Comanche	5,751	108	22	38	44	4	5,402	91	48	4,244	1,019
Coos	-	-	-	-	-	-	-	-	-	-	-
Costanoan	15	-	-	-	-	-	15	-	-	-	15
Cowitz	13	-	-	-	-	-	13	-	-	7	6
Cree	303	55	7	14	-	34	82	6	-	32	44
Creek											
Total	21,587	1,567	28	97	1,315	127	17,296	253	248	15,421	1,374
Creek	21,315	1,539	28	97	1,287	127	17,239	253	248	15,371	1,367
Eastern Creek	39	7	-	-	7	-	7	-	-	-	7
Lower Muskogee	178	16	-	-	16	-	-	-	-	-	-
Muskogee	-	-	-	-	-	-	-	-	-	-	-
Thlopthlocco	42	-	-	-	-	-	42	-	-	42	-
Other Creek	13	5	-	-	5	-	8	-	-	8	-
Croatan	105	-	-	-	-	-	22	-	-	-	22
Crow	223	28	-	7	21	-	171	24	-	92	55
Cupeno											
Total	11	-	-	-	-	-	7	-	-	7	-
Agua Caliente	11	-	-	-	-	-	7	-	-	7	-
Cupeno	-	-	-	-	-	-	-	-	-	-	-
Delaware											
Total	2,194	40	10	27	3	-	1,964	79	-	1,689	196
Delaware	2,177	30	-	27	3	-	1,964	79	-	1,689	196
Munsee	-	-	-	-	-	-	-	-	-	-	-
Sand Hill	17	10	10	-	-	-	-	-	-	-	-
Diegueno											
Total	6	6	-	6	-	-	-	-	-	-	-

[Continued]

★ 207 ★

American Indian Population, by Tribe and State, 1980: South Region, Chippewa-Iowa - II

[Continued]

Tribe	Total South Region	South Region (cont.)									
		East South Central Division					West South Central Division				
		Total East South Central	KY	TN	AL	MS	West South Central Total	AR	LA	OK	TX
Diegueno	6	6	-	6	-	-	-	-	-	-	-
Manzanita	-	-	-	-	-	-	-	-	-	-	-
San Pascual	-	-	-	-	-	-	-	-	-	-	-
Santa Ysabel	-	-	-	-	-	-	-	-	-	-	-
Other Diegueno	-	-	-	-	-	-	-	-	-	-	-
Eastern tribes (n.e.c.)											
Total	1,986	30	15	-	6	9	50	-	8	12	30
Moor	26	9	-	-	-	9	-	-	-	-	-
Nansemond	26	-	-	-	-	-	-	-	-	-	-
Natchez	10	-	-	-	-	-	10	-	-	5	5
Nipmuc	6	6	-	-	6	-	-	-	-	-	-
Southeastern Indians	1,871	15	15	-	-	-	32	-	-	7	25
Tunica	34	-	-	-	-	-	8	-	8	-	-
Other Eastern	13	-	-	-	-	-	-	-	-	-	-
Flathead	61	-	-	-	-	-	39	-	-	7	32
Fort Hall	7	-	-	-	-	-	7	-	-	-	7
Gabrieleno	7	-	-	-	-	-	-	-	-	-	-
Gros Ventres											
Total	47	5	5	-	-	-	42	-	-	29	13
Atsina	-	-	-	-	-	-	-	-	-	-	-
Gros Ventres	47	5	5	-	-	-	42	-	-	29	13
Haida	10	-	-	-	-	-	-	-	-	-	-
Haliwa	1,919	-	-	-	-	-	-	-	-	-	-
Hidatsa	17	-	-	-	-	-	17	-	-	17	-
Hitchiti	15	-	-	-	-	-	-	4	-	4	-
Hoopa	37	-	-	-	-	-	7	-	-	7	-
Houma	2,490	24	-	-	20	4	2,416	18	2,271	53	74
Iowa	258	-	-	-	-	-	245	-	-	196	49

Source: U.S. Bureau of the Census, *1980 Census of Population, Volume 2, Subject Reports, Characteristics of American Indians, by Tribes and Selected Areas: 1980*, PC80-2-1C, Section 1: Tables I-II, issued September 1989, U.S. Department of Commerce, U.S. Government Printing Office, Washington, D.C., pp. 1-53. *Notes:* (N.E.C.) stands for not elsewhere classified. A dash (-) represents zero or a percent which rounds to less than 0.1. 1. Reporting and/or processing problems may have affected the data for this tribe.

★ 208 ★

American Indian Population, by Tribe and State, 1980: South Region, Iroquois-Pomo - I

Data are estimates based on a sample and are the most recent available.

Tribe	Total South Region	South Region — South Atlantic Division									
		Total South Atlantic	DE	MD	DC	VA	WV	NC	SC	GA	FL
Iroquois											
Total	4,278	2,152	56	187	8	225	56	999	28	124	469
Cayuga	63	15	-	8	-	-	-	-	-	-	7
Iroquois (n.e.c.)	420	216	9	7	-	21	22	32	-	-	125
Mohawk[1]	1,067	631	34	78	8	150	6	83	9	106	157
Oneida	225	72	-	24	-	-	-	14	-	8	26
Onondaga	47	23	-	8	-	-	-	-	-	-	15
Seneca											
Total	796	247	5	47	-	41	28	21	4	10	91
Seneca	796	247	5	47	-	41	28	21	4	10	91
Seneca Nation	-	-	-	-	-	-	-	-	-	-	-
Tonawanda Seneca	-	-	-	-	-	-	-	-	-	-	-
Seneca-Cayuga	277	-	-	-	-	-	-	-	-	-	-
Tuscarora	943	884	8	15	-	-	-	824	15	-	22
Wyandot	440	64	-	-	-	13	-	25	-	-	26
Kalispel	-	-	-	-	-	-	-	-	-	-	-
Karok	-	-	-	-	-	-	-	-	-	-	-
Kaw	381	7	-	-	-	-	-	-	-	-	7
Kickapoo	1,193	-	-	-	-	-	-	-	-	-	-
Kiowa	5,555	55	-	22	-	-	-	19	14	-	-
Klamath	51	9	-	-	-	-	-	9	-	-	-
Konkow	3	-	-	-	-	-	-	-	-	-	-
Kootenai	16	-	-	-	-	-	-	-	-	-	-
Long Island											
Total	67	22	-	-	-	-	-	18	-	4	-
Matinecock	35	4	-	-	-	-	-	-	-	4	-
Montauk	32	18	-	-	-	-	-	18	-	-	-
Poosepatuck	-	-	-	-	-	-	-	-	-	-	-
Other Long Island	-	-	-	-	-	-	-	-	-	-	-
Luiseno											
Total	36	15	-	-	-	-	-	15	-	-	-
LaJolla	-	-	-	-	-	-	-	-	-	-	-
Luiseno	15	-	-	-	-	-	-	-	-	-	-
Pala	18	15	-	-	-	-	-	15	-	-	-
Pauma	-	-	-	-	-	-	-	-	-	-	-
Pechanga	3	-	-	-	-	-	-	-	-	-	-
Lumbee[2]	27,714	27,476	6	571	-	157	-	26,447	184	60	51
Lummi[2]	1,794	1,782	-	44	-	40	-	1,677	12	9	-
Maidu	9	-	-	-	-	-	-	-	-	-	-
Makah	-	-	-	-	-	-	-	-	-	-	-
Maliseet	7	7	-	-	-	-	-	-	-	-	7
Mandan	110	14	-	-	-	-	-	14	-	-	-

[Continued]

378

★ 208 ★

American Indian Population, by Tribe and State, 1980: South Region, Iroquois-Pomo - 1

[Continued]

Tribe	Total South Region	South Region									
		South Atlantic Division									
		Total South Atlantic	DE	MD	DC	VA	WV	NC	SC	GA	FL
Mattaponi	86	86	-	-	-	86	-	-	-	-	-
Menominee	145	77	-	36	-	-	-	-	-	-	41
Miami	413	43	-	-	-	-	-	-	8	-	35
Miccosukee[3]	36	20	-	-	-	-	-	-	-	-	20
Micmac[4]	15	13	-	-	-	6	-	-	-	7	-
Mission Indians	36	15	-	-	-	-	-	7	-	-	8
Miwok	43	-	-	-	-	-	-	-	-	-	-
Modoc	58	5	-	-	-	5	-	-	-	-	-
Mohegan	74	23	-	-	-	-	-	-	-	-	23
Mono	38	6	-	-	-	-	6	-	-	-	-
Nanticoke	458	416	396	-	-	14	-	-	-	-	6
Narragansett	-	-	-	-	-	-	-	-	-	-	-
Navajo	2,508	538	6	61	7	88	34	148	40	57	97
Nez Perce[3]	106	48	-	-	7	7	-	6	-	-	28
Nomalaki	24	-	-	-	-	-	-	-	-	-	-
Northwest tribes (n.e.c)											
Total	19	-	-	-	-	-	-	-	-	-	-
Columbia Wenatchee	5	-	-	-	-	-	-	-	-	-	-
Kalapuya	-	-	-	-	-	-	-	-	-	-	-
Tillamook	-	-	-	-	-	-	-	-	-	-	-
Other Northwest	14	-	-	-	-	-	-	-	-	-	-
Omaha	130	25	-	-	-	12	-	6	-	-	7
Oregon Athabaskan	51	9	-	-	-	-	-	-	-	9	-
Osage	3,687	108	-	15	-	23	-	18	7	13	32
Oto	1,090	55	-	31	-	-	-	-	-	-	24
Ottawa	444	115	-	-	-	26	-	5	-	4	80
Paiute[3]											
Total	191	34	13	6	-	15	-	-	-	-	-
Burns Paiute	-	-	-	-	-	-	-	-	-	-	-
Northern Paiute	-	-	-	-	-	-	-	-	-	-	-
Paiute	191	34	13	6	-	15	-	-	-	-	-
Pyramind Lake	-	-	-	-	-	-	-	-	-	-	-
Southern Paiute	-	-	-	-	-	-	-	-	-	-	-
Walker River	-	-	-	-	-	-	-	-	-	-	-
Other Paiute	-	-	-	-	-	-	-	-	-	-	-
Pamunkey	93	86	-	8	-	50	-	17	5	6	-
Papago											
Total	270	49	-	-	-	24	-	6	-	-	19
Papago	263	42	-	-	-	24	-	6	-	-	12
Other Papago	7	7	-	-	-	-	-	-	-	-	7
Passamaquoddy											
Total	21	21	-	-	-	-	-	6	-	-	15

[Continued]

★ 208 ★

American Indian Population, by Tribe and State, 1980: South Region, Iroquois-Pomo - I
[Continued]

Tribe	Total South Region	South Region									
		South Atlantic Division									
		Total South Atlantic	DE	MD	DC	VA	WV	NC	SC	GA	FL
Passamaquoddy	21	21	-	-	-	-	-	6	-	-	15
Other Passamaquoddy	-	-	-	-	-	-	-	-	-	-	-
Pawnee	1,389	47	-	-	9	18	14	6	-	-	-
Penobscot	117	78	-	14	-	40	-	-	15	-	9
Peoria	265	6	-	-	-	-	-	-	-	6	-
Pequot	12	5	-	-	-	-	-	-	-	5	-
Pima	132	63	3	-	-	16	-	13	-	9	22
Piscataway	478	478	-	470	-	-	-	-	8	-	-
Pit River	29	-	-	-	-	-	-	-	-	-	-
Pomo											
Total	107	77	-	-	-	-	-	72	-	-	5
Eastern Pomo	72	72	-	-	-	-	-	72	-	-	-
Kashaya	-	-	-	-	-	-	-	-	-	-	-
Northern Pomo	12	5	-	-	-	-	-	-	-	-	5
Pomo	23	-	-	-	-	-	-	-	-	-	-
Other Pomo	-	-	-	-	-	-	-	-	-	-	-

Source: U.S. Bureau of the Census, *1980 Census of Population, Volume 2, Subject Reports, Characteristics of American Indians, by Tribes and Selected Areas: 1980*, PC80-2-1C, Section 1: Tables I-II, issued September 1989, U.S. Department of Commerce, U.S. Government Printing Office, Washington, D.C., pp. 1-53. *Notes:* (N.E.C.) stands for not elsewhere classified. A dash (-) represents zero or a percent which rounds to less than 0.1. 1. Any Mohawk entry of "Ganienka" was miscoded to Wailaki. 2. Miscoding of entries of "Lummee," "Lummi," "Lumbee," or "Lumbi" may have affected the data for this tribe. 3. Reporting and/or processing may have affected the data for this tribe. 4. Any entry with the spelling "Micmac" was miscoded to Cheyenne River Sioux.

★ 209 ★

American Indian Population, by Tribe and State, 1980: South Region, Iroquois-Pomo - II

Data are estimates based on a sample and are the most recent available.

Tribe	Total South Region	South Region (cont.)									
		East South Central Division					West South Central Division				
		Total East South Central	KY	TN	AL	MS	West South Central Total	AR	LA	OK	TX
Iroquois											
Total	4,278	215	61	76	78	-	1,911	87	59	1,258	507
Cayuga	63	-	61	76	78	-	48	-	-	28	20
Iroquois (n.e.c.)	420	49	31	12	6	-	155	-	3	38	114
Mohawk[1]	1,067	124	7	50	67	-	312	35	12	128	137
Oneida	225	-	-	-	-	-	153	23	10	29	91
Onondaga	47	17	17	-	-	-	7	-	-	-	7

[Continued]

American Indian Population, by Tribe and State, 1980: South Region, Iroquois-Pomo - II
[Continued]

Tribe	Total South Region	South Region (cont.)									
		East South Central Division					West South Central Division				
		Total East South Central	KY	TN	AL	MS	West South Central Total	AR	LA	OK	TX
Seneca											
Total	796	14	6	8	-	-	535	23	34	436	42
Seneca	796	14	6	8	-	-	535	23	34	436	42
Seneca Nation	-	-	-	-	-	-	-	-	-	-	-
Tonawanda Seneca	-	-	-	-	-	-	-	-	-	-	-
Seneca-Cayuga	277	6	-	6	-	-	271	-	-	265	6
Tuscarora	943	-	-	-	-	-	59	-	-	20	39
Wyandot	440	5	-	-	5	-	371	6	-	314	51
Kalispel	-	-	-	-	-	-	-	-	-	-	-
Karok	-	-	-	-	-	-	-	-	-	-	-
Kaw	381	-	-	-	-	-	374	-	-	342	32
Kickapoo	1,193	42	-	-	42	-	1,151	2	-	953	196
Kiowa	5,555	70	5	33	2	30	5,430	48	6	5,004	372
Klamath	51	-	-	-	-	-	42			12	
Konkow	3	-	-	-	-	-	3	-	-	3	-
Kootenai	16	7	7	-	-	-	9	-	-	9	-
Long Island											
Total	67	-	-	-	-	-	45	-	45	-	-
Matinecock	35	-	-	-	-	31	-	-	31	-	-
Montauk	32	-	-	-	-	-	14	-	14	-	-
Poosepatuck	-	-	-	-	-	-	-	-	-	-	-
Other Long Island	-	-	-	-	-	-	-	-	-	-	-
Luiseno											
Total	36	-	-	-	-	-	21	-	-	18	3
LaJolla	-	-	-	-	-	-	-	-	-	-	-
Luiseno	15	-	-	-	-	-	15	-	-	15	-
Pala	18	-	-	-	-	-	3	-	-	-	3
Pauma	-	-	-	-	-	-	-	-	-	-	-
Pechanga	3	-	-	-	-	-	3	-	-	3	-
Lumbee[2]	27,714	84	21	40	23	-	154	31	51	7	65
Lummu[2]	1,794	-	-	-	-	-	12	2	-	10	-
Maidu	9	-	-	-	-	-	9	-	-	9	-
Makah	-	-	-	-	-	-	-	-	-	-	-
Maliseet	7	-	-	-	-	-	-	-	-	-	-
Mandan	110	-	-	-	-	-	96	12	-	2	82
Mattaponi	86	-	-	-	-	-	-	-	-	-	-
Menominee	145	12	12	-	-	-	56	4	-	24	28
Maimi	413	8	8	-	-	-	362	35	-	297	30
Miccosukee[3]	36	-	-	-	-	-	16	-	-	16	-
Micmac[4]	15	-	-	-	-	-	2	2	-	-	-
Mission Indians	36	-	-	-	-	-	21	-	3	1	17
Miwok	43	-	-	-	-	-	43	-	-	-	43

[Continued]

American Indian Population, by Tribe and State, 1980: South Region, Iroquois-Pomo - II

[Continued]

Tribe	Total South Region	South Region (cont.)									
		East South Central Division					West South Central Division				
		Total East South Central	KY	TN	AL	MS	West South Central Total	AR	LA	OK	TX
Modoc	58	-	-	-	-	-	53	-	-	35	18
Mohegan	74	32	-	-	32	-	19	-	-	13	6
Mono	38	-	-	-	-	-	32	-	-	-	32
Nanticoke	458	-	-	-	-	-	42	-	6	30	6
Narragansett	-	-	-	-	-	-	-	-	-	-	-
Navajo	2,508	107	8	31	13	55	1,863	41	95	890	837
Nez Perce[3]	106	12	6	-	-	6	46	13	-	26	7
Nomalaki	24	-	-	-	-	-	24	-	-	24	-
Northwest tribes (n.e.c)											
Total	19	5	-	5		-	14	-	-	14	-
Columbia Wenatchee	5	-	-	5	-	-	-	-	-	-	-
Kalapuya	-	-	-	-	-	-	-	-	-	-	-
Tillamook	-	-	-	-	-	-	-	-	-	-	-
Other Northwest	14	-	-	-	-	-	14	-	-	14	-
Omaha	130	5	5	-	-	-	100	5	-	48	47
Oregon Athabaskan	51	-	-	-	-	-	42	-	-	42	-
Osage	3,687	11	-	-	11	-	3,568	85	56	3,029	398
Oto	1,090	-	-	-	-	-	1,035	22	-	1,013	-
Ottawa	444	13	6	7	-	-	316	30	-	189	97
Paiute[3]											
Total	191	13	6	7	-	-	144	3	-	116	25
Burns Paiute	-	-	-	-	-	-	-	-	-	-	-
Northern Paiute	-	-	-	-	-	-	-	-	-	-	-
Paiute	191	13	6	7	-	-	144	3	-	116	25
Pyramind Lake	-	-	-	-	-	-	-	-	-	-	-
Southern Paiute	-	-	-	-	-	-	-	-	-	-	-
Walker River	-	-	-	-	-	-	-	-	-	-	-
Other Paiute	-	-	-	-	-	-	-	-	-	-	-
Pamunkey	93	7	-	-	7	-	-	-	-	-	-
Papago											
Total	270	7	7	-	-	-	214	-	-	93	121
Papago	263	7	7	-	-	-	214	-	-	93	121
Other Papago	7	-	-	-	-	-	-	-	-	-	-
Passamaquoddy											
Total	21	-	-	-	-	-	-	-	-	-	-
Passamaquoddy	21	-	-	-	-	-	-	-	-	-	-
Other Passamaquoddy	-	-	-	-	-	-	-	-	-	-	-
Pawnee	1,389	22	11	-	11	-	1,320	-	10	1,269	41
Penobscot	117	-	-	-	-	-	39	-	-	10	29
Peoria	265	-	-	-	-	-	259	6	-	253	-
Pequot	12	-	-	-	-	-	7	-	-	7	-
Pima	132	12	12	-	-	-	57	-	-	43	14

[Continued]

★ 209 ★

American Indian Population, by Tribe and State, 1980: South Region, Iroquois-Pomo - II

[Continued]

Tribe	Total South Region	South Region (cont.)									
		East South Central Division					West South Central Division				
		Total East South Central	KY	TN	AL	MS	West South Central Total	AR	LA	OK	TX
Piscataway	478	-	-	-	-	-	-	-	-	-	-
Pit River	29	-	-	-	-	-	29	8	-	11	10
Pomo											
Total	107	-	-	-	-	-	30	-	-	23	7
Eastern Pomo	72	-	-	-	-	-	-	-	-	-	-
Kashaya	-	-	-	-	-	-	-	-	-	-	-
Northern Pomo	12	-	-	-	-	-	7	-	-	-	7
Pomo	23	-	-	-	-	-	23	-	-	23	-
Other Pomo	-	-	-	-	-	-	-	-	-	-	-

Source: U.S. Bureau of the Census, *1980 Census of Population, Volume 2, Subject Reports, Characteristics of American Indians, by Tribes and Selected Areas: 1980,* PC80-2-1C, Section 1: Tables I-II, issued September 1989, U.S. Department of Commerce, U.S. Government Printing Office, Washington, D.C., pp. 1-53. *Notes:* (N.E.C.) stands for not elsewhere classified. A dash (-) represents zero or a percent which rounds to less than 0.1. 1. Any Mohawk entry of "Ganienka" was miscoded to Wailaki. 2. Miscoding of entries of "Lummee," "Lummi," "Lumbee," or "Lumbi" may have affected the data for this tribe. 3. Reporting and/or processing may have affected the data for this tribe. 4. Any entry with the spelling "Micmac" was miscoded to Cheyenne River Sioux.

★ 210 ★

American Indian Population, by Tribe and State, 1980: South Region, Ponca-Sioux - I

Data are estimates based on a sample and are the most recent available.

Tribe	Total South Region	South Region									
		South Atlantic Division									
		Total South Atlantic	DE	MD	DC	VA	WV	NC	SC	GA	FL
Ponca	1,568	-	-	-	-	-	-	-	-	-	-
Potawatomi											
Total	2,948	136	-	37	-	8	-	-	8	22	61
Citizen Band	299	-	-	-	-	-	-	-	-	-	-
Forest County	-	-	-	-	-	-	-	-	-	-	-
Huron Potawatomi	-	-	-	-	-	-	-	-	-	-	-
Potawatomie	2,620	136	-	37	-	8	-	-	8	22	61
Prairie Band	29	-	-	-	-	-	-	-	-	-	-
Other Potawatomi	-	-	-	-	-	-	-	-	-	-	-
Powhatan	78	27	-	-	6	-	-	21	-	-	-
Pueblo[1]											
Total	1,046	208	-	11	-	82	-	44	5	43	23
Acoma	29	6	-	-	-	6	-	-	-	-	-
Arizona Tewa	-	-	-	-	-	-	-	-	-	-	-
Cochiti	6	-	-	-	-	-	-	-	-	-	-

[Continued]

American Indian Population, by Tribe and State, 1980: South Region, Ponca-Sioux - I
[Continued]

| Tribe | Total South Region | South Region — South Atlantic Division | | | | | | | | | |
		Total South Atlantic	DE	MD	DC	VA	WV	NC	SC	GA	FL
Hopi	185	19	-	-	-	7	-	5	-	-	7
Isleta	37	21	-	-	-	21	-	-	-	-	-
Jemez	25	14	-	-	-	6	-	8	-	-	-
Keres (n.e.c.)	16	7	-	-	-	7	-	-	-	-	-
Laguna	92	23	-	-	-	15	-	-	-	7	1
Nambe	-	-	-	-	-	-	-	-	-	-	-
Picuris	-	-	-	-	-	-	-	-	-	-	-
Pojoaque	-	-	-	-	-	-	-	-	-	-	-
Pueblo (n.e.c.)	259	59	-	6	-	8	-	8	-	30	7
Sandia	1	-	-	-	-	-	-	-	-	-	-
San Felipe	-	-	-	-	-	-	-	-	-	-	-
San Ildefonso	-	-	-	-	-	-	-	-	-	-	-
San Juan	2	-	-	-	-	-	-	-	-	-	-
Santa Ana	12	-	-	-	-	-	-	-	-	-	-
Santa Clara[1]	-	-	-	-	-	-	-	-	-	-	-
Santo Domingo	-	-	-	-	-	-	-	-	-	-	-
Taos	15	8	-	-	-	-	-	-	-	-	8
Tesuque	-	-	-	-	-	-	-	-	-	-	-
Tewa	43	17	-	-	-	12	-	5	-	-	-
Tigua[1]	224	5	-	-	-	-	-	-	5	-	-
Zia	26	5	-	5	-	-	-	-	-	-	-
Zuni	75	24	-	-	-	-	-	18	-	6	-
Puget Sound Salish											
Total	128	56	-	34	7	-	-	6	-	-	9
Duwamish	4	-	-	-	-	-	-	-	-	-	-
Muckleshoot	5	-	-	-	-	-	-	-	-	-	-
Nisqually	-	-	-	-	-	-	-	-	-	-	-
Nooksack	-	-	-	-	-	-	-	-	-	-	-
Puget Sound Salish (n.e.c.)	-	-	-	-	-	-	-	-	-	-	-
Puyallup	7	-	-	-	-	-	-	-	-	-	-
Samish	20	-	-	-	-	-	-	-	-	-	-
Sauk-Sauiatte	-	-	-	-	-	-	-	-	-	-	-
Skokomish	6	6	-	-	-	-	-	6	-	-	-
Skykomish	-	-	-	-	-	-	-	-	-	-	-
Snohomish	-	-	-	-	-	-	-	-	-	-	-
Snoqualmie	-	-	-	-	-	-	-	-	-	-	-
Squaxin Island	-	-	-	-	-	-	-	-	-	-	-
Steilacoom	-	-	-	-	-	-	-	-	-	-	-
Stillaguamish	-	-	-	-	-	-	-	-	-	-	-
Suquamish	9	9	-	-	-	-	-	-	-	-	-
Swinomish	25	-	-	-	-	-	-	-	-	-	-
Tulalip	34	34	-	34	-	-	-	-	-	-	-

[Continued]

★ 210 ★

American Indian Population, by Tribe and State, 1980: South Region, Ponca-Sioux - I
[Continued]

Tribe	Total South Region	South Region									
		South Atlantic Division									
		Total South Atlantic	DE	MD	DC	VA	WV	NC	SC	GA	FL
Upper Skagit	18	7	-	-	7	-	-	-	-	-	-
Quapaw	429	22									
Quinault	-	-	6	-	-	-	-	-	-	-	16
Rappahannock	17	7	-	-	-	-	-	-	-	7	-
Sac and Fox Mesquakie	1,514	74	-	18	-	22	-	-	9	-	25
Salinan	-	-	-	-	-	-	-	-	-	-	-
Schaghticoke	5	5	-	-	-	-	-	-	-	-	5
Seminole[1]											
Total	6,823	1,262	-	29	-	58	-	40	20	89	1,026
Seminole	6,405	892	-	29	-	45	-	38	20	89	671
Seminole Nation of Oklahoma	46	8	-	-	-	-	-	2	-	-	6
Seminole Tribe of Florida	372	362	-	-	-	13	-	-	-	-	349
Other Seminole	-	-	-	-	-	-	-	-	-	-	-
Serrano	13	2	-	-	-	-	-	-	-	-	2
Shasta	6	-	-	-	-	-	-	-	-	-	-
Shawnee											
Total	2,335	174	-	25	-	16	31	12	-	17	73
Absentee Shawnee	304	16	-	-	-	16	-	-	-	-	-
Shawnee	2,031	158	-	25	-	-	31	12	-	17	73
Shinnecock	16	8	-	-	-	-	-	-	-	-	8
Shoshone											
Total	341	44	-	-	-	8	-	8	-	16	12
Goshute	-	-	-	-	-	-	-	-	-	-	-
Shoshone	306	32	-	-	-	8	-	8	-	16	-
Te-Moak Western Shoshone[1]	23	-	-	-	-	-	-	-	-	-	-
Yomba[1]	12	12	-	-	-	-	-	-	-	-	12
Other Shoshone	-	-	-	-	-	-	-	-	-	-	-
Siletz	11	-	-	-	-	-	-	-	-	-	-
Sioux											
Total	4,046	1,179	14	114	-	184	34	290	72	134	337
Blackfoot Sioux	26	6	-	-	-	6	-	-	-	-	-
Brule Sioux	-	-	-	-	-	-	-	-	-	-	-
Cheyenne River Sioux[2]	65	5	-	-	-	5	-	-	-	-	-
Crow River Sioux[2]	-	-	-	-	-	-	-	-	-	-	-
Dakota Sioux	74	24	-	-	-	-	-	24	-	-	-
Devil's Lake Sioux	-	-	-	-	-	-	-	-	-	-	-
Fladreau Santee	-	-	-	-	-	-	-	-	-	-	-
Fort Peck	-	-	-	-	-	-	-	-	-	-	-
Lower Brule Sioux	13	-	-	-	-	-	-	-	-	-	-
Mdewakanton Sioux	-	-	-	-	-	-	-	-	-	-	-
Oglala Sioux	144	21	-	6	-	-	-	9	-	-	6
Pine Ridge Sioux	-	-	-	-	-	-	-	-	-	-	-

[Continued]

★ 210 ★

American Indian Population, by Tribe and State, 1980: South Region, Ponca-Sioux - I
[Continued]

| Tribe | Total South Region | South Region | | | | | | | | | | |
| | | South Atlantic Division | | | | | | | | | | |
		Total South Atlantic	DE	MD	DC	VA	WV	NC	SC	GA	FL
Prior Lake Sioux	-	-	-	-	-	-	-	-	-	-	-
Rosebud Sioux	20	-	-	-	-	-	-	-	-	-	-
Santee Sioux	23	16	-	8	-	-	1	7	-	-	-
Sioux	3,518	1,040	14	100	-	173	33	244	42	134	300
Sisseton Sioux	20	9	-	-	-	-	-	-	-	-	9
Standing Rock Sioux	14	-	-	-	-	-	-	-	-	-	-
Teton Sioux	21	11	-	-	-	-	-	6	-	-	5
Wahpeton Sioux	-	-	-	-	-	-	-	-	-	-	-
Yankton Sioux	48	30	-	-	-	-	-	-	30	-	-
Yanktonai Sioux	8	5	-	-	-	-	-	-	-	-	5
Other Sioux	33	-	-	-	-	-	-	-	-	-	-

Source: U.S. Bureau of the Census, *1980 Census of Population, Volume 2, Subject Reports, Characteristics of American Indians, by Tribes and Selected Areas: 1980*, PC80-2-1C, Section 1: Tables I-II, issued September 1989, U.S. Department of Commerce, U.S. Government Printing Office, Washington, D.C., pp. 1-53. *Notes:* (N.E.C.) stands for not elsewhere classified. A dash (-) represents zero or a percent which rounds to less than 0.1. 1. Reporting and/or processing problems may have affected the data for this tribe. 2. Any entry with the spelling "Micmac" was miscoded to Cheyenne River Sioux.

★ 211 ★

American Indian Population, by Tribe and State, 1980: South Region, Ponca-Sioux - II

Data are estimates based on a sample and are the most recent available.

| Tribe | Total South Region | South Region (cont.) | | | | | | | | | |
| | | East South Central Division | | | | | West South Central Division | | | | |
		Total East South Central	KY	TN	AL	MS	West South Central Total	AR	LA	OK	TX
Ponca	1,568	47	-	5	-	42	1,521	6	13	1,424	78
Potawatomi											
Total	2,948	71	14	32	17	8	2,741	15	-	2,296	430
Citizen Band	299	-	-	-	-	-	299	-	-	287	12
Forest County	-	-	-	-	-	-	-	-	-	-	-
Huron Potawatomi	-	-	-	-	-	-	-	-	-	-	-
Potawatomie	2,620	71	14	32	17	8	2,413	15	-	1,986	412
Prairie Band	29	-	-	-	-	-	29	-	-	23	6
Other Potawatomi	-	-	-	-	-	-	-	-	-	-	-
Powhatan	78	8	-	8	-	-	43	-	16	-	27
Pueblo[1]											
Total	1,046	80	44	6	30	-	758	6	23	219	510
Acoma	29	7	7	-	-	-	16	-	-	10	6
Arizona Tewa	-	-	-	-	-	-	-	-	-	-	-
Cochiti	6	-	-	-	-	-	6	-	-	6	-
Hopi	185	7	1	6	-	-	159	6	23	57	73
Isleta	37	-	-	-	-	-	16	-	-	7	9
Jemez	25	-	-	-	-	-	11	-	-	11	-
Keres (n.e.c.)	16	-	-	-	-	-	9	-	-	-	9

[Continued]

★ 211 ★

American Indian Population, by Tribe and State, 1980: South Region, Ponca-Sioux - II
[Continued]

Tribe	Total South Region	Total East South Central	KY	TN	AL	MS	West South Central Total	AR	LA	OK	TX
		South Region (cont.)									
		East South Central Division					West South Central Division				
Laguna	92	22	-	-	22	-	47	-	-	28	19
Nambe	-	-	-	-	-	-	-	-	-	-	-
Picuris	-	-	-	-	-	-	-	-	-	-	-
Pojoaque	-	-	-	-	-	-	-	-	-	-	-
Pueblo (n.e.c.)	259	30	30	-	-	-	170	-	-	67	103
Sandia	-	-	-	-	-	-	-	-	-	-	-
San Felipe	-	-	-	-	-	-	-	-	-	-	-
San Ildefonso	-	-	-	-	-	-	-	-	-	-	-
San Juan	2	-	-	-	-	-	2	-	-	2	-
Santa Ana	12	-	-	-	-	-	12	-	-	12	-
Santa Clara[1]	-	-	-	-	-	-	-	-	-	-	-
Santo Domingo	-	-	-	-	-	-	-	-	-	-	-
Taos	15	-	-	-	-	-	7	-	-	7	-
Tesuque	-	-	-	-	-	-	-	-	-	-	-
Tewa	43	-	-	-	-	-	26	-	-	-	26
Tigua[1]	224	-	-	-	-	-	219	-	-	-	219
Zia	26	-	-	-	-	-	21	-	-	-	21
Zuni	75	14	6	-	8	-	37	-	-	12	25
Puget Sound Salish											
Total	128	37	-	12	-	25	35	-	-	18	17
Duwamish	4	4	-	4	-	-	-	-	-	-	-
Muckleshoot	5	-	-	-	-	-	5	-	-	-	5
Nisqually	-	-	-	-	-	-	-	-	-	-	-
Nooksack	-	-	-	-	-	-	-	-	-	-	-
Puget Sound Salish (n.e.c.)	-	-	-	-	-	-	-	-	-	-	-
Puyallup	7	-	-	-	-	-	7	-	-	-	7
Samish	20	8	-	8	-	-	12	-	-	12	-
Sauk-Sauiatte	-	-	-	-	-	-	-	-	-	-	-
Skokomish	6	-	-	-	-	-	-	-	-	-	-
Skykomish	-	-	-	-	-	-	-	-	-	-	-
Snohomish	-	-	-	-	-	-	-	-	-	-	-
Snoqualmie	-	-	-	-	-	-	-	-	-	-	-
Squaxin Island	-	-	-	-	-	-	-	-	-	-	-
Steilacoom	-	-	-	-	-	-	-	-	-	-	-
Stillaguamish	-	-	-	-	-	-	-	-	-	-	-
Suquamish	9	-	-	-	-	-	-	-	-	-	-
Swinomish	25	-	-	-	-	25	-	-	-	-	-
Tulalip	34	-	-	-	-	-	-	-	-	-	-
Upper Skagit	18	-	-	-	-	-	11	-	-	6	5
Quapaw	429	-	-	-	-	-	407	29	-	347	31
Quinault	17	-	-	-	-	-	10	-	4	-	6
Rappahannock	234	-	-	-	-	-	-	-	-	-	-
Sac and Fox Mesquakie	1,514	24	-	24	-	-	1,416	-	-	1,272	144
Salinan	-	-	-	-	-	-	-	-	-	-	-
Schaghticoke	5	-	-	-	-	-	-	-	-	-	-
Seminole[1]											
Total	6,823	81	33	13	31	4	5,480	27	94	5,037	322
Seminole	6,405	81	33	13	31	4	5,432	27	85	4,998	322
Seminole Nation of Oklahoma	46	-	-	-	-	-	38	-	-	38	-
Seminole Tribe of Florida	372	-	-	-	-	-	10	-	9	1	-
Other Seminole	-	-	-	-	-	-	-	-	-	-	-
Serrano	13	-	-	-	-	-	11	-	-	11	-
Shasta	6	-	-	-	-	-	6	-	-	-	6

[Continued]

★ 211 ★

American Indian Population, by Tribe and State, 1980: South Region, Ponca-Sioux - II

[Continued]

Tribe	Total South Region	South Region (cont.)									
		East South Central Division					West South Central Division				
		Total East South Central	KY	TN	AL	MS	West South Central Total	AR	LA	OK	TX
Shawnee											
Total	2,335	36	29	7	-	-	2,125	37	5	1,876	207
Absentee Shawnee	304	-	-	-	-	-	288	-	-	277	11
Shawnee	2,031	36	29	7	-	-	1,837	37	5	1,599	196
Shinnecock	16	-	-	-	-	-	8	-	-	-	8
Shoshone											
Total	341	48	19	14	12	3	249	17	19	153	60
Goshute	-	-	-	-	-	-	-	-	-	-	-
Shoshone	306	48	19	14	12	3	226	17	19	130	60
Te-Moak Western Shoshone[1]	23	-	-	-	-	-	23	-	-	23	-
Yomba[1]	12	-	-	-	-	-	-	-	-	-	-
Other Shoshone	-	-	-	-	-	-	-	-	-	-	-
Siletz	11	-	-	-	-	-	11	-	-	11	-
Sioux											
Total	4,046	291	85	66	70	50	2,576	200	93	1,024	1,259
Blackfoot Sioux	26	-	-	-	-	-	20	-	-	13	7
Brule Sioux	-	-	-	-	-	-	-	-	-	-	-
Cheyenne River Sioux[2]	65	-	-	-	-	-	60	-	-	34	26
Crow River Sioux[2]	-	-	-	-	-	-	-	-	-	-	-
Dakota Sioux	74	-	-	-	-	-	50	-	-	2	48
Devil's Lake Sioux	-	-	-	-	-	-	-	-	-	-	-
Fladreau Santee	-	-	-	-	-	-	-	-	-	-	-
Fort Peck	-	-	-	-	-	-	-	-	-	-	-
Lower Brule Sioux	13	-	-	-	-	-	13	-	6	-	7
Mdewakanton Sioux	-	-	-	-	-	-	-	-	-	-	-
Oglala Sioux	144	11	-	3	-	8	112	6	6	64	36
Pine Ridge Sioux	-	-	-	-	-	-	-	-	-	-	-
Prior Lake Sioux	19	-	-	-	-	-	7	-	-	7	-
Rosebud Sioux	20	-	-	-	-	-	20	-	-	20	-
Santee Sioux	23	-	-	-	-	-	7	7	-	-	-
Sioux	3,518	264	85	83	59	37	2,214	187	81	868	1,078
Sisseton Sioux	20	5	-	-	-	5	6	-	-	-	6
Standing Rock Sioux	14	8	-	-	8	-	6	-	-	-	6
Teton Sioux	21	3	-	-	3	-	7	-	-	-	7
Wahpeton Sioux	-	-	-	-	-	-	-	-	-	-	-
Yankton Sioux	48	-	-	-	-	-	18	-	-	-	18
Yanktonai Sioux	8	-	-	-	-	-	3	-	-	3	-
Other Sioux	33	-	-	-	-	-	33	-	-	13	20

Source: U.S. Bureau of the Census, *1980 Census of Population, Volume 2, Subject Reports, Characteristics of American Indians, by Tribes and Selected Areas: 1980,* PC80-2-1C, Section 1: Tables I-II, issued September 1989, U.S. Department of Commerce, U.S. Government Printing Office, Washington, D.C., pp. 1-53. *Notes:* (N.E.C.) stands for not elsewhere classified. A dash (-) represents zero or a percent which rounds to less than 0.1. 1. Reporting and/or processing problems may have affected the data for this tribe. 2. Any entry with the spelling "Micmac" was miscoded to Cheyenne River Sioux.

★ 212 ★

American Indian Population, by Tribe and State, 1980: South Region, Siuslaw-Yurok - I

Data are estimates based on a sample and are the most recent available.

Tribe	Total South Region	South Region									
		South Atlantic Division									
		Total South Atlantic	DE	MD	DC	VA	WV	NC	SC	GA	FL
Siuslaw	18	18	-	-	-	-	-	-	-	-	18
Spokane	14	14	-	-	-	6	-	-	-	-	8
Stockbridge	146	76	-	-	-	16	-	6	8	-	46
Tlingit	107	40	-	20	-	6	-	-	-	-	14
Tolowa	-	-	-	-	-	-	-	-	-	-	-
Tonkawa	212	-	-	-	-	-	-	-	-	-	-
Tsimishian	13	8	-	-	-	-	-	-	-	-	8
Umatilla	26	7	-	-	-	-	-	7	-	-	-
Ute											
Total	112	42	-	13	-	2	-	6	-	10	11
Uintah Ute	10	10	-	6	-	-	-	-	-	4	-
Ute	96	26	-	7	-	2	-	-	-	6	11
Ute Mountain Ute	6	6	-	-	-	-	-	6	-	-	-
Other Ute	-	-	-	-	-	-	-	-	-	-	-
Wailaki[1]	83	80	-	-	-	-	-	-	80	-	-
Walla-Walla	46	46	19	27	-	-	-	-	-	-	-
Wampanoag	23	17	-	6	-	-	-	11	-	-	-
Warm Springs	52	30	-	-	-	30	-	-	-	-	-
Washo											
Total	39	-	-	-	-	-	-	-	-	-	-
Washo	39	-	-	-	-	-	-	-	-	-	-
Other Washo	-	-	-	-	-	-	-	-	-	-	-
Wichita	502	7	-	-	-	-	-	-	-	7	-
Winnebago	134	11	-	-	-	-	-	-	-	-	11
Wintu	112	6	-	6	-	-	-	-	-	-	-
Wiyot	-	-	-	-	-	-	-	-	-	-	-
Yakima	85	7	-	-	-	-	-	-	-	-	7
Yaqui											
Total	75	43	-	-	-	-	-	-	6	3	34
Barrio Libre	69	43	-	-	-	-	-	-	6	3	34
Yaqui	6	-	-	-	-	-	-	-	-	-	-
Other Yaqui	-	-	-	-	-	-	-	-	-	-	-
Yavapai Apache	-	-	-	-	-	-	-	-	-	-	-
Yokuts											
Total	65	8	-	-	-	8	-	-	-	-	-
Chuckhansi	8	8	-	-	-	8	-	-	-	-	-
Tachi	-	-	-	-	-	-	-	-	-	-	-
Tule River	-	-	-	-	-	-	-	-	-	-	-
Yokuts	57	-	-	-	-	-	-	-	-	-	-
Yuchi	144	6	-	-	-	-	-	-	-	-	6
Yuman											
Total	300	75	-	-	-	24	-	-	-	4	47
Cocopah	-	-	-	-	-	-	-	-	-	-	-

[Continued]

★ 212 ★

American Indian Population, by Tribe and State, 1980: South Region, Siuslaw-Yurok - I
[Continued]

Tribe	Total South Region	South Region									
		South Atlantic Division									
		Total South Atlantic	DE	MD	DC	VA	WV	NC	SC	GA	FL
Havasupai	160	9	-	-	-	-	-	-	-	4	5
Hualapai	20	6	-	-	-	6	-	-	-	-	-
Maricopa	12	3	-	-	-	-	-	-	-	-	3
Mohave	36	18	-	-	-	18	-	-	-	-	-
Quechan	50	39	-	-	-	-	-	-	-	-	39
Yavapai	22	-	-	-	-	-	-	-	-	-	-
Yurok	88	14	-	-	8	-	-	-	-	6	-
Other specified tribes (n.e.c.)											
Total	39	31	-	-	-	5	-	-	26	-	-
Fort Berthold	-	-	-	-	-	-	-	-	-	-	-
Gila River	-	-	-	-	-	-	-	-	-	-	-
Grand Rhonde	-	-	-	-	-	-	-	-	-	-	-
Los Coyotes	-	-	-	-	-	-	-	-	-	-	-
Round Valley	-	-	-	-	-	-	-	-	-	-	-
Scotts Valley	-	-	-	-	-	-	-	-	-	-	-
Shoalwater	-	-	-	-	-	-	-	-	-	-	-
All other specified	39	31	-	-	-	5	-	-	26	-	-
Tribe not specified	8,266	3,268	17	279	23	142	142	1,672	140	237	616
Tribe not reported	107,713	53,155	516	4,079	590	4,821	1,159	21,908	3,162	5,189	11,731

Source: U.S. Bureau of the Census, *1980 Census of Population, Volume 2, Subject Reports, Characteristics of American Indians, by Tribes and Selected Areas: 1980*, PC80-2-1C, Section 1: Tables I-II, issued September 1989, U.S. Department of Commerce, U.S. Government Printing Office, Washington, D.C., pp. 1-53. *Notes:* (N.E.C.) stands for not elsewhere classified. A dash (-) represents zero or a percent which rounds to less than 0.1. 1. Any Mohawk entry of "Ganienka" was miscoded to Wailaki.

★ 213 ★

American Indian Population, by Tribe and State, 1980: South Region, Siuslaw-Yurok - II

Data are estimates based on a sample and are the most recent available.

Tribe	Total South Region	South Region (cont.)									
		East South Central Division					West South Central Division				
		Total East South Central	KY	TN	AL	MS	West South Central Total	AR	LA	OK	TX
Siuslaw	18	-	-	-	-	-	-	-	-	-	-
Spokane	14	-	-	-	-	-	-	-	-	-	-
Stockbridge	146	29	2	-	27	-	41	-	-	34	7
Tlingit	107	6	-	-	6	-	61	45	-	10	6
Tolowa	-	-	-	-	-	-	-	-	-	-	-
Tonkawa	212	-	-	-	-	-	212	-	-	209	3
Tsimishian	13	-	-	-	-	-	5	-	-	-	5
Umatilla	26	19	-	-	-	19	-	-	-	-	-

[Continued]

★ 213 ★

American Indian Population, by Tribe and State, 1980: South Region, Siuslaw-Yurok - II
[Continued]

Tribe	Total South Region	South Region (cont.)									
		East South Central Division					West South Central Division				
		Total East South Central	KY	TN	AL	MS	West South Central Total	AR	LA	OK	TX
Ute											
Total	112	6	6	-	-	-	64	-	-	51	13
Uintah Ute	10	-	-	-	-	-	-	-	-	-	-
Ute	96	6	6	-	-	-	64	-	-	51	13
Ute Mountain Ute	6	-	-	-	-	-	-	-	-	-	-
Other Ute	-	-	-	-	-	-	-	-	-	-	-
Wailaki[1]	83	-	-	-	-	-	3	-	-	3	-
Walla-Walla	46	-	-	-	-	-	-	-	-	-	-
Wampanoag	23	6	6	-	-	-	6	-	-	-	-
Warm Springs	52	-	-	-	-	-	22	-	-	22	-
Washo											
Total	39	7	-	-	7	-	32	-	-	2	30
Washo	39	7	-	-	7	-	32	-	-	2	30
Other Washo	-	-	-	-	-	-	-	-	-	-	-
Wichita	502	38	-	-	32	6	458	-	-	405	52
Winnebago	134	8	8	-	-	-	115	-	-	46	69
Wintu	112	-	-	-	-	-	106	36	-	7	63
Wiyot	-	-	-	-	-	-	-	-	-	-	-
Yakima	85	8	2	6	-	-	70	-	-	55	15
Yaqui											
Total	75	14	7	7	-	-	18	-	-	6	12
Barrio Libre	69	14	7	7	-	-	12	-	-	6	6
Yaqui	6	-	-	-	-	-	6	-	-	-	6
Other Yaqui	-	-	-	-	-	-	-	-	-	-	-
Yavapai Apache	-	-	-	-	-	-	-	-	-	-	-
Yokuts											
Total	65	23	-	-	-	23	34	-	-	6	28
Chuckhansi	8	-	-	-	-	-	-	-	-	-	-
Tachi	-	-	-	-	-	-	-	-	-	-	-
Tule River	-	-	-	-	-	-	-	-	-	-	-
Yokuts	57	23	-	-	-	23	34	-	-	6	28
Yuchi	144	-	-	-	-	-	138	-	-	138	-
Yuman											
Total	300	11	-	11	-	-	214	7	9	33	165
Cocopah	-	-	-	-	-	-	-	-	-	-	-
Havasupai	160	11	-	11	-	-	140	7	-	-	133
Hualapai	20	-	-	-	-	-	14	-	-	-	14
Maricopa	12	-	-	-	-	-	9	-	-	9	-
Mohave	36	-	-	-	-	-	18	-	-	-	18
Quechan	50	-	-	-	-	-	11	-	9	2	-
Yavapai	22	-	-	-	-	-	22	-	-	22	-
Yurok	88	-	-	-	7	67	74	-	-	7	67
Other specified tribes (n.e.c.)											
Total	39	-	-	-	-	-	8	-	-	2	6
Fort Berthold	-	-	-	-	-	-	-	-	-	-	-
Gila River	-	-	-	-	-	-	-	-	-	-	-
Grand Rhode	-	-	-	-	-	-	-	-	-	-	-
Los Coyotes	-	-	-	-	-	-	-	-	-	-	-
Round Valley	-	-	-	-	-	-	-	-	-	-	-
Scotts Valley	-	-	-	-	-	-	-	-	-	-	-
Shoalwater	-	-	-	-	-	-	-	-	-	-	-
All other specified	39	-	-	-	-	-	8	-	-	2	6

[Continued]

391

★ 213 ★

American Indian Population, by Tribe and State, 1980: South Region, Siuslaw-Yurok - II
[Continued]

| Tribe | Total South Region | South Region (cont.) | | | | | | | | | |
| | | East South Central Division | | | | | West South Central Division | | | | |
		Total East South Central	KY	TN	AL	MS	West South Central Total	AR	LA	OK	TX
Tribe not specified	8,266	521	209	112	107	93	4,477	322	214	1,864	2,077
Tribe not reported	107,713	11,203	1,438	3,291	3,999	2,475	43,355	2,904	5,767	20,441	14,243

Source: U.S. Bureau of the Census, *1980 Census of Population, Volume 2, Subject Reports, Characteristics of American Indians, by Tribes and Selected Areas: 1980,* PC80-2-1C, Section 1: Tables I-II, issued September 1989, U.S. Department of Commerce, U.S. Government Printing Office, Washington, D.C., pp. 1-53. *Notes:* (N.E.C.) stands for not elsewhere classified. A dash (-) represents zero or a percent which rounds to less than 0.1. 1. Any Mohawk entry of "Ganienka" was miscoded to Wailaki.

★ 214 ★

American Indian Population, by Tribe and State, 1980: West Region, Abenaki-Chinook - I

Data are estimates based on a sample and are the most recent available.

| Tribe | Total West Region | Mountain Divison | | | | | | | |
		Total Mountain	MT	ID	WY	CO	NM	AZ	UT
All American Indians	716,149	371,912	37,623	10,405	8,192	20,682	106,585	154,175	19,994
Abenaki (n.e.c)	62	7	-	-	-	-	-	7	-
Alabama Coushatta[1]	26	7	-	-	-	2	5	-	-
Alaska Native (n.e.c.)									
Total	516	94	24	-	-	16	-	18	27
Alaska Native	441	51	24	-	-	-	-	18	-
Sealaska	75	43	-	-	-	16	-	-	
Alaska Athabaskans									
Total	9,564	127	2	12	36	12	19	33	-
Alaskan Athaboskans	9,160	110	2	7	31	12	12	33	-
Doyon	180	-	-	-	-	-	-	-	-
Taniana	209	17	-	5	5	-	7	-	-
Other Alaskan	15	-							
Athabaskans	15	-	-	-	-	-	-	-	-
Aleut and Eskimo									
Total	533	50	6	-	-	2	14	22	-
Akutan	-	-	-	-	-	-	-	-	-
Aleut	173	7	-	-	-	-	7	-	-
Calista	78	20	-	-	-	-	-	14	-
Chugach	153	-	-	-	-	-	-	-	-
Eskimo	77	16	6	-	-	2	-	8	-
Kotzebue Sound	19	-	-	-	-	-	-	-	-
Other Aleut and Eskimo	33	7	-	-	-	-	7	-	-
Algoquian (n.e.c.)	565	114	23	6	-	29	56	-	-

[Continued]

★ 214 ★

American Indian Population, by Tribe and State, 1980: West Region, Abenaki-Chinook - I
[Continued]

Tribe	Total West Region	Mountain Divison							
		Total Mountain	MT	ID	WY	CO	NM	AZ	UT
Apache									
Total	27,654	19,231	89	99	165	716	3,734	13,867	284
Apache (n.e.c.)	16,599	8,873	85	94	133	693	702	6,744	214
Chiricahua	244	29	-	-	2	11	-	10	-
Fort Sill Apache	147	43	-	-	-	-	4	-	-
Jicarilla	1,552	1,534	-	-	-	6	1,517	6	5
Kiowa Apache	79	32	4	-	-	-	28	-	-
Mescalero	1,704	1,545	-	-	7	6	1,478	47	7
Payson Apache	45	-	-	-	-	-	-	-	-
San Carlos Apache	3,627	3,784	-	-	-	-	5	3,767	12
White Mountain Apache	3,457	3,391	-	5	23	-	-	3,293	46
Other Apache	-	-	-	-	-	-	-	-	-
Arapaho	3,168	2,502	62	11	2,149	144	15	97	24
Arikara	390	144	22	4	6	79	8	25	-
Assiniboine	3,696	3,110	2,889	19	-	18	4	67	73
Bannock	384	344	-	291	-	15	36	-	2
Blackfoot[1]	13,438	5,549	4,571	141	58	245	88	226	87
Brotherton	10	3	-	-	-	-	-	3	-
Caddo	295	68	-	-	-	38	18	12	-
Cahuilla									
Total	1,146	14	-	-	-	-	-	7	-
Cahuilla	848	14	-	-	-	-	-	7	-
Soboba	212	-	-	-	-	-	-	-	-
Torres-Martinez	42	-	-	-	-	-	-	-	-
Other Cahuilla	44	-	-	-	-	-	-	-	-
California tribes (n.e.c.)									
Total	478	-	-	-	-	-	-	-	-
Cahto	4	-	-	-	-	-	-	-	-
Digger	38	-	-	-	-	-	-	-	-
Mattole	29	-	-	-	-	-	-	-	-
Morongo	189	-	-	-	-	-	-	-	-
Wappo	64	-	-	-	-	-	-	-	-
Yuki	75	-	-	-	-	-	-	-	-
Other California	79	-	-	-	-	-	-	-	-
Canadian and Latin American	4,286	1,077	75	34	16	294	103	362	123
Catawba	98	78	7	-	14	33	18	-	6
Cayuse	144	2	-	2	-	-	-	-	-
Chehalis	259	-	-	-	-	-	-	-	-
Chemakuan									
Total	478	-	-	-	-	-	-	-	-
Hoh	95	-	-	-	-	-	-	-	-
Quileute	383	-	-	-	-	-	-	-	-
Other Chemehuevi	-	-	-	-	-	-	-	-	-

[Continued]

★ 214 ★

American Indian Population, by Tribe and State, 1980: West Region, Abenaki-Chinook - I
[Continued]

| Tribe | Total West Region | Mountain Divison | | | | | | | |
		Total Mountain	MT	ID	WY	CO	NM	AZ	UT
Chemehuevi	429	277	7	-	-	-	14	199	22
Cherokee									
Total	75,365	12,542	858	1,088	639	3,780	1,200	2,713	955
Cherokee	75,200	12,482	843	1,088	639	3,773	1,200	2,696	952
Eastern Cherokee	77	33	8	-	-	7	-	-	-
Etowah Cherokee	22	-	-	-	-	-	-	-	-
Tuscola	-	-	-	-	-	-	-	-	-
United Keetoowah	-	-	-	-	-	-	-	-	-
Western Cherokee	45	11	-	-	-	-	-	8	3
Other Cherokee	21	16	7	-	-	-	-	9	-
Cheyenne									
Total	4,819	3,666	2,661	49	73	355	285	100	43
Cheyenne	2,227	1,182	425	8	56	244	233	90	26
Northern Cheyenne	2,525	2,432	2,222	41	16	79	52	10	12
Southern Cheyenne	67	52	14	-	1	32	-	-	5
Chickahominy	26	19	-	-	-	-	-	19	-
Chicksaw	2,281	441	32	5	-	132	129	110	13
Chinook									
Total	1,212	37	8	13	-	-	4	-	-
Chinook	1,136	37	8	13	-	-	4	-	-
Clatsop	39	-	-	-	-	-	-	-	-
Columbia River Chinook	37	-	-	-	-	-	-	-	-
Other Chinook	-	-	-	-	-	-	-	-	-

Source: U.S. Bureau of the Census, *1980 Census of Population, Volume 2, Subject Reports, Characteristics of American Indians, by Tribes and Selected Areas: 1980,* PC80-2-1C, Section 1: Tables I-II, issued September 1989, U.S. Department of Commerce, U.S. Government Printing Office, Washington, D.C., pp. 1-53. *Notes:* (N.E.C.) stands for not elsewhere classified. A dash (-) represents zero or a percent which rounds to less than 0.1. 1. Reporting and/or processing problems may have affected the data for this tribe.

★ 215 ★

American Indian Population, by Tribe and State, 1980: West Region, Abenaki-Chinook - II

Data are estimates based on a sample and are the most recent available.

| Tribe | Total West Region | Pacific Division | | | | | | |
		Total Pacific	NV	WA	OR	CA	AK	HI
All American Indians	716,149	344,237	14,256	61,233	29,783	227,757	22,631	2,833
Abenaki (n.e.c)	62	7	-	12	-	24	-	19
Alabama Coushatta[1]	26	19	-	-	7	12	-	-

[Continued]

★ 215 ★

American Indian Population, by Tribe and State, 1980: West Region, Abenaki-Chinook - 11

[Continued]

Tribe	Total West Region	Pacific Division						
		Total Pacific	NV	WA	OR	CA	AK	HI
Alaska Native (n.e.c.)								
Total	516	422	9	263	70	50	32	7
Alaska Native	441	390	9	256	48	47	32	7
Sealaska	75	32	-	7	22	3	-	-
Alaska Athabaskans								
Total	9,564	9,437	13	198	186	304	8,744	5
Alaskan Athabaskans	9,160	9,050	13	195	176	235	8,439	5
Doyon	180	180	-	-	-	26	154	-
Taniana	209	192	-	3	10	28	151	-
Other Alaskan Athabaskans	15	15	-	-	-	15	-	-
Aleut and Eskimo								
Total	533	483	6	34	114	119	210	6
Akutan	-	-	-	-	-	-	-	-
Aleut	173	166	-	18	27	10	111	-
Calista	78	58	6	-	9	43	-	6
Chugach	153	153	-	5	39	37	72	-
Eskimo	77	61	-	-	33	12	16	-
Kotzebue Sound	19	19	-	-	6	13	-	-
Other Aleut and Eskimo	33	26	-	11	-	4	11	-
Algonquian (n.e.c.)	565	451	-	70	2	355	13	11
Apache								
Total	27,654	8,423	277	598	516	7,012	87	210
Apache (n.e.c.)	16,599	7,726	208	553	387	6,517	75	194
Chiricahua	244	215	6	4	5	180	10	16
Fort Sill Apache	147	104	39	12	84	8	-	-
Jicarilla	1,552	18	-	5	-	13	-	-
Kiowa Apache	79	47	-	-	-	45	2	-
Mescalero	1,704	159	-	3	-	156	-	-
Payson	45	45	-	-	-	-	45	-
San Carlos	3,827	43	-	-	14	29	-	-
White Mountain Apache	3,457	66	24	21	26	19	-	-
Other Apache	-	-	-	-	-	-	-	-
Arapaho	3,168	666	-	227	10	415	8	6
Arikara	390	246	-	45	12	183	-	6
Assiniboine	3,696	586	10	269	34	273	10	-
Bannock	384	40	-	6	-	34	-	-
Blackfoot[1]	13,438	7,889	133	1,950	757	4,990	108	84
Brotherton	10	7	-	-	7	-	-	-
Caddo	295	227	-	22	-	205	-	-
Cahuilla								
Total	1,146	1,132	7	32	-	1,100	-	-

[Continued]

★ 215 ★

American Indian Population, by Tribe and State, 1980: West Region, Abenaki-Chinook - II

[Continued]

Tribe	Total West Region	Pacific Division						
		Total Pacific	NV	WA	OR	CA	AK	HI
Cahuilla	848	834	7	6	-	828	-	-
Soboba	212	212	-	-	-	212	-	-
Torres-Martinez	42	42	-	-	-	42	-	-
Other Cahuilla	44	44	-	26	-	18	-	-
California tribes (n.e.c)								
Total	478	478	-	18	9	444	7	-
Cahto	4	4	-	-	-	4	-	-
Digger	38	38	-	14	-	24	-	-
Mattole	29	29	-	-	-	29	-	-
Morongo	189	189	-	-	-	189	-	-
Wappo	64	64	-	-	-	64	-	-
Yuki	75	75	-	-	2	66	7	-
Other California	79	79	-	4	7	68	-	-
Canadian and Latin American	4,286	3,209	-	4	7	68	-	-
Catawba	98	20	-	-	-	14	6	-
Cayuse	144	142	-	33	95	14	-	-
Chehalis	259	259	-	235	24	-	-	-
Chemakuan								
Total	478	478	-	466	6	6	-	-
Hoh	95	95	-	95	-	-	-	-
Quileute	383	383	-	371	6	6	-	-
Other Chemakuan	-	-	-	-	-	-	-	-
Chemehuevi	429	152	35	-	-	152	-	-
Cherokee								
Total	75,365	62,823	1,309	5,201	4,864	51,360	707	691
Cherokee	75,200	62,718	1,291	5,174	4,864	51,288	701	691
Eastern Cherokee	77	44	18	3	-	41	-	-
Etowah Cherokee	22	22	-	5	-	11	6	-
Tuscola	-	-	-	-	-	-	-	-
United Keetoowah	-	-	-	-	-	-	-	-
Western Cherokee	45	34	-	19	-	15	-	-
Other Cherokee	21	5	-	-	-	5	-	-
Cheyenne								
Total	4,819	1,153	100	179	172	697	17	88
Cheyenne	2,227	1,045	100	128	151	661	17	88
Northern Cheyenne	2,525	93	-	45	21	27	-	-
Southern Cheyenne	67	15	-	6	-	9	-	-
Chickahominy	26	7	-	-	7	-	-	-
Chickasaw	2,281	1,840	20	173	91	1,523	7	46
Chinook								
Total	1,212	1,175	12	247	788	140	-	-
Chinook	1,136	1,099	12	203	775	121	-	-
Clatsop	39	39	-	13	7	19	-	-

[Continued]

396

★ 215 ★

American Indian Population, by Tribe and State, 1980: West Region, Abenaki-Chinook - II

[Continued]

| Tribe | Total West Region | Pacific Division | | | | | | |
		Total Pacific	NV	WA	OR	CA	AK	HI
Columbia River Chinook	37	37	-	31	6	-	-	-
Other Chinook	-	-		-	-		-	-

Source: U.S. Bureau of the Census, *1980 Census of Population, Volume 2, Subject Reports, Characteristics of American Indians, by Tribes and Selected Areas: 1980,* PC80-2-1C, Section 1: Tables I-II, issued September 1989, U.S. Department of Commerce, U.S. Government Printing Office, Washington, D.C., pp. 1-53. *Notes:* (N.E.C.) stands for not elsewhere classified. A dash (-) represents zero or a percent which rounds to less than 0.1. 1. Reporting and/or processing problems may have affected the data for this tribe.

★ 216 ★

American Indian Population, by Tribe and State, 1980: West Region, Chippewa-Iowa - I

Data are estimates based on a sample and are the most recent available.

| Tribe | Total West Region | Mountain Division | | | | | | | |
		Total Mountain	MT	ID	WY	CO	NM	AZ	UT
Chippewa									
Total	12,447	4,639	2,578	293	194	528	199	458	221
Bad River	11	11	-	-	-	11	-	-	-
Bay Mills Chippewa	-	-	-	-	-	-	-	-	-
Bois Forte	-	-	-	-	-	-	-	-	-
Chippewa	11,752	4,372	2,476	254	179	491	193	458	195
Lac Courte Oreilles	-	-	-	-	-	-	-	-	-
Lac du Flambeau	-	-	-	-	-	-	-	-	-
Lake Superior	8	-	-	-	-	-	-	-	-
Leech Lake	-	-	-	-	-	-	-	-	-
Leelanau	28	-	-	-	-	-	-	-	-
Mille Lac	11	11	-	-	-	11	-	-	-
Minnesota Chippewa	74	6	4	-	-	-	-	-	2
Ontonagon	15	15	-	-	15	-	-	-	-
Red Cliff Chippewa	22	-	-	-	-	-	-	-	-
Red Lake Chippewa	40	6	-	-	-	6	-	-	-
Saginaw Chippewa	28	-	-	-	-	-	-	-	-
St. Croix Chippewa	-	-	-	-	-	-	-	-	-
Sault Ste. Marie Chippewa	136	54	-	39	-	9	6	-	-
Sokoagon Chippewa	42	42	-	-	-	-	-	-	-
Turtle Mountain	120	64	59	-	-	-	-	-	5
White Earth	142	58	39	-	-	-	-	-	19
Other Chippewa	18	-	-	-	-	-	-	-	-
Chitimacha	42	-	-	-	-	-	-	-	-

[Continued]

★ 216 ★

American Indian Population, by Tribe and State, 1980: West Region, Chippewa-Iowa - I

[Continued]

Tribe	Total West Region	Mountain Division							
		Total Mountain	MT	ID	WY	CO	NM	AZ	UT
Choctaw									
Total	11,241	2,041	41	135	64	431	328	727	48
Choctaw	11,183	2,017	41	135	64	407	328	727	48
Clifton Choctaw	58	24	-	-	-	24	-	-	-
Chumash[1]									
Total	1,426	56	-	-	-	12	12	32	-
Chumash	1,421	56	-	-	-	12	12	32	-
Other Chumash	5	-	-	-	-	-	-	-	-
Clallam									
Total	858	44	31	13	-	-	-	-	-
Clallam	592	44	31	13	-	-	-	-	-
Lower Elwah	43	-	-	-	-	-	-	-	-
Port Gamble Clallam	216	-	-	-	-	-	-	-	-
Other Clellam	7	-	-	-	-	-	-	-	-
Coeur d' Alene	684	194	26	156	-	7	-	-	5
Coharie	6	6	6	-	-	-	-	-	-
Colorado River	932	919	-	-	-	-	-	919	-
Colville	5,293	143	11	60	5	27	9	22	-
Comanche	2,472	833	25	34	42	206	192	215	107
Coos	128	-	-	-	-	-	-	-	-
Costanoan	473	9	-	-	-	-	-	-	6
Cowitz	936	10	-	-	10	-	-	-	-
Cree	5,223	3,875	3,661	94	7	36	7	34	21
Creek									
Total	4,663	966	1	31	24	173	242	391	28
Creek	4,600	956	1	31	18	169	242	391	28
Eastern Creek	4	4	-	-	-	4	-	-	-
Lower Muskogee	6	-	-	-	-	-	-	-	-
Muskogee	34	-	-	-	-	-	-	-	-
Thlopthlocco	19	6	-	-	6	-	-	-	-
Other Creek	-	-	-	-	-	-	-	-	-
Croatan	58	5	-	-	-	-	-	5	-
Crow	6,155	5,261	4,846	13	66	37	83	87	92
Cupeno									
Total	267	-	-	-	-	-	-	-	-
Agua Caliente	43	-	-	-	-	-	-	-	-
Cupeno	224	-	-	-	-	-	-	-	-
Delaware									
Total	1,134	386	8	108	18	129	73	23	18
Munsee	70	48	-	14	-	22	-	12	-
Sand Hill	-	-	-	-	-	-	-	-	-
Diegueno									
Total	1,376	54	-	43	-	-	-	11	-

[Continued]

★ 216 ★

American Indian Population, by Tribe and State, 1980: West Region, Chippewa-Iowa - I

[Continued]

Tribe	Total West Region	Mountain Division							
		Total Mountain	MT	ID	WY	CO	NM	AZ	UT
Diegueno	1,141	23	-	12	-	-	-	11	-
Manzanita	31	31	-	31	-	-	-	-	-
San Pascual	123	-	-	-	-	-	-	-	-
Santa Ysabel	47	-	-	-	-	-	-	-	-
Other Diegueno	34	-	-	-	-	-	-	-	-
Eastern tribes (n.e.c.)									
Total	287	58	14	-	39	5	-	-	-
Moor	-	-	-	-	-	-	-	-	-
Nansemond	6	-	-	-	-	-	-	-	-
Natchez	20	-	-	-	-	-	-	-	-
Nipmuc	4	-	-	-	-	-	-	-	-
Southeastern Indians	257	58	14	-	39	5	-	-	-
Tunica	-	-	-	-	-	-	-	-	-
Other Eastern	-	-	-	-	-	-	-	-	-
Flathead	4,788	3,491	3,177	92	35	17	33	83	11
Fort Hall	413	317	4	306	-	-	-	-	7
Gabrieleno	1,762	15	-	-	-	-	-	-	-
Gros Ventres									
Total	1,811	1,364	1,245	28	26	-	35	4	20
Atsina	-	-	-	-	-	-	-	-	-
Gros Ventres	1,811	1,364	1,245	28	26	-	35	4	20
Haida	1,393	11	-	-	-	4	7	-	-
Haliwa	17	17	-	-	-	-	-	-	17
Hidatsa	247	154	78	-	-	17	-	-	59
Hitchiti	7	-	-	-	-	-	-	-	-
Hoopa	1,907	15	-	-	-	-	9	-	6
Houma	71	-	-	-	-	-	-	-	-
Iowa	163	19	-	13	-	6	-	-	-

Source: U.S. Bureau of the Census, *1980 Census of Population, Volume 2, Subject Reports, Characteristics of American Indians, by Tribes and Selected Areas: 1980*, PC80-2-1C, Section 1: Tables I-II, issued September 1989, U.S. Department of Commerce, U.S. Government Printing Office, Washington, D.C., pp. 1-53. *Notes:* (N.E.C.) stands for not elsewhere classified. A dash (-) represents zero or a percent which rounds to less than 0.1. 1. Reporting and/or processing problems may have affected the data for this tribe.

★ 217 ★

American Indian Population, by Tribe and State, 1980: West Region, Chippewa-Iowa - II

Data are estimates based on a sample and are the most recent available.

| Tribe | Total West Region | Pacific Division | | | | | | |
		Total Pacific	NV	WA	OR	CA	AK	HI
Chippewa								
Total	12,447	7,808	168	2,334	1,365	3,879	132	98
Bad River	11	-	-	-	-	-	-	-
Bay Mills Chippewa	-	-	-	-	-	-	-	-
Bois Forte	-	-	-	-	-	-	-	-
Chippewa	11,752	7,380	126	2,211	1,307	3,632	132	98
Lac Courte Oreilles	-	-	-	-	-	-	-	-
Lac du Flambeau	-	-	-	-	-	-	-	-
Lake Superior	8	8	-	-	8	-	-	-
Leech Lake	-	-	-	-	-	-	-	-
Leelanau	28	28	-	-	-	28	-	-
Mille Lac	11	-	-	-	-	-	-	-
Minnesota Chippewa	74	68	-	25	2	41	-	-
Ontonagon	15	-	-	-	-	-	-	-
Red Cliff Chippewa	22	22	-	-	-	22	-	-
Red Lake Chippewa	40	34	-	34	-	-	-	-
Saginaw Chippewa	28	28	-	7	4	17	-	-
St. Croix Chippewa	-	-	-	-	-	-	-	-
Sault Ste. Marie Chippewa	136	82	-	5	33	44	-	-
Sokoagon Chippewa	42	-	42	-	-	-	-	-
Turtle Mountain	120	56	-	41	3	12	-	-
White Earth	142	84	-	11	-	73	-	-
Other Chippewa	18	18	-	-	8	10	-	-
Chitimacha	42	42	-	-	-	42	-	-
Choctaw								
Total	11,241	9,200	267	617	488	7,974	61	61
Choctaw	11,183	9,166	267	603	488	7,953	61	61
Clifton Choctaw	58	34	-	14	-	20	-	-
Chumash[1]								
Total	1,426	1,370	-	34	21	1,298	-	17
Other Chumash	1,421	1,365	-	-	-	5	-	-
Clallam								
Total	858	814	-	743	20	51	-	-
Clallam	592	548	-	477	20	51	-	-
Lower Elwah	43	43	-	43	-	-	-	-
Port Gamble Clallam	216	216	-	216	-	-	-	-
Other Clellam	7	7	-	7	-	-	-	-
Coeur d' Alene	684	490	-	394	51	45	-	-
Coharie	6	-	-	-	-	-	-	-
Colorado River	932	13	-	-	-	13	-	-
Colville	5,293	5,150	9	4,832	134	129	40	15
Comanche	2,472	1,639	12	89	144	1,383	2	21
Coos	128	128	-	-	109	18	1	-

[Continued]

American Indian Population, by Tribe and State, 1980: West Region, Chippewa-Iowa - 11
[Continued]

Tribe	Total West Region	Pacific Division						
		Total Pacific	NV	WA	OR	CA	AK	HI
Costanoan	473	464	3	11	-	453	-	-
Cowitz	936	926	-	735	102	86	3	-
Cree	5,223	1,348	15	566	172	544	47	19
Creek								
Total	4,663	3,697	76	358	267	3,038	26	8
Creek	4,600	3,644	76	351	261	2,998	26	8
Eastern Creek	4	-	-	-	-	-	-	-
Lower Muskogee	6	6	-	-	6	-	-	-
Muskogee	34	34	-	-	-	34	-	-
Thlopthlocco	19	13	-	7	-	6	-	-
Other Creek	-	-	-	-	-	-	-	-
Croatan	58	53	-	-	53	-	-	-
Crow	6,155	894	37	136	26	723	-	9
Cupeno								
Total	267	267	-	5	7	255	-	-
Agua Caliente	43	43	-	5	7	31	-	-
Cupeno	224	224	-	-	-	224	-	-
Delaware								
Total	1,134	386	9	147	77	516	-	8
Delaware	1,064	726	9	144	77	497	-	8
Munsee	70	22	-	3	-	19	-	-
Sand Hill	-	-	-	-	-	-	-	-
Diegueno								
Total	1,376	1,322	-	-	-	1,276	46	-
Diegueno	1,141	1,118	-	-	-	1,072	46	-
Manzanita	31	-	-	-	-	-	-	-
San Pascual	123	123	-	-	-	123	-	-
Santa Ysabel	47	47	-	-	-	34	-	-
Other Diegueno	34	34	-	-	-	34	-	-
Eastern tribes (n.e.c.)								
Total	287	229	-	6	-	215	-	8
Moor	-	-	-	-	-	-	-	-
Nansemond	6	6	-	-	-	6	-	-
Natchez	20	20	-	-	-	20	-	-
Nipmuc	4	4	-	-	-	4	-	-
Southeastern Indians	257	199	-	6	-	185	-	8
Tunica	-	-	-	-	-	-	-	-
Other Eastern	-	-	-	-	-	-	-	-
Flathead	4,788	1,297	43	837	240	187	33	-
Fort Hall	413	96	-	6	59	25	6	-
Gabrieleno	1,762	1,747	15	25	17	1,702	3	-
Gros Ventres								
Total	1,811	447	6	187	89	129	42	-

[Continued]

★ 217 ★

American Indian Population, by Tribe and State, 1980: West Region, Chippewa-Iowa - II
[Continued]

Tribe	Total West Region	Pacific Division						
		Total Pacific	NV	WA	OR	CA	AK	HI
Atsina	-	-	-	-	-	-	-	-
Gros Ventres	1,811	447	6	187	89	129	42	-
Haida	1,393	1,382	-	337	25	26	994	-
Haliwa	17	-	-	-	-	-	-	-
Hidatsa	247	93	-	38	-	50	5	-
Hitchiti	7	7	-	-	-	7	-	-
Hoopa	1,907	1,892	-	56	28	1,798	10	-
Houma	71	71	-	2	-	69	-	-
Iowa	163	144	-	22	-	122	-	-

Source: U.S. Bureau of the Census, *1980 Census of Population, Volume 2, Subject Reports, Characteristics of American Indians, by Tribes and Selected Areas: 1980,* PC80-2-1C, Section 1: Tables I-II, issued September 1989, U.S. Department of Commerce, U.S. Government Printing Office, Washington, D.C., pp. 1-53. *Notes:* (N.E.C.) stands for not elsewhere classified. A dash (-) represents zero or a percent which rounds to less than 0.1. 1. Reporting and/or processing problems may have affected the data for this tribe.

★ 218 ★

American Indian Population, by Tribe and State, 1980: West Region, Iroquois-Pomo - I

Data are estimates based on a sample and are the most recent available.

Tribe	Total West Region	Mountain Division							
		Total Mountain	MT	ID	WY	CO	NM	AZ	UT
Iroquois									
Total	5,364	1,282	64	81	49	295	149	347	136
Cayuga	90	31	7	-	-	-	-	-	24
Iroquois (n.e.c.)	1,486	292	20	6	-	75	-	104	22
Mohawk[1]	1,546	377	7	46	49	89	29	71	54
Oneida	725	238	24	29	-	72	70	28	7
Onondaga	55	10	-	-	-	-	6	-	-
Seneca									
Total	926	178	6	-	-	33	30	82	11
Seneca	919	178	6	-	-	33	30	82	11
Seneca Nation	7	-	-	-	-	-	-	-	-
Tonawanda Seneca	-	-	-	-	-	-	-	-	-
Seneca-Cayuga	75	47	-	-	-	14	8	25	-
Tuscarora	121	48	-	-	-	12	6	6	-
Wyandot	340	61	-	-	-	-	31	18	12
Kalispel	181	14	10	4	-	-	-	-	-
Karok	1,948	58	6	-	-	-	-	22	7

[Continued]

★ 218 ★

American Indian Population, by Tribe and State, 1980: West Region, Iroquois-Pomo - I
[Continued]

Tribe	Total West Region	Mountain Division							
		Total Mountain	MT	ID	WY	CO	NM	AZ	UT
Kaw	138	59	-	2	10	-	-	40	-
Kickapoo	303	105	11	-	13	14	14	34	19
Kiowa	1,386	522	5	10	34	71	131	185	77
Klamath	1,992	107	12	6	-	-	12	11	13
Konkow	326	17	-	-	-	-	-	-	8
Kootenai	362	260	152	84	2	-	-	-	22
Long Island									
Total	20	9	-	9	-	-	-	-	-
Matinecock	-	-	-	-	-	-	-	-	-
Montauk	9	9	-	9	-	-	-	-	-
Poosepatuck	-	-	-	-	-	-	-	-	-
Other Long Island	11	-	-	-	-	-	-	-	-
Luiseno									
Total	1,187	3	-	3	-	-	-	-	-
LaJolla	39	-	-	-	-	-	-	-	-
Luiseno	872	-	-	-	-	-	-	-	-
Pala	130	-	-	-	-	-	-	-	-
Pauma	36	3	-	3	-	-	-	-	-
Pechanga	110	-	-	-	-	-	-	-	-
Lumbee[2]	406	55	-	-	-	6	-	15	12
Maidu	1,124	56	-	-	6	-	-	9	-
Makah	1,026	3	-	3	-	-	-	-	-
Maliseet	17	-	-	-	-	-	-	-	-
Mandan	347	197	67	7	-	62	23	32	6
Mattaponi	24	7	-	-	-	-	-	-	7
Menominee	274	88	-	-	-	11	10	29	26
Maimi	334	122	-	27	-	44	-	33	-
Miccosukee[3]	15	-	-	-	-	-	-	-	-
Micmac[4]	100	34	-	-	-	2	12	13	-
Mission Indians	2,369	110	-	13	-	23	8	12	6
Miwok	2,060	37	6	6	2	-	-	-	7
Modoc	683	68	-	7	10	-	6	-	32
Mohegan	23	-	-	-	-	-	-	-	-
Mono	1,262	7	-	-	-	7	-	-	-
Nanticoke	10	2	-	-	-	2	-	-	-
Narragansett	72	-	-	-	-	-	-	-	-
Navajo	154,024	146,899	183	419	182	2,086	57,919	76,642	9,178
Nez Perce[1]	1,984	585	37	420	25	20	4	71	3
Nomalaki	204	9	-	-	-	-	-	-	-
Northwest tribes (n.e.c)									
Total	210	36	2	2	-	-	-	32	-
Columbia Wenatchee	15	-	-	-	-	-	-	-	-
Kalapuya	65	13	2	-	-	-	-	11	-

[Continued]

★ 218 ★

American Indian Population, by Tribe and State, 1980: West Region, Iroquois-Pomo - I
[Continued]

Tribe	Total West Region	Mountain Division							
		Total Mountain	MT	ID	WY	CO	NM	AZ	UT
Tillamook	82	9	-	-	-	-	-	9	-
Other Northwest	48	14	-	2	-	-	-	12	-
Omaha	458	218	15	59	-	9	26	103	6
Oregon Athabaskan	507	-	-	-	-	-	-	-	-
Osage	2,373	747	69	53	24	197	166	98	35
Oto	203	97	3	-	10	-	70	14	-
Ottawa	420	85	-	-	4	14	14	41	6
Paiute[1]									
Total	9,142	4,780	20	74	70	32	24	210	702
Burns Paiute	67	-	-	-	-	-	-	-	-
Northern Paiute	57	6	-	-	-	-	-	-	-
Paiute	8,777	4,578	20	69	70	32	24	210	593
Pyramind Lake	20	20	-	-	-	-	-	-	-
Southern Paiute	110	110	-	5	-	-	-	-	100
Walker River	34	34	-	-	-	-	-	-	-
Other Paiute	77	32	-	-	-	-	-	-	9
Pamunkey	78	29	-	-	-	21	-	-	8
Papago									
Total	12,840	11,840	-	-	-	30	3 2	1 1,509 1	35
Papago	12,827	11,833	-	-	-	30	3 2	1 1,502 1	35
Other Papago	13	7	-	-	-	-	-	7	-
Passamaquoddy									
Total	101	29	-	-	-	-	-	-	-
Passamaquoddy	101	29	-	-	-	-	-	-	-
Other Passamaquoddy	-	-	-	-	-	-	-	-	-
Pawnee	758	261	10	5	3	55	115	59	7
Penobscot	146	16	-	-	-	6	10	-	-
Peoria	223	11	-	-	-	-	5	6	-
Pequot	64	9	-	-	-	-	6	3	-
Pima	11,454	10,313	24	-	-	28	82	9,957	90
Piscataway	-	-	-	-	-	-	-	-	-
Pit River	1,231	5	-	-	-	-	-	-	-
Pomo									
Total	3,007	72	6	4	-	7	35	7	-
Eastern Pomo	-	-	-	-	-	-	-	-	-
Kashaya	50	-	-	-	-	-	-	-	-
Northern Pomo	40	-	-	-	-	-	-	-	-

[Continued]

★ 218 ★

American Indian Population, by Tribe and State, 1980: West Region, Iroquois-Pomo - I
[Continued]

| Tribe | Total West Region | Mountain Division | | | | | | | |
		Total Mountain	MT	ID	WY	CO	NM	AZ	UT
Pomo	2,882	69	3	4	-	7	35	7	-
Other Pomo	35	3	3	-	-	-	-	-	-

Source: U.S. Bureau of the Census, *1980 Census of Population, Volume 2, Subject Reports, Characteristics of American Indians, by Tribes and Selected Areas: 1980,* PC80-2-1C, Section 1: Tables I-II, issued September 1989, U.S. Department of Commerce, U.S. Government Printing Office, Washington, D.C., pp. 1-53. *Notes:* (N.E.C.) stands for not elsewhere classified. A dash (-) represents zero or a percent which rounds to less than 0.1. 1. Any Mohawk entry of "Ganienka" was miscoded to Wailaki. 2. Miscoding of entries of "Lummee," "Lummi," "Lumbee," or "Lumbi" may have affected the data for this tribe. 3. Reporting and/or processing may have affected the data for this tribe. 4. Any entry with the spelling "Micmac" was miscoded to Cheyenne River Sioux.

★ 219 ★

American Indian Population, by Tribe and State, 1980: West Region, Iroquois-Pomo - II

Data are estimates based on a sample and are the most recent available.

| Tribe | Total West Region | Pacific Division | | | | | | |
		Total Pacific	NV	WA	OR	CA	AK	HI
Iroquois								
Total	5,364	4,082	161	419	266	3,294	69	34
Cayuga	90	59	-	-	7	52	-	-
Iroquois (n.e.c.)	1,486	1,194	65	128	114	908	18	26
Mohawk[1]	1,546	1,169	32	112	44	1,006	4	3
Oneida	725	487	8	47	39	391	5	5
Onondaga	55	45	4	21	-	23	1	-
Seneca								
Total	926	748	16	90	26	591	41	-
Seneca	919	741	16	90	26	584	41	-
Seneca Nation	7	7	-	-	-	7	-	-
Tonawanda Seneca	-	-	-	-	-	-	-	-
Seneca-Cayuga	75	28	-	-	9	19	-	-
Tuscarora	121	73	24	-	8	65	-	-
Wyandot	340	279	12	21	19	239	-	-
Kalispel	181	167	-	163	-	4	-	-
Karok	1,948	1,890	23	113	261	1,511	5	-
Kaw	138	79	7	13	17	49	-	-
Kickapoo	303	198	-	18	49	125	6	-
Kiowa	1,386	864	9	39	116	700	2	7
Klamath	1,992	1,885	53	127	1,500	246	7	5
Konkow	326	309	0	-	13	296	-	-
Kootenai	362	102	-	34	26	42	-	-

[Continued]

★ 219 ★

American Indian Population, by Tribe and State, 1980: West Region, Iroquois-Pomo - II

[Continued]

Tribe	Total West Region	Pacific Division						
		Total Pacific	NV	WA	OR	CA	AK	HI
Long Island								
Total	20	11	-	-	-	11	-	-
Matinecock	-	-	-	-	-	-	-	-
Montauk	9	-	-	-	-	-	-	-
Poosepatuck	-	-	-	-	-	-	-	-
Other Long Island	11	11	-	-	-	11	-	-
Luiseno								
Total	1,187	1,184	-	45	3	1,136	-	-
LaJolla	39	39	-	-	-	39	-	-
Luiseno	872	872	-	5	-	867	-	-
Pala	130	130	-	33	3	94	-	-
Pauma	36	33	-	-	-	33	-	-
Pechanga	110	110	-	7	-	103	-	-
Lumbee[2]	406	351	22	45	6	243	27	30
Lummi[2]	2,259	2,259	-	2,115	55	86	-	-
Maidu	1,124	1,068	41	20	27	1,011	4	6
Makah	1,026	1,023	-	970	12	4	37	-
Maliseet	17	17	-	-	-	11	6	-
Mandan	347	150	-	23	2	110	5	10
Mattaponi	24	17	-	-	-	17	-	-
Menominee	274	186	12	20	28	133	5	-
Maimi	334	212	18	39	23	150	-	-
Miccosukee[3]	15	15	-	-	-	15	-	-
Micmac[4]	100	66	7	-	15	51	-	-
Mission Indians	2,369	2,259	48	31	12	2,213	3	-
Miwok	2,060	2,023	16	9	17	1,984	-	13
Modoc	683	615	13	68	220	327	-	-
Mohegan	23	23	-	8	-	15	-	-
Mono	1,262	1,255	-	15	21	1,192	27	-
Nanticoke	10	8	-	-	-	8	-	-
Narragansett	72	72	-	3	8	55	-	6
Navajo	154,024	7,125	290	485	411	6,030	77	122
Nex Perce[3]	1,984	1,399	5	644	321	407	5	22
Nomalaki	204	195	9	-	3	192	-	-
Northwest tribes (n.e.c)								
Total	210	174	-	28	101	40	5	-
Columbia Wenatchee	15	15	-	15	-	-	-	-
Kalapuya	65	52	-	-	34	18	-	-
Tillamook	82	73	-	-	57	16	-	-
Other Northwest	48	34	-	13	10	6	5	-
Omaha	458	240	-	5	6	197	4	28
Oregon Athabaskan	507	507	-	31	365	92	19	-
Osage	2,373	1,626	105	182	219	1,185	40	-

[Continued]

406

★ 219 ★

American Indian Population, by Tribe and State, 1980: West Region, Iroquois-Pomo - II

[Continued]

Tribe	Total West Region	Pacific Division						
		Total Pacific	NV	WA	OR	CA	AK	HI
Oto	203	106	-	10	10	86	-	-
Ottawa	420	335	6	24	28	279	4	-
Paiute[3]								
Total	9,142	4,362	3,648	116	536	3,679	15	16
Burns Paiute	67	67	-	4	63	-	-	-
Northern Paiute	57	51	6	-	3	48	-	-
Paiute	8,777	4,199	3,560	99	470	3,599	15	16
Pyramind Lake	20	-	20	-	-	-	-	-
Southern Paiute	110	-	5	-	-	-	-	-
Walker River	34	-	34	-	-	-	-	-
Other Paiute	77	45	23	13	-	32	-	-
Pamunkey	78	49	-	7	-	42	-	-
Papago								
Total	12,840	1,000	134	6	10	980	4	-
Papago	12,827	994	134	-	10	980	4	-
Other Papago	13	6	-	6	-	-	-	-
Passamaquoddy								
Total	101	72	29	-	7	57	8	-
Passamaquoddy	101	72	29	-	7	57	8	-
Other Passamaquoddy	-	-	-	-	-	-	-	-
Pawnee	758	497	7	71	50	374	2	-
Penobscot	146	130	-	42	3	85	-	-
Peoria	223	212	-	56	6	150	-	-
Pequot	64	55	-	-	3	52	-	-
Pima	11,454	1,141	132	41	64	1,036	-	-
Piscataway	-	-	-	-	-	-	-	-
Pit River	1,231	1,226	5	-	77	1,149	-	-
Pomo								
Total	3,007	2,935	13	70	42	2,817	-	6
Eastern Pomo	-	-	-	-	-	-	-	-
Kashaya	50	50	-	-	-	50	-	-
Northern Pomo	40	40	-	4	8	28	-	-
Pomo	2,882	2,813	13	55	34	2,718	-	6
Other Pomo	35	32	-	11	-	21	-	-

Source: U.S. Bureau of the Census, *1980 Census of Population, Volume 2, Subject Reports, Characteristics of American Indians, by Tribes and Selected Areas: 1980,* PC80-2-1C, Section 1: Tables I-II, issued September 1989, U.S. Department of Commerce, U.S. Government Printing Office, Washington, D.C., pp. 1-53. *Notes:* (N.E.C.) stands for not elsewhere classified. A dash (-) represents zero or a percent which rounds to less than 0.1. 1. Any Mohawk entry of "Ganienka" was miscoded to Wailaki. 2. Miscoding of entries of "Lummee," "Lummi," "Lumbee," or "Lumbi" may have affected the data for this tribe. 3. Reporting and/or processing may have affected the data for this tribe. 4. Any entry with the spelling "Micmac" was miscoded to Cheyenne River Sioux.

★ 220 ★

American Indian Population, by Tribe and State, 1980: West Region, Ponca-Sioux - I

Data are estimates based on a sample and are the most recent available.

Tribe	Total West Region	Mountain Division							
		Total Mountain	MT	ID	WY	CO	NM	AZ	UT
Ponca	130	94	-	-	-	8	11	10	-
Potawatomi									
Total	2,087	1,556	23	19	26	234	81	112	27
Citizen Band	100	56	-	-	-	35	9	-	-
Forest County	36	36	-	-	-	-	-	-	-
Huron Potawatomi	-	-	-	-	-	-	-	-	-
Potawatomie	1,921	1,455	23	19	26	199	72	112	6
Prairie Band	30	9	-	-	-	-	-	-	21
Other Potawatomi	-	-	-	-	-	-	-	-	-
Powhatan	76	76	-	-	-	-	-	-	-
Pueblo[1]									
Total	40,688	3,864	46	105	28	487	26,649	8,690	472
Acoma	2,978	227	-	33	-	-	2,588	101	16
Arizona Tewa	302	38	-	-	-	-	14	213	37
Cochiti	822	54	-	-	5	-	752	11	-
Hopi	8,592	995	1	10	-	79	294	6,969	171
Isleta	2,497	199	-	-	-	20	2,254	12	12
Jemez	1,359	50	-	-	-	-	1,235	57	17
Keres (n.e.c.)	672	1	-	-	9	14	648	-	-
Laguna	3,932	284	3	5	-	6	3,298	328	8
Nambe	256	10	-	-	-	-	234	12	-
Picuris	26	-	-	-	-	17	9	-	-
Pojoaque	37	-	-	-	-	37	-	-	-
Pueblo (n.e.c.)	2,078	1,108	35	27	-	207	485	95	97
Sandia	734	53	-	-	-	6	305	370	-
San Felipe	1,707	-	-	-	-	-	1,693	14	-
San Ildefonso	232	-	-	-	-	-	221	11	-
San Juan	423	12	-	-	-	-	387	5	-
Santa Ana	342	-	-	-	-	-	342	-	-
Santa Clara[1]	435	58	-	-	-	-	371	-	6
Santo Domingo	2,442	46	-	-	-	4	2,366	26	-
Taos	1,321	86	3	-	-	89	1,055	59	23
Tesuque	199	-	-	-	11	188	-	-	-
Tewa	1,981	198	-	30	3	27	1,465	212	34
Tigua[1]	335	212	-	-	-	-	111	12	-
Zia	668	51	-	-	-	-	617	-	-
Zuni	6,318	182	4	-	-	18	5,880	183	51
Puget Sound Salish									
Total	6,368	6,236	19	45	3	17	18	14	8
Duwamish	101	94	-	-	-	-	-	7	-
Muckleshoot	532	532	-	-	-	-	-	-	-
Nisqually	204	192	-	8	-	-	4	-	-
Nooksack	537	509	-	3	-	17	-	-	8

[Continued]

★ 220 ★

American Indian Population, by Tribe and State, 1980: West Region, Ponca-Sioux - 1

[Continued]

Tribe	Total West Region	Mountain Division							
		Total Mountain	MT	ID	WY	CO	NM	AZ	UT
Puget Sound Salish (n.e.c.)	49	49	-	-	-	-	-	-	-
Puyallup	600	592	-	-	-	-	-	-	-
Samish	91	91	-	-	-	-	-	-	-
Sauk-Sauiatte	135	135	-	-	-	-	-	-	-
Skokomish	475	469	6	-	-	-	-	-	-
Skykomish	57	55	2	-	-	-	-	-	-
Snohomish	491	478	6	-	-	-	-	-	-
Snoqualmie	236	236	-	-	-	-	-	-	-
Squaxin Island	313	310	-	-	3	-	-	-	-
Steilacoom	142	142	-	-	-	-	-	-	-
Stillaguamish	72	72	-	-	-	-	-	-	-
Suquamish	360	346	-	-	-	-	14	-	-
Swinomish	434	434	-	-	-	-	-	-	-
Tulalip	1,140	1,106	-	34	-	-	-	-	-
Upper Skagit	399	394	5	-	-	-	-	-	-
Quapaw	298	261	-	-	-	25	3	-	9
Quinault	1,625	1,607	18	-	-	-	-	-	-
Rappahannock	7	7	-	-	-	-	-	-	-
Sac and Fox Mesquakie	616	437	9	6	7	27	20	96	14
Salinan	278	271	-	-	-	-	-	-	-
Schaghticoke	-	-	-	-	-	-	-	-	-
Seminole[1]									
Total	1,961	1,670	6	5	-	48	52	99	37
Seminole	1,928	1,637	6	5	-	48	52	99	37
Seminole Nation of Oklahoma	27	27	-	-	-	-	-	-	-
Seminole Tribe of Florida	6	6	-	-	-	-	-	-	-
Other Seminole	-	-	-	-	-	-	-	-	-
Serrano	193	184	-	-	9	-	-	-	-
Shasta	298	292	-	-	-	6	-	-	-
Shawnee									
Total	971	704	6	18	-	29	151	56	-
Absentee Shawnee	42	33	-	-	-	-	-	9	-
Shawnee	929	671	6	18	-	29	151	47	-
Shinnecock	59	40	-	-	-	-	-	13	-
Shoshone									
Total	8,936	1,976	161	2,274	1,289	175	115	122	494
Goshute	122	-	-	5	-	-	-	-	70
Shoshone	8,604	1,913	161	2,267	1,280	157	80	110	419
Te-Moak Western Shoshone[1]	93	25	-	-	9	18	29	12	-
Yomba[1]	62	18	-	2	-	-	6	-	-
Other Shoshone	55	20	-	-	-	-	-	-	5
Siletz	687	620	-	67	-	-	-	-	-

[Continued]

★ 220 ★

American Indian Population, by Tribe and State, 1980: West Region, Ponca-Sioux - I

[Continued]

Tribe	Total West Region	Mountain Division							
		Total Mountain	MT	ID	WY	CO	NM	AZ	UT
Sioux									
Total	18,837	10,358	3,255	409	709	1,862	388	1,052	477
Blackfoot Sioux	161	109	49	-	-	-	-	-	3
Brule Sioux	93	51	-	-	-	-	25	-	8
Cheyenne River Sioux[2]	135	67	8	-	10	14	5	20	-
Crow River Sioux[2]	79	18	7	4	-	-	-	50	-
Dakota Sioux	155	150	-	-	-	-	-	5	-
Devil's Lake Sioux	16	11	-	-	-	-	-	5	-
Fladreau Santee	-	-	-	-	-	-	-	-	-
Fort Peck	128	-	114	-	-	-	-	-	-
Lower Brule Sioux	-	-	-	-	-	-	-	-	-
Mdewakanton Sioux	18	18	-	-	-	-	-	-	-
Oglala Sioux	1,134	544	156	-	31	193	95	80	24
Pine Ridge Sioux	-	-	-	-	-	-	-	-	-
Prior Lake Sioux	60	56	-	-	-	4	-	-	-
Rosebud Sioux	371	178	18	6	93	20	14	34	-
Santee Sioux	163	117	-	12	-	17	-	5	-
Sioux	15,695	8,620	2,850	381	563	1,539	243	817	413
Sisseton Sioux	94	58	17	-	-	11	-	-	8
Standing Rock Sioux	79	44	19	3	-	6	-	-	-
Teton Sioux	190	119	-	-	5	58	-	8	-
Wahpeton Sioux	17	7	10	-	-	-	-	-	-
Yankton Sioux	200	156	-	3	-	-	6	28	7
Yanktonai Sioux	26	12	7	-	7	-	-	-	-
Other Sioux	23	23	-	-	-	-	-	-	-

Source: U.S. Bureau of the Census, *1980 Census of Population, Volume 2, Subject Reports, Characteristics of American Indians, by Tribes and Selected Areas: 1980*, PC80-2-1C, Section 1: Tables I-II, issued September 1989, U.S. Department of Commerce, U.S. Government Printing Office, Washington, D.C., pp. 1-53. *Notes:* (N.E.C.) stands for not elsewhere classified. A dash (-) represents zero or a percent which rounds to less than 0.1. 1. Reporting and/or processing problems may have affected the data for this tribe. 2. Any entry with the spelling "Micmac" was miscoded to Cheyenne River Sioux.

★ 221 ★

American Indian Population, by Tribe and State, 1980: West Region, Ponca-Sioux - II

Data are estimates based on a sample and are the most recent available.

| Tribe | Total West Region | Pacific Division | | | | | | |
		Total Pacific	NV	WA	OR	CA	AK	HI
Ponca	130	94	7	42	18	25	9	-
Potawatomi								
Total	2,087	1,556	9	268	121	1,146	7	14
Citizen Band	100	56	-	13	17	26	-	-
Forest County	36	36	-	-	-	36	-	-
Huron Potawatomi	-	-	-	-	-	-	-	-
Potawatomie	1,921	1,455	9	246	104	1,084	7	14
Prairie Band	30	9	9	-	-	-	-	-
Other Potawatomi	-	-	-	-	-	-	-	-
Powhatan	76	76	-	13	-	63	-	-
Pueblo[1]								
Total	40,688	3,864	147	175	232	3,340	63	54
Acoma	2,978	227	13	7	-	220	-	-
Arizona Tewa	302	38	-	-	-	38	-	-
Cochiti	822	38	-	-	19	27	8	-
Hopi	8,592	995	73	29	52	888	7	19
Isleta	2,497	199	-	14	31	131	16	7
Jemez	1,359	50	-	-	-	46	4	-
Keres (n.e.c.)	672	1	-	1	-	-	-	-
Laguna	3,932	284	63	8	213	-	-	-
Nambe	256	10	-	-	10	-	-	-
Picuris	26	-	-	-	-	-	-	-
Pojoaque	37	-	-	-	-	-	-	-
Pueblo (n.e.c.)	2,078	1,108	24	31	51	1,004	14	8
Sandia	734	53	-	-	-	53	-	-
San Felipe	1,707	-	-	-	-	-	-	-
San Ildefonso	232	-	-	-	-	-	-	-
San Juan	423	12	19	-	-	12	-	-
Santa Ana	342	-	-	-	-	-	-	-
Santa Clara[1]	435	58	-	12	-	46	-	-
Santo Domingo	2,442	46	-	-	-	41	5	-
Taos	1,321	86	6	-	10	76	-	-
Tesuque	199	-	-	-	-	-	-	-
Tewa	1,981	198	12	6	6	179	-	7
Tigua[1]	335	212	-	5	-	207	-	-
Zia	668	51	-	-	42	9	-	-
Zuni	6,318	182	-	7	55	107	-	13
Puget Sound Salish								
Total	6,368	6,236	8	5,623	162	382	45	24
Duwamish	101	94	-	57	13	24	-	-
Muckleshoot	532	532	-	472	6	43	-	11
Nisqually	204	192	-	174	8	10	-	-
Nooksack	537	509	-	501	-	8	-	-

[Continued]

★ 221 ★

American Indian Population, by Tribe and State, 1980: West Region, Ponca-Sioux - II

[Continued]

Tribe	Total West Region	Pacific Division						
		Total Pacific	NV	WA	OR	CA	AK	HI
Puget Sound Salish (n.e.c.)	49	49	-	35	-	8	-	6
Puyallup	600	592	8	525	18	43	6	-
Samish	91	91	-	79	6	6	-	-
Sauk-Sauiatte	135	135	-	125	10	-	-	-
Skokomish	475	469	-	393	9	57	10	-
Skykomish	57	55	-	32	-	23	-	-
Snohomish	491	478	-	393	30	41	7	7
Snoqualmie	236	236	-	160	14	57	5	-
Squaxin Island	313	310	-	261	18	19	12	-
Steilacoom	142	142	-	137	-	5	-	-
Stillaguamish	72	72	-	67	5	-	-	-
Suquamish	360	346	-	383	2	4	2	-
Swinomish	434	434	-	423	-	11	-	-
Tulalip	1,140	1,106	-	1,078	13	12	3	-
Upper Skagit	399	394	-	373	10	11	-	-
Quapaw	298	261	-	99	11	144	7	-
Quinault	1,625	1,607	-	1,419	57	90	41	-
Rappahannock	7	7	-	-	-	7	-	-
Sac and Fox Mesquakie	616	437	-	70	20	334	2	11
Salinan	278	271	7	-	21	250	-	-
Schaghticoke	-	-	-	-	-	-	-	-
Seminole[1]								
Total	1,961	1,670	44	162	170	1,306	11	21
Seminole	1,928	1,637	44	143	170	1,292	11	12
Seminole Nation of Oklahoma	27	27	-	13	-	14	-	-
Seminole Tribe of Florida	6	6	-	6	-	-	-	-
Other Seminole	-	-	-	-	-	-	-	-
Serrano	193	184	-	-	-	184	-	-
Shasta	298	292	-	18	111	160	3	-
Shawnee								
Total	971	704	7	37	89	566	6	6
Absentee Shawnee	42	33	-	-	-	33	-	-
Shawnee	929	671	7	37	89	533	6	6
Shinnecock	59	40	6	-	-	33	2	5
Shoshone								
Total	8,936	1,976	2,330	254	147	1,482	71	22
Goshute	122	-	47	-	-	-	-	-
Shoshone	8,604	1,913	2,217	254	147	1,424	71	17
Te-Moak Western Shoshone[1]	93	25	-	-	-	25	-	-
Yomba[1]	62	18	36	-	-	13	-	5
Other Shoshone	55	20	30	-	-	20	-	-
Siletz	687	620	-	35	574	11	-	-

[Continued]

★ 221 ★

American Indian Population, by Tribe and State, 1980: West Region, Ponca-Sioux - II
[Continued]

Tribe	Total West Region	Pacific Division						
		Total Pacific	NV	WA	OR	CA	AK	HI
Sioux								
Total	18,837	10,358	327	2,148	1,348	6,587	180	95
Blackfoot Sioux	161	109	-	30	4	75	-	-
Brule Sioux	93	51	9	7	-	44	-	-
Cheyenne River Sioux[2]	135	67	11	42	-	25	-	-
Crow Creek Sioux	79	18	-	18	-	-	-	-
Dakota Sioux	155	150	-	39	4	107	-	-
Devil's Lake Sioux	16	11	-	-	-	11	-	-
Fladreau Santee	-	-	-	-	-	-	-	-
Fort Peck	128	-	-	-	-	-	-	-
Lower Brule Sioux	-	-	-	-	-	-	-	-
Mdewakanton Sioux	18	18	-	-	-	18	-	-
Oglala Sioux	1,134	544	11	134	28	374	8	-
Pine Ridge Sioux	-	-	-	-	-	-	-	-
Prior Lake Sioux	60	56	-	-	-	56	-	-
Rosebud Sioux	371	178	8	33	18	106	12	9
Santee Sioux	163	117	12	7	20	86	4	-
Sioux	15,695	8,620	' 269	1,779	1,211	5,388	156	86
Sisseton Sioux	94	58	-	6	12	40	-	-
Standing Rock Sioux	79	44	7	-	4	40	-	-
Teton Sioux	190	119	-	17	32	70	-	-
Wahpeton Sioux	17	7	-	-	-	7	-	-
Yankton Sioux	200	156	-	20	15	121	-	-
Yanktonai Sioux	26	12	-	6	-	6	-	-
Other Sioux	23	23	-	10	-	13	-	-

Source: U.S. Bureau of the Census, *1980 Census of Population, Volume 2, Subject Reports, Characteristics of American Indians, by Tribes and Selected Areas: 1980,* PC80-2-1C, Section 1: Tables I-II, issued September 1989, U.S. Department of Commerce, U.S. Government Printing Office, Washington, D.C., pp. 1-53. *Notes:* (N.E.C.) stands for not elsewhere classified. A dash (-) represents zero or a percent which rounds to less than 0.1. 1. Reporting and/or processing problems may have affected the data for this tribe. 2. Any entry with the spelling "Micmac" was miscoded to Cheyenne River Sioux.

★ 222 ★

American Indian Population, by Tribe and State, 1980: West Region, Siuslaw-Yurok - I

Data are estimates based on a sample and are the most recent available.

Tribe	Total West Region	Mountain Division							
		Total Mountain	MT	ID	WY	CO	NM	AZ	UT
Siuslaw	333	5	-	-	-	-	-	-	5
Spokane	1,739	83	21	26	-	-	-	14	22
Stockbridge	163	28	-	-	-	17	5	-	6
Tlingit	9,129	342	27	8	14	46	33	101	
Tolowa	394	9	-	-	-	-	9	-	-
Tonkawa	17	17	-	-	-	-	-	17	-
Tsimishian	1,513	28	-	-	-	-	-	14	7
Umatilla	914	21	-	14	-	-	-	-	-
Ute									
Total	5,572	4,853	23	51	26	1,889	146	79	2,626
Uintah Ute	26	21	-	-	-	-	-	-	21
Ute	4,846	4,201	16	51	26	1,323	93	74	2,605
Ute Mountain Ute	690	621	7	-	-	556	53	5	-
Other Ute	10	10	-	-	-	10	-	-	-
Wailaki[1]	489	4	-	-	-	-	4	-	-
Walla-Walla	216	-	-	-	-	-	-	-	-
Wampanoag	122	33	-	-	9	17	-	-	-
Warm Springs	1,271	17	-	-	-	-	-	6	-
Washo									
Total	1,369	840	3	40	-	-	4	-	28
Washo	1,332	803	3	14	-	-	4	-	28
Other Washo	37	37	-	26	-	-	-	-	-
Wichita	119	54	-	-	27	19	4	4	-
Winnebago	639	54	44	36	-	77	39	56	28
Wintu	1,923	76	19	-	-	12	-	-	16
Wiyot	238	-	-	-	-	-	-	-	-
Yakima	6,322	233	49	35	6	16	21	20	68
Yaqui									
Total	5,045	3,661	-	5	5	108	38	3,494	-
Barrio Libre	369	101	-	-	-	68	8	25	-
Yaqui	4,671	3,555	-	5	5	40	30	3,464	-
Other Yaqui	5	5	-	-	-	-	-	5	-
Yavapai Apache	127	119	-	-	-	-	-	119	-
Yokuts									
Total	1,667	48	-	-	-	6	15	20	-
Chuckhansi	525	6	-	-	-	6	-	-	-
Tachi	259	15	-	-	-	-	15	-	-
Tule River	398	-	-	-	-	-	-	-	-
Yokuts	485	27	-	-	-	-	20	-	-
Yuchi	72	15	-	-	-	-	15	-	-
Yuman									
Total	6,132	4,256	18	-	15	41	109	3,898	81
Cocopah	719	583	-	-	-	-	-	579	4

[Continued]

★ 222 ★

American Indian Population, by Tribe and State, 1980: West Region, Siuslaw-Yurok - I
[Continued]

Tribe	Total West Region	Mountain Division							
		Total Mountain	MT	ID	WY	CO	NM	AZ	UT
Havasupai	336	167	-	-	8	-	63	57	16
Hualapai	1,018	912	-	-	-	5	13	843	34
Maricopa	726	666	-	-	-	4	14	634	-
Mohave	1,416	901	11	-	-	27	11	840	-
Quechan	1,162	319	7	-	7	5	-	262	27
Yavapai	755	708	-	-	-	-	8	683	-
Yurok	2,820	39	3	-	6	6	-	-	-
Other specified tribes (n.e.c.)									
Total	380	163	90	-	-	5	-	42	11
Fort Berthold	19	19	19	-	-	-	-	-	-
Gila River	34	34	-	-	-	-	-	17	11
Grand Rhonde	60	5	-	-	-	-	-	-	5
Los Coyotes	44	-	-	-	-	-	-	-	-
Round Valley	25	-	-	-	-	-	-	-	-
Scotts Valley	65	65	65	-	-	-	-	-	-
Shoalwater	49	-	-	-	-	-	-	-	-
All other specified	84	40	6	-	-	5	-	20	-
Tribe not specified	15,288	3,399	265	155	66	428	712	1,206	427
Tribe not reported	122,980	45,717	5,725	2,596	1,844	4,452	11,876	14,389	2,205

Source: U.S. Bureau of the Census, *1980 Census of Population, Volume 2, Subject Reports, Characteristics of American Indians, by Tribes and Selected Areas: 1980*, PC80-2-1C, Section 1: Tables I-II, issued September 1989, U.S. Department of Commerce, U.S. Government Printing Office, Washington, D.C., pp. 1-53. *Notes:* (N.E.C.) stands for not elsewhere classified. A dash (-) represents zero or a percent which rounds to less than 0.1. 1. Any Mohawk entry of "Ganienka" was miscoded to Wailaki.

★ 223 ★

American Indian Population, by Tribe and State, 1980: West Region, Siuslaw-Yurok - II

Data are estimates based on a sample and are the most recent available.

Tribe	Total West Region	Pacific Division						
		Total Pacific	NV	WA	OR	CA	AK	HI
Siuslaw	333	328	-	8	271	49	-	-
Spokane	1,739	1,656	-	1,557	55	44	-	-
Stockbridge	163	135	-	31	26	78	-	-
Tlingit	9,129	8,787	64	1,415	270	330	6,764	8
Tolowa	394	385	-	-	70	315	-	-
Tonkawa	17	-	-	-	-	-	-	-
Tsimishian	1,513	1,485	7	224	68	25	1,168	-
Umatilla	914	893	7	169	660	60	4	-

[Continued]

★ 223 ★

American Indian Population, by Tribe and State, 1980: West Region, Siuslaw-Yurok - II

[Continued]

Tribe	Total West Region	Pacific Division						
		Total Pacific	NV	WA	OR	CA	AK	HI
Ute								
Total	5,572	719	13	74	119	500	26	-
Uintah Ute	26	5	-	-	5	-	-	-
Ute	4,846	645	13	74	114	431	26	-
Ute Mountain Ute	690	69	-	-	-	69	-	-
Other Ute	10	-	-	-	-	-	-	-
Wailaki[1]	489	485	-	6	30	449	-	-
Walla-Walla	216	216	-	37	154	25	-	-
Wampanoag	122	89	7	7	6	76	-	-
Warm Springs	1,271	1,254	11	168	1,000	75	11	-
Washo								
Total	1,369	529	765	27	9	493	-	-
Washo	1,332	529	754	27	9	493	-	-
Other Washo	37	-	11	-	-	-	-	-
Wichita	119	65	-	-	29	36	-	-
Winnebago	639	320	39	25	-	289	6	-
Wintu	1,923	1,847	29	135	84	1,619	3	6
Wiyot	238	238	-	-	11	227	-	-
Yakima	6,322	6,089	18	5,060	648	318	52	11
Yaqui								
Total	5,045	1,384	11	38	55	1,269	9	13
Barrio Libre	369	268	-	-	37	224	2	5
Yaqui	4,671	1,116	11	38	18	1,045	7	8
Other Yaqui	5	-	-	-	-	-	-	-
Yavapai Apache	127	8	-	-	-	8	-	-
Yokuts								
Total	1,667	1,619	7	8	40	1,571	-	-
Chuckhansi	525	519	-	8	19	492	-	-
Tachi	259	244	-	-	-	224	-	-
Tule River	398	398	-	-	-	398	-	-
Yokuts	485	458	7	-	21	437	-	-
Yuchi	72	57	-	2	-	55	-	-
Yuman								
Total	6,132	1,876	94	16	13	1,847	-	-
Cocopah	719	136	-	11	8	117	-	-
Havasupai	336	169	23	-	-	169	-	-
Hualapai	1,018	106	17	-	-	106	-	-
Maricopa	726	60	14	-	5	55	-	-
Mohave	1,416	515	12	-	-	515	-	-
Quechan	1,162	843	11	-	-	843	-	-
Yavapai	755	47	17	5	-	42	-	-
Yurok	2,820	2,781	24	111	234	2,422	-	14

[Continued]

★ 223 ★

American Indian Population, by Tribe and State, 1980: West Region, Siuslaw-Yurok - II

[Continued]

Tribe	Total West Region	Pacific Division						
		Total Pacific	NV	WA	OR	CA	AK	HI
Other specified tribes (n.e.c.)								
Total	380	217	15	121	24	72	-	-
Fort Berthold	19	-	-	-	-	-	-	-
Gila River	34	-	6	-	-	-	-	-
Grand Rhode	60	55	-	41	8	6	-	-
Los Coyotes	44	44	-	-	-	44	-	-
Round Valley	25	25	-	12	-	13	-	-
Scotts Valley	65	-	-	-	-	-	-	-
Shoalwater	49	49	-	49	-	-	-	-
All other specified	84	44	9	19	16	9	-	-
Tribe not specified	15,288	11,889	140	2,004	779	8,644	366	96
Tribe not reported	122,980	77,263	2,630	10,060	5,783	58,815	1,933	672

Source: U.S. Bureau of the Census, *1980 Census of Population, Volume 2, Subject Reports, Characteristics of American Indians, by Tribe and Selected Areas: 1980,* PC80-2-1C, Section 1: Tables I-II, issued September 1989, U.S. Department of Commerce, U.S. Government Printing Office, Washington, D.C., pp. 1-53. *Notes:* (N.E.C.) stands for not elsewhere classified. A dash (-) represents zero or a percent which rounds to less than 0.1. 1. Any Mohawk entry of "Ganienka" was miscoded to Wailaki.

Population Trends

★ 224 ★

American Indian Population, by State, 1900 - 1980

State	1900	1910	1920	1930	1940	1950	1960	1970	1980
Alabama	177	909	405	465	464	928	1,276	2,443	7,502
Alaska	13,152?	11,244	9,918?	10,955	11,283	14,089	14,444	16,276	21,869
Arizona	26,480	29,201	32,989	43,726	55,076	65,761	83,387	95,812	152,498
Arkansas	66	460	106	408	278	533	580	2,014	9,364
California	15,377	16,371	17,360	19,212	18,675	19,947	39,014	91,018	198,275
Colorado	1,437	1,482	1,383	1,395	1,360	1,567	4,238	8,336	17,734
Connecticut	153	152	159	162	201	333	923	2,222	4,431
Delaware	9	5	2	5	14	?	597	656	1,307
District of Columbia	22	68	37	40	190	330	587	956	996
Florida	358	74	518	587	690	1,011	2,504	6,677	19,134
Georgia	19	95	125	43	106	333	749	2,347	7,442
Hawaii	?	?	?	?	?	?	472	1,126	2,655
Idaho	4,226	3,488	3,098	3,638	3,537	3,800	5,231	6,687	10,418
Illinois	16	188	194	469	624	1,443	4,704	11,413	15,846

[Continued]

★ 224 ★

American Indian Population, by State, 1900 - 1980
[Continued]

State	1900	1910	1920	1930	1940	1950	1960	1970	1980
Indiana	243	279	125	285	223	438	948	3,887	7,682
Iowa	382	471	529	660	733	1,084	1,708	2,992	5,369
Kansas	2,130	2,444	2,276	2,454	1,165?	2,381	5,069	8,672	15,256
Kentucky	102	234	57	22	44	234	391	1,531	3,518
Louisiana	593	780	1,066	1,536	1,801	409?	3,587	5,294	11,969
Maine	798	892	839	1,012	1,251	1,522	1,879	2,195	4,057
Maryland	3	55	32	50	73	314	1,538	4,239	7,823
Massachusetts	587	688	555	874	769	1,201	2,118	4,475	7,483
Michigan	6,354	7,519	5,614	7,080	6,282	7,000	9,701	16,854	39,734
Minnesota	9,182	9,053	8,761	11,077	12,528	12,533	15,496	23,128	34,831
Mississippi	2,203	1,253	1,105	1,458	2,134	2,502	3,442	4,113	6,131
Missouri	130	313	171	578	330	547	1,723	5,405	12,129
Montana	11,343	10,745	10,956	14,798	16,841	16,606	21,181	27,130	37,598
Nebraska	3,322	3,502	2,888	3,256	3,401	3,954	5,545	6,624	9,145
Nevada	5,216	5,240	4,907	4,871	4,747	5,025	6,681	7,933	13,306
New Hampshire	22	34	23	64	50	74	135	361	1,297
New Jersey	63	168	100	213	211	621	1,699	4,706	8,176
New Mexico	13,144	20,573	19,512	28,941	34,510	41,901	56,255	72,788	107,338
New York	5,257	6,046	5,503	6,973	8,651	10,640	16,491	28,355	38,967
North Carolina	5,687	7,851	11,824	16,579	22,546	3,742?	38,129	44,406	64,536
North Dakota	6,968	6,486	6,254	8,387	10,114	10,766	11,736	14,369	20,120
Ohio	42	127	151	435	338	1,146	1,910	6,654	11,985
Oklahoma	64,445	74,825	57,337	92,725	63,125	53,769	64,689	98,468	169,292
Oregon	4,951	5,090	4,590	4,776	4,594	5,820	8,026	13,510	26,591
Pennsylvania	1,629	1,503	337	523	441	1,141	2,122	5,533	9,179
Rhode Island	35	234	110	318	196	385	932	1,390	2,872
South Carolina	121	331	304	959	1,234	554	1,098	2,241	5,665
South Dakota	20,225	19,137	16,384?	21,833	23,347	23,344	25,794	32,365	44,948
Tennessee	108	216	56	161	114	339	638	2,276	5,013
Texas	470	702	2,109	1,001	1,103	2,736	5,750	17,957	39,740
Utah	2,623	3,123	2,711	2,869	3,611	4,201	6,961	11,273	19,158
Vermont	5	26	24	36	16	30	57	229	968
Virginia	354	539	824	779	198	1,056	2,155	4,853	9,211
Washington	10,039	10,997	9,061	11,253	11,394	13,816	21,076	33,386	58,186
West Virginia	12	36	7	18	25	160	181	751	1,555
Wisconsin	8,372	10,142	9,611	11,548	12,265	12,196	14,297	18,924	29,320
Wyoming	1,686	1,486	1,343	1,845	2,349	3,237	4,020	4,980	7,057

Source: Russell Thornton, *American Indian Holocaust and Survival: A Population History Since 1492*, University of Oklahoma, Press, 1987, p. 162-163. Published by permission. Primary source: U.S. Bureau of the Census, *Indian Population of the United States and Alaska*, 1910. Washington, D.C.: U.S. Government Printing Office, 1915. p. 10, and 112; *The Indian Population of the United States and Alaska*, Washington, D.C.: U.S. Government Printing Office, 1937, p. 231; *General Population Characteristics: United States Summary*. PC80-1-B1, Pt. 1 Washington, D.C.: U.S. Government Printing Office, 1983, p. 3; *1980 Census of Population, Supplementary Report. American Indian Areas and Alaska Native Villages: 1980*. PC80-S1-13. Washington, D.C.: U.S. Government Printing Office, 1984, p. 14; Stanley and Thomas, "Current Demographics and Social Trends Among North American Indians," *Annals of the American Academy of Political and Social Science*, 1978, p. 114; Swagerty and Thornton, "Preliminary 1980 Census Counts for American Indians, Eskimos and Aleuts," *American Indian Culture and Research Journal*, 1982, pp. 92-93.

★ 225 ★

Changes in Population, 1980 to 1989

Numbers in thousands. Includes Armed Forces overseas.

Race/ethnicity	Population on July 1		Population change, 1980-89		Average annual percent change
	1989	1980	Number	Percent	
Total, all ages	248,762	227,757	21,005	9.2	1.0
American Indian, Eskimo, or Aleut[1]	1,737	1,429	308	21.6	2.2
Hispanic origin[2]	20,528	14,803	5,724	38.7	3.6
White	209,326	195,571	13,755	7.0	0.8
Black	30,788	26,903	3,885	14.4	1.5
Asian or Pacific Islander[1]	6,881	· 3,834	3,047	79.5	6.5

Source: Hollmann, Frederick W., *U.S. Population Estimates, by Age, Sex, Race, and Hispanic Origin: 1989*, U.S. Department of Commerce, Bureau of the Census, Current Population Reports, Population Estimates and Projections, series P-25, No.1057, March 1990, p. 2. *Notes:* 1. Resident population. 2. Persons of Hispanic origin may be of any race.

★ 226 ★

Native American Population Growth Compared With Other Groups, 1980 to 1990

Asian - 107.8
Hispanic - 53.0
Native American - 37.9
Black - 13.2
White - 6.0

There are now nearly 2 million Native Americans living in the United States.

Race and ethnicity	Population increase (%)
Asian	107.8
Hispanic[1]	53.0
Native American	37.9
Black	13.2
White	6.0

Source: USA TODAY, December 10, 1992, p. 11A. Primary source: U.S. Census Bureau. *Note:* 1. Hispanics may be of any race.

★ 227 ★

Percentage of the United States Indian Population Who Are Urban, 1890-1980

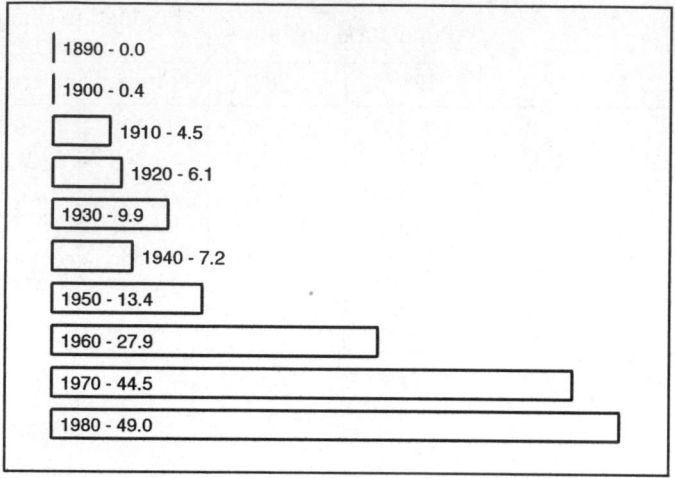

Year	Percent
1890	0.0
1900	0.4
1910	4.5
1920	6.1
1930	9.9
1940	7.2
1950	13.4
1960	27.9
1970	44.5
1980	49.0

Source: Russell Thornton, *American Indian Holocaust and Survival: A Population History Since 1492*, University of Oklahoma Press, 1987, p. 227. Published by permission. Primary source: Thornton, Sandefur, and Grasmick, *The Urbanization of American Indians: A Critical Bibliography*. Bloomington: Indiana University Press, 1982, p. 14. U.S. Bureau of the Census, *General Social and Economic Characteristics: United States Summary*. PC80-1-C1. Washington, D.C.: U.S. Government Printing Office, 1983, p. 92.

★ 228 ★

Percentage of Population Growth, by Race/Ethnicity, 1980 to 1990

Race and ethnicity	Percent
Asian	107.8
Hispanic[1]	53.0
Native American	37.9
Black	13.2
White	6.0

Source: USA TODAY, May 29, 1992, p. 7A. Primary source: U.S. Census Bureau. Note: 1. Persons of Hispanic origin may be of any race.

★ 229 ★

Population Projections for 2040

By the middle of the next century, minority groups will make up 47% of the total U.S. population.

Race/ethnicity	1992 (in millions)	Projected population for 2040 (in millions)
Total	254.9	382.7
Whites	190.6	201.8
Blacks	30.4	57.3
Hispanics[1]	24.1	80.7
Asians	7.9	38.8
Native Americans	1.9	4.1

Source: USA TODAY, December 4, 1992, p. 8A. Primary source: U.S. Census Bureau. Note: 1. Hispanics can be of any race.

Geographic Mobility

★ 230 ★

Geographic Mobility on Identified Reservations, 1980 - I

Data are the latest available.

Identified reservation	Persons 3 to 34 years old					Persons 16 to 19 years old -- percent not enrolled in school, not high school graduates	Persons 25 years and over	
	All persons	Percent enrolled in school					Percent completed less than 5 years of school	Percent high school graduates
		Total	5 to 19 years		20 to 34 years old			
			Total	Bureau of indian affairs or tribal school				
Total persons	219,396	54.9	49.3	24.4	2.6	27.1	16.2	43.2
Acoma Pueblo, New Mexico	1,411	44.9	39.6	42.9	1.6	48.3	9.0	53.0
Valencia County	1,411	44.9	39.6	42.9	1.6	48.3	9.0	53.0
Agua Caliente Reservation, California	-	-	-	-	-	-	-	-
Riverside County	-	-	-	-	-	-	-	-
Alabama-Coushatta Reservation, Texas	293	54.4	49.5	3.3	1.1	19.5	7.1	52.2
Polk County	293	54.4	49.5	3.3	1.1	19.5	71.	52.2
Alamo Reservation, New Mexico	724	42.8	39.2	19.5	1.2	57.9	48.3	20.0
Socorro County	724	42.8	39.2	19.5	1.2	57.9	48.3	20.0
Allegany Reservation, New York	549	60.0	51.0	1.2	3.7	16.7	2.9	56.8
Cattaraugus County	549	60.0	51.0	1.2	3.7	16.7	2.9	56.8
Alturas Rancheria, California	...	...	...	...	...	...	...	...
Modoc County	...	...	...	...	...	...	...	...
Annette Islands Reserve, Alaska	617	52.7	47.0	1.0	2.2	11.8	0.9	59.2
Prince of Wales-Outer Ketchikan Census Area	617	52.7	47.0	1.0	2.2	11.8	0.9	59.2
Augustine Reservation, California	-	-	-	-	-	-	-	-
Riverside County	-	-	-	-	-	-	-	-
Bad River Reservation, Wisconsin	420	62.2	53.3	0.5	3.7	9.8	2.9	51.1
Ashland County	420	62.2	53.3	0.5	3.7	9.8	2.9	51.1
Iron County	-	-	-	-	-	-	-	-
Barona Rancheria, California	146	45.2	37.5	-	-	48.2	2.2	52.5
San Diego County	146	45.2	37.5	-	-	48.2	2.2	52.5
Bay Mills Reservation, Michigan	189	56.4	46.2	2.9	5.5	28.9	-	58.7
Chippewa County	189	56.4	46.2	2.9	5.5	28.9	-	58.7
Benton Paiute Reservation, California	...	...	...	...	...	...	...	...
Mono County	...	...	...	...	...	...	...	...
Berry Creek Rancheria, California	-	-	-	-	-	-	-	-
Butte County	-	-	-	-	-	-	-	-
Big Bend Rancheria, California	...	...	...	...	...	...	...	...
Shasta County	...	...	...	...	...	...	...	...
Big Cypress Reservation, Florida	239	59.0	50.7	67.6	1.8	31.6	46.7	23.8
Hendry County	239	59.0	50.7	67.6	1.8	31.6	46.7	23.8
Big Lagoon Rancheria, California	...	...	...	...	...	...	...	...
Humboldt County	...	...	...	...	...	...	...	...
Big Pine Rancheria, California	189	51.3	46.9	1.3	1.7	9.3	0.9	74.0
Inyo County	189	51.3	46.9	1.3	1.7	9.3	0.9	74.0
Bishop Rancheria, California	492	50.2	43.9	-	1.8	19.4	2.9	56.1
Inyo County	492	50.2	43.9	-	1.8	19.4	2.9	56.1
Blackfeet Reservation, Montana	3,478	54.2	48.2	2.9	2.7	28.6	3.8	49.9
Glacier County	3,129	54.0	47.9	3.2	2.8	27.8	3.5	50.7

[Continued]

422

Geographic Mobility on Identified Reservations, 1980 - I

[Continued]

Identified reservation	Persons 3 to 34 years old					Persons 16 to 19 years old -- percent not enrolled in school, not high school graduates	Persons 25 years and over	
	All persons	Percent enrolled in school					Percent completed less than 5 years of school	Percent high school graduates
		Total	5 to 19 years		20 to 34 years old			
			Total	Bureau of indian affairs or tribal school				
Pondera County	349	55.5	50.4	-	1.4	35.4	6.9	41.4
Bois Forte Reservation (Nett Lake), Minnesota	270	61.1	51.5	4.3	0.7	40.8	4.1	40.5
Koochiching County	42	59.5	50.0	-	2.4	40.0	-	44.8
St. Louis County	228	61.4	51.8	5.1	0.4	40.9	5.0	39.5
Bridgeport Colony, California	31	57.6	53.7	20.2	3.9	28.3	17.0	43.5
Mono County	31	57.6	53.7	20.2	3.9	28.3	17.0	43.5
Brighton Reservation, Florida	205	60.7	49.1	1.1	1.1	29.3	44.4	35.7
Glades County	205	60.7	49.1	1.1	1.1	29.3	44.4	35.7
Burns Reservation, Oregon	97	57.7	47.4	8.7	2.1	33.3	6.8	32.9
Harney County	97	57.7	47.4	8.7	2.1	33.3	6.8	32.9
Cabazon Reservation, California	...	...	...	...	...	...	...	...
Riverside County	...	...	...	...	...	...	...	...
Cachil Dehe Rancheria, California	...	...	...	...	...	...	...	...
Colusa County	...	...	...	...	...	...	...	...
Cahuilla Reservation, California	...	...	...	...	...	...	...	...
Riverside County	...	...	...	...	...	...	...	...
Campo Reservation, California	47	56.4	56.4	-	-	51.0	22.7	28.0
San Diego County	47	56.4	56.4	-	-	51.0	22.7	28.0
Camp Verde Reservation, Arizona	107	58.9	49.5	1.9	3.7	43.8	5.6	40.8
Yavapai County	107	58.9	49.5	1.9	3.7	43.8	5.6	40.8
Canoncito Reservation, New Mexico	682	54.0	49.5	65.7	2.3	21.3	43.6	28.4
Bernalillo County	595	53.9	49.0	66.7	2.4	19.0	42.4	29.7
Sandoval County	-	-	-	-	-	-	-	-
Valencia County	87	54.3	52.9	59.3	1.3	39.5	52.4	19.6
Capitan Grande Reservation, California	-	-	-	-	-	-	-	-
San Diego County	-	-	-	-	-	-	-	-
Carson Colony, Nevada	140	43.1	41.3	-	1.8	8.5	6.8	50.7
Carson City	140	43.1	41.3	-	1.8	8.5	6.8	50.7
Catawba Reservation, South Carolina	644	47.9	42.1	1.3	5.0	26.0	11.5	35.7
York County	644	47.9	42.1	1.3	5.0	26.0	11.5	35.7
Cattaraugus Reservation, New York	1,092	59.4	51.4	1.5	2.5	25.9	2.4	51.7
Cattaragus County	222	58.0	49.9	1.0	2.5	34.4	3.2	47.8
Chautauqua County	...	...	...	...	...	...	...	...
Erie County	864	60.2	52.1	1.6	2.5	23.9	2.2	52.8
Cedarville Rancheria, California	...	...	...	...	...	...	...	...
Modoc County	...	...	...	...	...	...	...	...
Chehalis Reservation, Washington	129	62.8	44.2	3.6	9.7	34.5	4.4	52.7
Grays Harbor County	112	62.8	44.3	4.2	10.2	28.8	5.0	48.1
Thurston County	...	...	...	...	...	...	...	...
Chemehuevi Rerservation, California	...	...	...	...	...	...	...	...
San Bernardino County	...	...	...	...	...	...	...	...
Cheyenne River Reservation, South Dakota	997	57.4	50.0	83.8	3.0	38.8	2.2	40.9
Dewey County	496	57.2	50.6	80.0	2.3	32.2	1.8	49.2
Ziebach County	501	57.7	49.5	87.6	3.7	45.0	2.5	32.8
Chitimacha Reservation, Louisiana	114	53.6	51.4	50.8	2.2	49.7	23.8	36.7

[Continued]

★ 230 ★

Geographic Mobility on Identified Reservations, 1980 - I
[Continued]

Identified reservation	All persons	Persons 3 to 34 years old				Persons 16 to 19 years old -- percent not enrolled in school, not high school graduates	Persons 25 years and over	
			Percent enrolled in school					
		Total	5 to 19 years		20 to 34 years old		Percent completed less than 5 years of school	Percent high school graduates
			Total	Bureau of indian affairs or tribal school				
St. Mary Parish	114	53.6	51.4	50.8	2.2	49.7	23.8	36.7
Cochiti Pueblo, New Mexico	362	67.0	58.0	14.8	3.2	8.8	6.9	63.3
Sandoval County	362	67.0	58.0	14.8	3.2	8.8	6.9	63.3
Cocopah Reservation, Arizona	236	55.1	47.8	10.7	3.8	33.3	40.9	18.1
Yuma County	236	55.1	47.8	10.7	3.8	33.3	40.9	18.1
Coeur d'Alene Reservation, Idaho	363	59.0	52.7	42.6	2.7	23.1	4.2	57.0
Benewah County	275	55.7	49.5	48.0	2.9	29.4	2.4	63.3
Kootenai County	88	69.3	62.7	29.3	2.2	-	8.5	42.4
Cold Springs Rancheria, California	36	48.5	48.5	-	-	23.1	14.0	15.2
Fresno County	36	48.5	48.5	-	-	23.1	14.0	15.2
Colorado River Reservation, Arizona-California	1,246	54.1	47.3	4.8	2.8	30.2	4.2	52.4
Arizona	1,230	54.0	47.1	4.9	2.8	30.2	4.3	52.0
Yuma County	1,230	54.0	47.1	4.9	2.8	30.2	4.3	52.0
California	...	...	...	...	...	...	...	...
Riverside and San Bernardino Counties	...	...	...	...	...	...	...	...
Colville Reservation, Washington	2,298	52.2	46.4	9.2	3.5	28.9	3.7	56.2
Ferry County	547	53.6	48.4	5.7	1.5	18.3	3.3	51.4
Okanogan County	1,751	51.8	45.7	10.3	4.1	32.8	3.8	57.9
Cortina Rancheria, California	...	...	...	...	...	...	...	...
Colusa County	...	...	...	...	...	...	...	...
Coushatta Reservation, Louisiana	...	...	...	...	...	...	...	...
Allen Parish	...	...	...	...	...	...	...	...
Coyote Valley Rancheria, California	-	-	-	-	-	-	-	-
Mendocino County	-	-	-	-	-	-	-	-
Crow Reservation, Montana	2,580	54.9	47.8	5.0	3.4	24.1	2.5	52.1
Big Horn County	2,504	54.5	47.2	4.9	3.5	25.0	2.5	51.6
Yellowstone County	76	67.5	67.5	8.2	-	-	-	70.8
Crow Creek Reservation, South Dakota	997	56.5	51.2	54.4	1.0	28.1	1.4	43.4
Buffalo County	835	54.3	50.2	60.2	0.7	30.0	1.4	45.8
Hughes County	118	67.5	55.2	18.9	2.1	-	2.1	25.1
Hyde County	44	68.3	59.8	50.2	3.2	36.9	-	50.0
Cuyapaipe Reservation, California	...	...	...	...	...	...	...	...
San Diego County	...	...	...	...	...	...	...	...
Deer Creek Reservation, Minnesota	...	...	...	...	...	...	...	...
Itasca County	...	...	...	...	...	...	...	...
Dresslerville Colony, Nevada	89	52.4	43.6	6.9	-	33.0	8.9	77.0
Douglas County	89	52.4	43.6	6.9	-	33.0	8.9	77.0
Dry Creek Rancheria, California	28	57.1	50.0	7.1	3.6	57.1	10.5	26.3
Sonoma County	28	57.1	50.0	7.1	3.6	57.1	10.5	26.3
Duck Valley Reservation, Idaho-Nevada	563	60.1	54.3	2.3	2.0	9.2	8.9	47.1
Idaho	121	63.9	58.2	3.5	1.2	28.3	20.2	27.7
Owyhee County	121	63.9	58.2	3.5	1.2	28.3	20.2	27.7
Nevada	442	59.0	53.2	1.9	2.3	3.7	6.4	51.4
Elko County	442	59.0	53.2	1.9	2.3	3.7	6.4	51.4
Duckwater Reservation, Nevada	64	54.0	41.3	57.7	1.6	-	14.9	40.4

[Continued]

★ 230 ★

Geographic Mobility on Identified Reservations, 1980 - I
[Continued]

Identified reservation	Persons 3 to 34 years old					Persons 16 to 19 years old -- percent not enrolled in school, not high school graduates	Persons 25 years and over	
		Percent enrolled in school					Percent completed less than 5 years of school	Percent high school graduates
			5 to 19 years		20 to 34 years old			
	All persons	Total	Total	Bureau of indian affairs or tribal school				
Nye County	64	54.0	41.3	57.7	1.6	-	14.9	40.4
Eastern Cherokee Reservation, North Carolina	2,958	53.8	46.9	73.1	3.1	35.1	7.6	43.2
Cherokee County	33	53.9	44.5	-	9.4	25.4	1.9	34.9
Graham County	215	52.2	47.5	-	3.7	57.1	13.4	21.6
Haywood County	-	-	-	-	-	-	-	-
Jackson County	1,319	55.7	47.1	77.3	3.7	35.5	7.7	44.1
Swain County	1,392	52.4	46.6	82.1	2.3	32.0	7.0	45.9
Eastern Pequot Reservation, Connecticut	...	...	...	...	...	...	...	...
New London County	...	...	...	...	...	...	...	...
Ely Colony, Nevada	35	56.2	56.2	6.2	-	100.0	10.6	63.6
White Pine County	35	56.2	56.2	6.2	-	100.0	10.6	63.6
Enterprise Rancheria, California	...	...	...	...	...	...	...	...
Butte County	...	...	...	...	...	...	...	...
Fallon Colony, Nevada	24	57.1	57.1	-	-	59.2	19.8	43.4
Churchill County	24	57.1	57.1	-	-	59.2	19.8	43.4
Fallon Reservation, Nevada	156	66.4	57.2	1.4	5.1	5.8	5.7	63.5
Churchill County	156	66.4	57.2	1.4	5.1	5.8	5.7	63.5
Flandreau Reservation, South Dakota	112	57.7	48.7	15.0	4.5	29.8	3.2	77.6
Moody County	112	57.7	48.7	15.0	4.5	29.8	3.2	77.6
Flathead Reservation, Montana	2,361	49.7	45.7	3.8	2.7	25.2	4.4	57.0
Flathead County	...	...	...	...	...	...	...	...
Lake County	1,968	49.1	45.2	2.7	2.6	25.9	4.2	57.3
Missoula County	181	60.5	54.9	8.2	4.5	15.4	6.4	52.0
Sanders County	210	46.2	43.3	9.9	2.4	27.6	4.4	58.9
Fond du Lac Reservation, Minnesota	318	58.7	51.8	2.9	3.3	19.1	2.6	49.8
Carlton County	261	63.3	54.9	3.3	4.0	15.6	2.2	48.7
St. Louis County	57	38.0	38.0	-	-	34.3	5.6	57.1
Fort Apache Reservation, Arizona	4,702	54.7	49.9	15.5	1.8	29.1	4.5	34.1
Apache County	77	54.8	43.0	-	4.1	18.8	16.8	41.3
Gila County	826	54.5	50.2	12.3	2.2	30.7	3.0	31.6
Navajo County	3,799	54.8	49.9	16.5	1.6	29.0	4.6	34.5
Fort Belknap Reservation, Montana	1,255	56.2	48.7	4.4	3.9	22.3	2.6	53.1
Blaine County	1,158	56.5	48.7	4.7	4.0	22.7	2.7	53.2
Phillips County	97	52.7	49.4	-	3.3	18.0	1.6	52.4
Fort Berthold Reservation, North Dakota	1,726	57.0	50.9	6.5	3.1	25.9	4.6	53.3
Dunn County	271	55.2	48.9	3.4	2.9	9.4	7.3	47.7
McKenzie County	566	60.3	53.9	2.0	4.2	26.8	5.8	55.0
McLean County	280	57.5	50.3	18.7	1.2	22.9	1.3	62.2
Mercer County	35	48.6	45.5	13.6	-	-	3.4	39.7
Mountrail County	574	54.9	49.3	6.4	3.4	34.1	4.0	51.2
Ward County	-	-	-	-	-	-	-	-

Source: U.S. Bureau of the Census, Subject Reports, PC80-2-1D, Part 1, *American Indians, Eskimos, and Aleuts on Identified Reservations and in the Historic Areas of Oklahoma (Excluding Urbanized Areas)*, U.S. Government Printing Office, Washington, D.C., 1986, pp. 50-58. *Notes:* A dash "(-)" represents zero or a percent which rounds to less than 0.1. Also, a dash "(-)" is used because the number of supplementary questionnaires for the reservations was insufficient to produce reliable estimates. Three dots "..." means not applicable, or that the data are being withheld to avoid disclosure of information for individuals.

★ 231 ★

Geographic Mobility on Identified Reservations, 1980 - II

Data are the latest available.

Identified reservation	Persons 1 year and over						
	Total	Always lived on this reservation	Did not always live on this reservation				
			Total		Percent moved onto reservation in--		
					1979 or 1980	1975 to 1978	1974 or earlier
			Number	Percent			
Total persons	326,430	226,391	75,363	23.1	6.2	6.6	10.3
Acoma Pueblo, New Mexico	2,203	1,985	164	7.4	1.4	2.8	3.3
Valencia County	2,203	1,985	164	7.4	1.4	2.8	3.3
Agua Caliente Reservation, California	-	-	-	-	-	-	-
Riverside County	-	-	-	-	-	-	-
Alabama-Coushatta Reservation, Texas	490	365	118	24.0	1.2	7.6	15.2
Polk County	490	365	118	24.0	1.2	7.6	15.2
Alamo Reservation, New Mexico	1,027	587	35	3.4	1.4	1.2	0.9
Socorro County	1,027	587	35	3.4	1.4	1.2	0.9
Allegany Reservation, New York	907	567	286	31.5	9.5	9.4	12.5
Cattaraugus County	907	567	286	31.5	9.5	9.4	12.5
Alturas Rancheria, California	...	...	...	...	...	...	...
Modoc County	...	...	...	...	...	...	...
Annette Islands Reserve, Alaska	922	662	199	21.6	2.8	5.2	13.6
Prince of Wales-Outer Ketchikan Census Area	922	662	199	21.6	2.8	5.2	13.6
Augustine Reservation, California	-	-	-	-	-	-	-
Riverside County	-	-	-	-	-	-	-
Bad River Reservation, Wisconsin	684	224	455	66.6	13.2	29.1	24.3
Ashland County	684	224	455	66.6	13.2	29.1	24.3
Iron County	-	-	-	-	-	-	-
Barona Rancheria, California	213	135	77	36.3	8.3	17.5	10.4
San Diego County	213	135	77	36.3	8.3	17.5	10.4
Bay Mills Reservation, Michigan	269	160	108	39.9	5.2	13.3	21.4
Chippewa County	269	160	108	39.9	5.2	13.3	21.4
Benton Paiute Reservation, California	...	...	...	...	...	...	...
Mono County	...	...	...	...	...	...	...
Berry Creek Rancheria, California	-	-	-	-	-	-	-
Butte County	-	-	-	-	-	-	-
Big Bend Rancheria, California	...	...	...	...	...	...	...
Shasta County	...	...	...	...	...	...	...
Big Cypress Reservation, Florida	343	249	94	27.2	1.8	8.0	17.5
Hendry County	343	249	94	27.2	1.8	8.0	17.5
Big Lagoon Rancheria, California	...	...	...	...	...	...	...
Humboldt County	...	...	...	...	...	...	...
Big Pine Rancheria, California	262	31	220	84.2	42.6	9.5	32.1
Inyo County	262	31	220	84.2	42.6	9.5	32.1
Bishop Rancheria, California	757	338	395	52.2	12.7	14.7	24.8
Inyo County	757	338	395	52.2	12.7	14.7	24.8
Blackfeet Reservation, Montana	5,358	4,029	902	16.8	4.1	5.5	7.2
Glacier County	4,847	3,622	859	17.7	4.4	5.7	7.7
Pondera County	511	407	43	8.3	1.4	4.0	2.9
Bois Forte Reservation (Nett Lake), Minnesota	393	270	117	29.8	14.0	3.6	12.2
Koochiching County	62	46	16	25.8	16.1	-	9.7
St. Louis County	331	224	101	30.5	13.6	4.2	12.7
Bridgeport Colony, California	50	1	49	97.5	97.5	-	-
Mono County	50	1	49	97.5	97.5	-	-
Brighton Reservation, Florida	325	239	66	20.4	1.7	9.2	9.5
Glades County	325	239	66	20.4	1.7	9.2	9.5

[Continued]

★ 231 ★

Geographic Mobility on Identified Reservations, 1980 - II
[Continued]

Identified reservation	Persons 1 year and over						
	Total	Always lived on this reservation	Did not always live on this reservation				
			Total		Percent moved onto reservation in--		
			Number	Percent	1979 or 1980	1975 to 1978	1974 or earlier
Burns Reservation, Oregon	158	78	80	50.6	15.8	21.5	13.3
Harney County	158	78	80	50.6	15.8	21.5	13.3
Cabazon Reservation, California	...	...	...	...	...	...	...
Riverside County	...	...	...	...	...	...	...
Cachil Dehe Rancheria, California	...	...	...	...	...	...	...
Colusa County	...	...	...	...	...	...	...
Cahuilla Reservation, California	...	...	...	...	...	...	...
Riverside County	...	...	...	...	...	...	...
Campo Reservation, California	83	36	45	53.9	10.3	17.1	26.5
San Diego County	83	36	45	53.9	10.3	17.1	26.5
Camp Verde Reservation, Arizona	173	97	64	37.0	1.7	25.4	9.8
Yavapai County	173	97	64	37.0	1.7	25.4	9.8
Canoncito Reservation, New Mexico	935	823	99	10.6	4.5	2.4	3.6
Bernalillo County	811	716	86	10.6	4.7	2.6	3.3
Sandoval County	-	-	-	-	-	-	-
Valencia County	124	107	13	10.5	3.3	1.1	6.1
Capitan Grande Reservation, California	-	-	-	-	-	-	-
San Diego County	-	-	-	-	-	-	-
Carson Colony, Nevada	211	67	144	68.3	9.4	24.9	34.0
Carson City	211	67	144	68.3	9.4	24.9	34.0
Catawba Reservation, South Carolina	966	80	311	32.2	26.6	3.3	2.4
York County	966	80	311	32.2	26.6	3.3	2.4
Cattaraugus Reservation, New York	1,806	1,193	455	25.2	3.6	8.0	13.5
Cattaragus County	331	270	43	13.1	3.0	6.0	4.1
Chautauqua County	...	...	...	...	...	...	...
Erie County	1,465	916	412	28.1	3.8	8.5	15.8
Cedarville Rancheria, California	...	...	...	...	...	...	...
Modoc County	...	...	...	...	...	...	...
Chehalis Reservation, Washington	192	82	109	56.6	8.7	27.4	20.5
Grays Harbor County	170	75	94	55.4	8.0	26.1	21.3
Thurston County	...	...	...	...	...	...	...
Chemehuevi Rerservation, California	...	...	...	...	...	...	...
San Bernardino County	...	...	...	...	...	...	...
Cheyenne River Reservation, South Dakota	1,463	1,186	256	17.5	8.0	3.8	5.7
Dewey County	715	548	165	23.1	10.6	6.9	5.7
Ziebach County	748	637	90	12.1	5.6	0.8	5.7
Chitimacha Reservation, Louisiana	176	107	55	31.4	6.5	8.1	16.8
St. Mary Parish	176	107	55	31.4	6.5	8.1	16.8
Cochiti Pueblo, New Mexico	596	444	152	25.5	3.3	10.0	12.2
Sandoval County	596	444	152	25.5	3.3	10.0	12.2
Cocopah Reservation, Arizona	342	179	153	44.8	7.7	9.4	27.7
Yuma County	342	179	153	44.8	7.7	9.4	27.7
Coeur d'Alene Reservation, Idaho	549	207	296	54.0	13.7	16.1	24.2
Benewah County	402	149	221	54.9	12.7	19.8	22.4
Kootenai County	147	58	75	51.5	16.4	5.9	29.1
Cold Springs Rancheria, California	62	45	16	25.8	1.5	12.2	12.2
Fresno County	62	45	16	25.8	1.5	12.2	12.2
Colorado River Reservation, Arizona-California	1,885	847	736	39.0	12.7	7.6	18.7

[Continued]

427

★ 231 ★

Geographic Mobility on Identified Reservations, 1980 - II

[Continued]

Identified reservation	Persons 1 year and over						
	Total	Always lived on this reservation	Did not always live on this reservation		Percent moved onto reservation in--		
			Total		1979 or 1980	1975 to 1978	1974 or earlier
			Number	Percent			
Arizona	1,858	837	719	38.7	12.6	7.2	18.9
Yuma County	1,858	837	719	38.7	12.6	7.2	18.9
California	...	...	...	...	...	...	...
Riverside and San Bernardino Counties	...	...	...	...	...	...	...
Colville Reservation, Washington	3,481	1,723	1,714	49.2	12.7	15.2	21.4
Ferry County	884	454	423	47.9	7.1	16.2	24.5
Okanogan County	2,597	1,269	1,291	49.7	14.6	14.9	20.3
Cortina Rancheria, California	...	...	...	...	...	...	...
Colusa County	...	...	...	...	...	...	...
Coushatta Reservation, Louisiana	...	...	...	...	...	...	...
Allen Parish	...	...	...	...	...	...	...
Coyote Valley Rancheria, California	-	-	-	-	-	-	-
Mendocino County	-	-	-	-	-	-	-
Crow Reservation, Montana	3,833	2,706	996	26.0	8.9	6.5	10.6
Big Horn County	3,721	2,656	934	25.1	8.4	6.4	10.4
Yellowstone County	112	50	62	55.3	26.7	10.5	18.1
Crow Creek Reservation, South Dakota	1,449	981	414	28.6	7.4	7.6	13.5
Buffalo County	1,222	852	317	25.9	8.2	6.2	11.4
Hughes County	165	90	75	45.3	4.2	12.0	29.1
Hyde County	61	39	22	36.1	-	23.3	12.8
Cuyapaipe Reservation, California	...	...	...	...	...	...	...
San Diego County	...	...	...	...	...	...	...
Deer Creek Reservation, Minnesota	...	...	...	...	...	...	...
Itasca County	...	...	...	...	...	...	...
Dresslerville Colony, Nevada	122	82	39	32.3	9.0	7.7	15.6
Douglas County	122	82	39	32.3	9.0	7.7	15.6
Dry Creek Rancheria, California	43	19	24	55.8	27.9	2.3	25.6
Sonoma County	43	19	24	55.8	27.9	2.3	25.6
Duck Valley Reservation, Idaho-Nevada	909	604	283	31.1	8.6	7.5	14.9
Idaho	184	120	45	24.5	3.6	2.9	18.1
Owyhee County	184	120	45	24.5	3.6	2.9	18.1
Nevada	725	484	238	32.7	9.9	8.7	14.1
Elko County	725	484	238	32.7	9.9	8.7	14.1
duckwater Reservation, Nevada	102	33	69	67.3	23.8	15.8	27.7
Nye County	102	33	69	67.3	23.8	15.8	27.7
Eastern Cherokee Reservation, North Carolina	4,726	3,718	960	20.3	3.1	5.4	11.8
Cherokee County	76	27	45	58.8	3.8	41.8	13.2
Graham County	338	282	55	16.2	1.4	6.2	8.6
Haywood County	-	-	-	-	-	-	-
Jackson County	2,083	1,667	403	19.4	2.4	5.8	11.2
Swain County	2,229	1,741	457	20.5	3.9	3.8	12.8
Eastern Pequot Reservation, Connecticut	...	...	...	...	...	...	...
New London County	...	...	...	...	...	...	...
Ely Colony, Nevada	59	3	56	95.6	4.5	80.3	10.8
White Pine County	59	3	56	95.6	4.5	80.3	10.8
Enterprise Rancheria, California	...	...	...	...	...	...	...
Butte County	...	...	...	...	...	...	...
Fallon Colony, Nevada	46	14	32	70.6	21.1	-	49.5

[Continued]

★ 231 ★

Geographic Mobility on Identified Reservations, 1980 - II
[Continued]

Identified reservation	Persons 1 year and over						
	Total	Always lived on this reservation	Did not always live on this reservation				
			Total		Percent moved onto reservation in--		
			Number	Percent	1979 or 1980	1975 to 1978	1974 or earlier
Churchill County	46	14	32	70.6	21.1	-	49.5
Fallon Reservation, Nevada	257	93	155	60.5	17.0	12.6	30.9
Churchill County	257	93	155	60.5	17.0	12.6	30.9
Flandreau Reservation, South Dakota	158	38	120	75.8	32.6	23.1	20.1
Moody County	158	38	120	75.8	32.6	23.1	20.1
Flathead Reservation, Montana	3,528	1,462	1,484	42.1	9.9	11.6	20.5
Flathead County	...	...	...	...	...	...	...
Lake County	2,892	1,202	1,183	40.9	9.6	11.3	20.0
Missoula County	285	87	142	49.7	13.9	12.2	23.6
Sanders County	347	170	158	45.5	9.2	13.8	22.5
Fond du Lac Reservation, Minnesota	493	286	181	36.6	7.9	12.9	15.8
Carlton County	417	238	152	36.6	8.2	12.7	15.7
St. Louis County	76	48	28	36.9	6.2	14.1	16.6
Fort Apache Reservation, Arizona	6,653	5,560	651	9.8	4.1	2.4	3.3
Apache County	107	51	50	46.7	4.8	16.6	25.3
Gila County	1,191	1,036	68	5.7	3.0	0.4	2.4
Navajo County	5,354	4,473	533	10.0	4.3	2.5	3.1
Fort Belknap Reservation, Montana	1,820	1,026	586	32.2	6.6	13.6	12.0
Blaine County	1,664	931	549	33.0	6.6	14.6	11.7
Phillips County	156	95	37	23.8	5.7	2.6	15.5
Fort Berthold Reservation, North Dakota	2,542	1,602	798	31.4	10.9	9.6	10.8
dunn County	413	250	147	35.6	10.2	7.2	18.1
McKenzie County	804	557	245	30.5	10.2	11.8	8.5
McLean County	421	308	106	25.1	8.0	5.3	11.8
Mercer County	51	28	23	44.6	27.8	14.5	2.3
Mountrail County	854	459	278	32.6	12.5	10.6	9.5
Ward County	-	-	-	-	-	-	-

Source: U.S. Bureau of the Census, Subject Reports, PC80-2-1D, Part 1, *American Indians, Eskimos, and Aleuts on Identified Reservations and in the Historic Areas of Oklahoma (Excluding Urbanized Areas),* U.S. Government Printing Office, Washington, D.C., 1986, pp. 50-58. *Notes:* A dash "(-)" represents zero or a percent which rounds to less than 0.1. Also, a dash "(-)" is used because the number of supplementary questionnaires for the reservations was insufficient to produce reliable estimates. Three dots "..." means not applicable, or that the data are being withheld to avoid disclosure of information for individuals.

★ 232 ★

Geographic Mobility on Identified Reservations, 1980 - III

Data are the latest available.

Identified reservation	Persons 3 to 34 years old					Persons 16 to 19 years old -- percent not enrolled in school, not high school graduates	Persons 25 years and over	
	All persons	Percent enrolled in school					Percent completed less than 5 years of school	Percent high school graduates
		Total	5 to 19 years		20 to 34 years old			
			Total	Bureau of indian affairs or tribal school				
Fort Bidwell Reservation, California	52	58.4	48.3	4.1	6.0	25.0	2.7	62.5
Modoc County	52	58.4	48.3	4.1	6.0	25.0	2.7	62.5
Fort Hall Reservation, Idaho	1,583	53.7	49.1	7.3	1.9	26.0	10.4	39.5
Bannock County	450	51.5	46.8	10.5	2.0	27.2	10.7	37.8
Bingham County	1,032	54.8	50.2	6.5	1.9	25.9	9.1	40.5
Caribou County	-	-	-	-	-	-	-	-
Power County	101	51.5	48.1	2.2	2.3	22.9	21.9	36.4
Fort Independence Reservation, California	13	42.3	42.3	-	-	-	24.3	51.1
Inyo County	13	42.3	42.3	-	-	-	24.3	51.1
Fort McDermitt Reservation, Nevada-Oregon	318	58.4	51.7	2.7	1.8	18.8	6.9	28.9
Nevada	318	58.4	51.7	2.7	1.8	18.8	6.9	28.9
Humboldt County	318	58.4	51.7	2.7	1.8	18.8	6.9	28.9
Oregon	-	-	-	-	-	-	-	-
Malheur County	-	-	-	-	-	-	-	-
Fort McDowell Reservation, Arizona	215	41.3	37.5	19.7	1.1	42.9	11.3	48.3
Maricopa County	215	41.3	37.5	19.7	1.1	42.9	11.3	48.3
Fort Mojave Reservation, Arizona-California-Nevada	81	54.3	50.6	9.8	3.7	21.4	-	50.0
Arizona	81	54.3	50.6	9.8	3.7	21.4	-	50.0
Mohave County	81	54.3	50.6	9.8	3.7	21.4	-	50.0
California	-	-	-	-	-	-	-	-
San Bernardino County	-	-	-	-	-	-	-	-
Nevada	-	-	-	-	-	-	-	-
Clark County	-	-	-	-	-	-	-	-
Fort Peck Reservation, Montana	2,823	53.6	47.7	3.3	2.3	34.3	3.2	51.1
Daniels County	-	-	-	-	-	-	-	-
Roosevelt County	2,498	53.1	47.2	3.4	2.4	35.6	3.4	51.2
Sheridan County	-	-	-	-	-	-	-	-
Valley County	325	57.4	51.5	2.6	1.2	25.8	1.2	49.8
Fort Totten Reservation, North Dakota	1,496	58.1	49.9	55.1	3.2	39.8	3.8	38.7
Benson County	1,496	58.1	49.9	55.1	3.2	39.8	3.5	39.2
Eddy County	...	...	...	...	...	...	...	...
Nelson County	-	-	-	-	-	-	-	-
Ramsey County	...	...	...	...	...	...	...	...
Fort Yuma Reservation, Arizona-California	651	54.5	48.1	2.2	1.1	40.3	10.4	42.9
Arizona	67	47.3	43.2	-	-	83.1	39.4	10.3
Yuma County	67	47.3	43.2	-	-	83.1	39.4	10.3
California	584	55.3	48.7	2.4	1.2	37.2	4.7	49.3
Imperial County	584	55.3	48.7	2.4	1.2	37.2	4.7	49.3
Gila Bend Reservation, Arizona	-	-	-	-	-	-	-	-
Maricopa County	-	-	-	-	-	-	-	-
Gila River Reservation, Arizona	4,529	51.1	44.9	19.6	3.2	40.2	5.7	38.3
Maricopa County	1,310	51.1	44.9	22.6	2.6	39.7	5.6	40.2
Pinal County	3,219	51.1	44.9	18.3	3.4	40.4	5.8	37.5
Golden Hill Reservation, Connecticut	...	...	...	...	...	...	...	...
Fairfield County	...	...	...	...	...	...	...	...
Goshute Reservation, Nevada-Utah	46	29.5	29.5	-	-	100.0	48.1	19.3

[Continued]

★ 232 ★

Geographic Mobility on Identified Reservations, 1980 - III
[Continued]

Identified reservation	Persons 3 to 34 years old					Persons 16 to 19 years old -- percent not enrolled in school, not high school graduates	Persons 25 years and over	
	All persons	Percent enrolled in school					Percent completed less than 5 years of school	Percent high school graduates
		Total	5 to 19 years		20 to 34 years old			
			Total	Bureau of indian affairs or tribal school				
Nevada	...	...	...	...	...	...	...	...
White Pine County	...	...	...	...	...	...	...	...
Utah	31	18.2	18.2	-	-	-	57.9	15.8
Juab and Tooele Counties	31	18.2	18.2	-	-	-	57.9	15.8
Grand Portage Reservation, Minnesota	113	48.5	42.2	-	2.5	34.3	3.3	66.9
Cook County	113	48.5	42.2	-	2.5	34.3	3.3	66.9
Grindstone Creek Rancheria, California	42	54.0	40.6	-	8.3	74.8	4.8	33.2
Glenn County	42	54.0	40.6	-	8.3	74.8	4.8	33.2
Hannahville Community, Michigan	145	55.7	43.6	64.3	-	54.2	2.3	43.6
Menominee County	145	55.7	43.6	64.3	-	54.2	2.3	43.6
Hassanamisco Reservation, Massachusetts	...	...	...	...	...	...	...	...
Worcester County	...	...	...	...	...	...	...	...
Havasupai Reservation, Arizona	173	45.1	40.9	70.9	1.2	41.4	7.0	26.7
Coconino County	173	45.1	40.9	70.9	1.2	41.4	7.0	26.7
Hoh Reservation, Washington	29	38.7	34.4	12.4	-	78.9	-	29.9
Jefferson County	29	38.7	34.4	12.4	-	78.9	-	29.9
Hollywood Reservation, Florida	278	54.0	42.5	12.4	3.8	29.3	20.7	63.5
Broward County	278	54.0	42.5	12.4	3.8	29.3	20.7	63.5
Hoopa Valley Reservation, California	947	53.8	46.1	2.0	3.7	21.2	2.4	56.0
Humboldt County	947	53.8	46.1	2.0	3.7	21.2	2.4	56.0
Hoopa Valley Extension Reservation, California	236	50.7	48.0	-	0.5	20.0	2.1	41.2
Del Norte County	91	51.9	46.2	-	1.3	-	1.3	48.0
Humboldt County	145	50.0	49.2	-	-	28.2	2.6	36.9
Hopi Reservation, Arizona	4,007	57.5	50.2	56.1	3.3	15.1	21.0	41.7
Coconino County	771	62.4	52.7	40.5	4.9	11.9	33.0	32.5
Navajo County	3,237	56.3	49.6	60.0	2.9	16.0	18.1	43.9
Hopland Rancheria, California	-	-	-	-	-	-	-	-
Mendocino County	-	-	-	-	-	-	-	-
Hualapai Reservation, Arizona	557	52.6	42.8	15.4	2.5	15.6	2.1	53.1
Coconino and Mohave Counties	554	52.6	42.7	15.6	2.6	14.8	2.1	53.0
Yavapai County	...	...	...	...	...	...	...	...
Inaja-Cosmit Reservation, California	-	-	-	-	-	-	-	-
San Diego County	-	-	-	-	-	-	-	-
Indian Township Reservation, Maine	223	57.1	53.1	63.4	1.1	45.9	5.2	39.3
Washington County	223	57.1	53.1	63.4	1.1	45.9	5.2	39.3
Iowa Reservation, Kansas-Nebraska	24	36.1	32.0	-	4.1	-	-	41.9
Kansas	...	...	...	...	...	...	...	...
Brown County	...	...	...	...	...	...	...	...
Doniphan County	-	-	-	-	-	-	-	-
Nebraska	...	...	...	...	...	...	...	...
Richardson County	...	...	...	...	...	...	...	...
Isabella Reservation, Michigan	331	50.7	45.3	-	1.6	42.5	4.7	39.5
Isabella County	331	50.7	45.3	-	1.6	42.5	4.7	39.5
Isleta Pueblo, New Mexico	1,402	54.2	48.0	41.9	3.4	12.3	5.2	57.2
Bernalillo County	1,089	53.8	46.3	45.0	3.9	12.2	5.6	55.8
Torrance County	-	-	-	-	-	-	-	-

[Continued]

★ 232 ★

Geographic Mobility on Identified Reservations, 1980 - III

[Continued]

Identified reservation	Persons 3 to 34 years old					Persons 16 to 19 years old -- percent not enrolled in school, not high school graduates	Persons 25 years and over	
	All persons	Percent enrolled in school					Percent completed less than 5 years of school	Percent high school graduates
		Total	5 to 19 years		20 to 34 years old			
			Total	Bureau of indian affairs or tribal school				
Valencia County	313	55.9	53.5	32.3	1.5	12.7	3.4	62.3
Jackson Rancheria, California	...	...	...	...	...	...	...	...
Amador County	...	...	...	...	...	...	...	...
Jemez Pueblo, New Mexico	977	59.9	52.0	34.2	3.1	16.3	5.8	50.1
Sandoval County	977	59.9	52.0	34.2	3.1	16.3	5.8	50.1
Jicarilla Apache Reservation, New Mexico	1,161	50.1	45.7	7.5	2.1	24.1	9.7	55.5
Rio Arriba and Sandoval Counties	1,161	50.1	45.7	7.5	2.1	24.1	9.7	55.5
Kaibab Reservation, Arizona	63	46.6	41.6	7.8	3.4	24.7	16.1	61.2
Coconino County	-	-	-	-	-	-	-	-
Mohave County	63	46.6	41.6	7.8	3.4	24.7	16.1	61.2
Kalispel Reservation, Washington	73	49.3	45.2	-	-	73.3	11.4	48.6
Pend Oreille County	73	49.3	45.2	-	-	73.3	11.4	48.6
Kickapoo Reservation, Kansas	219	64.5	56.4	-	4.9	8.6	3.8	50.3
Brown County	219	64.5	56.4	-	4.9	8.6	3.8	50.3
Kootenai Reservation, Idaho	-	-	-	-	-	-	-	-
Boundary County	-	-	-	-	-	-	-	-
Lac Courte Oreilles Reservation, Wisconsin	730	60.7	51.1	42.1	3.7	26.3	2.7	50.2
Sawyer County	730	60.7	51.1	42.1	3.7	26.3	2.7	50.2
Lac du Flambeau Reservation, Wisconsin	696	62.2	56.8	1.5	2.2	27.2	0.4	44.3
Iron County	-	-	-	-	-	-	-	-
Oneida County	-	-	-	-	-	-	-	-
Vilas County	696	62.2	56.8	1.5	2.2	27.2	0.4	44.3
Laguna Pueblo, New Mexico	2,164	47.2	41.0	50.1	2.1	31.7	5.1	62.0
Bernalillo and Valencia Counties	2,164	47.2	41.0	50.1	2.1	31.7	5.1	62.0
Sandoval County	-	-	-	-	-	-	-	-
La Jolla Reservation, California	88	66.1	54.9	4.5	2.6	12.4	2.0	56.1
San Diego County	88	66.1	54.9	4.5	2.6	12.4	2.0	56.1
L'Anse Reservation, Michigan	373	63.7	56.0	2.8	5.1	15.3	3.0	42.1
Baraga County	373	63.7	56.0	2.8	5.1	15.3	3.0	42.1
La Posta Reservation, California	...	...	...	...	...	...	...	...
San Diego County	...	...	...	...	...	...	...	...
Las Vegas Colony, Nevada	66	46.2	40.7	-	-	58.8	8.7	25.2
Clark County	66	46.2	40.7	-	-	58.8	8.7	25.2
Laytonville Rancheria, California	68	52.9	51.5	-	1.5	50.0	6.8	29.5
Mendocino County	68	52.9	51.5	-	1.5	50.0	6.8	29.5
Leech Lake Reservation, Minnesota	1,698	59.5	52.4	5.4	2.2	33.2	4.2	49.2
Beltrami County	216	60.1	51.9	16.9	3.4	31.0	4.2	43.3
Cass and Hubbard Counties	1,028	58.9	52.2	4.0	2.0	34.3	3.3	53.8
Itasca County	454	60.6	53.1	3.0	2.0	31.8	6.3	40.1
Likely Rancheria, California	-	-	-	-	-	-	-	-
Modoc County	-	-	-	-	-	-	-	-
Lone Pine Rancheria, California	103	58.6	57.4	-	1.2	14.1	5.2	58.4
Inyo County	103	58.6	57.4	-	1.2	14.1	5.2	58.4
Lookout Rancheria, California	...	...	...	...	...	...	...	...
Modoc County	...	...	...	...	...	...	...	...

[Continued]

★ 232 ★

Geographic Mobility on Identified Reservations, 1980 - III
[Continued]

Identified reservation	All persons	Persons 3 to 34 years old				Persons 16 to 19 years old -- percent not enrolled in school, not high school graduates	Persons 25 years and over	
		Total	Percent enrolled in school				Percent completed less than 5 years of school	Percent high school graduates
			5 to 19 years		20 to 34 years old			
			Total	Bureau of indian affairs or tribal school				
Los Coyotes Reservation, California	27	38.3	38.3	-	-	-	-	60.2
San Diego County	27	38.3	-	-	-	-	-	60.2
Lovelock Colony, Nevada	64	64.1	64.1	-	-	-	3.6	50.3
Pershing County	64	64.1	64.1	-	-	-	3.6	50.3
Lower Brule Reservation, South Dakota	560	52.8	44.8	63.1	2.3	29.2	3.9	44.9
Lyman County	555	53.3	45.1	63.1	2.3	29.2	4.0	44.3
Stanley County	...	...	...	...	...	...	...	...
Lower Elwah Reservation, Washington	27	55.6	55.6	-	-	100.0	4.3	21.7
Clallam County	27	55.6	55.6	-	-	100.0	4.3	21.7
Lower Sioux Community, Minnesota	36	38.3	38.3	-	-	-	4.3	52.1
Redwood County	36	38.3	38.3	-	-	-	4.3	52.1
Lummi Reservation, Washington	854	59.1	50.5	5.7	5.4	34.1	2.6	54.4
Whatcom County	854	59.1	50.5	5.7	5.4	34.1	2.6	54.4
Makah Reservation, Washington	528	55.3	47.2	2.3	1.4	31.7	3.6	58.0
Clallam County	528	55.3	47.2	2.3	1.4	31.7	3.6	58.0
Manchester Rancheria, California	41	52.6	52.6	-	-	40.8	6.5	28.1
Mendocino County	41	52.6	52.6	-	-	40.8	6.5	28.1
Manzanita Reservation, California	...	...	...	...	...	...	...	...
San Diego County	...	...	...	...	...	...	...	...
Maricopa Reservation, Arizona	250	54.3	43.8	6.0	2.6	33.6	12.8	31.1
Pinal County	250	54.3	43.8	6.0	2.6	33.6	12.8	31.1
Mattaponi Reservation, Virgina	32	53.1	50.0	-	3.1	33.3	14.3	17.1
King William County	32	53.1	50.0	-	3.1	33.3	14.3	17.1
Menominee Reservation, Wisconsin	1,531	56.3	49.7	11.4	1.8	26.3	1.1	48.7
Menominee County	1,531	56.3	49.7	11.4	1.8	26.3	1.1	48.7
Mesa Grande Reservation, California	-	-	-	-	-	-	-	-
San Diego County	-	-	-	-	-	-	-	-

Source: U.S. Bureau of the Census, Subject Reports, PC80-2-1D, Part 1, *American Indians, Eskimos, and Aleuts on Identified Reservations and in the Historic Areas of Oklahoma (Excluding Urbanized Areas)*, U.S. Government Printing Office, Washington, D.C., 1986, pp. 50-58. *Notes:* A dash "(-)" represents zero or a percent which rounds to less than 0.1. Also, a dash "(-)" is used because the number of supplementary questionnaires for the reservations was insufficient to produce reliable estimates. Three dots "..." means not applicable, or that the data are being withheld to avoid disclosure of information for individuals.

★ 233 ★

Geographic Mobility on Identified Reservations, 1980 - IV

Data are the latest available.

Identified reservation		Persons 1 year and over					
		Always lived on this reservation	Did not always live on this reservation				
			Total		Percent moved onto reservation in--		
	Total				1979 or 1980	1975 to 1978	1974 or earlier
			Number	Percent			
Fort Bidwell Reservation, California	90	29	60	66.5	19.4	37.4	9.6
Modoc County	90	29	60	66.5	19.4	37.4	9.6
Fort Hall Reservation, Idaho	2,439	1,685	583	23.9	8.6	6.0	9.3
Bannock County	663	479	104	15.6	3.0	5.2	7.4
Bingham County	1,610	1,075	457	28.4	11.1	6.7	10.5
Caribou County	-	-	-	-	-	-	-
Power County	166	131	23	13.6	6.4	2.7	4.5
Fort Independence Reservation, California	32	4	26	82.2	9.7	12.3	60.3
Inyo County	32	4	26	82.2	9.7	12.3	60.3
Fort McDermitt Reservation, Nevada-Oregon	454	283	155	34.2	7.7	4.6	22.0
Nevada	454	283	155	34.2	7.7	4.6	22.0
Humboldt County	454	283	155	34.2	7.7	4.6	22.0
Oregon	-	-	-	-	-	-	-
Malheur County	-	-	-	-	-	-	-
Fort McDowell Reservation, Arizona	338	204	70	20.6	8.0	3.4	9.3
Maricopa County	338	204	70	20.6	8.0	3.4	9.3
Fort Mojave Reservation, Arizona-California-Nevada	124	4	102	82.3	3.2	18.5	60.5
Arizona	124	4	102	82.3	3.2	18.5	60.5
Mohave County	124	4	102	82.3	3.2	18.5	60.5
California	-	-	-	-	-	-	-
San Bernardino County	-	-	-	-	-	-	-
Nevada	-	-	-	-	-	-	-
Clark County	-	-	-	-	-	-	-
Fort Peck Reservation, Montana	4,097	2,501	1,377	33.6	8.4	9.9	15.3
Daniels County	-	-	-	-	-	-	-
Roosevelt County	3,635	2,202	1,236	34.0	8.8	9.8	15.4
Sheridan County	-	-	-	-	-	-	-
Valley County	461	299	141	30.6	5.7	11.0	14.0
Fort Totten Reservation, North Dakota	2,127	1,648	429	20.2	5.1	5.4	9.6
Benson County	2,118	1,639	429	20.2	5.2	5.4	9.7
Eddy County	...	...	...	...	...	...	...
Nelson County	-	-	-	-	-	-	-
Ramsey County	...	...	...	...	...	...	...
Fort Yuma Reservation, Arizona-California	1,054	554	281	26.7	13.2	5.7	7.8
Arizona	136	77	14	10.2	1.4	5.4	3.3
Yuma County	136	77	14	10.2	1.4	5.4	3.3
California	918	478	267	29.1	15.0	5.7	8.4
Imperial County	918	478	267	29.1	15.0	5.7	8.4
Gila Bend Reservation, Arizona	-	-	-	-	-	-	-
Maricopa County	-	-	-	-	-	-	-
Gila River Reservation, Arizona	6,707	5,163	1,355	20.2	7.7	4.3	8.2
Maricopa County	1,963	1,408	522	26.6	9.8	6.2	10.5
Pinal County	4,744	3,754	833	17.6	6.9	3.4	7.3
Golden Hill Reservation, Connecticut	...	...	...	...	...	...	...
Fairfield County	...	...	...	...	...	...	...
Goshute Reservation, Nevada-Utah	101	50	45	44.9	22.7	10.7	11.4
Nevada	...	...	...	...	...	...	...
White Pine County	...	...	...	...	...	...	...
Utah	77	40	31	40.7	25.9	3.7	11.1

[Continued]

★ 233 ★

Geographic Mobility on Identified Reservations, 1980 - IV
[Continued]

Identified reservation	Total	Always lived on this reservation	Persons 1 year and over				
			Did not always live on this reservation		Percent moved onto reservation in--		
			Total		1979 or 1980	1975 to 1978	1974 or earlier
			Number	Percent			
Juab and Tooele Counties	77	40	31	40.7	25.9	3.7	11.1
Grand Portage Reservation, Minnesota	186	34	146	78.1	27.6	22.7	27.7
Cook County	186	34	146	78.1	27.6	22.7	27.7
Grindstone Creek Rancheria, California	69	8	61	88.7	22.8	34.9	30.9
Glenn County	69	8	61	88.7	22.8	34.9	30.9
Hannahville Community, Michigan	199	161	39	19.5	3.9	2.5	13.1
Menominee County	199	161	39	19.5	3.9	2.5	13.1
Hassanamisco Reservation, Massachusetts	...	...	...	...	...	...	...
Worcester County	...	...	...	...	...	...	...
Havasupai Reservation, Arizona	258	194	37	14.2	2.9	2.6	8.7
Coconino County	258	194	37	14.2	2.9	2.6	8.7
Hoh Reservation, Washington	40	8	32	80.7	7.3	38.9	34.4
Jefferson County	40	8	32	80.7	7.3	38.9	34.4
Hollywood Reservation, Florida	398	212	168	42.3	21.5	5.7	15.1
Broward County	398	212	168	42.3	21.5	5.7	15.1
Hoopa Valley Reservation, California	1,440	728	577	40.1	9.2	9.0	21.9
Humboldt County	1,440	728	577	40.1	9.2	9.0	21.9
Hoopa Valley Extension Reservation, California	404	186	155	38.3	7.1	15.2	16.0
Del Norte County	151	52	82	54.1	8.8	28.3	16.9
Humboldt County	252	134	73	28.9	6.0	7.4	15.5
Hopi Reservation, Arizona	6,449	5,060	562	8.7	3.4	2.2	3.2
Coconino County	1,260	1,048	33	2.7	0.9	0.5	1.2
Navajo County	5,189	4,012	528	10.2	4.0	2.6	3.6
Hopland Rancheria, California	-	-	-	-	-	-	-
Mendocino County	-	-	-	-	-	-	-
Hualapai Reservation, Arizona	787	493	181	23.1	5.4	6.3	11.3
Coconino and Mohave Counties	783	493	181	23.1	5.4	6.3	11.3
Yavapai County	...	...	...	...	...	...	...
Inaja-Cosmit Reservation, California	-	-	-	-	-	-	-
San Diego County	-	-	-	-	-	-	-
Indian Township Reservation, Maine	315	197	116	36.7	5.8	16.5	14.4
Washington County	315	197	116	36.7	5.8	16.5	14.4
Iowa Reservation, Kansas-Nebraska	31	19	10	31.7	-	7.3	24.4
Kansas	...	...	...	...	...	...	...
Brown County	...	...	...	...	...	...	...
Doniphan County	-	-	-	-	-	-	-
Nebraska	...	...	...	...	...	...	...
Richardson County	...	...	...	...	...	...	...
Isabella Reservation, Michigan	495	160	307	62.0	21.1	18.6	22.3
Isabella County	495	160	307	62.0	21.1	18.6	22.3
Isleta Pueblo, New Mexico	2,228	1,515	634	28.5	3.1	6.0	19.3
Bernalillo County	1,734	1,159	541	31.2	3.4	6.9	20.9
Torrance County	-	-	-	-	-	-	-
Valencia County	494	356	93	18.8	2.2	2.8	13.7
Jackson Rancheria, California	...	...	...	...	...	...	...
Amador County	...	...	...	...	...	...	...
Jemez Pueblo, New Mexico	1,450	1,281	144	10.0	3.0	3.3	3.7
Sandoval County	1,450	1,281	144	10.0	3.0	3.3	3.7

[Continued]

★ 233 ★

Geographic Mobility on Identified Reservations, 1980 - IV
[Continued]

Identified reservation	Total	Always lived on this reservation	Did not always live on this reservation		Percent moved onto reservation in--		
			Total		1979 or 1980	1975 to 1978	1974 or earlier
			Number	Percent			
Jicarilla Apache Reservation, New Mexico	1,651	1,295	338	20.5	7.0	5.8	7.7
Rio Arriba and Sandoval Counties	1,651	1,295	338	20.5	7.0	5.8	7.7
Kaibab Reservation, Arizona	89	30	59	66.5	10.8	12.2	43.6
Coconino County	-	-	-	-	-	-	-
Mohave County	89	30	59	66.5	10.8	12.2	43.6
Kalispel Reservation, Washington	97	49	47	48.5	20.6	11.3	16.5
Pend Oreille County	97	49	47	48.5	20.6	11.3	16.5
Kickapoo Reservation, Kansas	352	75	277	78.8	21.9	22.6	34.2
Brown County	352	75	277	78.8	21.9	22.6	34.2
Kootenai Reservation, Idaho	-	-	-	-	-	-	-
Boundary County	-	-	-	-	-	-	-
Lac Courte Oreilles Reservation, Wisconsin	1,113	464	608	54.6	12.4	19.3	22.9
Sawyer County	1,113	464	608	54.6	12.4	19.3	22.9
Lac du Flambeau Reservation, Wisconsin	1,056	672	368	34.9	13.2	10.6	11.1
Iron County	-	-	-	-	-	-	-
Oneida County	-	-	-	-	-	-	-
Vilas County	1,056	672	368	34.9	13.2	10.6	11.1
Laguna Pueblo, New Mexico	3,452	2,128	1,280	37.1	8.8	9.2	19.1
Bernalillo and Valencia Counties	3,452	2,128	1,280	37.1	8.8	9.2	19.1
Sandoval County	-	-	-	-	-	-	-
La Jolla Reservation, California	133	22	105	79.0	23.1	35.6	20.2
San Diego County	133	22	105	79.0	23.1	35.6	20.2
L'Anse Reservation, Michigan	552	232	315	57.0	13.6	17.8	25.6
Baraga County	552	232	315	57.0	13.6	17.8	25.6
La Posta Reservation, California	...	...	...	...	...	...	...
San Diego County	...	...	...	...	...	...	...
Las Vegas Colony, Nevada	99	51	42	42.7	4.3	14.3	24.1
Clark County	99	51	42	42.7	4.3	14.3	24.1
Laytonville Rancheria, California	103	33	70	68.0	17.5	7.8	42.7
Mendocino County	103	33	70	68.0	17.5	7.8	42.7
Leech Lake Reservation, Minnesota	2,661	1,451	1,129	42.4	10.0	16.5	15.9
Beltrami County	321	169	144	44.9	8.8	23.6	12.5
Cass and Hubbard Counties	1,653	829	769	46.5	11.3	17.6	17.6
Itasca County	686	452	216	31.4	7.4	10.6	13.5
Likely Rancheria, California	-	-	-	-	-	-	-
Modoc County	-	-	-	-	-	-	-
Lone Pine Rancheria, California	165	74	91	55.3	24.9	12.9	17.6
Inyo County	165	74	91	55.3	24.9	12.9	17.6
Lookout Rancheria, California	...	...	...	...	...	...	...
Modoc County	...	...	...	...	...	...	...
Los Coyotes Reservation, California	41	19	23	55.1	20.0	17.5	17.7
San Diego County	41	19	23	55.1	20.0	17.5	17.7
Lovelock Colony, Nevada	109	54	48	44.2	5.3	16.2	22.6
Pershing County	109	54	48	44.2	5.3	16.2	22.6
Lower Brule Reservation, South Dakota	793	439	311	39.3	14.0	9.2	16.1
Lyman County	785	436	309	39.4	14.2	9.3	15.9
Stanley County	...	...	...	...	...	...	...
Lower Elwah Reservation, Washington	45	5	23	51.1	15.6	15.6	20.0

[Continued]

★ 233 ★

Geographic Mobility on Identified Reservations, 1980 - IV
[Continued]

Identified reservation	Total	Always lived on this reservation	Total		1979 or 1980	1975 to 1978	1974 or earlier
			Number	Percent			
Clallam County	45	5	23	51.1	15.6	15.6	20.0
Lower Sioux Community, Minnesota	71	57	13	18.9	10.2	6.3	2.4
Redwood County	71	57	13	18.9	10.2	6.3	2.4
Lummi Reservation, Washington	1,218	678	497	40.8	11.0	13.1	16.7
Whatcom County	1,218	678	497	40.8	11.0	13.1	16.7
Makah Reservation, Washington	764	390	340	44.6	8.2	17.1	19.3
Clallam County	764	390	340	44.6	8.2	17.1	19.3
Manchester Rancheria, California	73	31	42	57.4	9.7	1.5	46.2
Mendocino County	73	31	42	57.4	9.7	1.5	46.2
Manzanita Reservation, California	...	...	...	...	...	...	...
San Diego County	...	...	...	...	...	...	...
Maricopa Reservation, Arizona	364	262	98	27.0	3.8	5.3	18.0
Pinal County	364	262	98	27.0	3.8	5.3	18.0
Mattaponi Reservation, Virgina	60	28	32	53.3	-	26.7	26.7
King William County	60	28	32	53.3	-	26.7	26.7
Menominee Reservation, Wisconsin	2,299	1,349	537	23.4	4.6	8.4	10.4
Menominee County	2,299	1,349	537	23.4	4.6	8.4	10.4
Mesa Grande Reservation, California	-	-	-	-	-	-	-
San Diego County	-	-	-	-	-	-	-

Source: U.S. Bureau of the Census, Subject Reports, PC80-2-1D, Part 1, *American Indians, Eskimos, and Aleuts on Identified Reservations and in the Historic Areas of Oklahoma (Excluding Urbanized Areas)*, U.S. Government Printing Office, Washington, D.C., 1986, pp. 50-58. *Notes:* A dash "(-)" represents zero or a percent which rounds to less than 0.1. Also, a dash "(-)" is used because the number of supplementary questionnaires for the reservations was insufficient to produce reliable estimates. Three dots "..." means not applicable, or that the data are being withheld to avoid disclosure of information for individuals.

★ 234 ★

Geographic Mobility on Identified Reservations, 1980 - V

Data are the latest available.

Identified reservation	Persons 3 to 34 years old					Persons 16 to 19 years old -- percent not enrolled in school, not high school graduates	Persons 25 years and over	
	All persons	Percent enrolled in school					Percent completed less than 5 years of school	Percent high school graduates
		Total	5 to 19 years		20 to 34 years old			
			Total	Bureau of indian affairs or tribal school				
Mescalero Apache Reservation, New Mexico	1,340	53.6	49.3	3.4	2.3	24.9	5.6	52.3
Otero County	1,340	53.6	49.3	3.4	2.3	24.9	5.6	52.3
Miccosukee Reservation, Florida	184	34.8	27.7	66.7	2.7	56.0	60.2	19.4
Broward County	-	-	-	-	-	-	-	-
Dade County	184	34.8	27.7	66.7	2.7	56.0	60.2	19.4
Middletown Rancheria, California	28	50.0	50.0	-	-	-	17.6	58.8
Lake County	28	50.0	50.0	-	-	-	17.6	58.8
Mille Lacs Reservation, Minnesota	-	-	-	-	-	-	-	-
Aitkin County	-	-	-	-	-	-	-	-

[Continued]

★ 234 ★

Geographic Mobility on Identified Reservations, 1980 - V
[Continued]

Identified reservation	Persons 3 to 34 years old					Persons 16 to 19 years old -- percent not enrolled in school, not high school graduates	Persons 25 years and over	
	All persons	Percent enrolled in school					Percent completed less than 5 years of school	Percent high school graduates
		Total	5 to 19 years		20 to 34 years old			
			Total	Bureau of indian affairs or tribal school				
Kanabec County	-	-	-	-	-	-	-	-
Mille Lacs County	-	-	-	-	-	-	-	-
Pine County	-	-	-	-	-	-	-	-
Mississippi Choctaw Reservation	1,816	61.0	52.8	82.4	4.1	27.3	28.6	34.1
Attala County	-	-	-	-	-	-	-	-
Jones County	76	57.9	50.0	15.8	1.3	28.6	41.2	27.5
Kemper County	...	...	...	...	...	...	...	...
Leake County	344	65.2	55.5	75.1	5.2	24.9	27.9	32.2
Neshoba County	1,173	60.9	52.8	88.9	4.4	24.7	28.2	36.3
Newton County	221	55.6	49.3	81.3	2.1	44.8	25.3	28.1
Moapa River Reservation, Nevada	119	57.7	56.0	-	1.7	28.6	6.2	39.0
Clark County	119	57.7	56.0	-	1.7	28.6	6.2	39.0
Montgomery Creek Rancheria, California	...	...	...	...	...	...	...	...
Shasta County	...	...	...	...	...	...	...	...
Morongo Reservation, California	190	53.5	46.9	1.2	3.9	26.1	1.5	47.1
Riverside County	190	53.5	46.9	1.2	3.9	26.1	1.5	47.1
Muckleshoot Reservation, Washington	264	60.5	52.3	4.2	1.2	48.9	2.6	30.6
King County	264	60.5	52.3	4.2	1.2	48.9	2.6	30.6
Pierce County	-	-	-	-	-	-	-	-
Nambe Pueblo, New Mexico	121	41.7	34.6	8.5	3.8	25.2	13.1	70.2
Santa Fe County	121	41.7	34.6	8.5	3.8	25.2	13.1	70.2
Navajo Reservation, Arizona, New Mexico - Utah	69,722	55.4	50.9	28.6	2.3	24.3	37.4	34.1
Arizona	47,531	56.3	51.4	33.6	2.4	24.8	39.0	33.8
Apache County	25,175	55.6	50.8	25.6	2.6	24.7	36.7	35.5
Coconino County	10,401	58.3	52.6	30.5	1.9	23.4	37.6	36.3
Navajo County	11,955	55.9	51.6	52.7	2.2	26.2	45.2	27.7
New Mexico	19,102	52.4	48.7	15.4	2.3	22.9	31.6	36.7
McKinley County	6,447	47.9	45.1	9.2	1.5	28.6	28.9	38.2
San Juan County	12,655	54.6	50.5	18.3	2.7	20.2	33.0	35.9
Utah	3,089	60.4	56.2	29.4	1.4	27.0	52.0	22.7
San Juan County	3,089	60.4	56.2	29.4	1.4	27.0	52.0	22.7
Nez Perce Reservation, Idaho	949	58.4	52.8	4.8	2.7	15.1	3.6	59.9
Clearwater County	86	53.5	47.7	2.4	1.2	27.3	-	52.0
Idaho County	81	54.3	50.3	15.0	1.2	17.0	4.7	54.1
Lewis County	136	47.1	41.9	-	1.5	26.1	-	61.1
Nez Perce County	646	61.9	56.0	4.7	3.4	10.3	4.5	61.4
Nisqually Reservation, Washington	25	63.2	54.5	41.8	4.3	22.3	5.6	36.2
Pierce County	-	-	-	-	-	-	-	-
Thurston County	25	63.2	54.5	41.8	4.3	22.3	5.6	36.2
Nooksack Reservation, Washington	-	-	-	-	-	-	-	-
Whatcom County	-	-	-	-	-	-	-	-
Northern Cheyenne Reservation, Montana	2,038	59.0	50.5	25.6	4.3	23.8	7.4	52.0
Big Horn County	538	60.2	52.9	48.5	3.8	15.4	2.7	51.3
Rosebud County	1,500	58.5	49.6	16.8	4.4	26.4	9.2	52.3
Oil Springs Reservation, New York	-	-	-	-	-	-	-	-

[Continued]

★ 234 ★

Geographic Mobility on Identified Reservations, 1980 - V

[Continued]

Identified reservation	Persons 3 to 34 years old					Persons 16 to 19 years old -- percent not enrolled in school, not high school graduates	Persons 25 years and over	
	All persons	Percent enrolled in school					Percent completed less than 5 years of school	Percent high school graduates
		Total	5 to 19 years		20 to 34 years old			
			Total	Bureau of indian affairs or tribal school				
Allegany County	-	-	-	-	-	-	-	-
Cattaraugus County	-	-	-	-	-	-	-	-
Omaha Reservation, Iowa-Nebraska	789	60.1	53.0	9.6	1.9	21.0	6.7	35.2
Iowa	-	-	-	-	-	-	-	-
Monona County	-	-	-	-	-	-	-	-
Nebraska	789	60.1	53.0	9.6	1.9	21.0	6.7	35.2
Burt County	...	...	...	...	...	...	...	...
Cuming County	-	-	-	-	-	-	-	-
Thurston County	783	60.2	53.2	9.6	1.9	21.0	6.8	35.2
Oneida Reservation, Wisconsin	1,090	58.2	51.5	15.5	2.7	20.9	5.5	45.6
Brown County	412	56.4	52.7	8.1	2.0	27.1	6.0	44.3
Outagamie County	678	59.2	50.8	20.1	3.1	16.5	5.1	46.6
Onondaga Reservation, New York	-	-	-	-	-	-	-	-
Onondaga County	-	-	-	-	-	-	-	-
Ontonagon Reservation, Michigan	-	-	-	-	-	-	-	-
Ontonagon County	-	-	-	-	-	-	-	-
Osage Reservation, Oklahoma	2,678	51.6	46.7	0.4	2.3	20.1	2.3	65.9
Osage County	2,678	51.6	46.7	0.4	2.3	20.1	2.3	65.9
Ozette Reservation, Washington	...	...	...	...	...	...	...	...
Clallam County	...	...	...	...	...	...	...	...
Pala Reservation, California	275	51.8	44.0	5.5	3.5	22.1	1.0	60.0
San Diego County	275	51.8	44.0	5.5	3.5	22.1	1.0	60.0
Pamunkey Reservation, Virginia	11	81.8	72.7	-	9.1	-	9.4	15.6
King William County	11	81.8	72.7	-	9.1	-	9.4	15.6
Papago Reservation, Arizona	4,192	55.0	49.6	45.8	1.8	24.2	25.2	35.0
Maricopa County	67	65.6	60.7	97.3	-	100.0	44.6	12.6
Pima County	3,718	54.8	49.4	47.5	2.0	21.1	25.2	35.2
Pinal County	408	55.3	49.5	20.0	0.3	54.8	20.6	37.8
Pascua Yaqui Reservation, Arizona	370	52.2	49.0	1.2	0.6	49.1	24.7	14.9
Pima County	370	52.2	49.0	1.2	0.6	49.1	24.7	14.9
Pauma Reservation, California	55	54.9	38.6	-	12.3	41.4	2.0	64.8
San Diego County	55	54.9	38.6	-	12.3	41.4	2.0	64.8
Payson Community of Yavapai-Apache, Arizona	-	-	-	-	-	-	-	-
Gila County	-	-	-	-	-	-	-	-
Pechanga Reservation, California	71	48.5	40.0	-	2.9	35.7	-	49.0
Riverside County	71	48.5	40.0	-	2.9	35.7	-	49.0
Penobscot Reservation, Maine	264	57.0	48.3	1.6	7.2	20.0	-	62.4
Penobscot County	264	57.0	48.3	1.6	7.2	20.0	-	62.4
Picuris Pueblo, New Mexico	85	54.7	47.9	12.3	3.5	-	2.8	68.1
Taos County	85	54.7	47.9	12.3	3.5	-	2.8	68.1
Pine Creek Reservation, Michigan	...	...	...	...	...	...	...	...
Calhoun County	...	...	...	...	...	...	...	...
Pine Ridge Reservation, South Dakota	8,028	56.9	50.6	59.1	3.4	29.5	3.9	44.8
Jackson County	934	61.3	54.6	80.3	2.7	15.2	3.4	40.7
Shannon County	7,094	56.3	50.1	56.1	3.5	31.1	4.0	45.3
Pleasant Point Reservation, Maine	322	59.6	54.6	59.9	1.3	30.0	5.3	42.1

[Continued]

★ 234 ★

Geographic Mobility on Identified Reservations, 1980 - V
[Continued]

Identified reservation	All persons	Persons 3 to 34 years old				Persons 16 to 19 years old -- percent not enrolled in school, not high school graduates	Persons 25 years and over	
		Percent enrolled in school						
		Total	5 to 19 years		20 to 34 years old		Percent completed less than 5 years of school	Percent high school graduates
			Total	Bureau of indian affairs or tribal school				
Washington County	322	59.6	54.6	59.9	1.3	30.0	5.3	42.1
Pojoaque Pueblo, New Mexico	66	54.8	48.3	9.0	3.0	13.7	8.0	64.4
Santa Fe County	66	54.8	48.3	9.0	3.0	13.7	8.0	64.4
Poospatuck Reservation, New York	61	69.6	60.0	-	5.9		3.2	43.1
Suffolk County	61	69.6	60.0	-	5.9		3.2	43.1
Port Gamble Reservation, Washington	172	44.3	39.5	3.3	1.5	43.9	2.4	38.3
Kitsap County	172	44.3	39.5	3.3	1.5	43.9	2.4	38.3
Port Madison Reservation, Washington	90	37.9	33.5	5.0	1.5	44.9	2.0	75.3
Kitsap County	90	37.9	33.5	5.0	1.5	44.9	2.0	75.3
Potawatomi Reservation, Wisconsin	144	63.6	56.7	2.4	2.8	14.8	8.5	21.8
Forest County	144	63.6	56.7	2.4	2.8	14.8	8.5	21.8
Onconto County	-	-	-	-	-	-	-	-
Pottawatomi Reservation, Kansas	168	57.2	55.9	-	1.2	13.8	2.8	61.0
Jackson County	168	57.2	55.9	-	1.2	13.8	2.8	61.0
Prairie Island Community, Minnesota	52	44.2	38.5	-	1.9	50.0	5.1	35.9
Goodhue County	52	44.2	38.5	-	1.9	50.0	5.1	35.9
Puyallup Reservation, Washington	575	54.7	47.7	12.3	4.7	35.3	3.2	61.2
Pierce County	575	54.7	47.7	12.3	4.7	35.3	3.2	61.2
Pyramid Lake Reservation, Nevada	427	48.4	45.3	10.2	1.9	15.9	1.4	54.0
Lyon County	-	-	-	-	-	-	-	-
Storey County	-	-	-	-	-	-	-	-
Washoe County	427	48.4	45.3	10.2	1.9	15.9	1.4	54.0
Quileute Reservation, Washington	194	56.5	50.0	51.5	1.2	35.3	2.3	34.1
Clallam County	194	56.5	50.0	51.5	1.2	35.3	2.3	34.1
Quainault Reservation, Washington	635	53.4	47.8	9.3	2.8	28.9	0.6	47.5
Grays Harbor County	518	53.3	47.9	10.9	3.0	29.8	0.4	50.5
Jefferson County	117	53.6	47.0	2.0	1.8	24.9	1.9	31.9
Ramah Community, New Mexico	753	53.1	47.2	44.8	3.9	31.7	45.3	29.2
McKinley County	57	58.0	50.6	43.3	5.4	11.3	61.9	23.2
Valencia County	696	52.7	46.9	44.9	3.8	34.8	43.2	30.0
Ramona Reservation, California	-	-	-	-	-	-	-	-
Riverside County	-	-	-	-	-	-	-	-
Red Cliff Reservation, Wisconsin	394	59.9	53.8	-	3.3	21.0	2.2	35.3
Bayfield County	394	59.9	53.8	-	3.3	21.0	2.2	35.3
Red Lake Reservation, Minnesota	1,852	57.3	51.5	9.0	1.8	44.9	3.6	43.4
Beltrami County	1,813	57.5	51.6	9.2	1.9	45.1	3.6	43.9
Clearwater County	40	48.4	45.2	-	-	33.3	4.1	21.5
Koochiching County	-	-	-	-	-	-	-	-
Lake of the Woods County	-	-	-	-	-	-	-	-
Marshall County	-	-	-	-	-	-	-	-
Pennington County	-	-	-	-	-	-	-	-
Polk County	-	-	-	-	-	-	-	-
Red Lake County	-	-	-	-	-	-	-	-
Roseau County	-	-	-	-	-	-	-	-
Reno-Sparks Colony, Nevada	309	47.6	40.3	0.6	4.4	32.9	2.9	60.5
Washoe County	309	47.6	40.3	0.6	4.4	32.9	2.9	60.5

[Continued]

★ 234 ★

Geographic Mobility on Identified Reservations, 1980 - V
[Continued]

Identified reservation	Persons 3 to 34 years old					Persons 16 to 19 years old -- percent not enrolled in school, not high school graduates	Persons 25 years and over	
	All persons	Percent enrolled in school					Percent completed less than 5 years of school	Percent high school graduates
		Total	5 to 19 years		20 to 34 years old			
			Total	Bureau of indian affairs or tribal school				
Resighini Rancheria, California	...	...	...	...	...	...	...	...
Del Norte County	...	...	...	...	...	...	...	...
Rincon Reservation, California	189	59.4	49.8	2.8	5.2	27.3	3.5	54.0
San Diego County	189	59.4	49.8	2.8	5.2	27.3	3.5	54.0
Roaring Creek Rancheria, California	...	...	...	...	...	...	...	...
Shasta County	...	...	...	...	...	...	...	...
Rocky Boy's Reservation, Montana	1,036	60.1	54.2	9.0	2.7	23.5	9.7	41.7
Chouteau County	87	59.8	54.0	10.6	1.1	18.8	5.4	51.8
Hill County	949	60.2	54.2	8.8	2.9	24.0	10.1	40.6
Rosebud Reservation, South Dakota	3,749	52.5	47.9	18.5	3.4	32.6	3.3	50.2
Todd County	3,749	52.5	47.9	18.5	3.4	32.6	3.3	50.2
Round Valley Reservation, California	332	52.0	48.9	-	0.3	17.0	-	50.4
Mendocino County	332	52.0	48.9	-	0.3	17.0	-	50.4
Rumsey Rancheria, California	...	...	...	...	...	...	...	...
Yolo County	...	...	...	...	...	...	...	...
Sac and Fox Reservation, Iowa	303	59.4	54.8	33.3	2.0	22.1	6.6	42.6
Tama County	303	59.4	54.8	33.3	2.0	22.1	6.6	42.6
Sac and Fox Reservation, Kansas-Nebraska	...	...	...	...	...	...	...	...
Kansas	-	-	-	-	-	-	-	-
Brown County	-	-	-	-	-	-	-	-
Nebraska	...	...	...	...	...	...	...	...
Richardson County	...	...	...	...	...	...	...	...

Source: U.S. Bureau of the Census, Subject Reports, PC80-2-1D, Part 1, *American Indians, Eskimos, and Aleuts on Identified Reservations and in the Historic Areas of Oklahoma (Excluding Urbanized Areas)*, U.S. Government Printing Office, Washington, D.C., 1986, pp. 50-58. *Notes:* A dash "(-)" represents zero or a percent which rounds to less than 0.1. Also, a dash "(-)" is used because the number of supplementary questionnaires for the reservations was insufficient to produce reliable estimates. Three dots "..." means not applicable, or that the data are being withheld to avoid disclosure of information for individuals.

★ 235 ★

Geographic Mobility on Identified Reservations, 1980 - VI

Data are the latest available.

Identified reservations	Persons 1 year and over						
	Total	Always lived on this reservation	Did not always live on this reservation				
			Total		Percent moved onto reservation in--		
			Number	Percent	1979 or 1980	1975 to 1978	1974 or earlier
Mescalero Apache Reservation, New Mexico	1,854	498	148	8.0	1.9	2.4	3.7
Otero County	1,854	498	148	8.0	1.9	2.4	3.7
Miccosukee Reservation, Florida	263	161	88	33.5	6.5	7.6	19.4
Broward County	-	-	-	-	-	-	-
Dade County	263	161	88	33.5	6.5	7.6	19.4
Middletown Rancheria, California	38	14	24	63.2	39.5	10.5	13.2

[Continued]

★ 235 ★

Geographic Mobility on Identified Reservations, 1980 - VI
[Continued]

Identified reservations		Persons 1 year and over					
			Did not always live on this reservation				
		Always lived on this reservation	Total		Percent moved onto reservation in--		
	Total				1979 or 1980	1975 to 1978	1974 or earlier
			Number	Percent			
Lake County	38	14	24	63.2	39.5	10.5	13.2
Mille Lacs Reservation, Minnesota	-	-	-	-	-	-	-
Aitkin County	-	-	-	-	-	-	-
Kanabec County	-	-	-	-	-	-	-
Mille Lacs County	-	-	-	-	-	-	-
Pine County	-	-	-	-	-	-	-
Mississippi Choctaw Reservation	2,669	1,497	1,119	41.9	6.2	15.8	19.9
Attala County	-	-	-	-	-	-	-
Jones County	116	46	70	60.3	11.2	23.3	25.9
Kemper County	...	...	...	...	...	...	...
Leake County	516	302	201	39.0	1.8	10.1	27.1
Neshoba County	1,700	913	750	44.1	6.7	18.4	19.0
Newton County	333	232	98	29.4	8.8	9.4	11.2
Moapa River Reservation, Nevada	178	104	67	37.9	10.7	5.9	21.3
Clark County	178	104	67	37.9	10.7	5.9	21.3
Montgomery Creek Rancheria, California	...	...	...	...	...	...	...
Shasta County	...	...	...	...	...	...	...
Morongo Reservation, California	305	125	172	56.3	22.7	11.8	21.8
Riverside County	305	125	172	56.3	22.7	11.8	21.8
Muckleshoot Reservation, Washington	365	218	92	25.3	4.4	14.1	6.8
King County	365	218	92	25.3	4.4	14.1	6.8
Pierce County	-	-	-	-	-	-	-
Nambe Pueblo, New Mexico	185	81	32	17.5	4.7	2.2	10.6
Santa Fe County	185	81	32	17.5	4.7	2.2	10.6
Navajo Reservation, Arizona, New Mexico - Utah	101,355	83,040	10,380	10.2	2.8	2.2	5.3
Arizona	69,155	56,371	6,920	10.0	2.6	2.1	5.3
Apache County	36,937	29,183	4,150	11.2	2.4	2.3	6.5
Coconino County	14,759	12,484	1,055	7.1	3.4	1.6	2.1
Navajo County	17,459	14,703	1,716	9.8	2.2	2.1	5.5
New Mexico	27,794	22,869	3,030	10.9	3.1	2.4	5.3
McKinley County	9,264	6,584	1,445	15.6	2.9	3.3	9.4
San Juan County	18,530	16,285	1,585	8.6	3.2	2.0	3.3
Utah	4,406	3,801	430	9.8	3.2	2.3	4.2
San Juan County	4,406	3,801	430	9.8	3.2	2.3	4.2
Nez Perce Reservation, Idaho	1,472	746	667	45.3	13.4	13.8	18.1
Clearwater County	117	41	67	57.3	29.1	8.5	19.7
Idaho County	145	71	73	50.1	19.0	4.7	26.4
Lewis County	203	88	101	49.8	12.3	13.3	24.1
Nez Perce County	1,007	546	426	42.3	11.0	15.8	15.5
Nisqually Reservation, Washington	42	12	30	72.1	30.6	13.9	27.6
Pierce County	-	-	-	-	-	-	-
Thurston County	42	12	30	72.1	30.6	13.9	27.6
Nooksack Reservation, Washington	-	-	-	-	-	-	-
Whatcom County	-	-	-	-	-	-	-
Northern Cheyenne Reservation, Montana	2,963	1,972	743	25.1	8.6	8.0	8.5
Big Horn County	795	527	223	28.1	7.7	9.0	11.4
Rosebud County	2,168	1,446	520	24.0	8.9	7.7	7.4
Oil Springs Reservation, New York	-	-	-	-	-	-	-

[Continued]

★ 235 ★

Geographic Mobility on Identified Reservations, 1980 - VI
[Continued]

| Identified reservations | Total | Always lived on this reservation | Did not always live on this reservation | | Percent moved onto reservation in-- | | |
| | | | Total | | 1979 or 1980 | 1975 to 1978 | 1974 or earlier |
			Number	Percent			
Allegany County	-	-	-	-	-	-	-
Cattaraugus County	-	-	-	-	-	-	-
Omaha Reservation, Iowa-Nebraska	1,200	395	205	17.1	3.2	4.9	8.9
Iowa	-	-	-	-	-	-	-
Monona County	-	-	-	-	-	-	-
Nebraska	1,200	395	205	17.1	3.2	4.9	8.9
Burt County	...	...	...	...	...	...	...
Cuming County	-	-	-	-	-	-	-
Thurston County	1,192	395	205	17.2	3.2	5.0	9.0
Oneida Reservation, Wisconsin	1,768	817	834	47.1	9.0	16.9	21.3
Brown County	707	343	302	42.8	6.0	14.1	22.7
Outagamie County	1,061	474	531	50.1	10.9	18.8	20.3
Onondaga Reservation, New York	-	-	-	-	-	-	-
Onondaga County	-	-	-	-	-	-	-
Ontonagon Reservation, Michigan	-	-	-	-	-	-	-
Ontonagon County	-	-	-	-	-	-	-
Osage Reservation, Oklahoma	4,589	1,415	2,551	55.6	14.8	16.5	24.3
Osage County	4,589	1,415	2,551	55.6	14.8	16.5	24.3
Ozette Reservation, Washington	...	...	...	...	...	...	...
Clallam County	...	...	...	...	...	...	...
Pala Reservation, California	420	153	266	63.2	5.5	20.6	37.1
San Diego County	420	153	266	63.2	5.5	20.6	37.1
Pamunkey Reservation, Virginia	44	10	34	77.3	25.0	15.9	36.4
King William County	44	10	34	77.3	25.0	15.9	36.4
Papago Reservation, Arizona	6,597	5,161	1,304	19.8	4.9	5.2	9.7
Maricopa County	120	113	2	2.0	1.1	0.9	-
Pima County	5,848	4,526	1,215	20.8	4.8	5.5	10.4
Pinal County	630	522	87	13.8	6.0	2.9	4.9
Pascua Yaqui Reservation, Arizona	528	273	244	46.2	5.5	10.7	29.9
Pima County	528	273	244	46.2	5.5	10.7	29.9
Pauma Reservation, California	82	51	31	37.6	6.0	8.3	23.2
San Diego County	82	51	31	37.6	6.0	8.3	23.2
Payson Community of Yavapai-Apache, Arizona	-	-	-	-	-	-	-
Gila County	-	-	-	-	-	-	-
Pechanga Reservation, California	116	22	88	76.3	14.9	26.3	35.1
Riverside County	116	22	88	76.3	14.9	26.3	35.1
Penobscot Reservation, Maine	398	132	260	65.4	19.7	32.8	12.9
Penobscot County	398	132	260	65.4	19.7	32.8	12.9
Picuris Pueblo, New Mexico	136	64	63	46.6	15.3	23.5	7.8
Taos County	136	64	63	46.6	15.3	23.5	7.8
Pine Creek Reservation, Michigan	...	...	...	...	...	...	...
Calhoun County	...	...	...	...	...	...	...
Pine Ridge Reservation, South Dakota	11,472	8,596	2,145	18.7	4.9	6.5	7.3
Jackson County	1,331	870	336	25.2	6.4	9.9	8.9
Shannon County	10,141	7,726	1,810	17.8	4.7	6.1	7.1
Pleasant Point Reservation, Maine	491	262	217	44.2	9.0	16.4	18.8
Washington County	491	262	217	44.2	9.0	16.4	18.8
Pojoaque Pueblo, New Mexico	93	47	46	49.2	21.5	10.0	17.7
Santa Fe County	93	47	46	49.2	21.5	10.0	17.7

[Continued]

★ 235 ★

Geographic Mobility on Identified Reservations, 1980 - VI

[Continued]

Identified reservations	Total	Always lived on this reservation	Persons 1 year and over				
			Did not always live on this reservation				
			Total		Percent moved onto reservation in--		
					1979 or 1980	1975 to 1978	1974 or earlier
			Number	Percent			
Poospatuck Reservation, New York	92	37	45	49.0	-	3.7	45.3
Suffolk County	92	37	45	49.0	-	3.7	45.3
Port Gamble Reservation, Washington	256	108	139	54.5	7.1	16.3	31.2
Kitsap County	256	108	139	54.5	7.1	16.3	31.2
Port Madison Reservation, Washington	144	34	97	66.8	26.8	22.6	17.5
Kitsap County	144	34	97	66.8	26.8	22.6	17.5
Potawatomi Reservation, Wisconsin	212	131	81	37.9	10.5	13.2	14.3
Forest County	212	131	81	37.9	10.5	13.2	14.3
Onconto County	-	-	-	-	-	-	-
Pottawatomi Reservation, Kansas	328	111	213	65.1	11.4	30.1	23.6
Jackson County	328	111	213	65.1	11.4	30.1	23.6
Prairie Island Community, Minnesota	81	62	19	23.5	13.6	3.7	6.2
Goodhue County	81	62	19	23.5	13.6	3.7	6.2
Puyallup Reservation, Washington	846	133	642	76.0	29.1	23.3	23.6
Pierce County	846	133	642	76.0	29.1	23.3	23.6
Pyramid Lake Reservation, Nevada	692	378	310	44.8	12.6	17.4	14.7
Lyon County	-	-	-	-	-	-	-
Storey County	-	-	-	-	-	-	-
Washoe County	692	378	310	44.8	12.6	17.4	14.7
Quileute Reservation, Washington	256	173	77	30.3	8.6	9.2	12.4
Clallam County	256	173	77	30.3	8.6	9.2	12.4
Quainault Reservation, Washington	913	446	420	46.0	12.1	12.6	21.3
Grays Harbor County	752	359	358	47.6	13.3	12.3	22.0
Jefferson County	161	88	62	38.8	6.7	14.2	17.9
Ramah Community, New Mexico	1,110	932	114	10.3	2.9	3.3	4.0
McKinley County	101	84	16	16.0	5.9	7.4	2.6
Valencia County	1,009	848	98	9.7	2.6	2.9	4.2
Ramona Reservation, California	-	-	-	-	-	-	-
Riverside County	-	-	-	-	-	-	-
Red Cliff Reservation, Wisconsin	568	198	349	61.4	30.4	15.8	15.2
Bayfield County	568	198	349	61.4	30.4	15.8	15.2
Red Lake Reservation, Minnesota	2,736	2,102	556	20.3	4.9	5.7	9.7
Beltrami County	2,673	2,061	535	20.0	4.7	5.8	9.5
Clearwater County	63	41	22	34.6	14.5	-	20.1
Koochiching County	-	-	-	-	-	-	-
Lake of the Woods County	-	-	-	-	-	-	-
Marshall County	-	-	-	-	-	-	-
Pennington County	-	-	-	-	-	-	-
Polk County	-	-	-	-	-	-	-
Red Lake County	-	-	-	-	-	-	-
Roseau County	-	-	-	-	-	-	-
Reno-Sparks Colony, Nevada	446	221	214	48.1	15.5	6.0	26.7
Washoe County	446	221	214	48.1	15.5	6.0	26.7
Resighini Rancheria, California	...	...	...	...	...	...	...
Del Norte County	...	...	...	...	...	...	...
Rincon Reservation, California	290	81	198	68.2	10.1	17.9	40.2
San Diego County	290	81	198	68.2	10.1	17.9	40.2
Roaring Creek Rancheria, California	...	...	...	...	...	...	...
Shasta County	...	...	...	...	...	...	...

[Continued]

★ 235 ★

Geographic Mobility on Identified Reservations, 1980 - VI
[Continued]

Identified reservations	Persons 1 year and over						
	Total	Always lived on this reservation	Did not always live on this reservation				
			Total		Percent moved onto reservation in--		
			Number	Percent	1979 or 1980	1975 to 1978	1974 or earlier
Rocky Boy's Reservation, Montana	1,490	924	537	36.1	8.5	10.9	16.7
Chouteau County	127	68	57	44.9	4.7	14.2	26.0
Hill County	1,363	856	480	35.2	8.8	10.6	15.8
Rosebud Reservation, South Dakota	5,405	3,647	1,293	23.9	7.4	7.4	9.1
Todd County	5,405	3,647	1,293	23.9	7.4	7.4	9.1
Round Valley Reservation, California	516	279	226	43.8	12.6	20.7	10.5
Mendocino County	516	279	226	43.8	12.6	20.7	10.5
Rumsey Rancheria, California	...	...	...	...	...	...	...
Yolo County	...	...	...	...	...	...	...
Sac and Fox Reservation, Iowa	475	318	131	27.6	14.0	7.2	6.4
Tama County	475	318	131	27.6	14.0	7.2	6.4
Sac and Fox Reservation, Kansas-Nebraska	...	...	...	...	...	...	...
Kansas	-	-	-	-	-	-	-
Brown County	-	-	-	-	-	-	-
Nebraska	...	...	...	...	...	...	...
Richardson County	...	...	...	...	...	...	...

Source: U.S. Bureau of the Census, Subject Reports, PC80-2-1D, Part 1, *American Indians, Eskimos, and Aleuts on Identified Reservations and in the Historic Areas of Oklahoma (Excluding Urbanized Areas)*, U.S. Government Printing Office, Washington, D.C., 1986, pp. 50-58. *Notes:* A dash "(-)" represents zero or a percent which rounds to less than 0.1. Also, a dash "(-)" is used because the number of supplementary questionnaires for the reservations was insufficient to produce reliable estimates. Three dots "..." means not applicable, or that the data are being withheld to avoid disclosure of information for individuals.

★ 236 ★

Geographic Mobility on Identified Reservations, 1980 - VII

Data are the latest available.

Identified reservation	Persons 3 to 34 years old					Persons 16 to 19 years old -- percent not enrolled in school, not high school graduates	Persons 25 years and over	
	All persons	Percent enrolled in school					Percent completed less than 5 years of school	Percent high school graduates
		Total	5 to 19 years		20 to 34 years old			
			Total	Bureau of indian affairs or tribal school				
St. Croix Reservation, Wisconsin	255	56.5	53.0	3.6	1.4	33.9	11.0	35.1
Barron County	50	44.0	44.0	-	-	54.3	31.8	14.5
Burnett County	149	63.2	60.4	5.4	1.2	22.7	1.2	45.0
Polk County	56	49.7	41.4	-	3.4	70.3	20.5	25.5
St. Regis Mohawk Reservation, New York	980	58.0	49.6	0.4	5.5	17.4	9.1	38.2
Franklin County	980	58.0	49.6	0.4	5.5	17.4	9.1	38.2
Salt River Reservation, Arizona	1,720	47.5	41.4	33.3	3.2	44.1	3.3	47.5
Maricopa County	1,720	47.5	41.4	33.3	3.2	44.1	3.3	47.5
San Carlos Reservation, Arizona	3,957	53.6	49.2	11.7	2.1	30.7	8.8	37.1
Gila County	2,276	50.0	45.2	19.3	2.4	37.2	9.6	37.3
Graham County	1,681	58.5	54.8	3.3	1.8	21.7	7.5	36.9
Pinal County	-	-	-	-	-	-	-	-

[Continued]

Geographic Mobility on Identified Reservations, 1980 - VII

[Continued]

Identified reservation	Persons 3 to 34 years old					Persons 16 to 19 years old -- percent not enrolled in school, not high school graduates	Persons 25 years and over	
	All persons	Percent enrolled in school					Percent completed less than 5 years of school	Percent high school graduates
		Total	5 to 19 years		20 to 34 years old			
			Total	Bureau of indian affairs or tribal school				
Sandia Pueblo, New Mexico	137	54.3	45.5	6.6	4.4	20.0	4.6	63.5
Bernalillo County	-	-	-	-	-	-	-	-
Sandoval County	137	54.3	45.5	6.6	4.4	20.0	4.6	63.5
Sandy Lake Reservation, Minnesota	-	-	-	-	-	-	-	-
Aitkin County	-	-	-	-	-	-	-	-
San Felipe Pueblo, New Mexico	1,250	58.7	53.1	43.2	1.2	22.1	9.8	43.8
Sandoval County	1,250	58.7	53.1	43.2	1.2	22.1	9.8	43.8
San Ildefonso Pueblo, New Mexico	275	54.3	43.0	41.3	3.8	5.2	3.7	68.5
Sandoval County	-	-	-	-	-	-	-	-
Sante Fe County	275	54.3	43.0	41.3	3.8	5.2	3.7	68.5
San Juan Pueblo, New Mexico	524	53.3	47.0	23.9	2.5	24.8	5.1	58.6
Rio Arriba County	524	53.3	47.0	23.9	2.5	24.8	5.1	58.6
San Manuel Reservation, California	-	-	-	-	-	-	-	-
San Bernardino County	-	-	-	-	-	-	-	-
San Pasqual Reservation, California	75	48.7	40.2	3.7	4.2	77.7	2.1	54.9
San Diego County	75	48.7	40.2	3.7	4.2	77.7	2.1	54.9
Santa Ana Pueblo, New Mexico	244	51.1	44.6	6.8	3.4	13.9	5.6	59.5
Sandoval County	244	51.1	44.6	6.8	3.4	13.9	5.6	59.5
Santa Clara Pueblo, New Mexico	1,138	60.1	49.7	38.8	5.8	6.3	3.4	68.3
Rio Arriba County	1,119	60.8	50.3	38.9	5.9	6.3	3.4	67.9
Sandoval County	-	-	-	-	-	-	-	-
Sante Fe County	...	...	...	...	...	...	...	...
Santa Rosa Rancheria, California	80	49.0	37.6	-	-	48.9	13.7	32.9
Kings County	80	49.0	37.6	-	-	48.9	13.7	32.9
Santa Rosa Reservation, California	...	...	...	...	...	...	...	...
Riverside County	...	...	...	...	...	...	...	...
Santa Ynez Reservation, California	69	64.3	57.1	-	1.8	9.1	9.5	35.7
Santa Barbara County	69	64.3	57.1	-	1.8	9.1	9.5	35.7
Santa Ysabel Reservation, California	111	48.1	42.5	-	2.5	36.2	5.5	46.7
San Diego County	111	48.1	42.5	-	2.5	36.2	5.5	46.7
Santee Reservation, Nebraska	254	61.5	53.7	3.8	1.6	18.7	8.2	39.8
Knox County	254	61.5	53.7	3.8	1.6	18.7	8.2	39.8
Santo Domingo Pueblo, New Mexico	1,471	55.4	49.6	6.2	1.1	24.4	14.9	39.7
Sandoval County	1,471	55.4	49.6	6.2	1.1	24.4	14.9	39.7
Santa Fe County	-	-	-	-	-	-	-	-
San Xavier Reservation, Arizona	570	51.8	43.6	20.8	3.6	22.9	10.6	41.3
Pima County	570	51.8	43.6	20.8	3.6	22.9	10.6	41.3
Sauk-Suiattle Reservation, Washington	-	-	-	-	-	-	-	-
Snohomish County	-	-	-	-	-	-	-	-
Sault Ste. Marie Reservation, Michigan	-	-	-	-	-	-	-	-
Chippewa County	-	-	-	-	-	-	-	-
Schaghticoke Reservation, Michigan	...	...	...	...	...	...	...	...
Litchfield County	...	...	...	...	...	...	...	...
Shakopee Community, Minnesota	48	41.2	39.0	-	2.2	40.5	3.2	61.4
Scott County	48	41.2	39.0	-	2.2	40.5	3.2	61.4
Sheep Ranch Rancheria, California	...	...	...	...	...	...	...	...

[Continued]

★ 236 ★

Geographic Mobility on Identified Reservations, 1980 - VII
[Continued]

Identified reservation	Persons 3 to 34 years old					Persons 16 to 19 years old -- percent not enrolled in school, not high school graduates	Persons 25 years and over	
	All persons	Percent enrolled in school					Percent completed less than 5 years of school	Percent high school graduates
		Total	5 to 19 years		20 to 34 years old			
			Total	Bureau of indian affairs or tribal school				
Calaveras County	...	...	...	...	...	...	...	...
Sherwood Valley Rancheria, California	...	...	...	...	...	...	...	...
Mendocino County	...	...	...	...	...	...	...	...
Shingle Springs Rancheria, California	-	-	-	-	-	-	-	-
El Dorado County	-	-	-	-	-	-	-	-
Shinnecock Reservation, New York	95	53.0	48.6	-	4.3	32.6	-	48.6
Suffolk County	95	53.0	48.6	-	4.3	32.6	-	48.6
Shoalwater Reservation, Washington	...	...	...	...	...	...	...	...
Pacific County	...	...	...	...	...	...	...	...
Sisseton Reservation, North Dakota-South Dakota	1,672	56.4	52.5	3.8	1.5	38.8	5.5	45.7
North Dakota	-	-	-	-	-	-	-	-
Richland County	-	-	-	-	-	-	-	-
Sargent County	-	-	-	-	-	-	-	-
South Dakota	1,672	56.4	52.5	3.8	1.5	38.8	5.5	45.7
Codington County	...	...	...	...	...	...	...	...
Day County	201	57.4	53.0	5.1	0.6	33.7	10.6	29.3
Grant County	-	-	-	-	-	-	-	-
Marshall County	167	59.6	57.2	-	2.4	29.4	1.4	48.9
Roberts County	1,304	55.8	51.9	4.1	1.5	40.7	5.3	47.6
Skokomish Reservation, Washington	180	58.3	54.2	2.5	2.1	34.2	4.8	40.8
Mason County	180	58.3	54.2	2.5	2.1	34.2	4.8	40.8
Skull Valley Reservation, Utah	-	-	-	-	-	-	-	-
Tooele County	-	-	-	-	-	-	-	-
Soboba Reservation, California	151	52.4	42.6	-	2.4	20.7	3.5	54.4
Riverside County	151	52.4	42.6	-	2.4	20.7	3.5	54.4
Sokaogon Chippewa Community, Wisconsin	55	29.7	24.1	-	5.6	50.0	2.3	51.1
Forest County	55	29.7	24.1	-	5.6	50.0	2.3	51.1
Southern Paiute Reservation, Utah	124	54.8	49.9	-	4.9	25.2	21.5	20.7
Iron County	62	59.9	50.1	-	9.8	29.8	19.2	21.4
Millard County	34	57.9	57.9	-	-	-	9.2	35.6
Sevier County	28	40.0	40.0	-	-	-	35.7	7.1
Southern Ute Reservation, Colorado	591	60.6	54.1	1.3	2.3	19.4	4.5	65.9
Archuleta County	...	...	...	...	...	...	...	...
La Plata County	582	60.5	53.9	1.3	2.3	17.7	4.3	66.2
Montezuma County	-	-	-	-	-	-	-	-
Spokane Reservation, Washington	688	49.4	45.6	0.3	3.1	24.6	4.8	52.9
Lincoln County	-	-	-	-	-	-	-	-
Stevens County	688	49.4	45.6	0.3	3.1	24.6	4.8	52.9
Squaxin Island Reservation, Washington	23	21.7	21.7	-	-	100.0	16.7	50.0
Mason County	23	21.7	21.7	-	-	100.0	16.7	50.0
Standing Rock Reservation, North Dakota-South Dakota	2,974	51.6	46.6	24.4	1.5	29.3	2.0	50.8
North Dakota	1,505	53.4	49.0	22.4	2.1	19.1	1.2	57.8
Sioux County	1,505	53.4	49.0	22.4	2.1	19.1	1.2	57.8
South Dakota	1,469	49.7	44.2	26.8	0.9	37.4	2.7	45.0
Corson County	1,469	49.7	44.2	26.8	0.9	37.4	2.7	45.0
Stewart's Point Rancheria, California	42	53.7	48.8	50.0	-	11.1	6.1	12.1

[Continued]

★ 236 ★

Geographic Mobility on Identified Reservations, 1980 - VII

[Continued]

Identified reservation	Persons 3 to 34 years old					Persons 16 to 19 years old -- percent not enrolled in school, not high school graduates	Persons 25 years and over	
		Percent enrolled in school						
			5 to 19 years					
	All persons	Total	Total	Bureau of indian affairs or tribal school	20 to 34 years old		Percent completed less than 5 years of school	Percent high school graduates
Sonoma County	42	53.7	48.8	50.0	-	11.1	6.1	12.1
Stockbridge Reservation, Wisconsin	324	57.2	50.6	3.2	4.7	23.1	3.2	49.8
Shawano County	324	57.2	50.6	3.2	4.7	23.1	3.2	49.8
Sulphur Bank Reservation, California	74	50.4	43.4	4.0	-	33.3	13.2	25.0
Lake County	74	50.4	43.4	4.0	-	33.3	13.2	25.0
Summit Lake Reservation, Nevada	...	...	...	...	...	...	...	...
Humboldt County	...	...	...	...	...	...	...	...
Susanville Reservation, California	51	63.8	59.6	-	4.2	42.9	6.1	52.1
Lassen County	51	63.8	59.6	-	4.2	42.9	6.1	52.1
Swinomish Reservation, Washington	282	51.4	42.3	4.6	2.6	49.8	4.6	39.5
Skagit County	282	51.4	42.3	4.6	2.6	49.8	4.6	39.5
Sycuan Reservation, California	33	77.2	77.2	-	-	25.0	22.4	21.3
San Diego County	33	77.2	77.2	-	-	25.0	22.4	21.3
Tama Reservation, Georgia	17	44.0	44.0	-	-	-	6.3	43.8
Grady County	17	44.0	44.0	-	-	-	6.3	43.8
Toas Pueblo, New Mexico	551	60.4	52.6	53.4	3.2	7.1	13.8	51.7
Toas County	551	60.4	52.6	53.4	3.2	7.1	13.8	51.7
Te-Moak Reservation, Nevada	45	66.6	63.0	-	3.6	-	19.6	38.3
Elko County	45	66.6	63.0	-	3.6	-	19.6	38.3
Tesuque Pueblo, New Mexico	135	60.1	51.1	25.8	4.9	-	8.0	62.7
Sante Fe County	135	60.1	51.1	25.8	4.9	-	8.0	62.7
Tigua Reservation, Texas	255	55.3	46.3	0.8	3.1	38.9	21.0	15.0
El Paso County	255	55.3	46.3	0.8	3.1	38.9	21.0	15.0
Tonawanda Reservation, New York	223	54.9	50.1	-	4.3	41.6	4.6	49.9
Erie County	-	-	-	-	-	-	-	-
Genesee County	223	54.9	50.1	-	4.3	41.6	4.6	49.9
Niagara County	-	-	-	-	-	-	-	-
Torres-Martinez Reservation, California	-	-	-	-	-	-	-	-
Imperial County	-	-	-	-	-	-	-	-
Riverside County	-	-	-	-	-	-	-	-
Trinidad Rancheria, California	29	46.8	39.0	-	7.8	33.3	4.7	50.0
Humboldt County	29	46.8	39.0	-	7.8	33.3	4.7	50.0
Tulalip Reservation, Washington	496	55.4	48.0	3.9	4.4	44.5	2.3	50.2
Snohomish County	496	55.4	48.0	3.9	4.4	44.5	2.3	50.2
Tule River Reservation, California	307	56.2	49.6	3.5	0.6	35.9	5.1	35.6
Tulare County	307	56.2	49.6	3.5	0.6	35.9	5.1	35.6
Tunica-Biloxi Reservation, Louisiana	...	...	...	...	...	...	...	...
Avoyelles Parish	...	...	...	...	...	...	...	...
Tuolumne Rancheria, California	49	69.4	63.3	-	6.1	-	4.7	53.5
Tuolumne County	49	69.4	63.3	-	6.1	-	4.7	53.5
Turtle Mountain Reservatin, North Dakota	2,562	58.6	51.7	73.6	3.6	36.4	9.6	38.8
Rolette County	2,562	58.6	51.7	73.6	3.6	36.4	9.6	38.8
Tuscarora Reservation, New York	-	-	-	-	-	-	-	-
Niagara County	-	-	-	-	-	-	-	-
Twenty-Nine Palms Reservation, California	-	-	-	-	-	-	-	-

[Continued]

★ 236 ★

Geographic Mobility on Identified Reservations, 1980 - VII
[Continued]

Identified reservation	Persons 3 to 34 years old					Persons 16 to 19 years old -- percent not enrolled in school, not high school graduates	Persons 25 years and over	
	All persons	Percent enrolled in school					Percent completed less than 5 years of school	Percent high school graduates
		Total	5 to 19 years		20 to 34 years old			
			Total	Bureau of indian affairs or tribal school				
San Bernardino County	-	-	-	-	-	-	-	-
Uintah and Ouray Reservation, Utah	1,451	53.6	45.4	6.6	2.2	33.6	7.4	47.7
Carbon County	-	-	-	-	-	-	-	-
Duchesne County	279	54.2	49.3	1.1	1.6	42.3	11.4	58.3
Grand County	-	-	-	-	-	-	-	-
Uintah County	1,173	53.4	44.5	8.1	2.4	31.8	6.4	45.0
Utah County	-	-	-	-	-	-	-	-
Wasatch County	-	-	-	-	-	-	-	-
Umatilla Reservation, Oregon	539	60.9	52.9	4.7	4.8	17.2	3.5	56.5
Umatilla County	539	60.9	52.9	4.7	4.8	17.2	3.5	56.5
Union County	-	-	-	-	-	-	-	-
Upper Sioux Community, Minnesota	25	50.2	50.2	-	-	-	7.6	31.9
Yellow Medicine County	25	50.2	50.2	-	-	-	7.6	31.9
Upper Skagit Reservation, Washington	-	-	-	-	-	-	-	-
Skagit County	-	-	-	-	-	-	-	-
Ute Mountain Reservation, Colorado-New Mexico	750	48.7	42.6	4.0	1.1	22.5	23.0	16.7
Colorado	750	48.7	42.6	4.0	1.1	22.5	23.0	16.7
La Plata County	-	-	-	-	-	-	-	-
Montezuma County	750	48.7	42.6	4.0	1.1	22.5	23.0	16.7
New Mexico	-	-	-	-	-	-	-	-
San Juan County	-	-	-	-	-	-	-	-
Vermillion Lake Reservation, Minnesota	62	50.1	47.8	-	-	16.8	-	56.7
St. Louis County	62	50.1	47.8	-	-	16.8	-	56.7
Viejas Rancheria, California	81	51.7	48.4	3.2	-	20.4	8.7	44.4
San Diego County	81	51.7	48.4	3.2	-	20.4	8.7	44.4
Walker River Reservation, Nevada	284	59.9	52.8	4.0	2.8	20.0	3.5	53.5
Churchill County	-	-	-	-	-	-	-	-
Lyon County	-	-	-	-	-	-	-	-
Mineral County	284	59.9	52.8	4.0	2.8	20.0	3.5	53.5
Wampanoag Reservation, Massachusetts	-	-	-	-	-	-	-	-
Bristol County	-	-	-	-	-	-	-	-
Warm Springs Reservation, Oregon	1,399	55.7	47.8	7.0	2.7	28.8	4.7	60.0
Clackamas County	-	-	-	-	-	-	-	-
Jefferson County	1,178	55.1	46.6	7.3	2.6	28.7	3.9	61.9
Marion County	-	-	-	-	-	-	-	-
Wasco County	222	58.9	54.2	5.5	2.8	29.4	8.3	51.2
Washoe Reservation, Nevada	-	-	-	-	-	-	-	-
Douglas County	-	-	-	-	-	-	-	-
Western Pequot Reservation, Connecticut	...	...	...	...	...	...	...	...
New London County	...	...	...	...	...	...	...	...
White Earth Reservation, Minnesota	1,609	52.2	46.6	7.4	2.0	35.0	2.0	44.5
Becker County	785	51.8	45.6	7.1	1.9	36.0	2.3	42.5
Clearwater County	208	51.2	43.6	13.5	2.7	50.1	4.6	33.3
Mahnomen County	615	53.1	49.0	5.9	1.9	27.8	1.0	50.0
Wind River Reservation, Wyoming	2,737	51.8	47.2	20.5	2.7	31.0	2.6	47.1
Fremont County	2,725	52.0	47.5	20.5	2.7	30.6	2.6	47.3

[Continued]

★ 236 ★

Geographic Mobility on Identified Reservations, 1980 - VII
[Continued]

Identified reservation	Persons 3 to 34 years old					Persons 16 to 19 years old -- percent not enrolled in school, not high school graduates	Persons 25 years and over	
	All persons	Percent enrolled in school					Percent completed less than 5 years of school	Percent high school graduates
		Total	5 to 19 years		20 to 34 years old			
			Total	Bureau of indian affairs or tribal school				
Hot Springs County	...	...	...	...	...	...	...	...
Winnebago Reservation, Nebraska	693	58.3	50.0	5.6	3.2	23.0	2.8	55.1
Dixon County	...	...	...	...	...	...	...	...
Thurston County	692	58.2	50.1	5.6	3.2	23.0	2.6	55.2
Winnemucca Colony, Nevada	21	55.4	55.4	-	-	-	7.1	35.7
Humboldt County	21	55.4	55.4	-	-	-	7.1	35.7
Wisconsin Winnebago Reservation	259	63.2	54.9	5.1	4.6	34.4	3.0	50.9
Jackson County	31	59.7	59.7	-	-	-	-	28.9
Juneau County	64	57.4	52.8	4.3	4.6	39.1	10.8	30.8
Monroe County	...	...	...	...	...	...	...	...
Sauk County	73	58.9	55.9	-	-	46.7	-	57.4
Shawano County	...	...	...	...	...	...	...	...
Wood County	70	79.3	71.2	11.7	3.5	20.5	-	61.1
Woodfords Community, California	-	-	-	-	-	-	-	-
Alpine County	-	-	-	-	-	-	-	-
XL Ranch Reservation, California	...	...	...	...	...	...	...	...
Modoc County	...	...	...	...	...	...	...	...
Yakima Reservation, Washington	3,206	55.6	48.5	6.1	3.8	30.6	4.7	51.3
Klickitat County	53	41.5	34.0	-	3.8	-	-	68.4
Yakima County	3,153	55.9	48.8	6.2	3.8	31.0	4.7	51.2
Yankton Reservation, South Dakota	1,059	48.2	45.1	24.1	1.1	22.7	6.9	40.8
Charles Mix County	1,059	48.2	45.1	24.1	1.1	22.7	6.9	40.8
Yavapai Reservation, Arizona	42	66.7	47.6	-	16.7	-	7.4	55.6
Yavapai County	42	66.7	47.6	-	16.7	-	7.4	55.6
Yerington Reservation, Nevada	64	75.8	67.5	-	3.2	-	14.7	43.6
Lyon County	64	75.8	67.5	-	3.2	-	14.7	43.6
Yomba Reservation, Nevada	40	46.1	43.4	5.8	2.7	15.2	8.2	20.9
Nye County	40	46.1	43.4	5.8	2.7	15.2	8.2	20.9
Zia Pueblo, New Mexico	338	58.5	48.0	44.2	3.4	15.9	6.9	49.7
Sandoval County	338	58.5	48.0	44.2	3.4	15.9	6.9	49.7
Zuni Pueblo, New Mexico	4,168	53.0	48.9	5.2	2.2	30.2	5.6	38.3
McKinley County	4,168	53.0	48.9	5.2	2.2	30.2	5.6	38.3
Valencia County	-	-	-	-	-	-	-	-
San Felipe/Santa Ana Joint Area, New Mexico	-	-	-	-	-	-	-	-
Sandoval County	-	-	-	-	-	-	-	-
San Felipe/Santo Domingo Joint Area, New Mexico	88	64.5	49.3	-	10.1	35.4	-	64.2
Sandoval County	88	64.5	49.3	-	10.1	35.4	-	64.2
Other Reservation Lands in Montana	-	-	-	-	-	-	-	-
Big Horn County	-	-	-	-	-	-	-	-

Source: U.S. Bureau of the Census, Subject Reports, PC80-2-1D, Part 1, *American Indians, Eskimos, and Aleuts on Identified Reservations and in the Historic Areas of Oklahoma (Excluding Urbanized Areas)*, U.S. Government Printing Office, Washington, D.C., 1986, pp. 50-58. *Notes:* A dash "(-)" represents zero or a percent which rounds to less than 0.1. Also, a dash "(-)" is used because the number of supplementary questionnaires for the reservations was insufficient to produce reliable estimates. Three dots "..." means not applicable, or that the data are being withheld to avoid disclosure of information for individuals.

Geographic Mobility on Identified Reservations, 1980 - VIII

Data are the latest available.

Identified reservations	Persons 1 year and over						
	Total	Always lived on this reservation	Did not always live on this reservation				
			Total		Percent moved onto reservation in--		
			Number	Percent	1979 or 1980	1975 to 1978	1974 or earlier
St. Croix Reservation, Wisconsin	401	161	216	53.7	7.2	22.3	24.2
Barron County	82	52	30	37.0	3.8	6.9	26.3
Burnett County	241	68	151	62.8	8.3	24.6	29.9
Polk County	78	42	34	43.2	7.4	31.1	4.7
St. Regis Mohawk Reservation, New York	1,722	1,476	220	12.8	1.9	4.7	6.2
Franklin County	1,722	1,476	220	12.8	1.9	4.7	6.2
Salt River Reservation, Arizona	2,523	1,791	519	20.6	8.7	4.1	7.7
Maricopa County	2,523	1,791	519	20.6	8.7	4.1	7.7
San Carlos Reservation, Arizona	5,631	4,136	877	15.6	6.0	3.9	5.7
Gila County	3,322	2,535	613	18.5	7.0	4.7	6.8
Graham County	2,309	1,600	264	11.4	4.5	2.8	4.1
Pinal County	-	-	-	-	-	-	-
Sandia Pueblo, New Mexico	218	140	47	21.7	7.8	4.2	9.7
Bernalillo County	-	-	-	-	-	-	-
Sandoval County	218	140	47	21.7	7.8	4.2	9.7
Sandy Lake Reservation, Minnesota	-	-	-	-	-	-	-
Aitkin County	-	-	-	-	-	-	-
San Felipe Pueblo, New Mexico	1,742	1,663	67	3.9	0.6	0.5	2.8
Sandoval County	1,742	1,663	67	3.9	0.6	0.5	2.8
San Ildefonso Pueblo, New Mexico	470	351	110	23.4	3.7	3.7	16.0
Sandoval County	-	-	-	-	-	-	-
Sante Fe County	470	351	110	23.4	3.7	3.7	16.0
San Juan Pueblo, New Mexico	822	565	228	27.7	6.8	7.6	13.3
Rio Arriba County	822	565	228	27.7	6.8	7.6	13.3
San Manuel Reservation, California	-	-	-	-	-	-	-
San Bernardino County	-	-	-	-	-	-	-
San Pasqual Reservation, California	118	6	77	65.0	7.2	34.7	23.2
San Diego County	118	6	77	65.0	7.2	34.7	23.2
Santa Ana Pueblo, New Mexico	397	243	146	36.8	7.0	10.4	19.4
Sandoval County	397	243	146	36.8	7.0	10.4	19.4
Santa Clara Pueblo, New Mexico	1,780	1,036	662	37.2	9.5	8.7	19.0
Rio Arriba County	1,754	1,032	653	37.2	9.6	8.7	18.9
Sandoval County	-	-	-	-	-	-	-
Sante Fe County	...	...	...	...	...	...	...
Santa Rosa Rancheria, California	118	81	37	31.0	5.9	15.5	9.6
Kings County	118	81	37	31.0	5.9	15.5	9.6
Santa Rosa Reservation, California	...	...	...	...	...	...	...
Riverside County	...	...	...	...	...	...	...
Santa Ynez Reservation, California	119	34	83	70.1	29.9	7.2	33.0
Santa Barbara County	119	34	83	70.1	29.9	7.2	33.0
Santa Ysabel Reservation, California	173	36	118	68.0	14.4	23.2	30.4
San Diego County	173	36	118	68.0	14.4	23.2	30.4
Santee Reservation, Nebraska	402	62	115	28.7	7.8	10.3	10.5
Knox County	402	62	115	28.7	7.8	10.3	10.5
Santo Domingo Pueblo, New Mexico	2,087	1,720	360	17.2	3.6	3.7	10.0
Sandoval County	2,087	1,720	360	17.2	3.6	3.7	10.0
Santa Fe County	-	-	-	-	-	-	-
San Xavier Reservation, Arizona	817	487	314	38.5	7.7	12.2	18.6
Pima County	817	487	314	38.5	7.7	12.2	18.6

[Continued]

★ 237 ★

Geographic Mobility on Identified Reservations, 1980 - VIII
[Continued]

Identified reservations	Total	Always lived on this reservation	Persons 1 year and over				
			Did not always live on this reservation				
			Total		Percent moved onto reservation in--		
					1979 or 1980	1975 to 1978	1974 or earlier
			Number	Percent			
Sauk-Suiattle Reservation, Washington	-	-	-	-	-	-	-
Snohomish County	-	-	-	-	-	-	-
Sault Ste. Marie Reservation, Michigan	-	-	-	-	-	-	-
Chippewa County	-	-	-	-	-	-	-
Schaghticoke Reservation, Michigan	...	...	...	...	...	...	...
Litchfield County	...	...	...	...	...	...	...
Shakopee Community, Minnesota	73	8	54	74.8	5.6	14.7	54.5
Scott County	73	8	54	74.8	5.6	14.7	54.5
Sheep Ranch Rancheria, California	...	...	...	...	...	...	...
Calaveras County	...	...	...	...	...	...	...
Sherwood Valley Rancheria, California	...	...	...	...	...	...	...
Mendocino County	...	...	...	...	...	...	...
Shingle Springs Rancheria, California	-	-	-	-	-	-	-
El Dorado County	-	-	-	-	-	-	-
Shinnecock Reservation, New York	194	98	78	40.1	13.7	8.0	18.4
Suffolk County	194	98	78	40.1	13.7	8.0	18.4
Shoalwater Reservation, Washington	...	...	...	...	...	...	...
Pacific County	...	...	...	...	...	...	...
Sisseton Reservation, North Dakota-South Dakota	2,498	1,519	920	36.8	11.2	11.9	13.7
North Dakota	-	-	-	-	-	-	-
Richland County	-	-	-	-	-	-	-
Sargent County	-	-	-	-	-	-	-
South Dakota	2,498	1,519	920	36.8	11.2	11.9	13.7
Codington County	...	...	...	...	...	...	...
Day County	302	206	92	30.4	10.9	12.6	6.9
Grant County	-	-	-	-	-	-	-
Marshall County	249	118	126	50.5	7.6	27.3	15.6
Roberts County	1,944	1,193	702	36.1	11.7	9.9	14.5
Skokomish Reservation, Washington	295	200	88	29.8	8.4	12.8	8.6
Mason County	295	200	88	29.8	8.4	12.8	8.6
Skull Valley Reservation, Utah	-	-	-	-	-	-	-
Tooele County	-	-	-	-	-	-	-
Soboba Reservation, California	226	139	81	36.0	13.3	9.6	13.1
Riverside County	226	139	81	36.0	13.3	9.6	13.1
Sokaogon Chippewa Community, Wisconsin	93	52	41	44.4	15.2	16.3	13.0
Forest County	93	52	41	44.4	15.2	16.3	13.0
Southern Paiute Reservation, Utah	181	98	83	45.7	15.9	19.1	10.7
Iron County	91	55	36	39.6	19.5	5.3	14.8
Millard County	48	18	30	62.2	5.5	50.5	6.3
Sevier County	42	25	17	40.0	20.0	13.3	6.7
Southern Ute Reservation, Colorado	858	476	212	24.7	7.5	5.3	11.8
Archuleta County	...	...	...	...	...	...	...
La Plata County	846	475	202	23.8	7.3	5.4	11.2
Montezuma County	-	-	-	-	-	-	-
Spokane Reservation, Washington	1,019	395	622	61.1	11.6	21.2	28.2
Lincoln County	-	-	-	-	-	-	-
Stevens County	1,019	395	622	61.1	11.6	21.2	28.2
Squaxin Island Reservation, Washington	29	-	27	93.1	13.8	79.3	-
Mason County	29	-	27	93.1	13.8	79.3	-

[Continued]

★ 237 ★

Geographic Mobility on Identified Reservations, 1980 - VIII
[Continued]

Identified reservations	Total	Always lived on this reservation	Persons 1 year and over				
			Did not always live on this reservation				
			Total		Percent moved onto reservation in--		
			Number	Percent	1979 or 1980	1975 to 1978	1974 or earlier
Standing Rock Reservation, North Dakota-South Dakota	4,428	2,841	1,268	28.6	10.2	6.9	11.6
North Dakota	2,160	1,510	628	29.1	7.0	9.3	12.8
Sioux County	2,160	1,510	628	29.1	7.0	9.3	12.8
South Dakota	2,268	1,331	640	28.2	13.1	4.6	10.4
Corson County	2,268	1,331	640	28.2	13.1	4.6	10.4
Stewart's Point Rancheria, California	70	22	35	50.7	1.4	14.5	34.8
Sonoma County	70	22	35	50.7	1.4	14.5	34.8
Stockbridge Reservation, Wisconsin	561	72	422	75.1	11.7	19.9	43.5
Shawano County	561	72	422	75.1	11.7	19.9	43.5
Sulphur Bank Reservation, California	110	71	38	34.9	13.7	11.9	9.2
Lake County	110	71	38	34.9	13.7	11.9	9.2
Summit Lake Reservation, Nevada	...	...	...	...	...	...	...
Humboldt County	...	...	...	...	...	...	...
Susanville Reservation, California	83	13	46	55.0	6.5	33.5	15.0
Lassen County	83	13	46	55.0	6.5	33.5	15.0
Swinomish Reservation, Washington	413	163	246	59.6	18.7	7.8	33.0
Skagit County	413	163	246	59.6	18.7	7.8	33.0
Sycuan Reservation, California	54	17	37	68.8	-	6.6	62.2
San Diego County	54	17	37	68.8	-	6.6	62.2
Tama Reservation, Georgia	30	-	30	100.0	17.9	42.8	39.2
Grady County	30	-	30	100.0	17.9	42.8	39.2
Toas Pueblo, New Mexico	1,032	767	240	23.2	5.5	6.3	11.5
Toas County	1,032	767	240	23.2	5.5	6.3	11.5
Te-Moak Reservation, Nevada	91	27	64	70.0	1.4	24.7	43.9
Elko County	91	27	64	70.0	1.4	24.7	43.9
Tesuque Pueblo, New Mexico	232	158	63	27.0	5.6	8.0	13.3
Sante Fe County	232	158	63	27.0	5.6	8.0	13.3
Tigua Reservation, Texas	353	1	352	99.7	4.2	93.2	2.3
El Paso County	353	1	352	99.7	4.2	93.2	2.3
Tonawanda Reservation, New York	432	275	92	21.3	5.3	2.7	13.2
Erie County	-	-	-	-	-	-	-
Genesee County	432	275	92	21.3	5.3	2.7	13.2
Niagara County	-	-	-	-	-	-	-
Torres-Martinez Reservation, California	-	-	-	-	-	-	-
Imperial County	-	-	-	-	-	-	-
Riverside County	-	-	-	-	-	-	-
Trinidad Rancheria, California	46	1	40	87.9	10.0	21.9	56.0
Humboldt County	46	1	40	87.9	10.0	21.9	56.0
Tulalip Reservation, Washington	745	364	349	46.8	15.2	12.4	19.3
Snohomish County	745	364	349	46.8	15.2	12.4	19.3
Tule River Reservation, California	415	292	116	28.1	13.4	6.5	8.1
Tulare County	415	292	116	28.1	13.4	6.5	8.1
Tunica-Biloxi Reservation, Louisiana	...	...	...	...	...	...	...
Avoyelles Parish	...	...	...	...	...	...	...
Tuolumne Rancheria, California	81	17	64	79.0	18.5	23.5	37.0
Tuolumne County	81	17	64	79.0	18.5	23.5	37.0
Turtle Mountain Reservatin, North Dakota	3,881	2,728	1,100	28.3	7.1	5.8	15.5
Rolette County	3,881	2,728	1,100	28.3	7.1	5.8	15.5
Tuscarora Reservation, New York	-	-	-	-	-	-	-

[Continued]

453

★ 237 ★

Geographic Mobility on Identified Reservations, 1980 - VIII
[Continued]

Identified reservations	Total	Always lived on this reservation	Persons 1 year and over				
			Did not always live on this reservation				
			Total		Percent moved onto reservation in--		
			Number	Percent	1979 or 1980	1975 to 1978	1974 or earlier
Niagara County	-	-	-	-	-	-	-
Twenty-Nine Palms Reservation, California	-	-	-	-	-	-	-
San Bernardino County	-	-	-	-	-	-	-
Uintah and Ouray Reservation, Utah	2,110	1,280	440	20.9	6.9	4.6	9.3
Carbon County	-	-	-	-	-	-	-
Duchesne County	413	248	56	13.6	7.3	1.8	4.4
Grand County	-	-	-	-	-	-	-
Uintah County	1,697	1,032	384	22.6	6.8	5.3	10.6
Utah County	-	-	-	-	-	-	-
Wasatch County	-	-	-	-	-	-	-
Umatilla Reservation, Oregon	881	387	458	52.0	12.2	18.3	21.6
Umatilla County	881	387	458	52.0	12.2	18.3	21.6
Union County	-	-	-	-	-	-	-
Upper Sioux Community, Minnesota	52	8	44	84.0	8.1	17.9	57.9
Yellow Medicine County	52	8	44	84.0	8.1	17.9	57.9
Upper Skagit Reservation, Washington	-	-	-	-	-	-	-
Skagit County	-	-	-	-	-	-	-
Ute Mountain Reservation, Colorado-New Mexico	1,085	557	113	10.4	3.8	2.6	4.0
Colorado	1,085	557	113	10.4	3.8	2.6	4.0
La Plata County	-	-	-	-	-	-	-
Montezuma County	1,085	557	113	10.4	3.8	2.6	4.0
New Mexico	-	-	-	-	-	-	-
San Juan County	-	-	-	-	-	-	-
Vermillion Lake Reservation, Minnesota	104	23	79	75.8	32.1	16.1	27.6
St. Louis County	104	23	79	75.8	32.1	16.1	27.6
Viejas Rancheria, California	142	53	86	60.3	15.6	14.7	30.0
San Diego County	142	53	86	60.3	15.6	14.7	30.0
Walker River Reservation, Nevada	469	226	240	51.2	12.2	13.6	25.4
Churchill County	-	-	-	-	-	-	-
Lyon County	-	-	-	-	-	-	-
Mineral County	469	226	240	51.2	12.2	13.6	25.4
Wampanoag Reservation, Massachusetts	-	-	-	-	-	-	-
Bristol County	-	-	-	-	-	-	-
Warm Springs Reservation, Oregon	1,936	1,094	626	32.3	9.0	9.1	14.3
Clackamas County	-	-	-	-	-	-	-
Jefferson County	1,603	871	560	34.9	9.8	10.0	15.0
Marion County	-	-	-	-	-	-	-
Wasco County	332	222	66	20.0	5.0	4.5	10.5
Washoe Reservation, Nevada	-	-	-	-	-	-	-
Douglas County	-	-	-	-	-	-	-
Western Pequot Reservation, Connecticut	...	...	...	...	...	...	...
New London County	...	...	...	...	...	...	...
White Earth Reservation, Minnesota	2,481	1,505	953	38.4	7.0	15.6	15.8
Becker County	1,218	763	439	36.0	7.6	16.1	12.3
Clearwater County	306	236	68	22.1	7.5	11.3	3.3
Mahnomen County	956	505	446	46.7	6.0	16.3	24.4
Wind River Reservation, Wyoming	4,020	2,670	913	22.7	7.6	7.4	7.7
Fremont County	4,000	2,650	913	22.8	7.7	7.4	7.7

[Continued]

454

★ 237 ★

Geographic Mobility on Identified Reservations, 1980 - VIII
[Continued]

Identified reservations	Total	Always lived on this reservation	Persons 1 year and over				
			Did not always live on this reservation				
			Total		Percent moved onto reservation in--		
			Number	Percent	1979 or 1980	1975 to 1978	1974 or earlier
Hot Springs County	...	...	...	...	...	...	...
Winnebago Reservation, Nebraska	1,066	323	292	27.4	8.8	8.1	10.5
Dixon County	...	...	...	...	...	...	...
Thurston County	1,064	323	292	27.5	8.8	8.1	10.5
Winnemucca Colony, Nevada	32	8	24	74.3	43.6	-	30.7
Humboldt County	32	8	24	74.3	43.6	-	30.7
Wisconsin Winnebago Reservation	348	10	223	64.1	16.9	28.9	18.3
Jackson County	36	10	-	-	-	-	-
Juneau County	95	-	95	100.0	21.5	24.4	54.1
Monroe County	...	...	...	...	...	...	...
Sauk County	92	-	24	26.2	2.4	23.7	-
Shawano County	...	...	...	...	...	...	...
Wood County	93	-	93	100.0	32.7	53.8	13.5
Woodfords Community, California	-	-	-	-	-	-	-
Alpine County	-	-	-	-	-	-	-
XL Ranch Reservation, California	...	...	...	...	...	...	...
Modoc County	...	...	...	...	...	...	...
Yakima Reservation, Washington	4,810	2,982	1,472	30.6	6.2	8.8	15.6
Klickitat County	66	43	23	34.8	13.6	9.1	12.1
Yakima County	4,744	2,939	1,449	30.5	6.1	8.7	15.7
Yankton Reservation, South Dakota	1,581	861	645	40.8	12.1	16.4	12.4
Charles Mix County	1,581	861	645	40.8	12.1	16.4	12.4
Yavapai Reservation, Arizona	63	34	29	46.0	15.9	7.9	22.2
Yavapai County	63	34	29	46.0	15.9	7.9	22.2
Yerington Reservation, Nevada	107	42	64	60.1	1.0	12.6	46.5
Lyon County	107	42	64	60.1	1.0	12.6	46.5
Yomba Reservation, Nevada	56	28	28	49.2	18.5	14.7	16.1
Nye County	56	28	28	49.2	18.5	14.7	16.1
Zia Pueblo, New Mexico	499	457	40	8.1	1.9	1.9	4.3
Sandoval County	499	457	40	8.1	1.9	1.9	4.3
Zuni Pueblo, New Mexico	5,831	5,151	599	10.3	2.2	3.0	5.1
McKinley County	5,831	5,151	599	10.3	2.2	3.0	5.1
Valencia County	-	-	-	-	-	-	-
San Felipe/Santa Ana Joint Area, New Mexico	-	-	-	-	-	-	-
Sandoval County	-	-	-	-	-	-	-
San Felipe/Santo Domingo Joint Area, New Mexico	112	100	11	10.2	2.3	5.0	2.9
Sandoval County	112	100	11	10.2	2.3	5.0	2.9
Other Reservation Lands in Montana	-	-	-	-	-	-	-
Big Horn County	-	-	-	-	-	-	-

Source: U.S. Bureau of the Census, Subject Reports, PC80-2-1D, Part 1, *American Indians, Eskimos, and Aleuts on Identified Reservations and in the Historic Areas of Oklahoma (Excluding Urbanized Areas)*, U.S. Government Printing Office, Washington, D.C., 1986, pp. 50-58. *Notes:* A dash "(-)" represents zero or a percent which rounds to less than 0.1. Also, a dash "(-)" is used because the number of supplementary questionnaires for the reservations was insufficient to produce reliable estimates. Three dots "..." means not applicable, or that the data are being withheld to avoid disclosure of information for individuals.

Chapter 3
THE FAMILY

Households

★ 238 ★

Household and Family Characteristics, by Major Tribal Group, 1980: Abenaki-Pamunkey - I

Data are estimates based on a sample and are the most recent available.

Major Tribal Group	Household Type and Relationship									Persons in households		
	In households	Family householder	Non-Family householder		Spouse	Other relative	Non-relative	Persons per household	Persons per family	Households	1 Person	2 Persons
			Male	Female								
All American Indians	1,434,267	331,458	50,573	47,529	240,930	701,825	61,952	3.34	3.84	429,560	79,538	99,884
Abenaki (n.e.c)	814	183	30	32	140	365	64	3.32	3.76	245	50	57
Alabama Coushatta[1]	1,051	256	23	34	212	507	19	3.36	3.81	313	50	41
Alaska Native (n.e.c.)	554	124	27	14	96	267	24	3.36	3.94	165	50	75
Alaska Athabaskans	9,912	1,927	463	296	1,415	5,248	583	3.69	4.46	2,686	600	582
Aleut and Eskimo	631	156	27	27	97	294	30	3.00	3.51	210	35	60
Algonquian (n.e.c.)	1,685	449	107	75	239	745	70	2.67	3.19	631	142	145
Apache	34,241	7,296	1,430	739	5,034	17,736	2,006	3.62	4.12	9,456	1,657	2,016
Arapaho	4,283	895	147	69	617	2,389	166	3.86	4.36	1,111	145	186
Arikara	1,465	332	7	32	176	877	41	3.95	4.17	371	29	38
Assiniboine	3,906	780	103	106	563	2,219	135	3.95	4.57	989	188	149
Bannock	478	117	-	6	110	234	11	3.89	3.94	123	6	41
Blackfoot[1]	21,122	5,328	1,097	780	4,084	8,609	1,224	2.93	3.38	7,205	1,405	1,508
Brotherton	173	42	11	2	43	75	-	3.15	3.81	55	13	15
Caddo	1,670	396	42	51	280	835	66	3.42	3.82	489	87	138
Cahuilla	1,231	248	42	71	193	636	41	3.41	4.34	361	87	66
California tribes (n.e.c.)	568	143	53	10	72	258	32	2.76	3.31	206	42	85
Canadian and Latin American	7,577	1,744	511	256	1,272	3,226	568	3.02	3.58	2,511	539	569
Catawba	1,495	259	13	48	237	914	24	4.67	5.44	320	54	39
Cayuse	150	27	7	16	15	75	10	3.00	4.33	50	23	1
Chehalis	255	56	-	16	44	136	3	3.54	4.21	72	16	29
Chemakuan	473	84	10	2	31	319	27	4.93	5.17	96	12	33
Chemehuevi	462	90	-	7	89	226	50	4.76	4.50	97	7	10
Cherokee	226,258	58,531	9,623	10,656	47,399	90,006	10,043	2.87	3.35	78,810	16,770	21,304
Cheyenne	9,441	1,735	393	179	1,304	5,305	525	4.09	4.81	2,307	497	325
Chickahominy	838	185	31	15	191	411	5	3.63	4.25	231	39	66
Chickasaw	10,114	2,640	312	648	2,068	4,300	146	2.81	3.41	3,600	854	1,018
Chinook	1,339	284	71	42	167	714	61	3.37	4.10	397	106	80
Chippewa	71,302	15,288	2,207	1,949	10,164	37,963	3,371	3.67	4.15	19,444	3,307	4,023
Chitimacha	340	68	-	-	45	220	7	5.00	4.90	68	-	6
Choctaw	48,952	12,088	1,895	2,256	9,557	21,906	1,250	3.01	3.60	16,239	3,673	4,167
Chumash[1]	1,433	283	71	62	246	742	29	3.44	4.49	416	103	101
Clallam	893	161	51	28	138	476	39	3.72	4.81	240	66	62
Coeur d'Alene	668	105	36	6	70	362	89	4.54	5.11	147	30	28
Coharie	490	119	-	6	120	245	-	3.92	4.07	125	6	43
Colorado River	654	212	34	14	153	515	29	3.67	4.15	260	41	66
Colville	5,357	1,077	210	222	772	2,768	308	3.55	4.29	1,509	346	314
Comanche	8,720	2,172	429	259	1,419	4,229	212	3.05	3.60	2,660	533	719
Coos	128	22	4	11	17	74	-	3.46	5.14	37	11	9
Costanoan	506	97	13	14	58	314	10	4.08	4.84	124	27	13
Cowitz	936	214	33	53	221	393	22	3.12	3.87	300	76	65
Cree	6,290	1,281	220	200	878	3,447	264	3.70	4.38	1,701	328	315

[Continued]

456

Household and Family Characteristics, by Major Tribal Group, 1980: Abenaki-Pamunkey - I
[Continued]

Major Tribal Group	In households	Family householder	Non-Family householder		Spouse	Other relative	Non-relative	Persons per household	Persons per family	Persons in households		
			Male	Female						Households	1 Person	2 Persons
Creek	27,670	6,549	927	1,161	5,163	13,244	626	3.20	3.81	8,637	1,863	2,056
Croatan	182	54	-	12	14	90	12	2.76	2.93	66	12	12
Crow	6,885	1,374	165	98	924	4,147	177	4.21	4.69	1,637	221	217
Cupeno	283	58	20	23	30	135	17	2.80	3.84	101	37	12
Delaware	5,302	1,304	192	195	1,064	2,385	162	3.14	3.64	1,691	315	411
Diegueno	1,381	313	84	57	174	703	50	3.04	3.80	454	112	96
Eastern tribes (n.e.c.)	2,580	694	86	57	484	1,228	31	3.08	3.47	837	138	160
Flathead	4,755	1,078	177	128	710	2,414	248	3.44	3.90	1,383	255	330
Fort Hall	436	98	-	9	59	250	20	4.07	4.15	107	9	12
Gabrieleno	1,810	375	21	29	317	997	71	4.26	4.50	425	29	107
Gros Ventres	2,038	429	43	62	305	1,131	68	3.82	4.35	534	91	75
Haida	1,417	328	63	47	211	722	46	3.24	3.84	438	93	79
Haliwa	2,074	477	51	7	428	1,069	42	3.88	4.14	535	48	55
Hidatsa	1,510	278	33	20	171	926	82	4.56	4.95	331	43	48
Hitchiti	22	7	-	-	-	15	-	3.14	3.14	7	-	-
Hoopa	1,955	449	63	56	335	1,003	49	3.44	3.98	568	105	157
Houma	2,587	519	68	42	465	1,458	35	4.11	4.71	629	101	101
Iowa	931	161	56	61	140	466	27	3.12	4.35	298	101	97
Iroquois	37,292	8,705	1,434	1,561	6,279	17,373	1,940	3.19	3.72	11,700	2,333	2,858
Kalispel	181	42	7	4	11	108	9	3.42	3.83	53	11	6
Karok	1,943	437	75	94	266	983	83	3.21	3.86	606	140	122
Kaw	673	158	33	16	167	262	17	3.25	3.84	207	32	61
Kickapoo	2,128	513	56	51	327	1,131	50	3.43	3.84	620	80	148
Kiowa	7,009	1,448	132	124	1,161	3,951	193	4.11	4.53	1,704	208	336
Klamath	2,029	357	67	68	319	1,051	167	4.12	4.84	492	106	131
Konkow	321	127	15	7	52	120	-	2.15	2.35	149	7	43
Kootenai	367	89	21	5	60	126	66	3.19	3.09	115	16	55
Long Island	304	93	-	17	61	133	-	2.76	3.09	110	5	16
Luiseno	1,209	210	50	22	245	667	15	4.29	5.34	282	53	59
Lumbee[2]	28,192	6,448	543	474	5,011	15,201	515	3.78	4.13	7,465	889	1,259
Lummi[2]	4,036	898	50	56	606	2,270	156	4.02	4.20	1,004	78	172
Maidu	1,171	246	26	45	202	623	29	3.69	4.35	317	63	49
Makah	1,005	216	31	21	126	539	72	3.75	4.08	268	52	76
Maliseet	521	113	9	15	63	316	5	3.80	4.35	137	24	25
Mandan	964	186	52	20	128	526	52	3.74	4.52	258	52	62
Mattaponi	136	40	6	5	25	60	-	2.67	3.13	51	11	6
Menominee	6,879	1,167	102	125	783	3,386	316	4.22	4.57	1,394	153	241
Miami	2,290	577	57	99	325	1,180	52	3.12	3.61	733	134	174
Miccosukee[1]	46	14	7	-	9	16	-	2.19	2.79	21	7	-
Micmac[3]	1,079	189	41	24	168	545	112	4.25	4.77	254	48	75
Mission Indians	2,469	579	104	137	517	1,054	78	3.01	3.71	820	187	184
Miwok	2,107	478	66	75	397	1,015	76	3.40	3.95	619	112	209
Modoc	702	163	36	29	122	283	69	3.08	3.48	228	57	51
Mohegan	514	144	20	20	108	204	18	2.79	3.17	184	38	69
Mono	1,329	258	97	69	183	647	75	3.13	4.22	424	154	40
Nanticoke	983	286	51	50	204	355	37	2.54	2.95	387	78	128
Narragansett	2,046	511	70	84	281	1,053	47	3.08	3.61	665	126	185
Navajo	155,208	29,802	2,201	2,334	22,308	94,603	3,960	4.52	4.92	34,337	3,951	4,656
Nez Perce[1]	2,106	483	169	61	359	883	151	2.95	3.57	713	149	145
Nomalaki	228	48	11	-	28	141	-	3.86	4.52	59	11	5
Northwest tribes (n.e.c.)	276	108	27	16	37	85	3	1.83	2.13	151	32	48
Omaha	2,958	591	73	35	361	1,751	147	4.23	4.57	699	90	131
Oregon Athabaskan	615	161	24	9	103	296	22	3.17	3.48	194	33	41
Osage	6,727	1,639	406	393	1,227	2,869	193	2.76	3.50	2,438	696	707
Oto	1,469	341	21	25	239	744	99	3.80	3.88	387	39	120
Ottawa	6,331	1,335	196	162	1,044	3,341	263	3.74	4.28	1,693	288	443
Paiute[1]	9,294	2,036	311	289	1,263	5,046	349	3.53	4.10	2,636	488	574
Pamunkey	335	90	6	11	70	152	6	3.13	3.47	107	11	32

Source: U.S. Bureau of the Census, *1980 Census of Population, Volume 2, Subject Reports, Characteristics of American Indians, by Tribes and Selected Areas: 1980,* PC80-2-1C, Section 1: Tables I-II, issued September 1989, U.S. Department of Commerce, U.S. Government Printing Office, Washington, D.C., pp. 150-202. *Notes:* (N.E.C.) stands for not elsewhere classified. A dash (-) represents zero or a percent which rounds to less than 0.1. 1. Reporting and/or processing problems may have affected the data for this tribe. 2. Miscoding of entries of "Lummee," "Lummi," "Lumbee," or "Lumbi" may have affected the data for this tribe. 3. Any entry with the spelling "Micmac" was miscoded to Cheyenne River Sioux.

★ 239 ★

Household and Family Characteristics, by Major Tribal Group, 1980: Abenaki-Pamunkey - II

Data are estimates based on a sample and are the most recent available.

Major Tribal Group	Persons in Household (cont.)				Family Type, by Presence of Own Children					
					Families		Married-couple, families		Female householder, no husband present	
	3 Persons	4 Persons	5 Persons	6 or more persons	Total Families	With own children under 18 years	Total married coupled families	With own children under 18 years	Total female householder, no husband present	With own children under 18 years
All American Indians	77,090	72,179	46,948	53,921	331,458	218,575	238,304	156,041	75,390	53,164
Abenaki (n.e.c)	34	66	19	19	183	130	121	81	60	47
Alabama Coushatta[1]	29	80	29	84	256	184	212	161	21	16
Alaska Native (n.e.c.)	40	12	7	2	124	76	57	23	53	41
Alaskan Athabaskans	455	377	289	383	1,927	1,397	1,129	806	609	481
Aleut and Eskimo	47	27	28	13	156	106	108	66	38	38
Algonquian (n.e.c.)	83	106	76	79	449	347	327	229	91	89
Apache	1,659	1,294	1,128	1,711	7,296	5,213	5,022	3,569	1,837	1,381
Arapaho	200	162	153	265	895	625	523	388	345	228
Arikara	76	96	40	92	332	276	223	192	102	80
Assiniboine	199	175	117	161	780	523	526	383	208	118
Bannock	23	12	17	24	117	85	95	76	22	9
Blackfoot[1]	1,551	1,169	830	742	5,328	3,791	3,634	2,518	1,319	1,028
Brotherton	3	2	16	6	42	27	35	22	7	5
Caddo	64	62	67	71	396	231	287	163	103	68
Cahuilla	49	88	35	36	248	162	195	119	41	31
California tribes (n.e.c.)	11	34	9	25	143	95	95	59	41	29
Canadian and Latin American	520	457	217	209	1,744	1,290	1,198	894	423	322
Catawba	83	62	50	32	259	211	219	186	28	13
Cayuse	7	6	5	8	27	20	15	8	12	12
Chehalis	10	14	-	3	56	32	21	16	35	16
Chemakuan	-	8	8	35	84	58	27	23	57	35
Chemehuevi	33	29	8	10	90	82	30	22	49	49
Cherokee	14,283	13,017	7,900	5,536	58,531	36,320	43,952	26,462	12,110	8,550
Cheyenne	307	442	360	376	1,735	1,359	1,275	1,015	377	279
Chickahominy	28	26	34	38	185	104	150	94	35	10
Chickasaw	612	630	272	214	2,640	1,503	2,158	1,204	391	253
Chinook	62	69	37	43	284	197	203	144	62	45
Chippewa	3,483	3,359	2,370	2,902	15,288	11,263	9,655	6,929	4,618	3,738
Chitimacha	12	20	30	-	68	49	62	49	6	-
Choctaw	2,787	2,819	1,480	1,313	12,088	7,127	9,498	5,693	2,124	1,282
Chumash[1]	61	62	48	41	283	199	204	132	51	46
Clallam	34	28	26	24	161	122	98	80	63	42
Coeur d'Alene	19	8	46	16	105	76	44	31	55	39
Coharie	21	23	10	21	119	68	90	64	18	-
Colorado River	24	55	38	34	212	148	116	83	75	52
Colville	204	278	172	195	1,077	771	666	456	311	243
Comanche	566	412	331	299	2,172	1,383	1,580	989	468	335
Coos	4	7	-	6	22	13	15	6	7	7
Costanoan	21	32	26	5	97	79	69	64	23	10
Cowitz	50	67	25	17	214	159	181	136	28	18
Cree	291	305	230	232	1,281	988	861	643	359	299
Creek	1,576	1,592	814	736	6,549	4,050	5,031	3,054	1,273	882
Croatan	3	10	15	14	54	31	34	31	14	-
Crow	264	256	305	374	1,374	1,010	1,010	765	328	228
Cupeno	5	18	17	12	58	40	41	29	11	5
Delaware	372	320	144	129	1,304	781	1,011	618	238	140

[Continued]

★ 239 ★

Household and Family Characteristics, by Major Tribal Group, 1980: Abenaki-Pamunkey - II
[Continued]

Major Tribal Group	Persons in Household (cont.)				Family Type, by Presence of Own Children					
					Families		Married-couple, families		Female householder, no husband present	
	3 Persons	4 Persons	5 Persons	6 or more persons	Total Families	With own children under 18 years	Total married coupled families	With own children under 18 years	Total female householder, no husband present	With own children under 18 years
Diegueno	75	82	52	37	313	220	182	126	101	83
Eastern tribes (n.e.c.)	155	174	131	79	694	478	571	393	103	71
Flathead	246	204	120	228	1,078	623	713	392	313	205
Fort Hall	20	28	21	17	98	90	55	43	43	37
Gabrieleno	61	87	97	44	375	227	246	150	123	71
Gros Ventres	129	57	61	121	429	301	241	169	151	111
Haida	64	81	55	66	328	230	221	149	65	47
Haliwa	169	100	79	84	477	373	397	314	73	52
Hidatsa	81	48	24	87	278	194	176	121	96	68
Hitchiti	-	-	7	-	7	7	7	7	-	-
Hoopa	83	99	80	44	449	323	330	228	88	79
Houma	89	153	70	115	519	361	445	301	56	47
Iowa	36	31	21	12	181	89	127	57	47	30
Iroquois	2,264	1,795	1,195	1,255	8,705	5,749	6,040	3,946	2,135	1,541
Kalispel	15	7	6	8	42	26	23	13	12	6
Karok	151	79	65	49	437	292	325	220	83	49
Kaw	18	36	21	19	158	80	120	64	38	16
Kickapoo	126	93	79	94	513	337	337	233	154	95
Kiowa	347	319	284	210	1,448	959	1,087	760	331	199
Klamath	75	82	48	50	357	232	203	139	113	69
Konkow	47	17	7	28	127	78	77	42	33	19
Kootenai	4	29	5	6	89	45	52	23	21	13
Long Island	25	6	40	18	93	45	75	45	18	-
Luiseno	8	65	46	51	210	153	140	96	50	37
Lumbee[2]	1,434	1,611	1,053	1,219	6,448	4,583	4,692	3,515	1,463	942
Lummi[2]	181	253	176	144	898	615	616	458	230	140
Maidu	51	74	48	32	246	166	169	118	71	48
Makah	40	36	48	16	216	145	146	95	49	33
Maliseet	20	48	10	10	113	61	78	47	35	14
Mandan	51	31	14	48	165	118	126	88	60	30
Mattaponi	17	11	6	-	40	23	18	6	15	15
Menominee	228	247	211	314	1,167	825	713	521	341	246
Miami	105	152	78	90	577	418	518	376	47	30
Miccosukee[1]	10	-	-	4	14	8	10	4	4	4
Micmac[3]	44	30	6	51	189	139	128	84	61	55
Mission Indians	152	167	81	49	579	354	455	255	110	93
Miwok	86	100	58	54	478	251	358	189	43	31
Modoc	50	22	25	23	163	89	118	57	45	32
Mohegan	34	18	20	5	144	82	107	51	33	27
Mono	86	43	61	40	258	194	132	112	120	82
Nanticoke	87	50	30	14	286	122	230	114	39	8
Narragansett	113	80	69	92	511	330	300	152	189	165
Navajo	5,140	5,699	4,938	9,953	29,802	22,335	21,448	16,751	7,015	4,823
Nez Perce[1]	145	148	58	68	483	328	347	219	108	93
Nomalaki	-	20	10	13	48	38	27	17	21	21
Northwest tribes (n.e.c.)	30	25	8	8	108	58	84	48	24	10
Omaha	113	98	79	188	591	409	315	221	233	158
Oregon Athabaskan	27	58	21	14	161	108	130	88	20	10

[Continued]

★ 239 ★

Household and Family Characteristics, by Major Tribal Group, 1980: Abenaki-Pamunkey - II
[Continued]

| Major Tribal Group | Persons in Household (cont.) | | | | Family Type, by Presence of Own Children | | | | | |
| | | | | | Families | | Married-couple, families | | Female householder, no husband present | |
	3 Persons	4 Persons	5 Persons	6 or more persons	Total Families	With own children under 18 years	Total married coupled families	With own children under 18 years	Total female householder, no husband present	With own children under 18 years
Osage	410	338	219	68	1,639	929	1,280	731	285	182
Oto	66	62	32	68	341	188	242	133	78	54
Ottawa	305	297	207	153	1,335	931	888	612	336	248
Paiute[1]	428	486	347	313	2,036	1,282	1,193	762	713	467
Pamunkey	28	15	10	11	90	47	84	47	6	-

Source: U.S. Bureau of the Census, *1980 Census of Population, Volume 2, Subject Reports, Characteristics of American Indians, by Tribes and Selected Areas: 1980*, PC80-2-1C, Section 1: Tables I-II, issued September 1989, U.S. Department of Commerce, U.S. Government Printing Office, Washington, D.C., pp. 150-202. *Notes:* (N.E.C.) stands for not elsewhere classified. A dash (-) represents zero or a percent which rounds to less than 0.1. 1. Reporting and/or processing problems may have affected the data for this tribe. 2. Miscoding of entries of "Lummee," "Lummi," "Lumbee," or "Lumbi" may have affected the data for this tribe. 3. Any entry with the spelling "Micmac" was miscoded to Cheyenne River Sioux.

★ 240 ★

Household and Family Characteristics, by Major Tribal Group, 1980: Papago-Yurok - I

Data are estimates based on a sample and are the most recent available.

| Major Tribal Group | Household Type and Relationship | | | | | | | | | Persons in Households | | |
| | In households | Family householder | Non-Family householder | | Spouse | Other relative | Non-relative | Persons per household | Persons per family | Households | 1 Person | 2 Persons |
			Male	Female								
Papago	12,675	2,340	305	237	1,606	7,638	549	4.40	4.95	2,882	427	503
Passamaquoddy	1,710	385	64	42	138	997	84	3.48	3.95	491	88	83
Pawnee	2,375	559	116	60	395	1,139	106	3.23	3.74	735	148	229
Penobscot	1,355	381	92	54	173	531	124	2.57	2.85	527	124	137
Peoria	631	136	25	18	114	328	10	3.53	4.25	179	38	62
Pequot	431	95	39	32	54	180	31	2.60	3.46	166	62	16
Pima	11,237	2,121	249	191	1,292	6,765	619	4.39	4.80	2,561	345	345
Piscataway	478	89	15	5	81	281	7	4.39	5.07	109	12	8
Pit River	1,222	284	38	11	158	676	55	3.67	3.94	333	41	35
Pomo	3,077	570	68	48	490	1,726	175	4.49	4.89	686	95	134
Ponca	1,921	398	28	24	297	1,147	27	4.27	4.63	450	45	105
Potawatomi	9,464	2,238	309	335	1,873	4,414	295	3.28	3.81	2,882	533	739
Powhatan	314	108	7	49	19	131	-	1.91	2.39	164	50	39
Pueblo[1]	41,584	8,525	738	644	6,125	24,758	794	4.20	4.62	9,907	1,103	1,545
Puget Sound Salish	6,460	1,304	245	134	1,020	3,372	385	3.84	4.37	1,683	301	383
Quapaw	903	240	28	19	200	400	16	3.15	3.50	287	45	77
Quinault	1,618	316	51	31	251	872	97	4.07	4.55	398	61	104
Rappahannock	266	66	7	-	49	143	1	3.64	3.91	73	7	22
Sac and Fox Mesquakie	3,305	769	64	137	639	1,627	69	3.41	3.95	970	180	214
Salinan	271	56	7	-	43	160	5	4.30	4.63	63	7	12
Schaghticoke	199	44	5	25	27	98	-	2.69	3.84	74	15	15
Seminole[1]	10,004	2,254	446	323	1,658	4,969	354	3.31	3.94	3,023	655	648
Serrano	206	44	-	21	27	114	-	3.17	4.20	65	21	4
Shasta	315	76	11	23	73	109	23	2.86	3.39	110	28	26
Shawnee	4,215	1,094	183	135	867	1,853	83	2.99	3.49	1,412	268	367
Shinnecock	1,022	232	39	21	166	526	38	3.50	3.98	292	50	66
Shoshone	9,443	2,083	299	278	1,497	4,923	363	3.55	4.08	2,660	482	615
Siletz	691	132	45	20	60	389	45	3.51	4.40	197	42	54
Sioux	75,357	15,052	2,082	1,668	10,068	42,407	4,080	4.01	4.49	18,802	2,840	3,807
Siuslaw	326	86	11	7	73	149	-	3.13	3.58	104	11	28
Spokane	1,733	412	70	59	238	864	90	3.20	3.67	541	102	141
Stockbridge	1,508	375	92	83	253	650	55	2.74	3.41	550	147	132
Tlingit	9,379	1,827	225	307	1,504	5,006	510	3.98	4.56	2,359	400	526
Tolowa	396	85	-	-	31	265	15	4.66	4.48	85	-	18
Tonkawa	242	71	-	-	42	127	2	3.41	3.38	71	-	13

[Continued]

★ 240 ★

Household and Family Characteristics, by Major Tribal Group, 1980: Papago-Yurok - I
[Continued]

Major Tribal Group	In households	Family householder	Non-Family householder Male	Non-Family householder Female	Spouse	Other relative	Non-relative	Persons per household	Persons per family	Persons in Households Households	1 Person	2 Persons
Tsimshian	1,580	319	13	22	285	893	48	4.46	4.69	354	35	76
Umatilla	937	191	55	35	141	468	47	3.33	4.19	281	82	52
Ute	5,597	1,155	121	110	793	3,189	229	4.04	4.45	1,386	187	260
Wailaki[2]	583	87	-	23	140	304	29	5.30	6.10	110	23	52
Walla-Walla	262	71	3	-	41	147	-	3.54	3.65	74	3	25
Wampanoag	1,381	363	49	81	191	658	39	2.80	3.34	493	102	156
Warm Springs	1,275	266	-	25	111	774	99	4.38	4.33	291	17	16
Washo	1,358	294	87	36	212	693	36	3.26	4.08	417	111	91
Wichita	692	144	49	22	110	356	11	3.22	4.24	215	69	40
Winnebago	4,985	921	129	126	603	2,810	396	4.24	4.71	1,176	212	244
Wintu	2,025	380	53	60	428	1,045	59	4.11	4.88	493	100	136
Wiyot	234	50	19	6	35	113	11	3.12	3.96	75	15	19
Yakima	6,352	1,256	177	118	865	3,525	411	4.10	4.50	1,551	239	355
Yaqui	5,106	1,099	103	30	719	2,976	179	4.14	4.36	1,232	98	191
Yavapai Apache	135	29	-	-	21	85	-	4.66	4.66	29	-	14
Yokuts	1,731	280	68	40	248	973	122	4.46	5.36	388	93	89
Yuchi	225	31	18	10	59	88	19	3.81	5.74	59	21	33
Yuman	6,353	1,377	159	159	804	3,649	205	3.75	4.23	1,695	243	307
Yurok	2,903	657	115	97	455	1,453	126	3.34	3.90	869	179	181
Other specified tribes (n.e.c.)	422	69	21	16	69	224	23	3.98	5.25	106	27	25
All other specified	122	31	-	6	26	55	4	3.30	3.61	37	6	9
Tribe not specified	33,589	7,209	1,494	1,423	5,807	16,007	1,649	3.32	4.03	10,126	2,494	2,342
Tribe not reported	292,764	76,978	13,302	12,024	50,905	123,589	15,966	2.88	3.27	102,304	19,771	27,532

Source: U.S. Bureau of the Census, *1980 Census of Population, Volume 2, Subject Reports, Characteristics of American Indians, by Tribes and Selected Areas: 1980*, PC80-2-1C, Section 1: Tables I-II, issued September 1989, U.S. Department of Commerce, U.S. Government Printing Office, Washington, D.C., pp. 150-202. *Notes:* (N.E.C.) stands for not elsewhere classified. A dash (-) represents zero or a percent which rounds to less than 0.1. 1. Reporting and/or processing problems may have affected the data for this tribe. 2. Any Mohawk entry of "Ganienka" was miscoded to Wailaki.

★ 241 ★

Household and Family Characteristics, by Major Tribal Group, 1980: Papago-Yurok - II

Data are estimates based on a sample and are the most recent available.

Major Tribal Group	Persons in Households (cont.) 3 Persons	4 Persons	5 Persons	6 Persons	Family Type, by Presence of Own Children Families Total Families	With own children under 18 years	Married-couple, families Total married-coupled families	With own children under 18 years	Female householder, no husband present Total female householders, no husband present	With own children under 18 years
Papago	405	385	388	794	2,340	1,455	1,452	1,022	649	349
Passamaquoddy	100	99	51	70	385	313	230	175	129	112
Pawnee	155	102	50	51	559	286	392	182	129	80
Penobscot	97	97	27	45	381	257	320	213	54	37
Peoria	27	26	26	-	136	80	127	77	9	3
Pequot	30	23	21	4	95	85	57	47	34	34
Pima	416	477	407	571	2,121	1,416	1,069	752	837	552
Piscataway	7	31	27	24	89	58	82	51	-	-
Pit River	78	73	31	75	284	251	139	134	115	92
Pomo	123	96	127	111	570	383	367	261	151	107
Ponca	111	67	19	103	398	235	276	175	73	42
Potawatomi	473	547	336	254	2,238	1,520	1,784	1,192	394	303
Powhatan	43	18	14	-	108	58	89	45	13	13
Pueblo[1]	1,813	1,840	1,454	2,152	8,525	5,701	6,061	4,232	1,880	1,186
Puget Sound Salish	313	242	217	247	1,304	870	813	534	375	295

[Continued]

461

★ 241 ★

Household and Family Characteristics, by Major Tribal Group, 1980: Papago-Yurok - II
[Continued]

| Major Tribal Group | Persons in Households (cont.) | | | | Family Type, by Presence of Own Children | | | | | |
| | | | | | Families | | Married-couple, families | | Female householder, no husband present | |
	3 Persons	4 Persons	5 Persons	6 Persons	Total Families	With own children under 18 years	Total married-coupled families	With own children under 18 years	Total female householders, no husband present	With own children under 18 years
Quapaw	61	64	33	7	240	144	183	114	53	30
Quinault	86	35	40	72	316	213	208	129	89	65
Rappahannock	22	9	13	-	66	14	42	14	13	-
Sac and Fox Mesquakie	179	133	107	157	769	542	600	431	142	89
Salinan	2	16	11	15	56	40	42	26	14	14
Schaghticoke	3	16	16	9	44	44	36	36	8	8
Seminole[1]	576	545	294	305	2,254	1,485	1,602	1,078	468	293
Serrano	14	-	9	17	44	14	40	14	4	-
Shasta	19	23	8	6	76	49	51	35	8	8
Shawnee	299	227	131	120	1,094	701	789	516	282	166
Shinnecock	54	52	45	25	232	148	134	77	88	61
Shoshone	506	428	272	357	2,083	1,323	1,372	849	587	421
Siletz	12	29	34	26	132	82	70	45	59	37
Sioux	3,334	3,135	2,079	3,607	15,052	10,680	8,981	6,295	5,042	3,787
Siuslaw	27	19	16	3	86	60	66	52	9	2
Spokane	72	98	42	86	412	262	253	139	121	99
Stockbridge	89	107	43	32	375	234	281	168	83	57
Tlingit	354	395	373	311	1,827	1,319	1,249	889	423	348
Tolowa	29	13	13	12	85	39	35	14	11	11
Tonkawa	26	27	-	5	71	38	51	27	11	11
Tsimshian	70	47	66	60	319	210	218	160	64	39
Umatilla	62	34	20	31	191	138	110	68	76	65
Ute	217	247	169	306	1,155	819	822	610	240	183
Wailaki[2]	3	20	-	12	87	57	36	14	46	38
Walla-Walla	12	20	10	4	71	41	51	25	14	10
Wampanoag	56	102	55	22	363	218	240	136	110	82
Warm Springs	75	48	41	94	266	193	169	145	81	32
Washo	55	77	32	51	294	207	194	145	95	62
Wichita	18	35	14	39	144	79	113	67	31	12
Winnebago	194	206	123	197	921	650	523	371	340	256
Wintu	62	96	42	57	380	249	263	184	70	49
Wiyot	8	15	9	9	50	41	42	37	4	4
Yakima	246	235	199	277	1,256	838	775	510	421	282
Yaqui	199	201	181	362	1,099	808	780	625	202	120
Yavapai Apache	-	2	7	6	29	15	14	7	15	8
Yokuts	45	78	42	41	280	153	114	45	124	81
Yuchi	2	-	3	-	31	5	31	5	-	-
Yuman	316	231	200	398	1,377	825	894	586	401	201
Yurok	152	225	95	37	657	486	451	332	192	147
Other specified tribes (n.e.c.)	40	6	-	8	69	43	42	19	21	18
All other specified	17	-	-	5	31	21	29	19	2	2
Tribe not specified	1,767	1,619	899	1,005	7,209	4,591	5,168	3,236	1,629	1,163
Tribe not reported	19,522	17,066	9,552	8,861	76,978	48,031	58,688	35,997	14,272	9,

Source: U.S. Bureau of the Census, *1980 Census of Population, Volume 2, Subject Reports, Characteristics of American Indians, by Tribes and Selected Areas: 1980*, PC80-2-1C, Section 1: Tables I-II, issued September 1989, U.S. Department of Commerce, U.S. Government Printing Office, Washington, D.C., pp. 150-202. *Notes:* (N.E.C.) stands for not elsewhere classified. A dash (-) represents zero or a percent which rounds to less than 0.1. 1. Reporting and/or processing problems may have affected the data for this tribe. 2. Any Mohawk entry of "Ganienka" was miscoded to Wailaki.

★ 242 ★

Household Characteristics of Eighth Graders, 1990

Distribution of students is shown in percent for each race/ethnicity.

| Race/ethnicity | Single parent household[1] | Single parent/other relative | | | Two parent | | |
		Mother/ female guardian only in household	Father/ male guardian only in household	Other relative or non-relative only in household	Mother & father in household	Mother & guardian in household	Father & guardian in household
Total	22.3	16.5	2.6	3.2	63.6	11.5	2.6
American Indian and Native Alaskan	31.1	21.1	3.6	6.4	55.6	11.8	1.5
Asian and Pacific Islander	14.3	8.3	2.4	3.6	78.4	5.4	1.9
Hispanic	23.4	17.7	2.2	3.5	63.5	11.2	1.9
Black	46.5	36.1	2.1	8.3	38.4	13.3	1.9
White	17.7	12.9	2.7	2.1	67.9	11.6	2.9

Source: "Percentage of Eighth Graders from Different Types of Households, by Selected Background Characteristics," *A Profile of the American Eighth Grader*, 1990, p. 6. Primary source: U.S. Department of Education, National Center for Education Statistics. "National Education Longitudinal Study of 1988: Base Year Student Survey." *Notes:* 1. This column is the sum of columns 5, 6, and 7 (mother only, father only, and other relative or non-relative). "Other relative or non-relative" group is included in the single parent household category even though there is no parent in the home and it may include 2 people (e.g. grandparents).

Characteristics

★ 243 ★

Families With American Indian, Eskimo, or Aleut Members on Identified Reservations by Selected Characteristics, 1980: Acoma Pueblo - Eastern Pequot

Data are the latest available.

| Identified reservations | Families with one or more American Indian, Eskimo, or Aleut | | Families with American Indian, Eskimo, or Aleut householder or spouse | | | | Families with American Indian, Eskimo, or Aleut householder | | | | | Persons under 18 percent living with two parents |
	Total	Percent with own children under 18 years	Total	Percent with own children under 18 years	Percent with own children under 6 years	Persons per family	Total	Married couple	Female householder, no husband present	Percent with own children under 18 years	Persons per family	
Total persons	71,275	68.9	70,500	68.8	35.4	4.76	66,792	43,331	18,372	68.9	4.81	57.6
Acoma Pueblo, NM	410	64.4	410	64.4	28.6	5.43	400	274	94	64.5	5.45	57.3
Valencia County	410	64.4	410	64.4	28.6	5.43	400	274	94	64.5	5.45	57.3
Agua Caliente Reservation, CA	-	-	-	-	-	-	-	-	-	-	-	-
Riverside County	-	-	-	-	-	-	-	-	-	-	-	-
Alabama-Coushatta Reservation, TX	118	54.8	118	54.8	26.8	4.06	117	92	16	55.4	4.08	67.4
Polk County	118	54.8	118	54.8	26.8	4.06	117	92	16	55.4	4.08	67.4
Alamo Reservation, NM	192	78.5	192	78.5	49.2	5.50	192	164	17	78.5	5.50	75.9
Socorro County	192	78.5	192	78.5	49.2	5.50	192	164	17	78.5	5.50	75.9
Allegany Reservation, NY	270	61.6	259	61.0	27.8	3.83	229	151	61	59.0	3.89	55.0
Cattaraugus County	270	61.6	259	61.0	27.8	3.83	229	151	61	59.0	3.89	55.0
Alturas Rancheria, CA	...	...	...	...	...	...	...	...	...	...	...	...
Modoc County	...	...	...	...	...	...	...	...	...	...	...	...
Annette Islands Reserve, AK	227	67.1	227	67.1	39.4	4.39	208	163	24	66.8	4.42	74.7

[Continued]

★ 243 ★

Families With American Indian, Eskimo, or Aleut Members on Identified Reservations by Selected Characteristics, 1980: Acoma Pueblo - Eastern Pequot

[Continued]

Identified reservations	Families with one or more American Indian, Eskimo, or Aleut		Families with American Indian, Eskimo, or Aleut householder or spouse				Families with American Indian, Eskimo, or Aleut householder					Persons under 18 percent living with two parents
	Total	Percent with own children under 18 years	Total	Percent with own children under 18 years	Percent with own children under 6 years	Persons per family	Total	Married couple	Female householder, no husband present	Percent with own children under 18 years	Persons per family	
Prince of Wales-Outer- Ketchikan Census Area	227	67.1	227	67.1	39.4	4.39	208	163	24	66.8	4.42	74.7
Augustine Reservation, CA	-	-	-	-	-	-	-	-	-	-	-	-
Riverside County	-	-	-	-	-	-	-	-	-	-	-	-
Bad River Reservation, WI	166	64.1	166	64.1	32.6	4.22	151	92	45	62.5	4.28	54.6
Ashland County	166	64.1	166	64.1	32.6	4.22	151	92	45	62.5	4.28	54.6
Iron County	-	-	-	-	-	-	-	-	-	-	-	-
Barona Rancheria, CA	61	73.6	59	72.9	42.2	4.07	50	29	19	73.2	4.29	59.7
San Diego County	61	73.6	59	72.9	42.2	4.07	50	29	19	73.2	4.29	59.7
Bay Mills Reservation, MI	65	70.8	63	72.1	36.5	4.68	52	39	5	69.8	4.68	81.2
Chippewa County	65	70.8	63	72.1	36.5	4.68	52	39	5	69.8	4.68	81.2
Benton Paiute Reservation, CA	...	...	...	...	...	...	...	...	...	...	...	...
Mono County	...	...	...	...	...	...	...	...	...	...	...	...
Berry Creek Rancheria, CA	-	-	-	-	-	-	-	-	-	-	-	-
Butte County	-	-	-	-	-	-	-	-	-	-	-	-
Big Bend Rancheria, CA	...	...	...	...	...	...	...	...	...	...	...	...
Shasta County	...	...	...	...	...	...	...	...	...	...	...	...
Big Cypress Reservation, FL	71	66.2	71	66.2	24.3	4.73	65	37	22	63.4	4.70	49.8
Hendry County	71	66.2	71	66.2	24.3	4.73	65	37	22	63.4	4.70	49.8
Big Lagoon Rancheria, CA	...	...	...	...	...	...	...	...	...	...	...	...
Humboldt County	...	...	...	...	...	...	...	...	...	...	...	...
Big Pine Rancheria, CA	64	73.5	64	73.5	33.6	4.23	63	34	25	72.7	4.22	60.3
Inyo County	64	73.5	64	73.5	33.6	4.23	63	34	25	72.7	4.22	60.3
Bishop Rancheria, CA	186	65.1	180	64.0	32.6	4.16	163	95	57	63.9	4.09	59.6
Inyo County	186	65.1	180	64.0	32.6	4.16	163	95	57	63.9	4.09	59.6
Blackfeet Reservation, MT	1,362	69.2	1,340	69.1	36.8	4.30	1,203	850	257	69.7	4.49	64.8
Glacier County	1,266	68.8	1,244	68.7	36.7	4.21	1,109	776	239	69.2	4.40	64.7
Pondera County	96	74.4	96	74.4	39.0	5.47	94	74	18	76.1	5.54	66.0
Bois Forte Reservation (Nett Lake), MN	91	72.5	90	72.2	48.9	4.27	87	34	36	73.6	4.33	40.1
Koochiching County	12	50.0	12	50.0	25.0	4.92	12	8	2	50.0	4.92	60.0
St. Louis County	79	75.9	78	75.6	52.6	4.17	75	26	34	77.3	4.24	37.0
Bridgeport Colony , CA	13	55.4	13	55.4	18.5	3.33	12	4	7	50.8	3.10	39.4
Mono County	13	55.4	13	55.4	18.5	3.33	12	4	7	50.8	3.10	39.4
Brighton Reservation, FL	69	62.0	69	62.0	38.0	4.70	68	45	18	61.4	4.70	57.9
Glades County	69	62.0	69	62.0	38.0	4.70	68	45	18	61.4	4.70	57.9
Burns Reservation, OR	32	56.3	32	56.3	40.6	5.00	31	18	10	54.8	5.03	57.4
Harney County	32	56.3	32	56.3	40.6	5.00	31	18	10	54.8	5.03	57.4
Cabazon Reservation, CA	...	...	...	...	...	...	...	...	...	...	...	...
Riverside County	...	...	...	...	...	...	...	...	...	...	...	...
Cachil Dehe Rancheria, CA	...	...	...	...	...	...	...	...	...	...	...	...
Colusa County	...	...	...	...	...	...	...	...	...	...	...	...
Cahuilla Reservation, CA	7	50.0	7	50.0	33.3	4.11	7	6	-	50.0	4.11	...
Riverside County	7	50.0	7	50.0	33.3	4.11	7	6	-	50.0	4.11	...
Campo Reservation, CA	25	55.6	24	53.6	15.6	3.58	21	9	9	48.1	3.37	38.2
San Diego County	25	55.6	24	53.6	15.6	3.58	21	9	9	48.1	3.37	38.2
Camp Verde Reservation, AZ	40	65.0	40	65.0	50.0	4.42	40	26	13	65.0	4.42	56.8
Yavapai County	40	65.0	40	65.0	50.0	4.42	40	26	13	65.0	4.42	56.8
Canoncito Reservation, NM	194	81.1	194	81.1	41.4	4.87	192	141	45	81.8	4.88	67.7
Bernalillo County	168	80.8	168	80.8	43.0	4.90	167	123	38	81.6	4.91	67.8
Sandoval County	-	-	-	-	-	-	-	-	-	-	-	-
Valencia County	26	83.0	26	83.0	31.3	4.67	26	18	8	83.0	4.67	67.3
Capitan Grande Reservation, CA	-	-	-	-	-	-	-	-	-	-	-	-
San Diego County	-	-	-	-	-	-	-	-	-	-	-	-
Carson Colony, NV	56	50.3	56	50.3	25.4	3.88	53	27	18	50.4	3.90	49.7
Carson City	56	50.3	56	50.3	25.4	3.88	53	27	18	50.4	3.90	49.7
Catawba Reservation, SC	325	76.5	325	76.5	42.5	2.69	325	34	157	76.5	2.69	4.7
York County	325	76.5	325	76.5	42.5	2.69	325	34	157	76.5	2.69	4.7
Cattaraugus Reservation, NY	455	62.0	453	61.8	28.4	4.05	432	266	137	60.8	4.02	55.2
Cattaraugus County	75	65.2	75	65.2	32.4	4.46	74	47	23	66.2	4.48	54.8
Chautauqua County	...	...	...	...	...	...	...	...	...	...	...	...

[Continued]

Families With American Indian, Eskimo, or Aleut Members on Identified Reservations by Selected Characteristics, 1980: Acoma Pueblo - Eastern Pequot

[Continued]

Identified reservations	Families with one or more American Indian, Eskimo, or Aleut		Families with American Indian, Eskimo, or Aleut householder or spouse				Families with American Indian, Eskimo, or Aleut householder					Persons under 18 percent living with two parents
	Total	Percent with own children under 18 years	Total	Percent with own children under 18 years	Percent with own children under 6 years	Persons per family	Total	Married couple	Female householder, no husband present	Percent with own children under 18 years	Persons per family	
Erie County	375	61.3	373	61.1	27.5	3.98	353	215	113	59.6	3.94	55.0
Cedarville Rancheria, CA	...	...	...	...	...	...	...	...	...	...	...	...
Modoc County	...	...	...	...	...	...	...	...	...	...	...	...
Chehalis Reservation, WA	47	78.3	46	77.8	56.7	4.54	42	28	10	78.3	4.62	61.0
Grays Harbor County	43	76.3	42	75.7	54.9	4.43	38	26	9	75.9	4.50	60.4
Thurston County	...	...	...	...	...	...	...	...	...	...	...	...
Chemehuevi Reservation, CA	10	75.0	10	75.0	50.0	2.75	...	...	...	...	...	...
San Bernardino County	10	75.0	10	75.0	50.0	2.75	...	...	...	...	...	...
Cheyenne River Reservation, SD	289	70.7	289	70.7	39.9	5.32	261	162	71	69.9	5.37	53.8
Dewey County	153	70.9	153	70.9	39.2	4.98	133	85	32	70.0	5.04	62.0
Ziebach County	135	70.6	135	70.6	40.8	5.69	128	78	39	69.7	5.71	46.3
Chitimacha Reservation, LA	66	62.8	63	61.3	30.1	3.58	39	34	4	64.5	3.44	77.3
St. Mary Parish	66	62.8	63	61.3	30.1	3.58	39	34	4	64.5	3.44	77.3
Cochiti Pueblo, NM	133	56.9	132	57.5	20.3	4.54	132	85	31	57.5	4.54	63.9
Sandoval County	133	56.9	132	57.5	20.3	4.54	132	85	31	57.5	4.54	63.9
Cocopah Reservation, AZ	58	62.0	58	62.0	25.9	5.84	57	33	19	61.4	5.75	40.1
Yuma County	58	62.0	58	62.0	25.9	5.84	57	33	19	61.4	5.75	40.1
Coeur d'Alene Reservation, ID	130	69.0	128	68.5	34.0	4.28	118	65	42	67.5	4.26	42.1
Benewah County	94	72.5	92	71.9	36.8	4.38	87	48	30	70.3	4.34	43.0
Kootenai County	36	59.7	36	59.7	26.8	4.02	31	17	12	59.7	4.02	39.6
Cold Springs Rancheria, CA	11	62.1	11	62.1	29.1	5.35	11	2	6	62.1	5.35	17.2
Fresno County	11	62.1	11	62.1	29.1	5.35	11	2	6	62.1	5.35	17.2
Colorado River Reservation, AZ-CA	481	66.0	463	64.7	38.5	4.34	416	283	104	64.9	4.37	53.5
Arizona	469	66.8	452	65.5	39.2	4.38	408	277	102	65.7	4.40	54.0
Yuma County	469	66.8	452	65.5	39.2	4.38	408	277	102	65.7	4.40	54.0
California	12	31.1	12	31.1	12.6	2.62	8	6	2	26.8	2.54	...
Riverside and San Bernardino Cnts.	12	31.1	12	31.1	12.6	2.62	8	6	2	26.8	2.54	...
Colville Reservation, WA	908	65.6	890	65.7	34.9	4.02	822	503	239	66.7	4.05	54.7
Ferry County	247	56.7	245	56.7	30.6	3.76	224	152	49	58.9	3.83	59.2
Okanogan County	661	68.9	645	69.1	36.5	4.11	598	351	190	69.6	4.14	53.4
Cortina Rancheria, CA	...	...	...	...	...	...	...	...	...	...	...	...
Colusa County	...	...	...	...	...	...	...	...	...	...	...	...
Coushatta Reservation, LA	...	...	...	...	...	...	...	...	...	...	...	...
Allen Parish	...	...	...	...	...	...	...	...	...	...	...	...
Coyote Valley Rancheria, CA	-	-	-	-	-	-	-	-	-	-	-	-
Mendocino County	-	-	-	-	-	-	-	-	-	-	-	-
Crow Reservation, MT	783	70.5	774	70.7	31.1	5.21	743	546	174	70.8	5.23	57.4
Big Horn County	758	70.0	749	70.2	31.4	5.22	722	527	171	70.3	5.24	57.1
Yellowstone County	25	85.3	25	85.3	23.4	4.93	21	19	2	88.3	5.06	66.5
Crow Creek Reservation, SD	284	66.3	282	66.1	33.6	5.22	256	142	87	64.1	5.23	51.9
Buffalo County	246	65.9	243	65.6	29.9	5.08	220	116	79	63.8	5.10	47.5
Hughes County	28	63.7	28	63.7	52.4	6.08	26	21	4	61.9	6.17	75.9
Hyde County	11	81.5	11	81.5	68.5	61.4	...	...	...	...	...	...
Cuyapaipe Reservation, CA	...	...	...	...	...	...	...	...	...	...	...	...
San Diego County	...	...	...	...	...	...	...	...	...	...	...	...
Deer Creek Reservation, MN	...	...	...	...	...	...	...	...	...	...	...	...
Itasca County	...	...	...	...	...	...	...	...	...	...	...	...
Dresslerville Colony, NV	33	58.0	33	58.0	30.5	3.78	33	18	10	58.0	3.78	63.7
Douglas County	33	58.0	33	58.0	30.5	3.78	33	18	10	58.0	3.78	63.7
Dry Creek Rancheria, CA	...	...	...	...	...	...	...	...	...	...	...	...
Sonoma County	...	...	...	...	...	...	...	...	...	...	...	...
Duck Valley Reservation, ID-NV	195	58.1	194	57.8	25.6	4.61	187	116	53	57.5	4.65	47.2
Idaho	40	59.2	40	59.2	28.8	4.51	40	21	18	59.2	4.51	46.0
Owyhee County	40	59.2	40	59.2	28.8	4.51	40	21	18	59.2	4.51	46.0
Nevada	155	57.8	154	57.5	24.8	4.64	147	95	35	57.0	4.68	47.6
Elko County	155	57.8	154	57.5	24.8	4.64	147	95	35	57.0	4.68	47.6
Duckwater Reservation, NV	24	58.3	24	58.3	33.3	4.17	24	17	5	58.3	4.17	50.0
Nye County	24	58.3	24	58.3	33.3	4.17	24	17	5	58.3	4.17	50.0
Eastern Cherokee Reservation, NC	1,276	63.9	1,22	63.8	25.4	3.96	1,167	780	307	63.8	3.98	60.2
Cherokee County	33	45.7	32	47.1	19.0	3.29	25	14	10	44.1	3.32	39.2
Graham County	77	66.8	77	66.8	29.4	4.74	67	49	17	64.9	4.81	74.5

[Continued]

★ 243 ★

Families With American Indian, Eskimo, or Aleut Members on Identified Reservations by Selected Characteristics, 1980: Acoma Pueblo - Eastern Pequot

[Continued]

Identified reservations	Families with one or more American Indian, Eskimo, or Aleut		Families with American Indian, Eskimo, or Aleut householder or spouse				Families with American Indian, Eskimo, or Aleut householder					Persons under 18 percent living with two parents
	Total	Percent with own children under 18 years	Total	Percent with own children under 18 years	Percent with own children under 6 years	Persons per family	Total	Married couple	Female householder, no husband present	Percent with own children under 18 years	Persons per family	
Haywood County	-	-	-	-	-	-	-	-	-	-	-	-
Jackson County	567	64.4	562	64.5	25.0	3.88	525	358	125	64.0	3.88	60.3
Swain County	599	64.0	591	63.7	25.7	3.96	549	360	155	64.4	4.00	58.2
Eastern Pequot Reservation, CT	...	...	...	...	...	...	...	...	...	...	...	...
New London County	...	...	...	...	...	...	...	...	...	...	...	...

Source: U.S. Bureau of the Census, Subject Reports, PC80-2-1D, Part I, *American Indians, Eskimos, and Aleuts on Identified Reservations and in the Historic Areas of Oklahoma (Excluding Urbanized Areas)*, U.S. Government Printing Office, Washington, D.C., 1986, pp. 41-49. *Notes:* A dash (-) represents zero or a percent which rounds to less than 0.1. Also, a dash (-) is used because the number of supplementary questionnaires for the reservations was insufficient to produce reliable estimates. Three dots (...) means not applicable, or that the data are being withheld to avoid disclosure of information for individuals.

★ 244 ★

Families With American Indian, Eskimo, or Aleut Members on Identified Reservations by Selected Characteristics, 1980: Ely Colony - Lac du Flambeau

Data are the latest available.

Identified reservations	Families with one or more American Indian, Eskimo, or Aleut		Families with American Indian, Eskimo, or Aleut householder or spouse				Families with American Indian, Eskimo, or Aleut householder					Persons under 18 percent living with two parents
	Total	Percent with own children under 18 years	Total	Percent with own children under 18 years	Percent with own children under 6 years	Persons per family	Total	Married couple	Female householder, no husband present	Percent with own children under 18 years	Persons per family	
Ely Colony, NV	17	71.5	16	69.2	31.0	4.35	12	6	4	59.7	4.25	63.3
White Pine County	17	71.5	16	69.2	31.0	4.35	12	6	4	59.7	4.25	63.3
Enterprise Rancheria CA	...	...	...	...	...	...	...	...	...	...	...	...
Butte County	...	...	...	...	...	...	...	...	...	...	...	...
Fallon Colony, NV	11	47.0	11	47.0	-	3.82	11	4	7	47.0	3.82	26.7
Churchill County	11	47.0	11	47.0	-	3.82	11	4	7	47.0	3.82	26.7
Fallon Reservation, NV	62	54.2	61	53.4	12.1	4.27	58	37	14	51.6	4.25	48.1
Churchill County	62	54.2	61	53.4	12.1	4.27	58	37	14	51.6	4.25	48.1
Flandreau Reservation, SD	38	73.0	38	73.0	27.1	4.05	32	16	12	71.2	3.97	63.4
Moody County	38	73.0	38	73.0	27.1	4.05	32	16	12	71.2	3.97	63.4
Flathead Reservation, MT	1,114	68.6	1,060	67.8	36.5	4.05	857	602	206	68.5	4.11	58.5
Flathead County	...	...	...	...	...	...	...	...	...	...	...	...
Lake County	920	69.7	871	68.8	37.8	4.04	701	485	179	69.3	4.11	56.7
Missoula County	78	73.3	76	72.6	28.8	4.29	65	46	15	74.6	4.41	69.8
Sanders County	114	56.1	111	56.8	31.5	3.87	88	69	12	58.0	3.86	64.1
Fond du Lac Reservation, MN	145	65.4	143	65.0	28.6	4.13	109	63	33	68.9	4.38	63.9
Carlton County	118	66.6	116	66.1	30.7	4.08	98	57	31	70.1	4.26	60.1
St. Louis County	27	60.1	27	60.1	19.7	4.37	11	6	2	58.3	5.43	87.2
Fort Apache Reservation, AZ	1,301	75.7	1,229	75.8	38.5	5.20	1,262	862	317	75.6	5.28	58.0
Apache County	25	88.4	25	88.4	38.8	4.32	23	14	5	88.4	4.32	58.6
Gila County	227	73.5	227	73.5	31.9	5.25	227	156	62	73.5	5.25	64.7
Navajo County	1,050	75.8	1,048	76.0	40.0	5.21	1,010	692	250	75.8	5.30	56.6
Fort Belknap Reservation, MT	394	69.1	394	69.1	33.9	4.83	384	239	108	68.9	4.83	57.7
Blaine County	350	69.8	350	69.8	34.4	4.91	343	208	103	69.9	4.91	55.6
Phillips County	44	62.8	44	62.8	30.0	4.20	41	31	6	60.0	4.17	83.3
Fort Berthold Reservation, ND	559	69.5	555	69.3	34.0	4.78	499	304	162	69.7	4.92	51.1
Dunn County	91	68.3	90	67.9	33.1	4.78	77	60	13	69.2	4.87	62.8
Mckenzie County	161	74.7	161	74.7	35.5	5.16	153	91	59	74.5	5.12	46.3
Mclean County	90	61.1	90	61.1	28.4	4.92	84	51	27	64.0	5.08	52.9
Mercer County	12	49.6	12	49.6	28.8	4.29	11	7	4	55.0	4.54	42.0
Mountrail County	206	71.0	203	70.6	36.0	4.44	173	96	59	69.2	4.72	49.9
Ward County	-	-	-	-	-	-	-	-	-	-	-	-

[Continued]

★ 244 ★

Families With American Indian, Eskimo, or Aleut Members on Identified Reservations by Selected Characteristics, 1980: Ely Colony - Lac du Flambeau
[Continued]

Identified reservations	Families with one or more American Indian, Eskimo, or Aleut		Families with American Indian, Eskimo, or Aleut householder or spouse				Families with American Indian, Eskimo, or Aleut householder					Persons under 18 percent living with two parents
	Total	Percent with own children under 18 years	Total	Percent with own children under 18 years	Percent with own children under 6 years	Persons per family	Total	Married couple	Female householder, no husband present	Percent with own children under 18 years	Persons per family	
Fort Bidwell Reservation CA	19	61.0	19	61.0	34.1	4.58	19	11	7	61.0	4.58	52.6
Modoc County	19	61.0	19	61.0	34.1	4.58	19	11	7	61.0	4.58	52.6
Fort Hall Reservation, ID	583	59.6	573	59.1	29.0	4.41	539	338	156	57.7	4.40	53.7
Bannock County	156	53.9	151	52.9	24.5	4.64	145	88	42	51.9	4.65	51.5
Bingham County	391	61.6	387	61.1	30.5	4.25	364	226	112	60.2	4.25	53.2
Caribou County	-	-	-	-	-	-	-	-	-	-	-	-
Power County	35	62.7	35	62.7	31.4	5.15	30	24	2	55.6	4.98	66.9
Fort Independence												
Reservation CA	11	33.8	11	33.8	11.5	2.63	10	4	4	38.8	2.69	50.0
Inyo County	11	33.8	11	33.8	11.5	2.63	10	4	4	38.8	2.69	50.0
Fort McDermitt												
Reservation, NV-OR	82	61.1	82	61.1	18.8	5.57	81	50	26	60.6	5.56	41.6
Nevada	82	61.1	82	61.1	18.8	5.57	81	50	26	60.6	5.56	41.6
Humboldt County	82	61.1	82	61.1	18.8	5.57	81	50	26	60.6	5.56	41.6
Oregon	-	-	-	-	-	-	-	-	-	-	-	-
Malheur County	-	-	-	-	-	-	-	-	-	-	-	-
Fort McDowell Reservation, AZ	70	53.2	70	53.2	31.5	4.72	70	41	15	53.2	4.72	44.5
Maricopa County	70	53.2	70	53.2	31.5	4.72	70	41	15	53.2	4.72	44.5
Fort Mojave												
Reservation,												
AZ-CA-NV	30	76.7	30	76.7	46.7	4.33	30	21	8	76.7	4.33	51.7
Arizona	30	76.7	30	76.7	46.7	4.33	30	21	8	76.7	4.33	51.7
Mohave County	30	76.7	30	76.7	46.7	4.33	30	21	8	76.7	4.33	51.7
California	-	-	-	-	-	-	-	-	-	-	-	-
San Bernardino County	-	-	-	-	-	-	-	-	-	-	-	-
Nevada	-	-	-	-	-	-	-	-	-	-	-	-
Clark County	-	-	-	-	-	-	-	-	-	-	-	-
Fort Peck Reservation, MT	955	69.7	929	69.7	34.2	4.61	846	527	244	68.8	4.63	52.7
Daniels County	-	-	-	-	-	-	-	-	-	-	-	-
Roosevelt County	859	69.7	834	69.7	34.2	4.55	755	465	226	68.9	4.57	52.7
Sheridan County	-	-	-	-	-	-	-	-	-	-	-	-
Valley County	96	70.1	96	70.1	34.0	5.12	91	62	18	68.4	5.13	52.9
Fort Totten Reservation, ND	421	74.4	416	74.1	43.9	5.33	392	172	152	73.5	5.42	39.3
Benson County	417	75.0	412	74.7	44.3	5.35	389	170	152	74.2	5.45	39.3
Eddy County	...	...	...	...	...	...	...	...	...	...	...	...
Nelson County	-	-	-	-	-	-	-	-	-	-	-	...
Ramsey County	...	...	...	...	...	...	...	...	...	...	...	...
Fort Yuma Reservation, AZ-CA	266	58.8	260	58.7	26.5	4.31	238	125	92	57.1	4.37	52.1
Arizona	46	41.2	42	36.0	17.9	4.08	31	13	11	25.7	4.70	21.4
Yuma County	46	41.2	42	36.0	17.9	4.08	31	13	11	25.7	4.70	21.4
California	220	62.5	217	63.1	28.2	4.35	207	112	81	61.8	4.32	55.5
Imperial County	220	62.5	217	63.1	28.2	4.35	207	112	81	61.8	4.32	55.5
Gila Bend Reservation, AZ	-	-	-	-	-	-	-	-	-	-	-	-
Maricopa County	-	-	-	-	-	-	-	-	-	-	-	-
Gila River Reservation, AZ	1,399	63.9	1,396	63.9	30.9	4.78	1,371	705	455	63.2	4.78	41.4
Maricopa County	410	67.7	410	67.7	34.3	4.71	407	186	152	67.5	4.70	35.0
Pinal County	989	62.4	985	62.2	29.4	4.81	963	519	302	61.4	4.81	44.1
Golden Hill Reservation, CT	...	...	...	...	...	...	...	...	...	...	...	...
Fairfield County	...	...	...	...	...	...	...	...	...	...	...	...
Goshute Reservation, NV-UT	22	43.9	22	43.9	21.9	4.31	22	12	8	43.9	4.31	40.1
Nevada	...	...	...	...	...	...	...	...	...	...	...	...
White Pine County	...	...	...	...	...	...	...	...	...	...	...	...
Utah	17	33.3	17	33.3	16.7	4.17	17	9	6	33.3	4.17	33.3
Juab and Tooele Counties	17	33.3	17	33.3	16.7	4.17	17	9	6	33.3	4.17	33.3
Grand Portage Reservation, MN	55	55.0	55	55.0	33.4	3.55	51	34	15	51.2	3.56	55.6
Cook County	55	55.0	55	55.0	33.4	3.55	51	34	15	51.2	3.56	55.6
Grindstone Creek Rancheria CA	15	76.1	15	76.1	44.6	4.78	15	10	-	76.1	4.78	50.5
Glenn County	15	76.1	15	76.1	44.6	4.78	15	10	-	76.1	4.78	50.5
Hannahville Community, MI	33	89.6	33	89.6	44.8	5.87	33	20	9	89.6	5.87	49.1
Menominee County	33	89.6	33	89.6	44.8	5.87	33	20	9	89.6	5.87	49.1
Hassanamisco Reservation, MA	...	...	...	...	...	...	...	...	...	...	...	...
Worcester County	...	...	...	...	...	...	...	...	...	...	...	...
Havasupai Reservation, AZ	54	59.2	54	59.2	27.9	4.80	54	31	11	59.2	4.80	51.4
Coconino County	54	59.2	54	59.2	27.9	4.80	54	31	11	59.2	4.80	51.4

[Continued]

★ 244 ★

Families With American Indian, Eskimo, or Aleut Members on Identified Reservations by Selected Characteristics, 1980: Ely Colony - Lac du Flambeau

[Continued]

Identified reservations	Families with one or more American Indian, Eskimo, or Aleut		Families with American Indian, Eskimo, or Aleut householder or spouse				Families with American Indian, Eskimo, or Aleut householder					Persons under 18 percent living with two parents
	Total	Percent with own children under 18 years	Total	Percent with own children under 18 years	Percent with own children under 6 years	Persons per family	Total	Married couple	Female householder, no husband present	Percent with own children under 18 years	Persons per family	
Hoh Reservation, WA	8	100.0	8	100.0	45.6	5.06	8	5	3	100.0	5.06	33.2
Jefferson County	8	100.0	8	100.0	45.6	5.06	8	5	3	100.0	5.06	33.2
Hollywood Reservation, FL	106	69.6	104	70.7	45.8	4.03	96	38	41	71.5	4.10	42.9
Broward County	106	69.6	104	70.7	45.8	4.03	96	38	41	71.5	4.10	42.9
Hoopa Valley Reservation CA	385	61.7	377	61.2	32.2	3.85	355	206	96	63.1	3.88	53.8
Humboldt County	385	61.7	377	61.2	32.2	3.85	355	206	96	63.1	3.88	53.8
Hoopa Valley Extension Reservation CA	115	59.9	109	59.3	36.0	3.86	84	58	23	61.9	3.94	60.9
Del Norte County	50	59.9	47	60.4	36.1	3.61	38	23	14	61.7	3.59	47.9
Humboldt County	63	59.9	61	58.5	36.0	4.06	46	35	9	62.0	4.23	68.4
Hopi Reservation, AZ	1,266	62.9	1,263	62.8	25.8	5.06	1,257	914	281	62.8	5.07	61.5
Coconino County	236	60.6	236	60.6	21.5	5.32	236	170	56	60.6	5.32	62.5
Navajo County	1,030	63.5	1,026	63.3	26.8	5.00	1,021	743	225	63.4	5.01	61.2
Hopland Rancheria CA	-	-	-	-	-	-	-	-	-	-	-	-
Mendocino County	-	-	-	-	-	-	-	-	-	-	-	-
Hualapai Reservation, AZ	147	67.9	147	67.9	37.6	5.42	145	104	32	68.1	5.43	60.2
Coconino and Mohave Counties	146	67.6	146	67.6	37.9	5.41	144	103	32	67.9	5.43	59.9
Yavapai County	...	...	...	...	...	...	...	...	...	...	...	...
Inaja-Cosmit Reservation CA	-	-	-	-	-	-	-	-	-	-	-	-
San Diego County	-	-	-	-	-	-	-	-	-	-	-	-
Indian Township Reservation, ME	79	77.0	77	76.4	34.7	4.45	72	42	20	74.9	4.39	69.1
Washington County	79	77.0	77	76.4	34.7	4.45	72	42	20	74.9	4.39	69.1
Iowa Reservation, KS-NE	13	49.0	11	59.0	29.5	3.39	...	...	...	...	...	100.0
Kansas	11	40.0	...	...	...	...	...	...	...	...	...	...
Brown County	11	40.0	...	...	...	...	...	...	...	...	...	...
Doniphan County	-	-	-	-	-	-	-	-	-	-	-	-
Nebraska	...	...	...	...	...	...	...	...	...	...	...	...
Richardson County	...	...	...	...	...	...	...	...	...	...	...	...
Isabella Reservation, MI	133	67.6	120	66.0	39.0	4.35	104	52	46	65.4	4.52	46.2
Isabella County	133	67.6	120	66.0	39.0	4.35	104	52	46	65.4	4.52	46.2
Isleta Pueblo, NM	593	67.3	586	67.2	29.3	3.85	553	371	138	67.3	3.87	63.1
Bernalillo County	469	65.3	464	65.4	29.3	3.77	437	279	122	65.4	3.78	59.6
Torrace County	-	-	-	-	-	-	-	-	-	-	-	-
Valencia County	124	74.6	122	74.3	29.1	4.15	115	92	15	74.2	4.22	74.4
Jackson Rancheria CA	...	...	...	...	...	...	...	...	...	...	...	...
Amador County	...	...	...	...	...	...	...	...	...	...	...	...
Jemez Pueblo, NM	276	65.0	276	65.0	23.8	5.36	276	176	73	65.0	5.36	49.4
Sandoval County	276	65.0	276	65.0	23.8	5.36	276	176	73	65.0	5.36	49.4
Jicarilla Apache Reservation, NM Rio Arriba and Sandoval Counties	354	78.4	351	78.5	43.4	4.76	336	220	93	78.0	4.74	64.9
	354	78.4	351	78.5	43.4	4.76	336	220	93	78.0	4.74	64.9
Kaibab Reservation, AZ	20	61.1	20	61.1	38.8	4.30	20	15	3	61.1	4.30	67.7
Coconino County	-	-	-	-	-	-	-	-	-	-	-	-
Mohave County	20	61.1	20	61.1	38.8	4.30	20	15	3	61.1	4.30	67.7
Kalispel Reservation, WA	18	61.1	17	58.8	35.3	5.47	14	8	6	57.1	5.50	59.6
Pend Oreille County	18	61.1	17	58.8	35.3	5.47	14	8	6	57.1	5.50	59.6
Kickapoo Reservation, KS	95	67.4	93	66.7	28.3	4.02	83	55	24	65.4	4.13	66.9
Brown County	95	67.4	93	66.7	28.3	4.02	83	55	24	65.4	4.13	66.9
Kootenai Reservation, ID	-	-	-	-	-	-	-	-	-	-	-	-
Boundary County	-	-	-	-	-	-	-	-	-	-	-	-
Lac Courte Oreilles Reservation, WI	279	73.0	275	72.7	31.5	4.16	258	129	99	74.1	4.26	45.0
Sawyer County	279	73.0	275	72.7	31.5	4.16	258	129	99	74.1	4.26	45.0
Lac du Flambeau Reservation, WI	237	67.4	228	66.1	27.1	4.58	217	110	79	64.4	4.53	53.9
Iron County	-	-	-	-	-	-	-	-	-	-	-	-

[Continued]

★ 244 ★

Families With American Indian, Eskimo, or Aleut Members on Identified Reservations by Selected Characteristics, 1980: Ely Colony - Lac du Flambeau

[Continued]

Identified reservations	Families with one or more American Indian, Eskimo, or Aleut		Families with American Indian, Eskimo, or Aleut householder or spouse				Families with American Indian, Eskimo, or Aleut householder					Persons under 18 percent living with two parents
	Total	Percent with own children under 18 years	Total	Percent with own children under 18 years	Percent with own children under 6 years	Persons per family	Total	Married couple	Female householder, no husband present	Percent with own children under 18 years	Persons per family	
Oneida County	-	-	-	-	-	-	-	-	-	-	-	-
Vilas County	237	67.4	228	66.1	27.1	4.58	217	110	79	64.4	4.53	53.9

Source: U.S. Bureau of the Census, Subject Reports, PC80-2-1D, Part I, *American Indians, Eskimos, and Aleuts on Identified Reservations and in the Historic Areas of Oklahoma (Excluding Urbanized Areas)*, U.S. Government Printing Office, Washington, D.C., 1986, pp. 41-49. *Notes:* A dash (-) represents zero or a percent which rounds to less than 0.1. Also, a dash (-) is used because the number of supplementary questionnaires for the reservations was insufficient to produce reliable estimates. Three dots (...) means not applicable, or that the data are being withheld to avoid disclosure of information for individuals.

★ 245 ★

Families With American Indian, Eskimo, or Aleut Members on Identified Reservations by Selected Characteristics, 1980: Laguna Pueblo - Picuris Pueblo

Data are the latest available.

Identified reservations	Families with one or more American Indian, Eskimo, or Aleut		Families with American Indian, Eskimo, or Aleut householder or spouse				Families with American Indian, Eskimo, or Aleut householder					Persons under 18 percent living with two parents
	Total	Percent with own children under 18 years	Total	Percent with own children under 18 years	Percent with own children under 6 years	Persons per family	Total	Married couple	Female householder, no husband present	Percent with own children under 18 years	Persons per family	
Laguna Pueblo, NM	833	66.2	828	66.4	35.3	4.21	810	584	182	65.6	4.21	66.6
Bernalillo and Valencia Counties	833	66.2	828	66.4	35.3	4.21	810	584	182	65.6	4.21	66.6
Sandoval County	-	-	-	-	-	-	-	-	-	-	-	-
La Jolla Reservation, CA	33	80.2	32	79.4	46.0	4.10	30	21	8	78.6	4.14	69.8
San Diego County	33	80.2	32	79.4	46.0	4.10	30	21	8	78.6	4.14	69.8
L'Anse Reservation, MI	160	69.3	157	68.6	35.1	4.13	116	80	30	69.7	4.05	70.7
Baraga County	160	69.3	157	68.6	35.1	4.13	116	80	30	69.7	4.05	70.7
La Posta Reservation, CA	...	...	...	...	...	...	...	...	...	...	...	...
San Diego County	...	...	...	...	...	...	...	...	...	...	...	...
Las Vegas Colony, NV	21	88.7	21	88.7	45.7	4.97	18	8	9	87.0	4.70	32.0
Clark County	21	88.7	21	88.7	45.7	4.97	18	8	9	87.0	4.70	32.0
Laytonville Rancheria, CA	21	66.7	20	65.0	40.0	5.05	20	13	6	65.0	5.05	76.7
Mendocino County	21	66.7	20	65.0	40.0	5.05	20	13	6	65.0	5.05	76.7
Leech Lake Reservation, MN	639	68.4	621	69.5	32.3	4.44	559	323	187	69.8	4.50	48.3
Beltrami County	82	64.7	80	66.0	27.8	4.20	76	50	18	69.4	4.24	50.2
Cass and Hubbard Counties	405	68.6	393	68.4	31.6	4.32	350	184	136	68.9	4.38	44.3
Itasca County	153	73.9	148	74.1	36.7	4.88	133	89	33	72.5	4.96	56.6
Likely Rancheria, CA	-	-	-	-	-	-	-	-	-	-	-	-
Modoc County	-	-	-	-	-	-	-	-	-	-	-	-
Lone Pine Rancheria, CA	47	58.0	45	55.7	20.9	3.93	40	23	15	53.3	3.88	47.0
Inyo County	47	58.0	45	55.7	20.9	3.93	40	23	15	53.3	3.88	47.0
Lookout Rancheria, CA	...	...	...	...	...	...	...	...	...	...	...	...
Modoc County	...	...	...	...	...	...	...	...	...	...	...	...
Los Coyotes Reservation, CA	16	46.2	16	46.2	30.8	3.11	16	11	4	46.2	3.11	68.7
San Diego County	16	46.2	16	46.2	30.8	3.11	16	11	4	46.2	3.11	68.7
Lovelock Colony, NV	25	60.0	25	60.0	23.9	4.57	23	15	6	65.7	4.71	61.1
Pershing County	25	60.0	25	60.0	23.9	4.57	23	15	6	65.7	4.71	61.1
Lower Brule Reservation, SD	166	70.9	161	71.0	43.4	4.92	150	87	54	71.0	4.72	50.8
Lyman County	161	73.0	157	73.2	44.8	5.01	145	82	54	73.4	4.81	50.8
Stanley County	...	...	...	...	...	...	...	...	...	...	...	...
Lower Elwah Reservation, WA	10	50.0	10	50.0	10.0	4.70	10	6	2	50.0	4.70	50.0
Clallam County	10	50.0	10	50.0	10.0	4.70	10	6	2	50.0	4.70	50.0
Lower Sioux Community, MN	20	30.9	20	30.9	30.9	3.54	20	11	6	30.9	3.54	33.3

[Continued]

469

★ 245 ★

Families With American Indian, Eskimo, or Aleut Members on Identified Reservations by Selected Characteristics, 1980: Laguna Pueblo - Picuris Pueblo

[Continued]

Identified reservations	Families with one or more American Indian, Eskimo, or Aleut		Families with American Indian, Eskimo, or Aleut householder or spouse				Families with American Indian, Eskimo, or Aleut householder					Persons under 18 percent living with two parents
	Total	Percent with own children under 18 years	Total	Percent with own children under 18 years	Percent with own children under 6 years	Persons per family	Total	Married couple	Female householder, no husband present	Percent with own children under 18 years	Persons per family	
Redwood County	20	30.9	20	30.9	30.9	3.54	20	11	6	30.9	3.54	33.3
Lummi Reservation, WA	278	70.5	275	70.2	32.7	4.62	265	178	58	69.1	4.64	65.2
Whatcom County	278	70.5	275	70.2	32.7	4.62	265	178	58	69.1	4.64	65.2
Makah Reservation, WA	219	65.5	214	64.7	35.9	3.81	178	98	50	63.4	3.74	57.1
Clallam County	219	65.5	214	64.7	35.9	3.81	178	98	50	63.4	3.74	57.1
Manchester Rancheria, CA	16	45.9	16	45.9	7.0	4.78	14	8	4	53.4	5.15	55.8
Mendocino County	16	45.9	16	45.9	7.0	4.78	14	8	4	53.4	5.15	55.8
Manzanita Reservation, CA	...	...	...	...	...	...	...	...	...	...	...	...
San Diego County	...	...	...	...	...	...	...	...	...	...	...	...
Maricopa Reservation, AZ	63	67.4	63	67.4	25.1	5.78	63	42	14	67.4	5.78	54.0
Pinal County	63	67.4	63	67.4	25.1	5.78	63	42	14	67.4	5.78	54.0
Mattaponi Reservation, VA	21	38.1	21	38.1	14.3	3.19	16	14	2	43.8	3.50	63.2
King William County	21	38.1	21	38.1	14.3	3.19	16	14	2	43.8	3.50	63.2
Menominee Reservation, WI	480	68.4	477	68.6	32.0	4.94	451	269	130	69.9	4.94	54.5
Menominee County	480	68.4	477	68.6	32.0	4.94	451	269	130	69.9	4.94	54.5
Mesa Grande Reservation, CA	-	-	-	-	-	-	-	-	-	-	-	-
San Diego County	-	-	-	-	-	-	-	-	-	-	-	-
Mescalero Apache Reservation, NM	395	78.2	391	78.0	45.0	4.89	366	242	103	77.6	4.88	62.3
Otero County	395	78.2	391	78.0	45.0	4.89	366	242	103	77.6	4.88	62.3
Miccosukee Reservation, FL	57	73.7	57	73.7	35.1	4.53	57	43	14	73.7	4.53	64.8
Broward County	-	-	-	-	-	-	-	-	-	-	-	-
Dade County	57	73.7	57	73.7	35.1	4.53	57	43	14	73.7	4.53	64.8
Middletown Rancheria, CA	...	...	...	...	...	...	...	...	...	...	...	23.5
Lake County	...	...	...	...	...	...	...	...	...	...	...	23.5
Mille Lacs Reservation, MN	-	-	-	-	-	-	-	-	-	-	-	-
Aitkin County	-	-	-	-	-	-	-	-	-	-	-	-
Kanabec County	-	-	-	-	-	-	-	-	-	-	-	-
Mille Lacs County	-	-	-	-	-	-	-	-	-	-	-	-
Pine County	-	-	-	-	-	-	-	-	-	-	-	-
Mississippi Choctaw Reservation, MS	530	65.9	530	65.9	32.6	5.13	527	339	151	65.9	5.13	49.5
Attala County	-	-	-	-	-	-	-	-	-	-	-	-
Jones County	26	69.2	26	69.2	46.2	4.65	26	19	6	69.2	4.65	52.0
Kemper County	...	...	...	...	...	...	...	...	...	...	...	...
Leake County	97	59.9	97	59.9	22.1	5.41	96	58	24	60.5	5.44	47.8
Neshoba County	340	67.1	340	67.1	34.1	5.08	340	229	93	67.1	5.08	50.0
Newton County	66	68.1	66	68.1	35.3	5.14	64	32	28	67.3	5.17	49.3
Moapa River Reservation, NV	40	72.5	40	72.5	23.8	4.58	38	17	17	71.0	4.51	54.8
Clark County	40	72.5	40	72.5	23.8	4.58	38	17	17	71.0	4.51	54.8
Montgomery Creek Rancheria, CA	...	...	...	...	...	...	...	...	...	...	...	...
Shasta County	...	...	...	...	...	...	...	...	...	...	...	...
Morongo Reservation, CA	79	67.7	79	67.7	31.3	4.21	71	45	17	66.4	4.31	55.3
Riverside County	79	67.7	79	67.7	31.3	4.21	71	45	17	66.4	4.31	55.3
Muckleshoot Reservation, WA	66	75.6	64	77.8	39.1	6.16	60	41	10	76.6	6.31	66.7
King County	66	75.6	64	77.9	39.1	6.16	60	41	10	76.6	6.31	66.7
Pierce County	-	-	-	-	-	-	-	-	-	-	-	-
Nambe Pueblo, NM	66	53.4	63	53.1	23.1	3.38	52	30	9	56.7	3.72	60.1
Santa Fe County	66	53.4	63	53.1	23.1	3.38	52	30	9	56.7	3.72	60.1
Navajo Reservation, AZ-NM-UT	19,970	73.9	19,933	73.9	40.5	5.14	19,741	13,970	4,806	73.8	5.15	65.1
Arizona	13,524	74.2	13,497	74.2	40.8	5.17	13,354	9,376	3,339	74.0	5.18	65.1
Apache County	7,295	72.5	7,281	72.5	38.7	5.11	7,199	4,917	1,877	72.4	5.12	63.2
Coconino County	2,870	77.2	2,862	77.2	44.7	5.22	2,825	2,002	712	77.0	5.23	65.3
Navajo County	3,358	75.2	3,354	75.3	42.1	5.26	3,330	2,457	751	75.1	5.27	68.8
New Mexico	5,621	73.0	5,611	72.9	39.6	5.01	5,565	3,956	1,308	72.8	5.02	63.8
McKinley County	1,910	72.6	1,905	72.5	41.2	4.94	1,893	1,318	472	72.5	4.95	63.8
San Juan County	3,711	73.2	3,707	73.1	38.7	5.05	3,672	2,637	836	73.0	5.06	63.7
Utah	825	77.3	825	77.3	41.5	5.44	822	639	160	77.3	5.44	72.0
San Juan County	825	77.3	825	77.3	41.5	5.44	822	639	160	77.3	5.44	72.0
Nez Perce Reservation, ID	379	62.6	370	62.5	30.4	4.18	322	212	91	62.2	4.19	59.9
Clearwater County	40	60.0	36	58.3	33.3	3.58	26	16	8	61.5	3.69	39.2
Idaho County	43	56.2	42	55.3	34.6	3.79	36	27	6	53.5	3.91	64.3
Lewis County	59	62.7	57	63.2	29.8	3.86	50	35	14	62.0	3.82	60.0

[Continued]

Families With American Indian, Eskimo, or Aleut Members on Identified Reservations by Selected Characteristics, 1980: Laguna Pueblo - Picuris Pueblo

[Continued]

Identified reservations	Families with one or more American Indian, Eskimo, or Aleut		Families with American Indian, Eskimo, or Aleut householder or spouse				Families with American Indian, Eskimo, or Aleut householder					Persons under 18 percent living with two parents
	Total	Percent with own children under 18 years	Total	Percent with own children under 18 years	Percent with own children under 6 years	Persons per family	Total	Married couple	Female householder, no husband present	Percent with own children under 18 years	Persons per family	
Nez Perce County	237	64.1	235	64.3	29.4	4.43	210	134	63	63.8	4.38	61.7
Nisqually Reservation, WA	11	50.0	11	50.0	20.0	3.93	10	5	3	55.6	4.14	35.7
Pierce County	-	-	-	-	-	-	-	-	-	-	-	-
Thurston County	11	50.0	11	50.0	20.0	3.93	10	5	3	55.6	4.14	35.7
Nooksack Reservation, WA	-	-	-	-	-	-	-	-	-	-	-	-
Whatcom County	-	-	-	-	-	-	-	-	-	-	-	-
Northern Cheyenne Reservation, MT	650	76.5	645	76.7	41.6	4.72	613	407	172	76.8	4.76	59.5
Big Horn County	185	74.5	183	74.3	38.6	4.60	170	121	42	75.2	4.68	62.4
Rosebud County	465	77.3	462	77.6	42.8	4.76	443	286	130	77.4	4.78	58.3
Oil Springs Reservation, NY	-	-	-	-	-	-	-	-	-	-	-	-
Allegany County	-	-	-	-	-	-	-	-	-	-	-	-
Cattaraugus County	-	-	-	-	-	-	-	-	-	-	-	-
Omaha Reservation, IO-NE	252	60.0	246	60.0	28.9	4.86	239	122	97	60.8	4.89	40.1
Iowa	-	-	-	-	-	-	-	-	-	-	-	-
Monona County	-	-	-	-	-	-	-	-	-	-	-	-
Nebraska	252	60.0	246	60.0	28.9	4.86	239	122	97	60.8	4.89	40.1
Burt County	...	...	...	...	...	...	...	...	...	...	...	...
Cuming County	-	-	-	-	-	-	-	-	-	-	-	-
Thurston County	251	60.2	245	60.3	29.1	4.85	238	121	97	61.0	4.88	40.4
Oneida Reservation, WI	457	62.9	449	62.2	27.0	4.00	387	271	88	61.3	3.97	70.2
Brown County	186	54.6	180	53.1	17.0	3.92	159	116	30	50.0	4.00	75.5
Outagamie County	271	68.6	268	68.2	33.8	4.05	229	155	58	69.2	3.94	67.2
Onondaga Reservation, NY	-	-	-	-	-	-	-	-	-	-	-	-
Onondaga County	-	-	-	-	-	-	-	-	-	-	-	-
Ontonagon Reservation, MI	-	-	-	-	-	-	-	-	-	-	-	-
Ontonagon County	-	-	-	-	-	-	-	-	-	-	-	-
Osage Reservation, OK	1,783	53.3	1,685	52.5	26.1	3.35	1,165	915	200	51.9	3.41	72.1
Osage County	1,783	53.3	1,685	52.5	26.1	3.35	1,165	915	200	51.9	3.41	72.1
Ozette Reservation, WA	...	...	...	...	...	...	...	...	...	...	...	...
Clallam County	...	...	...	...	...	...	...	...	...	...	...	...
Pala Reservation, CA	121	60.8	120	60.5	32.5	3.89	111	61	34	62.2	3.94	53.4
San Diego County	121	60.8	120	60.5	32.5	3.89	111	61	34	62.2	3.94	53.4
Pamunkey Reservation, VA	14	28.6	14	28.6	7.1	2.79	14	10	2	28.6	2.79	72.7
King William County	14	28.6	14	28.6	7.1	2.79	14	10	2	28.6	2.79	72.7
Papago Reservation, AZ	1,291	58.1	1,286	58.2	29.1	5.07	1,283	693	417	58.1	5.08	48.4
Maricopa County	23	53.9	23	53.9	16.6	5.28	23	16	6	53.9	5.28	53.3
Pima County	1,144	58.4	1,139	58.5	29.2	5.09	1,136	598	385	58.4	5.09	48.0
Pinal County	124	56.3	124	56.3	31.2	4.90	124	79	26	56.3	4.90	51.8
Pascua Yaqui Reservation, AZ	92	77.5	91	77.2	40.8	6.11	87	64	19	77.6	6.10	51.4
Pima County	92	77.5	91	77.2	40.8	6.11	87	64	19	77.6	6.10	51.4
Pauma Reservation, CA	19	42.9	19	42.9	19.7	4.32	16	12	3	31.1	4.39	64.2
San Diego County	19	42.9	19	42.9	19.7	4.32	16	12	3	31.1	4.39	64.2
Payson Community Of Yavapai-Apache, AZ	-	-	-	-	-	-	-	-	-	-	-	-
Gila County	-	-	-	-	-	-	-	-	-	-	-	-
Pechanga Reservation, CA	30	56.7	30	56.7	30.0	4.03	25	14	9	60.0	4.12	50.0
Riverside County	30	56.7	30	56.7	30.0	4.03	25	14	9	60.0	4.12	50.0
Penobscot Reservation, ME	115	60.5	112	60.4	31.5	3.68	103	63	31	60.8	3.64	57.0
Penobscot County	115	60.5	112	60.4	31.5	3.68	103	63	31	60.8	3.64	57.0
Picuris Pueblo, NM	36	79.7	36	79.7	33.9	3.87	27	18	7	73.3	3.90	65.0
Taos County	36	79.7	36	79.7	33.9	3.87	27	18	7	73.3	3.90	65.0

Source: U.S. Bureau of the Census, Subject Reports, PC80-2-1D, Part I, *American Indians, Eskimos, and Aleuts on Identified Reservations and in the Historic Areas of Oklahoma (Excluding Urbanized Areas)*, U.S. Government Printing Office, Washington, D.C., 1986, pp. 41-49. *Notes:* A dash (-) represents zero or a percent which rounds to less than 0.1. Also, a dash (-) is used because the number of supplementary questionnaires for the reservations was insufficient to produce reliable estimates. Three dots (...) means not applicable, or that the data are being withheld to avoid disclosure of information for individuals.

★ 246 ★

Families With American Indian, Eskimo, or Aleut Members on Identified Reservations by Selected Characteristics, 1980: Pine Creek - Southern Paiute

Data are the latest available.

Identified reservations	Families with one or more American Indian, Eskimo, or Aleut		Families with American Indian, Eskimo, or Aleut householder or spouse				Families with American Indian, Eskimo, or Aleut householder					Persons under 18 percent living with two parents
	Total	Percent with own children under 18 years	Total	Percent with own children under 18 years	Percent with own children under 6 years	Persons per family	Total	Married couple	Female householder, no husband present	Percent with own children under 18 years	Persons per family	
Pine Creek Reservation, MI	1	100.0	1	100.0	-	9.00	...	...	...	...	...	...
Calhoun County	1	100.0	1	100.0	-	9.00	...	...	...	...	...	...
Pine Ridge Reservation, SD	2,118	71.6	2,111	71.5	37.3	5.57	2,050	1,198	680	71.5	5.63	46.0
Jackson County	233	72.8	233	72.8	43.2	5.95	210	137	57	71.2	6.17	64.4
Shannon County	1,885	71.5	1,877	71.3	36.5	5.52	1,840	1,061	624	71.5	5.56	43.5
Pleasant Point Reservation, ME	115	72.7	114	72.4	38.7	4.43	108	66	42	70.9	4.40	55.2
Washington County	115	72.7	114	72.4	38.7	4.43	108	66	42	70.9	4.40	55.2
Pojoaque Pueblo, NM	27	75.4	27	75.4	35.2	3.65	22	12	10	84.3	3.77	37.7
Santa Fe County	27	75.4	27	75.4	35.2	3.65	22	12	10	84.3	3.77	37.7
Poospatuck Reservation, NY	24	60.8	23	58.8	34.3	4.75	12	9	2	62.2	4.69	72.6
Suffolk County	24	60.8	23	58.8	34.3	4.75	12	9	2	62.2	4.69	72.6
Port Gamble Reservation, WA	64	70.7	64	70.7	41.7	4.23	61	32	21	69.4	4.19	50.1
Kitsap County	64	70.7	64	70.7	41.7	4.23	61	32	21	69.4	4.19	50.1
Port Madison Reservation, WA	54	56.8	46	53.9	29.6	3.16	38	26	9	56.7	3.24	60.2
Kitsap County	54	56.8	46	53.9	29.6	3.16	38	26	9	56.7	3.24	60.2
Potawatomi Reservation, WI	40	66.9	40	66.9	41.5	5.38	39	17	15	66.1	5.42	53.5
Forest County	40	66.9	40	66.9	41.5	5.38	39	17	15	66.1	5.42	53.5
Oconto County	-	-	-	-	-	-	-	-	-	-	-	-
Pottawatomi Reservation, KS	80	48.5	80	48.5	13.9	4.37	66	46	15	46.4	4.32	65.6
Jackson County	80	48.5	80	48.5	13.9	4.37	66	46	15	46.4	4.32	65.6
Prairie Island Community, MN	17	52.9	17	52.9	23.5	5.12	16	8	8	56.3	4.94	43.8
Goodhue County	17	52.9	17	52.9	23.5	5.12	16	8	8	56.3	4.94	43.8
Puyallup Reservation, WA	274	72.5	247	71.3	35.8	3.96	200	110	78	73.3	3.94	41.3
Pierce County	274	72.5	247	71.3	35.8	3.96	200	110	78	73.3	3.94	41.3
Pyramid Lake Reservation, NV	171	62.9	171	62.9	26.4	4.16	169	102	45	62.4	4.17	53.9
Lyon County	-	-	-	-	-	-	-	-	-	-	-	-
Storey County	-	-	-	-	-	-	-	-	-	-	-	-
Washoe County	171	62.9	171	62.9	26.4	4.16	169	102	45	62.4	4.17	53.9
Quileute Reservation, WA	55	76.8	55	76.8	47.8	4.92	48	28	12	73.3	4.74	71.0
Clallam County	55	76.8	55	76.8	47.8	4.92	48	28	12	73.3	4.74	71.0
Quinault Reservation, WA	217	73.3	215	73.8	35.6	4.41	201	117	48	72.5	4.40	55.3
Grays Harbor County	184	71.6	182	72.1	33.5	4.30	170	95	42	70.8	4.29	53.7
Jefferson County	33	83.1	33	83.1	46.7	5.02	31	22	6	82.0	5.02	61.7
Ramah Community, NM	231	66.0	231	66.0	31.7	4.63	231	129	84	66.0	4.63	62.7
McKinely County	19	51.0	19	51.0	22.8	4.55	19	7	8	51.0	4.55	34.7
Valencia County	212	67.4	212	67.4	32.5	4.64	212	122	75	67.4	4.64	65.0
Ramona Reservation, CA	-	-	-	-	-	-	-	-	-	-	-	-
Riverside County	-	-	-	-	-	-	-	-	-	-	-	-
Red Cliff Reservation, WI	133	70.1	128	69.0	43.5	4.58	116	88	25	68.0	4.60	69.8
Bayfield County	133	70.1	128	69.0	43.5	4.58	116	88	25	68.0	4.60	69.8
Red Lake Reservation, MN	589	67.9	586	68.0	33.2	4.69	578	317	205	68.1	4.70	45.1
Beltrami County	577	68.2	574	68.3	33.2	4.68	568	313	201	68.5	4.70	45.6
Clearwater County	11	52.3	11	52.3	30.9	5.18	10	4	4	47.3	4.84	20.5
Koochiching County	-	-	-	-	-	-	-	-	-	-	-	-
Lake of the Woods County	-	-	-	-	-	-	-	-	-	-	-	-
Marshall County	-	-	-	-	-	-	-	-	-	-	-	-
Pennington County	-	-	-	-	-	-	-	-	-	-	-	-
Polk County	-	-	-	-	-	-	-	-	-	-	-	-
Red Lake County	-	-	-	-	-	-	-	-	-	-	-	-
Roseau County	-	-	-	-	-	-	-	-	-	-	-	-
Reno-Sparks Colony, NV	105	67.2	104	66.9	22.0	4.17	101	61	29	65.8	4.11	54.8
Washoe County	105	67.2	104	66.9	22.0	4.17	101	61	29	65.8	4.11	54.8
Resighini Rancheria, CA	...	...	...	...	...	...	...	...	...	...	...	...
Del Norte County	...	...	...	...	...	...	...	...	...	...	...	...
Rincon Reservation, CA	75	57.4	75	57.4	25.9	4.27	67	43	15	56.3	4.31	49.4
San Diego County	75	57.4	75	57.4	25.9	4.27	67	43	15	56.3	4.31	49.4
Roaring Creek Rancheria, CA	...	...	...	...	...	...	...	...	...	...	...	...
Shasta County	...	...	...	...	...	...	...	...	...	...	...	...
Rocky Boy's Reservation, MT	299	76.1	299	76.1	35.8	5.23	296	204	76	76.2	5.24	57.4
Chouteau County	28	71.4	28	71.4	25.0	4.57	27	20	4	70.4	4.56	65.5
Hill County	271	76.6	271	76.6	36.9	5.29	269	184	72	76.8	5.31	56.7
Rosebud Reservation, SD	1,176	72.4	1,168	72.4	42.5	4.79	1,119	620	401	72.2	4.86	45.6

[Continued]

★ 246 ★

Families With American Indian, Eskimo, or Aleut Members on Identified Reservations by Selected Characteristics, 1980: Pine Creek - Southern Paiute

[Continued]

Identified reservations	Families with one or more American Indian, Eskimo, or Aleut		Families with American Indian, Eskimo, or Aleut householder or spouse				Families with American Indian, Eskimo, or Aleut householder					Persons under 18 percent living with two parents
	Total	Percent with own children under 18 years	Total	Percent with own children under 18 years	Percent with own children under 6 years	Persons per family	Total	Married couple	Female householder, no husband present	Percent with own children under 18 years	Persons per family	
Todd County	1,176	72.4	1,168	72.4	42.5	4.79	1,119	620	401	72.2	4.86	45.6
Round Valley Reservation, CA	130	64.5	130	64.5	35.2	4.07	124	74	40	66.6	4.12	5.65
Mendocino County	130	64.5	130	64.5	35.2	4.07	124	74	40	66.6	4.12	5.65
Rumsey Rancheria, CA	...	...	...	...	...	...	...	...	...	...	...	...
Yolo County	...	...	...	...	...	...	...	...	...	...	...	...
Sac and Fox Reservation, IA	89	57.4	89	57.4	31.1	5.47	89	63	16	57.4	5.47	60.4
Tama County	89	57.4	89	57.4	31.1	5.47	89	63	16	57.4	5.47	60.4
Sac and Fox Reservation, KS-NE	...	...	...	...	...	...	...	...	...	...	...	...
Kansas	-	-	-	-	-	-	-	-	-	-	-	-
Brown County	-	-	-	-	-	-	-	-	-	-	-	-
Nebraska	...	...	...	...	...	...	...	...	...	...	...	...
Richardson County	...	...	...	...	...	...	...	...	...	...	...	...
St. Croix Reservation, WI	84	49.5	82	48.1	19.5	4.70	82	50	24	48.1	4.70	39.0
Barron County	16	67.8	16	67.8	13.6	5.02	16	12	4	67.8	5.02	22.8
Burnett County	47	48.1	45	45.4	21.8	5.14	45	28	14	45.4	5.14	40.5
Polk County	21	38.6	21	38.6	19.2	3.54	21	11	5	38.6	3.54	53.4
St. Regis Mohawk Reservation, NY	413	59.6	412	59.5	25.6	4.04	412	301	81	59.5	4.04	65.9
Franklin County	413	59.6	412	59.5	25.6	4.04	412	301	81	59.5	4.04	65.9
Salt River Reservation, AZ	510	71.0	510	71.0	33.1	5.02	492	259	174	70.5	5.10	44.1
Maricopa County	510	71.0	510	71.0	33.1	5.02	492	259	174	70.5	5.10	44.1
San Carlos Reservation, AZ	1,070	71.7	1,067	71.6	33.2	5.30	1,054	668	297	71.3	5.33	54.2
Gila County	666	69.3	663	69.2	30.1	5.01	653	404	179	68.7	5.04	51.6
Graham County	404	75.5	404	75.5	38.4	5.79	402	265	118	75.7	5.78	57.2
Pinal County	-	-	-	-	-	-	-	-	-	-	-	-
Sandia Pueblo, NM	59	64.1	57	64.8	25.6	3.95	51	35	11	61.1	4.04	70.2
Bernalillo County	-	-	-	-	-	-	-	-	-	-	-	-
Sandoval County	59	64.1	57	64.8	25.6	3.95	51	35	11	61.1	4.04	70.2
Sandy Lake Reservation, MN	-	-	-	-	-	-	-	-	-	-	-	-
Aitkin County	-	-	-	-	-	-	-	-	-	-	-	-
San Felipe Pueblo, NM	275	63.3	274	63.1	26.3	6.51	273	146	87	62.9	6.53	40.5
Sandoval County	275	63.3	274	63.1	26.3	6.51	273	146	87	62.9	6.53	40.5
San Ildefonso Pueblo, NM	124	60.8	124	60.8	32.1	3.84	122	75	39	60.1	3.85	61.0
Sandoval County	-	-	-	-	-	-	-	-	-	-	-	-
Santa Fe County	124	60.8	124	60.8	32.1	3.84	122	75	39	60.1	3.85	61.0
San Juan Pueblo, NM	197	67.6	194	67.1	24.5	4.38	168	107	48	63.6	4.39	66.2
Rio Arriba County	197	67.6	194	67.1	24.5	4.38	168	107	48	63.6	4.39	66.2
San Manuel Reservation, CA	-	-	-	-	-	-	-	-	-	-	-	-
San Bernardino County	-	-	-	-	-	-	-	-	-	-	-	-
San Pasqual Reservation, CA	39	64.5	37	68.2	42.7	4.10	30	17	8	67.5	3.83	79.1
San Diego County	39	64.5	37	68.2	42.7	4.10	30	17	8	67.5	3.83	79.1
Santa Ana Pueblo, NM	93	62.3	93	62.3	21.4	4.31	93	63	25	62.3	4.31	54.9
Sandoval County	93	62.3	93	62.3	21.4	4.31	93	63	25	62.3	4.31	54.9
Santa Clara Pueblo, NM	476	63.1	474	63.0	33.4	4.11	451	331	92	63.2	4.18	64.2
Rio Arriba County	468	62.9	468	62.9	33.0	4.12	449	329	92	63.1	4.18	64.1
Sandoval County	-	-	-	-	-	-	-	-	-	-	-	-
Santa Fe County	8	75.0	...	...	...	...	...	...	...	...	...	...
Santa Rosa Rancheria, CA	23	81.5	23	81.5	60.6	5.75	19	7	8	78.2	5.84	26.2
Kings County	23	81.5	23	81.5	60.6	5.75	19	7	8	78.2	5.84	26.2
Santa Rosa Reservation, CA	...	...	...	...	...	...	...	...	...	...	...	...
Riverside County	...	...	...	...	...	...	...	...	...	...	...	...
Santa Ynez Reservation, CA	32	65.4	32	65.4	30.8	3.92	29	18	6	62.5	3.84	63.4
Santa Barbara County	32	65.4	32	65.4	30.8	3.92	29	18	6	62.5	3.84	63.4
Santa Ysabel Reservation, CA	42	64.5	40	62.3	23.9	4.26	40	24	7	62.3	4.26	58.1
San Diego County	42	64.5	40	62.3	23.9	4.26	40	24	7	62.3	4.26	58.1
Santee Reservation, NE	88	61.8	87	62.6	37.9	4.66	83	43	32	62.0	4.66	40.2
Knox County	88	61.8	87	62.6	37.9	4.66	83	43	32	62.0	4.66	40.2
Santo Domingo Pueblo, NM	325	64.7	325	64.7	28.0	6.53	325	206	84	64.7	6.53	57.0
Sandoval County	325	64.7	325	64.7	28.0	6.53	325	206	84	64.7	6.53	57.0
Santa Fe County	-	-	-	-	-	-	-	-	-	-	-	-
San Xavier Reservation, AZ	159	56.2	159	56.2	24.9	5.23	155	69	63	56.1	5.17	40.1
Pima County	159	56.2	159	56.2	24.9	5.23	155	69	63	56.1	5.17	40.1
Sauk-Suiattle Reservation, WA	-	-	-	-	-	-	-	-	-	-	-	-
Snohomish County	-	-	-	-	-	-	-	-	-	-	-	-

[Continued]

★ 246 ★

Families With American Indian, Eskimo, or Aleut Members on Identified Reservations by Selected Characteristics, 1980: Pine Creek - Southern Paiute

[Continued]

Identified reservations	Families with one or more American Indian, Eskimo, or Aleut		Families with American Indian, Eskimo, or Aleut householder or spouse				Families with American Indian, Eskimo, or Aleut householder					Persons under 18 percent living with two parents
	Total	Percent with own children under 18 years	Total	Percent with own children under 18 years	Percent with own children under 6 years	Persons per family	Total	Married couple	Female householder, no husband present	Percent with own children under 18 years	Persons per family	
Sault Ste. Marie Reservation, MI	-	-	-	-	-	-	-	-	-	-	-	-
Chippewa County	-	-	-	-	-	-	-	-	-	-	-	-
Schaghticoke Reservation, CT	...	...	...	...	...	...	...	...	...	...	...	...
Litchfield County	...	...	...	...	...	...	...	...	...	...	...	...
Shakopee Community, MN	25	61.7	25	61.7	39.0	3.84	21	16	4	55.0	3.58	93.4
Scott County	25	61.7	25	61.7	39.0	3.84	21	16	4	55.0	3.58	93.4
Sheep Ranch Rancheria, CA	...	...	...	...	...	...	...	...	...	...	...	...
Calveras County	...	...	...	...	...	...	...	...	...	...	...	...
Sherwood Valley Rancheria, CA	...	...	...	...	...	...	...	...	...	...	...	...
Mendocino County	...	...	...	...	...	...	...	...	...	...	...	...
Shingle Springs Rancheria, CA	-	-	-	-	-	-	-	-	-	-	-	-
El Dorado County	-	-	-	-	-	-	-	-	-	-	-	-
Shinnecock Reservation, NY	55	38.7	55	38.7	16.6	3.57	49	31	15	43.8	3.67	62.6
Suffolk County	55	38.7	55	38.7	16.6	3.57	49	31	15	43.8	3.67	62.6
Shoalwater Reservation, WA	8	26.1	7	30.5	15.3	3.71	7	3	1	30.5	3.71	...
Pacific County	8	26.1	7	30.5	15.3	3.71	7	3	1	30.5	3.71	...
Sisseton Reservation, ND-SD	552	71.5	543	71.8	45.9	4.72	505	234	195	71.8	4.69	42.6
North Dakota	-	-	-	-	-	-	-	-	-	-	-	-
Richland County	-	-	-	-	-	-	-	-	-	-	-	-
Sargent County	-	-	-	-	-	-	-	-	-	-	-	-
South Dakota	552	71.5	543	71.8	45.9	4.72	505	234	195	71.8	4.69	42.6
Codington County	...	...	...	...	...	...	...	...	...	...	...	...
Day County	60	70.2	60.	70.2	41.7	5.11	58	28	24	69.2	4.89	38.2
Grant County	-	-	-	-	-	-	-	-	-	-	-	-
Marshall County	57	74.1	57	74.1	58.4	4.75	57	37	13	74.1	4.75	49.4
Roberts County	434	71.4	426	71.8	44.8	4.66	390	169	159	71.9	4.66	42.4
Skokomish Reservation, WA	71	75.0	71	75.0	32.3	4.44	62	45	9	76.5	4.64	70.0
Mason County	71	75.0	71	75.0	32.3	4.44	62	45	9	76.5	4.64	70.0
Skull Valley Reservation, UT	-	-	-	-	-	-	-	-	-	-	-	-
Tooele County	-	-	-	-	-	-	-	-	-	-	-	-
Soboba Reservation, CA	55	79.0	55	79.0	39.3	4.21	51	29	16	79.2	4.20	54.2
Riverside County	55	79.0	55	79.0	39.3	4.21	51	29	16	79.2	4.20	54.2
Sokaogon Chippewa Community, WI	22	68.1	22	68.1	45.4	4.00	21	11	6	66.6	4.04	43.8
Forest County	22	68.1	22	68.1	45.4	4.00	21	11	6	66.6	4.04	43.8
Southern Paiute Reservation, UT	34	71.9	34	71.9	47.4	5.39	34	19	13	71.9	5.39	51.2
Iron County	18	81.6	18	71.6	50.0	4.99	18	9	8	71.6	4.99	48.1
Millard County	9	65.9	9	65.9	31.8	5.57	9	6	3	65.9	5.57	70.4
Sevier County	...	...	...	...	...	...	...	...	...	...	...	...

Source: U.S. Bureau of the Census, Subject Reports, PC80-2-1D, Part I, *American Indians, Eskimos, and Aleuts on Identified Reservations and in the Historic Areas of Oklahoma (Excluding Urbanized Areas),* U.S. Government Printing Office, Washington, D.C., 1986, pp. 41-49. *Notes:* A dash (-) represents zero or a percent which rounds to less than 0.1. Also, a dash (-) is used because the number of supplementary questionnaires for the reservations was insufficient to produce reliable estimates. Three dots (...) means not applicable, or that the data are being withheld to avoid disclosure of information for individuals.

★ 247 ★

Families With American Indian, Eskimo, or Aleut Members on Identified Reservations by Selected Characteristics, 1980: Southern Ute - Zuni Pueblo

Data are the latest available.

Identified Reservations	Families with one or more American Indian, Eskimo, or Aleut		Families with American Indian, Eskimo, or Aleut householder or spouse				Families with American Indian, Eskimo, or Aleut householder					Persons under 18 percent living with two parents
	Total	Percent with own children under 18 years	Total	Percent with own children under 18 years	Percent with own children under 6 years	Persons per family	Total	Married couple	Female householder, no husband present	Percent with own children under 18 years	Persons per family	
Southern Ute Reservation, CO	215	72.6	206	72.9	34.5	4.25	184	106	60	71.7	4.22	55.9
Archuleta County	...	...	...	...	...	...	...	...	...	...	...	...
La Plata County	213	72.3	204	72.6	34.8	4.21	183	105	60	71.5	4.19	55.2
Montezuma County	-	-	-	-	-	-	-	-	-	-	-	-
Spokane Reservation, WA	268	65.0	266	64.8	32.6	4.27	243	161	52	65.7	4.24	58.2
Lincoln County	-	-	-	-	-	-	-	-	-	-	-	-
Stevens County	268	65.0	266	64.8	32.6	4.27	243	161	52	65.7	4.24	58.2
Squaxin Island Reservation, WA	11	81.8	...	...	...	...	...	...	...	...	...	...
Mason County	11	81.8	...	...	...	...	...	...	...	...	...	...
Standing Rock Reservation, ND-SD	946	70.2	924	70.1	37.0	4.83	858	486	312	68.5	4.85	48.2
North Dakota	455	74.8	444	75.0	40.5	4.83	411	225	155	73.6	4.83	50.4
Sioux County	455	74.8	444	75.0	40.5	4.83	411	225	155	73.6	4.83	50.4
South Dakota	491	65.9	480	65.6	33.8	4.84	447	261	157	63.9	4.87	45.9
Corson County	491	65.9	480	65.6	33.8	4.84	447	261	157	63.9	4.87	45.9
Stewart's Point Rancheria, CA	13	69.2	13	69.2	30.8	5.31	12	8	2	75.0	5.58	64.0
Sonoma County	13	69.2	13	69.2	30.8	5.31	12	8	2	75.0	5.58	64.0
Stockbridge Reservation, WI	159	64.0	156	63.3	33.6	4.06	129	95	23	68.9	4.31	81.6
Shawano County	159	64.0	156	63.3	33.6	4.06	129	95	23	68.9	4.31	81.6
Sulphur Bank Rancheria, CA	21	75.2	21	75.2	56.1	5.36	21	14	6	75.2	5.36	58.1
Lake County	21	75.2	21	75.2	56.1	5.36	21	14	6	75.2	5.36	58.1
Summit Lake Reservation, NV	...	...	...	...	...	...	...	...	...	...	...	...
Humboldt County	...	...	...	...	...	...	...	...	...	...	...	...
Susanville Reservation, CA	20	54.7	20	54.7	15.9	4.07	19	7	8	52.1	3.95	37.6
Lassen County	20	54.7	20	54.7	15.9	4.07	19	7	8	52.1	3.95	37.6
Swinomish Reservation, WA	96	66.5	93	66.8	34.3	4.36	91	59	25	66.3	4.37	58.2
Skagit County	96	66.5	93	66.8	34.3	4.36	91	59	25	66.3	4.37	58.2
Sycuan Reservation, CA	11	71.4	11	71.4	41.8	5.06	10	5	2	66.9	4.93	66.1
San Diego County	11	71.4	11	71.4	41.8	5.06	10	5	2	66.9	4.93	66.1
Tama Reservation, GA	6	49.7	6	49.7	-	3.01	6	4	2	49.7	3.01	16.7
Grady County	6	49.7	6	49.7	-	3.01	6	4	2	49.7	3.01	16.7
Taos Pueblo, NM	265	50.2	263	49.9	16.8	3.79	258	198	49	50.0	3.80	63.2
Taos County	265	50.2	263	49.9	16.8	3.79	258	198	49	50.0	3.80	63.2
Te-Moak Reservation, NV	22	45.9	22	45.9	6.4	3.83	22	18	4	45.9	3.83	78.0
Elko County	22	45.9	22	45.9	6.4	3.83	22	18	4	45.9	3.83	78.0
Tesuque Pueblo, NM	56	62.0	56	62.0	28.9	4.26	52	34	15	58.8	4.19	65.4
Santa Fe County	56	62.0	56	62.0	28.9	4.26	52	34	15	58.8	4.19	65.4
Tigua Reservation, TX	101	78.2	100	78.0	51.0	4.52	100	79	16	78.0	4.52	75.3
El Paso County	101	78.2	100	78.0	51.0	4.52	100	79	16	78.0	4.52	75.3
Tonawanda Reservation, NY	101	50.8	99	50.8	17.3	4.07	95	59	25	50.2	4.05	70.5
Erie County	-	-	-	-	-	-	-	-	-	-	-	-
Genesee County	101	50.8	99	50.8	17.3	4.07	95	59	25	50.2	4.05	70.5
Niagara County	-	-	-	-	-	-	-	-	-	-	-	-
Torres-Martinez Reservation, CA	-	-	-	-	-	-	-	-	-	-	-	-
Imperial County	-	-	-	-	-	-	-	-	-	-	-	-
Riverside County	-	-	-	-	-	-	-	-	-	-	-	-
Trinidad Rancheria, CA	16	46.7	16	46.7	6.7	3.51	12	7	3	54.5	3.54	38.5
Humboldt County	16	46.7	16	46.7	6.7	3.51	12	7	3	54.5	3.54	38.5
Tulalip Reservation, WA	173	69.3	166	70.6	34.6	4.67	143	91	38	70.5	4.71	60.5
Snohomish County	173	69.3	166	70.6	34.6	4.67	143	91	38	70.5	4.71	60.5
Tule River Reservation, CA	97	90.4	95	90.2	44.7	4.38	93	53	34	90.0	4.39	47.9
Tulare County	97	90.4	95	90.2	44.7	4.38	93	53	34	90.0	4.39	47.9
Tunica-Biloxi Reservation, LA	...	...	...	...	...	...	...	...	...	...	...	...
Avoyelles Parish	...	...	...	...	...	...	...	...	...	...	...	...
Tuolumne Rancheria, CA	22	63.6	21	61.9	14.3	4.05	21	14	2	61.9	4.05	51.4
Tuolumne County	22	63.6	21	61.9	14.3	4.05	21	14	2	61.9	4.05	51.4
Turtle Mountain Reservation, ND	858	73.9	854	73.7	39.1	4.57	825	517	245	73.7	4.62	56.7
Rolette County	858	73.9	854	73.7	39.1	4.57	825	517	245	73.7	4.62	56.7
Tuscarora Reservation, NY	-	-	-	-	-	-	-	-	-	-	-	-
Niagara County	-	-	-	-	-	-	-	-	-	-	-	-
Twenty-Nine Palms Reservation, CA	-	-	-	-	-	-	-	-	-	-	-	-
San Bernardino County	-	-	-	-	-	-	-	-	-	-	-	-
Uintah and Ouray Reservation, UT	485	70.8	480	70.5	38.1	4.79	434	273	121	69.2	4.96	60.0

[Continued]

★ 247 ★

Families With American Indian, Eskimo, or Aleut Members on Identified Reservations by Selected Characteristics, 1980: Southern Ute - Zuni Pueblo

[Continued]

Identified reservations	Families with one or more American Indian, Eskimo, or Aleut		Families with American Indian, Eskimo, or Aleut householder or spouse				Families with American Indian, Eskimo, or Aleut householder					Persons under 18 percent living with two parents
	Total	Percent with own children under 18 years	Total	Percent with own children under 18 years	Percent with own children under 6 years	Persons per family	Total	Married couple	Female householder, no husband present	Percent with own children under 18 years	Persons per family	
Carbon County	-	-	-	-	-	-	-	-	-	-	-	-
Duchesne County	89	78.5	87	78.0	33.9	5.08	78	47	23	75.6	5.03	60.7
Grand County	-	-	-	-	-	-	-	-	-	-	-	-
Uintah County	395	69.1	393	68.9	39.1	4.72	355	226	98	67.8	4.94	59.9
Utah County	-	-	-	-	-	-	-	-	-	-	-	-
Wastach County	-	-	-	-	-	-	-	-	-	-	-	-
Umatilla Reservation, OR	235	54.8	228	54.4	26.5	4.16	196	119	61	53.1	4.27	49.2
Umatilla County	235	54.8	228	54.4	26.5	4.16	196	119	61	53.1	4.27	49.2
Union County	-	-	-	-	-	-	-	-	-	-	-	-
Upper Sioux Community, MN	14	29.0	14	29.0	29.0	3.35	12	6	6	17.0	3.27	50.6
Yellow Medicine County	14	29.0	14	29.0	29.0	3.35	12	6	6	17.0	3.27	50.6
Upper Skagit Reservation, WA	-	-	-	-	-	-	-	-	-	-	-	-
Skagit County	-	-	-	-	-	-	-	-	-	-	-	-
Ute Mountain Reservation, CO-NM	247	70.4	247	70.4	37.5	4.33	242	163	63	70.9	4.33	55.6
Colorado	247	70.4	247	70.4	37.5	4.33	242	163	63	70.9	4.33	55.6
La Plata County	-	-	-	-	-	-	-	-	-	-	-	-
Montezuma County	247	70.4	247	70.4	37.5	4.33	242	163	63	70.9	4.33	55.6
New Mexico	-	-	-	-	-	-	-	-	-	-	-	-
San Juan County	-	-	-	-	-	-	-	-	-	-	-	-
Vermillion Lake Reservation, MN	27	65.5	27	65.5	43.5	3.59	27	11	14	65.5	3.59	21.7
St. Louis County	27	65.5	27	65.5	43.5	3.59	27	11	14	65.5	3.59	21.7
Viejas Rancheria, CA	34	59.7	33	58.3	26.1	4.25	32	17	13	57.0	4.25	31.5
San Diego County	34	59.7	33	58.3	26.1	4.25	32	17	13	57.0	4.25	31.5
Walker River Reservation, NV	118	57.6	116	56.9	26.7	3.90	109	76	31	56.0	3.92	61.4
Churchill County	-	-	-	-	-	-	-	-	-	-	-	-
Lyon County	-	-	-	-	-	-	-	-	-	-	-	-
Mineral County	118	57.6	116	56.9	26.7	3.90	109	76	31	56.0	3.92	61.4
Wampanoag Reservation, MA	-	-	-	-	-	-	-	-	-	-	-	-
Bristol County	-	-	-	-	-	-	-	-	-	-	-	-
Warm Springs Reservation, OR	416	72.7	413	72.7	38.2	4.77	390	252	101	73.7	4.90	59.1
Clackamas County	-	-	-	-	-	-	-	-	-	-	-	-
Jefferson County	349	72.7	346	72.7	39.7	4.73	326	212	79	73.7	4.86	58.5
Marion County	-	-	-	-	-	-	-	-	-	-	-	-
Wasco County	67	72.8	67	72.8	35.5	5.02	64	40	22	74.1	5.09	61.9
Washoe Reservation, NV	-	-	-	-	-	-	-	-	-	-	-	-
Douglas County	-	-	-	-	-	-	-	-	-	-	-	-
Western Pequot Reservation, CT	...	...	...	...	...	...	...	...	...	...	...	...
New London County	...	...	...	...	...	...	...	...	...	...	...	...
White Earth Reservation, MN	662	64.2	639	64.8	34.4	4.24	520	320	147	65.2	4.22	55.7
Becker County	316	66.3	310	66.5	36.8	4.25	263	162	78	66.2	4.24	53.4
Clearwater County	69	68.6	66	67.2	35.8	4.80	57	28	16	70.4	4.97	51.3
Mahnomen County	277	60.7	264	62.1	31.3	4.08	201	130	53	62.5	3.99	60.1
Wind River Reservation, WY	892	65.7	877	65.7	34.9	4.94	796	538	201	66.3	5.09	57.1
Fremont County	886	65.9	872	65.9	35.1	4.95	791	533	201	66.5	5.10	57.1
Hot Springs County	...	...	...	...	...	...	...	...	...	...	...	...
Winnebago Reservation, NE	255	66.6	250	65.9	35.2	4.36	229	94	115	63.4	4.37	40.6
Dixon County	...	...	...	...	...	...	...	...	...	...	...	...
Thurston County	253	66.3	249	65.8	35.4	4.36	229	94	115	63.4	4.37	40.7
Winnemucca Colony, NV	8	66.7	8	66.7	16.7	4.54	8	5	3	66.7	4.54	44.4
Humboldt County	8	66.7	8	66.7	16.7	4.54	8	5	3	66.7	4.54	44.4
Wisconsin Winnebago Reservation	76	88.1	76	88.1	42.3	4.65	71	40	27	87.2	4.60	51.9
Jackson County	...	...	...	...	...	...	...	...	...	...	...	...
Juneau County	21	87.2	21	87.2	7.1	4.77	19	10	8	85.3	4.84	28.1
Monroe County	...	...	...	...	...	...	...	...	...	...	...	...
Sauk County	24	100.0	24	100.0	55.9	4.01	24	13	7	100.0	4.01	58.8
Shawano County	...	...	...	...	...	...	...	...	...	...	...	...
Wood County	19	89.5	19	89.5	51.9	5.16	17	9	7	88.1	4.93	56.4
Woodfords Community, CA	-	-	-	-	-	-	-	-	-	-	-	-
Alpine County	-	-	-	-	-	-	-	-	-	-	-	-
XL Ranch Reservation, CA	...	...	...	...	...	...	...	...	...	...	...	...
Modoc County	...	...	...	...	...	...	...	...	...	...	...	...
Yakima Reservation, WA	1,202	67.6	1,164	67.8	33.1	4.45	1,065	625	355	68.6	4.57	48.0
Klickitat County	16	87.5	15	93.3	73.3	4.53	12	10	-	91.7	4.58	90.9

[Continued]

★ 247 ★

Families With American Indian, Eskimo, or Aleut Members on Identified Reservations by Selected Characteristics, 1980: Southern Ute - Zuni Pueblo

[Continued]

Identified reservations	Families with one or more American Indian, Eskimo, or Aleut		Families with American Indian, Eskimo, or Aleut householder or spouse				Families with American Indian, Eskimo, or Aleut householder					Persons under 18 percent living with two parents
	Total	Percent with own children under 18 years	Total	Percent with own children under 18 years	Percent with own children under 6 years	Persons per family	Total	Married couple	Female householder, no husband present	Percent with own children under 18 years	Persons per family	
Yakima County	1,186	67.3	1,149	67.5	32.5	4.45	1,053	615	355	68.3	4.57	47.3
Yankton Reservation, SD	355	66.7	351	66.3	45.4	4.56	328	156	143	64.9	4.52	40.2
Charles Mix County	355	66.7	351	66.3	45.4	4.56	328	156	143	64.9	4.52	40.2
Yavapai Reservation, AZ	21	47.6	21	47.6	33.3	33.3	19	6	10	42.1	3.05	31.8
Yavapai County	21	47.6	21	47.6	33.3	33.3	19	6	10	42.1	3.05	31.8
Yerington Reservation, NV	28	69.7	28	69.7	11.4	3.93	26	17	8	72.0	4.00	49.3
Lyon County	28	69.7	28	69.7	11.4	3.93	26	17	8	72.0	4.00	49.3
Yomba Reservation, NV	10	60.3	10	60.3	19.9	5.46	10	8	1	60.3	5.46	52.3
Nye County	10	60.3	10	60.3	19.9	5.46	10	8	1	60.3	5.46	52.3
Zia Pueblo, NM	103	69.8	103	69.8	28.2	5.01	103	58	39	69.8	5.01	45.9
Sandoval County	103	69.8	103	69.8	28.2	5.01	103	58	39	69.8	5.01	45.9
Zuni Pueblo, NM	1,047	71.2	1,045	71.3	30.4	5.73	1,028	702	284	71.0	5.77	45.5
McKinley County	1,047	71.2	1,045	71.3	30.4	5.73	1,028	702	284	71.0	5.77	45.5
Valencia County	-	-	-	-	-	-	-	-	-	-	-	-
San Felipe/Santa Ana Joint Area, New Mexico	-	-	-	-	-	-	-	-	-	-	-	-
Sandoval County	-	-	-	-	-	-	-	-	-	-	-	-
San Felipe/Santo Domingo Joint Area, New Mexico	24	82.4	24	82.4	41.2	4.84	24	13	9	82.4	4.84	52.8
Sandoval County	24	82.4	24	82.4	41.2	4.84	24	13	9	82.4	4.84	52.8
Other reservation lands in MT	-	-	-	-	-	-	-	-	-	-	-	-
Big Horn County	-	-	-	-	-	-	-	-	-	-	-	-

Source: U.S. Bureau of the Census, Subject Reports, PC80-2-1D, Part I, *American Indians, Eskimos, and Aleuts on Identified Reservations and in the Historic Areas of Oklahoma (Excluding Urbanized Areas)*, U.S. Government Printing Office, Washington, D.C., 1986, pp. 41-49. *Notes:* A dash (-) represents zero or a percent which rounds to less than 0.1. Also, a dash (-) is used because the number of supplementary questionnaires for the reservations was insufficient to produce reliable estimates. Three dots (...) means not applicable, or that the data are being withheld to avoid disclosure of information for individuals.

Marriage

★ 248 ★

Marital Status of Selected Racial/Ethnic Groups Age 15 Years Old and Older, by Sex, 1930

Figures are shown in percent.

Color and nativity	Male					Female				
	Single	Married	Widowed	Divorced	Unknown	Single	Married	Widowed	Divorced	Unknown
All classes	34.1	60.0	4.6	1.1	0.2	26.4	61.1	11.1	1.3	0.1
Indian	36.8	54.5	6.9	1.6	0.2	24.3	61.6	12.0	2.0	0.2
White	34.2	60.1	4.5	1.1	0.2	26.7	61.4	10.5	1.2	0.1
Native	36.9	57.8	4.0	1.1	0.2	29.4	59.7	9.4	1.3	0.1
Foreign born	22.2	70.2	6.5	0.9	0.2	12.9	69.8	16.3	9.0	0.1

[Continued]

★ 248 ★

Marital Status of Selected Racial/Ethnic Groups Age 15 Years Old and Older, by Sex, 1930
[Continued]

Color and nativity	Male					Female				
	Single	Married	Widowed	Divorced	Unknown	Single	Married	Widowed	Divorced	Unknown
Negro	32.2	59.8	6.3	1.4	0.2	23.3	58.5	15.9	2.2	0.1
All other races	54.4	41.6	2.4	0.5	1.2	17.1	78.3	3.9	0.5	0.1

Source: Dr. Leon E. Truesdell, U.S. Department of Commerce, Bureau of the Census, Fifteenth Census of the United States: 1930, *The Indian Population of the United States and Alaska,* U.S. Government Printing Office, 1937, p. 122.

Child Care

★ 249 ★

Latchkey Children

```
┌─────────────────────────────────────────────────┐
│  ┌──────────────────────────────────────────┐    │
│  │ White - 18.6                             │    │
│  └──────────────────────────────────────────┘    │
│  ┌──────────────────────────────────────────┐    │
│  │ Black - 17.6                             │    │
│  └──────────────────────────────────────────┘    │
│  ┌───────────────────────────────────────┐       │
│  │ American Indian and Alaska Native - 13.8 │     │
│  └───────────────────────────────────────┘       │
│  ┌────────────────────────────────┐              │
│  │ Asian and Pacific Islander - 14.4 │           │
│  └────────────────────────────────┘              │
│  ┌──────────────────────────┐                    │
│  │ Hispanic - 12.4          │                    │
│  └──────────────────────────┘                    │
└─────────────────────────────────────────────────┘
```

Data reflect results of a 1988 survey of eighth graders. Affirmative responses are shown as percentages for each race/ethnicity.

Race and ethnicity	Usually no one home when returns home from school
Hispanic	12.4
American Indian and Alaska Native	13.8
Asian and Pacific Islander	14.4
Black	17.6
White	18.6

Source: "Percentage of Eighth Graders Who Usually Have No One Home When They Return Home From School, by Selected Background Characteristics," *A Profile of the American Eighth Grader,* 1990, p. 52. Primary source: U.S. Department of Education, National Center for Education Statistics, "National Education Longitudinal Study of 1988: Base Year Student Survey".

★ 250 ★

Time Spent by Eighth Graders at Home Alone

Figures represent results of a 1988 survey. Students' affirmative responses are shown in percent for each race/ethnicity.

Race/ethnicity	Number of hours				
	None Never happens	Less than 1 hour	1-2 hours	2-3 hours	More than 3 hours
Total	13.3	32.4	27.8	12.9	13.6
American Indian/Native Alaskan	16.0	30.8	21.1	13.3	18.8
Asian and Pacific Islander	16.7	29.0	25.8	12.6	15.9
Hispanic	20.7	29.0	22.8	11.2	16.3
Black	16.2	28.1	23.2	12.8	19.5
White	11.6	33.8	29.5	13.1	12.0

Source: "Percentage of Eighth Graders Spending Various Numbers of Hours After School Each Day at Home With No Adult Present, by Selected Background Characteristics," *A Profile of the American Eighth Grader,* 1990, p. 53. Primary source: U.S. Department of Education, National Center for Education Statistics, "National Education Longitudinal Study 1988: Base Year Student Survey".

Adolescents

★ 251 ★

Adolescent Suicide Attempts, by History of Family Attempts or Completions

22% of the sample reported knowledge of a suicide attempt or completion by a family member. Data are shown in percent and are based on a survey of 13,923 rural American Indian/Alaska Native adolescents living on or near reservations[1].

Youth suicide attempts	Family history	
	No attempts	Attempts/ completions
No attempts	86.8	69.7
Ever attempted suicide	13.2	30.3
Total	100.0	100.0

Source: The State of Native American Youth Health, February, 1992, Indian Health Service, Maternal and Child Health Bureau, and the Robert Wood Johnson Foundation, p. 32. *Notes:* 1. Caution: Sample was not random and does not fully represent all Native American/Alaska Native groups.

★ 252 ★

Adolescents Participating in Motor Vehicle Risk Behaviors

Data are shown in percent and are based on a survey of 13,923 rural American Indian/Alaska Native adolescents living on or near reservations[1].

Motor vehicle risk behaviors	Males		Females	
	Grades 7-9	Grades 10-12	Grades 7-9	Grades 10-12
Among those who drive, percent who have driven while under the influence of drugs/alcohol	30.9	44.8	22.2	34.1
Often or sometimes ride with a drinking/drug using driver	20.2	27.8	18.1	23.9
Believe it is OK to drive after three or more drinks	4.9	11.7	2.7	4.1
Ride a motorcycle more often than once a month	44.2	38.9	30.1	24.9
Among motorcyclists, percent who rarely or never wear a helmet when on a motorcycle	37.8	44.0	44.2	57.8
Rarely or never wear seatbelts in a car	45.6	46.7	42.8	42.6
Frequently ride in the back of a pickup truck	48.2	40.8	35.6	21.5
High risk for motor vehicle injuries[2]	11.8	15.9	8.7	7.9

Source: The State of Native American Youth Health, February, 1992, Indian Health Service, Maternal and Child Health Bureau, and the Robert Wood Johnson Foundation, p. 18. *Notes:* 1. Caution: Sample was not random and does not fully represent all Native American/Alaska Native groups. 2. High risk is based on respondents affirming four or more vehicle related risk factors.

★ 253 ★

Adolescents' School Performance, by Associated Behavior

Data show percentage of Native American youths who report above or below average school performance and selected risk behaviors. Data are based on a survey of 13,923 rural American Indian/Alaska Native adolescents living on or near reservations[1].

Risk behavior	Below average school performance	Above average school performance
Daily/weekly cigarette use	30.9	13.4
Daily/weekly alcohol use	19.6	8.5
Drink five times/drinks per sittings	54.7	41.9
Daily/weekly marijuana use	17.9	7.8
Ever had sexual intercourse	32.5	26.6

[Continued]

★ 253 ★

Adolescents' School Performance, by Associated Behavior
[Continued]

Risk behavior	Below average school performance	Above average school performance
Ever caused/gotten pregnant	3.7	4.2
Feel school people don't care	41.6	22.0
Feel family doesn't understand	35.6	19.8
Feel extremely hopeless	13.7	10.0
Would like to commit suicide	16.6	7.5
Have attempted suicide	22.2	14.9
Ever been sexually abused	11.3	10.1
Ever been physically abused	16.9	12.5

Source: The State of Native American Youth Health, February, 1992, Indian Health Service, Maternal and Child Health Bureau, and the Robert Wood Johnson Foundation, p. 10. *Notes:* 1. Caution: Sample was not random and does not fully represent all Native American/Alaska Native groups.

★ 254 ★

Characteristics of Adolescents Who Had Reported Emotional Stress in the Previous Month

Data are based on a survey of 13,923 rural American Indian/Alaska Native adolescents living on or near reservations[1].

Characteristic	High stress (N=750)	All adolescents (N=13,226)
Family relations		
Live in single parent or alternative family structures	60.3	54.1
Biological parents divorced or separated	36.4	31.3
Worries a great deal that parents will divorce	30.4	26.2
Feels family does not understand them	44.0	24.4
Physical/sexual abuse		
Reports have been sexually abused	21.9	10.1
Reports have been physically abused	31.7	13.3
School problems		
Reports doing below average in school	17.3	11.9
Frequently absent from school due to illness	12.8	7.6
Suicidal tendencies		
Has ever attempted suicide	44.6	16.9
Reports they would like to commit suicide or would if they had the chance	26.0	9.2

[Continued]

★ 254 ★

Characteristics of Adolescents Who Had Reported Emotional Stress in the Previous Month
[Continued]

Characteristic	High stress (N = 750)	All adolescents (N = 13,226)
Sexual risk taking		
Has had sexual intercourse	42.8	30.9
Has been pregnant or caused a pregnancy	10.8	6.1

Source: *The State of Native American Youth Health, February, 1992,* Indian Health Service, Maternal and Child Health Bureau, and the Robert Wood Johnson Foundation, p. 27. *Notes:* An (N) refers to the number of students answering in the affirmative. 1. Caution: Sample was not random and does not fully represent all Native American/Alaska Native groups.

★ 255 ★

Comparisons of Adolescents for High and Low Risk of Suicide

Data are shown in percent and are based on a survey of 13,923 rural American Indian/Alaska Native adolescents living on or near reservations[1].

	High (N = 2,171)	Low (N = 11,283)	Percent difference
Associated behaviors			
Heavy drinking	30.6	17.4	13.2
Marijuana weekly or daily	20.1	10.2	9.9
Had sexual intercourse	44.0	28.4	15.6
Caused/had pregnancy	10.2	5.3	4.9
Sexual/physical abuse	12.5	4.0	8.5
Induced vomiting weekly	7.6	3.2	4.3
Support system factors			
Family doesn't understand	39.3	21.3	18.0
Friend attempted suicide	26.6	16.4	10.2
Adults don't care	26.6	15.0	11.6
Friend completed suicide	18.9	7.6	11.3
Family member tried suicide	36.4	18.8	17.6

Source: *The State of Native American Youth Health, February, 1992,* Indian Health Service, Maternal and Child Health Bureau, and the Robert Wood Johnson Foundation, p. 33. *Notes:* For the purpose of better understanding who is at high risk for suicide, further analysis was undertaken for youths who; 1)attempted suicide within the past year; 2)think seriously about killing themselves; and have made repeated attempts, even though the attempts may have been more than a year ago. Eighty-four percent of youths surveyed do not have any of these elements of suicide history or ideation. Nine percent have one out of the three characteristics, five percent have two of the three, and two percent (N = 293) have all three characteristics. 1. Caution: Sample was not random and does not fully represent all Native American/Alaska Native groups. 2. An (N) indicates the number of adolescents in each group.

★ 256 ★

Delinquent Behaviors of Rural Adolescents

Data are shown in percent, by sex and grade, and are based on a survey of 13,923 rural American Indian/Alaska Native adolescents living on or near reservations[1].

Anti-social activity in past 12 months	Males		Females	
	Grades 7-9	Grades 10-12	Grades 7-9	Grades 10-12
Damaged, destroyed or vandalized property				
Once or twice	23.1	22.5	16.5	12.6
3 or more times	8.9	7.3	4.3	3.0
Stolen from a store/shoplifted				
Once or twice	18.5	22.6	16.3	16.1
3 or more times	10.8	9.8	7.4	6.9
Stolen from parents or other family members				
Once or twice	15.4	12.0	17.0	12.4
3 or more times	5.2	3.9	4.4	2.5
Ran away from home				
Once or twice	9.5	6.7	10.8	9.8
3 or more times	4.8	2.7	5.4	3.9

Source: The State of Native American Youth Health, February, 1992, Indian Health Service, Maternal and Child Health Bureau, and the Robert Wood Johnson Foundation, p. 23. *Notes:* 1. Caution: Sample was not random and does not fully represent all Native American/Alaska Native groups.

★ 257 ★

Reasons Given for Sexual Abstinence by Adolescents

Data are shown in percent and are based on a survey of 13,923 rural American Indian/Alaska Native adolescents living on or near reservations[1].

Reasons for sexual abstinence	Males	Females
Want to wait until older	42.7	45.5
Don't want risk of pregnancy	20.4	48.0
Want to wait until marriage	29.0	41.3
Not ready emotionally	16.2	37.1
Fear of disease	21.7	28.3
Parents' values are against it	8.0	23.8
No one has asked me to do it	14.1	7.9
Haven't met anyone yet	11.8	12.6
Haven't had the opportunity	7.1	5.3
Religious values are against it	4.0	7.0

Source: The State of Native American Youth Health, February, 1992, Indian Health Service, Maternal and Child Health Bureau, and the Robert Wood Johnson Foundation, p. 36. *Notes:* 1. Caution: Sample was not random and does not fully represent all Native American/Alaska Native groups.

★ 258 ★

Risk Behaviors and Perceived Health Status of Adolescents

Data are based on a survey of 13,923 rural American Indian/Alaska Native adolescents living on or near reservations[1].

Risk behavior	Perceived health status	
	Poor (N=264)	Good or excellent (N=10,386)
Ever attempted suicide	33.9	14.8
Below average school performance	34.8	9.2
Use three or more drugs at least monthly	10.6	4.7
Feel overweight	64.1	26.1
Sexually active	36.7	29.9
Experienced abuse	29.2	15.1

Source: The State of Native American Youth Health, February, 1992, Indian Health Service, Maternal and Child Health Bureau, and the Robert Wood Johnson Foundation, p. 12. Notes: An (N) refers to the number of students who reported a certain health status. 1. Caution: Sample was not random and does not fully represent all Native American/Alaska Native groups.

★ 259 ★

Sexual Activity Among Adolescents

Data are shown in percent and are based on a survey of 13,923 rural American Indian/Alaska Native adolescents living on or near reservations[1].

Frequency of sexual intercourse	Males	Females
Not sure	24.6	21.1
Once or twice	14.7	16.9
Rarely (a few times a year or less)	30.6	32.2
Sometimes (1-4 times per month)	22.6	20.4
Frequently (several times a week)	7.6	9.4

Source: The State of Native American Youth Health, February, 1992, Indian Health Service, Maternal and Child Health Bureau, and the Robert Wood Johnson Foundation, p. 35. Notes: 1. Caution: Sample was not random and does not fully represent all Native American/Alaska Native groups.

★ 260 ★

Student Reports of Risk Behaviors

Data show the percent of Native American youths who reported that the following activities occur on or off school grounds. Data are based on a survey of 13,923 rural American Indian/Alaska Native adolescents living on or near reservations[1].

Activity	Grades 7-9	Grades 10-12
Using drugs	23.4	48.4
Drinking	32.3	54.7
Inhaling paint, gas	12.2	8.3
Destroying things	22.2	26.2
Getting into fights	36.1	20.0
Stealing things	26.2	25.8

Source: The State of Native American Youth Health, February, 1992, Indian Health Service, Maternal and Child Health Bureau, and the Robert Wood Johnson Foundation, p. 10. Notes: 1. Caution: Sample was not random and does not fully represent all Native American/Alaska Native groups.

Native American Adolescents

★ 261 ★

Substance Abuse Among Adolescents

Data show the percent of youths who report trying the following substances. Results are based on a survey of 13,923 rural American Indian/Alaska Native adolescents living on or near reservations[1].

Substance	Grades 7-9		Grades 10-12	
	Males	Females	Males	Females
Cigarettes	41.6	46.3	50.1	54.2
Beer/Wine	45.3	45.3	74.0	69.1
Hard liquor	28.8	24.2	56.2	46.2
Chewing tobacco/snuff	44.8	29.4	49.3	25.1
Marijuana	32.9	29.5	51.7	48.4
Peyote	23.4	20.4	25.0	21.5
Inhalants	12.7	15.0	6.6	7.4
Amphetamines	7.8	7.7	13.8	12.7
Cocaine	4.6	4.1	8.9	6.7
Sedatives	3.6	3.2	3.9	3.8
Codine/morphine/other opiates	2.9	2.1	5.7	5.0
Psychedelics	4.3	2.9	9.3	6.3
Diet pills to lose weight	4.2	8.4	3.7	14.6
Look-a-like drugs	4.5	4.5	2.7	3.0
PCP/Angel dust	2.5	2.5	3.7	2.4

[Continued]

★ 261 ★

Substance Abuse Among Adolescents
[Continued]

Substance	Grades 7-9		Grades 10-12	
	Males	Females	Males	Females
Crack/rock cocaine	2.7	2.5	4.1	2.8
Heroin	1.6	1.2	1.1	1.0

Source: The State of Native American Youth Health, February, 1992, Indian Health Service, Maternal and Child Health Bureau, and the Robert Wood Johnson Foundation, p. 41. *Notes:* 1. Caution: Sample was not random and does not fully represent all Native American/Alaska Native groups.

★ 262 ★

Suicide Attempts Reported by Rural Native American Adolescents, by Sex and Grade: Females

```
7th - 10.9
8th - 10.4
9th - 9.8
10th - 13.0
11th - 13.2
12th - 16.2
```

Data are based on a survey of 13,923 rural American Indian/Alaska Native adolescents living on or near reservations.[1].

Grade	Percent
7th	10.9
8th	10.4
9th	9.8
10th	13.0
11th	13.2
12th	16.2

Source: The State of Native American Youth Health, February, 1992, Indian Health Service, Maternal and Child Health Bureau, and the Robert Wood Johnson Foundation, p. 31. *Notes:* 1. Caution: Sample was not truly random and does not fully represent all Native American/Alaska Native groups.

★ 263 ★

Suicide Attempts Reported by Rural Native American Adolescents, by Sex and Grade: Males

7th - 15.0
8th - 19.9
9th - 24.6
10th - 24.4
11th - 26.6
12th - 24.1

Data are based on a survey of 13,923 rural American Indian/Alaska Native adolescents living on or near reservations.[1].

Grade	Percent
7th	15.0
8th	19.9
9th	24.6
10th	24.4
11th	26.6
12th	24.1

Source: The State of Native American Youth Health, February, 1992, Indian Health Service, Maternal and Child Health Bureau, and the Robert Wood Johnson Foundation, p. 31. *Notes:* 1. Caution: Sample was not truly random and does not fully represent all Native American/Alaska Native groups.

★ 264 ★

Top Concerns of Rural Adolescents: Females

Data are based on a survey of 13,923 rural American Indian/Alaska Native adolescents living on or near reservations[1].

Concerns, by age group	%
Grades 7-9	
School performance	64.5
Parent dying	63.2
Losing best friend	61.6
Getting AIDS	49.7
Appearance/looks	48.6
Grades 10-12	
School performance	72.9
Parent dying	63.8
Losing best friend	57.1

[Continued]

★ 264 ★

Top Concerns of Rural Adolescents: Females
[Continued]

Concerns, by age group	%
Future employment	48.8
Getting AIDS	48.4

Source: The State of Native American Youth Health, February, 1992, Indian Health Service, Maternal and Child Health Bureau, and the Robert Wood Johnson Foundation, p. 26. *Notes:* 1. Caution: Sample was not random and does not fully represent all Native American/Alaska Native groups.

★ 265 ★

Top Concerns of Rural Adolescents: Males

Data are based on a survey of 13,923 rural American Indian/Alaska Native adolescents living on or near reservations[1].

Concerns, by age group	%
Grades 7-9	
Parent dying	55.3
School performance	51.1
Getting AIDS	49.3
Losing best friend	38.6
Body development	35.6
Grades 10-12	
Parent dying	55.4
School performance	54.6
Getting AIDS	48.6
Losing best friend	39.9
Future employment	37.7

Source: The State of Native American Youth Health, February, 1992, Indian Health Service, Maternal and Child Health Bureau, and the Robert Wood Johnson Foundation, p. 26. *Notes:* 1. Caution: Sample was not random and does not fully represent all Native American/Alaska Native groups.

★ 266 ★

Whom Adolescents Confide in When Physically or Sexually Abused

Data are shown in percent for those who did confide in someone. Results are based on a survey of 13,923 rural American Indian/Alaska Native adolescents living on or near reservations[1].

Abuse confidant	Physical abuse		Sexual abuse	
	Males (N=198)	Females (N=711)	Males (N=74)	Females (N=558)
Family member	67.6	59.6	49.3	67.9
Close friend	57.6	83.3	55.6	77.4
School counselor or teacher	25.7	27.5	22.6	16.5
Social worker	23.0	25.8	27.0	25.9
School nurse/public health nurse	13.1	9.6	17.6	8.3
Physician	11.9	6.8	19.1	7.7
Mental health counselor	11.4	11.8	18.6	13.8
Dorm aide or counselor	13.2	9.4	16.4	7.8
CHR Village Health aide	6.9	1.4	14.3	2.5
Minister or priest	9.1	4.8	14.7	4.8

Source: *The State of Native American Youth Health, February, 1992*, Indian Health Service, Maternal and Child Health Bureau, and the Robert Wood Johnson Foundation, p. 30. *Notes:* An (N) indicates the number of respondents. 1. Caution: Sample was not random and does not fully represent all Native American/Alaska Native groups.

Chapter 4
EDUCATION

Educational Attainment

★ 267 ★

Years of Education Completed

Years of formal education are shown, by number and percentage. Figures represent a random sample selected from the United States Indian population in 1981 which are representative of age, sex, region, and the population size of the counties in which the subjects lived.

Years of formal education	Total Indian population		Indians residing in the East		Indians residing in the West	
	Number	Percent	Number	Percent	Number	Percent
0	187	4.88	39	5.29	148	4.78
1-6	281	7.34	81	10.99	200	6.47
7	124	3.24	30	4.07	94	3.04
8	260	6.79	54	7.33	206	6.66
9	320	8.36	67	9.09	253	8.18
10-11	753	19.66	141	19.13	612	19.79
12	1,080	28.20	196	26.59	884	28.58
13-15	634	16.55	96	13.03	538	17.39
16	113	2.95	20	2.71	93	3.01
17+	78	2.04	13	1.76	65	2.10
Total	3,830	100.0	737	100.0	3,093	100.0
Percent of total population		100.0		19.24		80.76

Source: Rodney L. Brod and John M. McQuiston, "American Indian Adult Education and Literacy: The First National Survey," *Journal of American Indian Education*, Vol. 22, No. 2, January 1983, p. 4.

★ 268 ★

Years of School Completed by Persons 18 to 24 Years Old on Reservations, 1980 - I

Data are the latest available.

Identified reservation	Both sexes, 18 to 24 years old			Males, 18 to 24 years old			Females, 18 to 24 years old		
	Number of persons	Percent		Number of males	Percent		Number of females	Percent	
		High school graduates	4 or more years of college		High school graduates	4 or more years of college		High school graduates	4 or more years of college
American Indian, Eskimo and Aleut	45,446	50.0	0.6	22,393	47.4	0.4	23,053	52.6	0.7
Acoma Pueblo, New Mexico	338	73.0	0.4	160	69.5	-	178	76.1	0.8
Agua Caliente, California	-	-	-	-	-	-	-	-	-
Alabama-Coushatta, Texas	52	63.2	-	26	69.2	-	26	56.9	-
Alamo, New Mexico	153	34.9	-	69	30.5	-	84	38.6	-
Allegany, New York	100	59.5	2.7	52	62.1	-	49	56.6	5.6
Alturas Rancheria, California	...	...	...	...	...	...	...	...	...
Annette Islands Reserve, Alaska	136	62.8	-	67	56.2	-	69	69.2	-
Augustine, California	-	-	-	-	-	-	-	-	-
Bad River, Wisconsin	73	64.9	-	37	60.5	-	36	69.4	-
Barona Rancheria, California	34	43.7	-	16	50.6	-	18	37.8	-
Bay Mills, Michigan	53	52.6	-	35	49.9	-	18	57.9	-
Benton Paiute, California	...	...	...	...	...	...	...	...	...
Berry Creek Rancheria, California	-	-	-	-	-	-	-	-	-
Big Bend Rancheria, California	...	...	...	...	...	...	...	...	...
Big Cypress, Florida	45	31.4	5.1	25	12.9	-	21	53.4	11.1
Big Lagoon Rancheria, California	...	...	...	...	...	...	...	...	...
Big Pine Rancheria, California	40	76.6	3.5	21	74.5	-	19	78.8	7.3
Bishop Rancheria, California	106	58.8	-	55	56.0	-	52	61.6	-
Blackfeet, Montana	804	49.5	0.6	387	46.7	-	417	52.1	1.2
Bois Forte (Nett Lake), Minnesota	58	37.9	-	27	37.0	-	31	38.7	-
Bridgeport Colony, California	2	-	-	-	-	-	2	-	-
Brighton, Florida	40	74.1	-	25	71.6	-	15	78.2	-
Burns, Oregon	24	62.5	-	8	50.0	-	16	68.8	-
Cabazon, California	...	...	...	...	...	...	...	...	...
Cachil Dehe Rancheria, California	...	...	...	...	...	...	...	...	...
Cahuilla, California	...	...	...	...	...	...	...	...	...
Campo, California	8	28.1	-	6	-	-	2	100.0	-
Camp Verde, Arizona	21	38.1	-	11	18.2	-	10	60.0	-
Canoncito, New Mexico	147	44.0	2.3	76	33.6	2.3	71	55.1	1.5
Capitan Grande, California	-	-	-	-	-	-	-	-	-
Carson Colony, Nevada	30	53.6	-	14	42.6	-	16	63.0	-
Catawba, South Carolina	122	38.8	-	58	34.6	-	64	42.6	-
Cattaraugus, New York	239	41.6	-	123	38.4	-	116	44.9	-
Cedarville Rancheria, California	...	...	...	...	...	...	...	...	...
Chehalis, Washington	31	56.5	-	13	33.1	-	19	72.3	-
Chemehuevi, California	...	...	...	...	...	...	...	...	...
Cheyenne River, South Dakota	207	39.2	-	94	44.9	-	113	34.4	-
Chitimacha, Louisiana	25	39.3	-	15	45.9	-	9	28.2	-
Cochiti Pueblo, New Mexico	74	78.6	1.6	29	79.2	-	46	78.2	2.7
Cocopah, Arizona	49	37.5	-	21	33.3	-	27	40.8	-
Coeur d'Alene, Idaho	65	52.9	7.7	35	66.1	5.7	29	36.9	10.1
Cold Springs Rancheria, California	4	25.7	-	1	-	-	3	34.3	-
Colorado River, Arizona-California	258	56.8	0.8	133	62.4	0.7	125	50.9	0.8
Colville, Washington	477	58.1	2.3	242	58.5	2.9	235	57.7	1.7
Cortina Rancheria, California	...	...	...	...	...	...	...	...	...
Coushatta, Louisiana	...	...	...	...	...	...	...	...	...
Coyote Valley Rancheria, California	-	-	-	-	-	-	-	-	-
Crow, Montana	572	54.6	0.6	280	54.8	-	292	54.4	1.2
Crow Creek, South Dakota	204	53.0	2.1	99	62.1	1.9	105	44.2	2.3
Cuyapaipe, California	...	...	...	...	...	...	...	...	...
Deer Creek, Minnesota	...	...	...	...	...	...	...	...	...

[Continued]

★ 268 ★

Years of School Completed by Persons 18 to 24 Years Old on Reservations, 1980 - I
[Continued]

Identified reservation	Both sexes, 18 to 24 years old			Males, 18 to 24 years old			Females, 18 to 24 years old		
	Number of persons	Percent		Number of males	Percent		Number of females	Percent	
		High school graduates	4 or more years of college		High school graduates	4 or more years of college		High school graduates	4 or more years of college
Dresslerville Colony, Nevada	15	81.9	-	11	75.7	-	4	100.0	-
Dry Creek Rancheria, California	5	20.0	-	2	50.0	-	3	-	-
Duck Valley, Idaho-Nevada	109	68.7	2.1	47	63.5	-	61	72.8	3.8
Duckwater, Nevada	18	83.3	-	9	88.9	-	9	77.9	-
Eastern Cherokee, North Carolina	629	60.0	1.5	294	56.4	0.8	335	63.1	2.1
Eastern Pequot, Connecticut	...	...	...	...	...	...	...	...	...
Ely Colony, Nevada	7	61.1	-	5	51.2	-	1	100.0	-
Enterprise Rancheria, California	...	...	...	...	...	...	...	...	...
Fallon Colony, Nevada	5	23.2	-	2	-	-	2	50.0	-
Fallon, Nevada	44	61.8	-	25	51.8	-	19	74.6	-
Flandreau, South Dakota	20	55.2	-	7	43.0	-	13	61.7	-
Flathead, Montana	482	56.9	0.5	229	53.1	1.1	253	60.3	-
Fond du Lac, Minnesota	64	59.8	-	36	55.2	-	28	65.6	-
Fort Apache, Arizona	946	52.6	0.4	463	48.8	0.2	483	56.2	0.5
Fort Belknap, Montana	266	58.2	0.5	145	49.3	-	121	68.8	1.0
Fort Berthold, North Dakota	355	62.3	0.8	165	53.1	-	190	70.3	1.5
Fort Bidwell, California	11	27.2	-	2	50.0	-	9	22.2	-
Fort Hall, Idaho	336	48.5	0.8	170	34.3	-	166	63.0	1.6
Fort Independence, California	1	-	-	1	-	-	-	-	-
Fort McDermitt, Nevada-Oregon	62	47.9	-	32	50.2	-	29	45.3	-
Fort McDowell, Arizona	47	54.2	-	29	44.4	-	18	69.6	-
Fort Mojave, Arizona-California-Nevada	14	42.9	-	8	62.5	-	6	16.7	-
Fort Peck, Montana	577	46.0	0.2	297	42.6	0.4	280	49.7	-
Fort Totten, North Dakota	286	38.2	-	137	33.8	-	149	42.3	-
Fort Yuma, Arizona-California	120	43.7	-	57	44.5	-	63	42.9	-
Gila Bend, Arizona	-	-	-	-	-	-	-	-	-
Gila River, Arizona	981	47.5	0.1	487	44.1	-	494	50.9	0.3
Golden Hill, Connecticut	...	...	...	...	...	...	...	...	...
Goshute, Nevada-Utah	16	58.8	-	11	63.5	-	6	50.0	-
Grand Portage, Minnesota	22	50.4	-	16	43.2	-	7	67.0	-
Grindstone Creek Rancheria, California	14	46.5	-	7	57.3	-	6	33.9	-
Hannahville Community, Michigan	31	19.8	-	18	25.5	-	12	11.6	-
Hassanamisco, Massachusetts	...	...	...	...	...	...	...	...	...
Havasupai, Arizona	41	56.8	-	19	39.0	-	23	71.7	-
Hoh, Washington	6	-	-	-	-	-	6	-	-
Hollywood, Florida	64	46.5	-	30	46.3	-	34	46.7	-
Hoopa Valley, California	230	55.9	-	107	48.8	-	123	62.1	-
Hoopa Valley Extension, California	60	53.6	-	36	40.6	-	24	73.5	-
Hopi, Arizona	917	58.0	1.1	461	53.5	0.8	456	62.7	1.5
Hopland Rancheria, California	-	-	-	-	-	-	-	-	-
Hualapai, Arizona	137	60.7	-	72	53.5	-	65	68.8	-
Inaja-Cosmit, California	-	-	-	-	-	-	-	-	-
Indian Township, Maine	50	49.7	2.3	27	35.7	-	23	65.7	4.9
Iowa, Kansas-Nebraska	10	76.9	-	7	100.0	-	3	30.6	-
Isabella, Michigan	61	44.1	-	26	36.9	-	35	49.5	-

Source: U.S. Bureau of the Census, Subject Reports, PC80-2-1D, Part I, *American Indians, Eskimos, and Aleuts on Identified Reservations and in the Historic Areas of Oklahoma (Excluding Urbanized Areas),* U.S. Government Printing Office, Washington, D.C., 1986, pp. 209-247. *Notes:* A dash (-) represents zero or a percent which rounds to less than 0.1. Also, a dash (-) is used because the number of supplementary questionnaires for the areas was insufficient to produce reliable estimates. Three dots (...) means not applicable, or that the data are being withheld to avoid disclosure of information for individuals.

Years of School Completed by Persons 18 to 24 Years Old on Reservations, 1980 - II

Data are the latest available.

Identified reservation	Both sexes, 18 to 24 years old			Males, 18 to 24 years old			Females, 18 to 24 years old		
		Percent			Percent			Percent	
	Number of persons	High school graduates	4 or more years of college	Number of males	High school graduates	4 or more years of college	Number of females	High school graduates	4 or more years of college
Isleta Pueblo, New Mexico	315	71.3	1.1	154	70.4	-	161	72.2	2.1
Jackson Rancheria, California	...	...	...	...	...	...	...	...	...
Jemez Pueblo, New Mexico	204	61.3	1.6	93	55.0	3.5	111	66.7	-
Jicarilla Apache, New Mexico	236	66.1	-	128	62.6	-	108	70.3	-
Kaibab, Arizona	13	75.5	-	5	100.0	-	7	58.4	-
Kalispel, Washington	15	20.0	-	7	28.6	-	8	12.5	-
Kickapoo, Kansas	39	52.5	-	20	49.0	-	19	56.1	-
Kootenai, Idaho	-	-	-	-	-	-	-	-	-
Lac Courte Oreilles, Wisconsin	156	59.2	-	84	57.3	-	71	61.4	-
Lac du Flambeau, Wisconsin	110	47.4	-	49	59.1	-	61	37.9	-
Laguna Pueblo, New Mexico	470	73.3	1.6	243	69.9	0.5	228	76.9	2.7
La Jolla, California	12	46.0	-	4	25.8	-	8	57.8	-
L'Anse, Michigan	65	71.8	-	41	65.8	-	24	82.0	-
La Posta, California	...	...	...	...	...	...	...	...	...
Las Vegas Colony, Nevada	12	32.2	-	4	35.6	-	8	30.7	-
Laytonville Rancheria, California	16	37.5	6.3	9	22.2	-	7	57.1	14.3
Leech Lake, Minnesota	313	45.3	0.4	156	48.3	-	157	42.3	0.7
Likely Rancheria, California	-	-	-	-	-	-	-	-	-
Lone Pine Rancheria, California	19	76.8	-	6	100.0	-	13	66.9	-
Lookout Rancheria, California	...	...	...	...	...	...	...	...	...
Los Coyotes, California	10	55.8	-	5	25.9	-	6	80.3	-
Lovelock Colony, Nevada	9	77.4	-	7	69.4	-	2	100.0	-
Lower Brule, South Dakota	127	42.1	-	64	35.8	-	63	48.5	-
Lower Elwah, Washington	2	50.0	-	1	-	-	1	100.0	-
Lower Sioux Community, Minnesota	8	26.4	-	6	35.9	-	2	-	-
Lummi, Washington	177	45.8	-	100	36.8	-	77	57.6	-
Makah, Washington	97	52.4	1.3	51	53.2	2.4	45	51.6	-
Manchester Rancheria, California	14	30.9	-	8	50.5	-	5	-	-
Manzanita, California	...	...	...	...	...	...	...	...	...
Maricopa, Arizona	54	35.5	-	18	23.8	-	35	41.6	-
Mattaponi, Virginia	6	50.0	-	4	50.0	-	2	50.0	-
Menominee, Wisconsin	325	47.9	-	173	44.5	-	152	51.7	-
Mesa Grande, California	-	-	-	-	-	-	-	-	-
Mescalero Apache, New Mexico	267	46.4	-	113	46.7	-	154	46.1	-
Miccosukee, Florida	52	17.3	-	26	7.7	-	26	26.9	-
Middletown Rancheria, California	4	-	-	4	-	-	-	-	-
Mille Lacs, Minnesota	-	-	-	-	-	-	-	-	-
Mississippi Choctaw Reservation	327	50.1	0.8	163	43.7	0.7	164	56.6	1.0
Moapa River, Nevada	17	18.4	-	13	16.2	-	4	25.0	-
Montgomery Creek Rancheria, California	...	...	...	...	...	...	...	...	...
Morongo, California	45	35.2	-	23	36.7	-	22	33.7	-
Muckleshoot, Washington	48	35.0	-	29	27.4	-	19	46.5	-
Nambe Pueblo, New Mexico	28	71.0	-	16	68.7	-	12	74.2	-
Navajo, Arizona-New Mexico-Utah	14,380	43.6	0.5	6,983	41.2	0.4	7,397	45.9	0.6
Nez Perce, Idaho	179	55.2	-	89	52.7	-	90	57.6	-
Nisqually, Washington	4	67.5	-	2	50.0	-	1	100.0	-
Nooksack, Washington	-	-	-	-	-	-	-	-	-
Northern Cheyenne, Montana	387	57.9	1.2	165	57.9	0.7	223	58.0	1.5
Oil Springs, New York	-	-	-	-	-	-	-	-	-
Omaha, Iowa-Nebraska	147	50.1	-	68	59.5	-	79	42.2	-
Oneida, Wisconsin	236	66.5	-	123	59.7	-	113	73.8	-
Onondaga, New York	-	-	-	-	-	-	-	-	-
Ontonagon, Michigan	-	-	-	-	-	-	-	-	-

[Continued]

★ 269 ★

Years of School Completed by Persons 18 to 24 Years Old on Reservations, 1980 - II

[Continued]

Identified reservation	Both sexes, 18 to 24 years old			Males, 18 to 24 years old			Females, 18 to 24 years old		
	Number of persons	Percent		Number of males	Percent		Number of females	Percent	
		High school graduates	4 or more years of college		High school graduates	4 or more years of college		High school graduates	4 or more years of college
Osage, Oklahoma	544	65.6	1.8	291	65.6	1.6	254	65.5	2.1
Ozette, Washington	...	...	...	...	...	...	...	...	...
Pala, California	56	51.9	2.2	25	50.8	-	31	52.8	3.9
Pamunkey, Virginia	1	-	-	-	-	-	1	-	-
Papago, Arizona	796	60.9	0.1	378	57.0	-	418	64.3	0.3
Pascua Yaqui, Arizona	76	28.6	-	31	31.0	-	44	26.8	-
Pauma, California	11	58.2	-	6	40.5	-	5	79.8	-
Payson Community of Yavapai-Apache, Arizona	-	-	-	-	-	-	-	-	-
Pechanga, California	17	64.7	-	10	60.0	-	7	71.4	-
Penobscot, Maine	65	63.1	1.5	37	54.1	-	28	75.0	3.6
Picuris Pueblo, New Mexico	11	100.0	-	10	100.0	-	1	100.0	-
Pine Creek, Michigan	...	...	...	...	...	...	...	...	...
Pine Ridge, South Dakota	1,610	47.9	0.4	798	47.0	0.3	812	48.8	0.4
Pleasant Point, Maine	55	53.7	-	25	78.3	-	30	32.6	-
Pojoaque Pueblo, New Mexico	11	61.7	27.7	6	50.6	50.6	5	75.0	-
Poospatuck, New York	7	100.0	-	3	100.0	-	4	100.0	-
Port Gamble, Washington	46	51.0	-	25	46.1	-	21	56.6	-
Port Madison, Washington	25	46.1	-	14	63.0	-	11	24.8	-
Potawatomi, Wisconsin	28	39.3	-	15	33.3	-	13	46.2	-
Pottawatomi, Kansas	33	68.7	-	18	57.0	-	15	82.1	-
Prairie Island Community, Minnesota	10	60.0	-	5	40.0	-	5	80.0	-
Puyallup, Washington	103	60.0	-	47	56.9	-	56	62.6	-
Pyramid Lake, Nevada	95	71.5	3.2	56	71.9	2.6	39	71.1	4.0
Quileute, Washington	39	36.0	-	21	31.4	-	18	41.2	-
Quinault, Washington	148	44.9	-	78	47.3	-	71	42.2	-
Ramah Community, New Mexico	177	66.1	1.9	84	60.6	2.7	93	71.1	1.1
Ramona, California	-	-	-	-	-	-	-	-	-
Red Cliff, Wisconsin	71	51.6	2.3	39	39.3	-	32	66.6	5.2
Red Lake, Minnesota	366	39.9	-	181	37.5	-	185	42.3	-
Reno-Sparks Colony, Nevada	62	43.5	-	27	34.8	-	35	50.2	-
Resighini Rancheria, California	...	...	...	...	...	...	...	...	...
Rincon, California	30	34.0	-	13	33.1	-	17	34.7	-
Roaring Creek Rancheria, California	...	...	...	...	...	...	...	...	...
Rocky Boy's, Montana	197	45.8	-	95	41.6	-	103	49.7	-
Rosebud, South Dakota	698	53.8	1.2	330	53.9	0.8	369	53.7	1.5
Round Valley, California	57	63.6	1.7	26	65.4	3.6	30	2.0	-
Rumsey Rancheria, California	...	...	...	...	...	...	...	...	...
Sac and Fox, Iowa	61	45.0	-	37	37.0	-	24	57.4	-
Sac and Fox, Kansas-Nebraska	...	...	...	...	...	...	...	...	...
St. Croix, Wisconsin	50	34.6	-	28	32.8	-	23	36.9	-
St. Regis Mohawk, New York	219	71.7	3.6	123	64.9	3.3	96	80.4	4.0
Salt River, Arizona	390	46.6	-	198	43.4	-	192	49.9	-
San Carlos, Arizona	835	40.2	0.1	404	37.5	-	431	42.8	0.3
Sandia Pueblo, New Mexico	23	95.7	4.3	10	100.0	9.9	13	92.3	-
Sandy Lake, Minnesota	-	-	-	-	-	-	-	-	-
San Felipe Pueblo, New Mexico	259	48.2	-	116	43.6	-	143	52.0	-
San Ildefonso Pueblo, New Mexico	65	83.4	-	25	72.8	-	40	90.1	-
San Juan Pueblo, New Mexico	113	83.2	0.9	54	77.1	2.0	59	88.9	-
San Manuel, California	-	-	-	-	-	-	-	-	-
San Pasqual, California	18	17.7	-	9	25.0	-	10	11.0	-

[Continued]

★ 269 ★

Years of School Completed by Persons 18 to 24 Years Old on Reservations, 1980 - II
[Continued]

Identified reservation	Both sexes, 18 to 24 years old			Males, 18 to 24 years old			Females, 18 to 24 years old		
	Number of persons	Percent		Number of males	Percent		Number of females	Percent	
		High school graduates	4 or more years of college		High school graduates	4 or more years of college		High school graduates	4 or more years of college
Santa Ana Pueblo, New Mexico	56	81.4	-	32	79.5	-	24	84.0	-
Santa Clara Pueblo, New Mexico	232	78.0	-	130	82.4	-	102	72.5	-

Source: U.S. Bureau of the Census, Subject Reports, PC80-2-1D, Part I, *American Indians, Eskimos, and Aleuts on Identified Reservations and in the Historic Areas of Oklahoma (Excluding Urbanized Areas)*, U.S. Government Printing Office, Washington, D.C., 1986, pp. 209-247. *Notes:* A dash (-) represents zero or a percent which rounds to less than 0.1. Also, a dash (-) is used because the number of supplementary questionnaires for the areas was insufficient to produce reliable estimates. Three dots (...) means not applicable, or that the data are being withheld to avoid disclosure of information for individuals.

★ 270 ★

Years of School Completed by Persons 18 to 24 Years Old on Reservations, 1980 - III

Data are the latest available.

Identified reservations	Both sexes, 18 to 24 years old			Males, 18 to 24 years old			Females, 18 to 24 years old		
	Number of persons	Percent		Number of males	Percent		Number of females	Percent	
		High school graduates	4 or more years of college		High school graduates	4 or more years of college		High school graduates	4 or more years of college
Santa Rosa Rancheria, California	20	22.8	-	10	19.4	-	10	26.1	-
Santa Rosa, California	...	...	...	...	...	...	...	...	...
Santa Ynez, California	17	35.7	-	10	37.5	-	7	33.3	-
Santa Ysabel, California	33	49.4	4.0	14	48.2	-	19	50.3	7.0
Santee, Nebraska	52	43.9	-	28	36.9	-	24	52.1	-
Santo Domingo Pueblo, New Mexico	284	47.0	0.4	140	44.9	0.8	144	49.1	-
San Xavier, Arizona	124	59.6	1.1	67	53.5	-	57	66.9	2.4
Sauk-Suiattle, Washington	-	-	-	-	-	-	-	-	-
Sault Ste. Marie, Michigan	-	-	-	-	-	-	-	-	-
Schaghticoke, Connecticut	...	...	...	...	...	...	...	...	...
Shakopee Community, Minnesota	6	32.6	16.3	4	24.4	-	2	49.2	49.2
Sheep Ranch Rancheria, California	...	...	...	...	...	...	...	...	...
Sherwood Valley Rancheria, California	...	...	...	...	...	...	...	...	...
Shingle Springs Rancheria, California	-	-	-	-	-	-	-	-	-
Shinnecock, New York	16	77.4	9.1	8	100.0	17.7	8	53.3	-
Shoalwater, Washington	...	...	...	...	...	...	...	...	...
Sisseton, North Dakota-South Dakota	296	42.4	-	149	40.5	-	146	44.3	-
Skokomish, Washington	46	35.6	-	21	43.0	-	25	29.3	-
Skull Valley, Utah	-	-	-	-	-	-	-	-	-
Soboba, California	20	51.5	-	10	30.1	-	10	71.4	-
Sokaogon Chippewa Community, Wisconsin	17	41.0	5.9	8	49.9	-	9	33.2	11.2
Southern Paiute, Utah	25	51.6	-	13	40.4	-	12	62.9	-
Southern Ute, Colorado	92	59.3	1.3	52	44.0	-	40	79.3	2.9
Spokane, Washington	155	62.4	0.7	79	60.3	1.3	76	64.5	-
Squaxin Island, Washington	10	50.0	-	3	33.3	-	7	57.1	-
Standing Rock, North Dakota-South Dakota	580	54.4	0.8	287	57.2	-	293	51.8	1.5
Stewart's Point Rancheria, California	11	36.4	-	7	28.6	-	4	50.0	-
Stockbridge, Wisconsin	70	54.9	-	39	56.8	-	31	52.5	-
Sulphur Bank Rancheria, California	17	54.9	-	5	25.0	-	12	68.1	-
Summit Lake, Nevada	...	...	...	...	...	...	...	...	...
Susanville, California	12	36.4	-	6	66.7	-	5	-	-
Swinomish, Washington	62	57.9	-	32	78.9	-	30	35.8	-
Sycuan, California	5	-	-	3	-	-	2	-	-
Tama, Georgia	6	66.7	-	6	66.7	-	-	-	-
Taos Pueblo, New Mexico	115	66.0	-	68	60.0	-	46	74.9	-

[Continued]

★ 270 ★

Years of School Completed by Persons 18 to 24 Years Old on Reservations, 1980 - III
[Continued]

Identified reservations	Both sexes, 18 to 24 years old			Males, 18 to 24 years old			Females, 18 to 24 years old		
	Number of persons	Percent		Number of males	Percent		Number of females	Percent	
		High school graduates	4 or more years of college		High school graduates	4 or more years of college		High school graduates	4 or more years of college
Te-Moak, Nevada	11	85.5	-	5	66.7	-	6	100.0	-
Tesuque Pueblo, New Mexico	30	64.8	-	16	49.9	-	14	81.8	-
Tigua, Texas	63	42.9	3.2	30	40.0	3.3	33	45.5	3.0
Tonawanda, New York	44	51.4	-	22	41.8	-	22	61.1	-
Torres-Martinez, California	-	-	-	-	-	-	-	-	-
Trinidad Rancheria, California	7	100.0	-	2	100.0	-	5	100.0	-
Tulalip, Washington	104	37.3	0.9	60	40.7	-	44	32.7	2.2
Tule River, California	58	29.4	-	33	28.3	-	25	30.7	-
Tunicabiloxi, Louisiana	...	...	...	...	...	...	...	...	...
Tuolumne Rancheria, California	3	33.3	-	-	-	-	3	33.3	-
Turtle Mountain, North Dakota	509	46.0	0.4	237	44.2	-	272	47.6	0.8
Tuscarora, New York	-	-	-	-	-	-	-	-	-
Twenty-Nine Palms, California	-	-	-	-	-	-	-	-	-
Uintah and Ouray, Utah	305	35.5	-	130	33.9	-	175	36.7	-
Umatilla, Oregon	96	54.1	-	47	53.5	-	49	54.6	-
Upper Sioux Community, Minnesota	7	65.4	-	2	100.0	-	5	50.0	-
Upper Skagit, Washington	-	-	-	-	-	-	-	-	-
Ute Mountain, Colorado-New Mexico	226	48.6	-	121	46.1	-	105	51.4	-
Vermillion Lake, Minnesota	20	57.2	-	7	50.0	-	12	61.7	-
Viejas Rancheria, California	20	28.7	-	8	19.8	-	12	34.4	-
Walker River, Nevada	59	57.6	3.4	32	50.0	-	27	66.7	7.4
Wampanoag, Massachusetts	-	-	-	-	-	-	-	-	-
Warm Springs, Oregon	297	48.0	-	156	43.4	-	140	53.2	-
Washoe, Nevada	-	-	-	-	-	-	-	-	-
Western Pequot, Connecticut	...	...	...	...	...	...	...	...	...
White Earth, Minnesota	373	51.0	0.4	186	41.2	0.7	186	60.7	-
Wind River, Wyoming	591	57.0	0.5	298	52.5	-	293	61.6	0.9
Winnebago, Nebraska	124	58.2	-	55	56.8	-	69	59.2	-
Winnemucca Colony, Nevada	-	-	-	-	-	-	-	-	-
Wisconsin Winnebago Reservation	40	55.4	-	15	40.2	-	25	64.6	-
Woodfords Community, California	-	-	-	-	-	-	-	-	-
XL Ranch, California	...	...	...	...	...	...	...	...	...
Yakima, Washington	695	48.9	0.7	344	48.7	0.5	351	49.0	0.9
Yankton, South Dakota	219	56.7	-	110	52.8	-	109	60.6	-
Yavapai, Arizona	14	100.0	-	6	100.0	-	8	100.0	-
Yerington, Nevada	12	83.4	-	5	60.0	-	7	100.0	-
Yomba, Nevada	10	19.4	-	6	32.6	-	4	-	-
Zia Pueblo, New Mexico	72	58.8	1.5	34	54.3	3.3	38	62.8	-
Zuni Pueblo, New Mexico	918	49.6	0.4	446	42.9	0.5	471	56.0	0.3
San Felipe/Santa Ana Joint Area, New Mexico	-	-	-	-	-	-	-	-	-
San Felipe/Santo Domingo Joint Area, New Mexico	14	34.2	-	4	-	-	9	50.0	-
Other Reservation Lands in Montana	-	-	-	-	-	-	-	-	-

Source: U.S. Bureau of the Census, Subject Reports, PC80-2-1D, Part I, *American Indians, Eskimos, and Aleuts on Identified Reservations and in the Historic Areas of Oklahoma (Excluding Urbanized Areas)*, U.S. Government Printing Office, Washington, D.C., 1986, pp. 209-247. *Notes:* A dash (-) represents zero or a percent which rounds to less than 0.1. Also, a dash (-) is used because the number of supplementary questionnaires for the areas was insufficient to produce reliable estimates. Three dots (...) means not applicable, or that the data are being withheld to avoid disclosure of information for individuals.

★ 271 ★

Years of School Completed by Females 25 Years Old and Older on Reservations, 1980 - I

Data are the latest available.

Identified reservations	Total females, 25 years old and older	Elementary school		High school		College			Percent high school graduates	Median school years completed
		0 to 4 years	5 to 8 years	1 to 3 years	4 years	1 to 3 years	4 years	5 or more years		
American Indian, Eskimo and Aleut	70,884	12,064	13,971	14,838	19,617	8,270	1,434	690	42.3	10.8
Acoma Pueblo, New Mexico	526	38	83	137	184	67	10	7	51.0	12.0
Agua Caliente, California	-	-	-	-	-	-	-	-	-	-
Alabama-Coushatta, Texas	121	7	36	22	37	17	4	-	47.1	10.8
Alamo, New Mexico	183	90	26	29	29	9	-	-	20.8	5.2
Allegany, New York	231	5	45	44	91	40	6	-	59.4	12.2
Alturas Rancheria, California	...	...	...	...	...	...	...	...	...	...
Annette Islands Reserve, Alaska	191	1	26	64	73	21	5	2	52.6	12.1
Augustine, California	-	-	-	-	-	-	-	-	-	-
Bad River, Wisconsin	155	9	13	45	50	37	2	-	56.9	12.2
Barona Rancheria, California	45	2	5	18	16	3	-	-	43.0	11.6
Bay Mills, Michigan	40	-	8	9	18	5	-	-	58.1	12.2
Benton Paiute, California	...	...	...	...	...	...	...	...	...	...
Berry Creek Rancheria, California	-	-	-	-	-	-	-	-	-	-
Big Bend Rancheria, California	...	...	...	...	...	...	...	...	...	...
Big Cypress, Florida	76	37	15	5	14	4	1	-	24.7	5.2
Big Lagoon Rancheria, California	...	...	...	...	...	...	...	...	...	...
Big Pine Rancheria, California	59	1	6	11	35	6	-	-	69.5	12.3
Bishop Rancheria, California	186	3	37	46	77	19	2	1	53.7	12.1
Blackfeet, Montana	1,178	38	216	289	408	167	40	19	53.8	12.1
Bois Forte (Nett Lake), Minnesota	81	2	19	25	27	6	2	-	43.2	11.2
Bridgeport Colony, California	15	5	2	6	-	1	-	-	8.4	9.1
Brighton, Florida	78	38	4	7	19	7	2	1	36.9	5.8
Burns, Oregon	30	2	8	7	8	5	-	-	43.3	11.0
Cabazon, California	...	...	...	...	...	...	...	...	...	...
Cachil Dehe Rancheria, California	...	...	...	...	...	...	...	...	...	...
Cahuilla, California	...	...	...	...	...	...	...	...	...	...
Campo, California	22	7	4	8	4	-	-	-	19.4	9.2
Camp Verde, Arizona	38	3	4	12	14	5	-	-	50.0	12.0
Canoncito, New Mexico	186	101	20	18	35	8	3	-	24.7	3.9
Capitan Grande, California	-	-	-	-	-	-	-	-	-	-
Carson Colony, Nevada	54	1	7	23	14	7	-	1	42.5	11.6
Catawba, South Carolina	225	19	78	61	50	13	2	2	29.5	9.6
Cattaraugus, New York	474	3	86	119	144	102	14	5	56.0	12.2
Cedarville Rancheria, California	...	...	...	...	...	...	...	...	...	...
Chehalis, Washington	37	2	4	9	17	3	1	1	59.1	12.2
Chemehuevi, California	...	...	...	...	...	...	...	...	...	...
Cheyenne River, South Dakota	261	4	57	85	88	22	3	2	44.1	11.5
Chitimacha, Louisiana	35	9	7	5	13	1	-	-	40.8	10.1
Cochiti Pueblo, New Mexico	146	10	22	29	55	23	5	2	58.6	12.2
Cocopah, Arizona	71	27	22	7	12	2	-	-	20.0	6.4
Coeur d'Alene, Idaho	126	6	32	27	35	22	5	-	48.8	11.9
Cold Springs Rancheria, California	18	1	4	11	-	1	-	-	7.6	9.6
Colorado River, Arizona-California	410	17	80	103	125	72	10	3	51.3	12.0
Colville, Washington	773	30	141	193	257	131	12	9	52.9	12.1
Cortina Rancheria, California	...	...	...	...	...	...	...	...	...	...
Coushatta, Louisiana	...	...	...	...	...	...	...	...	...	...
Coyote Valley Rancheria, California	-	-	-	-	-	-	-	-	-	-
Crow, Montana	836	23	207	155	200	189	48	14	53.8	12.2
Crow Creek, South Dakota	269	1	62	90	77	38	-	-	42.9	10.9
Cuyapaipe, California	...	...	...	...	...	...	...	...	...	...
Deer Creek, Minnesota	...	...	...	...	...	...	...	...	...	...
Dresslerville Colony, Nevada	30	5	4	-	20	1	-	-	71.2	12.3

[Continued]

Years of School Completed by Females 25 Years Old and Older on Reservations, 1980 - I
[Continued]

Identified reservations	Total females, 25 years old and older	Elementary school		High school		College			Percent high school graduates	Median school years completed
		0 to 4 years	5 to 8 years	1 to 3 years	4 years	1 to 3 years	4 years	5 or more years		
Dry Creek Rancheria, California	12	2	6	3	1	-	-	-	8.3	8.3
Duck Valley, Idaho-Nevada	208	18	44	45	52	41	5	2	48.3	11.8
Duckwater, Nevada	24	2	6	6	7	3	-	-	41.7	10.7
Eastern Cherokee, North Carolina	1,154	75	249	315	380	112	13	10	44.6	11.2
Eastern Pequot, Connecticut	...	...	...	...	...	...	...	...	...	...
Ely Colony, Nevada	16	1	4	3	8	-	-	-	49.1	9.9
Enterprise Rancheria, California	...	...	...	...	...	...	...	...	...	...
Fallon Colony, Nevada	15	3	4	3	5	-	-	-	34.2	9.4
Fallon, Nevada	64	1	12	7	38	8	1	1	67.8	12.3
Flandreau, South Dakota	34	1	-	4	14	13	1	-	67.0	12.8
Flathead, Montana	784	35	152	155	298	114	21	10	56.4	12.2
Fond du Lac, Minnesota	113	2	26	26	44	16	-	-	52.8	12.1
Fort Apache, Arizona	1,380	66	412	462	308	113	17	3	31.9	10.1
Fort Belknap, Montana	367	11	56	88	109	79	21	4	58.1	12.3
Fort Berthold, North Dakota	554	25	115	118	163	94	34	6	53.5	12.1
Fort Bidwell, California	24	-	5	4	11	5	-	-	63.9	12.3
Fort Hall, Idaho	562	59	146	120	159	71	5	2	42.2	11.0
Fort Independence, California	10	2	2	2	4	1	-	-	53.5	12.1
Fort McDermitt, Nevada-Oregon	89	3	23	34	19	11	-	-	33.1	10.7
Fort McDowell, Arizona	79	7	11	20	28	12	1	-	52.1	12.1
Fort Mojave, Arizona-California-Nevada	30	-	1	14	10	5	-	-	50.0	12.0
Fort Peck, Montana	866	23	173	247	260	140	15	9	48.8	11.9
Fort Totten, North Dakota	398	10	105	131	101	38	10	2	38.2	10.9
Fort Yuma, Arizona-California	278	17	69	67	89	33	3	-	45.0	11.6
Gila Bend, Arizona	-	-	-	-	-	-	-	-	-	-
Gila River, Arizona	1,473	64	452	406	415	124	10	3	37.5	10.6
Golden Hill, Connecticut	...	...	...	...	...	...	...	...	...	...
Goshute, Nevada-Utah	26	14	9	-	3	-	-	-	11.5	4.5
Grand Portage, Minnesota	55	2	4	7	25	14	-	4	77.3	12.6
Grindstone Creek Rancheria, California	14	1	3	5	4	1	-	-	36.2	11.3
Hannahville Community, Michigan	23	-	6	10	2	4	-	-	29.9	10.3
Hassanamisco, Massachusetts	...	...	...	...	...	...	...	...	...	...
Havasupai, Arizona	56	4	19	14	19	1	-	-	35.5	10.3
Hoh, Washington	8	-	3	3	2	-	-	-	20.5	10.0
Hollywood, Florida	93	22	10	7	29	21	1	2	57.9	12.3
Hoopa Valley, California	319	6	34	101	130	33	7	7	55.5	12.1
Hoopa Valley Extension, California	103	4	14	40	35	8	-	1	43.0	11.5
Hopi, Arizona	1,540	326	286	318	411	161	29	8	39.6	10.5
Hopland Rancheria, California	-	-	-	-	-	-	-	-	-	-
Hualapai, Arizona	171	3	34	50	58	25	-	1	49.2	11.8
Inaja-Cosmit, California	-	-	-	-	-	-	-	-	-	-
Indian Township, Maine	52	4	25	7	13	2	1	-	30.8	8.8
Iowa, Kansas-Nebraska	5	-	2	2	-	-	-	-	-	10.0
Isabella, Michigan	114	2	45	23	33	10	-	1	38.2	10.2

Source: U.S. Bureau of the Census, Subject Reports, PC80-2-1D, Part I, *American Indians, Eskimos, and Aleuts on Identified Reservations and in the Historic Areas of Oklahoma (Excluding Urbanized Areas)*, U.S. Government Printing Office, Washington, D.C., 1986, pp. 209-247. *Notes:* A dash (-) represents zero or a percent which rounds to less than 0.1. Also, a dash (-) is used because the number of supplementary questionnaires for the areas was insufficient to produce reliable estimates. Three dots (...) means not applicable, or that the data are being withheld to avoid disclosure of information for individuals.

★ 272 ★

Years of School Completed by Females 25 Years Old and Older on Reservations, 1980 - II

Data are the latest available.

Identified reservation	Total females, 25 years old and older	Elementary school		High school		College			Percent high school graduates	Median school years completed
		0 to 4 years	5 to 8 years	1 to 3 years	4 years	1 to 3 years	4 years	5 or more years		
Isleta Pueblo, New Mexico	553	23	97	114	224	69	20	5	57.6	12.2
Jackson Rancheria, California	...	...	...	...	...	...	...	...	...	...
Jemez Pueblo, New Mexico	337	14	80	88	109	38	7	2	46.2	11.6
Jicarilla Apache, New Mexico	349	31	69	60	143	39	5	3	54.3	12.1
Kaibab, Arizona	17	1	3	2	7	3	-	-	62.3	12.3
Kalispel, Washington	17	3	4	5	5	-	-	-	29.4	9.5
Kickapoo, Kansas	82	3	12	26	29	12	-	-	49.9	11.9
Kootenai, Idaho	-	-	-	-	-	-	-	-	-	-
Lac Courte Oreilles, Wisconsin	246	1	45	68	78	44	7	2	53.5	12.1
Lac du Flambeau, Wisconsin	250	2	38	108	72	28	2	-	40.8	11.1
Laguna Pueblo, New Mexico	899	40	123	177	375	146	23	14	62.1	12.3
La Jolla, California	27	-	3	9	10	5	-	-	53.1	12.1
L'Anse, Michigan	115	4	28	31	27	19	4	1	44.9	11.5
La Posta, California	...	...	...	...	...	...	...	...	...	...
Las Vegas Colony, Nevada	29	1	6	18	3	-	1	-	13.1	9.8
Laytonville Rancheria, California	20	-	8	6	2	4	-	-	30.0	9.7
Leech Lake, Minnesota	590	16	131	116	221	90	12	4	55.2	12.1
Likely Rancheria, California	-	-	-	-	-	-	-	-	-	-
Lone Pine Rancheria, California	43	3	3	8	24	5	-	-	68.7	12.3
Lookout Rancheria, California	...	...	...	...	...	...	...	...	...	...
Los Coyotes, California	6	-	2	1	1	1	-	-	40.6	10.5
Lovelock Colony, Nevada	25	2	8	6	9	-	-	-	34.6	10.1
Lower Brule, South Dakota	154	3	35	44	54	16	3	-	47.0	11.6
Lower Elwah, Washington	10	1	3	2	3	1	-	-	40.0	10.0
Lower Sioux Community, Minnesota	21	-	8	2	11	-	-	-	51.3	12.0
Lummi, Washington	242	7	42	66	86	37	3	1	52.4	12.1
Makah, Washington	167	7	27	37	62	27	4	4	57.4	12.2
Manchester Rancheria, California	19	1	7	5	4	1	-	-	27.7	9.9
Manzanita, California	...	...	...	...	...	...	...	...	...	...
Maricopa, Arizona	71	6	31	9	22	1	1	-	34.3	8.9
Mattaponi, Virginia	19	2	6	7	4	-	-	-	21.1	10.2
Menominee, Wisconsin	484	5	107	143	168	50	6	5	47.3	11.7
Mesa Grande, California	-	-	-	-	-	-	-	-	-	-
Mescalero Apache, New Mexico	358	16	62	94	145	35	-	6	52.0	12.1
Miccosukee, Florida	52	33	4	4	8	2	-	1	21.2	12.1
Middletown Rancheria, California	4	-	-	2	2	-	-	-	50.0	12.0
Mille Lacs, Minnesota	-	-	-	-	-	-	-	-	-	-
Mississippi Choctaw Reservation	593	188	148	59	132	57	3	5	33.4	8.2
Moapa River, Nevada	39	1	9	14	11	3	-	-	37.5	10.9
Montgomery Creek Rancheria, California	...	...	...	...	...	...	...	...	...	...
Morongo, California	70	-	5	27	28	7	1	1	53.3	12.1
Muckleshoot, Washington	59	2	10	32	11	4	-	-	25.8	10.2
Nambe Pueblo, New Mexico	36	4	3	7	15	4	3	-	61.6	12.3
Navajo, Arizona-New Mexico-Utah	21,217	8,598	3,168	2,590	4,327	1,872	404	258	32.3	8.0
Nez Perce, Idaho	345	12	56	85	97	72	13	9	55.5	12.2
Nisqually, Washington	10	-	5	2	2	1	-	-	32.9	9.2
Nooksack, Washington	-	-	-	-	-	-	-	-	-	-
Northern Cheyenne, Montana	585	53	110	127	195	78	21	1	50.4	12.0
Oil Springs, New York	-	-	-	-	-	-	-	-	-	-
Omaha, Iowa-Nebraska	268	7	104	68	58	25	1	5	33.4	9.9
Oneida, Wisconsin	436	11	112	106	150	41	13	4	47.5	11.5
Onondaga, New York	-	-	-	-	-	-	-	-	-	-
Ontonagon, Michigan	-	-	-	-	-	-	-	-	-	-
Osage, Oklahoma	1,277	20	146	293	489	245	59	25	64.1	12.4

[Continued]

★ 272 ★

Years of School Completed by Females 25 Years Old and Older on Reservations, 1980 - II

[Continued]

Identified reservation	Total females, 25 years old and older	Elementary school		High school		College			Percent high school graduates	Median school years completed
		0 to 4 years	5 to 8 years	1 to 3 years	4 years	1 to 3 years	4 years	5 or more years		
Ozette, Washington	...	...	...	...	...	...	...	...	...	...
Pala, California	101	1	5	31	42	17	3	1	62.3	12.3
Pamunkey, Virginia	14	1	5	5	3	-	-	-	21.4	10.0
Papago, Arizona	1,572	402	413	224	418	92	17	6	33.9	8.8
Pascua Yaqui, Arizona	102	21	48	24	9	-	-	-	8.9	8.2
Pauma, California	23	-	2	6	6	8	-	2	66.1	12.6
Payson Community of Yavapai-Apache, Arizona	-	-	-	-	-	-	-	-	-	-
Pechanga, California	25	-	5	8	6	4	1	1	48.0	11.5
Penobscot, Maine	90	-	22	14	31	16	4	3	60.0	12.3
Picuris Pueblo, New Mexico	40	2	7	3	20	6	1	-	69.1	12.4
Pine Creek, Michigan	...	...	...	...	...	...	...	...	...	...
Pine Ridge, South Dakota	2,252	78	659	472	579	377	62	25	46.3	11.4
Pleasant Point, Maine	102	7	44	17	22	12	1	-	34.2	9.1
Pojoaque Pueblo, New Mexico	23	2	5	2	11	1	2	-	63.8	12.3
Poospatuck, New York	25	1	4	9	6	4	-	-	41.1	11.4
Port Gamble, Washington	46	3	9	21	9	4	-	-	28.4	10.1
Port Madison, Washington	31	1	1	7	12	10	-	-	68.9	12.5
Potawatomi, Wisconsin	38	6	14	10	5	2	1	-	21.3	8.9
Pottawatomi, Kansas	86	3	10	20	42	12	-	-	62.2	12.3
Prairie Island Community, Minnesota	20	1	5	6	5	2	-	1	40.0	11.3
Puyallup, Washington	208	6	34	36	84	37	7	3	62.3	12.3
Pyramid Lake, Nevada	162	1	36	47	54	17	2	5	47.9	11.9
Quileute, Washington	47	-	11	22	13	2	-	-	31.4	11.0
Quinault, Washington	176	1	34	52	54	28	7	-	50.4	12.0
Ramah Community, New Mexico	270	138	40	19	49	19	5	-	27.2	4.8
Ramona, California	-	-	-	-	-	-	-	-	-	-
Red Cliff, Wisconsin	98	2	19	37	33	5	2	-	40.3	11.2
Red Lake, Minnesota	545	12	131	148	219	31	2	1	46.6	11.6
Reno-Sparks Colony, Nevada	107	3	8	41	43	12	-	-	50.8	12.0
Resighini Rancheria, California	...	...	...	...	...	...	...	...	...	...
Rincon, California	69	-	12	20	15	19	2	-	52.5	12.1
Roaring Creek Rancheria, California	...	...	...	...	...	...	...	...	...	...
Rocky Boy's, Montana	298	28	80	64	59	45	19	3	42.4	10.8
Rosebud, South Dakota	1,129	32	259	267	331	194	29	17	50.6	12.0
Round Valley, California	123	-	21	35	48	17	1	1	54.6	12.1
Rumsey Rancheria, California	...	...	...	...	...	...	...	...	...	...
Sac and Fox, Iowa	91	5	20	23	30	12	-	-	46.5	11.6
Sac and Fox, Kansas-Nebraska	...	...	...	...	...	...	...	...	...	...
St. Croix, Wisconsin	84	7	32	14	25	5	-	1	37.3	10.3
St. Regis Mohawk, New York	447	34	147	86	104	65	12	-	40.4	10.5
Salt River, Arizona	561	16	106	183	183	70	2	1	45.7	11.6
San Carlos, Arizona	1,130	90	324	325	287	93	11	-	34.6	10.3
Sandia Pueblo, New Mexico	57	3	10	6	21	15	-	1	66.2	12.4
Sandy Lake, Minnesota	-	-	-	-	-	-	-	-	-	-
San Felipe Pueblo, New Mexico	364	22	98	80	112	39	11	1	44.8	11.1
San Ildefonso Pueblo, New Mexico	133	4	24	15	56	24	6	4	67.7	12.4
San Juan Pueblo, New Mexico	195	4	30	52	70	32	4	4	56.3	12.2
San Manuel, California	-	-	-	-	-	-	-	-	-	-
San Pasqual, California	26	-	3	8	10	3	-	2	57.8	12.2

[Continued]

★ 272 ★

Years of School Completed by Females 25 Years Old and Older on Reservations, 1980 - II

[Continued]

Identified reservation	Total females, 25 years old and older	Elementary school		High school		College			Percent high school graduates	Median school years completed
		0 to 4 years	5 to 8 years	1 to 3 years	4 years	1 to 3 years	4 years	5 or more years		
Santa Ana Pueblo, New Mexico	101	4	11	20	40	22	3	1	65.4	12.4
Santa Clara Pueblo, New Mexico	429	5	54	83	153	106	12	15	66.9	12.5

Source: U.S. Bureau of the Census, Subject Reports, PC80-2-1D, Part I, *American Indians, Eskimos, and Aleuts on Identified Reservations and in the Historic Areas of Oklahoma (Excluding Urbanized Areas),* U.S. Government Printing Office, Washington, D.C., 1986, pp. 209-247. *Notes:* A dash (-) represents zero or a percent which rounds to less than 0.1. Also, a dash (-) is used because the number of supplementary questionnaires for the areas was insufficient to produce reliable estimates. Three dots (...) means not applicable, or that the data are being withheld to avoid disclosure of information for individuals.

★ 273 ★

Years of School Completed by Females 25 Years Old and Older on Reservations, 1980 - III

Data are the latest available.

Identified reservation	Total females, 25 years old and older	Elementary school		High school		College			Percent high school graduates	Median school years completed
		0 to 4 years	5 to 8 years	1 to 3 years	4 years	1 to 3 years	4 years	5 or more years		
Santa Rosa Rancheria, California	22	3	7	4	6	2	-	-	36.8	9.8
Santa Rosa, California	...	...	...	...	...	...	...	...	...	...
Santa Ynez, California	27	1	5	7	12	1	-	-	50.0	12.0
Santa Ysabel, California	37	-	5	14	16	3	-	-	49.7	12.0
Santee, Nebraska	79	5	19	21	30	2	3	-	43.9	10.9
Santo Domingo Pueblo, New Mexico	445	70	79	149	118	28	1	-	33.1	10.4
San Xavier, Arizona	203	21	50	48	72	11	1	-	41.4	10.7
Sauk-Suiattle, Washington	-	-	-	-	-	-	-	-	-	-
Sault Ste. Marie, Michigan	-	-	-	-	-	-	-	-	-	-
Schaghticoke, Connecticut	...	...	...	...	...	...	...	...	...	...
Shakopee Community, Minnesota	15	1	1	2	8	2	-	-	69.7	12.4
Sheep Ranch Rancheria, California	...	...	...	...	...	...	...	...	...	...
Sherwood Valley Rancheria, California	...	...	...	...	...	...	...	...	...	...
Shingle Springs Rancheria, California	-	-	-	-	-	-	-	-	-	-
Shinnecock, New York	70	-	18	15	23	5	9	-	52.9	12.1
Shoalwater, Washington	...	...	...	...	...	...	...	...	...	...
Sisseton, North Dakota-South Dakota	524	27	109	132	187	53	15	2	48.9	11.9
Skokomish, Washington	61	2	14	18	23	5	-	-	44.9	11.2
Skull Valley, Utah	-	-	-	-	-	-	-	-	-	-
Soboba, California	49	1	7	10	17	12	1	-	61.7	12.3
Sokaogon Chippewa Community, Wisconsin	18	1	6	4	4	3	-	-	38.9	10.3
Southern Paiute, Utah	42	7	10	17	6	1	-	-	18.2	9.9
Southern Ute, Colorado	183	6	15	36	82	38	2	4	69.0	12.4
Spokane, Washington	215	11	44	53	84	20	1	1	49.5	11.9
Squaxin Island, Washington	1	1	-	-	-	-	-	-	-	4.5
Standing Rock, North Dakota-South Dakota	901	17	201	239	263	138	30	13	49.2	11.9
Stewart's Point Rancheria, California	16	2	3	10	-	-	1	-	6.2	10.5
Stockbridge, Wisconsin	150	2	40	33	56	19	-	-	49.9	12.0
Sulphur Bank Rancheria, California	16	3	5	4	3	1	-	-	25.1	10.0
Summit Lake, Nevada	...	...	...	...	...	...	...	...	...	...
Susanville, California	18	2	1	8	2	3	-	-	33.3	11.2
Swinomish, Washington	94	6	18	34	14	18	3	-	38.1	10.7

[Continued]

★ 273 ★

Years of School Completed by Females 25 Years Old and Older on Reservations, 1980 - III
[Continued]

Identified reservation	Total females, 25 years old and older	Elementary school		High school		College			Percent high school graduates	Median school years completed
		0 to 4 years	5 to 8 years	1 to 3 years	4 years	1 to 3 years	4 years	5 or more years		
Sycuan, California	10	2	2	5	-	2	-	-	16.2	9.5
Tama, Georgia	9	-	1	1	4	-	1	1	75.0	12.5
Taos Pueblo, New Mexico	287	33	36	70	113	33	2	-	51.7	12.0
Te-Moak, Nevada	23	5	4	2	9	2	-	-	49.8	12.0
Tesuque Pueblo, New Mexico	62	4	7	14	21	12	1	1	58.9	12.3
Tigua, Texas	46	14	10	16	2	4	-	-	13.0	8.8
Tonawanda, New York	136	6	32	28	45	15	7	2	51.2	12.0
Torres-Martinez, California	-	-	-	-	-	-	-	-	-	-
Trinidad Rancheria, California	10	-	2	1	2	3	-	1	65.9	12.7
Tulalip, Washington	163	4	27	44	55	27	5	-	53.8	12.1
Tule River, California	69	2	13	25	22	7	-	-	41.5	11.5
Tunicabiloxi, Louisiana	...	...	...	...	...	...	...	...	...	...
Tuolumne Rancheria, California	19	1	1	4	10	3	-	-	68.4	12.3
Turtle Mountain, North Dakota	800	59	200	191	178	127	39	6	43.7	11.1
Tuscarora, New York	-	-	-	-	-	-	-	-	-	-
Twenty-Nine Palms, California	-	-	-	-	-	-	-	-	-	-
Uintah and Ouray, Utah	450	29	89	114	145	50	12	12	48.5	11.8
Umatilla, Oregon	241	7	44	57	73	55	4	2	55.4	12.2
Upper Sioux Community, Minnesota	17	2	4	6	2	-	2	-	26.1	9.4
Upper Skagit, Washington	-	-	-	-	-	-	-	-	-	-
Ute Mountain, Colorado-New Mexico	217	47	60	68	37	5	-	-	19.4	9.1
Vermillion Lake, Minnesota	21	-	6	5	4	5	-	-	45.5	11.6
Viejas Rancheria, California	36	1	8	12	5	9	-	-	38.8	10.5
Walker River, Nevada	117	4	19	30	37	18	4	5	54.7	12.1
Wampanoag, Massachusetts	-	-	-	-	-	-	-	-	-	-
Warm Springs, Oregon	395	24	64	88	146	62	9	1	55.3	12.1
Washoe, Nevada	-	-	-	-	-	-	-	-	-	-
Western Pequot, Connecticut	...	...	...	...	...	...	...	...	...	...
White Earth, Minnesota	495	5	120	133	187	42	8	-	47.9	11.7
Wind River, Wyoming	852	17	182	290	229	119	10	6	42.6	11.4
Winnebago, Nebraska	256	4	33	67	100	32	12	8	59.4	12.2
Winnemucca Colony, Nevada	10	-	-	4	6	-	-	-	62.5	12.2
Wisconsin Winnebago Reservation	76	4	5	20	28	16	2	-	61.4	12.3
Woodfords Community, California	-	-	-	-	-	-	-	-	-	-
XL Ranch, California	...	...	...	...	...	...	...	...	...	...
Yakima, Washington	1,084	59	225	260	341	167	14	18	49.8	12.0
Yankton, South Dakota	347	18	88	99	113	20	6	2	40.8	11.1
Yavapai, Arizona	16	2	1	5	5	2	1	-	50.0	12.0
Yerington, Nevada	24	3	6	6	8	-	1	-	35.1	10.3
Yomba, Nevada	8	1	2	2	2	1	-	-	38.1	9.5
Zia Pueblo, New Mexico	113	9	22	30	36	14	1	1	46.1	11.6
Zuni Pueblo, New Mexico	1,236	63	332	423	309	97	8	2	33.8	10.4
San Felipe/Santa Ana Joint Area, New Mexico	-	-	-	-	-	-	-	-	-	-
San Felipe/Santo Domingo Joint Area, New Mexico	26	-	5	3	10	7	-	-	68.5	12.5
Other Reservation Lands in Montana	-	-	-	-	-	-	-	-	-	-

Source: U.S. Bureau of the Census, Subject Reports, PC80-2-1D, Part I, *American Indians, Eskimos, and Aleuts on Identified Reservations and in the Historic Areas of Oklahoma (Excluding Urbanized Areas)*, U.S. Government Printing Office, Washington, D.C., 1986, pp. 209-247. *Notes:* A dash (-) represents zero or a percent which rounds to less than 0.1. Also, a dash (-) is used because the number of supplementary questionnaires for the areas was insufficient to produce reliable estimates. Three dots (...) means not applicable, or that the data are being withheld to avoid disclosure of information for individuals.

★274★

Years of School Completed by Males 25 Years Old and Older on Reservations, 1980 - I

Data are the latest available.

Identified reservations	Total males, 25 years old and older	Elementary school		High school		College			Percent high school graduates	Median school years completed
		0 to 4 years	5 to 8 years	1 to 3 years	4 years	1 to 3 years	4 years	5 or more years		
American Indian, Eskimo and Aleut	64,744	9,876	13,054	13,297	18,760	7,601	1,388	768	44.0	11.1
Acoma Pueblo, New Mexico	442	50	74	74	177	55	7	5	55.3	12.1
Agua Caliente, California	-	-	-	-	-	-	-	-	-	-
Alabama-Coushatta, Texas	125	10	25	18	45	21	4	1	57.1	12.2
Alamo, New Mexico	194	92	41	23	27	8	2	-	19.2	5.4
Allegany, New York	225	9	41	53	86	27	6	3	54.1	12.1
Alturas Rancheria, California	...	...	...	...	...	...	...	...	...	...
Annette Islands Reserve, Alaska	230	2	28	51	93	42	7	6	64.7	12.4
Augustine, California	-	-	-	-	-	-	-	-	-	-
Bad River, Wisconsin	160	-	52	35	45	24	-	4	45.5	11.3
Barona Rancheria, California	47	-	3	15	23	5	1	-	61.5	12.2
Bay Mills, Michigan	62	-	12	13	23	11	2	-	59.1	12.2
Benton Paiute, California	...	...	...	...	...	...	...	...	...	...
Berry Creek Rancheria, California	-	-	-	-	-	-	-	-	-	-
Big Bend Rancheria, California	...	...	...	...	...	...	...	...	...	...
Big Cypress, Florida	71	32	12	11	14	2	-	-	22.9	6.8
Big Lagoon Rancheria, California	...	...	...	...	...	...	...	...	...	...
Big Pine Rancheria, California	51	-	4	7	33	6	1	-	79.2	12.4
Bishop Rancheria, California	166	7	21	40	68	20	9	1	58.7	12.2
Blackfeet, Montana	1,130	49	256	309	320	148	29	20	45.7	11.6
Bois Forte (Nett Lake), Minnesota	67	4	13	25	19	6	-	-	37.3	10.8
Bridgeport Colony, California	13	-	-	2	10	1	-	-	82.1	12.4
Brighton, Florida	65	25	6	12	15	6	1	-	34.3	9.4
Burns, Oregon	43	3	12	17	7	3	-	1	25.6	10.6
Cabazon, California	...	...	...	...	...	...	...	...	...	...
Cachil Dehe Rancheria, California	...	...	...	...	...	...	...	...	...	...
Cahuilla, California	...	...	...	...	...	...	...	...	...	...
Campo, California	16	2	4	3	4	2	-	-	40.0	11.5
Camp Verde, Arizona	33	1	6	16	8	-	2	-	30.3	11.2
Canoncito, New Mexico	164	51	32	27	44	6	-	3	32.6	8.9
Capitan Grande, California	-	-	-	-	-	-	-	-	-	-
Carson Colony, Nevada	47	6	3	10	20	7	1	-	60.2	12.2
Catawba, South Carolina	235	33	73	31	56	32	8	2	41.6	10.2
Cattaraugus, New York	394	17	91	103	118	47	13	5	46.4	11.4
Cedarville Rancheria, California	...	...	...	...	...	...	...	...	...	...
Chehalis, Washington	35	1	7	11	5	7	3	-	45.9	11.7
Chemehuevi, California	...	...	...	...	...	...	...	...	...	...
Cheyenne River, South Dakota	284	7	71	97	86	16	3	3	38.0	10.8
Chitimacha, Louisiana	38	9	10	6	7	2	2	-	32.8	8.9
Cochiti Pueblo, New Mexico	128	9	17	13	49	26	9	4	68.7	12.5
Cocopah, Arizona	75	32	22	8	7	5	-	-	16.2	6.7
Coeur d'Alene, Idaho	110	4	19	14	40	25	5	3	66.4	12.5
Cold Springs Rancheria, California	13	3	2	4	3	-	-	-	25.2	11.0
Colorado River, Arizona-California	401	17	66	103	134	68	7	6	53.6	12.1
Colville, Washington	804	27	151	149	290	141	36	10	59.3	12.3
Cortina Rancheria, California	...	...	...	...	...	...	...	...	...	...
Coushatta, Louisiana	...	...	...	...	...	...	...	...	...	...
Coyote Valley Rancheria, California	-	-	-	-	-	-	-	-	-	-
Crow, Montana	762	16	190	173	186	166	24	6	50.1	12.0
Crow Creek, South Dakota	243	6	54	76	70	29	5	3	44.0	11.6
Cuyapaipe, California	...	...	...	...	...	...	...	...	...	...
Deer Creek, Minnesota	...	...	...	...	...	...	...	...	...	...
Dresslerville Colony, Nevada	24	-	4	-	20	-	-	-	84.2	12.4

[Continued]

★ 274 ★

Years of School Completed by Males 25 Years Old and Older on Reservations, 1980 - I
[Continued]

Identified reservations	Total males, 25 years old and older	Elementary school		High school		College			Percent high school graduates	Median school years completed
		0 to 4 years	5 to 8 years	1 to 3 years	4 years	1 to 3 years	4 years	5 or more years		
Dry Creek Rancheria, California	7	-	1	2	3	1	-	-	57.1	12.2
Duck Valley, Idaho-Nevada	213	19	46	50	72	20	1	4	45.8	11.4
Duckwater, Nevada	23	5	5	4	4	5	-	-	39.1	10.3
Eastern Cherokee, North Carolina	1,061	93	248	277	328	90	13	12	41.7	10.9
Eastern Pequot, Connecticut	...	...	...	...	...	...	...	...	...	...
Ely Colony, Nevada	10	1	-	-	8	-	-	-	87.2	12.4
Enterprise Rancheria, California	...	...	...	...	...	...	...	...	...	...
Fallon Colony, Nevada	13	3	2	1	5	2	-	-	53.9	12.1
Fallon, Nevada	54	6	8	9	27	5	-	-	58.3	12.2
Flandreau, South Dakota	29	1	2	6	7	11	1	1	69.1	12.8
Flathead, Montana	830	36	162	155	296	116	41	24	57.5	12.2
Fond du Lac, Minnesota	105	4	22	30	37	9	3	-	46.6	11.1
Fort Apache, Arizona	1,261	52	355	395	333	107	14	5	36.4	10.7
Fort Belknap, Montana	372	8	126	58	116	52	7	4	48.2	11.5
Fort Berthold, North Dakota	467	22	95	102	162	70	10	6	53.0	12.1
Fort Bidwell, California	20	1	5	2	7	5	-	-	60.9	12.3
Fort Hall, Idaho	514	54	111	161	112	62	10	4	36.6	10.8
Fort Independence, California	15	5	2	1	4	3	-	-	49.4	11.9
Fort McDermitt, Nevada-Oregon	88	10	25	31	16	6	-	-	24.5	10.1
Fort McDowell, Arizona	89	12	15	22	30	8	1	1	45.0	11.2
Fort Mojave, Arizona-California-Nevada	20	-	4	6	7	3	-	-	50.0	12.0
Fort Peck, Montana	822	31	170	182	268	138	19	13	53.5	12.1
Fort Totten, North Dakota	369	19	115	90	86	54	4	1	39.3	10.8
Fort Yuma, Arizona-California	232	36	45	56	73	21	-	-	40.4	10.7
Gila Bend, Arizona	-	-	-	-	-	-	-	-	-	-
Gila River, Arizona	1,396	100	368	382	388	132	20	5	39.1	10.8
Golden Hill, Connecticut	...	...	...	...	...	...	...	...	...	...
Goshute, Nevada-Utah	39	17	5	8	10	-	-	-	24.4	5.6
Grand Portage, Minnesota	52	2	9	12	21	6	2	-	55.7	12.1
Grindstone Creek Rancheria, California	11	-	5	3	3	-	-	-	29.5	10.9
Hannahville Community, Michigan	32	1	5	9	12	3	-	2	53.4	12.1
Hassanamisco, Massachusetts	...	...	...	...	...	...	...	...	...	...
Havasupai, Arizona	60	5	16	28	10	1	-	-	18.4	9.9
Hoh, Washington	10	-	4	2	4	-	-	-	38.0	10.5
Hollywood, Florida	72	12	4	5	26	23	1	1	70.7	12.6
Hoopa Valley, California	314	9	28	100	120	46	5	6	56.5	12.2
Hoopa Valley Extension, California	94	-	23	35	18	15	2	2	39.3	11.2
Hopi, Arizona	1,394	289	232	260	402	154	43	15	44.0	10.9
Hopland Rancheria, California	-	-	-	-	-	-	-	-	-	-
Hualapai, Arizona	147	3	22	37	59	23	1	2	57.6	12.2
Inaja-Cosmit, California	-	-	-	-	-	-	-	-	-	-
Indian Township, Maine	66	2	25	8	22	7	-	1	45.9	11.0
Iowa, Kansas-Nebraska	3	-	-	-	3	-	-	-	100.0	12.5
Isabella, Michigan	98	8	19	31	30	8	2	-	41.1	10.9

Source: U.S. Bureau of the Census, Subject Reports, PC80-2-1D, Part I, *American Indians, Eskimos, and Aleuts on Identified Reservations and in the Historic Areas of Oklahoma (Excluding Urbanized Areas)*, U.S. Government Printing Office, Washington, D.C., 1986, pp. 209-247. *Notes:* A dash (-) represents zero or a percent which rounds to less than 0.1. Also, a dash (-) is used because the number of supplementary questionnaires for the areas was insufficient to produce reliable estimates. Three dots (...) means not applicable, or that the data are being withheld to avoid disclosure of information for individuals.

★ 275 ★

Years of School Completed by Males 25 Years Old and Older on Reservations, 1980 - II

Data are the latest available.

Identified reservation	Total males, 25 years old and older	Elementary school		High school		College			Percent high school graduates	Median school years completed
		0 to 4 years	5 to 8 years	1 to 3 years	4 years	1 to 3 years	4 years	5 or more years		
Isleta Pueblo, New Mexico	524	32	89	105	198	73	21	6	56.7	12.2
Jackson Rancheria, California	...	...	...	...	...	...	...	...	...	...
Jemez Pueblo, New Mexico	289	23	52	56	113	34	8	2	54.6	12.1
Jicarilla Apache, New Mexico	320	34	30	74	141	38	1	3	56.9	12.2
Kaibab, Arizona	26	6	1	3	11	3	1	-	60.5	12.2
Kalispel, Washington	18	1	2	3	4	8	-	-	66.7	12.8
Kickapoo, Kansas	85	3	26	13	25	17	-	1	50.8	12.0
Kootenai, Idaho	-	-	-	-	-	-	-	-	-	-
Lac Courte Oreilles, Wisconsin	222	11	49	59	75	21	4	3	46.5	11.6
Lac du Flambeau, Wisconsin	210	-	19	90	75	23	2	2	48.4	11.9
Laguna Pueblo, New Mexico	740	43	87	153	324	104	20	10	61.8	12.3
La Jolla, California	27	1	3	7	12	2	2	-	59.1	12.2
L'Anse, Michigan	109	3	33	31	30	12	-	1	39.1	10.9
La Posta, California	...	...	...	...	...	...	...	...	...	...
Las Vegas Colony, Nevada	17	3	5	1	6	2	-	-	46.8	11.6
Laytonville Rancheria, California	24	3	4	10	6	1	-	-	29.2	10.3
Leech Lake, Minnesota	551	31	161	123	180	37	10	8	42.8	10.7
Likely Rancheria, California	-	-	-	-	-	-	-	-	-	-
Lone Pine Rancheria, California	31	1	5	11	9	5	-	-	44.4	11.2
Lookout Rancheria, California	...	...	...	...	...	...	...	...	...	...
Los Coyotes, California	12	-	1	2	7	1	-	-	70.1	12.3
Lovelock Colony, Nevada	26	-	5	4	13	4	-	-	65.6	12.3
Lower Brule, South Dakota	127	8	18	45	33	11	3	7	42.4	11.3
Lower Elwah, Washington	13	-	3	9	1	-	-	-	7.7	9.6
Lower Sioux Community, Minnesota	20	2	5	2	11	-	-	-	53.0	12.1
Lummi, Washington	250	6	47	56	81	41	9	10	56.3	12.2
Makah, Washington	152	5	22	36	61	20	5	3	58.5	12.2
Manchester Rancheria, California	15	1	8	1	2	2	-	-	28.6	8.0
Manzanita, California	...	...	...	...	...	...	...	...	...	...
Maricopa, Arizona	83	14	22	24	17	7	-	-	28.4	9.6
Mattaponi, Virginia	16	3	8	3	2	-	-	-	12.5	9.6
Menominee, Wisconsin	484	5	117	120	178	54	9	1	50.1	12.0
Mesa Grande, California	-	-	-	-	-	-	-	-	-	-
Mescalero Apache, New Mexico	313	22	38	88	138	22	2	3	52.6	12.1
Miccosukee, Florida	51	29	7	6	5	3	-	1	17.6	1.0
Middletown Rancheria, California	13	3	-	2	6	2	-	-	61.5	12.3
Mille Lacs, Minnesota	-	-	-	-	-	-	-	-	-	-
Mississippi Choctaw Reservation	486	120	135	61	94	53	18	4	34.9	8.7
Moapa River, Nevada	39	4	8	11	12	4	-	-	40.6	10.7
Montgomery Creek Rancheria, California	...	...	...	...	...	...	...	...	...	...
Morongo, California	66	2	16	21	17	8	1	-	40.5	10.9
Muckleshoot, Washington	71	1	32	13	20	2	1	1	34.6	9.5
Nambe Pueblo, New Mexico	53	8	3	2	24	15	-	1	75.9	12.6
Navajo, Arizona-New Mexico-Utah	18,436	6,249	3,117	2,399	4,381	1,745	342	204	36.2	8.9
Nez Perce, Idaho	315	11	47	53	108	74	9	12	64.6	12.4
Nisqually, Washington	11	1	4	2	2	1	1	-	39.3	9.9
Nooksack, Washington	-	-	-	-	-	-	-	-	-	-
Northern Cheyenne, Montana	569	32	101	130	196	82	17	10	53.7	12.1
Oil Springs, New York	-	-	-	-	-	-	-	-	-	-
Omaha, Iowa-Nebraska	236	27	72	49	44	44	-	-	37.3	10.5
Oneida, Wisconsin	384	34	109	74	130	30	5	2	43.5	10.8
Onondaga, New York	-	-	-	-	-	-	-	-	-	-
Ontonagon, Michigan	-	-	-	-	-	-	-	-	-	-
Osage, Oklahoma	1,089	33	126	189	404	231	69	37	68.1	12.5

[Continued]

Years of School Completed by Males 25 Years Old and Older on Reservations, 1980 - II
[Continued]

Identified reservation	Total males, 25 years old and older	Elementary school		High school		College			Percent high school graduates	Median school years completed
		0 to 4 years	5 to 8 years	1 to 3 years	4 years	1 to 3 years	4 years	5 or more years		
Ozette, Washington	...	...	...	...	...	...	...	...	...	...
Pala, California	99	1	9	32	34	19	3	1	57.7	12.2
Pamunkey, Virginia	18	2	11	3	-	1	1	-	11.1	8.2
Papago, Arizona	1,495	369	333	252	443	87	8	3	36.2	9.5
Pascua Yaqui, Arizona	92	27	34	11	15	3	1	-	21.5	7.8
Pauma, California	20	1	2	5	7	4	2	-	63.3	12.4
Payson Community of Yavapai-Apache, Arizona	-	-	-	-	-	-	-	-	-	-
Pechanga, California	24	-	5	7	10	1	1	-	50.0	12.0
Penobscot, Maine	83	-	14	15	39	12	2	1	65.0	12.3
Picuris Pueblo, New Mexico	33	-	6	5	16	4	2	-	66.99	12.3
Pine Creek, Michigan	...	...	...	...	...	...	...	...	...	...
Pine Ridge, South Dakota	2,124	95	581	530	578	252	53	36	43.2	11.0
Pleasant Point, Maine	95	4	28	16	36	10	3	-	50.5	12.0
Pojoaque Pueblo, New Mexico	19	2	1	4	4	8	-	-	65.1	12.7
Poospatuck, New York	14	-	3	4	6	1	-	-	46.6	11.6
Port Gamble, Washington	60	-	14	19	19	6	3	-	45.9	11.3
Port Madison, Washington	39	-	4	3	18	12	-	2	80.4	12.7
Potawatomi, Wisconsin	45	1	17	17	9	1	-	-	22.1	9.7
Pottawatomi, Kansas	86	2	22	10	33	17	-	2	59.7	12.3
Prairie Island Community, Minnesota	19	1	5	7	4	2	-	-	31.6	10.2
Puyallup, Washington	140	5	24	30	45	30	3	4	58.2	12.3
Pyramid Lake, Nevada	163	3	18	43	64	26	3	5	60.1	12.3
Quileute, Washington	50	2	10	19	10	8	-	1	36.6	11.1
Quinault, Washington	199	1	39	69	46	39	2	2	45.0	11.7
Ramah Community, New Mexico	206	78	37	26	34	24	4	3	31.9	8.1
Ramona, California	-	-	-	-	-	-	-	-	-	-
Red Cliff, Wisconsin	126	3	37	47	20	20	-	-	31.3	10.6
Red Lake, Minnesota	543	27	137	162	179	31	4	4	40.1	10.7
Reno-Sparks Colony, Nevada	105	3	6	23	46	24	3	1	70.5	12.5
Resighini Rancheria, California	...	...	...	...	...	...	...	...	...	...
Rincon, California	61	4	11	11	19	9	5	1	55.8	12.2
Roaring Creek Rancheria, California	...	...	...	...	...	...	...	...	...	...
Rocky Boy's, Montana	268	27	77	54	68	32	7	2	40.9	10.4
Rosebud, South Dakota	1,038	39	241	241	300	169	27	21	49.8	12.0
Round Valley, California	109	-	22	37	39	8	2	1	45.8	11.6
Rumsey Rancheria, California	...	...	...	...	...	...	...	...	...	...
Sac and Fox, Iowa	100	8	26	27	29	8	2	-	39.1	10.8
Sac and Fox, Kansas-Nebraska	...	...	...	...	...	...	...	...	...	...
St. Croix, Wisconsin	91	13	38	11	22	7	1	-	33.1	8.8
St. Regis Mohawk, New York	444	48	155	82	101	42	10	6	36.0	10.1
Salt River, Arizona	480	19	74	149	161	70	6	1	49.7	12.0
San Carlos, Arizona	1,120	108	254	312	325	103	10	7	39.7	10.8
Sandia Pueblo, New Mexico	53	2	11	8	16	12	2	2	60.5	12.3
Sandy Lake, Minnesota	-	-	-	-	-	-	-	-	-	-
San Felipe Pueblo, New Mexico	300	43	59	70	80	42	5	1	42.7	11.3
San Ildefonso Pueblo, New Mexico	112	5	16	13	47	20	1	9	69.5	12.5
San Juan Pueblo, New Mexico	178	15	21	34	74	24	10	1	61.0	12.3
San Manuel, California	-	-	-	-	-	-	-	-	-	-
San Pasqual, California	26	1	4	7	8	5	-	-	52.1	12.1

[Continued]

★ 275 ★

Years of School Completed by Males 25 Years Old and Older on Reservations, 1980 - II
[Continued]

| Identified reservation | Total males, 25 years old and older | Elementary school | | High school | | College | | | Percent high school graduates | Median school years completed |
		0 to 4 years	5 to 8 years	1 to 3 years	4 years	1 to 3 years	4 years	5 or more years		
Santa Ana Pueblo, New Mexico	104	7	15	26	34	21	1	-	53.8	12.1
Santa Clara Pueblo, New Mexico	405	23	43	56	117	138	20	8	69.8	12.7

Source: U.S. Bureau of the Census, Subject Reports, PC80-2-1D, Part I, *American Indians, Eskimos, and Aleuts on Identified Reservations and in the Historic Areas of Oklahoma (Excluding Urbanized Areas)*, U.S. Government Printing Office, Washington, D.C., 1986, pp. 209-247. *Notes:* A dash (-) represents zero or a percent which rounds to less than 0.1. Also, a dash (-) is used because the number of supplementary questionnaires for the areas was insufficient to produce reliable estimates. Three dots (...) means not applicable, or that the data are being withheld to avoid disclosure of information for individuals.

★ 276 ★

Years of School Completed by Males 25 Years Old and Older on Reservations, 1980 - III

Data are the latest available.

| Identified reservation | Total males, 25 years old and older | Elementary school | | High school | | College | | | Percent high school graduates | Median school years completed |
		0 to 4 years	5 to 8 years	1 to 3 years	4 years	1 to 3 years	4 years	5 or more years		
Santa Rosa Rancheria, California	12	1	3	5	2	1	-	-	26.0	11.2
Santa Rosa, California	...	...	...	...	...	...	...	...	...	...
Santa Ynez, California	24	4	7	9	4	1	-	-	20.0	10.0
Santa Ysabel, California	43	4	6	13	13	4	1	-	44.1	11.5
Santee, Nebraska	83	8	22	23	25	2	1	2	35.9	10.5
Santo Domingo Pueblo, New Mexico	412	58	60	100	155	36	3	-	46.9	11.6
San Xavier, Arizona	167	18	49	31	58	10	-	-	41.1	10.7
Sauk-Suiattle, Washington	-	-	-	-	-	-	-	-	-	-
Sault Ste. Marie, Michigan	-	-	-	-	-	-	-	-	-	-
Schaghticoke, Connecticut	...	...	...	...	...	...	...	...	...	...
Shakopee Community, Minnesota	21	-	6	3	7	4	-	-	55.3	12.2
Sheep Ranch Rancheria, California	...	...	...	...	...	...	...	...	...	...
Sherwood Valley Rancheria, California	...	...	...	...	...	...	...	...	...	...
Shingle Springs Rancheria, California	-	-	-	-	-	-	-	-	-	-
Shinnecock, New York	48	-	8	20	8	7	5	-	42.3	11.3
Shoalwater, Washington	...	...	...	...	...	...	...	...	...	...
Sisseton, North Dakota-South Dakota	486	28	139	113	145	50	9	1	42.3	10.9
Skokomish, Washington	55	4	22	0	14	6	-	-	36.2	9.2
Skull Valley, Utah	-	-	-	-	-	-	-	-	-	-
Soboba, California	51	2	7	17	20	4	-	-	47.4	11.8
Sokaogon Chippewa Community, Wisconsin	25	-	6	4	8	6	-	1	59.9	12.3
Southern Paiute, Utah	28	8	5	8	4	2	1	-	24.4	9.3
Southern Ute, Colorado	172	10	20	35	73	30	2	2	62.7	12.3
Spokane, Washington	248	11	36	62	98	29	4	7	55.9	12.1
Squaxin Island, Washington	5	-	-	2	3	-	-	-	60.0	12.2
Standing Rock, North Dakota-South Dakota	879	19	198	201	299	122	30	10	52.5	12.1
Stewart's Point Rancheria, California	17	-	5	9	3	-	-	-	17.6	10.1
Stockbridge, Wisconsin	131	7	30	29	42	18	3	2	49.6	11.8
Sulphur Bank Rancheria, California	24	3	5	10	5	1	-	-	24.9	11.3
Summit Lake, Nevada	...	...	...	...	...	...	...	...	...	...
Susanville, California	21	-	2	4	8	4	2	-	68.1	12.5
Swinomish, Washington	95	3	25	29	19	15	2	3	40.9	10.7

[Continued]

★ 276 ★

Years of School Completed by Males 25 Years Old and Older on Reservations, 1980 - III
[Continued]

Identified reservation	Total males, 25 years old and older	Elementary school		High school		College			Percent high school graduates	Median school years completed
		0 to 4 years	5 to 8 years	1 to 3 years	4 years	1 to 3 years	4 years	5 or more years		
Sycuan, California	13	3	2	5	2	2	-	-	25.2	10.9
Tama, Georgia	9	1	4	2	1	-	-	-	12.5	8.8
Taos Pueblo, New Mexico	280	45	20	70	96	44	3	2	51.8	12.1
Te-Moak, Nevada	26	4	7	7	6	1	-	-	27.8	9.3
Tesuque Pueblo, New Mexico	53	5	7	5	17	17	2	-	67.1	12.5
Tigua, Texas	54	7	21	17	7	2	-	-	16.7	8.8
Tonawanda, New York	110	5	20	31	39	12	1	1	48.4	11.8
Torres-Martinez, California	-	-	-	-	-	-	-	-	-	-
Trinidad Rancheria, California	14	1	2	5	4	1	-	-	38.7	10.5
Tulalip, Washington	146	3	38	37	41	22	4	-	46.3	11.4
Tule River, California	74	5	18	29	15	5	3	-	30.0	9.9
Tunicabiloxi, Louisiana	...	...	...	...	...	...	...	...	...	...
Tuolumne Rancheria, California	24	1	5	8	9	-	1	-	41.7	11.7
Turtle Mountain, North Dakota	763	91	255	161	135	81	29	11	33.6	9.7
Tuscarora, New York	-	-	-	-	-	-	-	-	-	-
Twenty-Nine Palms, California	-	-	-	-	-	-	-	-	-	-
Uintah and Ouray, Utah	411	35	54	130	124	49	17	3	46.8	11.8
Umatilla, Oregon	193	9	31	42	81	25	2	4	57.8	12.2
Upper Sioux Community, Minnesota	10	-	4	2	-	4	-	-	41.4	9.6
Upper Skagit, Washington	-	-	-	-	-	-	-	-	-	-
Ute Mountain, Colorado-New Mexico	211	51	68	62	26	4	-	-	14.0	8.6
Vermillion Lake, Minnesota	20	-	4	2	8	2	3	-	68.7	12.4
Viejas Rancheria, California	30	4	3	7	11	4	-	-	51.2	12.0
Walker River, Nevada	109	4	23	25	33	16	4	4	52.3	12.1
Wampanoag, Massachusetts	-	-	-	-	-	-	-	-	-	-
Warm Springs, Oregon	375	12	45	75	142	76	14	11	64.8	12.4
Washoe, Nevada	-	-	-	-	-	-	-	-	-	-
Western Pequot, Connecticut	...	...	...	...	...	...	...	...	...	...
White Earth, Minnesota	541	16	166	135	156	55	12	2	41.4	10.6
Wind River, Wyoming	805	26	166	196	274	117	12	14	51.8	12.1
Winnebago, Nebraska	214	9	48	50	66	39	3	-	50.0	12.0
Winnemucca Colony, Nevada	8	1	3	4	-	-	-	-	-	9.0
Wisconsin Winnebago Reservation	56	-	16	19	14	6	-	-	36.6	11.3
Woodfords Community, California	-	-	-	-	-	-	-	-	-	-
XL Ranch, California	...	...	...	...	...	...	...	...	...	...
Yakima, Washington	957	37	162	251	292	167	26	22	53.0	12.1
Yankton, South Dakota	284	26	68	74	87	18	9	2	40.9	11.1
Yavapai, Arizona	11	-	1	3	4	3	-	-	63.6	12.4
Yerington, Nevada	22	3	5	2	11	-	-	-	53.2	12.1
Yomba, Nevada	16	1	5	8	2	-	-	-	12.3	9.7
Zia Pueblo, New Mexico	108	6	22	22	43	8	2	4	53.4	12.1
Zuni Pueblo, New Mexico	1,011	63	219	287	334	86	19	3	43.8	11.2
San Felipe/Santa Ana Joint Area, New Mexico	-	-	-	-	-	-	-	-	-	-
San Felipe/Santo Domingo Joint Area, New Mexico	16	-	-	7	6	2	1	-	57.1	12.2
Other Reservation Lands in Montana	-	-	-	-	-	-	-	-	-	-

Source: U.S. Bureau of the Census, Subject Reports, PC80-2-1D, Part I, *American Indians, Eskimos, and Aleuts on Identified Reservations and in the Historic Areas of Oklahoma (Excluding Urbanized Areas)*, U.S. Government Printing Office, Washington, D.C., 1986, pp. 209-247. *Notes:* A dash (-) represents zero or a percent which rounds to less than 0.1. Also, a dash (-) is used because the number of supplementary questionnaires for the areas was insufficient to produce reliable estimates. Three dots (...) means not applicable, or that the data are being withheld to avoid disclosure of information for individuals.

★ 277 ★

Years of School Completed by Persons 25 Years Old and Older, by Major Tribal Group, 1980: Abenaki-Pamunkey

Data are estimates based on a sample and are the most recent available.

Major Tribal Group	Persons 25 years old and older						Percent of high school graduates	Percent of college graduates
	Total	Elementary: 0 to 8 years	High School		College			
			1 to 3 years	4 years	1 to 3 years	4 or more years		
All American Indians	691,452	169,018	136,872	216,838	115,266	53,456	55.8	7.7
Abenaki (n.e.c)	402	138	38	157	31	38	56.2	9.5
Alabama Coushatta[1]	512	166	77	145	93	31	52.5	6.1
Alaska Native (n.e.c.)	273	41	60	109	34	29	63.0	10.6
Alaskan Athabaskans	4,359	1,593	624	1,408	582	152	49.1	3.5
Aleut and Eskimo	314	64	78	86	59	27	54.8	8.6
Algonquin (n.e.c.)	914	139	141	272	225	137	69.4	15.0
Apache	14,794	3,045	3,774	4,740	2,401	834	53.9	5.6
Arapaho	1,803	326	309	541	533	94	64.8	5.2
Arikara	604	104	112	231	118	39	64.2	6.5
Assiniboine	1,627	328	228	587	387	97	65.8	6.0
Bannock	222	59	53	40	43	27	49.5	12.2
Blackfoot[1]	10,731	1,762	2,234	3,669	2,145	921	62.8	8.6
Brotherton	99	4	19	36	19	21	76.6	21.2
Caddo	762	100	188	240	124	110	62.2	14.4
Cahuilla	562	75	134	203	110	40	62.8	7.1
California tribes (n.e.c.)	293	36	91	86	69	11	56.7	3.8
Canadian and Latin American	3,841	1,071	798	1,076	606	290	51.3	7.6
Catawba	575	165	127	166	83	34	49.2	5.9
Cayuse	73	14	27	16	16	-	43.8	-
Chehalis	103	11	15	38	33	6	74.8	5.8
Chemakuan	120	23	9	61	19	8	73.3	6.7
Chemehuevi	221	15	62	99	33	12	65.2	5.4
Cherokee	125,524	26,757	25,483	39,858	21,863	11,563	58.4	9.2
Cheyenne	3,835	732	789	1,278	759	277	60.3	7.2
Chickahominy	460	99	151	143	48	19	45.7	4.1
Chickasaw	5,590	1,085	983	1,785	1,100	637	63.0	11.4
Chinook	583	124	102	131	143	83	61.2	14.2
Chippewa	30,535	6,731	7,076	10,323	4,782	1,623	54.8	5.3
Chitimacha	119	12	8	74	20	5	83.2	4.2
Choctaw	26,033	5,902	4,752	8,335	4,406	2,638	59.1	10.1
Chumash[1]	674	59	206	221	165	23	60.7	3.4
Clallam	375	65	122	93	64	31	50.1	8.3
Coeur d'Alene	245	31	95	61	45	13	48.6	5.3
Coharie	258	75	56	98	25	4	49.2	1.6
Colorado River	433	104	103	116	92	18	52.2	4.2
Colville	2,344	361	508	802	526	147	62.9	6.3
Comanche	4,257	647	698	1,394	1,017	501	68.4	11.8

[Continued]

★ 277 ★

Years of School Completed by Persons 25 Years Old and Older, by Major Tribal Group, 1980:
Abenaki-Pamunkey
[Continued]

Major Tribal Group	Persons 25 years old and older							
	Total	Elementary: 0 to 8 years	High School		College		Percent of high school graduates	Percent of college graduates
			1 to 3 years	4 years	1 to 3 years	4 or more years		
Coos	49	4	18	21	6	-	55.1	-
Costanoan	237	33	74	79	36	15	54.9	6.3
Cowitz	539	45	148	213	84	49	64.2	9.1
Cree	2,699	603	582	876	400	238	56.1	8.8
Creek	13,837	2,476	2,354	4,635	2,856	1,516	65.1	11.0
Croatan	92	21	14	44	-	13	62.0	14.1
Crow	2,877	534	582	831	619	311	61.2	10.8
Cupeno	143	16	24	67	29	7	72.0	4.9
Delaware	2,810	426	566	846	641	331	64.7	11.8
Diegueno	630	154	170	166	108	32	48.6	5.1
Eastern tribes (n.e.c.)	1,315	459	268	342	143	103	44.7	7.8
Flathead	2,384	435	445	994	424	86	63.1	3.6
Fort Hall	179	52	42	41	39	5	47.5	2.8
Gabrieleno	838	103	140	356	181	58	71.0	6.9
Gros Ventres	856	134	149	312	216	75	68.1	8.5
Haida	667	57	175	282	131	22	65.2	3.3
Haliwa	1,010	378	229	343	50	10	39.9	1.0
Hidatsa	615	103	108	191	167	46	65.7	7.5
Hitchiti	10	-	-	3	7	-	100.0	-
Hoopa	769	73	171	324	139	62	68.3	8.1
Houma	1,080	732	123	182	26	17	20.8	1.6
Iowa	431	87	92	121	84	47	58.5	10.9
Iroquois	19,022	3,826	3,811	6,412	3,266	1,707	59.9	9.0
Kalispel	75	11	11	32	21	-	70.7	-
Karok	788	68	172	308	189	51	69.5	6.5
Kaw	375	50	80	114	121	10	65.3	2.7
Kickapoo	953	192	189	333	180	59	60.0	6.2
Kiowa	2,956	353	591	957	702	353	68.1	11.9
Klamath	778	103	237	309	96	33	56.3	4.2
Konkow	221	60	86	54	21	-	33.9	-
Kootenai	187	27	25	69	62	4	72.2	2.1
Long Island	198	41	28	73	39	17	65.2	8.6
Luiseno	530	55	136	194	129	16	64.0	3.0
Lumbee[2]	12,941	5,211	2,840	2,925	1,003	962	37.8	7.4
Lummi[2]	1,682	522	450	458	182	70	42.2	4.2
Maidu	567	79	204	191	76	17	50.1	3.0
Makah	419	48	106	164	71	30	63.2	7.2
Maliseet	228	63	56	75	16	18	47.8	7.9

[Continued]

★ 277 ★

Years of School Completed by Persons 25 Years Old and Older, by Major Tribal Group, 1980: Abenaki-Pamunkey

[Continued]

Major Tribal Group	Persons 25 years old and older							
	Total	Elementary: 0 to 8 years	High School		College		Percent of high school graduates	Percent of college graduates
			1 to 3 years	4 years	1 to 3 years	4 or more years		
Mandan	418	37	43	139	116	83	80.9	19.9
Mattaponi	69	34	7	22	6	-	40.6	-
Menominee	2,397	495	765	724	328	85	47.4	3.5
Miami	1,039	140	230	402	147	120	64.4	11.5
Miccosukee[1]	23	8	9	-	6	-	26.1	-
Micmac[3]	453	167	95	107	50	34	42.2	7.5
Mission Indians	1,410	275	445	472	171	47	48.9	3.3
Miwok	1,090	204	274	373	186	53	56.1	4.9
Modoc	413	30	50	220	91	22	80.6	5.3
Mohegan	287	85	57	86	28	31	50.5	10.8
Mono	663	104	187	254	118	20	59.1	3.0
Nanticoke	665	148	111	275	77	54	61.1	8.1
Narragansett	991	191	240	334	150	76	56.5	7.7
Navajo	59,615	27,908	7,916	14,446	7,092	2,253	39.9	3.8
Nez Perce[1]	1,069	171	86	407	212	193	76.0	18.1
Nomalaki	86	15	28	19	18	6	50.0	7.0
Northwest tribes (n.e.c.)	172	45	41	57	27	2	50.0	1.2
Omaha	1,275	262	354	442	184	33	51.7	2.6
Oregon Athabaskan	303	38	83	96	59	27	60.1	8.9
Osage	3,736	349	429	1,151	1,073	734	79.2	19.6
Oto	645	72	147	241	141	44	66.0	6.8
Ottawa	2,865	622	695	1,067	338	143	54.0	5.0
Paiute[1]	3,945	700	936	1,579	545	185	58.5	4.7
Pamunkey	195	11	50	61	42	31	68.7	15.9

Source: U.S. Bureau of the Census, *1980 Census of Population, Volume 2, Subject Reports, Characteristics of American Indians, by Tribes, and Selected Areas: 1980*, PC80-2-1C, Section 1: Tables I-II, issued September 1989, U.S. Department of Commerce, U.S. Government Printing Office, Washington, D.C., pp. 203-255. *Notes:* (N.E.C.) stands for not elsewhere classified. A dash (-) represents zero or a percent which rounds to less than 0.1. 1. Reporting and/or processing problems may have affected the data for this tribe. 2. Miscoding of entries of "Lummee," "Lummi," "Lumbee," or "Lumbi" may have affected the data for this tribe. 3. Any entry with the spelling "Micmac" was miscoded to Cheyenne River Sioux.

★ 278 ★

Years of School Completed by Persons 25 Years Old and Older, by Major Tribal Group, 1980: Papago-Yurok

Data are estimates based on a sample and are the most recent available.

Major Tribal Group	Persons 25 years old and older							
	Total	Elementary: 0 to 8 years	High School		College		Percent of high school graduates	Percent of college graduates
			1 to 3 years	4 years	1 to 3 years	4 or more years		
Papago	5,627	2,452	760	1,774	509	132	42.9	2.3
Passamaquoddy	620	246	113	171	74	16	42.1	2.6
Pawnee	1,270	135	191	457	320	167	74.3	13.1
Penobscot	684	112	103	242	141	86	68.6	12.6
Peoria	272	12	82	89	78	11	65.4	4.0
Pequot	227	17	31	90	40	49	79.9	21.6
Pima	4,535	1,120	1,341	1,335	641	98	45.7	2.2
Piscataway	207	90	57	56	4	-	29.0	-
Pit River	496	93	131	162	97	10	54.2	2.0
Pomo	1,230	183	354	453	204	86	58.0	8.7
Ponca	772	113	245	240	148	26	53.6	3.4
Potawatomi	4,759	683	985	1,796	851	444	65.0	9.3
Powhatan	176	27	27	38	27	57	69.3	32.4
Pueblo[1]	17,910	3,990	3,484	6,203	3,076	1,157	58.3	6.5
Puget Sound Salish	2,896	571	760	1,021	410	134	54.0	4.6
Quapaw	452	55	70	179	90	58	72.3	12.8
Quinault	652	136	187	187	118	24	50.5	3.7
Rappahannock	171	58	63	31	7	12	29.2	7.0
Sac and Fox Mesquakie	1,595	226	326	600	292	151	65.4	9.5
Salinan	140	22	37	62	19	-	57.9	-
Schaghticoke	93	8	40	39	-	6	48.4	6.5
Seminole[1]	4,885	983	757	1,644	1,087	414	64.4	8.5
Serrano	91	14	46	8	18	5	34.1	5.5
Shasta	182	33	34	55	41	19	63.2	10.4
Shawnee	2,251	361	350	851	454	235	68.4	10.4
Shinnecock	573	30	118	226	143	56	74.2	9.8
Shoshone	4,397	1,062	1,083	1,308	725	219	51.2	5.0
Siletz	299	27	72	152	39	9	66.9	3.0
Sioux	31,824	6,422	7,324	10,198	5,536	2,344	56.8	7.4
Siuslaw	199	55	49	69	26	-	47.7	-
Spokane	793	187	150	313	106	37	57.5	4.7
Stockbridge	821	167	141	325	132	56	62.5	6.8
Tlingit	4,001	663	751	1,615	771	201	64.7	5.0
Tolowa	168	25	33	43	29	38	65.5	22.6
Tonkawa	108	30	59	13	6	-	17.6	-
Tsimshian	710	85	189	270	135	31	61.4	4.4
Umatilla	424	74	93	165	70	22	60.6	5.2
Ute	2,339	503	619	740	346	131	52.0	5.6
Wailaki[2]	257	47	71	101	32	6	54.1	2.3

[Continued]

★ 278 ★

Years of School Completed by Persons 25 Years Old and Older, by Major Tribal Group, 1980: Papago-Yurok

[Continued]

Major Tribal Group	Persons 25 years old and older							
	Total	Elementary: 0 to 8 years	High School		College		Percent of high school graduates	Percent of college graduates
			1 to 3 years	4 years	1 to 3 years	4 or more years		
Walla-Walla	140	27	34	63	10	6	56.4	4.3
Wampanoag	660	120	109	294	77	60	65.3	9.1
Warm Springs	438	96	90	141	109	2	57.5	.5
Washo	691	233	84	251	100	23	54.1	3.3
Wichita	337	28	90	80	110	29	65.0	8.6
Winnebago	2,095	345	366	781	432	171	66.1	8.2
Wintu	907	106	269	302	193	37	58.7	4.1
Wiyot	115	15	35	46	19	-	56.5	-
Yakima	2,655	537	433	969	567	149	63.5	5.6
Yaqui	2,169	1,034	426	419	210	80	32.7	3.7
Yavapai Apache	40	7	13	-	13	7	50.0	17.5
Yokuts	844	240	231	179	163	31	44.2	3.7
Yuchi	108	15	25	44	24	-	63.0	-
Yuman	2,820	703	670	881	467	99	51.3	3.5
Yurok	1,360	151	280	608	221	100	68.3	7.4
Other specific tribes (n.e.c.)	167	27	33	31	40	36	64.1	21.6
All other specified	71	6	15	10	28	12	70.4	16.9
Tribe not specified	16,565	4,152	3,432	4,886	2,752	1,343	54.2	8.1
Tribe not reported	155,875	38,254	29,842	47,913	26,336	13,530	56.3	8.7

Source: U.S. Bureau of the Census, *1980 Census of Population, Volume 2, Subject Reports, Characteristics of American Indians, by Tribes and Selected Areas: 1980,* PC80-2-1C, Section 1: Tables I-II, issued September 1989, U.S. Department of Commerce, U.S. Government Printing Office, Washington, D.C., pp. 203-255. *Notes:* (N.E.C.) stands for not elsewhere classified. A dash (-) represents zero or a percent which rounds to less than 0.1. 1. Reporting and/or processing problems may have affected the data for this tribe. 2. Any Mohawk entry of "Ganienka" was miscoded to Wailaki.

★ 279 ★

Educational Goals

The percent of eighth graders aspiring to various academic levels is shown, by race/ethnicity, for 1988.

Race/ethnicity	Education levels					
	Won't finish high school	Will finish high school	Vocational trade, business after	Will attend college	Will finish college	Will attend graduate school
Total	1.5	10.5	9.4	13.1	42.8	22.7
American Indian and Native Alaskan	3.2	16.0	13.8	16.5	33.9	16.7
Asian and Pacific Islander	1.5	5.8	4.9	12.1	37.4	38.2

[Continued]

★ 279 ★

Educational Goals
[Continued]

Race/ethnicity	Education levels					
	Won't finish high school	Will finish high school	Vocational trade, business after	Will attend college	Will finish college	Will attend graduate school
Hispanic	2.6	14.8	10.7	17.1	33.2	21.5
Black	1.4	8.2	10.2	16.3	39.4	24.5
White	1.3	10.74	9.2	11.9	45.2	21.9

Source: "Percentage of Eighth Graders Aspiring to Various Education Levels, by Selected Student Characteristics," *A Profile of the American Eighth Grader*, 1990, p. 71. Primary source: U.S. Department of Education, National Center for Education Statistics, "National Education Longitudinal Study of 1988: Base Year Student Survey".

★ 280 ★

High School or Equivalency Completed

Figures indicate responses to the question "Did you receive a high school diploma or pass a high school equivalency exam?" The random sample selected from the United States Indian population in 1981 was representative of age, sex, region and the population size of the counties in which subjects lived.

	Nation		East		West	
	Number	Percent	Number	Percent	Number	Percent
Yes						
High school diploma	1,762	46.8	303	42.1	1,459	47.9
Equivalency test	381	10.1	67	9.3	314	10.3
No	1,622	43.1	349	48.5	1,273	41.8
Subtotal	3,765	98.3	719	97.6	3,046	98.5
Missing cases	65	1.7	18	2.4	47	1.5
Total	3,830	100.0	737	100.0	3,093	100.0

Source: Rodney L. Brod and John M. McQuiston, "American Indian Adult Education and Literacy: The First National Survey," *Journal of American Indian Education*, Vol. 22, No. 2, January 1983, p. 5.

★ 281 ★

High School Program Entry Plans

The percent of eighth graders planning to enroll in various types education programs is shown, by race/ethnicity, for 1988.

Race/ethnicity	High school programs					
	College preparatory Academic	Vocational technical business	General high school program	Specialized program	Other	Don't know
Total	29.2	18.0	14.3	5.4	8.1	25.1
American Indian and Native Alaskan	17.2	22.8	9.6	7.2	8.7	34.6
Asian and Pacific Islander	37.1	17.6	9.7	4.0	6.9	24.6
Hispanic	22.5	22.3	10.6	5.3	10.4	29.0
Black	24.7	25.9	9.7	5.6	10.9	23.1
White	30.9	15.94	16.0	5.5	7.2	24.6

Source: "Percentage of Eighth Graders Planning to Enroll in Various High School Programs by Selected Background Characteristics," *A Profile of the American Eighth Grader*, 1990, p. 66. Primary source: U.S. Department of Education, National Center for Education Statistics, "National Education Longitudinal Study of 1988: Base Year Student Survey".

★ 282 ★

Interval Between High School and College Graduation

Race/ethnicity	Percent							
	Less than or equal to:						More than	
	4 years		5 years		6 years		6 years	
	1977	1986	1977	1986	1977	1986	1977	1986
Total	53.8	45.5	70.9	65.5	77.1	73.0	22.9	27.0
American Indian	[1]	42.4	[1]	58.5	[1]	63.6	[1]	36.4
White, non-Hispanic	55.2	47.1	72.4	67.3	78.2	74.5	21.8	25.5
Black, non-Hispanic	42.3	31.8	58.2	51.6	67.3	61.6	32.7	38.4
Hispanic	31.4	33.5	48.4	51.6	55.7	62.9	44.3	37.1
Asian	48.2	35.4	66.5	57.4	76.9	66.7	23.1	33.3
Other	-	31.9	-	46.1	-	57.8	-	42.2

Source: "Time Between High School Graduation and Award of the Baccalaureate Degree, by Race/ Ethnicity, and Sex: Years of College Graduation 1977 and 1986," *The Condition of Education, 1991, Volume 2: Postsecondary Education*, 1991, p. 30. Primary source: U.S. Department of Education, National Center for Education Statistics, Recent College Graduate surveys. *Notes:* - stands for not available. 1. Too few sample observations for a reliable estimate.

★ 283 ★

Repetition of Grades in School

The percent of eighth graders who reported repeating various grades is shown, by race/ethnicity, for 1988.

Race/ethnicity	Repeated at least one grade[1]	Repeated exactly one grade[2]	Repeated 2 or more grades	Repeat K'drtn	Repeat 1st gr	Repeat 2nd gr	Repeat 3rd gr	Repeat 4th gr	Repeat 5th gr	Repeat 6th gr	Repeat 7th gr	Repeat 8th gr
Total	17.7	87.5	12.5	12.9	25.8	17.1	13.2	9.3	8.6	8.7	11.7	9.4
American Indian and Native Alaskan	28.8	86.8	13.2	16.3	21.3	19.1	9.8	17.4	13.8	6.7	15.1	12.1
Asian and Pacific Islander	11.5	92.6	7.4	17.2	19.8	22.7	12.7	7.5	8.5	5.8	4.1	13.0
Hispanic	22.6	84.8	15.2	9.1	25.4	14.2	18.1	13.3	10.6	10.7	10.8	10.9
Black	26.1	86.3	13.7	5.1	20.7	18.5	15.0	11.7	12.2	11.6	12.4	10.1
White	15.6	88.5	11.5	15.8	27.7	16.5	11.6	7.4	6.9	7.6	11.6	8.6

Source: "Percentage of Eighth Graders Who Report Repeating One or More Grades in School, by Year of Birth and Selected Background Characteristics," *A Profile of the American Eighth Grader*, 1990, p. 9. Primary source: U.S. Department of Education, National Center for Education Statistics, "National Education Longitudinal Study of 1988: Base Year Student survey". *Notes:* 1. Column one was calculated as the percentage of all children (entire population). 2. Columns 2-12 were calculated as percentages of children who repeated at least one grade (18% of population), and are not based on all children.

★ 284 ★

Risk Factors Among Eighth Graders

Percentage of students at risk is shown for each race/ethnicity in 1988.

Race/ethnicity	Risk factors						Percent with factors[1]			
	Parent is single	Parents have no high school diploma	Limited English proficiency	Income less than $15,000	Sibling has dropped out of school	Home alone more than 3 hours per day	Zero	One	Two	Three or more
Total	22.3	10.5	2.3	21.3	10.0	13.6	53.4	25.6	13.7	7.3
American Indian	31.1	13.4	8.6	40.1	15.1	18.6	31.4	32.3	22.2	14.1
White	17.7	6.2	0.8	14.1	8.8	12.0	61.5	24.2	10.1	4.2
Black	46.5	15.8	1.6	47.0	13.0	19.5	27.9	28.5	26.2	17.4
Hispanic[2]	23.4	33.4	8.8	37.5	16.0	16.3	30.5	30.8	22.5	16.2
Asian/Pacific Islander	14.2	8.8	7.1	17.8	6.1	15.9	57.9	26.0	10.1	6.2

Source: "Percentage of Eighth Graders With Various Risk Factors, by Race/Ethnicity: 1988," *The Condition of Education, 1991, Volume 1, Elementary and Secondary Education*, 1991, p. 74. Primary source: U.S. Department of Education, National Center for Education Statistics, National Educational Longitudinal Study of 1988, base year survey; *A Profile of the American Eighth Grader*, 1990. *Notes:* 1. Individuals who did not respond to any one of the six risk factors were excluded. Complete data were available for 92 percent of the sample. 2. Hispanics may be of any race.

School Enrollment

★ 285 ★

School Enrollment of Persons 3 to 34 Years Old on Identified Reservations, 1980 - I

Data are the latest available.

Identified reservation	Persons 3 to 34 years old					Persons 16 to 19 years old -- percent not enrolled in school, not high school graduates	Persons 25 years and over	
	All persons	Percent enrolled in school					Percent completed less than 5 years of school	Percent high school graduates
		Total	5 to 19 years		20 to 34 years old			
			Total	Bureau of indian affairs or tribal school				
Total persons	219,396	54.9	49.3	24.4	2.6	27.1	16.2	43.2
Acoma Pueblo, New Mexico	1,411	44.9	39.6	42.9	1.6	48.3	9.0	53.0
Valencia County	1,411	44.9	39.6	42.9	1.6	48.3	9.0	53.0
Agua Caliente Reservation, California	-	-	-	-	-	-	-	-
Riverside County	-	-	-	-	-	-	-	-
Alabama-Coushatta Reservation, Texas	293	54.4	49.5	3.3	1.1	19.5	7.1	52.2
Polk County	293	54.4	49.5	3.3	1.1	19.5	71.	52.2
Alamo Reservation, New Mexico	724	42.8	39.2	19.5	1.2	57.9	48.3	20.0
Socorro County	724	42.8	39.2	19.5	1.2	57.9	48.3	20.0
Allegany Reservation, New York	549	60.0	51.0	1.2	3.7	16.7	2.9	56.8
Cattaraugus County	549	60.0	51.0	1.2	3.7	16.7	2.9	56.8
Alturas Rancheria, California	...	...	...	...	...	...	...	...
Modoc County	...	...	...	...	...	...	...	...
Annette Islands Reserve, Alaska	617	52.7	47.0	1.0	2.2	11.8	0.9	59.2
Prince of Wales-Outer Ketchikan Census Area	617	52.7	47.0	1.0	2.2	11.8	0.9	59.2
Augustine Reservation, California	-	-	-	-	-	-	-	-
Riverside County	-	-	-	-	-	-	-	-
Bad River Reservation, Wisconsin	420	62.2	53.3	0.5	3.7	9.8	2.9	51.1
Ashland County	420	62.2	53.3	0.5	3.7	9.8	2.9	51.1
Iron County	-	-	-	-	-	-	-	-
Barona Rancheria, California	146	45.2	37.5	-	-	48.2	2.2	52.5
San Diego County	146	45.2	37.5	-	-	48.2	2.2	52.5
Bay Mills Reservation, Michigan	189	56.4	46.2	2.9	5.5	28.9	-	58.7
Chippewa County	189	56.4	46.2	2.9	5.5	28.9	-	58.7
Benton Paiute Reservation, California	...	...	...	...	...	...	...	...
Mono County	...	...	...	...	...	...	...	...
Berry Creek Rancheria, California	-	-	-	-	-	-	-	-
Butte County	-	-	-	-	-	-	-	-
Big Bend Rancheria, California	...	...	...	...	...	...	...	...
Shasta County	...	...	...	...	...	...	...	...
Big Cypress Reservation, Florida	239	59.0	50.7	67.6	1.8	31.6	46.7	23.8
Hendry County	239	59.0	50.7	67.6	1.8	31.6	46.7	23.8
Big Lagoon Rancheria, California	...	...	...	...	...	...	...	...
Humboldt County	...	...	...	...	...	...	...	...
Big Pine Rancheria, California	189	51.3	46.9	1.3	1.7	9.3	0.9	74.0
Inyo County	189	51.3	46.9	1.3	1.7	9.3	0.9	74.0
Bishop Rancheria, California	492	50.2	43.9	-	1.8	19.4	2.9	56.1
Inyo County	492	50.2	43.9	-	1.8	19.4	2.9	56.1
Blackfeet Reservation, Montana	3,478	54.2	48.2	2.9	2.7	28.6	3.8	49.9
Glacier County	3,129	54.0	47.9	3.2	2.8	27.8	3.5	50.7

[Continued]

517

★ 285 ★

School Enrollment of Persons 3 to 34 Years Old on Identified Reservations, 1980 - I

[Continued]

Identified reservation		Persons 3 to 34 years old				Persons 16 to 19 years old -- percent not enrolled in school, not high school graduates	Persons 25 years and over	
			Percent enrolled in school					
	All persons	Total	5 to 19 years		20 to 34 years old		Percent completed less than 5 years of school	Percent high school graduates
			Total	Bureau of indian affairs or tribal school				
Pondera County	349	55.5	50.4	-	1.4	35.4	6.9	41.4
Bois Forte Reservation (Nett Lake), Minnesota	270	61.1	51.5	4.3	0.7	40.8	4.1	40.5
Koochiching County	42	59.5	50.0	-	2.4	40.0	-	44.8
St. Louis County	228	61.4	51.8	5.1	0.4	40.9	5.0	39.5
Bridgeport Colony, California	31	57.6	53.7	20.2	3.9	28.3	17.0	43.5
Mono County	31	57.6	53.7	20.2	3.9	28.3	17.0	43.5
Brighton Reservation, Florida	205	60.7	49.1	1.1	1.1	29.3	44.4	35.7
Glades County	205	60.7	49.1	1.1	1.1	29.3	44.4	35.7
Burns Reservation, Oregon	97	57.7	47.4	8.7	2.1	33.3	6.8	32.9
Harney County	97	57.7	47.4	8.7	2.1	33.3	6.8	32.9
Cabazon Reservation, California	...	...	...	...	...	...	...	...
Riverside County	...	...	...	...	...	...	...	...
Cachil Dehe Rancheria, California	...	...	...	...	...	...	...	...
Colusa County	...	...	...	...	...	...	...	...
Cahuilla Reservation, California	...	...	...	...	...	...	...	...
Riverside County	...	...	...	...	...	...	...	...
Campo Reservation, California	47	56.4	56.4	-	-	51.0	22.7	28.0
San Diego County	47	56.4	56.4	-	-	51.0	22.7	28.0
Camp Verde Reservation, Arizona	107	58.9	49.5	1.9	3.7	43.8	5.6	40.8
Yavapai County	107	58.9	49.5	1.9	3.7	43.8	5.6	40.8
Canoncito Reservation, New Mexico	682	54.0	49.5	65.7	2.3	21.3	43.6	28.4
Bernalillo County	595	53.9	49.0	66.7	2.4	19.0	42.4	29.7
Sandoval County	-	-	-	-	-	-	-	-
Valencia County	87	54.3	52.9	59.3	1.3	39.5	52.4	19.6
Capitan Grande Reservation, California	-	-	-	-	-	-	-	-
San Diego County	-	-	-	-	-	-	-	-
Carson Colony, Nevada	140	43.1	41.3	-	1.8	8.5	6.8	50.7
Carson City	140	43.1	41.3	-	1.8	8.5	6.8	50.7
Catawba Reservation, South Carolina	644	47.9	42.1	1.3	5.0	26.0	11.5	35.7
York County	644	47.9	42.1	1.3	5.0	26.0	11.5	35.7
Cattaraugus Reservation, New York	1,092	59.4	51.4	1.5	2.5	25.9	2.4	51.7
Cattaragus County	222	58.0	49.9	1.0	2.5	34.4	3.2	47.8
Chautauqua County	...	...	...	...	...	...	...	...
Erie County	864	60.2	52.1	1.6	2.5	23.9	2.2	52.8
Cedarville Rancheria, California	...	...	...	...	...	...	...	...
Modoc County	...	...	...	...	...	...	...	...
Chehalis Reservation, Washington	129	62.8	44.2	3.6	9.7	34.5	4.4	52.7
Grays Harbor County	112	62.8	44.3	4.2	10.2	28.8	5.0	48.1
Thurston County	...	...	...	...	...	...	...	...
Chemehuevi Rerservation, California	...	...	...	...	...	...	...	...
San Bernardino County	...	...	...	...	...	...	...	...
Cheyenne River Reservation, South Dakota	997	57.4	50.0	83.8	3.0	38.8	2.2	40.9
Dewey County	496	57.2	50.6	80.0	2.3	32.2	1.8	49.2
Ziebach County	501	57.7	49.5	87.6	3.7	45.0	2.5	32.8
Chitimacha Reservation, Louisiana	114	53.6	51.4	50.8	2.2	49.7	23.8	36.7

[Continued]

★ 285 ★

School Enrollment of Persons 3 to 34 Years Old on Identified Reservations, 1980 - I
[Continued]

Identified reservation	Persons 3 to 34 years old					Persons 16 to 19 years old -- percent not enrolled in school, not high school graduates	Persons 25 years and over	
	All persons	Total	Percent enrolled in school				Percent completed less than 5 years of school	Percent high school graduates
			5 to 19 years		20 to 34 years old			
			Total	Bureau of indian affairs or tribal school				
St. Mary Parish	114	53.6	51.4	50.8	2.2	49.7	23.8	36.7
Cochiti Pueblo, New Mexico	362	67.0	58.0	14.8	3.2	8.8	6.9	63.3
Sandoval County	362	67.0	58.0	14.8	3.2	8.8	6.9	63.3
Cocopah Reservation, Arizona	236	55.1	47.8	10.7	3.8	33.3	40.9	18.1
Yuma County	236	55.1	47.8	10.7	3.8	33.3	40.9	18.1
Coeur d'Alene Reservation, Idaho	363	59.0	52.7	42.6	2.7	23.1	4.2	57.0
Benewah County	275	55.7	49.5	48.0	2.9	29.4	2.4	63.3
Kootenai County	88	69.3	62.7	29.3	2.2	-	8.5	42.4
Cold Springs Rancheria, California	36	48.5	48.5	-	-	23.1	14.0	15.2
Fresno County	36	48.5	48.5	-	-	23.1	14.0	15.2
Colorado River Reservation, Arizona-California	1,246	54.1	47.3	4.8	2.8	30.2	4.2	52.4
Arizona	1,230	54.0	47.1	4.9	2.8	30.2	4.3	52.0
Yuma County	1,230	54.0	47.1	4.9	2.8	30.2	4.3	52.0
California	...	...	...	...	...	...	...	...
Riverside and San Bernardino Counties	...	...	...	...	...	...	...	...
Colville Reservation, Washington	2,298	52.2	46.4	9.2	3.5	28.9	3.7	56.2
Ferry County	547	53.6	48.4	5.7	1.5	18.3	3.3	51.4
Okanogan County	1,751	51.8	45.7	10.3	4.1	32.8	3.8	57.9
Cortina Rancheria, California	...	...	...	...	...	...	...	...
Colusa County	...	...	...	...	...	...	...	...
Coushatta Reservation, Louisiana	...	...	...	...	...	...	...	...
Allen Parish	...	...	...	...	...	...	...	...
Coyote Valley Rancheria, California	-	-	-	-	-	-	-	-
Mendocino County	-	-	-	-	-	-	-	-
Crow Reservation, Montana	2,580	54.9	47.8	5.0	3.4	24.1	2.5	52.1
Big Horn County	2,504	54.5	47.2	4.9	3.5	25.0	2.5	51.6
Yellowstone County	76	67.5	67.5	8.2	-	-	-	70.8
Crow Creek Reservation, South Dakota	997	56.5	51.2	54.4	1.0	28.1	1.4	43.4
Buffalo County	835	54.3	50.2	60.2	0.7	30.0	1.4	45.8
Hughes County	118	67.5	55.2	18.9	2.1	-	2.1	25.1
Hyde County	44	68.3	59.8	50.2	3.2	36.9	-	50.0
Cuyapaipe Reservation, California	...	...	...	...	...	...	...	...
San Diego County	...	...	...	...	...	...	...	...
Deer Creek Reservation, Minnesota	...	...	...	...	...	...	...	...
Itasca County	...	...	...	...	...	...	...	...
Dresslerville Colony, Nevada	89	52.4	43.6	6.9	-	33.0	8.9	77.0
Douglas County	89	52.4	43.6	6.9	-	33.0	8.9	77.0
Dry Creek Rancheria, California	28	57.1	50.0	7.1	3.6	57.1	10.5	26.3
Sonoma County	28	57.1	50.0	7.1	3.6	57.1	10.5	26.3
Duck Valley Reservation, Idaho-Nevada	563	60.1	54.3	2.3	2.0	9.2	8.9	47.1
Idaho	121	63.9	58.2	3.5	1.2	28.3	20.2	27.7
Owyhee County	121	63.9	58.2	3.5	1.2	28.3	20.2	27.7
Nevada	442	59.0	53.2	1.9	2.3	3.7	6.4	51.4
Elko County	442	59.0	53.2	1.9	2.3	3.7	6.4	51.4
Duckwater Reservation, Nevada	64	54.0	41.3	57.7	1.6	-	14.9	40.4

[Continued]

★ 285 ★

School Enrollment of Persons 3 to 34 Years Old on Identified Reservations, 1980 - I
[Continued]

Identified reservation	Persons 3 to 34 years old					Persons 16 to 19 years old -- percent not enrolled in school, not high school graduates	Persons 25 years and over	
	All persons	Percent enrolled in school					Percent completed less than 5 years of school	Percent high school graduates
		Total	5 to 19 years		20 to 34 years old			
			Total	Bureau of indian affairs or tribal school				
Nye County	64	54.0	41.3	57.7	1.6	-	14.9	40.4
Eastern Cherokee Reservation, North Carolina	2,958	53.8	46.9	73.1	3.1	35.1	7.6	43.2
Cherokee County	33	53.9	44.5	-	9.4	25.4	1.9	34.9
Graham County	215	52.2	47.5	-	3.7	57.1	13.4	21.6
Haywood County	-	-	-	-	-	-	-	-
Jackson County	1,319	55.7	47.1	77.3	3.7	35.5	7.7	44.1
Swain County	1,392	52.4	46.6	82.1	2.3	32.0	7.0	45.9
Eastern Pequot Reservation, Connecticut	...	...	...	...	...	...	...	...
New London County	...	...	...	...	...	...	...	...
Ely Colony, Nevada	35	56.2	56.2	6.2	-	100.0	10.6	63.6
White Pine County	35	56.2	56.2	6.2	-	100.0	10.6	63.6
Enterprise Rancheria, California	...	...	...	...	...	...	...	...
Butte County	...	...	...	...	...	...	...	...
Fallon Colony, Nevada	24	57.1	57.1	-	-	59.2	19.8	43.4
Churchill County	24	57.1	57.1	-	-	59.2	19.8	43.4
Fallon Reservation, Nevada	156	66.4	57.2	1.4	5.1	5.8	5.7	63.5
Churchill County	156	66.4	57.2	1.4	5.1	5.8	5.7	63.5
Flandreau Reservation, South Dakota	112	57.7	48.7	15.0	4.5	29.8	3.2	77.6
Moody County	112	57.7	48.7	15.0	4.5	29.8	3.2	77.6
Flathead Reservation, Montana	2,361	49.7	45.7	3.8	2.7	25.2	4.4	57.0
Flathead County	...	...	...	...	...	...	...	...
Lake County	1,968	49.1	45.2	2.7	2.6	25.9	4.2	57.3
Missoula County	181	60.5	54.9	8.2	4.5	15.4	6.4	52.0
Sanders County	210	46.2	43.3	9.9	2.4	27.6	4.4	58.9
Fond du Lac Reservation, Minnesota	318	58.7	51.8	2.9	3.3	19.1	2.6	49.8
Carlton County	261	63.3	54.9	3.3	4.0	15.6	2.2	48.7
St. Louis County	57	38.0	38.0	-	-	34.3	5.6	57.1
Fort Apache Reservation, Arizona	4,702	54.7	49.9	15.5	1.8	29.1	4.5	34.1
Apache County	77	54.8	43.0	-	4.1	18.8	16.8	41.3
Gila County	826	54.5	50.2	12.3	2.2	30.7	3.0	31.6
Navajo County	3,799	54.8	49.9	16.5	1.6	29.0	4.6	34.5
Fort Belknap Reservation, Montana	1,255	56.2	48.7	4.4	3.9	22.3	2.6	53.1
Blaine County	1,158	56.5	48.7	4.7	4.0	22.7	2.7	53.2
Phillips County	97	52.7	49.4	-	3.3	18.0	1.6	52.4
Fort Berthold Reservation, North Dakota	1,726	57.0	50.9	6.5	3.1	25.9	4.6	53.3
Dunn County	271	55.2	48.9	3.4	2.9	9.4	7.3	47.7
McKenzie County	566	60.3	53.9	2.0	4.2	26.8	5.8	55.0
McLean County	280	57.5	50.3	18.7	1.2	22.9	1.3	62.2
Mercer County	35	48.6	45.5	13.6	-	-	3.4	39.7
Mountrail County	574	54.9	49.3	6.4	3.4	34.1	4.0	51.2
Ward County	-	-	-	-	-	-	-	-

Source: U.S. Bureau of the Census, Subject Reports, PC80-2-1D, Part 1, *American Indians, Eskimos, and Aleuts on Identified Reservations and in the Historic Areas of Oklahoma (Excluding Urbanized Areas),* U.S. Government Printing Office, Washington, D.C., 1986, pp. 50-58. *Notes:* A dash "(-)" represents zero or a percent which rounds to less than 0.1. Also, a dash "(-)" is used because the number of supplementary questionnaires for the reservations was insufficient to produce reliable estimates. Three dots "..." means not applicable, or that the data are being withheld to avoid disclosure of information for individuals.

★ 286 ★

School Enrollment of Persons 3 to 34 Years Old on Identified Reservations, 1980 - II

Data are the latest available.

Identified reservation	Persons 1 year and over						
	Total	Always lived on this reservation	Did not always live on this reservation				
			Total		Percent moved onto reservation in--		
			Number	Percent	1979 or 1980	1975 to 1978	1974 or earlier
Total persons	326,430	226,391	75,363	23.1	6.2	6.6	10.3
Acoma Pueblo, New Mexico	2,203	1,985	164	7.4	1.4	2.8	3.3
Valencia County	2,203	1,985	164	7.4	1.4	2.8	3.3
Agua Caliente Reservation, California	-	-	-	-	-	-	-
Riverside County	-	-	-	-	-	-	-
Alabama-Coushatta Reservation, Texas	490	365	118	24.0	1.2	7.6	15.2
Polk County	490	365	118	24.0	1.2	7.6	15.2
Alamo Reservation, New Mexico	1,027	587	35	3.4	1.4	1.2	0.9
Socorro County	1,027	587	35	3.4	1.4	1.2	0.9
Allegany Reservation, New York	907	567	286	31.5	9.5	9.4	12.5
Cattaraugus County	907	567	286	31.5	9.5	9.4	12.5
Alturas Rancheria, California	...	...	...	...	...	...	...
Modoc County	...	...	...	...	...	...	...
Annette Islands Reserve, Alaska	922	662	199	21.6	2.8	5.2	13.6
Prince of Wales-Outer Ketchikan Census Area	922	662	199	21.6	2.8	5.2	13.6
Augustine Reservation, California	-	-	-	-	-	-	-
Riverside County	-	-	-	-	-	-	-
Bad River Reservation, Wisconsin	684	224	455	66.6	13.2	29.1	24.3
Ashland County	684	224	455	66.6	13.2	29.1	24.3
Iron County	-	-	-	-	-	-	-
Barona Rancheria, California	213	135	77	36.3	8.3	17.5	10.4
San Diego County	213	135	77	36.3	8.3	17.5	10.4
Bay Mills Reservation, Michigan	269	160	108	39.9	5.2	13.3	21.4
Chippewa County	269	160	108	39.9	5.2	13.3	21.4
Benton Paiute Reservation, California	...	...	...	...	...	...	...
Mono County	...	...	...	...	...	...	...
Berry Creek Rancheria, California	-	-	-	-	-	-	-
Butte County	-	-	-	-	-	-	-
Big Bend Rancheria, California	...	...	...	...	...	...	...
Shasta County	...	...	...	...	...	...	...
Big Cypress Reservation, Florida	343	249	94	27.2	1.8	8.0	17.5
Hendry County	343	249	94	27.2	1.8	8.0	17.5
Big Lagoon Rancheria, California	...	...	...	...	...	...	...
Humboldt County	...	...	...	...	...	...	...
Big Pine Rancheria, California	262	31	220	84.2	42.6	9.5	32.1
Inyo County	262	31	220	84.2	42.6	9.5	32.1
Bishop Rancheria, California	757	338	395	52.2	12.7	14.7	24.8
Inyo County	757	338	395	52.2	12.7	14.7	24.8
Blackfeet Reservation, Montana	5,358	4,029	902	16.8	4.1	5.5	7.2
Glacier County	4,847	3,622	859	17.7	4.4	5.7	7.7
Pondera County	511	407	43	8.3	1.4	4.0	2.9
Bois Forte Reservation (Nett Lake), Minnesota	393	270	117	29.8	14.0	3.6	12.2
Koochiching County	62	46	16	25.8	16.1	-	9.7
St. Louis County	331	224	101	30.5	13.6	4.2	12.7
Bridgeport Colony, California	50	1	49	97.5	97.5	-	-
Mono County	50	1	49	97.5	97.5	-	-
Brighton Reservation, Florida	325	239	66	20.4	1.7	9.2	9.5
Glades County	325	239	66	20.4	1.7	9.2	9.5

[Continued]

School Enrollment of Persons 3 to 34 Years Old on Identified Reservations, 1980 - II
[Continued]

Identified reservation	Total	Always lived on this reservation	Did not always live on this reservation		Percent moved onto reservation in--		
			Total		1979 or 1980	1975 to 1978	1974 or earlier
			Number	Percent			
Burns Reservation, Oregon	158	78	80	50.6	15.8	21.5	13.3
Harney County	158	78	80	50.6	15.8	21.5	13.3
Cabazon Reservation, California	...	...	...	...	...	...	...
Riverside County	...	...	...	...	...	...	...
Cachil Dehe Rancheria, California	...	...	...	...	...	...	...
Colusa County	...	...	...	...	...	...	...
Cahuilla Reservation, California	...	...	...	...	...	...	...
Riverside County	...	...	...	...	...	...	...
Campo Reservation, California	83	36	45	53.9	10.3	17.1	26.5
San Diego County	83	36	45	53.9	10.3	17.1	26.5
Camp Verde Reservation, Arizona	173	97	64	37.0	1.7	25.4	9.8
Yavapai County	173	97	64	37.0	1.7	25.4	9.8
Canoncito Reservation, New Mexico	935	823	99	10.6	4.5	2.4	3.6
Bernalillo County	811	716	86	10.6	4.7	2.6	3.3
Sandoval County	-	-	-	-	-	-	-
Valencia County	124	107	13	10.5	3.3	1.1	6.1
Capitan Grande Reservation, California	-	-	-	-	-	-	-
San Diego County	-	-	-	-	-	-	-
Carson Colony, Nevada	211	67	144	68.3	9.4	24.9	34.0
Carson City	211	67	144	68.3	9.4	24.9	34.0
Catawba Reservation, South Carolina	966	80	311	32.2	26.6	3.3	2.4
York County	966	80	311	32.2	26.6	3.3	2.4
Cattaraugus Reservation, New York	1,806	1,193	455	25.2	3.6	8.0	13.5
Cattaragus County	331	270	43	13.1	3.0	6.0	4.1
Chautauqua County	...	...	...	...	...	...	...
Erie County	1,465	916	412	28.1	3.8	8.5	15.8
Cedarville Rancheria, California	...	...	...	...	...	...	...
Modoc County	...	...	...	...	...	...	...
Chehalis Reservation, Washington	192	82	109	56.6	8.7	27.4	20.5
Grays Harbor County	170	75	94	55.4	8.0	26.1	21.3
Thurston County	...	...	...	...	...	...	...
Chemehuevi Rerservation, California	...	...	...	...	...	...	...
San Bernardino County	...	...	...	...	...	...	...
Cheyenne River Reservation, South Dakota	1,463	1,186	256	17.5	8.0	3.8	5.7
Dewey County	715	548	165	23.1	10.6	6.9	5.7
Ziebach County	748	637	90	12.1	5.6	0.8	5.7
Chitimacha Reservation, Louisiana	176	107	55	31.4	6.5	8.1	16.8
St. Mary Parish	176	107	55	31.4	6.5	8.1	16.8
Cochiti Pueblo, New Mexico	596	444	152	25.5	3.3	10.0	12.2
Sandoval County	596	444	152	25.5	3.3	10.0	12.2
Cocopah Reservation, Arizona	342	179	153	44.8	7.7	9.4	27.7
Yuma County	342	179	153	44.8	7.7	9.4	27.7
Coeur d'Alene Reservation, Idaho	549	207	296	54.0	13.7	16.1	24.2
Benewah County	402	149	221	54.9	12.7	19.8	22.4
Kootenai County	147	58	75	51.5	16.4	5.9	29.1
Cold Springs Rancheria, California	62	45	16	25.8	1.5	12.2	12.2
Fresno County	62	45	16	25.8	1.5	12.2	12.2
Colorado River Reservation, Arizona-California	1,885	847	736	39.0	12.7	7.6	18.7

[Continued]

★ 286 ★

School Enrollment of Persons 3 to 34 Years Old on Identified Reservations, 1980 - II
[Continued]

Identified reservation		Persons 1 year and over					
	Total	Always lived on this reservation	Did not always live on this reservation				
			Total		Percent moved onto reservation in--		
			Number	Percent	1979 or 1980	1975 to 1978	1974 or earlier
Arizona	1,858	837	719	38.7	12.6	7.2	18.9
Yuma County	1,858	837	719	38.7	12.6	7.2	18.9
California	...	...	...	...	...	...	...
Riverside and San Bernardino Counties	...	...	...	...	...	...	...
Colville Reservation, Washington	3,481	1,723	1,714	49.2	12.7	15.2	21.4
Ferry County	884	454	423	47.9	7.1	16.2	24.5
Okanogan County	2,597	1,269	1,291	49.7	14.6	14.9	20.3
Cortina Rancheria, California	...	...	...	...	...	...	...
Colusa County	...	...	...	...	...	...	...
Coushatta Reservation, Louisiana	...	...	...	...	...	...	...
Allen Parish	...	...	...	...	...	...	...
Coyote Valley Rancheria, California	-	-	-	-	-	-	-
Mendocino County	-	-	-	-	-	-	-
Crow Reservation, Montana	3,833	2,706	996	26.0	8.9	6.5	10.6
Big Horn County	3,721	2,656	934	25.1	8.4	6.4	10.4
Yellowstone County	112	50	62	55.3	26.7	10.5	18.1
Crow Creek Reservation, South Dakota	1,449	981	414	28.6	7.4	7.6	13.5
Buffalo County	1,222	852	317	25.9	8.2	6.2	11.4
Hughes County	165	90	75	45.3	4.2	12.0	29.1
Hyde County	61	39	22	36.1	-	23.3	12.8
Cuyapaipe Reservation, California	...	...	...	...	...	...	...
San Diego County	...	...	...	...	...	...	...
Deer Creek Reservation, Minnesota	...	...	...	...	...	...	...
Itasca County	...	...	...	...	...	...	...
Dresslerville Colony, Nevada	122	82	39	32.3	9.0	7.7	15.6
Douglas County	122	82	39	32.3	9.0	7.7	15.6
Dry Creek Rancheria, California	43	19	24	55.8	27.9	2.3	25.6
Sonoma County	43	19	24	55.8	27.9	2.3	25.6
Duck Valley Reservation, Idaho-Nevada	909	604	283	31.1	8.6	7.5	14.9
Idaho	184	120	45	24.5	3.6	2.9	18.1
Owyhee County	184	120	45	24.5	3.6	2.9	18.1
Nevada	725	484	238	32.7	9.9	8.7	14.1
Elko County	725	484	238	32.7	9.9	8.7	14.1
Duckwater Reservation, Nevada	102	33	69	67.3	23.8	15.8	27.7
Nye County	102	33	69	67.3	23.8	15.8	27.7
Eastern Cherokee Reservation, North Carolina	4,726	3,718	960	20.3	3.1	5.4	11.8
Cherokee County	76	27	45	58.8	3.8	41.8	13.2
Graham County	338	282	55	16.2	1.4	6.2	8.6
Haywood County	-	-	-	-	-	-	-
Jackson County	2,083	1,667	403	19.4	2.4	5.8	11.2
Swain County	2,229	1,741	457	20.5	3.9	3.8	12.8
Eastern Pequot Reservation, Connecticut	...	...	...	...	...	...	...
New London County	...	...	...	...	...	...	...
Ely Colony, Nevada	59	3	56	95.6	4.5	80.3	10.8
White Pine County	59	3	56	95.6	4.5	80.3	10.8
Enterprise Rancheria, California	...	...	...	...	...	...	...
Butte County	...	...	...	...	...	...	...
Fallon Colony, Nevada	46	14	32	70.6	21.1	-	49.5

[Continued]

★ 286 ★

School Enrollment of Persons 3 to 34 Years Old on Identified Reservations, 1980 - II

[Continued]

Identified reservation	Persons 1 year and over						
	Total	Always lived on this reservation	Did not always live on this reservation				
			Total		Percent moved onto reservation in--		
			Number	Percent	1979 or 1980	1975 to 1978	1974 or earlier
Churchill County	46	14	32	70.6	21.1	-	49.5
Fallon Reservation, Nevada	257	93	155	60.5	17.0	12.6	30.9
Churchill County	257	93	155	60.5	17.0	12.6	30.9
Flandreau Reservation, South Dakota	158	38	120	75.8	32.6	23.1	20.1
Moody County	158	38	120	75.8	32.6	23.1	20.1
Flathead Reservation, Montana	3,528	1,462	1,484	42.1	9.9	11.6	20.5
Flathead County	...	...	...	...	...	...	...
Lake County	2,892	1,202	1,183	40.9	9.6	11.3	20.0
Missoula County	285	87	142	49.7	13.9	12.2	23.6
Sanders County	347	170	158	45.5	9.2	13.8	22.5
Fond du Lac Reservation, Minnesota	493	286	181	36.6	7.9	12.9	15.8
Carlton County	417	238	152	36.6	8.2	12.7	15.7
St. Louis County	76	48	28	36.9	6.2	14.1	16.6
Fort Apache Reservation, Arizona	6,653	5,560	651	9.8	4.1	2.4	3.3
Apache County	107	51	50	46.7	4.8	16.6	25.3
Gila County	1,191	1,036	68	5.7	3.0	0.4	2.4
Navajo County	5,354	4,473	533	10.0	4.3	2.5	3.1
Fort Belknap Reservation, Montana	1,820	1,026	586	32.2	6.6	13.6	12.0
Blaine County	1,664	931	549	33.0	6.6	14.6	11.7
Phillips County	156	95	37	23.8	5.7	2.6	15.5
Fort Berthold Reservation, North Dakota	2,542	1,602	798	31.4	10.9	9.6	10.8
Dunn County	413	250	147	35.6	10.2	7.2	18.1
McKenzie County	804	557	245	30.5	10.2	11.8	8.5
McLean County	421	308	106	25.1	8.0	5.3	11.8
Mercer County	51	28	23	44.6	27.8	14.5	2.3
Mountrail County	854	459	278	32.6	12.5	10.6	9.5
Ward County	-	-	-	-	-	-	-

Source: U.S. Bureau of the Census, Subject Reports, PC80-2-1D, Part 1, *American Indians, Eskimos, and Aleuts on Identified Reservations and in the Historic Areas of Oklahoma (Excluding Urbanized Areas)*, U.S. Government Printing Office, Washington, D.C., 1986, pp. 50-58. *Notes:* A dash "(-)" represents zero or a percent which rounds to less than 0.1. Also, a dash "(-)" is used because the number of supplementary questionnaires for the reservations was insufficient to produce reliable estimates. Three dots "..." means not applicable, or that the data are being withheld to avoid disclosure of information for individuals.

★ 287 ★

School Enrollment of Persons 3 to 34 Years Old on Identified Reservations, 1980 - III

Data are the latest available.

Identified reservation	Persons 3 to 34 years old					Persons 16 to 19 years old -- percent not enrolled in school, not high school graduates	Persons 25 years and over	
	All persons	Percent enrolled in school					Percent completed less than 5 years of school	Percent high school graduates
		Total	5 to 19 years		20 to 34 years old			
			Total	Bureau of indian affairs or tribal school				
Fort Bidwell Reservation, California	52	58.4	48.3	4.1	6.0	25.0	2.7	62.5
Modoc County	52	58.4	48.3	4.1	6.0	25.0	2.7	62.5
Fort Hall Reservation, Idaho	1,583	53.7	49.1	7.3	1.9	26.0	10.4	39.5
Bannock County	450	51.5	46.8	10.5	2.0	27.2	10.7	37.8
Bingham County	1,032	54.8	50.2	6.5	1.9	25.9	9.1	40.5
Caribou County	-	-	-	-	-	-	-	-
Power County	101	51.5	48.1	2.2	2.3	22.9	21.9	36.4
Fort Independence Reservation, California	13	42.3	42.3	-	-	-	24.3	51.1
Inyo County	13	42.3	42.3	-	-	-	24.3	51.1
Fort McDermitt Reservation, Nevada-Oregon	318	58.4	51.7	2.7	1.8	18.8	6.9	28.9
Nevada	318	58.4	51.7	2.7	1.8	18.8	6.9	28.9
Humboldt County	318	58.4	51.7	2.7	1.8	18.8	6.9	28.9
Oregon	-	-	-	-	-	-	-	-
Malheur County	-	-	-	-	-	-	-	-
Fort McDowell Reservation, Arizona	215	41.3	37.5	19.7	1.1	42.9	11.3	48.3
Maricopa County	215	41.3	37.5	19.7	1.1	42.9	11.3	48.3
Fort Mojave Reservation, Arizona-California-Nevada	81	54.3	50.6	9.8	3.7	21.4	-	50.0
Arizona	81	54.3	50.6	9.8	3.7	21.4	-	50.0
Mohave County	81	54.3	50.6	9.8	3.7	21.4	-	50.0
California	-	-	-	-	-	-	-	-
San Bernardino County	-	-	-	-	-	-	-	-
Nevada	-	-	-	-	-	-	-	-
Clark County	-	-	-	-	-	-	-	-
Fort Peck Reservation, Montana	2,823	53.6	47.7	3.3	2.3	34.3	3.2	51.1
Daniels County	-	-	-	-	-	-	-	-
Roosevelt County	2,498	53.1	47.2	3.4	2.4	35.6	3.4	51.2
Sheridan County	-	-	-	-	-	-	-	-
Valley County	325	57.4	51.5	2.6	1.2	25.8	1.2	49.8
Fort Totten Reservation, North Dakota	1,496	58.1	49.9	55.1	3.2	39.8	3.8	38.7
Benson County	1,496	58.1	49.9	55.1	3.2	39.8	3.5	39.2
Eddy County	...	...	...	...	...	...	...	...
Nelson County	-	-	-	-	-	-	-	-
Ramsey County	...	...	...	...	...	...	...	...
Fort Yuma Reservation, Arizona-California	651	54.5	48.1	2.2	1.1	40.3	10.4	42.9
Arizona	67	47.3	43.2	-	-	83.1	39.4	10.3
Yuma County	67	47.3	43.2	-	-	83.1	39.4	10.3
California	584	55.3	48.7	2.4	1.2	37.2	4.7	49.3
Imperial County	584	55.3	48.7	2.4	1.2	37.2	4.7	49.3
Gila Bend Reservation, Arizona	-	-	-	-	-	-	-	-
Maricopa County	-	-	-	-	-	-	-	-
Gila River Reservation, Arizona	4,529	51.1	44.9	19.6	3.2	40.2	5.7	38.3
Maricopa County	1,310	51.1	44.9	22.6	2.6	39.7	5.6	40.2
Pinal County	3,219	51.1	44.9	18.3	3.4	40.4	5.8	37.5
Golden Hill Reservation, Connecticut	...	...	...	...	...	...	...	...
Fairfield County	...	...	...	...	...	...	...	...
Goshute Reservation, Nevada-Utah	46	29.5	29.5	-	-	100.0	48.1	19.3

[Continued]

★ 287 ★

School Enrollment of Persons 3 to 34 Years Old on Identified Reservations, 1980 - III

[Continued]

Identified reservation	All persons	Persons 3 to 34 years old				Persons 16 to 19 years old -- percent not enrolled in school, not high school graduates	Persons 25 years and over	
		Percent enrolled in school						
		Total	5 to 19 years		20 to 34 years old		Percent completed less than 5 years of school	Percent high school graduates
			Total	Bureau of indian affairs or tribal school				
Nevada	...	...	...	...	...	...	...	...
White Pine County	...	...	...	...	...	...	...	...
Utah	31	18.2	18.2	-	-	-	57.9	15.8
Juab and Tooele Counties	31	18.2	18.2	-	-	-	57.9	15.8
Grand Portage Reservation, Minnesota	113	48.5	42.2	-	2.5	34.3	3.3	66.9
Cook County	113	48.5	42.2	-	2.5	34.3	3.3	66.9
Grindstone Creek Rancheria, California	42	54.0	40.6	-	8.3	74.8	4.8	33.2
Glenn County	42	54.0	40.6	-	8.3	74.8	4.8	33.2
Hannahville Community, Michigan	145	55.7	43.6	64.3	-	54.2	2.3	43.6
Menominee County	145	55.7	43.6	64.3	-	54.2	2.3	43.6
Hassanamisco Reservation, Massachusetts	...	...	...	...	...	...	...	...
Worcester County	...	...	...	...	...	...	...	...
Havasupai Reservation, Arizona	173	45.1	40.9	70.9	1.2	41.4	7.0	26.7
Coconino County	173	45.1	40.9	70.9	1.2	41.4	7.0	26.7
Hoh Reservation, Washington	29	38.7	34.4	12.4	-	78.9	-	29.9
Jefferson County	29	38.7	34.4	12.4	-	78.9	-	29.9
Hollywood Reservation, Florida	278	54.0	42.5	12.4	3.8	29.3	20.7	63.5
Broward County	278	54.0	42.5	12.4	3.8	29.3	20.7	63.5
Hoopa Valley Reservation, California	947	53.8	46.1	2.0	3.7	21.2	2.4	56.0
Humboldt County	947	53.8	46.1	2.0	3.7	21.2	2.4	56.0
Hoopa Valley Extension Reservation, California	236	50.7	48.0	-	0.5	20.0	2.1	41.2
Del Norte County	91	51.9	46.2	-	1.3	-	1.3	48.0
Humboldt County	145	50.0	49.2	-	-	28.2	2.6	36.9
Hopi Reservation, Arizona	4,007	57.5	50.2	56.1	3.3	15.1	21.0	41.7
Coconino County	771	62.4	52.7	40.5	4.9	11.9	33.0	32.5
Navajo County	3,237	56.3	49.6	60.0	2.9	16.0	18.1	43.9
Hopland Rancheria, California	-	-	-	-	-	-	-	-
Mendocino County	-	-	-	-	-	-	-	-
Hualapai Reservation, Arizona	557	52.6	42.8	15.4	2.5	15.6	2.1	53.1
Coconino and Mohave Counties	554	52.6	42.7	15.6	2.6	14.8	2.1	53.0
Yavapai County	...	...	...	...	...	...	...	...
Inaja-Cosmit Reservation, California	-	-	-	-	-	-	-	-
San Diego County	-	-	-	-	-	-	-	-
Indian Township Reservation, Maine	223	57.1	53.1	63.4	1.1	45.9	5.2	39.3
Washington County	223	57.1	53.1	63.4	1.1	45.9	5.2	39.3
Iowa Reservation, Kansas-Nebraska	24	36.1	32.0	-	4.1	-	-	41.9
Kansas	...	...	...	...	...	...	...	...
Brown County	...	...	...	...	...	...	...	...
Doniphan County	-	-	-	-	-	-	-	-
Nebraska	...	...	...	...	...	...	...	...
Richardson County	...	...	...	...	...	...	...	...
Isabella Reservation, Michigan	331	50.7	45.3	-	1.6	42.5	4.7	39.5
Isabella County	331	50.7	45.3	-	1.6	42.5	4.7	39.5
Isleta Pueblo, New Mexico	1,402	54.2	48.0	41.9	3.4	12.3	5.2	57.2
Bernalillo County	1,089	53.8	46.3	45.0	3.9	12.2	5.6	55.8
Torrance County	-	-	-	-	-	-	-	-

[Continued]

★ 287 ★

School Enrollment of Persons 3 to 34 Years Old on Identified Reservations, 1980 - III
[Continued]

Identified reservation	Persons 3 to 34 years old					Persons 16 to 19 years old -- percent not enrolled in school, not high school graduates	Persons 25 years and over	
	All persons	Total	Percent enrolled in school				Percent completed less than 5 years of school	Percent high school graduates
			5 to 19 years		20 to 34 years old			
			Total	Bureau of indian affairs or tribal school				
Valencia County	313	55.9	53.5	32.3	1.5	12.7	3.4	62.3
Jackson Rancheria, California	...	...	...	...	...	...	...	...
Amador County	...	...	...	...	...	...	...	...
Jemez Pueblo, New Mexico	977	59.9	52.0	34.2	3.1	16.3	5.8	50.1
Sandoval County	977	59.9	52.0	34.2	3.1	16.3	5.8	50.1
Jicarilla Apache Reservation, New Mexico	1,161	50.1	45.7	7.5	2.1	24.1	9.7	55.5
Rio Arriba and Sandoval Counties	1,161	50.1	45.7	7.5	2.1	24.1	9.7	55.5
Kaibab Reservation, Arizona	63	46.6	41.6	7.8	3.4	24.7	16.1	61.2
Coconino County	-	-	-	-	-	-	-	-
Mohave County	63	46.6	41.6	7.8	3.4	24.7	16.1	61.2
Kalispel Reservation, Washington	73	49.3	45.2	-	-	73.3	11.4	48.6
Pend Oreille County	73	49.3	45.2	-	-	73.3	11.4	48.6
Kickapoo Reservation, Kansas	219	64.5	56.4	-	4.9	8.6	3.8	50.3
Brown County	219	64.5	56.4	-	4.9	8.6	3.8	50.3
Kootenai Reservation, Idaho	-	-	-	-	-	-	-	-
Boundary County	-	-	-	-	-	-	-	-
Lac Courte Oreilles Reservation, Wisconsin	730	60.7	51.1	42.1	3.7	26.3	2.7	50.2
Sawyer County	730	60.7	51.1	42.1	3.7	26.3	2.7	50.2
Lac du Flambeau Reservation, Wisconsin	696	62.2	56.8	1.5	2.2	27.2	0.4	44.3
Iron County	-	-	-	-	-	-	-	-
Oneida County	-	-	-	-	-	-	-	-
Vilas County	696	62.2	56.8	1.5	2.2	27.2	0.4	44.3
Laguna Pueblo, New Mexico	2,164	47.2	41.0	50.1	2.1	31.7	5.1	62.0
Bernalillo and Valencia Counties	2,164	47.2	41.0	50.1	2.1	31.7	5.1	62.0
Sandoval County	-	-	-	-	-	-	-	-
La Jolla Reservation, California	88	66.1	54.9	4.5	2.6	12.4	2.0	56.1
San Diego County	88	66.1	54.9	4.5	2.6	12.4	2.0	56.1
L'Anse Reservation, Michigan	373	63.7	56.0	2.8	5.1	15.3	3.0	42.1
Baraga County	373	63.7	56.0	2.8	5.1	15.3	3.0	42.1
La Posta Reservation, California	...	...	...	...	...	...	...	...
San Diego County	...	...	...	...	...	...	...	...
Las Vegas Colony, Nevada	66	46.2	40.7	-	-	58.8	8.7	25.2
Clark County	66	46.2	40.7	-	-	58.8	8.7	25.2
Laytonville Rancheria, California	68	52.9	51.5	-	1.5	50.0	6.8	29.5
Mendocino County	68	52.9	51.5	-	1.5	50.0	6.8	29.5
Leech Lake Reservation, Minnesota	1,698	59.5	52.4	5.4	2.2	33.2	4.2	49.2
Beltrami County	216	60.1	51.9	16.9	3.4	31.0	4.2	43.3
Cass and Hubbard Counties	1,028	58.9	52.2	4.0	2.0	34.3	3.3	53.8
Itasca County	454	60.6	53.1	3.0	2.0	31.8	6.3	40.1
Likely Rancheria, California	-	-	-	-	-	-	-	-
Modoc County	-	-	-	-	-	-	-	-
Lone Pine Rancheria, California	103	58.6	57.4	-	1.2	14.1	5.2	58.4
Inyo County	103	58.6	57.4	-	1.2	14.1	5.2	58.4
Lookout Rancheria, California	...	...	...	...	...	...	...	...
Modoc County	...	...	...	...	...	...	...	...

[Continued]

★ 287 ★

School Enrollment of Persons 3 to 34 Years Old on Identified Reservations, 1980 - III

[Continued]

Identified reservation	Persons 3 to 34 years old					Persons 16 to 19 years old -- percent not enrolled in school, not high school graduates	Persons 25 years and over	
	All persons	Percent enrolled in school					Percent completed less than 5 years of school	Percent high school graduates
		Total	5 to 19 years		20 to 34 years old			
			Total	Bureau of indian affairs or tribal school				
Los Coyotes Reservation, California	27	38.3	38.3	-	-	-	-	60.2
San Diego County	27	38.3	-	-	-	-	-	60.2
Lovelock Colony, Nevada	64	64.1	64.1	-	-	-	3.6	50.3
Pershing County	64	64.1	64.1	-	-	-	3.6	50.3
Lower Brule Reservation, South Dakota	560	52.8	44.8	63.1	2.3	29.2	3.9	44.9
Lyman County	555	53.3	45.1	63.1	2.3	29.2	4.0	44.3
Stanley County	...	...	...	...	...	...	...	...
Lower Elwah Reservation, Washington	27	55.6	55.6	-	-	100.0	4.3	21.7
Clallam County	27	55.6	55.6	-	-	100.0	4.3	21.7
Lower Sioux Community, Minnesota	36	38.3	38.3	-	-	-	4.3	52.1
Redwood County	36	38.3	38.3	-	-	-	4.3	52.1
Lummi Reservation, Washington	854	59.1	50.5	5.7	5.4	34.1	2.6	54.4
Whatcom County	854	59.1	50.5	5.7	5.4	34.1	2.6	54.4
Makah Reservation, Washington	528	55.3	47.2	2.3	1.4	31.7	3.6	58.0
Clallam County	528	55.3	47.2	2.3	1.4	31.7	3.6	58.0
Manchester Rancheria, California	41	52.6	52.6	-	-	40.8	6.5	28.1
Mendocino County	41	52.6	52.6	-	-	40.8	6.5	28.1
Manzanita Reservation, California	...	...	...	...	...	...	...	...
San Diego County	...	...	...	...	...	...	...	...
Maricopa Reservation, Arizona	250	54.3	43.8	6.0	2.6	33.6	12.8	31.1
Pinal County	250	54.3	43.8	6.0	2.6	33.6	12.8	31.1
Mattaponi Reservation, Virgina	32	53.1	50.0	-	3.1	33.3	14.3	17.1
King William County	32	53.1	50.0	-	3.1	33.3	14.3	17.1
Menominee Reservation, Wisconsin	1,531	56.3	49.7	11.4	1.8	26.3	1.1	48.7
Menominee County	1,531	56.3	49.7	11.4	1.8	26.3	1.1	48.7
Mesa Grande Reservation, California	-	-	-	-	-	-	-	-
San Diego County	-	-	-	-	-	-	-	-

Source: U.S. Bureau of the Census, Subject Reports, PC80-2-1D, Part 1, *American Indians, Eskimos, and Aleuts on Identified Reservations and in the Historic Areas of Oklahoma (Excluding Urbanized Areas)*, U.S. Government Printing Office, Washington, D.C., 1986, pp. 50-58. *Notes:* A dash "(-)" represents zero or a percent which rounds to less than 0.1. Also, a dash "(-)" is used because the number of supplementary questionnaires for the reservations was insufficient to produce reliable estimates. Three dots "..." means not applicable, or that the data are being withheld to avoid disclosure of information for individuals.

School Enrollment of Persons 3 to 34 Years Old on Identified Reservations, 1980 - IV

Data are the latest available.

Identified reservation	Persons 1 year and over						
	Total	Always lived on this reservation	Did not always live on this reservation				
			Total		Percent moved onto reservation in--		
			Number	Percent	1979 or 1980	1975 to 1978	1974 or earlier
Fort Bidwell Reservation, California	90	29	60	66.5	19.4	37.4	9.6
Modoc County	90	29	60	66.5	19.4	37.4	9.6
Fort Hall Reservation, Idaho	2,439	1,685	583	23.9	8.6	6.0	9.3
Bannock County	663	479	104	15.6	3.0	5.2	7.4
Bingham County	1,610	1,075	457	28.4	11.1	6.7	10.5
Caribou County	-	-	-	-	-	-	-
Power County	166	131	23	13.6	6.4	2.7	4.5
Fort Independence Reservation, California	32	4	26	82.2	9.7	12.3	60.3
Inyo County	32	4	26	82.2	9.7	12.3	60.3
Fort McDermitt Reservation, Nevada-Oregon	454	283	155	34.2	7.7	4.6	22.0
Nevada	454	283	155	34.2	7.7	4.6	22.0
Humboldt County	454	283	155	34.2	7.7	4.6	22.0
Oregon	-	-	-	-	-	-	-
Malheur County	-	-	-	-	-	-	-
Fort McDowell Reservation, Arizona	338	204	70	20.6	8.0	3.4	9.3
Maricopa County	338	204	70	20.6	8.0	3.4	9.3
Fort Mojave Reservation, Arizona-California-Nevada	124	4	102	82.3	3.2	18.5	60.5
Arizona	124	4	102	82.3	3.2	18.5	60.5
Mohave County	124	4	102	82.3	3.2	18.5	60.5
California	-	-	-	-	-	-	-
San Bernardino County	-	-	-	-	-	-	-
Nevada	-	-	-	-	-	-	-
Clark County	-	-	-	-	-	-	-
Fort Peck Reservation, Montana	4,097	2,501	1,377	33.6	8.4	9.9	15.3
Daniels County	-	-	-	-	-	-	-
Roosevelt County	3,635	2,202	1,236	34.0	8.8	9.8	15.4
Sheridan County	-	-	-	-	-	-	-
Valley County	461	299	141	30.6	5.7	11.0	14.0
Fort Totten Reservation, North Dakota	2,127	1,648	429	20.2	5.1	5.4	9.6
Benson County	2,118	1,639	429	20.2	5.2	5.4	9.7
Eddy County	...	...	...	...	...	...	...
Nelson County	-	-	-	-	...	...	...
Ramsey County	...	...	...	...	...	...	...
Fort Yuma Reservation, Arizona-California	1,054	554	281	26.7	13.2	5.7	7.8
Arizona	136	77	14	10.2	1.4	5.4	3.3
Yuma County	136	77	14	10.2	1.4	5.4	3.3
California	918	478	267	29.1	15.0	5.7	8.4
Imperial County	918	478	267	29.1	15.0	5.7	8.4
Gila Bend Reservation, Arizona	-	-	-	-	-	-	-
Maricopa County	-	-	-	-	-	-	-
Gila River Reservation, Arizona	6,707	5,163	1,355	20.2	7.7	4.3	8.2
Maricopa County	1,963	1,408	522	26.6	9.8	6.2	10.5
Pinal County	4,744	3,754	833	17.6	6.9	3.4	7.3
Golden Hill Reservation, Connecticut	...	...	...	...	...	...	...
Fairfield County	...	...	...	...	...	...	...
Goshute Reservation, Nevada-Utah	101	50	45	44.9	22.7	10.7	11.4
Nevada	...	...	...	...	...	...	...
White Pine County	...	...	...	...	...	...	...
Utah	77	40	31	40.7	25.9	3.7	11.1

[Continued]

★ 288 ★

School Enrollment of Persons 3 to 34 Years Old on Identified Reservations, 1980 - IV

[Continued]

Identified reservation	Total	Always lived on this reservation	Persons 1 year and over				
			Did not always live on this reservation				
			Total		Percent moved onto reservation in--		
					1979 or 1980	1975 to 1978	1974 or earlier
			Number	Percent			
Juab and Tooele Counties	77	40	31	40.7	25.9	3.7	11.1
Grand Portage Reservation, Minnesota	186	34	146	78.1	27.6	22.7	27.7
Cook County	186	34	146	78.1	27.6	22.7	27.7
Grindstone Creek Rancheria, California	69	8	61	88.7	22.8	34.9	30.9
Glenn County	69	8	61	88.7	22.8	34.9	30.9
Hannahville Community, Michigan	199	161	39	19.5	3.9	2.5	13.1
Menominee County	199	161	39	19.5	3.9	2.5	13.1
Hassanamisco Reservation, Massachusetts	...	...	...	...	...	...	...
Worcester County	...	...	...	...	...	...	...
Havasupai Reservation, Arizona	258	194	37	14.2	2.9	2.6	8.7
Coconino County	258	194	37	14.2	2.9	2.6	8.7
Hoh Reservation, Washington	40	8	32	80.7	7.3	38.9	34.4
Jefferson County	40	8	32	80.7	7.3	38.9	34.4
Hollywood Reservation, Florida	398	212	168	42.3	21.5	5.7	15.1
Broward County	398	212	168	42.3	21.5	5.7	15.1
Hoopa Valley Reservation, California	1,440	728	577	40.1	9.2	9.0	21.9
Humboldt County	1,440	728	577	40.1	9.2	9.0	21.9
Hoopa Valley Extension Reservation, California	404	186	155	38.3	7.1	15.2	16.0
Del Norte County	151	52	82	54.1	8.8	28.3	16.9
Humboldt County	252	134	73	28.9	6.0	7.4	15.5
Hopi Reservation, Arizona	6,449	5,060	562	8.7	3.4	2.2	3.2
Coconino County	1,260	1,048	33	2.7	0.9	0.5	1.2
Navajo County	5,189	4,012	528	10.2	4.0	2.6	3.6
Hopland Rancheria, California	-	-	-	-	-	-	-
Mendocino County	-	-	-	-	-	-	-
Hualapai Reservation, Arizona	787	493	181	23.1	5.4	6.3	11.3
Coconino and Mohave Counties	783	493	181	23.1	5.4	6.3	11.3
Yavapai County	...	...	...	...	...	...	...
Inaja-Cosmit Reservation, California	-	-	-	-	-	-	-
San Diego County	-	-	-	-	-	-	-
Indian Township Reservation, Maine	315	197	116	36.7	5.8	16.5	14.4
Washington County	315	197	116	36.7	5.8	16.5	14.4
Iowa Reservation, Kansas-Nebraska	31	19	10	31.7	-	7.3	24.4
Kansas	...	...	...	...	...	...	...
Brown County	...	...	...	...	...	...	...
Doniphan County	-	-	-	-	-	-	-
Nebraska	...	...	...	...	...	...	...
Richardson County	...	...	...	...	...	...	...
Isabella Reservation, Michigan	495	160	307	62.0	21.1	18.6	22.3
Isabella County	495	160	307	62.0	21.1	18.6	22.3
Isleta Pueblo, New Mexico	2,228	1,515	634	28.5	3.1	6.0	19.3
Bernalillo County	1,734	1,159	541	31.2	3.4	6.9	20.9
Torrance County	-	-	-	-	-	-	-
Valencia County	494	356	93	18.8	2.2	2.8	13.7
Jackson Rancheria, California	...	...	...	...	...	...	...
Amador County	...	...	...	...	...	...	...
Jemez Pueblo, New Mexico	1,450	1,281	144	10.0	3.0	3.3	3.7
Sandoval County	1,450	1,281	144	10.0	3.0	3.3	3.7

[Continued]

★ 288 ★

School Enrollment of Persons 3 to 34 Years Old on Identified Reservations, 1980 - IV
[Continued]

Identified reservation	Persons 1 year and over						
	Total	Always lived on this reservation	Did not always live on this reservation				
			Total		Percent moved onto reservation in--		
			Number	Percent	1979 or 1980	1975 to 1978	1974 or earlier
Jicarilla Apache Reservation, New Mexico	1,651	1,295	338	20.5	7.0	5.8	7.7
Rio Arriba and Sandoval Counties	1,651	1,295	338	20.5	7.0	5.8	7.7
Kaibab Reservation, Arizona	89	30	59	66.5	10.8	12.2	43.6
Coconino County	-	-	-	-	-	-	-
Mohave County	89	30	59	66.5	10.8	12.2	43.6
Kalispel Reservation, Washington	97	49	47	48.5	20.6	11.3	16.5
Pend Oreille County	97	49	47	48.5	20.6	11.3	16.5
Kickapoo Reservation, Kansas	352	75	277	78.8	21.9	22.6	34.2
Brown County	352	75	277	78.8	21.9	22.6	34.2
Kootenai Reservation, Idaho	-	-	-	-	-	-	-
Boundary County	-	-	-	-	-	-	-
Lac Courte Oreilles Reservation, Wisconsin	1,113	464	608	54.6	12.4	19.3	22.9
Sawyer County	1,113	464	608	54.6	12.4	19.3	22.9
Lac du Flambeau Reservation, Wisconsin	1,056	672	368	34.9	13.2	10.6	11.1
Iron County	-	-	-	-	-	-	-
Oneida County	-	-	-	-	-	-	-
Vilas County	1,056	672	368	34.9	13.2	10.6	11.1
Laguna Pueblo, New Mexico	3,452	2,128	1,280	37.1	8.8	9.2	19.1
Bernalillo and Valencia Counties	3,452	2,128	1,280	37.1	8.8	9.2	19.1
Sandoval County	-	-	-	-	-	-	-
La Jolla Reservation, California	133	22	105	79.0	23.1	35.6	20.2
San Diego County	133	22	105	79.0	23.1	35.6	20.2
L'Anse Reservation, Michigan	552	232	315	57.0	13.6	17.8	25.6
Baraga County	552	232	315	57.0	13.6	17.8	25.6
La Posta Reservation, California	...	...	...	...	...	...	...
San Diego County	...	...	...	...	...	...	...
Las Vegas Colony, Nevada	99	51	42	42.7	4.3	14.3	24.1
Clark County	99	51	42	42.7	4.3	14.3	24.1
Laytonville Rancheria, California	103	33	70	68.0	17.5	7.8	42.7
Mendocino County	103	33	70	68.0	17.5	7.8	42.7
Leech Lake Reservation, Minnesota	2,661	1,451	1,129	42.4	10.0	16.5	15.9
Beltrami County	321	169	144	44.9	8.8	23.6	12.5
Cass and Hubbard Counties	1,653	829	769	46.5	11.3	17.6	17.6
Itasca County	686	452	216	31.4	7.4	10.6	13.5
Likely Rancheria, California	-	-	-	-	-	-	-
Modoc County	-	-	-	-	-	-	-
Lone Pine Rancheria, California	165	74	91	55.3	24.9	12.9	17.6
Inyo County	165	74	91	55.3	24.9	12.9	17.6
Lookout Rancheria, California	...	...	...	...	...	...	...
Modoc County	...	...	...	...	...	...	...
Los Coyotes Reservation, California	41	19	23	55.1	20.0	17.5	17.7
San Diego County	41	19	23	55.1	20.0	17.5	17.7
Lovelock Colony, Nevada	109	54	48	44.2	5.3	16.2	22.6
Pershing County	109	54	48	44.2	5.3	16.2	22.6
Lower Brule Reservation, South Dakota	793	439	311	39.3	14.0	9.2	16.1
Lyman County	785	436	309	39.4	14.2	9.3	15.9
Stanley County	...	...	...	...	...	...	...
Lower Elwah Reservation, Washington	45	5	23	51.1	15.6	15.6	20.0

[Continued]

★ 288 ★

School Enrollment of Persons 3 to 34 Years Old on Identified Reservations, 1980 - IV

[Continued]

Identified reservation		Persons 1 year and over					
	Total	Always lived on this reservation	Did not always live on this reservation				
			Total		Percent moved onto reservation in--		
			Number	Percent	1979 or 1980	1975 to 1978	1974 or earlier
Clallam County	45	5	23	51.1	15.6	15.6	20.0
Lower Sioux Community, Minnesota	71	57	13	18.9	10.2	6.3	2.4
Redwood County	71	57	13	18.9	10.2	6.3	2.4
Lummi Reservation, Washington	1,218	678	497	40.8	11.0	13.1	16.7
Whatcom County	1,218	678	497	40.8	11.0	13.1	16.7
Makah Reservation, Washington	764	390	340	44.6	8.2	17.1	19.3
Clallam County	764	390	340	44.6	8.2	17.1	19.3
Manchester Rancheria, California	73	31	42	57.4	9.7	1.5	46.2
Mendocino County	73	31	42	57.4	9.7	1.5	46.2
Manzanita Reservation, California	...	...	...	...	...	...	...
San Diego County	...	...	...	...	...	...	...
Maricopa Reservation, Arizona	364	262	98	27.0	3.8	5.3	18.0
Pinal County	364	262	98	27.0	3.8	5.3	18.0
Mattaponi Reservation, Virgina	60	28	32	53.3	-	26.7	26.7
King William County	60	28	32	53.3	-	26.7	26.7
Menominee Reservation, Wisconsin	2,299	1,349	537	23.4	4.6	8.4	10.4
Menominee County	2,299	1,349	537	23.4	4.6	8.4	10.4
Mesa Grande Reservation, California	-	-	-	-	-	-	-
San Diego County	-	-	-	-	-	-	-

Source: U.S. Bureau of the Census, Subject Reports, PC80-2-1D, Part 1, *American Indians, Eskimos, and Aleuts on Identified Reservations and in the Historic Areas of Oklahoma (Excluding Urbanized Areas)*, U.S. Government Printing Office, Washington, D.C., 1986, pp. 50-58. *Notes:* A dash "(-)" represents zero or a percent which rounds to less than 0.1. Also, a dash "(-)" is used because the number of supplementary questionnaires for the reservations was insufficient to produce reliable estimates. Three dots "..." means not applicable, or that the data are being withheld to avoid disclosure of information for individuals.

★ 289 ★

School Enrollment of Persons 3 to 34 Years Old on Identified Reservations, 1980 - V

Data are the latest available.

Identified reservation	Persons 3 to 34 years old					Persons 16 to 19 years old -- percent not enrolled in school, not high school graduates	Persons 25 years and over	
	All persons	Percent enrolled in school					Percent completed less than 5 years of school	Percent high school graduates
		Total	5 to 19 years		20 to 34 years old			
			Total	Bureau of indian affairs or tribal school				
Mescalero Apache Reservation, New Mexico	1,340	53.6	49.3	3.4	2.3	24.9	5.6	52.3
Otero County	1,340	53.6	49.3	3.4	2.3	24.9	5.6	52.3
Miccosukee Reservation, Florida	184	34.8	27.7	66.7	2.7	56.0	60.2	19.4
Broward County	-	-	-	-	-	-	-	-
Dade County	184	34.8	27.7	66.7	2.7	56.0	60.2	19.4
Middletown Rancheria, California	28	50.0	50.0	-	-	-	17.6	58.8
Lake County	28	50.0	50.0	-	-	-	17.6	58.8
Mille Lacs Reservation, Minnesota	-	-	-	-	-	-	-	-
Aitkin County	-	-	-	-	-	-	-	-

[Continued]

★ 289 ★

School Enrollment of Persons 3 to 34 Years Old on Identified Reservations, 1980 - V
[Continued]

Identified reservation	Persons 3 to 34 years old					Persons 16 to 19 years old -- percent not enrolled in school, not high school graduates	Persons 25 years and over	
	All persons	Percent enrolled in school					Percent completed less than 5 years of school	Percent high school graduates
		Total	5 to 19 years		20 to 34 years old			
			Total	Bureau of indian affairs or tribal school				
Kanabec County	-	-	-	-	-	-	-	-
Mille Lacs County	-	-	-	-	-	-	-	-
Pine County	-	-	-	-	-	-	-	-
Mississippi Choctaw Reservation	1,816	61.0	52.8	82.4	4.1	27.3	28.6	34.1
Attala County	-	-	-	-	-	-	-	-
Jones County	76	57.9	50.0	15.8	1.3	28.6	41.2	27.5
Kemper County	...	...	...	...	...	...	...	...
Leake County	344	65.2	55.5	75.1	5.2	24.9	27.9	32.2
Neshoba County	1,173	60.9	52.8	88.9	4.4	24.7	28.2	36.3
Newton County	221	55.6	49.3	81.3	2.1	44.8	25.3	28.1
Moapa River Reservation, Nevada	119	57.7	56.0	-	1.7	28.6	6.2	39.0
Clark County	119	57.7	56.0	-	1.7	28.6	6.2	39.0
Montgomery Creek Rancheria, California	...	...	...	...	...	...	...	...
Shasta County	...	...	...	...	...	...	...	...
Morongo Reservation, California	190	53.5	46.9	1.2	3.9	26.1	1.5	47.1
Riverside County	190	53.5	46.9	1.2	3.9	26.1	1.5	47.1
Muckleshoot Reservation, Washington	264	60.5	52.3	4.2	1.2	48.9	2.6	30.6
King County	264	60.5	52.3	4.2	1.2	48.9	2.6	30.6
Pierce County	-	-	-	-	-	-	-	-
Nambe Pueblo, New Mexico	121	41.7	34.6	8.5	3.8	25.2	13.1	70.2
Santa Fe County	121	41.7	34.6	8.5	3.8	25.2	13.1	70.2
Navajo Reservation, Arizona, New Mexico - Utah	69,722	55.4	50.9	28.6	2.3	24.3	37.4	34.1
Arizona	47,531	56.3	51.4	33.6	2.4	24.8	39.0	33.8
Apache County	25,175	55.6	50.8	25.6	2.6	24.7	36.7	35.5
Coconino County	10,401	58.3	52.6	30.5	1.9	23.4	37.6	36.3
Navajo County	11,955	55.9	51.6	52.7	2.2	26.2	45.2	27.7
New Mexico	19,102	52.4	48.7	15.4	2.3	22.9	31.6	36.7
McKinley County	6,447	47.9	45.1	9.2	1.5	28.6	28.9	38.2
San Juan County	12,655	54.6	50.5	18.3	2.7	20.2	33.0	35.9
Utah	3,089	60.4	56.2	29.4	1.4	27.0	52.0	22.7
San Juan County	3,089	60.4	56.2	29.4	1.4	27.0	52.0	22.7
Nez Perce Reservation, Idaho	949	58.4	52.8	4.8	2.7	15.1	3.6	59.9
Clearwater County	86	53.5	47.7	2.4	1.2	27.3	-	52.0
Idaho County	81	54.3	50.3	15.0	1.2	17.0	4.7	54.1
Lewis County	136	47.1	41.9	-	1.5	26.1	-	61.1
Nez Perce County	646	61.9	56.0	4.7	3.4	10.3	4.5	61.4
Nisqually Reservation, Washington	25	63.2	54.5	41.8	4.3	22.3	5.6	36.2
Pierce County	-	-	-	-	-	-	-	-
Thurston County	25	63.2	54.5	41.8	4.3	22.3	5.6	36.2
Nooksack Reservation, Washington	-	-	-	-	-	-	-	-
Whatcom County	-	-	-	-	-	-	-	-
Northern Cheyenne Reservation, Montana	2,038	59.0	50.5	25.6	4.3	23.8	7.4	52.0
Big Horn County	538	60.2	52.9	48.5	3.8	15.4	2.7	51.3
Rosebud County	1,500	58.5	49.6	16.8	4.4	26.4	9.2	52.3
Oil Springs Reservation, New York	-	-	-	-	-	-	-	-

[Continued]

★ 289 ★

School Enrollment of Persons 3 to 34 Years Old on Identified Reservations, 1980 - V
[Continued]

Identified reservation	Persons 3 to 34 years old					Persons 16 to 19 years old -- percent not enrolled in school, not high school graduates	Persons 25 years and over	
	All persons	Percent enrolled in school					Percent completed less than 5 years of school	Percent high school graduates
		Total	5 to 19 years		20 to 34 years old			
			Total	Bureau of indian affairs or tribal school				
Allegany County	-	-	-	-	-	-	-	-
Cattaraugus County	-	-	-	-	-	-	-	-
Omaha Reservation, Iowa-Nebraska	789	60.1	53.0	9.6	1.9	21.0	6.7	35.2
Iowa	-	-	-	-	-	-	-	-
Monona County	-	-	-	-	-	-	-	-
Nebraska	789	60.1	53.0	9.6	1.9	21.0	6.7	35.2
Burt County	...	...	...	...	...	...	...	...
Cuming County	-	-	-	-	-	-	-	-
Thurston County	783	60.2	53.2	9.6	1.9	21.0	6.8	35.2
Oneida Reservation, Wisconsin	1,090	58.2	51.5	15.5	2.7	20.9	5.5	45.6
Brown County	412	56.4	52.7	8.1	2.0	27.1	6.0	44.3
Outagamie County	678	59.2	50.8	20.1	3.1	16.5	5.1	46.6
Onondaga Reservation, New York	-	-	-	-	-	-	-	-
Onondaga County	-	-	-	-	-	-	-	-
Ontonagon Reservation, Michigan	-	-	-	-	-	-	-	-
Ontonagon County	-	-	-	-	-	-	-	-
Osage Reservation, Oklahoma	2,678	51.6	46.7	0.4	2.3	20.1	2.3	65.9
Osage County	2,678	51.6	46.7	0.4	2.3	20.1	2.3	65.9
Ozette Reservation, Washington	...	...	...	...	...	...	...	...
Clallam County	...	...	...	...	...	...	...	...
Pala Reservation, California	275	51.8	44.0	5.5	3.5	22.1	1.0	60.0
San Diego County	275	51.8	44.0	5.5	3.5	22.1	1.0	60.0
Pamunkey Reservation, Virginia	11	81.8	72.7	-	9.1	-	9.4	15.6
King William County	11	81.8	72.7	-	9.1	-	9.4	15.6
Papago Reservation, Arizona	4,192	55.0	49.6	45.8	1.8	24.2	25.2	35.0
Maricopa County	67	65.6	60.7	97.3	-	100.0	44.6	12.6
Pima County	3,718	54.8	49.4	47.5	2.0	21.1	25.2	35.2
Pinal County	408	55.3	49.5	20.0	0.3	54.8	20.6	37.8
Pascua Yaqui Reservation, Arizona	370	52.2	49.0	1.2	0.6	49.1	24.7	14.9
Pima County	370	52.2	49.0	1.2	0.6	49.1	24.7	14.9
Pauma Reservation, California	55	54.9	38.6	-	12.3	41.4	2.0	64.8
San Diego County	55	54.9	38.6	-	12.3	41.4	2.0	64.8
Payson Community of Yavapai-Apache, Arizona	-	-	-	-	-	-	-	-
Gila County	-	-	-	-	-	-	-	-
Pechanga Reservation, California	71	48.5	40.0	-	2.9	35.7	-	49.0
Riverside County	71	48.5	40.0	-	2.9	35.7	-	49.0
Penobscot Reservation, Maine	264	57.0	48.3	1.6	7.2	20.0	-	62.4
Penobscot County	264	57.0	48.3	1.6	7.2	20.0	-	62.4
Picuris Pueblo, New Mexico	85	54.7	47.9	12.3	3.5	-	2.8	68.1
Taos County	85	54.7	47.9	12.3	3.5	-	2.8	68.1
Pine Creek Reservation, Michigan	...	...	...	...	...	...	...	...
Calhoun County	...	...	...	...	...	...	...	...
Pine Ridge Reservation, South Dakota	8,028	56.9	50.6	59.1	3.4	29.5	3.9	44.8
Jackson County	934	61.3	54.6	80.3	2.7	15.2	3.4	40.7
Shannon County	7,094	56.3	50.1	56.1	3.5	31.1	4.0	45.3
Pleasant Point Reservation, Maine	322	59.6	54.6	59.9	1.3	30.0	5.3	42.1

[Continued]

★ 289 ★

School Enrollment of Persons 3 to 34 Years Old on Identified Reservations, 1980 - V
[Continued]

Identified reservation	All persons	Persons 3 to 34 years old				Persons 16 to 19 years old -- percent not enrolled in school, not high school graduates	Persons 25 years and over	
		Percent enrolled in school					Percent completed less than 5 years of school	Percent high school graduates
		Total	5 to 19 years		20 to 34 years old			
			Total	Bureau of indian affairs or tribal school				
Washington County	322	59.6	54.6	59.9	1.3	30.0	5.3	42.1
Pojoaque Pueblo, New Mexico	66	54.8	48.3	9.0	3.0	13.7	8.0	64.4
Santa Fe County	66	54.8	48.3	9.0	3.0	13.7	8.0	64.4
Poospatuck Reservation, New York	61	69.6	60.0	-	5.9	-	3.2	43.1
Suffolk County	61	69.6	60.0	-	5.9	-	3.2	43.1
Port Gamble Reservation, Washington	172	44.3	39.5	3.3	1.5	43.9	2.4	38.3
Kitsap County	172	44.3	39.5	3.3	1.5	43.9	2.4	38.3
Port Madison Reservation, Washington	90	37.9	33.5	5.0	1.5	44.9	2.0	75.3
Kitsap County	90	37.9	33.5	5.0	1.5	44.9	2.0	75.3
Potawatomi Reservation, Wisconsin	144	63.6	56.7	2.4	2.8	14.8	8.5	21.8
Forest County	144	63.6	56.7	2.4	2.8	14.8	8.5	21.8
Onconto County	-	-	-	-	-	-	-	-
Pottawatomi Reservation, Kansas	168	57.2	55.9	-	1.2	13.8	2.8	61.0
Jackson County	168	57.2	55.9	-	1.2	13.8	2.8	61.0
Prairie Island Community, Minnesota	52	44.2	38.5	-	1.9	50.0	5.1	35.9
Goodhue County	52	44.2	38.5	-	1.9	50.0	5.1	35.9
Puyallup Reservation, Washington	575	54.7	47.7	12.3	4.7	35.3	3.2	61.2
Pierce County	575	54.7	47.7	12.3	4.7	35.3	3.2	61.2
Pyramid Lake Reservation, Nevada	427	48.4	45.3	10.2	1.9	15.9	1.4	54.0
Lyon County	-	-	-	-	-	-	-	-
Storey County	-	-	-	-	-	-	-	-
Washoe County	427	48.4	45.3	10.2	1.9	15.9	1.4	54.0
Quileute Reservation, Washington	194	56.5	50.0	51.5	1.2	35.3	2.3	34.1
Clallam County	194	56.5	50.0	51.5	1.2	35.3	2.3	34.1
Quainault Reservation, Washington	635	53.4	47.8	9.3	2.8	28.9	0.6	47.5
Grays Harbor County	518	53.3	47.9	10.9	3.0	29.8	0.4	50.5
Jefferson County	117	53.6	47.0	2.0	1.8	24.9	1.9	31.9
Ramah Community, New Mexico	753	53.1	47.2	44.8	3.9	31.7	45.3	29.2
McKinley County	57	58.0	50.6	43.3	5.4	11.3	61.9	23.2
Valencia County	696	52.7	46.9	44.9	3.8	34.8	43.2	30.0
Ramona Reservation, California	-	-	-	-	-	-	-	-
Riverside County	-	-	-	-	-	-	-	-
Red Cliff Reservation, Wisconsin	394	59.9	53.8	-	3.3	21.0	2.2	35.3
Bayfield County	394	59.9	53.8	-	3.3	21.0	2.2	35.3
Red Lake Reservation, Minnesota	1,852	57.3	51.5	9.0	1.8	44.9	3.6	43.4
Beltrami County	1,813	57.5	51.6	9.2	1.9	45.1	3.6	43.9
Clearwater County	40	48.4	45.2	-	-	33.3	4.1	21.5
Koochiching County	-	-	-	-	-	-	-	-
Lake of the Woods County	-	-	-	-	-	-	-	-
Marshall County	-	-	-	-	-	-	-	-
Pennington County	-	-	-	-	-	-	-	-
Polk County	-	-	-	-	-	-	-	-
Red Lake County	-	-	-	-	-	-	-	-
Roseau County	-	-	-	-	-	-	-	-
Reno-Sparks Colony, Nevada	309	47.6	40.3	0.6	4.4	32.9	2.9	60.5
Washoe County	309	47.6	40.3	0.6	4.4	32.9	2.9	60.5

[Continued]

★ 289 ★

School Enrollment of Persons 3 to 34 Years Old on Identified Reservations, 1980 - V
[Continued]

Identified reservation	Persons 3 to 34 years old					Persons 16 to 19 years old -- percent not enrolled in school, not high school graduates	Persons 25 years and over	
	All persons	Percent enrolled in school					Percent completed less than 5 years of school	Percent high school graduates
		Total	5 to 19 years		20 to 34 years old			
			Total	Bureau of indian affairs or tribal school				
Resighini Rancheria, California	...	...	...	...	...	...	...	...
Del Norte County	...	...	...	...	...	...	...	...
Rincon Reservation, California	189	59.4	49.8	2.8	5.2	27.3	3.5	54.0
San Diego County	189	59.4	49.8	2.8	5.2	27.3	3.5	54.0
Roaring Creek Rancheria, California	...	...	...	...	...	...	...	...
Shasta County	...	...	...	...	...	...	...	...
Rocky Boy's Reservation, Montana	1,036	60.1	54.2	9.0	2.7	23.5	9.7	41.7
Chouteau County	87	59.8	54.0	10.6	1.1	18.8	5.4	51.8
Hill County	949	60.2	54.2	8.8	2.9	24.0	10.1	40.6
Rosebud Reservation, South Dakota	3,749	52.5	47.9	18.5	3.4	32.6	3.3	50.2
Todd County	3,749	52.5	47.9	18.5	3.4	32.6	3.3	50.2
Round Valley Reservation, California	332	52.0	48.9	-	0.3	17.0	-	50.4
Mendocino County	332	52.0	48.9	-	0.3	17.0	-	50.4
Rumsey Rancheria, California	...	...	...	...	...	...	...	...
Yolo County	...	...	...	...	...	...	...	...
Sac and Fox Reservation, Iowa	303	59.4	54.8	33.3	2.0	22.1	6.6	42.6
Tama County	303	59.4	54.8	33.3	2.0	22.1	6.6	42.6
Sac and Fox Reservation, Kansas-Nebraska	...	...	...	...	...	...	...	...
Kansas	-	-	-	-	-	-	-	-
Brown County	-	-	-	-	-	-	-	-
Nebraska	...	...	...	...	...	...	...	...
Richardson County	...	...	...	...	...	...	...	...

Source: U.S. Bureau of the Census, Subject Reports, PC80-2-1D, Part 1, *American Indians, Eskimos, and Aleuts on Identified Reservations and in the Historic Areas of Oklahoma (Excluding Urbanized Areas)*, U.S. Government Printing Office, Washington, D.C., 1986, pp. 50-58. *Notes:* A dash "(-)" represents zero or a percent which rounds to less than 0.1. Also, a dash "(-)" is used because the number of supplementary questionnaires for the reservations was insufficient to produce reliable estimates. Three dots "..." means not applicable, or that the data are being withheld to avoid disclosure of information for individuals.

★ 290 ★

School Enrollment of Persons 3 to 34 Years Old on Identified Reservations, 1980 - VI

Data are the latest available.

Identified reservations	Persons 1 year and over						
	Total	Always lived on this reservation	Did not always live on this reservation				
			Total		Percent moved onto reservation in--		
			Number	Percent	1979 or 1980	1975 to 1978	1974 or earlier
Mescalero Apache Reservation, New Mexico	1,854	498	148	8.0	1.9	2.4	3.7
Otero County	1,854	498	148	8.0	1.9	2.4	3.7
Miccosukee Reservation, Florida	263	161	88	33.5	6.5	7.6	19.4
Broward County	-	-	-	-	-	-	-
Dade County	263	161	88	33.5	6.5	7.6	19.4
Middletown Rancheria, California	38	14	24	63.2	39.5	10.5	13.2

[Continued]

★ 290 ★

School Enrollment of Persons 3 to 34 Years Old on Identified Reservations, 1980 - VI
[Continued]

Identified reservations	Total	Always lived on this reservation	Persons 1 year and over				
			Did not always live on this reservation				
			Total		Percent moved onto reservation in—		
			Number	Percent	1979 or 1980	1975 to 1978	1974 or earlier
Lake County	38	14	24	63.2	39.5	10.5	13.2
Mille Lacs Reservation, Minnesota	-	-	-	-	-	-	-
Aitkin County	-	-	-	-	-	-	-
Kanabec County	-	-	-	-	-	-	-
Mille Lacs County	-	-	-	-	-	-	-
Pine County	-	-	-	-	-	-	-
Mississippi Choctaw Reservation	2,669	1,497	1,119	41.9	6.2	15.8	19.9
Attala County	-	-	-	-	-	-	-
Jones County	116	46	70	60.3	11.2	23.3	25.9
Kemper County	...	...	...	...	...	...	...
Leake County	516	302	201	39.0	1.8	10.1	27.1
Neshoba County	1,700	913	750	44.1	6.7	18.4	19.0
Newton County	333	232	98	29.4	8.8	9.4	11.2
Moapa River Reservation, Nevada	178	104	67	37.9	10.7	5.9	21.3
Clark County	178	104	67	37.9	10.7	5.9	21.3
Montgomery Creek Rancheria, California	...	...	...	...	...	...	...
Shasta County	...	...	...	...	...	...	...
Morongo Reservation, California	305	125	172	56.3	22.7	11.8	21.8
Riverside County	305	125	172	56.3	22.7	11.8	21.8
Muckleshoot Reservation, Washington	365	218	92	25.3	4.4	14.1	6.8
King County	365	218	92	25.3	4.4	14.1	6.8
Pierce County	-	-	-	-	-	-	-
Nambe Pueblo, New Mexico	185	81	32	17.5	4.7	2.2	10.6
Santa Fe County	185	81	32	17.5	4.7	2.2	10.6
Navajo Reservation, Arizona, New Mexico - Utah	101,355	83,040	10,380	10.2	2.8	2.2	5.3
Arizona	69,155	56,371	6,920	10.0	2.6	2.1	5.3
Apache County	36,937	29,183	4,150	11.2	2.4	2.3	6.5
Coconino County	14,759	12,484	1,055	7.1	3.4	1.6	2.1
Navajo County	17,459	14,703	1,716	9.8	2.2	2.1	5.5
New Mexico	27,794	22,869	3,030	10.9	3.1	2.4	5.3
McKinley County	9,264	6,584	1,445	15.6	2.9	3.3	9.4
San Juan County	18,530	16,285	1,585	8.6	3.2	2.0	3.3
Utah	4,406	3,801	430	9.8	3.2	2.3	4.2
San Juan County	4,406	3,801	430	9.8	3.2	2.3	4.2
Nez Perce Reservation, Idaho	1,472	746	667	45.3	13.4	13.8	18.1
Clearwater County	117	41	67	57.3	29.1	8.5	19.7
Idaho County	145	71	73	50.1	19.0	4.7	26.4
Lewis County	203	88	101	49.8	12.3	13.3	24.1
Nez Perce County	1,007	546	426	42.3	11.0	15.8	15.5
Nisqually Reservation, Washington	42	12	30	72.1	30.6	13.9	27.6
Pierce County	-	-	-	-	-	-	-
Thurston County	42	12	30	72.1	30.6	13.9	27.6
Nooksack Reservation, Washington	-	-	-	-	-	-	-
Whatcom County	-	-	-	-	-	-	-
Northern Cheyenne Reservation, Montana	2,963	1,972	743	25.1	8.6	8.0	8.5
Big Horn County	795	527	223	28.1	7.7	9.0	11.4
Rosebud County	2,168	1,446	520	24.0	8.9	7.7	7.4
Oil Springs Reservation, New York	-	-	-	-	-	-	-

[Continued]

★ 290 ★

School Enrollment of Persons 3 to 34 Years Old on Identified Reservations, 1980 - VI

[Continued]

Identified reservations	Total	Always lived on this reservation	Persons 1 year and over				
			Did not always live on this reservation				
			Total		Percent moved onto reservation in--		
			Number	Percent	1979 or 1980	1975 to 1978	1974 or earlier
Allegany County	-	-	-	-	-	-	-
Cattaraugus County	-	-	-	-	-	-	-
Omaha Reservation, Iowa-Nebraska	1,200	395	205	17.1	3.2	4.9	8.9
Iowa	-	-	-	-	-	-	-
Monona County	-	-	-	-	-	-	-
Nebraska	1,200	395	205	17.1	3.2	4.9	8.9
Burt County	...	...	...	...	...	...	...
Cuming County	-	-	-	-	-	-	-
Thurston County	1,192	395	205	17.2	3.2	5.0	9.0
Oneida Reservation, Wisconsin	1,768	817	834	47.1	9.0	16.9	21.3
Brown County	707	343	302	42.8	6.0	14.1	22.7
Outagamie County	1,061	474	531	50.1	10.9	18.8	20.3
Onondaga Reservation, New York	-	-	-	-	-	-	-
Onondaga County	-	-	-	-	-	-	-
Ontonagon Reservation, Michigan	-	-	-	-	-	-	-
Ontonagon County	-	-	-	-	-	-	-
Osage Reservation, Oklahoma	4,589	1,415	2,551	55.6	14.8	16.5	24.3
Osage County	4,589	1,415	2,551	55.6	14.8	16.5	24.3
Ozette Reservation, Washington	...	...	...	...	...	...	...
Clallam County	...	...	...	...	...	...	...
Pala Reservation, California	420	153	266	63.2	5.5	20.6	37.1
San Diego County	420	153	266	63.2	5.5	20.6	37.1
Pamunkey Reservation, Virginia	44	10	34	77.3	25.0	15.9	36.4
King William County	44	10	34	77.3	25.0	15.9	36.4
Papago Reservation, Arizona	6,597	5,161	1,304	19.8	4.9	5.2	9.7
Maricopa County	120	113	2	2.0	1.1	0.9	-
Pima County	5,848	4,526	1,215	20.8	4.8	5.5	10.4
Pinal County	630	522	87	13.8	6.0	2.9	4.9
Pascua Yaqui Reservation, Arizona	528	273	244	46.2	5.5	10.7	29.9
Pima County	528	273	244	46.2	5.5	10.7	29.9
Pauma Reservation, California	82	51	31	37.6	6.0	8.3	23.2
San Diego County	82	51	31	37.6	6.0	8.3	23.2
Payson Community of Yavapai-Apache, Arizona	-	-	-	-	-	-	-
Gila County	-	-	-	-	-	-	-
Pechanga Reservation, California	116	22	88	76.3	14.9	26.3	35.1
Riverside County	116	22	88	76.3	14.9	26.3	35.1
Penobscot Reservation, Maine	398	132	260	65.4	19.7	32.8	12.9
Penobscot County	398	132	260	65.4	19.7	32.8	12.9
Picuris Pueblo, New Mexico	136	64	63	46.6	15.3	23.5	7.8
Taos County	136	64	63	46.6	15.3	23.5	7.8
Pine Creek Reservation, Michigan	...	...	...	...	...	...	...
Calhoun County	...	...	...	...	...	...	...
Pine Ridge Reservation, South Dakota	11,472	8,596	2,145	18.7	4.9	6.5	7.3
Jackson County	1,331	870	336	25.2	6.4	9.9	8.9
Shannon County	10,141	7,726	1,810	17.8	4.7	6.1	7.1
Pleasant Point Reservation, Maine	491	262	217	44.2	9.0	16.4	18.8
Washington County	491	262	217	44.2	9.0	16.4	18.8
Pojoaque Pueblo, New Mexico	93	47	46	49.2	21.5	10.0	17.7
Santa Fe County	93	47	46	49.2	21.5	10.0	17.7

[Continued]

★ 290 ★

School Enrollment of Persons 3 to 34 Years Old on Identified Reservations, 1980 - VI

[Continued]

Identified reservations	Total	Always lived on this reservation	Persons 1 year and over				
			Did not always live on this reservation		Percent moved onto reservation in--		
			Total		1979 or 1980	1975 to 1978	1974 or earlier
			Number	Percent			
Poospatuck Reservation, New York	92	37	45	49.0	-	3.7	45.3
Suffolk County	92	37	45	49.0	-	3.7	45.3
Port Gamble Reservation, Washington	256	108	139	54.5	7.1	16.3	31.2
Kitsap County	256	108	139	54.5	7.1	16.3	31.2
Port Madison Reservation, Washington	144	34	97	66.8	26.8	22.6	17.5
Kitsap County	144	34	97	66.8	26.8	22.6	17.5
Potawatomi Reservation, Wisconsin	212	131	81	37.9	10.5	13.2	14.3
Forest County	212	131	81	37.9	10.5	13.2	14.3
Onconto County	-	-	-	-	-	-	-
Pottawatomi Reservation, Kansas	328	111	213	65.1	11.4	30.1	23.6
Jackson County	328	111	213	65.1	11.4	30.1	23.6
Prairie Island Community, Minnesota	81	62	19	23.5	13.6	3.7	6.2
Goodhue County	81	62	19	23.5	13.6	3.7	6.2
Puyallup Reservation, Washington	846	133	642	76.0	29.1	23.3	23.6
Pierce County	846	133	642	76.0	29.1	23.3	23.6
Pyramid Lake Reservation, Nevada	692	378	310	44.8	12.6	17.4	14.7
Lyon County	-	-	-	-	-	-	-
Storey County	-	-	-	-	-	-	-
Washoe County	692	378	310	44.8	12.6	17.4	14.7
Quileute Reservation, Washington	256	173	77	30.3	8.6	9.2	12.4
Clallam County	256	173	77	30.3	8.6	9.2	12.4
Quainault Reservation, Washington	913	446	420	46.0	12.1	12.6	21.3
Grays Harbor County	752	359	358	47.6	13.3	12.3	22.0
Jefferson County	161	88	62	38.8	6.7	14.2	17.9
Ramah Community, New Mexico	1,110	932	114	10.3	2.9	3.3	4.0
McKinley County	101	84	16	16.0	5.9	7.4	2.6
Valencia County	1,009	848	98	9.7	2.6	2.9	4.2
Ramona Reservation, California	-	-	-	-	-	-	-
Riverside County	-	-	-	-	-	-	-
Red Cliff Reservation, Wisconsin	568	198	349	61.4	30.4	15.8	15.2
Bayfield County	568	198	349	61.4	30.4	15.8	15.2
Red Lake Reservation, Minnesota	2,736	2,102	556	20.3	4.9	5.7	9.7
Beltrami County	2,673	2,061	535	20.0	4.7	5.8	9.5
Clearwater County	63	41	22	34.6	14.5	-	20.1
Koochiching County	-	-	-	-	-	-	-
Lake of the Woods County	-	-	-	-	-	-	-
Marshall County	-	-	-	-	-	-	-
Pennington County	-	-	-	-	-	-	-
Polk County	-	-	-	-	-	-	-
Red Lake County	-	-	-	-	-	-	-
Roseau County	-	-	-	-	-	-	-
Reno-Sparks Colony, Nevada	446	221	214	48.1	15.5	6.0	26.7
Washoe County	446	221	214	48.1	15.5	6.0	26.7
Resighini Rancheria, California	...	...	...	...	...	...	...
Del Norte County	...	...	...	...	...	...	...
Rincon Reservation, California	290	81	198	68.2	10.1	17.9	40.2
San Diego County	290	81	198	68.2	10.1	17.9	40.2
Roaring Creek Rancheria, California	...	...	...	...	...	...	...
Shasta County	...	...	...	...	...	...	...

[Continued]

★ 290 ★

School Enrollment of Persons 3 to 34 Years Old on Identified Reservations, 1980 - VI

[Continued]

Identified reservations	Persons 1 year and over						
	Total	Always lived on this reservation	Did not always live on this reservation				
			Total		Percent moved onto reservation in--		
			Number	Percent	1979 or 1980	1975 to 1978	1974 or earlier
Rocky Boy's Reservation, Montana	1,490	924	537	36.1	8.5	10.9	16.7
Chouteau County	127	68	57	44.9	4.7	14.2	26.0
Hill County	1,363	856	480	35.2	8.8	10.6	15.8
Rosebud Reservation, South Dakota	5,405	3,647	1,293	23.9	7.4	7.4	9.1
Todd County	5,405	3,647	1,293	23.9	7.4	7.4	9.1
Round Valley Reservation, California	516	279	226	43.8	12.6	20.7	10.5
Mendocino County	516	279	226	43.8	12.6	20.7	10.5
Rumsey Rancheria, California	...	...	...	...	...	...	...
Yolo County	...	...	...	...	...	...	...
Sac and Fox Reservation, Iowa	475	318	131	27.6	14.0	7.2	6.4
Tama County	475	318	131	27.6	14.0	7.2	6.4
Sac and Fox Reservation, Kansas-Nebraska	...	...	...	...	...	...	...
Kansas	-	-	-	-	-	-	-
Brown County	-	-	-	-	-	-	-
Nebraska	...	...	...	...	...	...	...
Richardson County	...	...	...	...	...	...	...

Source: U.S. Bureau of the Census, Subject Reports, PC80-2-1D, Part 1, *American Indians, Eskimos, and Aleuts on Identified Reservations and in the Historic Areas of Oklahoma (Excluding Urbanized Areas)*, U.S. Government Printing Office, Washington, D.C., 1986, pp. 50-58. *Notes:* A dash "(-)" represents zero or a percent which rounds to less than 0.1. Also, a dash "(-)" is used because the number of supplementary questionnaires for the reservations was insufficient to produce reliable estimates. Three dots "..." means not applicable, or that the data are being withheld to avoid disclosure of information for individuals.

★ 291 ★

School Enrollment of Persons 3 to 34 Years Old on Identified Reservations, 1980 - VII

Data are the latest available.

Identified reservation	Persons 3 to 34 years old					Persons 16 to 19 years old -- percent not enrolled in school, not high school graduates	Persons 25 years and over	
	All persons	Percent enrolled in school					Percent completed less than 5 years of school	Percent high school graduates
		Total	5 to 19 years		20 to 34 years old			
			Total	Bureau of indian affairs or tribal school				
St. Croix Reservation, Wisconsin	255	56.5	53.0	3.6	1.4	33.9	11.0	35.1
Barron County	50	44.0	44.0	-	-	54.3	31.8	14.5
Burnett County	149	63.2	60.4	5.4	1.2	22.7	1.2	45.0
Polk County	56	49.7	41.4	-	3.4	70.3	20.5	25.5
St. Regis Mohawk Reservation, New York	980	58.0	49.6	0.4	5.5	17.4	9.1	38.2
Franklin County	980	58.0	49.6	0.4	5.5	17.4	9.1	38.2
Salt River Reservation, Arizona	1,720	47.5	41.4	33.3	3.2	44.1	3.3	47.5
Maricopa County	1,720	47.5	41.4	33.3	3.2	44.1	3.3	47.5
San Carlos Reservation, Arizona	3,957	53.6	49.2	11.7	2.1	30.7	8.8	37.1
Gila County	2,276	50.0	45.2	19.3	2.4	37.2	9.6	37.3
Graham County	1,681	58.5	54.8	3.3	1.8	21.7	7.5	36.9
Pinal County	-	-	-	-	-	-	-	-

[Continued]

School Enrollment of Persons 3 to 34 Years Old on Identified Reservations, 1980 - VII
[Continued]

Identified reservation	Persons 3 to 34 years old					Persons 16 to 19 years old -- percent not enrolled in school, not high school graduates	Persons 25 years and over	
	All persons	Percent enrolled in school					Percent completed less than 5 years of school	Percent high school graduates
		Total	5 to 19 years		20 to 34 years old			
			Total	Bureau of indian affairs or tribal school				
Sandia Pueblo, New Mexico	137	54.3	45.5	6.6	4.4	20.0	4.6	63.5
Bernalillo County	-	-	-	-	-	-	-	-
Sandoval County	137	54.3	45.5	6.6	4.4	20.0	4.6	63.5
Sandy Lake Reservation, Minnesota	-	-	-	-	-	-	-	-
Aitkin County	-	-	-	-	-	-	-	-
San Felipe Pueblo, New Mexico	1,250	58.7	53.1	43.2	1.2	22.1	9.8	43.8
Sandoval County	1,250	58.7	53.1	43.2	1.2	22.1	9.8	43.8
San Ildefonso Pueblo, New Mexico	275	54.3	43.0	41.3	3.8	5.2	3.7	68.5
Sandoval County	-	-	-	-	-	-	-	-
Sante Fe County	275	54.3	43.0	41.3	3.8	5.2	3.7	68.5
San Juan Pueblo, New Mexico	524	53.3	47.0	23.9	2.5	24.8	5.1	58.6
Rio Arriba County	524	53.3	47.0	23.9	2.5	24.8	5.1	58.6
San Manuel Reservation, California	-	-	-	-	-	-	-	-
San Bernardino County	-	-	-	-	-	-	-	-
San Pasqual Reservation, California	75	48.7	40.2	3.7	4.2	77.7	2.1	54.9
San Diego County	75	48.7	40.2	3.7	4.2	77.7	2.1	54.9
Santa Ana Pueblo, New Mexico	244	51.1	44.6	6.8	3.4	13.9	5.6	59.5
Sandoval County	244	51.1	44.6	6.8	3.4	13.9	5.6	59.5
Santa Clara Pueblo, New Mexico	1,138	60.1	49.7	38.8	5.8	6.3	3.4	68.3
Rio Arriba County	1,119	60.8	50.3	38.9	5.9	6.3	3.4	67.9
Sandoval County	-	-	-	-	-	-	-	-
Sante Fe County	...	...	...	...	...	...	...	...
Santa Rosa Rancheria, California	80	49.0	37.6	-	-	48.9	13.7	32.9
Kings County	80	49.0	37.6	-	-	48.9	13.7	32.9
Santa Rosa Reservation, California	...	...	...	...	...	...	...	...
Riverside County	...	...	...	...	...	...	...	...
Santa Ynez Reservation, California	69	64.3	57.1	-	1.8	9.1	9.5	35.7
Santa Barbara County	69	64.3	57.1	-	1.8	9.1	9.5	35.7
Santa Ysabel Reservation, California	111	48.1	42.5	-	2.5	36.2	5.5	46.7
San Diego County	111	48.1	42.5	-	2.5	36.2	5.5	46.7
Santee Reservation, Nebraska	254	61.5	53.7	3.8	1.6	18.7	8.2	39.8
Knox County	254	61.5	53.7	3.8	1.6	18.7	8.2	39.8
Santo Domingo Pueblo, New Mexico	1,471	55.4	49.6	6.2	1.1	24.4	14.9	39.7
Sandoval County	1,471	55.4	49.6	6.2	1.1	24.4	14.9	39.7
Santa Fe County	-	-	-	-	-	-	-	-
San Xavier Reservation, Arizona	570	51.8	43.6	20.8	3.6	22.9	10.6	41.3
Pima County	570	51.8	43.6	20.8	3.6	22.9	10.6	41.3
Sauk-Suiattle Reservation, Washington	-	-	-	-	-	-	-	-
Snohomish County	-	-	-	-	-	-	-	-
Sault Ste. Marie Reservation, Michigan	-	-	-	-	-	-	-	-
Chippewa County	-	-	-	-	-	-	-	-
Schaghticoke Reservation, Michigan	...	...	...	...	...	...	...	...
Litchfield County	...	...	...	...	...	...	...	...
Shakopee Community, Minnesota	48	41.2	39.0	-	2.2	40.5	3.2	61.4
Scott County	48	41.2	39.0	-	2.2	40.5	3.2	61.4
Sheep Ranch Rancheria, California	...	...	...	...	...	...	...	...

[Continued]

★ 291 ★

School Enrollment of Persons 3 to 34 Years Old on Identified Reservations, 1980 - VII

[Continued]

Identified reservation	Persons 3 to 34 years old					Persons 16 to 19 years old -- percent not enrolled in school, not high school graduates	Persons 25 years and over	
	All persons	Percent enrolled in school					Percent completed less than 5 years of school	Percent high school graduates
		Total	5 to 19 years		20 to 34 years old			
			Total	Bureau of indian affairs or tribal school				
Calaveras County	...	...	...	...	...	...	...	...
Sherwood Valley Rancheria, California	...	...	...	...	...	...	...	...
Mendocino County	...	...	...	...	...	...	...	...
Shingle Springs Rancheria, California	-	-	-	-	-	-	-	-
El Dorado County	-	-	-	-	-	-	-	-
Shinnecock Reservation, New York	95	53.0	48.6	-	4.3	32.6	-	48.6
Suffolk County	95	53.0	48.6	-	4.3	32.6	-	48.6
Shoalwater Reservation, Washington	...	...	...	...	...	...	...	...
Pacific County	...	...	...	...	...	...	...	...
Sisseton Reservation, North Dakota-South Dakota	1,672	56.4	52.5	3.8	1.5	38.8	5.5	45.7
North Dakota	-	-	-	-	-	-	-	-
Richland County	-	-	-	-	-	-	-	-
Sargent County	-	-	-	-	-	-	-	-
South Dakota	1,672	56.4	52.5	3.8	1.5	38.8	5.5	45.7
Codington County	...	...	...	...	...	...	...	...
Day County	201	57.4	53.0	5.1	0.6	33.7	10.6	29.3
Grant County	-	-	-	-	-	-	-	-
Marshall County	167	59.6	57.2	-	2.4	29.4	1.4	48.9
Roberts County	1,304	55.8	51.9	4.1	1.5	40.7	5.3	47.6
Skokomish Reservation, Washington	180	58.3	54.2	2.5	2.1	34.2	4.8	40.8
Mason County	180	58.3	54.2	2.5	2.1	34.2	4.8	40.8
Skull Valley Reservation, Utah	-	-	-	-	-	-	-	-
Tooele County	-	-	-	-	-	-	-	-
Soboba Reservation, California	151	52.4	42.6	-	2.4	20.7	3.5	54.4
Riverside County	151	52.4	42.6	-	2.4	20.7	3.5	54.4
Sokaogon Chippewa Community, Wisconsin	55	29.7	24.1	-	5.6	50.0	2.3	51.1
Forest County	55	29.7	24.1	-	5.6	50.0	2.3	51.1
Southern Paiute Reservation, Utah	124	54.8	49.9	-	4.9	25.2	21.5	20.7
Iron County	62	59.9	50.1	-	9.8	29.8	19.2	21.4
Millard County	34	57.9	57.9	-	-	-	9.2	35.6
Sevier County	28	40.0	40.0	-	-	-	35.7	7.1
Southern Ute Reservation, Colorado	591	60.6	54.1	1.3	2.3	19.4	4.5	65.9
Archuleta County	...	...	...	...	...	...	...	...
La Plata County	582	60.5	53.9	1.3	2.3	17.7	4.3	66.2
Montezuma County	-	-	-	-	-	-	-	-
Spokane Reservation, Washington	688	49.4	45.6	0.3	3.1	24.6	4.8	52.9
Lincoln County	-	-	-	-	-	-	-	-
Stevens County	688	49.4	45.6	0.3	3.1	24.6	4.8	52.9
Squaxin Island Reservation, Washington	23	21.7	21.7	-	-	100.0	16.7	50.0
Mason County	23	21.7	21.7	-	-	100.0	16.7	50.0
Standing Rock Reservation, North Dakota-South Dakota	2,974	51.6	46.6	24.4	1.5	29.3	2.0	50.8
North Dakota	1,505	53.4	49.0	22.4	2.1	19.1	1.2	57.8
Sioux County	1,505	53.4	49.0	22.4	2.1	19.1	1.2	57.8
South Dakota	1,469	49.7	44.2	26.8	0.9	37.4	2.7	45.0
Corson County	1,469	49.7	44.2	26.8	0.9	37.4	2.7	45.0
Stewart's Point Rancheria, California	42	53.7	48.8	50.0	-	11.1	6.1	12.1

[Continued]

★ 291 ★

School Enrollment of Persons 3 to 34 Years Old on Identified Reservations, 1980 - VII
[Continued]

Identified reservation	All persons	Persons 3 to 34 years old				Persons 16 to 19 years old -- percent not enrolled in school, not high school graduates	Persons 25 years and over	
		Percent enrolled in school						
		Total	5 to 19 years		20 to 34 years old		Percent completed less than 5 years of school	Percent high school graduates
			Total	Bureau of indian affairs or tribal school				
Sonoma County	42	53.7	48.8	50.0	-	11.1	6.1	12.1
Stockbridge Reservation, Wisconsin	324	57.2	50.6	3.2	4.7	23.1	3.2	49.8
Shawano County	324	57.2	50.6	3.2	4.7	23.1	3.2	49.8
Sulphur Bank Reservation, California	74	50.4	43.4	4.0	-	33.3	13.2	25.0
Lake County	74	50.4	43.4	4.0	-	33.3	13.2	25.0
Summit Lake Reservation, Nevada	...	...	...	...	...	...	...	...
Humboldt County	...	...	...	...	...	...	...	...
Susanville Reservation, California	51	63.8	59.6	-	4.2	42.9	6.1	52.1
Lassen County	51	63.8	59.6	-	4.2	42.9	6.1	52.1
Swinomish Reservation, Washington	282	51.4	42.3	4.6	2.6	49.8	4.6	39.5
Skagit County	282	51.4	42.3	4.6	2.6	49.8	4.6	39.5
Sycuan Reservation, California	33	77.2	77.2	-	-	25.0	22.4	21.3
San Diego County	33	77.2	77.2	-	-	25.0	22.4	21.3
Tama Reservation, Georgia	17	44.0	44.0	-	-	-	6.3	43.8
Grady County	17	44.0	44.0	-	-	-	6.3	43.8
Toas Pueblo, New Mexico	551	60.4	52.6	53.4	3.2	7.1	13.8	51.7
Toas County	551	60.4	52.6	53.4	3.2	7.1	13.8	51.7
Te-Moak Reservation, Nevada	45	66.6	63.0	-	3.6	-	19.6	38.3
Elko County	45	66.6	63.0	-	3.6	-	19.6	38.3
Tesuque Pueblo, New Mexico	135	60.1	51.1	25.8	4.9	-	8.0	62.7
Sante Fe County	135	60.1	51.1	25.8	4.9	-	8.0	62.7
Tigua Reservation, Texas	255	55.3	46.3	0.8	3.1	38.9	21.0	15.0
El Paso County	255	55.3	46.3	0.8	3.1	38.9	21.0	15.0
Tonawanda Reservation, New York	223	54.9	50.1	-	4.3	41.6	4.6	49.9
Erie County	-	-	-	-	-	-	-	-
Genesee County	223	54.9	50.1	-	4.3	41.6	4.6	49.9
Niagara County	-	-	-	-	-	-	-	-
Torres-Martinez Reservation, California	-	-	-	-	-	-	-	-
Imperial County	-	-	-	-	-	-	-	-
Riverside County	-	-	-	-	-	-	-	-
Trinidad Rancheria, California	29	46.8	39.0	-	7.8	33.3	4.7	50.0
Humboldt County	29	46.8	39.0	-	7.8	33.3	4.7	50.0
Tulalip Reservation, Washington	496	55.4	48.0	3.9	4.4	44.5	2.3	50.2
Snohomish County	496	55.4	48.0	3.9	4.4	44.5	2.3	50.2
Tule River Reservation, California	307	56.2	49.6	3.5	0.6	35.9	5.1	35.6
Tulare County	307	56.2	49.6	3.5	0.6	35.9	5.1	35.6
Tunica-Biloxi Reservation, Louisiana	...	...	...	...	...	...	...	...
Avoyelles Parish	...	...	...	...	...	...	...	...
Tuolumne Rancheria, California	49	69.4	63.3	-	6.1	-	4.7	53.5
Tuolumne County	49	69.4	63.3	-	6.1	-	4.7	53.5
Turtle Mountain Reservatin, North Dakota	2,562	58.6	51.7	73.6	3.6	36.4	9.6	38.8
Rolette County	2,562	58.6	51.7	73.6	3.6	36.4	9.6	38.8
Tuscarora Reservation, New York	-	-	-	-	-	-	-	-
Niagara County	-	-	-	-	-	-	-	-
Twenty-Nine Palms Reservation, California	-	-	-	-	-	-	-	-

[Continued]

543

★ 291 ★

School Enrollment of Persons 3 to 34 Years Old on Identified Reservations, 1980 - VII
[Continued]

Identified reservation	Persons 3 to 34 years old					Persons 16 to 19 years old -- percent not enrolled in school, not high school graduates	Persons 25 years and over	
	All persons	Percent enrolled in school					Percent completed less than 5 years of school	Percent high school graduates
		Total	5 to 19 years		20 to 34 years old			
			Total	Bureau of indian affairs or tribal school				
San Bernardino County	-	-	-	-	-	-	-	-
Uintah and Ouray Reservation, Utah	1,451	53.6	45.4	6.6	2.2	33.6	7.4	47.7
Carbon County	-	-	-	-	-	-	-	-
Duchesne County	279	54.2	49.3	1.1	1.6	42.3	11.4	58.3
Grand County	-	-	-	-	-	-	-	-
Uintah County	1,173	53.4	44.5	8.1	2.4	31.8	6.4	45.0
Utah County	-	-	-	-	-	-	-	-
Wasatch County	-	-	-	-	-	-	-	-
Umatilla Reservation, Oregon	539	60.9	52.9	4.7	4.8	17.2	3.5	56.5
Umatilla County	539	60.9	52.9	4.7	4.8	17.2	3.5	56.5
Union County	-	-	-	-	-	-	-	-
Upper Sioux Community, Minnesota	25	50.2	50.2	-	-	-	7.6	31.9
Yellow Medicine County	25	50.2	50.2	-	-	-	7.6	31.9
Upper Skagit Reservation, Washington	-	-	-	-	-	-	-	-
Skagit County	-	-	-	-	-	-	-	-
Ute Mountain Reservation, Colorado-New Mexico	750	48.7	42.6	4.0	1.1	22.5	23.0	16.7
Colorado	750	48.7	42.6	4.0	1.1	22.5	23.0	16.7
La Plata County	-	-	-	-	-	-	-	-
Montezuma County	750	48.7	42.6	4.0	1.1	22.5	23.0	16.7
New Mexico	-	-	-	-	-	-	-	-
San Juan County	-	-	-	-	-	-	-	-
Vermillion Lake Reservation, Minnesota	62	50.1	47.8	-	-	16.8	-	56.7
St. Louis County	62	50.1	47.8	-	-	16.8	-	56.7
Viejas Rancheria, California	81	51.7	48.4	3.2	-	20.4	8.7	44.4
San Diego County	81	51.7	48.4	3.2	-	20.4	8.7	44.4
Walker River Reservation, Nevada	284	59.9	52.8	4.0	2.8	20.0	3.5	53.5
Churchill County	-	-	-	-	-	-	-	-
Lyon County	-	-	-	-	-	-	-	-
Mineral County	284	59.9	52.8	4.0	2.8	20.0	3.5	53.5
Wampanoag Reservation, Massachusetts	-	-	-	-	-	-	-	-
Bristol County	-	-	-	-	-	-	-	-
Warm Springs Reservation, Oregon	1,399	55.7	47.8	7.0	2.7	28.8	4.7	60.0
Clackamas County	-	-	-	-	-	-	-	-
Jefferson County	1,178	55.1	46.6	7.3	2.6	28.7	3.9	61.9
Marion County	-	-	-	-	-	-	-	-
Wasco County	222	58.9	54.2	5.5	2.8	29.4	8.3	51.2
Washoe Reservation, Nevada	-	-	-	-	-	-	-	-
Douglas County	-	-	-	-	-	-	-	-
Western Pequot Reservation, Connecticut	...	...	...	...	...	...	...	...
New London County	...	...	...	...	...	...	...	...
White Earth Reservation, Minnesota	1,609	52.2	46.6	7.4	2.0	35.0	2.0	44.5
Becker County	785	51.8	45.6	7.1	1.9	36.0	2.3	42.5
Clearwater County	208	51.2	43.6	13.5	2.7	50.1	4.6	33.3
Mahnomen County	615	53.1	49.0	5.9	1.9	27.8	1.0	50.0
Wind River Reservation, Wyoming	2,737	51.8	47.2	20.5	2.7	31.0	2.6	47.1
Fremont County	2,725	52.0	47.5	20.5	2.7	30.6	2.6	47.3

[Continued]

★ 291 ★

School Enrollment of Persons 3 to 34 Years Old on Identified Reservations, 1980 - VII
[Continued]

Identified reservation	Persons 3 to 34 years old					Persons 16 to 19 years old -- percent not enrolled in school, not high school graduates	Persons 25 years and over	
	All persons	Percent enrolled in school					Percent completed less than 5 years of school	Percent high school graduates
		Total	5 to 19 years		20 to 34 years old			
			Total	Bureau of indian affairs or tribal school				
Hot Springs County	...	...	...	...	...	...	...	...
Winnebago Reservation, Nebraska	693	58.3	50.0	5.6	3.2	23.0	2.8	55.1
Dixon County	...	...	...	...	...	...	...	...
Thurston County	692	58.2	50.1	5.6	3.2	23.0	2.6	55.2
Winnemucca Colony, Nevada	21	55.4	55.4	-	-	-	7.1	35.7
Humboldt County	21	55.4	55.4	-	-	-	7.1	35.7
Wisconsin Winnebago Reservation	259	63.2	54.9	5.1	4.6	34.4	3.0	50.9
Jackson County	31	59.7	59.7	-	-	-	-	28.9
Juneau County	64	57.4	52.8	4.3	4.6	39.1	10.8	30.8
Monroe County	...	...	...	...	...	...	...	...
Sauk County	73	58.9	55.9	-	-	46.7	-	57.4
Shawano County	...	...	...	...	...	...	...	...
Wood County	70	79.3	71.2	11.7	3.5	20.5	-	61.1
Woodfords Community, California	-	-	-	-	-	-	-	-
Alpine County	-	-	-	-	-	-	-	-
XL Ranch Reservation, California	...	...	...	...	...	...	...	...
Modoc County	...	...	...	...	...	...	...	...
Yakima Reservation, Washington	3,206	55.6	48.5	6.1	3.8	30.6	4.7	51.3
Klickitat County	53	41.5	34.0	-	3.8	-	-	68.4
Yakima County	3,153	55.9	48.8	6.2	3.8	31.0	4.7	51.2
Yankton Reservation, South Dakota	1,059	48.2	45.1	24.1	1.1	22.7	6.9	40.8
Charles Mix County	1,059	48.2	45.1	24.1	1.1	22.7	6.9	40.8
Yavapai Reservation, Arizona	42	66.7	47.6	-	16.7	-	7.4	55.6
Yavapai County	42	66.7	47.6	-	16.7	-	7.4	55.6
Yerington Reservation, Nevada	64	75.8	67.5	-	3.2	-	14.7	43.6
Lyon County	64	75.8	67.5	-	3.2	-	14.7	43.6
Yomba Reservation, Nevada	40	46.1	43.4	5.8	2.7	15.2	8.2	20.9
Nye County	40	46.1	43.4	5.8	2.7	15.2	8.2	20.9
Zia Pueblo, New Mexico	338	58.5	48.0	44.2	3.4	15.9	6.9	49.7
Sandoval County	338	58.5	48.0	44.2	3.4	15.9	6.9	49.7
Zuni Pueblo, New Mexico	4,168	53.0	48.9	5.2	2.2	30.2	5.6	38.3
McKinley County	4,168	53.0	48.9	5.2	2.2	30.2	5.6	38.3
Valencia County	-	-	-	-	-	-	-	-
San Felipe/Santa Ana Joint Area, New Mexico	-	-	-	-	-	-	-	-
Sandoval County	-	-	-	-	-	-	-	-
San Felipe/Santo Domingo Joint Area, New Mexico	88	64.5	49.3	-	10.1	35.4	-	64.2
Sandoval County	88	64.5	49.3	-	10.1	35.4	-	64.2
Other Reservation Lands in Montana	-	-	-	-	-	-	-	-
Big Horn County	-	-	-	-	-	-	-	-

Source: U.S. Bureau of the Census, Subject Reports, PC80-2-1D, Part 1, *American Indians, Eskimos, and Aleuts on Identified Reservations and in the Historic Areas of Oklahoma (Excluding Urbanized Areas)*, U.S. Government Printing Office, Washington, D.C., 1986, pp. 50-58. *Notes:* A dash "(-)" represents zero or a percent which rounds to less than 0.1. Also, a dash "(-)" is used because the number of supplementary questionnaires for the reservations was insufficient to produce reliable estimates. Three dots "..." means not applicable, or that the data are being withheld to avoid disclosure of information for individuals.

★ 292 ★

School Enrollment of Persons 3 to 34 Years Old on Identified Reservations, 1980 - VIII

Data are the latest available.

Identified reservations	Total	Always lived on this reservation	Persons 1 year and over				
			Did not always live on this reservation		Percent moved onto reservation in--		
			Total		1979 or 1980	1975 to 1978	1974 or earlier
			Number	Percent			
St. Croix Reservation, Wisconsin	401	161	216	53.7	7.2	22.3	24.2
Barron County	82	52	30	37.0	3.8	6.9	26.3
Burnett County	241	68	151	62.8	8.3	24.6	29.9
Polk County	78	42	34	43.2	7.4	31.1	4.7
St. Regis Mohawk Reservation, New York	1,722	1,476	220	12.8	1.9	4.7	6.2
Franklin County	1,722	1,476	220	12.8	1.9	4.7	6.2
Salt River Reservation, Arizona	2,523	1,791	519	20.6	8.7	4.1	7.7
Maricopa County	2,523	1,791	519	20.6	8.7	4.1	7.7
San Carlos Reservation, Arizona	5,631	4,136	877	15.6	6.0	3.9	5.7
Gila County	3,322	2,535	613	18.5	7.0	4.7	6.8
Graham County	2,309	1,600	264	11.4	4.5	2.8	4.1
Pinal County	-	-	-	-	-	-	-
Sandia Pueblo, New Mexico	218	140	47	21.7	7.8	4.2	9.7
Bernalillo County	-	-	-	-	-	-	-
Sandoval County	218	140	47	21.7	7.8	4.2	9.7
Sandy Lake Reservation, Minnesota	-	-	-	-	-	-	-
Aitkin County	-	-	-	-	-	-	-
San Felipe Pueblo, New Mexico	1,742	1,663	67	3.9	0.6	0.5	2.8
Sandoval County	1,742	1,663	67	3.9	0.6	0.5	2.8
San Ildefonso Pueblo, New Mexico	470	351	110	23.4	3.7	3.7	16.0
Sandoval County	-	-	-	-	-	-	-
Sante Fe County	470	351	110	23.4	3.7	3.7	16.0
San Juan Pueblo, New Mexico	822	565	228	27.7	6.8	7.6	13.3
Rio Arriba County	822	565	228	27.7	6.8	7.6	13.3
San Manuel Reservation, California	-	-	-	-	-	-	-
San Bernardino County	-	-	-	-	-	-	-
San Pasqual Reservation, California	118	6	77	65.0	7.2	34.7	23.2
San Diego County	118	6	77	65.0	7.2	34.7	23.2
Santa Ana Pueblo, New Mexico	397	243	146	36.8	7.0	10.4	19.4
Sandoval County	397	243	146	36.8	7.0	10.4	19.4
Santa Clara Pueblo, New Mexico	1,780	1,036	662	37.2	9.5	8.7	19.0
Rio Arriba County	1,754	1,032	653	37.2	9.6	8.7	18.9
Sandoval County	-	-	-	-	-	-	-
Sante Fe County	...	...	...	...	...	...	...
Santa Rosa Rancheria, California	118	81	37	31.0	5.9	15.5	9.6
Kings County	118	81	37	31.0	5.9	15.5	9.6
Santa Rosa Reservation, California	...	...	...	...	...	...	...
Riverside County	...	...	...	...	...	...	...
Santa Ynez Reservation, California	119	34	83	70.1	29.9	7.2	33.0
Santa Barbara County	119	34	83	70.1	29.9	7.2	33.0
Santa Ysabel Reservation, California	173	36	118	68.0	14.4	23.2	30.4
San Diego County	173	36	118	68.0	14.4	23.2	30.4
Santee Reservation, Nebraska	402	62	115	28.7	7.8	10.3	10.5
Knox County	402	62	115	28.7	7.8	10.3	10.5
Santo Domingo Pueblo, New Mexico	2,087	1,720	360	17.2	3.6	3.7	10.0
Sandoval County	2,087	1,720	360	17.2	3.6	3.7	10.0
Santa Fe County	-	-	-	-	-	-	-
San Xavier Reservation, Arizona	817	487	314	38.5	7.7	12.2	18.6
Pima County	817	487	314	38.5	7.7	12.2	18.6

[Continued]

★ 292 ★

School Enrollment of Persons 3 to 34 Years Old on Identified Reservations, 1980 - VIII
[Continued]

Identified reservations	Persons 1 year and over						
	Total	Always lived on this reservation	Did not always live on this reservation				
			Total		Percent moved onto reservation in--		
			Number	Percent	1979 or 1980	1975 to 1978	1974 or earlier
Sauk-Suiattle Reservation, Washington	-	-	-	-	-	-	-
Snohomish County	-	-	-	-	-	-	-
Sault Ste. Marie Reservation, Michigan	-	-	-	-	-	-	-
Chippewa County	-	-	-	-	-	-	-
Schaghticoke Reservation, Michigan	...	...	...	...	...	...	...
Litchfield County	...	...	...	...	...	...	...
Shakopee Community, Minnesota	73	8	54	74.8	5.6	14.7	54.5
Scott County	73	8	54	74.8	5.6	14.7	54.5
Sheep Ranch Rancheria, California	...	...	...	...	...	...	...
Calaveras County	...	...	...	...	...	...	...
Sherwood Valley Rancheria, California	...	...	...	...	...	...	...
Mendocino County	...	...	...	...	...	...	...
Shingle Springs Rancheria, California	-	-	-	-	-	-	-
El Dorado County	-	-	-	-	-	-	-
Shinnecock Reservation, New York	194	98	78	40.1	13.7	8.0	18.4
Suffolk County	194	98	78	40.1	13.7	8.0	18.4
Shoalwater Reservation, Washington	...	...	...	...	...	...	...
Pacific County	...	...	...	...	...	...	...
Sisseton Reservation, North Dakota-South Dakota	2,498	1,519	920	36.8	11.2	11.9	13.7
North Dakota	-	-	-	-	-	-	-
Richland County	-	-	-	-	-	-	-
Sargent County	-	-	-	-	-	-	-
South Dakota	2,498	1,519	920	36.8	11.2	11.9	13.7
Codington County	...	...	...	...	...	...	...
Day County	302	206	92	30.4	10.9	12.6	6.9
Grant County	-	-	-	-	-	-	-
Marshall County	249	118	126	50.5	7.6	27.3	15.6
Roberts County	1,944	1,193	702	36.1	11.7	9.9	14.5
Skokomish Reservation, Washington	295	200	88	29.8	8.4	12.8	8.6
Mason County	295	200	88	29.8	8.4	12.8	8.6
Skull Valley Reservation, Utah	-	-	-	-	-	-	-
Tooele County	-	-	-	-	-	-	-
Soboba Reservation, California	226	139	81	36.0	13.3	9.6	13.1
Riverside County	226	139	81	36.0	13.3	9.6	13.1
Sokaogon Chippewa Community, Wisconsin	93	52	41	44.4	15.2	16.3	13.0
Forest County	93	52	41	44.4	15.2	16.3	13.0
Southern Paiute Reservation, Utah	181	98	83	45.7	15.9	19.1	10.7
Iron County	91	55	36	39.6	19.5	5.3	14.8
Millard County	48	18	30	62.2	5.5	50.5	6.3
Sevier County	42	25	17	40.0	20.0	13.3	6.7
Southern Ute Reservation, Colorado	858	476	212	24.7	7.5	5.3	11.8
Archuleta County	...	...	...	...	...	...	...
La Plata County	846	475	202	23.8	7.3	5.4	11.2
Montezuma County	-	-	-	-	-	-	-
Spokane Reservation, Washington	1,019	395	622	61.1	11.6	21.2	28.2
Lincoln County	-	-	-	-	-	-	-
Stevens County	1,019	395	622	61.1	11.6	21.2	28.2
Squaxin Island Reservation, Washington	29	-	27	93.1	13.8	79.3	-
Mason County	29	-	27	93.1	13.8	79.3	-

[Continued]

★ 292 ★

School Enrollment of Persons 3 to 34 Years Old on Identified Reservations, 1980 - VIII
[Continued]

Identified reservations	Total	Always lived on this reservation	Persons 1 year and over				
			Did not always live on this reservation				
			Total		Percent moved onto reservation in--		
			Number	Percent	1979 or 1980	1975 to 1978	1974 or earlier
Standing Rock Reservation, North Dakota-South Dakota	4,428	2,841	1,268	28.6	10.2	6.9	11.6
North Dakota	2,160	1,510	628	29.1	7.0	9.3	12.8
Sioux County	2,160	1,510	628	29.1	7.0	9.3	12.8
South Dakota	2,268	1,331	640	28.2	13.1	4.6	10.4
Corson County	2,268	1,331	640	28.2	13.1	4.6	10.4
Stewart's Point Rancheria, California	70	22	35	50.7	1.4	14.5	34.8
Sonoma County	70	22	35	50.7	1.4	14.5	34.8
Stockbridge Reservation, Wisconsin	561	72	422	75.1	11.7	19.9	43.5
Shawano County	561	72	422	75.1	11.7	19.9	43.5
Sulphur Bank Reservation, California	110	71	38	34.9	13.7	11.9	9.2
Lake County	110	71	38	34.9	13.7	11.9	9.2
Summit Lake Reservation, Nevada	...	...	...	...	...	...	...
Humboldt County	...	...	...	...	...	...	...
Susanville Reservation, California	83	13	46	55.0	6.5	33.5	15.0
Lassen County	83	13	46	55.0	6.5	33.5	15.0
Swinomish Reservation, Washington	413	163	246	59.6	18.7	7.8	33.0
Skagit County	413	163	246	59.6	18.7	7.8	33.0
Sycuan Reservation, California	54	17	37	68.8	-	6.6	62.2
San Diego County	54	17	37	68.8	-	6.6	62.2
Tama Reservation, Georgia	30	-	30	100.0	17.9	42.8	39.2
Grady County	30	-	30	100.0	17.9	42.8	39.2
Toas Pueblo, New Mexico	1,032	767	240	23.2	5.5	6.3	11.5
Toas County	1,032	767	240	23.2	5.5	6.3	11.5
Te-Moak Reservation, Nevada	91	27	64	70.0	1.4	24.7	43.9
Elko County	91	27	64	70.0	1.4	24.7	43.9
Tesuque Pueblo, New Mexico	232	158	63	27.0	5.6	8.0	13.3
Sante Fe County	232	158	63	27.0	5.6	8.0	13.3
Tigua Reservation, Texas	353	1	352	99.7	4.2	93.2	2.3
El Paso County	353	1	352	99.7	4.2	93.2	2.3
Tonawanda Reservation, New York	432	275	92	21.3	5.3	2.7	13.2
Erie County	-	-	-	-	-	-	-
Genesee County	432	275	92	21.3	5.3	2.7	13.2
Niagara County	-	-	-	-	-	-	-
Torres-Martinez Reservation, California	-	-	-	-	-	-	-
Imperial County	-	-	-	-	-	-	-
Riverside County	-	-	-	-	-	-	-
Trinidad Rancheria, California	46	1	40	87.9	10.0	21.9	56.0
Humboldt County	46	1	40	87.9	10.0	21.9	56.0
Tulalip Reservation, Washington	745	364	349	46.8	15.2	12.4	19.3
Snohomish County	745	364	349	46.8	15.2	12.4	19.3
Tule River Reservation, California	415	292	116	28.1	13.4	6.5	8.1
Tulare County	415	292	116	28.1	13.4	6.5	8.1
Tunica-Biloxi Reservation, Louisiana	...	...	...	...	...	...	...
Avoyelles Parish	...	...	...	...	...	...	...
Tuolumne Rancheria, California	81	17	64	79.0	18.5	23.5	37.0
Tuolumne County	81	17	64	79.0	18.5	23.5	37.0
Turtle Mountain Reservatin, North Dakota	3,881	2,728	1,100	28.3	7.1	5.8	15.5
Rolette County	3,881	2,728	1,100	28.3	7.1	5.8	15.5
Tuscarora Reservation, New York	-	-	-	-	-	-	-

[Continued]

★ 292 ★

School Enrollment of Persons 3 to 34 Years Old on Identified Reservations, 1980 - VIII
[Continued]

| Identified reservations | Total | Always lived on this reservation | Did not always live on this reservation | | Percent moved onto reservation in-- | | |
| | | | Total | | 1979 or 1980 | 1975 to 1978 | 1974 or earlier |
			Number	Percent			
Niagara County	-	-	-	-	-	-	-
Twenty-Nine Palms Reservation, California	-	-	-	-	-	-	-
San Bernardino County	-	-	-	-	-	-	-
Uintah and Ouray Reservation, Utah	2,110	1,280	440	20.9	6.9	4.6	9.3
Carbon County	-	-	-	-	-	-	-
Duchesne County	413	248	56	13.6	7.3	1.8	4.4
Grand County	-	-	-	-	-	-	-
Uintah County	1,697	1,032	384	22.6	6.8	5.3	10.6
Utah County	-	-	-	-	-	-	-
Wasatch County	-	-	-	-	-	-	-
Umatilla Reservation, Oregon	881	387	458	52.0	12.2	18.3	21.6
Umatilla County	881	387	458	52.0	12.2	18.3	21.6
Union County	-	-	-	-	-	-	-
Upper Sioux Community, Minnesota	52	8	44	84.0	8.1	17.9	57.9
Yellow Medicine County	52	8	44	84.0	8.1	17.9	57.9
Upper Skagit Reservation, Washington	-	-	-	-	-	-	-
Skagit County	-	-	-	-	-	-	-
Ute Mountain Reservation, Colorado-New Mexico	1,085	557	113	10.4	3.8	2.6	4.0
Colorado	1,085	557	113	10.4	3.8	2.6	4.0
La Plata County	-	-	-	-	-	-	-
Montezuma County	1,085	557	113	10.4	3.8	2.6	4.0
New Mexico	-	-	-	-	-	-	-
San Juan County	-	-	-	-	-	-	-
Vermillion Lake Reservation, Minnesota	104	23	79	75.8	32.1	16.1	27.6
St. Louis County	104	23	79	75.8	32.1	16.1	27.6
Viejas Rancheria, California	142	53	86	60.3	15.6	14.7	30.0
San Diego County	142	53	86	60.3	15.6	14.7	30.0
Walker River Reservation, Nevada	469	226	240	51.2	12.2	13.6	25.4
Churchill County	-	-	-	-	-	-	-
Lyon County	-	-	-	-	-	-	-
Mineral County	469	226	240	51.2	12.2	13.6	25.4
Wampanoag Reservation, Massachusetts	-	-	-	-	-	-	-
Bristol County	-	-	-	-	-	-	-
Warm Springs Reservation, Oregon	1,936	1,094	626	32.3	9.0	9.1	14.3
Clackamas County	-	-	-	-	-	-	-
Jefferson County	1,603	871	560	34.9	9.8	10.0	15.0
Marion County	-	-	-	-	-	-	-
Wasco County	332	222	66	20.0	5.0	4.5	10.5
Washoe Reservation, Nevada	-	-	-	-	-	-	-
Douglas County	-	-	-	-	-	-	-
Western Pequot Reservation, Connecticut	...	...	...	...	...	...	...
New London County	...	...	...	...	...	...	...
White Earth Reservation, Minnesota	2,481	1,505	953	38.4	7.0	15.6	15.8
Becker County	1,218	763	439	36.0	7.6	16.1	12.3
Clearwater County	306	236	68	22.1	7.5	11.3	3.3
Mahnomen County	956	505	446	46.7	6.0	16.3	24.4
Wind River Reservation, Wyoming	4,020	2,670	913	22.7	7.6	7.4	7.7
Fremont County	4,000	2,650	913	22.8	7.7	7.4	7.7

[Continued]

★ 292 ★

School Enrollment of Persons 3 to 34 Years Old on Identified Reservations, 1980 - VIII
[Continued]

Identified reservations	Total	Always lived on this reservation	Did not always live on this reservation				
			Total		Percent moved onto reservation in--		
			Number	Percent	1979 or 1980	1975 to 1978	1974 or earlier
Hot Springs County	...	...	...	...	...	...	...
Winnebago Reservation, Nebraska	1,066	323	292	27.4	8.8	8.1	10.5
Dixon County	...	...	...	...	...	...	...
Thurston County	1,064	323	292	27.5	8.8	8.1	10.5
Winnemucca Colony, Nevada	32	8	24	74.3	43.6	-	30.7
Humboldt County	32	8	24	74.3	43.6	-	30.7
Wisconsin Winnebago Reservation	348	10	223	64.1	16.9	28.9	18.3
Jackson County	36	10	-	-	-	-	-
Juneau County	95	-	95	100.0	21.5	24.4	54.1
Monroe County	...	...	...	...	...	...	...
Sauk County	92	-	24	26.2	2.4	23.7	-
Shawano County	...	...	...	...	...	...	...
Wood County	93	-	93	100.0	32.7	53.8	13.5
Woodfords Community, California	-	-	-	-	-	-	-
Alpine County	-	-	-	-	-	-	-
XL Ranch Reservation, California	...	...	...	...	...	...	...
Modoc County	...	...	...	...	...	...	...
Yakima Reservation, Washington	4,810	2,982	1,472	30.6	6.2	8.8	15.6
Klickitat County	66	43	23	34.8	13.6	9.1	12.1
Yakima County	4,744	2,939	1,449	30.5	6.1	8.7	15.7
Yankton Reservation, South Dakota	1,581	861	645	40.8	12.1	16.4	12.4
Charles Mix County	1,581	861	645	40.8	12.1	16.4	12.4
Yavapai Reservation, Arizona	63	34	29	46.0	15.9	7.9	22.2
Yavapai County	63	34	29	46.0	15.9	7.9	22.2
Yerington Reservation, Nevada	107	42	64	60.1	1.0	12.6	46.5
Lyon County	107	42	64	60.1	1.0	12.6	46.5
Yomba Reservation, Nevada	56	28	28	49.2	18.5	14.7	16.1
Nye County	56	28	28	49.2	18.5	14.7	16.1
Zia Pueblo, New Mexico	499	457	40	8.1	1.9	1.9	4.3
Sandoval County	499	457	40	8.1	1.9	1.9	4.3
Zuni Pueblo, New Mexico	5,831	5,151	599	10.3	2.2	3.0	5.1
McKinley County	5,831	5,151	599	10.3	2.2	3.0	5.1
Valencia County	-	-	-	-	-	-	-
San Felipe/Santa Ana Joint Area, New Mexico	-	-	-	-	-	-	-
Sandoval County	-	-	-	-	-	-	-
San Felipe/Santo Domingo Joint Area, New Mexico	112	100	11	10.2	2.3	5.0	2.9
Sandoval County	112	100	11	10.2	2.3	5.0	2.9
Other Reservation Lands in Montana	-	-	-	-	-	-	-
Big Horn County	-	-	-	-	-	-	-

Source: U.S. Bureau of the Census, Subject Reports, PC80-2-1D, Part 1, *American Indians, Eskimos, and Aleuts on Identified Reservations and in the Historic Areas of Oklahoma (Excluding Urbanized Areas)*, U.S. Government Printing Office, Washington, D.C., 1986, pp. 50-58. *Notes:* A dash "(-)" represents zero or a percent which rounds to less than 0.1. Also, a dash "(-)" is used because the number of supplementary questionnaires for the reservations was insufficient to produce reliable estimates. Three dots "..." means not applicable, or that the data are being withheld to avoid disclosure of information for individuals.

★ 293 ★

School Enrollment, by Sector

Percent of eighth graders enrolled in each school sector in 1988 is shown for each race/ethnicity.

Race/ethnicity	Public school	Catholic school	Independent school	Other private school
Total	87.9	7.5	1.0	3.6
American Indian and Native Alaskan	92.0	3.4	0.3	4.3
Asian and Pacific Islander	83.8	8.8	3.2	4.2
Hispanic	90.5	7.9	0.4	1.2
Black	92.9	5.7	0.5	0.9
White	86.7	7.8	1.1	4.4

Source: "Percentage of Eighth Graders Who Are Enrolled in Various School Sectors, by Selected Background Characteristics," *A Profile of the American Eighth Grader*, 1990, p. 19. Primary source: U.S. Department of Education, National Center for Education Statistics, "National Education Longitudinal Study of 1988: Base Year Student Survey".

★ 294 ★

Public School Enrollment Trends

Percent change in enrollment from 1976 to 1986 is shown for each race/ethnicity.

Race/ethnicity	Percent
American Indian, Aleut, Eskimo	-3.3
White, non-Hispanic	-12.9
Black, non-Hispanic	-2.2
Hispanic	44.7
Asian/Pacific Islander	116.4
Total	16.4

Source: "Percent Change Within Race/Ethnicity Group, 1976 to 1986," *The Condition of Education 1991, Volume 1, Elementary and Secondary Education*, 1991, p. 69. Primary source: U.S. Department of Education, Office of Civil Rights, *Directory of Elementary and Secondary School Districts and Schools in Selected Districts*: 1976-1977; and 1984 and 1986 Elementary and Secondary School Civil Rights Survey.

★ 295 ★

Public School Enrollment, 1976 and 1986

Percent distribution of enrolled students is shown, by race/ethnicity for 1976 and for 1986.

Race/ethnicity	1976	1986
Total minority	24.0	29.6
American Indian, Aleut, Eskimo	0.8	0.9
White, non-Hispanic	76.0	70.4
Black, non-Hispanic	15.5	16.1
Hispanic	6.4	9.9
Asian/Pacific Islander	1.2	2.8

Source: "Enrollment in Public Elementary and Secondary Education, by Race/Ethnicity: 1976 and 1986," *The Condition of Education 1991, Volume 1, Elementary and Secondary Education,* 1991, p. 69. Primary source: U.S. Department of Education, Office for Civil Rights, *Directory of Elementary and Secondary School Districts and Schools in Selected Districts*: 1976-1977; and 1984 and 1986 Elementary and Secondary School Civil Rights Survey.

★ 296 ★

Catholic School Enrollment, 1980-90

The enrollment of American Indian students reported by NCEA (the National Catholic Education Association) is shown.

Year	Total enrollment	NCEA Indian students	% of NCEA population
1990	2,475,439	9,743	(.39)
1989	2,498,870	10,279	(.41)
1988	2,623,031	9,200	(.35)
1987	2,734,000	9,300	(.34)
1986	2,821,000	9,700	(.34)
1985	2,901,000	9,100	(.31)
1984	2,968,154	9,700	(.33)
1983	3,026,200	10,700	(.35)
1982	3,094,000	10,000	(.32)
1981	3,106,378	9,700	(.31)
1980	3,140,051	10,000	(.32)

Source: Toward the Year 2000: Listening to the Voice of Native America, National Advisory Council on Indian Education, 17th Annual report to the United States Congress, Fiscal Year 1990, p. 66. Primary source: U.S. Department of Education, National Center for Education Statistics, Digest of Education Statistics 1990 - Enrollment in Educational Institutions 1869-70 to fall 2001. National Catholic Educational Association, 1989-90 Annual Report.

★ 297 ★

Nursery School and Kindergarten Enrollment on Reservations, by Type of School, 1980 - I

Data are the latest available and are for persons 3 years old and older.

Identified reservation	Nursery school						Kindergarten					
	Total	Tribal school	Bureau of Indian Affairs school	Other public school	Other private school	Not reported	Total	Tribal school	Bureau of Indian Affairs school	Other public school	Other private school	Not reported
American Indian, Eskimo and Aleut	7,478	2,449	923	2,105	417	1,585	8,577	715	1,833	4,639	307	1,083
Acoma Pueblo, New Mexico	54	34	9	2	-	10	48	10	30	1	-	7
Agua Caliente, California	-	-	-	-	-	-	-	-	-	-	-	-
Alabama-Coushatta, Texas	17	1	-	12	-	3	18	4	-	9	-	5
Alamo, New Mexico	7	1	-	-	4	2	27	1	5	-	8	13
Allegany, New York	33	5	-	1	14	12	18	-	-	17	-	1
Alturas Rancheria, California	...	...	...	...	...	...	...	...	...	...	...	...
Annette Islands Reserve, Alaska	32	-	-	29	-	3	16	-	-	15	-	2
Augustine, California	-	-	-	-	-	-	-	-	-	-	-	-
Bad River, Wisconsin	23	11	-	10	-	1	29	-	-	27	-	2
Barona Rancheria, California	10	6	-	-	1	2	6	-	-	6	-	-
Bay Mills, Michigan	10	-	-	2	-	8	9	-	-	9	-	-
Benton Paiute, California	...	...	...	...	...	...	...	...	...	...	...	...
Berry Creek Rancheria, California	-	-	-	-	-	-	-	-	-	-	-	-
Big Bend Rancheria, California	...	...	...	...	...	...	...	...	...	...	...	...
Big Cypress, Florida	19	-	-	17	-	2	12	-	12	-	-	-
Big Lagoon Rancheria, California	...	...	...	...	...	...	...	...	...	...	...	...
Big Pine Rancheria, California	6	3	-	1	1	1	2	-	-	2	-	-
Bishop Rancheria, California	25	2	-	23	-	-	13	-	-	10	1	2
Blackfeet, Montana	138	9	3	74	-	52	126	2	-	100	-	25
Bois Forte (Nett Lake), Minnesota	30	22	-	3	-	5	10	-	-	10	-	-
Bridgeport Colony, California	-	-	-	-	-	-	-	-	-	-	-	-
Brighton, Florida	22	14	6	1	1	-	9	-	-	9	-	-
Burns, Oregon	10	-	-	5	5	-	1	-	-	1	-	-
Cabazon, California	...	...	...	...	...	...	...	...	...	...	...	...
Cachil Dehe Rancheria, California	...	...	...	...	...	...	...	...	...	...	...	...
Cahuilla, California	...	...	...	...	...	...	...	...	...	...	...	...
Campo, California	-	-	-	-	-	-	1	-	-	1	-	-
Camp Verde, Arizona	5	-	-	4	-	1	4	-	-	3	1	-
Canoncito, New Mexico	15	9	2	-	-	4	20	-	19	-	-	1
Capitan Grande, California	-	-	-	-	-	-	-	-	-	-	-	-
Carson Colony, Nevada	-	-	-	-	-	-	5	-	-	5	-	-
Catawba, South Carolina	4	-	-	1	2	-	30	-	-	26	1	2
Cattaraugus, New York	73	35	-	24	-	14	44	-	-	35	1	8
Cedarville Rancheria, California	...	...	...	...	...	...	...	...	...	...	...	...
Chehalis, Washington	12	12	-	-	-	-	6	-	-	6	-	-
Chemehuevi, California	...	...	...	...	...	...	...	...	...	...	...	...
Cheyenne River, South Dakota	65	26	26	-	-	12	27	1	19	2	-	4
Chitimacha, Louisiana	-	-	-	-	-	-	6	3	-	-	-	3
Cochiti Pueblo, New Mexico	24	8	-	16	-	-	14	-	-	14	-	-
Cocopah, Arizona	14	10	-	2	-	2	8	1	-	7	-	-
Coeur d'Alene, Idaho	14	13	-	-	-	1	18	12	-	5	-	1
Cold Springs Rancheria, California	-	-	-	-	-	-	-	-	-	-	-	-
Colorado River, Arizona-California	66	16	4	25	5	16	50	-	1	42	-	7
Colville, Washington	77	7	1	53	1	15	93	2	-	85	-	5
Cortina Rancheria, California	...	...	...	...	...	...	...	...	...	...	...	...
Coushatta, Louisiana	...	...	...	...	...	...	...	...	...	...	...	...
Coyote Valley Rancheria, California	-	-	-	-	-	-	-	-	-	-	-	-
Crow, Montana	109	9	2	48	19	31	100	-	-	82	7	11
Crow Creek, South Dakota	59	46	3	2	2	6	27	3	11	12	2	-
Cuyapaipe, California	...	...	...	...	...	...	...	...	...	...	...	...
Deer Creek, Minnesota	...	...	...	...	...	...	...	...	...	...	...	...
Dresslerville Colony, Nevada	9	1	-	7	1	-	-	-	-	-	-	-
Dry Creek Rancheria, California	1	-	-	-	-	1	-	-	-	-	-	-
Duck Valley, Idaho-Nevada	26	13	-	9	-	3	16	-	-	15	-	1
Duckwater, Nevada	8	6	-	-	2	-	-	-	-	-	-	-
Eastern Cherokee, North Carolina	118	28	32	8	3	47	112	21	67	17	-	7
Eastern Pequot, Connecticut	...	...	...	...	...	...	...	...	...	...	...	...
Ely Colony, Nevada	-	-	-	-	-	-	2	-	-	1	-	1
Enterprise Rancheria, California	...	...	...	...	...	...	...	...	...	...	...	...
Fallon Colony, Nevada	-	-	-	-	-	-	-	-	-	-	-	-

[Continued]

★ 297 ★

Nursery School and Kindergarten Enrollment on Reservations, by Type of School, 1980 - I
[Continued]

Identified reservation	Nursery school						Kindergarten					
	Total	Tribal school	Bureau of Indian Affairs school	Other public school	Other private school	Not reported	Total	Tribal school	Bureau of Indian Affairs school	Other public school	Other private school	Not reported
Fallon, Nevada	7	1	2	1	-	2	6	-	-	6	-	-
Flandreau, South Dakota	5	-	-	4	-	1	3	-	-	2	-	1
Flathead, Montana	45	8	5	14	4	15	79	1	-	61	-	18
Fond du Lac, Minnesota	17	-	14	1	-	2	8	-	-	7	-	1
Fort Apache, Arizona	96	18	5	58	2	13	223	5	37	140	9	32
Fort Belknap, Montana	58	24	1	19	4	10	40	1	-	37	-	1
Fort Berthold, North Dakota	62	23	4	17	-	18	62	-	6	44	1	11
Fort Bidwell, California	2	-	-	-	-	2	2	-	-	2	-	-
Fort Hall, Idaho	45	9	2	25	3	6	66	2	1	50	1	12
Fort Independence, California	-	-	-	-	-	-	-	-	-	-	-	-
Fort McDermitt, Nevada-Oregon	18	1	-	11	-	6	9	-	-	8	-	1
Fort McDowell, Arizona	10	6	1	-	-	2	6	5	1	-	-	-
Fort Mojave, Arizona-California-Nevada	10	6	1	-	-	2	6	5	1	-	-	-
Fort Peck, Montana	132	32	22	44	1	33	114	-	2	95	1	16
Fort Totten, North Dakota	97	63	4	9	-	22	64	36	16	11	-	1
Fort Yuma, Arizona-California	43	10	3	22	2	6	14	-	-	11	1	2
Gila Bend, Arizona	-	-	-	-	-	-	-	-	-	-	-	-
Gila River, Arizona	156	69	32	38	5	13	169	21	48	82	-	19
Golden Hill, Connecticut	...	...	...	...	...	...	...	...	...	...	...	...
Goshute, Nevada-Utah	-	-	-	-	-	-	-	-	-	-	-	-
Grand Portage, Minnesota	7	-	-	7	-	-	8	-	-	8	-	-
Grindstone Creek Rancheria, California	2	-	-	2	-	-	-	-	-	-	-	-
Hannahville Community, Michigan	17	17	-	-	-	-	10	10	-	-	-	-
Hassanamisco, Massachusetts	...	...	...	...	...	...	...	...	...	...	...	...
Havasupai, Arizona	7	5	-	1	1	-	5	3	-	2	-	-
Hoh, Washington	2	2	-	-	-	-	-	-	-	-	-	-
Hollywood, Florida	8	8	-	-	-	-	23	12	-	7	1	2
Hoopa Valley, California	45	9	7	16	3	9	39	-	-	35	-	4
Hoopa Valley Extension, California	4	-	-	2	-	2	8	-	-	6	-	2
Hopi, Arizona	160	68	46	1	3	41	143	37	77	9	3	18
Hopland Rancheria, California	-	-	-	-	-	-	-	-	-	-	-	-
Hualapai, Arizona	46	23	-	9	-	13	12	-	-	9	-	3
Inaja-Cosmit, California	-	-	-	-	-	-	-	-	-	-	-	-
Indian Township, Maine	9	4	-	4	-	1	11	8	-	2	-	1
Iowa, Kansas-Nebraska	-	-	-	-	-	-	-	-	-	-	-	-
Isabella, Michigan	14	-	-	9	3	2	13	-	-	13	-	-

Source: U.S. Bureau of the Census, Subject Reports, PC80-2-1D, Part I, *American Indians, Eskimos, and Aleuts on Identified Reservations and in the Historic Areas of Oklahoma (Excluding Urbanized Areas)*, U.S. Government Printing Office, Washington, D.C., 1986, pp. 209-247. *Notes:* A dash (-) represents zero or a percent which rounds to less than 0.1. Also, a dash (-) is used because the number of supplementary questionnaires for the areas was insufficient to produce reliable estimates. Three dots (...) means not applicable, or that the data are being withheld to avoid disclosure of information for individuals.

★ 298 ★

Nursery School and Kindergarten Enrollment on Reservations, by Type of School, 1980 - II

Data are the latest available and are for persons 3 years old and older.

Identified reservation	Nursery school						Kindergarten					
	Total	Tribal school	Bureau of Indian Affairs school	Other public school	Other private school	Not reported	Total	Tribal school	Bureau of Indian Affairs school	Other public school	Other private school	Not reported
Isleta Pueblo, New Mexico	54	38	9	-	1	5	46	13	29	1	-	2
Jackson Rancheria, California	...	...	...	...	...	...	...	...	...	...	...	...
Jemez Pueblo, New Mexico	47	19	8	1	6	13	43	-	28	-	11	4
Jicarilla Apache, New Mexico	38	8	1	18	2	8	41	5	-	33	-	2
Kaibab, Arizona	-	-	-	-	-	-	8	-	-	8	-	-

[Continued]

Nursery School and Kindergarten Enrollment on Reservations, by Type of School, 1980 - II
[Continued]

Identified reservation	Nursery school						Kindergarten					
	Total	Tribal school	Bureau of Indian Affairs school	Other public school	Other private school	Not reported	Total	Tribal school	Bureau of Indian Affairs school	Other public school	Other private school	Not reported
Kalispel, Washington	3	-	-	3	-	-	3	-	-	3	-	-
Kickapoo, Kansas	11	-	-	5	2	4	14	-	-	14	-	-
Kootenai, Idaho	-	-	-	-	-	-	-	-	-	-	-	-
Lac Courte Oreilles, Wisconsin	52	40	2	10	-	-	17	6	-	3	8	-
Lac du Flambeau, Wisconsin	41	6	-	26	-	9	13	-	-	13	-	-
Laguna Pueblo, New Mexico	112	61	13	16	-	22	62	6	51	3	-	1
La Jolla, California	8	2	-	4	-	1	6	-	-	6	-	-
L'Anse, Michigan	15	-	-	12	1	1	12	-	-	12	-	-
La Posta, California	...	...	...	...	...	...	...	...	...	...	...	...
Las Vegas Colony, Nevada	4	-	-	4	-	-	4	-	-	4	-	-
Laytonville Rancheria, California	-	-	-	-	-	-	2	-	-	1	-	1
Leech Lake, Minnesota	97	21	13	37	2	25	61	-	-	52	2	7
Likely Rancheria, California	-	-	-	-	-	-	-	-	-	-	-	-
Lone Pine Rancheria, California	-	-	-	-	-	-	7	-	-	7	-	-
Lookout Rancheria, California	...	...	...	...	...	...	...	...	...	...	...	...
Los Coyotes, California	-	-	-	-	-	-	-	-	-	-	-	-
Lovelock Colony, Nevada	-	-	-	-	-	-	3	-	-	3	-	-
Lower Brule, South Dakota	40	23	9	-	-	8	20	11	6	2	2	-
Lower Elwah, Washington	-	-	-	-	-	-	-	-	-	-	-	-
Lower Sioux Community, Minnesota	-	-	-	-	-	-	5	-	-	5	-	-
Lummi, Washington	33	11	-	15	2	5	27	2	-	21	-	3
Makah, Washington	40	6	4	17	2	12	21	-	-	21	-	-
Manchester Rancheria, California	-	-	-	-	-	-	-	-	-	-	-	-
Manzanita, California	...	...	...	...	...	...	...	...	...	...	...	...
Maricopa, Arizona	23	14	-	-	6	3	6	-	1	5	-	-
Mattaponi, Virginia	-	-	-	-	-	-	-	-	-	-	-	-
Menominee, Wisconsin	89	12	4	29	23	22	46	-	1	26	6	13
Mesa Grande, California	-	-	-	-	-	-	-	-	-	-	-	-
Mescalero Apache, New Mexico	43	12	-	6	-	25	57	1	-	17	-	39
Miccosukee, Florida	9	9	-	-	-	-	3	3	-	-	-	-
Middletown Rancheria, California	-	-	-	-	-	-	-	-	-	-	-	-
Mille Lacs, Minnesota	-	-	-	-	-	-	-	-	-	-	-	-
Mississippi Choctaw Reservation	67	47	11	-	-	9	98	33	58	1	-	6
Moapa River, Nevada	-	-	-	-	-	-	4	-	-	3	-	1
Montgomery Creek Rancheria, California	...	...	...	...	...	...	...	...	...	...	...	...
Morongo, California	6	1	1	2	1	1	10	-	1	8	-	1
Muckleshoot, Washington	26	10	-	8	-	8	15	-	-	13	-	2
Nambe Pueblo, New Mexico	3	1	-	1	-	-	4	-	-	3	-	1
Navajo, Arizona-New Mexico-Utah	1,422	427	257	303	142	293	2,874	210	828	1,330	92	414
Nez Perce, Idaho	34	11	3	12	-	8	34	2	-	31	-	1
Nisqually, Washington	1	1	-	-	-	-	1	-	-	1	-	-
Nooksack, Washington	-	-	-	-	-	-	-	-	-	-	-	-
Northern Cheyenne, Montana	108	51	2	25	3	23	62	9	-	38	5	10
Oil Springs, New York	-	-	-	-	-	-	-	-	-	-	-	-
Omaha, Iowa-Nebraska	47	23	-	8	1	15	26	2	-	14	-	10
Oneida, Wisconsin	64	39	4	16	-	5	39	12	-	24	-	3
Onondaga, New York	-	-	-	-	-	-	-	-	-	-	-	-
Ontonagon, Michigan	-	-	-	-	-	-	-	-	-	-	-	-
Osage, Oklahoma	79	9	21	27	6	16	121	-	-	106	3	13
Ozette, Washington	...	...	...	...	...	...	...	...	...	...	...	...
Pala, California	12	1	-	8	3	-	11	-	-	5	7	-
Pamunkey, Virginia	-	-	-	-	-	-	-	-	-	-	-	-
Papago, Arizona	150	43	28	32	7	40	195	13	77	86	1	18
Pascua Yaqui, Arizona	6	-	-	6	-	-	8	-	-	8	-	-
Pauma, California	1	-	-	-	1	-	2	-	-	2	-	-
Payson Community of Yavapai-Apache, Arizona	-	-	-	-	-	-	-	-	-	-	-	-
Pechanga, California	3	-	1	2	-	-	4	-	-	2	1	1
Penobscot, Maine	6	-	-	-	6	-	13	-	-	13	-	-
Picuris Pueblo, New Mexico	4	2	-	-	-	2	4	-	1	3	-	-
Pine Creek, Michigan	...	...	...	...	...	...	...	...	...	...	...	...
Pine Ridge, South Dakota	302	114	58	32	30	68	268	25	133	40	29	41
Pleasant Point, Maine	16	12	-	3	1	-	18	12	-	1	-	5

[Continued]

★ 298 ★

Nursery School and Kindergarten Enrollment on Reservations, by Type of School, 1980 - II

[Continued]

Identified reservation	Nursery school						Kindergarten					
	Total	Tribal school	Bureau of Indian Affairs school	Other public school	Other private school	Not reported	Total	Tribal school	Bureau of Indian Affairs school	Other public school	Other private school	Not reported
Pojoaque Pueblo, New Mexico	3	2	-	-	-	1	2	-	-	2	-	-
Poospatuck, New York	1	-	-	1	-	-	3	-	-	2	-	1
Port Gamble, Washington	9	8	-	-	-	1	6	-	-	6	-	-
Port Madison, Washington	3	2	-	-	1	-	3	-	-	3	-	-
Potawatomi, Wisconsin	9	-	-	7	-	2	7	-	-	7	-	-
Pottawatomi, Kansas	-	-	-	-	-	-	-	-	-	-	-	-
Prairie Island Community, Minnesota	2	-	-	-	1	1	1	-	-	1	-	-
Puyallup, Washington	13	4	1	5	1	2	23	5	-	15	1	2
Pyramid Lake, Nevada	12	-	6	6	-	-	12	-	-	12	-	-
Quileute, Washington	8	8	-	-	-	-	12	9	-	2	-	-
Quinault, Washington	27	7	-	14	-	6	22	-	-	17	-	5
Ramah Community, New Mexico	16	2	1	1	7	5	25	7	5	2	8	3
Ramona, California	-	-	-	-	-	-	-	-	-	-	-	-
Red Cliff, Wisconsin	6	-	-	6	-	-	23	-	-	19	-	4
Red Lake, Minnesota	99	18	4	49	2	27	83	1	1	65	1	14
Reno-Sparks Colony, Nevada	9	4	-	4	1	-	10	-	-	10	-	-
Resighini Rancheria, California	...	...	...	...	...	...	...	...	...	...	...	...
Rincon, California	10	1	2	4	-	3	10	-	-	10	-	-
Roaring Creek Rancheria, California	...	...	...	...	...	...	...	...	...	...	...	...
Rocky Boy's, Montana	33	6	-	21	-	6	44	5	-	36	-	3
Rosebud, South Dakota	85	23	4	24	7	27	129	11	4	92	5	18
Round Valley, California	6	-	-	3	-	3	18	-	-	14	2	1
Rumsey Rancheria, California	...	...	...	...	...	...	...	...	...	...	...	...
Sac and Fox, Iowa	15	1	11	1	-	1	8	-	5	3	-	1
Sac and Fox, Kansas-Nebraska	...	...	...	...	...	...	...	...	...	...	...	...
St. Croix, Wisconsin	5	1	-	3	-	1	8	-	-	8	-	-
St. Regis Mohawk, New York	26	-	-	24	-	2	39	-	-	36	-	3
Salt River, Arizona	56	31	9	5	1	10	49	7	24	8	-	10
San Carlos, Arizona	97	45	9	13	4	26	153	16	15	60	46	15
Sandia Pueblo, New Mexico	6	-	1	4	-	1	5	1	1	2	-	1
Sandy Lake, Minnesota	-	-	-	-	-	-	-	-	-	-	-	-
San Felipe Pueblo, New Mexico	82	7	3	69	-	4	40	-	39	1	-	-
San Ildefonso Pueblo, New Mexico	25	21	-	2	-	3	-	-	-	-	-	-
San Juan Pueblo, New Mexico	18	10	3	4	-	1	25	1	8	14	-	3
San Manuel, California	-	-	-	-	-	-	-	-	-	-	-	-
San Pasqual, California	4	2	-	-	1	1	3	-	-	1	-	1
Santa Ana Pueblo, New Mexico	9	1	-	8	-	-	10	3	-	7	-	-
Santa Clara Pueblo, New Mexico	63	36	-	20	-	8	46	-	31	15	-	-

Source: U.S. Bureau of the Census, Subject Reports, PC80-2-1D, Part I, *American Indians, Eskimos, and Aleuts on Identified Reservations and in the Historic Areas of Oklahoma (Excluding Urbanized Areas)*, U.S. Government Printing Office, Washington, D.C., 1986, pp. 209-247. *Notes:* A dash (-) represents zero or a percent which rounds to less than 0.1. Also, a dash (-) is used because the number of supplementary questionnaires for the areas was insufficient to produce reliable estimates. Three dots (...) means not applicable, or that the data are being withheld to avoid disclosure of information for individuals.

★ 299 ★

Nursery School and Kindergarten Enrollment on Reservations, by Type of School, 1980 - III

Data are the latest available and are for persons 3 years old and older.

Identified reservation	Nursery school						Kindergarten					
	Total	Tribal school	Bureau of Indian Affairs school	Other public school	Other private school	Not reported	Total	Tribal school	Bureau of Indian Affairs school	Other public school	Other private school	Not reported
Santa Rosa Rancheria, California	9	1	-	8	-	-	2	-	-	2	-	-
Santa Rosa, California	...	...	...	...	...	...	...	...	...	...	...	...
Santa Ynez, California	4	-	-	2	1	-	5	-	-	5	-	-
Santa Ysabel, California	2	1	-	1	-	-	1	-	-	1	-	-
Santee, Nebraska	21	1	-	9	-	11	6	-	-	4	-	2
Santo Domingo Pueblo, New Mexico	66	9	-	53	-	5	109	-	2	106	-	2
San Xavier, Arizona	17	14	1	-	1	1	30	14	-	14	-	1
Sauk-Suiattle, Washington	-	-	-	-	-	-	-	-	-	-	-	-
Sault Ste. Marie, Michigan	-	-	-	-	-	-	-	-	-	-	-	-
Schaghticoke, Connecticut	...	...	...	...	...	...	...	...	...	...	...	...
Shakopee Community, Minnesota	-	-	-	-	-	-	1	-	-	-	-	1
Sheep Ranch Rancheria, California	...	...	...	...	...	...	...	...	...	...	...	...
Sherwood Valley Rancheria, California	...	...	...	...	...	...	...	...	...	...	...	...
Shingle Springs Rancheria, California	-	-	...	...	-	-	-	-	-	-	-	-
Shinnecock, New York	-	-	-	-	-	-	2	-	-	2	-	...
Shoalwater, Washington	...	...	...	...	...	...	...	...	...	...	...	...
Sisseton, North Dakota-South Dakota	53	6	19	17	-	11	59	-	2	50	-	6
Skokomish, Washington	6	3	-	2	-	-	9	-	-	9	-	-
Skull Valley, Utah	-	-	-	-	-	-	-	-	-	-	-	-
Soboba, California	8	6	1	1	-	-	6	-	-	6	-	-
Sokaogon Chippewa Community, Wisconsin	-	-	-	-	-	-	2	-	-	2	-	-
Southern Paiute, Utah	-	-	-	-	-	-	3	-	-	3	-	-
Southern Ute, Colorado	33	2	5	19	1	6	27	-	-	23	-	5
Spokane, Washington	4	-	-	3	1	-	22	-	-	22	-	-
Squaxin Island, Washington	-	-	-	-	-	-	1	-	-	1	-	-
Standing Rock, North Dakota-South Dakota	121	28	33	20	6	33	135	5	40	74	2	14
Stewart's Point Rancheria, California	1	-	-	-	1	-	1	-	-	1	-	-
Stockbridge, Wisconsin	12	6	-	6	-	-	13	-	-	13	-	-
Sulphur Bank Rancheria, California	5	-	-	4	-	1	2	-	-	2	-	-
Summit Lake, Nevada	...	...	...	...	...	...	...	...	...	...	...	...
Susanville, California	1	-	-	-	-	1	2	-	-	1	-	1
Swinomish, Washington	26	4	-	18	-	4	9	-	-	9	-	-
Sycuan, California	4	-	-	-	-	4	2	-	-	2	-	-
Tama, Georgia	-	-	-	-	-	-	-	-	-	-	-	-
Taos Pueblo, New Mexico	23	11	-	1	7	3	15	-	12	2	2	-
Te-Moak, Nevada	-	-	-	-	-	-	1	-	-	1	-	-
Tesuque Pueblo, New Mexico	3	3	-	-	-	-	6	2	-	-	1	3
Tigua, Texas	15	10	1	4	-	-	12	-	-	10	-	2
Tonawanda, New York	1	-	-	-	-	1	5	-	-	4	-	1
Torres-Martinez, California	-	-	-	-	-	-	-	-	-	-	-	-
Trinidad Rancheria, California	-	-	-	-	-	-	-	-	-	-	-	-
Tulalip, Washington	20	6	2	8	1	2	19	1	-	16	-	2
Tule River, California	17	-	2	13	-	2	10	-	-	8	-	2
Tunicabiloxi, Louisiana	...	...	...	...	...	...	...	...	...	...	...	...
Tuolumne Rancheria, California	-	-	-	-	-	-	-	-	-	-	-	-
Turtle Mountain, North Dakota	111	31	42	21	-	17	89	23	45	18	-	3
Tuscarora, New York	-	-	-	-	-	-	-	-	-	-	-	-
Twenty-Nine Palms, California	-	-	-	-	-	-	-	-	-	-	-	-
Uintah and Ouray, Utah	104	26	20	24	-	35	71	1	1	51	-	18
Umatilla, Oregon	22	9	3	7	-	4	34	1	1	30	-	1
Upper Sioux Community, Minnesota	-	-	-	-	-	-	-	-	-	-	-	-
Upper Skagit, Washington	-	-	-	-	-	-	-	-	-	-	-	-
Ute Mountain, Colorado-New Mexico	51	8	4	1	-	38	24	3	-	11	-	10
Vermillion Lake, Minnesota	6	-	1	3	-	2	-	-	-	-	-	-
Viejas Rancheria, California	-	-	-	-	-	-	4	-	-	3	-	1
Walker River, Nevada	14	3	2	1	7	1	6	-	-	6	-	-
Wampanoag, Massachusetts	-	-	-	-	-	-	-	-	-	-	-	-
Warm Springs, Oregon	79	31	3	27	-	17	63	11	-	42	1	9
Washoe, Nevada	-	-	-	-	-	-	-	-	-	-	-	-
Western Pequot, Connecticut	...	...	...	...	...	...	...	...	...	...	...	...
White Earth, Minnesota	69	18	5	26	-	20	54	-	-	48	-	6
Wind River, Wyoming	68	21	14	19	2	12	105	5	12	75	-	13

[Continued]

★ 299 ★

Nursery School and Kindergarten Enrollment on Reservations, by Type of School, 1980 - III
[Continued]

Identified reservation	Nursery school						Kindergarten					
	Total	Tribal school	Bureau of Indian Affairs school	Other public school	Other private school	Not reported	Total	Tribal school	Bureau of Indian Affairs school	Other public school	Other private school	Not reported
Winnebago, Nebraska	44	15	-	4	-	25	24	-	-	10	-	14
Winnemucca Colony, Nevada	-	-	-	-	-	-	-	-	-	-	-	-
Wisconsin Winnebago Reservation	16	3	-	6	-	7	20	-	-	12	-	7
Woodfords Community, California	-	-	-	-	-	-	-	-	-	-	-	-
XL Ranch, California	...	...	...	...	...	...	...	...	...	...	...	...
Yakima, Washington	122	49	12	28	6	27	100	8	3	78	2	9
Yankton, South Dakota	33	-	5	10	5	14	44	4	2	32	2	4
Yavapai, Arizona	2	-	-	2	-	-	2	-	-	2	-	-
Yerington, Nevada	3	-	-	2	-	1	-	-	-	-	-	-
Yomba, Nevada	-	-	-	-	-	-	-	-	-	-	-	-
Zia Pueblo, New Mexico	25	20	1	1	3	-	15	-	14	-	1	-
Zuni Pueblo, New Mexico	101	38	-	44	4	14	168	5	-	134	27	2
San Felipe/Santa Ana Joint Area, New Mexico	-	-	-	-	-	-	-	-	-	-	-	-
San Felipe/Santo Domingo Joint Area, New Mexico	6	-	-	6	-	-	7	-	-	7	-	-
Other Reservation Lands in Montana	-	-	-	-	-	-	-	-	-	-	-	-

Source: U.S. Bureau of the Census, Subject Reports, PC80-2-1D, Part I, *American Indians, Eskimos, and Aleuts on Identified Reservations and in the Historic Areas of Oklahoma (Excluding Urbanized Areas)*, U.S. Government Printing Office, Washington, D.C., 1986, pp. 209-247. *Notes:* A dash (-) represents zero or a percent which rounds to less than 0.1. Also, a dash (-) is used because the number of supplementary questionnaires for the areas was insufficient to produce reliable estimates. Three dots (...) means not applicable, or that the data are being withheld to avoid disclosure of information for individuals.

★ 300 ★

Elementary and Secondary School Enrollment Distribution in the 10 Largest States, by Race/Ethnicity, 1986 and 1989

Percent distributions are shown, by race/ethnicity and selected state, for 1986 and 1989.

State	Percent distribution, fall 1986						Percent distribution, fall 1989					
	Total	American Indian/ Alaskan Native	White[1]	Black[1]	Hispanic	Asian or Pacific Islander	Total	American Indian/ Alaskan Native	White[1]	Black[1]	Hispanic	Asian or Pacific Islander
United States	100.0	0.9	70.4	16.1	9.9	2.8	-	-	-	-	-	-
California	100.0	0.7	53.7	9.0	27.5	9.1	100.0	0.8	47.1	8.7	33.0	10.4
Florida	100.0	0.2	65.4	23.7	9.5	1.2	100.0	0.2	62.8	23.8	11.9	1.4
Illinois	100.0	0.1	69.8	18.7	9.2	2.3	100.0	0.1	66.0	21.9	9.3	2.6
Michigan	100.0	0.8	76.4	19.8	1.8	1.2	100.0	0.9	77.8	17.8	2.3	1.2
New Jersey	100.0	0.1	69.1	17.4	10.7	2.7	100.0	0.1	66.1	18.8	11.1	4.1
New York	100.0	0.2	68.4	16.5	12.3	2.7	100.0	0.3	62.1	20.5	13.2	3.9
North Carolina	100.0	1.7	68.4	28.9	0.4	0.6	100.0	1.6	66.5	30.4	0.7	0.8
Ohio	100.0	0.1	83.1	15.0	1.0	0.7	100.0	0.1	83.6	14.2	1.2	0.9
Pennsylvania	100.0	0.1	84.4	12.6	1.8	1.2	100.0	0.1	82.7	13.1	2.6	1.5
Texas	100.0	0.2	51.0	14.4	32.5	2.0	100.0	0.2	50.3	14.6	33.1	1.9

Source: "Enrollment in Public Elementary and Secondary Schools, by Race or Ethnicity and State: Fall 1986 and Fall 1989," *Digest of Education Statistics 1991, November 1991*, p. 58. Primary source: U.S. Department of Education, Office for Civil Rights, *1986 State Summaries of Elementary and Secondary School Civil Rights Survey*; and National Center for Education Statistics, "Common Core of Data" survey. (This table was prepared March 1991). *Notes:* The 1986-87 data were derived from the 1986 Elementary and Secondary School Civil Rights sample survey of public schools districts. State estimates may differ from other data sources because of variations in survey methodology. Because of rounding, details may not add to totals. A dash (-) stands for data not available. 1. Excludes persons of Hispanic origin.

★ 301 ★

Elementary and Secondary School Enrollment Rates in the 10 Largest States, 1986 and 1989

Percentage rates are shown, by selected states and race/ethnicity, for 1986 and 1989.

State	Percent distribution, fall 1986						Percent distribution, fall 1989					
	Total	American Indian/ Alaskan Native	White[1]	Black[1]	Hispanic	Asian or Pacific Islander	Total	American Indian/ Alaskan Native	White[1]	Black[1]	Hispanic	Asian or Pacific Islander
United States	100.0	0.9	70.4	16.1	9.9	2.8	-	-	-	-	-	-
California	100.0	0.7	53.7	9.0	27.5	9.1	100.0	0.8	47.1	8.7	33.0	10.4
Florida	100.0	0.2	65.4	23.7	9.5	1.2	100.0	0.2	62.8	23.8	11.9	1.4
Illinois	100.0	0.1	69.8	18.7	9.2	2.3	100.0	0.1	66.0	21.9	9.3	2.6
Michigan	100.0	0.8	76.4	19.8	1.8	1.2	100.0	0.9	77.8	17.8	2.3	1.2
New Jersey	100.0	0.1	69.1	17.4	10.7	2.7	100.0	0.1	66.1	18.5	11.1	4.1
New York	100.0	0.2	68.4	16.5	12.3	2.7	100.0	0.3	62.1	20.5	13.2	3.9
North Carolina	100.0	1.7	68.4	28.9	0.4	0.6	100.0	1.6	66.5	30.4	0.7	0.8
Ohio	100.0	0.1	83.1	15.0	1.0	0.7	100.0	0.1	83.6	14.2	1.2	0.9
Pennsylvania	100.0	0.1	84.4	12.6	1.8	1.2	100.0	0.1	82.7	13.1	2.6	1.5
Texas	100.0	0.2	51.0	14.4	32.5	2.0	100.0	0.2	50.3	14.6	33.1	1.9

Source: "Enrollment in Public Elementary and Secondary Schools, by race or Ethnicity and State: Fall 1986 and Fall 1989," *Digest of Education Statistics 1991*, November 1991, p. 58. Primary source: U.S. Department of Education, Office for Civil Rights, *1986 State Summaries of Elementary and Secondary School Civil Rights Survey*; and National Center for Education Statistics, "Common Core of Data" survey. (This table was prepared March 1991.) *Notes:* The 1986-87 data were derived from the 1986 Elementary and Secondary School Civil Rights sample survey of public school districts. State estimates may differ from other data sources because of variations in survey methodology. Because of rounding, details may not add to totals. A dash (-) indicates that data were not available in the original source. 1. Excludes persons of Hispanic origin.

★ 302 ★

Elementary School Enrollment on Reservations, by Type of School, 1980 - I

Data are the latest available.

Identified reservations	Total	Tribal school	Bureau of Indian Affairs day school	Bureau of Indian Affairs boarding school	Other public school	Other private school	Not reported
American Indian, Eskimo and Aleut	69,903	2,427	8,634	6,536	42,515	3,427	6,364
Acoma Pueblo, New Mexico	377	31	161	-	131	47	7
Agua Caliente, California	-	-	-	-	-	-	-
Alabama-Coushatta, Texas	91	-	-	-	83	-	8
Alamo, New Mexico	242	3	18	30	37	52	102
Allegany, New York	175	1	-	-	151	6	17
Alturas Rancheria, California	...	...	...	...	...	...	...
Annette Islands Reserve, Alaska	154	-	1	-	149	1	2
Augustine, California	-	-	-	-	-	-	-
Bad River, Wisconsin	118	-	-	-	73	45	-

[Continued]

★ 302 ★

Elementary School Enrollment on Reservations, by Type of School, 1980 - I
[Continued]

Identified reservations	Total	Tribal school	Bureau of Indian Affairs day school	Bureau of Indian Affairs boarding school	Other public school	Other private school	Not reported
Barona Rancheria, California	40	-	-	-	37	1	2
Bay Mills, Michigan	44	-	-	-	43	-	1
Benton Paiute, California	...	...	...	...	...	...	...
Berry Creek Rancheria, California	-	-	-	-	-	-	-
Big Bend Rancheria, California	...	...	...	...	...	...	...
Big Cypress, Florida	83	-	56	2	21	1	2
Big Lagoon Rancheria, California	...	...	...	...	...	...	...
Big Pine Rancheria, California	60	-	-	-	59	-	1
Bishop Rancheria, California	134	-	-	-	130	1	3
Blackfeet, Montana	1,059	2	2	3	890	6	156
Bois Forte (Nett Lake), Minnesota	87	-	-	-	83	-	4
Bridgeport Colony, California	10	-	-	-	10	-	-
Brighton, Florida	72	-	-	-	64	-	8
Burns, Oregon	33	-	-	-	28	-	5
Cabazon, California	...	...	...	...	...	...	...
Cachil Dehe Rancheria, California	...	...	...	...	...	...	...
Cahuilla, California	...	...	...	...	...	...	...
Campo, California	15	-	-	-	15	-	-
Camp Verde, Arizona	38	-	-	-	33	1	4
Canoncito, New Mexico	224	1	831	2	32	-	6
Capitan Grande, California	-	-	-	-	-	-	-
Carson Colony, Nevada	37	-	-	-	35	-	1
Catawba, South Carolina	188	5	-	-	172	4	8
Cattaraugus, New York	350	1	-	-	297	14	37
Cedarville Rancheria, California	...	...	...	...	...	...	...
Chehalis, Washington	35	1	-	-	33	-	1
Chemehuevi, California	...	...	...	...	...	...	...
Cheyenne River, South Dakota	316	5	224	39	30	10	8
Chitimacha, Louisiana	33	24	-	-	3	1	4
Cochiti Pueblo, New Mexico	124	1	-	8	113	1	-
Cocopah, Arizona	80	-	-	1	72	-	6
Coeur d'Alene, Idaho	120	65	-	-	48	-	7
Cold Springs Rancheria, California	9	-	-	-	9	-	-
Colorado River, Arizona-California	377	-	-	5	320	2	50
Colville, Washington	671	50	14	17	538	7	45
Cortina Rancheria, California	...	...	...	...	...	...	...
Coushatta, Louisiana	...	...	...	...	...	...	...
Coyote Valley Rancheria, California	-	-	-	-	-	-	-
Crow, Montana	721	5	5	-	550	74	88
Crow Creek, South Dakota	350	58	135	2	138	6	12
Cuyapaipe, California	...	...	...	...	...	...	...
Deer Creek, Minnesota	...	...	...	...	...	...	...

[Continued]

★ 302 ★

Elementary School Enrollment on Reservations, by Type of School, 1980 - I
[Continued]

Identified reservations	Total	Tribal school	Bureau of Indian Affairs day school	Bureau of Indian Affairs boarding school	Other public school	Other private school	Not reported
Dresslerville Colony, Nevada	22	-	-	-	18	-	4
Dry Creek Rancheria, California	9	-	-	-	9	-	-
Duck Valley, Idaho-Nevada	181	-	-	-	169	-	12
Duckwater, Nevada	15	14	-	-	-	1	-
Eastern Cherokee, North Carolina	897	136	515	4	206	1	35
Eastern Pequot, Connecticut	...	...	...	...	...	...	...
Ely Colony, Nevada	16	1	-	-	14	-	1
Enterprise Rancheria, California	...	...	...	...	...	...	...
Fallon Colony, Nevada	9	-	-	-	9	-	-
Fallon, Nevada	44	1	-	-	43	-	-
Flandreau, South Dakota	34	-	-	-	31	-	3
Flathead, Montana	698	2	-	-	556	1	139
Fond du Lac, Minnesota	100	-	-	-	94	-	5
Fort Apache, Arizona	1,608	4	239	19	1,097	115	135
Fort Belknap, Montana	393	-	1	4	276	64	48
Fort Berthold, North Dakota	550	11	13	1	480	8	37
Fort Bidwell, California	19	-	-	-	19	-	-
Fort Hall, Idaho	492	9	2	-	411	5	65
Fort Independence, California	1	-	-	-	1	-	-
Fort McDermitt, Nevada-Oregon	102	-	1	-	99	-	1
Fort McDowell, Arizona	50	-	-	1	41	-	7
Fort Mojave, Arizona-California-Nevada	26	-	-	-	20	-	6
Fort Peck, Montana	851	4	-	13	776	1	56
Fort Totten, North Dakota	505	194	87	12	177	2	32
Fort Yuma, Arizona-California	208	1	-	2	165	10	30
Gila Bend, Arizona	-	-	-	-	-	-	-
Gila River, Arizona	1,407	21	148	12	1,026	127	74
Golden Hill, Connecticut	...	...	...	...	...	...	...
Goshute, Nevada-Utah	13	-	-	-	10	-	3
Grand Portage, Minnesota	28	-	-	-	28	-	-
Grindstone Creek Rancheria, California	16	-	-	-	13	-	3
Hannahville Community, Michigan	41	31	-	-	8	3	-
Hassanamisco, Massachusetts	...	...	...	...	...	...	...
Havasupai, Arizona	45	28	-	3	6	-	8
Hoh, Washington	7	-	-	-	7	-	-
Hollywood, Florida	83	2	-	-	75	3	2
Hoopa Valley, California	268	2	-	-	236	1	29
Hoopa Valley Extension, California	70	-	-	-	56	3	11
Hopi, Arizona	1,234	60	410	274	243	37	211
Hopland Rancheria, California	-	-	-	-	-	-	-
Hualapai, Arizona	143	-	-	1	126	-	17
Inaja-Cosmit, California	-	-	-	-	-	-	-

[Continued]

★ 302 ★

Elementary School Enrollment on Reservations, by Type of School, 1980 - I
[Continued]

Identified reservations	Total	Tribal school	Bureau of Indian Affairs day school	Bureau of Indian Affairs boarding school	Other public school	Other private school	Not reported
Indian Township, Maine	75	66	-	-	9	-	-
Iowa, Kansas-Nebraska	8	-	-	-	8	-	-
Isabella, Michigan	95	-	-	-	87	3	5

Source: U.S. Bureau of the Census, Subject Reports, PC80-2-1D, Part I, *American Indians, Eskimos, and Aleuts on Identified Reservations and in the Historic Areas of Oklahoma (Excluding Urbanized Areas),* U.S. Government Printing Office, Washington, D.C., 1986, pp. 209-247. *Notes:* A dash (-) represents zero or a percent which rounds to less than 0.1. Also, a dash (-) is used because the number of supplementary questionnaires for the areas was insufficient to produce reliable estimates. Three dots (...) means not applicable, or that the data are being withheld to avoid disclosure of information for individuals.

★ 303 ★

Elementary School Enrollment on Reservations, by Type of School, 1980 - II

Data are the latest available.

Identified reservation	Total	Tribal school	Bureau of Indian Affairs day school	Bureau of Indian Affairs boarding school	Other public school	Other private school	Not reported
Isleta Pueblo, New Mexico	381	61	161	2	134	5	17
Jackson Rancheria, California	...	...	...	...	...	...	...
Jemez Pueblo, New Mexico	296	2	112	2	74	94	11
Jicarilla Apache, New Mexico	351	13	-	1	285	44	8
Kaibab, Arizona	13	-	-	-	13	-	-
Kalispel, Washington	24	-	-	-	23	-	1
Kickapoo, Kansas	62	-	-	-	49	3	11
Kootenai, Idaho	-	-	-	-	-	-	-
Lac Courte Oreilles, Wisconsin	259	101	-	-	87	61	9
Lac du Flambeau, Wisconsin	267	-	-	-	259	-	8
Laguna Pueblo, New Mexico	561	8	355	4	145	38	11
La Jolla, California	33	-	-	-	30	1	2
L'Anse, Michigan	123	-	-	-	113	9	1
La Posta, California	...	...	...	...	...	...	...
Las Vegas Colony, Nevada	14	-	-	-	14	-	-
Laytonville Rancheria, California	21	-	-	-	21	-	-
Leech Lake, Minnesota	602	21	2	1	519	8	50
Likely Rancheria, California	-	-	-	-	-	-	-
Lone Pine Rancheria, California	36	-	-	-	36	-	-
Lookout Rancheria, California	...	...	...	...	...	...	...
Los Coyotes, California	4	-	-	-	4	-	-

[Continued]

★ 303 ★

Elementary School Enrollment on Reservations, by Type of School, 1980 - II

[Continued]

Identified reservation	Total	Tribal school	Bureau of Indian Affairs day school	Bureau of Indian Affairs boarding school	Other public school	Other private school	Not reported
Lovelock Colony, Nevada	28	-	-	-	28	-	-
Lower Brule, South Dakota	160	-	97	3	27	18	15
Lower Elwah, Washington	12	-	-	-	8	-	4
Lower Sioux Community, Minnesota	7	-	-	-	7	-	-
Lummi, Washington	296	3	-	1	269	8	14
Makah, Washington	142	4	-	-	128	-	10
Manchester Rancheria, California	7	-	-	-	7	-	-
Manzanita, California	...	...	...	...	...	...	...
Maricopa, Arizona	71	-	2	-	67	-	1
Mattaponi, Virginia	11	-	-	-	10	-	1
Menominee, Wisconsin	478	12	-	12	293	85	76
Mesa Grande, California	-	-	-	-	-	-	-
Mescalero Apache, New Mexico	435	1	-	1	145	-	288
Miccosukee, Florida	42	28	-	1	10	-	3
Middletown Rancheria, California	11	-	-	-	9	-	2
Mille Lacs, Minnesota	-	-	-	-	-	-	-
Mississippi Choctaw Reservation	598	57	414	49	59	-	19
Moapa River, Nevada	44	-	-	-	40	-	3
Montgomery Creek Rancheria, California	...	...	...	...	...	...	...
Morongo, California	49	-	-	-	45	3	1
Muckleshoot, Washington	81	-	-	2	65	-	13
Nambe Pueblo, New Mexico	30	2	-	-	16	-	12
Navajo, Arizona-New Mexico-Utah	23,357	134	1,861	5,514	12,997	725	2,126
Nez Perce, Idaho	320	1	-	-	299	-	20
Nisqually, Washington	6	1	-	-	3	1	-
Nooksack, Washington	-	-	-	-	-	-	-
Northern Cheyenne, Montana	650	96	30	14	377	67	64
Oil Springs, New York	-	-	-	-	-	-	-
Omaha, Iowa-Nebraska	272	9	3	7	111	6	136
Oneida, Wisconsin	346	47	-	-	257	5	38
Onondaga, New York	-	-	-	-	-	-	-
Ontonagon, Michigan	-	-	-	-	-	-	-
Osage, Oklahoma	755	-	-	-	695	8	53
Ozette, Washington	...	...	...	...	...	...	...
Pala, California	73	4	-	-	37	31	1
Pamunkey, Virginia	4	-	-	-	4	-	-
Papago, Arizona	1,369	37	404	163	683	34	47
Pascua Yaqui, Arizona	136	-	-	1	134	-	1
Pauma, California	16	-	-	-	16	-	-
Payson Community of Yavapai-Apache, Arizona	-	-	-	-	-	-	-
Pechanga, California	17	-	-	-	11	3	3
Penobscot, Maine	80	-	-	-	75	1	4

[Continued]

★ 303 ★

Elementary School Enrollment on Reservations, by Type of School, 1980 - II

[Continued]

Identified reservation	Total	Tribal school	Bureau of Indian Affairs day school	Bureau of Indian Affairs boarding school	Other public school	Other private school	Not reported
Picuris Pueblo, New Mexico	30	1	-	1	15	11	2
Pine Creek, Michigan	...	...	...	...	...	...	...
Pine Ridge, South Dakota	2,712	240	1,251	77	519	437	187
Pleasant Point, Maine	114	85	-	-	20	2	6
Pojoaque Pueblo, New Mexico	21	3	-	-	16	-	3
Poospatuck, New York	23	-	-	-	18	-	5
Port Gamble, Washington	50	-	-	-	48	-	2
Port Madison, Washington	23	2	-	-	19	3	-
Potawatomi, Wisconsin	46	-	-	-	46	-	-
Pottawatomi, Kansas	66	-	-	-	66	-	-
Prairie Island Community, Minnesota	17	-	-	-	17	-	-
Puyallup, Washington	194	13	4	-	150	8	18
Pyramid Lake, Nevada	101	-	1	-	96	-	4
Quileute, Washington	59	38	-	-	18	-	2
Quinault, Washington	187	22	-	-	151	-	14
Ramah Community, New Mexico	247	47	57	3	48	71	20
Ramona, California	-	-	-	-	-	-	-
Red Cliff, Wisconsin	123	-	-	-	112	5	6
Red Lake, Minnesota	640	3	5	22	483	91	35
Reno-Sparks Colony, Nevada	86	-	-	1	76	2	7
Resighini Rancheria, California	...	...	...	...	...	...	...
Rincon, California	67	1	1	-	62	-	1
Roaring Creek Rancheria, California	...	...	...	...	...	...	...
Rocky Boy's, Montana	358	18	-	-	318	1	21
Rosebud, South Dakota	1,259	84	103	33	778	108	153
Round Valley, California	106	-	-	-	94	9	3
Rumsey Rancheria, California	...	...	...	...	...	...	...
Sac and Fox, Iowa	91	-	33	2	53	1	3
Sac and Fox, Kansas-Nebraska	...	...	...	...	...	...	...
St. Croix, Wisconsin	79	-	-	-	78	-	1
St. Regis Mohawk, New York	294	-	2	-	277	2	13
Salt River, Arizona	486	-	141	23	299	9	14
San Carlos, Arizona	1,292	4	80	14	742	262	190
Sandia Pueblo, New Mexico	40	1	-	-	22	10	7
Sandy Lake, Minnesota	-	-	-	-	-	-	-
San Felipe Pueblo, New Mexico	397	-	208	8	177	-	4
San Ildefonso Pueblo, New Mexico	83	7	30	-	43	-	3
San Juan Pueblo, New Mexico	129	-	32	4	74	1	18
San Manuel, California	-	-	-	-	-	-	-
San Pasqual, California	18	-	-	-	10	-	8

[Continued]

★ 303 ★

Elementary School Enrollment on Reservations, by Type of School, 1980 - II
[Continued]

Identified reservation	Total	Tribal school	Bureau of Indian Affairs day school	Bureau of Indian Affairs boarding school	Other public school	Other private school	Not reported
Santa Ana Pueblo, New Mexico	64	-	-	2	59	-	2
Santa Clara Pueblo, New Mexico	313	5	140	5	101	28	33

Source: U.S. Bureau of the Census, Subject Reports, PC80-2-1D, Part I, *American Indians, Eskimos, and Aleuts on Identified Reservations and in the Historic Areas of Oklahoma (Excluding Urbanized Areas)*, U.S. Government Printing Office, Washington, D.C., 1986, pp. 209-247. *Notes:* A dash (-) represents zero or a percent which rounds to less than 0.1. Also, a dash (-) is used because the number of supplementary questionnaires for the areas was insufficient to produce reliable estimates. Three dots (...) means not applicable, or that the data are being withheld to avoid disclosure of information for individuals.

★ 304 ★

Elementary School Enrollment on Reservations, by Type of School, 1980 - III

Data are the latest available.

Identified reservation	Total	Tribal school	Bureau of Indian Affairs day school	Bureau of Indian Affairs boarding school	Other public school	Other private school	Not reported
Santa Rosa Rancheria, California	21	-	-	-	21	-	-
Santa Rosa, California	...	...	...	...	...	...	...
Santa Ynez, California	20	-	-	-	20	-	-
Santa Ysabel, California	36	-	-	-	32	-	3
Santee, Nebraska	87	2	-	-	32	5	47
Santo Domingo Pueblo, New Mexico	405	2	3	12	379	2	9
San Xavier, Arizona	157	-	-	11	70	65	11
Sauk-Suiattle, Washington	-	-	-	-	-	-	-
Sault Ste. Marie, Michigan	-	-	-	-	-	-	-
Schaghticoke, Connecticut	...	...	...	...	...	...	...
Shakopee Community, Minnesota	11	-	-	-	4	-	7
Sheep Ranch Rancheria, California	...	...	...	...	...	...	...
Sherwood Valley Rancheria, California	...	...	...	...	...	...	...
Shingle Springs Rancheria, California	-	-	-	-	-	-	-
Shinnecock, New York	38	-	-	-	31	3	4
Shoalwater, Washington	...	...	...	...	...	...	...
Sisseton, North Dakota-South Dakota	602	1	-	9	573	1	18
Skokomish, Washington	57	-	-	-	55	1	1
Skull Valley, Utah	-	-	-	-	-	-	-
Soboba, California	43	-	-	-	41	2	-
Sokaogon Chippewa Community, Wisconsin	8	-	-	-	8	-	-
Southern Paiute, Utah	40	-	-	-	40	-	-
Southern Ute, Colorado	195	-	-	-	150	-	45

[Continued]

★ 304 ★

Elementary School Enrollment on Reservations, by Type of School, 1980 - III
[Continued]

Identified reservation	Total	Tribal school	Bureau of Indian Affairs day school	Bureau of Indian Affairs boarding school	Other public school	Other private school	Not reported
Spokane, Washington	195	-	-	-	192	-	3
Squaxin Island, Washington	4	-	-	-	4	-	-
Standing Rock, North Dakota-South Dakota	884	3	161	38	556	53	72
Stewart's Point Rancheria, California	13	9	-	-	3	-	1
Stockbridge, Wisconsin	97	-	-	-	96	-	1
Sulphur Bank Rancheria, California	25	-	-	-	20	-	5
Summit Lake, Nevada	...	...	...	...	...	...	...
Susanville, California	15	-	-	-	10	-	5
Swinomish, Washington	83	1	-	-	73	2	7
Sycuan, California	14	-	-	-	14	-	-
Tama, Georgia	4	-	-	-	4	-	-
Taos Pueblo, New Mexico	166	-	123	-	41	-	2
Te-Moak, Nevada	17	-	-	-	17	-	-
Tesuque Pueblo, New Mexico	38	2	11	1	12	2	9
Tigua, Texas	78	-	-	-	72	1	5
Tonawanda, New York	80	-	-	-	56	-	23
Torres-Martinez, California	-	-	-	-	-	-	-
Trinidad Rancheria, California	7	-	-	-	6	1	-
Tulalip, Washington	153	1	1	-	137	-	14
Tule River, California	101	-	-	-	90	1	10
Tunicabiloxi, Louisiana	...	...	...	...	...	...	...
Tuolumne Rancheria, California	22	-	-	-	22	-	-
Turtle Mountain, North Dakota	815	171	421	20	163	1	39
Tuscarora, New York	-	-	-	-	-	-	-
Twenty-Nine Palms, California	-	-	-	-	-	-	-
Uintah and Ouray, Utah	387	3	-	-	315	3	66
Umatilla, Oregon	168	1	-	-	154	-	13
Upper Sioux Community, Minnesota	9	-	-	-	5	4	-
Upper Skagit, Washington	-	-	-	-	-	-	-
Ute Mountain, Colorado-New Mexico	207	-	-	-	119	-	89
Vermillion Lake, Minnesota	16	-	-	-	16	-	-
Viejas Rancheria, California	23	-	-	-	20	-	2
Walker River, Nevada	92	1	-	-	90	1	-
Wampanoag, Massachusetts	-	-	-	-	-	-	-
Warm Springs, Oregon	424	13	2	1	360	1	46
Washoe, Nevada	-	-	-	-	-	-	-
Western Pequot, Connecticut	...	...	...	...	...	...	...
White Earth, Minnesota	481	34	-	-	417	9	22
Wind River, Wyoming	841	11	102	1	618	8	101
Winnebago, Nebraska	220	5	-	1	113	20	81
Winnemucca Colony, Nevada	7	-	-	-	7	-	-
Wisconsin Winnebago Reservation	101	-	6	-	63	2	30

[Continued]

★ 304 ★

Elementary School Enrollment on Reservations, by Type of School, 1980 - III
[Continued]

Identified reservation	Total	Tribal school	Bureau of Indian Affairs day school	Bureau of Indian Affairs boarding school	Other public school	Other private school	Not reported
Woodfords Community, California	-	-	-	-	-	-	-
XL Ranch, California	...	...	...	...	...	...	...
Yakima, Washington	995	22	-	6	883	22	63
Yankton, South Dakota	319	57	13	-	218	14	19
Yavapai, Arizona	10	-	-	-	9	1	-
Yerington, Nevada	31	-	-	-	25	-	6
Yomba, Nevada	10	-	-	-	10	-	-
Zia Pueblo, New Mexico	84	1	44	2	32	1	2
Zuni Pueblo, New Mexico	1,283	25	2	5	1,007	213	31
San Felipe/Santa Ana Joint Area, New Mexico	-	-	-	-	-	-	-
San Felipe/Santo Domingo Joint Area, New Mexico	25	-	-	-	23	-	2
Other Reservation Lands in Montana	-	-	-	-	-	-	-

Source: U.S. Bureau of the Census, Subject Reports, PC80-2-1D, Part I, *American Indians, Eskimos, and Aleuts on Identified Reservations and in the Historic Areas of Oklahoma (Excluding Urbanized Areas),* U.S. Government Printing Office, Washington, D.C., 1986, pp. 209-247. *Notes:* A dash (-) represents zero or a percent which rounds to less than 0.1. Also, a dash (-) is used because the number of supplementary questionnaires for the areas was insufficient to produce reliable estimates. Three dots (...) means not applicable, or that the data are being withheld to avoid disclosure of information for individuals.

★ 305 ★

High School Enrollment on Reservations, by Type of School, 1980 - I

Data are the latest available.

Identified reservation	High school enrollment							Persons 16 to 19 years old	
	Total	Tribal school	Bureau of Indian Affairs day school	Bureau of Indian Affairs boarding school	Other public school	Other private school	Not reported	Total number	Percent not enrolled in school, not high school graduated
American Indian, Eskimo and Aleut	29,597	1,331	1,499	3,377	19,488	1,081	2,821	33,104	27.1
Acoma Pueblo, New Mexico	121	-	-	3	111	3	4	230	48.3
Agua Caliente, California	-	-	-	-	-	-	-	-	-
Alabama-Coushatta, Texas	30	-	-	3	28	-	-	28	19.5
Alamo, New Mexico	33	1	1	1	15	-	15	103	57.9
Allegany, New York	90	5	-	-	71	1	13	82	16.7
Alturas Rancheria, California	...	...	...	...	...	...	...	...	...
Annette Islands Reserve, Alaska	119	-	2	3	108	1	5	96	11.8
Augustine, California	-	-	-	-	-	-	-	-	-
Bad River, Wisconsin	75	3	-	1	68	1	1	63	9.8
Barona Rancheria, California	11	-	-	-	11	-	-	16	48.2
Bay Mills, Michigan	33	-	-	1	31	-	-	41	28.9
Benton Paiute, California	...	...	...	...	...	...	...	...	...
Berry Creek Rancheria, California	-	-	-	-	-	-	-	-	-
Big Bend Rancheria, California	...	...	...	...	...	...	...	...	...
Big Cypress, Florida	25	-	1	11	12	-	1	34	31.6

[Continued]

★ 305 ★

High School Enrollment on Reservations, by Type of School, 1980 - I
[Continued]

Identified reservation	High school enrollment							Persons 16 to 19 years old	
	Total	Tribal school	Bureau of Indian Affairs day school	Bureau of Indian Affairs boarding school	Other public school	Other private school	Not reported	Total number	Percent not enrolled in school, not high school graduate
Big Lagoon Rancheria, California	...	...	...	...	...	...	...	...	...
Big Pine Rancheria, California	26	-	-	-	23	-	2	24	9.3
Bishop Rancheria, California	67	1	-	-	63	1	2	68	19.4
Blackfeet, Montana	488	16	3	17	381	2	69	559	28.6
Bois Forte (Nett Lake), Minnesota	35	1	-	-	32	-	2	49	40.8
Bridgeport Colony, California	7	-	-	3	1	2	-	8	28.3
Brighton, Florida	18	-	-	-	16	-	2	27	29.3
Burns, Oregon	11	-	-	4	7	-	-	15	33.3
Cabazon, California	...	...	...	...	...	...	...	...	...
Cachil Dehe Rancheria, California	...	...	...	...	...	...	...	...	...
Cahuilla, California	...	...	...	...	...	...	...	...	...
Campo, California	11	-	1	-	10	-	-	7	51.0
Camp Verde, Arizona	12	-	-	1	10	-	1	16	43.8
Canoncito, New Mexico	95	8	3	8	69	-	6	107	21.3
Capitan Grande, California	-	-	-	-	-	-	-	-	-
Carson Colony, Nevada	16	-	-	-	15	-	1	16	8.5
Catawba, South Carolina	78	15	-	-	56	-	7	59	26.0
Cattaraugus, New York	161	3	-	-	138	-	21	179	25.9
Cedarville Rancheria, California	...	...	...	...	...	...	...	...	...
Chehalis, Washington	14	-	-	-	14	-	-	21	24.5
Chemehuevi, California	...	...	...	...	...	...	...	...	...
Cheyenne River, South Dakota	152	19	28	78	16	2	9	166	38.8
Chitimacha, Louisiana	18	3	-	-	10	3	3	22	49.7
Cochiti Pueblo, New Mexico	59	-	-	18	39	3	-	66	8.8
Cocopah, Arizona	21	-	-	6	13	1	1	30	33.3
Coeur d'Alene, Idaho	51	3	-	1	41	-	6	47	23.1
Cold Springs Rancheria, California	8	-	-	-	3	-	5	8	23.1
Colorado River, Arizona-California	154	3	1	17	108	1	24	164	30.2
Colville, Washington	290	7	-	8	239	4	31	309	28.9
Cortina Rancheria, California	...	...	...	...	...	...	...	...	...
Coushatta, Louisiana	...	...	...	...	...	...	...	...	...
Coyote Valley Rancheria, California	-	-	-	-	-	-	-	-	-
Crow, Montana	403	8	3	38	303	14	38	431	24.1
Crow Creek, South Dakota	117	49	4	7	52	3	3	149	28.1
Cuyapaipe, California	...	...	...	...	...	...	...	...	...
Deer Creek, Minnesota	...	...	...	...	...	...	...	...	...
Dresslerville Colony, Nevada	16	-	-	3	13	-	-	12	33.0
Dry Creek Rancheria, California	5	1	-	-	4	-	-	7	57.1
Duck Valley, Idaho-Nevada	105	-	-	7	95	-	4	83	9.2
Duckwater, Nevada	10	-	-	-	10	-	-	13	-
Eastern Cherokee, North Carolina	369	85	192	1	75	-	16	473	35.1
Eastern Pequot, Connecticut	...	...	...	...	...	...	...	...	...
Ely Colony, Nevada	1	-	-	-	1	-	-	3	100.0
Enterprise Rancheria, California	...	...	...	...	...	...	...	...	...
Fallon Colony, Nevada	5	-	-	-	5	-	-	6	59.2
Fallon, Nevada	40	-	-	1	37	-	1	36	5.8
Flandreau, South Dakota	17	1	-	6	9	-	1	20	29.8
Flathead, Montana	295	32	3	4	205	1	50	323	25.2
Fond du Lac, Minnesota	48	-	-	1	45	1	1	50	19.1
Fort Apache, Arizona	586	4	9	65	411	29	67	660	29.1
Fort Belknap, Montana	164	1	2	14	124	-	23	211	22.3
Fort Berthold, North Dakota	248	5	6	11	204	2	20	278	25.9
Fort Bidwell, California	6	-	-	2	4	-	-	4	25.0

[Continued]

★ 305 ★

High School Enrollment on Reservations, by Type of School, 1980 - I
[Continued]

Identified reservation	High school enrollment							Persons 16 to 19 years old	
	Total	Tribal school	Bureau of Indian Affairs day school	Bureau of Indian Affairs boarding school	Other public school	Other private school	Not reported	Total number	Percent not enrolled in school, not high school graduated
Fort Hall, Idaho	215	25	1	14	138	1	35	232	26.0
Fort Independence, California	4	-	-	-	4	-	-	3	-
Fort McDermitt, Nevada-Oregon	54	-	-	3	46	1	4	43	18.8
Fort McDowell, Arizona	20	-	-	5	14	-	1	32	42.9
Fort Mojave, Arizona-California-Nevada	16	-	-	4	10	-	2	14	21.4
Fort Peck, Montana	369	2	-	10	317	5	35	439	34.3
Fort Totten, North Dakota	176	19	20	10	116	2	8	204	39.8
Fort Yuma, Arizona-California	84	-	-	3	57	2	22	89	40.3
Gila Bend, Arizona	-	-	-	-	-	-	-	-	-
Gila River, Arizona	459	12	2	134	282	3	26	666	40.2
Golden Hill, Connecticut	...	...	...	...	...	...	...	...	...
Goshute, Nevada-Utah	1	-	-	-	1	-	-	1	100.0
Grand Portage, Minnesota	7	-	-	-	7	-	-	20	34.3
Grindstone Creek Rancheria, California	2	-	-	-	2	-	-	4	74.8
Hannahville Community, Michigan	12	-	-	-	12	-	-	39	54.2
Hassanamisco, Massachusetts	...	...	...	...	...	...	...	...	...
Havasupai, Arizona	20	3	-	12	2	1	1	25	41.4
Hoh, Washington	2	-	-	-	2	-	-	8	78.9
Hollywood, Florida	29	10	-	4	11	3	1	35	29.3
Hoopa Valley, California	130	9	2	-	107	1	11	132	21.2
Hoopa Valley Extension, California	34	-	-	-	27	1	6	33	20.0
Hopi, Arizona	652	22	21	259	228	10	111	677	15.1
Hopland Rancheria, California	-	-	-	-	-	-	-	-	-
Hualapai, Arizona	82	2	-	36	32	2	10	84	15.6
Inaja-Cosmit, California	-	-	-	-	-	-	-	-	-
Indian Township, Maine	27	-	-	-	24	1	2	39	45.9
Iowa, Kansas-Nebraska	-	-	-	-	-	-	-	3	-
Isabella, Michigan	42	-	-	-	38	-	3	46	42.5

Source: U.S. Bureau of the Census, Subject Reports, PC80-2-1D, Part I, *American Indians, Eskimos, and Aleuts on Identified Reservations and in the Historic Areas of Oklahoma (Excluding Urbanized Areas),* U.S. Government Printing Office, Washington, D.C., 1986, pp. 209-247. *Notes:* A dash (-) represents zero or a percent which rounds to less than 0.1. Also, a dash (-) is used because the number of supplementary questionnaires for the areas was insufficient to produce reliable estimates. Three dots (...) means not applicable, or that the data are being withheld to avoid disclosure of information for individuals.

★ 306 ★

High School Enrollment on Reservations, by Type of School, 1980 - II

Data are the latest available.

Identified reservation	High school enrollment							Persons 16 to 19 years old	
	Total	Tribal school	Bureau of Indian Affairs day school	Bureau of Indian Affairs boarding school	Other public school	Other private school	Not reported	Total number	Percent not enrolled in school, not high school graduated
Isleta Pueblo, New Mexico	225	6	-	5	195	6	13	229	12.3
Jackson Rancheria, California	...	...	...	...	...	...	...	...	...
Jemez Pueblo, New Mexico	171	-	4	22	116	23	6	149	16.3
Jicarilla Apache, New Mexico	117	6	1	7	101	1	-	186	24.1

[Continued]

★ 306 ★

High School Enrollment on Reservations, by Type of School, 1980 - II
[Continued]

Identified reservation	High school enrollment							Persons 16 to 19 years old	
	Total	Tribal school	Bureau of Indian Affairs day school	Bureau of Indian Affairs boarding school	Other public school	Other private school	Not reported	Total number	Percent not enrolled in school, not high school graduated
Kaibab, Arizona	4	-	-	2	2	-	-	8	24.7
Kalispel, Washington	6	-	-	-	6	-	-	15	73.3
Kickapoo, Kansas	43	-	-	-	34	-	10	33	8.6
Kootenai, Idaho	-	-	-	-	-	-	-	-	-
Lac Courte Oreilles, Wisconsin	101	45	2	-	51	2	2	104	26.3
Lac du Flambeau, Wisconsin	96	-	-	2	89	-	4	99	27.2
Laguna Pueblo, New Mexico	225	-	1	5	200	8	11	289	31.7
La Jolla, California	11	-	-	2	8	1	-	9	12.4
L'Anse, Michigan	79	5	-	3	68	-	3	70	15.3
La Posta, California	...	...	...	...	...	...	...	...	...
Las Vegas Colony, Nevada	9	-	-	-	7	-	1	12	58.8
Laytonville Rancheria, California	11	-	-	-	10	-	1	10	50.0
Leech Lake, Minnesota	216	14	2	3	152	5	41	271	33.2
Likely Rancheria, California	-	-	-	-	-	-	-	-	-
Lone Pine Rancheria, California	14	-	-	-	14	-	-	16	14.1
Lookout Rancheria, California	...	...	...	...	...	...	...	...	...
Los Coyotes, California	6	-	-	-	6	-	-	7	-
Lovelock Colony, Nevada	10	-	-	-	10	-	-	2	-
Lower Brule, South Dakota	61	-	31	4	19	4	3	70	29.2
Lower Elwah, Washington	3	-	-	-	3	-	-	1	100.0
Lower Sioux Community, Minnesota	2	-	-	-	2	-	-	2	-
Lummi, Washington	110	10	-	9	87	1	3	124	34.1
Makah, Washington	89	2	1	-	80	1	4	93	31.7
Manchester Rancheria, California	14	-	-	-	13	-	1	16	40.8
Manzanita, California	...	...	...	...	...	...	...	...	...
Maricopa, Arizona	33	-	-	-	29	2	2	39	33.6
Mattaponi, Virginia	7	-	-	-	6	-	1	6	33.3
Menominee, Wisconsin	224	47	-	12	106	4	56	209	26.3
Mesa Grande, California	-	-	-	-	-	-	-	-	-
Mescalero Apache, New Mexico	151	2	1	12	53	1	82	172	24.9
Miccosukee, Florida	9	2	-	1	4	-	2	25	56.0
Middletown Rancheria, California	3	-	-	-	3	-	-	3	-
Mille Lacs, Minnesota	-	-	-	-	-	-	-	-	-
Mississippi Choctaw Reservation	288	29	116	63	67	3	10	278	27.3
Moapa River, Nevada	20	-	-	1	17	-	2	15	28.6
Montgomery Creek Rancheria, California	...	...	...	...	...	...	...	...	...
Morongo, California	31	-	-	-	25	-	6	35	26.1
Muckleshoot, Washington	33	-	-	1	25	-	7	53	48.9
Nambe Pueblo, New Mexico	9	-	-	1	5	-	3	12	25.2
Navajo, Arizona-New Mexico-Utah	9,697	119	144	1,464	6,686	366	918	10,907	24.3
Nez Perce, Idaho	150	12	2	5	118	1	12	133	15.1
Nisqually, Washington	7	5	-	-	2	-	-	11	22.3
Nooksack, Washington	-	-	-	-	-	-	-	-	-
Northern Cheyenne, Montana	302	74	17	15	99	54	43	292	23.8
Oil Springs, New York	-	-	-	-	-	-	-	-	-
Omaha, Iowa-Nebraska	113	5	1	7	42	-	59	117	21.0
Oneida, Wisconsin	159	17	-	4	119	6	13	163	20.9
Onondaga, New York	-	-	-	-	-	-	-	-	-
Ontonagon, Michigan	-	-	-	-	-	-	-	-	-
Osage, Oklahoma	350	-	-	-	318	7	25	403	20.1
Ozette, Washington	...	...	...	...	...	...	...	...	...
Pala, California	35	1	-	3	32	-	-	39	22.1
Pamunkey, Virginia	5	-	-	-	4	-	1	2	-

[Continued]

High School Enrollment on Reservations, by Type of School, 1980 - II

[Continued]

Identified reservation	High school enrollment							Persons 16 to 19 years old	
	Total	Tribal school	Bureau of Indian Affairs day school	Bureau of Indian Affairs boarding school	Other public school	Other private school	Not reported	Total number	Percent not enrolled in school, not high school graduated
Papago, Arizona	522	7	24	230	218	17	25	533	24.2
Pascua Yaqui, Arizona	42	1	-	-	39	1	1	57	49.1
Pauma, California	3	-	-	-	3	-	-	7	41.4
Payson Community of Yavapai-Apache, Arizona	-	-	-	-	-	-	-	-	-
Pechanga, California	8	-	-	-	8	-	-	14	35.7
Penobscot, Maine	33	2	-	-	26	2	3	35	20.0
Picuris Pueblo, New Mexico	5	-	-	-	5	-	-	6	-
Pine Creek, Michigan	...	...	...	...	...	...	...	...	...
Pine Ridge, South Dakota	1,028	125	429	96	100	205	73	1,165	29.5
Pleasant Point, Maine	40	6	-	-	24	9	1	53	30.0
Pojoaque Pueblo, New Mexico	6	-	-	-	5	-	1	9	13.7
Poospatuck, New York	10	-	-	-	10	-	-	7	-
Port Gamble, Washington	7	-	-	-	5	-	1	31	43.9
Port Madison, Washington	4	-	-	-	4	-	-	5	44.9
Potawatomi, Wisconsin	28	-	-	2	24	-	2	27	14.8
Pottawatomi, Kansas	28	-	-	-	24	-	4	29	13.8
Prairie Island Community, Minnesota	2	-	-	-	2	-	-	10	50.0
Puyallup, Washington	66	9	2	2	50	1	3	71	35.3
Pyramid Lake, Nevada	73	5	8	1	59	-	-	70	15.9
Quileute, Washington	27	-	-	3	20	-	3	41	35.3
Quinault, Washington	87	4	-	2	75	-	5	96	28.9
Ramah Community, New Mexico	82	17	22	2	9	19	14	110	31.7
Ramona, California	-	-	-	-	-	-	-	-	-
Red Cliff, Wisconsin	71	-	-	-	54	-	17	54	21.0
Red Lake, Minnesota	217	5	-	43	159	2	8	283	44.9
Reno-Sparks Colony, Nevada	30	-	-	-	29	-	1	39	32.9
Resighini Rancheria, California	...	...	...	...	...	...	...	...	...
Rincon, California	18	-	-	-	15	-	3	21	27.3
Roaring Creek Rancheria, California	...	...	...	...	...	...	...	...	...
Rocky Boy's, Montana	163	12	7	5	129	-	10	163	23.5
Rosebud, South Dakota	395	43	31	15	207	58	41	454	32.6
Round Valley, California	41	-	-	-	40	1	-	37	17.0
Rumsey Rancheria, California	...	...	...	...	...	...	...	...	...
Sac and Fox, Iowa	62	-	-	10	48	-	4	55	22.1
Sac and Fox, Kansas-Nebraska	...	...	...	...	...	...	...	...	...
St. Croix, Wisconsin	47	-	1	4	39	-	3	36	33.9
St. Regis Mohawk, New York	163	2	-	-	150	3	9	140	17.4
Salt River, Arizona	167	3	1	36	110	4	13	256	44.1
San Carlos, Arizona	528	9	9	86	296	39	89	614	30.7
Sandia Pueblo, New Mexico	16	-	-	1	11	3	1	20	20.0
Sandy Lake, Minnesota	-	-	-	-	-	-	-	-	-
San Felipe Pueblo, New Mexico	203	1	1	29	166	3	3	187	22.1
San Ildefonso Pueblo, New Mexico	31	2	-	5	23	1	-	35	5.2
San Juan Pueblo, New Mexico	89	3	3	7	71	1	4	91	24.8
San Manuel, California	-	-	-	-	-	-	-	-	-
San Pasqual, California	9	-	-	-	5	-	5	10	77.7
Santa Ana Pueblo, New Mexico	31	-	-	3	27	1	-	28	13.9
Santa Clara Pueblo, New Mexico	186	5	3	20	112	33	13	161	6.3

Source: U.S. Bureau of the Census, Subject Reports, PC80-2-1D, Part I, *American Indians, Eskimos, and Aleuts on Identified Reservations and in the Historic Areas of Oklahoma (Excluding Urbanized Areas),* U.S. Government Printing Office, Washington, D.C., 1986, pp. 209-247. *Notes:* A dash (-) represents zero or a percent which rounds to less than 0.1. Also, a dash (-) is used because the number of supplementary questionnaires for the areas was insufficient to produce reliable estimates. Three dots (...) means not applicable, or that the data are being withheld to avoid disclosure of information for individuals.

★ 307 ★

High School Enrollment on Reservations, by Type of School, 1980 - III

Data are the latest available.

| Identified reservations | High school enrollment | | | | | | | Persons 16 to 19 years old | |
	Total	Tribal school	Bureau of Indian Affairs day school	Bureau of Indian Affairs boarding school	Other public school	Other private school	Not reported	Total number	Percent not enrolled in school, not high school graduated
Santa Rosa Rancheria, California	9	-	-	-	9	-	-	16	48.9
Santa Rosa, California	...	...	...	...	...	...	...	...	...
Santa Ynez, California	16	-	-	-	16	-	-	13	9.1
Santa Ysabel, California	13	-	-	-	11	-	2	19	36.2
Santee, Nebraska	38	2	-	-	16	1	20	33	18.7
Santo Domingo Pueblo, New Mexico	223	3	7	16	192	4	3	179	24.4
San Xavier, Arizona	75	-	-	32	38	4	1	69	22.9
Sauk-Suiattle, Washington	-	-	-	-	-	-	-	-	-
Sault Ste. Marie, Michigan	-	-	-	-	-	-	-	-	-
Schaghticoke, Connecticut	...	...	...	...	...	...	...	...	...
Shakopee Community, Minnesota	6	-	-	-	3	-	3	5	40.5
Sheep Ranch Rancheria, California	...	...	...	...	...	...	...	...	...
Sherwood Valley Rancheria, California	...	...	...	...	...	...	...	...	...
Shingle Springs Rancheria, California	-	-	-	-	-	-	-	-	-
Shinnecock, New York	4	-	-	-	2	-	2	11	32.6
Shoalwater, Washington	...	...	...	...	...	...	...	...	...
Sisseton, North Dakota-South Dakota	212	11	-	6	185	-	10	233	38.8
Skokomish, Washington	29	1	-	-	27	-	1	28	34.2
Skull Valley, Utah	-	-	-	-	-	-	-	-	-
Soboba, California	18	-	-	-	18	-	-	11	20.7
Sokaogon Chippewa Community, Wisconsin	5	-	-	-	4	-	1	10	50.0
Southern Paiute, Utah	19	-	-	-	19	-	-	8	25.2
Southern Ute, Colorado	94	1	-	3	75	1	13	99	19.4
Spokane, Washington	97	-	-	-	94	1	2	106	24.6
Squaxin Island, Washington	-	-	-	-	-	-	-	2	100.0
Standing Rock, North Dakota-South Dakota	345	6	35	33	249	4	18	447	29.3
Stewart's Point Rancheria, California	7	1	-	-	-	-	6	9	11.1
Stockbridge, Wisconsin	49	3	-	-	46	-	-	49	23.1
Sulphur Bank Rancheria, California	5	-	-	1	4	-	-	8	33.3
Summit Lake, Nevada	...	...	...	...	...	...	...	...	...
Susanville, California	14	-	-	-	9	-	5	15	42.9
Swinomish, Washington	19	1	-	-	17	-	-	36	49.8
Sycuan, California	6	-	-	-	6	-	-	6	25.0
Tama, Georgia	4	-	-	-	4	-	-	4	-
Taos Pueblo, New Mexico	111	6	-	19	81	3	3	84	7.1
Te-Moak, Nevada	9	-	-	-	9	-	-	8	-
Tesuque Pueblo, New Mexico	28	-	-	3	18	2	4	25	-
Tigua, Texas	28	1	-	-	24	-	3	36	38.9
Tonawanda, New York	26	-	-	-	26	-	-	41	41.6
Torres-Martinez, California	-	-	-	-	-	-	-	-	-
Trinidad Rancheria, California	6	-	-	-	6	-	-	7	33.3
Tulalip, Washington	65	3	-	1	50	4	7	74	44.5
Tule River, California	43	-	-	5	37	-	1	45	35.9
Tunicabiloxi, Louisiana	...	...	...	...	...	...	...	...	...
Tuolumne Rancheria, California	11	-	-	-	11	-	-	4	-
Turtle Mountain, North Dakota	390	68	212	5	84	1	22	436	36.4
Tuscarora, New York	-	-	-	-	-	-	-	-	-
Twenty-Nine Palms, California	-	-	-	-	-	-	-	-	-
Uintah and Ouray, Utah	185	3	-	29	119	1	32	213	33.6
Umatilla, Oregon	89	8	1	4	72	1	4	86	17.2
Upper Sioux Community, Minnesota	4	-	-	-	4	-	-	4	-
Upper Skagit, Washington	-	-	-	-	-	-	-	-	-
Ute Mountain, Colorado-New Mexico	75	1	-	5	33	-	35	104	22.5

[Continued]

★ 307 ★

High School Enrollment on Reservations, by Type of School, 1980 - III
[Continued]

Identified reservations	High school enrollment							Persons 16 to 19 years old	
	Total	Tribal school	Bureau of Indian Affairs day school	Bureau of Indian Affairs boarding school	Other public school	Other private school	Not reported	Total number	Percent not enrolled in school, not high school graduated
Vermillion Lake, Minnesota	9	-	-	-	9	-	-	11	16.8
Viejas Rancheria, California	16	-	-	1	15	-	-	12	20.4
Walker River, Nevada	48	-	-	6	41	1	-	45	20.0
Wampanoag, Massachusetts	-	-	-	-	-	-	-	-	-
Warm Springs, Oregon	186	8	1	14	134	3	27	209	28.8
Washoe, Nevada	-	-	-	-	-	-	-	-	-
Western Pequot, Connecticut	...	...	...	...	...	...	...	...	...
White Earth, Minnesota	203	18	-	-	174	-	10	265	35.0
Wind River, Wyoming	341	31	63	38	167	8	33	405	31.0
Winnebago, Nebraska	93	2	1	7	45	2	36	97	23.0
Winnemucca Colony, Nevada	5	-	-	-	5	-	-	2	-
Visconsin Winnebago Reservation	23	-	1	3	13	-	5	23	34.4
Woodfords Community, California	-	-	-	-	-	-	-	-	-
XL Ranch, California	...	...	...	...	...	...	...	...	...
Yakima, Washington	456	47	2	12	356	5	34	488	30.6
Yankton, South Dakota	114	33	4	4	59	6	7	136	22.7
Yavapai, Arizona	5	-	-	-	5	-	-	5	-
Yerington, Nevada	11	-	-	-	10	-	1	14	-
Yomba, Nevada	7	-	-	1	5	1	-	7	15.2
Zia Pueblo, New Mexico	62	-	-	9	52	1	-	57	15.9
Zuni Pueblo, New Mexico	578	33	1	23	478	16	26	619	30.2
San Felipe/Santa Ana Joint Area, New Mexico	-	-	-	-	-	-	-	-	-
San Felipe/Santo Domingo Joint Area, New Mexico	25	-	-	-	23	-	2	9	35.4
Other Reservation Lands in Montana	-	-	-	-	-	-	-	-	-

Source: U.S. Bureau of the Census, Subject Reports, PC80-2-1D, Part I, *American Indians, Eskimos, and Aleuts on Identified Reservations and in the Historic Areas of Oklahoma (Excluding Urbanized Areas)*, U.S. Government Printing Office, Washington, D.C., 1986, pp. 209-247. *Notes:* A dash (-) represents zero or a percent which rounds to less than 0.1. Also, a dash (-) is used because the number of supplementary questionnaires for the areas was insufficient to produce reliable estimates. Three dots (...) means not applicable, or that the data are being withheld to avoid disclosure of information for individuals.

Academic Progress

★ 308 ★

Mathematics Credits Earned, 1982 and 1987

The percentage of high school graduates having taken courses in selected mathematics topics is shown, by sex and race/ethnicity, for 1982 and 1987.

Subject and student characteristic	1982	1987
All mathematics credits		
Male	2.64	3.06
Female	2.47	2.97
Native American	2.09	3.06
White	2.60	3.03

[Continued]

★ 308 ★

Mathematics Credits Earned, 1982 and 1987
[Continued]

Subject and student characteristic	1982	1987
Asian	3.14	3.70
Black	2.55	2.96
Hispanic	2.2	42.86
Basic mathematics		
Male	0.11	0.14
Female	0.08	0.12
Native American	0.26	0.10
White	0.07	0.09
Asian	0.08	0.09
Black	0.20	0.25
Hispanic	0.15	0.35
General mathematics		
Male	0.50	0.38
Female	0.40	0.30
Native American	0.49	0.48
White	0.37	0.29
Asian	0.33	0.22
Black	0.72	0.63
Hispanic	0.68	0.44
Algebra		
Male	0.55	0.66
Female	0.59	0.68
Native American	0.40	0.67
White	0.60	0.69
Asian	0.60	0.71
Black	0.47	0.59
Hispanic	0.45	0.59
Geometry		
Male	0.45	0.57
Female	0.46	0.59
Native American	0.25	0.45
White	0.51	0.62
Asian	0.68	0.75
Black	0.30	0.43
Hispanic	0.24	0.40
Calculus		
Male	0.05	0.07
Female	0.04	0.05
Native American	0.02	[1]
White	0.05	0.06
Asian	0.13	0.26

[Continued]

★ 308 ★

Mathematics Credits Earned, 1982 and 1987
[Continued]

Subject and student characteristic	1982	1987
Black	0.02	0.03
Hispanic	0.02	0.03

Source: National Science Board, *Science and Engineering Indicators - 1991*, Washington, D.C., U.S. Government Printing Office, 1991, (NSB 91-1) p. 218. Primary source: J. Tuma, A. Gifford, D. Harde, E.G. Hoachlander, and L. Horn. *Course Enrollment Patterns in Public Secondary Schools, 1969 to 1987* (Berkeley, CA: MPR Associates, Inc., 1989). *Notes:* (NA) stands for not available. 1. Less than .01 credits were taken.

★ 309 ★

Achievement Quartiles from Sixth to Eighth Grade

Data reflect results of a 1988 survey of eighth graders.

Race/ethnicity	Grade quartiles			
	Lowest quartile	25-49%	50-74%	Highest quartile
Total	24.9	22.2	24.6	28.3
American Indian and Native Alaskan	36.7	27.6	23.1	12.6
Asian and Pacific Islander	16.5	16.2	21.3	46.1
Hispanic	30.6	24.5	25.2	19.7
Black	28.8	28.3	26.3	16.6
White	23.4	20.9	24.4	31.2

Source: "Percentage of Eighth Graders Classified into Selected Quartiles Based on Self-Reported Grades From Grade Six Until Grade Eight, by Selected Background Characteristics," *A Profile of the American Eighth Grader*, 1990, p. 34. Primary source: U.S. Department of Education, National Center for Education Statistics, "National Education Longitudinal Study of 1988: Base Year Student Survey."

★ 310 ★

Achievement Scores of Eighth Graders in Selected Subjects, 1988

Standardized scores, are shown for selected subjects, by race/ethnicity.

Achievement test	Eighth graders' achievement, by standardized score[1]				
	American Indian	White	Black	Hispanic	Asian
History	44.2	51.6	45.0	45.9	51.9
Mathematics	44.7	51.8	43.8	45.7	53.6
Reading	44.3	51.7	44.6	46.0	51.2
Science	43.9	51.8	43.9	46.1	51.8

Source: "Eighth Graders Achievement on History, Mathematics, Reading, and Science Tests: 1988," *Digest of Education Statistics 1991*, November 1991, p. 122. Primary source: U.S. Department of Education, National Center for Education Statistics, "National Education Longitudinal Study of 1988" survey. (This table was prepared April 1991.) *Notes:* Because of rounding, details may not add to totals. 1. Standardized scores with a mean of 50 and standard deviation of 10.

★ 311 ★

Average Carnegie Units Completed by High School Graduates, by Curriculum Track, Sex, and Race/Ethnicity, 1982 and 1987

In this indicator Carnegie Units are divided among 3 curricular areas: Academic, vocational, and personal use. Within each area, courses are assigned as follows: 1. Academic mathematics (basic, general applied, pre- algebra, algebra I, geometry, advanced/other, advanced calculus); Science (survey, biology, chemistry, physics); English (survey, literature, composition, speech); social studies (American history, world history, American government, humanities/other); Fine arts (fine arts and crafts, music drama/dance); foreign languages (survey, English for speakers of other languages, years 1-4 by language); 2. Vocational, consumer and homemaking education, general labor market preparation (typewriting I, introductory industrial arts, work experience/career exploration, general labor market skills); specific labor market preparation (agriculture/renewable resources, business, marketing and distribution, health occupations, occupational home economics, trade and industry, technical and communications); 3. Personal use general skills, health (physical education); religion; military science.

Characteristic	Total carnegie units		Total academic units		Total vocational units		Total personal use units	
	1982	1987	1982	1987	1982	1987	1982	1987
Total	21.3	22.8	14.1	15.6	4.6	4.4	2.6	2.7
Sex								
Male	21.2	22.7	13.9	15.3	4.6	4.5	2.7	2.8
Female	21.5	22.9	14.3	16.0	4.6	4.4	2.5	2.6
Race/ethnicity								
American Indian	21.3	23.2	13.3	15.3	5.1	4.7	2.9	3.2
White	21.4	22.9	14.4	15.7	4.5	4.5	2.5	2.6
Black	21.0	22.1	13.6	15.0	4.8	4.5	2.6	2.7
Hispanic	21.1	22.5	12.9	15.1	5.3	4.3	2.9	3.2
Asian	22.1	23.9	15.8	17.8	3.1	2.9	3.1	3.2

Source: U.S. Department of Education, National Center for Education Statistics, *The Condition of Education, 1992*, Washington, D.C.: 1992, p. 246. Primary source: U.S. Department of Education, National Center for Education Statistics, *The 1969 Study of Academic Growth and Prediction*; *High School and Beyond*, base year study; *1987 High School Transcript Study*; *National Assessment of Vocational Education Statistics, The Secondary School Taxonomy, 1989.*

★ 312 ★

Average Vocational Carnegie Units, by Vocational Category Completed by High School Graduates and Sex: 1982 and 1987

Vocational Carnegie Units include: Consumer and homemaking education; General labor market preparation (typewriting 1, introductory industrial arts, work experience/career exploration, general labor market skills); Specific labor market preparation (agriculture/renewable resources, business, marketing and distribution, health occupations, occupational home economics, trade and industry, technical and communications).

Characteristic	Total		Career and home-maker education		General labor market preparation		Specific labor market preparation	
	1982	1987	1982	1987	1982	1987	1982	1987
Total	4.6	4.4	0.7	0.6	1.0	0.9	2.9	2.9
Sex								
Male	4.6	4.5	0.3	0.3	1.0	0.9	3.4	3.3
Female	4.6	4.4	1.0	0.9	1.1	1.0	2.6	2.6
Race/ethnicity								
American Indian	5.1	4.7	0.5	0.6	1.1	0.9	3.5	3.2
White	4.5	4.5	0.6	0.6	1.0	0.9	2.9	3.0
Black	4.8	4.5	0.9	0.7	1.0	1.0	2.9	2.8
Hispanic	5.3	4.3	0.9	0.6	1.2	1.0	3.2	2.7
Asian	3.1	2.9	0.3	0.3	0.9	0.7	1.9	1.9

Source: U.S. Department of Education, National Center for Education Statistics, *The Condition of Education, 1992,* Washington, D.C.: 1992, p. 247. Primary source: U.S. Department of Education, National Center for Education Statistics, *The 1969 Study of Academic Growth and Prediction; High School and Beyond,* base year study; 1987 *High School Transcript Study.*

★ 313 ★

Biology, Chemistry, and Physics and Science Proficiency

Data shown for students in grades 9-12, by race/ethnicity. Proficiencies are based on IRT (item response theory) scaling procedures. Progress is estimated on a scale of 0 to 500.

	One year or more			Less than one year		
	Percent of students	Average proficiency	Average content area proficiency	Percent of students	Average proficiency	Average content area proficiency
Biology						
American Indian	74 (10.0)[1]	290 (6.5)[1]	292 (6.9)[1]	26 (10.0)[1]	269 (15.2)[1]	270 (16.7)[1]
Hispanic	86 (2.7)	281 (2.8)	283 (2.8)	14 (2.7)	246 (5.5)	247 (6.6)
White	92 (1.2)	306 (1.2)	308 (1.1)	8 (1.2)	270 (2.6)	274 (3.0)
Black	91 (1.2)	259 (2.6)	265 (2.2)	9 (1.2)	233 (5.4)	240 (5.4)
Asian/Pacific Islander	89 (1.6)	311 (6.0)	312 (6.0)	11 (1.6)	297 (13.8)	298 (14.7)
Total	91 (1.0)	298 (1.2)	301 (1.1)	9 (1.0)	263 (1.8)	267 (2.1)
Chemistry						
American Indian	36 (6.8)[1]	304 (9.5)[1]	306 (8.0)[1]	64 (6.8)[1]	272 (4.8)[1]	267 (5.7)[1]
Hispanic	48 (3.0)	293 (3.5)	295 (4.5)	52 (3.0)	262 (2.8)	257 (4.1)
White	56 (1.4)	321 (1.2)	322 (1.6)	44 (1.4)	280 (1.4)	273 (1.8)

[Continued]

★ 313 ★

Biology, Chemistry, and Physics and Science Proficiency
[Continued]

	One year or more			Less than one year		
	Percent of students	Average proficiency	Average content area proficiency	Percent of students	Average proficiency	Average content area proficiency
Black	49 (3.3)	275 (2.6)	274 (2.9)	51 (3.3)	240 (2.8)	234 (4.1)
Asian/Pacific Islander	80 (7.3)	319 (3.8)	322 (5.1)	20 (7.3)	277 (6.4)	273 (9.4)
Total	55 (1.3)	314 (1.2)	314 (1.6)	45 (1.3)	273 (1.3)	266 (1.6)
Physics						
American Indian	19 (6.0)[1]	298 (17.8)[1]	304 (17.2)[1]	81 (6.0)[1]	281 (5.2)[1]	276 (4.6)[1]
Hispanic	26 (1.9)	293 (4.1)	294 (4.9)	74 (1.9)	271 (3.4)	268 (4.4)
White	29 (1.2)	329 (1.6)	334 (2.1)	71 (1.2)	293 (1.0)	287 (1.3)
Black	24 (2.8)	262 (4.5)	262 (5.7)	76 (2.8)	255 (2.6)	251 (3.5)
Asian/Pacific Islander	56 (5.0)	326 (6.2)	333 (7.8)	44 (5.0)	290 (4.2)	285 (5.7)
Total	29 (1.1)	319 (1.6)	323 (2.1)	71 (1.1)	286 (1.0)	280 (1.2)

Source: The 1990 Science Report Card: NAEP's Assessment of Fourth, Eighth, and Twelfth Graders, Lee R. Jones, Ina V.S. Mullis, Senta A. Raizen, Iris R. Weiss, Elizabeth A. Weston, Prepared by Educational Testing Service under contract with the National Center for Education Statistics, Office of Educational Research and Improvement, U.S. Department of Education, March, 1992, p. 73. *The 1990 Science Report Card NAEP's Assessment of Fourth, Eighth and Twelfth Graders*, (National Center for Education Statistics U.S. Department of Education, 1992). *Notes:* Achievement results were analyzed using item response theory (IRT) scaling procedures, which allowed the National Assessment of Educational Progress to estimate students' average proficiency on a scale ranging from 0 to 500. The standard errors of the estimated percentages and proficiencies appear in parentheses. It can be said with 95 percent certainty that for each population of interest, the value for the whole population is within plus or minus two standard errors of the estimate for the sample. 1. Interpret with caution - the nature of the sample does not allow accurate determination of the variability of these estimated statistics.

★ 314 ★

Mathematics Proficiency

Data reflect results of a 1988 survey of eighth graders.

Race/ethnicity	Percentage at each level of mathematics			
	Advanced	Intermediate	Basic	Below basic
American Indian	6.0	13.0	48.0	32.0
Asian	35.0	21.0	30.0	14.0
White	23.0	24.0	37.0	16.0
Hispanic	9.0	17.0	46.0	28.0
Black	6.0	16.0	48.0	30.0

Source: "Percentage of Eighth Graders Proficient at Each Mathematics Level, by Race," *A Profile of the American Eighth Grader*, 1990, p. 26. Primary source: U.S. Dept., Ed. NCES, NELS:88 BY.

★ 315 ★

SAT: Distribution of Test Takers, by Race/Ethnicity and Sex, 1976-1991

Distribution of students, by race/ethnicity and sex, is shown in percent.

| Year | Race/ethnicity | | | | | | | | Sex | |
	American Indian	White	Black	Mexican American	Puerto Rican	Other Hispanic	Asian American	Other	Male	Female
1976	0.3	85.0	8.2	1.0	0.7	-	2.2	2.0	49.5	50.5
1977	0.4	83.9	8.8	1.7	0.8	-	2.4	2.1	48.9	51.1
1978	0.4	83.0	9.0	1.7	1.0	-	2.6	2.3	48.4	51.6
1979	0.4	82.9	8.9	1.6	1.0	-	2.8	2.4	48.3	51.7
1980	0.5	82.1	9.1	1.7	1.1	-	3.2	2.3	48.3	51.7
1981	0.6	81.9	9.0	1.7	1.1	-	3.4	2.2	48.1	51.9
1982	0.5	81.7	8.9	1.8	1.2	-	3.8	2.2	48.2	51.8
1983	0.5	81.1	8.8	1.9	1.2	-	4.2	2.2	48.3	51.7
1984	0.5	80.3	9.1	2.0	1.3	-	4.5	2.3	48.2	51.8
1985	0.5	80.0	8.9	2.2	1.2	-	4.8	2.4	48.3	51.7
1986	-	-	-	-	-	-	-	-	48.1	51.9
1987	1.0	78.2	8.7	2.1	1.0	1.9	5.8	1.2	48.2	51.8
1988	1.2	77.0	9.2	2.2	1.1	1.9	6.1	1.3	48.0	52.0
1989	1.8	74.7	9.6	2.5	1.1	2.1	6.8	1.3	47.9	52.1
1990	1.1	73.4	10.0	2.8	1.2	2.5	7.6	1.5	47.8	52.2
1991	0.8	72.0	10.5	3.0	1.3	2.7	8.0	1.7	47.8	52.2

Source: U.S. Department of Education, National Center for Education Statistics, *The Condition of Education, 1992*, Washington, D.C.: 1992, p. 226. Primary source: College Entrance Examination Board, *National Report: College Bound Seniors, 1972-1991. Notes:* A dash (-) indicates that data were not available. The first year for which SAT scores by race/ethnic group are available is 1976.

★ 316 ★

SAT Scores, by Race/Ethnicity, 1992

```
┌─────────────────────────────────────────────────────┐
│  ┌──────────────────────────────────────────────┐   │
│  │ Asian - 945                                    │   │
│  └──────────────────────────────────────────────┘   │
│  ┌─────────────────────────────────────────────┐    │
│  │ White - 933                                   │    │
│  └─────────────────────────────────────────────┘    │
│  ┌──────────────────────────────────────┐           │
│  │ Native American - 837                  │           │
│  └──────────────────────────────────────┘           │
│  ┌─────────────────────────────────────┐            │
│  │ Other Hispanic - 816                  │            │
│  └─────────────────────────────────────┘            │
│  ┌────────────────────────────────────┐             │
│  │ Mexican - 797                        │             │
│  └────────────────────────────────────┘             │
│  ┌──────────────────────────────────┐               │
│  │ Puerto Rican - 772                 │               │
│  └──────────────────────────────────┘               │
│  ┌─────────────────────────────────┐                │
│  │ Black - 737                       │                │
│  └─────────────────────────────────┘                │
│              Chart shows data from column 1.          │
└─────────────────────────────────────────────────────┘
```

Average scores are shown with five year changes, by race/ethnicity, for 1992.

Race and ethnicity	1992	5-year change
Native American	837	+12
Mexican	797	-6
Puerto Rican	772	+12
Other Hispanic	816	-3
White	933	-3
Black	737	+9
Asian	945	+19

Source: USA TODAY, August 22, 1992, p. 1-D. Primary source: The College Board.

★ 317 ★

SAT Average Mathematics Scores, by Race/Ethnicity and Sex, 1976-1991

Year	All	Race/ethnicity								Sex	
		American Indian	White	Black	Mexican American	Puerto Rican	Other Hispanic	Asian American	Other	Male	Female
1976	472	420	493	354	410	401	-	518	458	497	446
1977	470	421	489	357	408	397	-	514	457	497	445
1978	468	419	485	354	402	388	-	510	450	494	444
1979	467	421	483	358	410	388	-	511	447	493	443
1980	466	426	482	360	413	394	-	509	449	491	443
1981	466	425	483	362	415	398	-	513	447	492	443
1982	467	424	483	366	416	403	-	513	449	493	443
1983	468	425	484	369	417	403	-	514	446	493	445
1984	471	427	487	373	420	405	-	519	450	495	449
1985	475	428	490	376	426	409	-	518	448	499	452
1986	475	-	-	-	-	-	-	-	-	501	451

[Continued]

580

★ 317 ★

SAT Average Mathematics Scores, by Race/Ethnicity and Sex, 1976-1991
[Continued]

| Year | All | Race/ethnicity | | | | | | | | Sex | |
		American Indian	White	Black	Mexican American	Puerto Rican	Other Hispanic	Asian American	Other	Male	Female
1987	476	432	489	377	424	400	432	521	455	500	453
1988	476	435	490	384	428	402	433	522	460	498	455
1989	476	428	491	386	430	406	436	525	467	500	454
1990	476	437	491	385	429	405	434	528	467	499	455
1991	474	437	489	385	427	406	431	530	466	497	453

Source: U.S. Department of Education, National Center for Education Statistics, *The Condition of Education, 1992*, Washington, D.C.: 1992, p. 227. Primary source: College Entrance Examination Board, *National Report: College Bound Sseniors, 1972-1991. Note:* A dash (-) indicates that date were not available.

★ 318 ★

SAT Average Verbal Scores, by Race/Ethnicity and Sex, 1976-1991

| Year | All | Race/ethnicity | | | | | | | | Sex | |
		American Indian	White	Black	Mexican American	Puerto Rican	Other Hispanic	Asian American	Other	Male	Female
1976	431	388	451	332	371	364	-	414	410	433	430
1977	429	390	448	330	370	355	-	405	402	431	427
1978	429	387	446	332	370	349	-	401	399	433	425
1979	427	386	444	330	370	345	-	396	393	431	423
1980	424	390	442	330	372	350	-	396	394	428	420
1981	424	391	442	332	373	353	-	397	388	430	418
1982	426	388	444	341	377	360	-	398	392	431	421
1983	425	388	443	339	375	358	-	395	386	430	420
1984	426	390	445	342	376	358	-	398	388	433	420
1985	431	392	449	346	382	368	-	404	391	437	425
1986	431	-	-	-	-	-	-	-	-	437	426
1987	430	393	447	351	379	360	387	405	405	435	425
1988	428	393	445	353	382	355	387	408	410	435	422
1989	427	384	446	351	381	360	389	409	414	434	421
1990	424	388	442	352	380	359	383	410	410	429	419
1991	422	393	441	351	377	361	382	411	411	426	418

Source: U.S. Department of Education, National Center for Education Statistics, *The Condition of Education, 1992*, Washington, D.C.: 1992, p. 227. Primary source: College Entrance Examination Board, *National Report: College Bound Seniors, 1972-1991. Note:* A dash (-) indicates that date were not available.

★ 319 ★

Science Credits Earned, 1982 and 1987

The percentage of high school graduates having taken courses in selected science topics is shown, by sex and race/ethnicity, for 1982 and 1987.

Subject and student characteristic	1982	1987
All science credits		
Male	2.23	2.53
Female	2.11	2.49
Native American	1.96	2.44
White	2.25	2.57
Asian	2.57	3.00
Black	2.04	2.31
Hispanic	1.78	2.20
Survey courses		
Male	0.78	0.78
Female	0.71	0.73
Native American	0.72	0.81
White	0.73	0.74
Asian	0.51	0.65
Black	0.82	0.90
Hispanic	0.77	0.77
Biology		
Male	0.89	1.04
Female	0.96	1.13
Native American	0.77	1.22
White	0.96	1.11
Asian	1.08	1.11
Black	0.88	1.00
Hispanic	0.79	1.05
Chemistry		
Male	0.35	0.47
Female	0.33	0.47
Native American	0.35	0.32
White	0.38	0.50
Asian	0.60	0.80
Black	0.25	0.31
Hispanic	0.15	0.28
Physics		
Male	0.21	0.25
Female	0.12	0.16
Native American	0.11	0.09
White	0.19	0.16
Asian	0.39	0.43

[Continued]

★ 319 ★

Science Credits Earned, 1982 and 1987
[Continued]

Subject and student characteristic	1982	1987
Black	0.09	0.11
Hispanic	0.06	0.09

Source: National Science Board, *Science and Engineering Indicators - 1991*, Washington, D.C., U.S. Government Printing Office, 1991, (NSB 91-1) p. 217. Primary source: J. Tuma, A. Gifford, D. Harde, E.G. Hoachlander, and L. Horn. *Course Enrollment Patterns in Public Secondary Schools, 1969 to 1987* (Berkeley, CA: MPR Associates, Inc., 1989).

★ 320 ★

Science Experiments and Projects

Data show percent of students providing affirmative responses to the question "Have you ever done experiments or projects at home or in school with...?"

	Plants or animals	Electricity	Chemicals	Rocks or minerals	Telescope	Thermometer or barometer
Grade 4						
American Indian	70 (3.4)	58 (3.6)	39 (4.7)	53 (3.0)	45 (3.9)	57 (3.5)
Hispanic	57 (1.6)	55 (1.9)	40 (1.5)	47 (1.8)	46 (2.0)	48 (1.8)
White	58 (1.0)	53 (1.5)	42 (1.0)	51 (1.4)	42 (0.9)	45 (1.3)
Black	53 (1.5)	53 (1.6)	38 (1.8)	47 (1.5)	40 (2.0)	49 (2.0)
Asian/Pacific Islander	64 (3.8)	52 (6.1)	38 (4.7)	48 (5.9)	46 (3.4)	37 (6.0)
Male	58 (1.0)	60 (1.4)	41 (1.1)	50 (1.2)	43 (1.1)	46 (1.4)
Female	57 (1.3)	46 (1.5)	41 (1.0)	51 (1.7)	41 (1.0)	46 (1.4)
Total	58 (0.8)	53 (1.2)	41 (0.7)	50 (1.2)	42 (0.8)	46 (1.1)
Grade 8						
American Indian	59 (14.4)[1]	60 (7.8)[1]	60 (12.5)[1]	58 (9.2)[1]	49 (5.0)[1]	56 (6.4)[1]
Hispanic	68 (1.8)	60 (2.3)	55 (1.9)	54 (2.5)	44 (1.7)	49 (2.5)
White	74 (1.2)	67 (1.4)	65 (1.6)	60 (1.5)	49 (1.1)	56 (1.5)
Black	64 (2.0)	58 (2.5)	57 (2.3)	51 (2.1)	36 (2.3)	47 (2.6)
Asian/Pacific Islander	73 (4.2)	70 (3.0)	64 (3.3)	54 (4.8)	36 (3.3)	46 (5.1)
Male	71 (1.2)	75 (1.2)	64 (1.5)	57 (1.4)	49 (1.2)	52 (1.3)
Female	73 (1.5)	54 (1.4)	61 (1.6)	59 (1.6)	45 (1.1)	56 (1.6)
Total	72 (1.1)	65 (1.2)	63 (1.4)	58 (1.3)	47 (0.9)	54 (1.2)
Grade 12						
American Indian	78 (7.0)[1]	72 (9.9)[1]	74 (7.2)[1]	61 (5.2)[1]	42 (8.5)[1]	62 (6.6)[1]
Hispanic	83 (1.9)	64 (2.2)	76 (1.8)	64 (2.5)	53 (2.4)	63 (2.1)
White	86 (0.7)	74 (1.1)	83 (0.8)	70 (1.0)	55 (1.0)	71 (1.2)
Black	79 (1.8)	65 (2.0)	77 (1.8)	62 (2.3)	51 (2.3)	63 (1.6)
Asian/Pacific Islander	84 (1.9)	74 (2.3)	81 (5.6)	63 (5.2)	49 (3.6)	74 (2.4)
Male	84 (0.9)	82 (0.9)	83 (0.7)	68 (1.2)	56 (1.1)	70 (1.1)

[Continued]

★ 320 ★

Science Experiments and Projects
[Continued]

	Plants or animals	Electricity	Chemicals	Rocks or minerals	Telescope	Thermometer or barometer
Female	85 (0.8)	63 (1.4)	80 (1.0)	68 (1.3)	52 (1.1)	69 (1.3)
Total	85 (0.7)	72 (1.0)	81 (0.7)	68 (1.0)	54 (0.8)	69 (1.0)

Source: The 1990 Science Report Card: NAEP's Assessment of Fourth, Eighth, and Twelfth Graders, Lee R. Jones, Ina V.S. Mullis, Senta A. Raizen, Iris R. Weiss, Elizabeth A. Weston, Prepared by Educational Testing Service under contract with the National Center for Education Statistics, Office of Educational Research and Improvement, U.S. Department of Education, March, 1992, p. 83. *The 1990 Science Report Card NAEP's Assessment of Fourth, Eighth and Twelfth Graders*, (National Center for Education Statistics U.S. Department of Education, 1992). *Notes:* 1. Interpret with caution - the nature of the sample does not allow accurate determination of the variability of these estimated statistics.

★ 321 ★

Science Experiments and Projects Performed by Students and Average Proficiencies

Percent of students reporting the number of projects or experiments done and their average proficiencies based on IRT (item response theory) scaling procedures. Progress is estimated on a scale of 0 to 500.

	Five or six		Three or four		One or two		None	
	% of students	Avg. profic.	% of students	Avg. profic.	% of students	Avg. profic.	% of students	Avg. profic.
Grade 4								
American Indian	17 (2.9)	231 (4.4)	56 (4.2)	225 (3.4)	22 (3.7)	224 (6.0)	5 (1.5)	233 (10.7)
Hispanic	12 (1.2)	216 (3.2)	51 (1.8)	210 (1.6)	31 (1.3)	215 (1.9)	6 (0.6)	215 (4.2)
White	16 (0.7)	246 (1.3)	44 (0.8)	240 (1.3)	32 (0.9)	243 (1.2)	8 (0.6)	243 (2.0)
Black	11 (0.9)	212 (3.4)	49 (1.6)	203 (2.0)	33 (1.4)	206 (1.6)	8 (0.9)	213 (3.0)
Asian/Pacific Islander	15 (5.5)	234 (7.9)	41 (3.4)	231 (4.0)	39 (5.5)	236 (6.1)	4 (1.6)	228 (10.9)
Male	16 (0.9)	243 (1.7)	47 (1.1)	230 (1.3)	31 (1.1)	235 (1.5)	6 (0.5)	237 (2.9)
Female	13 (0.8)	235 (2.0)	45 (1.1)	230 (1.4)	34 (1.0)	232 (1.3)	8 (0.8)	234 (2.4)
Total	15 (0.6)	239 (1.2)	46 (0.6)	230 (1.2)	32 (1.1)	234 (1.1)	7 (0.5)	235 (1.7)
Grade 8								
American Indian	34 (10.6)[1]	266 (5.6)[1]	35 (6.0)[1]	251 (10.7)[1]	20 (9.9)[1]	245 (6.0)[1]	11 (3.7)[1]	223 (9.1)[1]
Hispanic	28 (2.0)	253 (2.8)	40 (1.6)	242 (2.7)	26 (1.7)	234 (2.9)	7 (1.1)	222 (5.0)
White	38 (1.6)	283 (1.5)	37 (1.0)	272 (1.5)	20 (0.9)	262 (2.1)	5 (0.5)	246 (2.8)
Black	22 (1.9)	246 (3.6)	40 (2.0)	232 (2.4)	32 (1.5)	223 (3.2)	6 (1.1)	216 (6.5)
Asian/Pacific Islander	29 (3.1)	284 (4.5)	41 (3.2)	270 (4.1)	26 (3.2)	260 (6.1)	5 (1.6)	253 (18.2)
Male	36 (1.5)	278 (1.6)	38 (0.9)	264 (1.8)	20 (0.9)	252 (1.9)	6 (0.5)	239 (4.0)
Female	33 (1.6)	276 (1.8)	37 (1.2)	261 (1.2)	24 (1.0)	248 (2.1)	6 (0.6)	238 (3.1)
Total	35 (1.3)	277 (1.4)	38 (0.9)	262 (1.3)	22 (0.8)	250 (1.6)	6 (0.4)	238 (2.4)
Grade 12								
American Indian	47 (6.9)[1]	288 (6.6)[1]	31 (6.7)[1]	294 (7.0)[1]	12 (7.4)[1]	270 (5.6)[1]	10 (5.3)[1]	268 (7.5)[1]
Hispanic	46 (2.1)	283 (2.5)	34 (1.7)	270 (5.2)	16 (1.6)	258 (3.8)	4 (0.9)	238 (9.0)
White	58 (1.3)	311 (1.1)	28 (0.9)	298 (1.9)	10 (0.6)	282 (2.8)	4 (0.4)	270 (3.6)
Black	46 (2.2)	266 (2.8)	34 (1.7)	253 (3.6)	15 (1.3)	243 (3.9)	6 (0.8)	233 (6.7)
Asian/Pacific Islander	55 (4.1)	316 (8.6)	27 (2.7)	306 (7.3)	15 (2.1)	289 (7.5)	3 (1.2)	274 (32.2)
Male	59 (1.3)	308 (1.6)	27 (1.0)	293 (2.1)	10 (0.7)	277 (2.9)	4 (0.4)	266 (4.4)
Female	51 (1.5)	299 (1.3)	31 (1.0)	284 (1.8)	13 (0.9)	270 (2.4)	5 (0.4)	256 (3.8)
Total	55 (1.2)	304 (1.2)	29 (0.8)	288 (1.6)	12 (0.6)	273 (2.2)	4 (0.3)	260 (2.9)

Source: The 1990 Science Report Card: NAEP's Assessment of Fourth, Eighth, and Twelfth Graders, Lee R. Jones, Ina V.S. Mullis, Senta A. Raizen, Iris R. Weiss, Elizabeth A. Weston, Prepared by Educational Testing Service under contract with the National Center for Education Statistics, Office of Educational Research and Improvement, U.S. Department of Education, March, 1992, p. 84. *The 1990 Science Report Card NAEP's Assessment of Fourth, Eighth and Twelfth Graders*, (National Center for Education Statistics U.S. Department of Education, 1992). *Notes:* Achievement results were analyzed using item response theory (IRT) scaling procedures, which allowed the National Assessment of Educational Progress to estimate students' average proficiency on a scale ranging from 0 to 500. The standard errors of the estimated percentages and proficiencies appear in parentheses. It can be said with 95 percent certainty that for each population of interest, the value for the whole population is within plus or minus two standard errors of the estimate for the sample. 1. Interpret with caution - the nature of the sample does not allow accurate determination of the variability of these estimated statistics.

★ 322 ★

Science Instruction: Frequency Reported by 4th Graders

Frequency of instruction is shown in percent. Proficiency is based on IRT (item response theory) scaling procedures. Progress is estimated on a scale of 0 to 500.

Group	Almost every day		Several times a week		About once a week		Less than once a week		Never	
	% of students	Avg. profic.	% of students	Avg. profic.	% of students	Avg. profic.	% of students	Avg. profic.	% of students	Avg. profic.
American Indian	51 (5.0)	228 (3.6)	19 (3.0)	229 (6.8)	13 (3.8)	233 (6.9)	10 (3.2)	216 (8.6)	6 (2.8)	201 (7.6)
Hispanic	44 (3.4)	216 (2.1)	20 (1.5)	213 (2.2)	18 (1.9)	211 (3.0)	9 (1.0)	205 (2.9)	10 (1.4)	203 (4.0)
White	54 (2.1)	243 (1.1)	22 (1.1)	246 (1.6)	12 (1.1)	242 (1.7)	8 (0.8)	238 (2.2)	5 (0.8)	230 (3.3)
Black	46 (2.9)	209 (1.8)	20 (1.9)	207 (3.0)	17 (1.7)	203 (1.9)	10 (1.1)	201 (4.0)	7 (1.1)	192 (4.0)
Asian/Pacific Islander	39 (5.3)	240 (6.5)	24 (2.6)	230 (4.5)	21 (3.2)	230 (4.1)	8 (2.1)	232 (8.8)	9 (4.1)	223 (10.9)
Male	51 (1.9)	237 (1.3)	22 (1.1)	237 (2.2)	13 (1.1)	232 (1.9)	8 (0.7)	226 (2.7)	6 (0.8)	218 (3.2)
Female	51 (2.2)	234 (1.3)	20 (1.2)	235 (1.6)	15 (1.3)	228 (2.1)	8 (0.8)	227 (2.6)	5 (0.8)	216 (4.4)
Total	51 (1.9)	235 (1.1)	21 (0.9)	236 (1.5)	14 (1.0)	230 (1.5)	8 (0.7)	227 (2.0)	6 (0.7)	217 (2.8)

Source: The 1990 Science Report Card: NAEP's Assessment of Fourth, Eighth, and Twelfth Graders, Lee R. Jones, Ina V.S. Mullis, Senta A. Raizen, Iris R. Weiss, Elizabeth A. Weston, Prepared by Educational Testing Service under contract with the National Center for Education Statistics, Office of Educational Research and Improvement, U.S. Department of Education, March, 1992, p. 79. The 1990 Science Report Card NAEP's Assessment of Fourth, Eighth and Twelfth Graders, (National Center for Education Statistics, U.S. Department of Education, 1992). Notes: Achievement results were analyzed using item response theory (IRT) scaling procedures, which allowed the National Assessment of Educational Progress to estimate students' average proficiency on a scale ranging from 0 to 500. The standard errors of the estimated percentages and proficiencies appear in parentheses. It can be said with 95 percent certainty that for each population of interest, the value for the whole population is within plus or minus two standard errors of the estimate for the sample.

★ 323 ★

Student Attitudes Toward Science

Responses to the question "Do you like science?" Average proficiencies are based on IRT (item response theory) scaling procedures. Progress is estimated on a scale of 0 to 500.

	Yes		No	
	Percent of students	Average proficiency	Percent of students	Average proficiency
Grade 4				
American Indian	80 (4.1)	230 (3.1)	21 (4.1)	212 (5.1)
Hispanic	76 (1.4)	217 (1.5)	24 (1.4)	199 (2.5)
White	81 (0.9)	245 (1.1)	19 (0.9)	231 (1.5)
Black	75 (1.9)	208 (1.7)	25 (1.9)	199 (2.3)
Asian/Pacific Islander	78 (5.7)	238 (2.9)	22 (5.7)	217 (4.3)
Male	81 (1.0)	238 (1.2)	19 (1.0)	218 (2.0)
Female	78 (1.0)	235 (1.2)	22 (1.0)	222 (1.6)
Total	80 (0.8)	237 (1.0)	20 (0.8)	220 (1.4)
Grade 8				
American Indian	71 (5.9)[1]	254 (12.5)[1]	29 (5.9)[1]	246 (6.8)[1]
Hispanic	71 (2.1)	245 (2.7)	29 (2.1)	233 (2.9)
White	67 (1.1)	280 (1.2)	33 (1.1)	258 (1.6)
Black	70 (2.1)	235 (2.3)	30 (2.1)	223 (2.9)
Asian/Pacific Islander	70 (4.6)	277 (4.5)	31 (4.6)	256 (5.0)
Male	72 (1.1)	272 (1.5)	28 (1.1)	248 (2.0)
Female	64 (1.2)	266 (1.5)	36 (1.2)	253 (1.6)

[Continued]

★ 323 ★

Student Attitudes Toward Science
[Continued]

| | Yes | | No | |
	Percent of students	Average proficiency	Percent of students	Average proficiency
Total	68 (1.0)	269 (1.2)	32 (1.0)	251 (1.4)
Grade 12				
American Indian	71 (6.5)[1]	298 (5.3)[1]	29 (6.5)[1]	257 (6.0)[1]
Hispanic	68 (2.3)	279 (3.0)	32 (2.3)	261 (3.9)
White	66 (0.9)	312 (1.4)	34 (0.9)	284 (1.3)
Black	60 (1.8)	263 (2.9)	40 (1.8)	247 (3.0)
Asian/Pacific Islander	69 (3.5)	320 (7.8)	31 (3.5)	284 (5.0)
Male	74 (0.9)	307 (1.6)	26 (0.9)	275 (1.9)
Female	57 (1.1)	298 (1.3)	43 (1.1)	277 (1.4)
Total	65 (0.7)	303 (1.3)	35 (0.7)	276 (1.2)

Source: The 1990 Science Report Card: NAEP's Assessment of Fourth, Eighth, and Twelfth Graders, Lee R. Jones, Ina V.S. Mullis, Senta A. Raizen, Iris R. Weiss, Elizabeth A. Weston, Prepared by Educational Testing Service under contract with the National Center for Education Statistics, Office of Educational Research and Improvement, U.S. Department of Education, March, 1992, p. 81. *The 1990 Science Report Card NAEP's Assessment of Fourth, Eighth and Twelfth Graders*, (National Center for Education Statistics U.S. Department of Education, 1992). *Notes:* Achievement results were analyzed using item response theory (IRT) scaling procedures, which allowed the National Assessment of Educational Progress to estimate students' average proficiency on a scale ranging from 0 to 500. The standard errors of the estimated percentages and proficiencies appear in parentheses. It can be said with 95 percent certainty, that for each population of interest, the value for the whole population is within plus or minus two standard errors of the estimate for the sample. 1. Interpret with caution - the nature of the sample does not allow accurate determination of the variability of these estimated statistics.

★ 324 ★

Students in the Top and Bottom Thirds of Their Classes in Science

Percentages are shown, by race/ethnicity.

	American Indian	Hispanic	White	Black	Asian/ Pacific Islander
Grade 4					
Top one-third	27 (6.0)	15 (2.3)	38 (3.2)	8 (1.8)	25 (9.7)
Bottom one-third	33 (4.7)	53 (3.4)	18 (2.2)	73 (3.9)	39 (9.0)
Grade 8					
Top one-third	15 (11.8)[1]	13 (7.7)	31 (3.5)	11 (2.3)	36 (7.7)
Bottom one-third	59 (26.9)[1]	59 (5.9)	25 (3.4)	69 (4.7)	33 (8.5)

[Continued]

★ 324 ★

Students in the Top and Bottom Thirds of Their Classes in Science

[Continued]

	American Indian	Hispanic	White	Black	Asian/ Pacific Islander
Grade 12					
Top one-third	29 (8.4)[1]	22 (4.4)	41 (3.8)	13 (3.3)	37 (15.4)
Bottom onc-third	28 (11.2)[1]	47 (6.8)	16 (3.6)	64 (4.6)	17 (5.9)

Source: The 1990 Science Report Card: NAEP's Assessment of Fourth, Eighth, and Twelfth Graders, Lee R. Jones, Ina V.S. Mullis, Senta A. Raizen, Iris R. Weiss, Elizabeth A. Weston, Prepared by Educational Testing Service under contract with the National Center for Education Statistics, Office of Educational Research and Improvement, U.S. Department of Education, March, 1992, p. 20. The 1990 Science Report Card NAEP's Assessment of Fourth, Eighth and Twelfth Graders, (National Center for Education Statistics U.S. Department of Education, 1992). Notes: Achievement results were analyzed using item response theory (IRT) scaling procedures, which allowed the National Assessment of Educational Progress to estimate students' average proficiency on a scale ranging from 0 to 500. The standard errors of the estimated percentages and proficiencies appear in parentheses. It can be said with 95 percent certainty, that for each population of interest, the value for the whole population is within plus or minus two standard errors of the estimate for the sample. 1. Interpret with caution - the nature of the sample does not allow accurate determination of the variability of these estimated statistics.

★ 325 ★

Students' Average Science Proficiency, by Content Area

Proficiency is based on IRT (item response theory) scaling procedures. Progress is estimated on a scale of 0 to 500.

	Percent of students	Life sciences	Physical sciences	Earth and space sciences	Nature of science
Grade 4					
American Indian	2 (0.3)	222 (3.8)	229 (4.0)	228 (3.6)	226 (3.8)
Hispanic	11 (0.3)	209 (1.8)	213 (1.6)	215 (1.6)	212 (1.7)
White	70 (0.5)	238 (1.0)	245 (1.2)	243 (1.1)	242 (1.1)
Black	15 (0.4)	204 (1.6)	207 (2.0)	204 (1.5)	212 (1.7)
Asian/Pacific Islander	2 (0.3)	227 (4.1)	238 (3.9)	233 (3.6)	238 (3.5)
Grade 8					
American Indian	1 (0.5)[1]	252 (9.7)[1]	250 (7.8)[1]	257 (7.3)[1]	244 (15.6)[1]
Hispanic	10 (0.3)	242 (2.4)	241 (2.2)	242 (2.3)	236 (2.4)
White	71 (0.4)	273 (1.4)	271 (1.4)	276 (1.5)	270 (1.5)
Black	15 (0.4)	233 (2.3)	232 (2.3)	228 (2.6)	230 (2.7)
Asian/Pacific Islander	3 (0.4)	272 (4.0)	271 (3.9)	270 (4.3)	267 (5.2)
Grade 12					
American Indian	1 (0.2)[1]	287 (4.5)[1]	283 (5.6)[1]	289 (6.1)[1]	283 (9.6)[1]
Hispanic	8 (0.3)	275 (2.7)	271 (3.2)	270 (2.9)	277 (3.9)
White	73 (0.4)	305 (1.1)	300 (1.7)	301 (1.3)	307 (1.4)

[Continued]

★ 325 ★

Students' Average Science Proficiency, by Content Area
[Continued]

	Percent of students	Life sciences	Physical sciences	Earth and space sciences	Nature of science
Black	14 (0.5)	262 (2.0)	253 (3.1)	247 (2.8)	267 (3.0)
Asian/Pacific Islander	4 (0.2)	309 (7.1)	310 (8.3)	304 (6.6)	312 (6.9)

Source: The 1990 Science Report Card: NAEP's Assessment of Fourth, Eighth, and Twelfth Graders, Lee R. Jones, Ina V.S. Mullis, Senta A. Raizen, Iris R. Weiss, Elizabeth A. Weston, Prepared by Educational Testing Service under contract with the National Center for Education Statistics, Office of Educational Research and Improvement, U.S. Department of Education, March, 1992, p. 64. *The 1990 Science Report Card NAEP's Assessment of Fourth, Eighth and Twelfth Graders,* (National Center for Education Statistics U.S. Department of Education, 1992). *Notes:* Achievement results were analyzed using item response theory (IRT) scaling procedures, which allowed the National Assessment of Educational Progress to estimate students' average proficiency on a scale ranging from 0 to 500. The standard errors of the estimated percentages and proficiencies appear in parentheses. It can be said with 95 percent certainty that for each population of interest, the value for the whole population is within plus or minus two standard errors of the estimate for the sample. 1. Interpret with caution - the nature of the sample does not allow accurate determination of the variability of these estimated statistics.

★ 326 ★

Students' Science Proficiency

Students' average proficiency is shown, based on IRT (item response theory) scaling procedures. Progress is estimated on a scale of 0 to 500.

Race/ethnicity	Students		Proficiency	
	Percent	Standard error	Average score	Standard error
Grade 4				
American Indian	2	0.3	226	2.7
White	70	0.5	242	1.0
Black	15	0.4	205	1.5
Hispanic	11	0.3	212	1.5
Asian/Pacific Islander	2	0.3	233	3.0
Grade 8				
American Indian	1	0.5[1]	252	8.5[1]
White	71	0.4	273	1.4
Black	15	0.4	231	2.2
Hispanic	10	0.3	241	2.1
Asian/Pacific Islander	3	0.4	271	4.0
Grade 12				
American Indian	1	0.2[1]	286	4.6[1]
White	73	0.4	303	1.3
Black	14	0.5	256	2.4

[Continued]

★ 326 ★

Students' Science Proficiency

[Continued]

Race/ethnicity	Students		Proficiency	
	Percent	Standard error	Average score	Standard error
Hispanic	8	0.3	273	2.8
Asian/Pacific Islander	4	0.2	308	7.1

Source: The 1990 Science Report Card: NAEP's Assessment of Fourth, Eighth, and Twelfth Graders, Lee R. Jones, Ina V.S. Mullis, Senta A. Raizen, Iris R. Weiss, Elizabeth A. Weston, Prepared by Educational Testing Service under contract with the National Center for Education Statistics, Office of Educational Research and Improvement, U.S. Department of Education, March, 1992. Primary source: *The 1990 Science Report Card: NAEP's Assessment of Fourth, Eighth, and Twelfth Graders* (National Center for Education Statistics, U.S. Department of Education, 1992). *Notes:* Achievement results were analyzed using item response theory (IRT) scaling procedures, which allowed the National Assessment of Educational Progress to estimate students' average proficiency on a scale ranging from 0 to 500. It can be said with 95 percent certainty that for each population of interest, the value for the whole population is within plus or minus two standard errors of the estimate for the sample. 1. Interpret with caution-the nature of the sample does not allow accurate determination of the variability of these estimated statistics.

★ 327 ★

Students' Science Proficiency Levels

Percent of students at or above four proficiency levels based on IRT (item response theory) scaling procedures. Progress is estimated on a scale of 0 to 500.

	Level 200	Level 250	Level 300	Level 350
Grade 4				
American Indian	81 (5.3)	20 (4.8)	0 (0.0)	0 (0.0)
Hispanic	66 (2.4)	10 (1.2)	0 (0.0)	0 (0.0)
White	93 (0.8)	40 (1.6)	1 (0.3)	0 (0.0)
Black	58 (2.7)	5 (1.1)	0 (0.2)	0 (0.2)
Asian/Pacific Islander	88 (3.1)	29 (5.2)	2 (1.5)	0 (0.0)
Grade 8				
American Indian	92 (2.8)[1]	54 (11.6)[1]	8 (2.8)[1]	0 (0.0)[1]
Hispanic	87 (1.7)	42 (2.8)	5 (0.9)	0 (0.1)
White	97 (0.5)	74 (1.3)	23 (1.3)	1 (0.3)
Black	80 (2.5)	31 (2.5)	3 (0.8)	0 (0.1)
Asian/Pacific Islander	96 (1.9)	71 (4.8)	23 (4.1)	1 (0.6)
Grade 12				
American Indian	100 (0.7)[1]	89 (5.6)[1]	33 (9.3)[1]	2 (0.0)[1]
Hispanic	98 (0.8)	70 (3.4)	23 (2.9)	3 (1.0)
White	100 (0.1)	91 (0.8)	53 (1.4)	12 (0.9)

[Continued]

★ 327 ★

Students' Science Proficiency Levels
[Continued]

	Level 200	Level 250	Level 300	Level 350
Black	94 (1.4)	57 (3.0)	12 (2.0)	1 (0.6)
Asian/Pacific Islander	99 (1.4)	90 (3.2)	60 (7.4)	17 (5.0)

Source: The 1990 Science Report Card: NAEP's Assessment of Fourth, Eighth, and Twelfth Graders, Lee R. Jones, Ina V.S. Mullis, Senta A. Raizen, Iris R. Weiss, Elizabeth A. Weston, Prepared by Educational Testing Service under contract with the National Center for Education Statistics, Office of Educational Research and Improvement, U.S. Department of Education, March, 1992, p. 52. *The 1990 Science Report Card NAEP's Assessment of Fourth, Eighth and Twelfth Graders*, (National Center for Education Statistics U.S. Department of Education, 1992). *Notes:* Achievement results were analyzed using item response theory (IRT) scaling procedures, which allowed the National Assessment of Educational Progress to estimate students' average proficiency on a scale ranging from 0 to 500. The standard errors of the estimated percentages and proficiencies appear in parentheses. It can be said with 95 percent certainty that for each population of interest, the value for the whole population is within plus or minus two standard errors of the estimate for the sample. When the percentage of students is either 0 or 100, the standard error is inestimable. However, percentages 99.5 percent and greater were rounded to 100 percent and percentages less than 0.5 were rounded to 0 percent. 1. Interpret with caution - the nature of the sample does not allow accurate determination of the variability of these estimated statistics.

Extracurriculars

★ 328 ★

Extracurricular Activity, by Type

Figures represent percentage of eighth graders participating in selected outside-school activities. Data are shown, by race/ethnicity.

	Any Outside School Activity	Scouting	Boys' or Girls' Clubs	'Y' or Other Youth Group	4-H	Religious Youth Groups	Hobby Clubs	Neighborhood Clubs	Summer Program	Non-School Team Sports
Total	71.3	14.2	10.7	15.3	9.3	33.8	15.5	12.7	19.2	37.3
American Indian/Native Alaskan	60.9	17.3	18.0	15.7	10.0	27.5	20.6	17.6	22.0	34.1
Asian and Pacific Islander	67.9	13.1	9.1	12.7	4.7	27.4	16.7	11.8	24.2	32.0
Hispanic	60.3	10.9	13.2	13.9	6.1	24.6	15.5	13.3	19.5	31.3
Black	65.6	20.0	23.7	23.0	13.8	30.0	22.4	23.4	29.6	33.9
White	74.4	13.7	8.1	14.3	9.1	36.6	14.1	10.7	17.1	39.1

Source: "Percentage of Eighth Graders Participating This Year in Outside-School Activities, by Selected Background Characteristics," *A Profile of the American Eighth Grader*, 1990, p. 55. Primary source: U.S. Department of Education, National Center for Education Statistics, "National Education Longitudinal Study of 1988: Base Year Student Survey."

★ 329 ★

Homework vs. Non-Academic Activities

Average number of hours spent per week by eighth graders on outside reading, homework, and television watching, by race/ethnicity.

	Outside Reading	Homework	TV Total
American Indian and Native Alaskan	1.7	4.7	23.3
Asian and Pacific Islander	1.9	6.7	21.4
Hispanic	1.6	4.7	22.6
Black	1.6	5.2	27.6
White	1.9	5.7	20.8

Source: "Average Number of Hours Spent per Week on Outside Reading, Homework, and Television Watching, by Selected Background Characteristics," *A Profile of the American Eighth Grader*, 1990, p. 49 Primary source: U.S. Department of Education, National Center for Education Statistics, "National Education Longitudinal Study of 1988: Base Year Student Survey."

★ 330 ★

School Activities: Activities in School but Outside of Class

Data reflect results of a 1988 survey of eighth graders.

Race/ethnicity	Activity					
	School varsity sports	Intramural sports	Band/ orchestra/ chorus	Dance/ drama	Science fairs	Student newspaper/ yearbook
Total	47.9	42.5	39.8	31.4	28.3	21.5
American Indian and Native Alaskan	46.6	44.2	31.4	28.9	31.5	21.0
Asian and Pacific Islander	43.1	47.3	36.5	32.2	29.4	24.7
Hispanic	44.4	39.5	31.1	30.7	22.9	20.5
Black	48.3	45.0	42.2	30.9	33.8	27.5
White	48.4	42.2	40.9	31.5	27.9	20.5

Source: "Percentage of Eighth Graders Who Report Participating in Various School-Based Extracurricular Activities, by Selected Background Characteristics," *A Profile of the American Eighth Grader*, 1990, p. 41. Primary source: U.S. Department of Education, National Center for Education Statistics, "National Education Longitudinal Study of 1988: Base Year Student Survey".

School Environment

★ 331 ★

Drug Exposure in School

Data represent percentage of eighth graders who reported having been offered drugs during a single semester in 1988.

		Race/ethnicity				
	Total	American Indian	White	Black	Hispanic[1]	Asian/ Pacific Is.
Never	90.0	83.6	90.1	92.4	85.7	95.2
Once or twice	6.9	11.3	6.9	5.8	8.9	3.5
More than twice	3.1	5.1	3.0	1.8	5.3	1.3

Source: "Percent of Eighth Grade Students Offered Drugs at School During One Semester, by Race/ Ethnicity and School Type: 1988," *The Condition of Education 1991, Volume 1, Elementary and Secondary Education,* 1991, p. 78. Primary source: U.S. Department of Education, National Center for Education Statistics, National Educational Longitudinal Survey, base year survey, 1988 (student responses); Schools and Staffing Survey, base year survey, 1987-1988 (teacher responses), unpublished tabulations. *Notes:* Columns in the table may not sum to 100 due to rounding. 1. Hispanics may be of any race.

★ 332 ★

Percentage of High School Seniors Using Drugs, Alcohol in the Past Year, 1985-1989

Data have been combined for 1985 to 1989.

Type of drug	American Indian		White		Black		Mexican American		Puerto Rican/ Latin American		Asian American	
	Male	Female	Male	Female	Male	Female	Male	Female	Male	Female	Male	Female
Sample size	537	531	28,056	29,808	3,688	4,499	1,518	1,599	680	712	982	917

Percent who used within last 30 days

Type of drug	Male	Female	Male	Female	Male	Female	Male	Female	Male	Female	Male	Female
Marijuana	42.0	44.0	40.2	36.0	29.8	18.4	37.3	26.0	30.6	21.3	19.6	17.1
Inhalants[1]	9.6	4.4	8.8	5.2	2.6	2.2	6.0	4.3	5.1	2.9	4.8	3.2
Hallucinogens	10.0	9.0	8.3	5.0	1.9	0.6	5.9	2.2	6.5	2.1	3.0	2.2
LSD	7.8	7.2	7.0	3.9	1.3	0.3	5.2	1.6	3.4	1.1	2.5	1.9
Cocaine	14.2	15.5	11.9	9.3	6.1	2.6	14.7	7.6	15.6	8.2	5.8	5.7
Heroin	1.5	1.0	0.7	0.3	0.7	0.4	0.9	0.4	1.2	0.4	0.4	0.2
Other opiates[2]	7.4	5.7	6.5	5.3	1.9	1.2	3.2	2.1	3.0	1.6	3.1	2.1
Stimulants[2]	17.0	19.4	13.6	14.7	4.6	3.1	11.3	10.1	8.0	5.9	5.6	7.0
Sedatives[2]	8.8	6.4	5.3	4.4	2.2	1.2	4.7	2.7	4.6	2.6	3.4	2.6
Barbiturates[2]	7.2	6.2	4.4	3.8	1.9	1.1	4.1	2.4	4.0	2.5	2.6	2.3
Methaqualone[2]	4.8	2.2	2.5	1.4	0.9	0.3	1.2	0.5	2.3	0.5	1.5	0.9

[Continued]

★ 332 ★

Percentage of High School Seniors Using Drugs, Alcohol in the Past Year, 1985 1989
[Continued]

Type of drug	American Indian		White		Black		Mexican American		Puerto Rican/ Latin American		Asian American	
	Male	Female	Male	Female	Male	Female	Male	Female	Male	Female	Male	Female
Tranquilizers[2]	6.9	8.7	5.8	5.9	1.7	1.4	2.6	2.1	3.1	4.1	3.2	1.8
Alcohol	82.0	81.3	88.3	88.6	72.5	63.9	82.4	73.6	80.6	77.2	69.3	67.5

Source: U.S. Department of Education, National Center for Education Statistics, *The Condition of Education, 1992,* Washington, D.C.: 1992, p. 312. Primary source: U.S. Department of Health and Human Services; Alcohol, Drug Abuse, Mental Health Administration; National Institute on Drug Abuse, *Drug Use Among American High School Students, College Students, and Other Young Adults, 1991. Notes:* 1. Respondents represent four-fifths of sample size indicated. 2. Only drug use which was not under a doctor's orders are included here.

★ 333 ★

Percentage of High-School Seniors Who Reported Using Selected Drugs in the Past Year, 1985-1989

Drugs used in past 12 months	American Indian		White		Black		Mexican American		Puerto Rican/ Latin American		Asian American	
	Male	Female	Male	Female	Male	Female	Male	Female	Male	Female	Male	Female
Marijuana/hashish	42.0	44.0	40.2	36.0	29.8	18.4	37.3	26.0	30.6	21.3	19.6	17.1
Cocaine	14.2	15.5	11.9	9.3	6.1	2.6	14.7	7.6	15.6	7.6	5.8	5.7
Alcohol	82.0	81.3	88.3	88.6	72.5	63.9	82.4	73.6	80.6	77.2	69.3	67.5

Source: U.S. Department of Education, National Center for Education Statistics, *The Condition of Education, 1992,* Washington, D.C.: 1992, p. 118. Primary source: U.S. Department of Health and Human Services, Alcohol, Drug Use and Mental Health Administration, National Institute on Drug Abuse, *Drug Use Among American High School Students, College Students, and Other Young Adults, 1991.*

★ 334 ★

Percentage of High School Seniors Who Reported Using Drugs, Alcohol, or Cigarettes Daily in the Past Month, 1985-1989

Data have been combined for 1985 to 1989.

Type of drug	American Indian		White		Black		Mexican American		Puerto Rican/ Latin American		Asian American	
	Male	Female	Male	Female	Male	Female	Male	Female	Male	Female	Male	Female
Sample size	537	531	28,056	29,808	3,688	4,499	1,518	1,599	680	712	982	917
Percent who used daily in last 30 days												
Marijuana/hashish	8.2	4.3	5.1	2.1	2.8	0.9	4.2	1.1	3.5	0.5	1.7	0.5
Alcohol												
Daily	10.1	5.4	7.0	2.8	4.2	0.7	8.3	2.6	4.0	0.9	2.3	0.9
Five or more drinks in a row/last 2 weeks	48.1	33.7	48.1	31.3	24.0	9.3	45.3	23.6	31.4	14.5	19.4	10.7

[Continued]

★ 334 ★

Percentage of High School Seniors Who Reported Using Drugs, Alcohol, or Cigarettes Daily in the Past Month, 1985-1989

[Continued]

Type of drug	American Indian		White		Black		Mexican American		Puerto Rican/ Latin American		Asian American	
	Male	Female	Male	Female	Male	Female	Male	Female	Male	Female	Male	Female
Cigarettes	26.0	33.8	18.8	22.5	8.6	7.1	11.6	8.1	13.3	13.3	9.0	9.4
Half-pack or more per day	18.4	23.4	12.5	13.3	3.3	2.2	5.2	2.5	6.1	4.2	4.4	4.5

Source: U.S. Department of Education, National Center for Education Statistics, *The Condition of Education, 1992*, Washington, D.C.: 1992, p. 313. Primary source: U.S. Department of Health and Human Services; Alcohol, Drug Abuse, Mental Health Administration; National Institute on Drug Abuse, *Drug Use Among American High School Students, College Students, and Other Young Adults, 1991.*

★ 335 ★

Percentage of High School Seniors Who Reported Using Selected Drugs in the Past Month, 1985-1989

Data have been combined for 1985 to 1989.

Type of drug	American Indian		White		Black		Mexican American		Puerto Rican/ Latin American		Asian American	
	Male	Female	Male	Female	Male	Female	Male	Female	Male	Female	Male	Female
Sample size	537	531	28,056	29,808	3,688	4,499	1,518	1,599	680	712	982	917

Percent who used within last 30 days

Type of drug	Male	Female	Male	Female	Male	Female	Male	Female	Male	Female	Male	Female
Marijuana	27.6	23.9	25.0	19.8	18.5	9.9	22.0	13.6	18.9	9.6	9.7	8.1
Inhalants[1]	5.2	0.9	3.4	2.0	1.4	1.4	2.3	2.1	2.0	0.8	1.3	0.8
Hallucinogens	3.6	2.7	3.5	1.7	0.9	0.3	2.4	0.7	3.0	0.4	1.5	0.3
LSD	3.1	2.2	2.8	1.1	0.6	0.2	1.9	0.3	1.6	0.2	1.1	0.1
Cocaine	7.3	9.2	5.6	4.1	2.6	1.3	8.2	3.0	8.1	2.9	1.8	2.6
Heroin	1.1	0.4	0.3	0.1	0.5	0.3	0.3	0.2	0.9	0.2	0.1	0.0
Other opiates[2]	4.0	2.4	2.3	1.9	0.9	0.6	1.1	0.7	1.5	0.5	1.6	0.7
Stimulants[2]	8.1	10.3	5.6	6.0	1.9	1.3	4.9	4.8	3.1	1.2	2.1	3.6
Sedatives[2]	4.8	2.6	2.2	1.7	1.1	0.5	2.0	0.9	1.8	1.3	1.9	1.3
Barbiturates[2]	3.7	2.1	1.8	1.5	0.9	0.5	1.7	0.8	1.3	1.2	1.4	1.0
Methaqualone[2]	2.5	0.9	0.9	0.5	0.5	0.1	0.6	0.2	0.9	0.1	0.8	0.6
Tranquilizers[2]	3.1	2.2	1.9	2.0	0.8	0.5	0.8	0.9	0.6	1.5	1.7	0.9
Alcohol	69.0	60.2	72.3	66.6	49.2	32.8	65.0	50.5	55.4	43.0	43.7	34.2
Cigarettes	36.8	43.6	29.8	34.0	15.6	13.3	23.8	18.7	22.0	24.7	16.8	14.3

Source: U.S. Department of Education, National Center for Education Statistics, *The Condition of Education, 1992*, Washington, D.C.: 1992, p. 312. Primary source: U.S. Department of Health and Human Services; Alcohol, Drug Abuse, Mental Health Administration; National Institute on Drug Abuse, *Drug Use Among American High School Students, College Students, and Other Young Adults, 1991. Notes:* 1. Respondents represent four-fifths of sample size indicated. 2. Only drug use which was not under a doctor's orders are included here.

★ 336 ★

Percentage of Persons 12 to 19 Years Old Reporting Behavior Taken to Avoid Attacks in the Past 6 Months, 1989

Behavior taken to avoid attacks	Total	Race/ethnicity				
		American Indian	White	Black	Hispanic	Asian Pacific Islander
Stay home	1.2	3.2	1.1	1.0	2.5	0.3
Stay away from shortest route to school	1.5	1.0	1.0	2.4	3.0	4.3
Stay away from school entrances	1.3	0.0	1.0	2.1	1.4	3.5
Stay away from halls/stairs	2.1	1.2	1.7	2.9	3.0	3.3
Stay away from cafeteria	1.6	2.3	1.3	2.6	2.4	1.8
Stay away from restrooms	2.7	0.9	2.3	4.0	3.5	2.7
Stay away from other places inside school	1.1	2.0	0.8	1.7	1.6	2.3
Stay away from parking lot	1.3	2.1	1.1	1.6	2.1	2.8
Stay away from other places on grounds	1.7	0.9	1.6	1.8	2.6	2.3
Stay away from extracurricular activities	1.1	4.1	0.7	2.2	1.0	1.9

Source: U.S. Department of Education, National Center for Education Statistics, *The Condition of Education, 1992*, Washington, D.C.: 1992, p. 309. Primary source: U.S. Department of Justice, Office of Justice Programs, Bureau of Justice Statistics, *National Crime Survey, School Crime Supplement, 1989.*

★ 337 ★

Percentage of Twelve to Nineteen-Year Old Students Reporting Selected Criminal Activities in School, 1989

Activity within past 6 months	Total	Sex		Race/ethnicity					Control of school	
		Male	Female	American Indian	White	Black	Hispanic	Asian/Pacific Islander	Public	Private
Street gangs in school	15.4	15.8	14.9	11.0	11.7	19.9	31.8	29.2	16.5	4.4
Something taken directly by force	0.7	0.9	0.4	0.0	0.6	0.9	1.1	0.0	0.7	0.8
Something stolen from desk/locker/other	12.2	12.1	12.3	18.5	12.2	12.4	11.1	11.9	12.4	10.8
Physically attacked	2.9	4.0	1.8	7.0	2.9	2.7	3.6	1.0	3.0	2.1
Bring something to school to protect yourself	1.2	1.7	0.7	3.3	1.2	1.5	1.2	0.6	1.2	1.2
Teacher attacked or threatened with attack	16.3	17.0	15.5	14.9	16.1	19.7	14.2	10.2	17.4	5.2

Source: U.S. Department of Education, National Center for Education Statistics, *The Condition of Education, 1992*, Washington, D.C.: 1992, p. 116. Primary source: U.S. Department of Justice, Office of Justice Programs, Bureau of Justice Statistics, *National Crime Survey, 1989.*

★ 338 ★

Safety in the Schools

Figures represent percentages of 8th grade students reporting occurrence of each type of safety-related incident. Results of a 1988 survey are shown by race/ethnicity.

	I Fought with a Student	Something was Stolen from Me	Someone Offered to Sell Me Drugs	Someone Threatened to Hurt Me	I Don't Feel Safe at School
Total	22.5	49.1	10.0	27.8	11.8
American Indian and Native Alaskan	36.6	52.1	16.4	24.4	18.0
Asian and Pacific Islander	18.9	47.9	4.8	21.3	11.7
Hispanic	25.3	49.1	14.3	23.0	16.1
Black	30.3	57.5	7.6	24.9	18.0
White	20.6	47.6	9.9	29.3	9.9

Source: "Percentages of Eighth Graders Reporting Various Safety-Related Occurrences in Their School, by Selected Background Characteristics," *A Profile of the American Eighth Grader*, 1990, p. 45. Primary source: U.S. Department of Education, National Center for Education Statistics, "National Education Longitudinal Study of 1988: Base Year Student Survey."

★ 339 ★

Student/Teacher Perceptions of School Problems

Figures represent percentage of eighth grade students and teachers who consider each issue to be a serious problem. Data are shown, by race/ethnicity, for 1988.

	Total	Race/ethnicity				
		American Indian	White	Black	Hispanic[1]	Asian Pacific Is.
Eighth grade students						
Possession of weapons	11.3	15.3	9.7	16.8	13.7	14.3
Vandalism of school property	14.5	19.4	12.8	19.6	17.6	20.0
Physical conflicts among students	16.6	22.3	14.8	25.6	17.8	17.2
Physical abuse of teachers	7.9	9.6	7.0	9.6	10.4	11.3
Verbal abuse of teachers	11.5	13.0	10.9	14.1	13.0	11.3
Eighth grade teachers						
Possession of weapons	1.4	7.3	1.4	1.6	0.0	0.0
Vandalism of school property	4.9	9.5	4.6	8.5	7.3	2.5
Physical conflicts among students	7.0	7.3	6.8	12.2	1.8	0.0

[Continued]

★ 339 ★

Student/Teacher Perceptions of School Problems
[Continued]

	Total	Race/ethnicity				
		American Indian	White	Black	Hispanic[1]	Asian Pacific Is.
Physical abuse of teachers	1.7	7.3	1.6	1.9	0.0	0.0
Verbal abuse of teachers	10.1	20.9	10.0	10.6	9.7	6.9

Source: "Percent of Eighth Grade Students and Percent of Eighth Grade Teachers Who Consider Problems to be Serious, by Selected Personal and School Characteristics: 1988," *The Condition of Education 1991, Volume 1, Elementary and Secondary Education,* 1991, p. 80. Primary source: U.S. Department of Education, National Center for Education Statistics, National Education Longitudinal Survey, base year survey, 1988 (student response); Schools and Staffing Survey, base year survey, 1987-1988 (teacher responses). *Note:* 1. Hispanics may be of any race.

★ 340 ★

Student/Teacher Perceptions of Student Substance Abuse

Figures represent percentage of eighth grade students and teachers who view student substance abuse as a serious school problem. Data are shown, by race/ethnicity, for 1988.

	Total	Race/ethnicity				
		American Indian	White	Black	Hispanic[1]	Asian/ Pacific Is.
Students						
Alcohol	15.3	19.9	15.1	16.1	15.0	16.1
Drugs	14.2	20.0	13.3	16.3	16.5	16.5
Teachers						
Alcohol	7.5	17.3	7.6	7.0	4.7	0.0
Drugs	6.2	19.2	5.5	11.1	5.3	3.9

Source: "Percent of Eighth Grade Students and Percent of Eighth Grade Teachers Who Consider Student Drug and Alcohol Usage to be Serious School Problems, by Race/Ethnicity and School Type: 1988," *The Condition of Education 1991, Volume 1, Elementary and Secondary Education,* 1991, p. 78. Primary source: U.S. Department of Education, National Center for Education Statistics, National Longitudinal Survey, base year survey, 1988 (student responses); Schools and Staffing Survey, base year survey 1987-1988 (teacher responses), unpublished tabulations. *Note:* 1. Hispanics may be of any race.

School Personnel

★ 341 ★

School Teachers and Administrators, by Race/Ethnicity

Characteristics	Teachers				Administrators			
	Public school	Percent of total	Private school	Percent of total	Public school	Percent of total	Private school	Percent of total
Total	2,323,204	100.0	307,131	100.0	77,890	100.0	25,401	100.0
Race, ethnicity								
American Indian, Alaskan Native	24,670	1.1	2,827	0.9	821	1.1	-	-
Asian or Pacific Islander	21,307	0.9	3,987	1.3	434	0.6	-	-
Black	190,018	8.2	7,165	2.3	6,696	8.6	771	3.0
White	2,050,400	88.3	288,432	93.9	69,048	88.6	24,056	94.7
Not reported	36,810	1.6	4,719	1.5	890	1.1	-	-
Ethnic origin[1]								
Hispanic	67,084	2.9	8,569	2.8	2,483	3.2	629	2.5
Non-Hispanic	2,207,746	95.0	292,566	95.3	73,245	94.0	24,167	95.1
Not reported	48,374	2.1	5,995	2.0	2,162	2.8	604	2.4

Source: "Selected Characteristics of Teachers and School Administrators: School Year 1987-1988," *The Condition of Education 1991, Volume 1, Elementary and Secondary Education*, 1991, p. 96. Primary source: U.S. Department of Education, National Center for Education Statistics, Schools and Staffing Survey, Selected Characteristics of Public and Private School Administrators (Principals): 1987-88, 1990; Characteristics of Public and Private School Teachers, 1987-88, 1990. *Notes:* - means that there a too few sample cases for a reliable estimate. Details may not add to totals due to rounding, missing values in cells with too few sample cases, or item nonresponse. Cell entries may be underestimates due to item nonresponse. 1. Hispanics and non-Hispanics may be of any race.

★ 342 ★

School Teachers/Administrators: Degree Status and Experience of School Teachers, 1987-88

Data are shown for teachers in public and private elementary and secondary schools.

Selected characteristics	Total	Percent of teachers, by highest degree earned						Percent of teachers, by years of full-time teaching experience			
		No degree	Associate	Bachelor's	Master's	Education specialist	Doctor's	Less than 3	3 to 9	10 to 20	Over 20
Public schools											
Race/ethnicity											
White	1,994,389	0.2	0.4	52.1	40.3	6.2	0.8	0.8	26.6	44.4	21.0
Black	187,836	2	2	49.7	42.4	0.6	2	6.1	19.4	46.3	28.2
Hispanic	67,084	2	2	84.5	29.9	6.7	2	11.9	33.2	40.9	13.9
Asian or Pacific Islander	20,709	2	2	52.8	28.7	13.5	2	11.2	22.1	43.0	23.7
American Indian or Alaskan Native	23,998	2	2	50.1	40.5	7.5	2	5.7	24.3	49.7	20.2

[Continued]

★ 342 ★

School Teachers/Administrators: Degree Status and Experience of School Teachers, 1987-88
[Continued]

Selected characteristics	Total	Percent of teachers, by highest degree earned						Percent of teachers, by years of full-time teaching experience			
		No degree	Associate	Bachelor's	Master's	Education specialist	Doctor's	Less than 3	3 to 9	10 to 20	Over 20
Private schools											
Race/ethnicity											
White	281,152	2.9	1.3	61.2	30.3	2.7	1.6	18.4	37.7	30.2	13.8
Black	7,015	2	2	69.1	16.6	2	2	27.0	42.2	21.3	2
Hispanic	8,569	2	2	60.8	19.7	2	2	22.0	41.4	25.8	2
Asian or Pacific Islander	3,491	2	2	56.2	2	2	2	2	2	2	2
American Indian or Alaskan Native	2,747	2	2	93.7	2	2	2	2	2	2	2

Source: Teachers in Public and Private Elementary and Secondary Schools, by Selected Characteristics: 1987-88, *Digest of Education Statistics 1991*, November 1991, p. 73. Primary source: U.S. Department of Education, National Center for Education Statistics, "Schools and Staffing Survey, 1987-88." (This table was prepared June 1990.) *Notes:* 1. Total differs from data appearing in other tables because of varying survey processing procedures and time period coverages. 2. Too few sample cases (fewer than 30) for a reliable estimate.

★ 343 ★

School Teachers/Administrators: Degree Status, Experience, and Salary of School Principals, 1987-1988

Data are shown for principals in public and private elementary and secondary schools.

Selected characteristics	Total[1]	Percent of principals, by highest degree earned[2]				Average years of experience				Average annual salary of principals, by length of work		
		Bachelor's	Master's	Education specialist	Doctor's and first professional	As a principal	Other school position	As a teacher	Outside school position	10 months or less	11 months	12 months
Public schools												
Total	77,890	2.4	53.4	35.1	8.9	10.0	3.8	9.8	1.0	38,726	41,563	44,252
Race/ethnicity												
White[3]	69,048	2.5	53.7	35.0	8.6	10.1	3.6	9.6	1.0	38,136	41,397	44,319
Black[3]	6,696	5	51.4	36.9	11.5	8.8	4.8	11.8	1.2	42,796	42,843	43,319
Hispanic[4]	2,483	5	54.2	30.2	5	6.6	5.4	9.8	1.3	40,394	42,235	46,770
Asian or Pacific Islander[3]	434	5	52.8	33.4	5	7.7	4.5	10.8	0.4	41,581	5	5
American Indian or Alaskan Native[3]	821	5	51.2	5	5	9.9	4.6	9.1	1.3	5	5	43,706
Private schools												
Total	25,401	25.7	51.0	12.2	4.2	8.0	2.6	9.8	2.4	13,182	23,505	22,651
Race/ethnicity												
White[3]	24,056	25.9	51.0	12.3	6.1	8.0	2.6	9.8	2.3	12,853	23,582	22,746
Black[3]	771	5	5.6	5	5	6.8	4.1	10.2	2.6	5	5	21,895
Hispanic[4]	629	5	5	5	5	8.0	3.5	11.1	2.2	5	5	23,101

Source: Principals in Public and Private Elementary and Secondary Schools, by Selected Characteristics: 1987-88, *Digest of Education Statistics 1991*, November 1991, p. 91. Primary source: U.S. Department of Education, National Center for Education Statistics, "Schools and Staffing Survey, 1987-88." (This table was prepared May 1990.) *Notes:* Details may not add to 100 percent because of rounding and survey item nonresponse. 1. Total differs from data appearing in other tables because of varying survey processing procedures and time period coverages. 2. Percentages for those with less than a bachelor's degree are not shown. 3. Includes persons of Hispanic origin. 4. Persons of Hispanic origin may be of any race. 5. Too few sample cases (fewer than 30) for a reliable estimate.

★ 344 ★

School Teachers/Administrators: Salaries and Other Characteristics of School Teachers, 1987-1988

Data are shown for teachers in public and private elementary and secondary schools.

Selected characteristics	Total earned income	Base salary	Number of full-time teachers	School year supplement contract		Supplemental contract during school		Number of teachers with nonschool employment		
				Number of teachers	Supplemental salary	Number of teachers	Supplemental salary	School year only	Summer only	All year
Public schools										
Total	28,189	26,231	2,118,253	705,223	2,134	361,360	1,810	121,894	162,185	207,623
Race/ethnicity										
White, non-Hispanic	28,226	26,264	1,810,496	626,386	2,018	303,418	1,713	107,050	140,649	183,921
Black, non-Hispanic	27,786	25,976	177,055	39,144	3,184	34,880	2,227	8,752	12,176	13,619
Hispanic	27,234	25,103	63,129	19,271	2,877	13,356	2,581	2,595	4,578	4,432
Asian or Pacific Islander	30,262	28,499	19,314	5,514	2,331	3,563	1,990	1	1	1,432
American Indian or Alaskan Native	28,614	26,160	21,702	7,979	3,889	3,783	2,824	1	1,939	2,355
Private schools										
Total	18,318	16,562	250,524	48,559	2,026	39,231	2,163	18,046	29,708	29,999
Race/ethnicity										
White, non-Hispanic	18,244	16,521	229,429	45,357	2,035	34,054	2,124	16,659	27,592	28,292
Black, non-Hispanic	16,774	15,221	6,012	1	1	1,519	2,255	1	1	1
Hispanic	18,360	16,385	6,157	1	1	1	1	1	1	1
Asian or Pacific Islander	24,475	22,332	3,069	1	1	1	1	1	1	1
American Indian or Alaskan Native	20,217	18,325	2,468	1	1	1	1	1	1	1

Source: Average Salaries for Full-Time Teachers in Public Elementary and Secondary Schools, Characteristics: 1987-88, *Digest of Education Statistics 1991*, November 1991, p. 80. Primary source: U.S. Department of Education, National Center for Education Statistics, "Schools and Staffing Survey, 1987-88." (This table was prepared July 1990.) *Notes:* Details may not add to totals because of rounding or missing values in cells with too few cases or survey item nonresponse. 1. Too few sample cases (fewer than 30) for reliable estimate.

★ 345 ★

Staffing of BIA School Dormitories

The minimum staff/student ratios of schools operated by the BIA (Bureau of Indian Affairs) are shown for selected grades.

Grade	Ratio
Grades 1 to 6	
Weekdays:	
Mornings	1:30
During school hours	1:40
Evenings	1:30
Nights	1:40
Weekends:	
Mornings	1:30
Evenings	1:30
Nights	1:40
Grades 7 to 12	
Weekdays:	
Mornings	1:50
During school hours	1:80

[Continued]

★ 345 ★

Staffing of BIA School Dormitories
[Continued]

Grade	Ratio
Evenings	1:50
Nights	1:80
Weekends:	
Mornings	1:50
Evenings	1:50
Nights	1:80

Source: *Code of Federal Regulations: Indians*, Office of the Federal Register National Archives and Records Administration, April 1, 1991, p. 111.

★ 346 ★

Staffing of BIA Schools

Each BIA school must, meet the following minimum requirements of average daily membership.

Level	Student/teacher ratio
Kindergarten	20:1
1st grade-3rd grade	22:1
4th grade-high school	25:1

Source: *Code of Federal Regulations*, Vol. 25, April 1991, Office of the Federal Register National Archives and Records Administration, p. 99. *Notes:* Schools exceeding these specific staffing ratios for over 30 consecutive days during one school year must submit a justification for a request for a waiver to the Director through the Agency Superintendent for Education or Area Education Programs Administrator, as appropriate, which may be approved for a period not to exceed one school year and for the following reasons: Additional classroom space is not available for establishing another class; or the school, agency, area and Office of Indian Education Programs Applicant Supply File has been exhausted and the required teacher position cannot be filled. However, efforts to fill the vacancy must be continued.

Higher Education Enrollment

★ 347 ★

Enrollment - 1990

Data are based on enrollments for Fall 1990.

Control and level of institution, and sex	All students	American Indian/ Alaskan Native	White, Non-Hispanic	Black, Non-Hispanic	Hispanic	Asian or Pacific Islander	Race/ethnicity unknown	Nonresident alien
Total[1]	13,711,555	100,732	10,436,129	1,206,102	747,863	544,353	279,788	396,588
4-year	8,530,276	47,160	6,593,453	703,845	337,525	334,425	191,782	322,086
2-year	5,181,279	53,572	3,842,676	502,257	410,338	209,928	88,006	74,502
Public total	10,741,588	89,039	8,183,127	942,501	642,066	438,778	181,310	264,767
4-year	5,803,501	37,713	4,507,235	482,658	246,801	233,688	101,698	193,708
2-year	4,938,087	51,326	3,675,892	459,843	395,265	205,090	79,612	71,059
Private total	2,970,147	11,873	2,253,002	263,601	105,797	105,575	98,478	131,821
4-year	2,726,775	9,447	2,086,218	221,187	90,724	100,737	90,084	128,378
2-year	243,372	2,426	166,784	42,414	15,073	4,838	8,394	3,443

Source: Trends in Racial/Ethnic Enrollment in Higher Education: Fall 1980 Through Fall 1990, U.S. Department of Education, Office of Educational Research and Improvement, Postsecondary Education Statistics Division, Washington, D.C., p. 11. Primary source: U.S. Department of Education, National Center of Education Statistics, Integrated Postsecondary Education Data System "Fall Enrollment" survey 1990. *Notes:* Fall enrollment represents actual counts reported, or imputed, prior to distribution of "race/ethnicity unknown" category. 1. Total enrollment reflects student counts prior to the distribution of race/ethnicity unknown data. After the distribution procedure, total enrollment dropped slightly (to 13,710,150) due to rounding.

★ 348 ★

Enrollment, by State

Enrollment figures are shown for fall 1990.

State	Total	American Indian/ Alaskan Native	White, non-Hispanic	Black, non-Hispanic	Hispanic	Asian or Pacific Islander	Nonresident alien
Total	13,710,150	102,618	10,674,784	1,223,303	758,054	554,803	396,588
Alabama	247,117	591	190,920	48,180	1,138	1,699	4,589
Alaska	29,833	2,648	24,264	1,079	634	740	468
Arizona	264,735	8,845	205,676	7,585	29,618	6,116	6,895
Arkansas	90,425	438	75,157	12,188	431	740	1,471
California[1]	1,771,746	21,005	1,131,741	114,804	222,749	215,416	66,031
Colorado	231,547	2,315	194,943	6,943	17,319	5,417	4,610
Connecticut	169,480	433	144,265	9,952	5,648	4,362	4,820
Delaware	42,004	99	35,155	4,710	546	710	784
District of Columbia	80,669	270	40,977	24,770	2,406	3,222	9,024
Florida[1]	538,389	1,616	397,880	53,400	58,490	10,871	16,132
Georgia	251,810	548	189,189	49,199	2,740	4,241	5,893

[Continued]

★ 348 ★

Enrollment, by State
[Continued]

State	Total	American Indian/ Alaskan Native	White, non-Hispanic	Black, non-Hispanic	Hispanic	Asian or Pacific Islander	Nonresident alien
Hawaii[1]	53,772	162	16,132	1,457	1,002	31,356	3,663
Idaho	51,881	485	48,024	310	1,004	706	1,352
Illinois	729,246	2,245	541,347	89,218	48,932	32,353	15,151
Indiana[1]	283,015	720	251,389	15,323	4,380	3,913	7,290
Iowa	170,515	441	155,204	4,044	1,587	2,430	6,809
Kansas	163,478	1,969	143,116	6,798	3,538	2,717	5,340
Kentucky	177,852	506	162,549	10,491	738	1,343	2,225
Louisiana	186,599	856	130,361	44,738	3,448	2,683	4,513
Maine	57,186	398	55,487	296	195	418	392
Maryland	264,862	852	195,079	44,582	5,026	11,694	7,629
Massachusetts	418,874	1,220	349,516	18,376	12,501	16,144	21,117
Michigan	569,803	3,547	475,505	56,786	9,094	10,693	14,178
Minnesota	253,789	2,002	235,201	4,143	1,936	4,948	5,529
Mississippi	122,883	377	85,699	33,699	395	783	1,930
Missouri	289,407	1,132	250,758	23,050	3,434	4,487	6,546
Montana	35,876	2,427	32,200	114	280	120	735
Nebraska	112,831	729	104,620	2,723	1,559	1,178	2,022
Nevada	61,728	1,043	50,910	2,931	3,408	2,559	877
New Hampshire	59,510	229	55,522	669	490	760	840
New Jersey	323,947	776	241,666	33,113	21,642	14,340	12,410
New Mexico	85,596	4,596	52,573	2,176	23,635	1,125	1,491
New York	1,040,484	3,914	753,074	112,173	74,835	49,171	47,317
North Carolina	351,990	3,082	273,874	62,032	2,528	5,622	4,852
North Dakota	37,878	1,616	34,380	246	195	285	1,156
Ohio	555,702	1,422	482,201	45,270	5,467	7,356	13,986
Oklahoma	173,221	9,609	140,865	11,816	2,635	2,904	5,392
Oregon	166,641	1,694	145,797	2,153	2,990	6,321	7,686
Pennsylvania	604,060	1,011	523,157	44,009	7,709	13,588	14,586
Rhode Island	78,273	222	69,974	2,558	1,606	1,891	2,022
South Carolina	159,302	334	122,964	31,177	911	1,494	2,422
South Dakota[1]	34,208	1,912	31,106	250	94	198	648
Tennessee	226,238	476	186,541	31,240	1,302	2,283	4,396
Texas	901,437	3,006	617,626	80,458	148,296	27,907	24,144
Utah	121,303	1,322	110,150	661	2,233	2,243	4,694
Vermont	36,398	131	34,178	375	428	569	717
Virginia	353,442	860	280,786	49,566	4,803	11,400	6,027
Washington	263,278	3,854	225,213	7,361	6,122	15,424	5,304
West Virginia	84,790	139	78,795	3,160	360	688	1,648
Wisconsin	299,774	2,050	271,096	10,667	4,692	4,991	6,278
Wyoming	31,326	444	28,952	284	905	184	557

Source: Trends in Racial/Ethnic Enrollment in Higher Education: Fall 1980 Through Fall 1990, U.S. Department of Education, Office of Educational Research and Improvement, Postsecondary Education Statistics Division, Washington D.C., p. 6. Primary source: U.S. Department of Education, National Center for Education Statistics, Integrated Postsecondary Education System, "Fall Enrollment" survey, 1990. *Notes:* 1. High proportions of enrollment data for 2-year institutions of higher education were imputed for these states. Virtually no data for public 2- year institutions of higher education were submitted by California, Florida, or Hawaii.

★ 349 ★

Enrollment in Institutions of Higher Education in the 10 Largest States, 1988

Figures are shown, by race/ethnicity, nonresident alien status, and state.

State	Total	White, non-Hispanic	Minority enrollment, by race/ethnicity						Nonresident alien
			Total minority	Percent minority[1]	American Indian/ Alaskan Native	Black, non-Hispanic	Hispanic	Asian/Pacific Islander	
United States total	13,043,118	10,283,176	2,398,764	18.9	92,534	1,129,580	679,962	496,688	361,178
California	1,753,564	1,131,731	556,314	33.0	20,600	114,388	215,397	205,929	65,519
Florida	515,590	386,687	113,749	22.7	1,509	48,396	54,513	9,331	15,154
Illinois	688,974	521,510	153,644	22.8	1,972	83,090	40,784	27,798	13,820
Michigan	542,580	458,194	70,941	13.4	3,122	51,494	7,718	8,607	13,445
New Jersey	302,640	232,047	58,768	20.2	847	28,831	17,894	11,196	11,825
New York	1,007,411	742,572	229,401	23.6	3,619	111,000	70,739	44,043	35,438
North Carolina	332,521	260,563	67,489	20.6	2,620	58,267	2,249	4,353	4,469
Ohio	541,737	478,222	50,094	9.5	1,272	38,130	4,552	6,140	13,421
Pennsylvania	573,927	504,972	56,055	10.0	918	38,415	6,139	10,583	12,900
Texas	847,192	597,400	227,654	27.6	2,756	75,478	125,778	23,642	22,138

Source: "Total Enrollment in Institutions of Higher Education, by Race/Ethnicity of Student and by State: Fall 1988," *Digest of Education Statistics 1991,* November 1991, p. 201. Primary source: U.S. Department of Education, National Center for Education Statistics, Integrated Postsecondary Education Data System (IPEDS), "Fall Enrollment, 1988," survey. (This table was prepared March 1990.) *Notes:* Because of adjustments to underreported and nonreported racial/ethnic data, figures are slightly different from corresponding data in other tables. 1. Percent minority based on U.S. citizen enrollment (total enrollment less enrollment of nonresident aliens).

★ 350 ★

Enrollment in Institutions of Higher Education, 1980-90

The total number of students and the number of American Indian/Alaska Native students in two year or four year institutions is shown for 1980-90.

Year	All students	American Indian/Alaska Native Students		
		All students	In 4-yr Inst.	In 2-yr Inst.
1990	13,950,000	97,657[1]	43,905	53,711
1989	13,490,349	93,000	41,289	50,464
1988	13,043,124	90,000	41,000	50,000
1987	12,768,307	90,000	40,500	49,500
1986	12,503,511	90,133	39,658	49,573
1985	12,247,780	85,729[1]	38,578	47,151
1984	12,241,940	83,776	37,699	46,076
1983	12,464,780	87,252[1]	39,263	47,989
1982	12,425,780	88,000	39,000	49,000

[Continued]

★ 350 ★

Enrollment in Institutions of Higher Education, 1980-90
[Continued]

Year	All students	American Indian/Alaska Native Students		
		All students	In 4-yr Inst.	In 2-yr Inst.
1981	12,371,672	86,602[1]	38,971	47,631
1980	12,096,895	84,000	37,800	46,200

Source: Toward the Year 2000: Listening to the Voice of Native America, National Advisory Council on Indian Education, 17th Annual report to the United States Congress, Fiscal Year 1990, p. 68. Primary source: U.S. Department of Education, National Center for Education Statistics, Higher Education General Information Survey (HEGIS), "Fall Enrollment" survey 1970 to 1985; and Integrated Postsecondary Education Data System (IPEDS), "Fall Enrollment" survey, 1986, and "Early Estimates" survey, 1990. *Notes:* 1. Estimates are based on prior-year trends. The 1990 figures for American Indian/Alaska Natives may not be this high when final student counts are tabulated.

★ 351 ★

Enrollment Trends, by Level of Institution

Total fall enrollment and percent distributions are shown, by race/ethnicity, for 1980-90.

Level of institution and race/ethnicity	Numbers in thousands						Percent distribution of total enrollment					
	1980	1982	1984	1986	1988	1990	1980	1982	1984	1986	1988	1990
All institutions	12,087	12,388	12,235	12,504	13,043	13,710	100.0	100.0	100.0	100.0	100.0	100.0
White, non-Hispanic	9,833	9,997	9,815	9,921	10,283	10,675	81.4	80.7	80.2	79.3	78.8	77.9
Total minority	1,949	2,059	2,085	2,238	2,399	2,639	16.1	16.6	17.0	17.9	18.4	19.2
Black, non-Hispanic	1,107	1,101	1,076	1,082	1,130	1,223	9.2	8.9	8.8	8.7	8.7	8.9
Hispanic	472	519	535	618	680	758	3.9	4.2	4.4	4.9	5.2	5.5
Asian or Pacific Islander	286	351	390	448	497	555	2.4	2.8	3.2	3.6	3.8	4.0
American Indian or Alaskan Native	84	88	84	90	93	103	0.7	0.7	0.7	0.7	0.7	0.7
Nonresident alien	305	331	335	345	361	397	2.5	2.7	2.7	2.8	2.8	2.9
4-year institutions	7,565	7,648	7,708	7,824	8,175	8,529	62.6	61.7	63.0	62.6	62.7	62.2
White, non-Hispanic	6,275	6,306	6,301	6,337	6,582	6,757	51.9	50.9	51.5	50.7	50.5	49.3
Total minority	1,050	1,073	1,124	1,195	1,292	1,450	8.7	8.7	9.2	9.6	9.9	10.6
Black, non-Hispanic	634	612	617	615	656	715	5.2	4.9	5.0	4.9	5.0	5.2
Hispanic	217	229	246	278	296	344	1.8	1.8	2.0	2.2	2.3	2.5
Asian or Pacific Islander	162	193	223	262	297	343	1.3	1.6	1.8	2.1	2.3	2.5
American Indian or Alaskan Native	37	39	38	40	42	48	0.3	03	0.3	0.3	0.3	0.4
Nonresident alien	241	270	282	292	302	322	2.0	2.2	2.3	2.3	2.3	2.3
2-year institutions[1]	4,521	4,740	4,527	4,680	4,868	5,181	37.4	38.3	37.0	37.4	37.3	37.8
White, non-Hispanic	3,558	3,692	3,514	3,584	3,702	3,918	29.4	29.8	28.7	28.7	28.4	28.6
Total minority	899	987	961	1,043	1,107	1,189	7.4	8.0	7.9	8.3	8.5	8.7
Black, non-Hispanic	472	489	459	467	473	509	3.9	3.9	3.7	3.7	3.6	3.7
Hispanic	255	291	289	340	384	414	2.1	2.3	2.4	2.7	2.9	3.0
Asian or Pacific Islander	124	158	167	186	199	212	1.0	1.3	1.4	1.5	1.5	1.5
American Indian or Alaskan Native	47	49	46	51	50	54	0.4	0.4	0.4	0.4	0.4	0.4
Nonresident alien	64	61	53	53	60	75	0.5	0.5	0.4	0.4	0.5	0.5

Source: Trends in Racial/Ethnic Enrollment in Higher Education: Fall 1980 Through Fall 1990, U.S. Department of Education, Office of Educational Research and Improvement, Postsecondary Education Statistics Division, Washington, D.C., p. 3. Primary source: U.S. Department of Education, National Center for Education Statistics, Higher Education General Information Survey "Fall Enrollment in Colleges and Universities (1978-1984)" and Integrated Postsecondary Education Education Data System "Fall Enrollment" surveys (1986, 1988, and 1990.) *Notes:* Because of underreporting/nonreporting of racial/ethnic data, data prior to 1986 were estimated when possible. Also, due to rounding, detail may not add to totals.

★ 352 ★

Enrollment Trends, by Level of Study

Fall enrollment and percent distribution are shown biennially from 1980 through 1990.

Level of study and race/ethnicity	Number in thousands						Percent distribution by level of study					
	1980	1982	1984	1986	1988	1990	1980	1982	1984	1986	1988	1990
Undergraduate enrollment												
Total	10,560	10,875	10,610	10,798	11,304	11,863	100.0	100.0	100.0	100.0	100.0	100.0
White, non-Hispanic	8,556	8,749	8,484	8,558	8,907	9,231	81.0	80.5	80.0	79.3	78.8	77.8
Total minority	1,797	1,907	1,911	2,036	2,192	2,406	17.0	17.5	18.0	18.9	19.4	20.3
Black, non-Hispanic	1,028	1,028	995	996	1,039	1,124	9.7	9.4	9.4	9.2	9.2	9.5
Hispanic	438	485	495	563	631	702	4.1	4.5	4.7	5.2	5.6	5.9
Asian or Pacific Islander	253	313	343	393	437	485	2.4	2.9	3.2	3.6	3.9	4.1
American Indian or Alaskan Native	79	82	78	83	86	95	0.7	0.8	0.7	0.8	0.8	0.8
Nonresident alien	208	220	216	205	205	226	2.0	2.0	2.0	1.9	1.8	1.9
Graduate enrollment												
Total	1,250	1,235	1,344	1,435	1,472	1,574	100.0	100.0	100.0	100.0	100.0	100.0
White, non-Hispanic	1,030	1,002	1,087	1,133	1,153	1,221	82.4	81.1	80.9	78.9	78.4	77.6
Total minority	125	123	141	167	167	187	10.0	10.0	10.5	11.6	11.4	11.9
Black, non-Hispanic	66	61	67	72	76	84	5.3	4.9	5.0	5.0	5.2	5.3
Hispanic	27	27	32	46	39	46	2.2	2.2	2.4	3.2	2.7	2.9
Asian or Pacific Islander	28	30	37	43	46	52	2.2	2.5	2.8	3.0	3.1	3.3
American Indian or Alaskan Native	4	5	5	5	6	6	0.4	0.4	0.4	0.4	0.4	0.4
Nonresident alien	94	108	115	136	151	165	7.5	8.8	8.6	9.5	10.3	10.5
First-professional enrollment												
Total	277	278	278	270	267	274	100.0	100.0	100.0	100.0	100.0	100.0
White, non-Hispanic	248	246	243	231	223	222	89.5	88.5	87.4	85.3	83.6	81.3
Total minority	26	29	32	36	39	46	9.5	10.4	11.4	13.2	14.6	16.7
Black, non-Hispanic	13	13	13	14	14	16	4.6	4.7	4.8	5.2	5.4	5.8
Hispanic	7	7	8	9	9	10	2.4	2.5	2.9	3.4	3.5	3.8
Asian or Pacific Islander	6	8	9	11	14	18	2.2	2.9	3.4	4.2	5.4	6.7
American Indian or Alaskan Native	1	1	1	1	1	1	0.3	0.4	0.4	0.4	0.4	0.4
Nonresident alien	3	3	3	4	5	5	1.0	1.1	1.2	1.5	1.8	2.0

Source: Trends in Racial/Ethnic Enrollment in Higher Education: Fall 1980 Through Fall 1990, U.S. Department of Education, Office of Educational Research and Improvement, Postsecondary Education Statistics Division, Washington, D.C., p. 4. Primary source: U.S. Department of Education, National Center for Educational Statistics, Higher Education General Information Survey "Fall Enrollment in Colleges and Universities" (1978-1984) and Integrated Postsecondary Education Data System "Fall Enrollment" surveys (1986, 1988, and 1990). *Notes:* Because of underreporting/nonreporting, racial/ethnic data prior to 1986 were estimated when possible. Also, due to rounding, detail may not add to totals.

★ 353 ★

Enrollment Trends, by Sex and Race/Ethnicity

Total fall enrollment and percent distribution of students are shown biennially from 1980 through 1990.

Race/ethnicity and sex	Number, in thousands						Percent distribution					
	1980	1982	1984	1986	1988	1990	1980	1982	1984	1986	1988	1990
All students												
Total	12,087	12,388	12,235	12,504	13,043	13,710	100.0	100.0	100.0	100.0	100.0	100.0
American Indian or Alaskan Native	84	88	84	90	93	103	0.7	0.7	0.7	0.7	0.7	0.7
White, non-Hispanic	9,833	9,997	9,815	9,921	10,283	10,675	81.4	80.7	80.2	79.3	78.8	77.9
Black, non-Hispanic	1,107	1,101	1,076	1,082	1,130	1,223	9.2	8.9	8.8	8.7	8.7	8.9
Hispanic	472	519	535	618	680	758	3.9	4.2	4.4	4.9	5.2	5.5

[Continued]

★ 353 ★

Enrollment Trends, by Sex and Race/Ethnicity
[Continued]

Race/ethnicity and sex	Number, in thousands						Percent distribution					
	1980	1982	1984	1986	1988	1990	1980	1982	1984	1986	1988	1990
Asian or Pacific Islander	286	351	390	448	497	555	2.4	2.8	3.2	3.6	3.8	4.0
Nonresident alien	305	331	335	345	361	397	2.5	2.7	2.7	2.8	2.8	2.9
Men												
Total	5,868	5,999	5,859	5,885	5,998	6,239	48.5	48.4	47.9	47.1	46.0	45.5
American Indian or Alaskan Native	38	40	38	39	39	43	0.3	0.3	0.3	0.3	0.3	0.3
White, non-Hispanic	4,773	4,830	4,690	4,647	4,712	4,841	39.5	39.0	38.3	37.2	36.1	35.3
Black, non-Hispanic	464	458	437	436	443	476	3.8	3.7	3.6	3.5	3.4	3.5
Hispanic	232	252	254	290	310	344	1.9	2.0	2.1	2.3	2.4	2.5
Asian or Pacific Islander	151	189	210	239	259	287	1.3	1.5	1.7	1.9	2.0	2.1
Nonresident alien	211	230	231	233	235	248	1.7	1.9	1.9	1.9	1.8	1.8
Women												
Total	6,219	6,389	6,376	6,619	7,045	7,472	51.5	51.6	52.1	52.9	54.0	54.5
American Indian or Alaskan Native	46	48	46	51	53	60	0.4	0.4	0.4	0.4	0.4	0.4
White, non-Hispanic	5,060	5,167	5,125	5,273	5,572	5,834	41.9	41.7	41.9	42.2	42.7	42.6
Black, non-Hispanic	643	644	639	646	687	747	5.3	5.2	5.2	5.2	5.3	5.4
Hispanic	240	267	281	328	370	414	2.0	2.2	2.3	2.6	2.8	3.0
Asian or Pacific Islander	135	162	180	209	237	268	1.1	1.3	1.5	1.7	1.8	2.0
Nonresident alien	94	101	104	112	126	149	0.8	0.8	0.9	0.9	1.0	1.1

Source: Trends in Racial/Ethnic Enrollment in Higher Education: Fall 1980 Through Fall 1990, U.S. Department of Education, Office of Educational Research and Improvement, Postsecondary Education Statistics Division, Washington D.C., p. 6. Primary source: U.S. Department of Education, National Center for Education Statistics, Higher Education General Information Survey "Fall Enrollment in Colleges and Universities" (1978-1984) and Integrated Postsecondary Education Data System "Fall Enrollment" surveys (1986, 1988, and 1990). *Notes:* Because of underreporting of racial/ethnic data, data prior to 1986 were estimated when possible. Also, due to rounding, detail may not add to totals.

★ 354 ★

Enrollment Trends in Public and Private Higher Education Institutions

	Number in thousands				Percent distribution			
	1984	1986	1988	1990	1984	1986	1988	1990
All institutions	12,235	12,504	13,043	13,710	100.0	100.0	100.0	100.0
White, non-Hispanic	9,815	9,921	10,283	10,675	80.2	79.3	78.8	77.9
Black, non-Hispanic	1,076	1,082	1,130	1,223	8.8	8.7	8.7	8.9
Hispanic	535	618	680	758	4.4	4.9	5.2	5.5
Asian or Pacific Islander	390	448	497	555	3.2	3.6	3.8	4.0
American Indian or Alaskan Native	84	90	93	103	0.7	0.7	0.7	0.7
Nonresident alien	335	345	361	397	2.7	2.8	2.8	2.9
Public	9,458	9,714	10,156	10,741	77.3	77.7	77.9	78.3
White, non-Hispanic	7,543	7,654	7,964	8,340	61.6	61.2	61.1	60.8
Black, non-Hispanic	844	854	881	952	6.9	6.8	6.8	6.9
Hispanic	456	532	587	648	3.7	4.3	4.5	4.7
Asian or Pacific Islander	323	371	406	445	2.6	3.0	3.1	3.2

[Continued]

★ 354 ★

Enrollment Trends in Public and Private Higher Education Institutions
[Continued]

	Number in thousands				Percent distribution			
	1984	1986	1988	1990	1984	1986	1988	1990
American Indian or Alaskan Native	72	79	81	90	0.6	0.6	0.6	0.7
Nonresident alien	219	224	238	265	1.8	1.8	1.8	1.9
Private	2,777	2,790	2,887	2,970	22.7	22.3	22.1	21.7
White, non-Hispanic	2,272	2,267	2,319	2,335	18.6	18.1	17.8	17.0
Black, non-Hispanic	232	228	248	271	1.9	1.8	1.9	2.0
Hispanic	79	86	93	110	0.6	0.7	0.7	0.8
Asian or Pacific Islander	67	77	91	109	0.5	0.6	0.7	0.8
American Indian or Alaskan Native	11	11	11	12	0.1	0.1	0.1	0.1
Nonresident alien	116	120	123	132	0.9	1.0	0.9	1.0
Men	5,859	5,885	5,998	6,239	47.9	47.1	46.0	45.5
White, non-Hispanic	4,690	4,647	4,712	4,841	38.3	37.2	36.1	35.3
Black, non-Hispanic	437	436	443	476	3.6	3.5	3.4	3.5
Hispanic	254	290	310	344	2.1	2.3	2.4	2.5
Asian or Pacific Islander	210	239	259	287	1.7	1.9	2.0	2.1
American Indian or Alaskan Native	38	39	39	43	0.3	0.3	0.3	0.3
Nonresident alien	231	233	235	248	1.9	1.9	1.8	1.8
Women	6,376	6,619	7,045	7,472	52.1	52.9	54.0	54.5
White, non-Hispanic	5,125	5,273	5,572	5,834	41.9	42.2	42.7	42.6
Black, non-Hispanic	639	646	687	747	5.2	5.2	5.3	5.4
Hispanic	281	328	370	414	2.3	2.6	2.8	3.0
Asian or Pacific Islander	180	209	237	268	1.5	1.7	1.8	2.0
American Indian or Alaskan Native	46	51	53	60	0.4	0.4	0.4	0.4
Nonresident alien	104	112	126	149	0.9	0.9	1.0	1.1

Source: "Total Enrollment in Institutions of Higher Education, by Control of Institution, Race/Ethnicity and Sex: Biennially, Fall 1978 Through Fall 1988," *Trends in Racial/Ethnic Enrollment in Higher Education: Fall 1978 Through Fall 1988*, 1990, pp. 3-4. Primary source: U.S. Department of Education, National Center for Education Statistics, Higher Education General Information Survey "Fall Enrollment in Colleges and Universities" (1978-1984) and Integrated Postsecondary Education Data System "Fall Enrollment" surveys (1986 and 1988). *Notes:* Because of underreporting/nonreporting of racial/ethnic data, data prior to 1986 was estimated when possible. Also, due to rounding, detail may not add to totals.

★ 355 ★

Tribally Controlled Community Colleges, Enrollment 1980-1990

Numbers show full-time equivalent enrollment from 1980-1990.

	Fiscal years										
	1980	1981	1982	1983	1984	1985	1986	1987	1988	1989	1990
Blackfeet	83	184	211	176	179	174	207	213	263	315	268
Cheyenne	-	-	66	73	52	45	42	49	61	75	66
D-Q University	76	91	99	100	107	112	108	112	121	127	91
Dull Knife	93	73	104	146	190	178	95	100	116	155	106
Fond du Lac	-	-	-	-	-	-	-	-	-	115	162
Fort Belknap	-	-	-	-	-	76	85	89	114	123	120
Fort Berthold	-	46	49	41	63	61	106	113	115	120	145
Fort Peck	-	52	60	50	57	59	100	126	180	176	221
Lac Courte Oreilles	-	-	-	-	57	66	85	79	136	150	180
Little Big Horn	-	-	32	81	95	80	84	92	100	100	211
Little Hoop	35	21	41	39	57	66	83	85	86	100	238
Lummi (NWIC)	-	40	33	26	77	104	150	175	243	421	471
Nebraska	109	128	183	162	149	146	157	144	132	88	166
Oglala	282	282	331	371	421	480	467	473	710	701	629
Salish Kootenai	90	118	162	190	182	179	268	272	342	353	369
Sinte Gleska	173	197	181	194	252	269	291	278	316	373	339
Sisseton-Wapeton	-	72	84	71	116	126	110	87	81	105	123
Standing Rock	111	142	147	172	214	225	227	215	242	217	230
Stone Child	-	-	-	-	-	-	-	123	135	135	156
Turtle Mountain	107	159	198	172	191	225	259	240	300	338	376
Bay Mills[1]	-	-	-	-	-	-	-	-	-	65	169
Ganado[1]	131	84	49	130	157	182	135	-	-	-	-

Source: Roger Walke, *Federal Programs of Assistance to Native Americans: A Report Prepared for the Senate Select Committee on Indian Affairs of the United States Senate*, U.S. Government Printing Office, Washington, D.C., December 1991, p. 164. *Note:* 1. Ganado closed Fall 1986; Bay Mills Community College joined in 1989.

★ 356 ★

Science and Engineering Graduate Students, by Field and Racial/Ethnic Group, 1983-1990

The number of students is shown, by field of study and racial/ethnic group, for 1983-90.

Field[1]	1983	1984	1985	1986	1987	1988	1989	1990
Total, U.S. citizens								
Total science & engineering	278,994	279,554	283,741	286,279	287,606	284,243	287,681	299,110
Total sciences	214,676	213,916	215,725	215,349	216,457	215,893	219,731	227,938
Physical sciences	21,805	22,017	22,054	22,232	22,110	21,860	21,820	21,826
Mathematics	12,442	12,285	12,262	12,179	12,443	12,716	12,711	13,443
Computer sciences	18,068	19,451	22,386	23,419	23,409	23,717	23,122	23,778

[Continued]

★ 356 ★
Science and Engineering Graduate Students, by Field and Racial/Ethnic Group, 1983-1990
[Continued]

Field[1]	1983	1984	1985	1986	1987	1988	1989	1990
Environmental sciences	13,679	13,808	13,651	13,067	12,299	11,589	11,247	11,442
Life sciences	49,567	49,208	48,366	47,918	47,785	46,612	46,878	47,391
Psychology	39,605	39,685	39,811	40,047	41,346	42,726	44,652	46,819
Social sciences	59,510	57,462	57,195	56,487	57,065	56,673	59,301	63,239
Total engineering	64,318	65,638	68,016	70,930	71,149	68,350	67,950	71,172
Native American								
Total science & engineering	919	835	741	752	788	928	859	1,048
Total sciences	738	643	619	620	664	784	734	891
Physical sciences	45	77	35	48	46	52	44	63
Mathematics	32	23	22	32	48	32	34	20
Computer sciences	22	48	56	20	27	40	41	42
Environmental sciences	27	23	23	21	19	29	27	30
Life sciences	153	108	109	130	118	139	110	157
Psychology	136	116	136	135	153	179	181	236
Social sciences	323	248	238	234	253	313	297	343
Total engineering	181	192	122	132	124	144	125	157
White								
Total science & engineering	226,010	224,118	224,898	228,655	230,170	230,855	232,012	241,210
Total sciences	176,909	174,289	174,063	175,249	175,991	178,030	180,165	186,869
Physical sciences	18,657	18,595	18,338	18,565	18,098	18,292	18,328	18,570
Mathematics	10,293	9,976	9,818	9,547	9,695	10,188	10,174	10,705
Computer sciences	13,482	13,983	15,569	16,498	17,149	17,660	16,665	17,436
Environmental sciences	12,322	12,021	11,860	11,654	11,035	10,531	10,309	10,476
Life sciences	43,665	43,725	42,051	41,767	40,532	40,454	40,107	40,343
Psychology	32,665	32,143	32,741	33,285	34,872	36,120	37,815	39,511
Social sciences	45,825	43,846	43,686	43,933	44,610	44,785	46,767	49,828
Total engineering	49,101	49,829	50,835	53,406	54,179	52,828	51,847	54,341
Black								
Total science & engineering	11,045	10,781	10,587	10,580	10,510	11,246	11,779	12,891
Total sciences	9,634	9,306	9,165	9,071	9,075	9,713	10,131	11,081
Physical sciences	575	596	535	524	536	569	633	653
Mathematics	404	394	410	450	442	422	463	512
Computer sciences	564	561	609	686	750	825	838	984
Environmental sciences	111	108	122	98	95	108	96	125
Life sciences	1,296	1,295	1,332	1,238	1,194	1,304	1,372	1,441
Psychology	1,911	1,933	1,815	1,815	1,825	1,983	2,094	2,289

[Continued]

★ 356 ★

Science and Engineering Graduate Students, by Field and Racial/Ethnic Group, 1983-1990

[Continued]

Field[1]	1983	1984	1985	1986	1987	1988	1989	1990
Social sciences	4,773	4,419	4,342	4,260	4,233	4,502	4,635	5,077
Total engineering	1,411	1,475	1,422	1,509	1,435	1,533	1,648	1,810
Asian								
Total science & engineering	9,393	10,208	12,049	12,883	14,639	15,256	15,778	17,474
Total sciences	5,974	6,374	7,222	7,697	8,754	9,289	9,745	10,699
Physical sciences	748	891	937	912	1,047	1,213	1,141	1,217
Mathematics	564	565	625	707	771	759	710	900
Computer sciences	1,099	1,251	1,853	2,078	2,463	2,690	2,748	2,864
Environmental sciences	239	187	193	152	181	210	211	267
Life sciences	1,409	1,460	1,602	1,716	1,846	2,035	2,263	2,585
Psychology	532	545	559	619	728	752	821	964
Social sciences	1,383	1,475	1,453	1,513	1,718	1,630	1,851	1,902
Total engineering	3,419	3,834	4,827	5,186	5,885	5,967	6,033	6,775
Hispanic								
Total science & engineering	8,928	8,715	8,637	8,713	8,842	9,132	9,487	10,502
Total sciences	7,463	7,193	7,140	7,071	7,108	7,401	7,762	8,547
Physical sciences	563	535	599	629	591	624	680	641
Mathematics	331	292	262	270	266	328	305	370
Computer sciences	282	292	481	445	544	517	546	566
Environmental sciences	226	263	241	239	228	211	213	241
Life sciences	1,138	1,103	1,263	1,265	1,262	1,405	1,510	1,530
Psychology	1,814	1,903	1,613	1,709	1,669	1,728	1,756	2,159
Social sciences	3,109	2,805	2,681	2,514	2,548	2,588	2,752	3,040
Total engineering	1,465	1,522	1,497	1,642	1,734	1,731	1,725	1,955

Source: National Science Board, *Science and Engineering Indicators - 1991*, Washington D.C., U.S. Government Printing Office, 1991, (NSB 91-1) pp. 240- 241. Primary source: Science Resources Studies Division. National Science Foundation. *Selected Data on Graduate Students and Postdoctorates in Science and Engineering: Fall 1990*, NSF 91-320 (Washington, DC: NSF, 1991), unpublished tabulations; and annual series. *Notes:* Data on racial/ethnic groups are only available for U.S. citizens. 1. Total includes racial/ethnic group unknown.

Higher Education Degrees

★ 357 ★

Associate's Degrees Conferred, 1984-89

The total number of degrees conferred is shown, by sex and field of study.

Field of study	Men			Women			Total		
	84-85	86-87	88-89	84-85	86-87	88-89	84-85	86-87	88-89
Agriculture/Nat. Resources	41	36	29	12	15	6	53	51	35
Architecture/Envir. Design	2	1	2	2	3	2	4	4	4
Area and Ethnic Studies	0	3	2	5	3	4	5	6	6
Business and Management	234	203	193	562	608	589	796	811	782
Communications	4	9	13	7	13	9	11	22	22
Computer/Information Science	16	20	24	36	27	39	52	47	63
Education	23	33	42	78	101	85	101	134	127
Engineering	313	320	360	41	40	49	354	360	409
Fine and Applied Arts	74	96	63	42	89	42	116	185	105
Foreign Languages	0	6	5	0	5	5	0	11	10
Health Professions	45	51	50	327	352	360	372	403	410
Home Economics	9	17	15	54	37	61	63	54	76
Law	0	5	8	7	6	28	7	11	36
Letters	1	4	8	4	4	10	5	8	18
Library Science	0	0	1	0	0	2	0	0	3
Life Sciences	4	5	8	4	13	12	8	18	20
Mathematics	4	2	6	0	2	3	4	4	9
Military Sciences	0	1	0	0	0	0	0	1	0
Physical Sciences	7	3	1	7	3	2	14	6	3
Psychology	2	6	3	9	11	8	11	17	13
Public Affairs/Services	64	60	93	62	84	71	126	144	164
Social Sciences	10	18	15	25	34	29	35	52	44
Theology	0	0	0	1	1	2	1	1	2
Interdisciplinary Studies	345	364	372	470	482	585	815	846	957
Total	1,198	1,263	1,315	1,755	1,933	2,003	2,953	3,196	3,318

Source: Toward the Year 2000: Listening to the Voice of Native America, National Advisory Council on Indian Education, 17th Annual report to the United States Congress, Fiscal Year 1990, p. 71. Primary source: National Center for Education Statistics, "Race/Ethnicity Trends in Degrees Conferred by Institutions of Higher Education: 1978-79 through 1988-89," January 1991.

★ 358 ★

Bachelor's Degrees Conferred, by Race/Ethnicity, 1976-89

Distribution of bachelor's degrees awarded is shown in percent, by sex, year, and race/ethnicity.

Year and sex of student	Total	Percent distribution of degrees conferred					
		American Indian/ Alaskan Native	White, non-Hispanic	Black, non-Hispanic	Hispanic	Asian or Pacific Islander	Non-resident alien
1976-77							
Total[1]	100.0	0.4	88.0	6.4	2.0	1.5	1.7
Men	100.0	0.4	88.6	5.1	2.1	1.5	2.3
Women	100.0	0.4	87.3	7.9	2.0	1.5	1.0
1978-79							
Total[2]	100.0	0.4	87.3	6.6	2.2	1.7	1.9
Men	100.0	0.4	87.8	5.2	2.2	1.7	2.7
Women	100.0	0.4	86.7	8.0	2.2	1.6	1.1
1980-81							
Total[3]	100.0	0.4	86.4	6.5	2.3	2.0	2.4
Men	100.0	0.4	86.5	5.2	2.3	2.2	3.5
Women	100.0	0.4	86.2	7.8	2.4	1.9	1.3
1984-85							
Total[4]	100.0	0.4	85.3	5.9	2.7	2.6	3.0
Men	100.0	0.4	85.1	4.8	2.6	2.8	4.2
Women	100.0	0.5	85.5	7.0	2.7	2.4	1.9
1986-87							
Total[5]	100.0	0.4	84.9	5.7	2.7	3.3	3.0
Men	100.0	0.4	84.6	4.7	2.7	3.6	4.1
Women	100.0	0.4	85.2	6.7	2.8	3.0	1.9
1988-89							
Total[6]	100.0	0.4	84.5	5.7	2.9	3.8	2.7
Men	100.0	0.4	84.4	4.6	2.9	4.1	3.6
Women	100.0	0.4	84.6	6.7	3.0	3.5	1.8

Source: "Bachelor's Degrees Conferred by Institutions of Higher Education, by Racial/Ethnic Group and Sex of Student: 1976-77 to 1988-89, *"Digest of Education Statistics 1991*, November 1991, p. 264. Primary source: U.S. Department of Education, National Center for Education Statistics, "Degrees and Other Formal Awards Conferred" surveys, and Integrated Postsecondary Education Data System (IPEDS), "Completions" survey. (This table was prepared November 1990). *Notes:* 1. Excludes 1,121 men and 528 women whose racial/ethnic group was not available. 2. Excludes 1,279 men and 571 women whose racial/ethnic group was not available. 3. Excludes 258 men and 82 women whose racial/ethnic group was not available. 4. Excludes 6,380 men and 4,786 women whose racial/ethnic group was not available. 5. Reported racial/ethnic distributions of students by level of degree, field of degree, and sex were used to estimate race/ethnicity for students whose race/ethnicity was not reported. Excludes 74 men and 5 women whose racial/ethnic group and field of study were not available. 6. Reported racial/ethnic distributions of students by level of degrees, field of degree, and sex were used to estimate race/ethnicity for students whose race/ethnicity was not reported. Excludes 1,410 men and 1,018 women whose racial/ethnic group and field of study were not available.

★ 359 ★

Bachelor's Degrees Conferred, by Major Field of Study, 1988-89

The number of degrees conferred is shown, by major field of study and race/ethnicity, in the 1988-89 academic year.

Major field of study	Total	American Indian/ Alaskan Native	White non-Hispanic	Black non-Hispanic	Hispanic	Asian or Pacific Islander	Non-resident alien
All fields, total[1]	1,015,239	4,046	858,186	58,016	29,800	38,219	26,972
Agriculture and natural resources	13,488	70	12,248	311	222	240	397
Architecture and environmental design	9,191	39	7,421	281	359	430	661
Area and ethnic studies	3,949	25	3,055	237	171	333	128
Business and management	246,659	824	207,824	15,088	6,987	8,039	7,897
Communications	48,625	137	42,472	3,202	1,169	992	653
Computer and information sciences	30,637	94	22,515	2,557	902	2,355	2,214
Education	96,988	537	88,152	4,233	2,293	1,127	646
Engineering	66,296	179	50,783	2,094	1,937	6,159	5,144
Engineering technologies	18,977	106	15,726	1,143	521	853	628
Foreign languages	10,774	36	8,778	319	964	403	274
Health sciences	59,111	245	51,011	3,973	1,386	1,733	763
Home economics	14,717	51	12,846	894	284	462	180
Law	1,976	5	1,725	127	57	54	8
Letters	43,323	158	38,898	1,862	969	1,048	388
Liberal/general studies	23,459	157	19,699	1,721	1,064	544	274
Library and archival science	122	0	105	8	2	3	4
Life sciences	36,079	147	28,896	1,944	1,254	2,951	887
Mathematics	15,237	54	12,487	801	310	1,034	551
Military sciences	419	0	356	37	12	4	10
Multi/interdisciplinary studies	18,213	79	15,454	1,097	539	695	349
Parks and recreation	4,171	23	3,768	197	90	58	35
Philosophy and religion	6,411	25	5,713	224	160	174	115
Physical sciences	17,204	63	14,502	708	384	936	611
Protective services	14,626	74	11,501	2,106	686	182	77
Psychology	48,516	214	41,584	2,815	1,773	1,605	525
Public affairs	15,254	133	12,053	1,974	613	287	194
Social sciences	107,714	431	90,929	6,498	3,618	3,992	2,246
Theology	5,322	12	4,779	185	96	121	129
Visual and performing arts	37,781	128	32,906	1,380	978	1,405	984

Source: "Bachelor's Degrees Conferred by Institutions of Higher Education, by Racial/Ethnic Group, Major Field of Study, and Sex of Student: 1988-89," *Digest of Education Statistics 1991,* November 1991, pp. 265-266. Primary source: U.S. Department of Education, National Center for Education Statistics, Integrated Postsecondary Education Data System (IPEDS), "Completions" survey. (This table was prepared November 1990). *Notes:* To facilitate trend comparisons, certain aggregations have been made of the degree fields as reported in the IPEDS "Completions" survey: "Agriculture and natural resources" includes agribusiness and agriculture production, agricultural sciences, and renewable natural resources. "Business and management" includes business and management, business and office, marketing and distribution, and consumer and personal services; "Engineering and related technologies" includes engineering and related technologies, mechanics and repairers, and construction trades; "Physical sciences" includes physical sciences and science technologies; "Public affairs" includes public affairs and transportation and material moving; and "Visual and performing arts" includes visual and performing arts and precision production. 1. Reported racial/ethnic distributions of students by level of degree, field of degree, and sex were used to estimate race/ethnicity for students whose race/ethnicity was not reported. Excludes 1,410 men and 1,018 women whose racial/ethnic group and field of study were not available.

★ 360 ★

Bachelor's Degrees Held by Persons 25 Years Old and Older, by Race/Ethnicity

Asians - 37.0

Whites - 22.0

Blacks - 11.0

Hispanics - 9.0

Native Americans - 9.0

Race and ethnicity	Percent holding a bachelor's degree
Asians	37.0
Whites	22.0
Blacks	11.0
Hispanics	9.0
Native Americans	9.0

Source: USA TODAY, December 10, 1992, p. 11A. Primary source: U.S. Census Bureau.

★ 361 ★

Bachelor's Degrees Conferred in Science, by Selected Field and Race/Ethnicity, 1977-89

The number of degrees conferred is shown, by field of study and racial/ethnic group, for 1977-89.

Field[1]	1977	1979	1981	1985	1987	1989
Total, U.S. citizens and permanent residents						
Total science & engineering	326,418	322,195	322,189	345,400	339,934	336,582
Total sciences	280,325	264,192	253,803	257,992	254,800	257,857
Physical sciences	22,038	22,659	23,441	22,892	19,027	16,482
Mathematics	13,977	11,534	10,717	14,212	15,506	14,524
Computer sciences	6,161	8,392	14,455	36,692	35,943	27,721
Life sciences	74,230	71,442	64,560	55,479	51,729	48,561
Psychology	47,297	42,561	40,878	39,406	41,248	47,396
Social sciences	116,622	107,604	99,752	89,311	91,347	103,173
Total engineering	46,093	58,003	68,386	87,408	85,134	78,725
Native American						
Total science & engineering	1,155	1,187	1,202	1,484	1,350	1,323

[Continued]

★ 361 ★

Bachelor's Degrees Conferred in Science, by Selected Field and Race/Ethnicity, 1977-89
[Continued]

Field[1]	1977	1979	1981	1985	1987	1989
Total sciences	1,020	1,023	1,007	1,175	1,067	1,048
Physical sciences[2]	68	63	65	98	72	62
Mathematics	26	41	18	59	52	53
Computer sciences	15	11	21	139	112	90
Life sciences[3]	270	233	233	231	202	215
Psychology	167	177	196	201	180	420
Social sciences[4]	474	498	474	447	449	208
Total engineering[5]	135	164	195	309	283	275
White, non-Hispanic						
Total science & engineering	290,175	284,582	281,924	299,662	289,700	283,260
Total sciences	248,103	232,201	221,068	223,357	217,834	218,035
Physical sciences[2]	20,417	20,958	21,249	20,541	16,653	14,238
Mathematics	12,602	10,229	9,447	12,163	13,265	12,287
Computer sciences	5,508	7,404	12,566	31,321	29,181	21,711
Life sciences[3]	67,891	64,445	57,529	48,248	44,034	40,594
Psychology	41,494	36,648	34,718	33,959	35,761	40,506
Social sciences[4]	100,191	92,517	85,559	77,125	78,940	88,699
Total engineering[5]	42,072	52,651	60,856	76,305	71,866	65,225
Black, non-Hispanic						
Total science & engineering	19,455	18,743	18,828	18,075	18,279	18,405
Total sciences	18,070	16,968	16,379	14,933	14,859	15,251
Physical sciences[2]	692	704	911	830	823	697
Mathematics	712	652	585	770	834	792
Computer sciences	361	507	786	2,143	2,820	2,457
Life sciences[3]	2,724	2,837	2,650	2,417	2,185	2,225
Psychology	3,221	3,218	3,308	2,667	2,451	2,743
Social sciences[4]	10,360	9,050	8,139	6,106	5,746	6,337
Total engineering[5]	1,385	1,775	2,449	3,142	3,420	3,154
Asian						
Total science & engineering	6,096	7,080	9,027	13,791	17,612	19,734
Total sciences	4,885	5,222	5,961	8,784	11,234	12,831
Physical sciences[2]	377	439	599	763	804	922
Mathematics	316	324	392	885	1,034	1,019
Computer sciences	163	263	669	2,044	2,455	2,268
Life sciences[3]	1,558	1,788	1,807	2,197	2,844	3,146
Psychology	807	781	843	845	1,154	1,575

[Continued]

★ 361 ★

Bachelor's Degrees Conferred in Science, by Selected Field and Race/Ethnicity, 1977-89

[Continued]

Field[1]	1977	1979	1981	1985	1987	1989
Social sciences[4]	1,664	1,627	1,651	2,050	2,853	3,901
Total engineering[5]	1,211	1,858	3,066	5,007	6,378	6,903
Hispanic						
Total science & engineering	9,537	10,333	11,208	12,388	12,993	13,860
Total sciences	8,247	8,778	9,388	9,743	9,806	10,692
Physical sciences[2]	484	495	617	660	585	563
Mathematics	321	288	275	335	321	373
Computer sciences	114	207	413	1,045	1,375	1,195
Life sciences[3]	1,787	2,139	2,341	2,386	2,464	2,381
Psychology	1,608	1,737	1,813	1,734	1,702	2,152
Social sciences[4]	3,933	3,912	3,929	3,583	3,359	4,028
Total engineering[5]	1,290	1,555	1,820	2,645	3,187	3,168

Source: National Science Board, *Science and Engineering Indicators - 1991*, Washington D.C., U.S. Government Printing Office, 1991, (NSB 91-1) pp. 236- 237. Primary source: Science Resources Studies Division. National Science Foundation, unpublished tabulations from the Completion Survey conducted by the National Center for Education Statistics. *Notes:* Data by racial/ethnic group are collected on a biennial schedule: data are provided by institutions; imputations are done for some non-response. Racial/ethnic categories are designated on the survey form. These categories include U.S. citizens and foreign citizens on permanent visas. Data are not available by racial/ethnic group for foreign citizens on temporary visas. 1. Data on racial/ethnic groups are collected by broad fields of study only; therefore, these data cannot be adjusted to the exact field taxonomies used by the National Science Foundation. 2. Includes environmental sciences. 3. Excludes health sciences. 4. For 1977 to 1981, social sciences included Afro-American black cultural studies and American Indian studies. 5. Includes engineering technology. Racial/ethnic data for engineering technology can only be separated for 1985 and 1987.

★ 362 ★

Master's Degrees Conferred, 1978-89

The total number of degrees conferred, the number of American Indian/ Alaska Natives receiving degrees, and the percent received by American Indian/Alaska Natives are shown, by selected years, for 1978-89.

Year	Total degrees conferred	American Indian/Alaska Natives receiving degrees	% received by American Indian/ Alaska Natives
1988-89	308,872	1,133	.37
1986-87	289,341	1,104	.39
1984-85	280,421	1,256	.45
1980-81	294,183	1,034	.35
1978-79	301,707	999	.33

Source: Toward the Year 2000: Listening to the Voice of Native America, National Advisory Council on Indian Education, 17th Annual report to the United States Congress, Fiscal Year 1990, p. 81.

★ 363 ★

Master's Degree Distribution, by Race/Ethnicity, 1976-89

Distribution of degrees awarded is shown in percent, by sex, year, and race/ethnicity.

Year and sex of student	Percent distribution of degrees conferred						
	Total	American Indian/ Alaskan Native	White, non-Hispanic	Black, non-Hispanic	Hispanic	Asian or Pacific Islander	Non-resident alien
1976-77							
Total[1]	100.0	0.4	88.0	6.4	2.0	1.5	1.7
Men	100.0	0.4	88.6	5.1	2.1	1.5	2.3
Women	100.0	0.4	87.3	7.9	2.0	1.5	1.0
1978-79							
Total[2]	100.0	0.4	87.3	6.6	2.2	1.7	1.9
Men	100.0	0.4	87.8	5.2	2.2	1.7	2.7
Women	100.0	0.4	86.7	8.0	2.2	1.6	1.1
1980-81							
Total[3]	100.0	0.4	86.4	6.5	2.3	2.0	2.4
Men	100.0	0.4	86.5	5.2	2.3	2.2	3.5
Women	100.0	0.4	86.2	7.8	2.4	1.9	1.3
1984-85							
Total[4]	100.0	0.4	85.3	5.9	2.7	2.6	3.0

[Continued]

★ 363 ★

Master's Degree Distribution, by Race/Ethnicity, 1976-89
[Continued]

Year and sex of student	Total	American Indian/ Alaskan Native	White, non-Hispanic	Black, non-Hispanic	Hispanic	Asian or Pacific Islander	Non-resident alien
			Percent distribution of degrees conferred				
Men	100.0	0.4	85.1	4.8	2.6	2.8	4.2
Women	100.0	0.5	85.5	7.0	2.7	2.4	1.9
1986-87							
Total[5]	100.0	0.4	84.9	5.7	2.7	3.3	3.0
Men	100.0	0.4	84.6	4.7	2.7	3.6	4.1
Women	100.0	0.4	85.2	6.7	2.8	3.0	1.9
1988-89							
Total[6]	100.0	0.4	84.5	5.7	2.9	3.8	2.7
Men	100.0	0.4	84.4	4.6	2.9	4.1	3.6
Women	100.0	0.4	84.6	6.7	3.0	3.5	1.8

Source: "Master's Degrees Conferred by Institutions of Higher Education, by Racial/Ethnic Group and Sex of Student: 1976-77 to 1988-89, *"Digest of Education Statistics 1991*, November 1991, p. 267. Primary source: U.S. Department of Education, National Center for Education Statistics, "Degrees and Other Formal Awards Conferred" surveys, and Integrated Postsecondary Education Data System (IPEDS), "Completions" survey. (This table was prepared November 1990). *Notes:* 1. Excludes 387 men and 175 women whose racial/ethnic group was not available. 2. Excludes 733 men and 91 women whose racial/ethnic group was not available. 3. Excludes 1,377 men and 179 women whose racial/ethnic group was not available. 4. Excludes 3,973 men and 1,857 women whose racial/ethnic group was not available. 5. Reported racial/ethnic distributions of students by level of degree, field of degree, and sex were used to estimate race/ethnicity for students whose race/ethnicity was not reported. Excludes 99 men and 117 women whose racial/ethnic group and field of study were not available. 6. Reported racial/ethnic distributions of students by level of degrees, field of degree, and sex were used to estimate race/ethnicity for students whose race/ethnicity was not reported. Excludes 496 men and 394 women whose racial/ethnic group and field of study were not available.

★ 364 ★

Master's Degrees Conferred, by Major Field of Study, 1988-89

The number of degrees conferred is shown, by major field of study and race/ethnicity, for the 1988-89 academic year.

Major field of study	Total	American Indian/ Alaskan Native	White non-Hispanic	Black non-Hispanic	Hispanic	Asian or Pacific Islander	Non-resident alien
All fields, total[1]	308,872	1,133	241,607	14,076	7,270	10,714	34,072
Agriculture and natural resources	3,245	6	2,222	53	56	56	855
Architecture and environmental design	3,378	9	2,350	98	90	118	713
Area and ethnic studies	978	7	667	30	57	48	169
Business and management	73,154	197	57,445	3,077	1,581	2,962	7,892
Communications	4,233	14	3,328	215	70	99	507
Computer and information sciences	9,392	43	5,290	218	152	987	2,702
Education	82,238	386	70,827	5,272	2,157	1,064	2,532
Engineering	23,713	35	13,575	375	472	2,108	7,148
Engineering technologies	828	2	631	49	10	38	98
Foreign languages	1,911	3	1,271	21	158	46	412
Health sciences	119,255	85	16,235	854	398	563	1,120
Home economics	2,174	10	1,820	67	45	54	178
Law	2,098	4	1,050	73	41	62	868

[Continued]

★ 364 ★

Master's Degrees Conferred, by Major Field of Study, 1988-89
[Continued]

Major field of study	Total	American Indian/ Alaskan Native	White non-Hispanic	Black non-Hispanic	Hispanic	Asian or Pacific Islander	Non-resident alien
Letters	6,608	24	5,469	125	125	187	678
Liberal/general studies	1,408	6	1,248	31	39	24	60
Library and archival science	3,940	19	3,444	129	61	113	174
Life sciences	4,933	17	3,791	128	113	230	654
Mathematics	3,424	6	2,123	61	29	186	1,019
Military sciences	0	0	0	0	0	0	0
Multi/interdisciplinary studies	3,225	7	2,741	125	76	99	177
Parks and recreation	460	1	376	24	5	15	39
Philosophy and religion	1,274	2	1,054	51	32	36	99
Physical sciences	5,737	18	3,962	82	77	292	1,306
Protective services	1,046	1	826	138	15	12	54
Psychology	8,579	35	7,420	414	301	137	272
Public affairs	17,928	100	14,337	1,626	594	417	854
Social sciences	10,854	53	7,678	397	247	329	2,150
Theology	4,625	9	3,767	146	99	148	456
Visual and performing arts	8,234	34	6,660	197	170	287	886

Source: "Master's Degrees Conferred by Institutions of Higher Education, by Racial/Ethnic Group, Major Field of Study, and Sex of Student: 1988-89," *Digest of Education Statistics 1991*, November 1991, pp. 268-269. Primary source: U.S. Department of Education, National Center for Education Statistics, Integrated Postsecondary Education Data System (IPEDS), "Completions" survey. (This table was prepared November 1990). *Notes:* To facilitate trend comparisons, certain aggregations have been made of the degree fields as reported in the IPEDS "Completions" survey: "Agriculture and natural resources" includes agribusiness and agriculture production, agricultural sciences, and renewable natural resources. "Business and management" includes business and management, business and office, marketing and distribution, and consumer and personal services; "Engineering and related technologies" includes engineering and related technologies, mechanics and repairers, and construction trades; "Physical sciences" includes physical sciences and science technologies; "Public affairs" includes public affairs and transportation and material moving; and "Visual and performing arts" includes visual and performing arts and precision production. 1. Reported racial/ethnic distributions of students by level of degree, field of degree, and sex were used to estimate race/ethnicity for students whose race/ethnicity was not reported. Excludes 496 men and 394 women whose racial/ethnic group and field of study were not available.

★ 365 ★

Master's Degrees Conferred in Science, by Selected Field and Race/ Ethnicity, 1977-89

The number of degrees conferred is shown, by field of study and racial/ethnic group, for 1977-89.

Field[1]	1977	1979	1981	1985	1987	1989
Total, U.S. citizens and permanent residents						
Total science & engineering	55,054	50,201	48,711	50,994	50,720	51,872
Total sciences	42,359	38,784	36,909	36,094	34,773	35,510
Physical sciences	4,689	4,713	4,457	4,563	4,271	4,232
Mathematics	3,328	2,571	2,103	2,146	2,331	2,309
Computer sciences	2,432	2,528	3,239	5,233	5,848	6,061
Life sciences	9,748	9,697	8,954	7,624	6,963	6,561
Psychology	8,149	7,852	7,769	8,129	7,493	7,994
Social sciences	14,013	11,423	10,387	8,399	7,867	8,353
Total engineering	12,695	11,417	11,802	14,900	15,947	16,362

[Continued]

★ 365 ★

Master's Degrees Conferred in Science, by Selected Field and Race/ Ethnicity, 1977-89
[Continued]

Field[1]	1977	1979	1981	1985	1987	1989
Native American						
Total science & engineering	148	163	159	222	171	205
Total sciences	125	139	128	173	108	170
Physical sciences[2]	21	29	11	21	9	18
Mathematics	12	8	7	7	3	6
Computer sciences	3	16	12	41	22	39
Life sciences[3]	27	21	22	24	17	23
Psychology	26	20	32	37	35	33
Social sciences[4]	36	45	44	43	22	51
Total engineering[5]	23	24	31	49	63	35
White, non-Hispanic						
Total science & engineering	49,670	45,185	43,435	44,387	43,715	44,316
Total sciences	38,226	35,103	33,288	31,808	30,476	30,894
Physical sciences[2]	4,363	4,373	4,115	4,133	3,834	3,766
Mathematics	3,048	2,352	1,890	1,873	2,012	2,032
Computer sciences	2,208	2,273	2,818	4,303	4,717	4,786
Life sciences[3]	9,042	8,909	8,296	6,946	6,236	5,878
Psychology	7,201	7,078	7,019	7,220	6,698	7,075
Social sciences[4]	12,364	10,118	9,150	7,333	6,979	7,357
Total engineering[5]	11,444	10,082	10,147	12,579	13,239	13,422
Black, non-Hispanic						
Total science & engineering	2,266	1,988	1,787	1,755	1,803	1,688
Total sciences	2,026	1,742	1,527	1,396	1,370	1,287
Physical sciences[2]	94	86	107	89	79	78
Mathematics	133	71	67	53	73	59
Computer sciences	67	65	70	180	207	198
Life sciences[3]	257	296	244	226	245	177
Psychology	506	476	424	426	376	395
Social sciences[4]	969	748	615	422	390	380
Total engineering[5]	240	246	260	359	433	401
Asian						
Total science & engineering	1,693	1,895	2,132	3,276	3,475	4,100
Total sciences	956	1,045	1,053	1,703	1,783	2,073
Physical sciences[2]	142	160	153	213	227	278
Mathematics	90	104	97	164	183	178

[Continued]

★ 365 ★

Master's Degrees Conferred in Science, by Selected Field and Race/Ethnicity, 1977-89

[Continued]

Field[1]	1977	1979	1981	1985	1987	1989
Computer sciences	108	149	279	615	779	894
Life sciences[3]	246	309	212	254	247	276
Psychology	95	87	77	129	113	131
Social sciences[4]	275	236	235	328	234	316
Total engineering[5]	737	850	1,079	1,573	1,692	2,027
Hispanic						
Total science & engineering	1,277	970	1,198	1,354	1,556	1,563
Total sciences	1,026	755	913	1,014	1,036	1,086
Physical sciences[2]	69	65	71	107	122	92
Mathematics	45	36	42	49	60	34
Computer sciences	46	25	60	94	123	144
Life sciences[3]	176	162	180	174	218	207
Psychology	321	191	217	317	271	360
Social sciences[4]	269	276	343	273	242	249
Total engineering[5]	251	215	285	340	520	477

Source: National Science Board, *Science and Engineering Indicators - 1991*, Washington D.C., U.S. Government Printing Office, 1991, (NSB 91-1) pp. 245- 246. Primary source: Science Resources Studies Division, National Science Foundation, unpublished tabulations from the Completion Survey conducted by the National Center for Education Statistics. *Notes:* Data by racial/ethnic group are collected on a biennial schedule: data are provided by institutions; imputations are done for some non-response. Racial/ethnic categories are designated on the survey form. These categories include U.S. citizens and foreign citizens on permanent visas. Data are not available by racial/ethnic group for foreign citizens on temporary visas. 1. Data on racial/ethnic groups are collected by broad fields of study only; therefore, these data cannot be adjusted to the exact field taxonomies used by the National Science Foundation. 2. Includes environmental sciences. 3. Excludes health sciences. 4. For 1977 to 1981, social sciences included Afro-American black cultural studies and American Indian studies. 5. Includes engineering technology. Racial/ethnic data for engineering technology can only be separated for 1985 and 1987.

★ 366 ★

Doctoral Degrees Conferred, 1978-89

The total number of degrees conferred, the number of American Indian/ Alaska Natives receiving degrees, and the percent received by American Indian/Alaska Natives is shown, by selected years, for 1978-89.

Year	Total degrees conferred	American Indian/ Alaska Natives receiving degrees	% received by American Indian/ Alaska Natives
1988-89	35,692	84	.23
1986-87	34,033	104	.30
1984-85	32,307	119	.37
1980-81	32,839	130	.40
1978-79	32,664	104	.32

Source: Toward the Year 2000: Listening to the Voice of Native America, National Advisory Council on Indian Education, 17th Annual report to the United States Congress, Fiscal Year 1990, p. 81.

★ 367 ★

Doctoral Degrees Conferred, by Sex and Race/Ethnicity, 1976-89

The percentage of doctoral degrees awarded is shown, by sex and race/ethnicity.

Year and sex of student	Percent distribution of degrees conferred						
	Total	American Indian/ Alaskan Native	White, non-Hispanic	Black, non-Hispanic	Hispanic	Asian or Pacific Islander	Non-resident alien
1976-77							
Total[1]	100.0	0.3	81.1	3.8	1.6	2.0	11.3
Men	100.0	0.3	80.0	3.1	1.5	2.2	13.0
Women	100.0	0.3	84.3	6.0	1.7	1.5	6.2
1978-79							
Total[2]	100.0	0.3	80.0	3.9	1.3	2.5	12.0
Men	100.0	0.3	78.5	3.1	1.3	2.8	14.1
Women	100.0	0.4	83.9	5.8	1.6	1.8	6.6
1980-81							
Total[3]	100.0	0.4	78.9	3.9	1.4	2.7	12.8
Men	100.0	0.4	76.6	3.1	1.2	2.9	15.8
Women	100.0	0.3	83.9	5.6	1.7	2.2	6.2
1984-85							
Total[4]	100.0	0.4	74.1	3.6	2.1	3.4	16.5

[Continued]

★ 367 ★

Doctoral Degrees Conferred, by Sex and Race/Ethnicity, 1976-89

[Continued]

Year and sex of student	Total	Percent distribution of degrees conferred					
		American Indian/ Alaskan Native	White, non-Hispanic	Black, non-Hispanic	Hispanic	Asian or Pacific Islander	Non-resident alien
Men	100.0	0.3	70.5	2.6	2.0	3.8	20.8
Women	100.0	0.5	81.0	5.4	2.2	2.8	8.1
1986-87							
Total[5]	100.0	0.3	71.8	3.1	2.2	3.2	19.4
Men	100.0	0.3	67.2	2.2	2.0	3.6	24.8
Women	100.0	0.4	80.4	4.8	2.6	2.5	9.4
1988-89							
Total[6]	100.0	0.2	69.7	3.0	1.8	3.7	21.5
Men	100.0	0.2	64.3	2.2	1.6	4.2	27.5
Women	100.0	0.3	79.2	4.4	2.1	2.9	11.1

Source: "Doctor's Degrees Conferred by Institutions of Higher Education, by Racial/Ethnic Group and Sex of Student: 1976-77 to 1988-89, *"Digest of Education Statistics 1991,* November 1991, p. 270. Primary source: U.S. Department of Education, National Center for Education Statistics, "Degrees and Other Formal Awards Conferred" surveys, and Integrated Postsecondary Education Data System (IPEDS), "Completions" survey. (This table was prepared November 1990). *Notes:* 1. Excludes 106 men whose racial/ethnic group was not available. 2. Excludes 53 men and 2 women whose racial/ethnic group was not available. 3. Excludes 116 men and 3 women whose racial/ethnic group was not available. 4. Excludes 404 men and 232 women whose racial/ethnic group was not available. 5. Reported racial/ethnic distributions of students by level of degree, field of degree, and sex were used to estimate race/ethnicity for students whose race/ethnicity was not reported. Excludes 40 men and 47 women whose racial/ethnic group and field of study were not available. 6. Reported racial/ethnic distributions of students by level of degrees, field of degree, and sex were used to estimate race/ethnicity for students whose race/ethnicity was not reported. Excludes 54 men and 13 women whose racial/ethnic group and field of study were not available.

★ 368 ★

Doctoral Degrees Conferred, by Major Field of Study, 1988-89

The number of degrees conferred is shown, by major field study and race/ethnicity, in the 1988-89 academic year.

Major field of study	Total	American Indian/ Alaskan Native	White non-Hispanic	Black non-Hispanic	Hispanic	Asian or Pacific Islander	Non-resident alien
All fields, total[1]	35,692	84	24,895	1,071	625	1,337	7,680
Agriculture and natural resources	1,184	0	677	15	20	30	442
Architecture and environmental design	86	1	34	2	2	6	41
Area and ethnic studies	110	1	82	2	4	2	19
Business and management	1,150	2	746	20	14	57	311
Communications	248	0	177	16	4	2	49
Computer and information sciences	538	0	285	2	4	42	205
Education	6,783	25	5,445	450	162	128	573
Engineering	4,521	3	1,939	30	43	326	2,180
Engineering technologies	12	0	8	0	0	0	4
Foreign languages	422	0	282	14	32	7	87
Health sciences	1,439	2	1,107	39	15	47	229
Home economics	263	0	207	12	2	6	36
Law	76	0	24	4	0	2	46

[Continued]

★ 368 ★

Doctoral Degrees Conferred, by Major Field of Study, 1988-89
[Continued]

Major field of study	Total	American Indian/ Alaskan Native	White non-Hispanic	Black non-Hispanic	Hispanic	Asian or Pacific Islander	Non-resident alien
Letters	1,238	3	1,000	29	24	24	158
Liberal/general studies	32	0	25	6	0	0	1
Library and archival science	61	0	42	1	0	3	15
Life sciences	3,533	10	2,677	58	47	174	567
Mathematics	882	1	413	8	7	33	420
Military sciences	0	0	0	0	0	0	0
Multi/interdisciplinary studies	257	1	207	5	5	5	34
Parks and recreation	36	0	24	2	0	0	10
Philosophy and religion	464	0	377	9	9	12	57
Physical sciences	3,852	13	2,436	32	54	185	1,132
Protective services	27	0	24	3	0	0	0
Psychology	3,263	8	2,876	113	89	61	116
Public affairs	417	1	297	36	10	16	57
Social sciences	2,878	10	1,874	108	60	101	725
Theology	1,165	2	984	44	10	35	90
Visual and performing arts	755	1	626	11	8	33	76

Source: "Doctor's Degrees Conferred by Institutions of Higher Education, by Racial/Ethnic Group, Major Field of Study, and Sex of Student: 1988-89," *Digest of Education Statistics 1991*, November 1991, pp. 271-272. Primary source: U.S. Department of Education, National Center for Education Statistics, Integrated Postsecondary Education Data System (IPEDS), "Completions" survey. (This table was prepared November 1990). *Notes:* To facilitate trend comparisons, certain aggregations have been made of the degree fields as reported in the IPEDS "Completions" survey: "Agriculture and natural resources" includes agribusiness and agriculture production, agricultural sciences, and renewable natural resources; "business and management" includes business and management, business and office, marketing and distribution, and consumer and personal services; "engineering and related technologies" includes engineering and related technologies, mechanics and repairers, and construction trades; "physical sciences" includes physical sciences and science technologies; "public affairs" includes public affairs and transportation and material moving; and "visual and performing arts" includes visual and performing arts and precision production. 1. Reported racial/ethnic distributions of students by level of degree, field of degree, and sex were used to estimate race/ethnicity for students whose race/ethnicity was not reported. Excludes 54 men and 13 women whose racial/ethnic group and field of study were not available.

★ 369 ★

Doctoral Degrees Conferred in Science, by Selected Field and Racial/Ethnic Group, 1980-90

The number of degrees conferred is shown, by field of study and racial/ethnic group, for 1980-90.

Degree and Race/Ethnicity	1980	1981	1982	1983	1984	1985	1986	1987	1988	1989	1990
Total, all doctorates	26,512	26,342	25,619	25,634	25,251	24,694	24,513	24,561	24,911	25,024	25,844
Native American	75	85	77	82	74	96	99	115	94	94	93
White	22,462	22,470	22,143	22,245	21,864	21,297	21,224	21,116	21,455	21,568	22,345
Black	1,105	1,110	1,143	1,005	1,055	1,043	949	907	966	962	972
Asian	1,102	1,073	1,004	1,043	1,019	1,069	1,058	1,167	1,236	1,260	1,260
Hispanic	485	526	614	608	607	634	678	709	696	694	813
Total Science and Engineering	14,362	14,437	14,146	14,301	14,085	13,876	13,856	13,906	14,346	14,432	14,776
Native American	27	26	38	28	31	41	52	52	41	52	40
White	12,146	12,388	12,330	12,478	12,246	12,004	12,014	11,921	12,326	12,364	12,727
Black	319	332	336	322	357	357	318	308	346	352	340
Asian	866	821	765	778	774	808	807	921	913	979	968

[Continued]

★ 369 ★

Doctoral Degrees Conferred in Science, by Selected Field and Racial/Ethnic Group, 1980-90
[Continued]

Degree and Race/Ethnicity	1980	1981	1982	1983	1984	1985	1986	1987	1988	1989	1990
Hispanic	213	238	269	282	295	290	342	354	394	379	451
Total sciences	12,808	12,966	12,681	12,819	12,572	12,282	12,130	11,993	12,198	12,203	12,473
Native American	24	22	35	27	28	40	46	45	37	45	36
White	11,003	11,295	11,230	11,350	11,089	10,816	10,660	10,463	10,672	10,638	10,909
Black	301	313	316	293	342	323	294	283	315	319	300
Asian	588	536	519	581	524	527	545	594	580	619	623
Hispanic	186	222	233	253	261	268	307	320	331	331	398
Physical sciences	2,035	2,103	2,110	2,184	2,190	2,178	2,147	2,227	2,236	2,119	2,244
Native American	3	1	3	6	4	3	5	7	6	10	3
White	1,661	1,757	1,859	1,917	1,888	1,900	1,858	1,942	1,927	1,817	1,929
Black	16	24	26	25	34	27	25	20	33	31	27
Asian	164	149	131	136	144	150	146	143	137	155	161
Hispanic	27	30	25	26	47	30	40	56	63	59	70
Mathematics	582	525	499	457	443	418	402	396	386	428	416
Native American	0	1	1	0	3	0	1	0	2	0	1
White	496	448	437	395	380	350	343	319	332	369	367
Black	12	9	6	3	4	7	6	11	4	8	4
Asian	42	40	32	34	30	33	28	41	33	24	25
Hispanic	5	5	6	7	11	12	12	11	4	11	10
Computer sciences	169	188	155	207	195	213	249	275	326	396	396
Native American	0	0	1	1	0	0	0	3	1	2	0
White	143	162	136	174	163	177	193	229	265	319	334
Black	0	2	1	3	3	3	1	2	2	1	1
Asian	9	16	12	20	20	17	37	26	44	52	46
Hispanic	1	0	1	0	3	6	7	4	2	4	5
Environmental sciences	538	488	557	513	499	474	446	450	542	559	544
Native American	2	0	0	2	0	1	2	0	2	6	1
White	485	448	510	453	461	430	413	408	500	509	502
Black	1	4	3	1	3	4	1	2	3	4	2
Asian	22	14	27	26	19	21	14	18	15	23	17
Hispanic	4	6	7	11	2	6	5	5	8	9	13
Life sciences	4,035	4,050	4,104	4,009	4,059	3,982	3,868	3,774	3,933	3,951	3,967
Native American	6	7	10	5	11	17	17	13	12	9	7
White	3,511	3,566	3,678	3,608	3,646	3,572	3,445	3,313	3,484	3,475	3,505
Black	58	61	56	58	68	69	64	73	68	70	56
Asian	198	181	182	197	178	175	189	208	201	222	223
Hispanic	36	56	54	49	52	71	83	77	97	90	111
Psychology	2,909	3,158	2,923	3,108	2,986	2,864	2,831	2,806	2,728	2,738	2,589
Native American	6	9	16	9	6	10	9	16	7	11	18

[Continued]

★ 369 ★

Doctoral Degrees Conferred in Science, by Selected Field and Racial/Ethnic Group, 1980-90
[Continued]

Degree and Race/Ethnicity	1980	1981	1982	1983	1984	1985	1986	1987	1988	1989	1990
White	2,562	2,849	2,638	2,783	2,683	2,590	2,547	2,516	2,445	2,453	2,551
Black	119	113	115	112	121	105	109	93	103	97	110
Asian	50	41	31	44	43	44	41	47	47	55	51
Hispanic	54	66	74	94	84	69	89	95	93	93	103
Social sciences	2,540	2,454	2,333	2,341	2,200	2,153	2,187	2,065	2,047	2,012	2,047
Native American	7	4	4	4	4	9	12	6	7	7	6
White	2,145	2,065	1,972	2,020	1,868	1,797	1,861	1,736	1,719	1,696	1,721
Black	95	100	109	91	109	108	88	82	102	108	100
Asian	103	95	104	74	90	87	90	111	103	88	100
Hispanic	59	59	66	66	62	74	71	72	64	65	86
Total engineering	1,554	1,471	1,465	1,482	1,513	1,594	1,726	1,913	2,148	2,229	2,303
Native American	3	4	3	1	3	1	6	7	4	7	4
White	1,143	1,093	1,100	1,128	1,157	1,188	1,354	1,458	1,654	1,726	1,818
Black	18	19	20	29	15	34	24	25	31	33	40
Asian	278	285	246	247	250	281	262	327	333	360	345
Hispanic	27	16	36	29	34	22	35	34	63	48	53

Source: National Science Board, *Science and Engineering Indicators - 1991*, Washington, D.C., U.S. Government Printing Office, 1991, (NSB 91-1) pp. 248-249. Primary source: Science Resources Studies Division, National Science Foundation. *Selected Data on Science and Engineering Doctorate Awards, 1990*, NSF 91-310 (Washington, DC: NSF 1991). *Note:* Data are for U.S. citizens and permanent residents only.

★ 370 ★

First-Professional Degrees Conferred, 1978-89

The total number of degrees conferred, the number of American Indian/Alaska Natives receiving degrees, and the percent received by American Indian/Alaska Natives is shown, by selected years, for 1978-89.

Year	Total degrees conferred	AI/AN's receiving degrees	Percent received by AI/AN's
1988-89	70,758	268	.38
1986-87	71,617	304	.42
1984-85	75,057	248	.33
1980-81	71,340	192	.27
1978-79	68,503	216	.32

Source: Toward the Year 2000: Listening to the Voice of Native America, National Advisory Council on Indian Education, 17th Annual report to the United States Congress, Fiscal Year 1990, p. 82.

Higher Education Faculty

★ 371 ★

Faculty at Institutions of Higher Education, 1987 - I

Figures are shown, by the type of position and institution and race/ethnicity, for 1987.

Selected characteristics	Number in thousands	Percent total	Public research	Private research	Public doctoral	Private doctoral
Total (in thousands)	770	-	119	53	45	27
Percent	-	100	16	7	6	4
Percent distribution						
Total	-	100.0	100.0	100.0	100.0	100.0
Race						
White, non-Hispanic	690	90.0	91.0	85.0	93.0	91.0
Black, non-Hispanic	25	3.0	1.0	7.0	2.0	1
Hispanic	18	2.0	2.0	5.0	1.0	4.0
Asian	30	4.0	4.0	4.0	4.0	4.0
American Indian	6	1.0	1.0	1	1.0	1.0

Source: "Total Regular and Temporary Instructional Faculty in Institutions of Higher Education by Selected Characteristics and Type and Control of Institution: Fall 1987," *Digest of Education Statistics 1991*, p. 222. Primary source: U.S. Department of Education, National Center for Education Statistics, *National Survey of Postsecondary Faculty (NSOPF), 1988*. (This table was prepared June 1990). *Notes:* A dash (-) stands for not applicable. Data may not add to totals because of rounding or missing data. 1. Less than 0.5 percent.

★ 372 ★

Faculty at Institutions of Higher Education, 1987 - II

Figures are shown, by the type of position and institution and race/ethnicity, for 1987.

Selected characteristics	Public comprehensive	Private comprehensive	Liberal arts	Public 2- year	Private 2-year	Medical	Other
Total (in thousands)	130	130	130	201	6	35	32
Percent	17	17	17	26	1	5	4
Percent distribution							
Total	100.0	100.0	100.0	100.0	100.0	100.0	100.0
Race							
White, non-Hispanic	88.0	88.0	88.0	91.0	90.0	82.0	92.0
Black, non-Hispanic	3.0	3.0	3.0	3.0	4.0	2.0	4.0
Hispanic	2.0	2.0	2.0	4.0	2.0	1	1.0

[Continued]

★ 372 ★

Faculty at Institutions of Higher Education, 1987 - II
[Continued]

Selected characteristics	Public comprehensive	Private comprehensive	Liberal arts	Public 2- year	Private 2-year	Medical	Other
Asian	6.0	6.0	6.0	2.0	2.0	15.0	4.0
American Indian	1.0	1.0	1.0	1.0	2.0	1.0	[1]

Source: "Total Regular and Temporary Instructional Faculty in Institutions of Higher Education by Selected Characteristics and Type and Control of Institution: Fall 1987," *Digest of Education Statistics 1991*, p. 222. Primary source: U.S. Department of Education, National Center for Education Statistics, *National Survey of Postsecondary Faculty (NSOPF), 1988*. (This table was prepared June 1990). *Notes:* A dash (-) stands for not applicable. Data may not add to totals because of rounding or missing data. 1. Less than 0.5 percent.

★ 373 ★

Full-Time Faculty at Institutions of Higher Education, 1987 - I

Figures are shown, by the type of position and institution and race/ethnicity, for 1987.

Selected characteristics	Number in thousands	Percent total	Public research	Private research	Public doctoral	Private doctoral
Total (in thousands)	489	-	96	39	396	15
Percent	-	100.0	19.7	8.0	7.3	3.0
Percent distribution						
Total	-	100.0	100.0	100.0	100.0	100.0
Race						
White, non-Hispanic	438	89.5	90.4	85.4	92.0	91.3
Black, non-Hispanic	16	3.2	1.6	1.6	1.8	0.1
Hispanic	11	2.3	2.4	5.0	1.1	2.2
Asian	21	4.2	4.8	3.5	4.5	5.9
American Indian	3	0.7	0.7	[1]	0.6	0.5

Source: "Full-Time Regular Instructional Faculty in Institutions of Higher Education by Selected Characteristics and Type and Control of Institution: Fall 1987," *Digest of Education Statistics 1991*, November 1991, p. 220. Primary source: U.S. Department of Education, National Center for Education Statistics, *National Survey of Postsecondary Faculty (NSOPF), 1988*. This table was prepared June 1990. *Notes:* A dash (-) stands for not applicable. Data may not add to totals because of rounding or missing data. 1. Less than 0.5 percent.

★ 374 ★

Full-Time Faculty at Institutions of Higher Education, 1987 - II

Figures are shown, by the type of position and institution and race/ethnicity, for 1987.

Selected characteristics	Public comprehensive	Private comprehensive	Liberal arts	Public 2-year	Private 2-year	Medical	Other
Total (in thousands)	93	35	39	91	4	25	15
Percent	19.0	7.2	8.0	18.7	0.8	5.2	3.0
Percent distribution							
Total	100.0	100.0	100.0	100.0	100.0	100.0	100.0
Race							
White, non-Hispanic	88.0	91.2	86.9	91.0	94.1	85.3	95.1
Black, non-Hispanic	3.5	1.7	8.0	3.0	3.1	3.0	2.3
Hispanic	2.1	1.6	1.2	3.5	2.3	[1]	1.6
Asian	5.8	4.4	2.7	1.6	0.5	10.3	1.0
American Indian	0.6	1.1	1.2	0.9	[1]	1.4	[1]

Source: "Full-Time Regular Instructional Faculty in Institutions of Higher Education by Selected Characteristics and Type and Control of Institution: Fall 1987," *Digest of Education Statistics 1991*, November 1991, p. 220. Primary source: U.S. Department of Education, National Center for Education Statistics, *National Survey of Postsecondary Faculty (NSOPF), 1988*. This table was prepared June 1990. *Notes:* A dash (-) stands for not applicable. Data may not add to totals because of rounding or missing data. 1. Less than 0.5 percent.

★ 375 ★

Full-Time Faculty at Institutions of Higher Education, by Field, 1987-88 - I

Figures are shown, by the field and race/ethnicity of faculty member, for the 1987-88 academic year.

Faculty characteristics	Number in thousands	All fields	Agricultural and home economics	Business	Education	Engineering
Total, in thousands	489	-	13	37	35	25
Percentage	-	100.0	3.0	7.0	7.0	5.0
Percent distribution						
Total	489	100.0	100.0	100.0	100.0	100.0
Race/ethnicity						
White, non-Hispanic	438	90.0	94.0	88.0	88.0	87.0
Asian	21	4.0	2.0	6.0	1.0	11.0
Black, non-Hispanic	16	3.0	0.0	4.0	6.0	[1]
Hispanic	11	2.0	3.0	1.0	4.0	2.0
American Indian	4	1.0	1.0	1.0	1.0	[1]

Source: "Full-Time Regular Instructional Faculty in Institutions of Higher Education, by Faculty Characteristics and by Field: 1987-88," *Digest of Education Statistics 1991*, November 1991, p. 221. Primary source: U.S. Department of Education, *National Survey of Postsecondary Faculty (NSOPF), 1987-88*. This table was prepared April 1991. *Notes:* Because of rounding and survey item nonresponse, details may not add to totals. A dash (-) stands for not applicable. 1. Less than 0.5 percent.

★ 376 ★

Full-Time Faculty at Institutions of Higher Education, by Field, 1987-88 - II

Figures are shown, by the field and race/ethnicity of faculty member, for the 1987-88 academic year.

Faculty characteristics	Fine arts	Health	Humanities	Natural sciences	Social sciences	Other
Total, in thousands	32	85	62	84	53	64
Percentage	7.0	17.0	13.0	17.0	11.0	13.0
Percent distribution						
Total	100.0	100.0	100.0	100.0	100.0	100.0
Race/ethnicity						
White, non-Hispanic	92.0	88.0	90.0	91.0	90.0	89.0
Asian	1.0	7.0	2.0	6.0	2.0	3.0
Black, non-Hispanic	3.0	2.0	3.0	2.0	5.0	5.0
Hispanic	3.0	1.0	5.0	1.0	3.0	2.0
American Indian	[1]	1.0	1.0	[1]	1.0	1.0

Source: "Full-Time Regular Instructional Faculty in Institutions of Higher Education, by Faculty Characteristics and by Field: 1987-88," *Digest of Education Statistics 1991*, November 1991, p. 221. Primary source: U.S. Department of Education, National Survey of Postsecondary Faculty (NSOPF), 1987-88. This table was prepared April 1991. *Notes:* Because of rounding and survey item nonresponse, details may not add to totals. A dash (-) stands for not applicable. 1. Less than 0.5 percent.

★ 377 ★

Part-Time Faculty at Institutions of Higher Education, by Field, 1987 - I

Figures are shown, by the type of position and institution and race/ethnicity of faculty member, for the 1987 academic year.

Selected characteristics	Number in thousands	Percent total	Public research	Private research	Public doctoral	Private doctoral
Total (in thousands)	174	-	10	9	5	8
Percent	-	100.0	6.0	5.0	3.0	5.0
Percent distribution						
Total	-	100.0	100.0	100.0	100.0	100.0
Race						
White, non-Hispanic	156	90.0	98.0	83.0	94.0	91.0
Black, non-Hispanic	6	4.0	1.0	12.0	2.0	[2]
Hispanic	4	3.0	[2]	2.0	2.0	9.0

[Continued]

★ 377 ★

Part-Time Faculty at Institutions of Higher Education, by Field,
1987 - I
[Continued]

Selected characteristics	Number in thousands	Percent total	Public research	Private research	Public doctoral	Private doctoral
Asian	6	3.0	[2]	2.0	[2]	[2]
American Indian	2	1.0	1.0	2.0	2.0	[2]

Source: "Part-Time Regular Instructional Faculty in Institutions of Higher Education, by Selected Characteristics and Type and Control of Institution: Fall 1987," *Digest of Education Statistics 1991, November 1991,* p. 222. Primary source: U.S. Department of Education, National Center for Education Statistics, *National Survey of Postsecondary Faculty (NSOPF), 1988.* This table was prepared June 1990. *Notes:* A dash (-) stands for not applicable. Data may not add to totals because of rounding or missing data. 1. Too few cases for reliable estimate. 2. Less than 0.5 percent.

★ 378 ★

Part-Time Faculty at Institutions of Higher Education, by Field, 1987 - II

Figures are shown, by the type of position and institution and race/ethnicity of the faculty member, for the 1987 academic year.

Selected characteristics	Public comprehensive	Private comprehensive	Liberal arts	Public 2-year	Private 2-year	Medical	Other
Total (in thousands)	22	10	13	81	2	5	11
Percent	12.0	6.0	7.0	46.0	1.0	3.0	6.0
Percent distribution							
Total	100.0	100.0	100.0	100.0	100.0	100.0	100.0
Race							
White, non-Hispanic	84.0	97.0	82.0	92.0	[1]	[1]	97.0
Black, non-Hispanic	2.0	[2]	14.0	3.0	[1]	[1]	[2]
Hispanic	2.0	3.0	2.0	3.0	[1]	[1]	[2]
Asian	9.0	0.0	[2]	2.0	[1]	[1]	1.0
American Indian	4.0	[2]	1.0	0.0	[1]	[1]	[2]

Source: "Part-Time Regular Instructional Faculty in Institutions of Higher Education, by Selected Characteristics and Type and Control of Institution: Fall 1987," *Digest of Education Statistics 1991, November 1991,* p. 222. Primary source: U.S. Department of Education, National Center for Education Statistics, *National Survey of Postsecondary Faculty (NSOPF), 1988.* This table was prepared June 1990. *Notes:* A dash (-) stands for not applicable. Data may not add to totals because of rounding or missing data. 1. Too few cases for reliable estimate. 2. Less than 0.5 percent.

Higher Education Costs

★ 379 ★

Financial Aid Received by Undergraduates, 1986-87 - I

Figures are shown, by type of aid given and race/ethnicity.

Selected student characteristics	Enrollment of under-graduates[1] (000)	Any Aid			Grants		
		Total[2]	Federal	Non Federal	Total	Federal	Non Federal
Percent of all undergraduates receiving aid							
All undergraduates	11,185	48.6	34.5	32.7	36.4	24.6	25.9
Race/ethnicity							
American Indian	106	53.0	40.4	34.7	38.8	34.6	23.7
White, non-Hispanic	8,700	46.3	31.5	32.0	33.8	20.9	25.5
Black, non-Hispanic	1,047	66.7	55.5	37.6	55.7	47.0	30.1
Hispanic	759	51.8	40.9	31.6	39.9	33.1	24.6
Asian American	106	53.0	40.4	34.7	38.8	34.6	23.7
Average 1986-87 award for full-time, full-year undergraduate enrollment in fall 1986							
All full-time, full year undergraduates	6,068	3,674	2,862	2,130	2,533	1,538	1,966
Race/ethnicity							
American Indian	45	4,196	2,852	2,637	3,260	1,812	2,576
White, non-Hispanic	4,793	3,573	2,850	2,066	2,434	1,488	1,893
Black, non-Hispanic	537	4,023	3,036	2,273	2,695	1,704	2,157
Hispanic	361	3,692	2,699	2,139	2,656	1,494	2,083
Asian American	332	4,257	2,800	2,661	3,200	1,648	2,407
Average 1986-87 award for other undergraduates enrolled in fall 1986							
All other undergraduates[3]	5,117	1,971	2,108	1,102	1,376	1,186	978
Race/ethnicity							
American Indian	61	1,738	1,841	919	1,866	1,262	1,264
White, non-Hispanic	3,907	1,848	2,024	1,083	1,298	1,134	960
Black, non-Hispanic	510	2,266	2,226	1,060	1,487	1,279	907
Hispanic	398	2,260	2,373	1,099	1,521	1,229	1,048
Asian American	240	2,523	2,381	1,621	1,817	1,356	1,356

Source: "Percentage of Undergraduates Enrolled in Fall 1986 and Average Amount Awarded in 1986-87 per Student, by Type and Source of Aid and Selected Student Characteristics," *Digest of Education Statistics 1991, November 1991*, pp. 299-300. Primary source: U.S. Department of Education, National Center for Education Statistics, *National Postsecondary Student Aid Study*, unpublished data. (This table was prepared June 1991). *Notes:* A dash (-) indicates no data were available in the original source. Because of the rounding and/or the fact that some students receive aid from multiple sources, details may not add to totals. Data have been revised from previously published figures. 1. Numbers of undergraduates may not equal figures reported in other tables, since these data are based on a sample survey. 2. Includes students who reported they were awarded aid, but did not specify the source or type of aid. 3. Enrollment data include persons whose attendance status was not reported.

★ 380 ★

Financial Aid Received by Undergraduates, 1986-87 - II

Figures are shown, by type of aid given and race/ethnicity.

Selected student characteristics	Loans			Work study		
	Total	Federal	Non Federal	Total	Federal	Non Federal
Percent of all undergraduates receiving aid						
All undergraduates	24.1	23.0	1.7	6.1	4.3	2.1
Race/ethnicity						
American Indian	19.1	18.0	1.1	6.8	4.3	3.1
White, non-Hispanic	23.2	22.2	1.7	5.6	3.8	2.1
Black, non-Hispanic	34.9	32.6	2.8	9.8	8.1	2.1
Hispanic	24.0	23.4	1.1	5.8	4.3	1.5
Asian American	18.0	17.7	0.9	7.5	5.2	2.5
Average 1986-87 award for full-time, full-year undergraduate enrollment in fall 1986						
All full-time, full year undergraduates	2,349	2,322	1,690	1,061	962	1,135
Race/ethnicity						
American Indian	2,439	2,439	-	681	646	662
White, non-Hispanic	2,372	2,334	1,811	1,025	926	1,082
Black, non-Hispanic	2,207	2,242	1,128	1,162	1,020	1,445
Hispanic	2,395	2,360	1,945	1,179	1,158	1,197
Asian American	2,261	2,249	1,133	1,183	1,042	1,374
Percentage 1986-87 award for other undergraduates enrolled in fall 1986						
All other undergraduates[1]	2,051	2,060	1,358	1,001	934	975
Race/ethnicity						
American Indian	1,643	1,830	690	484	719	277
White, non-Hispanic	2,037	2,023	1,477	1,009	899	1,000
Black, non-Hispanic	1,984	2,068	906	1,108	1,009	1,352
Hispanic	2,230	2,257	973	838	991	586
Asian American	2,251	2,168	3,041	989	1,029	949

Source: "Percentage of Undergraduates Enrolled in Fall 1986 and Average Amount Awarded in 1986-87 per Student, by Type and Source of Aid and Selected Student Characteristics," *Digest of Education Statistics 1991, November 1991,* pp. 299-300. Primary source: U.S. Department of Education, National Center for Education Statistics, *National Postsecondary Student Aid Study,* unpublished data. (This table was prepared June 1991). *Notes:* A dash (-) indicates no data were available in the original source. Because of the rounding and/or the fact that some students receive aid from multiple sources, details may not add to totals. Data have been revised from previously published figures. 1. Enrollment data include persons whose attendance status was not reported.

Federal Government Support

★ 381 ★

Budget for the Office of Indian Education

Budget allocations are shown for FY 1988-90.

Program	Number of dollars		
	FY 1988 appropriation	FY 1989 appropriation	FY 1990 appropriation
Subpart 1			
Local Educational Agencies	45,670,000	49,248,000	50,825,000
Indian-Controlled Schools	3,500,000	3,500,000	3,451,000
Subpart 1 subtotal	49,170,000	52,748,000	54,276,000
Subpart 2			
Education Services for Indian Children	3,710,000	3,710,000	4,138,000
Planning, Pilot & Demonstration	1,935,000	1,935,000	1,841,000
Fellowships	1,600,000	1,600,000	1,587,000
Education Personnel Development	2,262,000	2,262,000	2,230,000
Resource & Evaluation Centers	2,200,000	2,300,000	2,268,000
Gifted & Talented Program	0	500,000	493,000[1]
Subpart 2 subtotal	11,707,000	12,307,000	12,307,000
Subpart 3			
Education Services for Adults	3,000,000	4,000,000	4,078,000
Planning, Pilot & Demonstration	0	0	0
Subpart 3 subtotal	3,000,000	4,000,000	4,078,000
Subpart 4			
Office of Indian Education	2,163,000	2,206,000	2,403,000
National Advisory Council on Indian Education	286,000	292,000	306,000
Subpart 4 subtotal	2,449,000	2,449,000	2,709,000
Indian Education Program Totals	66,326,000	71,553,000	73,620,000

Source: Toward the Year 2000: Listening to the Voice of Native America, National Advisory Council on Indian Education, (NACIE) 17th Annual Report to the United States Congress, Fiscal Year 1990, p. 53. Primary source: Office of Indian Education Budget Reports. *Notes:* 1. The Gifted and talented budget was reduced to $493,000 from $500,000 by the Gramm-Rudman Hollings sequester. The gifted and talented appropriation for fiscal year 1990 was carried over from fiscal year 1989.

★ 382 ★

Budgets for Federal Education Programs Which Serve the Indian Population

Program	($)
U.S. Department of Education	
Elementary and Secondary Education	
Indian Education Act	73,620,000
Impact Aid - Maintenance & Operations	243,690,065
Impact Aid - Construction	11,798,215
Adult and Vocational Education	
Vocational Education Set-Aside	11,009,952
Special Education and Rehabilitation Services	
Vocational Rehabilitation Set-Aside	3,821,000
Postsecondary Education	
Minority Science Improvement Program	803,106
Institutional Aid	6,585,342
Bilingual Education	14,194,000
Educational Research & Improvement	
Library Services for Tribes	2,419,120
Total	367,940,800
Operated by BIA but funded through Education Department	
Chapter 1 (Set-Aside)	27,344,592
Education of the Handicapped	19,034,529
Math and Science Handicapped Set-Aside	686,660
Drug-free Schools and Communities (Set-Aside)	5,332,000
Total	52,397,781
Other Department of Education Programs Serving Indians	
Chapter 1, ECIA[2]	79,334,000[1]
Subtotal	499,672,581
U.S. Department of the Interior Bureau of Indian Affairs	
School Operations	
ISEP[3] (Formula & Adjustments)	176,052,000
Institutionalized Handicapped	3,382,000
School Boards (Expense & Training)	1,183,200
Student Transportation	12,489,000
Solo Parent Program	131,000
Technical Support (Agency & MIS[4])	6,990,000
Indian School Program Adjustments	1,885,000
Tribal Departments of Education	99,000
Substance Abuse/Alcohol-Educ. Prog.	
School Counselors	2,330,000
Johnson O'Malley	23,252,000

[Continued]

★ 382 ★

Budgets for Federal Education Programs Which Serve the Indian Population
[Continued]

Program	($)
Continuing Education	
Postsecondary Schools	12,110,000
Special Higher Education Scholarships	2,131,000
Tribally Controlled Comm. Colleges (Operations & Endowment)	15,825,000
Mansfield University	395,000
Tribe/Agency Operations	
Scholarships	27,635,000
Adult Education	3,167,000
Tribal Colleges Snyder Act Supplement	904,000
BIA total	289,960,200
Other programs	
Office of Construction (Interior)	33,710,000
Indian Health Service Scholarships	8,799,000
Head Start (Health and Human Services)	48,256,821
Job Training Partnership Act (Dept. of Labor, American Indian/Alaska Native JPTA program)	57,910,602
Grand total	938,309,204

Source: *Toward the Year 2000: Listening to the Voice of Native America*, National Advisory Council on Indian Education, 17th Annual Report to the United States Congress, Fiscal Year 1990, p. 54. *Notes:* 1. Figures from the Office of Planning, Budget & Evaluation. 2. Education Consolidation and Improvement Act 3. Indian Schools Education Program 4. Management Information System.

★ 383 ★

Educational Fellowships Given by the Office of Indian Education, by Field

The number of fellows, total awards by field, and the average amount given per pupil is shown, FY 1990. 59 of the fellows were new, and 69 were continuing from the previous year.

Field	# fellows	Total award by field ($)	Av. per pupil award ($)
Business Administration	14	174,063	12,433
Clinical Psychology	9	118,149	13,128
Education	19	241,831	12,728
Engineering	20	173,729	8,686
Law	19	307,964	16,209
Medicine	23	357,953	15,563
Natural Resources	15	131,302	8,753

[Continued]

★ 383 ★

Educational Fellowships Given by the Office of Indian Education, by Field

[Continued]

Field	# fellows	Total award by field ($)	Av. per pupil award ($)
Psychology	9	95,663	10,629
Total	128	1,600,654	12,505

Source: *Toward the Year 2000: Listening to the Voice of Native America*, National Advisory Council on Indian Education, 17th Annual Report to the United States Congress, Fiscal Year 1990, p. 12. Primary source: Office of Indian Education, Fellowship Program.

★ 384 ★

Educational Personnel Recruitment

The dollars granted for the Educational Personnel Development Program[1] are shown, by state, FY 1990.

State	Amount ($)
California	
Humboldt State University, Arcata	190,654
Montana (3)	
Blackfeet Community College, Browning	67,628
Montana State University, Bozeman	283,540
Stone Child College, Box Elder	142,663
Montana total	493,831
New Mexico	
Ramah Navajo School Board, Inc., Pine Hill	49,902
Oklahoma (4)	
American Indian Research & Development, Norman	229,551
American Indian Resource Center, Talequah	156,879
Cross Cultural Education Center, Park Hill	247,627
Oklahoma total	634,057
Pennsylvania	
Pennsylvania State University, University Park	197,945
South Dakota (2)	
Oglala Lakota College, Kyle	213,188
Sinte Gleska College, Rosebud	101,487
South Dakota total	314,675
Wisconsin	
Menominee Indian Tribe of Wisconsin, Keshena	180,853

[Continued]

★ 384 ★

Educational Personnel Recruitment
[Continued]

State	Amount ($)
Wyoming	
Univ. of Wyoming, Student Educational Opp., Laramie	167,499
Educational Personnel Development total	2,229,416
Applications awarded	14

Source: Toward the Year 2000: Listening to the Voice of Native America, National Advisory Council on Indian Education, 17th Annual Report to the United States Congress, Fiscal Year 1990, pp. 43 & 44. Primary source: Office of Indian Education. *Notes:* 1. The Educational Personnel Development (EPD) Program provides training for American Indian/Alaska Native students for careers in education. The ultimate objective of the program is to train educational personnel to serve the Indian community. Under the authorizing legislation, awards are made primarily to universities for graduate programs in education. A majority of the projects offer graduate degrees in social work, educational administration, counseling, and doctoral degrees in educational development.

★ 385 ★

Educational Services for Indian Adults

Dollars granted under the Indian Education Act for special programs relating to adult education are shown, FY 1990.

State/ organization city	Grant amount ($)
Arizona (2)	
Cocopah Indian Tribe, Somerton	137,603
Native Americans for Community Action, Flagstaff	105,458
Arizona total	243,061
Colorado	
Denver Indian Center, Denver	134,134
Massachusetts	
Boston Indian Council, Boston	205,461
Michigan (3)	
Genesee Valley Indian Assn., Flint	50,824
Grand Traverse Band of Ottawa/Chipewa, Suttons Bay	169,886
Sault Ste. Marie Chippawa Indian, Sault Ste. Marie	77,688
Michigan total	298,398
Minnesota (4)	
American Indian OIC., Inc., Minneapolis	115,048
Heart of the Earth Survival School, Minneapolis	250,226
Migizi Communications, Inc., Minneapolis	218,725
Red School House, Inc., St. Paul	208,489

[Continued]

★ 385 ★

Educational Services for Indian Adults
[Continued]

State/ organization city	Grant amount ($)
Minnesota total	832,488
Nebraska	
Lincoln Indian Center, Lincoln	45,367
Montana (4)	
Dull Knife Memorial College	119,008
Fort Belknap Community Council, Harlem	128,389
Little Bighorn College, Crow Agency	138,255
Stonechild College, Box Elder	129,408
Montana total	515,060
New York (1)	
Seneca Nation of Indians, Irving	79,920
North Carolina (1)	
Cumberland Co. Assn. for Indian People, Fayetteville	143,021
Oklahoma (4)	
American Indian Resource Center, Tahlequah	128,337
Cherokee Nation of Oklahoma, Tahlequah	208,670
Miami Inter-Tribal Council, Miami	118,749
Sac and Fox Nation Education Dept., Stroud	156,870
Oklahoma total	611,870
South Dakota (2)	
Oglala Lakota College, Kyle	91,024
Sisseton-Wahpeton Sioux Tribe, Sisseton	89,377
South Dakota total	180,401
Utah	
Ute Indian Tribe, Ft. Duchesne	182,538
Washington (4)	
Nisqually Indian Tribe, Olympia	141,084
Seattle Indian Center, Seattle	143,686
Snoqualmie Tribal Learning Center, Seattle	134,991
United Indians of all Tribes, Seattle	186,520
Washington total	606,281

[Continued]

★ 385 ★

Educational Services for Indian Adults
[Continued]

State/ organization city	Grant amount ($)
Educational Services for Indian Adults total	4,078,000
Total Applications Awarded in FY 1990	30

Source: Toward the Year 2000: Listening to the Voice of Native America, National Advisory Council on Indian Education, 17th Annual Report to the United States Congress, Fiscal Year 1990, pp. 46 & 47. Primary source: Office of Indian Education.

Chapter 5
CULTURE AND TRADITION

Language

★ 386 ★

Percentage of American Indians With an American Indian Language as Their Mother Tongue, 1970

	Percent
All Indians	32
On reservations	58
By states and city (SMSA)[1]	
South Dakota	29
California	20
Los Angeles	24
San Francisco-Oakland	26
Washington	13
Seattle	14
Oklahoma	30
Oklahoma City	24
Tulsa	19
Arizona	76
Phoenix	34
Tucson	68
New Mexico	70
Albuquerque	39

Source: Russell Thornton, *American Indian Holocaust and Survival: A Population History Since 1492*, University of Oklahoma Press, 1987, p. 238. Published by permission. Primary source: U.S. Bureau of the Census, 1970 *Census of the Population, Subject Report, American Indians*. Final Report PC (2)- 1F. Washington, D.C.: U.S. Government Printing Office, p. 192. U.S. Department of Health, Education, and Welfare, *A Study of Selected Socio-Economic Characteristics of Ethnic Minorities Based on the 1970 Census*. Vol. 3, *American Indians*. Washington, D.C., p. 48. *Note:* 1. SMSA stands for Standard Metropolitan Statistical Area.

★ 387 ★

Language Spoken at Home and Ability to Speak English of Persons 5 to 17 Years Old, by Major Tribal Group, 1980: Abenaki - Pamunkey

Data are estimates based on a sample and are the most recent available.

Major Tribal Group	Total number of persons 5 to 17 years	Speak only English at home	Speak a language other than English at home	American Indian or Alaska Native language spoken at home			Other language spoken at home		
				Total	Speak English very well or well	Speak English not well or not at all	Total	Speak English very well or well	Speak English not well or not at all
All American Indians	413,614	318,263	95,351	79,476	67,138	12,338	15,875	13,911	1,964
Abenaki (n.e.c)	248	246	2	-	-	-	2	2	-
Alabama Coushatta[1]	303	172	131	124	93	31	7	7	-
Alaska Native (n.e.c.)	163	148	15	15	15	-	-	-	-
Alaskan Athabaskans	3,000	2,707	293	288	279	9	5	5	-
Aleut and Eskimo	161	161	-	-	-	-	-	-	-
Algonquian (n.e.c.)	475	461	14	7	7	-	7	7	-
Apache	10,867	6,070	4,797	4,239	3,887	352	558	504	54
Arapaho	1,236	1,169	67	50	50	-	17	17	-
Arikara	542	536	6	-	-	-	6	6	-
Assiniboine	1,241	1,136	105	91	82	9	14	8	6
Bannock	132	88	44	7	7	-	30	30	7
Blackfoot[1]	5,047	4,801	246	110	110	-	136	110	26
Brotherton	48	48	-	-	-	-	-	-	-
Caddo	542	534	8	8	8	-	-	-	-
Cahuilla	423	390	33	-	-	-	33	22	11
California tribes (n.e.c.)	175	160	15	13	6	7	2	2	-
Canadian and Latin American	1,983	1,373	610	5	5	-	605	531	74
Catawba	496	492	4	4	4	-	-	-	-
Cayuse	44	44	-	-	-	-	-	-	-
Chehalis	100	100	-	-	-	-	-	-	-
Chemakuan	125	70	55	55	55	-	-	-	-
Chemehuevi	127	120	7	-	-	-	7	7	-
Cherokee	55,667	52,486	3,181	1,881	1,735	146	1,300	1,185	115
Cheyenne	3,340	3,010	330	282	270	12	48	43	5
Chickahominy	232	223	9	-	-	-	9	9	-
Chickasaw	2,503	2,408	95	79	79	-	16	16	-
Chinook	445	397	48	36	36	-	12	5	7
Chippewa	23,686	22,339	1,347	1,059	1,012	47	288	263	25
Chitimacha	121	121	-	-	-	-	-	-	-
Choctaw	13,491	11,780	1,711	1,454	1,265	189	257	205	52
Chumash[1]	402	360	42	7	7	-	35	35	-
Clallam	217	217	-	-	-	-	-	-	-
Coeur d'Alene	254	243	11	-	-	-	11	-	11
Coharie	122	122	-	-	-	-	-	-	-
Colorado River	318	296	22	6	6	-	16	16	-
Colville	1,707	1,688	19	4	4	1	15	15	-
Comanche	2,553	2,374	179	85	85	-	94	87	7
Coos	59	59	-	-	-	-	-	-	-
Costanoan	164	102	62	-	-	-	62	44	18
Cowitz	251	251	-	-	-	-	-	-	-
Cree	2,269	1,950	319	309	278	31	10	10	-
Creek	7,940	7,696	244	218	180	38	26	26	-
Croatan	35	21	14	-	-	-	14	14	-
Crow	2,170	1,133	1,037	1,027	933	94	10	10	-
Cupeno	58	58	-	-	-	-	-	-	-
Delaware	1,233	1,168	45	8	8	-	37	37	-
Diegueno	445	403	42	16	16	-	26	21	5
Eastern tribes (n.e.c.)	733	699	34	6	6	-	28	21	7
Flathead	1,377	1,306	71	62	62	-	9	7	2
Fort Hall	170	134	36	30	30	-	6	6	-
Gabrieleno	584	478	86	5	5	-	81	81	-
Gros Ventres	609	597	12	-	-	-	12	12	-
Haida	421	382	39	31	31	-	8	8	-

[Continued]

★ 387 ★

Language Spoken at Home and Ability to Speak English of Persons 5 to 17 Years Old, by Major Tribal Group, 1980: Abenaki - Pamunkey

[Continued]

Major Tribal Group	Total number of persons 5 to 17 years	Speak only English at home	Speak a language other than English at home	American Indian or Alaska Native language spoken at home			Other language spoken at home		
				Total	Speak English very well or well	Speak English not well or not at all	Total	Speak English very well or well	Speak English not well or not at all
Haliwa	648	641	7	-	-	-	7	7	-
Hidatsa	500	452	48	39	39	-	9	9	-
Hitchiti	11	-	11	-	-	-	11	11	-
Hoopa	621	587	34	21	21	-	13	13	-
Houma	928	538	390	-	-	-	390	369	21
Iowa	276	269	7	-	-	-	7	-	7
Iroquois	10,562	9,843	719	554	540	14	165	151	14
Kalispel	54	54	-	-	-	-	-	-	-
Karok	639	594	45	27	27	-	18	18	-
Kaw	149	149	-	-	-	-	-	-	-
Kickapoo	662	587	75	75	63	12	-	-	-
Kiowa	2,450	2m367	83	69	60	9	14	14	-
Klamath	742	742	-	-	-	-	-	-	-
Konkow	49	49	-	-	-	-	-	-	-
Kootenai	75	60	15	15	15	-	-	-	-
Long Island	43	43	-	-	-	-	-	-	-
Luiseno	323	323	-	-	-	-	-	-	-
Lumbee[2]	8,903	8,852	51	3	3	-	48	37	11
Lummi[2]	1,169	1,159	30	19	19	-	11	11	-
Maidu	379	352	27	20	20	-	7	7	-
Makah	269	245	24	24	24	-	-	-	-
Maliseet	167	162	5	5	5	-	-	-	-
Mandan	351	358	23	8	8	-	15	15	-
Mattaponi	36	36	-	-	-	-	-	-	-
Menominee	2,095	2,044	51	34	34	-	17	17	-
Miami	769	753	16	8	8	-	8	8	-
Miccosukee[1]	27	11	16	16	16	-	-	-	-
Micmac[3]	340	314	26	20	20	-	6	6	-
Mission Indians	568	517	51	-	-	-	51	38	13
Miwok	530	509	21	5	5	-	16	16	-
Modoc	174	131	43	-	-	-	43	43	-
Mohegan	122	122	-	-	-	-	-	-	-
Mono	410	410	-	-	-	-	-	-	-
Nanticoke	192	190	2	-	-	-	2	2	-
Narragansett	636	636	-	-	-	-	-	-	-
Navajo	52,677	11,446	41,231	41,018	32,611	8,407	213	181	32
Nez Perce[1]	570	520	50	29	29	-	21	21	-
Nomalaki	82	82	-	-	-	-	-	-	-
Northwest tribes (n.e.c.)	46	27	19	6	6	-	13	-	13
Omaha	1,027	959	68	68	68	-	-	-	-
Oregon Athabaskan	172	172	-	-	-	-	-	-	-
Osage	1,656	1,595	61	17	17	-	44	44	-
Oto	438	433	5	5	5	-	-	-	-
Ottawa	2,185	2,026	159	134	115	19	25	23	2
Paiute[1]	2,785	2,524	261	222	216	6	39	39	-
Pamunkey	67	67	-	-	-	-	-	-	-

Source: U.S. Bureau of the Census, *1980 Census of Population, Volume 2, Subject Reports, Characteristics of American Indians, by Tribes and Selected Areas: 1980,* PC80-2-1C, Section 1: Tables I-II, issued September 1989, U.S. Department of Commerce, U.S. Government Printing Office, Washington, D.C., pp. 203-255. *Notes:* (N.E.C.) stands for not elsewhere classified. A dash (-) represents zero or a percent which rounds to less than 0.1. 1. Reporting and/or processing problems may have affected the data for this tribe. 2. Miscoding of entries of "Lummee," "Lummi," "Lumbee," or "Lumbi" may have affected the data for this tribe. 3. Any entry with the spelling "Micmac" was miscoded to Cheyenne River Sioux.

★ 388 ★

Language Spoken at Home and Ability to Speak English of Persons 5 to 17 Years Old, by Major Tribal Group, 1980: Papago - Yurok

Data are estimates based on a sample and are the most recent available.

Major Tribal Group	Total number of persons 5 to 17 years	Speak only English at home	Speak a language other than English at home	American Indian or Alaska Native language spoken at home			Other language spoken at home		
				Total	Speak English very well or well	Speak English not well or not at all	Total	Speak English very well or well	Speak English not well or not at all
Papago	4,285	1,845	2,440	2,277	1,994	283	163	144	19
Passamaquoddy	630	407	223	223	207	16	-	-	-
Pawnee	694	665	29	22	22	-	7	7	-
Penobscot	376	373	3	-	-	-	3	3	-
Peoria	260	260	-	-	-	-	-	-	-
Pequot	91	88	3	-	-	-	3	3	-
Pima	3,986	3,224	762	621	561	60	141	141	-
Piscataway	153	153	-	-	-	-	-	-	-
Pit River	475	434	41	37	28	9	4	-	4
Pomo	1,023	969	54	19	19	-	35	29	6
Ponca	630	580	50	40	35	5	10	10	-
Potawatomi	2,694	2,600	94	57	57	-	37	37	-
Powhatan	59	59	-	-	-	-	-	-	-
Pueblo[1]	12,815	5,311	7,504	6,924	6,023	901	580	556	24
Puget Sound Salish	1,975	1,885	90	77	77	-	13	4	9
Quapaw	222	222	-	-	-	-	-	-	-
Quinault	547	542	5	5	5	-	-	-	-
Rappahannock	51	51	-	-	-	-	-	-	-
Sac and Fox Mesquakie	993	877	116	112	86	26	4	4	-
Salinan	86	70	16	-	-	-	16	16	-
Schaghticoke	61	61	-	-	-	-	-	-	-
Seminole[1]	2,973	2,729	244	194	185	9	50	50	-
Serrano	52	52	-	-	-	-	-	-	-
Shasta	28	28	-	-	-	-	-	-	-
Shawnee	1,209	1,177	32	14	14	-	18	18	-
Shinnecock	206	201	5	-	-	-	5	5	-
Shoshone	2,928	2,342	586	494	455	39	92	67	25
Siletz	179	179	-	-	-	-	-	-	-
Sioux	25,529	21,608	3,921	3,643	3,472	171	278	289	9
Siuslaw	103	97	6	-	-	-	6	6	-
Spokane	501	480	21	14	14	-	7	7	-
Stockbridge	412	400	12	-	-	-	12	12	-
Tlingit	3,132	2,982	150	124	117	7	26	26	-
Tolowa	169	152	17	17	17	-	-	-	-
Tonkawa	81	81	-	-	-	-	-	-	-
Tsimshian	471	461	10	1	1	-	9	9	-
Umatilla	264	205	59	59	59	-	-	-	-
Ute	1,864	1,216	648	598	598	-	50	45	5
Wailaki[2]	198	188	8	8	-	8	-	-	-
Walla-Walla	84	84	-	-	-	-	-	-	-
Wampanoag	419	405	14	10	10	-	4	4	-
Warm Springs	493	442	51	47	47	-	4	-	4
Washo	318	292	26	21	21	-	5	5	-
Wichita	196	193	3	3	3	-	-	-	-
Winnebago	1,717	1,458	259	243	219	24	16	16	-
Wintu	713	696	17	5	5	-	12	12	-
Wiyot	70	70	-	-	-	-	-	-	-
Yakima	1,985	1,811	174	156	123	33	18	18	-
Yaqui	1,640	609	1,031	80	80	-	951	811	140
Yavapai Apache	48	33	15	15	15	-	-	-	-
Yokuts	512	482	30	15	15	-	15	15	-
Yuchi	59	59	-	-	-	-	-	-	-
Yuman	2,083	1,474	609	482	452	30	127	102	25
Yurok	830	797	33	17	17	-	16	16	-

[Continued]

★ 388 ★

Language Spoken at Home and Ability to Speak English of Persons 5 to 17 Years Old, by Major Tribal Group, 1980: Papago - Yurok

[Continued]

Major Tribal Group	Total number of persons 5 to 17 years	Speak only English at home	Speak a language other than English at home	American Indian or Alaska Native language spoken at home			Other language spoken at home		
				Total	Speak English very well or well	Speak English not well or not at all	Total	Speak English very well or well	Speak English not well or not at all
Other specified tribes (n.e.c.)	177	166	11	11	11	-	-	-	-
All other specified	43	38	5	5	5	-	-	-	-
Tribe not specified	9,072	7,554	1,518	521	448	73	997	819	178
Tribe not reported	72,137	56,887	15,250	8,188	6,976	1,212	7,062	6,091	971

Source: U.S. Bureau of the Census, *1980 Census of Population, Volume 2, Subject Reports, Characteristics of American Indians, by Tribes and Selected Areas: 1980,* PC80-2-1C, Section 1: Tables I-II, issued September 1989, U.S. Department of Commerce, U.S. Government Printing Office, Washington, D.C., pp. 203-255.
Notes: (N.E.C.) stands for not elsewhere classified. A dash (-) represents zero or a percent which rounds to less than 0.1. 1. Reporting and/or processing problems may have affected the data for this tribe. 2. Any Mohawk entry of "Ganienka" was miscoded to Wailaki.

★ 389 ★

Language Spoken at Home and Ability to Speak English of Persons 18 Years Old and Older, by Major Tribal Group, 1980: Abenaki - Pamunkey

Data are estimates based on a sample and are the most recent available.

Major Tribal Group	Total number of persons 18 years old and over	Speak only English at home	Speak a language other than English at home	American Indian or Alaska Native language spoken at home			Other language spoken at home		
				Total	Speak English very well or well	Speak English not well or not at all	Total	Speak English very well or well	Speak English not well or not at all
All American Indians	915,707	664,393	251,314	194,597	165,975	28,622	56,717	48,956	7,761
Abenaki (n.e.c)	508	433	75	14	14	-	61	46	15
Alabama Coushatta[1]	653	197	456	454	395	59	2	2	-
Alaska Native (n.e.c.)	371	339	32	8	8	-	24	24	-
Alaskan Athabaskans	5,874	4,133	1,741	1,675	1,485	190	66	60	6
Aleut and Eskimo	439	368	71	50	42	8	21	21	-
Algonquian (n.e.c.)	1,130	966	164	50	42	8	114	108	6
Apache	20,933	9,622	11,311	8,436	7,841	595	2,875	2,784	91
Arapaho	2,591	1,932	659	588	582	6	71	65	6
Arikara	845	720	125	102	102	-	23	23	-
Assiniboine	2,214	1,932	282	237	237	-	45	45	-
Bannock	289	161	128	48	39	9	80	80	-
Blackfoot[1]	15,070	13,337	1,733	885	837	48	848	799	49
Brotherton	122	122	-	-	-	-	-	-	-
Caddo	1,018	917	101	101	101	-	-	-	-
Cahuilla	681	538	143	24	24	-	119	112	7
California tribes (n.e.c.)	353	322	31	6	6	-	25	25	-
Canadian and Latin American	5,182	2,707	2,475	157	134	23	2,318	1,894	424
Catawba	763	746	17	5	5	-	12	12	-
Cayuse	98	68	30	30	23	7	-	-	-
Chehalis	154	150	4	4	4	-	-	-	-
Chemakuan	238	160	78	74	74	-	4	4	-
Chemehuevi	300	228	72	11	11	-	61	61	-
Cherokee	159,432	145,002	14,430	8,486	7,465	1,021	5,944	5,435	509
Cheyenne	5,374	3,572	1,802	1,653	1,536	117	149	143	6
Chickahominy	571	571	-	-	-	-	-	-	-
Chickasaw	6,974	6,325	649	553	514	39	96	80	16
Chinook	773	684	89	81	77	4	8	8	-
Chippewa	41,513	36,092	5,421	4,472	4,381	191	849	817	32

[Continued]

★ 389 ★

Language Spoken at Home and Ability to Speak English of Persons 18 Years Old and Older, by Major Tribal Group, 1980: Abenaki - Pamunkey

[Continued]

Major Tribal Group	Total number of persons 18 years old and over	Speak only English at home	Speak a language other than English at home	American Indian or Alaska Native language spoken at home			Other language spoken at home		
				Total	Speak English very well or well	Speak English not well or not at all	Total	Speak English very well or well	Speak English not well or not at all
Chitimacha	178	172	6	-	-	-	6	-	6
Choctaw	32,725	27,003	5,722	4,996	4,556	440	726	658	68
Chumash[1]	915	628	287	12	12	-	275	268	7
Clallam	531	507	24	24	24		-	-	-
Coeur d'Alene	339	291	48	24	24	-	24	14	10
Coharie	335	327	8	-	-	-	8	8	-
Colorado River	541	386	155	122	97	25	33	26	7
Colville	3,072	2,953	119	94	94	-	25	25	-
Comanche	5,656	4,661	995	614	612	2	381	360	21
Coos	58	49	9	5	5	-	4	-	4
Costanoan	296	201	95	-	-	-	95	88	7
Cowitz	626	622	4	2	2	-	2	2	-
Cree	3,683	2,839	844	696	631	65	148	126	22
Creek	17,580	14,650	2,930	2,613	2,461	152	317	310	7
Croatan	130	89	41	-	-	-	41	41	-
Crow	3,906	1,760	2,146	2,095	2,049	46	51	47	4
Cupeno	219	192	27	9	9	-	18	18	-
Delaware	3,597	3,398	199	94	94	-	105	98	7
Diegueno	819	608	211	97	87	10	114	114	-
Eastern tribes (n.e.c.)	1,681	1,543	138	12	5	7	126	98	28
Flathead	3,050	2,685	365	327	327	-	38	38	-
Fort Hall	233	159	74	74	74	-	-	-	-
Gabrieleno	1,099	663	436	6	6	-	430	408	22
Gros Ventres	1,212	1,066	126	112	104	8	14	14	-
Haida	681	755	126	100	100	-	26	26	-
Haliwa	1,215	1,202	13	-	-	-	13	13	-
Hidatsa	865	579	266	273	266	7	13	13	-
Hitchiti	10	8	2	2	2	-	-	-	-
Hoopa	1,121	992	129	102	95	7	27	27	-
Houma	1,406	398	1,008	17	17	-	991	889	102
Iowa	600	544	56	8	8	-	48	43	5
Iroquois	24,567	20,908	3,659	2,862	2,766	96	797	734	63
Kalispel	104	68	36	30	30	-	6	6	-
Karok	1,140	1,014	126	85	85	-	41	41	-
Kaw	479	456	23	11	11	-	12	12	-
Kickapoo	1,502	1,141	361	280	252	28	81	81	-
Kiowa	4,047	3,108	939	874	844	30	65	65	-
Klamath	1,137	1,070	67	60	60	-	7	7	-
Konkow	272	270	2	2	2	-	-	-	-
Kootenai	240	203	37	37	37	-	-	-	-
Long Island	253	226	27	-	-	-	27	27	-
Luiseno	772	650	122	26	26	-	96	87	9
Lumbee[2]	16,812	16,679	133	18	18	-	115	102	13
Lummi[2]	2,366	2,228	138	102	96	6	36	36	-
Maidu	694	540	154	126	116	10	28	28	-
Makah	615	559	56	48	27	21	8	8	-
Maliseet	301	180	121	119	119	-	2	2	-
Mandan	541	411	130	110	110	-	20	20	-
Mattaponi	87	87	-	-	-	-	-	-	-
Menominee	3,263	3,038	225	192	192	-	33	30	3
Miami	1,294	1,260	34	14	14	-	20	20	-
Miccosukee[1]	35	21	14	4	4	-	10	6	4
Micmac[3]	661	470	191	160	154	6	31	24	7
Mission Indians	1,768	1,297	471	60	60	-	411	382	29

[Continued]

647

★ 389 ★

Language Spoken at Home and Ability to Speak English of Persons 18 Years Old and Older, by Major Tribal Group, 1980: Abenaki - Pamunkey

[Continued]

Major Tribal Group	Total number of persons 18 years old and over	Speak only English at home	Speak a language other than English at home	American Indian or Alaska Native language spoken at home			Other language spoken at home		
				Total	Speak English very well or well	Speak English not well or not at all	Total	Speak English very well or well	Speak English not well or not at all
Miwok	1,352	1,262	90	47	47	-	43	43	-
Modoc	537	487	50	36	31	5	14	14	-
Mohegan	351	313	38	26	26	-	12	12	-
Mono	865	708	157	115	115	-	42	37	5
Nanticoke	753	728	25	7	7	-	18	10	8
Narragansett	1,233	1,186	47	14	14	-	33	33	-
Navajo	84,568	9,358	75,210	73,618	55,076	18,542	1,592	1,509	83
Nez Perce[1]	1,499	1,181	318	245	219	26	73	73	-
Nomalaki	130	130	-	-	-	-	-	-	-
Northwest tribes (n.e.c.)	221	145	76	28	25	3	48	33	15
Omaha	1,726	1,184	542	505	476	29	37	37	-
Oregon Athabaskan	401	382	19	12	12	-	7	7	-
Osage	4,613	4,330	283	144	144	-	139	137	2
Oto	915	828	87	59	51	8	28	28	-
Ottawa	3,763	3,170	593	490	452	38	103	95	8
Paiute[1]	5,619	4,418	1,201	1,047	975	72	154	154	-
Pamunkey	263	221	42	-	-	-	42	42	-

Source: U.S. Bureau of the Census, *1980 Census of Population, Volume 2, Subject Reports, Characteristics of American Indians, by Tribes and Selected Areas: 1980,* PC80-2-1C, Section 1: Tables I-II, issued September 1989, U.S. Department of Commerce, U.S. Government Printing Office, Washington, D.C., pp. 203-255. *Notes:* (N.E.C.) stands for not elsewhere classified. A dash (-) represents zero or a percent which rounds to less than 0.1. 1. Reporting and/or processing problems may have affected the data for this tribe. 2. Miscoding of entries of "Lummee," "Lummi," "Lumbee," or "Lumbi" may have affected the data for this tribe. 3. Any entry with the spelling "Micmac" was miscoded to Cheyenne River Sioux.

★ 390 ★

Language Spoken at Home and Ability to Speak English of Persons 18 Years Old and Older, by Major Tribal Group, 1980: Papago - Yurok

Data are estimates based on a sample and are the most recent available.

Major Tribal Group	Total number of persons 18 years old and over	Speak only English at home	Speak a language other than English at home	American Indian or Alaska Native language spoken at home			Other language spoken at home		
				Total	Speak English very well or well	Speak English not well or not at all	Total	Speak English very well or well	Speak English not well or not at all
Papago	7,601	1,470	6,131	5,793	4,638	1,155	338	305	33
Passamaquoddy	913	406	507	498	490	8	9	9	-
Pawnee	1,559	1,440	119	69	69	-	50	50	-
Penobscot	901	853	48	16	16	-	32	32	-
Peoria	343	330	13	13	6	7	-	-	-
Pequot	266	278	8	8	8	-	-	-	-
Pima	6,325	2,615	3,710	3,417	3,265	152	293	258	35
Piscataway	316	306	10	-	-	-	10	10	-
Pit River	655	678	77	60	50	10	17	10	7
Pomo	1,729	1,570	159	72	65	7	87	61	26
Ponca	1,140	857	247	229	217	12	18	18	-
Potawatomi	6,151	5,657	494	403	376	27	91	91	-
Powhatan	236	200	36	15	15	-	21	21	-
Pueblo[1]	24,748	5,990	18,758	17,278	16,171	1,107	1,480	1,389	111
Puget Sound Salish	3,810	3,504	306	200	184	16	106	106	-

[Continued]

★ 390 ★

Language Spoken at Home and Ability to Speak English of Persons 18 Years Old and Older, by Major Tribal Group, 1980: Papago - Yurok

[Continued]

Major Tribal Group	Total number of persons 18 years old and over	Speak only English at home	Speak a language other than English at home	American Indian or Alaska Native language spoken at home			Other language spoken at home		
				Total	Speak English very well or well	Speak English not well or not at all	Total	Speak English very well or well	Speak English not well or not at all
Quapaw	619	579	40	30	24	6	10	10	-
Quinault	959	921	38	32	32	-	6	6	-
Rappahannock	208	201	7	-	-	-	7	7	-
Sac and Fox Mesquakie	2,102	1,583	519	457	457	-	62	55	7
Salinan	196	150	48	-	-	-	48	48	-
Schaghticoke	111	106	5	-	-	-	5	5	-
Seminole[1]	6,347	4,670	1,677	1,409	1,242	167	268	251	17
Serrano	139	119	20	20	20	-	-	-	-
Shasta	248	242	6	-	-	-	6	6	-
Shawnee	2,806	2,486	320	226	214	12	94	81	13
Shinnecock	744	683	61	-	-	-	61	57	4
Shoshone	5,924	3,732	2,192	1,859	1,774	85	333	291	42
Siletz	435	421	14	6	6	-	8	-	8
Sioux	43,411	30,130	13,281	12,245	11,794	451	1,036	973	63
Siuslaw	218	215	3	3	3	-	-	-	-
Spokane	1,049	967	82	71	67	4	11	11	-
Stockbridge	1,005	949	56	11	11	-	45	45	-
Tlingit	5,363	4,335	1,028	976	936	40	52	46	6
Tolowa	199	152	47	45	45	-	2	2	-
Tonkawa	150	115	35	9	9	-	26	6	20
Tsimshian	964	858	106	106	102	4	-	-	-
Umatilla	553	491	62	57	57	-	5	5	-
Ute	3,220	1,405	1,815	1,601	1,485	116	214	206	8
Wailaki[2]	334	334	-	-	-	-	-	-	-
Walla-Walla	159	151	8	8	8	-	-	-	-
Wampanoag	898	866	32	26	26	-	6	6	-
Warm Springs	692	536	156	156	156	-	-	-	-
Washo	934	662	272	255	226	29	17	11	6
Wichita	436	390	46	38	38	-	8	8	-
Winnebago	2,819	1,933	886	875	844	31	11	9	2
Wintu	1,109	1,021	88	53	46	7	35	35	-
Wiyot	173	164	9	-	-	-	9	9	-
Yakima	3,699	3,008	691	579	561	18	112	94	18
Yaqui	2,944	564	2,380	480	323	157	1,900	1,632	268
Yavapai Apache	85	54	31	31	31	-	-	-	-
Yokuts	1,063	845	218	148	123	25	70	55	15
Yuchi	165	113	52	12	12	-	40	40	-
Yuman	3,809	1,832	1,977	1,590	1,403	187	387	325	62
Yurok	1,760	1,527	233	128	126	2	105	105	-
Other specified tribes (n.e.c.)	254	225	29	23	23	-	6	6	-
All other specified	85	68	17	11	11	-	6	6	-
Tribe not specified	21,557	16,897	4,660	1,580	1,403	177	3,080	2,582	498
Tribe not reported	204,367	161,498	42,869	18,934	16,345	2,589	23,935	19,186	4,749

Source: U.S. Bureau of the Census, *1980 Census of Population, Volume 2, Subject Reports, Characteristics of American Indians, by Tribes and Selected Areas: 1980,* PC80-2-1C, Section 1: Tables I-II, issued September 1989, U.S. Department of Commerce, U.S. Government Printing Office, Washington, D.C., pp. 203-255. *Notes:* (N.E.C.) stands for not elsewhere classified. A dash (-) represents zero or a percent which rounds to less than 0.1. 1. Reporting and/or processing problems may have affected the data for this tribe. 2. Any Mohawk entry of "Ganienka" was miscoded to Wailaki.

Employment

★ 391 ★

Traditional Occupations Held by Residents of Reservations, 1980: Acoma Pueblo - Isabella - I

Data are the latest available.

Identified reservation	Persons 16 years and over working in 1980 reference period	Traditional occupations										
		Tribal government occupations				Native healers	Sheep workers	Artists and performers				
		Total	Officials and administrators	Legislators	Judicial administrators			Total	Dancers	Drummers and singers	Painters	Potters
Total American Indian, Eskimo, and Aleut	89,697	834	563	200	71	31	276	290	6	3	70	211
Acoma Pueblo, NM	632	2	2	-	-	-	3	4	-	-	-	4
Agua Caliente, CA	-	-	-	-	-	-	-	-	-	-	-	-
Alabama-Coushatta, TX	234	-	-	-	-	-	-	10	1	1	1	6
Alamo, NM	204	-	-	-	-	-	-	-	-	-	-	-
Allegany, NY	381	2	2	-	-	-	-	-	-	-	-	-
Alturas Rancheria, CA	...	...	...	...	...	...	...	...	...	...	...	...
Annette Islands Reserve, AK	398	-	-	-	-	-	-	-	-	-	-	-
Augustine, CA	-	-	-	-	-	-	-	-	-	-	-	-
Bad River, WI	197	4	4	-	-	-	-	-	-	-	-	-
Barona Rancheria, CA	79	-	-	-	-	-	-	-	-	-	-	-
Bay Mills, MI	99	1	1	-	-	-	-	-	-	-	-	-
Benton Paiute, CA	...	...	...	...	...	...	...	...	...	...	...	...
Berry Creek Rancheria, CA	-	-	-	-	-	-	-	-	-	-	-	-
Big Bend Rancheria, CA	...	...	...	...	...	...	...	...	...	...	...	...
Big Cypress, FL	108	2	2	-	-	2	-	-	-	-	-	-
Big Lagoon Rancheria, CA	...	...	...	...	...	...	...	...	...	...	...	...
Big Pine Rancheria, CA	79	-	-	-	-	-	-	-	-	-	-	-
Bishop Rancheria, CA	276	1	1	-	-	-	-	-	-	-	-	-
Blackfeet, MT	1,665	16	7	7	2	-	2	-	-	-	-	-
Bois Forte (Nett Lake), MN	123	2	2	-	-	-	-	-	-	-	-	-
Bridgeport Colony, CA	23	-	-	-	-	-	-	-	-	-	-	-
Brighton, FL	132	-	-	-	-	-	-	-	-	-	-	-
Burns, Oregon	55	2	2	-	-	-	-	-	-	-	-	-
Cabazon, CA	...	...	...	...	...	...	...	...	...	...	...	...
Cachil Dehe Rancheria, CA	...	...	...	...	...	...	...	...	...	...	...	...
Cahuilla, CA	...	...	...	...	...	...	...	...	...	...	...	...
Campo, CA	17	-	-	-	-	-	-	-	-	-	-	-
Camp Verde, AZ	42	-	-	-	-	-	-	1	-	-	-	1
Canoncito, NM	156	1	1	-	-	-	-	-	-	-	-	-
Capitan Grande, CA	-	-	-	-	-	-	-	-	-	-	-	-
Carson Colony, NV	73	1	1	-	-	-	-	-	-	-	-	-
Catawba, SC	395	-	-	-	-	-	-	6	-	-	4	2
Cattaraugus, NY	559	3	2	-	1	-	-	-	-	-	-	-
Cedarville Rancheria, CA	...	...	...	...	...	...	...	...	...	...	...	...
Chehalis, WA	52	2	2	-	-	-	-	-	-	-	-	-
Chemehuevi, CA	...	...	...	...	...	...	...	...	...	...	...	...
Cheyenne River, SD	399	1	-	-	1	-	-	-	-	-	-	-
Chitimacha, LA	65	-	-	-	-	-	-	-	-	-	-	-
Cochiti Pueblo, NM	167	-	-	-	-	-	-	2	-	-	-	2
Cocopah, AZ	83	2	2	-	-	-	-	-	-	-	-	-
Coeur D'Alene, Idaho	146	-	-	-	-	-	-	-	-	-	-	-
Cold Springs Rancheria, CA	11	1	1	-	-	-	-	-	-	-	-	-
Colorado River, AZ-CA	650	8	5	-	3	-	-	1	-	-	-	1
Colville, WA	1,304	18	7	9	2	-	-	1	-	-	1	-
Cortina Rancheria, CA	...	...	...	...	...	...	...	...	...	...	...	...
Coushatta, LA	...	...	...	...	...	...	...	...	...	...	...	...
Coyote Valley Rancheria, CA	-	-	-	-	-	-	-	-	-	-	-	-
Crow, MT	1,039	16	12	-	3	-	-	-	-	-	-	-
Crow Creek, SD	322	2	-	2	-	-	-	1	-	-	1	-
Cuyapaipe, CA	...	...	...	...	...	...	...	...	...	...	...	...
Deer Creek, MN	...	...	...	...	...	...	...	...	...	...	...	...
Dresslerville Colony, NV	50	-	-	-	-	-	-	-	-	-	-	-
Dry Creek Rancheria, CA	4	-	-	-	-	-	-	-	-	-	-	-
Duck Valley, ID-NV	278	2	1	-	1	-	-	-	-	-	-	-
Duckwater, NV	40	-	-	-	-	-	-	-	-	-	-	-
Eastern Cherokee, NC	1,800	7	6	1	-	-	-	7	4	1	-	1
Eastern Pequot, CT	...	...	...	...	...	...	...	...	...	...	...	...
Ely Colony, NV	21	-	-	-	-	-	-	-	-	-	-	-

[Continued]

★ 391 ★

Traditional Occupations Held by Residents of Reservations, 1980: Acoma Pueblo - Isabella - I

[Continued]

Identified reservation	Persons 16 years and over working in 1980 reference period	Traditional occupations										
		Tribal government occupations				Native healers	Sheep workers	Artists and performers				
		Total	Officials and administrators	Legislators	Judicial administrators			Total	Dancers	Drummers and singers	Painters	Potters
Enterprise Rancheria, CA	...	...	...	...	...	...	...	...	...	...	...	...
Fallon Colony, NV	16	1	1	-	-	-	-	-	-	-	-	-
Fallon, NV	100	1	1	-	-	-	-	-	-	-	-	-
Flandreau, SD	60	-	-	-	-	-	-	-	-	-	-	-
Flathead, MT	1,216	10	9	1	-	-	-	-	-	-	-	-
Fond du Lac, MN	142	4	2	2	-	-	-	-	-	-	-	-
Fort Apache, AZ	1,837	2	1	1	-	-	-	1	-	-	1	-
Fort Belknap, MT	493	5	5	-	-	-	-	-	-	-	-	-
Fort Berthold, ND	740	14	9	5	-	-	-	-	-	-	-	-
Fort Bidwell, CA	19	-	-	-	-	-	-	-	-	-	-	-
Fort Hall, Idaho	675	5	3	2	-	-	-	-	-	-	-	-
Fort Independence, CA	16	-	-	-	-	-	-	-	-	-	-	-
Fort McDermitt, NV-OR	101	1	1	-	-	-	-	-	-	-	-	-
Fort McDowell, AZ	129	1	1	-	-	-	-	-	-	-	-	-
Fort Mojave, AZ-CA-NV	39	-	-	-	-	-	-	-	-	-	-	-
Fort Peck, MT	1,262	18	16	-	2	-	-	-	-	-	-	-
Fort Totten, ND	462	4	4	-	-	-	-	-	-	-	-	-
Fort Yuma, AZ-CA	339	3	3	-	-	-	-	-	-	-	-	-
Gila Bend, AZ	-	-	-	-	-	-	-	-	-	-	-	-
Gila River, AZ	1,762	19	12	4	4	1	-	-	-	-	-	-
Golden Hill, CT	...	...	...	...	...	...	...	...	...	...	...	...
Goshute, NV-UT	17	-	-	-	-	-	-	-	-	-	-	-
Grand Portage, MN	88	-	-	-	-	-	-	-	-	-	-	-
Grindstone Creek Rancheria, CA	20	-	-	-	-	-	-	-	-	-	-	-
Hannahville Community, MI	76	2	2	-	-	-	-	-	-	-	-	-
Hassanamisco, MA	...	...	...	...	...	...	...	...	...	...	...	...
Havasupai, AZ	86	1	1	-	-	-	-	-	-	-	-	-
Hoh, WA	14	-	-	-	-	-	-	-	-	-	-	-
Hollywood, FL	197	7	7	-	-	-	-	-	-	-	-	-
Hoopa Valley, CA	441	1	1	-	-	-	2	-	-	-	-	-
Hoopa Valley Extension, CA	100	1	-	-	1	-	-	-	-	-	-	-
Hopi, AZ	1,435	7	7	-	-	-	-	49	-	-	3	46
Hopland Rancheria, CA	-	-	-	-	2	-	-	-	-	-	-	-
Hualapai, AZ	236	3	1	-	2	-	-	-	-	-	-	-
Inaja-Cosmit, CA	-	-	-	-	-	-	-	-	-	-	-	-
Indian Township, ME	104	1	1	-	-	-	-	-	-	-	-	-
Iowa, KS-NE	15	-	-	-	-	-	-	-	-	-	-	-
Isabella, MI	146	-	-	-	-	-	-	-	-	-	-	-

Source: U.S. Bureau of the Census, Subject Reports, PC80-2-1D, Part II, *American Indians, Eskimos, and Aleuts on Identified Reservations and in the Historic Areas of Oklahoma (Excluding Urbanized Areas)*, U.S. Government Printing Office, Washington, D.C., 1986, pp. 482-520. *Notes:* A dash (-) represents zero or a percent which rounds to less than 0.1. Also, a dash (-) is used because the number of supplementary questionnaires for the areas was insufficient to produce reliable estimates. Three dots (...) means not applicable, or that the data are being withheld to avoid disclosure of information for individuals.

★ 392 ★

Traditional Occupations Held by Residents of Reservations, 1980: Acoma Pueblo - Isabella - II

Data are the latest available.

Identified reservation	Jewelers	Traditional occupations										
		Handworking occupations										
		Total	Basket makers	Beaders	Bustle makers	Carvers	Fan makers	Moccasin makers	Quilters	Rattle makers	Weavers	Other handworking occupations
American Indian, Eskimo, and Aleut	1,323	1,365	156	193	2	54	2	20	47	-	806	85
Acoma Pueblo, NM	-	-	-	-	-	-	-	-	-	-	-	-

[Continued]

651

★ 392 ★

Traditional Occupations Held by Residents of Reservations, 1980: Acoma Pueblo - Isabella - II

[Continued]

Identified reservation	Jewelers	Traditional occupations										
		Handworking occupations										
		Total	Basket makers	Beaders	Bustle makers	Carvers	Fan makers	Moccasin makers	Quilters	Rattle makers	Weavers	Other handworking occupations
Agua Caliente, CA	-	-	-	-	-	-	-	-	-	-	-	-
Alabama-Coushatta, TX	-	1	-	1	-	-	-	-	-	-	-	-
Alamo, NM	9	9	-	-	-	-	-	-	1	-	6	2
Allegany, NY	-	3	-	3	-	-	-	-	-	-	-	-
Alturas Rancheria, CA	...	...	...	...	...	...	...	...	...	...	...	...
Annette Islands Reserve, AK	-	-	-	-	-	-	-	-	-	-	-	-
Augustine, CA	-	-	-	-	-	-	-	-	-	-	-	-
Bad River, WI	-	-	-	-	-	-	-	-	-	-	-	-
Barona Rancheria, CA	-	-	-	-	-	-	-	-	-	-	-	-
Bay Mills, MI	-	-	-	-	-	-	-	-	-	-	-	-
Benton Paiute, CA	...	...	...	...	...	...	...	...	...	...	...	...
Berry Creek Rancheria, CA	-	-	-	-	-	-	-	-	-	-	-	-
Big Bend Rancheria, CA	...	...	...	...	...	...	...	...	...	...	...	...
Big Cypress, FL	-	1	-	-	-	-	-	-	-	-	-	1
Big Lagoon Rancheria, CA	...	...	...	...	...	...	...	...	...	...	...	...
Big Pine Rancheria, CA	-	-	-	-	-	-	-	-	-	-	...	-
Bishop Rancheria, CA	2	-	-	-	-	-	-	-	-	-	-	-
Blackfeet, MT	-	8	2	3	-	2	-	-	2	-	-	-
Bois Forte (Nett Lake), MN	-	-	-	-	-	-	-	-	-	-	-	-
Bridgeport Colony, CA	-	-	-	-	-	-	-	-	-	-	-	-
Brighton, FL	1	-	-	-	-	-	-	-	-	-	-	-
Burns, Oregon	-	-	-	-	-	-	-	-	-	-	-	-
Cabazon, CA	...	...	...	...	...	...	...	...	...	...	...	...
Cachil Dehe Rancheria, CA	...	...	...	...	...	...	...	...	...	...	...	...
Cahuilla, CA	...	...	...	...	...	...	...	...	...	...	...	...
Campo, CA	-	-	-	-	-	-	-	-	-	-	...	-
Camp Verde, AZ	-	2	-	-	-	-	-	-	-	-	-	-
Canoncito, NM	9	2	-	-	-	-	-	-	-	-	-	2
Capitan Grande, CA	-	-	-	-	-	-	-	-	-	-	-	-
Carson Colony, NV	-	-	-	-	-	-	-	-	-	-	-	-
Catawba, SC	-	-	-	-	-	-	-	-	-	-	-	-
Cattaraugus, NY	-	-	-	-	-	-	-	-	-	-	-	-
Cedarville Rancheria, CA	...	...	...	...	...	...	...	...	...	...	...	...
Chehalis, WA	-	1	-	1	-	-	-	-	-	-	-	-
Chemehuevi, CA	...	...	...	...	...	...	...	...	...	...	...	...
Cheyenne River, SD	-	2	-	2	-	-	-	-	-	-	-	-
Chitimacha, LA	-	-	-	-	-	-	-	-	-	-	-	-
Cochiti Pueblo, NM	6	-	-	-	-	-	-	-	-	-	-	-
Cocopah, AZ	-	-	-	-	-	-	-	-	-	-	-	-
Coeur D'Alene, Idaho	-	-	-	-	-	-	-	-	-	-	-	-
Cold Springs Rancheria, CA	-	-	-	-	-	-	-	-	-	-	-	-
Colorado River, AZ-CA	2	2	-	-	-	-	-	-	-	-	2	-
Colville, WA	2	6	-	4	-	-	-	-	-	-	2	-
Cortina Rancheria, CA	...	...	...	...	...	...	...	...	...	...	...	...
Coushatta, LA	...	...	...	...	...	...	...	...	...	...	...	...
Coyote Valley Rancheria, CA	-	-	-	-	-	-	-	-	-	-	-	-
Crow, MT	-	5	-	5	-	-	-	-	-	-	-	-
Crow Creek, SD	-	4	-	1	-	-	-	-	3	-	-	-
Cuyapaipe, CA	...	...	...	...	...	...	...	...	...	...	...	...
Deer Creek, MN	...	...	...	...	...	...	...	...	...	...	...	...
Dresslerville Colony, NV	-	-	-	-	-	-	-	-	-	-	-	-
Dry Creek Rancheria, CA	-	-	-	-	-	-	-	-	-	-	-	-
Duck Valley, ID-NV	-	-	-	-	-	-	-	-	-	-	-	-
Duckwater, NV	-	-	-	-	-	-	-	-	-	-	-	-
Eastern Cherokee, NC	2	61	20	6	-	8	2	4	6	-	-	15
Eastern Pequot, CT	...	...	...	...	...	...	...	...	...	...	...	...
Ely Colony, NV	-	-	-	-	-	-	-	-	-	-	...	...
Enterprise Rancheria, CA	...	...	...	...	...	...	...	...	...	...	...	...
Fallon Colony, NV	-	1	-	1	-	-	-	-	-	-	-	-
Fallon, NV	-	-	-	-	-	-	-	-	-	-	-	-

[Continued]

★ 392 ★

Traditional Occupations Held by Residents of Reservations, 1980: Acoma Pueblo - Isabella - II

[Continued]

| Identified reservation | Jewelers | Traditional occupations | | | | | | | | | | |
| | | Handworking occupations | | | | | | | | | | |
		Total	Basket makers	Beaders	Bustle makers	Carvers	Fan makers	Moccasin makers	Quilters	Rattle makers	Weavers	Other handworking occupations
Flandreau, SD	-	-	-	-	-	-	-	-	-	-	-	-
Flathead, MT	-	9	-	5	-	4	-	-	-	-	-	-
Fond du Lac, MN	-	3	-	-	-	-	-	-	-	-	1	2
Fort Apache, AZ	1	12	1	-	-	1	-	-	2	-	8	-
Fort Belknap, MT	-	1	-	-	-	-	-	-	1	-	-	-
Fort Berthold, ND	-	20	3	14	-	-	-	2	2	-	-	-
Fort Bidwell, CA	-	-	-	-	-	-	-	-	-	-	-	-
Fort Hall, Idaho	4	13	1	7	-	-	-	-	2	-	-	3
Fort Independence, CA	-	-	-	-	-	-	-	-	-	-	-	-
Fort McDermitt, NV-OR	-	-	-	-	-	-	-	-	-	-	-	-
Fort McDowell, AZ	1	3	-	-	-	1	-	-	-	-	-	2
Fort Mojave, AZ-CA-NV	-	-	-	-	-	-	-	-	-	-	-	-
Fort Peck, MT	-	6	1	3	-	-	-	-	1	-	-	-
Fort Totten, ND	-	5	-	5	-	-	-	-	-	-	-	-
Fort Yuma, AZ-CA	-	1	-	1	-	-	-	-	-	-	-	-
Gila Bend, AZ	-	-	-	-	-	-	-	-	-	-	-	-
Gila River, AZ	3	4	3	-	-	-	-	-	-	-	2	-
Golden Hill, CT	...	...	...	...	...	...	...	...	...	...	...	...
Goshute, NV-UT	-	-	-	-	-	-	-	-	-	-	-	-
Grand Portage, MN	-	2	-	2	-	-	-	-	-	-	-	-
Grindstone Creek Rancheria, CA	-	-	-	-	-	-	-	-	-	-	-	-
Hannahville Community, MI	-	-	-	-	-	-	-	-	-	-	-	-
Hassanamisco, MA	...	...	...	...	...	...	...	...	...	...	...	...
Havasupai, AZ	-	-	-	-	-	-	-	-	-	-	-	-
Hoh, WA	-	-	-	-	-	-	-	-	-	-	-	-
Hollywood, FL	-	6	-	3	-	-	-	-	-	-	1	3
Hoopa Valley, CA	2	-	-	-	-	-	-	-	-	-	-	-
Hoopa Valley Extension, CA	-	-	-	-	-	-	-	-	-	-	-	-
Hopi, AZ	26	69	3	-	-	11	-	-	-	-	34	20
Hopland Rancheria, CA	-	-	-	-	-	-	-	-	-	-	-	-
Hualapai, AZ	-	1	-	-	-	1	-	-	-	-	-	-
Inaja-Cosmit, CA	-	-	-	-	-	-	-	-	-	-	-	-
Indian Township, ME	-	-	-	-	-	-	-	-	-	-	-	-
Iowa, KS-NE	-	-	-	-	-	-	-	-	-	-	-	-
Isabella, MI	-	7	2	5	-	-	-	-	-	-	-	-

Source: U.S. Bureau of the Census, Subject Reports, PC80-2-1D, Part II, *American Indians, Eskimos, and Aleuts on Identified Reservations and in the Historic Areas of Oklahoma (Excluding Urbanized Areas)*, U.S. Government Printing Office, Washington, D.C., 1986, pp. 482-520. *Notes:* A dash (-) represents zero or a percent which rounds to less than 0.1. Also, a dash (-) is used because the number of supplementary questionnaires for the areas was insufficient to produce reliable estimates. Three dots (...) means not applicable, or that the data are being withheld to avoid disclosure of information for individuals.

★ 393 ★

Traditional Occupations Held by Residents of Reservations, 1980: Isleta - Santa Clara Pueblo - I

Data are the latest available.

Identified reservation	Persons 16 years and over working in 1980 reference period	Traditional occupations										
		Tribal governmental occupations				Native healers	Sheep workers	Artists and performers				
		Total	Officials and administrators	Legislators	Judicial administrators			Total	Dancers	Drummers and singers	Painters	Potters
Isleta Pueblo, NM	874	10	10	-	-	-	-	7	-	-	3	3
Jackson Rancheria, CA	...	...	...	...	...	...	...	...	...	...	...	...
Jemez Pueblo, NM	383	5	5	-	-	-	-	3	-	-	-	3
Jicarilla Apache, NM	656	1	-	-	1	-	4	-	-	-	-	-
Kaibab, AZ	42	3	3	-	-	-	-	-	-	-	-	-
Kalispel, WA	36	1	1	-	-	-	-	-	-	-	-	-
Kickapoo, KS	108	-	-	-	-	-	-	1	-	-	1	-
Kootenai, ID	-	-	-	-	-	-	-	-	-	-	-	-
Lac Courte Oreilles, WI	331	13	7	5	1	-	-	-	-	-	-	-
Lac du Flambeau, WI	322	4	4	-	-	-	-	-	-	-	-	-
Laguna Pueblo, NM	1,300	2	1	-	1	-	1	5	-	-	-	5
La Jolla, CA	43	-	-	-	-	-	-	-	-	-	-	-
L'Anse, MI	177	2	2	-	-	-	-	-	-	-	-	-
La Posta, CA	...	...	...	...	...	...	...	...	...	...	...	...
Las Vegas Colony, NV	35	-	-	-	-	-	-	-	-	-	-	-
Laytonville Rancheria, CA	24	-	-	-	-	-	-	-	-	-	-	-
Leech Lake, MN	728	11	11	-	-	-	-	-	-	-	-	-
Likely Rancheria, CA	-	-	-	-	-	-	-	-	-	-	-	-
Lone Pine Rancheria, CA	49	-	-	-	-	-	-	-	-	-	-	-
Lookout Rancheria, CA	...	...	...	...	...	...	...	...	...	...	...	...
Los Coyotes, CA	11	-	-	-	-	-	-	-	-	-	-	-
Lovelock Colony, NV	34	-	-	-	-	-	-	-	-	-	-	-
Lower Brule, SD	243	4	2	2	-	-	-	-	-	-	-	-
Lower Elwah, WA	17	-	-	-	-	-	-	-	-	-	-	-
Lower Sioux Community, MN	25	-	-	-	-	-	-	-	-	-	-	-
Lummi, WA	347	6	6	-	-	-	-	-	-	-	-	-
Makah, WA	318	10	8	2	-	-	-	-	-	-	-	-
Manchester Rancheria, CA	15	-	-	-	-	-	-	-	-	-	-	-
Manzanita, CA	...	...	...	...	...	...	...	...	...	...	...	...
Maricopa, AZ	95	1	1	-	-	-	-	-	-	-	-	-
Mattaponi, VA	23	-	-	-	-	-	-	-	-	-	-	-
Menominee, WI	699	16	13	1	2	-	-	-	-	-	-	-
Mesa Grande, CA	-	-	-	-	-	-	-	-	-	-	-	-
Mescalero Apache, NM	548	8	-	-	8	-	-	2	-	-	2	-
Miccosukee, Florida	134	-	-	-	-	-	-	-	-	-	-	-
Middletown Rancheria, CA	9	-	-	-	-	-	-	-	-	-	-	-
Mille Lacs, MN	-	-	-	-	-	-	-	-	-	-	-	-
Mississippi Choctaw Reservation, MS	909	11	8	1	1	-	-	-	-	-	-	-
Moapa River, NV	47	4	4	-	-	-	-	-	-	-	-	-
Montgomery Creek Rancheria, CA	...	...	...	...	...	...	...	...	...	...	...	...
Morongo, CA	96	-	-	-	-	-	-	-	-	-	-	-
Muckleshoot, WA	98	3	1	2	-	-	-	-	-	-	-	-
Nambe Pueblo, NM	82	4	4	-	-	-	-	1	-	-	-	1
Navajo, AZ-NM-UT	22,636	116	55	57	4	28	209	25	-	-	22	2
Nez Perce, ID	469	13	11	1	1	-	-	1	-	-	1	-
Nisqually, WA	13	-	-	-	-	-	-	-	-	-	-	-
Nooksack, WA	-	-	-	-	-	-	-	-	-	-	-	-
Northern Cheyenne, MT	839	16	5	10	1	-	-	-	-	-	-	-
Oil Springs, NY	-	-	-	-	-	-	-	-	-	-	-	-
Omaha, IO-NE	339	1	-	1	-	-	-	-	-	-	-	-
Oneida, WI	608	11	8	3	-	-	-	2	-	-	1	1
Onondaga, NY	-	-	-	-	-	-	-	-	-	-	-	-
Ontonagon, MI	-	-	-	-	-	-	-	-	-	-	-	-
Osage, OK	1,755	7	7	-	-	-	-	2	-	-	2	-
Ozette, WA	...	...	...	...	...	...	...	...	...	...	...	...
Pala, CA	142	-	-	-	-	-	-	-	-	-	-	-
Pamunkey, VA	19	1	1	-	-	-	-	3	-	-	-	3
Papago, AZ	1,607	6	6	-	-	-	1	2	-	-	1	1
Pascua Yaqui, AZ	110	3	3	-	-	-	-	-	-	-	-	-
Pauma, CA	26	-	-	-	-	-	-	-	-	-	-	-
Payson Comm. of Yavapai-Apache, AZ	-	-	-	-	-	-	-	-	-	-	-	-
Pechanga, CA	36	-	-	-	-	-	-	-	-	-	-	-
Penobscot, MA	127	7	6	-	1	-	-	-	-	-	-	-
Picuris Pueblo, NM	52	-	-	-	-	-	-	-	-	-	-	-
Pine Creek, MI	...	...	...	...	...	...	...	...	...	...	...	...
Pine Ridge, SD	2,482	56	22	28	6	-	-	3	-	-	1	1
Pleasant Point, MA	101	3	3	-	-	-	-	2	-	-	-	2
Pojoaque Pueblo, NM	41	-	-	-	-	-	-	-	-	-	-	-
Poospatuck, NY	13	-	-	-	-	-	-	-	-	-	-	-

[Continued]

★ 393 ★

Traditional Occupations Held by Residents of Reservations, 1980: Isleta - Santa Clara Pueblo - I

[Continued]

Identified reservation	Persons 16 years and over working in 1980 reference period	Traditional occupations										
		Tribal governmental occupations				Native healers	Sheep workers	Artists and performers				
		Total	Officials and administrators	Legislators	Judicial administrators			Total	Dancers	Drummers and singers	Painters	Potters
Port Gamble, WA	97	-	-	-	-	-	-	-	-	-	-	-
Port Madison, WA	56	-	-	-	-	-	-	2	-	-	-	2
Potawatomi, WI	61	4	4	-	-	-	-	-	-	-	-	-
Pottawatomi, KS	128	-	-	-	-	-	-	-	-	-	-	-
Prairie Island Community, MN	28	1	1	-	-	-	-	-	-	-	-	-
Puyallup, WA	237	2	2	-	-	-	-	-	-	-	-	-
Pyramid Lake, NV	226	2	2	-	-	-	-	-	-	-	-	-
Quileute, WA	69	-	-	-	-	-	-	-	-	-	-	-
Quinault, WA	324	4	3	-	1	-	-	-	-	-	-	-
Ramah Community, NM	335	2	1	1	-	-	11	1	-	-	1	-
Ramona, CA	-	-	-	-	-	-	-	-	-	-	-	-
Red Cliff, WI	149	4	4	-	-	-	-	-	-	-	-	-
Red Lake, MN	707	4	2	-	2	-	-	1	-	-	1	-
Reno-Sparks Colony, NV	186	1	1	-	-	-	-	2	-	-	2	-
Resighini Rancheria, CA	...	...	...	...	...	...	...	...	...	...	...	...
Rincon, CA	91	-	-	-	-	-	-	-	-	-	-	-
Roaring Creek Rancheria, CA	...	...	...	...	...	...	...	...	...	...	...	...
Rocky Boy's, MT	391	11	6	3	1	-	-	-	-	-	-	-
Rosebud, SD	1,279	11	9	2	-	-	-	3	-	-	-	3
Round Valley, CA	142	-	-	-	-	-	-	-	-	-	-	-
Rumsey Rancheria, CA	...	...	...	...	...	...	...	...	...	...	...	...
Sac and Fox, Iowa	141	-	-	-	-	-	-	-	-	-	-	-
Sac and Fox, KS-NE	...	-	...	...	...	...	...	...	...	...	...	...
St. Croix, WI	116	13	10	2	-	-	-	-	-	-	-	-
St. Regis Mohawk, NY	491	9	9	-	-	-	-	-	-	-	-	-
Salt River, AZ	880	1	-	1	-	-	-	4	-	-	4	-
San Carlos, AZ	1,442	14	7	5	2	-	-	1	-	-	1	-
Sandia Pueblo, NM	86	2	1	1	-	-	-	-	-	-	-	-
Sandy Lake, MN	-	-	-	-	-	-	-	-	-	-	-	-
San Felipe Pueblo, NM	469	4	4	-	-	-	-	1	-	-	1	-
San Ildefonso Pueblo, NM	197	-	-	-	-	-	-	23	-	-	-	23
San Juan Pueblo, NM	287	-	-	-	-	-	-	3	-	-	-	3
San Manuel, CA	-	-	-	-	-	-	-	-	-	-	-	-
San Pasqual, CA	34	-	-	-	-	-	-	-	-	-	-	-
Santa Ana Pueblo, NM	184	4	4	-	-	-	-	-	-	-	-	-
Santa Clara Pueblo, NM	706	8	8	-	-	-	-	64	-	-	3	61

Source: U.S. Bureau of the Census, Subject Reports, PC80-2-1D, Part II, *American Indians, Eskimos, and Aleuts on Identified Reservations and in the Historic Areas of Oklahoma (Excluding Urbanized Areas)*, U.S. Government Printing Office, Washington, D.C., 1986, pp. 482-520. *Notes:* A dash (-) represents zero or a percent which rounds to less than 0.1. Also, a dash (-) is used because the number of supplementary questionnaires for the areas was insufficient to produce reliable estimates. Three dots (...) means not applicable, or that the data are being withheld to avoid disclosure of information for individuals.

★ 394 ★

Traditional Occupations Held by Residents of Reservations, 1980: Isleta - Santa Clara Pueblo - II

Data are the latest available.

Identified reservation	Jewelers	Traditional occupations										
		Handworking occupations										
		Total	Basket makers	beaders	Bustle makers	Carvers	Fan makers	Moccasin makers	Quilters	Rattle makers	Weavers	Other handworking occupations
Isleta Pueblo, NM	6	1	-	-	-	-	-	-	-	-	1	-
Jackson Rancheria, CA	...	...	...	...	...	...	...	...	...	...	...	...
Jemez Pueblo, NM	3	-	-	-	-	-	-	-	-	-	-	-
Jicarilla Apache, NM	-	17	6	5	-	-	-	-	-	-	5	1
Kaibab, AZ	-	-	-	-	-	-	-	-	-	-	-	-
Kalispel, WA	-	-	-	-	-	-	-	-	-	-	-	-

[Continued]

★ 394 ★

Traditional Occupations Held by Residents of Reservations, 1980: Isleta - Santa Clara Pueblo - II

[Continued]

Identified reservation	Jewelers	Traditional occupations										
		Handworking occupations										
		Total	Basket makers	beaders	Bustle makers	Carvers	Fan makers	Moccasin makers	Quilters	Rattle makers	Weavers	Other handworking occupations
Kickapoo, KS	4	-	-	-	-	-	-	-	-	-	4	-
Kootenai, ID	-	-	-	-	-	-	-	-	-	-	-	-
Lac Courte Oreilles, WI	-	-	-	-	-	-	-	-	-	-	-	-
Lac du Flambeau, WI	-	-	-	-	-	-	-	-	-	-	-	-
Laguna Pueblo, NM	2	1	-	-	-	-	-	-	-	-	1	-
La Jolla, CA	-	-	-	-	-	-	-	-	-	-	-	-
L'Anse, MI	-	3	-	1	-	-	-	-	-	-	1	-
La Posta, CA	...	...	...	...	...	...	...	...	...	...	...	...
Las Vegas Colony, NV	-	-	-	-	-	-	-	-	-	-	-	-
Laytonville Rancheria, CA	-	-	-	-	-	-	-	-	-	-	-	-
Leech Lake, MN	-	1	-	-	-	-	-	-	-	-	1	-
Likely Rancheria, CA	-	-	-	-	-	-	-	-	-	-	-	-
Lone Pine Rancheria, CA	-	-	-	-	-	-	-	-	-	-	-	-
Lookout Rancheria, CA	...	...	...	...	...	...	...	...	...	...	...	...
Los Coyotes, CA	-	-	-	-	-	-	-	-	-	-	-	-
Lovelock Colony, NV	-	-	-	-	-	-	-	-	-	-	-	-
Lower Brule, SD	-	-	-	-	-	-	-	-	-	-	-	-
Lower Elwah, WA	-	-	-	-	-	-	-	-	-	-	-	-
Lower Sioux Community, MN	-	-	-	-	-	-	-	-	-	-	-	-
Lummi, WA	-	1	-	-	-	-	-	-	-	-	-	1
Makah, WA	1	6	2	-	-	3	-	-	-	-	-	-
Manchester Rancheria, CA	-	-	-	-	-	-	-	-	-	-	-	-
Manzanita, CA	...	...	...	...	...	...	...	...	...	...	...	...
Maricopa, AZ	-	-	-	-	-	-	-	-	-	-	-	-
Mattaponi, VA	-	-	-	-	-	-	-	-	-	-	-	-
Menominee, WI	-	3	-	1	-	-	-	-	-	-	-	1
Mesa Grande, CA	-	-	-	-	-	-	-	-	-	-	-	-
Mescalero Apache, NM	1	4	-	-	-	-	-	-	3	-	1	-
Miccosukee, Florida	1	3	-	-	1	1	-	-	-	-	-	1
Middletown Rancheria, CA	-	-	-	-	-	-	-	-	-	-	-	-
Mille Lacs, MN	-	-	-	-	-	-	-	-	-	-	-	-
Mississippi Choctaw Reservation, MS	-	2	-	1	-	-	-	-	1	-	-	-
Moapa River, NV	-	-	-	-	-	-	-	-	-	-	-	-
Montgomery Creek Rancheria, CA	...	...	...	...	...	...	...	...	...	...	...	...
Morongo, CA	-	-	-	-	-	-	-	-	-	-	-	-
Muckleshoot, WA	-	-	-	-	-	-	-	-	-	-	-	-
Nambe Pueblo, NM	-	-	-	-	-	-	-	-	-	-	-	-
Navajo, AZ-NM-UT	121	775	28	16	1	3	-	-	2	-	719	6
Nez Perce, ID	-	3	-	3	-	-	-	-	-	-	-	-
Nisqually, WA	-	1	-	1	-	-	-	-	-	-	-	-
Nooksack, WA	-	-	-	-	-	-	-	-	-	-	-	-
Northern Cheyenne, MT	-	5	-	5	-	-	-	-	-	-	-	-
Oil Springs, NY	-	-	-	-	-	-	-	-	-	-	-	-
Omaha, IO-NE	-	-	-	-	-	-	-	-	-	-	-	-
Oneida, WI	1	1	-	-	-	-	-	-	-	-	-	1
Onondaga, NY	-	-	-	-	-	-	-	-	-	-	-	-
Ontonagon, MI	-	-	-	-	-	-	-	-	-	-	-	-
Osage, OK	-	4	-	1	-	1	-	-	-	-	-	1
Ozette, WA	...	...	...	...	...	...	...	...	...	...	...	...
Pala, CA	-	-	-	-	-	-	-	-	-	-	-	-
Pamunkey, VA	-	-	-	-	-	-	-	-	-	-	-	-
Papago, AZ	-	55	54	-	-	-	-	-	-	-	1	-
Pascua Yaqui, AZ	-	-	-	-	-	-	-	-	-	-	-	-
Pauma, CA	-	1	-	1	-	-	-	-	-	-	-	-
Payson Comm. of Yavapai-Apache, AZ	-	-	-	-	-	-	-	-	-	-	-	-
Pechanga, CA	-	-	-	-	-	-	-	-	-	-	-	-
Penobscot, MA	-	2	1	-	-	1	-	-	-	-	-	-
Picuris Pueblo, NM	-	-	-	-	-	-	-	-	-	-	-	-
Pine Creek, MI	...	...	...	...	...	...	...	...	...	...	...	...
Pine Ridge, SD	3	30	-	11	-	-	-	9	5	-	-	5

[Continued]

★ 394 ★

Traditional Occupations Held by Residents of Reservations, 1980: Isleta - Santa Clara Pueblo - II
[Continued]

Identified reservation	Jewelers	Traditional occupations / Handworking occupations										
		Total	Basket makers	beaders	Bustle makers	Carvers	Fan makers	Moccasin makers	Quilters	Rattle makers	Weavers	Other handworking occupations
Pleasant Point, MA	-	-	-	-	-	-	-	-	-	-	-	-
Pojoaque Pueblo, NM	-	-	-	-	-	-	-	-	-	-	-	-
Poospatuck, NY	-	-	-	-	-	-	-	-	-	-	-	-
Port Gamble, WA	-	1	1	-	-	-	-	-	-	-	-	-
Port Madison, WA	-	-	-	-	-	-	-	-	-	-	-	-
Potawatomi, WI	-	6	-	6	-	-	-	-	-	-	-	-
Pottawatomi, KS	-	-	-	-	-	-	-	-	-	-	-	-
Prairie Island Community, MN	-	1	-	1	-	-	-	-	-	-	-	-
Puyallup, WA	-	-	-	-	-	-	-	-	-	-	-	-
Pyramid Lake, NV	3	-	-	-	-	-	-	-	-	-	-	-
Quileute, WA	-	-	-	-	-	-	-	-	-	-	-	-
Quinault, WA	-	1	1	-	-	-	-	-	-	-	-	-
Ramah Community, NM	4	9	4	-	-	2	-	-	-	-	4	-
Ramona, CA	-	-	-	-	-	-	-	-	-	-	-	-
Red Cliff, WI	-	-	-	-	-	-	-	-	-	-	-	-
Red Lake, MN	-	-	-	-	-	-	-	-	-	-	-	-
Reno-Sparks Colony, NV	2	1	-	1	-	-	-	-	-	-	-	-
Resighini Rancheria, CA	...	...	...	...	...	...	...	...	...	...	...	-
Rincon, CA	-	-	-	-	-	-	-	-	-	-	-	-
Roaring Creek Rancheria, CA	...	...	...	...	...	...	...	...	...	...	...	-
Rocky Boy's, MT	-	10	9	1	-	-	-	-	-	-	-	-
Rosebud, SD	-	5	-	1	-	-	-	-	4	-	-	-
Round Valley, CA	-	-	-	-	-	-	-	-	-	-	-	-
Rumsey Rancheria, CA	...	...	...	...	...	...	...	...	...	...	...	-
Sac and Fox, Iowa	-	1	-	1	-	-	-	-	-	-	-	-
Sac and Fox, KS-NE	...	...	...	...	...	...	...	...	...	...	...	-
St. Croix, WI	-	-	-	-	-	-	-	-	-	-	-	-
St. Regis Mohawk, NY	-	-	-	-	-	-	-	-	-	-	-	1
Salt River, AZ	2	1	-	-	-	-	-	-	-	-	-	-
San Carlos, AZ	7	7	6	-	-	-	-	-	-	-	1	-
Sandia Pueblo, NM	4	2	-	-	-	-	-	1	-	-	1	-
Sandy Lake, MN	-	-	-	-	-	-	-	-	-	-	-	-
San Felipe Pueblo, NM	9	-	-	-	-	-	-	-	-	-	-	-
San Ildefonso Pueblo, NM	7	-	-	-	-	-	-	-	-	-	-	-
San Juan Pueblo, NM	2	-	-	-	-	-	-	-	-	-	-	-
San Manuel, CA	-	-	-	-	-	-	-	-	-	-	-	-
San Pasqual, CA	-	-	-	-	-	-	-	-	-	-	-	-
Santa Ana Pueblo, NM	-	-	-	-	-	-	-	-	-	-	-	-
Santa Clara Pueblo, NM	10	-	-	-	-	-	-	-	-	-	-	-

Source: U.S. Bureau of the Census, Subject Reports, PC80-2-1D, Part II, *American Indians, Eskimos, and Aleuts on Identified Reservations and in the Historic Areas of Oklahoma (Excluding Urbanized Areas)*, U.S. Government Printing Office, Washington, D.C., 1986, pp. 482-520. *Notes:* A dash (-) represents zero or a percent which rounds to less than 0.1. Also, a dash (-) is used because the number of supplementary questionnaires for the areas was insufficient to produce reliable estimates. Three dots (...) means not applicable, or that the data are being withheld to avoid disclosure of information for individuals.

★ 395 ★

Traditional Occupations Held by Residents of Reservations, 1980: Santa Rosa Rancheria - Zuni Pueblo - I

Data are the latest available.

Identified reservation	Persons 16 years and over working in 1980 reference period	Traditional occupations										
		Tribal governmental occupations				Native healers	Sheep workers	Artists and performers				
		Total	Officials and administrators	Legislators	Judicial administrators			Total	Dancers	Drummers and singers	Painters	Potters
Santa Rosa Rancheria, CA	31	-	-	-	-	-	1	-	-	-	-	-
Santa Rosa, CA	...	...	...	...	...	...	...	...	...	...	...	...
Santa Ynez, CA	56	1	1	-	...	...	...	...	...	...	...	...
Santa Ysabel, CA	63	-	-	-	-	-	-	-	-	-	-	-
Santee, Nebraska	124	-	-	-	-	-	-	-	-	-	-	-
Santo Domingo Pueblo, NM	712	3	3	-	-	-	-	11	-	-	-	11
San Xavier, AZ	247	3	3	-	-	-	-	2	-	-	2	-
Sauk-Suiattle, WA	-	-	-	-	-	-	-	-	-	-	-	-
Sault Ste. Marie, MI	-	-	-	-	-	-	-	-	-	-	-	-
Schaghticoke, CT	...	...	...	...	...	...	...	...	...	...	...	...
Shakopee Community, MN	30	-	-	-	-	-	-	-	-	-	-	-
Sheep Ranch Rancheria, CA	...	...	...	...	...	...	...	...	...	...	...	...
Sherwood Valley Rancheria, CA	...	...	...	...	...	...	...	...	...	...	...	...
Shingle Springs Rancheria, CA	-	...	...	...	...	...	...	...	...	...	...	...
Shinnecock, NY	72	-	-	-	-	-	-	-	-	-	-	-
Shoalwater, WA	...	...	...	...	...	...	...	...	...	...	...	...
Sisseton, ND-SD	591	3	-	3	-	-	-	-	...	...	...	...
Skokomish, WA	61	1	1	-	-	-	-	-	-	-	-	-
Skull Valley, UT	-	-	-	-	-	-	-	-	-	-	-	-
Soboba, CA	57	-	-	-	-	-	-	-	-	-	-	-
Sokaogon Chippewa Community, WI	44	1	1	-	-	-	-	2	-	-	-	2
Southern Paiute, UT	50	-	-	-	-	-	-	-	-	-	-	-
Southern Ute, CO	291	6	3	3	-	-	1	2	-	1	1	-
Spokane, WA	451	10	6	2	2	-	-	-	-	-	-	-
Squaxin Island, WA	9	-	-	-	-	-	-	-	-	-	-	-
Standing Rock, ND-SD	1,077	14	3	8	3	-	-	-	-	-	-	-
Stewart's Point Rancheria, CA	20	-	-	-	-	-	-	-	-	-	-	-
Stockbridge, WI	207	2	2	-	-	-	-	-	-	-	-	-
Sulphur Bank Rancheria, CA	18	-	-	-	-	-	-	-	-	-	-	-
Summit Lake, NV	...	...	...	...	...	...	...	...	...	...	...	...
Susanville, CA	30	-	-	-	-	-	-	-	...	...	...	...
Swinomish, WA	139	2	2	-	-	-	-	-	-	-	-	-
Sycuan, CA	8	-	-	-	-	-	-	-	-	-	-	-
Tama, GA	17	1	1	-	-	-	-	-	-	-	-	-
Taos Pueblo, NM	307	-	-	-	-	-	-	2	-	-	-	2
Te-Moak, NV	38	-	-	-	-	-	-	-	-	-	-	-
Tesuque Pueblo, NM	83	1	1	-	-	-	-	-	-	-	-	-
Tigua, TX	105	-	-	-	-	-	-	3	-	-	-	3
Tonawanda, NY	168	-	-	-	-	-	-	-	-	-	-	-
Torres-Martinez, CA	-	-	-	-	-	-	-	-	-	-	-	-
Trinidad Rancheria, CA	20	-	-	-	-	-	-	-	-	-	-	-
Tulalip, WA	241	1	1	-	-	-	-	-	-	-	-	-
Tule River, CA	134	3	3	-	-	-	-	-	-	-	-	-
Tunicabiloxi, LA	...	...	...	...	...	...	...	...	...	...	...	...
Tuolumne Rancheria, CA	26	-	-	-	-	-	-	-	-	-	-	-
Turtle Mountain, ND	961	11	9	-	2	-	-	-	-	-	-	-
Tuscarora, NY	-	-	-	-	-	-	-	-	-	-	-	-
Twenty-Nine Palms, CA	-	-	-	-	-	-	-	-	-	-	-	-
Uintah and Ouray, UT	588	3	3	-	-	-	-	1	-	-	-	1
Umatilla, OR	297	8	8	-	-	-	-	-	-	-	-	-
Upper Sioux Community, MN	21	-	-	-	-	-	-	-	-	-	-	-
Upper Skagit, WA	-	-	-	-	-	-	-	-	-	-	-	-
Ute Mountain, CO-NM	308	1	-	1	-	-	-	8	-	-	4	4
Vermillion Lake, MN	27	-	-	-	-	-	-	-	-	-	-	-
Viejas Rancheria, CA	51	-	-	-	-	-	-	-	-	-	-	-
Walker River, NV	162	1	1	-	-	-	-	-	-	-	-	-
Wampanoag, MA	-	-	-	-	-	-	-	-	-	-	-	-
Warm Springs, OR	602	7	4	1	2	-	-	-	-	-	-	-
Washoe, NV	-	-	-	-	-	-	-	-	-	-	-	-
Western Pequot, CT	...	...	...	...	...	...	...	...	...	...	...	...
White Earth, MN	734	9	8	-	1	-	-	-	-	-	-	-
Wind River, WY	1,119	14	11	1	1	-	-	-	-	-	-	-
Winnebago, Nebraska	317	4	2	2	-	-	-	-	-	-	-	-
Winnemucca Colony, NV	9	-	-	-	-	-	-	-	-	-	-	-
Wisconsin Winnebago Reservation	105	-	-	-	-	-	-	-	-	-	-	-
Woodfords Community, CA	-	-	-	-	-	-	-	-	-	-	-	-
XL Ranch, CA	...	...	...	...	...	...	...	...	...	...	...	...
Yakima, WA	1,532	33	19	13	1	-	-	9	-	-	1	8
Yankton, SD	359	-	-	-	-	-	-	-	-	-	-	-

[Continued]

★ 395 ★

Traditional Occupations Held by Residents of Reservations, 1980: Santa Rosa Rancheria - Zuni Pueblo - I

[Continued]

Identified reservation	Persons 16 years and over working in 1980 reference period	Traditional occupations										
		Tribal governmental occupations				Native healers	Sheep workers	Artists and performers				
		Total	Officials and administrators	Legislators	Judicial administrators			Total	Dancers	Drummers and singers	Painters	Potters
Yavapai, AZ	28	1	1	-	-	-	-	-	-	-	-	-
Yerington, NV	40	1	1	-	-	-	-	-	-	-	-	-
Yomba, NV	20	-	-	-	-	-	-	-	-	-	-	-
Zia Pueblo, NM	179	6	6	-	-	-	-	-	-	-	-	-
Zuni Pueblo, NM	2,000	12	8	2	1	-	41	4	-	-	2	1
San Felipe/Santa Ana Joint Area, NM	-	-	-	-	-	-	-	-	-	-	-	-
San Felipe/Santo Domingo Joint Area, NM	26	-	-	-	-	-	-	-	-	-	-	-
Other Reservation Lands in MT	-	-	-	-	-	-	-	-	-	-	-	-

Source: U.S. Bureau of the Census, Subject Reports, PC80-2-1D, Part II, *American Indians, Eskimos, and Aleuts on Identified Reservations and in the Historic Areas of Oklahoma (Excluding Urbanized Areas)*, U.S. Government Printing Office, Washington, D.C., 1986, pp. 482-520. *Notes:* A dash (-) represents zero or a percent which rounds to less than 0.1. Also, a dash (-) is used because the number of supplementary questionnaires for the areas was insufficient to produce reliable estimates. Three dots (...) means not applicable, or that the data are being withheld to avoid disclosure of information for individuals.

★ 396 ★

Traditional Occupations Held by Residents of Reservations, 1980: Santa Rosa Rancheria - Zuni Pueblo - II

Data are the latest available.

Identified reservation	Jewelers	Traditional occupations										
		Handworking occupations										
		Total	Basket makers	Beaders	Bustle makers	Carvers	Fan makers	Moccasin makers	Quilters	Rattle makers	Weavers	Other handworking occupations
Santa Rosa Rancheria, CA	-	-	-	-	-	-	-	-	-	-	-	-
Santa Rosa, CA	...	...	...	...	...	...	...	...	...	...	...	-
Santa Ynez, CA	-	-	-	-	-	-	-	-	-	-	-	-
Santa Ysabel, CA	-	1	-	1	-	-	-	-	-	-	-	-
Santee, Nebraska	-	-	-	-	-	-	-	-	-	-	-	-
Santo Domingo Pueblo, NM	325	1	-	-	-	-	-	1	-	-	-	-
San Xavier, AZ	-	4	4	-	-	-	-	-	-	-	-	-
Sauk-Suiattle, WA	-	-	-	-	-	-	-	-	-	-	-	-
Sault Ste. Marie, MI	-	-	-	-	-	-	-	-	-	-	-	-
Schaghticoke, CT	...	...	...	...	...	...	...	...	...	...	...	-
Shakopee Community, MN	-	-	-	-	-	-	-	-	-	-	-	-
Sheep Ranch Rancheria, CA	...	...	...	...	...	...	...	...	...	...	...	-
Sherwood Valley Rancheria, CA	...	...	...	...	...	...	...	...	...	...	...	-
Shingle Springs Rancheria, CA	-	-	-	-	-	-	-	-	-	-	-	-
Shinnecock, NY	-	-	-	-	-	-	-	-	-	-	-	-
Shoalwater, WA	...	...	-	...	-	-	...	-	...	...	-	-
Sisseton, ND-SD	-	9	-	-	-	-	-	1	6	-	-	2
Skokomish, WA	-	-	-	-	-	-	-	-	-	-	-	-
Skull Valley, UT	-	-	-	-	-	-	-	-	-	-	-	-
Soboba, CA	-	-	-	-	-	-	-	-	-	-	-	-
Sokaogon Chippewa Community, WI	-	-	-	-	-	-	-	-	-	-	-	-
Southern Paiute, UT	-	2	-	-	-	-	-	-	-	-	-	2
Southern Ute, CO	1	-	-	-	-	-	-	-	-	-	-	-
Spokane, WA	-	4	-	4	-	-	-	-	-	-	-	-
Squaxin Island, WA	-	-	-	-	-	-	-	-	-	-	-	-
Standing Rock, ND-SD	-	9	-	2	-	-	-	-	5	-	2	-
Stewart's Point Rancheria, CA	-	-	-	-	-	-	-	-	-	-	-	-
Stockbridge, WI	-	-	-	-	-	-	-	-	-	-	-	-
Sulphur Bank Rancheria, CA	-	-	-	-	-	-	-	-	-	-	-	-
Summit Lake, NV	...	...	...	...	...	...	...	...	...	...	...	-

[Continued]

★ 396 ★

Traditional Occupations Held by Residents of Reservations, 1980: Santa Rosa Rancheria - Zuni Pueblo - II

[Continued]

| Identified reservation | Jewelers | Traditional occupations | | | | | | | | | | |
| | | Handworking occupations | | | | | | | | | | |
		Total	Basket makers	Beaders	Bustle makers	Carvers	Fan makers	Moccasin makers	Quilters	Rattle makers	Weavers	Other handworking occupations
Susanville, CA	-	-	-	-	-	-	-	-	-	-	-	-
Swinomish, WA	-	-	-	-	-	-	-	-	-	-	-	-
Sycuan, CA	-	-	-	-	-	-	-	-	-	-	-	-
Tama, GA	-	-	-	-	-	-	-	-	-	-	-	-
Taos Pueblo, NM	2	6	-	-	-	-	-	2	-	-	-	4
Te-Moak, NV	-	-	-	-	-	-	-	-	-	-	-	-
Tesuque Pueblo, NM	-	1	-	1	-	-	-	-	-	-	-	-
Tigua, TX	3	1	-	-	-	-	-	-	-	-	1	-
Tonawanda, NY	-	-	-	-	-	-	-	-	-	-	-	-
Torres-Martinez, CA	-	-	-	-	-	-	-	-	-	-	-	-
Trinidad Rancheria, CA	-	-	-	-	-	-	-	-	-	-	-	-
Tulalip, WA	-	4	-	-	-	3	-	-	-	-	-	1
Tule River, CA	-	-	-	-	-	-	-	-	-	-	-	-
Tunicabiloxi, LA	...	...	...	...	...	...	...	...	...	...	...	-
Tuolumne Rancheria, CA	1	-	-	-	-	-	-	-	-	-	-	-
Turtle Mountain, ND	-	1	-	1	-	-	-	-	-	-	-	-
Tuscarora, NY	-	-	-	-	-	-	-	-	-	-	-	-
Twenty-Nine Palms, CA	-	-	-	-	-	-	-	-	-	-	-	-
Uintah and Ouray, UT	-	1	1	-	-	-	-	-	-	-	-	-
Umatilla, OR	-	1	-	1	-	-	-	-	-	-	-	-
Upper Sioux Community, MN	-	-	-	-	-	-	-	-	-	-	-	-
Upper Skagit, WA	-	-	-	-	-	-	-	-	-	-	-	-
Ute Mountain, CO-NM	-	-	-	-	-	-	-	-	-	-	-	-
Vermillion Lake, MN	-	-	-	-	-	-	-	-	-	-	-	-
Viejas Rancheria, CA	-	-	-	-	-	-	-	-	-	-	-	-
Walker River, NV	-	-	-	-	-	-	-	-	-	-	-	-
Wampanoag, MA	-	-	-	-	-	-	-	-	-	-	-	-
Warm Springs, OR	1	10	-	10	-	-	-	-	-	-	-	-
Washoe, NV	-	-	-	-	-	-	-	-	-	-	-	-
Western Pequot, CT	...	...	...	...	...	...	...	...	...	...	...	-
White Earth, MN	-	6	3	-	-	-	-	-	1	-	2	-
Wind River, WY	3	16	-	15	-	-	-	-	-	-	1	-
Winnebago, Nebraska	-	-	-	-	-	-	-	-	-	-	-	-
Winnemucca Colony, NV	-	-	-	-	-	-	-	-	-	-	-	-
Wisconsin Winnebago Reservation	-	2	-	2	-	-	-	-	-	-	-	-
Woodfords Community, CA	-	-	-	-	-	-	-	-	-	-	-	-
XL Ranch, CA	...	...	...	...	...	...	...	...	...	...	...	-
Yakima, WA	2	9	-	6	-	2	-	-	-	-	-	-
Yankton, SD	-	1	-	-	-	-	-	-	-	-	-	1
Yavapai, AZ	-	-	-	-	-	-	-	-	-	-	-	-
Yerington, NV	-	-	-	-	-	-	-	-	-	-	-	-
Yomba, NV	-	-	-	-	-	-	-	-	-	-	-	-
Zia Pueblo, NM	-	-	-	-	-	-	-	-	-	-	-	-
Zuni Pueblo, NM	718	32	-	16	-	9	-	-	-	-	-	7
San Felipe/Santa Ana Joint Area, NM	-	-	-	-	-	-	-	-	-	-	-	-
San Felipe/Santo Domingo Joint Area, NM	5	-	-	-	-	-	-	-	-	-	-	-
Other Reservation Lands in MT	-	-	-	-	-	-	-	-	-	-	-	-

Source: U.S. Bureau of the Census, Subject Reports, PC80-2-1D, Part II, *American Indians, Eskimos, and Aleuts on Identified Reservations and in the Historic Areas of Oklahoma (Excluding Urbanized Areas)*, U.S. Government Printing Office, Washington, D.C., 1986, pp. 482-520. *Notes:* A dash (-) represents zero or a percent which rounds to less than 0.1. Also, a dash (-) is used because the number of supplementary questionnaires for the areas was insufficient to produce reliable estimates. Three dots (...) means not applicable, or that the data are being withheld to avoid disclosure of information for individuals.

Perceptions of Native Americans

★ 397 ★

Perceived Social Standing of Selected Racial/Ethnic Groups, 1964-89

In polls taken in 1964 and 1989, adults nationwide were asked to rate the "social standing" of the following groups in the United States, using a scale in which 1 was the lowest standing and 9 was the highest. The figures shown are averages.

Ethnic Group	1964	1989	Change
Native white Americans	7.25	7.03	0.22
People of my own ethnic background	6.16	6.57	0.41
British	6.37	6.46	0.09
Protestants	6.59	6.39	0.20
Catholics	6.36	6.33	0.03
French	5.73	6.07	0.34
Irish	5.94	6.05	0.11
Swiss	5.50	6.03	0.53
Swedes	5.41	5.99	0.58
Austrians	5.06	5.94	0.88
Dutch	5.60	5.90	0.30
Norwegians	5.48	5.87	0.39
Scotch	5.73	5.85	0.12
Germans	5.63	5.78	0.15
Southerners	5.25	5.77	0.52
Italians	5.03	5.69	0.66
Danes	5.20	5.63	0.43
French Canadians	5.08	5.62	0.54
Japanese	3.95	5.56	1.61
Jews	4.71	5.55	0.84
People of foreign ancestry	4.84	5.38	0.54
Finns	5.08	5.34	0.26
Greeks	4.31	5.09	0.78
Lithuanians	4.42	4.96	0.54
Spanish-Americans	4.81	4.79	0.02
Chinese	3.44	4.76	1.32
Hungarians	4.57	4.70	0.13
Czechs	4.40	4.64	0.24
Poles	4.54	4.63	0.09
Russians	3.88	4.58	0.70
Latin Americans	4.27	4.42	0.15
American Indians	4.04	4.27	0.23
Negroes[1]	2.75	4.17	1.42
"Wisians"[2]		4.12	
Mexicans	3.00	3.52	0.52

[Continued]

★ 397 ★

Perceived Social Standing of Selected Racial/Ethnic Groups, 1964-89

[Continued]

Ethnic Group	1964	1989	Change
Puerto Ricans	2.91	3.32	0.41
Gypsies	2.29	2.65	0.36

Source: The New York Times, January 8, 1992, p. A-10. Primary source: National Opinion Research Center. The 1989 survey included 1,537 adults. *Notes:* 1. Blacks were referred to as Negroes by the National Opinion Research Center in the 1989 survey to conform with the wording in the 1964 survey. 2. The Wisians, a fictitious group, were included in 1989.

Chapter 6

HEALTH AND HEALTH CARE

Births and Deaths

★ 398 ★

Life Expectancy at Birth

Decennial Census year	Indian and Alaska Native			U.S. White population		
	Both sexes	Male	Female	Both sexes	Male	Female
1980	71.1	67.1	75.1	74.4	70.7	78.1
1970	65.1	60.7	71.2	71.7	68.0	75.6
1960	61.7	60.0	65.7	70.6	67.4	74.1
1950	60.0	58.1	52.2	69.1	66.5	72.2
1940	51.0	51.3	51.9	64.2	62.1	66.6

Source: Trends in Indian Health, 1991, U.S. Department of Health and Human Services, Public Health Service, Indian Health Service, p. 56. *Notes:* Life expectancy at birth based upon 3 years of mortality experience centered in the decennial census year specified for the American Indian and Alaskan Native population and for the single year specified for the U.S. white population. Data for 1940 and 1950 for both population groups are for continental United States. American Indian and Alaskan Native data for 1960-1980 are for states in which IHS had responsibilities (1960 and 1970- 25 States, 1980-28 States) and U.S. white population 1960-1980 are for 50 states and the District of Columbia.

★ 399 ★

Live Births, by Selected Years, 1975-88

Data are based on the National Vital Statistics System.

Race/ethnicity	Number of live births				
	1970	1975	1980	1985	1988
All races	3,731,386	3,144,198	3,612,258	3,760,561	3,909,510
American Indian[1]	25,864	27,546	36,797	42,646	45,871
White	3,091,264	2,551,996	2,898,732	2,991,373	3,046,162
Black	572,362	511,581	589,616	608,193	671,976
Asian or Pacific Islander[2]	31,476	32,812	82,454	115,616	142,258
Chinese	7,824	8,413	12,792	17,880	22,904

[Continued]

★ 399 ★

Live Births, by Selected Years, 1975-88
[Continued]

Race/ethnicity	Number of live births				
	1970	1975	1980	1985	1988
Japanese	8,226	7,442	8,755	9,802	10,483
Filipino	8,874	11,233	15,086	21,482	24,612

Source: "Live Births, According to Race of Child and Selected Characteristics: United States, Selected Years 1970-88," *Health United States 1990*, 1991, pp. 58-59. Primary source: National Center for Health Statistics: Vital Statistics of the United States, Vol. 1, Natality, for data years 1970-88. Public Health Service. Washington. U.S. Government Printing Office. Data computed by the Division of Analysis from data compiled by the Division of Vital Statistics. *Notes:* 1. Includes Aleut and Eskimo. 2. Includes Chinese, Japanese, Filipino, Hawaiian (includes part Hawaiian), Guamian, and other Asian or Pacific Islander (starting in 1980).

★ 400 ★

Live Births, by Year

American Indians and Alaska Natives and U.S. all races, 1955-1988.

Calendar year	Indian and Alaska Native		Indian		Alaska Native		U.S. all races		U.S. other than White
	Number	Rate[1]	Number	Rate[1]	Number	Rate[1]	Number	Rate[1]	Rate[1]
1988	44,242		41,375		2,867				
1987	42,163	28.0	39,308	27.5	2,855	36.0	3,809,394	15.7	21.7
1986	41,020	27.9	38,312	27.5	2,708	36.5	3,756,547	15.6	21.4
1985	41,155	28.0	38,395	27.5	2,760	36.6	3,760,561	15.6	21.4
1984	39,679	28.4	37,050	27.9	2,629	37.6	3,669,141	15.5	21.2
1983	39,521	28.8	36,839	28.4	2,682	37.2	3,638,933	15.5	21.3
1982	38,560	28.5	36,099	28.1	2,461	36.3	3,680,537	15.9	21.9
1981	34,205	28.0	31,975	27.7	2,230	34.9	3,629,238	15.8	22.0
1980	33,937	27.0	31,742	26.7	2,195	33.7	3,612,258	15.9	22.5
1979	31,843	27.2	29,803	26.8	2,040	33.0	3,494,398	15.6	22.2
1978	29,857	27.0	27,922	26.7	1,935	32.0	3,333,279	15.0	21.6
1977	28,198	27.1	26,325	26.8	1,873	31.1	3,326,632	15.1	21.6
1976	26,748	26.9	24,989	26.7	1,759	30.8	3,167,788	14.6	20.8
1975	25,457	26.9	23,695	26.7	1,762	30.2	3,144,198	14.6	21.0
1974	24,301	27.3	22,653	27.0	1,648	30.4	3,159,958	14.8	21.2
1973	23,757	28.1	22,087	28.0	1,670	30.1	3,136,965	14.8	21.7
1972	23,752	29.7	22,154	29.6	1,598	31.2	3,258,411	15.6	22.8
1971	23,806	31.2	22,092	31.1	1,714	31.8	3,555,970	17.2	24.6
1970	22,746	32.0	21,100	32.0	1,646	32.0	3,731,386	18.4	25.1
1969	21,593	32.3	20,074	32.3	1,519	31.4	3,600,206	17.9	24.5
1968	21,602	32.2	20,066	32.2	1,536	32.3	3,501,564	17.6	24.5
1967	20,658	33.0	18,948	32.8	1,710	35.8	3,520,959	17.8	25.0
1966	21,100	34.5	19,154	34.1	1,946	39.7	3,606,274	18.4	26.1
1965	22,370	36.4	20,352	36.0	2,018	42.3	3,760,358	19.4	27.6
1964	22,782	38.4	20,794	37.9	1,988	44.4	4,027,490	21.1	29.2
1963	22,274	39.5	20,142	38.9	2,132	45.7	4,098,020	21.7	29.7
1962	21,866	40.8	19,770	40.2	2,096	47.2	4,167,362	22.4	30.5

[Continued]

★ 400 ★

Live Births, by Year
[Continued]

Calendar year	Indian and Alaska Native		Indian		Alaska Native		U.S. all races		U.S. other than White
	Number	Rate[1]	Number	Rate[1]	Number	Rate[1]	Number	Rate[1]	Rate[1]
1961	21,664	41.7	19,570	41.2	2,094	46.8	4,268,326	23.3	31.6
1960	21,154	42.1	19,188	41.7	1,966	46.4	4,257,850	23.7	32.1
1959	20,520	41.4	18,616	40.9	1,904	46.7	4,244,796	24.0	32.9
1958	19,371	40.3	17,428	39.7	1,943	47.4	4,203,812	24.3	33.0
1957	18,814	39.1	16,982	38.2	1,832	49.3	4,254,784	25.0	33.9
1956	17,947	38.2	21,604	37.2	1,907	49.5	4,168,090	24.9	33.9
1955	17,028	37.5	15,304	36.5	1,724	49.5	4,047,295	24.6	33.1
1954	16,691		15,042		1,649				

Source: Trends in Indian Health, 1991, U.S. Department of Health and Human Services, Public Health Service, Indian Health Service, p. 23. *Note:* 1. Rate per 1,000 population.

★ 401 ★

Live Births, by Selected Characteristic, 1970-87

Percent of live births is shown with various characteristics for selected years.

Race of child and characteristic	Percent of births									
	1970	1975	1980	1981	1982	1983	1984	1985	1986	1987
All races										
Birth weight:[1]										
Less than 2,500 grams	7.94	7.39	6.84	6.81	6.75	6.82	6.72	6.75	6.81	6.90
Less than 1,500 grams	1.17	1.16	1.15	1.16	1.18	1.19	1.19	1.21	1.21	1.24
Age of mother:										
Less than 18 years	6.3	7.6	5.8	5.4	5.2	5.0	4.8	4.7	4.8	4.8
18-19 years	11.3	11.3	9.8	9.4	9.0	8.7	8.3	8.0	7.8	7.6
Unmarried mothers	10.7	14.3	18.4	18.9	19.4	20.3	21.0	22.0	23.4	24.5
Education of mother:										
Less than 12 years	30.8	26.6	23.7	22.9	22.3	21.7	20.9	20.6	20.4	20.2
16 years or more	8.6	11.4	14.0	14.8	15.3	15.9	16.4	16.7	17.1	17.6
Prenatal care began:										
1st trimester	68.0	72.4	76.3	76.3	76.1	76.2	76.5	76.2	75.9	76.0
3rd trimester or no prenatal care	7.9	6.0	5.1	5.2	5.5	5.6	5.6	5.7	6.0	6.1
American Indian[2]										
Birth weight:[1]										
Less than 2,500 grams	7.99	6.61	6.47	6.27	6.17	6.43	6.16	5.88	6.16	6.24
Less than 1,500 grams	0.98	1.04	0.96	0.90	1.04	1.06	1.03	0.98	1.01	1.08
Age of mother:										
Less than 18 years	7.5	11.0	8.8	8.5	8.0	7.9	7.4	7.1	7.4	7.4
18-19 years	13.3	15.8	14.3	14.0	13.5	12.9	12.6	12.0	11.8	11.5
Unmarried mothers	19.8	27.9	33.5	35.2	36.3	38.7	39.8	40.7	42.3	44.9

[Continued]

★ 401 ★

Live Births, by Selected Characteristic, 1970-87
[Continued]

Race of child and characteristic	Percent of births									
	1970	1975	1980	1981	1982	1983	1984	1985	1986	1987
Education of mother:										
Less than 12 years	57.6	50.6	41.8	40.7	39.5	38.8	38.0	36.9	36.8	36.6
16 years or more	3.0	2.8	4.2	4.4	4.5	4.3	4.5	4.6	4.6	4.5
Prenatal care began:										
1st trimester	41.7	49.3	58.7	59.3	60.5	58.7	60.0	60.3	60.7	60.2
3rd trimester or no prenatal care	25.6	19.5	13.3	12.9	12.4	12.7	12.4	11.5	11.6	11.7
White										
Birth weight:[1]										
Less than 2,500 grams	6.84	6.26	5.70	5.67	5.63	5.67	5.59	5.64	5.64	5.68
Less than 1,500 grams	0.95	0.92	0.90	0.90	0.92	0.93	0.92	0.94	0.93	0.94
Age of mother:										
Less than 18 years	4.8	6.0	4.5	4.3	4.1	3.9	3.7	3.7	3.7	3.7
18-19 years	10.4	10.3	9.0	8.6	8.2	7.9	7.4	7.1	6.9	6.8
Unmarried mothers	5.7	7.3	11.0	11.6	12.1	12.8	13.4	14.5	15.7	16.7
Education of mother:										
Less than 12 years	27.0	25.0	20.7	19.9	19.3	18.7	18.0	17.8	17.6	17.3
16 years or more	9.5	12.7	15.6	16.4	17.0	17.7	18.4	18.7	19.2	19.9
Prenatal care began:										
1st trimester	72.4	75.9	79.3	79.4	79.3	79.4	79.6	79.4	79.2	79.4
3rd trimester	6.2	5.0	4.3	4.3	4.5	4.6	4.7	4.7	5.0	5.0
Black										
Birth weight:[1]										
Less than 2,500 grams	13.86	13.09	12.49	12.53	12.40	12.59	12.36	12.42	12.53	12.71
Less than 1,500 grams	2.40	2.37	2.44	2.47	2.51	2.55	2.56	2.65	2.66	2.73
Age of mother:										
Less than 18 years	14.7	16.1	12.2	11.4	11.1	10.9	10.6	10.3	10.4	10.5
18-19 years	16.6	16.8	14.3	13.9	13.5	13.4	13.1	12.7	12.4	12.1
Unmarried mothers	37.4	49.0	55.2	56.0	56.7	58.2	59.2	60.1	61.2	62.2
Education of mother:										
Less than 12 years	51.0	45.1	36.2	35.4	34.8	34.2	33.1	32.3	31.7	31.4
16 years or more	2.8	4.4	6.3	6.6	6.8	6.8	7.0	7.1	7.3	7.2
Prenatal care began:										
1st trimester	44.4	55.8	62.7	62.4	61.5	61.5	62.2	61.8	61.6	61.1
3rd trimester	16.6	10.5	8.8	9.1	9.6	9.7	9.6	10.0	10.6	11.1
Asian and Pacific Islander[3]										
Birth weight:[1]										
Less than 2,500 grams	8.43	7.04	6.55	6.61	6.63	6.51	6.53	6.11	6.38	6.3
Less than 1,500 grams	1.12	0.80	0.91	0.91	0.87	0.87	0.91	0.84	0.87	0.9
Age of mother:										
Less than 18 years	3.3	2.7	1.7	1.8	1.8	1.7	1.8	1.8	1.9	1.9
18-19 Years	7.1	5.8	4.3	4.4	4.4	3.9	3.8	3.7	3.7	3.6
Unmarried mothers	7.8	8.5	7.8	7.5	8.4	9.0	9.6	10.1	10.6	11.5

[Continued]

★ 401 ★

Live Births, by Selected Characteristic, 1970-87
[Continued]

Race of child and characteristic	Percent of births									
	1970	1975	1980	1981	1982	1983	1984	1985	1986	1987
Education of mother:										
Less than 12 years	21.7	18.5	20.0	21.9	22.2	20.7	19.3	18.5	17.3	17.3
16 years or more	20.0	27.5	30.2	29.0	28.9	29.7	30.2	30.1	31.1	31.6
Prenatal care began:										
1st trimester	67.8	73.9	74.7	74.4	74.4	74.9	75.6	75.0	75.6	75.7
3rd trimester	6.8	4.5	6.1	6.2	6.2	6.1	6.0	6.1	5.9	6.0

Source: Health Status of Minorities and Low-Income Groups: Third Edition, U.S. Department of Health and Human Services, Public Health Service, Health Resources and Services Administration, Government Printing Office, Washington, D.C., pp. 109-110. *Primary source:* National Center for Health Statistics. Health, United States 1988, Mar 1989, Department of Health and Human Services Pub. No. (PHS) 89-1232, Hyattsville, MD Table 7, p. 47, (2) National Center for Health Statistics. Monthly Vital Statistics Report, Advance Report of Final Natality Statistics, 1987, Vol. 38, No. 3 Supplement, Jun 29, 1989, Hyattsville, MD, Table 2, p. 16, Table 15, pp. 28-29, Table 18, p. 32, Table 21, p. 36, Tables 28 & 29, p. 40, Table 30, p. 41, and (3) Unpublished data from National Center for Health Statistics. *I Live births Notes:* Data on education of mother are not available from California, Texas, and Washington. Other States do not have data on marital status, education, and/or month prenatal care began for certain years before 1980. 1. Before 1979, data are for infants weighing 2,500 grams or less at birth. 2. Includes Chinese, Japanese, Filipino, Hawaiian (includes part Hawaiian), Guamian (1970 and 1975), and other Asian or Pacific Islander (starting in 1990). 3. Includes Aleut and Eskimo.

★ 402 ★

Live Birth Rates, by Order and Age of Mother

Age of mother	Total live births	Live birth order					
		1st child	2nd child	3rd child	4th child	5th child	6th + child
American Indians and Alaska Natives, 1986-1988							
All ages	127,062[1]	42,414	35,903	23,920	12,764	6,355	5,706
All ages	100.0	100.0	100.0	100.0	100.0	100.0	100.0
Under 20 years	19.0	41.9	14.6	4.2	1.1	0.3	-
20-24 years	35.0	36.9	44.4	36.6	23.6	13.4	4.4
25-29 years	26.2	14.8	27.1	35.9	38.9	37.6	23.5
30-34 years	14.0	5.0	11.0	17.3	26.2	31.9	38.4
35-39 years	4.9	1.2	2.6	5.2	9.0	14.3	26.0
40 years and over	0.9	0.2	0.3	0.8	1.3	2.5	7.7
U.S. all races, 1987							
All ages	3,793,386[2]	1,567,678	1,247,526	608,204	224,522	81,377	64,079
All ages	100.0	100.0	100.0	100.0	100.0	100.0	100.0
Under 20 years	12.5	23.3	7.0	2.6	1.1	0.4	0.1
20-24 years	28.4	33.0	29.3	22.6	17.1	11.8	4.7
25-29 years	32.1	27.8	35.4	36.2	34.0	30.5	20.4
30-34 years	20.1	12.4	21.8	27.9	31.4	34.1	34.5

[Continued]

★ 402 ★

Live Birth Rates, by Order and Age of Mother
[Continued]

Age of mother	Total live births	Live birth order					
		1st child	2nd child	3rd child	4th child	5th child	6th + child
35-39 years	6.5	3.2	5.9	9.6	14.0	19.0	29.5
40 years and over	1.0	0.4	0.6	1.2	2.3	4.2	10.9

Source: Trends in Indian Health, 1991, U.S. Department of Health and Human Services, Public Health Service, Indian Health Service, p. 25. *Notes:* Percentages may not sum to totals due to rounding. 1. Excludes 363 American Indian and Alaska Native Births with live birth order not reported. 2. Excludes 16,008 U.S. All Races births (0.6 percent) with birth order not reported.

★ 403 ★

Births - Low in Weight and Preterm, 1987

Race/ethnicity	Percent of live births	
	Low birth-weight infants[1]	Preterm births[2]
All races[3]	6.9	10.2
White	5.7	8.5
Black	12.7	18.0
American Indian[4]	6.2	11.7
Asian or Pacific Islander		
Chinese	5.0	7.1
Japanese	6.3	7.9
Hawaiian	6.6	10.7
Filipino	7.3	10.4
Other	6.4	10.5
Origin of mother[5]		
All origins[6]	7.0	10.4
Hispanic, total	6.2	11.0
Mexican	5.7	11.0
Puerto Rican	9.3	12.6
Cuban	5.9	8.9
Central and South American	5.7	10.3
Other and unknown Hispanic	6.9	11.0
Non-Hispanic[7]	7.1	10.3

[Continued]

★ 403 ★

Births - Low in Weight and Preterm, 1987
[Continued]

Race/ethnicity	Percent of live births	
	Low birth-weight infants[1]	Preterm births[2]
White	5.6	8.2
Black	12.9	11.4

Source: Health Status of Minorities and Low-Income Groups: Third Edition, U.S. Department of Health and Human Services, Public Health Service, Health Resources and Services Administration, Government Printing Office, Washington, D.C., p. 107. Primary source: (1) Unpublished data from the National Center for Health Statistics, (2) National Center for Health Statistics, Advance Report of Final Natality Statistics, 1987, Monthly Vital Statistics Report, Vol. 38, No. 3. Supplement, Jun 29, 1989, Department of Health and Human Services Pub. No. (PHS) 89-1120, Hyattsville, MD, Tables 27, 29, & 32, pp. 39, 40, & 43. *Notes:* 1. Birth weight of less than 2,500 grams (5 lb. 8 oz.). 2. Born prior to 37 completed weeks of gestation. 3. Includes births of other races not shown separately. 4. Includes births to Aleuts and Eskimos. 5. Data from 23 reporting states and the District of Columbia. 6. Includes origin not stated. 7. Includes races other than White and Black.

★ 404 ★

Births of Low Birth Weight

For American Indians and Alaska Natives, 1986-1988 and U.S. all races, 1987. Births were under 2,500 grams.

Age of mother	Indian and Alaska Native			U.S. all races		
	Total live births	Number low weight	Percent low weight	Total live births	Number low weight	Percent low weight
All ages	127,219[1]	7,774	6.1	3,809,394	262,344	6.9
Under 20 years	24,201	1,536	6.3	472,623	44,466	9.4
Under 15 years	471	35	7.4	10,311	1,412	13.7
15-19 years	23,730	1,501	6.3	462,312	43,054	9.3
20-24 years	44,515	2,491	5.6	1,075,856	76,562	7.1
25-29 years	33,318	1,959	5.9	1,216,080	74,309	6.1
30-34 years	17,804	1,222	6.9	760,695	46,979	6.2
35-39 years	6,248	462	7.4	247,984	17,169	6.9
40 years and over	1,133	104	9.2	36,156	2,859	7.9

Source: Trends in Indian Health, 1991, U.S. Department of Health and Human Services, Public Health Service, Indian Health Service, p. 24. *Notes:* 1. Excludes 206 American Indian and Alaska Native live births and 4,885 U.S. all races live births with birth weight was not stated.

★ 405 ★

Birth Malformations, 1981-86

Rate per 10,000 of major congenital malformations, 1981-86[1].

Malformation[2]	Rate per 10,000[2]				
	American Indians	Blacks	Hispanics	Asians	Whites
Anencephaly	3.6	2.1	4.4	4.4	3.0
Spina bifida without anencephaly	4.1	3.3	5.9	1.8	5.1
Hydrocephalus without spina bifida	10.8	8.1	4.6	4.8	5.4
Microcephalus	2.6	4.8	2.8	1.9	2.1
Ventricular septal defect	19.1	14.4	13.8	21.0	17.4
Atrial septal defect	4.1	2.1	1.2	2.5	2.1
Valve stenosis and atresia	8.2	5.9	1.9	2.8	3.2
Patent ductus arteriosus	33.5	49.9	20.7	25.1	26.5
Pulmonary artery stenosis	0	5.4	1.4	1.8	1.5
Cleft palate without cleft lip	9.8	3.7	3.7	4.6	5.9
Cleft lip with or without cleft palate	17.5	4.4	8.6	12.9	9.7
Clubfoot without CNS[3] defects	15.5	19.9	19.1	14.4	27.5
Hip dislocation without CNS[3] defects	31.4	13.8	24.0	25.0	32.3
Hypospadias	17.5	24.6	14.9	16.5	32.7
Rectal atresia and stenosis	4.6	2.8	3.0	3.8	3.7
Fetal alcohol syndrome	29.9	6.0	0.8	0.3	0.9
Down syndrome	6.7	6.5	11.6	11.3	8.5
Autosomal abnormalities, excluding Down syndrome	3.1	2.1	2.1	2.9	2.2
Total	222.0	179.9	144.4	157.8	189.8

Source: Health Status of Minorities and Low-Income Groups: Third Edition, U.S. Department of Health and Human Services, Public Health Service, Health Resources and Services Administration, Government Printing Office, Washington, D.C., p. 106. Primary source: Centers for Disease Control. G.F. Chavez, J.F. Cordero, J.E. Becerra, "Leading Malformations Among Minority Groups in the United States, 1981-86," *Morbidity and Mortality Weekly Report* 1988, 37 (No. SS-3), Table 1, p. 19. *Notes:* 1. Definitions of malformations. Anencephaly-Absence of top and back of the skull and most of the brain, usually causing still birth or newborn death; Spina bifida without anencephaly-Longitudinal gap in the spinal column, with serious consequences (e.g., paralysis) when the spinal cord and nerve roots in the gap segment are malformed; Hydrocephalus without spinal bifida-Expansion of the fluid-filled compartments within the brain, often at the expense of the brain tissue; Microcephalus-Very small brain, usually accompanied by mental retardation; Ventricular septal defect-Hole in the wall between the two main (lower) pumping chambers of the heart, often compromising heart efficiency; Atrial septal defect-Hole in the wall between the two auxiliary (upper) pumping chambers of the heart, often compromising heart efficiency; Valve stenosis and atresia-Absence or narrowing of a heart valve; Patent ductus arteriosus-Persistence of a heart-lung bypass vessel that is normal in the fetus, but that should begin to close immediately after birth for efficient heart-lung function; Pulmonary artery stenosis-Complete obstruction of the blood vessel(s) leading from the heart to the lungs; Cleft palate without cleft lip-Front- to-back cleft in the hard or soft palate or both (roof of the mouth), usually interfering with feeding and speech development; Cleft lip with or without cleft palate-Vertical cleft (single or double) in the upper lip; Clubfoot with CNS defects-Deformation of a (usually) fully developed foot and ankle; Hip dislocation without CNS defects-Dislocated or (more often) dislocatable hip joint, usually due to shallow socket; Hypospadias-Opening in the urethra in the base or shaft of the penis rather than at its tip; Rectal atresia and stenosis-Narrowing or complete impassability of the rectum; Fetal alcohol syndrome-A variable combination of mental deficiency, certain abnormal facial features, prenatal and subsequent growth retardation, and various physical malformations in offspring of women drinking heavily during pregnancy; Down syndrome-A variable pattern of mental retardation and physical abnormalities due to presence of an extra (third) copy of chromosome 21 (or a specific segment thereof) in all or, occasionally, some cells of the body; Autosomal abnormalities excluding Down syndrome-All other abnormalities in number or structure of any of the 22 nonsex chromosome pairs. 2. By organ and/or system. 3. Central nervous system.

★ 406 ★

Fertility Characteristics of American Indian Women, by Tribe, 1980: Abenaki-Chinook

Data are estimates based on a sample and are the most recent available.

Tribe	Fertility		
	Women 15 to 44 years	Children ever born	Children born per 1,000 women
All American Indians	375,884	634,619	1,688
Abenaki (n.e.c)	223	334	1,498
Alabama Coushatta[1]	146	202	1,384
Alaska Native (n.e.c.)			
Total	146	202	1,384
Alaska Native	125	147	1,176
Sealaska	21	55	2,619
Alaska Athabaskans			
Total	2,591	4,246	1,639
Alaskan Athabaskans	2,430	3,960	1,632
Doyon	71	137	1,930
Taniana	73	105	1,438
Other Alaskan Athabaskans	8	24	3,000
Aleut and Eskimo			
Total	162	292	1,802
Akutan	5	15	3,000
Aleut	67	83	1,239
Calista	16	46	2,875
Chugach	43	61	1,419
Eskimo	23	79	3,435
Kotzebue Sound	2	8	4,000
Other Aleut and Eskimo	6	-	-
Algonquian (n.e.c.)	419	809	1,931
Apache			
Total	9,358	11,134	1,742
Apache (n.e.c.)	6,392	11,134	1,742
Chiricahua	75	96	1,280
Fort Sill Apache	24	62	2,583
Jicarilla	406	743	1,830
Kiowa Apache	71	114	1,606
Mescalero	511	820	1,605
Payson	14	46	3,286
San Carlos	959	1,807	1,884
White Mountain Apache	906	1,621	1,789
Other Apache	-	-	-
Arapaho	1,135	2,203	1,941
Arikara	381	563	1,478
Assiniboine	995	2,042	2,052
Bannock	99	172	1,737
Blackfoot[1]	6,745	11,544	1,711

[Continued]

★ 406 ★

Fertility Characteristics of American Indian Women, by Tribe, 1980: Abenaki-Chinook

[Continued]

Tribe	Fertility		
	Women 15 to 44 years	Children ever born	Children born per 1,000 women
Caddo	486	885	1,780
California tribes (n.e.c.)			
Total	124	154	1,242
Cahto	2	4	2,000
Digger	6	12	2,000
Mattole	0	0	1,000
Morongo	45	14	311
Wappo	15	20	1,333
Yuki			
Other California tribes	25	67	2,680
Canadian and Latin American	2,165	3,372	1,558
Catawba	352	657	1,868
Cayuse	48	23	479
Chehalis	75	74	987
Chemakuan			
Total	124	252	2,032
Hoh	10	48	4,800
Quileute	114	204	1,789
Other Chemakuan	-	-	-
Chemehuevi	183	327	1,787
Cherokee			
Total	62,800	104,496	1,664
Cherokee	62,450	103,937	1,664
Eastern Cherokee	266	337	1,267
Etowah Cherokee	18	12	667
Tuscola	11	28	2,545
United Keetoowah	10	6	600
Western Cherokee	40	176	4,400
Other Cherokee	5	-	-
Cheyenne			
Total	2,311	4,180	1,809
Cheyenne	1,731	3,097	1,789
Northern Cheyenne	548	1,064	1,942
Southern Cheyenne	32	19	594
Chickahominy	246	377	1,533
Chickasaw	2,297	3,470	1,511
Chinook			
Total	284	439	1,546
Chinook	281	430	1,530
Clatsop	3	9	3,000

[Continued]

★ 406 ★

Fertility Characteristics of American Indian Women, by Tribe, 1980: Abenaki-Chinook

[Continued]

Tribe	Fertility		
	Women 15 to 44 years	Children ever born	Children born per 1,000 women
Columbia River Chinook	-	-	-
Other Chinook	-	-	-

Source: U.S. Bureau of the Census, *1980 Census of Population, Volume 2, Subject Reports, Characteristics of American Indians, by Tribes and Selected Areas: 1980*, PC80-2-1C, Section 1: Tables I-II, issued September 1989, U.S. Department of Commerce, U.S. Government Printing Office, Washington, D.C., pp. 150-202. *Notes:* (N.E.C.) stands for not elsewhere classified. A dash (-) represents zero or a percent which rounds to less than 0.1. 1. Reporting and/or processing problems may have affected the data for this tribe.

★ 407 ★

Fertility Characteristics of American Indian Women, by Tribe, 1980: Chippewa-Iowa

Data are estimates based on a sample and are the most recent available.

Tribe	Fertility		
	Women 15 to 44 years	Children ever born	Children born per 1,000 women
Chippewa			
Total	18,416	33,680	1,829
Bad River	65	90	1,385
Bay Mills Chippewa	95	228	2,400
Bois Forte	32	56	1,750
Chippewa	17,253	31,793	1,843
Lac Courte Oreilles	64	106	1,656
Lac du Flambeau	4	32	8,000
Lake Superior	24	32	3,333
Leech Lake	5	8	1,600
Leelanau	15	15	1,000
Mille Lac	13	13	1,000
Minnesota Chippewa	189	346	1,831
Ontonagon	17	27	1,588
Red Cliff Chippewa	24	38	1,583
Red Lake Chippewa	57	64	1,123
Saginaw Chippewa	74	118	1,595
St. Croix Chippewa	9	18	2,000
Sault Ste. Marie Chippewa	198	269	1,359
Sokoagon Chippewa	42	24	1,348
Turtle Mountain	132	125	1,453

[Continued]

★ 407 ★

Fertility Characteristics of American Indian Women, by Tribe, 1980: Chippewa-Iowa
[Continued]

Tribe	Fertility		
	Women 15 to 44 years	Children ever born	Children born per 1,000 women
White Earth	86	125	1,453
Other Chippewa	18	52	2,889
Chitimacha	85	148	1,741
Choctaw			
Total	11,973	19,809	1,654
Choctaw	11,870	19,655	1,656
Clifton Choctaw	103	154	1,495
Chumash[1]			
Total	362	495	1,367
Chumash	357	495	1,387
Other Chumash	5	-	-
Clallam			
Total	254	346	1,362
Clallam	215	262	1,219
Lower Elwah	-	-	-
Port Gamble Clallam	39	84	2,154
Other Clellam	-	-	-
Coeur d'Alene	134	293	2,187
Coharie	129	138	1,070
Colorado River	243	507	2,004
Colville	1,359	2,205	1,623
Comanche	2,224	3,392	1,525
Coos	18	55	3,056
Costanoan	125	188	1,504
Cowlitz	297	368	1,239
Cree	1,550	2,785	1,797
Creek			
Total	6,825	10,092	1,479
Creek	6,760	10,013	1,481
Eastern Creek	28	21	750
Lower Muskogee	25	34	1,360
Muskogee	6	12	2,000
Thiopthiocco	6	12	2,000
Other Creek	-	-	-
Croatan	39	25	641
Crow	1,661	2,565	1,544
Cupeno			
Total	93	139	1,495
Agua Caliente	21	27	1,286
Cupeno	72	112	1,556
Delaware			
Total	1,258	1,701	1,354

[Continued]

★ 407 ★

Fertility Characteristics of American Indian Women, by Tribe, 1980: Chippewa-Iowa

[Continued]

Tribe	Fertility		
	Women 15 to 44 years	Children ever born	Children born per 1,000 women
Delaware	1,092	1,422	1,302
Munsee	29	43	1,483
Sand Hill	135	236	1,748
Diegueno			
Total	376	744	1,979
Diegueno	322	612	1,901
Manzanita	7	21	3,000
San Pascual	28	62	2,214
Santa Ysabel	19	49	2,579
Other Diegueno	-	-	-
Eastern tribes (n.e.c.)			
Total	631	1,094	1,734
Moor	21	23	1,095
Nansemond	7	-	-
Natchez	5	-	-
Nipmuc	13	18	1,385
Southeastern Indians	580	1,053	1,816
Tunica	5	-	-
Other Eastern tribes	-	-	-
Flathead	1,214	2,406	1,982
Fort Hall	100	238	2,380
Gabrieleno	543	1,010	1,860
Gros Ventres			
Total	622	1,152	1,852
Atsina	13	10	769
Gros Ventres	609	1,142	1,875
Haida	319	502	1,574
Haliwa	551	1,040	1,854
Hidatsa	373	702	1,882
Hitchiti	2	2	1,000
Hoopa	622	825	1,326
Houma	475	1,409	2,968
Iowa	218	321	1,472

Source: U.S. Bureau of the Census, *1980 Census of Population, Volume 2, Subject Reports, Characteristics of American Indians, by Tribes and Selected Areas: 1980*, PC80-2-1C, Section 1: Tables I-II, issued September 1989, U.S. Department of Commerce, U.S. Government Printing Office, Washington, D.C., pp. 150-202. *Notes:* (N.E.C.) stands for not elsewhere classified. A dash (-) represents zero or a percent which rounds to less than 0.1. 1. Reporting and/or processing problems may have affected the data for this tribe.

★ 408 ★

Fertility Characteristics of American Indian Women, by Tribe, 1980: Iroquois-Pomo

Data are estimates based on a sample and are the most recent available.

Tribe	Fertility		
	Women 15 to 44 years	Children ever born	Children born per 1,000 women
Iroquois			
Total	10,127	116,058	1,586
Cayuga	204	309	1,515
Iroquois (n.e.c.)	1,212	1,699	1,402
Mohawk[1]	3,631	5,612	1,546
Oneida	2,075	3,508	1,691
Onondaga	241	426	1,768
Seneca			
Total	1,822	3,075	1,688
Seneca	1,767	2,957	1,673
Seneca Nation	9	18	2,000
Tonawanda Seneca	46	100	2,174
Seneca-Cayuga	109	151	1,385
Tuscarora	528	734	1,390
Wyandot	305	544	1,784
Kalispel	45	90	2,000
Karok	489	614	1,665
Kaw	192	277	1,443
Kickapoo	591	943	1,596
Kiowa	1,781	2,801	1,573
Klamath	508	856	1,685
Konkow	75	94	1,253
Kootenai	98	124	1,265
Long Island			
Total	53	17	321
Matinecock	17	5	294
Montauk	30	12	400
Poosepatuck	-	-	-
Other Long Island	6	-	-
Luiseno			
Total	353	718	2,034
LaJolla	15	70	4,667
Luiseno	249	439	1,763
Pala	44	115	2,614
Pauma	2	-	-
Pechanga	43	94	2,186
Lumbee[3]	7,090	13,336	1,881
Lummi[3]	993	1,777	1,790
Maidu	322	620	1,925
Makah	264	436	1,652
Maliseet	125	339	2,712
Mandan	218	445	2,041

[Continued]

★ 408 ★

Fertility Characteristics of American Indian Women, by Tribe, 1980: Iroquois-Pomo

[Continued]

Tribe	Fertility		
	Women 15 to 44 years	Children ever born	Children born per 1,000 women
Mattaponi	51	68	1,333
Menominee	1,453	3,041	2,093
Miami	433	484	1,118
Miccosukee[1]	22	43	1,955
Micmac[4]	320	605	1,891
Mission Indians	610	803	1,316
Miwok	538	796	1,480
Modoc	166	276	1,663
Mohegan	150	247	1,647
Mono	388	695	1,791
Nanticoke	217	320	1,475
Narragansett	576	1,178	2,045
Navajo	39,931	71,663	1,795
Nez Perce[3]	587	723	1,232
Nomalaki	80	161	2,013
Northwest tribes (n.e.c)			
Total	81	93	1,148
Columbia Wenatchee	26	16	615
Kalapuya	18	49	2,722
Tillamook	4	16	4,000
Other Northwest	33	12	364
Omaha	751	1,329	1,770
Oregon Athabaskan	114	97	851
Osage	1,653	2,137	1,293
Oto	335	647	1,926
Ottawa	1,702	2,758	1,620
Paiute[3]			
Total	2,476	4,224	1,706
Burns Paiute	14	24	1,714
Northern Paiute	10	15	1,500
Paiute	22,369	4,084	1,724
Pyramid Lake	6	9	1,500
Southern Paiute	28	51	1,621
Walker River	17	17	1,000
Other Paiute	32	24	750
Pamunkey	55	38	691
Papago			
Total	3,332	5,783	1,736
Papago	3,325	5,783	1,739
Other Papago	7	-	-
Passamaquoddy			
Total	471	967	2,053

[Continued]

★ 408 ★

Fertility Characteristics of American Indian Women, by Tribe, 1980: Iroquois-Pomo
[Continued]

Tribe	Fertility		
	Women 15 to 44 years	Children ever born	Children born per 1,000 women
Passamaquoddy	471	967	2,053
Other Passamaquoddy	-	-	-
Pawnee	684	1,219	1,782
Penobscot	282	529	1,876
Peoria	121	216	1,785
Pequot	75	68	907
Pima	3,038	5,778	1,902
Piscataway	128	181	1,414
Pit River	291	610	2,096
Pomo			
Total	790	1,389	1,758
Eastern Pomo	19	52	2,737
Kashaya	19	-	-
Northern Pomo	25	88	3,520
Pomo	713	1,249	1,752
Other Pomo	14	-	-

Source: U.S. Bureau of the Census, 1980 Census of Population, Volume 2, Subject Reports, Characteristics of American Indians, by Tribes and Selected Areas: 1980, PC80-2-1C, Section 1: Tables I-II, issued September 1989, U.S. Department of Commerce, U.S. Government Printing Office, Washington, D.C., pp. 150-202. Notes: (N.E.C.) stands for not elsewhere classified. A dash (-) represents zero or a percent which rounds to less than 0.1. 1. Any Mohawk entry of "Ganienka" was miscoded to Wailaki. 2. Miscoding of entries of "Lummee," "Lummi," "Lumbee," or "Lumbi" may have affected the data for this tribe. 3. Reporting and/or processing may have affected the data for this tribe. 4. Any entry with the spelling "Micmac" was miscoded to Cheyenne River Sioux.

★ 409 ★

Fertility Characteristics of American Indian Women, by Tribe, 1980: Ponca-Sioux

Data are estimates based on a sample and are the most recent available.

Tribe	Fertility		
	Women 15 to 44 years	Children ever born	Children born per 1,000 women
Ponca	493	843	1,710
Potawatomi			
Total	2,383	3,554	1,491
Citizen Band	130	180	1,385
Forest County	6	22	3,667
Huron Potawatomi	45	84	1,867

[Continued]

★ 409 ★

Fertility Characteristics of American Indian Women, by Tribe, 1980: Ponca-Sioux
[Continued]

Tribe	Fertility		
	Women 15 to 44 years	Children ever born	Children born per 1,000 women
Potawatomie	2,123	3,145	1,481
Prairie Band	70	111	1,586
Other Potawatomi	9	12	1,333
Powhatan	66	33	500
Pueblo[1]			
Total	10,652	17,460	1,639
Acoma	755	1,312	1,738
Arizona Tewa	57	108	1,895
Cochiti	248	299	1,206
Hopi	2,183	3,313	1,518
Isleta	607	883	1,455
Jemez	332	673	1,027
Keres (n.e.c.)	188	256	1,362
Laguna	957	1,508	1,576
Nambe	49	94	1,918
Picuris	-	-	-
Pojoaque	-	-	-
Pueblo (n.e.c.)	758	1,189	1,569
Sandia	161	262	1,627
San Felipe	476	846	1,777
San Ildefonso	42	46	1,095
San Juan	103	200	1,942
Santa Ana	106	150	1,415
Santa Clara[1]	140	203	1,450
Santo Domingo	549	940	1,712
Taos	348	520	1,494
Tesuque	49	48	980
Tewa	575	864	1,503
Tigua[1]	143	248	1,734
Zia	166	385	2,070
Zuni	1,640	3,113	1,898
Puget Sound Salish			
Total	1,640	3,267	1,992
Duwamish	16	22	1,375
Muckleshoot	150	294	1,960
Nisqually	78	159	2,038
Nooksack	118	215	1,822
Puget Sound Salish (n.e.c.)	29	56	1,931
Puyallup	139	278	2,000
Samish	15	42	2,800
Sauk-Suiattle	55	85	1,545
Skokomish	104	200	1,923

[Continued]

★ 409 ★

Fertility Characteristics of American Indian Women, by Tribe, 1980: Ponca-Sioux

[Continued]

Tribe	Fertility		
	Women 15 to 44 years	Children ever born	Children born per 1,000 women
Skykomish	5	10	2,000
Snohomish	122	107	877
Snoqualmie	64	135	2,109
Squaxin Island	99	234	2,364
Steilacoom	32	24	750
Stillaguamish	19	23	1,211
Suquamish	85	225	2,647
Swinomish	102	796	1,755
Tulalip	318	796	2,503
Upper Skagit	90	183	2,033
Quapaw	272	327	1,202
Quinault	453	771	1,702
Rappahannock	68	60	882
Sac and Fox Mesquakie	923	1,504	1,629
Salinan	47	137	2,915
Schaghticoke	44	69	1,568
Seminole[1]			
Total	2,639	4,087	1,549
Seminole	2,536	3,904	1,539
Seminole Nation of Oklahoma	22	36	1,636
Seminole Tribe of Florida	81	147	1,815
Other Seminole	-	-	-
Serrano	30	17	567
Shasta	78	111	1,423
Shawnee			
Total	1,158	1,655	1,429
Absentee Shawnee	91	91	1,000
Shawnee	1,067	1,564	1,466
Shinnecock	334	510	1,527
Shoshone			
Total	2,579	3,917	1,519
Goshute	45	59	1,311
Shoshone	2,450	3,606	1,472
Te-Moak Western Shoshone[1]	35	152	4,343
Yomba[1]	23	52	2,261
Other Shoshone	26	48	1,846
Siletz	169	211	1,249
Sioux			
Total	19,402	37,781	1,947
Blackfoot Sioux	72	93	1,292
Brule Sioux	33	84	2,545
Cheyenne River Sioux[2]	882	1,818	2,061

[Continued]

★ 409 ★

Fertility Characteristics of American Indian Women, by Tribe, 1980: Ponca-Sioux

[Continued]

Tribe	Fertility		
	Women 15 to 44 years	Children ever born	Children born per 1,000 women
Crow River Sioux[2]	274	595	2,172
Dakota Sioux	278	568	2,043
Devil's Lake Sioux	23	40	1,739
Fladreau Santee	19	50	2,632
Fort Peck	54	217	4,019
Lower Brule Sioux	146	383	2,623
Mdewakanton Sioux	35	79	2,257
Oglala Sioux	2,884	5,883	2,040
Pine Ridge Sioux	113	37	2,846
Prior Lake Sioux	43	83	1,930
Rosebud Sioux	1,256	2,617	2,084
Santee Sioux	289	538	1,862
Sioux	11,634	21,868	1,880
Sisseton Sioux	336	621	1,848
Standing Rock Sioux	461	887	1,924
Teton Sioux	131	168	1,282
Wahpeton Sioux	22	26	1,182
Yankton Sioux	453	1,015	2,241
Yanktonai Sioux	27	38	1,407
Other Sioux	37	73	1,973

Source: U.S. Bureau of the Census, *1980 Census of Population, Volume 2, Subject Reports, Characteristics of American Indians, by Tribes and Selected Areas: 1980*, PC80-2-1C, Section 1: Tables I-II, issued September 1989, U.S. Department of Commerce, U.S. Government Printing Office, Washington, D.C., pp. 150-202. *Notes:* (N.E.C.) stands for not elsewhere classified. A dash (-) represents zero or a percent which rounds to less than 0.1. 1. Reporting and/or processing problems may have affected the data for this tribe. 2. Any entry with the spelling "Micmac" was miscoded to Cheyenne River Sioux.

★ 410 ★

Fertility Characteristics of American Indian Women, by Tribe, 1980: Siuslaw-Yurok

Data are estimates based on a sample and are the most recent available.

Tribe	Fertility		
	Women 15 to 44 years	Children ever born	Children born per 1,000 women
Siuslaw	68	133	1,956
Spokane	429	541	1,261
Stockbridge	350	551	1,574
Tlingit	2,501	4,500	1,799
Tolowa	97	152	1,567
Tonkawa	64	166	2,594
Tsimishian	384	481	1,253
Umatilla	277	442	1,596
Ute			
Total	1,513	3,023	1,998
Uintah Ute	7	2	286
Ute	1,310	2,573	1,964
Ute Mountain Ute	196	448	2,286
Other Ute	-	-	-
Wailaki[1]	198	436	1,985
Walla-Walla	67	133	1,985
Wampanoag	306	483	1,578
Warm Springs	429	919	2,142
Washo			
Total	348	540	1,552
Washo	341	519	1,522
Other Washo	7	21	3,000
Wichita	143	286	2,000
Winnebago	1,318	2,044	1,551
Wintu	497	978	1,968
Wiyot	68	96	1,412
Yakima	1,692	2,904	1,716
Yaqui			
Total	1,274	2,138	1,678
Barrio Libre	108	145	1,343
Yaqui	1,166	1,993	1,709
Other Yaqui	-	-	-
Yavapai Apache	42	44	1,048
Yokuts			
Total	440	921	2,093
Chuckhansi	134	233	1,739
Tachi	58	281	4,845
Tule River	97	174	1,794
Yokuts	151	233	1,543
Yuchi	51	72	1,412
Yuman			
Total	1,652	3,044	1,843

[Continued]

682

★ 410 ★

Fertility Characteristics of American Indian Women, by Tribe, 1980: Siuslaw-Yurok
[Continued]

Tribe	Fertility		
	Women 15 to 44 years	Children ever born	Children born per 1,000 women
Cocopah	151	210	1,391
Havasupai	171	280	1,637
Hualapai	245	402	1,641
Maricopa	207	380	1,836
Mohave	323	714	2,211
Quechan	347	660	1,902
Yavapai	208	398	1,913
Yurok	724	1,112	1,536
Other specified tribes (n.e.c.)			
Total	150	156	1,040
Fort Berthold	10	12	1,200
Gila River	17	14	824
Grand Rhonde	15	20	1,333
Los Coyotes	13	25	1,923
Round Valley	2	8	4,000
Scotts Valley	17	21	1,235
Shoalwater	34	8	235
All other specified	42	48	1,143
Tribe not specified	8,357	13,680	1,637
Tribe not reported	76,329	120,407	1,577

Source: U.S. Bureau of the Census, *1980 Census of Population, Volume 2, Subject Reports, Characteristics of American Indians, by Tribes and Selected Areas: 1980*, PC80-2-1C, Section 1: Tables I-II, Issued September 1989, U.S. Department of Commerce, U.S. Government Printing Office, Washington, D.C., pp. 150-202. *Notes:* (N.E.C.) stands for not elsewhere classified. A dash (-) represents zero or a percent which rounds to less than 0.1. 1. Any Mohawk entry of "Ganienka" was miscoded to Wailaki.

★ 411 ★

Number and Percent Distribution of Deaths, by Age and Sex

American Indians, Alaskan Natives, 1986-1988, and selected U.S. populations, 1987.

Age group	American Indians and Alaska Natives						United States		
	Both sexes		Male		Female		All races	White	Black
	Number	Percent	Number	Percent	Number	Percent			
Totals	21,943	100.0	12,888	100.0	9,055	100.0	2,123,323	1,843,067	254,814
Under 1	1,236	5.6	679	5.3	557	6.2	1.8	1.4	4.5
1 to 4	329	1.5	190	1.5	139	1.5	0.4	0.3	0.7
5 to 14	329	1.5	207	1.6	122	1.3	0.4	0.4	0.7
15 to 24	1,610	7.3	1,228	9.5	382	4.2	1.8	1.6	2.9

[Continued]

★ 411 ★

Number and Percent Distribution of Deaths, by Age and Sex

[Continued]

Age group	American Indians and Alaska Natives						United States		
	Both sexes		Male		Female		United States		
	Number	Percent	Number	Percent	Number	Percent	All races	White	Black
25 to 34	1,839	8.4	1,302	10.1	537	5.9	2.7	2.3	5.6
35 to 44	1,821	8.3	1,230	9.5	591	6.5	3.5	2.9	6.9
45 to 54	2,272	10.4	1,422	11.0	850	9.4	5.5	4.9	9.0
55 to 64	3,077	14.0	1,782	13.8	1,295	14.3	12.9	12.4	15.9
65 to 74	3,812	17.4	2,142	16.6	1,670	18.4	22.9	23.1	21.9
75 to 84	3,463	15.8	1,745	13.5	1,718	19.0	27.5	28.6	20.4
85 and over	2,137	9.7	949	7.4	1,188	13.1	20.7	22.1	11.5
Age not stated	18	0.1	12	0.1	6	0.1	0.0[1]	0.0[1]	0.1

Source: Trends in Indian Health, 1991, U.S. Department of Health and Human Services, Public Health Service, Indian Health Service, p. 41. *Note:* Percents may not sum to 100.0 due to rounding.

★ 412 ★

Mortality Rates, by Age

Rate per 100,000 population for American Indians, Alaskan Natives, 1986- 1988, and selected U.S. populations, 1987.

Age group	Indian and Alaska Natives		U.S. rate			Ratio American Indian and Alaska Native to U.S. all races
	Number	Rate	All races	White	All other	
Under 1	1,236	1,161.9	1,018.5	845.1	1,757.0	1.1
1-4	329	87.6	51.6	46.4	73.6	1.7
5-14	329	33.7	25.6	24.1	31.8	1.3
15-24	1,610	157.9	99.4	93.8	124.9	1.6
25-34	1,839	248.1	133.2	115.7	225.7	1.9
35-44	1,821	372.1	214.1	184.2	396.7	1.7
45-54	2,272	648.6	498.0	451.9	786.7	1.3
55-64	3,077	1,210.6	1,241.3	1,182.1	1,677.2	1.0
65-74	3,812	2,438.0	2,751.3	2,688.9	3,286.6	0.9
75-84	3,463	5,195.6	6,282.5	6,247.8	6,629.7	0.8
85+	2,137	11,357.4	15,320.8	15,580.5	12,683.3	0.7

Source: Trends in Indian Health, 1991, U.S. Department of Health and Human Services, Public Health Service, Indian Health Service, p. 39. Primary source: U.S. Data by Race: National Center for Health Statistics, HHS, Monthly Vital Statistics Report, Vol. 38, No. 5, Supplement Advance Report- Final Mortality Statistics, 1987, and Final Mortality Statistics, 1987, NCHS Volume II, Part A, Table 1-10.

★ 413 ★

Mortality Rates, by Selected Causes

Age-adjusted rate per 100,000 population for American Indians, Alaskan Natives, and selected U.S. populations, 1988.

Cause of death	Indian and Alaska Native	United States			Ratio American Indian and Alaska Native to U.S. all
		All races	White	All other	races
All causes	574.3	535.5	509.8	692.5	1.1
Major cardiovascular disease	172.5	206.6	199.2	256.4	0.8
Diseases of heart	138.1	166.3	1615	197.8	0.8
Cerebrovascular diseases	26.4	29.7	27.5	45.6	0.9
Atherosclerosis	3.0	3.4	3.4	3.3	0.9
Hypertension	1.7	1.8	1.5	4.7	0.9
Malignant neoplasms	91.3	132.7	130.0	151.9	0.7
Accidents	80.8	35.	34.1	40.7	2.3
Motor vehicle	44.7	19.7	20.0	18.5	2.3
All other	36.1	15.3	14.1	22.2	2.4
Chronic liver disease and cirrhosis	30.4	9.0	8.4	12.9	3.4
Diabetes mellitus	25.8	10.1	9.0	18.7	2.6
Pneumonia and influenza	18.7	14.2	13.6	17.5	1.3
Suicide	14.5	11.4	12.2	6.9	1.3
Homicide	14.1	9.0	5.3	28.2	1.6
Chronic obstructive pulmonary diseases and allied conditions	13.8	19.4	19.8	14.8	0.7
Tuberculosis, all forms	2.5	0.5	0.3	1.9	5.0

Source: Trends in Indian Health, 1991, U.S. Department of Health and Human Services, Public Health Service, Indian Health Service, p. 38. Primary source: U.S. Mortality Rates: Monthly Vital Statistics Report, NCHS, DHHS Pub. No. (PHS) 91-1120, Vol. 39, No. 7, Supplement, Nov. 28, 1990, Table 12.

★ 414 ★

Death Rate Reductions: 1955-1988

Tuberculosis, all forms - 96.0	
Maternal - 91.0	
Conditions in the perinatal period - 88.0	
Postneonatal - 87.0	
Gastrointestinal diseases - 86.0	
Infant - 85.0	
Neonatal - 80.0	
Pneumonia and influenza - 71.0	
Congenital malformations - 57.0	
Accidents - 56.0	

Chart shows data from column 3.

Chart shows percentage decreases, as shown in column three of table.

Death rates	Calendar year 1955 rate	Calendar year 1987/88 rate	Percentage decrease
Infant[1]	62.7	9.7	85.0
Neonatal[1]	23.1	4.6	80.0
Postneonatal[1]	39.7	5.1	87.0
Maternal[2]	82.6	7.1	91.0
Conditions in the perinatal period[3]	67.6	8.2	88.0
Pneumonia and influenza[4]	64.4	18.7	71.0
Tuberculosis, all forms[4]	57.9	2.5	96.0
Gastrointestinal diseases[4]	15.4	2.1	86.0
Congenital malformations[4]	10.1	4.3	57.0
Accidents[4]	184.0	80.8	56.0

Source: Trends in Indian Health, 1991, U.S. Department of Health and Human Services, Public Health Service, Indian Health Service, p. 57. *Notes:* 1. Rates per 1,000 live births for 1954-1956 and 1986-1988. 2. Rates per 100,000 live births for 1957-1959 and 1986-1988. 3. Rate per 100,000 population (since all deaths occurred under age 5) for 1954-1956 and 1986-1988. 4. Single year age-adjusted rates per 100,000 population for 1988.

★ 415 ★

Leading Causes of Death

Rate per 100,000 population for American Indians, Alaskan Natives, 1986-1988.

Cause of death	Number	Rate
All causes	21,943	481.6
Diseases of the heart	5,078	111.5
Accidents	3,533	77.5
Motor vehicles	2,032	44.6

[Continued]

★ 415 ★

Leading Causes of Death

[Continued]

Cause of death	Number	Rate
Other accidents	1,501	32.9
Malignant neoplasms	3,011	66.1
Cerebrovascular diseases	1,003	22.0
Chronic liver disease and cirrhosis	934	20.5
Diabetes mellitus	798	17.5
Pneumonia and influenza	740	16.2
Homicide	654	14.4
Suicide	653	14.3
Chronic obstructive pulmonary diseases	474	10.4
All other causes	5,065	

Source: *Trends in Indian Health, 1991*, U.S. Department of Health and Human Services, Public Health Service, Indian Health Service, p. 36.

★ 416 ★

Leading Causes of Death, by Sex

Rate per 100,000 population for American Indians, Alaskan Natives, 1986-1988.

Cause of death	Number	Rate
Male		
All causes	12,888	573.9
Diseases of the heart	2,970	132.2
Accidents	2,597	115.6
Motor vehicles	1,454	64.7
Other accidents	1,143	50.9
Malignant neoplasms	1,519	67.6
Suicide	545	24.3
Chronic liver disease and cirrhosis	517	23.0
Homicide	508	22.6
Cerebrovascular diseases	473	21.1
Pneumonia and influenza	424	18.9
Diabetes mellitus	324	14.4
Chronic obstructive pulmonary diseases and allied conditions	305	13.6
All other causes	2,706	
Female		
All causes	9,055	392.0
Disease of the heart	2,108	91.3
Malignant neoplasms	1,492	64.6
Accidents	936	40.5
Motor vehicles	578	25.0
Other accidents	358	15.5

[Continued]

687

★ 416 ★

Leading Causes of Death, by Sex
[Continued]

Cause of death	Number	Rate
Cerebrovascular diseases	530	22.9
Diabetes mellitus	474	20.5
Chronic liver disease and cirrhosis	417	18.1
Pneumonia and influenza	316	13.7
Nephritis, nephrotic syndrome, and nephrosis	185	8.0
Chronic obstructive pulmonary diseases and allied conditions	169	7.3
Congenital anomalies	165	7.1
All other causes	2,263	

Source: Trends in Indian Health, 1991, U.S. Department of Health and Human Services, Public Health Service, Indian Health Service, p. 37.

★ 417 ★

Ten Leading Causes of Death, 1 to 14 Years of Age

Rate per 100,000 population for American Indians, Alaskan Natives, 1986-1988, and U.S. all races, 1987.

Cause of death	Indian and Alaska Native		U.S. all races Rate	Ratio American Indian and Alaska Native to U.S. all races
	Number	Rate		
All causes	658	48.6	33.3	1.5
Accidents	365	27.0	14.6	1.8
Motor vehicles	172	12.7	7.0	1.8
Other accidents	193	14.3	7.7	1.9
Congenital anomalies	36	2.7	2.8	1.0
Malignant neoplasms	34	2.5	3.5	0.7
Diseases of the heart	26	1.9	1.3	1.5
Homicide	26	1.9	1.5	1.3
Suicide	17	1.3	0.5	2.6
Pneumonia and influenza	16	1.2	0.6	2.0
Septicemia	5	0.4	0.3	1.3
Benign neoplasms	4	0.3	0.3	1.0
Anemias	4	0.3	0.2	1.5
All other causes	125			

Source: Trends in Indian Health, 1991, U.S. Department of Health and Human Services, Public Health Service, Indian Health Service, p. 31.

★ 418 ★

Ten Leading Causes of Death, 15 to 24 Years of Age

Rate per 100,000 population for American Indians, Alaskan Natives, 1986-1988, and U.S. all races, 1987.

Cause of death	Indian and Alaska Native		U.S. all races Rate	Ratio American Indian and Alaska Native to U.S. all races
	Number	Rate		
All causes	1,610	157.9	99.40	1.6
Accidents	908	89.1	48.9	1.8
Motor vehicles	650	63.8	37.8	1.7
Other accidents	258	25.3	11.1	2.3
Suicide	240	23.5	12.9	1.8
Homicide	215	21.1	14.0	1.5
Malignant neoplasms	29	2.8	5.1	0.5
Diseases of the heart	18	1.8	2.8	0.6
Chronic liver disease and cirrhosis	9	0.9	0.2	4.5
Cerebrovascular diseases	7	0.7	0.6	1.2
Pneumonia and influenza	6	0.6	0.7	0.9
Chronic obstructive pulmonary diseases and allied conditions	6	0.6	0.5	1.2
Congenital anomalies	6	0.6	1.3	0.5
All other causes	166			

Source: Trends in Indian Health, 1991, U.S. Department of Health and Human Services, Public Health Service, Indian Health Service, p. 32.

★ 419 ★

Ten Leading Causes of Death, 25 to 44 Years of Age

Rate per 100,000 population for American Indians, Alaskan Natives, 1986-1988, and U.S. all races, 1987.

Cause of death	Indian and Alaska Native		U.S. all races Rate	Ratio American Indian and Alaska Native to U.S. all races
	Number	Rate		
All causes	3,660	297.5	169.0	1.8
Accidents	1,330	108.1	35.4	3.1
Motor vehicles	820	66.6	21.1	3.2
Other accidents	510	41.4	14.3	2.9
Chronic liver disease and cirrhosis	342	27.8	5.9	4.7
Homicide	319	25.9	13.2	2.0
Suicide	309	25.1	15.2	1.7

[Continued]

★ 419 ★

Ten Leading Causes of Death, 25 to 44 Years of Age
[Continued]

Cause of death	Indian and Alaska Native		U.S. all races Rate	Ratio American Indian and Alaska Native to U.S. all races
	Number	Rate		
Diseases of the heart	296	24.1	20.5	1.2
Malignant neoplasms	226	18.4	26.2	0.7
Cerebrovascular diseases	72	5.9	4.4	1.3
Pneumonia and influenza	52	4.2	2.5	1.7
Diabetes mellitus	42	3.4	2.3	1.5
Nephritis, nephrotic syndrome and nephrosis	28	2.3	0.9	2.6
All other causes	644			

Source: Trends in Indian Health, 1991, U.S. Department of Health and Human Services, Public Health Service, Indian Health Service, p. 33.

★ 420 ★

Ten Leading Causes of Death, 45 to 64 Years of Age

Rate per 100,000 population for American Indians, Alaskan Natives, 1986-1988, and U.S. all races, 1987.

Cause of death	Indian and Alaska Native		U.S. all races Rate	Ratio American Indian and Alaska Native to U.S. all races
	Number	Rate		
All causes	5,349	884.9	859.4	1.0
Diseases of the heart	1,443	238.7	270.9	0.9
Malignant neoplasms	1,046	173.0	301.7	0.6
Accidents	507	83.9	32.7	2.6
Motor vehicles	250	41.4	15.5	2.7
Other accidents	257	42.5	17.2	2.5
Chronic liver disease and cirrhosis	450	74.4	25.8	2.9
Diabetes mellitus	307	50.8	18.0	2.8
Cerebrovascular diseases	212	35.1	35.7	1.0
Pneumonia and influenza	122	20.2	11.2	1.8
Chronic obstructive pulmonary diseases and allied conditions	100	16.5	27.8	0.6
Nephritis, nephrotic syndrome and nephrosis	99	16.4	6.2	2.6
Suicide	67	11.1	16.2	0.7
All other causes	996			

Source: Trends in Indian Health, 1991, U.S. Department of Health and Human Services, Public Health Service, Indian Health Service, p. 34.

★ 421 ★

Ten Leading Causes of Death, 65 Years Old and Older

Rate per 100,000 population for American Indians, Alaskan Natives, 1986- 1988, and U.S. all races, 1987.

Cause of death	Indian and Alaska Native		U.S. all races Rate	Ratio American Indian and Alaska Native to U.S. all races
	Number	Rate		
All causes	9,412	3,892.1	5,059.9	0.8
Diseases of the heart	3,258	1,347.2	2,074.6	0.6
Malignant neoplasms	1,673	691.8	1,059.8	0.7
Cerebrovascular diseases	698	288.6	435.0	0.7
Pneumonia and influenza	499	206.3	202.9	1.0
Diabetes mellitus	446	184.4	95.1	1.9
Accidents	359	148.5	86.6	1.7
Motor vehicles	19	49.2	22.7	2.2
Other accidents	240	99.2	63.9	1.6
Chronic obstructive pulmonary diseases and allied conditions	352	145.6	216.0	0.7
Suicide				
Homicide				
Nephritis,nephrotic syndrome and nephrosis	185	76.5	61.2	1.3
Chronic liver disease and cirrhosis	132	54.6	33.0	1.7
Septicemia	125	51.7	53.2	1.0
All other causes	1,685			

Source: *Trends in Indian Health, 1991*, U.S. Department of Health and Human Services, Public Health Service, Indian Health Service, p. 35.

Accidents and Injuries

★ 422 ★

Fatal Accidents, by Age and Sex

Rate per 100,000 population for American Indians, Alaskan Natives, 1986-1988, and U.S. all races, 1987.

Age group	Male				Female			
	Indian and Alaska Native		U.S. all races	Ratio Indian to U.S. all	Indian and Alaska Native		U.S. all races	Ratio Indian to U.S. all
	Number	Rate	Rate	races	Number	Rate	Rate	races
Motor vehicle accidents								
Under 1 year	12	22.6	5.0	4.5	6	11.3	5.6	2.0
1 to 4 years	45	24.2	7.6	3.2	34	17.9	6.1	2.9
5 to 14 years	54	11.0	9.1	1.2	39	8.0	4.8	1.7
15 to 24 years	493	97.0	55.5	1.7	157	30.7	19.7	1.6
25 to 34 years	384	104.7	36.8	2.8	148	39.5	11.5	3.4
35 to 44 years	208	86.2	25.6	3.4	80	32.2	9.3	3.5
45 to 54 years	112	65.7	21.8	3.0	50	27.8	9.2	3.0
55 to 64 years	64	52.2	21.7	2.4	24	18.3	10.2	1.8
65 to 74 years	47	65.6	24.6	2.7	15	17.7	13.7	1.3
78 to 84 years	29	99.1	42.7	2.3	21	56.1	21.3	2.6
85 years and over	4	53.2	57.1	0.9	3	26.6	15.4	1.7
Other accidents								
Under 1 year	21	39.5	22.1	1.8	18	33.8	17.5	1.9
1 to 4 years	66	35.5	16.7	2.1	31	16.3	9.8	1.7
5 to 14 years	73	14.9	7.6	2.0	23	4.7	2.9	1.6
15 to 24 years	216	42.5	18.6	2.3	42	8.2	3.5	2.3
25 to 34 years	233	63.5	23.6	2.7	49	13.1	4.8	2.7
35 to 44 years	186	77.1	23.8	3.2	42	16.9	5.2	3.3
45 to 54 years	102	59.9	23.4	2.6	24	13.3	6.4	2.1
55 to 64 years	101	82.3	30.3	2.7	30	22.8	10.6	2.2
65 to 74 years	81	113.0	42.6	2.7	37	43.7	21.1	2.1
75 to 84 years	36	123.1	103.3	1.2	28	74.9	62.0	1.2
85 years and over	24	319.3	297.9	1.1	34	300.9	196.2	1.5

Source: Trends in Indian Health, 1991, U.S. Department of Health and Human Services, Public Health Service, Indian Health Service, p. 44.

★ 423 ★

Fatal Accidents, by Year

Age-adjusted rate per 100,000 population for American Indians, Alaskan Natives, and U.S. all races, 1955-1988.

Calendar year	Indian and Alaska Native				U.S. all races			U.S. other than White		
	Total deaths	All accidents	Motor vehicle	Other	All accidents	Motor vehicle	Other	All accidents	Motor vehicle	Other
1988	1,177	80.8	44.7	36.1	35.0	19.7	15.3	40.7	18.5	22.2
1987	1,166	82.6	46.8	35.9	34.6	19.5	15.2	39.7	17.9	21.7
1986	1,185	83.2	47.7	35.5	35.2	19.4	15.7	39.9	18.1	21.7
1985	1,075	77.7	42.6	35.1	34.7	18.8	16.0	39.7	17.4	22.3
1984	1,078	81.2	41.9	39.3	35.0	19.1	15.9	38.5	16.6	21.9
1983	1,065	83.0	44.6	38.3	35.3	18.5	16.8	40.2	16.4	23.7
1982	1,135	94.7	49.9	44.8	36.6	19.3	17.3	40.8	16.8	23.9
1981	1,124	92.8	54.1	38.7	39.8	21.8	18.0	44.0	18.6	25.4
1980	1,255	107.3	61.3	46.0	42.3	22.9	19.5	49.5	20.3	29.3
1979	1,248	109.3	60.2	49.1	43.7	23.7	20.0	50.5	21.5	29.0
1978	1,302	127.4	71.5	55.9	44.3	23.4	20.9	52.6	22.4	30.1
1977	1,226	125.5	71.8	53.7	43.8	22.4	21.4	53.1	21.9	31.2
1976	1,215	131.9	74.5	57.4	43.2	21.5	21.7	53.2	21.9	31.3
1975	1,256	143.6	78.5	65.1	44.8	21.3	23.5	56.9	22.5	34.4
1974	1,110	138.7	72.9	65.7	46.0	21.8	24.2	58.5	23.2	35.3
1973	1,341	175.5	101.8	73.7	51.7	26.4	25.3	67.5	30.0	37.6
1972	1,254	173.2	99.7	73.5	52.0	27.0	25.0	68.8	30.6	38.1
1971	1,134	170.3	89.6	80.7	52.0	26.6	25.3	71.6	31.3	40.4
1970	1,107	181.8	98.5	83.3	53.7	27.4	26.3	72.8	30.9	41.9
1969	1,139	194.4	99.1	95.3	55.3	28.5	26.8	75.5	33.7	41.8
1968	1,051	183.0	94.5	88.5	55.1	28.4	26.7	77.0	33.3	43.7
1967	1,000	178.9	95.5	83.4	54.8	27.8	27.0	73.2	31.1	42.1
1966	1,003	185.2	92.4	92.8	55.6	28.3	27.3	75.8	31.6	44.1
1965	951	186.7	91.9	94.8	53.4	26.6	26.8	70.8	29.2	41.5
1964	912	208.5	97.3	111.1	52.0	25.7	26.3	68.4	27.5	40.8
1963	835	172.5	78.0	94.5	50.9	24.3	26.6	68.2	26.5	41.7
1962	744	176.2	87.6	88.6	49.7	23.1	26.6	66.5	25.2	41.3
1961	822	188.8	91.5	97.4	48.1	22.1	26.1	63.3	23.9	39.4
1960	773	186.1	91.9	94.6	49.9	22.5	27.4	67.3	24.4	42.9
1959	794	197.4	98.3	99.1	49.9	22.8	27.1	66.1	25.0	41.1
1958	709	172.3	87.4	84.9	49.8	22.5	27.3	66.7	24.7	42.0
1957	743	185.1	94.9	90.0	53.4	24.1	29.3	71.0	27.3	43.7
1956	794	195.5	106.2	89.4	54.4	25.2	29.2	72.0	29.5	42.5
1955	714	184.0	97.6	90.3	54.3	24.6	29.7	71.1	28.1	43.0

Source: Trends in Indian Health, 1991, U.S. Department of Health and Human Services, Public Health Service, Indian Health Service, p. 42. *Notes:* Estimated population methodology for the Indian population revised in 1976. Maine, New York and Pennsylvania included as Reservation States beginning 1979, Connecticut, Rhode Island and Texas in 1983 and Alabama in 1984. Decennial Census population counts used for 1960, 1970 and 1980.

★ 424 ★

Injury Death Rates of Persons 0 to 14 Years Old, by Leading Cause, 1980-85

Death rates, per 100,000 are shown, by injury cause and race/ethnicity, for 1980-85. Total deaths are shown in parentheses.

Injury Cause	Death rate per 100,000				
	All races[1]	Native American	White	Black	Oriental
All injuries	19.3	33.9	17.5	29.3	17.5
	(59,711)	(918)	(44,217)	(13,634)	(917)
Motor vehicle occupant	3.2	6.9	3.3	2.6	3.1
	(9,796)	(186)	(8,224)	(1,217)	(162)
Pedestrian, traffic	2.4	3.6	2.2	3.8	2.9
	(7,489)	(98)	(5,487)	(1,748)	(153)
Drowning	2.8	4.8	2.6	3.9	3.4
	(8,568)	(131)	(6,438)	(1,814)	(180)
House fire	2.3	3.3	1.6	6.0	1.0
	(7,021)	(90)	(4,080)	(2,795)	(51)
Fall	0.4	0.6	0.4	0.7	0.9
	(1,332)	(17)	(933)	(333)	(49)
Homocide	1.9	2.7	1.3	4.7	1.9
	(5,722)	(72)	(3,355)	(2,191)	(101)

Source: Health Status of Minorities and Low-Income Groups: Third Edition, U.S. Department of Health and Human Services, Public Health Service, Health Resources and Services Administration, Government Printing Office, Washington, D.C., p. 171. A.E. Waller, S.P. Baker A. Szocka, "Childhood Injury Deaths: National Analysis and Geographic Variations," American Journal of Public Health, Mar 1989, Vol. 79, No. 3, Table 2, p. 312 *Note:* 1. All races column includes cases where race was unknown.

★ 425 ★

Injury Death Ratios in Relation to Whites of Persons 0 to 14 Years Old, by Leading Cause, 1980-85

Injury death ratios in relation to whites are shown, by leading cause and race/ethnicity, for 1980-85.

Injury Cause	Ratio of Death Rate for This Group to Death Rate for Whites		
	Native American	Black	Asian/Pacific Islander
All Injuries	1.94	1.67	1.00
Motor vehicle occupant	2.09	0.79	0.94
Pedestrian, traffic	1.64	1.73	1.32
Drowning	1.85	1.50	1.31
House fire	2.06	3.75	0.63

[Continued]

★ 425 ★

Injury Death Ratios in Relation to Whites of Persons 0 to 14 Years Old, by Leading Cause, 1980-85
[Continued]

| Injury Cause | Ratio of Death Rate for This Group to Death Rate for Whites | | |
	Native American	Black	Asian/Pacific Islander
Fall	1.50	1.75	2.25
Homocide	2.08	3.62	1.46

Source: Health Status of Minorities and Low-Income Groups: Third Edition, U.S. Department of Health and Human Services, Public Health Service, Health Resources and Services Administration, Government Printing Office, Washington, D.C., p. 171. Calculated from data in A.E. Waller, S.P. Baker, A. Szocka, "Childhood Injury Deaths: National Analysis and Geographic Variations," *American Journal of Public Health*, Mar. 1989, Vol. 79, No. 3, Table 3, p. 312.

AIDS

★ 426 ★

AIDS Education of 8th and 10th Graders

Based on 1988 national study of 3,617 eighth and tenth graders. Percentages reflect responses to the question "Since the beginning of the 7th grade, have you received instruction in school on AIDS?"

	American Indian/ Alaskan	White	Black	Hispanic	Asian/ Pacific Islander	Other
Yes	50.1	33.3	40.2	39.4	30.2	38.4
No	24.8	48.7	41.9	32.1	39.5	38.8
Don't remember	25.1	18.0	18.0	28.6	30.3	22.8

Source: D. Michael Anderson and Gregory M. Christenson, "Ethnic Breakdown of AIDS Related Knowledge and Attitudes from the National Adolescent Student Health Survey," *Journal of Health Education*, Vol. 22, No. 1, January/February 1991, p. 31. Primary source: *The National Adolescent Student Health Survey: A Report on the Health of America's Youth.* 1989. Third Party Publishing Co., Oakland, CA; American School Health Association, Association for the Advancement of Health Education, Society for Public Health Education, Inc. (Subset of original data).

★ 427 ★

AIDS Incidence, by Race/Ethnicity, 1981-1988

Category	Racial/ethnic group (percent)					
	American Indian/Alaskan Native	White	Black	Hispanic	Asian/ Pacific Islander	Total
U.S. population	1.0	80.0	12.0	6.0	2.0	100.0
All AIDS cases	<1.0	59.0	27.0	13.0	1.0	100.0
Adult AIDS cases						
Male	<1.0	62.0	24.0	13.0	1.0	100.0
Female	<1.0	29.0	54.0	16.0	1.0	100.0
Pediatric cases	<1.0	25.0	55.0	20.0	<1.0	100.0

Source: "Racial/Ethnic Distribution of the U.S. Population Overall Compared With the Racial/Ethnic Distribution of AIDS Cases, 1981-1988," *Health Status of Minorities and Low-Income Groups: Third Edition,* 1991, p. 203. Primary source: Centers for Disease Control. AIDS and Human Immunodeficiency Virus Infection in the United States; 1988 Update. *Morbidity and Mortality Weekly Report,* May 12, 1989, Vol. 38, No. S-4, Table 2, p. 18. *Note:* Excluding U.S. territories.

★ 428 ★

AIDS Prevention Awareness of 8th and 10th Graders

Percentages reflect a 1988 national survey of 3,617 eighth and tenth graders.

	American Indian/ Alaskan	White	Black	Hispanic	Asian/ Pacific Islander	Other
Does this behavior make infection LESS likely?						
Using condoms (rubbers) during sex:						
Yes[1]	75.4	88.3	84.3	75.0	76.4	74.8
No	6.4	5.6	11.6	14.8	14.7	12.0
Don't know	18.2	6.1	4.0	10.2	8.9	13.3
Not having sex:						
Yes[1]	65.2	79.7	665	62.4	66.8	75.4
No	17.6	15.0	26.1	28.2	24.3	19.0
Don't know	17.3	5.4	7.4	9.4	8.9	5.6
Going to the bathroom after having sex:						
Yes	18.9	6.4	16.7	9.7	11.7	18.4
No[1]	42.9	61.8	55.1	57.3	52.3	54.5
Don't know	38.4	31.8	28.3	33.1	36.1	27.0

[Continued]

★ 428 ★

AIDS Prevention Awareness of 8th and 10th Graders
[Continued]

	American Indian/ Alaskan	White	Black	Hispanic	Asian/ Pacific Islander	Other
Washing after having sex:						
Yes	40.0	20.0	41.0	33.5	23.1	20.5
No[1]	33.1	52.5	41.0	36.4	49.5	46.1
Don't know	26.9	27.5	18.1	30.1	27.4	33.4

Source: D. Michael Anderson and Gregory M. Christenson, "Ethnic Breakdown of AIDS Related Knowledge and Attitudes from the National Adolescent Student Health Survey," *Journal of Health Education,* Vol. 22, No. 1, January/February 1991, p. 33. Primary source: *The National Adolescent Student Health Survey: A Report on the Health of America's Youth.* 1989. Third Party Publishing Co., Oakland, CA; American School Health Association, Association for the Advancement of Health Education, Society for Public Health Education, Inc. (Subset of original data). *Note:* 1. Indicates a correct response.

★ 429 ★

AIDS Risk Awareness of 8th and 10th Graders

Percentages reflect a 1988 national survey of 3,617 eighth and tenth graders.

	American Indian/ Alaskan	White	Black	Hispanic	Asian/ Pacific Islander	Other
Does this behavior make infection MORE likely?						
Having sexual intercourse with someone who has AIDS:						
Yes[1]	92.2	96.8	90.3	87.8	86.9	89.4
No	3.5	2.9	7.2	10.4	11.3	8.6
Don't know	4.3	0.3	2.5	1.8	1.8	2.0
Being in the same classroom with someone who has AIDS:						
Yes	0.0	4.3	5.9	5.0	3.8	5.1
No[1]	84.2	88.2	79.6	75.9	84.1	77.9
Don't know	15.8	7.6	14.5	19.1	21.1	17.0
Having more than one sex partner:						
Yes[1]	85.3	85.0	74.1	75.8	75.0	82.9
No	10.4	7.2	15.4	11.4	17.3	8.1
Don't know	4.3	7.7	10.6	12.9	7.7	9.1
Having sex with someone who has had several sex partners:						
Yes[1]	82.0	86.7	74.4	75.8	73.7	81.7
No	10.8	5.0	12.8	10.4	14.9	7.2
Don't know	7.2	8.3	12.9	13.8	11.5	11.1

[Continued]

★ 429 ★

AIDS Risk Awareness of 8th and 10th Graders
[Continued]

	American Indian/ Alaskan	White	Black	Hispanic	Asian/ Pacific Islander	Other
A male having sex with another male:						
Yes[1]	85.9	82.4	79.7	73.7	74.6	75.1
No	8.0	7.6	11.4	12.2	15.5	10.3
Don't know	6.1	10.0	8.8	14.1	9.9	14.6
Sharing drug needles:						
Yes[1]	79.3	93.8	86.8	85.9	83.3	80.2
No	6.4	3.3	8.4	10.7	14.0	11.5
Don't know	14.2	2.9	4.8	3.4	2.7	8.3
Donating blood:						
Yes	49.7	43.0	55.0	54.7	45.1	63.9
No[1]	19.0	43.3	27.4	31.3	44.8	28.4
Don't know	31.3	13.7	17.6	14.0	10.1	7.8

Source: D. Michael Anderson and Gregory M. Christenson, "Ethnic Breakdown of AIDS Related Knowledge and Attitudes from the National Adolescent Student Health Survey," *Journal of Health Education,* Vol. 22, No. 1, January/February 1991, p. 32. Primary source: *The National Adolescent Student Health Survey: A Report on the Health of America's Youth.* 1989. Third Party Publishing Co., Oakland, CA; American School Health Association, Association for the Advancement of Health Education, Society for Public Health Education, Inc. (Subset of original data). *Note:* 1. Indicates a correct response.

★ 430 ★

AIDS Transmission, by Category

Total number of AIDS cases from 1981-1988 is shown, by race/ethnicity. Percent distribution of those cases is shown for each patient group, by category of transmission.

Category	Total	Percent								
		Homosexual/ bisexual	IVDU[1]	Homosexual and IVDU	Heterosexual contact		Transfusion recipient	Coagulation disorder	Other risk factor	NIR[2]
					Sex with IVDU	Sex with person at risk (non IVDU)				
American Indian/Alaskan Native										
Adult										
Male	75	61	9	17	<1	<1	1	4	<1	7
Female	12[6]	-	-	-	-	-	-	-	-	-
Pediatric	2[6]	-	-	-	-	-	-	-	-	-
White										
Adult										
Male	45,359	81	5	8	<1	<1	2	1	<1	2
Female	1,948	-	40	-	12	13	26	1	<1	8
Pediatric	321	-	22[3]	-	10[4]	8[5]	29	19	9	3
Black										
Adult										
Male	17,618	45	34	8	1	<1	1	<1	5	4
Female	3,604	-	58	-	17	5	4	<1	8	7
Pediatric	707	-	47[3]	-	15[4]	4[5]	5	1	23	5

[Continued]

★ 430 ★

AIDS Transmission, by Category
[Continued]

Category	Total	Homosexual/ bisexual	IVDU[1]	Homosexual and IVDU	Sex with IVDU	Sex with person at risk (non IVDU)	Transfusion recipient	Coagulation disorder	Other risk factor	NIR[2]
						Percent				
					Heterosexual contact					
Hispanic										
Adult										
Male	10,773	48	37	8	<1	<1	1	1	<1	5
Female	1,360	-	54	-	29	5	5	<1	<1	7
Pediatric	308	-	50[3]	-	21[4]	4[5]	11	4	6	4
Asian/Pacific Islander										
Adult										
Male	440	82	2	2	<1	<1	6	2	<1	6
Female	42	-	19	-	10	19	36	<1	<1	17
Pediatric	6[6]	-	-	-	-	-	-	-	-	-

Source: "Adult and Pediatric AIDS Cases, by Transmission Category, Race/Ethnic Group, and Sex, 1981-1988," *Health Status of Minorities and Low-Income Groups: Third Edition*, 1991, p. 202. Primary source: Centers for Disease Control, "AIDS and Human Immunodeficiency Virus in the United States: 1988 Update." *Morbidity and Mortality Weekly Report*, May 12, 1989, Vol. 38, No. S-4, Table 3, p. 19. *Notes:* 1. IVDU stands for intravenous drug user. 2. NIR stands for no identified risk. 3. Mother with history of intravenous drug use. 4. Mother with history of sex with IVDU. 5. Mother with history of sex with person at risk for HIV (other than IVDU). 6. Small numbers make calculations of percentages of limited value.

★ 431 ★

AIDS, Basic Knowledge of 8th and 10th Graders

Percentages reflect a 1988 national survey of 3,617 eighth and tenth graders.

	American Indian/ Alaskan	White	Black	Hispanic	Asian/ Pacific Islander	Other
There is no known cure for AIDS:						
True[1]	73.7	88.9	84.0	82.5	82.3	75.8
False	19.8	4.1	6.7	9.0	8.4	7.8
Don't know	6.6	7.0	9.3	8.6	9.3	16.5
A test to determine whether a person has the AIDS virus is now available:						
True[1]	82.5	85.0	73.3	76.2	84.4	78.3
False	9.6	5.1	10.7	7.0	2.2	5.6
Don't know	8.0	9.9	16.1	16.8	13.4	16.1
A vaccine that protects people from getting the AIDS virus is available:						
True	8.8	8.5	17.6	14.2	8.8	13.0
False[1]	56.2	66.9	47.0	51.3	58.1	56.2
Don't know	35.0	24.7	35.5	34.5	33.4	30.8
A pregnant woman who has the AIDS virus can give AIDS to her baby:						
True[1]	62.1	80.8	84.3	85.0	79.9	71.7

[Continued]

★ 431 ★

AIDS, Basic Knowledge of 8th and 10th Graders
[Continued]

	American Indian/ Alaskan	White	Black	Hispanic	Asian/ Pacific Islander	Other
False	0.0	1.4	2.4	2.5	4.4	1.4
Don't know	37.9	17.8	13.3	12.5	15.8	26.9

Source: D. Michael Anderson and Gregory M. Christenson, "Ethnic Breakdown of AIDS Related Knowledge and Attitudes from the National Adolescent Student Health Survey," *Journal of Health Education,* Vol. 22, No. 1, January/February 1991, p. 33. Primary source: *The National Adolescent Student Health Survey: A Report on the Health of America's Youth.* 1989. Third Party Publishing Co., Oakland, CA; American School Health Association, Association for the Advancement of Health Education, Society for Public Health Education, Inc. (Subset of original data). *Note:* 1. Indicates a correct response.

Chronic Diseases

★ 432 ★

Deaths from Chronic Diseases, 1987

Number of deaths and age-adjusted death rates per 100,000 are shown, by selected major chronic disease.

Cause of death	Percent distribution			Age-adjusted rate[1]		
	Indian	Non-Hispanic White	Hispanic	Indian	Non-Hispanic White	Hispanic
All causes	100.0	100.0	100.0	932.7	792.9	809.6
Diseases of the heart	13.6	31.0	23.9	162.9	246.6	216.9
Cerebrovascular diseases	2.7	5.9	5.9	33.1	48.2	54.1
Malignant neoplasms, all sites	12.1	22.9	18.0	134.3	174.7	155.1
Chronic obstructive pulmonary diseases (COPD)	1.3	6.5	3.1	-	50.6	29.1
Pneumonia and influenza	3.3	3.2	3.3	39.3	26.9	30.6
Diabetes mellitus	4.4	1.9	3.5	51.0	15.2	30.4
Chronic liver disease and cirrhosis	4.8	1.3	3.3	39.1	9.4	25.1
Nephritis and nephrosis	1.2	0.9	1.1	-	7.2	-

Source: Health Status of Minorities and Low-Income Groups: Third Edition, U.S. Department of Health and Human Services, Public Health Service, Health Resources and Services Administration, Government Printing Office, Washington, D.C., p. 153. Primary source: State of New Mexico, Health and Environment Department, Selected Health Statistics, New Mexico 1987. Santa Fe, NM: *The Department,* May 1989, Tables 3.6 and 3.7. *Notes:* 1. Rates are per 100,000 and age-adjusted by direct method to the 1986 U.S. population.

★ 433 ★

Diabetes Mellitus Deaths and Mortality Rates, by Year

Age-adjusted rate per 100,000 population for American Indians, Alaskan Natives, and U.S. all races, 1955-1988.

Calendar year	Indian and Alaska Native		U.S. all races		U.S. other than White Rate	Ratio Indian to:	
	Number	Rate	Number	Rate		U.S. all races	U.S. other than White
1988	304	25.8	40,368	10.1	18.7	2.6	1.4
1987	265	23.4	38,532	9.8	17.9	2.4	1.3
1986	229	20.6	37,184	9.6	17.8	2.1	1.2
1985	247	22.9	36,969	9.6	16.1	2.4	1.4
1984	219	20.6	35,787	9.5	17.4	2.2	1.2
1983	210	20.5	36,246	9.9	17.8	2.1	1.2
1982	193	20.2	34,583	9.6	16.7	2.1	1.2
1981	191	20.8	34,642	9.8	17.9	2.1	1.2
1980	204	22.6	34,851	10.1	18.8	2.2	1.2
1979	170	19.2	33,192	10.0	18.5	1.9	1.0
1978	183	22.6	33,841	10.4	19.0	2.2	1.2
1977	161	21.1	32,989	10.4	19.5	2.0	1.1
1976	149	20.2	34,508	11.1	21.0	1.8	1.0
1975	145	20.8	35,230	11.6	21.7	1.8	1.0
1974	139	21.4	37,329	12.5	23.4	1.7	0.9
1973	157	25.6	38,208	13.2	25.3	1.9	1.0
1972	158	27.3	38,674	13.6	26.0	2.0	1.1
1971	166	30.1	28,256	13.8	27.5	2.2	1.1
1970	143	27.1	38,324	14.1	25.2	1.9	1.1
1969	127	21.1	38,541	14.5	27.7	1.5	0.8
1968	141	25.6	38,352	14.7	28.0	1.7	0.9
1967	107	23.3	35,049	13.7	24.5	1.7	1.0
1966	115	25.7	34,597	13.9	24.8	1.8	1.0
1965	110	25.4	33,174	13.5	23.6	1.9	1.1
1964	95	22.0	32,279	13.5	23.6	1.6	0.9
1963	115	29.9	32,465	13.8	23.1	2.2	1.3
1962	89	23.9	31,222	13.5	21.8	1.8	1.1
1961	70	19.6	30,098	13.3	21.0	1.5	0.9
1960	71	20.3	29,971	13.6	21.6	1.5	0.9
1959	82	26.1	28,080	13.4	19.4	1.9	1.3
1958	65	20.8	27,501	13.0	18.8	1.6	1.1
1957	62	19.6	27,180	13.5	18.2	1.5	1.1
1956	79	20.2	26,184	13.0	17.1	1.6	1.2
1955	64	17.0	25,488	13.0	16.5	1.3	1.0

Source: Trends in Indian Health, 1991, U.S. Department of Health and Human Services, Public Health Service, Indian Health Service, p. 54. *Notes:* Estimated population methodology for the American Indian and Alaska Native population revised in 1976. Maine, New York and Pennsylvania included as Reservation States beginning in 1979, Connecticut, Rhode Island and Texas in 1983 and Alabama in 1984. Decennial Census population counts used for 1960, 1970, and 1980.

★ 434 ★

Diabetes Prevalence Among Selected Groups

U.S. Population Group[1]	Percent rate	Rate relative to whites
American Indian[2]	9.1	1.5
Pima Indian[3]	43.4	7.0
White	6.2	1.0
Cuban	9.3	1.5
Black	10.2	1.6
Mexican American	13.0	2.1
Puerto Rican	13.4	2.2

Source: Diabetes: Status of the Disease Among American Indians, Blacks, and Hispanics, U.S. General Accounting Office, 1992, p. 4. Primary source: Hispanic Health and Nutrition Examination Survey 1982-84 (HHANES); National Health and Nutrition Examination Survey 1976-80 (NHANES); Indian Health Service, 1991; W.C. Knowler, et al., "Diabetes Mellitus in the Pima Indians: Incidence, Risk Factors and Pathogenesis," Diabetes/Metabolism Reviews, 6:1 (1990), 1-27. *Notes:* 1. Rates for Whites, Cubans, Blacks, Mexican Americans, and Puerto Ricans are based on previously diagnosed and undiagnosed cases of diabetes. Undiagnosed cases were detected by administering an oral glucose test to a subsample of the study population. Rates for American Indians and Pima Indians are based on previously diagnosed cases of diabetes. It is likely that there are fewer undiagnosed cases of diabetes in American Indians than other racial groups because of the numerous community education programs and free health care services that are available to American Indians. Thus, it is reasonable to compare the rates, although it is likely that the total prevalence of diabetes in American Indians and Pima Indians is higher than indicated in the table. 2. The rate for American Indians is based on persons 15 years of age and older, 1990 (age-adjusted to the 1980 U.S. population). It is likely that the prevalence rate for American Indians 20 to 74 years of age would be higher than the rate for persons 15 years of age and older because increasing age is a risk factor for diabetes. 3. The rate for Pima Indians is based on persons 25-64 years of age, 1981-88. The rates are not age-adjusted. The Pima Indians, who have the highest recorded prevalence rate of diabetes in the world, have been studied for over 25 years.

★ 435 ★

Gastrointestinal Disease Deaths and Mortality Rates, by Year

Age-adjusted rate per 100,000 population for American Indians, Alaskan Natives, and U.S. all races, 1955-1988.

Calendar year	Indian and Alaska Native		U.S. all races	Ratio Indian to U.S. all races
	Number	Rate	Rate	
1988	29	2.1	1.3	1.6
1987	15	1.1	1.3	0.8
1986	23	1.6	2.4	0.7
1985	15	1.1	2.3	0.5
1984	22	1.8	2.4	0.8
1983	30	2.6	2.5	1.0
1982	20	1.7	2.5	0.7
1981	26	2.3	2.5	0.9
1980	31	2.6	2.7	1.0

[Continued]

★ 435 ★

Gastrointestinal Disease Deaths and Mortality Rates, by Year
[Continued]

Calendar year	Indian and Alaska Native		U.S. all races Rate	Ratio Indian to U.S. all races
	Number	Rate		
1979	39	3.4	2.6	1.3
1978	34	2.7	1.9	1.4
1977	32	2.6	2.0	1.3
1976	43	3.9	2.1	1.9
1975	41	3.7	2.2	1.7
1974	52	4.9	2.4	2.0
1973	42	4.8	2.6	1.8
1972	56	6.4	2.7	2.4
1971	45	5.1	2.8	1.8
1970	66	7.8	2.9	2.7
1969	82	9.8	3.0	2.5
1968	104	9.9	3.1	3.2
1967	80	9.8	3.0	3.3
1966	107	11.6	3.0	3.9
1965	111	10.9	3.2	3.4
1964	100	9.6	3.3	2.9
1963	110	11.3	3.4	3.3
1962	155	16.2	3.4	4.8
1961	119	11.1	3.3	3.4
1960	152	14.2	3.4	4.2
1959	124	13.0	3.3	3.9
1958	159	15.4	3.5	4.4
1957	198	18.0	3.5	5.1
1956	137	13.9	3.4	4.1
1955	165	15.4	3.6	4.3

Source: Trends in Indian Health, 1991, U.S. Department of Health and Human Services, Public Health Service, Indian Health Service, p. 55. *Notes:* Maine, New York and Pennsylvania included as Reservation States beginning in 1979, Connecticut, Rhode Island and Texas in 1983 and Alabama in 1984. Starting in 1979 cause of death codes which define gastrointestinal deaths were revised to exclude ICD-9 code 557 (vascular insufficiency of intestine). Currently ICD-9 codes that define gastrointestinal deaths include: 004, 006, 008, 009, 535, 555, 558 and 562.

★ 436 ★

Malignant Neoplasm Deaths and Mortality Rates, by Year

Age-adjusted rate per 100,000 population for American Indians, Alaskan Natives, and U.S. all races, 1955-1988.

Calendar year	Indian and Alaska Native		U.S. all races		U.S. other than White Rate	Ratio Indian to:	
	Number	Rate	Number	Rate		U.S. all races	U.S. other than White
1988	1,081	91.3	485,048	132.7	151.9	0.7	0.6
1987	987	84.9	476,927	132.9	153.0	0.6	0.6
1986	942	83.4	469,376	133.2	154.1	0.6	0.5
1985	931	84.9	461,563	133.6	155.7	0.6	0.5
1984	941	88.4	453,492	133.5	157.8	0.7	0.6
1983	853	81.5	442,986	132.6	156.8	0.6	0.5
1982	780	80.3	433,795	132.5	157.0	0.6	0.5
1981	707	74.0	422,094	131.6	156.7	0.6	0.5
1980	720	76.4	416,509	132.8	158.2	0.6	0.5
1979	592	65.8	403,395	130.8	159.0	0.5	0.4
1978	646	77.0	396,992	133.8	159.1	0.6	0.5
1977	581	73.1	386,686	133.0	159.3	0.5	0.5
1976	551	73.3	377,312	132.3	156.3	0.6	0.5
1975	508	70.4	365,693	129.4	155.0	0.5	0.5
1974	526	77.7	360,472	131.8	156.6	0.6	0.5
1973	477	73.4	351,055	130.7	156.4	0.6	0.5
1972	461	76.1	345,618	130.7	152.2	0.6	0.5
1971	451	80.0	337,398	130.7	160.8	0.6	0.5
1970	421	80.5	330,730	129.9	148.3	0.6	0.5
1969	407	78.4	323,092	129.7	158.6	0.6	0.5
1968	383	75.7	318,547	130.2	158.3	0.6	0.5
1967	392	80.8	310,983	129.1	154.3	0.6	0.5
1966	386	83.0	303,736	128.4	152.7	0.6	0.5
1965	362	80.1	297,588	127.0	147.7	0.6	0.5
1964	376	83.5	289,577	126.6	145.6	0.7	0.6
1963	342	86.3	285,362	126.6	145.2	0.7	0.6
1962	330	86.1	278,562	125.6	140.9	0.7	0.6
1961	347	94.3	273,502	125.4	140.4	0.8	0.7
1960	325	91.1	267,627	125.8	139.3	0.7	0.7
1959	359	109.3	260,047	124.5	136.2	0.9	0.8
1958	293	89.9	254,426	124.6	135.3	0.7	0.7
1957	333	105.2	253,183	126.4	136.7	0.8	0.8
1956	333	104.5	247,357	126.3	136.2	0.8	0.8
1955	296	95.0	240,681	125.8	131.5	0.8	0.7

Source: Trends in Indian Health, 1991, U.S. Department of Health and Human Services, Public Health Service, Indian Health Service, p. 51. *Notes:* Estimated population methodology for the American Indian and Alaska Native population revised in 1976. Maine, New York and Pennsylvania included as Reservation States beginning in 1979, Connecticut, Rhode Island and Texas in 1983 and Alabama in 1984. Decennial Census population counts used for 1960, 1970, and 1980.

★ 437 ★

Malignant Neoplasm Mortality Rates, by Age and Sex

Rate per 100,000 population for American Indians, Alaskan Natives, and U.S. all races, 1955-1988.

Age group	Indian and Alaska Native			U.S. all races			U.S. Other than White		
	Both sexes	Male	Female	Both sexes	Male	Female	Both sexes	Male	Female
Under 5 years	3.3	3.3	3.3	3.6	3.8	3.3	3.1	3.5	2.8
5-14 years	2.0	2.0	2.0	3.3	3.8	2.8	2.8	2.9	2.7
15-24 years	2.8	3.0	2.7	5.1	6.0	4.1	5.6	6.3	5.0
25-34 years	10.1	6.0	14.2	12.4	12.1	12.7	14.1	13.1	15.0
35-44 years	30.9	28.2	33.5	43.5	39.1	47.8	59.8	55.4	63.5
45-54 years	112.5	108.6	116.2	164.3	169.1	159.7	216.2	250.1	187.7
55-64 years	256.5	260.0	253.3	447.0	528.4	374.5	525.8	672.7	405.9
65-74 years	542.3	636.3	462.8	843.6	1,084.0	652.5	918.7	1,286.2	640.6
75-84 years	888.2	1,090.6	729.9	1,298.4	1,850.2	967.4	1,388.9	2,072.2	954.5
85 years +	1,238.3	1,556.5	1,026.6	1,618.0	2,474.8	1,282.9	1,606.8	2,468.7	1,195.4

Source: Trends in Indian Health, 1991, U.S. Department of Health and Human Services, Public Health Service, Indian Health Service, p. 52.

★ 438 ★

Tuberculosis: Distribution of Cases, by Race

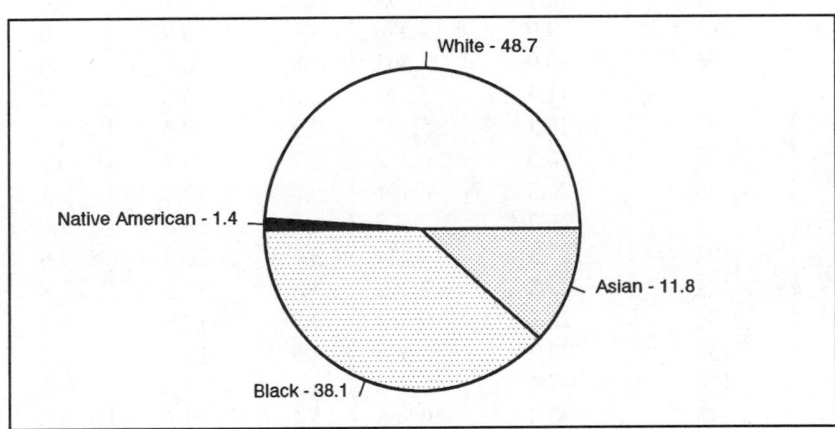

Race	Percent
Native American	1.4
White	48.7
Black	38.1
Asian	11.8

Source: USA TODAY, November 17, 1992, p. 4D.

★ 439 ★

Tuberculosis Deaths and Mortality Rates, by Year

Age-adjusted rate per 100,000 population for American Indians, Alaskan Natives, and U.S. all races, 1955-1988.

Calendar year	Indian and Alaska Native		U.S. all races		U.S. other than White Rate	Ratio Indian to:	
	Number	Rate	Number	Rate		U.S. all races	U.S. other than White
1988	30	2.5	1,921	0.5	1.9	5.0	1.3
1987	30	2.5	1,755	0.5	1.7	5.0	1.5
1986	26	2.1	1,782	0.5	1.9	4.2	1.1
1985	20	1.6	1,752	0.5	1.8	3.2	0.9
1984	20	1.8	1,729	0.5	2.0	3.6	0.9
1983	36	3.3	1,779	0.5	1.9	6.6	1.7
1982	22	2.0	1,807	0.6	2.0	3.3	1.0
1981	31	3.2	1,937	0.6	2.3	5.3	1.4
1980	36	3.6	1,978	0.6	2.4	6.0	1.5
1979	35	3.7	2,007	0.7	2.5	5.3	1.5
1978	43	5.2	2,914	1.0	3.1	5.2	1.7
1977	40	5.2	2,968	1.0	3.5·	5.2	1.5
1976	55	7.3	3,130	1.1	3.8	6.6	1.9
1975	64	8.6	3,333	1.2	4.0	7.2	2.2
1974	59	8.5	3,513	1.3	4.6	6.5	1.8
1973	52	8.1	3,875	1.5	5.2	5.4	1.6
1972	61	9.9	4,376	1.7	5.9	5.8	1.7
1971	56	10.0	4,501	1.8	6.6	5.6	1.5
1970	63	11.4	5,217	2.2	6.8	5.2	1.7
1969	86	16.1	5,567	2.3	8.0	7.0	2.0
1968	78	16.5	6,292	2.7	9.4	6.1	1.8
1967	90	24.3	6,901	3.0	10.1	8.1	2.4
1966	91	23.7	7,625	3.4	10.8	7.0	2.2
1965	104	27.3	7,934	3.6	10.9	7.6	2.5
1964	111	29.5	8,303	3.8	11.5	7.8	2.6
1963	130	28.9	9,311	4.3	12.8	6.7	2.3
1962	150	37.2	9,506	4.5	13.4	8.3	2.8
1961	120	35.2	10,470	4.8	14.0	7.3	2.5
1960	115	32.3	10,866	5.4	15.1	6.0	2.1
1959	163	43.0	11,456	5.8	16.6	7.4	2.6
1958	150	39.6	12,361	6.5	19.0	6.1	2.1
1957	186	41.0	13,324	7.1	20.0	5.8	2.1
1956	212	47.6	14,061	7.7	22.0	6.2	2.2
1955	253	57.9	14,940	8.4	24.1	6.9	2.4

Source: Trends in Indian Health, 1991, U.S. Department of Health and Human Services, Public Health Service, Indian Health Service, p. 53. *Notes:* Estimated population methodology revised in 1976. Maine, New York and Pennsylvania included as Reservation States beginning in 1979, Connecticut, Rhode Island and Texas in 1983 and Alabama in 1984. Decennial Census population counts used for 1960, 1970, and 1980.

Dental Health

★ 440 ★

Dental Services

Numbers of dental services provided by IHS, contact, tribal, and urban programs, FY 1955-1990.

Fiscal year	Number of services provided				% contract of total	% tribal and urban of total	% increase of total since 1955
	Total	IHS		Tribal and urban			
		Direct	Contract[1]				
1990	2,362,228	1,563,934	139,425	658,869	5.9	27.9	1,212.3
1989	2,207,082	1,466,812	132,918	607,352	6.0	27.5	1,126.2
1988	2,106,741	1,415,815	194,784	496,142	9.2	23.6	1,070.4
1987	2,130,690	1,397,262	191,639	541,789	9.0	25.4	1,083.7
1986	1,984,522	1,322,794	155,939	505,789	7.9	25.5	1,002.5
1985	1,914,820	1,276,623	210,508	427,689	11.0	22.3	963.8
1984	2,011,326	1,348,599	224,918	437,809	11.2	21.8	1,017.4
1983	1,907,336	1,325,187	149,741	432,408	7.9	22.7	959.6
1982	1,666,263	1,202,422	153,030	311,341	9.2	18.6	825.7
1981	1,801,982	1,319,913	182,880	299,189	10.1	16.6	901.1
1980	1,833,206	1,357,809	216,574	258,823	11.8	14.1	918.4
1979[2]	1,618,383	1,239,108	215,997	163,278	13.3	10.1	799.1
1978	1,099,019	885,019	214,000		19.5		510.6
1977	1,037,640	823,328	214,312		20.7		476.5
1976	975,647	798,709	176,938		18.1		442.0
1975	946,722	745,831	200,891		21.2		426.0
1974	927,701	775,747	151,954		16.4		415.4
1973	863,057	728,909	134,148		15.5		379.5
1972	844,724	718,176	126,548		15.0		369.3
1971	776,168	684,612	91,556		11.8		331.2
1970	737,206	646,580	90,626		12.3		309.6
1969	703,232	634,479	68,753		9.8		290.7
1968	681,745	613,084	68,661		10.1		278.7
1967	626,458	545,509	80,949		12.9		248.0
1966[2]	570,779	502,710	60,069		11.9		217.1
1965	572,079	495,006	77,073		13.5		217.8
1964	525,010	462,981	62,029		11.8		191.7
1963	453,906	398,452	55,454		12.2		152.2
1962	421,597	364,988	56,609		13.4		134.2
1961	403,528	348,776	54,752		13.6		124.2
1960[2]	364,423	307,248	57,175		15.7		102.5
1959	328,613	283,206	45,407		13.8		82.6
1958	282,372	282,372	-		-		56.9
1957	249,048	249,048	-		-		38.4

[Continued]

★ 440 ★

Dental Services
[Continued]

Fiscal year	Number of services provided				% contract of total	% tribal and urban of total	% increase of total since 1955
	Total	IHS		Tribal and urban			
		Direct	Contract[1]				
1956	219,353	219,353	-		-		21.9
1955	180,000	180,000	-	-	-		-

Source: Trends in Indian Health, 1991, U.S. Department of Health and Human Services, Public Health Service, Indian Health Service, p. 73.
Notes: 1. Beginning with FY 1979 this category excludes contract services purchased from the private sector by Tribes. 2. Data systems were modified in 1960, 1966 and 1978. In 1978 the IHS began to use the dental services coding list adopted by the American Dental Association (ADA). The ADA list identifies individual clinical services. Previously the IHS had reported specified clinical services combined into major dental service groupings. Excluded from the 1978 count are diagnostic and adjunctive services. Excluded from the clinical counts since 1979 are diagnostic services other than examinations, revisits and non-clinical adjunctive services.

★ 441 ★

Tooth Loss of Persons 5 to 17 Years Old

Mean DMFT (decayed, missing, and filled teeth) scores and the percent of DMFT due to decayed, missing and filled teeth are shown for Native American children in IHS (Indian Health Service) clinics. Data compare Native American children in 11 IHS areas (1983-84) to all American children (1979- 80).

Age 5-17	DMF teeth	Percent of DMFT		
		Percent decayed	Percent missing	Percent filled
Native Americans (IHS)	5.9	44	2.2	53
National (All Children)	2.9	19	2.4	79

Source: Health Status of Minorities and Low-Income Groups: Third Edition, U.S. Department of Health and Human Services, Public Health Service, Health Resources and Services Administration, Government Printing Office, Washington, D.C., p. 227. Department of Health and Human Services. Indian Health Service, "Findings from the Oral Health Survey: A Summary of Selected Data," p. 47. Comparative national figures are from the National Caries Prevalence Survey of 1979-80 conducted by the National Institute of Dental Research.

Infant Mortality

★ 442 ★

Infant Deaths, by Leading Cause

Rate per 1,000 live births for American Indians, Alaskan Natives, 1986- 1988, and U.S. all races, 1987.

Cause of death	Indian and Alaska Native		U.S. all races Rate	U.S. other than White	Ratio American Indian and Alaska Native to:	
	Number	Rate			U.S. all races	U.S. other than White
All causes	1,236	9.7	10.1	15.4	1.0	0.6
Sudden infant death syndrome	285	2.2	1.4	2.0	1.6	1.1
Congenital anomalies	237	1.9	2.1	2.1	0.9	0.9
Respiratory distress syndrome	69	0.5	0.9	1.2	0.6	0.4
Accidents	57	0.4	0.2	0.4	2.0	1.0
Disorders relating to short gestation and low birth weight	56	0.4	0.9	1.9	0.4	0.2
Pneumonia and influenza	45	0.4	0.2	0.3	2.0	1.3
Infections specific to thc perinatal period	29	0.2	0.2	0.4	1.0	0.5
Newborn affected by maternal complications of pregnancy	25	0.2	0.4	0.6	0.5	0.3
Newborn affected by complications of placenta, cord, and membranes	22	0.2	0.2	0.3	1.0	0.7
Intrauterine hypoxia and birth asphyxia	19	0.1	0.2	0.4	0.5	0.3
All other causes	392					

Source: Trends in Indian Health, 1991, U.S. Department of Health and Human Services, Public Health Service, Indian Health Service, p. 30. Primary source: National Center for Health Statistics (NCHS), U.S. infant mortality rates (all ages)—Monthly Vital Statistics Report, Vol. 38, No. 5, Supplement, September 26, 1989, Table 15: Infant mortality rates by age and race an published in Vital Statistics of the United States, 1987, Volume II, Part A, Mortality, Tables 2-6 and 2-16.

★ 443 ★

Infant Mortalities in Oklahoma, by Estimated Actual Indian Deaths Based on Matched Records, 1975-88

Death rates are shown per 1,000 live births. Matching (linking) of infant deaths to birth certificates from 1975 to 1988 indicates that infants born Indian had a 28 percent chance of being misclassified as another race (usually white) on the death certificate. Infants born white or black had less than a 1 percent chance of being misclassified.

Years	Reported born Indian	Estimated infant deaths	Reported live births	Estimated mortality rate	Reported mortality rate
1975-76	108	117.3	7,015	16.72	12.97
1977-78	108	118.6	7,660	15.48	13.71
1979-80	98	109.8	9,073	12.10	10.76
1981-82	110	126.2	10,568	11.93	8.80
1983-84	115	126.9	10,513	12.07	7.61
1985-86	101	110.5	10,310	10.72	5.40
1987-88	97	111.2	10,650	10.44	5.79
Totals	737	820.5	65,789	12.47	8.87

Source: Richard D. Kennedy, M.S. and Roger E. Deapen, Ph.D., "Differences Between Oklahoma Indian Infant Mortality and Other Races," *Public Health Reports*, Vol 106, No. 1, January-February 1991, p. 99.

★ 444 ★

Infant Mortalities in Oklahoma, by Matches for Race Classifications of Indians on Birth and Death Certificates, 1975-88

Misclassification of Indian deaths strongly alters the overall infant mortality rate for the Oklahoma Indian population form the currently reported 5.8 per 1,000 (1987-88) to an estimated actual rate of 10.4 per 1,000 for the same period.

Years	Identified Indian		Percent other race on death certificate
	On birth certificate	On death certificate	
1975-76	108	87	19.44
1977-78	108	98	9.26
1979-80	98	85	13.27
1981-82	110	81	26.36
1983-84	115	68	40.87
1985-86	101	52	48.51

[Continued]

★ 444 ★

Infant Mortalities in Oklahoma, by Matches for Race Classifications of Indians on Birth and Death Certificates, 1975-88

[Continued]

Years	Identified Indian		Percent other race on death certificate
	On birth certificate	On death certificate	
1987-88	97	57	41.24
Totals	737	528	28.35

Source: Richard D. Kennedy, M.S. and Roger E. Deapen, Ph.D., "Differences Between Oklahoma Indian Infant Mortality and Other Races," *Public Health Reports*, Vol. 106, No. 1, January-February 1991, p. 99.

★ 445 ★

Infant Mortalities in Oklahoma, by Race Classifications at Birth and at Death, 1975-88

Matching (linking) of infant deaths to birth certificates from 1975 to 1988 indicates that infants born Indian had a 28 percent chance of being misclassified as another race (usually white) on the death certificate. Infants born white or black had less than a 1 percent chance of being misclassified.

Race at death	Race at birth					
	Indian	White	Black	Other	Unknown	Total
Indian	484	37	2	4	1	528
White	246	5,549	26	35	18	5,874
Black	4	42	1,103	1	2	1,152
Other	0	7	2	49	0	58
Unknown	3	11	3	1	1	19
Total	737	5,646	1,136	90	22	7,631

Source: Richard D. Kennedy, M.S. and Roger E. Deapen, Ph.D., "Differences Between Oklahoma Indian Infant Mortality and Other Races," *Public Health Reports*, Vol. 106, No.1, January-February 1991, p.98.

★ 446 ★

Infant Mortalities in Oklahoma, by Race Classified at Birth and at Death, 1975-88

The registered race, at birth and death, is shown. Matching (linking) of infant deaths to birth certificates from 1975 to 1988 indicates that infants born Indian had a 28 percent chance of being misclassified as another race (usually white) on the death certificate. Infants born white or black had less than a 1 percent chance of being misclassified.

Years	Indian at birth White at death	Percent of Indians	White at birth Indian at death	Percent of whites	Indian at birth Black at death	Black at birth Indian at death
1975-76	25	23.1	6	0.6	1	0
1977-78	13	12.0	4	0.5	1	1
1979-80	18	18.4	6	0.7	1	0
1981-82	37	33.6	5	0.6	0	0
1983-84	53	46.1	7	0.9	1	1
1985-86	54	53.5	5	0.7	0	0
1987-88	46	47.4	4	0.7	0	0
Totals	246	33.4	37	0.7	4	2

Source: Richard D. Kennedy, M.S. and Roger E. Deapen, Ph.D., "Differences Between Oklahoma Indian Infant Mortality and Other Races," *Public Health Reports*, Vol. 106, No. 1, January-February 1991, p. 99.

★ 447 ★

Infant Mortality Rates in Oklahoma, 1975-88

Mortality rates per 1,000 live births are shown.

Years	All races	Indian	White	Black
1975-76	16.38	12.97	15.71	26.02
1977-78	13.98	13.71	13.01	21.43
1979-80	12.58	10.76	11.87	20.23
1981-82	12.05	8.80	11.87	17.40
1983-84	10.65	7.61	10.62	14.45
1985-86	10.55	5.40	10.35	18.19
1987-88	9.33	5.79	9.32	13.47
14 year average[1]	12.10	8.87	11.75	18.43

Source: Richard D. Kennedy, M.S. and Roger E. Deapen, Ph.D., "Differences Between Oklahoma Indian Infant Mortality and Other Races," *Public Health Reports*, Vol. 106, No. 1, January-February 1991, p. 98. *Notes:* 1. Computed by dividing all infant deaths from 1975 to 1988 by total number of live births for the same period.

★ 448 ★

Infant Mortality Rates, by Age

Rate per 1,000 live births for American Indians, Alaskan Natives, and U.S. all races, 1966-1987.

| Calendar year | Infant mortality rate | Neonatal | | | | Post neonatal 28 days- 11 months |
		Total	Under 1 day	1-6 days	7-27 days	
American Indians and Alaska Natives						
1986-1988	9.7	4.6	2.4	1.1	1.2	5.1
1985-1987	9.8	4.7	2.4	1.2	1.1	5.1
1984-1986	9.7	4.4	2.3	1.2	0.9	5.2
1983-1985	9.8	4.6	2.4	1.2	1.0	5.3
1982-1984	10.2	4.6	2.4	1.2	1.0	5.6
1981-1983	11.0	5.0	2.5	1.3	1.1	6.1
1980-1982	11.9	5.5	2.8	1.6	1.1	6.5
1979-1981	13.8	6.6	3.3	2.0	1.3	7.2
1978-1980	14.6	7.3	3.7	2.3	1.3	7.2
1977-1979	15.5	7.8	3.9	2.5	1.3	7.8
1976-1978	16.4	8.2	4.4	2.5	1.3	8.2
1975-1977	17.7	8.8	4.8	2.7	1.3	8.9
1974-1976	18.7	9.2	5.1	2.8	1.3	9.5
1973-1975	18.8	9.2	4.8	3.0	1.4	9.6
1972-1974	19.7	9.3	5.0	2.9	1.4	10.4
1971-1973	21.3	10.3	5.8	3.0	1.4	11.0
1970-1972	22.7	11.0	6.5	2.9	1.6	11.6
1969-1971	24.6	12.2	6.8	3.6	1.8	12.3
1968-1970	27.1	12.9	7.0	3.9	2.0	14.1
1967-1969	30.0	14.3	7.8	4.5	2.0	15.7
1966-1968	34.0	15.7	8.4	4.9	2.3	18.4
1965-1967	36.8	16.1	8.6	5.1	2.4	20.7
U.S. all races						
1987	10.1	6.5	3.8	1.6	1.1	3.6
1986	10.4	6.7	3.9	1.7	1.1	3.6
1985	10.6	7.0	4.0	1.8	1.1	3.7
1984	10.8	7.0	4.1	1.8	1.1	3.8
1983	11.2	7.3	4.3	1.9	1.2	3.9
1982	11.5	7.7	4.4	2.0	1.3	3.8
1981	11.9	8.0	4.5	2.3	1.3	3.9
1980	12.6	8.5	4.6	2.4	1.4	4.1
1979	13.1	8.9	4.8	2.7	1.4	4.2
1978	13.8	9.5	5.1	2.9	1.5	4.3
1977	14.1	9.9	5.3	3.1	1.5	4.2
1976	15.2	10.9	5.9	3.1	1.6	4.3
1975	16.1	11.6	6.3	3.7	1.6	4.5
1974	16.7	12.3	6.7	3.7	1.6	4.4
1973	17.7	13.0	7.2	4.2	1.5	4.7
1972	18.5	13.7	8.1	4.3	1.3	4.8
1971	19.1	14.2	8.2	4.6	1.4	4.9
1970	20.0	15.1	8.8	4.8	1.5	4.9
1969	20.9	15.6	9.2	4.9	1.5	5.3

[Continued]

★ 448 ★

Infant Mortality Rates, by Age

[Continued]

Calendar year	Infant mortality rate	Neonatal				Post neonatal 28 days- 11 months
		Total	Under 1 day	1-6 days	7-27 days	
1968	21.8	16.1	9.5	5.1	1.5	5.7
1967	22.4	16.5	9.6	5.3	1.6	5.9
1966	23.7	17.2	10.0	5.6	1.6	6.5

Source: Trends in Indian Health, 1991, U.S. Department of Health and Human Services, Public Health Service, Indian Health Service, p. 28.

★ 449 ★

Infant Mortality Rates, by Year

Rate per 1,000 live births for American Indians, Alaskan Natives, and U.S. all races, 1966-1987.

Calendar year	Indian and Alaska Native	Indian	Alaska Native	U.S. all races	U.S. other than White	U.S. Black	Ratio Indian and Alaska Native to:		
							U.S. all races	U.S. other than White	U.S. Black
1987	9.7	9.3	14.6	10.1	15.4	17.9	1.0	0.6	0.5
1986	9.8	9.5	13.9	10.4	15.7	18.0	0.9	0.6	0.5
1985	9.7	9.3	14.6	10.6	15.8	18.2	0.9	0.6	0.5
1984	9.8	9.4	16.0	10.8	16.1	18.4	0.9	0.6	0.5
1983	10.2	9.7	17.0	11.2	16.8	19.2	0.9	0.6	0.5
1982	11.0	10.6	16.3	11.5	17.3	19.6	1.0	0.6	0.6
1981	11.9	11.6	17.3	11.9	17.8	20.0	1.0	0.7	0.6
1980	13.8	13.4	20.4	12.6	19.1	21.4	1.1	0.7	0.6
1979	14.6	14.1	21.4	13.1	19.8	21.8	1.1	0.7	0.7
1978	15.5	15.1	20.5	13.8	21.1	23.1	1.1	0.7	0.7
1977	16.4	16.1	21.4	14.1	21.7	23.6	1.2	0.8	0.7
1976	17.7	17.4	21.9	15.2	23.5	25.5	1.2	0.8	0.7
1975	18.7	18.2	25.3	16.1	24.2	26.2	1.2	0.8	0.8
1974	18.8	18.4	24.0	16.7	24.9	26.8	1.1	0.8	0.7
1973	19.7	19.4	24.2	17.7	26.2	28.1	1.1	0.8	0.7
1972	21.3	21.1	24.1	18.5	27.7	29.6	1.2	0.8	0.7
1971	22.7	22.5	24.6	19.1	28.5	30.3	1.2	0.8	0.7
1970	24.6	24.3	28.1	20.0	30.9	32.6	1.2	0.8	0.8
1969	27.1	26.6	32.2	20.9	32.9	34.8	1.3	0.8	0.8
1968	30.0	28.9	42.6	21.8	34.5	36.2	1.4	0.9	0.8
1967	34.0	32.6	49.5	22.4	35.9	37.5	1.5	0.9	0.9
1966	36.8	38.4	57.6	23.7	38.8	40.2	1.6	0.9	0.9
1965	38.5	40.2	57.3	24.7	40.3	41.7	1.6	1.0	0.9
1964	40.0	38.4	56.9	24.8	41.1	42.3	1.6	1.0	0.9
1963	41.8	40.2	57.4	25.2	41.5	42.8	1.7	1.0	1.0
1962	44.1	42.3	60.4	25.3	41.4	42.6	1.7	1.1	1.0
1961	46.3	43.9	68.9	25.3	40.7	41.8	1.8	1.1	1.0
1960	48.0	45.5	72.1	26.0	43.2	44.3	1.8	1.1	1.1

[Continued]

★ 449 ★

Infant Mortality Rates, by Year

[Continued]

Calendar year	Indian and Alaska Native	Indian	Alaska Native	U.S. all races	U.S. other than White	U.S. Black	Ratio Indian and Alaska Native to:		
							U.S. all races	U.S. other than White	U.S. Black
1959	52.5	50.2	74.0	26.4	44.0	44.8	2.0	1.2	1.2
1958	55.8	53.7	75.2	27.1	45.7	46.3	2.0	1.2	1.2
1957	59.2	57.0	78.7	26.3	43.7	44.2	2.3	1.4	1.3
1956	60.7	58.5	80.9	26.0	42.1	42.4	2.3	1.4	1.4
1955	62.7	60.9	79.5	26.4	42.8	43.1	2.4	1.5	1.5

Source: Trends in Indian Health, 1991, U.S. Department of Health and Human Services, Public Health Service, Indian Health Service, p. 27. *Notes:* Indian and Alaska Native rates are 3-year rates centered in the year specified. All other rates are for the year specified.

★ 450 ★

Maternal Deaths and Death Rates

Rate per 100,000 live births for American Indians, Alaskan Natives, and U.S. all races, 1958-1988.

Calendar year	Indian and Alaska Native		U.S. all races		U.S. other than white	Ratio Indian to:	
	Number	Rate[1]	Number	Rate	Rate	U.S. all races	U.S. other than White
1988	5						
1987	2	7.1	251	6.6	12.0	1.1	0.6
1986	2	8.8	272	7.2	16.0	1.2	0.6
1985	7	8.2	295	7.8	18.1	1.1	0.5
1984	1	10.8	285	7.8	16.9	1.4	0.6
1983	5	7.6	290	8.0	16.3	1.0	0.5
1982	3	8.9	292	7.9	16.4	1.1	0.5
1981	2	7.5	309	8.5	17.3	0.9	0.4
1980	3	9.0	334	9.2	19.8	1.0	0.5
1979	4	11.4	336	9.6	22.7	1.2	0.5
1978	4	11.1	321	9.6	23.0	1.2	0.5
1977	2	8.3	373	11.2	26.0	0.7	0.3
1976	1	8.7	390	12.3	26.5	0.7	0.3
1975	4	11.8	340	12.8	29.0	0.9	0.4
1974	4	16.3	462	14.6	35.1	1.1	0.5
1973	4	23.7	477	15.2	34.6	1.6	0.7
1972	9	30.8	612	18.8	38.5	1.6	0.8
1971	9	35.0	668	18.8	45.3	1.9	0.8
1970	7	32.3	803	21.5	55.9	1.5	0.6
1969	6	32.8	801	22.2	55.7	1.5	0.6
1968	9	37.0	859	24.5	63.6	1.5	0.6
1967	7	49.1	987	28.0	69.5	1.8	0.7
1966	16	54.6	1,049	29.1	72.4	1.9	0.8
1965	12	63.4	1,189	31.6	83.7	2.0	0.8
1964	14	74.2	1,343	33.3	89.9	2.2	0.8
1963	24	83.7	1,466	35.8	96.9	2.3	0.8

[Continued]

★ 450 ★

Maternal Deaths and Death Rates
[Continued]

Calendar year	Indian and Alaska Native		U.S. all races		U.S. other than white	Ratio Indian to:	
	Number	Rate[1]	Number	Rate	Rate	U.S. all races	U.S. other than White
1962	18	89.7	1,465	35.2	95.9	2.5	0.9
1961	17	66.5	1,573	36.9	101.3	1.8	0.7
1960	8	67.9	1,579	37.1	97.9	1.8	0.7
1959	18	68.8	1,588	37.4	102.1	1.8	0.7
1958	16	82.6	1,581	37.6	101.8	2.2	0.8

Source: Trends in Indian Health, 1991, U.S. Department of Health and Human Services, Public Health Service, Indian Health Service, p. 26. *Notes:* 1. Indian and Alaska Native rates are 3-year rates centered in the year specified. All other rates are for the year specified.

★ 451 ★

Neonatal Deaths, by Leading Cause

Rate per 1,000 live births for American Indians, Alaskan Natives, 1986- 1988, and U.S. all races, 1987.

Cause of death	Indian and Alaska Native		U.S. all races Rate	U.S. other than White	Ratio American Indian and Alaska Native to:	
	Number	Rate			U.S. all races	U.S. other than White
All causes	587	4.6	6.5	10.0	0.7	0.5
Congenital anomalies	168	1.3	1.5	1.4	0.9	0.9
Respiratory distress syndrome	62	0.5	0.8	1.1	0.6	0.5
Disorders relating to short gestation and low birth weigh	54	0.4	0.9	1.9	0.4	0.2
Sudden infant death syndrome	30	0.2	01	0.2	2.0	1.0
Infections specific to the perinatal period	26	0.2	0.2	0.3	1.0	0.7
Newborn affected by maternal complications of pregnancy	25	0.2	0.2	0.3	1.0	0.7
Newborn affected by complications of placenta, cord, and membranes	22	0.2	0.2	0.3	1.0	0.7
Intrauterine hypoxia and birth asphyxia	18	0.1	0.2	0.3	0.5	0.3
Neonatal hemorrhage	9	0.1	0.2	0.1	1.0	1.0
Accidents	6	0.0	0.0	0.0	[1]	[1]
All other causes	167					

Source: Trends in Indian Health, 1991, U.S. Department of Health and Human Services, Public Health Service, Indian Health Service, p. 30. Primary source: National Center for Health Statistics (NCHS), U.S. infant mortality rates (all ages)—Monthly Vital Statistics Report, Vol. 38, No. 5, Supplement, September 26, 1989, Table 15: Infant mortality rates by age and race an published in Vital Statistics of the United States, 1987, Volume II, Part A, Mortality, Tables 2-6 and 2-16. *Note:* 1. Not applicable.

★ 452 ★

Postneonatal Deaths, by Leading Causes

Rate per 1,000 live births for American Indians, Alaskan Natives, 1986- 1988, and U.S. all races, 1987.

Cause of death	Indian and Alaska Native		U.S. all races Rate	U.S. other than White	Ratio American Indian and Alaska Native to:	
	Number	Rate			U.S. all races	U.S. other than White
All causes	649	5.1	3.6	5.4	1.4	0.9
Sudden infant death syndrome	255	2.0	1.3	1.8	1.5	0.1
Congenital anomalies	69	0.5	0.6	0.7	0.8	0.7
Accidents	51	0.4	0.2	0.3	2.0	1.3
Pneumonia and influenza	41	0.3	0.1	0.2	3.0	1.5
Meningitis	17	0.1	0.0	0.1	1	1.0
Septicemia	15	0.1	0.1	0.1	1.0	1.0
Homicide	11	0.1	0.1	0.1	1.0	1.0
Viral diseases	10	0.1	0.0	0.0	1	1
Gastritis, duodenitis, and non-infective enteritis and colitis	9	0.1	0.0	0.1	1	1.0
Respiratory distress syndrome	7	0.1	0.1	0.1	1.0	1.0
All other causes	164					

Source: Trends in Indian Health, 1991, U.S. Department of Health and Human Services, Public Health Service, Indian Health Service, p. 30. Primary source: National Center for Health Statistics (NCHS), U.S. infant mortality rates (all ages)—Monthly Vital Statistics Report, Vol. 38, No. 5, Supplement, September 26, 1989, Table 15: Infant mortality rates by age and race an published in Vital Statistics of the United States, 1987, Volume II, Part A, Mortality, Tables 2-6 and 2-16. *Note:* 1. Not applicable.

Mental Health

★ 453 ★

Suicide Deaths and Mortality Rates, by Year

Age-adjusted rate per 100,000 population for American Indians, Alaskan Natives, and U.S. all races, 1955-1988.

Calendar year	Indian and Alaskan Native		U.S. all races		U.S. other than White Rate	Ratio Indian to:	
	Number	Rate	Number	Rate		U.S. all races	U.S. other than White
1988	221	14.5	30,407	11.4	6.9	1.3	2.1
1987	221	15.0	30,796	11.7	6.9	1.3	2.2
1986	211	15.0	30,904	11.9	6.8	1.3	2.2
1985	204	14.1	29,453	11.5	6.7	1.2	2.1
1984	181	12.9	29,286	11.6	6.6	1.1	2.0
1983	196	14.7	28,295	11.4	6.4	1.3	2.3
1982	178	13.6	28,242	11.6	6.4	1.2	2.1

[Continued]

★ 453 ★

Suicide Deaths and Mortality Rates, by Year
[Continued]

Calendar year	Indian and Alaskan Native		U.S. all races		U.S. other than White Rate	Ratio Indian to:	
	Number	Rate	Number	Rate		U.S. all races	U.S. other than White
1981	191	15.5	27,596	11.5	6.8	1.3	2.3
1980	173	14.1	26,869	11.4	6.7	1.2	2.1
1979	188	16.1	27,204	11.7	7.9	1.4	2.0
1978	150	14.0	27,294	12.0	7.4	1.2	1.9
1977	199	20.5	28,681	12.9	7.8	1.6	2.6
1976	168	17.9	26,832	12.3	7.6	1.5	2.4
1975	180	21.2	27,063	12.6	7.5	1.7	2.8
1974	148	18.0	25,683	12.2	7.2	1.5	2.5
1973	149	19.8	25,118	12.0	7.2	1.7	2.8
1972	138	18.5	25,004	12.1	7.5	1.5	2.5
1971	135	19.9	24,092	11.9	7.0	1.7	2.8
1970	105	17.9	22,630	11.8	6.5	1.5	2.8
1969	94	16.8	22,364	11.3	6.3	1.5	2.7
1968	90	17.5	21,372	11.0	5.7	1.6	3.1
1967	94	16.2	21,325	11.1	6.1	1.5	2.7
1966	64	15.2	21,281	11.2	6.1	1.4	2.5
1965	65	12.9	21,507	11.4	6.1	1.1	2.1
1964	52	15.8	20,588	11.0	5.6	1.4	2.8
1963	66	15.6	20,825	11.3	6.0	1.4	2.6
1962	59	16.9	20,207	11.1	5.6	1.5	3.0
1961	61	16.7	18,999	10.5	5.6	1.6	3.0
1960	57	16.8	19,041	10.6	5.4	1.6	3.1
1959	57	17.0	18,633	10.6	5.5	1.6	3.1
1958	61	18.7	18,519	10.5	5.1	1.8	3.7
1957	58	17.6	16,632	9.6	4.7	1.8	3.7
1956	45	12.5	16,727	9.7	4.4	1.3	2.8
1955	39	11.9	16,760		4.3	1.2	2.8

Source: Trends in Indian Health, 1991, U.S. Department of Health and Human Services, Public Health Service, Indian Health Service, p. 45.
Notes: Estimated population methodology for the Indian population was revised in 1976. Maine, New York and Pennsylvania included as Reservation States beginning in 1979, Connecticut, Rhode Island and Texas in 1983 and Alabama in 1984. Decennial Census population counts used for 1960, 1970, and 1980.

★ 454 ★

Suicide Mortality Rates, by Age and Sex

Rate per 100,000 population for American Indians, Alaskan Natives, 1986-1988, and U.S. all races, 1987.

Age group	Indian and Alaskan Native			U.S. all races			U.S. Other than White		
	Both sexes	Male	Female	Both sexes	Male	Female	Both sexes	Male	Female
Under 5 years	-	-	-	-	-	-	-	-	-
5-14 years	1.7	2.9	0.6	0.7	1.1	0.3	0.5	0.7	0.2
15-24 years	23.5	40.7	6.5	12.9	21.3	4.3	8.7	14.4	3.0
25-34 years	28.7	49.6	8.3	15.4	24.8	5.9	11.7	20.1	4.0
35-44 years	19.6	30.3	9.3	15.0	22.9	7.2	9.5	16.4	3.6
45-54 years	13.1	21.7	5.0	15.9	23.8	8.5	7.6	12.7	3.3
55-64 years	8.3	12.2	4.6	16.6	26.6	7.7	6.2	10.5	2.6
65-74 years	9.0	16.7	2.4	19.4	34.8	7.2	9.4	17.6	3.1
75-84 years	7.5	13.7	2.7	25.8	57.1	7.0	9.6	21.5	2.1
85 years +	5.3	13.3	-	22.1	66.9	4.6	9.3	22.9	2.9

Source: *Trends in Indian Health, 1991*, U.S. Department of Health and Human Services, Public Health Service, Indian Health Service, p. 46. *Note:* - Represents zero.

Native American Adolescents

★ 455 ★

Nutritional Inadequacies of Adolescents

Data show the percent of adolescents who reported not consuming items from each food group on a daily basis. Data are based on a survey of 13,923 rural American Indian/Alaska Native adolescents living on or near reservations[1].

Food groups	Males	Females
Meat & meat substitutes	23.7	30.7
Dairy food	14.6	19.9
Bread & rice	30.4	29.2
Fruit & vegetables	14.4	12.8
Eats from all four groups daily	49.2	44.5
Misses 1-2 groups daily	42.7	46.3
Misses 3-4 groups daily	8.1	9.2

Source: *The State of Native American Youth Health, February, 1992*, Indian Health Service, Maternal and Child Health Bureau, and the Robert Wood Johnson Foundation, p. 14. *Notes:* 1. Caution: Sample was not random and does not fully represent all Native American/Alaska Native groups.

★ 456 ★

Physical Illnesses Reported by Rural Adolescents

Data are based on a survey of 13,923 rural American Indian/Alaska Native adolescents living on or near reservations[1].

Condition	Percent of total report-ing having the condition	Percent of total report-ing limitations from the condition
Nerve-sensory		
Hearing impairments	5.0	0.8
Speech problems	12.7	1.4
Vision problems	30.0	4.0
Learning disabilities	12.6	1.7
Emotional/somatic		
Seizures/convulsions	1.5	0.5
Nervous/emotional problems	16.4	2.4
Abdominal problems	27.1	2.0
Chronic		
Headaches	73.5	4.9
Respiratory problems	11.8	1.5
Diabetes	1.7	0.4
Allergies/hay fever	19.1	1.6
Other		
Mononucleosis	1.8	0.3
Concentration problems	27.0	2.7
Sexually transmitted diseases	1.8	0.4
Condition limiting school	8.4	8.4

Source: The State of Native American Youth Health, February, 1992, Indian Health Service, Maternal and Child Health Bureau, and the Robert Wood Johnson Foundation, p. 15. *Notes:* 1. Caution: Sample was not random and does not fully represent all Native American/Alaska Native groups.

★ 457 ★

Unhealthy Characteristics of Adolescents

Data are shown in percent and are based on a survey of 13,923 rural American Indian/Alaska Native adolescents living on or near reservations[1].

Characteristic	Males	Females	Total
Are obese	24.7	25.0	24.9
Eat red meat daily	41.4	37.1	39.2
Eat eggs daily	40.6	33.8	37.2
Eat fruit and vegetables less than daily	14.4	12.8	13.6
Eat junk food three or more times daily	39.6	42.3	41.0
Smoke cigarettes daily	10.8	12.5	11.7

[Continued]

★ 457 ★

Unhealthy Characteristics of Adolescents

[Continued]

Characteristic	Males	Females	Total
Use chewing tobacco daily	14.5	7.7	11.1
Never exercise	18.3	19.4	18.9
Have at least four of these problems	15.8	13.1	14.4

Source: The State of Native American Youth Health, February, 1992, Indian Health Service, Maternal and Child Health Bureau, and the Robert Wood Johnson Foundation, p. 13. *Notes:* 1. Caution: Sample was not random and does not fully represent all Native American/Alaska Native groups.

Substance Abuse

★ 458 ★

Alcohol Treatment Programs

State client treatment admissions are shown, by race/ethnicity and state.

State	Native American	White, not of Hispanic origin	Black, not of Hispanic origin	Hispanic	Asian or Pacific Islander	Other	Not reported	Total
Alabama	N/A	5,443	1,748	N/A	N/A	21	0	7,212
Alaska	4,828	4,100	141	0	0	335	70	9,474
Arizona	4,197	15,998	1,358	4,379	70	0	0	26,002
Arkansas	49	5,693	1,396	51	2	0	0	7,191
California	2,410	81,790	28,450	12,570	640	1,140	0	127,000
Colorado	3,016	33,505	3,400	14,696	165	54	0	54,836
Connecticut	N/A	9,418	3,320	1,294	N/A	69	5,435	19,536[1]
Delaware	0	2,756	1,250	81	2	0	24	4,113
District of Columbia	0	1,321	3,478	0	0	98	0	4,897
Florida	195	47,547	10,376	3,846	84	164	1,082	63,294
Georgia	22	17,927	8,343	77	9	49	0	26,427
Guam	1	34	0	3	84	0	0	122
Hawaii	119	1,120	55	66	648	306	14	2,328
Idaho	224	3,668	18	379	6	37	0	4,332
Illinois	186	28,726	15,720	2,665	124	0	0	47,421
Indiana	19	11,161	2,417	157	14	32	5	13,805
Iowa	236	16,808	535	308	35	31	254	18,207
Kansas	347	9,037	1,143	725	26	29	28	11,335
Kentucky	N/A	12,252	1,017	N/A	N/A	48	403	13,720
Louisiana	14	6,939	1,273	11	5	13	0	8,255
Maine	446	9,918	70	0	11	40	0	10,485
Maryland	N/A	12,264	5,688	N/A	N/A	244	6	18,202[2]
Massachusetts	333	46,942	4,273	2,373	127	1,157	0	55,205
Michigan	872	32,664	6,426	493	49	276	132	40,912

[Continued]

★ 458 ★

Alcohol Treatment Programs
[Continued]

State	Native American	White, not of Hispanic origin	Black, not of Hispanic origin	Hispanic	Asian or Pacific Islander	Other	Not reported	Total
Minnesota	8,519	35,305	3,032	1,253	74	88	353	48,624
Mississippi	42	4,635	3,412	0	0	0	0	8,089
Missouri	167	18,843	6,595	187	23	26	39	25,880
Montana	1,217	6,389	27	106	8	17	0	7,764
Nebraska	2,932	17,719	1,188	959	35	46	15	22,894
Nevada	693	8,837	1,036	635	51	116	0	11,368
New Hampshire	41	4,792	75	43	4	0	22	4,977
New Jersey	60	17,078	10,516	2,470	0	106	30	30,260
New Mexico	2,519	2,646	133	4,143	6	0	8	9,455
New York	1,033	100,036	42,741	13,489	0	1,011	2,581	160,891
North Carolina	342	19,135	9,506	87	0	83	77	29,230
North Dakota	408	2,485	4	8	2	6	25	2,938
Ohio	20	14,953	5,545	207	0	43	0	20,768
Oklahoma	1,521	9,041	1,173	259	19	0	0	12,013
Oregon	N/A	N/A	N/A	N/A	N/A	N/A	N/A	N/A
Pennsylvania	N/A	28,137	6,138	756	29	62	N/A	35,122
Puerto Rico	0	0	0	7,816	0	0	0	7,816
Rhode Island	6	2,215	260	131	2	67	6,186	8,867
South Carolina	37	17,884	7,444	71	8	1	2	25,447
South Dakota	1,687	4,671	65	0	0	65	0	6,488
Tennessee	9	4,093	1,121	9	4	8	0	5,244
Texas	122	8,113	1,768	4,066	25	4	0	14,098
Utah	2,071	9,411	277	1,499	87	27	89	13,461
Vermont	0	3,287	0	0	0	0	116	3,403
Virginia	78	29,355	10,064	797	80	754	807	41,935
Washington	N/A	N/A	N/A	N/A	N/A	N/A	N/A	N/A
West Virginia	4	10,775	764	5	1	0	3	11,549
Wisconsin	2,598	76,682	3,101	1,341	84	0	0	83,806
Wyoming	N/A	N/A	N/A	N/A	N/A	N/A	N/A	N/A
Total	43,640	873,545	217,880	84,511	2,643	6,673	17,806	1,246,698
Percent of total	3.5	70.0	17.5	6.8	.2	.5	1.4	100.0

Source: State Resource and Services Related to Alcohol and Other Drug Abuse Problems for Fiscal Year 1990, National Institute on Drug Abuse and The National Institute on Alcohol Abuse and Alcoholism, p. 26. State Alcohol and Drug Abuse Profile (SADAP), FY 1990; data are included for "only those programs which received at least some funds administered by the State Alcohol/Drug Agency during the State's Fiscal Year (FY) 1990." *Notes:* N/A stands for information not available. 1. Asian or Pacific Islander and Native American are included under Other. 2. Other includes all categories other than White and Black.

★ 459 ★

Alcoholism Deaths and Mortality Rates, 1969-88

Age adjusted rates are shown, per 100,000 population, for American Indians, Alaskan Natives, and U.S. all races.

Calendar year	Indian and Alaskan Native		U.S. all races		Ratio American Indian and Alaska Native to U.S. all races
	Number	Rate	Number	Rate	
1988	389	33.9	16,882	6.3	5.4
1987	288	25.9	15,513	6.0	4.3
1986	272	24.6	15,525	6.4	3.8
1985	281	26.1	15,844	6.2	4.2
1984	316	30.0	15,706	6.2	4.8
1983	293	28.9	15,424	6.1	4.7
1982	298	30.7	15,596	6.4	4.8
1981	338	35.8	16,745	7.0	5.2
1980	382	41.3	17,742	7.5	5.5
1979	398	45.1	17,064	7.4	6.1
1978	437	54.5	18,490	8.1	6.7
1977	429	55.5	18,437	8.3	6.7
1976	425	58.2	18,484	8.6	6.8
1975	403	62.2	18,190	8.6	7.2
1974	417	64.2	18,530	8.6	7.5
1973	399	66.1	17,791	8.6	7.7
1972	315	55.0	17,484	8.6	6.4
1971	334	62.9	16,891	8.4	7.5
1970	272	56.2	16,130	8.1	6.9
1969	267	56.6	15,138	7.7	7.4

Source: Trends in Indian Health, 1991, U.S. Department of Health and Human Services, Public Health Service, Indian Health Service, p. 49. *Notes:* For 1969-1978 includes deaths due to alcoholism, alcoholic psychoses and cirrhosis of the liver with mention of alcoholism. For 1979 and after includes deaths due to alcohol dependence syndrome, alcoholic psychoses and chronic liver disease and cirrhosis, specified as alcoholic. Population estimation methodology for the American Indian and Alaska Native population revised in 1976. Maine, New York and Pennsylvania included as Reservation States beginning in 1979, Connecticut, Rhode Island and Texas in 1983 and Alabama in 1984. Decennial Census population counts used for 1970 and 1980.

★ 460 ★

Alcoholism Mortality Rates, by Age and Sex

Rate per 100,000 population for American Indians, Alaskan Natives, and U.S. all races, 1955-1988.

Age group	Indian and Alaska Native			U.S. all races			U.S. Other than White		
	Both sexes	Male	Female	Both sexes	Male	Female	Both sexes	Male	Female
Under 5 years	-	-	-	-	-	-	-	-	-
5-14 years	-	-	-	-	-	-	-	-	-
15-24 years	1.0	0.8	1.2	0.1	0.1	0.1	0.3	0.2	0.4
25-34 years	19.3	21.8	16.8	2.3	3.2	1.4	5.7	7.9	3.7
35-44 years	50.1	65.5	35.1	8.5	12.9	4.2	22.1	34.2	11.9
45-54 years	76.5	96.8	57.3	15.8	24.4	7.6	32.6	53.1	15.4
55-64 years	72.0	95.4	50.2	20.5	33.1	9.4	33.0	55.4	14.7
65-74 years	47.3	79.5	20.1	16.0	27.0	7.3	19.8	34.8	8.4
75-84 years	36.0	58.1	18.7	8.9	17.5	3.8	12.1	24.8	4.0
85 years +	10.6	13.3	8.9	3.2	7.3	1.6	5.1	10.8	2.3

Source: Trends in Indian Health, 1991, U.S. Department of Health and Human Services, Public Health Service, Indian Health Service, p. 50.

★ 461 ★

Drug Treatment Program Enrollment

Percent distribution of clients is shown by race/ethnicity for each treatment modality. Data are shown for October 30, 1987.

Race/ethnicity	Detoxification	Maintenance	Drug free	Total
American Indian/Alaskan Native	1.0	0.3	1.3	1.0
White	64.8	41.1	62.8	57.8
Black	20.3	28.7	22.1	23.6
Hispanic	13.6	29.5	12.7	16.7
Asian	0.2	0.2	0.7	0.6
Other	0.0	0.2	0.4	0.3
Total	100.0	100.0	100.0	100.0

Source: "Percent Distribution of Drug Abuse Clients by Race/Ethnicity, by Treatment Modality in Single-Modality Drug Only and Combined Units: October 30, 1987," *Health Status of Minorities and Low-Income Groups: Third Edition*, 1991, p. 278. Primary source: National Institute on Drug Abuse and National Institute on Alcohol Abuse and Alcoholism, National Drug and Alcoholism Treatment Unit Survey (NDATUS), 1987 Final Report, Table 25, p. 41. *Note:* Percentages may not add to 100 percent because of rounding.

★ 462 ★

Initial Drug Abuse Treatment Contacts

Numbers show initial contacts to the IHS substance abuse treatment program, 1985-89.

Drug of abuse	Number of initial contacts				
	FY 1985	FY 1986	FY 1987	FY 1988	FY 1989
All drugs	1,333	1,487	1,457	1,854	2,346
Opiates	122	134	75	106	141
Barbiturates	81	67	63	102	73
Cocaine	31	56	108	144	268
Marijuana	851	938	932	1,134	1,309
Amphetamines	43	68	56	731	108
Hallucinogens	30	25	20	30	21
Multiple drugs excluding sniffing	113	139	136	201	318
Sniffing/inhalants	41	37	43	48	71
Sniffing and other drugs	21	23	24	16	37

Source: Trends in Indian Health, 1991, U.S. Department of Health and Human Services, Public Health Service, Indian Health Service, p. 77. Primary source: Alcoholism Treatment and Guidance System (ATGS).

★ 463 ★

Smoking Prevalence Among American Indians and Whites

Data are based on surveys conducted from 1987 to 1991.

Sex	Percent who smoked		Average number smoked per day	
	American Indians, Aleuts and Eskimos	Whites	American Indians, Aleuts and Eskimos	Whites
Both sexes	29.9	24.3	na	na
Men	33.4	25.7	19.4	21.4
Women	26.6	23.0	15.5	17.7

Source: Lakota Times, November 9, 1992, p. B5. Primary source: Centers for Disease Control and Prevention.

★ 464 ★

State Drug Treatment Programs

Number of drug client treatment admissions are shown, by race/ethnicity and state, for fiscal year 1990.

State	Native American	White, not of Hispanic origin	Black, not of Hispanic origin	Hispanic	Asian or Pacific Islander	Other	Not reported	Total
Alabama	N/A	3,734	2,642	N/A	N/A	18	705	7,099
Alaska	450	1,232	228	N/A	N/A	64	0	1,974
Arizona	343	6,367	1,091	2,120	28	0	0	9,949
Arkansas	6	1,819	1,112	15	3	0	0	2,955
California	811	44,576	15,002	23,596	1,759	0	58	85,802
Colorado	70	3,436	837	1,520	30	0	0	5,893
Connecticut	N/A	4,141	3,456	2,131	N/A	71	2,875	12,674[1]
Delaware	0	936	1,135	67	2	0	1	2,141
District of Columbia	0	207	6,545	0	0	137	0	6,889
Florida	114	16,885	11,221	2,753	45	0	0	31,018
Georgia	8	8,244	13,295	57	6	35	0	21,645
Guam	0	6	0	0	15	0	0	21
Hawaii	67	475	40	36	766	232	107	1,723
Idaho	61	2,031	10	105	10	19	0	2,236
Illinois	135	20,867	11,418	1,935	91	0	0	34,446
Indiana	9	5,305	1,149	75	7	15	0	6,560
Iowa	51	3,669	556	57	8	15	92	4,448
Kansas	71	2,345	1,247	108	9	9	164	3,953
Kentucky	N/A	4,429	829	N/A	N/A	17	170	5,445
Louisiana	14	4,387	1,966	4	4	8	0	6,383
Maine	26	1,401	17	0	0	10	0	1,454
Maryland	N/A	7,800	12,656	N/A	N/A	167	2	20,625[2]
Massachusetts	144	22,307	8,859	4,203	88	1,140	0	36,741
Michigan	221	13,891	13,072	255	33	204	109	27,785
Minnesota	941	7,269	1,453	156	33	47	13	9,912
Mississippi	6	2,031	2,402	0	0	0	0	4,439
Missouri	68	7,931	4,809	66	6	22	13	12,915
Montana	325	1,667	7	24	2	0	0	2,025
Nebraska	94	2,094	353	65	6	3	3	2,618
Nevada	40	2,162	441	204	22	27	0	2,896
New Hampshire	9	1,404	43	18	1	0	0	1,475
New Jersey	15	6,694	7,260	2,490	30	0	0	16,489
New Mexico	274	764	87	955	8	0	6	2,094
New York	155	20,522	19,977	10,915	75	438	37,112	89,194
North Carolina	210	6,356	5,541	22	0	16	20	12,165
North Dakota	15	191	0	3	1	0	1	211
Ohio	45	6,210	4,744	145	11	34	10,720	21,909
Oklahoma	353	3,707	1,057	102	5	0	0	5,224
Oregon	N/A	N/A	N/A	N/A	N/A	N/A	N/A	N/A
Pennsylvania	N/A	13,594	16,446	1,802	26	17	0	31,885
Puerto Rico	0	0	0	0	0	16,071	0	16,071
Rhode Island	7	2,876	425	187	4	57	2,096	5,652
South Carolina	8	3,889	3,833	20	2	1	0	7,753
South Dakota	991	2,744	38	0	0	38	0	3,811

[Continued]

★ 464 ★

State Drug Treatment Programs

[Continued]

State	Native American	White, not of Hispanic origin	Black, not of Hispanic origin	Hispanic	Asian or Pacific Islander	Other	Not reported	Total
Tennessee	10	1,902	832	2	3	5	0	2,754
Texas	55	8,280	6,301	5,484	32	39	0	20,191
Utah	57	2,132	84	227	9	2	21	2,532
Vermont	0	2,123	0	0	0	0	0	2,123
Virginia	36	12,740	9,009	261	29	66	529	22,670
Washington	N/A	N/A	N/A	N/A	N/A	N/A	N/A	N/A
West Virginia	2	1,263	287	2	0	0	0	1,554
Wisconsin	323	13,886	7,044	836	201	0	0	22,290
Wyoming	N/A	N/A	N/A	N/A	N/A	N/A	N/A	N/A
Total	6,640	314,921	200,856	63,023	3,410	19,044	54,817	662,711
Percent of total	1.0	47.5	30.3	9.5	.5	2.9	8.3	100.0

Source: State Resource and Services Related to Alcohol and Other Drug Abuse Problems for Fiscal Year 1990, The National Institute on Drug Abuse and The National Institute on Alcohol Abuse and Alcoholism, p. 33. State Alcohol and Drug Abuse Profile (SADAP), FY 1990; data are included for "only those programs which received at least some funds administered by the State Alcohol/Drug Agency during the State's Fiscal Year (FY) 1990." *Notes:* N/A stands for information not available. 1. Asian or Pacific Islander and Native American are included under Other. 2. Other includes all categories other than White and Black.

Venereal Disease

★ 465 ★

Gonorrhea Cases - IHS vs. Non-IHS Areas

Figures contrast reported gonorrhea cases in Indian Health Service service areas and non-service areas of selected states, 1988.

State	IHS service areas		Non-service areas	
	Number cases	Cases per 100,000	Number cases	Cases per 100,000
California	115	138.1	58	37.1
Colorado	7	215.5	15	77.4
Montana	181	445.1	6	78.4
North Carolina	18	277.3	158	232.9
North Dakota	81	370.3	9	220.9
South Dakota	224	437.6	29	585.0
Utah	15	131.3	16	126.7

Source: Kathleen E. Toomey, Alisa G. Oberschelp, and Joel R. Greenspan, "Sexually Transmitted Diseases and Native Americans: Trends in Reported Gonorrhea and Syphilis Morbidity, 1984-88," *Public Health Reports*, Vol. 104, No. 6, November/December 1989, p. 570.

★ 466 ★

Gonorrhea Cases in Selected States

Figures are given for the number of cases, and cases per 100,000, from 1984-1988.

State	Native Americans		Non-Native Americans	
	Number cases	Cases per 100,000	Number cases	Cases per 100,000
Alaska[1]	5,526	1,469.66	5,984	283.66
Arizona[1]	5,074	569.22	31,835	209.08
Colorado	139	131.25	30,905	194.32
Minnesota[1]	1,171	564.59	25,230	120.94
Montana[1]	1,350	595.78	2,114	54.98
New Mexico[1]	2,647	441.31	9,908	149.41
North Carolina[2]	867	241.41	163,231	531.56
North Dakota[1]	527	428.37	996	30.89
Oklahoma	2,401	247.38	50,898	331.86
Oregon	272	178.02	25,504	190.92
South Dakota[1]	1,680	637.53	1,985	61.18
Utah[3]	268	238.27	4,757	58.59
Washington[1]	1,751	508.78	43,390	199.78
13 States combined	23,673	500.83	396,737	247.52
United States	25,533	316.42	4,146,346	349.18

Source: Kathleen E. Toomey, Alisa G. Oberschelp, and Joel R. Greenspan, "Sexually Transmitted Diseases and Native Americans: Trends in Reported Gonorrhea and Syphilis Morbidity, 1984-88," *Public Health Reports*, Vol. 104, No. 6, November/December 1989, p. 568. *Notes:* 1. Rates for Native Americans exceeded 349 per 100,000 and were higher than rates for non-Native Americans. 2. Rates for non-Native Americans exceeded 349 per 100,000. 3. Rates for Native Americans exceeded rates for non-Native Americans.

★ 467 ★

Gonorrhea Cases, by Race/Ethnicity

| Blacks - 2,045 |
| Native Americans - 501 |
| Hispanics - 279 |
| Whites - 97 |

Figures are for 13 selected states from 1984-1988.

Race and ethnicity	Cases per 100,000
Native Americans	501
Blacks	2,045
Hispanics	279
Whites	97

Source: Kathleen E. Toomey, Alisa G. Oberschelp, and Joel R. Greenspan, "Sexually Transmitted Diseases and Native Americans: Trends in Reported Gonorrhea and Syphilis Morbidity, 1984-88," *Public Health Reports*, Vol. 104, No. 6, November/December 1989, p. 569.

★ 468 ★

Syphilis Cases in Selected States

Figures are given for 1984-1988.

State	Native Americans		Non-Native Americans	
	Number cases	Cases per 100,000	Number cases	Cases per 100,000
Alaska	7	1.83	23	1.10
Arizona	351	39.52	900	5.87
Colorado	981	8.73	694	4.36
Minnesota	24	12.05	175	0.84
Montana	6	2.64	25	0.65
New Mexico	102	17.06	304	4.58
North Carolina	14	3.91	3,657	11.89
North Dakota	3	2.73	15	0.46
Oklahoma	34	3.56	859	5.61
Oregon	15	9.60	973	7.23
South Dakota	3	1.14	16	0.49

[Continued]

★ 468 ★

Syphilis Cases in Selected States
[Continued]

State	Native Americans		Non-Native Americans	
	Number cases	Cases per 100,000	Number cases	Cases per 100,000
Utah	6	5.24	92	1.13
Washington	35	10.09	873	3.99

Source: Kathleen E. Toomey, Alisa G. Oberschelp, and Joel R. Greenspan, "Sexually Transmitted Diseases and Native Americans: Trends in Reported Gonorrhea and Syphilis Morbidity, 1984-88," *Public Health Reports*, Vol. 104, No. 6, November/December 1989, p. 569. *Notes:* Primary and secondary syphilis rates for Native Americans exceeded the rates for non-Native Americans in all States except Oklahoma and North Carolina.

Health Care

★ 469 ★

Health Care Facilities

Number of facilities operated by Indian Health Service and tribes as of October 1, 1990.

Type of facility	IHS	Tribal
Hospitals	43	7
Outpatient facilities	121	329
Health centers	66	89
School health centers	4	3
Health stations	51	64
Alaska village clinics	-	173

Source: Trends in Indian Health, 1991, U.S. Department of Health and Human Services, Public Health Service, Indian Health Service, p. 15. *Note:* A dash (-) represents zero.

★ 470 ★

Methods of Health Care on Identified Reservations, 1980 - I

Data are the latest available.

| | | Persons who received health care in last 12 months | | | | | | | | | |
| | | Usual place of health care -- percent | | | Health care paid by -- percent | | | | | Travel time to health care facility -- percent | |
Identified reservations	Total	Indian service clinic, health center or hospital	Private physician or dentist	Tribal clinic or hospital	Person or other family member	Private health insurance	Medicaid or Medicare	Indian Health Service or tribe	Other government services	Less than 30 minutes	30 minutes to 1 hour
Total persons	285,618	80.3	11.3	4.8	4.7	4.9	2.8	84.1	2.0	60.0	23.9
Acoma Pueblo, New Mexico	2,094	88.4	8.8	0.8	4.6	3.0	1.2	89.4	0.8	86.8	7.2
Valencia County	2,094	88.4	8.8	0.8	4.6	3.0	1.2	89.4	0.8	86.8	7.2
Agua Caliente Reservation, California	-	-	-	-	-	-	-	-	-	-	-
Riverside County	-	-	-	-	-	-	-	-	-	-	-
Alabama-Coushatta Reservation, Texas	349	0.7	78.3	1.8	60.0	16.9	4.2	2.9	12.4	72.7	13.4
Polk County	349	0.7	78.3	1.8	60.0	16.9	4.2	2.9	12.4	72.7	13.4
Alamo Reservation, New Mexico	410	28.6	5.2	8.1	1.0	1.5	3.9	88.3	3.6	6.6	6.9
Socorro County	410	28.6	5.2	8.1	1.0	1.5	3.9	88.3	3.6	6.6	6.9
Allegany Reservation, New York	771	65.7	15.8	15.3	5.6	22.3	13.1	56.7	0.6	76.4	21.4
Cattaraugus County	771	65.7	15.8	15.3	5.6	22.3	13.1	56.7	0.6	76.4	21.4
Alturas Rancheria, California	...	...	...	...	...	...	...	...	...	...	...
Modoc County	...	...	...	...	...	...	...	...	...	...	...
Annette Islands Reserve, Alaska	854	89.8	5.2	2.1	2.8	4.2	1.1	88.9	1.5	90.5	2.7
Prince of Wales-Outer Ketchikan Census Area	854	89.8	5.2	2.1	2.8	4.2	1.1	88.9	1.5	90.5	2.7
Augustine Reservation, California	-	-	-	-	-	-	-	-	-	-	-
Riverside County	-	-	-	-	-	-	-	-	-	-	-
Bad River Reservation, Wisconsin	648	0.3	90.5	7.7	1.0	11.4	41.7	42.0	4.0	91.0	7.8
Ashland County	648	0.3	90.5	7.7	1.0	11.4	41.7	42.0	4.0	91.0	7.8
Iron County	-	-	-	-	-	-	-	-	-	-	-
Barona Rancheria, California	179	27.0	68.0	-	25.6	38.9	30.8	2.1	1.3	12.5	64.4
San Diego County	179	27.0	68.0	-	25.6	38.9	30.8	2.1	1.3	12.5	64.4
Bay Mills Reservation, Michigan	255	83.3	3.2	-	-	13.4	4.2	81.7	0.7	14.5	79.3
Chippewa County	255	83.3	3.2	-	-	13.4	4.2	81.7	0.7	14.5	79.3
Benton Paiute Reservation, California	...	...	...	...	...	...	...	...	...	...	...
Mono County	...	...	...	...	...	...	...	...	...	...	...
Berry Creek Rancheria, California	-	-	-	-	-	-	-	-	-	-	-
Butte County	-	-	-	-	-	-	-	-	-	-	-
Big Bend Rancheria, California	...	...	...	...	...	...	...	...	...	...	...
Shasta County	...	...	...	...	...	...	...	...	...	...	...
Big Cypress Reservation, Florida	349	99.0	1.0	-	0.7	1.8	-	97.3	-	98.4	0.6
Hendry County	349	99.0	1.0	-	0.7	1.8	-	97.3	-	98.4	0.6
Big Lagoon Rancheria, California	...	...	...	...	...	...	...	...	...	...	...
Humboldt County	...	...	...	...	...	...	...	...	...	...	...
Big Pine Rancheria, California	255	1.3	4.4	93.3	3.3	2.2	7.1	86.3	-	24.6	74.9
Inyo County	255	1.3	4.4	93.3	3.3	2.2	7.1	86.3	-	24.6	74.9
Bishop Rancheria, California	700	11.7	9.0	76.1	3.8	16.6	12.3	59.8	5.2	97.1	0.7
Inyo County	700	11.7	9.0	76.1	3.8	16.6	12.3	59.8	5.2	97.1	0.7
Blackfeet Reservation, Montana	4,780	96.2	2.9	0.6	1.2	1.6	0.5	95.7	0.4	81.7	12.4
Glacier County	4,314	96.1	3.0	0.5	1.1	1.7	0.5	95.7	0.4	81.5	12.8
Pondera County	466	97.0	1.6	1.4	2.4	0.2	1.1	95.4	0.2	84.1	9.4
Bois Forte Reservation (Nett Lake), Minnesota	373	37.5	51.7	1.3	0.8	5.4	2.7	60.3	2.1	28.7	8.3
Koochiching County	54	46.3	5.6	7.4	-	25.9	5.6	55.6	5.6	11.1	29.6
St. Louis County	319	36.1	59.6	0.3	0.9	1.9	2.2	61.1	1.6	31.7	4.7
Bridgeport Colony, California	43	40.1	14.2	13.4	14.0	5.8	8.0	53.5	16.1	43.0	34.9
Mono County	43	40.1	14.2	13.4	14.0	5.8	8.0	53.5	16.1	43.0	34.9
Brighton Reservation, Florida	304	97.4	2.6	-	1.5	3.7	1.1	93.7	-	96.7	2.3
Glades County	304	97.4	2.6	-	1.5	3.7	1.1	93.7	-	96.7	2.3
Burns Reservation, Oregon	141	32.6	63.1	1.4	0.7	17.7	2.1	77.3	1.4	87.2	1.4
Harney County	141	32.6	63.1	1.4	0.7	17.7	2.1	77.3	1.4	87.2	1.4
Cabazon Reservation, California	...	...	...	...	...	...	...	...	...	...	...
Riverside County	...	...	...	...	...	...	...	...	...	...	...
Cachil Dehe Rancheria, California	...	...	...	...	...	...	...	...	...	...	...
Colusa County	...	...	...	...	...	...	...	...	...	...	...
Cahuilla Reservation, California	...	...	...	...	...	...	...	...	...	...	...
Riverside County	...	...	...	...	...	...	...	...	...	...	...
Campo Reservation, California	72	27.7	43.9	15.6	14.5	17.6	33.5	11.0	15.9	51.0	5.9
San Diego County	72	27.7	43.9	15.6	14.5	17.6	33.5	11.0	15.9	51.0	5.9
Camp Verde Reservation, Arizona	130	73.1	23.1	-	-	7.7	-	90.0	2.3	60.8	-
Yavapai County	130	73.1	23.1	-	-	7.7	-	90.0	2.3	60.8	-
Canoncito Reservation, New Mexico	937	98.1	1.4	0.4	0.9	0.5	0.5	97.9	-	68.9	22.2
Bernalillo County	813	97.8	1.7	0.4	1.1	0.6	0.5	97.6	-	72.5	18.0
Sandoval County	-	-	-	-	-	-	-	-	-	-	-
Valencia County	124	100.0	-	-	-	-	-	100.0	45.5	49.5	

[Continued]

731

★ 470 ★

Methods of Health Care on Identified Reservations, 1980 - I
[Continued]

Identified reservations	Total	Usual place of health care -- percent			Health care paid by -- percent					Travel time to health care facility -- percent	
		Indian service clinic, health center or hospital	Private physician or dentist	Tribal clinic or hospital	Person or other family member	Private health insurance	Medicaid or Medicare	Indian Health Service or tribe	Other government services	Less than 30 minutes	30 minutes to 1 hour
Capitan Grande Reservation, California	-	-	-	-	-	-	-	-	-	-	-
San Diego County	-	-	-	-	-	-	-	-	-	-	-
Carson Colony, Nevada	100	64.4	21.8	9.7	4.9	6.1	3.8	76.3	2.5	62.2	6.0
Carson City	100	64.4	21.8	9.7	4.9	6.1	3.8	76.3	2.5	62.2	6.0
Catawba Reservation, South Carolina	971	-	97.5	0.1	92.2	1.0	4.5	-	1.3	71.5	26.0
York County	971	-	97.5	0.1	92.2	1.0	4.5	-	1.3	71.5	26.0
Cattaraugus Reservation, New York	1,448	7.4	17.6	73.2	5.8	43.5	13.1	34.5	0.7	95.2	3.3
Cattaragus County	292	2.4	11.8	84.6	3.3	48.9	20.4	24.1	1.3	95.7	2.9
Chautauqua County	...	...	...	...	...	...	...	...	...	...	...
Erie County	1,154	8.7	19.1	70.3	6.4	42.2	11.3	37.2	0.6	95.0	3.4
Cedarville Rancheria, California	...	...	...	...	...	...	...	...	...	...	...
Modoc County	...	...	...	...	...	...	...	...	...	...	...
Chehalis Reservation, Washington	195	12.2	53.3	31.1	6.4	17.7	3.3	63.4	9.1	63.8	34.9
Grays Harbor County	171	13.9	53.4	30.0	6.7	19.6	3.8	59.5	10.4	63.0	35.6
Thurston County	...	...	...	...	...	...	...	...	...	...	...
Chemehuevi Rerservation, California	...	...	...	...	...	...	...	...	...	...	...
San Bernardino County	...	...	...	...	...	...	...	...	...	...	...
Cheyenne River Reservation, South Dakota	1,374	80.0	9.9	8.5	4.4	2.4	3.0	87.3	1.7	15.5	34.5
Dewey County	691	71.9	15.3	11.6	7.2	4.5	4.2	82.7	1.5	20.5	45.4
Ziebach County	684	88.1	4.4	5.4	1.5	0.3	1.7	92.0	2.0	10.5	23.3
Chitimacha Reservation, Louisiana	134	-	100.0	-	1.0	11.1	4.6	83.3	-	95.3	3.8
St. Mary Parish	134	-	100.0	-	1.0	11.1	4.6	83.3	-	95.3	3.8
Cochiti Pueblo, New Mexico	587	95.0	2.4	0.6	1.1	1.4	-	96.1	1.1	10.1	85.8
Sandoval County	587	95.0	2.4	0.6	1.1	1.4	-	96.1	1.1	10.1	85.8
Cocopah Reservation, Arizona	312	99.0	-	0.3	0.3	-	-	98.4	0.3	14.9	76.1
Yuma County	312	99.0	-	0.3	0.3	-	-	98.4	0.3	14.9	76.1
Coeur d'Alene Reservation, Idaho	486	41.1	49.1	2.8	2.8	9.8	3.1	81.7	1.6	27.6	56.9
Benewah County	363	39.5	49.6	3.7	1.7	9.2	3.9	83.4	1.4	23.8	56.5
Kootenai County	122	45.8	47.7	-	6.3	11.8	0.8	76.9	2.4	38.9	58.0
Cold Springs Rancheria, California	53	70.0	15.3	-	-	-	9.5	68.9	10.8	2.1	65.3
Fresno County	53	70.0	15.3	-	-	-	9.5	68.9	10.8	2.1	65.3
Colorado River Reservation, Arizona-California	1,492	92.8	5.1	0.8	2.2	2.7	0.6	92.7	1.2	83.2	14.8
Arizona	1,469	93.6	4.9	0.8	2.3	2.5	0.6	93.5	0.6	83.8	14.3
Yuma County	1,469	93.6	4.9	0.8	2.3	2.5	0.6	93.5	0.6	83.8	14.3
California	...	...	...	...	...	...	...	...	...	...	...
Riverside and San Bernardino Counties	...	...	...	...	...	...	...	...	...	...	...
Colville Reservation, Washington	3,259	59.0	35.9	1.7	3.4	11.5	1.8	80.6	1.7	72.5	13.4
Ferry County	836	63.8	33.7	1.7	2.2	11.2	2.4	82.7	1.0	46.4	17.0
Okanogan County	2,423	57.4	36.6	1.7	3.9	11.6	1.6	79.9	1.9	81.5	12.2
Cortina Rancheria, California	...	...	...	...	...	...	...	...	...	...	...
Colusa County	...	...	...	...	...	...	...	...	...	...	...
Coushatta Reservation, Louisiana	...	...	...	...	...	...	...	...	...	...	...
Allen Parish	...	...	...	...	...	...	...	...	...	...	...
Coyote Valley Rancheria, California	-	-	-	-	-	-	-	-	-	-	-
Mendocino County	-	-	-	-	-	-	-	-	-	-	-
Crow Reservation, Montana	3,767	95.1	3.4	0.7	1.5	1.9	0.4	94.9	0.5	50.5	34.6
Big Horn County	3,666	95.4	3.3	0.4	1.5	1.8	0.4	95.0	0.5	51.0	35.4
Yellowstone County	101	83.0	6.3	9.7	1.0	5.3	-	91.7	1.0	33.5	6.4
Crow Creek Reservation, South Dakota	1,351	84.1	12.6	1.0	2.6	7.1	2.7	84.6	1.5	64.4	29.5
Buffalo County	1,132	85.1	11.1	1.1	2.1	7.2	2.7	84.6	1.8	73.7	19.2
Hughes County	157	71.7	27.3	1.0	6.0	9.1	3.6	80.5	-	1.0	98.3
Hyde County	61	96.7	3.3	-	3.3	-	-	96.7	-	54.3	42.4
Cuyapaipe Reservation, California	...	...	...	...	...	...	...	...	...	...	...
San Diego County	...	...	...	...	...	...	...	...	...	...	...
Deer Creek Reservation, Minnesota	...	...	...	...	...	...	...	...	...	...	...
Itasca County	...	...	...	...	...	...	...	...	...	...	...
Dresslerville Colony, Nevada	111	87.7	11.2	-	8.3	-	-	90.6	-	85.1	8.3
Douglas County	111	87.7	11.2	-	8.3	-	-	90.6	-	85.1	8.3
Dry Creek Rancheria, California	42	88.1	11.9	-	2.4	2.4	61.9	31.0	-	2.4	59.5
Sonoma County	42	88.1	11.9	-	2.4	2.4	61.9	31.0	-	2.4	59.5
Duck Valley Reservation, Idaho-Nevada	797	97.6	1.0	0.2	0.7	1.2	1.2	96.2	0.4	95.1	1.0
Idaho	152	97.1	1.0	0.9	1.0	-	4.4	93.8	-	87.1	0.9
Owyhee County	152	97.1	1.0	0.9	1.0	-	4.4	93.8	-	87.1	0.9

[Continued]

★ 470 ★

Methods of Health Care on Identified Reservations, 1980 - I

[Continued]

		Persons who received health care in last 12 months									
		Usual place of health care -- percent			Health care paid by -- percent					Travel time to health care facility -- percent	
Identified reservations	Total	Indian service clinic, health center or hospital	Private physician or dentist	Tribal clinic or hospital	Person or other family member	Private health insurance	Medicaid or Medicare	Indian Health Service or tribe	Other government services	Less than 30 minutes	30 minutes to 1 hour
Nevada	646	97.7	1.1	-	0.7	1.4	0.4	96.7	0.5	97.0	1.1
Elko County	646	97.7	1.1	-	0.7	1.4	0.4	96.7	0.5	97.0	1.1

Source: U.S. Bureau of the Census, Subject Reports, PC80-2-1D, Part 1, *American Indians, Eskimos, and Aleuts on Identified Reservations and in the Historic Areas of Oklahoma (Excluding Urbanized Areas)*, U.S. Government Printing Office, Washington, D.C., 1986, pp. 59-67. *Notes:* Three dots (...) means not applicable, or that the data are being withheld to avoid disclosure of information for individuals. A dash (-) represents zero or a percent which rounds to less than 0.1. Also, a dash (-) is used because the number of supplementary questionnaires for the reservations was insufficient to produce reliable estimates.

★ 471 ★

Methods of Health Care on Identified Reservations, 1980 - II

Data are the latest available.

		Persons who received health care in last 12 months									
		Usual place of health care -- percent			Health care paid by -- percent					Travel time to health care facility -- percent	
Identified reservations	Total	Indian service clinic, health center or hospital	Private physician or dentist	Tribal clinic or hospital	Person or other family member	Private health insurance	Medicaid or Medicare	Indian Health Service or tribe	Other government services	Less than 30 minutes	30 minutes to 1 hour
Duckwater Reservation, Nevada	77	11.8	22.4	-	9.2	6.6	2.6	77.6	2.6	7.9	-
Nye County	77	11.8	22.4	-	9.2	6.6	2.6	77.6	2.6	7.9	-
Eastern Cherokee Reservation, North Carolina	4,524	93.7	4.5	1.0	2.5	2.1	0.7	93.8	0.5	85.2	11.9
Cherokee County	69	48.5	20.8	19.0	15.2	4.3	5.7	70.4	4.4	13.8	15.9
Graham County	345	88.1	3.2	8.4	2.3	0.6	0.5	94.7	1.1	47.3	39.3
Haywood County	-	-	-	-	-	-	-	-	-	-	-
Jackson County	1,944	95.4	4.0	-	2.5	1.9	0.8	94.2	0.3	90.1	8.9
Swain County	2,166	94.6	4.7	0.2	2.1	2.4	0.6	94.2	0.5	89.1	10.0
Eastern Pequot Reservation, Connecticut	...	...	...	...	...	...	...	...	...	...	...
New London County	...	...	...	...	...	...	...	...	...	...	...
Ely Colony, Nevada	48	15.8	-	-	7.8	5.2	3.0	73.7	2.7	92.5	-
White Pine County	48	15.8	-	-	7.8	5.2	3.0	73.7	2.7	92.5	-
Enterprise Rancheria, California	...	...	...	...	...	...	...	...	...	...	...
Butte County	...	...	...	...	...	...	...	...	...	...	...
Fallon Colony, Nevada	46	94.2	5.8	-	5.8	-	2.7	91.6	-	5.8	-
Churchill County	46	94.2	5.8	-	5.8	-	2.7	91.6	-	5.8	-
Fallon Reservation, Nevada	234	85.5	10.1	-	8.8	2.4	2.8	82.2	2.9	12.5	32.4
Churchill County	234	85.5	10.1	-	8.8	2.4	2.8	82.2	2.9	12.5	32.4
Flandreau Reservation, South Dakota	124	79.7	17.1	-	8.0	11.4	2.5	74.9	3.2	92.0	2.4
Moody County	124	79.7	17.1	-	8.0	11.4	2.5	74.9	3.2	92.0	2.4
Flathead Reservation, Montana	2,887	33.3	60.8	1.7	2.8	12.0	6.8	76.6	0.8	69.5	24.9
Flathead County	...	...	...	...	...	...	...	...	...	...	...
Lake County	2,357	30.5	62.8	1.7	3.0	11.1	7.4	76.9	0.8	74.8	21.9
Missoula County	226	37.8	59.9	1.8	0.4	21.2	4.5	71.1	1.8	43.7	55.0
Sanders County	301	52.5	45.5	1.0	3.3	12.6	4.3	78.4	0.3	48.5	25.9
Fond du Lac Reservation, Minnesota	438	4.1	79.1	1.7	4.8	22.6	5.0	45.7	13.0	85.9	11.7
Carlton County	360	3.5	86.3	2.1	4.1	21.7	5.2	45.9	13.7	87.6	9.6
St. Louis County	77	6.9	45.5	-	7.6	27.0	4.0	44.7	9.8	78.3	21.7
Fort Apache Reservation, Arizona	6,080	97.5	1.3	0.1	0.7	1.0	0.1	90.9	6.8	66.0	25.3
Apache County	102	88.6	8.3	-	3.1	1.2	5.7	88.6	-	13.8	80.7
Gila County	1,019	99.6	0.1	-	0.1	0.2	-	77.4	21.3	57.2	17.3
Navajo County	4,959	97.2	1.4	0.2	0.8	1.2	-	93.7	3.9	68.9	25.8
Fort Belknap Reservation, Montana	1,608	97.3	1.0	0.8	0.3	1.1	1.2	95.6	0.4	48.2	36.4
Blaine County	1,479	97.2	1.1	0.9	0.3	1.1	1.3	95.8	0.4	52.3	35.7
Phillips County	129	97.6	-	-	0.9	-	-	93.0	-	2.0	44.9
Fort Berthold Reservation, North Dakota	2,329	78.3	16.1	0.4	3.8	9.0	0.8	75.1	9.9	52.7	29.8
Dunn County	389	81.1	17.4	-	6.0	12.7	1.6	73.0	5.8	40.0	25.2
McKenzie County	781	84.4	13.7	0.2	4.9	4.1	0.6	85.3	4.4	48.5	33.0
McLean County	421	75.3	21.6	0.6	1.6	13.0	0.8	75.1	8.1	48.1	31.6
Mercer County	45	90.5	6.9	-	-	-	7.5	82.0	10.5	82.8	12.2

[Continued]

★ 471 ★

Methods of Health Care on Identified Reservations, 1980 - II
[Continued]

Identified reservations	Total	Usual place of health care -- percent			Health care paid by -- percent					Travel time to health care facility -- percent	
		Indian service clinic, health center or hospital	Private physician or dentist	Tribal clinic or hospital	Person or other family member	Private health insurance	Medicaid or Medicare	Indian Health Service or tribe	Other government services	Less than 30 minutes	30 minutes to 1 hour
Mountrail County	693	70.8	15.2	0.6	3.0	10.6	0.2	64.2	19.5	65.4	28.8
Ward County	-	-	-	-	-	-	-	-	-	-	-
Fort Bidwell Reservation, California	86	16.0	59.0	3.9	16.1	13.4	34.6	21.1	2.5	17.3	70.4
Modoc County	86	16.0	59.0	3.9	16.1	13.4	34.6	21.1	2.5	17.3	70.4
Fort Hall Reservation, Idaho	2,254	89.6	8.3	0.2	3.3	9.6	1.0	82.4	2.6	82.6	15.3
Bannock County	565	90.3	6.8	-	3.1	13.9	1.4	80.9	0.2	87.6	11.9
Bingham County	1,535	88.9	9.2	0.3	3.7	8.8	1.0	81.8	3.8	88.5	10.6
Caribou County	-	-	-	-	-	-	-	-	-	-	-
Power County	154	93.6	4.3	0.7	-	2.2	0.6	94.4	-	5.6	74.2
Fort Independence Reservation, California	21	18.3	62.3	12.3	15.4	25.1	27.7	24.7	7.1	28.9	26.6
Inyo County	21	18.3	62.3	12.3	15.4	25.1	27.7	24.7	7.1	28.9	26.6
Fort McDermitt Reservation, Nevada-Oregon	453	90.3	2.2	2.5	0.8	5.2	5.0	85.9	2.3	86.1	3.0
Nevada	453	90.3	2.2	2.5	0.8	5.2	5.0	85.9	2.3	86.1	3.0
Humboldt County	453	90.3	2.2	2.5	0.8	5.2	5.0	85.9	2.3	86.1	3.0
Oregon	-	-	-	-	-	-	-	-	-	-	-
Malheur County	-	-	-	-	-	-	-	-	-	-	-
Fort McDowell Reservation, Arizona	227	73.8	5.6	19.6	4.1	1.5	-	91.7	0.5	19.9	20.2
Maricopa County	227	73.8	5.6	19.6	4.1	1.5	-	91.7	0.5	19.9	20.2
Fort Mojave Reservation, Arizona-California-Nevada	109	0.9	0.9	-	0.9	-	-	97.2	0.9	99.1	-
Arizona	109	0.9	0.9	-	0.9	-	-	97.2	0.9	99.1	-
Mohave County	109	0.9	0.9	-	0.9	-	-	97.2	0.9	99.1	-
California	-	-	-	-	-	-	-	-	-	-	-
San Bernardino County	-	-	-	-	-	-	-	-	-	-	-
Nevada	-	-	-	-	-	-	-	-	-	-	-
Clark County	-	-	-	-	-	-	-	-	-	-	-
Fort Peck Reservation, Montana	3,843	92.7	4.8	1.3	1.1	2.2	1.8	93.3	1.0	84.5	12.6
Daniels County	-	-	-	-	-	-	-	-	-	-	-
Roosevelt County	3,404	92.8	4.6	1.4	1.1	2.3	1.6	93.4	1.0	89.6	8.2
Sheridan County	-	-	-	-	-	-	-	-	-	-	-
Valley County	439	92.5	6.3	0.7	1.1	1.5	3.0	93.3	0.7	45.4	46.9
Fort Totten Reservation, North Dakota	2,105	91.9	3.4	0.6	0.2	3.8	1.7	90.6	2.6	85.0	13.8
Benson County	2,100	92.0	3.4	0.6	0.2	3.8	1.7	90.6	2.6	84.9	13.9
Eddy County	...	...	...	...	...	...	...	...	...	...	...
Nelson County	-	-	-	-	-	-	-	-	-	-	-
Ramsey County	...	...	...	...	...	...	...	...	...	...	...
Fort Yuma Reservation, Arizona-California	839	95.1	2.5	0.2	1.5	0.8	1.0	94.5	1.9	98.1	1.3
Arizona	97	99.1	0.9	-	-	0.9	-	99.1	-	100.0	-
Yuma County	97	99.1	0.9	-	-	0.9	-	99.1	-	100.0	-
California	743	94.6	2.7	0.3	1.6	0.8	1.1	93.9	2.1	97.9	1.5
Imperial County	743	94.6	2.7	0.3	1.6	0.8	1.1	93.9	2.1	97.9	1.5
Gila Bend Reservation, Arizona	-	-	-	-	-	-	-	-	-	-	-
Maricopa County	-	-	-	-	-	-	-	-	-	-	-
Gila River Reservation, Arizona	5,882	93.3	1.8	4.1	1.2	0.7	0.2	96.7	0.7	67.2	23.6
Maricopa County	1,926	86.7	1.3	11.0	-	1.1	0.1	97.8	0.5	42.0	43.0
Pinal County	3,956	96.5	2.0	0.8	1.8	0.5	0.3	96.1	0.8	79.4	14.2
Golden Hill Reservation, Connecticut	...	...	...	...	...	...	...	...	...	...	...
Fairfield County	...	...	...	...	...	...	...	...	...	...	...
Goshute Reservation, Nevada-Utah	46	18.5	-	-	6.2	6.2	6.2	75.3	6.2	6.2	2.2
Nevada	...	...	...	...	...	...	...	...	...	...	...
White Pine County	...	...	...	...	...	...	...	...	...	...	...
Utah	34	25.0	-	-	8.3	8.3	8.3	66.7	8.3	8.3	-
Juab and Tooele Counties	34	25.0	-	-	8.3	8.3	8.3	66.7	8.3	8.3	-
Grand Portage Reservation, Minnesota	156	18.7	10.6	1.3	0.6	2.7	13.1	81.0	2.1	19.7	74.3
Cook County	156	18.7	10.6	1.3	0.6	2.7	13.1	81.0	2.1	19.7	74.3
Grindstone Creek Rancheria, California	52	13.0	70.1	-	4.4	-	49.7	43.8	-	2.1	56.9
Glenn County	52	13.0	70.1	-	4.4	-	49.7	43.8	-	2.1	56.9
Hannahville Community, Michigan	191	-	98.7	0.5	3.0	12.8	46.7	37.6	-	95.4	4.6
Menominee County	191	-	98.7	0.5	3.0	12.8	46.7	37.6	-	95.4	4.6
Hassanamisco Reservation, Massachusetts	...	...	...	...	...	...	...	...	...	...	...
Worcester County	...	...	...	...	...	...	...	...	...	...	...
Havasupai Reservation, Arizona	173	100.0	-	-	-	-	-	100.0	-	96.8	-
Coconino County	173	100.0	-	-	-	-	-	100.0	-	96.8	-
Hoh Reservation, Washington	43	71.9	22.4	-	-	-	-	100.0	-	3.0	93.4
Jefferson County	43	71.9	22.4	-	-	-	-	100.0	-	3.0	93.4
Hollywood Reservation, Florida	373	86.5	13.5	-	6.3	14.8	-	78.9	-	88.2	9.9

[Continued]

★ 471 ★

Methods of Health Care on Identified Reservations, 1980 - II

[Continued]

Identified reservations	Total	Usual place of health care -- percent			Health care paid by -- percent					Travel time to health care facility -- percent	
		Indian service clinic, health center or hospital	Private physician or dentist	Tribal clinic or hospital	Person or other family member	Private health insurance	Medicaid or Medicare	Indian Health Service or tribe	Other government services	Less than 30 minutes	30 minutes to 1 hour
Broward County	373	86.5	13.5	-	6.3	14.8	-	78.9	-	88.2	9.9
Hoopa Valley Reservation, California	1,253	10.2	12.2	68.4	10.6	29.1	23.0	22.3	4.7	86.3	3.1
Humboldt County	1,253	10.2	12.2	68.4	10.6	29.1	23.0	22.3	4.7	86.3	3.1
Hoopa Valley Extension Reservation, California	308	37.0	27.7	27.4	15.8	21.2	35.2	15.9	3.2	19.7	23.2
Del Norte County	133	46.1	50.2	-	27.5	23.4	27.6	6.8	3.4	21.0	37.6
Humboldt County	175	30.0	10.5	48.4	6.8	19.6	41.0	22.7	3.0	18.7	12.2
Hopi Reservation, Arizona	5,471	98.7	0.2	0.1	0.2	0.2	0.2	97.7	1.2	29.4	47.7
Coconino County	1,099	99.5	0.4	0.1	0.1	0.4	0.1	98.3	0.7	54.8	19.4
Navajo County	4,372	98.5	0.1	0.1	0.2	0.2	0.2	97.6	1.3	23.0	54.8
Hopland Rancheria, California	-	-	-	-	-	-	-	-	-	-	-
Mendocino County	-	-	-	-	-	-	-	-	-	-	-
Hualapai Reservation, Arizona	689	98.5	0.4	0.3	-	3.2	0.4	95.5	0.5	90.6	4.5
Coconino and Mohave Counties	689	98.5	0.4	0.3	-	3.2	0.4	95.5	0.5	90.6	4.5
Yavapai County	...	...	...	...	...	...	...	...	...	...	...
Inaja-Cosmit Reservation, California	-	-	-	-	-	-	-	-	-	-	-
San Diego County	-	-	-	-	-	-	-	-	-	-	-
Indian Township Reservation, Maine	323	57.0	42.2	-	0.8	3.1	30.0	42.3	23.5	61.9	32.2
Washington County	323	57.0	42.2	-	0.8	3.1	30.0	42.3	23.5	61.9	32.2

Source: U.S. Bureau of the Census, Subject Reports, PC80-2-1D, Part 1, *American Indians, Eskimos, and Aleuts on Identified Reservations and in the Historic Areas of Oklahoma (Excluding Urbanized Areas)*, U.S. Government Printing Office, Washington, D.C., 1986, pp. 59-67. *Notes:* Three dots (...) means not applicable, or that the data are being withheld to avoid disclosure of information for individuals. A dash (-) represents zero or a percent which rounds to less than 0.1. Also, a dash (-) is used because the number of supplementary questionnaires for the reservations was insufficient to produce reliable estimates.

★ 472 ★

Methods of Health Care on Identified Reservations, 1980 - III

Data are the latest available.

Identified reservations	Total	Usual place of health care -- percent			Health care paid by -- percent					Travel time to health care facility -- percent	
		Indian service clinic, health center or hospital	Private physician or dentist	Tribal clinic or hospital	Person or other family member	Private health insurance	Medicaid or Medicare	Indian Health Service or tribe	Other government services	Less than 30 minutes	30 minutes to 1 hour
Iowa Reservation, Kansas-Nebraska	24	9.3	90.7	-	62.8	9.3	-	27.9	-	-	100.0
Kansas	...	...	...	...	...	...	...	...	...	...	...
Brown County	...	...	...	...	...	...	...	...	...	...	...
Doniphan County	-	-	-	-	-	-	-	-	-	-	-
Nebraska	...	...	...	...	...	...	...	...	...	...	...
Richardson County	...	...	...	...	...	...	...	...	...	...	...
Isabella Reservation, Michigan	402	16.6	62.4	6.4	6.8	18.7	36.1	35.7	1.6	87.3	11.2
Isabella County	402	16.6	62.4	6.4	6.8	18.7	36.1	35.7	1.6	87.3	11.2
Isleta Pueblo, New Mexico	1,800	66.0	12.4	15.0	4.5	8.0	2.4	82.5	1.3	82.4	16.7
Bernalillo County	1,367	61.7	12.2	19.2	4.4	8.2	2.8	81.9	1.0	83.3	15.7
Torrance County	-	-	-	-	-	-	-	-	-	-	-
Valencia County	433	79.4	13.1	1.9	4.9	7.3	1.3	84.2	2.3	79.7	19.8
Jackson Rancheria, California	...	...	...	...	...	...	...	...	...	...	...
Amador County	...	...	...	...	...	...	...	...	...	...	...
Jemez Pueblo, New Mexico	1,252	96.6	1.8	0.6	0.4	1.5	1.0	95.8	0.8	82.9	3.4
Sandoval County	1,252	96.6	1.8	0.6	0.4	1.5	1.0	95.8	0.8	82.9	3.4
Jicarilla Apache Reservation, New Mexico	1,628	95.2	2.7	1.7	1.9	0.8	0.4	95.7	0.8	87.5	6.5
Rio Arriba and Sandoval Counties	1,628	95.2	2.7	1.7	1.9	0.8	0.4	95.7	0.8	87.5	6.5
Kaibab Reservation, Arizona	85	2.5	-	95.0	1.3	-	-	96.1	2.5	97.5	2.5
Coconino County	-	-	-	-	-	-	-	-	-	-	-
Mohave County	85	2.5	-	95.0	1.3	-	-	96.1	2.5	97.5	2.5
Kalispel Reservation, Washington	91	54.9	42.9	-	-	-	2.2	97.8	-	79.1	19.8
Pend Oreille County	91	54.9	42.9	-	-	-	2.2	97.8	-	79.1	19.8
Kickapoo Reservation, Kansas	344	80.2	16.8	0.4	8.0	4.6	3.7	77.8	2.8	75.5	22.6

[Continued]

★ 472 ★

Methods of Health Care on Identified Reservations, 1980 - III
[Continued]

Identified reservations	Total	Usual place of health care -- percent			Health care paid by -- percent					Travel time to health care facility -- percent	
		Indian service clinic, health center or hospital	Private physician or dentist	Tribal clinic or hospital	Person or other family member	Private health insurance	Medicaid or Medicare	Indian Health Service or tribe	Other government services	Less than 30 minutes	30 minutes to 1 hour
Brown County	344	80.2	16.8	0.4	8.0	4.6	3.7	77.8	2.8	75.5	22.6
Kootenai Reservation, Idaho	-	-	-	-	-	-	-	-	-	-	-
Boundary County	-	-	-	-	-	-	-	-	-	-	-
Lac Courte Oreilles Reservation, Wisconsin	974	18.4	59.3	14.6	0.8	2.4	26.7	53.8	14.4	64.1	30.0
Sawyer County	974	18.4	59.3	14.6	0.8	2.4	26.7	53.8	14.4	64.1	30.0
Lac du Flambeau Reservation, Wisconsin	999	24.6	4.7	65.3	1.1	3.8	13.9	73.7	5.2	97.4	1.3
Iron County	-	-	-	-	-	-	-	-	-	-	-
Oneida County	-	-	-	-	-	-	-	-	-	-	-
Vilas County	999	24.6	4.7	65.3	1.1	3.8	13.9	73.7	5.2	97.4	1.3
Laguna Pueblo, New Mexico	3,229	86.4	9.3	1.2	4.2	5.9	0.8	87.8	0.9	64.1	27.1
Bernalillo and Valencia Counties	3,229	86.4	9.3	1.2	4.2	5.9	0.8	87.8	0.9	64.1	27.1
Sandoval County	-	-	-	-	-	-	-	-	-	-	-
La Jolla Reservation, California	122	65.9	24.9	2.0	29.1	28.3	9.0	2.8	10.1	40.5	52.9
San Diego County	122	65.9	24.9	2.0	29.1	28.3	9.0	2.8	10.1	40.5	52.9
L'Anse Reservation, Michigan	527	10.3	49.4	39.4	5.1	25.1	16.2	51.9	0.6	89.4	7.6
Baraga County	527	10.3	49.4	39.4	5.1	25.1	16.2	51.9	0.6	89.4	7.6
La Posta Reservation, California	...	...	...	...	...	...	...	...	...	...	...
San Diego County	...	...	...	...	...	...	...	...	...	...	...
Las Vegas Colony, Nevada	81	74.7	23.8	-	-	15.8	1.8	79.2	3.2	92.5	6.0
Clark County	81	74.7	23.8	-	-	15.8	1.8	79.2	3.2	92.5	6.0
Laytonville Rancheria, California	86	22.1	36.0	-	10.5	33.7	51.2	3.5	-	33.7	27.9
Mendocino County	86	22.1	36.0	-	10.5	33.7	51.2	3.5	-	33.7	27.9
Leech Lake Reservation, Minnesota	2,549	77.8	16.0	0.8	2.6	7.0	6.8	74.7	8.5	63.1	31.2
Beltrami County	311	80.5	7.3	1.0	-	4.6	6.4	76.6	10.5	89.4	7.9
Cass and Hubbard Counties	1,583	90.2	7.8	0.7	2.0	3.7	6.6	86.2	1.4	72.7	21.0
Itasca County	655	46.4	40.0	0.9	5.3	16.0	7.5	46.0	24.4	27.6	66.8
Likely Rancheria, California	-	-	-	-	-	-	-	-	-	-	-
Modoc County	-	-	-	-	-	-	-	-	-	-	-
Lone Pine Rancheria, California	138	15.9	29.7	53.4	7.7	19.9	6.7	65.7	-	31.2	-
Inyo County	138	15.9	29.7	53.4	7.7	19.9	6.7	65.7	-	31.2	-
Lookout Rancheria, California	...	...	...	...	...	...	...	...	...	...	...
Modoc County	...	...	...	...	...	...	...	...	...	...	...
Los Coyotes Reservation, California	38	25.7	45.4	2.9	12.2	18.9	59.6	-	3.2	2.9	55.4
San Diego County	38	25.7	45.4	2.9	12.2	18.9	59.6	-	3.2	2.9	55.4
Lovelock Colony, Nevada	103	82.6	17.4	-	23.8	-	1.8	70.5	-	40.1	1.4
Pershing County	103	82.6	17.4	-	23.8	-	1.8	70.5	-	40.1	1.4
Lower Brule Reservation, South Dakota	764	84.8	6.2	2.4	1.7	4.9	1.2	86.3	5.5	82.4	13.0
Lyman County	764	84.8	6.2	2.4	1.7	4.9	1.2	86.3	5.5	82.4	13.0
Stanley County	...	...	...	...	...	...	...	...	...	...	...
Lower Elwah Reservation, Washington	36	58.3	36.1	-	2.8	-	-	88.9	8.3	97.2	2.8
Clallam County	36	58.3	36.1	-	2.8	-	-	88.9	8.3	97.2	2.8
Lower Sioux Community, Minnesota	65	-	-	-	-	-	-	94.0	2.7	76.1	11.0
Redwood County	65	-	-	-	-	-	-	94.0	2.7	76.1	11.0
Lummi Reservation, Washington	1,180	79.2	7.4	11.9	0.7	5.6	1.5	87.8	3.5	95.6	3.6
Whatcom County	1,180	79.2	7.4	11.9	0.7	5.6	1.5	87.8	3.5	95.6	3.6
Makah Reservation, Washington	761	83.4	4.9	10.2	0.5	2.8	0.4	93.3	2.3	91.9	1.6
Clallam County	761	83.4	4.9	10.2	0.5	2.8	0.4	93.3	2.3	91.9	1.6
Manchester Rancheria, California	57	27.0	41.9	-	9.4	16.2	70.6	-	-	27.1	7.5
Mendocino County	57	27.0	41.9	-	9.4	16.2	70.6	-	-	27.1	7.5
Manzanita Reservation, California	...	...	...	...	...	...	...	...	...	...	...
San Diego County	...	...	...	...	...	...	...	...	...	...	...
Maricopa Reservation, Arizona	345	97.6	2.0	-	2.0	-	-	97.0	-	2.0	80.3
Pinal County	345	97.6	2.0	-	2.0	-	-	97.0	-	2.0	80.3
Mattaponi Reservation, Virginia	48	18.8	77.1	-	47.9	12.5	16.7	18.8	-	45.8	33.3
King William County	48	18.8	77.1	-	47.9	12.5	16.7	18.8	-	45.8	33.3
Menominee Reservation, Wisconsin	1,788	3.3	12.7	58.9	3.1	26.0	30.3	33.5	3.1	83.1	14.2
Menominee County	1,788	3.3	12.7	58.9	3.1	26.0	30.3	33.5	3.1	83.1	14.2
Mesa Grande Reservation, California	-	-	-	-	-	-	-	-	-	-	-
San Diego County	-	-	-	-	-	-	-	-	-	-	-
Mescalero Apache Reservation, New Mexico	683	92.7	1.3	2.1	1.2	0.7	0.7	93.0	3.3	86.1	9.5
Otero County	683	92.7	1.3	2.1	1.2	0.7	0.7	93.0	3.3	86.1	9.5
Miccosukee Reservation, Florida	267	1.5	3.7	94.8	1.9	10.9	-	87.3	-	87.3	11.2
Broward County	-	-	-	-	-	-	-	-	-	-	-
Dade County	267	1.5	3.7	94.8	1.9	10.9	-	87.3	-	87.3	11.2
Middletown Rancheria, California	30	46.7	50.0	-	16.7	13.3	43.3	10.0	-	20.0	10.0
Lake County	30	46.7	50.0	-	16.7	13.3	43.3	10.0	-	20.0	10.0

[Continued]

★ 472 ★

Methods of Health Care on Identified Reservations, 1980 - III
[Continued]

| | | Persons who received health care in last 12 months | | | | | | | | | |
| Identified reservations | Total | Usual place of health care -- percent | | | Person or other family member | Health care paid by -- percent | | | | Travel time to health care facility -- percent | |
		Indian service clinic, health center or hospital	Private physician or dentist	Tribal clinic or hospital		Private health insurance	Medicaid or Medicare	Indian Health Service or tribe	Other government services	Less than 30 minutes	30 minutes to 1 hour
Mille Lacs Reservation, Minnesota	-	-	-	-	-	-	-	-	-	-	-
Aitkin County	-	-	-	-	-	-	-	-	-	-	-
Kanabec County	-	-	-	-	-	-	-	-	-	-	-
Mille Lacs County	-	-	-	-	-	-	-	-	-	-	-
Pine County	-	-	-	-	-	-	-	-	-	-	-
Mississippi Choctaw Reservation	2,316	86.9	3.8	3.2	2.3	1.7	1.6	89.4	4.7	53.4	31.8
Attala County	-	-	-	-	-	-	-	-	-	-	-
Jones County	123	13.0	6.5	-	1.6	-	7.3	9.8	81.3	0.8	95.1
Kemper County	...	...	...	...	...	...	...	...	...	...	...
Leake County	437	90.6	5.2	0.4	5.6	0.7	0.6	92.0	0.9	28.7	67.7
Neshoba County	1,498	92.8	2.2	4.2	1.1	1.8	1.0	95.6	0.4	71.3	8.6
Newton County	253	83.4	9.2	2.8	4.5	4.0	4.5	86.5	-	14.5	77.3
Moapa River Reservation, Nevada	115	94.5	2.6	-	1.1	3.8	-	91.6	0.9	0.9	12.2
Clark County	115	94.5	2.6	-	1.1	3.8	-	91.6	0.9	0.9	12.2
Montgomery Creek Rancheria, California	...	...	...	...	...	...	...	...	...	...	...
Shasta County	...	...	...	...	...	...	...	...	...	...	...
Morongo Reservation, California	247	15.8	29.4	51.8	23.3	8.1	7.3	49.1	4.1	84.9	10.8
Riverside County	247	15.8	29.4	51.8	23.3	8.1	7.3	49.1	4.1	84.9	10.8
Muckleshoot Reservation, Washington	292	26.4	26.8	37.9	-	12.0	10.9	71.5	4.1	81.6	17.0
King County	292	26.4	26.8	37.9	-	12.0	10.9	71.5	4.1	81.6	17.0
Pierce County	-	-	-	-	-	-	-	-	-	-	-
Nambe Pueblo, New Mexico	103	96.4	3.6	-	1.1	-	-	97.9	-	8.5	91.5
Santa Fe County	103	96.4	3.6	-	1.1	-	-	97.9	-	8.5	91.5
Navajo Reservation, Arizona-New Mexico-Utah	87,376	87.5	7.3	1.4	5.9	3.0	0.9	88.3	0.8	39.8	28.4
Arizona	59,265	90.7	4.6	1.3	4.8	1.9	0.1	91.4	0.8	39.7	25.2
Apache County	31,054	88.5	5.7	1.2	7.2	1.7	0.1	88.9	0.8	38.3	26.8
Coconino County	12,587	92.5	3.6	1.7	2.3	2.1	0.1	93.9	1.0	49.6	20.8
Navajo County	15,624	93.6	3.0	1.1	2.0	2.0	0.2	94.4	0.6	34.4	25.6
New Mexico	23,979	84.9	12.5	1.2	7.2	5.4	0.3	85.3	0.5	42.2	36.9
McKinley County	6,955	91.3	4.0	3.5	2.6	2.1	0.2	94.1	0.3	42.0	42.4
San Juan County	17,024	82.3	16.0	0.3	9.0	6.8	0.3	81.7	0.6	42.2	34.7
Utah	4,132	56.8	16.2	5.2	15.4	5.0	15.2	60.3	2.8	29.0	24.1
San Juan County	4,132	56.8	16.2	5.2	15.4	5.0	15.2	60.3	2.8	29.0	24.1

Source: U.S. Bureau of the Census, Subject Reports, PC80-2-1D, Part 1, *American Indians, Eskimos, and Aleuts on Identified Reservations and in the Historic Areas of Oklahoma (Excluding Urbanized Areas)*, U.S. Government Printing Office, Washington, D.C., 1986, pp. 59-67. *Notes:* Three dots ... means not applicable, or that the data are being withheld to avoid disclosure of information for individuals. A dash (-) represents zero or a percent which rounds to less than 0.1. Also, a dash (-) is used because the number of supplementary questionnaires for the reservations was insufficient to produce reliable estimates.

★ 473 ★

Methods of Health Care on Identified Reservations, 1980 - IV

Data are the latest available.

| | | Persons who received health care in last 12 months | | | | | | | | | |
| Identified reservations | Total | Usual place of health care -- percent | | | Person or other family member | Health care paid by -- percent | | | | Travel time to health care facility -- percent | |
		Indian service clinic, health center or hospital	Private physician or dentist	Tribal clinic or hospital		Private health insurance	Medicaid or Medicare	Indian Health Service or tribe	Other government services	Less than 30 minutes	30 minutes to 1 hour
Nez Perce Reservation, Idaho	1,385	72.8	25.0	1.4	2.5	9.8	3.9	82.0	1.1	84.5	11.7
Clearwater County	102	35.3	57.8	2.0	16.7	16.7	19.6	45.1	2.0	63.7	22.5
Idaho County	140	14.8	81.1	2.7	2.2	32.9	14.7	49.3	-	66.8	19.8
Lewis County	181	39.8	54.1	5.0	1.7	9.9	1.7	82.3	3.3	74.6	16.6
Nez Perce County	962	91.5	7.8	0.4	1.2	5.6	1.1	90.6	0.7	91.2	8.4
Nisqually Reservation, Washington	42	13.9	55.3	16.7	2.8	10.9	22.3	50.2	13.8	44.0	50.4
Pierce County	-	-	-	-	-	-	-	-	-	-	-
Thurston County	42	13.9	55.3	16.7	2.8	10.9	22.3	50.2	13.8	44.0	50.4
Nooksack Reservation, Washington	-	-	-	-	-	-	-	-	-	-	-

[Continued]

Methods of Health Care on Identified Reservations, 1980 - IV

[Continued]

Identified reservations	Total	Usual place of health care -- percent			Health care paid by -- percent					Travel time to health care facility -- percent	
		Indian service clinic, health center or hospital	Private physician or dentist	Tribal clinic or hospital	Person or other family member	Private health insurance	Medicaid or Medicare	Indian Health Service or tribe	Other government services	Less than 30 minutes	30 minutes to 1 hour
Whatcom County	-	-	-	-	-	-	-	-	-	-	-
Northern Cheyenne Reservation, Montana	2,746	94.7	2.9	1.0	1.5	2.6	1.2	93.3	0.7	74.5	13.0
Big Horn County	764	91.7	4.0	3.0	2.0	2.1	1.6	93.0	0.8	71.1	20.9
Rosebud County	1,981	95.8	2.5	0.2	1.3	2.7	1.0	93.5	0.7	75.9	9.9
Oil Springs Reservation, New York	-	-	-	-	-	-	-	-	-	-	-
Allegany County	-	-	-	-	-	-	-	-	-	-	-
Cattaraugus County	-	-	-	-	-	-	-	-	-	-	-
Omaha Reservation, Iowa-Nebraska	561	55.8	3.7	39.4	0.6	1.1	1.6	92.9	1.8	94.8	3.5
Iowa	-	-	-	-	-	-	-	-	-	-	-
Monona County	-	-	-	-	-	-	-	-	-	-	-
Nebraska	561	55.8	3.7	39.4	0.6	1.1	1.6	92.9	1.8	94.8	3.5
Burt County	...	...	...	...	...	...	...	...	...	...	...
Cuming County	-	-	-	-	-	-	-	-	-	-	-
Thurston County	561	55.8	3.7	39.4	0.6	1.1	1.6	92.9	1.8	94.8	3.5
Oneida Reservation, Wisconsin	1,485	18.3	48.6	30.1	8.8	29.6	11.6	34.8	13.1	82.3	16.8
Brown County	565	16.8	53.1	27.5	10.0	31.1	11.4	36.4	7.8	89.3	10.3
Outagamie County	920	19.2	45.7	31.7	8.0	28.7	11.8	33.7	16.3	78.0	20.9
Onondaga Reservation, New York	-	-	-	-	-	-	-	-	-	-	-
Onondaga County	-	-	-	-	-	-	-	-	-	-	-
Ontonagon Reservation, Michigan	-	-	-	-	-	-	-	-	-	-	-
Ontonagon County	-	-	-	-	-	-	-	-	-	-	-
Osage Reservation, Oklahoma	4,111	38.1	54.2	5.3	33.2	16.3	4.4	41.4	2.5	50.1	40.7
Osage County	4,111	38.1	54.2	5.3	33.2	16.3	4.4	41.4	2.5	50.1	40.7
Ozette Reservation, Washington	...	...	...	...	...	...	...	...	...	...	...
Clallam County	...	...	...	...	...	...	...	...	...	...	...
Pala Reservation, California	347	67.6	24.7	2.0	45.0	18.9	14.4	4.4	3.4	71.2	25.0
San Diego County	347	67.6	24.7	2.0	45.0	18.9	14.4	4.4	3.4	71.2	25.0
Pamunkey Reservation, Virginia	36	-	94.4	-	58.3	8.3	22.2	-	5.6	33.3	50.0
King William County	36	-	94.4	-	58.3	8.3	22.2	-	5.6	33.3	50.0
Papago Reservation, Arizona	6,039	98.1	1.0	0.1	0.5	0.6	0.1	96.8	1.6	51.5	21.6
Maricopa County	123	100.0	-	-	-	-	-	100.0	-	-	0.9
Pima County	5,390	98.7	0.3	0.1	0.2	0.3	0.1	97.3	1.6	56.0	18.3
Pinal County	526	90.5	8.1	-	3.7	3.5	-	90.5	1.8	17.8	60.1
Pascua Yaqui Reservation, Arizona	481	79.9	4.6	0.7	8.6	3.6	0.9	80.1	5.7	61.9	35.2
Pima County	481	79.9	4.6	0.7	8.6	3.6	0.9	80.1	5.7	61.9	35.2
Pauma Reservation, California	69	50.3	27.5	2.4	37.6	20.0	14.0	3.3	18.2	61.6	29.6
San Diego County	69	50.3	27.5	2.4	37.6	20.0	14.0	3.3	18.2	61.6	29.6
Payson Community of Yavapai-Apache, Arizona	-	-	-	-	-	-	-	-	-	-	-
Gila County	-	-	-	-	-	-	-	-	-	-	-
Pechanga Reservation, California	75	8.1	60.9	14.9	35.2	28.3	27.1	4.1	1.4	39.2	40.6
Riverside County	75	8.1	60.9	14.9	35.2	28.3	27.1	4.1	1.4	39.2	40.6
Penobscot Reservation, Maine	371	74.0	23.3	-	3.0	7.0	10.3	76.4	2.7	80.2	19.0
Penobscot County	371	74.0	23.3	-	3.0	7.0	10.3	76.4	2.7	80.2	19.0
Picuris Pueblo, New Mexico	103	93.7	1.3	3.4	1.6	1.3	1.0	94.7	-	8.6	61.7
Taos County	103	93.7	1.3	3.4	1.6	1.3	1.0	94.7	-	8.6	61.7
Pine Creek Reservation, Michigan	...	...	...	...	...	...	...	...	...	...	...
Calhoun County	...	...	...	...	...	...	...	...	...	...	...
Pine Ridge Reservation, South Dakota	10,179	93.4	3.4	0.6	2.0	1.1	1.1	92.5	2.4	50.4	27.9
Jackson County	1,057	89.4	7.5	0.4	3.0	0.8	2.0	90.2	4.0	59.9	21.1
Shannon County	9,122	93.9	3.0	0.6	1.9	1.1	1.0	92.8	2.3	49.3	28.6
Pleasant Point Reservation, Maine	349	33.1	60.8	0.4	1.1	8.3	30.9	48.1	11.2	59.7	29.1
Washington County	349	33.1	60.8	0.4	1.1	8.3	30.9	48.1	11.2	59.7	29.1
Pojoaque Pueblo, New Mexico	96	90.8	9.2	-	4.9	6.9	-	88.2	-	31.5	61.6
Santa Fe County	96	90.8	9.2	-	4.9	6.9	-	88.2	-	31.5	61.6
Poospatuck Reservation, New York	82	-	76.7	-	35.1	44.0	18.2	-	2.7	95.9	2.7
Suffolk County	82	-	76.7	-	35.1	44.0	18.2	-	2.7	95.9	2.7
Port Gamble Reservation, Washington	243	13.0	86.1	0.5	1.0	31.1	15.0	48.0	4.3	85.8	12.7
Kitsap County	243	13.0	86.1	0.5	1.0	31.1	15.0	48.0	4.3	85.8	12.7
Port Madison Reservation, Washington	134	25.1	66.3	1.0	6.9	22.2	4.0	59.7	5.8	85.7	9.6
Kitsap County	134	25.1	66.3	1.0	6.9	22.2	4.0	59.7	5.8	85.7	9.6
Potawatomi Reservation, Wisconsin	218	3.6	95.9	0.5	0.9	1.4	46.5	43.3	3.2	57.2	30.9
Forest County	218	3.6	95.9	0.5	0.9	1.4	46.5	43.3	3.2	57.2	30.9
Oconto County	-	-	-	-	-	-	-	-	-	-	-
Pottawatomi Reservation, Kansas	318	75.6	18.5	0.9	12.2	10.6	4.2	69.0	1.2	50.2	48.2
Jackson County	318	75.6	18.5	0.9	12.2	10.6	4.2	69.0	1.2	50.2	48.2
Prairie Island Community, Minnesota	83	2.4	39.8	-	2.4	13.3	15.7	61.4	7.2	14.5	83.1

[Continued]

★ 473 ★

Methods of Health Care on Identified Reservations, 1980 - IV
[Continued]

| Identified reservations | Total | Usual place of health care -- percent | | | Person or other family member | Health care paid by -- percent | | | | Travel time to health care facility -- percent | |
		Indian service clinic, health center or hospital	Private physician or dentist	Tribal clinic or hospital		Private health insurance	Medicaid or Medicare	Indian Health Service or tribe	Other government services	Less than 30 minutes	30 minutes to 1 hour
Goodhue County	83	2.4	39.8	-	2.4	13.3	15.7	61.4	7.2	14.5	83.1
Puyallup Reservation, Washington	733	30.3	35.3	23.7	5.5	21.5	6.8	43.5	19.9	89.8	9.1
Pierce County	733	30.3	35.3	23.7	5.5	21.5	6.8	43.5	19.9	89.8	9.1
Pyramid Lake Reservation, Nevada	605	74.4	21.0	0.8	10.0	8.9	1.5	74.8	1.4	5.0	12.7
Lyon County	-	-	-	-	-	-	-	-	-	-	-
Storey County	-	-	-	-	-	-	-	-	-	-	-
Washoe County	605	74.4	21.0	0.8	10.0	8.9	1.5	74.8	1.4	5.0	12.7
Quileute Reservation, Washington	249	16.6	27.2	54.5	3.1	5.5	-	90.6	-	66.2	28.9
Clallam County	249	16.6	27.2	54.5	3.1	5.5	-	90.6	-	66.2	28.9
Quainault Reservation, Washington	862	83.6	8.5	6.1	1.8	4.2	0.3	90.7	1.0	82.1	8.1
Grays Harbor County	716	85.9	7.7	4.4	2.0	4.9	0.2	91.3	0.3	84.2	9.3
Jefferson County	145	72.2	12.0	14.3	0.8	0.8	0.7	88.0	4.5	71.7	2.3
Ramah Community, New Mexico	839	85.2	0.8	10.6	1.2	1.5	2.1	90.4	3.2	47.8	39.8
McKinley County	77	94.4	1.9	-	1.9	-	4.7	91.7	-	5.4	69.6
Valencia County	762	84.2	0.7	11.7	1.1	1.7	1.9	90.3	3.6	52.1	36.8
Ramona Reservation, California	-	-	-	-	-	-	-	-	-	-	-
Riverside County	-	-	-	-	-	-	-	-	-	-	-
Red Cliff Reservation, Wisconsin	537	5.9	88.6	1.4	2.6	4.4	19.4	39.2	2.2	21.7	63.5
Bayfield County	537	5.9	88.6	1.4	2.6	4.4	19.4	39.2	2.2	21.7	63.5
Red Lake Reservation, Minnesota	2,351	95.4	1.3	1.2	0.1	1.7	3.8	89.9	1.6	76.6	19.5
Beltrami County	2,290	95.7	1.2	1.3	0.1	1.7	3.5	90.5	1.5	77.4	19.2
Clearwater County	61	86.3	3.7	-	3.7	1.8	16.3	70.1	8.0	45.4	32.8
Koochiching County	-	-	-	-	-	-	-	-	-	-	-
Lake of the Woods County	-	-	-	-	-	-	-	-	-	-	-
Marshall County	-	-	-	-	-	-	-	-	-	-	-
Pennington County	-	-	-	-	-	-	-	-	-	-	-
Polk County	-	-	-	-	-	-	-	-	-	-	-
Red Lake County	-	-	-	-	-	-	-	-	-	-	-
Roseau County	-	-	-	-	-	-	-	-	-	-	-
Reno-Sparks Colony, Nevada	383	52.4	36.5	-	16.4	15.2	1.6	58.9	6.4	50.9	10.3
Washoe County	383	52.4	36.5	-	16.4	15.2	1.6	58.9	6.4	50.9	10.3
Resighini Rancheria, California	...	...	...	...	...	...	...	...	...	...	...
Del Norte County	...	...	...	...	...	...	...	...	...	...	...
Rincon Reservation, California	231	45.7	42.4	7.8	41.2	24.8	8.2	5.4	-	61.6	32.2
San Diego County	231	45.7	42.4	7.8	41.2	24.8	8.2	5.4	-	61.6	32.2
Roaring Creek Rancheria, California	...	...	...	...	...	...	...	...	...	...	...
Shasta County	...	...	...	...	...	...	...	...	...	...	...
Rocky Boy's Reservation, Montana	1,490	98.2	1.1	0.4	0.7	0.3	0.9	97.1	0.3	83.8	15.7
Chouteau County	125	97.6	1.6	-	-	-	-	97.6	-	75.2	24.0
Hill County	1,365	98.2	1.0	0.5	0.8	0.3	1.0	97.1	0.3	84.6	15.0
Rosebud Reservation, South Dakota	4,697	83.7	12.6	0.7	6.4	3.8	4.4	82.6	1.6	64.2	27.5
Todd County	4,697	83.7	12.6	0.7	6.4	3.8	4.4	82.6	1.6	64.2	27.5
Round Valley Reservation, California	500	1.6	8.1	1.3	34.9	26.9	34.2	0.2	1.4	87.4	0.4
Mendocino County	500	1.6	8.1	1.3	34.9	26.9	34.2	0.2	1.4	87.4	0.4
Rumsey Rancheria, California	...	...	...	...	...	...	...	...	...	...	...
Yolo County	...	...	...	...	...	...	...	...	...	...	11.2
Sac and Fox Reservation, Iowa	423	2.1	95.0	-	3.3	11.3	10.8	66.4	0.8	86.8	11.2
Tama County	423	2.1	95.0	-	3.3	11.3	10.8	66.4	0.8	86.8	11.2
Sac and Fox Reservation, Kansas-Nebraska	...	...	...	...	...	...	...	...	...	...	...
Kansas	...	...	...	...	...	...	...	...	...	...	...
Brown County	-	-	-	-	-	-	-	-	-	-	-
Nebraska	...	...	...	...	...	...	...	...	...	...	...
Richardson County	...	...	...	...	...	...	...	...	...	...	...

Source: U.S. Bureau of the Census, Subject Reports, PC80-2-1D, Part 1, *American Indians, Eskimos, and Aleuts on Identified Reservations and in the Historic Areas of Oklahoma (Excluding Urbanized Areas)*, U.S. Government Printing Office, Washington, D.C., 1986, pp. 59-67. *Notes:* Three dots (...) means not applicable, or that the data are being withheld to avoid disclosure of information for individuals. A dash (-) represents zero or a percent which rounds to less than 0.1. Also, a dash (-) is used because the number of supplementary questionnaires for the reservations was insufficient to produce reliable estimates.

★ 474 ★

Methods of Health Care on Identified Reservations, 1980 - V

Data are the latest available.

		Persons who received health care in last 12 months									
Identified reservations	Total	Usual place of health care -- percent			Health care paid by -- percent					Travel time to health care facility -- percent	
		Indian service clinic, health center or hospital	Private physician or dentist	Tribal clinic or hospital	Person or other family member	Private health insurance	Medicaid or Medicare	Indian Health Service or tribe	Other government services	Less than 30 minutes	30 minutes to 1 hour
St. Croix Reservation, Wisconsin	371	11.9	76.8	3.7	2.6	8.1	27.4	25.9	29.6	78.0	19.4
Barron County	82	5.3	65.7	-	-	-	73.8	9.4	-	82.3	17.7
Burnett County	214	18.6	77.5	1.9	4.4	11.9	15.2	41.2	26.0	72.6	24.3
Polk County	74	-	87.0	13.0	-	5.9	11.5	-	72.6	89.1	7.3
St. Regis Mohawk Reservation, New York	1,639	86.2	10.3	2.8	1.5	20.6	4.7	71.4	0.8	94.8	4.3
Franklin County	1,639	86.2	10.3	2.8	1.5	20.6	4.7	71.4	0.8	94.8	4.3
Salt River Reservation, Arizona	2,191	57.5	1.5	40.7	0.9	0.5	0.1	97.7	0.1	52.2	43.7
Maricopa County	2,191	57.5	1.5	40.7	0.9	0.5	0.1	97.7	0.1	52.2	43.7
San Carlos Reservation, Arizona	4,942	96.6	1.9	0.4	0.8	1.0	0.1	96.5	0.8	90.8	6.6
Gila County	3,019	96.7	1.7	0.3	0.8	0.8	0.1	96.3	1.0	91.2	6.4
Graham County	1,922	96.5	2.1	0.5	0.8	1.4	0.2	96.7	0.5	90.2	7.0
Pinal County	-	-	-	-	-	-	-	-	-	-	-
Sandia Pueblo, New Mexico	185	74.4	14.3	10.3	2.8	8.8	1.1	84.1	1.1	59.4	38.4
Bernalillo County	-	-	-	-	-	-	-	-	-	-	-
Sandoval County	185	74.4	14.3	10.3	2.8	8.8	1.1	84.1	1.1	59.4	38.4
Sandy Lake Reservation, Minnesota	-	-	-	-	-	-	-	-	-	-	-
Aitkin County	-	-	-	-	-	-	-	-	-	-	-
San Felipe Pueblo, New Mexico	1,306	42.7	4.0	52.8	2.4	1.3	0.9	94.7	0.3	55.6	34.6
Sandoval County	1,306	42.7	4.0	52.8	2.4	1.3	0.9	94.7	0.3	55.6	34.6
San Ildefonso Pueblo, New Mexico	450	93.5	4.9	1.1	4.2	0.5	-	94.9	-	25.9	72.6
Sandoval County	-	-	-	-	-	-	-	-	-	-	-
Sante Fe County	450	93.5	4.9	1.1	4.2	0.5	-	94.9	-	25.9	72.6
San Juan Pueblo, New Mexico	767	79.3	5.3	14.7	2.7	1.4	1.0	93.5	0.2	17.1	64.0
Rio Arriba County	767	79.3	5.3	14.7	2.7	1.4	1.0	93.5	0.2	17.1	64.0
San Manuel Reservation, California	-	-	-	-	-	-	-	-	-	-	-
San Bernardino County	-	-	-	-	-	-	-	-	-	-	-
San Pasqual Reservation, California	81	70.9	19.9	3.9	31.3	24.2	13.2	3.9	-	86.8	11.9
San Diego County	81	70.9	19.9	3.9	31.3	24.2	13.2	3.9	-	86.8	11.9
Santa Ana Pueblo, New Mexico	340	52.3	17.6	27.5	2.2	15.7	1.9	79.4	0.9	33.4	65.9
Sandoval County	340	52.3	17.6	27.5	2.2	15.7	1.9	79.4	0.9	33.4	65.9
Santa Clara Pueblo, New Mexico	1,666	89.3	8.4	0.6	5.0	2.9	0.8	89.3	0.6	12.2	86.0
Rio Arriba County	1,639	89.3	8.4	0.6	5.0	3.0	89.3	0.6	11.8	86.3	
Sandoval County	-	-	-	-	-	-	-	-	-	-	-
Sante Fe County	...	...	...	...	...	...	...	...	...	...	...
Santa Rosa Rancheria, California	86	53.0	15.7	5.6	8.1	-	27.3	61.3	1.6	49.8	35.5
Kings County	86	53.0	15.7	5.6	8.1	-	27.3	61.3	1.6	49.8	35.5
Santa Rosa Reservation, California	...	...	...	...	...	...	...	...	...	...	...
Riverside County	...	...	...	...	...	...	...	...	...	...	...
Santa Ynez Reservation, California	91	4.1	93.2	-	28.4	20.3	25.7	24.3	-	66.2	32.4
Santa Barbara County	91	4.1	93.2	-	28.4	20.3	25.7	24.3	-	66.2	32.4
Santa Ysabel Reservation, California	131	44.0	42.4	-	25.9	12.3	45.3	5.6	4.4	18.9	64.0
San Diego County	131	44.0	42.4	-	25.9	12.3	45.3	5.6	4.4	18.9	64.0
Santee Reservation, Nebraska	167	36.8	22.1	38.8	1.9	14.5	2.5	77.4	3.7	69.0	21.1
Knox County	167	36.8	22.1	38.8	1.9	14.5	2.5	77.4	3.7	69.0	21.1
Santo Domingo Pueblo, New Mexico	1,734	82.1	0.9	14.4	0.2	0.1	2.6	94.1	2.2	56.5	40.9
Sandoval County	1,734	82.1	0.9	14.4	0.2	0.1	2.6	94.1	2.2	56.5	40.9
Santa Fe County	-	-	-	-	-	-	-	-	-	-	-
San Xavier Reservation, Arizona	777	94.0	3.9	-	1.5	3.0	0.3	93.5	0.7	91.2	6.8
Pima County	777	94.0	3.9	-	1.5	3.0	0.3	93.5	0.7	91.2	6.8
Sauk-Suiattle Reservation, Washington	-	-	-	-	-	-	-	-	-	-	-
Snohomish County	-	-	-	-	-	-	-	-	-	-	-
Sault Ste. Marie Reservation, Michigan	-	-	-	-	-	-	-	-	-	-	-
Chippewa County	-	-	-	-	-	-	-	-	-	-	-
Schaghticoke Reservation, Michigan	...	...	...	...	...	...	...	...	...	...	...
Litchfield County	...	...	...	...	...	...	...	...	...	...	...
Shakopee Community, Minnesota	63	7.9	86.8	-	1.7	19.1	-	63.4	14.2	96.6	3.4
Scott County	63	7.9	86.8	-	1.7	19.1	-	63.4	14.2	96.6	3.4
Sheep Ranch Rancheria, California	...	...	...	...	...	...	...	...	...	...	...
Calaveras County	...	...	...	...	...	...	...	...	...	...	...
Sherwood Valley Rancheria, California	...	...	...	...	...	...	...	...	...	...	...
Mendocino County	...	...	...	...	...	...	...	...	...	...	...
Shingle Springs Rancheria, California	-	-	-	-	-	-	-	-	-	-	-
El Dorado County	-	-	-	-	-	-	-	-	-	-	-
Shinnecock Reservation, New York	127	-	100.0	-	50.3	30.9	13.3	-	2.1	92.6	4.3
Suffolk County	127	-	100.0	-	50.3	30.9	13.3	-	2.1	92.6	4.3

[Continued]

★ 474 ★

Methods of Health Care on Identified Reservations, 1980 - V
[Continued]

Identified reservations	Total	Usual place of health care -- percent			Health care paid by -- percent					Travel time to health care facility -- percent	
		Indian service clinic, health center or hospital	Private physician or dentist	Tribal clinic or hospital	Person or other family member	Private health insurance	Medicaid or Medicare	Indian Health Service or tribe	Other government services	Less than 30 minutes	30 minutes to 1 hour
Shoalwater Reservation, Washington	...	...	...	...	...	...	...	...	...	...	...
Pacific County	...	...	...	...	...	...	...	...	...	...	...
Sisseton Reservation, North Dakota-South Dakota	2,347	89.4	5.3	0.4	1.9	1.5	2.1	88.9	4.6	75.4	22.0
North Dakota	-	-	-	-	-	-	-	-	-	-	-
Richland County	-	-	-	-	-	-	-	-	-	-	-
Sargent County	-	-	-	-	-	-	-	-	-	-	-
South Dakota	2,347	89.4	5.3	0.4	1.9	1.5	2.1	88.9	4.6	75.4	22.0
Codington County	...	...	...	...	...	...	...	...	...	...	...
Day County	294	89.2	5.5	-	2.6	0.9	2.8	88.4	5.3	15.4	83.9
Grant County	-	-	-	-	-	-	-	-	-	-	-
Marshall County	208	87.9	10.9	-	2.0	2.2	0.7	92.8	0.7	54.3	35.2
Roberts County	1,843	89.7	4.5	0.5	1.8	1.4	2.2	88.6	4.9	87.3	10.7
Skokomish Reservation, Washington	132	51.3	44.2	2.6	4.4	20.1	1.9	64.6	-	81.0	10.2
Mason County	132	51.3	44.2	2.6	4.4	20.1	1.9	64.6	-	81.0	10.2
Skull Valley Reservation, Utah	-	-	-	-	-	-	-	-	-	-	-
Tooele County	-	-	-	-	-	-	-	-	-	-	-
Soboba Reservation, California	225	58.9	10.6	29.5	11.8	4.7	8.9	72.7	1.0	87.7	10.0
Riverside County	225	58.9	10.6	29.5	11.8	4.7	8.9	72.7	1.0	87.7	10.0
Sokaogon Chippewa Community, Wisconsin	94	24.5	71.2	-	5.3	-	19.4	59.1	13.0	86.1	10.7
Forest County	94	24.5	71.2	-	5.3	-	19.4	59.1	13.0	86.1	10.7
Southern Paiute Reservation, Utah	131	4.5	77.4	-	58.0	12.1	17.5	3.2	8.1	77.2	8.2
Iron County	67	4.6	75.3	-	71.9	10.8	5.9	-	11.4	84.0	9.5
Millard County	33	-	81.9	-	41.4	22.0	28.0	-	4.6	45.8	13.5
Sevier County	31	9.1	7.3	-	45.5	4.5	31.8	13.6	4.5	95.5	-
Southern Ute Reservation, Colorado	688	86.0	7.1	5.6	2.2	9.8	1.9	84.1	1.4	88.3	10.9
Archuleta County	...	...	...	...	...	...	...	...	...	...	...
La Plata County	676	86.5	6.7	5.6	1.6	10.0	2.0	84.4	1.4	89.9	9.3
Montezuma County	-	-	-	-	-	-	-	-	-	-	-
Spokane Reservation, Washington	973	86.2	11.5	0.6	1.9	11.5	2.4	83.3	0.7	74.5	17.3
Lincoln County	-	-	-	-	-	-	-	-	-	-	-
Stevens County	973	86.2	11.5	0.6	1.9	11.5	2.4	83.3	0.7	74.5	17.3
Squaxin Island Reservation, Washington	26	15.4	80.8	-	-	3.8	-	76.9	19.2	65.4	34.6
Mason County	26	15.4	80.8	-	-	3.8	-	76.9	19.2	65.4	34.6
Standing Rock Reservation, North Dakota-South Dakota	3,993	93.5	3.8	0.4	1.6	3.5	1.2	91.7	1.8	65.7	28.9
North Dakota	2,095	94.9	3.9	0.3	0.9	4.6	0.3	92.8	1.1	81.6	14.6
Sioux County	2,095	94.9	3.9	0.3	0.9	4.6	0.3	92.8	1.1	81.6	14.6
South Dakota	1,898	92.0	3.6	0.6	2.3	2.3	2.2	90.5	2.5	48.1	44.7
Corson County	1,898	92.0	3.6	0.6	2.3	2.3	2.2	90.5	2.5	48.1	44.7
Stewart's Point Rancheria, California	60	96.6	3.4	-	-	37.3	16.9	44.1	-	22.0	1.7
Sonoma County	60	96.6	3.4	-	-	37.3	16.9	44.1	-	22.0	1.7
Stockbridge Reservation, Wisconsin	526	18.1	16.7	63.2	3.4	29.2	12.3	40.7	8.9	85.6	10.7
Shawano County	526	18.1	16.7	63.2	3.4	29.2	12.3	40.7	8.9	85.6	10.7
Sulphur Bank Reservation, California	95	10.7	78.7	-	1.2	15.8	1.4	14.8	1.3	1.4	76.1
Lake County	95	10.7	78.7	-	1.2	15.8	1.4	14.8	1.3	1.4	76.1
Summit Lake Reservation, Nevada	...	...	...	...	...	...	...	...	...	...	...
Humboldt County	...	...	...	...	...	...	...	...	...	...	...
Susanville Reservation, California	55	47.0	37.0	2.0	5.9	14.4	8.6	53.1	6.1	81.7	-
Lassen County	55	47.0	37.0	2.0	5.9	14.4	8.6	53.1	6.1	81.7	-
Swinomish Reservation, Washington	387	14.6	83.9	1.1	0.4	8.9	8.7	66.4	0.7	93.0	6.1
Skagit County	387	14.6	83.9	1.1	0.4	8.9	8.7	66.4	0.7	93.0	6.1
Sycuan Reservation, California	39	-	82.7	4.7	4.1	25.7	27.1	-	8.1	62.1	33.8
San Diego County	39	-	82.7	4.7	4.1	25.7	27.1	-	8.1	62.1	33.8
Tama Reservation, Georgia	24	-	86.4	-	72.7	-	4.5	-	13.6	31.9	36.3
Grady County	24	-	86.4	-	72.7	-	4.5	-	13.6	31.9	36.3
Taos Pueblo, New Mexico	969	96.5	1.2	1.2	0.5	0.4	1.9	96.5	0.4	94.0	5.1
Taos County	969	96.5	1.2	1.2	0.5	0.4	1.9	96.5	0.4	94.0	5.1
Te-Moak Reservation, Nevada	69	91.7	6.2	-	2.0	4.4	10.1	83.5	-	-	83.6
Elko County	69	91.7	6.2	-	2.0	4.4	10.1	83.5	-	-	83.6
Tesuque Pueblo, New Mexico	226	99.5	-	-	0.5	-	0.5	97.9	0.5	79.6	19.4
Sante Fe County	226	99.5	-	-	0.5	-	0.5	97.9	0.5	79.6	19.4

[Continued]

★ 474 ★

Methods of Health Care on Identified Reservations, 1980 - V
[Continued]

Identified reservations	Total	Usual place of health care -- percent			Health care paid by -- percent					Travel time to health care facility -- percent	
		Indian service clinic, health center or hospital	Private physician or dentist	Tribal clinic or hospital	Person or other family member	Private health insurance	Medicaid or Medicare	Indian Health Service or tribe	Other government services	Less than 30 minutes	30 minutes to 1 hour
Tigua Reservation, Texas	265	-	49.4	2.6	75.8	6.4	9.1	4.5	0.8	31.7	64.9
El Paso County	265	-	49.4	2.6	75.8	6.4	9.1	4.5	0.8	31.7	64.9

Source: U.S. Bureau of the Census, Subject Reports, PC80-2-1D, Part 1, *American Indians, Eskimos, and Aleuts on Identified Reservations and in the Historic Areas of Oklahoma (Excluding Urbanized Areas),* U.S. Government Printing Office, Washington, D.C., 1986, pp. 59-67. *Notes:* Three dots ... means not applicable, or that the data are being withheld to avoid disclosure of information for individuals. A dash (-) represents zero or a percent which rounds to less than 0.1. Also, a dash (-) is used because the number of supplementary questionnaires for the reservations was insufficient to produce reliable estimates.

★ 475 ★

Methods of Health Care on Identified Reservations, 1980 - VI

Data are the latest available.

Identified reservations	Total	Usual place of health care -- percent			Health care paid by -- percent					Travel time to health care facility -- percent	
		Indian service clinic, health center or hospital	Private physician or dentist	Tribal clinic or hospital	Person or other family member	Private health insurance	Medicaid or Medicare	Indian Health Service or tribe	Other government services	Less than 30 minutes	30 minutes to 1 hour
Tonawanda Reservation, New York	320	18.0	33.9	0.3	11.9	16.8	6.3	14.7	47.4	75.6	19.2
Erie County	-	-	-	-	-	-	-	-	-	-	-
Genesee County	320	18.0	33.9	0.3	11.9	16.8	6.3	14.7	47.4	75.6	19.2
Niagara County	-	-	-	-	-	-	-	-	-	-	-
Torres-Martinez Reservation, California	-	-	-	-	-	-	-	-	-	-	-
Imperial County	-	-	-	-	-	-	-	-	-	-	-
Riverside County	-	-	-	-	-	-	-	-	-	-	-
Trinidad Rancheria, California	42	97.3	2.7	-	-	5.4	5.4	86.8	2.5	86.6	10.7
Humboldt County	42	97.3	2.7		-	5.4	5.4	86.8	2.5	86.6	10.7
Tulalip Reservation, Washington	676	6.5	74.5	16.5	1.1	20.3	8.4	63.0	7.3	91.6	7.3
Snohomish County	676	6.5	74.5	16.5	1.1	20.3	8.4	63.0	7.3	91.6	7.3
Tule River Reservation, California	368	72.8	9.9	9.6	4.3	2.8	4.0	82.0	1.0	89.2	9.4
Tulare County	368	72.8	9.9	9.6	4.3	2.8	4.0	82.0	1.0	89.2	9.4
Tunica-Biloxi Reservation, Louisiana	...	...	...	...	...	...	...	...	...	...	...
Avoyelles Parish	...	...	...	...	...	...	...	...	...	...	...
Tuolumne Rancheria, California	71	67.6	25.4	5.6	5.6	29.6	18.3	43.7	-	93.0	5.6
Tuolumne County	71	67.6	25.4	5.6	5.6	29.6	18.3	43.7	-	93.0	5.6
Turtle Mountain Reservation, North Dakota	3,714	79.2	11.7	0.6	0.5	6.7	3.2	77.7	6.1	89.8	8.6
Rolette County	3,714	79.2	11.7	0.6	0.5	6.7	3.2	77.7	6.1	89.8	8.6
Tuscarora Reservation, New York	-	-	-	-	-	-	-	-	-	-	-
Niagara County	-	-	-	-	-	-	-	-	-	-	-
Twenty-Nine Palms Reservation, California	-	-	-	-	-	-	-	-	-	-	-
San Bernardino County	-	-	-	-	-	-	-	-	-	-	-
Uintah and Ouray Reservation, Utah	1,666	92.7	5.0	0.9	3.4	2.8	0.2	92.3	1.0	87.1	11.5
Carbon County	-	-	-	-	-	-	-	-	-	-	-
Duchesne County	305	88.9	7.2	3.9	1.0	6.4	-	91.1	1.5	93.9	6.1
Grand County	-	-	-	-	-	-	-	-	-	-	-
Uintah County	1,361	93.6	4.4	0.2	4.0	1.9	0.2	92.6	0.9	85.5	12.7
Utah County	-	-	-	-	-	-	-	-	-	-	-
Wasatch County	-	-	-	-	-	-	-	-	-	-	-
Umatilla Reservation, Oregon	800	83.6	11.5	4.0	2.6	3.2	2.2	88.1	2.1	88.8	9.5
Umatilla County	800	83.6	11.5	4.0	2.6	3.2	2.2	88.1	2.1	88.8	9.5
Union County	-	-	-	-	-	-	-	-	-	-	-
Upper Sioux Community, Minnesota	46	25.7	16.7	-	-	4.4	18.1	63.7	13.8	96.0	-
Yellow Medicine County	46	25.7	16.7	-	-	4.4	18.1	63.7	13.8	96.0	-
Upper Skagit Reservation, Washington	-	-	-	-	-	-	-	-	-	-	-
Skagit County	-	-	-	-	-	-	-	-	-	-	-
Ute Mountain Reservation, Colorado-New Mexico	667	85.6	3.9	9.7	4.0	0.5	0.8	93.8	0.2	86.0	9.2
Colorado	667	85.6	3.9	9.7	4.0	0.5	0.8	93.8	0.2	86.0	9.2
La Plata County	-	-	-	-	-	-	-	-	-	-	-

[Continued]

★ 475 ★

Methods of Health Care on Identified Reservations, 1980 - VI
[Continued]

Identified reservations	Total	Persons who received health care in last 12 months									
		Usual place of health care -- percent			Health care paid by -- percent					Travel time to health care facility -- percent	
		Indian service clinic, health center or hospital	Private physician or dentist	Tribal clinic or hospital	Person or other family member	Private health insurance	Medicaid or Medicare	Indian Health Service or tribe	Other government services	Less than 30 minutes	30 minutes to 1 hour
Montezuma County	667	85.6	3.9	9.7	4.0	0.5	0.8	93.8	0.2	86.0	9.2
New Mexico	-	-	-	-	-	-	-	-	-	-	-
San Juan County	-	-	-	-	-	-	-	-	-	-	-
Vermillion Lake Reservation, Minnesota	93	25.5	72.2	2.2	2.0	31.0	-	38.3	10.6	24.0	73.6
St. Louis County	93	25.5	72.2	2.2	2.0	31.0	-	38.3	10.6	24.0	73.6
Viejas Rancheria, California	99	12.4	76.1	3.7	31.0	8.3	20.5	6.6	20.3	46.8	46.1
San Diego County	99	12.4	76.1	3.7	31.0	8.3	20.5	6.6	20.3	46.8	46.1
Walker River Reservation, Nevada	463	94.8	2.2	0.2	0.9	0.9	0.6	95.2	2.4	94.8	2.2
Churchill County	-	-	-	-	-	-	-	-	-	-	-
Lyon County	-	-	-	-	-	-	-	-	-	-	-
Mineral County	463	94.8	2.2	0.2	0.9	0.9	0.6	95.2	2.4	94.8	2.2
Wampanoag Reservation, Massachusetts											
Bristol County	-	-	-	-	-	-	-	-	-	-	-
Warm Springs Reservation, Oregon	1,753	91.9	6.4	1.4	1.9	9.9	0.2	87.3	-	87.1	10.4
Clackamas County	-	-	-	-	-	-	-	-	-	-	-
Jefferson County	1,453	92.1	6.3	1.5	2.2	9.2	0.3	87.8	-	94.6	3.2
Marion County	-	-	-	-	-	-	-	-	-	-	-
Wasco County	300	91.3	6.9	0.9	0.4	13.2	-	85.2	-	50.8	45.6
Washoe Reservation, Nevada	-	-	-	-	-	-	-	-	-	-	-
Douglas County	-	-	-	-	-	-	-	-	-	-	-
Western Pequot Reservation, Connecticut	...	...	...	...	...	...	...	...	...	...	...
New London County	...	...	...	...	...	...	...	...	...	...	...
White Earth Reservation, Minnesota	2,361	81.7	14.5	2.0	2.4	5.9	4.7	81.6	4.6	72.4	22.2
Becker County	1,212	93.4	4.7	0.7	0.5	1.9	0.6	93.8	2.8	85.7	12.2
Clearwater County	233	50.0	38.8	7.7	6.8	6.6	26.8	46.1	8.6	34.3	42.5
Mahnomen County	917	74.2	21.4	2.3	3.8	11.2	4.5	74.4	5.9	64.4	30.2
Wind River Reservation, Wyoming	3,559	93.0	2.7	2.8	2.1	1.6	0.7	94.0	0.3	83.8	12.3
Fremont County	3,539	93.6	2.6	2.3	2.0	1.6	0.7	94.0	0.3	84.0	12.3
Hot Springs County	...	...	...	...	...	...	...	...	...	...	...
Winnebago Reservation, Nebraska	615	86.4	4.1	0.7	2.8	2.4	0.6	84.7	8.7	95.0	5.0
Dixon County	...	...	...	...	...	...	...	...	...	...	...
Thurston County	615	86.4	4.1	0.7	2.8	2.4	0.6	84.7	8.7	95.0	5.0
Winnemucca Colony, Nevada	33	63.5	23.8	-	27.7	-	7.7	64.6	-	51.9	-
Humboldt County	33	63.5	23.8	-	27.7	-	7.7	64.6	-	51.9	-
Wisconsin Winnebago Reservation	236	46.6	46.9	-	2.6	18.2	23.9	42.3	7.9	67.8	25.6
Jackson County	-	-	-	-	-	-	-	-	-	-	-
Juneau County	95	65.3	18.5	-	2.7	28.2	53.5	10.7	1.5	100.0	-
Monroe County	...	...	...	...	...	...	...	...	...	...	...
Sauk County	15	-	100.0	-	24.5	15.4	-	-	-	69.9	-
Shawano County	...	...	...	...	...	...	...	...	...	...	...
Wood County	95	50.7	49.3	-	-	14.9	-	66.9	18.2	58.0	42.0
Woodfords Community, California	-	-	-	-	-	-	-	-	-	-	-
Alpine County	-	-	-	-	-	-	-	-	-	-	-
XL Ranch Reservation, California	...	...	...	...	...	...	...	...	...	...	...
Modoc County	...	...	...	...	...	...	...	...	...	...	...
Yakima Reservation, Washington	4,406	77.5	16.3	4.8	3.7	10.1	2.1	80.8	2.0	71.7	25.9
Klickitat County	63	27.0	71.4	-	1.6	20.6	-	76.2	1.6	15.9	47.6
Yakima County	4,343	78.2	15.5	4.9	3.8	9.9	2.2	80.9	2.0	72.6	25.6
Yankton Reservation, South Dakota	1,519	89.4	4.2	0.1	2.8	1.3	1.3	90.8	3.5	67.3	29.8
Charles Mix County	1,519	89.4	4.2	0.1	2.8	1.3	1.3	90.8	3.5	67.3	29.8
Yavapai Reservation, Arizona	57	47.4	38.6	-	3.5	3.5	-	87.7	3.5	71.9	3.5
Yavapai County	57	47.4	38.6	-	3.5	3.5	-	87.7	3.5	71.9	3.5
Yerington Reservation, Nevada	110	93.0	7.0	-	-	5.0	-	90.3	2.0	3.0	92.1
Lyon County	110	93.0	7.0	-	-	5.0	-	90.3	2.0	3.0	92.1
Yomba Reservation, Nevada	55	87.3	3.6	-	1.8	-	-	87.3	5.5	3.6	1.8
Nye County	55	87.3	3.6	-	1.8	-	-	87.3	5.5	3.6	1.8
Zia Pueblo, New Mexico	441	89.2	2.9	3.4	1.1	1.7	2.0	93.0	1.8	83.6	12.9
Sandoval County	441	89.2	2.9	3.4	1.1	1.7	2.0	93.0	1.8	83.6	12.9
Zuni Pueblo, New Mexico	4,775	97.0	0.6	1.0	1.0	0.2	2.2	95.4	0.3	92.5	3.3
McKinley County	4,775	97.0	0.6	1.0	1.0	0.2	2.2	95.4	0.3	92.5	3.3
Valencia County	-	-	-	-	-	-	-	-	-	-	-
San Felipe/Santa Ana Joint Area, New Mexico	-	-	-	-	-	-	-	-	-	-	-
Sandoval County	-	-	-	-	-	-	-	-	-	-	-
San Felipe/Santo Domingo Joint Area, New Mexico	110	58.6	1.2	-	-	-	-	58.6	40.0	52.4	47.6
Sandoval County	110	58.6	1.2	-	-	-	-	58.6	40.0	52.4	47.6

[Continued]

★ 475 ★

Methods of Health Care on Identified Reservations, 1980 - VI
[Continued]

Identified reservations	Total	Persons who received health care in last 12 months									
		Usual place of health care -- percent			Health care paid by -- percent					Travel time to health care facility -- percent	
		Indian service clinic, health center or hospital	Private physician or dentist	Tribal clinic or hospital	Person or other family member	Private health insurance	Medicaid or Medicare	Indian Health Service or tribe	Other government services	Less than 30 minutes	30 minutes to 1 hour
Other Reservation Lands in Montana	-	-	-	-	-	-	-	-	-	-	-
Big Horn County	-	-	-	-	-	-	-	-	-	-	-

Source: U.S. Bureau of the Census, Subject Reports, PC80-2-1D, Part 1, *American Indians, Eskimos, and Aleuts on Identified Reservations and in the Historic Areas of Oklahoma (Excluding Urbanized Areas)*, U.S. Government Printing Office, Washington, D.C., 1986, pp. 59-67. *Notes:* Three dots (...) means not applicable, or that the data are being withheld to avoid disclosure of information for individuals. A dash (-) represents zero or a percent which rounds to less than 0.1. Also, a dash (-) is used because the number of supplementary questionnaires for the reservations was insufficient to produce reliable estimates.

Hospitalization

★ 476 ★

Institutionalized Populations on Reservations, Tribal Jurisdiction Statistical Areas, and Tribal Designated Statistical Areas

Reservation	State	In Nursing Homes	In Mental Hospitals	In College Dormitories	In Military Quarters	In Emergency Shelters	Visible in Streets
Agua Caliente Reservation	CA	208	4				
Allegany Reservation	NY	119					
Blackfeet Reservation	MT	36	24				
Cabazon Reservation	CA	16					
Coeur d'Alene Reservation and Trust Lands	ID	1					
Colorado River Reservation	CO	2	6	28			
Colville Reservation	WA	49					
Crow Creek Reservation	SD	12					
Devils Lake Sioux Reservation	ND	7					
Flathead Reservation	MT	229					
Fort Berthold Reservation	ND	118					
Fort Hall Reservation and Trust Lands	ID	13					
Fort McDowell Reservation	AZ	9					
Fort Peck Reservation	MT	71	3				
Gila River Reservation	AZ	72					
Hoopa Valley Reservation	CA	12					
Isabella Reservation and Trust Lands	MI	168	11				
Lac Courte Oreilles Reservation and Trust Lands	WI	14					
Lac du Flambeau Reservation	WI	14					
Laguna Pueblo and Trust Lands	NM	22					
Lake Traverse (Sisseton) Reservation		150	4	29			
L'Anse Reservation and Trust Lands	MI	59					
Leech Lake Reservation	MN	4					
Makah Reservation	WA	20					
Muckleshoot Reservation and Trust Lands	WA	10					
Navajo Reservation and Trust Lands, AZ--NM--UT		124	172	15			
Nez Perce Reservation	ID	61	20				
Omaha Reservation	NE	79					
Oneida (West) Reservation	WI	42	5				
Osage Reservation	OK	229	5				

[Continued]

★ 476 ★

Institutionalized Populations on Reservations, Tribal Jurisdiction Statistical Areas, and Tribal Designated Statistical Areas

[Continued]

Reservation	State	In Nursing Homes	In Mental Hospitals	In College Dormitories	In Military Quarters	In Emergency Shelters	Visible in Streets
Ozette Reservation	WA	12					
Pine Ridge Reservation and Trust Lands, NE--SD		48	51				
Pinoleville Rancheria	CA	5					
Puyallup Reservation and Trust Lands	WA	5					
Red Lake Reservation	MN	32					
Rocky Boy's Reservation and Trust Lands	MT	1					
Salt River Reservation	AZ	4	36				
San Carlos Reservation	AZ	26					
Santa Clara Pueblo	NM	108					
Southern Ute Reservation	CO	15					
Turtle Mountain Reservation and Trust Lands, ND--SD		11					
Uintah and Ouray Reservation	UT	38	3				
Umatilla Reservation	OR	53					
White Earth Reservation	MN	61					
Wind River Reservation	WY	118	32	19			
Yakima Reservation and Trust Lands	WA	164					
Yankton Reservation	SD	123	63				
Zuni Pueblo	AZ-NM	5					
Absentee Shawnee-Citizens Band of Potawatomi TJSA	OK	495	57				
Caddo-Wichita-Delaware TJSA	OK	90					
Cherokee TJSA	OK	3379	644	1088	21	154	3
Cheyenne-Arapaho TJSA	OK	1849	937	137			
Chickasaw TJSA	OK	3318	1029	103			
Choctaw TJSA	OK	2620	924	28			
Creek TJSA	OK	5339	279	4108	449	91	
Kaw TJSA	OK	121					
Kiowa-Comanche-Apache-Fort Sill Apache TJSA	OK	1944	483	7666	87	2	
Pawnee TJSA	OK	90	4				
Sac and Fox TJSA	OK	528	7	5			
Seminole TJSA	OK	327	5				
Tonkawa TJSA	OK	197	227				
Creek-Seminole Joint Area TJSA	OK	171					
Barrow	AK	9					
Bethel	AK	26					
Galena	AK	303					
King Salmon	AK	267					
Kotzebue	AK	33					
Ninilchik	AK	16	12	50	6		
St. Paul	AK	17					
Tanana	AK	13					
Apache Choctaw TDSA (state)	LA	256					
Coharie TDSA (state)	NC	1221	627	272	49		
Coquille Indian TDSA	OR	3673	55	5115	771	166	
Jena Band of Choctaw TDSA (state)	LA	761	388	378	10	23	
Klamath TDSA	OR	249	4	359	84	2	
Lumbee TDSA (state)	NC	166	639	1			
Meherrin TDSA (state)	NC	372	583	3			
Mohegan TDSA (state)	CT	144	6	10			
United Houma Nation TDSA (state)	LA	3659	38	734	157	260	44

Source: Census of Population and Housing, 1990: Summary Tape File 1 on CD-ROM, U.S. Bureau of the Census, Washington, D.C. 1991.

★ 477 ★

Ten Leading Causes of Hospitalization - Females

Indian Health Service and Tribal Direct and Contract General Hospitals, Fiscal Year 1989.

Diagnostic category	Female	
	Number of discharges	Percent of total
All categories	60,431	100.0
Obstetric deliveries and complications of pregnancy and puerperium	23,068	38.2
Respiratory system diseases	5,364	8.9
Digestive system diseases	5,180	8.6
Injuries and poisonings	4,030	6.7
Genitourinary system diseases	3,602	6.0
Symptoms and ill-defined conditions	2,796	4.6
Supplementary conditions	2,775	4.6
Circulatory system diseases	2,670	4.4
Endocrine, nutritional and metabolic diseases	1,996	3.3
Mental disorders	1,622	2.7
All other	7,328	12.1

Source: Trends in Indian Health, 1991, U.S. Department of Health and Human Services, Public Health Service, Indian Health Service, p. 64. Primary source: IHS Direct: On-Request Report 21. IHS Contract: On-Request Report 19. Tribal: Area submissions.

★ 478 ★

Ten Leading Causes of Hospitalization - Males

Indian Health Service and Tribal Direct and Contract General Hospitals, Fiscal Year 1989.

Diagnostic category	Male	
	Number of discharges	Percent of total
All categories	36,000	100.0
Injuries and poisonings	6,276	17.4
Respiratory system diseases	5,732	15.9
Digestive system diseases	4,376	12.2
Circulatory system diseases	2,947	8.2
Symptoms and ill-defined conditions	2,775	7.7
Mental disorders	2,574	7.2
Skin and subcutaneous tissue diseases	1,578	4.4
Supplementary conditions	1,573	4.4
Endocrine, nutritional and metabolic diseases	1,428	4.0

[Continued]

★ 478 ★

Ten Leading Causes of Hospitalization - Males
[Continued]

Diagnostic category	Male	
	Number of discharges	Percent of total
Nervous system and sense organs	1,403	3.9
All other	5,338	14.8

Source: Trends in Indian Health, 1991, U.S. Department of Health and Human Services, Public Health Service, Indian Health Service, p. 64. Primary source: IHS Direct: On-Request Report 21. IHS Contract: On-Request Report 19. Tribal: Area submissions.

Indian Health Service

★ 479 ★

IHS Service Population Trends, by Area

IHS (Indian Health Service) service population is shown, by service area, for fiscal years 1982 through 1992.

Area	1982[1]	1983	1984[2]	1985	1986	1987	1988	1989[3]	1990	1991	1992
All areas	871,167	902,701	936,942	961,881	986,551	1,011,837	1,038,121	1,073,886	1,102,001	1,131,013	1,160,896
(Growth factor)	-	(3.62)	(3.79)	(2.66)	(2.56)	(2.56)	(2.60)	(3.45)	(2.62)	(2.63)	(2.64)
Aberdeen	66,755	68,571	70,449	73,296	75,298	77,348	79,455	81,617	83,817	86,088	88,404
Alaska	67,582	69,493	71,499	73,599	75,798	78,088	80,478	82,960	85,538	88,211	90,981
Albuquerque	48,833	49,992	51,186	52,413	53,673	54,966	59,297	59,848	61,283	62,748	64,242
Bemidji	44,675	45,745	46,882	48,068	49,424	50,603	51,959	54,107	55,582	57,120	58,711
Billings	38,641	40,147	41,687	42,851	44,058	45,295	46,569	47,878	49,223	50,601	52,013
California	68,561	70,181	71,962	73,893	75,973	78,208	80,595	83,128	85,818	88,657	91,652
Nashville	28,116	30,309	35,430	35,972	36,527	37,098	37,686	42,468	43,148	43,844	44,556
Navajo	153,332	157,600	161,994	166,511	171,152	175,915	180,802	185,812	190,947	196,203	201,583
Oklahoma	180,419	185,229	189,395	193,661	198,038	202,519	207,105	211,799	216,593	221,497	226,506
Phoenix	78,218	80,256	82,417	84,709	87,123	89,661	92,319	96,626	99,561	102,631	105,842
Portland	79,050	87,795	96,249	98,693	100,836	103,036	105,293	107,606	109,966	112,386	114,865
Tucson	16,985	17,383	17,792	18,215	18,651	19,100	19,563	20,037	20,525	21,027	21,541

Source: Trends in Indian Health, 1991, U.S. Department of Health and Human Services, Public Health Service, Indian Health Service, p. 19. Estimates based on 1978-1987 vital events. *Notes:* 1. Includes Reservation States of Connecticut, Rhode Island, and Texas. 2. Includes Alabama. 3. Includes Massachusetts.

★ 480 ★

Indian Health Service Employees, by Race/Ethnicity, 1989

The number of full-time permanent Indian and non-Indian professional (direct patient care and direct patient care support activities) and administrative support staff employed by the Indian Health Service (IHS) during FY 89 is shown below. The data show that Indian people comprised 56.6 percent of the IHS professional and support staff as of September 30, 1989[1].

Category	Indians	Non-Indians	Total
Physicians	47	757	804
Dentists	18	295	313
Graduate Nurses	755	1,358	2,113
Physician Assistants	76	17	93
Practical Nurses	388	34	422
Nursing Assistants	289	5	294
Sanitarians/Engineering	39	127	166
Pharmacists	44	291	335
Social Worker	84	35	119
Health Educator	19	8	27
Nutritionists/Dietitians	16	77	93
Medical Clerks	276	5	281
Medical Records Librarians	46	21	67
Medical Records Technicians	271	7	278
Dental Auxiliaries	376	17	393
Medical Auxiliaries (Medical Aide, Physical Therapist, Occupational Therapist, Rehabilitation Therapist, Medical Technologist, Medical Technician, Medical Radiology Technician, Medical Machine Technician, Pharmacy Technician, Health Aid/Technician)	459	421	880
Speech Pathologist/Audiologist	3	4	7
All Others[2]	1,679	271	1,950
Total[3]	4,885	3,750	8,635

Source: Annual Report to Congress: Indian Civil Service Retirement Act, P.L. 96- 135, FY 89, p. 18. Notes: 1. Health professions are considered to be the MODVOPP—medicine, osteopathy, dentistry, engineers/sanitarians, optometry, podiatry, pharmacy, nursing, and various allied health professions. 2. Includes staff in the direct patient care and direct patient care support activities category. 3. Data are based on official personnel records. Data may vary in various professional and professional support categories from the Indian Health Service (IHS) program information since some positions are coded to other administrative and management occupational categories and do not reflect the professional category under which the incumbent was initially appointed.

★ 481 ★

Indian Health Service Employees, New Hires, 1989

The total number of health professionals and support staff hired in the IHS during FY 89, is shown.

Category	Indians Hired	Non-Indians Hired	Total
Physicians	23	581	604
Medical Records Librarians	6	3	9
Sanitarians/Engineers	10	39	49
Pharmacists	6	78	84
Physician Assistants	11	61	72
Graduate Nurses	165	503	668
Practical Nurses	66	24	90
Nutritionists/Dietitians	1	14	15
Dentists	11	131	142
Health Educators	2	2	4
Social Workers	11	15	26
Medical Clerks	120	6	126
Medical Record Technicians	98	8	106
Dental Auxiliaries	72	6	78
Medical Auxiliaries (Medical Aid, Physical Therapist, Occupational Therapist, Rehabilitation Therapist, Medical Technologist, Medical Technician, Medical Radiology Technician, Medical Machine Technician, Pharmacy Technician, Health Aid/Technician	156	169	325
Speech Pathologists/Audiologist	0	0	0
All Others[1]	280	105	385
Total[2]	1,038	1,745	2,783

Source: Annual Report to Congress: Indian Civil Service Retirement Act, P.L. 96- 135, FY 89, 19. Notes: During FY 89, the IHS continued its efforts to recruit, hire, and train Indian health professionals and support staff. During FY 89, approximately 3,537 health professionals and support staff were hired in the IHS. Of that number, 1,597 or 45.1 percent were Indian health professionals and support staff working in hospitals and Service Units in the IHS. 1. Includes staff in the direct patient care and direct patient care support activities category. 2. Data are based on official personnel records. Data may vary in various professional support categories from the IHS program information since some positions are coded to other administrative and management occupational categories and do not reflect the professional category under which the incumbent was initially appointed.

★ 482 ★

Indian Health Service Employees, Support Staff, 1989

Indian and non-Indian IHS administrative support staff as of September 30, 1989, is shown.

Organizational Identity	Indians	Non-Indians	Total
Headquarters and Area Offices	2,310	614	2,744

Source: *Annual Report to Congress: Indian Civil Service Retirement Act, P.L. 96- 135, FY 89*, p. 19.

IHS Facilities

★ 483 ★

Accreditation of IHS Health Centers

Indian Health Services Health Center accreditation status[1], January 1, 1991.

Area	IHS health centers			
	Total[2]	Accredited[1]	Not accredited	Accredited as a percent of total
All areas	56	53	3	95
Aberdeen	4	3	1	75
Alaska	1	1	0	100
Albuquerque	8	8	0	100
Bemidji	1	1	0	100
Billings	7	7	0	100
California	-	-	-	-
Nashville	-	-	-	-
Navajo	7	7	0	100
Oklahoma	11	9	2	82
Phoenix	6	6	0	100
Portland	11	11	0	100
Tucson	-	-	-	-

Source: *Trends in Indian Health, 1991*, U.S. Department of Health and Human Services, Public Health Service, Indian Health Service, p. 16. *Notes:* 1. Health centers are accredited by the Joint Commission on the Accreditation of Healthcare Organizations. 2. Excludes health centers not eligible for accreditation survey and under tribal management pursuant to Public Law 93-638.

★ 484 ★

Accreditation of IHS Labs

Indian Health Services laboratory accreditation status, December 31, 1990.[1]

Area	IHS health laboratories					IHS health center laboratories				
	Total	Accredited[1]	Not accredited	Percent accredited	Percent in proficiency testing program[2]	Total	Accredited[1]	Not accredited	Percent accredited	Percent in proficiency testing program[2]
All areas	43	43	0	100	100	47	41	6	87	100
Aberdeen	9	9	0	100	100	4	4	0	100	100
Alaska	3	3	0	100	100	-	-	-	-	-
Albuquerque	5	5	0	100	100	4	4	0	100	100
Bemidji	2	2	0	100	100	2	1	1	50	100
Billings	3	3	0	100	100	6	6	0	100	100
California	-	-	-	-	-	-	-	-	-	-
Nashville	1	1	0	100	100	-	-	-	-	-
Navajo	6	6	0	100	100	5	5	0	100	100
Oklahoma	5	5	0	100	100	11	7	4	64	100
Phoenix	8	8	0	100	100	3	3	0	100	100
Portland	-	-	-	-	-	11	11	0	100	100
Tucson	1	1	0	100	100	1	0	1	0	100

Source: Trends in Indian Health, 1991, U.S. Department of Health and Human Services, Public Health Service, Indian Health Service, p. 17. *Notes:* 1. Laboratories are accredited by the College of American Pathologists, the Joint Commission on the Accreditation of Healthcare Organizations and the Health Care Financing Administration, DHHS. Excludes laboratories under tribal management pursuant to Public Law 93-638. 2. Laboratories participating in the College of American Pathologist (CAP) national proficiency testing program.

★ 485 ★

Bed size - IHS vs. U.S. Hospitals

Indian Health Service hospitals, FY 1990, and U.S. Short-Stay hospitals, CY 1989.

Bed size	Number of hospitals		Percent of total	
	IHS[1]	U.S.	IHS	U.S.
All	43[2]	5,455	100.0[2]	100.0
6-24	14	239	33.3	4.4
25-49	18	949	42.9	17.4
50-99	7	1,288	16.7	23.6
100-199	3	1,331	7.1	24.4
200 +	-	1,648	-	30.2

Source: Trends in Indian Health, 1991, U.S. Department of Health and Human Services, Public Health Service, Indian Health Service, p. 66. Primary source: IHS - Monthly Report of Inpatient Services, September 1990. U.S. - Hospital Statistics, 1990-91 Edition, American Hospital Association, Table 5A. *Notes:* 1. Operated by IHS on September 30, 1990. 2. One IHS hospital closed inpatient services for renovation and showed no beds available by the end of FY 1990. Therefore, percent of total is based on 42 hospitals.

★ 486 ★

Discharge Rates - IHS vs. U.S. Hospitals

Indian Health Service and Tribal Direct and Contract General Hospitals, FY 1989 and U.S. General Short-Stay Hospitals, CY 1988.

Age at admission	Discharges per 1,000 population		% difference IHS rate to U.S. rate
	IHS	U.S.	
All ages	95.3	127.6	-25.3
Under 1 year	367.2	200.6	83.1
1-4 years	43.4	53.3	-18.6
5-14 years	22.3	30.5	-26.9
15-19 years	81.9	82.2	-0.4
20-24 years	129.5	120.6	7.4
25-44 years	107.7	105.2	2.4
45-+64 years	134.8	140.5	-4.1
65 years and over	208.7	334.1	-37.5

Source: Trends in Indian Health, 1991, U.S. Department of Health and Human Services, Public Health Service, Indian Health Service, p. 65. Primary source: IHS - Annual Reports 2C and 31. U.S. - Utilization of Short-Stay Hospitals, Annual Summary of the U.S., NCHS.

★ 487 ★

IHS Hospital Inpatient Workload, by Area and Facility

Workload statistics for IHS (Indian Health Service) hospitals are shown for fiscal year 1990, which ended in September.

	Beds available 09/30/90	Admissions	Discharges	Average daily census	Average length of stay	Newborns		Hospital days	
						Births	ADPL[1]	Adults & Pediatrics	Newborn
All IHS areas	1,699	65,972	66,048	825.2	4.6	12.516	78.3	301,207	28,565
Aberdeen area	277	7,835	7,834	86.8	4.0	732.000	5.1	31,682	1,858
Belcourt, ND	42	971	971	8.3	3.1	77	0.5	3,041	200
Eagle Butte, SD	27	915	922	8.6	3.4	101	0.5	3,1396	175
Fort Yates, ND	16	558	561	4.5	2.9	26	0.2	1,629	60
Pine Ridge, SD	46	1,811	1,802	16.9	3.4	357	2.9	6,164	1,056
Rapid City, SD	40	947	943	14.2	5.5	-	-	5,166	-
Rosebud, SD	35	1,323	1,317	11.0	3.0	166	1.0	4,009	359
Sisseton, SD	18	183	185	2.4	4.9	-	-	889	-
Wagner, SD	23	494	501	5.4	4.0	5	-	1,953	8
Winnebago, NB	30	633	632	15.6	9.0	-	-	5,695	
Alaska area	204	6,965	7,020	121.8	6.4	1,535	9.7	44,442	3,540
Anchorage, AK	140	4,510	4,566	99.3	8.0	972	6.0	36,229	2,190
Barrow, AK	14	590	590	4.0	2.5	96	0.5	1,458	166
Yukon-Kuskokwim-Delta, AK	50	1,865	1,864	18.5	3.6	467	3.2	6,755	1,184
Albuquerque Area	142	5,060	5,067	68.7	5.0	507	3.0	25,078	1,093
Acoma-Laguna, NM	25	607	608	8.4	5.1	-	-	3,073	-
Albuquerque, NM	28	925	921	12.7	5.0	-	-	4,629	-
Mescalero, NM	13	441	443	4.6	3.8	-	-	1,662	-

[Continued]

★487★

IHS Hospital Inpatient Workload, by Area and Facility
[Continued]

	Beds available 09/30/90	Admissions	Discharges	Average daily census	Average length of stay	Newborns		Hospital days	
						Births	ADPL[1]	Adults & Pediatrics	Newborn
Santa Fe, NM	39	1,922	1,925	29.9	5.7	338	2.2	10,914	809
Zuni, NM	37	1,165	1,170	13.2	4.1	169	0.8	4,800	284
Bemidji area	36	1,375	1,375	14.1	3.7	1	-	5,140	2
Cass Lake, MN	13	513	513	5.2	3.7	-	-	1,910	-
Red Lake, MN	23	862	862	8.8	3.7	1	-	3,230	2
Billings area	77	3,208	3,211	30.0	3.4	427	2.8	10,964	1,028
Browning. MT	27	1,389	1,391	12.1	3.2	188	1.2	4,416	430
Crow Agency, MT	34	1,395	1,394	13.8	3.6	239	1.6	5,019	598
Harlem, MT	16	424	426	4.2	3.6	-	-	1,529	-
Nashville area	35	1,118	1,115	16.9	5.5	7	-	6,163	14
Cherokee, NC	35	1,118	1,115	16.9	5.5	7	-	6,163	14
Navajo area	386	18,247	18,244	200.3	4.0	4,917	30.2	73,108	11,009
Chinle, AZ	60	2,858	2,854	33.3	4.2	757	4.1	12,143	1,493
Crownpoint, NM	39	1,057	1,060	9.9	3.4	261	1.3	3,627	466
Fort Defiance, AZ	40	2,063	2,061	24.1	4.3	649	4.5	8,782	1,652
Gallup, NM	112	5,115	5,121	62.6	4.5	1,236	7.8	22,836	2,850
Shiprock, NM	50	3,172	3,176	32.0	3.7	1,035	6.8	11,694	2,469
Tuba City, AZ	85	3,982	3,972	38.4	3.5	979	5.7	14,026	2,079
Oklahoma area	216	10,813	10,795	113.2	3.8	3,256	20.6	41,318	7,532
Carl Albert (ADA), OK	53	2,089	2,088	22.9	4.0	812	5.6	8,366	2,030
Claremore, OK	50	2,831	2,827	28.7	3.7	974	4.9	10,482	1,781
Clinton, OK	11	472	468	6.5	5.0	-	-	2,359	-
Lawton, OK	42	1,423	1,426	16.3	4.2	320	2.5	5,932	913
Wm. W. Hastings (Tahlequah)	60	3,998	3,986	38.8	3.5	1,150	7.7	14,179	2,808
Phoenix area	292	10,473	10,512	157.1	5.5	1,057	6.5	57,329	2,372
Fort Yuma (Winterhaven), CA	17	347	347	4.9	5.1	-	-	1,777	-
Hu-Hu-Kam (Sacaton), AZ	20	706	714	10.1	5.2	4	-	3,704	5
Keams Canyon, AZ	24	775	775	6.7	3.2	117	0.5	2,457	176
Owyhee, NV	15	147	149	2.3	5.8	-	-	857	-
Parker, AZ	20	334	338	5.0	5.4	-	-	1,810	-
Phoenix, AZ	147	6,009	6,035	102.5	6.2	737	5.2	37,397	1,893
San Carlos, AZ	-	5	6	0.1	5.4	4	-	27	4
Whiteriver, AZ	49	2,150	2,148	25.5	4.3	195	0.8	9,300	294
Tucson area	34	878	875	16.4	6.8	77	0.3	5,983	117
Sells, AZ	34	878	875	16.4	6.8	77	0.3	5,983	117

Source: Hospital Inpatient Workload Summary and Comparison with Previous Year, U.S. Department of Health, Public Health Service, Rockville, MD, 1990, p. 24. Primary source: Monthly Report of Inpatient Services (Form IHS-202-1). *Note:* 1. Average daily patient load.

★ 488 ★

IHS Hospital Inpatient Workload, by Year

Workload statistics for IHS (Indian Health Service) hospitals are shown, by fiscal year, from 1970 through 1990.

Fiscal Year	Number of hospitals	Available beds	ADPL[1]	Percent occupancy	Admissions	Hospital days	ALOS[2]	Births
1990	43	1,699	825.2	48.6	65,972	301,207	4.6	12,516
1989	43	1,731	872.8	50.4	71,243	318,587	4.5	13,148
1988	44	1,773	938.5	52.9	76,488	342,836	4.5	13,375
1987	45	1,907	959.8	50.3	76,244	350,342	4.6	13,108
1986	46	1,958	1,017.4	52.0	78,162	362,129	4.6	12,703
1985	47	2,066	1,052.4	50.9	78,423	381,185	4.9	12,645
1984	48	2,137	1,072.3	50.2	77,522	389,911	5.0	12,453
1983	48	2,148	1,119.3	52.1	78,027	406,179	5.2	12,700
1982	47	2,157	1,120.5	51.5	77,070	408,908	5.3	12,262
1981	48	2,179	1,193.3	54.4	81,387	435,651	5.4	11,566
1980	49	2,215	1,178.1	53.2	77,798	427,732	5.5	11,034
1979	48	2,205	1,191.7	54.0	75,174	434,976	5.8	10,583
1978	51	2,222	1,256.4	56.5	77,567	458,583	5.9	10,291
1977	51	2,286	1,302.4	57.0	78,424	475,325	6.1	10,420
1976	51	2,341	1,299.4	55.5	76,382	475,574	6.2	9,920
1975	51	2,452	1,329.8	54.2	74,594	485,374	6.5	9,768
1974	51	2,512	1,376.2	54.8	73,402	502,323	6.8	9,690
1973	51	2,589	1,498.7	56.2	75,245	547,050	7.1	9,844
1972	51	2,625	1,626.0	59.7	76,054	595,235	7.6	9,923
1971	51	2,650	1,627.0	60.3	70,729	593,929	8.0	9,753
1970	51	2,705	1,729.0	63.9	67,877	631,218	8.8	8,928

Source: Hospital Inpatient Workload Summary and Comparison with Previous Year, U.S. Department of Health, Public Health Service, Indian Health Service, Rockville, MD, 1990, p. 6. Primary source: Monthly Report of Inpatient Services (Form IHS-202-1). *Notes:* 1. Average daily patient load. 2. Average length of stay.

Outpatient Services

★ 489 ★

Estimated Population, Outpatient Clinical Impressions, and Inpatient Discharges

Indian Health Service direct and contract facilities, 1989.

	All ages	Percent distributions by age						
		Under 1 year	1-4 years	5-14 years	15-24 years	25-44 years	45-64 years	65 years and over
Estimated user population	100.0	2.0	11.6	21.8	18.8	28.5	11.8	5.6
Outpatient clinical impressions	100.0	7.4	11.7	12.2	15.1	26.6	17.9	9.1
Inpatient discharges	100.0	7.7	5.3	5.1	20.8	32.2	16.7	12.3
Inpatient days	100.0	7.5	3.4	3.9	15.4	29.2	22.0	18.7

Source: Trends in Indian Health, 1991, U.S. Department of Health and Human Services, Public Health Service, Indian Health Service, p. 70.

★ 490 ★

Community Health Representative Contacts

Community health representative[1] client contacts for leading health problems, FY 1990.

Health problem	Number	Percent distribution
Total client contacts[2]	3,171,444	100.0
Maternal/child health	416,072	13.1
Health promotion/disease prevention	383,949	12.1
Gerontological health care	293,267	9.2
Diabetes	280,670	8.9
Adverse environmental condition	251,167	7.9
Hypertension	195,234	6.2
Dental	141,239	4.5
Communicable disease	96,031	3.0
Cancer	56,290	1.8
Substance abuse	39,221	1.2
Community injury control	37,031	1.2
Mental health	25,766	0.8

[Continued]

★ 490 ★

Community Health Representative Contacts
[Continued]

Health problem	Number	Percent distribution
AIDS	20,046	0.6
Other general medical	935,461	29.5

Source: Trends in Indian Health, 1991, U.S. Department of Health and Human Services, Public Health Service, Indian Health Service, p. 89. *Notes:* 1. Community health representatives are Indians selected, employed, and supervised by their tribes. They are trained by IHS to provide specific health care services at the community level. The two leading health functions for community health representatives contacts in FY 1990 were resolving physical, economic and cultural barriers to health care (41 percent); and problem assessment, therapeutic and follow-up services (40 percent). 2. Estimated data based on CHR reports of actual client contacts completed during February, 1990 through September, 1990 and expanded to illustrate the workload for the entire fiscal year beginning October 1, 1989. The total number of contacts reported under setting, function and health care area varies as a result of the manner in which training and administration were reported in each category.

★ 491 ★

IHS Public Health Nursing Visits

Number and percent of visits, by program area, FY 1990.

Program area	Number of visits	Percent distribution
Total visits	344,278	100.0
Morbidity	140,374	40.8
Child health	48,866	14.2
Health promotion/disease prevention	48,519	14.1
Maternal health	39,237	11.4
Communicable disease	23,242	6.8
Mental health	21,462	6.2
School health	8,079	2.3
Accidents/trauma	7,845	2.3
General	6,653	1.9

Source: Trends in Indian Health, 1991, U.S. Department of Health and Human Services, Public Health Service, Indian Health Service, p. 82. Primary source: Indian Health Service, Community Health Activities Report No. 3, Fiscal Year 1990.

★ 492 ★

Outpatient Clinical Impressions for Leading Specific
Conditions: Females

Prenatal care - 168,817

Upper respiratory infection, common cold - 151,261

Diabetes mellitus - 125,370

Otitis media - 115,111

Hypertensive disease - 80,707

Tests only

Well child care - 65,453

Refractive error - 62,617

Physical examination - 58,362

Urinary tract infection - 50,354

Indian Health Service direct and contract facilities, FY 1989.

Condition	Number of clinical impressions
Prenatal care	168,817
Upper respiratory infection, common cold	151,261
Diabetes mellitus	125,370
Otitis media	115,111
Hypertensive disease	80,707
Tests only (lab, x-ray)	77,190
Well child care	65,453
Refractive error	62,617
Physical examination	58,362
Urinary tract infection	50,354

Source: Trends in Indian Health, 1991, U.S. Department of Health and Human Services, Public Health Service, Indian Health Service, p. 69. Primary source: Direct: *Annual report 1C*. Contract: *Annual report 3A*.

★ 493 ★

Outpatient Clinical Impressions for Leading Specific
Conditions: Males

Otitis media - 115,114

Upper respiratory infection, common cold - 108,689

Diabetes mellitus - 73,287

Hypertensive disease - 65,097

Well child care - 64,869

Laceration, open wound - 46,410

Refractive error - 39,343

Physical examination - 37,128

Respiratory allergy, asthma, hay fever - 35,540

Tests only

Indian Health Service direct and contract facilities, FY 1989.

Condition	Number of clinical impressions
Otitis media	115,114
Upper respiratory infection, common cold	108,689
Diabetes mellitus	73,287
Hypertensive disease	65,097
Well child care	64,869
Laceration, open wound	46,410
Refractive error	39,343
Physical examination	37,128
Respiratory allergy, asthma, hay fever	35,540
Tests only (lab, x-ray)	35,389

Source: Trends in Indian Health, 1991, U.S. Department of Health and Human Services, Public Health Service, Indian Health Service, p. 69. Primary source: Direct: Annual report 1C. Contract: Annual report 3A.

★ 494 ★

Outpatient Visits, by Type of Provider

Indian Health Service and Tribal Direct Facilities, FY 1990.

Type of provider	Number of visits	total
Total, all providers	4,634,945	100.0
Primary care providers	3,139,234	67.7
Physician	2,487,721	53.7
Physician assistant	345,214	7.4
Nurse practitioner	170,681	3.7
Contract physician	41,890	0.9
Nurse midwife	41,603	0.9
Pediatric nurse practitioner	17,731	0.4
All other	34,394	0.7
Other providers	1,495,711	32.3
Pharmacist	780,512	16.8
Clinic R.N.	176,626	3.8
Optometrist	117,856	2.5
Licensed Practical Nurse	54,603	1.2
Public Health Nurse	43,411	0.9
Physical therapist	43,011	0.9
All other	279,692	6.0

Source: *Trends in Indian Health, 1991*, U.S. Department of Health and Human Services, Public Health Service, Indian Health Service, p. 71. Primary source: Annual Report 1A.

Preventative Health Care

★ 495 ★

Nutritional Counseling

Number and percent of patient/client contacts to the IHS nutrition and dietetics program[1], FY 1990.

Purpose	Number	% distribution
Total contacts[2]	147,314	100.0
General nutrition	50,087	34.0
Diabetes	38,302	26.0
Weight control	20,624	14.0
Prenatal	13,258	9.0
Fat controlled	8,838	6.0

[Continued]

★ 495 ★

Nutritional Counseling
[Continued]

Purpose	Number	% distribution
Undernutrition	4,419	3.0
Alcohol related	2,946	2.0
Sodium controlled	2,062	1.0
Gestational Diabetes	1,915	1.0
Anemia	1,399	1.0
All other	3,464	2.0

Source: Trends in Indian Health, 1991, U.S. Department of Health and Human Services, Public Health Service, Indian Health Service, p. 81. *Notes:* 1. The Indian Health Service nutrition and dietetics program made approximately 223,500 patient/client contacts during FY 1990. The majority of contacts were in the hospital (40 percent) and the clinic (36 percent). Two-thirds of the nutrition and dietetics program contacts during FY 1990 were for clinical nutritional counseling. 2. Excludes activities that are not direct patient/client services, and activities associated with program planning, administration, evaluation, and continuing education.

★ 496 ★

Prenatal Care, 1986

The percentage of babies born to women obtaining early and late or no care is shown, by race/ethnicity, for 1986.

Care received	All races	American Indian	White	Black	Asian or Pacific Islander					
					Chinese	Japanese	Hawaiian	Filipino	Other	Total
Early	75.9	60.7	79.2	61.6	82.4	86.2	71.0	78.6	71.3	75.6
Late or none	6.0	11.6	5.0	10.6	4.0	2.8	6.5	4.3	7.6	6.0

Source: Health Status of Minorities and Low-Income Groups: Third Edition, U.S. Department of Health and Human Services, Public Health Service, Health Resources and Services Administration, Government Printing Office, Washington, D.C., p. 63. National Center for Health Statistics, Vital Statistics of the United States, 1986, Vol. 1, Natality, Department of Health and Human Services Pub. No. (PHS) 88-1113, Public Health Service, Hyattsville, MD, 1987.

★ 497 ★

Smoking During Pregnancy

Figures reflect results of a study of Native Americans and whites between the ages of 11 and 39 in the state of Washington from 1984 through 1988. Data were collected from Washington State birth certificates. Since 1984 the state has required the mother to specify whether or not she smoked at any time throughout her pregnancy.

Age and marital status	Native Americans			Whites		
	Number births[1]	Number smoked	Percent smoked	Number births[1]	Number smoked	Percent smoked
Total	7,089	2,820	39.8	286,379	73,307	25.6
Married	3,004	966	32.2	237,586	48,228	20.3
Unmarried	4,085	1,854	45.4	48,793	25,079	51.4
Less than 20 years	1,640	620	37.8	27,347	11,579	42.3
20-24 years	2,513	1,059	42.1	81,791	26,835	32.8
25-29 years	1,771	683	38.6	96,276	22,298	23.2
30-34 years	883	347	39.3	61,549	9,891	16.1
35-39 years	228	111	39.4	19,416	2,704	13.9

Source: Robert L. Davis, MD et al., "Smoking During Pregnancy Among Northwest Native Americans," *Public Health Reports*. January-February 1992, p. 67. *Notes:* 1. Excludes 17,147 white births and 533 Native American births for whom smoking status or marital status of mother was unknown.

★ 498 ★

Preventive Health Care by Adolescents

The percent of Native American youths who reported engaging in the following behaviors is shown. Data are based on a survey of 13,923 rural American Indian/Alaska Native adolescents living on or near reservations[1].

Preventive behavior	Male	Female
Physical exam in last two years	56.1	52.1
Seen medicine man or woman in last two years	21.5	19.0
Hearing exam in last two years	55.0	53.9
Eye exam in last two years	66.4	69.8
Dental exam within last year	46.3	52.1
Brush teeth daily	77.1	88.3
Strenuous exercise three times a week	50.6	38.0

Source: The State of Native American Youth Health, February, 1992, Indian Health Service, Maternal and Child Health Bureau, and the Robert Wood Johnson Foundation, p. 15. *Notes:* 1. Caution: Sample was not random and does not fully represent all Native American/Alaska Native groups.

Tribal Hospitals

★ 499 ★

Tribal Hospital Inpatient Workload, by Area and Facility

Workload statistics for tribally operated hospitals are shown for fiscal year 1990.

	Beds available 09/30/90	Admissions	Discharges	Average daily census	Average length of stay	Newborns		Hospital days	
						Births	ADPL[1]	Adults & pediatrics	Newborn
All IHS[2]	266	7,022	7,009	89.8	4.7	774	5.1	32,761	1,851
Alaska area	138	4,547	4,544	59.0	4.7	539	3.7	21,553	1,333
Kanakanak, AK	16	835	833	5.4	24	87	0.6	1,973	229
Maniilaq, AK	25	887	888	6.9	2.8	156	0.8	2,519	292
Mount Edgecumbe, AK	78	2,096	2,094	40.0	7.0	150	1.2	14,608	447
Norton Sound, AK[3]	19	729	729	6.7	3.4	146	1.0	2,453	365
Nashville area	37	927	927	11.0	4.4	-	-	4,033	-
Choctaw, MS	37	927	927	11.0	4.4	-	-	4,033	-
Oklahoma area	91	1,548	1,538	19.7	4.6	235	1.4	7,175	518
Creek Nation, OK	39	549	547	7.5	5.0	-	-	2,731	-
Talihina, OK	52	999	991	12.2	4.4	235	1.4	4,444	518

Source: Hospital Inpatient Workload Summary and Comparison with Previous Year, U.S. Department of Health, Public Health Service, Indian Health Service, Rockville, MD, 1990, p. 26. Primary source: Monthly Report of Inpatient Services (Form IHS-202-1). *Notes:* 1. Average daily patient load. 2. Indian Health Service. 3. Statistics derived from special Area Office.

VA Hospitals

★ 500 ★

Selected Data on Native American Veterans Who Used VA Hospitals, 1986

	Patients discharged during FY 1986	Patients remaining as of September 30, 1986
Total	4,366	220
VA Region		
Northeast	224	12
Mid Atlantic	166	6

[Continued]

★ 500 ★

Selected Data on Native American Veterans Who Used VA Hospitals, 1986
[Continued]

	Patients discharged during FY 1986	Patients remaining as of September 30, 1986
Southeast	73	8
Great Lakes	305	19
Midwest	2,116	110
West	458	31
Southwest	1,024	34
State of residence		
South Dakota	1,060	40
Oklahoma	510	14
Montana	294	21
Arizona	255	15
California	216	16
New York	185	12
New Mexico	183	8
Wisconsin	167	9
Minnesota	165	6
North Dakota	149	15
Nebraska	149	3
Washington	138	6
North Carolina	117	3
All other	778	52
Age		
Under 25 years	30	0
25-34	510	20
35-44	963	62
45-54	772	36
55-64	1,218	48
65-74	718	46
75-84	129	8
85 and over	26	0
Period of service[1]		
Spanish American War	0	0
World War I	18	0
World war II	1,550	74
Pre-Korean conflict	47	2
Korean conflict	790	41
Post-Korean conflict	330	15
Vietnam era	1,261	77
Post-Vietnam era	316	10
Other	54	1

[Continued]

★ 500 ★

Selected Data on Native American Veterans Who Used VA Hospitals, 1986

[Continued]

	Patients discharged during FY 1986	Patients remaining as of September 30, 1986
Service-connected disability status		
Service connected	363	15
Service connected, treated for nonservice-connected conditions	932	51
Nonservice connected	3,020	153
Non-veteran	51	1
Marital status		
Divorced	1,220	66
Married	1,790	81
Never married	736	44
Separated	219	11
Widowed	355	14
Unknown	46	4
Sex		
Male	4,268	217
Female	98	3
Attained length of stay		
30 days or less	3,728	155
31-60 days	473	21
61-90 days	64	12
91-365 days	85	17
366 days or more	16	15
Primary diagnosis (total)	4,366	220
Total psychoses	263	32
Psychoses other than drug or alcohol-related	188	22
Alcohol and drug-related psychoses	75	10
Total other psychiatric	1,045	37
Alcohol dependence/abuse	880	28
All other non-psychotic mental disorders, including drug dependence/abuse	165	9
Total medical and surgical	3,058	151
Heart diseases	379	9
Digestive diseases other than abdominal hernias or cirrhosis	263	16
Injuries and poisonings	233	6

[Continued]

★ 500 ★

Selected Data on Native American Veterans Who Used VA Hospitals, 1986
[Continued]

	Patients discharged during FY 1986	Patients remaining as of September 30, 1986
Factors other than disease or injury affecting health status and resulting in contact with health services	438	48
Malignant neoplasms	196	8
Musculoskeletal system diseases	170	7
Symptoms, signs and ill-defined conditions	171	4
Circulatory system diseases other than heart diseases or cerebrovascular diseases	121	7
All other medical or surgical	1,087	46

Source: U.S. Congress, Senate, Hearing Before the Select Committee on Indian Affairs, *Indian Veterans*, S. HRG. 101-549, U.S. Government Printing Office, Washington, D.C., pp. 211-212. *Notes:* 1. For veterans with multiple periods of service, the most recent period of service is reported.

Health Insurance

★ 501 ★

Medicaid Recipients in 1986

Race/ethnicity	Medicaid beneficiaries	
	Millions	Percent
American Indian, Asian, Alaskan Native, or Pacific Islander	0.7	2.9
Unknown	1.9	8.4
White, Non-Hispanic	11.9	52.8
Black, Non-Hispanic	6.2	27.4
Hispanic	1.9	8.4

Source: "Race/Ethnicity of Medicaid Beneficiaries, Fiscal Year 1986," *Health Status of Minorities and Low-Income Groups: Third Edition*, 1991, p. 351. Primary source: Congressional Research Service. Committee on Energy and Commerce, U.S. House of Representatives, "Medical Source Book: Background Data and Analysis," Nov 1988, U.S. Government Printing Office, Figure 1-6, p. 15. Racial characteristics not reported in Maine, Puerto Rico and the Virgin Islands.

Chapter 7
SOCIAL AND ECONOMIC CONDITIONS

Employment

★ 502 ★

Racial/Ethnic Distribution of the U.S. Workforce

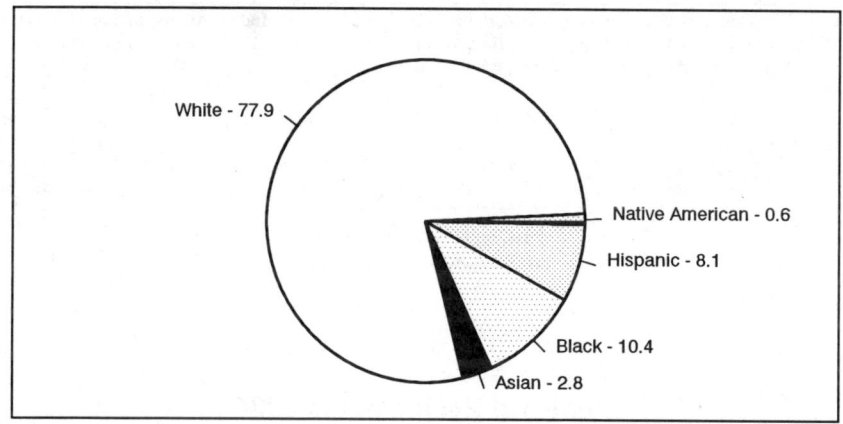

Characteristic	Percent
White	77.9
Black	10.4
Hispanic	8.1
Asian	2.8
Native American	0.6

Source: USA TODAY, January 29, 1993, p. 7A. Primary source: U.S. Census Bureau; Bureau of Labor Statistics; *USA TODAY* analysis of Census data.

★ 503 ★

Percentage Change in the Workforce, by Race/Ethnicity, 1980-1990

Characteristic	Percent	
	Men	Women
Whites	5.7	21.5
Blacks	16.2	29.8
Hispanics[1]	63.9	72.3
Asians	105.2	107.2
Native Americans	36.7	56.0
Total workforce	11.8	26.9

Source: USA TODAY, January 29, 1993, p. 7A. Note: 1. Hispanics may be of any race.

★ 504 ★

American Indian Labor Force Characteristics, by Major Tribal Group, 1980: Abenaki - Pamunkey

Data are estimates based on a sample and are the most recent available.

Major Tribal Group	Persons 16 years old and older	Total persons in labor force	Percent of persons 16 years old and older	Labor force				Total persons not in labor force
				Civilian labor force			Percent	
				Total civilian labor force	Employed persons	Unemployed persons	of civilian labor force	
All American Indians	985,937	580,380	58.9	556,776	492,988	73,788	13.0	405,557
Abenaki (n.e.c)	534	311	58.2	302	229	73	24.2	223
Alabama Coushatta[1]	714	480	67.2	473	454	19	4.0	234
Alaska Native (n.e.c.)	396	187	47.2	187	153	34	18.2	209
Alaskan Athabaskans	6,460	2,873	44.5	2,873	2,254	619	21.5	3,587
Aleut and Eskimo	469	347	74.0	333	285	48	14.4	122
Algonquian (n.e.c.)	1,219	817	67.0	785	649	138	17.3	402
Apache	22,741	13,429	59.1	12,951	11,094	1,857	14.3	9,312
Arapaho	2,818	1,578	56.0	1,531	1,229	302	19.7	1,240
Arikara	935	498	53.3	477	406	71	14.9	437
Assiniboine	2,418	1,336	55.3	1,315	1,108	207	15.7	1,082
Bannock	321	245	76.3	245	206	39	15.9	76
Blackfoot[1]	16,071	10,488	65.3	10,019	8,408	1,611	16.1	5,583
Brotherton	139	85	61.2	85	74	11	12.9	54
Caddo	1,133	664	58.6	664	621	43	6.5	469
Cahuilla	781	456	58.4	450	404	46	10.2	325
California tribes (n.e.c.)	433	288	66.5	280	256	24	8.6	145
Canadian and Latin American	5,582	3,482	62.4	3,374	2,974	400	11.9	2,100
Catawba	794	509	64.1	485	443	42	8.7	285
Cayuse	111	49	44.1	49	45	4	8.2	62
Chehalis	180	121	67.2	121	110	11	9.1	59
Chemakuan	251	150	59.8	150	132	18	12.0	101
Chemehuevi	336	209	62.2	209	193	16	7.7	127

[Continued]

★ 504 ★

American Indian Labor Force Characteristics, by Major Tribal Group, 1980:
Abenaki - Pamunkey
[Continued]

Major Tribal Group	Persons 16 years old and older	Labor force						Total persons not in labor force
		Total persons in labor force	Percent of persons 16 years old and older	Civilian labor force			Percent	
				Total civilian labor force	Employed persons	Unemployed persons	of civilian labor force	
Cherokee	169,389	104,494	61.7	101,570	90,227	11,343	11.2	64,895
Cheyenne	5,782	3,226	55.8	3,156	2,657	499	15.8	2,556
Chickahominy	642	384	59.8	374	368	6	1.6	258
Chickasaw	7,357	4,368	59.4	4,281	3,941	340	7.9	2,989
Chinook	824	436	52.9	422	394	28	6.6	388
Chippewa	45,525	26,484	58.2	26,039	21,121	4,918	18.9	19,041
Chitimacha	204	179	87.7	179	173	6	3.4	25
Choctaw	35,042	21,209	60.5	20,696	18,941	1,755	8.5	13,833
Chumash[1]	959	702	73.2	682	620	62	9.1	257
Clallam	576	296	51.4	296	251	45	15.2	280
Coeur d'Alene	353	201	56.9	201	170	31	15.4	152
Coharie	353	253	71.7	247	221	26	10.5	100
Colorado River	613	411	67.0	411	371	40	9.7	202
Colville	3,377	1,943	57.5	1,930	1,622	308	16.0	1,434
Comanche	6,080	3,725	61.3	3,567	3,076	491	13.8	2,355
Coos	58	42	72.4	42	38	4	9.5	16
Costanoan	318	215	67.6	215	203	12	5.6	103
Cowitz	697	443	63.6	443	405	38	8.6	254
Cree	4,056	2,307	56.9	2,222	1,867	355	16.0	1,749
Creek	18,881	11,453	60.7	11,303	10,345	958	8.5	7,428
Croatan	142	89	62.7	89	81	8	9.0	53
Crow	4,313	2,531	58.7	2,494	1,870	624	25.0	1,782
Cupeno	224	164	73.2	164	144	20	12.2	60
Delaware	3,859	2,454	63.6	2,422	2,226	196	8.1	1,405
Diegueno	871	463	53.2	463	384	79	17.1	408
Eastern tribes (n.e.c.)	1,802	1,094	60.7	1,077	947	130	12.1	708
Flathead	3,257	1,910	58.6	1,884	1,547	337	17.9	1,347
Fort Hall	252	154	61.1	147	128	19	12.9	98
Gabrieleno	1,216	771	63.4	771	679	92	11.9	445
Gros Ventres	1,343	648	48.3	638	529	109	17.1	695
Haida	990	604	61.0	589	431	158	26.8	386
Haliwa	1,331	845	63.5	821	763	58	7.1	486
Hidatsa	945	597	63.2	597	470	127	21.3	348
Hitchiti	10	8	80.0	8	8	-	-	2
Hoopa	1,236	727	58.8	727	566	141	19.4	509
Houma	1,527	838	54.9	822	777	45	5.5	689
Iowa	640	419	65.5	407	355	52	12.8	221
Iroquois	26,486	16,256	61.4	15,835	13,487	2,348	14.8	10,230
Kalispel	119	92	77.3	92	51	41	44.6	27
Karok	1,263	825	65.3	822	659	163	19.8	438
Kaw	505	312	61.8	312	282	30	9.6	193
Kickapoo	1,611	939	58.3	933	762	171	18.3	672
Kiowa	4,414	2,379	53.9	2,338	2,006	332	14.2	2,035
Klamath	1,195	663	55.5	641	520	121	18.9	532
Konkow	287	176	61.3	176	131	45	25.6	111
Kootenai	258	183	70.9	176	142	34	19.3	75
Long Island	253	157	62.1	157	157	-	-	96
Luiseno	820	513	62.6	500	437	63	12.6	307
Lumbee[2]	18,247	11,091	60.8	10,920	10,103	817	7.5	7,156

[Continued]

★ 504 ★

American Indian Labor Force Characteristics, by Major Tribal Group, 1980:
Abenaki - Pamunkey
[Continued]

Major Tribal Group	Persons 16 years old and older	Labor force						Total persons not in labor force
		Total persons in labor force	Percent of persons 16 years old and older	Civilian labor force			Percent	
				Total civilian labor force	Employed persons	Unemployed persons	of civilian labor force	
Lummi[2]	2,541	1,376	54.2	1,349	1,101	248	18.4	1,165
Maidu	726	461	63.5	454	329	125	27.5	265
Makah	659	400	60.7	393	343	50	12.7	259
Maliseet	324	232	71.6	226	185	41	18.1	92
Mandan	597	373	62.5	360	309	51	14.2	224
Mattaponi	100	55	55.0	55	48	7	12.7	45
Menominee	3,629	2,033	56.0	2,014	1,689	325	16.1	1,596
Miami	1,417	1,006	71.0	975	889	86	8.8	411
Miccosukee[1]	51	28	54.9	28	23	5	17.9	23
Micmac[3]	695	441	63.5	407	352	55	13.5	254
Mission Indians	1,890	1,192	63.1	1,192	1,073	119	10.0	698
Miwok	1,424	845	59.3	837	760	77	9.2	579
Modoc	572	350	61.2	331	299	32	9.7	222
Mohegan	369	208	56.4	206	189	17	8.3	161
Mono	955	550	57.6	528	464	64	12.1	405
Nanticoke	785	588	74.9	582	546	36	6.2	197
Narragansett	1,317	716	54.4	708	668	40	5.6	601
Navajo	93,210	44,692	47.9	44,059	37,828	6,231	14.1	48,518
Nez Perce[1]	1,625	920	56.6	913	780	133	14.6	705
Nomalaki	145	96	66.2	96	60	36	37.5	49
Northwest tribes (n.e.c.)	224	132	58.9	132	111	21	15.9	92
Omaha	1,950	1,066	54.7	1,059	828	231	21.8	884
Oregon Athabaskan	419	303	72.3	297	243	54	18.2	116
Osage	4,899	3,034	61.9	2,986	2,734	252	8.4	1,865
Oto	948	541	57.1	541	475	66	12.2	407
Ottawa	4,131	2,541	61.5	2,490	1,973	518	20.8	1,590
Paiute[1]	6,078	3,560	58.6	3,525	3,063	462	13.1	2,518
Pamunkey	276	223	80.8	223	215	8	3.6	53

Source: U.S. Bureau of the Census, *1980 Census of Population, Volume 2, Subject Reports, Characteristics of American Indians, by Tribes and Selected Areas: 1980*, PC80-2-1C, Section 1: Tables I-II, issued September 1989, U.S. Department of Commerce, U.S. Government Printing Office, Washington, D.C., pp. 256-308. *Notes:* (N.E.C.) stands for not elsewhere classified. A dash (-) represents zero or a percent which rounds to less than 0.1. 1. Reporting and/or processing problems may have affected the data for this tribe. 2. Miscoding of entries of "Lummee," "Lummi," "Lumbee," or "Lumbi" may have affected the data for this tribe. 3. Any entry with the spelling "Micmac" was miscoded to Cheyenne River Sioux.

★ 505 ★

American Indian Labor Force Characteristics, by Major Tribal Group, 1980: Papago - Yurok

Data are estimates based on a sample and are the most recent available.

Major Tribal Group	Persons 16 years old and older	Labor force		Civilian labor force				Total persons not in labor force
		Total persons in labor force	Percent of persons 16 years old and older	Total civilian labor force	Employed persons	Unemployed persons	Percent of civilian labor force	
Papago	8,243	4,099	49.7	4,025	3,466	559	13.9	4,144
Passamaquoddy	1,018	605	59.4	594	461	133	22.4	413
Pawnee	1,680	1,051	62.6	1,035	952	83	8.0	629
Penobscot	953	659	69.2	637	593	44	6.9	294
Peoria	368	222	60.3	222	193	29	13.1	146
Pequot	311	219	70.4	209	158	51	24.4	92
Pima	6,968	3,542	50.8	3,527	3,022	505	14.3	3,426
Piscataway	327	195	59.6	193	185	8	4.1	132
Pit River	735	359	48.8	357	224	133	37.3	376
Pomo	1,867	1,048	56.1	1,021	804	217	21.3	819
Ponca	1,185	613	51.7	607	539	68	11.2	572
Potawatomi	6,583	4,149	63.2	4,082	3,659	423	10.4	2,414
Powhatan	247	166	67.2	166	152	14	8.4	81
Pueblo[1]	26,976	15,048	55.8	14,782	12,619	2,163	14.6	11,928
Puget Sound Salish	4,218	2,198	52.1	2,134	1,811	323	15.1	2,020
Quapaw	645	422	65.4	416	380	36	8.7	223
Quinault	1,041	486	46.7	461	394	67	14.5	555
Rappahannock	222	113	50.9	113	113	-	-	109
Sac and Fox Mesquakie	2,325	1,371	59.0	1,347	1,192	155	11.5	954
Salinan	202	121	59.9	108	101	7	6.5	81
Schaghticoke	131	113	86.3	113	106	7	6.2	18
Seminole[1]	6,866	4,281	62.4	4,204	3,671	533	12.7	2,585
Serrano	152	80	52.6	80	75	5	6.3	72
Shasta	248	141	59.9	134	116	18	13.4	107
Shawnee	3,038	1,818	59.8	1,763	1,590	173	9.8	1,220
Shinnecock	783	556	71.0	533	485	48	9.0	227
Shoshone	6,511	3,528	54.2	3,470	3,004	466	13.4	2,983
Siletz	443	333	75.2	333	271	62	18.6	110
Sioux	47,626	26,296	55.2	25,627	21,076	4,551	17.8	21,330
Siuslaw	221	111	50.2	104	86	18	17.3	110
Spokane	1,161	679	58.5	679	534	145	21.4	482
Stockbridge	1,059	677	63.9	655	580	95	14.5	382
Tlingit	5,852	3,475	59.4	3,456	2,788	688	19.3	2,377
Tolowa	213	129	60.6	129	74	55	42.6	84
Tonkawa	150	91	60.7	91	89	2	2.2	59
Tsimshian	1,092	608	55.7	608	514	94	15.5	484
Umatilla	617	370	60.0	363	305	58	16.0	247
Ute	3,491	1,961	56.2	1,949	1,687	262	13.4	1,530
Wailaki[2]	375	132	35.2	132	108	24	18.2	243
Walla-Walla	183	87	47.5	87	65	22	25.3	96
Wampanoag	978	558	57.1	558	472	86	15.4	420
Warm Springs	786	408	51.9	408	342	66	16.2	378
Washo	1,004	541	53.9	521	448	73	14.0	463
Wachita	482	284	58.9	271	262	9	3.3	198
Winnebago	3,039	1,691	55.6	1,661	1,292	369	22.2	1,348
Wintu	1,251	676	54.0	676	541	135	20.0	575
Wiyot	189	119	63.0	119	105	14	11.8	70
Yakima	4,020	2,076	51.6	2,033	1,650	383	18.8	1,944

[Continued]

★ 505 ★

American Indian Labor Force Characteristics, by Major Tribal Group, 1980:
Papago - Yurok
[Continued]

Major Tribal Group	Persons 16 years old and older	Labor force							Total persons not in labor force
		Total persons in labor force	Percent of persons 16 years old and older	Civilian labor force					
				Total civilian labor force	Employed persons	Unemployed persons	Percent of civilian labor force		
Yaqui	3,255	1,813	55.7	1,792	1,425	367	20.5		1,442
Yavapai Apache	100	69	69.0	69	56	13	18.8		31
Yokuts	1,149	575	50.0	558	449	109	19.5		574
Yuchi	165	97	58.8	97	88	9	9.3		68
Yuman	4,088	2,239	54.8	2,177	1,887	290	13.3		1,849
Yurok	1,860	987	53.1	960	807	153	15.9		873
Other specified tribes (n.e.c.)	313	179	57.2	179	134	45	25.1		134
All other specified	102	60	58.8	60	54	6	10.0		42
Tribe not specified	22,986	13,849	60.2	13,479	11,683	1,796	13.3		9,137
Tribe not reported	216,672	134,830	62.2	131,050	116,148	14,902	11.4		81,842

Source: U.S. Bureau of the Census, *1980 Census of Population, Volume 2, Subject Reports, Characteristics of American Indians, by Tribes and Selected Areas: 1980,* PC80-2-1C, Section 1: Tables I-II, issued September 1989, U.S. Department of Commerce, U.S. Government Printing Office, Washington, D.C., pp. 256-308. *Notes:* (N.E.C.) stands for not elsewhere classified. A dash (-) represents zero or a percent which rounds to less than 0.1. 1. Reporting and/or processing problems may have affected the data for this tribe. 2. Any Mohawk entry of "Ganienka" was miscoded to Wailaki.

★ 506 ★

Unemployment Rates on the 10 Largest Indian Reservations, 1990

Reservation	Persons 16 & over	Total civilian labor force	Civilian unemployment rate (%)
Fort Apache (White Mountain Apache)	5,721	3,138	35.3
Pine Ridge & trust lands	6,108	2,930	32.7
Blackfeet	4,162	2,340	31.1
San Carlos Apache	4,228	1,819	31.0
Gila River	5,706	2,552	30.6
Navajo & trust lands	87,118	37,954	29.5
Rosebud & trust lands	4,481	2,266	29.5
Hopi & trust lands	4,522	2,170	26.8
Papago (Tohono O'odham)	5,361	1,936	23.4
Zuni Pueblo	4,600	2,962	13.8

Source: Lakota Times, August 12, 1992, p. A2. Primary source: 1990 Census of Population and Housing, U.S. Bureau of Census. *Note:* All data shown are for persons considered as Indian, Eskimo or Aleut.

★ 507 ★

Employment of Native Americans, by Major Industry and Major Tribal Group, 1980: Abenkai-Pamunkey - I

Data are estimates based on a sample and are the most recent available.

Major Tribal Group	Total employed persons, 16 years old and older	Agriculture, forestry, fisheries and mining	Construction	Manufacturing total	Nondurable goods	Durable goods	Transportation	Communications and other public utilities	Wholesale trade
All American Indians	492,968	28,228	41,500	96,522	34,751	61,771	19,923	14,261	14,042
Abenaki (n.e.c)	229	4	23	49	14	35	3	6	23
Alabama Coushatta[1]	454	25	30	139	25	114	31	23	-
Alaska Native (n.e.c.)	153	5	11	33	-	33	12	-	11
Alaskan Athabaskans	2,254	73	221	138	53	85	186	74	24
Aleut and Eskimo	285	12	22	59	11	48	19	16	-
Algonquian (n.e.c.)	649	32	63	103	11	92	20	-	-
Apache	11,094	761	845	1,841	524	1,317	424	303	257
Arapaho	1,229	131	71	94	18	76	24	40	15
Arikara	406	20	9	53	4	49	16	16	12
Assiniboine	1,108	29	50	99	40	59	38	14	19
Bannock	206	21	35	37	11	26	-	-	7
Blackfoot[1]	8,408	355	752	1,520	422	1,098	383	236	207
Brotherton	74	2	-	14	-	14	6	-	-
Caddo	621	10	54	108	58	50	13	5	23
Cahuilla	404	15	35	75	3	72	26	14	6
California tribes (n.e.c.)	256	11	11	51	24	27	26	2	5
Canadian and Latin American	2,974	160	186	806	284	522	111	76	116
Catawba	443	7	58	146	117	29	15	22	9
Cayuse	45	7	-	-	-	-	7	-	6
Chehalis	110	17	-	24	3	21	5	-	-
Chemakuan	132	14	-	4	-	4	-	13	-
Chemehuevi	193	18	13	29	11	18	5	-	-
Cherokee	90,227	4,459	8,089	19,345	6,685	12,660	4,310	2,494	3,213
Cheyenne	2,657	199	182	416	124	292	70	88	72
Chickahominy	368	13	22	112	73	39	52	17	15
Chickasaw	3,941	290	364	689	256	433	183	117	168
Chinook	394	33	32	91	4	87	6	12	-
Chippewa	21,121	766	1,554	4,150	1,067	2,083	778	459	636
Chitimacha	173	12	17	19	-	19	12	7	6
Choctaw	18,941	1,133	1,584	4,120	1,617	2,503	784	607	534
Chumash[1]	620	43	98	106	22	84	38	15	8
Clallam	251	20	12	64	36	28	12	3	-
Coeur d'Alene	170	12	32	37	19	18	-	-	5
Coharie	221	11	6	47	15	32	6	19	8
Colorado River	371	11	17	18	2	16	6	-	8
Colville	1,622	164	89	276	68	208	64	37	66
Comanche	3,076	125	328	606	196	410	128	47	126
Coos	38	6	-	4	-	4	5	6	-
Costanoan	203	3	11	79	30	49	13	-	20
Cowitz	405	-	26	102	27	75	8	2	25
Cree	1,867	101	172	244	70	174	83	59	84
Creek	10,345	594	862	2,007	757	1,250	419	289	286
Croatan	81	6	8	4	4	-	7	-	-
Crow	1,870	199	94	174	62	112	53	45	-
Cupeno	144	-	-	40	6	34	6	12	-
Delaware	2,226	119	194	478	160	318	77	29	120
Diegueno	384	12	31	34	8	26	12	27	27
Eastern tribes (n.e.c.)	947	32	223	265	91	174	37	16	22
Flathead	1,547	163	125	153	23	130	61	50	62
Fort Hall	128	21	-	26	19	7	11	6	7
Gabrieleno	679	19	71	143	25	118	29	27	15
Gros Ventres	529	41	47	44	14	30	9	19	-
Haida	431	17	19	64	22	42	8	17	20

[Continued]

★ 507 ★

Employment of Native Americans, by Major Industry and Major Tribal Group, 1980: Abcnkni-Pamunkey - I

[Continued]

Major Tribal Group	Total employed persons, 16 years old and older	Agriculture, forestry, fisheries and mining	Construction	Manufacturing			Transportation	Communications and other public utilities	Wholesale trade
				Manufacturing total	Nondurable goods	Durable goods			
Haliwa	763	26	141	327	201	126	19	21	9
Hidatsa	470	87	27	19	9	10	10	2	3
Hitchiti	8	-	7	-	-	-	-	-	-
Hoopa	586	12	36	103	21	82	6	-	11
Houma	777	143	51	155	36	119	141	15	21
Iowa	355	15	61	61	21	40	20	-	4
Iroquois	13,487	355	1,105	3,433	1,146	2,287	662	405	346
Kalispel	51	-	-	4	-	4	-	-	-
Karok	659	59	26	161	25	136	42	31	19
Kaw	262	9	11	48	15	33	11	8	21
Kickapoo	752	55	98	119	55	64	50	38	10
Kiowa	2,006	54	117	295	114	181	65	63	48
Klamath	520	29	16	128	34	94	9	8	-
Konkow	131	13	9	35	-	35	17	7	-
Kootenai	142	8	8	20	-	20	4	-	-
Long Island	157	-	-	46	5	41	22	-	-
Luiseno	437	17	57	85	-	85	12	16	20
Lumbee[2]	10,103	667	1,343	4,171	2,900	1,271	119	113	228
Lummi[2]	1,101	161	138	326	214	112	21	14	17
Maidu	329	50	17	81	6	75	8	28	-
Makah	343	16	24	67	11	56	-	3	15
Maliseet	185	25	6	80	59	21	-	7	13
Mandan	309	20	12	26	6	20	2	1	-
Mattaponi	48	-	16	20	2	18	-	-	-
Menominee	1,689	25	64	521	82	439	40	59	18
Miami	889	13	48	217	42	175	47	23	71
Miccosukee[1]	23	13	-	-	-	-	-	-	-
Micmac[3]	352	17	18	118	82	36	8	6	4
Mission Indians	1,073	31	77	205	42	163	33	23	54
Miwok	760	80	58	102	26	76	36	16	21
Modoc	299	26	6	65	14	51	14	4	6
Mohegan	189	-	-	78	29	49	6	-	7
Mono	464	60	33	56	21	35	16	7	25
Nanticoke	546	17	49	107	50	57	8	32	11
Narragansett	668	-	11	178	53	125	32	11	18
Navajo	37,828	3,445	3,226	3,362	1,016	2,346	1,242	1,917	419
Nez Perce[1]	780	89	65	71	10	61	28	39	15
Nomalaki	60	-	3	7	7	-	-	5	-
Northwest tribes (n.e.c.)	111	24	23	16	2	14	-	-	-
Omaha	828	22	53	115	27	88	32	20	20
Oregon Athabaskan	243	6	22	81	9	72	11	1	8
Osage	2,734	209	163	425	166	259	75	80	86
Oto	475	4	68	77	27	50	14	23	8
Ottawa	1,973	84	117	579	145	434	38	73	29
Paiute[1]	3,063	223	291	515	134	381	131	82	15
Pamunkey	215	-	6	59	11	48	6	-	8

Source: U.S. Bureau of the Census, *1980 Census of Population, Volume 2, Subject Reports, Characteristics of American Indians, by Tribes and Selected Areas: 1980,* PC80-2-1C, Section 1: Tables I-II, issued September 1989, U.S. Department of Commerce, U.S. Government Printing Office, Washington, D.C., pp. 256-308. *Notes:* (N.E.C.) stands for not elsewhere classified. A dash (-) represents zero or a percent which rounds to less than 0.1. 1. Reporting and/or processing problems may have affected the data for this tribe. 2. Miscoding of entries of "Lummee," "Lummi," "Lumbee," or "Lumbi" may have affected the data for this tribe. 3. Any entry with the spelling "Micmac" was miscoded to Cheyenne River Sioux.

★ 508 ★

Employment of Native Americans, by Major Industry and Major Tribal Group, 1980: Abenaki-Pamunkey - II

Data are estimates based on a sample and are the most recent available.

Major Tribal Group	Retail trade	Finance, insurance, and real estate	Business and repair services	Personal, entertainment, and recreation services	Professional and related services				Public administration
					Total professional and related services	Health services	Educational services	Other professional and related services	
All American Indians	63,395	16,681	20,090	22,709	98,670	35,466	44,130	19,074	56,967
Abenaki (n.e.c)	32	21	3	12	46	37	2	7	7
Alabama Coushatta[1]	38	13	22	9	58	27	9	22	66
Alaska Native (n.e.c.)	31	6	-	7	31	14	11	6	6
Alaskan Athabaskans	244	112	73	59	622	153	359	110	428
Aleut and Eskimo	11	15	15	14	76	38	32	6	26
Algonquian (n.e.c.)	133	29	36	54	138	48	69	21	41
Apache	1,333	366	493	526	2,171	706	1,036	429	1,774
Arapaho	84	27	23	51	401	91	214	96	268
Arikara	42	2	3	5	118	39	11	38	110
Assiniboine	194	6	44	42	302	154	96	52	271
Bannock	34	-	-	8	48	7	39	2	16
Blackfoot[1]	1,221	335	479	481	1,604	542	660	402	835
Brotherton	22	1	2	-	19	8	11	-	8
Caddo	124	21	26	17	175	95	66	14	45
Cahuilla	47	13	6	22	96	43	31	22	49
California tribes (n.e.c.)	38	-	5	14	52	26	26	-	41
Canadian and Latin American	477	121	141	163	430	182	154	94	187
Catawba	73	12	11	11	67	20	29	18	12
Cayuse	10	-	-	-	1	1	-	-	14
Chehalis	5	-	-	-	18	5	8	5	41
Chemakuan	6	-	-	8	20	-	20	-	67
Chemehuevi	26	13	-	19	47	29	18	-	23
Cherokee	14,296	3,694	4,262	4,453	16,066	6,671	6,309	3,086	5,546
Cheyenne	290	40	105	104	599	212	289	98	492
Chickahominy	27	5	-	13	55	28	19	8	37
Chickasaw	481	180	149	188	782	255	330	197	350
Chinook	66	14	6	19	69	13	29	27	46
Chippewa	2,720	625	732	1,026	4,579	1,903	1,847	829	3,096
Chitimacha	37	15	-	6	19	13	6	-	23
Choctaw	2,587	668	764	750	3,830	1,505	1,710	615	1,580
Chumash[1]	84	33	19	18	118	32	33	53	40
Clallam	53	-	-	-	48	17	31	-	8
Coeur d'Alene	22	-	5	-	17	7	5	5	40
Coharie	21	5	17	12	56	5	35	16	13
Colorado River	33	31	10	4	42	23	12	7	191
Colville	180	72	52	76	379	121	165	93	167
Comanche	437	54	142	95	576	215	256	105	412
Coos	7	5	-	-	-	-	-	-	5
Costanoan	24	-	17	9	21	13	8	-	6
Cowitz	106	21	29	3	66	17	16	33	17
Cree	263	18	69	184	289	62	196	31	301
Creek	1,275	497	381	445	2,310	863	1,084	363	980
Croatan	14	12	5	6	15	8	7	-	4
Crow	116	54	62	64	526	181	296	49	483
Cupeno	-	16	0	12	28	7	-	21	21
Delaware	313	108	74	114	370	158	155	57	230

[Continued]

★ 508 ★

Employment of Native Americans, by Major Industry and Major Tribal Group, 1980: Abenaki-Pamunkey - II

[Continued]

Major Tribal Group	Retail trade	Finance, insurance, and real estate	Business and repair services	Personal, entertainment, and recreation services	Professional and related services				Public administration
					Total professional and related services	Health services	Educational services	Other professional and related services	
Diegueno	27	59	7	30	73	35	24	14	66
Eastern tribes (n.e.c.)	84	8	17	36	144	40	73	31	63
Flathead	179	27	33	62	285	121	95	69	347
Fort Hall	10	5	-	15	19	4	7	8	8
Gabrieleno	59	69	42	4	159	71	54	34	42
Gros Ventres	33	5	24	37	157	60	61	36	113
Haida	44	33	6	7	119	24	58	37	77
Haliwa	57	24	11	6	73	28	37	8	49
Hidatsa	8	16	2	11	135	37	90	8	150
Hitchiti	-	-	-	-	-	-	-	-	1
Hoopa	72	23	28	23	128	37	50	41	144
Houma	68	12	21	38	79	15	40	24	33
Iowa	53	10	14	9	58	5	52	1	50
Iroquois	1,713	478	664	598	2,541	918	1,043	580	1,187
Kalispel	5	-	5	-	8	8	-	-	29
Karok	105	24	27	9	125	51	41	33	31
Kaw	38	17	17	15	49	33	7	9	38
Kickapoo	96	15	22	25	140	39	59	42	94
Kiowa	303	41	52	69	533	191	192	150	366
Klamath	72	31	12	44	100	22	56	22	71
Konkow	20	7	-	-	18	18	-	-	5
Kootenai	12	-	5	7	66	13	21	32	12
Long Island	21	11	-	9	41	13	22	6	7
Luiseno	37	14	21	18	56	20	29	7	84
Lumbee[2]	813	100	203	271	1,553	290	1,047	216	522
Lummi[2]	75	11	17	26	218	50	90	78	77
Maidu	35	6	10	14	75	15	35	25	5
Makah	52	27	14	12	55	18	28	9	58
Maliseet	25	-	-	17	9	-	9	-	3
Mandan	24	10	12	12	121	23	82	16	69
Mattaponi	6	-	-	-	6	-	6	-	-
Menominee	198	34	58	34	328	75	181	72	310
Miami	119	38	23	32	205	80	102	23	53
Miccosukee[1]	-	4	-	-	6	-	6	-	-
Micmac[3]	42	-	12	18	71	25	12	34	38
Mission Indians	250	39	36	48	209	72	97	40	68
Miwok	90	20	54	58	171	56	76	39	54
Modoc	85	4	8	15	60	29	25	6	6
Mohegan	18	29	13	-	26	14	12	-	12
Mono	32	21	-	28	125	67	40	18	61
Nanticoke	72	25	31	32	89	49	23	17	73
Narragansett	75	19	55	41	139	60	41	38	89
Navajo	3,712	580	1,117	1,327	10,384	2,540	6,489	1,355	7,097
Nez Perce[1]	95	25	25	51	168	46	61	61	109
Nomalaki	19	-	6	-	9	2	7	-	11
Northwest tribes (n.e.c.)	19	2	-	2	13	7	6	-	12
Omaha	72	26	40	61	235	102	52	81	132
Oregon Athabaskan	37	2	13	-	40	13	27	-	22

[Continued]

★ 508 ★

Employment of Native Americans, by Major Industry and Major Tribal Group, 1980: Abenaki-Pamunkey - II

[Continued]

Major Tribal Group	Retail trade	Finance, insurance, and real estate	Business and repair services	Personal, entertainment, and recreation services	Professional and related services				Public administration
					Total professional and related services	Health services	Educational services	Other professional and related services	
Osage	431	163	102	112	580	195	265	120	308
Oto	25	12	26	9	135	61	22	52	74
Ottawa	293	57	87	85	361	142	165	54	170
Paiute[1]	325	79	80	312	490	224	166	100	520
Pamunkey	28	13	22	10	40	7	33	-	23

Source: U.S. Bureau of the Census, *1980 Census of Population, Volume 2, Subject Reports, Characteristics of American Indians, by Tribes and Selected Areas: 1980,* PC80-2-1C, Section 1: Tables I-II, issued September 1989, U.S. Department of Commerce, U.S. Government Printing Office, Washington, D.C., pp. 256-308. *Notes:* (N.E.C.) stands for not elsewhere classified. A dash (-) represents zero or a percent which rounds to less than 0.1. 1. Reporting and/or processing problems may have affected the data for this tribe. 2. Miscoding of entries of "Lummee," "Lummi," "Lumbee," or "Lumbi" may have affected the data for this tribe. 3. Any entry with the spelling "Micmac" was miscoded to Cheyenne River Sioux.

★ 509 ★

Employment of Native Americans, by Major Industry and Major Tribal Group, 1980: Papago-Yurok - I

Data are estimates based on a sample and are the most recent available.

Major Tribal Group	Total employed persons, 16 years old and older	Agriculture forestry, fisheries, and mining	Construction	Manufacturing			Transporation	Communications and other public utilities	Wholesale trade
				Manufacturing total	Nondurable goods	Durable goods			
Papago	3,466	355	222	277	109	168	60	99	30
Passamaquoddy	461	26	26	118	50	68	21	7	13
Pawnee	952	46	76	163	56	107	24	24	32
Penobscot	593	12	60	114	30	84	30	16	5
Peoria	193	16	2	62	37	25	-	17	5
Pequot	158	-	-	59	6	53	6	7	-
Pima	3,022	358	125	405	95	312	22	107	54
Piscataway	185	-	44	-	-	-	-	4	8
Pit River	224	33	23	28	-	28	7	-	8
Pomo	804	42	56	246	28	218	15	33	13
Ponca	539	33	46	102	32	70	13	18	5
Potawatomi	3,659	150	268	774	254	520	157	142	198
Powhatan	152	-	15	15	-	15	8	9	9
Pueblo[1]	12,619	1,007	1,004	1,222	322	900	186	299	146
Puget Sound Salish	1,811	124	126	282	90	192	85	55	66
Quapaw	380	18	40	81	12	69	22	-	8
Quinault	394	49	34	103	28	75	15	2	-
Rappahannock	113	13	29	22	10	12	-	5	-
Sac and Fox Mesquakie	1,192	40	134	231	76	155	37	28	39
Salinan	101	15	7	21	7	14	5	-	6
Schaghticoke	106	-	18	19	-	19	10	-	16
Seminole[1]	3,671	160	317	779	387	392	111	122	123
Serrano	75	-	14	24	9	15	-	-	-
Shasta	116	5	6	42	5	37	-	-	10
Shawnee	1,590	55	107	327	97	230	55	38	60
Shinnecock	485	-	19	60	24	36	30	14	4
Shoshone	3,004	315	289	363	164	199	92	36	59
Siletz	271	15	13	65	7	58	7	-	-

[Continued]

★ 509 ★

Employment of Native Americans, by Major Industry and Major Tribal Group, 1980: Papago Yurok - I

[Continued]

Major Tribal Group	Total employed persons, 16 years old and older	Agriculture forestry, fisheries, and mining	Construction	Manufacturing			Transporation	Communications and other public utilities	Wholesale trade
				Manufacturing total	Nondurable goods	Durable goods			
Sioux	21,076	1,165	1,275	2,689	927	1,762	710	460	454
Siuslaw	86	-	-	47	5	42	-	8	-
Spokane	534	57	53	107	29	78	13	11	8
Stockbridge	560	2	37	139	33	106	44	15	16
Tlingit	2,788	150	166	390	129	261	256	47	49
Tolowa	74	2	7	5	5	-	7	-	-
Tonkawa	89	6	2	13	-	13	-	-	-
Tsimshian	514	41	16	91	21	70	70	25	2
Umatilla	305	12	14	56	32	24	27	-	-
Ute	1,667	118	124	281	39	242	31	29	53
Wailaki[2]	108	19	-	22	-	22	5	5	-
Walla-Walla	65	-	11	11	1	10	-	-	-
Wampanoag	472	22	40	50	8	42	11	24	34
Warm Springs	342	13	12	93	9	84	7	-	-
Washo	448	22	50	56	15	41	22	-	-
Wachita	262	10	10	50	34	16	19	7	16
Winnebago	1,292	41	61	261	94	167	23	46	25
Wintu	541	47	21	78	18	60	30	9	19
Wiyot	105	9	9	38	16	22	9	9	-
Yakima	1,650	204	112	267	44	223	38	34	29
Yaqui	1,425	142	121	184	42	142	52	55	75
Yavapai Apache	56	-	15	8	2	6	-	-	-
Yokuts	449	54	28	41	24	17	14	14	-
Yuchi	88	7	-	24	-	24	18	6	2
Yuman	1,887	76	122	247	130	117	21	72	25
Yurok	807	63	65	154	41	113	26	11	17
Other specified tribes (n.e.c.)	134	-	5	12	-	12	13	-	5
All other specified	54	-	5	5	-	5	-	-	-
Tribe not specified	11,683	561	956	2,577	924	1,653	397	408	377
Tribe not reported	116,148	5,942	10,523	26,382	10,184	16,198	5,328	3,297	3,998

Source: U.S. Bureau of the Census, *1980 Census of Population, Volume 2, Subject Reports, Characteristics of American Indians, by Tribes and Selected Areas: 1980*, PC80-2-1C, Section 1: Tables I-II, issued September 1989, U.S. Department of Commerce, U.S. Government Printing Office, Washington, D.C., pp. 256-308. *Notes:* (N.E.C.) stands for not elsewhere classified. A dash (-) represents zero or a percent which rounds to less than 0.1. 1. Reporting and/or processing problems may have affected the data for this tribe. 2. Any Mohawk entry of "Ganienka" was miscoded to Wailaki.

★ 510 ★

Employment of Native Americans, by Major Industry and Major Tribal Group, 1980: Papago-Yurok - II

Data are estimates based on a sample and are the most recent available.

Major Tribal Group	Retail trade	Finance insurance, and real estate	Business and repair services	Personal, entertainment, and recreation services	Professional and related services				Public administration
					Total professional and related services	Health services	Educational services	Other professional and related services	
Papago	237	80	67	204	921	226	546	149	914
Passamaquoddy	9	4	6	4	157	65	54	38	70
Pawnee	101	31	52	50	178	101	62	15	175
Penobscot	49	27	2	7	161	41	84	36	110
Peoria	31	14	6	10	30	13	7	10	-
Pequot	10	16	-	6	38	12	16	10	16
Pima	162	48	114	206	693	268	243	182	728
Piscataway	41	-	-	5	15	6	5	4	68
Pit River	18	5	12	5	49	19	30	-	36
Pomo	105	27	5	69	136	50	40	46	57
Ponca	69	28	11	25	131	42	51	38	58
Potawatomi	489	131	111	147	717	263	282	172	375
Powhatan	6	6	9	10	57	14	23	20	8
Pueblo[1]	1,089	310	569	503	3,387	1,116	1,692	579	2,897
Puget Sound Salish	219	92	40	46	364	96	148	120	312
Quapaw	59	16	27	23	69	26	22	21	19
Quinault	34	13	14	14	46	14	18	14	70
Rappahannock	-	-	12	-	9	-	9	-	23
Sac and Fox Mesquakie	98	57	48	16	257	128	65	64	207
Salinan	8	-	20	-	19	10	9	-	-
Schaghticoke	8	-	-	-	35	10	21	4	-
Seminole[1]	444	185	161	200	680	319	270	91	389
Serrano	6	-	12	9	5	-	5	-	5
Shasta	20	-	-	4	13	6	7	-	16
Shawnee	231	101	20	89	370	155	179	36	137
Shinnecock	44	32	35	28	157	103	31	23	62
Shoshone	364	42	96	170	583	190	276	117	575
Siletz	12	21	17	24	57	24	16	17	40
Sioux	2,228	664	714	899	4,423	1,877	2,501	1,145	4,295
Siuslaw	17	-	7	2	5	-	-	5	-
Spokane	23	27	19	22	92	22	30	40	102
Stockbridge	48	9	20	27	163	63	66	34	40
Tlingit	284	69	154	112	520	187	207	126	591
Tolowa	14	-	-	-	39	2	37	-	-
Tonkawa	-	-	-	-	15	15	-	-	53
Tsimshian	48	6	17	18	77	21	43	13	103
Umatilla	43	6	21	28	37	14	16	7	61
Ute	163	11	72	108	251	63	142	46	448
Wailaki[2]	17	12	-	7	21	9	-	12	-
Walla-Walla	7	5	-	9	12	-	12	-	10
Wampanoag	59	19	13	34	112	29	66	17	54
Warm Springs	10	14	20	23	57	6	10	41	93
Washo	35	3	17	47	76	21	38	17	120
Wachita	39	-	8	9	43	22	19	2	51
Winnebago	123	36	30	59	376	99	136	141	211
Wintu	87	22	54	61	80	30	44	6	33
Wiyot	5	-	-	15	5	-	5	-	6
Yakima	141	69	15	37	315	73	156	86	389

[Continued]

★ 510 ★

Employment of Native Americans, by Major Industry and Major Tribal Group, 1980: Papago-Yurok - II

[Continued]

| Major Tribal Group | Retail trade | Finance insurance, and real estate | Business and repair services | Personal, entertainment, and recreation services | Professional and related services | | | | Public administration |
					Total professional and related services	Health services	Educational services	Other professional and related services	
Yaqui	174	71	99	100	253	76	146	31	99
Yavapai Apache	7	-	-	-	26	12	7	7	-
Yokuts	63	20	18	18	124	46	49	29	55
Yuchi	23	-	-	-	-	-	-	-	8
Yuman	156	60	36	124	419	133	127	159	529
Yurok	90	24	58	46	160	55	100	5	93
Other specified tribes (n.e.c.)	29	-	6	6	32	3	23	6	26
All other specified	9	-	6	-	18	-	12	6	11
Tribe not specified	1,486	515	568	668	2,215	882	912	421	955
Tribe not reported	16,101	4,230	5,274	5,634	19,837	7,725	7,923	4,189	9,702

Source: U.S. Bureau of the Census, *1980 Census of Population, Volume 2, Subject Reports, Characteristics of American Indians, by Tribes and Selected Areas: 1980*, PC80-2-1C, Section 1: Tables I-II, issued September 1989, U.S. Department of Commerce, U.S. Government Printing Office, Washington, D.C., pp. 256-308. *Notes:* (N.E.C.) stands for not elsewhere classified. A dash (-) represents zero or a percent which rounds to less than 0.1. 1. Reporting and/or processing problems may have affected the data for this tribe. 2. Any Mohawk entry of "Ganienka" was miscoded to Wailaki.

★ 511 ★

Employment of Native Americans, by Major Occupation and Major Tribal Group, 1980: Abenaki-Pamunkey - I

Data are estimates based on a sample and are the most recent available.

| Major Tribal Group | Service occupations | | | | Farming, forestry, and fishing occupations | Precision production, craft, and repair occupations | Operators, fabricators, and laborers | | | |
	Total service occupations	Private household occupations	Protective service occupations	Service occupations, except protective and household			Operators, fabricators and laborers total	Machine operators, assemblers, and inspectors	Transportation and material moving occupations	Handlers, equipment cleaners, helpers, and laborers
All American Indians	88,597	3,213	9,948	75,436	18,040	74,436	114,325	52,408	29,402	32,515
Abenaki (n.e.c)	30	10	-	20	4	60	42	20	7	15
Alabama Coushatta[1]	70	-	9	61	19	51	181	59	57	65
Alaska Native (n.e.c.)	40	-	-	40	5	17	55	27	6	22
Alaskan Athabaskans	459	6	10	443	60	243	288	54	116	118
Aleut and Eskimo	46	6	2	38	7	48	58	33	23	2
Algonquian (n.e.c.)	119	12	-	107	28	117	77	29	25	23
Apache	2,310	73	407	1,830	377	1,555	2,616	1,008	766	842
Arapaho	278	4	47	227	51	138	207	87	47	73
Arikara	74	-	7	67	24	39	67	39	21	7
Assiniboine	349	7	15	327	18	92	193	61	24	108
Bannock	49	-	4	45	7	19	49	8	27	14
Blackfoot[1]	1,531	58	216	1,257	260	1,239	1,885	700	613	572
Brotherton	27	-	-	27	1	2	12	6	6	-
Caddo	169	8	10	151	9	85	92	42	16	34
Cahuilla	53	-	8	45	22	52	114	37	24	53
California tribes (n.e.c.)	39	9	-	30	25	28	61	33	18	10
Canadian and Latin American	641	14	51	576	132	418	861	405	212	244
Catawba	75	11	-	64	-	70	146	88	11	47
Cayuse	6	-	6	-	2	-	18	7	5	6
Chehalis	16	-	-	16	20	13	16	8	-	9
Chemakuan	28	-	13	15	-	17	-	-	-	-
Chemehuevi	49	-	-	49	18	15	45	18	6	21

[Continued]

★ 511 ★

Employment of Native Americans, by Major Occupation and Major Tribal Group, 1980: Abenaki-Pamunkey - I

[Continued]

Major Tribal Group	Service occupations				Farming, forestry, and fishing occupations	Precision production, craft, and repair occupations	Operators, fabricators, and laborers			
	Total service occupations	Private household occupations	Protective service occupations	Service occupations, except protective and household			Operators, fabricators and laborers total	Machine operators, assemblers, and inspectors	Transportation and material moving occupations	Handlers, equipment cleaners, helpers, and laborers
Cherokee	14,891	475	1,745	12,671	2,559	15,064	19,971	9,436	5,753	4,782
Cheyenne	506	5	59	442	96	357	589	280	162	147
Chickahominy	37	-	-	37	-	35	152	57	56	39
Chickasaw	588	28	83	477	128	666	839	319	310	210
Chinook	96	12	11	73	23	23	106	41	41	24
Chippewa	4,514	160	378	3,976	674	2,952	4,792	2,347	1,015	1,430
Chitimacha	17	-	-	17	-	37	41	11	30	-
Choctaw	3,149	68	347	2,734	774	2,897	4,497	2,104	1,243	1,150
Chumash[1]	117	-	22	95	28	47	199	61	72	66
Clallam	70	-	7	63	18	4	55	22	13	20
Coeur d'Alene	5	-	-	5	-	20	55	24	20	11
Coharie	42	-	-	42	11	41	55	39	9	7
Colorado River	75	-	6	69	23	69	56	9	15	32
Colville	287	5	7	275	144	128	306	119	88	99
Comanche	496	-	89	407	58	535	683	305	191	187
Coos	7	-	-	7	6	10	5	-	-	5
Costanoan	25	-	5	20	3	39	72	42	7	23
Cowitz	64	-	-	64	-	34	89	24	42	23
Cree	445	34	55	356	69	302	421	140	133	148
Creek	1,609	65	168	1,376	243	1,474	2,334	1,163	632	539
Croatan	9	-	3	6	-	8	4	-	-	4
Crow	355	-	47	308	105	178	252	78	96	78
Cupeno	32	6	8	18	6	12	53	37	6	10
Delaware	304	9	22	273	40	373	440	180	143	117
Diegueno	101	6	23	72	5	40	42	12	21	9
Eastern tribes (n.e.c.)	109	-	16	93	30	267	285	149	64	72
Flathead	328	-	30	298	171	170	336	85	108	143
Fort Hall	9	9	-	-	21	11	56	23	17	16
Gabrieleno	112	-	6	106	21	95	159	64	48	47
Gros Ventres	134	10	8	116	31	74	92	43	15	34
Haida	151	-	-	151	22	47	24	-	15	9
Haliwa	83	-	5	78	45	154	335	191	37	107
Hidatsa	86	-	7	79	83	32	44	19	4	21
Hitchiti	-	-	-	-	-	8	-	-	-	-
Hoopa	109	5	12	92	32	39	123	43	57	23
Houma	87	25	8	54	72	60	412	72	244	96
Iowa	45	-	11	34	15	48	87	21	23	43
Iroquois	2,555	127	256	1,872	317	2,027	3,294	1,869	610	815
Kalispel	33	-	10	23	-	-	14	-	-	14
Karok	143	4	8	131	63	48	160	58	36	66
Kaw	35	-	5	30	-	35	37	28	5	4
Kickapoo	95	-	-	95	39	133	173	106	39	28
Kiowa	280	11	29	240	19	183	394	186	95	113
Klamath	137	8	15	114	18	38	124	66	33	25
Konkow	36	-	5	31	11	16	56	29	14	13
Kootenai	20	-	-	20	6	7	35	7	15	13
Long Island	49	9	-	40	-	32	17	7	10	-
Luiseno	77	-	-	77	25	37	126	51	37	38
Lumbee[2]	1,162	74	145	943	692	1,895	3,909	2,732	834	843
Lummi[2]	151	-	-	151	125	214	301	201	47	53
Maidu	67	-	-	67	44	70	55	35	20	-
Makah	43	8	9	26	41	30	90	26	21	43
Maliseet	29	-	-	29	27	24	72	61	9	2
Mandan	32	6	2	24	18	26	33	9	12	12
Mattaponi	-	-	-	-	-	11	12	12	-	-
Menominee	272	9	29	234	78	214	489	275	49	165
Miami	144	-	16	128	7	123	199	104	61	34
Miccosukee[1]	-	-	-	-	4	-	-	-	-	-
Micmac[3]	79	2	9	68	16	45	93	63	18	12
Mission Indians	153	-	6	147	27	181	277	103	105	68
Miwok	180	26	-	154	39	127	143	32	46	65
Modoc	83	-	-	83	30	12	71	24	35	12
Mohegan	19	-	6	13	-	40	54	54	-	-
Mono	61	-	6	55	28	75	71	40	16	15
Nanticoke	87	18	9	60	15	81	122	50	33	39
Narragansett	178	11	7	160	-	79	126	82	31	13

[Continued]

★ 511 ★

Employment of Native Americans, by Major Occupation and Major Tribal Group, 1980: Abenaki-Pamunkey - I

[Continued]

Major Tribal Group	Service occupations				Farming, forestry, and fishing occupations	Precision production, craft, and repair occupations	Operators, fabricators, and laborers			
	Total service occupations	Private household occupations	Protective service occupations	Service occupations, except protective and household			Operators, fabricators and laborers total	Machine operators, assemblers, and inspectors	Transportation and material moving occupations	Handlers, equipment cleaners, helpers, and laborers
Navajo	8,232	94	746	7,392	802	6,270	8,785	3,262	2,159	3,364
Nez Perce[1]	175	-	16	159	85	108	121	45	39	37
Nomalaki	12	-	-	12	4	3	6	-	-	6
Northwest tribes (n.e.c.)	15	-	-	15	25	29	20	9	7	4
Omaha	200	8	28	164	25	73	188	82	78	28
Oregon Athabaskan	39	-	12	27	12	18	88	34	20	34
Osage	372	16	69	287	124	300	433	216	106	111
Oto	99	-	7	92	-	78	116	48	37	31
Ottawa	424	22	65	337	92	250	562	331	163	68
Paiute[1]	717	37	30	650	93	384	652	254	207	191
Pamunkey	45	-	13	32	-	26	42	27	-	15

Source: U.S. Bureau of the Census, *1980 Census of Population, Volume 2, Subject Reports, Characteristics of American Indians, by Tribes and Selected Areas: 1980,* PC80-2-1C, Section 1: Tables I-II, issued September 1989, U.S. Department of Commerce, U.S. Government Printing Office, Washington, D.C., pp. 256-308. *Notes:* (N.E.C.) stands for not elsewhere classified. A dash (-) represents zero or a percent which rounds to less than 0.1. 1. Reporting and/or processing problems may have affected the data for this tribe. 2. Miscoding of entries of "Lummee," "Lummi," "Lumbee," or "Lumbi" may have affected the data for this tribe. 3. Any entry with the spelling "Micmac" was miscoded to Cheyenne River Sioux.

★ 512 ★

Employment of Native Americans, by Major Occupation and Major Tribal Group, 1980: Abenaki-Pamunkey - II

Data are estimates based on a sample and are the most recent available.

Major Tribal Group	Employed persons 16 years old and older	Managerial and professional specialty occupations			Technical, sales, and administrative support occupations			
		Total	Executive, administrative and managerial occupations	Professional specialty occupations	Total	Technicians and related support occupations	Sales occupations	Administrative support occupations, including clerical
All American Indians	492,988	78,938	35,534	43,404	118,630	13,564	30,101	74,965
Abenaki (n.e.c)	229	36	22	14	57	29	13	15
Alabama Coushatta[1]	454	37	16	21	96	7	15	74
Alaska Native (n.e.c.)	153	21	12	9	15	3	-	12
Alaskan Athabaskans	2,254	460	213	247	744	76	149	519
Aleut and Eskimo	285	40	25	15	86	8	11	67
Algonquian (n.e.c.)	649	171	87	84	137	25	45	67
Apache	11,094	1,735	788	947	2,501	253	585	1,663
Arapaho	1,229	237	74	163	318	86	41	191
Arikara	406	89	35	54	113	13	21	79
Assiniboine	1,108	163	111	52	293	31	70	192
Bannock	206	46	17	29	36	4	23	9
Blackfoot[1]	8,408	1,456	721	735	2,037	209	538	1,290
Brotherton	74	4	1	3	28	9	13	6
Caddo	621	129	74	55	137	25	49	63
Cahuilla	404	80	26	54	83	27	12	44
California tribes (n.e.c.)	256	47	21	26	56	4	8	44
Canadian and Latin American	2,974	363	171	192	559	17	146	396

[Continued]

★ 512 ★

Employment of Native Americans, by Major Occupation and Major Tribal Group, 1980: Abenaki-Pamunkey - II

[Continued]

Major Tribal Group	Employed persons 16 years old and older	Managerial and professional specialty occupations			Technical, sales, and administrative support occupations			
		Total	Executive, administrative and managerial occupations	Professional specialty occupations	Total	Technicians and related support occupations	Sales occupations	Administrative support occupations, including clerical
Catawba	443	45	26	19	107	23	32	52
Cayuse	45	1	-	1	18	-	10	8
Chehalis	110	15	2	13	30	5	5	20
Chemakuan	132	8	8	-	79	-	6	73
Chemehuevi	193	21	6	15	45	-	34	11
Cherokee	90,227	14,883	7,204	7,679	22,859	2,379	7,403	13,077
Cheyenne	2,657	512	203	309	597	61	123	413
Chickahominy	368	37	28	9	107	15	-	92
Chickasaw	3,941	693	308	385	1,027	125	307	595
Chinook	394	66	26	40	80	-	16	64
Chippewa	21,121	3,157	1,523	1,634	5,032	521	1,060	3,451
Chitimacha	173	19	19	-	59	7	26	26
Choctaw	18,941	3,043	1,315	1,728	4,581	529	1,294	2,758
Chumash[1]	620	108	65	43	121	5	32	84
Clallam	251	34	-	34	70	-	20	50
Coeur d'Alene	170	50	31	19	40	6	9	25
Coharie	221	38	7	31	34	5	6	23
Colorado River	371	84	48	36	64	-	2	82
Colville	1,622	299	144	155	458	65	90	303
Comanche	3,076	562	237	325	742	80	203	459
Coos	38	-	-	-	10	-	-	10
Costanoan	203	26	-	26	38	5	14	19
Cowitz	405	83	43	40	135	-	74	61
Cree	1,867	327	157	170	303	21	80	202
Creek	10,345	1,954	773	1,181	2,731	359	615	1,757
Croatan	81	29	14	15	31	-	-	31
Crow	1,870	368	118	250	612	50	94	468
Cupeno	144	13	13	-	28	7	-	21
Delaware	2,226	469	213	256	600	81	223	296
Diegueno	384	56	37	19	105	16	19	70
Eastern tribes (n.e.c.)	947	106	27	79	150	30	54	66
Flathead	1,547	228	123	105	314	30	67	217
Fort Hall	128	9	5	4	22	4	7	11
Gabrieleno	679	87	53	34	205	37	61	107
Gros Ventres	529	75	40	35	123	7	26	90
Haida	431	52	21	31	135	26	27	82
Haliwa	763	28	7	21	118	-	21	97
Hidatsa	470	107	41	66	118	19	14	85
Hitchiti	8	-	-	-	-	-	-	-
Hoopa	586	119	43	76	164	9	34	121
Houma	777	41	11	30	105	26	36	43
Iowa	355	60	36	24	100	23	16	61
Iroquois	13,487	2,191	882	1,309	3,403	396	780	2,227
Kalispel	51	4	4	-	-	-	-	-
Karok	659	80	41	39	165	25	55	85
Kaw	262	54	31	23	121	10	27	84

[Continued]

★ 512 ★

Employment of Native Americans, by Major Occupation and Major Tribal Group, 1980.
Abenaki-Pamunkey - II
[Continued]

Major Tribal Group	Employed persons 16 years old and older	Managerial and professional specialty occupations			Technical, sales, and administrative support occupations			
		Total	Executive, administrative and managerial occupations	Professional specialty occupations	Total	Technicians and related support occupations	Sales occupations	Administrative support occupations, including clerical
Kickapoo	762	116	54	62	206	25	43	138
Kiowa	2,006	515	221	294	615	77	135	403
Klamath	520	62	18	44	141	-	39	102
Konkow	131	-	-	-	12	-	-	12
Kootenai	142	56	32	24	18	-	-	18
Long Island	157	5	-	5	54	7	19	28
Luiseno	437	65	45	20	107	17	6	84
Lumbee[2]	10,103	1,146	403	743	1,299	91	448	760
Lummi[2]	1,101	175	89	86	135	-	26	109
Maidu	329	48	29	19	45	5	11	29
Makah	343	54	21	33	85	6	17	62
Maliseet	185	23	14	9	10	-	3	7
Mandan	309	126	31	95	74	17	5	52
Mattaponi	48	8	8	-	17	-	11	6
Menominee	1,689	225	59	166	411	26	91	294
Miami	889	183	73	110	233	45	68	120
Miccosukee[1]	23	10	10	-	9	9	-	-
Micmac[3]	352	8	7	1	111	14	13	84
Mission Indians	1,073	116	45	17	319	35	102	182
Miwok	760	53	30	23	218	28	28	162
Modoc	299	34	24	10	69	6	27	36
Mohegan	189	37	17	20	39	6	5	28
Mono	464	76	28	48	153	18	27	108
Nanticoke	546	100	51	49	141	20	54	67
Narragansett	668	93	47	46	192	6	43	143
Navajo	37,828	5,685	1,890	3,795	8,054	918	1,548	5,588
Nez Perce[1]	780	174	102	72	117	21	32	64
Nomalaki	60	6	6	-	29	-	14	15
Northwest tribes (n.e.c.)	111	2	2	-	20	-	6	14
Omaha	828	177	99	78	165	26	39	100
Oregon Athabaskan	243	32	11	21	54	-	10	44
Osage	2,734	728	328	400	777	120	240	417
Oto	475	62	35	27	120	27	12	81
Ottawa	1,973	264	77	187	381	74	114	193
Paiute[1]	3,063	463	246	217	754	80	112	562
Pamunkey	215	51	30	21	51	-	17	34

Source: U.S. Bureau of the Census, *1980 Census of Population, Volume 2, Subject Reports, Characteristics of American Indians, by Tribes and Selected Areas: 1980,* PC80-2-1C, Section 1: Tables I-II, issued September 1989, U.S. Department of Commerce, U.S. Government Printing Office, Washington, D.C., pp. 256-308. *Notes:* (N.E.C.) stands for not elsewhere classified. A dash (-) represents zero or a percent which rounds to less than 0.1. 1. Reporting and/or processing problems may have affected the data for this tribe. 2. Miscoding of entries of "Lummee," "Lummi," "Lumbee," or "Lumbi" may have affected the data for this tribe. 3. Any entry with the spelling "Micmac" was miscoded to Cheyenne River Sioux.

★ 513 ★

Employment of Native Americans, by Major Occupation and Major Tribal Group, 1980: Papago-Yurok - I

Data are estimates based on a sample and are the most recent available.

Major Tribal Group	Service occupations				Farming, forestry, and fishing occupations	Precision production, craft, and repair occupations	Operators, fabricators and laborers			
	Total service occupations	Private household occupations	Protective service occupations	Service occupations, except protective and household			Operators, fabricators and laborers total	Machine operators, assemblers, and inspectors	Transporation and material moving occupations	Handlers, equipment cleaners, helpers, and laborers
Papago	890	90	41	759	293	216	895	268	184	443
Passamaquoddy	131	-	16	115	22	35	106	45	19	42
Pawnee	145	10	14	121	27	156	178	109	26	43
Penobscot	102	-	17	85	10	96	109	54	29	26
Peoria	44	-	6	38	10	23	48	29	14	5
Pequot	23	-	-	23	-	14	43	32	-	11
Pima	862	45	99	718	335	287	530	221	131	178
Piscataway	24	-	-	24	9	-	65	12	40	13
Pit River	38	-	-	38	32	26	58	7	40	11
Pomo	113	16	6	91	25	98	255	113	73	69
Ponca	138	-	6	132	33	92	125	42	18	65
Potawatomi	598	6	99	491	93	670	768	313	274	181
Powhatan	35	6	6	23	-	8	31	17	8	6
Pueblo[1]	2,511	178	387	1,946	331	1,669	2,120	685	526	909
Puget Sound Salish	330	12	23	295	150	181	342	93	161	88
Quapaw	41	-	6	35	16	80	68	43	17	8
Quinault	76	5	11	60	55	34	76	33	34	9
Rappahannock	1	-	-	1	-	5	57	24	-	33
Sac and Fox Mesquakie	182	4	13	165	54	175	248	108	57	83
Salinan	-	-	-	-	10	7	49	25	7	17
Schaghticoke	18	-	-	18	-	33	13	8	5	-
Seminole[1]	552	10	68	474	87	614	879	467	143	269
Serrano	9	9	-	-	5	14	24	24	-	-
Shasta	17	-	6	11	11	-	26	20	6	-
Shawnee	276	14	11	251	13	281	285	193	91	31
Shinnecock	110	6	35	69	7	53	66	33	33	-
Shoshone	559	17	44	498	145	406	778	258	216	304
Siletz	62	-	7	55	37	13	57	28	12	17
Sioux	4,750	148	598	4,004	1,053	2,317	3,793	1,522	1,084	1,187
Siuslaw	7	-	-	7	-	13	42	16	10	16
Spokane	137	7	25	105	16	58	139	39	54	46
Stockbridge	126	7	4	115	10	66	139	92	25	22
Tlingit	436	3	36	397	128	365	498	160	132	204
Tolowa	7	-	-	7	2	7	27	14	13	-
Tonkawa	17	-	-	17	6	-	26	13	11	2
Tsimshian	51	11	6	34	30	53	136	24	44	68
Umatilla	74	-	7	67	8	13	115	25	14	78
Ute	358	7	51	300	58	304	321	134	57	130
Wailaki[2]	22	7	-	15	15	5	27	7	15	5
Walla-Walla	28	-	5	23	-	7	19	10	4	5
Wampanoag	78	-	8	70	22	33	73	19	32	22
Warm Springs	58	-	8	50	7	9	93	43	20	30
Washo	104	5	17	82	27	58	96	36	26	34
Wichita	27	-	-	27	-	17	97	53	22	22
Winnebago	295	9	28	258	46	126	262	139	33	90
Wintu	122	3	14	105	43	15	117	47	34	36
Wiyot	6	-	-	6	13	14	38	29	9	-
Yakima	260	-	54	206	201	146	259	88	62	109
Yaqui	307	6	12	289	130	257	379	142	71	166
Yavapai Apache	19	-	-	19	-	8	9	2	-	7
Yokuts	84	-	17	67	44	41	101	21	48	32
Yuchi	-	-	-	-	7	13	38	19	6	13
Yuman	380	22	48	310	116	216	422	135	124	163
Yurok	156	2	12	142	68	115	133	59	31	43
Other specified tribes (n.e.c.)	11	-	-	11	7	15	11	-	6	5
All other specified	4	-	-	4	-	15	-	-	-	-
Tribe not specified	2,062	103	203	1,756	508	1,689	2,682	1,353	580	749
Tribe not reported	18,943	815	2,323	15,805	4,069	18,982	29,202	13,899	7,386	7,917

Source: U.S. Bureau of the Census, *1980 Census of Population, Volume 2, Subject Reports, Characteristics of American Indians, by Tribes and Selected Areas: 1980,* PC80-2-1C, Section 1: Tables I-II, issued September 1989, U.S. Department of Commerce, U.S. Government Printing Office, Washington, D.C., pp. 256-308. *Notes:* (N.E.C.) stands for not elsewhere classified. A dash (-) represents zero or a percent which rounds to less than 0.1. 1. Reporting and/or processing problems may have affected the data for this tribe. 2. Any Mohawk entry of "Ganienka" was miscoded to Wailaki.

★ 514 ★

Employment of Native Americans, by Major Occupation and Major Tribal Group, 1980: Papago-Yurok - II

Data are estimates based on a sample and are the most recent available.

Major Tribal Group	Employed persons 16 years old and older	Managerial and professional specialty occupations			Technical, sales, and administrative support occupations			
		Total	Executive administrative, and managerial occupations	Professional specialty occupations	Total	Technicians and related support occupations	Sales occupations	Administrative support occupations, including clerical
Papago	3,466	509	187	322	663	85	72	506
Passamaquoddy	461	72	28	44	95	28	4	63
Pawnee	952	181	68	113	265	21	33	211
Penobscot	593	117	64	53	159	26	26	107
Peoria	193	19	6	13	49	-	6	43
Pequot	158	32	8	24	46	7	8	31
Pima	3,022	394	181	213	614	132	56	426
Piscataway	185	18	12	6	69	4	-	65
Pit River	224	7	7	-	63	20	5	38
Pomo	804	105	38	67	208	21	60	127
Ponca	539	48	12	36	103	15	21	67
Potawatomi	3,659	675	287	388	857	124	232	501
Powhatan	152	56	27	29	22	-	4	18
Pueblo[1]	12,619	2,425	1,150	1,275	3,363	673	466	2,224
Puget Sound Salish	1,811	323	176	147	485	57	92	336
Quapaw	380	88	64	24	87	7	25	55
Quinault	394	39	11	28	114	17	20	77
Rappahannock	113	12	-	12	38	7	5	26
Sac and Fox Mesquakie	1,192	152	99	53	381	27	47	307
Salinan	101	9	-	9	26	-	5	21
Schaghticoke	106	7	1	6	35	-	16	19
Seminole[1]	3,671	555	237	318	984	111	224	649
Serrano	75	-	-	-	23	-	6	17
Shasta	116	22	6	16	40	8	19	13
Shawnee	1,590	306	175	131	429	70	113	246
Shinnecock	485	71	23	48	178	13	38	127
Shoshone	3,004	417	178	239	699	69	143	487
Siletz	271	25	12	13	77	4	-	73
Sioux	21,076	3,759	1,530	2,229	5,404	543	1,014	3,847
Siuslaw	86	9	9	-	15	-	10	5
Spokane	534	80	37	43	104	18	26	60
Stockbridge	560	87	36	51	132	24	44	64
Tlingit	2,788	475	295	180	888	69	88	731
Tolowa	74	19	-	19	12	-	-	12
Tonkawa	89	17	11	6	23	-	-	23
Tsimshian	514	99	37	62	145	27	21	97
Umatilla	305	52	5	47	43	14	-	29
Ute	1,687	279	148	131	367	68	89	210
Wailaki[2]	108	12	6	6	27	-	11	16
Walla-Walla	65	6	-	6	5	-	5	-
Wampanoag	472	100	35	65	168	8	44	114
Warm Springs	342	70	41	29	105	-	-	105
Washo	448	62	42	20	101	7	14	80
Wichita	262	51	33	18	70	20	6	44
Winnebago	1,292	244	116	128	319	26	51	242
Wintu	541	116	73	43	128	6	27	95

[Continued]

★ 514 ★

Employment of Native Americans, by Major Occupation and Major Tribal Group, 1980: Papago-Yurok - II
[Continued]

Major Tribal Group	Employed persons 16 years old and older	Managerial and professional specialty occupations			Technical, sales, and administrative support occupations			
		Total	Executive administrative, and managerial occupations	Professional specialty occupations	Total	Technicians and related support occupations	Sales occupations	Administrative support occupations, including clerical
Wiyot	104	9	9	-	25	-	5	20
Yakima	1,650	344	152	192	440	25	94	321
Yaqui	1,425	143	55	88	209	26	18	165
Yavapai Apache	56	14	7	7	6	6	-	-
Yokuts	449	82	41	41	97	32	27	38
Yuchi	88	-	-	-	30	-	10	20
Yuman	1,887	323	185	138	430	44	51	335
Yurok	807	174	78	96	161	7	44	110
Other specified tribes (n.e.c.)	134	54	23	31	38	4	9	23
All other specified	54	23	10	13	12	-	9	3
Tribe not specified	11,683	1,750	804	946	2,992	363	765	1,864
Tribe not reported	116,148	17,491	8,140	9,351	27,461	3,124	7,756	16,581

Source: U.S. Bureau of the Census, *1980 Census of Population, Volume 2, Subject Reports, Characteristics of American Indians, by Tribes and Selected Areas: 1980,* PC80-2-1C, Section 1: Tables I-II, issued September 1989, U.S. Department of Commerce, U.S. Government Printing Office, Washington, D.C., pp. 256-308. *Notes:* (N.E.C.) stands for not elsewhere classified. A dash (-) represents zero or a percent which rounds to less than 0.1. 1. Reporting and/or processing problems may have affected the data for this tribe. 2. Any Mohawk entry of "Ganienka" was miscoded to Wailaki.

★ 515 ★

Academic Employment of Doctoral Scientists and Engineers, by Selected Field and Race/Ethnicity, 1979 and 1989

The academic employment of doctoral scientists and engineers is shown, by race/ethnicity and field of study, for 1979 and 1989.

Field	1979					1989				
	Native American	White	Black	Asian	Hispanic	Native American	White	Black	Asian	Hispanic
Total science and engineering	267	138,162	1,721	9,966	2,019	387	177,232	3,299	16,420	3,893
Physical sciences	43	20,085	130	1,801	349	70	21,780	363	2,188	526
Math and computer sciences	-	12,054	128	998	207	32	16,390	169	1,998	428
Environmental sciences	-	4,991	-	176	71	-	6,774	24	383	193
Life sciences	46	43,310	523	3,507	627	80	59,576	927	5,537	1,095
Psychology	38	15,885	284	194	67	44	19,920	531	418	258
Social sciences	90	25,511	542	1,479	312	143	32,900	987	2,147	837
Other sciences	32	4,512	78	306	64	-	2,477	141	359	87
Engineering	-	11,814	35	1,505	322	-	17,415	157	3,390	469

Source: National Science Board, *Science and Engineering Indicators - 1991,* Washington, D.C., U.S. Government Printing Office, 1991, (NSB 91-1) pp. 376. Primary source: Science Resources Studies Division, National Science Foundation, *Characteristics of Doctoral Scientists and Engineers in the United States: 1989,* NSF 91-317. Detailed Statistical Tables (Washington, DC; NSF, 1991); and unpublished tabulations. *Note:* A dash (-) indicates that there are too few cases to estimate.

★ 516 ★

Agricultural Employees of Lands Under BIA Jurisdiction

Number of Employees engaged in agricultural production, excluding grazing and ranching, is shown, by land ownership.

Land ownership	Full-Time		Part-Time		Total
	Indian	Non-Indian	Indian	Non-Indian	
Tribal	1,749	2,479	4,240	518	8,986
Individual	1,812	4,632	3,985	1,310	11,739
Government	-	31	1	8	40
Assigned	3	25	25	-	53
Total	3,564	7,167	8,251	1,836	20,818

Source: Bureau of Indian Affairs Natural Resource Information System Inventory and Production Report, 1989, United States Department of the Interior, Report No. 55-38-X, p. 3. *Note:* A dash (-) indicates no data given in original source.

★ 517 ★

Doctoral Scientists and Engineers Active in Research and Development, by Selected Field and Race/Ethnicity, 1979 and 1989

The number of doctoral scientists and engineers active in research and development is shown, by race/ethnicity and field, for 1979 and 1989.

Field	1979					1989				
	Native American	White	Black	Asian	Hispanic	Native American	White	Black	Asian	Hispanic
Total science and engineering	206	89,395	866	8,173	1,257	302	133,976	2,055	14,627	3,154
Physical sciences	-	13,633	94	1,478	183	68	16,923	306	1,913	432
Math and computer sciences	-	7,199	51	751	131	28	11,264	115	1,636	321
Environmental sciences	-	3,856	-	160	56	-	6,016	22	337	174
Life sciences	46	32,117	340	3,151	520	66	48,732	659	5,042	1,005
Psychology	38	7,804	94	68	30	33	11,650	217	290	85
Social sciences	59	13,651	251	822	171	89	24,016	540	1,820	703
Other sciences	32	2,242	22	269	33	-	1,447	84	319	70
Engineering	-	8,893	-	1,474	133	-	13,928	112	3,270	364

Source: National Science Board, *Science and Engineering Indicators - 1991,* Washington, D.C., U.S. Government Printing Office, 1991, (NSB 91-1) pp. 376. Primary source: Science Resources Studies Division, National Science Foundation, *Characteristics of Doctoral Scientists and Engineers in the United States: 1989,* NSF 91-317. Detailed Statistical Tables (Washington, DC; NSF, 1991); and unpublished tabulations. *Note:* A dash (-) indicates that there are too few cases to estimate.

★ 518 ★

Employment Experience of Eighth Graders

The percentage of eighth graders who reported having worked at various jobs is shown, by race/ethnicity.

Race/Ethnicity	Have not worked for pay	Lawn work	Waiter/ odd jobs	Newspaper route	Baby-sitting	Farm/ manual labor	Clerk/ sales office
Total	19.6	14.7	16.1	5.4	32.5	8.5	3.2
American Indian and Native Alaskan	18.9	13.3	21.2	5.5	30.6	7.1	3.4
Pacific Islander	35.3	9.2	17.0	5.0	22.8	5.4	5.4
Hispanic	31.8	9.8	17.9	4.5	24.3	6.6	5.1
Black	25.4	14.0	18.9	4.4	28.4	4.4	4.5
White	16.0	15.9	15.1	5.8	35.0	9.6	2.6

Source: "Percentage of Eighth Graders Reporting Various Jobs Ever Worked for Pay, by Selected Background Characteristics," *A Profile of the American Eighth Grader*, p. 57. U.S. Department of Education, National Center for Education Statistics, "National Education Longitudinal Study of 1988: Base Year Survey".

★ 519 ★

Managerial and Professional Specialty Occupations Held by Residents of Reservations, 1980: Acoma Pueblo - Isabella

Data are the latest available.

Identified reservation	Persons 16 years and over working in 1980 reference period	Total	Executive, administrative, and managerial occupations			Professional specialty occupations						
			Total	Officials and administrators, public administration	Management related occupations	Total	Engineers and natural scientists	Engineers	Health diagnosing occupations	Health assessment and treating occupations	Teachers, librarians, and counselors	Teachers, elementary and secondary schools
Total American Indian, Eskimo, and Aleut	89,697	11,884	4,964	1,259	1,137	6,920	395	157	29	477	3,778	2,531
Acoma Pueblo, NM	632	56	26	6	5	30	3	1	-	1	16	13
Agua Caliente, CA	-	-	-	-	-	-	-	-	-	-	-	-
Alabama-Coushatta, TX	234	23	11	2	2	12	1	-	-	1	4	3
Alamo, NM	204	14	7	3	-	7	-	-	-	-	4	3
Allegany, NY	381	58	24	6	4	34	1	-	-	2	16	14
Alturas Rancheria, CA	...	...	...	...	...	...	...	...	...	...	...	...
Annette Islands Reserve, AK	398	46	18	1	1	28	2	2	-	2	17	15
Augustine, CA	-	-	-	-	-	-	-	-	-	-	-	-
Bad River, WI	197	35	22	14	-	13	1	-	-	-	10	5
Barona Rancheria, CA	79	7	2	-	-	4	-	-	-	-	3	1
Bay Mills, MI	99	15	10	6	1	5	4	-	-	-	-	-
Benton Paiute, CA	...	...	...	...	...	...	...	...	...	...	...	...
Berry Creek Rancheria, CA	-	-	-	-	-	-	-	-	-	-	-	-
Big Bend Rancheria, CA	...	...	...	...	...	...	...	...	...	...	...	...
Big Cypress, FL	108	12	5	2	1	7	-	-	-	-	6	3
Big Lagoon Rancheria, CA	...	...	...	...	...	...	...	...	...	...	...	...
Big Pine Rancheria, CA	79	9	5	4	-	5	-	-	-	-	5	2
Bishop Rancheria, CA	276	27	14	4	2	13	1	1	-	2	5	2
Blackfeet, MT	1,665	252	117	24	33	134	3	1	-	9	75	60
Bois Forte (Nett Lake), MN	123	24	11	6	-	13	5	2	-	-	4	4
Bridgeport Colony, CA	23	6	1	-	1	5	-	-	-	-	2	1
Brighton, FL	132	11	7	-	3	4	-	-	-	-	3	1
Burns, Oregon	55	11	1	-	-	10	-	-	-	-	6	3

[Continued]

★ 519 ★

Managerial and Professional Specialty Occupations Held by Residents of Reservations, 1980:
Acoma Pueblo - Isabella
[Continued]

Identified reservation	Persons 16 years and over working in 1980 reference period	Managerial and professional specialty occupations										
		Total	Executive, administrative, and managerial occupations			Professional specialty occupations						
			Total	Officials and administrators, public administration	Management related occupations	Total	Engineers and natural scientists	Engineers	Health diagnosing occupations	Health assessment and treating occupations	Teachers, librarians, and counselors	Teachers, elementary and secondary schools
Cabazon, CA	...	...	...	...	...	...	...	...	...	...	...	...
Cachil Dehe Rancheria, CA	...	...	...	...	...	...	...	...	...	...	...	...
Cahuilla, CA	...	...	...	...	...	...	...	...	...	...	...	...
Campo, CA	17	6	1	-	-	5	1	-	-	-	3	-
Camp Verde, AZ	42	6	2	-	1	4	-	-	-	-	4	1
Canoncito, NM	156	23	6	1	-	17	-	-	-	3	8	8
Capitan Grande, CA	-	-	-	-	-	-	-	-	-	-	-	-
Carson Colony, NV	73	4	4	1	1	-	-	-	-	-	-	-
Catawba, SC	395	21	12	-	2	9	2	-	-	-	4	-
Cattaraugus, NY	559	75	31	4	6	43	2	2	-	15	17	6
Cedarville Rancheria, CA	...	...	...	...	...	...	...	...	...	...	...	...
Chehalis, WA	52	11	6	1	3	5	-	-	-	-	4	2
Chemehuevi, CA	...	...	...	...	...	...	...	...	...	...	...	...
Cheyenne River, SD	399	38	21	13	1	17	2	1	-	3	3	2
Chitimacha, LA	65	5	4	-	3	1	-	-	-	1	-	-
Cochiti Pueblo, NM	167	45	14	6	5	31	-	-	-	1	20	3
Cocopah, AZ	83	8	2	2	-	6	-	-	-	-	2	2
Coeur D'Alene, Idaho	146	37	17	7	3	20	1	-	-	1	8	7
Cold Springs Rancheria, CA	11	-	-	-	-	-	-	-	-	-	-	-
Colorado River, AZ-CA	650	89	46	12	10	42	2	-	-	1	24	15
Colville, WA	1,304	219	105	30	23	114	11	2	1	-	54	15
Cortina Rancheria, CA	...	...	...	...	...	...	...	...	...	...	...	...
Coushatta, LA	...	-	...	...	...	...	...	...	...	...	...	...
Coyote Valley Rancheria, CA	...	-	-	...	...	-	-	-	-	-	-	-
Crow, MT	1,039	196	89	31	25	107	7	1	-	6	78	58
Crow Creek, SD	322	37	22	10	2	15	-	-	-	-	13	12
Cuyapaipe, CA	...	...	...	...	...	...	...	...	...	...	...	...
Deer Creek, MN	...	...	...	...	...	...	...	...	...	...	...	...
Dresslerville Colony, NV	50	8	6	1	-	2	-	-	-	-	2	-
Dry Creek Rancheria, CA	4	-	-	-	-	-	-	-	-	-	-	-
Duck Valley, ID-NV	278	33	20	7	1	13	-	-	-	3	6	5
Duckwater, NV	40	4	3	1	-	1	-	-	-	1	-	-
Eastern Cherokee, NC	1,800	193	105	15	7	88	4	4	-	8	43	22
Eastern Pequot, CT	...	...	...	...	...	...	...	...	...	...	...	...
Ely Colony, NV	21	1	-	-	-	1	-	-	-	-	1	1
Enterprise Rancheria, CA	...	...	...	...	...	...	...	...	...	...	...	-
Fallon Colony, NV	16	-	-	-	-	-	-	-	-	-	-	-
Fallon, NV	100	9	1	-	-	8	1	-	-	1	5	-
Flandreau, SD	60	5	3	1	-	2	-	-	-	-	2	1
Flathead, MT	1,216	198	100	22	30	98	10	5	1	7	49	20
Fond du Lac, MN	142	9	3	-	-	5	-	-	-	1	2	-
Fort Apache, AZ	1,837	167	73	17	17	95	7	5	1	8	42	30
Fort Belknap, MT	493	93	33	6	8	60	2	1	-	3	35	27
Fort Berthold, ND	740	102	41	21	4	62	-	-	1	9	37	23
Fort Bidwell, CA	19	9	8	-	5	1	-	-	-	-	1	-
Fort Hall, Idaho	675	101	46	17	5	55	2	2	-	8	24	14
Fort Independence, CA	16	1	1	-	1	-	-	-	-	-	-	-
Fort McDermitt, NV-OR	101	6	4	-	-	2	-	-	-	-	1	1
Fort McDowell, AZ	129	15	7	1	1	8	1	-	-	-	4	3
Fort Mojave, AZ-CA-NV	39	1	-	-	-	1	-	-	-	-	-	-
Fort Peck, MT	1,262	143	62	19	19	81	1	-	2	11	28	20
Fort Totten, ND	462	61	27	6	10	33	1	-	1	-	10	5
Fort Yuma, AZ-CA	339	48	23	14	6	24	-	-	-	2	14	8
Gila Bend, AZ	-	-	-	-	-	-	-	-	-	-	-	-
Gila River, AZ	1,762	157	59	13	21	99	1	1	-	15	50	26
Golden Hill, CT	...	...	...	...	...	...	...	...	...	...	...	...
Goshute, NV-UT	17	-	-	-	-	-	-	-	-	-	-	-
Grand Portage, MN	88	15	12	2	2	3	-	-	-	-	-	-
Grindstone Creek Rancheria, CA	20	1	-	-	-	1	-	-	-	-	-	-
Hannahville Community, MI	76	5	5	2	2	-	-	-	-	-	-	-
Hassanamisco, MA	...	...	...	...	...	...	...	...	...	...	...	...
Havasupai, AZ	86	15	5	2	-	11	-	-	-	-	10	8
Hoh, WA	14	5	-	-	-	5	5	-	-	-	-	-
Hollywood, FL	197	30	19	3	1	11	-	-	-	-	4	1
Hoopa Valley, CA	441	79	35	7	6	44	1	-	-	4	27	19
Hoopa Valley Extension, CA	100	12	5	-	3	7	-	-	-	1	5	1
Hopi, AZ	1,435	183	80	20	16	103	1	1	-	9	75	56
Hopland Rancheria, CA	-	-	-	-	-	-	-	-	-	-	-	-
Hualapai, AZ	236	27	7	6	-	20	-	-	-	1	10	5
Inaja-Cosmit, CA	-	-	-	-	-	-	-	-	-	-	-	-

[Continued]

★ 519 ★

Managerial and Professional Specialty Occupations Held by Residents of Reservations, 1980:
Acoma Pueblo - Isabella
[Continued]

Identified reservation	Persons 16 years and over working in 1980 reference period	Managerial and professional specialty occupations										
		Total	Executive, administrative, and managerial occupations			Professional specialty occupations						
			Total	Officials and administrators, public administration	Management related occupations	Total	Engineers and natural scientists	Engineers	Health diagnosing occupations	Health assessment and treating occupations	Teachers, librarians, and counselors	Teachers, elementary and secondary schools
Indian Township, ME	104	15	8	3	-	8	-	-	-	1	2	2
Iowa, KS-NE	15	1	-	-	-	1	-	-	-	-	-	-
Isabella, MI	146	11	1	-	-	10	-	-	-	4	-	-

Source: U.S. Bureau of the Census, Subject Reports, PC80-2-1D, Part II, *American Indians, Eskimos, and Aleuts on Identified Reservations and in the Historic Areas of Oklahoma (Excluding Urbanized Areas)*, U.S. Government Printing Office, Washington, D.C., 1986, pp. 482-520. *Notes:* A dash (-) represents zero or a percent which rounds to less than 0.1. Also, a dash (-) is used because the number of supplementary questionnaires for the areas was insufficient to produce reliable estimates. Three dots (...) means not applicable, or that the data are being withheld to avoid disclosure of information for individuals.

★ 520 ★

Managerial and Professional Specialty Occupations Held by Residents of Reservations, 1980:
Isleta - Santa Clara Pueblo

Data are the latest available.

Identified reservation	Persons 16 years and over working in 1980 reference period	Managerial and professional specialty occupations										
		Total	Executive, Administrative and managerial occupations			Professional specialty occupations						
			Total	Officials and administrators, public administration	Management related occupations	Total	Engineers and natural scientists	Engineers	Health diagnosing occupations	Health assessment and treating occupations	Teachers, librarians, and counselors	Teachers, elementary and secondary schools
Isleta Pueblo, NM	874	114	53	8	25	61	7	5	-	8	23	19
Jackson Rancheria, CA	...	...	...	...	...	...	...	...	...	...	...	...
Jemez Pueblo, NM	383	42	19	2	11	23	-	-	1	1	11	7
Jicarilla Apache, NM	656	92	49	19	5	43	4	-	-	3	23	11
Kaibab, AZ	42	9	1	-	-	8	-	-	-	-	3	-
Kalispel, WA	36	1	1	1	-	-	-	-	-	-	-	-
Kickapoo, KS	108	8	5	3	-	3	-	-	-	-	-	-
Kootenai, ID	-	-	-	-	-	-	-	-	-	-	-	-
Lac Courte Oreilles, WI	331	47	20	8	7	27	-	-	-	-	24	15
Lac du Flambeau, WI	322	54	25	4	5	29	6	-	-	2	13	8
Laguna Pueblo, NM	1,300	123	51	11	11	72	9	6	-	8	38	29
La Jolla, CA	43	9	4	-	-	6	-	-	-	-	5	2
L'Anse, MI	177	21	14	5	1	6	-	-	-	1	3	1
La Posta, CA	...	...	...	...	...	...	...	...	...	...	...	...
Las Vegas Colony, NV	35	3	3	1	1	-	-	-	-	-	-	-
Laytonville Rancheria, CA	24	-	-	-	-	-	-	-	-	-	-	-
Leech Lake, MN	728	125	49	21	16	77	2	-	-	2	42	22
Likely Rancheria, CA	-	-	-	-	-	-	-	-	-	-	-	-
Lone Pine Rancheria, CA	49	8	5	1	-	4	-	-	-	-	3	1
Lookout Rancheria, CA	...	...	...	...	...	...	...	...	...	...	...	...
Los Coyotes, CA	11	-	-	-	-	-	-	-	-	-	-	-
Lovelock Colony, NV	34	-	-	-	-	-	-	-	-	-	-	-
Lower Brule, SD	243	29	18	4	5	11	-	-	-	-	7	5
Lower Elwah, WA	17	3	-	-	-	3	2	-	-	-	1	-
Lower Sioux Community, MN	25	4	2	2	-	2	-	-	-	-	2	2
Lummi, WA	347	62	35	9	7	27	2	-	-	3	9	5
Makah, WA	318	49	15	2	4	34	6	1	-	1	19	14
Manchester Rancheria, CA	15	-	-	-	-	-	-	-	-	-	-	-
Manzanita, CA	...	...	...	...	...	...	...	...	...	...	...	...
Maricopa, AZ	95	6	2	-	-	4	-	-	-	-	2	2
Mattaponi, VA	23	-	-	-	-	-	-	-	-	-	-	-
Menominee, WI	699	89	35	9	6	54	4	-	-	1	30	13
Mesa Grande, CA	-	-	-	-	-	-	-	-	-	-	-	-
Mescalero Apache, NM	548	56	24	14	1	31	-	-	-	1	21	18
Miccosukee, Florida	134	17	11	3	2	6	-	-	-	-	3	-
Middletown Rancheria, CA	9	1	-	-	-	1	1	1	-	-	-	-
Mille Lacs, MN	-	-	-	-	-	-	-	-	-	-	-	-

[Continued]

★ 520 ★

Managerial and Professional Specialty Occupations Held by Residents of Reservations, 1980: Isleta - Santa Clara Pueblo

[Continued]

identified reservation	Persons 16 years and over working in 1980 reference period	Total	Executive, Administrative and managerial occupations			Professional specialty occupations						
			Total	Officials and administrators, public administration	Management related occupations	Total	Engineers and natural scientists	Engineers	Health diagnosing occupations	Health assessment and treating occupations	Teachers, librarians, and counselors	Teachers, elementary and secondary schools
ississippi Choctaw Reservation, MS	909	118	32	12	6	86	3	-	-	5	43	30
oapa River, NV	47	4	1	-	1	3	-	-	-	-	1	1
ontgomery Creek Rancheria, CA	...	...	...	...	...	...	...	...	...	...	...	...
orongo, CA	96	6	3	-	-	3	1	1	-	-	1	-
uckleshoot, WA	98	20	9	3	1	11	1	-	-	-	5	2
ambe Pueblo, NM	82	19	10	2	3	8	-	-	-	-	5	3
avajo, AZ-NM-UT	22,636	2,934	1,039	197	270	1,895	105	54	6	119	1,154	886
ez Perce, ID	469	66	31	8	8	35	2	-	-	1	22	18
isqually, WA	13	1	1	-	1	-	-	-	-	-	-	-
ooksack, WA	-	-	-	-	-	-	-	-	-	-	-	-
orthern Cheyenne, MT	839	146	53	1	18	93	6	-	-	4	53	32
il Springs, NY	-	-	-	-	-	-	-	-	-	-	-	-
maha, IO-NE	339	48	23	5	7	26	-	-	-	3	9	4
neida, WI	608	75	31	10	6	44	5	2	-	1	26	16
nondaga, NY	-	-	-	-	-	-	-	-	-	-	-	-
ntonagon, MI	-	-	-	-	-	-	-	-	-	-	-	-
sage, OK	1,755	240	111	14	22	129	13	10	5	19	59	42
zette, WA	...	...	...	...	...	...	...	...	...	...	...	...
ala, CA	142	21	10	4	-	11	-	-	-	2	9	5
amunkey, VA	19	-	-	-	-	-	-	-	-	-	-	-
apago, AZ	1,607	185	67	24	15	118	1	1	-	20	62	44
ascua Yaqui, AZ	110	9	6	4	-	3	-	-	-	-	3	1
auma, CA	26	9	6	4	-	3	-	-	-	-	3	-
ayson Comm. of Yavapai-Apache, AZ	-	-	-	-	-	-	-	-	-	-	-	-
echanga, CA	36	2	1	-	-	1	-	-	-	-	1	-
enobscot, MA	127	18	10	2	6	8	1	-	-	1	4	-
curis Pueblo, NM	52	12	5	4	-	6	-	-	-	-	4	4
ne Creek, MI	...	...	...	...	...	...	...	...	...	...	...	...
ne Ridge, SD	2,482	456	166	34	38	290	8	3	3	9	186	131
easant Point, MA	101	19	12	3	1	7	2	-	-	1	4	3
ojoaque Pueblo, NM	41	18	6	4	2	12	3	3	-	-	4	2
oospatuck, NY	13	1	1	-	-	-	-	-	-	-	-	-
ort Gamble, WA	97	9	3	3	-	7	2	-	-	-	3	2
ort Madison, WA	56	7	3	3	-	3	-	-	-	-	1	-
otawatomi, WI	61	7	2	-	1	5	-	-	-	-	2	-
ottawatomi, KS	128	19	13	6	2	5	-	-	-	-	-	-
airie Island Community, MN	28	1	-	-	-	1	-	-	-	1	1	1
uyallup, WA	237	28	13	-	2	16	1	-	1	2	3	2
yramid Lake, NV	226	47	19	11	1	28	16	1	-	-	6	6
uileute, WA	69	17	9	1	2	8	1	-	-	-	4	2
uinault, WA	324	55	32	6	3	23	2	-	-	-	7	4
amah Community, NM	335	61	22	6	2	39	3	3	-	3	24	17
amona, CA	-	-	-	-	-	-	-	-	-	-	-	-
ed Cliff, WI	149	23	13	8	-	11	2	2	-	-	-	-
ed Lake, MN	707	66	23	9	3	43	1	-	-	3	23	17
eno-Sparks Colony, NV	186	18	5	1	2	13	-	-	-	-	7	3
esighini Rancheria, CA	...	...	...	...	...	...	...	...	...	...	...	...
incon, CA	91	13	4	-	-	10	-	-	-	-	8	2
oaring Creek Rancheria, CA	...	...	...	...	...	...	...	...	...	...	...	...
ocky Boy's, MT	391	58	29	11	2	29	1	1	-	3	19	14
osebud, SD	1,279	244	86	22	21	158	2	1	1	12	89	48
ound Valley, CA	142	20	13	2	3	8	-	-	-	4	2	-
umsey Rancheria, CA	...	...	...	...	...	...	...	...	...	...	...	...
ac and Fox, Iowa	141	9	5	1	1	4	-	-	-	-	1	1
ac and Fox, KS-NE	...	...	...	...	...	...	...	...	...	...	...	...
. Croix, WI	116	9	4	2	2	5	-	-	1	2	3	3
. Regis Mohawk, NY	491	87	38	13	5	49	2	2	-	8	33	15
alt River, AZ	880	70	25	4	9	45	-	-	-	2	24	13
an Carlos, AZ	1,442	138	73	20	20	65	7	3	-	3	25	14
andia Pueblo, NM	86	9	3	-	-	6	2	2	-	-	1	-
andy Lake, MN	-	-	-	-	-	-	-	-	-	-	-	-
an Felipe Pueblo, NM	469	54	25	6	7	29	1	1	-	1	18	13
an Ildefonso Pueblo, NM	197	30	13	8	2	17	2	-	-	3	8	2
an Juan Pueblo, NM	287	51	20	2	6	31	-	-	-	3	19	7
an Manuel, CA	-	-	-	-	-	-	-	-	-	-	-	-
an Pasqual, CA	34	3	1	1	-	2	-	-	-	-	1	-

[Continued]

★ 520 ★

Managerial and Professional Specialty Occupations Held by Residents of Reservations, 1980: Isleta - Santa Clara Pueblo

[Continued]

Identified reservation	Persons 16 years and over working in 1980 reference period	Managerial and professional specialty occupations										
		Total	Executive, Administrative and managerial occupations			Professional specialty occupations						
			Total	Officials and administrators, public administration	Management related occupations	Total	Engineers and natural scientists	Engineers	Health diagnosing occupations	Health assessment and treating occupations	Teachers, librarians, and counselors	Teacher elementa and seconda schools
Santa Ana Pueblo, NM	184	24	10	1	6	14	-	-	-	1	7	4
Santa Clara Pueblo, NM	706	137	46	8	15	91	-	-	-	3	50	22

Source: U.S. Bureau of the Census, Subject Reports, PC80-2-1D, Part II, *American Indians, Eskimos, and Aleuts on Identified Reservations and in the Historic Areas Oklahoma (Excluding Urbanized Areas)*, U.S. Government Printing Office, Washington, D.C., 1986, pp. 482-520. *Notes:* A dash (-) represents zero or a percent which rounds less than 0.1. Also, a dash (-) is used because the number of supplementary questionnaires for the areas was insufficient to produce reliable estimates. Three dots (...) means applicable, or that the data are being withheld to avoid disclosure of information for individuals.

★ 521 ★

Managerial and Professional Specialty Occupations Held by Residents of Reservations, 1980: Santa Rosa Rancheria - Zuni Pueblo

Data are the latest available.

Identified reservation	Persons 16 years and over working in 1980 reference period	Managerial and professional specialty occupations										
		Total	Executive, Administrative and management occupations			Professional specialty occupations						
			Total	Offic. and admin. public admin.	Management related occupations	Total	Engineers and natural scientists	Engineers	Health diagnosing occupations	Health assessment and treating occupations	Teachers, librarians, and counselors	Teachers, elementary and secondary schools
Santa Rosa Rancheria, CA	31	1	-	-	-	1	1	-	-	-	-	-
Santa Rosa, CA	...	...	...	...	...	...	...	...	...	...	...	...
Santa Ynez, CA	56	5	4	2	-	1	-	-	-	-	-	-
Santa Ysabel, CA	63	11	3	1	-	9	-	-	-	3	6	5
Santee, Nebraska	124	25	11	5	1	13	-	-	-	-	8	6
Santo Domingo Pueblo, NM	712	34	11	4	5	23	1	-	-	1	15	8
San Xavier, AZ	247	17	9	3	5	8	-	-	-	1	6	3
Sauk-Suiattle, WA	-	-	-	-	-	-	-	-	-	-	-	-
Sault Ste. Marie, MI	-	-	-	-	-	-	-	-	-	-	-	-
Schaghticoke, CT	...	...	...	...	...	...	...	...	...	...	...	...
Shakopee Community, MN	30	2	-	-	-	2	-	-	-	1	1	-
Sheep Ranch Rancheria, CA	...	...	...	...	...	...	...	...	...	...	...	...
Sherwood Valley Rancheria, CA	...	...	...	...	...	...	...	...	...	...	...	...
Shingle Springs Rancheria, CA	-	-	-	-	-	-	-	-	-	-	-	-
Shinnecock, NY	72	20	11	2	2	9	2	-	-	-	3	-
Shoalwater, WA	...	...	...	...	...	...	...	...	...	...	...	...
Sisseton, ND-SD	591	83	36	11	5	47	-	-	-	4	9	9
Skokomish, WA	61	9	-	-	-	9	-	-	-	1	5	2
Skull Valley, UT	-	-	-	-	-	-	-	-	-	-	-	-
Soboba, CA	57	6	2	-	-	4	-	-	-	-	2	1
Sokaogon Chippewa Community, WI	44	12	3	2	-	9	-	-	-	-	3	-
Southern Paiute, UT	50	2	2	-	-	-	-	-	-	-	-	-
Southern Ute, CO	291	39	17	5	3	22	1	-	1	1	14	11
Spokane, WA	451	46	31	11	1	14	1	-	-	2	6	1
Squaxin Island, WA	9	1	1	-	1	-	-	-	-	-	-	-
Standing Rock, ND-SD	1,077	162	76	13	27	85	9	-	-	8	37	28
Stewart's Point Rancheria, CA	20	2	2	-	-	-	-	-	-	-	-	-
Stockbridge, WI	207	33	21	2	3	12	-	-	-	-	9	4
Sulphur Bank Rancheria, CA	18	2	1	1	-	1	-	-	-	-	1	1
Summit Lake, NV	...	...	...	...	...	...	...	...	...	...	...	...
Susanville, CA	30	1	-	-	-	1	-	-	-	-	1	-
Swinomish, WA	139	15	7	3	1	8	1	-	-	-	1	1
Sycuan, CA	8	-	-	-	-	-	-	-	-	-	-	-
Tama, GA	17	-	-	-	-	-	-	-	-	-	-	-
Taos Pueblo, NM	307	35	8	-	4	26	1	1	-	-	12	10
Te-Moak, NV	38	3	3	3	-	-	-	-	-	-	-	-
Tesuque Pueblo, NM	83	9	3	3	-	5	-	-	-	-	3	3

[Continued]

★ 521 ★

Managerial and Professional Specialty Occupations Held by Residents of Reservations, 1980: Santa Rosa Rancheria - Zuni Pueblo

[Continued]

Identified reservation	Persons 16 years and over working in 1980 reference period	Managerial and professional specialty occupations										
		Total	Executive, Administrative and management occupations			Professional specialty occupations						
			Total	Offic. and admin. public admin.	Management related occupations	Total	Engineers and natural scientists	Engineers	Health diagnosing occupations	Health assessment and treating occupations	Teachers, librarians, and counselors	Teachers, elementary and secondary schools
Tigua, TX	105	7	3	1	1	4	-	-	-	-	1	-
Tonawanda, NY	168	17	5	-	-	12	1	1	-	3	6	3
Torres-Martinez, CA	-	-	-	-	-	-	-	-	-	-	-	-
Trinidad Rancheria, CA	20	3	-	-	-	3	-	-	-	-	2	1
Tulalip, WA	241	32	16	4	3	16	1	-	-	-	5	4
Tule River, CA	134	23	13	-	3	10	-	-	-	-	5	2
Tunicabiloxi, LA	...	...	...	...	...	...	...	...	...	...	...	...
Tuolumne Rancheria, CA	26	3	1	-	-	2	1	-	-	-	1	1
Turtle Mountain, ND	961	166	65	18	7	101	1	-	1	9	58	51
Tuscarora, NY	-	-	-	-	-	-	-	-	-	-	-	-
Twenty-Nine Palms, CA	-	-	-	-	-	-	-	-	-	-	-	-
Uintah and Ouray, UT	588	121	64	26	19	57	1	1	-	-	42	33
Umatilla, OR	297	38	14	-	6	25	1	-	-	1	11	7
Upper Sioux Community, MN	21	6	2	-	-	4	-	-	-	-	4	-
Upper Skagit, WA	-	-	-	-	-	-	-	-	-	-	-	-
Ute Mountain, CO-NM	308	37	5	3	-	32	-	-	-	-	16	12
Vermillion Lake, MN	27	3	3	-	-	-	-	-	-	-	-	-
Viejas Rancheria, CA	51	9	4	-	2	5	-	-	-	-	5	-
Walker River, NV	162	22	11	-	-	11	-	-	-	3	6	5
Wampanoag, MA	-	-	-	-	-	-	-	-	-	-	-	-
Warm Springs, OR	602	127	64	21	18	63	7	3	-	1	20	13
Washoe, NV	-	-	-	-	-	-	-	-	-	-	-	-
Western Pequot, CT	...	...	...	...	...	...	...	...	...	...	...	...
White Earth, MN	734	71	36	11	5	35	2	-	-	-	21	10
Wind River, WY	1,119	145	59	12	19	86	4	3	-	7	50	35
Winnebago, Nebraska	317	72	35	10	14	36	1	-	-	4	9	4
Winnemucca Colony, NV	9	-	-	-	-	-	-	-	-	-	-	-
Wisconsin Winnebago Reservation	105	16	12	-	2	4	-	-	-	-	-	-
Woodfords Community, CA	-	-	-	-	-	-	-	-	-	-	-	-
XL Ranch, CA	...	...	...	...	...	...	...	...	...	...	...	...
Yakima, WA	1,532	235	80	13	24	155	20	7	-	6	69	41
Yankton, SD	359	43	28	8	6	15	-	-	-	-	9	4
Yavapai, AZ	28	1	-	-	-	1	-	-	-	-	1	-
Yerington, NV	40	2	2	1	1	-	-	-	-	-	-	-
Yomba, NV	20	2	2	1	1	-	-	-	-	-	-	-
Zia Pueblo, NM	179	26	9	4	4	17	3	1	-	1	7	5
Zuni Pueblo, NM	2,000	162	67	24	10	96	5	3	-	5	45	29
San Felipe/Santa Ana Joint Area, NM	-	-	-	-	-	-	-	-	-	-	-	-
San Felipe/Santo Domingo Joint Area, NM	26	6	2	-	-	4	-	-	-	-	4	4
Other Reservation Lands in MT	-	-	-	-	-	-	-	-	-	-	-	-

Source: U.S. Bureau of the Census, Subject Reports, PC80-2-1D, Part II, *American Indians, Eskimos, and Aleuts on Identified Reservations and in the Historic Areas of Oklahoma (Excluding Urbanized Areas)*, U.S. Government Printing Office, Washington, D.C., 1986, pp. 482-520. *Notes:* A dash (-) represents zero or a percent which rounds to less than 0.1. Also, a dash (-) is used because the number of supplementary questionnaires for the areas was insufficient to produce reliable estimates. Three dots (...) means not applicable, or that the data are being withheld to avoid disclosure of information for individuals.

★ 522 ★

Manufacturing Occupations Held by Residents of Reservations, 1980: Acoma Pueblo - Isabella

Data are the latest available.

Identified reservations	Persons 16 years and over working in 1980 reference period	Precision production, craft, and repair occupations				Operators, fabricators, and laborers						
		Total	Mechanics and repairers	Construction trades	Precision production occupations	Total	Machine operators and tenders, except precision	Fabricators, assemblers, inspectors, and samplers	Transportation occupations			Handlers, equipment cleaners, helpers, and laborers
									Total	Motor vehicle operators	Material moving equipment operators	
Total American Indian, Eskimo, and Aleut	89,697	10,414	2,130	5,488	1,830	17,358	2,628	1,716	4,940	2,856	2,017	8,073
Acoma Pueblo, NM	632	106	12	30	8	168	16	19	49	25	24	84
Agua Caliente, CA	-	-	-	-	-	-	-	-	-	-	-	-
Alabama-Coushatta, TX	234	24	6	10	2	80	27	14	17	8	8	22
Alamo, NM	204	24	4	16	3	59	15	1	11	9	8	22
Allegany, NY	381	59	4	44	10	77	18	9	21	9	9	28
Alturas Rancheria, CA	...	...	...	...	...	...	...	...	...	...	...	...
Annette Islands Reserve, AK	398	55	14	22	19	142	38	1	30	5	25	72
Augustine, CA	-	-	-	-	-	-	-	-	-	-	-	-
Bad River, WI	197	17	1	10	6	32	9	6	2	2	-	-
Barona Rancheria, CA	79	11	2	8	1	27	2	3	9	9	-	15
Bay Mills, MI	99	6	-	6	-	11	-	-	6	4	-	12
Benton Paiute, CA	...	...	...	...	...	...	...	...	...	...	...	5
Berry Creek Rancheria, CA	-	-	-	-	-	-	-	-	-	-	-	-
Big Bend Rancheria, CA	...	...	...	...	...	...	...	...	...	...	...	...
Big Cypress, FL	108	10	1	7	-	10	4	-	5	-	3	2
Big Lagoon Rancheria, CA	...	...	...	...	...	...	...	...	...	...	...	...
Big Pine Rancheria, CA	79	8	-	1	-	13	5	1	1	1	-	6
Bishop Rancheria, CA	276	50	7	16	6	64	12	-	16	7	9	35
Blackfeet, MT	1,665	185	13	136	33	284	71	17	69	37	32	127
Bois Forte (Nett Lake), MN	123	10	2	7	1	17	3	1	5	3	2	8
Bridgeport Colony, CA	23	1	-	1	-	2	-	-	-	-	-	2
Brighton, FL	132	16	-	10	4	25	7	-	16	7	9	3
Burns, Oregon	55	-	-	-	-	15	4	-	3	2	1	8
Cabazon, CA	...	...	...	...	...	...	...	...	...	...	...	...
Cachil Dehe Rancheria, CA	...	...	...	...	...	...	...	...	...	...	...	...
Cahuilla, CA	...	...	...	...	...	...	...	...	...	...	...	...
Campo, CA	17	1	-	1	-	4	-	-	1	-	-	...
Camp Verde, AZ	42	4	1	1	2	14	9	1	1	-	1	2
Canoncito, NM	156	24	7	7	9	26	-	1	-	-	-	4
Capitan Grande, CA	-	-	-	-	-	-	-	1	6	6	-	18
Carson Colony, NV	73	7	5	1	-	17	3	-	7	3	4	6
Catawba, SC	395	107	24	58	25	160	86	15	23	11	12	36
Cattaraugus, NY	559	119	5	91	23	103	36	7	26	7	16	34
Cedarville Rancheria, CA	...	...	...	...	...	...	...	...	...	...	...	...
Chehalis, WA	52	2	-	2	-	6	-	-	1	1	-	5
Chemehuevi, CA	...	...	...	...	...	...	...	...	...	...	...	...
Cheyenne River, SD	399	25	5	15	5	30	1	-	12	11	1	17
Chitimacha, LA	65	22	6	2	1	12	1	-	11	-	6	-
Cochiti Pueblo, NM	167	13	2	5	6	17	1	-	1	1	-	14
Cocopah, AZ	83	6	3	2	1	23	-	1	6	6	-	16
Coeur D'Alene, Idaho	146	8	1	7	-	13	2	1	3	-	3	7
Cold Springs Rancheria, CA	11	1	-	-	1	4	1	-	-	-	-	2
Colorado River, AZ-CA	650	69	30	22	17	100	18	5	35	22	13	42
Colville, WA	1,304	139	39	81	12	265	30	14	122	42	76	99
Cortina Rancheria, CA	...	...	...	...	...	...	...	...	...	...	...	...
Coushatta, LA	...	...	...	...	...	...	...	...	...	...	...	...
Coyote Valley Rancheria, CA	-	-	-	-	-	-	-	-	-	-	...	...
Crow, MT	1,039	76	13	40	14	133	2	8	56	21	36	66
Crow Creek, SD	322	21	-	14	7	44	2	2	13	13	-	28
Cuyapaipe, CA	...	...	...	...	...	...	...	...	...	...	...	...
Deer Creek, MN	...	...	...	...	...	...	...	...	...	...	...	...
Dresslerville Colony, NV	50	4	4	-	-	15	-	5	3	3	-	6
Dry Creek Rancheria, CA	4	1	-	1	-	1	1	-	-	-	-	-
Duck Valley, ID-NV	278	11	2	8	-	45	3	-	16	10	6	26
Duckwater, NV	40	-	-	-	-	12	-	-	6	1	5	6
Eastern Cherokee, NC	1,800	178	29	80	67	482	190	51	96	66	30	145
Eastern Pequot, CT	...	...	...	...	...	...	...	...	...	...	...	...
Ely Colony, NV	21	3	1	2	-	9	-	-	-	-	...	9
Enterprise Rancheria, CA	...	...	...	...	...	...	...	-	-	-	-	...
Fallon Colony, NV	16	4	-	1	1	1	-	-	1	1	-	...
Fallon, NV	100	8	5	4	-	14	1	-	7	1	6	6
Flandreau, SD	60	1	-	-	1	4	1	-	1	1	-	2
Flathead, MT	1,216	131	34	79	13	218	59	13	49	25	22	98
Fond du Lac, MN	142	22	6	6	8	41	9	6	4	2	1	22
Fort Apache, AZ	1,837	143	36	85	22	476	77	23	131	65	66	246
Fort Belknap, MT	493	55	13	29	3	67	1	2	24	13	11	40
Fort Berthold, ND	740	70	4	27	15	99	7	15	33	14	18	43
Fort Bidwell, CA	19	2	-	1	1	3	-	-	1	-	1	2

[Continued]

★ 522 ★

Manufacturing Occupations Held by Residents of Reservations, 1980: Acoma Pueblo - Isabella
[Continued]

Identified reservations	Persons 16 years and over working in 1980 reference period	Precision production, craft, and repair occupations				Operators, fabricators, and laborers						
		Total	Mechanics and repairers	Construction trades	Precision production occupations	Total	Machine operators and tenders, except precision	Fabricators, assemblers, inspectors, and samplers	Transportation occupations			Handlers, equipment cleaners, helpers, and laborers
									Total	Motor vehicle operators	Material moving equipment operators	
Fort Hall, Idaho	675	82	29	31	18	154	12	25	74	36	37	42
Fort Independence, CA	16	2	-	2	-	4	-	-	-	-	-	4
Fort McDermitt, NV-OR	101	22	-	6	15	16	4	3	3	-	3	5
Fort McDowell, AZ	129	10	4	1	5	42	10	3	14	5	9	16
Fort Mojave, AZ-CA-NV	39	-	-	-	-	6	-	1	3	2	1	2
Fort Peck, MT	1,262	178	27	103	34	225	54	19	52	36	15	100
Fort Totten, ND	462	41	3	25	14	104	24	33	22	17	6	25
Fort Yuma, AZ-CA	339	32	6	21	4	37	7	4	5	3	2	21
Gila Bend, AZ	-	-	-	-	-	-	-	-	-	-	-	-
Gila River, AZ	1,762	125	24	61	40	401	58	56	99	66	33	188
Golden Hill, CT	...	...	...	...	...	...	...	...	...	...	...	...
Goshute, NV-UT	17	1	-	-	1	4	-	3	-	-	-	1
Grand Portage, MN	88	4	-	4	-	12	2	1	4	3	1	5
Grindstone Creek Rancheria, CA	20	3	1	2	-	4	-	-	3	-	3	1
Hannahville Community, MI	76	11	7	4	-	9	-	2	2	2	-	5
Hassanamisco, MA	...	...	...	...	...	...	...	...	...	...	...	...
Havasupai, AZ	86	6	1	3	1	22	1	-	1	-	1	20
Hoh, WA	14	2	2	-	-	-	-	-	-	-	-	-
Hollywood, FL	197	6	-	6	-	28	1	2	3	1	1	22
Hoopa Valley, CA	441	36	14	18	5	88	12	3	38	24	14	34
Hoopa Valley Extension, CA	100	10	5	3	2	23	1	-	10	3	6	13
Hopi, AZ	1,435	154	36	94	23	189	23	7	62	43	18	97
Hopland Rancheria, CA	-	-	-	-	-	-	-	-	-	-	-	-
Hualapai, AZ	236	17	3	11	2	41	5	-	20	12	8	16
Inaja-Cosmit, CA	-	-	-	-	-	-	-	-	-	-	-	-
Indian Township, ME	104	8	3	2	3	28	3	-	5	5	-	21
Iowa, KS-NE	15	2	-	-	2	-	-	-	-	-	-	-
Isabella, MI	146	34	5	23	7	20	5	4	4	2	2	7

Source: U.S. Bureau of the Census, Subject Reports, PC80-2-1D, Part II, *American Indians, Eskimos, and Aleuts on Identified Reservations and in the Historic Areas of Oklahoma (Excluding Urbanized Areas)*, U.S. Government Printing Office, Washington, D.C., 1986, pp. 482-520. *Notes:* A dash (-) represents zero or a percent which rounds to less than 0.1. Also, a dash (-) is used because the number of supplementary questionnaires for the areas was insufficient to produce reliable estimates. Three dots (...) means not applicable, or that the data are being withheld to avoid disclosure of information for individuals.

★ 523 ★

Manufacturing Occupations Held by Residents of Reservations, 1980: Isleta - Santa Clara Pueblo

Data are the latest available.

Identified reservations	Persons 16 years and over working in 1980 reference period	Precision production, craft and repair occupations				Operators, fabricators and laborers						
		Total	Mechanics and repaires	Construction trades	Precision production occupations	Total	Machine operators and tenders, except precision	Fabricators, assemblers, inspectors, and samplers	Transportation occupations			Handlers, equipment cleaners, helpers, and laborers
									Total	Motor vehicle operators	Material moving equipment operators	
Isleta Pueblo, NM	874	130	18	71	41	155	29	22	36	25	11	68
Jackson Rancheria, CA	...	...	...	...	...	...	...	...	...	...	...	...
Jemez Pueblo, NM	383	35	11	17	7	102	20	5	14	8	6	63
Jicarilla Apache, NM	656	85	18	53	7	130	7	48	27	11	14	48
Kaibab, AZ	42	2	-	2	-	7	-	1	-	-	-	5
Kalispel, WA	36	2	2	-	-	18	1	2	2	1	1	13
Kickapoo, KS	108	8	-	6	2	31	7	-	9	-	9	15
Kootenai, ID	-	-	-	-	-	-	-	-	-	-	-	-
Lac Courte Oreilles, WI	331	39	4	35	-	45	-	6	8	8	-	32
Lac du Flambeau, WI	322	35	7	10	18	94	7	40	10	6	4	36
Laguna Pueblo, NM	1,300	273	111	50	30	476	34	30	259	159	96	153
La Jolla, CA	43	2	-	2	-	16	-	1	8	2	6	7
L'Anse, MI	177	35	8	23	1	41	6	11	8	6	2	16
La Posta, CA	...	...	...	...	...	...	...	...	...	...	...	...
Las Vegas Colony, NV	35	4	4	-	-	7	2	3	-	-	-	3
Laytonville Rancheria, CA	24	2	1	-	1	12	6	1	1	1	-	4
Leech Lake, MN	728	102	26	71	5	131	15	3	39	26	11	74

[Continued]

★ 523 ★

Manufacturing Occupations Held by Residents of Reservations, 1980: Isleta - Santa Clara Pueblo

[Continued]

Identified reservations	Persons 16 years and over working in 1980 reference period	Precision production, craft and repair occupations				Operators, fabricators and laborers						
		Total	Mechanics and repaires	Construction trades	Precision production occupations	Total	Machine operators and tenders, except precision	Fabricators, assemblers, inspectors, and samplers	Transportation occupations			Handlers, equipment cleaners, helpers, and laborers
									Total	Motor vehicle operators	Material moving equipment operators	
Likely Rancheria, CA	-	-	-	-	-	-	-	-	-	-	-	-
Lone Pine Rancheria, CA	49	-	-	-	-	8	-	-	1	-	1	7
Lookout Rancheria, CA	...	...	...	...	...	...	...	...	...	...	...	...
Los Coyotes, CA	11	-	-	-	-	5	-	-	5	1	4	-
Lovelock Colony, NV	34	9	2	3	1	9	2	1	-	-	-	6
Lower Brule, SD	243	22	8	12	2	34	-	-	13	8	5	20
Lower Elwah, WA	17	2	1	-	1	2	-	-	1	1	-	1
Lower Sioux Community, MN	25	12	-	12	-	4	4	-	-	-	-	-
Lummi, WA	347	27	7	11	8	36	4	4	6	3	2	22
Makah, WA	318	23	2	18	3	31	2	2	14	8	5	13
Manchester Rancheria, CA	15	-	-	-	-	1	-	-	-	-	-	1
Manzanita, CA	...	...	...	...	...	...	...	...	...	...	...	...
Maricopa, AZ	95	-	-	-	-	13	-	2	2	1	1	9
Mattaponi, VA	23	1	-	-	1	13	3	1	3	3	-	6
Menominee, WI	699	61	19	27	15	170	54	17	48	38	10	52
Mesa Grande, CA	-	-	-	-	-	-	-	-	-	-	-	-
Mescalero Apache, NM	548	57	7	42	7	88	3	7	24	17	7	54
Miccosukee, Florida	134	16	1	9	6	29	-	1	6	1	1	22
Middletown Rancheria, CA	9	1	1	-	-	2	-	-	-	-	-	2
Mille Lacs, MN	-	-	-	-	-	-	-	-	-	-	-	-
Mississippi Choctaw Reservation, MS	909	59	7	26	25	244	74	29	48	38	8	93
Moapa River, NV	47	7	2	2	3	6	1	1	1	1	-	2
Montgomery Creek Rancheria, CA	...	...	...	...	...	...	...	...	...	...	...	...
Morongo, CA	96	12	3	5	4	22	5	1	6	4	2	9
Muckleshoot, WA	98	14	-	13	-	5	2	-	-	-	-	3
Nambe Pueblo, NM	82	9	3	5	1	10	2	-	-	-	-	8
Navajo, AZ-NM-UT	22,636	3,241	750	1,607	451	4,387	423	501	1,379	744	620	2,084
Nez Perce, ID	469	46	12	28	6	105	28	7	26	12	13	44
Nisqually, WA	13	-	-	-	-	2	1	1	-	-	-	-
Nooksack, WA	-	-	-	-	-	-	-	-	-	-	-	-
Northern Cheyenne, MT	839	86	5	71	8	136	13	11	38	25	13	74
Oil Springs, NY	-	-	-	-	-	-	-	-	-	-	-	-
Omaha, IO-NE	339	22	1	17	4	51	4	8	14	10	4	25
Oneida, WI	608	72	24	25	23	190	55	24	32	19	13	79
Onondaga, NY	-	-	-	-	-	-	-	-	-	-	-	-
Ontonagon, MI	-	-	-	-	-	-	-	-	-	-	-	-
Osage, OK	1,755	315	31	110	72	340	51	66	118	73	44	105
Ozette, WA	...	...	...	...	...	...	...	...	...	...	...	...
Pala, CA	142	21	2	14	5	32	3	5	4	3	1	19
Pamunkey, VA	19	2	-	2	-	2	2	-	-	-	-	-
Papago, AZ	1,607	89	15	50	10	451	14	1	95	72	23	341
Pascua Yaqui, AZ	110	19	6	10	3	21	-	2	6	6	-	13
Pauma, CA	26	1	1	-	-	3	-	1	1	-	1	2
Payson Comm. of Yavapai-Apache, AZ	-	-	-	-	-	-	-	-	-	-	-	-
Pechanga, CA	36	3	-	1	2	10	1	2	3	1	2	4
Penobscot, MA	127	19	6	9	4	16	3	1	5	4	1	7
Picuris Pueblo, NM	52	2	-	2	-	13	-	-	1	-	1	12
Pine Creek, MI	...	...	...	...	...	...	...	...	...	...	...	...
Pine Ridge, SD	2,482	143	31	80	31	362	60	28	130	113	17	144
Pleasant Point, MA	101	6	-	6	-	6	1	-	-	-	-	4
Pojoaque Pueblo, NM	41	6	-	6	-	3	2	-	-	-	-	1
Poospatuck, NY	13	1	-	1	-	4	-	-	3	3	-	1
Port Gamble, WA	97	4	-	4	-	21	8	5	3	-	3	5
Port Madison, WA	56	8	1	5	1	10	1	2	6	2	1	1
Potawatomi, WI	61	6	1	3	2	6	2	-	1	1	-	3
Pottawatomi, KS	128	18	7	12	-	24	-	4	8	3	5	12
Prairie Island Community, MN	28	-	-	-	-	21	5	3	1	1	-	12
Puyallup, WA	237	21	8	13	-	44	17	10	8	6	1	9
Pyramid Lake, NV	226	28	3	19	4	43	3	5	12	5	8	23
Quileute, WA	69	3	-	2	1	15	1	1	5	1	3	8
Quinault, WA	324	7	2	3	1	53	19	2	6	2	3	27
Ramah Community, NM	335	48	6	40	1	43	2	3	17	12	4	20
Ramona, CA	-	-	-	-	-	-	-	-	-	-	-	-
Red Cliff, WI	149	11	-	7	4	19	2	5	5	5	-	7
Red Lake, MN	707	72	7	56	8	149	17	11	58	46	12	62
Reno-Sparks Colony, NV	186	16	3	8	5	44	11	5	8	5	3	20
Resighini Rancheria, CA	...	...	...	...	...	...	...	...	...	...	...	...
Rincon, CA	91	13	3	7	2	21	3	2	8	4	3	8
Roaring Creek Rancheria, CA	...	...	...	...	...	...	...	...	...	...	...	...
Rocky Boy's, MT	391	51	6	43	2	71	1	4	27	22	5	39
Rosebud, SD	1,279	100	17	62	21	153	11	5	40	35	5	97
Round Valley, CA	142	6	2	2	2	44	10	-	12	4	8	21

[Continued]

★ 523 ★

Manufacturing Occupations Held by Residents of Reservations, 1980: Isleta - Santa Clara Pueblo
[Continued]

Identified reservations	Persons 16 years and over working in 1980 reference period	Precision production, craft and repair occupations				Operators, fabricators and laborers						
		Total	Mechanics and repaires	Construction trades	Precision production occupations	Total	Machine operators and tenders, except precision	Fabricators, assemblers, inspectors, and samplers	Transportation occupations			Handlers, equipment cleaners, helpers, and laborers
									Total	Motor vehicle operators	Material moving equipment operators	
Rumsey Rancheria, CA	...	...	...	...	...	...	...	...	...	...	...	...
Sac and Fox, Iowa	141	30	6	18	6	30	4	1	6	3	2	19
Sac and Fox, KS-NE	...	...	...	...	...	...	...	...	...	...	...	...
St. Croix, WI	116	10	1	7	2	21	5	6	-	-	-	10
St. Regis Mohawk, NY	491	109	17	88	4	112	44	12	18	12	6	38
Salt River, AZ	880	73	16	38	19	166	31	29	49	28	21	57
San Carlos, AZ	1,442	198	38	75	48	306	27	6	76	47	29	197
Sandia Pueblo, NM	86	5	1	3	1	18	2	3	1	1	-	12
Sandy Lake, MN	-	-	-	-	-	-	-	-	-	-	-	-
San Felipe Pueblo, NM	469	66	4	58	5	81	27	12	7	7	-	35
San Ildefonso Pueblo, NM	197	12	5	4	2	18	-	-	4	2	2	14
San Juan Pueblo, NM	287	32	3	24	3	37	2	2	3	2	1	29
San Manuel, CA	-	-	-	-	-	-	-	-	-	-	-	-
San Pasqual, CA	34	7	-	5	2	6	1	-	3	-	3	2
Santa Ana Pueblo, NM	184	17	-	10	6	41	12	2	5	4	2	22
Santa Clara Pueblo, NM	706	56	5	36	15	79	8	-	15	3	13	56

Source: U.S. Bureau of the Census, Subject Reports, PC80-2-1D, Part II, *American Indians, Eskimos, and Aleuts on Identified Reservations and in the Historic Areas of Oklahoma (Excluding Urbanized Areas)*, U.S. Government Printing Office, Washington, D.C., 1986, pp. 482-520. *Notes:* A dash (-) represents zero or a percent which rounds to less than 0.1. Also, a dash (-) is used because the number of supplementary questionnaires for the areas was insufficient to produce reliable estimates. Three dots (...) means not applicable, or that the data are being withheld to avoid disclosure of information for individuals.

★ 524 ★

Manufacturing Occupations Held by Residents of Reservations, 1980: Santa Rosa Rancheria - Zuni Pueblo

Data are the latest available.

Identified reservations	Persons 16 years and over working in 1980 reference period	Precision production, craft, and repair occupations				Operators, fabricators, and laborers						
		Total	Mechanics and repairers	Construction trades	Precision production occupations	Total	Machine operators and tenders, except precision	Fabricators, assemblers, inspectors, and samplers	Transportation occupations			Handlers, equipment cleaners, helpers, and laborers
									Total	Motor vehicle operators	Material moving equipment operators	
Santa Rosa Rancheria, CA	31	4	2	1	-	1	-	-	-	-	-	1
Santa Rosa, CA	...	...	...	...	...	...	...	...	...	...	...	...
Santa Ynez, CA	56	4	1	2	-	6	2	1	-	-	-	2
Santa Ysabel, CA	63	6	1	3	1	14	-	-	5	1	4	9
Santee, Nebraska	124	12	1	7	4	23	-	17	2	1	1	4
Santo Domingo Pueblo, NM	712	66	7	16	44	96	18	4	23	15	8	52
San Xavier, AZ	247	22	6	6	2	50	7	12	12	7	5	19
Sauk-Suiattle, WA	-	-	-	-	-	-	-	-	-	-	-	-
Sault Ste. Marie, MI	-	-	-	-	-	-	-	-	-	-	-	-
Schaghticoke, CT	...	...	...	...	...	...	...	...	...	...	...	...
Shakopee Community, MN	30	2	-	1	12	12	3	2	1	1	-	5
Sheep Ranch Rancheria, CA	...	...	...	...	...	...	...	...	...	...	...	...
Sherwood Valley Rancheria, CA	...	...	...	...	...	...	...	...	...	...	...	...
Shingle Springs Rancheria, CA	-	-	-	-	-	-	-	-	-	-	-	-
Shinnecock, NY	72	7	3	4	-	4	2	-	-	-	-	2
Shoalwater, WA	...	...	...	...	...	...	...	...	...	...	...	...
Sisseton, ND-SD	591	80	10	60	9	107	7	9	21	20	1	69
Skokomish, WA	61	5	-	4	1	8	1	-	4	2	1	4
Skull Valley, UT	-	-	-	-	-	-	-	-	-	-	-	-
Soboba, CA	57	8	2	2	3	7	1	2	1	1	-	2
Sokaogon Chippewa Community, WI	44	6	1	5	-	7	-	-	-	-	-	7
Southern Paiute, UT	50	4	1	3	-	18	13	-	3	-	3	2
Southern Ute, CO	291	23	2	14	4	31	1	2	14	3	10	14
Spokane, WA	451	80	29	23	4	137	12	6	80	31	49	39
Squaxin Island, WA	9	-	-	-	-	2	-	-	-	-	-	2
Standing Rock, ND-SD	1,077	52	16	30	6	222	13	4	43	30	13	163
Stewart's Point Rancheria, CA	20	-	-	-	-	7	2	2	1	-	1	2

[Continued]

797

★ 524 ★

Manufacturing Occupations Held by Residents of Reservations, 1980: Santa Rosa Rancheria - Zuni Pueblo
[Continued]

Identified reservations	Persons 16 years and over working in 1980 reference period	Precision production, craft, and repair occupations				Operators, fabricators, and laborers						
		Total	Mechanics and repairers	Construction trades	Precision production occupations	Total	Machine operators and tenders, except precision	Fabricators, assemblers, inspectors, and samplers	Transportation occupations			Handlers, equipment cleaners, helpers, and laborers
									Total	Motor vehicle operators	Material moving equipment operators	
Stockbridge, WI	207	22	9	8	5	57	11	2	30	22	8	14
Sulphur Bank Rancheria, CA	18	4	-	1	2	2	-	-	1	-	-	1
Summit Lake, NV	...	...	...	...	...	...	...	...	...	...	...	...
Susanville, CA	30	2	1	1	-	6	-	-	1	1	-	5
Swinomish, WA	139	9	-	5	4	10	3	-	-	-	-	7
Sycuan, CA	8	2	2	-	-	-	-	-	-	-	-	-
Tama, GA	17	3	1	2	-	6	2	1	-	-	-	3
Taos Pueblo, NM	307	40	5	31	4	75	15	2	16	13	4	41
Te-Moak, NV	38	4	2	1	1	4	-	-	1	1	-	3
Tesuque Pueblo, NM	83	6	-	3	3	12	3	-	-	-	-	9
Tigua, TX	105	13	3	6	4	27	5	7	5	4	1	10
Tonawanda, NY	168	16	-	8	6	76	20	22	12	8	4	22
Torres-Martinez, CA	-	-	-	-	-	-	-	-	-	-	-	-
Trinidad Rancheria, CA	20	2	1	-	1	2	-	-	2	2	-	-
Tulalip, WA	241	22	9	10	3	41	7	6	2	5	20	10
Tule River, CA	134	7	2	5	-	19	-	-	8	4	4	10
Tunicabiloxi, LA	...	...	...	...	...	...	...	...	...	...	...	...
Tuolumne Rancheria, CA	26	2	-	2	-	6	2	-	2	-	2	2
Turtle Mountain, ND	961	146	17	107	22	191	23	49	48	39	8	71
Tuscarora, NY	-	-	-	-	-	-	-	-	-	-	-	-
Twenty-Nine Palms, CA	-	-	-	-	-	-	-	-	-	-	-	-
Uintah and Ouray, UT	588	63	14	41	7	84	22	6	21	6	15	35
Umatilla, OR	297	32	7	20	5	63	12	13	12	5	6	26
Upper Sioux Community, MN	21	2	-	-	2	6	-	4	-	-	-	2
Upper Skagit, WA	-	-	-	-	-	-	-	-	-	-	-	-
Ute Mountain, CO-NM	308	18	-	16	2	66	15	-	18	15	3	33
Vermillion Lake, MN	27	-	-	-	-	10	-	-	4	-	2	6
Viejas Rancheria, CA	51	5	3	2	-	13	1	3	2	1	1	7
Walker River, NV	162	25	11	10	3	29	6	3	8	4	4	12
Wampanoag, MA	-	-	-	-	-	-	-	-	-	-	-	-
Warm Springs, OR	602	14	1	10	3	116	44	10	29	8	21	33
Washoe, NV	-	-	-	-	-	-	-	-	-	-	-	-
Western Pequot, CT	...	...	...	...	...	...	...	...	...	...	...	...
White Earth, MN	734	130	21	90	20	124	20	8	36	21	15	60
Wind River, WY	1,119	147	31	63	15	202	22	10	49	27	21	122
Winnebago, Nebraska	317	27	4	17	6	41	2	12	10	3	6	17
Winnemucca Colony, NV	9	-	-	-	-	1	-	-	-	-	-	1
Wisconsin Winnebago Reservation	105	13	-	7	6	29	11	13	4	-	4	1
Woodfords Community, CA	-	-	-	-	-	-	-	-	-	-	-	-
XL Ranch, CA	...	...	...	...	...	...	...	...	...	...	...	...
Yakima, WA	1,532	143	31	69	41	222	48	24	69	33	35	80
Yankton, South Dakota	359	44	5	34	5	78	-	-	33	27	6	45
Yavapai, AZ	28	6	-	3	3	5	2	1	1	-	1	1
Yerington, NV	40	3	3	-	-	12	2	1	5	3	2	3
Yomba, NV	20	-	-	-	-	5	-	-	4	1	3	1
Zia Pueblo, NM	179	14	6	2	5	47	5	7	5	2	3	30
Zuni Pueblo, NM	2,000	178	21	91	66	122	21	1	29	15	12	70
San Felipe/Santa Ana Joint Area, NM	-	-	-	-	-	-	-	-	-	-	-	-
San Felipe/Santo Domingo Joint Area, NM	26	1	-	1	-	5	-	-	5	5	-	-
Other Reservation Lands in MT	-	-	-	-	-	-	-	-	-	-	-	-

Source: U.S. Bureau of the Census, Subject Reports, PC80-2-1D, Part II, *American Indians, Eskimos, and Aleuts on Identified Reservations and in the Historic Areas of Oklahoma (Excluding Urbanized Areas)*, U.S. Government Printing Office, Washington, D.C., 1986, pp. 482-520. *Notes:* A dash (-) represents zero or a percent which rounds to less than 0.1. Also, a dash (-) is used because the number of supplementary questionnaires for the areas was insufficient to produce reliable estimates. Three dots (...) means not applicable, or that the data are being withheld to avoid disclosure of information for individuals.

★ 525 ★

Service Farming, Forestry, and Fishing Occupations Held by Residents of Reservations, 1980: Acoma Pueblo - Isabella

Data are the latest available.

Identified reservation	Persons 16 years and over working in 1980 reference period	Service occupations							Farming, forestry and fishing occupations		
		Total	Private household occupations	Protective service occupations		Service occupations, except protective and household			Total	Farm operators and managers	Farm workers and related occupations
				Total	Police and fire-fighting	Total	Food service occupations	Cleaning and building service occupations			
Total American Indian, Eskimo, and Aleut	89,697	19,436	480	2,412	1,254	16,545	4,144	5,976	6,230	1,631	4,599
Acoma Pueblo, NM	632	128	2	12	8	114	29	35	3	-	3
Agua Caliente, CA	-	-	-	-	-	-	-	-	-	-	-
Alabama-Coushatta, TX	234	29	-	3	-	26	7	6	21	-	21
Alamo, NM	204	44	3	6	5	35	8	12	9	-	9
Allegany, NY	381	84	3	14	7	67	15	25	5	1	3
Alturas Rancheria, CA	...	...	...	...	...	...	...	...	...	...	...
Annette Islands Reserve, AK	398	58	1	2	-	55	25	19	46	-	46
Augustine, CA	-	-	-	-	-	-	-	-	-	-	-
Bad River, WI	197	49	-	15	10	34	5	19	12	-	12
Barona Rancheria, CA	79	16	-	4	4	11	1	5	4	-	4
Bay Mills, MI	99	24	-	5	2	19	-	11	15	-	15
Benton Paiute, CA	...	...	...	...	...	...	...	...	...	...	...
Berry Creek Rancheria, CA	-	-	-	-	-	-	-	-	-	-	-
Big Bend Rancheria, CA	...	...	...	...	...	...	...	...	...	...	...
Big Cypress, FL	108	32	-	1	-	30	7	10	17	-	17
Big Lagoon Rancheria, CA	...	...	...	...	...	...	...	...	...	...	...
Big Pine Rancheria, CA	79	20	-	2	-	18	1	11	4	-	4
Bishop Rancheria, CA	276	67	1	2	-	64	13	33	7	-	7
Blackfeet, MT	1,665	365	14	58	22	293	90	107	196	107	89
Bois Forte (Nett Lake), MN	123	16	-	2	2	14	7	4	12	-	12
Bridgeport Colony, CA	23	8	-	1	-	7	-	7	2	-	2
Brighton, FL	132	19	-	2	2	17	5	1	30	3	27
Burns, Oregon	55	16	2	1	1	13	2	10	6	-	6
Cabazon, CA	...	...	...	...	...	...	...	...	...	...	...
Cachil Dehe Rancheria, CA	...	...	...	...	...	...	...	...	...	...	...
Cahuilla, CA	...	...	...	...	...	...	...	...	...	...	...
Campo, CA	17	5	1	1	1	2	1	1	1	-	1
Camp Verde, AZ	42	9	-	2	1	7	1	3	-	-	-
Canoncito, NM	156	31	1	4	2	26	11	7	2	2	-
Capitan Grande, CA	-	-	-	-	-	-	-	-	-	-	-
Carson Colony, NV	73	13	-	4	-	10	2	6	2	-	2
Catawba, SC	395	46	-	5	2	42	11	15	2	-	2
Cattaraugus, NY	559	145	-	4	3	142	15	43	26	-	26
Cedarville Rancheria, CA	...	...	...	...	...	...	...	...	...	...	...
Chehalis, WA	52	13	-	1	-	12	5	1	7	1	5
Chemehuevi, CA	...	...	...	...	...	...	...	...	...	...	...
Cheyenne River, SD	399	144	1	18	9	125	36	18	105	83	22
Chitimacha, LA	65	14	1	-	-	13	4	4	1	-	1
Cochiti Pueblo, NM	167	44	2	5	-	37	6	17	-	-	-
Cocopah, AZ	83	15	-	4	4	11	2	5	9	-	9
Coeur D'Alene, Idaho	146	15	-	5	3	10	1	6	19	4	15
Cold Springs Rancheria, CA	11	4	-	-	-	4	-	1	-	-	-
Colorado River, AZ-CA	650	148	2	23	16	123	30	45	73	26	47
Colville, WA	1,304	153	5	17	8	131	47	45	213	36	177
Cortina Rancheria, CA	...	...	...	...	...	...	...	...	...	...	...
Coushatta, LA	...	...	...	...	...	...	...	...	...	...	...
Coyote Valley Rancheria, CA	-	-	-	-	-	-	-	-	-	-	-
Crow, MT	1,039	250	2	27	18	220	63	88	91	50	41
Crow Creek, SD	322	96	-	8	3	88	28	26	42	21	21
Cuyapaipe, CA	...	...	...	...	...	...	...	...	...	...	...
Deer Creek, MN	...	...	...	...	...	...	...	...	...	...	...
Dresslerville Colony, NV	50	8	-	4	4	4	-	-	-	-	-
Dry Creek Rancheria, CA	4	1	-	-	-	1	-	-	-	-	-
Duck Valley, ID-NV	278	80	1	7	7	73	13	26	45	32	13
Duckwater, NV	40	6	-	-	-	6	1	-	17	12	5

[Continued]

★ 525 ★

Service Farming, Forestry, and Fishing Occupations Held by Residents of Reservations, 1980: Acoma Pueblo - Isabella
[Continued]

Identified reservation	Persons 16 years and over working in 1980 reference period	Service occupations							Farming, forestry and fishing occupations		
		Total	Private household occupations	Protective service occupations		Service occupations, except protective and household			Total	Farm operators and managers	Farm workers and related occupations
				Total	Police and fire-fighting	Total	Food service occupations	Cleaning and building service occupations			
Eastern Cherokee, NC	1,800	452	4	47	21	401	90	158	78	1	77
Eastern Pequot, CT	...	...	...	...	...	...	...	...	...	...	...
Ely Colony, NV	21	6	-	-	-	6	-	4	-	-	-
Enterprise Rancheria, CA	...	...	...	...	...	...	...	...	...	...	...
Fallon Colony, NV	16	7	-	-	-	7	4	-	2	-	2
Fallon, NV	100	22	1	1	1	20	3	9	21	13	8
Flandreau, SD	60	36	-	1	1	35	4	9	3	-	3
Flathead, MT	1,216	215	4	19	13	191	53	51	194	67	127
Fond du Lac, MN	142	40	-	1	1	39	11	15	3	-	3
Fort Apache, AZ	1,837	479	4	74	47	402	105	144	133	-	133
Fort Belknap, MT	493	106	-	14	7	92	20	31	60	28	32
Fort Berthold, ND	740	204	3	38	28	163	40	59	83	57	26
Fort Bidwell, CA	19	-	-	-	-	-	-	-	-	-	-
Fort Hall, Idaho	675	106	3	22	12	81	17	27	75	36	39
Fort Independence, CA	16	3	-	-	-	3	-	3	-	-	-
Fort McDermitt, NV-OR	101	32	-	2	2	29	4	16	11	5	5
Fort McDowell, AZ	129	33	2	1	1	31	7	11	2	-	2
Fort Mojave, AZ-CA-NV	39	11	-	2	2	9	-	2	11	-	11
Fort Peck, MT	1,262	297	2	21	15	273	65	82	106	51	55
Fort Totten, ND	462	139	1	30	12	107	24	51	13	2	12
Fort Yuma, AZ-CA	339	89	4	9	8	76	17	29	37	1	36
Gila Bend, AZ	-	-	-	-	-	-	-	-	-	-	-
Gila River, AZ	1,762	431	17	64	40	350	68	107	239	21	219
Golden Hill, CT	...	...	...	...	...	...	...	...	...	...	...
Goshute, NV-UT	17	3	-	-	-	3	-	-	6	-	6
Grand Portage, MN	88	30	-	-	-	30	7	17	8	-	8
Grindstone Creek Rancheria, CA	20	2	-	-	-	2	-	1	3	-	3
Hannahville Community, MI	76	13	-	2	2	12	2	7	28	-	28
Hassanamisco, MA	...	...	...	...	...	...	...	...	...	...	...
Havasupai, AZ	86	24	-	2	0	21	8	9	2	1	1
Hoh, WA	14	4	-	-	-	4	-	2	2	-	2
Hollywood, FL	197	47	2	9	-	35	4	15	7	-	7
Hoopa Valley, CA	441	99	4	8	5	87	19	25	42	-	42
Hoopa Valley Extension, CA	100	20	-	1	1	19	4	9	12	-	12
Hopi, AZ	1,435	313	14	27	21	272	82	104	47	16	30
Hopland Rancheria, CA	-	-	-	-	-	-	-	-	-	-	-
Hualapai, AZ	236	60	-	18	15	42	9	14	27	-	27
Inaja-Cosmit, CA	-	-	-	-	-	-	-	-	-	-	-
Indian Township, ME	104	25	1	11	4	13	5	5	10	-	10
Iowa, KS-NE	15	2	2	-	-	-	-	-	8	5	2
Isabella, MI	146	34	4	2	1	28	6	10	6	2	4

Source: U.S. Bureau of the Census, Subject Reports, PC80-2-1D, Part II, *American Indians, Eskimos, and Aleuts on Identified Reservations and in the Historic Areas of Oklahoma (Excluding Urbanized Areas)*, U.S. Government Printing Office, Washington, D.C., 1986, pp. 482-520. *Notes:* A dash (-) represents zero or a percent which rounds to less than 0.1. Also, a dash (-) is used because the number of supplementary questionnaires for the areas was insufficient to produce reliable estimates. Three dots (...) means not applicable, or that the data are being withheld to avoid disclosure of information for individuals.

★ 526 ★

Service Farming, Forestry, and Fishing Occupations Held by Residents of Reservations, 1980: Isleta - Santa Clara Pueblo

Data are the latest available.

Identified reservation	Persons 16 years and over working in 1980 reference period	Service occupations							Farming, forestry, and fishing occupations		
		Total	Private household occupations	Protective service occupations		Service occupations, except protective and household			Total	Farm operators and managers	Farm workers and related occupations
				Total	Police and fire-fighting	Total	Food service occupations	Cleaning and building service occupations			
Isleta Pueblo, NM	874	160	19	33	16	109	12	57	37	7	30
Jackson Rancheria, CA	...	...	...	...	...	...	...	...	...	...	...
Jemez Pueblo, NM	383	74	5	8	3	62	18	23	21	-	21
Jicarilla Apache, NM	656	137	1	25	18	111	29	39	62	13	48
Kaibab, AZ	42	11	-	2	2	9	-	3	2	-	2
Kalispel, WA	36	5	-	2	2	3	-	-	-	-	-
Kickapoo, KS	108	23	2	1	1	20	5	6	10	4	6
Kootenai, ID	-	-	-	-	-	-	-	-	-	-	-
Lac Courte Oreilles, WI	331	85	6	9	-	70	28	23	29	-	29
Lac du Flambeau, WI	322	59	-	5	2	54	19	13	26	-	26
Laguna Pueblo, NM	1,300	169	12	34	12	123	37	41	25	12	13
La Jolla, CA	43	7	-	1	-	6	-	5	1	-	1
L'Anse, MI	177	37	1	5	4	30	4	17	1	-	1
La Posta, CA	...	...	...	...	...	...	...	...	...	...	...
Las Vegas Colony, NV	35	12	-	2	-	11	-	8	3	-	3
Laytonville Rancheria, CA	24	4	-	-	-	4	-	3	-	-	-
Leech Lake, MN	728	143	2	6	2	136	43	40	61	2	59
Likely Rancheria, CA	-	-	-	-	-	-	-	-	-	-	-
Lone Pine Rancheria, CA	49	23	-	-	-	23	8	14	-	-	-
Lookout Rancheria, CA	...	...	...	...	...	...	...	...	...	...	...
Los Coyotes, CA	11	2	1	1	-	-	-	-	1	-	1
Lovelock Colony, NV	34	6	-	-	-	6	-	2	5	-	5
Lower Brule, SD	243	57	4	4	4	49	14	11	41	25	15
Lower Elwah, WA	17	4	-	1	-	3	-	3	3	-	3
Lower Sioux Community, MN	25	-	-	-	-	-	-	-	-	-	-
Lummi, WA	347	67	3	8	2	56	7	28	81	1	76
Makah, WA	318	65	6	3	1	56	11	12	48	1	47
Manchester Rancheria, CA	15	10	-	-	-	10	3	5	1	-	1
Manzanita, CA	...	...	...	...	...	...	...	...	...	...	...
Maricopa, AZ	95	12	-	3	2	10	2	3	37	2	35
Mattaponi, VA	23	6	-	-	-	6	3	2	1	-	1
Menominee, WI	699	178	3	31	7	144	32	60	29	2	26
Mesa Grande, CA	-	-	-	-	-	-	-	-	-	-	-
Mescalero Apache, NM	548	155	1	26	11	129	20	40	75	-	75
Miccosukee, Florida	134	31	-	2	2	29	11	7	5	-	5
Middletown Rancheria, CA	9	2	1	-	-	1	-	1	2	-	2
Mille Lacs, MN	-	-	-	-	-	-	-	-	-	-	-
Mississippi Choctaw Reservation, MS	909	235	2	9	6	225	43	111	81	3	78
Moapa River, NV	47	7	-	1	-	6	4	-	14	1	13
Montgomery Creek Rancheria, CA	...	...	...	...	...	...	...	...	...	...	...
Morongo, CA	96	31	1	1	1	28	2	10	7	3	4
Muckleshoot, WA	98	21	-	5	4	16	-	10	9	-	9
Nambe Pueblo, NM	82	14	-	6	1	7	-	3	4	1	3
Navajo, AZ-NM-UT	22,636	4,567	66	453	213	4,048	1,197	1,469	645	223	423
Nez Perce, ID	469	77	2	4	1	71	20	32	34	6	28
Nisqually, WA	13	2	-	-	-	2	-	-	2	-	2
Nooksack, WA	-	-	-	-	-	-	-	-	-	-	-
Northern Cheyenne, MT	839	152	-	24	18	128	31	34	63	26	37
Oil Springs, NY	-	-	-	-	-	-	-	-	-	-	-
Omaha, IO-NE	339	128	-	27	4	101	21	42	25	8	16
Oneida, WI	608	112	3	5	3	104	26	26	26	6	20
Onondaga, NY	-	-	-	-	-	-	-	-	-	-	-
Ontonagon, MI	-	-	-	-	-	-	-	-	-	-	-
Osage, OK	1,755	289	4	55	22	229	72	75	99	63	36
Ozette, WA	...	...	...	...	...	...	...	...	...	...	...
Pala, CA	142	29	1	6	1	22	5	9	11	-	11
Pamunkey, VA	19	7	-	1	-	6	2	3	1	-	1
Papago, AZ	1,607	359	12	39	18	308	61	100	97	16	81
Pascua Yaqui, AZ	110	29	1	1	-	26	1	19	13	1	12
Pauma, CA	26	5	-	1	-	4	-	3	2	-	2
Payson Comm. of Yavapai-Apache, AZ	-	-	-	-	-	-	-	-	-	-	-
Pechanga, CA	36	11	-	-	-	11	1	10	3	-	3
Penobscot, MA	127	33	-	6	5	27	7	13	5	-	5
Picuris Pueblo, NM	52	15	-	2	2	13	2	3	1	-	1
Pine Creek, MI	...	...	...	...	...	...	...	...	...	...	...
Pine Ridge, SD	2,482	654	8	140	62	505	148	146	165	79	85
Pleasant Point, MA	101	29	1	5	3	23	4	2	12	-	12
Pojoaque Pueblo, NM	41	9	-	1	1	8	1	4	-	-	-
Poospatuck, NY	13	4	-	1	1	3	-	1	-	-	-

[Continued]

★ 526 ★

Service Farming, Forestry, and Fishing Occupations Held by Residents of Reservations, 1980: Isleta - Santa Clara Pueblo

[Continued]

Identified reservation	Persons 16 years and over working in 1980 reference period	Service occupations							Farming, forestry, and fishing occupations		
		Total	Private household occupations	Protective service occupations		Service occupations, except protective and household			Total	Farm operators and managers	Farm workers and related occupations
				Total	Police and fire-fighting	Total	Food service occupations	Cleaning and building service occupations			
Port Gamble, WA	97	18	-	5	4	12	2	4	22	1	20
Port Madison, WA	56	6	-	3	3	3	-	3	8	-	8
Potawatomi, WI	61	14	-	2	-	12	2	2	14	-	14
Pottawatomi, KS	128	24	-	1	1	23	4	3	7	3	4
Prairie Island Community, MN	28	1	-	-	-	1	-	-	-	-	-
Puyallup, WA	237	30	1	4	4	25	8	6	18	2	16
Pyramid Lake, NV	226	32	-	6	-	27	3	17	9	1	8
Quileute, WA	69	13	-	3	2	10	3	-	3	-	3
Quinault, WA	324	65	-	15	11	50	9	18	70	1	69
Ramah Community, NM	335	68	4	7	1	57	6	28	11	-	11
Ramona, CA	-	-	-	-	-	-	-	-	-	-	-
Red Cliff, WI	149	32	-	7	3	24	6	14	26	-	26
Red Lake, MN	707	144	2	26	14	116	19	36	73	9	64
Reno-Sparks Colony, NV	186	49	3	4	2	41	3	29	5	-	5
Resighini Rancheria, CA	...	...	...	...	...	...	...	...	...	...	...
Rincon, CA	91	16	1	2	2	13	1	8	7	2	5
Roaring Creek Rancheria, CA	...	...	...	...	...	...	...	...	...	...	...
Rocky Boy's, MT	391	82	-	12	8	70	20	17	31	7	24
Rosebud, SD	1,279	300	2	31	18	267	63	68	129	74	55
Round Valley, CA	142	29	4	1	1	24	3	9	20	1	19
Rumsey Rancheria, CA	...	...	...	...	...	...	...	...	...	...	...
Sac and Fox, Iowa	141	39	-	9	-	30	8	9	5	1	4
Sac and Fox, KS-NE	...	...	...	...	...	...	...	...	...	...	...
St. Croix, WI	116	38	-	8	-	30	2	15	4	-	4
St. Regis Mohawk, NY	491	102	2	25	17	75	20	31	9	4	6
Salt River, AZ	880	320	20	22	10	278	54	151	85	1	83
San Carlos, AZ	1,442	325	6	48	27	271	55	123	131	5	126
Sandia Pueblo, NM	86	16	1	2	1	13	3	3	1	1	-
Sandy Lake, MN	-	-	-	-	-	-	-	-	-	-	-
San Felipe Pueblo, NM	469	108	33	4	3	71	20	37	16	2	13
San Ildefonso Pueblo, NM	197	41	3	11	8	27	5	4	2	2	-
San Juan Pueblo, NM	287	87	8	8	7	71	22	34	5	1	4
San Manuel, CA	-	-	-	-	-	-	-	-	-	-	-
San Pasqual, CA	34	5	-	-	-	5	1	4	1	-	1
Santa Ana Pueblo, NM	184	41	4	5	2	32	10	10	3	1	2
Santa Clara Pueblo, NM	706	142	5	48	38	89	18	38	10	3	8

Source: U.S. Bureau of the Census, Subject Reports, PC80-2-1D, Part II, *American Indians, Eskimos, and Aleuts on Identified Reservations and in the Historic Areas of Oklahoma (Excluding Urbanized Areas)*, U.S. Government Printing Office, Washington, D.C., 1986, pp. 482-520. *Notes:* A dash (-) represents zero or a percent which rounds to less than 0.1. Also, a dash (-) is used because the number of supplementary questionnaires for the areas was insufficient to produce reliable estimates. Three dots (...) means not applicable, or that the data are being withheld to avoid disclosure of information for individuals.

★ 527 ★

Service Farming, Forestry, and Fishing Occupations Held by Residents of Reservations, 1980: Santa Rosa Rancheria - Zuni Pueblo

Data are the latest available.

Identified reservation	Persons 16 years and over working in 1980 reference period	Service occupations							Farming, forestry and fishing occupations		
		Total	Private household occupations	Protective service occupations		Service occupations except protective and household			Total	Farm operators and managers	Farm workers and related occupations
				Total	Police and fire-fighting	Total	Food service occupations	Cleaning and building service occupations			
Santa Rosa Rancheria, CA	31	-	-	-	-	7	1	5	12	-	12
Santa Rosa, CA	...	...	...	...	...	...	...	...	...	...	...
Santa Ynez, CA	56	21	-	-	-	21	6	9	11	-	11
Santa Ysabel, CA	63	10	-	2	2	7	3	2	10	-	10
Santee, Nebraska	124	40	1	2	1	37	14	14	11	1	10

[Continued]

Service Farming, Forestry, and Fishing Occupations Held by Residents of Reservations, 1980: Santa Rosa Rancheria - Zuni Pueblo

[Continued]

Identified reservation	Persons 16 years and over working in 1980 reference period	Service occupations							Farming, forestry and fishing occupations		
		Total	Private household occupations	Protective service occupations		Service occupations except protective and household			Total	Farm operators and managers	Farm workers and related occupations
				Total	Police and fire-fighting	Total	Food service occupations	Cleaning and building service occupations			
Santo Domingo Pueblo, NM	712	76	-	4	1	72	7	12	40	28	12
San Xavier, AZ	247	79	26	4	-	50	6	23	21	2	19
Sauk-Suiattle, WA	-	-	-	-	-	-	-	-	-	-	-
Sault Ste. Marie, MI	-	-	-	-	-	-	-	-	-	-	-
Schaghticoke, CT	...	...	...	...	...	...	...	...	...	...	...
Shakopee Community, MN	30	7	-	-	-	7	-	3	1	1	-
Sheep Ranch Rancheria, CA	...	...	...	...	...	...	...	...	...	...	...
Sherwood Valley Rancheria, CA	...	...	...	...	...	...	...	...	...	...	...
Shingle Springs Rancheria, CA	-	-	-	-	-	-	-	-	-	-	-
Shinnecock, NY	72	24	2	2	2	19	9	9	5	-	5
Shoalwater, WA	...	...	...	...	...	...	...	...	...	...	...
Sisseton, ND-SD	591	135	9	13	9	113	22	32	30	11	19
Skokomish, WA	61	7	-	1	1	6	1	3	16	-	16
Skull Valley, UT	-	-	-	-	-	-	-	-	-	-	-
Soboba, CA	57	19	-	-	-	19	-	10	3	-	3
Sokaogon Chippewa Community, WI	44	6	-	-	-	6	2	1	4	-	4
Southern Paiute, UT	50	7	-	-	-	7	2	1	8	-	8
Southern Ute, CO	291	69	-	12	8	57	13	25	19	3	16
Spokane, WA	451	66	-	13	4	52	7	25	26	6	20
Squaxin Island, WA	9	4	-	1	-	3	1	1	1	-	1
Standing Rock, ND-SD	1,077	311	8	43	15	259	76	75	113	66	47
Stewart's Point Rancheria, CA	20	4	-	-	-	4	-	2	7	-	7
Stockbridge, WI	207	41	-	3	2	38	3	24	12	1	11
Sulphur Bank Rancheria, CA	18	5	-	-	-	5	-	1	2	-	2
Summit Lake, NV	...	...	...	...	...	...	...	...	...	...	...
Susanville, CA	30	11	-	1	-	10	2	7	4	-	4
Swinomish, WA	139	31	2	2	-	27	7	4	53	-	53
Sycuan, CA	8	6	-	1	1	5	2	2	-	-	-
Tama, GA	17	3	-	1	1	2	2	-	1	1	-
Taos Pueblo, NM	307	71	7	13	11	51	8	16	19	1	18
Te-Moak, NV	38	11	1	-	-	9	-	8	12	-	12
Tesuque Pueblo, NM	83	30	4	3	2	24	6	6	-	-	-
Tigua, TX	105	34	-	3	-	31	5	21	3	1	2
Tonawanda, NY	168	21	2	1	-	17	6	4	4	-	4
Torres-Martinez, CA	-	-	-	-	-	-	-	-	-	-	-
Trinidad Rancheria, CA	20	8	-	1	-	7	2	2	2	-	2
Tulalip, WA	241	43	-	3	-	40	2	15	25	-	25
Tule River, CA	134	45	-	-	-	45	3	25	9	-	9
Tunicabiloxi, LA	...	...	...	...	...	...	...	...	...	...	...
Tuolumne Rancheria, CA	26	7	-	-	-	7	1	5	2	-	2
Turtle Mountain, ND	961	239	7	25	16	207	48	52	21	6	15
Tuscarora, NY	-	-	-	-	-	-	-	-	-	-	-
Twenty-Nine Palms, CA	-	-	-	-	-	-	-	-	-	-	-
Uintah and Ouray, UT	588	157	-	33	19	124	22	63	41	20	21
Umatilla, OR	297	50	3	1	-	46	6	14	25	3	22
Upper Sioux Community, MN	21	-	-	-	-	-	-	-	-	-	-
Upper Skagit, WA	-	-	-	-	-	-	-	-	-	-	-
Ute Mountain, CO-NM	308	96	-	25	21	70	7	24	17	8	9
Vermillion Lake, MN	27	8	-	2	2	6	4	-	-	-	-
Viejas Rancheria, CA	51	15	-	3	2	12	-	4	2	-	2
Walker River, NV	162	34	1	2	-	31	7	8	11	8	3
Wampanoag, MA	-	-	-	-	-	-	-	-	-	-	-
Warm Springs, OR	602	137	-	24	15	112	29	39	64	10	53
Washoe, NV	-	-	-	-	-	-	-	-	-	-	-
Western Pequot, CT	...	...	...	...	...	...	...	...	...	...	...
White Earth, MN	734	156	-	9	1	147	31	42	62	7	55
Wind River, WY	1,119	259	-	23	7	236	74	80	113	49	64
Winnebago, Nebraska	317	80	-	7	1	74	12	31	20	5	15
Winnemucca Colony, NV	9	5	-	-	-	5	-	4	-	-	-
Wisconsin Winnebago Reservation	105	16	-	-	-	16	3	12	-	-	-
Woodfords Community, CA	-	-	-	-	-	-	-	-	...	...	...
XL Ranch, CA	...	...	...	...	...	...	...	...	...	...	...
Yakima, WA	1,532	292	4	49	29	239	68	60	247	61	186
Yankton, South Dakota	359	96	1	6	5	88	27	21	12	4	8
Yavapai, AZ	28	6	-	1	1	5	-	1	1	-	1
Yerington, NV	40	5	-	-	-	5	2	1	11	2	9
Yomba, NV	20	3	-	-	-	3	-	2	6	-	6
Zia Pueblo, NM	179	52	8	3	3	41	8	16	9	-	9
Zuni Pueblo, NM	2,000	287	5	42	16	239	66	92	93	18	74
San Felipe/Santa Ana Joint Area, NM	-	-	-	-	-	-	-	-	-	-	-

[Continued]

★ 527 ★

Service Farming, Forestry, and Fishing Occupations Held by Residents of Reservations, 1980: Santa Rosa Rancheria - Zuni Pueblo

[Continued]

Identified reservation	Persons 16 years and over working in 1980 reference period	Service occupations								Farming, forestry and fishing occupations		
		Total	Private household occupations	Protective service occupations		Service occupations except protective and household				Total	Farm operators and managers	Farm workers and related occupations
				Total	Police and fire-fighting	Total	Food service occupations	Cleaning and building service occupations				
San Felipe/Santo Domingo Joint Area, NM	26	8	-	-	-	8	2	1	-	-	-	
Other Reservation Lands in MT	-	-	-	-	-	-	-	-	-	-	-	

Source: U.S. Bureau of the Census, Subject Reports, PC80-2-1D, Part II, *American Indians, Eskimos, and Aleuts on Identified Reservations and in the Historic Areas of Oklahoma (Excluding Urbanized Areas)*, U.S. Government Printing Office, Washington, D.C., 1986, pp. 482-520. *Notes:* A dash (-) represents zero or a percent which rounds to less than 0.1. Also, a dash (-) is used because the number of supplementary questionnaires for the areas was insufficient to produce reliable estimates. Three dots (...) means not applicable, or that the data are being withheld to avoid disclosure of information for individuals.

★ 528 ★

Technical, Sales, and Administrative Occupations Held by Residents of Reservations, 1980: Acoma Pueblo - Isabella

Data are the latest available.

Identified reservation	Persons 16 years and over working in 1980 reference period	Technical, sales, and administrative support occupations								
		Total	Health technologists and technicians	Technologists and technicians, except health	Sales occupations	Administrative support occupations, including clerical				
						Total	Computer equipment operators	Secretaries, stenographers, and typists	Financial records processing occupations	Mail and message distributing occupations
Total American Indian, Eskimo, and Aleut	89,697	20,256	900	1,544	2,264	15,547	118	4,919	1,023	201
Acoma Pueblo, NM	632	161	9	16	13	123	6	43	6	-
Agua Caliente, CA	-	-	-	-	-	-	-	-	-	-
Alabama-Coushatta, TX	234	47	5	3	18	21	-	5	5	-
Alamo, NM	204	35	2	-	1	32	2	6	1	-
Allegany, NY	381	94	2	9	7	76	3	26	11	1
Alturas Rancheria, CA	...	...	...	...	...	...	...	...	...	...
Annette Islands Reserve, AK	398	51	-	6	10	36	-	6	6	1
Augustine, CA	-	-	-	-	-	-	-	-	-	-
Bad River, WI	197	47	-	2	2	44	-	21	12	-
Barona Rancheria, CA	79	14	1	-	2	11	-	4	-	-
Bay Mills, MI	99	28	-	1	1	26	-	9	2	-
Benton Paiute, CA	...	...	...	...	...	...	...	...	...	...
Berry Creek Rancheria, CA	-	-	-	-	-	-	-	-	-	-
Big Bend Rancheria, CA	...	...	...	...	...	...	...	...	...	...
Big Cypress, FL	108	21	4	-	2	15	-	5	-	-
Big Lagoon Rancheria, CA	...	...	...	...	...	...	...	...	...	...
Big Pine Rancheria, CA	79	24	-	1	6	17	-	10	-	-
Bishop Rancheria, CA	276	58	2	2	5	48	-	14	8	-
Blackfeet, MT	1,665	357	16	25	43	273	2	100	26	2
Bois Forte (Nett Lake), MN	123	42	-	7	-	35	-	8	4	1
Bridgeport Colony, CA	23	2	-	1	-	1	-	-	-	-
Brighton, FL	132	30	3	2	3	21	-	5	1	-
Burns, Oregon	55	5	-	1	-	4	-	1	1	-
Cabazon, CA	...	...	...	...	...	...	...	...	...	...
Cachil Dehe Rancheria, CA	...	...	...	...	...	...	...	...	...	...
Cahuilla, CA	...	...	...	...	...	...	...	...	...	...
Campo, CA	17	1	-	-	-	1	-	1	-	-
Camp Verde, AZ	42	6	1	1	-	4	-	3	-	-
Canoncito, NM	156	38	1	3	4	30	-	2	2	-
Capitan Grande, CA	-	-	-	-	-	-	-	-	-	-

[Continued]

★ 528 ★

Technical, Sales, and Administrative Occupations Held by Residents of Reservations, 1980: Acoma Pueblo - Isabella

[Continued]

Identified reservation	Persons 16 years and over working in 1980 reference period	Technical, sales, and administrative support occupations								
		Total	Health technologists and technicians	Technologists and technicians, except health	Sales occupations	Administrative support occupations, including clerical				
						Total	Computer equipment operators	Secretaries, stenographers, and typists	Financial records processing occupations	Mail and message distributing occupations
Carson Colony, NV	73	28	4	4	6	15	-	9	1	-
Catawba, SC	395	53	1	7	15	30	-	3	4	-
Cattaraugus, NY	559	87	5	3	3	76	3	31	1	-
Cedarville Rancheria, CA	...	...	...	...	...	...	...	...	...	...
Chehalis, WA	52	11	-	1	4	5	-	1	-	-
Chemehuevi, CA	...	...	...	...	...	...	...	...	...	...
Cheyenne River, SD	399	54	1	-	3	50	-	12	8	-
Chitimacha, LA	65	11	3	1	1	6	-	2	-	-
Cochiti Pueblo, NM	167	40	1	6	-	34	3	13	4	-
Cocopah, AZ	83	19	1	1	1	16	-	4	1	-
Coeur D'Alene, Idaho	146	55	2	4	6	43	-	12	4	-
Cold Springs Rancheria, CA	11	1	-	-	-	1	-	-	-	-
Colorado River, AZ-CA	650	158	10	18	13	117	3	50	8	-
Colville, WA	1,304	287	5	41	36	205	1	83	13	1
Cortina Rancheria, CA	...	...	...	...	...	...	...	...	...	...
Coushatta, LA	...	...	...	...	...	...	...	...	...	...
Coyote Valley Rancheria, CA	-	-	-	-	-	-	-	-	-	-
Crow, MT	1,039	272	8	30	19	216	-	88	14	5
Crow Creek, SD	322	75	-	10	5	60	-	23	2	-
Cuyapaipe, CA	...	...	...	...	...	...	...	...	...	...
Deer Creek, MN	...	...	...	...	...	...	...	...	...	...
Dresslerville Colony, NV	50	16	-	-	4	12	-	-	1	-
Dry Creek Rancheria, CA	4	1	-	-	-	1	-	-	-	-
Duck Valley, ID-NV	278	62	6	6	-	50	-	18	9	2
Duckwater, NV	40	10	-	-	-	10	-	5	-	-
Eastern Cherokee, NC	1,800	340	17	29	79	215	1	66	11	6
Eastern Pequot, CT	...	...	...	...	...	...	...	...	...	...
Ely Colony, NV	21	1	-	-	-	1	-	1	-	-
Enterprise Rancheria, CA	...	...	...	...	...	...	...	...	...	...
Fallon Colony, NV	16	-	-	-	-	-	-	-	-	-
Fallon, NV	100	24	1	-	1	21	-	8	-	-
Flandreau, SD	60	11	-	-	-	11	-	5	1	-
Flathead, MT	1,216	241	5	24	44	168	3	49	19	5
Fond du Lac, MN	142	21	3	1	-	17	-	1	3	3
Fort Apache, AZ	1,837	422	33	16	72	300	1	92	10	2
Fort Belknap, MT	493	105	8	6	4	88	-	51	4	3
Fort Berthold, ND	740	148	-	11	4	132	-	61	3	-
Fort Bidwell, CA	19	4	1	-	-	3	-	2	-	-
Fort Hall, Idaho	675	136	7	16	13	100	1	42	4	-
Fort Independence, CA	16	6	-	-	1	5	-	2	-	-
Fort McDermitt, NV-OR	101	14	-	-	-	14	-	6	1	-
Fort McDowell, AZ	129	21	1	-	3	17	-	5	-	-
Fort Mojave, AZ-CA-NV	39	10	1	-	1	8	-	3	-	-
Fort Peck, MT	1,262	289	17	33	20	219	1	64	17	5
Fort Totten, ND	462	94	3	12	5	75	1	30	5	-
Fort Yuma, AZ-CA	339	93	13	6	6	68	-	24	5	1
Gila Bend, AZ	-	-	-	-	-	-	-	-	-	-
Gila River, AZ	1,762	382	30	35	24	293	4	93	11	1
Golden Hill, CT	...	...	...	...	...	...	...	...	...	...
Goshute, NV-UT	17	4	-	-	-	4	-	-	-	-
Grand Portage, MN	88	18	-	2	1	15	-	3	3	-
Grindstone Creek Rancheria, CA	20	6	1	-	-	5	-	-	3	-
Hannahville Community, MI	76	8	-	-	-	8	-	-	2	-
Hassanamisco, MA	...	...	...	...	...	...	...	...	4	...
Havasupai, AZ	86	15	1	1	2	11	-	-	4	-
Hoh, WA	14	1	-	-	-	1	-	1	-	-
Hollywood, FL	197	67	1	-	27	39	-	16	6	-
Hoopa Valley, CA	441	91	1	4	12	74	-	22	7	5

[Continued]

805

★ 528 ★

Technical, Sales, and Administrative Occupations Held by Residents of Reservations, 1980: Acoma Pueblo - Isabella
[Continued]

Identified reservation	Persons 16 years and over working in 1980 reference period	Technical, sales, and administrative support occupations								
		Total	Health technologists and technicians	Technologists and technicians, except health	Sales occupations	Administrative support occupations, including clerical				
						Total	Computer equipment operators	Secretaries, stenographers, and typists	Financial records processing occupations	Mail and message distributing occupations
Hoopa Valley Extension, CA	100	20	-	1	-	19	-	2	2	1
Hopi, AZ	1,435	399	21	12	53	313	1	99	16	3
Hopland Rancheria, CA	-	-	-	-	-	-	-	-	-	-
Hualapai, AZ	236	59	5	7	2	45	-	23	2	1
Inaja-Cosmit, CA	-	-	-	-	-	-	-	-	-	-
Indian Township, ME	104	16	-	1	1	13	-	5	-	-
Iowa, KS-NE	15	2	-	-	-	2	-	2	-	-
Isabella, MI	146	33	1	2	5	25	-	11	2	-

Source: U.S. Bureau of the Census, Subject Reports, PC80-2-1D, Part II, *American Indians, Eskimos, and Aleuts on Identified Reservations and in the Historic Areas of Oklahoma (Excluding Urbanized Areas),* U.S. Government Printing Office, Washington, D.C., 1986, pp. 482-520. *Notes:* A dash (-) represents zero or a percent which rounds to less than 0.1. Also, a dash (-) is used because the number of supplementary questionnaires for the areas was insufficient to produce reliable estimates. Three dots (...) means not applicable, or that the data are being withheld to avoid disclosure of information for individuals.

★ 529 ★

Technical, Sales, and Administrative Occupations Held by Residents of Reservations, 1980: Isleta - Santa Clara Pueblo

Data are the latest available.

Identified reservation	Persons 16 years and over working in 1980 reference period	Technical, sales, and administrative occupations								
		Total	Health technologists and technicians	Technologists and technicians, except health	Sales occupations	Administrative support occupations, including clerical				
						Total	Computer equipment operators	Secretaries, stenographers, and typists	Financial records processing occupations	Mail and message distributing occupations
Isleta Pueblo, NM	874	255	17	39	19	181	6	61	21	3
Jackson Rancheria, CA	...	...	...	...	...	...	...	...	...	...
Jemez Pueblo, NM	383	98	2	11	10	74	-	19	4	4
Jicarilla Apache, NM	656	128	4	7	13	104	3	47	8	-
Kaibab, AZ	42	9	-	2	-	6	-	1	3	-
Kalispel, WA	36	9	-	-	2	7	-	2	-	-
Kickapoo, KS	108	23	-	2	3	19	-	14	3	-
Kootenai, ID	-	-	-	-	-	-	-	-	-	-
Lac Courte Oreilles, WI	331	73	3	-	3	67	6	16	11	-
Lac du Flambeau, WI	322	50	1	-	-	49	-	13	7	-
Laguna Pueblo, NM	1,300	222	17	24	10	170	-	64	11	3
La Jolla, CA	43	7	-	-	1	6	-	2	1	-
L'Anse, MI	177	38	1	1	4	1	32	-	15	-
La Posta, CA	...	...	...	...	...	...	...	...	...	...
Las Vegas Colony, NV	35	7	-	-	3	4	-	1	-	-
Laytonville Rancheria, CA	24	6	-	-	-	6	-	-	1	-
Leech Lake, MN	728	153	14	6	10	123	-	54	6	2
Likely Rancheria, CA	-	-	-	-	-	-	-	-	-	-
Lone Pine Rancheria, CA	49	10	1	-	4	5	-	2	-	-
Lookout Rancheria, CA	...	...	...	...	...	...	...	...	...	...
Los Coyotes, CA	11	2	-	-	-	2	-	-	-	-
Lovelock Colony, NV	34	4	2	-	-	2	-	2	-	-
Lower Brule, SD	243	56	-	4	-	52	-	28	5	-
Lower Elwah, WA	17	3	-	1	1	1	-	1	-	-
Lower Sioux Community, MN	25	4	-	-	2	2	-	-	-	-
Lummi, WA	347	68	1	3	6	58	-	23	6	-
Makah, WA	318	83	-	7	12	65	-	24	7	1
Manchester Rancheria, CA	15	3	-	-	1	2	-	1	-	-
Manzanita, CA	...	...	...	...	...	...	...	...	...	...
Maricopa, AZ	95	25	-	2	3	20	-	6	-	-
Mattaponi, VA	23	2	-	-	1	1	-	-	1	-

[Continued]

★ 529 ★

Technical, Sales, and Administrative Occupations Held by Residents of Reservations, 1980: Isleta - Santa Clara Pueblo

[Continued]

Identified reservation	Persons 16 years and over working in 1980 reference period	Technical, sales, and administrative occupations								
		Total	Health technologists and technicians	Technologists and technicians, except health	Sales occupations	Administrative support occupations, including clerical				
						Total	Computer equipment operators	Secretaries, stenographers, and typists	Financial records processing occupations	Mail and message distributing occupations
Menominee, WI	699	154	2	15	19	118	3	30	16	1
Mesa Grande, CA	-	-	-	-	-	-	-	-	-	-
Mescalero Apache, NM	548	102	13	6	8	75	1	30	8	1
Miccosukee, Florida	134	32	2	2	6	22	-	9	2	-
Middletown Rancheria, CA	9	1	-	-	1	-	-	-	-	-
Mille Lacs, MN	-	-	-	-	-	-	-	-	-	-
Mississippi Choctaw Reservation, MS	909	159	5	10	5	139	4	34	5	1
Moapa River, NV	47	5	-	-	1	4	-	-	2	-
Montgomery Creek Rancheria, CA	...	...	...	...	...	...	...	...	...	...
Morongo, CA	96	18	-	-	6	12	-	4	-	-
Muckleshoot, WA	98	25	-	-	7	18	-	5	1	-
Nambe Pueblo, NM	82	22	-	6	-	15	-	10	2	-
Navajo, AZ-NM-UT	22,636	5,587	224	351	691	4,322	26	1,066	197	26
Nez Perce, ID	469	123	7	5	7	104	-	39	6	1
Nisqually, WA	13	3	-	-	-	3	-	-	-	-
Nooksack, WA	-	-	-	-	-	-	-	-	-	-
Northern Cheyenne, MT	839	235	12	20	4	199	-	66	13	13
Oil Springs, NY	-	-	-	-	-	-	-	-	-	-
Omaha, IO-NE	339	63	1	10	-	52	-	32	6	-
Oneida, WI	608	118	3	14	20	81	-	27	11	3
Onondaga, NY	-	-	-	-	-	-	-	-	-	-
Ontonagon, MI	-	-	-	-	-	-	-	-	-	-
Osage, OK	1,755	458	16	28	120	294	10	109	24	17
Ozette, WA	...	...	...	...	...	...	...	...	...	...
Pala, CA	142	29	-	1	3	25	-	15	-	1
Pamunkey, VA	19	3	-	-	-	3	-	-	1	-
Papago, AZ	1,607	361	20	21	16	305	-	81	17	-
Pascua Yaqui, AZ	110	16	1	-	-	14	-	6	-	-
Pauma, CA	26	5	-	-	-	5	-	1	-	-
Payson Comm. of Yavapai-Apache, AZ	-	-	-	-	-	-	-	-	-	-
Pechanga, CA	36	6	-	-	3	3	-	-	1	1
Penobscot, MA	127	26	1	4	1	20	-	6	4	-
Picuris Pueblo, NM	52	10	-	1	-	8	-	4	3	-
Pine Creek, MI	...	...	...	...	...	...	...	...	...	...
Pine Ridge, SD	2,482	609	26	37	39	507	-	133	24	11
Pleasant Point, MA	101	26	-	2	1	23	-	4	3	-
Pojoaque Pueblo, NM	41	6	1	1	-	3	-	1	-	-
Poospatuck, NY	13	2	-	1	-	1	-	-	-	-
Port Gamble, WA	97	23	-	-	5	18	-	8	6	-
Port Madison, WA	56	15	-	1	10	4	-	-	-	-
Potawatomi, WI	61	4	-	-	-	4	-	-	1	-
Pottawatomi, KS	128	35	3	-	7	26	-	12	-	4
Prairie Island Community, MN	28	3	-	-	1	2	-	-	-	-
Puyallup, WA	237	94	7	3	38	45	-	18	5	-
Pyramid Lake, NV	226	61	2	6	10	43	-	12	7	-
Quileute, WA	69	18	-	-	4	14	-	2	1	-
Quinault, WA	324	69	1	3	13	52	-	15	6	-
Ramah Community, NM	335	78	4	7	5	63	-	19	4	3
Ramona, CA	-	-	-	-	-	-	-	-	-	-
Red Cliff, WI	149	33	-	-	2	31	-	16	1	-
Red Lake, MN	707	198	11	13	6	168	1	54	13	1
Reno-Sparks Colony, NV	186	48	1	4	16	26	-	8	2	3
Resighini Rancheria, CA	...	...	...	...	...	...	...	...	...	...
Rincon, CA	91	21	-	2	2	16	-	6	-	-
Roaring Creek Rancheria, CA	...	...	...	...	...	...	...	...	...	...
Rocky Boy's, MT	391	77	2	11	5	60	-	28	6	-
Rosebud, SD	1,279	334	11	19	31	273	-	90	22	-
Round Valley, CA	142	24	1	-	2	21	-	5	6	-
Rumsey Rancheria, CA	...	...	...	...	...	...	...	...	...	...
Sac and Fox, Iowa	141	27	1	2	1	22	-	3	1	2
Sac and Fox, KS-NE	...	...	...	...	...	...	...	...	...	...
St. Croix, WI	116	22	-	3	-	19	-	6	4	-
St. Regis Mohawk, NY	491	62	-	8	6	48	-	16	4	-
Salt River, AZ	880	159	4	9	23	123	1	33	3	1
San Carlos, AZ	1,442	315	17	20	31	247	1	77	23	7
Sandia Pueblo, NM	86	28	1	4	2	21	-	13	1	-
Sandy Lake, MN	-	-	-	-	-	-	-	-	-	-
San Felipe Pueblo, NM	469	130	2	16	8	104	4	45	3	4
San Ildefonso Pueblo, NM	197	63	1	12	4	45	-	26	-	-
San Juan Pueblo, NM	287	71	5	8	7	51	-	21	2	2

[Continued]

807

★ 529 ★

Technical, Sales, and Administrative Occupations Held by Residents of Reservations, 1980: Isleta - Santa Clara Pueblo

[Continued]

Identified reservation	Persons 16 years and over working in 1980 reference period	Technical, sales, and administrative occupations								
		Total	Health technologists and technicians	Technologists and technicians, except health	Sales occupations	Administrative support occupations, including clerical				
						Total	Computer equipment operators	Secretaries, stenographers, and typists	Financial records processing occupations	Mail and message distributing occupations
San Manuel, CA	-	-	-	-	-	-	-	-	-	-
San Pasqual, CA	34	11	-	-	-	11	-	3	1	1
Santa Ana Pueblo, NM	184	54	3	10	1	39	1	13	2	-
Santa Clara Pueblo, NM	706	201	8	38	10	145	-	64	8	5

Source: U.S. Bureau of the Census, Subject Reports, PC80-2-1D, Part II, *American Indians, Eskimos, and Aleuts on Identified Reservations and in the Historic Areas of Oklahoma (Excluding Urbanized Areas)*, U.S. Government Printing Office, Washington, D.C., 1986, pp. 482-520. *Notes:* A dash (-) represents zero or a percent which rounds to less than 0.1. Also, a dash (-) is used because the number of supplementary questionnaires for the areas was insufficient to produce reliable estimates. Three dots (...) means not applicable, or that the data are being withheld to avoid disclosure of information for individuals.

★ 530 ★

Technical, Sales, and Administrative Occupations Held by Residents of Reservations, 1980: Santa Rosa Rancheria - Zuni Pueblo

Data are the latest available.

Identified reservation	Persons 16 years and over working in 1980 reference period	Technical, sales, and administrative occupations								
		Total	Health technologists and technicians	Technologists and technicians, except health	Sales occupations	Administrative support occupations, including clerical				
						Total	Computer equipment operators	Secretaries, stenographers, and typists	Financial records processing occupations	Mail and message distributing occupations
Santa Rosa Rancheria, CA	31	6	-	-	-	6	-	1	-	-
Santa Rosa, CA	...	...	...	...	...	...	...	...	...	...
Santa Ynez, CA	56	9	-	-	2	6	-	4	1	-
Santa Ysabel, CA	63	11	-	2	-	8	-	3	1	-
Santee, Nebraska	124	12	-	2	-	10	-	6	-	-
Santo Domingo Pueblo, NM	712	60	9	5	-	47	-	16	6	-
San Xavier, AZ	247	50	2	5	13	30	-	9	1	-
Sauk-Suiattle, WA	-	-	-	-	-	-	-	-	-	-
Sault Ste. Marie, MI	-	-	-	-	-	-	-	-	-	-
Schaghticoke, CT	...	...	...	...	...	...	...	...	...	...
Shakopee Community, MN	30	6	-	1	-	5	-	1	-	-
Sheep Ranch Rancheria, CA	...	...	...	...	...	...	...	...	...	...
Sherwood Valley Rancheria, CA	...	...	...	...	...	...	...	...	...	...
Shingle Springs Rancheria, CA	...	...	-	-	-	-	-	-	-	-
Shinnecock, NY	72	12	-	-	-	12	-	10	-	-
Shoalwater, WA	...	...	...	...	...	...	...	...	...	...
Sisseton, ND-SD	591	144	8	11	6	119	-	50	7	3
Skokomish, WA	61	13	1	-	2	10	-	6	-	-
Skull Valley, UT	-	-	-	-	-	-	-	-	-	-
Soboba, CA	57	14	4	1	-	9	-	1	-	1
Sokaogon Chippewa Community, WI	44	6	-	1	-	5	-	2	-	-
Southern Paiute, UT	50	10	-	1	1	8	-	3	-	-
Southern Ute, CO	291	101	3	16	1	80	-	28	-	-
Spokane, WA	451	82	1	15	12	54	-	27	5	1
Squaxin Island, WA	9	1	-	-	-	1	-	-	-	-
Standing Rock, ND-SD	1,077	194	7	17	5	165	-	61	5	-
Stewart's Point Rancheria, CA	20	-	-	-	-	-	-	-	-	-
Stockbridge, WI	207	41	2	-	5	33	-	11	8	-
Sulphur Bank Rancheria, CA	18	2	-	-	-	2	-	-	-	-
Summit Lake, NV	...	...	...	...	...	...	...	...	...	...
Susanville, CA	30	5	-	1	-	3	-	1	-	-
Swinomish, WA	139	20	-	1	2	16	-	-	6	-
Sycuan, CA	8	-	-	-	-	-	-	-	-	-
Tama, GA	17	2	-	-	2	-	-	-	-	-
Taos Pueblo, NM	307	57	5	2	9	41	-	3	6	2
Te-Moak, NV	38	4	-	-	-	4	-	1	1	-
Tesuque Pueblo, NM	83	24	-	3	4	17	-	9	2	-

[Continued]

★ 530 ★

Technical, Sales, and Administrative Occupations Held by Residents of Reservations, 1980: Santa Rosa Rancheria - Zuni Pueblo

[Continued]

Identified reservation	Persons 16 years and over working in 1980 reference period	Technical, sales, and administrative occupations								
		Total	Health technologists and technicians	Technologists and technicians, except health	Sales occupations	Administrative support occupations, including clerical				
						Total	Computer equipment operators	Secretaries, stenographers, and typists	Financial records processing occupations	Mail and message distributing occupations
Tigua, TX	105	14	-	1	3	10	-	2	1	-
Tonawanda, NY	168	35	-	5	7	24	-	6	1	-
Torres-Martinez, CA	-	-	-	-	-	-	-	-	-	-
Trinidad Rancheria, CA	20	2	-	-	1	1	-	-	1	-
Tulalip, WA	241	72	6	3	19	45	1	19	5	1
Tule River, CA	134	28	2	4	-	22	-	6	3	-
Tunicabiloxi, LA	...	...	...	...	...	...	...	...	...	...
Tuolumne Rancheria, CA	26	5	-	-	-	5	-	-	-	-
Turtle Mountain, ND	961	185	11	19	15	140	-	41	5	6
Tuscarora, NY	-	-	-	-	-	-	-	-	-	-
Twenty-Nine Palms, CA	-	-	-	-	-	-	-	-	-	-
Uintah and Ouray, UT	588	116	7	5	23	82	5	29	8	-
Umatilla, OR	297	81	5	10	14	53	-	27	2	1
Upper Sioux Community, MN	21	6	-	-	-	6	-	-	-	-
Upper Skagit, WA	-	-	-	-	-	-	-	-	-	-
Ute Mountain, CO-NM	308	65	-	11	3	51	-	14	-	-
Vermillion Lake, MN	27	5	-	-	-	5	-	5	-	-
Viejas Rancheria, CA	51	7	-	-	1	6	-	1	-	-
Walker River, NV	162	40	3	3	3	31	-	12	-	2
Wampanoag, MA	-	-	-	-	-	-	-	-	-	-
Warm Springs, OR	602	125	2	20	15	88	1	37	4	-
Washoe, NV	-	-	-	-	-	-	-	-	-	-
Western Pequot, CT	...	...	...	...	...	...	...	...	...	...
White Earth, MN	734	176	5	9	36	125	-	19	10	5
Wind River, WY	1,119	221	19	14	9	179	2	69	22	1
Winnebago, Nebraska	317	74	4	3	4	62	-	35	3	-
Winnemucca Colony, NV	9	3	-	-	1	2	-	2	-	-
Wisconsin Winnebago Reservation	105	30	2	3	2	24	-	3	-	-
Woodfords Community, CA	-	-	-	-	-	-	-	-	-	-
XL Ranch, CA	...	...	...	...	...	...	...	...	...	...
Yakima, WA	1,532	341	5	33	58	247	3	79	16	3
Yankton, SD	359	85	4	11	-	70	-	24	4	2
Yavapai, AZ	28	8	2	-	-	6	-	2	1	-
Yerington, NV	40	5	1	1	1	2	-	2	-	-
Yomba, NV	20	4	-	-	-	4	-	3	-	-
Zia Pueblo, NM	179	24	1	1	-	22	1	6	1	-
Zuni Pueblo, NM	2,000	352	27	23	39	263	-	78	12	-
San Felipe/Santa Ana Joint Area, NM	-	-	-	-	-	-	-	-	-	-
San Felipe/Santo Domingo Joint Area, NM	26	2	-	-	-	2	-	-	-	-
Other Reservation Lands in MT	-	-	-	-	-	-	-	-	-	-

Source: U.S. Bureau of the Census, Subject Reports, PC80-2-1D, Part II, *American Indians, Eskimos, and Aleuts on Identified Reservations and in the Historic Areas of Oklahoma (Excluding Urbanized Areas)*, U.S. Government Printing Office, Washington, D.C., 1986, pp. 482-520. *Notes:* A dash (-) represents zero or a percent which rounds to less than 0.1. Also, a dash (-) is used because the number of supplementary questionnaires for the areas was insufficient to produce reliable estimates. Three dots (...) means not applicable, or that the data are being withheld to avoid disclosure of information for individuals.

Income and Poverty

★ 531 ★

Median Annual Income of Full-Time State and Local Government Employees, by Race/Ethnicity, Sex and Profession, 1990: U.S. Summary

Race/ethnicity and sex	Median annual income ($)				
	Total	Officials/ administrators	Professionals	Technicians	Protective service
Both sexes					
Total	24,499	39,986	31,936	24,955	27,738
American Indian/Alaska Native	22,507	37,349	28,937	23,106	23,562
White	25,188	40,208	31,936	25,496	27,896
Black	22,011	37,911	29,485	22,806	25,705
Hispanic	23,764	38,071	31,694	24,955	30,719
Asian	31,462	45,315	38,796	28,548	35,104
Men					
Total	27,323	42,457	34,669	28,014	28,265
American Indian/Alaska Native	24,064	40,198	30,334	24,318	24,041
White	28,166	42,504	34,932	28,353	28,394
Black	23,351	41,081	30,682	25,047	26,155
Hispanic	25,998	41,529	33,932	27,306	31,030
Asian	34,111	45,857	40,653	30,485	35,297
Women					
Total	21,847	35,037	29,724	22,157	23,995
American Indian/Alaska Native	20,453	31,316	27,514	21,264	21,403
White	22,005	35,007	29,597	22,076	23,411
Black	20,963	35,036	28,901	21,643	24,481
Hispanic	21,578	32,742	29,902	23,074	28,645
Asian	28,962	44,042	37,316	26,705	33,527

Source: U.S. Equal Employment Opportunity Commission, *Job Patterns for Minorities and Women in State and Local Government, 1990*, U.S. Government Printing Office, 1991, p. 1-7.

★ 532 ★

Median Annual Income of Full-Time Local Government Employees, by Race/Ethnicity and Type of Government, 1990

Figures are shown in dollars.

Race/ethnicity and sex	County	City	Town	Special districts
Both sexes				
Total	22,066	26,258	27,306	27,209
American Indian/Alaska Native	20,472	24,376	27,083	30,525
White	22,145	27,645	27,407	28,270
Black	20,739	22,874	24,510	24,456
Hispanic	22,425	24,620	25,309	25,017
Asian	29,947	32,337	26,726	32,318
Men				
Total	24,208	28,048	29,317	30,380
American Indian/Alaska Native	22,057	25,643	28,179	33,322
White	24,510	29,298	29,426	31,614
Black	21,549	23,391	25,849	27,987
Hispanic	24,356	26,063	27,160	27,935
Asian	31,522	34,031	29,849	35,125
Women				
Total	20,141	22,711	21,599	22,218
American Indian/Alaska Native	19,066	22,061	22,857	24,296
White	19,816	22,707	21,584	23,452
Black	20,244	22,310	22,109	19,096
Hispanic	21,152	22,408	20,673	19,234
Asian	28,762	30,270	22,353	29,861

Source: U.S. Equal Employment Opportunity Commission, *Job Patterns for Minorities and Women in State and Local Government, 1990*, U.S. Government Printing Office, 1991, pp. 15, 18, 21 and 24. *Note:* This table includes some units that cross geographical boundaries.

★ 533 ★

Median Household Income and Poverty Status Compared to Whites, 1980 and 1990

Income characteristic	1980[1]	1990
Median household income ($)		
White	29,632	31,435
Native American	20,541	20,025
Percentage below poverty		
White	9.4	9.8
Native American	27.5	30.9

Source: USA TODAY, December 10, 1992, p. 11A. Primary source: U.S. Census Bureau *Note:* 1. Adjusted for inflation.

★ 534 ★

Child Poverty Rates in Urban Areas, 1989

Highest poverty rates are shown for each group, by urban area.

Race/ethnicity	Children living in poverty	
	City	Percent
Native Americans	Minneapolis, MN	66.0
Blacks	Erie, PA	62.0
Hispanics	Erie, PA	69.0
Asians	St. Paul, MN	69.0

Source: USA TODAY, August 12, 1992, p. 3-A. Primary source: Children's Defense Fund.

★ 535 ★

Poorest Counties in the United States, 1980 and 1990

Counties/parishes emboldened are those on Indian reservations. Note that those reservations in poverty actually got *poorer* over the last ten years and while two reservations are off the list, three more fell below the poverty line.

County/parish and year	Percent of people living below poverty
1990	
Shannon, SD	63.1
Starr, TX	60.0
Tunica, MS	56.8
East Carroll, LA	56.8
Holmes, MS	53.2
Owsley, KY	52.1
Ziebach, SD	51.1
Maverick, TX	50.4
Zavala, TX	50.4
Todd, SD	50.2
Issaquena, MS	49.3
Dimmit, TX	48.9
Menominee, WI	48.7
Presido, TX	48.1
Sharkey, MS	47.5
Sioux, ND	47.4
Lee, AR	47.3
Apache, AZ	47.1
Jefferson, MS	46.9
Tensas, LA	46.3
Humphreys, MS	45.9
Greene, AL	45.6
McCreary, KY	45.5
Coahoma, MS	45.5
Wilcox, AL	45.2
1980	
Tunica, MS	52.9
Starr, TX	50.6
Owsley, KY	48.3
Holmes, MS	46.9
Greene, AL	45.7
Wilcox, AL	45.3
Lowndes, AL	45.0
Humphreys, MS	44.7
Shannon, SD	44.7
Lee, AR	44.3
Sharkey, MS	44.0
Perry, AL	43.8

[Continued]

★ 535 ★

Poorest Counties in the United States, 1980 and 1990

[Continued]

County/parish and year	Percent of people living below poverty
Ziebach, SD	43.7
Todd, SD	43.5
Tallahatchie, MS	43.5
Hancock, TN	43.0
Madison, LA	42.7
Buffalo, SD	42.5
Clay, KY	42.4
East Carroll, LA	41.8
Corson, SD	41.5
Quitman, MS	41.4
Tensas, LA	41.2
Jefferson, MS	41.1
Clay, GA	40.7

Source: USA TODAY, November 30, 1992, p. 7A. Primary source: Census Bureau. *Notes:* In 1991, the Census Bureau considered a family of four with an income of $13,924 or below in poverty.

★ 536 ★

Poverty Status, by Race/Ethnicity, 1980 and 1990

Data are shown for 1980 (adjusted for inflation) and 1990.

Income characteristics	1980	1990
Median household income		
Native American	20,541	20,025
White	29,632	31,435
Black	18,340	19,758
Asian	33,463	36,784
Hispanic[1]	22,629	24,156
Percentage below poverty line		
Native American	27.5	30.9
White	9.4	9.8
Black	29.9	29.5
Asian	13.1	14.1
Hispanic[1]	23.5	25.3
Children below poverty line (%)		
Native American	32.5	37.6
White	11.0	12.3
Black	37.8	38.8

[Continued]

★ 536 ★

Poverty Status, by Race/Ethnicity, 1980 and 1990
[Continued]

Income characteristics	1980	1990
Asian	14.9	16.6
Hispanic[1]	29.1	31.0

Source: Margaret L. Udansky, "Income Equality Gap Widens for Minorities," *USA Today*, July 24, 1992, p. 3A. Census Bureau *Note:* 1. Hispanics may be of any race.

Public Assistance

★ 537 ★

Home Energy Assistance

Number of households receiving LIHEAP (Low Income Home Energy Assistance Program) assistance is shown, by tribe or tribal organization for each state. Data refer to FY1988[1].

Indian tribe or tribal organization	Type of Assistance			
	Heating	Cooling	Crisis	Weatherization
Total[2]	40,959	620	7,807	1,589
Alabama				
Mowa Band of Choctaws	338	-	16	-
Poarch Band of Creeks	150	55	27	-
Alaska				
Aleutian/Pribilof Islands Assn.	169	-	34	-
Assn. Village Council Pres.	1,743	-	202	50
C. Council Tlingit & Haida	639	-	202	-
Cook Inlet Tribal Council	975	-	500	-
Kenaitze	96	-	-	-
Ketchikan Indian Corp.	127	-	89	-
Orutsararmuit Native Council	288	-	-	-
Tanana Chiefs Conference	1,305	-	10	85
Arizona				
Colorado River	105[3]	[3]	7	-
Gila River	163[3]	[3]	95	13
Hopi	88	-	1	10
Navajo	7,305	-	286	278
Pascua Yaqui	-	-	104	-
Quechan (Ft. Yuma)	106	106	-	-
Salt River Pima-Maricopa	125	27	12	13
San Carlos Apache	168	-	19	16

[Continued]

★537★

Home Energy Assistance
[Continued]

Indian tribe or tribal organization	Type of Assistance			
	Heating	Cooling	Crisis	Weatherization
Tohono O'odham (Papago)	165	59	101	-
White Mountain Apache	366	-	46	25
California				
Berry Creek	33	-	13	4
Covelo (Round Valley)	183	-	-	-
Coyote Valley Pomo[4]	-	-	-	-
Hoopa Valley	176	-	-	-
ITC of California	373	155	54	-
Karuk	111[3]	[3]	41	2
La Jolla	43	-	9	-
Pit River	74	-	49	6
Quartz Valley[4]	-	-	-	-
Riverside-San B. Indian Health	91	-	137	2
Robinson	17	-	14	-
Santa Ysabel	23	-	-	-
Sherwood Valley	-	-	37	-
S. Cal. Tribal Chr. Assn.	59	-	-	1
S. Indian Health Council	48	-	42	-
Florida				
Seminole	58	-	-	-
Idaho				
Kootenai[4]	-	-	-	-
Nez Perce	132	-	28	-
Shoshone-Bannock (Ft. Hall)	-	-	172	-
Kansas				
United Tribes Kansas & SE Neb.	55	22	-	-
Maine				
Houlton Band of Maliseets	72	-	-	-
Passamaquoddy--Indian Township	131	-	50	-
Passamaquoddy--Pleasant Point	134	-	52	16
Penobscot	100	-	-	-
Massachusetts				
Mashpee Wampanoag	36	-	-	-
Michigan				
Grand Traverse Ottawa/Chippewa	136	-	-	-
ITC of Michigan	241	-	6	-
Sault Ste. Marie Chippewa	81	-	242	9

[Continued]

★ 537 ★

Home Energy Assistance
[Continued]

Indian tribe or tribal organization	Type of Assistance			
	Heating	Cooling	Crisis	Weatherization
Minnesota				
Mille Lacs Band of Chippewas	214	-	31	-
Mississippi				
Mississippi Choctaw	-	-	105	-
Montana				
Assiniboine & Sioux (Ft. Peck)	802	-	128	-
Blackfeet	1,467	-	-	-
Chippewa-Cree (Rocky Boy's)	332	-	-	-
Confederated Salish & Kootenai	806	-	42	-
Ft. Belknap	325	-	-	-
Northern Cheyenne	516	-	-	-
Dept. of Interior for Crow	586	-	-	-
Nebraska				
Winnebago[4]	-	-	-	-
Nevada				
Walker River Paiute	65	-	65	-
New Jersey				
Powhatan Renape	221	-	16	-
New Mexico				
Five Sandoval Pueblos	133	-	-	-
Jicarilla Apache	50	-	3	-
Pueblo of Laguna	78	-	-	-
Pueblo of Zuni	420			
New York				
Seneca	155	-	14	-
St. Regis Mohawk	225	-	51	-
North Carolina				
Lumbee	3,378	-	808	-
North Dakota				
Devils Lake Sioux (Ft. Totten)	308	-	43	-
Standing Rock Sioux	520	-	188	-
Three Affiliated (Ft. Berthold)	351	-	40	-
Turtle Mountain Chippewa	1,177	-	-	-
Oklahoma				
Apache[4]	-	-	-	-

[Continued]

817

★ 537 ★

Home Energy Assistance
[Continued]

Indian tribe or tribal organization	Type of Assistance			
	Heating	Cooling	Crisis	Weatherization
Caddo	24	5	19	-
Cherokee	1,584	15	13	-
Cheyenne-Arapaho	108	-	-	-
Chickasaw	195	112	78	-
Choctaw	192	-	679	-
Citizen Band Potawatomi	39	-	-	-
Comanche	117	13	43	-
Delaware	7	1	3	-
Kiowa	-	-	223	-
Otoe-Missouria	17	-	-	-
Pawnee	24	-	-	-
Sac & Fox	52	-	5	-
Seminole	136	-	-	-
Tonkawa	19	-	-	-
Rhode Island				
Narragansett[4]	-	-	-	-
South Dakota				
Cheyenne River Sioux	736	-	88	-
Crow Creek Sioux	196	-	-	-
Lower Brule Sioux	166	-	-	-
Ogala Sioux (Pine Ridge)	1,794	-	395	969
Rosebud Sioux	1,249	50	532	-
Sisseton-Wahpeton Sioux	487	-	70	-
Yankton Sioux	193	-	193	-
Utah				
Paiute	285	-	91	-
Ute (Uintah & Ouray)	177	-	16	-
Washington				
Colville	691	-	370	56
Confederated Yakima	1,143	-	436	-
Jamestown Klallam	21	-	6	-
Kalispel	18	-	2	-
Lower Elwha Klallam	54	-	7	18
Lummi	329	-	45	-
Makah	128	-	-	-
Muckelshoot	151	-	-	-
Nooksack	113	-	-	-
Port Gamble Klallam	53	-	8	-
Puyallup	232	-	124	5
Quinault	198	-	69	11
Small Tribes Org. W. Wash.	113	-	7	-

[Continued]

★ 537 ★

Home Energy Assistance
[Continued]

Indian tribe or tribal organization	Type of Assistance			
	Heating	Cooling	Crisis	Weatherization
South Puget I.P.A.	290	-	-	-
Spokane	271	-	19	-
Suquamish	24	-	-	-
Tulalip	220	-	1	-
Upper Skagit	52	-	24	-

Source: Low Income Home Energy Assistance Program: Report to Congress for FY89, U.S. Department of Health and Human Services, Family Support Administration, Office of Community Services, Office of Energy Assistance, October 29, 1992, ff. 101-105. *Notes:* 1. Information was provided by grantees' required reports on the number and income levels of households served. For grantees with at least one table cell filled, a dash (-) indicates that, according to information available to HHS, the respective grantee did not provide the type of assistance specified by the column heading. 2. Totals include households served by 108 of the 114 tribal grantees. 3. Combined heating and cooling assistance program. 4. Grantee did not report on number of households served.

★ 538 ★

Home Energy Grants

LIHEAP (Low Income Home Energy Assistance Program) allotments are shown in dollars, by tribe or tribal organization in each state. Data refer to FY1988.

Indian tribe or Tribal organization	Allotment $
Total	12,877,935
Alabama[1]	
Mowa Band of Choctaw Indians	41,627
Poarch Band of Creek Indians (includes Florida service population)[2,3]	27,668
Alaska[1]	
Aleutian/Pribilof Islands Association	114,765
Association of Village Council Presidents	807,240
Central Council of the Tlingit and Haida Tribes of Alaska	380,564
Cook Inlet Tribal Council	411,400
Kenaitze Indian Tribe	52,662
Ketchikan Indian Corporation	74,616
Orutsaramuit Native Council	145,002
Tanana Chiefs Conference	741,082
Arizona[1]	
Colorado River Indian Tribes (includes California service population)[2,3,4]	17,010
Gila River Indian Community[5]	49,376
Hopi Tribe[5]	52,877

[Continued]

819

★ 538 ★

Home Energy Grants
[Continued]

Indian tribe or Tribal organization	Allotment $
Navajo Nation (includes New Mexico and Utah service population)[2,6]	953,132
Pascua Yaqui Tribe[5]	11,237
Quechan Tribe of the Fort Yuma Indian Reservation (includes California service population)[2,3,4]	22,209
Salt River Pima-Maricopa Indian Community[5]	20,899
San Carlos Apache Tribe[5]	31,689
Tohono O'odham Nation (Papago tribe)[5]	66,971
White Mountain Apache Tribe[5]	41,553
California[1]	
Berry Creek Rancheria of Maidu Indians[7]	4,486
Covelo Indian Community of the Round Valley Reservation[7]	31,771
Coyote Valley Band of Pomo Indians[7]	6,043
Hoopa Valley Tribe[7]	15,565
Inter-Tribal Council of California, for 31 tribes:[7]	172,677
Big Lagoon Rancheria of Smith River Indians	641
Big Pine Band of Paiute Shoshone Indians	6,592
Big Sandy Rancheria of Mono Indians	1,831
Big Valley Rancheria of Pomo and Pit River Indians	7,142
Bridgeport Paiute Indian Colony	824
Cabazon Band of Mission Indians	92
Coast Indian Community of the Resighini Rancheria	1,831
Death Valley Timbi-Sha Shoshone Band	6,134
Dry Creek Rancheria of Pomo Indians	3,021
Elem Indian Colony of Pomo Indians of the Sulphur Bank Rancheria	1,190
Elk Valley Rancheria of Smith River Tolowa Indians	2,014
Fort Mojave Indian Tribe	7,050
Hopland Band of Pomo Indians	7,508
Kashia Band of Pomo Indians of the Stewart's Point Rancheria	5,585
Manchester Band of Pomo Indians of the Manchester-Point Arena Rancheria	11,811
Paiute-Shoshone Indians of the Bishop Community	15,016
Paiute-Shoshone Indians of the Lone Pine Community	4,029
Pauma Band of Mission Indians of the Pauma and Yuima Reservation	3,571
Pinoleville Rancheria of Pomo Indians	4,120
Redding Rancheria of Pomo Indians	1,740
Redwood Valley Rancheria of Pomo Indians	1,282
Rohnerville Rancheria	2,655
Santa Rosa Indian Community of the Santa Rosa Rancheria	4,669
Santa Ynez Band of Mission Indians	3,296
Smith River Rancheria	3,662

[Continued]

★ 538 ★

Home Energy Grants
[Continued]

Indian tribe or Tribal organization	Allotment $
Susanville Indian Rancheria	3,296
Table Mountain Rancheria	824
Tuolumne Band of Me-Wuk Indians	3,021
Utu Utu Gwaitu Paiute Tribe of the Benton Paiute Reservations	1,190
Woodfords Washo Community of the Washoe Tribe of Nevada and California	4,669
Yurok Tribe of the Hoopa Valley Reservation	52,371
Karuk Tribe of California[7]	32,046
La Jolla Band of Mission Indians[7]	7,508
Pit River Tribe of California[7]	41,385
Quartz Valley Rancheria of Karok, Shasta and Upper Klamath Indians[7]	4,303
Riverside-San Bernardino County Indian Health, Inc., for 8 tribes:[7]	29,665
Agua Caliente Band of Cahuilla Indians	3,021
Cahuilla Band of Mission Indians	1,648
Morongo Band of Cahuilla Mission Indians	9,888
Pechanga Band of Luiseno Mission Indians	4,669
San Manuel Band of Serrano Mission Indians	551
Santa Rosa Band of Mission Indians of the Santa Rosa Reservation	1,373
Soboba Band of Luiseno Mission Indians	5,402
Torres-Martinez Band of Mission Indians	3,113
Robinson Rancheria of Pomo Indians[7]	4,345
Santa Ysabel Band of Mission Indians[7]	3,937
Sherwood Valley Rancheria of Pomo Indians[7]	4,761
Southern California Tribal Chairmen's Assn. for 5 tribes:[7]	13,642
Cuyapaipe Community of Mission Indians	183
Inaja Band of Mission Indians of the Inaja and Cosmit Reservation	92
Los Coyotes Band of Mission Indians	1,099
Mesa Grande Band of Mission Indians	3,936
Rincon Band of Mission Indians	8,332
Southern Indian Health Council, for 6 tribes:[7]	11,170
Barona Band of Mission Indians	3,845
Campo Band of Mission Indians	2,656
Jamul Indian Village	549
La Posta Band of Mission Indians	92
Manzanita Band of Mission Indians	1,007
Viejas Band of Mission Indians	3,021
Florida[1]	
Seminole Tribe of Florida	3,954

[Continued]

★ 538 ★

Home Energy Grants
[Continued]

Indian tribe or Tribal organization	Allotment $
Idaho	
Kootenai Tribe of Idaho	825
Nez Perce Tribe of Idaho	34,614
Shoshone-Bannock Tribes of the Fort Hall Reservation	40,755
Kansas[1]	

United Tribes of Kansas and Southeast Nebraska, for 2 tribes:
    Iowa Tribe of Kansas and Nebraska
    Sac and Fox Tribe of Missouri[8]
	19,485

Maine[1]	
Houlton Band of Maliseet Indians	32,293
Passamaquoddy Tribe of Maine--Indian Township	51,668
Passamaquoddy Tribe of Maine--Pleasant Point	79,665
Penobscot Tribe of Maine	51,668
Massachusetts[1]	
Mashpee Wampanoag Tribe	20,000
Michigan	
Grand Traverse Band of Ottawa and Chippewa Indians	21,759
Inter-Tribal Council of Michigan, for 5 tribes:	30,867
Bay Mills Indian Community	4,554
Hannahville Indian Community	3,626
Keweenaw Bay Indian Community	11,048
Lac Vieux Desert Band of Chippewa Indians	5,560
Saginaw Chippewa Indian Tribe	6,073
Sault Ste. Marie Tribe of Chippewa Indians	100,444
Minnesota[1]	
Mille Lacs Band of the Minnesota Chippewa Tribe	121,519
Mississippi	
Mississippi Band of Choctaw Indians	12,235
Montana[1]	
Assiniboine and Sioux Tribes of the Fort Peck Reservation	333,596
Blackfeet Tribe	539,342
Chippewa-Cree Tribe of the Rocky Boy's Reservation	154,013
Confederated Salish and Kootenai Tribes of the Flathead Reservation	309,215
Fort Belknap Indian Community	164,320
Northern Cheyenne Tribe	203,765

[Continued]

★ 538 ★

Home Energy Grants
[Continued]

Indian tribe or Tribal organization	Allotment $
Funds transferred to Department of the Interior Bureau of Indian Affairs to serve Crow Tribe service population[9]	180,000
Nebraksa	
Winnebago Tribe	16,563
Nevada	
Walker River Paiute Tribe	6,083
New Jersey	
Powhatan Renape Nation, for 3 tribes:	93,569
Confederation of Nanticoke-Lenni Lenape Tribes	
Powhatan Renape Nation[10]	76,703
Ramapough Mountain Indian Tribe	16,866
New Mexico	
Five Sandoval Indian Pueblos, for 5 tribes:	29,376
Pueblo of Cochiti	5,023
Pueblo of Jemez	16,539
Pueblo of Sandia	1,851
Pueblo of Santa Ana	3,349
Pueblo of Zia	4,230
Jicarilla Apache Tribe	12,781
Pueblo of Laguna	16,977
Pueblo of Zuni	40,938
New York	
Seneca Nation of New York	47,676
St. Regis Band of Mohawk Indians[1]	120,000
North Carolina[1]	
Lumbee Regional Development Association (Lumbee Tribe)	247,898
North Dakota[1]	
Devils Lake Sioux Tribe	226,204
Standing Rock Sioux Tribe (includes South Dakota service population)[2,3,11]	388,095
Three Affiliated Tribes of the Fort Berthold Reservation	242,099
Turtle Mountain Band of Chippewa Indians	715,292
Oklahoma	
Apache Tribe of Oklahoma	2,067
Caddo Indian Tribe	4,775
Cherokee Nation of Oklahoma	275,900

[Continued]

★ 538 ★

Home Energy Grants
[Continued]

Indian tribe or Tribal organization	Allotment $
Cheyenne-Arapaho Tribes of Oklahoma	12,392
Chickasaw Nation of Oklahoma	38,337
Choctaw Nation of Oklahoma	112,531
Citizen Band of Potawatomi Indians of Oklahoma	4,655
Comanche Indian Tribe	16,502
Delaware Tribe of Western Oklahoma	1,076
Kiowa Indian Tribe	17,010
Otoe-Missouria Tribe	2,345
Pawnee Indian Tribe	2,744
Sac and Fox Tribe of Indians of Oklahoma	6,528
Seminole Nation of Oklahoma	13,432
Tonkawa Tribe	1,355
Rhode Island[1]	
Narragansett Indian Tribe	28,405
South Dakota[1]	
Cheyenne River Sioux Tribe[11]	213,106
Crow Creek Sioux Tribe	53,526
Lower Brule Sioux Tribe	35,174
Oglala Sioux Tribe of the Pine Ridge Reservation[11]	707,829
Rosebud Sioux Tribe[11]	413,476
Sisseton-Wahpeton Sioux Tribe	134,580
Yankton Sioux Tribe[11]	93,271
Utah[1]	
Paiute Indian Tribe of Utah	92,163
Ute Indian Tribe of the Unitah and Ouray Reservation	73,995
Washington[1]	
Colville Confederated Tribes[12]	316,862
Confederated Tribes and Bands of the Yamika Indian Nation[12]	325,321
Jamestown Band of Klallam Indians	7,628
Kalispel Indian Community[12]	7,285
Lower Elwha Band of the Klallam Indian Tribe	18,646
Lummi Indian Tribe	77,127
Makah Indian Tribe	60,176
Muckelshoot Indian Tribe[12]	53,857
Nooksack Indian Tribe	21,189
Port Gamble Klallam Tribe	12,713
Puyallup Tribe	86,027
Quinault Tribe	66,957
Small Tribes Organization of Western Washington,	37,834

[Continued]

★ 538 ★

Home Energy Grants
[Continued]

Indian tribe or Tribal organization	Allotment $
for 3 tribes:[12]	
Sauk-Suiattle Indian Tribe	
Shoalwater Bay Tribe	
Stillaguamish Tribe[8]	
South Puget Intertribal Planning Agency, for 4 tribes:	96,543
Confederated Tribes of the Chehalis Reservation	
Nisqually Indian Community	
Skokomish Indian Tribe	
Squaxin Island Tribe[8]	
Spokane Tribe of Indians[12]	66,820
Suquamish Indian Tribe of the Port Madison Reservation	7,628
Swinomish Indians of the Swinomish Reservation	32,631
Tulalip Tribes	57,634
Upper Skagit Indian Tribe	11,442

Source: Low Income Home Energy Assistance Program Report to Congress for FY1989, U.S. Department of Health and Human Services (HHS), Family Support Administration, Office of Community Services, Office of Energy Assistance, October 29, 1990, pp. 93-100. *Notes:* 1. Tribe-state agreement affects allotment amounts. 2. Multi-state tribal grant with set-asides from more than one state. 3. Tribe-state agreements affect service population in both states. 4. Agreements with Arizona and California increased tribe's LIHEAP allotment in lieu of Exxon oil overcharge funds. 5. Agreement with Arizona increased tribe's LIHEAP allotment in lieu of Exxon oil overcharge fund. 6. Tribe-state agreement affects Arizona service population only. 7. Agreement with California increased grantee's LIHEAP allotment in lieu of Exxon oil overcharge fund. 8. Agreement with state did not include tribe-by-tribe figures. 9. HHS withheld FY 1988 funds from Crow Tribe under section 2608 of LIHEAP statute. Of the $277,897 originally set aside Crow Tribe in FY 1988, HHS transferred $180,000 to DoI/BIA under Public Law 100-318, and awarded $97,897 to state of Montana, to serve eligible Indian households on Crow Reservation. 10. Because service areas of Powhatan Renape Nation and Nanticoke-Lenni Lenape Tribes overlap, tribe-by-tribe allotment amounts are not available. 11. Agreement with South Dakota increased tribe's LIHEAP allotment in lieu of Exxon oil overcharge funds. 12. Agreement with Washington state increased grantee's LIHEAP allotment in lieu of Exxon oil overcharge funds.

★ 539 ★

WIC Participation

Number of clinics under operation and average number of participants in WIC (Special Supplement Food Program for Women, Infants, and Children) are shown, by region, FY 1990.

Region	Clinics Operating in Sept.[1]	Average participation[2]			
		Women	Infants	Children	Total
Northeast					
Pleasant Point, ME	1	25	19	67	111
Indian Township, ME	1	19	15	66	100
Seneca Nation, NY	2	48	58	199	305
Southeast					
Seminole Tribe, FL	3	28	39	85	152
Miccosukee, FL	1	10	10	34	54

[Continued]

★ 539 ★

WIC Participation
[Continued]

Region	Clinics Operating in Sept.[1]	Average participation[2]			
		Women	Infants	Children	Total
Choctaw, MS	5	94	182	403	679
E. Cherokee, NC	193	183	154	404	741
Southcentral					
8 Northen Pueblo, NM	6	70	107	305	482
Isleta, NM	2	81	117	278	476
Pueblo of Zuni, NM	1	161	183	339	683
5 Sandovai, NM	5	76	76	292	444
Santo Domingo, NM	1	53	68	213	334
San Felipe, NM	3	47	51	203	301
ALC, NM	60	75	132	266	473
Choctaw, OK	13	365	507	1,072	7,944
Chickasaw Nation, OK	7	261	319	494	1,074
Tonkawa, OK	6	106	158	343	607
Cherokee, OK	12	885	1,447	2,324	4,656
Patawatomi, OK	6	181	298	491	970
Inter-Tribal, OK	2	56	87	33	176
WCD, OK	6	293	388	887	1,568
Northcentral					
Ute Mountain, CO	1	21	34	71	126
IITCD, NE	88	90	115	351	556
Standing Rock, ND	9	186	207	707	1,100
Fort Berthold, ND	5	90	87	299	476
North Dakota	93	3,021	3,249	8,687	14,957
Cheyenne River, SD	1	111	134	411	656
Rosebud, SD	8	303	302	882	1,487
Shoshone & Araphoe, WY	39	161	143	480	784
West					
Maunelak Assn., AK	11	88	97	183	368
Navajo Tribe, AZ	17	3,441	3,960	9,699	17,100
Inter Tribal, AZ	37	1,475	1,646	3,275	6,396
ITCN, NV	21	182	224	671	1,077

Source: Special Supplemental Food Program for Women, Infants, and Children (WIC) Racial Participation, April 1991, Food and Nutrition Service Financial Management Program Information Division Data Base, Monitoring Branch , November 1991. *Notes:* 1. WIC clinic data are obtained from the FNS191 racial/ethnic group participation (WIC) report. 2. Program participation and cost data are preliminary and subject to change as revised reports are received from state agencies.

★ 540 ★

WIC Participation, by Race/Ethnicity

Number of Participants in the WIC program (Special Supplemental Food Program for Women, Infants, and Children) is shown, by race/ethnicity for April 1990 and 1991.

Race/ethnicity	April 1990	April 1991	Difference (+/-)
American Indian or Alaska Native			
Women	18,867	19,663	796
Infants	23,848	24,840	992
Children	52,018	52,710	692
Total	94,733	97,213	2,480
Black			
Women	268,503	276,383	7,880
Infants	427,196	456,772	29,576
Children	623,870	650,913	27,043
Total	1,319,569	1,384,068	64,499
Hispanic			
Women	249,836	294,230	44,394
Infants	335,669	398,330	62,661
Children	414,569	435,500	20,931
Total	1,000,074	1,128,060	127,986
Asian or Pacific			
Women	24,231	25,958	1,727
Infants	36,507	39,278	2,771
Children	50,875	50,035	-840
Total	111,613	115,271	3,658
White			
Women	485,155	507,549	22,394
Infants	598,518	653,559	55,041
Children	973,950	994,542	20,592
Total	2,057,623	2,155,650	98,027
All groups			
Women	1,046,592	1,123,783	77,191
Infants	1,421,738	1,572,779	151,041
Children	2,115,282	2,183,700	68,418
Total	4,583,612	4,880,262	296,650

Source: Special Supplemental Food Program for Women, Infants, and Children (WIC) Racial Participation, April 1991, Food and Nutrition Service Financial Management Program Information Division Data Base, Monitoring Branch, November 1991. Primary source: Food and Nutrition Service Program Information Division, Data Base Monitoring Branch, November 5, 1991.

Housing

★ 541 ★

Housing and Household Characteristics of American Indian and Alaska Native Areas: 1990, Acoma-Colville - I

American Indian/Alaska Native Area State State	All housing units		Occupied housing units with American Indian, Eskimo, or Aleut householder				Family households		
			Owner occupied		Renter occupied				
						Mean contract rent (dollars), specified renter paying cash rent			Female house-holder, no husband present
			Total	Mean value (dollars) specified Owner	Total		Total	Married-couple family	
	Total	Occupied							
American Indian Reservation and Trust Lands[1,2]									
All areas	328,349	250,065	75,552	41,500	36,657	130	93,367	51,948	31,155
Acoma Pueblo and Trust Lands, NM	992	607	537	48,000	49	179	525	309	160
Acoma Pueblo, NM	992	607	537	48,000	49	179	525	309	160
Acoma Trust Lands, NM	-	-	-	-	-	-	-	-	-
Agua Caliente Reservation, CA	20,840	10,546	27	162,900	25	499	35	26	8
Alabama and Caushatta Reservation, TX	150	143	132	32,600	11	127	115	79	26
Alamo Navajo Reservation, NM	343	276	191	18,800	65	86	232	172	39
Allegany Reservation, NY	3,141	2,902	230	44,100	165	166	274	146	97
Alturas Rancheria, CA	7	3	3	65,000	-	-	2	-	2
Annette Islands Reserve, AK	529	449	270	69,000	78	222	261	181	61
Augustine Reservation, CA	-	-	-	-	-	-	-	-	-
Bad River Reservation, WI	465	349	159	32,300	126	96	212	92	99
Barona Rancheria, CA	151	146	71	91,100	19	121	82	57	15
Bay Mills Reservation, MI	138	126	66	27,300	38	134	87	51	27
Benton Paiute Reservation, CA	28	24	5	95,000	19	-	14	3	8
Berry Creek Rancheria, CA	2	1	-	-	1	-	1	1	-
Big Bend Rancheria, CA	3	2	1	95,000	1	-	1	-	-
Big Cypress Reservation, FL	161	149	125	44,900	17	141	106	36	52
Big Lagoon Rancheria, CA	7	7	7	-	-	-	5	3	-
Big Pine Rancheria, CA	156	141	84	79,500	12	107	83	37	43
Big Sandy Rancheria, CA	18	17	11	82,500	1	-	10	4	5
Big Valley Rancheria, CA	41	35	24	38,900	4	138	22	11	9
Bishop Rancheria, CA	507	472	205	63,700	115	158	234	129	74
Blackfeet Reservation, MT	3,004	2,333	969	41,100	903	113	1,571	930	479
Blue Lake Rancheria, CA	29	27	11	59,400	1	313	9	7	2
Bois Forte (Nett Lake) Reservation, MN	138	112	50	19,000	56	81	76	25	39

[Continued]

828

★ 541 ★

Housing and Household Characteristics of American Indian and Alaska Native Areas: 1990, Acoma-Colville - I

[Continued]

American Indian/Alaska Native Area State State	All housing units		Occupied housing units with American Indian, Eskimo, or Aleut householder				Family households		
			Owner occupied		Renter occupied				
						Mean contract rent (dollars), specified renter paying cash rent		Married-couple family	Female house-holder, no husband present
	Total	Occupied	Total	Mean value (dollars) specified Owner	Total		Total		
Bridgeport Colony, CA	21	18	-	-	15	185	9	1	7
Brighton Reservation, FL	210	176	105	46,300	24	149	97	59	31
Burns Paiute Reservation and Trust Lands, OR	48	44	16	43,000	26	263	33	11	17
Burns Paiute Reservation, OR	47	44	16	43,000	26	263	33	11	17
Burns Paiute Trust Lands, OR	1	-	-	-	-	-	-	-	-
Cabazon Reservation, CA	193	190	6	-	-	-	6	5	1
Cahuilla Reservation, CA	37	34	27	56,800	2	-	19	10	8
Campo Reservation, CA	109	97	39	34,300	11	-	33	12	17
Camp Verde Reservation, AZ	162	150	86	49,800	56	78	128	63	42
Canoncito Reservation, NM	295	275	230	20,800	40	57	237	135	83
Captain Grande Reservation, CA	-	-	-	-	-	-	-	-	-
Carson Colony, NV	86	78	64	62,200	10	113	63	25	29
Catawba Reservation (state), SC	55	54	49	31,200	2	-	40	34	4
Cattaragus Reservation, NY	788	708	477	41,700	200	173	482	225	195
Cedarville Rancheria, CA	5	4	2	12,500	2	-	1	-	1
Chehalis Reservation, WA	181	162	29	42,300	67	98	74	37	27
Chemehuevi Reservation, CA	734	160	15	73,300	19	92	27	12	12
Cheyenne River Reservation, SD	2,923	2,351	434	33,700	859	118	1,040	511	420
Chicken Ranch Rancheria, CA	37	33	2	85,000	1	-	2	1	-
Chitimacha Reservation, LA	102	93	75	42,900	7	238	71	46	20
Cochiti Pueblo, NM	527	430	155	54,700	18	307	140	87	36
Cacopah Reservation, AZ	130	126	66	36,800	32	106	81	40	32
Coer d'Alene Reservation and Trust Lands, ID	3,731	2,215	145	50,800	95	104	186	100	64
Coer d'Alene Reservation, ID	3,730	2,214	145	50,800	95	104	186	100	64
Coer d'Alene Trust Lands, ID	1	1	-	-	-	-	-	-	-
Cold Springs Rancheria, CA	61	55	7	63,600	35	77	38	11	18
Colorado River Reservation	4,768	2,659	419	49,200	233	193	526	288	182
Arizona	2,832	2,136	417	49,200	230	189	522	285	181
California	1,936	523	2	-	3	454	4	3	1

[Continued]

★ 541 ★

Housing and Household Characteristics of American Indian and Alaska Native Areas: 1990, Acoma-Colville - I

[Continued]

American Indian/Alaska Native Area State State	All housing units		Occupied housing units with American Indian, Eskimo, or Aleut householder				Family households		
			Owner occupied		Renter occupied				
					Total	Mean contract rent (dollars), specified renter paying cash rent	Total	Married-couple family	Female house-holder, no husband present
	Total	Occupied	Total	Mean value (dollars) specified Owner					
Calusa (Cachil Dehe) Rancheria, CA	9	9	-	-	9	-	6	1	3
Colville Reservation, WA	2,996	2,398	695	50,100	501	131	923	463	322

Source: Summary Population and Housing Characteristics, United States Summary, United States Bureau of the Census, CP H-1, pp. 417-432. *Notes:* A dash (-) indicates that no data were given in the original source. 1. Federal American Indian reservations are areas with boundaries established by treaty, statute, and/or executive or court order, and recognized by the federal government as territory in which American Indian tribes have jurisdiction. State reservations are lands held in trust by state governments for the use and benefit of a given tribe. The reservations and their boundaries were identified for the 1990 census by the Bureau of Indian Affairs (BIA), Department of Interior (for Federal reservations), and state governments (for state reservations). The names of American Indian reservations recognized by state governments, but not by the federal government, are followed by (state). Areas composed of reservation lands that are administered jointly and/or are claimed by two reservations, as identified by the BIA, are called "joint areas," and are treated as separate American Indian reservations for census purposes. Federal reservations may cross state boundaries, and federal and state reservations may cross county, county subdivision, and place boundaries. For reservations that cross state boundaries, only the portion of the reservations in a given state are shown in the data products for that state; the entire reservations are shown in data products for the United States. 2. Trust lands are property associated with a particular American Indian reservation or tribe, held in trust by the federal government. Trust lands may be held in trust either for a tribe (tribal trust lands) or for an individual member of a tribe (individual trust land). Trust lands recognized for the 1990 census comprised all tribal trust lands and inhabited individual trust lands located outside of a reservation boundary. As with other American Indian areas, trust lands may be located in more than one state. Only the trust lands in a given state are shown in the data products for that state; all trust lands associated with a reservation or tribe are shown in data products for the United States. The Census Bureau first reported data for tribal trust lands for the 1980 census.

★ 542 ★

Housing and Household Characteristics of American Indian and Alaska Native Areas: 1990, Acoma-Colville - II

American Indian/Alaska Native Area State	Households with American Indian, Eskimo, or Aleut householder Nonfamily households		Land area	
	Total	Householder living alone	Square kilometers	Square miles
American Indian Reservation and Trust Lands[1,2]				
All areas	18,842	16,165	284,185.0	109,723.9
Acoma Pueblo and Trust Lands, NM	61	49	1,079.3	416.7
Acoma Pueblo, NM	61	49	1,065.2	411.3
Acoma Trust Lands, NM	-	-	14.1	5.4
Agua Caliente Reservation, CA	17	12	128.4	49.6
Alabama and Caushatta Reservation, TX	28	28	18.1	7.0

[Continued]

★ 542 ★

Housing and Household Characteristics of American Indian and Alaska Native Areas:
1990, Acoma-Colville - II
[Continued]

American Indian/Alaska Native Area State	Households with American Indian, Eskimo, or Aleut householder Nonfamily households		Land area	
	Total	Householder living alone	Square kilometers	Square miles
Alamo Navajo Reservation, NM	24	20	256.5	99.0
Allegany Reservation, NY	121	102	106.2	41.0
Alturas Rancheria, CA	1	1	1	-
Annette Islands Reserve, AK	67	62	333.9	128.9
Augustine Reservation, CA	-	-	2.6	1.0
Bad River Reservation, WI	73	62	497.4	192.0
Barana Rancheria, CA	8	6	23.8	9.2
Bay Mills Reservation, MI	17	15	9.0	3.5
Benton Paiute Reservation, CA	10	9	.6	.2
Berry Creek Rancheria, CA	-	-	.1	.1
Big Bend Rancheria, CA	1	1	.2	.1
Big Cypress Reservation, FL	36	28	212.1	81.9
Big Lagoon Rancheria, CA	2	1	-	-
Big Pine Rancheria, CA	13	13	1.1	.4
Big Sandy Rancheria, CA	2	2	1.0	.4
Big Valley Rancheria, CA	6	4	.5	.2
Bishop Rancheria, CA	86	74	3.5	1.4
Blackfeet Reservation, MT	301	260	6,141.9	2,371.4
Blue Lake Rancheria, CA	3	2	.1	-
Bois Forte (Nett Lake) Reservation, MN	30	27	422.1	163.0

[Continued]

★ 542 ★

Housing and Household Characteristics of American Indian and Alaska Native Areas: 1990, Acoma-Colville - II
[Continued]

| American Indian/Alaska Native Area State | Households with American Indian, Eskimo, or Aleut householder Nonfamily households | | Land area | |
	Total	Householder living alone	Square kilometers	Square miles
Bridgeport Colony, CA	6	6	.2	.1
Brighton Reservation, FL	32	26	147.6	57.0
Burns Paiute Reservation and Trust Lands, OR	9	6	48.9	18.9
Burns Paiute Reservation, OR	9	6	3.3	1.3
Burns Paiute Trust Lands, OR	-	-	45.6	17.6
Cabazon Reservation, CA	-	-	8.7	3.4
Cahuilla Reservation, CA	10	9	74.2	28.6
Campo Reservation, CA	17	16	66.9	25.8
Camp Verde Reservation, AZ	14	14	2.5	1.0
Canoncito Reservation, NM	33	30	314.9	121.6
Captain Grande Reservation, CA	-	-	53.1	20.5
Carson Colony, NV	11	11	.6	.2
Catawba Reservation (state), SC	11	10	2.9	1.1
Cattaragus Reservation, NY	195	163	87.3	33.7
Cedarville Rancheria, CA	3	2	.1	-
Chehalis Reservation, WA	22	21	18.2	7.0
Chemehuevi Reservation, CA	7	7	128.2	49.5
Cheyenne River Reservation, SD	253	219	11,047.1	4,265.3
Chicken Ranch Rancheria, CA	1	1	.2	.1
Chitimacha Reservation, LA	11	10	1.1	.4
Cochiti Pueblo, NM	33	29	208.3	80.4

[Continued]

★ 542 ★

Housing and Household Characteristics of American Indian and Alaska Native Areas 1990, Acoma-Colville - II

[Continued]

American Indian/Alaska Native Area State	Households with American Indian, Eskimo, or Aleut householder Nonfamily households		Land area	
	Total	Householder living alone	Square kilometers	Square miles
Cacopah Reservation, AZ	17	10	25.9	10.0
Coer d'Alene Reservation and Trust Lands, ID	54	38	1,549.1	598.1
Coer d'Alene Reservation, ID	54	38	1,549.0	598.1
Coer d'Alene Trust Lands, ID	-	-	.1	-
Cold Springs Rancheria, CA	4	4	.4	.2
Colorado River Reservation	126	109	1,120.8	432.7
Arizona	125	108	932.1	359.9
California	1	1	188.7	72.9
Calusa (Cachil Dehe) Rancheria, CA	3	3	.9	.3
Colville Reservation, WA	273	211	5,482.0	2,116.6

Source: Summary Population and Housing Characteristics, United States Summary, United States Bureau of the Census, CP H-1, pp. 417-432. Notes: A dash (-) indicates that no data were given in the original source. 1. Federal American Indian reservations are areas with boundaries established by treaty, statute, and/or executive or court order, and recognized by the federal government as territory in which American Indian tribes have jurisdiction. State reservations are lands held in trust by state governments for the use and benefit of a given tribe. The reservations and their boundaries were identified for the 1990 census by the Bureau of Indian Affairs (BIA), Department of Interior (for Federal reservations), and state governments (for state reservations). The names of American Indian reservations recognized by state governments, but not by the federal government, are followed by (state). Areas composed of reservation lands that are administered jointly and/or are claimed by two reservations, as identified by the BIA, are called "joint areas," and are treated as separate American Indian reservations for census purposes. Federal reservations may cross state boundaries, and federal and state reservations may cross county, county subdivision, and place boundaries. For reservations that cross state boundaries, only the portion of the reservations in a given state are shown in the data products for that state; the entire reservations are shown in data products for the United States. 2. Trust lands are property associated with a particular American Indian reservation or tribe, held in trust by the federal government. Trust lands may be held in trust either for a tribe (tribal trust lands) or for an individual member of a tribe (individual trust land). Trust lands recognized for the 1990 census comprised all tribal trust lands and inhabited individual trust lands located outside of a reservation boundary. As with other American Indian areas, trust lands may be located in more than one state. Only the trust lands in a given state are shown in the data products for that state; all trust lands associated with a reservation or tribe are shown in data products for the United States. The Census Bureau first reported data for tribal trust lands for the 1980 census.

★ 543 ★

Housing and Household Characteristics of American Indian and Alaska Native Areas: 1990, Coos-Grindstone - I

American Indian/Alaska Native Area State	All housing units		Occupied housing units with American Indian, Eskimo, or Aleut householder				Family households		
			Owner occupied		Renter occupied				
						Mean contract rent (dollars), specified renter paying cash rent			Female house-holder, no husband present
	Total	Occupied	Total	Mean value (dollars) specified Owner	Total		Total	Married-couple family	
American Indian Reservation and Trust Land[1,2]									
Coos, Lower Umpaqua, and Siuslaw Reservation, OR	2	2	-	-	1	-	1	1	-
Cortina Rancherio, CA	11	10	7	60,800	1	-	3	3	-
Coushatta Reservation, LA	14	12	9	24,400	3	-	8	5	2
Cow Creek Reservation, OR	23	21	1	-	4	213	2	-	2
Coyote Valley Reservation, CA	42	35	4	109,400	28	83	29	16	9
Crow Reservation and Trust Lands, MT	2,091	1,675	653	40,000	424	122	978	636	278
Crow Reservation, MT	2,088	1,673	653	40,000	424	122	978	636	278
Crow Trust Lands, MT	3	2	-	-	-	-	-	-	-
Crow Creek Reservation, SD	489	434	112	20,900	240	116	311	131	123
Cuyapaipe Reservation, CA	-	-	-	-	-	-	-	-	-
Deer Creek Reservation, MN	135	66	1	-	-	-	1	-	-
Devils Lake Sioux Reservation, ND	1,317	972	251	34,900	376	129	549	231	247
Dresslerville Colony, NV	58	53	36	59,100	16	141	40	15	20
Dry Creek Rancheria, CA	12	6	9,000	1	-	7	2	5	
Duck Valley Reservation	420	344	234	43,300	83	101	240	118	89
Idaho	67	49	42	48,000	6	132	40	25	11
Nevada	353	295	192	42,400	77	98	200	93	78
Duckwater Reservation, NV	65	51	30	56,300	13	71	34	16	15
Eastern Cherokee Reservation, NC	2,370	2,104	1,445	52,300	341	114	1,432	890	442
Elk Valley Rancheria, CA	29	27	10	77,300	2	213	11	5	4
Ely Colony, NV	19	16	14	32,600	2	50	13	8	4
Enterprise Rancheria, CA	4	2	2	-	-	-	2	-	2
Fallon Colony, NV	55	51	19	53,300	31	69	38	17	20
Fallon Reservation, NV	147	129	99	60,100	21	96	97	48	35
Flanadreau Reservation, SD	97	84	50	55,700	28	105	65	31	27
Flathead Reservation, MT	10,399	7,874	1,045	54,000	687	144	1,285	773	392
Fond du Lac Reservation, MN	1,375	1,101	157	53,700	185	93	267	123	98
Fort Apache Reservation, AZ	3,240	2,480	1,577	32,700	655	123	1,974	1,227	607
Fort Belknap Reservation and Trust Lands, MT	856	716	357	43,200	299	88	537	286	192
Fort Belknap Reservation, MT	854	716	357	43,200	299	88	537	286	192
Fort Belknap Trust Lands, MT	2	-	-	-	-	-	-	-	-

[Continued]

★ 543 ★

Housing and Household Characteristics of American Indian and Alaska Native Areas: 1990, Coos Grindstone - I

[Continued]

American Indian/Alaska Native Area State	All housing units		Occupied housing units with American Indian, Eskimo, or Aleut householder				Family households		
			Owner occupied		Renter occupied				
					Total	Mean contract rent (dollars), specified renter paying cash rent	Total	Married-couple family	Female house-holder, no husband present
	Total	Occupied	Total	Mean value (dollars) specified Owner					
Fort Berthold Reservation, ND	2,738	1,760	380	36,400	468	118	673	315	271
Fort Bidwell Reservation, CA	51	36	18	46,000	17	58	27	12	12
Fort Hall Reservation and Trust Lands, ID	1,754	1,498	632	47,100	200	130	725	429	219
Fort Hall Reservation, ID	1,725	1,483	632	47,100	200	130	725	429	219
Fort Hall Trust Lands, ID	29	15	-	-	-	-	-	-	-
Fort Independence Reservation, CA	44	33	17	74,800	1	50	12	7	3
Fort McDermitt Reservation, NV	137	107	93	19,600	12	103	86	43	33
Oregon	-	-	-	-	-	-	-	-	-
Fort McDowell Reservation, AZ	179	164	110	43,900	30	131	117	60	38
Fort Mojave Reservation and Trust Lands,AZ-CA-NV	291	223	23	52,600	145	100	135	55	62
Fort Mojave Reservation	214	149	-	-	98	122	76	33	29
Arizona	194	133	-	-	98	122	76	33	29
California	20	16	-	-	-	-	-	-	-
Nevada	-	-	-	-	-	-	-	-	-
Fort Mojave Trust Lands, CA	77	74	23	52,600	47	75	59	22	33
Fort Peck Reservation, MT	3,983	3,443	777	40,200	814	129	1,318	688	468
Fort Yuma (Quechan) Reservation	959	780	240	43,600	91	160	249	129	100
Arizona	10	8	-	-	-	-	-	-	-
California	949	772	240	43,600	91	160	249	129	100
Gila Bend Reservation and Trust Lands, AZ	-	-	-	-	-	-	-	-	-
Gila Bend Reservation, AZ	-	-	-	-	-	-	-	-	-
Gila Bend Trust Lands, AZ	-	-	-	-	-	-	-	-	-
Gila River Reservation, AZ	2,649	2,428	1,540	22,600	755	110	1,973	856	827
Golden Hill Reservation, CT (state)	5	5	-	-	1	-	-	-	-
Goshute Reservation	48	29	5	52,500	24	50	21	10	10
Nevada	10	6	-	-	6	50	5	4	1
Utah	38	23	5	52,500	18	50	16	6	9
Grand Portage Reservation, MN	190	125	44	52,100	43	109	52	35	10
Grand Ronde Reservation, OR	21	20	1	37,500	-	-	1	1	-
Grand Traverse Reservation and Trust Lands, MI	76	69	24	79,800	37	111	45	15	25
Grand Traverse Reservation, MI	4	4	3	125,800	-	-	2	1	1
Grand Traverse Trust Lands, MI	72	65	21	69,200	37	111	43	14	24

[Continued]

★ 543 ★

Housing and Household Characteristics of American Indian and Alaska Native Areas: 1990, Coos-Grindstone - I

[Continued]

American Indian/Alaska Native Area State	All housing units		Occupied housing units with American Indian, Eskimo, or Aleut householder				Family households		
			Owner occupied		Renter occupied				
						Mean contract rent (dollars), specified renter paying cash rent			Female house-holder, no husband present
	Total	Occupied	Total	Mean value (dollars) specified Owner	Total		Total	Married-couple family	
Greenville Rancheria, CA	16	12	3	40,000	1	-	3	1	2
Grindstone Creek Rancheria, CA	24	24	15	36,100	8	59	20	11	5

Source: Summary Population and Housing Characteristics, United States Summary, United States Bureau of the Census, CP H-1, pp. 417-432. *Notes:* A dash (-) indicates that no data were given in the original source. 1. Federal American Indian reservations are areas with boundaries established by treaty, statute, and/or executive or court order, and recognized by the federal government as territory in which American Indian tribes have jurisdiction. State reservations are lands held in trust by state governments for the use and benefit of a given tribe. The reservations and their boundaries were identified for the 1990 census by the Bureau of Indian Affairs (BIA), Department of Interior (for Federal reservations), and state governments (for state reservations). The names of American Indian reservations recognized by state governments, but not by the federal government, are followed by (state). Areas composed of reservation lands that are administered jointly and/or are claimed by two reservations, as identified by the BIA, are called "joint areas," and are treated as separate American Indian reservations for census purposes. Federal reservations may cross state boundaries, and federal and state reservations may cross county, county subdivision, and place boundaries. For reservations that cross state boundaries, only the portion of the reservations in a given state are shown in the data products for that state; the entire reservations are shown in data products for the United States. 2. Trust lands are property associated with a particular American Indian reservation or tribe, held in trust by the federal government. Trust lands may be held in trust either for a tribe (tribal trust lands) or for an individual member of a tribe (individual trust land). Trust lands recognized for the 1990 census comprised all tribal trust lands and inhabited individual trust lands located outside of a reservation boundary. As with other American Indian areas, trust lands may be located in more than one state. Only the trust lands in a given state are shown in the data products for that state; all trust lands associated with a reservation or tribe are shown in data products for the United States. The Census Bureau first reported data for tribal trust lands for the 1980 census.

★ 544 ★

Housing and Household Characteristics of American Indian and Alaska Native Areas: 1990, Coos-Grindstone - II

American Indian/ Alaska Native Area State	Households with American Indian, Eskimo, or Aleut householder Nonfamily households		Land area	
	Total	Householder living alone	Square kilometers	Square miles
American Indian Reservation and Trust Lands[1,2]				
Coos, Lower Umpqua, and Siuslaw Reservation, OR	-	-	-	-
Cortina Rancherio, CA	5	5	3.1	1.2
Coushatta Reservation, LA	4	4	1.0	.4
Cow Creek Reservation, OR	3	3	.1	.1
Coyote Valley Reservation, CA	3	3	.3	.1

[Continued]

★ 544 ★

Housing and Household Characteristics of American Indian and Alaska Native Areas: 1990, Coos-Grindstone - II
[Continued]

American Indian/ Alaska Native Area State	Households with American Indian, Eskimo, or Aleut householder Nonfamily households		Land area	
	Total	Householder living alone	Square kilometers	Square miles
Crow Reservation and Trust Lands, MT	99	92	9,257.0	3,574.1
Crow Reservation, MT	99	92	9,177.8	3,543.5
Crow Trust Lands, MT	-	-	79.3	30.6
Crow Creek Reservation, SD	41	33	1,092.2	421.7
Cuyapaipe Reservation, CA	-	-	20.5	7.9
Deer Creek Reservation, MN	-	-	90.9	35.1
Devils Lake Sioux Reservation, ND	78	67	1,015.3	392.0
Dresslerville Colony, NV	12	10	.2	.1
Dry Creek Rancheria, CA	-	-	.3	.1
Duck Valley Reservation	77	66	1,310.0	505.8
Idaho	8	7	728.9	281.4
Nevada	69	59	581.0	224.3
Duckwater Reservation, NV	9	9	16.0	6.2
Eastern Cherokee Reservation, NC	354	294	210.1	81.1
Elk Valley Rancheria, CA	1	1	.4	.1
Ely Colony, NV	3	3	.4	.2
Enterprise Rancheria, CA	-	-	.2	.1
Fallon Colony, NV	12	11	.3	.1
Fallon Reservation, NV	23	17	33.1	12.8
Flanadreau Reservation, SD	13	13	9.0	3.5
Flathead Reservation, MT	447	376	5,019.8	1,938.2
Fond du Lac Reservation, MN	75	65	427.3	165.0

[Continued]

★ 544 ★

Housing and Household Characteristics of American Indian and Alaska Native Areas: 1990, Coos-Grindstone - II
[Continued]

American Indian/ Alaska Native Area State	Households with American Indian, Eskimo, or Aleut householder Nonfamily households		Land area	
	Total	Householder living alone	Square kilometers	Square miles
Fort Apache Reservation, AZ	258	201	6,805.7	2,627.7
Fort Belknap Reservation and Trust Lands, MT	119	107	2,625.8	1,013.8
Fort Belknap Reservation, MT	119	107	2,509.7	969.0
Fort Belknap Trust Lands, MT	-	-	116.1	44.8
Fort Berthold Reservation, ND	175	151	3,416.0	1,318.9
Fort Bidwell Reservation, CA	8	8	13.2	5.1
Fort Hall Reservation and Trust Lands, ID	107	94	2,110.6	814.9
Fort Hall Reservation, ID	107	94	2,109.5	814.5
Fort Hall Trust Lands, ID	-	-	1.1	.4
Fort Independence Reservation, CA	6	6	1.5	.6
Fort McDermitt Reservation, NV	19	18	67.8	26.2
Oregon	-	-	73.7	28.5
Fort McDowell Reservation, AZ	23	19	99.8	38.6
Fort Mojave Reservation and Trust Lands,AZ-CA-NV	33	26	132.9	51.3
Fort Mojave Reservation	22	16	132.7	51.2
Arizona	22	16	93.0	35.9
California	-	-	24.3	9.4
Nevada	-	-	15.5	6.0
Fort Mojave Trust Lands, CA	11	10	.2	.1
Fort Peck Reservation, MT	273	223	8,518.7	3,289.1
Fort Yuma (Quechan) Reservation	82	64	177.1	68.4
Arizona	-	-	7.8	3.0
California	82	64	169.3	65.4
Gila Bend Reservation and Trust Lands, AZ	-	-	1.9	.7
Gila Bend Reservation, AZ	-	-	1.7	.7
Gila Bend Trust Lands, AZ	-	-	.2	.1

[Continued]

★ 544 ★

Housing and Household Characteristics of American Indian and Alaska Native Areas: 1990, Coos-Grindstone - II
[Continued]

American Indian/ Alaska Native Area State	Households with American Indian, Eskimo, or Aleut householder Nonfamily households		Land area	
	Total	Householder living alone	Square kilometers	Square miles
Gila River Reservation, AZ	322	251	1,512.3	583.9
Golden Hill Reservation, CT (state)	1	-	.4	.2
Goshute Reservation	8	6	459.5	177.4
Nevada	1	1	284.5	109.8
Utah	7	5	175.1	67.6
Grand Portage Reservation, MN	35	26	189.5	73.2
Grand Ronde Reservation, OR	-	-	40.0	15.4
Grand Traverse Reservation and Trust Lands, MI	16	15	1.2	.5
Grand Traverse Reservation, MI	1	1	.1	-
Grand Traverse Trust Lands, MI	15	14	1.1	.4
Greenville Rancheria, CA	1	1	.3	.1
Grindstone Creek Rancheria, CA	3	2	.3	.1

Source: Summary Population and Housing Characteristics, United States Summary, United States Bureau of the Census, CP H-1, pp. 417-432. *Notes:* 1Federal American Indian reservations are areas with boundaries established by treaty, statute, and/or executive or court order, and recognized by the federal government as territory in which American Indian tribes have jurisdiction. State reservations are lands held in trust by state governments for the use and benefit of a given tribe. The reservations and their boundaries were identified for the 1990 census by the Bureau of Indian Affairs (BIA), Department of Interior (for federal reservations), and state governments (for state reservations). The names of American Indian reservations recognized by state governments, but not by the federal government, are followed by (state). Areas composed of reservation lands that are administered jointly and/or are claimed by two reservations, as identified by the BIA, are called "joint areas," and are treated as separate American Indian reservations for census purposes. Federal reservations may cross state boundaries, and federal and state reservations may cross county, county subdivision, and place boundaries. For reservations that cross state boundaries, only the portion of the reservations in a given state are shown in the data products for that state; the entire reservations are shown in data products for the United States. 2. Trust lands are property associated with a particular American Indian reservation or tribe, held in trust by the federal government. Trust lands may be held in trust either for a tribe (tribal trust lands) or for an individual member of a tribe (individual trust land). Trust lands recognized for the 1990 census comprised all tribal trust lands and inhabited individual trust lands located outside of a reservation boundary. As with other American Indian areas, trust lands may be located in more than one state. Only the trust lands in a given state are shown in the data products for that state; all trust lands associated with a reservation or tribe are shown in data products for the United States. The Census Bureau first reported data for tribal trust lands for the 1980 census.

★ 545 ★

Housing and Household Characteristics of American Indian and Alaska Native Areas: 1990, Hannahville-Lummi - I

American Indian/ Alaska Native Area State	All housing units		Occupied housing units with American Indian, Eskimo, or Aleut householder				Family households		
			Owner occupied		Renter occupied				
						Mean contract rent (dollars), specified renter paying cash rent		Married-couple family	Female house-holder, no husband present
	Total	Occupied	Total	Mean value (dollars) specified Owner	Total		Total		
American Indian Reservation and Trust Lands[1,2]									
Hannahville Community and Trust Lands, MI	46	43	8	37,500	34	77	36	17	14
Hannahville Community, MI	41	38	7	30,000	30	79	31	13	13
Hannahville Trust Lands, MI	5	5	1	52,500	4	50	5	4	1
Hassanamisco Reservation, MA (State)	1	1	-	-	1	-	-	-	-
Havasupai Reservation, AZ	142	104	74	82,500	19	163	82	57	17
Hoh Reservation, WA	36	29	21	61,000	3	118	15	5	7
Hollywood Reservation, FL	783	516	95	53,700	53	129	119	44	57
Hoopa Valley Reservation, CA	812	690	339	61,000	196	174	409	203	155
Hopi Reservation and Trust Lands, AZ	2,476	1,866	1,380	46,100	344	105	1,468	864	511
Hopland Rancheria, CA	62	59	15	57,400	29	129	34	10	22
Houlapai Reservation and Trust Lands, AZ	322	206	114	33,800	86	91	177	106	52
Hualapai Reservation, AZ	319	206	114	33,800	86	91	177	106	52
Hualapai Trust Lands, AZ	3	-	-	-	-	-	-	-	-
Inaja-Cosmit Reservation, CA	-	-	-	-	-	-	-	-	-
Indian Township Reservation, ME	232	184	81	56,600	88	100	131	65	49
Iowa Reservation	64	59	26	51,100	7	69	25	22	2
Kansas	59	55	24	51,100	7	69	23	20	2
Nebraska	5	4	2	-	-	-	2	2	-
Isabella Reservation and Trust Lands, MI	9,037	8,275	121	38,900	107	213	178	94	61
Isabella Reservation, MI	9,013	8,252	104	39,000	105	213	163	82	58
Isabella Trust Lands, MI	24	23	17	38,800	2	-	15	12	3
Isleta Pueblo, NM	1,032	888	762	67,600	69	115	659	370	199
Jackson Rancheria, CA	8	8	-	-	6	163	3	1	2
Jamestown Klallam Reservation and Trust Lands, WA	9	8	-	-	2	413	2	2	-
Jamestown Klallam Reservation, WA	2	2	-	-	2	413	2	2	-
Jamestown Klallam Trust Lands, WA	7	6	-	-	-	-	-	-	-
Jamul Village, CA	-	-	-	-	-	-	-	-	-
Jemez, NM	449	404	358	42,700	44	125	367	185	128
Jircarilla Apache Reservation, NM	905	702	363	43,800	244	117	503	250	175
Kaibab Reservation, AZ	72	57	25	64,100	10	72	26	14	8
Kalispel Reservation, WA	30	30	21	35,300	6	66	22	9	8
Karok Reservation and Trust Lands, CA	165	159	7	50,800	-	-	7	3	4
Karok Reservation, CA	-	-	-	-	-	-	-	-	-
Korak Trust Lands, CA	165	159	7	50,800	-	-	7	3	4

[Continued]

★ 545 ★

Housing and Household Characteristics of American Indian and Alaska Native Areas: 1990, Hannahville-Lummi - I

[Continued]

American Indian/ Alaska Native Area State	All housing units		Occupied housing units with American Indian, Eskimo, or Aleut householder				Family households		
			Owner occupied		Renter occupied				
						Mean contract rent (dollars), specified renter paying cash rent		Married-couple family	Female house-holder, no husband present
			Total	Mean value (dollars) specified Owner	Total		Total		
	Total	Occupied							
Kickapoo Reservation, KS	176	139	46	26,500	54	73	82	44	22
Kootenai Reservation, ID	20	18	16	40,900	1	50	15	10	3
Lac Courte Oreilles Reservation and Trust Lands, WI	1,791	796	199	46,700	324	90	411	178	187
Lac du Flambeau Reservation, WI	2,593	869	146	43,600	282	104	341	146	131
Lac Vieux Desert Reservation, MI	39	39	-	-	37	97	25	11	12
Laguna Pueblo and Trust Lands, NM	1,339	1,052	767	68,000	240	90	825	541	230
Laguna Pueblo, NM	1,338	1,052	767	68,000	240	90	825	541	230
Laguna Trust Lands, NM	1	-	-	-	-	-	-	-	-
La Jolla Reservation, CA	39	32	24	73,300	-	-	19	8	8
Lake Traverse (Sisseton) Reservation	5,422	3,855	213	43,200	526	111	570	219	258
North Dakota	92	87	-	-	1	-	1	1	-
South Dakota	5,330	3,768	213	43,200	525	111	569	218	258
L'Anse Reservation and Trust Lands, MI	1,522	1,248	120	38,700	138	173	180	87	74
L'Anse Reservation, MI	1,515	1,241	119	38,300	138	173	179	86	74
L'Anse Trust Lands, MI	7	7	1	67,500	-	-	1	1	-
La Posta Reservation, CA	8	7	3	107,500	-	-	-	-	-
Las Vegas Colony, NV	26	23	21	-	-	-	14	5	7
Laytonville Rancheria, CA	54	52	7	111,500	41	177	35	10	19
Leech Lake Reservation, MN	6,227	3,084	613	41,000	386	137	778	309	338
Likely Rancheria, CA	-	-	-	-	-	-	-	-	-
Lone Pine Rancheria, CA	95	86	44	85,200	15	132	40	21	16
Lookout Rancheria, CA	5	5	-	-	4	-	3	2	-
Los Coyotes Reservation, CA	21	21	4	95,000	10	-	9	6	2
Lovelock Colony, NV	35	33	13	33,200	16	62	17	4	7
Lower Brule Reservation, SD	351	282	99	32,900	138	110	195	97	72
Lower Elwha Reservation and Trust Lands, WA	47	44	40	59,000	2	463	34	11	14

[Continued]

★ 545 ★

Housing and Household Characteristics of American Indian and Alaska Native Areas: 1990, Hannahville-Lummi - I
[Continued]

American Indian/ Alaska Native Area State	All housing units		Occupied housing units with American Indian, Eskimo, or Aleut householder				Family households		
			Owner occupied		Renter occupied				
						Mean contract rent (dollars), specified renter paying cash rent			Female householder, no husband present
	Total	Occupied	Total	Mean value (dollars) specified Owner	Total		Total	Married-couple family	
Lower Sioux Community, MN	86	78	42	33,500	33	66	57	23	22
Lummi Reservation, WA	1,331	1,050	248	60,400	126	155	322	207	84

Source: Summary Population and Housing Characteristics, United States Summary, United States Bureau of the Census, CP H-1, pp. 417-432. *Notes:* A dash (-) indicates that no data were given in the original source. 1. Federal American Indian reservations are areas with boundaries established by treaty, statute, and/or executive or court order, and recognized by the federal government as territory in which American Indian tribes have jurisdiction. State reservations are lands held in trust by state governments for the use and benefit of a given tribe. The reservations and their boundaries were identified for the 1990 census by the Bureau of Indian Affairs (BIA), Department of Interior (for federal reservations), and state governments (for state reservations). The names of American Indian reservations recognized by state governments, but not by the federal government, are followed by (state). Areas composed of reservation lands that are administered jointly and/or are claimed by two reservations, as identified by the BIA, are called "joint areas," and are treated as separate American Indian reservations for census purposes. Federal reservations may cross state boundaries, and federal and state reservations may cross county, county subdivision, and place boundaries. For reservations that cross state boundaries, only the portion of the reservations in a given state are shown in the data products for that state; the entire reservations are shown in data products for the United States. 2. Trust lands are property associated with a particular American Indian reservation or tribe, held in trust by the federal government. Trust lands may be held in trust either for a tribe (tribal trust lands) or for an individual member of a tribe (individual trust land). Trust lands recognized for the 1990 census comprised all tribal trust lands and inhabited individual trust lands located outside of a reservation boundary. As with other American Indian areas, trust lands may be located in more than one state. Only the trust lands in a given state are shown in the data products for that state; all trust lands associated with a reservation or tribe are shown in data products for the United States. The Census Bureau first reported data for tribal trust lands for the 1980 census.

★ 546 ★

Housing and Household Characteristics of American Indian and Alaska Native Areas: 1990, Hannahville-Lummi - II

American Indian/ Alaska Native Area State	Households with American Indian, Eskimo, or Aleut householder Nonfamily households		Land area	
	Total	Householder living alone	Square kilometers	Square miles
American Indian reservation and Trust Lands[1,2]				
Hannahville Community and Trust Lands, MI	6	4	17.7	6.8
Hannahville Community, MI	6	4	14.4	5.6
Hannahville Trust Lands, MI	-	-	3.3	1.3
Hassanamisco Reservation, MA (State)	1	1	-	-
Havasupai Reservation, AZ	11	9	709.4	273.9
Hoh Reservation, WA	9	5	1.9	.7

[Continued]

★ 546 ★

Housing and Household Characteristics of American Indian and Alaska Native Areas: 1990, Hannahville-Lummi - II

[Continued]

American Indian/ Alaska Native Area State	Households with American Indian, Eskimo, or Aleut householder Nonfamily households		Land area	
	Total	Householder living alone	Square kilometers	Square miles
Hollywood Reservation, FL	29	20	1.9	.7
Hoopa Valley Reservation, CA	126	100	354.6	136.9
Hopi Reservation and Trust Lands, AZ	256	231	6,309.4	2,236.1
Hopi Reservation, AZ	256	231	6,308.5	2,435.7
Hopi Trust Lands, AZ	-	-	1.0	.4
Hopland Rancheria, CA	10	10	.2	.1
Houlapai Reservation and Trust Lands, AZ	23	13	4,146.5	1,601.0
Houlapai Reservation, AZ	23	13	4,120.1	1,590.8
Houlapai Trust Lands, AZ	-	-	26.4	10.2
Inaja-Cosmit Reservation, CA	-	-	3.5	1.3
Indian Township Reservation, ME	38	33	97.0	37.5
Iowa Reservation	8	8	50.5	19.5
Kansas	8	8	35.1	13.5
Nebraska	-	-	15.5	6.0
Isabella Reservation and Trust Lands, MI	50	37	563.3	217.5
Isabella Reservation, MI	46	34	561.6	216.8
Isabella Trust Lands, MI	4	3	1.8	.7
Isleta Pueblo, NM	172	146	849.6	328.0
Jackson Rancheria, CA	3	3	1.3	.5
Jamestown Klallam Reservation and Trust Lands, WA	-	-	.1	-
Jamestown Klallam Reservation, WA	-	-	-	-
Jamestown Klallam Trust Lands, WA	-	-	.1	-
Jamul Village, CA	-	-	.1	-
Jemez, NM	35	34	361.8	139.7
Jircarilla Apache Reservation, NM	104	85	3,331.8	1,286.4

[Continued]

★ 546 ★

Housing and Household Characteristics of American Indian and Alaska Native Areas: 1990, Hannahville-Lummi - II

[Continued]

American Indian/ Alaska Native Area State	Households with American Indian, Eskimo, or Aleut householder Nonfamily households		Land area	
	Total	Householder living alone	Square kilometers	Square miles
Kaibab Reservation, AZ	9	8	488.9	188.8
Kalispel Reservation, WA	5	5	18.8	7.3
Karok Reservation and Trust Lands, CA	-	-	1.7	.7
Karok Reservation, CA	-	-	-	-
Korak Trust Lands, CA	-	-	1.7	.6
Kickapoo Reservation, KS	18	16	77.2	29.8
Kootenai Reservation, ID	2	2	.1	-
Lac Courte Oreilles Reservation and Trust Lands, WI	112	95	277.2	107.0
Lac Courte Oreilles Reservation, WI	112	95	276.9	106.9
Lac Courte Oreilles Trust Lands, WI	-	-	.3	.1
Lac du Flambeau Reservation, WI	87	64	279.3	107.8
Lac Vieux Desert Reservation, MI	12	11	-	-
Laguna Pueblo and Trust Lands, NM	182	162	1,970.7	760.9
Laguna Pueblo, NM	182	162	1,963.4	758.1
Laguna Trust Lands, NM	-	-	7.4	2.8
La Jolla Reservation, CA	5	5	35.0	13.5
Lake Traverse (Sisseton) Reservation	169	143	3,754.8	1,449.7
North Dakota	-	-	269.8	104.2
South Dakota	169	143	3,485.0	1,345.6
L'Anse Reservation and Trust Lands, MI	78	72	238.4	92.0
L'Anse Reservation, MI	78	72	238.2	92.0
L'Anse Trust Lands, MI	-	-	.2	.1
La Posta Reservation, CA	3	3	16.5	6.4
Las Vegas Colony, NV	7	6	16.0	6.2
Laytonville Rancheria, CA	13	12	.8	.3

[Continued]

★ 546 ★

Housing and Household Characteristics of American Indian and Alaska Native Areas: 1990, Hannahville-Lummi - II
[Continued]

American Indian/ Alaska Native Area State	Households with American Indian, Eskimo, or Aleut householder Nonfamily households		Land area	
	Total	Householder living alone	Square kilometers	Square miles
Leech Lake Reservation, MN	221	171	2,518.4	972.4
Likely Rancheria, CA	-	-	-	-
Lone Pine Rancheria, CA	19	15	.9	.4
Lookout Rancheria, CA	1	1	.2	.1
Los Coyotes Reservation, CA	5	5	101.4	39.2
Lovelock Colony, NV	12	12	.1	-
Lower Brule Reservation, SD	42	37	877.3	338.7
Lower Elwha Reservation and Trust Lands, WA	8	8	1.8	.7
Lower Elwha Reservation, WA	8	8	1.7	.7
Lower Elwha Trust Lands, WA	-	-	.1	.1
Lower Sioux Community, MN	18	14	7.0	2.7
Lummi Reservation, WA	52	38	54.4	21.0

Source: Summary Population and Housing Characteristics, United States Summary, United States Bureau of the Census, CP H-1, pp. 417-432. *Notes:* A dash (-) indicates that no data were given in original source. 1. Federal American Indian reservations are areas with boundaries established by treaty, statute, and/or executive or court order, and recognized by the federal government as territory in which American Indian tribes have jurisdiction. State reservations are lands held in trust by state governments for the use and benefit of a given tribe. The reservations and their boundaries were identified for the 1990 census by the Bureau of Indian Affairs (BIA), Department of Interior (for federal reservations), and state governments (for state reservations). The names of American Indian reservations recognized by state governments, but not by the federal government, are followed by (state). Areas composed of reservation lands that are administered jointly and/or are claimed by two reservations, as identified by the BIA, are called "joint areas," and are treated as separate American Indian reservations for census purposes. Federal reservations may cross state boundaries, and federal and state reservations may cross county, county subdivision, and place boundaries. For reservations that cross state boundaries, only the portion of the reservations in a given state are shown in the data products for that state; the entire reservations are shown in data products for the United States. 2. Trust lands are property associated with a particular American Indian reservation or tribe, held in trust by the federal government. Trust lands may be held in trust either for a tribe (tribal trust lands) or for an individual member of a tribe (individual trust land). Trust lands recognized for the 1990 census comprised all tribal trust lands and inhabited individual trust lands located outside of a reservation boundary. As with other American Indian areas, trust lands may be located in more than one state. Only the trust lands in a given state are shown in the data products for that state; all trust lands associated with a reservation or tribe are shown in data products for the United States. The Census Bureau first reported data for tribal trust lands for the 1980 census.

★ 547 ★

Housing and Household Characteristics of American Indian and Alaska Native Areas: 1990, Makah-Papago - I

American Indian/ Alaska Native Area State	All housing units		Occupied housing units with American Indian, Eskimo, or Aleut householder				Family households		
			Owner occupied		Renter occupied				
						Mean contract rent (dollars), specified renter paying cash rent			Female householder, no husband present
	Total	Occupied	Total	Mean value (dollars) specified Owner	Total		Total	Married-couple family	
American Indian Reservation and Trust Lands[1,2]									
Makah Reservation, WA	593	414	250	56,900	67	111	227	121	69
Manchester (Point Arena) Rancheria, CA	60	58	12	72,300	40	117	42	16	21
Manzanita Reservation, CA	18	18	13	100,800	3	-	13	7	3
Maricopa (Ak-Chin) Reservation, AZ	109	107	88	27,100	8	-	87	60	17
Mashantucket Pequot Reservation, CT	35	26	15	122,100	5	287	15	12	2
Mattaponi Reservation, VA (state)	27	25	21	35,300	2	-	20	16	2
Menominee Reservation, WI	1,176	901	475	40,900	349	120	699	311	293
Mesa Grande Reservation, CA	40	34	25	260,000	2	-	18	11	4
Mescalero Apache Reservation, NM	721	653	175	37,800	420	155	529	276	194
Miccosukee Reservation, FL	15	15	14	32,800	1	137	15	6	7
Middletown Rancheria, CA	31	31	7	-	1	-	3	2	1
Mille Lacs Reservation, MN	187	131	90	34,200	29	82	94	28	48
Minnesota Chippewa Trust Lands, MN	31	14	9	49,000	2	-	9	4	3
Mississippi Choctaw Reservation and Trust Lands, MS	1,007	939	579	31,500	313	99	804	400	302
Mississippi Choctaw Reservation, MS	933	869	541	31,300	289	100	746	369	284
Mississippi Choctaw Trust Lands, MS	74	70	38	34,900	24	89	58	31	18
Maapa River Reservation, NV	112	107	46	47,200	18	102	49	27	19
Montgomery Creek Rancheria, CA	6	5	2	-	2	163	2	1	-
Morongo Reservation, CA	416	365	137	76,000	33	226	134	73	43
Muckleshoot Reservation and Trust Lands, WA	1,379	1,319	92	98,700	82	175	154	58	64
Nambe Pueblo and Trust Lands, NM	570	523	110	70,500	8	104	89	50	26
Narragansett Reservation, RI	9	9	3	146,700	1	875	4	3	1
Navajo Reservation and Trust Lands, AZ-NM-UT	55,467	36,250	26,679	31,600	7,407	144	29,015	18,036	8,296
Navajo Reservation	48,385	31,295	22,788	32,200	6,587	145	25,023	15,601	7,190
Arizona	34,847	22,093	15,901	33,300	4,689	156	17,473	10,905	5,029
New Mexico	11,485	7,872	5,795	30,800	1,748	118	6,463	3,943	1,885
Utah	2,053	1,330	1,092	21,500	150	137	1,087	753	276
Navajo Trust Lands	7,082	4,955	3,891	28,200	820	130	3,992	2,435	1,106
Arizona	8	5	2	-	-	-	1	1	-
New Mexico	7,074	4,950	3,889	28,200	820	130	3,991	2,434	1,106
Nez Perce Reservation, ID	6,920	6,122	397	52,200	184	162	471	290	135
Nisqually Reservation, WA	170	166	90	75,000	11	157	86	40	27
Nooksack Reservation and Trust Lands, WA	152	143	83	53,200	27	117	97	57	26

[Continued]

★ 547 ★

Housing and Household Characteristics of American Indian and Alaska Native Areas: 1990, Makah
Papago - I
[Continued]

American Indian/ Alaska Native Area State	All housing units		Occupied housing units with American Indian, Eskimo, or Aleut householder				Family households		
			Owner occupied		Renter occupied				Female house-holder, no husband present
				Mean value (dollars) specified Owner	Total	Mean contract rent (dollars), specified renter paying cash rent	Total	Married-couple family	
	Total	Occupied	Total						
Nooksack Reservation, WA	12	7	4	-	-	-	4	3	-
Nooksack Trust Lands, WA	140	136	79	53,200	27	117	93	54	26
Northern Cheyenne Reservation and Trust Lands, MT - SD	1,291	1,045	554	36,800	326	114	750	395	279
Northern Cheyenne Reservation, MT	1,1291	1,045	554	36,800	326	114	750	395	279
Northern Cheyenne Trust Lands, MT, SD	-	-	-	-	-	-	-	-	-
North Fork Rancheria, CA	2	2	-	-	-	-	-	-	-
Northwestern Shoshoni Reservation, UT	-	-	-	-	-	-	-	-	-
Oil Springs Reservation, NY	17	2	-	-	-	-	-	-	-
Omaha Reservation, NE	1,938	1,741	146	44,900	283	119	377	148	179
Oneido (East) Reservation, NY	20	12	11	-	1	363	10	4	4
Oneido (West) Reservation, WI	5,910	5,761	449	52,200	258	177	577	324	193
Onondaga Reservation, NY	221	221	1	112,500	-	-	1	1	-
Ontonagon Reservation, MI	-	-	-	-	-	-	-	-	-
Osage Reservation, OK	18,064	15,266	1,473	40,700	458	159	1,459	1,106	289
Ozette Reservation, WA	-	-	-	-	-	-	-	-	-
Paiute of Utah Reservation, UT	250	187	38	46,700	42	57	75	40	29
Pala Reservation, CA	315	296	152	59,600	17	176	130	71	48
Pamunkey Reservation (state), VA	34	27	25	35,000	-	-	14	14	-
Papago Reservation, AZ	2,535	2,186	1,552	23,900	534	111	1,732	680	711

Source: Summary Population and Housing Characteristics, United States Summary, United States Bureau of the Census, CP H-1, pp. 417-432. *Notes:* A dash (-) indicates that no data were given in the original source. 1. Federal American Indian reservations are areas with boundaries established by treaty, statute, and/or executive or court order, and recognized by the federal government as territory in which American Indian tribes have jurisdiction. State reservations are lands held in trust by state governments for the use and benefit of a given tribe. The reservations and their boundaries were identified for the 1990 census by the Bureau of Indian Affairs (BIA), Department of Interior (for federal reservations), and state governments (for state reservations). The names of American Indian reservations recognized by state governments, but not by the federal government, are followed by (state). Areas composed of reservation lands that are administered jointly and/or are claimed by two reservations, as identified by the BIA, are called "joint areas," and are treated as separate American Indian reservations for census purposes. Federal reservations may cross state boundaries, and federal and state reservations may cross county, county subdivision, and place boundaries. For reservations that cross state boundaries, only the portion of the reservations in a given state are shown in the data products for that state; the entire reservations are shown in data products for the United States. 2. Trust lands are property associated with a particular American Indian reservation or tribe, held in trust by the federal government. Trust lands may be held in trust either for a tribe (tribal trust lands) or for an individual member of a tribe (individual trust land). Trust lands recognized for the 1990 census comprised all tribal trust lands and inhabited individual trust lands located outside of a reservation boundary. As with other American Indian areas, trust lands may be located in more than one state. Only the trust lands in a given state are shown in the data products for that state; all trust lands associated with a reservation or tribe are shown in data products for the United States. The Census Bureau first reported data for tribal trust lands for the 1980 census.

★ 548 ★

Housing and Household Characteristics of American Indian and Alaska Native Areas: 1990, Makah-Papago - II

American Indian/ Alaska Native Area State	Households with American Indian, Eskimo, or Aleut householder Nonfamily households		Land area	
	Total	Householder living alone	Square kilometers	Square miles
American Indian Reservation and Trust Lands[1,2]				
Makah Reservation, WA	90	78	110.6	42.7
Manchester (Point Arena) Rancheria, CA	10	8	1.5	.6
Manzanita Reservation, CA	3	3	14.5	5.6
Maricopa (Ak-Chin) Reservation, AZ	9	9	85.2	32.9
Mashantucket Pequot Reservation, CT	5	3	5.0	1.9
Mattaponi Reservation, VA (state)	3	3	.3	.1
Menominee Reservation, WI	125	95	921.7	355.9
Mesa Grande Reservation, CA	9	9	30.7	11.9
Mescalero Apache Reservation, NM	66	57	1,862.5	719.1
Miccosukee Reservation, FL	-	-	331.3	127.9
Middletown Rancheria, CA	5	5	.5	.2
Mille Lacs Reservation, MN	25	21	13.8	5.3
Minnesota Chippewa Trust Lands, MN	2	1	1.9	.7
Mississippi Choctaw Reservation and Trust Lands, MS	88	50	85.5	33.0
Mississippi Choctaw Reservation, MS	84	48	75.3	29.1
Mississippi Choctaw Trust Lands, MS	4	2	10.3	4.0
Maapa River Reservation, NV	15	14	290.1	112.0
Montgomery Creek Rancheria, CA	2	2	.4	.1
Morongo Reservation, CA	36	26	127.4	49.2
Muckleshoot Reservation and Trust Lands, WA	20	13	15.9	6.1
Muckleshoot Trust Lands, WA	-	-	.1	.1

[Continued]

★ 548 ★

Housing and Household Characteristics of American Indian and Alaska Native Areas 1990, Makah-Papago - II

[Continued]

American Indian/ Alaska Native Area State	Households with American Indian, Eskimo, or Aleut householder Nonfamily households		Land area	
	Total	Householder living alone	Square kilometers	Square miles
Nambe Pueblo and Trust Lands, NM	29	26	83.7	32.3
Nambe Pueblo, NM	29	26	83.0	32.0
Nambe Trust Lands, NM	-	-	.8	.3
Narragansett Reservation, RI	-	-	8.7	3.4
Navajo Reservation and Trust Lands, AZ-NM-UT	5,071	4,626	63,263.4	24,426.0
Navajo Reservation	4,352	3,969	56,663.4	21,877.8
Arizona	3,117	2,849	41,342.2	15,962.2
New Mexico	1,080	982	10,132.9	3,912.3
Utah	155	138	5,188.3	2,003.2
Navajo Trust Lands	719	657	6,600.0	2,548.3
Arizona	1	1	23.3	9.0
New Mexico	718	656	6,576.6	2,539.2
Nez Perce Reservation, ID	110	86	3,095.4	1,195.1
Nisqually Reservation, WA	15	10	20.6	7.9
Nooksack Reservation and Trust Lands, WA	13	10	10.9	4.2
Nooksack Reservation, WA	-	-	1.8	.7
Nooksack Trust Lands, WA	13	10	9.1	3.5
Northern Cheyenne Reservation and Trust Lands, MT - SD	130	110	1,813.9	700.3
Northern Cheyenne Reservation, MT	130	110	1,805.6	697.1
Northern Cheyenne Trust Lands	-	-	8.2	3.2
Montana	-	-	5.6	2.1
South Dakota	-	-	2.7	1.0
North Fork Rancheria, CA	-	-	.3	.1
Northwestern Shoshoni Reservation, UT	-	-	.8	.3
Oil Springs Reservation, NY	-	-	2.5	1.0
Omaha Reservation	52	43	808.1	312.0
Iowa	-	-	22.9	8.9
Nebraska	52	43	785.2	303.2

[Continued]

★ 548 ★

Housing and Household Characteristics of American Indian and Alaska Native Areas: 1990, Makah-Papago - II
[Continued]

American Indian/ Alaska Native Area State	Households with American Indian, Eskimo, or Aleut householder Nonfamily households		Land area	
	Total	Householder living alone	Square kilometers	Square miles
Oneido (East) Reservation, NY	2	1	.2	.1
Oneido (West) Reservation, WI	130	110	264.9	102.3
Onondaga Reservation, NY	-	-	24.0	9.2
Ontonagon Reservation, MI	-	-	9.6	3.7
Osage Reservation, OK	472	443	5,808.7	2,242.7
Ozette Reservation, WA	-	-	3.2	1.2
Paiute of Utah Reservation, UT	5	5	132.1	51.0
Pala Reservation, CA	39	30	65.9	25.4
Pamunkey Reservation (state)	11	11	4.5	1.7
Papago Reservation, AZ	354	261	11,245.8	4,342.0

Source: Summary Population and Housing Characteristics, United States Summary, United States Bureau of the Census, CP H-1, pp. 417-432. *Notes:* A dash (-) indicates that no data were given in the original source. 1. Federal American Indian reservations are areas with boundaries established by treaty, statute, and/or executive or court order, and recognized by the federal government as territory in which American Indian tribes have jurisdiction. State reservations are lands held in trust by state governments for the use and benefit of a given tribe. The reservations and their boundaries were identified for the 1990 census by the Bureau of Indian Affairs (BIA), Department of Interior (for federal reservations), and state governments (for state reservations). The names of American Indian reservations recognized by state governments, but not by the federal government, are followed by (state). Areas composed of reservation lands that are administered jointly and/or are claimed by two reservations, as identified by the BIA, are called "joint areas," and are treated as separate American Indian reservations for census purposes. Federal reservations may cross state boundaries, and federal and state reservations may cross county, county subdivision, and place boundaries. For reservations that cross state boundaries, only the portion of the reservations in a given state are shown in the data products for that state; the entire reservations are shown in data products for the United States. 2. Trust lands are property associated with a particular American Indian reservation or tribe, held in trust by the federal government. Trust lands may be held in trust either for a tribe (tribal trust lands) or for an individual member of a tribe (individual trust land). Trust lands recognized for the 1990 census comprised all tribal trust lands and inhabited individual trust lands located outside of a reservation boundary. As with other American Indian areas, trust lands may be located in more than one state. Only the trust lands in a given state are shown in the data products for that state; all trust lands associated with a reservation or tribe are shown in data products for the United States. The Census Bureau first reported data for tribal trust lands for the 1980 census.

Housing and Household Characteristics of American Indian and Alaska Native Areas: 1990, Pascua-Rocky Boy - I

American Indian/ Alaska Native Area State	All housing units		Occupied housing units with American Indian, Eskimo, or Aleut householder				Family households		
			Owner occupied		Renter occupied				
						Mean contract rent (dollars), specified renter paying cash rent		Married-couple family	Female house-holder, no husband present
	Total	Occupied	Total	Mean value (dollars) specified Owner	Total		Total		
American Indian Reservation and Trust Lands[1,2]									
Pascua Yoqui Reservation, AZ	600	546	269	50,600	256	101	493	265	178
Passamaquaddy Trust Lands, ME	16	2	-	-	1	-	-	-	-
Paucatuck Eastern Peqquot Reservation, CT (state)	13	8	8	155,000	-	-	6	2	3
Pauma Reservation, CA	35	35	27	78,700	6	110	27	12	10
Payson (Yavapai-Apache) Community, AZ	28	27	23	73,900	4	213	22	18	3
Pechanga Reservation, CA	162	132	90	70,200	7	251	63	33	23
Penobscot Reservation and Trust Lands, ME	260	181	90	48,100	71	177	111	63	32
Penobscot Reservation, ME	182	176	90	48,100	71	177	111	63	32
Penobscot Trust Lands, ME	78	5	-	-	-	-	-	-	-
Picayune Rancheria, CA	11	10	4	9,000	-	-	3	1	-
Picuris Pueblo, NM	839	640	46	34,000	2	237	37	17	14
Pine Creek Reservation, MI (state)	15	11	8	10,200	2	-	5	2	3
Pine Ridge Reservation and Trust Lands, NE-SD	3,387	2,752	1,048	31,100	1,304	115	2,076	955	823
Pine Ridge Reservation, SD	3,158	2,571	964	32,200	1,251	116	1,951	883	783
Pine Ridge Trust Lands	229	181	84	20,500	53	103	125	72	40
Nebraska	10	9	2	-	-	-	2	1	-
South Dakota	219	172	82	20,500	53	103	123	71	40
Pinoleville Rancheria, CA	38	35	12	124,200	10	242	18	5	7
Pit River Trust Lands, CA	3	3	-	-	1	-	-	-	-
Pleasant Point Reservation, ME	183	180	118	55,100	50	98	134	56	61
Poarch Creek Reservation and Trust Lands, AL	81	77	5	55,800	61	77	46	29	17
Pojaaque Pueblo, NM	1,040	938	31	120,100	38	122	42	17	17
Poospatuck Reservation, NY (state)	46	45	29	175,200	2	313	23	13	6
Port Gamble Reservation, WA	158	151	59	38,400	39	133	89	48	26
Port Madison Reservation, WA	2,133	1,874	84	91,000	39	263	99	68	22
Potawatomi (Kansas) Reservation, KS	375	355	88	39,300	60	81	111	67	29
Potawatomi (Wisconsin) Reservation and Trust Lands, WI	84	75	55	18,500	16	67	56	19	22
Potawatomi (Wisconsin) Reservation, WI	84	75	55	18,500	16	67	56	19	22
Potawatomi (Wisconsin) Trust Lands, WI	-	-	-	-	-	-	-	-	-
Prarie Island Community, MN	24	22	7	26,700	13	128	17	4	9
Puyallup Reservation and Trust Lands, WA	12,873	11,950	139	70,100	141	323	215	105	88
Puyallup Reservation, WA	12,867	11,944	139	70,100	140	323	215	105	88
Puyallup Trust Lands, WA	6	6	-	-	1	-	-	-	-

[Continued]

851

★ 549 ★

Housing and Household Characteristics of American Indian and Alaska Native Areas: 1990, Pascua-Rocky Boy - I
[Continued]

American Indian/ Alaska Native Area State	All housing units		Occupied housing units with American Indian, Eskimo, or Aleut householder				Family households		
			Owner occupied		Renter occupied				
			Total	Mean value (dollars) specified Owner	Total	Mean contract rent (dollars), specified renter paying cash rent	Total	Married-couple family	Female house-holder, no husband present
	Total	Occupied							
Pyramid Lake Reservation, NV	580	504	193	58,200	113	146	239	115	98
Quartz Valley Rancheria, CA	52	46	8	32,500	2	263	6	5	-
Quileute Reservation, WA	130	115	76	44,100	22	177	70	39	22
Quinault Reservation, WA	475	358	184	40,800	91	163	232	122	70
Ramah Navajo Community, NM	83	48	47	18,000	-	-	38	17	14
Ramana Reservation, CA	1	-	-	-	-	-	-	-	-
Rankokus Reservation, NJ (state)	-	-	-	-	-	-	-	-	-
Red Cliff Reservation and Trust Lands, WI	343	259	118	38,100	98	104	172	95	56
Red Cliff Reservation, WI	343	259	118	38,100	98	104	172	95	56
Red Cliff Trust Lands, WI	-	-	-	-	-	-	-	-	-
Redding Rancheria, CA	33	31	17	121,400	8	300	17	8	6
Red Lake Reservation, MN	1,063	960	585	41,000	343	94	775	317	346
Redwood Valley Rancheria, CA	46	46	4	137,500	-	-	3	-	3
Reno-Sparks Colony, NV	67	67	54	53,500	12	165	58	24	29
Resighini Rancheria, CA	9	9	8	44,500	-	-	7	5	1
Rincon Reservation, CA	434	380	91	104,100	33	315	95	54	31
Roaring Creek Rancheria, CA	4	4	-	-	4	-	4	1	3
Robinson Rancheria, CA	31	31	14	44,100	11	80	24	4	17
Rocky Boy's Reservation and Trust Lands, MT	514	437	209	30,100	198	86	373	216	113
Rocky Boy's Reservation, MT	397	333	165	30,600	147	92	286	162	87
Rocky Boy's Trust Lands, MT	117	104	44	28,100	51	69	87	54	26

Source: Summary Population and Housing Characteristics, United States Summary, United States Bureau of the Census, CP H-1, pp. 417-432. *Notes:* A dash (-) indicates that no data were given in the original source. 1. Federal American Indian reservations are areas with boundaries established by treaty, statute, and/or executive or court order, and recognized by the federal government as territory in which American Indian tribes have jurisdiction. State reservations are lands held in trust by state governments for the use and benefit of a given tribe. The reservations and their boundaries were identified for the 1990 census by the Bureau of Indian Affairs (BIA), Department of Interior (for federal reservations), and state governments (for state reservations). The names of American Indian reservations recognized by state governments, but not by the federal government, are followed by (state). Areas composed of reservation lands that are administered jointly and/or are claimed by two reservations, as identified by the BIA, are called "joint areas," and are treated as separate American Indian reservations for census purposes. Federal reservations may cross state boundaries, and federal and state reservations may cross county, county subdivision, and place boundaries. For reservations that cross state boundaries, only the portion of the reservations in a given state are shown in the data products for that state; the entire reservations are shown in data products for the United States. 2. Trust lands are property associated with a particular American Indian reservation or tribe, held in trust by the federal government. Trust lands may be held in trust either for a tribe (tribal trust lands) or for an individual member of a tribe (individual trust land). Trust lands recognized for the 1990 census comprised all tribal trust lands and inhabited individual trust lands located outside of a reservation boundary. As with other American Indian areas, trust lands may be located in more than one state. Only the trust lands in a given state are shown in the data products for that state; all trust lands associated with a reservation or tribe are shown in data products for the United States. The Census Bureau first reported data for tribal trust lands for the 1980 census.

★ 550 ★

Housing and Household Characteristics of American Indian and Alaska Native Areas: 1990, Pascua-Rocky Boy - II

American Indian/ Alaska Native Area State	Households with American Indian, Eskimo, or Aleut householder Nonfamily households		Land area	
	Total	Householder living alone	Square kilometers	Square miles
American Indian Reservation and Trust Lands[1,2]				
Pascua Yoqui Reservation, AZ	32	22	3.7	1.4
Passamaquaddy Trust Lands, ME	1	1	379.8	146.7
Paucatuck Eastern Peqquot Reservation, CT (state)	2	1	.9	.3
Pauma Reservation, CA	6	4	24.3	9.4
Payson (Yavapai-Apache) Community, AZ	5	2	.3	.1
Pechanga Reservation, CA	34	31	18.2	7.0
Penobscot Reservation and Trust Lands, ME	50	44	260.8	100.7
Penobscot Reservation, ME	50	44	20.3	7.8
Penobscot Trust Lands, ME	-	-	240.5	92.9
Picayune Rancheria, CA	1	-	.3	.1
Picuris Pueblo, NM	11	10	70.9	27.4
Pine Creek Reservation, MI (state)	5	4	.5	.2
Pine Ridge Reservation and Trust Lands, NE-SD	276	225	8,983.3	3,468.4
Pine Ridge Reservation, SD	264	217	8,182.0	3,159.1
Pine Ridge Trust Lands	12	8	801.2	309.3
Nebraska	-	-	2.3	.9
South Dakota	12	8	798.9	308.5
Pinoleville Rancheria, CA	4	3	.4	.2
Pit River Trust Lands, CA	1	1	1.1	.4
Pleasant Point Reservation, ME	34	30	2.0	.8
Poarch Creek Reservation and Trust Lands, AL	20	20	1.1	.4
Poarch Creek Reservation, AL	20	20	1.0	.4
Poarch Creek Trust Lands, AL	-	-	-	-

[Continued]

★ 550 ★

Housing and Household Characteristics of American Indian and Alaska Native Areas: 1990, Pascua-Rocky Boy - II

[Continued]

American Indian/ Alaska Native Area State	Households with American Indian, Eskimo, or Aleut householder Nonfamily households		Land area	
	Total	Householder living alone	Square kilometers	Square miles
Pojaaque Pueblo, NM	27	23	54.5	21.1
Poospatuck Reservation, NY (state)	8	8	.2	.1
Port Gamble Reservation, WA	9	6	4.9	1.9
Port Madison Reservation, WA	24	20	30.3	11.7
Potawatomi (Kansas) Reservation, KS	37	33	311.1	120.1
Potawatomi (Wisconsin) Reservation and Trust Lands	15	10	48.6	18.8
Potawatomi (Wisconsin) Reservation, WI	15	10	48.2	18.6
Potawatomi (Wisconsin) Trust Lands, WI	-	-	.4	.2
Prarie Island Community, MN	3	2	2.1	.8
Puyallup Reservation and Trust Lands, WA	65	50	73.9	28.5
Puyallup Reservation, WA	64	49	73.9	28.5
Puyallup Trust Lands, WA	1	1	-	-
Pyramid Lake Reservation, NV	67	56	1,434.7	553.9
Quartz Valley Rancheria, CA	4	4	2.5	1.0
Quileute Reservation, WA	28	23	4.1	1.6
Quinault Reservation, WA	43	31	842.4	325.2
Ramah Navajo Community, NM	9	9	71.7	27.7
Ramana Reservation, CA	-	-	2.2	.9
Rankokus Reservation, NJ (state)	-	-	1.1	.4
Red Cliff Reservation and Trust Lands, WI	44	32	58.9	22.7
Red Cliff Reservation, WI	44	32	56.7	21.9
Red Cliff Trust Lands, WI	-	-	2.2	.9
Redding Rancheria, CA	8	7	.1	-

[Continued]

★ 550 ★

Housing and Household Characteristics of American Indian and Alaska Native Areas: 1990, Pascua-Rocky Boy - II

[Continued]

American Indian/ Alaska Native Area State	Households with American Indian, Eskimo, or Aleut householder Nonfamily households		Land area	
	Total	Householder living alone	Square kilometers	Square miles
Red Lake Reservation, MN	153	125	2,279.6	880.1
Redwood Valley Rancheria, CA	1	1	.3	.1
Reno-Sparks Colony, NV	8	7	8.2	3.2
Resighini Rancheria, CA	1	1	.9	.4
Rincon Reservation, CA	29	26	15.9	6.1
Roaring Creek Rancheria, CA	-	-	.3	.1
Robinson Rancheria, CA	1	1	.9	.4
Rocky Boy's Reservation and Trust Lands, MT	34	29	435.9	168.3
Rocky Boy's Reservation, MT	26	21	229.3	88.5
Rocky Boy's Trust Lands, MT	8	8	206.6	79.8

Source: Summary Population and Housing Characteristics, United States Summary, United States Bureau of the Census, CP H-1, pp. 417-432. *Notes:* A dash (-) indicates that no data were given in the original source. 1. Federal American Indian reservations are areas with boundaries established by treaty, statute, and/or executive or court order, and recognized by the federal government as territory in which American Indian tribes have jurisdiction. State reservations are lands held in trust by state governments for the use and benefit of a given tribe. The reservations and their boundaries were identified for the 1990 census by the Bureau of Indian Affairs (BIA), Department of Interior (for federal reservations), and state governments (for state reservations). The names of American Indian reservations recognized by state governments, but not by the federal government, are followed by (state). Areas composed of reservation lands that are administered jointly and/or are claimed by two reservations, as identified by the BIA, are called "joint areas," and are treated as separate American Indian reservations for census purposes. Federal reservations may cross state boundaries, and federal and state reservations may cross county, county subdivision, and place boundaries. For reservations that cross state boundaries, only the portion of the reservations in a given state are shown in the data products for that state; the entire reservations are shown in data products for the United States. 2. Trust lands are property associated with a particular American Indian reservation or tribe, held in trust by the federal government. Trust lands may be held in trust either for a tribe (tribal trust lands) or for an individual member of a tribe (individual trust land). Trust lands recognized for the 1990 census comprised all tribal trust lands and inhabited individual trust lands located outside of a reservation boundary. As with other American Indian areas, trust lands may be located in more than one state. Only the trust lands in a given state are shown in the data products for that state; all trust lands associated with a reservation or tribe are shown in data products for the United States. The Census Bureau first reported data for tribal trust lands for the 1980 census.

★ 551 ★

Housing and Household Characteristics of American Indian and Alaska Native Areas: 1990, Rohnerville-Soboba - I

American Indian/ Alaska Native Area State	All housing units		Occupied housing units with American Indian, Eskimo, or Aleut householder				Family households		
			Owner occupied		Renter occupied				
						Mean contract rent (dollars), specified renter paying cash rent			Female householder, no husband present
			Total	Mean value (dollars) specified Owner	Total		Total	Married-couple family	
	Total	Occupied							
American Indian Reservation and Trust Lands[1,2]									
Rohnerville Rancheria, CA	6	6	1	-	-	-	-	-	-
Rosebud Reservation and Trust Lands, SD	2,987	2,540	822	23,700	1,102	122	1,585	688	681
Rosebud Reservation, SD	2,572	2,210	705	23,700	951	124	1,373	588	595
Rosebud Trust Lands, SD	415	330	117	23,700	151	110	212	100	86
Round Valley Reservation and Trust Lands, CA	484	399	88	49,500	81	111	139	69	51
Round Valley Reservation, CA	484	399	88	49,500	81	111	139	69	51
Round Valley Trust Lands, CA	-	-	-	-	-	-	-	-	-
Rumsey Rancheria, CA	4	3	-	-	1	487	1	1	-
Sac and Fox (Iowa) Reservation, IA	154	139	102	22,100	33	120	113	66	37
Sac and Fox (KS-NE) Reservation and Trust Lands, KS-NE	81	71	16	56,800	1	50	10	7	2
Sac and Fox Reservation	79	70	15	56,800	1	50	10	7	2
Kansas	29	24	14	59,400	1	50	10	7	2
Nebraska	50	46	1	22,500	-	-	-	-	-
Sac and Fox (KS-NE) Trust Lands	2	1	1	-	-	-	-	-	-
Kansas	2	1	1	-	-	-	-	-	-
Nebraska	-	-	-	-	-	-	-	-	-
St. Croix Reservation, WI	163	147	43	40,100	95	133	103	46	47
St. Regis Mohawk Reservation, NY	754	634	561	45,000	64	184	485	342	106
Salt River Reservation, AZ	2,141	1,583	598	69,000	257	116	743	348	285
San Carlos Reservation, AZ	2,124	1,706	1,099	30,500	535	93	1,418	872	440
Sandia Pueblo, NM	1,440	1,294	92	52,300	16	245	87	54	22
Sandy Lake Reservation, MN	11	9	5	54,200	4	163	5	2	1
San Filipe Pueblo, NM	582	512	315	63,300	15	157	311	146	116
San Ildefonso Pueblo, NM	635	535	98	78,700	5	327	85	44	30
San Juan Pueblo, NM	1,885	1,667	320	55,700	36	144	301	165	98
San Manuel Reservation, CA	26	26	18	90,400	4	585	15	11	2
San Pasqual Reservation, CA	154	147	45	128,400	8	244	39	25	13
Santa Ana Pueblo, NM	248	153	113	50,300	6	-	104	69	31
Santa Clara Pueblo, NM	4,127	3,617	321	61,800	78	192	309	193	83
Santa Rosa Rancheria, CA	79	76	27	38,000	41	135	54	22	21
Santa Rosa Reservation, CA	14	14	7	13,500	5	163	10	4	6
Santa Ynez Reservation, CA	118	74	41	110,600	19	160	46	23	17
Santa Ysabel Reservation, CA	56	53	44	59,500	6	187	33	14	11

[Continued]

★ 551 ★

Housing and Household Characteristics of American Indian and Alaska Native Areas: 1990, Rohnerville-Soboba - I
[Continued]

American Indian/ Alaska Native Area State	All housing units		Occupied housing units with American Indian, Eskimo, or Aleut householder				Family households		
			Owner occupied		Renter occupied				
						Mean contract rent (dollars), specified renter paying cash rent	Total	Married-couple family	Female house-holder, no husband present
			Total	Mean value (dollars) specified Owner	Total				
	Total	Occupied							
Santee Reservation, NE	338	268	36	47,700	104	107	104	54	41
Santo Domingo Pueblo, NM	494	441	415	80,900	12	227	395	205	132
San Xavier Reservation, AZ	357	305	207	44,200	68	152	216	79	102
Saulk-Suiattle Reservation, WA	36	33	12	73,000	4	60	16	5	9
Sault Ste. Marie Reservation and Trust Lands, MI	220	215	16	48,500	122	105	113	57	48
Sault Ste. Marie Reservation, MI	105	105	2	40,000	75	108	62	29	30
Sault Ste. Marie Trust Lands, MI	115	110	14	49,800	47	101	51	28	18
Schaghticoke Reservation, CT (state)	6	5	4	-	-	-	1	1	-
Seminole Trust Lands, FL	32	32	25	44,800	2	50	22	12	7
Shakopee Community, MN	71	68	58	70,500	-	-	43	22	13
Sheep Ranch Rancheria, CA	-	-	-	-	-	-	-	-	-
Sherwood Valley Rancheria, CA	9	5	2	-	1	313	3	2	-
Shingle Springs Rancheria, CA	7	7	4	45,000	-	-	2	1	1
Shinnecock Reservation, NY (state)	173	135	110	86,100	11	458	85	59	18
Shoalwater Reservation, WA	79	44	19	68,200	3	50	20	11	6
Siletz Reservation, OR	1	1	-	-	-	-	-	-	-
Skokomish Reservation, WA	301	200	104	50,000	20	223	100	63	22
Skull Valley Reservation, UT	11	9	9	16,600	-	-	7	4	3
Smith River Rancheria, CA	41	31	16	54,200	4	296	18	10	6
Soboba Reservation, CA	119	113	70	55,300	24	143	71	34	24

Source: *Summary Population and Housing Characteristics, United States Summary*, United States Bureau of the Census, CP H-1, pp. 417-432. *Notes:* A dash (-) indicates that no data were given in the original source. 1. Federal American Indian reservations are areas with boundaries established by treaty, statute, and/or executive or court order, and recognized by the federal government as territory in which American Indian tribes have jurisdiction. State reservations are lands held in trust by state governments for the use and benefit of a given tribe. The reservations and their boundaries were identified for the 1990 census by the Bureau of Indian Affairs (BIA), Department of Interior (for federal reservations), and state governments (for state reservations). The names of American Indian reservations recognized by state governments, but not by the federal government, are followed by (state). Areas composed of reservation lands that are administered jointly and/or are claimed by two reservations, as identified by the BIA, are called "joint areas," and are treated as separate American Indian reservations for census purposes. Federal reservations may cross state boundaries, and federal and state reservations may cross county, county subdivision, and place boundaries. For reservations that cross state boundaries, only the portion of the reservations in a given state are shown in the data products for that state; the entire reservations are shown in data products for the United States. 2. Trust lands are property associated with a particular American Indian reservation or tribe, held in trust by the federal government. Trust lands may be held in trust either for a tribe (tribal trust lands) or for an individual member of a tribe (individual trust land). Trust lands recognized for the 1990 census comprised all tribal trust lands and inhabited individual trust lands located outside of a reservation boundary. As with other American Indian areas, trust lands may be located in more than one state. Only the trust lands in a given state are shown in the data products for that state; all trust lands associated with a reservation or tribe are shown in data products for the United States. The Census Bureau first reported data for tribal trust lands for the 1980 census.

★ 552 ★

Housing and Household Characteristics of American Indian and Alaska Native Areas: 1990, Rohnerville-Soboba - II

American Indian/ Alaska Native Area State	Households with American Indian, Eskimo, or Aleut householder Nonfamily households		Land area	
	Total	Householder living alone	Square kilometers	Square miles
American Indian Reservation and Trust Lands[1,2]				
Rohnerville Rancheria, CA	1	1	.1	-
Rosebud Reservation and Trust Lands, SD	339	287	5,114.3	1,974.6
Rosebud Reservation, SD	283	242	3,595.5	1,388.2
Rosebud Trust Lands, SD	56	45	1,518.8	586.4
Round Valley Reservation and Trust Lands, CA	30	28	245.8	94.9
Round Valley Reservation, CA	30	28	202.7	78.2
Round Valley Trust Lands, CA	-	-	43.1	16.6
Rumsey Rancheria, CA	-	-	.2	.1
Sac and Fox (Iowa) Reservation, IA	22	18	15.3	5.9
Sac and Fox (KS-NE) Reservation and Trust Lands, KS-NE	7	5	62.1	24.0
Sac and Fox Reservation	6	4	59.8	23.1
Kansas	5	3	20.0	7.7
Nebraska	1	1	39.8	15.3
Sac and Fox (KS-NE) Trust Lands	1	1	2.3	.9
Kansas	1	1	1.8	.7
Nebraska	-	-	.6	.2
St. Croix Reservation, WI	35	25	7.5	2.9
St. Regis Mohawk Reservation, NY	140	124	49.2	19.0
Salt River Reservation, AZ	112	89	207.2	80.0
San Carlos Reservation, AZ	216	188	7,538.5	2,910.6
Sandia Pueblo, NM	21	18	101.1	39.0
Sandy Lake Reservation, MN	4	4	1.0	.4
San Filipe Pueblo, NM	19	16	203.5	78.6
San Ildefonso Pueblo, NM	18	15	113.2	43.7

[Continued]

★ 552 ★

Housing and Household Characteristics of American Indian and Alaska Native Areas: 1990, Rohnerville-Soboba - II

[Continued]

American Indian/ Alaska Native Area State	Households with American Indian, Eskimo, or Aleut householder Nonfamily households		Land area	
	Total	Householder living alone	Square kilometers	Square miles
San Juan Pueblo, NM	55	51	69.1	26.7
San Manuel Reservation, CA	7	4	2.6	1.0
San Pasqual Reservation, CA	14	13	5.8	2.2
Santa Ana Pueblo, NM	15	14	262.2	101.2
Santa Clara Pueblo, NM	90	79	198.8	76.8
Santa Rosa Rancheria, CA	14	11	.7	.3
Santa Rosa Reservation, CA	2	1	44.2	17.1
Santa Ynez Reservation, CA	14	12	.4	.2
Santa Ysabel Reservation, CA	17	14	37.4	14.4
Santee Reservation, NE	36	33	447.9	172.9
Santo Domingo Pueblo, NM	32	31	277.8	107.2
San Xavier Reservation, AZ	59	53	288.6	111.4
Saulk-Suiattle Reservation, WA	-	-	.2	.1
Sault Ste. Marie Reservation and Trust Lands, MI	25	21	3.3	1.3
Sault Ste. Marie Reservation, MI	15	14	2.4	.9
Sault Ste. Marie Trust Lands, MI	10	7	1.0	.4
Schaghticoke Reservation, CT (state)	3	1	1.1	.4
Seminole Trust Lands, FL	5	4	.2	.1
Shakopee Community, MN	15	11	1.2	.5
Sheep Ranch Rancheria, CA	-	-	-	-
Sherwood Valley Rancheria, CA	-	-	1.2	.5

[Continued]

859

★ 552 ★

Housing and Household Characteristics of American Indian and Alaska Native Areas: 1990, Rohnerville-Soboba - II

[Continued]

American Indian/ Alaska Native Area State	Households with American Indian, Eskimo, or Aleut householder Nonfamily households		Land area	
	Total	Householder living alone	Square kilometers	Square miles
Shingle Springs Rancheria, CA	2	2	.7	.3
Shinnecock Reservation, NY (state)	36	36	3.4	1.3
Shoalwater Reservation, WA	2	2	3.2	1.2
Siletz Reservation, OR	-	-	14.9	5.8
Skokomish Reservation, WA	24	14	21.1	8.2
Skull Valley Reservation, UT	2	2	73.0	28.2
Smith River Rancheria, CA	2	2	.6	.2
Soboba Reservation, CA	23	20	23.5	9.1

Source: Summary Population and Housing Characteristics, United States Summary, United States Bureau of the Census, CP H-1, pp. 417-432. *Notes:* A dash (-) indicates that no data were given in the original source. 1. Federal American Indian reservations are areas with boundaries established by treaty, statute, and/or executive or court order, and recognized by the federal government as territory in which American Indian tribes have jurisdiction. State reservations are lands held in trust by state governments for the use and benefit of a given tribe. The reservations and their boundaries were identified for the 1990 census by the Bureau of Indian Affairs (BIA), Department of Interior (for federal reservations), and state governments (for state reservations). The names of American Indian reservations recognized by state governments, but not by the federal government, are followed by (state). Areas composed of reservation lands that are administered jointly and/or are claimed by two reservations, as identified by the BIA, are called "joint areas," and are treated as separate American Indian reservations for census purposes. Federal reservations may cross state boundaries, and federal and state reservations may cross county, county subdivision, and place boundaries. For reservations that cross state boundaries, only the portion of the reservations in a given state are shown in the data products for that state; the entire reservations are shown in data products for the United States. 2. Trust lands are property associated with a particular American Indian reservation or tribe, held in trust by the federal government. Trust lands may be held in trust either for a tribe (tribal trust lands) or for an individual member of a tribe (individual trust land). Trust lands recognized for the 1990 census comprised all tribal trust lands and inhabited individual trust lands located outside of a reservation boundary. As with other American Indian areas, trust lands may be located in more than one state. Only the trust lands in a given state are shown in the data products for that state; all trust lands associated with a reservation or tribe are shown in data products for the United States. The Census Bureau first reported data for tribal trust lands for the 1980 census.

★ 553 ★

Housing and Household Characteristics of American Indian and Alaska Native Areas, 1990, Sokaagon-Vermillion - I

American Indian/ Alaska Native Area State	All housing units		Occupied housing units with American Indian, Eskimo, or Aleut householder				Family households		
			Owner occupied		Renter occupied				
					Total	Mean contract rent (dollars), specified renter paying cash rent			Female house- holder, no husband present
			Total	Mean value (dollars) specified Owner			Total	Married- couple family	
	Total	Occupied							
American Indian Reservation and Trust Lands[1,2]									
Sokaagon Chippewa Community and Trust Lands, WI	123	108	15	33,800	78	89	68	27	29
Sokaagon Chippewa Community, WI	88	74	13	34,600	49	92	53	25	20
Sokaagon Chippewa Trust Lands, WI	35	34	2	27,500	29	73	15	2	9
Southern Ute Reservation, CO	3,320	2,684	182	64,900	128	155	254	132	91
Spokane Reservation, WA	565	464	240	50,100	137	88	303	163	90
Squaxin Island Reservation and Trust Lands, WA	54	46	36	57,600	1	90	33	21	11
Squaxin Island Reservation, WA	1	-	-	-	-	-	-	-	-
Squaxin Island Trust Lands	53	46	36	57,600	1	90	33	21	11
Standing Rock Reservation	2,732	2,325	320	21,100	813	125	947	439	371
Norh Dakota	1,175	1,022	188	23,600	476	134	555	241	226
South Dakota	1,557	1,303	132	18,000	337	112	392	198	145
Stewarts Point Rancheria, CA	19	19	4	32,500	14	50	13	9	4
Stillaguamish Reservation, WA	32	30	18	69,300	5	74	21	11	8
Stockbridge Reservation, WI	228	197	112	33,700	44	150	119	69	35
Sulphur Bank (El-Em) Rancheria, CA	23	23	9	81,700	14	213	21	9	6
Summit Lake Reservation, NV	12	4	4	9,000	-	-	2	2	-
Susanville Reservation, CA	161	154	45	67,000	7	81	41	20	17
Swinomish Reservation, WA	1,074	924	70	62,500	85	109	130	64	47
Sycuan Reservation, CA	1	1	-	-	-	-	-	-	-
Toble Bluff Rancheria, CA	18	18	13	28,800	3	50	12	1	7
Table Mountain Rancheria, CA	16	16	13	47,500	2	188	14	8	6
Tama Reservation , GA (state)	6	6	2	-	3	82	4	1	-
Taos Pueblo and Trust Lands, NM	2,678	1,944	356	64,300	66	197	316	186	88
Taos Pueblo, NM	2,650	1,919	356	64,300	66	197	316	186	88
Taos Trust Lands, NM	28	25	-	-	-	-	-	-	-
Te-Maak Reservation and Trust Lands, NV	353	316	203	57,200	87	115	233	95	106
Te-Maak Reservation, NV	338	303	192	57,400	85	116	223	89	102
Te-Maak Trust Lands, NV	15	13	11	46,300	2	50	10	6	4
Tesuque Pueblo and Trust Lands, NM	294	247	57	105,900	3	229	54	35	14
Tonawanda Reservation, NY	162	162	128	39,300	27	181	113	59	44
Torres-Martinez Reservation, CA	448	375	30	64,000	11	100	34	19	11
Trinidad Rancheria, CA	26	24	16	127,800	2	-	13	9	3
Tulalip Reservation, WA	4,026	2,524	197	77,700	114	215	255	163	66

[Continued]

861

★ 553 ★

Housing and Household Characteristics of American Indian and Alaska Native Areas: 1990, Sokaagon-Vermillion - I
[Continued]

American Indian/ Alaska Native Area State	All housing units		Occupied housing units with American Indian, Eskimo, or Aleut householder				Family households		
			Owner occupied		Renter occupied				
						Mean contract rent (dollars), specified renter paying cash rent		Married-couple family	Female house-holder, no husband present
	Total	Occupied	Total	Mean value (dollars) specified Owner	Total		Total		
Tule River Reservation, CA	212	205	155	35,700	40	102	163	51	86
Tunica-Biloxi Reservation, LA	12	12	8	30,000	1	-	7	5	1
Tuolumne Rancheria, CA	54	51	33	57,400	12	72	28	19	5
Turtle Mountain Reservation and Trust Lands, ND-SD	2,322	2,086	1,162	45,200	820	105	1,616	816	629
Turtle Mountain Reservation, ND	1,711	1,528	840	46,400	612	111	1,145	576	455
Turtle Mountain Trust Lands, ND	611	558	322	42,500	208	85	471	240	174
Tuscarara Reservation, NY	339	265	106	58,900	21	240	101	94	3
Twenty-Nine Palms Reservation, CA	-	-	-	-	-	-	-	-	-
Unitah and Quray Reservation, UT	7,545	4,938	416	30,900	235	147	566	299	205
Umatilla Reservation, OR	955	828	148	52,100	151	128	239	110	93
Upper Lake Rancheria, CA	23	21	-	-	7	313	5	1	4
Upper Sioux Community, MN	23	21	20	18,900	-	-	12	5	7
Upper Skagit Reservation, WA	53	50	44	62,800	3	71	39	16	17
Ute Mountain Reservation and Trust Lands, CO-NM-UT	422	349	260	27,500	74	106	296	151	100
Ute Mountain Reservation	417	347	260	27,500	74	106	296	151	100
Colorado	353	288	213	28,200	62	113	244	121	84
Utah	64	59	47	23,400	12	61	52	30	16
Ute Mountain Trust Lands, UT	5	2	-	-	-	-	-	-	-
Vermillion Lake Reservation,MN	127	30	11	49,300	16	50	16	9	6

Source: Summary Population and Housing Characteristics, United States Summary, United States Bureau of the Census, CP H-1, pp. 417-432. *Notes:* A dash (-) indicates that no data were given in the original source. 1. Federal American Indian reservations are areas with boundaries established by treaty, statute, and/or executive or court order, and recognized by the federal government as territory in which American Indian tribes have jurisdiction. State reservations are lands held in trust by state governments for the use and benefit of a given tribe. The reservations and their boundaries were identified for the 1990 census by the Bureau of Indian Affairs (BIA), Department of Interior (for federal reservations), and state governments (for state reservations). The names of American Indian reservations recognized by state governments, but not by the federal government, are followed by (state). Areas composed of reservation lands that are administered jointly and/or are claimed by two reservations, as identified by the BIA, are called "joint areas," and are treated as separate American Indian reservations for census purposes. Federal reservations may cross state boundaries, and federal and state reservations may cross county, county subdivision, and place boundaries. For reservations that cross state boundaries, only the portion of the reservations in a given state are shown in the data products for that state; the entire reservations are shown in data products for the United States. 2. Trust lands are property associated with a particular American Indian reservation or tribe, held in trust by the federal government. Trust lands may be held in trust either for a tribe (tribal trust lands) or for an individual member of a tribe (individual trust land). Trust lands recognized for the 1990 census comprised all tribal trust lands and inhabited individual trust lands located outside of a reservation boundary. As with other American Indian areas, trust lands may be located in more than one state. Only the trust lands in a given state are shown in the data products for that state; all trust lands associated with a reservation or tribe are shown in data products for the United States. The Census Bureau first reported data for tribal trust lands for the 1980 census.

★ 554 ★

Housing and Household Characteristics of American Indian and Alaska Native Areas: 1990, Sokaagon-Vermillion - II

American Indian/ Alaska Native Area State	Households with American Indian, Eskimo, or Aleut householder Nonfamily households		Land area	
	Total	Householder living alone	Square kilometers	Square miles
American Indian Reservation and Trust Lands[1,2]				
Sokaagon Chippewa Community and Trust Lands, WI	25	19	7.4	2.9
Sokaagon Chippewa Community, WI	9	5	6.3	2.4
Sokaagon Chippewa Trust Lands, WI	16	14	1.1	.4
Southern Ute Reservation, CO	56	45	2,741.7	1,058.6
Spokane Reservation, WA	74	61	615.2	237.5
Squaxin Island Reservation and Trust Lands, WA	4	4	6.5	2.5
Squaxin Island Reservation, WA	-	-	5.7	2.2
Squaxin Island Trust Lands	4	4	.8	.3
Standing Rock Reservation	186	161	9,239.2	3,567.3
Norh Dakota	109	94	2,834.0	1,094.2
South Dakota	77	67	6,405.2	2,473.1
Stewarts Point Rancheria, CA	5	5	.2	.1
Stillaguamish Reservation, WA	2	2	.1	-
Stockbridge Reservation, WI	37	32	90.1	34.8
Sulphur Bank (El-Em) Rancheria, CA	2	2	.2	.1
Summit Lake Reservation, NV	2	2	45.1	17.4
Susanville Reservation, CA	11	8	.6	.2
Swinomish Reservation, WA	25	19	29.6	11.4
Sycuan Reservation, CA	-	-	2.6	1.0
Table Bluff Rancheria, CA	4	3	.1	-
Table Mountain Rancheria, CA	1	1	.6	.2
Tama Reservation , GA (state)	1	1	.4	.1

[Continued]

★ 554 ★

Housing and Household Characteristics of American Indian and Alaska Native Areas: 1990, Sokaagon-Vermillion - II

[Continued]

American Indian/ Alaska Native Area State	Households with American Indian, Eskimo, or Aleut householder Nonfamily households		Land area	
	Total	Householder living alone	Square kilometers	Square miles
Taos Pueblo and Trust Lands, NM	106	98	404.3	156.1
Taos Pueblo, NM	106	98	401.1	154.9
Taos Trust Lands, NM	-	-	3.2	1.2
Te-Maak Reservation and Trust Lands, NV	57	49	72.1	27.8
Te-Maak Reservation, NV	54	46	43.1	16.6
Te-Maak Trust Lands, NV	32	3	29.0	11.2
Tesuque Pueblo and Trust Lands, NM	6	4	69.9	27.0
Tesuque Pueblo, NM	6	4	68.7	26.5
Tesuque Trust Lands, NM	-	-	1.2	.5
Tonawanda Reservation, NY	42	35	30.6	11.8
Torres-Martinez Reservation, CA	7	5	89.5	34.5
Trinidad Rancheria, CA	5	2	.3	.1
Tulalip Reservation, WA	56	44	91.1	35.2
Tule River Reservation, CA	32	26	218.7	84.4
Tunica-Biloxi Reservation, LA	2	2	.5	.2
Tuolumne Rancheria, CA	17	13	1.3	.5
Turtle Mountain Reservation and Trust Lands, ND-SD	366	323	359.4	138.8
Turtle Mountain Reservation, ND	307	273	181.1	69.9
Turtle Mountain Trust Lands	59	50	178.3	68.8
North Dakota	59	50	176.1	68.0
South Dakota	-	-	2.1	.8
Tuscarara Reservation, NY	26	25	24.1	9.3
Twenty-Nine Palms Reservation, CA	-	-	.6	.2
Unitah and Quray Reservation, UT	85	71	17,529.6	6,768.2
Umatilla Reservation, OR	60	48	702.0	271.1

[Continued]

★ 554 ★

Housing and Household Characteristics of American Indian and Alaska Native Areas, 1990, Sokaagon-Vermillion - II

[Continued]

American Indian/ Alaska Native Area State	Households with American Indian, Eskimo, or Aleut householder Nonfamily households		Land area	
	Total	Householder living alone	Square kilometers	Square miles
Upper Lake Rancheria, CA	2	2	1.8	.7
Upper Sioux Community, MN	8	8	3.1	1.2
Upper Skagit Reservation, WA	8	6	.4	.2
Ute Mountain Reservation and Trust Lands, CO-NM-UT	38	32	2,332.5	900.6
Ute Mountain Reservation	38	32	2,302.3	888.9
Colorado	31	26	1,854.4	716.0
New Mexico	-	-	418.0	161.4
Utah	7	6	29.9	11.5
Ute Mountain Trust Lands, UT	-	-	30.2	11.6
Vermillion Lake Reservation,MN	11	10	4.2	1.6

Source: Summary Population and Housing Characteristics, United States Summary, United States Bureau of the Census, CP H-1, pp. 417-432. *Notes:* A dash (-) indicates that no data were given in the original source. 1. Federal American Indian reservations are areas with boundaries established by treaty, statute, and/or executive or court order, and recognized by the federal government as territory in which American Indian tribes have jurisdiction. State reservations are lands held in trust by state governments for the use and benefit of a given tribe. The reservations and their boundaries were identified for the 1990 census by the Bureau of Indian Affairs (BIA), Department of Interior (for federal reservations), and state governments (for state reservations). The names of American Indian reservations recognized by state governments, but not by the federal government, are followed by (state). Areas composed of reservation lands that are administered jointly and/or are claimed by two reservations, as identified by the BIA, are called "joint areas," and are treated as separate American Indian reservations for census purposes. Federal reservations may cross state boundaries, and federal and state reservations may cross county, county subdivision, and place boundaries. For reservations that cross state boundaries, only the portion of the reservations in a given state are shown in the data products for that state; the entire reservations are shown in data products for the United States. 2. Trust lands are property associated with a particular American Indian reservation or tribe, held in trust by the federal government. Trust lands may be held in trust either for a tribe (tribal trust lands) or for an individual member of a tribe (individual trust land). Trust lands recognized for the 1990 census comprised all tribal trust lands and inhabited individual trust lands located outside of a reservation boundary. As with other American Indian areas, trust lands may be located in more than one state. Only the trust lands in a given state are shown in the data products for that state; all trust lands associated with a reservation or tribe are shown in data products for the United States. The Census Bureau first reported data for tribal trust lands for the 1980 census.

★ 555 ★

Housing and Household Characteristics of American Indian and Alaska Native Areas: 1990, Viejas-Crow/Northern Cheyenne - I

American Indian/ Alaska Native Area State	All housing units		Occupied housing units with American Indian, Eskimo, or Aleut householder				Family households		
			Owner occupied		Renter occupied				
	Total	Occupied	Total	Mean value (dollars) specified Owner	Total	Mean contract rent (dollars), specified renter paying cash rent	Total	Married-couple family	Female house-holder, no husband present
American Indian Reservation and Trust Lands[1,2]									
Viejas Rancheria, CA	156	136	49	62,800	14	264	50	21	20
Walker River Reservation, NV	283	238	160	45,800	44	112	154	88	44
Warm Springs Reservation and Trust Lands, OR	815	751	411	57,400	264	170	587	292	203
Warm Springs Reservation, OR	815	751	411	57,400	264	170	587	292	203
Warm Springs Trust Lands, OR	-	-	-	-	-	-	-	-	-
Washoe Reservation, NV	73	60	8	45,800	15	130	17	5	10
White Earth Reservation, MN	4,610	3,002	498	40,800	318	97	633	318	230
Wind River Reservation, WY	8,756	7,492	853	45,700	621	170	1,233	726	394
Winnebago Reservation, NE	849	755	125	32,500	186	130	252	100	121
Winnemucca Colony, NV	22	22	18	28,500	1	-	15	9	4
Wisconsin Winnebago Reservation and Trust Lands, WI	265	204	52	16,100	103	110	119	43	53
Wisconsin Winnebago Reservation, WI	170	131	23	16,500	95	107	97	33	47
Wisconsin Winnebago Trust Lands, WI	95	73	29	14,500	8	238	22	10	6
Woodfords Community, CA	6	6	-	-	-	-	-	-	-
XL Ranch Reservation, CA	14	14	2	52,500	9	169	5	4	-
Yakima Reservation and Trust Lands, WA	8,442	7,915	836	48,500	735	178	1,344	626	550
Yakima Reservation, WA	8,415	7,889	827	48,700	723	179	1,324	618	540
Yakima Trust Lands, WA	27	26	9	37,500	12	88	20	8	10
Yakatan Reservation, SD	2,479	2,143	169	35,700	321	100	385	174	156
Yavapai Reservation, AZ	53	49	36	52,900	9	313	40	26	14
Yerington Reservation and Trust Lands, NV	131	123	78	51,300	39	88	93	49	34
Yerington Reservation, NV	78	71	52	53,800	16	64	59	37	19
Yerlington Trust Lands, NV	53	52	26	47,100	23	103	34	12	15
Yomba Reservation, NV	36	26	3	-	20	101	19	14	4
Ysleta Del Sur Pueblo, TX	74	74	55	44,200	9	80	59	41	15
Yurok Reservation, CA	667	499	93	47,600	51	281	102	58	32
Zia Pueblo and Trust Lands, NM	167	143	133	55,800	10	250	134	81	43
Zuni Pueblo	1,901	1,648	1,159	55,500	306	103	1,364	831	458
Arizona	4	2	-	-	-	-	-	-	-

[Continued]

★ 555 ★

Housing and Household Characteristics of American Indian and Alaska Native Areas. 1990, Viejas-Crow/Northern Cheyenne - I

[Continued]

American Indian/ Alaska Native Area State	All housing units		Occupied housing units with American Indian, Eskimo, or Aleut householder				Family households		
			Owner occupied		Renter occupied				
					Total	Mean contract rent (dollars), specified renter paying cash rent	Total	Married-couple family	Female house-holder, no husband present
	Total	Occupied	Total	Mean value (dollars) specified Owner					
New Mexico	1,897	1,646	1,159	55,500	306	103	1,364	831	458
Crow/Northern Cheyenne Area, MT	4	2	-	-	-	-	-	-	-

Source: Summary Population and Housing Characteristics, United States Summary, United States Bureau of the Census, CP H-1, pp. 417-432. *Notes:* A dash (-) indicates that no data were given in the original source. 1. Federal American Indian reservations are areas with boundaries established by treaty, statute, and/or executive or court order, and recognized by the federal government as territory in which American Indian tribes have jurisdiction. State reservations are lands held in trust by state governments for the use and benefit of a given tribe. The reservations and their boundaries were identified for the 1990 census by the Bureau of Indian Affairs (BIA), Department of Interior (for federal reservations), and state governments (for state reservations). The names of American Indian reservations recognized by state governments, but not by the federal government, are followed by (state). Areas composed of reservation lands that are administered jointly and/or are claimed by two reservations, as identified by the BIA, are called "joint areas," and are treated as separate American Indian reservations for census purposes. Federal reservations may cross state boundaries, and federal and state reservations may cross county, county subdivision, and place boundaries. For reservations that cross state boundaries, only the portion of the reservations in a given state are shown in the data products for that state; the entire reservations are shown in data products for the United States. 2. Trust lands are property associated with a particular American Indian reservation or tribe, held in trust by the federal government. Trust lands may be held in trust either for a tribe (tribal trust lands) or for an individual member of a tribe (individual trust land). Trust lands recognized for the 1990 census comprised all tribal trust lands and inhabited individual trust lands located outside of a reservation boundary. As with other American Indian areas, trust lands may be located in more than one state. Only the trust lands in a given state are shown in the data products for that state; all trust lands associated with a reservation or tribe are shown in data products for the United States. The Census Bureau first reported data for tribal trust lands for the 1980 census.

★ 556 ★

Housing and Household Characteristics of American Indian and Alaska Native Areas: 1990, Viejas-Crow/Northern Cheyenne - II

American Indian/ Alaska Native Area State	Households with American Indian, Eskimo, or Aleut householder Nonfamily households		Land area	
	Total	Householder living alone	Square kilometers	Square miles
American Indian Reservation and Trust Lands[1,2]				
Viejas Rancheria, CA	13	7	6.6	2.5
Walker River Reservation, NV	50	40	1,384.2	534.4
Warm Springs Reservation and Trust Lands, OR	88	72	2,640.0	1,019.3
Warm Springs Reservation, OR	88	72	2,617.3	1,010.5
Warm Springs Trust Lands, OR	-	-	22.8	8.8
Washoe Reservation, NV	6	4	11.7	4.5

[Continued]

★ 556 ★

Housing and Household Characteristics of American Indian and Alaska Native Areas: 1990, Viejas-Crow/Northern Cheyenne - II

[Continued]

American Indian/ Alaska Native Area State	Households with American Indian, Eskimo, or Aleut householder Nonfamily households		Land area	
	Total	Householder living alone	Square kilometers	Square miles
White Earth Reservation, MN	183	160	2,818.9	1,088.4
Wind River Reservation, WY	241	196	8,990.8	3,471.4
Winnebago Reservation, NE	59	56	449.2	173.4
Winnemucca Colony, NV	4	3	1.4	.6
Wisconsin Winnebago Reservation and Trust Lands, WI	36	34	12.9	5.0
Wisconsin Winnebago Reservation, WI	21	20	3.3	1.3
Wisconsin Winnebago Trust Lands, WI	15	14	9.6	3.7
Woodfords Community, CA	-	-	1.4	.6
XL Ranch Reservation, CA	6	5	37.3	14.4
Yakima Reservation and Trust Lands, WA	227	170	5,536.3	2,137.6
Yakima Reservation, WA	226	170	5,450.1	2,104.3
Yakima Trust Lands, WA	1	-	86.3	33.3
Yakatan Reservation, SD	105	93	1,724.3	665.8
Yavapai Reservation, AZ	5	2	5.7	2.2
Yerington Reservation and Trust Lands, NV	24	23	6.6	2.6
Yerington Reservation, NV	9	9	6.6	2.5
Yerlington Trust Lands, NV	15	14	-	-
Yomba Reservation, NV	4	3	18.9	7.3
Ysleta Del Sur Pueblo, TX	5	5	.4	.2
Yurok Reservation, CA	42	33	219.5	84.7
Zia Pueblo and Trust Lands, NM	9	9	491.8	189.9
Zia Pueblo, NM	9	9	483.2	186.6
Zia Trust Lands, NM	-	-	8.6	3.3
Zuni Pueblo	101	95	1,694.5	654.3

[Continued]

★ 556 ★

Housing and Household Characteristics of American Indian and Alaska Native Areas: 1990, Viejas-Crow/Northern Cheyenne - II

[Continued]

American Indian/ Alaska Native Area State	Households with American Indian, Eskimo, or Aleut householder Nonfamily households		Land area	
	Total	Householder living alone	Square kilometers	Square miles
Arizona	-	-	45.8	17.7
New Mexico	101	95	1,648.7	636.6
San Felipe/Santa Ana joint area, NM	-	-	2.8	1.1
San Felipe/Santa Domingi joint area, NM	-	-	3.2	1.2
Crow/Northern Cheyenne Area, MT	-	-	48.2	18.6

Source: Summary Population and Housing Characteristics, United States Summary, United States Bureau of the Census, CP H-1, pp. 417-432. *Notes:* A dash (-) indicates that no data were given in the original source. 1. Federal American Indian reservations are areas with boundaries established by treaty, statute, and/or executive or court order, and recognized by the federal government as territory in which American Indian tribes have jurisdiction. State reservations are lands held in trust by state governments for the use and benefit of a given tribe. The reservations and their boundaries were identified for the 1990 census by the Bureau of Indian Affairs (BIA), Department of Interior (for Federal reservations), and state governments (for state reservations). The names of American Indian reservations recognized by state governments, but not by the federal government, are followed by (state). Areas composed of reservation lands that are administered jointly and/or are claimed by two reservations, as identified by the BIA, are called "joint areas," and are treated as separate American Indian reservations for census purposes. Federal reservations may cross state boundaries, and federal and state reservations may cross county, county subdivision, and place boundaries. For reservations that cross state boundaries, only the portion of the reservations in a given state are shown in the data products for that state; the entire reservations are shown in data products for the United States. 2. Trust lands are property associated with a particular American Indian reservation or tribe, held in trust by the federal government. Trust lands may be held in trust either for a tribe (tribal trust lands) or for an individual member of a tribe (individual trust land). Trust lands recognized for the 1990 census comprised all tribal trust lands and inhabited individual trust lands located outside of a reservation boundary. As with other American Indian areas, trust lands may be located in more than one state. Only the trust lands in a given state are shown in the data products for that state; all trust lands associated with a reservation or tribe are shown in data products for the United States. The Census Bureau first reported data for tribal trust lands for the 1980 census.

★ 557 ★

Housing and Household Characteristics of American Indian and Alaska Native Tribal Designated Statistical Areas: 1990 - I

American Indian/ Alaska Native Area State	All housing units		Occupied housing units with American Indian, Eskimo, or Aleut householder				Family households		
			Owner occupied		Renter occupied				
						Mean contract rent (dollars), specified renter paying cash rent			Female house-holder, no husband present
	Total	Occupied	Total	Mean value (dollars) specified Owner	Total		Total	Married-couple family	
Tribal Designated Statistical Area									
All areas	661,461	596,523	11,398	49,800	4,901	224	13,133	8,888	3,256
Apache Choctaw TDSA, LA (state)	12,789	8,361	166	34,800	33	154	160	125	21
Chickahominy TDSA, VA (state)	1,003	953	157	52,100	8	233	134	106	23

[Continued]

★ 557 ★

Housing and Household Characteristics of American Indian and Alaska Native Tribal Designated Statistical Areas: 1990 - I
[Continued]

American Indian/ Alaska Native Area State	All housing units		Occupied housing units with American Indian, Eskimo, or Aleut householder				Family households		
			Owner occupied		Renter occupied				
					Total	Mean contract rent (dollars), specified renter paying cash rent	Total	Married-couple family	Female house-holder, no husband present
	Total	Occupied	Total	Mean value (dollars) specified Owner					
Clifton Choctaw TDSA, LA (state)	154	138	48	28,800	8	136	44	36	7
Coharie TDSA, NC (state)	48,198	44,170	292	47,000	148	200	339	255	63
Coquille Indian TDSA, OR	170,539	160,912	855	59,800	953	312	1,285	866	320
Delaware-Muncie TDSA, KA (state)	102	92	4	-	-	-	2	2	-
Eastern Chickahominy TDSA, VA (state)	42	38	12	51,700	-	-	9	8	1
Florida Tribe of Eastern Creek TDSA, FL (state)	121	80	-	-	-	-	-	-	-
Haliwa-Saponi TDSA, NC (state)	2,273	2,079	488	40,000	220	110	577	397	128
Jena Bend of Choctaw TDSA, LA (state)	23,597	21,004	54	45,000	30	225	71	56	12
Klamath TDSA, OR	17,647	16,198	230	45,900	295	261	399	216	142
Lumbee TDSA, NC (state)	17,219	16,138	6,684	46,500	2,190	159	7,277	4,724	2,017
Meherrin TDSA, NC (state)	22,414	20,120	80	48,300	24	207	71	55	15
Mohegan TDSA, CT (state)	10,666	9,796	32	153,900	43	433	57	37	17
Panca TDSA, NE (state)	8	3	-	-	-	-	-	-	-
Ramapough TDSA, NJ (state)	234	227	41	107,900	19	526	49	27	14
United Houma Nation TDSA, LA (state)	321,862	290,302	1,852	46,500	854	251	2,263	1,686	396
Waccamaw Siouan TDSA, NC (state)	989	909	350	50,200	38	166	338	253	65
Wampanoag-Gay Head TDSA, MA	11,604	5,003	53	234,600	38	508	58	39	15

Source: Summary Population and Housing Characteristics, United States Summary, United States Bureau of the Census, CP H-1, pp. 417-432. *Notes:* A dash (-) indicates that no data were given in the original source. Alaska Native villages: (ANV's) constitute tribes, bands,clans, groups, villages, communities, or associations in Alaska that are recognized pursuant to the Alaska Native Claims Settlement Act of 1972, Public Law 92- 203. Because ANV's do not have legally designated boundaries, the Census Bureau has established Alaska Native village statistical areas (ANVSA's) for statistical purposes. For the 1990 census, the Census Bureau cooperated with officials of the nonprofit corporation within each participating Alaska Native Regional Corporation (ANRC), as well as other knowledgeable officials, to delineate boundaries that encompass the settles area associated with each ANV.

★ 558 ★

Housing and Household Characteristics of American Indian and Alaska Native Tribal Designated Statistical Areas: 1990 - II

| | Households with American Indian, Eskimo, or Aleut householder Nonfamily households | | Land area | |
	Total	Householder living alone	square kilometers	Square miles
Tribal Designated Statistical Area				
All areas	3,166	2,659	33,683.7	13,005.3
Apache Choctaw TDSA, LA (state)	39	38	2,241.2	865.3
Chickahominy TDSA, VA (state)	31	29	128.6	49.7
Clifton Choctaw TDSA, LA (state)	12	12	103.7	638.6
Coharie TDSA, NC (state)	101	94	1,654.1	638.6
Coquille Indian TDSA, OR	523	370	9,857.6	3,806.0
Delaware-Muncie TDSA, KA (state)	2	1	33.9	13.1
Eastern Chickahominy TDSA, VA (state)	3	3	5.2	2.0
Florida Tribe of Eastern Creek TDSA, FL (state)	-	-	5.8	2.2
Haliwa-Saponi TDSA, NC (state)	131	122	420.3	162.3
Jena Bend of Choctaw TDSA, LA (state)	13	11	1,824.2	704.3
Klamath TDSA, OR	126	98	281.9	108.8
Lumbee TDSA, NC (state)	1,597	1,385	1,010.7	390.2
Meherrin TDSA, NC (state)	33	30	3,664.9	1,415.0
Mohegan TDSA, CT (state)	18	14	38.3	14.8
Panca TDSA, NE (state)	-	-	15.9	6.1
Ramapough TDSA, NJ (state)	11	8	19.6	7.6
United Houma Nation TDSA, LA (state)	443	370	11,945.5	4,612.2

[Continued]

★ 558 ★

Housing and Household Characteristics of American Indian and Alaska Native Tribal Designated Statistical Areas: 1990 - II

[Continued]

	Households with American Indian, Eskimo, or Aleut householder Nonfamily households		Land area	
	Total	Householder living alone	square kilometers	Square miles
Waccamaw Siouan TDSA, NC (state)	50	46	163.5	63.1
Wampanoag-Gay Head TDSA, MA	33	28	268.9	103.8

Source: Summary Population and Housing Characteristics, United States Summary, United States Bureau of the Census, CP H-1, pp. 417-432.
Notes: A dash (-) indicates that no data were given in the original source. Alaska Native villages: (ANV's) constitute tribes, bands,clans, groups, villages, communities, or associations in Alaska that are recognized pursuant to the Alaska Native Claims Settlement Act of 1972, Public Law 92-203. Because ANV's do not have legally designated boundaries, the Census Bureau has established Alaska Native village statistical areas (ANVSA's) for statistical purposes. For the 1990 census, the Census Bureau cooperated with officials of the nonprofit corporation within each participating Alaska Native Regional Corporation (ANRC), as well as other knowledgeable officials, to delineate boundaries that encompass the settles area associated with each ANV.

★ 559 ★

Housing and Household Characteristics of American Indian and Alaska Native Tribal Jurisdiction Statistical Areas: 1990 - I

American Indian/ Alaska Native Area State	All housing units		Occupied housing units with American Indian, Eskimo, or Aleut householder				Family households		
			Owner occupied		Renter occupied				
					Total	Mean contract rent (dollars), specified renter paying cash rent	Total	Married-couple family	Female house-holder, no husband present
	Total	Occupied	Total	Mean value (dollars) specified Owner					
Tribal Jurisdiction Statistical Area									
All areas	919,372	790,869	40,936	42,400	20,436	206	47,349	34,763	9,970
Absentee Shawnee-Citizens Band of Patawatomi TJSA, OK	34,344	30,902	1,412	50,100	374	187	1,465	1,149	252
Caddo-Witchita-Delaware TJSA, OK	4,134	3,152	104	30,200	35	145	118	78	24
Cherokee TJSA, OK	179,618	149,922	14,159	41,300	6,149	201	15,828	11,980	2,989
Cheyenne-Arapaho TJSA, OK	65,927	55,376	912	42,600	804	196	1,391	917	380
Chickasaw TJSA, OK	117,781	99,380	4,530	39,900	2,128	185	5,105	3,832	988
Choctaw TJSA, OK	92,387	79,416	6,391	34,300	2,689	161	6,940	5,214	1,392
Creek TJSA, OK	282,719	251,317	8,828	51,300	5,561	254	10,615	7,767	2,280
Iowa TJSA, OK	1,799	1,493	52	31,900	12	172	59	43	9
Kaw TJSA, OK	5,678	5,090	161	52,500	47	226	163	129	27

[Continued]

★ 559 ★

Housing and Household Characteristics of American Indian and Alaska Native Tribal Jurisdiction Statistical Areas: 1990 - I

[Continued]

American Indian/ Alaska Native Area State	All housing units		Occupied housing units with American Indian, Eskimo, or Aleut householder				Family households		
			Owner occupied		Renter occupied				
					Total	Mean contract rent (dollars), specified renter paying cash rent		Married-couple family	Female householder, no husband present
			Total	Mean value (dollars) specified Owner			Total		
	Total	Occupied							
Kiowa-Comanche-Apache-Fort Sill Apache TJSA, OK	85,552	72,825	2,123	40,200	1,388	186	2,869	1,769	911
Otoe-Missouria TJSA, OK	1,186	1,005	65	25,700	65	81	101	52	39
Pawnee TJSA, OK	7,340	5,956	354	37,500	158	175	408	298	83
Sac and Fox TJSA, OK	23,170	20,208	928	39,500	454	171	1,102	765	278
Seminole TJSA, OK	10,382	8,784	657	27,200	409	163	853	537	244
Tankawa TJSA, OK	5,956	4,836	149	33,500	107	151	198	139	46
Creek-Seminole Joint Area TJSA, OK	1,022	881	104	25,500	55	110	127	87	28
Iowa-Sac and Fox Joint Area TJSA, OK	377	326	7	34,200	1	413	7	7	-

Source: Summary Population and Housing Characteristics, United States Summary, United States Bureau of the Census, CP H-1, pp. 417-432. *Notes:* A dash (-) indicates that no data were given in the original source. Tribal designated statistical areas: (TDSA's) are areas, delineated outside Oklahoma by federally- and state-recognized tribes without a land base or associated trust lands, to provide statistical areas for which the Census Bureau tabulates data. TDSA's represent areas generally containing the American Indian population over which federally-recognized tribes have jurisdiction and areas in which state tribes provide benefits and services to their members. The names of TDSA's delineated by state-recognized tribes are followed by (state). The Census Bureau did not recognize TDSA's before the 1990 census.

★ 560 ★

Housing and Household Characteristics of American Indian and Alaska Native Tribal Jurisdiction Statistical Areas: 1990 - II

American Indian/ Alaska Native Area State	Households with American Indian, Eskimo, or Aleut householder Nonfamily households		Land area	
	Total	Householder living alone	Square kilometers	Square miles
Tribal Jurisdiction Statistical Area				
All areas	14,023	12,376	126,389.7	48,799.1
Absentee Shawnee-Citizens Band of Patawatomi TJSA, OK	321	275	2,887.8	1,115.0
Caddo-Witchita-Delaware TJSA, OK	21	20	1,675.0	646.7
Cherokee TJSA, OK	4,480	3,976	17,354.2	6,700.4

[Continued]

★ 560 ★

Housing and Household Characteristics of American Indian and Alaska Native Tribal Jurisdiction Statistical Areas: 1990 - II
[Continued]

American Indian/ Alaska Native Area State	Households with American Indian, Eskimo, or Aleut householder Nonfamily households		Land area	
	Total	Householder living alone	Square kilometers	Square miles
Cheyenne-Arapaho TJSA, OK	325	263	21,037.6	8,122.6
Chickasaw TJSA, OK	1,553	1,381	18,916.7	7,303.7
Choctaw TJSA, OK	2,140	1,952	27,485.8	10,612.3
Creek TJSA, OK	3,774	3,270	12,038.7	4,648.2
Iowa TJSA, OK	5	5	804.4	310.6
Kaw TJSA, OK	45	36	791.6	305.6
Kiowa-Comanche-Apache-Fort Sill Apache TJSA, OK	642	551	16,944.1	6,542.1
Otoe-Missouria TJSA, OK	29	27	721.1	278.4
Pawnee TJSA, OK	104	93	1,318.4	509.0
Sac and Fox TJSA, OK	280	258	1,993.6	769.7
Seminole TJSA, OK	213	192	1,469.5	567.4
Tankawa TJSA, OK	58	50	659.4	254.6
Creek-Seminole Joint Area TJSA, OK	32	26	168.7	65.1
Iowa-Sac and Fox Joint Area TJSA, OK	1	1	123.1	47.5

Source: Summary Population and Housing Characteristics, United States Summary, United States Bureau of the Census, CP H-1, pp. 417-432. *Notes:* A dash (-) indicates that no data were given in the original source. Tribal designated statistical areas: (TDSA's) are areas, delineated outside Oklahoma by federally- and state-recognized tribes without a land base or associated trust lands, to provide statistical areas for which the Census Bureau tabulates data. TDSA's represent areas generally containing the American Indian population over which federally-recognized tribes have jurisdiction and areas in which state tribes provide benefits and services to their members. The names of TDSA's delineated by state-recognized tribes are followed by (state). The Census Bureau did not recognize TDSA's before the 1990 census.

★ 561 ★

Housing and Household Characteristics of American Indian and Alaska Native Village Statistical Areas: 1990 Akihok-Evansville - I

American Indian/ Alaska Native Area State	All housing units		Occupied housing units with American Indian, Eskimo, or Aleut householder				Family households		
			Owner occupied		Renter occupied				
						Mean contract rent (dollars), specified renter paying cash rent			Female house-holder, no husband present
	Total	Occupied	Total	Mean value (dollars) specified Owner	Total		Total	Married-couple family	
Alaska Native Village Statistical Area									
All Areas	28,744	22,334	8,508	66,000	3,311	343	9,277	5,700	2,201
Akhiok	35	19	11	65,500	6	90	13	9	2
Akiachak	130	113	72	45,000	30	50	89	64	14
Akiak	80	67	45	82,700	18	269	50	34	12
Akutan	34	31	22	77,000	1	50	14	6	4
Alakanuk	140	121	100	47,800	12	875	96	59	26
Alatna	14	13	12	22,200	-	-	6	-	4
Aleknagik	84	57	43	116,100	3	313	35	24	6
Alexander	28	16	-	-	2	-	2	2	-
Allakaket	61	46	42	21,100	2	263	34	20	8
Ambler	79	71	46	41,000	8	138	47	26	11
Anaktuvuk Pass	81	75	37	93,900	17	308	39	22	9
Andreafsky	138	110	62	42,800	19	289	65	40	18
Angoon	166	156	40	66,300	72	170	98	64	22
Aniak	175	159	37	62,900	53	235	68	44	15
Anvik	47	32	24	21,000	3	50	16	7	7
Arctic Villagae	50	36	26	23,100	7	157	21	8	9
Atka	41	30	23	68,500	2	-	21	14	5
Atkasook	64	52	30	87,500	14	300	37	23	7
Atmautluak	67	53	28	33,500	21	142	45	40	4
Barrow	933	835	190	93,900	221	513	327	184	107
Beaver	52	43	30	20,600	10	88	18	5	3
Belkofski	4	-	-	-	-	-	-	-	-
Bethel	1,624	1,432	311	82,600	394	491	536	279	199
Bill Moore's	3	-	-	-	-	-	-	-	-
Birch Creek	21	15	14	228,400	-	-	9	2	4
Brevig Mission	64	53	38	76,400	12	282	38	13	11
Buckland	70	69	46	58,300	17	146	57	37	15
Cantwell	85	62	5	87,500	7	113	9	5	1
Canyon Village	5	-	-	-	-	-	-	-	-
Chalkyitsik	52	33	29	16,800	2	300	18	10	5
Chefornak	79	64	51	93,400	7	-	53	40	8
Chenega	34	29	15	95,300	2	-	14	10	3
Chevak	164	147	90	59,300	37	76	90	51	24
Chignik	104	46	25	93,300	3	463	21	14	3
Chignik Lagoon	83	17	9	76,000	-	-	7	7	-
Chignik Lake	57	34	25	62,100	4	363	27	17	6
Chilkat	66	36	24	44,300	7	115	25	13	9
Chilkoot	110	90	8	93,300	2	694	8	7	-
Chistochina	34	20	10	31,100	-	-	8	3	4
Chitina	37	22	5	28,800	4	-	7	3	2
Chuathbaluk	33	28	18	57,100	5	50	18	8	3

[Continued]

★ 561 ★

Housing and Household Characteristics of American Indian and Alaska Native Village Statistical Areas: 1990 Akihok-Evansville - I
[Continued]

American Indian/ Alaska Native Area State	All housing units		Occupied housing units with American Indian, Eskimo, or Aleut householder				Family households		
			Owner occupied		Renter occupied				
					Total	Mean contract rent (dollars), specified renter paying cash rent	Total	Married-couple family	Female house-holder, no husband present
	Total	Occupied	Total	Mean value (dollars) specified Owner					
Chulloonawick	10	-	-	-	-	-	-	-	-
Circle	31	23	8	31,700	11	166	14	2	7
Clark's Point	55	18	10	87,700	6	-	13	7	6
Copper Center	244	166	38	62,800	14	250	36	17	11
Council	32	3	1	27,500	-	-	1	1	-
Craig	504	444	59	89,500	31	373	62	37	20
Crooked Creek	49	33	19	66,300	8	148	20	5	10
Deering	54	44	26	55,000	12	122	28	11	13
Dillingham	851	691	196	106,300	136	436	243	160	67
Dot Lake	23	18	8	69,400	2	-	7	2	2
Eagle	36	20	15	15,300	-	-	7	1	2
Eek	80	72	40	12,100	26	60	48	31	11
Egegik	66	48	23	76,000	5	-	13	6	4
Eklutna	139	123	13	78,800	4	354	10	3	5
Ekuk	65	1	-	-	1	-	1	-	1
Ekwok	39	30	25	91,700	1	725	19	15	3
Elim	121	73	53	51,400	11	182	52	27	13
Emmonak	172	161	104	62,700	33	312	114	65	24
English Bay	51	42	34	53,500	4	113	29	20	5
Evansville	44	32	7	28,400	1	-	6	2	4

Source: Summary Population and Housing Characteristics, United States Summary, United States Bureau of the Census, CP H-1, pp. 417-432. *Notes:* A dash (-) indicates that no data were given in original source. Alaska Native villages: (ANV's) constitute tribes, bands, clans, groups, villages, communities, or associations in Alaska that are recognized pursuant to the Alaska Native Claims Settlement Act of 1972, Public Law 92- 203. Because ANV's do not have legally designated boundaries, the Census Bureau has established Alaska Native village statistical areas (ANVSA's) for statistical purposes. For the 1990 census, the Census Bureau cooperated with officials of the nonprofit corporation within each participating Alaska Native Regional Corporation (ANRC), as well as other knowledgeable officials, to delineate boundaries that encompass the settles area associated with each ANV.

★ 562 ★

Housing and Household Characteristics of American Indian and Alaska Native Village Statistical Areas: 1990 Akhiok-Evansville - II

American Indian/ Alaska Native Area State	Households with American Indian, Eskimo, or Aleut householder Nonfamily households		Land area	
	Total	Householder living alone	Square kilometers	Square miles
Alaska Native Village Statistical Area				
All areas	2,542	2,146	23,368.7	9,022.7
Akhiok	4	4	19.0	7.3
Akiachak	13	13	60.0	23.2
Akiak	13	11	4.9	1.9
Akutan	9	6	35.1	13.6
Alakanuk	16	14	89.8	34.7
Alatna	6	6	6.1	2.4
Aleknagik	11	10	31.8	12.3
Alexander	-	-	147.0	56.8
Allakaket	10	10	5.6	2.1
Ambler	7	7	30.0	11.6
Anaktuvuk Pass	15	13	36.0	13.9
Andreafsky	16	12	6.5	2.5
Angoon	14	13	59.5	23.0
Aniak	22	17	12.2	4.7
Anvik	11	10	28.9	11.2
Arctic Villagae	12	11	173.7	67.1
Atko	4	4	260.7	100.7
Atkasook	7	4	106.8	41.2
Atmautluak	4	3	4.5	1.7
Barrow	84	69	48.3	18.6
Beaver	22	20	49.8	19.2
Belkofski	-	-	5.6	2.2
Bethel	169	122	114.7	44.3
Bill Moore's	-	-	4.2	1.6
Birch Creek	5	4	26.0	10.1
Brevig Mission	12	8	10.8	4.2
Buckland	6	6	3.6	1.4
Cantwell	3	3	113.3	43.7
Canyon Village	-	-	109.6	42.3
Chalkyitsik	13	12	5.3	2.0
Chefornak	5	5	83.0	32.1
Chenega	3	3	74.5	28.8
Chevak	37	35	4.0	1.5

[Continued]

★ 562 ★

Housing and Household Characteristics of American Indian and Alaska Native Village Statistical Areas: 1990 Akhiok-Evansville - II
[Continued]

American Indian/ Alaska Native Area State	Households with American Indian, Eskimo, or Aleut householder Nonfamily households		Land area	
	Total	Householder living alone	Square kilometers	Square miles
Chignik	7	7	30.3	11.7
Chignik Lagoon	2	1	31.8	12.3
Chignik Lake	2	2	47.6	18.4
Chilkat	6	4	5.0	1.9
Chilkoot	2	1	.9	.3
Chistochina	2	1	43.8	16.9
Chitina	2	1	74.1	28.6
Chuathbaluk	5	5	10.8	4.2
Chulloonawick	-	-	41.0	15.8
Circle	5	4	11.8	4.6
Clark's Point	3	3	9.8	3.8
Copper Center	16	15	55.2	21.3
Council	-	-	57.0	22.0
Craig	28	17	15.3	5.9
Crooked Creek	7	7	104.4	40.3
Deering	10	10	13.6	5.3
Dillingham	89	66	84.8	32.7
Dot Lake	3	3	2.4	.9
Eagle	8	8	87.5	33.8
Eek	18	15	2.7	1.0
Egegik	15	12	139.5	53.9
Eklutna	7	7	16.3	6.3
Ekuk	-	-	38.4	14.8
Ekwok	7	7	51.1	19.7
Elim	12	8	1,226.7	473.6
Emmonak	23	22	16.2	6.2
English Bay	9	8	19.6	7.6
Evansville	2	2	119.6	46.2

Source: Summary Population and Housing Characteristics, United States Summary, United States Bureau of the Census, CP H-1, pp. 417-432. *Notes:* A dash (-) indicates that no data were given in the original source. Alaska Native villages: (ANV's) constitute tribes, bands,clans, groups, villages, communities, or associations in Alaska that are recognized pursuant to the Alaska Native Claims Settlement Act of 1972, Public Law 92- 203. Because ANV's do not have legally designated boundaries, the Census Bureau has established Alaska Native village statistical areas (ANVSA's) for statistical purposes. For the 1990 census, the Census Bureau cooperated with officials of the nonprofit corporation within each participating Alaska Native Regional Corporation (ANRC), as well as other knowledgeable officials, to delineate boundaries that encompass the settles area associated with each ANV.

★ 563 ★

Housing and Household Characteristics of American Indian and Alaska Native Village Statistical Areas: 1990 Eyak-Port Heiden - I

American Indian/ Alaska Native Area State	All housing units		Occupied housing units with American Indian, Eskimo, or Aleut householder				Family households		
			Owner occupied		Renter occupied				
						Mean contract rent (dollars), specified renter paying cash rent		Married-couple family	Female house-holder, no husband present
	Total	Occupied	Total	Mean value (dollars) specified Owner	Total		Total		
Alaska Native Village Statistical Area									
Eyak	62	55	4	162,500	-	-	3	3	-
False Pass	36	23	14	78,300	3	513	11	6	4
Fort Yukon	272	205	137	40,600	24	140	118	48	46
Gakana	12	7	-	-	-	-	-	-	-
Galena	286	190	79	66,500	33	264	77	45	9
Gambell	132	120	101	50,400	8	700	94	55	14
Georgetown	4	-	-	-	-	-	-	-	-
Golavin	49	42	27	70,100	11	79	23	13	5
Goodnews Bay	72	66	54	19,000	7	191	50	25	15
Grayling	62	51	38	36,800	7	228	37	23	10
Grouse Creek Group	232	198	20	86,900	1	113	14	8	5
Gulkana	60	42	17	49,900	8	171	14	5	7
Hamilton	6	-	-	-	-	-	-	-	-
Healy Lake	47	14	12	15,800	-	-	10	5	2
Holy Cross	-	-	-	-	-	-	-	-	-
Hoonah	268	242	122	57,500	33	286	123	85	23
Hooper Bay	203	190	138	36,100	37	245	141	91	34
Hughes	29	22	15	17,000	6	-	12	7	3
Huslia	85	62	52	29,500	5	50	39	19	13
Hydaburgg	135	118	65	74,300	34	210	74	47	16
Igiugig	16	13	9	75,700	1	113	5	4	1
Iliamna	36	30	13	126,700	7	444	17	16	-
Inalik	41	41	8	25,100	29	-	31	16	6
Ivanof Bay	14	9	5	22,900	3	188	8	6	1
Kake	265	220	134	65,600	23	301	127	93	19
Kaktovik	82	67	32	83,800	18	405	36	25	2
Kalskag	51	48	22	35,200	13	169	26	14	4
Kaltag	74	63	50	41,100	4	166	43	24	8
Karluk	27	18	15	118,000	1	50	14	8	4
Kasaan	30	19	6	61,500	5	278	10	6	3
Kasigluk	105	89	48	71,400	31	84	72	56	13
Kiana	124	91	67	52,700	13	379	60	31	20
King Cove	127	88	40	79,800	9	563	40	32	7
King Salmon	228	158	16	219,700	9	575	18	14	4
Kipnuk	128	99	94	44,200	1	-	84	70	9
Kivalina	71	67	46	39,600	15	406	54	36	6
Klawack	281	241	71	95,600	40	324	91	63	17
Knik	178	105	8	37,100	1	113	7	3	2
Kobuk	24	18	11	51,900	3	-	10	3	6
Kokhanok	41	38	28	45,500	4	163	27	14	12
Koliganek	53	47	37	21,300	4	163	36	24	6
Kongiganak	67	60	53	16,400	2	-	52	35	9
Kotlik	109	101	77	67,600	15	291	83	69	9

[Continued]

★ 563 ★

Housing and Household Characteristics of American Indian and Alaska Native Village Statistical Areas: 1990 Eyak-Port Heiden - I
[Continued]

American Indian/ Alaska Native Area State	All housing units		Occupied housing units with American Indian, Eskimo, or Aleut householder				Family households		
			Owner occupied		Renter occupied				
			Total	Mean value (dollars) specified Owner	Total	Mean contract rent (dollars), specified renter paying cash rent	Total	Married-couple family	Female house-holder, no husband present
	Total	Occupied							
Kotzebue	911	764	231	112,200	250	637	384	215	113
Koyuk	70	61	45	53,900	9	137	45	24	15
Koyukuk	50	40	34	19,200	3	119	28	14	5
Kwethluk	138	127	95	51,000	19	325	99	71	15
Kwigillingok	78	62	52	22,000	5	875	53	49	4
Lake Minchumina	34	12	1	27,500	-	-	1	1	-
Larsen Bay	74	44	31	75,300	5	90	26	16	8
Levelock	46	39	15	57,500	16	215	21	15	2
Lime Village	17	14	10	15,900	3	513	8	5	2
Lower Kalskag	73	67	45	89,600	19	82	55	34	16
McGrath	207	175	21	54,900	46	180	46	25	16
Manley Hot Springs	115	46	5	49,200	-	-	5	2	2
Manokotak	107	90	67	61,200	17	332	76	58	14
Marshall	83	70	51	45,800	9	66	49	32	9
Mary's Igloo	8	-	-	-	-	-	-	-	-
Medfra	8	-	-	-	-	-	-	-	-
Mekoryuk	67	63	56	71,800	6	102	41	29	6
Mentasta Lake	51	33	12	75,300	8	157	13	6	5
Minto	95	66	59	74,700	5	50	47	22	13
Mountain Village	191	148	73	72,600	46	111	108	71	23
Naknek	276	208	55	133,800	15	361	48	39	2
Napaimute	9	1	1	67,500	-	-	1	-	1
Napakiak	105	81	39	77,000	34	141	61	36	13
Napaskiak	99	74	61	192,200	4	313	60	50	10
Nelson Lagoon	35	31	22	184,000	2	-	19	12	5
Nenana	190	140	50	62,700	11	335	39	18	12
Newhalen	40	36	27	86,100	6	423	30	21	4
New Stuyahok	95	88	60	74,000	20	106	71	54	11
Newtok	45	42	23	50,800	14	109	31	23	2
Nightmute	36	29	23	73,300	1	-	22	18	2
Nikolai	43	40	26	19,500	9	169	21	13	5
Nikolski	26	19	16	59,200	1	-	7	7	-
Ninilchik	5,203	3,761	87	85,400	40	311	88	65	14
Noatak	85	74	53	56,000	13	250	51	33	10
Nondalton	65	54	31	70,900	12	138	37	18	8
Noorvik	125	107	77	36,400	18	197	83	48	20
Northway	37	30	23	58,600	2	0	21	11	3
Nuiqsut	102	91	55	73,800	25	273	64	35	16
Nulato	117	90	72	55,000	11	54	66	34	18
Nunapitchuk	97	87	54	36,900	29	149	68	52	9
Ohogamiut	2	-	-	-	-	-	-	-	-
Old Harbor	112	87	70	51,800	6	229	57	31	15
Oscarville	21	15	11	143,100	2	50	11	8	2
Ouzinkie	82	68	53	98,200	6	333	45	29	9

[Continued]

★ 563 ★

Housing and Household Characteristics of American Indian and Alaska Native Village Statistical Areas: 1990 Eyak-Port Heiden - I

[Continued]

American Indian/ Alaska Native Area State	All housing units		Occupied housing units with American Indian, Eskimo, or Aleut householder				Family households		
			Owner occupied		Renter occupied				
						Mean contract rent (dollars), specified renter paying cash rent			Female house-holder, no husband present
	Total	Occupied	Total	Mean value (dollars) specified Owner	Total		Total	Married-couple family	
Paimiut	2	-	-	-	-	-	-	-	-
Pedro Bay	36	17	15	85,200	1	875	10	7	2
Pelican	98	81	7	157,100	12	352	14	7	6
Perryville	45	31	26	24,700	2	137	23	16	6
Pilot Point	57	17	12	151,800	1	-	12	10	-
Pilot Station	123	100	68	71,300	24	107	78	60	13
Pitkas Point	47	37	22	80,200	12	175	27	19	7
Platinum	45	22	18	20,400	1	-	14	6	3
Point Hope	174	143	56	84,200	65	184	107	61	27
Point Lay	48	44	19	101,000	18	246	26	11	4
Portage Creek	22	3	-	-	1	-	-	-	-
Port Graham	68	60	45	62,600	9	141	38	24	7
Port Heiden	61	42	22	105,000	6	113	20	12	4

Source: Summary Population and Housing Characteristics, United States Summary, United States Bureau of the Census, CP H-1, pp. 417-432. *Notes:* A dash (-) indicates that no data were given in the original source. Alaska Native villages: (ANV's) constitute tribes, bands,clans, groups, villages, communities, or associations in Alaska that are recognized pursuant to the Alaska Native Claims Settlement Act of 1972, Public Law 92- 203. Because ANV's do not have legally designated boundaries, the Census Bureau has established Alaska Native village statistical areas (ANVSA's) for statistical purposes. For the 1990 census, the Census Bureau cooperated with officials of the nonprofit corporation within each participating Alaska Native Regional Corporation (ANRC), as well as other knowledgeable officials, to delineate boundaries that encompass the settles area associated with each ANV.

★ 564 ★

Housing and Household Characteristics of American Indian and Alaska Native Village Statistical Areas: 1990 Eyak-Port Heiden - II

American Indian/ Alaska Native Area State	Households with American Indian, Eskimo, or Aleut householder Nonfamily households		Land area	
	Total	Householder living alone	Square kilometers	Square miles
Alaska Native Village Statistical Area				
Eyak	1	1	34.0	13.1
False Pass	6	5	38.3	14.8
Fort Yukon	43	42	17.6	6.8
Gakana	-	-	3.1	1.2
Galena	35	24	42.8	16.5

[Continued]

★ 564 ★

Housing and Household Characteristics of American Indian and Alaska Native Village Statistical Areas: 1990 Eyak-Port Heiden - II

[Continued]

American Indian/ Alaska Native Area State	Households with American Indian, Eskimo, or Aleut householder Nonfamily households		Land area	
	Total	Householder living alone	Square kilometers	Square miles
Gambell	15	14	28.8	11.1
Georgetown	-	-	64.2	24.8
Golavin	15	15	9.9	3.8
Goodnews Bay	11	8	8.4	3.2
Grayling	8	8	27.6	10.7
Grouse Creek Group	7	5	21.9	8.5
Gulkana	11	9	31.1	12.0
Hamilton	-	-	11.9	4.6
Healy Lake	2	2	412.7	159.3
Holy Cross	-	-	6.1	2.4
Hoonah	32	29	3.4	1.3
Hooper Bay	34	31	22.1	8.5
Hughes	9	9	6.4	2.5
Huslia	18	17	40.1	15.5
Hydaburgg	25	23	1.3	.5
Igiugig	5	5	70.8	27.3
Iliamna	3	2	57.1	22.1
Inalik	6	6	4.9	1.9
Ivanof Bay	-	-	28.8	11.1
Kake	30	27	20.7	8.0
Kaktovik	14	12	2.2	.8
Kalskag	9	8	9.8	3.8
Kaltag	11	11	56.6	21.9
Karluk	2	2	120.5	46.5
Kasaan	1	1	13.8	5.3
Kasigluk	7	7	48.8	18.9
Kiana	20	19	.8	.3
King Cove	9	7	7.5	2.9
King Salmon	7	6	568.1	219.3
Kipnuk	11	9	76.4	29.5
Kivalina	7	7	4.6	1.8
Klawack	20	16	.9	.3
Knik	2	2	25.2	9.7
Kobuk	4	4	42.4	16.4
Kokhanok	5	5	56.3	21.7

[Continued]

★ 564 ★

Housing and Household Characteristics of American Indian and Alaska Native Village Statistical Areas: 1990 Eyak-Port Heiden - II

[Continued]

American Indian/ Alaska Native Area State	Households with American Indian, Eskimo, or Aleut householder Nonfamily households		Land area	
	Total	Householder living alone	Square kilometers	Square miles
Koliganek	5	4	251.6	97.1
Kongiganak	3	3	29.5	11.4
Kotlik	9	7	9.1	3.5
Kotzebue	97	68	69.8	26.9
Koyuk	9	9	11.7	4.5
Koyukuk	9	8	15.5	6.0
Kwethluk	15	15	26.4	10.2
Kwigillingok	4	4	40.8	15.7
Lake Minchumina	-	-	189.4	73.1
Larsen Bay	10	6	13.4	5.2
Levelock	10	10	72.9	28.2
Lime Village	5	4	138.3	53.4
Lower Kalskag	9	7	3.3	1.3
McGrath	21	17	97.3	37.6
Manley Hot Springs	-	-	151.4	58.5
Manokotak	8	7	111.0	42.9
Marshall	11	9	11.6	4.5
Mary's Igloo	-	-	29.1	11.2
Medfra	-	-	52.2	20.1
Mekoryuk	21	21	19.1	7.4
Mentasta Lake	7	6	203.1	78.4
Minto	17	14	421.8	162.9
Mountain Village	11	9	11.3	4.3
Naknek	22	20	186.8	72.1
Napaimute	-	-	113.7	43.9
Napakiak	12	11	16.7	6.5
Napaskiak	5	5	11.4	4.4
Nelson Lagoon	5	4	634.7	245.1
Nenana	22	19	14.2	5.5
Newhalen	3	3	15.5	6.0
New Stuyahok	9	9	87.9	33.9
Newtok	6	6	18.8	7.3
Nightmute	2	2	251.7	97.2
Nikolai	14	12	12.8	4.9
Nikolski	10	10	228.9	88.4
Ninilchik	39	32	8,506.1	3,284.2

[Continued]

★ 564 ★

Housing and Household Characteristics of American Indian and Alaska Native Village Statistical Areas: 1990 Eyak-Port Heiden - II

[Continued]

American Indian/ Alaska Native Area State	Households with American Indian, Eskimo, or Aleut householder Nonfamily households		Land area	
	Total	Householder living alone	Square kilometers	Square miles
Noatak	15	13	45.8	17.7
Nondalton	6	5	21.5	8.3
Noorvik	12	10	.5	.2
Northway	4	4	10.9	4.2
Nuiqsut	16	15	21.5	8.3
Nulato	17	16	120.4	46.5
Nunapitchuk	15	13	16.0	6.2
Ohogamiut	-	-	17.4	6.7
Old Harbor	19	15	52.9	20.4
Oscarville	2	2	3.9	1.5
Ouzinkie	14	10	14.5	5.6
Paimiut	-	-	65.3	25.2
Pedro Bay	6	5	47.1	18.2
Pelican	5	4	.9	.3
Perryville	5	5	96.2	37.1
Pilot Point	1	1	172.8	66.7
Pilot Station	14	13	3.9	1.5
Pitkas Point	7	6	2.7	1.0
Platinum	5	4	115.4	44.6
Point Hope	14	10	14.5	5.6
Point Lay	11	8	45.0	17.4
Portage Creek	1	1	33.7	13.0
Port Graham	16	14	15.3	5.9
Port Heiden	8	5	132.3	51.1

Source: Summary Population and Housing Characteristics, United States Summary, United States Bureau of the Census, CP H-1, pp. 417-432. *Notes:* A dash (-) indicates that no data were given in the original source. Alaska Native villages: (ANV's) constitute tribes, bands,clans, groups, villages, communities, or associations in Alaska that are recognized pursuant to the Alaska Native Claims Settlement Act of 1972, Public Law 92- 203. Because ANV's do not have legally designated boundaries, the Census Bureau has established Alaska Native village statistical areas (ANVSA's) for statistical purposes. For the 1990 census, the Census Bureau cooperated with officials of the nonprofit corporation within each participating Alaska Native Regional Corporation (ANRC), as well as other knowledgeable officials, to delineate boundaries that encompass the settles area associated with each ANV.

★ 565 ★

Housing and Household Characteristics of American Indian and Alaska Native Village Statistical Areas: 1990 Port Lions-Sealaska - I

American Indian/ Alaska Native Area State	All housing units		Occupied housing units with American Indian, Eskimo, or Aleut householder				Family households		
			Owner occupied		Renter occupied				
						Mean contract rent (dollars), specified renter paying cash rent			Female house- holder, no husband present
			Total	Mean value (dollars) specified Owner	Total		Total	Married- couple family	
	Total	Occupied							
Alaska Native Village Statistical Area									
Port Lions	103	73	47	75,300	2	213	38	31	5
Quinhagak	136	127	83	49,300	32	64	100	66	20
Rampart	42	24	20	49,000	1	50	13	5	6
Red Devil	24	18	7	24,700	1	-	5	2	2
Ruby	92	61	30	51,200	10	225	22	15	3
Russian Mission	58	56	41	62,800	8	875	41	31	8
St. George	67	45	30	54,900	10	138	32	22	5
St. Mary's	16	8	4	29,200	1	-	4	3	-
St. Michael	78	69	43	29,500	12	90	47	28	12
St. Paul	177	154	102	86,300	21	414	102	71	17
Salamatof	424	264	7	66,700	14	322	10	5	5
Sand Point	272	242	110	92,200	30	451	99	72	15
Savaango	129	116	85	48,500	22	90	90	58	15
Saxman	105	99	57	109,700	13	398	58	32	18
Scammon Bay	99	85	67	58,700	12	71	61	35	15
Selawik	154	129	88	58,600	26	163	104	55	32
Seldovia	221	129	13	83,300	1	163	9	5	-
Shageluk	49	42	32	28,200	6	206	26	9	8
Shaktoolik	58	46	34	28,100	6	107	35	28	3
Sheldon Point	33	27	1	12,500	21	50	19	9	1
Shishmaref	136	119	80	71,600	28	176	84	41	24
Shungnak	68	54	40	57,200	7	163	39	24	8
Slana	33	25	1	-	-	-	-	-	-
Sleetmute	38	33	25	44,600	3	363	21	11	5
Soloman	4	4	4	27,500	-	-	1	-	-
South Naknek	90	39	25	78,300	5	159	25	15	7
Stebbins	87	86	68	40,300	9	155	69	43	13
Stevens Village	53	37	27	66,300	8	120	15	6	2
Stony River	27	19	12	65,000	4	363	9	3	5
Takotna	40	15	3	35,000	1	113	2	1	1
Tanacross	53	35	33	27,600	-	-	23	15	4
Tanana	169	123	47	53,000	39	117	57	27	22
Tatitlek	52	33	25	84,500	3	-	28	18	8
Tazlina	99	80	15	55,600	2	463	12	5	1
Telida	7	3	2	9,000	-	-	2	-	-
Teller	64	44	13	23,500	20	66	24	8	10
Tenakee Springs	139	51	3	111,700	3	88	3	3	-
Tetlin	47	28	23	12,400	1	-	18	7	7
Togiak	200	151	117	70,900	8	431	107	77	23
Tok	561	367	16	57,900	15	420	18	13	4
Toksook Bay	103	88	67	167,200	14	875	71	60	7
Tuluksak	90	74	58	42,700	7	-	58	42	11
Tuntutuliak	76	70	58	50,000	7	78	56	40	10

[Continued]

Housing and Household Characteristics of American Indian and Alaska Native Village Statistical Areas: 1990 Port Lions-Sealaska - I
[Continued]

American Indian/ Alaska Native Area State	All housing units		Occupied housing units with American Indian, Eskimo, or Aleut householder				Family households		
			Owner occupied		Renter occupied				
						Mean contract rent (dollars), specified renter paying cash rent			Female house-holder, no husband present
	Total	Occupied	Total	Mean value (dollars) specified Owner	Total		Total	Married-couple family	
Tunuak	92	78	59	61,800	13	163	57	42	6
Twin Hills	35	25	20	20,100	3	113	15	11	1
Tyonek	92	55	35	33,500	15	113	40	13	12
Ugashik	20	4	3	78,800	-	-	3	1	-
Ukivok	18	-	-	-	-	-	-	-	-
Unalakleet	240	207	120	70,500	38	359	128	77	28
Unalaska	675	575	53	118,100	16	643	48	22	17
Venetie	64	50	39	24,800	4	50	36	17	14
Wainwright	160	133	90	78,200	27	334	93	64	17
Wales	66	49	26	31,800	14	170	32	14	9
White Mountain	69	58	33	37,900	18	86	33	16	7
Wiseman	37	11	-	-	-	-	-	-	-
Yakutat	189	175	58	74,500	33	387	60	32	18
Alaska Native Regional Corporation									
Ahtna	2,714	1,161	134	59,000	54	231	127	63	36
Aleut	2,742	2,378	489	90,200	113	434	459	311	87
Arctic Slope	2,154	1,673	581	82,300	443	420	809	463	214
Bering Straits	3,684	2,371	986	54,900	495	482	1,161	638	294
Bristol Bay	3,204	2,110	964	82,300	303	377	993	686	204
Calista	6,228	4,973	2,666	62,800	1,122	322	3,097	2,030	691
Chugach	4,860	3,861	267	83,800	131	380	289	187	71
Cook Inlet	132,266	108,849	2,066	90,400	3,099	459	3,465	1,833	1,312
Dayon	39,783	31,271	1,724	51,300	1,313	364	2,048	976	740
Koniag	4,890	4,083	428	94,600	219	483	450	289	106
NANA	1,998	1,526	752	68,900	384	565	932	530	255
Sealaska	27,556	24,210	1,670	85,800	1,554	434	2,321	1,394	675

Source: Summary Population and Housing Characteristics, United States Summary, United States Bureau of the Census, CP H-1, pp. 417-432. *Notes:* A dash (-) indicates that no data were given in the original source. Alaska Native villages: (ANV's) constitute tribes, bands, clans, groups, villages, communities, or associations in Alaska that are recognized pursuant to the Alaska Native Claims Settlement Act of 1972, Public Law 92-203. Because ANV's do not have legally designated boundaries, the Census Bureau has established Alaska Native village statistical areas (ANVSA's) for statistical purposes. For the 1990 census, the Census Bureau cooperated with officials of the nonprofit corporation within each participating Alaska Native Regional Corporation (ANRC), as well as other knowledgeable officials, to delineate boundaries that encompass the settles area associated with each ANV.

★ 566 ★

Housing and Household Characteristics of American Indian and Alaska Native Village Statistical Areas: 1990 Port Lions-Sealaska - II

American Indian/ Alaska Native Area State	Households with American Indian, Eskimo, or Aleut householder Nonfamily households		Land area	
	Total	Householder living alone	Square kilometers	Square miles
Alaska Native Village Statistical Area				
Port Lions	11	11	17.1	6.6
Quinhagak	15	13	12.7	4.9
Rampart	8	6	604.3	233.3
Red Devil	3	3	60.8	23.5
Ruby	18	14	19.1	7.4
Russian Mission	8	8	13.2	5.1
St. George	8	7	90.4	34.9
St. Mary's	1	1	101.8	39.3
St. Michael	8	8	54.9	21.2
St. Paul	21	15	103.8	40.1
Salamatof	11	9	21.0	8.1
Sand Point	41	29	20.0	7.7
Savaango	17	17	19.0	7.3
Saxman	12	9	1.7	.6
Scammon Bay	18	16	1.9	.7
Selawik	10	10	7.4	2.9
Seldovia	5	5	.8	.3
Shageluk	12	10	24.8	9.6
Shaktoolik	5	4	4.1	1.6
Sheldon Point	3	2	34.3	13.2
Shishmaref	24	22	7.2	2.8
Shungnak	8	7	22.1	8.5
Slana	1	1	44.8	17.3
Sleetmute	7	7	71.6	27.6
Soloman	3	3	40.6	15.7
South Naknek	5	2	247.4	95.5
Stebbins	8	7	92.6	35.8
Stevens Village	20	16	22.6	8.7
Stony River	7	4	44.3	17.1
Takotna	2	2	37.7	14.5
Tanacross	10	10	203.1	78.4
Tanana	29	26	43.7	16.9
Tatitlek	-	-	14.5	5.6
Tazlina	5	4	33.1	12.8
Telida	-	-	155.9	60.2

[Continued]

887

★ 566 ★

Housing and Household Characteristics of American Indian and Alaska Native Village Statistical Areas: 1990 Port Lions-Sealaska - II

[Continued]

American Indian/ Alaska Native Area State	Households with American Indian, Eskimo, or Aleut householder Nonfamily households		Land area	
	Total	Householder living alone	Square kilometers	Square miles
Teller	9	7	.7	.3
Tenakee Springs	3	2	30.3	11.7
Tetlin	6	6	396.1	152.9
Togiak	18	14	116.0	44.8
Tok	13	11	344.4	133.0
Toksook Bay	10	9	83.5	32.2
Tuluksak	7	7	8.4	3.2
Tuntutuliak	9	6	69.8	26.9
Tunuak	15	15	11.0	4.3
Twin Hills	8	8	80.2	31.0
Tyonek	10	9	57.7	22.3
Ugashik	-	-	227.9	88.0
Ukivok	-	-	10.4	4.0
Unalakleet	30	27	7.5	2.9
Unalaska	21	14	30.3	11.7
Venetie	7	7	34.3	13.2
Wainwright	24	19	10.6	4.1
Wales	8	7	6.3	2.4
White Mountain	18	16	6.6	2.6
Wiseman	-	-	210.2	81.1
Yakutat	31	25	7.6	2.9
Alaska Native Regional Corporation				
Ahtna	61	52	74,003.2	28,572.7
Aleut	143	107	28,845.7	11,137.3
Arctic Slope	215	175	214,848.0	82,952.9
Bering Straits	320	280	59,602.5	23,012.6
Bristol Bay	274	228	103,862.4	40,101.3
Calista	691	586	143,477.1	55,396.6
Chugach	109	89	37,960.5	14,656.6
Cook Inlet	1,700	1,214	97,002.6	37,452.7
Dayon	989	822	515,427.9	199,006.9
Koniag	197	152	18,534.7	7,156.2

[Continued]

★ 566 ★

Housing and Household Characteristics of American Indian and Alaska Native Village Statistical Areas: 1990 Port Lions-Sealaska - II

[Continued]

American Indian/ Alaska Native Area State	Households with American Indian, Eskimo, or Aleut householder Nonfamily households		Land area	
	Total	Householder living alone	Square kilometers	Square miles
NANA	204	169	92,883.8	35,862.5
Sealaska	903	679	90,485.2	34,936.4

Source: Summary Population and Housing Characteristics, United States Summary, United States Bureau of the Census, CP H-1, pp. 417-432. *Notes:* A dash (-) indicates that no data were given in the original source. Alaska Native villages: (ANV's) constitute tribes, bands,clans, groups, villages, communities, or associations in Alaska that are recognized pursuant to the Alaska Native Claims Settlement Act of 1972, Public Law 92- 203. Because ANV's do not have legally designated boundaries, the Census Bureau has established Alaska Native village statistical areas (ANVSA's) for statistical purposes. For the 1990 census, the Census Bureau cooperated with officials of the nonprofit corporation within each participating Alaska Native Regional Corporation (ANRC), as well as other knowledgeable officials, to delineate boundaries that encompass the settles area associated with each ANV.

Housing Characteristics

★ 567 ★

Electric Lighting and Telephones in Occupied Housing Units on Reservations, 1980: Acoma Pueblo - La Jolla

Data are the latest available.

Identified reservation	Total	Electric lighting								Telephone			
		Yes							No	Yes	No		
		Public or private utility company	Rural electric cooperative	Bureau of Indian affairs electric system	Tribal system	Household generator	Other	No			Total	Within 1/4 mile	More than 1/4 mile
American Indian, Eskimo, or Aleut householder or spouse	68,371	35,706	20,886	3,596	7,866	112	205	12,903	35,894	45,379	23,812	21,567
American Indian, Eskimo, or Aleut householder	64,861	33,622	19,749	3,406	7,776	106	202	12,848	33,089	44,620	23,269	21,350
Acoma Pueblo, New Mexico	442	22	421	-	-	-	-	23	302	163	82	82
Agua Caliente, California	-	-	-	-	-	-	-	-	103	33	31	2
Alabama-Coushatta, Texas	136	2	134	-	-	-	-	-	2	206	4	202
Alamo, New Mexico	177	111	65	1	-	-	-	31	263	64	63	1
Allegany, New York	328	323	4	-	-	-	-	-				
Alturas Rancheria, California	...	...	...	...	...	...	...	...	...	...	...	...
Annette Islands Reserve, Alaska	262	136	67	-	57	-	2	-	208	54	49	4
Augustine, California	-	-	-	-	-	-	-	-	-	-	-	-
Bad River, Wisconsin	203	72	131	-	-	-	-	-	159	44	44	-
Barona Rancheria, California	67	67	-	-	-	-	-	-	54	13	13	-
Bay Mills, Michigan	75	2	74	-	-	-	-	2	53	24	24	-
Benton Paiute, California	...	...	...	...	...	...	...	...	...	...	...	-
Berry Creek Rancheria, California	-	-	-	-	-	-	-	-	-	-	-	...
Big Bend Rancheria, California	...	...	...	...	...	...	...	...	...	...	...	...

[Continued]

889

★ 567 ★

Electric Lighting and Telephones in Occupied Housing Units on Reservations, 1980: Acoma Pueblo - La Jolla
[Continued]

Identified reservation	Total	Electric lighting							Telephone			
		Yes						No	Yes	No		
		Public or private utility company	Rural electric cooperative	Bureau of Indian affairs electric system	Tribal system	Household generator	Other			Total	Within 1/4 mile	More than 1/4 mile
Big Cypress, Florida	90	-	90	-	-	-	-	3	31	62	23	39
Big Lagoon Rancheria, California	...	...	...	...	...	...	...	...	...	...	...	...
Big Pine Rancheria, California	76	76	-	-	-	-	-	-	55	21	18	3
Bishop Rancheria, California	238	235	3	-	-	-	-	2	193	47	46	1
Blackfeet, Montana	1,498	716	767	4	4	5	2	9	654	853	602	252
Bois Forte (Nett Lake), Minnesota	108	-	108	-	-	-	-	1	69	40	39	1
Bridgeport Colony, California	20	20	-	-	-	-	-	-	6	14	14	-
Brighton, Florida	75	8	67	-	-	-	-	-	35	40	39	1
Burns, Oregon	33	32	-	1	-	-	-	3	21	15	11	4
Cabazon, California	...	...	...	...	...	...	...	...	...	...	...	...
Cachil Dehe Rancheria, California	...	...	...	...	...	...	...	...	...	...	...	...
Cahuilla, California	14	1	13	-	-	-	-	-	4	11	1	9
Campo, California	27	23	3	-	-	-	-	2	13	15	8	8
Camp Verde, Arizona	44	44	-	-	-	-	-	2	18	28	28	-
Canoncito, New Mexico	144	46	96	1	1	-	-	71	46	169	51	118
Capitan Grande, California	-	-	-	-	-	-	-	-	-	-	-	-
Carson Colony, Nevada	65	65	-	-	-	-	-	-	42	23	23	-
Catawaba, South Carolina	273	132	141	-	-	-	-	2	193	82	75	6
Cattaraugus, New York	543	536	5	-	-	1	1	5	385	164	148	16
Cedarville Rancheria, California	...	...	...	...	...	...	...	...	...	...	...	...
Chehalis, Washington	55	55	-	-	-	-	-	-	42	13	13	-
Chemehuevi, California	10	10	-	-	-	-	-	-	8	2	2	-
Cheyenne River, South Dakota	307	1	306	-	-	-	-	22	174	155	128	28
Chitimacha, Louisiana	74	-	74	-	-	-	-	-	68	5	4	1
Cochiti Pueblo, New Mexico	149	149	-	-	-	-	-	1	98	52	43	9
Cocopah, Arizona	64	63	-	1	-	-	-	3	19	48	40	8
Coeur D'Alene, Idaho	168	111	55	-	-	1	1	3	112	59	48	11
Cold Springs Rancheria, California	13	13	-	-	-	-	-	-	1	12	9	3
Colorado River, Arizona-California	550	160	1	390	-	-	-	2	384	168	139	30
Colville, Washington	1,122	663	458	-	-	-	1	7	770	359	298	61
Cortina Rancheria, California	...	...	...	...	...	...	...	...	...	...	...	...
Coushatta, Louisiana	...	...	...	...	...	...	...	...	...	...	...	...
Coyote Valley Rancheria, California	-	-	-	-	-	-	-	-	-	-	-	...
Crow, Montana	833	173	658	1	-	-	-	-	494	339	226	113
Crow Creek, South Dakota	328	46	271	2	9	-	-	-	124	204	178	25
Cuyapaipe, California	...	...	...	...	...	...	...	...	...	...	...	...
Deer Creek, Minnesota	...	...	...	...	...	...	...	...	...	...	...	...
Dresslerville Colony, Nevada	34	34	-	-	-	-	-	-	21	13	4	9
Dry Creek Rancheria, California	...	...	...	...	...	...	...	...	...	...	...	...
Duck Valley, Idaho-Nevada	240	238	1	-	-	1	-	3	83	160	994	65
Duckwater, Nevada	27	-	27	-	-	-	-	-	7	20	16	4
Eastern Cherokee, North Carolina	1,468	1,408	52	8	-	-	-	5	881	593	495	97
Eastern Pequot, Connecticut	...	...	...	...	...	...	...	...	...	...	...	...
Ely Colony, Nevada	17	17	-	-	-	-	-	-	14	3	2	1
Enterprise Rancheria, California	...	...	...	...	...	...	...	...	...	...	...	...
Fallon Colony, Nevada	15	12	3	-	-	-	-	1	12	4	3	1
Fallon, Nevada	64	58	3	-	2	-	-	2	41	24	19	6
Flandreau, South Dakota	49	28	21	-	-	-	-	-	27	22	22	-
Flathead, Montana	1,271	331	23	905	7	1	3	8	892	386	348	38
Fond du Lac, Minnesota	167	143	24	-	-	-	1	4	137	35	33	1
Fort Apache, Arizona	1,336	440	888	-	1	1	5	147	335	1,148	579	569
Fort Belknap, Montana	444	220	221	1	2	-	-	8	155	297	132	165
Fort Berthold, North Dakota	627	147	478	-	2	-	-	5	377	255	195	60
Fort Bidwell, California	26	2	24	-	-	-	-	-	7	19	18	1
Fort Hall, Idaho	665	633	13	-	1	-	18	7	395	277	233	43
Fort Independence, California	17	17	-	-	-	-	-	-	13	4	4	-
Fort McDermitt, Nevada-California	93	4	89	-	-	-	-	1	32	62	26	36
Fort McDowell, Arizona	78	72	6	-	-	-	-	6	36	48	35	13

[Continued]

★ 567 ★

Electric Lighting and Telephones in Occupied Housing Units on Reservations, 1980: Acoma Pueblo - La Jolla
[Continued]

Identified reservation	Electric lighting								Telephone			
	Yes							No	Yes	No		
	Total	Public or private utility company	Rural electric cooperative	Bureau of Indian affairs electric system	Tribal system	Household generator	Other			Total	Within 1/4 mile	More than 1/4 mile
Fort Mojave, Arizona-California-Nevada	34	-	34	-	-	-	-	-	19	15	12	3
Fort Peck, Montana	1,102	831	261	1	4	4	1	1	675	428	391	37
Fort Totten, North Dakota	479	40	429	3	6	-	1	10	244	246	218	28
Fort Yuma, Arizona-California	333	327	5	2	-	-	-	6	166	173	151	22
Gila Bend, Arizona	-	-	-	-	-	-	-	-	-	-	-	-
Gila River, Arizona	1,515	654	12	843	2	-	3	98	444	1,169	627	542
Golden Hill, Connecticut	...	...	...	...	...	...	...	...	...	...	...	...
Goshute, Nevada-Utah	26	26	-	-	-	-	-	2	-	28	2	26
Grand Portage, Minnesota	71	2	69	-	-	-	-	7	57	21	18	3
Grindstone Creek Rancheria, California	16	16	-	-	-	-	-	1	5	12	12	-
Hannahville Community, Michigan	44	1	43	-	-	-	-	1	24	21	10	11
Hassanamisco, Massachusetts	...	...	...	...	...	...	...	...	...	...	...	...
Havasupai, Arizona	54	2	-	37	15	-	-	7	8	53	45	7
Hoh, Washington	14	14	-	-	-	-	-	-	7	7	7	-
Hollywood, Florida	125	125	-	-	-	-	-	-	63	62	62	-
Hoopa Valley, California	476	476	-	-	-	-	-	4	312	168	125	43
Hoopa Valley Extension, California	111	91	-	-	-	19	-	46	47	110	13	97
Hopi, Arizona	779	760	2	2	2	6	7	694	325	1,147	367	781
Hopland Rancheria, California	-	-	-	-	-	-	-	-	-	-	-	-
Hualapai, Arizona	156	45	110	1	-	-	-	4	65	95	63	32
Inaja-Cosmit, California	-	-	-	-	-	-	-	-	-	-	-	-
Indian Township, Maine	92	37	55	-	-	-	-	-	56	36	34	1
Iowa, Kansas-Nebraska	11	2	9	-	-	-	-	-	11	-	-	-
Isabella, Michigan	137	133	4	-	-	-	-	1	101	37	37	-
Isleta Pueblo, New Mexico	698	697	1	-	-	-	-	-	558	140	125	15
Jackson Rancheria, California	...	...	...	...	...	...	...	...	...	...	...	...
Jemez Pueblo, New Mexico	303	10	293	-	-	-	-	1	61	243	228	15
Jicarilla Apache, New Mexico	382	60	318	1	1	-	2	48	132	298	166	132
Kaibab, Arizona	24	24	-	-	-	-	-	1	8	17	14	3
Kalispel, Washington	20	15	5	-	-	-	-	1	7	14	2	12
Kickapoo, Kansas	101	58	43	-	-	-	-	1	53	50	42	7
Kootenai, Idaho	-	-	-	-	-	-	-	-	-	-	-	-
Lac Courte Oreilles, Wisconsin	301	134	167	-	-	-	-	3	196	108	98	9
Lac du Flambeau, Wisconsin	281	277	3	-	-	-	-	-	239	41	36	5
Laguna Pueblo, New Mexico	947	189	752	-	1	2	3	9	631	326	268	58
La Jolla, California	39	38	1	-	-	-	-	3	20	23	12	10

Source: U.S. Bureau of the Census, Subject Reports, PC80-2-1D, Part II, *American Indians, Eskimos, and Aleuts on Identified Reservations and in the Historic Areas of Oklahoma (Excluding Urbanized Areas)*, U.S. Government Printing Office, Washington, D.C., 1986, pp. 794-871. *Notes:* Three dots (...) means not applicable, or that the data are being withheld to avoid disclosure of information for individuals. A dash (-) represents zero or a percent which rounds to less than 0.1. Also, a dash (-) is used because the number of supplementary questionnaires for the reservations was insufficient to produce reliable estimates.

★ 568 ★

Electric Lighting and Telephones in Occupied Housing Units on Reservations, 1980: L'Anse - San Xavier

Data are the latest available.

Identified reservation	Total	Electric lighting								Telephone			
		Yes							No	Yes	No		
		Public or private utility company	Rural electric cooperative	Bureau of Indian affairs electric system	Tribal system	Household generator	Other	No			Total	Within 1/4 mile	More than 1/4 mile
L'Anse, Michigan	191	140	47	-	-	-	3	-	166	25	22	3
La Posta, California	...	...	...	...	...	...	...	...	...	...	...	...
Las Vegas Colony, Nevada	24	24	-	-	-	-	-	...	13	11	11	...
Laytonville Rancheria, California	26	26	-	-	-	-	-	-	14	12	11	1
Leech Lake, Minnesota	767	280	484	-	-	-	3	15	502	280	233	47
Likely Rancheria, California	-	-	-	-	-	-	-	-	-	-	-	-
Lone Pine Rancheria, California	55	55	-	-	-	-	-	2	39	17	17	-
Lookout Rancheria, California	...	...	...	...	...	...	...	...	...	...	...	...
Los Coyotes, California	10	4	6	-	-	-	-	7	7	10	1	8
Lovelock Colony, Nevada	37	37	-	-	-	-	-	-	19	18	18	-
Lower Brule, South Dakota	196	2	195	-	-	-	-	-	106	90	82	7
Lower Elwah, Washington	13	13	-	-	-	-	-	-	11	2	2	-
Lower Sioux Community, Minnesota	24	3	21	-	-	-	-	-	17	7	7	-
Lummi, Washington	304	301	1	-	-	-	1	2	216	90	83	6
Makah, Washington	270	270	-	-	-	-	-	1	222	49	45	4
Manchester Rancheria, California	20	20	-	-	-	-	-	-	13	7	5	2
Manzanita, California	...	...	...	...	...	...	...	...	...	...	...	...
Maricopa, Arizona	66	66	-	-	-	-	-	1	20	47	44	3
Mattaponi, Virgina	23	23	-	-	-	-	-	-	16	7	7	-
Menominee, Wisconsin	544	456	78	-	2	-	8	6	401	149	105	44
Mesa Grande, California	-	-	-	-	-	-	-	-	-	-	-	-
Mescalero Apache, New Mexico	442	127	310	-	3	1	-	7	177	272	131	141
Miccosukee, Florida	68	64	4	-	-	-	-	4	9	63	42	21
Middletown Rancheria, California	...	...	...	...	...	...	...	...	...	...	...	...
Mille Lacs, Minnesota	-	-	-	-	-	-	-	-	-	-	-	-
Mississippi Choctaw, Reservation	561	513	45	3	-	-	-	9	171	399	281	118
Moapa River, Nevada	43	43	-	-	-	-	-	-	25	18	17	1
Montgomery Creek Rancheria, California	...	...	...	...	...	...	...	...	...	...	...	...
Morongo, California	98	98	-	-	-	-	-	1	76	23	22	1
Muckleshoot, Washington	71	71	-	-	-	-	-	2	49	24	23	1
Nambe Pueblo, New Mexico	72	45	28	-	-	-	-	-	36	36	33	3
Navajo, Arizona-New Mexico-Utah	12,090	4,779	180	307	6,698	56	70	10,214	4,598	17,706	4,571	13,135
Nez Perce, Idaho	452	428	24	-	-	-	-	-	313	139	118	22
Nisqually, Washington	13	13	-	-	-	-	-	-	7	6	4	2
Nooksack, Washington	-	-	-	-	-	-	-	-	-	-	-	-
Northern Cheyenne, Montana	740	105	634	-	1	-	-	8	323	425	270	155
Oil Springs, New York	-	-	-	-	-	-	-	-	-	-	-	-
Omaha, Iowa-Nebraska	291	217	71	-	2	-	-	1	113	179	163	16
Oneida, Wisconsin	567	563	4	-	-	-	-	1	479	88	88	-
Onondaga, New York	-	-	-	-	-	-	-	-	-	-	-	-
Ontonagon, Michigan	-	-	-	-	-	-	-	-	-	-	-	-
Osage, Oklahoma	2,007	1,550	454	3	-	-	1	1	1,812	197	177	20
Ozette, Washington	...	...	...	...	...	...	...	...	...	...	...	...
Pala, California	138	136	1	-	-	-	-	7	105	40	36	4
Pamunkey, Virginia	27	27	-	-	-	-	-	-	24	3	3	-
Papago, Arizona	1,186	242	5	94	826	5	15	339	194	1,331	517	814
Pascua Yaqui, Arizona	81	25	56	-	-	-	-	-	48	33	32	1
Pauma, California	24	24	-	-	-	-	-	3	20	7	4	3
Payson Community of Yavapai-Apache, Arizona	-	-	-	-	-	-	-	-	-	-	-	-
Pechanga, California	24	24	-	-	-	-	-	10	17	17	12	5
Penobscot, Maine	141	141	-	-	-	-	-	1	106	36	34	2
Picuris Pueblo, New Mexico	42	10	32	-	-	-	-	-	14	28	28	-
Pine Creek, Michigan	10	10	-	-	-	-	-	-	8	3	3	-
Pine Ridge, South Dakota	2,142	731	1,267	80	62	-	2	187	817	1,512	984	527
Pleasant Point, Maine	138	138	-	-	-	-	-	1	75	65	65	-
Pojoaque Pueblo, New Mexico	36	27	9	-	-	-	-	-	32	4	4	-
Poospatuck, New York	28	28	-	-	-	-	-	-	19	9	9	-
Port Gamble, Washington	76	76	-	-	-	-	-	-	49	27	27	-

[Continued]

★ 568 ★

Electric Lighting and Telephones in Occupied Housing Units on Reservations, 1980: L'Anse – San Xavier
[Continued]

| Identified reservation | Total | Electric lighting | | | | | | | | Telephone | | | |
| | | Yes | | | | | | | No | Yes | No | | |
		Public or private utility company	Rural electric cooperative	Bureau of Indian affairs electric system	Tribal system	Household generator	Other	No			Total	Within 1/4 mile	More than 1/4 mile
Port Madison, Washington	62	59	-	-	-	1	2	1	49	14	13	1	
Potawatomi, Wisconsin	46	46	-	-	-	-	-	-	18	28	14	14	
Pottawatomi, Kansas	102	19	83	-	-	-	-	-	82	20	15	4	
Prairie Island Community, Minnesota	20	-	20	-	-	-	-	-	13	7	4	3	
Puyallup, Washington	279	279	-	-	-	-	-	-	246	32	30	3	
Pyramid Lake, Nevada	204	202	1	-	-	-	-	2	49	157	102	54	
Quileute, Washington	62	62	-	-	-	-	-	-	46	16	16	-	
Quinault, Washington	255	252	2	-	-	-	1	-	174	81	76	4	
Ramah Community, New Mexico	103	63	33	-	1	1	4	193	39	257	54	203	
Ramona, California	-	-	-	-	-	-	-	-	-	-	-	-	
Red Cliff, Wisconsin	152	150	1	-	-	-	-	-	126	25	20	5	
Red Lake, Minnesota	680	13	666	1	-	-	-	-	403	278	235	43	
Reno-Sparks Colony, Nevada	123	123	-	-	-	-	-	-	95	28	21	7	
Resighini Rancheria, California	...	...	...	...	...	...	...	...	...	...	...	...	
Rincon, California	83	82	1	-	-	-	-	-	72	11	9	1	
Roaring Creek Rancheria, California	...	...	...	...	...	...	...	...	...	...	...	...	
Rocky Boy's, Montana	317	9	308	-	-	-	-	1	126	192	154	38	
Rosebud, South Dakota	1,334	108	1,062	151	11	-	1	34	512	856	622	234	
Round Valley, California	166	166	-	-	-	-	-	2	95	73	63	10	
Rumsey Rancheria, California	...	...	...	...	...	...	...	...	...	...	...	...	
Sac and Fox, Iowa	100	27	73	-	-	-	-	4	50	54	46	8	
Sac and Fox, Kansas-Nebraska	...	...	...	...	...	...	...	...	...	...	...	...	
St. Croix, Wisconsin	99	13	86	-	-	-	-	2	64	38	34	3	
St. Regis Mohawk, New York	511	502	6	-	-	-	3	1	436	76	67	9	
Salt River, Arizona	568	561	6	-	-	-	1	17	182	403	339	64	
San Carlos, Arizona	1,144	258	154	713	13	3	2	72	201	1,015	474	540	
Sandia Pueblo, New Mexico	73	71	2	-	-	-	-	-	45	28	23	5	
Sandy Lake, Minnesota	-	-	-	-	-	-	-	-	-	-	-	-	
San Felipe Pueblo, New Mexico	281	279	-	-	-	-	1	1	158	123	114	9	
San Ildefonso Pueblo, New Mexico	134	46	88	-	-	-	-	-	102	32	30	3	
San Juan Pueblo, New Mexico	245	166	77	-	1	-	-	-	121	124	111	13	
San Manuel, California	-	-	-	-	-	-	-	-	-	-	-	-	
San Pasqual, California	46	45	-	-	-	1	-	1	38	8	6	2	
Santa Ana Pueblo, New Mexico	98	98	-	-	-	-	-	-	62	36	36	-	
Santa Clara Pueblo, New Mexico	424	247	178	-	-	-	-	-	298	126	113	13	
Santa Rosa Rancheria, California	26	26	-	-	-	-	-	-	11	15	15	-	
Santa Rosa, California	...	...	...	...	...	...	...	...	...	...	...	...	
Santa Ynez, California	40	40	-	-	-	-	-	-	35	5	4	1	
Santa Ysabel, California	37	35	1	-	-	1	-	21	26	32	23	10	
Santee, Nebraska	101	70	30	-	1	-	-	1	44	58	49	9	
Santo Domingo Pueblo, New Mexico	336	336	-	-	-	-	-	3	39	300	273	27	
San Xavier, Arizona	169	90	79	-	-	-	-	17	82	104	84	20	

Source: U.S. Bureau of the Census, Subject Reports, PC80-2-1D, Part II, *American Indians, Eskimos, and Aleuts on Identified Reservations and in the Historic Areas of Oklahoma (Excluding Urbanized Areas)*, U.S. Government Printing Office, Washington, D.C., 1986, pp. 794-871. *Notes:* Three dots (...) means not applicable, or that the data are being withheld to avoid disclosure of information for individuals. A dash (-) represents zero or a percent which rounds to less than 0.1. Also, a dash (-) is used because the number of supplementary questionnaires for the reservations was insufficient to produce reliable estimates.

Electric Lighting and Telephones in Occupied Housing Units on Reservations, 1980: Sauk-Sauiattle - Zuni Pueblo

Data are the latest available.

| Identified reservation | Total | Electric lighting | | | | | | | | Telephone | | | |
| | | Yes | | | | | | | | Yes | No | | |
		Public or private utility company	Rural electric cooperative	Bureau of Indian affairs electric system	Tribal system	Household generator	Other	No			Total	Within 1\4 mile	More than 1\4 mile
Sauk-Sauiattle, Washington	-	-	-	-	-	-	-	-	-	-	-	-	-
Sault Ste. Marie, Michigan	-	-	-	-	-	-	-	-	-	-	-	-	-
Schaghti-Coke, Connecticut	...	...	...	...	...	...	...	...	...	...	...	...	...
Shakopee Community, Minnesota	27	-	27	-	-	-	-	-	21	6	4	1	
Sheep Ranch Rancheria, California	...	...	...	...	...	...	...	...	...	...	...	...	...
Sherwood Valley Rancheria, California	...	...	...	...	...	...	...	...	...	...	...	...	...
Shingle Springs Rancheria, California	-	-	-	-	-	-	-	-	-	-	-	-	-
Shinnecock, New York	76	74	2	-	-	-	-	-	72	4	4	-	
Shoalwater, Washington	11	11	-	-	-	-	-	-	8	2	2	-	
Sisseton, North Dakota-South Dakota	623	262	326	2	33	-	-	11	360	275	243	31	
Skokomish, Washington	80	80	-	-	-	-	-	-	45	35	34	1	
Skull Valley, Utah	-	-	-	-	-	-	-	-	-	-	-	-	
Soboba, California	69	69	-	-	-	-	-	2	40	31	28	3	
Sokaogon Chippewa Community, Wisconsin	31	31	-	-	-	-	-	-	8	23	17	6	
Southern Paiute, Utah	39	39	-	-	-	-	-	1	22	18	18	-	
Southern Ute, Colorado	251	131	120	-	-	-	-	2	131	122	93	29	
Spokane, Washington	333	332	1	-	-	-	-	3	183	153	117	36	
Squaxin Island, Washington	...	...	...	...	...	...	...	...	...	...	...	...	...
Standing Rock, North Dakota-South Dakota	1,034	297	646	15	53	-	23	40	373	701	523	178	
Stewart's Point Rancheria, California	14	14	-	-	-	-	-	2	3	13	11	2	
Stockbridge, Wisconsin	194	62	129	-	3	-	-	2	154	42	38	4	
Sulphur Bank Rancheria, California	24	24	-	-	-	-	-	-	11	13	13	-	
Summit Lake, Nevada	...	...	...	...	...	...	...	...	...	...	...	...	...
Susanville, California	23	23	-	-	-	-	-	-	16	7	7	-	
Swinomish, Washington	99	99	-	-	-	-	-	7	46	60	50	10	
Sycuan, California	16	16	-	-	-	-	-	-	9	7	7	-	
Tama, Georgia	16	-	16	-	-	-	-	-	2	14	13	1	
Taos Pueblo, New Mexico	169	11	151	4	3	-	-	149	97	221	100	121	
Te-Moak, Nevada	29	-	29	-	-	-	-	-	9	20	4	16	
Tesuque Peublo, New Mexico	57	57	-	-	-	-	-	-	32	25	24	1	
Tigua, Texas	103	103	-	-	-	-	-	-	62	41	41	-	
Tonawanda, New York	131	131		-	-	-	-	4	98	37	32	5	
Torres-Martinez, California	-	-	-	-	-	-	-	-	-	-	-	-	
Trinidad Rancheria, California	18	18	-	-	-	-	-	-	16	2	1	1	
Tulalip, Washington	207	207	-	-	-	-	-	1	158	51	51	-	
Tule River, California	105	100	-	5	-	-	-	12	38	79	63	16	
Tunica-Biloxi, Louisiana	...	...	...	...	...	...	...	...	...	...	...	...	...
Tuolumne Rancheria, California	24	24	-	-	-	-	-	1	17	8	7	1	
Turtle Mountain, North Dakota	1,007	295	702	7	2	-	1	6	730	283	263	20	
Tuscarora, New York	-	-	-	-	-	-	-	-	-	-	-	-	
Twenty-Nine Palms, California	-	-	-	-	-	-	-	-	-	-	-	-	
Uintah and Ouray, Utah	526	486	40	-	-	-	-	1	314	213	187	26	
Umatilla, Oregon	269	162	107	-	-	-	-	-	209	60	47	13	
Upper Sioux Community, Minnesota	20	-	20	-	-	-	-	-	14	6	6	-	
Upper Skagit, Washington	-	-	-	-	-	-	-	-	-	-	-	-	
Ute Mountain, Colorado-New Mexico	291	180	106	3	2	-	-	3	66	228	156	72	
Vermillion Lake, Minnesota	32	-	32	-	-	-	-	-	14	18	13	5	
Viejas Rancheria, California	43	43	-	-	-	-	-	-	30	12	12	-	
Walker River, Nevada	147	147	-	-	-	-	-	1	92	56	32	24	
Wampanoag, Massachusetts	-	-	-	-	-	-	-	-	-	-	-	-	
Warm Springs, Oregon	476	428	36	-	12	-	-	1	325	152	107	45	
Washoe, Nevada	-	-	-	-	-	-	-	-	-	-	-	-	
Western Pequot, Connecticut	...	...	...	...	...	...	...	...	...	...	...	...	...
White Earth, Minnesota	735	220	514	-	-	-	2	7	542	200	176	24	
Wind River, Wyoming	997	224	770	-	2	-	1	6	584	420	313	106	
Winnebago, Nebraska	294	243	46	-	1	-	4	1	147	148	133	15	
Winnemucca Colony, Nevada	11	11	-	-	-	-	-	-	3	8	8	-	
Wisconsin Winnebago, Reservation	78	5	72	-	-	-	-	5	57	26	25	2	

[Continued]

★ 569 ★

Electric Lighting and Telephones in Occupied Housing Units on Reservations, 1980: Sauk Sauiattle - Zuni Pueblo

[Continued]

Identified reservation	Total	Electric lighting								Telephone			
		Yes							No	Yes	No		
		Public or private utility company	Rural electric cooperative	Bureau of Indian affairs electric system	Tribal system	Household generator	Other	No			Total	Within 1\4 mile	More than 1\4 mile
Woodfords Community, California	-	-	-	-	-	-	-	-	-	-	-	-	-
XL Ranch, California	...	...	...	...	...	...	...	...	...	...	...	...	...
Yakima, Washington	1,348	1,015	328	1	2	-	2	2	812	538	467	71	
Yankton, South Dakota	396	237	159	-	-	-	-	21	224	194	181	13	
Yavapai, Arizona	22	22	-	-	-	-	-	-	10	12	11	1	
Yerington, Nevada	31	31	-	-	-	-	-	-	17	14	14	-	
Yomba, Nevada	12	11	1	-	-	-	-	1	-	13	2	11	
Zia Pueblo, New Mexico	103	1	102	-	-	-	-	-	66	37	37	-	
Zuni Pueblo, New Mexico	1,073	83	978	1	10	-	1	28	699	401	336	65	
San Felipe/Santa Ana Joint Area, New Mexico	-	-	-	-	-	-	-	-	-	-	-	-	
San Felipe/Santo Domingo Joint Area, New Mexico	23	23	-	-	-	-	-	-	1	22	20	1	
Other Reservation Lands in Montana	-	-	-	-	-	-	-	-	-	-	-	-	

Source: U.S. Bureau of the Census, Subject Reports, PC80-2-1D, Part II, *American Indians, Eskimos, and Aleuts on Identified Reservations and in the Historic Areas of Oklahoma (Excluding Urbanized Areas)*, U.S. Government Printing Office, Washington, D.C., 1986, pp. 794-871. *Notes:* Three dots (...) means not applicable, or that the data are being withheld to avoid disclosure of information for individuals. A dash (-) represents zero or a percent which rounds to less than 0.1. Also, a dash (-) is used because the number of supplementary questionnaires for the reservations was insufficient to produce reliable estimates.

★ 570 ★

Exterior Wall Materials Used in Occupied Housing Units on Reservations, 1980: Acoma Pueblo - La Jolla

Data are the latest available.

Identified reservations	Occupied housing units								
	Total	Exterior wall materials used							
		Siding or shingles (wood or aluminum)	Brick, concrete, block, stone or stucco	Logs	Asphalt siding or tar paper	Cloth or tent	Mud, adobe, or sod	Metal	Other
American Indian, Eskimo, or Aleut householder or spouse	81,273	43,537	23,444	3,383	2,270	39	3,612	3,803	1,186
American Indian, Eskimo, or Aleut householder	77,709	41,056	22,805	3,321	2,210	39	3,583	3,543	1,152
Acoma Pueblo, New Mexico	465	70	247	-	-	-	105	30	13
Agua Caliente, California	-	-	-	-	-	-	-	-	-
Alabama-Coushatta, Texas	136	13	122	-	-	-	-	-	1
Alamo, New Mexico	209	33	75	2	6	-	69	8	15
Allegany, New York	328	295	13	-	7	-	-	11	1
Alturas Rancheria, California	5	...	...	...	...	...	...	...	...
Annette Islands Reserve, Alaska	262	239	-	-	3	-	-	20	-
Augustine, California	-	-	-	-	-	-	-	-	-
Bad River, Wisconsin	203	165	11	2	2	-	-	23	-
Barona Rancheria, California	67	17	48	-	-	-	3	-	-
Bay Mills, Michigan	77	47	1	-	5	-	-	23	1
Benton Paiute, California	7	...	...	...	...	...	...	...	...
Berry Creek Rancheria, California	-	-	-	-	-	-	-	-	-
Big Bend Rancheria, California	5	...	...	...	...	...	...	...	...
Big Cypress, Florida	93	45	46	-	-	-	-	-	2

[Continued]

★ 570 ★

Exterior Wall Materials Used in Occupied Housing Units on Reservations, 1980: Acoma Pueblo - La Jolla
[Continued]

Identified reservations	Total	Occupied housing units							
		Exterior wall materials used							
		Siding or shingles (wood or aluminum)	Brick, concrete, block, stone or stucco	Logs	Asphalt siding or tar paper	Cloth or tent	Mud, adobe, or sod	Metal	Other
Big Lagoon Rancheria, California	2	...	...	...	...	...	...	...	...
Big Pine Rancheria, California	76	14	61	-	-	-	-	1	-
Bishop Rancheria, California	240	78	130	-	2	-	-	26	5
Blackfeet, Montana	1,507	1,216	111	49	42	-	-	83	6
Bois Forte (Nett Lake), Minnesota	109	107	-	-	1	-	-	1	-
Bridgeport Colony, California	20	19	-	-	-	-	-	1	-
Brighton, Florida	75	7	61	-	1	-	-	5	-
Burns, Oregon	36	36	-	-	-	-	-	-	-
Cabazon, California	4	...	...	...	...	...	...	...	...
Cachil Dehe Rancheria, California	6	...	...	...	...	...	...	...	...
Cahuilla, California	14	8	1	-	-	-	-	-	5
Campo, California	29	21	3	-	2	-	-	2	-
Camp Verde, Arizona	46	1	40	-	-	-	-	-	5
Canoncito, New Mexico	215	53	114	-	10	-	28	10	-
Capitan Grande, California	-	-	-	-	-	-	-	-	-
Carson Colony, Nevada	65	60	3	-	3	-	-	-	-
Catawaba, South Carolina	275	210	54	-	2	-	-	9	-
Cattaraugus, New York	548	451	10	-	30	-	-	43	15
Cedarville Rancheria, California	4	...	...	...	...	...	...	...	...
Chehalis, Washington	55	48	-	-	-	-	-	7	-
Chemehuevi, California	10	2	8	-	-	-	-	-	-
Cheyenne River, South Dakota	329	269	16	3	15	-	-	19	8
Chitimacha, Louisiana	74	61	10	-	2	-	-	-	1
Cochiti Pueblo, New Mexico	150	1	128	-	-	-	20	-	-
Cocopah, Arizona	67	10	55	-	-	-	1	1	-
Coeur D'Alene, Idaho	171	127	2	1	4	-	-	35	2
Cold Springs Rancheria, California	13	12	1	-	-	-	-	-	-
Colorado River, Arizona-California	552	161	355	-	2	-	8	22	4
Colville, Washington	1,129	900	22	21	24	-	-	152	11
Cortina Rancheria, California	1	...	...	...	...	...	...	...	...
Coushatta, Louisiana	5	...	...	...	...	...	...	...	...
Coyote Valley Rancheria, California	-	-	-	-	-	-	-	-	-
Crow, Montana	833	741	19	12	11	-	-	37	13
Crow Creek, South Dakota	328	280	2	-	27	-	-	14	5
Cuyapaipe, California	1	...	...	...	...	...	...	...	...
Deer Creek, Minnesota	2	...	...	...	...	...	...	...	...
Dresslerville Colony, Nevada	34	15	1	-	4	-	-	13	-
Dry Creek Rancheria, California	9	...	...	...	...	...	...	...	...
Duck Valley, Idaho-Nevada	243	204	13	3	16	-	-	3	2
Duckwater, Nevada	27	24	2	-	-	-	-	1	-
Eastern Cherokee, North Carolina	1,473	786	565	18	9	-	-	66	29
Eastern Pequot, Connecticut	9	...	...	...	...	...	...	...	...
Ely Colony, Nevada	17	-	-	-	-	-	-	-	-
Enterprise Rancheria, California	2	...	...	...	...	...	...	...	...
Fallon Colony, Nevada	16	13	-	-	-	-	-	3	-
Fallon, Nevada	66	54	3	-	2	-	-	7	-
Flandreau, South Dakota	49	46	2	-	-	-	-	1	-
Flathead, Montana	1,279	1,037	69	42	31	-	-	93	7
Fond du Lac, Minnesota	172	152	-	-	3	-	-	17	-
Fort Apache, Arizona	1,483	1,146	255	9	13	-	3	26	33

[Continued]

★ 570 ★

Exterior Wall Materials Used in Occupied Housing Units on Reservations, 1980: Acoma Pueblo - La Jolla
[Continued]

Identified reservations	Occupied housing units								
		Exterior wall materials used							
	Total	Siding or shingles (wood or aluminum)	Brick, concrete, block, stone or stucco	Logs	Asphalt siding or tar paper	Cloth or tent	Mud, adobe, or sod	Metal	Other
Fort Belknap, Montana	452	390	5	12	17	-	-	25	3
Fort Berthold, North Dakota	632	580	14	4	7	-	-	26	1
Fort Bidwell, California	26	26	-	-	-	-	-	-	-
Fort Hall, Idaho	672	541	65	10	2	-	-	50	5
Fort Independence, California	17	14	1	-	-	-	-	1	-
Fort McDermitt, Nevada-California	94	82	1	-	5	-	-	5	-
Fort McDowell, Arizona	84	32	39	-	2	-	1	6	2
Fort Mojave, Arizona-California-Nevada	34	33	1	-	-	-	-	-	-
Fort Peck, Montana	1,103	931	79	10	27	-	-	48	7
Fort Totten, North Dakota	489	448	14	5	6	-	2	12	3
Fort Yuma, Arizona-California	339	67	220	2	1	-	6	37	7
Gila Bend, Arizona	-	-	-	-	-	-	-	-	-
Gila River, Arizona	1,612	437	660	1	2	1	431	52	27
Golden Hill, Connecticut	1	...	...	...	...	...	...	...	...
Goshute, Nevada-Utah	28	25	-	3	-	-	-	-	-
Grand Portage, Minnesota	78	71	3	1	2	-	-	-	-
Grindstone Creek Rancheria, California	17	14	-	-	-	-	-	3	-
Hannahville Community, Michigan	45	30	5	-	2	-	1	6	-
Hassanamisco, Massachusetts	1	...	...	...	...	...	...	...	...
Havasupai, Arizona	61	53	1	-	7	-	-	-	-
Hoh, Washington	14	10	-	1	-	-	-	3	-
Hollywood, Florida	125	47	78	-	-	-	-	-	-
Hoopa Valley, California	480	427	2	-	4	-	-	46	1
Hoopa Valley Extension, California	157	138	2	-	2	2	-	10	3
Hopi, Arizona	1,473	217	948	115	24	-	135	30	3
Hopland Rancheria, California	-	-	-	-	-	-	-	-	-
Hualapai, Arizona	160	49	99	-	1	-	1	8	2
Inaja-Cosmit, California	-	-	-	-	-	-	-	-	-
Indian Township, Maine	92	61	20	-	1	-	-	8	1
Iowa, Kansas-Nebraska	11	-	9	-	1	-	-	1	-
Isabella, Michigan	138	121	7	-	2	-	-	7	1
Isleta Pueblo, New Mexico	698	27	393	1	-	-	213	41	22
Jackson Rancheria, California	4	...	...	...	...	...	...	...	...
Jemez Pueblo, New Mexico	304	15	183	-	-	-	100	5	1
Jicarilla Apache, New Mexico	430	269	98	23	9	3	1	22	5
Kaibab, Arizona	25	17	8	-	-	-	-	-	-
Kalispel, Washington	21	18	3	-	-	-	-	-	-
Kickapoo, Kansas	103	47	54	-	-	-	-	2	-
Kootenai, Idaho	-	-	-	-	-	-	-	-	-
Lac Courte Oreilles, Wisconsin	304	278	-	9	3	-	-	14	-
Lac du Flambeau, Wisconsin	281	273	4	2	-	-	-	-	1
Laguna Pueblo, New Mexico	956	121	548	-	2	-	230	38	17
La Jolla, California	43	32	3	-	-	-	2	5	1

Source: U.S. Bureau of the Census, Subject Reports, PC80-2-1D, Part II, *American Indians, Eskimos, and Aleuts on Identified Reservations and in the Historic Areas of Oklahoma (Excluding Urbanized Areas)*, U.S. Government Printing Office, Washington, D.C., 1986, pp. 794-871. *Notes:* Three dots (...) means not applicable, or that the data are being withheld to avoid disclosure of information for individuals. A dash (-) represents zero or a percent which rounds to less than 0.1. Also, a dash (-) is used because the number of supplementary questionnaires for the reservations was insufficient to produce reliable estimates.

★ 571 ★

Exterior Wall Materials Used in Occupied Housing Units on Reservations, 1980: L'Anse - San Xavier

Data are the latest available.

Identified reservations	Total	Occupied housing units							
		Exterior wall materials used							
		Siding or shingles (wood or aluminum)	Brick, concrete block, stone, or stucco	Logs	Asphalt siding or tar paper	Cloth or tent	Mud, adobe, or sod	Metal	Other
L'Anse, Michigan	191	161	11	3	5	-	-	4	7
La Posta, California	1	...	...	...	...	...	...	...	...
Las Vegas Colony, Nevada	24	6	-	-	-	-	-	18	-
Laytonville Rancheria, California	26	26	-	-	-	-	-	-	-
Leech Lake, Minnesota	782	710	13	4	23	-	-	31	1
Likely Rancheria, California	-	-	-	-	-	-	-	-	-
Lone Pine Rancheria, California	56	14	41	-	-	-	-	1	-
Lookout Rancheria, California	3	...	...	...	...	...	...	...	...
Los Coyotes, California	17	14	3	-	-	-	-	-	-
Lovelock Colony, Nevada	37	28	4	-	-	-	-	5	-
Lower Brule, South Dakota	196	154	39	-	-	-	-	3	-
Lower Elwah, Washington	13	13	-	-	-	-	-	-	-
Lower Sioux Community, Minnesota	24	20	-	-	-	-	-	4	-
Lummi, Washington	306	273	5	-	1	-	-	27	-
Makah, Washington	271	258	-	-	-	-	-	8	5
Manchester Rancheria, California	20	20	-	-	-	-	-	-	-
Manzanita, California	5	...	...	...	...	...	...	...	...
Maricopa, Arizona	67	15	43	-	-	-	10	-	-
Mattaponi, Virgina	23	17	2	-	3	-	-	1	-
Menominee, Wisconsin	550	490	6	24	6	-	-	21	3
Mesa Grande, California	-	-	-	-	-	-	-	-	-
Mescalero Apache, New Mexico	449	168	253	4	2	-	13	3	6
Miccosukee, Florida	72	47	4	-	1	11	-	4	5
Middletown Rancheria, California	8	...	...	...	...	...	...	...	...
Mille Lacs, Minnesota	-	-	-	-	-	-	-	-	-
Mississippi Choctaw, Reservation	570	232	311	1	1	-	-	25	-
Moapa River, Nevada	43	-	38	-	2	-	-	1	2
Montgomery Creek Rancheria, California	1	...	...	...	...	...	...	...	...
Morongo, California	99	15	69	-	-	-	1	14	-
Muckleshoot, Washington	73	64	-	-	-	-	-	8	-
Nambe Pueblo, New Mexico	72	5	50	-	-	-	8	9	-
Navajo, Arizona-New Mexico-Utah	22,304	6,522	9,685	2,482	1,300	11	833	981	489
Nez Perce, Idaho	452	386	10	1	9	-	-	43	3
Nisqually, Washington	13	10	-	-	-	-	-	3	-
Nooksack, Washington	-	-	-	-	-	-	-	-	-
Northern Cheyenne, Montana	748	621	40	29	24	-	1	26	8
Oil Springs, New York	-	-	-	-	-	-	-	-	-
Omaha, Iowa-Nebraska	291	177	97	2	-	-	-	15	-
Oneida, Wisconsin	568	503	26	1	21	-	-	14	3
Onondaga, New York	-	-	-	-	-	-	-	-	-
Ontonagon, Michigan	-	-	-	-	-	-	-	-	-
Osage, Oklahoma	2,009	1,265	612	10	36	-	-	75	11
Ozette, Washington	2	...	...	...	...	...	...	...	...
Pala, California	145	72	46	-	-	-	4	22	1
Pamunkey, Virginia	27	24	3	-	-	-	-	-	-
Papago, Arizona	1,525	122	832	5	1	-	470	18	77
Pascua Yaqui, Arizona	81	1	72	-	-	-	6	-	2
Pauma, California	27	13	2	-	-	-	4	6	2
Payson Community of Yavapai-Apache, Arizona	-	-	-	-	-	-	-	-	-
Pechanga, California	34	32	1	-	-	-	1	-	-

[Continued]

★ 571 ★

Exterior Wall Materials Used in Occupied Housing Units on Reservations, 1980:
L'Anse - San Xavier
[Continued]

Identified reservations	Total	Occupied housing units							
		Exterior wall materials used							
		Siding or shingles (wood or aluminum)	Brick, concrete block, stone, or stucco	Logs	Asphalt siding or tar paper	Cloth or tent	Mud, adobe, or sod	Metal	Other
Penobscot, Maine	142	113	-	-	6	-	-	-	23
Picuris Pueblo, New Mexico	42	-	35	-	-	-	6	1	-
Pine Creek, Michigan	10	5	-	-	3	-	-	3	-
Pine Ridge, South Dakota	2,328	1,674	213	158	131	-	4	141	7
Pleasant Point, Maine	140	100	40	-	-	-	-	-	-
Pojoaque Pueblo, New Mexico	36	2	33	-	-	-	1	-	-
Poospatuck, New York	28	23	1	-	2	-	-	1	-
Port Gamble, Washington	76	69	-	-	-	-	-	7	-
Port Madison, Washington	63	51	5	1	1	-	-	5	-
Potawatomi, Wisconsin	46	45	-	-	-	-	-	1	-
Pottawatomi, Kansas	102	75	23	-	-	-	-	2	2
Prairie Island Community, Minnesota	20	20	-	-	-	-	-	-	-
Puyallup, Washington	279	244	13	-	7	-	-	12	3
Pyramid Lake, Nevada	206	178	17	-	8	-	-	1	1
Quileute, Washington	62	61	-	-	-	-	-	1	-
Quinault, Washington	255	224	-	2	-	-	-	24	5
Ramah Community, New Mexico	296	132	32	88	24	2	9	6	4
Ramona, California	-	-	-	-	-	-	-	-	-
Red Cliff, Wisconsin	152	124	-	7	-	-	-	20	-
Red Lake, Minnesota	680	625	9	11	8	-	1	22	4
Reno-Sparks Colony, Nevada	123	110	5	-	1	-	-	3	4
Resighini Rancheria, California	7	...	...	...	...	...	...	...	...
Rincon, California	83	30	43	-	-	-	8	2	-
Roaring Creek Rancheria, California	4	...	...	...	...	...	...	...	...
Rocky Boy's, Montana	318	281	14	7	12	-	-	4	-
Rosebud, South Dakota	1,368	1,201	71	20	7	-	-	60	9
Round Valley, California	168	135	2	-	-	-	-	31	-
Rumsey Rancheria, California	3	...	...	...	...	...	...	...	...
Sac and Fox, Iowa	104	99	-	-	-	-	-	5	-
Sac and Fox, Kansas-Nebraska	2	...	...	...	...	...	...	...	...
St. Croix, Wisconsin	101	87	2	9	2	-	-	1	-
St. Regis Mohawk, New York	513	464	3	-	5	-	-	39	1
Salt River, Arizona	585	151	282	-	5	-	94	26	27
San Carlos, Arizona	1,216	704	437	23	2	-	-	35	15
Sandia Pueblo, New Mexico	73	6	52	-	-	-	13	-	1
Sandy Lake, Minnesota	-	-	-	-	-	-	-	-	-
San Felipe Pueblo, New Mexico	282	-	157	-	-	-	108	16	1
San Ildefonso Pueblo, New Mexico	134	13	62	-	-	-	53	2	5
San Juan Pueblo, New Mexico	245	57	117	2	-	-	56	11	1
San Manuel, California	-	-	-	-	-	-	-	-	-
San Pasqual, California	47	38	4	-	-	-	-	-	4
Santa Ana Pueblo, New Mexico	98	1	66	-	-	-	31	-	-
Santa Clara Pueblo, New Mexico	424	20	317	-	-	-	82	2	4
Santa Rosa Rancheria, California	26	3	23	-	-	-	-	-	-
Santa Rosa, California	6	...	...	...	...	...	...	...	...
Santa Ynez, California	40	21	19	-	-	-	-	-	-
Santa Ysabel, California	59	53	4	-	-	-	-	1	-
Santee, Nebraska	102	88	6	-	-	-	2	6	-

[Continued]

899

★ 571 ★

Exterior Wall Materials Used in Occupied Housing Units on Reservations, 1980: L'Anse - San Xavier

[Continued]

Identified reservations	Occupied housing units								
		Exterior wall materials used							
	Total	Siding or shingles (wood or aluminum)	Brick, concrete block, stone, or stucco	Logs	Asphalt siding or tar paper	Cloth or tent	Mud, adobe, or sod	Metal	Other
Santo Domingo Pueblo, New Mexico	339	6	239	2	-	-	53	13	27
San Xavier, Arizona	186	-	148	-	-	-	29	6	2

Source: U.S. Bureau of the Census, Subject Reports, PC80-2-1D, Part II, *American Indians, Eskimos, and Aleuts on Identified Reservations and in the Historic Areas of Oklahoma (Excluding Urbanized Areas)*, U.S. Government Printing Office, Washington, D.C., 1986, pp. 794-871. *Notes:* Three dots (...) means not applicable, or that the data are being withheld to avoid disclosure of information for individuals. A dash (-) represents zero or a percent which rounds to less than 0.1. Also, a dash (-) is used because the number of supplementary questionnaires for the reservations was insufficient to produce reliable estimates.

★ 572 ★

Exterior Wall Materials Used in Occupied Housing Units on Reservations, 1980: Sauk-Sauiattle - Zuni Pueblo

Data are the latest available.

Identified reservations	Occupied housing units								
		Exterior wall materials used							
	Total	Siding or shingles (wood or aluminum)	Brick, concrete, block, stone, or stucco	Logs	Asphalt siding or tar paper	Cloth or tent	Mud, adobe, or sod	Metal	Other
Sauk-Sauiattle, Washington	-	-	-	-	-	-	-	-	-
Sault Ste. Marie, Michigan	-	-	-	-	-	-	-	-	-
Schaghti-Coke, Connecticut	3	...	...	...	...	...	...	...	...
Shakopee Community, Minnesota	27	27	-	-	-	-	-	-	-
Sheep Ranch Rancheria, California	1	...	...	...	...	...	...	...	...
Sherwood Valley Rancheria, California	7	...	...	...	...	...	...	...	...
Shingle Springs Rancheria, California	-	-	-	-	-	-	...	-	-
Shinnecock, New York	76	69	-	-	4	-	-	2	2
Shoalwater, Washington	11	8	-	-	-	-	-	1	1
Sisseton, North Dakota-South Dakota	635	342	270	-	10	-	-	11	2
Skokomish, Washington	80	74	-	-	1	-	-	5	-
Skull Valley, Utah	-	-	-	-	-	-	-	-	-
Soboba, California	71	30	40	-	-	-	1	-	-
Sokaogon Chippewa Community, Wisconsin	31	24	-	2	1	-	-	4	-
Southern Paiute, Utah	40	40	-	-	-	-	-	-	-
Southern Ute, Colorado	253	60	181	2	3	-	2	4	1
Spokane, Washington	336	301	1	5	2	-	-	24	3
Squaxin Island, Washington	9	...	...	...	...	...	...	...	...
Standing Rock, North Dakota-South Dakota	1,074	892	83	16	5	-	-	57	20
Stewart's Point Rancheria, California	16	10	-	-	-	-	-	6	-
Stockbridge, Wisconsin	195	140	17	4	6	-	-	26	2
Sulphur Bank Rancheria, California	24	24	-	-	-	-	-	-	-
Summit Lake, Nevada	7	...	...	...	...	...	...	...	...
Susanville, California	23	15	3	-	-	-	-	3	2

[Continued]

★ 572 ★

Exterior Wall Materials Used in Occupied Housing Units on Reservations, 1980: Sauk-Sauiattle - Zuni Pueblo

[Continued]

Identified reservations	Occupied housing units								
		Exterior wall materials used							
	Total	Siding or shingles (wood or aluminum)	Brick, concrete, block, stone, or stucco	Logs	Asphalt siding or tar paper	Cloth or tent	Mud, adobe, or sod	Metal	Other
Swinomish, Washington	106	99	1	-	-	-	-	6	-
Sycuan, California	16	11	5	-	-	-	-	-	-
Tama, Georgia	16	16	-	-	-	-	-	-	-
Taos Pueblo, New Mexico	318	9	87	-	-	-	218	3	1
Te-Moak, Nevada	29	29	-	-	-	-	-	-	-
Tesuque Peublo, New Mexico	57	-	45	-	-	-	9	-	3
Tigua, Texas	103	-	102	-	-	-	1	-	-
Tonawanda, New York	135	94	1	3	20	-	-	11	6
Torres-Martinez, California	-	-	-	-	-	-	-	-	-
Trinidad Rancheria, California	18	15	-	-	-	-	-	3	-
Tulalip, Washington	209	203	1	-	2	1	-	1	-
Tule River, California	117	88	29	-	-	-	-	-	-
Tunica-Biloxi, Louisiana	3	...	...	...	...	...	...	...	...
Tuolumne Rancheria, California	25	23	-	-	-	-	-	-	2
Turtle Mountain, North Dakota	1,013	821	83	4	6	2	-	95	4
Tuscarora, New York	-	-	-	-	-	-	-	-	-
Twenty-Nine Palms, California	-	-	-	-	-	-	-	-	-
Uintah and Ouray, Utah	528	377	103	1	14	-	5	19	9
Umatilla, Oregon	269	249	5	2	4	-	-	9	-
Upper Sioux Community, Minnesota	20	10	-	-	-	-	-	10	-
Upper Skagit, Washington	-	-	-	-	-	-	-	-	1
Ute Mountain, Colorado-New Mexico	294	214	75	-	2	-	-	1	1
Vermillion Lake, Minnesota	32	30	-	-	-	-	-	2	-
Viejas Rancheria, California	43	41	1	-	-	-	-	1	-
Walker River, Nevada	148	135	10	-	1	-	-	2	-
Wampanoag, Massachusetts	-	-	-	-	-	-	-	-	-
Warm Springs, Oregon	477	420	15	2	6	-	-	28	6
Washoe, Nevada	-	-	-	-	-	-	-	-	-
Western Pequot, Connecticut	7	...	...	...	...	...	...	...	...
White Earth, Minnesota	743	638	18	4	26	-	-	47	10
Wind River, Wyoming	1,004	726	66	72	54	3	-	73	10
Winnebago, Nebraska	295	122	163	-	1	-	1	8	-
Winnemucca Colony, Nevada	11	11	-	-	-	-	-	-	-
Wisconsin Winnebago, Reservation	83	75	-	-	-	-	-	8	-
Woodfords Community, California	-	-	-	-	-	-	-	-	-
XL Ranch, California	9	...	...	...	...	...	...	...	...
Yakima, Washington	1,350	1,189	118	-	18	-	-	21	4
Yankton, South Dakota	417	361	46	2	5	-	-	1	2
Yavapai, Arizona	22	14	8	-	-	-	-	-	-
Yerington, Nevada	31	31	-	-	-	-	-	-	-
Yomba, Nevada	13	1	10	1	-	-	-	1	-
Zia Pueblo, New Mexico	103	3	66	-	-	-	25	-	9
Zuni Pueblo, New Mexico	1,100	238	703	-	8	-	87	63	1
San Felipe/Santa Ana Joint Area, New Mexico	-	-	-	-	-	-	-	-	-

[Continued]

★ 572 ★

Exterior Wall Materials Used in Occupied Housing Units on Reservations, 1980: Sauk-Sauiattle - Zuni Pueblo

[Continued]

Identified reservations	Occupied housing units								
		Exterior wall materials used							
	Total	Siding or shingles (wood or aluminum)	Brick, concrete, block, stone, or stucco	Logs	Asphalt siding or tar paper	Cloth or tent	Mud, adobe, or sod	Metal	Other
San Felipe/Santo Domingo Joint Area, New Mexico	23	-	23	-	-	-	-	-	-
Other Reservation Lands in Montana	-	-	-	-	-	-	-	-	-

Source: U.S. Bureau of the Census, Subject Reports, PC80-2-1D, Part II, *American Indians, Eskimos, and Aleuts on Identified Reservations and in the Historic Areas of Oklahoma (Excluding Urbanized Areas),* U.S. Government Printing Office, Washington, D.C., 1986, pp. 794-871. *Notes:* Three dots (...) means not applicable, or that the data are being withheld to avoid disclosure of information for individuals. A dash (-) represents zero or a percent which rounds to less than 0.1. Also, a dash (-) is used because the number of supplementary questionnaires for the reservations was insufficient to produce reliable estimates.

★ 573 ★

Floor Materials in Occupied Housing Units on Reservations, 1980: Acoma Pueblo - La Jolla

Data are the latest available.

Identified reservation	Occupied housing units						
		Floor materials					
	Total	Wood	Asphalt, linoleum, or vinyl tiles	Stone, concrete, brick, clay or ceramic tile	Metal	Earth, gravel, or sand	Other
American Indian, Eskimo, or Aleut householder or spouse	81,273	33,200	26,438	15,177	725	4,839	894
American Indian, Eskimo, or Aleut householder	77,709	31,020	25,560	14,808	669	4,821	831
Acoma Pueblo, New Mexico	465	121	99	151	11	79	4
Agua Caliente, California	-	-	-	-	-	-	-
Alabama-Coushatta, Texas	136	13	91	32	-	-	-
Alamo, New Mexico	208	51	21	131	1	2	2
Allegany, New York	328	221	99	7	-	-	1
Alturas Rancheria, California	5	...	...	...	...	...	...
Annette Islands Reserve, Alaska	262	178	82	-	-	-	1
Augustine, California	-	-	-	-	-	-	-
Bad River, Wisconsin	203	70	122	11	-	-	-
Barona Rancheria, California	67	13	24	28	2	-	-
Bay Mills, Michigan	77	51	26	-	-	-	-
Benton Paiute, California	7	...	...	...	...	...	...
Berry Creek Rancheria, California	-	-	-	-	-	-	-
Big Bend Rancheria, California	5	...	...	...	...	...	...
Big Cypress, Florida	93	17	1	62	-	14	-
Big Lagoon Rancheria, California	2	...	...	...	...	...	...
Big Pine Rancheria, California	76	10	16	51	-	-	...

[Continued]

★ 573 ★

Floor Materials in Occupied Housing Units on Reservations, 1980: Acoma Pueblo - La Jolla
[Continued]

Identified reservation	Occupied housing units						
		Floor materials					
	Total	Wood	Asphalt, linoleum, or vinyl tiles	Stone, concrete, brick, clay or ceramic tile	Metal	Earth, gravel, or sand	Other
Bishop Rancheria, California	240	102	65	72	1	-	-
Blackfeet, Montana	1,507	672	790	28	-	-	16
Bois Forte (Nett Lake), Minnesota	109	15	93	-	-	-	1
Bridgeport Colony, California	20	19	1	-	-	-	-
Brighton, Florida	75	9	41	22	3	-	-
Burns, Oregon	36	30	6	-	-	-	-
Cabazon, California	4	...	...	...	...	...	...
Cachil Dehe Rancheria, California	6	...	...	...	...	...	...
Cahuilla, California	14	10	1	2	-	-	-
Campo, California	29	20	3	4	1	-	-
Camp Verde, Arizona	46	3	39	4	-	-	-
Canoncito, New Mexico	215	41	23	125	-	25	-
Capitan Grande, California	-	-	-	-	-	-	-
Carson Colony, Nevada	65	60	5	-	-	-	-
Catawaba, South Carolina	275	255	6	13	-	-	-
Cattaraugus, New York	548	486	19	37	3	-	4
Cedarville Rancheria, California	4	...	...	...	...	...	...
Chehalis, Washington	55	23	32	-	-	-	-
Chemehuevi, California	10	2	8	-	-	-	-
Cheyenne River, South Dakota	329	125	196	6	-	-	3
Chitimacha, Louisiana	74	18	56	-	-	-	-
Cochiti Pueblo, New Mexico	150	14	62	62	-	12	-
Cocopah, Arizona	67	4	38	21	-	4	-
Coeur D'Alene, Idaho	171	75	79	-	14	-	3
Cold Springs Rancheria, California	13	9	4	-	-	-	-
Colorado River, Arizona-California	552	90	243	211	8	-	1
Colville, Washington	1,129	956	119	9	33	-	12
Cortina Rancheria, California	1	...	...	...	...	...	...
Coushatta, Louisiana	5	...	...	...	...	...	...
Coyote Valley Rancheria, California	-	-	-	-	-	-	-
Crow, Montana	833	552	259	13	9	-	-
Crow Creek, South Dakota	328	22	291	13	-	-	2
Cuyapaipe, California	1	...	...	...	...	...	...
Deer Creek, Minnesota	2	...	...	...	...	...	...
Dresslerville Colony, Nevada	34	22	9	-	4	-	-
Dry Creek Rancheria, California	9	...	...	...	...	...	...
Duck Valley, Idaho-Nevada	243	66	174	2	-	1	-
Duckwater, Nevada	27	2	25	-	-	-	-
Eastern Cherokee, North Carolina	1,473	635	95	695	23	-	25
Eastern Pequot, Connecticut	9	...	...	...	...	...	...
Ely Colony, Nevada	17	16	1	-	-	-	-

[Continued]

★ 573 ★

Floor Materials in Occupied Housing Units on Reservations, 1980: Acoma Pueblo - La Jolla
[Continued]

Identified reservation	Occupied housing units						
		Floor materials					
	Total	Wood	Asphalt, linoleum, or vinyl tiles	Stone, concrete, brick, clay or ceramic tile	Metal	Earth, gravel, or sand	Other
Enterprise Rancheria, California	2	...	...	...	...	...	...
Fallon Colony, Nevada	16	3	13	-	-	-	-
Fallon, Nevada	66	18	42	2	3	-	-
Flandreau, South Dakota	49	13	35	1	-	-	-
Flathead, Montana	1,279	954	253	20	19	-	33
Fond du Lac, Minnesota	172	122	44	-	4	-	1
Fort Apache, Arizona	1,483	623	338	505	9	5	3
Fort Belknap, Montana	452	185	259	3	-	-	6
Fort Berthold, North Dakota	632	437	180	9	7	-	-
Fort Bidwell, California	26	24	2	-	-	-	-
Fort Hall, Idaho	672	526	104	24	16	1	1
Fort Independence, California	17	14	1	-	1	-	-
Fort McDermitt, Nevada-California	94	24	67	1	-	-	2
Fort McDowell, Arizona	84	18	11	49	5	1	-
Fort Mojave, Arizona-California-Nevada	34	-	33	1	-	-	-
Fort Peck, Montana	1,103	335	688	37	6	-	38
Fort Totten, North Dakota	489	210	182	96	-	2	-
Fort Yuma, Arizona-California	339	70	147	97	9	9	7
Gila Bend, Arizona	-	-	-	-	-	-	-
Gila River, Arizona	1,612	158	352	905	10	168	20
Golden Hill, Connecticut	1	...	...	...	...	...	...
Goshute, Nevada-Utah	28	26	-	2	-	-	-
Grand Portage, Minnesota	78	70	2	6	-	-	-
Grindstone Creek Rancheria, California	17	1	16	-	-	-	-
Hannahville Community, Michigan	45	42	-	1	-	-	1
Hassanamisco, Massachusetts	1	...	...	...	...	...	...
Havasupai, Arizona	61	6	50	5	-	-	-
Hoh, Washington	14	5	1	-	-	-	8
Hollywood, Florida	125	15	78	33	-	-	-
Hoopa Valley, California	480	267	191	5	1	-	16
Hoopa Valley Extension, California	157	97	54	1	3	2	-
Hopi, Arizona	1,473	475	230	578	5	180	6
Hopland Rancheria, California	-	-	-	-	-	-	-
Hualapai, Arizona	160	50	34	76	-	-	-
Inaja-Cosmit, California	-	-	-	-	-	-	-
Indian Township, Maine	92	75	9	4	3	-	-
Iowa, Kansas-Nebraska	11	10	1	-	-	-	-
Isabella, Michigan	138	74	50	13	1	-	-
Isleta Pueblo, New Mexico	698	143	26	355	20	151	3
Jackson Rancheria, California	4	...	...	...	...	...	...
Jemez Pueblo, New Mexico	304	29	7	88	-	180	-

[Continued]

★ 573 ★

Floor Materials in Occupied Housing Units on Reservations, 1980: Acoma Pueblo - La Jolla

[Continued]

| Identified reservation | Occupied housing units | | | | | | |
| | Total | Floor materials | | | | | |
		Wood	Asphalt, linoleum, or vinyl tiles	Stone, concrete, brick, clay or ceramic tile	Metal	Earth, gravel, or sand	Other
Jicarilla Apache, New Mexico	430	164	229	22	-	6	10
Kaibab, Arizona	25	24	-	1	-	-	-
Kalispel, Washington	21	17	2	1	-	-	1
Kickapoo, Kansas	103	95	5	-	3	-	-
Kootenai, Idaho	-	-	-	-	-	-	-
Lac Courte Oreilles, Wisconsin	304	192	108	1	-	-	2
Lac du Flambeau, Wisconsin	281	221	57	2	-	-	-
Laguna Pueblo, New Mexico	956	252	115	414	15	148	13
La Jolla, California	43	29	7	7	-	-	-

Source: U.S. Bureau of the Census, Subject Reports, PC80-2-1D, Part II, *American Indians, Eskimos, and Aleuts on Identified Reservations and in the Historic Areas of Oklahoma (Excluding Urbanized Areas)*, U.S. Government Printing Office, Washington, D.C., 1986, pp. 794-871. *Notes:* Three dots (...) means not applicable, or that the data are being withheld to avoid disclosure of information for individuals. A dash (-) represents zero or a percent which rounds to less than 0.1. Also, a dash (-) is used because the number of supplementary questionnaires for the reservations was insufficient to produce reliable estimates.

★ 574 ★

Floor Materials in Occupied Housing Units on Reservations, 1980: L'Anse - San Xavier

Data are the latest available.

| Identified reservations | Occupied housing units | | | | | | |
| | Total | Floor materials | | | | | |
		Wood	Asphalt, linoleum, or vinyl tiles	Stone, concrete, brick, clay, or ceramic tile	Metal	Earth, gravel, or sand	Other
L'Anse, Michigan	191	167	5	4	1	-	13
La Posta, California	1	...	...	...	...	...	...
Las Vegas Colony, Nevada	24	18	5	1	-	-	-
Laytonville Rancheria, California	26	-	24	2	-	-	-
Leech Lake, Minnesota	782	630	118	17	14	-	3
Likely Rancheria, California	-	-	-	-	-	-	-
Lone Pine Rancheria, California	56	29	1	26	-	-	-
Lookout Rancheria, California	3	...	...	...	...	...	...
Los Coyotes, California	17	11	1	-	2	-	3
Lovelock Colony, Nevada	37	11	26	-	-	-	-
Lower Brule, South Dakota	196	21	167	-	-	-	8
Lower Elwah, Washington	13	13	-	-	-	-	-
Lower Sioux Community, Minnesota	24	18	-	-	6	-	-
Lummi, Washington	306	167	131	1	2	-	4

[Continued]

★ 574 ★

Floor Materials in Occupied Housing Units on Reservations, 1980: L'Anse - San Xavier
[Continued]

Identified reservations	Occupied housing units						
		Floor materials					
	Total	Wood	Asphalt, linoleum, or vinyl tiles	Stone, concrete, brick, clay, or ceramic tile	Metal	Earth, gravel, or sand	Other
Makah, Washington	271	155	105	-	2	-	8
Manchester Rancheria, California	20	20	-	-	-	-	-
Manzanita, California	5	...	...	...	...	...	...
Maricopa, Arizona	67	5	36	19	-	7	-
Mattaponi, Virgina	23	20	1	-	2	-	-
Menominee, Wisconsin	550	342	187	6	14	-	-
Mesa Grande, California	-	-	-	-	-	-	-
Mescalero Apache, New Mexico	449	131	212	102	-	-	4
Miccosukee, Florida	72	43	8	12	-	9	-
Middletown Rancheria, California	8	...	...	...	...	...	...
Mille Lacs, Minnesota	-	-	-	-	-	-	-
Mississippi Choctaw, Reservation	570	156	306	100	7	-	1
Moapa River, Nevada	43	-	37	6	-	-	-
Montgomery Creek Rancheria, California	1	...	...	...	...	...	...
Morongo, California	99	41	22	34	-	-	2
Muckleshoot, Washington	73	65	5	-	2	-	1
Nambe Pueblo, New Mexico	72	16	29	25	1	1	-
Navajo, Arizona-New Mexico-Utah	22,304	5,397	7,770	5,880	171	2,865	220
Nez Perce, Idaho	452	206	196	33	7	-	10
Nisqually, Washington	13	-	-	-	-	-	-
Nooksack, Washington	-	-	-	-	-	-	-
Northern Cheyenne, Montana	748	230	501	11	1	1	5
Oil Springs, New York	-	-	-	-	-	-	-
Omaha, Iowa-Nebraska	291	189	69	33	-	-	-
Oneida, Wisconsin	568	461	52	44	9	-	2
Onondaga, New York	-	-	-	-	-	-	-
Ontonagon, Michigan	-	-	-	-	-	-	-
Osage, Oklahoma	2,009	1,520	130	314	33	-	12
Ozette, Washington	2	...	...	...	...	...	...
Pala, California	145	64	55	25	2	-	1
Pamunkey, Virginia	27	22	5	-	-	-	-
Papago, Arizona	1,525	49	341	673	11	410	41
Pascua Yaqui, Arizona	81	-	17	62	-	2	-
Pauma, California	27	11	16	-	-	-	-
Payson Community of Yavapai-Apache, Arizona	-	-	-	-	-	-	-
Pechanga, California	34	30	2	2	-	-	-
Penobscot, Maine	142	83	-	59	-	-	-
Picuris Pueblo, New Mexico	42	10	6	26	-	-	-
Pine Creek, Michigan	10	5	3	-	3	-	-
Pine Ridge, South Dakota	2,328	1,410	860	42	10	-	7
Pleasant Point, Maine	140	116	2	20	-	-	1

[Continued]

★ 574 ★

Floor Materials in Occupied Housing Units on Reservations, 1980: L'Anse - San Xavier

[Continued]

Identified reservations	Occupied housing units						
		Floor materials					
	Total	Wood	Asphalt, linoleum, or vinyl tiles	Stone, concrete, brick, clay, or ceramic tile	Metal	Earth, gravel, or sand	Other
Pojoaque Pueblo, New Mexico	36	4	4	29	-	-	-
Poospatuck, New York	28	19	7	-	-	-	1
Port Gamble, Washington	76	65	10	-	1	-	-
Port Madison, Washington	63	56	4	1	3	-	-
Potawatomi, Wisconsin	46	19	26	1	-	-	-
Pottawatomi, Kansas	102	78	9	2	13	-	-
Prairie Island Community, Minnesota	20	5	15	-	-	-	-
Puyallup, Washington	279	239	29	8	-	-	3
Pyramid Lake, Nevada	206	118	60	22	7	-	-
Quileute, Washington	62	52	10	-	-	-	-
Quinault, Washington	255	58	180	1	1	-	14
Ramah Community, New Mexico	296	135	98	19	1	41	1
Ramona, California	-	-	-	-	-	-	-
Red Cliff, Wisconsin	152	144	8	-	-	-	-
Red Lake, Minnesota	680	305	357	7	5	-	7
Reno-Sparks Colony, Nevada	123	98	22	1	1	-	-
Resighini Rancheria, California	7	...	...	...	...	...	...
Rincon, California	83	27	39	16	-	-	-
Roaring Creek Rancheria, California	4	...	...	...	...	...	...
Rocky Boy's, Montana	318	21	285	7	2	-	2
Rosebud, South Dakota	1,368	874	446	20	3	2	23
Round Valley, California	168	43	125	-	-	-	-
Rumsey Rancheria, California	3	...	...	...	...	...	...
Sac and Fox, Iowa	104	82	19	3	-	-	-
Sac and Fox, Kansas-Nebraska	2	...	...	...	...	...	...
St. Croix, Wisconsin	101	60	41	-	-	-	-
St. Regis Mohawk, New York	513	226	282	2	2	-	1
Salt River, Arizona	585	119	171	208	15	71	1
San Carlos, Arizona	1,216	634	113	446	9	7	8
Sandia Pueblo, New Mexico	73	3	12	47	-	8	2
Sandy Lake, Minnesota	-	-	-	-	-	-	-
San Felipe Pueblo, New Mexico	282	1	238	36	1	5	-
San Ildefonso Pueblo, New Mexico	134	39	28	41	8	10	8
San Juan Pueblo, New Mexico	245	63	33	118	1	28	2
San Manuel, California	-	-	-	-	-	-	-
San Pasqual, California	47	37	5	1	1	-	2
Santa Ana Pueblo, New Mexico	98	4	41	32	-	22	-
Santa Clara Pueblo, New Mexico	424	71	61	262	-	30	-
Santa Rosa Rancheria, California	26	7	11	7	-	-	-
Santa Rosa, California	6	...	...	...	...	...	...
Santa Ynez, California	40	8	12	20	-	-	-

[Continued]

★ 574 ★

Floor Materials in Occupied Housing Units on Reservations, 1980: L'Anse - San Xavier

[Continued]

Identified reservations	Occupied housing units						
	Total	Floor materials					
		Wood	Asphalt, linoleum, or vinyl tiles	Stone, concrete, brick, clay, or ceramic tile	Metal	Earth, gravel, or sand	Other
Santa Ysabel, California	59	56	-	3	-	-	-
Santee, Nebraska	102	32	51	13	1	2	3
Santo Domingo Pueblo, New Mexico	339	13	179	38	-	93	15
San Xavier, Arizona	186	7	28	147	-	4	-

Source: U.S. Bureau of the Census, Subject Reports, PC80-2-1D, Part II, *American Indians, Eskimos, and Aleuts on Identified Reservations and in the Historic Areas of Oklahoma (Excluding Urbanized Areas)*, U.S. Government Printing Office, Washington, D.C., 1986, pp. 794-871. *Notes:* Three dots (...) means not applicable, or that the data are being withheld to avoid disclosure of information for individuals. A dash (-) represents zero or a percent which rounds to less than 0.1. Also, a dash (-) is used because the number of supplementary questionnaires for the reservations was insufficient to produce reliable estimates.

★ 575 ★

Floor Materials in Occupied Housing Units on Reservations, 1980: Sauk-Sauiattle - Zuni Pueblo

Data are the latest available.

Identified reservation	Occupied housing units						
	Total	Floor materials					
		Wood	Asphalt, linoleum, or vinyl tiles	Stone, concrete, brick, clay or ceramic tile	Metal	Earth, gravel, or sand	Other
Sauk-Sauiattle, Washington	-	-	-	-	-	-	-
Sault Ste. Marie, Michigan	-	-	-	-	-	-	-
Schaghti-Coke, Connecticut	3	...	...	...	...	...	...
Shakopee Community, Minnesota	27	27	-	-	-	-	-
Sheep Ranch Rancheria, California	1	...	...	...	...	...	...
Sherwood Valley Rancheria, California	7	...	...	...	...	...	...
Shingle Springs Rancheria, California	-	-	-	-	-	-	-
Shinnecock, New York	76	72	2	-	-	-	2
Shoalwater, Washington	11	7	2	1	-	-	-
Sisseton, North Dakota-South Dakota	635	319	283	28	4	-	2
Skokomish, Washington	80	54	24	1	1	-	-
Skull Valley, Utah	-	-	-	-	-	-	-
Soboba, California	71	30	22	18	-	-	1
Sokaogon Chippewa Community, Wisconsin	31	19	10	-	1	-	1
Southern Paiute, Utah	40	39	1	-	-	-	-
Southern Ute, Colorado	253	103	135	11	-	2	2
Spokane, Washington	336	321	9	2	4	-	-
Squaxin Island, Washington	9	...	...	...	...	...	...
Standing Rock, North Dakota-South Dakota	1,074	882	158	15	8	-	11

[Continued]

★ 575 ★

Floor Materials in Occupied Housing Units on Reservations, 1980: Sauk-Suiattle - Zuni Pueblo
[Continued]

Identified reservation	Occupied housing units						
		Floor materials					
	Total	Wood	Asphalt, linoleum, or vinyl tiles	Stone, concrete, brick, clay or ceramic tile	Metal	Earth, gravel, or sand	Other
Stewart's Point Rancheria, California	16	7	6	3	-	-	-
Stockbridge, Wisconsin	195	132	47	17	-	-	-
Sulphur Bank Rancheria, California	24	19	5	-	-	-	-
Summit Lake, Nevada	7	...	...	...	...	...	...
Susanville, California	23	2	18	-	-	-	3
Swinomish, Washington	106	21	85	-	-	-	-
Sycuan, California	16	5	9	2	-	-	-
Tama, Georgia	16	14	2	-	-	-	-
Taos Pueblo, New Mexico	318	35	119	45	6	101	12
Te-Moak, Nevada	29	3	26	-	-	-	-
Tesuque Peublo, New Mexico	57	17	3	31	-	6	-
Tigua, Texas	103	1	102	-	-	-	-
Tonawanda, New York	135	125	7	2	-	-	-
Torres-Martinez, California	-	-	-	-	-	-	-
Trinidad Rancheria, California	18	15	-	3	-	-	-
Tulalip, Washington	209	126	69	13	-	1	-
Tule River, California	117	59	7	49	2	-	-
Tunica-Biloxi, Louisiana	3	...	...	...	...	...	...
Tuolumne Rancheria, California	25	23	2	-	-	-	-
Turtle Mountain, North Dakota	1,013	393	581	12	11	-	18
Tuscarora, New York	-	-	-	-	-	-	-
Twenty-Nine Palms, California	-	-	-	-	-	-	-
Uintah and Ouray, Utah	528	176	345	6	-	-	1
Umatilla, Oregon	269	60	191	11	4	-	3
Upper Sioux Community, Minnesota	20	20	-	-	-	-	-
Upper Skagit, Washington	-	-	-	-	-	-	-
Ute Mountain, Colorado-New Mexico	294	74	127	92	-	-	-
Vermillion Lake, Minnesota	32	4	28	-	-	-	-
Viejas Rancheria, California	43	34	5	2	1	-	-
Walker River, Nevada	148	46	98	4	-	-	-
Wampanoag, Massachusetts	-	-	-	-	-	-	-
Warm Springs, Oregon	477	359	92	6	16	-	4
Washoe, Nevada	-	-	-	-	-	-	-
Western Pequot, Connecticut	7	...	...	...	...	...	...
White Earth, Minnesota	743	575	100	22	16	-	30
Wind River, Wyoming	1,004	542	410	37	8	-	7
Winnebago, Nebraska	295	132	126	36	-	1	-
Winnemucca Colony, Nevada	11	10	1	-	-	-	-
Wisconsin Winnebago, Reservation	83	9	74	-	-	-	-
Woodfords Community, California	-	-	-	-	-	-	-
XL Ranch, California	9	...	...	...	...	...	...

[Continued]

★ 575 ★

Floor Materials in Occupied Housing Units on Reservations, 1980: Sauk-Sauiattle - Zuni Pueblo

[Continued]

Identified reservation	Occupied housing units						
		Floor materials					
	Total	Wood	Asphalt, linoleum, or vinyl tiles	Stone, concrete, brick, clay or ceramic tile	Metal	Earth, gravel, or sand	Other
Yakima, Washington	1,350	729	504	32	6	-	79
Yankton, South Dakota	417	115	283	4	-	-	15
Yavapai, Arizona	22	6	7	9	-	-	-
Yerington, Nevada	31	31	-	-	-	-	-
Yomba, Nevada	13	5	7	1	-	-	-
Zia Pueblo, New Mexico	103	3	4	55	-	40	1
Zuni Pueblo, New Mexico	1,100	386	351	270	6	77	12
San Felipe/Santa Ana Joint Area, New Mexico	-	-	-	-	-	-	-
San Felipe/Santo Domingo Joint Area, New Mexico	23	-	4	19	-	-	-
Other Reservation Lands in Montana	-	-	-	-	-	-	-

Source: U.S. Bureau of the Census, Subject Reports, PC80-2-1D, Part II, *American Indians, Eskimos, and Aleuts on Identified Reservations and in the Historic Areas of Oklahoma (Excluding Urbanized Areas),* U.S. Government Printing Office, Washington, D.C., 1986, pp. 794-871. *Notes:* Three dots (...) means not applicable, or that the data are being withheld to avoid disclosure of information for individuals. A dash (-) represents zero or a percent which rounds to less than 0.1. Also, a dash (-) is used because the number of supplementary questionnaires for the reservations was insufficient to produce reliable estimates.

★ 576 ★

Heating Equipment in Occupied Housing Units on Reservations, 1980: Acoma Pueblo - La Jolla

Data are the latest available.

Identified reservation	Occupied housing units									
		Heating equipment								
	Total	Steam or hot water	Central warm air furnace	Electric heat pump	Other built-in electric units	Floor, wall or pipeless furnace	Room heaters with flue	Room heaters without flue	Fireplaces, stoves, or portable room heaters	None
American Indian, Eskimo, or Aleut householder or spouse	81,273	1,886	23,713	2,072	8,421	1,371	11,276	3,341	28,299	894
American Indian, Eskimo, or Aleut householder	77,709	1,794	22,213	1,959	8,015	1,228	10,738	3,184	27,701	877
Acoma Pueblo, New Mexico	465	4	113	-	3	-	81	11	253	-
Agua Caliente, California	-	-	-	-	-	-	-	-	-	-
Alabama-Coushatta, Texas	136	-	87	-	-	-	41	-	8	-
Alamo, New Mexico	208	-	7	-	-	19	17	3	158	4
Allegany, New York	328	129	102	7	13	9	34	7	26	-
Alturas Rancheria, California	5	...	...	...	...	...	...	...	...	...
Annette Islands Reserve, Alaska	262	24	58	21	77	-	25	8	47	-
Augustine, California	-	-	-	-	-	-	-	-	-	-
Bad River, Wisconsin	203	-	132	-	11	1	23	10	16	-
Barona Rancheria, California	67	-	38	1	3	-	3	1	19	1
Bay Mills, Michigan	77	-	3	-	-	2	6	38	27	1
Benton Paiute, California	7	...	...	...	...	...	...	...	...	...
Berry Creek Rancheria, California	-	-	-	-	-	-	-	-	-	-
Big Bend Rancheria, California	5	...	...	...	...	...	...	...	...	...
Big Cypress, Florida	93	-	16	2	1	1	12	-	12	48

[Continued]

★ 576 ★

Heating Equipment in Occupied Housing Units on Reservations, 1980: Acoma Pueblo - La Jolla
[Continued]

Identified reservation	Total	Occupied housing units								
		Heating equipment								
		Steam or hot water	Central warm air furnace	Electric heat pump	Other built-in electric units	Floor, wall or pipeless furnace	Room heaters with flue	Room heaters without flue	Fireplaces, stoves, or portable room heaters	None
Big Lagoon Rancheria, California	2	...	...	...	...	...	...	...	...	...
Big Pine Rancheria, California	76	-	53	-	-	-	11	2	10	-
Bishop Rancheria, California	240	3	72	3	5	-	43	3	110	2
Blackfeet, Montana	1,507	135	395	78	240	32	290	104	224	10
Bois Forte (Nett Lake), Minnesota	109	-	83	-	7	-	13	-	6	-
Bridgeport Colony, California	20	-	20	-	-	-	-	-	-	-
Brighton, Florida	75	-	24	-	1	1	20	6	18	4
Burns, Oregon	36	-	1	-	11	-	2	1	21	-
Cabazon, California	4	...	...	...	...	...	...	...	...	...
Cachil Dehe Rancheria, California	6	...	...	...	...	...	...	...	...	...
Cahuilla, California	14	-	-	-	-	-	9	-	5	-
Campo, California	29	-	1	2	2	-	1	-	22	-
Camp Verde, Arizona	46	-	1	-	-	-	39	-	3	3
Canoncito, New Mexico	215	2	28	-	6	1	23	5	150	-
Capitan Grande, California	-	-	-	-	-	-	-	-	-	-
Carson Colony, Nevada	65	1	51	-	1	-	4	-	8	-
Catawaba, South Carolina	275	1	112	10	18	6	76	19	33	-
Cattaraugus, New York	548	58	211	5	31	7	138	63	35	-
Cedarville Rancheria, California	4	...	...	...	...	...	...	...	...	...
Chehalis, Washington	55	-	12	1	30	-	2	1	9	-
Chemehuevi, California	10	-	4	-	-	-	6	-	-	-
Cheyenne River, South Dakota	329	1	119	12	56	5	49	16	70	-
Chitimacha, Louisiana	74	-	53	-	-	3	2	15	1	-
Cochiti Pueblo, New Mexico	150	-	90	-	2	3	36	4	16	-
Cocopah, Arizona	67	5	38	1	-	-	9	-	9	5
Coeur D'Alene, Idaho	171	-	50	7	67	4	15	3	25	-
Cold Springs Rancheria, California	13	-	-	-	-	1	-	-	12	-
Colorado River, Arizona-California	552	5	320	52	16	14	51	10	61	23
Colville, Washington	1,129	-	348	30	413	9	62	24	243	-
Cortina Rancheria, California	1	...	...	...	...	...	...	...	...	...
Coushatta, Louisiana	5	...	...	...	...	...	...	...	...	...
Coyote Valley Rancheria, California	-	-	-	-	-	-	-	-	-	-
Crow, Montana	833	4	455	4	29	38	126	43	135	-
Crow Creek, South Dakota	328	4	118	18	87	-	79	16	4	1
Cuyapaipe, California	1	...	...	...	...	...	...	...	...	...
Deer Creek, Minnesota	2	...	...	...	...	...	...	...	...	...
Dresslerville Colony, Nevada	34	3	22	-	1	-	-	-	8	-
Dry Creek Rancheria, California	9	...	...	...	...	...	...	...	...	...
Duck Valley, Idaho-Nevada	243	2	23	1	66	-	30	52	67	1
Duckwater, Nevada	27	-	20	-	-	-	5	-	2	-
Eastern Cherokee, North Carolina	1,473	2	325	13	69	2	270	85	704	2
Eastern Pequot, Connecticut	9	...	...	...	...	...	...	...	...	...
Ely Colony, Nevada	17	-	-	-	3	1	12	-	1	-
Enterprise Rancheria, California	2	...	...	...	...	...	...	...	...	...
Fallon Colony, Nevada	16	-	1	-	1	-	3	7	4	-
Fallon, Nevada	66	-	17	3	19	-	11	6	7	2
Flandreau, South Dakota	49	-	43	1	-	-	3	2	-	-
Flathead, Montana	1,279	22	417	30	181	29	125	76	398	-
Fond du Lac, Minnesota	172	1	135	-	2	1	19	3	10	-
Fort Apache, Arizona	1,483	4	403	14	124	21	303	43	552	18
Fort Belknap, Montana	452	6	267	30	46	1	51	13	37	1
Fort Berthold, North Dakota	632	26	359	25	99	11	69	19	23	3
Fort Bidwell, California	26	-	1	-	16	-	-	-	9	-

[Continued]

★ 576 ★

Heating Equipment in Occupied Housing Units on Reservations, 1980: Acoma Pueblo - La Jolla
[Continued]

Identified reservation	Total	Occupied housing units								
		Heating equipment								
		Steam or hot water	Central warm air furnace	Electric heat pump	Other built-in electric units	Floor, wall or pipeless furnace	Room heaters with flue	Room heaters without flue	Fireplaces, stoves, or portable room heaters	None
Fort Hall, Idaho	672	-	121	63	175	21	138	47	105	1
Fort Independence, California	17	-	9	-	-	-	4	-	4	-
Fort McDermitt, Nevada-California	94	-	17	2	34	1	9	4	25	1
Fort McDowell, Arizona	84	-	29	4	5	1	11	3	26	5
Fort Mojave, Arizona-California-Nevada	34	-	4	1	-	-	1	-	28	-
Fort Peck, Montana	1,103	31	622	34	110	49	200	26	25	4
Fort Totten, North Dakota	489	3	95	33	207	1	123	10	13	4
Fort Yuma, Arizona-California	339	5	126	44	36	-	39	5	68	17
Gila Bend, Arizona	-	-	-	-	-	-	-	-	-	-
Gila River, Arizona	1,612	12	394	95	114	11	125	95	700	67
Golden Hill, Connecticut	1	...	...	...	...	...	...	...	...	...
Goshute, Nevada-Utah	28	-	-	-	2	-	3	-	23	-
Grand Portage, Minnesota	78	5	33	-	2	-	2	21	15	-
Grindstone Creek Rancheria, California	17	-	-	1	5	-	1	-	10	-
Hannahville Community, Michigan	45	3	10	-	-	5	5	2	18	1
Hassanamisco, Massachusetts	1	...	...	...	...	...	...	...	...	...
Havasupai, Arizona	61	-	-	-	34	3	2	1	19	1
Hoh, Washington	14	-	1	1	11	-	-	-	-	-
Hollywood, Florida	125	1	29	-	56	-	3	3	3	30
Hoopa Valley, California	480	-	39	13	21	2	51	14	339	-
Hoopa Valley Extension, California	157	-	9	2	9	3	2	4	120	7
Hopi, Arizona	1,473	22	94	34	20	3	84	32	1,178	6
Hopland Rancheria, California	-	-	-	-	-	-	-	-	-	-
Hualapai, Arizona	160	1	36	1	2	1	21	5	92	1
Inaja-Cosmit, California	-	-	-	-	-	-	-	-	-	-
Indian Township, Maine	92	2	70	-	6	-	2	-	10	-
Iowa, Kansas-Nebraska	11	-	8	-	-	-	1	-	2	-
Isabella, Michigan	138	6	46	2	2	2	49	11	19	-
Isleta Pueblo, New Mexico	698	-	248	2	6	7	265	39	129	1
Jackson Rancheria, California	4	...	...	...	...	...	...	...	...	...
Jemez Pueblo, New Mexico	304	1	81	-	2	-	16	11	192	-
Jicarilla Apache, New Mexico	430	16	236	3	11	3	60	5	93	5
Kaibab, Arizona	25	-	5	-	13	-	-	-	7	-
Kalispel, Washington	21	-	6	3	-	-	5	1	6	-
Kickapoo, Kansas	103	2	83	-	-	1	7	-	9	-
Kootenai, Idaho	-	-	-	-	-	-	-	-	-	-
Lac Courte Oreilles, Wisconsin	304	9	191	2	-	4	52	10	37	-
Lac du Flambeau, Wisconsin	281	11	195	2	10	4	23	20	15	-
Laguna Pueblo, New Mexico	956	5	449	4	15	6	195	87	195	1
La Jolla, California	43	-	1	2	2	-	3	3	25	6

Source: U.S. Bureau of the Census, Subject Reports, PC80-2-1D, Part II, *American Indians, Eskimos, and Aleuts on Identified Reservations and in the Historic Areas of Oklahoma (Excluding Urbanized Areas)*, U.S. Government Printing Office, Washington, D.C., 1986, pp. 794-871. *Notes:* Three dots (...) means not applicable, or that the data are being withheld to avoid disclosure of information for individuals. A dash (-) represents zero or a percent which rounds to less than 0.1. Also, a dash (-) is used because the number of supplementary questionnaires for the reservations was insufficient to produce reliable estimates.

Heating Equipment in Occupied Housing Units on Reservations, 1980: L'Anse - San Xavier

Data are the latest available.

Identified reservation	Occupied housing units	Occupied housing units								
		Heating equipment								
	Occupied housing units	Steam or hot water	Central warm air furnace	Electric heat pump	Other built-in electric units	Floor, wall or pipeless furnace	Room heaters with flue	Room heaters without flue	Fireplaces, stoves, or portable room heaters	None
L'Anse, Michigan	191	29	102	-	6	5	18	6	25	-
La Posta, California	1	...	...	...	...	...	...	...	...	...
Las Vegas Colony, Nevada	24	-	3	1	5	1	9	4	1	-
Laytonville Rancheria, California	26	-	-	-	3	-	3	1	19	-
Leech Lake, Minnesota	782	25	336	7	113	38	68	13	182	-
Likely Rancheria, California	-	-	-	-	-	-	-	-	-	-
Lone Pine Rancheria, California	56	-	32	-	-	-	10	-	14	-
Lookout Rancheria, California	3	...	...	...	...	...	...	...	...	...
Los Coyotes, California	17	-	-	3	-	1	7	-	6	-
Lovelock Colony, Nevada	37	-	13	-	-	-	9	-	15	-
Lower Brule, South Dakota	196	29	124	-	22	2	17	-	2	-
Lower Elwah, Washington	13	-	2	-	5	-	-	1	5	-
Lower Sioux Community, Minnesota	24	-	8	-	-	-	14	2	-	-
Lummi, Washington	306	1	36	11	137	2	50	9	58	2
Makah, Washington	271	-	51	24	138	-	10	10	38	-
Manchester Rancheria, California	20	2	1	-	-	1	2	-	13	1
Manzanita, California	5	...	...	...	...	...	...	...	...	...
Maricopa, Arizona	67	-	40	2	-	2	7	-	14	1
Mattaponi, Virgina	23	1	10	1	2	-	6	1	1	-
Menominee, Wisconsin	550	5	397	4	11	1	88	12	33	-
Mesa Grande, California	-	-	-	-	-	-	-	-	-	-
Mescalero Apache, New Mexico	449	1	338	-	40	2	30	6	32	-
Miccosukee, Florida	72	-	4	-	11	2	1	1	-	53
Middletown Rancheria, California	8	...	...	...	...	...	...	...	...	...
Mille Lacs, Minnesota	-	-	-	-	-	-	-	-	-	-
Mississippi Choctaw, Reservation	570	8	218	7	66	2	98	72	94	5
Moapa River, Nevada	43	-	-	39	3	-	-	-	1	-
Montgomery Creek Rancheria, California	1	...	...	...	...	...	...	...	...	...
Morongo, California	99	-	48	1	-	20	12	3	10	4
Muckleshoot, Washington	73	-	15	2	9	2	7	5	30	3
Nambe Pueblo, New Mexico	72	3	46	6	-	-	8	-	9	-
Navajo, Arizona-New Mexico-Utah	22,304	343	3,262	356	1,065	153	2,271	547	14,076	230
Nez Perce, Idaho	452	1	87	18	198	18	34	3	89	3
Nisqually, Washington	13	-	-	1	1-	-	1	-	1	-
Nooksack, Washington	-	-	-	-	-	-	-	-	-	-
Northern Cheyenne, Montana	748	29	411	18	101	6	53	17	112	1
Oil Springs, New York	-	-	-	-	-	-	-	-	-	-
Omaha, Iowa-Nebraska	291	1	162	-	9	9	81	11	18	-
Oneida, Wisconsin	568	48	363	1	11	6	85	25	28	1
Onondaga, New York	-	-	-	-	-	-	-	-	-	-
Ontonagon, Michigan	-	-	-	-	-	-	-	-	-	-
Osage, Oklahoma	2,009	16	897	30	66	296	302	256	144	1
Ozette, Washington	2	...	...	...	...	...	...	...	...	...
Pala, California	145	-	43	2	10	7	39	9	25	10
Pamunkey, Virginia	27	-	13	-	1	-	12	-	1	-
Papago, Arizona	1,525	8	171	28	21	13	168	73	1,003	41
Pascua Yaqui, Arizona	81	1	36	-	-	4	2	5	33	-
Pauma, California	27	-	2	-	-	4	1	2	16	1
Payson Community of Yavapai-Apache, Arizona	-	-	-	-	-	-	-	-	-	-
Pechanga, California	34	-	7	-	-	3	3	1	15	5
Penobscot, Maine	142	96	24	1	-	-	20	1	-	-
Picuris Pueblo, New Mexico	42	-	9	-	2	-	13	4	14	-
Pine Creek, Michigan	10	-	5	-	-	-	5	-	-	-

[Continued]

★ 577 ★

Heating Equipment in Occupied Housing Units on Reservations, 1980: L'Anse - San Xavier
[Continued]

Identified reservation	Occupied housing units	Occupied housing units								
		Heating equipment								
		Steam or hot water	Central warm air furnace	Electric heat pump	Other built-in electric units	Floor, wall or pipeless furnace	Room heaters with flue	Room heaters without flue	Fireplaces, stoves, or portable room heaters	None
Pine Ridge, South Dakota	2,328	62	809	65	202	13	458	123	578	20
Pleasant Point, Maine	140	37	88	-	2	-	5	3	6	-
Pojoaque Pueblo, New Mexico	36	-	24	3	-	-	7	-	3	-
Poospatuck, New York	28	8	10	4	2	-	1	-	2	-
Port Gamble, Washington	76	-	5	-	23	-	1	-	47	-
Port Madison, Washington	63	2	13	1	24	-	3	1	18	-
Potawatomi, Wisconsin	46	-	-	-	-	1	19	12	13	1
Pottawatomi, Kansas	102	-	50	-	-	-	26	2	24	-
Prairie Island Community, Minnesota	20	-	-	-	-	-	17	-	3	-
Puyallup, Washington	279	-	87	15	78	9	63	11	16	-
Pyramid Lake, Nevada	206	-	133	-	3	-	37	5	27	2
Quileute, Washington	62	-	3	-	49	1	2	1	6	-
Quinault, Washington	255	1	49	5	181	-	3	1	14	-
Ramah Community, New Mexico	296	2	13	6	21	1	8	22	220	4
Ramona, California	-	-	-	-	-	-	-	-	-	-
Red Cliff, Wisconsin	152	41	41	2	3	1	18	23	22	-
Red Lake, Minnesota	680	2	331	17	88	12	94	24	110	2
Reno-Sparks Colony, Nevada	123	4	93	-	8	-	7	8	3	-
Resighini Rancheria, California	7	...	...	...	...	...	...	...	...	...
Rincon, California	83	1	17	6	6	3	16	5	27	2
Roaring Creek Rancheria, California	4	...	...	...	...	...	...	...	...	...
Rocky Boy's, Montana	318	-	163	8	78	8	55	1	5	-
Rosebud, South Dakota	1,368	13	499	106	252	14	256	31	190	7
Round Valley, California	168	-	46	2	2	2	24	5	85	1
Rumsey Rancheria, California	3	...	...	...	...	...	...	...	...	...
Sac and Fox, Iowa	104	-	37	-	-	7	6	29	24	-
Sac and Fox, Kansas-Nebraska	2	...	...	...	...	...	...	...	...	...
St. Croix, Wisconsin	101	2	73	-	1	-	8	-	17	-
St. Regis Mohawk, New York	513	14	340	1	10	2	83	21	41	-
Salt River, Arizona	585	-	133	26	87	10	49	52	201	27
San Carlos, Arizona	1,216	18	253	40	91	12	282	111	290	118
Sandia Pueblo, New Mexico	73	-	60	-	1	1	4	-	6	1
Sandy Lake, Minnesota	-	-	-	-	-	-	-	-	-	-
San Felipe Pueblo, New Mexico	282	1	17	1	12	1	91	1	157	-
San Ildefonso Pueblo, New Mexico	134	-	59	-	2	-	57	4	12	-
San Juan Pueblo, New Mexico	245	1	142	2	3	-	45	13	37	1
San Manuel, California	-	-	-	-	-	-	-	-	-	-
San Pasqual, California	47	1	22	3	-	-	7	2	8	2
Santa Ana Pueblo, New Mexico	98	-	47	-	5	8	6	1	30	-
Santa Clara Pueblo, New Mexico	424	4	287	-	-	6	66	11	50	-
Santa Rosa Rancheria, California	26	-	2	-	-	-	3	-	20	2
Santa Rosa, California	6	...	...	...	...	...	...	...	...	...
Santa Ynez, California	40	-	20	-	-	9	7	-	4	-
Santa Ysabel, California	59	-	-	2	-	-	13	3	41	-
Santee, Nebraska	102	-	82	2	-	6	6	1	5	-
Santo Domingo Pueblo, New Mexico	339	-	32	-	2	21	70	24	190	-
San Xavier, Arizona	186	3	21	18	24	-	23	2	90	4

Source: U.S. Bureau of the Census, Subject Reports, PC80-2-1D, Part II, *American Indians, Eskimos, and Aleuts on Identified Reservations and in the Historic Areas of Oklahoma (Excluding Urbanized Areas)*, U.S. Government Printing Office, Washington, D.C., 1986, pp. 794-871. *Notes:* Three dots (...) means not applicable, or that the data are being withheld to avoid disclosure of information for individuals. A dash (-) represents zero or a percent which rounds to less than 0.1. Also, a dash (-) is used because the number of supplementary questionnaires for the reservations was insufficient to produce reliable estimates.

★ 578 ★

Heating Equipment in Occupied Housing Units on Reservations, 1980: Sauk-Sauiattle - Zuni Pueblo

Data are the latest available.

Identified reservation	Total	Occupied housing units								
		Heating equipment								
		Steam or hot water	Central warm air furnace	Electric heat pump	Other built-in electric units	Floor, wall, or pipeless furnace	Room heaters with flue	Room heaters without flue	Fireplaces, stoves, or portable room heaters	None
Sauk-Sauiattle, Washington	-	-	-	-	-	-	-	-	-	-
Sault Ste. Marie, Michigan	-	-	-	-	-	-	-	-	-	-
Schaghti-Coke, Connecticut	3	...	...	...	...	...	...	...	...	...
Shakopee Community, Minnesota	27	-	24	2	-	-	1	-	-	-
Sheep Ranch Rancheria, California	1	...	...	...	...	...	...	...	...	...
Sherwood Valley Rancheria, California	7	...	...	...	...	...	...	...	...	...
Shingle Springs Rancheria, California	-	-	-	-	-	-	-	-	-	-
Shinnecock, New York	76	13	15	-	14	-	15	-	19	-
Shoalwater, Washington	11	-	2	-	7	-	-	-	1	-
Sisseton, North Dakota-South Dakota	635	6	96	15	319	19	97	34	48	1
Skokomish, Washington	80	-	4	-	48	-	7	8	14	-
Skull Valley, Utah	-	-	-	-	-	-	-	-	-	-
Soboba, California	71	-	21	1	2	3	24	-	17	3
Sokaogon Chippewa Community, Wisconsin	31	-	5	-	-	-	7	9	8	1
Southern Paiute, Utah	40	-	-	1	18	-	1	3	16	1
Southern Ute, Colorado	253	5	111	13	27	11	51	4	29	1
Spokane, Washington	336	-	149	43	64	1	14	4	61	-
Squaxin Island, Washington	9	...	...	...	...	...	...	...	...	...
Standing Rock, North Dakota-South Dakota	1,074	98	473	42	143	26	152	36	94	10
Stewart's Point Rancheria, California	16	-	7	-	-	-	-	1	8	-
Stockbridge, Wisconsin	195	16	111	3	-	8	25	14	19	-
Sulphur Bank Rancheria, California	24	-	-	3	20	-	-	-	1	-
Summit Lake, Nevada	7	...	...	...	...	...	...	...	...	...
Susanville, California	23	-	-	-	2	-	5	-	16	-
Swinomish, Washington	106	-	30	-	48	-	-	1	28	-
Sycuan, California	16	-	4	2	2	2	4	-	4	-
Tama, Georgia	16	-	2	-	-	-	7	5	2	-
Taos Pueblo, New Mexico	318	-	24	5	5	-	72	12	200	-
Te-Moak, Nevada	29	-	8	4	-	-	14	3	-	-
Tesuque Peublo, New Mexico	57	-	7	-	-	-	29	1	20	-
Tigua, Texas	103	1	100	-	-	-	2	-	-	-
Tonawanda, New York	135	-	25	1	3	1	72	9	24	-
Torres-Martinez, California	-	-	-	-	-	-	-	-	-	-
Trinidad Rancheria, California	18	2	-	-	1	-	2	-	12	-
Tulalip, Washington	209	-	25	2	136	2	10	3	30	-
Tule River, California	117	-	12	-	5	-	-	2	97	-
Tunica-Biloxi, Louisiana	3	...	...	...	...	...	...	...	...	...
Tuolumne Rancheria, California	25	-	2	-	-	2	1	-	19	1
Turtle Mountain, North Dakota	1,013	95	281	27	251	13	215	58	73	1
Tuscarora, New York	-	-	-	-	-	-	-	-	-	-
Twenty-Nine Palms, California	-	-	-	-	-	-	-	-	-	-
Uintah and Ouray, Utah	528	7	179	16	101	19	129	17	59	2
Umatilla, Oregon	269	-	71	17	73	5	22	10	69	1
Upper Sioux Community, Minnesota	20	-	6	-	-	14	-	-	-	-
Upper Skagit, Washington	-	-	-	-	-	-	-	-	-	-
Ute Mountain, Colorado-New Mexico	294	3	66	14	83	5	37	20	66	-
Vermillion Lake, Minnesota	32	-	19	-	6	-	5	-	2	-
Viejas Rancheria, California	43	-	5	-	-	9	9	3	15	3
Walker River, Nevada	148	2	85	-	6	1	9	12	33	-
Wampanoag, Massachusetts	-	-	-	-	-	-	-	-	-	-
Warm Springs, Oregon	477	10	105	32	203	4	64	14	44	1

[Continued]

★ 578 ★

Heating Equipment in Occupied Housing Units on Reservations, 1980: Sauk-Sauiattle - Zuni Pueblo
[Continued]

| Identified reservation | Occupied housing units | | | | | | | | | |
| | Total | Heating equipment | | | | | | | | |
		Steam or hot water	Central warm air furnace	Electric heat pump	Other built-in electric units	Floor, wall, or pipeless furnace	Room heaters with flue	Room heaters without flue	Fireplaces, stoves, or portable room heaters	None
Washoe, Nevada	-	-	-	-	-	-	-	-	-	-
Western Pequot, Connecticut	7	...	...	...	...	...	...	...	...	...
White Earth, Minnesota	743	12	277	8	49	16	139	27	211	2
Wind River, Wyoming	1,004	89	245	21	137	30	318	72	90	4
Winnebago, Nebraska	295	41	194	2	-	11	28	1	17	-
Winnemucca Colony, Nevada	11	-	10	-	-	-	1	-	-	-
Wisconsin Winnebago, Reservation	83	7	35	-	-	-	32	2	7	-
Woodfords Community, California	-	-	-	-	-	-	-	-	-	-
XL Ranch, California	9	...	...	...	...	...	...	...	...	...
Yakima, Washington	1,350	11	277	117	493	21	149	74	205	3
Yankton, South Dakota	417	20	159	17	77	16	81	9	32	5
Yavapai, Arizona	22	1	7	2	3	2	6	1	-	-
Yerington, Nevada	31	-	22	1	2	1	-	-	5	-
Yomba, Nevada	13	-	2	-	-	-	1	4	5	1
Zia Pueblo, New Mexico	103	-	29	-	-	-	13	1	60	-
Zuni Pueblo, New Mexico	1,100	3	381	40	65	14	112	32	452	2
San Felipe/Santa Ana Joint Area, New Mexico	-	-	-	-	-	-	-	-	-	-
San Felipe/Santo Domingo Joint Area, New Mexico	23	-	14	-	4	-	5	-	-	-
Other Reservation Lands in Montana	-	-	-	-	-	-	-	-	-	-

Source: U.S. Bureau of the Census, Subject Reports, PC80-2-1D, Part II, *American Indians, Eskimos, and Aleuts on Identified Reservations and in the Historic Areas of Oklahoma (Excluding Urbanized Areas)*, U.S. Government Printing Office, Washington, D.C., 1986, pp. 794-871. *Notes:* Three dots (...) means not applicable, or that the data are being withheld to avoid disclosure of information for individuals. A dash (-) represents zero or a percent which rounds to less than 0.1. Also, a dash (-) is used because the number of supplementary questionnaires for the reservations was insufficient to produce reliable estimates.

★ 579 ★

Kitchen Facilities in Occupied Housing Units on Reservations, 1980: Acoma Pueblo - La Jolla

Data are the latest available.

Identified reservations	Occupied housing units										
	Total	Owner-occupied housing units					Renter occupied housing units				
		Total	Complete kitchen facilities	Incomplete kitchen facilities			Total	Complete kitchen facilities	Incomplete kitchen facilities		
				Total	Refrigerator	No refrigerator			Total	Refrigerator	No refrigerator
American Indian, Eskimo, or Aleut householder or spouse	81,273	54,138	39,035	15,103	4,771	10,332	27,135	22,245	4,891	1,695	3,195
American Indian, Eskimo, or Aleut householder	77,709	51,468	36,467	15,001	4,700	10,301	26,241	21,388	4,852	1,663	3,189
Acoma Pueblo, New Mexico	465	427	383	44	25	19	38	23	15	7	8
Agua Caliente, California	-	-	-	-	-	-	-	-	-	-	-
Alabama-Coushatta, Texas	136	127	126	1	1	-	9	...	...	...	...
Alamo, New Mexico	208	177	103	74	37	37	31	21	10	5	5
Allegany, New York	328	213	208	5	4	1	115	113	1	1	-
Alturas Rancheria, California	5	...	...	...	...	...	...	...	...	...	...
Annette Islands Reserve, Alaska	262	216	216	-	-	-	46	45	1	1	-
Augustine, California	-	-	-	-	-	-	-	-	-	-	-
Bad River, Wisconsin	203	114	104	10	10	-	89	77	12	12	-
Barona Rancheria, California	67	53	53	-	-	-	14	14	-	-	-
Bay Mills, Michigan	77	63	57	6	3	3	14	14	-	-	-
Benton Paiute, California	7	...	...	...	...	...	...	...	-	-	-
Berry Creek Rancheria, California	-	-	-	-	-	-	-	-	-	-	-
Big Bend Rancheria, California	5	...	...	...	...	...	...	...	-	-	-
Big Cypress, Florida	93	82	62	20	15	5	11	11	-	-	-
Big Lagoon Rancheria, California	2	...	...	...	...	...	...	-	-	-	-

[Continued]

Kitchen Facilities In Occupied Housing Units on Reservations, 1980: Acoma Pueblo — La Jolla

[Continued]

Identified reservations	Total	Occupied housing units									
		Owner-occupied housing units					Renter occupied housing units				
		Total	Complete kitchen facilities	Incomplete kitchen facilities			Total	Complete kitchen facilities	Incomplete kitchen facilities		
				Total	Refrigerator	No refrigerator			Total	Refrigerator	No refrigerator
Big Pine Rancheria, California	76	72	72	-	-	-	4	...	...	...	...
Bishop Rancheria, California	240	155	150	4	2	2	86	84	1	-	1
Blackfeet, Montana	1,507	1,061	1,009	51	44	7	446	404	42	32	11
Bois Forte (Nett Lake), Minnesota	109	50	46	4	4	-	59	57	2	1	1
Bridgeport Colony, California	20	-	-	-	-	-	20	19	1	-	1
Brighton, Florida	75	61	61	-	-	-	14	12	1	-	1
Burns, Oregon	36	11	11	-	-	-	25	22	3	-	3
Cabazon, California	4	...	...	...	...	...	...	-	-	-	-
Cachil Dehe Rancheria, California	6	...	...	...	...	...	...	...	...	...	...
Cahuilla, California	14	13	8	5	5	-	1	...	...	...	...
Campo, California	29	18	13	4	2	2	11	8	3	1	2
Camp Verde, Arizona	46	42	40	2	2	-	4	...	...	...	...
Canoncito, New Mexico	215	191	103	88	22	66	24	15	9	7	2
Capitan Grande, California	-	-	-	-	-	-	-	-	-	-	-
Carson Colony, Nevada	65	56	53	3	3	-	9	...	...	...	...
Catawaba, South Carolina	275	167	149	18	16	2	108	105	3	3	-
Cattaraugus, New York	548	405	300	105	88	17	144	105	38	34	4
Cedarville Rancheria, California	4	...	...	...	...	...	...	...	...	...	...
Chehalis, Washington	55	49	49	-	-	-	6	...	...	...	...
Chemehuevi, California	10	4	...	...	...	...	6	...	...	...	...
Cheyenne River, South Dakota	329	184	119	65	47	18	145	123	22	18	5
Chitimacha, Louisiana	74	61	61	-	-	-	13	13	-	-	-
Cochiti Pueblo, New Mexico	150	145	144	1	-	1	5	...	...	...	...
Cocopah, Arizona	67	43	43	-	-	-	24	18	6	2	4
Coeur D'Alene, Idaho	171	120	115	5	1	4	51	50	1	1	-
Cold Springs Rancheria, California	13	11	11	-	-	-	2	...	...	...	...
Colorado River, Arizona-California	552	292	284	8	6	2	260	247	13	6	7
Colville, Washington	1,129	748	739	9	8	1	381	368	13	11	2
Cortina Rancheria, California	1	...	...	...	...	...	...	-	-	-	-
Coushatta, Louisiana	5	...	...	...	...	...	...	-	-	-	-
Coyote Valley Rancheria, California	-	-	-	-	-	-	-	-	-	-	-
Crow, Montana	833	602	555	47	43	4	231	207	24	23	1
Crow Creek, South Dakota	328	111	100	11	7	4	217	208	9	6	3
Cuyapaipe, California	1	...	-	-	-	-	...	-	-	-	-
Deer Creek, Minnesota	2	...	...	...	...	...	...	-	-	-	-
Dresslerville Colony, Nevada	34	29	29	-	-	-	5	...	...	...	...
Dry Creek Rancheria, California	9	...	...	...	...	...	...	...	...	...	...
Duck Valley, Idaho-Nevada	243	179	141	38	30	9	64	41	23	17	5
Duckwater, Nevada	27	23	23	-	-	-	4	...	...	...	...
Eastern Cherokee, North Carolina	1,473	1,235	1,217	18	12	6	238	229	9	5	4
Eastern Pequot, Connecticut	9	...	...	...	...	...	...	-	-	-	-
Ely Colony, Nevada	17	12	12	-	-	-	5	...	...	...	...
Enterprise Rancheria, California	2	...	...	...	...	...	...	-	-	-	-
Fallon Colony, Nevada	16	15	15	-	-	-	1	...	...	...	...
Fallon, Nevada	66	59	54	5	3	1	7	...	...	...	...
Flandreau, South Dakota	49	37	37	-	-	-	12	12	-	-	-
Flathead, Montana	1,279	881	865	16	12	4	397	385	12	8	4
Fond du Lac, Minnesota	172	111	103	8	6	1	61	57	4	3	1
Fort Apache, Arizona	1,483	1,009	778	230	81	149	475	367	108	36	71
Fort Belknap, Montana	452	224	206	18	17	1	228	216	12	11	1
Fort Berthold, North Dakota	632	329	285	44	38	7	303	285	18	12	7
Fort Bidwell, California	26	2	...	...	...	...	24	24	-	-	-
Fort Hall, Idaho	672	500	459	41	36	5	172	161	11	9	2
Fort Independence, California	17	17	17	-	-	-	-	-	-	-	-
Fort McDermitt, Nevada-California	94	84	70	14	8	6	10	6	4	4	-
Fort McDowell, Arizona	84	59	49	10	5	5	25	15	10	6	4
Fort Mojave, Arizona-California-Nevada	34	3	...	...	...	...	31	31	-	-	-
Fort Peck, Montana	1,103	614	598	16	14	2	488	479	10	3	6
Fort Totten, North Dakota	489	225	202	23	19	4	264	247	17	11	6
Fort Yuma, Arizona-California	339	235	223	12	9	3	104	98	6	2	4
Gila Bend, Arizona	-	-	-	-	-	-	-	-	-	-	-
Gila River, Arizona	1,612	1,054	883	172	110	62	558	450	107	69	38
Golden Hill, Connecticut	1	...	-	-	-	-	...	...	...	...	...
Goshute, Nevada-Utah	28	14	4	10	7	2	14	2	12	9	2
Grand Portage, Minnesota	78	42	36	6	-	6	36	36	-	-	-
Grindstone Creek Rancheria, California	17	2	...	...	...	...	15	15	-	-	-
Hannahville Community, Michigan	45	10	9	1	-	1	35	30	5	5	-
Hassanamisco, Massachusetts	1	...	-	-	-	-	...	...	...	...	...
Havasupai, Arizona	61	47	42	5	2	3	14	11	3	-	3
Hoh, Washington	14	13	13	-	-	-	1	...	...	...	...
Hollywood, Florida	125	52	52	-	-	-	73	71	1	1	-
Hoopa Valley, California	480	326	319	6	6	154	146	8	6	2	
Hoopa Valley Extension, California	157	121	113	7	1	6	36	32	4	-	4
Hopi, Arizona	1,473	1,100	435	665	298	367	373	147	226	57	168

[Continued]

★ 579 ★

Kitchen Facilities in Occupied Housing Units on Reservations, 1980: Acoma Pueblo - La Jolla
[Continued]

Identified reservations	Occupied housing units										
	Total	Owner-occupied housing units						Renter occupied housing units			
		Total	Complete kitchen facilities	Incomplete kitchen facilities			Total	Complete kitchen facilities	Incomplete kitchen facilities		
				Total	Refrigerator	No refrigerator			Total	Refrigerator	No refrigerator
Hopland Rancheria, California	-	-	-	-	-	-	-	-	-	-	-
Hualapai, Arizona	160	115	104	10	6	4	45	32	14	10	3
Inaja-Cosmit, California	-	-	-	-	-	-	-	-	-	-	-
Indian Township, Maine	92	64	60	4	1	3	28	28	-	-	-
Iowa, Kansas-Nebraska	11	10	10	-	-	-	1	...	...	...	...
Isabella, Michigan	138	65	58	7	7	1	73	70	3	3	-
Isleta Pueblo, New Mexico	698	653	641	12	10	2	45	44	1	1	-
Jackson Rancheria, California	4	...	...	...	...	...	...	-	-	-	-
Jemez Pueblo, New Mexico	304	264	255	9	8	1	40	33	7	7	-
Jicarilla Apache, New Mexico	430	271	197	74	21	54	159	137	22	9	13
Kaibab, Arizona	25	12	10	2	2	-	13	11	2	1	1
Kalispel, Washington	21	17	17	-	-	-	4	...	...	...	...
Kickapoo, Kansas	103	75	71	4	2	1	28	28	-	-	-
Kootenai, Idaho	-	-	-	-	-	-	-	-	-	-	-
Lac Courte Oreilles, Wisconsin	304	123	108	15	15	-	181	171	10	7	3
Lac du Flambeau, Wisconsin	281	112	106	6	6	-	169	163	6	6	-
Laguna Pueblo, New Mexico	956	794	742	52	45	7	163	151	12	10	2
La Jolla, California	43	31	25	6	5	1	12	10	2	-	2

Source: U.S. Bureau of the Census, *Subject Reports,* PC80-2-1D, Part II, *American Indians, Eskimos, and Aleuts on Identified Reservations and in the Historic Areas of Oklahoma (Excluding Urbanized Areas),* U.S. Government Printing Office, Washington, D.C., 1986, pp. 794-871. *Notes:* Three dots (...) means not applicable, or that the data are being withheld to avoid disclosure of information for individuals. A dash (-) represents zero or a percent which rounds to less than 0.1. Also, a dash (-) is used because the number of supplementary questionnaires for the reservations was insufficient to produce reliable estimates.

★ 580 ★

Kitchen Facilities in Occupied Housing Units on Reservations, 1980: L'Anse - San Xavier

Data are the latest available.

Identified reservations	Occupied housing units										
	Total	Owner-occupied housing units						Renter occupied housing units			
		Total	Complete kitchen facilities	Incomplete kitchen facilities			Total	Complete kitchen facilities	Incomplete kitchen facilities		
				Total	Refrigerator	No refrigerator			Total	Refrigerator	No refrigerator
L'Anse, Michigan	191	125	125	-	-	-	66	66	-	-	-
La Posta, California	1	...	-	-	-	-	...	...	...	...	...
Las Vegas Colony, Nevada	24	21	20	1	1	-	3	...	...	...	...
Laytonville Rancheria, California	26	5	...	...	...	...	21	21	-	-	-
Leech Lake, Minnesota	782	508	460	48	40	8	274	235	38	33	5
Likely Rancheria, California	-	-	-	-	-	-	-	-	-	-	-
Lone Pine Rancheria, California	56	52	50	2	2	-	4	...	...	...	...
Lookout Rancheria, California	3	...	-	-	-	-	...	...	...	...	...
Los Coyotes, California	17	12	11	1	-	1	5	...	...	...	...
Lovelock Colony, Nevada	37	28	26	2	2	-	9	...	...	...	...
Lower Brule, South Dakota	196	80	78	2	2	-	116	116	-	-	-
Lower Elwah, Washington	13	6	...	...	...	...	7	...	...	...	...
Lower Sioux Community, Minnesota	24	24	24	-	-	-	-	-	-	-	-
Lummi, Washington	306	203	197	6	5	1	103	98	5	5	-
Makah, Washington	271	221	219	2	-	2	50	50	-	-	-
Manchester Rancheria, California	20	1	...	...	...	...	19	18	1	1	-
Manzanita, California	5	...	-	-	-	-	...	-	-	-	-
Maricopa, Arizona	67	6	...	...	...	...	61	50	11	8	3
Mattaponi, Virgina	23	13	13	-	-	-	10	10	-	-	-
Menominee, Wisconsin	550	368	347	21	16	5	182	175	7	7	-
Mesa Grande, California	-	-	-	-	-	-	-	-	-	-	-
Mescalero Apache, New Mexico	449	152	150	1	-	1	297	296	1	1	-
Miccosukee, Florida	72	24	5	19	12	7	48	18	30	19	11
Middletown Rancheria, California	8	...	...	...	...	...	...	...	...	...	...
Mille Lacs, Minnesota	-	-	-	-	-	-	-	-	-	-	-
Mississippi Choctaw, Reservation	570	341	314	27	16	11	229	211	18	15	3
Moapa River, Nevada	43	16	16	-	-	-	27	27	-	-	-
Montgomery Creek Rancheria, California	1	...	-	-	-	-	...	...	...	...	...
Morongo, California	99	84	84	-	-	-	15	13	2	1	1
Muckleshoot, Washington	73	55	49	6	5	2	18	15	2	1	1
Nambe Pueblo, New Mexico	72	60	58	2	1	1	13	10	2	2	-

[Continued]

★ 580 ★

Kitchen Facilities in Occupied Housing Units on Reservations, 1980: L'Anse - San Xavier
[Continued]

Identified reservations	Total	Owner-occupied housing units					Renter occupied housing units				
		Total	Complete kitchen facilities	Incomplete kitchen facilities			Total	Complete kitchen facilities	Incomplete kitchen facilities		
				Total	Refrigerator	No refrigerator			Total	Refrigerator	No refrigerator
Navajo, Arizona-New Mexico-Utah	22,304	15,059	5,231	9,828	1,587	8,241	7,245	4,676	2,570	340	2,229
Nez Perce, Idaho	452	276	271	5	4	1	176	166	9	6	3
Nisqually, Washington	13	13	13	-	-	-	-	-	-	-	-
Nooksack, Washington	-	-	-	-	-	-	-	-	-	-	-
Northern Cheyenne, Montana	748	477	452	25	12	12	271	251	20	17	2
Oil Springs, New York	-	-	-	-	-	-	-	-	-	-	-
Omaha, Iowa-Nebraska	291	90	77	14	11	2	201	185	16	13	3
Oneida, Wisconsin	568	374	355	21	18	3	194	182	12	12	-
Onondaga, New York	-	-	-	-	-	-	-	-	-	-	-
Ontonagon, Michigan	-	-	-	-	-	-	-	-	-	-	-
Osage, Oklahoma	2,009	1,311	1,494	17	14	3	498	491	8	2	6
Ozette, Washington	2	...	...	...	...	...	...	...	...	...	...
Pala, California	145	116	106	10	4	6	29	27	2	-	2
Pamunkey, Virginia	27	25	22	3	3	-	2	...	...	...	...
Papago, Arizona	1,525	1,110	479	631	309	321	416	208	208	90	118
Pascua Yaqui, Arizona	81	78	78	-	-	-	3	...	...	...	...
Pauma, California	27	19	18	1	1	-	8	...	...	...	...
Payson Community of Yavapai-Apache, Arizona	-	-	-	-	-	-	-	-	-	-	-
Pechanga, California	34	30	24	6	1	5	4	...	...	...	...
Penobscot, Maine	142	117	116	1	-	1	25	24	1	1	-
Picuris Pueblo, New Mexico	42	37	33	4	2	1	5	...	...	...	...
Pine Creek, Michigan	10	-	-	-	-	-	10	10	-	-	-
Pine Ridge, South Dakota	2,328	1,048	577	471	321	150	1,281	1,110	171	100	71
Pleasant Point, Maine	140	122	120	1	-	1	18	18	-	-	-
Pojoaque Pueblo, New Mexico	36	34	34	-	-	-	2	...	...	...	...
Poospatuck, New York	28	25	23	1	1	-	3	...	...	...	...
Port Gamble, Washington	76	49	49	-	-	-	27	27	-	-	-
Port Madison, Washington	63	45	44	1	-	1	18	17	1	-	1
Potawatomi, Wisconsin	46	23	20	2	2	-	23	19	5	5	-
Pottawatomi, Kansas	102	70	64	6	6	-	32	25	7	7	-
Prairie Island Community, Minnesota	20	7	...	...	...	...	13	12	1	1	-
Puyallup, Washington	279	129	128	2	2	-	149	148	1	1	-
Pyramid Lake, Nevada	206	183	181	2	1	1	23	23	-	-	-
Quileute, Washington	62	50	49	1	1	-	12	12	-	-	-
Quinault, Washington	255	182	181	1	1	-	73	66	7	7	-
Ramah Community, New Mexico	296	161	26	135	14	121	135	41	94	10	84
Ramona, California	-	-	-	-	-	-	-	-	-	-	-
Red Cliff, Wisconsin	152	75	71	4	4	-	77	71	6	2	3
Red Lake, Minnesota	680	495	444	52	48	4	185	169	17	17	-
Reno-Sparks Colony, Nevada	123	92	91	1	1	-	31	31	-	-	-
Resighini Rancheria, California	7	...	...	...	...	...	...	...	...	...	...
Rincon, California	83	71	66	5	3	1	12	12	-	-	-
Roaring Creek Rancheria, California	4	...	-	-	-	-	...	...	...	...	...
Rocky Boy's, Montana	318	194	188	6	4	2	124	123	1	1	-
Rosebud, South Dakota	1,368	724	650	74	44	30	644	598	45	34	12
Round Valley, California	168	116	115	1	-	1	52	49	3	2	1
Rumsey Rancheria, California	3	...	...	...	...	...	...	...	...	...	...
Sac and Fox, Iowa	104	70	32	38	33	5	34	14	20	18	1
Sac and Fox, Kansas-Nebraska	2	...	...	...	...	...	...	...	...	...	...
St. Croix, Wisconsin	101	25	23	3	2	1	76	70	6	6	-
St. Regis Mohawk, New York	513	471	441	30	30	-	42	31	11	11	-
Salt River, Arizona	585	451	379	72	52	20	134	70	64	50	14
San Carlos, Arizona	1,216	909	631	278	160	118	307	217	90	41	49
Sandia Pueblo, New Mexico	73	59	57	1	1	-	14	12	2	1	1
Sandy Lake, Minnesota	-	-	-	-	-	-	-	-	-	-	-
San Felipe Pueblo, New Mexico	282	236	200	36	36	-	45	35	11	11	-
San Ildefonso Pueblo, New Mexico	134	102	102	-	-	-	32	32	-	-	-
San Juan Pueblo, New Mexico	245	202	195	7	3	4	43	39	4	4	-
San Manuel, California	-	-	-	-	-	-	-	-	-	-	-
San Pasqual, California	47	37	36	1	1	-	10	10	-	-	-
Santa Ana Pueblo, New Mexico	98	93	87	6	6	-	5	...	...	...	...
Santa Clara Pueblo, New Mexico	424	372	359	13	11	2	53	53	-	-	-
Santa Rosa Rancheria, California	26	18	18	-	-	-	8	...	...	...	...
Santa Rosa, California	6	...	...	...	...	...	...	-	-	-	-
Santa Ynez, California	40	31	31	-	-	-	9	...	...	...	...
Santa Ysabel, California	59	40	33	7	1	6	19	14	4	-	4
Santee, Nebraska	102	11	9	2	1	1	91	86	5	2	3

[Continued]

919

★ 580 ★

Kitchen Facilities in Occupied Housing Units on Reservations, 1980: L'Anse - San Xavier
[Continued]

Identified reservations	Total	Occupied housing units									
		Owner-occupied housing units						Renter occupied housing units			
		Total	Complete kitchen facilities	Incomplete kitchen facilities			Total	Complete kitchen facilities	Incomplete kitchen facilities		
				Total	Refrigerator	No refrigerator			Total	Refrigerator	No refrigerator
Santo Domingo Pueblo, New Mexico	339	310	268	42	35	7	29	19	10	5	5
San Xavier, Arizona	186	151	129	22	6	16	35	21	14	12	1

Source: U.S. Bureau of the Census, Subject Reports, PC80-2-1D, Part II, *American Indians, Eskimos, and Aleuts on Identified Reservations and in the Historic Areas of Oklahoma (Excluding Urbanized Areas),* U.S. Government Printing Office, Washington, D.C., 1986, pp. 794-871. *Notes:* Three dots (...) means not applicable, or that the data are being withheld to avoid disclosure of information for individuals. A dash (-) represents zero or a percent which rounds to less than 0.1. Also, a dash (-) is used because the number of supplementary questionnaires for the reservations was insufficient to produce reliable estimates.

★ 581 ★

Kitchen Facilities in Occupied Housing Units on Reservations, 1980: Sauk-Sauiattle - Zuni Pueblo

Data are the latest available.

Identified reservations	Total	Occupied housing units									
		Owner-occupied housing units						Renter occupied housing units			
		Total	Complete kitchen facilities	Incomplete kitchen facilities			Total	Complete kitchen facilities	Incomplete kitchen facilities		
				Total	Refrigerator	No refrigerator			Total	Refrigerator	No refrigerator
Sauk-Suiattle, Washington	-	-	-	-	-	-	-	-	-	-	-
Sault Ste. Marie, Michigan	-	-	-	-	-	-	-	-	-	-	-
Schaghti-Coke, Connecticut	3	...	...	...	...	...	...	...	...	...	...
Shakopee Community, Minnesota	27	26	24	2	2	-	1	...	...	...	...
Sheep Ranch Rancheria, California	1	...	...	...	...	...	...	-	-	-	-
Sherwood Valley Rancheria, California	7	...	...	...	...	...	...	...	...	...	...
Shingle Springs Rancheria, California	-	-	-	-	-	-	-	-	-	-	-
Shinnecock, New York	76	70	67	4	4	-	6	...	...	...	...
Shoalwater, Washington	11	10	10	-	-	-	1	...	...	...	...
Sisseton, North Dakota-South Dakota	635	197	175	22	17	5	438	414	24	21	3
Skokomish, Washington	80	70	69	1	-	1	10	9	1	1	-
Skull Valley, Utah	-	-	-	-	-	-	-	-	-	-	-
Soboba, California	71	61	58	3	-	3	10	7	3	2	1
Sokaogon Chippewa Community, Wisconsin	31	18	17	1	1	-	13	10	2	1	1
Southern Paiute, Utah	40	37	28	10	10	-	3	...	...	...	...
Southern Ute, Colorado	253	156	151	5	4	1	97	96	1	-	1
Spokane, Washington	336	267	257	10	7	3	69	63	6	5	1
Squaxin Island, Washington	9	...	...	...	...	...	...	...	...	...	...
Standing Rock, North Dakota-South Dakota	1,074	399	266	133	79	54	675	607	67	45	23
Stewart's Point Rancheria, California	16	3	...	...	...	...	13	11	2	-	2
Stockbridge, Wisconsin	195	123	114	9	3	6	72	62	11	11	-
Sulphur Bank Rancheria, California	24	21	19	3	3	-	3	...	...	...	...
Summit Lake, Nevada	7	...	-	-	-	-	...	...	...	...	...
Susanville, California	23	20	20	-	-	-	3	...	...	...	...
Swinomish, Washington	106	70	65	6	1	5	36	36	-	-	-
Sycuan, California	16	14	14	-	-	-	2	...	...	...	...
Tama, Georgia	16	9	...	...	...	...	7	...	...	...	...
Taos Pueblo, New Mexico	318	284	76	208	110	99	34	7	27	10	17
Te-Moak, Nevada	29	12	12	-	-	-	17	16	1	1	-
Tesuque Peublo, New Mexico	57	52	44	8	5	3	5	...	...	...	...
Tigua, Texas	103	102	102	-	-	-	1	...	...	...	...
Tonawanda, New York	135	102	102	-	-	-	1	...	...	...	...
Torres-Martinez, California	-	-	-	-	-	-	-	-	-	-	-
Trinidad Rancheria, California	18	15	14	1	1	-	3	...	...	...	...
Tulalip, Washington	209	124	124	-	-	-	85	79	5	4	1
Tule River, California	117	105	98	7	2	4	12	12	-	-	-
Tunica-Biloxi, Louisiana	3	...	...	...	...	...	...	...	...	...	...
Tuolumne Rancheria, California	25	18	17	1	-	1	7	...	...	...	...
Turtle Mountain, North Dakota	1,013	615	504	111	104	7	398	363	35	28	7
Tuscarora, New York	-	-	-	-	-	-	-	-	-	-	-
Twenty-Nine Palms, California	-	-	-	-	-	-	-	-	-	-	-
Uintah and Ouray, Utah	528	396	373	23	17	6	132	127	5	4	1
Umatilla, Oregon	269	160	158	2	1	1	109	109	-	-	-
Upper Sioux Community, Minnesota	20	18	18	-	-	-	2	...	...	...	...
Upper Skagit, Washington	-	-	-	-	-	-	-	-	-	-	-

[Continued]

★ 581 ★

Kitchen Facilities in Occupied Housing Units on Reservations, 1980: Sauk-Sauiattle - Zuni Pueblo
[Continued]

Identified reservations	Total	Owner-occupied housing units						Renter occupied housing units				
		Total	Complete kitchen facilities	Incomplete kitchen facilities				Total	Complete kitchen facilities	Incomplete kitchen facilities		
				Total	Refrigerator	No refrigerator				Total	Refrigerator	No refrigerator
Ute Mountain, Colorado-New Mexico	294	208	191	17	14	3		86	73	13	7	7
Vermillion Lake, Minnesota	32	15	6	9	9	-		17	15	2	2	-
Viejas Rancheria, California	43	26	25	1	-	1		17	16	1	1	-
Walker River, Nevada	148	116	107	9	9	-		32	23	9	8	1
Wampanoag, Massachusetts	-	-	-	-	-	-		-	-	-	-	-
Warm Springs, Oregon	477	275	268	7	4	3		202	198	4	4	-
Washoe, Nevada	-	-	-	-	-	-		-	-	-	-	-
Western Pequot, Connecticut	7	...	...	...	...	...		-	-	-	-	-
White Earth, Minnesota	743	515	488	27	24	3		228	208	20	19	1
Wind River, Wyoming	1,004	679	609	70	67	4		324	291	33	24	9
Winnebago, Nebraska	295	104	97	7	7	-		191	184	7	5	2
Winnemucca Colony, Nevada	11	10	10	-	-	-		1	...	...	...	...
Wisconsin Winnebago, Reservation	83	23	21	2	2	-		60	56	4	-	4
Woodfords Community, California	-	-	-	-	-	-		-	-	-	-	-
XL Ranch, California	9	...	...	-	-	-		...	...	...	...	...
Yakima, Washington	1,350	831	813	18	16	2		519	505	14	10	4
Yankton, South Dakota	417	139	124	14	3	11		279	251	28	13	15
Yavapai, Arizona	22	18	18	-	-	-		4	...	...	...	...
Yerington, Nevada	31	29	29	-	-	-		2	...	...	...	...
Yomba, Nevada	13	1	...	...	...	...		12	5	7	5	2
Zia Pueblo, New Mexico	103	86	85	1	-	1		17	16	1	1	-
Zuni Pueblo, New Mexico	1,100	751	662	89	53	36		349	334	15	12	3
San Felipe/Santa Ana Joint Area, New Mexico	-	-	-	-	-	-		-	-	-	-	-
San Felipe/Santo Domingo Joint Area, New Mexico	23	-	-	-	-	-		23	23	-	-	-
Other Reservation Lands in Montana	-	-	-	-	-	-		-	-	-	-	-

Source: U.S. Bureau of the Census, Subject Reports, PC80-2-1D, Part II, *American Indians, Eskimos, and Aleuts on Identified Reservations and in the Historic Areas of Oklahoma (Excluding Urbanized Areas)*, U.S. Government Printing Office, Washington, D.C., 1986, pp. 794-871. *Notes:* Three dots (...) means not applicable, or that the data are being withheld to avoid disclosure of information for individuals. A dash (-) represents zero or a percent which rounds to less than 0.1. Also, a dash (-) is used because the number of supplementary questionnaires for the reservations was insufficient to produce reliable estimates.

★ 582 ★

Plumbing Facilities in Occupied Housing Units on Reservations, 1980: Acoma Pueblo-La Jolla - I

Data are the latest available.

Identified reservation	Occupied housing units	Owner-occupied housing units							
		Complete plumbing for exclusive use			Lacking complete plumbing for exclusive use				
		Total	Total	1.01 or more persons per room	Total	1.01 or more persons per room			
						Total	Complete plumbing but used by another household	Some, but not all plumbing facilities	No plumbing facilities
American Indian, Eskimo, or Aleut householder or spouse	81,273	54,138	39,325	11,741	14,814	9,719	53	1,246	8,419
American Indian, Eskimo, or Aleut householder	77,709	51,468	36,751	11,319	14,717	9,660	50	1,236	8,374
Acoma Pueblo, New Mexico	465	427	375	174	52	37	2	12	23
Agua Caliente, California	-	-	-	-	-	-	-	-	-
Alabama-Coushatta, Texas	136	127	126	21	1	-	-	-	-
Alamo, New Mexico	208	177	98	54	79	57	1	17	38
Allegany, New York	328	213	208	14	5	2	-	-	2
Alturas Rancheria, California	5	...	...	...	...	...	...	...	...
Annette Islands Reserve, Alaska	262	216	214	45	2	-	-	-	-
Augustine, California	-	-	-	-	-	-	-	-	-
Bad River, Wisconsin	203	114	100	6	14	-	-	-	-
Barona Rancheria, California	67	53	53	9	-	-	-	-	-

[Continued]

921

★ 582 ★

Plumbing Facilities in Occupied Housing Units on Reservations, 1980: Acoma Pueblo-La Jolla - I

[Continued]

Identified reservation	Occupied housing units	Owner-occupied housing units							
		Total	Complete plumbing for exclusive use		Lacking complete plumbing for exclusive use				
						1.01 or more persons per room			
			Total	1.01 or more persons per room	Total	Total	Complete plumbing but used by another household	Some, but not all plumbing facilities	No plumbing facilities
Bay Mills, Michigan	77	63	61	11	2	-	-	-	-
Benton Paiute, California	7	...	...	...	...	...	...	...	...
Berry Creek Rancheria, California	-	-	-	-	-	-	-	...	...
Big Bend Rancheria, California	5	...	...	...	...	...	-	-	-
Big Cypress, Florida	93	82	65	29	17	8	-	...	...
Big Lagoon Rancheria, California	2	...	...	...	...	...	...	...	8
Big Pine Rancheria, California	76	72	72	9	-	...	...	...	...
Bishop Rancheria, California	240	155	150	28	4	-	-	-	-
Blackfeet, Montana	1,507	1,061	1,015	209	45	8	-	4	4
Bois Forte (Nett Lake), Minnesota	109	50	48	5	2	-	-	-	-
Bridgeport Colony, California	20	-	-	-	-	-	-	-	-
Brighton, Florida	75	61	61	11	-	-	-	-	-
Burns, Oregon	36	11	11	4	-	-	-	-	-
Cabazon, California	4	...	...	...	...	...	...	...	...
Cachil Dehe Rancheria, California	6	...	...	...	...	...	...	...	...
Cahuilla, California	14	13	8	0	5	-	-	-	...
Campo, California	29	18	12	5	6	2	-	-	-
Camp Verde, Arizona	46	42	39	11	3	1	-	1	2
Canoncito, New Mexico	215	191	108	51	83	57	-	4	53
Capitan Grande, California	-	-	-	-	-	-	-	-	-
Carson Colony, Nevada	65	56	53	3	3	1	-	1	-
Catawaba, South Carolina	275	167	143	6	24	2	-	-	2
Cattaraugus, New York	548	405	303	52	102	17	1	6	10
Cedarville Rancheria, California	4	...	...	...	...	...	...	...	...
Chehalis, Washington	55	49	49	7	-	-	-	-	-
Chemehuevi, California	10	4	...	...	...	...	...	...	...
Cheyenne River, South Dakota	329	184	124	39	60	34	-	6	28
Chitimacha, Louisiana	74	61	61	7	-	-	-	-	-
Cochiti Pueblo, New Mexico	150	145	145	39	-	-	-	-	-
Cocopah, Arizona	67	43	42	25	1	1	-	1	-
Coeur D'Alene, Idaho	171	120	118	15	2	-	-	-	-
Cold Springs Rancheria, California	13	11	11	6	-	-	-	-	-
Colorado River, Arizona-California	552	292	289	80	3	1	-	-	1
Colville, Washington	1,129	748	738	86	10	3	-	2	1
Cortina Rancheria, California	1	...	...	...	.	.	.	.	..
Coushatta, Louisiana	2	...	...	...	...	...	...	..	..
Coyote Valley Rancheria, California	-	-	-	-	-	-	-	...	...
Crow, Montana	833	602	558	221	44	23	1	8	14
Crow Creek, South Dakota	328	111	98	18	13	6	-	3	3
Cuyapaipe, California	1	...	-	-	-	-	-	-	-
Deer Creek, Minnesota	2	...	...	...	...	...	...	...	...
Dresslerville Colony, Nevada	34	29	29	5	-	-	-	-	-
Dry Creek Rancheria, California	9	...	...	...	...	...	...	...	...
Duck Valley, Idaho-Nevada	243	179	128	42	51	19	2	3	13
Duckwater, Nevada	27	23	23	4	-	-	-	-	-
Eastern Cherokee, North Carolina	1,473	1,235	1,219	145	16	7	-	-	7
Eastern Pequot, Connecticut	9	...	...	...	...	...	...	...	...
Ely Colony, Nevada	17	12	2	-	-	-	-	-	-
Enterprise Rancheria, California	2	...	...	...	...	...	...	...	...
Fallon Colony, Nevada	16	15	15	4	-	-	-	-	-
Fallon, Nevada	66	59	59	15	-	-	-	-	-
Flandreau, South Dakota	49	37	37	3	-	-	-	-	-
Flathead, Montana	1,279	881	864	97	17	5	1	2	2
Fond du Lac, Minnesota	172	111	100	17	10	-	-	-	-
Fort Apache, Arizona	1,483	1,009	847	456	161	86	-	28	58
Fort Belknap, Montana	452	224	215	73	10	2	-	-	2

[Continued]

★ 582 ★

Plumbing Facilities in Occupied Housing Units on Reservations, 1980: Acoma Pueblo-La Jolla - I
[Continued]

Identified reservation	Occupied housing units	Owner-occupied housing units							
		Total	Complete plumbing for exclusive use		Lacking complete plumbing for exclusive use				
						1.01 or more persons per room			
			Total	1.01 or more persons per room	Total	Total	Complete plumbing but used by another household	Some, but not all plumbing facilities	No plumbing facilities
Fort Berthold, North Dakota	632	329	287	69	42	18	-	4	14
Fort Bidwell, California	26	2	...	...	...	...	...	...	...
Fort Hall, Idaho	672	500	460	131	40	14	1	7	7
Fort Independence, California	17	17	17	-	-	-	-	-	-
Fort McDermitt, Nevada-California	94	84	66	32	18	11	-	7	4
Fort McDowell, Arizona	84	59	51	16	8	5	-	-	5
Fort Mojave, Arizona-California-Nevada	34	3	...	...	...	...	...	...	...
Fort Peck, Montana	1,103	614	599	136	15	4	-	1	3
Fort Totten, North Dakota	489	225	210	79	15	6	-	-	6
Fort Yuma, Arizona-California	339	235	220	63	15	2	-	1	1
Gila Bend, Arizona	-	-	-	-	-	-	-	-	-
Gila River, Arizona	1,612	1,054	872	341	182	84	1	35	48
Golden Hill, Connecticut	1	...	-	-	-	-	-	-	-
Goshute, Nevada-Utah	28	14	4	1	10	-	-	-	-
Grand Portage, Minnesota	78	42	36	2	6	-	-	-	-
Grindstone Creek Rancheria, California	17	2	...	...	...	...	...	...	...
Hannahville Community, Michigan	45	10	9	3	1	-	-	-	-
Hassanamisco, Massachusetts	1	...	-	-	-	-	-	-	-
Havasupai, Arizona	61	47	43	24	4	2	-	1	1
Hoh, Washington	14	13	13	2	-	-	-	-	-
Hollywood, Florida	125	52	52	7	-	-	-	-	-
Hoopa Valley, California	480	326	316	56	9	-	-	-	-
Hoopa Valley Extension, California	157	121	114	20	7	1	-	-	1
Hopi, Arizona	1,473	1,100	420	174	680	463	1	22	440
Hopland Rancheria, California	-	-	-	-	-	-	-	-	-
Hualapai, Arizona	160	115	108	53	6	3	-	-	3
Inaja-Cosmit, California	-	-	-	-	-	-	-	-	-
Indian Township, Maine	92	64	59	11	5	-	-	-	-
Iowa, Kansas-Nebraska	11	64	59	11	5	-	-	-	-
Isabella, Michigan	138	65	58	12	7	-	-	-	-
Isleta Pueblo, New Mexico	698	653	647	97	5	1	-	1	-
Jackson Rancheria, California	4	...	...	...	...	...	...	...	...
Jemez Pueblo, New Mexico	304	264	259	130	5	3	-	1	2
Jicarilla Apache, New Mexico	430	271	201	74	70	25	-	4	22
Kaibab, Arizona	25	12	12	6	-	-	-	-	-
Kalispel, Washington	21	-	17	4	-	-	-	-	-
Kickapoo, Kansas	103	75	74	7	1	-	-	-	-
Kootenai, Idaho	-	-	-	-	-	-	-	-	-
Lac Courte Oreilles, Wisconsin	304	123	108	31	15	2	-	2	-
Lac du Flambeau, Wisconsin	281	112	99	24	13	6	-	3	3
Laguna Pueblo, New Mexico	956	794	748	176	45	21	-	11	9
La Jolla, California	43	31	23	6	8	5	1	2	2

Source: U.S. Bureau of the Census, Subject Reports, PC80-2-1D, Part II, *American Indians, Eskimos, and Aleuts on Identified Reservations and in the Historic Areas of Oklahoma (Excluding Urbanized Areas)*, U.S. Government Printing Office, Washington, D.C., 1986, pp. 794-871. *Notes:* Three dots (...) means not applicable, or that the data are being withheld to avoid disclosure of information for individuals. A dash (-) represents zero or a percent which rounds to less than 0.1. Also, a dash (-) is used because the number of supplementary questionnaires for the reservations was insufficient to produce reliable estimates.

★ 583 ★

Plumbing Facilities in Occupied Housing Units on Reservations, 1980: Acoma Pueblo-La Jolla - II

Data are the latest available.

Identified reservation	Renter-occupied housing units								Piped water in building (all units)			
	Total	Complete plumbing for exclusive use		Lacking complete plumbing for exclusive use					Total	No piped water		
		Total	1.01 or more persons per room	Total	1.01 or more persons per room					Total	Source of water within 100 yards of building	Source of water more than 100 yards
					Total	Complete plumbing but used by another household	Some, but not all plumbing facilities	No plumbing facilities				
American Indian, Eskimo or Aleut householder or spouse	27,135	22,361	7,033	4,774	3,050	52	390	2,607	64,200	17,074	4,990	12,084
American Indian, Eskimo, or Aleut householder	26,241	21,505	6,867	4,736	3,031	47	382	2,601	60,736	16,973	4,926	12,047
Acoma Pueblo, New Mexico	38	19	13	19	13	-	5	8	412	53	19	33
Agua Caliente, California	-	-	-	-	-	-	-	-	-	-	-	-
Alabama-Coushatta, Texas	9	...	...	...	...	...	...	...	136	-	-	-
Alamo, New Mexico	31	21	7	10	6	-	2	3	141	67	37	31
Allegany, New York	115	111	14	3	1	1	-	-	324	4	4	-
Alturas Rancheria, California	...	...	...	...	...	...	...	...	...	...	...	...
Annette Islands Reserve, Alaska	46	44	10	2	-	-	-	-	262			
Augustine, California	-	-	-	-	-	-	-	-	-	-	-	-
Bad River, Wisconsin	89	77	15	12	4	-	-	4	181	22	9	13
Barona Rancheria, California	14	14	3	-	-	-	-	-	67			
Bay Mills, Michigan	14	13	5	1	1	-	1	-	75	2	2	-
Benton Paiute, California	...	...	...	...	...	...	...	...	...	...	...	...
Berry Creek Rancheria, California	-	-	-	-	-	-	-	-	-	-	-	-
Big Bend Rancheria, California	...	...	...	...	...	...	...	...	...	...	...	...
Big Cypress, Florida	11	11	3	-	-	-	-	-	77	16	16	-
Big Lagoon Rancheria, California	...	-	-	-	-	-	-	-	...	...	...	...
Big Pine Rancheria, California	4	...	...	...	...	...	...	...	76	-	-	...
Bishop Rancheria, California	86	84	15	2	2	-	2	-	236	4	2	2
Blackfeet, Montana	446	409	80	37	22	2	6	14	1,448	59	31	27
Bois Forte (Nett Lake), Minnesota	59	57	10	2	-	-	-	-	105	4	1	3
Bridgeport Colony, California	20	20	-	-	-	-	-	-	20	-	-	-
Brighton, Florida	14	14	2	-	-	-	-	-	75	-	-	-
Burns, Oregon	25	22	8	3	-	-	-	-	33	3	-	3
Cabazon, California	...	-	-	-	-	-	-	-	...	...	...	...
Cachil Dehe Rancheria, California	...	...	...	...	...	...	...	...	...	...	...	...
Cahuilla, California	1	...	...	...	...	...	...	...	9	5	1	4
Campo, California	11	7	2	4	1	-	1	-	22	7	6	1
Camp Verde, Arizona	4	...	...	...	...	...	...	...	42	4	3	1
Canoncito, New Mexico	24	15	5	9	7	-	-	7	130	85	29	56
Capitan Grande, California	-	-	-	-	-	-	-	-	-	-	-	-
Carson Colony, Nevada	9	...	...	...	...	...	...	...	64	1	1	-
Catawaba, South Carolina	108	102	5	6	1	-	1	-	256	19	9	10
Cattaraugus, New York	144	106	15	37	11	-	3	8	430	118	77	41
Cedarville Rancheria, California	...	...	...	...	...	...	...	...	...	...	...	...
Chehalis, Washington	6	...	...	...	...	...	...	...	54	1	-	1
Chemehuevi, California	6	...	...	...	...	...	...	...	6	4	2	2
Cheyenne River, South Dakota	145	127	60	18	5	-	-	5	261	68	6	62
Chitimacha, Louisiana	13	13	-	-	-	-	-	-	74	-	-	-
Cochiti Pueblo, New Mexico	5	...	...	...	...	...	...	...	150	-	-	-
Cocopah, Arizona	24	19	9	5	2	-	2	-	63	4	4	-
Coeur D'Alene, Idaho	51	50	9	1	1	-	-	1	169	2	1	1
Cold Springs Rancheria, California	2	...	...	...	...	...	...	...	13	-	-	-
Colorado River, Arizona-California	260	257	48	3	2	-	-	2	547	5	1	4
Colville, Washington	381	369	61	12	1	-	-	1	1,118	11	6	5
Cortina Rancheria, California	...	-	-	-	-	-	-	-	...	...	...	...
Coushatta, Louisiana	...	-	-	-	-	-	-	-	...	...	...	...
Coyote Valley Rancheria, California	-	-	-	-	-	-	-	-	-	-	-	-
Crow, Montana	231	213	62	18	7	-	3	4	786	47	28	19
Crow Creek, South Dakota	217	213	75	4	4	-	-	4	313	15	4	11
Cuyapaipe, California	...	...	...	...	...	...	...	...	...	...	...	...
Deer Creek, Minnesota	...	-	-	-	-	-	-	-	...	...	...	...
Dresslerville Colony, Nevada	5	...	...	...	...	...	...	...	30	4	4	-
Dry Creek Rancheria, California	...	...	...	...	...	...	...	...	...	...	...	...
Duck Valley, Idaho-Nevada	64	34	3	30	12	-	7	6	194	49	46	2
Duckwater, Nevada	4	...	...	...	...	...	...	...	27	-	-	-
Eastern Cherokee, North Carolina	238	231	24	8	1	-	1	-	1,460	14	13	1
Eastern Pequot, Connecticut	...	-	-	-	-	-	-	-	...	...	...	...
Ely Colony, Nevada	5	...	...	...	...	...	...	...	17	-	-	-
Enterprise Rancheria, California	...	-	-	-	-	-	-	-	...	...	...	...
Fallon Colony, Nevada	1	...	...	...	...	...	...	...	16	-	-	-
Fallon, Nevada	7	...	...	...	...	...	...	...	66	-	-	-
Flandreau, South Dakota	12	12	-	-	-	-	-	-	49	-	-	-
Flathead, Montana	397	384	54	13	2	1	-	1	1,264	15	8	7
Fond du Lac, Minnesota	61	57	11	4	-	-	-	-	161	11	8	3

[Continued]

★ 583 ★

Plumbing Facilities in Occupied Housing Units on Reservations, 1980: Acoma Pueblo-La Jolla - II
[Continued]

Identified reservation	Renter-occupied housing units								Piped water in building (all units)			
	Total	Complete plumbing for exclusive use		Lacking complete plumbing for exclusive use					Total	No piped water		
		Total	1.01 or more persons per room	Total	1.01 or more persons per room					Total	Source of water within 100 yards of building	Source of water more than 100 yards
					Total	Complete plumbing but used by another household	Some, but not all plumbing facilities	No plumbing facilities				
Fort Apache, Arizona	475	398	131	77	41	1	11	29	1,296	187	164	25
Fort Belknap, Montana	228	220	94	7	-	-	-	-	436	16	9	7
Fort Berthold, North Dakota	303	287	89	16	4	-	-	4	580	52	12	40
Fort Bidwell, California	24	24	4	-	-	-	-	-	26	-	-	-
Fort Hall, Idaho	172	158	37	14	8	-	3	5	639	33	29	4
Fort Independence, California	-	-	-	-	-	-	-	-	17	-	-	-
Fort McDermitt, Nevada-California	10	6	-	4	4	-	-	4	80	14	9	4
Fort McDowell, Arizona	25	15	6	10	6	-	-	6	66	18	11	6
Fort Mojave, Arizona-California-Nevada	31	31	12	-	-	-	-	-	34	-	-	-
Fort Peck, Montana	488	479	133	10	1	-	-	1	1,088	15	11	4
Fort Totten, North Dakota	264	239	72	25	10	7	1	1	466	24	13	10
Fort Yuma, Arizona-California	104	96	23	8	-	-	-	-	326	13	11	1
Gila Bend, Arizona	-	-	-	-	-	-	-	-	-	-	-	-
Gila River, Arizona	558	443	173	114	75	1	25	48	1,432	180	128	52
Golden Hill, Connecticut	...	...	...	...	...	...	...	...	...	...	...	...
Goshute, Nevada-Utah	14	2	-	12	6	-	-	6	6	22	9	12
Grand Portage, Minnesota	36	32	3	3	2	2	-	-	73	4	-	4
Grindstone Creek Rancheria, California	15	14	3	1	-	-	-	-	17	-	-	-
Hannahville Community, Michigan	35	32	15	2	-	-	-	-	43	2	-	2
Hassanamisco, Massachusetts	...	...	...	...	...	...	...	...	...	...	...	...
Havasupai, Arizona	14	13	9	1	1	-	-	1	56	5	5	-
Hoh, Washington	1	...	...	...	...	...	...	...	14	-	-	-
Hollywood, Florida	73	73	6	-	-	-	-	-	125	-	-	-
Hoopa Valley, California	154	149	17	5	2	-	1	1	476	4	3	1
Hoopa Valley Extension, California	36	29	9	7	6	-	3	3	151	6	2	4
Hopi, Arizona	373	137	46	236	183	-	13	170	617	856	226	629
Hopland Rancheria, California	-	-	-	-	-	-	-	-	-	-	-	-
Hualapai, Arizona	45	33	15	13	8	-	4	4	146	14	13	1
Inaja-Cosmit, California	-	-	-	-	-	-	-	-	-	-	-	-
Indian Township, Maine	28	27	1	1	-	-	-	-	92	-	-	-
Iowa, Kansas-Nebraska	1	...	...	...	...	...	...	...	11	-	-	-
Isabella, Michigan	73	67	19	6	2	-	2	-	128	10	9	1
Isleta Pueblo, New Mexico	45	41	12	4	1	-	1	-	696	2	2	-
Jackson Rancheria, California	...	...	-	-	-	-	-	-	...	...	...	...
Jemez Pueblo, New Mexico	40	35	15	5	5	-	1	4	295	9	6	3
Jicarilla Apache, New Mexico	159	140	39	19	5	-	-	5	353	77	38	40
Kaibab, Arizona	13	13	4	-	-	-	-	-	25	-	-	-
Kalispel, Washington	4	...	...	...	...	...	...	...	20	1	1	-
Kickapoo, Kansas	28	28	4	-	-	-	-	-	101	1	-	1
Kootenai, Idaho	-	-	-	-	-	-	-	-	-	-	-	-
Lac Courte Oreilles, Wisconsin	181	174	21	7	2	-	2	-	289	14	14	-
Lac du Flambeau, Wisconsin	169	156	32	13	1	-	-	1	273	7	1	6
Laguna Pueblo, New Mexico	163	147	23	16	7	-	2	5	930	27	22	4
La Jolla, California	12	8	4	4	-	-	-	-	37	6	2	3

Source: U.S. Bureau of the Census, Subject Reports, PC80-2-1D, Part II, *American Indians, Eskimos, and Aleuts on Identified Reservations and in the Historic Areas of Oklahoma (Excluding Urbanized Areas)*, U.S. Government Printing Office, Washington, D.C., 1986, pp. 794-871. *Notes:* Three dots (...) means not applicable, or that the data are being withheld to avoid disclosure of information for individuals. A dash (-) represents zero or a percent which rounds to less than 0.1. Also, a dash (-) is used because the number of supplementary questionnaires for the reservations was insufficient to produce reliable estimates.

★ 584 ★

Plumbing Facilities in Occupied Housing Units on Reservations, 1980: L'Anse-San Xavier - I

Data are the latest available.

Identified reservation	Occupied housing units	Owner-occupied housing units							
		Total	Complete plumbing for exclusive use		Lacking complete plumbing for exclusive use				
					Total	1.01 or more persons per room			
			Total	1.01 or more persons per room		Total	Complete plumbing but used by another household	Some, but not all plumbing facilities	No plumbing facilities
L'Anse, Michigan	191	125	124	16	1	-	-	-	-
La Posta, California	1	...	-	-	-	-	-	-	-
Las Vegas Colony, Nevada	24	21	21	11	-	-	-	-	-
Laytonville Rancheria, California	26	5	...	...	...	...	...	...	...
Leech Lake, Minnesota	782	508	461	93	47	8	-	4	5
Likely Rancheria, California	-	-	-	-	-	-	-	-	-
Lone Pine Rancheria, California	56	52	50	4	2	-	-	-	-
Lookout Rancheria, California	3	...	-	-	-	-	-	-	-
Los Coyotes, California	17	12	8	-	4	1	-	-	1
Lovelock Colony, Nevada	37	28	28	7	-	-	-	-	-
Lower Brule, South Dakota	196	80	78	16	2	2	-	2	-
Lower Elwah, Washington	13	6	...	...	...	...	...	...	...
Lower Sioux Community, Minnesota	24	24	24	3	-	-	-	-	-
Lummi, Washington	306	203	194	40	9	2	-	1	1
Makah, Washington	271	221	221	33	-	-	-	-	-
Manchester Rancheria, California	20	1	...	...	...	...	...	...	...
Manzanita, California	5	...	...	...	...	...	...	...	...
Maricopa, Arizona	67	6	...	...	...	...	...	...	...
Mattaponi, Virgina	23	13	12	2	1	-	-	-	-
Menominee, Wisconsin	550	368	345	86	23	7	-	1	5
Mesa Grande, California	-	-	-	-	-	-	-	-	-
Mescalero Apache, New Mexico	449	152	149	33	2	-	-	-	-
Miccosukee, Florida	72	24	4	4	20	11	1	-	10
Middletown Rancheria, California	8	...	...	...	...	...	...	...	...
Mille Lacs, Minnesota	-	-	-	-	-	-	-	-	-
Mississippi Choctaw, Reservation	570	341	316	129	25	10	-	6	4
Moapa River, Nevada	43	16	16	3	-	-	-	-	-
Montgomery Creek Rancheria, California	1	...	-	-	-	-	-	-	-
Morongo, California	99	84	84	13	-	-	-	-	-
Muckleshoot, Washington	73	55	45	14	10	6	2	1	3
Nambe Pueblo, New Mexico	72	60	59	6	1	-	-	-	-
Navajo, Arizona-New Mexico-Utah	22,304	15,059	5,544	3,184	9,515	7,069	19	593	6,458
Nez Perce, Idaho	452	276	268	42	8	2	2	-	-
Nisqually, Washington	13	13	13	1	-	-	-	-	-
Nooksack, Washington	-	-	-	-	-	-	-	-	-
Northern Cheyenne, Montana	748	477	460	131	17	7	-	4	3
Oil Springs, New York	-	-	-	-	-	-	-	-	-
Omaha, Iowa-Nebraska	291	90	70	16	20	9	-	5	4
Oneida, Wisconsin	368	374	354	40	20	4	-	2	2
Onondaga, New York	-	-	-	-	-	-	-	-	-
Ontonagon, Michigan	-	-	-	-	-	-	-	-	-
Osage, Oklahoma	2,009	1,511	1,502	60	9	3	-	1	2
Ozette, Washington	2	...	...	...	...	...	...	...	...
Pala, California	145	116	111	19	5	1	-	-	1
Pamunkey, Virginia	27	25	22	-	3	-	-	-	-
Papago, Arizona	1,525	1,110	438	189	672	375	-	140	235
Pascua Yaqui, Arizona	81	78	78	50	-	-	-	-	-
Pauma, California	27	19	19	1	-	-	-	-	-
Payson Community of Yavapai-Apache, Arizona	-	-	-	-	-	-	-	-	-
Pechanga, California	34	30	22	6	8	2	-	2	-

[Continued]

Plumbing Facilities in Occupied Housing Units on Reservations, 1980: L'Anse-San Xavier - I
[Continued]

Identified reservation	Occupied housing units	Owner-occupied housing units							
		Total	Complete plumbing for exclusive use		Lacking complete plumbing for exclusive use				
					Total	1.01 or more persons per room			
			Total	1.01 or more persons per room		Total	Complete plumbing but used by another household	Some, but not all plumbing facilities	No plumbing facilities
Penobscot, Maine	142	117	114	11	3	1	-	1	-
Picuris Pueblo, New Mexico	42	37	34	6	2	2	-	-	2
Pine Creek, Michigan	10	-	-	-	-	-	-	-	-
Pine Ridge, South Dakota	2,328	1,048	590	217	458	284	2	12	270
Pleasant Point, Maine	140	122	119	13	3	-	-	-	-
Pojoaque Pueblo, New Mexico	36	34	34	1	-	-	-	-	-
Poospatuck, New York	28	25	25	4	-	-	-	-	-
Port Gamble, Washington	76	49	49	8	-	-	-	-	-
Port Madison, Washington	63	45	44	2	1	-	-	-	-
Potawatomi, Wisconsin	46	23	20	11	2	-	-	-	-
Pottawatomi, Kansas	102	70	66	7	4	3	-	-	3
Prairie Island Community, Minnesota	20	7	...	...	...	...	...	...	...
Puyallup, Washington	279	129	129	5	-	-	-	-	-
Pyramid Lake, Nevada	206	193	177	26	6	2	-	2	-
Quileute, Washington	62	50	50	36	-	-	-	-	-
Quinault, Washington	255	182	181	25	1	1	-	1	-
Ramah Community, New Mexico	296	161	30	15	131	90	-	3	87
Ramona, California	-	-	-	-	-	-	-	-	-
Red Cliff, Wisconsin	152	75	71	9	4	2	-	-	2
Red Lake, Minnesota	680	495	453	134	42	18	-	5	13
Reno-Sparks Colony, Nevada	123	92	92	17	-	-	-	-	-
Resighini Rancheria, California	7	...	...	...	...	...	...	...	...
Rincon, California	83	71	69	17	2	1	-	1	-
Roaring Creek Rancheria, California	4	...	-	-	-	-	-	-	-
Rocky Boy's, Montana	318	194	191	76	3	1	-	-	1
Rosebud, South Dakota	1,368	724	645	196	79	35	-	12	23
Round Valley, California	168	116	115	20	1	-	-	-	-
Rumsey Rancheria, California	3	...	...	...	...	...	...	...	...
Sac and Fox, Iowa	104	70	36	18	34	13	1	1	11
Sac and Fox, Kansas-Nebraska	2	...	...	...	...	...	...	...	...
St. Croix, Wisconsin	101	25	21	1	4	-	-	-	-
St. Regis Mohawk, New York	513	471	441	62	30	7	-	2	5
Salt River, Arizona	585	451	375	136	76	45	2	13	30
San Carlos, Arizona	1,216	909	589	331	320	201	6	81	115
Sandia Pueblo, New Mexico	73	59	59	5	-	-	-	-	-
Sandy Lake, Minnesota	-	-	-	-	-	-	-	-	-
San Felipe Pueblo, New Mexico	282	236	205	133	31	26	-	4	21
San Ildefonso Pueblo, New Mexico	134	102	102	11	-	-	-	-	-
San Juan Pueblo, New Mexico	245	202	193	31	9	3	-	1	1
San Manuel, California	-	-	-	-	-	-	-	-	-
San Pasqual, California	47	37	37	11	-	-	-	-	-
Santa Ana Pueblo, New Mexico	98	93	87	15	6	1	-	-	1
Santa Clara Pueblo, New Mexico	424	372	367	76	4	2	-	-	2
Santa Rosa Rancheria, California	26	18	18	9	-	-	-	-	-
Santa Rosa, California	6	...	...	...	...	...	...	...	...
Santa Ynez, California	40	31	31	5	-	-	-	-	-
Santa Ysabel, California	59	40	32	9	8	-	-	-	-
Santee, Nebraska	102	11	9	1	2	2	-	1	1

[Continued]

927

★ 584 ★

Plumbing Facilities in Occupied Housing Units on Reservations, 1980: L'Anse-San Xavier - I
[Continued]

Identified reservation	Owner-occupied housing units								
	Occupied housing units	Total	Complete plumbing for exclusive use		Lacking complete plumbing for exclusive use				
					Total	1.01 or more persons per room			
			Total	1.01 or more persons per room		Total	Complete plumbing but used by another household	Some, but not all plumbing facilities	No plumbing facilities
Santo Domingo Pueblo, New Mexico	339	310	251	164	59	45	-	31	14
San Xavier, Arizona	186	151	109	38	42	19	-	11	7

Source: U.S. Bureau of the Census, Subject Reports, PC80-2-1D, Part II, *American Indians, Eskimos, and Aleuts on Identified Reservations and in the Historic Areas of Oklahoma (Excluding Urbanized Areas)*, U.S. Government Printing Office, Washington, D.C., 1986, pp. 794-871. *Notes:* Three dots (...) means not applicable, or that the data are being withheld to avoid disclosure of information for individuals. A dash (-) represents zero or a percent which rounds to less than 0.1. Also, a dash (-) is used because the number of supplementary questionnaires for the reservations was insufficient to produce reliable estimates.

★ 585 ★

Plumbing Facilities in Occupied Housing Units on Reservations, 1980: L'Anse-San Xavier - II

Data are the latest available.

Identified reservation	Renter-occupied housing units								Piped water in building (all units)			
	Total	Complete plumbing for exclusive use		Lacking complete plumbing for exclusive use					Total	No piped water		
					1.01 or more persons per room						Source of water within 100 yards of building	Source of water more than 100 yards
		Total	1.01 or more persons per room	Total	Total	Complete plumbing but used by another household	Some, but not all plumbing facilities	No plumbing facilities		Total		
L'Anse, Michigan	66	64	9	2	-	-	-	-	191	-	-	-
La Posta, California	...	...	...	...	...	...	...	...	...	...	...	...
Las Vegas Colony, Nevada	3	...	...	...	...	...	...	...	24	-	-	-
Laytonville Rancheria, California	21	21	4	-	-	-	-	-	26	-	-	-
Leech Lake, Minnesota	274	230	57	44	14	2	11	1	725	57	37	20
Likely Rancheria, California	-	-	-	-	-	-	-	-	-	-	-	-
Lone Pine Rancheria, California	4	...	...	...	...	...	...	...	55	2	2	-
Lookout Rancheria, California	...	...	...	...	...	...	...	...	...	...	...	...
Los Coyotes, California	5	...	...	...	...	...	...	...	13	4	4	-
Lovelock Colony, Nevada	9	...	...	...	...	...	...	...	37	-	-	-
Lower Brule, South Dakota	116	116	33	-	-	-	-	-	196	-	-	-
Lower Elwah, Washington	7	...	...	...	...	...	...	...	13	-	-	-
Lower Sioux Community, Minnesota	-	-	-	-	-	-	-	-	24	-	-	-
Lummi, Washington	103	94	21	9	-	-	-	-	300	6	6	-
Makah, Washington	50	50	10	-	-	-	-	-	271	-	-	-
Manchester Rancheria, California	19	14	4	5	1	-	1	-	19	1	1	-
Manzanita, California	...	-	-	-	-	-	-	-	...	...	...	...
Maricopa, Arizona	61	51	30	11	6	-	-	6	57	10	10	-
Mattaponi, Virgina	10	7	1	3	-	-	-	-	23	-	-	-
Menominee, Wisconsin	182	166	59	16	3	-	-	3	527	23	16	6
Mesa Grande, California	-	-	-	-	-	-	-	-	-	-	-	-
Mescalero Apache, New Mexico	297	295	66	2	2	1	-	1	448	1	1	-
Miccosukee, Florida	48	22	14	26	21	1	-	20	28	44	43	1
Middletown Rancheria, California	...	...	...	...	...	...	...	...	...	...	...	...
Mille Lacs, Minnesota	-	-	-	-	-	-	-	-	-	-	-	-
Mississippi Choctaw, Reservation	229	221	85	8	1	-	-	1	548	22	17	5
Moapa River, Nevada	27	27	5	-	-	-	-	-	43	-	-	-
Montgomery Creek Rancheria, California	...	...	...	...	...	...	...	...	...	...	...	...
Morongo, California	15	13	5	2	-	-	-	-	98	1	1	-
Muckleshoot, Washington	18	17	8	1	1	-	-	1	67	6	3	2
Nambe Pueblo, New Mexico	13	13	2	-	-	-	-	-	71	1	1	-
Navajo, Arizona-New Mexico-Utah	7,245	4,751	2,313	2,494	1,929	21	148	1,760	11,020	11,284	1,511	9,773
Nez Perce, Idaho	176	166	33	9	1	-	-	1	442	10	9	1
Nisqually, Washington	-	-	-	-	-	-	-	-	13	-	-	-
Nooksack, Washington	-	-	-	-	-	-	-	-	-	-	-	-

[Continued]

928

Plumbing Facilities in Occupied Housing Units on Reservations, 1980: L'Anse San Xavier   II

[Continued]

Identified reservation	Renter-occupied housing units								Piped water in building (all units)			
	Total	Complete plumbing for exclusive use		Lacking complete plumbing for exclusive use					Total	No piped water		
		Total	1.01 or more persons per room	Total	1.01 or more persons per room					Total	Source of water within 100 yards of building	Source of water more than 100 yards
					Total	Complete plumbing but used by another household	Some, but not all plumbing facilities	No plumbing facilities				
Northern Cheyenne, Montana	271	256	68	15	9	-	4	4	727	20	14	7
Oil Springs, New York	-	-	-	-	-	-	-	-	-	-	-	-
Omaha, Iowa-Nebraska	201	187	63	14	4	-	1	3	267	24	17	7
Oneida, Wisconsin	194	183	18	11	-	-	-	-	547	21	17	4
Onondaga, New York	-	-	-	-	-	-	-	-	-	-	-	-
Ontonagon, Michigan	-	-	-	-	-	-	-	-	-	-	-	-
Osage, Oklahoma	498	493	41	5	-	-	-	-	2,003	6	2	5
Ozette, Washington	...	...	...	...	...	...	...	...	140	...	...	...
Pala, California	29	27	5	2	-	-	-	-	25	5	5	-
Pamunkey, Virginia	2	...	...	...	...	...	...	...	...	2	2	-
Papago, Arizona	416	202	64	214	115	2	30	82	896	629	491	138
Pascua Yaqui, Arizona	3	...	...	...	...	...	...	...	80	1	1	-
Pauma, California	8	...	...	...	...	...	...	...	26	1	1	-
Payson Community of Yavapai-Apache, Arizona	-	-	-	-	-	-	-	-	-	-	-	-
Pechanga, California	4	...	...	...	...	...	...	...	28	6	2	4
Penobscot, Maine	25	24	-	1	-	-	-	-	141	1	1	-
Picuris Pueblo, New Mexico	5	...	...	...	...	...	...	...	40	2	2	-
Pine Creek, Michigan	10	8	-	3	-	-	-	-	10	-	-	-
Pine Ridge, South Dakota	1,281	1,112	544	168	103	3	5	94	1,752	577	431	146
Pleasant Point, Maine	18	18	2	-	-	-	-	-	138	1	1	-
Pojoaque Pueblo, New Mexico	2	...	...	...	...	...	...	...	36	-	-	-
Poospatuck, New York	3	...	...	...	...	...	...	...	28	-	-	-
Port Gamble, Washington	27	27	5	-	-	-	-	-	76	-	-	-
Port Madison, Washington	18	17	1	1	-	-	-	-	61	3	3	-
Potawatomi, Wisconsin	23	20	9	4	1	-	-	1	40	6	2	4
Pottawatomi, Kansas	32	32	8	-	-	-	-	-	98	4	3	2
Prairie Island Community, Minnesota	13	12	3	1	-	-	-	-	18	2	2	-
Puyallup, Washington	149	148	20	1	-	-	-	-	279	-	-	-
Pyramid Lake, Nevada	23	23	4	-	-	-	-	-	206	-	-	-
Quileute, Washington	12	12	9	-	-	-	-	-	62	-	-	-
Quinault, Washington	73	72	18	1	1	-	1	-	255	-	-	-
Ramah Community, New Mexico	135	41	13	94	60	-	-	60	72	224	11	213
Ramona, California	-	-	-	-	-	-	-	-	-	-	-	-
Red Cliff, Wisconsin	77	73	12	3	2	-	-	2	145	7	1	6
Red Lake, Minnesota	185	171	56	14	4	-	-	4	633	47	21	26
Reno-Sparks Colony, Nevada	31	31	7	-	-	-	-	-	123	-	-	-
Resighini Rancheria, California	...	...	...	...	...	...	...	...	83	...	...	...
Rincon, California	12	12	5	-	-	-	-	-				
Roaring Creek Rancheria, California	...	...	...	...	...	...	...	...	...	...	...	...
Rocky Boy's, Montana	124	123	31	1	-	-	-	-	314	4	3	1
Rosebud, South Dakota	644	598	150	46	8	-	1	7	1,274	94	53	40
Round Valley, California	52	49	3	3	-	-	-	-	164	4	3	1
Rumsey Rancheria, California	...	-	-	-	-	-	-	-	...	...	...	...
Sac and Fox, Iowa	34	16	7	18	10	-	-	10	55	49	39	9
Sac and Fox, Kansas-Nebraska	...	...	...	...	...	...	...	...	...	...	...	...
St. Croix, Wisconsin	76	70	16	6	2	-	-	2	93	9	4	5
St. Regis Mohawk, New York	42	31	5	11	3	-	-	3	481	32	19	12
Salt River, Arizona	134	74	30	60	40	-	5	35	477	108	102	6
San Carlos, Arizona	307	211	109	96	58	-	24	34	946	270	208	62
Sandia Pueblo, New Mexico	14	13	2	1	1	-	-	1	72	1	-	1
Sandy Lake, Minnesota	-	-	-	-	-	-	-	-	-	-	-	-
San Felipe Pueblo, New Mexico	45	33	10	12	9	-	-	9	246	36	30	6
San Ildefonso Pueblo, New Mexico	32	32	6	-	-	-	-	-	134	-	-	-
San Juan Pueblo, New Mexico	43	39	9	4	-	-	-	-	240	5	3	3
San Manuel, California	-	-	-	-	-	-	-	-	47	-	-	-
San Pasqual, California	10	10	1	-	-	-	-	-	93	5	5	-
Santa Ana Pueblo, New Mexico	5	...	...	...	...	...	...	...	...	...	...	...
Santa Clara Pueblo, New Mexico	53	53	15	-	-	-	-	-	420	4	4	-
Santa Rosa Rancheria, California	8	...	...	...	...	...	...	...	26	-	-	-
Santa Rosa, California	...	-	-	-	-	-	-	-	40	...	...	...
Santa Ynez, California	9	...	...	...	...	...	...	...				
Santa Ysabel, California	19	14	3	4	3	-	1	1	49	10	8	2
Santee, Nebraska	91	82	22	9	3	-	2	1	96	6	6	-

[Continued]

★ 585 ★

Plumbing Facilities in Occupied Housing Units on Reservations, 1980: L'Anse-San Xavier - II
[Continued]

Identified reservation	Renter-occupied housing units								Piped water in building (all units)			
	Total	Complete plumbing for exclusive use		Lacking complete plumbing for exclusive use					Total	No piped water		
		Total	1.01 or more persons per room	Total	1.01 or more persons per room					Total	Source of water within 100 yards of building	Source of water more than 100 yards
					Total	Complete plumbing but used by another household	Some, but not all plumbing facilities	No plumbing facilities				
Santo Domingo Pueblo, New Mexico	29	14	12	15	15	-	6	8	309	30	28	3
San Xavier, Arizona	25	18	10	17	13	-	8	5	166	20	15	5

Source: U.S. Bureau of the Census, Subject Reports, PC80-2-1D, Part II, *American Indians, Eskimos, and Aleuts on Identified Reservations and in the Historic Areas of Oklahoma (Excluding Urbanized Areas)*, U.S. Government Printing Office, Washington, D.C., 1986, pp. 794-871. *Notes:* Three dots (...) means not applicable, or that the data are being withheld to avoid disclosure of information for individuals. A dash (-) represents zero or a percent which rounds to less than 0.1. Also, a dash (-) is used because the number of supplementary questionnaires for the reservations was insufficient to produce reliable estimates.

★ 586 ★

Plumbing Facilities in Occupied Housing Units on Reservations, 1980: Sauk-Sauiattle - Zuni Pueblo - I

Data are the latest available.

Identified reservation	Owner-occupied housing units								
	Occupied housing units	Total	Complete plumbing for exclusive use		Lacking complete plumbing for exclusive use				
			Total	1.01 or more persons per room	Total	1.01 or more persons per room			
						Total	Complete plumbing but used by another household	Some, but not all plumbing facilities	No plumbing facilities
Sauk-Suiattle, Washington	-	-	-	-	-	-	-	-	-
Sault Ste. Marie, Michigan	-	-	-	-	-	-	-	-	-
Schaghti-Coke, Connecticut	...	...	...	...	...	...	...	...	...
Shakopee Community, Minnesota	26	26	25	3	1	-	-	-	-
Sheep Ranch Rancheria, California	...	...	...	...	...	...	...	...	...
Sherwood Valley Rancheria, California	...	...	...	...	...	...	...	...	...
Shingle Springs Rancheria, California	-	-	-	-	-	-	-	-	...
Shinnecock, New York	70	70	67	-	4	-	-	-	6
Shoalwater, Washington	10	10	10	-	-	-	-	-	-
Sisseton, North Dakota-South Dakota	197	197	178	35	19	7	-	2	4
Skokomish, Washington	70	70	70	17	-	-	-	-	-
Skull Valley, Utah	-	-	-	-	-	-	-	-	-
Soboba, California	61	61	56	6	5	2	-	-	2
Sokaogon Chippewa Community, Wisconsin	18	18	17	5	1	-	-	-	-
Southern Paiute, Utah	37	37	28	8	10	7	-	1	5
Southern Ute, Colorado	156	156	152	26	4	1	-	-	1
Spokane, Washington	267	267	257	41	10	1	-	1	-
Squaxin Island, Washington	...	...	...	...	...	...	...	...	...
Standing Rock, North Dakota-South Dakota	399	399	269	78	130	58	-	19	39
Stewart's Point Rancheria, California	3	3	...	...	...	...	...	...	...
Stockbridge, Wisconsin	123	123	114	10	9	1	-	-	1
Sulphur Bank Rancheria, California	21	21	19	7	3	3	-	-	3
Summit Lake, Nevada	...	...	-	-	-	-	-	-	-
Susanville, California	20	20	19	4	1	-	-	-	-
Swinomish, Washington	70	70	65	14	6	-	-	-	-
Sycuan, California	14	14	14	2	-	-	-	-	-

[Continued]

★ 586 ★

Plumbing Facilities in Occupied Housing Units on Reservations, 1980: Sauk-Saniattle - Zuni Pueblo - I

[Continued]

Identified reservation	Occupied housing units	Total	Owner-occupied housing units						
			Complete plumbing for exclusive use		Lacking complete plumbing for exclusive use				
					Total	1.01 or more persons per room			
			Total	1.01 or more persons per room		Total	Complete plumbing but used by another household	Some, but not all plumbing facilities	No plumbing facilities
Tama, Georgia	9	9	...	...	...	...	...	...	...
Taos Pueblo, New Mexico	284	284	73	14	211	76	-	6	70
Te-Moak, Nevada	12	12	12	-	-	-	-	-	-
Tesuque Peublo, New Mexico	52	52	45	10	6	1	-	1	-
Tigua, Texas	102	102	102	20	-	-	-	-	-
Tonawanda, New York	111	111	63	3	48	7	-	-	7
Torres-Martinez, California	-	-	-	-	-	-	-	-	-
Trinidad Rancheria, California	15	15	15	2	-	-	-	-	-
Tulalip, Washington	124	124	124	23	-	-	-	-	-
Tule River, California	105	105	98	32	7	2	-	2	-
Tunica-Biloxi, Louisiana	...	...	...	...	...	...	...	...	...
Tuolumne Rancheria, California	18	18	18	3	-	-	-	-	-
Turtle Mountain, North Dakota	615	615	514	134	100	34	-	1	32
Tuscarora, New York	-	-	-	-	-	-	-	-	-
Twenty-Nine Palms, California	-	-	-	-	-	-	-	-	-
Uintah and Ouray, Utah	396	396	377	120	18	12	-	-	12
Umatilla, Oregon	160	160	157	24	3	2	-	2	-
Upper Sioux Community, Minnesota	18	18	18	-	-	-	-	-	-
Upper Skagit, Washington	-	-	-	-	-	-	-	-	-
Ute Mountain, Colorado-New Mexico	208	208	196	53	12	6	-	1	5
Vermillion Lake, Minnesota	15	15	6	2	9	-	-	-	-
Viejas Rancheria, California	26	26	22	6	4	-	-	-	-
Walker River, Nevada	116	116	106	11	10	-	-	-	-
Wampanoag, Massachusetts	-	-	-	-	-	-	-	-	-
Warm Springs, Oregon	275	275	269	56	6	3	-	-	3
Washoe, Nevada	-	-	-	-	-	-	-	-	-
Western Pequot, Connecticut	...	...	...	...	...	...	...	...	...
White Earth, Minnesota	515	515	484	73	31	10	-	1	9
Wind River, Wyoming	679	679	624	227	55	19	1	4	14
Winnebago, Nebraska	104	104	95	14	9	3	-	2	1
Winnemucca Colony, Nevada	10	10	10	4	-	-	-	-	-
Wisconsin Winnebago, Reservation	23	23	21	7	2	-	-	-	-
Woodfords Community, California	-	-	-	-	-	-	-	-	-
XL Ranch, California	..	...	-	-	-	-	-	-	-
Yakima, Washington	831	831	820	182	11	5	-	3	3
Yankton, South Dakota	139	139	126	32	13	-	-	-	-
Yavapai, Arizona	18	18	18	3	-	-	-	-	-
Yerington, Nevada	29	29	29	4	-	-	-	-	-
Yomba, Nevada	1	1	...	...	...	...	...	...	...
Zia Pueblo, New Mexico	86	86	85	36	1	1	-	-	1
Zuni Pueblo, New Mexico	751	751	595	253	156	74	5	52	16
San Felipe/Santa Ana Joint Area, New Mexico	-	-	-	-	-	-	-	-	-

[Continued]

931

★ 586 ★

Plumbing Facilities in Occupied Housing Units on Reservations, 1980: Sauk-Sauiattle - Zuni Pueblo - I

[Continued]

Identified reservation	Owner-occupied housing units								
	Occupied housing units	Total	Complete plumbing for exclusive use		Lacking complete plumbing for exclusive use				
					Total	1.01 or more persons per room			
			Total	1.01 or more persons per room		Total	Complete plumbing but used by another household	Some, but not all plumbing facilities	No plumbing facilities
San Felipe/Santo Domingo Joint Area, New Mexico	-	-	-	-	-	-	-	-	-
Other Reservation Lands in Montana	-	-	-	-	-	-	-	-	-

Source: U.S. Bureau of the Census, Subject Reports, PC80-2-1D, Part II, *American Indians, Eskimos, and Aleuts on Identified Reservations and in the Historic Areas of Oklahoma (Excluding Urbanized Areas)*, U.S. Government Printing Office, Washington, D.C., 1986, pp. 794-871. *Notes:* Three dots (...) means not applicable, or that the data are being withheld to avoid disclosure of information for individuals. A dash (-) represents zero or a percent which rounds to less than 0.1. Also, a dash (-) is used because the number of supplementary questionnaires for the reservations was insufficient to produce reliable estimates.

★ 587 ★

Plumbing Facilities in Occupied Housing Units on Reservations, 1980: Sauk-Sauiattle - Zuni Pueblo - II

Data are the latest available.

Identified reservation	Renter-occupied housing units								Piped water in building (all units)			
	Total	Complete plumbing for exclusive use		Lacking complete plumbing for exclusive use					Total	No piped water		
						1.01 or more persons per room						
		Total	1.01 or more persons per room	Total	Total	Complete plumbing but used by another household	Some, but not all plumbing facilities	No plumbing facilities		Total	Source of water within 100 yards of building	Source of water more than 100 yards
Sauk-Suiattle, Washington	-	-	-	-	-	-	-	-	-	-	-	-
Sault Ste. Marie, Michigan	-	-	-	-	-	-	-	-	-	-	-	-
Schaghti-Coke, Connecticut	...	...	...	...	...	...	...	...	...	...	...	...
Shakopee Community, Minnesota	1	...	...	...	...	...	...	...	26	1	1	-
Sheep Ranch Rancheria, California	...	-	-	-	...	...	...	...	...	...	...	...
Sherwood Valley Rancheria, California	...	...	...	...	...	...	...	...	...	...	...	...
Shingle Springs Rancheria, California	-	-	-	-	...	...	...	-	-	-	-	-
Shinnecock, New York	6	...	...	...	...	...	...	...	74	2	2	-
Shoalwater, Washington	1	...	...	...	...	...	...	...	11	-	-	-
Sisseton, North Dakota-South Dakota	438	414	106	23	7	1	-	5	606	29	21	8
Skokomish, Washington	10	10	3	-	-	-	-	-	80	-	-	-
Skull Valley, Utah	-	-	-	-	-	-	-	-	-	-	-	-
Soboba, California	10	9	2	1	-	-	-	-	68	3	3	-
Sokaogon Chippewa Community, Wisconsin	13	10	3	2	1	-	1	-	28	3	1	2
Southern Paiute, Utah	3	...	...	...	...	...	...	...	30	10	10	-
Southern Ute, Colorado	97	96	11	1	-	-	-	-	249	4	2	2
Spokane, Washington	69	65	10	4	1	-	1	-	325	11	6	5
Squaxin Island, Washington	...	...	...	...	...	...	...	...	...	...	...	...
Standing Rock, North Dakota-South Dakota	675	605	223	69	33	-	17	16	911	163	107	55
Stewart's Point Rancheria, California	13	13	6	-	-	-	-	-	16	-	-	-
Stockbridge, Wisconsin	72	63	8	9	3	-	-	3	180	16	8	8
Sulphur Bank Rancheria, California	3	...	...	...	...	...	...	...	21	3	3	-
Summit Lake, Nevada	...	...	...	...	...	...	...	...	...	...	...	...
Susanville, California	3	...	...	...	...	...	...	...	23	-	-	...
Swinomish, Washington	36	36	4	-	-	-	-	-	101	6	3	3
Sycuan, California	2	...	...	...	...	...	...	...	16	-	-	-
Tama, Georgia	7	...	...	...	...	...	...	...	16	-	-	-
Taos Pueblo, New Mexico	34	7	-	27	9	-	-	9	84	234	193	42
Te-Moak, Nevada	17	16	3	1	-	-	-	-	29	-	-	-
Tesuque Peublo, New Mexico	5	...	...	...	...	...	...	...	56	1	1	-
Tigua, Texas	1	...	...	...	...	...	...	...	103	-	-	-

[Continued]

★ 587 ★

Plumbing Facilities in Occupied Housing Units on Reservations, 1980: Sauk Suiattle - Zuni Pueblo - II

[Continued]

Identified reservation	Renter-occupied housing units								Piped water in building (all units)			
	Total	Complete plumbing for exclusive use		Lacking complete plumbing for exclusive use					Total	No piped water		
		Total	1.01 or more persons per room	Total	1.01 or more persons per room					Total	Source of water within 100 yards of building	Source of water more than 100 yards
					Total	Complete plumbing but used by another household	Some, but not all plumbing facilities	No plumbing facilities				
Tonawanda, New York	24	10	-	14	2	-	-	2	82	53	38	15
Torres-Martinez, California	-	-	-	-	-	-	-	-	-	-	-	-
Trinidad Rancheria, California	3	...	...	...	...	...	...	...	18	-	-	-
Tulalip, Washington	85	81	16	4	2	-	-	2	205	4	4	-
Tule River, California	12	12	2	-	-	-	-	-	112	4	-	4
Tunica-Biloxi, Louisiana	...	-	-	-	-	-	-	-	...	...	...	...
Tuolumne Rancheria, California	7	...	...	...	...	...	...	...	25	-	-	-
Turtle Mountain, North Dakota	398	350	69	48	17	5	2	10	895	118	52	66
Tuscarora, New York	-	-	-	-	-	-	-	-	-	-	-	-
Twenty-Nine Palms, California	-	-	-	-	-	-	-	-	-	-	-	-
Uintah and Ouray, Utah	132	127	39	5	1	-	-	1	511	17	9	8
Umatilla, Oregon	109	108	16	1	1	-	1	-	269	-	-	-
Upper Sioux Community, Minnesota	2	...	...	...	...	...	...	...	20	-	-	-
Upper Skagit, Washington	-	-	-	-	-	-	-	-	-	-	-	-
Ute Mountain, Colorado-New Mexico	86	84	25	2	-	-	-	-	284	9	1	8
Vermillion Lake, Minnesota	17	17	2	-	-	-	-	-	25	7	5	2
Viejas Rancheria, California	17	15	7	2	-	-	-	-	43	-	-	-
Walker River, Nevada	32	23	2	9	2	-	-	2	135	13	10	3
Wampanoag, Massachusetts	-	-	-	-	-	-	-	-	-	-	-	-
Warm Springs, Oregon	202	199	41	2	-	-	-	-	471	6	4	2
Washoe, Nevada	-	-	-	-	-	-	-	-	-	-	-	-
Western Pequot, Connecticut	...	-	-	-	-	-	-	-	...	...	...	...
White Earth, Minnesota	228	205	40	23	2	-	1	1	703	39	27	12
Wind River, Wyoming	324	304	102	21	4	-	-	4	934	70	47	23
Winnebago, Nebraska	191	180	27	11	2	-	-	2	282	13	5	8
Winnemucca Colony, Nevada	1	...	...	...	...	...	...	...	11	-	-	-
Wisconsin Winnebago, Reservation	60	56	15	4	-	-	-	-	77	6	4	2
Woodfords Community, California	-	-	-	-	-	-	-	-	-	-	-	-
XL Ranch, California	...	...	...	...	...	...	...	...	...	...	...	...
Yakima, Washington	519	494	126	25	9	1	3	5	1,338	12	10	2
Yankton, South Dakota	279	262	58	17	3	-	3	-	392	25	9	16
Yavapai, Arizona	4	...	...	...	...	...	...	...	22	-	-	-
Yerington, Nevada	2	...	...	...	...	...	...	...	31	-	-	-
Yomba, Nevada	12	6	3	6	1	-	1	-	6	7	6	1
Zia Pueblo, New Mexico	17	16	7	1	1	-	1	-	101	2	2	-
Zuni Pueblo, New Mexico	349	337	122	12	7	-	3	4	1,039	61	34	27
San Felipe/Santa Ana Joint Area, New Mexico	-	-	-	-	-	-	-	-	-	-	-	-
San Felipe/Santo Domingo Joint Area, New Mexico	23	23	15	-	-	-	-	-	23	-	-	-
Other Reservation Lands in Montana	-	-	-	-	-	-	-	-	-	-	-	-

Source: U.S. Bureau of the Census, Subject Reports, PC80-2-1D, Part II, *American Indians, Eskimos, and Aleuts on Identified Reservations and in the Historic Areas of Oklahoma (Excluding Urbanized Areas)*, U.S. Government Printing Office, Washington, D.C., 1986, pp. 794-871. Notes: Three dots (...) means not applicable, or that the data are being withheld to avoid disclosure of information for individuals. A dash (-) represents zero or a percent which rounds to less than 0.1. Also, a dash (-) is used because the number of supplementary questionnaires for the reservations was insufficient to produce reliable estimates.

933

★ 588 ★

Source of Water and Sewage Disposal Method for Occupied Housing Units on Reservations, 1980: Acoma Pueblo - La Jolla

Data are the latest available.

Identified reservation	Source of water							Sewage disposal				
	Public system private company, or tribal community system	Individual well			Private cistern	Creek spring, river, lake, or pond	Other means	Public sewer	Septic tank or cesspool	Chemical toilet	Outhouse or privy	Other means
		Total	Drilled	Dug								
American Indian, Eskimo, or Aleut householder or spouse	55,485	19,076	16,714	2,362	589	2,578	3,545	34,330	28,362	359	16,925	1,297
American Indian, Eskimo, or Aleut householder	53,400	17,818	15,540	2,278	558	2,445	3,488	32,890	26,370	346	16,836	1,266
Acoma Pueblo, New Mexico	427	22	10	11	1	-	14	169	231	1	48	16
Agua Caliente, California	-	-	-	-	-	-	-	-	-	-	-	-
Alabama-Coushatta, Texas	136	-	-	-	-	-	-	2	134	-	-	-
Alamo, New Mexico	132	49	43	6	1	21	6	36	115	1	49	7
Allegany, New York	273	53	49	4	1	1	-	95	229	-	4	-
Alturas Rancheria, California	...	...	...	...	...	...	...	...	...	...	...	...
Annette Islands Reserve, Alaska	262	-	-	-	-	-	-	259	2	-	-	2
Augustine, California	-	-	-	-	-	-	-	-	-	-	-	-
Bad River, Wisconsin	115	76	68	8	-	-	12	110	63	3	17	10
Barona Rancheria, California	67	-	-	-	-	-	-	-	67	-	-	-
Bay Mills, Michigan	21	53	53	-	-	-	3	-	77	-	-	-
Benton Paiute, California	...	...	...	...	...	...	...	...	...	...	...	...
Berry Creek Rancheria, California	-	-	-	-	-	-	-	-	-	-	-	-
Big Bend Rancheria, California	...	...	...	...	...	...	...	...	...	...	...	...
Big Cypress, Florida	91	2	2	-	-	-	-	25	54	-	4	11
Big Lagoon Rancheria, California	...	...	...	...	...	...	...	...	...	...	...	...
Big Pine Rancheria, California	74	2	2	-	-	-	-	40	35	-	1	-
Bishop Rancheria, California	239	-	-	-	-	-	1	224	10	1	4	1
Blackfeet, Montana	909	495	447	48	15	44	44	829	599	4	60	15
Bois Forte (Nett Lake), Minnesota	97	10	8	2	-	2	-	59	44	-	6	-
Bridgeport Colony, California	20	-	-	-	-	-	-	20	-	-	-	-
Brighton, Florida	73	1	1	-	-	-	1	21	53	-	-	1
Burns, Oregon	36	-	-	-	-	-	-	33	-	-	3	-
Cabazon, California	...	...	...	...	...	...	...	...	...	...	...	...
Cachil Dehe Rancheria, California	...	...	...	...	...	...	...	...	...	...	...	...
Cahuilla, California	-	13	12	1	-	1	-	-	11	-	3	-
Campo, California	-	28	21	6	-	1	-	-	22	-	7	-
Camp Verde, Arizona	46	-	-	-	-	-	-	40	2	-	3	1
Canoncito, New Mexico	165	34	32	2	5	-	11	16	101	-	85	13
Capitan Grande, California	-	-	-	-	-	-	-	-	-	-	-	-
Carson Colony, Nevada	60	5	5	-	-	-	-	64	-	-	-	1
Catawaba, South Carolina	115	150	145	5	2	5	3	100	150	-	23	3
Cattaraugus, New York	19	473	402	71	-	49	7	15	399	6	118	10
Cedarville Rancheria, California	...	...	...	...	...	...	...	...	...	...	...	...
Chehalis, Washington	30	24	24	-	-	-	-	11	44	-	-	-
Chemehuevi, California	10	-	-	-	-	-	-	-	10	-	-	-
Cheyenne River, South Dakota	132	43	36	7	82	48	24	124	121	-	81	3
Chitimacha, Louisiana	74	-	-	-	-	-	-	74	-	-	-	-
Cochiti Pueblo, New Mexico	150	-	-	-	-	-	-	150	-	-	-	-
Cocopah, Arizona	67	-	-	-	-	-	-	7	55	-	5	-
Coeur D'Alene, Idaho	107	59	56	3	-	4	1	108	60	-	3	1
Cold Springs Rancheria, California	13	-	-	-	-	-	-	1	11	-	1	-
Colorado River, Arizona-California	265	277	250	27	-	-	10	269	276	-	5	2
Colville, Washington	686	398	368	30	4	37	4	409	705	3	8	4
Cortina Rancheria, California	...	...	...	...	...	...	...	...	...	...	...	...
Coushatta, Louisiana	...	...	...	...	...	...	...	...	...	...	...	...
Coyote Valley Rancheria, California	-	-	-	-	-	-	-	-	-	-	-	-
Crow, Montana	413	383	365	18	8	5	23	398	398	3	30	4
Crow Creek, South Dakota	253	56	47	9	2	4	13	191	126	-	6	5
Cuyapaipe, California	...	...	...	...	...	...	...	...	...	...	...	...
Deer Creek, Minnesota	...	...	...	...	...	...	...	...	...	...	...	...
Dresslerville Colony, Nevada	34	-	-	-	-	-	-	-	30	-	-	4
Dry Creek Rancheria, California	...	...	...	...	...	...	...	...	...	...	...	...
Duck Valley, Idaho-Nevada	90	142	133	9	-	3	7	46	139	-	57	1
Duckwater, Nevada	18	9	9	-	-	-	-	-	27	-	-	-

[Continued]

934

★ 588 ★

Source of Water and Sewage Disposal Method for Occupied Housing Units on Reservations, 1980:
Acoma Pueblo - La Jolla
[Continued]

Identified reservation	Source of water							Sewage disposal				
	Public system private company, or tribal community system	Individual well			Private cistern	Creek spring, river, lake, or pond	Other means	Public sewer	Septic tank or cesspool	Chemical toilet	Outhouse or privy	Other means
		Total	Drilled	Dug								
Eastern Cherokee, North Carolina	418	302	265	37	25	622	106	273	1,182	-	11	8
Eastern Pequot, Connecticut	...	...	...	...	...	...	...	...	...	...	...	...
Ely Colony, Nevada	17	-	-	-	-	-	-	17	-	-	-	-
Enterprise Rancheria, California	...	...	...	...	...	...	...	...	...	...	...	...
Fallon Colony, Nevada	16	-	-	-	-	-	-	-	16	-	-	-
Fallon, Nevada	66	-	-	-	-	-	-	-	65	-	1	-
Flandreau, South Dakota	47	1	1	-	1	-	-	26	23	-	-	-
Flathead, Montana	673	524	497	26	2	63	17	496	722	3	13	44
Fond du Lac, Minnesota	35	123	110	14	-	-	13	27	132	4	6	3
Fort Apache, Arizona	1,436	28	25	3	5	9	5	873	277	4	296	34
Fort Belknap, Montana	230	196	185	11	4	13	8	201	220	1	25	5
Fort Berthold, North Dakota	370	169	144	25	18	37	39	377	196	1	50	8
Fort Bidwell, California	26	-	-	-	-	-	-	-	15	-	-	11
Fort Hall, Idaho	193	472	440	30	-	3	3	182	444	1	32	12
Fort Independence, California	17	-	-	-	-	-	-	-	17	-	-	-
Fort McDermitt, Nevada-California	81	6	6	-	-	1	6	3	74	-	16	1
Fort McDowell, Arizona	84	-	-	-	-	-	-	1	65	3	13	3
Fort Mojave, Arizona-California-Nevada	34	-	-	-	-	-	-	34	1	-	-	-
Fort Peck, Montana	912	175	153	21	-	7	9	911	167	6	13	6
Fort Totten, North Dakota	251	222	200	22	3	2	11	231	226	2	18	12
Fort Yuma, Arizona-California	299	36	36	-	-	1	2	45	277	2	11	4
Gila Bend, Arizona	-	-	-	-	-	-	-	-	-	-	-	-
Gila River, Arizona	1,565	10	7	2	-	2	35	437	957	5	205	7
Golden Hill, Connecticut	...	...	...	...	...	...	...	...	...	...		
Goshute, Nevada-Utah	2	6	6	-	-	20	-	2	4	-	22	-
Grand Portage, Minnesota	66	5	4	2	-	7	-	33	40	-	4	-
Grindstone Creek Rancheria, California	16	1	1	-	-	-	-	17	-	-	-	-
Hannahville Community, Michigan	-	44	43	1	-	-	1	-	41	-	4	-
Hassanamisco, Massachusetts	...	...	...	...	...	...	...	...	...	...	...	...
Havasupai, Arizona	36	-	-	-	-	25	-	-	56	-	4	1
Hoh, Washington	4	-	-	-	-	10	-	-	13	1	-	-
Hollywood, Florida	125	-	-	-	-	-	-	123	1	-	-	-
Hoopa Valley, California	247	112	91	21	2	113	6	15	460	-	-	5
Hoopa Valley Extension, California	46	11	9	2	2	93	5	7	141	-	5	3
Hopi, Arizona	921	195	112	83	4	103	249	456	132	44	818	24
Hopland Rancheria, California	-	-	-	-	-	-	-	-	-	-	-	-
Hualapai, Arizona	152	2	2	-	-	2	4	125	16	-	18	1
Inaja-Cosmit, California	-	-	-	-	-	-	-	-	-	-	-	-
Indian Township, Maine	90	2	2	-	-	-	-	88	4	-	-	-
Iowa, Kansas-Nebraska	-	11	11	-	-	-	-	-	11	-	-	-
Isabella, Michigan	80	55	55	-	-	1	1	54	75	-	5	5
Isleta Pueblo, New Mexico	692	4	3	1	-	-	1	403	289	2	2	2
Jackson Rancheria, California	...	...	...	...	...	...	...	...	...	...	...	...
Jemez Pueblo, New Mexico	302	-	-	-	-	-	2	284	11	-	4	6
Jicarilla Apache, New Mexico	352	20	16	4	7	4	47	308	38	-	82	3
Kaibab, Arizona	23	1	1	-	-	-	1	22	1	-	2	-
Kalispel, Washington	4	15	14	1	-	2	-	-	20	-	-	1
Kickapoo, Kansas	100	2	2	-	-	1	-	17	84	-	1	-
Kootenai, Idaho	-	-	-	-	-	-	-	-	-	-	-	-
Lac Courte Oreilles, Wisconsin	142	130	128	1	-	-	32	29	262	-	9	3
Lac du Flambeau, Wisconsin	233	42	42	-	-	3	3	190	88	-	3	-
Laguna Pueblo, New Mexico	947	-	-	-	5	-	4	696	227	1	30	3
La Jolla, California	35	-	-	-	-	1	7	1	34	-	7	1

Source: U.S. Bureau of the Census, Subject Reports, PC80-2-1D, Part II, *American Indians, Eskimos, and Aleuts on Identified Reservations and in the Historic Areas of Oklahoma (Excluding Urbanized Areas)*, U.S. Government Printing Office, Washington, D.C., 1986, pp. 794-871. *Notes:* Three dots (...) means not applicable, or that the data are being withheld to avoid disclosure of information for individuals. A dash (-) represents zero or a percent which rounds to less than 0.1. Also, a dash (-) is used because the number of supplementary questionnaires for the reservations was insufficient to produce reliable estimates.

★ 589 ★

Source of Water and Sewage Disposal Method for Occupied Housing Units on Reservations, 1980: L'Anse - San Xavier

Data are the latest available.

Identified reservation	Source of water							Sewage disposal				
	Public system, private company, or tribal community system	Individual well			Private cistern	Creek, spring, river, lake, or pond	Other means	Public sewer	Septic tank or cesspool	Chemical toilet	Outhouse or privy	Other means
		Total	Drilled	Dug								
L'Anse, Michigan	112	76	74	2	1	-	1	96	89	1	3	1
La Posta, California	...	...	...	...	...	...	...	...	...	...	...	...
Las Vegas Colony, Nevada	24	-	-	-	-	-	-	24	-	-	-	-
Laytonville Rancheria, California	25	1	1	-	-	-	-	1	25	-	-	-
Leech Lake, Minnesota	253	508	485	22	1	6	15	133	587	-	55	7
Likely Rancheria, California	-	-	-	-	-	-	-	-	-	-	-	-
Lone Pine Rancheria, California	56	-	-	-	-	-	-	53	2	-	2	-
Lookout Rancheria, California	...	...	...	...	...	...	...	...	...	...	...	...
Los Coyotes, California	12	3	3	-	-	2	-	-	13	-	3	1
Lovelock Colony, Nevada	35	2	2	-	-	-	-	35	2	-	-	-
Lower Brule, South Dakota	152	41	40	1	3	-	-	155	37	-	-	4
Lower Elwah, Washington	-	13	13	-	-	-	-	-	13	-	-	-
Lower Sioux Community, Minnesota	-	24	22	2	-	-	-	-	24	-	-	-
Lummi, Washington	275	30	25	4	-	1	-	57	239	-	7	3
Makah, Washington	259	12	9	3	-	-	-	256	14	-	1	-
Manchester Rancheria, California	20	-	-	-	-	-	-	6	14	-	-	-
Manzanita, California	...	...	...	...	...	...	...	...	...	...	...	...
Maricopa, Arizona	67	-	-	-	-	-	-	4	50	-	12	-
Mattaponi, Virgina	-	22	22	-	1	-	-	-	20	-	3	-
Menominee, Wisconsin	310	213	193	19	1	1	25	278	233	2	33	5
Mesa Grande, California	-	-	-	-	-	-	-	-	-	-	-	-
Mescalero Apache, New Mexico	436	5	5	-	1	4	3	258	190	-	1	-
Miccosukee, Florida	43	28	27	1	-	-	1	-	40	16	1	15
Middletown Rancheria, California	...	...	...	...	...	...	...	...	...	...	...	...
Mille Lacs, Minnesota	-	-	-	-	-	-	-	-	-	-	-	-
Mississippi Choctaw, Reservation	524	31	19	12	1	4	10	143	380	-	35	12
Moapa River, Nevada	43	-	-	-	-	-	-	43	-	-	-	-
Montgomery Creek Rancheria, California	...	...	...	...	...	...	...	...	...	...	...	...
Morongo, California	99	-	-	-	-	-	-	2	92	-	1	3
Muckleshoot, Washington	52	19	19	-	-	2	-	10	53	4	6	-
Nambe Pueblo, New Mexico	70	2	2	-	-	-	-	51	19	-	3	-
Navajo, Arizona-New Mexico-Utah	15,153	4,110	3,199	911	267	672	2,103	7,480	3,134	129	11,043	518
Nez Perce, Idaho	297	127	123	4	2	24	2	287	154	-	8	3
Nisqually, Washington	5	6	3	3	-	1	-	-	12	-	-	1
Nooksack, Washington	-	-	-	-	-	-	-	-	-	-	-	-
Northern Cheyenne, Montana	448	272	254	18	3	11	14	429	276	1	39	2
Oil Springs, New York	-	-	-	-	-	-	-	-	-	-	-	-
Omaha, Iowa-Nebraska	242	40	24	15	-	4	6	226	30	-	32	3
Oneida, Wisconsin	208	354	340	14	1	-	5	159	381	2	16	11
Onondaga, New York	-	-	-	-	-	-	-	-	-	-	-	-
Ontonagon, Michigan	-	-	-	-	-	-	-	-	-	-	-	-
Osage, Oklahoma	1,649	281	248	33	15	48	15	1,182	810	2	4	11
Ozette, Washington	...	...	...	...	...	...	...	...	...	...	...	...
Pala, California	135	9	8	1	-	-	1	91	43	1	8	2
Pamunkey, Virginia	-	26	21	5	-	-	1	-	25	-	1	1
Papago, Arizona	1,423	85	74	11	-	3	14	396	267	6	817	39
Pascua Yaqui, Arizona	81	-	-	-	-	-	-	1	78	-	2	-
Pauma, California	22	5	5	-	-	-	-	-	24	-	3	-
Payson Community of Yavapai-Apache, Arizona	-	-	-	-	-	-	-	-	-	-	-	-
Pechanga, California	33	1	1	-	-	-	-	-	27	-	4	3
Penobscot, Maine	140	1	1	-	-	-	1	140	1	-	-	1
Picuris Pueblo, New Mexico	37	5	2	4	-	-	-	37	3	-	2	-
Pine Creek, Michigan	-	10	10	-	-	-	-	-	10	-	-	-
Pine Ridge, South Dakota	1,246	955	884	72	7	56	65	1,159	533	10	595	32
Pleasant Point, Maine	140	-	-	-	-	-	-	137	2	-	1	-
Pojoaque Pueblo, New Mexico	34	2	2	-	-	-	-	9	27	-	-	-
Poospatuck, New York	-	28	26	2	-	-	-	-	28	-	-	-
Port Gamble, Washington	76	-	-	-	-	-	-	9	67	-	-	-

[Continued]

★ 589 ★

Source of Water and Sewage Disposal Method for Occupied Housing Units on Reservations, 1980: L'Anse - San Xavier

[Continued]

Identified reservation	Public system, private company, or tribal community system	Source of water			Private cistern	Creek, spring, river, lake, or pond	Other means	Sewage disposal				
		Individual well						Public sewer	Septic tank or cesspool	Chemical toilet	Outhouse or privy	Other means
		Total	Drilled	Dug								
Port Madison, Washington	44	15	14	1	-	-	3	27	35	-	-	1
Potawatomi, Wisconsin	16	27	27	-	-	1	2	-	41	-	4	1
Pottawatomi, Kansas	67	22	15	8	2	2	9	2	98	-	2	-
Prairie Island Community, Minnesota	-	20	18	2	-	-	-	-	17	-	2	1
Puyallup, Washington	239	36	33	3	-	-	3	200	79	-	-	-
Pyramid Lake, Nevada	193	11	11	-	-	2	-	17	183	-	7	-
Quileute, Washington	61	-	-	-	-	1	-	61	1	-	-	-
Quinault, Washington	238	11	9	2	-	5	-	222	33	-	-	-
Ramah Community, New Mexico	179	22	10	11	1	3	91	48	18	1	221	8
Ramona, California	-	-	-	-	-	-	-	-	-	-	-	-
Red Cliff, Wisconsin	107	42	42	-	-	-	2	139	5	2	5	-
Red Lake, Minnesota	312	340	327	12	3	5	21	187	436	12	39	5
Reno-Sparks Colony, Nevada	123	-	-	-	-	-	-	122	1	-	-	-
Resighini Rancheria, California	...	...	...	...	...	...	...	...	...	...	...	...
Rincon, California	75	8	8	-	-	-	-	3	79	-	1	-
Roaring Creek Rancheria, California	...	...	...	...	...	...	...	...	...	...	...	...
Rocky Boy's, Montana	102	208	171	36	1	5	2	72	238	2	4	1
Rosebud, South Dakota	923	397	343	54	8	3	38	915	346	3	86	18
Round Valley, California	51	102	99	3	2	8	4	8	154	-	5	-
Rumsey Rancheria, California	...	...	...	...	...	...	...	...	...	...	...	...
Sac and Fox, Iowa	69	34	32	2	-	-	1	1	54	-	49	-
Sac and Fox, Kansas-Nebraska	...	...	...	...	...	...	...	...	...	...	...	...
St. Croix, Wisconsin	9	88	86	2	-	-	4	-	91	-	7	4
St. Regis Mohawk, New York	109	387	350	37	-	1	15	3	474	5	22	9
Salt River, Arizona	582	-	-	-	-	-	3	24	423	4	119	15
San Carlos, Arizona	1,172	24	19	5	-	8	12	673	232	14	269	28
Sandia Pueblo, New Mexico	66	3	3	-	2	-	1	69	3	-	1	-
Sandy Lake, Minnesota	-	-	-	-	-	-	-	-	-	-	-	-
San Felipe Pueblo, New Mexico	264	2	2	-	8	2	4	191	46	-	43	2
San Ildefonso Pueblo, New Mexico	114	18	16	2	1	-	1	92	42	-	-	-
San Juan Pueblo, New Mexico	237	7	7	-	-	-	-	131	108	1	2	3
San Manuel, California	-	-	-	-	-	-	-	-	-	-	-	-
San Pasqual, California	34	13	13	-	-	-	-	1	45	-	-	1
Santa Ana Pueblo, New Mexico	98	-	-	-	-	-	-	82	9	-	4	3
Santa Clara Pueblo, New Mexico	406	18	16	2	-	-	-	366	57	-	-	2
Santa Rosa Rancheria, California	23	3	3	-	-	-	-	-	26	-	-	-
Santa Rosa, California	...	...	...	...	...	...	...	...	...	...	...	...
Santa Ynez, California	40	-	-	-	-	-	-	-	40	-	-	-
Santa Ysabel, California	33	18	18	-	-	6	2	-	50	-	9	-
Santee, Nebraska	81	22	13	8	-	-	-	77	18	-	7	-
Santo Domingo Pueblo, New Mexico	334	2	2	-	-	2	1	299	6	5	19	10
San Xavier, Arizona	180	6	6	-	-	-	-	86	52	-	44	4

Source: U.S. Bureau of the Census, Subject Reports, PC80-2-1D, Part II, *American Indians, Eskimos, and Aleuts on Identified Reservations and in the Historic Areas of Oklahoma (Excluding Urbanized Areas)*, U.S. Government Printing Office, Washington, D.C., 1986, pp. 794-871. *Notes:* Three dots (...) means not applicable, or that the data are being withheld to avoid disclosure of information for individuals. A dash (-) represents zero or a percent which rounds to less than 0.1. Also, a dash (-) is used because the number of supplementary questionnaires for the reservations was insufficient to produce reliable estimates.

Source of Water and Sewage Disposal Method for Occupied Housing Units on Reservations, 1980: Sauk-Sauiattle - Zuni Pueblo

Data are the latest available.

Identified reservation	Source of water: Public system, private company, tribal or community system	Individual well Total	Drilled	Dug	Private cistern	Creek, spring, river, lake, or pond	Other means	Sewage disposal: Public sewer	Septic tank or cesspool	Chemical toilet	Outhouse or privy	Other means
Sauk-Sauiattle, Washington	-	-	-	-	-	-	-	-	-	-	-	-
Sault Ste. Marie, Michigan	-	-	-	-	-	-	-	-	-	-	-	-
Schaghti-Coke, Connecticut	-	-	-	-	-	-	-	-	-	-	-	-
Shakopee Community, Minnesota	14	13	13	-	-	-	...	...	26	...	1	...
Sheep Ranch Rancheria, California	...	...	...	...	...	...	...	...	...	...	...	...
Sherwood Valley Rancheria, California	...	...	...	...	...	...	...	...	...	...	...	...
Shingle Springs Rancheria, California	-	-	-	-	-	-	-	-	-	-	-	-
Shinnecock, New York	2	74	67	7	-	-	-	-	74	-	-	2
Shoalwater, Washington	11	-	-	-	-	-	-	-	11	-	-	-
Sisseton, North Dakota-South Dakota	456	150	125	25	6	9	13	402	206	5	11	11
Skokomish, Washington	20	60	59	1	-	-	-	2	78	-	-	-
Skull Valley, Utah	-	-	-	-	-	-	-	-	-	-	-	-
Soboba, California	70	-	-	-	-	1	-	2	65	-	3	-
Sokaogon Chippewa Community, Wisconsin	1	28	26	2	-	-	2	-	29	-	2	-
Southern Paiute, Utah	40	-	-	-	-	-	-	30	-	-	10	-
Southern Ute, Colorado	144	101	100	1	1	2	5	136	111	-	4	1
Spokane, Washington	77	246	239	7	3	9	1	15	313	-	4	4
Squaxin Island, Washington	...	...	...	...	...	...	...	...	...	...	...	...
Standing Rock, North Dakota-South Dakota	749	274	241	33	2	13	36	687	212	3	152	19
Stewart's Point Rancheria, California	16	-	-	-	-	-	-	-	16	-	-	-
Stockbridge, Wisconsin	58	123	108	15	2	5	7	53	121	-	19	2
Sulphur Bank Rancheria, California	21	-	-	-	-	-	3	21	-	-	-	3
Summit Lake, Nevada	...	...	...	...	...	...	...	...	...	...	...	...
Susanville, California	23	-	-	-	-	-	-	22	-	...	-	1
Swinomish, Washington	82	20	16	3	-	5	-	79	21	-	6	-
Sycuan, California	16	-	-	-	-	-	-	-	16	-	-	-
Tama, Georgia	16	-	-	-	-	-	-	1	15	-	-	-
Taos Pueblo, New Mexico	12	167	75	92	1	129	8	6	75	-	232	5
Te-Moak, Nevada	-	29	29	-	-	-	-	-	29	-	-	-
Tesuque Peublo, New Mexico	54	3	3	-	-	-	-	50	7	-	-	-
Tigua, Texas	101	2	2	-	-	-	-	102	1	-	-	-
Tonawanda, New York	9	121	78	43	-	5	-	1	77	1	55	-
Torres-Martinez, California	-	-	-	-	-	-	-	-	-	-	-	-
Trinidad Rancheria, California	18	-	-	-	-	-	-	-	18	-	-	-
Tulalip, Washington	175	30	25	5	-	1	2	83	121	-	3	1
Tule River, California	108	2	2	-	-	4	2	52	56	-	9	-
Tunica-Biloxi, Louisiana	...	...	...	...	...	...	...	...	...	...	...	...
Tuolumne Rancheria, California	24	1	1	-	-	-	-	-	24	-	1	-
Turtle Mountain, North Dakota	470	481	416	65	12	7	43	425	471	10	79	28
Tuscarora, New York	-	-	-	-	-	-	-	-	-	-	-	-
Twenty-Nine Palms, California	-	-	-	-	-	-	-	-	-	-	-	-
Uintah and Ouray, Utah	476	40	39	1	-	4	8	320	193	5	8	1
Umatilla, Oregon	106	159	151	8	1	2	-	94	171	-	3	1
Upper Sioux Community, Minnesota	-	20	18	2	-	-	-	-	20	-	-	-
Upper Skagit, Washington	-	-	-	-	-	-	-	-	-	-	-	-
Ute Mountain, Colorado-New Mexico	260	11	11	-	4	7	12	241	38	-	14	1
Vermillion Lake, Minnesota	11	17	17	-	-	5	-	11	12	-	5	5
Viejas Rancheria, California	35	6	6	-	-	-	2	-	43	-	-	-
Walker River, Nevada	79	66	62	4	-	-	3	10	126	1	10	1
Wampanoag, Massachusetts	-	-	-	-	-	-	-	-	-	-	-	-
Warm Springs, Oregon	403	43	42	1	1	24	6	345	122	1	8	1
Washoe, Nevada	-	-	-	-	-	-	-	-	-	-	-	-
Western Pequot, Connecticut	...	...	...	...	...	...	...	...	...	...	...	...
White Earth, Minnesota	352	361	332	29	2	9	18	245	453	...	23	22
Wind River, Wyoming	599	376	359	17	1	10	17	324	604	3	59	14
Winnebago, Nebraska	247	38	27	11	-	4	6	206	76	-	13	-
Winnemucca Colony, Nevada	11	-	-	-	-	-	-	11	-	-	-	-
Wisconsin Winnebago, Reservation	45	32	32	-	-	6	-	5	72	-	6	-
Woodfords Community, California	-	-	-	-	-	-	-	-	-	-	-	-
XL Ranch, California	...	...	...	...	...	...	...	...	...	...	...	...
Yakima, Washington	543	792	759	32	3	7	5	557	778	...	11	4
Yankton, South Dakota	359	47	38	9	-	-	11	241	143	-	27	6
Yavapai, Arizona	22	-	-	-	-	-	-	22	-	-	-	-
Yerington, Nevada	17	14	14	-	-	-	-	-	31	-	-	-
Yomba, Nevada	-	11	9	2	-	2	-	-	7	-	6	-
Zia Pueblo, New Mexico	103	-	-	-	-	-	-	99	1	-	-	2
Zuni Pueblo, New Mexico	1,055	17	9	8	-	6	23	990	30	1	49	30
San Felipe/Santa Ana Joint Area, New Mexico	-	-	-	-	-	-	-	-	-	-	-	-

[Continued]

★ 590 ★

Source of Water and Sewage Disposal Method for Occupied Housing Units on Reservations, 1980: Sauk-Sauiattle - Zuni Pueblo

[Continued]

Identified reservation	Source of water							Sewage disposal				
	Public system, private company, tribal or community system	Individual well			Private cistern	Creek, spring, river, lake, or pond	Other means	Public sewer	Septic tank or cesspool	Chemical toilet	Outhouse or privy	Other means
		Total	Drilled	Dug								
San Felipe/Santo Domingo Joint Area, New Mexico	11	-	-	-	12	-	-	11	12	-	-	-
Other Reservation Lands in Montana	-	-	-	-	-	-	-	-	-	-	-	-

Source: U.S. Bureau of the Census, Subject Reports, PC80-2-1D, Part II, *American Indians, Eskimos, and Aleuts on Identified Reservations and in the Historic Areas of Oklahoma (Excluding Urbanized Areas)*, U.S. Government Printing Office, Washington, D.C., 1986, pp. 794-871. *Notes:* Three dots (...) means not applicable, or that the data are being withheld to avoid disclosure of information for individuals. A dash (-) represents zero or a percent which rounds to less than 0.1. Also, a dash (-) is used because the number of supplementary questionnaires for the reservations was insufficient to produce reliable estimates.

Mortgages

★ 591 ★

Mortgage Approval and Denial Rates, by Race/ Ethnicity and Income, 1991

Percentage of conventional home mortgage applications approved or denied by race of applicant in 1991.

Race and ethnicity	Lower income		Upper income	
	Percent approved	Percent denied	Percent approved	Percent denied
American Indian	53.9	38.6	73.4	15.7
White	61.7	31.5	81.0	9.7
Black	44.9	48.2	66.0	23.2
Hispanic	54.0	37.1	68.5	19.8
Asian	68.5	20.2	74.3	13.6
Joint[1]	59.2	33.2	76.8	12.6
Other	63.0	28.1	70.4	16.6

Source: Wall Street Journal, October 28, p. A-10. Primary source: Federal Reserve Board. *Notes:* Lower income is defined as less than 80% and upper income greater than 120% of median family income of the metropolitan statistical area in which the property is located. 1. White/minority.

★ 592 ★

Mortgage Denial Rates of Largest Lenders, by Race/Ethnicity, 1991

Lenders are ranked by number of applications.

Lender	State	Total applications	White rejection rate	Minority to white rejection ratio			
				Native American	Hispanic	Black	Asian
Green Tree Acceptance	MN	144,519	68.71	1.09	1.05	1.16	1.06
Security Pacific Housing Service	CA	93,599	54.19	1.12	1.09	1.16	0.97
Norwest Mortgage	IA	65,210	5.23	1.73	2.18	2.68	1.22
American Residential Mortgage	CA	48,854	41.74	1.14	1.15	1.02	1.00
Home Savings of America	CA	36,392	18.69	0.96	1.30	1.94	0.99
Sears Mortgage	IL	35,844	3.03	1.65	1.98	2.94	0.96
Margaretten & Company	NJ	32,182	5.33	4.79	1.16	3.14	1.15
Bank of America	CA	28,922	31.68	1.29	1.63	1.47	1.02
Great Western Bank	CA	26,951	16.36	1.04	1.12	1.55	0.98
Fleet National Bank	RI	22,368	11.07	1.45	1.73	2.48	1.39
GMAC Mortgage	PA	22,036	6.57	3.23	2.48	3.70	1.29
Imco Realty Services	CA	21,518	11.80	1.84	1.78	2.10	1.26
Oakwood Acceptance	NC	20,643	44.56	1.12	1.30	1.36	-
United Savings Association	TX	19,643	8.81	2.06	1.68	1.96	1.13
The Prudential Home Mortgage	MD	18,192	16.38	1.67	1.72	2.53	1.43
Directors Mortgage Loan	CA	17,372	12.37	2.05	1.40	2.23	1.21
CTX Mortgage	TX	16,671	7.32	1.18	1.92	3.15	1.40
World Savings and Loan	CA	16,360	16.24	1.12	1.29	1.96	0.72
Security Pacific National Bank	CA	15,858	14.98	1.53	1.53	1.53	1.23
Washington Mutual Savings	WA	15,439	20.98	2.30	2.11	1.58	0.92

Source: Wall Street Journal, November 30, 1992, p. A5. *Note:* A dash (-) indicates fewer than 50 applications.

★ 593 ★

Mortgage Lending Distribution, by Race/Ethnicity

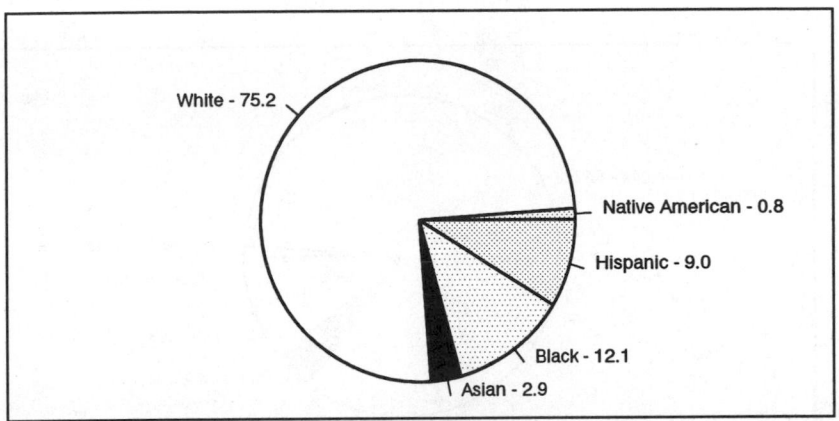

Shares of the U.S. population based on 1990 census data.

Characteristic	Percent
White[1]	75.2
Black	12.1
Hispanic	9.0
Asian	2.9
Native American	0.8

Source: Wall Street Journal, November 30, 1992, p. A4. *Note:* 1. White includes a small number from "other" races.

★ 594 ★

Mortgage Lending Distribution, by Race/Ethnicity: Amounts Approved

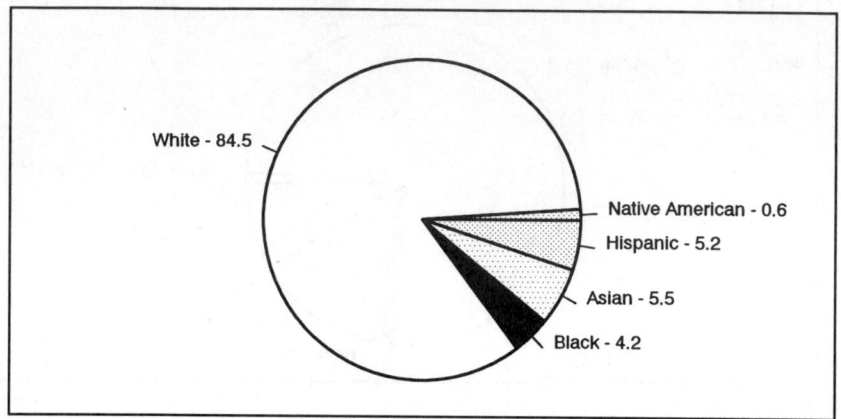

Each group's share of total mortgage money lent is shown; shares are based on 1991 data reported to the Federal Reserve.

Characteristic	Percent
White[1]	84.5
Asian	5.5
Hispanic	5.2
Black	4.2
Native American	0.6

Source: Wall Street Journal, November 30, 1992, p. A4. *Note:* 1. White includes a small number from "other" races.

★ 595 ★

Mortgage Lending Distribution, by Race/Ethnicity: Approved Applications

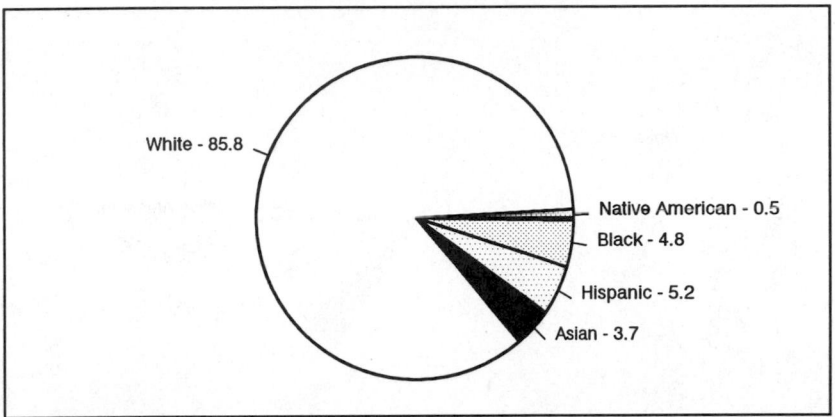

Each group's share of all loans approved is based on 1991 data reported to the Federal Reserve.

Characteristic	Percent
White[1]	85.8
Hispanic	5.2
Black	4.8
Asian	3.7
Native American	0.5

Source: Wall Street Journal, November 30, 1992, p. A4. *Note:* 1. White includes a small number from "other" races.

★ 596 ★

Mortgage Lending Distribution, by Race/Ethnicity:
Mortgage Applications

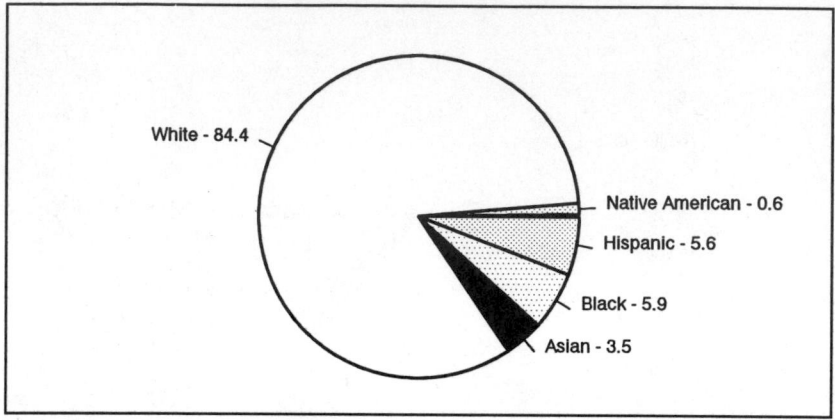

Shares based on 1991 data reported to the Federal Reserve.

Characteristic	Percent
White[1]	84.4
Black	5.9
Hispanic	5.6
Asian	3.5
Native American	0.6

Source: Wall Street Journal, November 30, 1992, p. A4. *Note:* 1. White includes a small number from "other" races.

Chapter 8

BUSINESS AND INDUSTRY

Businesses

★ 597 ★

Average Small Business Revenues in the U.S., by Sex and Race/Ethnicity, 1987

Ownership	Men	Women
White	189,000	70,000
Asian/Pacific Islander	107,000	64,000
Hispanic	66,000	88,000
African-American	50,000	41,000
American Indian/Alaska Native	47,000	32,000

Source: Alaska Business Monthly, June, 1992, p. 50. Primary source: U.S. Bureau of the Census.

★ 598 ★

Women in Corporate Management

The percent of women managers is shown, by race/ethnicity.

Ethnic group	Percent
Native American	0.5
White	96.7
Asian	1.9
African-American	0.9

Source: Dawn M. Baskerville, "Breaking Through the Glass Ceiling," *Black Enterprise* 22 (August 1991), p. 37. Primary source: Heldrick and Struggles, *The Corporate Woman Officer*, Chicago, 1986.

★ 599 ★

Minority-Owned Firms, 1987

Figures are shown for 1987, by race/ethnicity.

Ethnic group	Number of firms	% of all U.S. firms	1987 revenues (billions)	% of all U.S. revenues
American Indian and Alaskan	21,380	0.2	0.9	0.1
Black	424,165	3.1	19.8	1.0
Hispanic	422,373	3.1	24.7	1.2
Asian/Pacific	355,331	2.6	33.1	1.7

Source: USA TODAY, June 17, 1992, p. 4-B. Primary source: Economic Census (latest available data).

★ 600 ★

Minority-Owned Firms, by Type, 1987

Data are shown for 1987.

Industry division, legal form of organization, and minority	All firms		Firms with paid employees				Relative standard error of estimate (%) for column -			
	Firms (number) A	Sales and receipts ($1,000) B	Firms (number) C	Sales and receipts ($1,000) D	Employees (number) E	Annual payroll ($1,000) F	A	B	C	D
All industries	1,213,750	77,839,943	248,149	56,463,624	836,483	9,508,592	-	-	-	-
Subchapter S corporations	42,212	23,300,949	30,783	22,137,767	291,319	4,056,980	-	-	-	-
Minority men	25,528	15,658,873	18,740	14,905,851	188,706	2,692,533	-	-	-	-
Minority women	16,684	7,642,076	12,043	7,231,916	102,613	1,364,447	-	-	-	-
American Indian and Alaska Native	360	138,126	242	128,463	2,088	27,654	3	1	3	1
Black	12,565	7,741,387	8,669	7,389,781	102,504	1,498,206	-	-	-	-
Hispanic	13,374	7,265,356	9,628	6,871,684	85,102	1,239,896	-	-	1	-
Asian and Pacific Islander	16,475	8,402,698	12,656	7,977,348	105,402	1,347,721	-	-	-	-
Individual proprietorships	1,129,705	46,164,026	196,600	27,818,283	426,636	4,406,130	-	-	-	-
Minority men	773,846	38,282,773	157,353	23,971,930	353,914	3,756,446	-	-	-	-
Minority women	355,859	7,881,253	39,247	3,846,353	72,722	649,684	-	-	1	1
American Indian and Alaska Native	20,454	674,173	3,247	396,429	5,864	71,237	1	1	3	2
Black	400,339	10,056,751	57,398	5,210,241	91,671	986,628	-	-	-	-
Hispanic	396,769	15,169,291	67,552	9,112,214	147,544	1,705,000	-	-	1	-
Asian and Pacific Islander	320,161	20,570,018	69,663	13,276,736	185,065	1,677,348	-	-	1	-
Partnerships	41,833	8,374,968	20,766	6,507,574	118,528	1,045,482	-	-	-	-
Minority men	26,067	5,905,347	13,428	4,610,225	80,807	731,690	-	-	1	-
Minority women	15,766	2,469,621	7,338	1,897,319	37,721	313,792	-	-	1	1
American Indian and Alaska Native	566	98,980	250	77,897	1,004	10,380	2	2	3	2
Black	11,261	1,964,738	4,748	1,530,398	26,292	276,271	-	-	-	-

[Continued]

★ 600 ★

Minority-Owned Firms, by Type, 1987
[Continued]

Industry division, legal form of organization, and minority	All firms		Firms with paid employees				Relative standard error of estimate (%) for column -			
	Firms (number) A	Sales and receipts ($1,000) B	Firms (number) C	Sales and receipts ($1,000) D	Employees (number) E	Annual payroll ($1,000) F	A	B	C	D
Hispanic	12,230	2,296,953	5,728	1,745,534	32,200	298,446	1	-	1	-
Asian and Pacific Islander	18,695	4,151,610	10,399	3,247,254	60,878	476,848	-	-	1	-

Source: "Statistics for Minority-Owned Firms by Minority, Industry, Division, and Legal Form of Organization: 1987," *Minority-Owned Businesses*, p. 80. Primary source: 1987 Survey of Minority-Owned Businesses. *Minority-Owned Businesses*. Washington, D.C.: U.S. Government Printing Office, 1990. Detail may not add to total because of rounding and because a firm may be included in more than one minority group. This table is based on the 1972 SIC system.

★ 601 ★

Minority-Owned Firms: Business Ownership, by Sex

Data are shown for 1987.

Minority	Firms (number)	Sales and receipts ($1,000,000)	% of all minority-owned firms by gender	
			Firms	Sales and receipts
All minority firms	1,213,750	77,840	100.0	100.0
Men	825,443	59,847	100.0	100.0
American Indian and Alaska Native	15,072	711	1.8	1.2
Black	265,889	13,377	32.0	22.1
Hispanic	307,348	20,442	36.9	33.8
Asian and Pacific Islander	243,442	25,988	29.3	42.9
Women	388,309	17,993	100.0	100.0
American Indian and Alaskan Native	6,308	200	1.6	1.1
Black	158,278	6,531	40.4	35.9
Hispanic	115,025	4,328	29.4	23.8
Asian and Pacific Islander	111,889	7,136	28.6	39.2

Source: "Minority-Owned Firms by Gender," *Minority-Owned Businesses*, p. 2. Primary source: 1987 Survey of Minority-Owned Businesses. *Minority-Owned Businesses*, Washington, D.C.: U.S. Government Printing Office, 1990. *Notes:* Detail in this table does not add to total because of duplication of some firms. Firms that were owned equally by two or more minorities are included in the data for each minority group but counted only once at total levels.

★ 602 ★

Minority-Owned Firms: Employment Size

Employment size and minority	Firms (number) A	Sales and receipts ($1,000) B	Employees (number) C	Annual payroll ($1,000) D	Relative standard error of estimate (%) for column A	B
All industries	1,213,750	77,839,943	836,483	9,508,592	-	-
With no paid employees	965,601	21,376,319	-	-	-	-
Minority men	635,920	16,358,957	-	-	-	-
Minority women	329,681	5,017,362	-	-	-	1
American Indian and Alaska Native	17,641	308,490	-	-	1	2
Black	353,350	5,632,	456	-	-	-
Hispanic	339,465	7,002,168	-	-	-	1
Asian and Pacific Islander	262,613	8,622,988	-	-	-	-
With paid employees	248,149	56,463,624	836,483	9,508,592	-	-
Minority men	189,521	43,488,036	623,427	7,180,669	-	-
Minority women	58,628	12,975,588	213,056	2,327,923	1	-
American Indian and Alaska Native	3,739	602,789	8,956	109,271	3	1
Black	70,815	14,130,420	220,467	2,761,105	-	-
Hispanic	82,908	17,729,432	264,846	3,243,342	1	-
Asian and Pacific Islander	92,718	24,501,338	351,345	3,501,917	-	-
No employees[1]	90,794	6,324,443	-	1,055,951	1	1
Minority men	71,210	5,275,213	-	893,258	1	1
Minority women	19,584	1,049,230	-	162,693	1	1
American Indian and Alaska Native	1,894	103,948	-	19,252	5	4
Black	31,414	1,495,861	-	295,167	-	-
Hispanic	33,717	2,300,522	-	457,870	1	1
Asian and Pacific Islander	24,372	2,461,292	-	290,507	1	1
1 to 4 employees	113,295	17,677,566	218,776	2,128,328	-	-
Minority men	85,291	13,901,557	165,046	1,648,380	-	-
Minority women	28,004	3,776,009	53,730	479,948	1	1
American Indian and Alaska Native	1,365	190,813	2,646	25,810	3	2
Black	29,238	3,565,200	54,936	541,404	-	-
Hispanic	35,239	5,208,198	68,367	696,933	1	-
Asian and Pacific Islander	48,466	8,867,263	94,757	883,105	-	-
5 to 9 employees	26,114	9,887,070	168,495	1,571,332	-	-
Minority men	19,626	7,652,265	126,728	1,192,794	-	-
Minority women	6,488	2,234,805	41,767	378,538	1	1
American Indian and Alaska Native	286	112,284	1,870	20,160	3	1
Black	6,060	1,984,302	38,851	385,923	-	-

[Continued]

948

★ 602 ★

Minority-Owned Firms: Employment Size
[Continued]

Employment size and minority	Firms (number) A	Sales and receipts ($1,000) B	Employees (number) C	Annual payroll ($1,000) D	Relative standard error of estimate (%) for column	
					A	B
Hispanic	8,221	3,075,801	53,181	526,090	1	-
Asian and Pacific Islander	11,788	4,801,877	76,139	654,046	1	-
10 to 19 employees	11,566	7,430,113	151,985	1,407,438	-	-
Minority men	8,697	5,748,744	114,252	1,063,083	-	-
Minority women	2,869	1,681,369	37,733	344,355	1	-
American Indian and Alaska Native	136	91,447	1,755	16,654	-	-
Black	2,443	1,650,580	31,978	338,183	-	-
Hispanic	3,671	2,433,738	48,330	491,931	1	-
Asian and Pacific Islander	5,419	3,316,649	71,301	573,764	1	-
20 to 49 employees	4,914	6,671,271	142,516	1,442,486	-	-
Minority men	3,636	4,902,599	105,178	1,054,968	-	-
Minority women	1,278	1,768,672	37,338	387,518	-	-
American Indian and Alaska Native	49	70,164	1,396	15,979	-	-
Black	1,143	1,933,049	33,630	415,857	-	-
Hispanic	1,582	2,126,435	46,142	477,564	1	-
Asian and Pacific Islander	2,187	2,601,780	62,820	552,254	-	-
50 to 99 employees	1,033	4,103,812	69,809	824,387	-	-
Minority men	745	2,968,384	50,200	572,507	1	-
Minority women	288	1,135,428	19,609	251,880	-	-
American Indian and Alaska Native	4	7,743	271	2,482	-	-
Black	328	1,493,038	22,363	306,820	-	-
Hispanic	349	1,370,194	23,335	269,919	-	-
Asian and Pacific Islander	368	1,296,402	24,885	262,097	1	-
100 employees or more	433	4,369,349	84,902	1,078,670	-	-
Minority men	316	3,039,274	62,023	755,679	-	-
Minority women	117	1,330,075	22,879	322,991	-	-
American Indian and Alaska Native	5	26,390	1,018	8,934	-	-
Black	189	2,008,390	38,709	477,751	-	-
Hispanic	129	1,214,544	25,491	323,035	-	-
Asian and Pacific Islander	118	1,156,075	21,443	286,144	-	-

Source: "Statistics for Minority-Owned Firms by Minority and Employment Size of Firm: 1987," *Minority-Owned Businesses*, pp. 82-83. Primary source: 1987 Survey of Minority-Owned Businesses. *Minority-Owned Businesses*, Washington, D.C.: U.S. Government Printing Office, 1990. *Notes:* Detail may not add to total because of rounding and because a firm may be included in more than one minority group. 1. Firms reported annual payroll but did not report any employees on their payroll during specified period in 1987.

★ 603 ★

Minority-Owned Firms: Sales and Receipts

Data are shown for 1987.

Receipts size and minority	All firms		Firms with paid employees				Relative standard error of estimate (%) for column -			
	Firms (number) A	Sales and receipts ($1,000) B	Firms (number) C	Sales and receipts ($1,000) D	Employees (number) E	Annual payroll ($1,000) F	A	B	C	D
All industries	1,213,750	77,839,943	248,149	56,463,624	836,483	9,508,592	-	-	-	-
Less than $5,000	357,180	767,373	6,191	18,018	1,356	13,264	-	-	2	2
Minority men	212,340	459,143	4,010	11,738	875	8,714	-	-	3	3
Minority women	144,840	308,230	2,181	6,280	481	4,550	-	1	4	4
American Indian and Alaska Native	7,621	16,163	94	287	14	150	2	3	24	29
Black	149,446	316,631	2,812	8,051	501	5,674	-	-	-	-
Hispanic	120,717	261,704	2,030	6,067	406	4,273	1	1	5	6
Asian and Pacific Islander	81,973	178,337	1,286	3,701	446	3,212	1	1	6	6
$5,000 to $9,999	202,669	1,365,675	11,094	77,435	2,208	27,831	-	-	2	2
Minority men	126,505	856,227	7,588	52,934	1,431	18,970	1	1	2	2
Minority women	76,164	509,448	3,506	24,501	777	8,861	1	1	3	3
American Indian and Alaska Native	3,971	26,520	318	2,178	28	757	3	4	13	13
Black	77,874	524,276	4,860	33,893	830	12,377	-	-	-	-
Hispanic	74,711	504,776	3,555	24,696	674	8,879	1	1	4	4
Asian and Pacific Islander	47,618	320,333	2,446	17,283	702	6,092	1	1	4	4
$10,000 to $24,999	251,749	3,920,362	30,368	510,301	12,744	136,941	-	-	1	1
Minority men	172,921	2,719,467	21,981	371,110	8,370	99,747	-	-	1	1
Minority women	78,828	1,200,895	8,387	139,191	4,374	37,194	1	1	2	2
American Indian and Alaska Native	4,153	63,104	651	10,834	173	2,754	3	3	8	8
Black	91,566	1,416,051	12,445	206,391	4,901	56,803	-	-	-	-
Hispanic	92,386	1,430,591	10,742	180,700	3,876	49,395	1	1	2	2
Asian and Pacific Islander	65,521	1,039,524	6,771	116,147	3,884	176,848	1	1	2	2
$25,000 to $49,999	147,247	5,162,808	39,875	1,452,814	33,125	338,811	-	-	1	1
Minority men	111,523	9,918,201	29,829	1,089,678	22,616	255,013	1	1	1	1
Minority women	35,724	1,244,607	10,046	363,136	10,509	83,798	1	1	1	1
American Indian and Alaska Native	2,085	72,868	635	22,976	507	5,307	4	4	7	7
Black	46,583	1,616,585	13,807	496,718	11,582	121,062	-	-	-	-
Hispanic	52,737	1,849,069	14,686	535,844	11,180	129,340	1	1	2	2
Asian and Pacific Islander	47,112	1,667,594	11,031	407,377	10,197	85,360	1	1	2	2
$50,000 to $99,999	109,235	7,672,302	50,833	3,672,971	78,494	746,614	-	-	1	1
Minority men	85,576	6,014,686	38,962	2,818,375	55,505	569,968	1	1	1	1
Minority women	23,659	1,657,616	11,871	854,596	22,989	176,646	1	1	1	1
American Indian and Alaska Native	1,848	127,880	791	54,899	1,060	13,011	5	5	5	5
Black	29,482	2,044,481	14,353	1,019,898	23,194	231,730	-	-	-	-
Hispanic	36,589	2,554,350	17,642	1,266,051	25,711	277,329	1	1	1	1
Asian and Pacific Islander	42,235	3,011,371	18,446	1,360,951	29,192	230,816	1	1	1	1
$100,000 to $199,999	75,530	10,575,649	50,825	7,223,250	144,597	1,344,961	1	1	1	1
Minority men	60,282	8,437,235	40,166	5,708,013	107,865	1,050,795	1	1	1	1
Minority women	15,248	2,138,414	10,659	1,515,237	36,732	294,166	1	1	1	1
American Indian and Alaska Native	957	132,186	628	87,231	1,575	17,173	5	5	5	5
Black	15,942	2,201,517	11,086	1,552,069	33,591	330,816	-	-	-	-
Hispanic	23,711	3,308,844	15,927	2,251,181	43,490	467,072	1	1	1	1

[Continued]

★ 603 ★

Minority-Owned Firms: Sales and Receipts
[Continued]

Receipts size and minority	All firms		Firms with paid employees				Relative standard error of estimate (%) for column -			
	Firms (number) A	Sales and receipts ($1,000) B	Firms (number) C	Sales and receipts ($1,000) D	Employees (number) E	Annual payroll ($1,000) F	A	B	C	D
Asian and Pacific Islander	35,671	5,039,149	23,670	3,401,617	67,305	543,159	1	1	1	1
$200,000 to $249,999	16,738	3,726,447	13,087	2,916,812	54,561	537,175	1	1	1	1
Minority men	13,576	3,023,041	10,507	2,342,444	41,677	424,906	1	1	1	1
Minority women	3,162	703,406	2,580	574,368	12,884	112,269	2	2	2	2
American Indian and Alaska Native	154	34,425	124	27,711	455	5,623	6	6	7	7
Black	3,116	693,241	2,491	554,446	10,752	115,103	-	-	-	-
Hispanic	5,105	1,137,501	4,052	902,989	16,715	190,127	2	2	2	2
Asian and Pacific Islander	8,484	1,888,270	6,511	1,452,094	26,986	229,835	2	2	2	2
$250,000 to $499,999	32,089	11,012,084	26,713	9,216,396	160,815	1,636,006	-	-	-	-
Minority men	25,873	8,870,936	21,398	7,375,467	122,942	1,280,040	-	-	-	-
Minority women	6,216	2,141,148	5,315	1,840,929	37,873	355,966	1	1	1	1
American Indian and Alaska Native	355	124,565	277	97,409	1,604	17,723	1	1	2	2
Black	5,843	2,009,503	4,994	1,727,663	30,931	342,475	-	-	-	-
Hispanic	9,581	3,290,917	8,078	2,789,838	50,969	566,462	1	1	1	1
Asian and Pacific Islander	16,584	5,683,919	13,595	4,683,806	78,949	725,621	-	-	-	-
$500,000 to $999,999	13,164	9,041,044	11,697	8,051,763	126,253	1,333,349	-	-	-	-
Minority men	10,570	7,257,529	9,358	6,442,079	98,296	1,038,699	-	-	-	-
Minority women	2,594	1,783,515	2,339	1,609,684	27,957	294,650	1	1	1	1
American Indian and Alaska Native	154	105,787	143	98,922	1,317	16,037	1	1	1	1
Black	2,366	1,636,463	2,134	1,474,381	25,295	290,403	-	-	-	-
Hispanic	4,292	2,933,649	3,843	2,635,973	41,930	474,069	-	-	-	-
Asian and Pacific Islander	6,476	4,448,267	5,687	3,916,417	58,886	565,818	-	-	-	1
$1,000,000 or more	8,149	24,596,199	7,466	23,323,864	222,330	3,393,640	-	-	-	-
Minority men	6,275	18,290,528	5,722	17,276,198	163,850	2,433,817	-	-	-	-
Minority women	1,874	6,305,671	1,744	6,047,666	58,480	959,823	-	-	-	-
American Indian and Alaska Native	82	207,781	78	200,342	2,223	30,736	-	-	-	-
Black	1,947	7,304,128	1,833	7,056,910	78,890	1,254,662	-	-	-	-
Hispanic	2,544	7,460,199	2,353	7,136,093	69,895	1,076,396	-	-	-	-
Asian and Pacific Islander	3,657	9,847,562	3,275	9,141,945	74,798	1,083,042	-	-	-	-

Source: "Statistics for Minority-Owned Firms by Minority, Industry, and Receipts Size of Firm: 1987," *Minority-Owned Businesses*, p. 81. Primary source: 1987 Survey of Minority-Owned Businesses. *Minority-Owned Businesses*, Washington, D.C.: U.S. Government Printing Office, 1990. Detail may not add to total because of rounding and because a firm may be included in more than one minority group.

★ 604 ★

Minority-Owned Firms: Trends in Business Ownership, 1982-1987

Minority	Firms (number)			Sales and receipts ($1,000,000)		
	1982	1987	% change	1982	1987	% change
All minorities	741,640	1,213,750	63.7	34,454	77,454	125.9
American Indian and Alaska Native	13,573	21,380	57.5	495	911	84.4
Black	308,260	424,165	37.6	9,619	19,763	105.5
Hispanic	233,975	422,373	80.5	11,759	24,732	110.3
Asian and Pacific Islander	187,691	355,331	89.3	12,654	33,124	161.8

Source: "Comparison of Business Ownership by Minority Group: 1987 and 1982," *Minority-Owned Businesses*, p. 2. Primary source: 1987 Survey of Minority-Owned Businesses, *Minority-Owned Businesses*. Washington, D.C.: U.S. Government Printing Office, 1990. *Notes:* Detail in this table does not add to total because of duplication of some firms. Firms that were owned equally by two or more minorities are in the data for each minority group but counted only once at total levels. Figures for 1982 have been adjusted for comparability to 1987 data.

★ 605 ★

Minority-Owned Firms: Trends in Firm Ownership, 1982-87

The number of firms owned and the percent change, from 1982 to 1987, are shown, by race/ethnicity.

Race/ethnicity	Number of firms		Percent change
	1982	1987	
American Indian and Alaska Native	13,573	21,380	57.5
Black	308,260	424,165	37.6
Hispanic	233,975	422,373	80.5
Asian and Pacific Islander	187,691	355,331	89.3
All minorities	741,640	1,213,750	63.7
All U.S. firms (including minorities)	12,000,000	13,700,000	14.2

Source: *Wall Street Journal*, April 3, 1992, p. R-4. Primary source: Bureau of the Census.

★ 606 ★

Minority-Owned Firms: Trends in Firm Sales, 1982-87

Firm sales and the percent change from 1982 to 1987, are shown, by race/ethnicity.

Race/ethnicity	Total sales (in millions of dollars)		Percent change
	1982	1987	
American Indian and Alaska Native	495	911	84.0
Black	9,619	19,763	105.5
Hispanic	11,759	24,732	110.3
Asian and Pacific Islander	12,654	33,124	161.8
All minorities	34,454	77,840	125.9
All U.S. firms	967,500	1,994,800	106.2

Source: Wall Street Journal, April 3, 1992, p. R-4. Primary source: Bureau of the Census.

★ 607 ★

Minority-Owned Firms: Firm Ownership per 1,000 Population, 1982-87

The number of firms owned, per 1,000 population, is shown, by race/ethnicity, for 1982-87.

Race/ethnicity	1982	1987	Percent change 1982-87
American Indian	8.8	11.8	34.1
Native American	7.4	10.3	39.2
Aleut	58.5	54.0	7.7
Eskimo	36.8	44.4	20.7
Blacks	11.3	14.6	29.2
Hispanics	14.3	20.9	46.2
Mexican	13.7	18.8	37.2
Puerto Rican	6.3	10.9	73.0
Cuban	41.4	62.9	51.9
Other Hispanic	14.2	22.9	61.3
Asian[1]	43.2	57.0	31.9
Asian Indian	51.3	75.7	47.6
Chinese	49.1	63.4	29.1
Japanese	59.3	66.1	11.5
Korean	68.0	102.4	50.6
Vietnamese	14.6	49.6	239.7
Filipino	25.5	32.8	28.6

[Continued]

★ 607 ★

Minority-Owned Firms: Firm Ownership per 1,000 Population, 1982-87

[Continued]

Race/ethnicity	1982	1987	Percent change 1982-87
Hawaiian	16.6	21.5	29.5
Non-Minority	61.9	67.1	8.4

Source: American Demographics, January 1992, p. 34. Primary source: Bureau of the Census, 1982 and 1987 Economic Census and population estimates. *Note:* 1. Data include Pacific Islanders.

★ 608 ★

Minority-Owned Firms: Percent Distribution, by Industry

Percentages are shown for 1987.

Industry	American Indian and Alaskan Native	Black	Hispanic	Asian and Pacific Islander
Agricultural services, forestry fishing, and mining	10.0	20.0	45.0	26.0
Construction	3.0	34.0	52.0	12.0
Manufacturing	3.0	27.0	37.0	34.0
Transportation and public utilities	1.0	48.0	35.0	16.0
Wholesale trade	1.0	21.0	38.0	40.0
Retail trade	1.0	29.0	31.0	39.0
Finance, insurance, and real estate	1.0	35.0	29.0	36.0
Services	1.0	37.0	33.0	29.0
Industries not classified	2.0	38.0	36.0	25.0

Source: "Minority-Owned Firms by Industry Division: 1987," *Minority-Owned Businesses*, p. 8. Primary source: 1987 Survey of Minority-Owned Businesses. *Minority-Owned Businesses*. Washington, D.C.: U.S. Government Printing Office, 1990. Percent distributions may not add to 100, since duplication of firms exists among minority groups.

★ 609 ★

Minority-Owned Firms: All Industries

The number of firms, employees, sales and receipts, and annual payroll is shown for all industries, by sex and race/ethnicity, for 1987. Dollars are shown in thousands.

Characteristic	All firms		Firms with paid employees				Relative standard error of estimate % for column			
	Firms (number) A	Sales and receipts ($1,000) B	Firms (number) C	Sales and receipts ($1,000) D	Employees (number) E	Annual payroll ($1,000) F	A	B	C	D
All industries	1,213,750	77,839,943	248,149	56,463,624	836,483	9,506,592	-	-	-	-
Minority men	825,441	59,846,993	189,521	43,488,036	623,427	7,180,669	-	-	-	-
Minority women	388,309	17,992,950	58,628	12,975,588	213,056	2,327,923	-	-	1	-
American Indian and Alaska Native	21,380	911,279	3,739	602,789	8,956	109,271	1	1	3	1
Men	15,072	711,166	2,881	468,016	6,660	85,144	1	1	3	1
Women	6,306	200,113	858	134,773	2,296	24,127	3	20	5	2
Black	424,165	19,762,876	70,815	14,130,420	220,467	2,761,105	-	-	-	-
Men	265,887	13,232,364	51,518	9,289,084	147,520	1,820,396	-	-	-	-
Women	158,278	6,530,512	19,297	4,841,336	72,947	940,709	-	-	-	-
Hispanic	422,373	24,731,600	82,908	17,729,432	264,846	3,243,342	-	-	1	-
Men	307,348	20,403,191	66,907	14,715,111	210,749	2,653,099	-	-	1	-
Women	115,025	4,328,409	16,001	3,014,321	54,097	590,243	1	1	1	1
Asian and Pacific Islander	355,331	33,124,326	92,718	24,501,338	351,345	3,501,917	-	-	-	-
Men	243,442	25,988,493	69,675	19,370,068	264,873	2,698,681	-	-	-	-
Women	111,889	7,135,833	23,043	5,131,270	86,472	803,326	1	-	1	-

Source: 1987 Economic Census: Survey of Minority-Owned Business Enterprises, Summary, U.S. Department of Commerce, Bureau of the Census, 1991. *Notes:* A dash (-) represents or rounds to zero. Details may not add to total because of rounding and because a firm may be included in more than one minority group.

★ 610 ★

Minority-Owned Firms: Agricultural Services

Data are shown for 1987. Trade groups are based on the 1972 Standard Industrial Classification (SIC) system.

Receipts size and minority	All firms		Firms with paid employees				Relative standard error of estimate % for column			
	Firms (number) A	Sales and receipts ($1,000) B	Firms (number) C	Sales and receipts ($1,000) D	Employees (number) E	Annual payroll ($1,000) F	A	B	C	D
Agricultural services, forestry, and fishing	36,864	1,372,297	7,087	858,401	21,706	260,062	-	1	2	1
Minority men	33,861	1,238,555	6,497	770,464	19,701	235,241	1	1	2	1
Minority women	3,003	133,742	590	87,937	2,005	24,821	4	4	6	4
American Indian and Alaska Native	3,661	104,446	371	30,109	486	8,950	2	5	12	8
Men	3,204	93,986	329	28,357	460	8,480	3	5	13	8
Women	457	10,460	42	1,752	26	470	12	23	39	19
Black	7,316	216,742	1,662	144,276	3,078	38,046	-	-	-	-
Men	6,645	176,988	1,482	112,995	2,564	31,652	-	-	-	-
Women	671	39,754	180	31,281	514	6,394	-	-	-	-
Hispanic	16,365	694,937	3,331	479,658	14,449	163,569	1	1	3	2

[Continued]

★ 610 ★

Minority-Owned Firms: Agricultural Services

[Continued]

Receipts size and minority	All firms		Firms with paid employees				Relative standard error of estimate % for column			
	Firms (number) A	Sales and receipts ($1,000) B	Firms (number) C	Sales and receipts ($1,000) D	Employees (number) E	Annual payroll ($1,000) F	A	B	C	D
Men	15,211	645,694	3,096	446,248	13,309	150,316	1	1	3	2
Women	1,154	49,243	235	33,410	1,140	13,253	6	7	11	9
Asian and Pacific Islander	9,726	365,309	1,760	211,467	3,976	52,155	1	2	4	3
Men	8,975	330,533	1,622	189,712	3,635	47,386	1	2	4	3
Women	751	34,776	138	21,755	341	4,769	8	8	15	8
Agricultural services (SIC 07)	27,366	1,098,190	5,818	766,864	21,083	241,874	1	1	2	1
Minority men	25,241	994,220	5,363	689,959	19,131	218,459	1	1	2	1
Minority women	2,125	103,970	455	76,905	1,952	23,415	4	3	6	4
American Indian and Alaska Native	444	19,081	75	12,534	339	4,120	9	2	14	2
Black	6,155	189,980	1,474	134,886	2,984	36,210	-	-	-	-
Hispanic	14,752	648,290	3,210	464,607	14,197	160,618	1	2	3	2
Asian and Pacific Islander	6,184	248,865	1,093	161,548	3,836	43,482	2	2	4	3
Forestry (SIC 08)	728	21,520	186	13,316	317	3,486	-	-	-	-
Minority men	665	20,100	172	12,724	309	3,378	-	-	-	-
Minority women	63	1,420	14	592	8	108	-	-	-	-
American Indian and Alaska Native	89	1,368	12	803	30	266	-	-	-	-
Black	417	11,416	119	6,129	85	1,274	-	-	-	-
Hispanic	184	8,263	45	6,065	195	1,882	-	-	-	-
Asian and Pacific Islander	43	861	11	664	17	160	-	-	-	-
Fishing, hunting, and trapping (SIC 09)	8,770	252,587	1,083	78,221	306	14,702	1	3	7	6
Minority men	7,955	224,235	962	67,781	261	13,404	1	3	7	7
Minority women	815	28,352	121	10,440	45	1,298	8	12	23	16
American Indian and Alaska Native	3,128	83,997	284	16,772	117	4,564	3	6	16	14
Black	744	15,346	69	3,261	9	562	-	-	-	-
Hispanic	1,429	38,384	76	8,986	57	1,069	3	3	13	4
Asian and Pacific Islander	3,499	115,583	656	49,255	123	8,513	2	5	8	9

Source: "Statistics for Minority-Owned Firms by Major Industry Group: 1987," *Minority-Owned Businesses*, p. 9. Primary source: 1987 Survey of Minority-Owned Businesses. *Minority-Owned Businesses*, Washington, D.C., U.S. Government Printing Office, 1990. Arranged by the editors. Details may not add to total because of rounding and because a firm may be included in more than one minority group. *Note:* A dash (-) represents zero.

★ 611 ★

Minority-Owned Firms: Farm Operators

Figures are shown in thousands.

Race/ethnicity	All farms		Farms with sales of of $10,000 and over	
	1982	1987	1982	1987
Total operators	2,241	2,088	1,143	1,060
American Indian, Eskimos, and Aleuts	7	7	2	2
White	2,187	2,043	1,127	1,046
Black	33	23	7	4
Asian or Pacific Islander	8	8	5	5
Other	6	7	2	2
Operators of Hispanic origin[1]	16	17	6	6

Source: "Farm Operators-Tenure and Characteristics: 1982 and 1987," *Statistical Abstract of the United States,* p. 647. Primary source: U.S. Bureau of the Census, *1987 Census of Agriculture,* Vol. 1. *Notes:* 1. Operators of Hispanic origin may be of any race. 2. Excludes not reported.

★ 612 ★

Minority-Owned Firms: Mining

Data are shown for 1987. Trade groups are based on the 1972 Standard Industrial Classification (SIC) system.

Major industry group and minority	All firms		Firms with paid employees				Relative standard error of estimate % for column			
	Firms (number)	Sales and receipts ($1,000)	Firms (number)	Sales and receipts ($1,000)	Employees (number)	Annual payroll ($1,000)	A	B	C	D
	A	B	C	D	E	F				
Mining	1,613	103,075	147	76,961	859	14,532	3	1	3	1
Minority men	1,289	80,189	111	58,331	621	10,451	3	2	3	1
Minority women	324	22,886	36	18,630	238	4,081	7	1	7	-
American Indian and Alaska Native	106	4,062	8	1,882	28	522	11	5	-	-
Men	82	3,491	7	(D)	(D)	(D)	11	1	-	(D)
Women	24	571	1	(D)	(D)	(D)	31	37	-	(D)
Black	322	54,071	48	46,013	401	7,003	-	-	-	-
Men	221	38,462	29	31,906	222	3,750	-	-	-	-
Women	101	15,609	19	14,107	179	3,253	-	-	-	-
Hispanic	829	29,836	72	18,498	332	5,272	4	4	6	3
Men	684	25,109	62	15,763	291	4,678	4	5	6	3
Women	145	4,727	10	2,735	41	594	13	5	24	1
Asian and Pacific Islander	360	15,114	19	10,568	98	1,735	7	3	-	-
Men	303	13,128	13	(D)	(D)	(D)	8	4	-	(D)
Women	57	1,986	6	(D)	(D)	(D)	16	4	-	(D)
Metal mining	41	(D)	8	359	15	75	-	(D)	-	-
Minority men	38	(D)	7	(D)	(D)	(D)	-	(D)	-	(D)
Minority women	3	14	1	(D)	(D)	(D)	-	-	-	(D)

[Continued]

★ 612 ★

Minority-Owned Firms: Mining
[Continued]

Major industry group and minority	All firms		Firms with paid employees				Relative standard error of estimate % for column			
	Firms (number) A	Sales and receipts ($1,000) B	Firms (number) C	Sales and receipts ($1,000) D	Employees (number) E	Annual payroll ($1,000) F	A	B	C	D
American Indian and Alaska Native	11	(D)	2	(D)	(D)	(D)	-	(D)	-	(D)
Black	6	75	3	52	2	13	-	-	-	-
Hispanic	16	244	1	(D)	(D)	(D)	-	-	-	(D)
Asian and Pacific Islander	9	274	2	(D)	(D)	(D)	-	-	-	(D)
Anthracite mining	3	23	-	-	-	-	-	-	-	-
Minority men	1	(D)	-	-	-	-	-	(D)	-	-
Minority women	2	(D)	-	-	-	-	-	(D)		
American Indian and Alaska Native	-	-	-	-	-	-	-	-	-	-
Black	3	23	-	-	-	-	-	-	-	-
Hispanic	-	-	-	-	-	-	-	-	-	-
Asian and Pacific Islander	-	-	-	-	-	-	-	-	-	-
Bituminous coal and lignite mining	19	(D)	9	5,074	87	1,447	-	(D)	-	-
Minority men	16	4,311	6	(D)	(D)	(D)	-	-	-	(D)
Minority women	3	(D)	3	(D)	(D)	(D)	-	(D)	-	(D)
American Indian and Alaska Native	3	(D)	-	-	-	-	-	(D)	-	-
Black	9	3,968	6	(D)	(D)	(D)	-	-	-	(D)
Hispanic	4	58	1	(D)	(D)	(D)	-	-	-	(D)
Asian and Pacific Islander	3	(D)	2	(D)	(D)	(D)	-	(D)	-	(D)
Oil and gas extraction	1,448	73,870	100	54,299	543	9,737	3	2	4	1
Minority men	1,149	54,774	75	39,274	361	6,326	3	2	5	1
Minority women	299	19,096	25	15,025	182	3,411	7	2	10	-
American Indian and Alaska Native	80	2,441	5	(D)	(D)	(D)	14	9	-	(D)
Black	270	39,946	26	36,922	241	5,089	-	-	-	-
Hispanic	763	22,917	57	12,283	257	4,098	5	5	8	4
Asian and Pacific Islander	338	8,573	12	(D)	(D)	(D)	7	6	-	(D)
Nonmetallic minerals, except fuels	102	22,382	30	17,229	214	3,273	-	-	-	-
Minority men	85	(D)	23	(D)	(D)	(D)	-	(D)	-	(D)
Minority women	17	(D)	7	(D)	(D)	(D)	-	(D)	-	(D)
American Indian and Alaska Native	12	(D)	1	(D)	(D)	(D)	-	(D)	-	(D)
Black	34	10,039	13	(D)	(D)	(D)	-	-	-	(D)
Hispanic	46	6,617	13	(D)	(D)	(D)	-	-	-	(D)
Asian and Pacific Islander	10	(D)	3	(D)	(D)	(D)	-	(D)	-	(D)

Source: "Statistics for Minority-Owned Firms by Major Industry Group: 1987," *Minority-Owned Businesses*, pp. 9-10. Primary source: 1987 Survey of Minority-Owned Businesses. *Minority-Owned Businesses*, Washington, D.C., U.S. Government Printing Office, 1990. Arranged by the editors. Details may not add to total because of rounding and because a firm may be included in more than one minority group. (D) stands for data withheld to avoid disclosure of competitive information. *Note:* A dash (-) represents zero.

★ 613 ★

Minority-Owned Firms: Construction

Data are shown for 1987. Trade groups are based on the 1972 Standard Industrial Classification (SIC) system.

Major industry group and minority	SIC code	All firms		Firms with paid employees				Relative standard error of estimate % for column			
		Firms (number) A	Sales and receipts ($1,000) B	Firms (number) C	Sales and receipts ($1,000) D	Employees (number) E	Annual payroll ($1,000) F	A	B	C	D
Construction		107,650	6,903,022	29,721	5,196,718	69,878	1,222,932	-	-	1	-
Minority men		101,791	5,933,726	27,594	4,384,423	59,918	1,037,318	-	-	1	-
Minority women		5,859	969,296	2,127	812,295	9,960	185,614	2	1	2	-
American Indian and Alaska Native		2,832	155,784	835	(D)	(D)	(D)	3	2	5	(D)
Men		2,606	132,389	769	102,303	1,445	25,038	3	3	5	3
Women		226	23,395	66	(D)	(D)	(D)	10	5	11	(D)
Black		36,763	2,174,399	11,081	1,668,952	27,427	424,665	-	-	-	-
Men		34,455	1,697,563	10,078	1,266,771	21,966	325,833	-	-	-	-
Women		2,308	476,836	1,003	402,181	5,461	98,832	-	-	-	-
Hispanic		55,516	3,438,706	14,717	2,646,244	34,684	631,477	-	1	2	1
Men		53,092	3,117,491	13,901	2,365,673	31,241	565,954	1	1	2	1
Women		2,424	321,217	816	280,571	3,443	65,523	5	2	6	1
Asian and Pacific Islander		13,391	1,224,190	3,330	(D)	(D)	(D)	1	1	2	(D)
Men		12,419	1,067,003	3,067	720,819	5,995	137,159	1	1	2	1
Women		972	157,187	263	(D)	(D)	(D)	5	1	7	(D)
General building contractors	15	17,236	1,981,974	5,846	1,575,624	14,984	280,998	1	1	2	1
Minority men		16,074	1,618,344	5,311	1,367,321	12,821	235,519	1	1	2	1
Minority women		1,162	363,630	535	308,303	2,163	45,479	4	1	4	1
American Indian and Alaska Native		461	34,219	175	28,153	251	5,269	6	5	11	5
Black		6,285	635,702	2,291	516,768	5,227	92,940	-	-	-	-
Hispanic		7,990	860,943	2,522	689,809	7,271	138,470	1	1	3	1
Asian and Pacific Islander		2,632	486,113	909	374,588	2,491	51,694	2	1	3	1
Heavy construction contractors	16	1,683	389,244	668	361,861	4,582	79,241	1	-	2	-
Minority men		1,546	357,742	588	331,703	4,216	70,387	2	-	2	-
Minority women		137	31,502	80	30,158	366	8,854	8	1	8	1
American Indian and Alaska Native		93	(D)	38	15,549	178	3,902	3	(D)	-	-
Black		638	155,949	275	144,259	2,118	32,911	-	-	-	-
Hispanic		859	205,100	318	192,606	2,137	39,942	2	1	5	1
Asian and Pacific Islander		107	(D)	40	15,996	208	3,746	10	(D)	4	2
Special trade contractors	17	87,920	4,209,682	23,008	3,102,746	49,530	844,885	-	-	1	1
Minority men		83,514	3,700,436	21,538	2,658,510	42,296	718,565	-	1	1	1
Minority women		4,406	509,246	1,470	444,236	7,234	126,320	3	1	3	1
American Indian and Alaska Native		2,268	97,410	619	72,247	1,166	19,299	3	3	6	4
Black		29,631	1,313,819	8,462	972,180	19,817	292,741	-	-	-	-
Hispanic		46,383	2,266,204	11,803	1,691,285	25,032	446,520	1	1	2	1
Asian and Pacific Islander		10,331	579,278	2,308	404,939	4,035	95,933	1	1	33	1
Subdividers and developers, n.e.c.	6552	811	322,122	199	156,487	782	17,808	2	-	2	-
Minority men		657	257,204	157	126,889	585	12,847	1	1	2	-
Minority women		154	64,918	42	29,598	197	4,961	6	-	3	1
American Indian and Alaska Native		10	(D)	3	(D)	(D)	(D)	-	(D)	-	(D)
Black		209	68,929	53	35,745	265	6,073	-	-	-	-

[Continued]

★ 613 ★

Minority-Owned Firms: Construction
[Continued]

Major industry group and minority	SIC code	All firms		Firms with paid employees				Relative standard error of estimate % for column			
		Firms (number) A	Sales and receipts ($1,000) B	Firms (number) C	Sales and receipts ($1,000) D	Employees (number) E	Annual payroll ($1,000) F	A	B	C	D
Hispanic		284	106,461	74	72,544	244	6,545	2	1	4	1
Asian and Pacific Islander		321	(D)	73	(D)	(D)	(D)	3	(D)	4	(D)

Source: "Statistics for Minority-Owned Firms by Major Industry Group: 1987," *Minority-Owned Businesses*, p. 10. Primary source: 1987 Survey of Minority-Owned Businesses. *Minority-Owned Businesses*, Washington, D.C., U.S. Government Printing Office, 1990. Arranged by the editors. *Notes:* (D) stands for data withheld to avoid disclosure of competitive information. Details may not add to total because of rounding and because a firm may be included in more than one minority group. n.e.c. stands for not elsewhere classified. A dash (-) represents zero.

★ 614 ★

Minority-Owned Firms: Manufacturing

Data are shown for 1987. Trade groups are based on the 1972 Standard Industrial Classification (SIC) system.

Major industry group and minority	SIC code	All firms		Firms with paid employees				Relative standard error of estimate % for column			
		Firms (number) A	Sales and receipts ($1,000) B	Firms (number) C	Sales and receipts ($1,000) D	Employees (number) E	Annual payroll ($1,000) F	A	B	C	D
Manufacturing		29,879	3,961,128	10,126	3,584,420	76,741	946,089	-	-	1	-
Minority men		21,464	2,885,678	7,677	2,590,911	53,640	661,987	1	-	1	-
Minority women		8,415	1,075,450	2,449	993,509	23,101	284,102	1	-	2	-
American Indian and Alaska Native		911	63,563	148	(D)	(D)	(D)	4	1	5	(D)
Men		666	44,690	125	37,721	922	10,231	4	1	6	1
Women		245	18,873	23	(D)	(D)	(D)	10	3	6	(D)
Black		8,004	1,023,104	2,612	927,105	13,684	244,038	-	-	-	-
Men		6,349	639,407	2,111	563,806	8,719	146,829	-	-	-	-
Women		1,655	383,697	501	363,299	4,965	97,209	-	-	-	-
Hispanic		11,090	1,449,913	3,760	1,308,124	26,261	333,969	1	-	2	-
Men		8,358	1,085,513	2,890	967,467	18,468	242,123	1	1	2	1
Women		2,732	361,400	870	340,657	7,793	91,846	3	1	4	1
Asian and Pacific Islander		10,121	1,461,396	3,701	(D)	(D)	(D)	1	-	1	(D)
Men		6,253	1,135,387	2,616	1,041,615	26,077	269,851	1	-	2	-
Women		3,868	326,009	1,085	(D)	(D)	(D)	2	1	3	(D)
Food and kindred products	20	1,326	318,238	479	293,678	4,124	47,078	1	-	2	-
Minority men		871	252,347	360	233,092	3,200	35,092	2	1	2	-
Minority women		457	65,891	119	60,586	924	11,986	4	-	4	-
American Indian and Alaska Native		9	314	2	(D)	(D)	(D)	-	-	-	(D)
Black		286	60,595	70	57,181	699	11,019	-	-	-	-
Hispanic		589	151,632	240	140,141	2,100	23,442	3	1	3	1
Asian and Pacific Islander		459	110,276	170	(D)	(D)	(D)	2	-	-	(D)
Tobacco manufactures	21	7	860	7	860	32	180	-	-	-	-
Minority men		7	860	7	860	32	180	-	-	-	-
Minority women		-	-	-	-	-	-	-	-	-	-
American Indian and Alaska Native		-	-	-	-	-	-	-	-	-	-
Black		-	-	-	-	-	-	-	-	-	-

[Continued]

960

★ 614 ★

Minority-Owned Firms: Manufacturing
[Continued]

Major industry group and minority	SIC code	All firms		Firms with paid employees				Relative standard error of estimate % for column			
		Firms (number) A	Sales and receipts ($1,000) B	Firms (number) C	Sales and receipts ($1,000) D	Employees (number) E	Annual payroll ($1,000) F	A	B	C	D
Hispanic		7	860	7	860	32	180	-	-	-	-
Asian and Pacific Islander		-	-	-	-	-	-	-	-	-	-
Textile mill products	22	477	53,088	126	47,306	1,000	12,328	1	-	-	-
Minority men		225	35,093	72	31,285	581	6,852	-	-	-	-
Minority women		252	17,995	54	16,021	419	5,476	2	-	-	-
American Indian and Alaska Native		13	262	2	(D)	(D)	(D)	-	-	-	(D)
Black		74	9,954	25	9,384	115	3,070	-	-	-	-
Hispanic		188	21,361	56	18,894	437	5,229	1	-	-	-
Asian and Pacific Islander		208	22,337	47	(D)	(D)	(D)	3	-	-	(D)
Apparel and other textile products	23	6,536	847,492	2,720	794,509	36,611	278,739	1	1	2	1
Minority men		2,913	496,559	1,540	469,085	22,578	170,394	2	1	2	1
Minority women		3,623	350,933	1,180	325,424	14,033	108,345	2	1	3	1
American Indian and Alaska Native		76	(D)	6	(D)	(D)	(D)	14	(D)	24	(D)
Black		552	64,671	146	60,859	1,360	16,392	-	-	-	-
Hispanic		1,713	278,810	833	267,198	10,294	84,350	2	1	4	1
Asian and Pacific Islander		4,265	(D)	1,781	(D)	(D)	(D)	1	(D)	2	(D)
Lumber and wood products	24	5,046	344,167	1,838	278,091	5,056	68,168	1	-	1	1
Minority men		4,697	294,054	1,703	234,657	4,234	55,632	1	1	1	1
Minority women		349	50,113	135	43,434	822	12,536	4	1	6	1
American Indian and Alaska Native		274	22,230	78	18,796	407	5,155	7	2	10	1
Black		3,720	211,281	1,438	163,852	2,932	41,362	-	-	-	-
Hispanic		840	86,082	250	74,287	1,410	17,883	3	2	5	2
Asian and Pacific Islander		228	25,214	77	21,654	314	3,848	8	3	17	3
Furniture and fixtures	25	1,090	146,586	386	132,487	2,490	32,053	2	1	3	1
Minority men		931	127,483	340	114,921	2,151	26,779	2	1	4	1
Minority women		159	19,103	46	17,566	339	5,274	10	1	7	-
American Indian and Alaska Native		21	702	2	(D)	(D)	(D)	19	17	-	(D)
Black		226	29,812	65	27,429	545	7,960	-	-	-	-
Hispanic		657	88,946	249	80,165	1,617	19,810	3	1	5	1
Asian and Pacific Islander		202	28,309	73	(D)	(D)	(D)	3	-	-	(D)
Paper and allied products	26	195	(D)	51	(D)	(D)	(D)	-	(D)	-	(D)
Minority men		140	65,742	42	64,389	657	12,621	-	-	-	-
Minority women		55	(D)	9	(D)	(D)	(D)	-	(D)	-	(D)
American Indian and Alaska Native		2	(D)	-	-	-	-	-	(D)	-	-
Black		55	26,230	17	25,666	287	5,154	-	-	-	-
Hispanic		87	11,499	19	10,553	111	1,742	-	-	-	-
Asian and Pacific Islander		55	(D)	15	(D)	(D)	(D)	-	(D)	-	(D)
Printing and publishing	27	4,823	523,128	1,626	462,676	6,394	115,930	1	1	3	1
Minority men		3,652	359,175	1,246	314,458	4,551	76,998	2	1	3	1
Minority women		1,171	163,953	380	148,218	1,843	38,932	4	2	6	2
American Indian and Alaska Native		50	2,501	11	2,192	58	680	19	1	-	-
Black		1,394	126,488	360	109,971	1,629	35,538	-	-	-	-

[Continued]

★ 614 ★

Minority-Owned Firms: Manufacturing

[Continued]

Major industry group and minority	SIC code	All firms		Firms with paid employees				Relative standard error of estimate % for column			
		Firms (number) A	Sales and receipts ($1,000) B	Firms (number) C	Sales and receipts ($1,000) D	Employees (number) E	Annual payroll ($1,000) F	A	B	C	D
Hispanic		1,886	179,062	575	158,977	2,409	41,942	3	2	5	2
Asian and Pacific Islander		1,532	226,151	690	202,036	2,474	41,491	3	2	5	2
Chemicals and allied products	28	241	96,977	89	91,600	890	17,021	1	-	-	-
Minority men		195	87,925	74	83,257	806	14,815	2	-	-	-
Minority women		46	9,052	15	8,343	84	2,206	-	-	-	-
American Indian and Alaska Native		4	146	2	(D)	(D)	(D)	-	-	-	(D)
Black		65	57,468	23	56,511	498	10,329	-	-	-	-
Hispanic		72	20,157	28	19,432	179	3,135	-	-	-	-
Asian and Pacific Islander		100	19,206	36	(D)	(D)	(D)	3	-	-	(D)
Petroleum and coal products	29	8	(D)	6	(D)	(D)	(D)	-	(D)	-	(D)
Minority men		6	(D)	4	(D)	(D)	(D)	-	(D)	-	(D)
Minority women		2	(D)	2	(D)	(D)	(D)	-	(D)	-	(D)
American Indian and Alaska Native		-	-	-	-	-	-	-	-	-	-
Black		1	(D)	-	-	-	-	-	(D)	-	-
Hispanic		3	(D)	2	(D)	(D)	(D)	-	(D)	-	(D)
Asian and Pacific Islander		4	(D)	4	(D)	(D)	(D)	-	(D)	-	(D)
Rubber and miscellaneous plastics products	30	350	91,535	129	88,197	1,190	21,539	-	-	-	-
Minority men		260	74,426	101	71,610	870	16,501	-	-	-	-
Minority women		90	17,109	28	16,587	320	5,038	-	-	-	-
American Indian and Alaska Native		5	251	1	(D)	(D)	(D)	-	-	-	(D)
Black		71	11,844	29	11,383	214	4,231	-	-	-	-
Hispanic		176	50,765	62	48,960	698	12,891	-	-	-	-
Asian and Pacific Islander		101	30,244	38	(D)	(D)	(D)	-	-	-	(D)
Leather and leather products	31	362	35,834	92	31,313	590	7,701	3	-	-	-
Minority men		248	28,972	73	25,335	460	5,665	3	1	-	-
Minority women		114	6,862	19	5,978	130	2,036	6	-	-	-
American Indian and Alaska Native		18	212	2	(D)	(D)	(D)	-	-	-	(D)
Black		42	5,187	10	4,860	117	1,503	-	-	-	-
Hispanic		194	22,108	53	20,053	362	5,038	-	-	-	-
Asian and Pacific Islander		112	8,497	29	(D)	(D)	(D)	9	2	-	(D)
Stone, clay, and glass products	32	909	93,326	208	83,612	922	17,061	2	1	2	-
Minority men		595	63,485	172	56,673	654	11,906	3	1	3	-
Minority women		314	29,841	36	26,939	268	5,155	3	1	4	-
American Indian and Alaska Native		60	2,040	7	1,493	16	225	12	2	-	-
Black		193	30,428	61	29,637	349	5,742	-	-	-	-
Hispanic		400	38,880	106	33,782	370	7,203	3	1	5	1
Asian and Pacific Islander		263	22,175	35	18,717	187	3,897	9	1	-	-
Primary metal industry	33	219	97,553	66	(D)	(D)	(D)	4	-	-	(D)
Minority men		187	(D)	48	37,065	799	8,784	5	(D)	-	-
Minority women		32	(D)	18	(D)	(D)	(D)	-	(D)	-	(D)
American Indian and Alaska Native		10	(D)	2	(D)	(D)	(D)	-	(D)	-	(D)
Black		54	8,122	12	7,420	76	772	-	-	-	-

[Continued]

★ 614 ★

Minority-Owned Firms: Manufacturing
[Continued]

Major industry group and minority	SIC code	All firms		Firms with paid employees				Relative standard error of estimate % for column			
		Firms (number) A	Sales and receipts ($1,000) B	Firms (number) C	Sales and receipts ($1,000) D	Employees (number) E	Annual payroll ($1,000) F	A	B	C	D
Hispanic		104	53,897	32	(D)	(D)	(D)	-	-	-	(D)
Asian and Pacific Islander		51	(D)	20	(D)	(D)	(D)	19	(D)	-	(D)
Fabricated metal products	34	1,835	285,963	591	259,079	3,714	75,695	2	1	5	1
Minority men		1,563	189,915	485	166,400	2,527	44,356	2	1	5	1
Minority women		272	96,048	106	92,679	1,187	31,339	9	1	14	1
American Indian and Alaska Native		91	2,153	6	1,356	16	239	10	3	-	-
Black		338	116,191	106	111,785	1,271	33,167	-	-	-	-
Hispanic		1,140	107,976	386	91,969	1,792	28,303	2	2	7	2
Asian and Pacific Islander		275	60,548	94	54,614	651	14,166	3	1	5	1
Machinery, except electrical	35	2,003	249,327	701	222,707	3,074	63,193	2	1	4	1
Minority men		1,774	218,975	612	194,888	2,534	52,772	2	1	5	1
Minority women		229	30,352	89	27,819	540	10,421	10	2	9	2
American Indian and Alaska Native		34	4,090	8	3,635	44	1,042	11	6	17	6
Black		271	45,711	95	42,566	672	15,800	-	-	-	-
Hispanic		1,148	120,136	420	104,482	1,521	27,146	3	2	7	2
Asian and Pacific Islander		562	82,936	188	75,561	899	20,320	4	2	6	2
Electric and electronic equipment	36	1,037	314,557	250	298,577	4,333	79,415	1	-	3	-
Minority men		700	224,892	204	211,605	3,455	59,544	2	1	4	-
Minority women		337	89,665	46	86,972	878	19,871	5	-	3	-
American Indian and Alaska Native		8	4,250	3	4,236	59	630	31	-	-	-
Black		136	113,567	34	112,422	1,594	26,054	-	-	-	-
Hispanic		295	39,990	67	37,233	670	13,168	1	-	-	-
Asian and Pacific Islander		601	156,903	147	144,768	2,011	39,582	3	1	5	1
Transportation equipment	37	236	161,229	113	156,009	2,063	39,334	-	-	-	-
Minority men		197	146,418	89	141,533	1,761	34,806	-	-	-	-
Minority women		39	14,811	24	14,476	302	4,528	-	-	-	-
American Indian and Alaska Native		7	694	4	(D)	(D)	(D)	-	-	-	(D)
Black		57	69,685	24	68,917	902	18,396	-	-	-	-
Hispanic		129	74,747	66	70,875	938	17,821	-	-	-	-
Asian and Pacific Islander		48	17,023	22	(D)	(D)	(D)	-	-	-	(D)
Instruments and related products	38	187	26,979	78	(D)	(D)	(D)	-	-	-	(D)
Minority men		156	21,765	65	(D)	(D)	(D)	-	-	-	(D)
Minority women		31	5,214	13	4,706	59	1,082	-	-	-	-
American Indian and Alaska Native		3	14	-	-	-	-	-	-	-	-
Black		31	11,291	12	10,829	122	3,391	-	-	-	-
Hispanic		68	5,581	21	(D)	(D)	(D)	-	-	-	(D)
Asian and Pacific Islander		86	10,096	45	9,258	135	2,077	-	-	-	-
Miscellaneous manufacturing industries	39	2,990	170,602	570	124,418	1,920	27,606	2	2	4	1
Minority men		2,147	129,528	440	93,440	1,460	20,545	3	2	5	1
Minority women		843	41,074	130	30,978	460	7,061	5	2	9	1
American Indian and Alaska Native		226	4,266	12	2,320	57	530	9	14	-	-
Black		438	(D)	85	16,433	302	4,158	-	(D)	-	-

[Continued]

★ 614 ★

Minority-Owned Firms: Manufacturing

[Continued]

Major industry group and minority	SIC code	All firms		Firms with paid employees				Relative standard error of estimate % for column			
		Firms (number) A	Sales and receipts ($1,000) B	Firms (number) C	Sales and receipts ($1,000) D	Employees (number) E	Annual payroll ($1,000) F	A	B	C	D
Hispanic		1,394	(D)	288	53,451	858	11,821	3	(D)	7	3
Asian and Pacific Islander		969	68,340	190	54,365	741	11,650	4	2	7	1

Source: "Statistics for Minority-Owned Firms by Major Industry Group: 1987," *Minority-Owned Businesses*, pp. 10-12. Primary source: 1987 Survey of Minority-Owned Businesses. *Minority-Owned Businesses*, Washington, D.C., U.S. Government Printing Office, 1990. Arranged by the editors. *Notes:* (D) stands for data withheld to avoid disclosure of competitive information. Details may not add to total because of rounding and because a firm may be included in more than one minority group. A dash (-) represents zero.

★ 615 ★

Minority-Owned Firms: Transportation and Utilities

Data are shown for 1987. Trade groups are based on the 1972 Standard Industrial Classification (SIC) system.

Major industry group and minority	All firms		Firms with paid employees				Relative standard error of estimate % for column			
	Firms (number) A	Sales and receipts ($1,000) B	Firms (number) C	Sales and receipts ($1,000) D	Employees (number) E	Annual payroll ($1,000) F	A	B	C	D
Transportation and public utilities	76,229	3,665,10,233	10,223	1,955,168	20,795	335,242	-	-	1	-
Minority men	68,052	3,052,314	8,710	1,482,705	15,900	262,551	-	-	1	1
Minority women	8,177	613,368	1,513	472,463	4,895	72,691	2	1	3	1
American Indian and Alaska Native	917	44,286	161	22,979	280	3,990	5	4	9	4
Men	764	38,602	136	19,981	241	3,490	5	4	10	4
Women	153	5,684	25	2,998	39	500	12	8	15	2
Black	36,958	1,573,342	4,987	786,091	9,910	153,959	-	-	-	-
Men	33,165	1,279,210	4,295	554,535	7,305	115,165	-	-	-	-
Women	3,793	294,132	692	231,556	2,605	38,794	-	-	-	-
Hispanic	26,955	1,380,981	3,989	725,484	8,006	135,592	1	1	3	1
Men	24,230	1,207,449	3,459	597,628	6,437	111,669	1	1	3	1
Women	2,725	173,532	530	127,856	1,569	23,923	4	2	7	2
Asian and Pacific Islander	11,940	691,480	1,154	432,638	2,750	45,784	1	1	3	1
Men	10,359	545,809	878	318,035	2,032	35,732	1	1	4	1
Women	1,581	145,671	276	114,603	718	10,052	4	2	6	1
Local and interurban passenger transit	22,037	454,980	1,106	86,151	2,722	23,571	1	1	3	1
Minority men	20,072	411,789	863	68,298	2,109	18,678	1	1	3	1
Minority women	1,965	43,191	243	17,853	613	4,893	3	3	6	3
American Indian and Alaska Native	95	2,941	13	1,357	40	265	13	12	26	-
Black	11,566	218,209	700	53,266	1,746	14,621	-	-	-	-
Hispanic	4,522	105,763	260	20,340	744	6,188	2	2	10	3
Asian and Pacific Islander	6,049	132,832	159	12,092	235	2,770	2	2	15	5
Trucking and warehousing	39,556	2,060,753	7,044	966,322	10,952	196,536	-	1	2	1
Minority men	37,005	1,842,679	6,372	811,677	8,818	161,792	-	1	2	1
Minority women	2,551	218,074	672	154,645	2,134	36,744	3	2	5	1
American Indian and Alaska Native	590	32,189	125	15,359	185	2,900	6	5	11	6
Black	19,663	1,010,229	3,632	465,617	5,504	98,309	-	-	-	-

[Continued]

★ 615 ★

Minority-Owned Firms: Transportation and Utilities
[Continued]

Major industry group and minority	All firms		Firms with paid employees				Relative standard error of estimate % for column			
	Firms (number) A	Sales and receipts ($1,000) B	Firms (number) C	Sales and receipts ($1,000) D	Employees (number) E	Annual payroll ($1,000) F	A	B	C	D
Hispanic	17,304	906,583	2,936	426,794	4,499	85,692	1	1	4	2
Asian and Pacific Islander	2,214	121,853	377	61,832	786	12,228	3	2	6	3
Water transportation	339	37,000	89	31,814	572	7,820	1	-	-	-
Minority men	286	30,222	69	26,035	512	7,020	1	-	-	-
Minority women	53	6,778	20	5,779	60	800	7	1	-	-
American Indian and Alaska Native	12	695	3	452	10	127	-	-	-	-
Black	83	9,042	26	7,687	160	2,307	-	-	-	-
Hispanic	156	19,598	40	17,539	327	4,223	3	-	-	-
Asian and Pacific Islander	91	7,836	22	6,282	77	1,198	-	-	-	-
Transportation by air	462	29,332	51	15,919	239	4,279	3	-	-	-
Minority men	395	16,523	39	7,404	100	1,697	3	-	-	-
Minority women	67	12,809	12	8,515	139	2,582	5	-	-	-
American Indian and Alaska Native	30	865	6	414	4	63	31	6	-	-
Black	117	11,485	12	7,860	121	2,447	-	-	-	-
Hispanic	222	10,895	23	4,022	67	1,116	2	-	-	-
Asian and Pacific Islander	101	6,154	10	3,623	47	653	8	-	-	-
Pipe lines, except natural gas	1	(D)	-	-	-	-	-	(D)	-	-
Minority men	1	(D)	-	-	-	-	-	(D)	-	-
Minority women	-	-	-	-	-	-				
American Indian and Alaska Native	-	-	-	-	-	-	-	-	-	-
Black	-	-	-	-	-	-	-	-	-	-
Hispanic	-	-	-	-	-	-	-	-	-	-
Asian and Pacific Islander	1	(D)	-	-	-	-	-	(D)	-	-
Transportation services	10,665	895,539	1,479	706,588	4,018	62,172	1	-	2	-
Minority men	7,757	587,323	990	439,876	2,513	41,317	1	1	3	1
Minority women	2,908	308,216	489	266,712	1,505	20,855	2	1	3	1
American Indian and Alaska Native	134	6,296	8	4,711	34	494	13	3	-	-
Black	4,053	222,757	405	166,710	920	14,303	-	-	-	-
Hispanic	3,617	284,684	542	219,512	1,683	25,970	2	1	4	1
Asian and Pacific Islander	2,959	387,708	536	320,159	1,419	22,289	2	1	4	1
Communication	2,062	150,568	274	125,340	1,992	35,207	2	1	7	-
Minority men	1,537	130,548	219	109,567	1,583	28,928	2	1	8	-
Minority women	525	20,020	55	15,773	409	6,279	5	2	13	-
American Indian and Alaska Native	36	682	2	(D)	(D)	(D)	9	13	-	(D)
Black	896	81,785	118	71,953	1,334	20,779	-	-	-	-
Hispanic	756	38,852	115	28,851	533	10,451	4	2	16	1
Asian and Pacific Islander	385	32,355	40	(D)	(D)	(D)	5	1	5	(D)
Electric, gas, and sanitary services	1,107	(D)	180	23,034	300	3,657	2	(D)	5	1
Minority men	999	(D)	158	19,848	265	3,119	2	(D)	5	2
Minority women	108	4,280	22	3,186	35	538	6	4	16	5
American Indian and Alaska Native	20	618	4	(D)	(D)	(D)	-	-	-	(D)
Black	580	19,835	94	12,998	125	1,466	-	-	-	-

[Continued]

965

★ 615 ★

Minority-Owned Firms: Transportation and Utilities
[Continued]

Major industry group and minority	All firms		Firms with paid employees				Relative standard error of estimate % for column			
	Firms (number) A	Sales and receipts ($1,000) B	Firms (number) C	Sales and receipts ($1,000) D	Employees (number) E	Annual payroll ($1,000) F	A	B	C	D
Hispanic	378	14,606	73	8,426	153	1,952	4	3	11	4
Asian and Pacific Islander	140	(D)	10	(D)	(D)	(D)	10	(D)	-	(D)

Source: "Statistics for Minority-Owned Firms by Major Industry Group: 1987," *Minority-Owned Businesses*, p. 13. Primary source: 1987 Survey of Minority-Owned Businesses. *Minority-Owned Businesses*, Washington, D.C., U.S. Government Printing Office, 1990. Arranged by the editors. Details may not add to total because of rounding and because a firm may be included in more than one minority group. (D) stands for data withheld to avoid disclosure of competitive information. *Note:* A dash (-) represents zero.

★ 616 ★

Minority-Owned Firms: Wholesale Trade

Data are shown for 1987. Trade groups are based on the 1972 Standard Industrial Classification (SIC) system.

Major industry group and minority	All firms		Firms with paid employees				Relative standard error of estimate % for column--			
	Firms (number) A	Sales and receipts ($1,000) B	Firms (number) C	Sales and receipts ($1,000) D	Employees (number) E	Annual payroll ($1,000) F	A	B	C	D
Wholesale trade	26,432	7,950,013	6,216	6,216	6,489,777	24,455	1	-	1	-
Minority men	20,685	6,087,858	4,812	4,844,929	17,588	323,063	1	-	1	-
Minority women	5,747	1,862,155	1,404	1,644,845	6,867	127,794	2	-	2	-
American Indian and Alaska Native	360	36,058	93	26,490	192	2,755	8	3	16	2
Men	292	29,709	75	20,846	159	2,283	10	3	20	3
Women	68	6,349	18	5,644	33	472	16	2	19	1
Black	5,519	1,327,479	1,256	1,169,608	6,156	115,944	-	-	-	-
Men	4,016	821,228	850	702,267	3,589	64,940	-	-	-	-
Women	1,503	506,251	406	467,341	2,567	51,004	-	-	-	-
Hispanic	10,154	2,445,416	2,309	1,991,736	9,119	157,537	1	-	2	-
Men	8,292	2,011,404	1,888	1,616,146	7,204	123,920	1	-	2	-
Women	1,862	434,012	421	375,590	1,915	33,617	4	1	4	1
Asian and Pacific Islander	10,654	4,188,852	2,622	3,337,014	9,192	177,221	1	-	2	-
Men	8,259	3,251,019	2,031	2,524,919	6,727	133,214	1	-	2	-
Women	2,395	937,833	591	812,095	2,465	44,007	4	1	3	1
Wholesale trade--durable goods	13,219	3,463,935	3,281	2,784,804	11,909	231,471	1	-	2	-
Minority men	10,513	2,673,962	2,519	2,100,024	8,764	169,669	1	-	2	-
Minority women	2,706	789,973	762	684,780	3,145	61,802	3	1	3	1
American Indian and Alaska Native	247	24,294	60	18,867	158	2,251	11	3	20	2
Black	2,792	628,729	731	559,469	3,309	63,196	-	-	-	-
Hispanic	5,080	1,056,969	1,218	851,385	4,744	84,530	1	1	2	1
Asian and Pacific Islander	5,238	1,775,057	1,305	1,367,633	3,789	82,773	2	1	3	1
Wholesale trade--nondurable goods	13,213	4,486,078	2,935	3,704,973	12,546	219,386	1	-	1	-
Minority men	10,172	3,413,896	2,293	2,744,905	8,824	153,394	1	-	2	-
Minority women	3,041	1,072,182	642	960,068	3,722	65,992	2	1	2	1

[Continued]

★ 616 ★

Minority-Owned Firms: Wholesale Trade
[Continued]

Major industry group and minority	All firms		Firms with paid employees				Relative standard error of estimate % for column--			
	Firms (number) A	Sales and receipts ($1,000) B	Firms (number) C	Sales and receipts ($1,000) D	Employees (number) E	Annual payroll ($1,000) F	A	B	C	D
American Indian and Alaska Native	113	11,764	33	7,623	34	504	12	5	27	6
Black	2,727	698,750	525	610,139	2,847	52,748	-	-	-	-
Hispanic	5,074	1,388,447	1,091	1,140,351	4,375	73,007	1	1	3	-
Asian and Pacific Islander	5,416	2,413,795	1,317	1,969,381	5,403	94,448	1	-	2	-

Source: "Statistics for Minority-Owned Firms by Major Industry Group: 1987," *Minority-Owned Businesses*, pp. 13-14. Primary source: 1987 Survey of Minority-Owned Businesses. *Minority-Owned Businesses*, Washington, D.C., U.S. Government Printing Office, 1990. Arranged by the editors. *Note:* A dash (-) represents zero.

★ 617 ★

Minority-Owned Firms: Retail Trade

Major industry group and minority	SIC code	All firms		Firms with paid employees				Relative standard error of estimate % for column			
		Firms (number) A	Sales and receipts ($1,000) B	Firms (number) C	Sales and receipts ($1,000) D	Employees (number) E	Annual payroll ($1,000) F	A	B	C	D
Retail trade		226,140	26,903,914	72,310	21,614,740	319,048	2,522,579	-	-	-	-
Minority men		144,463	20,599,037	51,973	16,584,089	233,254	1,849,591	-	-	-	-
Minority women		81,677	6,304,877	20,337	5,030,651	85,794	672,988	1	-	1	-
Black		66,229	5,889,654	14,293	4,861,485	62,530	571,450	-	-	-	-
Men		36,389	3,812,061	9,274	3,124,476	39,383	350,570	-	-	-	-
Women		29,840	2,077,593	5,019	1,737,009	23,147	220,880	-	-	-	-
Hispanic		69,911	7,643,850	20,348	6,095,890	90,584	745,662	-	-	1	-
Men		46,179	6,216,518	15,114	5,011,191	70,394	590,518	1	-	1	-
Women		23,732	1,427,332	5,234	1,084,699	20,190	155,144	1	1	2	1
American Indian and Alaska Native		3,090	268,086	837	210,191	2,427	20,170	3	2	4	1
Men		1,683	202,941	534	163,835	1,730	14,722	4	2	5	2
Women		1,407	65,145	303	46,356	697	5,448	6	4	8	3
Asian and Pacific Islander		88,761	13,315,753	37,399	10,613,682	165,865	1,204,132	-	-	1	-
Men		61,356	10,514,603	27,390	8,398,758	123,261	905,725	1	-	1	-
Women		27,405	2,801,150	10,009	2,214,924	42,604	298,407	1	-	1	-
Building materials and garden supplies	52	2,690	467,932	971	407,114	3,737	49,022	1	1	2	1
Minority men		2,235	319,659	774	269,565	2,358	29,695	2	1	3	1
Minority women		455	148,273	197	137,549	1,379	19,327	5	1	3	1
Black		650	190,291	249	180,137	1,592	23,695	-	-	-	-
Hispanic		1,331	160,841	468	132,177	1,341	16,137	2	2	4	2
American Indian and Alaska Native		61	5,578	17	4,509	35	733	13	4	8	5
Asian and Pacific Islander		687	120,497	255	99,097	837	9,432	3	2	5	2
General merchandise stores	53	4,792	313,788	840	175,190	1,820	16,640	1	1	3	1
Minority men		3,359	219,268	607	113,058	1,129	9,512	2	2	4	1
Minority women		1,433	94,520	233	62,132	691	7,128	4	2	6	2
Black		1,064	44,343	194	26,097	306	2,569	-	-	-	-
Hispanic		1,152	54,795	146	30,974	406	3,237	3	2	10	2

[Continued]

★617★

Minority-Owned Firms: Retail Trade

[Continued]

Major industry group and minority	SIC code	All firms		Firms with paid employees				Relative standard error of estimate % for column			
		Firms (number) A	Sales and receipts ($1,000) B	Firms (number) C	Sales and receipts ($1,000) D	Employees (number) E	Annual payroll ($1,000) F	A	B	C	D
American Indian and Alaska Native		72	8,394	29	6,658	47	385	15	7	15	9
Asian and Pacific Islander		2,564	210,192	481	113,638	1,080	10,612	2	2	5	2
Food stores	54	35,747	6,617,891	13,650	4,915,955	47,917	388,722	-	-	1	-
Minority men		27,146	5,288,873	10,467	3,923,594	37,116	301,489	1	-	1	-
Minority women		8,601	1,329,018	3,183	992,361	10,801	87,233	1	1	2	1
Black		8,952	1,001,462	2,664	719,575	7,946	65,389	-	-	-	-
Hispanic		9,599	1,835,802	3,569	1,383,998	14,010	1418,064	1	1	2	1
American Indian and Alaska Native		301	54,320	108	42,230	356	2,526	9	4	5	2
Asian and Pacific Islander		17,263	3,785,579	7,430	2,810,796	26,075	206,260	1	1	1	1
Automotive dealers and service stations	55	12,275	6,156,369	6,027	5,646,224	26,348	379,555	1	-	1	-
Minority men		10,982	5,122,074	5,329	4,654,304	21,890	304,893	1	-	1	-
Minority women		1,293	1,034,295	698	991,920	4,458	74,662	3	-	3	-
Black		3,690	2,155,680	1,689	2,041,434	9,370	160,026	-	-	-	-
Hispanic		5,627	2,100,213	2,475	1,853,478	9,378	128,153	1	-	2	-
American Indian and Alaska Native		222	65,257	88	55,793	330	3,754	8	1	5	1
Asian and Pacific Islander		2,831	1,880,502	1,825	1,735,791	7,540	90,595	1	-	1	-
Apparel and accessory stores	56	12,687	1,043,144	4,026	754,812	11,225	85,000	1	1	2	1
Minority men		7,416	702,997	2,420	508,514	7,176	54,025	1	1	2	1
Minority women		5,271	340,147	1,606	246,298	4,049	30,975	2	2	3	2
Black		3,061	140,187	771	103,529	1,743	14,959	-	-	-	-
Hispanic		3,472	230,806	1,021	165,431 2	,651	21,258	2	2	3	2
American Indian and Alaska Native		85	5,994	36	4,992 8	8	516	11	4	14	4
Asian and Pacific Islander		6,208	677,045	2,242	489,078 6	,847	49,087	1	1	2	1
Furniture and home furnishings stores	57	7,536	961,045	2,399	756,200	6,338	79,599	1	1	1	1
Minority men		5,629	719,876	1,792	551,983	4,677	57,735	1	1	2	1
Minority women		1,907	241,169	607	204,217	1,661	21,864	3	1	3	1
Black		2,106	187,063	620	152,601	1,452	20,005	-	-	-	-
Hispanic		2,992	349,024	979	279,512	2,771	34,466	1	1	3	1
American Indian and Alaska Native		86	7,915	32	6,373	63	792	10	11	13	13
Asian and Pacific Islander		2,421	428,044	790	327,452	2,111	24,914	2	1	3	1
Eating and drinking places	58	52,202	6,324,180	30,586	5,620,474	186,687	1,198,209	-	-	1	-
Minority men		36,015	4,622,949	21,451	4,106,449	134,485	865,079	1	-	1	-
Minority women		16,187	1,701,231	9,135	1,514,025	52,202	333,130	1	1	1	1
Black		11,834	1,084,468	4,747	918,321	32,343	204,696	-	-	-	-
Hispanic		14,003	1,645,412	7,872	1,449,268	50,662	330,987	1	1	1	1
American Indian and Alaska Native		464	35,251	286	29,492	1,083	6,224	8	7	9	6
Asian and Pacific Islander		26,280	3,599,887	17,887	3,258,630	103,743	663,861	-	-	1	1
Miscellaneous retail	59	98,211	5,019,565	13,811	3,338,771	34,976	325,832	-	1	1	1
Minority men		51,681	3,603,341	9,133	2,456,622	24,423	227,163	1	1	1	1
Minority women		46,530	1,416,224	4,678	882,149	10,553	98,669	1	1	2	1
Black		34,870	1,086,160	3,359	719,791	7,778	80,111	-	-	-	-
Hispanic		31,735	1,266,957	3,818	801,052	9,365	93,360	1	1	3	1

[Continued]

★ 617 ★

Minority-Owned Firms: Retail Trade
[Continued]

Major industry group and minority	SIC code	All firms		Firms with paid employees				Relative standard error of estimate % for column			
		Firms (number) A	Sales and receipts ($1,000) B	Firms (number) C	Sales and receipts ($1,000) D	Employees (number) E	Annual payroll ($1,000) F	A	B	C	D
American Indian and Alaska Native		1,799	85,377	241	60,144	425	5,240	5	4	10	3
Asian and Pacific Islander		30,507	2,614,007	6,489	1,779,200	17,632	149,371	1	1	2	1

Source: "Statistics for Minority-Owned Firms by Major Industry Group: 1987," *Minority-Owned Businesses,* pp. 14-15. Primary source: 1987 Survey of Minority-Owned Businesses. *Minority-Owned Businesses,* Washington, D.C.: U.S. Government Printing Office, 1990. Arranged by the editors. Details may not add to total because of rounding and because a firm may be included in more than one minority group. *Notes:* This table is based on the 1972 SIC system. A Dash (-) indicates data were unavailable.

★ 618 ★

Minority-Owned Firms: Finance, Insurance, and Real Estate

Data are shown for 1987. Trade groups are based on the 1972 Standard Industrial Classification (SIC) system.

Major industry group and minority	SIC code	All firms		Firms with paid employees				Relative standard error of estimate % for column			
		Firms (number) A	Sales and receipts ($1,000) B	Firms (number) C	Sales and receipts ($1,000) D	Employees (number) E	Annual payroll ($1,000) F	A	B	C	D
Finance, insurance, and real estate		76,442	2,759,980	7,340	1,364,515	17,066	252,776	-	-	1	-
Minority men		47,936	1,942,427	5,388	997,955	12,337	179,468	1	1	1	1
Minority women		28,506	817,553	1,952	366,560	4,729	73,308	1	1	3	1
American Indian and Alaska Native		614	20,192	71	(D)	(D)	(D)	7	7	19	(D)
Men		389	11,508	44	4,420	167	2,021	9	11	21	6
Women		225	8,684	27	(D)	(D)	(D)	13	7	37	(D)
Black		26,989	804,252	2,514	464,389	5,938	94,718	-	-	-	-
Men		15,971	478,540	1,783	267,282	3,607	51,137	-	-	-	-
Women		11,018	325,712	731	197,107	2,331	43,581	-	-	-	-
Hispanic		22,106	864,282	2,236	433,851	4,960	80,882	1	1	2	1
Men		14,565	673,894	1,702	361,560	3,977	67,008	1	1	3	1
Women		7,541	190,388	534	72,291	983	13,874	2	2	5	3
Asian and Pacific Islander		27,297	1,086,855	2,558	(D)	(D)	(D)	1	1	3	(D)
Men		17,340	787,749	1,887	369,408	4,639	60,104	1	1	3	1
Women		9,957	299,106	671	(D)	(D)	(D)	2	2	6	(D)
Banking	60	86	(D)	82	88,897	881	14,146	-	(D)	-	-
Minority men		56	71,995	54	(D)	(D)	(D)	-	-	-	(D)
Minority women		30	(D)	28	(D)	(D)	(D)	-	(D)	-	(D)
American Indian and Alaska Native		1	(D)	1	(D)	(D)	(D)	-	(D)	-	(D)
Black		35	17,402	34	(D)	(D)	(D)	-	-	-	(D)
Hispanic		34	13,858	31	(D)	(D)	(D)	-	-	-	(D)
Asian and Pacific Islander		18	(D)	18	(D)	(D)	(D)	-	(D)	-	(D)
Credit agencies other than banks	61	175	(D)	141	30,116	624	9,775	-	(D)	-	-
Minority men		114	21,509	91	20,568	438	5,945	-	-	-	-
Minority women		61	(D)	50	9,548	186	3,830	-	(D)	-	-
American Indian and Alaska Native		1	(D)	1	(D)	(D)	(D)	-	(D)	-	(D)
Black		45	13,429	35	12,926	283	5,015	-	-	-	-
Hispanic		91	10,925	78	10,507	175	2,595	-	-	-	-

[Continued]

969

★ 618 ★

Minority-Owned Firms: Finance, Insurance, and Real Estate

[Continued]

Major industry group and minority	SIC code	All firms — Firms (number) A	All firms — Sales and receipts ($1,000) B	Firms with paid employees — Firms (number) C	Firms with paid employees — Sales and receipts ($1,000) D	Firms with paid employees — Employees (number) E	Firms with paid employees — Annual payroll ($1,000) F	RSE % A	RSE % B	RSE % C	RSE % D
Asian and Pacific Islander		40	6,852	27	(D)	(D)	(D)	-	-	-	(D)
Security, commodity brokers and services	62	1,981	165,577	192	112,452	394	22,174	2	1	6	-
Minority men		1,521	147,545	153	101,256	334	19,776	2	1	8	-
Minority women		460	18,032	39	11,196	60	2,398	6	7	6	1
American Indian and Alaska Native		30	(D)	12	369	3	54	34	(D)	58	35
Black		711	22,723	62	11,031	77	2,856	-	-	-	-
Hispanic		525	89,792	67	69,857	173	12,707	4	1	12	1
Asian and Pacific Islander		733	(D)	52	31,234	142	6,559	4	(D)	13	-
Insurance carriers	63	78	13,132	38	(D)	(D)	(D)	-	-	-	(D)
Minority men		49	6,472	21	5,516	99	1,523	-	-	-	-
Minority women		29	6,660	17	(D)	(D)	(D)	-	-	-	(D)
American Indian and Alaska Native		-	-	-	-	-	-	-	-	-	-
Black		36	6,220	16	4,532	52	611	-	-	-	-
Hispanic		33	5,086	15	4,567	71	1,115	-	-	-	-
Asian and Pacific Islander		9	1,826	7	(D)	(D)	(D)	-	-	-	(D)
Insurance agents, brokers, and services	64	20,793	576,848		305,429	3,979	62,749	1	1	2	1
Minority men		16,220	461,412	2,119	235,115	3,075	45,780	1	1	2	1
Minority women		4,573	115,436	457	70,314	904	16,969	2	2	6	2
American Indian and Alaska Native		152	5,051	20	2,321	40	500	15	21	27	1
Black		7,956	188,690	992	112,760	1,454	24,998	-	-	-	-
Hispanic		6,013	209,229	926	122,195	1,668	24,434	2	2	4	2
Asian and Pacific Islander		6,829	175,748	646	68,808	830	13,009	2	3	6	4
Real estate	65 pt.	46,253	1,671,457	3,864	772,820	10,604	133,755	-	1	2	1
Minority men		24,561	1,072,191	2,596	529,643	7,440	90,765	1	1	2	1
Minority women		20,692	599,266	1,268	243,177	3,164	42,990	1	1	3	1
American Indian and Alaska Native		370	12,746	33	7,710	150	1,668	10	7	31	7
Black		15,552	505,936	1,182	292,454	3,662	54,274	-	-	-	-
Hispanic		12,872	472,278	971	203,480	2,611	35,073	1	1	3	1
Asian and Pacific Islander		16,794	692,242	1,704	273,705	4,224	43,195	1	1	3	2
Combined real estate, insurance, etc.	66	7,959	189,043	430	35,734	333	6,138	1	2	5	3
Minority men		5,335	144,625	344	28,356	256	4,541	2	2	5	4
Minority women		2,624	44,418	86	7,378	77	1,597	3	5	10	9
American Indian and Alaska Native		59	1,212	4	411	9	96	21	34	-	-
Black		2,624	47,360	190	12,893	128	2,533	-	-	-	-
Hispanic		2,509	59,371	142	9,570	99	1,695	2	3	11	9
Asian and Pacific Islander		2,815	81,980	96	13,195	104	1,894	2	4	14	6
Holding and other investment officers	67 pt.	117	21,487	17	(D)	(D)	(D)	2	3	-	(D)
Minority men		80	16,678	10	(D)	(D)	(D)	4	3	-	(D)
Minority women		37	4,809	7	936	10	231	5	1	-	-
American Indian and Alaska Native		1	(D)	-	-	-	-	-	(D)	-	-
Black		30	2,492	3	(D)	(D)	(D)	-	-	-	(D)

[Continued]

★ 618 ★

Minority-Owned Firms: Finance, Insurance, and Real Estate
[Continued]

Major industry group and minority	SIC code	All firms		Firms with paid employees				Relative standard error of estimate % for column			
		Firms (number) A	Sales and receipts ($1,000) B	Firms (number) C	Sales and receipts ($1,000) D	Employees (number) E	Annual payroll ($1,000) F	A	B	C	D
Hispanic		29	3,743	6	(D)	(D)	(D)	-	-	-	(D)
Asian and Pacific Islander		59	(D)	8	(D)	(D)	(D)	4	(D)	-	(D)

Source: "Statistics for Minority-Owned Firms by Major Industry Group: 1987," *Minority-Owned Businesses*, pp. 15-16. Primary source: 1987 Survey of Minority-Owned Businesses. *Minority-Owned Businesses*, Washington, D.C., U.S. Government Printing Office, 1990. Arranged by the editors. *Notes:* (D) stands for data withheld to avoid disclosures of competitive information. Details may not add to total because of rounding and because a firm may be included in more than one minority group.

★ 619 ★

Minority-Owned Firms: Services

Detail may not add to total because of rounding and because a firm may be included in more than one minority group. Data are shown for 1987. Industry groups are based on the 1972 Standard Industrial Classification (SIC) system.

Major industry group and minority	All firms		Firms with paid employees				Relative standard error of estimate (percent) for column --			
	Firms (Number) A	Sales and receipts ($1,000) B	Firms (numbers) C	Sales and receipts ($1,000) D	Employees (Number) E	Annual Payroll ($1,000) F	A	B	C	D
Services	562,559	21,990,719	98,110	14,577,051	280,181	3,384,329	-	-	-	-
Minority men	337,630	16,279,824	71,314	11,152,064	205,861	2,520,901	-	-	-	-
Minority women	224,929	5,710,895	26,796	3,424,987	74,320	863,428	-	-	1	-
American Indian and Alaska Native	7,604	178,165	1,073	108,396	2,297	24,390	2	2	5	2
Men	4,422	121,878	744	76,074	1,409	16,262	3	3	6	3
Women	3,182	56,287	329	32,322	888	8,128	4	4	9	4
Black	209,547	6,120,084	29,963	3,888,212	89,700	1,077,437	-	-	-	-
Men	111,576	3,862,054	19,783	2,521,990	58,855	702,653	-	-	-	-
Women	97,971	2,258,030	10,180	1,366,222	30,845	374,784	-	-	-	-
Hispanic	184,372	6,031,406	29,750	3,774,117	74,427	941,588	-	-	1	1
Men	118,156	4,793,242	22,738	3,109,238	57,664	754,106	1	1	1	1
Women	66,216	1,238,164	7,012	664,879	16,763	187,482	1	1	2	1
Asian and Pacific Islander	165,342	9,880,868	38,176	6,962,276	117,946	1,387,293	-	-	1	-
Men	106,053	7,653,846	28,671	5,551,402	90,947	1,080,001	1	-	1	-
Women	59,289	2,227,022	9,505	1,410,874	26,999	307,292	1	1	2	1
Hotels and other lodging places	10,499	1,588,435	5,345	1,346,880	32,345	234,823	1	-	1	1
Minority men	7,498	1,245,764	4,134	1,060,050	25,073	180,130	1	1	1	1
Minority women	3,001	342,671	1,211	286,830	7,272	54,693	2	1	2	1
American Indian and Alaska Native	102	5,734	34	5,090	98	788	15	3	10	3
Black	1,734	128,256	553	94,028	2,698	22,334	-	-	-	-
Hispanic	973	112,551	315	92,996	2,284	23,342	4	1	6	1
Asian and Pacific Islander	7,809	1,366,121	4,507	1,177,169	27,682	192,406	1	1	1	1
Personal services	138,765	3,162,616	20,732	1,669,271	46,675	427,226	-	1	1	1
Minority men	68,771	1,927,822	12,067	1,097,981	29,342	270,185	1	1	1	1
Minority women	69,994	1,234,794	8,665	571,290	17,333	157,041	1	1	2	1
American Indian and Alaska Native	1,719	26,547	223	14,128	519	4,388	5	6	11	9
Black	56,772	959,696	6,246	427,283	12,108	109,773	-	-	-	-
Hispanic	44,872	893,064	6,111	430,645	13,688	129,379	1	1	2	2
Asian and Pacific Islander	36,392	1,318,400	8,304	819,467	21,249	190,277	1	1	2	1
Business services	166,666	4,510,917	19,755	2,592,828	63,552	799,677	-	-	1	1
Minority men	107,207	3,232,646	14,513	1,832,968	46,225	574,717	-	1	1	1
Minority women	59,459	1,278,271	5,242	759,860	17,327	224,960	1	1	2	1
American Indian and Alaska Native	2,532	48,601	319	23,585	545	6,238	5	5	12	5
Black	59,177	1,570,161	8,021	1,047,390	32,636	373,456	-	-	-	-

[Continued]

★ 619 ★

Minority-Owned Firms: Services
[Continued]

Major industry group and minority	All firms		Firms with paid employees				Relative standard error of estimate (percent) for column --			
	Firms (Number) A	Sales and receipts ($1,000) B	Firms (numbers) C	Sales and receipts ($1,000) D	Employees (Number) E	Annual Payroll ($1,000) F	A	B	C	D
Hispanic	59,948	1,419,790	6,716	747,056	18,979	235,949	1	1	2	1
Asian and Pacific Islander	46,066	1,523,290	4,847	814,432	12,913	202,894	1	1	3	1
Auto repair, services, and garages	32,861	1,765,545	9,328	1,302,474	19,942	270,583	-	1	1	1
Minority men	30,814	1,580,288	8,503	1,142,551	17,218	230,066	1	1	1	1
Minority women	2,047	185,257	825	159,923	2,724	40,517	3	2	4	2
American Indian and Alaska Native	538	20,704	134	14,111	226	2,710	8	7	11	8
Black	11,801	426,584	2,767	271,836	4,543	57,223	-	-	-	-
Hispanic	15,824	836,738	4,522	622,052	9,749	139,178	1	1	2	1
Asian and Pacific Islander	5,072	499,491	2,022	405,607	5,592	74,176	2	1	2	1
Miscellaneous repair services	17,321	623,735	3,431	394,622	6,736	89,471	1	1	2	1
Minority men	15,834	557,412	3,050	344,546	5,839	76,923	1	1	3	1
Minority women	1,487	66,323	381	50,076	897	12,548	4	3	6	3
American Indian and Alaska Native	300	11,105	53	8,023	103	1,144	9	5	12	6
Black	5,197	154,027	895	101,433	1,827	25,996	-	-	-	-
Hispanic	8,337	302,456	1,837	193,150	3,130	43,812	1	2	4	2
Asian and Pacific Islander	3,601	163,272	685	97,614	1,786	19,569	2	2	5	2
Motion pictures	1,939	109,396	263	76,501	882	14,296	2	1	4	1
Minority men	1,371	78,202	188	52,916	712	9,050	2	1	5	1
Minority women	568	31,194	75	23,585	170	5,246	5	2	7	1
American Indian and Alaska Native	34	1,691	5	(D)	(D)	(D)	20	9	-	(D)
Black	733	61,911	72	48,867	358	9,006	-	-	-	-
Hispanic	694	24,880	107	14,278	344	2,877	3	3	7	2
Asian and Pacific Islander	505	22,730	82	(D)	(D)	(D)	5	4	10	(D)
Amusement and recreation services	28,430	858,082	2,256	484,502	5,451	99,085	1	1	3	1
Minority men	21,653	619,237	1,729	316,275	4,079	72,178	1	1	3	1
Minority women	6,777	238,845	527	168,227	1,372	26,907	2	1	6	-
American Indian and Alaska Native	556	15,698	57	11,602	212	1,663	8	3	23	2
Black	13,250	502,847	965	316,336	2,021	62,094	-	-	-	-
Hispanic	9,528	203,812	800	89,891	1,518	19,948	2	3	8	4
Asian and Pacific Islander	5,307	142,451	467	70,229	1,736	16,188	2	3	7	3
Health services	80,753	6,399,878	23,508	4,727,372	66,568	889,621	-	-	1	1
Minority men	42,337	5,006,101	18,591	3,912,273	53,320	719,672	1	1	1	1
Minority women	38,416	1,393,777	4,917	815,099	13,248	169,949	1	1	2	1
American Indian and Alaska Native	488	20,840	91	13,417	205	2,293	10	11	18	11
Black	30,026	1,350,606	5,251	924,048	18,078	216,304	-	-	-	-
Hispanic	16,322	1,326,215	5,089	999,789	13,982	197,965	1	1	2	1
Asian and Pacific Islander	34,590	3,754,983	13,292	2,830,922	34,917	481,271	1	1	1	1
Legal services	10,887	809,756	3,572	608,052	7,121	120,514	1	1	1	1
Minority men	7,787	653,896	2,890	501,305	5,664	99,312	1	1	1	1
Minority women	3,100	155,860	682	106,747	1,457	21,202	2	1	3	2
American Indian and Alaska Native	169	11,153	52	8,400	105	1,916	8	4	10	2
Black	4,920	336,218	1,541	253,249	3,040	51,576	-	-	-	-
Hispanic	3,690	286,713	1,356	216,577	2,545	41,187	1	1	2	2
Asian and Pacific Islander	2,186	179,585	635	131,954	1,406	26,223	2	1	3	2
Educational services	10,124	173,474	574	104,556	2,764	34,429	1	1	3	-
Minority men	4,436	70,581	280	32,864	875	9,822	2	2	5	1
Minority women	5,688	102,893	294	71,692	1,889	24,607	2	1	5	1
American Indian and Alaska Native	210	1,051	3	214	4	38	12	7	-	-
Black	3,561	64,545	216	43,466	1,120	16,839	-	-	-	-
Hispanic	2,797	54,119	157	36,409	975	10,684	2	1	6	1
Asian and Pacific Islander	3,662	54,389	199	24,526	669	6,892	2	2	8	1
Social services	26,356	410,281	3,480	244,196	10,095	77,449	1	1	1	1
Minority men	4,121	128,058	844	95,455	3,916	31,745	3	1	3	1
Minority women	22,235	282,223	2,636	148,741	6,179	45,704	1	1	2	1

[Continued]

★ 619 ★

Minority-Owned Firms: Services
[Continued]

Major industry group and minority	All firms		Firms with paid employees				Relative standard error of estimate (percent) for column --			
	Firms (Number) A	Sales and receipts ($1,000) B	Firms (numbers) C	Sales and receipts ($1,000) D	Employees (Number) E	Annual Payroll ($1,000) F	A	B	C	D
American Indian and Alaska Native	451	3,842	28	1,413	85	545	10	8	-	-
Black	13,210	224,137	2,229	139,407	6,005	47,262	-	-	-	-
Hispanic	8,840	100,321	697	45,344	1,886	13,215	2	2	7	4
Asian and Pacific Islander	4,038	84,553	549	59,699	2,225	17,039	3	2	4	1
Museums, botanical, zoological gardens	-	-	-	-	-	-	-	-	-	-
Minority men	-	-	-	-	-	-	-	-	-	-
Minority women	-	-	-	-	-	-	-	-	-	-
American Indian and Alaska Native	-	-	-	-	-	-	-	-	-	-
Black	-	-	-	-	-	-	-	-	-	-
Hispanic	-	-	-	-	-	-	-	-	-	-
Asian and Pacific Islander	-	-	-	-	-	-	-	-	-	-
Miscellaneous services	37,958	1,576,604	5,866	1,025,797	18,050	327,155	1	1	2	1
Minority men	25,801	1,179,817	4,525	762,880	13,598	247,101	1	1	2	1
Minority women	12,157	398,787	1,341	262,917	4,452	80,054	2	1	4	1
American Indian and Alaska Native	505	11,199	74	(D)	(D)	(D)	9	8	21	(D)
Black	9,166	341,096	1,207	220,869	5,266	85,574	-	-	-	-
Hispanic	12,547	470,747	2,043	285,930	5,347	84,052	1	1	3	1
Asian and Pacific Islander	16,114	771,603	2,587	(D)	(D)	(D)	1	1	3	(D)

Source: "Statistics for Minority-Owned Firms by Major Industry Group: 1987," *Minority-Owned Businesses,* pp. 16-17. Primary source: 1987 Survey of Minority-Owned Businesses. *Minority-Owned Businesses,* Washington, D.C., U.S. Government Printing Office, 1990. Arranged by the editors. *Note:* A dash (-) represents zero.

★ 620 ★

Minority-Owned Firms: Unclassified Firms

Data are shown for 1987.

Race/ethnicity	All firms		Firms with paid employees				Relative standard error of estimate % for column			
	Firms (number) A	Sales and receipts ($1,000) B	Firms (number) C	Sales and receipts ($1,000) D	Employees (number) E	Annual payroll ($1,000) F	A	B	C	D
Industries not classified	69,942	2,230,113	6,869	745,873	5,754	119,194	-	1	2	2
Minority men	48,270	1,747,385	5,445	622,165	4,607	100,098	1	1	2	2
Minority women	21,672	482,728	1,424	123,708	1,147	19,096	1	2	4	4
American Indian and Alaska Native	1,285	36,637	142	14,001	119	2,353	5	9	18	12
Men	964	31,972	118	(D)	(D)	(D)	7	10	19	(D)
Women	321	4,665	24	(D)	(D)	(D)	12	11	46	(D)
Black	26,518	579,749	2,399	174,289	1,643	33,845	-	-	-	-
Men	17,100	426,851	1,833	143,056	1,310	27,867	-	-	-	-
Women	9,418	152,898	566	31,233	333	5,978	-	-	-	-
Hispanic	25,075	752,271	2,396	255,830	2,024	47,794	1	2	4	3
Men	18,581	623,877	2,057	224,197	1,764	42,807	1	2	5	4
Women	6,494	128,394	339	31,633	260	4,987	3	4	12	12
Asian and Pacific Islander	17,739	894,509	1,999	306,801	2,028	36,011	1	1	4	3

[Continued]

★ 620 ★

Minority-Owned Firms: Unclassified Firms

[Continued]

Race/ethnicity	All firms		Firms with paid employees				Relative standard error of estimate % for column			
	Firms (number) A	Sales and receipts ($1,000) B	Firms (number) C	Sales and receipts ($1,000) D	Employees (number) E	Annual payroll ($1,000) F	A	B	C	D
Men	12,125	689,416	1,500	(D)	(D)	(D)	2	2	5	(D)
Women	5,614	205,093	499	(D)	(D)	(D)	3	3	9	(D)

Source: "Statistics for Minority-Owned Firms by Major Industry Group: 1987," *Minority-Owned Businesses*, p. 17. Primary source: 1987 Survey of Minority-Owned Businesses. *Minority-Owned Businesses*, Washington, D.C.: U.S. Government Printing Office, 1990. Arranged by the editors. Details may not add to total because of rounding and because a firm may be included in more than one minority group. (D) stands for data withheld to avoid disclosure of competitive information. *Note:* A dash (-) indicates data were not available.

★ 621 ★

Minority-Owned Firms: Midwestern States

Data are shown for 1987.

Geographic area and minority	All firms		Firms with paid employees				Relative standard error of estimate % for column			
	Firms (number) A	Sales and receipts ($1,000) B	Firms (number) C	Sales and receipts ($1,000) D	Employees (number) E	Annual payroll ($1,000) F	A	B	C	D
Illinois	43,247	3,106,646	8,631	2,271,936	30,662	356,981	-	-	1	-
Minority men	28,696	2,204,476	6,417	1,585,935	21,731	242,495	1	1	1	-
Minority women	14,551	902,170	2,214	686,001	8,931	114,486	1	1	2	1
American Indian and Alaska Native	193	7,213	48	(D)	(D)	(D)	14	10	26	(D)
Men	122	6,033	33	3,564	31	527	18	12	30	15
Women	71	1,180	15	(D)	(D)	(D)	24	17	53	(D)
Black	19,011	1,100,204	3,014	816,022	10,655	138,699	-	-	-	-
Men	11,608	693,830	2,146	495,536	6,799	81,077	-	-	-	-
Women	7,403	406,374	868	320,486	3,856	57,622	-	-	-	-
Hispanic	9,636	588,646	1,712	416,569	5,890	68,893	1	1	3	1
Men	6,778	422,253	1,338	288,645	4,463	47,511	2	1	3	1
Women	2,858	166,393	374	127,924	1,427	21,382	3	2	7	2
Asian and Pacific Islander	14,679	1,437,700	3,904	(D)	(D)	(D)	1	1	2	(D)
Men	10,352	1,099,540	2,931	812,551	10,574	114,746	1	1	2	1
Women	4,327	338,160	973	(D)	(D)	(D)	3	2	4	(D)
Indiana	9,063	660,646	2,111	534,487	9,871	102,775	1	-	1	-
Minority men	5,744	493,768	1,526	402,946	6,991	74,615	1	-	1	-
Minority women	3,319	166,878	585	131,541	2,880	28,160	1	1	2	1
American Indian and Alaska Native	90	3,221	15	2,361	33	331	12	5	16	-
Men	57	2,788	10	2,100	23	246	14	5	24	-
Women	33	433	5	261	10	85	21	10	-	-
Black	5,867	349,643	1,110	281,611	4,715	53,703	-	-	-	-
Men	3,563	241,909	761	195,440	2,882	33,585	-	-	-	-
Women	2,304	107,734	349	86,171	1,833	20,118	-	-	-	-
Hispanic	1,427	106,111	300	85,099	1,455	16,541	3	1	3	-
Men	1,016	93,216	250	77,746	1,310	15,111	3	1	4	-
Women	411	12,895	50	7,353	145	1,430	6	2	10	-
Asian and Pacific Islander	1,718	205,485	699	168,918	3,744	33,100	2	1	2	1
Men	1,132	157,786	512	129,413	2,814	26,189	2	1	2	1

[Continued]

★ 621 ★

Minority-Owned Firms: Midwestern States
[Continued]

Geographic area and minority	All firms		Firms with paid employees				Relative standard error of estimate % for column			
	Firms (number) A	Sales and receipts ($1,000) B	Firms (number) C	Sales and receipts ($1,000) D	Employees (number) E	Annual payroll ($1,000) F	A	B	C	D
Women	586	47,699	187	39,505	930	6,911	4	3	5	2
Iowa	1,785	119,792	490	101,511	2,344	18,255	1	1	2	1
Minority men	1,129	84,799	345	72,466	1,448	11,874	2	1	3	1
Minority women	656	34,993	145	29,045	896	6,381	3	1	4	1
American Indian and Alaska Native	43	1,302	8	764	11	110	17	19	18	18
Men	25	687	4	485	2	53	20	3	-	-
Women	18	615	4	279	9	57	30	40	37	50
Black	703	44,795	142	38,013	722	7,158	-	-	-	-
Men	449	31,835	104	27,027	327	4,039	-	-	-	-
Women	254	12,960	38	10,986	395	3,119	-	-	-	-
Hispanic	475	20,210	111	16,662	489	3,534	3	1	3	1
Men	308	12,403	77	9,715	328	2,216	3	1	4	1
Women	167	7,807	34	6,947	161	1,318	6	1	-	-
Asian and Pacific Islander	574	53,931	232	46,453	1,136	7,544	4	2	4	2
Men	350	40,062	161	35,412	796	5,622	5	2	5	3
Women	224	13,869	71	11,041	338	1,922	7	3	7	2
Kansas	5,164	300,722	1,166	237,248	4,627	48,993	1	-	2	-
Minority men	3,351	232,133	889	186,913	3,471	38,034	2	1	3	-
Minority women	1,813	68,589	277	50,335	1,156	10,959	3	1	4	1
American Indian and Alaska Native	231	(D)	33	5,426	79	631	14	(D)	23	2
Men	135	6,474	27	4,955	53	570	16	5	28	2
Women	96	(D)	6	471	26	61	21	(D)	-	-
Black	2,323	154,448	403	127,424	2,132	28,094	-	-	-	-
Men	1,451	122,595	307	104,092	1,893	24,081	-	-	-	-
Women	872	31,853	96	23,332	239	4,013	-	-	-	-
Hispanic	1,541	62,275	335	43,035	1,027	9,405	3	1	4	1
Men	1,088	44,752	265	29,071	575	5,457	4	2	6	1
Women	453	17,523	70	13,964	452	3,948	7	2	3	-
Asian and Pacific Islander	1,135	(D)	406	62,750	1,437	11,146	4	(D)	5	1
Men	721	59,768	299	49,940	979	8,172	6	2	5	1
Women	414	(D)	107	12,810	458	2,974	8	(D)	11	3
Michigan	21,032	1,230,777	4,131	922,413	15,975	170,356	-	-	-	-
Minority men	12,992	904,046	2,982	691,324	11,120	125,797	1	1	1	1
Minority women	8,040	326,731	1,149	231,089	4,855	44,559	1	1	2	1
American Indian and Alaska Native	305	(D)	42	(D)	(D)	(D)	10	(D)	13	(D)
Men	214	6,909	29	4,915	62	844	12	5	15	4
Women	91	(D)	13	(D)	(D)	(D)	21	(D)	27	(D)
Black	13,708	701,335	2,241	524,583	8,485	91,991	-	-	-	-
Men	8,112	489,595	1,553	372,031	5,561	63,416	-	-	-	-
Women	5,596	211,740	688	152,552	2,924	28,575	-	-	-	-
Hispanic	2,654	126,046	464	87,743	1,560	20,945	1	1	3	1
Men	1,788	104,064	354	75,333	1,260	18,420	2	1	3	1
Women	866	21,982	110	12,410	300	2,525	3	3	8	4
Asian and Pacific Islander	4,424	(D)	1,402	(D)	(D)	(D)	2	(D)	3	(D)
Men	2,916	313,276	1,058	248,593	4,347	44,348	3	2	3	2
Women	1,508	(D)	344	(D)	(D)	(D)	5	(D)	6	(D)

[Continued]

★ 621 ★

Minority-Owned Firms: Midwestern States
[Continued]

Geographic area and minority	All firms		Firms with paid employees				Relative standard error of estimate % for column			
	Firms (number) A	Sales and receipts ($1,000) B	Firms (number) C	Sales and receipts ($1,000) D	Employees (number) E	Annual payroll ($1,000) F	A	B	C	D
Minnesota	4,188	324,316	906	260,880	5,098	53,716	1	-	1	-
Minority men	2,690	226,943	625	179,651	3,068	34,980	1	-	2	-
Minority women	1,498	97,373	281	81,229	2,030	18,736	2	1	4	1
American Indian and Alaska Native	340	18,054	56	13,088	248	2,773	6	2	8	1
Men	227	14,003	39	9,981	186	2,295	7	2	9	1
Women	113	4,051	17	3,107	62	478	11	3	16	2
Black	1,448	124,915	224	101,434	1,727	21,557	-	-	-	-
Men	926	77,179	163	61,213	859	10,576	-	-	-	-
Women	522	47,736	61	40,221	868	10,981	-	-	-	-
Hispanic	751	29,061	122	20,341	299	3,598	3	1	5	-
Men	528	17,745	87	10,694	178	2,148	4	2	4	1
Women	223	11,316	35	9,647	121	1,450	7	1	12	1
Asian and Pacific Islander	1,684	153,953	509	126,937	2,842	25,965	2	1	2	1
Men	1,026	118,957	338	96,232	1,852	20,059	3	1	3	1
Women	658	34,996	171	28,705	990	5,906	4	2	5	2
Missouri	11,215	549,921	2,388	400,435	8,348	79,486	-	-	1	-
Minority men	7,111	404,289	1,729	301,724	6,018	61,214	1	1	1	1
Minority women	4,104	145,632	659	98,711	2,330	18,272	1	1	2	1
American Indian and Alaska Native	137	2,145	16	994	34	282	11	11	28	15
Men	94	1,485	11	563	18	179	13	14	39	23
Women	43	660	5	431	16	103	19	15	29	15
Black	7,832	336,094	1,306	239,602	4,831	50,354	-	-	-	-
Men	4,848	240,162	929	179,274	3,430	39,526	-	-	-	-
Women	2,984	95,932	377	60,328	1,401	10,828	-	-	-	-
Hispanic	1,247	49,677	258	32,830	765	8,022	3	2	5	2
Men	852	37,905	194	24,350	545	5,714	4	2	5	2
Women	395	11,772	64	8,480	220	2,308	7	2	9	1
Asian and Pacific Islander	2,056	164,617	824	129,157	2,757	21,347	2	1	2	1
Men	1,354	125,975	605	98,370	2,037	15,884	2	2	3	2
Women	702	38,642	219	30,787	720	5,463	4	2	5	2
Nebraska	1,921	81,448	423	63,608	1,555	12,345	1	-	2	-
Minority men	1,204	60,507	307	47,160	1,094	9,246	2	1	2	1
Minority women	717	20,941	116	16,448	461	3,099	3	1	1	-
American Indian and Alaska Native	66	1,611	18	947	18	204	11	9	21	16
Men	44	1,288	13	720	15	167	13	11	29	20
Women	22	323	5	227	3	37	20	3	-	-
Black	863	30,826	160	24,289	612	4,832	-	-	-	-
Men	483	21,338	104	16,984	451	3,738	-	-	-	-
Women	380	9,488	56	7,305	161	1,094	-	-	-	-
Hispanic	619	19,391	122	14,557	413	3,414	3	1	3	1
Men	421	16,759	104	12,907	343	3,054	3	1	4	1
Women	198	2,632	18	1,650	70	360	7	3	-	-
Asian and Pacific Islander	385	29,776	125	23,893	513	3,905	5	1	3	-
Men	261	21,220	87	16,588	286	2,288	6	1	5	1
Women	124	8,556	38	7,305	227	1,617	11	1	4	1
North Dakota	472	31,545	123	26,048	395	3,752	2	-	2	-
Minority men	344	19,866	95	15,327	299	2,413	2	-	-	-
Minority women	128	11,679	28	10,721	96	1,339	4	-	9	-

[Continued]

★ 621 ★

Minority-Owned Firms: Midwestern States

[Continued]

Geographic area and minority	All firms		Firms with paid employees				Relative standard error of estimate % for column			
	Firms (number) A	Sales and receipts ($1,000) B	Firms (number) C	Sales and receipts ($1,000) D	Employees (number) E	Annual payroll ($1,000) F	A	B	C	D
American Indian and Alaska Native	210	(D)	57	(D)	(D)	(D)	3	(D)	4	(D)
Men	151	8,686	40	(D)	(D)	(D)	3	1	-	(D)
Women	59	(D)	17	9,159	35	960	8	(D)	15	-
Black	57	1,207	9	670	8	96	-	-	-	-
Men	37	(D)	7	(D)	(D)	(D)	-	(D)	-	(D)
Women	20	(D)	2	(D)	(D)	(D)	-	(D)	-	(D)
Hispanic	88	2,167	14	1,279	35	315	2	-	-	-
Men	66	(D)	12	(D)	(D)	(D)	2	(D)	-	(D)
Women	22	(D)	2	(D)	(D)	(D)	-	(D)	-	(D)
Asian and Pacific Islander	119	(D)	43	(D)	(D)	(D)	5	(D)	-	(D)
Men	91	8,250	36	6,670	181	1,265	5	-	-	-
Women	28	(D)	7	(D)	(D)	(D)	11	(D)	-	(D)
Ohio	21,902	1,207,885	4,360	907,907	16,847	180,419	1	1	1	1
Minority men	13,762	909,518	3,214	698,066	11,518	130,162	1	1	1	1
Minority women	8,140	298,367	1,146	209,841	5,329	50,257	1	1	2	1
American Indian and Alaska Native	152	(D)	22	(D)	(D)	(D)	15	(D)	9	(D)
Men	87	4,370	11	3,341	35	360	18	4	-	-
Women	65	(D)	11	(D)	(D)	(D)	24	(D)	18	(D)
Black	15,983	625,665	2,548	439,841	8,888	96,243	-	-	-	-
Men	9,715	430,099	1,842	300,745	5,142	58,637	-	-	-	-
Women	6,268	195,566	706	139,096	3,746	37,606	-	-	-	1
Hispanic	1,989	191,797	420	164,503	2,263	31,382	4	1	6	1
Men	1,379	178,534	363	157,745	2,092	30,171	4	1	7	1
Women	592	13,263	57	6,758	171	1,211	8	7	17	8
Asian and Pacific Islander	3,859	(D)	1,392	(D)	(D)	(D)	2	(D)	2	(D)
Men	2,618	299,921	1,017	238,830	4,297	41,463	3	2	3	2
Women	1,241	(D)	375	(D)	(D)	(D)	5	(D)	6	(D)
South Dakota	539	25,488	153	19,858	328	2,798	2	-	2	-
Minority men	380	18,356	108	13,593	254	2,141	2	-	2	-
Minority women	159	7,132	45	6,265	74	657	4	1	5	1
American Indian and Alaska Native	267	11,166	75	8,240	153	1,366	3	1	3	-
Men	199	9,106	57	6,528	126	1,181	4	1	3	-
Women	68	2,060	18	1,712	27	185	8	2	8	1
Black	63	4,832	14	4,391	35	418	-	-	-	-
Men	41	(D)	10	(D)	(D)	(D)	-	(D)	-	(D)
Women	22	(D)	4	(D)	(D)	(D)	-	(D)	-	(D)
Hispanic	109	4,262	27	3,071	43	506	1	-	-	-
Men	86	(D)	19	(D)	(D)	(D)	2	(D)	-	(D)
Women	23	(D)	8	(D)	(D)	(D)	-	(D)	-	(D)
Asian and Pacific Islander	108	5,714	39	4,607	110	707	6	1	5	1
Men	62	4,443	24	3,638	88	534	6	1	-	-
Women	46	1,271	15	969	22	173	10	3	13	3
Wisconsin	4,689	417,655	1,154	343,643	5,921	58,166	1	1	2	1
Minority men	3,043	313,228	833	255,633	3,825	36,610	2	1	2	1
Minority women	1,646	104,427	321	88,010	2,096	21,556	3	1	5	1
American Indian and Alaska Native	307	(D)	89	18,280	520	3,808	10	(D)	14	5
Men	219	17,325	64	14,925	488	3,561	10	5	14	6
Women	88	(D)	25	3,355	32	247	24	(D)	37	2

[Continued]

★ 621 ★

Minority-Owned Firms: Midwestern States
[Continued]

Geographic area and minority	All firms		Firms with paid employees				Relative standard error of estimate % for column			
	Firms (number) A	Sales and receipts ($1,000) B	Firms (number) C	Sales and receipts ($1,000) D	Employees (number) E	Annual payroll ($1,000) F	A	B	C	D
Black	2,381	190,696	477	159,597	2,552	28,726	-	-	-	-
Men	1,474	124,027	334	101,710	1,066	11,860	-	-	-	-
Women	907	66,669	143	57,887	1,486	16,866	-	-	-	-
Hispanic	894	73,541	184	61,897	683	6,919	3	1	4	1
Men	612	61,712	136	52,099	548	5,624	3	1	5	1
Women	282	11,829	48	9,798	135	1,295	7	3	10	2
Asian and Pacific Islander	1,144	(D)	417	105,222	2,198	18,928	4	(D)	5	2
Men	766	111,350	309	87,632	1,745	15,743	5	2	5	2
Women	378	(D)	108	17,590	453	3,185	10	(D)	13	5

Source: "Statistics for Minority-Owned Firms by State: 1987," *Minority-Owned Businesses*, pp. 18-28. Primary source: 1987 Survey of Minority-Owned Businesses. *Minority-Owned Businesses*, Washington, D.C., U.S. Government Printing Office, 1990. Arranged by the editors. Details may not add to total because of rounding and because a firm may be included in more than one minority group. (D) stands for data withheld to avoid disclosure of competitive information. *Note:* A dash (-) represents zero.

★ 622 ★

Minority-Owned Firms: Northeastern States

Geographic area and industry division	All firms		Firms with paid employees				Relative standard error of estimate % for column			
	Firms (number)	Sales and receipts ($1,000)	Firms (number)	Sales and receipts ($1,000)	Employees (number)	Annual payroll ($1,000)				
Connecticut	8,236	620,841	1,765	449,393	5,626	76,850	1	1	1	-
Minority men	5,421	465,269	1,307	333,261	4,131	54,660	1	1	2	-
Minority women	2,815	155,572	458	116,132	1,495	22,190	2	1	3	1
American Indian and Alaska Native	88	(D)	9	785	13	155	14	(D)	23	19
Men	68	1,522	7	(D)	(D)	(D)	15	16	29	(D)
Women	20	(D)	2	(D)	(D)	(D)	30	(D)	-	(D)
Black	4,061	225,718	724	162,610	1,936	28,798	-	-	-	-
Men	2,493	157,903	503	113,908	1,275	18,826	-	-	-	-
Women	1,568	67,815	221	48,702	661	9,972	-	-	-	-
Hispanic	2,235	175,520	397	118,141	1,610	19,580	3	2	5	1
Men	1,603	148,314	319	100,913	1,307	14,379	3	2	5	1
Women	632	27,206	78	17,228	303	5,201	6	5	11	7
Asian and Pacific Islander	1,963	(D)	650	171,402	2,123	29,085	2	(D)	3	1
Men	1,314	160,687	489	(D)	(D)	(D)	3	1	3	(D)
Women	649	(D)	161	(D)	(D)	(D)	5	(D)	6	(D)
Maine	496	43,772	143	33,339	811	7,736	2	-	1	-
Minority men	330	38,286	104	29,650	714	6,894	2	-	1	-
Minority women	168	5,486	39	3,689	97	842	3	1	-	-
American Indian and Alaska Native	68	3,956	16	3,012	46	541	7	1	-	-
Men	43	2,724	10	2,194	23	350	6	-	-	-
Women	25	1,232	6	818	23	191	15	4	-	-
Black	131	5,151	31	3,706	80	675	-	-	-	-
Men	77	2,831	20	2,130	47	415	-	-	-	-
Women	54	2,320	11	1,576	33	260	-	-	-	-
Hispanic	139	12,061	42	9,504	173	1,768	2	-	3	-

[Continued]

★ 622 ★

Minority-Owned Firms: Northeastern States
[Continued]

Geographic area and industry division	All firms		Firms with paid employees				Relative standard error of estimate % for column			
	Firms (number)	Sales and receipts ($1,000)	Firms (number)	Sales and receipts ($1,000)	Employees (number)	Annual payroll ($1,000)				
Men	98	11,409	31	9,145	165	1,631	3	-	5	-
Women	41	652	11	359	8	137	-	-	-	-
Asian and Pacific Islander	165	22,786	56	17,260	514	4,772	3	-	-	-
Men	116	21,403	44	16,223	480	4,515	4	-	-	-
Women	49	1,383	12	1,037	34	257	7	2	-	-
Massachusetts	11,180	714,391	1,856	502,212	7,186	99,228	1	1	2	1
Minority men	7,041	505,79	1,359	346,994	4,662	69,567	1	1	2	1
Minority women	4,139	208,602	497	155,218	2,524	29,661	2	1	3	1
American Indian and Alaska Native	132	4,557	24	(D)	(D)	(D)	13	7	23	(D)
Men	102	3,907	20	2,433	42	742	15	7	27	6
Women	30	650	4	(D)	(D)	(D)	27	21	34	(D)
Black	4,761	251,946	628	182,043	2,683	41,186	-	-	-	-
Men	2,886	154,712	465	104,940	1,512	26,367	-	-	-	-
Women	1,875	97,234	163	77,103	1,171	14,819	-	-	-	-
Hispanic	2,636	173,969	411	118,907	1,346	19,736	2	1	3	1
Men	1,756	154,291	329	109,913	1,201	18,425	2	1	4	1
Women	880	19,678	82	8,994	145	1,311	3	6	8	4
Asian and Pacific Islander	3,784	292,291	803	(D)	(D)	(D)	2	1	3	(D)
Men	2,371	199,744	552	133,140	1,950	26,141	3	2	4	2
Women	1,413	92,547	251	(D)	(D)	(D)	4	2	6	(D)
New Hampshire	801	84,946	174	68,166	688	10,050	2	-	2	-
Minority men	523	51,037	126	38,082	431	5,862	3	1	3	-
Minority women	278	33,909	48	30,086	257	4,188	4	1	-	-
American Indian and Alaska Native	29	(D)	3	625	2	54	11	(D)	-	-
Men	24	1,254	3	625	2	54	13	1	-	-
Women	5	(D)	-	-	-	-	-	(D)	-	-
Black	229	31,198	49	27,295	246	4,179	-	-	-	-
Men	141	6,918	26	4,385	77	935	-	-	-	-
Women	88	24,280	23	22,910	169	3,244	-	-	-	-
Hispanic	244	12,818	49	8,248	120	1,333	4	2	5	2
Men	167	9,001	41	5,199	80	1,100	5	2	6	3
Women	77	3,817	8	3,049	40	233	8	4	-	-
Asian and Pacific Islander	304	(D)	74	32,034	320	4,485	5	(D)	4	-
Men	196	34,452	57	27,909	272	3,774	6	1	5	-
Women	108	(D)	17	4,125	48	711	10	(D)	-	-
New Jersey	38,914	3,075,652	7,181	2,119,310	22,765	326,973	-	-	1	-
Minority men	26,511	2,158,010	5,233	1,424,051	14,948	206,961	1	1	1	1
Minority women	12,403	917,642	1,948	695,259	7,817	120,012	1	1	2	1
American Indian and Alaska Native	135	(D)	17	5,467	42	328	15	(D)	19	8
Men	68	7,455	9	5,154	32	260	18	7	16	9
Women	67	(D)	8	313	10	68	23	(D)	35	24
Black	14,556	995,614	2,169	731,490	8,969	138,762	-	-	-	-
Men	9,123	514,016	1,500	330,719	4,882	64,672	-	-	-	-
Women	5,433	481,598	669	400,771	4,087	74,090	-	-	-	-
Hispanic	12,094	902,004	2,226	598,775	6,167	87,642	1	1	2	1
Men	8,991	733,236	1,714	481,002	4,618	67,051	1	1	2	1
Women	3,103	168,768	512	117,773	1,549	20,591	2	2	4	2
Asian and Pacific Islander	12,530	(D)	2,846	804,173	7,828	103,840	1	(D)	2	1
Men	8,593	921,973	2,061	617,690	5,536	76,368	1	1	2	1

[Continued]

★ 622 ★

Minority-Owned Firms: Northeastern States
[Continued]

Geographic area and industry division	All firms		Firms with paid employees				Relative standard error of estimate % for column			
	Firms (number)	Sales and receipts ($1,000)	Firms (number)	Sales and receipts ($1,000)	Employees (number)	Annual payroll ($1,000)				
Women	3,937	(D)	785	186,483	2,292	27,472	3	(D)	4	2
New York	99,148	6,553,732	15,658	4,377,469	49,823	720,487	-	-	1	-
Minority men	64,353	4,721,673	11,233	3,105,769	34,884	503,172	1	1	1	1
Minority women	34,795	1,832,059	4,425	1,271,700	14,939	217,315	1	1	2	1
American Indian and Alaska Native	445	25,008	95	15,048	251	3,663	11	10	20	11
Men	273	20,352	69	11,903	206	2,880	13	11	23	11
Women	172	4,656	26	3,145	45	783	20	23	39	31
Black	36,289	1,886,038	4,438	1,315,458	16,799	258,234	-	-	-	-
Men	20,834	1,184,246	3,025	796,586	10,321	151,197	-	-	-	-
Women	15,455	701,792	1,413	518,872	6,478	107,037	-	-	-	-
Hispanic	28,254	1,555,801	4,334	944,513	12,745	186,100	1	1	2	1
Men	20,222	1,245,276	3,279	755,775	9,507	145,512	1	1	3	1
Women	8,032	310,525	1,055	188,738	3,238	40,588	2	2	4	3
Asian and Pacific Islander	35,812	3,192,830	7,061	2,167,260	21,367	287,376	1	1	2	1
Men	24,118	2,337,569	5,035	1,576,506	15,583	211,006	1	1	2	1
Women	11,694	855,261	2,026	590,754	5,784	76,370	2	2	4	2
Pennsylvania	21,464	1,920,686	4,711	1,461,277	17,475	210,076	1	-	1	-
Minority men	14,191	1,372,696	3,561	1,026,754	12,252	148,701	1	1	2	1
Minority women	7,273	547,990	1,150	434,523	5,223	61,375	1	1	3	-
American Indian and Alaska Native	140	(D)	34	(D)	(D)	(D)	24	(D)	31	(D)
Men	70	3,089	25	992	31	176	25	39	41	19
Women	70	(D)	9	(D)	(D)	(D)	31	(D)	16	(D)
Black	11,728	747,417	1,970	568,904	7,325	93,781	-	-	-	-
Men	7,352	493,809	1,399	364,807	4,782	58,317	-	-	-	-
Women	4,376	253,608	571	204,097	2,543	35,464	-	-	-	-
Hispanic	2,650	247,081	531	182,890	1,880	27,091	2	1	3	1
Men	1,897	214,586	423	160,928	1,561	24,047	3	2	4	1
Women	753	32,495	108	21,962	319	3,044	4	3	6	2
Asian and Pacific Islander	7,049	(D)	2,193	(D)	(D)	(D)	2	(D)	3	(D)
Men	4,932	665,353	1,728	502,726	5,934	66,701	2	1	3	1
Women	2,117	(D)	465	(D)	(D)	(D)	5	(D)	6	(D)
Rhode Island	1,353	98,188	292	69,396	1,350	11,434	2	-	1	-
Minority men	937	75,194	212	52,487	997	7,633	2	-	2	-
Minority women	416	22,994	80	16,909	353	3,801	3	1	-	-
American Indian and Alaska Native	36	(D)	3	278	4	40	15	(D)	-	-
Men	22	964	2	(D)	(D)	(D)	19	12	-	(D)
Women	14	(D)	1	(D)	(D)	(D)	24	(D)	-	(D)
Black	489	18,209	70	11,988	356	2,957	-	-	-	-
Men	322	13,306	49	(D)	(D)	(D)	-	-	-	(D)
Women	167	4,903	21	(D)	(D)	(D)	-	-	-	(D)
Hispanic	426	40,471	97	27,116	292	3,503	2	1	4	1
Men	322	32,427	78	21,218	182	1,786	3	1	5	1
Women	104	8,044	19	5,898	110	1,717	6	2	-	-
Asian and Pacific Islander	436	(D)	129	30,581	706	5,032	4	(D)	-	-
Men	298	29,999	90	23,121	550	3,925	5	1	-	-
Women	138	(D)	39	7,460	156	1,107	9	(D)	-	-
Vermont	326	24,679	93	19,572	324	3,903	-	-	-	-
Minority men	209	18,806	65	14,655	227	3,026	-	-	-	-

[Continued]

★ 622 ★

Minority-Owned Firms: Northeastern States

[Continued]

Geographic area and industry division	All firms		Firms with paid employees				Relative standard error of estimate % for column			
	Firms (number)	Sales and receipts ($1,000)	Firms (number)	Sales and receipts ($1,000)	Employees (number)	Annual payroll ($1,000)				
Minority women	117	5,873	28	4,917	97	877	-	-	-	-
American Indian and Alaska Native	9	(D)	-	-	-	-	-	(D)	-	-
Men	6	120	-	-	-	-	-	-	-	-
Women	3	(D)	-	-	-	-	-	(D)	-	-
Black	98	6,682	27	5,626	84	1,076	-	-	-	-
Men	64	6,358	16	(D)	(D)	(D)	-	-	-	(D)
Women	34	3,324	11	(D)	(D)	(D)	-	-	-	(D)
Hispanic	118	5,383	24	3,367	48	569	-	-	-	-
Men	83	4,917	21	(D)	(D)	(D)	-	-	-	(D)
Women	35	466	3	(D)	(D)	(D)	-	-	-	(D)
Asian and Pacific Islander	102	(D)	42	10,579	192	2,258	-	(D)	-	-
Men	57	10,421	28	8,868	144	1,979	-	-	-	-
Women	45	(D)	14	1,711	48	279	-	(D)	-	-

Source: "Statistics for Minority-Owned Firms by State: 1987," *Minority-Owned Businesses,* pp. 18-28. Primary source: 1987 Survey of Minority-Owned Businesses. *Minority-Owned Businesses,* Washington, D.C.: U.S. Government Printing Office, 1990. Arranged by the editors. Details may not add to total because of rounding and because a firm may be included in more than one minority group. (D) stands for data withheld to avoid disclosure of competitive information. *Note:* A dash (-) indicates data were unavailable.

★ 623 ★

Minority-Owned Firms: Southern States

Data are shown for 1987.

Geographic area and minority	All firms		Firms with paid employees				Relative standard error of estimate % for column			
	Firms (number) A	Sales and receipts ($1,000) B	Firms (number) C	Sales and receipts ($1,000) D	Employees (number) E	Annual payroll ($1,000) F	A	B	C	D
Alabama	11,458	599,258	2,870	454,103	7,913	79,622	-	-	1	-
Minority men	7,654	454,182	2,187	351,113	5,677	56,020	-	-	-	-
Minority women	3,804	145,076	683	102,990	2,236	23,602	1	1	2	-
American Indian and Alaska Native	90	5,053	26	3,830	36	882	15	11	18	3
Men	70	4,898	22	3,730	32	859	19	11	20	3
Women	20	155	4	100	4	23	15	8	35	10
Black	10,085	439,966	2,337	320,594	5,562	59,450	-	-	-	-
Men	6,709	326,577	1,784	241,576	3,892	41,089	-	-	-	-
Women	3,376	113,389	553	79,018	1,670	18,361	-	-	-	-
Hispanic	397	30,006	97	23,366	647	4,855	3	1	3	-
Men	259	24,650	81	21,079	586	4,454	3	1	3	-
Women	138	5,356	16	2,287	61	401	6	3	-	-
Asian and Pacific Islander	917	125,771	417	107,553	1,691	14,642	5	1	4	1
Men	637	98,549	303	84,975	1,174	9,685	5	1	5	1
Women	280	27,222	114	22,578	517	4,957	10	3	9	2
Arkansas	5,371	284,537	1,181	215,133	3,648	36,982	-	-	1	-
Minority men	3,686	202,968	917	149,044	2,774	28,371	1	-	1	-
Minority women	1,685	81,569	264	66,089	874	8,611	1	-	2	-

[Continued]

981

★ 623 ★

Minority-Owned Firms: Southern States

[Continued]

Geographic area and minority	All firms		Firms with paid employees				Relative standard error of estimate % for column			
	Firms (number)	Sales and receipts ($1,000)	Firms (number)	Sales and receipts ($1,000)	Employees (number)	Annual payroll ($1,000)	A	B	C	D
	A	B	C	D	E	F	A	B	C	D
American Indian and Alaska Native	91	3,141	11	1,694	32	219	12	4	14	6
Men	75	2,085	9	(D)	(D)	(D)	18	2	-	(D)
Women	16	1,056	2	(D)	(D)	(D)	18	2	-	(D)
Black	4,392	214,596	844	161,034	2,304	26,772	-	-	-	-
Men	2,953	146,669	658	105,938	1,685	19,912	-	-	-	-
Women	1,439	67,927	186	55,096	619	6,860	-	-	-	-
Hispanic	324	13,808	73	10,271	289	2,961	3	1	4	1
Men	230	11,007	59	(D)	(D)	(D)	4	1	5	(D)
Women	94	2,801	14	(D)	(D)	(D)	7	2	10	(D)
Asian and Pacific Islander	567	53,064	253	42,134	1,023	7,030	3	1	3	1
Men	430	43,256	191	34,145	862	5,818	4	1	4	1
Women	137	9,808	62	7,989	161	1,212	9	3	8	1
Delaware	2,039	127,249	478	93,477	1,950	19,585	1	-	-	-
Minority men	1,286	79,062	328	54,504	1,077	10,792	1	-	-	-
Minority women	753	48,187	150	38,973	873	8,793	1	-	1	-
American Indian and Alaska Native	43	(D)	7	664	13	178	11	(D)	-	-
Men	29	770	6	(D)	(D)	(D)	10	2	-	(D)
Women	14	(D)	1	(D)	(D)	(D)	25	(D)	-	(D)
Black	1,399	77,701	290	58,971	1,189	13,547	-	-	-	-
Men	869	43,060	198	29,012	559	6,598	-	-	-	-
Women	530	34,641	92	29,959	630	6,949	-	-	-	-
Hispanic	184	6,230	30	3,135	67	740	2	1	-	-
Men	130	4,728	24	2,218	33	482	-	-	-	-
Women	54	1,502	6	917	34	258	5	2	-	-
Asian and Pacific Islander	436	(D)	155	31,477	699	5,383	2	(D)	1	-
Men	273	31,177	102	(D)	(D)	(D)	3	-	-	(D)
Women	163	(D)	53	(D)	(D)	(D)	5	(D)	3	(D)
District of Columbia	9,722	602,789	1,412	478,635	6,046	89,017	-	-	-	-
Minority men	5,922	410,338	983	330,141	4,375	65,216	-	-	-	-
Minority women	3,850	192,451	429	148,494	1,671	23,801	-	-	1	-
American Indian and Alaska Native	28	865	2	(D)	(D)	(D)	21	5	-	(D)
Men	16	803	2	(D)	(D)	(D)	27	5	-	(D)
Women	12	62	-	-	-	-	35	34	-	-
Black	8,275	411,941	956	309,028	4,085	61,239	-	-	-	-
Men	5,021	272,015	666	205,493	2,952	44,429	-	-	-	-
Women	3,254	139,926	290	103,535	1,133	16,810	-	-	-	-
Hispanic	762	63,948	128	53,255	725	12,584	2	-	3	-
Men	446	50,703	91	43,328	611	10,857	3	-	3	-
Women	316	13,245	37	9,927	114	1,727	5	1	7	-
Asian and Pacific Islander	779	132,546	337	(D)	(D)	(D)	2	-	1	(D)
Men	484	91,897	229	(D)	(D)	(D)	3	-	-	(D)
Women	295	40,649	108	36,138	447	5,472	4	-	2	-
Florida	97,961	7,085,085	17,335	5,306,895	66,757	826,522	-	-	1	-
Minority men	69,121	5,541,004	12,741	4,127,260	48,311	627,190	-	-	1	-
Minority women	28,840	1,544,081	4,594	1,179,635	18,446	199,332	1	1	1	1
American Indian and Alaska Native	349	(D)	72	(D)	(D)	(D)	11	(D)	20	(D)
Men	184	11,893	38	9,857	103	1,148	15	6	28	6
Women	165	(D)	34	(D)	(D)	(D)	16	(D)	29	(D)

[Continued]

982

★ 623 ★

Minority Owned Firms. Southern States
[Continued]

Geographic area and minority	All firms		Firms with paid employees				Relative standard error of estimate % for column			
	Firms (number) A	Sales and receipts ($1,000) B	Firms (number) C	Sales and receipts ($1,000) D	Employees (number) E	Annual payroll ($1,000) F	A	B	C	D
Black	25,527	1,211,648	4,919	829,865	13,583	161,949	-	-	-	-
Men	15,976	766,466	3,502	502,475	8,538	106,221	-	-	-	-
Women	9,551	445,182	1,417	327,390	5,045	55,728	-	-	-	-
Hispanic	64,413	4,949,151	9,924	3,743,959	42,375	563,088	-	-	1	-
Men	47,832	4,035,364	7,462	3,033,185	31,806	442,897	1	-	2	-
Women	16,581	913,787	2,462	710,774	10,569	120,191	2	1	2	1
Asian and Pacific Islander	8,553	(D)	2,670	(D)	(D)	(D)	2	(D)	2	(D)
Men	5,722	771,264	1,909	612,066	8,593	86,309	2	1	3	1
Women	2,831	(D)	761	(D)	(D)	(D)	3	(D)	4	(D)
Georgia	27,350	1,789,953	6,103	1,396,438	19,888	235,494	-	-	1	-
Minority men	17,974	1,322,369	4,639	1,035,932	15,254	179,657	-	-	1	-
Minority women	9,376	467,584	1,464	360,506	4,634	55,837	1	-	1	-
American Indian and Alaska Native	129	5,715	39	(D)	(D)	(D)	13	7	21	(D)
Men	97	4,229	30	2,126	42	638	16	10	26	14
Women	32	1,486	9	(D)	(D)	(D)	21	7	27	(D)
Black	21,283	1,179,730	4,079	916,426	12,306	163,527	-	-	-	-
Men	13,682	828,199	3,062	642,456	9,162	119,503	-	-	-	-
Women	7,601	351,531	1,017	273,970	3,144	44,024	-	-	-	-
Hispanic	1,931	145,252	480	115,841	2,375	27,796	3	1	5	1
Men	1,343	124,175	377	100,623	2,028	24,533	3	1	5	1
Women	588	21,077	103	15,218	347	3,263	6	3	12	3
Asian and Pacific Islander	4,092	463,354	1,533	(D)	(D)	(D)	2	1	2	(D)
Men	2,916	368,263	1,190	292,615	4,063	35,346	2	1	2	1
Women	1,176	95,091	343	(D)	(D)	(D)	4	2	5	(D)
Kentucky	4,979	233,007	1,010	174,534	3,518	33,088	1	1	1	-
Minority men	3,145	166,903	712	123,435	2,485	24,286	1	1	1	-
Minority women	1,834	66,104	298	51,099	1,033	8,802	2	1	3	1
American Indian and Alaska Native	24	1,705	7	1,575	17	203	10	1	-	-
Men	19	1,629	6	(D)	(D)	(D)	11	-	-	(D)
Women	5	76	1	(D)	(D)	(D)	28	17	-	(D)
Black	3,738	120,201	617	85,628	1,706	17,882	-	-	-	-
Men	2,330	73,993	418	48,960	1,084	11,888	-	-	-	-
Women	1,408	46,208	199	36,668	622	5,994	-	-	-	-
Hispanic	359	16,562	68	9,319	153	1,354	3	1	5	1
Men	249	12,326	54	(D)	(D)	(D)	4	1	6	(D)
Women	110	4,236	14	(D)	(D)	(D)	6	2	10	(D)
Asian and Pacific Islander	875	95,656	324	78,987	1,660	13,882	4	1	3	1
Men	557	79,485	237	66,076	1,276	11,.297	5	2	2	1
Women	318	16,171	87	12,911	384	2,858	10	3	11	3
Louisiana	20,766	841,624	3,868	554,426	8,662	96,918	-	-	1	1
Minority men	14,672	598,995	2,983	376,639	6,008	65,637	-	1	1	1
Minority women	6,094	242,629	885	177,787	2,654	31,281	1	-	1	-
American Indian and Alaska Native	225	(D)	50	(D)	(D)	(D)	12	(D)	25	(D)
Men	182	6,658	38	3,802	37	909	13	20	29	30
Women	43	(D)	12	(D)	(D)	(D)	24	(D)	47	(D)
Black	15,331	531,548	2,611	346,946	5,259	62,283	-	-	-	-
Men	10,585	348,017	1,948	210,202	3,431	39,018	-	-	-	-
Women	4,766	183,531	663	136,744	1,828	23,265	-	-	-	-

[Continued]

★ 623 ★

Minority-Owned Firms: Southern States
[Continued]

Geographic area and minority	All firms		Firms with paid employees				Relative standard error of estimate % for column			
	Firms (number) A	Sales and receipts ($1,000) B	Firms (number) C	Sales and receipts ($1,000) D	Employees (number) E	Annual payroll ($1,000) F	A	B	C	D
Hispanic	2,697	136,083	505	91,532	1,434	17,406	2	1	3	1
Men	1,983	108,285	414	71,688	1,004	12,519	2	1	3	1
Women	714	27,798	91	19,844	430	4,887	3	1	6	1
Asian and Pacific Islander	2,583	(D)	717	(D)	(D)	(D)	3	(D)	5	(D)
Men	1,988	139,325	594	93,607	1,569	13,27	3	3	5	3
Women	595	(D)	123	(D)	(D)	(D)	7	(D)	9	(D)
Maryland	32,445	1,605,358	5,352	1,086,549	15,505	197,205	-	1	1	1
Minority men	19,751	1,122,431	3,894	758,975	10,876	133,767	1	1	1	1
Minority women	12,694	482,927	1,458	327,574	4,629	63,438	1	1	3	1
American Indian and Alaska Native	123	9,411	25	8,035	96	1,451	18	5	11	4
Men	73	7,589	19	6,605	86	1,348	22	5	15	5
Women	50	1,822	6	1,430	10	103	32	11	-	-
Black	21,678	719,715	2,689	451,643	7,248	92,740	-	-	-	-
Men	12,383	508,379	1,920	334,432	5,152	69,185	-	-	-	-
Women	9,295	211,336	769	117,211	2,096	23,555	-	-	-	-
Hispanic	2,931	185,308	509	137,111	1,431	25,929	1	1	3	-
Men	1,882	117,413	389	84,162	991	15,451	2	1	3	1
Women	1,049	67,895	120	52,949	440	10,478	3	1	11	1
Asian and Pacific Islander	7,831	701,690	2,172	498,724	6,817	78,945	2	1	3	1
Men	5,492	495,143	1,600	338,639	4,691	48,410	2	2	3	2
Women	2,339	206,547	572	160,085	2,126	30,535	4	3	7	2
Mississippi	11,122	683,679	2,871	528,060	8,291	76,249	-	-	1	1
Minority men	7,849	506,013	2,203	388,563	6,056	54,992	-	1	1	1
Minority women	3,273	177,666	668	139,497	2,235	21,257	1	1	2	1
American Indian and Alaska Native	50	(D)	10	1,666	13	152	24	(D)	37	12
Men	42	1,207	7	(D)	(D)	(D)	28	13	50	(D)
Women	8	(D)	3	(D)	(D)	(D)	24	(D)	45	(D)
Black	9,667	531,929	2,249	410,481	5,760	60,171	-	-	-	-
Men	6,743	385,089	1,712	295,171	4,080	42,141	-	-	-	-
Women	2,924	146,840	537	115,310	1,680	18,030	-	-	-	-
Hispanic	308	12,490	70	6,509	147	1,073	3	2	5	3
Men	228	10,442	58	(D)	(D)	(D)	3	2	6	(D)
Women	80	2,048	12	(D)	(D)	(D)	7	3	12	(D)
Asian and Pacific Islander	1,128	(D)	551	110,700	2,404	15,069	3	(D)	5	3
Men	858	110,221	431	87,470	1,873	11,945	4	3	6	3
Women	270	(D)	120	23,230	531	3,124	11	(D)	13	6
North Carolina	24,149	1,136,114	5,394	839,087	16,531	165,884	-	-	1	-
Minority men	16,399	815,151	4,146	600,512	12,011	120,145	-	1	1	1
Minority women	7,750	320,963	1,248	238,575	4,520	45,739	1	1	2	-
American Indian and Alaska Native	1,758	(D)	547	63,434	1,151	14,140	4	(D)	6	3
Men	1,373	79,362	467	58,486	1,016	13,075	4	3	6	3
Women	385	(D)	80	4,948	135	1,065	10	(D)	17	10
Black	19,487	746,112	3,843	529,118	10,930	114,331	-	-	-	-
Men	13,079	505,561	2,930	349,987	7,866	78,968	-	-	-	-
Women	6,408	240,551	913	179,131	3,064	35,363	-	-	-	-
Hispanic	918	92,903	179	80,052	695	10,751	3	1	5	1
Men	614	65,503	128	56,796	466	8,574	4	1	6	1
Women	304	27,400	51	23,256	229	2,177	6	1	7	-

[Continued]

★ 623 ★

Minority-Owned Firms: Southern States
[Continued]

Geographic area and minority	All firms		Firms with paid employees				Relative standard error of estimate % for column			
	Firms (number) A	Sales and receipts ($1,000) B	Firms (number) C	Sales and receipts ($1,000) D	Employees (number) E	Annual payroll ($1,000) F	A	B	C	D
Asian and Pacific Islander	2,069	(D)	855	168,937	3,807	27,024	3	(D)	3	2
Men	1,385	166,700	638	136,563	2,692	19,728	4	2	4	2
Women	684	(D)	217	32,374	1,115	7,296	7	(D)	7	3
Oklahoma	8,659	299,270	1,431	195,387	4,248	39,143	1	1	2	1
Minority men	5,804	227,772	1,072	147,600	3,052	27,873	1	1	2	1
Minority women	2,855	71,498	359	47,787	1,196	11,270	2	2	4	2
American Indian and Alaska Native	2,051	57,294	268	33,812	456	5,489	3	2	6	3
Men	1,501	47,875	225	27,963	353	4,549	3	3	7	4
Women	550	9,419	43	5,849	103	940	7	4	11	2
Black	3,461	93,903	489	58,677	1,423	14,730	-	-	-	-
Men	2,187	63,532	361	37,334	882	8,805	-	-	-	-
Women	1,274	30,371	128	21,343	541	5,925	-	-	-	-
Hispanic	1,516	50,409	243	33,883	725	6,958	3	1	5	-
Men	1,087	40,004	190	27,186	493	5,002	3	1	5	1
Women	429	10,405	53	6,697	232	1,956	7	4	12	1
Asian and Pacific Islander	1,700	98,174	440	69,191	1,645	12,007	3	2	4	2
Men	1,087	76,804	300	55,239	1,325	9,537	4	2	5	2
Women	613	21,370	140	13,952	320	2,470	6	6	9	7
South Carolina	14,155	546,465	3,039	372,719	8,765	78,842	-	-	-	-
Minority men	9,612	412,355	2,373	283,381	6,885	61,198	-	-	-	-
Minority women	4,543	134,110	666	89,338	1,880	17,644	1	1	2	1
American Indian and Alaska Native	47	3,832	15	3,049	79	568	11	2	9	2
Men	41	3,108	11	(D)	(D)	(D)	13	2	12	(D)
Women	6	724	4	(D)	(D)	(D)	-	-	-	(D)
Black	12,815	444,201	2,567	290,463	6,888	65,975	-	-	-	-
Men	8,720	335,572	2,025	221,207	5,478	51,753	-	-	-	-
Women	4,095	108,629	542	69,256	1,410	14,222	-	-	-	-
Hispanic	393	15,997	79	9,294	216	1,932	4	2	6	1
Men	252	12,408	57	(D)	(D)	(D)	4	1	7	(D)
Women	141	3,589	22	(D)	(D)	(D)	9	6	9	(D)
Asian and Pacific Islander	918	83,892	386	71,316	1,621	10,653	4	2	3	2
Men	607	62,411	285	53,976	1,227	7,665	5	1	3	1
Women	311	21,481	101	17,340	394	2,988	8	5	10	5
Tennessee	12,606	600,234	2,785	427,083	8,381	74,766	-	-	1	-
Minority men	8,322	442,295	2,099	313,495	6,451	56,827	-	1	1	1
Minority women	4,284	157,939	686	113,588	1,930	17,939	1	1	1	1
American Indian and Alaska Native	90	(D)	18	2,314	30	240	12	(D)	21	9
Men	64	3,119	15	2,239	27	228	13	7	19	8
Women	26	(D)	3	75	3	12	24	(D)	81	81
Black	10,423	386,078	1,929	260,582	4,902	50,139	-	-	-	-
Men	6,712	263,319	1,425	173,859	3,676	36,463	-	-	-	-
Women	3,711	122,759	504	86,723	1,226	13,676	-	-	-	-
Hispanic	554	35,187	134	21,055	345	3,954	3	1	3	1
Men	415	30,985	110	18,866	304	3,528	3	1	3	1
Women	139	4,202	24	2,189	41	426	6	3	8	5
Asian and Pacific Islander	1,574	(D)	713	144,233	3,125	20,648	2	(D)	2	1
Men	1,161	146,014	556	119,174	2,456	16,760	2	2	3	2
Women	413	(D)	157	25,059	669	3,888	5	(D)	6	3

[Continued]

★ 623 ★

Minority-Owned Firms: Southern States

[Continued]

Geographic area and minority	All firms		Firms with paid employees				Relative standard error of estimate % for column			
	Firms (number) A	Sales and receipts ($1,000) B	Firms (number) C	Sales and receipts ($1,000) D	Employees (number) E	Annual payroll ($1,000) F	A	B	C	D
Texas	152,409	6,961,063	32,113	4,835,241	77,983	851,079	-	-	1	-
Minority men	109,456	5,702,720	25,603	4,008,148	62,070	703,712	-	-	1	-
Minority women	42,953	1,258,343	6,510	827,093	15,913	147,367	1	1	2	1
American Indian and Alaska Native	929	28,116	167	(D)	(D)	(D)	8	5	14	(D)
Men	618	21,619	130	14,679	337	3,199	9	6	16	6
Women	311	6,497	37	(D)	(D)	(D)	13	11	27	(D)
Black	35,725	1,084,014	5,570	679,204	12,374	137,101	-	-	-	-
Men	22,946	798,775	4,099	504,496	9,059	103,415	-	-	-	-
Women	12,779	285,239	1,471	174,708	3,315	33,686	-	-	-	-
Hispanic	94,754	4,108,076	20,845	2,886,579	49,942	555,868	-	1	1	1
Men	71,996	3,495,544	17,278	2,478,732	41,125	479,386	1	1	1	1
Women	22,758	612,532	3,567	407,847	8,817	76,482	1	2	3	2
Asian and Pacific Islander	21,753	1,787,067	5,704	(D)	(D)	(D)	1	1	2	(D)
Men	14,408	1,420,025	4,234	1,038,064	12,591	126,550	1	1	2	1
Women	7,345	367,042	1,470	(D)	(D)	(D)	2	2	4	(D)
Virginia	29,555	1,549,881	6,237	1,161,164	19,866	251,178	-	1	1	1
Minority men	19,503	1,137,589	4,688	839,131	12,900	167,215	1	1	1	1
Minority women	10,052	412,292	1,549	322,033	6,966	83,963	1	1	3	1
American Indian and Alaska Native	190	(D)	42	(D)	(D)	(D)	16	(D)	25	(D)
Men	68	4,886	22	3,885	44	1,154	15	16	19	20
Women	122	(D)	20	(D)	(D)	(D)	24	(D)	48	(D)
Black	18,781	810,569	3,530	610,435	11,094	143,513	-	-	-	-
Men	12,188	587,934	2,725	439,327	7,178	92,927	-	-	-	-
Women	6,593	222,635	805	171,108	3,916	50,586	-	-	-	-
Hispanic	2,716	140,917	483	103,186	1,605	28,485	2	1	3	1
Men	1,735	104,832	375	76,429	1,175	22,418	2	1	3	1
Women	981	36,085	108	26,757	430	6,067	3	1	10	1
Asian and Pacific Islander	7,973	(D)	2,209	(D)	(D)	(D)	2	(D)	3	(D)
Men	5,580	451,185	1,584	330,230	4,604	53,310	2	2	3	2
Women	2,393	(D)	625	(D)	(D)	(D)	4	(D)	6	(D)
West Virginia	1,446	127,700	428	109,604	1,391	14,994	1	1	1	1
Minority men	941	108,673	331	95,580	1,100	12,686	1	1	2	1
Minority women	505	19,027	97	14,024	291	2,308	2	2	3	2
American Indian and Alaska Native	28	1,438	8	1,015	15	144	15	1	-	-
Men	16	1,139	5	(D)	(D)	(D)	-	-	-	(D)
Women	12	299	3	(D)	(D)	(D)	36	3	-	(D)
Black	727	38,930	107	32,959	264	4,130	-	-	-	-
Men	430	33,090	82	29,124	196	3,521	-	-	-	-
Women	297	5,840	25	3,835	68	609	-	-	-	-
Hispanic	177	13,847	46	10,323	126	1,417	1	-	-	-
Men	130	12,960	40	(D)	(D)	(D)	1	-	-	(D)
Women	47	887	6	(D)	(D)	(D)	-	-	-	(D)
Asian and Pacific Islander	523	74,821	271	66,568	995	9,470	3	2	2	2

[Continued]

★ 623 ★

Minority-Owned Firms: Southern States
[Continued]

Geographic area and minority	All firms		Firms with paid employees				Relative standard error of estimate % for column			
	Firms (number) A	Sales and receipts ($1,000) B	Firms (number) C	Sales and receipts ($1,000) D	Employees (number) E	Annual payroll ($1,000) F	A	B	C	D
Men	369	62,653	207	56,939	783	7,850	4	2	3	2
Women	154	12,168	64	9,629	212	1,620	7	3	5	3

Source: "Statistics for Minority-Owned Firms by State: 1987," *Minority-Owned Businesses,* pp. 18-28. Primary source: 1987 Survey of Minority-Owned Businesses. *Minority-Owned Businesses,* Washington, D.C., U.S. Government Printing Office, 1990. Arranged by the editors. Details may not add to total because of rounding and because a firm may be included in more than one minority group. (D) stands for data withheld to avoid disclosure of competitive information. *Note:* A dash (-) represents zero.

★ 624 ★

Minority-Owned Firms: Western States

Data are shown for 1987.

Geographic area and minority	All firms		Firms with paid employees				Relative standard error of estimate % for column			
	Firms (number) A	Sales and receipts ($1,000) B	Firms (number) C	Sales and receipts ($1,000) D	Employees (number) E	Annual payroll ($1,000) F	A	B	C	D
Alaska	6,011	236,742	818	118,135	1,756	23,894	2	2	6	2
Minority men	4,553	193,273	636	99,240	1,451	20,670	2	2	8	2
Minority women	1,458	43,469	182	18,895	305	3,224	5	7	12	3
American Indian and Alaska Native	4,006	117,726	405	37,182	320	6,229	3	4	11	5
Men	3,256	98,566	325	30,933	257	5,465	3	4	13	6
Women	750	19,160	80	6,249	63	764	9	13	23	5
Black	507	14,444	81	9,050	200	2,181	-	-	-	-
Men	285	10,461	57	6,925	158	1,747	-	-	-	-
Women	222	3,983	24	2,125	42	434	-	-	-	-
Hispanic	502	27,412	86	18,099	282	3,926	5	3	11	2
Men	316	19,498	48	13,976	216	3,176	6	1	3	-
Women	186	7,914	38	4,123	66	750	9	9	25	8
Asian and Pacific Islander	1,028	78,378	250	54,286	957	11,591	7	3	10	1
Men	711	65,501	208	47,747	822	10,298	8	3	12	2
Women	317	12,877	42	6,539	135	1,293	14	12	-	-
Arizona	14,960	904,314	3,384	679,621	15,025	126,476	1	1	2	1
Minority men	10,191	714,866	2,721	535,350	12,055	101,134	1	1	3	1
Minority women	4,769	189,448	663	144,271	2,970	25,342	3	2	5	1
American Indian and Alaska Native	872	50,276	165	41,613	491	4,364	5	3	11	3
Men	648	38,471	132	31,381	417	3,521	6	3	13	2
Women	224	11,805	33	10,232	74	843	11	8	19	8
Black	1,811	91,439	319	68,032	1,601	14,161	-	-	-	-
Men	1,154	56,333	241	38,594	1,196	9,901	-	-	-	-
Women	657	35,106	78	29,438	405	4,260	-	-	-	-
Hispanic	9,845	513,125	2,206	384,281	8,969	78,329	1	1	3	1
Men	6,802	423,294	1,834	320,696	7,304	63,870	2	1	4	1
Women	3,043	89,831	372	63,585	1,665	14,459	4	3	7	2
Asian and Pacific Islander	2,526	253,109	736	187,903	3,988	867	2	1	2	1
Men	1,658	200,048	554	146,733	3,161	24,081	3	1	3	1

[Continued]

987

★ 624 ★

Minority-Owned Firms: Western States
[Continued]

Geographic area and minority	All firms		Firms with paid employees				Relative standard error of estimate % for column			
	Firms (number) A	Sales and receipts ($1,000) B	Firms (number) C	Sales and receipts ($1,000) D	Employees (number) E	Annual payroll ($1,000) F	A	B	C	D
Women	868	53,061	182	41,170	827	5,786	5	3	5	2
California	324,584	25,022,349	72,765	18,244,209	264,410	2,953,274	-	-	1	-
Minority men	226,601	20,201,916	57,261	14,890,888	207,144	2,355,317	-	-	1	-
Minority women	97,983	4,820,433	15,504	3,353,321	57,266	597,957	1	1	1	1
American Indian and Alaska Native	3,280	162,179	631	109,621	1,572	21,332	5	4	8	4
Men	2,173	126,118	501	87,086	1,213	17,417	5	5	10	5
Women	1,107	36,061	130	22,535	359	3,915	8	6	16	6
Black	47,728	2,364,024	7,614	1,618,988	22,631	340,281	-	-	-	-
Men	29,627	1,621,645	5,466	1,103,238	16,174	238,186	-	-	-	-
Women	18,101	742,379	2,148	515,750	6,457	102,095	-	-	-	-
Hispanic	132,212	8,119,853	26,886	5,786,143	89,722	1,136,230	-	-	1	-
Men	95,254	6,772,518	22,127	4,886,061	72,588	939,893	1	-	1	1
Women	36,958	1,347,335	4,759	900,082	17,134	196,337	1	1	3	1
Asian and Pacific Islander	144,353	14,620,377	38,273	10,907,652	153,519	1,490,434	-	-	1	-
Men	101,562	11,871,690	29,653	8,957,609	119,360	1,187,089	1	-	1	-
Women	42,791	2,748,687	8,620	1,950,043	34,159	303,345	1	1	2	1
Colorado	15,762	725,030	3,196	530,568	9,704	103,027	1	1	2	1
Minority men	10,314	546,308	2,372	397,272	7,080	77,051	1	1	3	1
Minority women	5,448	178,722	824	133,296	2,624	25,976	2	2	4	2
American Indian and Alaska Native	351	14,084	38	(D)	(D)	(D)	12	4	17	(D)
Men	226	12,332	31	9,770	104	1,087	14	5	21	1
Women	125	1,752	7	(D)	(D)	(D)	19	17	-	(D)
Black	2,871	105,849	414	69,259	1,051	15,794	-	-	-	-
Men	1,751	70,180	291	44,068	715	11,906	-	-	-	-
Women	1,120	35,669	123	25,191	336	3,888	-	-	-	-
Hispanic	9,516	394,410	1,813	290,756	4,601	56,903	2	2	4	2
Men	6,381	305,643	1,402	226,079	3,480	42,751	2	2	4	2
Women	3,135	88,767	411	64,677	1,121	14,152	4	4	8	4
Asian and Pacific Islander	3,192	215,875	952	(D)	(D)	(D)	2	2	3	(D)
Men	2,066	162,137	665	119,259	2,859	21,769	3	2	4	2
Women	1,126	53,738	287	(D)	(D)	(D)	4	3	6	(D)
Hawaii	32,705	1,721,407	4,618	1,157,349	15,671	184,967	-	1	2	1
Minority men	21,137	1,284,297	3,309	876,968	10,875	139,234	1	1	2	1
Minority women	11,568	437,110	1,309	280,381	4,796	45,753	2	2	3	2
American Indian and Alaska Native	106	6,239	16	5,512	48	675	21	3	15	2
Men	81	5,897	15	(D)	(D)	(D)	23	3	16	(D)
Women	25	342	1	(D)	(D)	(D)	54	10	-	(D)
Black	399	12,310	52	7,429	147	1,286	-	-	-	-
Men	254	8,125	41	(D)	(D)	(D)	-	-	-	(D)
Women	145	4,185	11	(D)	(D)	(D)	-	-	-	(D)
Hispanic	1,226	58,098	177	41,838	542	5,923	4	2	6	2
Men	822	50,190	135	37,597	459	5,200	5	2	8	2
Women	404	7,908	42	4,241	83	723	8	6	9	7
Asian and Pacific Islander	31,300	1,656,030	4,427	1,109,366	15,046	178,004	-	1	2	1
Men	20,186	1,228,047	3,158	833,809	10,367	133,163	1	1	2	1
Women	11,114	427,983	1,269	275,557	4,479	44,841	2	2	4	2

[Continued]

★ 624 ★

Minority-Owned Firms: Western States
[Continued]

Geographic area and minority	All firms		Firms with paid employees				Relative standard error of estimate % for column			
	Firms (number) A	Sales and receipts ($1,000) B	Firms (number) C	Sales and receipts ($1,000) D	Employees (number) E	Annual payroll ($1,000) F	A	B	C	D
Idaho	1,541	70,760	362	53,922	1,173	10,286	2	1	4	1
Minority men	1,121	60,989	297	47,283	1,032	9,114	3	1	4	1
Minority women	420	9,771	65	6,639	141	1,172	5	3	8	3
American Indian and Alaska Native	80	6,965	17	(D)	(D)	(D)	11	-	-	(D)
Men	61	5,801	13	5,011	42	843	12	-	-	-
Women	19	1,164	4	(D)	(D)	(D)	25	2	-	(D)
Black	94	4,776	26	3,583	98	630	-	-	-	-
Men	67	3,026	16	1,981	69	352	-	-	-	-
Women	27	1,750	10	1,602	29	278	-	-	-	-
Hispanic	974	30,594	187	20,880	270	4,008	3	1	7	1
Men	731	26,000	153	17,965	220	3,564	3	1	8	1
Women	243	4,594	34	2,915	50	444	7	4	11	2
Asian and Pacific Islander	433	30,671	143	(D)	(D)	(D)	5	1	4	(D)
Men	286	27,365	118	23,096	714	4,503	5	1	3	1
Women	147	3,306	25	(D)	(D)	(D)	10	6	20	(D)
Montana	989	46,819	236	36,276	763	6,238	2	1	2	-
Minority men	674	37,159	183	28,988	569	4,746	3	1	2	-
Minority women	315	9,660	53	7,288	194	1,492	5	1	7	-
American Indian and Alaska Native	405	16,510	83	12,619	157	1,609	5	2	7	-
Men	281	13,163	62	10,147	119	1,220	5	2	7	1
Women	124	3,347	21	2,472	38	389	10	4	18	1
Black	77	6,944	21	6,255	123	1,027	-	-	-	-
Men	45	4,054	15	3,798	61	403	-	-	-	-
Women	32	2,890	6	2,457	62	624	-	-	-	-
Hispanic	304	10,107	61	6,416	114	995	2	1	-	-
Men	215	9,026	53	5,951	95	890	2	1	-	-
Women	89	1,081	8	465	19	105	4	2	-	-
Asian and Pacific Islander	207	13,317	72	11,020	371	2,613	6	1	-	-
Men	135	10,953	54	9,126	296	2,239	6	1	-	-
Women	72	2,364	18	1,894	75	374	14	1	-	-
Nevada	4,116	271,038	915	201,131	4,072	42,892	1	-	2	-
Minority men	2,741	216,537	686	162,556	6,300	35,970	2	1	3	-
Minority women	1,375	54,501	229	38,575	772	6,922	3	1	4	1
American Indian and Alaska Native	150	8,712	33	6,967	75	897	11	2	11	2
Men	101	6,289	20	4,952	31	492	14	3	18	2
Women	49	2,423	13	2,015	44	405	19	3	-	-
Black	1,002	38,608	182	27,916	592	4,925	-	-	-	-
Men	591	24,798	120	18,124	427	3,274	-	-	-	-
Women	411	13,810	62	9,792	165	1,651	-	-	-	-
Hispanic	1,767	141,608	385	109,257	2,250	26,056	3	1	5	-
Men	1,274	124,395	322	97,961	2,017	23,858	3	1	6	-
Women	493	17,213	63	11,296	233	2,198	7	3	5	1
Asian and Pacific Islander	1,245	83,915	320	58,251	1,197	11,264	3	1	4	1
Men	818	62,405	228	42,418	855	8,536	4	1	4	1
Women	427	21,510	92	15,833	342	2,728	7	2	10	1
New Mexico	16,963	828,247	4,279	625,462	12,868	114,331	1	1	2	1
Minority men	12,174	688,118	3,523	529,463	10,273	94,535	1	1	2	1
Minority women	4,789	140,129	756	95,999	2,595	19,796	2	2	5	2

[Continued]

989

★ 624 ★

Minority-Owned Firms: Western States

[Continued]

Geographic area and minority	All firms		Firms with paid employees				Relative standard error of estimate % for column			
	Firms (number) A	Sales and receipts ($1,000) B	Firms (number) C	Sales and receipts ($1,000) D	Employees (number) E	Annual payroll ($1,000) F	A	B	C	D
American Indian and Alaska Native	1,258	37,474	151	(D)	(D)	(D)	5	3	11	(D)
Men	782	25,051	98	17,916	276	3,378	7	3	9	3
Women	476	12,423	53	(D)	(D)	(D)	9	5	26	(D)
Black	587	27,133	110	20,762	481	4,284	-	-	-	-
Men	374	14,437	76	10,733	246	2,161	-	-	-	-
Women	213	12,696	34	10,029	235	2,123	-	-	-	-
Hispanic	14,299	702,098	3,716	529,176	10,680	97,036	1	1	2	1
Men	10,450	600,900	3,126	463,471	8,776	82,502	1	1	2	1
Women	3,849	101,198	590	65,705	1,904	14,534	3	3	6	2
Asian and Pacific Islander	897	66,611	330	(D)	(D)	(D)	5	2	4	(D)
Men	619	50,911	242	40,108	1,025	6,898	6	3	5	4
Women	278	15,700	88	(D)	(D)	(D)	11	3	8	(D)
Oregon	5,725	476,830	1,575	379,657	6,651	57,417	1	1	2	1
Minority men	3,735	372,305	1,178	299,810	4,897	43,763	2	1	2	1
Minority women	1,990	104,525	397	79,847	1,754	13,654	3	2	3	1
American Indian and Alaska Native	333	19,200	47	14,242	217	2,790	8	4	13	1
Men	187	15,781	32	12,751	189	2,608	10	2	16	1
Women	146	3,419	15	1,491	28	182	13	19	25	7
Black	848	34,136	134	24,189	448	4,456	-	-	-	-
Men	510	20,417	85	13,982	279	2,805	-	-	-	-
Women	338	13,719	49	10,207	169	1,651	-	-	-	-
Hispanic	1,598	109,642	403	89,053	1,445	15,363	3	1	5	1
Men	1,118	84,628	325	68,964	1,194	12,859	4	1	5	1
Women	480	25,014	78	20,089	251	2,504	7	2	9	-
Asian and Pacific Islander	3,007	331,950	1,002	269,264	4,644	37,664	2	1	2	1
Men	1,962	269,254	744	221,050	3,328	28,302	2	1	3	1
Women	1,045	62,696	258	48,214	1,316	9,362	4	2	4	2
Utah	2,722	125,866	543	89,343	1,987	16,101	2	1	4	1
Minority men	1,718	104,670	448	77,636	1,578	13,930	3	1	4	1
Minority women	1,004	21,196	95	11,707	409	2,171	6	3	9	2
American Indian and Alaska Native	110	(D)	16	2,648	40	615	15	(D)	25	2
Men	66	3,066	12	2,544	40	596	17	2	31	2
Women	44	(D)	4	104	-	19	29	(D)	35	38
Black	202	8,615	35	5,619	110	1,212	-	-	-	-
Men	125	5,109	23	3,829	79	987	-	-	-	-
Women	77	3,506	12	1,790	31	225	-	-	-	-
Hispanic	1,300	47,255	228	31,506	657	6,056	3	2	7	1
Men	842	40,578	204	28,612	497	5,471	4	1	8	1
Women	458	6,677	24	2,894	160	585	8	7	-	-
Asian and Pacific Islander	1,129	(D)	270	50,313	1,196	8,338	4	(D)	5	1
Men	697	56,765	215	43,394	978	6,996	5	1	5	1
Women	432	(D)	55	6,919	218	1,342	10	(D)	16	4
Washington	13,408	1,103,835	3,413	899,335	14,242	141,891	1	1	2	-
Minority men	8,838	869,808	2,571	716,871	11,219	109,176	1	1	2	1
Minority women	4,570	234,027	842	182,464	3,023	32,715	2	1	4	1
American Indian and Alaska Native	682	47,803	126	36,180	314	6,057	9	4	19	3
Men	442	34,572	93	24,825	211	3,380	10	5	23	3
Women	240	13,231	33	11,355	103	2,677	17	5	31	4

[Continued]

★ 624 ★

Minority-Owned Firms: Western States

[Continued]

Geographic area and minority	All firms		Firms with paid employees				Relative standard error of estimate % for column			
	Firms (number) A	Sales and receipts ($1,000) B	Firms (number) C	Sales and receipts ($1,000) D	Employees (number) E	Annual payroll ($1,000) F	A	B	C	D
Black	2,583	175,671	436	148,082	2,212	29,085	-	-	-	-
Men	1,561	99,348	301	81,986	1,518	17,708	-	-	-	-
Women	1,022	76,323	135	66,096	694	11,377	-	-	-	-
Hispanic	2,686	141,196	553	108,472	2,333	21,424	2	1	2	-
Men	1,859	122,980	463	96,785	1,988	19,009	2	1	2	1
Women	827	18,216	90	11,687	345	2,415	4	2	4	1
Asian and Pacific Islander	7,559	744,585	2,322	611,190	9,455	86,223	2	1	2	1
Men	5,042	617,577	1,731	517,630	7,569	69,939	2	1	3	1
Women	2,517	127,008	591	93,560	1,886	16,284	4	3	6	2
Wyoming	885	39,712	229	29,973	799	6,431	1	-	2	-
Minority men	585	27,238	167	19,817	509	4,388	2	-	2	-
Minority women	300	12,474	62	10,156	290	2,043	3	-	3	-
American Indian and Alaska Native	79	(D)	17	2,273	61	666	3	(D)	-	-
Men	50	2,649	12	1,816	48	564	4	-	-	-
Women	29	(D)	5	457	13	102	-	(D)	-	-
Black	81	3,512	11	2,605	56	785	-	-	-	-
Men	51	1,776	8	1,006	15	224	-	-	-	-
Women	30	1,736	3	1,599	41	561	-	-	-	-
Hispanic	584	21,736	134	15,838	381	3,146	2	1	3	-
Men	394	13,909	94	9,307	207	2,034	2	1	3	1
Women	190	7,827	40	6,531	174	1,112	5	1	5	-
Asian and Pacific Islander	154	(D)	68	9,361	307	1,850	1	(D)	-	-
Men	102	9,319	54	7,792	245	1,582	-	-	-	-
Women	52	(D)	14	1,569	62	268	4	(D)	-	-

Source: "Statistics for Minority-Owned Firms by State: 1987," *Minority-Owned Businesses*, pp. 18-28. Primary source: 1987 Survey of Minority-Owned Businesses. *Minority-Owned Businesses*, Washington, D.C., U.S. Government Printing Office, 1990. Arranged by the editors. Details may not add to total because of rounding and because a firm may be included in more than one minority group. (D) stands for data withheld to avoid disclosure of competitive information. *Note:* A dash (-) represents zero.

★ 625 ★

Native American Owned Firms: Comparison to Minority and U.S. Firms - 1987

Data include American Indian, Aleut, and Eskimo business owners.

Industry	Native-owned firms (number)	Native sales and receipts ($ thous.)	Percent of -			
			Minority-owned		All U.S.	
			Firms	Sales and receipts ($ thous.)	Firms	Sales and receipts ($ thous.)
All industries	21,380	911,279	1.76	1.17	0.16	0.05
Agriculture, forestry, and fishing	3,661	104,446	9.93	7.61	1.03	0.51
Mining	106	4,062	6.57	3.94	0.09	0.03
Construction	2,832	155,784	2.63	2.26	0.17	0.07
Manufacturing	911	63,563	3.05	1.60	0.21	0.03

[Continued]

★ 625 ★

Native American Owned Firms: Comparison to Minority and U.S. Firms - 1987
[Continued]

Industry	Native-owned firms (number)	Native sales and receipts ($ thous.)	Percent of -			
			Minority-owned		All U.S.	
			Firms	Sales and receipts ($ thous.)	Firms	Sales and receipts ($ thous.)
Transportation and public utilities	917	44,286	1.20	1.21	0.15	0.06
Wholesale trade	360	36,058	1.36	0.45	0.08	0.01
Retail trade	3,090	268,086	1.37	1.00	0.14	0.05
Finance, insurance, and real estate	614	20,192	0.80	0.73	0.05	0.02
Services	7,604	178,165	1.35	0.81	0.13	0.04
Industries not classified	1,285	36,637	1.84	1.64	0.18	0.09

Source: Derived from *1987 Economic Census: Survey of Minority-Owned Business Enterprises, Summary,* U.S. Department of Commerce, Bureau of the Census, MB87-4, 1991. *Note:* Percentages may not add to 100 due to rounding.

★ 626 ★

Native American Owned Firms, by Group and Legal Form of Organization

The number of firms owned and sales receipts, in thousands of dollars, are shown, by Native American group and legal form of organization.

Industry division, legal form of organization, and Native American group	All firms		Firms with paid employees				Relative standard error of estimate (percent) for column--			
	Firms (number) A	Sales and receipts ($1,000) B	Firms (number) C	Sales and receipts ($1,000) D	Employees (number) E	Annual payroll ($1,000) F	A	B	C	D
All industries	376,711	34,035,605	96,457	25,104,127	360,301	3,611,188	-	-	-	-
Subchapter S corporations	16,835	8,540,824	12,898	8,105,811	107,490	1,375,375	-	-	-	-
Aleut	13	5,611	6	(D)	(D)	(D)	-	-	-	(D)
Eskimo	14	9,398	13	(D)	(D)	(D)	14	1	16	(D)
American Indian	333	123,117	223	114,378	1,991	25,363	3	1	3	1
Individual proprietorships	340,615	21,244,191	72,910	13,673,165	190,929	1,748,585	-	-	1	-
Aleut	1,109	44,151	106	14,617	148	3,377	8	9	21	15
Eskimo	2,317	41,148	261	11,077	87	1,730	5	7	16	9
American Indian	17,028	588,874	2,880	370,735	5,629	66,130	2	1	3	1
Partnerships	19,261	4,250,590	10,649	3,325,151	61,882	487,228	-	-	1	-
Aleut	21	3,539	4	(D)	(D)	(D)	7	7	-	(D)
Eskimo	22	4,008	6	(D)	(D)	(D)	-	-	-	(D)
American Indian	523	91,433	240	74,371	951	9,652	3	2	3	2

Source: 1987 Economic Census: Survey of Minority-Owned Business Enterprises, Asian Americans, American Indians, and Other Minorities, U.S. Department of Commerce, Bureau of the Census, p. 104. *Notes:* A dash (-) represents zero. (D) stands for data withheld to avoid disclosure for individual companies.

★ 627 ★

Native American Owned Firms: Percent Distribution by Industry

Data include American Indian, Aleut, and Eskimo business owners.

Industry	Number of firms	Share of firms (percent)	Sales and receipts ($000)	Share of sales (percent)
All industries	21,380	100.0	911,279	100.0
Agriculture, forestry, and fishing	3,661	17.1	104,446	11.5
Mining	106	0.5	4,062	0.4
Construction	2,832	13.2	155,784	17.1
Manufacturing	911	4.3	63,563	7.0
Transportation and public utilities	917	4.3	44,286	4.9
Wholesale trade	360	1.7	36,058	4.0
Retail trade	3,090	14.5	268,086	29.4
Finance, insurance, and real estate	614	2.9	20,192	2.2
Services	7,604	35.6	178,165	19.6
Industries not classified	1,285	6.0	36,637	4.0

Source: Derived from *1987 Economic Census: Survey of Minority-Owned Business Enterprises, Summary*, U.S. Department of Commerce, Bureau of the Census, MB87-4. *Note:* Percentages rounded to nearest tenth. Detail may not add to 100%.

★ 628 ★

Native American Owned Firms, by Major Industry Group, 1987

The number of firms owned and sales receipts, in thousands of dollars, are shown, by Native American group and major industry, for 1987. This table is based on the 1972 Standard Industrial Classification (SIC) system.

Major industry group and minority	All firms		Firms with paid employees				Relative standard error of estimated (percent)[1] for column-			
	Firms (number) A	Sales and receipts ($1,000) B	Firms (number) C	Sales and receipts ($1,000) D	Employees (number) E	Annual payroll ($1,000) F	A	B	C	D
All Industries										
American Indian	17,884	803,424	3,343	559,484	8,571	101,145	1	1	3	1
Aleut	1,143	53,301	116	20,094	212	4,519	8	7	19	11
Eskimo	2,353	54,554	280	23,211	173	3,607	5	5	15	4
Agricultural services, forestry, and fishing										
American Indian	1,377	46,965	162	20,132	438	5,997	6	7	14	8
Aleut	671	34,207	52	7,743	48	2,196	10	10	32	20
Eskimo	1,613	23,274	157	2,234	-	757	5	10	23	37
Agricultural services	444	19,081	75	12,534	339	4,120	9	2	14	2
Forestry	89	1,368	12	803	30	266	-	-	-	-
Fishing, hunting and trapping	3,128	83,997	284	16,772	117	4,564	3	6	16	14
Mining										
American Indian	100	4,003	8	1,882	28	522	11	5	-	-
Aleut	-	-	-	-	-	-	-	-	-	-

[Continued]

★ 628 ★

Native American Owned Firms, by Major Industry Group, 1987
[Continued]

Major industry group and minority	All firms		Firms with paid employees				Relative standard error of estimated (percent)[1] for column-			
	Firms (number)	Sales and receipts ($1,000)	Firms (number)	Sales and receipts ($1,000)	Employees (number)	Annual payroll ($1,000)	A	B	C	D
	A	B	C	D	E	F				
Eskimo	6	59	-	-	-	-	-	-	-	-
Metal mining	11	(D)	2	(D)	(D)	(D)	-	(D)	-	(D)
Anthracite mining	-	-	-	-	-	-	-	-	-	-
Bituminous coal and lignite mining	3	(D)	-	-	-	-	-	(D)	-	(D)
Oil and gas extraction	80	2,441	5	(D)	(D)	(D)	14	9	-	(D)
Nonmetallic minerals, except fuels	12	(D)	1	(D)	(D)	(D)	-	(D)	-	(D)
Construction										
American Indian	2,749	148,012	823	116,258	1,594	28,524	3	3	5	3
Aleut	40	590	6	268	8	32	30	22	57	23
Eskimo	43	7,182	6	(D)	(D)	(D)	18	2	-	(D)
General building contractors	461	34,219	175	28,153	251	5,269	6	5	11	5
Heavy construction contractors	93	(D)	38	15,549	178	3,902	3	(D)	-	-
Special trade contractors	2,268	97,410	619	72,247	1,166	19,299	3	3	6	4
Subdividers and developers, n.e.c.	10	(D)	3	(D)	(D)	(D)	-	(D)	-	(D)
Manufacturing										
American Indian	875	60,221	144	51,452	1,275	13,472	4	1	6	1
Aleut	8	(D)	2	(D)	(D)	(D)	31	(D)	-	(D)
Eskimo	28	(D)	2	(D)	(D)	(D)	27	(D)	-	(D)
Food and kindred products	9	314	2	(D)	(D)	(D)	-	-	-	(D)
Tobacco manufacturers	-	-	-	-	-	-	-	-	-	-
Textile mill products	13	262	2	(D)	(D)	(D)	-	-	-	(D)
Apparel and other textile products	76	(D)	6	(D)	(D)	(D)	14	(D)	24	(D)
Lumber and wood products	274	22,230	78	18,796	407	5,155	7	2	10	1
Furniture and fixtures	21	702	2	(D)	(D)	(D)	19	17	-	(D)
Paper and allied products	2	(D)	-	-	-	-	-	(D)	-	-
Printing and publishing	50	2,501	11	2,192	58	680	19	1	-	-
Chemicals and allied products	4	146	2	(D)	(D)	(D)	-	-	-	(D)
Petroleum and coal products	-	-	-	-	-	-	-	-	-	-
Rubber and miscellaneous plastic products	5	251	1	(D)	(D)	(D)	-	-	-	(D)
Leather and leather products	18	212	2	(D)	(D)	(D)	-	-	-	(D)
Stone, clay and glass products	60	2,040	7	1,493	16	225	12	2	-	-
Primary metal industries	10	(D)	2	(D)	(D)	(D)	-	(D)	-	(D)
Fabricated metal products	91	2,153	6	1,356	16	239	10	3	-	-
Machinery, except electrical	34	4,090	8	3,635	44	1,042	11	6	17	6
Electric and electronic equipment	8	4,250	3	4,236	59	630	31	-	-	-
Transportation equipment	7	694	4	(D)	(D)	(D)	-	-	-	(D)
Instruments and related products	3	14	-	-	-	-	-	-	-	-
Miscellaneous manufacturing industries	226	4,266	12	2,320	57	530	9	14	-	-
Transportation and public utilities										
American Indian	819	41,675	152	22,483	270	3,881	5	4	9	4
Aleut	48	1,680	2	(D)	(D)	(D)	30	18	-	(D)
Eskimo	50	931	7	(D)	(D)	(D)	23	17	48	(D)
Local and interurban passenger transit	95	2,941	13	1,357	40	265	13	12	26	-
Trucking and warehousing	590	32,189	125	15,359	185	2,900	6	5	11	6
Water transportation	12	695	3	452	10	127	-	-	-	-
Transportation by air	30	865	6	414	4	63	31	6	-	-
Pipe lines, except natural gas	-	-	-	-	-	-	-	-	-	-
Transportation services	134	6,296	8	4,711	34	494	13	3	-	-
Communication	36	682	2	(D)	(D)	(D)	9	13	-	(D)
Electric, gas and sanitary services	20	618	4	(D)	(D)	(D)	-	-	-	-

[Continued]

994

★ 628 ★

Native American Owned Firms, by Major Industry Group, 1987
[Continued]

Major industry group and minority	All firms		Firms with paid employees				Relative standard error of estimated (percent)[1] for column-			
	Firms (number) A	Sales and receipts ($1,000) B	Firms (number) C	Sales and receipts ($1,000) D	Employees (number) E	Annual payroll ($1,000) F	A	B	C	D
Wholesale trade										
American Indian	340	34,585	91	(D)	(D)	(D)	9	3	17	(D)
Aleut	10	(D)	1	(D)	(D)	(D)	42	(D)	-	(D)
Eskimo	10	(D)	1	(D)	(D)	(D)	-	(d)	-	(D)
Wholesale trade-durable goods	247	24,294	60	18,867	158	2,251	11	3	20	2
Wholesale trade-nondurable goods	113	11,764	33	7,623	34	504	12	5	27	6
Retail trade										
American Indian	2,842	250,240	768	197,629	2,287	19,098	4	2	4	2
Aleut	91	5,564	27	3,688	28	339	24	20	37	27
Eskimo	157	12,282	42	8,874	112	733	17	3	20	1
Building materials and garden supplies	61	5,578	17	4,509	35	733	13	4	8	5
General merchandise stores	72	8,394	29	6,658	47	385	15	7	15	9
Food stores	301	54,320	108	42,230	356	2,526	9	4	5	2
Automotive dealers and service stations	222	65,257	88	55,793	330	3,754	8	1	5	1
Apparel and accessory stores	85	5,994	36	4,992	88	516	11	4	14	4
Furniture and home furnishings stores	86	7,915	32	6,373	63	792	10	11	13	13
Eating and drinking places	464	35,251	286	29,492	1,083	6,224	8	7	9	6
Miscellaneous retail	1,799	85,377	241	60,144	425	5,240	5	4	10	3
Finance, insurance and real estate										
American Indian	562	17,999	69	10,903	198	2,370	8	6	20	5
Aleut	29	1,238	2	(D)	(D)	(D)	40	55	-	(D)
Eskimo	23	955	-	-	-	-	46	82	-	-
Banking	1	(D)	1	(D)	(D)	(D)	-	(D)	-	(D)
Credit agencies other than banks	1	(D)	1	(D)	(D)	(D)	-	(D)	-	(D)
Security, commodity brokers and services	30	(D)	12	369	3	54	34	(D)	58	35
Insurance carriers	-	-	-	-	-	-	-	-	-	-
Insurance agents, brokers, and service	152	5,051	20	2,321	40	500	15	21	27	1
Real estate	370	12,746	33	7,710	150	1,668	10	7	31	7
Combined real estate, insurance, etc.	59	1,212	4	411	9	96	21	34	-	-
Holding and other investment offices	1	(D)	-	-	-	-	-	(D)	-	-
Services										
American Indian	7,132	168,784	1,007	102,075	2,218	22,837	2	3	5	3
Aleut	210	3,547	13	2,007	38	496	17	10	11	3
Eskimo	262	5,834	53	4,314	41	1,057	16	11	26	13
Hotels and other lodging places	102	5,734	34	5,090	98	788	15	3	10	3
Personal services	1,719	26,547	223	14,128	519	4,388	5	6	11	9
Business services	2,532	48,601	319	23,585	545	6,238	5	5	12	5
Auto repair, services and garages	538	20,704	134	14,111	226	2,710	8	7	11	8
Miscellaneous repair services	300	11,105	53	8,023	103	1,144	9	5	12	6
Motion pictures	34	1,691	5	(D)	(D)	(D)	20	9	-	(D)
Amusement and recreation services	556	15,698	57	11,602	212	1,663	8	3	23	2
Health services	488	20,840	91	13,417	205	2,293	10	11	18	11
Legal services	169	11,153	52	8,400	105	1,916	8	4	10	2
Educational services	210	1,051	3	214	4	38	12	7	-	-
Social services	451	3,842	28	1,413	85	545	10	8	-	-
Museums, botanical, zoological gardens	-	-	-	-	-	-	-	-	-	-
Miscellaneous services	505	11,109	74	(D)	(D)	(D)	9	8	21	(D)
Industries not classified										
American Indian	1,088	30,940	119	11,496	72	1,712	6	9	18	10

[Continued]

★ 628 ★

Native American Owned Firms, by Major Industry Group, 1987
[Continued]

Major industry group and minority	All firms		Firms with paid employees				Relative standard error of estimated (percent)[1] for column-			
	Firms (number) A	Sales and receipts ($1,000) B	Firms (number) C	Sales and receipts ($1,000) D	Employees (number) E	Annual payroll ($1,000) F	A	B	C	D
Aleut	36	2,296	11	1,732	40	505	45	57	86	74
Eskimo	161	3,401	12	773	7	136	15	26	80	19

Source: Economic Census: Survey of Minority-Owned Business Enterprises, Asian Americans, American Indians, and Other Minorities, U.S. Department of Commerce, Bureau of the Census, pp. 12-17. *Notes:* A dash (-) stands for zero. A (D) indicates data were withheld to avoid disclosure of individual companies.

★ 629 ★

Native American Owned Firms, by State, 1987 - I

The number of firms owned and sales receipts, in thousands of dollars, are shown, by Native American group and state, for 1987.

Geographic area and Native American Group	All firms		Firms with paid employees				Relative standard error of estimated (percent)[1] for column-			
	Firms (number) A	Sales and receipts ($1,000) B	Firms (number) C	Sales and receipts ($1,000) D	Employees (number) E	Annual payroll ($1,000) F	A	B	C	D
United States										
American Indian	17,884	803,424	3,343	559,484	8,571	101,145	1	1	3	1
Aleut	1,143	53,301	116	20,094	212	4,519	8	7	19	11
Eskimo	2,353	54,554	280	23,211	173	3,607	5	5	15	4
Alabama										
American Indian	89	(D)	25	(D)	(D)	(D)	15	(D)	19	(D)
Aleut	1	(D)	1	(D)	(D)	(D)	-	(D)	-	(D)
Eskimo	-	-	-	-	-	-	-	-	-	-
Alaska										
American Indian	1,039	39,329	102	15,123	129	1,747	8	9	19	6
Aleut	821	37,253	63	9,072	83	2,234	9	9	26	17
Eskimo	2,146	41,144	240	12,987	108	2,248	5	6	16	7
Arizona										
American Indian	843	49,801	160	41,206	488	4,291	5	3	11	3
Aleut	11	(D)	1	(D)	(D)	(D)	86	(D)	-	(D)
Eskimo	18	(D)	4	(D)	(D)	(D)	39	(D)	87	(D)
Arkansas										
American Indian	91	3,141	11	1,694	32	219	12	4	14	6
Aleut	-	-	-	-	-	-	-	-	-	-
Eskimo	-	-	-	-	-	-	-	-	-	-
California										
American Indian	3,087	148,305	599	99,692	1,511	19,873	5	4	9	4
Aleut	112	5,103	28	(D)	(D)	(D)	25	35	49	(D)
Eskimo	81	8,771	4	(D)	(D)	(D)	30	9	35	(D)
Colorado										
American Indian	343	13,807	37	10,275	108	1,051	12	5	18	1
Aleut	2	(D)	1	(D)	(D)	(D)	-	(D)	-	(D)
Eskimo	6	(D)	-	-	-	-	59	(D)	-	-

[Continued]

★ 629 ★

Native American Owned Firms, by State, 1987 - I
[Continued]

Geographic area and Native American Group	All firms		Firms with paid employees				Relative standard error of estimated (percent)[1] for column-			
	Firms (number) A	Sales and receipts ($1,000) B	Firms (number) C	Sales and receipts ($1,000) D	Employees (number) E	Annual payroll ($1,000) F	A	B	C	D
Connecticut										
American Indian	87	2,087	9	785	13	155	14	13	23	19
Aleut	1	(D)	-	-	-	-	-	(D)	-	-
Eskimo	-	-	-	-	-	-	-	-	-	-
Delaware										
American Indian	42	1,177	7	664	13	178	11	1	-	-
Aleut	-	-	-	-	-	-	-	-	-	-
Eskimo	1	(D)	-	-	-	-	-	(D)	-	-
District of Columbia										
American Indian	28	865	2	(D)	(D)	(D)	21	5	-	(D)
Aleut	-	-	-	-	-	-	-	-	-	-
Eskimo	-	-	-	-	-	-	-	-	-	-
Florida										
American Indian	348	18,250	71	14,639	219	2,677	11	8	20	9
Aleut	1	(D)	1	(D)	(D)	(D)	-	(D)	-	(D)
Eskimo	-	-	-	-	-	-	-	-	-	-
Georgia										
American Indian	122	5,282	33	2,925	42	637	13	8	21	11
Aleut	-	-	-	-	-	-	-	-	-	-
Eskimo	7	433	6	(D)	(D)	(D)	64	9	75	(D)
Hawaii										
American Indian	89	6,201	16	5,512	48	675	22	3	15	2
Aleut	6	6	-	-	-	-	92	92	-	-
Eskimo	11	32	-	-	-	-	86	59	-	-
Idaho										
American Indian	76	6,786	16	5,836	53	948	11	-	-	-
Aleut	-	-	-	-	-	-	-	-	-	-
Eskimo	4	179	1	(D)	(D)	(D)	-	-	-	(D)
Illinois										
American Indian	182	6,876	39	3,720	40	558	15	11	29	14
Aleut	2	(D)	1	(D)	(D)	(D)	-	(D)	-	(D)
Eskimo	9	(D)	8	78	6	38	63	(D)	71	59
Indiana										
American Indian	84	3,203	15	2,361	33	331	12	5	16	-
Aleut	3	15	-	-	-	-	83	83	-	-
Eskimo	3	3	-	-	-	-	81	81	-	-
Iowa										
American Indian	43	1,302	8	764	11	110	17	19	18	18
Aleut	-	-	-	-	-	-	-	-	-	-
Eskimo	-	-	-	-	-	-	-	-	-	-
Kansas										
American Indian	225	7,643	33	5,426	79	631	14	5	23	2
Aleut	6	(D)	-	-	-	-	90	(D)	-	-
Eskimo	-	-	-	-	-	-	-	-	-	-

[Continued]

★ 629 ★

Native American Owned Firms, by State, 1987 - I
[Continued]

Geographic area and Native American Group	All firms		Firms with paid employees				Relative standard error of estimated (percent)[1] for column-			
	Firms (number) A	Sales and receipts ($1,000) B	Firms (number) C	Sales and receipts ($1,000) D	Employees (number) E	Annual payroll ($1,000) F	A	B	C	D
Kentucky										
American Indian	24	1,705	7	1,575	17	203	10	1	-	-
Aleut	-	-	-	-	-	-	-	-	-	-
Eskimo	-	-	-	-	-	-	-	-	-	-
Louisiana										
American Indian	221	7,585	49	4,456	48	1,072	12	17	25	26
Aleut	2	(D)	1	(D)	(D)	(D)	-	(D)	-	(D)
Eskimo	2	(D0	-	-	-	-	71	(D)	-	-
Maine										
American Indian	68	3,956	15	3,012	46	541	7	1	-	-
Aleut	-	-	-	-	-	-	-	-	-	-
Eskimo	-	-	-	-	-	-	-	-	-	-
Maryland										
American Indian	123	9,411	25	8,035	96	1,451	18	5	11	4
Aleut	-	-	-	-	-	-	-	-	-	-
Eskimo	-	-	-	-	-	-	-	-	-	-
Massachusetts										
American Indian	132	4,557	24	(D)	(D)	(D)	13	7	23	(D)
Aleut	-	-	-	-	-	-	-	-	-	-
Eskimo	-	-	-	-	-	-	-	-	-	-
Michigan										
American Indian	304	8,512	41	5,626	85	999	10	7	14	7
Aleut	-	-	-	-	-	-	-	-	-	-
Eskimo	1	(D)	1	(D)	(D)	(D)	-	(D)	-	(D)
Minnesota										
American Indian	333	17,984	56	13,088	248	2,773	6	2	8	1
Aleut	7	70	-	-	-	-	49	55	-	-
Eskimo	-	-	-	-	-	-	-	-	-	-

Source: 1987 Economic Census: Survey of Minority-Owned Business Enterprises, Asian Americans, American Indians, and Other Minorities, U.S. Department of Commerce, Bureau of the Census, pp. 27-35. *Notes:* A dash (-) stands for zero. A (D) indicates data were withheld to avoid disclosure of individual companies.

★ 630 ★

Native American Owned Firms, by State, 1987 - II

The number of firms owned and sales receipts, in thousands of dollars, are shown, by Native American group and state, for 1987.

Geographic area and Native American Group	All firms		Firms with paid employees				Relative standard error of estimated (percent)[1] for column-			
	Firms (number) A	Sales and receipts ($1,000) B	Firms (number) C	Sales and receipts ($1,000) D	Employees (number) E	Annual payroll ($1,000) F	A	B	C	D
Mississippi										
American Indian	49	2,260	10	1,666	13	152	25	9	37	12
Aleut	-	-	-	-	-	-	-	-	-	-
Eskimo	1	(D)	-	-	-	-	-	-	-	-
Missouri										
American Indian	133	(D)	15	(D)	(D)	(D)	11	(D)	30	(D)
Aleut	1	(D)	1	(D)	(D)	(D)	-	(D)	-	(D)
Eskimo	3	3	-	-	-	-	82	82	-	-
Montana										
American Indian	405	16,510	83	12,619	157	1,609	5	2	7	-
Aleut	-	-	-	-	-	-	-	-	-	-
Eskimo	-	-	-	-	-	-	-	-	-	-
Nebraska										
American Indian	66	1,611	18	947	18	204	11	9	21	16
Aleut	-	-	-	-	-	-	-	-	-	-
Eskimo	-	-	-	-	-	-	-	-	-	-
Nevada										
American Indian	146	8,552	33	6,967	75	897	11	2	11	2
Aleut	-	-	-	-	-	-	-	-	-	-
Eskimo	4	160	-	-	-	-	92	92	-	-
New Hampshire										
American Indian	27	1,263	3	625	2	54	11	1	-	-
Aleut	2	(D)	-	-	-	-	-	(D)	-	-
Eskimo	-	-	-	-	-	-	-	-	-	-
New Jersey										
American Indian	131	6,104	15	(D)	(D)	(D)	15	8	21	(D)
Aleut	3	(D)	1	(D)	(D)	(D)	-	(D)	-	(D)
Eskimo	1	(D)	1	(D)	(D)	(D)	-	(D)	-	(D)
New Mexico										
American Indian	1,247	37,002	150	26,486	502	5,269	5	3	11	3
Aleut	3	(D)	1	(D)	(D)	(D)	44	(D)	-	(D)
Eskimo	8	(D)	-	-	-	-	94	(D)	-	-
New York										
American Indian	425	24,468	85	14,518	251	3,553	11	10	19	10
Aleut	10	10	-	-	-	-	95	95	-	-
Eskimo	10	530	10	530	-	110	95	95	95	95
North Carolina										
American Indian	1,757	89,708	547	63,434	1,515	14,140	4	3	6	3
Aleut	-	-	-	-	-	-	-	-	-	-
Eskimo	1	(D)	-	-	-	-	-	(D)	-	-
North Dakota										
American Indian	208	18,273	56	15,868	117	1,708	3	-	4	-
Aleut	-	-	-	-	-	-	-	-	-	-
Eskimo	2	(D)	1	(D)	(D)	(D)	-	(D)	-	(D)

[Continued]

★ 630 ★

Native American Owned Firms, by State, 1987 - II
[Continued]

Geographic area and Native American Group	All firms		Firms with paid employees				Relative standard error of estimated (percent)[1] for column-			
	Firms (number) A	Sales and receipts ($1,000) B	Firms (number) C	Sales and receipts ($1,000) D	Employees (number) E	Annual payroll ($1,000) F	A	B	C	D
Ohio										
American Indian	149	6,352	20	(D)	(D)	(D)	15	4	10	(D)
Aleut	2	(D)	1	(D)	(D)	(D)	-	(D)	-	(D)
Eskimo	1	(D)	1	(D)	(D)	(D)	-	(D)	-	(D)
Oklahoma										
American Indian	2,044	57,062	268	33,812	456	5,489	3	2	6	3
Aleut	3	228	-	-	-	-	84	84	-	-
Eskimo	4	4	-	-	-	-	88	88	-	-
Oregon										
American Indian	306	19,078	47	14,242	217	2,790	9	4	13	1
Aleut	20	101	-	-	-	-	34	45	-	-
Eskimo	7	21	-	-	-	-	53	51	-	-
Pennsylvania										
American Indian	139	(D)	33	14,115	354	3,698	24	(D)	31	1
Aleut	-	-	-	-	-	-	-	-	-	-
Eskimo	1	(D)	1	(D)	(D)	(D)	-	(D)	-	(D)
Rhode Island										
American Indian	36	(D)	3	278	4	40	15	(D)	-	-
Aleut	-	-	-	-	-	-	-	-	-	-
Eskimo	-	-	-	-	-	-	-	-	-	-
South Carolina										
American Indian	47	3,832	15	3,049	79	568	11	2	9	2
Aleut	-	-	-	-	-	-	-	-	-	-
Eskimo	-	-	-	-	-	-	-	-	-	-
South Dakota										
American Indian	267	11,166	75	8,240	153	1,366	3	1	3	-
Aleut	-	-	-	-	-	-	-	-	-	-
Eskimo	-	-	-	-	-	-	-	-	-	-
Tennessee										
American Indian	89	3,338	18	2,314	30	240	12	6	21	9
Aleut	-	-	-	-	-	-	-	-	-	-
Eskimo	1	(D)	-	-	-	-	-	(D)	-	-
Texas										
American Indian	872	27,049	165	17,916	387	3,847	8	5	14	6
Aleut	57	1,067	2	(D)	(D)	(D)	38	35	-	(D)
Eskimo	-	-	-	-	-	-	-	-	-	-
Utah										
American Indian	109	3,347	16	2,648	40	615	15	3	25	2
Aleut	1	(D)	-	-	-	-	-	(D)	-	-
Eskimo	-	-	-	-	-	-	-	-	-	-
Vermont										
American Indian	9	(D)	-	-	-	-	-	(D)	-	-
Aleut	-	-	-	-	-	-	-	-	-	-
Eskimo	-	-	-	-	-	-	-	-	-	-

[Continued]

★ 630 ★

Native American Owned Firms, by State, 1987 - II
[Continued]

Geographic area and Native American Group	All firms		Firms with paid employees				Relative standard error of estimated (percent)[1] for column-			
	Firms (number) A	Sales and receipts ($1,000) B	Firms (number) C	Sales and receipts ($1,000) D	Employees (number) E	Annual payroll ($1,000) F	A	B	C	D
Virginia										
American Indian	188	7,080	41	5,375	91	1,454	16	12	26	15
Aleut	1	(D)	1	(D)	(D)	(D)	-	(D)	-	(D)
Eskimo	1	(D)	-	-	-	-	-	(D)	-	-
Washington										
American Indian	602	42,976	112	33,256	295	5,500	10	4	21	3
Aleut	64	3,609	12	(D)	(D)	(D)	27	11	31	(D)
Eskimo	16	1,218	2	(D)	(D)	(D)	59	1	-	(D)
West Virginia										
American Indian	28	1,438	8	1,015	15	144	15	1	-	-
Aleut	-	-	-	-	-	-	-	-	-	-
Eskimo	-	-	-	-	-	-	-	-	-	-
Wisconsin										
American Indian	306	21,087	89	18,280	520	3,808	10	4	14	5
Aleut	-	-	-	-	-	-	-	-	-	-
Eskimo	1	(D)	-	-	-	-	-	(D)	-	-
Wyoming										
American Indian	76	3,299	17	2,273	61	666	3	-	-	-
Aleut	1	(D)	-	-	-	-	-	(D)	-	-
Eskimo	2	(D)	-	-	-	-	-	(D)	-	-

Source: 1987 Economic Census: Survey of Minority-Owned Business Enterprises, Asian Americans, American Indians, and Other Minorities, U.S. Department of Commerce, Bureau of the Census, pp. 27-35. *Notes:* A dash (-) stands for zero. A (D) indicates data were withheld to avoid disclosure of individual companies.

★ 631 ★

Native American Owned Firms: Ownership for Selected Metropolitan Areas, 1987 - I

The number of firms owned and sales and receipts, in thousands, are shown, by Native American group and statistical area[1].

Geographic area	All firms		Firms with paid employees				Relative standard of estimate (percent)[1] for column -			
	Firms (number) A	Sales and receipts ($1,000) B	Firms (number) C	Sales and receipts ($1,000) D	Employees (number) E	Annual payroll ($1,000) F	A	B	C	D
Albuquerque, NM MSA										
Aleut	2	(D)	0	0	0	0	66	(D)	0	0
Eskimo	0	0	0	0	0	0	0	0	0	0
American Indian	180	10,065	25	7,913	182	1,559	14	7	8	4
Anaheim-Santa Ana, CA PMSA										
Aleut	0	0	0	0	0	0	0	0	0	0
Eskimo	4	1,032	3	(D)	(D)	(D)	35	9	47	(D)
American Indian	293	15,644	53	7,828	178	1,814	15	17	29	13
Anchorage, AK MSA										
Aleut	75	2,244	6	736	6	222	31	39	0	0

[Continued]

★ 631 ★

Native American Owned Firms: Ownership for Selected Metropolitan Areas, 1987 - I
[Continued]

Geographic area	All firms		Firms with paid employees				Relative standard of estimate (percent)[1] for column -			
	Firms (number) A	Sales and receipts ($1,000) B	Firms (number) C	Sales and receipts ($1,000) D	Employees (number) E	Annual payroll ($1,000) F	A	B	C	D
Eskimo	132	4,438	8	2,797	26	656	21	7	0	0
American Indian	116	7,571	10	5,439	23	197	21	11	0	0
Atlanta, GA MSA										
Aleut	0	0	0	0	0	0	0	0	0	0
Eskimo	0	0	0	0	0	0	0	0	0	0
American Indian	68	(D)	14	(D)	(D)	(D)	19	(D)	37	(D)
Austin, TX MSA										
Aleut	0	0	0	0	0	0	0	0	0	0
Eskimo	0	0	0	0	0	0	0	0	0	0
American Indian	34	1,086	8	940	14	236	35	20	47	23
Bakersfield, CA MSA										
Aleut	10	1,030	10	1,030	0	50	95	95	95	95
Eskimo	0	0	0	0	0	0	0	0	0	0
American Indian	86	4,656	5	3,605	181	1,614	26	13	28	13
Baltimore, MD MSA										
Aleut	0	0	0	0	0	0	0	0	0	0
Eskimo	0	0	0	0	0	0	0	0	0	0
American Indian	63	4,879	13	4,335	71	1,074	28	6	19	5
Bellingham, WA MSA										
Aleut	20	390	0	0	0	0	67	67	0	0
Eskimo	1	(D)	1	(D)	(D)	(D)	0	(D)	0	(D)
American Indian	36	1,450	21	1,347	11	193	56	43	92	47
Boston, MA PSMA										
Aleut	0	0	0	0	0	0	0	0	0	0
Eskimo	0	0	0	0	0	0	0	0	0	0
American Indian	61	1,925	10	(D)	(D)	(D)	22	6	45	(D)
Boulder-Longmont, CO PMSA										
Aleut	0	0	0	0	0	0	0	0	0	0
Eskimo	0	0	0	0	0	0	0	0	0	0
American Indian	38	2,108	5	(D)	(D)	(D)	34	12	0	(D)
Charlotte-Gastonia-Rock Hill, NC-SC MSA										
Aleut	0	0	0	0	0	0	0	0	0	0
Eskimo	0	0	0	0	0	0	0	0	0	0
American Indian	113,3,936	29	2,550	45	489	18	9	27	10	
Chicago, IL PMSA										
Aleut	1	(D)	1	(D)	(D)	(D)	0	(D)	0	(D)
Eskimo	3	(D)	2	(D)	(D)	(D)	48	(D)	72	(D)
American Indian	120	4,443	25	2,219	20	288	19	15	38	19
Columbus, OH MSA										
Aleut	0	0	0	0	0	0	0	0	0	0
Eskimo	0	0	0	0	0	0	0	0	0	0
American Indian	36	705	2	(D)	(D)	(D)	29	6	0	(D)

[Continued]

★ 631 ★

Native American Owned Firms: Ownership for Selected Metropolitan Areas, 1987   I
[Continued]

Geographic area	All firms		Firms with paid employees				Relative standard of estimate (percent)[1] for column -			
	Firms (number) A	Sales and receipts ($1,000) B	Firms (number) C	Sales and receipts ($1,000) D	Employees (number) E	Annual payroll ($1,000) F	A	B	C	D
Dallas, TX PMSA										
Aleut	6	54	0	0	0	0	92	92	0	0
Eskimo	0	0	0	0	0	0	0	0	0	0
American Indian	185	7,463	44	5,973	111	1,504	16	7	29	7
Denver, CO PMSA										
Aleut	1	(D)	1	(D)	(D)	(D)	0	(D)	0	(D)
Eskimo	6	(D)	0	0	0	0	59	(D)	0	0
American Indian	161	2,557	16	902	31	186	19	20	31	9
Detroit, MI PMSA										
Aleut	0	0	0	0	0	0	0	0	0	0
Eskimo	1	(D)	1	(D)	(D)	(D)	0	(D)	0	(D)
American Indian	109	4,222	16	3,068	45	293	18	7	23	6
El Paso, TX MSA										
Aleut	4	8	0	0	0	0	87	87	0	0
Eskimo	0	0	0	0	0	0	0	0	0	0
American Indian	50	1,833	22	1,368	18	352	34	32	46	38
Fayetteville, NC MSA										
Aleut	0	0	0	0	0	0	0	0	0	0
Eskimo	0	0	0	0	0	0	0	0	0	0
American Indian	84	7,735	30	6,519	91	1,007	20	5	24	6
Fort Smith, AR-OK MSA										
Aleut	0	0	0	0	0	0	0	0	0	0
Eskimo	0	0	0	0	0	0	0	0	0	0
American Indian	63	1,278	7	(D)	(D)	(D)	19	7	49	(D)
Fort Worth-Arlington, TX PMSA										
Aleut	0	0	0	0	0	0	0	0	0	0
Eskimo	0	0	0	0	0	0	0	0	0	0
American Indian	73	(D)	13	(D)	(D)	(D)	25	(D)	48	(D)
Fresno, CA MSA										
Aleut	0	0	0	0	0	0	0	0	0	0
Eskimo	1	(D)	0	0	0	0	0	(D)	0	0
American Indian	42	(D)	18	1,523	34	438	39	(D)	54	13
Greensboro-Winston-Salem-High Point, NC MSA										
Aleut	0	0	0	0	0	0	0	0	0	0
Eskimo	0	0	0	0	0	0	0	0	0	0
American Indian	55	5,047	16	4,099	74	971	23	9	31	9

Source: 1987 Economic Census: Survey of Minority-Owned Business Enterprises, Asian Americans, American Indians, and Other Minorities, U.S. Department of Commerce, Bureau of the Census, MB87-3, 1991. *Notes:* A (D) indicates data were withheld to avoid disclosing data from individual companies. 1. The metropolitan statistical areas (MSA's) for which data are shown are among those defined by the Office of Management and Budget as of June 30, 1987. An MSA is an integrated economic and social unit with a population nucleus of at least 50,000 inhabitants. Each MSA consists of one or more counties meeting standards of metropolitan character; in New England, cities and towns, rather than counties, are the component geographic units. An MSA with a population of 1 million or more may be subdivided into primary metropolitan statistical areas (PMSA's). A PSMA consists of a large urbanized county or a cluster of counties (cities and towns in New England) that demonstrates very strong internal economic and social links separate from the ties to other portions of its MSA. Where PMSA's are defined, the MSA of which they are component parts is redesignated a consolidated metropolitan statistical area (CMSA).

★ 632 ★

Native American Owned Firms: Ownership for Selected Metropolitan Areas, 1987 - II

The number of firms owned and sales and receipts, in thousands, are shown, by Native American group and statistical area[1].

Geographic area	All firms		Firms with paid employees				Relative standard of estimate (percent)[1] for column -			
	Firms (number)	Sales and receipts ($1,000)	Firms (number)	Sales and receipts ($1,000)	Employees (number)	Annual payroll ($1,000)	A	B	C	D
	A	B	C	D	E	F				
Honolulu, HI MSA										
Aleut	6	6	0	0	0	0	92	92	0	0
Eskimo	11	32	0	0	0	0	86	59	0	0
American Indian	55	5,125	13	(D)	(D)	(D)	28	3	19	(D)
Houma-Thibodaux, LA MSA										
Aleut	0	0	0	0	0	0	0	0	0	0
Eskimo	0	0	0	0	0	0	0	0	0	0
American Indian	120	3,429	23	1,836	11	614	17	36	41	62
Houston, TX PMSA										
Aleut	11	308	0	0	0	0	86	92	0	0
Eskimo	0	0	0	0	0	0	0	0	0	0
American Indian	103	1,940	8	(D)	(D)	(D)	23	17	25	(D)
Kansas City, MO-KS MSA										
Aleut	0	0	0	0	0	0	0	0	0	0
Eskimo	0	0	0	0	0	0	0	0	0	0
American Indian	63	1,310	13	595	17	199	19	18	35	25
Las Cruces, NM MSA										
Aleut	1	(D)	1	(D)	(D)	(D)	0	(D)	0	(D)
Eskimo	0	0	0	0	0	0	0	0	0	0
American Indian	43	490	2	(D)	(D)	(D)	35	26	70	(D)
Las Vegas, NV MSA										
Aleut	0	0	0	0	0	0	0	0	0	0
Eskimo	4	160	0	0	0	0	92	92	0	0
American Indian	46	880	6	(D)	(D)	(D)	28	8	0	(D)
Lawton, OK MSA										
Aleut	0	0	0	0	0	0	0	0	0	0
Eskimo	0	0	0	0	0	0	0	0	0	0
American Indian	41	787	13	523	24	103	24	24	39	36
Los Angeles-Long Beach, CA PMSA										
Aleut	44	1,116	0	0	0	0	41	65	0	0
Eskimo	30	900	0	0	0	0	55	87	0	0
American Indian	722	37,045	148	24,328	238	3,626	10	7	19	8
Miami-Hialeah, FL PMSA										
Aleut	1	(D)	1	(D)	(D)	(D)	0	(D)	0	(D)
Eskimo	0	0	0	0	0	0	0	0	0	0
American Indian	49	1,027	5	280	13	98	32	53	40	30
Milwaukee, WI PSMA										
Aleut	0	0	0	0	0	0	0	0	0	0
Eskimo	0	0	0	0	0	0	0	0	0	0
American Indian	70	2,034	19	1,727	19	217	26	6	50	6
Minneapolis-St. Paul, MN-WI MSA										
Aleut	7	70	0	0	0	0	49	55	0	0
Eskimo	0	0	0	0	0	0	0	0	0	
American Indian	136	11,162	25	9,338	200	2,261	9	1	14	1

[Continued]

★ 632 ★

Native American Owned Firms: Ownership for Selected Metropolitan Areas, 1987 - II
[Continued]

Geographic area	All firms		Firms with paid employees				Relative standard of estimate (percent)[1] for column -			
	Firms (number) A	Sales and receipts ($1,000) B	Firms (number) C	Sales and receipts ($1,000) D	Employees (number) E	Annual payroll ($1,000) F	A	B	C	D
Modesto, CA MSA										
Aleut	2	(D)	2	(D)	(D)	(D)	71	(D)	71	(D)
Eskimo	0	0	0	0	0	0	0	0	0	0
American Indian	48	1,555	18	1,052	14	230	35	27	54	39
Nassau-Suffolk, NY PMSA										
Aleut	0	0	0	0	0	0	0	0	0	0
Eskimo	10	530	10	530	0	110	95	95	95	95
American Indian	24	4,776	14	3,963	46	794	25	23	25	26
New Orleans, LA MSA										
Aleut	2	(D)	1	(D)	(D)	(D)	0	(D)	0	(D)
Eskimo	0	0	0	0	0	0	0	0	0	0
American Indian	52	2,224	7	1,092	25	283	25	18	20	1
New York, NY PMSA										
Aleut	0	0	0	0	0	0	0	0	0	0
Eskimo	0	0	0	0	0	0	0	0	0	0
American Indian	180	6,444	23	(D)	(D)	(D)	18	23	43	(D)
Norfolk-Virginia Beach-Newport News, VA MSA										
Aleut	0	0	0	0	0	0	0	0	0	0
Eskimo	1	(D)	0	0	0	0	0	(D)	0	0
American Indian	34	1,405	9	1,290	13	634	35	54	42	59
Oakland, CA PMSA										
Aleut	3	15	0	0	0	0	82	82	0	0
Eskimo	0	0	0	0	0	0	0	0	0	0
American Indian	205	8,892	17	7,719	82	1,853	20	9	21	10
Oklahoma City, OK MSA										
Aleut	0	0	0	0	0	0	0	0	0	0
Eskimo	0	0	0	0	0	0	0	0	0	0
American Indian	320	8,406	32	4,339	75	870	9	8	12	13
Orlando, FL MSA										
Aleut	0	0	0	0	0	0	0	0	0	0
Eskimo	0	0	0	0	0	0	0	0	0	0
American Indian	48	2,509	17	2,208	21	431	30	41	47	46
Oxnard-Ventura, CA PMSA										
Aleut	12	1,702	10	(D)	(D)	(D)	80	77	95	(D)
Eskimo	0	0	0	0	0	0	0	0	0	0
American Indian	53	3,049	7	2,229	32	408	35	19	35	22
Philadelphia, PA-NJ PMSA										
Aleut	0	0	0	0	0	0	0	0	0	0
Eskimo	0	0	0	0	0	0	0	0	0	0
American Indian	60	14,797	16	(D)	(D)	(D)	28	6	18	(D)
Phoenix, AZ MSA										
Aleut	1	(D)	1	(D)	(D)	(D)	0	(D)	0	(D)

[Continued]

★ 632 ★

Native American Owned Firms: Ownership for Selected Metropolitan Areas, 1987 - II
[Continued]

Geographic area	All firms		Firms with paid employees				Relative standard of estimate (percent)[1] for column -			
	Firms (number)	Sales and receipts ($1,000)	Firms (number)	Sales and receipts ($1,000)	Employees (number)	Annual payroll ($1,000)	A	B	C	D
	A	B	C	D	E	F				
Eskimo	4	28	0	0	0	0	87	87	0	0
American Indian	198	13,728	30	11,628	132	866	11	2	27	2

Source: 1987 Economic Census: Survey of Minority-Owned Business Enterprises, Asian Americans, American Indians, and Other Minorities, U.S. Department of Commerce, Bureau of the Census, MB87-3, 1991. *Notes:* A (D) indicates data were withheld to avoid disclosing data from individual companies. 1. The metropolitan statistical areas (MSA's) for which data are shown are among those defined by the Office of Management and Budget as of June 30, 1987. An MSA is an integrated economic and social unit with a population nucleus of at least 50,000 inhabitants. Each MSA consists of one or more counties meeting standards of metropolitan character; in New England, cities and towns, rather than counties, are the component geographic units. An MSA with a population of 1 million or more may be subdivided into primary metropolitan statistical areas (PMSA's). A PSMA consists of a large urbanized county or a cluster of counties (cities and towns in New England) that demonstrates very strong internal economic and social links separate from the ties to other portions of its MSA. Where PMSA's are defined, the MSA of which they are component parts is redesignated a consolidated metropolitan statistical area (CMSA).

★ 633 ★

Native American Owned Firms: Ownership for Selected Metropolitan Areas, 1987 - III

The number of firms owned and sales and receipts, in thousands, are shown, by Native American group and statistical area[1].

Geographic area	All firms		Firms with paid employees				Relative standard of estimate (percent)[1] for column -			
	Firms (number)	Sales and receipts ($1,000)	Firms (number)	Sales and receipts ($1,000)	Employees (number)	Annual payroll ($1,000)	A	B	C	D
	A	B	C	D	E	F				
Portland, OR PMSA										
Aleut	17	95	0	0	0	0	38	47	0	0
Eskimo	6	(D)	0	0	0	0	15	2	38	(D)
American Indian	103	6,512	10	(D)	(D)	(D)	15	2	38	(D)
Raleigh-Durham, NC MSA										
Aleut	0	0	0	0	0	0	0	0	0	0
Eskimo	0	0	0	0	0	0	0	0	0	0
American Indian	53	1,564	13	1,036	12	324	26	31	38	44
Reno, NV MSA										
Aleut	0	0	0	0	0	0	0	0	0	0
Eskimo	0	0	0	0	0	0	0	0	0	0
American Indian	31	1,322	7	808	16	145	16	0	0	0
Richmond-Petersburg, VA MSA										
Aleut	0	0	0	0	0	0	0	0	0	0
Eskimo	0	0	0	0	0	0	0	0	0	0
American Indian	35	2,490	15	2,393	48	485	31	1	16	1
Riverside-San Bernadino, CA PMSA										
Aleut	4	68	0	0	0	0	87	87	0	0
Eskimo	4	36	0	0	0	0	87	87	0	0
American Indian	211	9,124	58	6,857	83	1,352	19	16	32	19
Rochester, NY MSA										
Aleut	10	10	0	0	0	0	95	95	0	0
Eskimo	0	0	0	0	0	0	0	0	0	0
American Indian	27	593	1	(D)	(D)	(D)	49	67	0	(D)

[Continued]

★ 633 ★

Native American Owned Firms: Ownership for Selected Metropolitan Areas, 1987 - III
[Continued]

Geographic area	All firms		Firms with paid employees				Relative standard of estimate (percent)[1] for column -			
	Firms (number)	Sales and receipts ($1,000)	Firms (number)	Sales and receipts ($1,000)	Employees (number)	Annual payroll ($1,000)	A	B	C	D
	A	B	C	D	E	F				
Sacramento, CA MSA										
Aleut	0	0	0	0	0	0	0	0	0	0
Eskimo	0	0	0	0	0	0	0	0	0	0
American Indian	197	9,366	41	5,258	98	1,126	18	25	31	31
St. Louis, MO-IL MSA										
Aleut	1	(D)	1	(D)	(D)	(D)	0	(D)	0	(D)
Eskimo	0	0	0	0	0	0	0	0	0	0
American Indian	36	(D)	4	116	2	18	22	(D)	35	44
Salinas-Seaside-Monterey, CA MSA										
Aleut	0	0	0	0	0	0	0	0	0	0
Eskimo	10	90	0	0	0	0	95	95	0	0
American Indian	46	3,846	4	3,530	22	323	37	13	35	14
Salt Lake City-Ogden, UT MSA										
Aleut	1	(D)	0	0	0	0	0	(D)	0	0
Eskimo	0	0	0	0	0	0	0	0	0	0
American Indian	46	694	7	481	15	86	24	10	20	2
San Antonio, TX MSA										
Aleut	11	148	1	(D)	(D)	(D)	86	13	0	(D)
Eskimo	0	0	0	0	0	0	0	0	0	0
American Indian	61	530	3	260	13	72	35	12	47	20
San Diego, CA MSA										
Aleut	13	404	3	364	9	69	74	35	47	37
Eskimo	18	222	0	0	0	0	67	71	0	0
American Indian	374	13,718	66	7,960	78	1,104	14	17	29	19
San Francisco, CA PMSA										
Aleut	11	(D)	1	(D)	(D)	(D)	86	(D)	0	(D)
Eskimo	0	0	0	0	0	0	0	0	0	0
American Indian	131	4,149	13	1,977	27	350	22	27	46	42
San Jose, CA PMSA										
Aleut	0	0	0	0	0	0	0	0	0	0
Eskimo	0	0	0	0	0	0	0	0	0	0
American Indian	173	6,393	35	4,331	138	1,621	22	19	30	12
Santa Barbara-Santa Maria-Lompoc, CA MSA										
Aleut	2	(D)	2	(D)	(D)	(D)	71	(D)	71	(D)
Eskimo	0	0	0	0	0	0	0	0	0	0
American Indian	29	4,355	12	4,284	31	303	43	4	56	4
Santa Cruz, CA PMSA										
Aleut	0	0	0	0	0	0	0	0	0	0
Eskimo	0	0	0	0	0	0	0	0	0	0
American Indian	40	753	5	442	4	109	55	33	49	23
Santa Fe, NM MSA										
Aleut	0	0	0	0	0	0	0	0	0	0
Eskimo	0	0	0	0	0	0	0	0	0	0
American Indian	58	4,354	12	3,553	21	653	25	3	0	0

[Continued]

★ 633 ★

Native American Owned Firms: Ownership for Selected Metropolitan Areas, 1987 - III
[Continued]

Geographic area	All firms		Firms with paid employees				Relative standard of estimate (percent)[1] for column -			
	Firms (number) A	Sales and receipts ($1,000) B	Firms (number) C	Sales and receipts ($1,000) D	Employees (number) E	Annual payroll ($1,000) F	A	B	C	D
Santa Rosa-Petaluma, CA PMSA										
Aleut	1	(D)	0	0	0	0	0	(D)	0	0
Eskimo	11	(D)	1	(D)	(D)	(D)	86	(D)	0	(D)
American Indian	48	1,807	15	1,631	15	305	40	27	64	29
Seattle, WA PMSA										
Aleut	18	2,031	7	921	4	303	27	4	49	7
Eskimo	2	(D)	0	0	0	0	0	(D)	0	0
American Indian	243	15,006	29	10,905	78	2,548	16	10	33	2
Spokane, WA MSA										
Aleut	10	80	0	0	0	0	95	95	0	0
Eskimo	0	0	0	0	0	0	0	0	0	0
American Indian	44	1,034	4	(D)	(D)	(D)	38	11	33	(D)
Stockton, CA MSA										
Aleut	0	0	0	0	0	0	0	0	0	0
Eskimo	0	0	0	0	0	0	0	0	0	0
American Indian	53	2,090	2	(D)	(D)	(D)	36	16	0	(D)
Syracuse, NY MSA										
Aleut	0	0	0	0	0	0	0	0	0	0
Eskimo	0	0	0	0	0	0	0	0	0	0
American Indian	32	472	1	(D)	(D)	(D)	47	55	0	(D)

Source: 1987 Economic Census: Survey of Minority-Owned Business Enterprises, Asian Americans, American Indians, and Other Minorities, U.S. Department of Commerce, Bureau of the Census, MB87-3, 1991. *Notes:* A (D) indicates data were withheld to avoid disclosing data from individual companies. 1. The metropolitan statistical areas (MSA's) for which data are shown are among those defined by the Office of Management and Budget as of June 30, 1987. An MSA is an integrated economic and social unit with a population nucleus of at least 50,000 inhabitants. Each MSA consists of one or more counties meeting standards of metropolitan character; in New England, cities and towns, rather than counties, are the component geographic units. An MSA with a population of 1 million or more may be subdivided into primary metropolitan statistical areas (PMSA's). A PSMA consists of a large urbanized county or a cluster of counties (cities and towns in New England) that demonstrates very strong internal economic and social links separate from the ties to other portions of its MSA. Where PMSA's are defined, the MSA of which they are component parts is redesignated a consolidated metropolitan statistical area (CMSA).

★ 634 ★

Native American Owned Firms: Ownership for Selected Metropolitan Areas, 1987 - IV

The number of firms owned and sales and receipts, in thousands, are shown, by Native American group and statistical area[1].

Geographic area	All firms		Firms with paid employees				Relative standard of estimate (percent)[1] for column -			
	Firms (number) A	Sales and receipts ($1,000) B	Firms (number) C	Sales and receipts ($1,000) D	Employees (number) E	Annual payroll ($1,000) F	A	B	C	D
Tacoma, WA PMSA										
Aleut	5	(D)	3	279	2	4	40	(D)	47	66
Eskimo	11	(D)	1	(D)	(D)	(D)	85	(D)	0	(D)
American Indian	17	5,252	8	5,149	53	541	18	2	30	2
Tampa-St. Petersburg-Clearwater, FL MSA										
Aleut	0	0	0	0	0	0	0	0	0	0

[Continued]

★ 634 ★

Native American Owned Firms: Ownership for Selected Metropolitan Areas, 1987 - IV
[Continued]

Geographic area	All firms		Firms with paid employees				Relative standard of estimate (percent)[1] for column -			
	Firms (number) A	Sales and receipts ($1,000) B	Firms (number) C	Sales and receipts ($1,000) D	Employees (number) E	Annual payroll ($1,000) F	A	B	C	D
Eskimo	0	0	0	0	0	0	0	0	0	0
American Indian	54	901	14	(D)	(D)	(D)	29	44	72	(D)
Tucson, AZ MSA										
Aleut	10	10	0	0	0	0	95	95	0	0
Eskimo	0	0	0	0	0	0	0	0	0	0
American Indian	61	6,392	15	5,688	33	365	19	13	34	14
Tulsa, OK MSA										
Aleut	0	0	0	0	0	0	0	0	0	0
Eskimo	4	4	0	0	0	0	88	88	0	0
American Indian	540	11,113	64	5,559	77	1,055	7	5	13	4
Washington, DC-MD VA MSA										
Aleut	1	(D)	1	(D)	(D)	(D)	0	(D)	0	(D)
Eskimo	0	0	0	0	0	0	0	0	0	0
American Indian	176	5,546	23	3,226	37	403	16	7	41	6
Wichita, KS MSA										
Aleut	6	(D)	0	0	0	0	90	(D)	0	0
Eskimo	0	0	0	0	0	0	0	0	0	0
American Indian	42	3,363	8	2,638	16	197	23	1	0	0
Yakima, WA MSA										
Aleut	0	0	0	0	0	0	0	0	0	0
Eskimo	0	0	0	0	0	0	0	0	0	0
American Indian	48	4,359	16	2,039	28	301	34	12	49	24

Source: 1987 Economic Census: Survey of Minority-Owned Business Enterprises, Asian Americans, American Indians, and Other Minorities, U.S. Department of Commerce, Bureau of the Census, MB87-3, 1991. *Notes:* A (D) indicates data were withheld to avoid disclosing data from individual companies. 1. The metropolitan statistical areas (MSA's) for which data are shown are among those defined by the Office of Management and Budget as of June 30, 1987. An MSA is an integrated economic and social unit with a population nucleus of at least 50,000 inhabitants. Each MSA consists of one or more counties meeting standards of metropolitan character; in New England, cities and towns, rather than counties, are the component geographic units. An MSA with a population of 1 million or more may be subdivided into primary metropolitan statistical areas (PMSA's). A PSMA consists of a large urbanized county or a cluster of counties (cities and towns in New England) that demonstrates very strong internal economic and social links separate from the ties to other portions of its MSA. Where PMSA's are defined, the MSA of which they are component parts is redesignated a consolidated metropolitan statistical area (CMSA).

Casinos and Gaming

★ 635 ★

Indian Gaming in the United States

Source: National Indian Gaming Association.

★ 636 ★

Tribal Casinos, by Year Started

| 1990 - 14 |
| 1991 - 9 |
| 1992 - 28 |
| ☐ Pending - 3 |

Three casinos are currently pending.

Year	Number started
1990	14
1991	9
1992	28
Pending	3

Source: USA TODAY, December 4, 1992, p. 1A. Primary source: National Indian Gaming Association.

★ 637 ★

Annual Revenues from Bingo, by Area, 1987

Area	Annual gross revenue
Aberdeen	5,076,083
Albuquerque	1,200,000
Anadarko	2,887,428
Billings	339,381
Eastern	65,000,000
Juneau	0
Minneapolis	40,450,000
Muskogee	18,776,029
Navajo	0
Phoenix	unknown
Portland	15,000,000
Sacramento	106,900,000

Source: U.S., Congress, Senate, Hearing Before the Select Committee on Indian Affairs, *Gaming Activities on Indian Reservations and Lands*, S. Hrg. 100- 341, U.S. Government Printing Office, Washington, D.C., 1988, p. 238.

★ 638 ★

Minnesota: Expenditures of Gaming Facilities, 1991

Figures are shown in millions of dollars.

Expenditure type	Amount
Salaries and wages	27.6
Payroll taxes and benefits	4.2
Payroll-related total	31.8
Advertising and promotion	7.1
Utilities	.9
Other operating	49.2
Operations-related total	57.2
Total	89.0

Source: U.S. Congress, Senate, Hearing Before the Select Committee on Indian Affairs, *Implementation of the Indian Gaming Regulatory Act*, S. HRG. 102- 660, Pt. 2, U.S. Government Printing Office, Washington, D.C., 1992, p. 283. *Notes:* Participating members include the following tribes: Bois Forte, Leech Lake, Lower Sioux, Mille Lacs Chippewa, Prairie Island Sioux, and Shakopee Sioux.

★ 639 ★

Minnesota: How Gambling Facilities Compare With Minnesota's Largest Corporate Employers

Tribal gaming includes all gaming groups together[1].

Company name	Rank	Minnesota employment
3M	1	23,000
Dayton Hudson Corporation	2	21,650
Northwest Airlines Inc.	3	17,600
Mayo Foundation	4	16,500
Health One Corp.	5	11,000
Honeywell Inc.	6	11,000
IBM Corporation	7	9,300
Lifespan Inc.	8	8,800
Norwest Corporation	9	8,151
Unisys Corporation	10	8,000
U.S. West	11	7,316
Fairview Hospital & Health Services	12	7,000
Northern States Power Company	13	7,000
First Bank System Inc.	14	6,426
Fingerhut Corporation	15	5,800
Kmart Corporation	16	5,700
Health East Corp.	17	5,050
Control Data Corporation	18	4,864
J.C. Penney Company Inc.	19	4,800

[Continued]

★ 639 ★

Minnesota: How Gambling Facilities Compare With Minnesota's Largest Corporate Employers
[Continued]

Company name	Rank	Minnesota employment
Tribal gaming	*	4,730
Burlington Northern Railroad Inc.	20	4,500
United Parcel Service	21	4,200
The Prudential	22	4,100
Sears, Roebuck and Company	23	4,033
Gateway/Rainbow Foods Inc.	24	4,000
Anderson Corporation	25	3,960

Source: U.S. Congress, Senate, Hearing Before the Select Committee on Indian Affairs, *Implementation of the Indian Gaming Regulatory Act*, S. HRG. 102- 660, Pt. 2, U.S. Government Printing Office, Washington, D.C., 1992, p. 16. Primary source: Minnesota Department of Trade and Economic Development, *Report of Minnesota's Largest Corporate Employers*, September 10, 1991. *Notes:* 1. Participating members include the following tribes: Bois Forte, Leech Lake, Lower Sioux, Mille Lacs Chippewa, Prairie Island Sioux, and Shakopee Sioux.

★ 640 ★

Minnesota: Out-of-State Visitor Expenditures at Gaming Facilities, 1991

Data include bus visitors only.

Expenditure type	In-state expenditure
Lodging	9,350,000
Meals	1,813,000
Miscellaneous	1,364,000
Total expenditures	12,527,000

Source: U.S. Congress, Senate, Hearing Before the Select Committee on Indian Affairs, *Implementation of the Indian Gaming Regulatory Act*, S. HRG. 102- 660, Pt. 2, U.S. Government Printing Office, Washington, D.C., 1992, p. 23. *Notes:* Participating members include the following tribes: Bois Forte, Leech Lake, Lower Sioux, Mille Lacs Chippewa, Prairie Island Sioux, and Shakopee Sioux.

★ 641 ★

Minnesota: Reported Revenues from Gaming, 1991

Figures are shown in millions of dollars.

Revenue sources	Amount
Video	99.3
Blackjack	28.5
Bingo and pull-tabs	11.0
Concessions & other	4.2
Total	143.0

Source: U.S. Congress, Senate, Hearing Before the Select Committee on Indian Affairs, *Implementation of the Indian Gaming Regulatory Act*, S. Hrg. 102- 660, Pt. 2, U.S. Government Printing Office, Washington, D.C., 1992, p. 282. *Notes:* Participating members include the following tribes: Bois Forte, Leech Lake, Lower Sioux, Mille Lacs Chippewa, Prairie Island Sioux, and Shakopee Sioux.

★ 642 ★

Oneida Tribe of Wisconsin: Reported Growth from Gaming Enterprises, 1976 to 1992

	1976	1992
Employment	150	1000+
Tribal members (%)		80.0
Non-tribal members (%)		20.0
Rate of unemployment (%)	40.1	17.9
Land holding (acres)	2,500	6,000
Nongaming enterprises		Radisson Hotel
		4 convenience stores
		Environmental lab
		Farm

Source: U.S. Congress, Senate, Hearing Before the Select Committee on Indian Affairs, *Implementation of the Indian Gaming Regulatory Act*, S. HRG. 102- 660, Pt. 2, U.S. Government Printing Office, Washington, D.C., 1992, pp. 302-303.

Minerals

★ 643 ★

U.S. Coal Mining Acreage from Indian Leases

U.S. Total - 60,791	
New Mexico - 30,055	
Arizona - 29,237	
Montana - 1,500	

Chart shows data from column 3.

Figures are shown for 1990, by state. Chart shows royalties in thousands of dollars.

State	Acres leased	Production (thousand short tons)	Royalties[1] ($ thou.)
New Mexico	36,026	12,174	30,055
Arizona	64,858	12,621	29,237
Montana	14,746	2,731	1,500
U.S. Total	115,630	27,526	60,791

Source: *Coal Data: A Reference, November 1991*, Energy Information Administration, Office of Coal, Nuclear, Electric and Alternate Fuels, U.S. Department of Energy, Washington, D.C., p. 49. Primary source: U.S. Department of the Interior, Minerals Management Service, Royalty Management Program, *Mineral Revenues: The 1990 Report on Receipts from Federal and Indian Leases.* Notes: Totals may not equal sum of components because of independent rounding. 1. Current dollars.

★ 644 ★

Coal Leases on Indian Lands, 1981-90

Year	Number of leases	Acres
1981	5	115,630
1982	6	155,918
1983	6	155,918
1984	6	155,918
1985	7	195,918
1986	6	155,630
1987	7	195,918
1988	7	155,918

[Continued]

★ 644 ★

Coal Leases on Indian Lands, 1981-90

[Continued]

Year	Number of leases	Acres
1989	8	156,141
1990	6	115,630

Source: Mineral Revenues 1990, Report on Receipts from Federal and Indian Leases, U.S. Department of the Interior, Minerals Management Service, Royalty Management Program, p. 101.

★ 645 ★

Coal Leases on Indian Lands, by State

Figures shown are for 1990.

State	Number	Acres
Arizona	3	64,858
Montana	1	14,746
New Mexico	2	36,026
Total	6	115,630

Source: Mineral Revenues 1990, Report on Receipts from Federal and Indian Leases, U.S. Department of the Interior, Minerals Management Service, Royalty Management Program, p. 100.

★ 646 ★

Mineral Leases on Federal and Indian Lands

Figures are shown for 1990.

Leases	U.S. total	Indian	Federal offshore	Federal onshore	Federal and Indian total
Oil in barrels (x000,000)					
Production volume	2,665	15	324	146	485
% U.S. total		0.6	12.1	5.5	18.2
Gas in Mcf (x000,000)					
Production volume	18,469	127	5,093	1,201	6,421
% U.S. total		0.7	27.6	6.5	34.8
Coal in tons (x000,000)					
Production volume	1,029	28	-	253	281
% U.S. total		2.7	-	24.6	27.3

[Continued]

★ 646 ★

Mineral Leases on Federal and Indian Lands
[Continued]

Leases	U.S. total	Indian	Federal offshore	Federal onshore	Federal and Indian total
Lead in tons (x000)					
Production volume	522	-	-	281	281
% U.S. total		-	-	53.8	53.8
Phosphate in tons (x000)					
Production volume	51,084	1,114	-	4,722	5,836
% U.S. total		2.2	-	9.2	11.4
Potash in tons (x000)					
Production volume	3,132	-	-	2,093	2,093
% U.S. total		-	-	66.8	66.8
Sodium in tons (x000)					
Production volume	10,478	-	-	4,736	4,736
% U.S. total		-	-	45.2	45.2

Source: Mineral Revenues 1990, Report on Receipts from Federal and Indian Leases, U.S. Department of the Interior, Minerals Management Service, Royalty Management Program, p. 26. Primary source: *Mineral Commodity Summaries 1991*, Bureau of Mines, and *Monthly Energy Review*, April 1991, Department of Energy, for U.S. totals; certain other data are estimated in part by the Minerals Management Service. *Notes:* 1990 U.S. production data are estimated. Data by calendar year are rounded: oil, including crude oil and condensate, in millions of barrels; natural gas in millions of Mcf; coal, including anthracite, bituminous, and lignite, in millions of short tons; and lead, phosphate, potash, and sodium in thousands of short tons.

★ 647 ★

Mineral Leases on Indian Lands, Summary

Data show royalty revenues collected from federal and Indian mineral leases in the U.S. from 1920-90. Data do not include rents and bonuses.

	Oil production (mil. bbl.)	Gas production (mil. Mcf)	Coal production (Mil. short tons)	Other production
1920-90				
Volume	1.299	4,138	456	N/A
Value ($)	8,648	3,679	5,284	2,084
Royalties ($)	1,232	485	325	228
1987				
Volume	19	108	24	N/A
Value ($)	322	183	443	51
Royalties ($)	46	22	30	6

[Continued]

★ 647 ★

Mineral Leases on Indian Lands, Summary
[Continued]

	Oil production (mil. bbl.)	Gas production (mil. Mcf)	Coal production (Mil. short tons)	Other production
1988				
Volume	17	103	26	N/A
Value ($)	247	175	490	55
Royalties ($)	36	22	47	7
1989				
Volume	15	114	27	N/A
Value ($)	270	191	499	79
Royalties ($)	41	25	48	9
1990				
Volume	15	127	28	N/A
Value ($)	330	220	532	2,084
Royalties ($)	52	30	61	228

Source: Mineral Revenues 1990, Report on Receipts from Federal and Indian Leases, U.S. Department of the Interior, Minerals Management Service, Royalty Management Program, pp. 16-17. Primary source: U.S. Geological Survey and the Minerals Management Service, Department of the Interior. *Note:* Data are rounded. N/A stands for not available.

★ 648 ★

Mineral Leases on Indian Lands

Revenues from 1981-90.

Year	Royalties ($)	Rents ($)	Total ($)
1981	161,473,757	D/I	161,473,757
1982	162,726,747	4,656,065	167,382,812
1983	156,373,198	3,621,550	159,994,748
1984	128,386,900	3,576,549	131,963,449
1985	139,424,708	3,372,750	142,797,458
1986	105,028,658	3,018,833	108,047,491
1987	104,787,583	1,206,406	105,993,989
1988	112,282,668	1,255,603	113,538,271
1989	122,429,802	1,454,523	123,884,325
1990	151,992,888	438,483	152,431,371

Source: Mineral Revenues 1990, Report on Receipts from Federal and Indian Leases, U.S. Department of the Interior, Minerals Management Service, Royalty Management Program, p. 8. Primary source: Bureau of Indian Affairs. *Notes:* D/I indicates that data are incomplete for the revenue source during the time period. Standard Indian leases do not contain royalty provisions. Most Indian leases retain rental provisions after the lease is producing. Indian rent revenues represent fiscal year data from Bureau of Indian Affairs (BIA) records for 1982-87. Indian rent revenues represent calendar year data from Minerals Management Service (MMS) records for producing during the period 1988-90. Indian bonus revenues are collected by the BIA.

★ 649 ★

Mineral Lease Terms on Indian Lands

Terms are shown as of 1990.

Type of lease	Customary royalty rate	Annual rental & other fees	Duration of lease	Size of lease	Bonding requirements
Oil & gas leases	Varied. Generally, new leases provide for 20% or more on production. Older leases are generally 12-1/2% or 16-2/3%.	Varied. Amounts range from $1.25 per acre to $30 per acre. Rents may or may not be recoupable against royalties.	Generally the primary term is 5 years or less.	Varied. Range from fraction of an acre to over 200,000 acres.	Lease: $500 to $2,000 depending on acreage. Nationwide: $75,000.
Coal leases	Varies according to terms and amendments. Generally 6% to 12%.	Varied. Average rental rate per acre is $2. Advance royalty payable up to $1 million annually.	Varies by lease terms.	Varied.	Lease: $500 to $2,000, depending on acreage. State: $75,000 or as determined by the Secretary.
Other mineral leases (Copper, gold, lead, silver tungsten, zinc and other ores and metals)	Varies by commodity and lease terms. Ranges from $.29 per unit to $.075 per unit and from 10% to 22-1/2%.	Varies from $1 per acre to $5 per acre. Flat amount of rental or advance royalty due regardless of lease size. Can range from $2,000 to $1.2 million annually.	Varies by lease from 1 year to 20 years.	1 acre to 40,000 acres.	Lease: As determined. State: $15,000. Nationwide: $75,000.

Source: Mineral Revenues 1990, Report on Receipts from Federal and Indian Leases, U.S. Department of the Interior, Minerals Management Service, Royalty Management Program, pp. 111-114. *Notes:* Lease terms may be extended or modified for various reasons as authorized by regulations. A $10 fee is required to file, transfer, or assign an Indian lease. A comparable fee is required to file, transfer, or assign certain other lease commodities.

★ 650 ★

Mineral Revenues on Indian Lands, 1937-90

Volume, sales value, and royalties, by state and commodity, from Indian mineral leases, 1937-90.

State/commodity	1937-85	1986	1987	1988	1989	1990	1937-90
Alaska							
Gas in Mcf							
Volume	277,556	0	0	0	0	0	277,556
Sales volume ($)	39,269	0	0	0	0	0	39,269
Royalties ($)	6,541	0	0	0	0	0	6,541
Arizona							
Oil in barrels							
Volume	19,048,598	164,464	135,709	108,734	126,408	117,987	19,701,900
Sales volume ($)	107,434,182	2,589,452	2,330,655	1,654,596	2,185,278	2,429,422	118,623,585
Royalties ($)	17,445,680	423,267	381,290	272,042	360,929	402,942	19,286,150
Gas in Mcf							
Volume	12,842,337	17,294	15,254	7,517	7,640	12,441	12,902,483
Sales value ($)	2,704,000	11,760	14,963	8,042	10,418	14,700	2,763,883
Royalties($)	339,720	1,446	1,870	1,005	1,302	1,844	347,187
Coal in tons							
Volume	129,124,096	11,550,000	11,602,674	12,318,335	11,118,215	12,621,393	188,334,713
Sales value ($)	1,400,031,309	184,684,500	124,925,051	238,341,308	226,502,328	243,469,458	2,417,953,954
Royalties ($)	50,553,214	9,078,969	5,887,427	21,7369,989	19,374,672	29,236,716	135,870,987

[Continued]

★ 650 ★

Mineral Revenues on Indian Lands, 1937-90
[Continued]

State/commodity	1937-85	1986	1987	1988	1989	1990	1937-90
Other products							
Sales value ($)	307,035,583	12,161,076	17,927,276	18,141,340	34,554,658	30,679,027	420,498,960
Royalties ($)	30,118,571	1,212,695	2,176,490	2,944,098	4,495,482	4,155,102	45,102,438
Total royalties							
All minerals ($)	98,457,185	10,716,377	8,447,077	24,957,134	24,232,385	33,796,604	200,605,762
California							
Other products							
Sales value ($)	22,701,952	2,771,676	3,724,398	3,780,110	792,547	10,398,711	44,169,394
Royalties ($)	2,293,287	346,460	446,928	452,022	46,546	1,291,546	4,876,789
Royalties							
All minerals ($)	2,293,287	346,460	446,928	452,022	46,546	1,291,546	4,876,789
Colorado							
Oil in barrels							
Volume	3,654,759	588,257	318,938	298,018	136,452	124,430	5,120,854
Sales value ($)	31,737,548	10,310,421	5,198,591	4,785,313	2,293,182	2,543,710	56,868,765
Royalties ($)	4,704,789	1,749,512	954,293	766,856	329,878	332,234	8,837,562
Gas in Mcf							
Volume	513,764,410	17,829,157	18,989,709	20,743,420	24,288,051	36,584,090	632,198,837
Sales value ($)	280,076,318	34,846,076	37,125,686	37,274,001	36,961,936	56,451,514	482,735,531
Royalties ($)	35,387,180	4,511,366	4,787,410	4,663,647	4,643,232	6,599,683	60,592,518
Coal in tons							
Volume	1,659	0	0	0	0	0	1,659
Sales value ($)	7,723	0	0	0	0	0	7,723
Royalties ($)	198	0	0	0	0	0	198
Other products							
Sales value ($)	2,300,305	589,285	355,423	99,965	679,729	2,363,452	6,388,159
Royalties ($)	277,259	102,132	54,367	12,344	82,662	279,369	808,133
Total royalties							
All minerals	40,369,426	6,363,010	5,796,070	5,442,847	5,055,772	7,211,286	70,238,411
Florida							
Oil in barrels							
Volume	4,688	0	0	0	0	0	4,688
Sales value ($)	51,367	0	0	0	0	0	51,367
Royalties ($)	6,422	0	0	0	0	0	6,422
Other products							
Sales value ($)	451,024	0	0	0	0	0	451,024

[Continued]

★ 650 ★

Mineral Revenues on Indian Lands, 1937-90
[Continued]

State/commodity	1937-85	1986	1987	1988	1989	1990	1937-90
Royalties ($)	45,103	0	0	0	0	0	45,103
Total royalties							
All minerals	51,525	0	0	0	0	0	51,525
Idaho							
Other products							
Sales value ($)	180,087,533	20,026,962	18,231,839	20,562,230	22,681,048	16,439,381	278,028,993
Royalties	15,620,361	2,461,808	2,278,980	2,365,726	2,430,332	1,764,968	26,922,175
Total royalties							
All minerals ($)	15,620,361	2,461,808	2,278,980	2,365,726	2,430,332	1,746,968	26,922,175
Michigan							
Oil in barrels							
Volume	37,822	2,127	1,307	1,502	1,911	1,588	46,257
Sales value ($)	334,636	37,483	22,638	24,240	33,718	35,474	488,189
Royalties ($)	43,127	6,432	2,982	3,550	5,072	5,163	66,326
Gas in Mcf							
Volume	0	1,030	108	22,072	416	98	23,724
Sales value ($)	0	670	63	21,189	1,016	273	23,211
Royalties ($)	0	28	8	2,649	126	34	2,845
Total royalties							
All minerals ($)	43,127	6,460	2,990	6,199	5,248	5,197	69,171
Minnesota							
Other products							
Sales value ($)	178,461	0	0	0	0	0	178,461
Royalties ($)	6,455	0	0	0	0	0	6,455
Total royalties							
All minerals	6,455	0	0	0	0	0	6,455
Montana							
Oil in barrels							
Volume	88,199,829	1,591,378	1,259,170	1,053,218	994,782	1,038,722	94,137,099
Sales value ($)	505,566,025	24,436,384	20,179,391	14,936,681	16,531,892	21,939,267	603,589,640
Royalties ($)	68,490,633	3,324,434	2,846,750	2,232,566	2,567,636	3,402,852	82,864,871
Gas in Mcf							
Volume	24,134,005	1,412,892	1,177,288	1,407,422	1,171,877	1,372,922	30,676,406
Sales value ($)	21,640,203	3,236,678	2,178,272	2,313,424	2,015,268	2,639,673	34,023,518
Royalties ($)	3,281,820	461,908	313,201	330,412	284,935	367,577	5,039,853

[Continued]

★ 650 ★

Mineral Revenues on Indian Lands, 1937-90
[Continued]

State/commodity	1937-85	1986	1987	1988	1989	1990	1937-90
Coal in tons							
Volume	41,814,690	1,168,836	1,231,669	1,926,826	2,614,973	2,730,964	51,487,958
Sales value ($)	339,530,820	13,378,181	10,987,034	14,990,558	18,855,032	18,422,448	416,164,073
Royalties ($)	20,982,894	812,464	708,859	1,126,593	1,489,332	1,499,932	26,620,074
Other products							
Sales value ($)	17,235,190	101,786	4,872	14,601	25,988	29,315	17,411,752
Royalties ($)	1,015,355	15,890	700	910	1,037	1,924	1,035,716
Total royalties							
All minerals ($)	93,770,702	4,614,696	3,869,510	3,690,481	4,342,940	5,272,185	115,560,514
Nevada							
Other products							
Sales value ($)	3,330,226	1,748,149	1,292,587	1,956,496	1,802,314	1,276,614	11,406,886
Royalties ($)	325,924	157,822	102,684	156,701	150,129	103,042	1,006,302
Total royalties							
All minerals ($)	325,924	167,822	102,684	156,701	150,129	103,042	1,006,302
New Mexico							
Oil in barrels							
Volume	101,537,542	1,803,995	2,363,197	1,932,611	1,490,661	1,358,619	110,486,625
Sales value ($)	669,222,293	20,201,618	38,333,688	26,333,852	26,409,382	30,130,817	810,331,650
Royalties ($)	93,150,355	2,743,651	5,115,260	3,587,417	3,499,813	4,175,026	112,271,522
Gas in Mcf							
Volume	1,613,422,067	16,225,790	16,571,091	19,053,982	24,707,624	38,505,580	1,728,486,134
Sales value ($)	1,155,855,959	47,300,933	35,469,326	36,611,000	42,749,789	67,979,864	1,385,966,871
Royalties ($)	150,956,195	6,176,038	4,695,317	4,809,241	5,458,029	8,406,848	180,501,668
Coal in tons							
Volume	147,188,950	10,210,329	11,157,838	11,984,923	13,249,499	12,173,961	205,965,500
Sales value ($)	1,136,426,894	209,236,271	306,648,588	237,139,427	253,595,409	269,740,481	2,412,787,070
Royalties ($)	37,801,422	19,585,540	23,885,088	23,825,185	26,813,923	30,054,848	161,966,006
Other products							
Sales value ($)	699,428,292	3,223,336	2,749,069	4,732,756	13,064,068	6,087,903	729,285,424
Royalties ($)	100,781,031	399,487	343,865	585,752	1,602,034	948,599	104,660,768
Total royalties							
All minerals ($)	382,689,003	28,904,716	34,039,530	32,807,595	37,373,799	43,585,321	559,399,964
North Dakota							
Oil in barrels							
Volume	8,934,463	94,303	114,391	127,483	93,598	122,459	9,486,697

[Continued]

★ 650 ★

Mineral Revenues on Indian Lands, 1937-90
[Continued]

State/commodity	1937-85	1986	1987	1988	1989	1990	1937-90
Sales value ($)	46,025,910	1,420,936	1,944,077	1,896,403	1,587,414	2,635,200	55,509,940
Royalties ($)	6,096,236	191,603	272,804	275,635	230,633	395,625	7,462,536
Gas in Mcf							
Volume	10,474,796	30,002	190,826	140,620	136,706	185,369	11,158,319
Sales value ($)	1,642,755	24,256	124,586	125,150	77,684	174,895	2,169,326
Royalties ($)	211,370	3,324	15,824	16,334	10,165	23,732	280,749
Coal in tons							
Volume	2,921	0	0	0	0	0	2,921
Sales value ($)	8,834	0	0	0	0	0	8,834
Royalties ($)	540	0	0	0	0	0	540
Other products							
Sales value ($)	5,006,608	1,335	23,955	137,263	82,662	95,961	5,347,784
Royalties ($)	380,308	167	2,994	13,412	8,828	12,191	417,900
Total royalties							
All minerals ($)	6,688,454	195,094	291,622	305,381	249,626	431,548	8,161,725
Oklahoma							
Oil in barrels							
Volume	358,704,177	4,086,478	3,764,771	3,221,375	2,926,504	2,447,881	375,151,186
Sale value ($)	1,647,616,913	51,392,515	65,121,512	49,782,893	51,139,525	52,876,286	1,927,929,644
Royalties ($)	208,370,481	8,046,769	8,433,077	6,523,640	7,063,189	7,957,300	246,394,456
Gas in Mcf							
Volume	832,554,807	45,096,525	57,375,400	45,578,928	40,978,372	37,303,356	1,058,887,388
Sales value ($)	195,755,788	102,710,719	81,475,935	71,473,941	65,413,470	60,351,360	1,177,181,213
Royalties ($)	105,346,113	10,172,241	8,636,325	8,464,378	8,105,099	9,300,449	150,024,605
Coal in tons							
Volume	9,375,686	0	0	0	0	0	9,375,686
Sales value ($)	37,232,091	0	0	0	0	0	37,232,091
Royalties ($)	1,050,777	0	0	0	0	0	1,050,777
Other products							
Sales value ($)	313,427,795	1,321,352	2,602,963	2,742,994	3,315,661	3,632,751	327,043,516
Royalties ($)	24,070,366	139,978	303,188	202,080	255,916	338,679	25,310,207
Total royalties							
All minerals ($)	338,837,737	18,358,988	17,372,590	15,190,098	15,424,204	17,596,428	422,780,045
South Dakota							
Oil in barrels							
Volume	75,669	841	6,375	6,389	5,781	6,888	101,943

[Continued]

★ 650 ★

Mineral Revenues on Indian Lands, 1937-90
[Continued]

State/commodity	1937-85	1986	1987	1988	1989	1990	1937-90
Sales value ($)	1,155,700	17,038	88,770	72,719	81,431	121,475	1,537,133
Royalties ($)	198,061	3,408	17,754	14,544	16,243	24,295	274,305
Coal in tons							
Volume	15,876	0	0	0	0	0	15,876
Sales value ($)	72,302	0	0	0	0	0	72,302
Royalties ($)	3,175	0	0	0	0	0	3,175
Other products							
Sales value ($)	5,950,624	0	0	0	0	0	5,950,624
Royalties ($)	474,609	0	0	0	0	0	474,609
Total royalties							
All minerals ($)	675,845	3,408	17,754	14,544	16,243	24,295	752,089
Texas							
Oil in barrels							
Volume	0	0	0	0	29,655	129,948	159,603
Sales value ($)	0	0	0	0	548,322	2,964,277	3,512,599
Royalties ($)	0	0	0	0	68,540	555,390	623,930
Gas in Mcf							
Volume	0	0	0	0	256,610	1,329,895	1,586,505
Sales value ($)	0	0	0	0	397,745	2,433,707	2,831,452
Royalties ($)	0	0	0	0	50,116	443,073	493,189
Total royalties							
All minerals ($)	0	0	0	0	118,656	998,463	1,117,119
Utah							
Oil in barrels							
Volume	391,226,853	8,182,235	7,800,045	7,161,520	6,762,666	7,193,799	428,327,118
Sales value ($)	2,923,143,699	128,820,858	138,514,859	109,382,351	125,647,412	161,668,148	3,587,177,327
Royalties ($)	439,742,797	18,824,315	19,858,199	18,919,988	24,880,001	538,442,670	
Gas in Mcf							
Volume	273,532,962	6,896,952	6,953,376	4,828,629	6,419,454	4,820,609	303,451,982
Sales value ($)	214,590,288	16,523,387	13,800,057	9,691,972	13,196,980	12,849,810	280,652,494
Royalties ($)	32,654,170	2,322,417	2,015,060	1,586,466	2,005,646	2,187,760	42,771,519
Other products							
Sales value ($)	163,306,625	6,771,898	3,480,708	2,774,385	1,753,902	2,658,367	180,745,885
Royalties ($)	10,082,362	985,901	499,509	311,171	206,018	297,327	12,382,288
Total royalties							
All minerals ($)	482,479,329	22,132,633	22,372,768	18,115,007	21,131,652	27,365,088	593,596,477

[Continued]

★ 650 ★

Mineral Revenues on Indian Lands, 1937-90

[Continued]

State/commodity	1937-85	1986	1987	1988	1989	1990	1937-90
Washington							
Gas in Mcf							
Volume	2,939	0	0	0	0	0	2,939
Sales value ($)	1,170	0	0	0	0	0	1,170
Royalties ($)	146	0	0	0	0	0	146
Other products							
Sales value ($)	48,660,404	63,732	33,456	33,261	27,620	520,108	49,338,581
Royalties ($)	5,021,901	7,967	4,182	4,264	3,615	49,958	5,091,887
Total royalties							
All minerals ($)	5,002,047	7,967	4,182	4,264	3,615	49,958	5,092,033
Wisconsin							
Other products							
Sales value ($)	40,711	0	0	0	0	0	40,711
Royalties ($)	3,271	0	0	0	0	0	3,271
Total royalties							
All minerals ($)	3,271	0	0	0	0	0	3,271
Wyoming							
Oil in barrels							
Volume	241,326,302	3,463,830	3,225,966	2,965,278	2,903,945	2,775,325	256,660,646
Sale value ($)	1,251,394,952	45,987,552	50,040,829	38,141,657	43,644,439	53,113,393	1,482,322,822
Royalties ($)	176,985,399	7,106,979	7,931,388	6,153,059	7,773,964	10,076,457	216,027,246
Gas in Mcf							
Volume	306,965,458	10,215,245	6,272,923	11,330,346	16,485,447	6,825,391	358,094,810
Sales value ($)	210,688,160	22,678,369	12,418,389	17,838,303	29,708,116	16,831,502	310,162,839
Royalties ($)	31,257,771	3,615,217	1,775,283	2,617,909	4,071,330	2,419,975	45,760,485
Other products							
Sales value ($)	6,161,853	213,547	263,178	54,103	9,689	3,811	6,706,181
Royalties ($)	580,334	27,023	38,227	3,701	411	527	650,223
Total royalties							
All minerals ($)	208,823,504	10,749,219	9,744,898	8,774,669	11,848,705	12,496,959	262,437,954
Indian Totals							
Oil in barrels							
Volume	1,212,750,702	19,977,908	18,989,869	16,876,128	15,472,363	15,317,646	1,299,384,616
Sales value ($)	7,183,683,225	295,214,257	321,775,010	247,010,705	269,801,995	330,457,469	8,647,942,661
Royalties ($)	1,015,233,980	42,420,370	45,813,797	36,046,679	40,835,885	52,207,285	1,232,557,996

[Continued]

★ 650 ★

Mineral Revenues on Indian Lands, 1937-90
[Continued]

State/commodity	1937-85	1986	1987	1988	1989	1990	1937-90
Gas in Mcf							
Volume	3,587,971,337	97,724,887	107,545,975	103,112,936	114,452,197	126,939,751	4,137,747,083
Sales value ($)	2,682,993,910	227,332,848	182,607,277	175,357,022	190,532,422	219,727,298	3,678,550,777
Royalties ($)	359,441,026	27,263,985	22,240,298	22,492,041	24,632,980	29,750,975	485,821,305
Coal in tons							
Volume	327,523,878	22,929,165	23,992,181	26,230,084	26,982,687	27,526,318	455,184,313
Sales value ($)	2,913,309,973	407,298,952	442,560,673	490,471,293	498,952,769	531,632,387	5,284,226,047
Royalties ($)	110,392,220	29,476,973	30,481,374	46,691,767	47,677,927	60,791,496	325,511,757
Other products							
Sales value ($)	1,775,303,186	48,994,134	50,689,724	55,029,504	78,790,386	74,185,401	2,082,992,335
Royalties ($)	191,096,497	5,867,330	6,252,114	7,052,181	9,283,010	9,243,132	228,794,264
Total royalties							
All minerals ($)	1,676,163,723	105,028,658	104,787,583	112,282,668	122,429,802	151,992,888	2,272,685,322

Source: Mineral Revenues 1990, Report on Receipts from Federal and Indian Leases, U.S. Department of the Interior, Minerals Management Service, Royalty Management Program, pp. 75-81.

★ 651 ★

Mineral Revenues on Indian Lands, by Commodity

Volume, sales value, and royalties, by commodity and state, from Indian mineral leases.

Leases	Production volume	Sales value ($)	Royalties received ($)
Chat			
Oklahoma	256,983	256,983	77,081
Coal			
Arizona	12,621,393	243,469,458	29,236,716
Montana	2,730,964	18,422,448	1,499,932
New Mexico	12,173,961	269,740,481	30,054,840
Subtotal	27,526,318	531,632,387	60,791,496
Copper			
Arizona	48,854	24,049,508	3,117,029
Gas			
Arizona	12,441	14,700	1,844
Colorado	36,584,090	56,451,514	6,599,683
Michigan	98	273	34
Montana	1,372,922	2,639,673	367,577

[Continued]

★ 651 ★

Mineral Revenues on Indian Lands, by Commodity
[Continued]

Leases	Production volume	Sales value ($)	Royalties received ($)
New Mexico	38,505,580	67,979,864	8,406,848
North Dakota	185,369	174,895	23,732
Oklahoma	37,303,356	60,351,360	9,300,449
Texas	1,329,895	2,433,707	443,073
Utah	4,820,609	12,849,810	2,167,760
Wyoming	6,825,391	16,831,502	2,419,975
Subtotal	126,939,751	219,727,298	29,750,975
Gas lost			
New Mexico	(25,537)	(44,123)	(5,066)
Gas plant products			
Colorado	6,095,554	2,363,452	279,369
Montana	97,262	29,315	1,824
New Mexico	215,827	991,443	92,407
North Dakota	496,195	95,961	12,191
Oklahoma	8,424,762	2,291,872	218,015
Utah	8,822,610	2,651,449	296,449
Wyoming	14,767	3,811	527
Subtotal	24,166,977	8,427,303	900,782
Helium			
New Mexico	327,445	123,789	20,632
Limestone			
Oklahoma	144,593	571,142	15,905
Oil			
Arizona	117,987	2,429,422	402,942
Colorado	124,430	2,543,710	332,234
Michigan	1,588	35,474	5,163
Montana	1,038,722	21,939,267	3,402,862
New Mexico	1,358,619	30,130,817	4,175,026
North Dakota	122,459	2,635,200	395,625
Oklahoma	2,447,381	52,876,286	7,957,300
South Dakota	6,388	121,475	24,296
Texas	129,948	2,964,277	555,390
Utah	7,192,799	161,668,148	24,880,001
Wyoming	2,775,325	53,113,393	10,076,457
Subtotal	15,317,646	330,457,469	52,207,285
Oil lost			
Utah	(521)	(6,918)	(878)

[Continued]

★ 651 ★

Mineral Revenues on Indian Lands, by Commodity
[Continued]

Leases	Production volume	Sales value ($)	Royalties received ($)
Phosphate			
Idaho	1,113,726	16,439,381	1,764,968
Sand and gravel			
Arizona	1,895,922	5,848,527	1,022,410
California	1,776,588	10,398,711	1,291,546
Nevada	317,921	1,276,614	103,041
New Mexico	1,419,120	5,016,794	840,627
Oklahoma	231,219	512,754	27,678
Washington	159,332	520,108	49,958
Subtotal	5,800,102	23,573,508	3,335,260
Silica sand			
Arizona	35,085	780,992	15,663
Total		1,156,002,555	151,992,888

Source: *Mineral Revenues 1990, Report on Receipts from Federal and Indian Leases*, U.S. Department of the Interior, Minerals Management Service, Royalty Management Program, pp. 82-83.

★ 652 ★

Royalties from Mineral Leases on Indian Lands

Royalties are shown, by type, from 1981-90.

Lease	1981	1982	1983	1984	1985	1986	1987	1988	1989	1990
Oil royalties	103,919,408	92,559,824	89,727,647	75,973,022	75,025,974	42,420,370	45,813,797	36,046,679	40,835,885	52,207,285
Gas royalties	36,880,307	54,378,374	50,287,896	37,295,148	35,853,169	27,263,985	22,240,298	22,492,041	24,632,980	29,750,975
Coal royalties	8,604,304	8,527,548	9,416,941	7,613,759	23,403,336	29,476,973	30,481,374	46,691,767	47,677,927	60,791,496
Other royalties	12,069,738	7,261,001	6,940,714	7,504,971	5,142,229	5,867,330	6,252,114	7,052,181	9,283,010	9,243,132
Rents	D/I	4,656,065	3,621,550	3,576,549	3,372,750	3,018,833	1,206,406	1,255,603	1,454,523	438,483
Totals	161,473,757	167,382,812	159,994,748	131,963,449	142,797,458	108,047,491	105,993,989	113,538,271	123,884,325	152,431,371

Source: *Mineral Revenues 1990, Report on Receipts from Federal and Indian Leases*, U.S. Department of the Interior, Minerals Management Service, Royalty Management Program, pp. 11-14. Primary source: D/I indicates that data are incomplete for the revenue source during the time period. Indian rent revenues represent fiscal year data from Bureau of Indian Affairs (BIA) records for 1982-87. Indian rent revenues represent calendar year data from Mineral Management Services (MMS) records for producing leases during the period 1988-90. Indian bonus revenues are collected by the BIA.

★ 653 ★

Oil and Gas Leases, 1981-90

Year	Number	Acres
1981	3,563	1,287,144
1982	3,778	1,222,699
1983	3,865	1,236,562
1984	4,392	1,594,148
1985	4,601	1,842,803
1986	4,701	1,647,920
1987	4,819	1,625,772
1988	4,349	1,600,469
1989	4,223	1,565,123
1990	4,137	1,607,407

Source: *Mineral Revenues 1990, Report on Receipts from Federal and Indian Leases*, U.S. Department of the Interior, Minerals Management Service, Royalty Management Program, p. 99.

★ 654 ★

Oil and Gas Leases on Indian Lands, by State

Figures are shown for 1990.

State	Number	Acres
Alaska	1	2,560
Arizona	10	66,211
Colorado	141	434,419
Michigan	3	60
Montana	460	115,225
New Mexico	438	497,962
North Dakota	35	6,817
Oklahoma	2,199	192,190
South Dakota	1	160
Texas	8	2,625
Utah	745	236,291
Wyoming	96	52,887
Total	4,137	1,607,407

Source: *Mineral Revenues 1990, Report on Receipts from Federal and Indian Leases*, U.S. Department of the Interior, Minerals Management Service, Royalty Management Program, p. 98.

★ 655 ★

Other Minerals Leased on Indian Lands, by State

Figures are shown for 1990.

State/mineral	Leases	Acres
Arizona		
Copper	2	2,554
Sand-gravel	8	574
Sand-silica	1	640
California		
Sand-gravel	3	1,322
Idaho		
Phosphate	16	4,476
Nevada		
Sand-gravel	1	100
New Mexico		
Sand-gravel	5	1,593
Oklahoma		
Chat	6	655
Limestone	1	18
Sand-gravel	2	256
Washington		
Sand-gravel	2	77
Total	47	12,265

Source: Mineral Revenues 1990, Report on Receipts from Federal and Indian Leases, U.S. Department of the Interior, Minerals Management Service, Royalty Management Program, p. 102.

Tobacco

★ 656 ★

Tax Exempt Cigarette Sales on Indian Reservations

Number of packs sold and state tax revenue losses are shown, by state, FY 1983[1].

State	Sales (thousands of packs)	Percent of total sales	Revenue loss (in thousands of dollars)
United States, total	189,822	0.6	43,130
Alabama	0	0	0
Alaska	0	0	0
Arizona	27,397	8.6	4,657

[Continued]

★ 656 ★

Tax Exempt Cigarette Sales on Indian Reservations
[Continued]

State	Sales (thousands of packs)	Percent of total sales	Revenue loss (in thousands of dollars)
Arkansas	0	0	0
California	115[3]	[4]	17
Colorado	Minimal	-	-
Connecticut	0	0	0
Delaware	0	0	0
Washington D.C.	0	0	0
Florida	59,777	4.5	15,542
Georgia	0	0	0
Hawaii	0	0	0
Idaho	5,399	5.0	707
Illinois	0	0	0
Indiana	0	0	0
Iowa	0	0	0
Kansas	180	[4]	34
Kentucky	0	0	0
Louisiana	0	0	0
Maine	0	0	0
Maryland	0	0	0
Massachusetts	0	0	0
Michigan	169	[4]	42
Minnesota	2,026	0.4	486
Mississippi	0	0	0
Missouri	0	0	0
Montana	15,902	17.4	2,544
Nebraska	4,002	2.3	880
Nevada	3,324	2.4	690
New Hampshire	0	0	0
New Jersey	0	0	0
New Mexico	13,476	10.3	2,021
New York	6,356	0.3	1,525
North Carolina	0	0	0
North Dakota	1,050	1.3	231
Ohio	0	0	0
Oklahoma	9,295	2.1	1,673
Oregon	500	0.2	94
Pennsylvania	0	0	0
Rhode Island	0	0	0
South Carolina	0	0	0
South Dakota	139[5]	0.2	21
Tennessee	0	0	0
Texas	0	0	0
Utah	NA[6]	-	-
Vermont	0	0	0
Virginia	0	0	0

[Continued]

★ 656 ★

Tax Exempt Cigarette Sales on Indian Reservations
[Continued]

State	Sales (thousands of packs)	Percent of total sales	Revenue loss (in thousands of dollars)
Washington	21,427	4.9	6,214
West Virginia	0	0	0
Wisconsin	19,132	3.8	5,740
Wyoming	156[1,7]	0.2	122

Source: Cigarette Tax Evasion: A Second Look, Advisory Commission on Intergovernment Relations, Washington, D.C., March 1985, Table 3-9. Primary source: Compiled by ACIR staff from data provided by state revenue departments. *Notes:* The data for Indian reservations were provided by state tax administrators. In the case of South Dakota, the information was obtained from the Minnesota revenue department as the Indians in South Dakota are supplied by a Minnesota wholesaler. 1. Montana and Nebraska figures are for CY 1983. Wyoming number is for FY 1984. 2. Losses are based on state cigarette and sales tax rates as of November 1, 1983. 3. Minimum estimate. 4. Less than 0.1 percent. 5. Total sales on Indian reservations are 1,384,400 packs. Only this small amount is not taxed. 6. NA is not explained in the original text. 7. Total sales are 260,000 packs; 40 percent are taxed.

Chapter 9
LAND AND WATER MANAGEMENT

Land Ownership

★ 657 ★

Federally Recognized Reservations, by Acreage, State, and Population, 1990 - I

Reservation	State	Acreage	Tribal land	Population	Indians
Poarch Creek	AL	213	213	212	149
Camp Verde	AZ	653	653	618	569
Cocopah	AZ	6,009	6,009	515	436
Fort Apache	AZ	1,664,972	1,664,972	10,394	9,825
Fort McDowell	AZ	24,680	24,680	640	560
Fort Yuma	AZ-CA	43,561	35,435	2,084	1,160
Gila Bend	AZ	10,404	10,404	0	0
Gila River	AZ	371,933	274,278	9,540	9,116
Havasupai	AZ	188,077	188,077	423	400
Hopi	AZ	1,561,213	1,560,993	7,360	7,061
Hualapai	AZ	992,463	992,463	822	802
Kaibab	AZ	120,413	120,413	165	102
Maricopa (AK-Chin)	AZ	21,840	21,840	446	405
Tohono O'Odham (Papago)	AZ	2,774,450	2,773,850	8,730	8,480
Pascua Yaqui	AZ	895	895	2,412	2,284
Payson Community	AZ	85	85	102	97
Salt River	AZ	50,506	26,072	4,852	3,533
San Carlos	AZ	1,826,541	1,826,541	7,294	7,110
San Juan Southern Paiute	AZ	0	0	204	204
San Xavier	AZ	71,095	30,412	1,172	1,073
Yavapai	AZ	1,398	1,398	176	134
Colorado River	AZ-CA	225,995	220,116	7,865	2,345
Fort Mojave	AZ-CA-NV	32,697	32,697	758	592
Navajo	AZ-NM-UT	15,662,413	14,715,093	148,451	143,405
Aqua Caliente Reservation	CA	23,173	2,139	20,206	117
Alturas Rancheria	CA	20	20	5	5
Augustine Reservation	CA	502	342	0	0
Barona Rancheria	CA	5,181	5,181	537	373
Benton Paiute Reservation	CA	160	160	63	52

[Continued]

★ 657 ★

Federally Recognized Reservations, by Acreage, State, and Population, 1990 - I

[Continued]

Reservation	State	Acreage	Tribal land	Population	Indians
Berry Creek Rancheria	CA	33	33	2	2
Big Bend Rancheria	CA	40	40	3	3
Big Lagoon Rancheria	CA	20	9	22	19
Big Pine Reservation	CA	279	279	452	331
Big Sandy Reservation	CA	76	...	51	38
Big Valley Reservation	CA	38	38	108	90
Bishop Reservation	CA	875	875	1,408	935
Blue Lake Rancheria	CA	4	0	58	30
Bridgeport Indian Colony	CA	40	40	49	37
Buena Vista	CA	0	...	1	1
Cabazon Reservation	CA	1,382	954	819	20
Cahuilla Reservation	CA	18,884	18,272	104	82
Campo Reservation	CA	15,480	15,010	281	143
Capitain Grande Reservation	CA	15,753	15,753	0	0
Cedarville Rancheria	CA	20	17	8	6
Chemehuevi Reservation	CA	30,654		358	95
Chicken Ranch Rancheria	CA	3	3	73	10
Cloverdale Rancheria	CA	0	0	1	1
Cold Springs Rancheria	CA	155	155	192	159
Colusa Rancheria	CA	273	278	22	19
Cortina Rancheria	CA	640	640	30	22
Coyote Valley Rancheria	CA	58	58	135	122
Cuyapaipe Reservation	CA	4,103	4,100	0	0
Dry Creek Rancheria	CA	75	75	75	38
Elk Valley Rancheria	CA	0	0	77	32
Enterprise Rancheria	CA	40	40	5	5
Fort Bidwell Reservation	CA	3,335	3,335	118	107
Fort Independence Reservation	CA	234	234	69	38
Greenville Rancheria	CA	0		24	7
Grindstone Rancheria	CA	80	80	103	102
Hoopa Valley	CA	85,445	85,432	2,143	1,733
Hopland Rancheria	CA	48	22	189	142
Inaja-Cosmit Reservation	CA	852	852	0	0
Jackson Rancheria	CA	331	331	21	13
Jamul Indian Village	CA	6	6	0	0
Karuk Tribe	CA	243	11	421	33
La Jolla Reservation	CA	8,541	7,588	152	121
La Posta Reservation	CA	3,556	3,672	10	3
Laytonville Rancheria	CA	200	200	142	129
Likely Rancheria	CA	1	1	0	0
Lone Pine Reservation	CA	237	237	244	168
Lookout Rancheria	CA	40	40	17	12
Los Coyotes Rancheria	CA	25,049	25,049	58	42
Manchester Point Rancheria	CA	363	363	200	178

[Continued]

★ 657 ★

Federally Recognized Reservations, by Acreage, State, and Population, 1990 - I

[Continued]

Reservation	State	Acreage	Tribal land	Population	Indians
Manzanita Reservation	CA	3,579	3,579	84	47
Mesa Grande Reservation	CA	20	120	96	72
Middletown Rancheria	CA	109	109	79	18
Montgomery Creek Rancheria	CA	72	72	11	9
Mooretown	CA	0	0	225	79
Morongo Reservation	CA	32,362	30,968	1,072	1,070
North Fork Rancheria	CA	80	0	4	0
Pala Reservation	CA	11,893	10,319	1,071	563
Pauma & Yulma Reservation	CA	5,877	5,877	148	137
Pechanga reservation	CA	4,394	2,626	398	289
Picayune Rancheria	CA	29	0	32	15
Pinoleville Rancheria	CA	3	0	130	77
Potter Valley Rancheria	CA	3		1	1
Quartz Valley Rancheria	CA	24	0	124	19
Ramona Reservation	CA	560	560	0	0
Redding Rancheria	CA	31	0	101	79
Redwood Valley Rancheria	CA	170	170	142	14
Resighini Rancheria	CA	228	228	28	26
Rincon Reservation	CA	4,276	3,612	1,352	379
Roaring Creek Rancheria	CA	80	80	18	18
Robinson Rancheria	CA	103	68	139	113
Rohnerville Rancheria	CA	0	0	8	8
Round Valley Reservation	CA	30,538	13,601	1,183	577
Rumsey Rancheria	CA	185	185	8	4
San Manuel Reservation	CA	658	658	80	56
San Pasqual Reservation	CA	1,380	1,380	512	212
Santa Rosa Rancheria	CA	170	179	323	284
Santa Rosa Reservation	CA	11,093	11,093	50	37
Santa Ynez Reservation	CA	127	127	279	213
Santa Ysabel Reservation	CA	15,527	15,527	169	150
Sheep Ranch Rancheria	CA	1	1	0	0
Sherwood Valley Rancheria	CA	350	292	15	9
Shingle Springs Rancheria	CA	160	160	18	7
Smith River Rancheria	CA	30	0	104	72
Soboba Reservation	CA	5,916	5,036	369	308
Stewart's Point Rancheria	CA	40	40	91	86
Sulphur Bank Rancheria	CA	50	50	93	90
Susanville Rancheria	CA	150	150	454	154
Sycuan Reservation	CA	640	371	4	0
Table Bluff Rancheria	CA	...	0	48	43
Table Mountain Rancheria	CA	61	37	51	48
Timbi-Sha W. Shoshone	CA	40	40	55	55
Torres-Martinez Reservation	CA	24,024	18,223	4,462	143
Trinidad Rancheria	CA	47	44	78	59

[Continued]

★ 657 ★

Federally Recognized Reservations, by Acreage, State, and Population, 1990 - I

[Continued]

Reservation	State	Acreage	Tribal land	Population	Indians
Tule River Reservation	CA	55,356	55,356	798	745
Tuolumne Rancheria	CA	336	336	135	107
Twenty-Nine Palms Reservation	CA	402	402	0	0
Upper Lake Rancheria	CA	19	0	76	28
Viejas Reservation	CA	1,609	1,609	411	227
XL Ranch	CA	9,255	9,255	35	27
Yurok Tribe	CA	3,669	3,669	1,357	463
Southern Ute	CO	310,002	307,561	7,804	1,044
Ute Mountain	CO-NM-UT	477,850	477,850	1,320	1,264
Mashantucket Pequot	CT	1,201	1,201	83	55
Big Cypress	FL	42,728	42,728	484	447
Brighton	FL	35,805	35,805	524	402
Hollywood	FL	481	481	1,394	481
Miccosukee	FL	75,146	74,812	94	94
Sac & Fox	IA	3,540	3,535	577	564
Omaha	IA-NE	26,792	9,596	5,227	1,908
Coeur d'Alene	ID	67,981	21,268	5,802	749
Duck Valley	ID	289,819	289,819	1,101	1,022
Fort Hall	ID	522,510	260,837	5,114	3,035
Kootenai	ID	2,072	18	65	61
Nez Perce	ID	85,661	36,409	16,160	1,863
Iowa	KS	1,072	866	172	83
Kickapoo	KS	6,660	3,505	478	370
Pottawatomi	KS	21,479	2,939	279	502
Sac & Fox	KS-NE	354	309	210	49
Chitimacha	LA	283	283	286	212
Coushatta	LA	154	154	36	33
Tunica-Biloxi	LA	134	134	29	16
Indian Township	ME	23,000	23,000	617	541
Penobscot	ME	127,838	60,143	517	430
Pleasant Point	ME	200	200	572	523
Bay Mills	MI	2,209	2,209	461	403
Grand Traverse	MI	...	...	228	208

Source: George Russell, *The American Indian in Question*, Phoenix: Thunderbird Enterprises, Copyright 1992, pp. 13-18. Published with permission. *Notes:* Three dots (...) indicates that data were not available at the time of the original source's publication.

★ 658 ★

Federally Recognized Reservations, by Acreage, State, and Population, 1990 - II

Reservation	State	Acreage	Tribal land	Population	Indians
Hannahville Community	MI	3,411	3,411	181	173
Isabella	MI	138,240	676	22,944	795
Lac Vieux Desert	MI	104	104	124	119
L'Anse	MI	13,765	5,764	3,293	724
Sault Ste. Marie	MI	293	293	768	554
Nett Lake	MN	41,864	30,354	358	346
Deer Creek	MN	...	...	186	6
Fond du Lac	MN	21,932	4,898	3,229	1,106
Grand Portage	MN	44,844	37,679	306	207
Leech Lake	MN	27,853	15,530	8,669	3,390
Lower Sioux Community	MN	1,745	1,745	259	225
Mille Lacs	MN	3,863	3,795	470	428
Prairie Island Community	MN	571	571	60	56
Red Lake	MN	564,452	564,452	3,699	3,602
Sandy Lake	MN	...	...	37	36
Shakopee	MN	293	293	203	153
Upper Sioux Community	MN	745	745	49	43
Vermillion Lake	MN	...	...	91	87
White Earth	MN	56,078	54,125	8,727	2,759
Mississippi Choctaw	MS	17,926	17,715	4,073	3,932
Blackfeet	MT	937,838	302,072	8,849	7,025
Crow	MT	1,517,406	408,444	6,370	4,724
Flathead	MT	627,070	581,907	21,259	5,130
Fort Belknap	MT	588,756	188,017	2,508	2,338
Fort Peck	MT	904,683	391,769	10,595	5,782
Rocky Boy's	MT	108,334	108,334	1,954	1,882
Northern Cheyenne	MT	436,948	318,072	3,923	3,542
Santee Sioux	NE	9,358	6,943	758	425
Winnebago	NE	27,538	4,241	2,341	1,156
Eastern Cherokee	NC	56,573	56,461	6,527	5,388
Devils Lake Sioux	ND	53,239	16,229	3,588	2,676
Fort Behold	ND	419,362	69,509	5,395	2,999
Turtle Mountain	ND	33,319	8,618	7,106	6,772
Acoma Pueblo	NM	263,611	263,291	2,590	2,551
Alamo (Navajo)	NM	63,108	43,335	1,271	1,228
Canoncito	NM	76,813	68,144	1,189	1,177
Cochiti Pueblo	NM	50,669	50,669	1,342	666
Isleta Pueblo	NM	211,034	211,026	2,915	2,699
Jemez Pueblo	NM	89,619	89,617	1,750	1,738
Jicarilla Apache	NM	823,580	823,580	2,617	2,375
Laguna Pueblo	NM	461,099	458,933	3,731	3,634
Mescalero Apache	NM	460,678	460,678	2,695	2,516
Nambe Pueblo	NM	19,076	19,076	1,402	329
Picuris Pueblo	NM	14,947	14,947	1,882	147
Pojoaque Pueblo	NM	11,602	11,602	2,556	177

[Continued]

★ 658 ★

Federally Recognized Reservations, by Acreage, State, and Population, 1990 - II

[Continued]

Reservation	State	Acreage	Tribal land	Population	Indians
Ramah Community	NM	146,953	99,353	194	191
Sandia Pueblo	NM	22,871	22,871	3,971	358
San Felipe Pueblo	NM	48,930	48,859	2,434	1,859
San Ildefonso Pueblo	NM	26,196	26,196	1,499	347
SAn Juan Pueblo	NM	12,237	12,235	5,209	1,276
Santa Ana Pueblo	NM	61,414	61,414	593	481
Santa Clara Pueblo	NM	45,748	45,744	10,193	1,246
Santo Domingo Pueblo	NM	69,260	69,260	2,992	2,947
Taos Pueblo	NM	95,341	95,334	4,745	1,212
Tesuque Pueblo	NM	16,813	16,811	697	232
Zia Pueblo	NM	117,680	117,680	637	637
Zuni Pueblo	NM-AZ	409,182	406,969	7,412	7,073
Carson Colony	NV	160	160	248	235
Dresslerville Colony	NV	40	40	152	144
Duckwater	NV	3,815	3,815	135	115
Ely Colony	NV	100	100	59	52
Fallon Colony & Res	NV	8,180	3,540	546	506
Fort McDermitt	NV-OR	16,497	16,352	396	387
Las Vegas Colony	NV	3,723	3,723	80	72
Lovelock Colony	NV	20	20	94	80
Moapa River	NV	71,955	71,955	375	190
Pyramid Lake	NV	476,689	476,689	1,388	959
Reno-Sparks Colony	NV	29	29	264	262
Summit Lake	NV	10,863	10,098	7	6
Te-Moak	NV	13,050	13,050	949	831
Walker River	NV	323,406	313,690	802	620
Washoe	NV	3,672	3,672	157	65
Winnemucca Colony	NV	340	340	67	61
Yerington	NV	1,632	1,632	428	324
Yomba	NV	4,718	4,718	95	88
Goshute	NV-UT	7,489	7,489	99	98
Allegany	NY	30,984	...	7,315	1,062
Cattaraugus	NY	22,013	...	2,178	2,051
Oil Springs	NY	640	...	5	0
Oneida	NY	32	...	37	37
Onondaga	NY	7,300	...	771	2
St. Regis Mohawk	NY	14,640	...	1,978	1,923
Tonawanda	NY	495	...	501	453
Tuscarora	NY	5,778	...	772	310
Osage	OK	168,794	675	41,645	6,161
Burns Paiute	OR	11,466	932	163	151
Coos, Lower Umpqua & Siuslaw	OR	6	6	4	1
Cow Creek	OR	28	28	58	11
Grand Ronde	OR	9,811	9,811	57	1

[Continued]

★ 658 ★

Federally Recognized Reservations, by Acreage, State, and Population, 1990 - II
[Continued]

Reservation	State	Acreage	Tribal land	Population	Indians
Siletz	OR	3,673	3,673	5	0
Umatilla	OR	85,256	16,643	2,502	1,029
Warm Springs	OR	643,507	592,143	3,076	2,820
Narragansett	RI	...	...	31	17
Cheyenne River	SD	1,395,905	954,398	7,743	5,100
Crow Creek	SD	125,483	65,018	1,756	1,531
Flandreau Santee Sioux	SD	2,183	3,183	279	249
Lower Brule	SD	130,239	104,244	1,123	994
Pine Ridge	SD-NE	1,780,444	709,112	12,215	11,182
Standing Rock	SD-ND	847,254	356,039	7,956	4,870
Lake Traverse (Sisseton)	SD-ND	105,543	17,104	10,733	2,821
Rosebud	SD	954,572	529,954	9,696	8,043
Yankton	SD	36,559	16,706	6,269	1,994
Alabama-Coushatta	TX	4,600	4,600	478	477
Ysleta Del Sur Pueblo	TX	...	...	292	211
Northwestern Shoshoni	UT	...	...	0	0
Paiute	UT	425	425	645	323
Skull Valley	UT	17,445	17,284	32	32
Uintah & Ouray	UT	1,021,558	1,007,238	17,224	2,650
Chehalis	WA	2,076	76	491	308
Colville	WA	1,063,043	1,023,640	6,957	3,788
Hoh	WA	443	443	96	74
Jamestown Klallam	WA	11	8	22	4
Kalispel	WA	4,557	1,970	100	91
Lower Elwah	WA	427	427	137	130
Lummi	WA	7,678	635	3,147	1,594
Makah	WA	27,244	24,967	1,214	940
Muckleshoot	WA	1,275	106	3,841	864
Nisqually	WA	930	195	578	365
Nooksack	WA	1	1	556	412
Ozette	WA	719	719	12	0
Port Gamble	WA	1,303	1,303	552	377
Port Madison	WA	2,872	86	4,834	388
Puyallup	WA	103	73	32,406	937
Quileute	WA	814	804	381	303
Quinault	WA	129,221	7,466	1,216	943
Sauk-Suiettle	WA	23	23	124	69
Shoalwater	WA	335	335	131	66
Skokomish	WA	2,987	162	614	431
Spokane	WA	133,302	105,383	1,502	1,229
Squaxin Island	WA	971	145	157	127
Stillaquamish	WA	...	...	113	96
Swinomish	WA	3,602	565	2,282	585
Tulalip	WA	10,667	7,511	7,103	1,204

[Continued]

★ 658 ★

Federally Recognized Reservations, by Acreage, State, and Population, 1990 - II

[Continued]

Reservation	State	Acreage	Tribal land	Population	Indians
Upper Skagit	WA	74	74	180	162
Yakima	WA	1,130,286	904,411	27,668	6,307
Bad River	WI	56,558	23,451	1,070	868
Lac Courte Oreilles	WI	48,139	22,062	2,408	1,771
Lac du Flambeau	WI	44,726	30,344	2,434	1,432
Menominee	WI	222,552	222,552	3,397	3,182
Oneida	WI	2,751	2,366	18,033	2,447
Potawatomi	WI	11,692	11,292	1,082	266
Red Cliff	WI	7,495	5,458	857	727
St. Croix	WI	1,940	1,940	505	462
Sokaogon Chippewa Community	WI	1,694	1,694	357	311
Stockbridge	WI	15,603	15,447	581	447
Wisconsin Winnebago	WI	4,245	632	700	570
Wind River	WY	1,888,558	1,793,420	21,851	5,676

Source: George Russell, *The American Indian in Question*, Phoenix: Thunderbird Enterprises, Copyright 1992, pp. 13-18. Published with permission. *Notes:* Three dots (...) indicates that data were not available at the time of the original sources publication.

★ 659 ★

How Some Sovereign Nations Compare in Size to Selected Indian Areas

Indian areas are shown in boldface type.

Nation/Tribe	Square miles
Navajo	21,838
Costa Rica	19,575
Dominican Republic	18,816
Bhutan	18,147
Denmark	16,619
Switzerland	15,941
Netherlands	14,125
Taiwan	13,886
Belgium	11,781
Lesotho	11,716
Albania	11,100
Equatorial Guinea	10,852
Burundi	10,747
Haiti	10,714
Rwanda	10,166

[Continued]

★ 659 ★

How Some Sovereign Nations Compare in Size to Selected Indian Areas
[Continued]

Nation/Tribe	Square miles
El Salvador	8,260
Israel	7,993
Fiji	7,055
Swaziland	6,704
Kuwait	6,178
Qatar	6,000
Papago	4,460
Jamaica	4,411
Lebanon	4,015
Gambia	4,005
Hopi	3,862
Cyprus	3,572
White Mountain Apache	2,947
Wind River tribes	2,947
San Carlos Apache	2,855
Pine Ridge Sioux	2,600
Crow tribe	2,434
Cheyenne River Sioux	2,210
Yakima tribe	1,711
Uintah and Ouray	1,581
Colville tribe	1,569
Hualapai tribe	1,551
Fort Peck Sioux	1,534
Rosebud Sioux	1,526
Blackfeet tribe	1,420
Standing Rock Sioux	1,320
Jicarilla Apache tribe	1,159
Trinidad and Tobago	1,979
Western Samoa	1,130
Fort Belknap	1,027
Luxembourg	999
Flathead tribe	960
Ute Mountain Ute	917
Red Lake Chippewa	882
Warm Springs tribe	881
Fort Hall Shoshone	817
Pyramid Lake Paiute	742
Mauritius	720

[Continued]

★ 659 ★

How Some Sovereign Nations Compare in Size to
Selected Indian Areas
[Continued]

Nation/Tribe	Square miles
Mescalero Apache	719
Northern Cheyenne	678
Laguna Pueblo	652
Fort Berthold	651
Zuni Pueblo	636
Sisseston	629
Pima	582
Walker River	500
Tonga	269
Bahrain	231
Singapore	226
Quinault	200
Kaibab Piute	188
Andorra	179
Barbados	166
Rocky Boy's Chippewa-Cree	162
Nez Perce	137
Hoopa Valley	134
Malta	122
Maldives	112
Coeur d'Alene	108
Liechtenstein	62
San Marino	23.50
Nauru	8
Monaco	.60
Vatican City	.17

Source: Vine Deloria, Jr., *Behind the Trail of Broken Treaties: An Indian Declaration of Independence,* University of Texas Press, Austin, pp. 166- 168. Published by Permission.

★ 660 ★

Land Ownership of Lands Under BIA Jurisdiction, by Selected Reservation and Indian Ownership, 1991

The number of tracts owned is shown, by selected reservation and type of ownership, 1991.

Reservation	Number of tracts owned solely by -			Number tracts with multiple owners		Total tracts
	One Indian	Tribe	Others	At least one Indian owner	No Indian owners	
Blackfeet	1,640	1,800	18	3,571	7	7,036
Cheyenne River	2,103	5,549	11	2,809	2	10,474
Colville	771	2,744	17	1,884	66	5,482
Crow	2,244	823	44	3,696	3	6,810
Fort Berthold	1,831	4,243	16	2,610	8	8,708
Fort Peck	1,928	1,232	7	3,702	27	6,896
Pine Ridge	2,409	3,435	85	4,726	6	10,661
Rosebud	629	2,766	7	2,961	47	6,410
Standing Rock	1,483	2,363	6	5,402	13	9,267
Turtle Mountain	401	101	5	409	1	917
Wind River	845	1,186	22	2,128	47	4,228
Yakima	916	2,892	15	2,236	30	6,089
Total	17,200	29,134	253	36,134	257	82,978

Source: Indian Programs: Profile of the Land Ownership at 12 Reservations, United States General Accounting Office, GAO/RCED-92-96BR, February 1992, p. 12.

★ 661 ★

Land Tract Owners on Selected Reservations, 1991

The number of Indian owners is shown, by selected reservation and tribal membership status, for 1991.

Reservation	Indian Owners		
	Members	Non-Members	Total[1]
Blackfeet	4,715	508	5,223
Cheyenne River	4,586	514	5,100
Colville	3,665	499	4,164
Crow	3,143	144	3,287
Fort Berthold	3,232	137	3,369
Fort Peck	5,743	728	6,471
Pine Ridge	12,910	2,490	15,400
Rosebud	9,811	2,226	12,037
Standing Rock	10,333	1,254	11,587
Turtle Mountain	4,524	126	4,650
Wind River	3,904	888	4,792

[Continued]

★ 661 ★

Land Tract Owners on Selected Reservations, 1991
[Continued]

Reservation	Indian Owners		
	Members	Non-Members	Total[1]
Yakima	3,508	273	3,781
Total	70,074	9,787	79,861

Source: Indian Programs: Profile of Land Ownership at 12 Reservations, United States General Accounting Office, GAO/RCED-92-96BR, February 1992, p. 24. *Notes:* 1. Coding errors in the BIA database led to some double counting of the Indian owners; therefore, the total number of Indian owners is slightly overstated.

★ 662 ★

Land Tract Ownership Records, by Selected Reservation and Size of Ownership Interest, 1991

The number of ownership records the BIA maintains is shown, by selected reservation and size of ownership interest, for 1991. As shown in the table, over 620,000 (about 67 percent) of the Indian individual ownership records are for interests of 2 percent or less.

Reservation	Number of records with percentage ownership interest of -						Total Indian records[1]
	100	51-99	26-50	11-25	3-10	2 or less	
Blackfeet	1,541	203	1,957	6,673	24,325	69,224	113,923
Cheyenne River	2,028	70	2,198	5,748	12,011	14,487	36,542
Colville	776	151	1,173	2,443	6,859	14,323	25,725
Crow	2,078	465	2,449	7,239	22,931	74,498	109,660
Fort Berthold	1,891	170	1,510	4,909	14,356	38,793	61,629
Fort Peck	1,932	195	2,444	6,710	19,000	47,040	77,321
Pine Ridge	2,198	209	2,855	8,212	24,559	81,881	119,914
Rosebud	566	72	1,203	4,024	14,968	73,758	94,591
Standing Rock	1,326	134	2,854	10,153	36,743	95,570	146,780
Turtle Mountain	423	43	251	795	2,250	9,760	13,522
Wind River	804	187	923	3,012	13,087	65,950	83,963
Yakima	914	226	1,302	3,622	12,174	25,228	43,465
Total	16,477	2,125	21,119	63,540	203,263	620,511	927,035

Source: Indian Programs: Profile of the Land Ownership at 12 Reservations, United States General Accounting Office, GAO/RCED-92-96BR, February 1992, p. 23. *Notes:* 1. This distribution excludes historical records for original allottees no longer having any ownership interests in the land and for 24 other Indians with less than one ten-millionth of one percent ownership interests.

★ 663 ★

Land Tract Ownership Records, by Selected Reservation and Type of Ownership Interest, 1991

The number of ownership records the BIA maintains is shown, by selected reservation and type of ownership, for 1991.

Reservation	Number of ownership records				Total ownership records
	Tribal interests	Individual Indians	Non-Indians	Other[1]	
Blackfeet	5,235	115,514	2,784	789	124,322
Cheyenne River	9,005	37,182	377	32	46,596
Colville	4,949	28,471	1,381	107	34,908
Crow	3,120	111,825	783	724	116,452
Fort Berthold	7,684	64,096	582	62	72,424
Fort Peck	2,572	79,110	2,021	50	83,753
Pine Ridge	16,660	121,126	800	156	138,742
Rosebud	24,309	95,684	1,169	108	121,270
Standing Rock	9,526	147,517	2,065	243	159,351
Turtle Mountain	494	13,699	504	20	14,717
Wind River	4,548	86,128	1,245	895	92,816
Yakima	6,226	47,808	212	85	54,331
Total	94,328	948,160	13,923	3,271	1,059,682

Source: Indian Programs: Profile of the Land Ownership at 12 Reservations, United States General Accounting Office, GAO/RCED-92-96BR, February 1992, p. 22. *Note:* 1. Other includes corporations and government.

★ 664 ★

Land Tract Ownership Records, by Selected Reservation and Type of Surface, 1991[1]

The number of ownership records the BIA maintains is shown, by selected reservation and type of surface, for 1991.

Reservation	Number of records maintained for tract ownership of -			Total ownership records[2]
	Surface only	Subsurface only	Both surface & subsurface	
Blackfeet	64,924	36,662	22,708	124,294
Cheyenne River	7,842	23,180	15,574	46,596
Colville	5,459	19,970	9,577	34,906
Crow	38,487	33,544	44,406	116,437
Fort Berthold	25,614	41,011	5,799	72,424
Fort Peck	12,239	38,090	33,424	83,753
Pine Ridge	11,521	24,206	103,015	138,742
Rosebud	19,645	37,620	64,005	121,270
Standing Rock	18,658	80,027	60,666	159,351

[Continued]

★ 664 ★

Land Tract Ownership Records, by Selected Reservation and Type of Surface, 1991
[Continued]

Reservation	Number of records maintained for tract ownership of -			Total ownership records[2]
	Surface only	Subsurface only	Both surface & subsurface	
Turtle Mountain	3,297	3,722	7,698	14,717
Wind River	25,496	52,753	14,564	92,813
Yakima	952	6,739	46,598	54,289
Total	234,134	397,524	427,934	1,059,592

Source: Indian Programs: Profile of the Land Ownership at 12 Reservations, United States General Accounting Office, GAO/RCED-92-96BR, February 1992, p. 21. *Notes:* 1. Land held for individual Indians and tribes includes both surface and subsurface (oil, gas, and mineral) components. These are accounted for as separate tracts when their ownership differs; they are otherwise treated as one tract. The BIA does not maintain records for land tracts that have been sold or transferred to non-Indian ownership and are, therefore, no longer the responsibility of the Interior Department. 2. Excludes 90 records where the tract resource code was not specified.

★ 665 ★

Land Tracts Under BIA Jurisdiction, by Selected Reservation and Degree of Individual Indian Ownership Interests, 1991

Figures are shown, by selected reservation, for 1991. To illustrate extreme cases of an Indian individual having ownership interest in many tracts, this table shows both the number of tracts and the number of separate ownership interests held by an Indian individual at each of the 12 reservations. It also shows the number of tracts where the Indian individual's interest is 2 percent or less.

Reservation	Number of tracts	Ownership interests	Number of tracts with ownership of 2 percent or less
Blackfeet	113	301	68
Cheyenne River	41	93	23
Colville	19	75	3
Crow	241	616	151
Fort Berthold	82	203	30
Fort Peck	73	191	2
Pine Ridge	44	199	19
Rosebud	50	150	36
Standing Rock	112	195	70
Turtle Mountain	2	58	0

[Continued]

★ 665 ★

Land Tracts Under BIA Jurisdiction, by Selected Reservation and Degree of Individual Indian Ownership Interests, 1991
[Continued]

Reservation	Number of tracts	Ownership interests	Number of tracts with ownership of 2 percent or less
Wind River	194	413	98
Yakima	95	121	34

Source: Indian Programs: Profile of the Land Ownership at 12 Reservations, United States General Accounting Office, GAO/RCED-92-96BR, February 1992, p. 18.

★ 666 ★

Land Tracts Under BIA Jurisdiction, by Selected Reservation and Individual Indian Ownership With Multiple Tract Ownership, 1991

The number of consolidated interests is shown, by selected reservation, for 1991.

Reservation	Number of Indians with ownership in -								Total Indian owners
	1 tract	2 tracts	3-5 tracts	6-10 tracts	11-25 tracts	26-50 tracts	51-100 tracts	Over 100 tracts	
Blackfeet	794	464	730	939	1,260	787	217	30	5,221
Cheyenne River	1,282	635	1,391	973	717	90	5	0	5,093
Colville	1,408	623	878	562	568	40	1	0	4,080
Crow	618	303	405	295	568	569	441	85	3,284
Fort Berthold	494	309	456	555	965	471	112	0	3,362
Fort Peck	1,585	1,001	1,080	860	1,392	463	50	2	6,433
Pine Ridge	4,346	2,056	3,229	2,791	2,597	368	13	0	15,400
Rosebud	3,025	2,196	2,582	2,038	1,808	373	12	0	12,034
Standing Rock	2,741	1,296	2,523	1,428	2,180	1,241	165	6	11,580
Turtle Mountain	2,120	1,314	1,052	163	1	0	0	0	4,650
Wind River	726	668	842	728	1,066	644	158	8	4,840
Yakima	962	439	599	626	798	294	15	0	3,733
Total	20,101	11,304	15,767	11,958	13,920	5,340	1,189	131	79,710

Source: Indian Programs: Profile of the Land Ownership at 12 Reservations, United States General Accounting Office, GAO/RCED-92-96BR, February 1992, p. 17.

★ 667 ★

Land Tracts Under BIA Jurisdiction, by Selected Reservation and Largest Number of Owners on a Single Tract, 1991

Figures are shown for selected reservations in 1991.

Reservation	Indian owners	Other owners	Total owners	Indian interests of 2 percent or or less	Tribal affiliations represented
Blackfeet	242	43	285	240	3
Cheyenne River	223	10	233	214	9
Colville	120	18	138	112	6
Crow	345	2	347	338	4
Fort Berthold	243	23	266	229	7
Fort Peck	335	10	345	326	12
Pine Ridge	407	12	419	406	9
Rosebud	367	7	374	364	6
Standing Rock	531	11	542	523	16
Turtle Mountain	335	27	362	331	6
Wind River	317	5	322	310	5
Yakima	160	2	162	148	3

Source: Indian Programs: Profile of the Land Ownership at 12 Reservations, United States General Accounting Office, GAO/RCED-92-96BR, February 1992, p. 16.

★ 668 ★

Land Tracts Under BIA Jurisdiction, by Selected Reservation and Number of Indian Owners, 1991

The number of tracts owned is shown, by selected reservation and number of Indian owners, for 1991.

Reservation	Number of tracts with -							Total tracts
	Two Indian owners	3-10 Indian owners	11-25 Indian owners	26-50 Indian owners	51-100 Indian owners	101-300 Indian owners	Over 300 Indian owners	
Blackfeet	381	1,141	960	667	351	71	0	3,571
Cheyenne River	535	1,416	645	177	30	6	0	2,809
Colville	476	753	435	163	52	5	0	1,884
Crow	490	1,403	933	481	261	122	6	3,696
Fort Berthold	352	999	675	377	174	33	0	2,610
Fort Peck	635	1,447	987	422	179	31	1	3,702
Pine Ridge	634	1,840	1,234	588	283	145	2	4,726
Rosebud	296	1,021	770	468	266	135	5	2,961
Standing Rock	411	1,958	1,640	858	414	111	10	5,402
Turtle Mountain	81	139	102	40	25	21	1	409

[Continued]

★ 668 ★

Land Tracts Under BIA Jurisdiction, by Selected Reservation and Number of Indian Owners, 1991

[Continued]

Reservation	Number of tracts with -							Total tracts
	Two Indian owners	3-10 Indian owners	11-25 Indian owners	26-50 Indian owners	51-100 Indian owners	101-300 Indian owners	Over 300 Indian owners	
Wind River	169	561	611	371	270	145	1	2,128
Yakima	297	875	636	332	86	10	0	2,236
Total	4,757	13,553	9,628	4,944	2,391	835	26	36,134

Source: Indian Programs: Profile of the Land Ownership at 12 Reservations, United States General Accounting Office, GAO/RCED-92-96BR, February 1992, p. 14.

★ 669 ★

Land Tracts Under BIA Jurisdiction, by Selected Reservation and Shared Ownership, 1991

The number of tracts owned is shown, by selected reservation and shared ownership, for 1991.

Reservation	Number of tracts owned by -				Total tracts
	Indians only	Indians and the tribe	Indians and non-Indians	Indians, tribe, and non-Indians	
Blackfeet	1,830	646	534	561	3,571
Cheyenne River	2,097	430	241	41	2,809
Colville	741	533	404	206	1,884
Crow	2,564	631	265	236	3,969
Fort Berthold	1,543	646	206	215	2,610
Fort Peck	2,265	294	826	317	3,702
Pine Ridge	2,546	1,672	176	332	4,726
Rosebud	1,120	1,168	177	496	2,961
Standing Rock	3,000	1,072	683	647	5,402
Turtle Mountain	258	23	70	58	409
Wind River	979	565	178	406	2,128
Yakima	1,141	972	42	81	2,236
Total	20,084	8,652	3,802	3,596	36,134

Source: Indian Programs: Profile of the Land Ownership at 12 Reservations, United States General Accounting Office, GAO/RCED-92-96BR, February 1992, p. 13.

★ 670 ★

Land Tracts Under BIA Jurisdiction, by Selected Reservation and Size of Consolidated Indian Ownership, 1991

The number of consolidated interests is shown, by selected reservation and size of interest, for 1991. As the table shows, 431,074, or over 60 percent, of the consolidated Indian ownership is represented by interests of 2 percent or less.

Reservation	Number of consolidated ownership interests totaling -						Total
	100 percent	51-99 percent	26-50 percent	11-25 percent	3-10 percent	2 percent or less	
Blackfeet	1,709	416	1,935	6,306	20,983	48,899	80,248
Cheyenne River	2,119	194	2,188	5,386	9,402	10,257	29,546
Colville	854	249	1,066	2,093	5,787	10,180	20,229
Crow	2,189	755	2,225	6,941	18,503	48,094	78,707
Fort Berthold	1,981	340	1,384	4,813	11,890	26,494	46,902
Fort Peck	2,062	513	2,394	6,076	15,606	29,789	56,440
Pine Ridge	2,324	451	2,884	7,339	20,845	60,986	94,829
Rosebud	612	190	1,238	3,819	12,993	55,552	74,404
Standing Rock	1,444	371	3,008	9,852	32,140	70,372	117,187
Turtle Mountain	432	103	242	734	1,685	6,437	9,633
Wind River	892	255	891	3,078	11,325	46,437	62,878
Yakima	1,057	271	1,259	3,550	9,845	17,577	33,559
Total	17,675	4,108	20,714	59,987	171,004	431,074	704,562

Source: Indian Programs: Profile of the Land Ownership at 12 Reservations, United States General Accounting Office, GAO/RCED-92-96BR, February 1992, p. 19.

★ 671 ★

Land Tracts Under BIA Jurisdiction, by Selected Reservation and Smallest Individual Indian Ownership Interests, 1991

This table shows extreme examples of fractioned ownership at each reservation in terms of the size of the ownership interest. For each reservation, it shows the smallest interest held by an Indian individual and identifies the land equivalent of that ownership interest. In some cases, the land size equivalent is smaller than the dimensions of this page.

Reservation	Tract acreage	Percentage ownership of tract	Land equivalent of ownership interest	
			Square feet	Inches
Blackfeet	80.00	0.0002900	10.11	38.1 x 38.1
Cheyenne River	647.21	0.0004962	139.89	142.0 x 142.0
Colville	160.00	0.0006955	48.47	83.5 x 83.5
Crow	160.00	0.0000100	.70	10.0 x 10.0
Fort Berthold	80.00	0.0002624	9.15	36.3 x 36.3
Fort Peck	40.00	0.0001200	2.09	17.4 x 17.4
Pine Ridge	474.14	0.0000047	0.97	11.8 x 11.8

[Continued]

★ 671 ★

Land Tracts Under BIA Jurisdiction, by Selected Reservation and Smallest Individual Indian Ownership Interests, 1991

[Continued]

Reservation	Tract acreage	Percentage ownership of tract	Land equivalent of ownership interest	
			Square feet	Inches
Rosebud	320.00	0.0000047	0.66	9.7 x 9.7
Standing Rock	320.00	0.0000025	0.35	7.1 x 7.1
Turtle Mountain	7.50	0.0000192	0.06	2.9 x 2.9
Wind River	80.00	0.0000100	.35	7.1 x 7.1
Yakima	80.00	0.0001929	6.72	31.1 x 31.1

Source: Indian Programs: Profile of the Land Ownership at 12 Reservations, United States General Accounting Office, GAO/RCED-92-96BR, February 1992, p. 20. *Notes:* Smallest ownership share represents the smallest share that is at least one ten-millionth of one percent. Attempts to identify ownership interest smaller than one ten-millionth of one percent were not made.

★ 672 ★

Land Tracts Under BIA Jurisdiction, by Selected Reservation and Two Percent or Less Consolidated Indian Ownership, 1991

The number of tracts owned is shown, by selected reservation and consolidated Indian ownership interests of two percent or less per tract, for 1991. The Indian Land Consolidation Act generally provides that ownership interests of 2 percent or less will transfer, or escheat, to the tribe upon the death of an Indian.

Reservation tracts	Number of tracts with Indian interests of 2 percent or less								Total
	None	One	2-10	11-25	26-50	51-100	101-300	Over 300	
Blackfeet	1,722	42	602	468	453	247	37	0	3,571
Cheyenne River	2,055	26	381	258	68	20	1	0	2,809
Colville	1,237	18	306	226	69	27	1	0	1,884
Crow	2,013	41	690	389	280	189	91	3	3,696
Fort Berthold	1,501	28	394	335	236	91	25	0	2,610
Fort Peck	2,159	53	669	481	214	103	22	1	3,702
Pine Ridge	2,570	46	847	559	374	214	115	1	4,726
Rosebud	1,256	40	534	506	292	216	113	4	2,961
Standing Rock	2,594	41	1,126	787	523	240	85	6	5,402
Turtle Mountain	235	4	67	38	25	22	17	1	409
Wind River	731	64	416	360	253	212	91	1	2,128
Yakima	1,211	45	446	320	169	37	8	0	2,236
Total	19,284	448	6,478	4,727	2,956	1,618	606	17	36,134

Source: Indian Programs: Profile of the Land Ownership at 12 Reservations, United States General Accounting Office, GAO/RCED-92-96BR, February 1992, p. 15.

★ 673 ★

Land Tracts Under BIA Jurisdiction, by Selected Reservation, 1991[1]

The number and acreage of tracts are shown, by selected reservation and selected characteristics, for 1991.

Reservation	Number of acres	Number of tracts	Number of tracts			Acreage of tracts		Average tract acreage
			Less than 40 acres	40-159 acres	160 acres or more	Smallest tract	Largest tract	
Blackfeet	1,238,021	7,036	792	3,434	2,810	0.001	5,365.7	176
Cheyenne River	2,004,773	10,474	449	2,830	7,195	0.001	2,800.0	191
Colville	1,233,098	5,482	1,195	2,027	2,260	0.050	6,133.0	225
Crow	1,680,246	6,810	957	2,899	2,954	0.030	23,025.0	247
Fort Berthold	1,190,544	8,708	728	4,192	3,788	0.010	827.5	137
Fort Peck	1,390,345	6,896	1,204	2,355	3,337	0.001	2,994.4	202
Pine Ridge	2,050,492	10,661	694	2,744	7,223	0.001	1,000.6	192
Rosebud	1,134,906	6,410	197	1,242	4,971	0.001	1,735.7	177
Standing Rock	1,244,016	9,267	3,018	1,854	4,395	0.010	2,290.0	134
Turtle Mountain	42,453	917	528	335	54	0.145	471.5	46
Wind River	2,158,925	4,228	1,256	2,437	535	0.310	662,515.2	511
Yakima	1,149,734	6,089	1,212	2,658	2,219	0.060	3,200.0	189
Total	16,517,553	82,978	12,230	29,007	41,741	-	-	199

Source: Indian Programs: Profile of the Land Ownership at 12 Reservations, United States General Accounting Office, GAO/RCED-92-96BR, February 1992, p. 9. Notes: A dash (-) stands for not applicable. 1. Because BIA maintains separate tract records for surface and subsurface resources when ownership is different, the number of acres shown in the table does not always represent surface acres.

★ 674 ★

Land Tracts Under BIA Jurisdiction, by Surface and Subsurface Use and Selected Reservation, 1991

The number of tracts is shown, by surface and subsurface use and selected reservation, for 1991.

Reservation	Tracts			Total tracts managed[1]
	Surface only	Subsurface only	Both surface and subsurface	
Blackfeet	3,204	1,417	2,412	7,033
Cheyenne River	2,457	3,501	4,516	10,474
Colville	880	1,369	3,231	5,480
Crow	3,195	1,406	2,205	6,806
Fort Berthold	2,169	5,436	1,130	8,708
Fort Peck	1,717	2,405	2,774	6,896
Pine Ridge	1,282	1,713	7,666	10,661
Rosebud	870	1,375	4,165	6,410
Standing Rock	1,473	3,911	3,883	9,267
Turtle Mountain	193	168	556	917
Wind River	1,414	1,394	1,417	4,225

[Continued]

★ 674 ★

Land Tracts Under BIA Jurisdiction, by Surface and Subsurface Use and Selected Reservation, 1991
[Continued]

Reservation	Tracts			Total tracts managed[1]
	Surface only	Subsurface only	Both surface and subsurface	
Yakima	252	299	5,531	6,082
Total	19,106	24,394	39,456	82,959

Source: Indian Programs: Profile of the Land Ownership at 12 Reservations, United States General Accounting Office, GAO/RCED-92-96BR, February 1992, p. 10. *Notes:* 1. Excludes 19 tracts for which the BIA database did not specify the resource type (i.e., surface, subsurface, or both).

Land Use

★ 675 ★

Acreage of Indian Lands, by State

Acreages are shown, by ownership and state, for 1990.

State	Ownership			Total
	Tribal	Individual	Government	
Alabama	213.00	0.00	0.00	213.00
Alaska	86,773.00	884,099.50	0.09	970,872.59
Arizona	19,775,958.14	311,579.05	90,697.55	20,178,234.74
Arkansas	0.00	2.78	0.00	2.78
California	520,048.66	66,769.39	808.04	587,626.09
Colorado	795,210.99	2,804.68	32.14	798,047.81
Connecticut	1,637.79	0.00	0.00	1,637.79
Florida	153,874.24	0.00	333.33	154,207.57
Idaho	609,621.91	327,300.63	32,531.88	969,454.42
Iowa	3,550.00	0.00	0.00	3,550.00
Kansas	7,218.54	23,762.60	1.00	30,982.14
Louisiana	414.59	0.00	0.00	414.59
Maine	163,570.15	0.00	0.00	163,570.15
Massachusetts	157.00	0.00	0.00	157.00
Michigan	14,410	9,276.28	0.00	23,687.18
Minnesota	779,137.52	50,337.60	103.10	829,578.22
Mississippi	20,486.16	0.00	192.41	20,678.57
Missouri	0.00	374.37	0.00	374.37
Montana	2,671,416.07	2,868,123.84	11,802.80	5,551,342.71
Nebraska	2,141,995.79	43,208.37	6.79	2,185,210.95
Nevada	1,147,087.55	78,528.56	4,945.91	1,230,562.02
New Mexico	7,252,325.70	630,293.42	270,276.14	8,152,895.26

[Continued]

★ 675 ★

Acreage of Indian Lands, by State
[Continued]

| State | Ownership | | | Total |
	Tribal	Individual	Government	
New York	118,199.40	0.00	0.00	118,199.40
North Carolina	56,508.87	0.00	112.16	56,621.03
North Dakota	214,005.96	627,288.84	623.57	841,918.37
Oklahoma	96,838.56	1,000,164.91	2,297.96	1,099,301.45
Oregon	660,366.77	135,052.36	378.08	795,797.21
Rhode Island	1,800.00	0.00	0.00	1,800.00
South Dakota	2,399,530.95	2,121,188.19	1,605.27	4,522,324.41
Texas	4,628.98	0.00	0.00	4,628.98
Utah	2,286,447.57	32,838.09	87.45	2,319,373.11
Washington	2,097,842.03	467,785.11	3,163.64	2,568,790.78
Wisconsin	338,097.10	80,345.36	1.00	418,443.46
Wyoming	1,908,095.44	101,537.25	1,296.15	2,010,928.84
State totals	46,327,469.33	9,862,661.18	421,296.48	56,611,426.99

Source: Bureau of Indian Affairs.

★ 676 ★

Acreage of Indian Lands, by State and Area Office, 1990

Acreages are shown, by ownership, state, and area office, for 1990.

| Area/state | Ownership | | | Total |
	Tribal	Individual	Government	
Aberdeen Area				
South Dakota	2,399,530.95	2,121,188.19	1,605.27	4,522,324.41
North Dakota	214,005.96	627,288.84	623.57	841,918.37
Nebraska	2,141,671.00	42,976.14	6.79	2,184,653.93
Aberdeen total	4,755,207.91	2,791,453.17	2,235.63	7,548,896.71
Albuquerque area				
Arizona	10,085.70	54,699.17	126.82	64,911.69
New Mexico	3,673,320.44	8,578.05	-	3,681,898.49
Utah	5,921.08	8,578.05	-	14,499.13
Colorado	795,210.99	2,408.88	32.14	797,652.01
Texas	-	-	-	-
Albuquerque total	4,484,538.21	74,264.15	158.96	4,558,961.32
Anadarko area				
Oklahoma	28,513.57	411,159.74	1,472.34	441,145.65
Texas	4,628.98	-	-	4,628.98
Kansas	7,218.54	23,762.60	1.00	30,982.14
Nebraska	324.79	232.23	-	557.02
Colorado	-	395.80	-	395.80

[Continued]

★ 676 ★

Acreage of Indian Lands, by State and Area Office, 1990
[Continued]

Area/state	Ownership			Total
	Tribal	Individual	Government	
Anadarko total	40,685.88	435,550.37	1,473.34	477,709.59
Billings area				
Montana	2,089,509.37	2,867,723.84	11,079.68	4,968,312.89
Wyoming	1,908,095.44	101,537.25	1,296.15	2,010,928.84
Billings total	3,997,604.81	2,969,261.09	12,375.83	6,979,241.73
Muskogee Area				
Oklahoma	68,324.99	589,005.17	825.64	658,155.80
Arizona	-	0.35	-	0.35
Arkansas	-	2.78	-	2.78
Missouri	-	374.37	-	374.37
Montana	-	400.00	-	400.00
New Mexico	-	0.16	-	0.16
Muskogee total	68,324.99	589,782.83	825.64	658,933.46
Navajo area				
Arizona	9,989,462.71	85,620.37	753.90	10,075,836.98
New Mexico	3,579,005.26	621,715.21	229,482.64	4,430,203.11
Utah	1,184,783.66	9,741.80	5.99	1,194,531.45
Navajo total	14,753,251.63	717,077.38	230,242.53	15,700,571.54
Eastern area				
North Carolina	56,508.87	-	112.16	56,621.03
New York	118,199.40	-	-	118,199.40
Florida	153,874.24	-	333.33	154,207.57
Mississippi	20,486.16	-	192.41	20,678.57
Louisiana	414.59	-	-	414.59
Alabama	213.00	-	-	213.00
Maine	163,570.15	-	-	163,570.15
Connecticut	1,637.79	-	-	1,637.79
Rhode Island	1,800.00	-	-	1,800.00
Massachusetts	157.00	-	-	157.00
Eastern total	516,861.20	0.00	637.90	517,499.10
Minneapolis area				
Wisconsin	338,097.10	80,345.36	1.00	418,443.46
Minnesota	779,137.52	50,337.60	103.10	829,578.22
Michigan	14,410.90	9,276.28	-	23,687.18
Iowa	3,550.00	-	-	3,550.00
Minneapolis total	1,135,195.52	139,959.24	104.10	1,275,258.86
Phoenix area				
Arizona	9,776,409.73	171,259.16	89,816.83	10,037,485.72
Nevada	1,147,087.55	78,528.56	4,945.91	1,230,562.02

[Continued]

★ 676 ★

Acreage of Indian Lands, by State and Area Office, 1990
[Continued]

Area/state	Ownership			Total
	Tribal	Individual	Government	
Utah	1,095,742.83	14,518.24	81.46	1,110,342.53
California	114,876.55	8,704.00	84.92	123,665.47
Oregon	16,936.00	-	-	16,936.00
Idaho	145,545.00	-	-	145,545.00
New Mexico	-	-	40,793.50	40,793.50
Phoenix total	12,296,597.66	273,009.96	135,722.62	12,705,330.24
Portland area				
Washington	2,097,842.03	467,785.11	3,163.64	2,568,790.78
Oregon	643,430.77	135,052.36	378.08	778,861.21
Idaho	464,076.91	327,300.63	32,531.88	823,909.42
Montana	581,906.70	-	723.12	582,629.82
Portland total	3,787,256.41	930,138.10	36,796.72	4,754,191.23
Sacramento area				
California	405,172.11	58,065.39	723.12	463,960.62
Sacramento total	405,172.11	58,065.39	723.12	463,960.62
Juneau area				
Alaska	86,773.00	884,099.50	0.09	970,872.59
Juneau total	86,773.00	884,099.50	0.09	970,872.59
Total	46,327,469.33	9,862,661.18	421,296.48	56,611,426.99

Source: Bureau of Indian Affairs *Note:* A dash (-) represents zero.

★ 677 ★

Development of Indian Trust Lands

Data are shown for FY 1989.

Development	Unit	Completed in 1989
Soil		
Brush Control	Acre	52,613
Contouring	Acre	173,072
Cover Crop	Acre	66,669
Cropping System	Acre	948,536
Deep Plowing	Acre	71,183
Dune Control	Acre	68
Fencing	Mile	1,300
Fertilizers	Ton	229,302
	Acre	576,868

[Continued]

★ 677 ★

Development of Indian Trust Lands
[Continued]

Development	Unit	Completed in 1989
Gully Control	Acre	12,403
Pest Control	Acre	160,378
Planting Trees, etc.	Number	5,359,908
Forest Development	Acre	16,475
Residue Management	Acre	581,047
Rough Tillage	Acre	154,233
Seeding and Sodding	Acre	13,779
Strip Cropping	Acre	12,570
Weed Control	Acre	519,650
Wildlife Stocking	Project	1,013,783
Soil Amendments	Acre	11,974
Sub total (cost only)	Dollars	9,975,811
Water conservation		
Bank Protection	Mile	95
Canals and Ditches	Mile	475
	Cu Yd	352,125
Conduits and Drops	Cu Yd	89,295
	Number	321
Detentions	Number	252
	Cu Yd	21,326
Dikes	Mile	25
	Cu Yd	1,500
Diversions	Number	2,118
	Cu Yd	76,205
Drainage	Acre	240
Leveling	Acre	11,569
Ponds	Cu Yd	241,638
	Number	184
	Ac Ft	171
Terraces	Mile	157
Upland Water Wasteways	Acre	43
Water Developments	Number	304
Water Distribution	Acre	33,361
Water Spreading	Acre	341
Sub Total (cost only)		831,745
Total		10,807,556

Source: Bureau of Indian Affairs Natural Resource Information System Inventory and Production Report, 1989, United States Department of the Interior, Report No. 55-38-X, p. 8.

★ 678 ★

Grazing on Lands Under BIA Jurisdiction

Number of acres grazed in range units is shown, by ownership and land use class.

Land use class	Tribal owned	Indian owned	Individually used	Liquid damaged	Government owned	Total	On & off
Indian	30,322,695	2,392,180	352,586	531	664,602	33,732,594	1,997,574
Non-Indian	1,136,572	806,234	132,807	374	4,628	2,080,615	348,162
Total	31,459,267	3,198,414	485,393	905	669,230	35,813,209	2,345,736

Source: Bureau of Indian Affairs Natural Resource Information System Inventory and Production Report, 1989, United States Department of the Interior, Report No. 55-38-X, p. 10.

★ 679 ★

Livestock on Lands Under BIA Jurisdiction

The number of livestock is shown, by type and land use class.

Land use class	Cattle	Horses	Sheep & goats	Game animals
Indian	315,776	35,977	312,303	31,622
Non-Indian	76,274	1,977	1,637	-
Total	392,050	37,954	313,939	31,622

Source: Bureau of Indian Affairs Natural Resource Information System Inventory and Production Report, 1989, United States Department of the Interior, Report No. 55-38-X, p. 10. *Note:* A dash (-) indicates no data were given in original source.

★ 680 ★

Ownership and Use of Lands Under BIA Jurisdiction

Numbers are shown in acres.

Ownership	Open grazing	Forest grazing	Commercial forestlands	Non-commercial forestlands	Dry farming	Irrigation projects	Private irrigation	Wild lands excluding timber	Other uses non-agricultural	Total[1]
Tribally owned										
Indian use	24,567,982	9,050,414	5,527,776	6,154,803	312,780	169,920	70,302	2,267,086	320,330	39,390,979
Non-Indian use	1,203,773	355,131	4,551	2,861	168,246	128,826	21,191	50,994	95,735	1,676,177
Idle	342,359	82,289	-	88	115,415	49,399	35,581	8,858	144,290	695,990
Total	26,114,114	9,487,834	5,532,327	6,157,752	596,441	348,145	127,074	2,326,938	560,355	41,763,146
Individually owned										
Indian use	3,724,752	414,300	817,855	593,687	341,735	70,533	104,423	929,820	365,002	6,947,807
Non-Indian use	2,613,214	94,870	4,252	46,336	967,787	142,413	26,378	4,536	20,767	3,825,683
Idle	98,503	2,862	205	4,647	86,883	55,782	11,191	-	39,730	296,941

[Continued]

★ 680 ★

Ownership and Use of Lands Under BIA Jurisdiction
[Continued]

Ownership	Open grazing	Forest grazing	Commercial forestlands	Non-commercial forestlands	Dry farming	Irrigation projects	Private irrigation	Wild lands excluding timber	Other uses non-agricultural	Total[1]
Total	6,436,469	512,032	822,312	644,670	1,396,405	268,728	141,992	934,356	425,499	11,070,431
Government owned										
Indian use	297,105	4,776	2,610	4,153	87	215	-	29,902	21,147	355,219
Non-Indian use	19,966	358	-	-	2,339	206	-	42,123	1,514	66,148
Idle	-	-	4,000	1,060	1,585	120	-	-	354	7,119
Total	317,071	5,134	6,610	5,213	4,011	541	-	72,025	23,015	428,486
Totals										
Indian use	28,589,839	9,469,490	8,803	49,197	1,138,372	271,445	47,569	97,653	118,016	5,568,008
Non-Indian use	3,836,953	450,359	8,803	49,197	1,138,372	271,445	47,569	97,653	118,016	5,568,008
Idle	440,862	85,151	4,205	5,795	203,883	105,301	46,772	8,858	184,374	1,000,050
Total	32,867,654	10,005,000	6,361,249	6,807,635	1,996,857	617,414	269,066	33,333,319	1,008,869	53,262,063
Other	776,978	113,619	94,262	23,496	12,113	16,767	7,653	48,434	4,771	984,474
Grand Total	33,644,632	10,118,619	6,455,511	6,831,131	2,008,970	634,181	276,719	3,381,753	1,013,640	54,246,537

Source: Bureau of Indian Affairs Natural Resource Information System Inventory and Production Report, 1989, United States Department of the Interior, Report No. 55-38-X, p. 1.
Notes: A dash (-) indicates no data given in original source. 1. Total excludes forest grazing.

★ 681 ★

Ownership and Use of Lands Under BIA Jurisdiction in Arizona

Numbers are shown in acres.

Ownership	Open grazing	Forest grazing	Commercial forestlands	Non-commercial forestlands	Dry farming	Irrigation projects	Private irrigation	Wild lands excluding timber	Other uses non-agricultural	Total[1]
Tribally owned										
Indian use	13,277,999	4,539,833	1,232,771	3,320,824	14,949	51,211	13,105	949,556	99,801	18,960,216
Non-Indian use	9,554	532	-	532	-	70,258	1,650	4,331	14,555	100,880
Idle	92,480	-	-	-	84,874	29,124	11,450	28,370	1,176	247,474
Total	13,380,033	4,540,365	1,232,771	3,321,356	99,823	150,593	26,205	982,257	115,532	19,308,570
Individually owned										
Indian use	97,026	20,236	3,600	16,636	400	8,876	8,300	27,406	1,978	164,222
Non-Indian use	-	-	-	-	250	12,786	5,981	73	3,176	22,266
Idle	9,920	-	-	-	-	22,070	7,409	18,760	1,638	59,825
Total	106,946	20,236	3,600	16,636	650	43,740	21,690	46,259	6,792	246,313
Government owned										
Indian use	-	-	-	-	-	-	-	-	1,938	1,938
Non-Indian use	-	-	-	-	-	-	-	-	-	-
Idle	-	-	-	-	-	120	-	-	-	120
Total	-	-	-	-	-	120	-	-	-	120
Totals										
Indian use	13,375,025	4,560,069	1,234,371	3,337,460	15,349	60,087	21,405	976,962	103,717	19,126,376
Non-Indian use	9,554	532	-	532	250	83,044	7,631	4,404	17,731	123,146
Idle	102,400	-	-	-	84,874	51,322	18,859	47,150	2,814	307,419
Total	13,486,279	4,560,601	1,236,371	3,337,992	100,473	194,453	47,895	1,028,516	124,262	19,556,941
Other	-	-	-	-	-	-	-	-	-	-
Grand Total	13,486,979	4,560,601	1,236,371	3,337,992	100,473	194,453	47,895	1,028,516	124,262	19,556,941

Source: Bureau of Indian Affairs Natural Resource Information System Inventory and Production Report, 1989, United States Department of the Interior, Report No. 55-38-X, p. 1. *Notes:* A dash (-) indicates no data given in original source. 1. Total excludes Forest Grazing.

★ 682 ★

Ownership and Use of Lands Under BIA Jurisdiction in California

Numbers are shown in acres.

Ownership	Open grazing	Forest grazing	Commercial forestlands	Non-commercial forestlands	Dry farming	Irrigation projects	Private irrigation	Wild lands excluding timber	Other uses non-agricultural	Total[1]
Tribally owned										
Indian use	111,075	75,499	210,950	33,092	532	3,810	320	94,814	23,013	477,606
Non-Indian use	5,825	-	-	-	3,560	166	6,771	31,945	9,726	57,993
Idle	70,487	-	-	-	1,171	480	4,413	7,019	2,736	86,306
Total	187,387	75,499	210,950	33,092	5,263	4,456	11,504	133,778	35,475	621,905
Individually owned										
Indian use	8,605	1,520	11,763	218	2,141	1,373	275	-	2,521	26,896
Non-Indian use	1,040	-	-	-	1,737	6,859	750	568	372	11,326
Idle	458	-	-	-	-	63	160	-	637	1,318
Total	10,103	1,520	11,763	218	3,878	8,295	1,185	568	3,530	39,540
Government owned										
Indian use	-	-	-	-	-	-	-	2	147	149
Non-Indian use	-	-	-	-	-	-	-	-	8	8
Idle	-	-	-	-	-	-	-	-	91	91
Total	-	-	-	-	-	-	-	2	246	248
Totals										
Indian use	119,680	77,019	222,713	33,310	2,673	5,183	595	94,816	25,681	504,651
Non-Indian use	6,865	-	-	-	5,297	7,025	7,521	32,513	10,106	69,327
Idle	70,945	-	-	-	1,171	543	4,573	7,019	3,464	87,715
Total	197,490	77,019	222,713	33,310	9,141	12,751	12,689	134,348	39,251	661,693
Other	1,868	-	-	-	-	-	-	-	584	2,452
Grand Total	199,358	77,019	222,713	33,310	9,141	12,751	12,689	134,348	39,835	664,145

Source: Bureau of Indian Affairs Natural Resource Information System Inventory and Production Report, 1989, United States Department of the Interior, Report No. 55-38-X, p. 1. *Notes:* A dash (-) indicates no data given in original source. 1. Total excludes Forest Grazing.

★ 683 ★

Ownership and Use of Lands Under BIA Jurisdiction in Colorado

Numbers are shown in acres.

Ownership	Open grazing	Forest grazing	Commercial forestlands	Non-commercial forestlands	Dry farming	Irrigation projects	Private irrigation	Wild lands excluding timber	Other uses non-agricultural	Total[1]
Tribally owned										
Indian use	408,039	129,415	65,293	226,298	-	5,289	984	92,088	3,272	801,263
Non-Indian use	11,582	26,060	-	-	300	8,863	-	-	593	21,338
Idle	7,870	-	-	-	-	-	-	-	-	7,870
Total	427,491	155,475	65,293	226,298	300	14,152	984	92,088	3,865	830,471
Individually owned										
Indian use	243	-	-	-	-	773	-	-	94	1,110
Non-Indian use	690	-	-	-	-	1,011	-	-	73	1,774
Idle	-	-	-	-	-	-	-	-	-	-
Total	933	-	-	-	-	1,784	-	-	167	2,884
Government owned										
Indian use	-	-	-	-	-	-	-	-	-	-
Non-Indian use	-	-	-	-	-	-	-	-	32	32
Idle	-	-	-	-	-	-	-	-	-	-

[Continued]

★ 683 ★

Ownership and Use of Lands Under BIA Jurisdiction in Colorado
[Continued]

Ownership	Open grazing	Forest grazing	Commercial forestlands	Non-commercial forestlands	Dry farming	Irrigation projects	Private irrigation	Wild lands excluding timber	Other uses non-agricultural	Total[1]
Total	-	-	-	-	-	-	-	-	32	32
Totals										
Indian use	408,282	129,415	65,293	226,298	-	6,062	984	92,088	3,366	802,373
Non-Indian use	12,272	26,060	-	-	300	9,874	-	-	698	23,144
Idle	7,870	-	-	-	-	-	-	-	-	7,870
Total	428,424	155,475	65,293	226,298	300	15,936	984	92,088	4,064	833,387
Other	29,531	20,000	-	-	-	3,070	290	-	-	32,891
Grand Total	457,955	175,475	65,293	226,298	300	19,006	1,274	92,088	4,064	866,278

Source: Bureau of Indian Affairs Natural Resource Information System Inventory and Production Report, 1989, United States Department of the Interior, Report No. 55-38-X, p. 1. *Notes:* A dash (-) indicates no data given in original source. 1. Total excludes Forest Grazing.

★ 684 ★

Ownership and Use of Lands Under BIA Jurisdiction in Florida

Numbers are shown in acres.

Ownership	Open grazing	Forest grazing	Commercial forestlands	Non-commercial forestlands	Dry farming	Irrigation projects	Private irrigation	Wild lands excluding timber	Other uses non-agricultural	Total[1]
Tribally owned										
Indian use	29,437	-	6,760	37,100	-	-	27,511	52,512	410	153,730
Non-Indian use	-	-	-	-	-	-	-	-	-	-
Idle	-	-	-	-	-	-	-	-	-	-
Total	29,437	-	6,760	37,100	-	-	27,511	52,512	410	153,730
Individually owned										
Indian use	-	-	-	-	-	-	-	-	-	-
Non-Indian use	-	-	-	-	-	-	-	-	-	-
Idle	-	-	-	-	-	-	-	-	-	-
Total	-	-	-	-	-	-	-	-	-	-
Government owned										
Indian use	-	-	-	-	-	-	-	-	-	-
Non-Indian use	-	-	-	-	-	-	-	-	-	-
Idle	-	-	-	-	-	-	-	-	-	-
Total	-	-	-	-	-	-	-	-	-	-
Totals										
Indian use	29,437	-	6,760	37,100	-	-	27,511	52,512	410	153,730
Non-Indian use	-	-	-	-	-	-	-	-	-	-
Idle	-	-	-	-	-	-	-	-	-	-
Total	29,437	-	6,760	37,100	-	-	27,511	52,512	410	153,730
Other	960	-	-	-	-	-	-	8,640	-	9,600
Grand Total	30,397	-	6,760	37,100	-	-	27,511	61,152	410	163,330

Source: Bureau of Indian Affairs Natural Resource Information System Inventory and Production Report, 1989, United States Department of the Interior, Report No. 55-38-X, p. 1. *Notes:* A dash (-) indicates no data given in original source. 1. Total excludes Forest Grazing.

★ 685 ★

Ownership and Use of Lands Under BIA Jurisdiction in Iowa

Numbers are shown in acres.

Ownership	Open grazing	Forest grazing	Commercial forestlands	Non-commercial forestlands	Dry farming	Irrigation projects	Private irrigation	Wild lands excluding timber	Other uses non-agricultural	Total[1]
Tribally owned										
Indian use	-	-	-	1,976	500	-	-	250	250	2,976
Non-Indian use	-	-	-	-	-	390	-	-	-	390
Idle	-	-	-	-	-	-	-	-	-	-
Total	-	-	-	1,976	500	390	-	250	250	3,366
Individually owned										
Indian use	-	-	-	-	-	-	-	-	-	-
Non-Indian use	-	-	-	-	-	-	-	-	-	-
Idle	-	-	-	-	-	-	-	-	-	-
Total	-	-	-	-	-	-	-	-	-	-
Government owned										
Indian use	-	-	-	-	-	-	-	-	-	-
Non-Indian use	-	-	-	-	-	-	-	-	-	-
Idle	-	-	-	-	-	-	-	-	-	-
Total	-	-	-	-	-	-	-	-	-	-
Totals										
Indian use	-	-	-	1,976	500	-	-	250	250	2,976
Non-Indian use	-	-	-	-	-	390	-	-	-	390
Idle	-	-	-	-	-	-	-	-	-	-
Total	-	-	-	1,976	500	390	-	250	250	3,366
Other										
Grand Total	-	-	-	1,976	500	390	-	250	250	3,366

Source: Bureau of Indian Affairs Natural Resource Information System Inventory and Production Report, 1989, United States Department of the Interior, Report No. 55-38-X, p. 1. *Notes:* A dash (-) indicates no data given in original source. 1. Total excludes Forest Grazing.

★ 686 ★

Ownership and Use of Lands Under BIA Jurisdiction in Kansas

Numbers are shown in acres.

Ownership	Open grazing	Forest grazing	Commercial forestlands	Non-commercial forestlands	Dry farming	Irrigation projects	Private irrigation	Wild lands excluding timber	Other uses non-agricultural	Total[1]
Tribally owned										
Indian use	1,400	-	-	236	2,588	-	-	-	2,129	6,353
Non-Indian use	860	-	-	-	234	-	-	-	-	1,094
Idle	119	-	-	-	113	-	-	-	-	232
Total	2,379	-	-	236	2,935	-	-	-	2,129	7,679
Individually owned										
Indian use	1,169	-	-	13	652	-	-	-	5,001	6,835
Non-Indian use	9,015	48	-	107	4,589	-	-	-	262	13,973
Idle	613	-	-	80	23	-	-	-	-	716
Total	10,797	48	-	200	5,264	-	-	-	5,263	21,524
Government owned										
Indian use	-	-	-	-	-	-	-	-	-	-
Non-Indian use	-	-	-	-	-	-	-	-	-	-
Idle	-	-	-	-	-	-	-	-	-	-

[Continued]

★ 686 ★

Ownership and Use of Lands Under BIA Jurisdiction in Kansas
[Continued]

Ownership	Open grazing	Forest grazing	Commercial forestlands	Non-commercial forestlands	Dry farming	Irrigation projects	Private irrigation	Wild lands excluding timber	Other uses non-agricultural	Total[1]
Total	-	-	-	-	-	-	-	-	-	-
Totals										
Indian use	2,569	-	-	249	3,240	-	-	-	7,130	13,188
Non-Indian use	9,875	48	-	107	4,823	-	-	-	262	15,067
Idle	732	-	-	80	136	-	-	-	-	948
Total	13,176	48	-	436	8,199	-	-	-	7,392	29,203
Other	-	-	-	-	-	-	-	-	-	-
Grand Total	13,176	48	-	436	8,199	-	-	-	7,392	29,203

Source: Bureau of Indian Affairs Natural Resource Information System Inventory and Production Report, 1989, United States Department of the Interior, Report No. 55-38-X, p. 1. *Notes:* A dash (-) indicates no data given in original source. 1. Total excludes Forest Grazing.

★ 687 ★

Ownership and Use of Lands Under BIA Jurisdiction in Maine

Numbers are shown in acres.

Ownership	Open grazing	Forest grazing	Commercial forestlands	Non-commercial forestlands	Dry farming	Irrigation projects	Private irrigation	Wild lands excluding timber	Other uses non-agricultural	Total[1]
Tribally owned										
Indian use	-	-	191,796	17,845	2,070	-	-	1,515	900	214,126
Non-Indian use	-	-	-	-	-	-	-	-	-	-
Idle	-	-	-	-	-	-	-	-	-	-
Total	-	-	191,796	17,845	2,070	-	-	1,515	900	214,126
Individually owned										
Indian use	-	-	-	-	-	-	3,455	-	-	3,455
Non-Indian use	-	-	-	-	-	-	-	-	-	-
Idle	-	-	-	-	-	-	-	-	-	-
Total	-	-	-	-	-	-	3,455	-	-	3,455
Government owned										
Indian use	-	-	-	-	-	-	-	-	-	-
Non-Indian use	-	-	-	-	-	-	-	-	-	-
Idle	-	-	-	-	-	-	-	-	-	-
Total	-	-	-	-	-	-	-	-	-	-
Totals										
Indian use	-	-	191,796	17,845	2,070	-	3,455	1,515	900	217,581
Non-Indian use	-	-	-	-	-	-	-	-	-	-
Idle	-	-	-	-	-	-	-	-	-	-
Total	-	-	191,796	17,845	2,070	-	3,455	1,515	900	217,581
Other	-	-	-	-	-	-	3,455	-	-	3,455
Grand Total	-	-	191,796	17,845	2,070	-	6,910	1,515	900	221,036

Source: Bureau of Indian Affairs Natural Resource Information System Inventory and Production Report, 1989, United States Department of the Interior, Report No. 55-38-X, p. 1. *Notes:* A dash (-) indicates no data given in original source. 1. Total excludes Forest Grazing.

★ 688 ★

Ownership and Use of Lands Under BIA Jurisdiction in Michigan

Numbers are shown in acres.

Ownership	Open grazing	Forest grazing	Commercial forestlands	Non-commercial forestlands	Dry farming	Irrigation projects	Private irrigation	Wild lands excluding timber	Other uses non-agricultural	Total[1]
Tribally owned										
Indian use	-	-	10,258	60	-	-	-	-	3,248	13,566
Non-Indian use	-	-	-	-	-	-	-	-	-	-
Idle	-	-	-	-	-	-	-	-	-	-
Total	-	-	10,258	60	-	-	-	-	3,248	13,566
Individually owned										
Indian use	-	-	7,349	240	-	-	-	-	1,593	9,182
Non-Indian use	-	-	-	-	-	-	-	-	-	-
Idle	-	-	-	-	-	-	-	-	-	-
Total	-	-	7,349	240	-	-	-	-	1,593	9,182
Government owned										
Indian use	-	-	-	-	-	-	-	-	-	-
Non-Indian use	-	-	-	-	-	-	-	-	-	-
Idle	-	-	-	-	-	-	-	-	-	-
Total	-	-	-	-	-	-	-	-	-	-
Totals										
Indian use	-	-	17,607	300	-	-	-	-	4,841	22,748
Non-Indian use	-	-	-	-	-	-	-	-	-	-
Idle	-	-	-	-	-	-	-	-	-	-
Total	-	-	17,607	300	-	-	-	-	-	-
Other	-	-	-	-	-	-	-	-	-	-
Grand Total	-	-	17,607	300	-	-	-	-	4,841	22,748

Source: *Bureau of Indian Affairs Natural Resource Information System Inventory and Production Report, 1989*, United States Department of the Interior, Report No. 55-38-X, p. 1. *Notes:* A dash (-) indicates no data given in original source. 1. Total excludes Forest Grazing.

★ 689 ★

Ownership and Use of Lands Under BIA Jurisdiction in Minnesota

Numbers are shown in acres.

Ownership	Open grazing	Forest grazing	Commercial forestlands	Non-commercial forestlands	Dry farming	Irrigation projects	Private irrigation	Wild lands excluding timber	Other uses non-agricultural	Total[1]
Tribally owned										
Indian use	2,304	10	467,369	101,894	10,014	710	-	130,842	15,045	728,178
Non-Indian use	-	-	-	-	1,569	-	-	-	3,000	4,459
Idle	864	-	-	-	-	-	-	-	1,096	1,960
Total	3,168	10	467,369	101,894	11,583	710	-	130,842	19,141	1,960
Individually owned										
Indian use	-	-	29,546	2,253	-	-	-	3,311	589	35,699
Non-Indian use	-	-	-	-	-	-	-	-	-	-
Idle	-	-	-	-	40	-	-	-	-	40
Total	-	-	29,546	2,253	40	-	-	3,311	589	35,739
Government owned										
Indian use	-	-	79	-	-	-	-	-	4	83
Non-Indian use	-	-	-	-	-	-	-	-	-	-
Idle	-	-	-	-	-	-	-	-	-	-

[Continued]

★ 689 ★

Ownership and Use of Lands Under BIA Jurisdiction in Minnesota

[Continued]

Ownership	Open grazing	Forest grazing	Commercial forestlands	Non-commercial forestlands	Dry farming	Irrigation projects	Private irrigation	Wild lands excluding timber	Other uses non-agricultural	Total[1]
Total	-	-	79	-	-	-	-	-	4	83
Totals										
Indian use	2,304	10	496,994	104,147	10,014	710	-	134,153	15,638	763,960
Non-Indian use	-	-	-	-	1,569	-	-	-	3,000	4,569
Idle	864	-	-	-	40	-	-	-	1,096	2,000
Total	3,168	10	496,994	104,147	11,623	710	-	134,153	19,734	770,529
Other	-	-	8,911	2,917	60	-	-	354	85	35,739
Grand Total	3,168	10	505,905	107,064	11,683	710	-	134,507	19,819	782,856

Source: Bureau of Indian Affairs Natural Resource Information System Inventory and Production Report, 1989, United States Department of the Interior, Report No. 55-38-X, p. 1. *Notes:* A dash (-) indicates no data given in original source. 1. Total excludes Forest Grazing.

★ 690 ★

Ownership and Use of Lands Under BIA Jurisdiction in Mississippi

Numbers are shown in acres.

Ownership	Open grazing	Forest grazing	Commercial forestlands	Non-commercial forestlands	Dry farming	Irrigation projects	Private irrigation	Wild lands excluding timber	Other uses non-agricultural	Total[1]
Tribally owned										
Indian use	701	60	16,220	160	514	-	-	-	2,873	20,468
Non-Indian use	-	-	-	-	-	-	-	-	-	-
Idle	-	-	-	-	-	-	-	-	-	-
Total	701	60	16,220	160	514	-	-	-	2,873	20,468
Individually owned										
Indian use	-	-	-	-	-	-	-	-	-	-
Non-Indian use	-	-	-	-	-	-	-	-	-	-
Idle	-	-	-	-	-	-	-	-	-	-
Total	-	-	-	-	-	-	-	-	-	-
Government owned										
Indian use	-	-	28	-	-	-	-	-	99	127
Non-Indian use	-	-	-	-	-	-	-	-	-	-
Idle	-	-	-	-	-	-	-	-	-	-
Total	-	-	28	-	-	-	-	-	99	127
Totals										
Indian use	701	60	16,248	160	514	-	-	-	2,972	20,595
Non-Indian use	-	-	-	-	-	-	-	-	-	-
Idle	-	-	-	-	-	-	-	-	-	-
Total	701	60	16,248	160	514	-	-	-	2,972	20,595
Other	-	-	-	-	-	-	-	-	-	-
Grand Total	701	60	16,248	160	514	-	-	-	2,972	20,595

Source: Bureau of Indian Affairs Natural Resource Information System Inventory and Production Report, 1989, United States Department of the Interior, Report No. 55-38-X, p. 1. *Notes:* A dash (-) indicates no data given in original source. 1. Total excludes Forest Grazing.

★ 691 ★

Ownership and Use of Lands Under BIA Jurisdiction in Montana

Numbers are shown in acres.

Ownership	Open grazing	Forest grazing	Commercial forestlands	Non-commercial forestlands	Dry farming	Irrigation projects	Private irrigation	Wild lands excluding timber	Other uses non-agricultural	Total[1]
Tribally owned										
Indian use	947,546	479,610	477,926	380,891	167,465	15,308	1,928	44,507	26,402	2,061,973
Non-Indian use	289,144	42,232	-	-	42,279	4,661	325	-	393	336,802
Idle	59,539	-	-	-	662	1,126	-	-	1,792	63,119
Total	1,296,229	521,842	477,926	380,891	210,406	21,095	2,253	44,507	28,587	2,461,894
Individually owned										
Indian use	1,055,343	33,006	55,769	75,228	239,682	25,855	5,993	12,613	3,895	1,474,378
Non-Indian use	916,172	10,502	-	-	411,071	32,749	3,453	-	3,545	1,366,990
Idle	58,311	-	-	-	23,419	28,858	1,024	-	178	111,790
Total	2,029,826	43,508	55,769	75,228	674,172	87,462	10,470	12,613	7,618	2,953,158
Government owned										
Indian use	397	342	-	125	87	293	-	-	7,690	8,592
Non-Indian use	120	-	-	-	112	110	-	-	1	343
Idle	-	-	-	-	-	40	-	-	-	40
Total	517	342	-	125	199	443	-	-	7,691	8,975
Totals										
Indian use	2,003,286	512,958	533,695	456,244	407,234	41,456	7,921	57,120	37,987	3,544,943
Non-Indian use	1,205,436	52,734	-	-	453,462	37,520	3,778	-	3,939	1,704,135
Idle	117,850	-	-	-	24,081	30,024	1,024	-	1,970	174,949
Total	3,326,572	565,692	533,695	456,244	884,777	109,000	12,723	57,120	43,896	5,424,027
Other	60,607	6,067	6,067	-	1,658	42,751	200	-	70	111,353
Grand Total	3,387,179	571,759	539,762	456,244	886,435	151,751	12,923	57,120	43,966	5,535,380

Source: Bureau of Indian Affairs Natural Resource Information System Inventory and Production Report, 1989, United States Department of the Interior, Report No. 55-38-X, p. 1. *Notes:* A dash (-) indicates no data given in original source. 1. Total excludes Forest Grazing.

★ 692 ★

Ownership and Use of Lands Under BIA Jurisdiction in Nebraska

Numbers are shown in acres.

Ownership	Open grazing	Forest grazing	Commercial forestlands	Non-commercial forestlands	Dry farming	Irrigation projects	Private irrigation	Wild lands excluding timber	Other uses non-agricultural	Total[1]
Tribally owned										
Indian use	5,718	19	3,606	1,083	6,185	-	-	1,210	2,156	19,958
Non-Indian use	25	-	-	-	2,049	2,855	-	4,728	777	10,434
Idle	-	-	-	-	-	586	-	-	-	586
Total	5,743	19	3,606	1,083	8,234	3,441	-	5,938	2,933	30,978
Individually owned										
Indian use	24	31	1,459	720	2,154	-	-	2,658	902	7,917
Non-Indian use	6,203	79	4,172	952	12,165	-	-	3,998	1,167	28,657
Idle	-	-	-	-	-	-	-	-	-	-
Total	6,227	110	5,631	1,672	14,319	-	-	6,656	2,069	36,574
Government owned										
Indian use	-	-	-	-	-	-	-	-	-	-
Non-Indian use	-	-	-	-	-	-	-	-	-	-
Idle	-	-	-	-	-	-	-	-	-	-

[Continued]

★ 692 ★

Ownership and Use of Lands Under BIA Jurisdiction in Nebraska

[Continued]

Ownership	Open grazing	Forest grazing	Commercial forestlands	Non-commercial forestlands	Dry farming	Irrigation projects	Private irrigation	Wild lands excluding timber	Other uses non-agricultural	Total[1]
Total	-	-	-	-	-	-	-	-	-	-
Totals										
Indian use	5,742	50	5,065	1,803	8,339	-	-	3,868	3,058	27,875
Non-Indian use	6,228	79	4,172	952	14,214	2,855	-	8,726	1,944	39,091
Idle	-	-	-	-	-	584	-	-	-	584
Total	11,970	129	9,237	2,755	22,553	3,441	-	12,594	5,002	67,552
Other	-	-	-	-	-	-	-	-	-	-
Grand Total	11,970	129	9,237	2,755	22,553	3,441	-	12,594	5,002	67,552

Source: Bureau of Indian Affairs Natural Resource Information System Inventory and Production Report, 1989, United States Department of the Interior, Report No. 55-38-X, p. 1. *Notes:* A dash (-) indicates no data given in original source. 1. Total excludes Forest Grazing.

★ 693 ★

Ownership and Use of Lands Under BIA Jurisdiction in Nevada

Numbers are shown in acres.

Ownership	Open grazing	Forest grazing	Commercial forestlands	Non-commercial forestlands	Dry farming	Irrigation projects	Private irrigation	Wild lands excluding timber	Other uses non-agricultural	Total[1]
Tribally owned										
Indian use	930,291	3,000	-	17,341	2,717	28,142	159	10,121	8,716	997,487
Non-Indian use	12,160	-	-	-	-	-	465	-	-	12,625
Idle	72,873	-	-	-	-	8,917	62	-	143,073	224,925
Total	1,015,324	3,000	-	17,341	2,717	37,059	686	10,121	151,789	1,235,037
Individually owned										
Indian use	4,210	-	-	-	-	4,197	-	-	1,207	9,614
Non-Indian use	-	-	-	-	-	-	-	-	-	-
Idle	4,028	-	-	-	-	540	-	-	120	4,688
Total	8,238	-	-	-	-	4,737	-	-	1,327	4,688
Government owned										
Indian use	-	-	-	-	-	-	-	-	964	964
Non-Indian use	-	-	-	-	-	-	-	-	-	-
Idle	42,880	-	-	3,000	-	-	-	-	-	45,880
Total	42,880	-	-	3,000	-	-	-	-	964	46,844
Totals										
Indian use	934,501	3,000	-	17,341	2,717	32,339	159	10,121	10,887	1,008,065
Non-Indian use	12,160	-	-	-	-	-	465	-	-	12,625
Idle	119,781	-	-	3,000	-	9,457	62	-	143,193	275,493
Total	1,066,442	3,000	-	20,341	2,717	41,796	686	10,121	154,080	1,296,183
Other	-	-	-	-	-	-	-	-	-	-
Grand Total	1,066,442	3,000	-	20,341	2,717	41,796	686	10,121	154,080	1,296,183

Source: Bureau of Indian Affairs Natural Resource Information System Inventory and Production Report, 1989, United States Department of the Interior, Report No. 55-38-X, p. 1. *Notes:* A dash (-) indicates no data given in original source. 1. Total excludes Forest Grazing.

★ 694 ★

Ownership and Use of Lands Under BIA Jurisdiction in New Mexico

Numbers are shown in acres.

Ownership	Open grazing	Forest grazing	Commercial forestlands	Non-commercial forestlands	Dry farming	Irrigation projects	Private irrigation	Wild lands excluding timber	Other uses non-agricultural	Total[1]
Tribally owned										
Indian use	4,961,369	1,698,649	653,073	1,101,502	4,569	16,130	10,724	205,062	53,067	7,005,496
Non-Indian use	15,874	-	-	-	452	-	600	3,183	14,220	34,329
Idle	-	-	-	-	1,056	13,127	11,564	-	8,490	34,237
Total	4,977,243	1,698,649	653,073	1,101,502	6,077	29,257	22,888	208,245	75,777	7,074,062
Individually owned										
Indian use	563,237	120,070	10,705	109,365	975	80	-	5,101	2,000	691,463
Non-Indian use	-	-	-	-	-	-	-	-	-	-
Idle	-	-	-	-	-	-	-	-	-	-
Total	563,237	120,070	10,705	109,365	975	80	-	5,101	2,000	691,463
Government owned										
Indian use	217,840	4,000	-	4,000	-	-	-	-	8,219	230,059
Non-Indian use	-	-	-	-	-	-	-	-	6	6
Idle	-	-	-	-	-	-	-	-	-	-
Total	217,840	4,000	-	4,000	-	-	-	-	8,225	230,065
Totals										
Indian use	5,742,446	1,822,719	663,778	1,214,867	5,544	16,210	10,724	210,163	63,286	7,927,018
Non-Indian use	15,874	-	-	-	452	-	600	3,183	14,226	34,335
Idle	-	-	-	-	1,056	13,127	11,564	-	8,490	34,237
Total	5,758,320	1,822,719	663,778	1,214,867	7,052	29,337	22,888	213,346	86,002	7,995,590
Other	65,442	-	-	-	-	6	-	80	-	65,528
Grand Total	5,823,762	1,822,719	663,778	1,214,867	7,052	29,343	22,888	213,426	86,002	8,061,118

Source: Bureau of Indian Affairs Natural Resource Information System Inventory and Production Report, 1989, United States Department of the Interior, Report No. 55-38-X, p. 1. *Notes:* A dash (-) indicates no data given in original source. 1. Total excludes Forest Grazing.

★ 695 ★

Ownership and Use of Lands Under BIA Jurisdiction in North Carolina

Numbers are shown in acres.

Ownership	Open grazing	Forest grazing	Commercial forestlands	Non-commercial forestlands	Dry farming	Irrigation projects	Private irrigation	Wild lands excluding timber	Other uses non-agricultural	Total[1]
Tribally owned										
Indian use	410	190	45,000	-	400	-	-	-	-	45,810
Non-Indian use	-	-	-	-	-	-	-	-	-	-
Idle	210	-	-	-	175	-	-	-	-	385
Total	620	190	45,000	-	575	-	-	-	-	46,195
Individually owned										
Indian use	-	-	-	-	-	-	-	-	-	-
Non-Indian use	-	-	-	-	-	-	-	-	-	-
Idle	-	-	-	-	-	-	-	-	-	-
Total	-	-	-	-	-	-	-	-	-	-
Government owned										
Indian use	-	-	-	-	-	-	-	-	-	-
Non-Indian use	-	-	-	-	-	-	-	-	-	-
Idle	-	-	-	-	-	-	-	-	-	-

[Continued]

★ 695 ★

Ownership and Use of Lands Under BIA Jurisdiction in North Carolina
[Continued]

Ownership	Open grazing	Forest grazing	Commercial forestlands	Non-commercial forestlands	Dry farming	Irrigation projects	Private irrigation	Wild lands excluding timber	Other uses non-agricultural	Total[1]
Total	-	-	-	-	-	-	-	-	-	-
Totals										
Indian use	410	190	45,000	-	400	-	-	-	-	45,810
Non-Indian use	-	-	-	-	-	-	-	-	-	-
Idle	210	-	-	-	175	-	-	-	-	385
Total	620	190	45,000	-	575	-	-	-	-	46,195
Other	-	-	-	-	-	-	-	-	-	-
Grand Total	620	190	45,000	-	575	-	-	-	-	46,195

Source: Bureau of Indian Affairs Natural Resource Information System Inventory and Production Report, 1989, United States Department of the Interior, Report No. 55-38-X, p. 1. *Notes:* A dash (-) indicates no data given in original source. 1. Total excludes Forest Grazing.

★ 696 ★

Ownership and Use of Lands Under BIA Jurisdiction in North Dakota

Numbers are shown in acres.

Ownership	Open grazing	Forest grazing	Commercial forestlands	Non-commercial forestlands	Dry farming	Irrigation projects	Private irrigation	Wild lands excluding timber	Other uses non-agricultural	Total[1]
Tribally owned										
Indian use	250,482	19,972	17,352	26,759	14,207	963	80	4,476	5,286	319,605
Non-Indian use	141,549	652	-	4,744	11,984	2,040	-	-	478	160,797
Idle	-	-	-	1,102	65,040	-	-	525	695	67,362
Total	392,031	20,624	17,352	32,607	91,231	3,003	80	5,001	6,459	547,764
Individually owned										
Indian use	489,580	13,730	10,604	8,483	24,611	37	-	2,984	18,978	555,277
Non-Indian use	248,654	2,735	-	-	81,255	-	-	-	1,523	331,432
Idle	25,536	-	-	-	1,908	-	-	-	368	27,812
Total	763,770	16,465	10,604	8,483	107,774	37	-	2,984	20,869	914,521
Government owned										
Indian use	100	101	100	-	-	-	-	-	339	539
Non-Indian use	-	-	-	-	-	-	-	-	191	191
Idle	-	-	-	-	-	-	-	-	-	-
Total	100	101	100	-	-	-	-	-	530	730
Totals										
Indian use	740,162	33,803	28,056	35,242	38,818	1,000	80	7,400	24,603	875,421
Non-Indian use	390,203	3,387	-	4,746	93,239	2,040	-	-	2,192	492,420
Idle	25,536	-	-	1,102	66,948	-	-	525	1,063	95,174
Total	1,155,901	37,190	28,056	41,090	199,005	3,040	80	7,985	27,858	1,463,015
Other	-	-	-	-	-	-	-	-	-	-
Grand Total	1,155,901	37,190	28,056	41,090	199,005	3,040	80	7,985	27,858	1,463,015

Source: Bureau of Indian Affairs Natural Resource Information System Inventory and Production Report, 1989, United States Department of the Interior, Report No. 55-38-X, p. 1. *Notes:* A dash (-) indicates no data given in original source. 1. Total excludes Forest Grazing.

★ 697 ★

Ownership and Use of Lands Under BIA Jurisdiction in Oklahoma

Numbers are shown in acres.

Ownership	Open grazing	Forest grazing	Commercial forestlands	Non-commercial forestlands	Dry farming	Irrigation projects	Private irrigation	Wild lands excluding timber	Other uses non-agricultural	Total[1]
Tribally owned										
Indian use	28,825	58,883	69,268	6,596	2,695	-	-	-	7,032	114,416
Non-Indian use	31,945	9,963	-	3,153	27,060	-	-	-	30,181	92,339
Idle	9,026	-	-	10,415	168	-	-	-	2,372	21,981
Total	69,796	68,846	69,268	20,164	29,923	-	-	-	39,585	228,736
Individually owned										
Indian use	203,590	34,244	40,326	98,279	22,725	2,600		-	13,579	381,099
Non-Indian use	610,281	82,874	-	46,809	179,865	6,012	110	-	22,643	865,720
Idle	10,003	-	-	2,506	5,290	16	-	-	8,785	26,600
Total	823,874	117,118	40,326	147,594	207,880	8,628	110	-	45,007	1,273,419
Government owned										
Indian use	-	60	60	-	-	-	-	-	673	733
Non-Indian use	-	179	179	-	10	-	-	-	6	195
Idle	-	-	-	-	-	-	-	-	349	349
Total	-	239	239	-	10	-	-	-	1,028	1,277
Totals										
Indian use	232,415	93,187	109,654	104,875	25,420	2,600	-	-	21,284	496,248
Non-Indian use	642,226	93,016	179	49,962	206,935	6,012	110	-	52,830	958,254
Idle	19,029	-	-	12,921	5,458	16	-	-	11,506	48,930
Total	893,670	186,203	109,833	167,758	237,813	8,628	110	-	85,620	1,503,432
Other	49	9	20	18	-	-	-	-	-	87
Grand Total	893,719	186,212	109,853	167,776	237,813	8,628	110	-	85,620	1,503,519

Source: Bureau of Indian Affairs Natural Resource Information System Inventory and Production Report, 1989, United States Department of the Interior, Report No. 55-38-X, p. 1. *Notes:* A dash (-) indicates no data given in original source. 1. Total excludes Forest Grazing.

★ 698 ★

Ownership and Use of Lands Under BIA Jurisdiction in Oregon

Numbers are shown in acres.

Ownership	Open grazing	Forest grazing	Commercial forestlands	Non-commercial forestlands	Dry farming	Irrigation projects	Private irrigation	Wild lands excluding timber	Other uses non-agricultural	Total[1]
Tribally owned										
Indian use	180,222	328,277	369,664	35,314	1,225	260	29	20,375	4,139	611,228
Non-Indian use	7,415	51,592	-	-	358	-	-	1,350	1,200	10,323
Idle	1,279	-	-	-	8,875	301	27	-	-	10,482
Total	188,916	379,869	369,664	35,314	10,458	561	56	21,725	5,339	632,033
Individually owned										
Indian use	44,050	18,053	15,277	3,131	710	160	47	867	1,538	65,780
Non-Indian use	35,250	-	80	-	25,142	-	373	-	527	61,372
Idle	5,058	-	-	-	4,322	691	-	-	-	10,071
Total	84,358	18,053	15,357	3,131	30,174	851	420	867	2,065	137,223
Government owned										
Indian use	-	-	-	-	-	-	-	-	16	16
Non-Indian use	-	-	-	-	-	-	-	-	122	122
Idle	-	-	-	-	-	-	-	-	-	-

[Continued]

★ 698 ★

Ownership and Use of Lands Under BIA Jurisdiction in Oregon

[Continued]

Ownership	Open grazing	Forest grazing	Commercial forestlands	Non-commercial forestlands	Dry farming	Irrigation projects	Private irrigation	Wild lands excluding timber	Other uses non-agricultural	Total[1]
Total	-	-	-	-	-	-	-	-	138	138
Totals										
Indian use	224,272	346,330	384,941	38,445	1,935	420	76	21,242	5,693	677,024
Non-Indian use	42,665	51,592	80	-	25,500	-	373	1,350	1,849	71,817
Idle	6,337	-	-	-	13,197	992	27	-	-	20,553
Total	273,274	397,922	385,021	38,445	40,632	1,412	476	22,592	7,542	769,394
Other	4,226	-	-	-	-	180	200	50	-	4,656
Grand Total	277,500	397,922	385,021	38,445	40,632	1,592	676	22,642	7,542	774,050

Source: Bureau of Indian Affairs Natural Resource Information System Inventory and Production Report, 1989, United States Department of the Interior, Report No. 55-38-X, p. 1. *Notes:* A dash (-) indicates no data given in original source. 1. Total excludes Forest Grazing.

★ 699 ★

Ownership and Use of Lands Under BIA Jurisdiction in South Dakota

Numbers are shown in acres.

Ownership	Open grazing	Forest grazing	Commercial forestlands	Non-commercial forestlands	Dry farming	Irrigation projects	Private irrigation	Wild lands excluding timber	Other uses non-agricultural	Total[1]
Tribally owned										
Indian use	1,634,931	35,026	26,417	174,195	26,706	12,598	181	127,217	38,283	2,040,528
Non-Indian use	241,015	-	-	-	44,496	8,403	1,426	5,198	3,273	304,011
Idle	74,734	-	-	-	11,346	-	50	-	25,166	111,296
Total	1,950,680	35,026	26,417	174,195	82,548	21,201	1,657	132,415	66,722	2,455,835
Individually owned										
Indian use	1,078,217	6,899	15,558	77,368	36,046	806	1,384	40,668	18,995	1,269,042
Non-Indian use	485,397	-	-	-	119,790	100	310	-	373	605,970
Idle	109,520	-	-	-	5,995	-	-	-	25,000	140,515
Total	1,673,134	6,899	15,558	77,368	161,831	906	1,694	40,668	44,368	2,015,527
Government owned										
Indian use	35,604	-	300	-	-	30	-	-	1,615	37,549
Non-Indian use	964	-	-	-	-	-	-	-	111	1,075
Idle	-	-	-	-	-	-	-	-	-	-
Total	36,568	-	300	-	-	30	-	-	1,726	38,624
Totals										
Indian use	2,748,752	41,925	42,275	251,563	62,752	13,434	1,565	167,885	58,893	3,347,119
Non-Indian use	727,376	-	-	-	164,286	8,703	1,736	5,198	3,757	911,056
Idle	184,254	-	-	-	17,341	-	50	-	50,166	251,811
Total	3,660,382	41,925	42,275	251,563	244,379	22,137	3,351	173,083	112,816	4,509,984
Other	-	-	-	-	-	-	-	-	-	-
Grand Total	3,660,382	41,925	42,275	251,563	244,379	22,137	3,351	173,083	112,816	4,509,986

Source: Bureau of Indian Affairs Natural Resource Information System Inventory and Production Report, 1989, United States Department of the Interior, Report No. 55-38-X, p. 1. *Notes:* A dash (-) indicates no data given in original source. 1. Total excludes Forest Grazing.

★ 700 ★

Ownership and Use of Lands Under BIA Jurisdiction in Texas

Numbers are shown in acres.

Ownership	Open grazing	Forest grazing	Commercial forestlands	Non-commercial forestlands	Dry farming	Irrigation projects	Private irrigation	Wild lands excluding timber	Other uses non-agricultural	Total[1]
Tribally owned										
Indian use	-	-	-	-	-	-	-	-	-	-
Non-Indian use	-	-	4,542	-	-	-	-	-	-	4,542
Idle	-	-	-	-	-	-	-	-	-	-
Total	-	-	4,542	-	-	-	-	-	-	4,542
Individually owned										
Indian use	-	-	-	-	-	-	-	-	-	-
Non-Indian use	-	-	-	-	-	-	-	-	-	-
Idle	-	-	-	-	-	-	-	-	-	-
Total	-	-	-	-	-	-	-	-	-	-
Government owned										
Indian use	-	-	-	-	-	-	-	-	-	-
Non-Indian use	-	-	-	-	-	-	-	-	-	-
Idle	-	-	-	-	-	-	-	-	-	-
Total	-	-	-	-	-	-	-	-	-	-
Totals										
Indian use	-	-	-	-	-	-	-	-	-	-
Non-Indian use	-	-	4,542	-	-	-	-	-	-	4,542
Idle	-	-	-	-	-	-	-	-	-	-
Total	-	-	4,542	-	-	-	-	-	-	4,542
Other	-	-	-	-	-	-	-	-	-	-
Grand Total	-	-	4,542	-	-	-	-	-	-	4,542

Source: Bureau of Indian Affairs Natural Resource Information System Inventory and Production Report, 1989, United States Department of the Interior, Report No. 55-38-X, p. 1. *Notes:* A dash (-) indicates no data given in original source. 1. Total excludes Forest Grazing.

★ 701 ★

Ownership and Use of Lands Under BIA Jurisdiction in Utah

Numbers are shown in acres.

Ownership	Open grazing	Forest grazing	Commercial forestlands	Non-commercial forestlands	Dry farming	Irrigation projects	Private irrigation	Wild lands excluding timber	Other uses non-agricultural	Total[1]
Tribally owned										
Indian use	1,052,592	734,903	29,216	705,585	231	13,989	947	240,042	11,045	2,053,647
Non-Indian use	111,311	-	-	-	-	6,673	1,420	-	952	120,356
Idle	172,884	-	-	-	220	2,085	2,992	-	-	178,181
Total	1,336,787	734,903	29,216	705,585	451	22,747	5,359	240,042	11,997	2,352,184
Individually owned										
Indian use	18,552	560	560	2,285	218	1,870	80	-	177	23,742
Non-Indian use	1,079	-	-	-	301	5,420	255	-	-	7,055
Idle	2,127	-	-	-	-	1,240	140	-	-	3,507
Total	21,758	560	560	2,285	519	8,530	475	-	177	34,304
Government owned										
Indian use	40	-	-	-	-	-	-	-	285	325
Non-Indian use	-	-	-	-	-	-	-	-	2	2
Idle	-	-	-	-	-	-	-	-	-	-

[Continued]

★ 701 ★

Ownership and Use of Lands Under BIA Jurisdiction in Utah

[Continued]

Ownership	Open grazing	Forest grazing	Commercial forestlands	Non-commercial forestlands	Dry farming	Irrigation projects	Private irrigation	Wild lands excluding timber	Other uses non-agricultural	Total[1]
Total	40	-	-	-	-	-	-	-	287	327
Totals										
Indian use	1,071,184	735,463	29,776	707,870	449	15,859	1,027	240,042	11,507	2,077,714
Non-Indian use	112,390	-	-	-	301	12,093	1,675	-	954	127,413
Idle	175,011	-	-	-	220	3,325	3,132	-	-	181,688
Total	1,358,585	735,463	29,776	707,870	970	31,277	5,834	240,042	12,461	2,386,815
Other	176,095	-	-	-	-	-	-	-	-	176,095
Grand Total	1,534,680	735,463	29,776	707,870	970	31,277	5,834	240,042	12,461	

Source: Bureau of Indian Affairs Natural Resource Information System Inventory and Production Report, 1989, United States Department of the Interior, Report No. 55-38-X, p. 1. *Notes:* A dash (-) indicates no data given in original source. 1. Total excludes Forest Grazing.

★ 702 ★

Ownership and Use of Lands Under BIA Jurisdiction in Washington

Numbers are shown in acres.

Ownership	Open grazing	Forest grazing	Commercial forestlands	Non-commercial forestlands	Dry farming	Irrigation projects	Private irrigation	Wild lands excluding timber	Other uses non-agricultural	Total[1]
Tribally owned										
Indian use	489,232	1,111,205	1,216,335	220,808	4,304	2,401	1,654	71,105	23,917	2,029,756
Non-Indian use	41,640	224,967	-	-	2,321	20,744	1,061	-	1,067	66,833
Idle	7,071	-	-	-	666	8,010	1,994	-	241	17,982
Total	537,943	1,336,172	1,216,335	220,808	7,291	31,155	4,709	71,105	25,225	2,114,571
Individually owned										
Indian use	89,194	75,353	246,572	17,310	6,261	12,423	1,665	10,925	7,363	391,713
Non-Indian use	12,065	15,081	-	-	12,256	71,592	1,459	-	3,967	101,339
Idle	19,795	814	-	-	9,744	22,733	120	-	833	53,225
Total	121,054	91,248	246,572	17,310	28,261	106,748	3,244	10,925	12,163	546,277
Government owned										
Indian use	1,843	-	2,082	16	-	-	-	-	8	3,969
Non-Indian use	-	-	-	-	-	-	-	-	31	31
Idle	-	-	-	-	-	-	-	-	-	-
Total	1,843	-	2,082	16	-	-	-	-	39	3,980
Totals										
Indian use	580,269	1,186,558	1,464,989	238,134	10,565	14,824	3,319	82,030	31,288	2,425,418
Non-Indian use	53,705	240,048	-	-	14,577	92,336	2,520	-	5,065	168,203
Idle	26,866	814	-	-	10,410	30,743	2,114	-	1,074	71,207
Total	660,840	1,427,420	1,464,989	238,134	35,552	137,903	7,953	82,030	37,427	2,664,828
Other	135,462	93,560	229,575	20,579	6,496	62,040	2,956	39,310	4,440	500,858
Grand Total	796,302	1,520,980	1,694,564	258,713	42,048	199,943	10,909	121,340	41,867	3,165,686

Source: Bureau of Indian Affairs Natural Resource Information System Inventory and Production Report, 1989, United States Department of the Interior, Report No. 55-38-X, p. 1. *Notes:* A dash (-) indicates no data given in original source. 1. Total excludes Forest Grazing.

★ 703 ★

Ownership and Use of Lands Under BIA Jurisdiction in Wisconsin

Numbers are shown in acres.

Ownership	Open grazing	Forest grazing	Commercial forestlands	Non-commercial forestlands	Dry farming	Irrigation projects	Private irrigation	Wild lands excluding timber	Other uses non-agricultural	Total[1]
Tribally owned										
Indian use	1,013	-	327,457	12,082	390	-	-	21,272	3,936	366,150
Non-Indian use	-	-	-	-	-	-	-	-	1,013	1,013
Idle	-	-	-	-	-	-	-	-	-	-
Total	1,013	-	327,457	12,082	390	-	-	21,272	4,949	367,163
Individually owned										
Indian use	-	-	89,948	5,459	9	-	-	5,995	360	101,771
Non-Indian use	-	-	-	-	-	-	-	-	-	-
Idle	-	-	-	-	-	-	-	-	-	-
Total	-	-	89,948	5,459	9	-	-	5,995	360	101,771
Government owned										
Indian use	-	-	-	-	-	-	-	-	-	-
Non-Indian use	-	-	-	-	-	-	-	-	-	-
Idle	-	-	-	-	-	-	-	-	-	-
Total	-	-	-	-	-	-	-	-	-	-
Totals										
Indian use	1,013	-	417,405	17,541	399	-	-	27,267	4,296	467,921
Non-Indian use	-	-	-	-	-	-	-	-	1,103	1,013
Idle	-	-	-	-	-	-	-	-	-	-
Total	1,103	-	417,405	17,541	399	-	-	27,267	5,309	468,934
Other	-	-	-	-	-	-	-	-	-	-
Grand Total	1,013	-	417,405	17,541	399	-	-	27,267	5,309	468,934

Source: Bureau of Indian Affairs Natural Resource Information System Inventory and Production Report, 1989, United States Department of the Interior, Report No. 55-38-X, p. 1. *Notes:* A dash (-) indicates no data given in original source. 1. Total excludes Forest Grazing.

★ 704 ★

Ownership of Lands Under BIA Jurisdiction: 1881 to 1970

Numbers are shown in thousands of acres, by land ownership and year.

Year	Total	Indian		Government owned
		Trust allotted	Tribal	
1970	55,408	10,698	39,642	5,068
1969	55,351	10,757	39,641	4,952
1968	55,427	10,894	39,586	4,947
1967	55,413	11,019	39,443	4,951
1966	55,294	11,121	39,251	4,922
1965	55,319	11,287	39,097	4,935
1964	55,134	11,450	38,975	4,709
1963	55,196	11,607	38,877	4,713
1962	55,247	11,763	38,814	4,669

[Continued]

★ 704 ★

Ownership of Lands Under BIA Jurisdiction: 1001 to 1970

[Continued]

| Year | Total | Indian | | Government owned |
		Trust allotted	Tribal	
1961	57,107	11,958	40,538	4,612
1960	58,080	12,235	41,226	4,618
1959	56,870	12,560	39,676	4,634
1958	57,023	12,896	42,304	1,823
1957	53,331	13,223	39,549	558
1956	53,376	13,328	39,465	583
1955	53,771	13,662	39,487	622
1954	54,108	13,652	39,882	574
1953	55,406	14,251	40,178	977
1949	56,005	16,534	38,608	863
1946	56,567	17,143	37,524	1,901
1945	55,364	16,796	37,251	1,317
1944	56,577	17,474	37,233	1,869
1943	55,657	17,441	36,957	1,258
1942	55,410	17,503	36,602	1,305
1941	55,392	17,762	36,276	1,354
1940	55,406	17,574	36,047	1,786
1939	54,839	17,594	35,402	1,842
1938	-	-	-	-
1937	34,620	-	34,620	-
1936	51,057	-	51,057	-
1935	50,696	-	50,696	-
1934	49,388	-	49,388	-
1933	52,651	-	47,398	-
1932	46,795	-	46,795	-
1930	32,097	-	32,097	-
1929	32,015	-	32,015	-
1928	30,262	-	30,262	-
1927	31,420	-	31,420	-
1926	31,791	-	31,791	-
1925	31,582	-	31,582	-
1924	34,948	-	34,948	-
1923	34,988	-	34,988	-
1922	34,979	-	34,979	-
1921	35,502	-	35,502	-
1920	72,661	37,159	35,502	-

[Continued]

★ 704 ★

Ownership of Lands Under BIA Jurisdiction: 1881 to 1970

[Continued]

| Year | Total | Indian | | Government owned |
		Trust allotted	Tribal	
1919	72,546	36,986	35,560	-
1918	71,094	36,861	34,233	-
1917	71,306	35,740	35,566	-
1916	71,978	35,565	36,413	-
1915	68,103	34,768	33,334	-
1914	69,900	34,072	35,828	-
1913	72,147	33,571	38,576	-
1912	71,917	32,414	39,503	-
1911	72,535	32,272	40,263	-
1910	72,146	31,094	41,052	-
1909	49,566	-	49,566	-
1908	52,013	-	52,013	-
1907	53,549	-	53,549	-
1906	55,831	-	55,831	-
1905	58,202	-	58,202	-
1904	72,392	-	72,392	-
1903	83,426	8,823	74,603	-
1902	75,149	-	75,149	-
1901	76,117	-	-	-
1900	84,602	6,737	77,865	-
1899	-	-	-	-
1898	-	-	-	-
1897	82,770	-	82,770	-
1896	83,405	-	83,405	-
1895	84,571	-	84,571	-
1894	85,581	-	85,581	-
1893	85,873	-	85,873	-
1892	92,478	-	92,478	-
1891	91,146	-	91,146	-
1890	104,314	-	104,314	-
1889	116,386	-	116,386	-
1888	118,484	-	118,484	-
1887	136,395	-	136,395	-
1886	135,978	-	135,978	-
1885	137,725	-	137,725	-
1884	137,767	-	137,767	-

[Continued]

★ 704 ★

Ownership of Lands Under BIA Jurisdiction 1881 to 1970
[Continued]

Year	Total	Indian		Government owned
		Trust allotted	Tribal	
1882	143,526	-	143,526	-
1881	155,632	-	155,632	-

Source: Historical Statistics of the United States, Colonial Times to 1970, Part I, U.S. Department of Commerce, Bureau of the Census, Washington, D.C., 1975, p. 430. *Note:* A dash (-) indicates no data were given in original source.

★ 705 ★

Products Grown on Indian Lands - Indian Operated

The gross value of products grown on Indian Lands is shown, by land use and ownership.

Land use	Dry farmed, range & forest				Irrigated				Total	
	Owned		Leased		Owned		Leased			
	Acres	Value	Acres	Value	Acres	Value	Acres	Value	Acres	Value
Row crops	18,816	2,305,196	15,333	1,494,527	39,691	27,485,533	3,272,739	18,438,324	3,346,579	49,723,580
Small grains	123,260	8,630,973	165,337	10,661,266	16,515	3,498,571	35,061	4,807,780	340,173	27,598,590
Forage-hay-pasture	75,008	2,762,715	53,767	2,469,975	111,882	15,487,323	105,186	12,036,924	345,843	32,756,937
Horticulture	4,648	3,091,355	277	1,040	2,809	2,579,470	2,146	378,497	9,880	6,050,362
Soil improvement	2,467	6,400	2,167	50,800	146	11,040	200	11,000	4,980	79,240
Fallow	83,802	3,810	109,854	-	14,060	165	35,522	-	243,238	3,975
Outdoor rec. wild	2,302,017	4,329,169	100,000	-	39	6,000	-	-	2,402,056	4,335,169
Native hay	28,071	521,330	32,796	37,325	300	54,000	200	36,000	61,367	648,655
Timber stumpage value	1,983,631	128,752,576	-	-	-	-	-	-	1,983,631	128,752,576
Timber log value	799,413	126,880,640	-	-	-	-	-	-	799,413	126,880,640
Grazing	16,628,635	38,919,326	8,776,818	30,896,799	5,324	142,565	3,362	97,425	25,414,139	70,056,115
Acquaculture	221,393	143,000	-	-	-	-	-	-	221,393	143,000
Wild rice	19,137	1,395,950	-	-	350	150,000	-	-	19,487	1,545,950
Grapes	-	-	-	-	53	90,805	-	-	53	90,805
Avocados	-	-	-	-	-	-	-	-	-	-
Pecans	10	20,000	-	-	320	-	-	-	330	20,000
Specialty crops	28,599	179,778	-	-	3,544	3,044,120	209	174,670	32,352	33,398,568
Total	22,318,907	317,942,218	9,256,349	45,611,732	195,033	52,549,592	3,454,625	35,980,620	35,224,914	452,084,162

Source: Bureau of Indian Affairs Natural Resource Information System Inventory and Production Report, 1989, United States Department of the Interior, Report No. 55-38-X, p. 4. *Note:* A dash (-) indicates no data were given in original source.

★ 706 ★

Products Grown on Indian Lands - Non-Indian Operated

The gross value of products grown on Indian Lands is shown, by land use and ownership.

Land Use	Dry farmed, range & forest		Irrigated		Total		Grand total	
	Acres	Value	Acres	Value	Acres	Value	Acres	Value
Row crops	130,099	20,193,390	87,377	61,646,599	217,476	81,839,989	3,564,055	131,563,569
Small grains	623,392	51,574,139	75,272	20,832,646	698,664	72,406,785	1,038,837	100,005,375
Forage-hay-pasture	147,779	4,817,027	95,509	36,241,567	243,288	41,058,594	589,131	73,815,531
Horticulture	390	97,450	8,182	29,830,754	8,572	29,928,204	18,452	35,978,566
Soil improvement	9,649	43,600	518	36,800	10,167	80,400	15,147	159,640
Fallow	247,912	-	14,508	-	262,420	-	505,658	3,975
Outdoor rec. wild	1,115	349,515	-	-	1,115	349,515	2,403,171	4,684,684
Native hay	16,465	474,251	-	-	16,465	474,251	77,832	1,122,906
Timber stumpage value	17,690	2,743,873	-	-	17,690	2,743,873	2,001,321	131,496,449
Timber log value	16,886	492,001	-	-	16,886	492,001	816,299	127,372,641
Grazing	3,512,592	31,283,821	12,980	276,520	3,525,572	31,560,341	28,939,711	101,616,456
Acquaculture	130	-	214	100,000	344	100,000	221,737	243,000
Wild rice	-	-	-	-	-	-	19,487	1,545,950
Grapes	-	-	110	150,381	110	150,381	163	241,186
Avocados	-	-	-	-	-	-	-	-
Pecans & other	-	-	-	-	-	-	330	20,000
Specialty crops	1,569	264,675	12,730	36,822,501	14,299	37,087,176	46,651	40,485,744
Total	4,725,668	112,333,742	307,400	185,937,768	5,033,068	298,271,510	40,257,982	750,355,672

Source: Bureau of Indian Affairs Natural Resource Information System Inventory and Production Report, 1989, United States Department of the Interior, Report No. 55-38-X, p. 4. Note: A dash (-) indicates no data were given in original source.

★ 707 ★

Surface Water on Lands Under BIA Jurisdiction

Type of water	Number	Surface acres	Miles	Shore line miles
Natural lakes and ponds	5,690	1,001,825	-	5,845
Reservoirs & impoundments	17,537	507,139	-	4,573
Perennial streams	4,047	384	14,279	6,500
Coastal	349	-	39	330
Total	27,623	1,509,348	14,318	17,248

Source: Bureau of Indian Affairs Natural Resource Information System Inventory and Production Report, 1989, United States Department of the Interior, Report No. 55-38-X, p. 3. Note: A dash (-) indicates no data given in original source.

★ 708 ★

Use of Lands Under BIA Jurisdiction

Numbers are shown in acres.

Land use	Acres
Rangeland	33,896,080
Forestland	12,592,472
Dry Farmland	2,145,737
Irrigated Farmland	999,281
Wildlands	3,169,669
Other	944,151
Potential Irrigation[1]	1,123,570
Total	53,747,390

Source: Bureau of Indian Affairs Natural Resource Information System Inventory and Production Report, 1989, United States Department of the Interior, Report No. 55-38-X, p. 2. *Note:* 1. Total excludes Potential Irrigation.

Environmental Issues

★ 709 ★

BIA Dam Safety

67 BIA dams, by combined hazard/safety classifications, task force rank among all of the Department of Interior's high- and significant-hazard dams, and relative rank among the BIA's priority dams.

Dam/rating	Interior rank	Relative BIA rank	Area office
High hazard dams/unsatisfactory safety rating			
Ganado	12	4	Navajo
Round Rock	14	6	Navajo
Black Lake	34	16	Portland
Pablo	42	22	Portland/ Flathead
Ponca	96	41	Aberdeen
High Hazard dams/poor safety rating			
Black Rock	4	1	Albuquerque
Dulce	6	2	Albuquerque
Bonneau	9	3	Billings
Washakie	21	7	Billings
McDonald	22	8	Portland/ Flathead

[Continued]

★ 709 ★

BIA Dam Safety
[Continued]

Dam/rating	Interior rank	Relative BIA rank	Area office
Santa Ana	23	9	Albuquerque
Lower Dry Fork	26	11	Portland/ Flathead
Tula Stone	29	13	Phoenix
Weber	31	14	Phoenix
Jocko	33	15	Portland/ Flathead
Many Farms	35	17	Navajo
Standing Rock	36	18	Aberdeen
Acomita	38	19	Albuquerque
Rosebud	47	24	Aberdeen
White Clay	56	29	Aberdeen
He Dog	61	31	Aberdeen
Upper Dry Fork	66	33	Portland/ Flathead
Oglala	72	37	Aberdeen
Barmelee	95	40	Aberdeen
Crow	117	45	Portland/ Flathead
Tabor	129	47	Portland/ Flathead
Assayi	186	53	Navajo
Elgo	242	57	Phoenix
Lower Two Medicine	274	62	Billings

Significant-hazard dams/unsatisfactory safety rating[1]

Significant-hazard dams/poor safety rating

Equalizer	25	10	Portland
Crow Creek	27	12	Aberdeen
Tsaile	206	54	Navajo

High-hazard dams/conditionally poor safety rating

Captain Tom	39	20	Navajo
Lower Mundo	40	21	Albuquerque
Wheatfields	53	28	Navajo
Kicking Horse	69	34	Portland
Lake Mescalero	71	36	Albuquerque
Cutter	113	44	Navajo
Wild Horse	243	58	Phoenix
Hubbart	248	59	Portland/ Flathead
Bottle Hollow	254	60	Phoenix
Willow Creek	322	64	Billings

[Continued]

★ 709 ★

BIA Dam Safety
[Continued]

Dam/rating	Interior rank	Relative BIA rank	Area office
Significant-hazard dams/conditionally poor safety rating			
Indian Lake	45	23	Portland
High-hazard dam/fair or satisfactory safety rating			
Ninepipe (Fair)	137	49	Portland/ Flathead
Little Bitteroot (Satisfactory)	157	50	Portland
Red Lake (Fair)	237	56	Navajo
Mission (Fair)	267	61	Portland/ Flathead
Significant-hazard dams/fair or satisfactory safety rating			
Headgate Rock (fair)	335	65	Phoenix
Tat Momolikot (Satisfactory)	354	67	Phoenix
High-hazard dams/no safety rating			
Canyon Diablo	13	5	Navajo
Indian Scout Lake	50	26	Aberdeen
Agency	60	30	Billings
East Fork	49	25	Billings
Kyle	89	39	Aberdeen
Ghost Hawk	169	51	Aberdeen
Ring Thunder	173	52	Aberdeen
Allen	227	55	Aberdeen
Blackfoot	275	63	Portland
Blue Canyon	348	66	Navajo
Significant-hazard dams/no safety rating			
Ray Lake	63	32	Billings
La Jara	70	35	Albuquerque
Wanblee	74	38	Aberdeen
Hell Roaring	110	46	Portland
Twin (Turtle) Lake	130	48	Portland
Low-or unclassified hazard dams			
Pasture Canyon	51	27	Phoenix
Tuve	98	42	Phoenix
Wauneka	104	43	Navajo

Source: *Indian Programs: BIA and Indian Tribes Are Taking Action to Address Dam Safety Concerns*, United States General Accounting Office, February, 1992, pp. 16-18. *Note:* 1. None in this category.

★ 710 ★

Coal Mining Effluent Limitations

Performance standards apply to each coal mining operation on Indian lands on or after December 16, 1977. Figures are given in milligrams per liter, except for pH.

Effluent characteristics	Maximum allowable[1]	Average of daily values for 30 consecutive discharge days[1]
Iron, total	7.0	3.5
Manganese, total	4.0	2.0
Total suspended solids[2]	70.0	35.0
pH[3]	Within the range 6.0 to 9.0	-

Source: Code of Federal Regulations, Vol. 25, April 1991 Office of the Federal Register National Archives and Records Administration, p. 558. *Notes:* Discharges from areas disturbed by surface coal mining and reclamation operations must meet all applicable Federal and Tribal laws and regulations and, at a minimum, the above numerical of effluent limitations. 1. Based on representative sampling. 2. In Arizona, Colorado, Montana, New Mexico, North Dakota, South dakota, Utah, and Wyoming, total suspended solids limitations will be determined on a case-by-case basis, but they must not be greater than 45 mg/l (maximum allowable) and 30 mg/l (average of daily value for 30 consecutive discharge days) based on a representative sampling. 3. Where the application of neutralization and sedimentation treatment technology results in inability to comply with the maganese limitations set forth, the regulatory authority may allow the pH level in the discharge to exceed to a small extent the upper limit of 9.0 in order that the manganese limitations will be achieved.

★ 711 ★

Concerns About Transporting Nuclear Waste Materials Near or Across Indian Lands - I

"The Nuclear Regulatory Commission identified fifteen Indian tribal jurisdictions that are transitted by or adjacent to designated spent-fuel shipping routes. These tribes have an obvious and immediate interest in the possibility of a transportation incident involving radioactive materials. With the assistance of the National Congress of American Indians, fifteen of these tribal jurisdictions were chosen for inclusion in the survey. All were contacted by project staff, and twelve agreed to participate." This table presents highlights from this survey, showing some of the more poignant questions asked and responses by the participating tribes.

Tribe	Question 1: Lead agency for radiological assessment at the scene	Question 2: Document identifying lead agency	Question 3: Document identifying support agency	Question 4: Local jurisdictions exercising own emergency response authority	Question 5: Written emergency response plan
Acoma Pueblo	Rely entirely on New Mexico state and county public safety authorities	New Mexico disaster protocol	County call list	None	No
Navajo Nation	Navajo Nation Emergency Response Commission and Navajo Environmental Protection Administration	In process of development	No documentation; cooperative agreements being sought with state and local jurisdictions in Arizona, New Mexico, and Utah	Highway rights-of-way in affected state	In process

[Continued]

★ 711 ★

Concerns About Transporting Nuclear Waste Materials Near or Across Indian Lands - I
[Continued]

Tribe	Question 1: Lead agency for radiological assessment at the scene	Question 2: Document identifying lead agency	Question 3: Document identifying support agency	Question 4: Local jurisdictions exercising own emergency response authority	Question 5: Written emergency response plan
Nez Perce Tribe	None	None	None	None	No
Onondaga Nation	None	None	None	None	No
Pyramid Lake Paiute Tribe	Bureau of Indian Affairs police	Nevada DOT calls appropriate state agency	None	None	No
San Filipe Pueblo	Bureau of Indian Affairs police, county fire dept.	Informal agreement, tribal authorities call state and local police	None	None	No, one in discussion
Sandia Pueblo	Bureau of Indian Affairs, Indian Health Service, and volunteer fire department	None	None	Some pockets of private land	No
Seneca Nation	None assigned, most likely Health Department of the Seneca	No documentation	Received SARA Title III grant for training; will include several tribal agencies	None	No plan
Shoshone-Bannock Tribes	Tribal police	Plan in process; participating with 8 local jurisdictions under SARA Title III to create regional umbrella plan	SARA hazmat plan will be appendix to Tribal Basic Emergency Plan also in process	No autonomous jurisdictions within reservation, but private industrial operation has its own personnel; concurrent jurisdiction with state on highway rights-of-way	Draft plan in process
Te-Moak Tribe	Bureau of Indian Affairs police	None	None	None	No
Umatilla Indian Reservation	No designed agency, but have public health and safety agencies that would be involved	None	None	No autonomous jurisdictions within reservation, but Possessory and Usage Rights Area extends into 4 states; situation unclear	No, use Indian Health Service Plan
Yakima Indian Nation	Tribal police	No official document	No	Indian Health Service (1 staff member)	No

Source: Frank J. Vilardo, Eric L. Mitter, James A. Palmer, Henry C. Briggs, and Julie Fesenmaier, *Survey of State and Tribal Emergency Response Capabilities for Radiological Transportation Incidents,* Division of Safeguards and Transportation, Office of Nuclear Material Safety and Safeguards, U.S. Nuclear Regulatory Commission, Washington, D.C., NRC FIN D1054, p. 4-4 to 4-5.

★ 712 ★

Concerns About Transporting Nuclear Waste Materials Near or Across Indian Lands - II

"The Nuclear Regulatory Commission identified fifteen Indian tribal jurisdictions that are transitted by or adjacent to designated spent-fuel shipping routes. These tribes have an obvious and immediate interest in the possibility of a transportation incident involving radioactive materials. With the assistance of the National Congress of American Indians, fifteen of these tribal jurisdictions were chosen for inclusion in the survey. All were contacted by project staff, and twelve agreed to participate." This table presents highlights from this survey, showing some of the more poignant questions asked and responses by the participating tribes.

Tribe	Question 22: Professional specialists available to contribute their expertise for emergency response	Question 23: and 24 Portable radiation-detection equipment (type and location)	Question 25: Dedicated emergency response vehicles	Question 26: Emergency field kits	Question 27: Communications network
Acoma Pueblo	No trained personnel	2 or 3 devices received 2 years ago; no one knows how to use them	None	None	Telephone/radio with State
Navajo Nation	2 health-physics technicians and 1 radiation monitor	All equipment at one location: 1 each Low-, medium-, and high-range beta-gamma instrument 3 low-energy gamma detectors 6 alpha-particle detectors, 3 instruments that determine concentration of radon decay products Also, certified sources and equipment for calibration	None	None	Tribal public safety
Nez Perce Tribe	No trained personnel	No detection instruments	None	None	None
Onondaga Nation	No trained personnel	No detection instruments	None	None	None
Pyramid Lake Paiute Tribe	No trained personnel	No detection instruments	None	None	Radio from Bureau of Indian Affairs police to county dispatch
San Felipe Pueblo	1 communications specialist and 1 site coordinator	No detection instruments	None	None	Radio contact with state authorities
Sandia Pueblo	No trained personnel	No dectection instruments	None	None	Fire and police radio link to Bureau of Indian Affairs
Seneca Nation	No trained personnel	No dectection instruments	None	First aid only	Tribal police and fire radio
Shoshone-Bannock Tribes	2 radiation monitors and 2 communication specialists	Bureau of Indian Affairs has 2 portable instruments, but these have never been taken out of their boxes	None	First aid only	Tribal police base station and portable units; access to state net
Te-Moak Tribe	No trained personnel	No detection instruments	None	None	None
Umatilla Indian Reservation	Sanitarian on temporary assignment to Indian Health Service is trained as radiation monitor	Beta-gamma detectors and alpha-particle detectors are available at one location	None	Not tribe's	None
Yakima Indian Nation	No trained personnel	No detection instruments	None	None	Tribal police radio

Source: Frank J. Vilardo, Eric L. Mitter, James A. Palmer, Henry C. Briggs, and Julie Fesenmaier, *Survey of State and Tribal Emergency Response Capabilities for Radiological Transportation Incidents,* Division of Safeguards and Transportation, Office of Nuclear Material Safety and Safeguards, U.S. Nuclear Regulatory Commission, Washington, D.C., NRC FIN D1054, p. 4-27.

★ 713 ★

Concerns About Transporting Nuclear Waste Materials Near or Across Indian Lands - III

"The Nuclear Regulatory Commission identified fifteen Indian tribal jurisdictions that are transitted by or adjacent to designated spent-fuel shipping routes. These tribes have an obvious and immediate interest in the possibility of a transportation incident involving radioactive materials. With the assistance of the National Congress of American Indians, fifteen of these tribal jurisdictions were chosen for inclusion in the survey. All were contacted by project staff, and twelve agreed to participate." This table presents highlights from this survey, showing some of the more poignant questions asked and responses by the participating tribes.

Tribe	Question 28: Number of trained radiological emergrency response teams	Question 29: Number of team members trained in radiological emergency response proced-dures (RERO or equivalent)	Question 30: Location of trained radiological emergency response team
Acoma Pueblo	0	0	Not applicable
Navajo Nation	0	0	Not applicable
Nez Perce Tribe	0	0	Not applicable
Onondaga Nation	0	0	Not applicable
Pyramid Lake Paiute Tribe	0	0	Not applicable
San Felipe Pueblo	0	0	Not applicable
Sandia Pueblo	0	0	Not applicable
Seneca Nation	0	0	Not applicable
Shoshone-Bannock Tribes	0	0	Not applicable
Te-Moak Tribe	0	0	Not applicable
Umatilla Indian Reservation	0	1[1]	Only 1 trained person
Yakima Indian Nation	0	0	Not applicable

Source: Frank J. Vilardo, Eric L. Mitter, James A. Palmer, Henry C. Briggs, and Julie Fesenmaier, *Survey of State and Tribal Emergency Response Capabilities for Radiological Transportation Incidents*, Division of Safeguards and Transportation, Office of Nuclear Material Safety and Safeguards, U.S. Nuclear Regulatory Commission, Washington, D.C., NRC FIN D1054, p. 4-20. *Note:* 1. An employee of the Indian Health Service on temporary assignment.

★ 714 ★

IHS Sanitation Facilities Funding

Number of Indian homes funded by IHS (Indian Health Service) to receive funding for sanitation facilities.

Fiscal Year	Total First Service	First Service and Upgrade	Existing First Services	HUD First Service[1]	HIP First Service[2]	Tribal and Other[3]	Total Upgrade
1990	2,500	2,620	671	1,213	294	323	121
1989	6,806	10,362	2,223	1,835	718	2,031	3,556
1988	5,557	8,017	966	2,529	581	1,481	2,460
1987	5,824	6,863	543	3,697	344	1,241	1,039
1986	5,736	7,365	390	2,428	617	2,302	1,629
1985	4,538	8,082	173	2,240	562	1,563	3,544
1984	3,913	6,839	155	1,413	705	1,640	2,927
1983	5,146	10,006	1,834	1,119	1,264	930	4,860
1982	8,573	10,107	771	5,848	588	1,396	1,535
1981	6,580	9,218	674	4,290	507	1,109	2,639
1980	6,619	9,434	715	4,355	607	943	2,815
1979	6,885	8,380	1,198	3,814	657	1,216	1,496
1978	3,332	3,654	480	1,273	800	779	322
1977	14,374	22,518	6,017	5,039	1,417	1,903	8,144
1976	7,427	9,885	666	4,613	733	1,416	2,458
1975	6,043	8,521	1,642	2,430	855	1,117	2,478
1974	6,253	8,534	2,656	2,019	750	1,009	2,281
1973	7,704	9,231	2,638	3,426	1,080	560	1,527
1972	8,767	11,304	2,413	4,860	705	790	2,537
1971	5,196	6,951	902	3,010	733	551	1,755
1970	6,835	7,770	2,058	3,840	620	318	935
1969	6,358	6,246	4,032	1,421	445	460	888
1968	4,923	5,315	3,581	747	455	141	392
1967	4,042	5,140	3,042	702	118	181	1,098
1966	4,259	4,526	2,635	1,023	102	500	267
1965	4,079	4,573	3,668	340	71	-	494
1964	6,142	6,482	5,836	164	142	-	341
1963	5,608	6,151	5,578	-	20	10	543
1962	3,413	3,418	3,362	51	-	1	5
1961	2,624	2,671	2,614	-	-	10	47
1960	60	60	60	-	-	-	-

Source: Trends in Indian Health 1991, U.S. Department of Health and Human Services, Public Health Service, Indian Health Service, p. 91. *Notes:* 1. HUD stands for Dept. of Housing and Urban Development. 2. HIP stands for Housing Development Program, which is administered by the Bureau of Indian Affairs. 3. Other includes State, FmHa, etc.

★ 715 ★

North American Buffalo Population History, Aboriginal Times to 1983

Date	Population
Aboriginal times	60,000,000
1800	40,000,000
1850	20,000,000
1865	15,000,000
1870	14,000,000
1875	1,000,000
1880	395,000
1885	20,000
1889	1,091
1895	800
1900	1,024
1902	1,940
1907	18,797
1983	50,000

Source: Russell Thornton, *American Indian Holocaust and Survival: A Population History Since 1492*, University of Oklahoma Press, 1987, 52. Published by permission. Russell Thornton, *We Shall Live Again: The 1870 and 1890 Ghost Dance Movements as Demographic Revitalization*, Cambridge University Press, 1986, p. 27. Published by permission. Primary source: U.S. Department of the Interior, *The American Bison in the Unites States and Canada*. Senate Document, no. 445. Washington, D.C.: U.S. Government Printing Office, 1902, p. 3; Seton, *Life Histories of Northern Animals*. Vol. 1. New York: Charles Scribner and Sons, 1909, p. 300; *Lives of Game Animals*. Vol. 3, Pt. 2. Garden City, New York: Doubleday, Deson and Company, 1929, pp. 655-657, 670; Walker, *Walker's Manuals of the World*. Vol. 2. 4th ed. Baltimore: The Johns Hopkins University Press, 1983, p. 1255.

★ 716 ★

Pest Control Funding

Figures show Federal dollars spent as mandated by the Federal Insecticide, Fungicide, and Rodenticide Act.

Fiscal year	Enforcement	Certification and train-ing[1]	Pesticide program initiatives[2]
1986	9,703,400	2,600,000	-
1987	8,703,400	2,500,000	-
1988	8,703,400	4,000,000	-
1989	8,803,400	4,000,000	-
1990	12,803,400	4,500,000	7,000,000

Source: Roger Walke, *Federal Programs of Assistance to Native Americans: A Report Prepared for the Senate Select Committee on Indian Affairs of the United States Senate*, U.S. Government Printing Office, Washington, D.C., December 1991, p. 246. *Notes:* 1. Training dollars go to an interagency agreement with USDA for all pesticide applicator training (approx. $1.68 million of the total). 2. Pesticide Program Initiatives for FY 1990 include groundwater, endangered species, and worker protection activities.

★ 717 ★

Pollution: Air Pollution on Reservations, 1986[1]

Results are based on a joint survey by the EPA and Americans for Indian Opportunity. Usable responses were received from 48 of the 74 reservations surveyed.[2] 369,500 persons, or just over half of current on-reserve population, were covered, representing 42 million acres (approximately 79% of all trust acreage).

Source of pollution	Times cited as source
Fossil fuel fired power plants	10
Residential heating	8
Wood stoves	1
Coal stoves	2
Mining	6
Lumber/sawmills	6
Landfills/dumps	6
Open-burning incinerators	5
Nuclear power plants	5
Minerals processing	5
Highways	4
Sand & gravel mines	3
Petroleum refineries	3
Gas & oil companies	3
Dust from agricultural cropland	3

[Continued]

★ 717 ★

Pollution. Air Pollution on Reservations, 1986

[Continued]

Source of pollution	Times cited as source
Cities/nearby urban areas	3
Vehicle emissions	2
Unpaved roads	2
Road & other construction	2
Prescribed burning (incl. timber, slash, grass)	2
Paper mills	2
Coal mines	2
Wood-fired industrial heating	1
Wild fires	1
Wild burning	1
Waste wood incinerators	1
Uranium mine	1
Uranium mill tailing project	1
Thermoelectric power plant	1
Synthetic gas plant	1
Surface mining	1
Steel mills	1
Small industry	1
Rock crushers	1
Pulp mills	1
PCB plants	1
Oil wells flaring sour gas	1
Northwest pipeline processing plant	1
Laguna Jackpile	1
Foundries	1
CO_2 processing plant	1
Copper mine	1
Coal-fired generator	1
Chemical waste dumps	1
Chemical companies	1
Cement plants	1
Aluminum plants	1

[Continued]

★ 717 ★

Pollution: Air Pollution on Reservations, 1986
[Continued]

Source of pollution	Times cited as source
Agriculture field burning	1
Agricultural spraying	1

Source: Survey of American Indian Environmental Protection Needs on Reservation Lands: 1986, p. 37-38, United States Environmental Protection Agency, September 1986, Submitted to the Environmental Protection Agency by Americans for Indian Opportunity. *Notes:* 1. There are no significant sources of air pollution on/near Rosebud and Zuni. 2. Responses received from the following reservations: Seneca, St. Regis-Mohawk, Choctaw, Leech Lake, White Earth, Menominee, Stockbridge- Munsee, Forest County Potowatomi, Sault Ste. Marie, Isabella & Saganing, Acoma Pueblo, Isleta Pueblo, Zuni Pueblo, Zia Pueblo, Winnebago, Southern Ute, Fort Belknap, Fort Peck, Northern Cheyenne, Rocky Boy's, Fort Berthold, Standing Rock Sioux, Cheyenne River Sioux, Pine Ridge, Yankton Sioux, Lower Brule, Rosebud Sioux, Lake Traverse, Hopi, Navajo, San Carlos, Hualapai, Pyramid Lake-Paiute, Ely Colony Shoshone, Hoopa Valley, Benton Paiute, Cabazon Rancheria, Colusa Rancheria, Rincon Rancheria, Santa Rosa Rancheria, Berry Creek Rancheria, Susanville Rancheria, Fort Hall, Umatilla, Warm Springs, Colville, Quinault, and Yakima .

★ 718 ★

Pollution: Environmental Protection Programs on Reservations, 1986

Results are based on a joint survey by the EPA and Americans for Indian Opportunity. Usable responses were received from 48 of the 74 reservations surveyed.[1] 369,500 persons, or just over half of current on-reserve population, were covered, representing 42 million acres (approximately 79% of all trust acreage).

Type of program	Number of reservations
Air quality monitoring	19
Water quality monitoring	27
Soil analysis	18
Developing tribal environmental standards	21
Enforcing tribal environmental standards	18
Animal control	19
Protection of endangered species	19
Sanitation & waste disposal	21
Environmental rehabilitation/reclamation	13
Emergency preparedness/evacuation	14
Other	
Pesticide/insecticide regulation/certification/ enforcement	6
Fungicide monitoring	1
Radiation monitoring	1
Hazardous waste inventory	1
Noise control	1

[Continued]

★ 718 ★

Pollution: Environmental Protection Programs on Reservations, 1986

[Continued]

Type of program	Number of reservations
Mining regulation	2
Developing codes to control future development	1
Injury control	1
Archaeological protection	2
Mississippi Headwaters Conservation Plan	1

Source: Survey of American Indian Environmental Protection Needs on Reservation Lands: 1986, p. 30, United States Environmental Protection Agency, September 1986, Submitted to the Environmental Protection Agency by Americans for Indian Opportunity. *Notes:* 1. Responses received from the following reservations: Seneca, St. Regis-Mohawk, Choctaw, Leech Lake, White Earth, Menominee, Stockbridge- Munsee, Forest County Potowatomi, Sault Ste. Marie, Isabella & Saganing, Acoma Pueblo, Isleta Pueblo, Zuni Pueblo, Zia Pueblo, Winnebago, Southern Ute, Fort Belknap, Fort Peck, Northern Cheyenne, Rocky Boy's, Fort Berthold, Standing Rock Sioux, Cheyenne River Sioux, Pine Ridge, Yankton Sioux, Lower Brule, Rosebud Sioux, Lake Traverse, Hopi, Navajo, San Carlos, Hualapai, Pyramid Lake-Paiute, Ely Colony Shoshone, Hoopa Valley, Benton Paiute, Cabazon Rancheria, Colusa Rancheria, Rincon Rancheria, Santa Rosa Rancheria, Berry Creek Rancheria, Susanville Rancheria, Fort Hall, Umatilla, Warm Springs, Colville, Quinault, and Yakima .

★ 719 ★

Pollution: Solid Waste Disposal on Reservations, 1986

Results are based on a joint survey by the EPA and Americans for Indian Opportunity. Usable responses were received from 48 of the 74 reservations surveyed.[1] 369,500 persons, or just over half of current on-reserve population, were covered, representing 42 million acres (approximately 79% of all trust acreage).

Type of disposal	Number of reservations
Community dump site	24
Community landfill	18
Incineration	
Community[2]	10
Individual	17
Other	
People make own dump sites within their own land use areas (Navaho)	1
Illegal/unauthorized open dumps/ roadside dumps/isolated vacant lots/ surface dumping	8
County contract	1

[Continued]

★ 719 ★

Pollution: Solid Waste Disposal on Reservations, 1986
[Continued]

Type of disposal	Number of reservations
Off-reservation landfill in neighboring community	7
Tribal transfer system to off-reservation system	1
Privately owned landfill and contractor	1

Source: Survey of American Indian Environmental Protection Needs on Reservation Lands: 1986, p. 30, United States Environmental Protection Agency, September 1986, Submitted to the Environmental Protection Agency by Americans for Indian Opportunity. *Notes:* 1. Responses received from the following reservations: Seneca, St. Regis-Mohawk, Choctaw, Leech Lake, White Earth, Menominee, Stockbridge- Munsee, Forest County Potowatomi, Sault Ste. Marie, Isabella & Saganing, Acoma Pueblo, Isleta Pueblo, Zuni Pueblo, Zia Pueblo, Winnebago, Southern Ute, Fort Belknap, Fort Peck, Northern Cheyenne, Rocky Boy's, Fort Berthold, Standing Rock Sioux, Cheyenne River Sioux, Pine Ridge, Yankton Sioux, Lower Brule, Rosebud Sioux, Lake Traverse, Hopi, Navajo, San Carlos, Hualapai, Pyramid Lake-Paiute, Ely Colony Shoshone, Hoopa Valley, Benton Paiute, Cabazon Rancheria, Colusa Rancheria, Rincon Rancheria, Santa Rosa Rancheria, Berry Creek Rancheria, Susanville Rancheria, Fort Hall, Umatilla, Warm Springs, Colville, Quinault, and Yakima. 2. e.g. PHS hospital, schools .

★ 720 ★

Pollution: Uncontrolled Toxic Waste Sites in Top States for American Indians

Areas are ranked, by number of American Indians.

State	Indians living in waste site areas	Number of sites in state	Number in thousands total population in state			Percentage of group which lives in waste site areas		
			Indian	White	All	Indian	White	All
California	109	916	227	15,845	23,660	43.1	43.9	46.2
Oklahoma	95	451	171	2,574	3,025	55.6	61.3	62.0
Arizona	45	217	154	2,028	2,718	28.9	51.9	53.6
New Mexico	36	165	107	690	1,303	34.0	69.6	66.0
Washington	36	461	61	3,734	4,132	58.9	69.1	69.2

Source: Commission for Racial Justice, United Church of Christ, *Toxic Wastes and Race in the United States: A National Report on the Racial and Socio- Economic Characteristics of Communities with Hazardous Waste Sites*, 1987, p. 59.

★ 721 ★

Pollution: Water Pollution on Reservations, 1986

Results are based on a joint survey by the EPA and Americans for Indian Opportunity. Usable responses were received from 48 of the 74 reservations surveyed.[1] 369,500 persons, or just over half of current on-reserve population, were covered, representing 42 million acres (approximately 79% of all trust acreage).

Source of pollution	Number of times cited as a source	
	Actual	Potential
Sewage treatment plants	10	20
Water treatment plants	1	14
Oxidation ponds	6	17
Municipal discharges	10	13
Industrial discharges	4	14
Domestic wastes (sewage)	12	22
Oil spills	3	12
Hazardous materials spills	3	20
Landfill leachate	6	24
Urban run-off (overland & storm sewer)	8	14
Agricultural run-off (cropland run-off animal waste, streambank erosion)	18	11
Sediment run-off (construction)	8	12
Sediment run-off (mining)	8	10
Sediment run-off (timber production and harvesting	8	8
Pesticide/herbicide/nutrient run-off	13	15
Toxicant build-up (pesticide usage)	5	16
On-lot disposal	1	8
Other		
Salt H_2O disposal	-	1
Drilling fluids	-	1
Gas	1	-
Hazardous waste disposal	1	-
Open solid waste dumps	1	-
Nuclear waste	-	1
Acid rain	1	-

Source: *Survey of American Indian Environmental Protection Needs on Reservation Lands: 1986*, p. 30, United States Environmental Protection Agency, September 1986, Submitted to the Environmental Protection Agency by Americans for Indian Opportunity. *Notes:* A dash (-) indicates no data in original source. 1. Responses received from the following reservations: Seneca, St. Regis-Mohawk, Choctaw, Leech Lake, White Earth, Menominee, Stockbridge- Munsee, Forest County Potowatomi, Sault Ste. Marie, Isabella & Saganing, Acoma Pueblo, Isleta Pueblo, Zuni Pueblo, Zia Pueblo, Winnebago, Southern Ute, Fort Belknap, Fort Peck, Northern Cheyenne, Rocky Boy's, Fort Berthold, Standing Rock Sioux, Cheyenne River Sioux, Pine Ridge, Yankton Sioux, Lower Brule, Rosebud Sioux, Lake Traverse, Hopi, Navajo, San Carlos, Hualapai, Pyramid Lake-Paiute, Ely Colony Shoshone, Hoopa Valley, Benton Paiute, Cabazon Rancheria, Colusa Rancheria, Rincon Rancheria, Santa Rosa Rancheria, Berry Creek Rancheria, Susanville Rancheria, Fort Hall, Umatilla, Warm Springs, Colville, Quinault, and Yakima .

★ 722 ★

Soil Conservation Service Programs, 1990

The estimated dollar value of assistance given to Native Americans by Soil Conservation Service (SCS) programs is shown, by the type of assistance, for FY 1990.

Type of Assistance	Amount ($)
Conservation operations (CO-01) technical assistance	5,000,000
Resource conservation and development program activities	150,000
Flood prevention (Watershed Program PL-566)	3,500,000
Soil Survey	750,000
Total	9,400,000

Source: U.S. Senate, Select Committee on Indian Affairs, *Federal Programs of Assistance to Native Americans*, 102d Cong., 1st sess., December 1991, p. 33. *Notes:* Assistance provided includes, but is not limited to, conservation planning on cropland, pastureland, and rangeland; assistance to apply rangeland management and improvement practices; irrigation water development structures and management; brush control; erosion control structures; agriculture; forestry salinity control; land treatment for watershed programs activities; no-till conservation tillage; and soil interpretations for various land uses. Soil Conservation Service assistance was provided to 4,104 Native Americans in 28 States in 1989. Of those, 1,026 had applied one or more conservation practices.

Chapter 10
GOVERNMENT RELATIONS

Employment

★ 723 ★

Number of Full-Time State and Local Government Employees, by Sex and Race/Ethnicity, 1990: Officials and Administrators

Annual salary	Total		Indian		White		Black		Hispanic		Asian	
	Number	Percent	Number	Percent	Number	Percent	Number	Percent	Number	Percent	Number	Percent
Male												
100-7,900	2,401	77.6	1	0.0	2,239	72.4	125	4.0	30	1.0	6	0.2
8,000-11,900	1,366	56.1	4	0.2	1,182	48.6	140	5.8	36	1.5	4	0.2
12,000-15,900	2,114	42.5	8	0.2	1,821	36.6	186	3.7	88	1.8	11	0.2
16,000-19,900	4,921	49.6	19	0.2	4,280	43.1	401	4.0	210	2.1	11	0.1
20,000-24,900	11,637	56.5	43	0.2	10,287	49.9	882	4.3	388	1.9	37	0.2
25,000-32,900	31,735	57.9	127	0.2	27,559	50.3	2,773	5.1	1,090	2.0	186	0.3
33,000-42,900	51,491	66.7	232	0.3	45,336	58.7	3,883	5.0	1,557	2.0	483	0.6
43,000-Plus	100,076	79.1	304	0.2	88,209	69.8	6,900	5.5	2,941	2.3	1,722	1.4
Total	205,741	68.7	738	0.2	180,913	60.4	15,290	5.1	6,340	2.1	2,460	0.8
Female												
100-7,900	693	22.4	2	0.1	641	20.7	42	1.4	5	0.2	3	0.1
8,000-11,900	1,067	43.9	22	0.9	941	38.7	71	2.9	31	1.3	2	0.1
12,000-15,900	2,856	57.5	12	0.2	2,542	51.1	209	4.2	86	1.7	7	0.1
16,000-19,900	5,000	50.4	31	0.3	4,339	43.7	464	4.7	151	1.5	15	0.2
20,000-24,900	8,960	43.5	47	0.2	7,578	36.8	923	4.5	384	1.9	28	0.1
25,000-32,900	23,046	42.1	95	0.2	16,491	30.1	5,016	9.2	1,252	2.3	192	0.4
33,000-42,900	25,718	33.3	106	0.1	20,015	25.9	4,281	5.5	982	1.3	334	0.4
43,000-Plus	26,360	20.9	63	0.0	20,550	16.3	4,187	3.3	846	0.7	734	0.6
Total	93,720	31.3	378	0.1	73,097	24.4	15,193	5.1	3,737	1.2	1,315	0.4
Total												
100-7,900	3,094	100.0	3	0.1	2,880	93.1	167	5.4	35	1.1	9	0.3
8,000-11,900	2,433	100.0	26	1.1	2,123	87.3	211	8.7	67	2.8	6	0.2
12,000-15,900	4,970	100.0	20	0.4	4,363	87.8	395	7.9	174	3.5	18	0.4
16,000-19,900	9,921	100.0	50	0.5	8,619	86.9	865	8.7	361	3.6	26	0.3
20,000-24,900	20,597	100.0	90	0.4	17,865	86.7	1,805	8.8	772	3.7	65	0.3
25,000-32,900	54,781	100.0	222	0.4	44,050	80.4	7,789	14.2	2,342	4.3	378	0.7
33,000-42,900	77,209	100.0	388	0.4	65,351	84.6	8,164	10.6	2,539	3.3	817	1.1
43,000-Plus	126,456	100.0	367	0.3	108,759	86.0	11,087	8.8	3,787	3.0	2,456	1.9
Total	299,461	100.0	1,116	0.4	254,010	84.8	30,483	10.2	10,077	3.4	3,775	1.3

Source: U.S. Equal Employment Opportunity Commission, *Job Patterns for Minorities and Women in State and Local Government, 1990*, U.S. Government Printing Office, 1990, p. 4.

★ 724 ★

Number of Full-Time State and Local Government Employees, by Sex and Race/Ethnicity, 1990: Professionals

Annual salary	Total		Indian		White		Black		Hispanic		Asian	
	Number	Percent	Number	Percent	Number	Percent	Number	Percent	Number	Percent	Number	Percent
Male												
100-7,900	1,866	54.0	11	0.3	1,656	47.9	110	3.2	57	1.6	32	0.9
8,000-11,900	1,265	39.2	5	0.2	1,095	33.9	128	4.0	21	0.7	16	0.5
12,000-15,900	5,035	32.4	32	0.2	3,900	25.1	827	5.3	251	1.6	25	0.2
16,000-19,900	24,557	35.8	173	0.3	19,063	27.8	3,943	5.8	1,162	1.7	216	0.3
20,000-24,900	72,267	38.6	612	0.3	56,607	30.2	10,663	5.7	3,346	1.8	1,039	0.6
25,000-32,900	163,673	43.8	932	0.2	134,457	36.0	17,067	4.6	7,025	1.9	4,192	1.1
33,000-42,900	181,345	54.3	747	0.2	150,791	45.2	14,839	4.4	7,519	2.3	7,449	2.2
43,000-Plus	147,867	71.7	397	0.2	124,245	60.2	8,008	3.9	5,745	2.8	9,472	4.6
Total	597,875	50.2	2,909	0.2	491,814	41.3	55,585	4.7	25,126	2.1	22,441	1.9
Female												
100-7,900	1,589	46.0	0	0.0	1,271	36.8	245	7.1	47	1.4	26	0.8
8,000-11,900	1,961	60.8	7	0.2	1,521	47.1	373	11.6	44	1.4	16	0.5
12,000-15,900	10,499	67.6	73	0.5	7,848	50.5	2,002	12.9	509	3.3	67	0.4
16,000-19,900	43,966	64.2	323	0.5	32,443	47.3	8,853	12.9	2,067	3.0	280	0.4
20,000-24,900	114,876	61.4	639	0.3	85,927	45.9	22,299	11.9	4,868	2.6	1,143	0.6
25,000-32,900	210,247	56.2	915	0.2	160,725	43.0	34,996	9.4	8,246	2.2	5,365	1.4
33,000-42,900	152,582	45.7	490	0.1	111,248	33.3	24,756	7.4	6,739	2.0	9,349	2.8
43,000-Plus	58,372	28.3	212	0.1	41,736	20.2	8,150	4.0	2,656	1.3	5,618	2.7
Total	594,092	49.8	2,659	0.2	442,719	37.1	101,674	8.5	25,176	2.1	21,864	1.8
Total												
100-7,900	3,455	100.0	11	0.3	2,927	84.7	355	10.3	104	3.0	58	1.7
8,000-11,900	3,226	100.0	12	0.4	2,616	81.1	501	15.5	65	2.0	32	1.0
12,000-15,900	15,534	100.0	105	0.7	11,748	75.6	2,829	18.2	760	4.9	92	0.6
16,000-19,900	68,523	100.0	496	0.7	51,506	75.2	12,796	18.7	3,229	4.7	496	0.7
20,000-24,900	187,143	100.0	1,251	0.7	142,534	76.2	32,962	17.6	8,214	4.4	2,182	1.2
25,000-32,900	373,920	100.0	1,847	0.5	295,182	78.9	52,063	13.9	15,271	4.1	9,557	2.6
33,000-42,900	333,927	100.0	1,237	0.4	262,039	78.5	39,595	11.9	14,258	4.3	16,798	5.0
43,000-Plus	206,239	100.0	609	0.3	165,981	80.5	16,158	7.8	8,401	4.1	15,090	7.3
Total	1,191,967	100.0	5,568	0.5	934,533	78.4	157,259	13.2	50,302	4.2	44,305	3.7

Source: U.S. Equal Employment Opportunity Commission, *Job Patterns for Minorities and Women in State and Local Government, 1990*, U.S. Government Printing Office, 1990, p. 5.

★ 725 ★

Number of Full-Time State and Local Government Employees, by Sex and Race/Ethnicity, 1990: Protective Service

Annual salary	Total		Indian		White		Black		Hispanic		Asian	
	Number	Percent	Number	Percent	Number	Percent	Number	Percent	Number	Percent	Number	Percent
Male												
100-7,900	3,541	63.1	61	1.1	2,842	50.6	478	8.5	145	2.6	15	0.3
8,000-11,900	6,512	68.2	56	0.6	4,921	51.5	1,148	12.0	364	3.8	23	0.2
12,000-15,900	35,914	75.8	253	0.5	26,288	55.5	7,741	16.3	1,523	3.2	109	0.2
16,000-19,900	98,924	82.7	960	0.8	76,332	63.8	16,400	13.7	4,963	4.1	269	0.2
20,000-24,900	146,292	84.8	740	0.4	115,610	67.0	22,569	13.1	6,881	4.0	492	0.3

[Continued]

★ 725 ★

Number of Full-Time State and Local Government Employees, by Sex and Race/Ethnicity, 1990: Protective Service

[Continued]

Annual salary	Total		Indian		White		Black		Hispanic		Asian	
	Number	Percent	Number	Percent	Number	Percent	Number	Percent	Number	Percent	Number	Percent
25,000-32,900	226,986	89.9	962	0.4	183,608	71.9	29,483	11.6	11,719	4.6	1,214	0.5
33,000-42,900	196,812	90.7	658	0.3	155,404	71.6	23,060	10.6	15,285	7.0	2,405	1.1
43,000-Plus	52,641	92.3	166	0.3	42,809	75.1	4,305	7.6	4,539	8.0	822	1.4
Total	767,622	86.8	3,856	0.4	607,814	68.8	105,184	11.9	45,419	5.1	5,349	0.6
Female												
100-7,900	2,073	36.9	12	0.2	1,348	24.0	602	10.7	107	1.9	4	0.1
8,000-11,900	3,039	31.8	15	0.2	2,243	23.5	628	6.6	149	1.6	4	0.0
12,000-15,900	11,449	24.2	78	0.2	7,524	15.9	3,442	7.3	381	0.8	24	0.1
16,000-19,900	20,667	17.3	185	0.2	13,872	11.6	5,634	4.7	918	0.8	58	0.0
20,000-24,900	26,222	15.2	164	0.1	16,756	9.7	8,110	4.7	1,132	0.7	60	0.0
25,000-32,900	28,268	11.1	140	0.1	16,888	6.6	9,287	3.6	1,758	0.7	195	0.1
33,000-42,900	20,274	9.3	65	0.0	11,393	5.2	6,475	3.0	2,047	0.9	294	0.1
43,000-Plus	4,363	7.7	13	0.0	2,813	4.9	971	1.7	484	0.8	82	0.1
Total	116,355	13.2	672	0.1	72,837	8.2	35,149	4.0	6,976	0.8	721	0.1
Total												
100-7,900	5,614	100.0	73	1.3	4,190	74.6	1,080	19.2	252	4.5	19	0.3
8,000-11,900	9,551	100.0	71	0.7	7,164	75.0	1,776	18.6	513	5.4	27	0.3
12,000-15,900	47,363	100.0	331	0.7	33,812	71.4	11,183	23.6	1,904	4.0	133	0.3
16,000-19,900	119,591	100.0	1,145	1.0	90,204	75.4	22,034	18.4	5,881	4.9	327	0.3
20,000-24,900	172,514	100.0	904	0.5	132,366	76.7	30,679	17.8	8,013	4.6	552	0.3
25,000-32,900	255,254	100.0	1,102	0.4	200,496	78.5	38,770	15.2	13,477	5.3	1,409	0.6
33,000-42,900	217,086	100.0	723	0.3	166,797	76.8	29,535	13.6	17,332	8.0	2,699	1.2
43,000-Plus	57,004	100.0	179	0.3	45,622	80.0	5,276	9.3	5,023	8.8	904	1.6
Total	883,977	100.0	4,528	0.5	680,651	77.0	140,333	15.9	52,395	5.9	6,070	0.7

Source: U.S. Equal Employment Opportunity Commission, *Job Patterns for Minorities and Women in State and Local Government, 1990*, U.S. Government Printing Office, 1990, p. 7.

★ 726 ★

Number of Full-Time State and Local Government Employees, by Sex and Race/Ethnicity, 1990: Technicians

Annual salary	Total		Indian		White		Black		Hispanic		Asian	
	Number	Percent	Number	Percent	Number	Percent	Number	Percent	Number	Percent	Number	Percent
Male												
100-7,900	701	43.7	1	0.1	597	37.2	70	4.4	25	1.6	8	0.5
8,000-11,900	2,760	36.0	12	0.2	2,096	27.3	402	5.2	240	3.1	10	0.1
12,000-15,900	14,966	38.0	127	0.3	11,114	28.2	2,638	6.7	998	2.5	89	0.2
16,000-19,900	35,024	43.5	318	0.4	27,465	34.1	4,828	6.0	2,028	2.5	385	0.5
20,000-24,900	61,716	50.3	418	0.3	49,090	40.0	7,505	6.1	3,525	2.9	1,178	1.0
25,000-32,900	89,203	63.9	403	0.3	73,108	52.3	8,617	6.2	4,728	3.4	2,347	1.7
33,000-42,900	61,736	82.1	249	0.3	52,071	69.2	4,726	6.3	2,984	4.0	1,706	2.3
43,000-Plus	31,438	90.1	110	0.3	26,462	75.8	2,202	6.3	1,829	5.2	835	2.4
Total	297,544	59.3	1,638	0.3	242,003	48.2	30,988	6.2	16,357	3.3	6,558	1.3
Female												
100-7,900	902	56.3	6	0.4	738	46.0	122	7.6	24	1.5	12	0.7
8,000-11,900	4,917	64.0	29	0.4	3,491	45.5	930	12.1	440	5.7	27	0.4

[Continued]

★ 726 ★

Number of Full-Time State and Local Government Employees, by Sex and Race/Ethnicity, 1990: Technicians
[Continued]

Annual salary	Total		Indian		White		Black		Hispanic		Asian	
	Number	Percent	Number	Percent	Number	Percent	Number	Percent	Number	Percent	Number	Percent
12,000-15,900	24,413	62.0	115	0.3	17,134	43.5	5,795	14.7	1,223	3.1	146	0.4
16,000-19,900	45,568	56.5	266	0.3	32,376	40.2	10,098	12.5	2,325	2.9	503	0.6
20,000-24,900	61,063	49.7	275	0.2	40,956	33.4	14,389	11.7	3,708	3.0	1,735	1.4
25,000-32,900	50,471	36.1	208	0.1	34,734	24.9	9,414	6.7	3,649	2.6	2,466	1.8
33,000-42,900	13,495	17.9	60	0.1	9,535	12.7	2,099	2.8	1,012	1.3	789	1.0
43,000-Plus	3,453	9.9	12	0.0	2,521	7.2	499	1.4	202	0.6	219	0.6
Total	204,282	40.7	971	0.2	141,485	28.2	43,346	8.6	12,583	2.5	5,897	1.2
Total												
100-7,900	1,603	100.0	7	0.4	1,335	83.3	192	12.0	49	3.1	20	1.2
8,000-11,900	7,677	100.0	41	0.5	5,587	72.8	1,332	17.4	680	8.9	37	0.5
12,000-15,900	39,379	100.0	242	0.6	28,248	71.7	8,433	21.4	2,221	5.6	235	0.6
16,000-19,900	80,592	100.0	584	0.7	59,841	74.3	14,926	18.5	4,353	5.4	888	1.1
20,000-24,900	122,779	100.0	693	0.6	90,046	73.3	21,894	17.8	7,233	5.9	2,913	2.4
25,000-32,900	139,674	100.0	611	0.4	107,842	77.2	18,031	12.9	8,377	6.0	4,813	3.4
33,000-42,900	75,231	100.0	309	0.4	61,606	81.9	6,825	9.1	3,996	5.3	2,495	3.3
43,000-Plus	34,891	100.0	122	0.3	28,983	83.1	2,701	7.7	2,031	5.8	1,054	3.0
Total	501,826	100.0	2,609	0.5	383,488	76.4	74,334	14.8	28,940	5.8	12,455	2.5

Source: U.S. Equal Employment Opportunity Commission, *Job Patterns for Minorities and Women in State and Local Government, 1990,* U.S. Government Printing Office, 1990, p. 6.

★ 727 ★

Number of Full-Time State and Local Government Employees, by Sex and Race/Ethnicity, 1990: U.S. Summary

Annual salary	Total		American Indian Alaska Native		White		Black		Hispanic		Asian	
	Number	Percent	Number	Percent	Number	Percent	Number	Percent	Number	Percent	Number	Percent
Male												
100-7,900	18,886	49.8	149	0.4	14,733	38.8	2,970	7.8	920	2.4	114	0.3
8,000-11,900	69,181	37.9	498	0.3	39,724	21.8	22,740	12.5	5,945	3.3	274	0.2
12,000-15,900	229,659	39.5	1,934	0.3	146,625	25.2	61,961	10.7	17,884	3.1	1,255	0.2
16,000-19,900	406,326	46.5	3,184	0.4	284,873	32.6	86,471	9.9	28,324	3.2	3,474	0.4
20,000-24,900	583,235	51.9	3,422	0.3	435,728	38.8	99,904	8.9	36,948	3.3	7,233	0.6
25,000-32,900	786,335	62.6	3,962	0.3	609,236	48.5	112,876	9.0	46,865	3.7	13,396	1.1
33,000-42,900	603,595	71.6	2,707	0.3	483,250	57.3	65,685	7.8	36,957	4.4	14,996	1.8
43,000-Plus	374,137	78.6	1,236	0.3	311,370	65.4	29,563	6.2	17,885	3.8	14,083	3.0
Total	3,071,354	57.2	17,092	0.3	2,335,539	43.3	482,170	9.0	191,728	3.6	54,825	1.0
Female												
100-7,900	19,069	50.2	100	0.3	14,586	38.4	3,520	9.3	762	2.0	101	0.3
8,000-11,900	113,129	62.1	620	0.3	75,196	41.2	30,540	16.8	6,249	3.4	524	0.3
12,000-15,900	351,550	60.5	2,201	0.4	241,407	41.5	85,723	14.7	20,084	3.5	2,135	0.4
16,000-19,900	467,700	53.5	2,662	0.3	318,643	36.5	111,412	12.7	29,602	3.4	5,381	0.6
20,000-24,900	540,928	48.1	2,594	0.2	365,502	32.5	127,721	11.4	34,273	3.0	10,838	1.0
25,000-32,900	468,883	37.4	2,204	0.2	333,124	26.5	93,613	7.5	26,371	2.1	13,571	1.1
33,000-42,900	239,252	28.4	870	0.1	170,135	20.2	43,104	5.1	13,122	1.6	12,021	1.4
43,000-Plus	101,901	21.4	385	0.1	74,165	15.6	15,954	3.4	4,567	1.0	6,830	1.4
Total	2,302,412	42.8	11,636	0.2	1,592,758	29.6	511,587	9.5	135,030	2.5	51,401	1.0

[Continued]

★ 727 ★

Number of Full-Time State and Local Government Employees, by Sex and Race/Ethnicity, 1990: U.S. Summary
[Continued]

Annual salary	Total		American Indian Alaska Native		White		Black		Hispanic		Asian	
	Number	Percent	Number	Percent	Number	Percent	Number	Percent	Number	Percent	Number	Percent
Total												
100-7,900	37,955	100.0	249	0.7	29,319	77.2	6,490	17.1	1,682	4.4	215	0.6
8,000-11,900	182,310	100.0	1,118	0.6	114,920	63.0	53,280	29.2	12,194	6.7	798	0.4
12,000-15,900	581,209	100.0	4,135	0.7	388,032	66.8	147,684	25.4	37,968	6.5	3,390	0.6
16,000-19,900	874,026	100.0	5,846	0.7	603,516	69.1	197,883	22.6	57,926	6.6	8,855	1.0
20,000-24,900	1,124,163	100.0	6,016	0.5	801,230	71.3	227,625	20.2	71,221	6.3	18,071	1.6
25,000-32,900	1,255,218	100.0	6,166	0.5	942,360	75.1	206,489	16.5	73,236	5.8	26,967	2.1
33,000-42,900	842,847	100.0	3,577	0.4	653,385	77.5	108,789	12.9	50,079	5.9	27,017	3.2
43,000-Plus	476,038	100.0	1,621	0.3	385,535	81.0	45,517	9.6	22,452	4.7	20,913	4.4
Total	5,373,766	100.0	28,728	0.5	3,918,297	72.9	993,757	18.5	326,758	6.1	106,226	2.0

Source: U.S. Equal Employment Opportunity Commission, *Job Patterns for Minorities and Women in State and Local Government, 1990,* U.S. Government Printing Office, 1991, p. 1.

★ 728 ★

Number of Part-Time State and Local Government Employees, by Job Category, 1990

Job category	Total		Indian		White		Black		Hispanic		Asian	
	Number	Percent	Number	Percent	Number	Percent	Number	Percent	Number	Percent	Number	Percent
Male												
Officials/administrators	14,052	60.7	52	0.2	12,159	52.5	999	4.3	558	2.4	284	1.2
Professionals	50,679	31.9	245	0.2	41,006	25.8	4,780	3.0	2,020	1.3	2,628	1.7
Technicians	29,642	40.3	233	0.3	23,849	32.5	2,762	3.8	1,689	2.3	1,109	1.5
Protective service workers	71,537	70.0	348	0.3	62,879	61.6	5,067	5.0	2,737	2.7	506	0.5
Paraprofessionals	73,755	36.4	381	0.2	53,124	26.2	12,698	6.3	5,750	2.8	1,802	0.9
Administrative support	48,840	22.4	943	0.4	35,654	16.3	7,119	3.3	3,171	1.5	1,953	0.9
Skilled craft workers	26,333	68.4	257	0.7	20,098	52.2	3,934	10.2	1,698	4.4	346	0.9
Service-maintenance	180,025	61.0	1,321	0.4	133,741	45.3	30,469	10.3	12,073	4.1	2,421	0.8
Total	494,863	44.5	3,780	0.3	382,510	34.4	67,828	6.1	29,696	2.7	11,049	1.0
Female												
Officials/administrators	9,108	39.3	34	0.1	7,062	30.5	1,089	4.7	688	3.0	235	1.0
Professionals	108,057	68.1	380	0.2	92,059	58.0	8,575	5.4	3,174	2.0	3,869	2.4
Technicians	43,828	59.7	209	0.3	34,719	47.3	5,284	7.2	2,338	3.2	1,278	1.7
Protective service workers	30,605	30.0	145	0.1	24,516	24.0	4,733	4.6	1,070	1.0	141	0.1
Paraprofessionals	128,628	63.6	653	0.3	97,163	48.0	21,553	10.6	7,264	3.6	1,995	1.0
Administrative support	169,596	77.6	911	0.4	131,857	60.4	22,502	10.3	10,265	4.7	4,061	1.9
Skilled craft workers	12,151	31.6	69	0.2	9,649	25.1	1,781	4.6	537	1.4	115	0.3
Service-maintenance	115,018	39.0	768	0.3	86,117	29.2	20,292	6.9	6,253	2.1	1,588	0.5
Total	616,991	55.5	3,169	0.3	483,142	43.5	85,809	7.7	31,589	2.8	13,282	1.2
Total												
Officials/administrators	23,160	100.0	86	0.4	19,221	83.0	2,088	9.0	1,246	5.4	519	2.2
Professionals	158,736	100.0	625	0.4	133,065	83.8	13,355	8.4	5,194	3.3	6,497	4.1
Technicians	73,470	100.0	442	0.6	58,568	79.7	8,046	11.0	4,027	5.5	2,387	3.2
Protective service workers	102,142	100.0	493	0.5	87,395	85.6	9,800	9.6	3,807	3.7	647	0.6
Paraprofessionals	202,383	100.0	1,034	0.5	150,287	74.3	34,251	16.9	13,014	6.4	3,797	1.9
Administrative support	218,436	100.0	1,854	0.8	167,511	76.7	29,621	13.6	13,436	6.2	6,014	2.8

[Continued]

★ 728 ★

Number of Part-Time State and Local Government Employees, by Job Category, 1990
[Continued]

Job category	Total		Indian		White		Black		Hispanic		Asian	
	Number	Percent	Number	Percent	Number	Percent	Number	Percent	Number	Percent	Number	Percent
Skilled craft workers	38,484	100.0	326	0.8	29,747	77.3	5,715	14.9	2,235	5.8	461	1.2
Service-maintenance	295,043	100.0	2,089	0.7	219,858	74.5	50,761	17.2	18,326	6.2	4,009	1.4
Total	1,111,854	100.0	6,949	0.6	865,652	77.9	153,637	13.8	61,285	5.5	24,331	2.2

Source: U.S. Equal Employment Opportunity Commission, *Job Patterns for Minorities and Women in State and Local Government, 1990*, U.S. Government Printing Office, 1991, p. 2.

★ 729 ★

Number of Full-Time Local Government Employees, by Sex and Income Level, 1990: Cities

Annual salary	Total		Indian		White		Black		Hispanic		Asian	
	Number	Percent	Number	Percent	Number	Percent	Number	Percent	Number	Percent	Number	Percent
Male												
100-7,900	5,732	56.0	73	0.7	4,261	41.6	1,081	10.6	292	2.9	25	0.2
8,000-11,900	22,655	59.7	161	0.4	10,596	27.9	9,228	24.3	2,617	6.9	53	0.1
12,000-15,900	74,004	60.3	492	0.4	41,058	33.4	23,853	19.4	8,292	6.8	309	0.3
16,000-19,900	145,888	61.8	853	0.4	90,394	38.3	39,933	16.9	13,633	5.8	1,075	0.5
20,000-24,900	210,384	64.7	1,015	0.3	143,760	44.2	45,441	14.0	17,580	5.4	2,588	0.8
25,000-32,900	300,364	76.4	1,337	0.3	222,911	56.7	48,139	12.2	22,403	5.7	5,574	1.4
33,000-42,900	249,284	82.7	978	0.3	194,102	64.4	30,294	10.0	17,646	5.9	6,264	2.1
43,000-Plus	137,875	85.5	494	0.3	112,563	69.8	11,846	7.3	8,320	5.2	4,652	2.9
Total	1,146,186	72.2	5,403	0.3	819,645	51.6	209,815	13.2	90,783	5.7	20,540	1.3
Female												
100-7,900	4,501	44.0	21	0.2	3,044	29.7	1,231	12.0	190	1.9	15	0.1
8,000-11,900	15,273	40.3	86	0.2	9,164	24.2	4,886	12.9	1,083	2.9	54	0.1
12,000-15,900	48,776	39.7	295	0.2	32,403	26.4	12,249	10.0	3,609	2.9	220	0.2
16,000-19,900	90,017	38.2	446	0.2	51,675	21.9	29,141	12.4	7,775	3.3	980	0.4
20,000-24,900	114,987	35.3	506	0.2	60,366	18.6	41,698	12.8	9,754	3.0	2,663	0.8
25,000-32,900	92,670	23.6	455	0.1	55,592	14.1	25,112	6.4	7,222	1.8	4,289	1.1
33,000-42,900	52,255	17.3	208	0.1	30,728	10.2	14,308	4.7	3,687	1.2	3,324	1.1
43,000-Plus	23,337	14.5	96	0.1	14,965	9.3	4,918	3.1	1,389	0.9	1,969	1.2
Total	441,816	27.8	2,113	0.1	257,937	16.2	133,543	8.4	34,709	2.2	13,514	0.9
Total												
100-7,900	10,233	100.0	94	0.9	7,305	71.4	2,312	22.6	482	4.7	40	0.4
8,000-11,900	37,928	100.0	247	0.7	19,760	52.1	14,114	37.2	3,700	9.8	107	0.3
12,000-15,900	122,780	100.0	787	0.6	73,461	59.8	36,102	29.4	11,901	9.7	529	0.4
16,000-19,900	235,905	100.0	1,299	0.6	142,069	60.2	69,074	29.3	21,408	9.1	2,055	0.9
20,000-24,900	325,371	100.0	1,521	0.5	204,126	62.7	87,139	26.8	27,334	8.4	5,251	1.6
25,000-32,900	393,034	100.0	1,792	0.5	278,503	70.9	73,251	18.6	29,625	7.5	9,863	2.5
33,000-42,900	301,539	100.0	1,186	0.4	224,830	74.6	44,602	14.8	21,333	7.1	9,588	3.2
43,000-Plus	161,212	100.0	590	0.4	127,528	79.1	16,764	10.4	9,709	6.0	6,621	4.1
Total	1,588,002	100.0	7,516	0.5	1,077,582	67.9	343,358	21.6	125,492	7.9	34,054	2.1

Source: U.S. Equal Employment Opportunity Commission, *Job Patterns for Minorities and Women in State and Local Government, 1990*, U.S. Government Printing Office, 1990, p. 18.

★ 730 ★

Number of Full-Time Local Government Employees, by Sex and Income Level, 1990:
Counties

Annual salary	Total		Indian		White		Black		Hispanic		Asian	
	Number	Percent	Number	Percent	Number	Percent	Number	Percent	Number	Percent	Number	Percent
Male												
100-7,900	9,303	46.0	51	0.3	7,597	37.6	1,213	6.0	397	2.0	45	0.2
8,000-11,900	22,698	32.3	206	0.3	15,844	22.6	5,116	7.3	1,451	2.1	81	0.1
12,000-15,900	65,587	33.9	622	0.3	49,090	25.4	11,579	6.0	3,969	2.1	327	0.2
16,000-19,900	100,803	41.8	523	0.3	79,383	32.9	13,658	5.7	6,144	2.5	995	0.4
20,000-24,900	121,749	47.3	682	0.3	96,663	37.6	15,006	5.8	7,538	2.9	1,860	0.7
25,000-32,900	123,477	53.1	677	0.3	98,827	42.5	13,811	5.9	7,813	3.4	2,349	1.0
33,000-42,900	86,811	58.7	416	0.3	70,430	47.6	7,710	5.2	5,766	3.9	2,489	1.7
43,000-Plus	71,248	71.2	288	0.3	60,346	60.3	4,337	4.3	3,977	4.0	2,300	2.3
Total	601,676	47.6	3,565	0.3	478,180	37.9	72,430	5.7	37,055	2.9	10,446	0.8
Female												
100-7,900	10,916	54.0	68	0.3	8,929	44.2	1,366	6.8	494	2.4	59	0.3
8,000-11,900	47,468	67.7	212	0.3	36,419	51.9	8,283	11.8	2,364	3.4	190	0.3
12,000-15,900	127,950	66.1	747	0.4	100,510	51.9	19,003	9.8	6,964	3.6	726	0.4
16,000-19,900	140,565	58.2	685	0.3	104,572	43.3	23,469	9.7	9,929	4.1	1,910	0.8
20,000-24,900	135,381	52.7	596	0.2	95,344	37.1	24,535	9.5	11,432	4.4	3,474	1.4
25,000-32,900	109,069	46.9	453	0.2	80,673	34.7	17,319	7.4	7,503	3.2	3,121	1.3
33,000-42,900	61,198	41.3	244	0.2	43,233	29.2	9,105	6.2	4,446	3.0	4,170	2.8
43,000-Plus	28,846	28.8	99	0.1	21,556	21.5	3,551	3.5	1,637	1.6	2,003	2.0
Total	661,393	52.4	3,104	0.2	491,236	38.9	106,681	8.4	44,769	3.5	15,653	1.2
Total												
100-7,900	20,219	100.0	119	0.6	16,526	81.7	2,579	12.8	891	4.4	104	0.5
8,000-11,900	70,166	100.0	418	0.6	52,263	74.5	13,399	19.1	3,815	5.4	271	0.4
12,000-15,900	193,537	100.0	1,369	0.7	149,600	77.3	30,582	15.8	10,933	5.6	1,053	0.5
16,000-19,900	241,368	100.0	1,308	0.5	183,955	76.2	37,127	15.4	16,073	6.7	2,905	1.2
20,000-24,900	257,130	100.0	1,278	0.5	192,007	74.7	39,541	15.4	18,970	7.4	5,334	2.1
25,000-32,900	232,546	100.0	1,130	0.5	179,500	77.2	31,130	13.4	15,316	6.6	5,470	2.4
33,000-42,900	148,009	100.0	660	0.4	113,663	76.8	16,815	11.4	10,212	6.9	6,659	4.5
43,000-Plus	100,094	100.0	387	0.4	81,902	81.8	7,888	7.9	5,614	5.6	4,303	4.3
Total	1,263,069	100.0	6,669	0.5	969,416	76.8	179,061	14.2	81,824	6.5	26,099	2.1

Source: U.S. Equal Employment Opportunity Commission, *Job Patterns for Minorities and Women in State and Local Government, 1990,* U.S. Government Printing Office, 1990, p. 15.

★ 731 ★

Number of Full-Time Local Government Employees, by Sex and Income Level, 1990:
Special Districts

Annual salary	Total		Indian		White		Black		Hispanic		Asian	
	Number	Percent	Number	Percent	Number	Percent	Number	Percent	Number	Percent	Number	Percent
Male												
100-7,900	975	42.7	8	0.4	533	23.4	202	8.9	205	9.0	27	1.2
8,000-11,900	5,390	25.7	12	0.1	1,969	9.4	2,343	11.2	1,004	4.8	52	0.3
12,000-15,900	9,800	25.6	26	0.1	4,517	11.8	3,885	10.1	1,228	3.2	144	0.4
16,000-19,900	13,550	33.1	64	0.2	7,133	17.4	4,870	11.9	1,268	3.1	215	0.5
20,000-24,900	25,352	47.6	174	0.3	15,382	28.9	6,964	13.1	2,366	4.4	466	0.9

[Continued]

★ 731 ★

Number of Full-Time Local Government Employees, by Sex and Income Level, 1990: Special Districts
[Continued]

Annual salary	Total		Indian		White		Black		Hispanic		Asian	
	Number	Percent	Number	Percent	Number	Percent	Number	Percent	Number	Percent	Number	Percent
25,000-32,900	66,905	62.7	351	0.3	41,296	38.7	18,912	17.7	5,053	4.7	1,293	1.2
33,000-42,900	44,961	68.1	497	0.8	32,404	49.1	7,329	11.1	3,415	5.2	1,315	2.0
43,000-Plus	33,190	79.0	170	0.4	24,112	57.4	6,147	14.6	1,310	3.1	1,451	3.5
Total	200,123	54.0	1,302	0.4	127,346	34.4	50,652	13.7	15,850	4.3	4,973	1.3
Female												
100-7,900	307	57.3	7	0.3	875	38.3	353	15.5	62	2.7	10	0.4
8,000-11,900	15,565	74.3	31	0.1	8,678	41.4	5,395	25.7	1,384	6.6	77	0.4
12,000-15,900	28,540	74.4	63	0.2	16,077	41.9	10,089	26.3	1,997	5.2	314	0.8
16,000-19,900	27,445	66.9	76	0.2	16,809	41.1	8,529	20.8	1,647	4.0	324	0.8
20,000-24,900	27,906	52.4	149	0.3	19,002	35.8	6,611	12.4	1,524	2.9	570	1.1
25,000-32,900	39,812	37.3	150	0.1	27,783	26.0	8,700	8.2	1,910	1.8	1,269	1.2
33,000-42,900	21,047	31.9	94	0.1	15,672	23.7	3,398	5.1	778	1.2	1,105	1.7
43,000-Plus	8,844	21.0	40	0.1	6,294	15.0	1,800	4.3	247	0.6	463	1.1
Total	170,466	46.0	610	0.2	111,300	30.0	44,875	12.1	9,549	2.6	4,132	1.1
Total												
100-7,900	2,282	100.0	15	0.7	1,408	61.7	555	24.3	267	11.7	37	1.6
8,000-11,900	20,955	100.0	43	0.2	10,647	50.8	7,738	36.9	2,388	11.4	139	0.7
12,000-15,900	38,340	100.0	89	0.2	20,594	53.7	13,974	36.4	3,225	8.4	458	1.2
16,000-19,900	40,995	100.0	140	0.3	24,002	58.5	13,399	32.7	2,915	7.1	539	1.3
20,000-24,900	53,258	100.0	322	0.6	34,434	64.7	13,575	25.5	3,890	7.3	1,036	1.9
25,000-32,900	106,717	100.0	501	0.5	69,079	64.7	27,612	25.9	6,963	6.5	2,562	2.4
33,000-42,900	66,008	100.0	501	0.9	48,076	72.8	10,727	16.3	4,194	6.4	2,420	3.7
43,000-Plus	42,034	100.0	210	0.5	30,403	72.3	7,947	18.9	1,557	2.7	1,914	4.6
Total	370,589	100.0	1,912	0.5	238,646	64.4	95,527	25.8	25,399	6.9	9,105	2.5

Source: U.S. Equal Employment Opportunity Commission, *Job Patterns for Minorities and Women in State and Local Government, 1990,* U.S. Government Printing Office, 1990, p. 24.

★ 732 ★

Number of Full-Time Local Government Employees, by Sex and Income Level, 1990: Towns

Annual salary	Total		Indian		White		Black		Hispanic		Asian	
	Number	Percent	Number	Percent	Number	Percent	Number	Percent	Number	Percent	Number	Percent
Male												
100-7,900	619	60.7	0	0.0	608	59.6	10	1.0	1	0.1	0	0.0
8,000-11,900	367	39.6	3	0.3	350	37.8	10	1.1	3	0.3	1	0.1
12,000-15,900	1,477	34.2	3	0.1	1,355	31.4	92	2.1	27	0.6	0	0.0
16,000-19,900	4,904	43.8	13	0.1	4,593	41.1	229	2.0	62	0.6	7	0.1
20,000-24,900	13,968	66.1	22	0.1	13,269	62.8	541	2.6	124	0.6	12	0.1
25,000-32,900	25,120	83.4	39	0.1	24,221	80.5	627	2.1	200	0.7	33	0.1
33,000-42,900	16,599	89.4	23	0.1	16,145	87.0	313	1.7	102	0.5	16	0.1
43,000-Plus	6,726	92.4	10	0.1	6,607	90.8	75	1.0	23	0.3	11	0.2
Total	69,780	73.8	113	0.1	67,148	71.0	1,897	2.0	542	0.6	80	0.1
Female												
100-7,900	401	39.3	1	0.1	397	38.9	2	0.2	1	0.1	0	0.0
8,000-11,900	559	60.4	0	0.0	532	57.5	12	1.3	12	1.3	3	0.3
12,000-15,900	2,839	65.8	4	0.1	2,712	62.8	94	2.2	25	0.6	4	0.1
16,000-19,900	6,284	56.2	4	0.0	6,067	54.2	146	1.3	46	0.4	21	0.2

[Continued]

★ 732 ★

Number of Full-Time Local Government Employees, by Sex and Income Level, 1990: Towns
[Continued]

Annual salary	Total		Indian		White		Black		Hispanic		Asian	
	Number	Percent	Number	Percent	Number	Percent	Number	Percent	Number	Percent	Number	Percent
20,000-24,900	7,167	33.9	7	0.0	6,842	32.4	249	1.2	52	0.2	17	0.1
25,000-32,900	4,985	16.6	9	0.0	4,776	15.9	149	0.5	33	0.1	18	0.1
33,000-42,900	1,961	10.6	1	0.0	1,902	10.2	48	0.3	7	0.0	3	0.0
43,000-Plus	553	7.6	0	0.0	523	7.2	18	0.2	6	0.1	6	0.1
Total	24,749	26.2	26	0.0	23,751	25.1	718	0.8	182	0.2	72	0.1
Total												
100-7,900	1,020	100.0	1	0.1	1,005	98.5	12	1.2	2	0.2	0	0.0
8,000-11,900	926	100.0	3	0.3	882	95.2	22	2.4	15	1.6	4	0.4
12,000-15,900	4,316	100.0	7	0.2	4,067	94.2	186	4.3	52	1.2	4	0.1
16,000-19,900	11,188	100.0	17	0.2	10,660	95.3	375	3.4	108	1.0	28	0.3
20,000-24,900	21,135	100.0	29	0.1	20,111	95.2	790	3.7	176	0.8	29	0.1
25,000-32,900	30,105	100.0	48	0.2	28,997	96.3	776	2.6	233	0.8	51	0.2
33,000-42,900	18,560	100.0	24	0.1	18,047	97.2	361	1.9	109	0.6	19	0.1
43,000-Plus	7,279	100.0	10	0.1	7,130	98.0	93	1.3	29	0.4	17	0.2
Total	94,529	100.0	139	0.1	90,899	96.2	2,615	2.8	724	0.8	152	0.2

Source: U.S. Equal Employment Opportunity Commission, *Job Patterns for Minorities and Women in State and Local Government, 1990,* U.S. Government Printing Office, 1990, p. 21.

Military Personnel

★ 733 ★

Estimates of the Armed Forces Overseas, by Age and Sex, 1991

Data are shown in thousands.

Age	Total U.S.			American Indian, Eskimo, and Aleut		
	Total	Male	Female	Total	Male	Female
All ages	511.6	452.2	59.3	3.0	2.6	0.5
Under 20	36.7	32.2	4.5	0.3	0.2	0.0
17	0.1	0.1	0.0	0.0	0.0	0.0
18	8.3	7.2	1.1	0.1	0.0	0.0
19	28.3	24.9	3.4	0.2	0.2	0.0
20-24	177.4	156.0	21.5	1.1	0.9	0.2
20	40.5	35.7	4.8	0.3	0.2	0.1
21	40.1	35.5	4.6	0.3	0.2	0.0
22	34.9	30.7	4.2	0.2	0.2	0.0
23	31.5	27.4	4.0	0.2	0.1	0.0
24	30.5	26.7	3.9	0.2	0.1	0.0

[Continued]

★ 733 ★

Estimates of the Armed Forces Overseas, by Age and Sex, 1991
[Continued]

Age	Total U.S.			American Indian, Eskimo, and Aleut		
	Total	Male	Female	Total	Male	Female
25-29	126.2	109.5	16.6	0.6	0.5	0.1
25	29.6	25.8	3.8	0.2	0.1	0.0
26	27.6	24.0	3.6	0.1	0.1	0.0
27	24.7	21.4	3.3	0.1	0.1	0.0
28	23.0	19.9	3.1	0.1	0.1	0.0
29	21.3	18.5	2.8	0.1	0.1	0.0
30-34	83.3	73.1	10.1	0.4	0.4	0.1
30	19.5	17.0	2.5	0.1	0.1	0.0
31	17.7	15.5	2.2	0.1	0.1	0.0
32	16.6	14.6	2.0	0.1	0.1	0.0
33	15.2	13.4	1.8	0.1	0.1	0.0
34	14.2	12.6	1.6	0.1	0.1	0.0
35-39	55.2	50.2	5.0	0.4	0.4	0.1
35	13.3	12.0	1.4	0.1	0.1	0.0
36	12.3	11.2	1.2	0.1	0.1	0.0
37	11.5	10.4	1.1	0.1	0.1	0.0
38	9.8	9.0	0.8	0.1	0.1	0.0
39	8.3	7.7	0.6	0.1	0.1	0.0
40-44	25.0	23.6	1.4	0.2	0.2	0.0
40	7.2	6.8	0.4	0.1	0.0	0.0
41	6.0	5.6	0.4	0.0	0.0	0.0
42	5.1	4.8	0.3	0.0	0.0	0.0
43	4.3	4.1	0.2	0.0	0.0	0.0
44	2.5	2.4	0.1	0.0	0.0	0.0
45-49	6.4	6.1	0.2	0.0	0.0	0.0
45	2.0	1.9	0.1	0.0	0.0	0.0
46	1.6	1.5	0.1	0.0	0.0	0.0
47	1.3	1.3	0.0	0.0	0.0	0.0
48	0.8	0.8	0.0	0.0	0.0	0.0
49	0.6	0.6	0.0	0.0	0.0	0.0
50-64	1.4	1.4	0.1	0.0	0.0	0.0

★ 734 ★

Veteran Status, by Major Tribal Group, 1980: Abanaki - Pamunkey

Data are estimates based on a sample and are the most recent available.

Major Tribal Group	Civilian persons 16 years old and older	Veterans		Male Veterans	
		Number of veterans	Percent of civilian persons 16 years old and older	Number of male veterans	Percent of civilian males 16 years old and older
All American Indians	972,333	154,863	15.9	147,351	31.5
Abenaki (n.e.c)	525	67	12.8	58	27.5
Alabama Coushatta[1]	707	79	11.2	79	21.6
Alaska Native (n.e.c.)	396	58	14.6	41	23.7
Alaskan Athabaskans	6,460	720	11.1	689	22.1
Aleut and Eskimo	455	78	17.1	72	29.9
Algonquian (n.e.c.)	1,187	266	22.4	253	38.8
Apache	22,263	3,616	16.2	3,476	31.1
Arapaho	2,771	317	11.4	301	22.7
Arikara	914	143	15.6	140	34.4
Assiniboine	2,397	435	18.1	377	35.5
Bannock	321	43	13.4	43	26.9
Blackfoot[1]	15,602	3,023	19.4	2,826	37.9
Brotherton	139	33	23.7	33	51.6
Caddo	1,133	185	16.3	172	36.1
Cahuilla	775	155	20.0	139	36.9
California tribes (n.e.c.)	425	76	17.9	63	25.9
Canadian and Latin American	5,474	769	14.0	727	26.6
Catawba	770	137	17.8	137	41.6
Cayuse	111	22	19.8	22	64.7
Chehalis	180	22	12.2	22	33.3
Chemakuan	251	10	4.0	10	8.7
Chemehuevi	336	45	13.4	45	41.7
Cherokee	166,465	30,672	18.4	29,206	38.1
Cheyenne	5,712	1,078	18.9	1,049	36.9
Chickahominy	632	95	15.0	95	33.6
Chickasaw	7,270	1,308	18.0	1,223	35.5
Chinook	610	147	18.1	147	36.2
Chippewa	45,080	7,693	17.1	7,344	34.0
Chitimacha	204	29	14.2	29	26.4
Choctaw	34,529	6,105	17.7	5,832	35.0
Chumash[1]	939	162	17.3	150	32.7
Clallam	576	64	11.1	64	28.6
Coeur d'Alene	353	62	17.6	53	34.2
Coharie	347	44	12.7	44	28.0
Colorado River	613	92	15.0	92	30.5
Colville	3,364	408	12.1	408	26.1

[Continued]

1105

★ 734 ★

Veteran Status, by Major Tribal Group, 1980: Abanaki - Pamunkey
[Continued]

Major Tribal Group	Civilian persons 16 years old and older	Veterans		Male Veterans	
		Number of veterans	Percent of civilian persons 16 years and older	Number of male veterans	Percent of civilian males 16 years old and older
Comanche	5,922	1,303	22.0	1,267	41.3
Coos	58	11	19.0	11	47.8
Costanoan	318	43	13.5	43	32.8
Cowitz	697	118	16.9	118	45.0
Cree	3,971	720	18.1	710	34.5
Creek	18,731	3,433	18.3	3,289	37.1
Croatan	142	16	11.3	16	21.3
Crow	4,276	639	14.9	624	29.0
Cupeno	224	26	11.6	26	28.3
Delaware	3,627	763	19.9	715	38.5
Diegueno	871	114	13.1	114	26.9
Eastern tribes (n.e.c.)	1,785	256	14.3	256	27.5
Flathead	3,231	577	17.9	566	35.9
Fort Hall	245	8	3.3	8	7.9
Gabrieleno	1,216	192	15.8	192	37.2
Gros Ventres	1,333	213	16.0	201	35.8
Haida	975	125	12.8	119	23.1
Haliwa	1,307	98	7.5	98	15.6
Hidatsa	945	152	16.1	150	32.8
Hitchiti	10	7	70.0	7	87.5
Hoopa	1,236	189	15.3	173	30.6
Houma	1,511	101	6.7	93	10.8
Iowa	628	89	14.2	89	27.5
Iroquois	26,065	4,426	17.0	4,103	33.5
Onondaga	581	65	11.2	61	20.7
Seneca	4,886	1,042	21.3	951	40.2
Seneca-Cayuga	229	47	20.5	39	43.8
Tuscarora	1,375	173	12.6	169	26.0
Wyandot	787	227	28.8	219	57.3
Kalispel	119	10	8.4	10	13.7
Karok	1,260	218	17.3	200	30.2
Kaw	505	88	17.4	83	40.5
Kickapoo	1,605	251	15.6	238	29.2
Kiowa	4,373	716	16.4	695	33.0
Klamath	1,173	116	9.9	114	22.1
Konkow	287	48	16.7	46	30.5
Kootenai	251	45	17.9	42	34.7

[Continued]

★ 734 ★

Veteran Status, by Major Tribal Group, 1980: Abenaki - Pamunkey
[Continued]

Major Tribal Group	Civilian persons 16 years old and older	Veterans		Male Veterans	
		Number of veterans	Percent of civilian persons 16 years and older	Number of male veterans	Percent of civilian males 16 years old and older
Long Island	253	58	22.9	52	49.5
Luiseno	807	90	11.2	74	21.1
Lumbee[2]	18,076	1,419	7.9	1,357	16.0
Lummi[2]	2,514	255	10.1	226	19.2
Maidu	719	115	16.0	115	39.4
Makah	652	82	12.6	82	25.1
Maliseet	318	82	25.8	82	50.6
Mandan	584	130	22.3	115	38.2
Mattaponi	100	12	12.0	12	27.3
Menominee	3,610	544	15.1	519	30.2
Miami	1,386	263	19.0	263	34.6
Miccosukee[1]	51	-	-	-	-
Micmac[3]	661	77	11.6	61	21.6
Mission Indians	1,890	344	18.2	318	34.3
Miowk	1,416	227	16.0	211	30.4
Modoc	553	130	23.5	114	37.3
Mohegan	367	67	18.3	62	40.3
Mono	933	149	16.0	149	38.2
Nanticoke	779	129	16.6	122	32.2
Narragansett	1,309	195	14.9	195	39.6
Navajo	92,577	6,478	7.0	6,192	14.3
Nez Perce[1]	1,618	258	15.9	246	27.5
Nomalaki	145	4	2.8	4	6.9
Northwest tribes (n.e.c.)	224	54	24.1	54	38.8
Omaha	1,943	261	13.4	260	27.7
Oregon Athabaskan	413	98	23.7	97	37.9
Osage	4,851	1,057	21.8	997	42.6
Oto	948	191	20.1	179	38.3
Ottawa	4,060	718	17.6	671	36.1
Paiute[1]	6,043	813	13.5	785	28.9
Pamunkey	276	73	26.4	73	47.7

Source: U.S. Bureau of the Census, *1980 Census of Population, Volume 2, Subject Reports, Characteristics of American Indians, by Tribes and Selected Areas: 1980*, PC80-2-1C, Section 1: Tables I-II, issued September 1989, U.S. Department of Commerce, U.S. Government Printing Office, Washington, D.C., pp. 203-255. *Notes:* (N.E.C.) stands for not elsewhere classified. A dash (-) represents zero or a percent which rounds to less than 0.1. 1. Reporting and/or processing problems may have affected the data for this tribe. 2. Miscoding of entries of "Lummee," "Lummi," "Lumbee," or "Lumbi" may have affected the data for this tribe. 3. Any entry with the spelling "Micmac" was miscoded to Cheyenne River Sioux.

★ 735 ★

Veteran Status, by Major Tribal Group, 1980: Papago - Yurok

Data are estimates based on a sample and are the most recent available.

Major Tribal Group	Civilian persons 16 years old and older	Veterans		Male Veterans	
		Number of veterans	Percent of civilian persons 16 years old and older	Number of male veterans	Percent of civlian males 16 years old and older
Papago	8,169	583	7.1	566	14.9
Passamaquoddy	1,007	154	15.3	135	26.9
Pawnee	1,664	367	22.1	342	43.3
Penobscot	931	232	24.9	213	41.3
Peoria	368	75	20.4	75	39.1
Pequot	301	44	14.6	35	24.3
Pima	6,953	735	10.6	712	22.6
Piscataway	325	34	10.5	34	20.1
Pit River	733	59	8.0	55	14.5
Pomo	1,840	241	13.1	234	30.7
Ponca	1,179	227	19.3	212	35.1
Potawatomi	6,496	1,195	18.4	1,134	36.9
Powhatan	247	63	25.5	56	47.1
Pueblo[1]	26,710	2,785	10.4	2,678	20.9
Puget Sound Salish	94	17	18.1	17	36.2
Quapaw	639	124	19.4	124	45.1
Quinault	1,016	109	10.7	109	23.5
Rappahannock	232	27	12.2	27	26.2
Sac and Fox Mesquakie	2,301	424	18.4	378	36.6
Salinan	189	7	3.7	7	6.8
Schaghticoke	131	12	9.2	12	16.9
Seminole[1]	6,789	1,354	19.9	1,289	38.1
Serrano	152	2	1.3	2	2.3
Shasta	241	30	12.4	30	25.6
Shawnee	2,983	556	18.6	530	39.7
Shinnecock	760	130	17.1	121	36.0
Shoshone	6,453	870	13.5	850	28.4
Siletz	443	104	23.5	100	45.0
Sioux	46,957	7,955	16.9	7,544	34.0
Siuslaw	214	60	28.0	60	55.6
Spokane	1,161	299	25.8	285	48.6
Stockbridge	1,037	228	22.0	222	43.5
Tlingit	5,833	933	16.0	886	32.4
Tolowa	213	57	26.8	57	46.7
Tonkawa	150	18	12.0	18	23.4
Tsimshian	1,092	142	13.0	122	24.3
Umatilla	610	95	15.6	95	34.3
Ute	3,479	541	15.6	514	30.0

[Continued]

★ 735 ★

Veteran Status, by Major Tribal Group, 1980: Papago — Yurok
[Continued]

Major Tribal Group	Civilian persons 16 years old and older	Veterans		Male Veterans	
		Number of veterans	Percent of civilian persons 16 years old and older	Number of male veterans	Percent of civlian males 16 years old and older
Wailaki[2]	375	37	9.9	37	30.8
Walla-Walla	183	47	25.7	37	41.6
Wampanoag	978	172	17.6	172	40.6
Warm Springs	786	58	7.4	58	19.3
Washo	984	162	16.5	147	31.8
Wichita	469	114	24.3	114	44.9
Winnebago	3,009	504	16.7	479	36.1
Wintu	1,251	207	16.5	191	34.9
Wiyot	189	38	20.1	38	38.4
Yakima	3,977	492	12.4	484	27.3
Yaqui	3,234	453	14.0	437	27.4
Yavapai Apache	100	7	7.0	7	13.5
Yokuts	1,132	118	10.4	97	18.9
Yuchi	165	20	12.1	20	31.3
Yuman	4,026	486	12.1	475	25.1
Yurok	1,833	276	15.1	268	33.0
Other specified tribes (n.e.c.)	313	59	18.8	55	40.7
All other specified	102	19	18.6	15	36.6
Tribe not specified	22,616	3,467	15.3	3,225	30.1
Tribe not reported	212,892	38,915	18.3	36,994	34.1

Source: U.S. Bureau of the Census, *1980 Census of Population, Volume 2, Subject Reports, Characteristics of American Indians, by Tribes and Selected Areas: 1980*, PC80-2-1C, Section 1: Tables I-II, issued September 1989, U.S. Department of Commerce, U.S. Government Printing Office, Washington, D.C., pp. 203-255. *Notes:* (N.E.C.) stands for not elsewhere classified. A dash (-) represents zero or a percent which rounds to less than 0.1. 1. Reporting and/or processing problems may have affected the data for this tribe. 2. Any Mohawk entry of "Ganienka" was miscoded to Wailaki.

Federal Expenditures

★ 736 ★

Department of Interior Expenditures on Education 1965-91

Expenditures are shown in thousands of dollars, for 1965-91.

Program	1965	1970	1975	1980	1985	1988	1989	1990	1991[1]
Total	130,096	140,705	220,392	318,170	389,810	379,645	379,381	445,267	429,383
Mineral Leasing Act and other funds									
Payments to States - estimated education share	11,075	12,294	27,389	62,636	127,369	92,227	114,414	123,811	141,792
Payments to counties - estimated education share	10,731	16,359	29,494	48,953	59,016	34,922	54,804	102,522	47,111
Indian Education									
Bureau of Indian Affairs schools	92,603	95,850	141,056	178,112	177,265	231,512	186,643	192,841	215,049
Johnson O'Malley assistance[2]	15,534	16,080	22,251	28,081	25,675	20,400	23,000	25,556	24,931
Education expenses for children of employees									
Yellowstone National Park	153	122	202	388	485	584	520	538	500

Source: Federal Support for Education: Fiscal Years 1980 to 1991, National Center for Education Statistics, Survey Report, December 1991, p. 35. *Notes:* 1. Data are estimated. 2. This program provides funding for supplemental programs for eligible Indian students in public schools.

★ 737 ★

Federal Forestry Assistance

Senior community service - 1800

Fiscal and plant management surveys - 279

Miscellaneous forestry assistance - 223

Rural planning fire protection - 125

Youth conservation corps - 111

Land management planning - 67.5

Other - 58

Estimates are for the amount of assistance given to Native Americans and Alaska Natives in FY 1989. The total was $3.3 million.

Type	Amount ($ 000)
Fiscal and plant management surveys	279
Youth conservation corps	111
Senior community service	1800
Miscellaneous forestry assistance	223
Land management planning	67.5
Rural planning fire protection	125
Other[1]	58

Source: Roger Walke, *Federal Programs of Assistance to Native Americans: A Report Prepared for the Senate Select Committee on Indian Affairs of the United States Senate,* U.S. Government Printing Office, Washington, D.C., December 1991, p. 38. *Notes:* 1. Includes urban forestry ($9,000), long-range planning ($16,000) and watershed planning ($33,000).

★ 738 ★

Federal Programs of Assistance to Native Americans, 1988-90 - I

Obligations represent actual dollars spent; appropriations are total amounts allotted at the beginning of the year.

Government agency and program	Appropriations ($)			Obligations ($)		
	1988	1989	1990	1988	1989	1990
Food and Nutrition Service						
Food Distribution Program on Indian Reservations	56,099	57,854	60,140	55,680	57,079	60,140
Nutrition Program for the Elderly (Title VI)	138,009	141,293	143,482	137,558	140,863	143,482
Food Stamp Program	12,678,507,000	12,915,329,000	15,969,589,000	12,338,327,000	12,859,527,000	15,522,412,000
National School Lunch Program	3,068,167	3,025,352	3,115,124	2,934,996	3,082,247	3,213,869
School Breakfast Program	479,819	514,498	563,926	473,190	513,032	564,367
Special Milk Program for Children	21,500	19,925	20,309	22,119	19,905	20,943

[Continued]

Federal Programs of Assistance to Native Americans, 1988-90 - I
[Continued]

Government agency and program	Appropriations ($)			Obligations ($)		
	1988	1989	1990	1988	1989	1990
Summer Food Service Program	137,649	147,824	170,872	136,312	146,672	163,344
Child and Adult Care Food Program	599,836	655,932	757,288	613,076	677,431	716,866
Supplemental Food Program for Women, Infants and Children (WIC)	1,802,363	1,929,362	2,126,000	1,802,430	1,928,926	2,126,398
Agricultural Stabilization and Conservation Service (ASCS)						
Forestry Incentives Program	N/A	N/A	N/A	N/A	N/A	N/A
Agricultural Conservation Program	N/A	N/A	N/A	N/A	N/A	N/A
Emergency Conservation Program	N/A	N/A	N/A	N/A	N/A	N/A
Water Bank Program	N/A	N/A	N/A	N/A	N/A	N/A
Wool and Mohair Payment Program	N/A	N/A	N/A	N/A	N/A	N/A
Indian Acute Distress Donation Program	N/A	N/A	N/A	N/A	N/A	N/A
Livestock Feed Program	N/A	N/A	N/A	N/A	N/A	N/A
Conservation Reserve Program	N/A	N/A	N/A	N/A	N/A	N/A
Natural Resources and Environment						
Soil Conservation Service	N/A	N/A	N/A	N/A	N/A	N/A
Soil Survey Program	N/A	N/A	N/A	N/A	N/A	N/A
Technical Assistance Program	N/A	N/A	N/A	N/A	N/A	N/A
Great Plains Conservation Programs	N/A	N/A	N/A	N/A	N/A	N/A
Resource Conservation and Development Program	N/A	N/A	N/A	N/A	N/A	N/A
Soil and Water Conservation Program	N/A	N/A	N/A	N/A	N/A	N/A
Watershed Projects	N/A	N/A	N/A	N/A	N/A	N/A
Forest Service						
Range Management Program	N/A	N/A	N/A	N/A	N/A	N/A
Special Land Use Program	N/A	N/A	N/A	N/A	N/A	N/A
Senior Community Service Employment Program	N/A	N/A	N/A	N/A	N/A	N/A
Cooperative Forest Management Program	N/A	N/A	N/A	N/A	N/A	N/A
Forest Products Utilization Program	N/A	N/A	N/A	N/A	N/A	N/A
Forest Pest Management Program	N/A	N/A	N/A	N/A	N/A	N/A
Forestry Incentives Program	N/A	N/A	N/A	N/A	N/A	N/A
Free Use Timber Program	N/A	N/A	N/A	N/A	N/A	N/A
Job Corps Civilian Conservation Program	N/A	N/A	N/A	N/A	N/A	N/A
Rural Community Fire Protection Program	N/A	N/A	N/A	N/A	N/A	N/A
Small Community and Rural Development						
Farmers Home Administration (FMHA)						
Indian Out Reach Program	N/A	N/A	N/A	N/A	N/A	N/A
Indian Land Acquisition Loans	2,000,000	2,000,000	N/A	461,330	120,000	N/A
Farm Ownership Loan Program	755,000,000	819,000,000	N/A	477,000,000	400,100,000	N/A
Farm Ownership Loans for Socially Disadvantaged Persons	N/A	N/A	10,913,300	N/A	N/A	11,149,680
Farm Operating Loan Program	3,050,000,000	3,531,000,000	N/A	1,793,000,000	1,735,000,000	N/A
Water and Waste Disposal Systems for Rural Communities						
Grants	109,395,000	116,895,000	N/A	119,359,170	122,698,510	N/A
Loans	330,380,000	332,880,000	N/A	330,380,000	332,879,900	N/A
Watershed Protection and Flood Prevention Loans	8,000,000	8,000,000	N/A	148,200	0	N/A
Resource Conservation and Development Loans	1,207,000	600,000	N/A	0	0	N/A
Industrial Development Grants	6,500,000	6,500,000	N/A	6,500,000	6,500,000	N/A
Community Facility Loans	95,700,000	95,700,000		95,700,000	95,700,000	N/A
Direct	N/A	N/A	94,381,000	N/A	N/A	N/A
Guarantee	N/A	N/A	23,229,000	N/A	N/A	N/A
Rural Housing Loan Program	N/A	N/A	1,310,804,000	N/A	N/A	N/A
Rural Housing Site Development Loans	600,000	600,000	N/A	N/A	400,000	N/A
Rental and Cooperative Housing Loan Program	515,100,000	554,900,000	571,900,000	N/A	544,900,000	N/A
Housing Preservation Grant Program	19,140,000	19,140,000	19,140,000	N/A	N/A	N/A
Business and Industrial Loans Program	95,700,000	295,700,000	165,000,000	95,400,000	99,100,000	N/A
Rural Electrification Administration (REA)						
Rural Electrification Loan Program	N/A	N/A	N/A	N/A	N/A	N/A
Rural Telephone Loan Bank	N/A	N/A	N/A	N/A	N/A	N/A
Rural Telephone Bank Loan Program	N/A	N/A	N/A	N/A	N/A	N/A
Rural Economic Development Loan and Grant Program	N/A	N/A	N/A	N/A	N/A	N/A
Department of Commerce						
Office of Intergovernmental Affairs	N/A	N/A	N/A	N/A	N/A	N/A

[Continued]

★ 738 ★

Federal Programs of Assistance to Native Americans, 1988-90 - I
[Continued]

Government agency and program	Appropriations ($)			Obligations ($)		
	1988	1989	1990	1988	1989	1990
Economic Development Administration (EDA)						
Planning Assistance	22,995,000	22,995,000	N/A	22,751,000	22,956,000	N/A
Public Works Impact Program	N/A	N/A	N/A	N/A	N/A	N/A
Public Works and Development Facilities Assistance	126,000,000	126,400,000	N/A	123,613,000	123,843,000	N/A
Loan Guarantees for Business Development	150,000,000	150,000,000	N/A	0	2,508,000	N/A
Technical Assistance	1,916,000	1,916,000	N/A	1,962,000	1,849,000	N/A
Special Economic Development and Adjustment Assistance	24,657,000	24,657,000	N/A	24,673,000	27,156,000	N/A
EDA Regional Offices	N/A	N/A	N/A	N/A	N/A	N/A
Minority Business Development Agency						
Indian Business Development Center (IBDC) Program	1,495,000	1,495,000	1,495,000	1,495,000	1,495,000	1,495,000
MBDA Regional Offices	N/A	N/A	N/A	N/A	N/A	N/A
National Oceanic and Atmospheric Administration						
Anadromous Fish Grants	N/A	N/A	N/A	N/A	N/A	N/A
Alaska Eskimo Whaling Commission Grants	427,950	350,000	350,000	427,950	330,000	330,000
National Telecommunications and Information Administration						
Public Telecommunications Facilities Program	18,000,000	18,000,000	N/A	19,000,000	22,000,000	N/A
Department of Defense						
National Guard Programs for Benefit to American Indians						
American Indian Program	N/A	N/A	N/A	N/A	N/A	N/A
Procurement Technical Assistant Program	500,000	500,000	600,000	500,000	500,000	N/A
Department of the Army	N/A	N/A	N/A	N/A	N/A	N/A
Corps of Engineers						
Missouri River Division						
Development of Shoreline Recreation Potential at Lake Oahe	8,000	6,000	4,000	N/A	N/A	N/A
Development of Shoreline Recreation Potential at Lake Sakakawea	10,000	10,000	5,000	N/A	N/A	N/A
Natural Resource Work at Lake Oahe	N/A	N/A	24,000	N/A	N/A	N/A
Native American Loop Trail	N/A	N/A	N/A	N/A	N/A	N/A
Crow Creek Sioux Wildlife Mitigation Contract	N/A	45,000	90,000	N/A	N/A	N/A
Lower Brule Sioux Wildlife Mitigation Contract	N/A	45,000	90,000	N/A	N/A	N/A

Source: Roger Walke, *Federal Programs of Assistance to Native Americans: A Report Prepared for the Senate Select Committee on Indian Affairs of the United States Senate,* S. Prt. 102-62, United States Government Printing Office, Washington, D.C., December 1991, pp. 1-83. *Notes:* (N/A) indicates that information was not available. 1. The allotments awarded to tribes/tribal organizations is taken from a percentage of state's allotment. 2. Referred to as draw downs in the original source.

★ 739 ★

Federal Programs of Assistance to Native Americans, 1988-90 - II

Obligations represent actual dollars spent; appropriations are total amounts allotted at the beginning of the year.

Government agency and program	Appropriations ($)			Obligations ($)		
	1988	1989	1990	1988	1989	1990
Department of Defense (cont.)						
North Pacific Division						
Grays Harbor Navigation Improvement	N/A	N/A	990,000	N/A	N/A	N/A
Puyallup River, WA	N/A	31,000	38,000	N/A	N/A	N/A
Howard A. Hanson Dam Flood Control and Low Flow Enhancement	N/A	N/A	N/A	N/A	N/A	N/A
Elwha Flood Damage Reduction Project	162,000	950,000	N/A	N/A	N/A	N/A
Neah Bay Shore Projection Project	N/A	15,000	290,000	N/A	N/A	N/A
Cultural Resources Curation Centers	26,000	42,000	114,000	N/A	N/A	N/A
Wildlife Mitigation at the Chief Joseph Dam	200,000	200,000	200,000	N/A	N/A	N/A
North Central Division						
Upper Mississippi Headwaters (St. Paul Monitoring Equipment)	120,000	120,000	120,000	N/A	N/A	N/A
Upper Mississippi Headwaters (St. Paul District Low Flow Plan)	230,000	230,000	230,000	N/A	N/A	N/A
Upper Mississippi Nine Foot Channel	2,000	2,000	2,000	N/A	N/A	N/A
Mission Project Cemetery Stabilization	48,000	48,000	48,000	N/A	N/A	N/A
Indian Business Initiative	N/A	N/A	N/A	N/A	N/A	N/A

[Continued]

1113

Federal Programs of Assistance to Native Americans, 1988-90 - II
[Continued]

Government agency and program	Appropriations ($)			Obligations ($)		
	1988	1989	1990	1988	1989	1990
Department of the Air Force						
Special Emphasis Program	N/A	N/A	N/A	N/A	N/A	N/A
Air Force Distinguished EEO Awards	N/A	N/A	N/A	N/A	N/A	N/A
Department of Education						
Indian education - Formula Grants to Local Education Agencies						
and Tribal Schools	45,670,000	49,248,000	50,828,000	N/A	N/A	N/A
Indian Education - Special Programs and Projects	7,907,000	8,307,000	8,200,000	N/A	N/A	N/A
Indian Education - Adult Indian Education	3,000,000	4,000,000	4,078,000	N/A	N/A	N/A
Indian Education - Grants to Indian - Controlled Schools	3,500,000	3,500,000	3,451,000	N/A	N/A	N/A
Indian Education - Fellowships for Indian Students	1,600,000	1,600,000	1,587,000	N/A	N/A	N/A
Indian Education - Technical Assistance Centers	2,200,000	2,268,000	2,268,000	2,200,000	2,268,000	2,268,000
Additional Education Department Programs						
Office of Vocational and Adult Education						
Vocational Education - Indians and Hawaiian Natives						
Indians	N/A	10,808,990	11,010,277	N/A	N/A	N/A
Hawaiians	N/A	2,161,798	2,202,055	N/A	N/A	N/A
Office of Elementary and Secondary Education						
Native Hawaiian Model Curriculum Development - Kamehameha						
Elementary Education Program (KEEP)	N/A	N/A	N/A	N/A	395,200	494,000
Native Hawaiian Family - Based Education Centers	N/A	N/A	N/A	N/A	1,778,400	2,765,000
Native Hawaiian Gifted and Talented	N/A	N/A	N/A	N/A	790,000	741,000
Office of Special Education and Rehabilitative Services						
Native Hawaiian Special Education	N/A	N/A	N/A	N/A	494,000	741,000
Office of Educational Research and Improvement						
Library Services for Indian Tribes and Hawaiian Natives	N/A	N/A	N/A	N/A	2,448,700	2,419,120
Jacob K. Javits Gifted and Talented Students	N/A	N/A	N/A	N/A	7,900,000	8,880,000
Department to Energy						
Weatherization Assistance Programs	161,000,000	161,000,000	N/A	N/A	N/A	N/A
Office of Minority Economic Impact						
Minority Financial Institution Deposit Program	N/A	N/A	N/A	N/A	N/A	N/A
Minority Undergraduate Training for Energy Related Careers						
Training Program (MUTEC)	N/A	N/A	1,000,000	N/A	N/A	N/A
Minority Honors Training Program	402,000	402,000	417,000	N/A	N/A	N/A
Bid or Proposal Loan Program	N/A	N/A	N/A	N/A	N/A	N/A
State Energy Conservation Program (SECP)	N/A	N/A	N/A	9,519,000	9,519,000	9,555,000
Energy Extension Service (EES)	N/A	N/A	N/A	3,968,000	3,844,050	3,983,000
Institutional Conservation Program (ICP)	25,100,000	25,100,000	25,200,000	N/A	N/A	N/A
Department of Energy Regional and Local Contacts	N/A	N/A	N/A	N/A	N/A	N/A
Department of Health and Human Services						
Office of Human Development Services						
Administration for Children, Youth and Families						
Head Start	1,202,324,000	1,235,000,000	1,386,315,000	38,570,020	41,520,689	46,983,000
Child Welfare Services	239,350,000	246,679,000	252,647,751	239,350,000	246,679,000	252,647,751
Administration for Native Americans	29,679,000	29,975,000	31,710,574	29,679,000	29,974,988	31,710,574
Office of Policy, Planning and Legislation						
Family Violence Prevention and Services	8,138,000	8,219,000	8,273,000	8,138,000	8,227,000	8,273,000
Administration on Aging						
American Indian Native Programs	7,500,000	9,345,000	11,107,970	7,500,000	9,345,000	11,170,970
Native Hawaiian Program	N/A	1,365,000	1,433,000	N/A	N/A	N/A
Title VI - Grants for Native Americans						
Public Health Service						
Indian Health Service						
Health Management Development Program	N/A	N/A	N/A	13,064,189	15,688,238	16,500,000
Health Professions Recruitment Program for Indians	575,000	625,000	640,000	N/A	625,000	640,000
Health Professions Preparatory and Pregradute						
Scholarship Program for Indians	2,058,000	2,119,000	2,160,000	N/A	1,327,596	2,160,000
Health Professions Scholarship Program for Indians	3,926,000	4,058,000	4,883,000	N/A	4,644,781	4,883,000
Indian Health service - Direct Services	928,824,500	1,002,623,500	1,185,910,000	N/A	N/A	N/A
National Institutes of Health						
Minority Biomedical Research Support Program (MBRS)	28,500,000	28,100,000	29,700,000	N/A	N/A	N/A

[Continued]

★ 739 ★

Federal Programs of Assistance to Native Americans, 1988-90 - II
[Continued]

Government agency and program	Appropriations ($)			Obligations ($)		
	1988	1989	1990	1988	1989	1990
Family Support Administration						
Office of Community Services						
Low Income Home Energy Assistance Program (LIHEAP)	1,532,000,000	1,383,000,000	1,393,000,000	N/A	N/A	N/A
Community Services Block Grant Programs (CSBG)[1,2]	1,793,022	1,687,048	1,689,827	729,325	1,683,328	2,453,739
Department of Housing and Urban Development						
Indian Housing Program	130,400,000	96,000,000	N/A	N/A	N/A	N/A
Comprehensive Improvement Assistance Program (CIAP)						
Modernization for Public Housing Agencies and Indians Authorities	54,000,000	43,000,000	N/A	N/A	N/A	N/A
Operating Subsidies for Public Housing Agencies and Indian housing Authorities	50,000,000	50,500,000	54,400,000	N/A	N/A	N/A
Community Development Block Grants for Indian Tribes and Alaskan Native Villages	25,500,000	27,000,000	26,200,000	27,000,000	N/A	N/A
Federal Housing Administration (FHA)						
Section 248 Mortgage Insurance on Indian Reservations	N/A	N/A	N/A	N/A	N/A	N/A
Section 247 Mortgage Insurance for Hawaiian Homelands	N/A	N/A	N/A	N/A	N/A	N/A
Indian Program Field Offices of the Department of Housing and Urban Development	N/A	N/A	N/A	N/A	N/A	N/A
Department of the Interior						
Bureau of Indian Affairs						
Office of Administration						
Indian Property Acquisition - Transfer of Federally Owned Buildings, Improvements and or Facilities (Public Law 991 Transfer)	N/A	N/A	N/A	N/A	N/A	N/A
Indian Property Acquisition - Transfer of Indian School Properties (Public Law 47 Transfer)	N/A	N/A	N/A	N/A	N/A	N/A
Office of Indian Education Programs						
Indian Education - Contracts/Grants with Indian Tribal Organizations	N/A	N/A	N/A	55,268,100	57,285,500	68,563,300
Indian Education - Federal Schools (Indian Schools)	N/A	N/A	N/A	177,890,000	175,286,000	187,596,000
Indian Education - Higher Education Grant Program	N/A	N/A	N/A	30,680,000	30,436,000	29,766,000
Adult Education	N/A	N/A	N/A	3,141,000	3,138,000	3,181,000
Johnson O'Malley Educational Assistance	N/A	N/A	N/A	20,400,000	23,000,000	23,252,000

Source: Roger Walke, *Federal Programs of Assistance to Native Americans: A Report Prepared for the Senate Select Committee on Indian Affairs of the United States Senate,* S. Prt. 102-62, United States Government Printing Office, Washington, D.C., December 1991, pp. 83-162. *Notes:* (N/A) indicates that information was not available. 1. The allotments awarded to tribes/tribal organizations is taken from a percentage of state's allotment. 2. Referred to as draw downs in the original source. 1. The allotments awarded to tribes/tribal organizations is taken from a percentage of state's allotment. 2. Referred to as draw downs in the original source.

★ 740 ★

Federal Programs of Assistance to Native Americans, 1988-90 - III

Obligations represent actual dollars spent; appropriations are total amounts allotted at the beginning of the year.

Government agency and program	Appropriations ($)			Obligations ($)		
	1988	1989	1990	1988	1989	1990
Department of the Interior (cont.)						
Tribally Controlled Community Colleges (TCCC)	N/A	N/A	N/A	12,836,000	13,800,000	17,124,000
Office of Tribal Services						
Indian Housing Assistance - Housing Improvement Program (HIP)	22,827,000	22,823,000	22,463,000	N/A	N/A	N/A
Indian Judicial Services - Contracts with Indian Tribal Organizations	N/A	N/A	N/A	9,061,000	9,399,000	10,527,000
Indian Law Enforcement Services	51,223,000	52,713,000	55,126,000	N/A	N/A	N/A
Self-Determination Grants - Indian Tribal Governments	N/A	N/A	13,500,000	N/A	N/A	N/A
Social Services - General Assistance	N/A	N/A	N/A	50,443,000	51,025,000	52,630,000
Social Services - Child and Family Services	N/A	N/A	N/A	17,602,000	18,899,000	24,488,000
Social Services - Indian Child Welfare Act Title II Grants	N/A	N/A	N/A	N/A	N/A	N/A

[Continued]

★ 740 ★

Federal Programs of Assistance to Native Americans, 1988-90 - III
[Continued]

Government agency and program	Appropriations ($)			Obligations ($)		
	1988	1989	1990	1988	1989	1990
Social Services - Child Welfare Assistance	N/A	N/A	N/A	15,943,000	16,792,000	16,402,000
Office of Trust and Economic Development						
Financial Assistance - Guaranteed Loan Program	N/A	3,400,000	4,800,000	N/A	N/A	43,600,000
Financial Assistance - Direct Loan Program	N/A	N/A	N/A	N/A	N/A	8,900,000
Financial Assistance - Expect Assistance Fund	N/A	N/A	N/A	N/A	N/A	716,485
Financial Assistance - Indian Business Development Grant Program	7,000,000	7,000,000	7,000,000	N/A	6,907,159	N/A
Division of Energy and Minerals - Minerals Resource Inventory Program	7,885,000	5,724,000	4,997,000	7,742,478	5,643,638	4,997,000
Environmental Services Staff - Indian Lands - Environmental Quality Services	1,259,000	1,321,000	1,727,000	1,259,000	1,321,000	1,727,000
Division of Forestry - Indian Forests - Management, Protection and Development	N/A	32,617,000	35,965,000	N/A	32,617,000	35,965,000
Division of Forestry - Indian Forests - Fire Suppression and Emergency Pre-Suppression	N/A	N/A	29,645,000	N/A	43,645,000	43,744,000
Division of Real Estate Services	26,967,000	27,482,000	26,311,000	22,153,331	26,845,330	25,546,764
Division of Real Estate Services - Appraisals	3,645,000	3,311,000	3,435,000	3,361,595	3,165,272	3,163,208
Division of Water and Land Resources - Indian Lands - Range Management	24,982,000	26,701,000	24,542,000	24,595,000	26,102,000	23,457,000
Division of Water and Land Resources - Indian Lands - Soil and Moisture Conservation	24,982,000	21,701,000	24,542,000	24,595,000	26,102,000	23,457,000
Area Offices - Bureau of Indian Affairs						
Indian Arts and Crafts Board						
Indian Arts and Crafts Development	N/A	N/A	N/A	912,000	900,000	912,000
Minerals Management Services (MMS)						
Royalty Management Program	N/A	N/A	N/A	N/A	N/A	N/A
Bureau of Land Management	N/A	N/A	N/A	N/A	N/A	N/A
Land Conveyances and Exchanges Benefiting American Indians	N/A	N/A	N/A	N/A	N/A	N/A
Surveys of Indian Lands	N/A	N/A	N/A	N/A	N/A	N/A
Employment of Wildlife Control Work	N/A	N/A	N/A	N/A	N/A	N/A
Management of Indian Mineral Leases	N/A	N/A	N/A	N/A	N/A	N/A
Bureau of Reclamation	N/A	N/A	N/A	N/A	N/A	N/A
Office of Native Americans Affairs	N/A	N/A	N/A	N/A	N/A	N/A
Department of Justice						
Civil Rights Division	N/A	N/A	N/A	N/A	N/A	N/A
Community Relations Service	N/A	N/A	N/A	N/A	N/A	N/A
Office of Justice Programs						
Office of Juvenile Justice and Delinquency Prevention (OJJDP)	N/A	N/A	N/A	N/A	N/A	N/A
Office for Victims of Crime (OVC)						
Children's Justice Act Discretionary Grant Program for Native Americans	0	0	531,000	N/A	N/A	531,000
Discretionary Grant Assistance to Victims of Federal Crime in Indian Country	0	1,000,000	700,000	N/A	1,700,000	1,700,00
Department of Labor						
Employment and Training Administration	59,713,000	58,996,000	58,193,000	59,713,000	58,996,000	58,193,000
Office of Special Targeted Programs	59,713,000	58,996,000	58,193,000	59,713,000	58,996,000	58,193,000
Indian and Native American Employment and Training Programs	59,713,000	58,996,000	58,193,000	59,713,000	58,996,000	58,193,000
Department of Transportation						
Federal Highway Administration						
Indian Employment and Contracting Preference	N/A	N/A	N/A	N/A	N/A	N/A
Supportive Services	N/A	N/A	N/A	N/A	N/A	N/A
Indian Reservation Road Program	80,000,000	80,000,000	80,000,000	80,000,000	78,500,000	77,640,000
National Highway Traffic Safety Administration						
American Indian Highway Safety Program	528,295	541,630	548,850	N/A	N/A	N/A

[Continued]

★ 740 ★

Federal Programs of Assistance to Native Americans, 1988-90 - III
[Continued]

Government agency and program	Appropriations ($)			Obligations ($)		
	1988	1989	1990	1988	1989	1990
Urban Mass Transportation Administration						
Section 6 Program - Research, Development and Demonstration						
Projects	9,000,000	7,000,000	8,000,000	N/A	N/A	393,417
Section 18 Program - Formula Grants	65,000,000	65,000,000	66,000,000	N/A	N/A	11,000,000
Section 20 Program - Human Resource Programs	1,500,000	1,000,000	1,000,000	N/A	N/A	139,433
United States Coast Guard						
Cooperative Education Program (CO-OP)	N/A	N/A	N/A	N/A	N/A	N/A
Minority Officer Recruiting Effort (M.O.R.E)	N/A	N/A	N/A	N/A	N/A	N/A
Federal Aviation Administration						
Disadvantaged Business Enterprise Program (DBE)	N/A	N/A	N/A	N/A	N/A	N/A
Action						
Vista (Volunteers in Service to America)	19,828,000	21,647,000	23,615,000	19,769,000	21,589,000	N/A
Student Community Service Program (SCS)	1,310 000	1,352,000	893,000	N/A	N/A	N/A
Program Demonstration and Development Division						
Minigrant Program	158,000	150,000	0	N/A	N/A	N/A
Volunteer Demonstration Program	621,000	754,000	0	N/A	N/A	N/A
Technical Assistance Program	124,000	46,000	0	N/A	N/A	N/A
Drug Alliance Program	1,541,000	1,600,000	1,314,000	N/A	N/A	N/A
Retired Senior Volunteer Program (RSVP)	30,608,000	30,862,000	31,487,000	N/A	N/A	N/A
Foster Grandparent Program (FGP)	57,413,000	58,928,000	59,623,000	N/A	N/A	N/A
Senior Companion Program (SCP)	23,104,000	25,135,000	26,692,000	N/A	N/A	N/A
Environmental Protection Agency						
Office of Air and Radiation						
Air Pollution Control Program Support	N/A	N/A	N/A	N/A	N/A	N/A
Air Pollution Control Manpower Training	N/A	N/A	N/A	240,000	400,000	200,000
Air Pollution Control - Technical Training	N/A	N/A	N/A	241,000	241,000	245,000
Air Pollution Control - National Ambient Air and Source						
Emission Data	N/A	N/A	N/A	1,170,000	1,085,000	1,485,000
Air Information Center	N/A	N/A	N/A	43,000	32,000	32,000
Office of Pesticides and Toxic Substances						
Pesticides use Regulation Program	N/A	N/A	N/A	N/A	N/A	N/A
Office of Solid Waste and Emergency Response						
Solid Waste Management - Assistance Grants	N/A	N/A	N/A	0	2,800,000	3,950,000
Office of Water						
Municipal Wastewater Treatment Construction Grants Program	N/A	11,000,000	4,705,000	1,596,854	1,596,854	1,596,854
Wetlands Protection Program on Indian Lands	N/A	25,000	30,000	N/A	N/A	N/A
Indian Water Quality Management Programs	N/A	N/A	N/A	489,898	489,898	489,898
Indian Public Water Supply Program	N/A	669,000	786,000	N/A	40,000	N/A
National Pollutant Discharge Elimination System Permits and						
State Sludge Management Program on Indian Lands	N/A	N/A	N/A	N/A	N/A	N/A
Indian Underground Injection Control Program	N/A	525,000	558,900	N/A	N/A	N/A

Source: Roger Walke, *Federal Programs of Assistance to Native Americans: A Report Prepared for the Senate Select Committee on Indian Affairs of the United States Senate,* S. Prt. 102-62, United States Government Printing Office, Washington, D.C., December 1991, pp. 165-256. *Notes:* (N/A) indicates that information was not available. 1. The allotments awarded to tribes/tribal organizations is taken from a percentage of state's allotment. 2. Referred to as draw downs in the original source.

★ 741 ★

Federal Programs of Assistance to Native Americans, 1988-90 - IV

Obligations represent actual dollars spent; appropriations are total amounts allotted at the beginning of the year.

Government agency and program	Appropriations ($)			Obligations ($)		
	1988	1989	1990	1988	1989	1990
Environmental Protection Agency (cont.)						
Indian Ground Water Protection Program	N/A	N/A	N/A	N/A	N/A	N/A
Equal Employment Opportunity Commission	N/A	N/A	N/A	N/A	N/A	N/A
Tribal Employment Rights Office Program (TERO)	N/A	N/A	N/A	N/A	N/A	N/A
Federal Emergency Management Agency	N/A	N/A	N/A	N/A	N/A	N/A
Emergency Management Assistance Program	54,123,000	58,123,000	61,123,000	54,160,038	58,116,000	N/A
Disaster Assistance Program	120,000,000	1,208,000,000	1,185,159,000	189,608,000	138,563,000	N/A
Sara Title III 305(A) Training Grants	142,000	0	150,000	142,000	N/A	150,000
U.S. Fire Administration						
National Fire Information Reporting System (NFIRS) Pilot						
Initiative with Amerind Risk Management Corp	N/A	N/A	N/A	N/A	N/A	N/A
National Community Volunteer Fire Prevention Program -						
Projects with an Indian Focus on Inclusion	N/A	N/A	N/A	N/A	N/A	N/A
Fema Regional Office	N/A	N/A	N/A	N/A	N/A	N/A
State Officials Responsible for Disaster Operations	N/A	N/A	N/A	N/A	N/A	N/A
Legal Services Corporation	7,022,000	7,022,000	7,304,000	N/A	N/A	N/A
National Endowment for the Arts	167,731,000	165,081,000	158,567,000	N/A	N/A	N/A
National Endowment for the Humanities	140,435,000	153,000,000	156,910,000	N/A	N/A	N/A
National Science Foundation						
Comprehensive Programs						
Career Access Opportunities in Science and Technology (ACCESS)	N/A	N/A	N/A	N/A	7,000,000	N/A
Alliances for Minority Participation (AMP)	N/A	N/A	N/A	N/A	N/A	N/A
Programs for Students						
Research Assistantships for Minority High School Students (RAMHSS)	N/A	N/A	N/A	N/A	27,035	N/A
Research Careers for Minority Scholars (RCMS)	N/A	N/A	N/A	N/A	2,000,000	N/A
Creativity Awards for Graduate Study in Engineering for Women,						
Minorities, and Disabled Persons	N/A	N/A	N/A	N/A	N/A	N/A
Minority Graduate Fellowship Program (MGF)	N/A	N/A	N/A	N/A	2,400,000	N/A
Postdoctoral and Faculty Research Opportunities						
Minority Postdoctoral Research Fellowships - Biological,						
Behavioral and Social Sciences Directorate	N/A	N/A	N/A	N/A	N/A	N/A
Minority Research Initiative Program (MRI)	N/A	N/A	N/A	N/A	3,400,000	N/A
Research Improvement in Minority Institutions Program (RIMI)	N/A	N/A	N/A	N/A	4,850,000	N/A
Minority Research Centers of Excellence (MRCE)	N/A	N/A	N/A	N/A	5,800,000	N/A
Computer and Information Science and Engineering (CISE) -						
Institutional Infrastructure in Minority Institutions	N/A	N/A	N/A	N/A	1,100,000	N/A
Nuclear Regulatory Commission	N/A	N/A	N/A	N/A	N/A	N/A
Office of Personnel Management						
Training Assistance to American Indian Tribal Organizations	N/A	N/A	N/A	N/A	N/A	N/A
Inter-Governmental Mobility of Federal, State, and Local Employees	N/A	N/A	N/A	N/A	N/A	N/A
Small Business Administration						
Minority Small Business and Capital Ownership Development	N/A	N/A	N/A	N/A	N/A	N/A
Minority Business Development - Procurement Assistance	N/A	N/A	N/A	N/A	N/A	N/A
Management and Technical Assistance for Disadvantaged Businesses	N/A	N/A	N/A	N/A	N/A	N/A
8(A) Participant Loans	0	5,000,000	5,000,000	N/A	N/A	N/A
Office of Business Development	46,133,000	51,338,000	5,122,000	45,912,000	51,338,000	5,122,000
Economic Injury Disaster Loans	N/A	N/A	N/A	5,708,600	78,762,500	N/A
Physical Disaster Loans	N/A	N/A	N/A	245,000,000	146,000,000	N/A
Economic Opportunity Loans						
Direct	N/A	N/A	N/A	17,100,000	17,100,000	17,000
Guarantee	N/A	N/A	N/A	32,800,000	33,900,000	0
Small Business Loans						
Direct	N/A	N/A	N/A	0	0	0
Guarantee	N/A	N/A	N/A	2,421,300,000	2,606,600,000	3,200,000,000
Veterans Loans Program	N/A	N/A	N/A	16,900,000	16,800,000	17,000,000
Handicapped Assistance Loans						
Direct	N/A	N/A	N/A	11,700,000	11,900,000	12,000,000
Guarantee	N/A	N/A	N/A	200,000	1,600,668	0
State and Local Development Company Loans	N/A	N/A	50,000,000	39,096,312	44,120,000	N/A
Certified Development Company Loans	450,000,000	365,000,000	422,228,000	291,986,000	329,247,000	N/A
Office of Women's Business Ownership	N/A	N/A	N/A	N/A	2,000,000	2,000,000
Small Business Pollution Control Loan Program	N/A	N/A	N/A	N/A	N/A	N/A

[Continued]

★ 741 ★

Federal Programs of Assistance to Native Americans, 1988-90 - IV
[Continued]

Government agency and program	Appropriations ($)			Obligations ($)		
	1988	1989	1990	1988	1989	1990
Procurement Assistance	15,635,000	15,444,000	16,223,000	15,635,000	15,444,000	16,223,000
Procurement Automated Source System	1,145,000	1,200,000	1,138,000	1,145,000	1,200,000	1,138,000
Small Business Development Centers	N/A	N/A	N/A	N/A	44,908,000	49,338,000
Surety Bond Guarantees	N/A	N/A	N/A	N/A	1,151,562,493	1,250,000,000
Small Business Investment Companies (SBIC)						
Direct	N/A	N/A	N/A	35,900,000	36,000,000	N/A
Guarantee	N/A	N/A	N/A	117,500,000	50,200,000	N/A
Service Corps of Retired Executives (SCORE)	2,120,000	2,500,000	2,500,000	2,120,000	2,500,000	2,500,000
Smithsonian Institution						
National American Resources at the Smithsonian Institution						
National Museum of National History/National Museum of Man	N/A	N/A	N/A	N/A	N/A	N/A
National Anthropological Archives	N/A	N/A	N/A	N/A	N/A	N/A
National Museum of American History	N/A	N/A	N/A	N/A	N/A	N/A
Office of Folklife Programs						
Office of Elementary and Secondary Education	N/A	N/A	N/A	N/A	N/A	N/A
Office of Fellowships and Grants	N/A	N/A	N/A	N/A	N/A	N/A
Quincentenary Programs	N/A	N/A	N/A	N/A	N/A	N/A

Source: Roger Walke, *Federal Programs of Assistance to Native Americans: A Report Prepared for the Senate Select Committee on Indian Affairs of the United States Senate,* S. Prt. 102-62, United States Government Printing Office, Washington, D.C., December 1991, pp. 256-326. *Notes:* (N/A) indicates that information was not available. 1. The allotments awarded to tribes/tribal organizations is taken from a percentage of state's allotment. 2. Referred to as draw downs in the original source.

★ 742 ★

Food Stamp Participation, by State

Participating American Indian or Alaskan Native households as of July 1988.

State	Number
Alabama	209
Alaska	3,633
Arizona	14,076
Arkansas	102
California	4,639
Colorado	924
Connecticut	28
Delaware	13
Florida	176
Georgia	42
Idaho	515
Illinois	576
Indiana	75
Iowa	348
Kansas	448
Kentucky	45
Louisiana	506
Maine	270
Maryland	240
Massachusetts	182
Michigan	1,545

[Continued]

★ 742 ★

Food Stamp Participation, by State
[Continued]

State	Number
Minnesota	4,917
Mississippi	363
Missouri	21
Montana	3,520
Nebraska	1,153
Nevada	409
New Hampshire	1
New Jersey	111
New Mexico	6,545
New York	1,720
North Carolina	3,325
North Dakota	2,150
Ohio	878
Oklahoma	8,195
Oregon	1,520
Pennsylvania	221
Rhode Island	60
South Carolina	90
South Dakota	5,046
Tennessee	120
Texas	771
Utah	1,692
Vermont	27
Virginia	165
Washington	4,647
West Virginia	26
Wisconsin	2,881
Wyoming	820
Washington, D.C.	4

Source: Roger Walke, *Federal Programs of Assistance to Native Americans: A Report Prepared for the Senate Select Committee on Indian Affairs of the United States Senate,* U.S. Government Printing Office, Washington, D.C., December 1991, p. 12. *Note:* U.S. total: 79,990 (1.2 percent of total caseload).

★ 743 ★

Projects and Funding for Diabetes Research by the U.S. Government, 1991

Type of research and population group	Projects		Funding	
	Number	%	($000)	%
Human (total)[1]				
American Indian	46	28	7,458	21
Black	15	9	4,145	11
Hispanic	4	2	1,671	5
Multiracial[2]	19	12	5,965	17
White	77	47	16,728	46
Total	163	100	36,089	100
Prevention behavioral				
American Indian	5	36	358	8
Black	5	36	2,048	47
Hispanic	0	0	70[3]	2
Multiracial[3]	1	7	285	7
White	3	21	1,600	37
Total	14	100	4,361	100
Clinical[1]				
American Indian	35	28	6,042	25
Black	6	5	1,095	4
Hispanic	1	<1	293	1
Multiracial[3]	12	10	2,559	11
White	69	55	14,246	58
Total	125	100	24,537	100
Epidemiologic				
American Indian	6	26	1,058	15
Black	4	17	1,002	14
Hispanic	3	13	1,308	18
Multiracial[3]	6	26	3,121	44
White	4	17	666	9
Total	23	100	7,155	100

Source: Diabetes: Status of the Disease Among American Indians, Blacks, and Hispanics, U.S. General Accounting Office, 1992, p. 13. *Primary source:* National Institute of Diabetes and Digestive and Kidney Diseases, 1991. *Notes:* 1. Totals for human and clinical research categories include two projects ($122,000) that were targeted to another population group; the human research for whites includes another type of project ($216,000). 2. Involved only non-white populations. 3. The amount from two multiracial projects that targeted Hispanics.

★ 744 ★

Projects Benefiting Indians

Bureau of Reclamation programs specifically designed to benefit Indians are shown for FY 1990. See notes at the end of table for an explanation of abbreviations.

Project and State	Tribe	Benefit
Minidoka, Idaho, Wyoming	Bannock-Shoshone, Fort Hall Reservation	Irrigation 132,000 AF and recreation
Owyhee, Idaho, Oregon, Nevada	Shoshone-Paiute, Duck Valley Reservation	Irrigation 72,000 AF
Yakima, Washington	Yakima	Irrigation 350,000 AF
Chief Joseph Dam, Washington	Colville and Wapate	Irrigation
Colville, Washington	Colville	Supplement municipal
Fort Hall Reservation, Idaho	Bannock Shoshone	Facility rehabilitation & irrigation study
South Fork Reservation, Nevada	Shoshone	Diversion study for reservation needs
Umatilla, Oregon	Confederated Tribes	Planning study for fish improvement
Colville Reservation, Washington	Yakima	Comprehensive multi-purpose river basin study
Upper John Day, Oregon	Umatilla	Fishery improvement study
Grande Ronde River Basin, Oregon	Do.	Fish habitat improvement study
Lower Deschutes River Basin, Oregon	Do.	Do.
Indigenous Anadromous Fish Habitat, Oregon	Nez Perce	Fish enhancement study
Warm Springs Reservation, Oregon	Reservation Tribes	Irrigation study 2,500 acres
Flathead Indian Irrigation, Montana	Kootenai, Salish	BR/BIA operation and maintenance
Cannonball Unit North Dakota	Standing Rock Reservation	Irrigation study 27,450 acres
Shell Creek, North Dakota	Fort Berthold Reservation	Irrigation study 4,500 acres
Independence, North Dakota	Independence Reservation	Irrigation study 4,130 acres
Fort Berthold, North Dakota	Fort Berthold Reservation	Irrigation study 9,400 acres
Old Agency, North Dakota	Old Agency Reservation	Irrigation study 9,210 acres
Garrison Diversion Unit, North Dakota	Fort Totten Reservation	Irrigation study 5,000 acres
Boysen Dam, Wyoming	Wind River Reservation	Flood protection
Fremont Unit, Wyoming	Do.	Irrigation study 56,000 acres
Shoshone Unit, Wyoming	Do.	Irrigation study 16,000 acres
Hudson Beach Unit, Wyoming	Do.	Irrigation study 5,700 acres
Little Wind River Unit (Coolidge Extension), Wyoming	Do.	Irrigation study 34,000 acres
Fresno Dam, Montana	Fort Belknap Reservation	Additional water and potential 14,000 acre development
Rocky Boy Reservation, Montana	Rocky Boy Reservation	5,000 acre development
Farmer Creek Unit, Montana	Fort Peck Reservation	Irrigation 1,600 acres
Hardin Unit, Montana	Crow Reservation	45,800 acre development
Spokane Indian, Washington	Spokane	Irrigation 1,800 acres
Yellowtail Dam, Montana	Crow Reservation	Flood protection
Crow Unit, Montana	Do.	1,200 acre development
Battlefield Unit, Montana	Do.	Do.
Custer Bench (Dunmore) Unit, Montana	Do.	11,400 acre development
Wyola Unit, Montana	Do.	3,600 acre development
Benteen Flat, Montana	Do.	1,600 acre development
Little Horn, Montana	Do.	14,000 acre development
North Cheyenne Tongue River Pumping, Montana	Northern Cheyenne	Irrigation 5,000 acres
Shadehill Unit, S. Dakota	Standing Rock Reservation	Flood protection and 9,000 acre development
Grand River Unit, S. Dakota	Do.	16,500 acre development
Moreau River Unit Bixby Reservoir, S. Dakota	Cheyenne River Reservation	27,500 acre development
Cheyenne River Pumping, S. Dakota	Do.	25,300 acre development
Angostura Dam, S. Dakota	Pine Ridge and Rosebud Reservations	Flood protection
White River Unit, S. Dakota	Do.	42,000 acre development
Pine Ridge Unit, S. Dakota	Do.	12,700 acre development
Joe Creek Unit, S. Dakota	Crow Creek Reservation	4,400 acre development
Culdesc Unit, S. Dakota	Do.	5,400 acre development
Fort Thompson Unit, S. Dakota	Do.	7,500 acre development
La Roche Unit, S. Dakota	Lower Brule Reservation	1,800 acre development
Red Cloud Unit (Iron Nation), S. Dakota	Do.	1,700 acre development
Big Bend Unit (Grass Rope), S. Dakota	Do.	4,300 acre development
Fort Hale, S. Dakota	Do.	2,100 acre development
Tower Unit, S. Dakota	Yankton Reservation	2,000 acre development
Greenwood Unit, S. Dakota	Do.	4,900 acre development
Wagner Unit, S. Dakota	Do.	1,700 acre development
Kiamichi, Oklahoma	Choctaw, Chickasaw	Hydropower study
Southeast Oklahoma, Oklahoma	Do.	Water supply study
East Central Oklahoma, Oklahoma	Shawnee, Creek, Seminole, Pottawatomie, Iowa, Sac, Kickapoo, Fox, Pawnee, Otoe, Ponca	Do.
Gallup-Navajo, New Mexico	Navajo Reservation	Water supply planning
San Juan Chama, New Mexico	San Juan Reservation	Planning
Jicarilla, New Mexico	Jicarilla Apache Reservation	Irrigation study

[Continued]

★ 744 ★

Projects Benefiting Indians

[Continued]

Project and State	Tribe	Benefit
Upper Rio Grande Basin, New Mexico	Pueblo Tribes	Irrigation
San Juan Chama (Pojoaque Tributary Unit), New Mexico	Do.	Do.
Rio Grande, Texas	Isleta Pueblo	Do.
Trinity River Management Program, California	Hoopa	Restoring fishery
Bonneville Unit, Utah	Ute	Multipurpose being constructed
Delores, Colorado	Do.	Do.
Flaming Gorge, Utah	Do.	Multipurpose operation
Florida, Colorado	Do.	Do.
Moon Lake, Utah	Do.	Do.
Navajo Indian Irrigation, New Mexico	Navajo	Multipurpose being constructed
Navajo Unit, New Mexico	Do.	Multipurpose operation
Pine River, Colorado	Ute	Do.
Uintah Unit, Utah	Do.	Multipurpose planning
Uintah Basin, Utah	Do.	Do.
Upalco, Utah	Do.	Multipurpose being constructed
Central Arizona Project (CAP), Arizona	Ak-Chin, Camp Verde Yavapai-Apache Communities, Fort McDowell Mohave-Apache Tribe, Gila River Indian Community, Papago Tribe, Asaqua-Yaqui Tribes, Salt River Pima-Maricopa Comm., San Carlos-Apache Tribe, Tonto-Apache Tribe, Yavapai-Prescott Tribes	Multipurpose
Headgate Rock Hydroelectric, Arizona/California	Colorado River Tribes	Hydroelectric power studies
Pima County, Santa Cruz River Ground Water, Colorado	San Javier Reservation	Ground water studies
Water Settlement Public Law 97-293, Arizona	Tohono O'odham Tribe (Papago)	Irrigation
Water Rights Settlement Public Law 98-530, Arizona	Ak-Chin Community	Do.
Water Rights Settlement Public Law 101-618, Nevada	Fallon Paiute-Shoshone and Pyramid Lake Paiute Tribes	Irrigation and fisheries
Water Rights Settlement Public Law 100-585, Colorado and New Mexico	Southern Ute and Ute Mountain Ute Tribes	Irrigation and water supply

Source: Roger Walke, *Federal Programs of Assistance to Native Americans: A Report Prepared for the Senate Select Committee on Indian Affairs of the United States Senate*, U.S. Government Printing Office, Washington, D.C., December 1991, p. 190. *Note:* (AF) stands for acre-feet; (Do.) means ditto.

Government Representation

★ 745 ★

Areas Legally Controlled by Indigenous Peoples for Selected Countries, 1992

Country	Area legally controlled (thous. square kilometers)	Share of national territory (percent)
Papua New Guinea	449	97
Fiji	15	83
Ecuador	190	41
Nicaragua	59	40
Sweden	137	31

[Continued]

★ 745 ★

Areas Legally Controlled by Indigenous Peoples for Selected Countries, 1992

[Continued]

Country	Area legally controlled (thous. square kilometers)	Share of national territory (percent)
Venezuela	234	26
Colombia	260	23
Canada	2,222	22
Panama	15	20
Australia	895	12
Mexico	160	8
Brazil	573	7
New Zealand	16	6
United States	365	4
Costa Rica	2	4

Source: Alan Thein Durning, *Guardians of the Land: indigenous Peoples and the Health of the Earth,* Worldwatch Paper 112, Worldwatch Institute, 1992, p. 24. Primary source: Worldwatch Institute. Legal ambiguities from Plant, "Land Rights for Indigenous and Tribal Peoples," and from Ronald Wixman, "Manipulating Territory, Undermining Rights," Cultural Survival Quarterly, Winter 1992. Table 3 assembled from scores of sources, including: Papau New Guinea from Owen J. Lynch, "Towards Conservations Partnerships in Papau New Guinea" (draft), World Resources Institute, Washington, D.C., July 1992; Fiji from Brij Lal, "Politics and Society in Post-Coup Fiji," Cultural Survival Quarterly, Vol. 15, No. 2, 1991: Ecuador from Plant, "Land Rights for Indigenous and Tribal Peoples," and from Douglas Farah, "Ecuador Cedes Amazon Lands to Indians," Washington Post, May 4, 1992; Sweden from Beach, "Saami of Lapland"; Colombia from Peter Bunyard, The Colombian Amazon: Politics for the Protection of its Indigenous Peoples and Their Environment (Cornwall, U.K.: Ecological Press, 1989); Canada from INA Canada, Schedule of Indian Bands, Reserves, and Settlements (Hull, Quebec: 1990), from INA, "Information Sheet No. 9," Ottawa, February 1992, and from INA, "Comprehensive Land Claims in Canada," Ottawa, December 1991; Australia from Libby, Hawke's Law, and from Burger, Report from the Frontier; Panama from Mac Chapin, program director of resource management, Cultural Survival, Arlington, Va., private communication, June 22, 1992; Mexico from Stefano Varese, professor, University of California, Davis private communication, September 22, 1992; Brazil from Carlos Alberta Ricardo, Ecumenical Center for Documentation and Information, Sao Paulo, Brazil, private communication, February 25, 1992; New Zealand from Asiaweek, December 23-30, 1988; Nicaragua from Bernard Nietschmann, professor, University of California, Berkeley, private communication, September 15, 1992; United States from Pickett, private communication; Costa Rica from Marcos Guevara Berger and Ruben Chacon Castro, "Territorios Indios en Costa Rica: Origenes, Situacion y Perspectivas," unpublished, January 1992; Venezuela from John Frechione, "The Yekuana of Southern Venezuela," Cultural Survival Quarterly, Vol. 8, No. 4, 1984, from Nelly Arvelo-Jimenez and Andrew L. Cousins, "False Promises," Cultural Survial Quarterly, Winter 1992, and from APPEN Features, "Venezuela: Yanomami Indians Demand Their Land," Asia-Pacific People's Environment Network, Penang, Malaysia, 1990; India from Council for Advancement of People's Action and Rural Technology, "People's Action," July 1990. *Notes:* 1. Figures are in most cases liberal. They include area over which, in principle, indigenous peoples have exclusive rights to use land and water bodies. Does not imply recognized indigenous ownership (many states retain ownership if indigenous reserves), or rights to minerals or petroleum (which states often retain). Does not necessarily imply effective state backing and full enforcement of rights. Some indigenous peoples' rights to use resources are limited (for example, Sweden recognizes indigenous peoples' rights only to graze reindeer). Figures generally exclude private, individually owned farms of indigenous peoples, as in Andean countries and Mexico.

★ 746 ★

Native Americans, Women, and Other Minorities in Congress, 1991 and 1993

Data include non-voting delegates.

Group	1991	1993
Women	31	54
Blacks	25	39
Hispanics	4	19
Asians	6	9
Native Americans	1	1

Source: USA TODAY, December 7, 1992. Primary source: *USA Today* research.

Chapter 11

LAW AND LAW ENFORCEMENT

Arrests

★ 747 ★

Arrests for Selected Offenses

By offense charged and race, United States, 1989. (10,479 agencies; 1989 estimated population 199,394,000).

Offense charged	Total	Percent[1]				
		Total	American Indian or Alaskan Native	White	Black	Asian or Pacific Islander
Total	11,224,528	100.0	1.0	67.3	30.8	0.8
Murder and nonnegligent manslaughter	17,944	100.0	0.7	42.2	56.4	0.8
Forcible rape	30,470	100.0	0.8	51.7	46.6	0.8
Robbery	133,683	100.0	0.4	34.0	65.0	0.7
Aggravated assault	353,868	100.0	0.9	57.5	40.9	0.8
Burglary	355,913	100.0	0.8	66.0	32.3	0.9
Larceny-theft	1,252,117	100.0	1.0	64.4	33.3	1.2
Motor vehicle theft	182,634	100.0	0.8	55.4	42.5	1.3
Arson	14,631	100.0	0.8	74.1	24.5	0.6
Violent crime[2]	535,965	100.0	0.7	50.8	47.7	0.7
Property crime[3]	1,805,295	100.0	1.0	63.9	34.0	1.1
Total crime index[4]	2,341,260	100.0	0.9	60.9	37.1	1.0

Source: "Arrests," *Sourcebook of Criminal Justice Statistics—1990,* 1991, pp. 424-426. Primary source: U.S. Department of Justice, Federal Bureau of Investigation, *Crime in the United States, 1989* (Washington, DC: USGPO, 1990), pp. 190-192. *Notes:* 1. Because of rounding, percents may not add to total. 2. Violent crimes are offenses of murder, forcible rape, robbery, and aggravated assault. 3. Property crimes are offenses of burglary, larceny-theft, motor vehicle theft, and arson. 4. Includes arson.

★ 748 ★

Arrests for Selected Offenses, by Age Group

Persons under 18 and 18 and over arrested for selected offenses in 1989. By offense charged, age group, and race, United States, 1989.

Offense charged	Arrests under 18 Total	Percent[1] under 18					Arrests 18 older	Percent[1] 18 and over				
		Total	American Indian or Alaskan Native	White	Black	Asian or Pacific Islander		Total	American Indian or Alaskan Native	White	Black	Asian or Pacific Islander
Total	1,740,461	100.0	1.0	69.5	28.1	1.4	9,484,067	100.0	1.0	67.0	31.3	0.7
Murder and nonnegligent manslaughter	2,202	100.0	0.5	37.0	61.2	1.3	15,742	100.0	0.7	42.9	55.7	0.7
Forcible rape	4,696	100.0	0.7	49.3	49.1	0.8	25,774	100.0	0.9	52.2	46.2	0.8
Robbery	30,776	100.0	0.3	32.7	65.7	1.2	102,907	100.0	0.4	34.4	64.7	0.5
Aggravated assault	46,899	100.0	0.7	52.6	45.6	1.0	306,969	100.0	0.9	58.2	40.1	0.7
Burglary	113,489	100.0	1.0	74.3	23.2	1.6	242,424	100.0	0.7	62.2	36.6	0.5
Larceny-theft	359,206	100.0	1.2	71.6	25.4	1.8	892,911	100.0	0.9	61.6	36.5	0.9
Motor vehicle theft	74,658	100.0	1.1	55.2	41.7	2.0	107,976	100.0	0.6	55.6	43.0	0.8
Arson	6,349	100.0	0.9	82.3	16.0	0.8	8,282	100.0	0.6	67.8	31.1	0.4
Violent crime[2]	84,573	100.0	0.6	44.8	53.5	1.1	451,392	100.0	0.8	51.9	46.6	0.7
Property crime[3]	553,702	100.0	1.2	70.0	27.0	1.8	1,251,593	100.0	0.9	61.2	37.1	0.8
Total crime index[4]	638,275	100.0	1.1	66.7	30.5	1.7	1,702,985	100.0	0.9	58.7	39.6	0.8

Source: "Arrests," *Sourcebook of Criminal Justice Statistics—1990*, 1991, pp. 424-426. Primary source: U.S. Department of Justice, Federal Bureau of Investigation, *Crime in the United States, 1989* (Washington, DC: USGPO, 1990), pp. 190-192. *Notes:* 1. Because of rounding, percents may not add to total. 2. Violent crimes are offenses of murder, forcible rape, robbery, and aggravated assault. 3. Property crimes are offenses of burglary, larceny-theft, motor vehicle theft, and arson. 4. Includes arson.

★ 749 ★

Arrests in Cities, for Selected Offenses

Number of arrests made in U.S. cities are shown, by offense and by race/ethnicity. Data, for 1989, are based on 7,221 agencies and an estimated population of 137,838,000.

Offense charged	Total arrests	Percent[1]				
		Total	American Indian or Alaskan Native	White	Black	Asian or Pacific Islander
Total	8,765,633	100.0	1.0	64.1	34.0	0.9
Murder or nonnegligent manslaughter	14,196	100.0	0.5	34.8	63.8	0.9
Forcible rape	23,215	100.0	0.7	45.7	52.6	0.9
Robbery	119,855	100.0	0.3	32.3	66.6	0.7
Aggravated assault	280,450	100.0	0.7	53.6	44.8	0.8
Burglary	269,822	100.0	0.7	61.8	36.5	0.9
Larceny-theft	1,071,489	100.0	1.1	63.2	34.5	1.2
Motor vehicle theft	150,090	100.0	0.7	51.7	46.2	1.4
Arson	10,840	100.0	0.7	70.7	27.9	0.6
Violent crime[2]	437,716	100.0	0.6	46.8	51.8	0.8

[Continued]

★ 749 ★

Arrests in Cities, for Selected Offenses
[Continued]

Offense charged	Total arrests	Percent[1]				
		Total	American Indian or Alaskan Native	White	Black	Asian or Pacific Islander
Property crime[3]	1,502,241	100.0	1.0	61.8	36.0	1.2
Total crime index[4]	1,939,957	100.0	0.9	58.4	39.6	1.1

Source: "Arrests in Cities," *Sourcebook of Criminal Justice Statistics—1990*, 1991, pp. 428-430. Primary source: U.S. Department of Justice, Federal Bureau of Investigation, *Crime in the United States, 1989* (Washington, DC: USGPO, 1990), pp. 199-201. *Notes:* 1. Because of rounding, percents may not add to total. 2. Violent crimes are offenses of murder, forcible rape, robbery, and aggravated assault. 3. Property crimes are offenses of burglary, larceny-theft, motor vehicle theft, and arson. 4. Includes arson.

★ 750 ★

Arrests in Cities, by Age Group

Persons in cities under 18 and 18 and over arrested for selected offenses in 1989, by offense charged and race, United States, 1989.

Offense charged	Arrests under 18 Total	Percent[1] under 18					Arrests 18 and older Total	Percent[1] 18 and over				
		Total	American Indian or Alaskan Native	White	Black	Asian or Pacific Islander		Total	American Indian or Alaskan Native	White	Black	Asian or Pacific Islander
Total	1,476,210	100.0	0.9	67.2	30.4	1.5	7,289,423	100.0	1.0	63.4	34.8	0.8
Murder and nonnegligent manslaughter	1,935	100.0	0.5	33.6	64.5	1.4	12,261	100.0	0.4	35.0	63.7	0.8
Forcible rape	3,732	100.0	0.5	43.7	54.8	1.0	19,483	100.0	0.8	46.1	52.2	0.9
Robbery	28,656	100.0	0.3	31.7	66.7	1.3	91,199	100.0	0.4	32.5	66.6	0.6
Aggravated assault	40,138	100.0	0.7	50.0	48.3	1.0	240,312	100.0	0.8	54.2	44.3	0.8
Burglary	86,408	100.0	0.8	70.8	26.7	1.7	183,414	100.0	0.7	57.6	41.2	0.6
Larceny-theft	315,665	100.0	1.3	70.6	26.3	1.8	755,824	100.0	1.0	60.1	37.9	1.0
Motor vehicle theft	63,210	100.0	1.0	52.2	44.8	2.1	86,880	100.0	0.5	51.3	47.3	0.9
Arson	5,029	100.0	0.9	80.7	17.6	0.7	5,811	100.0	0.6	62.0	36.8	0.6
Violent crime[2]	74,461	100.0	0.5	42.2	56.1	1.1	363,255	100.0	0.6	47.7	50.9	0.7
Property crime[3]	470,312	100.0	1.2	68.3	28.7	1.8	1,031,929	100.0	0.9	58.9	39.3	0.9
Total crime index[4]	544,773	100.0	1.1	64.7	32.5	1.7	1,395,184	100.0	0.8	56.0	42.3	0.8

Source: "Arrests in Cities," *Sourcebook of Criminal Justice Statistics—1990*, 1991, pp. 428-430. Primary source: U.S. Department of Justice, Federal Bureau of Investigation, *Crime in the United States, 1989* (Washington, DC: USGPO, 1990), pp. 199-201. *Notes:* 1. Because of rounding, percents may not add to total. 2. Violent crimes are offenses of murder, forcible rape, robbery, and aggravated assault. 3. Property crimes are offenses of burglary, larceny-theft, and arson. 4. Includes arson.

★ 751 ★

Arrests in Rural Counties

By offense charged and race, 1989. (2,280 agencies; 1989 estimated population 24,300,000).

Offense charged	Total	Percent[1]				
		Total	American Indian or Alaskan Native	White	Black	Asian or Pacific Islander
Total	846,861	100.0	2.2	82.6	14.3	0.9
Murder and nonnegligent manslaughter	1,400	100.0	3.0	71.8	24.7	0.5
Forcible rape	2,632	100.0	2.1	72.0	25.3	0.6
Robbery	2,474	100.0	1.5	56.3	41.4	0.8
Aggravated assault	25,597	100.0	3.2	72.8	23.3	0.7
Burglary	33,137	100.0	2.4	81.6	15.0	0.9
Larceny-theft	48,224	100.0	1.3	79.5	17.7	1.5
Motor vehicle theft	8,700	100.0	2.8	84.0	11.4	1.8
Arson	1,379	100.0	1.7	86.1	12.0	0.2
Violent crime[2]	32,103	100.0	3.0	71.4	24.9	0.7
Property crime[3]	91,440	100.0	1.9	80.8	16.0	1.3
Total crime index[4]	123,543	100.0	2.2	78.4	18.3	1.2

Source: "Arrests in Rural Counties," *Sourcebook of Criminal Justice Statistics—1990*, 1991, pp. 436-438. Primary source: U.S. Department of Justice, Federal Bureau of Investigation, *Crime in the United States, 1989* (Washington, D.C.: USGPO, 1990), pp. 217-219. *Notes:* 1. Because of rounding, percents may not add to total. 2. Violent crimes are offenses of murder, forcible rape, robbery, and aggravated assault. 3. Property crimes are offenses of burglary, larceny-theft, motor vehicle theft, and arson. 4. Includes arson.

★ 752 ★

Arrests in Rural Counties, by Age Group

Persons in rural counties under 18 and 18 and over arrested for selected offenses in 1989. By offense charged, age group, and race, 1989.

Offense charged	Total	Percent[1] under 18					Total	Percent[1] 18 and over				
		Total	American Indian or Alaskan Native	White	Black	Asian or Pacific Islander		Total	American Indian or Alaskan Native	White	Black	Asian or Pacific Islander
Total	81,028	100.0	3.0	87.2	7.0	2.9	765,833	100.0	2.1	82.1	15.1	0.7
Murder and nonnegligent manslaughter	78	100.0	2.6	70.5	26.9	-	1,322	100.0	3.0	71.9	24.6	0.5
Forcible rape	287	100.0	2.8	75.3	21.3	0.7	2,345	100.0	2.0	71.6	25.8	0.6
Robbery	213	100.0	3.8	66.7	27.2	2.3	2,261	100.0	1.3	55.4	42.7	0.6
Aggravated assault	1,534	100.0	4.4	73.1	20.4	2.1	24,063	100.0	3.1	72.8	23.5	0.6
Burglary	10,063	100.0	4.0	87.8	6.6	1.6	23,074	100.0	1.8	79.0	18.7	0.6
Larceny-theft	10,443	100.0	2.0	85.9	8.7	3.5	37,781	100.0	1.1	77.7	20.1	1.0
Motor vehicle theft	3,038	100.0	4.1	85.9	6.6	3.4	5,662	100.0	2.1	83.0	14.0	1.0
Arson	335	100.0	1.5	93.7	4.5	0.3	1,044	100.0	1.7	83.7	14.4	0.2
Violent crime[2]	2,112	100.0	4.0	72.7	21.4	1.8	29,991	100.0	2.9	71.3	25.2	0.6

[Continued]

★ 752 ★

Arrests in Rural Counties, by Age Group

[Continued]

Offense charged	Total	Percent[1] under 18					Total	Percent[1] 18 and over				
		Total	American Indian Alaskan Native	White	Black	Asian or Pacific Islander		Total	American Indian or Alaskan Native	White	Black	Asian or Pacific Islander
Property crime[3]	23,879	100.0	3.1	86.8	7.5	2.6	67,561	100.0	1.4	78.7	19.0	0.8
Total crime index[4]	25,991	100.0	3.2	85.6	8.6	2.6	97,552	100.0	1.9	76.4	20.9	0.8

Source: "Arrests in Rural Counties," *Sourcebook of Criminal Justice Statistics—1990,* 1991, pp. 436-438. Primary source: U.S. Department of Justice, Federal Bureau of Investigation, *Crime in the United States, 1989* (Washington, DC: USGPO, 1990), pp. 217-219. *Notes:* 1. Because of rounding, percents may not add to total. 2. Violent crimes are offenses of murder, forcible rape, robbery, and aggravated assault. 3. Property crimes are offenses of burglary, larceny-theft, motor vehicle theft, and arson. 4. Includes arson.

★ 753 ★

Arrests in Suburban Areas

By offense charged and race, 1989. (4,948 agencies; 1989 estimated population 79,592,000).

Offense charged	Total arrests	Percent[1]				
		Total	American Indian or Alaskan Native	White	Black	Asian or Pacific Islander
Total	3,715,103	100.0	0.4	78.8	20.3	0.4
Murder and nonnegligent manslaughter	3,676	100.0	0.5	64.2	34.9	0.4
Forcible rape	8,999	100.0	0.5	68.4	30.7	0.4
Robbery	24,192	100.0	0.4	47.4	51.9	0.4
Aggravated assault	99,065	100.0	0.5	71.8	27.2	0.5
Burglary	111,210	100.0	0.4	77.3	21.8	0.5
Larceny-theft	409,568	100.0	0.5	71.8	26.9	0.8
Motor vehicle theft	45,841	100.0	0.5	69.9	29.0	0.7
Arson	5,216	100.0	0.3	84.8	14.3	0.6
Violent crime[2]	135,932	100.0	0.5	67.0	32.0	0.5
Property crime[3]	571,835	100.0	0.5	72.8	25.9	0.7
Total crime index[4]	707,767	100.0	0.5	71.7	27.1	0.7

Source: "Arrests in Suburban Areas," *Sourcebook of Criminal Justice Statistics—1990,* 1991, pp. 432-434. Primary source: U.S. Department of Justice, Federal Bureau of Investigation, *Crime in the United States, 1989* (Washington, DC: USGPO, 1990), pp. 226-228. *Notes:* 1. Because of rounding, percents may not add to total. 2. Violent crimes are offenses of murder, forcible rape, robbery, and aggravated assault. 3. Property crimes are offenses of burglary, larceny-theft, motor vehicle theft, and arson. 4. Includes arson.

★ 754 ★

Arrests in Suburban Areas, by Age Group

Persons in suburban areas under 18 and 18 and over arrested for selected offenses in 1989. By offense charged, age group, and race, 1989.

Offense charged	Arrests under 18 Total	Percent[1] under 18					Arrests 18 and over Total	Percent[1] 18 and over				
		Total	American Indian or Alaskan Native	White	Black	Asian or Pacific Islander		Total	American Indian or Alaskan Native	White	Black	Asian or Pacific Islander
Total	584,571	100.0	0.4	81.4	17.5	0.6	3,130,532	100.0	0.4	78.3	20.8	0.4
Murder and nonnegligent manslaughter	334	100.0	0.6	58.7	39.8	0.9	3,342	100.0	0.5	64.7	34.4	0.4
Forcible rape	1,389	100.0	0.4	68.7	30.7	0.2	7,610	100.0	0.5	68.3	30.7	0.5
Robbery	4,565	100.0	0.4	47.8	51.3	0.5	19,627	100.0	0.4	47.3	52.0	0.4
Aggravated assault	12,623	100.0	0.3	67.5	31.7	0.6	86,442	100.0	0.6	72.4	26.6	0.5
Burglary	38,850	100.0	0.4	82.8	16.1	0.7	72,360	100.0	0.4	74.3	24.9	0.3
Larceny-theft	123,596	100.0	0.6	78.2	20.2	1.0	285,972	100.0	0.4	69.0	29.8	0.8
Motor vehicle theft	18,443	100.0	0.5	69.6	28.9	1.0	27,398	100.0	0.4	70.1	29.0	0.4
Arson	2,585	100.0	0.4	89.5	9.1	0.9	2,631	100.0	0.2	80.1	19.5	0.2
Violent crime[2]	18,911	100.0	0.3	62.7	36.5	0.6	117,021	100.0	0.5	67.7	31.3	0.5
Property crime[3]	183,474	100.0	0.5	78.5	20.0	0.9	388,361	100.0	0.4	70.2	28.7	0.7
Total crime index[4]	202,385	100.0	0.5	77.0	21.6	0.9	505,382	100.0	0.5	69.6	29.3	0.6

Source: "Arrests in Suburban Areas," *Sourcebook of Criminal Justice Statistics—1990,* 1991, pp. 432-434. Primary source: U.S. Department of Justice, Federal Bureau of Investigation, *Crime in the United States, 1989* (Washington, DC: USGPO, 1990), pp. 226-228. *Notes:* Includes suburban city and county law enforcement agencies within metropolitan areas. Excludes central cities. Suburban cities and counties are also included in other groups. 1. Because of rounding, percents may not add to total. 2. Violent crimes are offenses of murder, forcible rape, robbery, and aggravated assault. 3. Property crimes are offenses of burglary, larceny-theft, motor vehicle theft, and arson. 4. Includes arson.

Crime

★ 755 ★

Homicide Rates, by Year

Age-adjusted rate per 100,000 population for American Indians, Alaskan Natives, and U.S. all races, 1955-1988.

Calendar year	Indian and Alaskan Native		U.S. all races		U.S. other than White Rate	Ratio Indian to:	
	Number	Rate	Number	Rate		U.S. all races	U.S. other than White
1988	214	14.1	22,032	9.0	28.2	1.6	0.5
1987	199	14.1	21,103	8.6	26.4	1.6	0.5
1986	240	16.3	21,731	9.0	27.2	1.8	0.6
1985	191	14.3	19,893	8.3	24.4	1.7	0.6
1984	189	14.5	19,796	8.4	24.9	1.7	0.6
1983	217	16.4	20,191	8.6	26.4	1.9	0.6
1982	188	14.9	22,358	9.7	30.0	1.5	0.5
1981	207	17.9	23,646	10.4	33.3	1.7	0.5
1980	212	18.1	24,278	10.8	35.0	1.7	0.5

[Continued]

★ 755 ★

Homicide Rates, by Year

[Continued]

Calendar year	Indian and Alaskan Native		U.S. all races		U.S. other than White Rate	Ratio Indian to:	
	Number	Rate	Number	Rate		U.S. all races	U.S. other than White
1979	209	18.9	22,550	10.4	36.0	1.8	0.5
1978	218	21.2	20,432	9.6	33.4	2.2	0.6
1977	197	20.9	19,968	9.6	34.5	2.2	0.6
1976	185	21.6	19,554	9.5	36.4	2.3	0.6
1975	185	21.9	21,310	10.5	41.1	2.1	0.5
1974	203	26.4	21,465	10.8	44.5	2.4	0.6
1973	196	27.2	20,465	10.5	44.4	2.6	0.6
1972	159	23.2	19,638	10.3	46.6	2.3	0.5
1971	149	24.5	18,787	10.0	46.8	2.5	0.5
1970	125	23.8	16,848	9.1	41.3	2.6	0.6
1969	132	22.5	15,477	8.6	40.5	2.6	0.6
1968	116	22.2	14,686	8.2	38.8	2.7	0.6
1967	110	20.3	13,425	7.7	36.3	2.6	0.6
1966	79	20.3	11,606	6.7	31.9	3.0	0.6
1965	102	19.7	10,712	6.3	29.8	3.1	0.7
1964	84	23.6	9,814	5.8	27.6	4.1	0.9
1963	85	22.3	9,225	5.5	26.6	4.1	0.8
1962	80	21.0	9,013	5.5	26.3	3.8	0.8
1961	63	20.9	8,578	5.3	24.9	3.9	0.8
1960	80	19.5	8,464	5.3	25.8	3.7	0.8
1959	62	20.5	8,159	5.1	25.8	4.0	0.8
1958	69	20.4	7,815	4.9	25.3	4.2	0.8
1957	73	21.8	7,641	4.9	25.9	4.4	0.8
1956	76	21.7	7,629	5.0	26.5	4.3	0.8
1955	77	23.8	7,418	4.8	25.7	5.0	0.9

Source: Trends in Indian Health, 1991, U.S. Department of Health and Human Services, Public Health Service, Indian Health Service, p. 47.
Notes: Estimated population methodology for the Indian population revised in 1976. Maine, New York and Pennsylvania included as Reservation States beginning in 1979, Connecticut, Rhode Island and Texas in 1983 and Alabama in 1984. Decennial Census population counts used for 1960, 1970, and 1980.

★ 756 ★

Homicide Rates, by Victim Age and Sex

Rate per 100,000 population for American Indians, Alaskan Natives, and U.S. all races, 1955-1988.

Age group	Indian and Alaskan Native			U.S. all races			U.S. Other than White		
	Both sexes	Male	Female	Both sexes	Male	Female	Both sexes	Male	Female
Under 1 year	12.2	18.8	5.6	7.2	8.0	6.4	16.3	16.8	15.8
1-4 years	4.8	4.3	5.3	2.3	2.2	2.4	5.0	4.0	6.0
5-14 years	0.8	1.0	0.6	1.2	1.4	1.0	2.8	3.8	1.8
15-24 years	21.1	32.1	10.2	14.0	21.9	6.0	43.2	71.2	15.5
25-34 years	27.4	44.7	10.4	15.1	23.3	6.9	47.6	79.6	18.5

[Continued]

★ 756 ★

Homicide Rates, by Victim Age and Sex
[Continued]

Age group	Indian and Alaskan Native			U.S. all races			U.S. Other than White		
	Both sexes	Male	Female	Both sexes	Male	Female	Both sexes	Male	Female
35-44 years	23.7	38.6	9.3	10.8	17.1	4.8	35.1	62.3	12.0
45-54 years	11.7	19.4	4.4	7.7	12.1	3.6	22.1	37.9	9.0
55-64 years	8.7	13.0	4.6	5.5	8.8	2.5	16.3	28.1	6.7
65-74 years	6.4	12.6	1.2	4.3	6.2	2.8	13.6	23.5	6.1
75-84 years	9.0	17.1	2.7	4.8	6.8	3.6	15.2	25.1	8.9
85 years +	5.3	13.3	1	5.1	7.4	4.2	14.4	25.3	9.2

Source: Trends in Indian Health, 1991, U.S. Department of Health and Human Services, Public Health Service, Indian Health Service, p. 48. *Note:* 1. Represents zero.

★ 757 ★

Weapons Used in Homicides, by Race of Victim, 1966-88

Percent distribution of weapons used is shown for each race.

Weapon	American Indian/ Alaskan Native (N=237)	Asian/ Pacific Islander (N=329)	Black (N=15,419)	White (N=13,520)
Handgun	29.0	51.0	57.0	47.0
Other firearm	16.0	12.0	15.0	17.0
Knife	32.0	21.0	20.0	22.0
Personal	9.0	7.0	3.0	5.0
Other	14.0	9.0	5.0	9.0

Source: "Weapons Used in Homicides Among Victims 15-34 Years of Age, According to Type of Weapon and Race of Victim: United States, 1966-88," *Health United States 1990*, 1991, p. 17. Primary source: Federal Bureau of Investigation, Supplemental Homicide Reporting System. *Note:* Numbers of victims are in paretheses.

Law Officers

★ 758 ★

Assaults on Federal Government Officers

Numbers indicate total reported assaults in 1990.

	Number of assaults
Most	
Immigration and Naturalization	409
U.S. Attorney	269
Bureau of Prisons	185
Least	
Internal Revenue Service	3
Bureau of Indian Affairs	5
Postal Inspectors	6

Source: USA Today, April 30, 1992. Primary source: Federal Bureau of Investigation.

★ 759 ★

Native American Representation in Federal Law Enforcement Occupations, 1991

The estimated number of persons needed to reach full representation per capita population is shown, for selected groups.

Agency	Occupation series[1]	American Indian		Hispanic		White		Black		Asian	
		Men	Women	Men	Women	Men	Women	Men	Women	Men	Women
Drug Enforcement Administration	1811		3		10		101	23	56		
Federal Bureau of Investigation	1811	34	6	45	36			476	206		4
U.S. Immigration and Naturalization Service	1801	.82	2			19	37	13	.34	4	2
	1802		2			200	155		.62	30	15
	1811	5	2			120	22	66	29		
	1869	17	3			482	242	282	96	18	4
	2181	.23	.01	.37	.05		3	.96	.18		.03
U.S. Marshals Service	0082	3	.84	11	3			39	16	3	2
	1811		.89	3	6		19	14	37	11	3
Bureau of Alcohol, Tobacco and Firearms	1811	7	3		3		2	29	25	4	
U.S. Customs Service	1801	2	.65		6		42	15	15	.63	2
	1811	5	4		6		20	171	65		3
	2181	2	.06	.75	.26		8	3	.87	4	.14
Internal Revenue Service	1811	5	3	72		69		128	7		

[Continued]

★ 759 ★

Native American Representation in Federal Law Enforcement Occupations, 1991

[Continued]

Agency	Occupation series[1]	American Indian		Hispanic		White		Black		Asian	
		Men	Women	Men	Women	Men	Women	Men	Women	Men	Women
U.S. Secret Service	0083	7	2	33	9		50			8	2
	1811	5	2	20	14		66	61	38		2
U.S. Postal Service	1811	6	2	39	11			27	12		

Source: United States General Accounting Office, GAO/T-GGD-93-2, *Federal Affirmative Employment: Status of Women and Minority Representation in Federal Law Enforcement Occupations,* October 1, 1992, p. 10. *Notes:* Except when the estimated number was less than 1 person, each fraction of a person was rounded to the next whole person; for example, 21.6 was rounded to 22 people. 1. Occupation series represent the following groups: 0082, U.S. Marshal; 0083, Police; 1801, General inspection, investigation, and compliance; 1802, Compliance inspection and support; 1811, Criminal investigation; 1896, Border Patrol Agent; 2181, Aircraft operation.

★ 760 ★

Police Officers in New York City, by Race/Ethnicity, 1992

Race/ethnicity	Number of officers
Native American	28
White	20,098
Black	3,121
Hispanic	3,688
Asian-Pacific Islander	219

Source: USA TODAY, October 7, 1992, p. 8A. Primary source: USA TODAY research.

Legal Aid

★ 761 ★

Federally Funded Legal Aid

The Legal Services Corporation receives an annual appropriation. A specific amount of the appropriation is allocated to Native American programs and components.

	Fiscal year		
	1988	1989	1990[1]
LSC total	305,500,000	308,555,000	321,000,000
Native American	7,022,000	7,022,000	7,304,000

Source: Roger Walke, *Federal Programs of Assistance to Native Americans: A Report Prepared for the Senate Select Committee on Indian Affairs of the United States Senate,* U.S. Government Printing Office, Washington, D.C., December 1991, p. 272. *Notes:* 1. The 1990 funding levels are based on Public Law 101-162. They do not reflect sequestration required by applicable Executive orders issued pursuant to Public Law 100-119, and the Balanced Budget and Emergency Deficit Control Reaffirmation Act of 1987 (the so-called "Gramm-Rudman- Hollings") sequestration reductions. The final sequestration reduction was approximately 1.4 percent.

Prisons

★ 762 ★

Prisoners on Death Row

Numbers of prisoners are shown, by race/ethnicity and jurisdiction, April 24, 1991.

Jurisdiction	Total	Race/ethnicity					
		Native American	Hispanic	White	Black	Asian	Unknown
United States	2,457	45	170	1,243	966	15	18
Federal civil	0	-	-	-	-	-	-
U.S. military	5	0	0	1	4	0	0
Alabama	109	0	0	57[1,2,3]	51[4,5]	1	0
Arizona	96	3	16	65[3,6]	12[7]	0	0
Arkansas	35	1[3]	1	20	13[3]	0	0
California	299	11	38	136[4,8]	100	5	9
Colorado	2	0	1	1	0	0	0
Connecticut	2	0	0	2	0	0	0
Delaware	7	0	0	2	5	0	0

[Continued]

★ 762 ★

Prisoners on Death Row
[Continued]

Jurisdiction	Total	Race/ethnicity					
		Native American	Hispanic	White	Black	Asian	Unknown
Florida	295	2	26	162[2,4,7]	104[6]	1	0
Georgia	113	0	0	59[2,6]	54	0	0
Idaho	21	0	1	20	0	0	0
Illinois	136	0	8	41	86[3,6]	0	1
Indiana	53	0	1	32[3,6]	19[6,7]	0	1
Kentucky	27	0	0	22[6]	5[9]	0	0
Louisiana	34	0	1	15	17[5]	0	1
Maryland	16	0	0	2	14	0	0
Mississippi	52	0	1	21[3,9]	30[4,9]	0	0
Missouri	73	1	0	39[6,9]	33[3,9]	0	0
Montana	6	2	0	4	0	0	0
Nebraska	12	1	0	8[3]	3	0	0
Nevada	60	0	6	37	17[6]	0	0
New Hampshire	0	-	-	-	-	-	-
New Jersey	13	0	1	4	8	0	0
New Mexico	2	1	0	1	0	0	0
North Carolina	99	5	1	51[5,10]	42	0	0
Ohio	99	2	3	41	53	0	0
Oklahoma	122	9[3]	2	80[1,3,5]	27[6]	1	3
Oregon	20	1	2	15	2	0	0
Pennsylvania	132	0	5	45	78[2,3,6]	1	3
South Carolina	43	0	0	22[6]	21	0	0
South Dakota	0	-	-	-	-	-	-
Tennessee	85	2	0	57[6]	25[3]	1	0
Texas	335	5	55[9]	149[1,5,7]	122[3,6,11]	4	0
Utah	11	0	1	7[3]	3	0	0
Virginia	45	0	0	23	22	0	0
Washington	9	0	0	7	1	1	0
Wyoming	2	0	0	2	0	0	0

Source: Sourcebook of Criminal Justice Statistics - 1990, U.S. Department of Justice, Office of Justice Programs, Bureau of Justice Statistics, U.S. G.P.O., Washington, D.C., p. 674. Primary source: Table constructed by Sourcebook staff from data provided by the NAACP Legal Defense and Educational Fund, Inc. *Notes:* The NAACP Legal Defense and Educational Fund, Inc. periodically collects data on persons on death row. As of Apr. 24, 1991, 36 jurisdictions, the Federal government, and the United States military had capital punishment laws, and 34 jurisdictions and the United States military had at least 1 prisoner under sentence of death. Between Jan. 1, 1973 and Apr. 24, 1991, an estimated 1,091 convictions or sentences have been reversed or vacated on grounds other than constitutional. Between Jan. 1, 1973 and May 30, 1990, and estimated 558 death sentences have been vacated as unconstitutional. 1. Includes three females. 2. Includes three people who were juveniles at the time of the offense. 3. Includes one person sentenced to death in the state but serving another sentence in another state. 4. Includes two females. 5. Includes two people who were juveniles at the time of the offense. 6. Includes one female. 7. Includes two people sentenced to death in the state but serving another sentence in another state. 8. Includes three people sentenced to death in the state but serving another sentence in another state. 9. Includes one person who was a juvenile at the time of the offense. 10. Includes two females. 11. Includes four people who were juveniles at the time of the offense.

★ 763 ★

Adults on Probation, by Race, 1989

Regions and jurisdictions	Probation population 12/31/89	Number of adults on probation				
		American Indian/ Alaska Native	White	Black	Asian/ Pacific Islander	Other, unknown, or not reported
U.S. total	2,520,479	13,387	1,173,870	512,395	4,281	816,546
Federal	59,146	746	43,436	13,753	1,106	105
State	2,461,333	12,641	1,130,434	498,642	3,175	816,441
Northeast	443,794	351	171,155	82,625	644	189,019
Connecticut	42,842	-	29,990	12,852	-	-
Maine	6,851	70	6,721	50	10	-
Massachusetts	88,529	-	-	-	-	88,529
New Hampshire	2,991	-	2,841	-	-	150
New Jersey	66,753	-	-	-	-	66,753
New York	128,707	281	63,554	44,187	371	20,314
Pennsylvania	89,491	0	62,677	25,509	263	1,042
Rhode Island	12,231	-	-	-	-	12,231
Vermont	5,399	-	5,372	27	-	0
Midwest	542,765	4,827	224,397	67,709	647	245,185
Illinois	93,944	-	-	-	-	93,944
Indiana	61,861	-	-	-	-	61,861
Iowa	13,722	-	-	-	-	13,722
Kansas	22,525	276	17,713	4,369	94	73
Michigan	121,436	998	56,506	9,023	188	54,721
Minnesota	58,648	2,139	48,265	4,748	-	3,496
Missouri	45,251	40	33,375	11,505	30	301
Nebraska	12,627	495	10,228	1,389	185	330
North Dakota	1,652	166	1,468	12	6	0
Ohio	78,223	26	34,774	29,842	58	13,523
South Dakota	2,716	-	-	-	-	2,716
Wisconsin	30,160	687	22,068	6,821	86	498
South	986,508	3,482	611,892	336,438	775	33,921
Alabama	26,475	-	11,188	15,239	48	0
Arkansas	17,572	4	11,133	6,287	3	145
Delaware	9,701	16	5,616	4,064	5	0
District of Colombia	10,351	-	517	9,834	-	-
Florida	192,495	130	135,715	49,649	271	6,730
Georgia	125,441	73	66,280	59,040	5	43
Kentucky	8,062	-	-	-	-	8,062
Louisiana	32,295	-	15,710	16,377	-	208
Maryland	84,456	84	42,607	40,583	337	845
Mississippi	7,333	4	3,193	4,127	9	0
North Carolina	72,325	1,612	37,470	32,720	66	457
Oklahoma	24,240	1,558	17,174	5,472	30	6
South Carolina	29,652	-	15,657	13,880	-	115
Tennessee	30,906	-	6,563	7,257	-	17,086

[Continued]

★ 763 ★

Adults on Probation, by Race, 1989
[Continued]

Regions and jurisdictions	Probation population 12/31/89	Number of adults on probation				
		American Indian/ Alaska Native	White	Black	Asian/ Pacific Islander	Other, unknown, or not reported
Texas	291,156	-	227,100	64,056	-	-
Virginia	19,085	-	11,451	7,413	-	221
West Virginia	4,963	1	4,518	440	1	3
West	488,266	3,981	122,990	11,870	1,109	348,316
Alaska	3,335	828	2,170	302	35	0
Arizona	27,650	-	-	-	-	27,650
California	285,018	-	-	-	-	285,018
Colorado	26,378	37	18,248	2,220	14	5,859
Hawaii	11,377	-	-	-	-	11,377
Idaho	4,025	137	3,823	54	11	0
Montana	3,459	416	3,001	31	5	6
Nevada	7,324	92	5,340	1,290	39	563
New Mexico	5,660	231	3,828	244	0	1,357
Oregon	31,878	606	29,548	1,660	64	-
Utah	5,524	140	4,961	196	57	170
Washington	74,254	1,494	52,071	5,873	884	13,932
Wyoming	2,384	-	-	-	-	2,384

Source: U.S. Department of Justice, Office of Justice Programs, Bureau of Justice Statistics, *Correctional Populations in the United States, 1989*, NCJ-130445, October 1991, p. 31. *Notes:* 1. The state estimated all numbers in the detailed categories. 2. The state estimated all data.

★ 764 ★

Prisoners Under State and Federal Correctional Authority

Number of prisoners is shown, by race, region, and jurisdiction, December 31, 1989.

Region and jurisdiction	Total	American Indian or Alaska Native	White	Black	Asian or Pacific Islander	Unknown Race
United States, total	712,563	5,994	343,550	334,952	2,480	25,587
Federal institutions, total	59,171	1,065	39,483	18,092	464	67
State institutions, total	653,392	4,929	304,067	316,860	2,016	25,520
Northeast	113,965	197	52,619	56,888	206	4,055
Connecticut[1,2]	9,301	8	2,661	4,458	9	2,165
Maine	1,455	15	1,423	17	0	0
Massachusetts[2,3]	7,524	12	4,091	2,770	34	617
New Hampshire	1,166	0	1,116	47	3	0
New Jersey	19,439	6	6,535	11,979	13	906

[Continued]

★ 764 ★

Prisoners Under State and Federal Correctional Authority

[Continued]

Region and jurisdiction	Total	American Indian or Alaska Native	White	Black	Asian or Pacific Islander	Unknown Race
New York	51,227	137	25,368	25,249	124	349
Pennsylvania	20,469	14	8,897	11,525	15	18
Rhode Island[1]	2,479	5	1,623	843	8	0
Vermont[1,4]	905	NA	905	NA	NA	NA
Midwest	136,338	1,165	64,826	67,071	76	3,200
Illinois[2,3]	24,712	27	7,529	14,881	16	2,259
Indiana[3]	12,341	24	7,612	4,704	1	0
Iowa[2,3]	3,584	42	2,722	777	6	37
Kansas[2]	5,616	69	3,396	1,856	21	274
Michigan[2,3]	31,639	112	12,669	18,319	16	523
Minnesota[2]	3,103	246	1,909	854	3	91
Missouri	13,921	26	7,433	6,453	7	2
Nebraska	2,393	83	1,527	769	0	14
North Dakota	451	68	378	4	1	0
Ohio[4]	30,538	0	14,764	15,774	0	0
South Dakota	1,252	320	898	34	0	0
Wisconsin	6,788	148	3,989	2,646	5	0
South	262,115	1,177	97,444	151,892	189	11,413
Alabama	13,907	4	5,324	8,575	3	1
Arkansas[4]	6,409	1	3,060	3,313	0	35
Delaware[1]	3,458	2	1,210	2,198	4	44
District of Columbia[1,3,4]	10,039	0	152	9,872	0	15
Florida[2,3]	39,999	11	16,909	22,270	16	793
Georgia[3]	20,885	14	7,110	13,694	1	66
Kentucky	8,289	1	5,762	2,526	0	0
Louisiana	17,257	0	4,797	12,460	0	0
Maryland	16,514	7	4,276	12,211	0	20
Mississippi	7,911	10	2,393	5,481	10	17
North Carolina[3]	17,454	416	6,721	10,129	13	175
Oklahoma[2]	11,608	691	6,742	3,861	0	314
South Carolina	15,720	9	5,689	9,986	2	34
Tennessee[5]	10,630	NA	5,654	4,519	NA	457
Texas[2,3]	44,022	4	14,220	20,314	117	9,367
Virginia	16,477	6	6,112	10,262	22	75
West Virginia[3]	1,536	1	1,313	221	1	0
West	140,974	2,390	89,178	41,009	1,545	6,852
Alaska[1]	2,744	878	1,508	329	29	0
Arizona[3]	13,251	421	10,616	2,197	13	4
California[3]	87,297	NA	50,897	32,241	NA	4,159
Colorado[4]	6,908	69	5,028	1,612	22	177
Hawaii[1,2,4]	2,470	18	665	147	1,308	332

[Continued]

★ 764 ★

Prisoners Under State and Federal Correctional Authority

[Continued]

Region and jurisdiction	Total	American Indian or Alaska Native	White	Black	Asian or Pacific Islander	Unknown Race
Idaho	1,850	93	1,659	26	10	62
Montana	1,328	242	1,059	25	2	0
Nevada[2]	5,112	52	2,737	1,510	45	768
New Mexico	2,932	106	2,487	328	5	6
Oregon[4]	6,744	155	5,224	952	18	395
Utah	2,394	54	2,055	208	26	51
Washington[2]	6,928	250	4,439	1,377	66	796
Wyoming[2,3]	1,016	52	804	57	1	102

Source: Sourcebook of Criminal Justice - 1990, U.S. Department of Justice, Office of Justice Programs, Bureau of Justice Statistics, U.S. G.P.O., Washington, D.C., p. 609. Primary source: U.S. Department of Justice Bureau of Justice Statistics. *Correctional Populations in the United States, 1989*, NCJ: 130445 (Washington, D.C. USGPO, 1991). Table 5.6. *Notes:* NA stands for not available. 1. Figures include both jail and prison inmates: jails and prisons are combined in one system. 2. Hispanic prisoners were classified as persons of unknown race. 3. All data for Arizona, California, the District of Columbia, Georgia,Illinois, Indiana, Iowa, Massachusetts, Michigan, North Carolina, Texas, West Virginia (men), and Wyoming are custody rather than jurisdiction counts. Florida's counts are based on custody data. 4. Racial group membership of the population was estimated. 5. Tennessee reported persons whose race is neither black or white under "other race," here reported under "unknown race".

★ 765 ★

Runaway and Homeless Center Use

Use of runaway and homeless centers by youth in fiscal year 1989. Data shown, by race/ethnicity and by sex, for the U.S.

Race, ethnicity	Total (N=34,819)	Female (N=19,670)	Male (N=15,149)
American Indian or Alaskan Native	2.6	2.8	2.4
Asian or Pacific Islander	3.7	4.0	3.4
Black, non-Hispanic	19.5	18.8	20.5
White, non-Hispanic	64.8	65.1	64.4
Hispanic	9.4	9.3	9.4

Source: "Youth Served by Runaway and Homeless Centers," *Sourcebook of Criminal Justice Statistics—1990*, 1991, p. 577. Primary source: U.S. Department of Health and Human Services, Office of Human Development Services, "Annual Report to the Congress on the Runaway and Homeless Youth Program, Fiscal Year 1989," pp. 56, 57, 59. Washington, DC: U.S. Department of Health and Human Services. (Mimeographed). Table adapted by *Sourcebook* staff.

Chapter 12
CANADA

Population

★ 766 ★

Persons of Aboriginal Origin as a Proportion of the Total Canadian Population, Canada, 1986

| Region | Aboriginal Population | | | | Total Canadian Population |
| | On-Reserve | | Off-Reserve | | |
	Number	%	Number	%	
Atlantic	8,060	0.4	26,345	1.2	2,255,095
Quebec	21,600	0.3	59,325	0.9	6,454,490
Ontario	26,135	0.3	141,220	1.6	9,001,165
Manitoba	27,375	2.6	57,840	5.5	1,049,315
Saskatchewan	27,025	2.7	50,620	5.1	996,695
Alberta	18,845	0.8	85,065	3.6	2,340,265
British Columbia	30,045	1.1	96,260	3.4	2,849,585
Territories	580	0.8	34,925	46.3	75,375
Canada	159,665	0.6	551,605	2.2	25,022,010

Source: Canada's Off-Reserve Aboriginal Population: A Statistical Overview, Social Trends Directorate, Department of the Secretary of State of Canada, 1991, p. A-2. Primary source: For Aboriginal population: Statistics Canada, *A Profile of the Aboriginal Residing in Selected Off Reserve Areas,* prepared by the Aboriginal Data and Native Issues Unit of the Housing, Family and Social Statistics Division, February 1990; for total Canadian population: Statistics Canada, *1986 Census, Special Tabulations from the Small Area Database,* compiled for the Department of the Secretary of State. *Notes:* Sum of components may not always add to totals due to rounding and/or data suppression.

★ 767 ★

Persons of Aboriginal Origin and Total Canadian
Population, by Region, Canada, 1986

Region	Aboriginal Population				Total Canadian Population	
	On-Reserve		Off-Reserve			
	Number	%	Number	%	Number	%
Atlantic	8,060	5.0	26,345	4.8	2,255,095	9.0
Quebec	21,600	13.5	59,325	10.8	6,454,490	25.8
Ontario	26,135	16.4	141,220	25.6	9,001,165	36.0
Manitoba	27,375	17.1	57,840	10.5	1,049,315	4.2
Saskatchewan	27,025	16.9	50,620	9.2	996,695	4.0
Alberta	18,845	11.8	85,065	15.4	2,340,265	9.4
British Columbia	30,045	18.8	96,260	17.5	2,849,585	11.4
Territories	580	0.4	34,925	6.3	75,375	0.3
Canada	159,665	100.0	551,605	100.0	25,022,010	100.0

Source: Canada's Off-Reserve Aboriginal Population: A Statistical Overview, Social Trends Directorate, Department of the Secretary of State of Canada, 1991, p. A-2. Primary source: For Aboriginal population: Statistics Canada, *A Profile of the Aboriginal Residing in Selected Off Reserve Areas*, prepared by the Aboriginal Data and Native Issues Unit of the Housing, Family and Social Statistics Division, February 1990; for total Canadian population Statistics Canada, *1986 Census, Special Tabulations from the Small Area Database* compiled for the Department of the Secretary of State. *Notes:* Sum of components may not always add to totals due to rounding and/or data suppression.

★ 768 ★

Persons of Aboriginal Origin and Total Canadian
Population, by Age Group, Canada, 1986

Percent distributions are shown, by age group.

Group/Region	Age Group				
	0-14	15-24	25-44	45-64	65+
On-Reserve					
Atlantic	36.2	23.6	25.9	11.0	4.0
Quebec	37.6	23.3	23.3	11.2	4.7
Ontario	35.6	20.2	25.8	13.1	5.4
Manitoba	42.2	22.1	21.8	9.7	4.2
Saskatchewan	43.7	21.8	20.8	9.8	4.0
Alberta	41.0	22.4	23.5	9.8	3.6
British Columbia	33.0	21.1	27.7	13.4	5.9
Territories	29.3	21.6	28.4	11.2	11.2
Canada	38.5	21.8	24.0	11.2	4.7

[Continued]

★ 768 ★

Persons of Aboriginal Origin and Total Canadian Population, by Age Group, Canada, 1986
[Continued]

Group/Region	Age Group				
	0-14	15-24	25-44	45-64	65+
Off-Reserve					
Atlantic	35.2	22.5	30.3	9.7	2.2
Quebec	28.1	18.7	38.4	11.8	3.1
Ontario	34.4	20.7	33.4	9.6	2.0
Manitoba	37.4	21.7	28.6	9.6	2.6
Saskatchewan	41.9	21.8	25.2	8.2	2.9
Alberta	39.0	21.7	29.4	7.8	2.1
British Columbia	35.9	20.6	32.1	9.5	2.0
Territories	38.0	23.2	24.6	10.6	3.6
Canada	35.9	21.0	31.2	9.5	2.4
Total Canadian population					
Atlantic	23.3	18.1	31.0	17.3	10.3
Quebec	20.8	16.4	33.6	20.0	9.3
Ontario	20.8	16.6	32.1	20.3	10.2
Manitoba	22.4	16.8	30.4	18.6	11.8
Saskatchewan	24.6	16.7	28.8	17.9	12.0
Alberta	24.0	17.3	34.7	16.6	7.4
British Columbia	20.7	15.3	32.7	19.9	11.4
Territories	30.5	19.0	35.1	12.4	3.0
Canada	21.5	16.6	32.5	19.4	10.0

Source: Canada's Off-Reserve Aboriginal Population: A Statistical Overview, Social Trends Analysis Directorate, Department of the Secretary of State of Canada, 1991, p. A-3. Primary source: For Aboriginal population: Statistics Canada, *A Profile of the Aboriginal Population Residing in Selected Off Reserve Areas*, prepared by the Aboriginal Data and Native Issues Unit of the Housing, Family and Social Statistics Division, February 1990; for total Canadian population: Statistics Canada, *1986 Census, Special Tabulations from the Small Area Database* compiled for the Department of the Secretary of State. *Notes:* Sum of components may not always add to totals due to rounding and/or date suppression.

★ 769 ★

Population by Age Group and Sex for Selected Aboriginal Origins for Canada, 1986[1,2]

Age group and sex	Total Aboriginal origins[3]		Aboriginal origins only[4]		Aboriginal and non-Aboriginal origins[5]		Total Canada[6]	
	Number	Percent	Number	Percent	Number	Percent	Number	Percent
Total	711,720	100.0	379,225	100.0	332,500	100.0	25,022,005	100.0
Male	349,265	49.1	187,100	49.3	162,165	48.8	12,368,455	49.4
Female	362,460	50.9	192,125	50.7	170,335	51.2	12,653,550	50.6
Age less than 15	259,770	36.5	134,630	35.5	125,145	37.6	5,387,905	21.5
Male	132,130	18.6	68,600	18.1	63,535	19.1	2,762,200	11.0
Female	127,640	17.9	66,030	17.4	61,610	18.5	2,625,705	10.5
Age 15-24	150,970	21.2	82,675	21.8	68,300	20.5	4,161,195	16.6
Male	73,405	10.3	40,845	10.8	32,565	9.8	2,104,400	8.4
Female	77,560	10.9	41,830	11.0	35,735	10.7	2,056,795	8.2
Age 25-39	177,295	24.9	86,275	22.8	91,020	27.4	6,520,935	26.1
Male	83,395	11.7	41,025	10.8	42,370	12.7	3,235,875	12.9
Female	93,905	13.2	45,255	11.9	48,650	14.6	3,285,055	13.1
Age 40-54	76,930	10.8	43,900	11.6	33,030	9.9	4,144,710	16.6
Male	37,905	5.3	21,330	5.6	16,580	5.0	2,078,385	8.3
Female	39,020	5.5	22,570	6.0	16,450	4.9	2,066,325	8.3
Age 55-64	26,160	3.7	17,030	4.5	9,130	2.7	2,312,105	9.2
Male	12,570	1.8	8,125	2.1	4,440	1.3	1,115,525	4.5
Female	13,595	1.9	8,900	2.3	4,690	1.4	1,196,585	4.8
Age 65 and over	20,595	2.9	14,715	3.9	5,875	1.8	2,495,160	10.0
Male	9,860	1.4	7,185	1.9	2,675	0.8	1,072,070	4.3
Female	10,740	1.5	7,535	2.0	3,205	1.0	1,423,085	5.7

Source: Aboriginal Peoples Output Program, 1986 Census, Statistics Canada, *A Data Book on Canada's Aboriginal Population from the 1986 Census of Canada*, March, 1989, p. 1. Primary source: 1986 Census of Canada *Notes:* 1. Aboriginal origins are derived from the ethnic origin question which asks whether respondents are North American Indian, Metis or Inuit. 2. All 1986 figures exclude the population estimated at about 45,000 on 136 incompletely enumerated Indian reserves and settlements throughout Canada. 3. Total aboriginal origins - are the sum of persons who reported: (a) a single aboriginal (e.g., North American Indian, Metis or Inuit), and, (b) multiple aboriginal origins, that is those who reported: - at least one aboriginal origin with any other non-aboriginal (e.g., Metis and French), or - two or more aboriginal origins only. 4. Aboriginal origins only - is the sum of persons reporting an aboriginal origin as a single response, and those reporting two or more aboriginal origins (e.g., North American Indian and Metis). 5. Aboriginal and non-aboriginal origins - refers to persons reporting an aboriginal origin (North American Indian, Metis or Inuit) and one or more non-aboriginal origins (e.g., British, French). 6. Total Canada and total province or territory (columns 4 and 5) - refers to the total populations of Canada and the relevant province and territory, excluding the institutional population.

★ 770 ★

Population by Age Group and Sex for Detailed Aboriginal Origins for Canada, 1986 - I[1,2]

Age group and sex	Total Aboriginal origins[3]		North American Indian only		North American Indian and non-Aboriginal[4]		Metis only	
	Number	Percent	Number	Percent	Number	Percent	Number	Percent
Total	711,720	100.0	286,225	100.0	239,400	100.0	59,745	100.0
Male	349,265	49.1	140,550	49.1	116,465	48.6	29,875	50.0
Female	362,460	50.9	145,680	50.9	122,930	51.3	29,865	50.0
Age less than 15	259,770	36.5	101,375	35.4	89,115	37.2	19,770	33.1
Male	132,130	18.6	51,495	18.0	45,420	19.0	10,185	17.0
Female	127,640	17.9	49,875	17.4	43,690	18.2	9,580	16.0
Age 15-24	150,970	21.2	61,605	21.5	48,725	20.4	13,385	22.4
Male	73,405	10.3	30,315	10.6	22,955	9.6	6,705	11.2
Female	77,560	10.9	31,290	10.9	25,770	10.8	6,680	11.2
Age 25-39	177,295	24.9	66,160	23.1	67,785	28.3	13,570	22.7
Male	83,395	11.7	31,180	10.9	31,460	13.1	6,610	11.1
Female	93,905	13.2	34,975	12.2	36,330	15.2	6,960	11.6
Age 40-54	76,930	10.8	32,940	11.5	23,735	9.9	7,510	12.6
Male	37,905	5.3	15,980	5.6	11,855	5.0	3,695	6.2
Female	39,020	5.5	16,955	5.9	11,885	5.0	3,820	6.4
Age 55-64	26,160	3.7	12,710	4.4	6,305	2.6	3,095	5.2
Male	12,570	1.8	5,955	2.1	3,095	1.3	1,550	2.6
Female	13,595	1.9	6,755	2.4	3,210	1.3	1,550	2.6
Age 65 and over	20,595	2.9	11,445	4.0	3,730	1.6	2,420	4.1
Male	9,860	1.4	5,615	2.0	1,680	0.7	1,135	1.9
Female	10,740	1.5	5,830	2.0	2,045	0.9	1,285	2.2

Source: Aboriginal Peoples Output Program, 1986 Census, Statistics Canada, *A Data Book on Canada's Aboriginal Population from the 1986 Census of Canada,* March, 1989, p. 2. Primary source: 1986 Census of Canada *Notes:* A dash (-) represents zero or a percentage which rounds to less than .05 percent. 1. Aboriginal origins are derived from the ethnic origin question which asks whether respondents are North American Indian, Metis or Inuit. 2. All 1986 figures exclude the population estimated at about 45,000 on 136 incompletely enumerated Indian reserves and settlements throughout Canada. 3. Total aboriginal origins - are the sum of persons who reported: (a) a single aboriginal (e.g., North American Indian, Metis or Inuit), and, (b) multiple aboriginal origins, that is those who reported: - at least one aboriginal origin with any other non-aboriginal (e.g., Metis and French), or - two or more aboriginal origins only. 4. Non-aboriginal in these columns - refers to persons who report one or more non-aboriginal origins such as British, French, etc., in combination with one of the aboriginal origins such as North American Indian.

★ 771 ★

Population by Age Group and Sex for Detailed Aboriginal Origins for Canada, 1986 - II[1,2]

Age group and sex	Metis and non-Aboriginal[3]		Inuit only		Inuit and non-Aboriginal[3]		Other multiple Aboriginal origins[4]	
	Number	Percent	Number	Percent	Number	Percent	Number	Percent
Total	68,895	100.0	27,290	100.0	6,175	100.0	23,995	100.0
Male	33,310	48.3	13,840	50.7	3,095	50.1	12,125	50.5
Female	35,585	51.7	13,450	49.3	3,075	49.8	11,870	49.5
Age less than 15	26,460	38.4	10,790	39.5	2,510	40.6	9,745	40.6
Male	13,445	19.5	5,580	20.4	1,220	19.8	4,780	19.9
Female	13,010	18.9	5,210	19.1	1,295	21.0	4,975	20.7
Age 15-24	14,520	21.1	6,420	23.5	1,485	24.0	4,830	20.1
Male	6,960	10.1	3,250	11.9	720	11.7	2,500	10.4
Female	7,565	11.0	3,170	11.6	760	12.3	2,355	9.7
Age 25-39	16,980	24.6	5,335	19.5	1,315	21.3	6,155	25.7
Male	7,685	11.2	2,660	9.7	700	11.3	3,100	12.9
Female	9,295	13.5	2,680	9.8	615	10.0	3,055	12.7
Age 40-54	6,910	10.0	2,960	10.8	580	9.4	2,285	9.5
Male	3,350	4.9	1,440	5.3	320	5.2	1,260	5.3
Female	3,565	5.2	1,515	5.6	255	4.1	1,025	4.3
Age 55-64	2,295	3.3	1,055	3.9	150	2.4	545	2.3
Male	1,070	1.6	555	2.0	70	1.1	275	1.1
Female	1,225	1.8	505	1.9	80	1.3	270	1.1
Age 65 and over	1,730	2.5	730	2.7	130	2.1	415	1.7
Male	800	1.2	355	1.3	65	1.1	205	0.9
Female	930	1.3	370	1.4	70	1.1	210	0.9

Source: Aboriginal Peoples Output Program, 1986 Census, Statistics Canada, *A Data Book on Canada's Aboriginal Population from the 1986 Census of Canada,* March, 1989, p. 2. Primary source: 1986 Census of Canada *Notes:* A dash (-) represents zero or a percentage which rounds to less than .05 percent. 1. Aboriginal origins are derived from the ethnic origin question which asks whether respondents are North American Indian, Metis or Inuit. 2. All 1986 figures exclude the population estimated at about 45,000 on 136 incompletely enumerated Indian reserves and settlements throughout Canada. 3. Non-aboriginal in these columns - refers to persons who report one or more non-aboriginal origins such as British, French, etc., in combination with one of the aboriginal origins such as North American Indian. 4. Other multiple aboriginal origins - refer to the sum of those persons reporting two or more aboriginal origins with or without a non-aboriginal origin.

★ 772 ★

Population by Age Group and Sex for Detailed Aboriginal Origins for Alberta, 1986 - I[1,2]

Age group and sex	Total Aboriginal origins[3]		North American Indian only		North American Indian and non-Aboriginal[4]		Metis only	
	Number	Percent	Number	Percent	Number	Percent	Number	Percent
Total	103,930	100.0	34,490	100.0	28,470	100.0	16,880	100.0
Male	50,930	49.0	16,605	48.1	13,905	48.8	8,535	50.6
Female	53,000	51.0	17,890	51.9	14,570	51.2	8,350	49.5
Age less than 15	40,875	39.3	13,550	39.3	11,450	40.2	5,800	34.4
Male	20,700	19.9	6,840	19.8	5,790	20.3	3,055	18.1
Female	20,175	19.4	6,710	19.5	5,665	19.9	2,745	16.3
Age 15-24	22,655	21.8	7,740	22.4	6,115	21.5	3,750	22.2
Male	10,855	10.4	3,710	10.8	2,685	9.4	1,905	11.3
Female	11,800	11.4	4,025	11.7	3,425	12.0	1,845	10.9
Age 25-39	25,345	24.4	7,635	22.1	8,035	28.2	3,930	23.3
Male	11,850	11.4	3,995	9.8	3,910	13.7	1,865	11.0
Female	13,495	13.0	4,240	12.3	4,130	14.5	2,065	12.2
Age 40-54	9,630	9.3	3,435	10.0	2,140	7.5	1,950	11.6
Male	4,770	4.6	1,600	4.6	1,140	4.0	960	5.7
Female	4,860	4.7	1,835	5.3	995	3.5	985	5.8
Age 55-64	2,955	2.8	1,095	3.2	485	1.7	765	4.5
Male	1,500	1.4	535	1.6	255	0.9	415	2.5
Female	1,460	1.4	560	1.6	230	0.8	350	2.1
Age 65 and over	2,470	2.4	1,040	3.0	250	0.9	685	4.1
Male	1,260	1.2	525	1.5	120	0.4	335	2.0
Female	1,210	1.2	515	1.5	130	0.5	345	2.0

Source: Aboriginal Peoples Output Program, 1986 Census, Statistics Canada, *A Data Book on Canada's Aboriginal Population from the 1986 Census of Canada,* March, 1989, p. 218. Primary source: 1986 Census of Canada *Notes:* A dash (-) represents zero or a percentage which rounds to less than .05 percent. 1. Aboriginal origins are derived from the ethnic origin question which asks whether respondents are North American Indian, Metis or Inuit. 2. All 1986 figures exclude the population estimated at about 45,000 on 136 incompletely enumerated Indian reserves and settlements throughout Canada. 3. Total aboriginal origins - are the sum of persons who reported: (a) a single aboriginal (e.g., North American Indian, Metis or Inuit), and, (b) multiple aboriginal origins, that is those who reported: - at least one aboriginal origin with any other non-aboriginal (e.g., Metis and French), or - two or more aboriginal origins only. 4. Non-aboriginal in these columns - refers to persons who report one or more non-aboriginal origins such as British, French, etc., in combination with one of the aboriginal origins such as North American Indian.

★ 773 ★

Population by Age Group and Sex for Detailed Aboriginal Origins for Alberta, 1986 - II[1,2]

Age group and sex	Metis and non-Aboriginal[3]		Inuit only		Inuit and non-Aboriginal[3]		Other multiple Aboriginal origins[4]	
	Number	Percent	Number	Percent	Number	Percent	Number	Percent
Total	17,265	100.0	295	100.0	445	100.0	6,080	100.0
male	8,440	48.9	150	50.8	205	46.1	3,095	50.9
female	8,820	51.1	145	49.2	240	53.9	2,985	49.1
Age less than 15	7,265	42.1	90	30.5	165	37.1	2,555	42.0
male	3,695	21.4	40	13.6	95	21.3	1,190	19.6
female	3,570	20.7	50	16.9	70	15.7	1,370	22.5
Age 15-24	3,665	21.2	95	32.2	130	29.2	1,165	19.2
male	1,805	10.5	55	18.6	60	13.5	630	10.4
female	1,855	10.7	40	13.6	70	15.7	540	8.9
Age 25-39	4,055	23.5	55	18.6	100	22.5	1,535	25.2
male	1,780	10.3	30	10.2	40	9.0	825	13.6
female	2,270	13.1	25	8.5	60	13.5	705	11.6
Age 40-54	1,475	8.5	50	16.9	20	4.5	565	9.3
male	725	4.2	25	8.5	-	-	315	5.2
female	750	4.3	30	10.2	20	4.5	245	4.0
Age 55-64	455	2.6	-	-	20	4.5	135	2.2
male	225	1.3	-	-	-	-	65	1.1
female	225	1.3	-	-	15	3.4	70	1.2
Age 65 and over	350	2.0	-	-	15	3.4	130	2.1
male	205	1.2	-	-	-	-	70	1.2
female	150	0.9	-	-	-	-	55	0.9

Source: Aboriginal Peoples Output Program, 1986 Census, Statistics Canada, *A Data Book on Canada's Aboriginal Population from the 1986 Census of Canada*, March, 1989, p. 218. Primary source: 1986 Census of Canada *Notes:* A dash (-) represents zero or a percentage which rounds to less than .05 percent. 1. Aboriginal origins are derived from the ethnic origin question which asks whether respondents are North American Indian, Metis or Inuit. 2. All 1986 figures exclude the population estimated at about 45,000 on 136 incompletely enumerated Indian reserves and settlements throughout Canada. 3. Non-aboriginal in these columns - refers to persons who report one or more non-aboriginal origins such as British, French, etc., in combination with one of the aboriginal origins such as North American Indian. 4. Other multiple aboriginal origins - refer to the sum of those persons reporting two or more aboriginal origins with or without a non-aboriginal origin.

★ 774 ★

Population by Age Group and Sex for Detailed Aboriginal Origins for British Columbia, 1986 - I[1,2]

Age group and sex	Total Aboriginal origins[3]		North American Indian only		North American Indian and non-Aboriginal[4]		Metis only	
	Number	Percent	Number	Percent	Number	Percent	Number	Percent
Total	126,625	100.0	56,955	100.0	53,560	100.0	3,930	100.0
Male	62,985	49.7	28,240	49.6	26,690	49.8	1,905	48.5
Female	63,645	50.3	28,720	50.4	26,875	50.2	2,025	51.5
Age less than 15	44,445	35.1	17,935	31.5	21,260	39.7	920	23.4
Male	22,890	18.1	9,285	16.3	10,960	20.5	470	12.0
Female	21,560	17.0	8,650	15.2	10,295	19.2	450	11.5
Age 15-24	26,135	20.6	12,290	21.6	10,450	19.5	920	23.4
Male	13,115	10.4	6,170	10.8	5,240	9.8	420	10.7
Female	13,025	10.3	6,120	10.7	5,215	9.7	500	12.7
Age 25-39	32,730	25.8	14,155	24.9	14,240	26.6	1,025	26.1
Male	15,560	12.3	6,670	11.7	6,795	12.7	465	11.8
Female	17,170	13.6	7,480	13.1	7,440	13.9	560	14.2
Age 40-54	14,590	11.5	7,340	12.9	5,125	9.6	745	19.0
Male	7,185	5.7	3,570	6.3	2,510	4.7	380	9.7
Female	7,405	5.8	3,770	6.6	2,615	4.9	360	9.2
Age 55-64	5,040	4.0	2,875	5.0	1,535	2.9	200	5.1
Male	2,430	1.9	1,350	2.4	770	1.4	105	2.7
Female	2,605	2.1	1,520	2.7	765	1.4	95	2.4
Age 65 and over	3,680	2.9	2,365	4.2	955	1.8	120	3.1
Male	1,805	1.4	1,190	2.1	415	0.8	65	1.7
Female	1,875	1.5	1,180	2.1	535	1.0	55	1.4

Source: Aboriginal Peoples Output Program, 1986 Census, Statistics Canada, *A Data Book on Canada's Aboriginal Population from the 1986 Census of Canada*, March, 1989, p. 242. Primary source: 1986 Census of Canada *Notes:* A dash (-) represents zero or a percentage which rounds to less than .05 percent. 1. Aboriginal origins are derived from the ethnic origin question which asks whether respondents are North American Indian, Metis or Inuit. 2. All 1986 figures exclude the population estimated at about 45,000 on 136 incompletely enumerated Indian reserves and settlements throughout Canada. 3. Total aboriginal origins - are the sum of persons who reported: (a) a single aboriginal (e.g., North American Indian, Metis or Inuit), and, (b) multiple aboriginal origins, that is those who reported: - at least one aboriginal origin with any other non-aboriginal (e.g., Metis and French), or - two or more aboriginal origins only. 4. Non-aboriginal in these columns - refers to persons who report one or more non-aboriginal origins such as British, French, etc., in combination with one of the aboriginal origins such as North American Indian.

★ 775 ★

Population by Age Group and Sex for Detailed Aboriginal Origins for British Columbia, 1986 - II[1,2]

Age group and sex	Metis and non-Aboriginal[3]		Inuit only		Inuit and non-Aboriginal[3]		Other multiple Aboriginal origins[4]	
	Number	Percent	Number	Percent	Number	Percent	Number	Percent
Total	9,135	100.0	240	100.0	500	100.0	2,310	100.0
Male	4,515	49.4	140	58.3	275	55.0	1,220	52.8
Female	4,620	50.6	100	41.7	220	44.0	1,080	46.8
Age less than 15	3,330	36.5	75	31.3	170	34.0	765	33.1
Male	1,665	18.2	50	20.8	75	15.0	390	16.9
Female	1,660	18.2	25	10.4	100	20.0	375	16.2
Age 15-24	1,800	19.7	80	33.3	140	28.0	465	20.1
Male	910	10.0	50	20.8	80	16.0	245	10.6
Female	890	9.7	30	12.5	60	12.0	215	9.3
Age 25-39	2,455	26.9	45	18.8	110	22.0	695	30.1
Male	1,150	12.6	35	14.6	80	16.0	370	16.0
Female	1,305	14.3	10	4.2	35	7.0	330	14.3
Age 40-54	1,035	11.3	25	10.4	65	13.0	260	11.3
Male	530	5.8	-	-	30	6.0	160	6.9
Female	505	5.5	20	8.3	35	7.0	95	4.1
Age 55-64	325	3.6	-	-	-	-	90	3.9
Male	155	1.7	-	-	-	-	40	1.7
Female	165	1.8	-	-	-	-	50	2.2
Age 65 and over	195	2.1	-	-	-	-	25	1.1
Male	105	1.1	-	-	-	-	15	0.6
Female	90	1.0	-	-	-	-	-	-

Source: Aboriginal Peoples Output Program, 1986 Census, Statistics Canada, *A Data Book on Canada's Aboriginal Population from the 1986 Census of Canada*, March, 1989, p. 242. Primary source: 1986 Census of Canada *Notes:* A dash (-) represents zero or a percentage which rounds to less than .05 percent. 1. Aboriginal origins are derived from the ethnic origin question which asks whether respondents are North American Indian, Metis or Inuit. 2. All 1986 figures exclude the population estimated at about 45,000 on 136 incompletely enumerated Indian reserves and settlements throughout Canada. 3. Non-aboriginal in these columns - refers to persons who report one or more non-aboriginal origins such as British, French, etc., in combination with one of the aboriginal origins such as North American Indian. 4. Other multiple aboriginal origins - refer to the sum of those persons reporting two or more aboriginal origins with or without a non-aboriginal origin.

★ 776 ★

Population by Age Group and Sex for Detailed Aboriginal Origins for Manitoba, 1986 - I[1,2]

Age group and sex	Total Aboriginal origins[3]		North American Indian only		North American Indian and non-Aboriginal[4]		Metis only	
	Number	Percent	Number	Percent	Number	Percent	Number	Percent
Total	85,235	100.0	40,960	100.0	10,510	100.0	14,270	100.0
Male	41,860	49.1	20,140	49.2	5,275	50.2	7,185	50.4
Female	43,370	50.9	20,825	50.8	5,240	49.9	7,090	49.7
Age less than 15	33,185	38.9	16,600	40.5	4,155	39.5	4,940	34.6
Male	16,890	19.8	8,480	20.7	2,215	21.1	2,530	17.7
Female	16,295	19.1	8,115	19.8	1,935	18.4	2,405	16.9
Age 15-24	18,620	21.8	8,980	21.9	2,260	21.5	3,100	21.7
Male	9,080	10.7	4,430	10.8	1,025	9.8	1,605	11.2
Female	9,540	11.2	4,545	11.1	1,230	11.7	1,490	10.4
Age 25-39	18,720	22.0	8,305	20.3	2,725	25.9	3,025	21.2
Male	8,720	10.2	3,820	9.3	1,305	12.4	1,485	10.4
Female	10,000	11.7	4,485	10.9	1,425	13.6	1,540	10.8
Age 40-54	8,945	10.5	4,100	10.0	955	9.1	1,840	12.9
Male	4,315	5.1	1,950	4.8	515	4.9	840	5.9
Female	4,630	5.4	2,150	5.2	445	4.2	1,000	7.0
Age 55-64	3,100	3.6	1,525	3.7	245	2.3	780	5.5
Male	1,550	1.8	705	1.7	130	1.2	410	2.9
Female	1,550	1.8	815	2.0	110	1.0	375	2.6
Age 65 and over	2,660	3.1	1,455	3.6	175	1.7	595	4.2
Male	1,315	1.5	740	1.8	85	0.8	305	2.1
Female	1,350	1.6	710	1.7	90	0.9	285	2.0

Source: Aboriginal Peoples Output Program, 1986 Census, Statistics Canada, *A Data Book on Canada's Aboriginal Population from the 1986 Census of Canada*, March, 1989, p. 172. Primary source: 1986 Census of Canada *Notes:* A dash (-) represents zero or a percentage which rounds to less than .05 percent. 1. Aboriginal origins are derived from the ethnic origin question which asks whether respondents are North American Indian, Metis or Inuit. 2. All 1986 figures exclude the population estimated at about 45,000 on 136 incompletely enumerated Indian reserves and settlements throughout Canada. 3. Total aboriginal origins - are the sum of persons who reported: (a) a single aboriginal (e.g., North American Indian, Metis or Inuit), and, (b) multiple aboriginal origins, that is those who reported: - at least one aboriginal origin with any other non-aboriginal (e.g., Metis and French), or - two or more aboriginal origins only. 4. Non-aboriginal in these columns - refers to persons who report one or more non-aboriginal origins such as British, French, etc., in combination with one of the aboriginal origins such as North American Indian.

★ 777 ★

Population by Age Group and Sex for Detailed Aboriginal Origins for Manitoba, 1986 - II[1,2]

Age group and sex	Metis and non-Aboriginal[3]		Inuit only		Inuit and non-Aboriginal[3]		Other multiple Aboriginal origins[4]	
	Number	Percent	Number	Percent	Number	Percent	Number	Percent
Total	14,605	100.0	185	100.0	200	100.0	4,505	100.0
Male	6,955	47.6	60	32.4	85	42.5	2,170	48.2
Female	7,650	52.4	120	64.9	115	57.5	2,330	51.7
Age less than 15	5,500	37.7	80	43.2	80	40.0	1,830	40.6
Male	2,720	18.6	25	13.5	30	15.0	885	19.6
Female	2,780	19.0	55	29.7	50	25.0	935	20.8
Age 15-24	3,170	21.7	50	27.0	60	30.0	1,005	22.3
Male	1,480	10.1	20	10.8	25	12.5	490	10.9
Female	1,690	11.6	30	16.2	35	17.5	520	11.5
Age 25-39	3,525	24.1	35	18.9	45	22.5	1,060	23.5
Male	1,605	11.0	10	5.4	20	10.0	475	10.5
Female	1,920	13.1	25	13.5	30	15.0	590	13.1
Age 40-54	1,575	10.8	-	-	10	5.0	460	10.2
Male	760	5.2	-	-	-	-	240	5.3
Female	815	5.6	-	-	-	-	215	4.8
Age 55-64	465	3.2	-	-	-	-	90	2.0
Male	255	1.7	-	-	-	-	50	1.1
Female	205	1.4	-	-	-	-	40	0.9
Age 65 and over	370	2.5	-	-	-	-	60	1.3
Male	140	1.0	-	-	-	-	30	0.7
Female	235	1.6	-	-	-	-	20	0.4

Source: Aboriginal Peoples Output Program, 1986 Census, Statistics Canada, *A Data Book on Canada's Aboriginal Population from the 1986 Census of Canada*, March, 1989, p. 172. Primary source: 1986 Census of Canada *Notes:* A dash (-) represents zero or a percentage which rounds to less than .05 percent. 1. Aboriginal origins are derived from the ethnic origin question which asks whether respondents are North American Indian, Metis or Inuit. 2. All 1986 figures exclude the population estimated at about 45,000 on 136 incompletely enumerated Indian reserves and settlements throughout Canada. 3. Non-aboriginal in these columns - refers to persons who report one or more non-aboriginal origins such as British, French, etc., in combination with one of the aboriginal origins such as North American Indian. 4. Other multiple aboriginal origins - refer to the sum of those persons reporting two or more aboriginal origins with or without a non-aboriginal origin.

Population by Age Group and Sex for Detailed Aboriginal Origins for New Brunswick, 1986 - I[1,2]

Age group and sex	Total Aboriginal origins[3]		North American Indian only		North American Indian and non-Aboriginal[4]		Metis only	
	Number	Percent	Number	Percent	Number	Percent	Number	Percent
Total	9,375	100.0	3,680	100.0	4,830	100.0	190	100.0
Male	4,710	50.2	1,900	51.6	2,350	48.7	105	55.3
Female	4,670	49.8	1,780	48.4	2,480	51.3	85	44.7
Age less than 15	3,390	36.2	1,175	31.9	1,870	38.7	80	42.1
Male	1,690	18.0	610	16.6	905	18.7	30	15.8
Female	1,695	18.1	570	15.5	960	19.9	45	23.7
Age 15-24	2,170	23.1	825	22.4	1,190	24.6	60	31.6
Male	1,115	11.9	450	12.2	565	11.7	45	23.7
Female	1,060	11.3	375	10.2	620	12.8	15	7.9
Age 25-39	2,285	24.4	890	24.2	1,130	23.4	45	23.7
Male	1,100	11.7	445	12.1	515	10.7	20	10.5
Female	1,185	12.6	445	12.1	615	12.7	20	10.5
Age 40-54	1,015	10.8	440	12.0	490	10.1	-	-
Male	570	6.1	230	6.3	305	6.3	-	-
Female	445	4.7	215	5.8	190	3.9		
Age 55-64	310	3.3	215	5.8	90	1.9	-	-
Male	140	1.5	95	2.6	40	0.8	-	-
Female	170	1.8	115	3.1	50	1.0	-	-
Age 65 and over	210	2.2	135	3.7	55	1.1	-	-
Male	95	1.0	75	2.0	10	0.2	-	-
Female	115	1.2	65	1.8	40	0.8	-	-

Source: Aboriginal Peoples Output Program, 1986 Census, Statistics Canada, *A Data Book on Canada's Aboriginal Population from the 1986 Census of Canada*, March, 1989, p. 98. Primary source: 1986 Census of Canada *Notes:* A dash (-) represents zero or a percentage which rounds to less than .05 percent. 1. Aboriginal origins are derived from the ethnic origin question which asks whether respondents are North American Indian, Metis or Inuit. 2. All 1986 figures exclude the population estimated at about 45,000 on 136 incompletely enumerated Indian reserves and settlements throughout Canada. 3. Total aboriginal origins - are the sum of persons who reported: (a) a single aboriginal (e.g., North American Indian, Metis or Inuit), and, (b) multiple aboriginal origins, that is those who reported: - at least one aboriginal origin with any other non-aboriginal (e.g., Metis and French), or - two or more aboriginal origins only. 4. Non-aboriginal in these columns - refers to persons who report one or more non-aboriginal origins such as British, French, etc., in combination with one of the aboriginal origins such as North American Indian.

★ 779 ★

Population by Age Group and Sex for Detailed Aboriginal Origins for New Brunswick, 1986 - II[1,2]

Age group and sex	Metis and non-Aboriginal[3]		Inuit only		Inuit and non-Aboriginal[3]		Other multiple Aboriginal origins[4]	
	Number	Percent	Number	Percent	Number	Percent	Number	Percent
Total	365	100.0	15	100.0	105	100.0	190	100.0
Male	205	56.2	-	-	35	33.3	100	52.6
Female	165	45.2	-	-	65	61.9	85	44.7
Age less than 15	115	31.5	-	-	45	42.9	85	44.7
Male	65	17.8	-	-	10	9.5	50	26.3
Female	45	12.3	-	-	40	38.1	30	15.8
Age 15-24	50	13.7	-	-	25	23.8	25	13.2
Male	30	8.2	-	-	20	19.0	-	-
Female	30	8.2	-	-	-	-	20	10.5
Age 25-39	130	35.6	-	-	20	19.0	70	36.8
Male	75	20.5	-	-	-	-	40	21.1
Female	55	15.1	-	-	15	14.3	30	15.8
Age 40-54	60	16.4	-	-	-	-	-	-
Male	30	8.2	-	-	-	-	-	-
Female	35	9.6	-	-	-	-	-	-
Age 55-64	-	-	-	-	-	-	-	-
Male	-	-	-	-	-	-	-	-
Female	-	-	-	-	-	-	-	-
Age 65 and over	10	2.7	-	-	-	-	-	-
Male	-	-	-	-	-	-	-	-
Female	-	-	-	-	-	-	-	-

Source: Aboriginal Peoples Output Program, 1986 Census, Statistics Canada, *A Data Book on Canada's Aboriginal Population from the 1986 Census of Canada*, March, 1989, p. 98. Primary source: 1986 Census of Canada *Notes:* A dash (-) represents zero or a percentage which rounds to less than .05 percent. 1. Aboriginal origins are derived from the ethnic origin question which asks whether respondents are North American Indian, Metis or Inuit. 2. All 1986 figures exclude the population estimated at about 45,000 on 136 incompletely enumerated Indian reserves and settlements throughout Canada. 3. Non-aboriginal in these columns - refers to persons who report one or more non-aboriginal origins such as British, French, etc., in combination with one of the aboriginal origins such as North American Indian. 4. Other multiple aboriginal origins - refer to the sum of those persons reporting two or more aboriginal origins with or without a non-aboriginal origin.

★ 780 ★

Population by Age Group and Sex for Detailed Aboriginal Origins for Newfoundland, 1986 - I[1,2]

Age group and sex	Total Aboriginal origins[3]		North American Indian only		North American Indian and non-Aboriginal[4]		Metis only	
	Number	Percent	Number	Percent	Number	Percent	Number	Percent
Total	9,555	100.0	1,745	100.0	2,695	100.0	270	100.0
Male	4,925	51.5	835	47.9	1,425	52.9	135	50.0
Female	4,635	48.5	910	52.1	1,265	46.9	130	48.1
Age less than 15	3,400	35.6	685	39.3	960	35.6	50	18.5
Male	1,780	18.6	335	19.2	550	20.4	25	9.3
Female	1,620	17.0	345	19.8	415	15.4	20	7.4
Age 15-24	2,105	22.0	395	22.6	560	20.8	65	24.1
Male	1,105	11.6	180	10.3	270	10.0	35	13.0
Female	995	10.4	215	12.3	295	10.9	25	9.3
Age 25-39	2,360	24.7	390	22.3	785	29.1	50	18.5
Male	1,190	12.5	180	10.3	395	14.7	30	11.1
Female	1,165	12.2	210	12.0	390	14.5	20	7.4
Age 40-54	970	10.2	165	9.5	195	7.2	50	18.5
Male	510	5.3	85	4.9	120	4.5	20	7.4
Female	460	4.8	80	4.6	75	2.8	25	9.3
Age 55-64	455	4.8	70	4.0	120	4.5	25	9.3
Male	240	2.5	45	2.6	60	2.2	10	3.7
Female	220	2.3	30	1.7	60	2.2	-	-
Age 65 and over	270	2.8	35	2.0	70	2.6	40	14.8
Male	95	1.0	-	-	30	1.1	-	-
Female	170	1.8	25	1.4	35	1.3	30	11.1

Source: Aboriginal Peoples Output Program, 1986 Census, Statistics Canada, *A Data Book on Canada's Aboriginal Population from the 1986 Census of Canada,* March, 1989, p. 26. Primary source: 1986 Census of Canada *Notes:* A dash (-) represents zero or a percentage which rounds to less than .05 percent. 1. Aboriginal origins are derived from the ethnic origin question which asks whether respondents are North American Indian, Metis or Inuit. 2. All 1986 figures exclude the population estimated at about 45,000 on 136 incompletely enumerated Indian reserves and settlements throughout Canada. 3. Total aboriginal origins - are the sum of persons who reported: (a) a single aboriginal (e.g., North American Indian, Metis or Inuit), and, (b) multiple aboriginal origins, that is those who reported: - at least one aboriginal origin with any other non-aboriginal (e.g., Metis and French), or - two or more aboriginal origins only. 4. Non-aboriginal in these columns - refers to persons who report one or more non-aboriginal origins such as British, French, etc., in combination with one of the aboriginal origins such as North American Indian.

★ 781 ★

Population by Age Group and Sex for Detailed Aboriginal Origins for Newfoundland, 1986 - II[1,2]

Age group and sex	Metis and non-Aboriginal[3]		Inuit only		Inuit and non-Aboriginal[3]		Other multiple Aboriginal origins[4]	
	Number	Percent	Number	Percent	Number	Percent	Number	Percent
Total	680	100.0	1,815	100.0	1,750	100.0	610	100.0
Male	380	55.9	915	50.4	880	50.3	350	57.4
Female	300	44.1	900	49.6	870	49.7	260	42.6
Age less than 15	165	24.3	640	35.3	675	38.6	205	33.6
Male	100	14.7	320	17.6	335	19.1	105	17.2
Female	70	10.3	320	17.6	340	19.4	100	16.4
Age 15-24	160	23.5	370	20.4	400	22.9	145	23.8
Male	90	13.2	210	11.6	220	12.6	100	16.4
Female	75	11.0	165	9.1	175	10.0	45	7.4
Age 25-39	175	25.7	420	23.1	400	22.9	140	23.0
Male	105	15.4	210	11.6	195	11.1	70	11.5
Female	70	10.3	210	11.6	210	12.0	60	9.8
Age 40-54	115	16.9	230	12.7	155	8.9	65	10.7
Male	50	7.4	105	5.8	85	4.9	35	5.7
Female	65	9.6	120	6.6	70	4.0	25	4.1
Age 55-64	45	6.6	100	5.5	75	4.3	30	4.9
Male	30	4.4	50	2.8	30	1.7	20	3.3
Female	20	2.9	50	2.8	45	2.6	-	-
Age 65 and over	20	2.9	50	2.8	45	2.6	15	2.5
Male	-	-	20	1.1	15	0.9	-	-
Female	-	-	35	1.9	30	1.7	15	2.5

Source: Aboriginal Peoples Output Program, 1986 Census, Statistics Canada, *A Data Book on Canada's Aboriginal Population from the 1986 Census of Canada*, March, 1989, p. 26. Primary source: 1986 Census of Canada *Notes:* A dash (-) represents zero or a percentage which rounds to less than .05 percent. 1. Aboriginal origins are derived from the ethnic origin question which asks whether respondents are North American Indian, Metis or Inuit. 2. All 1986 figures exclude the population estimated at about 45,000 on 136 incompletely enumerated Indian reserves and settlements throughout Canada. 3. Non-aboriginal in these columns - refers to persons who report one or more non-aboriginal origins such as British, French, etc., in combination with one of the aboriginal origins such as North American Indian. 4. Other multiple aboriginal origins - refer to the sum of those persons reporting two or more aboriginal origins with or without a non-aboriginal origin.

★ 782 ★

Population by Age Group and Sex for Detailed Aboriginal Origins for Northwest Territories, 1986 - I[1,2]

Age group and sex	Total Aboriginal origins[3]		North American Indian only		North American Indian and non-Aboriginal[4]		Metis only	
	Number	Percent	Number	Percent	Number	Percent	Number	Percent
Total	30,530	100.0	7,585	100.0	845	100.0	2,200	100.0
Male	15,640	51.2	3,875	51.1	490	58.0	1,120	50.9
Female	14,885	48.8	3,715	49.0	360	42.6	1,085	49.3
Age less than 15	11,855	38.8	2,515	33.2	320	37.9	775	35.2
Male	6,070	19.9	1,275	16.8	175	20.7	380	17.3
Female	5,780	18.9	1,240	16.3	150	17.8	395	18.0
Age 15-24	7,080	23.2	1,690	22.3	175	20.7	470	21.4
Male	3,650	12.0	885	11.7	110	13.0	230	10.5
Female	3,435	11.3	805	10.6	65	7.7	240	10.9
Age 25-39	6,005	19.7	1,565	20.6	200	23.7	520	23.6
Male	3,025	9.9	765	10.1	130	15.4	265	12.0
Female	2,980	9.8	800	10.5	70	8.3	255	11.6
Age 40-54	3,300	10.8	940	12.4	120	14.2	260	11.8
Male	1,690	5.5	480	6.3	70	8.3	160	7.3
Female	1,610	5.3	460	6.1	50	5.9	100	4.5
Age 55-64	1,180	3.9	375	4.9	25	3.0	90	4.1
Male	625	2.0	200	2.6	-	-	40	1.8
Female	560	1.8	175	2.3	20	2.4	50	2.3
Age 65 and over	1,105	3.6	505	6.7	-	-	80	3.6
Male	585	1.9	265	3.5	-	-	40	1.8
Female	520	1.7	240	3.2	-	-	40	1.8

Source: Aboriginal Peoples Output Program, 1986 Census, Statistics Canada, *A Data Book on Canada's Aboriginal Population from the 1986 Census of Canada,* March, 1989, p. 266. Primary source: 1986 Census of Canada *Notes:* A dash (-) represents zero or a percentage which rounds to less than .05 percent. 1. Aboriginal origins are derived from the ethnic origin question which asks whether respondents are North American Indian, Metis or Inuit. 2. All 1986 figures exclude the population estimated at about 45,000 on 136 incompletely enumerated Indian reserves and settlements throughout Canada. 3. Total aboriginal origins - are the sum of persons who reported: (a) a single aboriginal (e.g., North American Indian, Metis or Inuit), and, (b) multiple aboriginal origins, that is those who reported: - at least one aboriginal origin with any other non-aboriginal (e.g., Metis and French), or - two or more aboriginal origins only. 4. Non-aboriginal in these columns - refers to persons who report one or more non-aboriginal origins such as British, French, etc., in combination with one of the aboriginal origins such as North American Indian.

★ 783 ★

Population by Age Group and Sex for Detailed Aboriginal Origins for Northwest Territories, 1986 - II[1,2]

Age group and sex	Metis and non-Aboriginal[3]		Inuit only		Inuit and non-Aboriginal[3]		Other multiple Aboriginal origins[4]	
	Number	Percent	Number	Percent	Number	Percent	Number	Percent
Total	765	100.0	17,380	100.0	750	100.0	995	100.0
Male	385	50.3	8,810	50.7	400	53.3	560	56.3
Female	375	49.0	8,570	49.3	355	47.3	440	44.2
Age less than 15	300	39.2	7,060	40.6	465	62.0	410	41.2
Male	140	18.3	3,625	20.9	250	33.3	235	23.6
Female	165	21.6	3,440	19.8	220	29.3	170	17.1
Age 15-24	165	21.6	4,210	24.2	140	18.7	230	23.1
Male	105	13.7	2,105	12.1	70	9.3	145	14.6
Female	55	7.2	2,105	12.1	75	10.0	80	8.0
Age 25-39	200	26.1	3,235	18.6	85	11.3	200	20.1
Male	100	13.1	1,605	9.2	60	8.0	100	10.0
Female	100	13.1	1,630	9.4	25	3.3	100	10.1
Age 40-54	75	9.8	1,790	10.3	40	5.3	85	8.5
Male	30	3.9	890	5.1	15	2.0	45	4.5
Female	45	5.9	900	5.2	20	2.7	30	3.0
Age 55-64	15	2.0	615	3.5	10	1.3	50	5.0
Male	10	1.3	335	1.9	-	-	10	1.0
Female	-	-	275	1.6	-	-	20	2.0
Age 65 and over	-	-	470	2.7	10	1.3	30	3.0
Male	-	-	255	1.5	-	-	10	1.0
Female	-	-	215	1.2	-	-	-	-

Source: Aboriginal Peoples Output Program, 1986 Census, Statistics Canada, *A Data Book on Canada's Aboriginal Population from the 1986 Census of Canada*, March, 1989, p. 266. Primary source: 1986 Census of Canada *Notes:* A dash (-) represents zero or a percentage which rounds to less than .05 percent. 1. Aboriginal origins are derived from the ethnic origin question which asks whether respondents are North American Indian, Metis or Inuit. 2. All 1986 figures exclude the population estimated at about 45,000 on 136 incompletely enumerated Indian reserves and settlements throughout Canada. 3. Non-aboriginal in these columns - refers to persons who report one or more non-aboriginal origins such as British, French, etc., in combination with one of the aboriginal origins such as North American Indian. 4. Other multiple aboriginal origins - refer to the sum of those persons reporting two or more aboriginal origins with or without a non-aboriginal origin.

★ 784 ★

Population by Age Group and Sex for Detailed Aboriginal Origins for Nova Scotia, 1986 - I[1,2]

Age group and sex	Total Aboriginal origins[3]		North American Indian only		North American Indian and non-Aboriginal[4]		Metis only	
	Number	Percent	Number	Percent	Number	Percent	Number	Percent
Total	14,225	100.0	5,570	100.0	7,240	100.0	255	100.0
Male	7,005	49.2	2,810	50.4	3,535	48.8	125	49.0
Female	7,220	50.8	2,760	49.6	3,705	51.2	130	51.0
Age less than 15	4,965	34.9	1,905	34.2	2,650	36.6	70	27.5
Male	2,565	18.0	970	17.4	1,390	19.2	35	13.7
Female	2,400	16.9	930	16.7	1,260	17.4	30	11.8
Age 15-24	3,250	22.8	1,275	22.9	1,510	20.9	65	25.5
Male	1,450	10.2	630	11.3	620	8.6	35	13.7
Female	1,805	12.7	640	11.5	885	12.2	30	11.8
Age 25-39	3,770	26.5	1,330	23.9	2,090	28.9	60	23.5
Male	1,825	12.8	670	12.0	970	13.4	35	13.7
Female	1,945	13.7	665	11.9	1,120	15.5	20	7.8
Age 40-54	1,395	9.8	620	11.1	655	9.0	25	9.8
Male	770	5.4	325	5.8	395	5.5	-	-
Female	625	4.4	290	5.2	260	3.6	25	9.8
Age 55-64	470	3.3	205	3.7	225	3.1	15	5.9
Male	220	1.5	115	2.1	95	1.3	-	-
Female	245	1.7	95	1.7	130	1.8	15	5.9
Age 65 and over	370	2.6	235	4.2	120	1.7	10	3.9
Male	175	1.2	105	1.9	60	0.8	-	-
Female	195	1.4	135	2.4	55	0.8	-	-

Source: Aboriginal Peoples Output Program, 1986 Census, Statistics Canada, *A Data Book on Canada's Aboriginal Population from the 1986 Census of Canada,* March, 1989, p. 74. Primary source: 1986 Census of Canada *Notes:* A dash (-) represents zero or a percentage which rounds to less than .05 percent. 1. Aboriginal origins are derived from the ethnic origin question which asks whether respondents are North American Indian, Metis or Inuit. 2. All 1986 figures exclude the population estimated at about 45,000 on 136 incompletely enumerated Indian reserves and settlements throughout Canada. 3. Total aboriginal origins - are the sum of persons who reported: (a) a single aboriginal (e.g., North American Indian, Metis or Inuit), and, (b) multiple aboriginal origins, that is those who reported: - at least one aboriginal origin with any other non-aboriginal (e.g., Metis and French), or - two or more aboriginal origins only. 4. Non-aboriginal in these columns - refers to persons who report one or more non-aboriginal origins such as British, French, etc., in combination with one of the aboriginal origins such as North American Indian.

★ 785 ★

Population by Age Group and Sex for Detailed Aboriginal Origins for Nova Scotia, 1986 - II[1,2]

Age group and sex	Metis and non-Aboriginal[3]		Inuit only		Inuit and non-Aboriginal[3]		Other multiple Aboriginal origins[4]	
	Number	Percent	Number	Percent	Number	Percent	Number	Percent
Total	625	100.0	135	100.0	155	100.0	240	100.0
Male	260	41.6	60	44.4	60	38.7	145	60.4
Female	365	58.4	70	51.9	90	58.1	95	39.6
Age less than 15	170	27.2	55	40.7	40	25.8	80	33.3
Male	80	12.8	20	14.8	20	12.9	40	16.7
Female	95	15.2	25	18.5	20	12.9	30	12.5
Age 15-24	235	37.6	25	18.5	50	32.3	95	39.6
Male	80	12.8	-	-	10	6.5	55	22.9
Female	150	24.0	20	14.8	35	22.6	40	16.7
Age 25-39	145	23.2	40	29.6	30	19.4	65	27.1
Male	70	11.2	20	14.8	-	-	40	16.7
Female	75	12.0	20	14.8	20	12.9	20	8.3
Age 40-54	55	8.8	15	11.1	25	16.1	-	-
Male	15	2.4	-	-	20	12.9	-	-
Female	40	6.4	-	-	10	6.5	-	-
Age 55-64	15	2.4	-	-	-	-	-	-
Male	-	-	-	-	-	-	-	-
Female	-	-	-	-	-	-	-	-
Age 65 and over	15	2.4	-	-	-	-	-	-
Male	-	-	-	-	-	-	-	-
Female	-	-	-	-	-	-	-	-

Source: Aboriginal Peoples Output Program, 1986 Census, Statistics Canada, *A Data Book on Canada's Aboriginal Population from the 1986 Census of Canada*, March, 1989, p. 74. Primary source: 1986 Census of Canada *Notes:* A dash (-) represents zero or a percentage which rounds to less than .05 percent. 1. Aboriginal origins are derived from the ethnic origin question which asks whether respondents are North American Indian, Metis or Inuit. 2. All 1986 figures exclude the population estimated at about 45,000 on 136 incompletely enumerated Indian reserves and settlements throughout Canada. 3. Non-aboriginal in these columns - refers to persons who report one or more non-aboriginal origins such as British, French, etc., in combination with one of the aboriginal origins such as North American Indian. 4. Other multiple aboriginal origins - refer to the sum of those persons reporting two or more aboriginal origins with or without a non-aboriginal origin.

★ 786 ★

Population by Age Group and Sex for Detailed Aboriginal Origins for Ontario, 1986 - I[1,2]

Age group and sex	Total Aboriginal origins[3]		North American Indian only		North American Indian and non-Aboriginal[4]		Metis only	
	Number	Percent	Number	Percent	Number	Percent	Number	Percent
Total	167,375	100.0	51,165	100.0	95,415	100.0	3,720	100.0
Male	80,975	48.4	24,725	48.3	46,010	48.2	1,855	49.9
Female	86,395	51.6	26,440	51.7	49,405	51.8	1,860	50.0
Age less than 15	57,835	34.6	15,785	30.9	34,655	36.3	1,070	28.8
Male	29,525	17.6	7,995	15.6	17,665	18.5	550	14.8
Female	28,310	16.9	7,785	15.2	16,990	17.8	520	14.0
Age 15-24	34,460	20.6	10,395	20.3	19,515	20.5	880	23.7
Male	16,655	10.0	5,160	10.1	9,335	9.8	460	12.4
Female	17,805	10.6	5,235	10.2	10,175	10.7	420	11.3
Age 25-39	45,500	27.2	12,820	25.1	27,165	28.5	895	24.1
Male	20,825	12.4	5,980	11.7	12,230	12.8	430	11.6
Female	24,670	14.7	6,840	13.4	14,935	15.7	465	12.5
Age 40-54	19,400	11.6	6,915	13.5	10,230	10.7	540	14.5
Male	9,365	5.6	3,215	6.3	4,975	5.2	270	7.3
Female	10,035	6.0	3,700	7.2	5,250	5.5	270	7.3
Age 55-64	5,970	3.6	2,840	5.6	2,450	2.6	195	5.2
Male	2,670	1.6	1,240	2.4	1,165	1.2	85	2.3
Female	3,300	2.0	1,605	3.1	1,285	1.3	115	3.1
Age 65 and over	4,210	2.5	2,410	4.7	1,400	1.5	135	3.6
Male	1,935	1.2	1,135	2.2	640	0.7	55	1.5
Female	2,280	1.4	1,275	2.5	765	0.8	75	2.0

Source: Aboriginal Peoples Output Program, 1986 Census, Statistics Canada, *A Data Book on Canada's Aboriginal Population from the 1986 Census of Canada,* March, 1989, p. 146. Primary source: 1986 Census of Canada *Notes:* A dash (-) represents zero or a percentage which rounds to less than .05 percent. 1. Aboriginal origins are derived from the ethnic origin question which asks whether respondents are North American Indian, Metis or Inuit. 2. All 1986 figures exclude the population estimated at about 45,000 on 136 incompletely enumerated Indian reserves and settlements throughout Canada. 3. Total aboriginal origins - are the sum of persons who reported: (a) a single aboriginal (e.g., North American Indian, Metis or Inuit), and, (b) multiple aboriginal origins, that is those who reported: - at least one aboriginal origin with any other non-aboriginal (e.g., Metis and French), or - two or more aboriginal origins only. 4. Non-aboriginal in these columns - refers to persons who report one or more non-aboriginal origins such as British, French, etc., in combination with one of the aboriginal origins such as North American Indian.

★ 787 ★

Population by Age Group and Sex for Detailed Aboriginal Origins for Ontario, 1986 - II[1,2]

Age group and sex	Metis and non-Aboriginal[3]		Inuit only		Inuit and non-Aboriginal[3]		Other multiple Aboriginal origins[4]	
	Number	Percent	Number	Percent	Number	Percent	Number	Percent
Total	10,615	100.0	680	100.0	1,590	100.0	4,195	100.0
Male	5,135	48.4	375	55.1	805	50.6	2,075	49.5
Female	5,480	51.6	300	44.1	785	49.4	2,115	50.4
Age less than 15	3,835	36.1	190	27.9	640	40.3	1,655	39.5
Male	2,050	19.3	135	19.9	305	19.2	820	19.5
Female	1,785	16.8	55	8.1	335	21.1	830	19.8
Age 15-24	2,340	22.0	125	18.4	405	25.5	810	19.3
Male	1,045	9.8	65	9.6	180	11.3	405	9.7
Female	1,295	12.2	60	8.8	220	13.8	405	9.7
Age 25-39	2,795	26.3	210	30.9	365	23.0	1,255	29.9
Male	1,265	11.9	105	15.4	210	13.2	610	14.5
Female	1,535	14.5	100	14.7	155	9.7	645	15.4
Age 40-54	1,080	10.2	100	14.7	155	9.7	380	9.1
Male	560	5.3	50	7.4	95	6.0	205	4.9
Female	520	4.9	55	8.1	60	3.8	175	4.2
Age 55-64	395	3.7	10	1.5	25	1.6	50	1.2
Male	145	1.4	-	-	10	0.6	20	0.5
Female	250	2.4	-	-	10	0.6	25	0.6
Age 65 and over	165	1.6	40	5.9	-	-	45	1.1
Male	70	0.7	10	1.5	-	-	20	0.5
Female	100	0.9	25	3.7	-	-	30	0.7

Source: Aboriginal Peoples Output Program, 1986 Census, Statistics Canada, *A Data Book on Canada's Aboriginal Population from the 1986 Census of Canada,* March, 1989, p. 146. Primary source: 1986 Census of Canada *Notes:* A dash (-) represents zero or a percentage which rounds to less than .05 percent. 1. Aboriginal origins are derived from the ethnic origin question which asks whether respondents are North American Indian, Metis or Inuit. 2. All 1986 figures exclude the population estimated at about 45,000 on 136 incompletely enumerated Indian reserves and settlements throughout Canada. 3. Non-aboriginal in these columns - refers to persons who report one or more non-aboriginal origins such as British, French, etc., in combination with one of the aboriginal origins such as North American Indian. 4. Other multiple aboriginal origins - refer to the sum of those persons reporting two or more aboriginal origins with or without a non-aboriginal origin.

★ 788 ★

Population by Age Group and Sex for Detailed Aboriginal Origins for Prince Edward Island, 1986 - I[1,2]

Age group and sex	Total Aboriginal origins[3]		North American Indian only		North American Indian and non-Aboriginal[4]		Metis only	
	Number	Percent	Number	Percent	Number	Percent	Number	Percent
Total	1,290	100.0	375	100.0	720	100.0	35	100.0
Male	650	50.4	190	50.7	355	49.3	-	-
Female	640	49.6	180	48.0	365	50.7	30	85.7
Age less than 15	445	34.5	135	36.0	250	34.7	20	57.1
Male	205	15.9	70	18.7	100	13.9	-	-
Female	245	19.0	70	18.7	145	20.1	15	42.9
Age 15-24	315	24.4	75	20.0	185	25.7	-	-
Male	140	10.9	30	8.0	80	11.1	-	-
Female	175	13.6	40	10.7	105	14.6	-	-
Age 25-39	325	25.2	90	24.0	200	27.8	-	-
Male	185	14.3	45	12.0	110	15.3	-	-
Female	140	10.9	40	10.7	80	11.1	-	-
Age 40-54	120	9.3	40	10.7	60	8.3	-	-
Male	65	5.0	20	5.3	30	4.2	-	-
Female	50	3.9	20	5.3	30	4.2	-	-
Age 55-64	50	3.9	20	5.3	20	2.8	-	-
Male	35	2.7	15	4.0	20	2.8	-	-
Female	10	0.8	-	-	-	-	-	-
Age 65 and over	35	2.7	15	4.0	10	1.4	-	-
Male	20	1.6	10	2.7	-	-	-	-
Female	10	0.8	-	-	-	-	-	-

Source: Aboriginal Peoples Output Program, 1986 Census, Statistics Canada, *A Data Book on Canada's Aboriginal Population from the 1986 Census of Canada*, March, 1989, p. 50. Primary source: 1986 Census of Canada *Notes:* A dash (-) represents zero or a percentage which rounds to less than .05 percent. 1. Aboriginal origins are derived from the ethnic origin question which asks whether respondents are North American Indian, Metis or Inuit. 2. All 1986 figures exclude the population estimated at about 45,000 on 136 incompletely enumerated Indian reserves and settlements throughout Canada. 3. Total aboriginal origins - are the sum of persons who reported: (a) a single aboriginal (e.g., North American Indian, Metis or Inuit), and, (b) multiple aboriginal origins, that is those who reported: - at least one aboriginal origin with any other non-aboriginal (e.g., Metis and French), or - two or more aboriginal origins only. 4. Non-aboriginal in these columns - refers to persons who report one or more non-aboriginal origins such as British, French, etc., in combination with one of the aboriginal origins such as North American Indian.

★ 789 ★

Population by Age Group and Sex for Detailed Aboriginal Origins for Prince Edward Island, 1986 - II[1,2]

Age group and sex	Metis and non-Aboriginal[3]		Inuit only		Inuit and non-Aboriginal[3]		Other multiple Aboriginal origins[4]	
	Number	Percent	Number	Percent	Number	Percent	Number	Percent
Total	110	100.0	-	-	20	100.0	25	100.0
Male	70	63.6	-	-	10	50.0	-	-
Female	40	36.4	-	-	10	50.0	20	80.0
Age less than 15	35	31.8	-	-	-	-	-	-
Male	25	22.7	-	-	-	-	-	-
Female	15	13.6	-	-	-	-	-	-
Age 15-24	35	31.8	-	-	-	-	-	-
Male	20	18.2	-	-	-	-	-	-
Female	15	13.6	-	-	-	-	-	-
Age 25-39	20	18.2	-	-	-	-	-	-
Male	-	-	-	-	-	-	-	-
Female	-	-	-	-	-	-	-	-
Age 40-54	10	9.1	-	-	-	-	-	-
Male	15	13.6	-	-	-	-	-	-
Female	-	-	-	-	-	-	-	-
Age 55-64	-	-	-	-	-	-	-	-
Male	-	-	-	-	-	-	-	-
Female	-	-	-	-	-	-	-	-
Age 65 and over	-	-	-	-	-	-	-	-
Male	-	-	-	-	-	-	-	-
Female	-	-	-	-	-	-	-	-

Source: Aboriginal Peoples Output Program, 1986 Census, Statistics Canada, *A Data Book on Canada's Aboriginal Population from the 1986 Census of Canada*, March, 1989, p. 50. Primary source: 1986 Census of Canada *Notes:* A dash (-) represents zero or a percentage which rounds to less than .05 percent. 1. Aboriginal origins are derived from the ethnic origin question which asks whether respondents are North American Indian, Metis or Inuit. 2. All 1986 figures exclude the population estimated at about 45,000 on 136 incompletely enumerated Indian reserves and settlements throughout Canada. 3. Non-aboriginal in these columns - refers to persons who report one or more non-aboriginal origins such as British, French, etc., in combination with one of the aboriginal origins such as North American Indian. 4. Other multiple aboriginal origins - refer to the sum of those persons reporting two or more aboriginal origins with or without a non-aboriginal origin.

★ 790 ★

Population by Age Group and Sex for Detailed Aboriginal Origins for Quebec, 1986 - I[1,2]

Age group and sex	Total Aboriginal origins[3]		North American Indian only		North American Indian and non-Aboriginal[4]		Metis only	
	Number	Percent	Number	Percent	Number	Percent	Number	Percent
Total	80,945	100.0	37,150	100.0	25,105	100.0	5,700	100.0
Male	39,150	48.4	18,330	49.3	11,535	45.9	2,940	51.6
Female	41,795	51.6	18,820	50.7	13,570	54.1	2,760	48.4
Age less than 15	24,780	30.6	11,400	30.7	7,200	28.7	1,600	28.1
Male	12,530	15.5	5,765	15.5	3,525	14.0	875	15.4
Female	12,250	15.1	5,635	15.2	3,680	14.7	725	12.7
Age 15-24	16,110	19.9	7,720	20.8	4,570	18.2	1,260	22.1
Male	7,570	9.4	3,720	10.0	1,930	7.7	665	11.7
Female	8,550	10.6	4,000	10.8	2,645	10.5	590	10.4
Age 25-39	23,510	29.0	10,075	27.1	8,900	35.5	1,480	26.0
Male	11,175	13.8	4,980	13.4	3,980	15.9	740	13.0
Female	12,340	15.2	5,095	13.7	4,925	19.6	735	12.9
Age 40-54	10,035	12.4	4,600	12.4	3,020	12.0	765	13.4
Male	4,905	6.1	2,300	6.2	1,435	5.7	390	6.8
Female	5,130	6.3	2,305	6.2	1,590	6.3	370	6.5
Age 55-64	3,680	4.5	1,760	4.7	900	3.6	380	6.7
Male	1,740	2.1	810	2.2	455	1.8	185	3.2
Female	1,940	2.4	950	2.6	450	1.8	195	3.4
Age 65 and over	2,825	3.5	1,590	4.3	505	2.0	225	3.9
Male	1,240	1.5	755	2.0	220	0.9	80	1.4
Female	1,585	2.0	835	2.2	285	1.1	145	2.5

Source: Aboriginal Peoples Output Program, 1986 Census, Statistics Canada, *A Data Book on Canada's Aboriginal Population from the 1986 Census of Canada*, March, 1989, p. 122. Primary source: 1986 Census of Canada *Notes:* A dash (-) represents zero or a percentage which rounds to less than .05 percent. 1. Aboriginal origins are derived from the ethnic origin question which asks whether respondents are North American Indian, Metis or Inuit. 2. All 1986 figures exclude the population estimated at about 45,000 on 136 incompletely enumerated Indian reserves and settlements throughout Canada. 3. Total aboriginal origins - are the sum of persons who reported: (a) a single aboriginal (e.g., North American Indian, Metis or Inuit), and, (b) multiple aboriginal origins, that is those who reported: - at least one aboriginal origin with any other non-aboriginal (e.g., Metis and French), or - two or more aboriginal origins only. 4. Non-aboriginal in these columns - refers to persons who report one or more non-aboriginal origins such as British, French, etc., in combination with one of the aboriginal origins such as North American Indian.

★ 791 ★

Population by Age Group and Sex for Detailed Aboriginal Origins for Quebec, 1986 - II[1,2]

Age group and sex	Metis and non-Aboriginal[3]		Inuit only		Inuit and non-Aboriginal[3]		Other multiple Aboriginal origins[4]	
	Number	Percent	Number	Percent	Number	Percent	Number	Percent
Total	4,565	100.0	6,470	100.0	580	100.0	1,370	100.0
Male	2,095	45.9	3,280	50.7	275	47.4	690	50.4
Female	2,470	54.1	3,190	49.3	300	51.7	680	49.6
Age less than 15	1,315	28.8	2,570	39.7	210	36.2	485	35.4
Male	700	15.3	1,340	20.7	95	16.4	230	16.8
Female	620	13.6	1,225	18.9	110	19.0	255	18.6
Age 15-24	835	18.3	1,430	22.1	95	16.4	205	15.0
Male	410	9.0	720	11.1	20	3.4	90	6.6
Female	425	9.3	705	10.9	70	12.1	105	7.7
Age 25-39	1,170	25.6	1,285	19.9	135	23.3	470	34.3
Male	520	11.4	640	9.9	70	12.1	245	17.9
Female	645	14.1	640	9.9	65	11.2	230	16.8
Age 40-54	650	14.2	730	11.3	90	15.5	170	12.4
Male	265	5.8	355	5.5	65	11.2	100	7.3
Female	390	8.5	380	5.9	25	4.3	75	5.5
Age 55-64	300	6.6	300	4.6	-	-	30	2.2
Male	115	2.5	150	2.3	-	-	25	1.8
Female	190	4.2	155	2.4	-	-	-	-
Age 65 and over	295	6.5	155	2.4	40	6.9	15	1.1
Male	90	2.0	70	1.1	20	3.4	-	-
Female	200	4.4	85	1.3	25	4.3	15	1.1

Source: Aboriginal Peoples Output Program, 1986 Census, Statistics Canada, *A Data Book on Canada's Aboriginal Population from the 1986 Census of Canada*, March, 1989, p. 122. Primary source: 1986 Census of Canada *Notes:* A dash (-) represents zero or a percentage which rounds to less than .05 percent. 1. Aboriginal origins are derived from the ethnic origin question which asks whether respondents are North American Indian, Metis or Inuit. 2. All 1986 figures exclude the population estimated at about 45,000 on 136 incompletely enumerated Indian reserves and settlements throughout Canada. 3. Non-aboriginal in these columns - refers to persons who report one or more non-aboriginal origins such as British, French, etc., in combination with one of the aboriginal origins such as North American Indian. 4. Other multiple aboriginal origins - refer to the sum of those persons reporting two or more aboriginal origins with or without a non-aboriginal origin.

★ 792 ★

Population by Age Group and Sex for Detailed Aboriginal Origins for Saskatchewan, 1986 - I[1,2]

Age group and sex	Total Aboriginal origins[3]		North American Indian only		North American Indian and non-Aboriginal[4]		Metis only	
	Number	Percent	Number	Percent	Number	Percent	Number	Percent
Total	77,650	100.0	43,390	100.0	8,455	100.0	12,220	100.0
Male	38,010	49.0	21,375	49.3	4,145	49.0	5,945	48.6
Female	39,635	51.0	22,010	50.7	4,310	51.0	6,270	51.3
Age less than 15	33,000	42.5	18,850	43.4	3,690	43.6	4,410	36.1
Male	16,510	21.3	9,460	21.8	1,815	21.5	2,225	18.2
Female	16,495	21.2	9,390	21.6	1,875	22.2	2,185	17.9
Age 15-24	16,925	21.8	9,540	22.0	1,825	21.6	2,795	22.9
Male	8,095	10.4	4,570	10.5	910	10.8	1,305	10.7
Female	8,830	11.4	4,965	11.4	920	10.9	1,490	12.2
Age 25-39	15,515	20.0	8,110	18.7	1,945	23.0	2,515	20.6
Male	7,380	9.5	3,870	8.9	945	11.2	1,250	10.2
Female	8,135	10.5	4,240	9.8	995	11.8	1,265	10.4
Age 40-54	6,970	9.0	3,895	9.0	660	7.8	1,315	10.8
Male	3,500	4.5	1,995	4.6	325	3.8	645	5.3
Female	3,470	4.5	1,900	4.4	330	3.9	675	5.5
Age 55-64	2,710	3.5	1,550	3.6	165	2.0	645	5.3
Male	1,290	1.7	760	1.8	75	0.9	295	2.4
Female	1,415	1.8	795	1.8	90	1.1	350	2.9
Age 65 and over	2,530	3.3	1,435	3.3	170	2.0	540	4.4
Male	1,240	1.6	720	1.7	80	0.9	235	1.9
Female	1,290	1.7	715	1.6	90	1.1	305	2.5

Source: Aboriginal Peoples Output Program, 1986 Census, Statistics Canada, *A Data Book on Canada's Aboriginal Population from the 1986 Census of Canada,* March, 1989, p. 194. Primary source: 1986 Census of Canada *Notes:* A dash (-) represents zero or a percentage which rounds to less than .05 percent. 1. Aboriginal origins are derived from the ethnic origin question which asks whether respondents are North American Indian, Metis or Inuit. 2. All 1986 figures exclude the population estimated at about 45,000 on 136 incompletely enumerated Indian reserves and settlements throughout Canada. 3. Total aboriginal origins - are the sum of persons who reported: (a) a single aboriginal (e.g., North American Indian, Metis or Inuit), and, (b) multiple aboriginal origins, that is those who reported: - at least one aboriginal origin with any other non-aboriginal (e.g., Metis and French), or - two or more aboriginal origins only. 4. Non-aboriginal in these columns - refers to persons who report one or more non-aboriginal origins such as British, French, etc., in combination with one of the aboriginal origins such as North American Indian.

★ 793 ★

Population by Age Group and Sex for Detailed Aboriginal Origins for Saskatchewan, 1986 - II[1,2]

Age group and sex	Metis and non-Aboriginal[3]		Inuit only		Inuit and non-Aboriginal[3]		Other multiple Aboriginal origins[4]	
	Number	Percent	Number	Percent	Number	Percent	Number	Percent
Total	10,080	100.0	40	100.0	60	100.0	3,405	100.0
Male	4,180	47.7	25	62.5	45	75.0	1,675	49.2
Female	5,270	52.3	20	50.0	15	25.0	1,740	51.1
Age less than 15	4,400	43.7	10	25.0	-	-	1,640	48.2
Male	2,200	21.8	-	-	-	-	795	23.3
Female	2,200	21.8	-	-	-	-	840	24.7
Age 15-24	2,050	20.3	10	25.0	35	58.3	665	19.5
Male	970	9.6	-	-	25	41.7	315	9.3
Female	1,085	10.8	-	-	-	-	360	10.6
Age 25-39	2,280	22.6	-	-	10	16.7	650	19.1
Male	985	9.8	-	-	10	16.7	325	9.5
Female	1,300	12.9	-	-	-	-	325	9.5
Age 40-54	770	7.6	-	-	10	16.7	310	9.1
Male	370	3.7	-	-	-	-	160	4.7
Female	400	4.0	-	-	-	-	150	4.4
Age 55-64	280	2.8	10	25.0	-	-	60	1.8
Male	115	1.1	-	-	-	-	30	0.9
Female	165	1.6	-	-	-	-	15	0.4
Age 65 and over	295	2.9	-	-	-	-	80	2.3
Male	165	1.6	-	-	-	-	35	1.0
Female	130	1.3	-	-	-	-	50	1.5

Source: Aboriginal Peoples Output Program, 1986 Census, Statistics Canada, *A Data Book on Canada's Aboriginal Population from the 1986 Census of Canada,* March, 1989, p. 194. Primary source: 1986 Census of Canada *Notes:* A dash (-) represents zero or a percentage which rounds to less than .05 percent. 1. Aboriginal origins are derived from the ethnic origin question which asks whether respondents are North American Indian, Metis or Inuit. 2. All 1986 figures exclude the population estimated at about 45,000 on 136 incompletely enumerated Indian reserves and settlements throughout Canada. 3. Non-aboriginal in these columns - refers to persons who report one or more non-aboriginal origins such as British, French, etc., in combination with one of the aboriginal origins such as North American Indian. 4. Other multiple aboriginal origins - refer to the sum of those persons reporting two or more aboriginal origins with or without a non-aboriginal origin.

★ 794 ★

Population by Age Group and Sex for Detailed Aboriginal Origins for Yukon Territory, 1986 - I[1,2]

Age group and sex	Total Aboriginal origins[3]		North American Indian only		North American Indian and non-Aboriginal[4]		Metis only	
	Number	Percent	Number	Percent	Number	Percent	Number	Percent
Total	4,995	100.0	3,160	100.0	1,545	100.0	80	100.0
Male	2,430	48.6	1,530	48.4	750	48.5	20	25.0
Female	2,565	51.4	1,630	51.6	790	51.1	65	81.3
Age less than 15	1,600	32.0	835	26.4	650	42.1	35	43.8
Male	785	15.7	405	12.8	330	21.4	-	-
Female	810	16.2	430	13.6	325	21.0	30	37.5
Age 15-24	1,135	22.7	695	22.0	370	23.9	20	25.0
Male	590	11.8	375	11.9	180	11.7	-	-
Female	545	10.9	320	10.1	185	12.0	15	18.8
Age 25-39	1,230	24.6	795	25.2	380	24.6	15	18.8
Male	565	11.3	360	11.4	170	11.0	-	-
Female	670	13.4	435	13.8	205	13.3	-	-
Age 40-54	565	11.3	435	13.8	90	5.8	-	-
Male	255	5.1	210	6.6	35	2.3	-	-
Female	300	6.0	225	7.1	55	3.6	-	-
Age 55-64	240	4.8	185	5.9	35	2.3	-	-
Male	130	2.6	85	2.7	25	1.6	-	-
Female	110	2.2	100	3.2	15	1.0	-	-
Age 65 and over	230	4.6	215	6.8	10	0.6	-	-
Male	105	2.1	95	3.0	-	-	-	-
Female	130	2.6	120	3.8	-	-	-	-

Source: Aboriginal Peoples Output Program, 1986 Census, Statistics Canada, *A Data Book on Canada's Aboriginal Population from the 1986 Census of Canada,* March, 1989, p. 290. Primary source: 1986 Census of Canada *Notes:* A dash (-) represents zero or a percentage which rounds to less than .05 percent. 1. Aboriginal origins are derived from the ethnic origin question which asks whether respondents are North American Indian, Metis or Inuit. 2. All 1986 figures exclude the population estimated at about 45,000 on 136 incompletely enumerated Indian reserves and settlements throughout Canada. 3. Total aboriginal origins - are the sum of persons who reported: (a) a single aboriginal (e.g., North American Indian, Metis or Inuit), and, (b) multiple aboriginal origins, that is those who reported: - at least one aboriginal origin with any other non-aboriginal (e.g., Metis and French), or - two or more aboriginal origins only. 4. Non-aboriginal in these columns - refers to persons who report one or more non-aboriginal origins such as British, French, etc., in combination with one of the aboriginal origins such as North American Indian.

★ 795 ★

Population by Age Group and Sex for Detailed Aboriginal Origins for Yukon Territory, 1986 - II[1,2]

Age group and sex	Metis and non-Aboriginal[3]		Inuit only		Inuit and non-Aboriginal[3]		Other multiple Aboriginal origins[4]	
	Number	Percent	Number	Percent	Number	Percent	Number	Percent
Total	85	100.0	35	100.0	20	100.0	65	100.0
Male	60	70.6	15	42.9	20	100.0	40	61.5
Female	25	29.4	25	71.4	-	-	30	46.2
Age less than 15	30	35.3	-	-	10	50.0	35	53.8
Male	20	23.5	-	-	-	-	10	15.4
Female	10	11.8	-	-	-	-	-	-
Age 15-24	20	23.5	-	-	-	-	10	15.4
Male	10	11.8	-	-	-	-	-	-
Female	-	-	-	-	-	-	-	-
Age 25-39	25	29.4	-	-	-	-	-	-
Male	15	17.6	-	-	-	-	-	-
Female	-	-	-	-	-	-	-	-
Age 40-54	-	-	10	28.6	-	-	-	-
Male	-	-	-	-	-	-	-	-
Female	-	-	10	28.6	-	-	-	-
Age 55-64	-	-	-	-	-	-	-	-
Male	-	-	-	-	-	-	-	-
Female	-	-	-	-	-	-	-	-
Age 65 and over	-	-	-	-	-	-	-	-
Male	-	-	-	-	-	-	-	-
Female	-	-	-	-	-	-	-	-

Source: Aboriginal Peoples Output Program, 1986 Census, Statistics Canada, *A Data Book on Canada's Aboriginal Population from the 1986 Census of Canada*, March, 1989, p. 290. Primary source: 1986 Census of Canada *Notes:* A dash (-) represents zero or a percentage which rounds to less than .05 percent. 1. Aboriginal origins are derived from the ethnic origin question which asks whether respondents are North American Indian, Metis or Inuit. 2. All 1986 figures exclude the population estimated at about 45,000 on 136 incompletely enumerated Indian reserves and settlements throughout Canada. 3. Non-aboriginal in these columns - refers to persons who report one or more non-aboriginal origins such as British, French, etc., in combination with one of the aboriginal origins such as North American Indian. 4. Other multiple aboriginal origins - refer to the sum of those persons reporting two or more aboriginal origins with or without a non-aboriginal origin.

Geographic Mobility

★ 796 ★

Persons of Aboriginal Origin and Total Canadian Population, by Geographic Mobility, Canada 1986

Region	Movers[1]				Total	Total Population Age 5+
	Migrants[2]		Non-Migrants[3]			
	Number	%	Number	%		
On-Reserve						
Atlantic	440	21.3	1,630	78.7	2,070	7,065
Quebec	810	17.4	3,835	82.6	4,645	18,925
Ontario	1,955	27.8	5,075	72.1	7,035	23,010
Manitoba	2,065	20.8	7,840	79.2	9,905	23,265
Saskatchewan	2,810	24.9	8,500	75.2	11,300	22,775
Alberta	1,375	22.1	4,870	78.1	6,235	16,050
British Columbia	3,480	31.6	7,520	68.4	11,000	26,820
Territories	75	27.8	200	74.1	270	535
Canada	13,015	24.8	39,455	75.2	52,465	138,440
Off-Reserve						
Atlantic	5,130	47.5	5,670	52.5	10,800	22,955
Quebec	13,575	44.6	16,870	55.4	30,450	53,310
Ontario	33,940	45.8	40,245	54.2	74,185	123,840
Manitoba	11,180	36.6	19,360	63.4	30,540	50,135
Saskatchewan	12,080	46.4	13,935	53.6	26,020	42,840
Alberta	22,690	46.0	26,595	54.0	49,290	72,570
British Columbia	25,685	46.2	29,965	53.8	55,650	83,990
Territories	4,890	30.6	11,085	69.4	15,975	30,100
Canada	129,165	44.1	163,740	55.9	292,905	479,745
Total Canadian Population						
Atlantic	308,680	43.7	397,990	56.3	706,675	2,087,960
Quebec	1,046,115	42.4	1,422,260	57.6	2,468,375	6,017,415
Ontario	1,686,535	45.3	2,037,830	54.7	3,724,365	8,361,215
Manitoba	150,560	36.2	264,890	63.8	415,450	968,905
Saskatchewan	175,060	45.9	206,495	54.1	381,545	910,185
Alberta	494,885	45.2	599,685	54.8	1,094,575	2,133,860
British Columbia	631,260	48.4	672,050	51.6	1,303,310	2,643,040

[Continued]

★ 796 ★

Persons of Aboriginal Origin and Total Canadian Population, by Geographic Mobility, Canada 1986
[Continued]

Region	Movers[1]				Total	Total Population Age 5+
	Migrants[2]		Non-Migrants[3]			
	Number	%	Number	%		
Territories	20,760	49.8	20,950	50.2	41,710	66,670
Canada	4,513,855	44.5	5,622,150	55.5	10,136,010	23,189,250

Source: Canada's Off-Reserve Aboriginal Population: A Statistical Overview, Social Trends Analysis Directorate, Department of the Secretary of State of Canada, 1991, p. A-5. Primary source: For Aboriginal population: Statistics Canada, A Profile of the Aboriginal Population Residing in Selected Off Reserve Areas, prepared by the Aboriginal Data and Native Issues Unit of the Housing, Family and Social Statistics Division, February 1990; for total Canadian population: Statistics Canada, 1986, Census, Special Tabulations from the Small Area Database compiled for the Department of the Secretary of State. Notes: Sum of components may not always add to totals due to rounding and/or data suppression. 1. Movers are "persons who, on Census Day, were living in a different dwelling than the one they occupied five years earlier", 2. Non-Migrants are "movers who, on Census Day, were living within the same Census sub-division (C.S.D.) they resided in five years earlier", 3. Migrants are "movers who, on Census Day, were residing in a different C.S.D. or outside Canada five years earlier". [Census Canada 1986 Dictionary, Statistics Canada, 1987:40].

★ 797 ★

Population 5 Years and Over, by Mobility Status and Sex for Detailed Aboriginal Origins for Canada, 1986 - I[1,2]

Mobility status	Total Aboriginal origins[3]		North American Indian only		North American Indian and non-Aboriginal[4]		Metis only	
	Number	Percent	Number	Percent	Number	Percent	Number	Percent
Total population (age 5 & over)	618,200	100.0	251,145	100.0	205,775	100.0	53,220	100.0
Male	301,445	48.8	122,785	48.9	99,165	48.2	26,470	49.7
Female	316,755	51.2	128,355	51.1	106,610	51.8	26,755	50.3
Total non-migrants[5]	476,020	77.0	204,785	81.5	146,335	71.1	41,515	78.0
Male	235,145	38.0	102,160	40.7	71,040	34.5	20,715	38.9
Female	240,870	39.0	102,625	40.9	75,290	36.6	20,800	39.1
Non-movers[6]	272,830	44.1	125,030	49.8	79,180	38.5	23,020	43.3
Male	136,960	22.2	63,180	25.2	38,765	18.8	11,870	22.3
Female	135,865	22.0	61,855	24.6	40,415	19.6	11,155	21.0
Movers[7]	203,190	32.9	79,755	31.8	67,155	32.6	18,490	34.7
Male	98,185	15.9	38,985	15.5	32,275	15.7	8,840	16.6
Female	105,005	17.0	40,077	16.2	34,880	17.0	9,650	18.1
Total migrants[8]	142,185	23.0	46,350	18.5	59,440	28.9	11,710	22.0
Male	66,295	10.7	20,625	8.2	28,125	13.7	5,755	10.8
Female	75,885	12.3	25,730	10.2	31,320	15.2	5,955	11.2

[Continued]

★ 797 ★

Population 5 Years and Over, by Mobility Status and Sex for Detailed Aboriginal Origins for Canada, 1986 - I
[Continued]

Mobility status	Total Aboriginal origins[3]		North American Indian only		North American Indian and non-Aboriginal[4]		Metis only	
	Number	Percent	Number	Percent	Number	Percent	Number	Percent
Migrants - same province or territory[9]	105,605	17.1	36,700	14.6	43,165	21.0	8,435	15.8
Male	48,675	7.9	16,280	6.5	20,190	9.8	4,090	7.7
Female	56,925	9.2	20,415	8.1	22,980	11.2	4,340	8.2
Migrants - from different province or territory or outside Canada	36,580	5.9	9,650	3.8	16,270	7.9	3,275	6.2
Male	17,625	2.9	4,340	1.7	7,935	3.9	1,665	3.1
Female	18,960	3.1	5,305	2.1	8,340	4.1	1,610	3.0

Source: Aboriginal Peoples Output Program, 1986 Census, Statistics Canada, *A Data Book on Canada's Aboriginal Population from the 1986 Census of Canada*, March, 1989, p. 12. Primary source: 1986 Census of Canada *Notes:* A dash (-) represents zero or a percentage which rounds to less than .05 percent. 1. Aboriginal origins are derived from the ethnic question which asks whether respondents are forth American Indian, Metis or Inuit. 2. All 1986 figures exclude the population estimated at about 45,000 on 136 incompletely enumerated Indian reserves and settlements throughout Canada. 3. Total Aboriginal Origins - are the sum of persons who reported: (a) a single aboriginal (e.g., North American Indian, Metis or Inuit) and, (b) multiple aboriginal origins, that is those who reported: - at least one aboriginal origin with any other non-aboriginal (e.g., Metis and French), or - two or more aboriginal origins only. 4. Non-aboriginal in these columns - refers to persons who report one or more non-aboriginal origins such as British, French, etc., in combination with one of the aboriginal origins such as North American Indian. 5. Non-migrants - refers to persons who on census day were living in the same census subdivision (or community) as they did five years earlier, though they may have changed dwellings. Non-migrants are the sum of non- movers and movers. 6. Non-movers - refers to persons who lived in the same dwelling on census day as the one they occupied five years earlier. 7. Movers - refers to persons who on census day occupied a different dwelling five years earlier, but did not change census subdivisions, that is, they did not move from their community. 8. Total migrants - refers to persons who on census day were living in a different census subdivision (or community) from the one they were living in five years earlier. 9. Migrants - same province or territory - refers to persons who, on census day, were living in a different census subdivision (or community) for the one they were living in five years earlier, but had not changed their province or territory. 10. Migrants - from different province, territory or outside Canada - refers to persons who five years earlier were living either in a different province or territory, or outside Canada.

★ 798 ★

Population 5 Years and Over, by Mobility Status and Sex for Detailed Aboriginal Origins for Canada, 1986 - II[1,2]

Mobility status	Metis and non-Aboriginal[3]		Inuit only		Inuit and non-Aboriginal[3]		Other multiple Aboriginal origins[4]	
	Number	Percent	Number	Percent	Number	Percent	Number	Percent
Total population (age 5 & over)	59,165	100.0	23,365	100.0	5,205	100.0	20,335	100.0
Male	28,350	47.9	11,780	50.4	2,630	50.5	10,270	50.5
Female	30,815	52.1	11,585	49.6	2,575	49.5	10,060	49.5
Total non-migrants[5]	44,035	74.4	20,525	87.8	3,910	75.1	14,915	73.3
Male	21,195	35.8	10,445	44.7	1,950	37.5	7,645	37.6
Female	22,840	38.6	10,080	43.1	1,960	37.7	7,280	35.8
Non-movers[6]	23,770	40.2	11,485	49.2	2,295	44.1	8,040	39.5

[Continued]

★ 798 ★

Population 5 Years and Over, by Mobility Status and Sex for Detailed Aboriginal Origins for Canada, 1986 - II
[Continued]

Mobility status	Metis and non-Aboriginal[3]		Inuit only		Inuit and non-Aboriginal[3]		Other multiple Aboriginal origins[4]	
	Number	Percent	Number	Percent	Number	Percent	Number	Percent
Male	11,900	20.1	5,900	25.3	1,130	21.7	4,220	20.8
Female	11,870	20.1	5,590	23.9	1,165	22.4	3,825	18.8
Movers[7]	20,265	34.3	9,035	38.7	1,615	31.0	6,880	33.8
Male	9,295	15.7	4,545	19.5	820	15.8	3,420	16.8
Female	10,965	18.5	4,490	19.2	795	15.3	3,455	17.0
Total migrants[8]	15,125	25.6	2,840	12.2	1,300	25.0	5,405	26.6
Male	7,150	12.1	1,335	5.7	680	13.1	2,625	12.9
Female	7,975	13.5	1,505	6.4	620	11.9	2,790	13.7
Migrants - same province or territory[9]	10,480	17.7	2,255	9.7	830	15.9	3,735	18.4
Male	4,800	8.1	1,075	4.6	435	8.4	1,780	8.8
Female	5,675	9.6	1,175	5.0	390	7.5	1,945	9.6
Migrants - from different province or territory or outside Canada	4,650	7.9	590	2.5	465	8.9	1,670	8.2
Male	2,350	4.0	245	1.0	235	4.5	835	4.1
Female	2,300	3.9	335	1.4	225	4.3	835	4.1

Source: Aboriginal Peoples Output Program, 1986 Census, Statistics Canada, *A Data Book on Canada's Aboriginal Population from the 1986 Census of Canada,* March, 1989, p. 12. Primary source: 1986 Census of Canada *Notes:* A dash (-) represents zero or a percentage which rounds to less than .05 percent. 1. Aboriginal origins are derived from the ethnic question which asks whether respondents are forth American Indian, Metis or Inuit. 2. All 1986 figures exclude the population estimated at about 45,000 on 136 incompletely enumerated Indian reserves and settlements throughout Canada. 3. Non-aboriginal in these columns - refers to persons who report one or more non-aboriginal origins such as British, French, etc., in combination with one of the aboriginal origins such as North American Indian. 4. Other Multiple Aboriginal origins - refers to the sum of those persons reporting two or more aboriginal origins with or without a non- aboriginal origin. 5. Non-migrants - refers to persons who on census day were living in the same census subdivision (or community) as they did five years earlier, though they may have changed dwellings. Non-migrants are the sum of non- movers and movers. 6. Non-movers - refers to persons who lived in the same dwelling on census day as the one they occupied five years earlier. 7. Movers - refers to persons who on census day occupied a different dwelling five years earlier, but did not change census subdivisions, that is, they did not move from their community. 8. Total migrants - refers to persons who on census day were living in a different census subdivision (or community) from the one they were living in five years earlier. 9. Migrants - same province or territory - refers to persons who, on census day, were living in a different census subdivision (or community) from the one they were living in five years earlier, but had not changed their province or territory. 10. Migrants - from different province, territory or outside Canada - refers to persons who five years earlier were living either in a different province or territory, or outside Canada.

★ 799 ★

Population 5 Years and Over, by Mobility Status and Sex for Detailed Aboriginal Origins for Alberta, 1986 - I[1,2]

Mobility status	Total Aboriginal origins[3]		North American Indian only		North American Indian and non-Aboriginal[4]		Metis only	
	Number	Percent	Number	Percent	Number	Percent	Number	Percent
Total population								
(age 5 & over)	88,630	100.0	29,695	100.0	23,685	100.0	15,025	100.0
Male	43,350	48.9	14,285	48.1	11,545	48.7	7,500	49.9
Female	45,275	51.1	15,405	51.9	12,140	51.3	7,525	50.1
Total non-migrants[5]	64,565	72.8	23,385	78.8	15,530	65.6	11,395	75.8
Male	31,890	36.0	11,450	38.6	7,650	32.3	5,745	38.2
Female	32,675	36.9	11,935	40.2	7,880	33.3	5,645	37.6
Non-movers[6]	33,100	37.3	13,360	45.0	6,615	27.9	5,730	38.1
Male	16,700	18.8	6,650	22.4	3,285	13.9	2,955	19.7
Female	16,400	18.5	6,710	22.6	3,335	14.1	2,775	18.5
Movers[7]	31,465	35.5	10,025	33.8	8,915	37.6	5,665	37.7
Male	15,190	17.1	4,800	16.2	4,365	18.4	2,790	18.6
Female	16,270	18.4	5,220	17.6	4,550	19.2	2,875	19.1
Total migrants[8]	24,065	27.2	6,310	21.2	8,160	34.5	3,630	24.2
Male	11,460	12.9	2,835	9.5	3,895	16.4	1,755	11.7
Female	12,600	14.2	3,475	11.7	4,265	18.0	1,875	12.5
Migrants - same province								
or territory[9]	15,895	17.9	4,375	14.7	4,645	19.6	2,670	17.8
Male	7,515	8.5	2,005	6.8	2,180	9.2	1,265	8.4
Female	8,380	9.5	2,370	8.0	2,465	10.4	1,400	9.3
Migrants - from different								
province or territory or								
outside Canada	8,170	9.2	1,930	6.5	3,510	14.8	965	6.4
Male	3,945	4.5	825	2.8	1,715	7.2	490	3.3
Female	4,220	4.8	1,110	3.7	1,800	7.6	470	3.1

Source: Aboriginal Peoples Output Program, 1986 Census, Statistics Canada, *A Data Book on Canada's Aboriginal Population from the 1986 Census of Canada*, March, 1989, p. 228. Primary source: 1986 Census of Canada *Notes:* A dash (-) represents zero or a percentage which rounds to less than .05 percent. 1. Aboriginal origins are derived from the ethnic question which asks whether respondents are forth American Indian, Metis or Inuit. 2. All 1986 figures exclude the population estimated at about 45,000 on 136 incompletely enumerated Indian reserves and settlements throughout Canada. 3. Total Aboriginal Origins - are the sum of persons who reported: (a) a single aboriginal (e.g., North American Indian, Metis or Inuit) and, (b) multiple aboriginal origins, that is those who reported: - at least one aboriginal origin with any other non-aboriginal (e.g., Metis and French), or - two or more aboriginal origins only. 4. Non-aboriginal in these columns - refers to persons who report one or more non-aboriginal origins such as British, French, etc., in combination with one of the aboriginal origins such as North American Indian. 5. Non-migrants - refers to persons who on census day were living in the same census subdivision (or community) as they did five years earlier, though they may have changed dwellings. Non-migrants are the sum of non- movers and movers. 6. Non-movers - refers to persons who lived in the same dwelling on census day as the one they occupied five years earlier. 7. Movers - refers to persons who on census day occupied a different dwelling five years earlier, but did not change census subdivisions, that is, they did not move from their community. 8. Total migrants - refers to persons who on census day were living in a different census subdivision (or community) from the one they were living in five years earlier. 9. Migrants - same province or territory - refers to persons who, on census day, were living in a different census subdivision (or community) for the one they were living in five years earlier, but had not changed their province or territory. 10. Migrants - from different province, territory or outside Canada - refers to persons who five years earlier were living either in a different province or territory, or outside Canada.

★ 800 ★

Population 5 Years and Over, by Mobility Status and Sex for Detailed Aboriginal Origins for Alberta, 1986 - 11[10]

Mobility status	Metis and non-Aboriginal[3]		Inuit only		Inuit and non-Aboriginal[3]		Other multiple Aboriginal origins[4]	
	Number	Percent	Number	Percent	Number	Percent	Number	Percent
Total population								
(age 5 & over)	14,480	100.0	295	100.0	390	100.0	5,050	100.0
Male	7,095	49.0	145	49.2	180	46.2	2,595	51.4
Female	7,390	51.0	145	49.2	210	53.8	2,465	48.8
Total non-migrants[5]	10,130	70.0	150	50.8	230	59.0	3,750	74.3
Male	4,935	34.1	85	28.8	90	23.1	1,925	38.1
Female	5,195	35.9	65	22.0	135	34.6	1,815	35.9
Non-movers[6]	5,210	36.0	60	20.3	75	19.2	2,050	40.6
Male	2,645	18.3	45	15.3	20	5.1	1,100	21.8
Female	2,565	17.7	15	5.1	60	15.4	945	18.7
Movers[7]	4,925	34.0	90	30.5	150	38.5	1,695	33.6
Male	2,290	15.8	45	15.3	75	19.2	830	16.4
Female	2,630	18.2	50	16.9	75	19.2	870	17.2
Total migrants[8]	4,35O	30.0	140	47.5	165	42.3	1,310	25.9
Male	2,155	14.9	60	20.3	85	21.8	665	13.2
Female	2,195	15.2	85	28.8	75	19.2	635	12.6
Migrants - same province or territory[9]	3,105	21.4	65	22.0	65	16.7	955	18.9
Male	1,490	10.3	25	8.5	45	11.5	500	9.9
Female	1,615	11.2	30	10.2	20	5.1	465	9.2
Migrants - from different province or territory or outside Canada	1,245	8.6	70	23.7	100	25.6	345	6.8
Male	670	4.6	35	11.9	45	11.5	170	3.4
Female	575	4.0	40	13.6	50	12.8	175	3.5

Source: Aboriginal Peoples Output Program, 1986 Census, Statistics Canada, *A Data Book on Canada's Aboriginal Population from the 1986 Census of Canada*, March, 1989, p. 228. Primary source: 1986 Census of Canada *Notes:* A dash (-) represents zero or a percentage which rounds to less than .05 percent. 1. Aboriginal origins are derived from the ethnic question which asks whether respondents are forth American Indian, Metis or Inuit. 2. All 1986 figures exclude the population estimated at about 45,000 on 136 incompletely enumerated Indian reserves and settlements throughout Canada. 3. Non-aboriginal in these columns - refers to persons who report one or more non-aboriginal origins such as British, French, etc., in combination with one of the aboriginal origins such as North American Indian. 4. Other Multiple Aboriginal origins - refers to the sum of those persons reporting two or more aboriginal origins with or without a non- aboriginal origin. 5. Non-migrants - refers to persons who on census day were living in the same census subdivision (or community) as they did five years earlier, though they may have changed dwellings. Non-migrants are the sum of non- movers and movers. 6. Non-movers - refers to persons who lived in the same dwelling on census day as the one they occupied five years earlier. 7. Movers - refers to persons who on census day occupied a different dwelling five years earlier, but did not change census subdivisions, that is, they did not move from their community. 8. Total migrants - refers to persons who on census day were living in a different census subdivision (or community) from the one they were living in five years earlier. 9. Migrants - same province or territory - refers to persons who, on census day, were living in a different census subdivision (or community) from the one they were living in five years earlier, but had not changed their province or territory. 10. Migrants - from different province, territory or outside Canada - refers to persons who five years earlier were living either in a different province or territory, or outside Canada.

★ 801 ★

Population 5 Years and Over, by Mobility Status and Sex for Detailed Aboriginal Origins for British Columbia, 1986 - I[1,2]

Mobility status	Total Aboriginal origins[3]		North American Indian only		North American Indian and non-Aboriginal[4]		Metis only	
	Number	Percent	Number	Percent	Number	Percent	Number	Percent
Total population								
(age 5 & over)	110,815	100.0	50,985	100.0	45,575	100.0	3,645	100.0
Male	54,745	49.4	25,110	49.2	22,595	49.6	1,720	47.2
Female	56,070	50.6	25,875	50.8	22,980	50.4	1,920	52.7
Total non-migrants[5]	81,650	73.7	39,920	78.3	31,900	70.0	2,675	73.4
Male	40,955	37.0	20,060	39.3	16,105	35.3	1,265	34.7
Female	40,695	36.7	19,855	38.9	15,800	34.7	1,415	38.8
Non-movers[6]	44,165	39.9	22,740	44.6	16,710	36.7	1,325	36.4
Male	22,340	20.2	11,515	22.6	8,435	18.5	665	18.2
Female	21,820	19.7	11,225	22.0	8,270	18.1	665	18.2
Movers[7]	37,485	33.8	17,170	33.7	15,190	33.3	1,355	37.2
Male	18,610	16.8	8,545	16.8	7,670	16.8	605	16.6
Female	18,870	17.0	8,625	16.9	7,520	16.5	745	20.4
Total migrants[8]	29,170	26.3	11,070	21.7	13,675	30.0	970	26.6
Male	13,785	12.4	5,050	9.9	6,485	14.2	460	12.6
Female	15,380	13.9	6,020	11.8	7,185	15.8	510	14.0
Migrants - same province								
or territory[9]	22,350	20.2	9,255	18.2	10,480	23.0	510	14.0
Male	10,360	9.3	4,210	8.3	4,895	10.7	240	6.6
Female	11,995	10.8	5,050	9.9	5,585	12.3	265	7.3
Migrants - from different								
province or territory								
or outside Canada	6,815	6.1	1,815	3.6	3,195	7.0	460	12.6
Male	3,430	3.1	840	1.6	1,595	3.5	210	5.8
Female	3,390	3.1	980	1.9	1,595	3.5	240	6.6

Source: Aboriginal Peoples Output Program, 1986 Census, Statistics Canada, *A Data Book on Canada's Aboriginal Population from the 1986 Census of Canada,* March, 1989, p. 252. Primary source: 1986 Census of Canada *Notes:* A dash (-) represents zero or a percentage which rounds to less than .05 percent. 1. Aboriginal origins are derived from the ethnic question which asks whether respondents are forth American Indian, Metis or Inuit. 2. All 1986 figures exclude the population estimated at about 45,000 on 136 incompletely enumerated Indian reserves and settlements throughout Canada. 3. Total Aboriginal Origins - are the sum of persons who reported: (a) a single aboriginal (e.g., North American Indian, Metis or Inuit) and, (b) multiple aboriginal origins, that is those who reported: - at least one aboriginal origin with any other non-aboriginal (e.g., Metis and French), or - two or more aboriginal origins only. 4. Non-aboriginal in these columns - refers to persons who report one or more non-aboriginal origins such as British, French, etc., in combination with one of the aboriginal origins such as North American Indian. 5. Non-migrants - refers to persons who on census day were living in the same census subdivision (or community) as they did five years earlier, though they may have changed dwellings. Non-migrants are the sum of non- movers and movers. 6. Non-movers - refers to persons who lived in the same dwelling on census day as the one they occupied five years earlier. 7. Movers - refers to persons who on census day occupied a different dwelling five years earlier, but did not change census subdivisions, that is, they did not move from their community. 8. Total migrants - refers to persons who on census day were living in a different census subdivision (or community) from the one they were living in five years earlier. 9. Migrants - same province or territory - refers to persons who, on census day, were living in a different census subdivision (or community) for the one they were living in five years earlier, but had not changed their province or territory. 10. Migrants - from different province, territory or outside Canada - refers to persons who five years earlier were living either in a different province or territory, or outside Canada.

★ 802 ★

Population 5 Years and Over, by Mobility Status and Sex for Detailed Aboriginal Origins for British Columbia, 1986 - II[1,2]

Mobility status	Metis and non-Aboriginal[3]		Inuit only		Inuit and non-Aboriginal[3]		Other multiple Aboriginal origins[4]	
	Number	Percent	Number	Percent	Number	Percent	Number	Percent
Total population								
(age 5 & over)	7,955	100.0	185	100.0	435	100.0	2,035	100.0
Male	3,900	49.0	100	54.1	250	57.5	1,065	52.3
Female	4,050	50.9	80	43.2	185	42.5	965	47.4
Total non-migrants[5]	5,470	68.8	120	64.9	295	67.8	1,275	62.7
Male	2,635	33.1	60	32.4	155	35.6	680	33.4
Female	2,835	35.6	55	29.7	135	31.0	595	29.2
Non-movers[6]	2,640	33.2	55	29.7	105	24.1	585	28.7
Male	1,340	16.8	25	13.5	55	12.6	305	15.0
Female	1,290	16.2	30	16.2	50	11.5	285	14.0
Movers[7]	2,830	35.6	65	35.1	190	43.7	685	33.7
Male	1,290	16.2	40	21.6	100	23.0	375	18.4
Female	1,545	19.4	25	13.5	90	20.7	315	15.5
Total migrants[8]	2,480	31.2	65	35.1	145	33.3	760	37.3
Male	1,270	16.0	35	18.9	95	21.8	395	19.4
Female	1,215	15.3	30	16.2	50	11.5	370	18.2
Migrants - same province or territory[9]	1,575	19.8	25	13.5	80	18.4	425	20.9
Male	755	9.5	-	-	50	11.5	180	8.8
Female	820	10.3	15	8.1	25	5.7	240	11.8
Migrants - from different province or territory or outside Canada	910	11.4	40	21.6	60	13.8	340	16.7
Male	505	6.3	30	16.2	40	9.2	205	10.1
Female	395	5.0	15	8.1	20	4.6	135	6.6

Source: Aboriginal Peoples Output Program, 1986 Census, Statistics Canada, *A Data Book on Canada's Aboriginal Population from the 1986 Census of Canada*, March, 1989, p. 252. Primary source: 1986 Census of Canada *Notes:* A dash (-) represents zero or a percentage which rounds to less than .05 percent. 1. Aboriginal origins are derived from the ethnic question which asks whether respondents are forth American Indian, Metis or Inuit. 2. All 1986 figures exclude the population estimated at about 45,000 on 136 incompletely enumerated Indian reserves and settlements throughout Canada. 3. Non-aboriginal in these columns - refers to persons who report one or more non-aboriginal origins such as British, French, etc., in combination with one of the aboriginal origins such as North American Indian. 4. Other Multiple Aboriginal origins - refers to the sum of those persons reporting two or more aboriginal origins with or without a non- aboriginal origin. 5. Non-migrants - refers to persons who on census day were living in the same census subdivision (or community) as they did five years earlier, though they may have changed dwellings. Non-migrants are the sum of non- movers and movers. 6. Non-movers - refers to persons who lived in the same dwelling on census day as the one they occupied five years earlier. 7. Movers - refers to persons who on census day occupied a different dwelling five years earlier, but did not change census subdivisions, that is, they did not move from their community. 8. Total migrants - refers to persons who on census day were living in a different census subdivision (or community) from the one they were living in five years earlier. 9. Migrants - same province or territory - refers to persons who, on census day, were living in a different census subdivision (or community) from the one they were living in five years earlier, but had not changed their province or territory. 10. Migrants - from different province, territory or outside Canada - refers to persons who five years earlier were living either in a different province or territory, or outside Canada.

★ 803 ★

Population 5 Years and Over, by Mobility Status and Sex for Detailed Aboriginal Origins for Manitoba, 1986 - I[1,2]

Mobility status	Total Aboriginal origins[3]		North American Indian only		North American Indian and non-Aboriginal[4]		Metis only	
	Number	Percent	Number	Percent	Number	Percent	Number	Percent
Total population								
(age 5 & over)	73,400	100.0	34,945	100.0	8,890	100.0	12,745	100.0
Male	35,790	48.8	17,115	49.0	4,370	49.2	6,400	50.2
Female	37,610	51.2	17,825	51.0	4,525	50.9	6,345	49.8
Total non-migrants[5]	60,160	82.0	29,480	84.4	6,680	75.1	10,330	81.1
Male	29,650	40.4	14,745	42.2	3,320	37.3	5,125	40.2
Female	30,505	41.6	14,740	42.2	3,360	37.8	5,200	40.8
Non-movers[6]	32,955	44.9	16,675	47.7	3,465	39.0	5,540	43.5
Male	16,870	23.0	8,565	24.5	1,800	20.2	2,870	22.5
Female	16,080	21.9	8,110	23.2	1,665	18.7	2,665	20.9
Movers[7]	27,200	37.1	12,810	36.7	3,215	36.2	4,790	37.6
Male	12,780	17.4	6,180	17.7	1,520	17.1	2,255	17.7
Female	14,420	19.6	6,630	19.0	1,695	19.1	2,535	19.9
Total migrants[8]	13,245	18.0	5,465	15.6	2,215	24.9	2,415	18.9
Male	6,135	8.4	2,375	6.8	1,045	11.8	1,270	10.0
Female	7,105	9.7	3,090	8.8	1,170	13.2	1,145	9.0
Migrants - same province								
or territory[9]	9,695	13.2	4,465	12.8	1,220	13.7	1,870	14.7
Male	4,475	6.1	1,945	5.6	605	6.8	965	7.6
Female	5,220	7.1	2,520	7.2	615	6.9	900	7.1
Migrants - from different								
province or territory								
or outside Canada	3,550	4.8	1,000	2.9	995	11.2	545	4.3
Male	1,660	2.3	430	1.2	450	5.1	300	2.4
Female	1,885	2.6	565	1.6	555	6.2	-	-

Source: Aboriginal Peoples Output Program, 1986 Census, Statistics Canada, *A Data Book on Canada's Aboriginal Population from the 1986 Census of Canada,* March, 1989, p. 182. Primary source: 1986 Census of Canada *Notes:* A dash (-) represents zero or a percentage which rounds to less than .05 percent. 1. Aboriginal origins are derived from the ethnic question which asks whether respondents are forth American Indian, Metis or Inuit. 2. All 1986 figures exclude the population estimated at about 45,000 on 136 incompletely enumerated Indian reserves and settlements throughout Canada. 3. Total Aboriginal Origins - are the sum of persons who reported: (a) a single aboriginal (e.g., North American Indian, Metis or Inuit) and, (b) multiple aboriginal origins, that is those who reported: - at least one aboriginal origin with any other non-aboriginal (e.g., Metis and French), or - two or more aboriginal origins only. 4. Non-aboriginal in these columns - refers to persons who report one or more non-aboriginal origins such as British, French, etc., in combination with one of the aboriginal origins such as North American Indian. 5. Non-migrants - refers to persons who on census day were living in the same census subdivision (or community) as they did five years earlier, though they may have changed dwellings. Non-migrants are the sum of non- movers and movers. 6. Non-movers - refers to persons who lived in the same dwelling on census day as the one they occupied five years earlier. 7. Movers - refers to persons who on census day occupied a different dwelling five years earlier, but did not change census subdivisions, that is, they did not move from their community. 8. Total migrants - refers to persons who on census day were living in a different census subdivision (or community) from the one they were living in five years earlier. 9. Migrants - same province or territory - refers to persons who, on census day, were living in a different census subdivision (or community) for the one they were living in five years earlier, but had not changed their province or territory. 10. Migrants - from different province, territory or outside Canada - refers to persons who five years earlier were living either in a different province or territory, or outside Canada.

★ 804 ★

Population 5 Years and Over, by Mobility Status and Sex for Detailed Aboriginal Origins for Manitoba, 1986 - II[1,2]

Mobility status	Metis and non-Aboriginal[3]		Inuit only		Inuit and non-Aboriginal[3]		Other multiple Aboriginal origins[4]	
	Number	Percent	Number	Percent	Number	Percent	Number	Percent
Total population								
(age 5 & over)	12,655	100.0	165	100.0	185	100.0	3,815	100.0
Male	5,950	47.0	45	27.3	80	43.2	1,835	48.1
Female	6,705	53.0	115	69.7	100	54.1	1,980	51.9
Total non-migrants[5]	10,280	81.2	105	63.6	105	56.8	3,175	83.2
Male	4,840	38.2	30	18.2	45	24.3	1,540	40.4
Female	5,435	42.9	70	42.4	60	32.4	1,635	42.9
Non-movers[6]	5,445	43.0	25	15.2	-	-	1,795	47.1
Male	2,715	21.5	-	-	-	-	905	23.7
Female	2,730	21.6	20	12.1	-	-	890	23.3
Movers[7]	4,835	38.2	75	45.5	95	51.4	1,375	36.0
Male	2,130	16.8	20	12.1	35	18.9	640	16.8
Female	2,705	21.4	50	30.3	60	32.4	745	19.5
Total migrants[8]	2,375	18.8	60	36.4	80	43.2	635	16.6
Male	1,105	8.7	20	12.1	35	18.9	290	7.6
Female	1,275	10.1	40	24.2	40	21.6	350	9.2
Migrants - same province or territory[9]	1,630	12.9	-	-	-	-	480	12.6
Male	730	5.8	-	-	-	-	210	5.5
Female	905	7.2	-	-	-	-	270	7.1
Migrants - from different province or territory or outside Canada	-	-	-	-	-	-	-	-
Male	-	-	-	-	-	-	-	-
Female	-	-	-	-	-	-	-	-

Source: Aboriginal Peoples Output Program, 1986 Census, Statistics Canada, *A Data Book on Canada's Aboriginal Population from the 1986 Census of Canada*, March, 1989, p. 182. Primary source: 1986 Census of Canada *Notes:* A dash (-) represents zero or a percentage which rounds to less than .05 percent. 1. Aboriginal origins are derived from the ethnic question which asks whether respondents are North American Indian, Metis or Inuit. 2. All 1986 figures exclude the population estimated at about 45,000 on 136 incompletely enumerated Indian reserves and settlements throughout Canada. 3. Non-aboriginal in these columns - refers to persons who report one or more non-aboriginal origins such as British, French, etc., in combination with one of the aboriginal origins such as North American Indian. 4. Other Multiple Aboriginal origins - refers to the sum of those persons reporting two or more aboriginal origins with or without a non- aboriginal origin. 5. Non-migrants - refers to persons who on census day were living in the same census subdivision (or community) as they did five years earlier, though they may have changed dwellings. Non-migrants are the sum of non- movers and movers. 6. Non-movers - refers to persons who lived in the same dwelling on census day as the one they occupied five years earlier. 7. Movers - refers to persons who on census day occupied a different dwelling five years earlier, but did not change census subdivisions, that is, they did not move from their community. 8. Total migrants - refers to persons who on census day were living in a different census subdivision (or community) from the one they were living in five years earlier. 9. Migrants - same province or territory - refers to persons who, on census day, were living in a different census subdivision (or community) from the one they were living in five years earlier, but had not changed their province or territory. 10. Migrants - from different province, territory or outside Canada - refers to persons who five years earlier were living either in a different province or territory, or outside Canada.

★ 805 ★

Population 5 Years and Over, by Mobility Status and Sex for Detailed Aboriginal Origins for New Brunswick, 1986 - I[1,2]

Mobility status	Total Aboriginal origins[3]		North American Indian only		North American Indian and non-Aboriginal[4]		Metis only	
	Number	Percent	Number	Percent	Number	Percent	Number	Percent
Total population								
(age 5 & over)	8,120	100.0	3,235	100.0	4,160	100.0	145	100.0
Male	4,125	50.8	1,690	52.2	2,045	49.2	85	58.6
Female	4,000	49.3	1,550	47.9	2,110	50.7	65	44.8
Total non-migrants[5]	6,620	81.5	2,845	87.9	3,230	77.6	125	86.2
Male	3,435	42.3	1,515	46.8	1,605	38.6	75	51.7
Female	3,185	39.2	1,335	41.3	1,625	39.1	55	37.9
Non-movers[6]	4,545	56.0	2,135	66.0	2,035	48.9	115	79.3
Male	2,390	29.4	1,160	35.9	1,000	24.0	70	48.3
Female	2,155	26.5	970	30.0	1,035	24.9	45	31.0
Movers[7]	2,075	25.6	715	22.1	1,195	28.7	-	-
Male	1,045	12.9	350	10.8	605	14.5	-	-
Female	1,030	12.7	360	11.1	590	14.2	-	-
Total migrants[8]	1,505	18.5	395	12.2	925	22.2	25	17.2
Male	690	8.5	180	5.6	445	10.7	10	6.9
Female	815	10.0	215	6.6	480	11.5	10	6.9
Migrants - same province								
or territory[9]	780	9.6	200	6.2	495	11.9	10	6.9
Male	315	3.9	70	2.2	210	5.0	10	6.9
Female	465	5.7	125	3.9	285	6.9	-	-
Migrants - from different								
province or territory								
or outside Canada	725	8.9	190	5.9	435	10.5	-	-
Male	370	4.6	105	3.2	230	5.5	-	-
Female	350	4.3	90	2.8	200	4.8	-	-

Source: Aboriginal Peoples Output Program, 1986 Census, Statistics Canada, *A Data Book on Canada's Aboriginal Population from the 1986 Census of Canada*, March, 1989, p. 108. Primary source: 1986 Census of Canada *Notes:* A dash (-) represents zero or a percentage which rounds to less than .05 percent. 1. Aboriginal origins are derived from the ethnic question which asks whether respondents are forth American Indian, Metis or Inuit. 2. All 1986 figures exclude the population estimated at about 45,000 on 136 incompletely enumerated Indian reserves and settlements throughout Canada. For an estimate of the unenumerated population and list of incompletely enumerated reserves in each affected province, see Appendix 1 and 2. 3. Non-aboriginal in these columns - refers to persons who report one or more non-aboriginal origins such as British, French, etc., in combination with one of the aboriginal origins such as North American Indian. 4. Other Multiple Aboriginal origins - refer to the sum of those persons reporting two or more aboriginal origins with or without a non-aboriginal origin. 5. Non-migrants - refer to persons who on census day were living in the same census subdivision (or community) as they did five years earlier, though they may have changed dwellings. Non-migrants are the sum of non- movers and movers. 6. Non-movers - refer to persons who lived in the same dwelling on census day as the one they occupied five years earlier. 7. Movers - refer to persons who on census day occupied a different dwelling five years earlier, but did not change census subdivisions, that is, they did not move from their community. 8. Total migrants - refer to persons who on census day were living in a different census subdivision (or community) from the one they were living in five years earlier. 9. Migrants - same province or territory - refer to persons who, on census day, were living in a different census subdivision (or community) for the one they were living in five years earlier, but had not changed their province or territory. 10. Migrants - from different province, territory or outside Canada - refer to persons who five years earlier were living either in a different province or territory, or outside Canada.

★ 806 ★

Population 5 Years and Over, by Mobility Status and Sex for Detailed Aboriginal Origins for New Brunswick, 1986 - II[1,2]

Mobility status	Metis and non-Aboriginal[3]		Inuit only		Inuit and non-Aboriginal[3]		Other multiple Aboriginal origins[4]	
	Number	Percent	Number	Percent	Number	Percent	Number	Percent
Total population								
(age 5 & over)	325	100.0	15	100.0	85	100.0	150	100.0
male	185	56.9	-	-	35	41.2	70	46.7
female	140	43.1	-	-	50	58.8	75	50.0
Total non-migrants[5]	235	72.3	10	66.7	70	82.4	95	63.3
male	155	47.7	-	-	30	35.3	55	36.7
female	75	23.1	-	-	40	47.1	45	30.0
Non-movers[6]	145	44.6	-	-	45	52.9	65	43.3
male	95	29.2	-	-	25	29.4	40	26.7
female	45	13.8	-	-	15	17.6	25	16.7
Movers[7]	85	26.2	-	-	25	29.4	30	20.0
male	55	16.9	-	-	-	-	10	6.7
female	30	9.2	-	-	20	23.5	15	10.0
Total migrants[8]	95	29.2	-	-	20	23.5	55	36.7
male	30	9.2	-	-	15	17.6	20	13.3
female	65	20.0	-	-	-	-	30	20.0
Migrants - same province or territory[9]	40	12.3	-	-	10	11.8	10	6.7
male	10	3.1	-	-	-	-	-	-
female	15	4.6	-	-	-	-	10	6.7
Migrants - from different province or								
territory or outside Canada	55	16.9	-	-	-	-	35	23.3
male	15	4.6	-	-	-	-	20	13.3
female	40	12.3	-	-	-	-	15	10.0

Source: Aboriginal Peoples Output Program, 1986 Census, Statistics Canada, *A Data Book on Canada's Aboriginal Population from the 1986 Census of Canada*, March, 1989, p. 108. Primary source: 1986 Census of Canada *Notes:* A dash (-) represents zero or a percentage which rounds to less than .05 percent. 1. Aboriginal origins are derived from the ethnic question which asks whether respondents are forth American Indian, Metis or Inuit. 2. All 1986 figures exclude the population estimated at about 45,000 on 136 incompletely enumerated Indian reserves and settlements throughout Canada. For an estimate of the unenumerated population and list of incompletely enumerated reserves in each affected province, see Appendix 1 and 2. 3. Non-aboriginal in these columns - refers to persons who report one or more non-aboriginal origins such as British, French, etc., in combination with one of the aboriginal origins such as North American Indian. 4. Other Multiple Aboriginal origins - refer to the sum of those persons reporting two or more aboriginal origins with or without a non-aboriginal origin. 5. Non-migrants - refer to persons who on census day were living in the same census subdivision (or community) as they did five years earlier, though they may have changed dwellings. Non-migrants are the sum of non-movers and movers. 6. Non-movers - refer to persons who lived in the same dwelling on census day as the one they occupied five years earlier. 7. Movers - refer to persons who on census day occupied a different dwelling five years earlier, but did not change census subdivisions, that is, they did not move from their community. 8. Total migrants - refer to persons who on census day were living in a different census subdivision (or community) from the one they were living in five years earlier. 9. Migrants - same province or territory - refer to persons who, on census day, were living in a different census subdivision (or community) for the one they were living in five years earlier, but had not changed their province or territory. 10. Migrants - from different province, territory or outside Canada - refer to persons who five years earlier were living either in a different province or territory, or outside Canada.

★ 807 ★

Population 5 Years and Over, by Mobility Status and Sex for Detailed Aboriginal Origins for Newfoundland, 1986 - I[1,2]

Mobility status	Total Aboriginal origins[3]		North American Indian only		North American Indian and non-Aboriginal[4]		Metis only	
	Number	Percent	Number	Percent	Number	Percent	Number	Percent
Total population								
(age 5 & over)	8,415	100.0	1,485	100.0	2,400	100.0	240	100.0
Male	4,345	51.6	720	48.5	1,280	53.3	115	47.9
Female	4,075	48.4	765	51.5	1,125	46.9	125	52.1
Total non-migrants[5]	7,395	87.9	1,350	90.9	1,935	80.6	220	91.7
Male	3,790	45.0	645	43.4	1,025	42.7	115	47.9
Female	3,600	42.8	700	47.1	910	37.9	105	43.8
Non-movers[6]	5,630	66.9	1,035	69.7	1,500	62.5	150	62.5
Male	2,925	34.8	525	35.4	800	33.3	80	33.3
Female	2,705	32.1	515	34.7	700	29.2	70	29.2
Movers[7]	1,760	20.9	310	20.9	440	18.3	70	29.2
Male	865	10.3	125	8.4	230	9.6	35	14.6
Female	900	10.7	190	12.8	210	8.8	35	14.6
Total migrants[8]	1,025	12.2	135	9.1	465	19.4	15	6.3
Male	550	6.5	70	4.7	255	10.6	-	-
Female	475	5.6	65	4.4	215	9.0	20	8.3
Migrants - same province								
or territory[9]	695	8.3	90	6.1	240	10.0	15	6.3
Male	350	4.2	45	3.0	120	5.0	-	-
Female	345	4.1	40	2.7	120	5.0	15	6.3
Migrants - from different								
province or territory								
or outside Canada	325	3.9	45	3.0	220	9.2	-	-
Male	195	2.3	25	1.7	130	5.4	-	-
Female	135	1.6	25	1.7	90	3.8	-	-

Source: Aboriginal Peoples Output Program, 1986 Census, Statistics Canada, *A Data Book on Canada's Aboriginal Population from the 1986 Census of Canada*, March, 1989, p. 36. Primary source: 1986 Census of Canada *Notes:* A dash (-) represents zero or a percentage which rounds to less than .05 percent. 1. Aboriginal origins are derived from the ethnic question which asks whether respondents are forth American Indian, Metis or Inuit. 2. All 1986 figures exclude the population estimated at about 45,000 on 136 incompletely enumerated Indian reserves and settlements throughout Canada. 3. Total Aboriginal Origins - are the sum of persons who reported: (a) a single aboriginal (e.g., North American Indian, Metis or Inuit) and, (b) multiple aboriginal origins, that is those who reported: - at least one aboriginal origin with any other non-aboriginal (e.g., Metis and French), or - two or more aboriginal origins only. 4. Non-aboriginal in these columns - refers to persons who report one or more non-aboriginal origins such as British, French, etc., in combination with one of the aboriginal origins such as North American Indian. 5. Non-migrants - refers to persons who on census day were living in the same census subdivision (or community) as they did five years earlier, though they may have changed dwellings. Non-migrants are the sum of non- movers and movers. 6. Non-movers - refers to persons who lived in the same dwelling on census day as the one they occupied five years earlier. 7. Movers - refers to persons who on census day occupied a different dwelling five years earlier, but did not change census subdivisions, that is, they did not move from their community. 8. Total migrants - refers to persons who on census day were living in a different census subdivision (or community) from the one they were living in five years earlier. 9. Migrants - same province or territory - refers to persons who, on census day, were living in a different census subdivision (or community) for the one they were living in five years earlier, but had not changed their province or territory. 10. Migrants - from different province, territory or outside Canada - refers to persons who five years earlier were living either in a different province or territory, or outside Canada.

★ 808 ★

Population 5 Years and Over, by Mobility Status and Sex for Detailed Aboriginal Origins for Newfoundland, 1986 - II[1,2]

Mobility status	Metis and non-Aboriginal[3]		Inuit only		Inuit and non-Aboriginal[3]		Other multiple Aboriginal origins[4]	
	Number	Percent	Number	Percent	Number	Percent	Number	Percent
Total population								
(age 5 & over)	640	100.0	1,600	100.0	1,480	100.0	570	100.0
Male	355	55.5	815	50.9	735	49.7	325	57.0
Female	285	44.5	780	48.8	745	50.3	245	43.0
Total non-migrants[5]	550	85.9	1,515	94.7	1,315	88.9	510	89.5
Male	315	49.2	765	47.8	640	43.2	285	50.0
Female	235	36.7	755	47.2	670	45.3	220	38.6
Non-movers[6]	420	65.6	1,185	74.1	1,015	68.6	315	55.3
Male	230	35.9	600	37.5	505	34.1	180	31.6
Female	190	29.7	585	36.6	515	34.8	135	23.7
Movers[7]	130	20.3	325	20.3	295	19.9	185	32.5
Male	80	12.5	160	10.0	140	9.5	95	16.7
Female	50	7.8	170	10.6	155	10.5	80	14.0
Total migrants[8]	90	14.1	85	5.3	170	11.5	55	9.6
Male	40	6.3	55	3.4	90	6.1	35	6.1
Female	50	7.8	30	1.9	80	5.4	15	2.6
Migrants - same province or territory[9]	70	10.9	75	4.7	155	10.5	40	7.0
Male	30	4.7	50	3.1	85	5.7	20	3.5
Female	40	6.3	25	1.6	65	4.4	20	3.5
Migrants - from different province or territory or outside Canada	20	3.1	-	-	15	1.0	-	-
Male	15	2.3	-	-	-	-	-	-
Female	-	-	-	-	-	-	-	-

Source: Aboriginal Peoples Output Program, 1986 Census, Statistics Canada, *A Data Book on Canada's Aboriginal Population from the 1986 Census of Canada*, March, 1989, p. 36. Primary source: 1986 Census of Canada *Notes:* A dash (-) represents zero or a percentage which rounds to less than .05 percent. 1. Aboriginal origins are derived from the ethnic question which asks whether respondents are forth American Indian, Metis or Inuit. 2. All 1986 figures exclude the population estimated at about 45,000 on 136 incompletely enumerated Indian reserves and settlements throughout Canada. 3. Non-aboriginal in these columns - refers to persons who report one or more non-aboriginal origins such as British, French, etc., in combination with one of the aboriginal origins such as North American Indian. 4. Other Multiple Aboriginal origins - refers to the sum of those persons reporting two or more aboriginal origins with or without a non- aboriginal origin. 5. Non-migrants - refers to persons who on census day were living in the same census subdivision (or community) as they did five years earlier, though they may have changed dwellings. Non-migrants are the sum of non- movers and movers. 6. Non-movers - refers to persons who lived in the same dwelling on census day as the one they occupied five years earlier. 7. Movers - refers to persons who on census day occupied a different dwelling five years earlier, but did not change census subdivisions, that is, they did not move from their community. 8. Total migrants - refers to persons who on census day were living in a different census subdivision (or community) from the one they were living in five years earlier. 9. Migrants - same province or territory - refers to persons who, on census day, were living in a different census subdivision (or community) from the one they were living in five years earlier, but had not changed their province or territory. 10. Migrants - from different province, territory or outside Canada - refers to persons who five years earlier were living either in a different province or territory, or outside Canada.

★ 809 ★

Population 5 Years and Over, by Mobility Status and Sex for Detailed Aboriginal Origins for Northwest Territories, 1986 - I[1,2]

Mobility status	Total Aboriginal origins[3]		North American Indian only		North American Indian and non-Aboriginal[4]		Metis only	
	Number	Percent	Number	Percent	Number	Percent	Number	Percent
Total population								
(age 5 & over)	26,255	100.0	6,720	100.0	710	100.0	1,960	100.0
Male	13,400	51.0	3,400	50.6	415	58.5	1,000	51.0
Female	12,850	48.9	3,320	49.4	295	41.5	960	49.0
Total non-migrants[5]	22,505	85.7	5,955	88.6	415	58.5	1,480	75.5
Male	11,590	44.1	3,090	46.0	240	33.8	760	38.8
Female	10,915	41.6	2,870	42.7	175	24.6	720	36.7
Non-movers[6]	12,680	48.3	4,205	62.6	235	33.1	820	41.8
Male	6,615	25.2	2,230	33.2	130	18.3	440	22.4
Female	6,070	23.1	1,975	29.4	105	14.8	380	19.4
Movers[7]	9,820	37.4	1,745	26.0	175	24.6	660	33.7
Male	4,970	18.9	860	12.8	105	14.8	320	16.3
Female	4,845	18.5	890	13.2	75	10.6	340	17.3
Total migrants[8]	3,750	14.3	765	11.4	300	42.3	480	24.5
Male	1,815	6.9	310	4.6	180	25.4	240	12.2
Female	1,930	7.4	450	6.7	120	16.9	240	12.2
Migrants - same province								
or territory[9]	2,720	10.4	535	8.0	115	16.2	270	13.8
Male	1,295	4.9	215	3.2	65	9.2	130	6.6
Female	1,420	5.4	330	4.9	50	7.0	140	7.1
Migrants - from different								
province or territory								
or outside Canada	1,020	3.9	230	3.4	180	25.4	205	10.5
Male	510	1.9	105	1.6	115	16.2	110	5.6
Female	510	1.9	125	1.9	65	9.2	95	4.8

Source: Aboriginal Peoples Output Program, 1986 Census, Statistics Canada, *A Data Book on Canada's Aboriginal Population from the 1986 Census of Canada,* March, 1989, p. 276. Primary source: 1986 Census of Canada *Notes:* A dash (-) represents zero or a percentage which rounds to less than .05 percent. 1. Aboriginal origins are derived from the ethnic question which asks whether respondents are forth American Indian, Metis or Inuit. 2. All 1986 figures exclude the population estimated at about 45,000 on 136 incompletely enumerated Indian reserves and settlements throughout Canada. 3. Total Aboriginal Origins - are the sum of persons who reported: (a) a single aboriginal (e.g., North American Indian, Metis or Inuit) and, (b) multiple aboriginal origins, that is those who reported: - at least one aboriginal origin with any other non-aboriginal (e.g., Metis and French), or - two or more aboriginal origins only. 4. Non-aboriginal in these columns - refers to persons who report one or more non-aboriginal origins such as British, French, etc., in combination with one of the aboriginal origins such as North American Indian. 5. Non-migrants - refers to persons who on census day were living in the same census subdivision (or community) as they did five years earlier, though they may have changed dwellings. Non-migrants are the sum of non- movers and movers. 6. Non-movers - refers to persons who lived in the same dwelling on census day as the one they occupied five years earlier. 7. Movers - refers to persons who on census day occupied a different dwelling five years earlier, but did not change census subdivisions, that is, they did not move from their community. 8. Total migrants - refers to persons who on census day were living in a different census subdivision (or community) from the one they were living in five years earlier. 9. Migrants - same province or territory - refers to persons who, on census day, were living in a different census subdivision (or community) for the one they were living in five years earlier, but had not changed their province or territory. 10. Migrants - from different province, territory or outside Canada - refers to persons who five years earlier were living either in a different province or territory, or outside Canada.

★ 810 ★

Population 5 Years and Over, by Mobility Status and Sex for Detailed Aboriginal Origins for Northwest Territories, 1986 - II[1,2]

Mobility status	Metis and non-Aboriginal[3]		Inuit only		Inuit and non-Aboriginal[3]		Other multiple Aboriginal origins[4]	
	Number	Percent	Number	Percent	Number	Percent	Number	Percent
Total population								
(age 5 & over)	650	100.0	14,805	100.0	555	100.0	860	100.0
Male	335	51.5	7,480	50.5	290	52.3	475	55.2
Female	310	47.7	7,325	49.5	260	46.8	385	44.8
Total non-migrants[5]	445	68.5	13,115	88.6	450	81.1	635	73.8
Male	220	33.8	6,685	45.2	230	41.4	365	42.4
Female	225	34.6	6,435	43.5	225	40.5	275	32.0
Non-movers[6]	225	34.6	6,625	44.7	250	45.0	320	37.2
Male	115	17.7	3,405	23.0	125	22.5	165	19.2
Female	110	16.9	3,220	21.7	125	22.5	150	17.4
Movers[7]	220	33.8	6,495	43.9	200	36.0	320	37.2
Male	110	16.9	3,280	22.2	110	19.8	190	22.1
Female	110	16.9	3,215	21.7	95	17.1	120	14.0
Total migrants[8]	205	31.5	1,690	11.4	105	18.9	215	25.0
Male	115	17.7	795	5.4	65	11.7	110	12.8
Female	90	13.8	895	6.0	40	7.2	105	12.2
Migrants - same province or territory[9]	95	14.6	1,495	10.1	75	13.5	120	14.0
Male	70	10.8	720	4.9	50	9.0	55	6.4
Female	15	2.3	775	5.2	25	4.5	55	6.4
Migrants - from different province or								
territory or outside Canada	105	16.2	185	1.2	25	4.5	90	10.5
Male	45	6.9	70	0.5	10	1.8	45	5.2
Female	65	10.0	110	0.7	-	-	35	4.1

Source: Aboriginal Peoples Output Program, 1986 Census, Statistics Canada, *A Data Book on Canada's Aboriginal Population from the 1986 Census of Canada*, March, 1989, p. 276. Primary source: 1986 Census of Canada *Notes:* A dash (-) represents zero or a percentage which rounds to less than .05 percent. 1. Aboriginal origins are derived from the ethnic question which asks whether respondents are forth American Indian, Metis or Inuit. 2. All 1986 figures exclude the population estimated at about 45,000 on 136 incompletely enumerated Indian reserves and settlements throughout Canada. 3. Non-aboriginal in these columns - refers to persons who report one or more non-aboriginal origins such as British, French, etc., in combination with one of the aboriginal origins such as North American Indian. 4. Other Multiple Aboriginal origins - refers to the sum of those persons reporting two or more aboriginal origins with or without a non- aboriginal origin. 5. Non-migrants - refers to persons who on census day were living in the same census subdivision (or community) as they did five years earlier, though they may have changed dwellings. Non-migrants are the sum of non- movers and movers. 6. Non-movers - refers to persons who lived in the same dwelling on census day as the one they occupied five years earlier. 7. Movers - refers to persons who on census day occupied a different dwelling five years earlier, but did not change census subdivisions, that is, they did not move from their community. 8. Total migrants - refers to persons who on census day were living in a different census subdivision (or community) from the one they were living in five years earlier. 9. Migrants - same province or territory - refers to persons who, on census day, were living in a different census subdivision (or community) from the one they were living in five years earlier, but had not changed their province or territory. 10. Migrants - from different province, territory or outside Canada - refers to persons who five years earlier were living either in a different province or territory, or outside Canada.

★ 811 ★

Population 5 Years and Over, by Mobility Status and Sex for Detailed Aboriginal Origins for Nova Scotia, 1986 - I[1,2]

Mobility status	Total Aboriginal origins[3]		North American Indian only		North American Indian and non-Aboriginal[4]		Metis only	
	Number	Percent	Number	Percent	Number	Percent	Number	Percent
Total population								
(age 5 & over)	12,415	100.0	4,905	100.0	6,270	100.0	235	100.0
Male	6,080	49.0	2,435	49.6	3,065	48.9	120	51.1
Female	6,335	51.0	2,465	50.3	3,205	51.1	110	46.8
Total non-migrants[5]	9,760	78.6	4,320	88.1	4,555	72.6	175	74.5
Male	4,785	38.5	2,170	44.2	2,210	35.2	90	38.3
Female	4,975	40.1	2,145	43.7	2,340	37.3	85	36.2
Non-movers[6]	6,560	52.8	3,150	64.2	2,870	45.8	110	46.8
Male	3,320	26.7	1,580	32.2	1,465	23.4	55	23.4
Female	3,240	26.1	1,575	32.1	1,405	22.4	55	23.4
Movers[7]	3,205	25.8	1,170	23.9	1,680	26.8	75	31.9
Male	1,470	11.8	590	12.0	740	11.8	35	14.9
Female	1,735	14.0	575	11.7	935	14.9	40	17.0
Total migrants[8]	2,650	21.3	585	11.9	1,720	27.4	55	23.4
Male	1,290	10.4	265	5.4	855	13.6	30	12.8
Female	1,360	11.0	320	6.5	860	13.7	25	10.6
Migrants - same province								
or territory[9]	1,235	9.9	295	6.0	845	13.5	-	-
Male	570	4.6	125	2.5	395	6.3	-	-
Female	670	5.4	170	3.5	455	7.3	-	-
Migrants - from different								
province or territory								
or outside Canada	1,415	11.4	290	5.9	870	13.9	40	17.0
Male	725	5.8	140	2.9	465	7.4	20	8.5
Female	685	5.5	150	3.1	410	6.5	20	8.5

Source: Aboriginal Peoples Output Program, 1986 Census, Statistics Canada, *A Data Book on Canada's Aboriginal Population from the 1986 Census of Canada,* March, 1989, p. 84. Primary source: 1986 Census of Canada *Notes:* A dash (-) represents zero or a percentage which rounds to less than .05 percent. 1. Aboriginal origins are derived from the ethnic question which asks whether respondents are forth American Indian, Metis or Inuit. 2. All 1986 figures exclude the population estimated at about 45,000 on 136 incompletely enumerated Indian reserves and settlements throughout Canada. 3. Total Aboriginal Origins - are the sum of persons who reported: (a) a single aboriginal (e.g., North American Indian, Metis or Inuit) and, (b) multiple aboriginal origins, that is those who reported: - at least one aboriginal origin with any other non-aboriginal (e.g., Metis and French), or - two or more aboriginal origins only. 4. Non-aboriginal in these columns - refers to persons who report one or more non-aboriginal origins such as British, French, etc., in combination with one of the aboriginal origins such as North American Indian. 5. Non-migrants - refers to persons who on census day were living in the same census subdivision (or community) as they did five years earlier, though they may have changed dwellings. Non-migrants are the sum of non- movers and movers. 6. Non-movers - refers to persons who lived in the same dwelling on census day as the one they occupied five years earlier. 7. Movers - refers to persons who on census day occupied a different dwelling five years earlier, but did not change census subdivisions, that is, they did not move from their community. 8. Total migrants - refers to persons who on census day were living in a different census subdivision (or community) from the one they were living in five years earlier. 9. Migrants - same province or territory - refers to persons who, on census day, were living in a different census subdivision (or community) for the one they were living in five years earlier, but had not changed their province or territory. 10. Migrants - from different province, territory or outside Canada - refers to persons who five years earlier were living either in a different province or territory, or outside Canada.

★ 812 ★

Population 5 Years and Over, by Mobility Status and Sex for Detailed Aboriginal Origins for Nova Scotia, 1986 - II[1,2]

Mobility status	Metis and non-Aboriginal[3]		Inuit only		Inuit and non-Aboriginal[3]		Other multiple Aboriginal origins[4]	
	Number	Percent	Number	Percent	Number	Percent	Number	Percent
Total population								
(age 5 & over)	560	100.0	110	100.0	135	100.0	200	100.0
Male	225	40.2	50	45.5	55	40.7	125	62.5
Female	335	59.8	60	54.5	80	59.3	80	40.0
Total non-migrants[5]	440	78.6	80	72.7	95	70.4	100	50.0
Male	180	32.1	30	27.3	35	25.9	65	32.5
Female	255	45.5	50	45.5	55	40.7	25	12.5
Non-movers[6]	270	48.2	70	63.6	40	29.6	40	20.0
Male	135	24.1	30	27.3	25	18.5	30	15.0
Female	130	23.2	35	31.8	20	14.8	15	7.5
Movers[7]	175	31.3	10	9.1	50	37.0	40	20.0
Male	45	8.0	-	-	-	-	35	17.5
Female	125	22.3	10	9.1	40	29.6	-	-
Total migrants[8]	120	21.4	30	27.3	45	33.3	95	47.5
Male	45	8.0	20	18.2	20	14.8	50	25.0
Female	75	13.4	15	13.6	25	18.5	40	20.0
Migrants - same province or territory[9]	30	5.4	-	-	-	-	35	17.5
Male	-	-	-	-	-	-	15	7.5
Female	25	4.5	-	-	-	-	-	-
Migrants - from different province or territory or outside Canada	85	15.2	25	22.7	45	33.3	50	25.0
Male	35	6.3	15	13.6	20	14.8	25	12.5
Female	50	8.9	10	9.1	25	18.5	15	7.5

Source: Aboriginal Peoples Output Program, 1986 Census, Statistics Canada, *A Data Book on Canada's Aboriginal Population from the 1986 Census of Canada*, March, 1989, p. 84. Primary source: 1986 Census of Canada *Notes:* A dash (-) represents zero or a percentage which rounds to less than .05 percent. 1. Aboriginal origins are derived from the ethnic question which asks whether respondents are forth American Indian, Metis or Inuit. 2. All 1986 figures exclude the population estimated at about 45,000 on 136 incompletely enumerated Indian reserves and settlements throughout Canada. 3. Non-aboriginal in these columns - refers to persons who report one or more non-aboriginal origins such as British, French, etc., in combination with one of the aboriginal origins such as North American Indian. 4. Other Multiple Aboriginal origins - refers to the sum of those persons reporting two or more aboriginal origins with or without a non- aboriginal origin. 5. Non-migrants - refers to persons who on census day were living in the same census subdivision (or community) as they did five years earlier, though they may have changed dwellings. Non-migrants are the sum of non- movers and movers. 6. Non-movers - refers to persons who lived on census day as the one they occupied five years earlier. 7. Movers - refers to persons who on census day occupied a different dwelling five years earlier, but did not change census subdivisions, that is, they did not move from their community. 8. Total migrants - refers to persons who on census day were living in a different census subdivision (or community) from the one they were living in five years earlier. 9. Migrants - same province or territory - refers to persons who, on census day, were living in a different census subdivision (or community) from the one they were living in five years earlier, but had not changed their province or territory. 10. Migrants - from different province, territory or outside Canada - refers to persons who five years earlier were living either in a different province or territory, or outside Canada.

★ 813 ★

Population 5 Years and Over, by Mobility Status and Sex for Detailed Aboriginal Origins for Ontario, 1986 - I[1,2]

Mobility status	Total Aboriginal origins[3]		North American Indian only		North American Indian and non-Aboriginal[4]		Metis only	
	Number	Percent	Number	Percent	Number	Percent	Number	Percent
Total population								
(age 5 & over)	146,850	100.0	46,080	100.0	82,655	100.0	3,385	100.0
Male	70,240	47.8	22,140	48.0	39,275	47.5	1,680	49.6
Female	76,610	52.2	23,945	52.0	43,385	52.5	1,705	50.4
Total non-migrants[5]	110,950	75.6	37,525	81.4	60,265	72.9	2,595	76.7
Male	53,480	36.4	18,155	39.4	28,715	34.7	1,290	38.1
Female	57,470	39.1	19,370	42.0	31,545	38.2	1,305	38.6
Non-movers[6]	65,630	44.7	24,670	53.5	33,460	40.5	1,570	46.4
Male	31,925	21.7	12,085	26.2	15,990	19.3	850	25.1
Female	33,700	22.9	12,580	27.3	17,465	21.1	715	21.1
Movers[7]	45,325	30.9	12,855	27.9	26,810	32.4	1,020	30.1
Male	21,555	14.7	6,070	13.2	12,725	15.4	435	12.9
Female	23,765	16.2	6,780	14.7	14,080	17.0	585	17.3
Total migrants[8]	35,895	24.4	8,555	18.6	22,390	27.1	790	23.3
Male	16,760	11.4	3,980	8.6	10,555	12.8	390	11.5
Female	19,140	13.0	4,575	9.9	11,835	14.3	400	11.8
Migrants - same province or territory[9]	28,035	19.1	6,685	14.5	17,780	21.5	510	15.1
Male	13,160	9.0	3,090	6.7	8,430	10.2	255	7.5
Female	14,870	10.1	3,590	7.8	9,355	11.3	250	7.4
Migrants - from different province or territory or outside Canada	7,865	5.4	1,875	4.1	4,610	5.6	275	8.1
Male	3,590	2.4	890	1.9	2,135	2.6	135	4.0
Female	4,270	2.9	985	2.1	2,485	3.0	145	4.3

Source: Aboriginal Peoples Output Program, 1986 Census, Statistics Canada, *A Data Book on Canada's Aboriginal Population from the 1986 Census of Canada,* March, 1989, p. 156. Primary source: 1986 Census of Canada *Notes:* A dash (-) represents zero or a percentage which rounds to less than .05 percent. 1. Aboriginal origins are derived from the ethnic question which asks whether respondents are forth American Indian, Metis or Inuit. 2. All 1986 figures exclude the population estimated at about 45,000 on 136 incompletely enumerated Indian reserves and settlements throughout Canada. 3. Total Aboriginal Origins - are the sum of persons who reported: (a) a single aboriginal (e.g., North American Indian, Metis or Inuit) and, (b) multiple aboriginal origins, that is those who reported: - at least one aboriginal origin with any other non-aboriginal (e.g., Metis and French), or - two or more aboriginal origins only. 4. Non-aboriginal in these columns - refers to persons who report one or more non-aboriginal origins such as British, French, etc., in combination with one of the aboriginal origins such as North American Indian. 5. Non-migrants - refers to persons who on census day were living in the same census subdivision (or community) as they did five years earlier, though they may have changed dwellings. Non-migrants are the sum of non- movers and movers. 6. Non-movers - refers to persons who lived in the same dwelling on census day as the one they occupied five years earlier. 7. Movers - refers to persons who on census day occupied a different dwelling five years earlier, but did not change census subdivisions, that is, they did not move from their community. 8. Total migrants - refers to persons who on census day were living in a different census subdivision (or community) from the one they were living in five years earlier. 9. Migrants - same province or territory - refers to persons who, on census day, were living in a different census subdivision (or community) for the one they were living in five years earlier, but had not changed their province or territory. 10. Migrants - from different province, territory or outside Canada - refers to persons who five years earlier were living either in a different province or territory, or outside Canada.

★ 814 ★

Population 5 Years and Over, by Mobility Status and Sex for Detailed Aboriginal Origins for Ontario, 1986 - II[1,2]

Mobility status	Metis and non-Aboriginal[3]		Inuit only		Inuit and non-Aboriginal[3]		Other multiple Aboriginal origins[4]	
	Number	Percent	Number	Percent	Number	Percent	Number	Percent
Total population								
(age 5 & over)	9,205	100.0	620	100.0	1,330	100.0	3,575	100.0
Male	4,390	47.7	315	50.8	675	50.8	1,760	49.2
Female	4,815	52.3	300	48.4	650	48.9	1,810	50.6
Total non-migrants[5]	6,670	72.5	420	67.7	930	69.9	2,550	71.3
Male	3,270	35.5	230	37.1	495	37.2	1,325	37.1
Female	3,400	36.9	190	30.6	435	32.7	1,230	34.4
Non-movers[6]	3,785	41.1	265	42.7	515	38.7	1,370	38.3
Male	1,890	20.5	130	21.0	250	18.8	735	20.6
Female	1,895	20.6	130	21.0	270	20.3	635	17.8
Movers[7]	2,880	31.3	160	25.8	420	31.6	1,185	33.1
Male	1,375	14.9	100	16.1	245	18.4	595	16.6
Female	1,500	16.3	55	8.9	170	12.8	585	16.4
Total migrants[8]	2,535	27.5	195	31.5	400	30.1	1,020	28.5
Male	1,115	12.1	85	13.7	190	14.3	440	12.3
Female	1,415	15.4	110	17.7	210	15.8	590	16.5
Migrants - same province or territory[9]	1,850	20.1	130	21.0	320	24.1	765	21.4
Male	830	9.0	65	10.5	145	10.9	340	9.5
Female	1,015	11.0	65	10.5	165	12.4	420	11.7
Migrants - from different province or territory or outside Canada	685	7.4	60	9.7	85	6.4	245	6.9
Male	290	3.2	20	3.2	40	3.0	90	2.5
Female	400	4.3	45	7.3	45	3.4	155	4.3

Source: Aboriginal Peoples Output Program, 1986 Census, Statistics Canada, *A Data Book on Canada's Aboriginal Population from the 1986 Census of Canada*, March, 1989, p. 156. Primary source: 1986 Census of Canada *Notes:* A dash (-) represents zero or a percentage which rounds to less than .05 percent. 1. Aboriginal origins are derived from the ethnic question which asks whether respondents are forth American Indian, Metis or Inuit. 2. All 1986 figures exclude the population estimated at about 45,000 on 136 incompletely enumerated Indian reserves and settlements throughout Canada. 3. Non-aboriginal in these columns - refers to persons who report one or more non-aboriginal origins such as British, French, etc., in combination with one of the aboriginal origins such as North American Indian. 4. Other Multiple Aboriginal origins - refers to the sum of those persons reporting two or more aboriginal origins with or without a non- aboriginal origin. 5. Non-migrants - refers to persons who on census day were living in the same census subdivision (or community) as they did five years earlier, though they may have changed dwellings. Non-migrants are the sum of non- movers and movers. 6. Non-movers - refers to persons who lived in the same dwelling on census day as the one they occupied five years earlier. 7. Movers - refers to persons who on census day occupied a different dwelling five years earlier, but did not change census subdivisions, that is, they did not move from their community. 8. Total migrants - refers to persons who on census day were living in a different census subdivision (or community) from the one they were living in five years earlier. 9. Migrants - same province or territory - refers to persons who, on census day, were living in a different census subdivision (or community) from the one they were living in five years earlier, but had not changed their province or territory. 10. Migrants - from different province, territory or outside Canada - refers to persons who five years earlier were living either in a different province or territory, or outside Canada.

★ 815 ★

Population 5 Years and Over, by Mobility Status and Sex for Detailed Aboriginal Origins for Prince Edward Island, 1986 - I[1,2]

Mobility status	Total Aboriginal origins[3]		North American Indian only		North American Indian and non-Aboriginal[4]		Metis only	
	Number	Percent	Number	Percent	Number	Percent	Number	Percent
Total population								
(age 5 & over)	1,075	100.0	310	100.0	610	100.0	25	100.0
Male	555	51.6	155	50.0	315	51.6	-	-
Female	515	47.9	150	48.4	290	47.5	15	60.0
Total non-migrants[5]	680	63.3	225	72.6	380	62.3	-	-
Male	360	33.5	110	35.5	195	32.0	-	-
Female	325	30.2	110	35.5	185	30.3	-	-
Non-movers[6]	415	38.6	135	43.5	225	36.9	-	-
Male	225	20.9	60	19.4	120	19.7	-	-
Female	195	18.1	75	24.2	100	16.4		
Movers[7]	265	24.7	90	29.0	160	26.2	-	-
Male	135	12.6	50	16.1	75	12.3	-	-
Female	130	12.1	40	12.9	85	13.9	-	-
Total migrants[8]	390	36.3	90	29.0	230	37.7	15	60.0
Male	200	18.6	45	14.5	120	19.7	-	-
Female	190	17.7	40	12.9	110	18.0	15	60.0
Migrants - same province								
or territory[9]	150	14.0	15	4.8	100	16.4	-	-
Male	85	7.9	15	4.8	55	9.0	-	-
Female	70	6.5	-	-	40	6.6	-	-
Migrants - from different								
province or territory								
or outside Canada	240	22.3	65	21.0	125	20.5	15	60.0
Male	105	9.8	20	6.5	60	9.8	-	-
Female	120	11.2	25	8.1	60	9.8	15	60.0

Source: Aboriginal Peoples Output Program, 1986 Census, Statistics Canada, *A Data Book on Canada's Aboriginal Population from the 1986 Census of Canada,* March, 1989, p. 60. Primary source: 1986 Census of Canada *Notes:* A dash (-) represents zero or a percentage which rounds to less than .05 percent. 1. Aboriginal origins are derived from the ethnic question which asks whether respondents are forth American Indian, Metis or Inuit. 2. All 1986 figures exclude the population estimated at about 45,000 on 136 incompletely enumerated Indian reserves and settlements throughout Canada. 3. Total Aboriginal Origins - are the sum of persons who reported: (a) a single aboriginal (e.g., North American Indian, Metis or Inuit) and, (b) multiple aboriginal origins, that is those who reported: - at least one aboriginal origin with any other non-aboriginal (e.g., Metis and French), or - two or more aboriginal origins only. 4. Non-aboriginal in these columns - refers to persons who report one or more non-aboriginal origins such as British, French, etc., in combination with one of the aboriginal origins such as North American Indian. 5. Non-migrants - refers to persons who on census day were living in the same census subdivision (or community) as they did five years earlier, though they may have changed dwellings. Non-migrants are the sum of non- movers and movers. 6. Non-movers - refers to persons who lived in the same dwelling on census day as the one they occupied five years earlier. 7. Movers - refers to persons who on census day occupied a different dwelling five years earlier, but did not change census subdivisions, that is, they did not move from their community. 8. Total migrants - refers to persons who on census day were living in a different census subdivision (or community) from the one they were living in five years earlier. 9. Migrants - same province or territory - refers to persons who, on census day, were living in a different census subdivision (or community) for the one they were living in five years earlier, but had not changed their province or territory. 10. Migrants - from different province, territory or outside Canada - refers to persons who five years earlier were living either in a different province or territory, or outside Canada.

★ 816 ★

Population 5 Years and Over, by Mobility Status and Sex for Detailed Aboriginal Origins for Prince Edward Island, 1986 - II[1,2]

Mobility status	Metis and non-Aboriginal[3]		Inuit only		Inuit and non-Aboriginal[3]		Other multiple Aboriginal origins[4]	
	Number	Percent	Number	Percent	Number	Percent	Number	Percent
Total population (age 5 & over)	90	100.0	-	-	20	100.0	20	100.0
Male	55	61.1	-	-	15	75.0	-	-
Female	35	38.9	-	-	-	-	15	75.0
Total non-migrants[5]	55	61.1	-	-	-	-	15	75.0
Male	35	38.9	-	-	-	-	-	-
Female	15	16.7	-	-	-	-	10	50.0
Non-movers[6]	35	38.9	-	-	-	-	15	75.0
Male	25	27.8	-	-	-	-	-	-
Female	-	-	-	-	-	-	10	50.0
Movers[7]	20	22.2	-	-	-	-	-	-
Male	10	11.1	-	-	-	-	-	-
Female	-	-	-	-	-	-	-	-
Total migrants[8]	30	33.3	-	-	20	100.0	-	-
Male	15	16.7	-	-	15	75.0	-	-
Female	15	16.7	-	-	-	-	-	-
Migrants - same province or territory[9]	-	-	-	-	15	75.0	-	-
Male	-	-	-	-	-	-	-	-
Female	-	-	-	-	-	-	-	-
Migrants - from different province or territory or outside Canada	25	27.8	-	-	-	-	-	-
Male	10	11.1	-	-	-	-	-	-
Female	15	16.7	-	-	-	-	-	-

Source: Aboriginal Peoples Output Program, 1986 Census, Statistics Canada, *A Data Book on Canada's Aboriginal Population from the 1986 Census of Canada*, March, 1989, p. 60. Primary source: 1986 Census of Canada *Notes:* A dash (-) represents zero or a percentage which rounds to less than .05 percent. 1. Aboriginal origins are derived from the ethnic question which asks whether respondents are forth American Indian, Metis or Inuit. 2. All 1986 figures exclude the population estimated at about 45,000 on 136 incompletely enumerated Indian reserves and settlements throughout Canada. 3. Non-aboriginal in these columns - refers to persons who report one or more non-aboriginal origins such as British, French, etc., in combination with one of the aboriginal origins such as North American Indian. 4. Other Multiple Aboriginal origins - refers to the sum of those persons reporting two or more aboriginal origins with or without a non- aboriginal origin. 5. Non-migrants - refers to persons who on census day were living in the same census subdivision (or community) as they did five years earlier, though they may have changed dwellings. Non-migrants are the sum of non- movers and movers. 6. Non-movers - refers to persons who lived in the same dwelling on census day as the one they occupied five years earlier. 7. Movers - refers to persons who on census day occupied a different dwelling five years earlier, but did not change census subdivisions, that is, they did not move from their community. 8. Total migrants - refers to persons who on census day were living in a different census subdivision (or community) from the one they were living in five years earlier. 9. Migrants - same province or territory - refers to persons who, on census day, were living in a different census subdivision (or community) from the one they were living in five years earlier, but had not changed their province or territory. 10. Migrants - from different province, territory or outside Canada - refers to persons who five years earlier were living either in a different province or territory, or outside Canada.

★ 817 ★

Population 5 Years and Over, by Mobility Status and Sex for Detailed Aboriginal Origins for Quebec, 1986 - I[1,2]

Mobility status	Total Aboriginal origins[3]		North American Indian only		North American Indian and non-Aboriginal[4]		Metis only	
	Number	Percent	Number	Percent	Number	Percent	Number	Percent
Total population								
(age 5 & over)	72,235	100.0	33,330	100.0	22,475	100.0	5,150	100.0
Male	34,740	48.1	16,420	49.3	10,180	45.3	2,685	52.1
Female	37,495	51.9	16,910	50.7	12,290	54.7	2,465	47.9
Total non-migrants[5]	57,850	80.1	28,490	85.5	16,050	71.4	4,000	77.7
Male	28,390	39.3	14,385	43.2	7,360	32.7	2,055	39.9
Female	29,460	40.8	14,105	42.3	8,690	38.7	1,940	37.7
Non-movers[6]	37,145	51.4	19,670	59.0	9,150	40.7	2,390	46.4
Male	18,645	25.8	10,050	30.2	4,280	19.0	1,280	24.9
Female	18,495	25.6	9,620	28.9	4,870	21.7	1,110	21.6
Movers[7]	20,710	28.7	8,820	26.5	6,900	30.7	1,610	31.3
Male	9,745	13.5	4,335	13.0	3,075	13.7	780	15.1
Female	10,965	15.2	4,485	13.5	3,825	17.0	830	16.1
Total migrants[8]	14,390	19.9	4,840	14.5	6,430	28.6	1,155	22.4
Male	6,350	8.8	2,030	6.1	2,825	12.6	630	12.2
Female	8,040	11.1	2,810	8.4	3,605	16.0	525	10.2
Migrants - same province								
or territory[9]	12,410	17.2	4,305	12.9	5,540	24.6	1,015	19.7
Male	5,445	7.5	1,800	5.4	2,440	10.9	540	10.5
Female	6,965	9.6	2,515	7.5	3,105	13.8	475	9.2
Migrants - from different								
province or territory								
or outside Canada	1,980	2.7	530	1.6	890	4.0	135	2.6
Male	905	1.3	235	0.7	380	1.7	80	1.6
Female	1,075	1.5	300	0.9	505	2.2	50	1.0

Source: Aboriginal Peoples Output Program, 1986 Census, Statistics Canada, *A Data Book on Canada's Aboriginal Population from the 1986 Census of Canada,* March, 1989, p. 132. Primary source: 1986 Census of Canada *Notes:* A dash (-) represents zero or a percentage which rounds to less than .05 percent. 1. Aboriginal origins are derived from the ethnic question which asks whether respondents are forth American Indian, Metis or Inuit. 2. All 1986 figures exclude the population estimated at about 45,000 on 136 incompletely enumerated Indian reserves and settlements throughout Canada. 3. Total Aboriginal Origins - are the sum of persons who reported: (a) a single aboriginal (e.g., North American Indian, Metis or Inuit) and, (b) multiple aboriginal origins, that is those who reported: - at least one aboriginal origin with any other non-aboriginal (e.g., Metis and French), or - two or more aboriginal origins only. 4. Non-aboriginal in these columns - refers to persons who report one or more non-aboriginal origins such as British, French, etc., in combination with one of the aboriginal origins such as North American Indian. 5. Non-migrants - refers to persons who on census day were living in the same census subdivision (or community) as they did five years earlier, though they may have changed dwellings. Non-migrants are the sum of non- movers and movers. 6. Non-movers - refers to persons who lived in the same dwelling on census day as the one they occupied five years earlier. 7. Movers - refers to persons who on census day occupied a different dwelling five years earlier, but did not change census subdivisions, that is, they did not move from their community. 8. Total migrants - refers to persons who on census day were living in a different census subdivision (or community) from the one they were living in five years earlier. 9. Migrants - same province or territory - refers to persons who, on census day, were living in a different census subdivision (or community) for the one they were living in five years earlier, but had not changed their province or territory. 10. Migrants - from different province, territory or outside Canada - refers to persons who five years earlier were living either in a different province or territory, or outside Canada.

★ 818 ★

Population 5 Years and Over, by Mobility Status and Sex for Detailed Aboriginal Origins for Quebec, 1986 - II[1,2]

Mobility status	Metis and non-Aboriginal[3]		Inuit only		Inuit and non-Aboriginal[3]		Other multiple Aboriginal origins[4]	
	Number	Percent	Number	Percent	Number	Percent	Number	Percent
Total population								
(age 5 & over)	4,060	100.0	5,510	100.0	505	100.0	1,200	100.0
Male	1,830	45.1	2,775	50.4	245	48.5	605	50.4
Female	2,230	54.9	2,730	49.5	260	51.5	600	50.0
Total non-migrants[5]	3,160	77.8	4,975	90.3	385	76.2	795	66.3
Male	1,445	35.6	2,535	46.0	195	38.6	410	34.2
Female	1,715	42.2	2,440	44.3	185	36.6	385	32.1
Non-movers[6]	1,995	49.1	3,180	57.7	210	41.6	545	45.4
Male	970	23.9	1,645	29.9	105	20.8	315	26.3
Female	1,030	25.4	1,540	27.9	105	20.8	240	20.0
Movers[7]	1,160	28.6	1,790	32.5	175	34.7	250	20.8
Male	480	11.8	885	16.1	95	18.8	95	7.9
Female	680	16.7	905	16.4	85	16.8	150	12.5
Total migrants[8]	905	22.3	535	9.7	125	24.8	405	33.8
Male	385	9.5	245	4.4	50	9.9	190	15.8
Female	520	12.8	290	5.3	70	13.9	215	17.9
Migrants - same province or territory[9]	715	17.6	425	7.7	85	16.8	325	27.1
Male	290	7.1	190	3.4	35	6.9	155	12.9
Female	430	10.6	230	4.2	50	9.9	165	13.8
Migrants - from different province or territory or outside Canada	190	4.7	110	2.0	45	8.9	75	6.3
Male	90	2.2	50	0.9	20	4.0	35	2.9
Female	85	2.1	55	1.0	25	5.0	40	3.3

Source: Aboriginal Peoples Output Program, 1986 Census, Statistics Canada, *A Data Book on Canada's Aboriginal Population from the 1986 Census of Canada*, March, 1989, p. 132. Primary source: 1986 Census of Canada *Notes:* A dash (-) represents zero or a percentage which rounds to less than .05 percent. 1. Aboriginal origins are derived from the ethnic question which asks whether respondents are forth American Indian, Metis or Inuit. 2. All 1986 figures exclude the population estimated at about 45,000 on 136 incompletely enumerated Indian reserves and settlements throughout Canada. 3. Non-aboriginal in these columns - refers to persons who report one or more non-aboriginal origins such as British, French, etc., in combination with one of the aboriginal origins such as North American Indian. 4. Other Multiple Aboriginal origins - refers to the sum of those persons reporting two or more aboriginal origins with or without a non- aboriginal origin. 5. Non-migrants - refers to persons who on census day were living in the same census subdivision (or community) as they did five years earlier, though they may have changed dwellings. Non-migrants are the sum of non- movers and movers. 6. Non-movers - refers to persons who lived in the same dwelling on census day as the one they occupied five years earlier. 7. Movers - refers to persons who on census day occupied a different dwelling five years earlier, but did not change census subdivisions, that is, they did not move from their community. 8. Total migrants - refers to persons who on census day were living in a different census subdivision (or community) from the one they were living in five years earlier. 9. Migrants - same province or territory - refers to persons who, on census day, were living in a different census subdivision (or community) from the one they were living in five years earlier, but had not changed their province or territory. 10. Migrants - from different province, territory or outside Canada - refers to persons who five years earlier were living either in a different province or territory, or outside Canada.

★ 819 ★

Population 5 Years and Over, by Mobility Status and Sex for Detailed Aboriginal Origins for Saskatchewan, 1986 - I[1,2]

Mobility status	Total Aboriginal origins[3]		North American Indian only		North American Indian and non-Aboriginal[4]		Metis only	
	Number	Percent	Number	Percent	Number	Percent	Number	Percent
Total population								
(age 5 & over)	65,615	100.0	36,600	100.0	7,045	100.0	10,605	100.0
Male	31,950	48.7	17,930	49.0	3,470	49.3	5,135	48.4
Female	33,670	51.3	18,670	51.0	3,580	50.8	5,475	51.6
Total non-migrants[5]	50,730	77.3	29,065	79.4	4,575	64.9	8,465	79.8
Male	25,235	38.5	14,695	40.2	2,215	31.4	4,160	39.2
Female	25,495	38.9	14,370	39.3	2,360	33.5	4,305	40.6
Non-movers[6]	28,295	43.1	16,035	43.8	2,475	35.1	5,240	49.4
Male	14,115	21.5	8,135	22.2	1,215	17.2	2,585	24.4
Female	14,180	21.6	7,905	21.6	1,260	17.9	2,655	25.0
Movers[7]	22,430	34.2	13,030	35.6	2,105	29.9	3,225	30.4
Male	11,120	16.9	6,560	17.9	1,005	14.3	1,575	14.9
Female	11,315	17.2	6,465	17.7	1,100	15.6	1,645	15.5
Total migrants[8]	14,890	22.7	7,535	20.6	2,470	35.1	2,145	20.2
Male	6,710	10.2	3,235	8.8	1,250	17.7	975	9.2
Female	8,180	12.5	4,300	11.7	1,215	17.2	1,170	11.0
Migrants - same province								
or territory[9]	10,905	16.6	6,055	16.5	1,410	20.0	1,555	14.7
Male	4,745	7.2	2,570	7.0	660	9.4	670	6.3
Female	6,165	9.4	3,485	9.5	745	10.6	885	8.3
Migrants - from different								
province or territory or								
outside Canada	3,985	6.1	1,475	4.0	1,060	15.0	585	5.5
Male	1,970	3.0	660	1.8	585	8.3	295	2.8
Female	2,010	3.1	820	2.2	470	6.7	285	2.7

Source: Aboriginal Peoples Output Program, 1986 Census, Statistics Canada, *A Data Book on Canada's Aboriginal Population from the 1986 Census of Canada,* March, 1989, p. 204. Primary source: 1986 Census of Canada *Notes:* A dash (-) represents zero or a percentage which rounds to less than .05 percent. 1. Aboriginal origins are derived from the ethnic question which asks whether respondents are forth American Indian, Metis or Inuit. 2. All 1986 figures exclude the population estimated at about 45,000 on 136 incompletely enumerated Indian reserves and settlements throughout Canada. 3. Total Aboriginal Origins - are the sum of persons who reported: (a) a single aboriginal (e.g., North American Indian, Metis or Inuit) and, (b) multiple aboriginal origins, that is those who reported: - at least one aboriginal origin with any other non-aboriginal (e.g., Metis and French), or - two or more aboriginal origins only. 4. Non-aboriginal in these columns - refers to persons who report one or more non-aboriginal origins such as British, French, etc., in combination with one of the aboriginal origins such as North American Indian. 5. Non-migrants - refers to persons who on census day were living in the same census subdivision (or community) as they did five years earlier, though they may have changed dwellings. Non-migrants are the sum of non- movers and movers. 6. Non-movers - refers to persons who lived in the same dwelling on census day as the one they occupied five years earlier. 7. Movers - refers to persons who on census day occupied a different dwelling five years earlier, but did not change census subdivisions, that is, they did not move from their community. 8. Total migrants - refers to persons who on census day were living in a different census subdivision (or community) from the one they were living in five years earlier. 9. Migrants - same province or territory - refers to persons who, on census day, were living in a different census subdivision (or community) for the one they were living in five years earlier, but had not changed their province or territory. 10. Migrants - from different province, territory or outside Canada - refers to persons who five years earlier were living either in a different province or territory, or outside Canada.

★ 820 ★

Population 5 Years and Over, by Mobility Status and Sex for Detailed Aboriginal Origins for Saskatchewan, 1986 - II[1,2]

Mobility status	Metis and non-Aboriginal[3]		Inuit only		Inuit and non-Aboriginal[3]		Other multiple Aboriginal origins[4]	
	Number	Percent	Number	Percent	Number	Percent	Number	Percent
Total population								
(age 5 & over)	8,470	100.0	40	100.0	55	100.0	2,795	100.0
Male	3,980	47.0	25	62.5	45	81.8	1,365	48.8
Female	4,495	53.1	15	37.5	15	27.3	1,425	51.0
Total non-migrants[5]	6,580	77.7	30	75.0	40	72.7	1,980	70.8
Male	3,140	37.1	15	37.5	35	63.6	970	34.7
Female	3,440	40.6	10	25.0	-	-	1,005	36.0
Non-movers[6]	3,585	42.3	15	37.5	30	54.5	920	32.9
Male	1,725	20.4	-	-	20	36.4	435	15.6
Female	1,865	22.0	10	25.0	-	-	480	17.2
Movers[7]	2,995	35.4	10	25.0	10	18.2	1,065	38.1
Male	1,415	16.7	10	25.0	15	27.3	535	19.1
Female	1,575	18.6	-	-	-	-	520	18.6
Total migrants[8]	1,890	22.3	10	25.0	20	36.4	820	29.3
Male	840	9.9	-	-	-	-	395	14.1
Female	1,050	12.4	-	-	-	-	425	15.2
Migrants - same province or territory[9]	1,340	15.8	-	-	-	-	535	19.1
Male	560	6.6	-	-	-	-	265	9.5
Female	780	9.2	-	-	-	-	270	9.7
Migrants - from different province or territory or outside Canada	550	6.5	-	-	20	36.4	290	10.4
Male	280	3.3	-	-	-	-	135	4.8
Female	275	3.2	-	-	-	-	150	5.4

Source: Aboriginal Peoples Output Program, 1986 Census, Statistics Canada, *A Data Book on Canada's Aboriginal Population from the 1986 Census of Canada*, March, 1989, p. 204. Primary source: 1986 Census of Canada *Notes:* A dash (-) represents zero or a percentage which rounds to less than .05 percent. 1. Aboriginal origins are derived from the ethnic question which asks whether respondents are forth American Indian, Metis or Inuit. 2. All 1986 figures exclude the population estimated at about 45,000 on 136 incompletely enumerated Indian reserves and settlements throughout Canada. 3. Non-aboriginal in these columns - refers to persons who report one or more non-aboriginal origins such as British, French, etc., in combination with one of the aboriginal origins such as North American Indian. 4. Other Multiple Aboriginal origins - refers to the sum of those persons reporting two or more aboriginal origins with or without a non- aboriginal origin. 5. Non-migrants - refers to persons who on census day were living in the same census subdivision (or community) as they did five years earlier, though they may have changed dwellings. Non-migrants are the sum of non- movers and movers. 6. Non-movers - refers to persons who lived in the same dwelling on census day as the one they occupied five years earlier. 7. Movers - refers to persons who on census day occupied a different dwelling five years earlier, but did not change census subdivisions, that is, they did not move from their community. 8. Total migrants - refers to persons who on census day were living in a different census subdivision (or community) from the one they were living in five years earlier. 9. Migrants - same province or territory - refers to persons who, on census day, were living in a different census subdivision (or community) from the one they were living in five years earlier, but had not changed their province or territory. 10. Migrants - from different province, territory or outside Canada - refers to persons who five years earlier were living either in a different province or territory, or outside Canada.

★ 821 ★

Population 5 Years and Over, by Mobility Status and Sex for Detailed Aboriginal Origins for Yukon Territory, 1986 - I[1,2]

Mobility status	Total Aboriginal origins[3]		North American Indian only		North American Indian and non-Aboriginal[4]		Metis only	
	Number	Percent	Number	Percent	Number	Percent	Number	Percent
Total population								
(age 5 & over)	4,385	100.0	2,840	100.0	1,295	100.0	65	100.0
Male	2,135	48.7	1,385	48.8	615	47.5	15	23.1
Female	2,250	51.3	1,455	51.2	680	52.5	45	69.2
Total non-migrants[5]	3,165	72.2	2,230	78.5	820	63.3	40	61.5
Male	1,590	36.3	1,130	39.8	395	30.5	15	23.1
Female	1,575	35.9	1,100	38.7	420	32.4	30	46.2
Non-movers[6]	1,710	39.0	1,205	42.4	445	34.4	25	38.5
Male	890	20.3	620	21.8	240	18.5	15	23.1
Female	820	18.7	590	20.8	210	16.2	15	23.1
Movers[7]	1,460	33.3	1,015	35.7	375	29.0	15	23.1
Male	700	16.0	510	18.0	160	12.4	-	-
Female	760	17.3	510	18.0	215	16.6	10	15.4
Total migrants[8]	1,215	27.7	610	21.5	475	36.7	20	30.8
Male	545	12.4	255	9.0	220	17.0	-	-
Female	670	15.3	360	12.7	260	20.1	20	30.8
Migrants - same province								
or territory[9]	730	16.6	410	14.4	300	23.2	-	-
Male	350	8.0	190	6.7	150	11.6	-	-
Female	380	8.7	220	7.7	155	12.0	-	-
Migrants - from different								
province or territory or								
outside Canada	485	11.1	195	6.9	170	13.1	20	30.8
Male	190	4.3	60	2.1	65	5.0	-	-
Female	290	6.6	135	4.8	100	7.7	15	23.1

Source: Aboriginal Peoples Output Program, 1986 Census, Statistics Canada, *A Data Book on Canada's Aboriginal Population from the 1986 Census of Canada,* March, 1989, p. 300. Primary source: 1986 Census of Canada *Notes:* A dash (-) represents zero or a percentage which rounds to less than .05 percent. 1. Aboriginal origins are derived from the ethnic question which asks whether respondents are forth American Indian, Metis or Inuit. 2. All 1986 figures exclude the population estimated at about 45,000 on 136 incompletely enumerated Indian reserves and settlements throughout Canada. 3. Total Aboriginal Origins - are the sum of persons who reported: (a) a single aboriginal (e.g., North American Indian, Metis or Inuit) and, (b) multiple aboriginal origins, that is those who reported: - at least one aboriginal origin with any other non-aboriginal (e.g., Metis and French), or - two or more aboriginal origins only. 4. Non-aboriginal in these columns - refers to persons who report one or more non-aboriginal origins such as British, French, etc., in combination with one of the aboriginal origins such as North American Indian. 5. Non-migrants - refers to persons who on census day were living in the same census subdivision (or community) as they did five years earlier, though they may have changed dwellings. Non-migrants are the sum of non- movers and movers. 6. Non-movers - refers to persons who lived in the same dwelling on census day as the one they occupied five years earlier. 7. Movers - refers to persons who on census day occupied a different dwelling five years earlier, but did not change census subdivisions, that is, they did not move from their community. 8. Total migrants - refers to persons who on census day were living in a different census subdivision (or community) from the one they were living in five years earlier. 9. Migrants - same province or territory - refers to persons who, on census day, were living in a different census subdivision (or community) for the one they were living in five years earlier, but had not changed their province or territory. 10. Migrants - from different province, territory or outside Canada - refers to persons who five years earlier were living either in a different province or territory, or outside Canada.

★ 822 ★

Population 5 Years and Over, by Mobility Status and Sex for Detailed Aboriginal Origins for Yukon Territory, 1986 - II[1,2]

Mobility status	Metis and non-Aboriginal[3]		Inuit only		Inuit and non-Aboriginal[3]		Other multiple Aboriginal origins[4]	
	Number	Percent	Number	Percent	Number	Percent	Number	Percent
Total population								
(age 5 & over)	80	100.0	35	100.0	20	100.0	50	100.0
Male	55	68.8	10	28.6	15	75.0	30	60.0
Female	25	31.3	20	57.1	-	-	20	40.0
Total non-migrants[5]	30	37.5	-	-	-	-	30	60.0
Male	25	31.3	-	-	-	-	15	30.0
Female	-	-	-	-	-	-	20	40.0
Non-movers[6]	20	25.0	-	-	-	-	-	-
Male	25	18.8	-	-	-	-	-	-
Female	-	-	-	-	-	-	-	-
Movers[7]	15	18.8	-	-	-	-	30	60.0
Male	-	-	-	-	-	-	15	30.0
Female	-	-	-	-	-	-	15	30.0
Total migrants[8]	50	62.5	25	71.4	15	75.0	10	20.0
Male	30	37.5	10	28.6	15	75.0	-	-
Female	20	25.0	20	57.1	-	-	-	-
Migrants - same province or territory[9]	10	12.5	-	-	-	-	-	-
Male	10	12.5	-	-	-	-	-	-
Female	-	-	-	-	-	-	-	-
Migrants - from different province or territory or outside Canada	40	50.0	25	71.4	-	-	-	-
Male	20	25.0	-	-	-	-	-	-
Female	20	25.0	10	28.6	-	-	-	-

Source: Aboriginal Peoples Output Program, 1986 Census, Statistics Canada, *A Data Book on Canada's Aboriginal Population from the 1986 Census of Canada*, March, 1989, p. 300. Primary source: 1986 Census of Canada *Notes:* A dash (-) represents zero or a percentage which rounds to less than .05 percent. 1. Aboriginal origins are derived from the ethnic question which asks whether respondents are forth American Indian, Metis or Inuit. 2. All 1986 figures exclude the population estimated at about 45,000 on 136 incompletely enumerated Indian reserves and settlements throughout Canada. 3. Non-aboriginal in these columns - refers to persons who report one or more non-aboriginal origins such as British, French, etc., in combination with one of the aboriginal origins such as North American Indian. 4. Other Multiple Aboriginal origins - refers to the sum of those persons reporting two or more aboriginal origins with or without a non- aboriginal origin. 5. Non-migrants - refers to persons who on census day were living in the same census subdivision (or community) as they did five years earlier, though they may have changed dwellings. Non-migrants are the sum of non- movers and movers. 6. Non-movers - refers to persons who lived in the same dwelling on census day as the one they occupied five years earlier. 7. Movers - refers to persons who on census day occupied a different dwelling five years earlier, but did not change census subdivisions, that is, they did not move from their community. 8. Total migrants - refers to persons who on census day were living in a different census subdivision (or community) from the one they were living in five years earlier. 9. Migrants - same province or territory - refers to persons who, on census day, were living in a different census subdivision (or community) from the one they were living in five years earlier, but had not changed their province or territory. 10. Migrants - from different province, territory or outside Canada - refers to persons who five years earlier were living either in a different province or territory, or outside Canada.

The Family

★ 823 ★

Population 15 Years and Over, by Marital Status and Sex for Detailed Aboriginal Origins for Canada, 1986 - I[1,2]

Marital status	Total Aboriginal origins[3]		North American Indian only		North American Indian and non-Aboriginal[4]		Metis only	
	Number	Percent	Number	Percent	Number	Percent	Number	Percent
Total	451,950	100.0	184,850	100.0	150,285	100.0	39,980	100.0
Male	217,135	48.0	89,050	48.2	71,045	47.3	19,690	49.2
Female	234,820	52.0	95,800	51.8	79,235	52.7	20,285	50.7
Single	168,995	37.4	71,590	38.7	52,040	34.6	16,015	40.1
Male	90,290	20.0	38,520	20.8	26,980	18.0	8,835	22.1
Female	78,705	17.4	33,070	17.9	25,065	16.7	7,180	18.0
Married	229,800	50.8	91,070	49.3	81,225	54.0	18,365	45.9
Male	109,345	24.2	43,010	23.3	38,855	25.9	8,920	22.3
Female	120,455	26.7	48,065	26.0	42,370	28.2	9,445	23.6
Separated	18,995	4.2	7,695	4.2	6,465	4.3	1,995	5.0
Male	7,080	1.6	2,990	1.6	2,240	1.5	755	1.9
Female	11,910	2.6	4,705	2.5	4,225	2.8	1,240	3.1
Divorced	17,955	4.0	5,625	3.0	7,460	5.0	1,870	4.7
Male	6,540	1.4	2,135	1.2	2,515	1.7	800	2.0
Female	11,410	2.5	3,490	1.9	4,945	3.3	1,070	2.7
Widowed	16,205	3.6	8,870	4.8	3,095	2.1	1,740	4.4
Male	3,870	0.9	2,395	1.3	455	0.3	380	1.0
Female	12,335	2.7	6,475	3.5	2,635	1.8	1,355	3.4

Source: Aboriginal Peoples Output Program, 1986 Census, Statistics Canada, *A Data Book on Canada's Aboriginal Population from the 1986 Census of Canada*, March, 1989, p. 4. Primary source: 1986 Census of Canada *Notes:* A dash (-) represents zero or a percentage which rounds to less than .05 percent. 1. Aboriginal origins are derived from the ethnic origin question which asks whether respondents are North American Indian, Metis or Inuit. 2. All 1986 figures exclude the population estimated at about 45,000 on 136 incompletely enumerated Indian reserves and settlements throughout Canada. 3. Total aboriginal origins - are the sum of persons who reported: (a) a single aboriginal (e.g., North American Indian, Metis or Inuit), and, (b) multiple aboriginal origins, that is those who reported: - at least one aboriginal origin with any other non-aboriginal (e.g., Metis and French), or - two or more aboriginal origins only. 4. Non-aboriginal in these columns - refers to persons who report one or more non-aboriginal origins such as British, French, etc., in combination with one of the aboriginal origins such as North American Indian.

★ 824 ★

Population 15 Years and Over, by Marital Status and Sex for Detailed Aboriginal Origins for Canada, 1986 - II[1,2]

Marital status	Metis and non-Aboriginal[3]		Inuit only		Inuit and non-Aborigina[3]		Other multiple Aboriginal origins[4]	
	Number	Percent	Number	Percent	Number	Percent	Number	Percent
Total	42,435	100.0	16,500	100.0	3,660	100.0	14,240	100.0
male	19,865	46.8	8,255	50.0	1,880	51.4	7,345	51.6
female	22,575	53.2	8,240	49.9	1,785	48.8	6,900	48.5
Single	15,235	35.9	6,940	42.1	1,490	40.7	5,695	40.0
male	8,075	19.0	3,845	23.3	825	22.5	3,220	22.6
female	7,160	16.9	3,095	18.8	670	18.3	2,470	17.3
Married	22,210	52.3	8,300	50.3	1,835	50.1	6,805	47.8
male	10,225	24.1	3,940	23.9	915	25.0	3,485	24.5
female	11,985	28.2	4,355	26.4	920	25.1	3,320	23.3
Separated	1,650	3.9	305	1.8	120	3.3	770	5.4
male	615	1.4	145	0.9	65	1.8	270	1.9
female	1,030	2.4	155	0.9	50	1.4	505	3.5
Divorced	2,000	4.7	190	1.2	130	3.6	675	4.7
male	655	1.5	70	0.4	70	1.9	290	2.0
female	1,345	3.2	125	0.8	55	1.5	380	2.7
Widowed	1,345	3.2	770	4.7	90	2.5	305	2.1
male	295	0.7	260	1.6	-	-	75	0.5
female	1,050	2.5	515	3.1	80	2.2	225	1.6

Source: Aboriginal Peoples Output Program, 1986 Census, Statistics Canada, *A Data Book on Canada's Aboriginal Population from the 1986 Census of Canada*, March, 1989, p. 4. Primary source: 1986 Census of Canada *Notes:* A dash represents zero or a percentage which rounds to less than .05 percent. 1. Aboriginal origins are derived from the ethnic origin question which asks whether respondents are North American Indian, Metis or Inuit. 2. All 1986 figures exclude the population estimated at about 45,000 on 136 incompletely enumerated Indian reserves and settlements throughout Canada. For an estimate of the unenumerated population and list of incompletely enumerated reserves in each affected province, see Appendix 1 and 2. 3. Total aboriginal origins - are the sum of persons who reported: (a) a single aboriginal (e.g., North American Indian, Metis or Inuit), and, (b) multiple aboriginal origins, that is those who reported: - at least one aboriginal origin with any other non-aboriginal (e.g., Metis and French), or - two or more aboriginal origins only. 4. Non-aboriginal in these columns - refers to persons who report one or more non-aboriginal origins such as British, French, etc., in combination with one of the aboriginal origins such as North American Indian. 5. Other multiple aboriginal origins - refers to the sum of those persons reporting two or more aboriginal origins with or without a non-aboriginal origin.

★ 825 ★

Population 15 Years and Over, by Marital Status and Sex for Detailed Aboriginal Origins for Alberta, 1986 - I[1,2]

Marital status	Total Aboriginal origins[3]		North American Indian only		North American Indian and non-Aboriginal[4]		Metis only	
	Number	Percent	Number	Percent	Number	Percent	Number	Percent
Total	63,055	100.0	20,940	100.0	17,020	100.0	11,085	100.0
Male	30,230	47.9	9,765	46.6	8,110	47.6	5,480	49.4
Female	32,825	52.1	11,175	53.4	8,905	52.3	5,600	50.5
Single	24,090	38.2	8,755	41.8	5,700	33.5	4,430	40.0
Male	12,905	20.5	4,560	21.8	2,930	17.2	2,470	22.3
Female	11,185	17.7	4,200	20.1	2,770	16.3	1,965	17.7
Married	31,585	50.1	9,750	46.6	9,555	56.1	5,090	45.9
Male	14,740	23.4	4,380	20.9	4,580	26.9	2,465	22.2
Female	16,845	26.7	5,370	25.6	4,975	29.2	2,625	23.7
Separated	2,815	4.5	1,035	4.9	675	4.0	560	5.1
Male	1,010	1.6	355	1.7	255	1.5	175	1.6
Female	1,800	2.9	675	3.2	420	2.5	385	3.5
Divorced	2,660	4.2	530	2.5	855	5.0	590	5.3
Male	1,110	1.8	240	1.1	330	1.9	260	2.3
Female	1,545	2.5	290	1.4	525	3.1	335	3.0
Widowed	1,905	3.0	865	4.1	240	1.4	405	3.7
Male	465	0.7	225	1.1	15	0.1	115	1.0
Female	1,445	2.3	635	3.0	225	1.3	290	2.6

Source: Aboriginal Peoples Output Program, 1986 Census, Statistics Canada, *A Data Book on Canada's Aboriginal Population from the 1986 Census of Canada*, March, 1989, p. 220. Primary source: 1986 Census of Canada *Notes:* A dash (-) represents zero or a percentage which rounds to less than .05 percent. 1. Aboriginal origins are derived from the ethnic origin question which asks whether respondents are North American Indian, Metis or Inuit. 2. All 1986 figures exclude the population estimated at about 45,000 on 136 incompletely enumerated Indian reserves and settlements throughout Canada. 3. Total aboriginal origins - are the sum of persons who reported: (a) a single aboriginal (e.g., North American Indian, Metis or Inuit), and, (b) multiple aboriginal origins, that is those who reported: - at least one aboriginal origin with any other non-aboriginal (e.g., Metis and French), or - two or more aboriginal origins only. 4. Non-aboriginal in these columns - refers to persons who report one or more non-aboriginal origins such as British, French, etc., in combination with one of the aboriginal origins such as North American Indian.

★ 826 ★

Population 15 Years and Over, by Marital Status and Sex for Detailed Aboriginal Origins for Alberta, 1986 - II[1,2]

Marital status	Metis and non-Aboriginal[3]		Inuit only		Inuit and non-Aboriginal[3]		Other multiple Aboriginal origins[4]	
	Number	Percent	Number	Percent	Number	Percent	Number	Percent
Total	9,995	100.0	205	100.0	280	100.0	3,530	100.0
Male	4,745	47.5	115	56.1	110	39.3	1,905	54.0
Female	5,255	52.6	100	48.8	175	62.5	1,620	45.9
Single	3,615	36.2	115	56.1	120	42.9	1,345	38.1
Male	1,985	19.9	75	36.6	65	23.2	820	23.2
Female	1,630	16.3	45	22.0	55	19.6	525	14.9
Married	5,255	52.6	70	34.1	125	44.6	1,735	49.2
Male	2,365	23.7	20	9.8	40	14.3	890	25.2
Female	2,890	28.9	50	24.4	85	30.4	850	24.1
Separated	365	3.7	15	7.3	-	-	160	4.5
Male	135	1.4	15	7.3	-	-	70	2.0
Female	235	2.4	-	-	-	-	85	2.4
Divorced	455	4.6	-	-	25	8.9	195	5.5
Male	170	1.7	-	-	-	-	105	3.0
Female	280	2.8	-	-	25	8.9	90	2.5
Widowed	305	3.1	-	-	15	5.4	80	2.3
Male	95	1.0	-	-	-	-	15	0.4
Female	215	2.2	-	-	10	3.6	65	1.8

Source: Aboriginal Peoples Output Program, 1986 Census, Statistics Canada, *A Data Book on Canada's Aboriginal Population from the 1986 Census of Canada*, March, 1989, p. 220. Primary source: 1986 Census of Canada *Notes:* A dash (-) represents zero or a percentage which rounds to less than .05 percent. 1. Aboriginal origins are derived from the ethnic origin question which asks whether respondents are North American Indian, Metis or Inuit. 2. All 1986 figures exclude the population estimated at about 45,000 on 136 incompletely enumerated Indian reserves and settlements throughout Canada. 3. Non-aboriginal in these columns - refers to persons who report one or more non-aboriginal origins such as British, French, etc., in combination with one of the aboriginal origins such as North American Indian. 4. Other multiple aboriginal origins - refers to the sum of those persons reporting two or more aboriginal origins with or without a non-aboriginal origin.

★ 827 ★

Population 15 Years and Over, by Marital Status and Sex for Detailed Aboriginal Origins for British Columbia, 1986 - I[1,2]

Marital status	Total Aboriginal origins[3]		North American Indian only		North American Indian and non-Aboriginal[4]		Metis only	
	Number	Percent	Number	Percent	Number	Percent	Number	Percent
Total	82,180	100.0	39,020	100.0	32,305	100.0	3,010	100.0
Male	40,090	48.8	18,950	48.6	15,725	48.7	1,435	47.7
Female	42,085	51.2	20,070	51.4	16,575	51.3	1,575	52.3
Single	31,200	38.0	15,340	39.3	11,740	36.3	1,190	39.5
Male	17,575	21.4	8,750	22.4	6,520	20.2	620	20.6
Female	13,630	16.6	6,590	16.9	5,210	16.1	570	18.9
Married	39,925	48.6	18,500	47.4	16,345	50.6	1,280	42.5
Male	18,680	22.7	8,250	21.1	7,920	24.5	610	20.3
Female	21,245	25.9	10,250	26.3	8,430	26.1	675	22.4
Separated	4,190	5.1	1,895	4.9	1,570	4.9	240	8.0
Male	1,645	2.0	805	2.1	555	1.7	100	3.3
Female	2,550	3.1	1,090	2.8	1,020	3.2	145	4.8
Divorced	4,005	4.9	1,480	3.8	1,875	5.8	190	6.3
Male	1,435	1.7	590	1.5	595	1.8	80	2.7
Female	2,570	3.1	890	2.3	1,275	3.9	115	3.8
Widowed	2,855	3.5	1,810	4.6	770	2.4	105	3.5
Male	760	0.9	560	1.4	135	0.4	25	0.8
Female	2,095	2.5	1,255	3.2	635	2.0	75	2.5

Source: Aboriginal Peoples Output Program, 1986 Census, Statistics Canada, *A Data Book on Canada's Aboriginal Population from the 1986 Census of Canada*, March, 1989, p. 244. Primary source: 1986 Census of Canada *Notes:* A dash (-) represents zero or a percentage which rounds to less than .05 percent. 1. Aboriginal origins are derived from the ethnic origin question which asks whether respondents are North American Indian, Metis or Inuit. 2. All 1986 figures exclude the population estimated at about 45,000 on 136 incompletely enumerated Indian reserves and settlements throughout Canada. 3. Total aboriginal origins - are the sum of persons who reported: (a) a single aboriginal (e.g., North American Indian, Metis or Inuit), and, (b) multiple aboriginal origins, that is those who reported: - at least one aboriginal origin with any other non-aboriginal (e.g., Metis and French), or - two or more aboriginal origins only. 4. Non-aboriginal in these columns - refers to persons who report one or more non-aboriginal origins such as British, French, etc., in combination with one of the aboriginal origins such as North American Indian.

★ 828 ★

Population 15 Years and Over, by Marital Status and Sex for Detailed Aboriginal Origins for British Columbia, 1986 - II[1,2]

Marital status	Metis and non-Aboriginal[3]		Inuit only		Inuit and non-Aboriginal[3]		Other multiple Aboriginal origins[4]	
	Number	Percent	Number	Percent	Number	Percent	Number	Percent
Total	5,805	100.0	165	100.0	330	100.0	1,540	100.0
Male	2,850	49.1	90	54.5	205	62.1	840	54.5
Female	2,960	51.0	75	45.5	125	37.9	705	45.8
Single	2,060	35.5	80	48.5	130	39.4	670	43.5
Male	1,140	19.6	55	33.3	90	27.3	395	25.6
Female	920	15.8	25	15.2	45	13.6	270	17.5
Married	2,955	50.9	60	36.4	160	48.5	615	39.9
Male	1,415	24.4	35	21.2	100	30.3	355	23.1
Female	1,540	26.5	25	15.2	55	16.7	265	17.2
Separated	315	5.4	-	-	10	3.0	160	10.4
Male	125	2.2	-	-	-	-	55	3.6
Female	190	3.3	-	-	-	-	100	6.5
Divorced	355	6.1	-	-	15	4.5	85	5.5
Male	140	2.4	-	-	-	-	30	1.9
Female	220	3.8	-	-	-	-	55	3.6
Widowed	125	2.2	15	9.1	10	3.0	15	1.0
Male	35	0.6	-	-	-	-	-	-
Female	90	1.6	15	9.1	10	3.0	-	-

Source: Aboriginal Peoples Output Program, 1986 Census, Statistics Canada, *A Data Book on Canada's Aboriginal Population from the 1986 Census of Canada*, March, 1989, p. 244. Primary source: 1986 Census of Canada *Notes:* A dash (-) represents zero or a percentage which rounds to less than .05 percent. 1. Aboriginal origins are derived from the ethnic origin question which asks whether respondents are North American Indian, Metis or Inuit. 2. All 1986 figures exclude the population estimated at about 45,000 on 136 incompletely enumerated Indian reserves and settlements throughout Canada. 3. Non-aboriginal in these columns - refers to persons who report one or more non-aboriginal origins such as British, French, etc., in combination with one of the aboriginal origins such as North American Indian. 4. Other multiple aboriginal origins - refers to the sum of those persons reporting two or more aboriginal origins with or without a non-aboriginal origin.

★ 829 ★

Population 15 Years and Over, by Marital Status and Sex for Detailed Aboriginal Origins for Manitoba, 1986 - I[1,2]

Marital status	Total Aboriginal origins[3]		North American Indian only		North American Indian and non-Aboriginal[4]		Metis only	
	Number	Percent	Number	Percent	Number	Percent	Number	Percent
Total	52,050	100.0	24,360	100.0	6,355	100.0	9,330	100.0
Male	24,970	48.0	11,655	47.8	3,060	48.2	4,650	49.8
Female	27,075	52.0	12,705	52.2	3,295	51.8	4,680	50.2
Single	20,430	39.3	9,580	39.3	2,395	37.7	3,935	42.2
Male	10,770	20.7	5,040	20.7	1,215	19.1	2,205	23.6
Female	9,665	18.6	4,545	18.7	1,180	18.6	1,725	18.5
Married	25,815	49.6	12,255	50.3	3,340	52.6	4,115	44.1
Male	12,350	23.7	5,800	23.8	1,655	26.0	1,970	21.1
Female	13,460	25.9	6,460	26.5	1,690	26.6	2,145	23.0
Separated	2,065	4.0	900	3.7	285	4.5	460	4.9
Male	745	1.4	340	1.4	90	1.4	190	2.0
Female	1,325	2.5	565	2.3	195	3.1	270	2.9
Divorced	1,735	3.3	535	2.2	215	3.4	415	4.4
Male	635	1.2	175	0.7	85	1.3	175	1.9
Female	1,100	2.1	360	1.5	125	2.0	235	2.5
Widowed	2,005	3.9	1,090	4.5	115	1.8	410	4.4
Male	480	0.9	310	1.3	10	0.2	105	1.1
Female	1,525	2.9	780	3.2	105	1.7	300	3.2

Source: Aboriginal Peoples Output Program, 1986 Census, Statistics Canada, *A Data Book on Canada's Aboriginal Population from the 1986 Census of Canada*, March, 1989, p. 174. Primary source: 1986 Census of Canada *Notes:* A dash (-) represents zero or a percentage which rounds to less than .05 percent. 1. Aboriginal origins are derived from the ethnic origin question which asks whether respondents are North American Indian, Metis or Inuit. 2. All 1986 figures exclude the population estimated at about 45,000 on 136 incompletely enumerated Indian reserves and settlements throughout Canada. 3. Total aboriginal origins - are the sum of persons who reported: (a) a single aboriginal (e.g., North American Indian, Metis or Inuit), and, (b) multiple aboriginal origins, that is those who reported: - at least one aboriginal origin with any other non-aboriginal (e.g., Metis and French), or - two or more aboriginal origins only. 4. Non-aboriginal in these columns - refers to persons who report one or more non-aboriginal origins such as British, French, etc., in combination with one of the aboriginal origins such as North American Indian.

★ 830 ★

Population 15 Years and Over, by Marital Status and Sex for Detailed Aboriginal Origins for Manitoba, 1986 - II[1,2]

Marital status	Metis and non-Aboriginal[3]		Inuit only		Inuit and non-Aboriginal[3]		Other multiple Aboriginal origins[4]	
	Number	Percent	Number	Percent	Number	Percent	Number	Percent
Total	9,105	100.0	100	100.0	120	100.0	2,675	100.0
Male	4,235	46.5	35	35.0	55	45.8	1,285	48.0
Female	4,870	53.5	70	70.0	60	50.0	1,390	52.0
Single	3,260	35.8	55	55.0	55	45.8	1,150	43.0
Male	1,710	18.8	20	20.0	20	16.7	555	20.7
Female	1,550	17.0	30	30.0	35	29.2	590	22.1
Married	4,785	52.6	35	35.0	55	45.8	1,225	45.8
Male	2,265	24.9	15	15.0	30	25.0	620	23.2
Female	2,525	27.7	20	20.0	25	20.8	605	22.6
Separated	285	3.1	-	-	-	-	125	4.7
Male	80	0.9	-	-	-	-	45	1.7
Female	210	2.3	-	-	-	-	80	3.0
Divorced	440	4.8	-	-	-	-	130	4.9
Male	135	1.5	-	-	-	-	-	-
Female	300	3.3	-	-	-	-	65	2.4
Widowed	335	3.7	-	-	-	-	50	1.9
Male	45	0.5	-	-	-	-	-	-
Female	290	3.2	-	-	-	-	45	1.7

Source: Aboriginal Peoples Output Program, 1986 Census, Statistics Canada, *A Data Book on Canada's Aboriginal Population from the 1986 Census of Canada*, March, 1989, p. 174. Primary source: 1986 Census of Canada *Notes:* A dash (-) represents zero or a percentage which rounds to less than .05 percent. 1. Aboriginal origins are derived from the ethnic origin question which asks whether respondents are North American Indian, Metis or Inuit. 2. All 1986 figures exclude the population estimated at about 45,000 on 136 incompletely enumerated Indian reserves and settlements throughout Canada. 3. Non-aboriginal in these columns - refers to persons who report one or more non-aboriginal origins such as British, French, etc., in combination with one of the aboriginal origins such as North American Indian. 4. Other multiple aboriginal origins - refers to the sum of those persons reporting two or more aboriginal origins with or without a non- aboriginal origin.

★ 831 ★

Population 15 Years and Over, by Marital Status and Sex for Detailed Aboriginal Origins for New Brunswick, 1986 - I[1,2]

Marital status	Total Aboriginal origins[3]		North American Indian only		North American Indian and non-Aboriginal[4]		Metis only	
	Number	Percent	Number	Percent	Number	Percent	Number	Percent
Total	5,990	100.0	2,505	100.0	2,960	100.0	110	100.0
Male	3,020	50.4	1,295	51.7	1,440	48.6	70	63.6
Female	2,970	49.6	1,210	48.3	1,515	51.2	35	31.8
Single	2,160	36.1	965	38.5	1,050	35.5	45	40.9
Male	1,200	20.0	555	22.2	545	18.4	40	36.4
Female	960	16.0	415	16.6	505	17.1	-	-
Married	3,125	52.2	1,165	46.5	1,645	55.6	50	45.5
Male	1,600	26.7	610	24.4	835	28.2	25	22.7
Female	1,530	25.5	555	22.2	810	27.4	25	22.7
Separated	235	3.9	125	5.0	95	3.2	-	-
Male	90	1.5	55	2.2	20	0.7	-	-
Female	145	2.4	65	2.6	75	2.5	-	-
Divorced	280	4.7	135	5.4	110	3.7	-	-
Male	85	1.4	45	1.8	30	1.0	-	-
Female	195	3.3	90	3.6	75	2.5	-	-
Widowed	195	3.3	120	4.8	65	2.2	-	-
Male	40	0.7	30	1.2	10	0.3	-	-
Female	155	2.6	90	3.6	55	1.9	-	-

Source: Aboriginal Peoples Output Program, 1986 Census, Statistics Canada, *A Data Book on Canada's Aboriginal Population from the 1986 Census of Canada*, March, 1989, p. 100. Primary source: 1986 Census of Canada *Notes:* A dash (-) represents zero or a percentage which rounds to less than .05 percent. 1. Aboriginal origins are derived from the ethnic origin question which asks whether respondents are North American Indian, Metis or Inuit. 2. All 1986 figures exclude the population estimated at about 45,000 on 136 incompletely enumerated Indian reserves and settlements throughout Canada. 3. Total aboriginal origins - are the sum of persons who reported: (a) a single aboriginal (e.g., North American Indian, Metis or Inuit), and, (b) multiple aboriginal origins, that is those who reported: - at least one aboriginal origin with any other non-aboriginal (e.g., Metis and French), or - two or more aboriginal origins only. 4. Non-aboriginal in these columns - refers to persons who report one or more non-aboriginal origins such as British, French, etc., in combination with one of the aboriginal origins such as North American Indian.

★ 832 ★

Population 15 Years and Over, by Marital Status and Sex for Detailed Aboriginal Origins for New Brunswick, 1986 - II[1,2]

Marital status	Metis and non-Aboriginal[3]		Inuit only		Inuit and non-Aboriginal[3]		Other multiple Aboriginal origins[4]	
	Number	Percent	Number	Percent	Number	Percent	Number	Percent
Total	260	100.0	-	-	55	100.0	100	100.0
Male	135	51.9	-	-	30	54.5	45	45.0
Female	120	46.2	-	-	30	54.5	55	55.0
Single	55	21.2	-	-	15	27.3	25	25.0
Male	35	13.5	-	-	15	27.3	15	15.0
Female	15	5.8	-	-	-	-	15	15.0
Married	165	63.5	-	-	35	63.6	65	65.0
Male	85	32.7	-	-	-	-	30	30.0
Female	75	28.8	-	-	25	45.5	40	40.0
Separated	15	5.8	-	-	-	-	-	-
Male	15	5.8	-	-	-	-	-	-
Female	-	-	-	-	-	-	-	-
Divorced	20	7.7	-	-	-	-	-	-
Male	-	-	-	-	-	-	-	-
Female	15	5.8	-	-	-	-	-	-
Widowed	-	-	-	-	-	-	-	-
Male	-	-	-	-	-	-	-	-
Female	-	-	-	-	-	-	-	-

Source: Aboriginal Peoples Output Program, 1986 Census, Statistics Canada, *A Data Book on Canada's Aboriginal Population from the 1986 Census of Canada*, March, 1989, p. 100. Primary source: 1986 Census of Canada *Notes:* A dash (-) represents zero or a percentage which rounds to less than .05 percent. 1. Aboriginal origins are derived from the ethnic origin question which asks whether respondents are North American Indian, Metis or Inuit. 2. All 1986 figures exclude the population estimated at about 45,000 on 136 incompletely enumerated Indian reserves and settlements throughout Canada. 3. Non-aboriginal in these columns - refers to persons who report one or more non-aboriginal origins such as British, French, etc., in combination with one of the aboriginal origins such as North American Indian. 4. Other multiple aboriginal origins - refers to the sum of those persons reporting two or more aboriginal origins with or without a non- aboriginal origin.

Population 15 Years and Over, by Marital Status and Sex for Detailed Aboriginal Origins for Newfoundland, 1986 - I[1,2]

Marital status	Total Aboriginal origins[3]		North American Indian only		North American Indian and non-Aboriginal[4]		Metis only	
	Number	Percent	Number	Percent	Number	Percent	Number	Percent
Total	6,160	100.0	1,060	100.0	1,730	100.0	220	100.0
male	3,140	51.0	495	46.7	875	50.6	110	50.0
female	3,020	49.0	560	52.8	850	49.1	105	47.7
Single	2,395	38.9	380	35.8	650	37.6	85	38.6
male	1,350	21.9	190	17.9	320	18.5	45	20.5
female	1,045	17.0	190	17.9	330	19.1	35	15.9
Married	3,230	52.4	595	56.1	960	55.5	90	40.9
male	1,605	26.1	290	27.4	505	29.2	60	27.3
female	1,620	26.3	305	28.8	455	26.3	30	13.6
Separated	160	2.6	15	1.4	45	2.6	-	-
male	95	1.5	-	-	25	1.4	-	-
female	60	1.0	10	0.9	15	0.9	-	-
Divorced	105	1.7	20	1.9	40	2.3	-	-
male	40	0.6	-	-	20	1.2	-	-
female	70	1.1	15	1.4	25	1.4	-	-
Widowed	270	4.4	50	4.7	35	2.0	35	15.9
male	50	0.8	-	-	-	-	-	-
female	225	3.7	40	3.8	25	1.4	35	15.9

Source: Aboriginal Peoples Output Program, 1986 Census, Statistics Canada, *A Data Book on Canada's Aboriginal Population from the 1986 Census of Canada*, March, 1989, p. 28. Primary source: 1986 Census of Canada *Notes:* A dash represents zero or a percentage which rounds to less than .05 percent. 1. Aboriginal origins are derived from the ethnic origin question which asks whether respondents are North American Indian, Metis or Inuit. 2. All 1986 figures exclude the population estimated at about 45,000 on 136 incompletely enumerated Indian reserves and settlements throughout Canada. For an estimate of the unenumerated population and list of incompletely enumerated reserves in each affected province, see Appendix 1 and 2. 3. Total aboriginal origins - are the sum of persons who reported: (a) a single aboriginal (e.g., North American Indian, Metis or Inuit), and, (b) multiple aboriginal origins, that is those who reported: - at least one aboriginal origin with any other non-aboriginal (e.g., Metis and French), or - two or more aboriginal origins only. 4. Non-aboriginal in these columns - refers to persons who report one or more non-aboriginal origins such as British, French, etc., in combination with one of the aboriginal origins such as North American Indian. 5. Other multiple aboriginal origins - refer to the sum of those persons reporting two or more aboriginal origins with or without a non-aboriginal origin.

★ 834 ★

Population 15 Years and Over, by Marital Status and Sex for Detailed Aboriginal Origins for Newfoundland, 1986 - II[1,2]

Marital status	Metis and non-Aboriginal[3]		Inuit only		Inuit and non-Aboriginal[3]		Other multiple Aboriginal origins[4]	
	Number	Percent	Number	Percent	Number	Percent	Number	Percent
Total	515	100.0	1,175	100.0	1,070	100.0	395	100.0
Male	280	54.4	595	50.6	545	50.9	240	60.8
Female	230	44.7	575	48.9	530	49.5	150	38.0
Single	220	42.7	450	38.3	440	41.1	170	43.0
Male	145	28.2	275	23.4	250	23.4	120	30.4
Female	75	14.6	170	14.5	190	17.8	50	12.7
Married	240	46.6	610	51.9	555	51.9	180	45.6
Male	115	22.3	275	23.4	260	24.3	100	25.3
Female	125	24.3	335	28.5	290	27.1	70	17.7
Separated	25	4.9	35	3.0	25	2.3	15	3.8
Male	20	3.9	15	1.3	20	1.9	-	-
Female	-	-	15	1.3	-	-	-	-
Divorced	-	-	15	1.3	15	1.4	-	-
Male	-	-	-	-	-	-	-	-
Female	-	-	-	-	-	-	-	-
Widowed	20	3.9	65	5.5	45	4.2	20	5.1
Male	-	-	20	1.7	-	-	-	-
Female	20	3.9	40	3.4	40	3.7	20	5.1

Source: Aboriginal Peoples Output Program, 1986 Census, Statistics Canada, *A Data Book on Canada's Aboriginal Population from the 1986 Census of Canada*, March, 1989, p. 28. Primary source: 1986 Census of Canada *Notes:* A dash (-) represents zero or a percentage which rounds to less than .05 percent. 1. Aboriginal origins are derived from the ethnic origin question which asks whether respondents are North American Indian, Metis or Inuit. 2. All 1986 figures exclude the population estimated at about 45,000 on 136 incompletely enumerated Indian reserves and settlements throughout Canada. 3. Non-aboriginal in these columns - refers to persons who report one or more non-aboriginal origins such as British, French, etc., in combination with one of the aboriginal origins such as North American Indian. 4. Other multiple aboriginal origins - refers to the sum of those persons reporting two or more aboriginal origins with or without a non- aboriginal origin.

★ 835 ★

Population 15 Years and Over, by Marital Status and Sex for Detailed Aboriginal Origins for Northwest Territories, 1986 - I[1,2]

Marital status	Total Aboriginal origins[3]		North American Indian only		North American Indian and non-Aboriginal[4]		Metis only	
	Number	Percent	Number	Percent	Number	Percent	Number	Percent
Total	18,675	100.0	5,075	100.0	525	100.0	1,425	100.0
Male	9,570	51.2	2,595	51.1	315	60.0	740	51.9
Female	9,105	48.8	2,480	48.9	210	40.0	685	48.1
Single	7,940	42.5	2,345	46.2	200	38.1	565	39.6
Male	4,550	24.4	1,365	26.9	135	25.7	320	22.5
Female	3,390	18.2	975	19.2	65	12.4	245	17.2
Married	9,330	50.0	2,320	45.7	275	52.4	710	49.8
Male	4,445	23.8	1,085	21.4	130	24.8	360	25.3
Female	4,885	26.2	1,245	24.5	145	27.6	345	24.2
Separated	390	2.1	110	2.2	-	-	75	5.3
Male	185	1.0	50	1.0	-	-	35	2.5
Female	205	1.1	55	1.1	-	-	40	2.8
Divorced	200	1.1	40	0.8	25	4.8	35	2.5
Male	90	0.5	10	0.2	25	4.8	15	1.1
Female	110	0.6	30	0.6	-	-	20	1.4
Widowed	815	4.4	250	4.9	20	3.8	40	2.8
Male	300	1.6	80	1.6	15	2.9	-	-
Female	520	2.8	170	3.3	-	-	40	2.8

Source: Aboriginal Peoples Output Program, 1986 Census, Statistics Canada, *A Data Book on Canada's Aboriginal Population from the 1986 Census of Canada*, March, 1989, p. 268. Primary source: 1986 Census of Canada *Notes:* A dash (-) represents zero or a percentage which rounds to less than .05 percent. 1. Aboriginal origins are derived from the ethnic origin question which asks whether respondents are North American Indian, Metis or Inuit. 2. All 1986 figures exclude the population estimated at about 45,000 on 136 incompletely enumerated Indian reserves and settlements throughout Canada. 3. Total aboriginal origins - are the sum of persons who reported: (a) a single aboriginal (e.g., North American Indian, Metis or Inuit), and, (b) multiple aboriginal origins, that is those who reported: - at least one aboriginal origin with any other non-aboriginal (e.g., Metis and French), or - two or more aboriginal origins only. 4. Non-aboriginal in these columns - refers to persons who report one or more non-aboriginal origins such as British, French, etc., in combination with one of the aboriginal origins such as North American Indian.

★ 836 ★

Population 15 Years and Over, by Marital Status and Sex for Detailed Aboriginal Origins for Northwest Territories, 1986 - II[1,2]

Marital status	Metis and non-Aboriginal[3]		Inuit only		Inuit and non-Aboriginal[3]		Other multiple Aboriginal origins[4]	
	Number	Percent	Number	Percent	Number	Percent	Number	Percent
Total	460	100.0	10,320	100.0	280	100.0	585	100.0
Male	250	54.3	5,190	50.3	155	55.4	320	54.7
Female	205	44.6	5,135	49.8	130	46.4	265	45.3
Single	190	41.3	4,215	40.8	160	57.1	260	44.4
Male	135	29.3	2,320	22.5	85	30.4	185	31.6
Female	55	12.0	1,895	18.4	75	26.8	85	14.5
Married	225	48.9	5,405	52.4	105	37.5	280	47.9
Male	100	21.7	2,585	25.0	65	23.2	125	21.4
Female	130	28.3	2,820	27.3	40	14.3	165	28.2
Separated	15	3.3	160	1.6	-	-	15	2.6
Male	-	-	80	0.8	-	-	-	-
Female	-	-	85	0.8	-	-	15	2.6
Divorced	20	4.3	70	0.7	-	-	-	-
Male	-	-	35	0.3	-	-	-	-
Female	15	3.3	35	0.3	-	-	-	-
Widowed	-	-	470	4.6	-	-	15	2.6
Male	-	-	175	1.7	-	-	10	1.7
Female	-	-	295	2.9	-	-	-	-

Source: Aboriginal Peoples Output Program, 1986 Census, Statistics Canada, *A Data Book on Canada's Aboriginal Population from the 1986 Census of Canada*, March, 1989, p. 268. Primary source: 1986 Census of Canada *Notes:* A dash (-) represents zero or a percentage which rounds to less than .05 percent. 1. Aboriginal origins are derived from the ethnic origin question which asks whether respondents are North American Indian, Metis or Inuit. 2. All 1986 figures exclude the population estimated at about 45,000 on 136 incompletely enumerated Indian reserves and settlements throughout Canada. 3. Non-aboriginal in these columns - refers to persons who report one or more non-aboriginal origins such as British, French, etc., in combination with one of the aboriginal origins such as North American Indian. 4. Other multiple aboriginal origins - refers to the sum of those persons reporting two or more aboriginal origins with or without a non- aboriginal origin.

★ 837 ★

Population 15 Years and Over, by Marital Status and Sex for Detailed Aboriginal Origins for Nova Scotia, 1986 - I[1,2]

Marital status	Total Aboriginal origins[3]		North American Indian only		North American Indian and non-Aboriginal[4]		Metis only	
	Number	Percent	Number	Percent	Number	Percent	Number	Percent
Total	9,260	100.0	3,665	100.0	4,590	100.0	185	100.0
Male	4,440	47.9	1,835	50.1	2,145	46.7	85	45.9
Female	4,815	52.0	1,825	49.8	2,445	53.3	95	51.4
Single	3,560	38.4	1,590	43.4	1,520	33.1	85	45.9
Male	1,815	19.6	870	23.7	710	15.5	50	27.0
Female	1,745	18.8	720	19.6	810	17.6	35	18.9
Married	4,680	50.5	1,565	42.7	2,635	57.4	80	43.2
Male	2,310	24.9	775	21.1	1,320	28.8	35	18.9
Female	2,365	25.5	790	21.6	1,315	28.6	45	24.3
Separated	300	3.2	135	3.7	130	2.8	-	-
Male	90	1.0	60	1.6	30	0.7	-	-
Female	210	2.3	80	2.2	105	2.3	-	-
Divorced	360	3.9	145	4.0	195	4.2	-	-
Male	145	1.6	65	1.8	75	1.6	-	-
Female	220	2.4	80	2.2	125	2.7	-	-
Widowed	360	3.9	235	6.4	105	2.3	10	5.4
Male	85	0.9	70	1.9	15	0.3	-	-
Female	275	3.0	160	4.4	95	2.1	10	5.4

Source: Aboriginal Peoples Output Program, 1986 Census, Statistics Canada, *A Data Book on Canada's Aboriginal Population from the 1986 Census of Canada*, March, 1989, p. 76. Primary source: 1986 Census of Canada *Notes:* A dash (-) represents zero or a percentage which rounds to less than .05 percent. 1. Aboriginal origins are derived from the ethnic origin question which asks whether respondents are North American Indian, Metis or Inuit. 2. All 1986 figures exclude the population estimated at about 45,000 on 136 incompletely enumerated Indian reserves and settlements throughout Canada. 3. Total aboriginal origins - are the sum of persons who reported: (a) a single aboriginal (e.g., North American Indian, Metis or Inuit), and, (b) multiple aboriginal origins, that is those who reported: - at least one aboriginal origin with any other non-aboriginal (e.g., Metis and French), or - two or more aboriginal origins only. 4. Non-aboriginal in these columns - refers to persons who report one or more non-aboriginal origins such as British, French, etc., in combination with one of the aboriginal origins such as North American Indian.

★ 838 ★

Population 15 Years and Over, by Marital Status and Sex for Detailed Aboriginal Origins for Nova Scotia, 1986 - II[1,2]

Marital status	Metis and non-Aboriginal[3]		Inuit only		Inuit and non-Aboriginal[3]		Other multiple Aboriginal origins[4]	
	Number	Percent	Number	Percent	Number	Percent	Number	Percent
Total	455	100.0	80	100.0	110	100.0	165	100.0
Male	180	39.6	40	50.0	40	36.4	100	60.6
Female	270	59.3	45	56.3	70	63.6	60	36.4
Single	195	42.9	35	43.8	55	50.0	80	48.5
Male	95	20.9	15	18.8	15	13.6	45	27.3
Female	100	22.0	20	25.0	40	36.4	20	12.1
Married	235	51.6	45	56.3	45	40.9	70	42.4
Male	85	18.7	20	25.0	20	18.2	55	33.3
Female	150	33.0	20	25.0	30	27.3	15	9.1
Separated	-	-	-	-	-	-	15	9.1
Male	-	-	-	-	-	-	-	-
Female	-	-	-	-	-	-	10	6.1
Divorced	-	-	-	-	-	-	-	-
Male	-	-	-	-	-	-	-	-
Female	-	-	-	-	-	-	-	-
Widowed	15	3.3	-	-	-	-	-	-
Male	-	-	-	-	-	-	-	-
Female	10	2.2	-	-	-	-	-	-

Source: Aboriginal Peoples Output Program, 1986 Census, Statistics Canada, *A Data Book on Canada's Aboriginal Population from the 1986 Census of Canada*, March, 1989, p. 76. Primary source: 1986 Census of Canada *Notes:* A dash (-) represents zero or a percentage which rounds to less than .05 percent. 1. Aboriginal origins are derived from the ethnic origin question which asks whether respondents are North American Indian, Metis or Inuit. 2. All 1986 figures exclude the population estimated at about 45,000 on 136 incompletely enumerated Indian reserves and settlements throughout Canada. 3. Non-aboriginal in these columns - refers to persons who report one or more non-aboriginal origins such as British, French, etc., in combination with one of the aboriginal origins such as North American Indian. 4. Other multiple aboriginal origins - refers to the sum of those persons reporting two or more aboriginal origins with or without a non- aboriginal origin.

★ 839 ★

Population 15 Years and Over, by Marital Status and Sex for Detailed Aboriginal Origins for Ontario, 1986 - I[1,2]

Marital status	Total Aboriginal origins[3]		North American Indian only		North American Indian and non-Aboriginal[4]		Metis only	
	Number	Percent	Number	Percent	Number	Percent	Number	Percent
Total	109,540	100.0	35,380	100.0	60,760	100.0	2,645	100.0
Male	51,455	47.0	16,730	47.3	28,345	46.7	1,310	49.5
Female	58,085	53.0	18,655	52.7	32,420	53.4	1,340	50.7
Single	37,380	34.1	12,320	34.8	20,305	33.4	980	37.1
Male	19,635	17.9	6,600	18.7	10,485	17.3	550	20.8
Female	17,750	16.2	5,715	16.2	9,820	16.2	435	16.4
Married	58,335	53.3	17,830	50.4	33,605	55.3	1,245	47.1
Male	27,535	25.1	8,465	23.9	15,800	26.0	630	23.8
Female	30,800	28.1	9,360	26.5	17,805	29.3	615	23.3
Separated	5,515	5.0	1,925	5.4	2,920	4.8	155	5.9
Male	1,935	1.8	675	1.9	995	1.6	55	2.1
Female	3,575	3.3	1,245	3.5	1,920	3.2	100	3.8
Divorced	4,690	4.3	1,290	3.6	2,735	4.5	155	5.9
Male	1,615	1.5	495	1.4	890	1.5	50	1.9
Female	3,080	2.8	800	2.3	1,845	3.0	105	4.0
Widowed	3,615	3.3	2,020	5.7	1,195	2.0	110	4.2
Male	725	0.7	485	1.4	170	0.3	20	0.8
Female	2,885	2.6	1,535	4.3	1,030	1.7	85	3.2

Source: Aboriginal Peoples Output Program, 1986 Census, Statistics Canada, *A Data Book on Canada's Aboriginal Population from the 1986 Census of Canada*, March, 1989, p. 148. Primary source: 1986 Census of Canada *Notes:* A dash (-) represents zero or a percentage which rounds to less than .05 percent. 1. Aboriginal origins are derived from the ethnic origin question which asks whether respondents are North American Indian, Metis or Inuit. 2. All 1986 figures exclude the population estimated at about 45,000 on 136 incompletely enumerated Indian reserves and settlements throughout Canada. 3. Total aboriginal origins - are the sum of persons who reported: (a) a single aboriginal (e.g., North American Indian, Metis or Inuit), and, (b) multiple aboriginal origins, that is those who reported: - at least one aboriginal origin with any other non-aboriginal (e.g., Metis and French), or - two or more aboriginal origins only. 4. Non-aboriginal in these columns - refers to persons who report one or more non-aboriginal origins such as British, French, etc., in combination with one of the aboriginal origins such as North American Indian.

★ 840 ★

Population 15 Years and Over, by Marital Status and Sex for Detailed Aboriginal Origins for Ontario, 1986 - II[1,2]

Marital status	Metis and non-Aboriginal[3]		Inuit only		Inuit and non-Aboriginal[3]		Other multiple Aboriginal origins[4]	
	Number	Percent	Number	Percent	Number	Percent	Number	Percent
Total	6,780	100.0	485	100.0	950	100.0	2,530	100.0
Male	3,090	45.6	235	48.5	500	52.6	1,255	49.6
Female	3,690	54.4	250	51.5	450	47.4	1,285	50.8
Single	2,325	34.3	170	35.1	325	34.2	965	38.1
Male	1,180	17.4	100	20.6	190	20.0	535	21.1
Female	1,145	16.9	70	14.4	135	14.2	430	17.0
Married	3,645	53.8	210	43.3	535	56.3	1,275	50.4
Male	1,680	24.8	90	18.6	255	26.8	615	24.3
Female	1,965	29.0	120	24.7	280	29.5	655	25.9
Separated	305	4.5	35	7.2	30	3.2	135	5.3
Male	115	1.7	15	3.1	20	2.1	50	2.0
Female	190	2.8	20	4.1	-	-	90	3.6
Divorced	300	4.4	45	9.3	50	5.3	120	4.7
Male	80	1.2	25	5.2	35	3.7	45	1.8
Female	225	3.3	15	3.1	20	2.1	70	2.8
Widowed	205	3.0	30	6.2	10	1.1	40	1.6
Male	35	0.5	-	-	-	-	15	0.6
Female	170	2.5	25	5.2	-	-	25	1.0

Source: Aboriginal Peoples Output Program, 1986 Census, Statistics Canada, *A Data Book on Canada's Aboriginal Population from the 1986 Census of Canada*, March, 1989, p. 148. Primary source: 1986 Census of Canada *Notes:* A dash (-) represents zero or a percentage which rounds to less than .05 percent. 1. Aboriginal origins are derived from the ethnic origin question which asks whether respondents are North American Indian, Metis or Inuit. 2. All 1986 figures exclude the population estimated at about 45,000 on 136 incompletely enumerated Indian reserves and settlements throughout Canada. 3. Non-aboriginal in these columns - refers to persons who report one or more non-aboriginal origins such as British, French, etc., in combination with one of the aboriginal origins such as North American Indian. 4. Other multiple aboriginal origins - refers to the sum of those persons reporting two or more aboriginal origins with or without a non- aboriginal origin.

★ 841 ★

Population 15 Years and Over, by Marital Status and Sex for Detailed Aboriginal Origins for Prince Edward Island, 1986 - I[1,2]

Marital status	Total Aboriginal origins[3]		North American Indian only		North American Indian and non-Aboriginal[4]		Metis only	
	Number	Percent	Number	Percent	Number	Percent	Number	Percent
Total	840	100.0	235	100.0	475	100.0	15	100.0
Male	450	53.6	120	51.1	255	53.7	-	-
Female	395	47.0	115	48.9	220	46.3	10	66.7
Single	295	35.1	100	42.6	155	32.6	-	-
Male	165	19.6	60	25.5	75	15.8	-	-
Female	135	16.1	35	14.9	80	16.8	-	-
Married	420	50.0	110	46.8	250	52.6	20	133.3
Male	240	28.6	50	21.3	160	33.7	-	-
Female	175	20.8	55	23.4	90	18.9	10	66.7
Separated	70	8.3	15	6.4	35	7.4	-	-
Male	20	2.4	-	-	-	-	-	-
Female	45	5.4	-	-	35	7.4	-	-
Divorced	25	3.0	-	-	25	5.3	-	-
Male	15	1.8	-	-	-	-	-	-
Female	15	1.8	-	-	10	2.1	-	-
Widowed	30	3.6	15	6.4	-	-	-	-
Male	-	-	-	-	-	-	-	-
Female	20	2.4	-	-	-	-	-	-

Source: Aboriginal Peoples Output Program, 1986 Census, Statistics Canada, *A Data Book on Canada's Aboriginal Population from the 1986 Census of Canada*, March, 1989, p. 52. Primary source: 1986 Census of Canada *Notes:* A dash (-) represents zero or a percentage which rounds to less than .05 percent. 1. Aboriginal origins are derived from the ethnic origin question which asks whether respondents are North American Indian, Metis or Inuit. 2. All 1986 figures exclude the population estimated at about 45,000 on 136 incompletely enumerated Indian reserves and settlements throughout Canada. 3. Total aboriginal origins - are the sum of persons who reported: (a) a single aboriginal (e.g., North American Indian, Metis or Inuit), and, (b) multiple aboriginal origins, that is those who reported: - at least one aboriginal origin with any other non-aboriginal (e.g., Metis and French), or - two or more aboriginal origins only. 4. Non-aboriginal in these columns - refers to persons who report one or more non-aboriginal origins such as British, French, etc., in combination with one of the aboriginal origins such as North American Indian.

★ 842 ★

Population 15 Years and Over, by Marital Status and Sex for Detailed Aboriginal Origins for Prince Edward Island, 1986 - II[1,2]

Marital status	Metis and non-Aboriginal[3]		Inuit only		Inuit and non-Aboriginal[3]		Other multiple Aboriginal origins[4]	
	Number	Percent	Number	Percent	Number	Percent	Number	Percent
Total	70	100.0	-	-	20	100.0	15	100.0
Male	50	71.4	-	-	15	75.0	-	-
Female	25	35.7	-	-	-	-	15	100.0
Single	25	35.7	-	-	-	-	10	66.7
Male	15	21.4	-	-	-	-	-	-
Female	-	-	-	-	-	-	10	66.7
Married	25	35.7	-	-	-	-	-	-
Male	15	21.4	-	-	-	-	-	-
Female	10	14.3	-	-	-	-	-	-
Separated	-	-	-	-	-	-	-	-
Male	-	-	-	-	-	-	-	-
Female	-	-	-	-	-	-	-	-
Divorced	-	-	-	-	-	-	-	-
Male	-	-	-	-	-	-	-	-
Female	-	-	-	-	-	-	-	-
Widowed	10	14.3	-	-	-	-	-	-
Male	-	-	-	-	-	-	-	-
Female	-	-	-	-	-	-	-	-

Source: Aboriginal Peoples Output Program, 1986 Census, Statistics Canada, *A Data Book on Canada's Aboriginal Population from the 1986 Census of Canada*, March, 1989, p. 52. Primary source: 1986 Census of Canada *Notes:* A dash (-) represents zero or a percentage which rounds to less than .05 percent. 1. Aboriginal origins are derived from the ethnic origin question which asks whether respondents are North American Indian, Metis or Inuit. 2. All 1986 figures exclude the population estimated at about 45,000 on 136 incompletely enumerated Indian reserves and settlements throughout Canada. 3. Non-aboriginal in these columns - refers to persons who report one or more non-aboriginal origins such as British, French, etc., in combination with one of the aboriginal origins such as North American Indian. 4. Other multiple aboriginal origins - refers to the sum of those persons reporting two or more aboriginal origins with or without a non- aboriginal origin.

★ 843 ★

Population 15 Years and Over, by Marital Status and Sex for Detailed Aboriginal Origins for Quebec, 1986 - I[1,2]

Marital status	Total Aboriginal origins[3]		North American Indian only		North American Indian and non-Aboriginal[4]		Metis only	
	Number	Percent	Number	Percent	Number	Percent	Number	Percent
Total	56,165	100.0	25,755	100.0	17,905	100.0	4,100	100.0
Male	26,620	47.4	12,560	48.8	8,010	44.7	2,060	50.2
Female	29,540	52.6	13,190	51.2	9,890	55.2	2,040	49.8
Single	19,550	34.8	8,750	34.0	5,990	33.5	1,445	35.2
Male	9,965	17.7	4,600	17.9	2,780	15.5	855	20.9
Female	9,590	17.1	4,155	16.1	3,210	17.9	590	14.4
Married	30,605	54.5	14,440	56.1	9,810	54.8	2,120	51.7
Male	14,935	26.6	7,240	28.1	4,635	25.9	1,035	25.2
Female	15,665	27.9	7,200	28.0	5,175	28.9	1,080	26.3
Separated	1,290	2.3	515	2.0	505	2.8	120	2.9
Male	470	0.8	175	0.7	185	1.0	55	1.3
Female	820	1.5	340	1.3	325	1.8	65	1.6
Divorced	2,630	4.7	930	3.6	1,170	6.5	210	5.1
Male	845	1.5	315	1.2	350	2.0	90	2.2
Female	1,785	3.2	615	2.4	815	4.6	120	2.9
Widowed	2,085	3.7	1,110	4.3	425	2.4	210	5.1
Male	405	0.7	235	0.9	60	0.3	35	0.9
Female	1,675	3.0	880	3.4	370	2.1	180	4.4

Source: Aboriginal Peoples Output Program, 1986 Census, Statistics Canada, *A Data Book on Canada's Aboriginal Population from the 1986 Census of Canada*, March, 1989, p. 124. Primary source: 1986 Census of Canada *Notes:* A dash (-) represents zero or a percentage which rounds to less than .05 percent. 1. Aboriginal origins are derived from the ethnic origin question which asks whether respondents are North American Indian, Metis or Inuit. 2. All 1986 figures exclude the population estimated at about 45,000 on 136 incompletely enumerated Indian reserves and settlements throughout Canada. 3. Total aboriginal origins - are the sum of persons who reported: (a) a single aboriginal (e.g., North American Indian, Metis or Inuit), and, (b) multiple aboriginal origins, that is those who reported: - at least one aboriginal origin with any other non-aboriginal (e.g., Metis and French), or - two or more aboriginal origins only. 4. Non-aboriginal in these columns - refers to persons who report one or more non-aboriginal origins such as British, French, etc., in combination with one of the aboriginal origins such as North American Indian.

★ 844 ★

Population 15 Years and Over, by Marital Status and Sex for Detailed Aboriginal Origins for Quebec, 1986 - II[1,2]

Marital status	Metis and non-Aboriginal[3]		Inuit only		Inuit and non-Aboriginal[3]		Other multiple Aboriginal origins[4]	
	Number	Percent	Number	Percent	Number	Percent	Number	Percent
Total	3,250	100.0	3,900	100.0	370	100.0	890	100.0
Male	1,400	43.1	1,940	49.7	180	48.6	465	52.2
Female	1,850	56.9	1,960	50.3	190	51.4	425	47.8
Single	1,135	34.9	1,795	46.0	145	39.2	290	32.6
Male	525	16.2	970	24.9	55	14.9	175	19.7
Female	605	18.6	825	21.2	90	24.3	115	12.9
Married	1,720	52.9	1,825	46.8	175	47.3	520	58.4
Male	775	23.8	890	22.8	100	27.0	265	29.8
Female	945	29.1	935	24.0	75	20.3	255	28.7
Separated	55	1.7	50	1.3	30	8.1	15	1.7
Male	25	0.8	15	0.4	10	2.7	-	-
Female	35	1.1	30	0.8	20	5.4	-	-
Divorced	195	6.0	45	1.2	15	4.1	50	5.6
Male	50	1.5	-	-	-	-	20	2.2
Female	145	4.5	45	1.2	-	-	30	3.4
Widowed	145	4.5	180	4.6	-	-	-	-
Male	25	0.8	55	1.4	-	-	-	-
Female	120	3.7	125	3.2	-	-	-	-

Source: Aboriginal Peoples Output Program, 1986 Census, Statistics Canada, *A Data Book on Canada's Aboriginal Population from the 1986 Census of Canada*, March, 1989, p. 124. Primary source: 1986 Census of Canada *Notes:* A dash (-) represents zero or a percentage which rounds to less than .05 percent. 1. Aboriginal origins are derived from the ethnic origin question which asks whether respondents are North American Indian, Metis or Inuit. 2. All 1986 figures exclude the population estimated at about 45,000 on 136 incompletely enumerated Indian reserves and settlements throughout Canada. 3. Non-aboriginal in these columns - refers to persons who report one or more non-aboriginal origins such as British, French, etc., in combination with one of the aboriginal origins such as North American Indian. 4. Other multiple aboriginal origins - refers to the sum of those persons reporting two or more aboriginal origins with or without a non- aboriginal origin.

★ 845 ★

Population 15 Years and Over, by Marital Status and Sex for Detailed Aboriginal Origins for Saskatchewan, 1986 - I[1,2]

Marital status	Total Aboriginal origins[3]		North American Indian only		North American Indian and non-Aboriginal[4]		Metis only	
	Number	Percent	Number	Percent	Number	Percent	Number	Percent
Total	44,645	100.0	24,535	100.0	4,760	100.0	7,810	100.0
Male	21,500	48.2	11,915	48.6	2,325	48.8	3,730	47.8
Female	23,145	51.8	12,620	51.4	2,440	51.3	4,080	52.2
Single	18,530	41.5	10,505	42.8	1,930	40.5	3,225	41.3
Male	9,530	21.3	5,355	21.7	1,025	21.5	1,670	21.4
Female	8,995	20.1	5,145	21.0	905	19.0	1,545	19.8
Married	21,235	47.6	11,510	46.9	2,380	50.0	3,545	45.4
Male	10,250	23.0	5,635	23.0	1,140	23.9	1,715	22.0
Female	10,980	24.6	5,875	23.9	1,240	26.1	1,835	23.5
Separated	1,840	4.1	935	3.8	165	3.5	380	4.9
Male	725	1.6	410	1.7	60	1.3	145	1.9
Female	1,115	2.5	525	2.1	105	2.2	235	3.0
Divorced	1,150	2.6	440	1.8	180	3.8	250	3.2
Male	485	1.1	170	0.7	90	1.9	120	1.5
Female	665	1.5	275	1.1	90	1.9	130	1.7
Widowed	1,900	4.3	1,150	4.7	110	2.3	410	5.2
Male	505	1.1	350	1.4	15	0.3	75	1.0
Female	1,390	3.1	805	3.3	90	1.9	335	4.3

Source: Aboriginal Peoples Output Program, 1986 Census, Statistics Canada, *A Data Book on Canada's Aboriginal Population from the 1986 Census of Canada*, March, 1989, p. 196. Primary source: 1986 Census of Canada *Notes:* A dash (-) represents zero or a percentage which rounds to less than .05 percent. 1. Aboriginal origins are derived from the ethnic origin question which asks whether respondents are North American Indian, Metis or Inuit. 2. All 1986 figures exclude the population estimated at about 45,000 on 136 incompletely enumerated Indian reserves and settlements throughout Canada. 3. Total aboriginal origins - are the sum of persons who reported: (a) a single aboriginal (e.g., North American Indian, Metis or Inuit), and, (b) multiple aboriginal origins, that is those who reported: - at least one aboriginal origin with any other non-aboriginal (e.g., Metis and French), or - two or more aboriginal origins only. 4. Non-aboriginal in these columns - refers to persons who report one or more non-aboriginal origins such as British, French, etc., in combination with one of the aboriginal origins such as North American Indian.

★ 846 ★

Population 15 Years and Over, by Marital Status and Sex for Detailed Aboriginal Origins for Saskatchewan, 1986 - II[1,2]

Marital status	Metis and non-Aboriginal[3]		Inuit only		Inuit and non-Aboriginal[3]		Other multiple Aboriginal origins[4]	
	Number	Percent	Number	Percent	Number	Percent	Number	Percent
Total	5,685	100.0	30	100.0	55	100.0	1,775	100.0
Male	2,605	45.8	15	50.0	35	63.6	870	49.0
Female	3,075	54.1	10	33.3	15	27.3	895	50.4
Single	2,125	37.4	15	50.0	35	63.6	700	39.4
Male	1,085	19.1	10	33.3	20	36.4	360	20.3
Female	1,040	18.3	-	-	-	-	340	19.2
Married	2,940	51.7	15	50.0	25	45.5	820	46.2
Male	1,310	23.0	-	-	15	27.3	430	24.2
Female	1,620	28.5	10	33.3	-	-	390	22.0
Separated	250	4.4	-	-	-	-	115	6.5
Male	85	1.5	-	-	-	-	30	1.7
Female	165	2.9	-	-	-	-	85	4.8
Divorced	200	3.5	-	-	-	-	85	4.8
Male	70	1.2	-	-	-	-	30	1.7
Female	125	2.2	-	-	-	-	45	2.5
Widowed	175	3.1	-	-	-	-	55	3.1
Male	50	0.9	-	-	-	-	15	0.8
Female	125	2.2	-	-	-	-	35	2.0

Source: Aboriginal Peoples Output Program, 1986 Census, Statistics Canada, *A Data Book on Canada's Aboriginal Population from the 1986 Census of Canada*, March, 1989, p. 196. Primary source: 1986 Census of Canada *Notes:* A dash (-) represents zero or a percentage which rounds to less than .05 percent. 1. Aboriginal origins are derived from the ethnic origin question which asks whether respondents are North American Indian, Metis or Inuit. 2. All 1986 figures exclude the population estimated at about 45,000 on 136 incompletely enumerated Indian reserves and settlements throughout Canada. 3. Non-aboriginal in these columns - refers to persons who report one or more non-aboriginal origins such as British, French, etc., in combination with one of the aboriginal origins such as North American Indian. 4. Other multiple aboriginal origins - refers to the sum of those persons reporting two or more aboriginal origins with or without a non- aboriginal origin.

★ 847 ★

Population 15 Years and Over, by Marital Status and Sex for Detailed Aboriginal Origins for Yukon Territory, 1986 - I[1,2]

Marital status	Total Aboriginal origins[3]		North American Indian only		North American Indian and non-Aboriginal[4]		Metis only	
	Number	Percent	Number	Percent	Number	Percent	Number	Percent
Total	3,395	100.0	2,325	100.0	890	100.0	45	100.0
Male	1,640	48.3	1,120	48.2	425	47.8	15	33.3
Female	1,755	51.7	1,200	51.6	470	52.8	30	66.7
Single	1,455	42.9	960	41.3	410	46.1	20	44.4
Male	835	24.6	570	24.5	220	24.7	-	-
Female	620	18.3	390	16.8	185	20.8	20	44.4
Married	1,525	44.9	1,035	44.5	415	46.6	20	44.4
Male	655	19.3	435	18.7	175	19.7	10	22.2
Female	870	25.6	600	25.8	240	27.0	10	22.2
Separated	135	4.0	100	4.3	25	2.8	-	-
Male	65	1.9	55	2.4	10	1.1	-	-
Female	65	1.9	45	1.9	15	1.7	-	-
Divorced	115	3.4	70	3.0	35	3.9	-	-
Male	40	1.2	25	1.1	15	1.7	-	-
Female	70	2.1	45	1.9	25	2.8	-	-
Widowed	170	5.0	160	6.9	-	-	-	-
Male	45	1.3	40	1.7	-	-	-	-
Female	130	3.8	115	4.9	-	-	-	-

Source: Aboriginal Peoples Output Program, 1986 Census, Statistics Canada, *A Data Book on Canada's Aboriginal Population from the 1986 Census of Canada*, March, 1989, p. 292. Primary source: 1986 Census of Canada *Notes:* A dash (-) represents zero or a percentage which rounds to less than .05 percent. 1. Aboriginal origins are derived from the ethnic origin question which asks whether respondents are North American Indian, Metis or Inuit. 2. All 1986 figures exclude the population estimated at about 45,000 on 136 incompletely enumerated Indian reserves and settlements throughout Canada. 3. Total aboriginal origins - are the sum of persons who reported: (a) a single aboriginal (e.g., North American Indian, Metis or Inuit), and, (b) multiple aboriginal origins, that is those who reported: - at least one aboriginal origin with any other non-aboriginal (e.g., Metis and French), or - two or more aboriginal origins only. 4. Non-aboriginal in these columns - refers to persons who report one or more non-aboriginal origins such as British, French, etc., in combination with one of the aboriginal origins such as North American Indian.

★ 848 ★

Population 15 Years and Over, by Marital Status and Sex for Detailed Aboriginal Origins for Yukon Territory, 1986 - II[1,2]

Marital status	Metis and non-Aboriginal[3]		Inuit only		Inuit and non-Aboriginal[3]		Other multiple Aboriginal origins[4]	
	Number	Percent	Number	Percent	Number	Percent	Number	Percent
Total	65	100.0	30	100.0	10	100.0	40	100.0
Male	40	61.5	-	-	-	-	-	-
Female	15	23.1	20	66.7	-	-	10	25.0
Single	30	46.2	-	-	-	-	10	25.0
Male	20	30.8	-	-	-	-	-	-
Female	15	23.1	-	-	-	-	-	-
Married	20	30.8	20	66.7	-	-	-	-
Male	20	30.8	-	-	-	-	-	-
Female	-	-	10	33.3	-	-	-	-
Separated	-	-	-	-	-	-	-	-
Male	-	-	-	-	-	-	-	-
Female	-	-	-	-	-	-	-	-
Divorced	-	-	-	-	-	-	-	-
Male	-	-	-	-	-	-	-	-
Female	-	-	-	-	-	-	-	-
Widowed	-	-	-	-	-	-	-	-
Male	-	-	-	-	-	-	-	-
Female	-	-	-	-	-	-	-	-

Source: Aboriginal Peoples Output Program, 1986 Census, Statistics Canada, *A Data Book on Canada's Aboriginal Population from the 1986 Census of Canada,* March, 1989, p. 292. Primary source: 1986 Census of Canada *Notes:* A dash (-) represents zero or a percentage which rounds to less than .05 percent. 1. Aboriginal origins are derived from the ethnic origin question which asks whether respondents are North American Indian, Metis or Inuit. 2. All 1986 figures exclude the population estimated at about 45,000 on 136 incompletely enumerated Indian reserves and settlements throughout Canada. 3. Non-aboriginal in these columns - refers to persons who report one or more non-aboriginal origins such as British, French, etc., in combination with one of the aboriginal origins such as North American Indian. 4. Other multiple aboriginal origins - refers to the sum of those persons reporting two or more aboriginal origins with or without a non- aboriginal origin.

★ 849 ★

Population 15 Years and Over, by Marital Status and Sex for Selected Aboriginal Origins for Canada, 1986[1,2]

Marital status	Total Aboriginal origins[3]		Aboriginal origins only[4]		Aboriginal and non-Aboriginal origins[5]		Total Canada[6]	
	Number	Percent	Number	Percent	Number	Percent	Number	Percent
Total	451,950	100.0	244,595	100.0	207,355	100.0	19,634,100	100.0
Male	217,135	48.0	118,500	48.4	98,630	47.6	9,606,255	48.9
Female	234,820	52.0	126,095	51.6	108,725	52.4	10,027,850	51.1
Single	168,995	37.4	95,990	39.2	73,005	35.2	5,328,645	27.1
Male	90,290	20.0	51,925	21.2	38,365	18.5	2,927,480	14.9
Female	78,705	17.4	44,060	18.0	34,640	16.7	2,401,170	12.2
Married	229,800	50.8	119,115	48.7	110,690	53.4	11,983,765	61.0
Male	109,345	24.2	56,490	23.1	52,855	25.5	5,995,330	30.5
Female	120,455	26.7	62,625	25.6	57,835	27.9	5,988,430	30.5
Separated	18,995	4.2	10,230	4.2	8,765	4.2	510,715	2.6
Male	7,080	1.6	3,975	1.6	3,115	1.5	220,730	1.1
Female	11,910	2.6	6,255	2.6	5,655	2.7	289,985	1.5
Divorced	17,955	4.0	7,795	3.2	10,155	4.9	686,525	3.5
Male	6,540	1.4	3,050	1.2	3,495	1.7	274,750	1.4
Female	11,410	2.5	4,750	1.9	6,660	3.2	411,750	2.1
Widowed	16,205	3.6	11,470	4.7	4,740	2.3	1,124,450	5.7
Male	3,870	0.9	3,070	1.3	805	0.4	187,935	1.0
Female	12,335	2.7	8,400	3.4	3,935	1.9	936,515	4.8

Source: Aboriginal Peoples Output Program, 1986 Census, Statistics Canada, *A Data Book on Canada's Aboriginal Population from the 1986 Census of Canada*, March, 1989, p. 316. Primary source: 1986 Census of Canada *Notes:* 1. Aboriginal origins are derived from the ethnic origin question which asks whether respondents are North American Indian, Metis or Inuit. 2. All 1986 figures exclude the population estimated at about 45,000 on 136 incompletely enumerated Indian reserves and settlements throughout Canada. 3. Total aboriginal origins - are the sum of persons who reported: (a) a single aboriginal (e.g., North American Indian, Metis or Inuit), and, (b) multiple aboriginal origins, that is those who reported: - at least one aboriginal origin with any other non-aboriginal (e.g., Metis and French), or - two or more aboriginal origins only. 4. Aboriginal origins only - is the sum of persons reporting an aboriginal origin as a single response, and those reporting two or more aboriginal origins (e.g., North American Indian and Metis). 5. Aboriginal and non-aboriginal origins - refers to persons reporting an aboriginal origin (North American Indian, Metis or Inuit) and one or more non-aboriginal origins (e.g., British, French). 6. Total Canada and total province or territory (columns 4 and 5) - refers to the total populations of Canada and the relevant province and territory, excluding the institutional population.

Education

★ 850 ★

Persons of Aboriginal Origin and Total Canadian Population, by Highest Level of Education, Canada, 1986

Group/Region	Highest Level of Education								Total Population Age 15+
	Less Than Grade 9		Grades 9-13 (w/o HS Degree)		High School Degree		Post-Secondary Degree		
	Number	%	Number	%	Number	%	Number	%	
On-Reserve									
Atlantic	1,890	36.3	1,525	29.3	230	4.4	1,565	30.0	5,210
Quebec	6,805	50.4	4,050	30.0	465	3.4	2,185	16.2	13,505
Ontario	5,955	35.3	6,455	38.3	1,080	6.4	3,365	20.0	16,855
Manitoba	8,275	52.3	5,535	35.0	300	1.9	1,720	10.9	15,830
Saskatchewan	7,720	50.6	4,705	30.9	245	1.6	2,575	16.9	15,245
Alberta	4,865	43.6	3,880	34.8	330	3.0	2,085	18.7	11,160
British Columbia	7,255	35.3	7,730	37.8	1,145	5.6	4,340	21.2	20,470
Territories	200	48.2	135	32.5	10	2.4	70	16.9	415
Canada	42,965	43.4	34,010	34.5	3,790	3.8	17,870	18.1	98,635
Off-Reserve									
Atlantic	4,225	24.8	4,960	29.1	1,445	8.5	6,415	37.6	17,045
Quebec	9,470	22.2	9,855	23.1	5,675	13.3	17,665	41.4	42,665
Ontario	11,240	12.1	32,650	35.2	11,335	12.2	37,460	40.4	92,685
Manitoba	9,535	26.3	14,450	39.9	2,180	6.0	10,050	27.8	36,215
Saskatchewan	8,935	30.4	10,140	34.5	1,350	4.6	8,980	30.5	29,405
Alberta	9,985	19.2	20,175	38.9	4,110	7.9	17,635	34.0	51,905
British Columbia	9,320	15.1	23,485	38.1	6,180	10.0	22,725	36.8	61,710
Territories	11,505	53.2	5,430	25.1	690	3.2	4,020	18.6	21,645
Canada	74,220	21.0	121,150	34.3	32,970	9.3	124,965	35.4	353,305
Total Canadian population									
Atlantic	374,825	21.7	533,020	30.8	162,525	9.4	659,790	38.1	1,730,160
Quebec	1,223,125	23.9	1,013,360	19.8	803,690	15.7	2,074,810	40.6	5,114,985
Ontario	1,040,500	14.6	2,030,990	28.5	946,425	13.3	3,114,895	43.7	7,132,810
Manitoba	147,925	18.2	269,690	33.1	73,820	9.1	322,490	39.6	813,925
Saskatchewan	144,125	19.2	247,190	32.9	64,725	8.6	295,065	39.3	751,105
Alberta	192,885	10.8	541,825	30.5	191,675	10.8	852,995	47.9	1,779,380
British Columbia	256,880	11.4	672,260	29.8	264,315	11.7	1,065,860	47.2	2,259,315

[Continued]

★ 850 ★

Persons of Aboriginal Origin and Total Canadian Population, by Highest Level of Education, Canada, 1986

[Continued]

Group/Region	Highest Level of Education				High School Degree		Post-Secondary Degree		Total Population Age 15+
	Less Than Grade 9		Grades 9-13 (w/o HS Degree)						
	Number	%	Number	%	Number	%	Number	%	
Territories	13,480	25.7	12,875	24.6	4,040	7.7	22,025	42.0	52,420
Canada	3,393,725	17.3	5,321,230	27.1	2,511,220	12.8	8,407,935	42.8	19,634,110

Source: Canada's Off-Reserve Aboriginal Population: A Statistical Overview, Social Trends Analysis Directorate, Department of the Secretary of State of Canada, 1991, p. A-6. Primary source: For Aboriginal population: Statistics Canada, *A Profile of the Aboriginal Population Residing in Selected Off Reserve Areas*, prepared by the Aboriginal Data and Native Issues Unit of the Housing, Family and Social Statistics Division, February 1990; for total Canadian population: Statistics Canada, *1986, Census, Special Tabulations from the Small Area Database*, compiled for the Department of the Secretary of State. *Notes:* Sum of components may not always add to totals due to rounding and/or data suppression.

★ 851 ★

Population 15 Years and Over, by Highest Level of Schooling and Sex for Detailed Aboriginal Origins for Canada, 1986 - I[1,2]

Highest level of schooling	Total Aboriginal origins[3]		North American Indian only		North American Indian non-Aboriginal[4]		Metis only	
	Number	Percent	Number	Percent	Number	Percent	Number	Percent
Total population								
aged 15+	451,950	100.0	184,855	100.0	150,280	100.0	39,975	100.0
Male	217,130	48.0	89,050	48.2	71,050	47.3	19,690	49.3
Female	234,820	52.0	95,800	51.8	79,240	52.7	20,285	50.7
Less than grade 9[5]	117,190	25.9	67,575	36.6	14,950	9.9	13,925	34.8
Male	58,020	12.8	33,210	18.0	7,495	5.0	6,880	17.2
Female	59,165	13.1	34,365	18.6	7,450	5.0	7,050	17.6
Grades 9-13 without certificate	155,160	34.3	64,235	34.7	49,770	33.1	15,560	38.9
Male	74,490	16.5	30,720	16.6	23,750	15.8	7,685	19.2
Female	80,675	17.9	33,510	18.1	26,020	17.3	7,875	19.7
Grades 9-13 with certificate	36,760	8.1	9,975	5.4	18,375	12.2	2,180	5.5
Male	16,030	3.5	4,535	2.5	7,820	5.2	930	2.3
Female	20,740	4.6	5,445	2.9	10,550	7.0	1,250	3.1
Trades certificate or diploma	10,760	2.4	3,830	2.1	4,095	2.7	910	2.3
Male	7,020	1.6	2,425	1.3	2,830	1.9	585	1.5
Female	3,660	0.8	1,405	0.8	1,265	0.8	320	0.8

[Continued]

★ 851 ★

Population 15 Years and Over, by Highest Level of Schooling and Sex for Detailed Aboriginal Origins for Canada, 1986 - I

[Continued]

Highest level of schooling	Total Aboriginal origins[3]		North American Indian only		North American Indian non-Aboriginal[4]		Metis only	
	Number	Percent	Number	Percent	Number	Percent	Number	Percent
Other non-university without certificate[6]	34,670	7.7	12,705	6.9	13,790	9.2	2,555	6.4
Male	15,460	3.4	5,685	3.1	6,050	4.0	1,160	2.9
Female	19,210	4.3	7,015	3.8	7,740	5.2	1,395	3.5
Other non-university with certificate	52,650	11.7	15,565	8.4	24,685	16.4	3,205	8.0
Male	25,505	5.6	7,610	4.1	11,525	7.7	1,665	4.2
Female	27,145	6.0	7,960	4.3	13,155	8.8	1,540	3.9
University without degree[7]	29,215	6.5	8,550	4.6	14,370	9.6	1,250	3.1
Male	13,170	2.9	3,770	2.0	6,630	4.4	600	1.5
Female	16,045	3.6	4,780	2.6	7,735	5.1	650	1.6
University with degree	15,625	3.5	2,415	1.3	10,250	6.8	395	1.0
Male	7,445	1.7	1,090	0.6	4,940	3.3	195	0.5
Female	8,180	1.8	1,325	0.7	5,305	3.5	205	0.5

Source: Aboriginal Peoples Output Program, 1986 Census, Statistics Canada, *A Data Book on Canada's Aboriginal Population from the 1986 Census of Canada*, March, 1989, p. 14. Primary source: 1986 Census of Canada. *Notes:* (NA) stands for not applicable. A dash (-) represents zero or a percentage less than .05 percent. 1. Aboriginal origins are derived from the ethnic origin question which asks whether respondents are North American Indian, Metis or Inuit. 2. All 1986 figures exclude the population estimated at about 45,000 on 136 incompletely enumerated Indian reserves and settlements throughout Canada. 3. Total Aboriginal origins - are the sum of persons who reported: (a) a single aboriginal (e.g., North American Indian, Metis or Inuit) and, (b) multiple aboriginal origins, that is those who reported: - at least one aboriginal origin with any other non-aboriginal (e.g., Metis and French), or - two or more aboriginal origins only. 4. Non-aboriginal in these columns - refers to persons who reported one or more non-aboriginal origins such as British, French, etc., in combination with one of the aboriginal origins such as North American Indian. 5. Includes "no schooling or kindergarten only." 6. Includes both post-secondary non-university courses requiring secondary school graduation such as community colleges or CEGEPS and courses taken in other institutions such as trade schools or vocational centers which may not require secondary school graduation. 7. Includes those with both university and other non-university education, as well as those university only.

★ 852 ★

Population 15 Years and Over, by Highest Level of Schooling and Sex for Detailed Aboriginal Origins for Canada, 1986 - II[1,2]

Highest level of schooling	Metis and non-Aboriginal[3]		Inuit only		Inuit and non-Aboriginal[3]		Other multiple Aboriginal origins[4]	
	Number	Percent	Number	Percent	Number	Percent	Number	Percent
Total population aged 15+	42,435	100.0	16,500	100.0	3,660	100.0	14,245	100.0
Male	19,865	46.8	8,255	50.0	1,875	51.2	7,345	51.6
Female	22,570	53.2	8,240	49.9	1,785	48.8	6,895	48.4
Less than grade 9[5]	7,215	17.0	9,880	59.9	795	21.7	2,850	20.0
Male	3,730	8.8	4,765	28.9	415	11.3	1,530	10.7

[Continued]

★ 852 ★

Population 15 Years and Over, by Highest Level of Schooling and Sex for Detailed Aboriginal Origins for Canada, 1986 - II
[Continued]

Highest level of schooling	Metis and non-Aboriginal[3]		Inuit only		Inuit and non-Aboriginal[3]		Other multiple Aboriginal origins[4]	
	Number	Percent	Number	Percent	Number	Percent	Number	Percent
Female	3,485	8.2	5,120	31.0	380	10.4	1,315	9.2
Grades 9-13 without certificate	15,965	37.6	3,795	23.0	1,215	33.2	4,630	32.5
Male	7,500	17.7	1,875	11.4	615	16.8	2,340	16.4
Female	8,460	19.9	1,915	11.6	600	16.4	2,295	16.1
Grades 9-13 with certificate	4,170	9.8	530	3.2	405	11.1	1,125	7.9
Male	1,705	4.0	295	1.8	215	5.9	525	3.7
Female	2,465	5.8	230	1.4	190	5.2	600	4.2
Trades certificate or diploma	1,075	2.5	270	1.6	105	2.9	390	2.7
Male	675	1.6	180	1.1	45	1.2	285	2.0
Female	405	1.0	90	0.5	60	1.6	110	0.8
Other non-university without certificate[6]	3,510	8.3	755	4.6	225	6.1	1,140	8.0
Male	1,520	3.6	410	2.5	105	2.9	535	3.8
Female	1,985	4.7	350	2.1	115	3.1	605	4.2
Other non-university with certificate	5,775	13.6	955	5.8	485	13.3	1,975	13.9
Male	2,725	6.4	590	3.6	265	7.2	1,125	7.9
Female	3,050	7.2	370	2.2	215	5.9	850	6.0
University without degree[7]	3,200	7.5	280	1.7	300	8.2	1,265	8.9
Male	1,290	3.0	130	0.8	165	4.5	575	4.0
Female	1,915	4.5	145	0.9	135	3.7	685	4.8
University with degree	1,530	3.6	40	0.2	125	3.4	865	6.1
Male	715	1.7	20	0.1	50	1.4	435	3.1
Female	810	1.9	20	0.1	80	2.2	430	3.0

Source: Aboriginal Peoples Output Program, 1986 Census, Statistics Canada, *A Data Book on Canada's Aboriginal Population from the 1986 Census of Canada*, March, 1989, p. 14. Primary source: 1986 Census of Canada. *Notes:* (NA) stands for not applicable. A dash (-) represents zero or a percentage less than .05 percent. 1. Aboriginal origins are derived from the ethnic origin question which asks whether respondents are North American Indian, Metis or Inuit. 2. All 1986 figures exclude the population estimated at about 45,000 on 136 incompletely enumerated Indian reserves and settlements throughout Canada. For an estimate of the unenumerated population and list of incompletely enumerated reserves in each affected province, see Appendix 1 and 2. 3. Total Aboriginal origins - are the sum of persons who reported: (a) a single aboriginal (e.g., North American Indian, Metis or Inuit) and, (b) multiple aboriginal origins, that is those who reported: - at least one aboriginal origin with any other non-aboriginal (e.g., Metis and French), or - two or more aboriginal origins only. 4. Other Multiple Aboriginal origins - refer to the sum of those persons reporting two or more aboriginal origins with or without a non-aboriginal origin. 5. Includes "no schooling or kindergarten only." 6. Includes both post-secondary non-university courses requiring secondary school graduation such as community colleges or CEGEPS, and courses taken in other institutions such as trade schools or vocational centers which may not require secondary school graduation. 7. Includes those with both university and other non-university education, as well as those with university only.

★ 853 ★

Population 15 Years and Over, by Highest Level of Schooling and Sex for Detailed Aboriginal Origins for Alberta, 1986 - I[1,2]

Highest level of schooling	Total Aboriginal origins[3]		North American Indian only		North American Indian non-Aboriginal[4]		Metis only	
	Number	Percent	Number	Percent	Number	Percent	Number	Percent
Total population								
Aged 15+	63,055	100.0	20,940	100.0	17,020	100.0	11,085	100.0
Male	30,230	47.9	9,765	46.6	8,115	47.7	5,480	49.4
Female	32,825	52.1	11,175	53.4	8,905	52.3	5,600	50.5
Less than grade 9[5]	14,850	23.6	7,595	36.3	1,185	7.0	3,760	33.9
Male	7,575	12.0	3,815	18.2	620	3.6	1,915	17.3
Female	7,275	11.5	3,785	18.1	560	3.3	1,850	16.7
Grades 9-13 without certificate	24,050	38.1	7,635	36.5	6,100	35.8	4,810	43.4
Male	11,275	17.9	3,420	16.3	2,835	16.7	2,375	21.4
Female	12,775	20.3	4,220	20.2	3,265	19.2	2,440	22.0
Grades 9-13 with certificate	4,435	7.0	840	4.0	1,845	10.8	445	4.0
Male	1,875	3.0	355	1.7	730	4.3	195	1.8
Female	2,565	4.1	485	2.3	1,115	6.6	245	2.2
Trades certificate or diploma	1,325	2.1	375	1.8	385	2.3	190	1.7
Male	900	1.4	235	1.1	285	1.7	130	1.2
Female	425	0.7	135	0.6	105	0.6	65	0.6
Other non-university without certificate[6]	5,535	8.8	1,760	8.4	1,785	10.5	735	6.6
Male	2,385	3.8	790	3.8	830	4.9	275	2.5
Female	3,150	5.0	975	4.7	960	5.6	460	4.1
Other non-university with certificate	7,455	11.8	1,670	8.0	2,910	17.1	850	7.7
Male	3,675	5.8	720	3.4	1,490	8.8	435	3.9
Female	3,775	6.0	955	4.6	1,425	8.4	420	3.8
University without degree[7]	3,515	5.6	865	4.1	1,585	9.3	210	1.9
Male	1,690	2.7	370	1.8	775	4.6	110	1.0
Female	1,825	2.9	490	2.3	810	4.8	95	0.9
University with degree	1,885	3.0	195	0.9	1,220	7.2	75	0.7

[Continued]

★ 853 ★

Population 15 Years and Over, by Highest Level of Schooling and Sex for Detailed Aboriginal Origins for Alberta, 1986 - I

[Continued]

Highest level of schooling	Total Aboriginal origins[3]		North American Indian only		North American Indian non-Aboriginal[4]		Metis only	
	Number	Percent	Number	Percent	Number	Percent	Number	Percent
Male	850	1.3	60	0.3	545	3.2	50	0.5
Female	1,035	1.6	130	0.6	670	3.9	25	0.2

Source: Aboriginal Peoples Output Program, 1986 Census, Statistics Canada, *A Data Book on Canada's Aboriginal Population from the 1986 Census of Canada*, March , 1989, p. 230. Primary source: 1986 Census of Canada *Notes:* (NA) stands for not applicable. A dash (-) represents zero or a percentage less than .05 percent. 1. Aboriginal origins are derived from the ethnic origin question which asks whether respondents are North American Indian, Metis or Inuit. 2. All 1986 figures exclude the population estimated at about 45,000 on 136 incompletely enumerated Indian reserves and settlements throughout Canada. 3. Total Aboriginal origins - are the sum of persons who reported: (a) a single aboriginal (e.g., North American Indian, Metis or Inuit) and, (b) multiple aboriginal origins, that is those who reported: - at least one aboriginal origin with any other non-aboriginal (e.g., Metis and French), or - two or more aboriginal origins only. 4. Non-aboriginal in these columns - refers to persons who reported one or more non-aboriginal origins such as British, French, etc., in combination with one of the aboriginal origins such as North American Indian. 5. Includes "no schooling or kindergarten only." 6. Includes both post-secondary non-university courses requiring secondary school graduation such as community colleges or CEGEPS and courses taken in other institutions such as trade schools or vocational centers which may not require secondary school graduation. 7. Includes those with both university and other non-university education, as well as those university only.

★ 854 ★

Population 15 Years and Over, by Highest Level of Schooling and Sex for Detailed Aboriginal Origins for Alberta, 1986 - II[1,2]

Highest level of schooling	Metis and non-Aboriginal[3]		Inuit only		Inuit and non-Aboriginal[3]		Other multiple Aboriginal origins[4]	
	Number	Percent	Number	Percent	Number	Percent	Number	Percent
Total population								
Aged 15+	9,995	100.0	210	100.0	285	100.0	3,525	100.0
Male	4,745	47.5	110	52.4	110	38.6	1,905	54.0
Female	5,255	52.6	95	45.2	175	61.4	1,620	46.0
Less than grade 9[5]	1,540	15.4	55	26.2	10	3.5	705	20.0
Male	800	8.0	20	9.5	-	-	400	11.3
Female	735	7.4	35	16.7	-	-	305	8.7
Grades 9-13 without certificate	4,115	41.2	65	31.0	110	38.6	1,215	34.5
Male	1,960	19.6	40	19.0	40	14.0	605	17.2
Female	2,160	21.6	25	11.9	65	22.8	610	17.3
Grades 9-13 with certificate	995	10.0	20	9.5	35	12.3	260	7.4
Male	415	4.2	15	7.1	25	8.8	145	4.1
Female	580	5.8	-	-	10	3.5	120	3.4
Trades certificate or diploma	210	2.1	-	-	10	3.5	140	4.0
Male	120	1.2	-	-	-	-	120	3.4
Female	90	0.9	-	-	-	-	30	0.9

[Continued]

★ 854 ★

Population 15 Years and Over, by Highest Level of Schooling and Sex for Detailed Aboriginal Origins for Alberta, 1986 - II

[Continued]

Highest level of schooling	Metis and non-Aboriginal[3]		Inuit only		Inuit and non-Aboriginal[3]		Other multiple Aboriginal origins[4]	
	Number	Percent	Number	Percent	Number	Percent	Number	Percent
Other non-university without certificate[6]	890	8.9	20	9.5	20	7.0	310	8.8
Male	355	3.6	-	-	-	-	125	3.5
Female	535	5.4	15	7.1	15	5.3	190	5.4
Other non-university with certificate	1,475	14.8	20	9.5	25	8.8	490	13.9
Male	710	7.1	10	4.8	-	-	310	8.8
Female	765	7.7	-	-	25	8.8	190	5.4
University without degree[7]	560	5.6	25	11.9	25	8.8	240	6.8
Male	285	2.9	15	7.1	-	-	115	3.3
Female	280	2.8	-	-	15	5.3	125	3.5
University with degree	215	2.2	-	-	30	10.5	155	4.4
Male	100	1.0	-	-	-	-	90	2.6
Female	110	1.1	-	-	30	10.5	65	1.8

Source: Aboriginal Peoples Output Program, 1986 Census, Statistics Canada, *A Data Book on Canada's Aboriginal Population from the 1986 Census of Canada*, March, 1989, p. 230. Primary source: 1986 Census of Canada *Notes:* (NA) stands for not applicable. A dash (-) represents zero or a percentage less than .05 percent. 1. Aboriginal origins are derived from the ethnic origin question which asks whether respondents are North American Indian, Metis or Inuit. 2. All 1986 figures exclude the population estimated at about 45,000 on 136 incompletely enumerated Indian reserves and settlements throughout Canada. For an estimate of the unenumerated population and list of incompletely enumerated reserves in each affected province, see Appendix 1 and 2. 3. Total Aboriginal origins - are the sum of persons who reported: (a) a single aboriginal (e.g., North American Indian, Metis or Inuit) and, (b) multiple aboriginal origins, that is those who reported: - at least one aboriginal origin with any other non-aboriginal (e.g., Metis and French), or - two or more aboriginal origins only. 4. Other Multiple Aboriginal origins - refer to the sum of those persons reporting two or more aboriginal origins with or without a non-aboriginal origin. 5. Includes "no schooling or kindergarten only." 6. Includes both post-secondary non-university courses requiring secondary school graduation such as community colleges or CEGEPS, and courses taken in other institutions such as trade schools or vocational centers which may not require secondary school graduation. 7. Includes those with both university and other non-university education, as well as those with university only.

★ 855 ★

Population 15 Years and Over, by Highest Level of Schooling and Sex for Detailed Aboriginal Origins for British Columbia, 1986 - I[1,2]

Highest level of schooling	Total Aboriginal origins[3]		North American Indian only		North American Indian non-Aboriginal[4]		Metis only	
	Number	Percent	Number	Percent	Number	Percent	Number	Percent
Total population								
Aged 15+	82,175	100.0	39,020	100.0	32,305	100.0	3,005	100.0
Male	40,095	48.8	18,950	48.6	15,730	48.7	1,435	47.8
Female	42,085	51.2	20,070	51.4	16,575	51.3	1,575	52.4
Less than grade 9[5]	16,580	20.2	11,725	30.0	2,930	9.1	915	30.4
Male	8,440	10.3	5,870	15.0	1,565	4.8	465	15.5

[Continued]

★ 855 ★

Population 15 Years and Over, by Highest Level of Schooling and Sex for Detailed Aboriginal Origins for British Columbia, 1986 - I
[Continued]

Highest level of schooling	Total Aboriginal origins[3]		North American Indian only		North American Indian non-Aboriginal[4]		Metis only	
	Number	Percent	Number	Percent	Number	Percent	Number	Percent
Female	8,135	9.9	5,850	15.0	1,370	4.2	445	14.8
Grades 9-13 without certificate	31,215	38.0	15,360	39.4	11,860	36.7	1,230	40.9
Male	15,610	19.0	7,615	19.5	6,035	18.7	570	19.0
Female	15,605	19.0	7,745	19.8	5,820	18.0	660	22.0
Grades 9-13 with certificate	7,330	8.9	2,515	6.4	3,835	11.9	195	6.5
Male	3,160	3.8	1,205	3.1	1,595	4.9	55	1.8
Female	4,170	5.1	1,310	3.4	2,235	6.9	135	4.5
Trades certificate or diploma	1,605	2.0	590	1.5	740	2.3	80	2.7
Male	1,095	1.3	350	0.9	535	1.7	50	1.7
Female	515	0.6	240	0.6	205	0.6	25	0.8
Other non-university without certificate[6]	7,395	9.0	3,260	8.4	3,170	9.8	225	7.5
Male	3,295	4.0	1,400	3.6	1,365	4.2	140	4.7
Female	4,105	5.0	1,865	4.8	1,805	5.6	95	3.2
Other non-university with certificate	10,580	12.9	3,965	10.2	5,100	15.8	230	7.7
Male	5,015	6.1	1,830	4.7	2,400	7.4	110	3.7
Female	5,565	6.8	2,140	5.5	2,700	8.4	125	4.2
University without degree[7]	5,045	6.1	1,285	3.3	2,905	9.0	100	3.3
Male	2,190	2.7	555	1.4	1,285	4.0	30	1.0
Female	2,855	3.5	730	1.9	1,620	5.0	65	2.2
University with degree	2,430	3.0	330	0.8	1,765	5.5	30	1.0
Male	1,295	1.6	130	0.3	950	2.9	-	-
Female	1,135	1.4	195	0.5	810	2.5	25	0.8

Source: Aboriginal Peoples Output Program, 1986 Census, Statistics Canada, *A Data Book on Canada's Aboriginal Population from the 1986 Census of Canada*, March , 1989, p. 254. Primary source: 1986 Census of Canada *Notes:* (NA) stands for not applicable. A dash (-) represents zero or a percentage less than .05 percent. 1. Aboriginal origins are derived from the ethnic origin question which asks whether respondents are North American Indian, Metis or Inuit. 2. All 1986 figures exclude the population estimated at about 45,000 on 136 incompletely enumerated Indian reserves and settlements throughout Canada. 3. Total Aboriginal origins - are the sum of persons who reported: (a) a single aboriginal (e.g., North American Indian, Metis or Inuit) and, (b) multiple aboriginal origins, that is those who reported: - at least one aboriginal origin with any other non-aboriginal (e.g., Metis and French), or - two or more aboriginal origins only. 4. Non-aboriginal in these columns - refers to persons who reported one or more non-aboriginal origins such as British, French, etc., in combination with one of the aboriginal origins such as North American Indian. 5. Includes "no schooling or kindergarten only." 6. Includes both post-secondary non-university courses requiring secondary school graduation such as community colleges or CEGEPS and courses taken in other institutions such as trade schools or vocational centers which may not require secondary school graduation. 7. Includes those with both university and other non-university education, as well as those university only.

★ 856 ★

Population 15 Years and Over, by Highest Level of Schooling and Sex for Detailed Aboriginal Origins for British Columbia, 1986 - II[1,2]

Highest level of schooling	Metis and non-Aboriginal[3]		Inuit only		Inuit and non-Aboriginal[3]		Other multiple Aboriginal origins[4]	
	Number	Percent	Number	Percent	Number	Percent	Number	Percent
Total population								
Aged 15+	5,805	100.0	165	100.0	330	100.0	1,545	100.0
Male	2,850	49.1	90	54.5	205	62.1	835	54.0
Female	2,955	50.9	75	45.5	125	37.9	705	45.6
Less than grade 9[5]	690	11.9	35	21.2	35	10.6	255	16.5
Male	385	6.6	-	-	15	4.5	145	9.4
Female	305	5.3	30	18.2	20	6.1	110	7.1
Grades 9-13 without certificate	2,120	36.5	50	30.3	145	43.9	445	28.8
Male	1,015	17.5	15	9.1	100	30.3	260	16.8
Female	1,110	19.1	30	18.2	50	15.2	185	12.0
Grades 9-13 with certificate	580	10.0	35	21.2	30	9.1	145	9.4
Male	195	3.4	35	21.2	15	4.5	55	3.6
Female	380	6.5	-	-	15	4.5	85	5.5
Trades certificate or diploma	160	2.8	-	-	-	-	35	2.3
Male	120	2.1	-	-	-	-	30	1.9
Female	40	0.7	-	-	-	-	-	-
Other non-university without certificate[6]	550	9.5	20	12.1	25	7.6	135	8.7
Male	290	5.0	15	9.1	10	3.0	75	4.9
Female	260	4.5	-	-	15	4.5	60	3.9
Other non-university with certificate	935	16.1	-	-	60	18.2	285	18.4
Male	475	8.2	-	-	40	12.1	155	10.0
Female	450	7.8	-	-	15	4.5	125	8.1
University without degree[7]	560	9.6	10	6.1	15	4.5	180	11.7
Male	235	4.0	-	-	10	3.0	70	4.5
Female	330	5.7	-	-	-	-	110	7.1
University with degree	210	3.6	-	-	10	3.0	75	4.9

[Continued]

★ 856 ★

Population 15 Years and Over, by Highest Level of Schooling and Sex for Detailed Aboriginal Origins for British Columbia, 1986 - II

[Continued]

Highest level of schooling	Metis and non-Aboriginal[3]		Inuit only		Inuit and non-Aboriginal[3]		Other multiple Aboriginal origins[4]	
	Number	Percent	Number	Percent	Number	Percent	Number	Percent
Male	135	2.3	-	-	-	-	50	3.2
Female	75	1.3	-	-	-	-	25	1.6

Source: Aboriginal Peoples Output Program, 1986 Census, Statistics Canada, *A Data Book on Canada's Aboriginal Population from the 1986 Census of Canada*, March, 1989, p. 254. Primary source: 1986 Census of Canada *Notes:* (NA) stands for not applicable. A dash (-) represents zero or a percentage less than .05 percent. 1. Aboriginal origins are derived from the ethnic origin question which asks whether respondents are North American Indian, Metis or Inuit. 2. All 1986 figures exclude the population estimated at about 45,000 on 136 incompletely enumerated Indian reserves and settlements throughout Canada. For an estimate of the unenumerated population and list of incompletely enumerated reserves in each affected province, see Appendix 1 and 2. 3. Total Aboriginal origins - are the sum of persons who reported: (a) a single aboriginal (e.g., North American Indian, Metis or Inuit) and, (b) multiple aboriginal origins, that is those who reported: - at least one aboriginal origin with any other non-aboriginal (e.g., Metis and French), or - two or more aboriginal origins only. 4. Other Multiple Aboriginal origins - refer to the sum of those persons reporting two or more aboriginal origins with or without a non-aboriginal origin. 5. Includes "no schooling or kindergarten only." 6. Includes both post-secondary non-university courses requiring secondary school graduation such as community colleges or CEGEPS, and courses taken in other institutions such as trade schools or vocational centers which may not require secondary school graduation. 7. Includes those with both university and other non-university education, as well as those with university only.

★ 857 ★

Population 15 Years and Over, by Highest Level of Schooling and Sex for Detailed Aboriginal Origins for Manitoba, 1986 - I[1,2]

Highest level of schooling	Total Aboriginal origins[3]		North American Indian only		North American Indian non-Aboriginal[4]		Metis only	
	Number	Percent	Number	Percent	Number	Percent	Number	Percent
Total population								
Aged 15+	52,050	100.0	24,360	100.0	6,360	100.0	9,330	100.0
Male	24,970	48.0	11,660	47.9	3,060	48.1	4,650	49.8
Female	27,075	52.0	12,705	52.2	3,300	51.9	4,680	50.2
Less than grade 9[5]	17,815	34.2	10,785	44.3	810	12.7	3,620	38.8
Male	8,735	16.8	5,190	21.3	435	6.8	1,785	19.1
Female	9,080	17.4	5,595	23.0	375	5.9	1,840	19.7
Grades 9-13 without certificate	19,990	38.4	8,915	36.6	2,240	35.2	3,820	40.9
Male	9,535	18.3	4,200	17.2	1,020	16.0	1,950	20.9
Female	10,450	20.1	4,715	19.4	1,215	19.1	1,870	20.0
Grades 9-13 with certificate	2,480	4.8	610	2.5	620	9.7	420	4.5
Male	1,070	2.1	295	1.2	280	4.4	190	2.0
Female	1,410	2.7	310	1.3	335	5.3	230	2.5
Trades certificate or diploma	750	1.4	250	1.0	155	2.4	125	1.3
Male	440	0.8	130	0.5	100	1.6	70	0.8
Female	305	0.6	120	0.5	60	0.9	55	0.6

[Continued]

★ 857 ★

Population 15 Years and Over, by Highest Level of Schooling and Sex for Detailed Aboriginal Origins for Manitoba, 1986 - I

[Continued]

Highest level of schooling	Total Aboriginal origins[3]		North American Indian only		North American Indian non-Aboriginal[4]		Metis only	
	Number	Percent	Number	Percent	Number	Percent	Number	Percent
Other non-university without certificate[6]	2,765	5.3	1,015	4.2	545	8.6	435	4.7
Male	1,290	2.5	470	1.9	245	3.9	210	2.3
Female	1,475	2.8	545	2.2	300	4.7	225	2.4
Other non-university with certificate	3,800	7.3	1,045	4.3	980	15.4	525	5.6
Male	1,940	3.7	565	2.3	495	7.8	245	2.6
Female	1,865	3.6	475	1.9	485	7.6	280	3.0
University without degree[7]	3,255	6.3	1,375	5.6	685	10.8	305	3.3
Male	1,445	2.8	655	2.7	310	4.9	170	1.8
Female	1,815	3.5	720	3.0	375	5.9	135	1.4
University with degree	1,205	2.3	365	1.5	320	5.0	85	0.9
Male	520	1.0	140	0.6	170	2.7	35	0.4
Female	690	1.3	230	0.9	155	2.4	50	0.5

Source: Aboriginal Peoples Output Program, 1986 Census, Statistics Canada, *A Data Book on Canada's Aboriginal Population from the 1986 Census of Canada*, March , 1989, p. 184. Primary source: 1986 Census of Canada *Notes:* (NA) stands for not applicable. A dash (-) represents zero or a percentage less than .05 percent. 1. Aboriginal origins are derived from the ethnic origin question which asks whether respondents are North American Indian, Metis or Inuit. 2. All 1986 figures exclude the population estimated at about 45,000 on 136 incompletely enumerated Indian reserves and settlements throughout Canada. 3. Total Aboriginal origins - are the sum of persons who reported: (a) a single aboriginal (e.g., North American Indian, Metis or Inuit) and, (b) multiple aboriginal origins, that is those who reported: - at least one aboriginal origin with any other non-aboriginal (e.g., Metis and French), or - two or more aboriginal origins only. 4. Non-aboriginal in these columns - refers to persons who reported one or more non-aboriginal origins such as British, French, etc., in combination with one of the aboriginal origins such as North American Indian. 5. Includes "no schooling or kindergarten only." 6. Includes both post-secondary non-university courses requiring secondary school graduation such as community colleges or CEGEPS and courses taken in other institutions such as trade schools or vocational centers which may not require secondary school graduation. 7. Includes those with both university and other non-university education, as well as those university only.

★ 858 ★

Population 15 Years and Over, by Highest Level of Schooling and Sex for Detailed Aboriginal Origins for Manitoba, 1986 - II[1,2]

Highest level of schooling	Metis and non-Aboriginal[3]		Inuit only		Inuit and non-Aboriginal[3]		Other multiple Aboriginal origins[4]	
	Number	Percent	Number	Percent	Number	Percent	Number	Percent
Total population								
Aged 15+	9,105	100.0	100	100.0	115	100.0	2,680	100.0
Male	4,235	46.5	35	35.0	55	47.8	1,285	47.9
Female	4,870	53.5	65	65.0	65	56.5	1,390	51.9
Less than grade 9[5]	1,930	21.2	20	20.0	-	-	640	23.9
Male	995	10.9	-	-	-	-	325	12.1

[Continued]

★ 858 ★

Population 15 Years and Over, by Highest Level of Schooling and Sex for Detailed Aboriginal Origins for Manitoba, 1986 - II

[Continued]

Highest level of schooling	Metis and non-Aboriginal[3]		Inuit only		Inuit and non-Aboriginal[3]		Other multiple Aboriginal origins[4]	
	Number	Percent	Number	Percent	Number	Percent	Number	Percent
Female	935	10.3	25	25.0	-	-	310	11.6
Grades 9-13 without certificate	3,855	42.3	40	40.0	45	39.1	1,075	40.1
Male	1,795	19.7	20	20.0	15	13.0	540	20.1
Female	2,055	22.6	20	20.0	30	26.1	540	20.1
Grades 9-13 with certificate	710	7.8	-	-	-	-	130	4.9
Male	260	2.9	-	-	-	-	45	1.7
Female	445	4.9	-	-	-	-	80	3.0
Trades certificate or diploma	185	2.0	-	-	-	-	25	0.9
Male	120	1.3	-	-	-	-	15	0.6
Female	65	0.7	-	-	-	-	-	-
Other non-university without certificate[6]	580	6.4	-	-	10	8.7	180	6.7
Male	270	3.0	-	-	-	-	85	3.2
Female	310	3.4	-	-	-	-	95	3.5
Other non-university with certificate	925	10.2	25	25.0	30	26.1	275	10.3
Male	450	4.9	15	15.0	15	13.0	155	5.8
Female	480	5.3	15	15.0	15	13.0	125	4.7
University without degree[7]	635	7.0	10	10.0	25	21.7	220	8.2
Male	225	2.5	-	-	15	13.0	70	2.6
Female	410	4.5	10	10.0	-	-	150	5.6
University with degree	290	3.2	-	-	-	-	140	5.2
Male	125	1.4	-	-	-	-	50	1.9
Female	165	1.8	-	-	-	-	85	3.2

Source: Aboriginal Peoples Output Program, 1986 Census, Statistics Canada, *A Data Book on Canada's Aboriginal Population from the 1986 Census of Canada*, March, 1989, p. 184. Primary source: 1986 Census of Canada *Notes:* (NA) stands for not applicable. A dash (-) represents zero or a percentage less than .05 percent. 1. Aboriginal origins are derived from the ethnic origin question which asks whether respondents are North American Indian, Metis or Inuit. 2. All 1986 figures exclude the population estimated at about 45,000 on 136 incompletely enumerated Indian reserves and settlements throughout Canada. For an estimate of the unenumerated population and list of incompletely enumerated reserves in each affected province, see Appendix 1 and 2. 3. Total Aboriginal origins - are the sum of persons who reported: (a) a single aboriginal (e.g., North American Indian, Metis or Inuit) and, (b) multiple aboriginal origins, that is those who reported: - at least one aboriginal origin with any other non-aboriginal (e.g., Metis and French), or - two or more aboriginal origins only. 4. Other Multiple Aboriginal origins - refer to the sum of those persons reporting two or more aboriginal origins with or without a non-aboriginal origin. 5. Includes "no schooling or kindergarten only." 6. Includes both post-secondary non-university courses requiring secondary school graduation such as community colleges or CEGEPS, and courses taken in other institutions such as trade schools or vocational centers which may not require secondary school graduation. 7. Includes those with both university and other non-university education, as well as those with university only.

Population 15 Years and Over, by Highest Level of Schooling and Sex for Detailed Aboriginal Origins for New Brunswick, 1986 - I[1,2]

Highest level of schooling	Total Aboriginal origins[3]		North American Indian only		North American Indian non-Aboriginal[4]		Metis only	
	Number	Percent	Number	Percent	Number	Percent	Number	Percent
Total population								
Aged 15+	5,990	100.0	2,505	100.0	2,960	100.0	105	100.0
Male	3,020	50.4	1,295	51.7	1,445	48.8	70	66.7
Female	2,970	49.6	1,215	48.5	1,515	51.2	35	33.3
Less than grade 9[5]	1,455	24.3	865	34.5	490	16.6	15	14.3
Male	775	12.9	445	17.8	265	9.0	-	-
Female	680	11.4	420	16.8	230	7.8	-	-
Grades 9-13 without certificate	1,780	29.7	725	28.9	890	30.1	55	52.4
Male	855	14.3	370	14.8	385	13.0	30	28.6
Female	925	15.4	355	14.2	510	17.2	15	14.3
Grades 9-13 with certificate	635	10.6	190	7.6	380	12.8	-	-
Male	305	5.1	75	3.0	205	6.9	-	-
Female	330	5.5	110	4.4	175	5.9	-	-
Trades certificate or diploma	130	2.2	55	2.2	70	2.4	-	-
Male	100	1.7	40	1.6	50	1.7	-	-
Female	30	0.5	15	0.6	15	0.5	-	-
Other non-university without certificate[6]	375	6.3	165	6.6	150	5.1	15	14.3
Male	160	2.7	80	3.2	60	2.0	-	-
Female	215	3.6	80	3.2	85	2.9	-	-
Other non-university with certificate	645	10.8	195	7.8	390	13.2	10	9.5
Male	355	5.9	120	4.8	205	6.9	-	-
Female	295	4.9	80	3.2	190	6.4	-	-
University without degree[7]	670	11.2	245	9.8	380	12.8	-	-
Male	320	5.3	125	5.0	165	5.6	-	-
Female	345	5.8	120	4.8	215	7.3	-	-
University with degree	295	4.9	65	2.6	210	7.1	-	-

[Continued]

★ 859 ★

Population 15 Years and Over, by Highest Level of Schooling and Sex for Detailed Aboriginal Origins for New Brunswick, 1986 - I
[Continued]

Highest level of schooling	Total Aboriginal origins[3]		North American Indian only		North American Indian non-Aboriginal[4]		Metis only	
	Number	Percent	Number	Percent	Number	Percent	Number	Percent
Male	145	2.4	35	1.4	110	3.7	-	-
Female	145	2.4	30	1.2	100	3.4	-	-

Source: Aboriginal Peoples Output Program, 1986 Census, Statistics Canada, *A Data Book on Canada's Aboriginal Population from the 1986 Census of Canada*, March , 1989, p. 110. Primary source: 1986 Census of Canada *Notes:* (NA) stands for not applicable. A dash (-) represents zero or a percentage less than .05 percent. 1. Aboriginal origins are derived from the ethnic origin question which asks whether respondents are North American Indian, Metis or Inuit. 2. All 1986 figures exclude the population estimated at about 45,000 on 136 incompletely enumerated Indian reserves and settlements throughout Canada. 3. Total Aboriginal origins - are the sum of persons who reported: (a) a single aboriginal (e.g., North American Indian, Metis or Inuit) and, (b) multiple aboriginal origins, that is those who reported: - at least one aboriginal origin with any other non-aboriginal (e.g., Metis and French), or - two or more aboriginal origins only. 4. Non-aboriginal in these columns - refers to persons who reported one or more non-aboriginal origins such as British, French, etc., in combination with one of the aboriginal origins such as North American Indian. 5. Includes "no schooling or kindergarten only." 6. Includes both post-secondary non-university courses requiring secondary school graduation such as community colleges or CEGEPS and courses taken in other institutions such as trade schools or vocational centers which may not require secondary school graduation. 7. Includes those with both university and other non-university education, as well as those university only.

★ 860 ★

Population 15 Years and Over, by Highest Level of Schooling and Sex for Detailed Aboriginal Origins for New Brunswick, 1986 - II[1,2]

Highest level of schooling	Metis and non-Aboriginal[3]		Inuit only		Inuit and non-Aboriginal[3]		Other multiple Aboriginal origins[4]	
	Number	Percent	Number	Percent	Number	Percent	Number	Percent
Total population								
Aged 15+	255	100.0	-	-	55	100.0	100	100.0
Male	140	54.9	-	-	25	45.5	45	45.0
Female	120	47.1	-	-	30	54.5	55	55.0
Less than grade 9[5]	50	19.6	-	-	15	27.3	15	15.0
Male	40	15.7	-	-	-	-	-	-
Female	10	3.9	-	-	-	-	10	10.0
Grades 9-13 without certificate	65	25.5	-	-	20	36.4	30	30.0
Male	30	11.8	-	-	10	18.2	15	15.0
Female	30	11.8	-	-	-	-	20	20.0
Grades 9-13 with certificate	45	17.6	-	-	10	18.2	-	-
Male	15	5.9	-	-	-	-	-	-
Female	30	11.8	-	-	10	18.2	-	-
Trades certificate or diploma	-	-	-	-	-	-	-	-
Male	-	-	-	-	-	-	-	-
Female	-	-	-	-	-	-	-	-

[Continued]

★ 860 ★

Population 15 Years and Over, by Highest Level of Schooling and Sex for Detailed Aboriginal Origins for New Brunswick, 1986 - II
[Continued]

Highest level of schooling	Metis and non-Aboriginal[3]		Inuit only		Inuit and non-Aboriginal[3]		Other multiple Aboriginal origins[4]	
	Number	Percent	Number	Percent	Number	Percent	Number	Percent
Other non-university without certificate[6]	25	9.8	-	-	-	-	15	15.0
Male	-	-	-	-	-	-	-	-
Female	20	7.8	-	-	-	-	10	10.0
Other non-university with certificate	25	9.8	-	-	-	-	20	20.0
Male	10	3.9	-	-	-	-	10	10.0
Female	10	3.9	-	-	-	-	-	-
University without degree[7]	30	11.8	-	-	-	-	15	15.0
Male	20	7.8	-	-	-	-	-	-
Female	-	-	-	-	-	-	-	-
University with degree	-	-	-	-	-	-	-	-
Male	-	-	-	-	-	-	-	-
Female	-	-	-	-	-	-	-	-

Source: Aboriginal Peoples Output Program, 1986 Census, Statistics Canada, *A Data Book on Canada's Aboriginal Population from the 1986 Census of Canada*, March , 1989, p. 110. Primary source: 1986 Census of Canada *Notes:* (NA) stands for not applicable. A dash (-) represents zero or a percentage less than .05 percent. 1. Aboriginal origins are derived from the ethnic origin question which asks whether respondents are North American Indian, Metis or Inuit. 2. All 1986 figures exclude the population estimated at about 45,000 on 136 incompletely enumerated Indian reserves and settlements throughout Canada. For an estimate of the unenumerated population and list of incompletely enumerated reserves in each affected province, see Appendix 1 and 2. 3. Total Aboriginal origins - are the sum of persons who reported: (a) a single aboriginal (e.g., North American Indian, Metis or Inuit) and, (b) multiple aboriginal origins, that is those who reported: - at least one aboriginal origin with any other non-aboriginal (e.g., Metis and French), or - two or more aboriginal origins only. 4. Other Multiple Aboriginal origins - refer to the sum of those persons reporting two or more aboriginal origins with or without a non-aboriginal origin. 5. Includes "no schooling or kindergarten only." 6. Includes both post-secondary non-university courses requiring secondary school graduation such as community colleges or CEGEPS, and courses taken in other institutions such as trade schools or vocational centers which may not require secondary school graduation. 7. Includes those with both university and other non-university education, as well as those with university only.

★ 861 ★

Population 15 Years and Over, by Highest Level of Schooling and Sex for Detailed Aboriginal Origins for Newfoundland, 1986 - I[1,2]

Highest level of schooling	Total Aboriginal origins[3]		North American Indian only		North American Indian non-Aboriginal[4]		Metis only	
	Number	Percent	Number	Percent	Number	Percent	Number	Percent
Total population								
Aged 15+	6,160	100.0	1,060	100.0	1,730	100.0	220	100.0
Male	3,140	51.0	495	46.7	875	50.6	110	50.0
Female	3,015	48.9	560	52.8	855	49.4	110	50.0
Less than grade 9[5]	2,330	37.8	505	47.6	435	25.1	65	29.5
Male	1,200	19.5	240	22.6	275	15.9	30	13.6

[Continued]

★ 861 ★

Population 15 Years and Over, by Highest Level of Schooling and Sex for Detailed Aboriginal Origins for Newfoundland, 1986 - I

[Continued]

Highest level of schooling	Total Aboriginal origins[3]		North American Indian only		North American Indian non-Aboriginal[4]		Metis only	
	Number	Percent	Number	Percent	Number	Percent	Number	Percent
Female	1,130	18.3	270	25.5	160	9.2	35	15.9
Grades 9-13 without certificate	1,795	29.1	355	33.5	470	27.2	85	38.6
Male	830	13.5	140	13.2	200	11.6	40	18.2
Female	970	15.7	220	20.8	270	15.6	45	20.5
Grades 9-13 with certificate	420	6.8	50	4.7	150	8.7	20	9.1
Male	195	3.2	30	2.8	50	2.9	-	-
Female	220	3.6	15	1.4	105	6.1	15	6.8
Trades certificate or diploma	105	1.7	-	-	35	2.0	-	-
Male	70	1.1	-	-	30	1.7	-	-
Female	35	0.6	-	-	-	-	-	-
Other non-university without certificate[6]	235	3.8	20	1.9	95	5.5	-	-
Male	130	2.1	15	1.4	35	2.0	-	-
Female	110	1.8	-	-	55	3.2	-	-
Other non-university with certificate	725	11.8	75	7.1	305	17.6	30	13.6
Male	425	6.9	45	4.2	150	8.7	25	11.4
Female	305	5.0	25	2.4	150	8.7	-	-
University without degree[7]	450	7.3	50	4.7	185	10.7	-	-
Male	260	4.2	25	2.4	120	6.9	-	-
Female	185	3.0	20	1.9	65	3.8	-	-
University with degree	90	1.5	-	-	60	3.5	-	-
Male	30	0.5	-	-	20	1.2	-	-
Female	60	1.0	-	-	35	2.0	-	-

Source: Aboriginal Peoples Output Program, 1986 Census, Statistics Canada, *A Data Book on Canada's Aboriginal Population from the 1986 Census of Canada*, March , 1989, p. 38. Primary source: 1986 Census of Canada *Notes:* (NA) stands for not applicable. A dash (-) represents zero or a percentage less than .05 percent. 1. Aboriginal origins are derived from the ethnic origin question which asks whether respondents are North American Indian, Metis or Inuit. 2. All 1986 figures exclude the population estimated at about 45,000 on 136 incompletely enumerated Indian reserves and settlements throughout Canada. 3. Total Aboriginal origins - are the sum of persons who reported: (a) a single aboriginal (e.g., North American Indian, Metis or Inuit) and, (b) multiple aboriginal origins, that is those who reported: - at least one aboriginal origin with any other non-aboriginal (e.g., Metis and French), or - two or more aboriginal origins only. 4. Non-aboriginal in these columns - refers to persons who reported one or more non-aboriginal origins such as British, French, etc., in combination with one of the aboriginal origins such as North American Indian. 5. Includes "no schooling or kindergarten only." 6. Includes both post-secondary non-university courses requiring secondary school graduation such as community colleges or CEGEPS and courses taken in other institutions such as trade schools or vocational centers which may not require secondary school graduation. 7. Includes those with both university and other non-university education, as well as those university only.

★ 862 ★

Population 15 Years and Over, by Highest Level of Schooling and Sex for Detailed Aboriginal Origins for Newfoundland, 1986 - II[1,2]

Highest level of schooling	Metis and non-Aboriginal[3]		Inuit only		Inuit and non-Aboriginal[3]		Other multiple Aboriginal origins[4]	
	Number	Percent	Number	Percent	Number	Percent	Number	Percent
Total population								
Aged 15+	515	100.0	1,170	100.0	1,070	100.0	395	100.0
Male	285	55.3	595	50.9	540	50.5	235	59.5
Female	230	44.7	580	49.6	525	49.1	160	40.5
Less than grade 9[5]	145	28.2	700	59.8	380	35.5	95	24.1
Male	75	14.6	330	28.2	180	16.8	70	17.7
Female	75	14.6	375	32.1	200	18.7	25	6.3
Grades 9-13 without certificate	175	34.0	270	23.1	315	29.4	115	29.1
Male	90	17.5	145	12.4	165	15.4	55	13.9
Female	85	16.5	125	10.7	150	14.0	70	17.7
Grades 9-13 with certificate	45	8.7	40	3.4	85	7.9	30	7.6
Male	15	2.9	25	2.1	55	5.1	20	5.1
Female	30	5.8	15	1.3	35	3.3	-	-
Trades certificate or diploma	35	6.8	-	-	25	2.3	-	-
Male	25	4.9	-	-	-	-	-	-
Female	-	-	-	-	20	1.9	-	-
Other non-university without certificate[6]	20	3.9	45	3.8	45	4.2	-	-
Male	20	3.9	25	2.1	30	2.8	-	-
Female	-	-	-	-	-	-	-	-
Other non-university with certificate	60	11.7	85	7.3	90	8.4	90	22.8
Male	35	6.8	55	4.7	45	4.2	60	15.2
Female	20	3.9	30	2.6	40	3.7	35	8.9
University without degree[7]	25	4.9	20	1.7	115	10.7	55	13.9
Male	25	4.9	-	-	55	5.1	35	8.9
Female	-	-	15	1.3	60	5.6	25	6.3
University with degree	10	1.9	-	-	15	1.4	-	-

[Continued]

★ 862 ★

Population 15 Years and Over, by Highest Level of Schooling and Sex for Detailed Aboriginal Origins for Newfoundland, 1986 - II

[Continued]

Highest level of schooling	Metis and non-Aboriginal[3]		Inuit only		Inuit and non-Aboriginal[3]		Other multiple Aboriginal origins[4]	
	Number	Percent	Number	Percent	Number	Percent	Number	Percent
Male	-	-	-	-	-	-	-	-
Female	10	1.9	-	-	10	0.9	-	-

Source: Aboriginal Peoples Output Program, 1986 Census, Statistics Canada, *A Data Book on Canada's Aboriginal Population from the 1986 Census of Canada*, March, 1989, p. 38. Primary source: 1986 Census of Canada *Notes:* (NA) stands for not applicable. A dash (-) represents zero or a percentage less than .05 percent. 1. Aboriginal origins are derived from the ethnic origin question which asks whether respondents are North American Indian, Metis or Inuit. 2. All 1986 figures exclude the population estimated at about 45,000 on 136 incompletely enumerated Indian reserves and settlements throughout Canada. For an estimate of the unenumerated population and list of incompletely enumerated reserves in each affected province, see Appendix 1 and 2. 3. Total Aboriginal origins - are the sum of persons who reported: (a) a single aboriginal (e.g., North American Indian, Metis or Inuit) and, (b) multiple aboriginal origins, that is those who reported: - at least one aboriginal origin with any other non-aboriginal (e.g., Metis and French), or - two or more aboriginal origins only. 4. Other Multiple Aboriginal origins - refer to the sum of those persons reporting two or more aboriginal origins with or without a non-aboriginal origin. 5. Includes "no schooling or kindergarten only." 6. Includes both post-secondary non-university courses requiring secondary school graduation such as community colleges or CEGEPS, and courses taken in other institutions such as trade schools or vocational centers which may not require secondary school graduation. 7. Includes those with both university and other non-university education, as well as those with university only.

★ 863 ★

Population 15 Years and Over, by Highest Level of Schooling and Sex for Detailed Aboriginal Origins for Northwest Territories, 1986 - I[1,2]

Highest level of schooling	Total Aboriginal origins[3]		North American Indian only		North American Indian non-Aboriginal[4]		Metis only	
	Number	Percent	Number	Percent	Number	Percent	Number	Percent
Total population								
Aged 15+	18,675	100.0	5,070	100.0	525	100.0	1,425	100.0
Male	9,570	51.2	2,595	51.2	315	60.0	745	52.3
Female	9,105	48.8	2,475	48.8	210	40.0	685	48.1
Less than grade 9[5]	10,725	57.4	3,005	59.3	120	22.9	425	29.8
Male	5,480	29.3	1,620	32.0	65	12.5	215	15.1
Female	5,245	28.1	1,385	27.3	50	9.5	205	14.4
Grades 9-13 without certificate	4,310	23.1	1,080	21.3	155	29.5	535	37.5
Male	2,115	11.3	485	9.6	100	19.0	270	18.9
Female	2,190	11.7	595	11.7	55	10.5	255	17.9
Grades 9-13 with certificate	485	2.6	95	1.9	15	2.9	85	6.0
Male	205	1.1	40	0.8	-	-	30	2.1
Female	285	1.5	55	1.1	15	2.9	55	3.9
Trades certificate or diploma	310	1.7	55	1.1	15	2.9	55	3.9
Male	215	1.2	30	0.6	-	-	45	3.2
Female	95	0.5	25	0.5	-	-	15	1.1

[Continued]

★ 863 ★

Population 15 Years and Over, by Highest Level of Schooling and Sex for Detailed Aboriginal Origins for Northwest Territories, 1986 - I

[Continued]

Highest level of schooling	Total Aboriginal origins[3]		North American Indian only		North American Indian non-Aboriginal[4]		Metis only	
	Number	Percent	Number	Percent	Number	Percent	Number	Percent
Other non-university without certificate[6]	875	4.7	285	5.6	35	6.7	65	4.6
Male	460	2.5	140	2.8	10	1.9	35	2.5
Female	410	2.2	140	2.8	20	3.8	30	2.1
Other non-university with certificate	1,550	8.3	455	9.0	110	21.0	195	13.7
Male	890	4.8	245	4.8	75	14.3	100	7.0
Female	660	3.5	210	4.1	40	7.6	95	6.7
University without degree[7]	320	1.7	85	1.7	30	5.7	50	3.5
Male	150	0.8	30	0.6	20	3.8	35	2.5
Female	170	0.9	50	1.0	15	2.9	20	1.4
University with degree	100	0.5	10	0.2	40	7.6	20	1.4
Male	55	0.3	-	-	30	5.7	-	-
Female	45	0.2	-	-	10	1.9	-	-

Source: Aboriginal Peoples Output Program, 1986 Census, Statistics Canada, *A Data Book on Canada's Aboriginal Population from the 1986 Census of Canada*, March , 1989, p. 278. Primary source: 1986 Census of Canada *Notes:* (NA) stands for not applicable. A dash (-) represents zero or a percentage less than .05 percent. 1. Aboriginal origins are derived from the ethnic origin question which asks whether respondents are North American Indian, Metis or Inuit. 2. All 1986 figures exclude the population estimated at about 45,000 on 136 incompletely enumerated Indian reserves and settlements throughout Canada. 3. Total Aboriginal origins - are the sum of persons who reported: (a) a single aboriginal (e.g., North American Indian, Metis or Inuit) and, (b) multiple aboriginal origins, that is those who reported: - at least one aboriginal origin with any other non-aboriginal (e.g., Metis and French), or - two or more aboriginal origins only. 4. Non-aboriginal in these columns - refers to persons who reported one or more non-aboriginal origins such as British, French, etc., in combination with one of the aboriginal origins such as North American Indian. 5. Includes "no schooling or kindergarten only." 6. Includes both post-secondary non-university courses requiring secondary school graduation such as community colleges or CEGEPS and courses taken in other institutions such as trade schools or vocational centers which may not require secondary school graduation. 7. Includes those with both university and other non-university education, as well as those university only.

★ 864 ★

Population 15 Years and Over, by Highest Level of Schooling and Sex for Detailed Aboriginal Origins for Northwest Territories, 1986 - II[1,2]

Highest level of schooling	Metis and non-Aboriginal[3]		Inuit only		Inuit and non-Aboriginal[3]		Other multiple Aboriginal origins[4]	
	Number	Percent	Number	Percent	Number	Percent	Number	Percent
Total population Aged 15+	460	100.0	10,320	100.0	280	100.0	590	100.0
Male	250	54.3	5,190	50.3	155	55.4	325	55.1
Female	210	45.7	5,130	49.7	130	46.4	265	44.9
Less than grade 9[5]	95	20.7	6,705	65.0	115	41.1	255	43.2
Male	65	14.1	3,300	32.0	65	23.2	150	25.4

[Continued]

★ 864 ★

Population 15 Years and Over, by Highest Level of Schooling and Sex for Detailed Aboriginal Origins for Northwest Territories, 1986 - II

[Continued]

Highest level of schooling	Metis and non-Aboriginal[3]		Inuit only		Inuit and non-Aboriginal[3]		Other multiple Aboriginal origins[4]	
	Number	Percent	Number	Percent	Number	Percent	Number	Percent
Female	30	6.5	3,405	33.0	50	17.9	110	18.6
Grades 9-13 without certificate	145	31.5	2,185	21.2	15	5.4	125	21.2
Male	85	18.5	1,055	10.2	-	-	70	11.9
Female	55	12.0	1,130	10.9	-	-	55	9.3
Grades 9-13 with certificate	45	9.8	195	1.9	20	7.1	35	5.9
Male	15	3.3	95	0.9	20	7.1	-	-
Female	30	6.5	100	1.0	-	-	25	4.2
Trades certificate or diploma	25	5.4	135	1.3	-	-	25	4.2
Male	20	4.3	95	0.9	-	-	20	3.4
Female	-	-	40	0.4	-	-	-	-
Other non-university without certificate[6]	20	4.3	400	3.9	15	5.4	55	9.3
Male	10	2.2	220	2.1	-	-	30	5.1
Female	15	3.3	175	1.7	-	-	25	4.2
Other non-university with certificate	75	16.3	595	5.8	-	-	80	13.6
Male	30	6.5	375	3.6	-	-	35	5.9
Female	50	10.9	220	2.1	-	-	40	6.8
University without degree[7]	30	6.5	100	1.0	-	-	15	2.5
Male	20	4.3	40	0.4	-	-	-	-
Female	15	3.3	60	0.6	-	-	-	-
University with degree	20	4.3	-	-	-	-	-	-
Male	-	-	-	-	-	-	-	-
Female	15	3.3	-	-	-	-	-	-

Source: Aboriginal Peoples Output Program, 1986 Census, Statistics Canada, *A Data Book on Canada's Aboriginal Population from the 1986 Census of Canada*, March , 1989, p. 278. Primary source: 1986 Census of Canada *Notes:* (NA) stands for not applicable. A dash (-) represents zero or a percentage less than .05 percent. 1. Aboriginal origins are derived from the ethnic origin question which asks whether respondents are North American Indian, Metis or Inuit. 2. All 1986 figures exclude the population estimated at about 45,000 on 136 incompletely enumerated Indian reserves and settlements throughout Canada. For an estimate of the unenumerated population and list of incompletely enumerated reserves in each affected province, see Appendix 1 and 2. 3. Total Aboriginal origins - are the sum of persons who reported: (a) a single aboriginal (e.g., North American Indian, Metis or Inuit) and, (b) multiple aboriginal origins, that is those who reported: - at least one aboriginal origin with any other non-aboriginal (e.g., Metis and French), or - two or more aboriginal origins only. 4. Other Multiple Aboriginal origins - refer to the sum of those persons reporting two or more aboriginal origins with or without a non-aboriginal origin. 5. Includes "no schooling or kindergarten only." 6. Includes both post-secondary non-university courses requiring secondary school graduation such as community colleges or CEGEPS, and courses taken in other institutions such as trade schools or vocational centers which may not require secondary school graduation. 7. Includes those with both university and other non-university education, as well as those with university only.

★ 865 ★

Population 15 Years and Over, by Highest Level of Schooling and Sex for Detailed Aboriginal Origins for Nova Scotia, 1986 - I[1,2]

Highest level of schooling	Total Aboriginal origins[3]		North American Indian only		North American Indian non-Aboriginal[4]		Metis only	
	Number	Percent	Number	Percent	Number	Percent	Number	Percent
Total population								
Aged 15+	9,260	100.0	3,665	100.0	4,595	100.0	185	100.0
Male	4,445	48.0	1,840	50.2	2,145	46.7	90	48.6
Female	4,815	52.0	1,825	49.8	2,445	53.2	100	54.1
Less than grade 9[5]	2,095	22.6	1,265	34.5	610	13.3	90	48.6
Male	1,060	11.4	665	18.1	275	6.0	55	29.7
Female	1,040	11.2	600	16.4	340	7.4	35	18.9
Grades 9-13 without certificate	2,625	28.3	1,010	27.6	1,300	28.3	40	21.6
Male	1,090	11.8	475	13.0	505	11.0	-	-
Female	1,535	16.6	535	14.6	795	17.3	30	16.2
Grades 9-13 with certificate	565	6.1	140	3.8	340	7.4	-	-
Male	255	2.8	65	1.8	170	3.7	-	-
Female	310	3.3	75	2.0	170	3.7	-	-
Trades certificate or diploma	285	3.1	90	2.5	170	3.7	-	-
Male	170	1.8	55	1.5	105	2.3	-	-
Female	120	1.3	35	1.0	65	1.4	-	-
Other non-university without certificate[6]	590	6.4	220	6.0	290	6.3	10	5.4
Male	310	3.3	110	3.0	160	3.5	-	-
Female	280	3.0	110	3.0	135	2.9	-	-
Other non-university with certificate	1,645	17.8	560	15.3	960	20.9	-	-
Male	895	9.7	300	8.2	515	11.2	-	-
Female	745	8.0	260	7.1	450	9.8	-	-
University without degree[7]	935	10.1	330	9.0	520	11.3	25	13.5
Male	420	4.5	150	4.1	220	4.8	10	5.4
Female	515	5.6	175	4.8	295	6.4	15	8.1
University with degree	520	5.6	55	1.5	395	8.6	-	-

[Continued]

★ 865 ★

Population 15 Years and Over, by Highest Level of Schooling and Sex for Detailed Aboriginal Origins for Nova Scotia, 1986 - I
[Continued]

Highest level of schooling	Total Aboriginal origins[3]		North American Indian only		North American Indian non-Aboriginal[4]		Metis only	
	Number	Percent	Number	Percent	Number	Percent	Number	Percent
Male	245	2.6	15	0.4	200	4.4	-	-
Female	275	3.0	40	1.1	195	4.2	-	-

Source: Aboriginal Peoples Output Program, 1986 Census, Statistics Canada, *A Data Book on Canada's Aboriginal Population from the 1986 Census of Canada*, March , 1989, p. 86. Primary source: 1986 Census of Canada *Notes:* (NA) stands for not applicable. A dash (-) represents zero or a percentage less than .05 percent. 1. Aboriginal origins are derived from the ethnic origin question which asks whether respondents are North American Indian, Metis or Inuit. 2. All 1986 figures exclude the population estimated at about 45,000 on 136 incompletely enumerated Indian reserves and settlements throughout Canada. 3. Total Aboriginal origins - are the sum of persons who reported: (a) a single aboriginal (e.g., North American Indian, Metis or Inuit) and, (b) multiple aboriginal origins, that is those who reported: - at least one aboriginal origin with any other non-aboriginal (e.g., Metis and French), or - two or more aboriginal origins only. 4. Non-aboriginal in these columns - refers to persons who reported one or more non-aboriginal origins such as British, French, etc., in combination with one of the aboriginal origins such as North American Indian. 5. Includes "no schooling or kindergarten only." 6. Includes both post-secondary non-university courses requiring secondary school graduation such as community colleges or CEGEPS and courses taken in other institutions such as trade schools or vocational centers which may not require secondary school graduation. 7. Includes those with both university and other non-university education, as well as those university only.

★ 866 ★

Population 15 Years and Over, by Highest Level of Schooling and Sex for Detailed Aboriginal Origins for Nova Scotia, 1986 - II[1,2]

Highest level of schooling	Metis and non-Aboriginal[3]		Inuit only		Inuit and non-Aboriginal[3]		Other multiple Aboriginal origins[4]	
	Number	Percent	Number	Percent	Number	Percent	Number	Percent
Total population								
Aged 15+	460	100.0	85	100.0	115	100.0	170	100.0
Male	185	40.2	40	47.1	40	34.8	105	61.8
Female	275	59.8	45	52.9	70	60.9	60	35.3
Less than grade 9[5]	65	14.1	30	35.3	40	34.8	-	-
Male	40	8.7	-	-	10	8.7	-	-
Female	30	6.5	20	23.5	25	21.7	-	-
Grades 9-13 without certificate	185	40.2	20	23.5	25	21.7	50	29.4
Male	55	12.0	15	17.6	-	-	30	17.6
Female	125	27.2	-	-	30	26.1	20	11.8
Grades 9-13 with certificate	65	14.1	-	-	-	-	-	-
Male	15	3.3	-	-	-	-	-	-
Female	50	10.9	-	-	-	-	-	-
Trades certificate or diploma	15	3.3	10	11.8	-	-	-	-
Male	-	-	10	11.8	-	-	-	-
Female	-	-	-	-	-	-	-	-

[Continued]

★ 866 ★

Population 15 Years and Over, by Highest Level of Schooling and Sex for Detailed Aboriginal Origins for Nova Scotia, 1986 - II

[Continued]

Highest level of schooling	Metis and non-Aboriginal[3]		Inuit only		Inuit and non-Aboriginal[3]		Other multiple Aboriginal origins[4]	
	Number	Percent	Number	Percent	Number	Percent	Number	Percent
Other non-university without								
certificate[6]	30	6.5	-	-	10	8.7	30	17.6
Male	-	-	-	-	10	8.7	25	14.7
Female	25	5.4	-	-	-	-	-	-
Other non-university with certificate	65	14.1	10	11.8	15	13.0	20	11.8
Male	50	10.9	-	-	10	8.7	10	5.9
Female	20	4.3	-	-	-	-	-	-
University without degree[7]	25	5.4	-	-	-	-	25	14.7
Male	10	2.2	-	-	-	-	20	11.8
Female	15	3.3	-	-	-	-	-	-
University with degree	15	3.3	-	-	15	13.0	30	17.6
Male	-	-	-	-	-	-	10	5.9
Female	-	-	-	-	10	8.7	15	8.5

Source: Aboriginal Peoples Output Program, 1986 Census, Statistics Canada, *A Data Book on Canada's Aboriginal Population from the 1986 Census of Canada*, March , 1989, p. 86. Primary source: 1986 Census of Canada *Notes:* (NA) stands for not applicable. A dash (-) represents zero or a percentage less than .05 percent. 1. Aboriginal origins are derived from the ethnic origin question which asks whether respondents are North American Indian, Metis or Inuit. 2. All 1986 figures exclude the population estimated at about 45,000 on 136 incompletely enumerated Indian reserves and settlements throughout Canada. For an estimate of the unenumerated population and list of incompletely enumerated reserves in each affected province, see Appendix 1 and 2. 3. Total Aboriginal origins - are the sum of persons who reported: (a) a single aboriginal (e.g., North American Indian, Metis or Inuit) and, (b) multiple aboriginal origins, that is those who reported: - at least one aboriginal origin with any other non-aboriginal (e.g., Metis and French), or - two or more aboriginal origins only. 4. Other Multiple Aboriginal origins - refer to the sum of those persons reporting two or more aboriginal origins with or without a non-aboriginal origin. 5. Includes "no schooling or kindergarten only." 6. Includes both post-secondary non-university courses requiring secondary school graduation such as community colleges or CEGEPS, and courses taken in other institutions such as trade schools or vocational centers which may not require secondary school graduation. 7. Includes those with both university and other non-university education, as well as those with university only.

★ 867 ★

Population 15 Years and Over, by Highest Level of Schooling and Sex for Detailed Aboriginal Origins for Ontario, 1986 - I[1,2]

Highest level of schooling	Total Aboriginal origins[3]		North American Indian only		North American Indian non-Aboriginal[4]		Metis only	
	Number	Percent	Number	Percent	Number	Percent	Number	Percent
Total population								
Aged 15+	109,540	100.0	35,380	100.0	60,760	100.0	2,645	100.0
Male	51,450	47.0	16,725	47.3	28,345	46.7	1,305	49.3
Female	58,085	53.0	18,650	52.7	32,415	53.3	1,340	50.7
Less than grade 9[5]	17,195	15.7	10,185	28.8	5,160	8.5	610	23.1
Male	7,925	7.2	4,670	13.2	2,450	4.0	240	9.1

[Continued]

★ 867 ★

Population 15 Years and Over, by Highest Level of Schooling and Sex for Detailed Aboriginal Origins for Ontario, 1986 - I
[Continued]

Highest level of schooling	Total Aboriginal origins[3]		North American Indian only		North American Indian non-Aboriginal[4]		Metis only	
	Number	Percent	Number	Percent	Number	Percent	Number	Percent
Female	9,270	8.5	5,515	15.6	2,710	4.5	370	14.0
Grades 9-13 without certificate	39,105	35.7	13,330	37.7	20,860	34.3	1,145	43.3
Male	18,820	17.2	6,440	18.2	9,905	16.3	605	22.9
Female	20,285	18.5	6,895	19.5	10,955	18.0	540	20.4
Grades 9-13 with certificate	12,415	11.3	2,670	7.5	8,155	13.4	255	9.6
Male	5,440	5.0	1,170	3.3	3,530	5.8	140	5.3
Female	6,975	6.4	1,500	4.2	4,630	7.6	115	4.3
Trades certificate or diploma	2,910	2.7	880	2.5	1,645	2.7	100	3.8
Male	2,065	1.9	615	1.7	1,185	2.0	65	2.5
Female	840	0.8	265	0.7	465	0.8	25	0.9
Other non-university without certificate[6]	9,030	8.2	2,545	7.2	5,415	8.9	170	6.4
Male	3,850	3.5	1,065	3.0	2,325	3.8	80	3.0
Female	5,175	4.7	1,475	4.2	3,095	5.1	85	3.2
Other non-university with certificate	15,490	14.1	3,570	10.1	10,000	16.5	235	8.9
Male	6,915	6.3	1,705	4.8	4,340	7.1	105	4.0
Female	8,570	7.8	1,865	5.3	5,665	9.3	130	4.9
University without degree[7]	7,900	7.2	1,630	4.6	5,345	8.8	100	3.8
Male	3,750	3.4	760	2.1	2,575	4.2	60	2.3
Female	4,155	3.8	875	2.5	2,770	4.6	45	1.7
University with degree	5,495	5.0	575	1.6	4,175	6.9	35	1.3
Male	2,685	2.5	305	0.9	2,040	3.4	10	0.4
Female	2,810	2.6	270	0.8	2,130	3.5	25	0.9

Source: Aboriginal Peoples Output Program, 1986 Census, Statistics Canada, *A Data Book on Canada's Aboriginal Population from the 1986 Census of Canada*, March , 1989, p. 158. Primary source: 1986 Census of Canada *Notes:* (NA) stands for not applicable. A dash (-) represents zero or a percentage less than .05 percent. 1. Aboriginal origins are derived from the ethnic origin question which asks whether respondents are North American Indian, Metis or Inuit. 2. All 1986 figures exclude the population estimated at about 45,000 on 136 incompletely enumerated Indian reserves and settlements throughout Canada. 3. Total Aboriginal origins - are the sum of persons who reported: (a) a single aboriginal (e.g., North American Indian, Metis or Inuit) and, (b) multiple aboriginal origins, that is those who reported: - at least one aboriginal origin with any other non-aboriginal (e.g., Metis and French), or - two or more aboriginal origins only. 4. Non-aboriginal in these columns - refers to persons who reported one or more non-aboriginal origins such as British, French, etc., in combination with one of the aboriginal origins such as North American Indian. 5. Includes "no schooling or kindergarten only." 6. Includes both post-secondary non-university courses requiring secondary school graduation such as community colleges or CEGEPS and courses taken in other institutions such as trade schools or vocational centers which may not require secondary school graduation. 7. Includes those with both university and other non-university education, as well as those university only.

★ 868 ★

Population 15 Years and Over, by Highest Level of Schooling and Sex for Detailed Aboriginal Origins for Ontario, 1986 - II[1,2]

Highest level of schooling	Metis and non-Aboriginal[3]		Inuit only		Inuit and non-Aboriginal[3]		Other multiple Aboriginal origins[4]	
	Number	Percent	Number	Percent	Number	Percent	Number	Percent
Total population								
Aged 15+	6,775	100.0	485	100.0	950	100.0	2,540	100.0
Male	3,085	45.5	235	48.5	500	52.6	1,250	49.2
Female	3,690	54.5	250	51.5	445	46.8	1,285	50.6
Less than grade 9[5]	795	11.7	85	17.5	95	10.0	270	10.6
Male	345	5.1	45	9.3	60	6.3	125	4.9
Female	450	6.6	40	8.2	35	3.7	150	5.9
Grades 9-13 without certificate	2,385	35.2	185	38.1	390	41.1	805	31.7
Male	1,175	17.3	80	16.5	205	21.6	415	16.3
Female	1,215	17.9	105	21.6	185	19.5	395	15.6
Grades 9-13 with certificate	780	11.5	75	15.5	170	17.9	315	12.4
Male	335	4.9	50	10.3	95	10.0	130	5.1
Female	445	6.6	30	6.2	75	7.9	185	7.3
Trades certificate or diploma	170	2.5	10	2.1	35	3.7	65	2.6
Male	125	1.8	-	-	20	2.1	50	2.0
Female	50	0.7	-	-	15	1.6	15	0.6
Other non-university without certificate[6]	580	8.6	65	13.4	55	5.8	200	7.9
Male	245	3.6	30	6.2	10	1.1	90	3.5
Female	340	5.0	35	7.2	45	4.7	105	4.1
Other non-university with certificate	1,125	16.6	25	5.2	150	15.8	385	15.2
Male	480	7.1	-	-	80	8.4	195	7.7
Female	645	9.5	20	4.1	70	7.4	190	7.5
University without degree[7]	535	7.9	25	5.2	45	4.7	220	8.7
Male	185	2.7	15	3.1	25	2.6	135	5.3
Female	350	5.2	15	3.1	20	2.1	90	3.5
University with degree	415	6.1	10	2.1	10	1.1	270	10.6

[Continued]

★ 868 ★

Population 15 Years and Over, by Highest Level of Schooling and Sex for Detailed Aboriginal Origins for Ontario, 1986 - II

[Continued]

Highest level of schooling	Metis and non-Aboriginal[3]		Inuit only		Inuit and non-Aboriginal[3]		Other multiple Aboriginal origins[4]	
	Number	Percent	Number	Percent	Number	Percent	Number	Percent
Male	200	3.0	-	-	-	-	120	4.7
Female	215	3.2	-	-	-	-	155	6.1

Source: Aboriginal Peoples Output Program, 1986 Census, Statistics Canada, *A Data Book on Canada's Aboriginal Population from the 1986 Census of Canada*, March, 1989, p. 158. Primary source: 1986 Census of Canada *Notes:* (NA) stands for not applicable. A dash (-) represents zero or a percentage less than .05 percent. 1. Aboriginal origins are derived from the ethnic origin question which asks whether respondents are North American Indian, Metis or Inuit. 2. All 1986 figures exclude the population estimated at about 45,000 on 136 incompletely enumerated Indian reserves and settlements throughout Canada. For an estimate of the unenumerated population and list of incompletely enumerated reserves in each affected province, see Appendix 1 and 2. 3. Total Aboriginal origins - are the sum of persons who reported: (a) a single aboriginal (e.g., North American Indian, Metis or Inuit) and, (b) multiple aboriginal origins, that is those who reported: - at least one aboriginal origin with any other non-aboriginal (e.g., Metis and French), or - two or more aboriginal origins only. 4. Other Multiple Aboriginal origins - refer to the sum of those persons reporting two or more aboriginal origins with or without a non-aboriginal origin. 5. Includes "no schooling or kindergarten only." 6. Includes both post-secondary non-university courses requiring secondary school graduation such as community colleges or CEGEPS, and courses taken in other institutions such as trade schools or vocational centers which may not require secondary school graduation. 7. Includes those with both university and other non-university education, as well as those with university only.

★ 869 ★

Population 15 Years and Over, by Highest Level of Schooling and Sex for Detailed Aboriginal Origins for Quebec, 1986 - I[1,2]

Highest level of schooling	Total Aboriginal origins[3]		North American Indian only		North American Indian non-Aboriginal[4]		Metis only	
	Number	Percent	Number	Percent	Number	Percent	Number	Percent
Total population								
Aged 15+	56,165	100.0	25,750	100.0	17,900	100.0	4,105	100.0
Male	26,620	47.4	12,565	48.8	8,010	44.7	2,065	50.3
Female	29,540	52.6	13,185	51.2	9,890	55.3	2,040	49.7
Less than grade 9[5]	16,275	29.0	9,580	37.2	2,285	12.8	1,255	30.6
Male	7,815	13.9	4,635	18.0	1,085	6.1	630	15.3
Female	8,460	15.1	4,945	19.2	1,205	6.7	625	15.2
Grades 9-13 without certificate	13,905	24.8	7,055	27.4	3,620	20.2	1,280	31.2
Male	6,595	11.7	3,435	13.3	1,600	8.9	615	15.0
Female	7,305	13.0	3,620	14.1	2,020	11.3	660	16.1
Grades 9-13 with certificate	6,140	10.9	2,315	9.0	2,545	14.2	480	11.7
Male	2,650	4.7	1,050	4.1	1,020	5.7	205	5.0
Female	3,480	6.2	1,270	4.9	1,520	8.5	275	6.7
Trades certificate or diploma	2,435	4.3	1,180	4.6	760	4.2	190	4.6
Male	1,440	2.6	720	2.8	450	2.5	105	2.6
Female	995	1.8	455	1.8	305	1.7	85	2.1

[Continued]

★ 869 ★

Population 15 Years and Over, by Highest Level of Schooling and Sex for Detailed Aboriginal Origins for Quebec, 1986 - I

[Continued]

Highest level of schooling	Total Aboriginal origins[3]		North American Indian only		North American Indian non-Aboriginal[4]		Metis only	
	Number	Percent	Number	Percent	Number	Percent	Number	Percent
Other non-university without certificate[6]	4,390	7.8	1,745	6.8	1,810	10.1	265	6.5
Male	2,130	3.8	900	3.5	825	4.6	135	3.3
Female	2,260	4.0	845	3.3	980	5.5	125	3.0
Other non-university with certificate	6,675	11.9	2,345	9.1	3,120	17.4	440	10.7
Male	3,285	5.8	1,170	4.5	1,440	8.0	280	6.8
Female	3,390	6.0	1,175	4.6	1,685	9.4	160	3.9
University without degree[7]	3,625	6.5	1,025	4.0	1,975	11.0	110	2.7
Male	1,500	2.7	415	1.6	835	4.7	45	1.1
Female	2,125	3.8	610	2.4	1,145	6.4	65	1.6
University with degree	2,720	4.8	510	2.0	1,790	10.0	85	2.1
Male	1,190	2.1	240	0.9	750	4.2	45	1.1
Female	1,525	2.7	275	1.1	1,035	5.8	40	1.0

Source: Aboriginal Peoples Output Program, 1986 Census, Statistics Canada, *A Data Book on Canada's Aboriginal Population from the 1986 Census of Canada*, March , 1989, p. 134. Primary source: 1986 Census of Canada *Notes:* (NA) stands for not applicable. A dash (-) represents zero or a percentage less than .05 percent. 1. Aboriginal origins are derived from the ethnic origin question which asks whether respondents are North American Indian, Metis or Inuit. 2. All 1986 figures exclude the population estimated at about 45,000 on 136 incompletely enumerated Indian reserves and settlements throughout Canada. 3. Total Aboriginal origins - are the sum of persons who reported: (a) a single aboriginal (e.g., North American Indian, Metis or Inuit) and, (b) multiple aboriginal origins, that is those who reported: - at least one aboriginal origin with any other non-aboriginal (e.g., Metis and French), or - two or more aboriginal origins only. 4. Non-aboriginal in these columns - refers to persons who reported one or more non-aboriginal origins such as British, French, etc., in combination with one of the aboriginal origins such as North American Indian. 5. Includes "no schooling or kindergarten only." 6. Includes both post-secondary non-university courses requiring secondary school graduation such as community colleges or CEGEPS and courses taken in other institutions such as trade schools or vocational centers which may not require secondary school graduation. 7. Includes those with both university and other non-university education, as well as those university only.

★ 870 ★

Population 15 Years and Over, by Highest Level of Schooling and Sex for Detailed Aboriginal Origins for Quebec, 1986 - II[1,2]

Highest level of schooling	Metis and non-Aboriginal[3]		Inuit only		Inuit and non-Aboriginal[3]		Other multiple Aboriginal origins[4]	
	Number	Percent	Number	Percent	Number	Percent	Number	Percent
Total population Aged 15+	3,250	100.0	3,900	100.0	365	100.0	885	100.0
Male	1,400	43.1	1,935	49.6	180	49.3	465	52.5
Female	1,850	56.9	1,965	50.4	185	50.7	425	48.0
Less than grade 9[5]	685	21.1	2,245	57.6	105	28.8	115	13.0
Male	285	8.8	1,050	26.9	70	19.2	60	6.8

[Continued]

★ 870 ★

Population 15 Years and Over, by Highest Level of Schooling and Sex for Detailed Aboriginal Origins for Quebec, 1986 - II
[Continued]

Highest level of schooling	Metis and non-Aboriginal[3]		Inuit only		Inuit and non-Aboriginal[3]		Other multiple Aboriginal origins[4]	
	Number	Percent	Number	Percent	Number	Percent	Number	Percent
Female	400	12.3	1,195	30.6	40	11.0	55	6.2
Grades 9-13 without certificate	750	23.1	950	24.4	50	13.7	205	23.2
Male	355	10.9	500	12.8	15	4.1	85	9.6
Female	395	12.2	450	11.5	35	9.6	120	13.6
Grades 9-13 with certificate	505	15.5	150	3.8	40	11.0	105	11.9
Male	250	7.7	75	1.9	-	-	50	5.6
Female	255	7.8	80	2.1	30	8.2	50	5.6
Trades certificate or diploma	135	4.2	100	2.6	20	5.5	50	5.6
Male	65	2.0	65	1.7	-	-	30	3.4
Female	70	2.2	40	1.0	15	4.1	25	2.8
Other non-university without certificate[6]	250	7.7	200	5.1	25	6.8	100	11.3
Male	85	2.6	105	2.7	15	4.1	60	6.8
Female	165	5.1	90	2.3	15	4.1	35	4.0
Other non-university with certificate	390	12.0	175	4.5	65	17.8	145	16.4
Male	175	5.4	105	2.7	30	8.2	80	9.0
Female	210	6.5	70	1.8	35	9.6	65	7.3
University without degree[7]	320	9.8	70	1.8	40	11.0	80	9.0
Male	95	2.9	45	1.2	20	5.5	45	5.1
Female	225	6.9	30	0.8	20	5.5	40	4.5
University with degree	220	6.8	-	-	20	5.5	85	9.6
Male	90	2.8	-	-	15	4.1	60	6.8
Female	135	4.2	-	-	-	-	30	3.4

Source: Aboriginal Peoples Output Program, 1986 Census, Statistics Canada, *A Data Book on Canada's Aboriginal Population from the 1986 Census of Canada*, March , 1989, p. 134. Primary source: 1986 Census of Canada *Notes:* (NA) stands for not applicable. A dash (-) represents zero or a percentage less than .05 percent. 1. Aboriginal origins are derived from the ethnic origin question which asks whether respondents are North American Indian, Metis or Inuit. 2. All 1986 figures exclude the population estimated at about 45,000 on 136 incompletely enumerated Indian reserves and settlements throughout Canada. For an estimate of the unenumerated population and list of incompletely enumerated reserves in each affected province, see Appendix 1 and 2. 3. Total Aboriginal origins - are the sum of persons who reported: (a) a single aboriginal (e.g., North American Indian, Metis or Inuit) and, (b) multiple aboriginal origins, that is those who reported: - at least one aboriginal origin with any other non-aboriginal (e.g., Metis and French), or - two or more aboriginal origins only. 4. Other Multiple Aboriginal origins - refer to the sum of those persons reporting two or more aboriginal origins with or without a non-aboriginal origin. 5. Includes "no schooling or kindergarten only." 6. Includes both post-secondary non-university courses requiring secondary school graduation such as community colleges or CEGEPS, and courses taken in other institutions such as trade schools or vocational centers which may not require secondary school graduation. 7. Includes those with both university and other non-university education, as well as those with university only.

★ 871 ★

Population 15 Years and Over, by Highest Level of Schooling and Sex for Detailed Aboriginal Origins for Prince Edward Island, 1986 - I[1,2]

Highest level of schooling	Total Aboriginal origins[3]		North American Indian only		North American Indian non-Aboriginal[4]		Metis only	
	Number	Percent	Number	Percent	Number	Percent	Number	Percent
Total population								
Aged 15+	840	100.0	235	100.0	475	100.0	20	100.0
Male	450	53.6	120	51.1	255	53.7	-	-
Female	395	47.0	110	46.8	220	46.32	10	50.0
Less than grade 9[5]	225	26.8	90	38.3	90	18.9	-	-
Male	140	16.7	55	23.4	55	11.58	-	-
Female	85	10.1	30	12.8	30	6.3	-	-
Grades 9-13 without certificate	280	33.3	80	34.0	170	35.8	-	-
Male	115	13.7	30	12.8	70	14.7	-	-
Female	165	19.6	45	19.1	100	21.1	-	-
Grades 9-13 with certificate	50	6.0	-	-	35	7.37	-	-
Male	30	3.6	-	-	15	3.16	-	-
Female	25	3.0	-	-	20	4.21	-	-
Trades certificate or diploma	15	1.8	15	6.4	-	-	-	-
Male	10	1.2	-	-	-	-	-	-
Female	-	-	-	-	-	-	-	-
Other non-university without								
certificate[6]	55	6.5	15	6.4	35	7.4	-	-
Male	20	2.4	-	-	-	-	-	-
Female	40	4.8	15	6.4	25	5.3	-	-
Other non-university with certificate	100	11.9	20	8.5	65	13.7	-	-
Male	70	8.3	10	4.26	50	10.5	-	-
Female	35	4.2	10	4.26	15	3.16	-	-
University without degree[7]	80	9.5	20	8.5	50	10.5	-	-
Male	40	4.8	-	-	25	5.3	-	-
Female	45	5.4	-	-	25	5.3	-	-
University with degree	30	3.6	-	-	25	5.3	-	-

[Continued]

★ 871 ★

Population 15 Years and Over, by Highest Level of Schooling and Sex for Detailed Aboriginal Origins for Prince Edward Island, 1986 - I

[Continued]

Highest level of schooling	Total Aboriginal origins[3]		North American Indian only		North American Indian non-Aboriginal[4]		Metis only	
	Number	Percent	Number	Percent	Number	Percent	Number	Percent
Male	30	3.6	-	-	25	5.3	-	-
Female	-	-	-	-	-	-	-	-

Source: Aboriginal Peoples Output Program, 1986 Census, Statistics Canada, *A Data Book on Canada's Aboriginal Population from the 1986 Census of Canada*, March , 1989, p. 62. Primary source: 1986 Census of Canada *Notes:* (NA) stands for not applicable. A dash (-) represents zero or a percentage less than .05 percent. 1. Aboriginal origins are derived from the ethnic origin question which asks whether respondents are North American Indian, Metis or Inuit. 2. All 1986 figures exclude the population estimated at about 45,000 on 136 incompletely enumerated Indian reserves and settlements throughout Canada. 3. Total Aboriginal origins - are the sum of persons who reported: (a) a single aboriginal (e.g., North American Indian, Metis or Inuit) and, (b) multiple aboriginal origins, that is those who reported: - at least one aboriginal origin with any other non-aboriginal (e.g., Metis and French), or - two or more aboriginal origins only. 4. Non-aboriginal in these columns - refers to persons who reported one or more non-aboriginal origins such as British, French, etc., in combination with one of the aboriginal origins such as North American Indian. 5. Includes "no schooling or kindergarten only." 6. Includes both post-secondary non-university courses requiring secondary school graduation such as community colleges or CEGEPS and courses taken in other institutions such as trade schools or vocational centers which may not require secondary school graduation. 7. Includes those with both university and other non-university education, as well as those university only.

★ 872 ★

Population 15 Years and Over, by Highest Level of Schooling and Sex for Detailed Aboriginal Origins for Prince Edward Island, 1986 - II[1,2]

Highest level of schooling	Metis and non-Aboriginal[3]		Inuit only		Inuit and non-Aboriginal[3]		Other multiple Aboriginal origins[4]	
	Number	Percent	Number	Percent	Number	Percent	Number	Percent
Total population								
Aged 15+	70	100.0	-	-	20	100.0	15	100.0
Male	45	64.3	-	-	15	75.0	-	-
Female	25	35.7	-	-	-	-	15	100.0
Less than grade 9[5]	35	50.0	-	-	-	-	-	-
Male	30	42.9	-	-	-	-	-	-
Female	-	-	-	-	-	-	-	-
Grades 9-13 without certificate	20	28.6	-	-	-	-	-	-
Male	-	-	-	-	-	-	-	-
Female	10	14.3	-	-	-	-	-	-
Grades 9-13 with certificate	-	-	-	-	-	-	-	-
Male	-	-	-	-	-	-	-	-
Female	-	-	-	-	-	-	-	-
Trades certificate or diploma	-	-	-	-	-	-	-	-
Male	-	-	-	-	-	-	-	-
Female	-	-	-	-	-	-	-	-

[Continued]

★ 872 ★

Population 15 Years and Over, by Highest Level of Schooling and Sex for Detailed Aboriginal Origins for Prince Edward Island, 1986 - II

[Continued]

Highest level of schooling	Metis and non-Aboriginal[3]		Inuit only		Inuit and non-Aboriginal[3]		Other multiple Aboriginal origins[4]	
	Number	Percent	Number	Percent	Number	Percent	Number	Percent
Other non-university without certificate[6]	-	-	-	-	-	-	-	-
Male	-	-	-	-	-	-	-	-
Female	-	-	-	-	-	-	-	-
Other non-university with certificate	10	14.3	-	-	-	-	-	-
Male	-	-	-	-	-	-	-	-
Female	-	-	-	-	-	-	-	-
University without degree[7]	-	-	-	-	-	-	-	-
Male	-	-	-	-	-	-	-	-
Female	-	-	-	-	-	-	-	-
University with degree	-	-	-	-	-	-	-	-
Male	-	-	-	-	-	-	-	-
Female	-	-	-	-	-	-	-	-

Source: Aboriginal Peoples Output Program, 1986 Census, Statistics Canada, *A Data Book on Canada's Aboriginal Population from the 1986 Census of Canada*, March , 1989, p. 62. Primary source: 1986 Census of Canada *Notes:* (NA) stands for not applicable. A dash (-) represents zero or a percentage less than .05 percent. 1. Aboriginal origins are derived from the ethnic origin question which asks whether respondents are North American Indian, Metis or Inuit. 2. All 1986 figures exclude the population estimated at about 45,000 on 136 incompletely enumerated Indian reserves and settlements throughout Canada. For an estimate of the unenumerated population and list of incompletely enumerated reserves in each affected province, see Appendix 1 and 2. 3. Total Aboriginal origins - are the sum of persons who reported: (a) a single aboriginal (e.g., North American Indian, Metis or Inuit) and, (b) multiple aboriginal origins, that is those who reported: - at least one aboriginal origin with any other non-aboriginal (e.g., Metis and French), or - two or more aboriginal origins only. 4. Other Multiple Aboriginal origins - refer to the sum of those persons reporting two or more aboriginal origins with or without a non-aboriginal origin. 5. Includes "no schooling or kindergarten only." 6. Includes both post-secondary non-university courses requiring secondary school graduation such as community colleges or CEGEPS, and courses taken in other institutions such as trade schools or vocational centers which may not require secondary school graduation. 7. Includes those with both university and other non-university education, as well as those with university only.

★ 873 ★

Population 15 Years and Over, by Highest Level of Schooling and Sex for Detailed Aboriginal Origins for Saskatchewan, 1986 - I[1,2]

Highest level of schooling	Total Aboriginal origins[3]		North American Indian only		North American Indian non-Aboriginal[4]		Metis only	
	Number	Percent	Number	Percent	Number	Percent	Number	Percent
Total population								
Aged 15 +	44,650	100.0	24,535	100.0	4,765	100.0	7,810	100.0
Male	21,505	48.2	11,915	48.6	2,330	48.9	3,725	47.7
Female	23,145	51.8	12,620	51.4	2,435	51.1	4,085	52.3
Less than grade 9[5]	16,650	37.3	11,095	45.2	755	15.8	3,160	40.5
Male	8,395	18.8	5,585	22.8	375	7.9	1,525	19.5

[Continued]

★ 873 ★

Population 15 Years and Over, by Highest Level of Schooling and Sex for Detailed Aboriginal Origins for Saskatchewan, 1986 - I
[Continued]

Highest level of schooling	Total Aboriginal origins[3]		North American Indian only		North American Indian non-Aboriginal[4]		Metis only	
	Number	Percent	Number	Percent	Number	Percent	Number	Percent
Female	8,260	18.5	5,505	22.4	380	8.0	1,635	20.9
Grades 9-13 without certificate	14,850	33.3	7,865	32.1	1,750	36.7	2,530	32.4
Male	7,025	15.7	3,715	15.1	910	19.1	1,200	15.4
Female	7,825	17.5	4,150	16.9	840	17.6	1,330	17.0
Grades 9-13 with certificate	1,590	3.6	460	1.9	340	7.1	270	3.5
Male	740	1.7	195	0.8	175	3.7	105	1.3
Female	855	1.9	260	1.1	165	3.5	165	2.1
Trades certificate or diploma	770	1.7	330	1.3	105	2.2	150	1.9
Male	495	1.1	225	0.9	65	1.4	105	1.3
Female	270	0.6	105	0.4	40	0.8	45	0.6
Other non-university without certificate[6]	3,140	7.0	1,495	6.1	365	7.7	620	7.9
Male	1,295	2.9	620	2.5	130	2.7	265	3.4
Female	1,840	4.1	870	3.5	230	4.8	355	4.5
Other non-university with certificate	3,525	7.9	1,400	5.7	580	12.2	670	8.6
Male	1,805	4.0	760	3.1	290	6.1	355	4.5
Female	1,720	3.9	640	2.6	285	6.0	315	4.0
University without degree[7]	3,285	7.4	1,610	6.6	635	13.3	340	4.4
Male	1,365	3.1	665	2.7	285	6.0	135	1.7
Female	1,915	4.3	940	3.8	345	7.2	205	2.6
University with degree	845	1.9	300	1.2	240	5.0	65	0.8
Male	390	0.9	150	0.6	90	1.9	30	0.4
Female	455	1.0	145	0.6	150	3.1	35	0.4

Source: Aboriginal Peoples Output Program, 1986 Census, Statistics Canada, *A Data Book on Canada's Aboriginal Population from the 1986 Census of Canada*, March , 1989, p. 206. Primary source: 1986 Census of Canada *Notes:* (NA) stands for not applicable. A dash (-) represents zero or a percentage less than .05 percent. 1. Aboriginal origins are derived from the ethnic origin question which asks whether respondents are North American Indian, Metis or Inuit. 2. All 1986 figures exclude the population estimated at about 45,000 on 136 incompletely enumerated Indian reserves and settlements throughout Canada. 3. Total Aboriginal origins - are the sum of persons who reported: (a) a single aboriginal (e.g., North American Indian, Metis or Inuit) and, (b) multiple aboriginal origins, that is those who reported: - at least one aboriginal origin with any other non-aboriginal (e.g., Metis and French), or - two or more aboriginal origins only. 4. Non-aboriginal in these columns - refers to persons who reported one or more non-aboriginal origins such as British, French, etc., in combination with one of the aboriginal origins such as North American Indian. 5. Includes "no schooling or kindergarten only." 6. Includes both post-secondary non-university courses requiring secondary school graduation such as community colleges or CEGEPS and courses taken in other institutions such as trade schools or vocational centers which may not require secondary school graduation. 7. Includes those with both university and other non-university education, as well as those university only.

★ 874 ★

Population 15 Years and Over, by Highest Level of Schooling and Sex for Detailed Aboriginal Origins for Saskatchewan, 1986 - II[1,2]

Highest level of schooling	Metis and non-Aboriginal[3]		Inuit only		Inuit and non-Aboriginal[3]		Other multiple Aboriginal origins[4]	
	Number	Percent	Number	Percent	Number	Percent	Number	Percent
Total population								
Aged 15+	5,680	100.0	30	100.0	50	100.0	1,765	100.0
Male	2,605	45.9	15	50.0	35	70.0	870	49.3
Female	3,080	54.2	15	50.0	15	30.0	900	51.0
Less than grade 9[5]	1,170	20.6	-	-	-	-	475	26.9
Male	670	11.8	-	-	-	-	240	13.6
Female	505	8.9	-	-	-	-	235	13.3
Grades 9-13 without certificate	2,130	37.5	15	50.0	15	30.0	550	31.2
Male	920	16.2	-	-	-	-	270	15.3
Female	1,210	21.3	15	50.0	-	-	275	15.6
Grades 9-13 with certificate	400	7.0	-	-	10	20.0	100	5.7
Male	185	3.3	-	-	10	20.0	55	3.1
Female	220	3.9	-	-	-	-	50	2.8
Trades certificate or diploma	135	2.4	-	-	-	-	50	2.8
Male	70	1.2	-	-	-	-	30	1.7
Female	65	1.1	-	-	-	-	20	1.1
Other non-university without certificate[6]	550	9.7	-	-	-	-	100	5.7
Male	235	4.1	-	-	-	-	35	2.0
Female	315	5.5	-	-	-	-	70	4.0
Other non-university with certificate	685	12.1	-	-	-	-	185	10.5
Male	285	5.0	-	-	-	-	120	6.8
Female	405	7.1	-	-	-	-	75	4.2
University without degree[7]	475	8.4	-	-	15	30.0	205	11.6
Male	185	3.3	-	-	15	30.0	70	4.0
Female	285	5.0	-	-	-	-	130	7.4
University with degree	135	2.4	-	-	-	-	100	5.7

[Continued]

★ 874 ★

Population 15 Years and Over, by Highest Level of Schooling and Sex for Detailed Aboriginal Origins for Saskatchewan, 1986 - II

[Continued]

Highest level of schooling	Metis and non-Aboriginal[3]		Inuit only		Inuit and non-Aboriginal[3]		Other multiple Aboriginal origins[4]	
	Number	Percent	Number	Percent	Number	Percent	Number	Percent
Male	55	1.0	-	-	-	-	50	2.8
Female	80	1.4	-	-	-	-	45	2.5

Source: Aboriginal Peoples Output Program, 1986 Census, Statistics Canada, *A Data Book on Canada's Aboriginal Population from the 1986 Census of Canada*, March, 1989, p. 206. Primary source: 1986 Census of Canada *Notes:* (NA) stands for not applicable. A dash (-) represents zero or a percentage less than .05 percent. 1. Aboriginal origins are derived from the ethnic origin question which asks whether respondents are North American Indian, Metis or Inuit. 2. All 1986 figures exclude the population estimated at about 45,000 on 136 incompletely enumerated Indian reserves and settlements throughout Canada. For an estimate of the unenumerated population and list of incompletely enumerated reserves in each affected province, see Appendix 1 and 2. 3. Total Aboriginal origins - are the sum of persons who reported: (a) a single aboriginal (e.g., North American Indian, Metis or Inuit) and, (b) multiple aboriginal origins, that is those who reported: - at least one aboriginal origin with any other non-aboriginal (e.g., Metis and French), or - two or more aboriginal origins only. 4. Other Multiple Aboriginal origins - refer to the sum of those persons reporting two or more aboriginal origins with or without a non-aboriginal origin. 5. Includes "no schooling or kindergarten only." 6. Includes both post-secondary non-university courses requiring secondary school graduation such as community colleges or CEGEPS, and courses taken in other institutions such as trade schools or vocational centers which may not require secondary school graduation. 7. Includes those with both university and other non-university education, as well as those with university only.

★ 875 ★

Population 15 Years and Over, by Highest Level of Schooling and Sex for Detailed Aboriginal Origins for Yukon Territory, 1986 - I[1,2]

Highest level of schooling	Total Aboriginal origins[3]		North American Indian only		North American Indian non-Aboriginal[4]		Metis only	
	Number	Percent	Number	Percent	Number	Percent	Number	Percent
Total population								
Aged 15+	3,395	100.0	2,325	100.0	895	100.0	45	100.0
Male	1,640	48.3	1,125	48.4	425	47.5	15	33.3
Female	1,755	51.7	1,200	51.6	465	52.0	30	66.7
Less than grade 9[5]	985	29.0	885	38.1	70	7.8	-	-
Male	470	13.8	425	18.3	30	3.4	-	-
Female	515	15.2	460	19.8	40	4.5	-	-
Grades 9-13 without certificate	1,255	37.0	830	35.7	360	40.2	25	55.6
Male	615	18.1	400	17.2	185	20.7	-	-
Female	640	18.9	425	18.3	175	19.6	15	33.3
Grades 9-13 with certificate	215	6.3	90	3.9	115	12.8	-	-
Male	100	2.9	50	2.2	45	5.0	-	-
Female	115	3.4	40	1.7	70	7.8	-	-
Trades certificate or diploma	30	0.9	20	0.9	-	-	-	-
Male	15	0.4	10	0.4	-	-	-	-
Female	10	0.3	10	0.4	-	-	-	-

[Continued]

★ 875 ★

Population 15 Years and Over, by Highest Level of Schooling and Sex for Detailed Aboriginal Origins for Yukon Territory, 1986 - I
[Continued]

Highest level of schooling	Total Aboriginal origins[3]		North American Indian only		North American Indian non-Aboriginal[4]		Metis only	
	Number	Percent	Number	Percent	Number	Percent	Number	Percent
Other non-university without certificate[6]	295	8.7	175	7.5	105	11.7	-	-
Male	135	4.0	85	3.7	45	5.0	-	-
Female	155	4.6	95	4.1	55	6.1	-	-
Other non-university with certificate	465	13.7	275	11.8	155	17.3	15	33.3
Male	245	7.2	135	5.8	80	8.9	-	-
Female	220	6.5	135	5.8	75	8.4	-	-
University without degree[7]	130	3.8	40	1.7	75	8.4	-	-
Male	45	1.3	10	0.4	20	2.2	-	-
Female	85	2.5	30	1.3	50	5.6	-	-
University with degree	35	1.0	-	-	10	1.1	-	-
Male	20	0.6	-	-	-	-	-	-
Female	10	0.3	-	-	-	-	-	-

Source: Aboriginal Peoples Output Program, 1986 Census, Statistics Canada, *A Data Book on Canada's Aboriginal Population from the 1986 Census of Canada*, March , 1989, p. 302. Primary source: 1986 Census of Canada *Notes:* (NA) stands for not applicable. A dash (-) represents zero or a percentage less than .05 percent. 1. Aboriginal origins are derived from the ethnic origin question which asks whether respondents are North American Indian, Metis or Inuit. 2. All 1986 figures exclude the population estimated at about 45,000 on 136 incompletely enumerated Indian reserves and settlements throughout Canada. 3. Total Aboriginal origins - are the sum of persons who reported: (a) a single aboriginal (e.g., North American Indian, Metis or Inuit) and, (b) multiple aboriginal origins, that is those who reported: - at least one aboriginal origin with any other non-aboriginal (e.g., Metis and French), or - two or more aboriginal origins only. 4. Non-aboriginal in these columns - refers to persons who reported one or more non-aboriginal origins such as British, French, etc., in combination with one of the aboriginal origins such as North American Indian. 5. Includes "no schooling or kindergarten only." 6. Includes both post-secondary non-university courses requiring secondary school graduation such as community colleges or CEGEPS and courses taken in other institutions such as trade schools or vocational centers which may not require secondary school graduation. 7. Includes those with both university and other non-university education, as well as those university only.

★ 876 ★

Population 15 Years and Over, by Highest Level of Schooling and Sex for Detailed Aboriginal Origins for Yukon Territory, 1986 - II[1,2]

Highest level of schooling	Metis and non-Aboriginal[3]		Inuit only		Inuit and non-Aboriginal[3]		Other multiple Aboriginal origins[4]	
	Number	Percent	Number	Percent	Number	Percent	Number	Percent
Total population								
Aged 15+	60	100.0	25	100.0	15	100.0	35	100.0
Male	45	75.0	-	-	-	-	20	57.1
Female	20	33.3	20	80.0	-	-	10	42.9
Less than grade 9[5]	15	25.0	-	-	-	-	-	-
Male	10	16.7	-	-	-	-	-	-

[Continued]

★ 876 ★

Population 15 Years and Over, by Highest Level of Schooling and Sex for Detailed Aboriginal Origins for Yukon Territory, 1986 - II

[Continued]

Highest level of schooling	Metis and non-Aboriginal[3]		Inuit only		Inuit and non-Aboriginal[3]		Other multiple Aboriginal origins[4]	
	Number	Percent	Number	Percent	Number	Percent	Number	Percent
Female	-	-	-	-	-	-	-	-
Grades 9-13 without certificate	25	41.7	-	-	-	-	-	-
Male	15	25.0	-	-	-	-	-	-
Female	15	25.0	-	-	-	-	-	-
Grades 9-13 with certificate	-	-	-	-	-	-	-	-
Male	-	-	-	-	-	-	-	-
Female	-	-	-	-	-	-	-	-
Trades certificate or diploma	-	-	-	-	-	-	-	-
Male	-	-	-	-	-	-	-	-
Female	-	-	-	-	-	-	-	-
Other non-university without certificate[6]	-	-	-	-	-	-	-	-
Male	-	-	-	-	-	-	-	-
Female	-	-	-	-	-	-	-	-
Other non-university with certificate	-	-	-	-	-	-	-	-
Male	-	-	-	-	-	-	-	-
Female	-	-	-	-	-	-	-	-
University without degree[7]	-	-	-	-	-	-	-	-
Male	-	-	-	-	-	-	-	-
Female	-	-	-	-	-	-	-	-
University with degree	-	-	-	-	-	-	-	-
Male	-	-	-	-	-	-	-	-
Female	-	-	-	-	-	-	-	-

Source: Aboriginal Peoples Output Program, 1986 Census, Statistics Canada, *A Data Book on Canada's Aboriginal Population from the 1986 Census of Canada*, March , 1989, p. 302. Primary source: 1986 Census of Canada *Notes:* (NA) stands for not applicable. A dash (-) represents zero or a percentage less than .05 percent. 1. Aboriginal origins are derived from the ethnic origin question which asks whether respondents are North American Indian, Metis or Inuit. 2. All 1986 figures exclude the population estimated at about 45,000 on 136 incompletely enumerated Indian reserves and settlements throughout Canada. For an estimate of the unenumerated population and list of incompletely enumerated reserves in each affected province, see Appendix 1 and 2. 3. Total Aboriginal origins - are the sum of persons who reported: (a) a single aboriginal (e.g., North American Indian, Metis or Inuit) and, (b) multiple aboriginal origins, that is those who reported: - at least one aboriginal origin with any other non-aboriginal (e.g., Metis and French), or - two or more aboriginal origins only. 4. Other Multiple Aboriginal origins - refer to the sum of those persons reporting two or more aboriginal origins with or without a non-aboriginal origin. 5. Includes "no schooling or kindergarten only." 6. Includes both post-secondary non-university courses requiring secondary school graduation such as community colleges or CEGEPS, and courses taken in other institutions such as trade schools or vocational centers which may not require secondary school graduation. 7. Includes those with both university and other non-university education, as well as those with university only.

Culture and Tradition

★ 877 ★

Cultural Areas of the Indians of Canada

Culture Area	Location	Linguistic groups involved
Algonkian	Eastern and Central Woodlands	Algonkian
Iroquoian	Southeastern Ontario	Iroquoian
Mackenzie River	Mackenzie River System and woodlands north of Churchill River	Athapaskan
Plains	Canadian Prairies	Algonkian Athapaskan
Plateau	Interior Plateau of British Columbia and Yukon	Salishan Athapaskan Tlingit Tagish Kootenayan[1]
Pacific Coast	Coast of British Columbia	Tsimshian Haida Salishan

Source: Indian and Inuit Affairs Program, Membership Division, *Adoption and the Indian Child,* Indian and Northern Affairs Canada, n.p., n.d., pp. 9-10. *Notes:* 1. The Kootenayans originally lived on the prairies but were driven in to the mountainous area of southeastern British Columbia by hostile Indians. When first encountered by the early fur traders their culture was still partly oriented to the Plains although they had been forced to adjust economically to their new environment.

★ 878 ★

Persons of Aboriginal Origin and Total Canadian Population, by Official Language, Canada Without Quebec, 1986

Group	English Only		French Only		French and English		Neither French nor English		Total
	Number	%	Number	%	Number	%	Number	%	
On-reserve	129,530	93.5	15	0.0	7,635	5.5	7,635	5.5	138,515
Off-reserve	446,025	90.6	670	0.1	36,520	7.4	9,055	1.8	492,270
Total Canadian population (w/o Quebec)	16,347,835	88.0	149,170	0.8	1,829,415	9.9	241,100	1.3	18,567,515

Source: Canada's Off-Reserve Aboriginal Population: A Statistical Overview, Social Trends Analysis Directorate, Department of the Secretary of State of Canada, 1991, p. A-7. For Aboriginal population: Statistics Canada, *A Profile of the Aboriginal Population Residing in Selected Off Reserve Areas*, prepared by the Aboriginal Data and Native Issues Unit of the Housing, Family and Social Statistics Division, February 1990; For total Canadian population: Statistics Canada, 1986 Census, *Special Tabulations from the Small Area Database*, compiled for the Department of the Secretary of State. *Notes:* Sum of components may not always add to totals due to rounding and/or data suppression.

★ 879 ★

Persons of Aboriginal Origin and Total Canadian Population, by Official Language, Quebec Only, 1986

Group	English Only		French Only		Neither French and English		French nor English		Total
	Number	%	Number	%	Number	%	Number	%	
On-reserve	6,060	28.0	8,640	40.0	2,720	12.6	4,185	19.4	21,605
Off-reserve	6,745	11.4	27,425	46.2	22,535	38.0	2,630	4.4	59,335
Total Quebec population	369,065	5.7	3,808,560	59.0	2,226,745	34.5	50,115	0.8	6,454,490

Source: Canada's Off-Reserve Aboriginal Population: A Statistical Overview, Social Trends Analysis Directorate, Department of the Secretary of State of Canada, 1991, p. A-7. For Aboriginal population: Statistics Canada, *A Profile of the Aboriginal Population Residing in Selected Off Reserve Areas*, prepared by the Aboriginal Data and Native Issues Unit of the Housing, Family and Social Statistics Division, February 1990; For total Canadian population: Statistics Canada, *1986 Census, Special Tabulations from the Small Area Database*, compiled for the Department of the Secretary of State. *Notes:* Sum of components may not always add to totals due to rounding and/or data suppression.

★ 880 ★

Persons of Aboriginal Origin, by Language Spoken at Home, Canada, 1986

Group/Region	Aboriginal languages								Other languages	Total population
	Algonquian languages				Athapaskan languages	West Coast languages	Other Aboriginal languages	Total		
	Inuit	Cree	Other Algonq.	Total						
On-Reserve										
Atlantic	0	0	3,950	3,950	0	0	0	3,985	4,065	8,060
Quebec	300	7,955	5,935	13,920	0	0	115	14,360	7,185	21,610
Ontario	0	395	4,860	5,250	0	0	0	5,260	20,730	26,115
Manitoba	0	10,430	1,995	12,445	475	0	2,020	14,960	12,385	27,405
Saskatchewan	0	8,075	720	8,785	1,880	0	10	10,705	16,230	26,995
Alberta	0	2,995	550	3,550	1,035	0	420	5,000	13,755	18,820
British Columbia	0	20	0	20	945	320	75	1,380	28,380	30,075
Territories	0	0	0	0	30	0	0	35	530	590
Canada	300	29,870	18,010	47,920	4,365	320	2,640	55,685	103,260	159,655
Off-Reserve										
Atlantic	230	0	765	765	0	0	45	1,010	25,385	26,380
Quebec	4,830	610	415	990	0	0	240	6,035	53,365	59,335
Ontario	20	335	785	1,120	0	0	165	1,300	140,080	141,260
Manitoba	10	2,405	695	3,080	15	0	55	3,145	54,745	57,830
Saskatchewan	0	3,685	240	3,945	2,010	0	30	5,960	44,755	50,655
Alberta	0	3,455	155	3,600	130	20	60	3,820	81,355	85,110
British Columbia	0	145	10	160	310	230	165	845	96,015	96,550
Territories	12,135	30	0	35	3,195	15	0	15,390	19,580	34,935
Canada	17,225	10,665	3,065	13,695	5,660	265	760	37,705	515,280	552,055

Source: Canada's Off-Reserve Aboriginal Population: A Statistical Overview, Social Trends Analysis Directorate, Department of the Secretary of State of Canada, 1991, p. A-9. Statistics Canada, *1986 Census, Special Tabulations from the Small Area Database*, compiled for the Department of the Secretary State. *Notes:* Sum of components may not always add to totals due to rounding and/or data suppression.

★ 881 ★

Persons of Aboriginal Origin, by Mother Tongue, Canada, 1986

Group/Region	Aboriginal languages								Other languages	Total population
	Algonquian languages				Athapaskan languages	West Coast languages	Other Aboriginal languages	Total		
	Inuit	Cree	Other Algonq.	Total						
On-Reserve										
Atlantic	0	0	4,550	4,530	0	0	85	4,655	3,350	8,045
Quebec	350	9,170	6,425	15,610	0	0	265	16,225	5,325	21,620
Ontario	0	415	7,080	7,535	0	0	185	7,780	18,265	26,150

[Continued]

★ 881 ★

Persons of Aboriginal Origin, by Mother Tongue, Canada, 1986
[Continued]

Group/Region	Aboriginal languages								Other languages	Total population
	Algonquian languages				Athapaskan languages	West Coast languages	Other Aboriginal languages	Total		
	Inuit	Cree	Other Algonq.	Total						
Manitoba	0	11,720	2,915	14,705	570	0	2,210	17,515	9,855	27,365
Saskatchewan	0	10,315	1,000	11,360	2,140	0	90	13,670	13,315	27,030
Alberta	0	4,615	1,270	5,900	1,165	0	625	7,760	11,060	18,820
British Columbia	0	95	0	95	1,600	1,945	365	4,160	25,485	30,040
Territories	0	0	0	0	95	40	30	175	420	585
Canada	350	36,330	23,240	59,735	5,570	1,985	3,855	71,940	87,075	159,655
Off-Reserve										
Atlantic	720	0	945	980	0	0	100	1,755	24,680	26,395
Quebec	5,095	785	590	1,360	15	0	330	6,805	52,590	59,325
Ontario	105	1,040	2,150	3,150	10	0	815	4,025	137,300	141,220
Manitoba	65	4,000	2,100	6,035	75	0	310	6,460	51,405	57,870
Saskatchewan	0	6,755	540	7,250	2,245	0	300	9,720	40,945	50,615
Alberta	0	6,850	640	7,480	425	45	315	8,230	76,875	85,110
British Columbia	0	745	100	845	710	1,210	1,015	3,630	93,350	96,585
Territories	14,460	115	20	130	4,975	60	120	19,750	15,175	34,935
Canada	20,485	20,290	7,085	27,230	8,455	1,315	3,305	60,375	492,320	552,055

Source: Canada's Off-Reserve Aboriginal Population: A Statistical Overview, Social Trends Analysis Directorate, Department of the Secretary of State of Canada, 1991, p. A-8. Statistics Canada, *1986 Census, Special Tabulations from the Small Area Database*, compiled for the Department of the Secretary State. *Notes:* Sum of components may not always add to totals due to rounding and/or data suppression.

★ 882 ★

Population, by Home Language and Sex for Detailed Aboriginal Origins for Canada, 1986 - I[1,2]

Home language	Total aboriginal origins[3]		North American Indian only		North American Indian and non-aboriginal[4]		Metis only	
	Number	Percent	Number	Percent	Number	Percent	Number	Percent
Total	711,725	100.0	286,230	100.0	239,395	100.0	59,745	100.0
Male	349,265	49.1	140,545	49.1	116,465	48.6	29,875	50.0
Female	362,460	50.9	145,680	50.9	122,930	51.4	29,870	50.0
English only	514,210	72.2	165,530	57.8	211,570	88.4	44,775	74.9
Male	251,355	35.3	79,850	27.9	103,810	43.4	22,260	37.3
Female	262,860	36.9	85,675	29.9	107,760	45.0	22,520	37.7
French only	47,565	6.7	15,220	5.3	19,855	8.3	5,440	9.1
Male	22,700	3.2	7,420	2.6	9,075	3.8	2,820	4.7

[Continued]

★ 882 ★

Population, by Home Language and Sex for Detailed Aboriginal Origins for Canada, 1986 - I

[Continued]

Home language	Total aboriginal origins[3]		North American Indian only		North American Indian and non-aboriginal[4]		Metis only	
	Number	Percent	Number	Percent	Number	Percent	Number	Percent
Female	24,860	3.5	7,800	2.7	10,780	4.5	2,620	4.4
Aboriginal only[5]	93,195	13.1	68,930	24.1	1,045	0.4	4,255	7.1
Male	47,830	6.7	35,450	12.4	480	0.2	2,165	3.6
Female	45,365	6.4	33,475	11.7	570	0.2	2,085	3.5
Other language[6]	240	-	100	-	65	-	20	-
Male	125	-	50	-	30	-	10	-
Female	115	-	45	-	35	-	-	-
Multiple languages[7]	56,515	7.9	36,450	12.7	6,860	2.9	5,260	8.8
Male	27,255	3.8	17,770	6.2	3,065	1.3	2,620	4.4
Female	29,260	4.1	18,680	6.5	3,790	1.6	2,640	4.4

Source: Aboriginal Peoples Output Program, 1986 Census, Statistics Canada, *A Data Book on Canada's Aboriginal Population from the 1986 Census of Canada*, March, 1989, p. 8. Primary source: 1986 Census of Canada *Notes:* A dash (-) represents zero or a percentage which rounds to less than .05 percent. 1. Aboriginal origins are derived from the ethnic origin question which asks whether respondents are North American Indian, Metis or Inuit. 2. All 1986 figures exclude the population estimated at about 45,000 on 136 incompletely enumerated Indian reserves and settlements throughout Canada. 3. Total Aboriginal origins - are the sum of persons who reported: (a) a single aboriginal (e.g., North American Indian, Metis or Inuit) and, (b) multiple aboriginal origins, that is those who reported: - at least one aboriginal origin with any other non-aboriginal (e.g., Metis or French), or - two or more aboriginal origins only. 4. Non-aboriginal in these columns - refers to persons who report one or more non-aboriginal origins such as British, French, etc., in combination with one of the aboriginal origins such as North American Indian. 5. Aboriginal only - refers to persons reporting only one aboriginal language (e.g. Cree) as the language spoken most often at home. 6. Other language - refers to persons reporting only one aboriginal language, which is not English or French, as their home language. 7. Multiple languages - refers to persons reporting more than one aboriginal and/or non-aboriginal language as their home language.

★ 883 ★

Population, by Home Language and Sex for Detailed Aboriginal Origins for Canada, 1986 - II[1,2]

Home language	Metis and non-Aboriginal[3]		Inuit only		Inuit and non-Aboriginal[3]		Other multiple Aboriginal origins[4]	
	Number	Percent	Number	Percent	Number	Percent	Number	Percent
Total	68,895	100.0	27,290	100.0	6,175	100.0	23,995	100.0
Male	33,310	48.3	13,840	50.7	3,095	50.1	12,125	50.5
Female	35,585	51.7	13,450	49.3	3,075	49.8	11,870	49.5
English only	60,820	88.3	6,650	24.4	5,235	84.8	19,635	81.8
Male	29,515	42.8	3,375	12.4	2,630	42.6	9,910	41.3
Female	31,300	45.4	3,275	12.0	2,605	42.2	9,720	40.5
French only	4,715	6.8	785	2.9	380	6.2	1,155	4.8
Male	2,215	3.2	415	1.5	190	3.1	570	2.4

[Continued]

★ 883 ★

Population, by Home Language and Sex for Detailed Aboriginal Origins for Canada, 1986 - II
[Continued]

Home language	Metis and non-Aboriginal[3]		Inuit only		Inuit and non-Aboriginal[3]		Other multiple Aboriginal origins[4]	
	Number	Percent	Number	Percent	Number	Percent	Number	Percent
Female	2,500	3.6	375	1.4	185	3.0	595	2.5
Aboriginal only[5]	315	0.5	17,355	63.6	185	3.0	1,105	4.6
Male	155	0.2	8,890	32.6	100	1.6	585	2.4
Female	155	0.2	8,470	31.0	90	1.5	520	2.2
Other language[6]	15	-	10	-	20	0.3	-	-
Male	-	-	-	-	10	0.2	-	-
Female	-	-	-	-	10	0.2	-	-
Multiple languages[7]	3,030	4.4	2,485	9.1	355	5.7	2,085	8.7
Male	1,415	2.1	1,160	4.3	170	2.8	1,055	4.4
Female	1,620	2.4	1,325	4.9	185	3.0	1,030	4.3

Source: Aboriginal Peoples Output Program, 1986 Census, Statistics Canada, *A Data Book on Canada's Aboriginal Population from the 1986 Census of Canada*, March, 1989, p. 8. Primary source: 1986 Census of Canada *Notes:* A dash (-) represents zero or a percentage which rounds to less than .05 percent. 1. Aboriginal origins are derived from the ethnic origin question which asks whether respondents are North American Indian, Metis or Inuit. 2. All 1986 figures exclude the population estimated at about 45,000 on 136 incompletely enumerated Indian reserves and settlements throughout Canada. 3. Non-aboriginal in these columns - refers to persons who report one or more non-aboriginal origins such as British, French, etc., in combination with one of the aboriginal origins such as North American Indian. 4. Other multiple aboriginal origins - refer to the sum of those persons reporting two or more aboriginal origins with or without a non-aboriginal origin. 5. Aboriginal only - refers to persons reporting only one aboriginal language (e.g. Cree) as the language spoken most often at home. 6. Other language - refers to persons reporting only one aboriginal language, which is not english or french, as their home language. 7. Multiple languages - refers to persons reporting more than one aboriginal and/or non-aboriginal language as their home language.

★ 884 ★

Population, by Home Language and Sex for Detailed Aboriginal Origins for Alberta, 1986 - I[1,2]

Home language	Total aboriginal origins[3]		North American Indian only		North American Indian and non-aboriginal[4]		Metis only	
	Number	Percent	Number	Percent	Number	Percent	Number	Percent
Total	103,930	100.0	34,490	100.0	28,470	100.0	16,880	100.0
Male	50,930	49.0	16,605	48.1	13,905	48.8	8,535	50.6
Female	53,000	51.0	17,885	51.9	14,570	51.2	8,350	49.5
English only	84,620	81.4	20,875	60.5	27,585	96.9	13,805	81.8
Male	41,190	39.6	9,740	28.2	13,490	47.4	6,985	41.4
Female	43,430	41.8	11,135	32.3	14,095	49.5	6,820	40.4
French only	125	0.1	15	-	40	0.1	-	-
Male	85	0.1	-	-	20	0.1	-	-

[Continued]

★ 884 ★

Population, by Home Language and Sex for Detailed Aboriginal Origins for Alberta, 1986 - I
[Continued]

Home language	Total aboriginal origins[3]		North American Indian only		North American Indian and non-aboriginal[4]		Metis only	
	Number	Percent	Number	Percent	Number	Percent	Number	Percent
Female	45	-	-	-	25	0.1	-	-
Aboriginal only[5]	8,825	8.5	6,880	19.9	90	0.3	1,550	9.2
Male	4,615	4.4	3,590	10.4	50	0.2	810	4.8
Female	4,205	4.0	3,285	9.5	45	0.2	740	4.4
Other language[6]	45	-	20	0.1	-	-	-	-
Male	25	-	-	-	-	-	-	-
Female	20	-	15	-	-	-	-	-
Multiple languages[7]	10,315	9.9	6,700	19.4	745	2.6	1,525	9.0
Male	5,010	4.8	3,260	9.5	340	1.2	740	4.4
Female	5,300	5.1	3,440	10.0	405	1.4	785	4.7

Source: Aboriginal Peoples Output Program, 1986 Census, Statistics Canada, *A Data Book on Canada's Aboriginal Population from the 1986 Census of Canada,* March, 1989, p. 224. Primary source: 1986 Census of Canada *Notes:* A dash (-) represents zero or a percentage which rounds to less than .05 percent. 1. Aboriginal origins are derived from the ethnic origin question which asks whether respondents are North American Indian, Metis or Inuit. 2. All 1986 figures exclude the population estimated at about 45,000 on 136 incompletely enumerated Indian reserves and settlements throughout Canada. 3. Total Aboriginal origins - are the sum of persons who reported: (a) a single aboriginal (e.g., North American Indian, Metis or Inuit) and, (b) multiple aboriginal origins, that is those who reported: - at least one aboriginal origin with any other non-aboriginal (e.g., Metis or French), or - two or more aboriginal origins only. 4. Non-aboriginal in these columns - refers to persons who report one or more non-aboriginal origins such as British, French, etc., in combination with one of the aboriginal origins such as North American Indian. 5. Aboriginal only - refers to persons reporting only one aboriginal language (e.g. Cree) as the language spoken most often at home. 6. Other language - refers to persons reporting only one aboriginal language, which is not English or French, as their home language. 7. Multiple languages - refers to persons reporting more than one aboriginal and/or non-aboriginal language as their home language.

★ 885 ★

Population, by Home Language and Sex for Detailed Aboriginal Origins for Alberta, 1986 - II[1,2]

Home language	Metis and non-Aboriginal[3]		Inuit only		Inuit and non-Aboriginal[3]		Other multiple Aboriginal origins[4]	
	Number	Percent	Number	Percent	Number	Percent	Number	Percent
Total	17,260	100.0	300	100.0	445	100.0	6,080	100.0
Male	8,440	48.9	150	50.0	205	46.1	3,090	50.8
Female	8,820	51.1	145	48.3	240	53.9	2,985	49.1
English only	16,555	95.9	255	85.0	410	92.1	5,125	84.3
Male	8,095	46.9	115	38.3	190	42.7	2,580	42.4
Female	8,460	49.0	140	46.7	225	50.6	2,555	42.0
French only	55	0.3	-	-	-	-	-	-
Male	40	0.2	-	-	-	-	-	-

[Continued]

★ 885 ★

Population, by Home Language and Sex for Detailed Aboriginal Origins for Alberta, 1986 - II

[Continued]

Home language	Metis and non-Aboriginal[3]		Inuit only		Inuit and non-Aboriginal[3]		Other multiple Aboriginal origins[4]	
	Number	Percent	Number	Percent	Number	Percent	Number	Percent
Female	10	0.1	-	-	-	-	-	-
Aboriginal only[5]	105	0.6	-	-	-	-	195	3.2
Male	55	0.3	-	-	-	-	110	1.8
Female	50	0.3	-	-	-	-	80	1.3
Other language[6]	-	-	-	-	-	-	-	-
Male	-	-	-	-	-	-	-	-
Female	-	-	-	-	-	-	-	-
Multiple languages[7]	535	3.1	20	6.7	30	6.7	755	12.4
Male	235	1.4	15	5.0	15	3.4	400	6.6
Female	300	1.7	-	-	15	3.4	350	5.8

Source: Aboriginal Peoples Output Program, 1986 Census, Statistics Canada, *A Data Book on Canada's Aboriginal Population from the 1986 Census of Canada*, March, 1989, p. 224. Primary source: 1986 Census of Canada *Notes:* A dash (-) represents zero or a percentage which rounds to less than .05 percent. 1. Aboriginal origins are derived from the ethnic origin question which asks whether respondents are North American Indian, Metis or Inuit. 2. All 1986 figures exclude the population estimated at about 45,000 on 136 incompletely enumerated Indian reserves and settlements throughout Canada. 3. Non-aboriginal in these columns - refers to persons who report one or more non-aboriginal origins such as British, French, etc., in combination with one of the aboriginal origins such as North American Indian. 4. Other multiple aboriginal origins - refer to the sum of those persons reporting two or more aboriginal origins with or without a non-aboriginal origin. 5. Aboriginal only - refers to persons reporting only one aboriginal language (e.g. Cree) as the language spoken most often at home. 6. Other language - refers to persons reporting only one aboriginal language, which is not english or french, as their home language. 7. Multiple languages - refers to persons reporting more than one aboriginal and/or non-aboriginal language as their home language.

★ 886 ★

Population, by Home Language and Sex for Detailed Aboriginal Origins for British Columbia, 1986 - I[1,2]

Home language	Total aboriginal origins[3]		North American Indian only		North American Indian and non-aboriginal[4]		Metis only	
	Number	Percent	Number	Percent	Number	Percent	Number	Percent
Total	126,625	100.0	56,960	100.0	53,560	100.0	3,930	100.0
Male	62,985	49.7	28,235	49.6	26,685	49.8	1,905	48.5
Female	63,645	50.3	28,720	50.4	26,875	50.2	2,025	51.5
English only	119,080	94.0	50,830	89.2	52,870	98.7	3,600	91.6
Male	59,245	46.8	25,160	44.2	26,420	49.3	1,735	44.1
Female	59,840	47.3	25,675	45.1	26,445	49.4	1,865	47.5
French only	165	0.1	30	0.1	50	0.1	-	-
Male	85	0.1	20	-	20	-	-	-

[Continued]

★ 886 ★

Population, by Home Language and Sex for Detailed Aboriginal Origins for British Columbia, 1986 - I
[Continued]

Home language	Total aboriginal origins[3]		North American Indian only		North American Indian and non-aboriginal[4]		Metis only	
	Number	Percent	Number	Percent	Number	Percent	Number	Percent
Female	85	0.1	10	-	35	0.1	-	-
Aboriginal only[5]	2,230	1.8	2,115	3.7	60	0.1	50	1.3
Male	1,130	0.9	1,070	1.9	15	-	45	1.1
Female	1,100	0.9	1,045	1.8	45	0.1	-	-
Other language[6]	20	-	10	-	-	-	-	-
Male	10	-	-	-	-	-	-	-
Female	10	-	-	-	-	-	-	-
Multiple languages[7]	5,120	4.0	3,975	7.0	580	1.1	270	6.9
Male	2,520	2.0	1,990	3.5	225	0.4	115	2.9
Female	2,605	2.1	1,980	3.5	350	0.7	155	3.9

Source: Aboriginal Peoples Output Program, 1986 Census, Statistics Canada, *A Data Book on Canada's Aboriginal Population from the 1986 Census of Canada*, March, 1989, p. 248. Primary source: 1986 Census of Canada *Notes:* A dash (-) represents zero or a percentage which rounds to less than .05 percent. 1. Aboriginal origins are derived from the ethnic origin question which asks whether respondents are North American Indian, Metis or Inuit. 2. All 1986 figures exclude the population estimated at about 45,000 on 136 incompletely enumerated Indian reserves and settlements throughout Canada. 3. Total Aboriginal origins - are the sum of persons who reported: (a) a single aboriginal (e.g., North American Indian, Metis or Inuit) and, (b) multiple aboriginal origins, that is those who reported: - at least one aboriginal origin with any other non-aboriginal (e.g., Metis or French), or - two or more aboriginal origins only. 4. Non-aboriginal in these columns - refers to persons who report one or more non-aboriginal origins such as British, French, etc., in combination with one of the aboriginal origins such as North American Indian. 5. Aboriginal only - refers to persons reporting only one aboriginal language (e.g. Cree) as the language spoken most often at home. 6. Other language - refers to persons reporting only one aboriginal language, which is not English or French, as their home language. 7. Multiple languages - refers to persons reporting more than one aboriginal and/or non-aboriginal language as their home language.

★ 887 ★

Population, by Home Language and Sex for Detailed Aboriginal Origins for British Columbia, 1986 - II[1,2]

Home language	Metis and non-Aboriginal[3]		Inuit only		Inuit and non-Aboriginal[3]		Other multiple Aboriginal origins[4]	
	Number	Percent	Number	Percent	Number	Percent	Number	Percent
Total	9,135	100.0	245	100.0	500	100.0	2,305	100.0
Male	4,515	49.4	140	57.1	275	55.0	1,225	53.1
Female	4,620	50.6	100	40.8	220	44.0	1,080	46.9
English only	8,890	97.3	225	91.8	485	97.0	2,175	94.4
Male	4,395	48.1	125	51.0	270	54.0	1,150	49.9
Female	4,500	49.3	100	40.8	215	43.0	1,035	44.9
French only	55	0.6	-	-	-	-	15	0.7
Male	30	0.3	-	-	-	-	-	-

[Continued]

★ 887 ★

Population, by Home Language and Sex for Detailed Aboriginal Origins for British Columbia, 1986 - II

[Continued]

Home language	Metis and non-Aboriginal[3]		Inuit only		Inuit and non-Aboriginal[3]		Other multiple Aboriginal origins[4]	
	Number	Percent	Number	Percent	Number	Percent	Number	Percent
Female	25	0.3	-	-	-	-	-	-
Aboriginal only[5]	-	-	-	-	-	-	-	-
Male	-	-	-	-	-	-	-	-
Female	-	-	-	-	-	-	-	-
Other language[6]	-	-	-	-	-	-	-	-
Male	-	-	-	-	-	-	-	-
Female	-	-	-	-	-	-	-	-
Multiple languages[7]	180	2.0	15	6.1	-	-	105	4.6
Male	95	1.0	15	6.1	-	-	65	2.8
Female	90	1.0	-	-	-	-	35	1.5

Source: Aboriginal Peoples Output Program, 1986 Census, Statistics Canada, *A Data Book on Canada's Aboriginal Population from the 1986 Census of Canada*, March, 1989, p. 248. Primary source: 1986 Census of Canada *Notes:* A dash (-) represents zero or a percentage which rounds to less than .05 percent. 1. Aboriginal origins are derived from the ethnic origin question which asks whether respondents are North American Indian, Metis or Inuit. 2. All 1986 figures exclude the population estimated at about 45,000 on 136 incompletely enumerated Indian reserves and settlements throughout Canada. 3. Non-aboriginal in these columns - refers to persons who report one or more non-aboriginal origins such as British, French, etc., in combination with one of the aboriginal origins such as North American Indian. 4. Other multiple aboriginal origins - refer to the sum of those persons reporting two or more aboriginal origins with or without a non-aboriginal origin. 5. Aboriginal only - refers to persons reporting only one aboriginal language (e.g. Cree) as the language spoken most often at home. 6. Other language - refers to persons reporting only one aboriginal language, which is not english or french, as their home language. 7. Multiple languages - refers to persons reporting more than one aboriginal and/or non-aboriginal language as their home language.

★ 888 ★

Population, by Home Language and Sex for Detailed Aboriginal Origins for Manitoba, 1986 - I[1,2]

Home language	Total aboriginal origins[3]		North American Indian only		North American Indian and non-aboriginal[4]		Metis only	
	Number	Percent	Number	Percent	Number	Percent	Number	Percent
Total	85,235	100.0	40,960	100.0	10,510	100.0	14,270	100.0
Male	41,860	49.1	20,135	49.2	5,275	50.2	7,180	50.3
Female	43,370	50.9	20,825	50.8	5,235	49.8	7,090	49.7
English only	55,660	65.3	16,795	41.0	9,795	93.2	11,975	83.9
Male	26,895	31.6	7,865	19.2	4,915	46.8	6,015	42.2
Female	28,765	33.7	8,920	21.8	4,880	46.4	5,960	41.8
French only	915	1.1	50	0.1	50	0.5	240	1.7
Male	485	0.6	35	0.1	40	0.4	115	0.8

[Continued]

★ 888 ★

Population, by Home Language and Sex for Detailed Aboriginal Origins for Manitoba, 1986 - I
[Continued]

Home language	Total aboriginal origins[3]		North American Indian only		North American Indian and non-aboriginal[4]		Metis only	
	Number	Percent	Number	Percent	Number	Percent	Number	Percent
Female	425	0.5	10	-	10	0.1	120	0.8
Aboriginal only[5]	18,105	21.2	16,660	40.7	195	1.9	740	5.2
Male	9,350	11.0	8,630	21.1	85	0.8	380	2.7
Female	8,750	10.3	8,030	19.6	110	1.0	365	2.6
Other language[6]	20	-	-	-	-	-	-	-
Male	-	-	-	-	-	-	-	-
Female	-	-	-	-	-	-	-	-
Multiple languages[7]	10,545	12.4	7,455	18.2	470	4.5	1,320	9.3
Male	5,120	6.0	3,600	8.8	245	2.3	675	4.7
Female	5,420	6.4	3,855	9.4	225	2.1	645	4.5

Source: Aboriginal Peoples Output Program, 1986 Census, Statistics Canada, *A Data Book on Canada's Aboriginal Population from the 1986 Census of Canada*, March, 1989, p. 178. Primary source: 1986 Census of Canada *Notes:* A dash (-) represents zero or a percentage which rounds to less than .05 percent. 1. Aboriginal origins are derived from the ethnic origin question which asks whether respondents are North American Indian, Metis or Inuit. 2. All 1986 figures exclude the population estimated at about 45,000 on 136 incompletely enumerated Indian reserves and settlements throughout Canada. 3. Total Aboriginal origins - are the sum of persons who reported: (a) a single aboriginal (e.g., North American Indian, Metis or Inuit) and, (b) multiple aboriginal origins, that is those who reported: - at least one aboriginal origin with any other non-aboriginal (e.g., Metis or French), or - two or more aboriginal origins only. 4. Non-aboriginal in these columns - refers to persons who report one or more non-aboriginal origins such as British, French, etc., in combination with one of the aboriginal origins such as North American Indian. 5. Aboriginal only - refers to persons reporting only one aboriginal language (e.g. Cree) as the language spoken most often at home. 6. Other language - refers to persons reporting only one aboriginal language, which is not English or French, as their home language. 7. Multiple languages - refers to persons reporting more than one aboriginal and/or non-aboriginal language as their home language.

★ 889 ★

Population, by Home Language and Sex for Detailed Aboriginal Origins for Manitoba, 1986 - II[1,2]

Home language	Metis and non-Aboriginal[3]		Inuit only		Inuit and non-Aboriginal[3]		Other multiple Aboriginal origins[4]	
	Number	Percent	Number	Percent	Number	Percent	Number	Percent
Total	14,605	100.0	185	100.0	200	100.0	4,505	100.0
Male	6,955	47.6	60	32.4	85	42.5	2,175	48.3
Female	7,650	52.4	120	64.9	115	57.5	2,335	51.8
English only	13,190	90.3	160	86.5	200	100.0	3,545	78.7
Male	6,275	43.0	55	29.7	85	42.5	1,690	37.5
Female	6,920	47.4	110	59.5	115	57.5	1,855	41.2
French only	540	3.7	-	-	-	-	-	-
Male	280	1.9	-	-	-	-	-	-

[Continued]

★ 889 ★

Population, by Home Language and Sex for Detailed Aboriginal Origins for Manitoba, 1986 - II

[Continued]

Home language	Metis and non-Aboriginal[3]		Inuit only		Inuit and non-Aboriginal[3]		Other multiple Aboriginal origins[4]	
	Number	Percent	Number	Percent	Number	Percent	Number	Percent
Female	260	1.8	-	-	-	-	-	-
Aboriginal only[5]	65	0.4	-	-	-	-	435	9.7
Male	40	0.3	-	-	-	-	220	4.9
Female	30	0.2	-	-	-	-	210	4.7
Other language[6]	-	-	-	-	-	-	-	-
Male	-	-	-	-	-	-	-	-
Female	-	-	-	-	-	-	-	-
Multiple languages[7]	810	5.5	15	8.1	-	-	475	10.5
Male	365	2.5	-	-	-	-	235	5.2
Female	445	3.0	-	-	-	-	240	5.3

Source: Aboriginal Peoples Output Program, 1986 Census, Statistics Canada, *A Data Book on Canada's Aboriginal Population from the 1986 Census of Canada*, March, 1989, p. 178. Primary source: 1986 Census of Canada *Notes:* A dash (-) represents zero or a percentage which rounds to less than .05 percent. 1. Aboriginal origins are derived from the ethnic origin question which asks whether respondents are North American Indian, Metis or Inuit. 2. All 1986 figures exclude the population estimated at about 45,000 on 136 incompletely enumerated Indian reserves and settlements throughout Canada. 3. Non-aboriginal in these columns - refers to persons who report one or more non-aboriginal origins such as British, French, etc., in combination with one of the aboriginal origins such as North American Indian. 4. Other multiple aboriginal origins - refer to the sum of those persons reporting two or more aboriginal origins with or without a non-aboriginal origin. 5. Aboriginal only - refers to persons reporting only one aboriginal language (e.g. Cree) as the language spoken most often at home. 6. Other language - refers to persons reporting only one aboriginal language, which is not english or french, as their home language. 7. Multiple languages - refers to persons reporting more than one aboriginal and/or non-aboriginal language as their home language.

★ 890 ★

Population, by Home Language and Sex for Detailed Aboriginal Origins for New Brunswick, 1986 - I[1,2]

Home language	Total aboriginal origins[3]		North American Indian only		North American Indian and non-aboriginal[4]		Metis only	
	Number	Percent	Number	Percent	Number	Percent	Number	Percent
Total	9,380	100.0	3,685	100.0	4,830	100.0	185	100.0
Male	4,705	50.2	1,905	51.7	2,355	48.8	100	54.1
Female	4,670	49.8	1,780	48.3	2,475	51.2	85	45.9
English only	6,815	72.7	1,810	49.1	4,335	89.8	120	64.9
Male	3,425	36.5	920	25.0	2,150	44.5	55	29.7
Female	3,390	36.1	885	24.0	2,185	45.2	65	35.1
French only	440	4.7	95	2.6	210	4.3	55	29.7
Male	255	2.7	65	1.8	110	2.3	45	24.3

[Continued]

★ 890 ★

Population, by Home Language and Sex for Detailed Aboriginal Origins for New Brunswick, 1986 - I

[Continued]

Home language	Total aboriginal origins[3]		North American Indian only		North American Indian and non-aboriginal[4]		Metis only	
	Number	Percent	Number	Percent	Number	Percent	Number	Percent
Female	190	2.0	30	0.8	100	2.1	15	8.1
Aboriginal only[5]	1,365	14.6	1,330	36.1	40	0.8	-	-
Male	710	7.6	695	18.9	15	0.3	-	-
Female	655	7.0	635	17.2	15	0.3	-	-
Other language[6]	-	-	-	-	-	-	-	-
Male	-	-	-	-	-	-	-	-
Female	-	-	-	-	-	-	-	-
Multiple languages[7]	745	7.9	450	12.2	245	5.1	-	-
Male	315	3.4	220	6.0	75	1.6	-	-
Female	430	4.6	230	6.2	165	3.4	-	-

Source: Aboriginal Peoples Output Program, 1986 Census, Statistics Canada, *A Data Book on Canada's Aboriginal Population from the 1986 Census of Canada*, March, 1989, p. 104. Primary source: 1986 Census of Canada *Notes:* A dash (-) represents zero or a percentage which rounds to less than .05 percent. 1. Aboriginal origins are derived from the ethnic origin question which asks whether respondents are North American Indian, Metis or Inuit. 2. All 1986 figures exclude the population estimated at about 45,000 on 136 incompletely enumerated Indian reserves and settlements throughout Canada. 3. Total Aboriginal origins - are the sum of persons who reported: (a) a single aboriginal (e.g., North American Indian, Metis or Inuit) and, (b) multiple aboriginal origins, that is those who reported: - at least one aboriginal origin with any other non-aboriginal (e.g., Metis or French), or - two or more aboriginal origins only. 4. Non-aboriginal in these columns - refers to persons who report one or more non-aboriginal origins such as British, French, etc., in combination with one of the aboriginal origins such as North American Indian. 5. Aboriginal only - refers to persons reporting only one aboriginal language (e.g. Cree) as the language spoken most often at home. 6. Other language - refers to persons reporting only one aboriginal language, which is not English or French, as their home language. 7. Multiple languages - refers to persons reporting more than one aboriginal and/or non-aboriginal language as their home language.

★ 891 ★

Population, by Home Language and Sex for Detailed Aboriginal Origins for New Brunswick, 1986 - II[1,2]

Home language	Metis and non-Aboriginal[3]		Inuit only		Inuit and non-Aboriginal[3]		Other multiple Aboriginal origins[4]	
	Number	Percent	Number	Percent	Number	Percent	Number	Percent
Total	370	100.0	15	100.0	105	100.0	190	100.0
Male	205	55.4	-	-	35	33.3	95	50.0
Female	165	44.6	-	-	65	61.9	90	47.4
English only	265	71.6	-	-	100	95.6	170	89.5
Male	160	43.2	-	-	40	38.1	90	47.4
Female	110	29.7	-	-	60	57.1	85	44.7
French only	70	18.9	-	-	-	-	-	-
Male	40	10.8	-	-	-	-	-	-

[Continued]

★ 891 ★

Population, by Home Language and Sex for Detailed Aboriginal Origins for New Brunswick, 1986 - II

[Continued]

Home language	Metis and non-Aboriginal[3]		Inuit only		Inuit and non-Aboriginal[3]		Other multiple Aboriginal origins[4]	
	Number	Percent	Number	Percent	Number	Percent	Number	Percent
Female	35	9.5	-	-	-	-	-	-
Aboriginal only[5]	-	-	-	-	-	-	-	-
Male	-	-	-	-	-	-	-	-
Female	-	-	-	-	-	-	-	-
Other language[6]	-	-	-	-	-	-	-	-
Male	-	-	-	-	-	-	-	-
Female	-	-	-	-	-	-	-	-
Multiple languages[7]	30	8.1	-	-	-	-	-	-
Male	-	-	-	-	-	-	-	-
Female	20	5.4	-	-	-	-	-	-

Source: Aboriginal Peoples Output Program, 1986 Census, Statistics Canada, *A Data Book on Canada's Aboriginal Population from the 1986 Census of Canada,* March, 1989, p. 104. Primary source: 1986 Census of Canada *Notes:* A dash (-) represents zero or a percentage which rounds to less than .05 percent. 1. Aboriginal origins are derived from the ethnic origin question which asks whether respondents are North American Indian, Metis or Inuit. 2. All 1986 figures exclude the population estimated at about 45,000 on 136 incompletely enumerated Indian reserves and settlements throughout Canada. 3. Non-aboriginal in these columns - refers to persons who report one or more non-aboriginal origins such as British, French, etc., in combination with one of the aboriginal origins such as North American Indian. 4. Other multiple aboriginal origins - refer to the sum of those persons reporting two or more aboriginal origins with or without a non-aboriginal origin. 5. Aboriginal only - refers to persons reporting only one aboriginal language (e.g. Cree) as the language spoken most often at home. 6. Other language - refers to persons reporting only one aboriginal language, which is not english or french, as their home language. 7. Multiple languages - refers to persons reporting more than one aboriginal and/or non-aboriginal language as their home language.

★ 892 ★

Population, by Home Language and Sex for Detailed Aboriginal Origins for Newfoundland, 1986 - I[1,2]

Home language	Total aboriginal origins[3]		North American Indian only		North American Indian and non-aboriginal[4]		Metis only	
	Number	Percent	Number	Percent	Number	Percent	Number	Percent
Total	9,555	100.0	1,745	100.0	2,690	100.0	265	100.0
Male	4,925	51.5	835	47.9	1,425	53.0	135	50.9
Female	4,635	48.5	910	52.1	1,270	47.2	130	49.1
English only	8,005	83.8	815	46.7	2,660	89.9	265	100.0
Male	4,150	43.4	380	21.8	1,410	52.4	135	50.9
Female	3,860	40.4	440	25.2	1,250	46.5	130	49.1
French only	-	-	-	-	-	-	-	-
Male	-	-	-	-	-	-	-	-

[Continued]

★ 892 ★

Population, by Home Language and Sex for Detailed Aboriginal Origins for Newfoundland, 1986 - I
[Continued]

Home language	Total aboriginal origins[3]		North American Indian only		North American Indian and non-aboriginal[4]		Metis only	
	Number	Percent	Number	Percent	Number	Percent	Number	Percent
Female	-	-	-	-	-	-	-	-
Aboriginal only[5]	900	9.4	660	37.8	-	-	-	-
Male	455	4.8	320	18.3	-	-	-	-
Female	440	4.6	335	19.2	-	-	-	-
Other language[6]	-	-	-	-	-	-	-	-
Male	-	-	-	-	-	-	-	-
Female	-	-	-	-	-	-	-	-
Multiple languages[7]	640	6.7	275	15.8	15	0.6	-	-
Male	315	3.3	135	7.7	10	0.4	-	-
Female	330	3.5	135	7.7	-	-	-	-

Source: Aboriginal Peoples Output Program, 1986 Census, Statistics Canada, *A Data Book on Canada's Aboriginal Population from the 1986 Census of Canada*, March, 1989, p. 32. Primary source: 1986 Census of Canada *Notes:* A dash (-) represents zero or a percentage which rounds to less than .05 percent. 1. Aboriginal origins are derived from the ethnic origin question which asks whether respondents are North American Indian, Metis or Inuit. 2. All 1986 figures exclude the population estimated at about 45,000 on 136 incompletely enumerated Indian reserves and settlements throughout Canada. 3. Total Aboriginal origins - are the sum of persons who reported: (a) a single aboriginal (e.g., North American Indian, Metis or Inuit) and, (b) multiple aboriginal origins, that is those who reported: - at least one aboriginal origin with any other non-aboriginal (e.g., Metis or French), or - two or more aboriginal origins only. 4. Non-aboriginal in these columns - refers to persons who report one or more non-aboriginal origins such as British, French, etc., in combination with one of the aboriginal origins such as North American Indian. 5. Aboriginal only - refers to persons reporting only one aboriginal language (e.g. Cree) as the language spoken most often at home. 6. Other language - refers to persons reporting only one aboriginal language, which is not English or French, as their home language. 7. Multiple languages - refers to persons reporting more than one aboriginal and/or non-aboriginal language as their home language.

★ 893 ★

Population, by Home Language and Sex for Detailed Aboriginal Origins for Newfoundland, 1986 - II[1,2]

Home language	Metis and non-Aboriginal[3]		Inuit only		Inuit and non-Aboriginal[3]		Other multiple Aboriginal origins[4]	
	Number	Percent	Number	Percent	Number	Percent	Number	Percent
Total	680	100.0	1,810	100.0	1,745	100.0	615	100.0
Male	380	55.9	915	50.6	880	50.4	350	56.9
Female	300	44.1	900	49.7	870	49.9	260	42.3
English only	670	98.5	1,280	70.7	1,710	98.0	600	97.6
Male	375	55.1	645	35.6	860	49.3	340	55.3
Female	290	42.6	640	35.4	855	49.0	255	41.5
French only	-	-	-	-	-	-	-	-
Male	-	-	-	-	-	-	-	-

[Continued]

★ 893 ★

Population, by Home Language and Sex for Detailed Aboriginal Origins for Newfoundland, 1986 - II

[Continued]

Home language	Metis and non-Aboriginal[3]		Inuit only		Inuit and non-Aboriginal[3]		Other multiple Aboriginal origins[4]	
	Number	Percent	Number	Percent	Number	Percent	Number	Percent
Female	-	-	-	-	-	-	-	-
Aboriginal only[5]	-	-	225	12.4	-	-	-	-
Male	-	-	125	6.9	-	-	-	-
Female	-	-	95	5.2	-	-	-	-
Other language[6]	-	-	-	-	-	-	-	-
Male	-	-	-	-	-	-	-	-
Female	-	-	-	-	-	-	-	-
Multiple languages[7]	-	-	305	16.9	30	1.7	-	-
Male	-	-	145	8.0	15	0.9	-	-
Female	-	-	160	8.8	15	0.9	-	-

Source: Aboriginal Peoples Output Program, 1986 Census, Statistics Canada, *A Data Book on Canada's Aboriginal Population from the 1986 Census of Canada*, March, 1989, p. 32. Primary source: 1986 Census of Canada *Notes:* A dash (-) represents zero or a percentage which rounds to less than .05 percent. 1. Aboriginal origins are derived from the ethnic origin question which asks whether respondents are North American Indian, Metis or Inuit. 2. All 1986 figures exclude the population estimated at about 45,000 on 136 incompletely enumerated Indian reserves and settlements throughout Canada. 3. Non-aboriginal in these columns - refers to persons who report one or more non-aboriginal origins such as British, French, etc., in combination with one of the aboriginal origins such as North American Indian. 4. Other multiple aboriginal origins - refer to the sum of those persons reporting two or more aboriginal origins with or without a non-aboriginal origin. 5. Aboriginal only - refers to persons reporting only one aboriginal language (e.g. Cree) as the language spoken most often at home. 6. Other language - refers to persons reporting only one aboriginal language, which is not english or french, as their home language. 7. Multiple languages - refers to persons reporting more than one aboriginal and/or non-aboriginal language as their home language.

★ 894 ★

Population, by Home Language and Sex for Detailed Aboriginal Origins for Northwest Territories, 1986 - I[1,2]

Home language	Total aboriginal origins[3]		North American Indian only		North American Indian and non-aboriginal[4]		Metis only	
	Number	Percent	Number	Percent	Number	Percent	Number	Percent
Total	30,530	100.0	7,585	100.0	845	100.0	2,200	100.0
Male	15,640	51.2	3,875	51.1	490	58.0	1,120	50.9
Female	14,890	48.8	3,715	49.0	360	42.6	1,080	49.1
English only	12,065	39.5	3,455	45.6	770	91.1	2,005	91.1
Male	6,160	20.2	1,665	22.0	465	55.0	1,015	46.1
Female	5,900	19.3	1,785	23.5	310	36.7	985	44.8
French only	45	0.1	15	0.2	-	-	15	0.7
Male	30	0.1	20	0.3	-	-	-	-

[Continued]

★ 894 ★

Population, by Home Language and Sex for Detailed Aboriginal Origins for Northwest Territories, 1986 - I

[Continued]

Home language	Total aboriginal origins[3]		North American Indian only		North American Indian and non-aboriginal[4]		Metis only	
	Number	Percent	Number	Percent	Number	Percent	Number	Percent
Female	15	-	-	-	-	-	-	-
Aboriginal only[5]	15,295	50.1	3,045	40.1	30	3.6	55	2.5
Male	7,945	26.0	1,660	21.9	15	1.8	20	0.9
Female	7,350	24.1	1,390	18.3	15	1.8	35	1.6
Other language[6]	10	-	-	-	-	-	-	-
Male	-	-	-	-	-	-	-	-
Female	-	-	-	-	-	-	-	-
Multiple languages[7]	3,110	10.2	1,065	14.0	40	4.7	130	5.9
Male	1,490	4.9	525	6.9	-	-	75	3.4
Female	1,620	5.3	540	7.1	30	3.6	55	2.5

Source: Aboriginal Peoples Output Program, 1986 Census, Statistics Canada, *A Data Book on Canada's Aboriginal Population from the 1986 Census of Canada*, March, 1989, p. 272. Primary source: 1986 Census of Canada *Notes:* A dash (-) represents zero or a percentage which rounds to less than .05 percent. 1. Aboriginal origins are derived from the ethnic origin question which asks whether respondents are North American Indian, Metis or Inuit. 2. All 1986 figures exclude the population estimated at about 45,000 on 136 incompletely enumerated Indian reserves and settlements throughout Canada. 3. Total Aboriginal origins - are the sum of persons who reported: (a) a single aboriginal (e.g., North American Indian, Metis or Inuit) and, (b) multiple aboriginal origins, that is those who reported: - at least one aboriginal origin with any other non-aboriginal (e.g., Metis or French), or - two or more aboriginal origins only. 4. Non-aboriginal in these columns - refers to persons who report one or more non-aboriginal origins such as British, French, etc., in combination with one of the aboriginal origins such as North American Indian. 5. Aboriginal only - refers to persons reporting only one aboriginal language (e.g. Cree) as the language spoken most often at home. 6. Other language - refers to persons reporting only one aboriginal language, which is not English or French, as their home language. 7. Multiple languages - refers to persons reporting more than one aboriginal and/or non-aboriginal language as their home language.

★ 895 ★

Population, by Home Language and Sex for Detailed Aboriginal Origins for Northwest Territories, 1986 - II[1,2]

Home language	Metis and non-Aboriginal[3]		Inuit only		Inuit and non-Aboriginal[3]		Other multiple Aboriginal origins[4]	
	Number	Percent	Number	Percent	Number	Percent	Number	Percent
Total	760	100.0	17,385	100.0	750	100.0	995	100.0
Male	385	50.7	8,815	50.7	400	53.3	560	56.3
Female	375	49.3	8,570	49.3	350	46.7	435	43.7
English only	745	98.0	3,765	21.7	440	58.7	880	88.4
Male	380	50.0	1,895	10.9	235	31.3	495	49.7
Female	365	48.0	1,865	10.7	205	27.3	385	38.7
French only	-	-	-	-	-	-	-	-
Male	-	-	-	-	-	-	-	-

[Continued]

★ 895 ★

Population, by Home Language and Sex for Detailed Aboriginal Origins for Northwest Territories, 1986 - II

[Continued]

Home language	Metis and non-Aboriginal[3]		Inuit only		Inuit and non-Aboriginal[3]		Other multiple Aboriginal origins[4]	
	Number	Percent	Number	Percent	Number	Percent	Number	Percent
Female	-	-	-	-	-	-	-	-
Aboriginal only[5]	-	-	11,965	68.8	155	20.7	35	3.5
Male	-	-	6,145	35.3	80	10.7	20	2.0
Female	-	-	5,820	33.5	80	10.7	10	1.0
Other language[6]	-	-	-	-	-	-	-	-
Male	-	-	-	-	-	-	-	-
Female	-	-	-	-	-	-	-	-
Multiple languages[7]	-	-	1,640	9.4	160	21.3	70	7.0
Male	-	-	770	4.4	85	11.3	25	2.5
Female	-	-	870	5.0	75	10.0	45	4.5

Source: Aboriginal Peoples Output Program, 1986 Census, Statistics Canada, *A Data Book on Canada's Aboriginal Population from the 1986 Census of Canada*, March, 1989, p. 272. Primary source: 1986 Census of Canada *Notes:* A dash (-) represents zero or a percentage which rounds to less than .05 percent. 1. Aboriginal origins are derived from the ethnic origin question which asks whether respondents are North American Indian, Metis or Inuit. 2. All 1986 figures exclude the population estimated at about 45,000 on 136 incompletely enumerated Indian reserves and settlements throughout Canada. 3. Non-aboriginal in these columns - refers to persons who report one or more non-aboriginal origins such as British, French, etc., in combination with one of the aboriginal origins such as North American Indian. 4. Other multiple aboriginal origins - refer to the sum of those persons reporting two or more aboriginal origins with or without a non-aboriginal origin. 5. Aboriginal only - refers to persons reporting only one aboriginal language (e.g. Cree) as the language spoken most often at home. 6. Other language - refers to persons reporting only one aboriginal language, which is not english or french, as their home language. 7. Multiple languages - refers to persons reporting more than one aboriginal and/or non-aboriginal language as their home language.

★ 896 ★

Population, by Home Language and Sex for Detailed Aboriginal Origins for Nova Scotia, 1986 - I[1,2]

Home language	Total aboriginal origins[3]		North American Indian only		North American Indian and non-aboriginal[4]		Metis only	
	Number	Percent	Number	Percent	Number	Percent	Number	Percent
Total	14,225	100.0	5,570	100.0	7,245	100.0	255	100.0
Male	7,005	49.2	2,815	50.5	3,535	48.8	125	49.0
Female	7,220	50.8	2,760	49.6	3,705	51.1	130	51.0
English only	10,740	75.5	2,410	43.3	7,025	97.0	255	100.0
Male	5,235	36.8	1,190	21.4	3,430	47.3	125	49.0
Female	5,500	38.7	1,220	21.9	3,595	49.6	130	51.0
French only	60	0.4	-	-	35	0.5	-	-
Male	35	0.2	-	-	25	0.3	-	-

[Continued]

Population, by Home Language and Sex for Detailed Aboriginal Origins for Nova Scotia, 1986 - I

[Continued]

Home language	Total aboriginal origins[3]		North American Indian only		North American Indian and non-aboriginal[4]		Metis only	
	Number	Percent	Number	Percent	Number	Percent	Number	Percent
Female	25	0.2	-	-	15	0.2	-	-
Aboriginal only[5]	2,705	19.0	2,670	47.9	30	0.4	-	-
Male	1,400	9.8	1,380	24.8	25	0.3	-	-
Female	1,305	9.2	1,295	23.2	15	0.2	-	-
Other language[6]	-	-	-	-	-	-	-	-
Male	-	-	-	-	-	-	-	-
Female	-	-	-	-	-	-	-	-
Multiple languages[7]	710	5.0	480	8.6	150	2.1	-	-
Male	325	2.3	240	4.3	60	0.8	-	-
Female	385	2.7	240	4.3	85	1.2	-	-

Source: Aboriginal Peoples Output Program, 1986 Census, Statistics Canada, *A Data Book on Canada's Aboriginal Population from the 1986 Census of Canada*, March, 1989, p. 80. Primary source: 1986 Census of Canada *Notes:* A dash (-) represents zero or a percentage which rounds to less than .05 percent. 1. Aboriginal origins are derived from the ethnic origin question which asks whether respondents are North American Indian, Metis or Inuit. 2. All 1986 figures exclude the population estimated at about 45,000 on 136 incompletely enumerated Indian reserves and settlements throughout Canada. 3. Total Aboriginal origins - are the sum of persons who reported: (a) a single aboriginal (e.g., North American Indian, Metis or Inuit) and, (b) multiple aboriginal origins, that is those who reported: - at least one aboriginal origin with any other non-aboriginal (e.g., Metis or French), or - two or more aboriginal origins only. 4. Non-aboriginal in these columns - refers to persons who report one or more non-aboriginal origins such as British, French, etc., in combination with one of the aboriginal origins such as North American Indian. 5. Aboriginal only - refers to persons reporting only one aboriginal language (e.g. Cree) as the language spoken most often at home. 6. Other language - refers to persons reporting only one aboriginal language, which is not English or French, as their home language. 7. Multiple languages - refers to persons reporting more than one aboriginal and/or non-aboriginal language as their home language.

Population, by Home Language and Sex for Detailed Aboriginal Origins for Nova Scotia, 1986 - II[1,2]

Home language	Metis and non-Aboriginal[3]		Inuit only		Inuit and non-Aboriginal[3]		Other multiple Aboriginal origins[4]	
	Number	Percent	Number	Percent	Number	Percent	Number	Percent
Total	625	100.0	135	100.0	150	100.0	250	100.0
Male	260	41.6	65	48.1	60	40.0	145	58.0
Female	360	57.6	70	51.9	90	60.0	95	38.0
English only	590	94.4	110	81.5	140	93.3	210	84.0
Male	245	39.2	60	44.4	60	40.0	130	52.0
Female	345	55.2	55	40.7	80	53.3	80	32.0
French only	15	2.4	-	-	-	-	-	-
Male	-	-	-	-	-	-	-	-

[Continued]

★ 897 ★

Population, by Home Language and Sex for Detailed Aboriginal Origins for Nova Scotia, 1986 - II
[Continued]

Home language	Metis and non-Aboriginal[3]		Inuit only		Inuit and non-Aboriginal[3]		Other multiple Aboriginal origins[4]	
	Number	Percent	Number	Percent	Number	Percent	Number	Percent
Female	-	-	-	-	-	-	-	-
Aboriginal only[5]	-	-	-	-	-	-	-	-
Male	-	-	-	-	-	-	-	-
Female	-	-	-	-	-	-	-	-
Other language[6]	-	-	-	-	-	-	-	-
Male	-	-	-	-	-	-	-	-
Female	-	-	-	-	-	-	-	-
Multiple languages[7]	20	3.2	25	18.5	15	10.0	20	8.0
Male	-	-	-	-	-	-	-	-
Female	-	-	20	14.8	15	10.0	15	6.0

Source: Aboriginal Peoples Output Program, 1986 Census, Statistics Canada, *A Data Book on Canada's Aboriginal Population from the 1986 Census of Canada*, March, 1989, p. 80. Primary source: 1986 Census of Canada *Notes:* A dash (-) represents zero or a percentage which rounds to less than .05 percent. 1. Aboriginal origins are derived from the ethnic origin question which asks whether respondents are North American Indian, Metis or Inuit. 2. All 1986 figures exclude the population estimated at about 45,000 on 136 incompletely enumerated Indian reserves and settlements throughout Canada. 3. Non-aboriginal in these columns - refers to persons who report one or more non-aboriginal origins such as British, French, etc., in combination with one of the aboriginal origins such as North American Indian. 4. Other multiple aboriginal origins - refer to the sum of those persons reporting two or more aboriginal origins with or without a non-aboriginal origin. 5. Aboriginal only - refers to persons reporting only one aboriginal language (e.g. Cree) as the language spoken most often at home. 6. Other language - refers to persons reporting only one aboriginal language, which is not english or french, as their home language. 7. Multiple languages - refers to persons reporting more than one aboriginal and/or non-aboriginal language as their home language.

★ 898 ★

Population, by Home Language and Sex for Detailed Aboriginal Origins for Ontario, 1986 - I[1,2]

Home language	Total aboriginal origins[3]		North American Indian only		North American Indian and non-aboriginal[4]		Metis only	
	Number	Percent	Number	Percent	Number	Percent	Number	Percent
Total	167,375	100.0	51,165	100.0	95,420	100.0	3,720	100.0
Male	80,980	48.4	24,725	48.3	46,010	48.2	1,855	49.9
Female	86,395	51.6	26,440	51.7	49,410	51.8	1,860	50.0
English only	149,490	89.3	39,595	77.4	91,010	95.4	3,425	92.1
Male	72,115	43.1	18,880	36.9	43,930	46.0	1,710	46.0
Female	77,380	46.2	20,715	40.5	47,085	49.3	1,715	46.1
French only	2,850	1.7	275	0.5	1,760	1.8	100	2.7
Male	1,415	0.8	120	0.2	855	0.9	65	1.7

[Continued]

★ 898 ★

Population, by Home Language and Sex for Detailed Aboriginal Origins for Ontario, 1986 - I

[Continued]

Home language	Total aboriginal origins[3]		North American Indian only		North American Indian and non-aboriginal[4]		Metis only	
	Number	Percent	Number	Percent	Number	Percent	Number	Percent
Female	1,430	0.9	150	0.3	900	0.9	35	0.9
Aboriginal only[5]	6,560	3.9	6,355	12.4	85	0.1	25	0.7
Male	3,395	2.0	3,305	6.5	40	-	10	0.3
Female	3,165	1.9	3,055	6.0	45	-	15	0.4
Other language[6]	60	-	25	-	15	-	10	0.3
Male	25	-	-	-	-	-	-	-
Female	35	-	20	-	-	-	-	-
Multiple languages[7]	8,410	5.0	4,910	9.6	2,545	2.7	155	4.2
Male	4,025	2.4	2,410	4.7	1,180	1.2	65	1.7
Female	4,385	2.6	2,505	4.9	1,370	1.4	85	2.3

Source: Aboriginal Peoples Output Program, 1986 Census, Statistics Canada, *A Data Book on Canada's Aboriginal Population from the 1986 Census of Canada*, March, 1989, p. 152. Primary source: 1986 Census of Canada *Notes:* A dash (-) represents zero or a percentage which rounds to less than .05 percent. 1. Aboriginal origins are derived from the ethnic origin question which asks whether respondents are North American Indian, Metis or Inuit. 2. All 1986 figures exclude the population estimated at about 45,000 on 136 incompletely enumerated Indian reserves and settlements throughout Canada. 3. Total Aboriginal origins - are the sum of persons who reported: (a) a single aboriginal (e.g., North American Indian, Metis or Inuit) and, (b) multiple aboriginal origins, that is those who reported: - at least one aboriginal origin with any other non-aboriginal (e.g., Metis or French), or - two or more aboriginal origins only. 4. Non-aboriginal in these columns - refers to persons who report one or more non-aboriginal origins such as British, French, etc., in combination with one of the aboriginal origins such as North American Indian. 5. Aboriginal only - refers to persons reporting only one aboriginal language (e.g. Cree) as the language spoken most often at home. 6. Other language - refers to persons reporting only one aboriginal language, which is not English or French, as their home language. 7. Multiple languages - refers to persons reporting more than one aboriginal and/or non-aboriginal language as their home language.

★ 899 ★

Population, by Home Language and Sex for Detailed Aboriginal Origins for Ontario, 1986 - II[1,2]

Home language	Metis and non-Aboriginal[3]		Inuit only		Inuit and non-Aboriginal[3]		Other multiple Aboriginal origins[4]	
	Number	Percent	Number	Percent	Number	Percent	Number	Percent
Total	10,610	100.0	680	100.0	1,590	100.0	4,190	100.0
Male	5,135	48.4	370	54.4	800	50.3	2,075	49.5
Female	5,480	51.6	305	44.9	785	49.4	2,120	50.6
English only	9,620	90.7	600	88.2	1,495	94.0	3,745	89.4
Male	4,635	43.7	350	51.5	755	47.5	1,860	44.4
Female	4,980	46.9	250	36.8	735	46.2	1,885	45.0
French only	475	4.5	-	-	35	2.2	195	4.7
Male	250	2.4	-	-	20	1.3	105	2.5

[Continued]

★ 899 ★

Population, by Home Language and Sex for Detailed Aboriginal Origins for Ontario, 1986 - II

[Continued]

Home language	Metis and non-Aboriginal[3]		Inuit only		Inuit and non-Aboriginal[3]		Other multiple Aboriginal origins[4]	
	Number	Percent	Number	Percent	Number	Percent	Number	Percent
Female	230	2.2	-	-	15	0.9	95	2.3
Aboriginal only[5]	10	0.1	30	4.4	-	-	45	1.1
Male	-	-	-	-	-	-	25	0.6
Female	-	-	30	4.4	-	-	20	0.5
Other language[6]	-	-	-	-	-	-	-	-
Male	-	-	-	-	-	-	-	-
Female	-	-	-	-	-	-	-	-
Multiple languages[7]	510	4.8	40	5.9	60	3.8	185	4.4
Male	250	2.4	20	2.9	25	1.6	80	1.9
Female	260	2.5	20	2.9	35	2.2	110	2.6

Source: Aboriginal Peoples Output Program, 1986 Census, Statistics Canada, *A Data Book on Canada's Aboriginal Population from the 1986 Census of Canada,* March, 1989, p. 152. Primary source: 1986 Census of Canada *Notes:* A dash (-) represents zero or a percentage which rounds to less than .05 percent. 1. Aboriginal origins are derived from the ethnic origin question which asks whether respondents are North American Indian, Metis or Inuit. 2. All 1986 figures exclude the population estimated at about 45,000 on 136 incompletely enumerated Indian reserves and settlements throughout Canada. 3. Non-aboriginal in these columns - refers to persons who report one or more non-aboriginal origins such as British, French, etc., in combination with one of the aboriginal origins such as North American Indian. 4. Other multiple aboriginal origins - refer to the sum of those persons reporting two or more aboriginal origins with or without a non-aboriginal origin. 5. Aboriginal only - refers to persons reporting only one aboriginal language (e.g. Cree) as the language spoken most often at home. 6. Other language - refers to persons reporting only one aboriginal language, which is not english or french, as their home language. 7. Multiple languages - refers to persons reporting more than one aboriginal and/or non-aboriginal language as their home language.

★ 900 ★

Population, by Home Language and Sex for Detailed Aboriginal Origins for Prince Edward Island, 1986 - I[1,2]

Home language	Total aboriginal origins[3]		North American Indian only		North American Indian and non-aboriginal[4]		Metis only	
	Number	Percent	Number	Percent	Number	Percent	Number	Percent
Total	1,290	100.0	375	100.0	720	100.0	35	100.0
Male	645	50.0	195	52.0	355	49.3	-	-
Female	640	49.6	185	49.3	365	50.7	25	71.4
English only	1,230	95.3	345	92.0	710	98.6	35	100.0
Male	630	48.8	175	46.7	350	48.6	-	-
Female	605	46.9	165	44.0	360	50.0	30	85.7
French only	-	-	-	-	-	-	-	-
Male	-	-	-	-	-	-	-	-

[Continued]

★ 900 ★

Population, by Home Language and Sex for Detailed Aboriginal Origins for Prince Edward Island, 1986 - I

[Continued]

Home language	Total aboriginal origins[3]		North American Indian only		North American Indian and non-aboriginal[4]		Metis only	
	Number	Percent	Number	Percent	Number	Percent	Number	Percent
Female	-	-	-	-	-	-	-	-
Aboriginal only[5]	25	1.9	20	5.3	-	-	-	-
Male	15	1.2	10	2.7	-	-	-	-
Female	10	0.8	10	2.7	-	-	-	-
Other language[6]	-	-	-	-	-	-	-	-
Male	-	-	-	-	-	-	-	-
Female	-	-	-	-	-	-	-	-
Multiple languages[7]	20	1.6	10	2.7	-	-	-	-
Male	-	-	-	-	-	-	-	-
Female	15	1.2	-	-	-	-	-	-

Source: Aboriginal Peoples Output Program, 1986 Census, Statistics Canada, *A Data Book on Canada's Aboriginal Population from the 1986 Census of Canada*, March, 1989, p. 56. Primary source: 1986 Census of Canada *Notes:* A dash (-) represents zero or a percentage which rounds to less than .05 percent. 1. Aboriginal origins are derived from the ethnic origin question which asks whether respondents are North American Indian, Metis or Inuit. 2. All 1986 figures exclude the population estimated at about 45,000 on 136 incompletely enumerated Indian reserves and settlements throughout Canada. 3. Total Aboriginal origins - are the sum of persons who reported: (a) a single aboriginal (e.g., North American Indian, Metis or Inuit) and, (b) multiple aboriginal origins, that is those who reported: - at least one aboriginal origin with any other non-aboriginal (e.g., Metis or French), or - two or more aboriginal origins only. 4. Non-aboriginal in these columns - refers to persons who report one or more non-aboriginal origins such as British, French, etc., in combination with one of the aboriginal origins such as North American Indian. 5. Aboriginal only - refers to persons reporting only one aboriginal language (e.g. Cree) as the language spoken most often at home. 6. Other language - refers to persons reporting only one aboriginal language, which is not English or French, as their home language. 7. Multiple languages - refers to persons reporting more than one aboriginal and/or non-aboriginal language as their home language.

★ 901 ★

Population, by Home Language and Sex for Detailed Aboriginal Origins for Prince Edward Island, 1986 - II[1,2]

Home language	Metis and non-Aboriginal[3]		Inuit only		Inuit and non-Aboriginal[3]		Other multiple Aboriginal origins[4]	
	Number	Percent	Number	Percent	Number	Percent	Number	Percent
Total	110	100.0	-	-	25	100.0	25	100.0
Male	70	63.6	-	-	15	60.0	-	-
Female	35	31.8	-	-	10	40.0	20	80.0
English only	100	90.9	-	-	15	60.0	25	100.0
Male	70	63.6	-	-	15	60.0	-	-
Female	30	27.3	-	-	-	-	20	80.0
French only	-	-	-	-	-	-	-	-
Male	-	-	-	-	-	-	-	-

[Continued]

★ 901 ★

Population, by Home Language and Sex for Detailed Aboriginal Origins for Prince Edward Island, 1986 - II
[Continued]

Home language	Metis and non-Aboriginal[3]		Inuit only		Inuit and non-Aboriginal[3]		Other multiple Aboriginal origins[4]	
	Number	Percent	Number	Percent	Number	Percent	Number	Percent
Female	-	-	-	-	-	-	-	-
Aboriginal only[5]	-	-	-	-	-	-	-	-
Male	-	-	-	-	-	-	-	-
Female	-	-	-	-	-	-	-	-
Other language[6]	-	-	-	-	-	-	-	-
Male	-	-	-	-	-	-	-	-
Female	-	-	-	-	-	-	-	-
Multiple languages[7]	-	-	-	-	-	-	-	-
Male	-	-	-	-	-	-	-	-
Female	-	-	-	-	-	-	-	-

Source: Aboriginal Peoples Output Program, 1986 Census, Statistics Canada, *A Data Book on Canada's Aboriginal Population from the 1986 Census of Canada*, March, 1989, p. 56. Primary source: 1986 Census of Canada *Notes:* A dash (-) represents zero or a percentage which rounds to less than .05 percent. 1. Aboriginal origins are derived from the ethnic origin question which asks whether respondents are North American Indian, Metis or Inuit. 2. All 1986 figures exclude the population estimated at about 45,000 on 136 incompletely enumerated Indian reserves and settlements throughout Canada. 3. Non-aboriginal in these columns - refers to persons who report one or more non-aboriginal origins such as British, French, etc., in combination with one of the aboriginal origins such as North American Indian. 4. Other multiple aboriginal origins - refer to the sum of those persons reporting two or more aboriginal origins with or without a non-aboriginal origin. 5. Aboriginal only - refers to persons reporting only one aboriginal language (e.g. Cree) as the language spoken most often at home. 6. Other language - refers to persons reporting only one aboriginal language, which is not english or french, as their home language. 7. Multiple languages - refers to persons reporting more than one aboriginal and/or non-aboriginal language as their home language.

★ 902 ★

Population, by Home Language and Sex for Detailed Aboriginal Origins for Quebec, 1986 - I[1,2]

Home language	Total aboriginal origins[3]		North American Indian only		North American Indian and non-aboriginal[4]		Metis only	
	Number	Percent	Number	Percent	Number	Percent	Number	Percent
Total	80,945	100.0	37,150	100.0	25,105	100.0	5,700	100.0
Male	39,150	48.4	18,330	49.3	11,535	45.9	2,940	51.6
Female	41,790	51.6	18,825	50.7	13,570	54.1	2,760	48.4
English only	10,675	13.2	3,310	8.9	5,700	22.7	375	6.6
Male	5,255	6.5	1,660	4.5	2,775	11.1	190	3.3
Female	5,420	6.7	1,645	4.4	2,925	11.7	185	3.2
French only	42,750	52.8	14,735	39.7	17,675	70.4	4,945	86.8
Male	20,210	25.0	7,155	19.3	7,990	31.8	2,550	44.7

[Continued]

1286

★ 902 ★

Population, by Home Language and Sex for Detailed Aboriginal Origins for Quebec, 1986 - I

[Continued]

Home language	Total aboriginal origins[3]		North American Indian only		North American Indian and non-aboriginal[4]		Metis only	
	Number	Percent	Number	Percent	Number	Percent	Number	Percent
Female	22,535	27.8	7,580	20.4	9,685	38.6	2,390	41.9
Aboriginal only[5]	20,395	25.2	15,020	40.4	75	0.3	60	1.1
Male	10,295	12.7	7,550	20.3	40	0.2	25	0.4
Female	10,095	12.5	7,470	20.1	45	0.2	35	0.6
Other language[6]	25	-	-	-	-	-	-	-
Male	-	-	-	-	-	-	-	-
Female	15	-	-	-	-	-	-	-
Multiple languages[7]	7,095	8.8	4,075	11.0	1,650	6.6	325	5.7
Male	3,375	4.2	1,955	5.3	735	2.9	175	3.1
Female	3,725	4.6	2,120	5.7	910	3.6	150	2.6

Source: Aboriginal Peoples Output Program, 1986 Census, Statistics Canada, *A Data Book on Canada's Aboriginal Population from the 1986 Census of Canada*, March, 1989, p. 128. Primary source: 1986 Census of Canada *Notes:* A dash (-) represents zero or a percentage which rounds to less than .05 percent. 1. Aboriginal origins are derived from the ethnic origin question which asks whether respondents are North American Indian, Metis or Inuit. 2. All 1986 figures exclude the population estimated at about 45,000 on 136 incompletely enumerated Indian reserves and settlements throughout Canada. 3. Total Aboriginal origins - are the sum of persons who reported: (a) a single aboriginal (e.g., North American Indian, Metis or Inuit) and, (b) multiple aboriginal origins, that is those who reported: - at least one aboriginal origin with any other non-aboriginal (e.g., Metis or French), or - two or more aboriginal origins only. 4. Non-aboriginal in these columns - refers to persons who report one or more non-aboriginal origins such as British, French, etc., in combination with one of the aboriginal origins such as North American Indian. 5. Aboriginal only - refers to persons reporting only one aboriginal language (e.g. Cree) as the language spoken most often at home. 6. Other language - refers to persons reporting only one aboriginal language, which is not English or French, as their home language. 7. Multiple languages - refers to persons reporting more than one aboriginal and/or non-aboriginal language as their home language.

★ 903 ★

Population, by Home Language and Sex for Detailed Aboriginal Origins for Quebec, 1986 - II[1,2]

Home language	Metis and non-Aboriginal[3]		Inuit only		Inuit and non-Aboriginal[3]		Other multiple Aboriginal origins[4]	
	Number	Percent	Number	Percent	Number	Percent	Number	Percent
Total	4,570	100.0	6,470	100.0	575	100.0	1,370	100.0
Male	2,095	45.8	3,280	50.7	275	47.8	695	50.7
Female	2,470	54.0	3,190	49.3	300	52.2	680	49.6
English only	665	14.6	160	2.5	160	27.8	300	21.9
Male	315	6.9	85	1.3	70	12.2	155	11.3
Female	355	7.8	80	1.2	95	16.5	140	10.2
French only	3,415	74.7	770	11.9	335	58.3	870	63.5
Male	1,515	33.2	400	6.2	170	29.6	425	31.0

[Continued]

★ 903 ★

Population, by Home Language and Sex for Detailed Aboriginal Origins for Quebec, 1986 - II

[Continued]

Home language	Metis and non-Aboriginal[3]		Inuit only		Inuit and non-Aboriginal[3]		Other multiple Aboriginal origins[4]	
	Number	Percent	Number	Percent	Number	Percent	Number	Percent
Female	1,895	41.5	370	5.7	170	29.6	445	32.5
Aboriginal only[5]	-	-	5,120	79.1	30	5.2	90	6.6
Male	-	-	2,610	40.3	20	3.5	55	4.0
Female	-	-	2,505	38.7	10	1.7	30	2.2
Other language[6]	-	-	-	-	-	-	-	-
Male	-	-	-	-	-	-	-	-
Female	-	-	-	-	-	-	-	-
Multiple languages[7]	480	10.5	420	6.5	45	7.8	110	8.0
Male	260	5.7	185	2.9	25	4.3	45	3.3
Female	220	4.8	235	3.6	20	3.5	50	3.6

Source: Aboriginal Peoples Output Program, 1986 Census, Statistics Canada, *A Data Book on Canada's Aboriginal Population from the 1986 Census of Canada*, March, 1989, p. 128. Primary source: 1986 Census of Canada *Notes:* A dash (-) represents zero or a percentage which rounds to less than .05 percent. 1. Aboriginal origins are derived from the ethnic origin question which asks whether respondents are North American Indian, Metis or Inuit. 2. All 1986 figures exclude the population estimated at about 45,000 on 136 incompletely enumerated Indian reserves and settlements throughout Canada. 3. Non-aboriginal in these columns - refers to persons who report one or more non-aboriginal origins such as British, French, etc., in combination with one of the aboriginal origins such as North American Indian. 4. Other multiple aboriginal origins - refer to the sum of those persons reporting two or more aboriginal origins with or without a non-aboriginal origin. 5. Aboriginal only - refers to persons reporting only one aboriginal language (e.g. Cree) as the language spoken most often at home. 6. Other language - refers to persons reporting only one aboriginal language, which is not english or french, as their home language. 7. Multiple languages - refers to persons reporting more than one aboriginal and/or non-aboriginal language as their home language.

★ 904 ★

Population, by Home Language and Sex for Detailed Aboriginal Origins for Saskatchewan, 1986 - I[1,2]

Home language	Total aboriginal origins[3]		North American Indian only		North American Indian and non-aboriginal[4]		Metis only	
	Number	Percent	Number	Percent	Number	Percent	Number	Percent
Total	77,650	100.0	43,385	100.0	8,455	100.0	12,215	100.0
Male	38,015	49.0	21,375	49.3	4,140	49.0	5,950	48.7
Female	39,635	51.0	22,010	50.7	4,310	51.0	6,270	51.3
English only	51,145	65.9	22,405	51.6	7,600	89.9	8,830	72.3
Male	24,785	31.9	10,810	24.9	3,760	44.5	4,265	34.9
Female	26,365	34.0	11,595	26.7	3,845	45.5	4,570	37.4
French only	195	0.3	-	-	20	0.2	85	0.7
Male	100	0.1	-	-	15	0.2	30	0.2

[Continued]

★ 904 ★

Population, by Home Language and Sex for Detailed Aboriginal Origins for Saskatchewan, 1986 - I

[Continued]

Home language	Total aboriginal origins[3]		North American Indian only		North American Indian and non-aboriginal[4]		Metis only	
	Number	Percent	Number	Percent	Number	Percent	Number	Percent
Female	95	0.1	-	-	-	-	50	0.4
Aboriginal only[5]	16,665	21.5	14,055	32.4	425	5.0	1,770	14.5
Male	8,450	10.9	7,190	16.6	195	2.3	875	7.2
Female	8,215	10.6	6,865	15.8	225	2.7	900	7.4
Other language[6]	45	0.1	15	-	25	0.3	-	-
Male	30	-	-	-	15	0.2	-	-
Female	15	-	-	-	15	0.2	-	-
Multiple languages[7]	9,600	12.4	6,915	15.9	385	4.6	1,530	12.5
Male	4,650	6.0	3,365	7.8	160	1.9	775	6.3
Female	4,950	6.4	3,545	8.2	225	2.7	755	6.2

Source: Aboriginal Peoples Output Program, 1986 Census, Statistics Canada, *A Data Book on Canada's Aboriginal Population from the 1986 Census of Canada,* March, 1989, p. 200. Primary source: 1986 Census of Canada *Notes:* A dash (-) represents zero or a percentage which rounds to less than .05 percent. 1. Aboriginal origins are derived from the ethnic origin question which asks whether respondents are North American Indian, Metis or Inuit. 2. All 1986 figures exclude the population estimated at about 45,000 on 136 incompletely enumerated Indian reserves and settlements throughout Canada. 3. Total Aboriginal origins - are the sum of persons who reported: (a) a single aboriginal (e.g., North American Indian, Metis or Inuit) and, (b) multiple aboriginal origins, that is those who reported: - at least one aboriginal origin with any other non-aboriginal (e.g., Metis or French), or - two or more aboriginal origins only. 4. Non-aboriginal in these columns - refers to persons who report one or more non-aboriginal origins such as British, French, etc., in combination with one of the aboriginal origins such as North American Indian. 5. Aboriginal only - refers to persons reporting only one aboriginal language (e.g. Cree) as the language spoken most often at home. 6. Other language - refers to persons reporting only one aboriginal language, which is not English or French, as their home language. 7. Multiple languages - refers to persons reporting more than one aboriginal and/or non-aboriginal language as their home language.

★ 905 ★

Population, by Home Language and Sex for Detailed Aboriginal Origins for Saskatchewan, 1986 - II[1,2]

Home language	Metis and non-Aboriginal[3]		Inuit only		Inuit and non-Aboriginal[3]		Other multiple Aboriginal origins[4]	
	Number	Percent	Number	Percent	Number	Percent	Number	Percent
Total	10,080	100.0	45	100.0	55	100.0	3,405	100.0
Male	4,810	47.7	20	44.4	45	81.8	1,675	49.2
Female	5,275	52.3	15	33.3	20	36.4	1,740	51.1
English only	9,435	93.6	40	88.9	60	109.1	2,775	81.5
Male	4,515	44.8	20	44.4	40	72.7	1,370	40.2
Female	4,920	48.8	20	44.4	20	36.4	1,400	41.1
French only	80	0.8	-	-	-	-	-	-
Male	55	0.5	-	-	-	-	-	-

[Continued]

★ 905 ★

Population, by Home Language and Sex for Detailed Aboriginal Origins for Saskatchewan, 1986 - II

[Continued]

Home language	Metis and non-Aboriginal[3]		Inuit only		Inuit and non-Aboriginal[3]		Other multiple Aboriginal origins[4]	
	Number	Percent	Number	Percent	Number	Percent	Number	Percent
Female	20	0.2	-	-	-	-	-	-
Aboriginal only[5]	130	1.3	-	-	-	-	285	8.4
Male	55	0.5	-	-	-	-	140	4.1
Female	70	0.7	-	-	-	-	155	4.6
Other language[6]	-	-	-	-	-	-	-	-
Male	-	-	-	-	-	-	-	-
Female	-	-	-	-	-	-	-	-
Multiple languages[7]	440	4.4	-	-	-	-	330	9.7
Male	185	1.8	-	-	-	-	160	4.7
Female	255	2.5	-	-	-	-	170	5.0

Source: Aboriginal Peoples Output Program, 1986 Census, Statistics Canada, *A Data Book on Canada's Aboriginal Population from the 1986 Census of Canada*, March, 1989, p. 200. Primary source: 1986 Census of Canada *Notes:* A dash (-) represents zero or a percentage which rounds to less than .05 percent. 1. Aboriginal origins are derived from the ethnic origin question which asks whether respondents are North American Indian, Metis or Inuit. 2. All 1986 figures exclude the population estimated at about 45,000 on 136 incompletely enumerated Indian reserves and settlements throughout Canada. 3. Non-aboriginal in these columns - refers to persons who report one or more non-aboriginal origins such as British, French, etc., in combination with one of the aboriginal origins such as North American Indian. 4. Other multiple aboriginal origins - refer to the sum of those persons reporting two or more aboriginal origins with or without a non-aboriginal origin. 5. Aboriginal only - refers to persons reporting only one aboriginal language (e.g. Cree) as the language spoken most often at home. 6. Other language - refers to persons reporting only one aboriginal language, which is not english or french, as their home language. 7. Multiple languages - refers to persons reporting more than one aboriginal and/or non-aboriginal language as their home language.

★ 906 ★

Population, by Home Language and Sex for Detailed Aboriginal Origins for Yukon Territory, 1986 - I[1,2]

Home language	Total aboriginal origins[3]		North American Indian only		North American Indian and non-aboriginal[4]		Metis only	
	Number	Percent	Number	Percent	Number	Percent	Number	Percent
Total	4,995	100.0	3,165	100.0	1,545	100.0	75	100.0
Male	2,430	48.6	1,530	48.3	755	48.9	20	26.7
Female	2,565	51.4	1,630	51.5	790	51.1	60	80.0
English only	4,680	93.7	2,895	91.5	1,510	97.7	80	106.7
Male	2,270	45.4	1,405	44.4	725	46.9	15	20.0
Female	2,415	48.3	1,485	46.9	785	50.8	60	80.0
French only	-	-	-	-	-	-	-	-
Male	-	-	-	-	-	-	-	-

[Continued]

★ 906 ★

Population, by Home Language and Sex for Detailed Aboriginal Origins for Yukon Territory, 1986 - I

[Continued]

Home language	Total aboriginal origins[3]		North American Indian only		North American Indian and non-aboriginal[4]		Metis only	
	Number	Percent	Number	Percent	Number	Percent	Number	Percent
Female	-	-	-	-	-	-	-	-
Aboriginal only[5]	120	2.4	120	3.8	-	-	-	-
Male	60	1.2	60	1.9	-	-	-	-
Female	65	1.3	65	2.1	-	-	-	-
Other language[6]	-	-	-	-	-	-	-	-
Male	-	-	-	-	-	-	-	-
Female	-	-	-	-	-	-	-	-
Multiple languages[7]	190	3.8	150	4.7	30	1.9	-	-
Male	105	2.1	65	2.1	25	1.6	-	-
Female	85	1.7	80	2.5	-	-	-	-

Source: Aboriginal Peoples Output Program, 1986 Census, Statistics Canada, *A Data Book on Canada's Aboriginal Population from the 1986 Census of Canada*, March, 1989, p. 296. Primary source: 1986 Census of Canada *Notes:* A dash (-) represents zero or a percentage which rounds to less than .05 percent. 1. Aboriginal origins are derived from the ethnic origin question which asks whether respondents are North American Indian, Metis or Inuit. 2. All 1986 figures exclude the population estimated at about 45,000 on 136 incompletely enumerated Indian reserves and settlements throughout Canada. 3. Total Aboriginal origins - are the sum of persons who reported: (a) a single aboriginal (e.g., North American Indian, Metis or Inuit) and, (b) multiple aboriginal origins, that is those who reported: - at least one aboriginal origin with any other non-aboriginal (e.g., Metis or French), or - two or more aboriginal origins only. 4. Non-aboriginal in these columns - refers to persons who report one or more non-aboriginal origins such as British, French, etc., in combination with one of the aboriginal origins such as North American Indian. 5. Aboriginal only - refers to persons reporting only one aboriginal language (e.g. Cree) as the language spoken most often at home. 6. Other language - refers to persons reporting only one aboriginal language, which is not English or French, as their home language. 7. Multiple languages - refers to persons reporting more than one aboriginal and/or non-aboriginal language as their home language.

★ 907 ★

Population, by Home Language and Sex for Detailed Aboriginal Origins for Yukon Territory, 1986 - II[1,2]

Home language	Metis and non-Aboriginal[3]		Inuit only		Inuit and non-Aboriginal[3]		Other multiple Aboriginal origins[4]	
	Number	Percent	Number	Percent	Number	Percent	Number	Percent
Total	90	100.0	40	100.0	25	100.0	65	100.0
Male	60	66.7	15	37.5	15	60.0	35	53.8
Female	30	33.3	20	50.0	-	-	30	46.2
English only	80	88.9	35	87.5	20	80.0	60	92.3
Male	50	55.6	15	37.5	20	80.0	35	53.8
Female	25	27.8	20	50.0	-	-	30	46.2
French only	-	-	-	-	-	-	-	-
Male	-	-	-	-	-	-	-	-

[Continued]

★ 907 ★

Population, by Home Language and Sex for Detailed Aboriginal Origins for Yukon Territory, 1986 - II
[Continued]

Home language	Metis and non-Aboriginal[3]		Inuit only		Inuit and non-Aboriginal[3]		Other multiple Aboriginal origins[4]	
	Number	Percent	Number	Percent	Number	Percent	Number	Percent
Female	-	-	-	-	-	-	-	-
Aboriginal only[5]	-	-	-	-	-	-	-	-
Male	-	-	-	-	-	-	-	-
Female	-	-	-	-	-	-	-	-
Other language[6]	-	-	-	-	-	-	-	-
Male	-	-	-	-	-	-	-	-
Female	-	-	-	-	-	-	-	-
Multiple languages[7]	-	-	-	-	-	-	-	-
Male	-	-	-	-	-	-	-	-
Female	-	-	-	-	-	-	-	-

Source: Aboriginal Peoples Output Program, 1986 Census, Statistics Canada, *A Data Book on Canada's Aboriginal Population from the 1986 Census of Canada,* March, 1989, p. 296. Primary source: 1986 Census of Canada *Notes:* A dash (-) represents zero or a percentage which rounds to less than .05 percent. 1. Aboriginal origins are derived from the ethnic origin question which asks whether respondents are North American Indian, Metis or Inuit. 2. All 1986 figures exclude the population estimated at about 45,000 on 136 incompletely enumerated Indian reserves and settlements throughout Canada. 3. Non-aboriginal in these columns - refers to persons who report one or more non-aboriginal origins such as British, French, etc., in combination with one of the aboriginal origins such as North American Indian. 4. Other multiple aboriginal origins - refer to the sum of those persons reporting two or more aboriginal origins with or without a non-aboriginal origin. 5. Aboriginal only - refers to persons reporting only one aboriginal language (e.g. Cree) as the language spoken most often at home. 6. Other language - refers to persons reporting only one aboriginal language, which is not english or french, as their home language. 7. Multiple languages - refers to persons reporting more than one aboriginal and/or non-aboriginal language as their home language.

Employment

★ 908 ★

Work Status of Persons of Aboriginal Origin and the Total Canadian Population, Canada, 1986

Group/Region	Work Activity				
	Full Time and Full Year		Part Time and Part Year		Total
	Number	%	Number	%	
On-Reserve					
Atlantic	1,380	60.4	905	39.6	2,285
Quebec	4,945	75.4	1,615	24.6	6,560
Ontario	9,285	89.8	1,050	10.2	10,335
Manitoba	3,815	52.6	3,440	47.4	7,255

[Continued]

★ 908 ★

Work Status of Persons of Aboriginal Origin and the Total Canadian Population, Canada, 1986
[Continued]

Group/Region	Work Activity				
	Full Time and Full Year		Part Time and Part Year		Total
	Number	%	Number	%	
Saskatchewan	3,665	55.9	2,890	44.1	6,555
Alberta	5,500	87.2	810	12.8	6,310
British Columbia	6,645	55.2	5,375	44.7	12,020
Territories	805	100.0	0	0.0	805
Canada	36,045	69.7	15,700	30.3	51,745
Off-Reserve					
Atlantic	3,880	35.5	7,035	64.5	10,915
Quebec	12,475	46.9	14,110	53.1	26,585
Ontario	30,445	46.5	35,035	53.5	65,480
Manitoba	7,740	37.8	12,725	62.2	20,465
Saskatchewan	4,720	31.4	10,315	68.6	15,035
Alberta	11,530	34.9	21,460	65.1	32,990
British Columbia	11,620	32.1	24,595	67.9	36,215
Territories	4,030	30.3	9,285	69.7	13,315
Canada	86,435	39.1	134,560	60.9	220,995
Total Canadian population[1]					
Atlantic	533,090	49.5	544,390	50.5	1,077,475
Quebec	1,944,955	61.0	1,243,655	39.0	3,188,610
Ontario	3,186,795	63.0	1,874,120	37.0	5,069,910
Manitoba	332,385	59.6	225,435	40.4	557,820
Saskatchewan	287,910	55.7	229,100	44.3	517,015
Alberta	784,280	58.8	548,875	41.2	1,333,150
British Columbia	815,230	55.0	666,130	45.0	1,481,370
Territories	21,490	53.4	18,750	46.6	40,240
Canada	7,906,135	59.6	5,350,450	40.4	13,256,585

Source: *Canada's Off-Reserve Aboriginal Population: A Statistical Overview*, Social Trends Analysis Directorate, Department of the Secretary of State of Canada, 1991, p. A-11. For Aboriginal population: Statistics Canada, *A Profile of the Aboriginal Population Residing in Selected Off Reserve Areas*, prepared by the Aboriginal Data and Native Issues Unit of the Housing, Family and Social Statistics Division, February 1990; For the total Canadian population: Statistics Canada, 1986 Census, *Special Tabulations from the Small Area Database* compiled for the Department of the Secretary of State. *Notes:* Sum of components may not always add to totals due to rounding and/or data suppression. 1. Experienced Labour Force: Persons 15 years of age and over who worked between January 1, 1985 and June 3, 1986.

★ 909 ★

Employment Status of Persons of Aboriginal Origin and the Total Canadian Population, Canada, 1986

Region	In the Labour Force			Not in the Labour Force	Total Population Age 15 Yrs +	Partici- pation Rate (%)	Unem- ployment Rate (%)
	Employed	Unemployed	Total				
On-Reserve							
Atlantic	1,200	890	2,085	3,110	5,195	40.1	42.7
Quebec	3,430	1,925	5,355	8,140	13,505	39.7	35.9
Ontario	6,170	2,170	8,340	8,515	16,855	49.5	26.0
Manitoba	3,775	2,420	6,200	9,630	15,835	39.2	39.0
Saskatchewan	3,725	1,880	5,595	9,640	15,230	36.7	33.6
Alberta	3,095	1,580	4,680	6,480	11,155	42.0	33.8
British Columbia	6,250	3,975	10,225	10,235	20,460	50.0	38.9
Territories	125	70	195	225	415	47.0	35.9
Canada	27,770	14,900	42,665	55,975	98,650	43.2	34.9
Off-Reserve							
Atlantic	8,055	2,770	10,830	6,225	17,060	63.5	25.6
Quebec	23,360	4,900	28,255	14,410	42,660	66.2	17.3
Ontario	58,180	8,435	66,615	26,070	92,685	71.9	12.7
Manitoba	16,585	4,830	21,410	14,810	36,215	59.1	22.6
Saskatchewan	11,965	4,640	16,615	12,800	29,415	56.5	27.9
Alberta	26,455	7,175	33,625	18,270	51,900	64.8	21.3
British Columbia	29,335	10,950	40,285	21,435	61,720	65.3	27.2
Territories	8,895	3,335	12,230	9,420	21,655	56.5	27.3
Canada	182,830	47,045	229,875	123,440	353,310	65.1	20.5
Total Canadian population							
Atlantic	869,980	185,005	1,054,985	675,190	1,730,170	61.0	17.5
Quebec	2,795,955	417,935	3,213,885	1,901,100	5,114,990	62.8	13.0
Ontario	4,585,150	337,095	4,922,240	2,210,570	7,132,810	69.0	6.8
Manitoba	500,740	41,480	542,220	271,710	813,935	66.6	7.7
Saskatchewan	461,510	40,235	501,745	249,340	751,090	66.8	8.0
Alberta	1,166,480	125,880	1,292,360	487,015	1,779,375	72.6	9.7
British Columbia	1,289,430	194,755	1,484,185	775,125	2,259,310	65.7	13.1
Territories	32,960	5,265	38,235	14,190	52,420	72.9	13.8
Canada	11,702,220	1,347,645	13,049,860	6,584,240	19,634,100	66.5	10.3

Source: Canada's Off-Reserve Aboriginal Population: A Statistical Overview, Social Trends Analysis Directorate, Department of the Secretary of State of Canada, 1991, p. A-10. For Aboriginal population: Statistics Canada, *A Profile of the Aboriginal Population Residing in Selected Off Reserve Areas*, prepared by the Aboriginal Data and Native Issues Unit of the Housing, Family and Social Statistics Division, February 1990; For total Canadian population: Statistics Canada, *1986 Census, Special Tabulations from the Small Area Database* compiled for the Department of the Secretary of State. *Notes:* Sum of components may not always add to totals due to rounding and/or data suppression.

★ 910 ★

Persons of Aboriginal Origin and the Total Canadian Population, Employment, by Industrial Sector, Canada, 1986

| Group/Region | Agricult. & related | Industrial Sector | | | | | | | | Industry Total |
		Fishing, Lodging Mining & related	Manufact. Industries	Construct. Industries	Transport. Storage Commun. & related	Trade Industries	Finance Insurance & related	Gov't Services	Other Service Industr.	
On-Reserve										
Atlantic	45	320	320	295	130	350	110	1,495	885	3,975
Quebec	95	505	610	680	450	930	520	2,630	2,285	8,705
Ontario	500	1,010	1,705	1,075	715	1,630	1,075	3,755	4,245	15,700
Manitoba	205	925	470	1,380	610	915	290	2,025	3,555	10,380
Saskatchewan	775	510	220	1,105	500	615	255	2,185	2,855	9,015
Alberta	580	810	460	1,185	560	975	480	2,100	3,400	10,550
British Columbia	685	2,465	1,885	685	515	1,150	675	4,460	3,520	16,040
Territories	10	385	75	315	215	420	290	845	705	3,260
Canada	2,890	6,930	5,745	6,715	3,670	6,990	3,690	19,485	21,495	77,625
Off-Reserve										
Atlantic	200	685	1,140	610	635	1,380	155	2,205	3,240	10,250
Quebec	360	580	4,450	1,355	2,250	4,275	780	2,805	9,740	26,595
Ontario	1,150	1,795	13,335	3,670	5,195	9,985	1,675	5,985	22,150	64,940
Manitoba	680	1,080	2,230	1,720	1,605	2,460	425	2,390	7,315	19,910
Saskatchewan	980	920	750	1,485	1,015	1,650	200	2,200	5,750	14,950
Alberta	970	2,920	2,410	3,435	2,775	4,470	555	2,880	11,560	32,245
British Columbia	920	3,845	5,100	2,315	3,010	5,065	705	3,010	12,565	36,535
Territories	40	1,265	195	840	1,250	1,320	35	2,900	3,525	11,370
Canada	5,310	13,090	29,610	15,435	17,760	30,870	4,535	24,385	75,800	216,795
Total Canadian population[1]										
Atlantic	28,705	71,185	153,360	74,820	87,845	190,745	40,240	129,485	348,235	1,124,620
Quebec	86,855	61,145	661,505	178,225	250,790	585,860	173,120	247,705	1,098,365	3,343,575
Ontario	158,835	57,250	1,131,405	295,280	353,915	906,220	312,360	361,505	1,685,775	5,262,535
Manitoba	49,065	8,655	70,295	33,490	54,515	100,200	29,195	49,635	190,400	585,440
Saskatchewan	101,465	15,635	29,860	32,560	39,595	91,825	23,450	40,255	170,240	544,880
Alberta	98,330	90,735	106,510	98,835	111,550	236,655	69,955	106,205	475,745	1,394,520
British Columbia	45,325	74,835	189,300	96,515	135,060	272,335	87,655	107,205	551,905	1,506,130
Territories	220	4,330	805	2,930	4,865	5,465	1,320	9,545	12,585	42,085
Canada	568,795	383,765	2,343,030	812,650	1,038,130	2,389,335	737,295	1,051,530	4,533,255	13,857,775

Source: Canada's Off-Reserve Aboriginal Population: A Statistical Overview, Social Trends Analysis Directorate, Department of the Secretary of State of Canada, 1991, p. A-13. Primary source: For Aboriginal population: Statistics Canada, *A Profile of the Aboriginal Population Residing in Selected Off Reserve Areas*, prepared by the Aboriginal Data and Native Issues Unit of the Housing, Family and Social Statistics Division, February 1990; for total Canadian population: Statistics Canada, 1986 Census, *Special Tabulations from the Small Area Database* compiled for the Department of the Secretary of State. *Notes:* Sum of components may not always add to totals due to rounding and/or data suppression. 1. Experienced Labour Force: Persons 15 years of age and over who worked between January 1, 1985 and June 3, 1986.

★ 911 ★

Persons of Aboriginal Origin and the Total Canadian Population, by Occupational Group, Canada, 1986

Group/Region	Occupational Group										Total
	Managr. Admin. & related	Profess. & related	Clerical & related	Sales Occups.	Services Occups.	Prim. Occups.	Process. Occups.	Product Fabric. & Assemb.	Constr. Trades	Other Occups.	
On-Reserve											
Atlantic	95	370	165	10	265	95	0	80	420	235	2,290
Quebec	365	965	690	140	920	655	50	150	1,040	455	5,930
Ontario	155	1,350	725	120	980	1,005	180	540	1,595	970	9,305
Manitoba	190	1,215	570	100	960	805	30	40	1,355	815	7,115
Saskatchewan	115	910	250	0	630	870	20	65	1,085	585	6,350
Alberta	255	640	495	75	705	650	20	135	805	870	5,420
British Columbia	120	1,000	500	120	770	2,640	405	40	645	1,090	11,145
Territories	0	25	0	0	50	10	0	0	15	25	245
Canada	1,295	6,475	3,395	565	5,280	6,730	705	1,050	6,960	5,045	47,800
Off-Reserve											
Atlantic	815	1,745	1,740	690	2,450	1,090	865	715	1,105	1,275	11,940
Quebec	2,780	5,100	5,775	2,200	4,420	1,125	1,260	2,895	1,665	2,640	29,370
Ontario	5,795	9,775	13,055	5,640	12,515	3,450	2,590	7,810	4,315	8,070	71,335
Manitoba	1,465	3,485	3,495	1,460	4,635	2,265	795	1,535	2,265	2,815	23,175
Saskatchewan	1,310	2,725	2,350	1,160	4,080	2,105	515	1,055	2,205	1,935	17,615
Alberta	2,085	4,215	6,220	2,710	8,300	2,960	910	2,290	3,910	4,545	37,370
British Columbia	2,895	5,460	6,520	3,405	8,455	5,365	2,550	2,760	3,190	4,650	41,430
Territories	935	2,040	2,195	425	2,905	1,160	175	650	1,900	2,120	14,385
Canada	18,080	34,545	41,350	17,690	47,760	19,520	9,660	19,710	20,555	28,050	246,620
Total Canadian population[1]											
Atlantic	88,860	169,170	177,635	90,750	170,355	90,950	70,405	70,360	88,755	107,385	1,124,605
Quebec	349,790	576,080	622,225	296,585	421,485	126,740	147,945	366,380	175,625	260,715	3,343,570
Ontario	567,075	842,725	1,017,000	487,065	658,175	197,840	162,260	595,890	279,545	454,965	5,262,535
Manitoba	53,210	96,345	102,965	52,045	81,450	53,450	13,120	48,470	35,105	48,890	585,440
Saskatchewan	47,975	80,260	81,935	46,965	73,745	103,740	8,280	28,520	34,680	38,775	544,880
Alberta	139,105	229,560	258,290	133,480	196,145	118,045	25,285	88,895	92,460	113,255	1,394,520
British Columbia	150,460	244,855	274,810	157,840	242,510	96,810	56,755	110,395	95,590	131,095	1,560,130
Territories	4,860	7,365	7,155	2,045	6,735	2,410	520	2,335	4,090	4,565	42,085
Canada	1,401,330	2,246,365	2,542,010	1,266,780	1,850,595	790,390	484,560	1,311,250	804,850	1,159,650	13,857,775

Source: Canada's Off-Reserve Aboriginal Population: A Statistical Overview, Social Trends Analysis Directorate, Department of the Secretary of State of Canada, 1991, p. A-12. Primary source: Statistics Canada, 1986 Census, *Special Tabulations from the Small Area Database* compiled for the Department of the Secretary of State. *Notes:* Sum of components may not always add to totals due to rounding and/or data suppression. 1. Experienced Labour Force: Persons 15 years of age and over who worked between January 1, 1985 and June 3, 1986.

★912★

Population 15 Years and Over by Labor Force Activity and Sex for Detailed Aboriginal Origins for Canada, 1986 - I[1,2]

Labor force activity	Total Aboriginal origins[3]		North American Indian only		North American Indian non-Aboriginal[4]		Metis only	
	Number	Percent	Number	Percent	Number	Percent	Number	Percent
Total population age 15+	451,950	100.0	184,855	100.0	150,280	100.0	39,975	100.0
Male	217,135	48.0	89,050	48.2	71,045	47.3	19,690	49.3
Female	234,815	52.0	95,805	51.8	79,235	52.7	20,285	50.7
Employed[5]	210,605	46.6	62,265	33.7	93,440	62.2	15,695	39.3
Male	116,860	25.9	35,650	19.3	50,420	33.6	9,105	22.8
Female	93,745	20.7	26,620	14.4	43,020	28.6	6,595	16.5
Unemployed[6]	61,940	13.7	28,090	15.2	17,095	11.4	6,395	16.0
Male	35,820	7.9	17,355	9.4	8,720	5.8	3,965	9.9
Female	26,125	5.8	10,740	5.8	8,375	5.6	2,430	6.1
Total in labor force[7]	272,545	60.3	90,360	48.9	110,535	73.6	22,095	55.3
Male	152,675	33.8	53,010	28.7	59,140	39.4	13,070	32.7
Female	119,870	26.5	37,355	20.2	51,395	34.2	9,025	22.6
Not in labor force[8]	179,405	39.7	94,490	51.1	39,745	26.4	17,880	44.7
Male	64,455	14.3	36,040	19.5	11,910	7.9	6,620	16.6
Female	114,950	25.4	58,450	31.6	27,840	18.5	11,265	28.2
Unemployment rate[9]	NA	22.7	NA	31.1	NA	15.5	NA	28.9
Male	NA	23.5	NA	32.7	NA	14.7	NA	30.3
Female	NA	21.5	NA	28.8	NA	16.3	NA	26.9
Participation rate[10]	NA	60.3	NA	48.9	NA	73.6	NA	55.3
Male	NA	70.3	NA	59.5	NA	83.2	NA	66.4
Female	NA	51.0	NA	39.0	NA	64.9	NA	44.5

Source: Aboriginal Peoples Output Program, 1986 Census, Statistics Canada, *A Data Book on Canada's Aboriginal Population from the 1986 Census of Canada*, March, 1989, p. 16. Primary source: 1986 Census of Canada. *Notes:* (NA) stands for not applicable. A dash (-) represents zero or a percentage less than .05 percent. 1. Aboriginal origins are derived from the ethnic origin question which asks whether respondents are North American Indian, Metis or Inuit. 2. All 1986 figures exclude the population estimated at about 45,000 on 136 incompletely enumerated Indian reserves and settlements throughout Canada. 3. Total Aboriginals—are the sum of persons who reported: (a) a single aboriginal (e.g., North American Indian, Metis, or Inuit) and (b) multiple aboriginal origins, that is those who reported:at least one aboriginal origin with any other non-aboriginal origin (e.g. Metis and French) or twoor more aboriginal origins only. *F 4. Non-aboriginal in these columns—refers to persons who reported one or more non-aboriginal origins such as British, French, etc., in combination with oneof the aboriginal origins such as North American Indian. 5. Employed—refers to persons 15 years of age and over who, during the week prior to June 3, 1986: (a) did any work at all excluding housework or other maintenance or repairs around the home and volunteer work; or (b) were absent from their job or business because of own temporary illnessor disability, vacation, labor dispute at their place of work, or were absent for other reasons. 6. Unemployed—refers to persons 15 years of age and over who, during the week prior to enumeration: (a) were without work, had actively looked for work in the past four weeks and were available for work; or (b) had been on lay-off and expected to return to their job; or (c) had definite arrangements to start a new job in four weeks or less. 7. Total in Labor Force (in reference week)—refers to persons 15 years of age and over who either employed or unemployed during the week prior to enumeration (June 3, 1986). 8. Nor in labor force—refers to those persons 15 years of age and over who, in the week prior to enumeration, were unwilling or unable to offer or supply their labor services under conditions existing in the labor market. It includes persons who looked for work during the last four weeks bwho were not available to work in the reference week, as well as persons who did not work, did nothave a new job to start in four weeks or less, were not on temporary layoff or did not look for woin the four weeks prior to enumeration. 9. Unemployment rate—refers to the unemployed labor force expressed as a percentage of the total labor force (in reference week) in an area, group, or category. 10. Participation rate—refers to the total labor force (in reference week) expressed as a percentage of the total population 15 years of age and over, excluding institutional residents, inan area, group, or category.

★ 913 ★

Population 15 Years and Over by Labor Force Activity and Sex for Detailed Aboriginal Origins for Canada, 1986 - II[1,2]

Labor force activity	Metis and non-Aboriginal[3]		Inuit only		Inuit and non-Aboriginal[3]		Other multiple Aboriginal origins[4]	
	Number	Percent	Number	Percent	Number	Percent	Number	Percent
Total population aged 15+	42,440	100.0	16,500	100.0	3,660	100.0	14,245	100.0
Male	19,865	46.8	8,260	50.1	1,880	51.4	7,345	51.6
Female	22,575	53.2	8,245	50.0	1,785	48.8	6,895	48.4
Employed[5]	23,505	55.4	6,160	37.3	1,915	52.3	7,620	53.5
Male	12,540	29.5	3,495	21.2	1,070	29.2	4,570	32.1
Female	10,960	25.8	2,665	16.2	845	23.1	3,045	21.4
Unemployed[6]	5,430	12.8	2,350	14.2	550	15.0	2,015	14.1
Male	2,865	6.8	1,420	8.6	320	8.7	1,170	8.2
Female	2,565	6.0	935	5.7	225	6.1	855	6.0
Total in labor force[7]	28,935	68.2	8,515	51.6	2,465	67.3	9,640	67.7
Male	15,405	36.3	4,915	29.8	1,395	38.1	5,740	40.3
Female	13,525	31.9	3,600	21.8	1,070	29.2	3,905	27.4
Not in labor force[8]	13,505	31.8	7,985	48.4	1,195	32.7	4,600	32.3
Male	4,460	10.5	3,345	20.3	485	13.3	1,605	11.3
Female	9,050	21.3	4,645	28.2	715	19.5	2,995	21.0
Unemployment rate[9]	NA	18.8	NA	27.6	NA	22.3	NA	20.9
Male	NA	18.6	NA	28.9	NA	22.9	NA	20.3
Female	NA	19.0	NA	26.0	NA	21.0	NA	21.8
Participation rate[10]	NA	68.2	NA	51.6	NA	67.3	NA	67.6
Male	NA	77.5	NA	59.5	NA	74.2	NA	78.1
Female	NA	59.9	NA	43.7	NA	59.9	NA	56.6

Source: Aboriginal Peoples Output Program, 1986 Census, Statistics Canada, *A Data Book on Canada's Aboriginal Population from the 1986 Census of Canada*, March, 1989, p. 16. Primary source: 1986 Census of Canada. *Notes:* (NA) stands for not applicable. A dash (-) represents zero or a percentage less than .05 1. Aboriginal origins are derived from the ethnic origin question which asks whether respondents are North American Indian, Metis or Inuit. 2. All 1986 figures exclude the population estimated at about 45,000 on 136 incompletely enumerated Indian reserves and settlements throughout Canada. 3. Non-aboriginal in these columns—refers to persons who reported one or more non-aboriginal origins such as British, French, etc., in combination with one of the aboriginal origins such as North American Indian. 4. Other Multiple Aboriginal origins—refer to the sum of those persons reporting two or more aboriginal origins with or without a non-aboriginal origin. 5. Employed—refers to persons 15 years of age and over who, during the week prior to June 3, 1986: (a) did any work at all excluding housework or other maintenance or repairs around the home and volunteer work; or (b) were absent from their job or business because of own temporary illnessor disability, vacation, labor dispute at their place of work, or were absent for other reasons. 6. Unemployed—refers to persons 15 years of age and over who, during the week prior to enumeration: (a) were without work, had actively looked for work in the past four weeks and were available for work; or (b) had been on lay-off and expected to return to their job; or (c) had definite arrangements to start a new job in four weeks or less. 7. Total in Labor Force (in reference week)—refers to persons 15 years of age and over who either employed or unemployed during the week prior to enumeration (June 3, 1986). 8. Not in labor force—refers to those persons 15 years of age and over who, in the week prior to enumeration, were unwilling or unable to offer or supply their labor services under conditions existing in the labor market. It includes persons who looked for work during the last four weeks bwho were not available to work in the reference week, as well as persons who did not work, did nothave a new job to start in four weeks or less, were not on temporary layoff or did not look for woin the four weeks prior to enumeration. 9. Unemployment rate—refers to the unemployed labor force expressed as a percentage of the total labor force (in reference week) in an area, group, or category. 10. Participation rate—refers to the total labor force (in reference week) expressed as a percentage of the total population 15 years of age and over, excluding institutional residents, inan area, group, or category.

★ 914 ★

Population 15 Years and Over by Labor Force Activity and Sex for Detailed Aboriginal Origins for Alberta, 1986 - I[1,2]

Labor force activity	Total Aboriginal origins[3]		North American Indian only		North American Indian non-Aboriginal[4]		Metis only	
	Number	Percent	Number	Percent	Number	Percent	Number	Percent
Total population aged 15+	63,055	100.0	20,945	100.0	17,020	100.0	11,080	100.0
Male	30,230	47.9	9,770	46.6	8,115	47.7	5,480	49.5
Female	32,825	52.1	11,175	53.4	8,905	52.3	5,600	50.5
Employed [5]	29,555	46.9	6,635	31.7	11,020	64.7	4,160	37.5
Male	16,300	25.9	3,660	17.5	5,965	35.0	2,365	21.3
Female	13,255	21.0	2,975	14.2	5,055	29.7	1,790	16.2
Unemployed[6]	8,755	13.9	3,185	15.2	1,955	11.5	1,765	15.9
Male	5,040	8.0	1,920	9.2	1,030	6.1	1,065	9.6
Female	3,710	5.9	1,270	6.1	925	5.4	700	6.3
Total in labor force[7]	38,305	60.7	9,820	46.9	12,975	76.2	5,925	53.5
Male	21,340	33.8	5,575	26.6	6,995	41.1	3,435	31.0
Female	16,970	26.9	4,240	20.2	5,980	35.1	2,490	22.5
Not in labor force[8]	24,750	39.3	11,120	53.1	4,045	23.8	5,160	46.6
Male	8,895	14.1	4,190	20.0	1,120	6.6	2,050	18.5
Female	15,860	25.2	6,930	33.1	2,930	17.2	3,105	28.0
Unemployment rate[9]	NA	23.0	NA	32.0	NA	15.0	NA	30.0
Male	NA	24.0	NA	34.0	NA	15.0	NA	31.0
Female	NA	22.0	NA	30.0	NA	15.0	NA	28.0
Participation rate[10]	NA	61.0	NA	47.0	NA	76.0	NA	53.0
Male	NA	71.0	NA	57.0	NA	86.0	NA	63.0
Female	NA	52.0	NA	38.0	NA	67.0	NA	44.0

Source: Aboriginal Peoples Output Program, 1986 Census, Statistics Canada, *A Data Book on Canada's Aboriginal Population from the 1986 Census of Canada*, March, 1989, p. 232. Primary source: 1986 Census of Canada. *Notes:* (NA) stands for not applicable. A dash (-) represents zero or a percentage less than .05 percent. 1. Aboriginal origins are derived from the ethnic origin question which asks whether respondents are North American Indian, Metis or Inuit. 2. All 1986 figures exclude the population estimated at about 45,000 on 136 incompletely enumerated Indian reserves and settlements throughout Canada. 3. Total Aboriginals—are the sum of persons who reported: (a) a single aboriginal (e.g., North American Indian, Metis, or Inuit) and (b) multiple aboriginal origins, that is those who reported:at least one aboriginal origin with any other non-aboriginal origin (e.g. Metis and French) or twoor more aboriginal origins only. 4. Non-aboriginal in these columns—refers to persons who reported one or more non-aboriginal origins such as British, French, etc., in combination with one of the aboriginal origins such as North American Indian. 5. Employed—refers to persons 15 years of age and over who, during the week prior to June 3, 1986: (a) did any work at all excluding housework or other maintenance or repairs around the home and volunteer work; or (b) were absent from their job or business because of own temporary illnessor disability, vacation, labor dispute at their place of work, or were absent for other reasons. 6. Unemployed—refers to persons 15 years of age and over who, during the week prior to enumeration: (a) were without work, had actively looked for work in the past four weeks and were available for work; or (b) had been on lay-off and expected to return to their job; or (c) had definite arrangements to start a new job in four weeks or less. 7. Total in Labor Force (in reference week)—refers to persons 15 years of age and over who were either employed or unemployed during the week prior to enumeration (June 3, 1986). 8. Nor in labor force—refers to those persons 15 years of age and over who, in the week prior to enumeration, were unwilling or unable to offer or supply their labor services under conditions existing in the labor market. It includes persons who looked for work during the last four weeks bwho were not available to work in the reference week, as well as persons who did not work, did nothave a new job to start in four weeks or less, were not on temporary layoff or did not look for woin the four weeks prior to enumeration. 9. Unemployment rate—refers to the unemployed labor force expressed as a percentage of the total labor force (in reference week) in an area, group, or category. 10. Participation rate—refers to the total labor force (in reference week) expressed as a percentage of the total population 15 years of age and over, excluding institutional residents, inan area, group, or category.

★ 915 ★

Population 15 Years and Over by Labor Force Activity and Sex for Detailed Aboriginal Origins for Alberta, 1986 - II[1,2]

Labor force activity	Metis and non-Aboriginal[3]		Inuit only		Inuit and non-Aboriginal[3]		Other multiple Aboriginal origins[4]	
	Number	Percent	Number	Percent	Number	Percent	Number	Percent
Total population								
Aged 15+	9,995	100.0	210	100.0	280	100.0	3,525	100.0
Male	4,745	47.5	115	54.8	110	39.3	1,905	54.0
Female	5,255	52.6	95	45.2	175	62.5	1,625	46.1
Employed[5]	5,535	55.4	100	47.6	165	58.9	1,935	54.9
Male	2,960	29.6	65	31.0	65	23.2	1,210	34.3
Female	2,575	25.8	30	14.3	100	35.7	720	20.4
Unemployed[6]	1,285	12.9	30	14.3	20	7.1	505	14.3
Male	715	7.2	20	9.5	-	-	285	8.1
Female	570	5.7	15	7.1	15	5.4	225	6.4
Total in labor force[7]	6,820	68.2	135	64.3	185	66.1	2,445	69.4
Male	3,675	36.8	85	40.5	70	25.0	1,495	42.1
Female	3,145	31.5	45	21.4	120	42.9	955	27.1
Not in labor force[8]	3,180	31.8	75	35.7	95	33.9	1,080	30.6
Male	1,070	10.7	20	9.5	40	14.3	405	11.5
Female	2,110	21.1	50	23.8	55	19.6	675	19.1
Unemployment rate[9]	NA	19.0	NA	22.0	NA	11.0	NA	20.6
Male	NA	19.0	NA	24.0	NA	-	NA	19.0
Female	NA	18.0	NA	33.0	NA	13.0	NA	23.5
Participation rate[10]	NA	68.0	NA	64.0	NA	66.0	NA	69.3
Male	NA	77.0	NA	74.0	NA	64.0	NA	78.4
Female	NA	60.0	NA	47.0	NA	69.0	NA	58.7

Source: Aboriginal Peoples Output Program, 1986 Census, Statistics Canada, *A Data Book on Canada's Aboriginal Population from the 1986 Census of Canada*, March, 1989, p. 232. Primary source: 1986 Census of Canada. *Notes:* (NA) stands for not applicable. A dash (-) represents zero or a percentage less than .05 percent. 1. Aboriginal origins are derived from the ethnic origin question which asks whether respondents are North American Indian, Metis or Inuit. 2. All 1986 figures exclude the population estimated at about 45,000 on 136 incompletely enumerated Indian reserves and settlements throughout Canada. 3. Non-aboriginal in these columns—refers to persons who reported one or more non-aboriginal origins such as British, French, etc., in combination with one of the aboriginal origins such as North American Indian. 4. Other Multiple Aboriginal origins—refer to the sum of those persons reporting two or more aboriginal origins with or without a non-aboriginal origin. 5. Employed—refers to persons 15 years of age and over who, during the week prior to June 3, 1986: (a) did any work at all excluding housework or other maintenance or repairs around the home and volunteer work; or (b) were absent from their job or business because of own temporary illnessor disability, vacation, labor dispute at their place of work, or were absent for other reasons. 6. Unemployed—refers to persons 15 years of age and over who, during the week prior to enumeration: (a) were without work, had actively looked for work in the past four weeks and were available for work; or (b) had been on lay-off and expected to return to their job; or (c) had definite arrangements to start a new job in four weeks or less. 7. Total in Labor Force (in reference week)—refers to persons 15 years of age and over who either employed or unemployed during the week prior to enumeration (June 3, 1986). 8. Not in labor force—refers to those persons 15 years of age and over who, in the week prior to enumeration, were unwilling or unable to offer or supply their labor services under conditions existing in the labor market. It includes persons who looked for work during the last four weeks bwho were not available to work in the reference week, as well as persons who did not work, did nothave a new job to start in four weeks or less, were not on temporary layoff or did not look for woin the four weeks prior to enumeration. 9. Unemployment rate—refers to the unemployed labor force expressed as a percentage of the total labor force (in reference week) in an area, group, or category. 10. Participation rate—refers to the total labor force (in reference week) expressed as a percentage of the total population 15 years of age and over, excluding institutional residents, inan area, group, or category.

★ 916 ★

Population 15 Years and Over by Labor Force Activity and Sex for Detailed Aboriginal Origins for British Columbia, 1986 - I[1,2]

Labor force activity	Total Aboriginal origins[3]		North American Indian only		North American Indian non-Aboriginal[4]		Metis only	
	Number	Percent	Number	Percent	Number	Percent	Number	Percent
Total population aged 15+	82,175	100.0	39,020	100.0	32,305	100.0	3,010	100.0
Male	40,095	48.8	18,950	48.6	15,730	48.7	1,435	47.7
Female	42,085	51.2	20,070	51.4	16,580	51.3	1,575	52.3
Employed[5]	35,585	43.3	12,280	31.5	18,115	56.1	1,030	34.2
Male	19,910	24.2	7,080	18.1	9,940	30.8	580	19.3
Female	15,675	19.1	5,200	13.3	8,180	25.3	455	15.1
Unemployed[6]	14,925	18.2	8,045	20.6	4,870	15.1	655	21.8
Male	8,895	10.8	4,960	12.7	2,705	8.4	380	12.6
Female	6,030	7.3	3,085	7.9	2,160	6.7	275	9.1
Total in labor force[7]	50,505	61.5	20,320	52.1	22,980	71.1	1,685	56.0
Male	28,810	35.1	12,040	30.9	12,645	39.1	960	31.9
Female	21,695	26.4	8,285	21.2	10,340	32.0	730	24.3
Not in labor force[8]	31,670	38.5	18,700	47.9	9,320	28.9	1,325	44.0
Male	11,280	13.7	6,910	17.7	3,085	9.5	475	15.8
Female	20,390	24.8	11,785	30.2	6,235	19.3	845	28.1
Unemployment rate[9]	NA	30.0	NA	40.0	NA	21.0	NA	39.0
Male	NA	31.0	NA	41.0	NA	21.0	NA	40.0
Female	NA	28.0	NA	37.0	NA	21.0	NA	38.0
Participation rate[10]	NA	61.0	NA	52.0	NA	71.0	NA	56.0
Male	NA	72.0	NA	64.0	NA	80.0	NA	67.0
Female	NA	52.0	NA	41.0	NA	62.0	NA	46.0

Source: Aboriginal Peoples Output Program, 1986 Census, Statistics Canada, *A Data Book on Canada's Aboriginal Population from the 1986 Census of Canada*, March, 1989, p. 256. Primary source: 1986 Census of Canada. *Notes:* (NA) stands for not applicable. A dash (-) represents zero or a percentage less than .05 percent. 1. Aboriginal origins are derived from the ethnic origin question which asks whether respondents are North American Indian, Metis or Inuit. 2. All 1986 figures exclude the population estimated at about 45,000 on 136 incompletely enumerated Indian reserves and settlements throughout Canada. 3. Total Aboriginals—are the sum of persons who reported: (a) a single aboriginal (e.g., North American Indian, Metis, or Inuit) and (b) multiple aboriginal origins, that is those who reported:at least one aboriginal origin with any other non-aboriginal origin (e.g. Metis and French) or twoor more aboriginal origins only. 4. Non-aboriginal in these columns—refers to persons who reported one or more non-aboriginal origins such as British, French, etc., in combination with one of the aboriginal origins such as North American Indian. 5. Employed—refers to persons 15 years of age and over who, during the week prior to June 3, 1986: (a) did any work at all excluding housework or other maintenance or repairs around the home and volunteer work; or (b) were absent from their job or business because of own temporary illnessor disability, vacation, labor dispute at their place of work, or were absent for other reasons. 6. Unemployed—refers to persons 15 years of age and over who, during the week prior to enumeration: (a) were without work, had actively looked for work in the past four weeks and were available for work; or (b) had been on lay-off and expected to return to their job; or (c) had definite arrangements to start a new job in four weeks or less. 7. Total in Labor Force (in reference week)—refers to persons 15 years of age and over who either employed or unemployed during the week prior to enumeration (June 3, 1986). 8. Nor in labor force—refers to those persons 15 years of age and over who, in the week prior to enumeration, were unwilling or unable to offer or supply their labor services under conditions existing in the labor market. It includes persons who looked for work during the last four weeks bwho were not available to work in the reference week, as well as persons who did not work, did nothave a new job to start in four weeks or less, were not on temporary layoff or did not look for woin the four weeks prior to enumeration. 9. Unemployment rate—refers to the unemployed labor force expressed as a percentage of the total labor force (in reference week) in an area, group, or category. 10. Participation rate—refers to the total labor force (in reference week) expressed as a percentage of the total population 15 years of age and over, excluding institutional residents, inan area, group, or category.

★917★

Population 15 Years and Over by Labor Force Activity and Sex for Detailed Aboriginal Origins for British Columbia, 1986 - II[1,2]

Labor force activity	Metis and non-Aboriginal[3]		Inuit only		Inuit and non-Aboriginal[3]		Other multiple Aboriginal origins[4]	
	Number	Percent	Number	Percent	Number	Percent	Number	Percent
Total population								
aged 15+	5,805	100.0	165	100.0	330	100.0	1,535	100.0
Male	2,845	49.0	90	54.5	205	62.1	835	54.4
Female	2,960	51.0	75	45.5	120	36.4	705	45.9
Employed[5]	3,170	54.6	50	30.3	160	48.5	785	51.1
Male	1,700	29.3	40	24.2	105	31.8	480	31.3
Female	1,470	25.3	-	-	60	18.2	300	19.5
Unemployed[6]	1,005	17.3	25	15.2	70	21.2	255	16.6
Male	625	10.8	-	-	60	18.2	160	10.4
Female	385	6.6	15	9.1	10	3.0	95	6.2
Total in labor force[7]	4,175	71.9	70	42.4	230	69.7	1,035	67.4
Male	2,320	40.0	45	27.3	160	48.5	645	42.0
Female	1,855	32.0	25	15.2	70	21.2	395	25.7
Not in labor force[8]	1,625	28.0	95	57.6	100	30.3	515	33.6
Male	525	9.0	45	27.3	40	12.1	190	12.4
Female	1,105	19.0	50	30.3	60	18.2	315	20.5
Unemployment rate[9]	NA	24.0	NA	36.0	NA	30.0	NA	24.6
Male	NA	27.0	NA	-	NA	38.0	NA	24.8
Female	NA	21.0	NA	60.0	NA	14.0	NA	24.0
Participation rate[10]	NA	72.0	NA	42.0	NA	70.0	NA	67.4
Male	NA	82.0	NA	50.0	NA	78.0	NA	77.2
Female	NA	63.0	NA	33.0	NA	58.0	NA	56.0

Source: Aboriginal Peoples Output Program, 1986 Census, Statistics Canada, *A Data Book on Canada's Aboriginal Population from the 1986 Census of Canada*, March, 1989, p. 256. Primary source: 1986 Census of Canada. *Notes:* (NA) stands for not applicable. A dash (-) represents zero or a percentage less than .05 percent. 1. Aboriginal origins are derived from the ethnic origin question which asks whether respondents are North American Indian, Metis or Inuit. 2. All 1986 figures exclude the population estimated at about 45,000 on 136 incompletely enumerated Indian reserves and settlements throughout Canada. 3. Non-aboriginal in these columns—refers to persons who reported one or more non-aboriginal origins such as British, French, etc., in combination with one of the aboriginal origins such as North American Indian. 4. Other Multiple Aboriginal origins—refer to the sum of those persons reporting two or more aboriginal origins with or without a non-aboriginal origin. 5. Employed—refers to persons 15 years of age and over who, during the week prior to June 3, 1986: (a) did any work at all excluding housework or other maintenance or repairs around the home and volunteer work; or (b) were absent from their job or business because of own temporary illnessor disability, vacation, labor dispute at their place of work, or were absent for other reasons. 6. Unemployed—refers to persons 15 years of age and over who, during the week prior to enumeration: (a) were without work, had actively looked for work in the past four weeks and were available for work; or (b) had been on lay-off and expected to return to their job; or (c) had definite arrangements to start a new job in four weeks or less. 7. Total in Labor Force (in reference week)—refers to persons 15 years of age and over who either employed or unemployed during the week prior to enumeration (June 3, 1986). 8. Not in labor force—refers to those persons 15 years of age and over who, in the week prior to enumeration, were unwilling or unable to offer or supply their labor services under conditions existing in the labor market. It includes persons who looked for work during the last four weeks bwho were not available to work in the reference week, as well as persons who did not work, did nothave a new job to start in four weeks or less, were not on temporary layoff or did not look for woin the four weeks prior to enumeration. 9. Unemployment rate—refers to the unemployed labor force expressed as a percentage of the total labor force (in reference week) in an area, group, or category. 10. Participation rate—refers to the total labor force (in reference week) expressed as a percentage of the total population 15 years of age and over, excluding institutional residents, inan area, group, or category.

★ 918 ★

Population 15 Years and Over by Labor Force Activity and Sex for Detailed Aboriginal Origins for Manitoba, 1986 - I[1,2]

Labor force activity	Total Aboriginal origins[3]		North American Indian only		North American Indian non-Aboriginal[4]		Metis only	
	Number	Percent	Number	Percent	Number	Percent	Number	Percent
Total population aged 15+	52,050	100.0	24,360	100.0	6,355	100.0	9,330	100.0
Male	24,970	48.0	11,655	47.8	3,060	48.2	4,650	49.8
Female	27,075	52.0	12,705	52.2	3,300	51.9	4,680	50.2
Employed[5]	20,360	39.1	6,645	27.3	3,830	60.3	3,445	36.9
Male	11,550	22.2	3,830	15.7	2,115	33.3	2,045	21.9
Female	8,810	16.9	2,815	11.6	1,715	27.0	1,400	15.0
Unemployed[6]	7,255	13.9	3,680	15.1	645	10.1	1,450	15.5
Male	4,455	8.6	2,360	9.7	370	5.8	940	10.1
Female	2,800	5.4	1,315	5.4	275	4.3	505	5.4
Total in labor force[7]	27,605	53.0	10,325	42.4	4,475	70.4	4,890	52.4
Male	16,000	30.7	6,190	25.4	2,485	39.1	2,990	32.0
Female	11,610	22.3	4,135	17.0	1,990	31.3	1,910	20.5
Not in labor force[8]	24,440	47.0	14,035	57.6	1,885	29.7	4,440	47.6
Male	8,970	17.2	5,465	22.4	570	9.0	1,660	17.8
Female	15,465	29.7	8,570	35.2	1,310	20.6	2,775	29.7
Unemployment rate[9]	NA	26.3	NA	35.6	NA	14.4	NA	29.7
Male	NA	27.8	NA	38.1	NA	14.9	NA	31.4
Female	NA	24.1	NA	31.8	NA	13.8	NA	26.4
Participation rate[10]	NA	53.0	NA	42.4	NA	70.4	NA	52.4
Male	NA	64.1	NA	53.1	NA	81.2	NA	64.3
Female	NA	42.9	NA	32.5	NA	60.3	NA	40.8

Source: Aboriginal Peoples Output Program, 1986 Census, Statistics Canada, *A Data Book on Canada's Aboriginal Population from the 1986 Census of Canada,* March, 1989, p. 186. Primary source: 1986 Census of Canada. *Notes:* (NA) stands for not applicable. A dash (-) represents zero or a percentage less than .05 percent. 1. Aboriginal origins are derived from the ethnic origin question which asks whether respondents are North American Indian, Metis or Inuit. 2. All 1986 figures exclude the population estimated at about 45,000 on 136 incompletely enumerated Indian reserves and settlements throughout Canada. 3. Total Aboriginals—are the sum of persons who reported: (a) a single aboriginal (e.g., North American Indian, Metis, or Inuit) and (b) multiple aboriginal origins, that is those who reported:at least one aboriginal origin with any other non-aboriginal origin (e.g. Metis and French) or twoor more aboriginal origins only. 4. Non-aboriginal in these columns—refers to persons who reported one or more non-aboriginal origins such as British, French, etc., in combination with one of the aboriginal origins such as North American Indian. 5. Employed—refers to persons 15 years of age and over who, during the week prior to June 3, 1986: (a) did any work at all excluding housework or other maintenance or repairs around the home and volunteer work; or (b) were absent from their job or business because of own temporary illnessor disability, vacation, labor dispute at their place of work, or were absent for other reasons. 6. Unemployed—refers to persons 15 years of age and over who, during the week prior to enumeration: (a) were without work, had actively looked for work in the past four weeks and were available for work; or (b) had been on lay-off and expected to return to their job; or (c) had definite arrangements to start a new job in four weeks or less. 7. Total in Labor Force (in reference week)—refers to persons 15 years of age and over who either employed or unemployed during the week prior to enumeration (June 3, 1986). 8. Nor in labor force—refers to those persons 15 years of age and over who, in the week prior to enumeration, were unwilling or unable to offer or supply their labor services under conditions existing in the labor market. It includes persons who looked for work during the last four weeks bwho were not available to work in the reference week, as well as persons who did not work, did nothave a new job to start in four weeks or less, were not on temporary layoff or did not look for woin the four weeks prior to enumeration. 9. Unemployment rate—refers to the unemployed labor force expressed as a percentage of the total labor force (in reference week) in an area, group, or category. 10. Participation rate—refers to the total labor force (in reference week) expressed as a percentage of the total population 15 years of age and over, excluding institutional residents, inan area, group, or category.

★ 919 ★

Population 15 Years and Over by Labor Force Activity and Sex for Detailed Aboriginal Origins for Manitoba, 1986 - II[1,2]

Labor force activity	Metis and non-Aboriginal[3]		Inuit only		Inuit and non-Aboriginal[3]		Other multiple Aboriginal origins[4]	
	Number	Percent	Number	Percent	Number	Percent	Number	Percent
Total population aged 15+	9,105	100.0	100	100.0	115	100.0	2,675	100.0
Male	4,235	46.5	35	35.0	55	47.8	1,285	48.0
Female	4,870	53.5	70	70.0	65	56.6	1,390	52.0
Employed[5]	5,045	55.4	55	55.0	80	69.6	1,260	47.1
Male	2,770	30.4	25	25.0	50	43.5	705	26.4
Female	2,270	24.9	25	25.0	30	26.1	545	20.4
Unemployed[6]	1,055	11.6	15	15.0	-	-	405	15.1
Male	520	5.7	-	-	-	-	250	9.3
Female	535	5.9	-	-	-	-	155	5.8
Total in labor force[7]	6,100	67.0	70	70.0	85	73.9	1,660	62.1
Male	3,295	36.2	35	35.0	55	47.8	955	35.7
Female	2,805	30.8	35	35.0	35	30.4	705	26.4
Not in labor force[8]	3,005	33.0	30	30.0	30	26.1	1,015	37.9
Male	940	10.3	-	-	-	-	335	12.5
Female	2,065	22.7	30	30.0	30	26.1	685	25.6
Unemployment rate[9]	NA	17.3	NA	21.4	NA	-	NA	24.3
Male	NA	15.8	NA	-	NA	-	NA	26.1
Female	NA	19.1	NA	-	NA	-	NA	21.9
Participation rate[10]	NA	67.0	NA	70.0	NA	73.9	NA	62.0
Male	NA	77.8	NA	100.0	NA	100.0	NA	74.3
Female	NA	57.6	NA	50.0	NA	53.8	NA	50.7

Source: Aboriginal Peoples Output Program, 1986 Census, Statistics Canada, *A Data Book on Canada's Aboriginal Population from the 1986 Census of Canada*, March, 1989, p. 186. Primary source: 1986 Census of Canada. *Notes:* (NA) stands for not applicable. A dash (-) represents zero or a percentage less than .05 percent. 1. Aboriginal origins are derived from the ethnic origin question which asks whether respondents are North American Indian, Metis or Inuit. 2. All 1986 figures exclude the population estimated at about 45,000 on 136 incompletely enumerated Indian reserves and settlements throughout Canada. 3. Non-aboriginal in these columns—refers to persons who reported one or more non-aboriginal origins such as British, French, etc., in combination with one of the aboriginal origins such as North American Indian. 4. Other Multiple Aboriginal origins—refer to the sum of those persons reporting two or more aboriginal origins with or without a non-aboriginal origin. 5. Employed—refers to persons 15 years of age and over who, during the week prior to June 3, 1986: (a) did any work at all excluding housework or other maintenance or repairs around the home and volunteer work; or (b) were absent from their job or business because of own temporary illnessor disability, vacation, labor dispute at their place of work, or were absent for other reasons. 6. Unemployed—refers to persons 15 years of age and over who, during the week prior to enumeration: (a) were without work, had actively looked for work in the past four weeks and were available for work; or (b) had been on lay-off and expected to return to their job; or (c) had definite arrangements to start a new job in four weeks or less. 7. Total in Labor Force (in reference week)—refers to persons 15 years of age and over who either employed or unemployed during the week prior to enumeration (June 3, 1986). 8. Not in labor force—refers to those persons 15 years of age and over who, in the week prior to enumeration, were unwilling or unable to offer or supply their labor services under conditions existing in the labor market. It includes persons who looked for work during the last four weeks bwho were not available to work in the reference week, as well as persons who did not work, did nothave a new job to start in four weeks or less, were not on temporary layoff or did not look for woin the four weeks prior to enumeration. 9. Unemployment rate—refers to the unemployed labor force expressed as a percentage of the total labor force (in reference week) in an area, group, or category. 10. Participation rate—refers to the total labor force (in reference week) expressed as a percentage of the total population 15 years of age and over, excluding institutional residents, inan area, group, or category.

★ 920 ★

Population 15 Years and Over by Labor Force Activity and Sex for Detailed Aboriginal Origins for New Brunswick, 1986 - I[1,2]

Labor force activity	Total Aboriginal origins[3]		North American Indian only		North American Indian non-Aboriginal[4]		Metis only	
	Number	Percent	Number	Percent	Number	Percent	Number	Percent
Total population aged 15+	5,995	100.0	2,505	100.0	2,960	100.0	110	100.0
Male	3,020	50.4	1,295	51.7	1,445	48.8	70	63.6
Female	2,970	49.5	1,210	48.3	1,515	51.2	40	36.4
Employed[5]	2,260	37.7	645	25.7	1,435	48.5	50	45.5
Male	1,350	22.5	375	15.0	875	29.6	30	27.3
Female	910	15.2	270	10.8	565	19.1	20	18.2
Unemployed[6]	1,115	18.6	525	21.0	450	15.2	25	22.7
Male	645	10.8	325	13.0	220	7.4	20	18.2
Female	475	7.9	200	8.0	230	7.8	-	-
Total in labor force[7]	3,375	56.3	1,165	46.5	1,890	63.9	70	63.6
Male	1,990	33.2	695	27.7	1,095	37.0	50	45.5
Female	1,385	23.1	470	18.8	795	26.9	25	22.7
Not in labor force[8]	2,620	43.7	1,335	53.3	1,075	36.3	40	36.4
Male	1,025	17.1	595	23.8	350	11.8	25	22.7
Female	1,590	26.5	740	29.5	720	24.3	15	13.6
Unemployment rate[9]	NA	33.0	NA	45.0	NA	24.0	NA	36.0
Male	NA	32.0	NA	47.0	NA	20.0	NA	40.0
Female	NA	34.0	NA	43.0	NA	29.0	NA	-
Participation rate[10]	NA	56.0	NA	47.0	NA	64.0	NA	64.0
Male	NA	66.0	NA	54.0	NA	76.0	NA	71.0
Female	NA	47.0	NA	39.0	NA	52.0	NA	63.0

Source: Aboriginal Peoples Output Program, 1986 Census, Statistics Canada, *A Data Book on Canada's Aboriginal Population from the 1986 Census of Canada,* March, 1989, p. 112. Primary source: 1986 Census of Canada. *Notes:* (NA) stands for not applicable. A dash (-) represents zero or a percentage less than .05 percent. 1. Aboriginal origins are derived from the ethnic origin question which asks whether respondents are North American Indian, Metis or Inuit. 2. All 1986 figures exclude the population estimated at about 45,000 on 136 incompletely enumerated Indian reserves and settlements throughout Canada. 3. Total Aboriginals—are the sum of persons who reported: (a) a single aboriginal (e.g., North American Indian, Metis, or Inuit) and (b) multiple aboriginal origins, that is those who reported:at least one aboriginal origin with any other non-aboriginal origin (e.g. Metis and French) or twoor more aboriginal origins only. 4. Non-aboriginal in these columns—refers to persons who reported one or more non-aboriginal origins such as British, French, etc., in combination with oneof the aboriginal origins such as North American Indian. 5. Employed—refers to persons 15 years of age and over who, during the week prior to June 3, 1986: (a) did any work at all excluding housework or other maintenance or repairs around the home and volunteer work; or (b) were absent from their job or business because of own temporary illnessor disability, vacation, labor dispute at their place of work, or were absent for other reasons. 6. Unemployed—refers to persons 15 years of age and over who, during the week prior to enumeration: (a) were without work, had actively looked for work in the past four weeks and were available for work; or (b) had been on lay-off and expected to return to their job; or (c) had definite arrangements to start a new job in four weeks or less. 7. Total in Labor Force (in reference week)—refers to persons 15 years of age and over who either employed or unemployed during the week prior to enumeration (June 3, 1986). 8. Nor in labor force—refers to those persons 15 years of age and over who, in the week prior to enumeration, were unwilling or unable to offer or supply their labor services under conditions existing in the labor market. It includes persons who looked for work during the last four weeks bwho were not available to work in the reference week, as well as persons who did not work, did nothave a new job to start in four weeks or less, were not on temporary layoff or did not look for woin the four weeks prior to enumeration. 9. Unemployment rate—refers to the unemployed labor force expressed as a percentage of the total labor force (in reference week) in an area, group, or category. 10. Participation rate—refers to the total labor force (in reference week) expressed as a percentage of the total population 15 years of age and over, excluding institutional residents, inan area, group, or category.

★ 921 ★

Population 15 Years and Over by Labor Force Activity and Sex for Detailed Aboriginal Origins for New Brunswick, 1986 - II[1,2]

Labor force activity	Metis and non-Aboriginal[3]		Inuit only		Inuit and non-Aboriginal[3]		Other multiple Aboriginal origins[4]	
	Number	Percent	Number	Percent	Number	Percent	Number	Percent
Total population aged 15+	260	100.0	-	-	60	100.0	100	100.0
Male	135	51.9	-	-	25	41.7	45	45.0
Female	120	46.2	-	-	30	50.0	55	55.0
Employed[5]	80	30.8	-	-	20	33.3	30	30.0
Male	50	19.2	-	-	-	-	15	15.0
Female	30	11.5	-	-	15	25.0	10	10.0
Unemployed[6]	85	32.7	-	-	10	16.7	20	20.0
Male	60	23.1	-	-	-	-	15	15.0
Female	30	11.5	-	-	-	-	-	-
Total in labor force[7]	170	65.4	-	-	35	58.3	45	45.0
Male	110	42.3	-	-	15	25.0	30	30.0
Female	60	23.1	-	-	25	41.7	15	15.0
Not in labor force[8]	85	32.7	-	-	30	50.0	50	50.0
Male	25	9.6	-	-	15	25.0	15	15.0
Female	60	23.1	-	-	-	-	40	40.0
Unemployment rate[9]	NA	50.0	NA	-	NA	29.0	NA	44.4
Male	NA	55.0	NA	-	NA	-	NA	50.0
Female	NA	50.0	NA	-	NA	-	NA	-
Participation rate[10]	NA	65.0	NA	-	NA	58.0	NA	45.0
Male	NA	81.0	NA	-	NA	60.0	NA	66.6
Female	NA	50.0	NA	-	NA	83.0	NA	27.2

Source: Aboriginal Peoples Output Program, 1986 Census, Statistics Canada, *A Data Book on Canada's Aboriginal Population from the 1986 Census of Canada,* March, 1989, p. 112. Primary source: 1986 Census of Canada. *Notes:* (NA) stands for not applicable. A dash (-) represents zero or a percentage less than .05 percent. 1. Aboriginal origins are derived from the ethnic origin question which asks whether respondents are North American Indian, Metis or Inuit. 2. All 1986 figures exclude the population estimated at about 45,000 on 136 incompletely enumerated Indian reserves and settlements throughout Canada. 3. Non-aboriginal in these columns—refers to persons who reported one or more non-aboriginal origins such as British, French, etc., in combination with one of the aboriginal origins such as North American Indian. 4. Other Multiple Aboriginal origins—refer to the sum of those persons reporting two or more aboriginal origins with or without a non-aboriginal origin. 5. Employed—refers to persons 15 years of age and over who, during the week prior to June 3, 1986: (a) did any work at all excluding housework or other maintenance or repairs around the home and volunteer work; or (b) were absent from their job or business because of own temporary illnessor disability, vacation, labor dispute at their place of work, or were absent for other reasons. 6. Unemployed—refers to persons 15 years of age and over who, during the week prior to enumeration: (a) were without work, had actively looked for work in the past four weeks and were available for work; or (b) had been on lay-off and expected to return to their job; or (c) had definite arrangements to start a new job in four weeks or less. 7. Total in Labor Force (in reference week)—refers to persons 15 years of age and over who either employed or unemployed during the week prior to enumeration (June 3, 1986). 8. Not in labor force—refers to those persons 15 years of age and over who, in the week prior to enumeration, were unwilling or unable to offer or supply their labor services under conditions existing in the labor market. It includes persons who looked for work during the last four weeks bwho were not available to work in the reference week, as well as persons who did not work, did nothave a new job to start in four weeks or less, were not on temporary layoff or did not look for woin the four weeks prior to enumeration. 9. Unemployment rate—refers to the unemployed labor force expressed as a percentage of the total labor force (in reference week) in an area, group, or category. 10. Participation rate—refers to the total labor force (in reference week) expressed as a percentage of the total population 15 years of age and over, excluding institutional residents, inan area, group, or category.

★ 922 ★

Population 15 Years and Over by Labor Force Activity and Sex for Detailed Aboriginal Origins for Newfoundland, 1986 - I[1,2]

Labor force activity	Total Aboriginal origins[3]		North American Indian only		North American Indian non-Aboriginal[4]		Metis only	
	Number	Percent	Number	Percent	Number	Percent	Number	Percent
Total population								
aged 15+	6,160	100.0	1,055	100.0	1,730	100.0	215	100.0
Male	3,145	51.1	495	46.9	875	50.6	110	51.2
Female	3,015	48.9	565	53.6	855	49.4	110	51.2
Employed[5]	2,245	36.4	310	29.4	790	45.7	75	34.9
Male	1,285	20.9	175	16.6	445	25.7	55	25.6
Female	960	15.6	135	12.8	345	19.9	20	9.3
Unemployed[6]	1,240	20.1	180	17.1	390	22.5	55	25.6
Male	775	12.6	110	10.4	260	15.0	25	11.6
Female	470	7.6	70	6.6	135	7.8	25	11.6
Total in labor force[7]	3,485	56.6	490	46.4	1,175	67.9	125	58.1
Male	2,060	33.4	285	27.0	695	40.2	80	37.2
Female	1,425	23.1	205	19.4	475	27.5	50	23.3
Not in labor force[8]	2,670	43.3	565	53.6	550	31.8	90	41.9
Male	1,080	17.5	215	20.4	175	10.1	30	14.0
Female	1,585	25.7	355	33.6	375	21.7	55	25.6
Unemployment rate[9]	NA	36.0	NA	37.0	NA	33.0	NA	44.0
Male	NA	38.0	NA	39.0	NA	37.0	NA	31.0
Female	NA	33.0	NA	34.0	NA	28.0	NA	50.0
Participation rate[10]	NA	57.0	NA	46.0	NA	68.0	NA	58.0
Male	NA	66.0	NA	58.0	NA	79.0	NA	73.0
Female	NA	47.0	NA	36.0	NA	56.0	NA	45.0

Source: Aboriginal Peoples Output Program, 1986 Census, Statistics Canada, *A Data Book on Canada's Aboriginal Population from the 1986 Census of Canada*, March, 1989, p. 40. Primary source: 1986 Census of Canada. *Notes:* (NA) stands for not applicable. A dash (-) represents zero or a percentage less than .05 percent. 1. Aboriginal origins are derived from the ethnic origin question which asks whether respondents are North American Indian, Metis or Inuit. 2. All 1986 figures exclude the population estimated at about 45,000 on 136 incompletely enumerated Indian reserves and settlements throughout Canada. 3. Total Aboriginals—are the sum of persons who reported: (a) a single aboriginal (e.g., North American Indian, Metis, or Inuit) and (b) multiple aboriginal origins, that is those who reported:at least one aboriginal origin with any other non-aboriginal origin (e.g. Metis and French) or twoor more aboriginal origins only. 4. Non-aboriginal in these columns—refers to persons who reported one or more non-aboriginal origins such as British, French, etc., in combination with one of the aboriginal origins such as North American Indian. 5. Employed—refers to persons 15 years of age and over who, during the week prior to June 3, 1986: (a) did any work at all excluding housework or other maintenance or repairs around the home and volunteer work; or (b) were absent from their job or business because of own temporary illnessor disability, vacation, labor dispute at their place of work, or were absent for other reasons. 6. Unemployed—refers to persons 15 years of age and over who, during the week prior to enumeration: (a) were without work, had actively looked for work in the past four weeks and were available for work; or (b) had been on lay-off and expected to return to their job; or (c) had definite arrangements to start a new job in four weeks or less. 7. Total in Labor Force (in reference week)—refers to persons 15 years of age and over who either employed or unemployed during the week prior to enumeration (June 3, 1986). 8. Nor in labor force—refers to those persons 15 years of age and over who, in the week prior to enumeration, were unwilling or unable to offer or supply their labor services under conditions existing in the labor market. It includes persons who looked for work during the last four weeks bwho were not available to work in the reference week, as well as persons who did not work, did nothave a new job to start in four weeks or less, were not on temporary layoff or did not look for woin the four weeks prior to enumeration. 9. Unemployment rate—refers to the unemployed labor force expressed as a percentage of the total labor force (in reference week) in an area, group, or category. 10. Participation rate—refers to the total labor force (in reference week) expressed as a percentage of the total population 15 years of age and over, excluding institutional residents, inan area, group, or category.

★ 923 ★

Population 15 Years and Over by Labor Force Activity and Sex for Detailed Aboriginal Origins for Newfoundland, 1986 - II[1,2]

Labor force activity	Metis and non-Aboriginal[3]		Inuit only		Inuit and non-Aboriginal[3]		Other multiple Aboriginal origins[4]	
	Number	Percent	Number	Percent	Number	Percent	Number	Percent
Total population aged 15+	515	100.0	1,170	100.0	1,075	100.0	395	100.0
Male	285	55.3	595	50.9	545	50.7	235	59.5
Female	230	44.7	575	49.1	530	49.3	150	38.0
Employed[5]	160	31.1	330	28.2	410	38.1	160	40.5
Male	105	20.4	160	13.7	225	20.9	120	30.4
Female	55	10.7	175	15.0	185	17.2	45	11.4
Unemployed[6]	85	16.5	215	18.4	235	21.9	75	19.0
Male	50	9.7	135	11.5	150	14.0	35	8.9
Female	30	5.8	80	6.8	85	7.9	35	8.9
Total in labor force[7]	245	47.6	550	47.0	645	60.0	245	62.0
Male	160	31.1	295	25.2	375	34.9	155	39.2
Female	90	17.5	255	21.8	270	25.1	80	20.3
Not in labor force[8]	265	51.5	625	53.4	430	40.0	145	36.7
Male	125	24.3	300	25.6	170	15.8	70	17.7
Female	140	27.2	325	27.8	260	24.2	70	17.7
Unemployment rate[9]	NA	35.0	NA	39.0	NA	36.0	NA	30.6
Male	NA	31.0	NA	46.0	NA	40.0	NA	22.5
Female	NA	33.0	NA	31.0	NA	31.0	NA	43.7
Participation rate[10]	NA	48.0	NA	47.0	NA	60.0	NA	62.0
Male	NA	56.0	NA	50.0	NA	69.0	NA	65.9
Female	NA	39.0	NA	44.0	NA	51.0	NA	53.3

Source: Aboriginal Peoples Output Program, 1986 Census, Statistics Canada, *A Data Book on Canada's Aboriginal Population from the 1986 Census of Canada*, March, 1989, p. 40. Primary source: 1986 Census of Canada. *Notes:* (NA) stands for not applicable. A dash (-) represents zero or a percentage less than .05 percent. 1. Aboriginal origins are derived from the ethnic origin question which asks whether respondents are North American Indian, Metis or Inuit. 2. All 1986 figures exclude the population estimated at about 45,000 on 136 incompletely enumerated Indian reserves and settlements throughout Canada. 3. Non-aboriginal in these columns—refers to persons who reported one or more non-aboriginal origins such as British, French, etc., in combination with one of the aboriginal origins such as North American Indian. 4. Other Multiple Aboriginal origins—refer to the sum of those persons reporting two or more aboriginal origins with or without a non-aboriginal origin. 5. Employed—refers to persons 15 years of age and over who, during the week prior to June 3, 1986: (a) did any work at all excluding housework or other maintenance or repairs around the home and volunteer work; or (b) were absent from their job or business because of own temporary illnessor disability, vacation, labor dispute at their place of work, or were absent for other reasons. 6. Unemployed—refers to persons 15 years of age and over who, during the week prior to enumeration: (a) were without work, had actively looked for work in the past four weeks and were available for work; or (b) had been on lay-off and expected to return to their job; or (c) had definite arrangements to start a new job in four weeks or less. 7. Total in Labor Force (in reference week)—refers to persons 15 years of age and over who either employed or unemployed during the week prior to enumeration (June 3, 1986). 8. Not in labor force—refers to those persons 15 years of age and over who, in the week prior to enumeration, were unwilling or unable to offer or supply their labor services under conditions existing in the labor market. It includes persons who looked for work during the last four weeks bwho were not available to work in the reference week, as well as persons who did not work, did nothave a new job to start in four weeks or less, were not on temporary layoff or did not look for woin the four weeks prior to enumeration. 9. Unemployment rate—refers to the unemployed labor force expressed as a percentage of the total labor force (in reference week) in an area, group, or category. 10. Participation rate—refers to the total labor force (in reference week) expressed as a percentage of the total population 15 years of age and over, excluding institutional residents, inan area, group, or category.

★ 924 ★

Population 15 Years and Over by Labor Force Activity and Sex for Detailed Aboriginal Origins for Northwest Territories, 1986 - I[1,2]

Labor force activity	Total Aboriginal origins[3]		North American Indian only		North American Indian non-Aboriginal[4]		Metis only	
	Number	Percent	Number	Percent	Number	Percent	Number	Percent
Total population aged 15+	18,675	100.0	5,070	100.0	530	100.0	1,425	100.0
Male	9,570	51.2	2,595	51.2	320	60.4	740	51.9
Female	9,110	48.8	2,475	48.8	210	39.6	685	48.1
Employed[5]	7,500	40.2	1,755	34.6	360	67.9	750	52.6
Male	4,155	22.2	925	18.2	230	43.4	415	29.1
Female	3,350	17.9	830	16.4	135	25.5	335	23.5
Unemployed[6]	2,695	14.4	660	13.0	45	8.5	190	13.3
Male	1,710	9.2	460	9.1	30	5.7	120	8.4
Female	990	5.3	205	4.0	15	2.8	70	4.9
Total in labor force[7]	10,205	54.6	2,420	47.7	405	76.4	935	65.6
Male	5,865	31.4	1,385	27.3	260	49.1	530	37.2
Female	4,335	23.2	1,035	20.4	150	28.3	405	28.4
Not in labor force[8]	8,475	45.4	2,655	52.4	120	22.6	490	34.4
Male	3,705	19.8	1,210	23.9	60	11.3	210	14.7
Female	4,770	25.5	1,440	28.4	65	12.3	280	19.6
Unemployment rate[9]	NA	26.0	NA	27.0	NA	11.0	NA	20.0
Male	NA	29.0	NA	33.0	NA	12.0	NA	23.0
Female	NA	23.0	NA	20.0	NA	10.0	NA	17.0
Participation rate[10]	NA	55.0	NA	48.0	NA	76.0	NA	66.0
Male	NA	61.0	NA	53.0	NA	81.0	NA	72.0
Female	NA	48.0	NA	42.0	NA	71.0	NA	59.0

Source: Aboriginal Peoples Output Program, 1986 Census, Statistics Canada, *A Data Book on Canada's Aboriginal Population from the 1986 Census of Canada,* March, 1989, p. 280. Primary source: 1986 Census of Canada. *Notes:* (NA) stands for not applicable. A dash (-) represents zero or a percentage less than .05 percent. 1. Aboriginal origins are derived from the ethnic origin question which asks whether respondents are North American Indian, Metis or Inuit. 2. All 1986 figures exclude the population estimated at about 45,000 on 136 incompletely enumerated Indian reserves and settlements throughout Canada. 3. Total Aboriginals—are the sum of persons who reported: (a) a single aboriginal (e.g., North American Indian, Metis, or Inuit) and (b) multiple aboriginal origins, that is those who reported at least one aboriginal origin with any other non-aboriginal origin (e.g. Metis and French) or twoor more aboriginal origins only. 4. Non-aboriginal in these columns—refers to persons who reported one or more non-aboriginal origins such as British, French, etc., in combination with one of the aboriginal origins such as North American Indian. 5. Employed—refers to persons 15 years of age and over who, during the week prior to June 3, 1986: (a) did any work at all excluding housework or other maintenance or repairs around the home and volunteer work; or (b) were absent from their job or business because of own temporary illnessor disability, vacation, labor dispute at their place of work, or were absent for other reasons. 6. Unemployed—refers to persons 15 years of age and over who, during the week prior to enumeration: (a) were without work, had actively looked for work in the past four weeks and were available for work; or (b) had been on lay-off and expected to return to their job; or (c) had definite arrangements to start a new job in four weeks or less. 7. Total in Labor Force (in reference week)—refers to persons 15 years of age and over who either employed or unemployed during the week prior to enumeration (June 3, 1986). 8. Nor in labor force—refers to those persons 15 years of age and over who, in the week prior to enumeration, were unwilling or unable to offer or supply their labor services under conditions existing in the labor market. It includes persons who looked for work during the last four weeks bwho were not available to work in the reference week, as well as persons who did not work, did nothave a new job to start in four weeks or less, were not on temporary layoff or did not look for woin the four weeks prior to enumeration. 9. Unemployment rate—refers to the unemployed labor force expressed as a percentage of the total labor force (in reference week) in an area, group, or category. 10. Participation rate—refers to the total labor force (in reference week) expressed as a percentage of the total population 15 years of age and over, excluding institutional residents, inan area, group, or category.

★ 925 ★

Population 15 Years and Over by Labor Force Activity and Sex for Detailed Aboriginal Origins for Northwest Territories, 1986 - II[1,2]

Labor force activity	Metis and non-Aboriginal[3]		Inuit only		Inuit and non-Aboriginal[3]		Other multiple Aboriginal origins[4]	
	Number	Percent	Number	Percent	Number	Percent	Number	Percent
Total population aged 15+	460	100.0	10,325	100.0	285	100.0	585	100.0
Male	250	54.3	5,190	50.3	155	54.4	325	55.6
Female	210	45.7	5,130	49.7	130	45.6	265	45.3
Employed[5]	290	63.0	3,860	37.4	135	47.4	360	61.5
Male	145	31.5	2,170	21.0	80	28.1	190	32.5
Female	145	31.5	1,690	16.4	55	19.3	155	26.5
Unemployed[6]	55	12.0	1,620	15.7	40	14.0	90	15.4
Male	40	8.7	990	9.6	25	8.8	40	6.8
Female	-	-	630	6.1	20	7.0	45	7.7
Total in labor force[7]	345	75.0	5,485	53.1	175	61.4	440	75.2
Male	190	41.3	3,160	30.6	105	36.8	240	41.0
Female	155	33.7	2,325	22.5	70	24.6	195	33.3
Not in labor force[8]	115	25.0	4,835	46.8	110	38.6	150	25.6
Male	65	14.1	2,030	18.7	50	17.5	85	14.5
Female	50	10.9	2,810	27.2	55	19.3	65	11.1
Unemployment rate[9]	NA	16.0	NA	30.0	NA	23.0	NA	20.4
Male	NA	21.0	NA	31.0	NA	24.0	NA	16.6
Female	NA	-	NA	27.0	NA	29.0	NA	23.0
Participation rate[10]	NA	75.0	NA	53.0	NA	61.0	NA	75.2
Male	NA	76.0	NA	61.0	NA	68.0	NA	73.8
Female	NA	74.0	NA	45.0	NA	54.0	NA	73.5

Source: Aboriginal Peoples Output Program, 1986 Census, Statistics Canada, *A Data Book on Canada's Aboriginal Population from the 1986 Census of Canada*, March, 1989, p. 280. Primary source: 1986 Census of Canada. *Notes:* (NA) stands for not applicable. A dash (-) represents zero or a percentage less than .05 percent. 1. Aboriginal origins are derived from the ethnic origin question which asks whether respondents are North American Indian, Metis or Inuit. 2. All 1986 figures exclude the population estimated at about 45,000 on 136 incompletely enumerated Indian reserves and settlements throughout Canada. 3. Non-aboriginal in these columns—refers to persons who reported one or more non-aboriginal origins such as British, French, etc., in combination with one of the aboriginal origins such as North American Indian. 4. Other Multiple Aboriginal origins—refer to the sum of those persons reporting two or more aboriginal origins with or without a non-aboriginal origin. 5. Employed—refers to persons 15 years of age and over who, during the week prior to June 3, 1986: (a) did any work at all excluding housework or other maintenance or repairs around the home and volunteer work; or (b) were absent from their job or business because of own temporary illnessor disability, vacation, labor dispute at their place of work, or were absent for other reasons. 6. Unemployed—refers to persons 15 years of age and over who, during the week prior to enumeration: (a) were without work, had actively looked for work in the past four weeks and were available for work; or (b) had been on lay-off and expected to return to their job; or (c) had definite arrangements to start a new job in four weeks or less. 7. Total in Labor Force (in reference week)—refers to persons 15 years of age and over who either employed or unemployed during the week prior to enumeration (June 3, 1986). 8. Not in labor force—refers to those persons 15 years of age and over who, in the week prior to enumeration, were unwilling or unable to offer or supply their labor services under conditions existing in the labor market. It includes persons who looked for work during the last four weeks bwho were not available to work in the reference week, as well as persons who did not work, did nothave a new job to start in four weeks or less, were not on temporary layoff or did not look for woin the four weeks prior to enumeration. 9. Unemployment rate—refers to the unemployed labor force expressed as a percentage of the total labor force (in reference week) in an area, group, or category. 10. Participation rate—refers to the total labor force (in reference week) expressed as a percentage of the total population 15 years of age and over, excluding institutional residents, inan area, group, or category.

★ 926 ★

Population 15 Years and Over by Labor Force Activity and Sex for Detailed Aboriginal Origins for Nova Scotia, 1986 - I[1,2]

Labor force activity	Total Aboriginal origins[3]		North American Indian only		North American Indian non-Aboriginal[4]		Metis only	
	Number	Percent	Number	Percent	Number	Percent	Number	Percent
Total population								
aged 15+	9,260	100.0	3,665	100.0	4,595	100.0	185	100.0
Male	4,440	47.9	1,840	50.2	2,145	46.7	85	45.9
Female	4,820	52.1	1,825	49.8	2,445	53.2	95	51.4
Employed[5]	4,370	47.2	1,040	28.4	2,810	61.2	75	40.5
Male	2,435	26.3	540	14.7	1,615	35.1	45	24.3
Female	1,940	21.0	505	13.8	1,200	26.1	35	18.9
Unemployed[6]	1,070	11.6	445	12.1	465	10.1	25	13.5
Male	570	6.2	285	7.8	205	4.5	25	13.5
Female	505	5.5	165	4.5	260	5.7	-	-
Total in labor force[7]	5,450	58.9	1,490	40.7	3,275	71.3	105	56.8
Male	3,005	32.5	820	22.4	1,815	39.5	60	32.4
Female	2,440	26.3	665	18.1	1,460	31.8	40	21.6
Not in labor force[8]	3,815	41.2	2,175	59.3	1,315	28.6	80	43.2
Male	1,435	15.5	1,015	27.7	335	7.3	25	13.5
Female	2,375	25.6	1,160	31.7	980	21.3	55	29.7
Unemployment rate[9]	NA	20.0	NA	30.0	NA	14.0	NA	24.0
Male	NA	19.0	NA	35.0	NA	11.0	NA	42.0
Female	NA	21.0	NA	25.0	NA	18.0	NA	-
Participation rate[10]	NA	59.0	NA	41.0	NA	71.0	NA	57.0
Male	NA	68.0	NA	45.0	NA	85.0	NA	71.0
Female	NA	51.0	NA	36.0	NA	60.0	NA	42.0

Source: Aboriginal Peoples Output Program, 1986 Census, Statistics Canada, *A Data Book on Canada's Aboriginal Population from the 1986 Census of Canada*, March, 1989, p. 88. Primary source: 1986 Census of Canada. *Notes:* (NA) stands for not applicable. A dash (-) represents zero or a percentage less than .05 percent. 1. Aboriginal origins are derived from the ethnic origin question which asks whether respondents are North American Indian, Metis or Inuit. 2. All 1986 figures exclude the population estimated at about 45,000 on 136 incompletely enumerated Indian reserves and settlements throughout Canada. 3. Total Aboriginals—are the sum of persons who reported: (a) a single aboriginal (e.g., North American Indian, Metis, or Inuit) and (b) multiple aboriginal origins, that is those who reported:at least one aboriginal origin with any other non-aboriginal origin (e.g. Metis and French) or twoor more aboriginal origins only. 4. Non-aboriginal in these columns—refers to persons who reported one or more non-aboriginal origins such as British, French, etc., in combination with one of the aboriginal origins such as North American Indian. 5. Employed—refers to persons 15 years of age and over who, during the week prior to June 3, 1986: (a) did any work at all excluding housework or other maintenance or repairs around the home and volunteer work; or (b) were absent from their job or business because of own temporary illnessor disability, vacation, labor dispute at their place of work, or were absent for other reasons. 6. Unemployed—refers to persons 15 years of age and over who, during the week prior to enumeration: (a) were without work, had actively looked for work in the past four weeks and were available for work; or (b) had been on lay-off and expected to return to their job; or (c) had definite arrangements to start a new job in four weeks or less. 7. Total in Labor Force (in reference week)—refers to persons 15 years of age and over who either employed or unemployed during the week prior to enumeration (June 3, 1986). 8. Nor in labor force—refers to those persons 15 years of age and over who, in the week prior to enumeration, were unwilling or unable to offer or supply their labor services under conditions existing in the labor market. It includes persons who looked for work during the last four weeks bwho were not available to work in the reference week, as well as persons who did not work, did nothave a new job to start in four weeks or less, were not on temporary layoff or did not look for woin the four weeks prior to enumeration. 9. Unemployment rate—refers to the unemployed labor force expressed as a percentage of the total labor force (in reference week) in an area, group, or category. 10. Participation rate—refers to the total labor force (in reference week) expressed as a percentage of the total population 15 years of age and over, excluding institutional residents, inan area, group, or category.

★ 927 ★

Population 15 Years and Over by Labor Force Activity and Sex for Detailed Aboriginal Origins for Nova Scotia, 1986 - II[1,2]

Labor force activity	Metis and non-Aboriginal[3]		Inuit only		Inuit and non-Aboriginal[3]		Other multiple Aboriginal origins[4]	
	Number	Percent	Number	Percent	Number	Percent	Number	Percent
Total population aged 15+	455	100.0	85	100.0	110	100.0	170	100.0
Male	185	40.7	35	41.2	45	40.9	100	58.8
Female	275	60.4	45	52.9	70	63.6	60	35.3
Employed[5]	220	48.4	35	41.2	75	68.2	115	67.6
Male	105	23.1	25	29.4	30	27.3	80	47.1
Female	120	26.4	-	-	45	40.9	25	14.7
Unemployed[6]	80	17.6	15	17.6	-	-	25	14.7
Male	40	8.8	-	-	-	-	-	-
Female	45	9.9	15	17.6	-	-	15	8.8
Total in labor force[7]	305	67.0	50	58.8	85	77.3	140	82.4
Male	140	30.8	30	35.3	35	31.8	90	52.9
Female	160	35.2	20	23.5	45	40.9	50	29.4
Not in labor force[8]	150	33.0	30	35.3	30	27.3	20	11.8
Male	40	8.8	-	-	-	-	-	-
Female	110	24.2	25	29.4	25	22.7	-	-
Unemployment rate[9]	NA	26.0	NA	30.0	NA	-	NA	17.8
Male	NA	29.0	NA	-	NA	-	NA	-
Female	NA	28.0	NA	75.0	NA	-	NA	30.0
Participation rate[10]	NA	67.0	NA	59.0	NA	77.0	NA	82.3
Male	NA	76.0	NA	86.0	NA	78.0	NA	90.0
Female	NA	58.0	NA	44.0	NA	64.0	NA	83.3

Source: Aboriginal Peoples Output Program, 1986 Census, Statistics Canada, *A Data Book on Canada's Aboriginal Population from the 1986 Census of Canada,* March, 1989, p. 88. Primary source: 1986 Census of Canada. *Notes:* (NA) stands for not applicable. A dash (-) represents zero or a percentage less than .05 percent. 1. Aboriginal origins are derived from the ethnic origin question which asks whether respondents are North American Indian, Metis or Inuit. 2. All 1986 figures exclude the population estimated at about 45,000 on 136 incompletely enumerated Indian reserves and settlements throughout Canada. 3. Non-aboriginal in these columns—refers to persons who reported one or more non-aboriginal origins such as British, French, etc., in combination with one of the aboriginal origins such as North American Indian. 4. Other Multiple Aboriginal origins—refer to the sum of those persons reporting two or more aboriginal origins with or without a non-aboriginal origin. 5. Employed—refers to persons 15 years of age and over who, during the week prior to June 3, 1986: (a) did any work at all excluding housework or other maintenance or repairs around the home and volunteer work; or (b) were absent from their job or business because of own temporary illnessor disability, vacation, labor dispute at their place of work, or were absent for other reasons. 6. Unemployed—refers to persons 15 years of age and over who, during the week prior to enumeration: (a) were without work, had actively looked for work in the past four weeks and were available for work; or (b) had been on lay-off and expected to return to their job; or (c) had definite arrangements to start a new job in four weeks or less. 7. Total in Labor Force (in reference week)—refers to persons 15 years of age and over who either employed or unemployed during the week prior to enumeration (June 3, 1986). 8. Not in labor force—refers to those persons 15 years of age and over who, in the week prior to enumeration, were unwilling or unable to offer or supply their labor services under conditions existing in the labor market. It includes persons who looked for work during the last four weeks bwho were not available to work in the reference week, as well as persons who did not work, did nothave a new job to start in four weeks or less, were not on temporary layoff or did not look for woin the four weeks prior to enumeration. 9. Unemployment rate—refers to the unemployed labor force expressed as a percentage of the total labor force (in reference week) in an area, group, or category. 10. Participation rate—refers to the total labor force (in reference week) expressed as a percentage of the total population 15 years of age and over, excluding institutional residents, inan area, group, or category.

★ 928 ★

Population 15 Years and Over by Labor Force Activity and Sex for Detailed Aboriginal Origins for Ontario, 1986 - I[1,2]

Labor force activity	Total Aboriginal origins[3]		North American Indian only		North American Indian non-Aboriginal[4]		Metis only	
	Number	Percent	Number	Percent	Number	Percent	Number	Percent
Total population aged 15+	109,540	100.0	35,380	100.0	60,760	100.0	2,645	100.0
Male	51,450	47.0	16,725	47.3	28,345	46.7	1,305	49.3
Female	58,085	53.0	18,650	52.7	32,415	53.3	1,340	50.7
Employed[5]	64,355	58.8	15,410	43.6	40,895	67.3	1,370	51.8
Male	34,865	31.8	8,675	24.5	21,700	35.7	800	30.2
Female	29,490	26.9	6,730	19.0	19,195	31.6	570	21.6
Unemployed[6]	10,600	9.7	4,145	11.7	5,195	8.6	285	10.8
Male	5,330	4.9	2,385	6.7	2,385	3.9	175	6.6
Female	5,275	4.8	1,765	5.0	2,810	4.6	105	4.0
Total in labor force[7]	74,955	68.4	19,555	55.3	46,090	75.9	1,655	62.6
Male	40,195	36.7	11,060	31.3	24,085	39.6	975	36.9
Female	34,760	31.7	8,495	24.0	22,005	36.2	680	25.7
Not in labor force[8]	34,585	31.6	15,825	44.7	14,675	24.2	995	37.6
Male	11,260	10.3	5,665	16.0	4,260	7.0	330	12.5
Female	23,320	21.3	10,160	28.7	10,410	17.1	660	25.0
Unemployment rate[9]	NA	14.0	NA	21.0	NA	11.0	NA	17.0
Male	NA	13.0	NA	22.0	NA	10.0	NA	18.0
Female	NA	15.0	NA	21.0	NA	13.0	NA	15.0
Participation rate[10]	NA	68.0	NA	55.0	NA	76.0	NA	63.0
Male	NA	78.0	NA	66.0	NA	85.0	NA	75.0
Female	NA	60.0	NA	46.0	NA	68.0	NA	51.0

Source: Aboriginal Peoples Output Program, 1986 Census, Statistics Canada, *A Data Book on Canada's Aboriginal Population from the 1986 Census of Canada,* March, 1989, p. 160. Primary source: 1986 Census of Canada. *Notes:* (NA) stands for not applicable. A dash (-) represents zero or a percentage less than .05 percent. 1. Aboriginal origins are derived from the ethnic origin question which asks whether respondents are North American Indian, Metis or Inuit. 2. All 1986 figures exclude the population estimated at about 45,000 on 136 incompletely enumerated Indian reserves and settlements throughout Canada. 3. Total Aboriginals—are the sum of persons who reported: (a) a single aboriginal (e.g., North American Indian, Metis, or Inuit) and (b) multiple aboriginal origins, that is those who reported:at least one aboriginal origin with any other non-aboriginal origin (e.g. Metis and French) or twoor more aboriginal origins only. 4. Non-aboriginal in these columns—refers to persons who reported one or more non-aboriginal origins such as British, French, etc., in combination with one of the aboriginal origins such as North American Indian. 5. Employed—refers to persons 15 years of age and over who, during the week prior to June 3, 1986: (a) did any work at all excluding housework or other maintenance or repairs around the home and volunteer work; or (b) were absent from their job or business because of own temporary illnessor disability, vacation, labor dispute at their place of work, or were absent for other reasons. 6. Unemployed—refers to persons 15 years of age and over who, during the week prior to enumeration: (a) were without work, had actively looked for work in the past four weeks and were available for work; or (b) had been on lay-off and expected to return to their job; or (c) had definite arrangements to start a new job in four weeks or less. 7. Total in Labor Force (in reference week)—refers to persons 15 years of age and over who either employed or unemployed during the week prior to enumeration (June 3, 1986). 8. Nor in labor force—refers to those persons 15 years of age and over who, in the week prior to enumeration, were unwilling or unable to offer or supply their labor services under conditions existing in the labor market. It includes persons who looked for work during the last four weeks bwho were not available to work in the reference week, as well as persons who did not work, did nothave a new job to start in four weeks or less, were not on temporary layoff or did not look for woin the four weeks prior to enumeration. 9. Unemployment rate—refers to the unemployed labor force expressed as a percentage of the total labor force (in reference week) in an area, group, or category. 10. Participation rate—refers to the total labor force (in reference week) expressed as a percentage of the total population 15 years of age and over, excluding institutional residents, inan area, group, or category.

★ 929 ★

Population 15 Years and Over by Labor Force Activity and Sex for Detailed Aboriginal Origins for Ontario, 1986 - II[1,2]

Labor force activity	Metis and non-Aboriginal[3]		Inuit only		Inuit and non-Aboriginal[3]		Other multiple Aboriginal origins[4]	
	Number	Percent	Number	Percent	Number	Percent	Number	Percent
Total population aged 15+	6,780	100.0	485	100.0	950	100.0	2,540	100.0
Male	3,085	45.5	235	48.5	500	52.6	1,260	49.6
Female	3,690	54.4	250	51.5	450	47.4	1,285	50.6
Employed[5]	4,205	62.0	245	50.0	625	65.8	1,610	63.4
Male	2,230	32.9	150	30.9	370	38.9	940	37.0
Female	1,970	29.1	95	19.6	255	26.8	670	26.4
Unemployed[6]	610	9.0	40	8.2	85	8.9	240	9.4
Male	205	3.0	25	5.2	40	4.2	115	4.5
Female	400	5.9	20	4.1	50	5.3	125	4.9
Total in labor force[7]	4,810	70.9	285	58.8	710	74.7	1,845	72.6
Male	2,440	36.0	175	36.1	410	43.2	1,050	41.3
Female	2,375	35.0	115	23.7	305	32.1	800	31.5
Not in labor force[8]	1,965	29.0	200	41.2	235	24.7	685	27.0
Male	650	9.6	60	12.4	95	10.0	200	7.9
Female	1,320	19.5	135	27.8	140	14.7	485	19.1
Unemployment rate[9]	NA	13.0	NA	14.0	NA	12.0	NA	13.0
Male	NA	8.0	NA	14.0	NA	10.0	NA	10.9
Female	NA	17.0	NA	17.0	NA	16.0	NA	15.6
Participation rate[10]	NA	71.0	NA	59.0	NA	75.0	NA	72.6
Male	NA	79.0	NA	74.0	NA	82.0	NA	83.3
Female	NA	64.0	NA	46.0	NA	68.0	NA	62.2

Source: Aboriginal Peoples Output Program, 1986 Census, Statistics Canada, *A Data Book on Canada's Aboriginal Population from the 1986 Census of Canada*, March, 1989, p. 160. Primary source: 1986 Census of Canada. *Notes:* (NA) stands for not applicable. A dash (-) represents zero or a percentage less than .05 percent. 1. Aboriginal origins are derived from the ethnic origin question which asks whether respondents are North American Indian, Metis or Inuit. 2. All 1986 figures exclude the population estimated at about 45,000 on 136 incompletely enumerated Indian reserves and settlements throughout Canada. 3. Non-aboriginal in these columns—refers to persons who reported one or more non-aboriginal origins such as British, French, etc., in combination with one of the aboriginal origins such as North American Indian. 4. Other Multiple Aboriginal origins—refer to the sum of those persons reporting two or more aboriginal origins with or without a non-aboriginal origin. 5. Employed—refers to persons 15 years of age and over who, during the week prior to June 3, 1986: (a) did any work at all excluding housework or other maintenance or repairs around the home and volunteer work; or (b) were absent from their job or business because of own temporary illnessor disability, vacation, labor dispute at their place of work, or were absent for other reasons. 6. Unemployed—refers to persons 15 years of age and over who, during the week prior to enumeration: (a) were without work, had actively looked for work in the past four weeks and were available for work; or (b) had been on lay-off and expected to return to their job; or (c) had definite arrangements to start a new job in four weeks or less. 7. Total in Labor Force (in reference week)—refers to persons 15 years of age and over who either employed or unemployed during the week prior to enumeration (June 3, 1986). 8. Not in labor force—refers to those persons 15 years of age and over who, in the week prior to enumeration, were unwilling or unable to offer or supply their labor services under conditions existing in the labor market. It includes persons who looked for work during the last four weeks bwho were not available to work in the reference week, as well as persons who did not work, did nothave a new job to start in four weeks or less, were not on temporary layoff or did not look for woin the four weeks prior to enumeration. 9. Unemployment rate—refers to the unemployed labor force expressed as a percentage of the total labor force (in reference week) in an area, group, or category. 10. Participation rate—refers to the total labor force (in reference week) expressed as a percentage of the total population 15 years of age and over, excluding institutional residents, inan area, group, or category.

★ 930 ★

Population 15 Years and Over by Labor Force Activity and Sex for Detailed Aboriginal Origins for Prince Edwards Island, 1986 - I[1,2]

Labor force activity	Total Aboriginal origins[3]		North American Indian only		North American Indian non-Aboriginal[4]		Metis only	
	Number	Percent	Number	Percent	Number	Percent	Number	Percent
Total population								
Aged 15+	840	100.0	240	100.0	475	100.0	15	100.0
Male	445	53.0	125	52.1	255	53.7	-	-
Female	395	47.0	110	45.8	220	46.3	10	66.7
Employed[5]	385	45.8	80	33.3	235	49.5	10	66.7
Male	200	23.8	45	18.8	120	25.3	-	-
Female	185	22.0	40	16.7	110	23.2	10	66.7
Unemployed[6]	225	26.8	65	27.1	140	29.5	-	-
Male	140	16.7	40	16.7	90	18.9	-	-
Female	80	9.5	25	10.4	45	9.5	-	-
Total in labor force[7]	605	72.0	150	62.5	370	77.9	10	66.7
Male	340	40.5	85	35.4	215	45.3	-	-
Female	270	32.1	65	27.1	155	32.6	15	100.0
Not in labor force[8]	230	27.4	85	35.4	105	22.1	-	-
Male	105	12.5	40	16.7	35	7.4	-	-
Female	130	15.5	45	18.8	65	13.7	-	-
Unemployment rate[9]	NA	37.0	NA	43.0	NA	38.0	NA	-
Male	NA	41.0	NA	47.0	NA	42.0	NA	-
Female	NA	30.0	NA	38.0	NA	29.0	NA	-
Participation rate[10]	NA	72.0	NA	63.0	NA	78.0	NA	67.0
Male	NA	76.0	NA	68.0	NA	84.0	NA	-
Female	NA	68.0	NA	59.0	NA	70.0	NA	150.0

Source: Aboriginal Peoples Output Program, 1986 Census, Statistics Canada, *A Data Book on Canada's Aboriginal Population from the 1986 Census of Canada,* March, 1989, p. 64. Primary source: 1986 Census of Canada. *Notes:* (NA) stands for not applicable. A dash (-) represents zero or a percentage less than .05 percent. 1. Aboriginal origins are derived from the ethnic origin question which asks whether respondents are North American Indian, Metis or Inuit. 2. All 1986 figures exclude the population estimated at about 45,000 on 136 incompletely enumerated Indian reserves and settlements throughout Canada. 3. Total Aboriginals—are the sum of persons who reported: (a) a single aboriginal (e.g., North American Indian, Metis, or Inuit) and (b) multiple aboriginal origins, that is those who reported:at least one aboriginal origin with any other non-aboriginal origin (e.g. Metis and French) or twoor more aboriginal origins only. 4. Non-aboriginal in these columns—refers to persons who reported one or more non-aboriginal origins such as British, French, etc., in combination with one of the aboriginal origins such as North American Indian. 5. Employed—refers to persons 15 years of age and over who, during the week prior to June 3, 1986: (a) did any work at all excluding housework or other maintenance or repairs around the home and volunteer work; or (b) were absent from their job or business because of own temporary illnessor disability, vacation, labor dispute at their place of work, or were absent for other reasons. 6. Unemployed—refers to persons 15 years of age and over who, during the week prior to enumeration: (a) were without work, had actively looked for work in the past four weeks and were available for work; or (b) had been on lay-off and expected to return to their job; or (c) had definite arrangements to start a new job in four weeks or less. 7. Total in Labor Force (in reference week)—refers to persons 15 years of age and over who either employed or unemployed during the week prior to enumeration (June 3, 1986). 8. Nor in labor force—refers to those persons 15 years of age and over who, in the week prior to enumeration, were unwilling or unable to offer or supply their labor services under conditions existing in the labor market. It includes persons who looked for work during the last four weeks bwho were not available to work in the reference week, as well as persons who did not work, did nothave a new job to start in four weeks or less, were not on temporary layoff or did not look for woin the four weeks prior to enumeration. 9. Unemployment rate—refers to the unemployed labor force expressed as a percentage of the total labor force (in reference week) in an area, group, or category. 10. Participation rate—refers to the total labor force (in reference week) expressed as a percentage of the total population 15 years of age and over, excluding institutional residents, inan area, group, or category.

★ 931 ★

Population 15 Years and Over by Labor Force Activity and Sex for Detailed Aboriginal Origins for Prince Edward Island, 1986 - II[1,2]

Labor force activity	Metis and non-Aboriginal[3]		Inuit only		Inuit and non-Aboriginal[3]		Other multiple Aboriginal origins[4]	
	Number	Percent	Number	Percent	Number	Percent	Number	Percent
Total population								
aged 15+	70	100.0	-	-	20	100.0	20	100.0
Male	45	64.3	-	-	15	75.0	-	-
Female	25	35.7	-	-	-	-	20	100.0
Employed[5]	30	42.9	-	-	15	75.0	-	-
Male	20	28.6	-	-	15	75.0	-	-
Female	15	21.4	-	-	-	-	-	-
Unemployed[6]	15	21.4	-	-	-	-	-	-
Male	10	14.3	-	-	-	-	-	-
Female	-	-	-	-	-	-	-	-
Total in labor force[7]	45	64.3	-	-	20	100.0	-	-
Male	25	35.7	-	-	10	50.0	-	-
Female	20	28.6	-	-	-	-	-	-
Not in labor force[8]	30	42.9	-	-	-	-	10	50.0
Male	20	28.6	-	-	-	-	-	-
Female	-	-	-	-	-	-	10	50.0
Unemployment rate[9]	NA	33.0	NA	-	NA	-	NA	-
Male	NA	40.0	NA	-	NA	-	NA	-
Female	NA	-	NA	-	NA	-	NA	-
Participation rate[10]	NA	64.0	NA	-	NA	100.0	NA	-
Male	NA	56.0	NA	-	NA	67.0	NA	-
Female	NA	80.0	NA	-	NA	-	NA	-

Source: Aboriginal Peoples Output Program, 1986 Census, Statistics Canada, *A Data Book on Canada's Aboriginal Population from the 1986 Census of Canada*, March, 1989, p. 64. Primary source: 1986 Census of Canada. *Notes:* (NA) stands for not applicable. A dash (-) represents zero or a percentage less than .05 percent. 1. Aboriginal origins are derived from the ethnic origin question which asks whether respondents are North American Indian, Metis or Inuit. 2. All 1986 figures exclude the population estimated at about 45,000 on 136 incompletely enumerated Indian reserves and settlements throughout Canada. 3. Non-aboriginal in these columns—refers to persons who reported one or more non-aboriginal origins such as British, French, etc., in combination with one of the aboriginal origins such as North American Indian. 4. Other Multiple Aboriginal origins—refer to the sum of those persons reporting two or more aboriginal origins with or without a non-aboriginal origin. 5. Employed—refers to persons 15 years of age and over who, during the week prior to June 3, 1986: (a) did any work at all excluding housework or other maintenance or repairs around the home and volunteer work; or (b) were absent from their job or business because of own temporary illnessor disability, vacation, labor dispute at their place of work, or were absent for other reasons. 6. Unemployed—refers to persons 15 years of age and over who, during the week prior to enumeration: (a) were without work, had actively looked for work in the past four weeks and were available for work; or (b) had been on lay-off and expected to return to their job; or (c) had definite arrangements to start a new job in four weeks or less. 7. Total in Labor Force (in reference week)—refers to persons 15 years of age and over who either employed or unemployed during the week prior to enumeration (June 3, 1986). 8. Not in labor force—refers to those persons 15 years of age and over who, in the week prior to enumeration, were unwilling or unable to offer or supply their labor services under conditions existing in the labor market. It includes persons who looked for work during the last four weeks bwho were not available to work in the reference week, as well as persons who did not work, did nothave a new job to start in four weeks or less, were not on temporary layoff or did not look for woin the four weeks prior to enumeration. 9. Unemployment rate—refers to the unemployed labor force expressed as a percentage of the total labor force (in reference week) in an area, group, or category. 10. Participation rate—refers to the total labor force (in reference week) expressed as a percentage of the total population 15 years of age and over, excluding institutional residents, inan area, group, or category.

★ 932 ★

Population 15 Years and Over by Labor Force Activity and Sex for Detailed Aboriginal Origins for Quebec, 1986 - I[1,2]

Labor force activity	Total Aboriginal origins[3]		North American Indian only		North American Indian non-Aboriginal[4]		Metis only	
	Number	Percent	Number	Percent	Number	Percent	Number	Percent
Total population aged 15+	56,160	100.0	25,750	100.0	17,900	100.0	4,105	100.0
Male	26,620	47.4	12,565	48.8	8,010	44.7	2,060	50.2
Female	29,545	52.6	13,185	51.2	9,885	55.2	2,040	49.7
Employed[5]	26,790	47.7	10,235	39.7	10,790	60.3	1,870	45.6
Male	14,930	26.6	6,010	23.3	5,685	31.8	1,100	26.8
Female	11,860	21.1	4,220	16.4	5,105	28.5	770	18.8
Unemployed[6]	6,825	12.2	3,150	12.2	2,170	12.1	600	14.6
Male	3,770	6.7	1,945	7.6	945	5.3	405	9.9
Female	3,060	5.4	1,205	4.7	1,225	6.8	190	4.6
Total in labor force[7]	33,615	59.9	13,385	52.0	12,960	72.4	2,470	60.2
Male	18,695	33.3	7,955	30.9	6,630	37.0	1,510	36.8
Female	14,920	26.6	5,425	21.1	6,335	35.4	960	23.4
Not in labor force[8]	22,550	40.2	12,365	48.0	4,940	27.6	1,635	39.8
Male	7,925	14.1	4,605	17.9	1,385	7.7	555	13.5
Female	14,625	26.0	7,760	30.1	3,560	19.9	1,075	26.2
Unemployment rate[9]	NA	20.0	NA	24.0	NA	17.0	NA	24.0
Male	NA	20.0	NA	24.0	NA	14.0	NA	27.0
Female	NA	21.0	NA	22.0	NA	19.0	NA	20.0
Participation rate[10]	NA	60.0	NA	52.0	NA	72.0	NA	60.0
Male	NA	70.0	NA	63.0	NA	83.0	NA	73.0
Female	NA	50.0	NA	41.0	NA	64.0	NA	47.0

Source: Aboriginal Peoples Output Program, 1986 Census, Statistics Canada, *A Data Book on Canada's Aboriginal Population from the 1986 Census of Canada,* March, 1989, p. 136. Primary source: 1986 Census of Canada. *Notes:* (NA) stands for not applicable. A dash (-) represents zero or a percentage less than .05 percent. 1. Aboriginal origins are derived from the ethnic origin question which asks whether respondents are North American Indian, Metis or Inuit. 2. All 1986 figures exclude the population estimated at about 45,000 on 136 incompletely enumerated Indian reserves and settlements throughout Canada. 3. Total Aboriginals—are the sum of persons who reported: (a) a single aboriginal (e.g., North American Indian, Metis, or Inuit) and (b) multiple aboriginal origins, that is those who reported:at least one aboriginal origin with any other non-aboriginal origin (e.g. Metis and French) or twoor more aboriginal origins only. 4. Non-aboriginal in these columns—refers to persons who reported one or more non-aboriginal origins such as British, French, etc., in combination with one of the aboriginal origins such as North American Indian. 5. Employed—refers to persons 15 years of age and over who, during the week prior to June 3, 1986: (a) did any work at all excluding housework or other maintenance or repairs around the home and volunteer work; or (b) were absent from their job or business because of own temporary illnessor disability, vacation, labor dispute at their place of work, or were absent for other reasons. 6. Unemployed—refers to persons 15 years of age and over who, during the week prior to enumeration: (a) were without work, had actively looked for work in the past four weeks and were available for work; or (b) had been on lay-off and expected to return to their job; or (c) had definite arrangements to start a new job in four weeks or less. 7. Total in Labor Force (in reference week)—refers to persons 15 years of age and over who either employed or unemployed during the week prior to enumeration (June 3, 1986). 8. Nor in labor force—refers to those persons 15 years of age and over who, in the week prior to enumeration, were unwilling or unable to offer or supply their labor services under conditions existing in the labor market. It includes persons who looked for work during the last four weeks bwho were not available to work in the reference week, as well as persons who did not work, did nothave a new job to start in four weeks or less, were not on temporary layoff or did not look for woin the four weeks prior to enumeration. 9. Unemployment rate—refers to the unemployed labor force expressed as a percentage of the total labor force (in reference week) in an area, group, or category. 10. Participation rate—refers to the total labor force (in reference week) expressed as a percentage of the total population 15 years of age and over, excluding institutional residents, inan area, group, or category.

★ 933 ★

Population 15 Years and Over by Labor Force Activity and Sex for Detailed Aboriginal Origins for Quebec, 1986 - II[1,2]

Labor force activity	Metis and non-Aboriginal[3]		Inuit only		Inuit and non-Aboriginal[3]		Other multiple Aboriginal origins[4]	
	Number	Percent	Number	Percent	Number	Percent	Number	Percent
Total population aged 15+	3,250	100.0	3,900	100.0	365	100.0	890	100.0
Male	1,400	43.1	1,935	49.6	180	49.3	460	51.7
Female	1,850	56.9	1,960	50.3	185	50.7	420	47.2
Employed[5]	1,685	51.8	1,460	37.4	205	56.2	540	60.7
Male	850	26.2	845	21.7	110	30.1	325	36.5
Female	835	25.7	620	15.9	90	24.7	220	24.7
Unemployed[6]	370	11.4	375	9.6	55	15.1	110	12.4
Male	165	5.1	215	5.5	15	4.1	65	7.3
Female	205	6.3	155	4.0	40	11.0	40	4.5
Total in labor force[7]	2,060	63.4	1,835	47.1	255	69.9	655	73.6
Male	1,020	31.4	1,065	27.3	130	35.6	395	44.4
Female	1,035	31.8	770	19.7	130	35.6	255	28.7
Not in labor force[8]	1,195	36.8	2,065	52.9	110	30.1	240	27.0
Male	380	11.7	875	22.4	55	15.1	75	8.4
Female	815	25.1	1,190	30.5	55	15.1	165	18.5
Unemployment rate[9]	NA	18.0	NA	20.0	NA	22.0	NA	16.7
Male	NA	16.0	NA	20.0	NA	12.0	NA	16.4
Female	NA	20.0	NA	20.0	NA	31.0	NA	15.6
Participation rate[10]	NA	63.0	NA	47.0	NA	70.0	NA	73.5
Male	NA	73.0	NA	55.0	NA	72.0	NA	85.8
Female	NA	56.0	NA	39.0	NA	70.0	NA	60.7

Source: Aboriginal Peoples Output Program, 1986 Census, Statistics Canada, *A Data Book on Canada's Aboriginal Population from the 1986 Census of Canada*, March, 1989, p. 136. Primary source: 1986 Census of Canada. *Notes:* (NA) stands for not applicable. A dash (-) represents zero or a percentage less than .05 percent. 1. Aboriginal origins are derived from the ethnic origin question which asks whether respondents are North American Indian, Metis or Inuit. 2. All 1986 figures exclude the population estimated at about 45,000 on 136 incompletely enumerated Indian reserves and settlements throughout Canada. 3. Non-aboriginal in these columns—refers to persons who reported one or more non-aboriginal origins such as British, French, etc., in combination with one of the aboriginal origins such as North American Indian. 4. Other Multiple Aboriginal origins—refer to the sum of those persons reporting two or more aboriginal origins with or without a non-aboriginal origin. 5. Employed—refers to persons 15 years of age and over who, during the week prior to June 3, 1986: (a) did any work at all excluding housework or other maintenance or repairs around the home and volunteer work; or (b) were absent from their job or business because of own temporary illnessor disability, vacation, labor dispute at their place of work, or were absent for other reasons. 6. Unemployed—refers to persons 15 years of age and over who, during the week prior to enumeration: (a) were without work, had actively looked for work in the past four weeks and were available for work; or (b) had been on lay-off and expected to return to their job; or (c) had definite arrangements to start a new job in four weeks or less. 7. Total in Labor Force (in reference week)—refers to persons 15 years of age and over who either employed or unemployed during the week prior to enumeration (June 3, 1986). 8. Not in labor force—refers to those persons 15 years of age and over who, in the week prior to enumeration, were unwilling or unable to offer or supply their labor services under conditions existing in the labor market. It includes persons who looked for work during the last four weeks bwho were not available to work in the reference week, as well as persons who did not work, did nothave a new job to start in four weeks or less, were not on temporary layoff or did not look for woin the four weeks prior to enumeration. 9. Unemployment rate—refers to the unemployed labor force expressed as a percentage of the total labor force (in reference week) in an area, group, or category. 10. Participation rate—refers to the total labor force (in reference week) expressed as a percentage of the total population 15 years of age and over, excluding institutional residents, inan area, group, or category.

★ 934 ★

Population 15 Years and Over by Labor Force Activity and Sex for Detailed Aboriginal Origins for Saskatchewan, 1986 - I[1,2]

Labor force activity	Total Aboriginal origins[3]		North American Indian only		North American Indian non-Aboriginal[4]		Metis only	
	Number	Percent	Number	Percent	Number	Percent	Number	Percent
Total population aged 15+	44,645	100.0	24,535	100.0	4,765	100.0	7,810	100.0
Male	21,500	48.2	11,915	48.6	2,330	48.9	3,730	47.8
Female	23,145	51.8	12,620	51.4	2,435	51.1	4,080	52.2
Employed[5]	15,690	35.1	6,345	25.9	2,630	55.2	2,830	36.2
Male	9,160	20.5	3,910	15.9	1,490	31.3	1,665	21.3
Female	6,530	14.6	2,435	9.9	1,140	23.9	1,170	15.0
Unemployed[6]	6,520	14.6	3,495	14.2	610	12.8	1,340	17.2
Male	4,065	9.1	2,270	9.3	385	8.1	810	10.4
Female	2,455	5.5	1,225	5.0	225	4.7	535	6.9
Total in labor force[7]	22,205	49.7	9,840	40.1	3,240	68.0	4,175	53.5
Male	13,230	29.6	6,180	25.2	1,875	39.3	2,475	31.7
Female	8,980	20.1	3,655	14.9	1,365	28.6	1,695	21.7
Not in labor force[8]	22,435	50.3	14,700	59.9	1,525	32.0	3,635	46.5
Male	8,275	18.5	5,735	23.4	450	9.4	1,255	16.1
Female	14,165	31.7	8,965	36.5	1,075	22.6	2,385	30.5
Unemployment rate[9]	NA	29.0	NA	36.0	NA	19.0	NA	32.0
Male	NA	31.0	NA	37.0	NA	21.0	NA	33.0
Female	NA	27.0	NA	34.0	NA	16.0	NA	32.0
Participation rate[10]	NA	50.0	NA	40.0	NA	68.0	NA	63.0
Male	NA	62.0	NA	52.0	NA	80.0	NA	66.0
Female	NA	39.0	NA	29.0	NA	56.0	NA	42.0

Source: Aboriginal Peoples Output Program, 1986 Census, Statistics Canada, *A Data Book on Canada's Aboriginal Population from the 1986 Census of Canada*, March, 1989, p. 208. Primary source: 1986 Census of Canada. *Notes:* (NA) stands for not applicable. A dash (-) represents zero or a percentage less than .05 percent. 1. Aboriginal origins are derived from the ethnic origin question which asks whether respondents are North American Indian, Metis or Inuit. 2. All 1986 figures exclude the population estimated at about 45,000 on 136 incompletely enumerated Indian reserves and settlements throughout Canada. 3. Total Aboriginals—are the sum of persons who reported: (a) a single aboriginal (e.g., North American Indian, Metis, or Inuit) and (b) multiple aboriginal origins, that is those who reported:at least one aboriginal origin with any other non-aboriginal origin (e.g. Metis and French) or twoor more aboriginal origins only. 4. Non-aboriginal in these columns—refers to persons who reported one or more non-aboriginal origins such as British, French, etc., in combination with one of the aboriginal origins such as North American Indian. 5. Employed—refers to persons 15 years of age and over who, during the week prior to June 3, 1986: (a) did any work at all excluding housework or other maintenance or repairs around the home and volunteer work; or (b) were absent from their job or business because of own temporary illnessor disability, vacation, labor dispute at their place of work, or were absent for other reasons. 6. Unemployed—refers to persons 15 years of age and over who, during the week prior to enumeration: (a) were without work, had actively looked for work in the past four weeks and were available for work; or (b) had been on lay-off and expected to return to their job; or (c) had definite arrangements to start a new job in four weeks or less. 7. Total in Labor Force (in reference week)—refers to persons 15 years of age and over who either employed or unemployed during the week prior to enumeration (June 3, 1986). 8. Nor in labor force—refers to those persons 15 years of age and over who, in the week prior to enumeration, were unwilling or unable to offer or supply their labor services under conditions existing in the labor market. It includes persons who looked for work during the last four weeks bwho were not available to work in the reference week, as well as persons who did not work, did nothave a new job to start in four weeks or less, were not on temporary layoff or did not look for woin the four weeks prior to enumeration. 9. Unemployment rate—refers to the unemployed labor force expressed as a percentage of the total labor force (in reference week) in an area, group, or category. 10. Participation rate—refers to the total labor force (in reference week) expressed as a percentage of the total population 15 years of age and over, excluding institutional residents, inan area, group, or category.

★ 935 ★

Population 15 Years and Over by Labor Force Activity and Sex for Detailed Aboriginal Origins for Saskatchewan, 1986 - II[1,2]

Labor force activity	Metis and non-Aboriginal[3]		Inuit only		Inuit and non-Aboriginal[3]		Other multiple Aboriginal origins[4]	
	Number	Percent	Number	Percent	Number	Percent	Number	Percent
Total population								
aged 15+	5,680	100.0	30	100.0	50	100.0	1,770	100.0
Male	2,610	46.0	20	66.7	40	80.0	870	49.2
Female	3,075	54.1	15	50.0	15	30.0	900	50.8
Employed[5]	3,040	53.5	-	-	30	60.0	800	45.2
Male	1,585	27.9	-	-	25	50.0	480	27.1
Female	1,460	25.7	-	-	-	-	330	18.6
Unemployed[6]	765	13.5	-	-	10	20.0	285	16.1
Male	405	7.1	-	-	10	20.0	175	9.9
Female	360	6.3	-	-	-	-	115	6.5
Total in labor force[7]	3,805	67.0	15	50.0	40	80.0	1,090	61.6
Male	1,995	35.1	15	50.0	35	70.0	650	36.7
Female	1,815	32.0	-	-	-	-	445	25.1
Not in labor force[8]	1,870	32.9	15	50.0	15	30.0	680	38.4
Male	615	10.8	-	-	-	-	220	12.4
Female	1,255	22.1	15	50.0	-	-	455	25.7
Unemployment rate[9]	NA	20.0	NA	-	NA	25.0	NA	26.1
Male	NA	20.0	NA	-	NA	29.0	NA	26.9
Female	NA	20.0	NA	-	NA	-	NA	25.8
Participation rate[10]	NA	67.0	NA	50.0	NA	80.0	NA	61.5
Male	NA	76.0	NA	75.0	NA	88.0	NA	74.7
Female	NA	59.0	NA	-	NA	-	NA	49.4

Source: Aboriginal Peoples Output Program, 1986 Census, Statistics Canada, *A Data Book on Canada's Aboriginal Population from the 1986 Census of Canada*, March, 1989, p. 208. Primary source: 1986 Census of Canada. *Notes:* (NA) stands for not applicable. A dash (-) represents zero or a percentage less than .05 percent. 1. Aboriginal origins are derived from the ethnic origin question which asks whether respondents are North American Indian, Metis or Inuit. 2. All 1986 figures exclude the population estimated at about 45,000 on 136 incompletely enumerated Indian reserves and settlements throughout Canada. 3. Non-aboriginal in these columns—refers to persons who reported one or more non-aboriginal origins such as British, French, etc., in combination with one of the aboriginal origins such as North American Indian. 4. Other Multiple Aboriginal origins—refer to the sum of those persons reporting two or more aboriginal origins with or without a non-aboriginal origin. 5. Employed—refers to persons 15 years of age and over who, during the week prior to June 3, 1986: (a) did any work at all excluding housework or other maintenance or repairs around the home and volunteer work; or (b) were absent from their job or business because of own temporary illnessor disability, vacation, labor dispute at their place of work, or were absent for other reasons. 6. Unemployed—refers to persons 15 years of age and over who, during the week prior to enumeration: (a) were without work, had actively looked for work in the past four weeks and were available for work; or (b) had been on lay-off and expected to return to their job; or (c) had definite arrangements to start a new job in four weeks or less. 7. Total in Labor Force (in reference week)—refers to persons 15 years of age and over who either employed or unemployed during the week prior to enumeration (June 3, 1986). 8. Not in labor force—refers to those persons 15 years of age and over who, in the week prior to enumeration, were unwilling or unable to offer or supply their labor services under conditions existing in the labor market. It includes persons who looked for work during the last four weeks bwho were not available to work in the reference week, as well as persons who did not work, did nothave a new job to start in four weeks or less, were not on temporary layoff or did not look for woin the four weeks prior to enumeration. 9. Unemployment rate—refers to the unemployed labor force expressed as a percentage of the total labor force (in reference week) in an area, group, or category. 10. Participation rate—refers to the total labor force (in reference week) expressed as a percentage of the total population 15 years of age and over, excluding institutional residents, inan area, group, or category.

★ 936 ★

Population 15 Years and Over by Labor Force Activity and Sex for Detailed Aboriginal Origins for Yukon Territory, 1986 - I[1,2]

Labor force activity	Total Aboriginal origins[3]		North American Indian only		North American Indian non-Aboriginal[4]		Metis only	
	Number	Percent	Number	Percent	Number	Percent	Number	Percent
Total population								
aged 15+	3,400	100.0	2,325	100.0	895	100.0	45	100.0
Male	1,640	48.2	1,125	48.4	425	47.5	15	33.3
Female	1,755	51.6	1,200	51.6	470	52.5	35	77.8
Employed[5]	1,520	44.7	885	38.1	530	59.2	25	55.6
Male	720	21.2	425	18.3	245	27.4	-	-
Female	800	23.5	465	20.0	280	31.3	15	33.3
Unemployed[6]	705	20.7	510	21.9	165	18.4	15	33.3
Male	425	12.5	310	13.3	100	11.2	-	-
Female	280	8.2	200	8.6	65	7.3	10	22.2
Total in labor force[7]	2,230	65.6	1,395	60.0	690	77.1	45	100.0
Male	1,145	33.7	735	31.6	345	38.5	15	33.3
Female	1,080	31.8	665	28.6	350	39.1	30	66.7
Not in labor force[8]	1,170	34.4	930	40.0	200	22.3	-	-
Male	490	14.4	390	16.8	80	8.9	-	-
Female	680	20.0	535	23.0	120	13.4	-	-
Unemployment rate[9]	NA	32.0	NA	37.0	NA	24.0	NA	33.0
Male	NA	37.0	NA	42.0	NA	29.0	NA	-
Female	NA	26.0	NA	30.0	NA	19.0	NA	33.0
Participation rate[10]	NA	66.0	NA	60.0	NA	77.0	NA	100.0
Male	NA	70.0	NA	65.0	NA	81.0	NA	100.0
Female	NA	62.0	NA	55.0	NA	74.0	NA	86.0

Source: Aboriginal Peoples Output Program, 1986 Census, Statistics Canada, *A Data Book on Canada's Aboriginal Population from the 1986 Census of Canada,* March, 1989, p. 304. Primary source: 1986 Census of Canada. *Notes:* (NA) stands for not applicable. A dash (-) represents zero or a percentage less than .05 percent. 1. Aboriginal origins are derived from the ethnic origin question which asks whether respondents are North American Indian, Metis or Inuit. 2. All 1986 figures exclude the population estimated at about 45,000 on 136 incompletely enumerated Indian reserves and settlements throughout Canada. 3. Total Aboriginals—are the sum of persons who reported: (a) a single aboriginal (e.g., North American Indian, Metis, or Inuit) and (b) multiple aboriginal origins, that is those who reported:at least one aboriginal origin with any other non-aboriginal origin (e.g. Metis and French) or twoor more aboriginal origins only. 4. Non-aboriginal in these columns—refers to persons who reported one or more non-aboriginal origins such as British, French, etc., in combination with one of the aboriginal origins such as North American Indian. 5. Employed—refers to persons 15 years of age and over who, during the week prior to June 3, 1986: (a) did any work at all excluding housework or other maintenance or repairs around the home and volunteer work; or (b) were absent from their job or business because of own temporary illnessor disability, vacation, labor dispute at their place of work, or were absent for other reasons. 6. Unemployed—refers to persons 15 years of age and over who, during the week prior to enumeration: (a) were without work, had actively looked for work in the past four weeks and were available for work; or (b) had been on lay-off and expected to return to their job; or (c) had definite arrangements to start a new job in four weeks or less. 7. Total in Labor Force (in reference week)—refers to persons 15 years of age and over who either employed or unemployed during the week prior to enumeration (June 3, 1986). 8. Nor in labor force—refers to those persons 15 years of age and over who, in the week prior to enumeration, were unwilling or unable to offer or supply their labor services under conditions existing in the labor market. It includes persons who looked for work during the last four weeks bwho were not available to work in the reference week, as well as persons who did not work, did nothave a new job to start in four weeks or less, were not on temporary layoff or did not look for woin the four weeks prior to enumeration. 9. Unemployment rate—refers to the unemployed labor force expressed as a percentage of the total labor force (in reference week) in an area, group, or category. 10. Participation rate—refers to the total labor force (in reference week) expressed as a percentage of the total population 15 years of age and over, excluding institutional residents, inan area, group, or category.

★ 937 ★

Population 15 Years and Over by Labor Force Activity and Sex for Detailed Aboriginal Origins for Yukon Territory, 1986 - II[1,2]

Labor force activity	Metis and non-Aboriginal[3]		Inuit only		Inuit and non-Aboriginal[3]		Other multiple Aboriginal origins[4]	
	Number	Percent	Number	Percent	Number	Percent	Number	Percent
Total population aged 15+	60	100.0	25	100.0	15	100.0	35	100.0
Male	45	75.0	-	-	-	-	-	-
Female	15	25.0	20	80.0	-	-	15	42.9
Employed[5]	30	50.0	15	60.0	-	-	30	85.7
Male	15	25.0	-	-	-	-	-	-
Female	15	25.0	-	-	-	-	-	-
Unemployed[6]	10	16.7	-	-	-	-	-	-
Male	15	25.0	-	-	-	-	-	-
Female	-	-	-	-	-	-	-	-
Total in labor force[7]	45	75.0	20	80.0	-	-	30	85.7
Male	30	50.0	-	-	-	-	-	-
Female	15	25.0	15	60.0	-	-	-	-
Not in labor force[8]	15	25.0	-	-	10	66.7	-	-
Male	10	16.7	-	-	-	-	-	-
Female	-	-	-	-	-	-	-	-
Unemployment rate[9]	NA	22.0	NA	-	NA	-	NA	-
Male	NA	50.0	NA	-	NA	-	NA	-
Female	NA	-	NA	-	NA	-	NA	-
Participation rate[10]	NA	75.0	NA	80.0	NA	-	NA	85.7
Male	NA	67.0	NA	-	NA	-	NA	-
Female	NA	100.0	NA	75.0	NA	-	NA	-

Source: Aboriginal Peoples Output Program, 1986 Census, Statistics Canada, *A Data Book on Canada's Aboriginal Population from the 1986 Census of Canada*, March, 1989, p. 304. Primary source: 1986 Census of Canada. *Notes:* (NA) stands for not applicable. A dash (-) represents zero or a percentage less than .05 percent. 1. Aboriginal origins are derived from the ethnic origin question which asks whether respondents are North American Indian, Metis or Inuit. 2. All 1986 figures exclude the population estimated at about 45,000 on 136 incompletely enumerated Indian reserves and settlements throughout Canada. 3. Non-aboriginal in these columns—refers to persons who reported one or more non-aboriginal origins such as British, French, etc., in combination with one of the aboriginal origins such as North American Indian. 4. Other Multiple Aboriginal origins—refer to the sum of those persons reporting two or more aboriginal origins with or without a non-aboriginal origin. 5. Employed—refers to persons 15 years of age and over who, during the week prior to June 3, 1986: (a) did any work at all excluding housework or other maintenance or repairs around the home and volunteer work; or (b) were absent from their job or business because of own temporary illnessor disability, vacation, labor dispute at their place of work, or were absent for other reasons. 6. Unemployed—refers to persons 15 years of age and over who, during the week prior to enumeration: (a) were without work, had actively looked for work in the past four weeks and were available for work; or (b) had been on lay-off and expected to return to their job; or (c) had definite arrangements to start a new job in four weeks or less. 7. Total in Labor Force (in reference week)—refers to persons 15 years of age and over who either employed or unemployed during the week prior to enumeration (June 3, 1986). 8. Not in labor force—refers to those persons 15 years of age and over who, in the week prior to enumeration, were unwilling or unable to offer or supply their labor services under conditions existing in the labor market. It includes persons who looked for work during the last four weeks bwho were not available to work in the reference week, as well as persons who did not work, did nothave a new job to start in four weeks or less, were not on temporary layoff or did not look for woin the four weeks prior to enumeration. 9. Unemployment rate—refers to the unemployed labor force expressed as a percentage of the total labor force (in reference week) in an area, group, or category. 10. Participation rate—refers to the total labor force (in reference week) expressed as a percentage of the total population 15 years of age and over, excluding institutional residents, inan area, group, or category.

★ 938 ★

Population 15 Years and Over, by Occupation and Sex for Selected Aboriginal Origin for Canada, 1986[1,2]

Marital status	Total Aboriginal origins[3]		Aboriginal origins only[4]		Aboriginal and non-Aboriginal origins[5]		Total Canada[6]	
	Number	Percent	Number	Percent	Number	Percent	Number	Percent
Total in labor force	272,545	100.0	122,720	100.0	149,825	100.0	13,049,860	100.0
Male	152,675	56.0	72,000	58.7	80,675	53.8	7,441,170	57.0
Female	119,865	44.0	50,725	41.3	69,145	46.2	5,608,690	43.0
Managerial, Administrative and related	18,345	6.7	6,950	5.7	11,395	7.6	1,341,970	10.3
Male	10,790	4.0	4,405	3.6	6,385	4.3	919,690	7.0
Female	7,550	2.8	2,545	2.1	5,005	3.3	422,275	3.2
Natural sciences, engineering, and mathematics	5,360	2.0	1,445	1.2	3,915	2.6	447,800	3.4
Male	4,165	1.5	1,155	0.9	3,005	2.0	369,420	2.8
Female	1,200	0.4	285	0.2	910	0.6	78,380	0.6
Social sciences and related fields	8,535	3.1	5,095	4.2	3,440	2.3	246,460	1.9
Male	2,905	1.1	1,750	1.4	1,150	0.8	103,900	0.8
Female	5,630	2.1	3,340	2.7	2,295	1.5	142,565	1.1
Religion	465	0.2	150	0.1	315	0.2	34,100	0.3
Male	320	0.1	120	0.1	205	0.1	25,970	0.2
Female	140	0.1	30	-	110	0.1	8,225	0.1
Teaching and related	8,430	3.1	3,980	3.2	4,450	3.0	543,640	4.2
Male	2,610	1.0	1,010	0.8	1,600	1.1	207,450	1.6
Female	5,815	2.1	2,975	2.4	2,845	1.9	336,190	2.6
Medicine and Health	8,345	3.1	2,665	2.2	5,685	3.8	614,090	4.7
Male	1,300	0.5	365	0.3	935	0.6	130,270	1.0
Female	7,050	2.6	2,295	1.9	4,755	3.2	483,820	3.7
Artistic, literary, and recreational and related fields	4,895	1.8	2,090	1.7	2,805	1.9	207,790	1.6
Male	2,775	1.0	1,270	1.0	1,500	1.0	120,230	0.9
Female	2,120	0.8	820	0.7	1,305	0.9	87,560	0.7
Clerical and related	39,545	14.5	13,910	11.3	25,635	17.1	2,318,620	17.8
Male	8,075	3.0	2,955	2.4	5,120	3.4	494,410	3.8
Female	31,465	11.5	10,955	8.9	20,510	13.7	1,824,210	14.0
Sales	15,890	5.8	4,455	3.6	11,430	7.6	1,153,160	8.8
Male	7,395	2.7	1,955	1.6	5,445	3.6	641,750	4.9
Female	8,500	3.1	2,500	2.0	5,995	4.0	511,405	3.9
Service	43,080	15.8	18,905	15.4	24,175	16.1	1,617,520	12.4
Male	15,980	5.9	6,645	5.4	9,335	6.2	742,615	5.7
Female	27,095	9.9	12,260	10.0	14,840	9.9	874,910	6.7
Farming, horticultural and animal husbandry	8,330	3.1	4,060	3.3	4,270	2.8	508,310	3.9
Male	6,490	2.4	3,290	2.7	3,200	2.1	383,970	2.9
Female	1,840	0.7	775	0.6	1,065	0.7	124,340	1.0
Fishing, trapping and related	3,045	1.1	2,220	1.8	825	0.6	45,950	0.4
Male	2,860	1.0	2,095	1.7	760	0.5	41,645	0.3
Female	185	0.1	120	0.1	65	-	4,305	-

[Continued]

1323

Population 15 Years and Over, by Occupation and Sex for Selected Aboriginal Origins for Canada, 1986
[Continued]

Marital status	Total Aboriginal origins[3]		Aboriginal origins only[4]		Aboriginal and non-Aboriginal origins[5]		Total Canada[6]	
	Number	Percent	Number	Percent	Number	Percent	Number	Percent
Forestry and logging	7,105	2.6	4,675	3.8	2,435	1.6	89,750	0.7
Male	6,620	2.4	4,375	3.6	2,245	1.5	83,570	0.6
Female	490	0.2	300	0.2	185	0.1	6,175	-
Mining and quarrying including oil and gas field	2,735	1.0	1,320	1.1	1,451	1.0	67,145	0.5
Male	2,690	1.0	1,285	1.0	1,405	0.9	65,830	0.5
Female	50	-	35	-	15	-	1,315	-
Processing	9,180	3.4	4,290	3.5	4,890	3.3	446,800	3.4
Male	6,795	2.5	3,065	2.5	3,730	2.5	336,985	2.6
Female	2,390	0.9	1,230	1.0	1,160	0.8	109,820	0.8
Machining and related	4,980	1.8	1,800	1.5	3,180	2.1	280,735	2.2
Male	4,520	1.7	1,665	1.4	2,855	1.9	261,000	2.0
Female	455	0.2	130	0.1	325	0.2	19,725	0.2
Product fabricating, assembling and repairing	14,090	5.2	5,060	4.1	9,035	6.0	955,150	7.3
Male	10,810	4.0	3,530	2.9	7,285	4.9	725,155	5.6
Female	3,275	1.2	1,525	1.2	1,745	1.2	229,995	1.8
Construction and trades	23,405	8.6	13,415	10.9	9,995	6.7	753,480	5.8
Male	22,510	8.3	12,870	10.5	9,640	6.4	735,385	5.6
Female	895	0.3	540	0.4	355	0.2	18,090	0.1
Transportation and equipment operating	11,290	4.1	4,770	3.9	6,520	4.4	468,825	3.6
Male	9,830	3.6	4,145	3.4	5,685	3.8	432,440	3.3
Female	1,460	0.5	630	0.5	835	0.6	36,390	0.3
Material handling and related, not elsewhere classified	5,780	2.1	22,600	18.4	3,180	2.1	236,475	1.8
Male	4,900	1.8	2,205	1.8	2,690	1.8	182,185	1.4
Female	880	0.3	390	0.3	490	0.3	54,290	0.4
Other crafts and equipment operating	2,665	1.9	855	0.7	1,805	1.2	146,960	1.1
Male	1,955	0.7	665	0.5	1,290	0.9	113,495	0.9
Female	710	0.3	190	0.2	520	0.3	33,465	0.3
Occupations not elsewhere classified	8,480	3.1	5,240	4.3	3,240	2.2	215,495	1.7
Male	7,170	2.6	4,445	3.6	2,720	1.8	176,940	1.4
Female	1,305	0.5	795	0.6	520	0.3	38,560	0.3
All occupations	253,980	93.2	109,950	89.6	144,035	96.1	12,740,230	97.6
Male	143,470	52.6	65,280	53.2	78,190	52.2	7,294,215	55.9
Female	110,510	40.5	44,665	36.4	65,850	44.0	5,446,015	41.7
Occupation - not applicable[7]	18,565	6.8	12,775	10.4	5,785	3.9	309,635	2.4

[Continued]

★ 938 ★

Population 15 Years and Over, by Occupation and Sex for Selected Aboriginal Origins for Canada, 1986
[Continued]

Marital status	Total Aboriginal origins[3]		Aboriginal origins only[4]		Aboriginal and non-Aboriginal origins[5]		Total Canada[6]	
	Number	Percent	Number	Percent	Number	Percent	Number	Percent
Male	9,205	3.4	6,720	5.5	2,490	1.8	146,950	1.1
Female	9,360	3.4	6,060	4.9	3,330	2.2	162,680	1.2

Source: Aboriginal Peoples Output Program, 1986 Census, Statistics Canada, *A Data Book on Canada's Aboriginal Population from the 1986 Census of Canada*, March, 1989, pp. 17-19. Primary source: 1986 Census of Canada *Notes:* A dash represents zero or a percentage which rounds to less than .05 percent. 1. Aboriginal origins are derived from the ethnic origin question which asks whether respondents are North American Indian, Metis or Inuit. 2. All 1986 figures exclude the population estimated at about 45,000 on 136 incompletely enumerated Indian reserves and settlements throughout Canada. 3. Total aboriginal origins - are the sum of persons who reported: (a) a single aboriginal (e.g., North American Indian, Metis or Inuit), and, (b) multiple aboriginal origins, that is those who reported: - at least one aboriginal origin with any other non-aboriginal (e.g., Metis and French), or - two or more aboriginal origins only. 4. Aboriginal origins only - is the sum of persons reporting an aboriginal origin as a single response, and those reporting two or more aboriginal origins (e.g., North American Indian and Metis). 5. Aboriginal and non-aboriginal origins - refers to persons reporting an aboriginal origin (North American Indian, Metis or Inuit) and one or more non-aboriginal origins (e.g., British, French). 6. Total Canada and total province or territory (columns 4 and 5) - refers to the total populations of Canada and the relevant province and territory, excluding the institutional population. 7. Occupation - not applicable - refers to unemployed persons who had never worked or who had last worked prior to January 1, 1985.

★ 939 ★

Population 15 Years and Over, by Occupation and Sex for Detailed Aboriginal Origins for Canada, 1986 - I[1,2]

Occupation	Total Aboriginal origins[3]		North American Indian only		North American and non-Aboriginal[4]		Metis only	
	Number	Percent	Number	Percent	Number	Percent	Number	Percent
Total in labor force	272,545	100.0	90,360	100.0	110,535	100.0	22,095	100.0
Male	152,675	56.0	53,005	58.7	59,140	53.5	13,070	59.2
Female	119,865	44.0	37,355	41.3	51,395	46.5	9,025	40.8
Managerial, administrative, and related	18,345	6.7	5,275	5.8	8,805	8.0	1,065	4.8
Male	10,790	4.0	3,370	3.7	4,935	4.5	645	2.9
Female	7,550	2.8	1,905	2.1	3,870	3.5	420	1.9
Natural sciences, engineering and mathematics	5,360	2.0	1,045	1.2	3,095	2.8	265	1.2
Male	4,165	1.5	835	0.9	2,370	2.1	205	0.9
Female	1,200	0.4	205	0.2	725	0.7	55	0.2
Social sciences and related fields	8,535	3.1	4,185	4.6	2,415	2.2	630	2.9
Male	2,905	1.1	1,450	1.6	755	0.7	195	0.9
Female	5,630	2.1	2,735	3.0	1,655	1.5	435	2.0
Religion	465	0.2	120	0.1	220	0.2	15	0.1
Male	320	0.1	95	0.1	180	0.2	-	-
Female	140	0.1	30	-	40	-	-	-
Teaching and related	8,430	3.1	3,010	3.3	3,310	3.0	420	1.9
Male	2,610	1.0	695	0.8	1,200	1.1	185	0.8
Female	5,815	2.1	2,310	2.6	2,110	1.9	240	1.1
Medicine and health	8,345	3.1	2,100	2.3	4,335	3.9	440	2.0
Male	1,300	0.5	275	0.3	740	0.7	55	0.2
Female	7,050	2.6	1,820	2.0	3,595	3.3	385	1.7

[Continued]

Population 15 Years and Over, by Occupation and Sex for Detailed Aboriginal Origins for Canada, 1986 - I

[Continued]

Occupation	Total Aboriginal origins[3]		North American Indian only		North American and non-Aboriginal[4]		Metis only	
	Number	Percent	Number	Percent	Number	Percent	Number	Percent
Artistic, literary, recreational and related fields	4,895	1.8	1,420	1.6	2,190	2.0	260	1.2
Male	2,775	1.0	940	1.0	1,170	1.1	170	0.8
Female	2,120	0.8	480	0.5	1,025	0.9	90	0.4
Clerical and related	39,545	14.5	10,015	11.1	19,520	17.7	2,460	11.1
Male	8,075	3.0	2,050	2.3	3,805	3.4	510	2.3
Female	31,465	11.5	7,965	8.8	15,715	14.2	1,950	8.8
Sales	15,890	5.8	3,225	3.6	8,605	7.8	915	4.1
Male	7,395	2.7	1,370	1.5	4,085	3.7	405	1.8
Female	8,500	3.1	1,855	2.1	4,520	4.1	505	2.3
Service	43,080	15.8	13,090	14.5	17,480	15.8	4,090	18.5
Male	15,980	5.9	4,785	5.3	7,045	6.4	1,255	5.7
Female	27,095	9.9	8,310	9.2	10,430	9.4	2,840	12.9
Farming, horticultural and animal husbandry	8,330	3.1	3,005	3.3	2,870	2.6	930	4.2
Male	6,490	2.4	2,445	2.7	2,080	1.9	745	3.4
Female	1,840	0.7	565	0.6	790	0.7	190	0.9
Fishing, trapping and related	3,045	1.1	1,850	2.0	575	0.5	200	0.9
Male	2,860	1.0	1,745	1.9	530	0.5	195	0.9
Female	185	0.1	105	0.1	40	-	-	-
Forestry and logging	7,105	2.6	3,880	4.3	1,675	1.5	680	3.1
Male	6,620	2.4	3,610	4.0	1,525	1.4	650	2.9
Female	490	0.2	270	0.3	155	0.1	25	0.1
Mining and quarrying including oil and gas field	2,735	1.0	755	0.8	835	0.8	395	1.8
Male	2,690	1.0	735	0.8	825	0.7	390	1.8
Female	50	-	20	-	-	-	-	-
Processing	9,180	3.4	3,315	3.7	3,730	3.4	760	3.4
Male	6,795	2.5	2,345	2.6	2,835	2.6	580	2.6
Female	2,390	0.9	970	1.1	890	0.8	180	0.8
Machining and related	4,980	1.8	1,380	1.5	2,395	2.2	340	1.5
Male	4,520	1.7	1,280	1.4	2,150	1.9	325	1.5
Female	455	0.2	105	0.1	245	0.2	15	0.1
Product fabricating, assembling, and repairing	14,090	5.2	3,625	4.0	7,060	6.4	1,000	4.5
Male	10,810	4.0	2,500	2.8	5,690	5.1	745	3.4
Female	3,275	1.2	1,125	1.2	1,370	1.2	255	1.2
Construction and trades	23,405	8.6	9,795	10.8	6,525	5.9	2,575	11.7
Male	22,510	8.3	9,395	10.4	6,310	5.7	2,475	11.2
Female	895	0.3	400	0.4	215	0.2	100	0.5
Transportation and equipment operating	11,290	4.1	3,080	3.4	4,875	4.4	1,035	4.7
Male	9,830	3.6	2,635	2.9	4,315	3.9	895	4.1
Female	1,460	0.5	445	0.5	565	0.5	150	0.7

[Continued]

★ 939 ★

Population 15 Years and Over, by Occupation and Sex for Detailed Aboriginal Origins for Canada, 1986 - I

[Continued]

Occupation	Total Aboriginal origins[3]		North American Indian only		North American and non-Aboriginal[4]		Metis only	
	Number	Percent	Number	Percent	Number	Percent	Number	Percent
Material handling and related, not elsewhere classified	5,780	2.1	1,840	2.0	2,435	2.2	525	2.4
Male	4,900	1.8	1,530	1.7	2,045	1.9	475	2.1
Female	880	0.3	310	0.3	390	0.4	50	0.2
Other crafts and equipment operating	2,665	1.0	575	0.6	1,425	1.3	160	0.7
Male	1,955	0.7	440	0.5	995	0.9	140	0.6
Female	710	0.3	140	0.2	425	0.4	25	0.1
Occupations not elsewhere classified	8,480	3.1	3,785	4.2	2,145	1.9	995	4.5
Male	7,170	2.6	3,170	3.5	1,810	1.6	875	4.0
Female	1,305	0.5	615	0.7	330	0.3	120	0.5
All occupations	253,980	93.2	80,385	89.0	106,500	96.3	20,165	91.3
Male	143,470	52.6	47,690	52.8	57,390	51.9	12,115	54.8
Female	110,510	40.5	32,690	36.2	49,105	44.4	8,050	36.4
Occupation - not applicable[5]	18,565	6.8	9,975	11.0	4,035	3.7	1,935	8.8
Male	9,205	3.4	5,315	5.9	1,745	1.6	955	4.3
Female	9,360	3.4	4,665	5.2	2,290	2.1	975	4.4

Source: Aboriginal Peoples Output Program, 1986 Census, Statistics Canada, *A Data Book on Canada's Aboriginal Population from the 1986 Census of Canada*, March, 1989, pp. 20-22. Primary source: 1986 Census of Canada. *Notes:* A dash (-) represents zero or a percentage less than .05 percent. 1. Aboriginal origins are derived from the ethnic origin question which asks whether respondents are North American Indian, Metis or Inuit. 2. All 1986 figures exclude the population estimated at about 45,000 on 136 incompletely enumerated Indian reserves and settlements throughout Canada. 3. Total Aboriginal origins—are sum of persons who reported: (A) a single aboriginal (e.g., North American Indian, Metis or Inuit) and, (B) multiple aboriginal origins, that is those who reported: at least one aboriginal origin with any other non-aboriginal (e.g., Metis and French), or two or more aboriginal origins only. 4. Non-aboriginal in these columns—refers to persons who reported one or more non-aboriginal origins such as British, French, etc., in combination with one of the aboriginal origins such as North American Indian. 5. Occupation—not applicable—refers to unemployed persons who had never worked or who last worked prior to January 1, 1985.

★ 940 ★

Population 15 Years and Over, by Occupation and Sex for Detailed Aboriginal Origins for Canada, 1986 - II[1,2]

Occupation	Metis and non-Aboriginal[3]		Inuit only		Inuit and non-Aboriginal[3]		Other multiple Aboriginal origins[4]	
	Number	Percent	Number	Percent	Number	Percent	Number	Percent
Total in labor force	28,935	100.0	8,515	100.0	2,465	100.0	9,645	100.0
Male	15,410	53.5	4,920	57.8	1,395	56.6	5,740	59.5
Female	13,530	46.8	3,595	42.2	1,070	43.4	3,900	40.4
Managerial, administrative, and related	1,855	6.4	535	6.3	210	8.5	565	5.9
Male	1,045	3.6	355	4.2	140	5.7	310	3.2
Female	840	2.9	185	2.2	70	2.8	255	2.6
Natural sciences, engineering and mathematics	550	1.9	125	1.5	60	2.4	220	2.3
Male	430	1.5	105	1.2	35	1.4	185	1.9
Female	120	0.4	20	0.2	30	1.2	30	0.3

[Continued]

★ 940 ★

Population 15 Years and Over, by Occupation and Sex for Detailed Aboriginal Origins for Canada, 1986 - II

[Continued]

Occupation	Metis and non-Aboriginal[3]		Inuit only		Inuit and non-Aboriginal[3]		Other multiple Aboriginal origins[4]	
	Number	Percent	Number	Percent	Number	Percent	Number	Percent
Social sciences and related fields	675	2.3	190	2.2	50	2.0	390	4.0
Male	240	0.8	80	0.9	25	1.0	155	1.6
Female	400	1.5	110	1.3	25	1.0	235	2.4
Religion	85	0.3	15	0.2	-	-	15	0.2
Male	15	0.1	15	0.2	-	-	15	0.2
Female	70	0.2	-	-	-	-	-	-
Teaching and related	755	2.6	470	5.5	65	2.6	400	4.1
Male	250	0.9	120	1.4	15	0.6	150	1.6
Female	505	1.7	350	4.1	45	1.8	250	2.6
Medicine and health	1,040	3.6	100	1.2	65	2.6	270	2.8
Male	130	0.4	30	0.4	20	0.8	50	0.5
Female	915	3.2	75	0.9	40	1.6	220	2.3
Artistic, literary, recreational and related fields	425	1.5	390	4.6	35	1.4	180	1.9
Male	235	0.8	150	1.8	20	0.8	80	0.8
Female	190	0.7	240	2.8	15	0.6	80	0.8
Clerical and related	4,575	15.8	1,220	14.3	400	16.2	1,350	14.0
Male	910	3.1	350	4.1	105	4.3	335	3.5
Female	3,665	12.7	870	10.2	290	11.8	1,010	10.5
Sales	2,180	7.5	250	2.9	130	5.3	595	6.2
Male	1,015	3.5	135	1.6	55	2.2	325	3.4
Female	1,160	4.0	115	1.4	75	3.0	270	2.8
Service	5,110	17.7	1,400	16.4	440	17.8	1,465	15.2
Male	1,610	5.6	485	5.7	175	7.1	630	6.5
Female	3,500	12.1	915	10.7	270	11.0	830	8.6
Farming, horticultural and animal husbandry	1,110	3.8	65	0.8	30	1.2	315	3.3
Male	875	3.0	50	0.6	20	0.8	280	2.9
Female	235	0.8	10	0.1	15	0.6	30	0.3
Fishing, trapping and related	125	0.4	135	1.6	70	2.8	85	0.9
Male	120	0.4	125	1.5	55	2.2	85	0.9
Female	-	-	-	-	10	0.4	-	-
Forestry and logging	555	1.9	35	0.4	55	2.2	235	2.4
Male	525	1.8	35	0.4	55	2.2	230	2.4
Female	30	0.1	-	-	-	-	-	-
Mining and quarrying including oil and gas field	460	1.6	135	1.6	15	0.6	140	1.5
Male	450	1.6	135	1.6	15	0.6	140	1.5
Female	-	-	-	-	-	-	-	-
Processing	885	3.1	165	1.9	95	3.9	225	2.3
Male	660	2.3	100	1.2	75	3.0	205	2.1
Female	225	0.8	65	0.8	25	1.0	20	0.2

[Continued]

★ 940 ★

Population 15 Years and Over, by Occupation and Sex for Detailed Aboriginal Origins for Canada, 1986 - II

[Continued]

Occupation	Metis and non-Aboriginal[3]		Inuit only		Inuit and non-Aboriginal[3]		Other multiple Aboriginal origins[4]	
	Number	Percent	Number	Percent	Number	Percent	Number	Percent
Machining and related	585	2.0	60	0.7	55	2.2	160	1.7
Male	520	1.8	50	0.6	45	1.8	135	1.4
Female	65	0.2	10	0.1	-	-	15	0.2
Product fabricating, assembling, and repairing	1,415	4.9	385	4.5	155	6.3	445	4.6
Male	1,125	3.9	255	3.0	130	5.3	365	3.8
Female	285	1.0	135	1.6	20	0.8	80	0.8
Construction and trades	2,580	8.9	875	10.3	115	4.7	955	9.9
Male	2,465	8.5	840	9.9	110	4.5	920	9.5
Female	110	0.4	35	0.4	-	-	25	0.3
Transportation and equipment operating	1,125	3.9	580	6.8	145	5.9	445	4.6
Male	935	3.2	560	6.6	125	5.1	375	3.9
Female	195	0.7	25	0.3	20	0.8	70	0.7
Material handling and related, not elsewhere classified	545	1.9	200	2.3	35	1.4	200	2.1
Male	475	1.6	180	2.1	30	1.2	170	1.8
Female	70	0.2	20	0.2	-	-	25	0.3
Other crafts and equipment operating	275	1.0	115	1.4	25	1.0	95	1.0
Male	205	0.7	85	1.0	20	0.8	75	0.8
Female	70	0.2	25	0.3	-	-	15	0.2
Occupations not elsewhere classified	775	2.7	370	4.3	90	3.7	325	3.4
Male	645	2.2	330	3.9	75	3.0	255	2.6
Female	125	0.4	35	0.4	15	0.6	65	0.7
All occupations	27,715	95.8	7,815	91.8	2,325	94.3	9,080	94.1
Male	14,885	51.4	4,555	53.5	1,335	54.2	5,490	56.9
Female	12,830	44.3	3,260	38.3	990	40.2	3,590	37.2
Occupation - not applicable[5]	1,225	4.2	700	8.2	140	5.7	555	5.8
Male	525	1.8	360	4.2	60	2.4	250	2.6
Female	700	2.4	340	4.0	85	3.4	310	3.2

Source: Aboriginal Peoples Output Program, 1986 Census, Statistics Canada, *A Data Book on Canada's Aboriginal Population from the 1986 Census of Canada*, March, 1989, pp. 20-22. Primary source: 1986 Census of Canada. *Notes:* A dash (-) represents zero or a percentage less than .05 percent. 1. Aboriginal origins and derived from the ethnic origin question which asks whether respondents are North American Indian, Metis or Inuit. 2. All 1986 figures exclude the population estimated at about 45,000 on 136 incompletely enumerated Indian reserves and settlements throughout Canada. 3. Non-aboriginal in these columns—refers to persons who reported one or more non-aboriginal origins such as British, French, etc., in combination with one of the aboriginal origins such as North American Indian. 4. Other multiple aboriginal origins—refer to the sum of those persons reporting two or more aboriginal origins with or without a non-aboriginal origin. 5. Occupation—not applicable—refers to unemployed persons who had never worked or who had last worked prior to January 1, 1985.

★ 941 ★

Population 15 Years and Over, by Occupation and Sex for Detailed Aboriginal Origins for Alberta, 1986 - I[1,2]

Occupation	Total Aboriginal origins[3]		North American Indian only		North American and non-Aboriginal[4]		Metis only	
	Number	Percent	Number	Percent	Number	Percent	Number	Percent
Total in labor force	38,305	100.0	9,820	100.0	12,975	100.0	5,930	100.0
Male	21,335	55.7	5,575	56.8	6,995	53.9	3,435	57.9
Female	16,965	44.3	4,240	43.2	5,980	46.1	2,495	42.1
Managerial, administrative, and related	2,205	5.8	475	4.8	935	7.2	215	3.6
Male	1,385	3.6	290	3.0	635	4.9	130	2.2
Female	820	2.1	190	1.9	305	2.4	85	1.4
Natural sciences, engineering and mathematics	735	1.9	75	0.8	385	3.0	75	1.3
Male	575	1.5	65	0.7	310	2.4	45	0.8
Female	160	0.4	15	0.2	80	0.6	25	0.4
Social sciences and related fields	1,145	3.0	525	5.3	250	1.9	170	2.9
Male	375	1.0	165	1.7	60	0.5	60	1.0
Female	765	2.0	365	3.7	190	1.5	105	1.8
Religion	50	0.1	-	-	35	0.3	-	-
Male	35	0.1	-	-	20	0.2	-	-
Female	15	-	-	-	15	0.1	-	-
Teaching and related	925	2.4	250	2.5	315	2.4	80	1.3
Male	265	0.7	45	0.5	105	0.8	40	0.7
Female	655	1.7	210	2.1	210	1.6	45	0.8
Medicine and health	975	2.5	240	2.4	400	3.1	100	1.7
Male	145	0.4	45	0.5	70	0.5	-	-
Female	830	2.2	195	2.0	335	2.6	95	1.6
Artistic, literary, recreational and related fields	455	1.2	70	0.7	255	2.0	50	0.8
Male	265	0.7	45	0.5	145	1.1	40	0.7
Female	185	0.5	25	0.3	105	0.8	10	0.2
Clerical and related	5,810	15.2	1,185	12.1	2,385	18.4	660	11.1
Male	960	2.5	155	1.6	440	3.4	90	1.5
Female	4,850	12.7	1,030	10.5	1,950	15.0	570	9.6
Sales	2,385	6.2	310	3.2	1,155	8.9	255	4.3
Male	1,085	2.8	145	1.5	510	3.9	105	1.8
Female	1,300	3.4	165	1.7	645	5.0	160	2.7
Service	7,060	18.4	1,750	17.8	2,270	17.5	1,280	21.6
Male	2,250	5.9	590	6.0	780	6.0	340	5.7
Female	4,815	12.6	1,160	11.8	1,495	11.5	940	15.9
Farming, horticultural and animal husbandry	1,510	3.9	525	5.3	430	3.3	205	3.5
Male	1,270	3.3	480	4.9	310	2.4	180	3.0
Female	235	0.6	40	0.4	115	0.9	25	0.4
Fishing, trapping and related	20	0.1	-	-	-	-	-	-
Male	20	0.1	-	-	-	-	-	-
Female	-	-	-	-	-	-	-	-
Forestry and logging	590	1.5	295	3.0	40	0.3	140	2.4
Male	565	1.5	280	2.9	35	0.3	135	2.3

[Continued]

★ 941 ★

Population 15 Years and Over, by Occupation and Sex for Detailed Aboriginal Origins for Alberta, 1986 - I

[Continued]

Occupation	Total Aboriginal origins[3]		North American Indian only		North American and non-Aboriginal[4]		Metis only	
	Number	Percent	Number	Percent	Number	Percent	Number	Percent
Female	20	0.1	115	0.2	-	-	-	-
Mining and quarrying including oil and gas field	775	2.0	110	1.1	290	2.2	125	2.1
Male	765	2.0	105	1.1	285	2.2	125	2.1
Female	10	-	-	-	-	-	-	-
Processing	850	2.2	185	1.9	310	2.4	175	3.0
Male	665	1.7	150	1.5	265	2.0	130	2.2
Female	180	0.5	35	0.4	45	0.3	50	0.8
Machining and related	670	1.7	125	1.3	240	1.8	100	1.7
Male	640	1.7	110	1.1	235	1.8	95	1.6
Female	25	0.1	10	0.1	-	-	-	-
Product fabricating, assembling, and repairing	1,550	4.0	270	2.7	660	5.1	220	3.7
Male	1,350	3.5	195	2.0	595	4.6	190	3.2
Female	200	0.5	75	0.8	65	0.5	35	0.6
Construction and trades	4,095	10.7	1,200	12.2	945	7.3	900	15.2
Male	3,905	10.2	1,140	11.6	920	7.1	830	14.0
Female	190	0.5	65	0.7	25	0.2	70	1.2
Transportation and equipment operating	1,820	4.8	365	3.7	630	4.9	275	4.6
Male	1,570	4.1	300	3.1	570	4.4	245	4.1
Female	255	0.7	65	0.7	65	0.5	30	0.5
Material handling and related, not elsewhere classified	720	1.9	130	1.3	235	1.8	145	2.4
Male	640	1.7	110	1.1	205	1.6	125	2.1
Female	80	0.2	15	0.2	25	0.2	25	0.4
Other crafts and equipment operating	385	1.0	70	0.7	165	1.3	45	0.8
Male	305	0.8	65	0.7	120	0.9	40	0.7
Female	80	0.2	-	-	45	0.3	-	-
Occupations not elsewhere classified	1,590	4.2	605	6.2	305	2.4	370	6.2
Male	1,370	3.6	525	5.3	265	2.0	325	5.5
Female	220	0.6	75	0.8	35	0.3	45	0.8
All occupations	36,310	94.8	8,770	89.3	12,630	97.3	5,590	94.3
Male	20,400	53.3	5,015	51.1	6,880	53.0	3,275	55.2
Female	15,910	41.5	3,750	38.2	5,750	44.3	2,315	39.0
Occupation - not applicable[5]	1,995	5.2	1,050	10.7	345	2.7	340	5.7

[Continued]

★ 941 ★

Population 15 Years and Over, by Occupation and Sex for Detailed Aboriginal Origins for Alberta, 1986 - I
[Continued]

Occupation	Total Aboriginal origins[3]		North American Indian only		North American and non-Aboriginal[4]		Metis only	
	Number	Percent	Number	Percent	Number	Percent	Number	Percent
Male	935	2.4	560	5.7	120	0.9	155	2.6
Female	1,060	2.8	490	5.0	230	1.8	180	3.0

Source: Aboriginal Peoples Output Program, 1986 Census, Statistics Canada, *A Data Book on Canada's Aboriginal Population from the 1986 Census of Canada*, March, 1989, pp. 236-238. Primary source: 1986 Census of Canada. *Notes:* A dash (-) represents zero or a percentage less than .05 percent. 1. Aboriginal origins are derived from the ethnic origin question which asks whether respondents are North American Indian, Metis or Inuit. 2. All 1986 figures exclude the population estimated at about 45,000 on 136 incompletely enumerated Indian reserves and settlements throughout Canada. 3. Total Aboriginal origins—are sum of persons who reported: (A) a single aboriginal (e.g., North American Indian, Metis or Inuit) and, (B) multiple aboriginal origins, that is those who reported: at least one aboriginal origin with any other non-aboriginal (e.g., Metis and French), or two or more aboriginal origins only. 4. Non-aboriginal in these columns—refers to persons who reported one or more non-aboriginal origins such as British, French, etc., in combination with one of the aboriginal origins such as North American Indian. 5. Occupation—not applicable—refers to unemployed persons who had never worked or who last worked prior to January 1, 1985.

★ 942 ★

Population 15 Years and Over, by Occupation and Sex for Detailed Aboriginal Origins for Alberta, 1986 - II[1,2]

Occupation	Metis and non-Aboriginal[3]		Inuit only		Inuit and non-Aboriginal[3]		Other multiple Aboriginal origins[4]	
	Number	Percent	Number	Percent	Number	Percent	Number	Percent
Total in labor force	6,820	100.0	130	100.0	185	100.0	2,445	100.0
Male	3,675	53.9	90	69.2	70	37.8	1,500	61.3
Female	3,145	46.1	40	30.8	120	64.9	950	38.9
Managerial, administrative, and related	430	6.3	20	15.4	15	8.1	105	4.3
Male	270	4.0	15	11.5	-	-	35	1.4
Female	160	2.3	-	-	15	8.1	55	2.2
Natural sciences, engineering and mathematics	110	1.6	15	11.5	-	-	60	2.5
Male	85	1.2	15	11.5	-	-	50	2.0
Female	20	0.3	-	-	-	-	10	0.4
Social sciences and related fields	130	1.9	-	-	-	-	65	2.7
Male	50	0.7	-	-	-	-	35	1.4
Female	85	1.2	-	-	-	-	20	0.8
Religion	-	-	-	-	-	-	-	-
Male	-	-	-	-	-	-	-	-
Female	-	-	-	-	-	-	-	-
Teaching and related	140	2.1	-	-	10	5.4	120	4.9
Male	35	0.5	-	-	-	-	45	1.8
Female	105	1.5	-	-	10	5.4	80	3.3
Medicine and health	180	2.6	-	-	-	-	50	2.0
Male	20	0.3	-	-	-	-	-	-
Female	155	2.3	-	-	-	-	40	1.6
Artistic, literary, recreational and related fields	60	0.9	-	-	-	-	-	-

[Continued]

★ 942 ★

Population 15 Years and Over, by Occupation and Sex for Detailed Aboriginal Origins for Alberta, 1986 - II
[Continued]

Occupation	Metis and non-Aboriginal[3]		Inuit only		Inuit and non-Aboriginal[3]		Other multiple Aboriginal origins[4]	
	Number	Percent	Number	Percent	Number	Percent	Number	Percent
Male	30	0.4	-	-	-	-	-	-
Female	35	0.5	-	-	-	-	-	-
Clerical and related	1,225	18.0	-	-	25	13.5	315	12.9
Male	205	3.0	-	-	-	-	70	2.9
Female	1,020	15.0	-	-	25	13.5	250	10.2
Sales	520	7.6	-	-	20	10.8	125	5.1
Male	270	4.0	-	-	-	-	35	1.4
Female	250	3.7	-	-	-	-	70	2.9
Service	1,230	18.0	35	26.9	60	32.4	430	17.6
Male	305	4.5	20	15.4	30	16.2	190	7.8
Female	930	13.6	15	11.5	30	16.2	240	9.8
Farming, horticultural and animal husbandry	240	3.5	-	-	-	-	110	4.5
Male	190	2.8	-	-	-	-	110	4.5
Female	50	0.7	-	-	-	-	-	-
Fishing, trapping and related	-	-	-	-	-	-	-	-
Male	-	-	-	-	-	-	-	-
Female	-	-	-	-	-	-	-	-
Forestry and logging	60	0.9	-	-	-	-	60	2.5
Male	55	0.8	-	-	-	-	55	2.2
Female	-	-	-	-	-	-	-	-
Mining and quarrying including oil and gas field	185	2.7	-	-	-	-	65	2.7
Male	185	2.7	-	-	-	-	70	2.9
Female	-	-	-	-	-	-	-	-
Processing	140	2.1	-	-	-	-	45	1.8
Male	100	1.5	-	-	-	-	30	1.2
Female	40	0.6	-	-	-	-	-	-
Machining and related	140	2.1	-	-	-	-	55	2.2
Male	135	2.0	-	-	-	-	55	2.2
Female	-	-	-	-	-	-	-	-
Product fabricating, assembling, and repairing	265	3.9	-	-	-	-	110	4.5
Male	250	3.7	-	-	-	-	100	4.1
Female	15	0.2	-	-	-	-	15	0.6
Construction and trades	765	11.2	10	7.7	-	-	275	11.2
Male	740	10.9	10	7.7	-	-	270	11.0
Female	25	0.4	-	-	-	-	-	-
Transportation and equipment operating	375	5.5	-	-	10	5.4	155	6.3
Male	310	4.5	-	-	10	5.4	130	5.3
Female	70	1.0	-	-	-	-	25	1.0

[Continued]

★ 942 ★

Population 15 Years and Over, by Occupation and Sex for Detailed Aboriginal Origins for Alberta, 1986 - II
[Continued]

Occupation	Metis and non-Aboriginal[3]		Inuit only		Inuit and non-Aboriginal[3]		Other multiple Aboriginal origins[4]	
	Number	Percent	Number	Percent	Number	Percent	Number	Percent
Material handling and related, not elsewhere classified	145	2.1	-	-	-	-	75	3.1
Male	130	1.9	-	-	-	-	55	2.2
Female	10	0.1	-	-	-	-	-	-
Other crafts and equipment operating	85	1.2	-	-	-	-	20	0.8
Male	65	1.0	-	-	-	-	15	0.6
Female	20	0.3	-	-	-	-	-	-
Occupations not elsewhere classified	215	3.2	-	-	-	-	90	3.7
Male	165	2.4	-	-	-	-	75	3.1
Female	45	0.7	-	-	-	-	10	0.4
All occupations	6,660	97.7	120	92.3	185	100.0	2,360	96.5
Male	3,610	52.9	80	61.5	70	37.8	1,470	60.1
Female	3,050	44.7	35	26.9	120	64.9	890	36.4
Occupation - not applicable[5]	165	2.4	10	7.7	-	-	85	3.5
Male	65	1.0	-	-	-	-	20	0.8
Female	95	1.4	-	-	-	-	55	2.2

Source: Aboriginal Peoples Output Program, 1986 Census, Statistics Canada, *A Data Book on Canada's Aboriginal Population from the 1986 Census of Canada,* March, 1989, pp. 236-238. Primary source: 1986 Census of Canada. *Notes:* A dash (-) represents zero or a percentage less than .05 percent. 1. Aboriginal origins and derived from the ethnic origin question which asks whether respondents are North American Indian, Metis or Inuit. 2. All 1986 figures exclude the population estimated at about 45,000 on 136 incompletely enumerated Indian reserves and settlements throughout Canada. 3. Non-aboriginal in these columns—refers to persons who reported one or more non-aboriginal origins such as British, French, etc., in combination with one of the aboriginal origins such as North American Indian. 4. Other multiple aboriginal origins—refer to the sum of those persons reporting two or more aboriginal origins with or without a non-aboriginal origin. 5. Occupation—not applicable—refers to unemployed persons who had never worked or who had last worked prior to January 1, 1985.

★ 943 ★

Population 15 Years and Over, by Occupation and Sex for Detailed Aboriginal Origins for British Columbia, 1986 - I[1,2]

Occupation	Total Aboriginal origins[3]		North American Indian only		North American and non-Aboriginal[4]		Metis only	
	Number	Percent	Number	Percent	Number	Percent	Number	Percent
Total in labor force	50,510	100.0	20,325	100.0	22,985	100.0	1,685	100.0
Male	28,810	57.0	12,035	59.2	12,640	55.0	955	56.7
Female	21,700	43.0	8,285	40.8	10,340	45.0	730	43.3
Managerial, administrative, and related	2,855	5.7	910	4.5	1,525	6.6	105	6.2
Male	1,670	3.3	515	2.5	890	3.9	70	4.2
Female	1,180	2.3	395	1.9	640	2.8	30	1.8
Natural sciences, engineering and mathematics	760	1.5	210	1.0	450	2.0	15	0.9
Male	610	1.2	175	0.9	360	1.6	-	-
Female	150	0.3	35	0.2	90	0.4	-	-
Social sciences and related fields	1,470	2.9	825	4.1	505	2.2	40	2.4

[Continued]

★ 943 ★

Population 15 Years and Over, by Occupation and Sex for Detailed Aboriginal Origins for British Columbia, 1986 - I

[Continued]

Occupation	Total Aboriginal origins[3]		North American Indian only		North American and non-Aboriginal[4]		Metis only	
	Number	Percent	Number	Percent	Number	Percent	Number	Percent
Male	460	0.9	230	1.1	180	0.8	-	-
Female	1,015	2.0	595	2.9	330	1.4	30	1.8
Religion	60	0.1	20	0.1	40	0.2	-	-
Male	45	0.1	15	0.1	30	0.1	-	-
Female	15	-	-	-	10	-	-	-
Teaching and related	1,325	2.6	550	2.7	645	2.8	20	1.2
Male	380	0.8	95	0.5	215	0.9	-	-
Female	945	1.9	455	2.2	430	1.9	15	0.9
Medicine and health	1,370	2.7	380	1.9	715	3.1	40	2.4
Male	240	0.5	60	0.3	145	0.6	10	0.6
Female	1,130	2.2	325	1.6	570	2.5	30	1.8
Artistic, literary, recreational and related fields	735	1.5	280	1.4	340	1.5	15	0.9
Male	370	0.7	170	0.8	150	0.7	15	0.9
Female	355	0.7	110	0.5	195	0.8	-	-
Clerical and related	6,260	12.4	1,715	8.4	3,620	15.7	175	10.4
Male	975	1.9	280	1.4	560	2.4	30	1.8
Female	5,285	10.5	1,430	7.0	3,060	13.3	145	8.6
Sales	3,075	6.1	630	3.1	1,920	8.4	75	4.5
Male	1,480	2.9	230	1.1	965	4.2	45	2.7
Female	1,590	3.1	395	1.9	950	4.1	35	2.1
Service	7,555	15.0	2,625	12.9	3,735	16.2	325	19.3
Male	2,670	5.3	845	4.2	1,375	6.0	110	6.5
Female	4,885	9.7	1,785	8.8	2,365	10.3	215	12.8
Farming, horticultural and animal husbandry	1,660	3.3	780	3.8	690	3.0	45	2.7
Male	1,245	2.5	580	2.9	510	2.2	30	1.8
Female	415	0.8	205	1.0	175	0.8	15	0.9
Fishing, trapping and related	1,440	2.9	1,080	5.3	315	1.4	10	0.6
Male	1,340	2.7	1,005	4.9	290	1.3	15	0.9
Female	100	0.2	75	0.4	20	0.1	-	-
Forestry and logging	3,195	6.3	1,755	8.6	1,060	4.6	105	6.2
Male	2,965	5.9	1,630	8.0	980	4.3	105	6.2
Female	225	0.4	125	0.6	85	0.4	-	-
Mining and quarrying including oil and gas field	335	0.7	115	0.6	140	0.6	30	1.8
Male	335	0.7	115	0.6	140	0.6	30	1.8
Female	-	-	-	-	-	-	-	-
Processing	2,610	5.2	1,385	6.8	990	4.3	35	2.1
Male	1,835	3.6	860	4.2	780	3.4	30	1.8
Female	775	1.5	525	2.6	215	0.9	-	-
Machining and related	660	1.3	210	1.0	310	1.3	20	1.2

[Continued]

★ 943 ★

Population 15 Years and Over, by Occupation and Sex for Detailed Aboriginal Origins for British Columbia, 1986 - I

[Continued]

Occupation	Total Aboriginal origins[3]		North American Indian only		North American and non-Aboriginal[4]		Metis only	
	Number	Percent	Number	Percent	Number	Percent	Number	Percent
Male	640	1.3	200	1.0	295	1.3	20	1.2
Female	20	-	-	-	-	-	-	-
Product fabricating, assembling, and repairing	1,910	3.8	485	2.4	1,055	4.6	60	3.6
Male	1,645	3.3	400	2.0	950	4.1	50	3.0
Female	265	0.5	85	0.4	100	0.4	10	0.6
Construction and trades	3,385	6.7	1,505	7.4	1,280	5.6	110	6.5
Male	3,215	6.4	1,425	7.0	1,225	5.3	110	6.5
Female	165	0.3	80	0.4	50	0.2	-	-
Transportation and equipment operating	1,820	3.6	500	2.5	1,035	4.5	70	4.2
Male	1,595	3.2	430	2.1	915	4.0	60	3.6
Female	220	0.4	70	0.3	120	0.5	-	-
Material handling and related, not elsewhere classified	1,470	2.9	650	3.2	645	2.8	60	3.6
Male	1,295	2.6	570	2.8	565	2.5	60	3.6
Female	180	0.4	80	0.4	80	0.3	-	-
Other crafts and equipment operating	315	0.6	85	0.4	195	0.8	-	-
Male	215	0.4	55	0.3	150	0.7	-	-
Female	105	0.2	35	0.2	50	0.2	-	-
Occupations not elsewhere classified	1,290	2.6	810	4.0	325	1.4	50	3.0
Male	1,100	2.2	675	3.3	290	1.3	45	2.7
Female	195	0.4	140	0.7	35	0.2	-	-
All occupations	45,560	90.2	17,510	86.2	21,545	93.7	1,420	84.3
Male	26,340	52.1	10,570	52.0	11,960	52.0	850	50.4
Female	19,220	38.1	6,940	34.1	9,580	41.7	565	33.5
Occupation - not applicable[5]	4,950	9.8	2,810	13.8	1,440	6.3	265	15.7
Male	2,470	4.9	1,470	7.2	680	3.0	110	6.5
Female	2,475	4.9	1,345	6.6	760	3.3	165	9.8

Source: Aboriginal Peoples Output Program, 1986 Census, Statistics Canada, *A Data Book on Canada's Aboriginal Population from the 1986 Census of Canada*, March, 1989, pp. 260-262. Primary source: 1986 Census of Canada. *Notes:* A dash (-) represents zero or a percentage less than .05 percent. 1. Aboriginal origins are derived from the ethnic origin question which asks whether respondents are North American Indian, Metis or Inuit. 2. All 1986 figures exclude the population estimated at about 45,000 on 136 incompletely enumerated Indian reserves and settlements throughout Canada. 3. Total Aboriginal origins—are sum of persons who reported: (A) a single aboriginal (e.g., North American Indian, Metis or Inuit) and, (B) multiple aboriginal origins, that is those who reported: at least one aboriginal origin with any other non-aboriginal (e.g., Metis and French), or two or more aboriginal origins only. 4. Non-aboriginal in these columns—refers to persons who reported one or more non-aboriginal origins such as British, French, etc., in combination with one of the aboriginal origins such as North American Indian. 5. Occupation—not applicable—refers to unemployed persons who had never worked or who last worked prior to January 1, 1985.

Population 15 Years and Over, by Occupation and Sex for Detailed Aboriginal Origins for British Columbia, 1986 - II[1,2]

Occupation	Metis and non-Aboriginal[3]		Inuit only		Inuit and non-Aboriginal[3]		Other multiple Aboriginal origins[4]	
	Number	Percent	Number	Percent	Number	Percent	Number	Percent
Total in labor force	4,175	100.0	70	100.0	230	100.0	1040	100.0
Male	2,320	55.6	45	64.3	165	71.7	640	61.5
Female	1,855	44.4	25	35.7	65	28.3	390	37.5
Managerial, administrative, and related	235	5.6	-	-	30	13.0	45	4.3
Male	135	3.2	-	-	30	13.0	30	2.9
Female	105	2.5	-	-	-	-	15	1.4
Natural sciences, engineering and mathematics	70	1.7	-	-	-	-	15	1.4
Male	45	1.1	-	-	-	-	15	1.4
Female	15	0.4	-	-	-	-	-	-
Social sciences and related fields	60	1.4	-	-	-	-	35	3.4
Male	25	0.6	-	-	-	-	15	1.4
Female	30	0.7	-	-	-	-	20	1.9
Religion	-	-	-	-	-	-	-	-
Male	-	-	-	-	-	-	-	-
Female	-	-	-	-	-	-	-	-
Teaching and related	95	2.3	-	-	-	-	10	1.0
Male	55	1.3	-	-	-	-	-	-
Female	40	1.0	-	-	-	-	-	-
Medicine and health	180	4.3	-	-	-	-	50	4.8
Male	20	0.5	-	-	-	-	-	-
Female	160	3.8	-	-	-	-	45	4.3
Artistic, literary, recreational and related fields	50	1.2	-	-	-	-	30	2.9
Male	25	0.6	-	-	-	-	15	1.4
Female	30	0.7	-	-	-	-	15	1.4
Clerical and related	560	13.4	-	-	45	19.6	130	12.5
Male	85	2.0	-	-	-	-	-	-
Female	475	11.4	-	-	35	15.2	125	12.0
Sales	335	8.0	-	-	-	-	105	10.1
Male	160	3.8	-	-	-	-	70	6.7
Female	175	4.2	-	-	-	-	40	3.8
Service	705	16.9	-	-	35	15.2	115	11.1
Male	235	5.6	-	-	20	8.7	85	8.2
Female	470	11.3	-	-	15	6.5	25	2.4
Farming, horticultural and animal husbandry	95	2.3	-	-	-	-	35	3.4
Male	80	1.9	-	-	-	-	35	3.4
Female	20	0.5	-	-	-	-	-	-
Fishing, trapping and related	30	0.7	-	-	-	-	-	-
Male	25	0.6	-	-	-	-	-	-
Female	-	-	-	-	-	-	-	-
Forestry and logging	175	4.2	-	-	25	10.9	65	6.3
Male	165	4.0	-	-	30	13.0	60	5.8

[Continued]

★ 944 ★

Population 15 Years and Over, by Occupation and Sex for Detailed Aboriginal Origins for British Columbia, 1986 - II

[Continued]

Occupation	Metis and non-Aboriginal[3]		Inuit only		Inuit and non-Aboriginal[3]		Other multiple Aboriginal origins[4]	
	Number	Percent	Number	Percent	Number	Percent	Number	Percent
Female	15	0.4	-	-	-	-	-	-
Mining and quarrying including oil and gas field	50	1.2	-	-	-	-	-	-
Male	50	1.2	-	-	-	-	-	-
Female	-	-	-	-	-	-	-	-
Processing	160	3.8	-	-	-	-	30	2.9
Male	135	3.2	-	-	-	-	30	2.9
Female	25	0.6	-	-	-	-	-	-
Machining and related	110	2.6	-	-	-	-	-	-
Male	105	2.5	-	-	-	-	-	-
Female	-	-	-	-	-	-	-	-
Product fabricating, assembling, and repairing	255	6.1	-	-	-	-	45	4.3
Male	205	4.9	-	-	-	-	35	3.4
Female	50	1.2	-	-	-	-	10	1.0
Construction and trades	360	8.6	-	-	-	-	120	11.5
Male	325	7.8	-	-	-	-	120	11.5
Female	30	0.7	-	-	-	-	-	-
Transportation and equipment operating	140	3.4	15	21.4	15	6.5	35	3.4
Male	120	2.9	20	28.6	10	4.3	35	3.4
Female	25	0.6	-	-	-	-	-	-
Material handling and related, not elsewhere classified	100	2.4	-	-	-	-	-	-
Male	85	2.0	-	-	-	-	-	-
Female	15	0.4	-	-	-	-	-	-
Other crafts and equipment operating	30	0.7	-	-	-	-	-	-
Male	10	0.2	-	-	-	-	-	-
Female	20	0.5	-	-	-	-	-	-
Occupations not elsewhere classified	90	2.2	-	-	-	-	10	1.0
Male	80	1.9	-	-	-	-	10	1.0
Female	-	-	-	-	-	-	-	-
All occupations	3,880	92.9	60	85.7	190	82.6	950	91.3
Male	2,170	52.0	45	64.3	135	58.7	610	58.7
Female	1,710	41.0	15	21.4	55	23.9	345	33.2
Occupation - not applicable[5]	295	7.1	-	-	40	17.4	85	8.2

[Continued]

★ 944 ★

Population 15 Years and Over, by Occupation and Sex for Detailed Aboriginal Origins for British Columbia, 1986 - II

[Continued]

Occupation	Metis and non-Aboriginal[3]		Inuit only		Inuit and non-Aboriginal[3]		Other multiple Aboriginal origins[4]	
	Number	Percent	Number	Percent	Number	Percent	Number	Percent
Male	155	3.7	-	-	35	15.2	30	2.9
Female	140	3.4	-	-	10	4.3	50	4.8

Source: Aboriginal Peoples Output Program, 1986 Census, Statistics Canada, *A Data Book on Canada's Aboriginal Population from the 1986 Census of Canada*, March, 1989, pp. 260-262. Primary source: 1986 Census of Canada. *Notes:* A dash (-) represents zero or a percentage less than .05 percent. 1. Aboriginal origins and derived from the ethnic origin question which asks whether respondents are North American Indian, Metis or Inuit. 2. All 1986 figures exclude the population estimated at about 45,000 on 136 incompletely enumerated Indian reserves and settlements throughout Canada. 3. Non-aboriginal in these columns—refers to persons who reported one or more non-aboriginal origins such as British, French, etc., in combination with one of the aboriginal origins such as North American Indian. 4. Other multiple aboriginal origins—refer to the sum of those persons reporting two or more aboriginal origins with or without a non-aboriginal origin. 5. Occupation—not applicable—refers to unemployed persons who had never worked or who had last worked prior to January 1, 1985.

★ 945 ★

Population 15 Years and Over, by Occupation and Sex for Detailed Aboriginal Origins for Manitoba, 1986 - I[1,2]

Occupation	Total Aboriginal origins[3]		North American Indian only		North American and non-Aboriginal[4]		Metis only	
	Number	Percent	Number	Percent	Number	Percent	Number	Percent
Total in labor force	27,605	100.0	10,325	100.0	4,475	100.0	4,890	100.0
Male	16,000	58.0	6,190	60.0	2,485	55.5	2,990	61.1
Female	11,605	42.0	4,140	40.1	1,985	44.4	1,905	39.0
Managerial, administrative, and related	1,515	5.5	590	5.7	290	6.5	195	4.0
Male	955	3.5	420	4.1	195	4.4	110	2.2
Female	555	2.0	170	1.6	90	2.0	85	1.7
Natural sciences, engineering and mathematics	365	1.3	95	0.9	75	1.7	45	0.9
Male	305	1.1	85	0.8	75	1.7	35	0.7
Female	60	0.2	15	0.1	-	-	-	-
Social sciences and related fields	1,310	4.7	705	6.8	160	3.6	205	4.2
Male	440	1.6	245	2.4	80	1.8	35	0.7
Female	870	3.2	460	4.5	80	1.8	175	3.6
Religion	40	0.1	30	0.3	-	-	-	-
Male	30	0.1	20	0.2	-	-	-	-
Female	10	-	-	-	-	-	-	-
Teaching and related	920	3.3	400	3.9	135	3.0	135	2.8
Male	310	1.1	125	1.2	60	1.3	55	1.1
Female	610	2.2	280	2.7	75	1.7	75	1.5
Medicine and health	870	3.2	295	2.9	215	4.8	95	1.9
Male	115	0.4	30	0.3	35	0.8	-	-
Female	755	2.7	260	2.5	175	3.9	85	1.7
Artistic, literary, recreational and related fields	385	1.4	160	1.5	85	1.9	50	1.0
Male	225	0.8	95	0.9	40	0.9	35	0.7

[Continued]

★ 945 ★

Population 15 Years and Over, by Occupation and Sex for Detailed Aboriginal Origins for Manitoba, 1986 - I

[Continued]

Occupation	Total Aboriginal origins[3]		North American Indian only		North American and non-Aboriginal[4]		Metis only	
	Number	Percent	Number	Percent	Number	Percent	Number	Percent
Female	165	0.6	65	0.6	40	0.9	15	0.3
Clerical and related	3,505	12.7	955	9.2	815	18.2	485	9.9
Male	935	3.4	265	2.6	170	3.8	165	3.4
Female	2,570	9.3	695	6.7	640	14.3	320	6.5
Sales	1,320	4.8	280	2.7	275	6.1	165	3.4
Male	575	2.1	105	1.0	125	2.8	70	1.4
Female	745	2.7	170	1.6	155	3.5	95	1.9
Service	4,380	15.9	1,545	15.0	755	16.9	820	16.8
Male	1,505	5.5	545	5.3	295	6.6	270	5.5
Female	2,875	10.4	1,000	9.7	460	10.3	550	11.2
Farming, horticultural and animal husbandry	990	3.6	235	2.3	165	3.7	285	5.8
Male	830	3.0	205	2.0	130	2.9	230	4.7
Female	165	0.6	35	0.3	30	0.7	60	1.2
Fishing, trapping and related	655	2.4	360	3.5	45	1.0	130	2.7
Male	635	2.3	350	3.4	40	0.9	125	2.6
Female	20	0.1	-	-	-	-	-	-
Forestry and logging	565	2.0	200	1.9	20	0.4	170	3.5
Male	555	2.0	200	1.9	20	0.4	170	3.5
Female	-	-	-	-	-	-	-	-
Mining and quarrying including oil and gas field	300	1.1	70	0.7	50	1.1	85	1.7
Male	295	1.1	70	0.7	55	1.2	85	1.7
Female	-	-	-	-	-	-	-	-
Processing	695	2.5	210	2.0	105	2.3	140	2.9
Male	575	2.1	165	1.6	100	2.2	120	2.5
Female	120	0.4	45	0.4	0	0	15	0.3
Machining and related	365	1.3	95	0.9	90	2.0	65	1.3
Male	340	1.2	95	0.9	90	2.0	60	1.2
Female	30	0.1	-	-	-	-	-	-
Product fabricating, assembling, and repairing	1,020	3.7	255	2.5	180	4.0	220	4.5
Male	690	2.5	155	1.5	130	2.9	145	3.0
Female	335	1.2	100	1.0	50	1.1	75	1.5
Construction and trades	3,015	10.9	1,375	13.3	355	7.9	550	11.2
Male	2,920	10.6	1,325	12.8	350	7.8	535	10.9
Female	95	0.3	45	0.4	-	-	15	0.3
Transportation and equipment operating	980	3.6	320	3.1	185	4.1	190	3.9
Male	815	3.0	275	2.7	155	3.5	145	3.0
Female	175	0.6	50	0.5	30	0.7	45	0.9
Material handling and related, not elsewhere classified	530	1.9	160	1.5	95	2.1	145	3.0

[Continued]

★ 945 ★

Population 15 Years and Over, by Occupation and Sex for Detailed Aboriginal Origins for Manitoba, 1986 - I

[Continued]

Occupation	Total Aboriginal origins[3]		North American Indian only		North American and non-Aboriginal[4]		Metis only	
	Number	Percent	Number	Percent	Number	Percent	Number	Percent
Male	475	1.7	145	1.4	75	1.7	125	2.6
Female	60	0.2	15	0.1	15	0.3	15	0.3
Other crafts and equipment operating	265	1.0	55	0.5	80	1.8	50	1.0
Male	175	0.6	40	0.4	35	0.8	25	0.5
Female	85	0.3	15	0.1	45	1.0	20	0.4
Occupations not elsewhere classified	1,120	4.1	495	4.8	145	3.2	195	4.0
Male	1,000	3.6	440	4.3	130	2.9	170	3.5
Female	125	0.5	55	0.5	15	0.3	20	0.4
All occupations	25,115	91.0	8,885	86.1	4,320	96.5	4,415	90.3
Male	14,690	53.2	5,415	52.4	2,405	53.7	2,720	55.6
Female	10,425	37.8	3,475	33.7	1,915	42.8	1,695	34.7
Occupation - not applicable[5]	2,490	9.0	1,440	13.9	155	3.5	480	9.8
Male	1,310	4.7	780	7.6	75	1.7	270	5.5
Female	1,180	4.3	665	6.4	80	1.8	210	4.3

Source: Aboriginal Peoples Output Program, 1986 Census, Statistics Canada, *A Data Book on Canada's Aboriginal Population from the 1986 Census of Canada*, March, 1989, pp. 188-190. Primary source: 1986 Census of Canada. *Notes:* A dash (-) represents zero or a percentage less than .05 percent. 1. Aboriginal origins are derived from the ethnic origin question which asks whether respondents are North American Indian, Metis or Inuit. 2. All 1986 figures exclude the population estimated at about 45,000 on 136 incompletely enumerated Indian reserves and settlements throughout Canada. 3. Total Aboriginal origins—are sum of persons who reported: (A) a single aboriginal (e.g., North American Indian, Metis or Inuit) and, (B) multiple aboriginal origins, that is those who reported: at least one aboriginal origin with any other non-aboriginal (e.g., Metis and French), or two or more aboriginal origins only. 4. Non-aboriginal in these columns—refers to persons who reported one or more non-aboriginal origins such as British, French, etc., in combination with one of the aboriginal origins such as North American Indian. 5. Occupation—not applicable—refers to unemployed persons who had never worked or who last worked prior to January 1, 1985.

★ 946 ★

Population 15 Years and Over, by Occupation and Sex for Detailed Aboriginal Origins for Manitoba, 1986 - II[1,2]

Occupation	Metis and non-Aboriginal[3]		Inuit only		Inuit and non-Aboriginal[3]		Other multiple Aboriginal origins[4]	
	Number	Percent	Number	Percent	Number	Percent	Number	Percent
Total in labor force	6,100	100.0	70	100.0	85	100.0	1,660	100.0
Male	3,295	54.0	35	50.0	55	64.7	960	57.8
Female	2,805	46.0	35	50.0	30	35.3	705	42.5
Managerial, administrative, and related	360	5.9	-	-	-	-	85	5.1
Male	190	3.1	-	-	-	-	-	-
Female	165	2.7	-	-	-	-	-	-
Natural sciences, engineering and mathematics	120	2.0	-	-	-	-	-	-
Male	100	1.6	-	-	-	-	-	-
Female	25	0.4	-	-	-	-	-	-
Social sciences and related fields	165	2.7	-	-	-	-	60	3.6
Male	60	1.0	-	-	-	-	-	-

[Continued]

★ 946 ★

Population 15 Years and Over, by Occupation and Sex for Detailed Aboriginal Origins for Manitoba, 1986 - II

[Continued]

Occupation	Metis and non-Aboriginal[3]		Inuit only		Inuit and non-Aboriginal[3]		Other multiple Aboriginal origins[4]	
	Number	Percent	Number	Percent	Number	Percent	Number	Percent
Female	100	1.6	-	-	-	-	55	3.3
Religion	-	-	-	-	-	-	-	-
Male	-	-	-	-	-	-	-	-
Female	-	-	-	-	-	-	-	-
Teaching and related	165	2.7	-	-	-	-	80	4.8
Male	45	0.7	-	-	-	-	-	-
Female	120	2.0	-	-	-	-	55	3.3
Medicine and health	205	3.4	-	-	-	-	-	-
Male	25	0.4	-	-	-	-	-	-
Female	185	3.0	-	-	-	-	-	-
Artistic, literary, recreational and related fields	25	0.4	-	-	-	-	-	-
Male	45	0.7	-	-	-	-	-	-
Female	65	1.1	-	-	-	-	-	-
Clerical and related	1,010	16.6	-	-	25	29.4	215	13.0
Male	260	4.3	-	-	10	11.8	-	-
Female	750	12.3	-	-	10	11.8	145	8.7
Sales	485	8.0	-	-	-	-	110	6.6
Male	210	3.4	-	-	-	-	-	-
Female	270	4.4	-	-	-	-	-	-
Service	1,020	16.7	-	-	35	41.2	210	12.7
Male	315	5.2	-	-	20	23.5	55	3.3
Female	705	11.6	-	-	15	17.6	150	9.0
Farming, horticultural and animal husbandry	270	4.4	-	-	-	-	-	-
Male	240	3.9	-	-	-	-	-	-
Female	30	0.5	-	-	-	-	-	-
Fishing, trapping and related	65	1.1	-	-	-	-	55	3.3
Male	65	1.1	-	-	-	-	50	3.0
Female	-	-	-	-	-	-	-	-
Forestry and logging	130	2.1	-	-	-	-	35	2.1
Male	130	2.1	-	-	-	-	35	2.1
Female	-	-	-	-	-	-	-	-
Mining and quarrying including oil and gas field	70	1.1	-	-	-	-	-	-
Male	70	1.1	-	-	-	-	-	-
Female	-	-	-	-	-	-	-	-
Processing	200	3.3	-	-	-	-	-	-
Male	145	2.4	-	-	-	-	-	-
Female	50	0.8	-	-	-	-	-	-
Machining and related	95	1.6	-	-	-	-	-	-
Male	80	1.3	-	-	-	-	-	-

[Continued]

★ 946 ★

Population 15 Years and Over, by Occupation and Sex for Detailed Aboriginal Origins for Manitoba, 1986 - II
[Continued]

Occupation	Metis and non-Aboriginal[3]		Inuit only		Inuit and non-Aboriginal[3]		Other multiple Aboriginal origins[4]	
	Number	Percent	Number	Percent	Number	Percent	Number	Percent
Female	15	0.2	-	-	-	-	-	-
Product fabricating, assembling, and repairing	285	4.7	-	-	10	11.8	-	-
Male	190	3.1	-	-	-	-	-	-
Female	90	1.5	-	-	-	-	-	-
Construction and trades	535	8.8	20	28.6	-	-	170	10.2
Male	515	8.4	20	28.6	-	-	160	9.6
Female	15	0.2	-	-	-	-	-	-
Transportation and equipment operating	215	3.5	10	14.3	-	-	-	-
Male	180	3.0	15	21.4	-	-	-	-
Female	30	0.5	-	-	-	-	-	-
Material handling and related, not elsewhere classified	105	1.7	-	-	-	-	-	-
Male	85	1.4	-	-	-	-	-	-
Female	20	0.3	-	-	-	-	-	-
Other crafts and equipment operating	50	0.8	-	-	-	-	-	-
Male	35	0.6	-	-	-	-	-	-
Female	15	0.2	-	-	-	-	-	-
Occupations not elsewhere classified	220	3.6	-	-	-	-	65	3.9
Male	205	3.4	-	-	-	-	50	3.0
Female	15	0.2	-	-	-	-	-	-
All occupations	5,830	95.6	60	85.7	85	100.0	1,515	91.3
Male	3,190	52.3	35	50.0	50	58.8	885	53.3
Female	2,645	43.4	30	42.9	30	35.3	635	38.3
Occupation - not applicable[5]	265	4.3	-	-	-	-	145	8.7
Male	105	1.7	-	-	-	-	75	4.5
Female	160	2.6	-	-	-	-	65	3.9

Source: Aboriginal Peoples Output Program, 1986 Census, Statistics Canada, *A Data Book on Canada's Aboriginal Population from the 1986 Census of Canada*, March, 1989, pp. 188-190. Primary source: 1986 Census of Canada. *Notes:* A dash (-) represents zero or a percentage less than .05 percent. 1. Aboriginal origins and derived from the ethnic origin question which asks whether respondents are North American Indian, Metis or Inuit. 2. All 1986 figures exclude the population estimated at about 45,000 on 136 incompletely enumerated Indian reserves and settlements throughout Canada. 3. Non-aboriginal in these columns—refers to persons who reported one or more non-aboriginal origins such as British, French, etc., in combination with one of the aboriginal origins such as North American Indian. 4. Other multiple aboriginal origins—refer to the sum of those persons reporting two or more aboriginal origins with or without a non-aboriginal origin. 5. Occupation—not applicable—refers to unemployed persons who had never worked or who had last worked prior to January 1, 1985.

★ 947 ★

Population 15 Years and Over, by Occupation and Sex for Detailed Aboriginal Origins for New Brunswick, 1986 - I[1,2]

Occupation	Total Aboriginal origins[3]		North American Indian only		North American and non-Aboriginal[4]		Metis only	
	Number	Percent	Number	Percent	Number	Percent	Number	Percent
Total in labor force	3,375	100.0	1,165	100.0	1,890	100.0	70	100.0
Male	1,990	59.0	695	59.7	1,095	57.9	45	64.3
Female	1,380	40.9	475	40.8	795	42.1	25	35.7
Managerial, administrative, and related	270	8.0	100	8.6	135	7.1	15	21.4
Male	165	4.9	70	6.0	80	4.2	-	-
Female	105	3.1	30	2.6	55	2.9	-	-
Natural sciences, engineering and mathematics	55	1.6	10	0.9	35	1.9	-	-
Male	50	1.5	-	-	30	1.6	-	-
Female	-	-	-	-	-	-	-	-
Social sciences and related fields	115	3.4	70	6.0	40	2.1		
Male	50	1.5	30	2.6	-	-	-	-
Female	65	1.9	35	3.0	25	1.3	-	-
Religion	-	-	-	-	-	-	-	-
Male	-	-	-	-	-	-	-	-
Female	-	-	-	-	-	-	-	-
Teaching and related	100	3.0	40	3.4	55	2.9	-	-
Male	50	1.5	15	1.3	30	1.6	-	-
Female	60	1.8	25	2.1	25	1.3	-	-
Medicine and health	105	3.1	20	1.7	80	4.2	-	-
Male	15	0.4	-	-	20	1.1	-	-
Female	85	2.5	20	1.7	60	3.2	-	-
Artistic, literary, recreational and related fields	65	1.9	15	1.3	50	2.6	-	-
Male	20	0.6	-	-	15	0.8	-	-
Female	40	1.2	-	-	30	1.6	-	-
Clerical and related	410	12.1	130	11.2	255	13.5	-	-
Male	80	2.4	20	1.7	55	2.9	-	-
Female	330	9.8	115	9.9	205	10.8	-	-
Sales	175	5.2	30	2.6	135	7.1	-	-
Male	95	2.8	10	0.9	75	4.0	-	-
Female	80	2.4	15	1.3	60	3.2	-	-
Service	590	17.5	185	15.9	370	19.6	15	21.4
Male	305	9.0	105	9.0	185	9.8	-	-
Female	280	8.3	75	6.4	185	9.8	-	-
Farming, horticultural and animal husbandry	70	2.1	-	-	60	3.2	-	-
Male	55	1.6	-	-	45	2.4	-	-
Female	15	0.4	-	-	15	0.8	-	-
Fishing, trapping and related	20	0.6	-	-	10	0.5	-	-
Male	15	0.4	-	-	10	0.5	-	-
Female	-	-	-	-	-	-	-	-
Forestry and logging	95	2.8	25	2.1	65	3.4	-	-
Male	95	2.8	30	2.6	65	3.4	-	-

[Continued]

★ 947 ★

Population 15 Years and Over, by Occupation and Sex for Detailed Aboriginal Origins for New Brunswick, 1986 - I
[Continued]

Occupation	Total Aboriginal origins[3]		North American Indian only		North American and non-Aboriginal[4]		Metis only	
	Number	Percent	Number	Percent	Number	Percent	Number	Percent
Female	-	-	-	-	-	-	-	-
Mining and quarrying including oil and gas field	10	0.3	-	-	10	0.5	-	-
Male	10	0.3	-	-	15	0.8	-	-
Female	-	-	-	-	-	-	-	-
Processing	105	3.1	15	1.3	75	4.0	-	-
Male	75	2.2	-	-	55	2.9	-	-
Female	25	0.7	-	-	20	1.1	-	-
Machining and related	35	1.0	10	0.9	25	1.3	-	-
Male	35	1.0	10	0.9	25	1.3	-	-
Female	-	-	-	-	-	-	-	-
Product fabricating, assembling, and repairing	165	4.9	35	3.0	125	6.6	-	-
Male	135	4.0	20	1.7	115	6.1	-	-
Female	30	0.9	10	0.9	10	0.5	-	-
Construction and trades	305	9.0	155	13.3	105	5.6	15	21.4
Male	285	8.4	140	12.0	100	5.3	20	28.6
Female	20	0.6	15	1.3	-	-	-	-
Transportation and equipment operating	150	4.4	50	4.3	95	5.0	-	-
Male	145	4.3	45	3.9	90	4.8	-	-
Female	10	0.3	-	-	-	-	-	-
Material handling and related, not elsewhere classified	20	0.6	10	0.9	15	0.8	-	-
Male	25	0.7	10	0.9	15	0.8	-	-
Female	-	-	-	-	-	-	-	-
Other crafts and equipment operating	20	0.6	-	-	10	0.5	-	-
Male	20	0.6	-	-	15	0.8	-	-
Female	-	-	-	-	-	-	-	-
Occupations not elsewhere classified	105	3.1	40	3.4	45	2.4	-	-
Male	95	2.8	40	3.4	35	1.9	-	-
Female	15	0.4	-	-	-	-	-	-
All occupations	3,010	89.2	965	82.8	1,795	95.0	70	100.0
Male	1,835	54.4	590	50.6	1,060	56.1	45	64.3
Female	1,175	34.8	370	31.8	730	38.6	15	21.4
Occupation - not applicable[5]	365	10.8	200	17.2	100	5.3	-	-

[Continued]

★ 947 ★

Population 15 Years and Over, by Occupation and Sex for Detailed Aboriginal Origins for New Brunswick, 1986 - I

[Continued]

Occupation	Total Aboriginal origins[3]		North American Indian only		North American and non-Aboriginal[4]		Metis only	
	Number	Percent	Number	Percent	Number	Percent	Number	Percent
Male	155	4.6	105	9.0	30	1.6	-	-
Female	205	6.1	100	8.6	65	3.4	-	-

Source: Aboriginal Peoples Output Program, 1986 Census, Statistics Canada, *A Data Book on Canada's Aboriginal Population from the 1986 Census of Canada,* March, 1989, pp. 116-118. Primary source: 1986 Census of Canada. *Notes:* A dash (-) represents zero or a percentage less than .05 percent. 1. Aboriginal origins are derived from the ethnic origin question which asks whether respondents are North American Indian, Metis or Inuit. 2. All 1986 figures exclude the population estimated at about 45,000 on 136 incompletely enumerated Indian reserves and settlements throughout Canada. 3. Total Aboriginal origins—are sum of persons who reported: (A) a single aboriginal (e.g., North American Indian, Metis or Inuit) and, (B) multiple aboriginal origins, that is those who reported: at least one aboriginal origin with any other non-aboriginal (e.g., Metis and French), or two or more aboriginal origins only. 4. Non-aboriginal in these columns—refers to persons who reported one or more non-aboriginal origins such as British, French, etc., in combination with one of the aboriginal origins such as North American Indian. 5. Occupation—not applicable—refers to unemployed persons who had never worked or who last worked prior to January 1, 1985.

★ 948 ★

Population 15 Years and Over, by Occupation and Sex for Detailed Aboriginal Origins for New Brunswick, 1986 - II[1,2]

Occupation	Metis and non-Aboriginal[3]		Inuit only		Inuit and non-Aboriginal[3]		Other multiple Aboriginal origins[4]	
	Number	Percent	Number	Percent	Number	Percent	Number	Percent
Total in labor force	170	100.0	-	-	30	100.0	45	100.0
Male	110	64.7	-	-	10	33.3	30	66.7
Female	60	35.3	-	-	25	83.3	15	33.3
Managerial, administrative, and related	-	-	-	-	10	33.3	15	33.3
Male	-	-	-	-	-	-	15	33.3
Female	-	-	-	-	10	33.3	-	-
Natural sciences, engineering and mathematics	15	8.8	-	-	-	-	-	-
Male	15	8.8	-	-	-	-	-	-
Female	-	-	-	-	-	-	-	-
Social sciences and related fields	-	-	-	-	-	-	-	-
Male	-	-	-	-	-	-	-	-
Female	-	-	-	-	-	-	-	-
Religion	-	-	-	-	-	-	-	-
Male	-	-	-	-	-	-	-	-
Female	-	-	-	-	-	-	-	-
Teaching and related	-	-	-	-	-	-	-	-
Male	-	-	-	-	-	-	-	-
Female	-	-	-	-	-	-	-	-
Medicine and health	-	-	-	-	-	-	-	-
Male	-	-	-	-	-	-	-	-
Female	-	-	-	-	-	-	-	-
Artistic, literary, recreational and related fields	-	-	-	-	-	-	-	-

[Continued]

★ 948 ★

Population 15 Years and Over, by Occupation and Sex for Detailed Aboriginal Origins for New Brunswick, 1986 - II

[Continued]

Occupation	Metis and non-Aboriginal[3]		Inuit only		Inuit and non-Aboriginal[3]		Other multiple Aboriginal origins[4]	
	Number	Percent	Number	Percent	Number	Percent	Number	Percent
Male	-	-	-	-	-	-	-	-
Female	-	-	-	-	-	-	-	-
Clerical and related	25	14.7	-	-	-	-	-	-
Male	10	5.9	-	-	-	-	-	-
Female	15	8.8	-	-	-	-	-	-
Sales	-	-	-	-	-	-	-	-
Male	-	-	-	-	-	-	-	-
Female	-	-	-	-	-	-	-	-
Service	-	-	-	-	-	-	15	33.3
Male	-	-	-	-	-	-	-	-
Female	-	-	-	-	-	-	-	-
Farming, horticultural and animal husbandry	-	-	-	-	-	-	-	-
Male	-	-	-	-	-	-	-	-
Female	-	-	-	-	-	-	-	-
Fishing, trapping and related	-	-	-	-	-	-	-	-
Male	-	-	-	-	-	-	-	-
Female	-	-	-	-	-	-	-	-
Forestry and logging	-	-	-	-	-	-	-	-
Male	-	-	-	-	-	-	-	-
Female	-	-	-	-	-	-	-	-
Mining and quarrying including oil and gas field	-	-	-	-	-	-	-	-
Male	-	-	-	-	-	-	-	-
Female	-	-	-	-	-	-	-	-
Processing	-	-	-	-	-	-	-	-
Male	-	-	-	-	-	-	-	-
Female	-	-	-	-	-	-	-	-
Machining and related	-	-	-	-	-	-	-	-
Male	-	-	-	-	-	-	-	-
Female	-	-	-	-	-	-	-	-
Product fabricating, assembling, and repairing	-	-	-	-	-	-	-	-
Male	-	-	-	-	-	-	-	-
Female	-	-	-	-	-	-	-	-
Construction and trades	25	14.7	-	-	-	-	-	-
Male	30	17.6	-	-	-	-	-	-
Female	-	-	-	-	-	-	-	-
Transportation and equipment operating	-	-	-	-	-	-	-	-
Male	-	-	-	-	-	-	-	-
Female	-	-	-	-	-	-	-	-

[Continued]

★ 948 ★

Population 15 Years and Over, by Occupation and Sex for Detailed Aboriginal Origins for New Brunswick, 1986 - II

[Continued]

Occupation	Metis and non-Aboriginal[3]		Inuit only		Inuit and non-Aboriginal[3]		Other multiple Aboriginal origins[4]	
	Number	Percent	Number	Percent	Number	Percent	Number	Percent
Material handling and related, not elsewhere classified	-	-	-	-	-	-	-	-
Male	-	-	-	-	-	-	-	-
Female	-	-	-	-	-	-	-	-
Other crafts and equipment operating	-	-	-	-	-	-	-	-
Male	-	-	-	-	-	-	-	-
Female	-	-	-	-	-	-	-	-
Occupations not elsewhere classified	15	8.8	-	-	-	-	-	-
Male	10	5.9	-	-	-	-	-	-
Female	-	-	-	-	-	-	-	-
All occupations	120	70.6	-	-	30	100.0	40	88.9
Male	95	55.9	-	-	10	33.3	25	55.6
Female	30	17.6	-	-	15	50.0	10	22.2
Occupation - not applicable[5]	50	29.4	-	-	-	-	-	-
Male	20	11.8	-	-	-	-	-	-
Female	25	14.7	-	-	-	-	-	-

Source: Aboriginal Peoples Output Program, 1986 Census, Statistics Canada, *A Data Book on Canada's Aboriginal Population from the 1986 Census of Canada*, March, 1989, pp. 116-118. Primary source: 1986 Census of Canada. *Notes:* A dash (-) represents zero or a percentage less than .05 percent. 1. Aboriginal origins and derived from the ethnic origin question which asks whether respondents are North American Indian, Metis or Inuit. 2. All 1986 figures exclude the population estimated at about 45,000 on 136 incompletely enumerated Indian reserves and settlements throughout Canada. 3. Non-aboriginal in these columns—refers to persons who reported one or more non-aboriginal origins such as British, French, etc., in combination with one of the aboriginal origins such as North American Indian. 4. Other multiple aboriginal origins—refer to the sum of those persons reporting two or more aboriginal origins with or without a non-aboriginal origin. 5. Occupation—not applicable—refers to unemployed persons who had never worked or who had last worked prior to January 1, 1985.

★ 949 ★

Population 15 Years and Over, by Occupation and Sex for Detailed Aboriginal Origins for Newfoundland, 1986 - I[1,2]

Occupation	Total Aboriginal origins[3]		North American Indian only		North American and non-Aboriginal[4]		Metis only	
	Number	Percent	Number	Percent	Number	Percent	Number	Percent
Total in labor force	3,490	100.0	495	100.0	1,180	100.0	130	100.0
Male	2,060	59.0	285	57.6	695	58.9	80	61.5
Female	1,430	41.0	205	41.4	480	40.7	50	38.5
Managerial, administrative, and related	190	5.4	10	2.0	80	6.8	-	-
Male	120	3.4	0	0	55	4.7	-	-
Female	70	2.0	-	-	35	3.0	-	-
Natural sciences, engineering and mathematics	60	1.7	-	-	25	2.1	-	-
Male	45	1.3	-	-	25	2.1	-	-
Female	15	0.4	-	-	-	-	-	-
Social sciences and related fields	95	2.7	10	2.0	35	3.0	-	-

[Continued]

★ 949 ★

Population 15 Years and Over, by Occupation and Sex for Detailed Aboriginal Origins for Newfoundland, 1986 - I

[Continued]

Occupation	Total Aboriginal origins[3]		North American Indian only		North American and non-Aboriginal[4]		Metis only	
	Number	Percent	Number	Percent	Number	Percent	Number	Percent
Male	35	1.0	-	-	10	0.8	-	-
Female	65	1.9	-	-	25	2.1	-	-
Religion	10	0.3	-	-	-	-	-	-
Male	15	0.4	-	-	-	-	-	-
Female	-	-	-	-	-	-	-	-
Teaching and related	130	3.7	15	3.0	45	3.8	-	-
Male	30	0.9	-	-	10	0.8	-	-
Female	100	2.9	15	3.0	30	2.5	-	-
Medicine and health	100	2.9	-	-	50	4.2	-	-
Male	-	-	-	-	-	-	-	-
Female	85	2.4	-	-	50	4.2	-	-
Artistic, literary, recreational and								
related fields	95	2.7	20	4.0	35	3.0	-	-
Male	75	2.1	-	-	35	3.0	-	-
Female	30	0.9	-	-	-	-	-	-
Clerical and related	455	13.0	60	12.1	170	14.4	-	-
Male	120	3.4	15	3.0	25	2.1	-	-
Female	330	9.5	45	9.1	140	11.9	-	-
Sales	120	3.4	40	8.1	25	2.1	-	-
Male	40	1.1	15	3.0	-	-	-	-
Female	75	2.1	30	6.1	20	1.7	-	-
Service	485	13.9	65	13.1	145	12.3	-	-
Male	215	6.2	20	4.0	70	5.9	-	-
Female	270	7.7	45	9.1	75	6.4	-	-
Farming, horticultural and animal husbandry	20	0.6	-	-	15	1.3	-	-
Male	15	0.4	-	-	-	-	-	-
Female	-	-	-	-	-	-	-	-
Fishing, trapping and related	175	5.0	15	3.0	60	5.1	-	-
Male	155	4.4	15	3.0	55	4.7	-	-
Female	15	0.4	-	-	-	-	-	-
Forestry and logging	125	3.6	35	7.1	55	4.7	-	-
Male	125	3.6	35	7.1	55	4.7	-	-
Female	-	-	-	-	-	-	-	-
Mining and quarrying including oil and								
gas field	15	0.4	-	-	-	-	-	-
Male	20	0.6	-	-	-	-	-	-
Female	-	-	-	-	-	-	-	-
Processing	275	7.9	40	8.1	95	8.1	30	23.1
Male	150	4.3	15	3.0	65	5.5	-	-
Female	125	3.6	20	4.0	35	3.0	25	19.2
Machining and related	10	0.3	-	-	-	-	-	-

[Continued]

★ 949 ★

Population 15 Years and Over, by Occupation and Sex for Detailed Aboriginal Origins for Newfoundland, 1986 - I
[Continued]

Occupation	Total Aboriginal origins[3]		North American Indian only		North American and non-Aboriginal[4]		Metis only	
	Number	Percent	Number	Percent	Number	Percent	Number	Percent
Male	10	0.3	-	-	-	-	-	-
Female	-	-	-	-	-	-	-	-
Product fabricating, assembling, and repairing	125	3.6	-	-	70	5.9	-	-
Male	105	3.0	-	-	65	5.5	-	-
Female	20	0.6	-	-	10	0.8	-	-
Construction and trades	325	9.3	60	12.1	65	5.5	40	30.8
Male	320	9.2	60	12.1	65	5.5	40	30.8
Female	-	-	-	-	-	-	-	-
Transportation and equipment operating	90	2.6	-	-	25	2.1	20	15.4
Male	90	2.6	-	-	30	2.5	20	15.4
Female	-	-	-	-	-	-	-	-
Material handling and related, not elsewhere classified	45	1.3	-	-	20	1.7	-	-
Male	45	1.3	-	-	15	1.3	-	-
Female	-	-	-	-	-	-	-	-
Other crafts and equipment operating	65	1.9	-	-	-	-	-	-
Male	55	1.6	-	-	-	-	-	-
Female	-	-	-	-	-	-	-	-
Occupations not elsewhere classified	240	6.9	45	9.1	70	5.9	-	-
Male	175	5.0	35	7.1	60	5.1	-	-
Female	60	1.7	-	-	15	1.3	-	-
All occupations	3,265	96.3	455	91.9	1,105	93.6	125	96.2
Male	1,960	56.2	265	53.5	665	56.4	80	61.5
Female	1,305	37.4	190	38.4	440	37.3	45	34.6
Occupation - not applicable[5]	220	6.3	30	6.1	75	6.4	-	-
Male	105	3.0	20	4.0	35	3.0	-	-
Female	120	3.4	15	3.0	40	3.4	-	-

Source: Aboriginal Peoples Output Program, 1986 Census, Statistics Canada, *A Data Book on Canada's Aboriginal Population from the 1986 Census of Canada*, March, 1989, pp. 44-46. Primary source: 1986 Census of Canada. *Notes:* A dash (-) represents zero or a percentage less than .05 percent. 1. Aboriginal origins are derived from the ethnic origin question which asks whether respondents are North American Indian, Metis or Inuit. 2. All 1986 figures exclude the population estimated at about 45,000 on 136 incompletely enumerated Indian reserves and settlements throughout Canada. 3. Total Aboriginal origins—are sum of persons who reported: (A) a single aboriginal (e.g., North American Indian, Metis or Inuit) and, (B) multiple aboriginal origins, that is those who reported: at least one aboriginal origin with any other non-aboriginal (e.g., Metis and French), or two or more aboriginal origins only. 4. Non-aboriginal in these columns—refers to persons who reported one or more non-aboriginal origins such as British, French, etc., in combination with one of the aboriginal origins such as North American Indian. 5. Occupation—not applicable—refers to unemployed persons who had never worked or who last worked prior to January 1, 1985.

★ 950 ★

Population 15 Years and Over, by Occupation and Sex for Detailed Aboriginal Origins for Newfoundland, 1986 - II[1,2]

Occupation	Metis and non-Aboriginal[3]		Inuit only		Inuit and non-Aboriginal[3]		Other multiple Aboriginal origins[4]	
	Number	Percent	Number	Percent	Number	Percent	Number	Percent
Total in labor force	245	100.0	550	100.0	645	100.0	250	100.0
Male	160	65.3	300	54.5	375	58.1	155	62.0
Female	85	34.7	255	46.4	265	41.1	80	32.0
Managerial, administrative, and related	10	4.1	35	6.4	35	5.4	20	8.0
Male	-	-	20	3.6	25	3.9	15	6.0
Female	-	-	15	2.7	10	1.6	-	-
Natural sciences, engineering and mathematics	-	-	10	1.8	20	3.1	-	-
Male	-	-	-	-	-	-	-	-
Female	-	-	-	-	10	1.6	-	-
Social sciences and related fields	15	6.1	20	3.6	15	2.3	-	-
Male	-	-	-	-	-	-	-	-
Female	10	4.1	10	1.8	-	-	-	-
Religion	-	-	-	-	-	-	-	-
Male	-	-	-	-	-	-	-	-
Female	-	-	-	-	-	-	-	-
Teaching and related	-	-	25	4.5	35	5.4	-	-
Male	-	-	-	-	10	1.6	-	-
Female	-	-	20	3.6	25	3.9	-	-
Medicine and health	-	-	15	2.7	15	2.3	-	-
Male	-	-	-	-	-	-	-	-
Female	-	-	15	2.7	15	2.3	-	-
Artistic, literary, recreational and related fields	-	-	25	4.5	-	-	-	-
Male	-	-	-	-	-	-	-	-
Female	-	-	20	3.6	-	-	-	-
Clerical and related	35	14.3	45	8.2	90	14.0	35	14.0
Male	20	8.2	-	-	45	7.0	-	-
Female	25	10.2	35	6.4	50	7.8	30	12.0
Sales	-	-	15	2.7	20	3.1	-	-
Male	-	-	-	-	15	2.3	-	-
Female	-	-	-	-	-	-	-	-
Service	50	20.4	80	14.5	115	17.8	30	12.0
Male	30	12.2	25	4.5	40	6.2	20	8.0
Female	20	8.2	50	9.1	75	11.6	-	-
Farming, horticultural and animal husbandry	-	-	-	-	-	-	-	-
Male	-	-	-	-	-	-	-	-
Female	-	-	-	-	-	-	-	-
Fishing, trapping and related	-	-	30	5.5	60	9.3	-	-
Male	-	-	25	4.5	50	7.8	-	-
Female	-	-	-	-	-	-	-	-
Forestry and logging	-	-	-	-	-	-	10	4.0
Male	-	-	-	-	-	-	-	-

[Continued]

★ 950 ★

Population 15 Years and Over, by Occupation and Sex for Detailed Aboriginal Origins for Newfoundland, 1986 - II

[Continued]

Occupation	Metis and non-Aboriginal[3]		Inuit only		Inuit and non-Aboriginal[3]		Other multiple Aboriginal origins[4]	
	Number	Percent	Number	Percent	Number	Percent	Number	Percent
Female	-	-	-	-	-	-	-	-
Mining and quarrying including oil and gas field	-	-	-	-	-	-	-	-
Male	-	-	-	-	-	-	-	-
Female	-	-	-	-	-	-	-	-
Processing	15	6.1	60	10.9	25	3.9	15	6.0
Male	-	-	30	5.5	15	2.3	-	-
Female	-	-	25	4.5	-	-	-	-
Machining and related	-	-	-	-	-	-	-	-
Male	-	-	-	-	-	-	-	-
Female	-	-	-	-	-	-	-	-
Product fabricating, assembling, and repairing	-	-	-	-	30	4.7	-	-
Male	-	-	-	-	25	3.9	-	-
Female	-	-	-	-	-	-	-	-
Construction and trades	30	12.2	50	9.1	55	8.5	35	14.0
Male	25	10.2	50	9.1	55	8.5	30	12.0
Female	-	-	-	-	-	-	-	-
Transportation and equipment operating	15	6.1	10	1.8	20	3.1	-	-
Male	15	6.1	-	-	20	3.1	-	-
Female	-	-	-	-	-	-	-	-
Material handling and related, not elsewhere classified	-	-	15	2.7	-	-	-	-
Male	-	-	10	1.8	-	-	-	-
Female	-	-	-	-	-	-	-	-
Other crafts and equipment operating	15	6.1	20	3.6	10	1.6	-	-
Male	15	6.1	15	2.7	-	-	-	-
Female	-	-	-	-	-	-	-	-
Occupations not elsewhere classified	-	-	45	8.2	45	7.0	30	12.0
Male	-	-	25	4.5	30	4.7	20	8.0
Female	-	-	20	3.6	15	2.3	-	-
All occupations	225	91.8	515	93.6	605	93.8	230	92.0
Male	150	61.2	280	50.9	360	55.8	145	58.0
Female	80	32.7	240	43.6	240	37.2	65	26.0
Occupation - not applicable[5]	20	8.2	35	6.4	40	6.2	15	6.0

[Continued]

★ 950 ★

Population 15 Years and Over, by Occupation and Sex for Detailed Aboriginal Origins for Newfoundland, 1986 - II

[Continued]

Occupation	Metis and non-Aboriginal[3]		Inuit only		Inuit and non-Aboriginal[3]		Other multiple Aboriginal origins[4]	
	Number	Percent	Number	Percent	Number	Percent	Number	Percent
Male	15	6.1	20	3.6	15	2.3	-	-
Female	-	-	15	2.7	25	3.9	-	-

Source: Aboriginal Peoples Output Program, 1986 Census, Statistics Canada, *A Data Book on Canada's Aboriginal Population from the 1986 Census of Canada,* March, 1989, pp. 44-46. Primary source: 1986 Census of Canada. *Notes:* A dash (-) represents zero or a percentage less than .05 percent. 1. Aboriginal origins and derived from the ethnic origin question which asks whether respondents are North American Indian, Metis or Inuit. 2. All 1986 figures exclude the population estimated at about 45,000 on 136 incompletely enumerated Indian reserves and settlements throughout Canada. 3. Non-aboriginal in these columns—refers to persons who reported one or more non-aboriginal origins such as British, French, etc., in combination with one of the aboriginal origins such as North American Indian. 4. Other multiple aboriginal origins—refer to the sum of those persons reporting two or more aboriginal origins with or without a non-aboriginal origin. 5. Occupation—not applicable—refers to unemployed persons who had never worked or who had last worked prior to January 1, 1985.

★ 951 ★

Population 15 Years and Over, by Occupation and Sex for Detailed Aboriginal Origins for Northwest Territories, 1986 - I[1,2]

Occupation	Total Aboriginal origins[3]		North American Indian only		North American and non-Aboriginal[4]		Metis only	
	Number	Percent	Number	Percent	Number	Percent	Number	Percent
Total in labor force	10,200	100.0	2,420	100.0	405	100.0	935	100.0
Male	5,865	57.5	1,385	57.2	260	64.2	530	56.7
Female	4,335	42.5	1,035	42.8	150	37.0	405	43.3
Managerial, administrative, and related	715	7.0	155	6.4	45	11.1	100	10.7
Male	440	4.3	100	4.1	25	6.2	65	7.0
Female	280	2.7	60	2.5	20	4.9	30	3.2
Natural sciences, engineering and mathematics	210	2.1	55	2.3	20	4.9	20	2.1
Male	190	1.9	50	2.1	20	4.9	15	1.6
Female	20	0.2	-	-	-	-	-	-
Social sciences and related fields	300	2.9	90	3.7	20	4.9	35	3.7
Male	100	1.0	25	1.0	15	3.7	-	-
Female	200	2.0	70	2.9	-	-	30	3.2
Religion	15	0.1	-	-	-	-	-	-
Male	10	0.1	-	-	-	-	-	-
Female	-	-	-	-	-	-	-	-
Teaching and related	490	4.8	110	4.5	-	-	20	2.1
Male	105	1.0	15	0.6	-	-	-	-
Female	390	3.8	95	3.9	-	-	20	2.1
Medicine and health	95	0.9	40	1.7	-	-	10	1.1
Male	-	-	-	-	-	-	-	-
Female	90	0.9	40	1.7	-	-	10	1.1
Artistic, literary, recreational and related fields	305	3.0	35	1.4	-	-	15	1.6
Male	120	1.2	15	0.6	-	-	-	-

[Continued]

★ 951 ★

Population 15 Years and Over, by Occupation and Sex for Detailed Aboriginal Origins for Northwest Territories, 1986 - I

[Continued]

Occupation	Total Aboriginal origins[3]		North American Indian only		North American and non-Aboriginal[4]		Metis only	
	Number	Percent	Number	Percent	Number	Percent	Number	Percent
Female	180	1.8	20	0.8	-	-	15	1.6
Clerical and related	1,495	14.7	295	12.2	70	17.3	155	16.6
Male	320	3.1	50	2.1	10	2.5	-	-
Female	1,175	11.5	245	10.1	60	14.8	150	16.0
Sales	245	2.4	45	1.9	25	6.2	25	2.7
Male	120	1.2	15	0.6	15	3.7	-	-
Female	130	1.3	30	1.2	-	-	20	2.1
Service	1,730	17.0	470	19.4	35	8.6	125	13.4
Male	555	5.4	125	5.2	20	4.9	40	4.3
Female	1,170	11.5	345	14.3	20	4.9	85	9.1
Farming, horticultural and animal husbandry	30	0.3	-	-	-	-	-	-
Male	25	0.2	-	-	-	-	-	-
Female	-	-	-	-	-	-	-	-
Fishing, trapping and related	225	2.2	95	3.9	10	2.5	-	-
Male	215	2.1	90	3.7	10	2.5	-	-
Female	-	-	-	-	-	-	-	-
Forestry and logging	115	1.1	90	3.7	-	-	10	1.1
Male	115	1.1	85	3.5	-	-	10	1.1
Female	-	-	-	-	-	-	-	-
Mining and quarrying including oil and gas field	340	3.3	135	5.6	-	-	45	4.8
Male	325	3.2	125	5.2	-	-	45	4.8
Female	15	0.1	10	0.4	-	-	-	-
Processing	105	1.0	10	0.4	-	-	15	1.6
Male	65	0.6	10	0.4	-	-	-	-
Female	40	0.4	-	-	-	-	-	-
Machining and related	70	0.7	-	-	-	-	15	1.6
Male	65	0.6	-	-	-	-	15	1.6
Female	-	-	-	-	-	-	-	-
Product fabricating, assembling, and repairing	390	3.8	50	2.1	30	7.4	30	3.2
Male	260	2.5	25	1.0	15	3.7	30	3.2
Female	135	1.3	25	1.0	10	2.5	-	-
Construction and trades	1,150	11.3	270	11.2	40	9.9	160	17.1
Male	1,120	11.0	270	11.2	40	9.9	155	16.6
Female	30	0.3	-	-	-	-	-	-
Transportation and equipment operating	670	6.6	110	4.5	35	8.6	45	4.8
Male	630	6.2	110	4.5	35	8.6	35	3.7
Female	45	0.4	-	-	-	-	10	1.1
Material handling and related, not elsewhere classified	210	2.1	35	1.4	-	-	15	1.6

[Continued]

1354

★ 951 ★

Population 15 Years and Over, by Occupation and Sex for Detailed Aboriginal Origins for Northwest Territories, 1986 - I

[Continued]

Occupation	Total Aboriginal origins[3]		North American Indian only		North American and non-Aboriginal[4]		Metis only	
	Number	Percent	Number	Percent	Number	Percent	Number	Percent
Male	190	1.9	35	1.4	-	-	15	1.6
Female	25	0.2	-	-	-	-	-	-
Other crafts and equipment operating	95	0.9	10	0.4	15	3.7	-	-
Male	80	0.8	10	0.4	15	3.7	-	-
Female	15	0.1	-	-	-	-	-	-
Occupations not elsewhere classified	460	4.5	135	5.6	-	-	40	4.3
Male	440	4.3	135	5.6	-	-	40	4.3
Female	15	0.1	-	-	-	-	-	-
All occupations	9,460	92.7	2,260	93.4	400	98.8	890	95.2
Male	5,500	53.9	1,300	53.7	255	63.0	520	55.6
Female	3,955	38.8	965	39.9	145	35.8	375	40.1
Occupation - not applicable[5]	745	7.3	160	6.6	-	-	40	4.3
Male	360	3.5	85	3.5	-	-	15	1.6
Female	385	3.8	70	2.9	-	-	25	2.7

Source: Aboriginal Peoples Output Program, 1986 Census, Statistics Canada, *A Data Book on Canada's Aboriginal Population from the 1986 Census of Canada*, March, 1989, pp. 284-286. Primary source: 1986 Census of Canada. *Notes:* A dash (-) represents zero or a percentage less than .05 percent. 1. Aboriginal origins are derived from the ethnic origin question which asks whether respondents are North American Indian, Metis or Inuit. 2. All 1986 figures exclude the population estimated at about 45,000 on 136 incompletely enumerated Indian reserves and settlements throughout Canada. 3. Total Aboriginal origins—are sum of persons who reported: (A) a single aboriginal (e.g., North American Indian, Metis or Inuit) and, (B) multiple aboriginal origins, that is those who reported: at least one aboriginal origin with any other non-aboriginal (e.g., Metis and French), or two or more aboriginal origins only. 4. Non-aboriginal in these columns—refers to persons who reported one or more non-aboriginal origins such as British, French, etc., in combination with one of the aboriginal origins such as North American Indian. 5. Occupation—not applicable—refers to unemployed persons who had never worked or who last worked prior to January 1, 1985.

★ 952 ★

Population 15 Years and Over, by Occupation and Sex for Detailed Aboriginal Origins for Northwest Territories, 1986 - II[1,2]

Occupation	Metis and non-Aboriginal[3]		Inuit only		Inuit and non-Aboriginal[3]		Other multiple Aboriginal origins[4]	
	Number	Percent	Number	Percent	Number	Percent	Number	Percent
Total in labor force	345	100.0	5,485	100.0	175	100.0	440	100.0
Male	185	53.6	3,160	57.6	105	60.0	240	54.5
Female	160	46.4	2,320	42.3	70	40.0	200	45.5
Managerial, administrative, and related	45	13.0	325	5.9	20	11.4	20	4.5
Male	10	2.9	200	3.6	15	8.6	15	3.4
Female	30	8.7	120	2.2	-	-	-	-
Natural sciences, engineering and mathematics	-	-	90	1.6	-	-	-	-
Male	-	-	75	1.4	-	-	-	-
Female	-	-	10	0.2	-	-	-	-
Social sciences and related fields	-	-	130	2.4	-	-	-	-
Male	-	-	45	0.8	-	-	-	-

[Continued]

★ 952 ★

Population 15 Years and Over, by Occupation and Sex for Detailed Aboriginal Origins for Northwest Territories, 1986 - II

[Continued]

Occupation	Metis and non-Aboriginal[3]		Inuit only		Inuit and non-Aboriginal[3]		Other multiple Aboriginal origins[4]	
	Number	Percent	Number	Percent	Number	Percent	Number	Percent
Female	-	-	75	1.4	-	-	-	-
Religion	-	-	-	-	-	-	-	-
Male	-	-	-	-	-	-	-	-
Female	-	-	-	-	-	-	-	-
Teaching and related	20	5.8	315	5.7	-	-	-	-
Male	-	-	70	1.3	-	-	-	-
Female	10	2.9	245	4.5	-	-	-	-
Medicine and health	-	-	25	0.5	-	-	-	-
Male	-	-	-	-	-	-	-	-
Female	-	-	20	0.4	-	-	-	-
Artistic, literary, recreational and related fields	-	-	240	4.4	-	-	-	-
Male	-	-	100	1.8	-	-	-	-
Female	-	-	140	2.6	-	-	-	-
Clerical and related	75	21.7	820	14.9	20	11.4	65	14.8
Male	15	4.3	225	4.1	-	-	-	-
Female	60	17.4	595	10.8	15	8.6	65	14.8
Sales	-	-	130	2.4	-	-	-	-
Male	-	-	65	1.2	-	-	-	-
Female	-	-	65	1.2	-	-	-	-
Service	50	14.5	915	16.7	40	22.9	100	22.7
Male	20	5.8	320	5.8	10	5.7	25	5.7
Female	30	8.7	590	10.8	25	14.3	70	15.9
Farming, horticultural and animal husbandry	-	-	15	0.3	-	-	-	-
Male	-	-	15	0.3	-	-	-	-
Female	-	-	-	-	-	-	-	-
Fishing, trapping and related	-	-	95	1.7	-	-	-	-
Male	-	-	95	1.7	-	-	-	-
Female	-	-	-	-	-	-	-	-
Forestry and logging	-	-	-	-	-	-	-	-
Male	-	-	-	-	-	-	-	-
Female	-	-	-	-	-	-	-	-
Mining and quarrying including oil and gas field	20	5.8	130	2.4	-	-	-	-
Male	20	5.8	120	2.2	-	-	-	-
Female	-	-	-	-	-	-	-	-
Processing	-	-	65	1.2	-	-	-	-
Male	-	-	30	0.5	-	-	-	-
Female	-	-	30	0.5	-	-	-	-
Machining and related	-	-	35	0.6	-	-	10	2.3
Male	-	-	30	0.5	-	-	10	2.3

[Continued]

Population 15 Years and Over, by Occupation and Sex for Detailed Aboriginal Origins for Northwest Territories, 1986 - II

[Continued]

Occupation	Metis and non-Aboriginal[3]		Inuit only		Inuit and non-Aboriginal[3]		Other multiple Aboriginal origins[4]	
	Number	Percent	Number	Percent	Number	Percent	Number	Percent
Female	-	-	-	-	-	-	-	-
Product fabricating, assembling, and repairing	20	5.8	230	4.2	-	-	15	3.4
Male	20	5.8	140	2.6	-	-	15	3.4
Female	-	-	90	1.6	-	-	-	-
Construction and trades	35	10.1	595	10.8	10	5.7	40	9.1
Male	35	10.1	575	10.5	10	5.7	45	10.2
Female	-	-	25	0.5	-	-	-	-
Transportation and equipment operating	25	7.2	395	7.2	15	8.6	35	8.0
Male	15	4.3	375	6.8	20	11.4	40	9.1
Female	-	-	20	0.4	-	-	-	-
Material handling and related, not elsewhere classified	-	-	140	2.6	-	-	15	3.4
Male	-	-	125	2.3	-	-	-	-
Female	-	-	15	0.3	-	-	-	-
Other crafts and equipment operating	-	-	55	1.0	-	-	-	-
Male	-	-	40	0.7	-	-	-	-
Female	-	-	15	0.3	-	-	-	-
Occupations not elsewhere classified	-	-	235	4.3	-	-	25	5.7
Male	-	-	225	4.1	-	-	15	3.4
Female	-	-	10	0.2	-	-	-	-
All occupations	335	97.1	4,980	90.8	170	97.1	420	95.5
Male	185	53.6	2,910	53.1	100	57.1	230	52.3
Female	150	43.5	2,060	37.6	65	37.1	190	43.2
Occupation - not applicable[5]	-	-	505	9.2	-	-	20	4.5
Male	-	-	245	4.5	-	-	10	2.3
Female	-	-	260	4.7	-	-	-	-

Source: Aboriginal Peoples Output Program, 1986 Census, Statistics Canada, *A Data Book on Canada's Aboriginal Population from the 1986 Census of Canada*, March, 1989, pp. 284-286. Primary source: 1986 Census of Canada. *Notes:* A dash (-) represents zero or a percentage less than .05 percent. 1. Aboriginal origins and derived from the ethnic origin question which asks whether respondents are North American Indian, Metis or Inuit. 2. All 1986 figures exclude the population estimated at about 45,000 on 136 incompletely enumerated Indian reserves and settlements throughout Canada. 3. Non-aboriginal in these columns—refers to persons who reported one or more non-aboriginal origins such as British, French, etc., in combination with one of the aboriginal origins such as North American Indian. 4. Other multiple aboriginal origins—refer to the sum of those persons reporting two or more aboriginal origins with or without a non-aboriginal origin. 5. Occupation—not applicable—refers to unemployed persons who had never worked or who had last worked prior to January 1, 1985.

★ 953 ★

Population 15 Years and Over, by Occupation and Sex for Detailed Aboriginal Origins for Nova Scotia, 1986 - I[1,2]

Occupation	Total Aboriginal origins[3]		North American Indian only		North American and non-Aboriginal[4]		Metis only	
	Number	Percent	Number	Percent	Number	Percent	Number	Percent
Total in labor force	5,445	100.0	1,490	100.0	3,275	100.0	105	100.0
Male	3,005	55.2	820	55.0	1,815	55.4	65	61.9
Female	2,440	44.8	665	44.6	1,465	44.7	40	38.1
Managerial, administrative, and related	365	6.7	105	7.0	230	7.0	-	-
Male	195	3.6	65	4.4	110	3.4	-	-
Female	175	3.2	40	2.7	125	3.8	-	-
Natural sciences, engineering and mathematics	150	2.8	25	1.7	100	3.1	-	-
Male	125	2.3	25	1.7	85	2.6	-	-
Female	20	0.4	-	-	15	0.5	-	-
Social sciences and related fields	195	3.6	105	7.0	70	2.1	-	-
Male	65	1.2	35	2.3	30	0.9	-	-
Female	130	2.4	75	5.0	40	1.2	-	-
Religion	-	-	-	-	-	-	-	-
Male	-	-	-	-	-	-	-	-
Female	-	-	-	-	-	-	-	-
Teaching and related	180	3.3	70	4.7	100	3.1	-	-
Male	75	1.4	10	0.7	50	1.5	-	-
Female	105	1.9	50	3.4	55	1.7	-	-
Medicine and health	195	3.6	30	2.0	150	4.6	-	-
Male	15	0.3	-	-	15	0.5	-	-
Female	180	3.3	30	2.0	130	4.0	-	-
Artistic, literary, recreational and related fields	105	1.9	20	1.3	65	2.0	-	-
Male	75	1.4	15	1.0	55	1.7	-	-
Female	30	0.6	-	-	15	0.5	-	-
Clerical and related	805	14.8	195	13.1	505	15.4	10	9.5
Male	155	2.8	35	2.3	100	3.1	-	-
Female	655	12.0	160	10.7	405	12.4	15	14.3
Sales	275	5.1	30	2.0	210	6.4	-	-
Male	140	2.6	20	1.3	110	3.4	-	-
Female	135	2.5	15	1.0	110	3.1	-	-
Service	1,135	20.8	235	15.8	755	23.1	20	19.0
Male	600	11.0	105	7.0	425	13.0	-	-
Female	540	9.9	130	8.7	335	10.2	20	19.0
Farming, horticultural and animal husbandry	95	1.7	15	1.0	40	1.2	25	23.8
Male	70	1.3	15	1.0	30	0.9	20	19.0
Female	20	0.4	-	-	10	0.3	-	-
Fishing, trapping and related	40	0.7	-	-	30	0.9	-	-
Male	35	0.6	-	-	20	0.6	-	-
Female	-	-	-	-	-	-	-	-
Forestry and logging	90	1.7	50	3.4	25	0.8	-	-
Male	85	1.6	50	3.4	25	0.8	-	-

[Continued]

★ 953 ★

Population 15 Years and Over, by Occupation and Sex for Detailed Aboriginal Origins for Nova Scotia, 1986 - I

[Continued]

Occupation	Total Aboriginal origins[3]		North American Indian only		North American and non-Aboriginal[4]		Metis only	
	Number	Percent	Number	Percent	Number	Percent	Number	Percent
Female	-	-	-	-	-	-	-	-
Mining and quarrying including oil and gas field	-	-	-	-	-	-	-	-
Male	-	-	-	-	-	-	-	-
Female	-	-	-	-	-	-	-	-
Processing	250	4.6	30	2.0	170	5.2	-	-
Male	140	2.6	15	1.0	110	3.4	-	-
Female	110	2.0	15	1.0	60	1.8	-	-
Machining and related	65	1.2	10	0.7	45	1.4	-	-
Male	45	0.8	-	-	40	1.2	-	-
Female	15	0.3	-	-	-	-	-	-
Product fabricating, assembling, and repairing	245	4.5	50	3.4	165	5.0	-	-
Male	165	3.0	25	1.7	125	3.8	-	-
Female	75	1.4	30	2.0	40	1.2	-	-
Construction and trades	520	9.6	215	14.4	260	7.9	-	-
Male	500	9.2	205	13.8	250	7.6	-	-
Female	20	0.4	-	-	-	-	-	-
Transportation and equipment operating	210	3.9	60	4.0	120	3.7	10	9.5
Male	205	3.8	55	3.7	120	3.7	10	9.5
Female	-	-	-	-	-	-	-	-
Material handling and related, not elsewhere classified	60	1.1	15	1.0	50	1.5	-	-
Male	60	1.1	15	1.0	45	1.4	-	-
Female	-	-	-	-	-	-	-	-
Other crafts and equipment operating	60	1.1	20	1.3	45	1.4	-	-
Male	40	0.7	-	-	30	0.9	-	-
Female	25	0.5	15	1.0	15	0.5	-	-
Occupations not elsewhere classified	105	1.9	55	3.7	30	0.9	-	-
Male	85	1.6	45	3.0	25	0.8	-	-
Female	15	0.3	10	0.7	-	-	-	-
All occupations	5,170	94.9	1,335	89.6	3,175	96.9	105	100.0
Male	2,905	53.4	740	49.7	1,805	55.1	65	61.9
Female	2,270	41.7	590	39.6	1,370	41.8	40	38.1
Occupation - not applicable[5]	275	5.1	160	10.7	100	3.1	-	-

[Continued]

★ 953 ★

Population 15 Years and Over, by Occupation and Sex for Detailed Aboriginal Origins for Nova Scotia, 1986 - I
[Continued]

Occupation	Total Aboriginal origins[3]		North American Indian only		North American and non-Aboriginal[4]		Metis only	
	Number	Percent	Number	Percent	Number	Percent	Number	Percent
Male	100	1.8	80	5.4	10	0.3	-	-
Female	175	3.2	75	5.0	90	2.7	-	-

Source: Aboriginal Peoples Output Program, 1986 Census, Statistics Canada, *A Data Book on Canada's Aboriginal Population from the 1986 Census of Canada*, March, 1989, pp. 92-94. Primary source: 1986 Census of Canada. *Notes:* A dash (-) represents zero or a percentage less than .05 percent. 1. Aboriginal origins are derived from the ethnic origin question which asks whether respondents are North American Indian, Metis or Inuit. 2. All 1986 figures exclude the population estimated at about 45,000 on 136 incompletely enumerated Indian reserves and settlements throughout Canada. 3. Total Aboriginal origins—are sum of persons who reported: (A) a single aboriginal (e.g., North American Indian, Metis or Inuit) and, (B) multiple aboriginal origins, that is those who reported: at least one aboriginal origin with any other non-aboriginal (e.g., Metis and French), or two or more aboriginal origins only. 4. Non-aboriginal in these columns—refers to persons who reported one or more non-aboriginal origins such as British, French, etc., in combination with one of the aboriginal origins such as North American Indian. 5. Occupation—not applicable—refers to unemployed persons who had never worked or who last worked prior to January 1, 1985.

★ 954 ★

Population 15 Years and Over, by Occupation and Sex for Detailed Aboriginal Origins for Nova Scotia, 1986 - II[1,2]

Occupation	Metis and non-Aboriginal[3]		Inuit only		Inuit and non-Aboriginal[3]		Other multiple Aboriginal origins[4]	
	Number	Percent	Number	Percent	Number	Percent	Number	Percent
Total in labor force	305	100.0	50	100.0	85	100.0	140	100.0
Male	140	45.9	30	60.0	35	41.2	90	64.3
Female	160	52.5	20	40.0	45	52.9	45	32.1
Managerial, administrative, and related	15	4.9	-	-	-	-	10	7.1
Male	10	3.3	-	-	-	-	15	10.7
Female	-	-	-	-	-	-	-	-
Natural sciences, engineering and mathematics	-	-	-	-	-	-	-	-
Male	-	-	-	-	-	-	-	-
Female	-	-	-	-	-	-	-	-
Social sciences and related fields	10	3.3	-	-	-	-	-	-
Male	-	-	-	-	-	-	-	-
Female	10	3.3	-	-	-	-	-	-
Religion	-	-	-	-	-	-	-	-
Male	-	-	-	-	-	-	-	-
Female	-	-	-	-	-	-	-	-
Teaching and related	-	-	-	-	-	-	-	-
Male	-	-	-	-	-	-	-	-
Female	-	-	-	-	-	-	-	-
Medicine and health	10	3.3	-	-	-	-	-	-
Male	-	-	-	-	-	-	-	-
Female	10	3.3	-	-	-	-	-	-
Artistic, literary, recreational and related fields	-	-	-	-	-	-	-	-

[Continued]

★ 954 ★

Population 15 Years and Over, by Occupation and Sex for Detailed Aboriginal Origins for Nova Scotia, 1986 - II

[Continued]

Occupation	Metis and non-Aboriginal[3]		Inuit only		Inuit and non-Aboriginal[3]		Other multiple Aboriginal origins[4]	
	Number	Percent	Number	Percent	Number	Percent	Number	Percent
Male	-	-	-	-	-	-	-	-
Female	-	-	-	-	-	-	-	-
Clerical and related	45	14.8	-	-	15	17.6	25	17.9
Male	-	-	-	-	-	-	10	7.1
Female	45	14.8	-	-	-	-	-	-
Sales	20	6.6	-	-	-	-	-	-
Male	-	-	-	-	-	-	-	-
Female	20	6.6	-	-	-	-	-	-
Service	75	24.6	-	-	15	17.6	25	17.9
Male	40	13.1	-	-	-	-	25	17.9
Female	35	11.5	-	-	-	-	-	-
Farming, horticultural and animal husbandry	15	4.9	-	-	-	-	-	-
Male	-	-	-	-	-	-	-	-
Female	-	-	-	-	-	-	-	-
Fishing, trapping and related	-	-	-	-	-	-	-	-
Male	-	-	-	-	-	-	-	-
Female	-	-	-	-	-	-	-	-
Forestry and logging	10	3.3	-	-	-	-	-	-
Male	10	3.3	-	-	-	-	-	-
Female	-	-	-	-	-	-	-	-
Mining and quarrying including oil and gas field	-	-	-	-	-	-	-	-
Male	-	-	-	-	-	-	-	-
Female	-	-	-	-	-	-	-	-
Processing	20	6.6	-	-	25	29.4	-	-
Male	-	-	-	-	-	-	-	-
Female	20	6.6	-	-	15	17.6	-	-
Machining and related	-	-	-	-	-	-	-	-
Male	-	-	-	-	-	-	-	-
Female	-	-	-	-	-	-	-	-
Product fabricating, assembling, and repairing	10	3.3	-	-	-	-	-	-
Male	-	-	-	-	-	-	-	-
Female	-	-	-	-	-	-	-	-
Construction and trades	20	6.6	-	-	-	-	10	7.1
Male	20	6.6	-	-	-	-	10	7.1
Female	-	-	-	-	-	-	-	-
Transportation and equipment operating	10	3.3	-	-	-	-	-	-
Male	10	3.3	-	-	-	-	-	-
Female	-	-	-	-	-	-	-	-

[Continued]

★ 954 ★

Population 15 Years and Over, by Occupation and Sex for Detailed Aboriginal Origins for Nova Scotia, 1986 - II

[Continued]

Occupation	Metis and non-Aboriginal[3]		Inuit only		Inuit and non-Aboriginal[3]		Other multiple Aboriginal origins[4]	
	Number	Percent	Number	Percent	Number	Percent	Number	Percent
Material handling and related, not elsewhere classified	-	-	-	-	-	-	-	-
Male	-	-	-	-	-	-	-	-
Female	-	-	-	-	-	-	-	-
Other crafts and equipment operating	-	-	-	-	-	-	-	-
Male	-	-	-	-	-	-	-	-
Female	-	-	-	-	-	-	-	-
Occupations not elsewhere classified	-	-	10	20.0	-	-	-	-
Male	-	-	10	20.0	-	-	-	-
Female	-	-	-	-	-	-	-	-
All occupations	295	96.7	50	100.0	80	94.1	135	96.4
Male	135	44.3	30	60.0	35	41.2	90	64.3
Female	160	52.5	20	40.0	45	52.9	40	28.6
Occupation - not applicable[5]	10	3.3	-	-	-	-	-	-
Male	-	-	-	-	-	-	-	-
Female	-	-	-	-	-	-	-	-

Source: Aboriginal Peoples Output Program, 1986 Census, Statistics Canada, *A Data Book on Canada's Aboriginal Population from the 1986 Census of Canada,* March, 1989, pp. 92-94. Primary source: 1986 Census of Canada. *Notes:* A dash (-) represents zero or a percentage less than .05 percent. 1. Aboriginal origins and derived from the ethnic origin question which asks whether respondents are North American Indian, Metis or Inuit. 2. All 1986 figures exclude the population estimated at about 45,000 on 136 incompletely enumerated Indian reserves and settlements throughout Canada. 3. Non-aboriginal in these columns—refers to persons who reported one or more non-aboriginal origins such as British, French, etc., in combination with one of the aboriginal origins such as North American Indian. 4. Other multiple aboriginal origins—refer to the sum of those persons reporting two or more aboriginal origins with or without a non-aboriginal origin. 5. Occupation—not applicable—refers to unemployed persons who had never worked or who had last worked prior to January 1, 1985.

★ 955 ★

Population 15 Years and Over, by Occupation and Sex for Detailed Aboriginal Origins for Ontario, 1986 - I[1,2]

Occupation	Total Aboriginal origins[3]		North American Indian only		North American and non-Aboriginal[4]		Metis only	
	Number	Percent	Number	Percent	Number	Percent	Number	Percent
Total in labor force	74,955	100.0	19,555	100.0	46,090	100.0	1,650	100.0
Male	40,195	53.6	11,060	56.6	24,080	52.2	975	59.1
Female	34,765	46.4	8,495	43.4	22,005	47.7	675	40.9
Managerial, administrative, and related	5,730	7.6	1,155	5.9	3,845	8.3	90	5.5
Male	3,120	4.2	695	3.6	2,045	4.4	40	2.4
Female	2,605	3.5	460	2.4	1,800	3.9	50	3.0
Natural sciences, engineering and mathematics	1,905	2.5	255	1.3	1,445	3.1	25	1.5
Male	1,440	1.9	185	0.9	1,105	2.4	15	0.9
Female	465	0.6	70	0.4	340	0.7	-	-
Social sciences and related fields	1,990	2.7	900	4.6	875	1.9	30	1.8

[Continued]

★ 955 ★

Population 15 Years and Over, by Occupation and Sex for Detailed Aboriginal Origins for Ontario, 1986 - I
[Continued]

Occupation	Total Aboriginal origins[3]		North American Indian only		North American and non-Aboriginal[4]		Metis only	
	Number	Percent	Number	Percent	Number	Percent	Number	Percent
Male	660	0.9	335	1.7	225	0.5	-	-
Female	1,330	1.8	565	2.9	650	1.4	20	1.2
Religion	120	0.2	40	0.2	65	0.1	-	-
Male	100	0.1	30	0.2	65	0.1	-	-
Female	20	-	10	0.1	-	-	-	-
Teaching and related	2,060	2.7	520	2.7	1,300	2.8	30	1.8
Male	740	1.0	140	0.7	485	1.1	25	1.5
Female	1,320	1.8	375	1.9	815	1.8	-	-
Medicine and health	2,620	3.5	505	2.6	1,835	4.0	30	1.8
Male	415	0.6	55	0.3	295	0.6	-	-
Female	2,210	2.9	455	2.3	1,545	3.4	20	1.2
Artistic, literary, recreational and related fields	1,455	1.9	345	1.8	885	1.9	35	2.1
Male	835	1.1	260	1.3	480	1.0	15	0.9
Female	615	0.8	90	0.5	400	0.9	15	0.9
Clerical and related	12,555	16.8	2,445	12.5	8,640	18.7	210	12.7
Male	2,765	3.7	560	2.9	1,845	4.0	70	4.2
Female	9,790	13.1	1,890	9.7	6,790	14.7	140	8.5
Sales	5,125	6.8	780	4.0	3,655	7.9	65	3.9
Male	2,240	3.0	330	1.7	1,605	3.5	20	1.2
Female	2,880	3.8	455	2.3	2,050	4.4	45	2.7
Service	11,345	15.1	2,865	14.7	6,955	15.1	270	16.4
Male	4,345	5.8	1,035	5.3	2,800	6.1	60	3.6
Female	7,005	9.3	1,830	9.4	4,155	9.0	210	12.7
Farming, horticultural and animal husbandry	1,780	2.4	500	2.6	1,015	2.2	40	2.4
Male	1,205	1.6	335	1.7	685	1.5	35	2.1
Female	570	0.8	170	0.9	330	0.7	-	-
Fishing, trapping and related	115	0.2	50	0.3	50	0.1	-	-
Male	110	0.1	50	0.3	45	0.1	-	-
Female	-	-	-	-	-	-	-	-
Forestry and logging	1,205	1.6	745	3.8	290	0.6	55	3.3
Male	1,055	1.4	655	3.3	240	0.5	45	2.7
Female	150	0.2	90	0.5	45	0.1	-	-
Mining and quarrying including oil and gas field	540	0.7	190	1.0	240	0.5	35	2.1
Male	530	0.7	185	0.9	235	0.5	35	2.1
Female	-	-	-	-	-	-	-	-
Processing	2,560	3.4	815	4.2	1,385	3.0	85	5.2
Male	1,940	2.6	600	3.1	1,050	2.3	65	3.9
Female	615	0.8	215	1.1	340	0.7	20	1.2
Machining and related	2,100	2.8	565	2.9	1,320	2.9	25	1.5

[Continued]

★ 955 ★

Population 15 Years and Over, by Occupation and Sex for Detailed Aboriginal Origins for Ontario, 1986 - I

[Continued]

Occupation	Total Aboriginal origins[3]		North American Indian only		North American and non-Aboriginal[4]		Metis only	
	Number	Percent	Number	Percent	Number	Percent	Number	Percent
Male	1,805	2.4	515	2.6	1,110	2.4	25	1.5
Female	295	0.4	50	0.3	210	0.5	-	-
Product fabricating, assembling, and repairing	5,800	7.7	1,315	6.7	3,770	8.2	145	8.8
Male	4,225	5.6	860	4.4	2,845	6.2	90	5.5
Female	1,575	2.1	460	2.4	920	2.0	60	3.6
Construction and trades	5,415	7.2	2,190	11.2	2,570	5.6	180	10.9
Male	5,170	6.9	2,075	10.6	2,475	5.4	175	10.6
Female	250	0.3	115	0.6	95	0.2	-	-
Transportation and equipment operating	3,300	4.4	650	3.3	2,195	4.8	115	7.0
Male	2,770	3.7	510	2.6	1,895	4.1	100	6.1
Female	525	0.7	135	0.7	300	0.7	15	0.9
Material handling and related, not elsewhere classified	1,820	2.4	450	2.3	1,150	2.5	35	2.1
Male	1,385	1.8	290	1.5	920	2.0	25	1.5
Female	435	0.6	160	0.8	230	0.5	-	-
Other crafts and equipment operating	920	1.2	155	0.8	660	1.4	30	1.8
Male	660	0.9	90	0.5	475	1.0	25	1.5
Female	260	0.3	60	0.3	190	0.4	-	-
Occupations not elsewhere classified	2,120	2.8	915	4.7	990	2.1	60	3.6
Male	1,630	2.2	685	3.5	790	1.7	50	3.0
Female	485	0.6	230	1.2	195	0.4	10	0.6
All occupations	72,565	96.8	18,355	93.9	45,135	97.9	1,605	97.3
Male	39,150	52.2	10,465	53.5	23,720	51.5	960	58.2
Female	33,415	44.6	7,890	40.3	21,415	46.5	645	39.1
Occupation - not applicable[5]	2,390	3.2	1,205	6.2	955	2.1	45	2.7
Male	1,040	1.4	600	3.1	365	0.8	15	0.9
Female	1,345	1.8	605	3.1	590	1.3	35	2.1

Source: Aboriginal Peoples Output Program, 1986 Census, Statistics Canada, *A Data Book on Canada's Aboriginal Population from the 1986 Census of Canada,* March, 1989, pp. 164-166. Primary source: 1986 Census of Canada. *Notes:* A dash (-) represents zero or a percentage less than .05 percent. 1. Aboriginal origins are derived from the ethnic origin question which asks whether respondents are North American Indian, Metis or Inuit. 2. All 1986 figures exclude the population estimated at about 45,000 on 136 incompletely enumerated Indian reserves and settlements throughout Canada. 3. Total Aboriginal origins—are sum of persons who reported: (A) a single aboriginal (e.g., North American Indian, Metis or Inuit) and, (B) multiple aboriginal origins, that is those who reported: at least one aboriginal origin with any other non-aboriginal (e.g., Metis and French), or two or more aboriginal origins only. 4. Non-aboriginal in these columns—refers to persons who reported one or more non-aboriginal origins such as British, French, etc., in combination with one of the aboriginal origins such as North American Indian. 5. Occupation—not applicable—refers to unemployed persons who had never worked or who last worked prior to January 1, 1985.

★ 956 ★

Population 15 Years and Over, by Occupation and Sex for Detailed Aboriginal Origins for Ontario, 1986 - II[1,2]

Occupation	Metis and non-Aboriginal[3]		Inuit only		Inuit and non-Aboriginal[3]		Other multiple Aboriginal origins[4]	
	Number	Percent	Number	Percent	Number	Percent	Number	Percent
Total in labor force	4,810	100.0	280	100.0	715	100.0	1,845	100.0
Male	2,440	50.7	170	60.7	410	57.3	1,050	56.9
Female	2,375	49.4	115	41.1	305	42.7	795	43.1
Managerial, administrative, and related	400	8.3	20	7.1	55	7.7	155	8.4
Male	200	4.2	10	3.6	45	6.3	90	4.9
Female	205	4.3	-	-	15	2.1	65	3.5
Natural sciences, engineering and mathematics	110	2.3	-	-	25	3.5	50	2.7
Male	70	1.5	-	-	20	2.8	40	2.2
Female	35	0.7	-	-	-	-	-	-
Social sciences and related fields	115	2.4	-	-	10	1.4	50	2.7
Male	50	1.0	-	-	-	-	25	1.4
Female	65	1.4	-	-	-	-	25	1.4
Religion	15	0.3	-	-	-	-	-	-
Male	-	-	-	-	-	-	-	-
Female	-	-	-	-	-	-	-	-
Teaching and related	150	3.1	-	-	-	-	55	3.0
Male	55	1.1	-	-	-	-	25	1.4
Female	95	2.0	-	-	-	-	25	1.4
Medicine and health	165	3.4	15	5.4	-	-	55	3.0
Male	30	0.6	-	-	-	-	15	0.8
Female	145	3.0	10	3.6	-	-	40	2.2
Artistic, literary, recreational and related fields	115	2.4	15	5.4	-	-	50	2.7
Male	55	1.1	-	-	-	-	15	0.8
Female	60	1.2	-	-	-	-	35	1.9
Clerical and related	765	15.9	50	17.9	120	16.8	315	17.1
Male	150	3.1	15	5.4	15	2.1	115	6.2
Female	620	12.9	40	14.3	100	14.0	205	11.1
Sales	390	8.1	20	7.1	60	8.4	145	7.9
Male	175	3.6	15	5.4	10	1.4	80	4.3
Female	220	4.6	-	-	45	6.3	70	3.8
Service	810	16.8	25	8.9	105	14.7	310	16.8
Male	305	6.3	-	-	25	3.5	105	5.7
Female	505	10.5	15	5.4	75	10.5	200	10.8
Farming, horticultural and animal husbandry	140	2.9	15	5.4	10	1.4	45	2.4
Male	100	2.1	10	3.6	-	-	35	1.9
Female	45	0.9	-	-	-	-	-	-
Fishing, trapping and related	-	-	-	-	-	-	-	-
Male	-	-	-	-	-	-	-	-
Female	-	-	-	-	-	-	-	-
Forestry and logging	85	1.8	-	-	25	3.5	10	0.5
Male	80	1.7	-	-	25	3.5	10	0.5

[Continued]

★ 956 ★

Population 15 Years and Over, by Occupation and Sex for Detailed Aboriginal Origins for Ontario, 1986 - II

[Continued]

Occupation	Metis and non-Aboriginal[3]		Inuit only		Inuit and non-Aboriginal[3]		Other multiple Aboriginal origins[4]	
	Number	Percent	Number	Percent	Number	Percent	Number	Percent
Female	-	-	-	-	-	-	-	-
Mining and quarrying including oil and gas field	65	1.4	-	-	-	-	-	-
Male	65	1.4	-	-	-	-	-	-
Female	-	-	-	-	-	-	-	-
Processing	150	3.1	10	3.6	45	6.3	55	3.0
Male	115	2.4	15	5.4	45	6.3	50	2.7
Female	40	0.8	-	-	-	-	-	-
Machining and related	115	2.4	-	-	30	4.2	40	2.2
Male	90	1.9	-	-	30	4.2	35	1.9
Female	25	0.5	-	-	-	-	-	-
Product fabricating, assembling, and repairing	360	7.5	35	12.5	65	9.1	100	5.4
Male	270	5.6	25	8.9	55	7.7	80	4.3
Female	95	2.0	-	-	10	1.4	15	0.8
Construction and trades	285	5.9	20	7.1	35	4.9	135	7.3
Male	265	5.5	15	5.4	30	4.2	125	6.8
Female	20	0.4	-	-	-	-	-	-
Transportation and equipment operating	195	4.1	25	8.9	55	7.7	65	3.5
Male	145	3.0	20	7.1	40	5.6	55	3.0
Female	55	1.1	-	-	10	1.4	-	-
Material handling and related, not elsewhere classified	120	2.5	-	-	20	2.8	35	1.9
Male	100	2.1	-	-	15	2.1	30	1.6
Female	20	0.4	-	-	-	-	-	-
Other crafts and equipment operating	50	1.0	10	3.6	-	-	-	-
Male	45	0.9	-	-	-	-	-	-
Female	-	-	-	-	-	-	-	-
Occupations not elsewhere classified	80	1.7	-	-	20	2.8	55	3.0
Male	45	0.9	-	-	15	2.1	40	2.2
Female	35	0.7	-	-	-	-	15	0.8
All occupations	4,705	97.8	280	100.0	695	97.2	1,795	97.3
Male	2,400	49.9	165	58.9	405	56.6	1,035	56.1
Female	2,305	47.9	115	41.1	295	41.3	760	41.2
Occupation - not applicable[5]	110	2.3	-	-	15	2.1	50	2.7

[Continued]

★ 956 ★

Population 15 Years and Over, by Occupation and Sex for Detailed Aboriginal Origins for Ontario, 1986 - II

[Continued]

Occupation	Metis and non-Aboriginal[3]		Inuit only		Inuit and non-Aboriginal[3]		Other multiple Aboriginal origins[4]	
	Number	Percent	Number	Percent	Number	Percent	Number	Percent
Male	35	0.7	-	-	-	-	20	1.1
Female	70	1.5	-	-	10	1.4	40	2.2

Source: Aboriginal Peoples Output Program, 1986 Census, Statistics Canada, *A Data Book on Canada's Aboriginal Population from the 1986 Census of Canada,* March, 1989, pp. 164-166. Primary source: 1986 Census of Canada. *Notes:* A dash (-) represents zero or a percentage less than .05 percent. 1. Aboriginal origins and derived from the ethnic origin question which asks whether respondents are North American Indian, Metis or Inuit. 2. All 1986 figures exclude the population estimated at about 45,000 on 136 incompletely enumerated Indian reserves and settlements throughout Canada. 3. Non-aboriginal in these columns—refers to persons who reported one or more non-aboriginal origins such as British, French, etc., in combination with one of the aboriginal origins such as North American Indian. 4. Other multiple aboriginal origins—refer to the sum of those persons reporting two or more aboriginal origins with or without a non-aboriginal origin. 5. Occupation—not applicable—refers to unemployed persons who had never worked or who had last worked prior to January 1, 1985.

★ 957 ★

Population 15 Years and Over, by Occupation and Sex for Detailed Aboriginal Origins for Prince Edward Island, 1986 - I[1,2]

Occupation	Total Aboriginal origins[3]		North American Indian only		North American and non-Aboriginal[4]		Metis only	
	Number	Percent	Number	Percent	Number	Percent	Number	Percent
Total in labor force	605	100.0	150	100.0	370	100.0	10	100.0
Male	340	56.2	80	53.3	220	59.5	-	-
Female	265	43.8	65	43.3	155	41.9	10	100.0
Managerial, administrative, and related	45	7.4	10	6.7	20	5.4	-	-
Male	-	-	-	-	-	-	-	-
Female	35	5.8	-	-	15	4.1	-	-
Natural sciences, engineering and mathematics	10	1.7	-	-	-	-	-	-
Male	15	2.5	-	-	-	-	-	-
Female	-	-	-	-	-	-	-	-
Social sciences and related fields	30	5.0	10	6.7	-	-	-	-
Male	15	2.5	-	-	-	-	-	-
Female	15	2.5	-	-	-	-	-	-
Religion	10	1.7	-	-	10	2.7	-	-
Male	10	1.7	-	-	10	2.7	-	-
Female	-	-	-	-	-	-	-	-
Teaching and related	25	4.1	-	-	-	-	-	-
Male	-	-	-	-	-	-	-	-
Female	20	3.3	-	-	-	-	-	-
Medicine and health	20	3.3	-	-	20	5.4	-	-
Male	-	-	-	-	-	-	-	-
Female	15	2.5	-	-	15	4.1		
Artistic, literary, recreational and related fields	-	-	-	-	-	-	-	-
Male	-	-	-	-	-	-	-	-

[Continued]

★ 957 ★

Population 15 Years and Over, by Occupation and Sex for Detailed Aboriginal Origins for Prince Edward Island, 1986 - I

[Continued]

Occupation	Total Aboriginal origins[3]		North American Indian only		North American and non-Aboriginal[4]		Metis only	
	Number	Percent	Number	Percent	Number	Percent	Number	Percent
Female	-	-	-	-	-	-	-	-
Clerical and related	40	6.6	15	10.0	25	6.8	-	-
Male	-	-	-	-	-	-	-	-
Female	35	5.8	15	10.0	25	6.8	-	-
Sales	20	3.3	-	-	10	2.7	-	-
Male	-	-	-	-	-	-	-	-
Female	15	2.5	-	-	-	-	-	-
Service	95	15.7	15	10.0	65	17.6	-	-
Male	50	8.3	-	-	40	10.8	-	-
Female	40	6.6	-	-	25	6.8	-	-
Farming, horticultural and animal husbandry	35	5.8	-	-	20	5.4	-	-
Male	20	3.3	-	-	10	2.7	-	-
Female	-	-	-	-	-	-	-	-
Fishing, trapping and related	55	9.1	10	6.7	30	8.1	-	-
Male	45	7.4	-	-	30	8.1	-	-
Female	-	-	-	-	-	-	-	-
Forestry and logging	25	4.1	-	-	15	4.1	-	-
Male	15	2.5	-	-	10	2.7	-	-
Female	-	-	-	-	-	-	-	-
Mining and quarrying including oil and gas field	-	-	-	-	-	-	-	-
Male	-	-	-	-	-	-	-	-
Female	-	-	-	-	-	-	-	-
Processing	25	4.1	-	-	25	6.8	-	-
Male	-	-	-	-	-	-	-	-
Female	15	2.5	-	-	15	4.1	-	-
Machining and related	-	-	-	-	-	-	-	-
Male	-	-	-	-	-	-	-	-
Female	-	-	-	-	-	-	-	-
Product fabricating, assembling, and repairing	35	5.8	10	6.7	25	6.8	-	-
Male	35	5.8	-	-	20	5.4	-	-
Female	-	-	-	-	-	-	-	-
Construction and trades	30	5.0	20	13.3	-	-	-	-
Male	30	5.0	10	6.7	-	-	-	-
Female	-	-	-	-	-	-	-	-
Transportation and equipment operating	20	3.3	-	-	15	4.1	-	-
Male	15	2.5	-	-	15	4.1	-	-
Female	-	-	-	-	-	-	-	-
Material handling and related, not elsewhere classified	-	-	-	-	-	-	-	-

[Continued]

★957★

Population 15 Years and Over, by Occupation and Sex for Detailed Aboriginal Origins for Prince Edward Island, 1986 - I
[Continued]

Occupation	Total Aboriginal origins[3]		North American Indian only		North American and non-Aboriginal[4]		Metis only	
	Number	Percent	Number	Percent	Number	Percent	Number	Percent
Male	-	-	-	-	-	-	-	-
Female	-	-	-	-	-	-	-	-
Other crafts and equipment operating	-	-	-	-	-	-	-	-
Male	-	-	-	-	-	-	-	-
Female	-	-	-	-	-	-	-	-
Occupations not elsewhere classified	25	4.1	-	-	15	4.1	-	-
Male	25	4.1	-	-	15	4.1	-	-
Female	-	-	-	-	-	-	-	-
All occupations	555	91.7	125	83.3	345	93.2	10	100.0
Male	310	51.2	60	40.0	200	54.1	-	-
Female	240	39.7	55	36.7	140	37.8	10	100.0
Occupation - not applicable[5]	55	9.1	25	16.7	30	8.1	-	-
Male	35	5.8	15	10.0	15	4.1	-	-
Female	25	4.1	10	6.7	10	2.7	-	-

Source: Aboriginal Peoples Output Program, 1986 Census, Statistics Canada, *A Data Book on Canada's Aboriginal Population from the 1986 Census of Canada,* March, 1989, pp. 68-70. Primary source: 1986 Census of Canada. *Notes:* A dash (-) represents zero or a percentage less than .05 percent. 1. Aboriginal origins are derived from the ethnic origin question which asks whether respondents are North American Indian, Metis or Inuit. 2. All 1986 figures exclude the population estimated at about 45,000 on 136 incompletely enumerated Indian reserves and settlements throughout Canada. 3. Total Aboriginal origins—are sum of persons who reported: (A) a single aboriginal (e.g., North American Indian, Metis or Inuit) and, (B) multiple aboriginal origins, that is those who reported: at least one aboriginal origin with any other non-aboriginal (e.g., Metis and French), or two or more aboriginal origins only. 4. Non-aboriginal in these columns—refers to persons who reported one or more non-aboriginal origins such as British, French, etc., in combination with one of the aboriginal origins such as North American Indian. 5. Occupation—not applicable—refers to unemployed persons who had never worked or who last worked prior to January 1, 1985.

★958★

Population 15 Years and Over, by Occupation and Sex for Detailed Aboriginal Origins for Prince Edward Island, 1986 - II[1,2]

Occupation	Metis and non-Aboriginal[3]		Inuit only		Inuit and non-Aboriginal[3]		Other multiple Aboriginal origins[4]	
	Number	Percent	Number	Percent	Number	Percent	Number	Percent
Total in labor force	45	100.0	-	-	20	100.0	-	-
Male	25	55.6	-	-	15	75.0	-	-
Female	20	44.4	-	-	-	-	-	-
Managerial, administrative, and related	-	-	-	-	-	-	-	-
Male	-	-	-	-	-	-	-	-
Female	-	-	-	-	-	-	-	-
Natural sciences, engineering and mathematics	-	-	-	-	-	-	-	-
Male	-	-	-	-	-	-	-	-
Female	-	-	-	-	-	-	-	-
Social sciences and related fields	-	-	-	-	-	-	-	-
Male	-	-	-	-	-	-	-	-

[Continued]

Population 15 Years and Over, by Occupation and Sex for Detailed Aboriginal Origins for Prince Edward Island, 1986 - II

[Continued]

Occupation	Metis and non-Aboriginal[3]		Inuit only		Inuit and non-Aboriginal[3]		Other multiple Aboriginal origins[4]	
	Number	Percent	Number	Percent	Number	Percent	Number	Percent
Female	-	-	-	-	-	-	-	-
Religion	-	-	-	-	-	-	-	-
Male	-	-	-	-	-	-	-	-
Female	-	-	-	-	-	-	-	-
Teaching and related	-	-	-	-	-	-	-	-
Male	-	-	-	-	-	-	-	-
Female	-	-	-	-	-	-	-	-
Medicine and health	-	-	-	-	-	-	-	-
Male	-	-	-	-	-	-	-	-
Female	-	-	-	-	-	-	-	-
Artistic, literary, recreational and related fields	-	-	-	-	-	-	-	-
Male	-	-	-	-	-	-	-	-
Female	-	-	-	-	-	-	-	-
Clerical and related	-	-	-	-	-	-	-	-
Male	-	-	-	-	-	-	-	-
Female	-	-	-	-	-	-	-	-
Sales	-	-	-	-	-	-	-	-
Male	-	-	-	-	-	-	-	-
Female	-	-	-	-	-	-	-	-
Service	-	-	-	-	-	-	-	-
Male	-	-	-	-	-	-	-	-
Female	-	-	-	-	-	-	-	-
Farming, horticultural and animal husbandry	-	-	-	-	-	-	-	-
Male	-	-	-	-	-	-	-	-
Female	-	-	-	-	-	-	-	-
Fishing, trapping and related	10	22.2	-	-	-	-	-	-
Male	10	22.2	-	-	-	-	-	-
Female	-	-	-	-	-	-	-	-
Forestry and logging	-	-	-	-	-	-	-	-
Male	-	-	-	-	-	-	-	-
Female	-	-	-	-	-	-	-	-
Mining and quarrying including oil and gas field	-	-	-	-	-	-	-	-
Male	-	-	-	-	-	-	-	-
Female	-	-	-	-	-	-	-	-
Processing	-	-	-	-	-	-	-	-
Male	-	-	-	-	-	-	-	-
Female	-	-	-	-	-	-	-	-
Machining and related	-	-	-	-	-	-	-	-
Male	-	-	-	-	-	-	-	-

[Continued]

★ 958 ★

Population 15 Years and Over, by Occupation and Sex for Detailed Aboriginal Origins for Prince Edward Island, 1986 - II

[Continued]

Occupation	Metis and non-Aboriginal[3]		Inuit only		Inuit and non-Aboriginal[3]		Other multiple Aboriginal origins[4]	
	Number	Percent	Number	Percent	Number	Percent	Number	Percent
Female	-	-	-	-	-	-	-	-
Product fabricating, assembling, and repairing	-	-	-	-	-	-	-	-
Male	-	-	-	-	-	-	-	-
Female	-	-	-	-	-	-	-	-
Construction and trades	-	-	-	-	-	-	-	-
Male	-	-	-	-	-	-	-	-
Female	-	-	-	-	-	-	-	-
Transportation and equipment operating	-	-	-	-	-	-	-	-
Male	-	-	-	-	-	-	-	-
Female	-	-	-	-	-	-	-	-
Material handling and related, not elsewhere classified	-	-	-	-	-	-	-	-
Male	-	-	-	-	-	-	-	-
Female	-	-	-	-	-	-	-	-
Other crafts and equipment operating	-	-	-	-	-	-	-	-
Male	-	-	-	-	-	-	-	-
Female	-	-	-	-	-	-	-	-
Occupations not elsewhere classified	-	-	-	-	-	-	-	-
Male	-	-	-	-	-	-	-	-
Female	-	-	-	-	-	-	-	-
All occupations	45	100.0	-	-	20	100.0	-	-
Male	25	55.6	-	-	15	75.0	-	-
Female	20	44.4	-	-	-	-	-	-
Occupation - not applicable[5]	-	-	-	-	-	-	-	-
Male	-	-	-	-	-	-	-	-
Female	-	-	-	-	-	-	-	-

Source: Aboriginal Peoples Output Program, 1986 Census, Statistics Canada, *A Data Book on Canada's Aboriginal Population from the 1986 Census of Canada*, March, 1989, pp. 68-70. Primary source: 1986 Census of Canada. *Notes:* A dash (-) represents zero or a percentage less than .05 percent. 1. Aboriginal origins and derived from the ethnic origin question which asks whether respondents are North American Indian, Metis or Inuit. 2. All 1986 figures exclude the population estimated at about 45,000 on 136 incompletely enumerated Indian reserves and settlements throughout Canada. 3. Non-aboriginal in these columns—refers to persons who reported one or more non-aboriginal origins such as British, French, etc., in combination with one of the aboriginal origins such as North American Indian. 4. Other multiple aboriginal origins—refer to the sum of those persons reporting two or more aboriginal origins with or without a non-aboriginal origin. 5. Occupation—not applicable—refers to unemployed persons who had never worked or who had last worked prior to January 1, 1985.

★ 959 ★

Population 15 Years and Over, by Occupation and Sex for Detailed Aboriginal Origins for Quebec, 1986 - I[1,2]

Occupation	Total Aboriginal origins[3]		North American Indian only		North American and non-Aboriginal[4]		Metis only	
	Number	Percent	Number	Percent	Number	Percent	Number	Percent
Total in labor force	33,615	100.0	13,385	100.0	12,965	100.0	2,465	100.0
Male	18,700	55.6	7,955	59.4	6,630	51.1	1,505	61.1
Female	14,915	44.4	5,430	40.6	6,335	48.9	960	38.9
Managerial, administrative, and related	3,010	9.0	1,070	8.0	1,405	10.8	160	6.5
Male	1,820	5.4	735	5.5	745	5.7	95	3.9
Female	1,185	3.5	335	2.5	655	5.1	65	2.6
Natural sciences, engineering and mathematics	850	2.5	225	1.7	460	3.5	60	2.4
Male	605	1.8	175	1.3	295	2.3	55	2.2
Female	240	0.7	45	0.3	170	1.3	-	-
Social sciences and related fields	750	2.2	310	2.3	320	2.5	10	0.4
Male	295	0.9	140	1.0	105	0.8	-	-
Female	455	1.4	175	1.3	210	1.6	-	-
Religion	105	0.3	20	0.1	20	0.2	-	-
Male	35	0.1	10	0.1	20	0.2	-	-
Female	70	0.2	-	-	-	-	-	-
Teaching and related	1,405	4.2	490	3.7	590	4.6	45	1.8
Male	440	1.3	125	0.9	210	1.6	20	0.8
Female	965	2.9	370	2.8	385	3.0	25	1.0
Medicine and health	1,375	4.1	380	2.8	765	5.9	65	2.6
Male	295	0.9	75	0.6	160	1.2	15	0.6
Female	1,090	3.2	300	2.2	610	4.7	50	2.0
Artistic, literary, recreational and related fields	895	2.7	285	2.1	400	3.1	45	1.8
Male	445	1.3	155	1.2	185	1.4	30	1.2
Female	445	1.3	130	1.0	215	1.7	15	0.6
Clerical and related	5,750	17.1	2,120	15.8	2,460	19.0	375	15.2
Male	1,305	3.9	515	3.8	510	3.9	85	3.4
Female	4,445	13.2	1,605	12.0	1,960	15.1	290	11.8
Sales	2,135	6.4	780	5.8	950	7.3	145	5.9
Male	1,115	3.3	375	2.8	505	3.9	95	3.9
Female	1,020	3.0	405	3.0	445	3.4	50	2.0
Service	4,480	13.3	1,725	12.9	1,650	12.7	355	14.4
Male	2,055	6.1	840	6.3	800	6.2	145	5.9
Female	2,430	7.2	885	6.6	855	6.6	205	8.3
Farming, horticultural and animal husbandry	540	1.6	165	1.2	205	1.6	65	2.6
Male	405	1.2	125	0.9	160	1.2	40	1.6
Female	135	0.4	40	0.3	50	0.4	20	0.8
Fishing, trapping and related	80	0.2	50	0.4	20	0.2	-	-
Male	70	0.2	45	0.3	10	0.1	-	-
Female	10	-	-	-	-	-	-	-
Forestry and logging	645	1.9	395	3.0	85	0.7	90	3.7
Male	600	1.8	370	2.8	70	0.5	90	3.7

[Continued]

★ 959 ★

Population 15 Years and Over, by Occupation and Sex for Detailed Aboriginal Origins for Quebec, 1986 - I

[Continued]

Occupation	Total Aboriginal origins[3]		North American Indian only		North American and non-Aboriginal[4]		Metis only	
	Number	Percent	Number	Percent	Number	Percent	Number	Percent
Female	45	0.1	30	0.2	15	0.1	-	-
Mining and quarrying including oil and gas field	125	0.4	70	0.5	25	0.2	15	0.6
Male	120	0.4	70	0.5	25	0.2	-	-
Female	-	-	-	-	-	-	-	-
Processing	1,215	3.6	450	3.4	470	3.6	160	6.5
Male	950	2.8	385	2.9	345	2.7	125	5.1
Female	260	0.8	75	0.6	130	1.0	40	1.6
Machining and related	690	2.1	295	2.2	265	2.0	50	2.0
Male	645	1.9	280	2.1	255	2.0	50	2.0
Female	45	0.1	15	0.1	-	-	-	-
Product fabricating, assembling, and repairing	2,115	6.3	850	6.4	855	6.6	170	6.9
Male	1,630	4.8	605	4.5	715	5.5	130	5.3
Female	485	1.4	245	1.8	140	1.1	35	1.4
Construction and trades	2,185	6.5	1,270	9.5	480	3.7	125	5.1
Male	2,125	6.3	1,225	9.2	475	3.7	120	4.9
Female	65	0.2	45	0.3	-	-	-	-
Transportation and equipment operating	1,295	3.9	540	4.0	390	3.0	170	6.9
Male	1,200	3.6	505	3.8	360	2.8	150	6.1
Female	100	0.3	35	0.3	30	0.2	20	0.8
Material handling and related, not elsewhere classified	545	1.6	230	1.7	190	1.5	35	1.4
Male	470	1.4	200	1.5	155	1.2	30	1.2
Female	70	0.2	30	0.2	30	0.2	-	-
Other crafts and equipment operating	400	1.2	120	0.9	200	1.5	30	1.2
Male	300	0.9	110	0.8	120	0.9	30	1.2
Female	105	0.3	-	-	80	0.6	-	-
Occupations not elsewhere classified	506	1.5	225	1.7	130	1.0	35	1.4
Male	435	1.3	190	1.4	120	0.9	30	1.2
Female	70	0.2	40	0.3	-	-	-	-
All occupations	31,115	92.6	12,080	90.3	12,325	95.1	2,230	90.5
Male	17,380	51.7	7,245	54.1	6,330	48.8	1,360	55.2
Female	13,735	40.9	4,845	36.2	5,995	46.2	865	35.1
Occupation - not applicable[5]	2,500	7.4	1,305	9.7	635	4.9	245	9.9

[Continued]

★ 959 ★

Population 15 Years and Over, by Occupation and Sex for Detailed Aboriginal Origins for Quebec, 1986 - I
[Continued]

Occupation	Total Aboriginal origins[3]		North American Indian only		North American and non-Aboriginal[4]		Metis only	
	Number	Percent	Number	Percent	Number	Percent	Number	Percent
Male	1,325	3.9	715	5.3	295	2.3	145	5.9
Female	1,180	3.5	590	4.4	335	2.6	95	3.9

Source: Aboriginal Peoples Output Program, 1986 Census, Statistics Canada, *A Data Book on Canada's Aboriginal Population from the 1986 Census of Canada*, March, 1989, pp. 140-142. Primary source: 1986 Census of Canada. *Notes:* A dash (-) represents zero or a percentage less than .05 percent. 1. Aboriginal origins are derived from the ethnic origin question which asks whether respondents are North American Indian, Metis or Inuit. 2. All 1986 figures exclude the population estimated at about 45,000 on 136 incompletely enumerated Indian reserves and settlements throughout Canada. 3. Total Aboriginal origins—are sum of persons who reported: (A) a single aboriginal (e.g., North American Indian, Metis or Inuit) and, (B) multiple aboriginal origins, that is those who reported: at least one aboriginal origin with any other non-aboriginal (e.g., Metis and French), or two or more aboriginal origins only. 4. Non-aboriginal in these columns—refers to persons who reported one or more non-aboriginal origins such as British, French, etc., in combination with one of the aboriginal origins such as North American Indian. 5. Occupation—not applicable—refers to unemployed persons who had never worked or who last worked prior to January 1, 1985.

★ 960 ★

Population 15 Years and Over, by Occupation and Sex for Detailed Aboriginal Origins for Quebec, 1986 - II[1,2]

Occupation	Metis and non-Aboriginal[3]		Inuit only		Inuit and non-Aboriginal[3]		Other multiple Aboriginal origins[4]	
	Number	Percent	Number	Percent	Number	Percent	Number	Percent
Total in labor force	2,055	100.0	1,835	100.0	255	100.0	655	100.0
Male	1,020	49.6	1,060	57.8	125	49.0	395	60.3
Female	1,040	50.6	775	42.2	125	49.0	235	38.9
Managerial, administrative, and related	175	8.5	135	7.4	30	11.8	40	6.1
Male	95	4.6	95	5.2	25	9.8	40	6.1
Female	85	4.1	35	1.9	-	-	-	-
Natural sciences, engineering and mathematics	60	2.9	15	0.8	-	-	35	5.3
Male	45	2.2	-	-	-	-	35	5.3
Female	10	0.5	-	-	-	-	-	-
Social sciences and related fields	35	1.7	30	1.6	-	-	35	5.3
Male	15	0.7	15	0.8	-	-	10	1.5
Female	20	1.0	15	0.8	-	-	25	3.8
Religion	65	3.2	-	-	-	-	-	-
Male	-	-	-	-	-	-	-	-
Female	60	2.9	-	-	-	-	-	-
Teaching and related	100	4.9	120	6.5	-	-	50	7.6
Male	25	1.2	40	2.2	-	-	25	3.8
Female	75	3.6	80	4.4	-	-	25	3.8
Medicine and health	85	4.1	40	2.2	20	7.8	15	2.3
Male	20	1.0	20	1.1	-	-	-	-
Female	70	3.4	20	1.1	20	7.8	10	1.5
Artistic, literary, recreational and related fields	50	2.4	95	5.2	-	-	10	1.5

[Continued]

★ 960 ★

Population 15 Years and Over, by Occupation and Sex for Detailed Aboriginal Origins for Quebec, 1986 - II
[Continued]

Occupation	Metis and non-Aboriginal[3]		Inuit only		Inuit and non-Aboriginal[3]		Other multiple Aboriginal origins[4]	
	Number	Percent	Number	Percent	Number	Percent	Number	Percent
Male	25	1.2	35	1.9	-	-	10	1.5
Female	20	1.0	65	3.5	-	-	-	-
Clerical and related	335	16.3	270	14.7	55	21.6	125	19.1
Male	65	3.2	100	5.4	15	5.9	30	4.6
Female	270	13.1	175	9.5	40	15.7	100	15.3
Sales	150	7.3	75	4.1	15	5.9	10	1.5
Male	80	3.9	45	2.5	-	-	10	1.5
Female	70	3.4	30	1.6	-	-	-	-
Service	335	16.3	315	17.2	25	9.8	70	10.7
Male	125	6.1	90	4.9	20	7.8	30	4.6
Female	210	10.2	225	12.3	-	-	30	4.6
Farming, horticultural and animal husbandry	60	2.9	20	1.1	-	-	-	-
Male	45	2.2	20	1.1	-	-	-	-
Female	15	0.7	-	-	-	-	-	-
Fishing, trapping and related	-	-	-	-	-	-	-	-
Male	-	-	-	-	-	-	-	-
Female	-	-	-	-	-	-	-	-
Forestry and logging	35	1.7	-	-	-	-	25	3.8
Male	35	1.7	-	-	-	-	30	4.6
Female	-	-	-	-	-	-	-	-
Mining and quarrying including oil and gas field	10	0.5	-	-	-	-	-	-
Male	10	0.5	-	-	-	-	-	-
Female	-	-	-	-	-	-	-	-
Processing	80	3.9	25	1.4	-	-	15	2.3
Male	65	3.2	25	1.4	-	-	20	3.1
Female	10	0.5	-	-	-	-	-	-
Machining and related	50	2.4	20	1.1	-	-	-	-
Male	35	1.7	15	0.8	-	-	-	-
Female	10	0.5	-	-	-	-	-	-
Product fabricating, assembling, and repairing	80	3.9	90	4.9	25	9.8	55	8.4
Male	65	3.2	50	2.7	20	7.8	30	4.6
Female	15	0.7	35	1.9	-	-	-	-
Construction and trades	95	4.6	175	9.5	-	-	30	4.6
Male	95	4.6	165	9.0	-	-	30	4.6
Female	-	-	-	-	-	-	-	-
Transportation and equipment operating	45	2.2	120	6.5	20	7.8	15	2.3
Male	40	1.9	115	6.3	15	5.9	15	2.3
Female	-	-	-	-	-	-	-	-

[Continued]

★ 960 ★

Population 15 Years and Over, by Occupation and Sex for Detailed Aboriginal Origins for Quebec, 1986 - II
[Continued]

Occupation	Metis and non-Aboriginal[3]		Inuit only		Inuit and non-Aboriginal[3]		Other multiple Aboriginal origins[4]	
	Number	Percent	Number	Percent	Number	Percent	Number	Percent
Material handling and related, not elsewhere classified	50	2.4	40	2.2	-	-	-	-
Male	40	1.9	40	2.2	-	-	-	-
Female	-	-	-	-	-	-	-	-
Other crafts and equipment operating	15	0.7	30	1.6	-	-	-	-
Male	10	0.5	25	1.4	-	-	-	-
Female	-	-	-	-	-	-	-	-
Occupations not elsewhere classified	35	1.7	70	3.8	-	-	-	-
Male	30	1.5	60	3.3	-	-	-	-
Female	-	-	-	-	-	-	-	-
All occupations	1,935	94.2	1,710	93.2	230	90.2	605	92.4
Male	965	47.0	985	53.7	120	47.1	365	55.7
Female	975	47.4	725	39.5	105	41.2	235	35.9
Occupation - not applicable[5]	120	5.8	125	6.8	30	11.8	45	6.9
Male	55	2.7	80	4.4	-	-	20	3.1
Female	65	3.2	50	2.7	25	9.8	20	3.1

Source: Aboriginal Peoples Output Program, 1986 Census, Statistics Canada, *A Data Book on Canada's Aboriginal Population From the 1986 Census of Canada*, March, 1989, pp. 140-142. Primary source: 1986 Census of Canada. *Notes:* A dash (-) represents zero or a percentage less than .05 percent. 1. Aboriginal origins and derived from the ethnic origin question which asks whether respondents are North American Indian, Metis or Inuit. 2. All 1986 figures exclude the population estimated at about 45,000 on 136 incompletely enumerated Indian reserves and settlements throughout Canada. 3. Non-aboriginal in these columns—refers to persons who reported one or more non-aboriginal origins such as British, French, etc., in combination with one of the aboriginal origins such as North American Indian. 4. Other multiple aboriginal origins—refer to the sum of those persons reporting two or more aboriginal origins with or without a non-aboriginal origin. 5. Occupation—not applicable—refers to unemployed persons who had never worked or who had last worked prior to January 1, 1985.

★ 961 ★

Population 15 Years and Over, by Occupation and Sex for Detailed Aboriginal Origins for Saskatchewan, 1986 - I[1,2]

Occupation	Total Aboriginal origins[3]		North American Indian only		North American and non-Aboriginal[4]		Metis only	
	Number	Percent	Number	Percent	Number	Percent	Number	Percent
Total in labor force	22,210	100.0	9,835	100.0	3,240	100.0	4,175	100.0
Male	13,230	59.6	6,180	62.8	1,880	58.0	2,480	59.4
Female	8,985	40.5	3,655	37.2	1,360	42.0	1,700	40.7
Managerial, administrative, and related	1,310	5.9	610	6.2	250	7.7	175	4.2
Male	840	3.8	435	4.4	135	4.2	110	2.6
Female	465	2.1	170	1.7	115	3.5	65	1.6
Natural sciences, engineering and mathematics	225	1.0	65	0.7	70	2.2	25	0.6
Male	190	0.9	60	0.6	45	1.4	25	0.6
Female	40	0.2	-	-	25	0.8	-	-
Social sciences and related fields	1,020	4.6	525	5.3	110	3.4	140	3.4

[Continued]

★ 961 ★

Population 15 Years and Over, by Occupation and Sex for Detailed Aboriginal Origins for Saskatchewan, 1986 - I

[Continued]

Occupation	Total Aboriginal origins[3]		North American Indian only		North American and non-Aboriginal[4]		Metis only	
	Number	Percent	Number	Percent	Number	Percent	Number	Percent
Male	405	1.8	230	2.3	30	0.9	70	1.7
Female	610	2.7	290	2.9	80	2.5	65	1.6
Religion	30	0.1	10	0.1	10	0.3	-	-
Male	25	0.1	-	-	10	0.3	-	-
Female	-	-	-	-	-	-	-	-
Teaching and related	820	3.7	505	5.1	100	3.1	95	2.3
Male	220	1.0	115	1.2	30	0.9	30	0.7
Female	600	2.7	385	3.9	75	2.3	60	1.4
Medicine and health	595	2.7	195	2.0	85	2.6	90	2.2
Male	40	0.2	15	0.2	-	-	-	-
Female	555	2.5	180	1.8	80	2.5	80	1.9
Artistic, literary, recreational and related fields	360	1.6	170	1.7	60	1.9	35	0.8
Male	300	1.4	150	1.5	45	1.4	30	0.7
Female	65	0.3	20	0.2	15	0.5	-	-
Clerical and related	2,170	9.8	765	7.8	440	13.6	365	8.7
Male	445	2.0	150	1.5	85	2.6	60	1.4
Female	1,730	7.8	615	6.3	360	11.1	310	7.4
Sales	930	4.2	255	2.6	210	6.5	155	3.7
Male	435	2.0	100	1.0	130	4.0	65	1.6
Female	500	2.3	155	1.6	80	2.5	90	2.2
Service	3,760	16.9	1,330	13.5	595	18.4	870	20.8
Male	1,350	6.1	520	5.3	235	7.3	280	6.7
Female	2,410	10.9	810	8.2	355	11.0	590	14.1
Farming, horticultural and animal husbandry	1,585	7.1	750	7.6	215	6.6	265	6.3
Male	1,320	5.9	675	6.9	175	5.4	205	4.9
Female	265	1.2	75	0.8	40	1.2	65	1.6
Fishing, trapping and related	205	0.9	150	1.5	-	-	30	0.7
Male	195	0.9	140	1.4	-	-	25	0.6
Female	-	-	-	-	-	-	-	-
Forestry and logging	380	1.7	215	2.2	15	0.5	100	2.4
Male	360	1.6	210	2.1	15	0.5	85	2.0
Female	15	0.1	-	-	-	-	-	-
Mining and quarrying including oil and gas field	245	1.1	50	0.5	55	1.7	65	1.6
Male	245	1.1	45	0.5	55	1.7	70	1.7
Female	-	-	-	-	-	-	-	-
Processing	460	2.1	150	1.5	85	2.6	100	2.4
Male	365	1.6	120	1.2	65	2.0	95	2.3
Female	100	0.5	30	0.3	20	0.6	-	-
Machining and related	305	1.4	55	0.6	100	3.1	65	1.6

[Continued]

1377

★ 961 ★

Population 15 Years and Over, by Occupation and Sex for Detailed Aboriginal Origins for Saskatchewan, 1986 - I

[Continued]

Occupation	Total Aboriginal origins[3]		North American Indian only		North American and non-Aboriginal[4]		Metis only	
	Number	Percent	Number	Percent	Number	Percent	Number	Percent
Male	290	1.3	55	0.6	95	2.9	65	1.6
Female	20	0.1	-	-	-	-	-	-
Product fabricating, assembling, and repairing	670	3.0	260	2.6	120	3.7	130	3.1
Male	520	2.3	185	1.9	105	3.2	100	2.4
Female	150	0.7	80	0.8	20	0.6	25	0.6
Construction and trades	2,630	11.8	1,300	13.2	315	9.7	490	11.7
Male	2,585	11.6	1,280	13.0	315	9.7	480	11.5
Female	45	0.2	20	0.2	-	-	-	-
Transportation and equipment operating	800	3.6	415	4.2	90	2.8	145	3.5
Male	685	3.1	345	3.5	85	2.6	125	3.0
Female	115	0.5	75	0.8	-	-	15	0.4
Material handling and related, not elsewhere classified	310	1.4	140	1.4	30	0.9	90	2.2
Male	300	1.4	125	1.3	30	0.9	90	2.2
Female	15	0.1	10	0.1	-	-	-	-
Other crafts and equipment operating	125	0.6	45	0.5	35	1.1	-	-
Male	105	0.5	45	0.5	35	1.1	-	-
Female	15	0.1	-	-	-	-	-	-
Occupations not elsewhere classified	830	3.7	380	3.9	55	1.7	230	5.5
Male	730	3.3	340	3.5	45	1.4	200	4.8
Female	100	0.5	50	0.5	-	-	25	0.6
All occupations	19,770	89.0	8,350	84.9	3,070	94.8	3,670	87.9
Male	11,945	53.8	5,345	54.3	1,780	54.9	2,230	53.4
Female	7,825	35.2	3,000	30.5	1,285	39.7	1,440	34.5
Occupation - not applicable[5]	2,440	11.0	1,490	15.1	165	5.1	505	12.1
Male	1,285	5.8	835	8.5	95	2.9	245	5.9
Female	1,155	5.2	655	6.7	70	2.2	260	6.2

Source: Aboriginal Peoples Output Program, 1986 Census, Statistics Canada, *A Data Book on Canada's Aboriginal Population from the 1986 Census of Canada,* March, 1989, pp. 212-214. Primary source: 1986 Census of Canada. *Notes:* A dash (-) represents zero or a percentage less than .05 percent. 1. Aboriginal origins are derived from the ethnic origin question which asks whether respondents are North American Indian, Metis or Inuit. 2. All 1986 figures exclude the population estimated at about 45,000 on 136 incompletely enumerated Indian reserves and settlements throughout Canada. 3. Total Aboriginal origins—are sum of persons who reported: (A) a single aboriginal (e.g., North American Indian, Metis or Inuit) and, (B) multiple aboriginal origins, that is those who reported: at least one aboriginal origin with any other non-aboriginal (e.g., Metis and French), or two or more aboriginal origins only. 4. Non-aboriginal in these columns—refers to persons who reported one or more non-aboriginal origins such as British, French, etc., in combination with one of the aboriginal origins such as North American Indian. 5. Occupation—not applicable—refers to unemployed persons who had never worked or who last worked prior to January 1, 1985.

★ 962 ★

Population 15 Years and Over, by Occupation and Sex for Detailed Aboriginal Origins for Saskatchewan, 1986 - II[1,2]

Occupation	Metis and non-Aboriginal[3]		Inuit only		Inuit and non-Aboriginal[3]		Other multiple Aboriginal origins[4]	
	Number	Percent	Number	Percent	Number	Percent	Number	Percent
Total in labor force	3,810	100.0	15	100.0	40	100.0	1,090	100.0
Male	1,995	52.4	15	100.0	35	87.5	655	60.1
Female	1,815	47.6	-	-	-	-	440	40.4
Managerial, administrative, and related	200	5.2	-	-	-	-	65	6.0
Male	135	3.5	-	-	-	-	20	1.8
Female	70	1.8	-	-	-	-	35	3.2
Natural sciences, engineering and mathematics	45	1.2	-	-	-	-	-	-
Male	40	1.0	-	-	-	-	-	-
Female	-	-	-	-	-	-	-	-
Social sciences and related fields	135	3.5	-	-	-	-	115	10.6
Male	40	1.0	-	-	-	-	40	3.7
Female	100	2.6	-	-	-	-	75	6.9
Religion	-	-	-	-	-	-	-	-
Male	-	-	-	-	-	-	-	-
Female	-	-	-	-	-	-	-	-
Teaching and related	65	1.7	-	-	-	-	50	4.6
Male	35	0.9	-	-	-	-	-	-
Female	35	0.9	-	-	-	-	45	4.1
Medicine and health	195	5.1	-	-	-	-	25	2.3
Male	10	0.3	-	-	-	-	25	2.3
Female	180	4.7	-	-	-	-	25	2.3
Artistic, literary, recreational and related fields	70	1.8	-	-	-	-	25	2.3
Male	50	1.3	-	-	-	-	15	1.4
Female	15	0.4	-	-	-	-	-	-
Clerical and related	490	12.9	-	-	-	-	100	9.2
Male	105	2.8	-	-	-	-	35	3.2
Female	385	10.1	-	-	-	-	65	6.0
Sales	255	6.7	-	-	-	-	45	4.1
Male	105	2.8	-	-	-	-	30	2.8
Female	150	3.9	-	-	-	-	20	1.8
Service	810	21.3	15	100.0	-	-	140	12.8
Male	235	6.2	10	66.7	-	-	65	6.0
Female	580	15.2	-	-	-	-	75	6.9
Farming, horticultural and animal husbandry	280	7.3	-	-	-	-	65	6.0
Male	205	5.4	-	-	-	-	55	5.0
Female	80	2.1	-	-	-	-	-	-
Fishing, trapping and related	10	0.3	-	-	-	-	-	-
Male	10	0.3	-	-	-	-	-	-
Female	-	-	-	-	-	-	-	-
Forestry and logging	35	0.9	-	-	-	-	15	1.4
Male	40	1.0	-	-	-	-	10	0.9

[Continued]

1379

★ 962 ★

Population 15 Years and Over, by Occupation and Sex for Detailed Aboriginal Origins for Saskatchewan, 1986 - II

[Continued]

Occupation	Metis and non-Aboriginal[3]		Inuit only		Inuit and non-Aboriginal[3]		Other multiple Aboriginal origins[4]	
	Number	Percent	Number	Percent	Number	Percent	Number	Percent
Female	-	-	-	-	-	-	-	-
Mining and quarrying including oil and gas field	55	1.4	-	-	-	-	-	-
Male	60	1.6	-	-	-	-	-	-
Female	-	-	-	-	-	-	-	-
Processing	100	2.6	-	-	-	-	10	0.9
Male	65	1.7	-	-	-	-	15	1.4
Female	35	0.9	-	-	-	-	-	-
Machining and related	70	1.8	-	-	-	-	15	1.4
Male	65	1.7	-	-	-	-	10	0.9
Female	-	-	-	-	-	-	-	-
Product fabricating, assembling, and repairing	120	3.1	-	-	-	-	25	2.3
Male	110	2.9	-	-	-	-	15	1.4
Female	15	0.4	-	-	-	-	-	-
Construction and trades	415	10.9	-	-	-	-	115	10.6
Male	400	10.5	-	-	-	-	115	10.6
Female	10	0.3	-	-	-	-	-	-
Transportation and equipment operating	100	2.6	-	-	-	-	40	3.7
Male	90	2.4	-	-	-	-	25	2.3
Female	15	0.4	-	-	-	-	-	-
Material handling and related, not elsewhere classified	30	0.8	-	-	-	-	20	1.8
Male	35	0.9	-	-	-	-	15	1.4
Female	-	-	-	-	-	-	-	-
Other crafts and equipment operating	15	0.4	-	-	-	-	15	1.4
Male	20	0.5	-	-	-	-	-	-
Female	-	-	-	-	-	-	-	-
Occupations not elsewhere classified	110	2.9	-	-	10	25.0	30	2.8
Male	95	2.5	-	-	10	25.0	30	2.8
Female	20	0.5	-	-	-	-	-	-
All occupations	3,630	95.3	15	100.0	40	100.0	1,000	91.7
Male	1,935	50.8	15	100.0	35	87.5	605	55.5
Female	1,695	44.5	-	-	-	-	395	36.2
Occupation - not applicable[5]	180	4.7	-	-	-	-	95	8.7

[Continued]

★ 962 ★

Population 15 Years and Over, by Occupation and Sex for Detailed Aboriginal Origins for Saskatchewan, 1986 - II

[Continued]

Occupation	Metis and non-Aboriginal[3]		Inuit only		Inuit and non-Aboriginal[3]		Other multiple Aboriginal origins[4]	
	Number	Percent	Number	Percent	Number	Percent	Number	Percent
Male	60	1.6	-	-	-	-	50	4.6
Female	120	3.1	-	-	-	-	45	4.1

Source: Aboriginal Peoples Output Program, 1986 Census, Statistics Canada, *A Data Book on Canada's Aboriginal Population from the 1986 Census of Canada,* March, 1989, pp. 212-214. Primary source: 1986 Census of Canada. *Notes:* A dash (-) represents zero or a percentage less than .05 percent. 1. Aboriginal origins and derived from the ethnic origin question which asks whether respondents are North American Indian, Metis or Inuit. 2. All 1986 figures exclude the population estimated at about 45,000 on 136 incompletely enumerated Indian reserves and settlements throughout Canada. 3. Non-aboriginal in these columns—refers to persons who reported one or more non-aboriginal origins such as British, French, etc., in combination with one of the aboriginal origins such as North American Indian. 4. Other multiple aboriginal origins—refer to the sum of those persons reporting two or more aboriginal origins with or without a non-aboriginal origin. 5. Occupation—not applicable—refers to unemployed persons who had never worked or who had last worked prior to January 1, 1985.

★ 963 ★

Population 15 Years and Over, by Occupation and Sex for Detailed Aboriginal Origins for Yukon Territory, 1986 - I[1,2]

Occupation	Total Aboriginal origins[3]		North American Indian only		North American and non-Aboriginal[4]		Metis only	
	Number	Percent	Number	Percent	Number	Percent	Number	Percent
Total in labor force	2,225	100.0	1,395	100.0	690	100.0	45	100.0
Male	1,145	51.5	730	52.3	345	50.0	10	22.2
Female	1,080	48.5	665	47.7	345	50.0	30	66.7
Managerial, administrative, and related	135	6.1	85	6.1	40	5.8	-	-
Male	60	2.7	40	2.9	15	2.2	-	-
Female	75	3.4	45	3.2	20	2.9	-	-
Natural sciences, engineering and mathematics	30	1.3	20	1.4	10	1.4	-	-
Male	15	0.7	10	0.7	-	-	-	-
Female	15	0.7	-	-	-	-	-	-
Social sciences and related fields	120	5.4	100	7.2	15	2.2	-	-
Male	15	0.7	15	1.1	-	-	-	-
Female	105	4.7	90	6.5	15	2.2	-	-
Religion	-	-	-	-	-	-	-	-
Male	-	-	-	-	-	-	-	-
Female	-	-	-	-	-	-	-	-
Teaching and related	55	2.5	45	3.2	-	-	-	-
Male	-	-	-	-	-	-	-	-
Female	45	2.0	45	3.2	-	-	-	-
Medicine and health	25	1.1	15	1.1	15	2.2	-	-
Male	-	-	-	-	-	-	-	-
Female	30	1.3	15	1.1	15	2.2	-	-
Artistic, literary, recreational and related fields	45	2.0	25	1.8	15	2.2	-	-
Male	35	1.6	20	1.4	10	1.4	-	-

[Continued]

★ 963 ★

Population 15 Years and Over, by Occupation and Sex for Detailed Aboriginal Origins for Yukon Territory, 1986 - I

[Continued]

Occupation	Total Aboriginal origins[3]		North American Indian only		North American and non-Aboriginal[4]		Metis only	
	Number	Percent	Number	Percent	Number	Percent	Number	Percent
Female	-	-	-	-	-	-	-	-
Clerical and related	290	13.0	130	9.3	135	19.6	15	33.3
Male	25	1.1	10	0.7	10	1.4	-	-
Female	265	11.9	120	8.6	125	18.1	15	33.3
Sales	80	3.6	35	2.5	35	5.1	-	-
Male	55	2.5	20	1.4	30	4.3	-	-
Female	25	1.1	20	1.4	-	-	-	-
Service	460	20.7	280	20.1	140	20.3	10	22.2
Male	80	3.6	45	3.2	30	4.3	-	-
Female	380	17.1	240	17.2	115	16.7	15	33.3
Farming, horticultural and animal husbandry	20	0.9	15	1.1	-	-	-	-
Male	20	0.9	15	1.1	-	-	-	-
Female	-	-	-	-	-	-	-	-
Fishing, trapping and related	15	0.7	15	1.1	-	-	-	-
Male	15	0.7	10	0.7	-	-	-	-
Female	-	-	-	-	-	-	-	-
Forestry and logging	75	3.4	65	4.7	10	1.4	-	-
Male	70	3.1	65	4.7	10	1.4	-	-
Female	-	-	-	-	-	-	-	-
Mining and quarrying including oil and gas field	40	1.8	15	1.1	15	2.2	-	-
Male	35	1.6	10	0.7	20	2.9	-	-
Female	-	-	-	-	-	-	-	-
Processing	35	1.6	20	1.4	10	1.4	-	-
Male	25	1.1	20	1.4	-	-	-	-
Female	15	0.7	-	-	-	-	-	-
Machining and related	-	-	-	-	-	-	-	-
Male	-	-	-	-	-	-	-	-
Female	-	-	-	-	-	-	-	-
Product fabricating, assembling, and repairing	60	2.7	35	2.5	15	2.2	-	-
Male	50	2.2	20	1.4	20	2.9	-	-
Female	15	0.7	15	1.1	-	-	-	-
Construction and trades	345	15.5	245	17.6	90	13.0	-	-
Male	325	14.6	240	17.2	85	12.3	-	-
Female	15	0.7	-	-	-	-	-	-
Transportation and equipment operating	130	5.8	65	4.7	55	8.0	-	-
Male	120	5.4	60	4.3	45	6.5	-	-
Female	10	0.4	-	-	-	-	-	-
Material handling and related, not elsewhere classified	25	1.1	20	1.4	-	-	-	-

[Continued]

★ 963 ★

Population 15 Years and Over, by Occupation and Sex for Detailed Aboriginal Origins for Yukon Territory, 1986 - I

[Continued]

Occupation	Total Aboriginal origins[3]		North American Indian only		North American and non-Aboriginal[4]		Metis only	
	Number	Percent	Number	Percent	Number	Percent	Number	Percent
Male	20	0.9	15	1.1	-	-	-	-
Female	-	-	-	-	-	-	-	-
Other crafts and equipment operating	10	0.4	-	-	15	2.2	-	-
Male	-	-	-	-	-	-	-	-
Female	15	0.7	-	-	10	1.4	-	-
Occupations not elsewhere classified	95	4.3	60	4.3	30	4.3	-	-
Male	85	3.8	55	3.9	30	4.3	-	-
Female	-	-	-	-	-	-	-	-
All occupations	2,095	94.2	1,300	93.2	665	96.4	40	88.9
Male	1,065	47.9	675	48.4	325	47.1	15	33.3
Female	1,025	46.1	620	44.4	340	49.3	25	55.6
Occupation - not applicable[5]	135	6.1	100	7.2	25	3.6	-	-
Male	85	3.8	60	4.3	20	2.9	-	-
Female	50	2.2	45	3.2	-	-	-	-

Source: Aboriginal Peoples Output Program, 1986 Census, Statistics Canada, *A Data Book on Canada's Aboriginal Population from the 1986 Census of Canada*, March, 1989, pp. 308-310. Primary source: 1986 Census of Canada. *Notes:* A dash (-) represents zero or a percentage less than .05 percent. 1. Aboriginal origins are derived from the ethnic origin question which asks whether respondents are North American Indian, Metis or Inuit. 2. All 1986 figures exclude the population estimated at about 45,000 on 136 incompletely enumerated Indian reserves and settlements throughout Canada. 3. Total Aboriginal origins—are sum of persons who reported: (A) a single aboriginal (e.g., North American Indian, Metis or Inuit) and, (B) multiple aboriginal origins, that is those who reported: at least one aboriginal origin with any other non-aboriginal (e.g., Metis and French), or two or more aboriginal origins only. 4. Non-aboriginal in these columns—refers to persons who reported one or more non-aboriginal origins such as British, French, etc., in combination with one of the aboriginal origins such as North American Indian. 5. Occupation—not applicable—refers to unemployed persons who had never worked or who last worked prior to January 1, 1985.

★ 964 ★

Population 15 Years and Over, by Occupation and Sex for Detailed Aboriginal Origins for Yukon Territory, 1986 - II[1,2]

Occupation	Metis and non-Aboriginal[3]		Inuit only		Inuit and non-Aboriginal[3]		Other multiple Aboriginal origins[4]	
	Number	Percent	Number	Percent	Number	Percent	Number	Percent
Total in labor force	50	100.0	25	100.0	-	-	30	100.0
Male	30	60.0	-	-	-	-	-	-
Female	15	30.0	15	60.0	-	-	-	-
Managerial, administrative, and related	-	-	-	-	-	-	-	-
Male	-	-	-	-	-	-	-	-
Female	-	-	-	-	-	-	-	-
Natural sciences, engineering and mathematics	-	-	-	-	-	-	-	-
Male	-	-	-	-	-	-	-	-
Female	-	-	-	-	-	-	-	-
Social sciences and related fields	-	-	-	-	-	-	-	-
Male	-	-	-	-	-	-	-	-

[Continued]

★ 964 ★

Population 15 Years and Over, by Occupation and Sex for Detailed Aboriginal Origins for Yukon Territory, 1986 - II

[Continued]

Occupation	Metis and non-Aboriginal[3]		Inuit only		Inuit and non-Aboriginal[3]		Other multiple Aboriginal origins[4]	
	Number	Percent	Number	Percent	Number	Percent	Number	Percent
Female	-	-	-	-	-	-	-	-
Religion	-	-	-	-	-	-	-	-
Male	-	-	-	-	-	-	-	-
Female	-	-	-	-	-	-	-	-
Teaching and related	-	-	-	-	-	-	-	-
Male	-	-	-	-	-	-	-	-
Female	-	-	-	-	-	-	-	-
Medicine and health	-	-	-	-	-	-	-	-
Male	-	-	-	-	-	-	-	-
Female	-	-	-	-	-	-	-	-
Artistic, literary, recreational and related fields	-	-	-	-	-	-	-	-
Male	-	-	-	-	-	-	-	-
Female	-	-	-	-	-	-	-	-
Clerical and related	-	-	-	-	-	-	-	-
Male	-	-	-	-	-	-	-	-
Female	-	-	-	-	-	-	-	-
Sales	-	-	-	-	-	-	-	-
Male	-	-	-	-	-	-	-	-
Female	-	-	-	-	-	-	-	-
Service	15	30.0	-	-	-	-	-	-
Male	-	-	-	-	-	-	-	-
Female	15	30.0	-	-	-	-	-	-
Farming, horticultural and animal husbandry	-	-	-	-	-	-	-	-
Male	-	-	-	-	-	-	-	-
Female	-	-	-	-	-	-	-	-
Fishing, trapping and related	-	-	-	-	-	-	-	-
Male	-	-	-	-	-	-	-	-
Female	-	-	-	-	-	-	-	-
Forestry and logging	-	-	-	-	-	-	-	-
Male	-	-	-	-	-	-	-	-
Female	-	-	-	-	-	-	-	-
Mining and quarrying including oil and gas field	-	-	-	-	-	-	-	-
Male	-	-	-	-	-	-	-	-
Female	-	-	-	-	-	-	-	-
Processing	-	-	-	-	-	-	-	-
Male	-	-	-	-	-	-	-	-
Female	-	-	-	-	-	-	-	-
Machining and related	-	-	-	-	-	-	-	-
Male	-	-	-	-	-	-	-	-

[Continued]

1384

★ 964 ★

Population 15 Years and Over, by Occupation and Sex for Detailed Aboriginal Origins for Yukon Territory, 1986 - II
[Continued]

Occupation	Metis and non-Aboriginal[3]		Inuit only		Inuit and non-Aboriginal[3]		Other multiple Aboriginal origins[4]	
	Number	Percent	Number	Percent	Number	Percent	Number	Percent
Female	-	-	-	-	-	-	-	-
Product fabricating, assembling, and repairing	-	-	-	-	-	-	-	-
Male	-	-	-	-	-	-	-	-
Female	-	-	-	-	-	-	-	-
Construction and trades	-	-	-	-	-	-	-	-
Male	-	-	-	-	-	-	-	-
Female	-	-	-	-	-	-	-	-
Transportation and equipment operating	-	-	-	-	-	-	-	-
Male	-	-	-	-	-	-	-	-
Female	-	-	-	-	-	-	-	-
Material handling and related, not elsewhere classified	-	-	-	-	-	-	-	-
Male	-	-	-	-	-	-	-	-
Female	-	-	-	-	-	-	-	-
Other crafts and equipment operating	-	-	-	-	-	-	-	-
Male	-	-	-	-	-	-	-	-
Female	-	-	-	-	-	-	-	-
Occupations not elsewhere classified	-	-	-	-	-	-	-	-
Male	-	-	-	-	-	-	-	-
Female	-	-	-	-	-	-	-	-
All occupations	45	90.0	20	80.0	-	-	25	83.3
Male	30	60.0	-	-	-	-	-	-
Female	15	30.0	15	60.0	-	-	-	-
Occupation - not applicable[5]	-	-	-	-	-	-	-	-
Male	-	-	-	-	-	-	-	-
Female	-	-	-	-	-	-	-	-

Source: Aboriginal Peoples Output Program, 1986 Census, Statistics Canada, *A Data Book on Canada's Aboriginal Population from the 1986 Census of Canada,* March, 1989, pp. 308-310. Primary source: 1986 Census of Canada. *Notes:* A dash (-) represents zero or a percentage less than .05 percent. 1. Aboriginal origins and derived from the ethnic origin question which asks whether respondents are North American Indian, Metis or Inuit. 2. All 1986 figures exclude the population estimated at about 45,000 on 136 incompletely enumerated Indian reserves and settlements throughout Canada. 3. Non-aboriginal in these columns—refers to persons who reported one or more non-aboriginal origins such as British, French, etc., in combination with one of the aboriginal origins such as North American Indian. 4. Other multiple aboriginal origins—refer to the sum of those persons reporting two or more aboriginal origins with or without a non-aboriginal origin. 5. Occupation—not applicable—refers to unemployed persons who had never worked or who had last worked prior to January 1, 1985.

Income

★ 965 ★

Family Income Level of Persons of Aboriginal Origin and the Total Canadian Population, Canada, 1985

Group/Region	Without Family Income	With Family Income							Grand Total
		Less than $10,000	$10,000 $14,999	$15,000 $24,999	$25,000 $34,999	$35,000 $44,999	$45,000 & over	Total	
On-Reserve									
Atlantic	10	2,205	980	1,165	530	280	165	5,335	5,385
Quebec	40	2,730	2,810	5,435	3,420	1,900	1,700	18,025	18,095
Ontario	45	4,135	2,985	4,445	2,900	1,450	1,110	17,150	17,245
Manitoba	25	5,445	4,310	6,160	2,930	1,125	785	20,855	20,890
Saskatchewan	0	4,470	4,145	5,370	2,410	1,145	930	18,560	18,590
Alberta	0	2,825	2,400	3,780	2,130	1,125	1,105	13,390	13,375
British Columbia	30	3,235	2,740	3,445	2,240	1,220	1,315	14,370	14,435
Territories	0	0	0	0	0	0	0	0	0
Canada	150	25,045	20,370	29,800	16,560	8,245	7,110	107,685	108,015
Off-Reserve									
Atlantic	60	4,455	3,110	5,655	4,550	3,465	3,195	24,410	24,425
Quebec	170	7,695	5,560	10,180	9,635	7,800	9,200	50,040	50,180
Ontario	275	17,260	11,365	20,385	25,020	21,575	30,060	125,535	125,755
Manitoba	150	12,930	6,385	9,850	8,340	5,685	6,675	49,765	49,905
Saskatchewan	150	10,985	7,825	10,185	7,085	4,310	4,965	45,260	45,385
Alberta	120	13,130	9,525	14,930	11,265	9,635	14,520	72,975	73,110
British Columbia	205	16,865	13,080	15,340	14,515	12,240	17,095	88,960	89,125
Territories	20	5,585	4,110	6,700	4,700	3,520	5,595	30,210	30,240
Canada	1,150	88,905	60,960	93,225	85,110	68,230	91,305	487,155	488,125
Total Canadian population									
Atlantic	2,360	181,700	193,765	437,900	412,935	316,870	419,015	1,962,195	1,964,540
Quebec	14,995	467,860	436,665	971,125	1,102,315	957,035	1,522,695	5,457,685	5,472,680
Ontario	17,285	427,865	407,855	1,041,730	1,356,585	1,430,190	2,987,010	7,651,230	7,668,515
Manitoba	1,970	67,860	69,145	158,130	172,555	153,670	250,070	871,435	873,360
Saskatchewan	1,150	76,320	76,750	159,655	154,440	139,370	232,905	839,445	840,590
Alberta	4,115	134,300	120,180	299,875	331,805	335,840	736,800	1,958,805	1,962,915
British Columbia	6,805	169,770	182,575	367,845	416,030	429,950	778,340	2,344,515	2,351,320
Territories	50	6,715	5,115	9,415	8,830	8,730	23,245	62,050	62,095
Canada	48,675	1,532,385	1,492,040	3,445,675	3,955,500	3,771,660	6,950,085	21,147,360	21,196,030

Source: Canada's Off-Reserve Aboriginal Population: A Statistical Overview, Social Trends Analysis Directorate, Department of the Secretary of State of Canada, 1991, p. A-15; Primary source: Statistics Canada, 1986 Census, *Special Tabulations from the Small Area Database* compiled for the Department of the Secretary of State. *Notes:* Sum of components may not always add to totals due to rounding and/or data suppression.

★ 966 ★

Individual Income Level of Persons of Aboriginal Origin and the Total Canadian Population, Canada, 1985

Group/Region	Without Income	Individuals with Income							Grand Total
		Less than $5,000	$5,000 $9,999	$10,000 $14,999	$15,000 $19,999	$20,000 $24,999	$25,000 & over	Total	
On-Reserve									
Atlantic	1,450	1,800	1,000	405	270	155	185	3,740	5,190
Quebec	3,260	3,280	3,265	1,450	915	603	695	10,245	13,505
Ontario	4,110	4,250	3,995	1,745	965	680	1,150	12,740	16,850
Manitoba	4,165	5,040	3,200	1,550	900	480	510	11,690	15,835
Saskatchewan	3,915	4,630	3,195	1,555	915	475	545	11,315	15,230
Alberta	2,150	3,605	2,430	1,185	750	460	575	9,005	11,155
British Columbia	4,250	6,295	4,515	2,015	1,145	885	1,350	16,205	20,455
Territories	80	140	115	40	20	15	10	335	415
Canada	23,365	29,040	21,720	9,945	5,880	3,765	4,935	75,270	98,635
Off-Reserve									
Atlantic	3,450	3,875	3,390	1,930	1,465	1,000	1,885	13,610	17,060
Quebec	6,845	7,800	8,275	5,035	4,385	3,465	6,865	35,815	42,660
Ontario	13,890	20,330	15,220	10,055	8,460	7,265	17,460	78,795	92,685
Manitoba	7,190	9,595	7,080	3,900	2,785	1,975	3,700	29,025	36,215
Saskatchewan	6,260	8,000	5,880	3,180	1,950	1,455	2,695	23,155	29,415
Alberta	9,090	12,510	9,570	6,080	3,970	3,310	7,375	42,810	51,900
British Columbia	11,440	15,465	11,015	6,690	4,295	3,585	9,230	50,280	61,720
Territories	5,225	5,665	3,775	2,030	1,195	1,075	2,700	16,430	21,655
Canada	63,385	83,240	64,200	38,900	28,505	23,145	51,950	289,925	353,310
Total Canadian population									
Atlantic	285,260	310,465	359,480	218,960	167,255	114,705	274,045	1,444,915	1,730,175
Quebec	786,490	806,885	973,490	602,810	504,320	413,210	1,027,790	4,328,505	5,114,995
Ontario	776,215	1,192,025	1,121,950	848,585	720,130	618,155	1,855,745	6,356,600	7,132,815
Manitoba	93,440	144,680	154,125	106,670	83,745	65,685	165,605	720,495	813,935
Saskatchewan	88,535	138,500	143,265	96,430	71,885	58,705	153,775	662,555	751,090
Alberta	197,960	291,015	285,440	214,270	167,080	152,235	462,370	1,581,415	1,779,375
British Columbia	277,815	377,625	395,165	271,035	202,445	181,635	553,585	1,981,500	2,259,315
Territories	7,540	9,595	7,160	5,055	3,770	3,920	15,380	44,870	52,410
Canada	2,513,260	3,270,800	3,440,070	2,363,805	1,929,635	1,608,245	4,508,285	17,120,835	19,634,095

Source: Canada's Off-Reserve Aboriginal Population: A Statistical Overview, Social Trends Analysis Directorate, Department of the Secretary of State of Canada, 1991, p. A-14. Primary source: For Aboriginal population: Statistics Canada, *Profile of the Aboriginal Population Residing in Selected Off Reserve Areas*, prepared by the Aboriginal Data and Native Issues Unit of the Housing, Family and Social Statistics Division, February 1990; for total Canadian population: Statistics Canada, 1986 Census, *Special Tabulations from the Small Area Database* compiled for the Department of the Secretary of State. *Notes:* Sum of components may not always add to totals due to rounding and/or data suppression.

★ 967 ★

Dependency Ratios of Persons of Aboriginal Origin and the Total Canadian Population, Canada, 1986

Dependency ratios[1] are shown, by region.

Region	Aboriginal Population		Total Canadian population
	On-Reserve	Off-Reserve	
Atlantic	66	60	51
Quebec	73	45	43
Ontario	69	57	45
Manitoba	86	67	52
Saskatchewan	91	81	58
Alberta	80	70	46
British Columbia	63	61	47
Territories	66	71	50
Canada	76	62	46

Source: Canada's Off-Reserve Aboriginal Population: A Statistical Overview, Social Trends Analysis Directorate, Department of the Secretary of State of Canada, 1991, p. A-4 Primary source: For Aboriginal population: Statistics Canada, *A Profile of the Aboriginal Population Residing in Selected Off Reserve Areas*, prepared by the Aboriginal Data and Native Issues Unit of the Housing and Social Statistics Division, February 1990; for total Canadian population: Statistics Canada, *1986 Census, Special Tabulations from the Small Area Database*, compiled for the Department of the Secretary of State. *Notes:* 1. The dependency ratio is a ratio of the dependent (i.e. with virtually no wage-earning potential) population to the independent (i.e. with wage- earning capabilities) population. The term dependency implies that those in the former population require some support, either directly or indirectly, from those in the latter. In this case, wage-earning potential is approximated using the working age. Thus, the ratio is calculated by dividing the combined total to those aged 0-14 and 65 and over by those aged 15 to 64 years. The result is then multiplied by 100 to obtain a ratio per 100.

★ 968 ★

Population 15 Years and Over, by Total Income Group and Sex for Detailed Aboriginal Origins for Canada, 1986 - I[1,2]

Income is shown in Canadian dollars.

Income group[3]	Total Aboriginal origins[4]		North American Indian only		North American Indian and non-Aboriginal[5]		Metis only	
	Number	Percent	Number	Percent	Number	Percent	Number	Percent
Total population aged 15 and over	451,955	100.0	184,850	100.0	150,285	100.0	39,975	100.0
Male	217,130	48.0	89,055	48.2	71,045	47.3	19,690	49.3
Female	234,815	52.0	95,805	51.8	79,240	52.7	20,285	50.7
No income	86,745	19.2	41,470	22.4	22,140	14.7	8,515	21.3
Male	28,110	6.2	13,490	7.3	6,480	4.3	3,160	7.9
Female	58,640	13.0	27,980	15.1	15,660	10.4	5,355	13.4

[Continued]

★ 968 ★

Population 15 Years and Over, by Total Income Group and Sex for Detailed Aboriginal Origins for Canada, 1986 - 1

[Continued]

Income group[3]	Total Aboriginal origins[4]		North American Indian only		North American Indian and non-Aboriginal[5]		Metis only	
	Number	Percent	Number	Percent	Number	Percent	Number	Percent
Less than $3,000								
(including losses)	74,530	16.5	33,500	18.1	21,185	14.1	6,900	17.3
Male	33,025	7.3	16,405	8.9	7,910	5.3	3,100	7.8
Female	41,505	9.2	17,909	9.7	13,275	8.8	3,800	9.5
$3,000 to $6,999	72,460	16.0	33,320	18.0	20,910	13.9	6,995	17.5
Male	31,915	7.1	15,850	8.6	7,995	5.3	3,265	8.2
Female	40,545	9.0	17,470	9.5	12,915	8.6	3,735	9.3
$7,000 to $9,999	51,200	11.3	23,370	12.6	14,370	9.6	5,235	13.1
Male	21,820	4.8	10,730	5.8	5,395	3.6	2,310	5.8
Female	29,380	6.5	12,645	6.8	8,975	6.0	2,925	7.3
$10,000 to $14,999	48,845	10.8	19,260	10.4	17,235	11.5	4,190	10.5
Male	23,965	5.3	9,975	5.4	7,840	5.2	2,140	5.4
Female	24,885	5.5	9,285	5.0	9,395	6.3	2,050	5.1
$15,000 to $19,999	34,390	7.6	11,705	6.3	14,140	9.4	2,545	6.4
Male	18,055	4.0	6,605	3.6	6,770	4.5	1,530	3.8
Female	16,330	3.6	5,105	2.8	7,370	4.9	1,015	2.5
$20,000 to $29,999	46,305	10.2	13,725	7.4	20,715	13.8	3,285	8.2
Male	29,475	6.5	8,980	4.9	12,780	8.5	2,200	5.5
Female	16,830	3.7	4,745	2.6	7,935	5.3	1,085	2.7
$30,000 to $49,999	32,410	7.2	7,575	4.1	16,750	11.1	1,950	4.9
Male	26,330	5.8	6,230	3.4	13,405	8.9	1,665	4.2
Female	6,080	1.3	1,345	0.7	3,345	2.2	285	0.7
$50,000 and over	5,065	1.1	925	0.5	2,840	1.9	365	0.9
Male	4,435	1.0	785	0.4	2,480	1.7	325	0.8
Female	630	0.1	140	0.1	355	0.2	45	0.1
			Average income[6]					
Total	12,899		10,538		15,706		11,244	

[Continued]

★ 968 ★

Population 15 Years and Over, by Total Income Group and Sex for Detailed Aboriginal Origins for Canada, 1986 - I

[Continued]

Income group[3]	Total Aboriginal origins[4]		North American Indian only		North American Indian and non-Aboriginal[5]		Metis only	
	Number	Percent	Number	Percent	Number	Percent	Number	Percent
Male	15,760		12,302		19,940		13,657	
Female	9,828		8,574		11,405		8,573	

Source: Aboriginal Peoples Output Program, 1986 Census, Statistics Canada, *A Data Book on Canada's Aboriginal Population from the 1986 Census of Canada*, March, 1989, p. 239. Primary source: 1986 Census of Canada. *Notes:* A dash (-) represents zero or a percentage which rounds to less than .05 percent. 1. Aboriginal origins are derived from the ethnic origin question which asks whether respondents are North American Indian, Metis or Inuit. 2. All 1986 figures exclude the population estimated at about 45,000 on 136 incompletely enumerated Indian reserves and settlements throughout Canada. 3. Total income—refers to income from all sources such as total wages and salaries, net nonfarm self-employed income, net farm self-employed income, family allowances, federal child tax credits, Old Age Security Pension Plan and Guaranteed Income Supplement, benefits and interest on bonds, deposits, savings certificates and other investment income, retirement pensions, superannuation and annuities, and other money income. Also shown in the table is a category for "No income" which refers to the population aged 15 and over who did not receive any income during 1985. 4. Total Aboriginal origins—are the sum of persons who reported: (a) a single aboriginal (e.g., North American Indian, Metis or Inuit) and, (b) multiple aboriginal origins, that is those who reported: - at least one aboriginal origin with any other non-aboriginal (e.g., Metis and French), or—two or more aboriginal origins only. 5. Non-aboriginal in these columns—refers to persons who report one or more non-aboriginal origins such as British, French, etc., in combination with one of the aboriginal origins such as North American Indian. 6. Average income - refers to the average of total income from all sources (e.g., total wages and salaries net nonfarm self-employed income, net self-employed income, family allowances, federal child tax credits, Old Age Security Pension Plan and Guaranteed Income Supplement, benefits from Unemployment Insurance, other income from government sources, dividends and interest on bonds, savings certificates and other investment income, retirement pensions, superannuation and annuities, and other money income). Average income excludes persons with no income in 1985.

★ 969 ★

Population 15 Years and Over, by Total Income Group and Sex for Detailed Aboriginal Origins for Canada, 1986 - II[1,2]

Income is shown in Canadian dollars.

Income group[3]	Metis and non-Aboriginal[4]		Inuit only		Inuit and non-Aboriginal[4]		Other multiple Aboriginal origins[5]	
	Number	Percent	Number	Percent	Number	Percent	Number	Percent
Total population aged 15 and over	42,435	100.0	16,500	100.0	3,660	100.0	14,240	100.0
Male	19,865	46.8	8,260	50.1	1,880	51.4	7,350	51.6
Female	22,575	53.2	8,240	49.9	1,780	48.6	6,895	48.4
No income	7,195	17.0	4,355	26.4	780	21.3	2,295	16.1
Male	2,360	5.6	1,555	9.4	280	7.7	780	5.5
Female	4,835	11.4	2,805	17.0	500	13.7	1,505	10.6
Less than $3,000 (including losses)	6,625	15.6	3,285	19.9	505	13.8	2,520	17.7
Male	2,695	6.4	1,480	9.0	210	5.7	1,220	8.6
Female	3,930	9.3	1,800	10.9	300	8.2	1,305	9.2
$3,000 to $6,999	6,065	14.3	2,430	14.7	635	17.3	2,100	14.7
Male	2,325	5.5	1,240	7.5	260	7.1	980	6.9
Female	3,735	8.8	1,190	7.2	375	10.2	1,120	7.9
$7,000 to $9,999	4,775	11.3	1,640	9.9	350	9.6	1,465	10.3

[Continued]

★ 969 ★

Population 15 Years and Over, by Total Income Group and Sex for Detailed Aboriginal Origins for Canada, 1986 - II
[Continued]

Income group[3]	Metis and non-Aboriginal[4]		Inuit only		Inuit and non-Aboriginal[4]		Other multiple Aboriginal origins[5]	
	Number	Percent	Number	Percent	Number	Percent	Number	Percent
Male	1,795	4.2	835	5.1	185	5.1	570	4.0
Female	2,975	7.0	805	4.9	165	4.5	895	6.3
$10,000 to $14,999	4,910	11.6	1,445	8.8	385	10.5	1,435	10.1
Male	2,180	5.1	850	5.2	210	5.7	770	5.4
Female	2,725	6.4	590	3.6	175	4.8	660	4.6
$15,000 to $19,999	3,620	8.5	950	5.8	240	6.6	1,185	8.3
Male	1,790	4.2	615	3.7	115	3.1	630	4.4
Female	1,830	4.3	340	2.1	125	3.4	545	3.8
$20,000 to $29,999	5,060	11.9	1,440	8.7	380	10.4	1,710	12.0
Male	3,180	7.5	940	5.7	290	7.9	1,105	7.8
Female	1,875	4.4	505	3.1	85	2.3	600	4.2
$30,000 to $49,999	3,615	8.5	860	5.2	325	8.9	1,325	9.3
Male	3,020	7.1	660	4.0	270	7.4	1,070	7.5
Female	595	1.4	200	1.2	55	1.5	250	1.8
$50,000 and over	575	1.4	85	0.5	60	1.6	205	1.4
Male	515	1.2	75	0.5	55	1.5	200	1.4
Female	60	0.1	10	0.1	-	-	10	0.1

Average income[6]

Total	13,925	11,099	13,882	14,036
Male	17,666	13,076	17,401	17,725
Female	10,233	8,663	9,503	7,597

Source: Aboriginal Peoples Output Program, 1986 Census, Statistics Canada, *A Data Book on Canada's Aboriginal Population from the 1986 Census of Canada,* March, 1989, p. 239. Primary source: 1986 Census of Canada. *Notes:* A dash (-) represents zero or a percentage which rounds to less than .05 percent. 1. Aboriginal origins are derived from the ethnic origin question which asks whether respondents are North American Indian, Metis or Inuit. 2. All 1986 figures exclude the population estimated at about 45,000 on 136 incompletely enumerated Indian reserves and settlements throughout Canada. 3. Total income—refers to income from all sources such as total wages and salaries, net nonfarm self-employed income, net farm self-employed income, family allowances, federal child tax credits, Old Age Security Pension Plan and Guaranteed Income Supplement, benefits and interest on bonds, deposits, savings certificates and other investment income, retirement pensions, superannuation and annuities, and other money income. Also shown in the table is a category for "No income" which refers to the population aged 15 and over who did not receive any income during 1985. 4. Non-aboriginal in these columns—refers to persons who report one or more non-aboriginal origins such as British, French, etc., in combination with one of the aboriginal origins such as North American Indian. 5. Other Multiple Aboriginal Origins—refer to the sum of those persons reporting two or more aboriginal origins with or without a non-aboriginal origin. 6. Average income—refers to the average of total income from all sources (e.g., total wages and salaries net nonfarm self-employed income, net self-employed income, family allowances, federal child tax credits, Old Age Security Pension Plan and Guaranteed Income Supplement, benefits from Unemployment Insurance, other income from government sources, dividends and interest on bonds, savings certificates and other investment income, retirement pensions, superannuation and annuities, and other money income). Average income excludes persons with no income in 1985.

★ 970 ★

Population 15 Years and Over, by Total Income Group and Sex for Detailed Aboriginal Origins for Alberta, 1986 - I[1,2]

Income is shown in Canadian dollars.

Income group[3]	Total Aboriginal origins[4]		North American Indian only		North American Indian and non-Aboriginal[5]		Metis only	
	Number	Percent	Number	Percent	Number	Percent	Number	Percent
Total population aged 15 and over	63,055	100.0	20,940	100.0	17,020	100.0	11,080	100.0
Male	30,230	47.9	9,765	46.6	8,115	47.7	5,480	49.5
Female	32,825	52.1	11,175	53.4	8,905	52.3	5,600	50.5
No income	11,240	17.8	4,325	20.7	2,185	12.8	2,365	21.3
Male	3,995	6.3	1,455	6.9	665	3.9	980	8.8
Female	7,245	11.5	2,870	13.7	1,520	8.9	1,385	12.5
Less than $3,000 (including losses)	10,960	17.4	4,195	20.0	2,380	14.0	2,085	18.8
Male	4,950	7.9	2,050	9.8	870	5.1	975	8.8
Female	6,010	9.5	2,150	10.3	1,505	8.8	1,110	10.0
$3,000 to $6,999	9,690	15.4	3,790	18.1	2,375	14.0	1,675	15.1
Male	4,035	6.4	1,720	8.2	815	4.8	820	7.4
Female	5,655	9.0	2,070	9.9	1,560	9.2	855	7.7
$7,000 to $9,999	7,470	11.8	2,795	13.3	1,480	8.7	1,575	14.2
Male	3,285	5.2	1,305	6.2	590	3.5	710	6.4
Female	4,190	6.6	1,500	7.2	890	5.2	865	7.8
$10,000 to $14,999	7,270	11.5	2,275	10.9	2,030	11.9	1,345	12.1
Male	3,220	5.1	1,050	5.0	830	4.9	585	5.3
Female	4,045	6.4	1,225	5.9	1,205	7.1	765	6.9
$15,000 to $19,999	4,720	7.5	1,295	6.2	1,665	9.8	535	4.8
Male	2,355	3.7	665	3.2	820	4.8	280	2.5
Female	2,360	3.7	630	3.0	850	5.0	255	2.3
$20,000 to $29,999	6,240	9.9	1,405	6.7	2,535	14.9	795	7.2
Male	3,840	6.1	855	4.1	1,545	9.1	515	4.6
Female	2,400	3.8	555	2.7	990	5.8	275	2.5
$30,000 to $49,999	4,370	6.9	725	3.5	1,825	10.7	560	5.1
Male	3,550	5.6	550	2.6	1,490	8.8	485	4.4
Female	820	1.3	170	0.8	330	1.9	80	0.7
$50,000 and over	1,105	1.8	125	0.6	545	3.2	150	1.4
Male	1,000	1.6	115	0.5	484	2.8	130	1.2
Female	100	0.2	-	-	55	0.3	10	0.1

[Continued]

★ 970 ★

Population 15 Years and Over, by Total Income Group and Sex for Detailed Aboriginal Origins for Alberta, 1986 - I
[Continued]

Income group[3]	Total Aboriginal origins[4]		North American Indian only		North American Indian and non-Aboriginal[5]		Metis only	
	Number	Percent	Number	Percent	Number	Percent	Number	Percent
Average income[6]								
Total	13,027		9,931		16,534		11,211	
Male	16,143		11,353		21,520		13,568	
Female	9,832		8,508		11,508		8,697	

Source: Aboriginal Peoples Output Program, 1986 Census, Statistics Canada, *A Data Book on Canada's Aboriginal Population from the 1986 Census of Canada*, March, 1989, p. 240. Primary source: 1986 Census of Canada. *Notes:* A dash (-) represents zero or a percentage which rounds to less than .05 percent. 1. Aboriginal origins are derived from the ethnic origin question which asks whether respondents are North American Indian, Metis or Inuit. 2. All 1986 figures exclude the population estimated at about 45,000 on 136 incompletely enumerated Indian reserves and settlements throughout Canada. 3. Total income—refers to income from all sources such as total wages and salaries, net nonfarm self-employed income, net farm self-employed income, family allowances, federal child tax credits, Old Age Security Pension Plan and Guaranteed Income Supplement, benefits and interest on bonds, deposits, savings certificates and other investment income, retirement pensions, superannuation and annuities, and other money income. Also shown in the table is a category for "No income" which refers to the population aged 15 and over who did not receive any income during 1985. 4. Total Aboriginal origins—are the sum of persons who reported: (a) a single aboriginal (e.g., North American Indian, Metis or Inuit) and, (b) multiple aboriginal origins, that is those who reported: - at least one aboriginal origin with any other non-aboriginal (e.g., Metis and French), or—two or more aboriginal origins only. 5. Non-aboriginal in these columns—refers to persons who report one or more non-aboriginal origins such as British, French, etc., in combination with one of the aboriginal origins such as North American Indian. 6. Average income - refers to the average of total income from all sources (e.g., total wages and salaries net nonfarm self-employed income, net self-employed income, family allowances, federal child tax credits, Old Age Security Pension Plan and Guaranteed Income Supplement, benefits from Unemployment Insurance, other income from government sources, dividends and interest on bonds, savings certificates and other investment income, retirement pensions, superannuation and annuities, and other money income). Average income excludes persons with no income in 1985.

★ 971 ★

Population 15 Years and Over, by Total Income Group and Sex for Detailed Aboriginal Origins for Alberta, 1986 - II[1,2]

Income is shown in Canadian dollars.

Income group[3]	Metis and non-Aboriginal[4]		Inuit only		Inuit and non-Aboriginal[4]		Other multiple Aboriginal origins[5]	
	Number	Percent	Number	Percent	Number	Percent	Number	Percent
Total population aged 15 and over	9,995	100.0	205	100.0	280	100.0	3,520	100.0
Male	4,745	47.5	115	56.1	110	39.3	1,905	54.1
Female	5,250	52.5	95	46.3	175	62.5	1,625	46.2
No income	1,715	17.2	60	29.3	55	19.6	535	15.2
Male	635	6.4	25	12.2	30	10.7	200	5.7
Female	1,080	10.8	30	14.6	25	8.9	335	9.5
Less than $3,000 (including losses)	1,635	16.4	40	19.5	40	14.3	585	16.6
Male	720	7.2	15	7.3	-	-	300	8.5
Female	910	9.1	25	12.2	30	10.7	280	8.0
$3,000 to $6,999	1,225	12.3	25	12.2	50	17.9	545	15.5
Male	405	4.1	-	-	-	-	260	7.4

[Continued]

★ 971 ★

Population 15 Years and Over, by Total Income Group and Sex for Detailed Aboriginal Origins for Alberta, 1986 - II
[Continued]

Income group[3]	Metis and non-Aboriginal[4]		Inuit only		Inuit and non-Aboriginal[4]		Other multiple Aboriginal origins[5]	
	Number	Percent	Number	Percent	Number	Percent	Number	Percent
Female	825	8.3	15	7.3	50	17.9	280	8.0
$7,000 to $9,999	1,200	12.0	30	14.6	40	14.3	345	9.8
Male	485	4.9	20	9.8	25	8.9	155	4.4
Female	710	7.1	15	7.3	20	7.1	190	5.4
$10,000 to $14,999	1,215	12.2	20	9.8	30	10.7	355	10.1
Male	535	5.4	-	-	10	3.6	210	6.0
Female	675	6.8	-	-	15	5.4	155	4.4
$15,000 to $19,999	880	8.8	-	-	10	3.6	320	9.1
Male	435	4.4	-	-	-	-	155	4.4
Female	450	4.5	-	-	10	3.6	170	4.8
$20,000 to $29,999	1,075	10.8	20	9.8	30	10.7	385	10.9
Male	645	6.5	20	0.8	20	7.1	240	6.8
Female	430	4.3	-	-	10	3.6	145	4.1
$30,000 to $49,999	855	8.6	-	-	20	7.1	380	10.8
Male	690	6.9	-	-	-	-	325	9.2
Female	160	1.6	-	-	10	3.6	60	1.7
$50,000 and over	200	2.0	-	-	-	-	70	2.0
Male	190	1.9	-	-	-	-	60	1.7
Female	10	0.1	-	-	-	-	-	-
Average income[6]								
Total	14,238		12,899		13,561		14,740	
Male	18,201		18,807		16,860		20,058	
Female	10,338		4,689		11,801		11,422	

Source: Aboriginal Peoples Output Program, 1986 Census, Statistics Canada, *A Data Book on Canada's Aboriginal Population from the 1986 Census of Canada,* March, 1989, p. 240. Primary source: 1986 Census of Canada. *Notes:* A dash (-) represents zero or a percentage which rounds to less than .05 percent. 1. Aboriginal origins are derived from the ethnic origin question which asks whether respondents are North American Indian, Metis or Inuit. 2. All 1986 figures exclude the population estimated at about 45,000 on 136 incompletely enumerated Indian reserves and settlements throughout Canada. 3. Total income—refers to income from all sources such as total wages and salaries, net nonfarm self-employed income, net farm self-employed income, family allowances, federal child tax credits, Old Age Security Pension Plan and Guaranteed Income Supplement, benefits and interest on bonds, deposits, savings certificates and other investment income, retirement pensions, superannuation and annuities, and other money income. Also shown in the table is a category for "No income" which refers to the population aged 15 and over who did not receive any income during 1985. 4. Non-aboriginal in these columns—refers to persons who report one or more non-aboriginal origins such as British, French, etc., in combination with one of the aboriginal origins such as North American Indian. 5. Other Multiple Aboriginal Origins—refer to the sum of those persons reporting two or more aboriginal origins with or without a non-aboriginal origin. 6. Average income—refers to the average of total income from all sources (e.g., total wages and salaries net nonfarm self-employed income, net self-employed income, family allowances, federal child tax credits, Old Age Security Pension Plan and Guaranteed Income Supplement, benefits from Unemployment Insurance, other income from government sources, dividends and interest on bonds, savings certificates and other investment income, retirement pensions, superannuation and annuities, and other money income). Average income excludes persons with no income in 1985.

★972★

Population 15 Years and Over, by Total Income Group and Sex for Detailed Aboriginal Origins for British Columbia, 1986 - I[1,2]

Income is shown in Canadian dollars.

Income group[3]	Total Aboriginal origins[4]		North American Indian only		North American Indian and non-Aboriginal[5]		Metis only	
	Number	Percent	Number	Percent	Number	Percent	Number	Percent
Total population aged 15 and over	82,180	100.0	39,020	100.0	32,305	100.0	3,010	100.0
Male	40,095	48.8	18,955	48.6	15,725	48.7	1,435	47.7
Female	42,085	51.2	20,070	51.4	16,575	51.3	1,580	52.5
No income	15,690	19.1	8,325	21.3	5,415	16.8	645	21.4
Male	5,085	6.2	2,675	6.9	1,760	5.4	185	6.1
Female	10,605	12.9	5,640	14.5	3,655	11.3	460	15.3
Less than $3,000								
(including losses)	13,390	16.3	6,885	17.6	4,710	14.6	475	15.8
Male	5,985	7.3	3,315	8.5	1,905	5.9	195	6.5
Female	7,405	9.0	3,570	9.1	2,805	8.7	280	9.3
$3,000 to $6,999	14,680	17.9	8,030	20.6	4,870	15.1	630	20.9
Male	7,005	8.5	4,040	10.4	2,120	6.6	330	11.0
Female	7,675	9.3	3,990	10.2	2,750	8.5	305	10.1
$7,000 to $9,999	9,220	11.2	5,015	12.9	3,170	9.8	315	10.5
Male	3,925	4.8	2,215	5.7	1,280	4.0	120	4.0
Female	5,285	6.4	2,805	7.2	1,895	5.9	195	6.5
$10,000 to $14,999	8,705	10.6	3,885	10.0	3,640	11.3	300	10.0
Male	4,025	4.9	1,890	4.8	1,635	5.1	120	4.0
Female	4,680	5.7	1,990	5.1	2,000	6.2	180	6.0
$15,000 to $19,999	5,440	6.6	2,155	5.5	2,555	7.9	130	4.3
Male	2,750	3.3	1,215	3.1	1,155	3.6	75	2.5
Female	2,695	3.3	935	2.4	1,400	4.3	50	1.7
$20,000 to $29,999	7,670	9.3	2,715	7.0	3,745	11.6	275	9.1
Male	4,860	5.9	1,790	4.6	2,285	7.1	190	6.3
Female	2,805	3.4	930	2.4	1,455	4.5	90	3.0
$30,000 to $49,999	6,390	7.8	1,760	4.5	3,575	11.1	205	6.8
Male	5,530	6.7	1,595	4.1	2,995	9.3	190	6.3
Female	860	1.0	170	0.4	580	1.8	20	0.7
$50,000 and over	995	1.2	250	0.6	620	1.9	35	1.2
Male	920	1.1	215	0.6	580	1.8	35	1.2
Female	75	0.1	35	0.1	40	0.1	-	-

[Continued]

★ 972 ★

Population 15 Years and Over, by Total Income Group and Sex for Detailed Aboriginal Origins for British Columbia, 1986 - I

[Continued]

Income group[3]	Total Aboriginal origins[4]		North American Indian only		North American Indian and non-Aboriginal[5]		Metis only	
	Number	Percent	Number	Percent	Number	Percent	Number	Percent
				Average income[6]				
Total	12,774		10,405		15,171		12,095	
Male	15,884		12,426		19,372		15,675	
Female	9,317		8,124		10,631		8,082	

Source: Aboriginal Peoples Output Program, 1986 Census, Statistics Canada, *A Data Book on Canada's Aboriginal Population from the 1986 Census of Canada*, March, 1989, p. 264. Primary source: 1986 Census of Canada. *Notes:* A dash (-) represents zero or a percentage which rounds to less than .05 percent. 1. Aboriginal origins are derived from the ethnic origin question which asks whether respondents are North American Indian, Metis or Inuit. 2. All 1986 figures exclude the population estimated at about 45,000 on 136 incompletely enumerated Indian reserves and settlements throughout Canada. 3. Total income—refers to income from all sources such as total wages and salaries, net nonfarm self-employed income, net farm self-employed income, family allowances, federal child tax credits, Old Age Security Pension Plan and Guaranteed Income Supplement, benefits and interest on bonds, deposits, savings certificates and other investment income, retirement pensions, superannuation and annuities, and other money income. Also shown in the table is a category for "No income" which refers to the population aged 15 and over who did not receive any income during 1985. 4. Total Aboriginal origins—are the sum of persons who reported: (a) a single aboriginal (e.g., North American Indian, Metis or Inuit) and, (b) multiple aboriginal origins, that is those who reported: - at least one aboriginal origin with any other non-aboriginal (e.g., Metis and French), or—two or more aboriginal origins only. 5. Non-aboriginal in these columns—refers to persons who report one or more non-aboriginal origins such as British, French, etc., in combination with one of the aboriginal origins such as North American Indian. 6. Average income - refers to the average of total income from all sources (e.g., total wages and salaries net nonfarm self-employed income, net self-employed income, family allowances, federal child tax credits, Old Age Security Pension Plan and Guaranteed Income Supplement, benefits from Unemployment Insurance, other income from government sources, dividends and interest on bonds, savings certificates and other investment income, retirement pensions, superannuation and annuities, and other money income). Average income excludes persons with no income in 1985.

★ 973 ★

Population 15 Years and Over, by Total Income Group and Sex for Detailed Aboriginal Origins for British Columbia, 1986 - II[1,2]

Income is shown in Canadian dollars.

Income group[3]	Metis and non-Aboriginal[4]		Inuit only		Inuit and non-Aboriginal[4]		Other multiple Aboriginal origins[5]	
	Number	Percent	Number	Percent	Number	Percent	Number	Percent
Total population aged 15 and over	5,805	100.0	165	100.0	330	100.0	1,545	100.0
Male	2,850	49.1	90	54.5	205	62.1	840	54.4
Female	2,955	50.9	75	45.5	125	37.9	710	46.0
No income	980	16.9	40	24.2	70	21.2	215	13.9
Male	340	5.9	15	9.1	30	9.1	80	5.2
Female	645	11.1	25	15.2	40	12.1	135	8.7
Less than $3,000 (including losses)	910	15.7	35	21.2	60	18.2	320	20.7
Male	345	5.9	15	9.1	45	13.6	170	11.0
Female	565	9.7	25	15.2	10	3.0	150	9.7
$3,000 to $6,999	825	14.2	20	12.1	65	19.7	235	15.2
Male	365	6.3	20	12.1	40	12.1	105	6.8

[Continued]

★973★

Population 15 Years and Over, by Total Income Group and Sex for Detailed Aboriginal Origins for British Columbia, 1986 - II

[Continued]

Income group[3]	Metis and non-Aboriginal[4]		Inuit only		Inuit and non-Aboriginal[4]		Other multiple Aboriginal origins[5]	
	Number	Percent	Number	Percent	Number	Percent	Number	Percent
Female	460	7.9	-	-	25	7.6	140	9.1
$7,000 to $9,999	535	9.2	20	12.1	20	6.1	135	8.7
Male	225	3.9	-	-	10	3.0	60	3.9
Female	310	5.3	10	6.1	-	-	75	4.9
$10,000 to $14,999	645	11.1	30	18.2	30	9.1	175	11.3
Male	245	4.2	15	9.1	10	3.0	105	6.8
Female	400	6.9	15	9.1	20	6.1	75	4.9
$15,000 to $19,999	465	8.0	-	-	-	-	120	7.8
Male	230	4.0	-	-	-	-	65	4.2
Female	235	4.0	-	-	-	-	55	3.6
$20,000 to $29,999	715	12.3	10	6.1	35	10.6	175	11.3
Male	450	7.8	10	6.1	30	9.1	115	7.4
Female	265	4.6	-	-	-	-	55	3.6
$30,000 to $49,999	695	12.0	-	-	25	7.6	120	7.8
Male	610	10.5	-	-	25	7.6	110	7.1
Female	85	1.5	-	-	-	-	-	-
$50,000 and over	40	0.7	-	-	10	3.0	30	1.9
Male	40	0.7	-	-	10	3.0	30	1.9
Female	-	-	-	-	-	-	-	-

Average income[6]

Total	14,688	8,557	13,623	12,719
Male	18,944	10,429	15,367	16,633
Female	10,070	5,896	9,862	9,309

Source: Aboriginal Peoples Output Program, 1986 Census, Statistics Canada, *A Data Book on Canada's Aboriginal Population from the 1986 Census of Canada,* March, 1989, p. 240 Primary source: 1986 Census of Canada. *Notes:* A dash (-) represents zero or a percentage which rounds to less than .05 percent. 1. Aboriginal origins are derived from the ethnic origin question which asks whether respondents are North American Indian, Metis or Inuit. 2. All 1986 figures exclude the population estimated at about 45,000 on 136 incompletely enumerated Indian reserves and settlements throughout Canada. 3. Total income—refers to income from all sources such as total wages and salaries, net nonfarm self-employed income, net farm self-employed income, family allowances, federal child tax credits, Old Age Security Pension Plan and Guaranteed Income Supplement, benefits and interest on bonds, deposits, savings certificates and other investment income, retirement pensions, superannuation and annuities, and other money income. Also shown in the table is a category for "No income" which refers to the population aged 15 and over who did not receive any income during 1985. 4. Non-aboriginal in these columns—refers to persons who report one or more non-aboriginal origins such as British, French, etc., in combination with one of the aboriginal origins such as North American Indian. 5. Other Multiple Aboriginal Origins—refer to the sum of those persons reporting two or more aboriginal origins with or without a non-aboriginal origin. 6. Average income—refers to the average of total income from all sources (e.g., total wages and salaries net nonfarm self-employed income, net self-employed income, family allowances, federal child tax credits, Old Age Security Pension Plan and Guaranteed Income Supplement, benefits from Unemployment Insurance, other income from government sources, dividends and interest on bonds, savings certificates and other investment income, retirement pensions, superannuation and annuities, and other money income). Average income excludes persons with no income in 1985.

★974★

Population 15 Years and Over, by Total Income Group and Sex for Detailed Aboriginal Origins for Manitoba, 1986 - I[1,2]

Income is shown in Canadian dollars.

Income group[3]	Total Aboriginal origins[4]		North American Indian only		North American Indian and non-Aboriginal[5]		Metis only	
	Number	Percent	Number	Percent	Number	Percent	Number	Percent
Total population aged 15 and over	52,050	100.0	24,360	100.0	6,360	100.0	9,330	100.0
Male	24,970	48.0	11,655	47.8	3,060	48.1	4,650	49.8
Female	27,075	52.0	12,705	52.2	3,300	51.9	4,680	50.2
No income	11,330	21.8	6,085	25.0	980	15.4	2,115	22.7
Male	3,730	7.2	1,890	7.8	330	5.2	835	8.9
Female	7,600	14.6	4,195	17.2	650	10.2	1,280	13.7
Less than $3,000 (including losses)	9,915	19.0	5,205	21.4	925	14.5	1,680	18.0
Male	4,685	9.0	2,655	10.9	360	5.7	800	8.6
Female	5,230	10.0	2,545	10.4	565	8.9	875	9.4
$3,000 to $6,999	9,115	17.5	4,530	18.6	1,035	16.3	1,790	19.2
Male	4,100	7.9	2,195	9.0	375	5.9	770	8.3
Female	5,015	9.6	2,340	9.6	665	10.5	1,015	10.9
$7,000 to $9,999	5,890	11.3	2,770	11.4	585	9.2	1,170	12.5
Male	2,540	4.9	1,370	5.6	220	3.5	520	5.6
Female	3,345	6.4	1,395	5.7	365	5.7	650	7.0
$10,000 to $14,999	5,445	10.5	2,445	10.0	745	11.7	880	9.4
Male	2,885	5.5	1,385	5.7	325	5.1	465	5.0
Female	2,560	4.9	1,060	4.4	415	6.5	415	4.4
$15,000 to $19,999	3,690	7.1	1,390	5.7	615	9.7	665	7.1
Male	2,115	4.1	845	3.5	290	4.6	455	4.9
Female	1,570	3.0	545	2.2	330	5.2	210	2.3
$20,000 to $29,999	4,210	8.1	1,335	5.5	770	12.1	725	7.8
Male	2,820	5.4	835	3.4	550	8.6	515	5.5
Female	1,385	2.7	500	2.1	215	3.4	205	2.2
$30,000 to $49,999	2,165	4.2	565	2.3	610	9.6	270	2.9
Male	1,815	3.5	440	1.8	530	8.3	230	2.5
Female	350	0.7	125	0.5	80	1.3	35	0.4
$50,000 and over	290	0.6	40	0.2	90	1.4	40	0.4
Male	275	0.5	40	0.2	80	1.3	40	0.4
Female	15	-	-	-	-	-	-	-

[Continued]

★ 974 ★

Population 15 Years and Over, by Total Income Group and Sex for Detailed Aboriginal Origins for Manitoba, 1986 - I

[Continued]

Income group[3]	Total Aboriginal origins[4]		North American Indian only		North American Indian and non-Aboriginal[5]		Metis only	
	Number	Percent	Number	Percent	Number	Percent	Number	Percent
	Average income[6]							
Total	10,672		8,829		14,302		10,032	
Male	12,784		9,854		18,624		12,147	
Female	8,368		7,562		9,851		7,658	

Source: Aboriginal Peoples Output Program, 1986 Census, Statistics Canada, *A Data Book on Canada's Aboriginal Population from the 1986 Census of Canada*, March, 1989, p. 192. Primary source: 1986 Census of Canada. *Notes:* A dash (-) represents zero or a percentage which rounds to less than .05 percent. 1. Aboriginal origins are derived from the ethnic origin question which asks whether respondents are North American Indian, Metis or Inuit. 2. All 1986 figures exclude the population estimated at about 45,000 on 136 incompletely enumerated Indian reserves and settlements throughout Canada. 3. Total income—refers to income from all sources such as total wages and salaries, net nonfarm self-employed income, net farm self-employed income, family allowances, federal child tax credits, Old Age Security Pension Plan and Guaranteed Income Supplement, benefits and interest on bonds, deposits, savings certificates and other investment income, retirement pensions, superannuation and annuities, and other money income. Also shown in the table is a category for "No income" which refers to the population aged 15 and over who did not receive any income during 1985. 4. Total Aboriginal origins—are the sum of persons who reported: (a) a single aboriginal (e.g., North American Indian, Metis or Inuit) and, (b) multiple aboriginal origins, that is those who reported: - at least one aboriginal origin with any other non-aboriginal (e.g., Metis and French), or—two or more aboriginal origins only. 5. Non-aboriginal in these columns—refers to persons who report one or more non-aboriginal origins such as British, French, etc., in combination with one of the aboriginal origins such as North American Indian. 6. Average income - refers to the average of total income from all sources (e.g., total wages and salaries net nonfarm self-employed income, net self-employed income, family allowances, federal child tax credits, Old Age Security Pension Plan and Guaranteed Income Supplement, benefits from Unemployment Insurance, other income from government sources, dividends and interest on bonds, savings certificates and other investment income, retirement pensions, superannuation and annuities, and other money income). Average income excludes persons with no income in 1985.

★ 975 ★

Population 15 Years and Over, by Total Income Group and Sex for Detailed Aboriginal Origins for Manitoba, 1986 - II[1,2]

Income is shown in Canadian dollars.

Income group[3]	Metis and non-Aboriginal[4]		Inuit only		Inuit and non-Aboriginal[4]		Other multiple Aboriginal origins[5]	
	Number	Percent	Number	Percent	Number	Percent	Number	Percent
Total population aged 15 and over	9,105	100.0	100	100.0	120	100.0	2,680	100.0
male	4,235	46.5	35	35.0	55	45.8	1,280	47.8
female	4,870	53.5	65	65.0	65	54.2	1,395	52.1
No income	1,600	17.6	25	25.0	-	-	525	19.6
male	490	5.4	-	-	-	-	180	6.7
female	1,110	12.2	20	20.0	-	-	345	12.9
Less than $3,000 (including losses)	1,540	16.9	10	10.0	25	20.8	530	19.8
male	660	7.2	-	-	-	-	205	7.6
female	880	9.7	-	-	20	16.7	330	12.3
$3,000 to $6,999	1,265	13.9	15	15.0	30	25.0	445	16.6
male	515	5.7	-	-	10	8.3	230	8.6

[Continued]

★ 975 ★

Population 15 Years and Over, by Total Income Group and Sex for Detailed Aboriginal Origins for Manitoba, 1986 - II
[Continued]

Income group[3]	Metis and non-Aboriginal[4]		Inuit only		Inuit and non-Aboriginal[4]		Other multiple Aboriginal origins[5]	
	Number	Percent	Number	Percent	Number	Percent	Number	Percent
female	745	8.2	-	-	20	16.7	225	8.4
$7,000 to $9,999	1,100	12.1	10	10.0	-	-	240	9.0
male	350	3.8	-	-	-	-	75	2.8
female	745	8.2	10	10.0	-	-	175	6.5
$10,000 to $14,999	1,065	11.7	20	20.0	15	12.5	270	10.1
male	515	5.7	20	20.0	10	8.3	170	6.3
female	555	6.1	-	-	-	-	110	4.1
$15,000 to $19,999	820	9.0	-	-	-	-	185	6.9
male	405	4.4	-	-	-	-	115	4.3
female	415	4.6	-	-	-	-	65	2.4
$20,000 to $29,999	1,035	11.4	10	10.0	-	-	315	11.8
male	705	7.7	-	-	-	-	200	7.5
female	325	3.6	10	10.0	-	-	125	4.7
$30,000 to $49,999	575	6.3	-	-	-	-	140	5.2
male	495	5.4	-	-	-	-	-	-
female	85	0.9	-	-	-	-	-	-
$50,000 and over	110	1.2	-	-	-	-	-	-
male	100	1.1	-	-	-	-	-	-
female	-	-	-	-	-	-	-	-

Average income[6]

Total	12,873		10,041		10,879		11,739	
male	16,303		10,007		16,461		14,997	
female	9,456		10,069		6,240		8,868	

Source: Aboriginal Peoples Output Program, 1986 Census, Statistics Canada, *A Data Book on Canada's Aboriginal Population from the 1986 Census of Canada,* March, 1989, p. 192. Primary source: 1986 Census of Canada. *Notes:* A dash (-) represents zero or a percentage which rounds to less than .05 percent. 1. Aboriginal origins are derived from the ethnic origin question which asks whether respondents are North American Indian, Metis or Inuit. 2. All 1986 figures exclude the population estimated at about 45,000 on 136 incompletely enumerated Indian reserves and settlements throughout Canada. 3. Total income—refers to income from all sources such as total wages and salaries, net nonfarm self-employed income, net farm self-employed income, family allowances, federal child tax credits, Old Age Security Pension Plan and Guaranteed Income Supplement, benefits and interest on bonds, deposits, savings certificates and other investment income, retirement pensions, superannuation and annuities, and other money income. Also shown in the table is a category for "No income" which refers to the population aged 15 and over who did not receive any income during 1985. 4. Non-aboriginal in these columns—refers to persons who report one or more non-aboriginal origins such as British, French, etc., in combination with one of the aboriginal origins such as North American Indian. 5. Other Multiple Aboriginal Origins—refer to the sum of those persons reporting two or more aboriginal origins with or without a non-aboriginal origin. 6. Average income—refers to the average of total income from all sources (e.g., total wages and salaries net nonfarm self-employed income, net self-employed income, family allowances, federal child tax credits, Old Age Security Pension Plan and Guaranteed Income Supplement, benefits from Unemployment Insurance, other income from government sources, dividends and interest on bonds, savings certificates and other investment income, retirement pensions, superannuation and annuities, and other money income). Average income excludes persons with no income in 1985.

★ 976 ★

Population 15 Years and Over, by Total Income Group and Sex for Detailed Aboriginal Origins for New Brunswick, 1986 - 1ᵃᵃ

Income is shown in Canadian dollars.

Income group[3]	Total Aboriginal origins[4]		North American Indian only		North American Indian and non-Aboriginal[5]		Metis only	
	Number	Percent	Number	Percent	Number	Percent	Number	Percent
Total population aged 15 and over	5,990	100.0	2,505	100.0	2,960	100.0	110	100.0
Male	3,015	50.3	1,295	51.7	1,445	48.8	70	63.6
Female	2,975	49.7	1,215	48.5	1,515	51.2	35	31.8
No income	1,355	22.6	610	24.4	615	20.8	30	27.3
Male	465	7.8	240	9.6	165	5.6	20	18.2
Female	890	14.9	365	14.6	455	15.4	-	-
Less than $3,000 (including losses)	1,210	20.2	605	24.2	485	16.4	30	27.3
Male	580	9.7	345	13.8	205	6.9	10	9.1
Female	625	10.4	260	10.4	285	9.6	20	18.2
$3,000 to $6,999	925	15.4	440	17.6	425	14.4	15	13.6
Male	385	6.4	190	7.6	170	5.7	-	-
Female	540	9.0	255	10.2	260	8.8	-	-
$7,000 to $9,999	655	10.9	310	12.4	285	9.6	-	-
Male	300	5.0	155	6.2	105	3.5	-	-
Female	355	5.9	155	6.2	175	5.9	-	-
$10,000 to $14,999	570	9.5	205	8.2	320	10.8	10	9.1
Male	355	5.9	120	4.8	190	6.4	15	13.6
Female	220	3.7	80	3.2	130	4.4	-	-
$15,000 to $19,999	420	7.0	150	6.0	240	8.1	10	9.1
Male	225	3.8	80	3.2	130	4.4	-	-
Female	190	3.2	65	2.6	115	3.9	-	-
$20,000 to $29,999	570	9.5	130	5.2	385	13.0	10	9.1
Male	460	7.7	105	4.2	310	10.5	-	-
Female	110	1.8	25	1.0	75	2.5	-	-
$30,000 to $49,999	265	4.4	55	2.2	175	5.9	-	-
Male	225	3.8	50	2.0	155	5.2	-	-
Female	35	0.6	-	-	20	0.7	-	-
$50,000 and over	20	0.3	-	-	15	0.5	-	-
Male	20	0.3	-	-	15	0.5	-	-
Female	-	-	-	-	-	-	-	-

[Continued]

★ 976 ★

Population 15 Years and Over, by Total Income Group and Sex for Detailed Aboriginal Origins for New Brunswick, 1986 - I
[Continued]

Income group[3]	Total Aboriginal origins[4]		North American Indian only		North American Indian and non-Aboriginal[5]		Metis only	
	Number	Percent	Number	Percent	Number	Percent	Number	Percent
	Average income[6]							
Total	11,081		8,522		13,175		8,838	
Male	13,625		9,947		16,638		10,613	
Female	7,959		6,744		9,001		6,280	

Source: Aboriginal Peoples Output Program, 1986 Census, Statistics Canada, *A Data Book on Canada's Aboriginal Population from the 1986 Census of Canada*, March, 1989, p. 120. Primary source: 1986 Census of Canada. *Notes:* A dash (-) represents zero or a percentage which rounds to less than .05 percent. 1. Aboriginal origins are derived from the ethnic origin question which asks whether respondents are North American Indian, Metis or Inuit. 2. All 1986 figures exclude the population estimated at about 45,000 on 136 incompletely enumerated Indian reserves and settlements throughout Canada. 3. Total income—refers to income from all sources such as total wages and salaries, net nonfarm self-employed income, net farm self-employed income, family allowances, federal child tax credits, Old Age Security Pension Plan and Guaranteed Income Supplement, benefits and interest on bonds, deposits, savings certificates and other investment income, retirement pensions, superannuation and annuities, and other money income. Also shown in the table is a category for "No income" which refers to the population aged 15 and over who did not receive any income during 1985. 4. Total Aboriginal origins—are the sum of persons who reported: (a) a single aboriginal (e.g., North American Indian, Metis or Inuit) and, (b) multiple aboriginal origins, that is those who reported: - at least one aboriginal origin with any other non-aboriginal (e.g., Metis and French), or—two or more aboriginal origins only. 5. Non-aboriginal in these columns—refers to persons who report one or more non-aboriginal origins such as British, French, etc., in combination with one of the aboriginal origins such as North American Indian. 6. Average income - refers to the average of total income from all sources (e.g., total wages and salaries net nonfarm self-employed income, net self-employed income, family allowances, federal child tax credits, Old Age Security Pension Plan and Guaranteed Income Supplement, benefits from Unemployment Insurance, other income from government sources, dividends and interest on bonds, savings certificates and other investment income, retirement pensions, superannuation and annuities, and other money income). Average income excludes persons with no income in 1985.

★ 977 ★

Population 15 Years and Over, by Total Income Group and Sex for Detailed Aboriginal Origins for New Brunswick, 1986 - II[1,2]

Income is shown in Canadian dollars.

Income group[3]	Metis and non-Aboriginal[4]		Inuit only		Inuit and non-Aboriginal[4]		Other multiple Aboriginal origins[5]	
	Number	Percent	Number	Percent	Number	Percent	Number	Percent
Total population aged 15 and over	260	100.0	-	-	60	100.0	100	100.0
Male	140	53.8	-	-	25	41.7	45	45.0
Female	120	46.2	-	-	35	58.3	55	55.0
No income	55	21.2	-	-	15	25.0	25	25.0
Male	10	3.8	-	-	10	16.7	-	-
Female	35	13.5	-	-	-	-	15	15.0
Less than $3,000								
(including losses)	55	21.2	-	-	10	16.7	20	20.0
Male	20	7.7	-	-	-	-	-	-
Female	35	13.5	-	-	-	-	15	15.0
$3,000 to $6,999	20	7.7	-	-	10	16.7	15	15.0
Male	-	-	-	-	-	-	-	-

[Continued]

★977★

Population 15 Years and Over, by Total Income Group and Sex for Detailed Aboriginal Origins for New Brunswick, 1986 - II

[Continued]

Income group[3]	Metis and non-Aboriginal[4]		Inuit only		Inuit and non-Aboriginal[4]		Other multiple Aboriginal origins[5]	
	Number	Percent	Number	Percent	Number	Percent	Number	Percent
Female	10	3.8	-	-	-	-	10	10.0
$7,000 to $9,999	50	19.2	-	-	-	-	10	10.0
Male	30	11.5	-	-	-	-	15	15.0
Female	20	7.7	-	-	-	-	-	-
$10,000 to $14,999	20	7.7	-	-	-	-	-	-
Male	15	5.8	-	-	-	-	-	-
Female	-	-	-	-	-	-	-	-
$15,000 to $19,999	-	-	-	-	-	-	-	-
Male	-	-	-	-	-	-	-	-
Female	-	-	-	-	-	-	-	-
$20,000 to $29,999	30	11.5	-	-	-	-	15	15.0
Male	25	9.6	-	-	-	-	15	15.0
Female	-	-	-	-	-	-	-	-
$30,000 to $49,999	25	9.6	-	-	-	-	-	-
Male	20	7.7	-	-	-	-	-	-
Female	-	-	-	-	-	-	-	-
$50,000 and over	-	-	-	-	-	-	-	-
Male	-	-	-	-	-	-	-	-
Female	-	-	-	-	-	-	-	-

Average income[6]

Total	12,212		-		-		11,561	
Male	15,513		-		-		14,548	
Female	7,203		-		-		8,769	

Source: Aboriginal Peoples Output Program, 1986 Census, Statistics Canada, *A Data Book on Canada's Aboriginal Population from the 1986 Census of Canada*, March, 1989, p. 120. Primary source: 1986 Census of Canada. *Notes:* A dash (-) represents zero or a percentage which rounds to less than .05 percent. 1. Aboriginal origins are derived from the ethnic origin question which asks whether respondents are North American Indian, Metis or Inuit. 2. All 1986 figures exclude the population estimated at about 45,000 on 136 incompletely enumerated Indian reserves and settlements throughout Canada. 3. Total income—refers to income from all sources such as total wages and salaries, net nonfarm self-employed income, net farm self-employed income, family allowances, federal child tax credits, Old Age Security Pension Plan and Guaranteed Income Supplement, benefits and interest on bonds, deposits, savings certificates and other investment income, retirement pensions, superannuation and annuities, and other money income. Also shown in the table is a category for "No income" which refers to the population aged 15 and over who did not receive any income during 1985. 4. Non-aboriginal in these columns—refers to persons who report one or more non-aboriginal origins such as British, French, etc., in combination with one of the aboriginal origins such as North American Indian. 5. Other Multiple Aboriginal Origins—refer to the sum of those persons reporting two or more aboriginal origins with or without a non-aboriginal origin. 6. Average income—refers to the average of total income from all sources (e.g., total wages and salaries net nonfarm self-employed income, net self-employed income, family allowances, federal child tax credits, Old Age Security Pension Plan and Guaranteed Income Supplement, benefits from Unemployment Insurance, other income from government sources, dividends and interest on bonds, savings certificates and other investment income, retirement pensions, superannuation and annuities, and other money income). Average income excludes persons with no income in 1985.

★ 978 ★

Population 15 Years and Over, by Total Income Group and Sex for Detailed Aboriginal Origins for Newfoundland, 1986 - I[1,2]

Income is shown in Canadian dollars.

Income group[3]	Total Aboriginal origins[4]		North American Indian only		North American Indian and non-Aboriginal[5]		Metis only	
	Number	Percent	Number	Percent	Number	Percent	Number	Percent
Total population aged 15 and over	6,160	100.0	1,060	100.0	1,730	100.0	215	100.0
Female	3,145	51.1	495	46.7	880	50.9	110	51.2
Female	3,015	48.9	560	52.8	850	49.1	105	48.8
No income	1,365	22.2	290	27.4	370	21.4	25	11.6
Female	420	6.8	70	6.6	110	6.4	-	-
Female	945	15.3	220	20.8	265	15.3	20	9.3
Less than $3,000 (including losses)	945	15.3	180	17.0	185	10.7	20	9.3
Female	430	7.0	85	8.0	60	3.5	15	7.0
Female	505	8.2	95	9.0	125	7.2	-	-
$3,000 to $6,999	1,065	17.3	195	18.4	255	14.7	30	14.0
Female	495	8.0	80	7.5	135	7.8	-	-
Female	570	9.3	110	10.4	120	6.9	25	11.6
$7,000 to $9,999	845	13.7	165	15.6	240	13.9	60	27.9
Female	415	6.7	90	8.5	120	6.9	25	11.6
Female	430	7.0	75	7.1	120	6.9	30	14.0
$10,000 to $14,999	685	11.1	90	8.5	215	12.4	30	14.0
Female	455	7.4	65	6.1	155	9.0	10	4.7
Female	225	3.7	25	2.4	60	3.5	20	9.3
$15,000 to $19,999	465	7.5	80	7.5	185	10.7	15	7.0
Female	340	5.5	65	6.1	125	7.2	15	7.0
Female	125	2.0	20	1.9	60	3.5	-	-
$20,000 to $29,999	460	7.5	30	2.8	180	10.4	10	4.7
Female	310	5.0	20	1.9	105	6.1	10	4.7
Female	150	2.4	10	0.9	75	4.3	-	-
$30,000 to $49,999	320	5.2	20	1.9	90	5.2	20	9.3
Female	260	4.2	15	1.4	60	3.5	20	9.3
Female	55	0.9	-	-	30	1.7	-	-
$50,000 and over	20	0.3	-	-	-	-	-	-
Female	15	0.2	-	-	-	-	-	-
Female	-	-	-	-	-	-	-	-

[Continued]

★ 978 ★

Population 15 Years and Over, by Total Income Group and Sex for Detailed Aboriginal Origins for Newfoundland, 1986 - I

[Continued]

Income group[3]	Total Aboriginal origins[4]		North American Indian only		North American Indian and non-Aboriginal[5]		Metis only	
	Number	Percent	Number	Percent	Number	Percent	Number	Percent
	Average income[6]							
Total	11,098		8,694		12,832		11,860	
Female	13,152		10,632		14,847		15,662	
Female	8,392		6,271		10,217		7,296	

Source: Aboriginal Peoples Output Program, 1986 Census, Statistics Canada, *A Data Book on Canada's Aboriginal Population from the 1986 Census of Canada*, March, 1989, p. 48. Primary source: 1986 Census of Canada. *Notes:* A dash (-) represents zero or a percentage which rounds to less than .05 percent. 1. Aboriginal origins are derived from the ethnic origin question which asks whether respondents are North American Indian, Metis or Inuit. 2. All 1986 figures exclude the population estimated at about 45,000 on 136 incompletely enumerated Indian reserves and settlements throughout Canada. 3. Total income—refers to income from all sources such as total wages and salaries, net nonfarm self-employed income, net farm self-employed income, family allowances, federal child tax credits, Old Age Security Pension Plan and Guaranteed Income Supplement, benefits and interest on bonds, deposits, savings certificates and other investment income, retirement pensions, superannuation and annuities, and other money income. Also shown in the table is a category for "No income" which refers to the population aged 15 and over who did not receive any income during 1985. 4. Total Aboriginal origins—are the sum of persons who reported: (a) a single aboriginal (e.g., North American Indian, Metis or Inuit) and, (b) multiple aboriginal origins, that is those who reported: - at least one aboriginal origin with any other non-aboriginal (e.g., Metis and French), or—two or more aboriginal origins only. 5. Non-aboriginal in these columns—refers to persons who report one or more non-aboriginal origins such as British, French, etc., in combination with one of the aboriginal origins such as North American Indian. 6. Average income - refers to the average of total income from all sources (e.g., total wages and salaries net nonfarm self-employed income, net self-employed income, family allowances, federal child tax credits, Old Age Security Pension Plan and Guaranteed Income Supplement, benefits from Unemployment Insurance, other income from government sources, dividends and interest on bonds, savings certificates and other investment income, retirement pensions, superannuation and annuities, and other money income). Average income excludes persons with no income in 1985.

★ 979 ★

Population 15 Years and Over, by Total Income Group and Sex for Detailed Aboriginal Origins for Newfoundland, 1986 - II[1,2]

Income is shown in Canadian dollars.

Income group[3]	Metis and non-Aboriginal[4]		Inuit only		Inuit and non-Aboriginal[4]		Other multiple Aboriginal origins[5]	
	Number	Percent	Number	Percent	Number	Percent	Number	Percent
Total population aged 15 and over	515	100.0	1,170	100.0	1,070	100.0	395	100.0
Male	280	54.4	590	50.4	545	50.9	240	60.8
Female	230	44.7	575	49.1	525	49.1	150	38.0
No income	115	22.3	255	21.8	250	23.4	60	15.2
Male	40	7.8	90	7.7	80	7.5	25	6.3
Female	70	13.6	165	14.1	170	15.9	35	8.9
Less than $3,000 (including losses)	60	11.7	245	20.9	155	14.5	80	20.3
Male	35	6.8	120	10.3	65	6.1	55	13.9
Female	30	5.8	130	11.1	90	8.4	25	6.3
$3,000 to $6,999	85	16.5	260	22.2	185	17.3	50	12.7
Male	40	7.8	125	10.7	75	7.0	35	8.9

[Continued]

★ 979 ★

Population 15 Years and Over, by Total Income Group and Sex for Detailed Aboriginal Origins for Newfoundland, 1986 - II
[Continued]

Income group[3]	Metis and non-Aboriginal[4]		Inuit only		Inuit and non-Aboriginal[4]		Other multiple Aboriginal origins[5]	
	Number	Percent	Number	Percent	Number	Percent	Number	Percent
Female	50	9.7	130	11.1	110	10.3	20	5.1
$7,000 to $9,999	55	10.7	140	12.0	115	10.7	60	15.2
Male	20	3.9	80	6.8	65	6.1	10	2.5
Female	30	5.8	60	5.1	55	5.1	50	12.7
$10,000 to $14,999	45	8.7	135	11.5	125	11.7	40	10.1
Male	35	6.8	80	6.8	75	7.0	25	6.3
Female	10	1.9	55	4.7	45	4.2	10	2.5
$15,000 to $19,999	40	7.8	55	4.7	65	6.1	20	5.1
Male	35	6.8	40	3.4	40	3.7	20	5.1
Female	-	-	15	1.3	25	2.3	-	-
$20,000 to $29,999	70	13.6	55	4.7	95	8.9	15	3.8
Male	50	9.7	40	3.4	75	7.0	-	-
Female	15	2.9	15	1.3	20	1.9	-	-
$30,000 to $49,999	40	7.8	25	2.1	70	6.5	55	13.9
Male	30	5.8	25	2.1	55	5.1	45	11.4
Female	-	-	-	-	15	1.4	-	-
$50,000 and over	-	-	-	-	-	-	-	-
Male	-	-	-	-	-	-	-	-
Female	-	-	-	-	-	-	-	-

Average income[6]

Total	13,704	8,352	11,795	11,840
Male	15,599	9,682	14,470	13,428
Female	10,793	6,703	8,358	8,457

Source: Aboriginal Peoples Output Program, 1986 Census, Statistics Canada, *A Data Book on Canada's Aboriginal Population from the 1986 Census of Canada,* March, 1989, p. 48. Primary source: 1986 Census of Canada. *Notes:* A dash (-) represents zero or a percentage which rounds to less than .05 percent. 1. Aboriginal origins are derived from the ethnic origin question which asks whether respondents are North American Indian, Metis or Inuit. 2. All 1986 figures exclude the population estimated at about 45,000 on 136 incompletely enumerated Indian reserves and settlements throughout Canada. 3. Total income—refers to income from all sources such as total wages and salaries, net nonfarm self-employed income, net farm self-employed income, family allowances, federal child tax credits, Old Age Security Pension Plan and Guaranteed Income Supplement, benefits and interest on bonds, deposits, savings certificates and other investment income, retirement pensions, superannuation and annuities, and other money income. Also shown in the table is a category for "No income" which refers to the population aged 15 and over who did not receive any income during 1985. 4. Non-aboriginal in these columns—refers to persons who report one or more non-aboriginal origins such as British, French, etc., in combination with one of the aboriginal origins such as North American Indian. 5. Other Multiple Aboriginal Origins—refer to the sum of those persons reporting two or more aboriginal origins with or without a non-aboriginal origin. 6. Average income—refers to the average of total income from all sources (e.g., total wages and salaries net nonfarm self-employed income, net self-employed income, family allowances, federal child tax credits, Old Age Security Pension Plan and Guaranteed Income Supplement, benefits from Unemployment Insurance, other income from government sources, dividends and interest on bonds, savings certificates and other investment income, retirement pensions, superannuation and annuities, and other money income). Average income excludes persons with no income in 1985.

★ 980 ★

Population 15 Years and Over, by Total Income Group and Sex for Detailed Aboriginal Origins for Northwest Territories, 1986 - I[1,2]

Income is shown in Canadian dollars.

Income group[3]	Total Aboriginal origins[4]		North American Indian only		North American Indian and non-Aboriginal[5]		Metis only	
	Number	Percent	Number	Percent	Number	Percent	Number	Percent
Total population aged 15 and over	18,675	100.0	5,075	100.0	525	100.0	1,425	100.0
Male	9,570	51.2	2,600	51.2	320	61.0	740	51.9
Female	9,105	48.8	2,475	48.8	210	40.0	680	47.7
No income	4,715	25.2	1,295	25.5	70	13.3	260	18.2
Male	1,710	9.2	480	9.5	40	7.6	105	7.4
Female	3,000	16.1	820	16.2	35	6.7	155	10.9
Less than $3,000 (including losses)	3,405	18.2	900	17.7	50	9.5	170	11.9
Male	1,630	8.7	440	8.7	30	5.7	75	5.3
Female	1,780	9.5	455	9.0	20	3.8	100	7.0
$3,000 to $6,999	2,710	14.5	825	16.3	60	11.4	185	13.0
Male	1,410	7.6	460	9.1	30	5.7	70	4.9
Female	1,300	7.0	365	7.2	30	5.7	110	7.7
$7,000 to $9,999	1,955	10.5	670	13.2	55	10.5	130	9.1
Male	1,075	5.8	360	7.1	25	4.8	75	5.3
Female	880	4.7	310	6.1	30	5.7	55	3.9
$10,000 to $14,999	1,690	9.0	475	9.4	40	7.6	130	9.1
Male	995	5.3	285	5.6	15	2.9	80	5.6
Female	695	3.7	190	3.7	20	3.8	50	3.5
$15,000 to $19,999	975	5.2	225	4.4	25	4.8	115	8.1
Male	595	3.2	135	2.7	15	2.9	50	3.5
Female	385	2.1	90	1.8	-	-	65	4.6
$20,000 to $29,999	1,630	8.7	370	7.3	75	14.3	175	12.3
Male	965	5.2	195	3.8	40	7.6	100	7.0
Female	670	3.6	175	3.4	35	6.7	75	5.3
$30,000 to $49,999	1,430	7.7	295	5.8	125	23.8	220	15.4
Male	1,065	5.7	220	4.3	90	17.1	155	10.9
Female	360	1.9	80	1.6	35	6.7	60	4.2
$50,000 and over	170	0.9	25	0.5	25	4.8	40	2.8
Male	130	0.7	25	0.5	25	4.8	30	2.1
Female	30	0.2	-	-	-	-	15	1.1

[Continued]

★ 980 ★

Population 15 Years and Over, by Total Income Group and Sex for Detailed Aboriginal Origins for Northwest Territories, 1986 - I
[Continued]

Income group[3]	Total Aboriginal origins[4]		North American Indian only		North American Indian and non-Aboriginal[5]		Metis only	
	Number	Percent	Number	Percent	Number	Percent	Number	Percent
	Average income[7]							
Total	12,377		10,841		22,474		17,807	
Male	14,157		11,946		26,337		20,541	
Female	10,083		9,434		16,486		14,492	

Source: Aboriginal Peoples Output Program, 1986 Census, Statistics Canada, *A Data Book on Canada's Aboriginal Population from the 1986 Census of Canada*, March, 1989, p. 288. Primary source: 1986 Census of Canada. *Notes:* A dash (-) represents zero or a percentage which rounds to less than .05 percent. 1. Aboriginal origins are derived from the ethnic origin question which asks whether respondents are North American Indian, Metis or Inuit. 2. All 1986 figures exclude the population estimated at about 45,000 on 136 incompletely enumerated Indian reserves and settlements throughout Canada. 3. Total income—refers to income from all sources such as total wages and salaries, net nonfarm self-employed income, net farm self-employed income, family allowances, federal child tax credits, Old Age Security Pension Plan and Guaranteed Income Supplement, benefits and interest on bonds, deposits, savings certificates and other investment income, retirement pensions, superannuation and annuities, and other money income. Also shown in the table is a category for "No income" which refers to the population aged 15 and over who did not receive any income during 1985. 4. Total Aboriginal origins—are the sum of persons who reported: (a) a single aboriginal (e.g., North American Indian, Metis or Inuit) and, (b) multiple aboriginal origins, that is those who reported: - at least one aboriginal origin with any other non-aboriginal (e.g., Metis and French), or—two or more aboriginal origins only. 5. Non-aboriginal in these columns—refers to persons who report one or more non-aboriginal origins such as British, French, etc., in combination with one of the aboriginal origins such as North American Indian. 6. Average income - refers to the average of total income from all sources (e.g., total wages and salaries net nonfarm self-employed income, net self-employed income, family allowances, federal child tax credits, Old Age Security Pension Plan and Guaranteed Income Supplement, benefits from Unemployment Insurance, other income from government sources, dividends and interest on bonds, savings certificates and other investment income, retirement pensions, superannuation and annuities, and other money income). Average income excludes persons with no income in 1985.

★ 981 ★

Population 15 Years and Over, by Total Income Group and Sex for Detailed Aboriginal Origins for Northwest Territories, 1986 - II[1,2]

Income is shown in Canadian dollars.

Income group[3]	Metis and non-Aboriginal[4]		Inuit only		Inuit and non-Aboriginal[4]		Other multiple Aboriginal origins[5]	
	Number	Percent	Number	Percent	Number	Percent	Number	Percent
Total population aged 15 and over	460	100.0	10,320	100.0	285	100.0	590	100.0
Male	250	54.3	5,190	50.3	155	54.4	320	54.2
Female	210	45.7	5,135	49.8	130	45.6	265	44.9
No income	75	16.3	2,840	27.5	85	29.8	80	13.6
Male	30	6.5	980	9.5	40	14.0	30	5.1
Female	50	10.9	1,860	18.0	45	15.8	40	6.8
Less than $3,000 (including losses)	35	7.6	2,125	20.6	40	14.0	90	15.3
Male	30	6.5	985	9.5	15	5.3	55	9.3
Female	-	-	1,145	11.1	20	7.0	35	5.9
$3,000 to $6,999	40	8.7	1,470	14.2	45	15.8	85	14.4
Male	15	3.3	760	7.4	20	7.0	55	9.3

[Continued]

★ 981 ★

Population 15 Years and Over, by Total Income Group and Sex for Detailed Aboriginal Origins for Northwest Territories, 1986 - II

[Continued]

Income group[3]	Metis and non-Aboriginal[4]		Inuit only		Inuit and non-Aboriginal[4]		Other multiple Aboriginal origins[5]	
	Number	Percent	Number	Percent	Number	Percent	Number	Percent
Female	25	5.4	715	6.9	25	8.8	40	6.8
$7,000 to $9,999	25	5.4	990	9.6	20	7.0	60	10.2
Male	15	3.3	550	5.3	10	3.5	30	5.1
Female	-	-	445	4.3	15	5.3	25	4.2
$10,000 to $14,999	65	14.1	895	8.7	15	5.3	75	12.7
Male	40	8.7	540	5.2	-	-	30	5.1
Female	30	6.5	355	3.4	-	-	40	6.8
$15,000 to $19,999	30	6.5	530	5.1	20	7.0	25	4.2
Male	15	3.3	350	3.4	-	-	15	2.5
Female	10	2.2	180	1.7	-	-	15	2.5
$20,000 to $29,999	70	15.2	835	8.1	30	10.5	80	13.6
Male	35	7.6	530	5.1	20	7.0	40	6.8
Female	35	7.6	305	3.0	-	-	40	6.8
$30,000 to $49,999	110	23.9	585	5.7	30	10.5	65	11.0
Male	65	14.1	465	4.5	25	8.8	40	6.8
Female	45	9.8	125	1.2	-	-	15	2.5
$50,000 and over	-	-	45	0.4	-	-	15	2.5
Male	-	-	35	0.3	-	-	10	1.7
Female	-	-	-	-	-	-	-	-

Average income[6]

Total	21,347		10,915		15,719		15,708	
Male	20,691		12,813		19,771		16,893	
Female	22,247		8,475		10,175		14,208	

Source: Aboriginal Peoples Output Program, 1986 Census, Statistics Canada, *A Data Book on Canada's Aboriginal Population from the 1986 Census of Canada,* March, 1989, p. 288. Primary source: 1986 Census of Canada. *Notes:* A dash (-) represents zero or a percentage which rounds to less than .05 percent. 1. Aboriginal origins are derived from the ethnic origin question which asks whether respondents are North American Indian, Metis or Inuit. 2. All 1986 figures exclude the population estimated at about 45,000 on 136 incompletely enumerated Indian reserves and settlements throughout Canada. 3. Total income—refers to income from all sources such as total wages and salaries, net nonfarm self-employed income, net farm self-employed income, family allowances, federal child tax credits, Old Age Security Pension Plan and Guaranteed Income Supplement, benefits and interest on bonds, deposits, savings certificates and other investment income, retirement pensions, superannuation and annuities, and other money income. Also shown in the table is a category for "No income" which refers to the population aged 15 and over who did not receive any income during 1985. 4. Non-aboriginal in these columns—refers to persons who report one or more non-aboriginal origins such as British, French, etc., in combination with one of the aboriginal origins such as North American Indian. 5. Other Multiple Aboriginal Origins—refer to the sum of those persons reporting two or more aboriginal origins with or without a non-aboriginal origin. 6. Average income—refers to the average of total income from all sources (e.g., total wages and salaries net nonfarm self-employed income, net self-employed income, family allowances, federal child tax credits, Old Age Security Pension Plan and Guaranteed Income Supplement, benefits from Unemployment Insurance, other income from government sources, dividends and interest on bonds, savings certificates and other investment income, retirement pensions, superannuation and annuities, and other money income). Average income excludes persons with no income in 1985.

★ 982 ★

Population 15 Years and Over, by Total Income Group and Sex for Detailed Aboriginal Origins for Nova Scotia, 1986 - I[1,2]

Income is shown in Canadian dollars.

Income group[3]	Total Aboriginal origins[4]		North American Indian only		North American Indian and non-Aboriginal[5]		Metis only	
	Number	Percent	Number	Percent	Number	Percent	Number	Percent
Total population aged 15 and over	9,255	100.0	3,665	100.0	4,590	100.0	185	100.0
Male	4,455	48.0	1,840	50.2	2,145	46.7	85	45.9
Female	4,815	52.0	1,825	49.8	2,440	53.2	100	54.1
No income	2,100	22.7	1,080	29.5	825	18.0	30	16.2
Male	605	6.5	410	11.2	145	3.2	10	5.4
Female	1,495	16.2	665	18.1	680	14.8	20	10.8
Less than $3,000 (including losses)	1,565	16.9	715	19.5	620	13.5	40	21.6
Male	705	7.6	410	11.2	220	4.8	-	-
Female	855	9.2	310	8.5	405	8.8	30	16.2
$3,000 to $6,999	1,395	15.1	670	18.3	580	12.6	40	21.6
Male	675	7.3	355	9.7	255	5.6	35	18.9
Female	715	7.7	315	8.6	320	7.0	-	-
$7,000 to $9,999	1,010	10.9	390	10.6	480	10.5	15	8.1
Male	400	4.3	195	5.3	155	3.4	-	-
Female	615	6.6	195	5.3	325	7.1	15	8.1
$10,000 to $14,999	950	10.3	310	8.5	530	11.5	10	5.4
Male	510	5.5	170	4.6	275	6.0	-	-
Female	435	4.7	140	3.8	255	5.6	10	5.4
$15,000 to $19,999	795	8.6	220	6.0	510	11.1	25	13.5
Male	470	5.1	135	3.7	280	6.1	15	8.1
Female	330	3.6	85	2.3	225	4.9	-	-
$20,000 to $29,999	890	9.6	205	5.6	610	13.3	15	8.1
Male	610	6.6	105	2.9	445	9.7	15	8.1
Female	280	3.0	100	2.7	165	3.6	-	-
$30,000 to $49,999	485	5.2	65	1.8	385	8.4	-	-
Male	405	4.4	50	1.4	325	7.1	-	-
Female	80	0.9	15	0.4	60	1.3	-	-
$50,000 and over	75	0.8	-	-	55	1.2	-	-
Male	70	0.8	-	-	45	1.0	-	-
Female	-	-	-	-	-	-	-	-

[Continued]

★ 982 ★

Population 15 Years and Over, by Total Income Group and Sex for Detailed Aboriginal Origins for Nova Scotia, 1986 - I

[Continued]

Income group[3]	Total Aboriginal origins[4]		North American Indian only		North American Indian and non-Aboriginal[5]		Metis only	
	Number	Percent	Number	Percent	Number	Percent	Number	Percent
	Average income[6]							
Total	12,096		8,771		14,697		10,273	
Male	14,494		9,105		18,397		13,902	
Female	9,328		8,360		10,497		6,562	

Source: Aboriginal Peoples Output Program, 1986 Census, Statistics Canada, *A Data Book on Canada's Aboriginal Population from the 1986 Census of Canada*, March, 1989, p. 96. Primary source: 1986 Census of Canada. *Notes:* A dash (-) represents zero or a percentage which rounds to less than .05 percent. 1. Aboriginal origins are derived from the ethnic origin question which asks whether respondents are North American Indian, Metis or Inuit. 2. All 1986 figures exclude the population estimated at about 45,000 on 136 incompletely enumerated Indian reserves and settlements throughout Canada. 3. Total income—refers to income from all sources such as total wages and salaries, net nonfarm self-employed income, net farm self-employed income, family allowances, federal child tax credits, Old Age Security Pension Plan and Guaranteed Income Supplement, benefits and interest on bonds, deposits, savings certificates and other investment income, retirement pensions, superannuation and annuities, and other money income. Also shown in the table is a category for "No income" which refers to the population aged 15 and over who did not receive any income during 1985. 4. Total Aboriginal origins—are the sum of persons who reported: (a) a single aboriginal (e.g., North American Indian, Metis or Inuit) and, (b) multiple aboriginal origins, that is those who reported: - at least one aboriginal origin with any other non-aboriginal (e.g., Metis and French), or—two or more aboriginal origins only. 5. Non-aboriginal in these columns—refers to persons who report one or more non-aboriginal origins such as British, French, etc., in combination with one of the aboriginal origins such as North American Indian. 6. Average income - refers to the average of total income from all sources (e.g., total wages and salaries net nonfarm self-employed income, net self-employed income, family allowances, federal child tax credits, Old Age Security Pension Plan and Guaranteed Income Supplement, benefits from Unemployment Insurance, other income from government sources, dividends and interest on bonds, savings certificates and other investment income, retirement pensions, superannuation and annuities, and other money income). Average income excludes persons with no income in 1985.

★ 983 ★

Population 15 Years and Over, by Total Income Group and Sex for Detailed Aboriginal Origins for Nova Scotia, 1986 - II[1,2]

Income is shown in Canadian dollars.

Income group[3]	Metis and non-Aboriginal[4]		Inuit only		Inuit and non-Aboriginal[4]		Other multiple Aboriginal origins[5]	
	Number	Percent	Number	Percent	Number	Percent	Number	Percent
Total population aged 15 and over	460	100.0	85	100.0	110	100.0	160	100.0
Male	180	39.1	40	47.1	45	40.9	100	62.5
Female	275	59.8	45	52.9	70	63.6	60	37.5
No income	105	22.8	25	29.4	30	27.3	-	-
Male	30	6.5	-	-	-	-	-	-
Female	80	17.4	15	17.6	30	27.3	-	-
Less than $3,000 (including losses)	90	19.6	25	29.4	30	27.3	40	25.0
Male	35	7.6	-	-	10	9.1	20	12.5
Female	55	12.0	15	17.6	20	18.2	-	-
$3,000 to $6,999	60	13.0	10	11.8	-	-	20	12.5
Male	20	4.3	-	-	-	-	-	-

[Continued]

★ 983 ★

Population 15 Years and Over, by Total Income Group and Sex for Detailed Aboriginal Origins for Nova Scotia, 1986 - II

[Continued]

Income group[3]	Metis and non-Aboriginal[4]		Inuit only		Inuit and non-Aboriginal[4]		Other multiple Aboriginal origins[5]	
	Number	Percent	Number	Percent	Number	Percent	Number	Percent
Female	40	8.7	10	11.8	-	-	15	9.4
$7,000 to $9,999	65	14.1	-	-	10	9.1	40	25.0
Male	15	3.3	-	-	-	-	25	15.6
Female	50	10.9	-	-	-	-	20	12.5
$10,000 to $14,999	50	10.9	-	-	20	18.2	20	12.5
Male	30	6.5	-	-	15	13.6	20	12.5
Female	25	5.4	-	-	-	-	-	-
$15,000 to $19,999	10	2.2	20	23.5	-	-	10	6.3
Male	-	-	20	23.5	-	-	10	6.3
Female	-	-	-	-	-	-	-	-
$20,000 to $29,999	50	10.9	-	-	-	-	-	-
Male	35	7.6	-	-	-	-	-	-
Female	15	3.3	-	-	-	-	-	-
$30,000 to $49,999	15	3.3	-	-	-	-	-	-
Male	15	3.3	-	-	-	-	-	-
Female	-	-	-	-	-	-	-	-
$50,000 and over	-	-	-	-	-	-	-	-
Male	-	-	-	-	-	-	-	-
Female	-	-	-	-	-	-	-	-

Average income[6]

	Metis and non-Aboriginal	Inuit only	Inuit and non-Aboriginal	Other multiple Aboriginal origins
Total	11,354	7,598	12,346	9,558
Male	16,173	12,044	13,707	12,300
Female	7,497	2,827	10,912	5,253

Source: Aboriginal Peoples Output Program, 1986 Census, Statistics Canada, *A Data Book on Canada's Aboriginal Population from the 1986 Census of Canada,* March, 1989, p. 96. Primary source: 1986 Census of Canada. *Notes:* A dash (-) represents zero or a percentage which rounds to less than .05 percent. 1. Aboriginal origins are derived from the ethnic origin question which asks whether respondents are North American Indian, Metis or Inuit. 2. All 1986 figures exclude the population estimated at about 45,000 on 136 incompletely enumerated Indian reserves and settlements throughout Canada. 3. Total income—refers to income from all sources such as total wages and salaries, net nonfarm self-employed income, net farm self-employed income, family allowances, federal child tax credits, Old Age Security Pension Plan and Guaranteed Income Supplement, benefits and interest on bonds, deposits, savings certificates and other investment income, retirement pensions, superannuation and annuities, and other money income. Also shown in the table is a category for "No income" which refers to the population aged 15 and over who did not receive any income during 1985. 4. Non-aboriginal in these columns—refers to persons who report one or more non-aboriginal origins such as British, French, etc., in combination with one of the aboriginal origins such as North American Indian. 5. Other Multiple Aboriginal Origins—refer to the sum of those persons reporting two or more aboriginal origins with or without a non-aboriginal origin. 6. Average income—refers to the average of total income from all sources (e.g., total wages and salaries net nonfarm self-employed income, net self-employed income, family allowances, federal child tax credits, Old Age Security Pension Plan and Guaranteed Income Supplement, benefits from Unemployment Insurance, other income from government sources, dividends and interest on bonds, savings certificates and other investment income, retirement pensions, superannuation and annuities, and other money income). Average income excludes persons with no income in 1985.

★ 984 ★

Population 15 Years and Over, by Total Income Group and Sex for Detailed Aboriginal Origins for Ontario, 1986 - 1[1]

Income is shown in Canadian dollars.

Income group[3]	Total Aboriginal origins[4]		North American Indian only		North American Indian and non-Aboriginal[5]		Metis only	
	Number	Percent	Number	Percent	Number	Percent	Number	Percent
Total population aged 15 and over	109,540	100.0	35,380	100.0	60,760	100.0	2,645	100.0
Male	51,455	47.0	16,725	47.3	28,345	46.7	1,305	49.3
Female	58,085	53.0	18,655	52.7	32,420	53.4	1,340	50.7
No income	18,005	16.4	7,565	21.4	8,250	13.6	520	19.7
Male	5,310	4.8	2,320	6.6	2,295	3.8	170	6.4
Female	12,690	11.6	5,245	14.8	5,955	9.8	350	13.2
Less than $3,000 (including losses)	16,585	15.1	5,755	16.3	8,820	14.5	485	18.3
Male	6,345	5.8	2,470	7.0	3,180	5.2	165	6.2
Female	10,235	9.3	3,290	9.3	5,640	9.3	320	12.1
$3,000 to $6,999	15,640	14.3	5,885	16.6	7,735	12.7	420	15.9
Male	6,130	5.6	2,610	7.4	2,725	4.5	190	7.2
Female	9,510	8.7	3,275	9.3	5,015	8.3	230	8.7
$7,000 to $9,999	11,575	10.6	4,555	12.9	5,665	9.3	315	11.9
Male	4,545	4.1	2,095	5.9	1,985	3.3	160	6.0
Female	7,025	6.4	2,460	7.0	3,685	6.1	155	5.9
$10,000 to $14,999	11,800	10.8	3,640	10.3	6,810	11.2	190	7.2
Male	5,660	5.2	1,965	5.6	3,085	5.1	105	4.0
Female	6,135	5.6	1,675	4.7	3,725	6.1	90	3.4
$15,000 to $19,999	9,430	8.6	2,495	7.1	5,875	9.7	235	8.9
Male	4,540	4.1	1,310	3.7	2,700	4.4	115	4.3
Female	4,885	4.5	1,180	3.3	3,180	5.2	120	4.5
$20,000 to $29,999	13,900	12.7	3,190	9.0	8,970	14.8	235	8.9
Male	8,725	8.0	2,085	5.9	5,470	9.0	180	6.8
Female	5,175	4.7	1,105	3.1	3,500	5.8	55	2.1
$30,000 to $49,999	11,020	10.1	2,085	5.9	7,490	12.3	230	8.7
Male	8,845	8.1	1,700	4.8	5,935	9.8	210	7.9
Female	2,175	2.0	385	1.1	1,555	2.6	15	0.6
$50,000 and over	1,590	1.5	210	0.6	1,145	1.9	10	0.4
Male	1,345	1.2	170	0.5	975	1.6	-	-
Female	245	0.2	45	0.1	170	0.3	-	-

[Continued]

★ 984 ★

Population 15 Years and Over, by Total Income Group and Sex for Detailed Aboriginal Origins for Ontario, 1986 - I

[Continued]

Income group[3]	Total Aboriginal origins[4]		North American Indian only		North American Indian and non-Aboriginal[5]		Metis only	
	Number	Percent	Number	Percent	Number	Percent	Number	Percent
				Average income[6]				
Total	14,370		11,715		16,258		12,541	
Male	18,513		14,023		20,784		16,193	
Female	10,885		9,235		11,802		8,350	

Source: Aboriginal Peoples Output Program, 1986 Census, Statistics Canada, *A Data Book on Canada's Aboriginal Population from the 1986 Census of Canada*, March, 1989, p. 168. Primary source: 1986 Census of Canada. *Notes:* A dash (-) represents zero or a percentage which rounds to less than .05 percent. 1. Aboriginal origins are derived from the ethnic origin question which asks whether respondents are North American Indian, Metis or Inuit. 2. All 1986 figures exclude the population estimated at about 45,000 on 136 incompletely enumerated Indian reserves and settlements throughout Canada. 3. Total income—refers to income from all sources such as total wages and salaries, net nonfarm self-employed income, net farm self-employed income, family allowances, federal child tax credits, Old Age Security Pension Plan and Guaranteed Income Supplement, benefits and interest on bonds, deposits, savings certificates and other investment income, retirement pensions, superannuation and annuities, and other money income. Also shown in the table is a category for "No income" which refers to the population aged 15 and over who did not receive any income during 1985. 4. Total Aboriginal origins—are the sum of persons who reported: (a) a single aboriginal (e.g., North American Indian, Metis or Inuit) and, (b) multiple aboriginal origins, that is those who reported: - at least one aboriginal origin with any other non-aboriginal (e.g., Metis and French), or—two or more aboriginal origins only. 5. Non-aboriginal in these columns—refers to persons who report one or more non-aboriginal origins such as British, French, etc., in combination with one of the aboriginal origins such as North American Indian. 6. Average income - refers to the average of total income from all sources (e.g., total wages and salaries net nonfarm self-employed income, net self-employed income, family allowances, federal child tax credits, Old Age Security Pension Plan and Guaranteed Income Supplement, benefits from Unemployment Insurance, other income from government sources, dividends and interest on bonds, savings certificates and other investment income, retirement pensions, superannuation and annuities, and other money income). Average income excludes persons with no income in 1985.

★ 985 ★

Population 15 Years and Over, by Total Income Group and Sex for Detailed Aboriginal Origins for Ontario, 1986 - II[1,2]

Income is shown in Canadian dollars.

Income group[3]	Metis and non-Aboriginal[4]		Inuit only		Inuit and non-Aboriginal[4]		Other multiple Aboriginal origins[5]	
	Number	Percent	Number	Percent	Number	Percent	Number	Percent
Total population aged 15 and over	6,780	100.0	490	100.0	950	100.0	2,535	100.0
Male	3,085	45.5	235	48.0	500	52.6	1,250	49.3
Female	3,695	54.5	250	51.0	445	46.8	1,285	50.7
No income	1,045	15.4	80	16.3	155	16.3	385	15.2
Male	335	4.9	15	3.1	55	5.8	105	4.1
Female	710	10.5	65	13.3	100	10.5	265	10.5
Less than $3,000 (including losses)	945	13.9	45	9.2	125	13.2	405	16.0
Male	320	4.7	25	5.1	40	4.2	150	5.9
Female	630	9.3	25	5.1	80	8.4	260	10.3
$3,000 to $6,999	1,045	15.4	70	14.3	175	18.4	315	12.4
Male	390	5.8	45	9.2	50	5.3	135	5.3

[Continued]

★ 985 ★

Population 15 Years and Over, by Total Income Group and Sex for Detailed Aboriginal Origins for Ontario, 1986 - II
[Continued]

Income group[3]	Metis and non-Aboriginal[4]		Inuit only		Inuit and non-Aboriginal[4]		Other multiple Aboriginal origins[5]	
	Number	Percent	Number	Percent	Number	Percent	Number	Percent
Female	660	9.7	25	5.1	125	13.2	185	7.3
$7,000 to $9,999	650	9.6	70	14.3	75	7.9	230	9.1
Male	190	2.8	15	3.1	40	4.2	70	2.8
Female	465	6.9	60	12.2	35	3.7	170	6.7
$10,000 to $14,999	815	12.0	35	7.1	100	10.5	215	8.5
Male	335	4.9	10	2.0	55	5.8	100	3.9
Female	485	7.2	20	4.1	40	4.2	105	4.1
$15,000 to $19,999	495	7.3	30	6.1	75	7.9	225	8.9
Male	240	3.5	20	4.1	45	4.7	110	4.3
Female	260	3.8	-	-	30	3.2	110	4.3
$20,000 to $29,999	925	13.6	100	20.4	110	11.6	375	14.8
Male	575	8.5	70	14.3	90	9.5	260	10.3
Female	350	5.2	30	6.1	25	2.6	115	4.5
$30,000 to $49,999	735	10.8	40	8.2	120	12.6	325	12.8
Male	620	9.1	15	3.1	105	11.1	255	10.1
Female	110	1.6	25	5.1	15	1.6	75	3.0
$50,000 and over	120	1.8	15	3.1	15	1.6	65	2.6
Male	95	1.4	20	4.1	15	1.6	65	2.6
Female	20	0.3	-	-	-	-	-	-

Average income[6]

Total	15,171	18,197	15,224	16,590
Male	19,748	22,002	20,172	21,353
Female	10,945	13,685	8,938	11,238

Source: Aboriginal Peoples Output Program, 1986 Census, Statistics Canada, *A Data Book on Canada's Aboriginal Population from the 1986 Census of Canada,* March, 1989, p. 168. Primary source: 1986 Census of Canada. *Notes:* A dash (-) represents zero or a percentage which rounds to less than .05 percent. 1. Aboriginal origins are derived from the ethnic origin question which asks whether respondents are North American Indian, Metis or Inuit. 2. All 1986 figures exclude the population estimated at about 45,000 on 136 incompletely enumerated Indian reserves and settlements throughout Canada. 3. Total income—refers to income from all sources such as total wages and salaries, net nonfarm self-employed income, net farm self-employed income, family allowances, federal child tax credits, Old Age Security Pension Plan and Guaranteed Income Supplement, benefits and interest on bonds, deposits, savings certificates and other investment income, retirement pensions, superannuation and annuities, and other money income. Also shown in the table is a category for "No income" which refers to the population aged 15 and over who did not receive any income during 1985. 4. Non-aboriginal in these columns—refers to persons who report one or more non-aboriginal origins such as British, French, etc., in combination with one of the aboriginal origins such as North American Indian. 5. Other Multiple Aboriginal Origins—refer to the sum of those persons reporting two or more aboriginal origins with or without a non-aboriginal origin. 6. Average income—refers to the average of total income from all sources (e.g., total wages and salaries net nonfarm self-employed income, net self-employed income, family allowances, federal child tax credits, Old Age Security Pension Plan and Guaranteed Income Supplement, benefits from Unemployment Insurance, other income from government sources, dividends and interest on bonds, savings certificates and other investment income, retirement pensions, superannuation and annuities, and other money income). Average income excludes persons with no income in 1985.

★ 986 ★

Population 15 Years and Over, by Total Income Group and Sex for Detailed Aboriginal Origins for Prince Edward Island, 1986 - I[1,2]

Income is shown in Canadian dollars.

Income group[3]	Total Aboriginal origins[4]		North American Indian only		North American Indian and non-Aboriginal[5]		Metis only	
	Number	Percent	Number	Percent	Number	Percent	Number	Percent
Total population aged 15 and over	840	100.0	235	100.0	475	100.0	15	100.0
Male	445	53.0	125	53.2	255	53.7	-	-
Female	395	47.0	110	46.8	220	46.3	10	66.7
No income	80	9.5	20	8.5	40	8.4	-	-
Male	25	3.0	-	-	10	2.1	-	-
Female	60	7.1	15	6.4	30	6.3	-	-
Less than $3,000 (including losses)	150	17.9	55	23.4	75	15.8	-	-
Male	75	8.9	30	12.8	40	8.4	-	-
Female	75	8.9	20	8.5	40	8.4	-	-
$3,000 to $6,999	160	19.0	50	21.3	105	22.1	-	-
Male	80	9.5	30	12.8	40	8.4	-	-
Female	80	9.5	20	8.5	60	12.6	-	-
$7,000 to $9,999	135	16.1	40	17.0	75	15.8	-	-
Male	70	8.3	20	8.5	35	7.4	-	-
Female	65	7.7	20	8.5	40	8.4	-	-
$10,000 to $14,999	135	16.1	45	19.1	55	11.6	-	-
Male	70	8.3	25	10.6	30	6.3	-	-
Female	60	7.1	20	8.5	25	5.3	-	-
$15,000 to $19,999	55	6.5	15	6.4	35	7.4	-	-
Male	30	3.6	-	-	30	6.3	-	-
Female	30	3.6	10	4.3	-	-	-	-
$20,000 to $29,999	100	11.9	-	-	70	14.7	-	-
Male	80	9.5	-	-	60	12.6	-	-
Female	20	2.4	-	-	10	2.1	-	-
$30,000 to $49,999	15	1.8	-	-	10	2.1	-	-
Male	10	1.2	-	-	10	2.1	-	-
Female	-	-	-	-	-	-	-	-
$50,000 and over	-	-	-	-	-	-	-	-
Male	-	-	-	-	-	-	-	-
Female	-	-	-	-	-	-	-	-

[Continued]

★ 986 ★

Population 15 Years and Over, by Total Income Group and Sex for Detailed Aboriginal Origins for Prince Edward Island, 1986 - I
[Continued]

Income group[3]	Total Aboriginal origins[4]		North American Indian only		North American Indian and non-Aboriginal[5]		Metis only	
	Number	Percent	Number	Percent	Number	Percent	Number	Percent
	Average income[6]							
Total	10,662		7,796		11,745		-	
Male	11,780		7,163		13,810		-	
Female	9,262		8,575		9,150		-	

Source: Aboriginal Peoples Output Program, 1986 Census, Statistics Canada, *A Data Book on Canada's Aboriginal Population from the 1986 Census of Canada*, March, 1989, p. 72. Primary source: 1986 Census of Canada. *Notes:* A dash (-) represents zero or a percentage which rounds to less than .05 percent. 1. Aboriginal origins are derived from the ethnic origin question which asks whether respondents are North American Indian, Metis or Inuit. 2. All 1986 figures exclude the population estimated at about 45,000 on 136 incompletely enumerated Indian reserves and settlements throughout Canada. 3. Total income—refers to income from all sources such as total wages and salaries, net nonfarm self-employed income, net farm self-employed income, family allowances, federal child tax credits, Old Age Security Pension Plan and Guaranteed Income Supplement, benefits and interest on bonds, deposits, savings certificates and other investment income. Also shown in the table is a category for "No income" which refers to the population aged 15 and over who did not receive any income during 1985. 4. Total Aboriginal origins—are the sum of persons who reported: (a) a single aboriginal (e.g., North American Indian, Metis or Inuit) and, (b) multiple aboriginal origins, that is those who reported: - at least one aboriginal origin with any other non-aboriginal (e.g., Metis and French), or—two or more aboriginal origins only. 5. Non-aboriginal in these columns—refers to persons who report one or more non-aboriginal origins such as British, French, etc., in combination with one of the aboriginal origins such as North American Indian. 6. Average income - refers to the average of total income from all sources (e.g., total wages and salaries net nonfarm self-employed income, net self-employed income, family allowances, federal child tax credits, Old Age Security Pension Plan and Guaranteed Income Supplement, benefits from Unemployment Insurance, other income from government sources, dividends and interest on bonds, savings certificates and other investment income, retirement pensions, superannuation and annuities, and other money income). Average income excludes persons with no income in 1985.

★ 987 ★

Population 15 Years and Over, by Total Income Group and Sex for Detailed Aboriginal Origins for Prince Edward Island, 1986 - II[1,2]

Income is shown in Canadian dollars.

Income group[3]	Metis and non-Aboriginal[4]		Inuit only		Inuit and non-Aboriginal[4]		Other multiple Aboriginal origins[5]	
	Number	Percent	Number	Percent	Number	Percent	Number	Percent
Total population aged 15 and over	70	100.0	-	-	20	100.0	20	100.0
Male	50	71.4	-	-	15	75.0	-	-
Female	25	35.7	-	-	-	-	15	75.0
No income	-	-	-	-	-	-	15	75.0
Male	-	-	-	-	-	-	-	-
Female	-	-	-	-	-	-	15	75.0
Less than $3,000 (including losses)	-	-	-	-	-	-	-	-
Male	-	-	-	-	-	-	-	-
Female	-	-	-	-	-	-	-	-
$3,000 to $6,999	-	-	-	-	-	-	-	-
Male	-	-	-	-	-	-	-	-

[Continued]

★ 987 ★

Population 15 Years and Over, by Total Income Group and Sex for Detailed Aboriginal Origins for Prince Edward Island, 1986 - II

[Continued]

Income group[3]	Metis and non-Aboriginal[4]		Inuit only		Inuit and non-Aboriginal[4]		Other multiple Aboriginal origins[5]	
	Number	Percent	Number	Percent	Number	Percent	Number	Percent
Female	-	-	-	-	-	-	-	-
$7,000 to $9,999	20	28.6	-	-	-	-	-	-
Male	15	21.4	-	-	-	-	-	-
Female	-	-	-	-	-	-	-	-
$10,000 to $14,999	15	21.4	-	-	-	-	-	-
Male	-	-	-	-	-	-	-	-
Female	10	14.3	-	-	-	-	-	-
$15,000 to $19,999	-	-	-	-	-	-	-	-
Male	-	-	-	-	-	-	-	-
Female	-	-	-	-	-	-	-	-
$20,000 to $29,999	10	14.3	-	-	-	-	-	-
Male	10	14.3	-	-	-	-	-	-
Female	-	-	-	-	-	-	-	-
$30,000 to $49,999	-	-	-	-	-	-	-	-
Male	-	-	-	-	-	-	-	-
Female	-	-	-	-	-	-	-	-
$50,000 and over	-	-	-	-	-	-	-	-
Male	-	-	-	-	-	-	-	-
Female	-	-	-	-	-	-	-	-

Average income[6]

Total	10,286		-		-		-	
Male	10,579		-		-		-	
Female	9,801		-		-		-	

Source: Aboriginal Peoples Output Program, 1986 Census, Statistics Canada, *A Data Book on Canada's Aboriginal Population from the 1986 Census of Canada,* March, 1989, p. 72. Primary source: 1986 Census of Canada. *Notes:* A dash (-) represents zero or a percentage which rounds to less than .05 percent. 1. Aboriginal origins are derived from the ethnic origin question which asks whether respondents are North American Indian, Metis or Inuit. 2. All 1986 figures exclude the population estimated at about 45,000 on 136 incompletely enumerated Indian reserves and settlements throughout Canada. 3. Total income—refers to income from all sources such as total wages and salaries, net nonfarm self-employed income, net farm self-employed income, family allowances, federal child tax credits, Old Age Security Pension Plan and Guaranteed Income Supplement, benefits and interest on bonds, deposits, savings certificates and other investment income, retirement pensions, superannuation and annuities, and other money income. Also shown in the table is a category for "No income" which refers to the population aged 15 and over who did not receive any income during 1985. 4. Non-aboriginal in these columns—refers to persons who report one or more non-aboriginal origins such as British, French, etc., in combination with one of the aboriginal origins such as North American Indian. 5. Other Multiple Aboriginal Origins—refer to the sum of those persons reporting two or more aboriginal origins with or without a non-aboriginal origin. 6. Average income—refers to the average of total income from all sources (e.g., total wages and salaries net nonfarm self-employed income, net self-employed income, family allowances, federal child tax credits, Old Age Security Pension Plan and Guaranteed Income Supplement, benefits from Unemployment Insurance, other income from government sources, dividends and interest on bonds, savings certificates and other investment income, retirement pensions, superannuation and annuities, and other money income). Average income excludes persons with no income in 1985.

★ 988 ★

Population 15 Years and Over, by Total Income Group and Sex for Detailed Aboriginal Origins for Quebec, 1986 - I[1,2]

Income is shown in Canadian dollars.

Income group[3]	Total Aboriginal origins[4]		North American Indian only		North American Indian and non-Aboriginal[5]		Metis only	
	Number	Percent	Number	Percent	Number	Percent	Number	Percent
Total population aged 15 and over	56,165	100.0	25,750	100.0	17,905	100.0	4,105	100.0
Male	26,620	47.4	12,560	48.8	8,010	44.7	2,060	50.2
Female	29,540	52.6	13,190	51.2	9,890	55.2	2,040	49.7
No income	10,105	18.0	5,190	20.2	2,465	13.8	740	18.0
Male	2,925	5.2	1,510	5.9	625	3.5	225	5.5
Female	7,185	12.8	3,680	14.3	1,840	10.3	520	12.7
Less than $3,000 (including losses)	7,085	12.6	3,335	13.0	1,950	10.9	485	11.8
Male	3,015	5.4	1,575	6.1	630	3.5	235	5.7
Female	4,075	7.3	1,755	6.8	1,320	7.4	260	6.3
$3,000 to $6,999	8,920	15.9	4,200	16.3	2,665	14.9	795	19.4
Male	3,675	6.5	1,815	7.0	980	5.5	325	7.9
Female	5,245	9.3	2,390	9.3	1,680	9.4	470	11.4
$7,000 to $9,999	6,620	11.8	3,405	13.2	1,782	10.0	580	14.1
Male	2,645	4.7	1,400	5.4	665	3.7	260	6.3
Female	3,965	7.1	2,010	7.8	1,115	6.2	315	7.7
$10,000 to $14,999	6,480	11.5	3,025	11.7	2,200	12.3	485	11.8
Male	3,255	5.8	1,625	6.3	950	5.3	295	7.2
Female	3,230	5.8	1,405	5.5	1,245	7.0	190	4.6
$15,000 to $19,999	5,300	9.4	2,115	8.2	2,030	11.3	355	8.6
Male	2,975	5.3	1,300	5.0	1,020	5.7	235	5.7
Female	2,325	4.1	810	3.1	1,010	5.6	120	2.9
$20,000 to $29,999	7,030	12.5	2,900	11.3	2,640	14.7	435	10.6
Male	4,525	8.1	2,025	7.9	1,540	8.6	295	7.2
Female	2,505	4.5	875	3.4	1,105	6.2	140	3.4
$30,000 to $49,999	4,110	7.3	1,415	5.5	1,940	10.8	200	4.9
Male	3,180	5.7	1,175	4.6	1,400	7.8	170	4.1
Female	930	1.7	245	1.0	535	3.0	30	0.7
$50,000 and over	510	0.9	170	0.7	245	1.4	30	0.7
Male	430	0.8	145	0.6	200	1.1	25	0.6
Female	80	0.1	30	0.1	45	0.3	-	-

[Continued]

★ 988 ★

Population 15 Years and Over, by Total Income Group and Sex for Detailed Aboriginal Origins for Quebec, 1986 - I
[Continued]

Income group[3]	Total Aboriginal origins[4]		North American Indian only		North American Indian and non-Aboriginal[5]		Metis only	
	Number	Percent	Number	Percent	Number	Percent	Number	Percent
				Average income[6]				
Total	13,931		13,078		15,746		12,302	
Male	16,927		15,948		19,427		14,819	
Female	10,755		9,739		12,364		9,265	

Source: Aboriginal Peoples Output Program, 1986 Census, Statistics Canada, *A Data Book on Canada's Aboriginal Population from the 1986 Census of Canada*, March, 1989, p. 144. Primary source: 1986 Census of Canada. *Notes:* A dash (-) represents zero or a percentage which rounds to less than .05 percent.

★ 989 ★

Population 15 Years and Over, by Total Income Group and Sex for Detailed Aboriginal Origins for Quebec, 1986 - II[1,2]

Income is shown in Canadian dollars.

Income group[3]	Metis and non-Aboriginal[4]		Inuit only		Inuit and non-Aboriginal[4]		Other multiple Aboriginal origins[5]	
	Number	Percent	Number	Percent	Number	Percent	Number	Percent
Total population aged 15 and over	3,250	100.0	3,900	100.0	365	100.0	885	100.0
Male	1,400	43.1	1,940	49.7	180	49.3	470	53.1
Female	1,850	56.9	1,960	50.3	185	50.7	425	48.0
No income	490	15.1	1,025	26.3	80	21.9	120	13.6
Male	110	3.4	420	10.8	20	5.5	10	1.1
Female	375	11.5	600	15.4	65	17.8	100	11.3
Less than $3,000 (including losses)	455	14.0	730	18.7	25	6.8	110	12.4
Male	195	6.0	305	7.8	-	-	75	8.5
Female	265	8.2	425	10.9	15	4.1	40	4.5
$3,000 to $6,999	540	16.6	545	14.0	55	15.1	125	14.1
Male	175	5.4	285	7.3	35	9.6	55	6.2
Female	370	11.4	260	6.7	20	5.5	70	7.9
$7,000 to $9,999	340	10.5	365	9.4	40	11.0	105	11.9
Male	120	3.7	155	4.0	20	5.5	25	2.8
Female	220	6.8	205	5.3	30	8.2	70	7.9
$10,000 to $14,999	350	10.8	310	7.9	35	9.6	80	9.0
Male	160	4.9	175	4.5	-	-	30	3.4

[Continued]

★ 989 ★

Population 15 Years and Over, by Total Income Group and Sex for Detailed Aboriginal Origins for Quebec, 1986 - II
[Continued]

Income group[3]	Metis and non-Aboriginal[4]		Inuit only		Inuit and non-Aboriginal[4]		Other multiple Aboriginal origins[5]	
	Number	Percent	Number	Percent	Number	Percent	Number	Percent
Female	185	5.7	135	3.5	25	6.8	40	4.5
$15,000 to $19,999	365	11.2	290	7.4	35	9.6	120	13.6
Male	160	4.9	160	4.1	15	4.1	80	9.0
Female	200	6.2	135	3.5	20	5.5	30	3.4
$20,000 to $29,999	475	14.6	415	10.6	40	11.0	120	13.6
Male	280	8.6	270	6.9	35	9.6	65	7.3
Female	195	6.0	145	3.7	-	-	40	4.5
$30,000 to $49,999	210	6.5	205	5.3	40	11.0	105	11.9
Male	165	5.1	150	3.8	35	9.6	75	8.5
Female	50	1.5	55	1.4	-	-	15	1.7
$50,000 and over	30	0.9	15	0.4	15	4.1	10	1.1
Male	30	0.9	15	0.4	10	2.7	15	1.7
Female	-	-	-	-	-	-	-	-
	Average income[6]							
Total	13,605		11,654		17,209		15,880	
Male	16,728		13,642		21,671		18,437	
Female	10,877		9,437		11,236		12,363	

Source: Aboriginal Peoples Output Program, 1986 Census, Statistics Canada, *A Data Book on Canada's Aboriginal Population from the 1986 Census of Canada,* March, 1989, p. 144. Primary source: 1986 Census of Canada. *Notes:* A dash (-) represents zero or a percentage which rounds to less than .05 percent. 1. Aboriginal origins are derived from the ethnic origin question which asks whether respondents are North American Indian, Metis or Inuit. 2. All 1986 figures exclude the population estimated at about 45,000 on 136 incompletely enumerated Indian reserves and settlements throughout Canada. 3. Total income—refers to income from all sources such as total wages and salaries, net nonfarm self-employed income, net farm self-employed income, family allowances, federal child tax credits, Old Age Security Pension Plan and Guaranteed Income Supplement, benefits and interest on bonds, deposits, savings certificates and other investment income, retirement pensions, superannuation and annuities, and other money income. Also shown in the table is a category for "No income" which refers to the population aged 15 and over who did not receive any income during 1985. 4. Non-aboriginal in these columns—refers to persons who report one or more non-aboriginal origins such as British, French, etc., in combination with one of the aboriginal origins such as North American Indian. 5. Other Multiple Aboriginal Origins—refer to the sum of those persons reporting two or more aboriginal origins with or without a non-aboriginal origin. 6. Average income—refers to the average of total income from all sources (e.g., total wages and salaries net nonfarm self-employed income, net self-employed income, family allowances, federal child tax credits, Old Age Security Pension Plan and Guaranteed Income Supplement, benefits from Unemployment Insurance, other income from government sources, dividends and interest on bonds, savings certificates and other investment income, retirement pensions, superannuation and annuities, and other money income). Average income excludes persons with no income in 1985.

★ 990 ★

Population 15 Years and Over, by Total Income Group and Sex for Detailed Aboriginal Origins for Saskatchewan, 1986 - I[1,2]

Income is shown in Canadian dollars.

Income group[3]	Total Aboriginal origins[4]		North American Indian only		North American Indian and non-Aboriginal[5]		Metis only	
	Number	Percent	Number	Percent	Number	Percent	Number	Percent
Total population aged 15 and over	44,645	100.0	24,540	100.0	4,765	100.0	7,810	100.0
Male	21,505	48.2	11,915	48.6	2,325	48.8	3,725	47.7
Female	23,145	51.8	12,620	51.4	2,435	51.1	4,080	52.2
No income	10,175	22.8	6,255	25.5	810	17.0	1,770	22.7
Male	3,600	8.1	2,255	9.2	295	6.2	620	7.9
Female	6,575	14.7	3,995	16.3	515	10.8	1,150	14.7
Less than $3,000 (including losses)	8,750	19.6	5,230	21.3	855	17.9	1,415	18.1
Male	4,330	9.7	2,815	11.5	345	7.2	625	8.0
Female	4,415	9.9	2,415	9.8	510	10.7	790	10.1
$3,000 to $6,999	7,565	16.9	4,240	17.3	695	14.6	1,425	18.2
Male	3,625	8.1	2,115	8.6	300	6.3	715	9.2
Female	3,945	8.8	2,130	8.7	390	8.2	715	9.2
$7,000 to $9,999	5,390	12.1	2,910	11.9	470	9.9	1,070	13.7
Male	2,430	5.4	1,370	5.6	200	4.2	440	5.6
Female	2,960	6.6	1,535	6.3	275	5.8	630	8.1
$10,000 to $14,999	4,735	10.6	2,640	10.8	515	10.8	800	10.2
Male	2,350	5.3	1,280	5.2	275	5.8	465	6.0
Female	2,385	5.3	1,355	5.5	240	5.0	340	4.4
$15,000 to $19,999	2,865	6.4	1,425	5.8	330	6.9	450	5.8
Male	1,550	3.5	775	3.2	170	3.6	270	3.5
Female	1,310	2.9	650	2.6	160	3.4	180	2.3
$20,000 to $29,999	3,285	7.4	1,270	5.2	590	12.4	595	7.6
Male	2,135	4.8	885	3.6	365	7.7	365	4.7
Female	1,150	2.6	385	1.6	225	4.7	230	2.9
$30,000 to $49,999	1,615	3.6	485	2.0	415	8.7	240	3.1
Male	1,260	2.8	355	1.4	325	6.8	195	2.5
Female	355	0.8	135	0.6	95	2.0	45	0.6
$50,000 and over	270	0.6	85	0.3	85	1.8	45	0.6
Male	215	0.5	65	0.3	55	1.2	35	0.4
Female	55	0.1	15	0.1	30	0.6	-	-

[Continued]

★ 990 ★

Population 15 Years and Over, by Total Income Group and Sex for Detailed Aboriginal Origins for Saskatchewan, 1986 - I

[Continued]

Income group[3]	Total Aboriginal origins[4]		North American Indian only		North American Indian and non-Aboriginal[5]		Metis only	
	Number	Percent	Number	Percent	Number	Percent	Number	Percent
	Average income[6]							
Total	10,346		8,917		13,862		10,092	
Male	11,853		9,712		16,816		11,754	
Female	8,717		8,027		10,728		8,330	

Source: Aboriginal Peoples Output Program, 1986 Census, Statistics Canada, *A Data Book on Canada's Aboriginal Population from the 1986 Census of Canada*, March, 1989, p. 216. Primary source: 1986 Census of Canada. *Notes:* A dash (-) represents zero or a percentage which rounds to less than .05 percent. 1. Aboriginal origins are derived from the ethnic origin question which asks whether respondents are North American Indian, Metis or Inuit. 2. All 1986 figures exclude the population estimated at about 45,000 on 136 incompletely enumerated Indian reserves and settlements throughout Canada. 3. Total income—refers to income from all sources such as total wages and salaries, net nonfarm self-employed income, net farm self-employed income, family allowances, federal child tax credits, Old Age Security Pension Plan and Guaranteed Income Supplement, benefits and interest on bonds, deposits, savings certificates and other investment income, retirement pensions, superannuation and annuities, and other money income. Also shown in the table is a category for "No income" which refers to the population aged 15 and over who did not receive any income during 1985. 4. Total Aboriginal origins—are the sum of persons who reported: (a) a single aboriginal (e.g., North American Indian, Metis or Inuit) and, (b) multiple aboriginal origins, that is those who reported: - at least one aboriginal origin with any other non-aboriginal (e.g., Metis and French), or—two or more aboriginal origins only. 5. Non-aboriginal in these columns—refers to persons who report one or more non-aboriginal origins such as British, French, etc., in combination with one of the aboriginal origins such as North American Indian. 6. Average income - refers to the average of total income from all sources (e.g., total wages and salaries net nonfarm self-employed income, net self-employed income, family allowances, federal child tax credits, Old Age Security Pension Plan and Guaranteed Income Supplement, benefits from Unemployment Insurance, other income from government sources, dividends and interest on bonds, savings certificates and other investment income, retirement pensions, superannuation and annuities, and other money income). Average income excludes persons with no income in 1985.

★ 991 ★

Population 15 Years and Over, by Total Income Group and Sex for Detailed Aboriginal Origins for Saskatchewan, 1986 - II[1,2]

Income is shown in Canadian dollars.

Income group[3]	Metis and non-Aboriginal[4]		Inuit only		Inuit and non-Aboriginal[4]		Other multiple Aboriginal origins[5]	
	Number	Percent	Number	Percent	Number	Percent	Number	Percent
Total population aged 15 and over	5,680	100.0	30	100.0	55	100.0	1,770	100.0
Male	2,610	46.0	20	66.7	35	63.6	875	49.4
Female	3,075	54.1	10	33.3	15	27.3	900	50.8
No income	990	17.4	-	-	-	-	340	19.2
Male	320	5.6	-	-	-	-	110	6.2
Female	675	11.9	-	-	-	-	225	12.7
Less than $3,000 (including losses)	885	15.6	15.	50.0	-	-	335	18.9
Male	340	6.0	15	50.0	-	-	190	10.7
Female	545	9.6	-	-	-	-	145	8.2
$3,000 to $6,999	945	16.6	10	33.3	10	18.2	245	13.8
Male	385	6.8	-	-	15	27.3	100	5.6

[Continued]

★ 991 ★

Population 15 Years and Over, by Total Income Group and Sex for Detailed Aboriginal Origins for Saskatchewan, 1986 - II

[Continued]

Income group[3]	Metis and non-Aboriginal[4]		Inuit only		Inuit and non-Aboriginal[4]		Other multiple Aboriginal origins[5]	
	Number	Percent	Number	Percent	Number	Percent	Number	Percent
Female	560	9.9	10	33.3	-	-	135	7.6
$7,000 to $9,999	730	12.9	-	-	-	-	205	11.6
Male	325	5.7	-	-	-	-	90	5.1
Female	405	7.1	-	-	-	-	115	6.5
$10,000 to $14,999	615	10.8	-	-	-	-	170	9.6
Male	265	4.7	-	-	-	-	65	3.7
Female	350	6.2	-	-	-	-	105	5.9
$15,000 to $19,999	505	8.9	-	-	-	-	150	8.5
Male	270	4.8	-	-	-	-	65	3.7
Female	240	4.2	-	-	-	-	75	4.2
$20,000 to $29,999	595	10.5	-	-	15	27.3	220	12.4
Male	360	6.3	-	-	10	18.2	150	8.5
Female	240	4.2	-	-	-	-	65	3.7
$30,000 to $49,999	360	6.3	-	-	-	-	100	5.6
Male	295	5.2	-	-	-	-	80	4.5
Female	55	1.0	-	-	-	-	25	1.4
$50,000 and over	55	1.0	-	-	-	-	-	-
Male	55	1.0	-	-	-	-	-	-
Female	-	-	-	-	-	-	-	-

Average income[6]

Total	12,647		-		-		12,363	
Male	15,859		-		-		14,205	
Female	9,589		-		-		10,323	

Source: Aboriginal Peoples Output Program, 1986 Census, Statistics Canada, *A Data Book on Canada's Aboriginal Population from the 1986 Census of Canada,* March, 1989, p. 216. Primary source: 1986 Census of Canada. *Notes:* A dash (-) represents zero or a percentage which rounds to less than .05 percent. 1. Aboriginal origins are derived from the ethnic origin question which asks whether respondents are North American Indian, Metis or Inuit. 2. All 1986 figures exclude the population estimated at about 45,000 on 136 incompletely enumerated Indian reserves and settlements throughout Canada. 3. Total income—refers to income from all sources such as total wages and salaries, net nonfarm self-employed income, net farm self-employed income, family allowances, federal child tax credits, Old Age Security Pension Plan and Guaranteed Income Supplement, benefits and interest on bonds, deposits, savings certificates and other investment income, retirement pensions, superannuation and annuities, and other money income. Also shown in the table is a category for "No income" which refers to the population aged 15 and over who did not receive any income during 1985. 4. Non-aboriginal in these columns—refers to persons who report one or more non-aboriginal origins such as British, French, etc., in combination with one of the aboriginal origins such as North American Indian. 5. Other Multiple Aboriginal Origins—refer to the sum of those persons reporting two or more aboriginal origins with or without a non-aboriginal origin. 6. Average income—refers to the average of total income from all sources (e.g., total wages and salaries net nonfarm self-employed income, net self-employed income, family allowances, federal child tax credits, Old Age Security Pension Plan and Guaranteed Income Supplement, benefits from Unemployment Insurance, other income from government sources, dividends and interest on bonds, savings certificates and other investment income, retirement pensions, superannuation and annuities, and other money income). Average income excludes persons with no income in 1985.

★ 992 ★

Population 15 Years and Over, by Total Income Group and Sex for Detailed Aboriginal Origins for Yukon Territory, 1986 - 1[10]

Income is shown in Canadian dollars.

Income group[6]	Total Aboriginal origins[4]		North American Indian only		North American Indian and non-Aboriginal[5]		Metis only	
	Number	Percent	Number	Percent	Number	Percent	Number	Percent
Total population aged 15 and over	3,400	100.0	2,325	100.0	890	100.0	40	100.0
Male	1,640	48.2	1,125	48.4	425	47.8	15	37.5
Female	1,755	51.6	1,205	51.8	470	52.8	30	75.0
No income	590	17.4	425	18.3	120	13.5	-	-
Male	240	7.1	170	7.3	50	5.6	-	-
Female	345	10.1	255	11.0	75	8.4	-	-
Less than $3,000 (including losses)	580	17.1	435	18.7	120	13.5	-	-
Male	285	8.4	205	8.8	65	7.3	-	-
Female	295	8.7	235	10.1	50	5.6	-	-
$3,000 to $6,999	595	17.5	460	19.8	115	12.9	-	-
Male	305	9.0	245	10.5	55	6.2	-	-
Female	290	8.5	215	9.2	65	7.3	-	-
$7,000 to $9,999	435	12.8	345	14.8	80	9.0	-	-
Male	180	5.3	155	6.7	15	1.7	-	-
Female	255	7.5	195	8.4	55	6.2	-	-
$10,000 to $14,999	380	11.2	230	9.9	140	15.7	-	-
Male	180	5.3	115	4.9	55	6.2	-	-
Female	200	5.9	115	4.9	80	9.0	-	-
$15,000 to $19,999	240	7.1	150	6.5	75	8.4	-	-
Male	115	3.4	65	2.8	25	2.8	-	-
Female	130	3.8	80	3.4	45	5.1	-	-
$20,000 to $29,999	320	9.4	160	6.9	135	15.2	-	-
Male	150	4.4	80	3.4	65	7.3	-	-
Female	170	5.0	85	3.7	75	8.4	-	-
$30,000 to $49,999	235	6.9	110	4.7	110	12.4	-	-
Male	170	5.0	85	3.7	80	9.0	-	-
Female	60	1.8	25	1.1	25	2.8	-	-
$50,000 and over	15	0.4	-	-	-	-	-	-
Male	10	0.3	-	-	-	-	-	-
Female	-	-	-	-	-	-	-	-

[Continued]

1425

★ 992 ★

Population 15 Years and Over, by Total Income Group and Sex for Detailed Aboriginal Origins for Yukon Territory, 1986 - I
[Continued]

Income group[6]	Total Aboriginal origins[4]		North American Indian only		North American Indian and non-Aboriginal[5]		Metis only	
	Number	Percent	Number	Percent	Number	Percent	Number	Percent
				Average income[6]				
Total	11,762		10,226		15,154		18,900	
Male	12,777		11,038		16,907		18,336	
Female	10,754		9,408		13,495		19,232	

Source: Aboriginal Peoples Output Program, 1986 Census, Statistics Canada, *A Data Book on Canada's Aboriginal Population from the 1986 Census of Canada,* March, 1989, p. 312. Primary source: 1986 Census of Canada. *Notes:* A dash (-) represents zero or a percentage which rounds to less than .05 percent. 1. Aboriginal origins are derived from the ethnic origin question which asks whether respondents are North American Indian, Metis or Inuit. 2. All 1986 figures exclude the population estimated at about 45,000 on 136 incompletely enumerated Indian reserves and settlements throughout Canada. 3. Total income—refers to income from all sources such as total wages and salaries, net nonfarm self-employed income, net farm self-employed income, family allowances, federal child tax credits, Old Age Security Pension Plan and Guaranteed Income Supplement, benefits and interest on bonds, deposits, savings certificates and other investment income, retirement pensions, superannuation and annuities, and other money income. Also shown in the table is a category for "No income" which refers to the population aged 15 and over who did not receive any income during 1985. 4. Total Aboriginal origins—are the sum of persons who reported: (a) a single aboriginal (e.g., North American Indian, Metis or Inuit) and, (b) multiple aboriginal origins, that is those who reported: - at least one aboriginal origin with any other non-aboriginal (e.g., Metis and French), or—two or more aboriginal origins only. 5. Non-aboriginal in these columns—refers to persons who report one or more non-aboriginal origins such as British, French, etc., in combination with one of the aboriginal origins such as North American Indian. 6. Average income - refers to the average of total income from all sources (e.g., total wages and salaries net nonfarm self-employed income, net self-employed income, family allowances, federal child tax credits, Old Age Security Pension Plan and Guaranteed Income Supplement, benefits from Unemployment Insurance, other income from government sources, dividends and interest on bonds, savings certificates and other investment income, retirement pensions, superannuation and annuities, and other money income). Average income excludes persons with no income in 1985.

★ 993 ★

Population 15 Years and Over, by Total Income Group and Sex for Detailed Aboriginal Origins for Yukon Territory, 1986 - II[1,2]

Income is shown in Canadian dollars.

Income group[3]	Metis and non-Aboriginal[4]		Inuit only		Inuit and non-Aboriginal[4]		Other multiple Aboriginal origins[5]	
	Number	Percent	Number	Percent	Number	Percent	Number	Percent
Total population aged 15 and over	60	100.0	25	100.0	10	100.0	35	100.0
Male	40	66.7	-	-	-	-	-	-
Female	20	33.3	20	80.0	-	-	10	28.6
No income	20	33.3	-	-	-	-	-	-
Male	15	25.0	-	-	-	-	-	-
Female	-	-	-	-	-	-	-	-
Less than $3,000 (including losses)	-	-	-	-	-	-	15	42.9
Male	-	-	-	-	-	-	-	-
Female	-	-	-	-	-	-	-	-
$3,000 to $6,999	-	-	10	40.0	-	-	-	-
Male	-	-	-	-	-	-	-	-

[Continued]

1426

★ 993 ★

Population 15 Years and Over, by Total Income Group and Sex for Detailed Aboriginal Origins for Yukon Territory, 1986 - II
[Continued]

Income group[3]	Metis and non-Aboriginal[4]		Inuit only		Inuit and non-Aboriginal[4]		Other multiple Aboriginal origins[5]	
	Number	Percent	Number	Percent	Number	Percent	Number	Percent
Female	-	-	10	40.0	-	-	-	-
$7,000 to $9,999	-	-	-	-	-	-	-	-
Male	-	-	-	-	-	-	-	-
Female	-	-	-	-	-	-	-	-
$10,000 to $14,999	-	-	-	-	-	-	-	-
Male	-	-	-	-	-	-	-	-
Female	-	-	-	-	-	-	-	-
$15,000 to $19,999	-	-	-	-	-	-	-	-
Male	-	-	-	-	-	-	-	-
Female	-	-	-	-	-	-	-	-
$20,000 to $29,999	-	-	-	-	-	-	-	-
Male	-	-	-	-	-	-	-	-
Female	-	-	-	-	-	-	-	-
$30,000 to $49,999	-	-	-	-	-	-	-	-
Male	-	-	-	-	-	-	-	-
Female	-	-	-	-	-	-	-	-
$50,000 and over	-	-	-	-	-	-	-	-
Male	-	-	-	-	-	-	-	-
Female	-	-	-	-	-	-	-	-
Average income[6]								
Total	-	-	-	-	-	-	-	-
Male	-	-	-	-	-	-	-	-
Female	-	-	-	-	-	-	-	-

Source: Aboriginal Peoples Output Program, 1986 Census, Statistics Canada, *A Data Book on Canada's Aboriginal Population from the 1986 Census of Canada*, March, 1989, p. 312. Primary source: 1986 Census of Canada. *Notes:* A dash (-) represents zero or a percentage which rounds to less than .05 percent. 1. Aboriginal origins are derived from the ethnic origin question which asks whether respondents are North American Indian, Metis or Inuit. 2. All 1986 figures exclude the population estimated at about 45,000 on 136 incompletely enumerated Indian reserves and settlements throughout Canada. 3. Total income—refers to income from all sources such as total wages and salaries, net nonfarm self-employed income, net farm self-employed income, family allowances, federal child tax credits, Old Age Security Pension Plan and Guaranteed Income Supplement, benefits and interest on bonds, deposits, savings certificates and other investment income, retirement pensions, superannuation and annuities, and other money income. Also shown in the table is a category for "No income" which refers to the population aged 15 and over who did not receive any income during 1985. 4. Non-aboriginal in these columns—refers to persons who report one or more non-aboriginal origins such as British, French, etc., in combination with one of the aboriginal origins such as North American Indian. 5. Other Multiple Aboriginal Origins—refer to the sum of those persons reporting two or more aboriginal origins with or without a non-aboriginal origin. 6. Average income—refers to the average of total income from all sources (e.g., total wages and salaries net nonfarm self-employed income, net self-employed income, family allowances, federal child tax credits, Old Age Security Pension Plan and Guaranteed Income Supplement, benefits from Unemployment Insurance, other income from government sources, dividends and interest on bonds, savings certificates and other investment income, retirement pensions, superannuation and annuities, and other money income). Average income excludes persons with no income in 1985.

History

★ 994 ★

Origins of the Population in Canada, 1871 to 1971

Native Americans and Inuits are shown in bold letters.

Origin[1]	1871	1881	1901	1911	1921	1931	1941	1951	1961	1971
British	2,110,502	2,548,514	3,063,195	3,999,195	4,868,738	5,381,071	5,715,904	6,709,685	7,996,669	9,624,115
English	706,369	881,301	1,260,899	1,871,268	2,545,358	2,741,419	2,968,402	3,630,344	4,195,175	-
Irish	846,414	957,403	988,721	1,074,738	1,107,803	1,230,808	1,267,702	1,439,635	1,753,351	-
Scottish	549,946	699,863	800,154	1,027,015	1,173,625	1,346,350	1,403,974	1,547,470	1,902,302	-
Other	7,773	9,947	13,421	26,060	41,952	62,494	75,826	92,236	145,841	-
Other European	1,322,813	1,598,386	2,107,327	3,006,502	3,699,846	4,753,242	5,526,964	6,872,889	9,657,195	11,139,800
French	1,089,940	1,298,929	1,649,371	2,061,719	2,452,743	2,927,990	3,483,038	4,319,167	5,540,346	6,180,120
Austrian	-	-	10,947[2]	44,036	107,671	48,639	37,715	32,231	106,535	42,120
Belgian	-	-	2,994	9,664	20,234	27,585	29,711	35,148	61,382	51,135
Czech and Slovak	-	-	-	-	8,840	30,401	42,912	63,959	73,061	81,870
Danish	-[3]	-[3]	-[3]	-[3]	21,124	34,118	37,439	42,671	85,473	75,725
Finnish	-	-	2,502	15,500	21,494	43,885	41,683	43,745	59,436	59,215
German	202,991	254,319	310,501	403,417	294,635	473,544	464,682	619,995	1,049,599	1,317,200
Greek	39	-	291	3,614	5,740	9,444	11,692	13,966	56,475	124,475
Hungarian	-	-	1,549[4]	11,648	13,181	40,582	54,598	60,460	126,220	131,890
Icelandic	-[3]	-[3]	-[3]	-[3]	15,876	19,382	21,050	23,307	30,623	27,905
Italian	1,035	1,849	10,834	45,963	66,769	98,173	112,625	152,245	450,351	730,820
Jewish	125	667	16,131	76,199	126,196	156,726	170,241	181,670	173,344	296,945
Lithuanian	-	-	-	-	1,970	5,876	7,789	16,224	27,629	24,535
Netherlander	29,662	30,412	33,845	55,961	117,505	148,962	212,863	264,267	429,679	425,945
Norwegian	-[3]	-[3]	-[3]	-[3]	68,856	93,243	100,718	119,266	148,681	179,290
Polish	-	-	6,285	33,652	53,403	145,503	167,485	219,845	323,517	316,430
Romanian	-	-	354[5]	5,883	13,470	29,056	24,689	23,601	43,805	27,375
Russian	607[6]	1,227[6]	19,825	44,376	100,064	88,148	83,708	91,279	119,168	64,475
Scandinavian[7]	1,623	5,223	31,042	112,682	167,359	228,049	244,603	283,024	386,534	384,795
Swedish	-[3]	-[3]	-[3]	-[3]	61,503	81,306	85,396	97,780	121,757	101,870
Ukrainian	-	-	5,682	75,432	106,721	225,113	305,929[8]	395,043	473,337	580,660
Yugoslavic	-	-	-	-	3,906	16,174	21,214	21,404	68,587	104,955
Other	3,791	5,760	5,174	6,756	17,945	9,392	9,787	35,616	88,190	194,850
Asiatic	4	4,383	23,731	43,213	65,914	84,548	74,064	72,827	121,753	285,540
Chinese	-	4,383	17,312	27,831	39,587	46,519	34,627	32,528	58,197	118,815
Japanese	-	-	4,738	9,067	15,868	23,342	23,149	21,663	29,157	37,260
Other	4	-	1,681	6,315	10,459	14,687	16,288	18,636	34,399	129,460
Other origins	52,442	173,527	177,062	157,847	153,451	157,925	189,723	354,028	462,630	518,850
Native Indian and										
Inuit (Eskimo)	**23,037**	**108,547**	**127,941**	**105,611**	**113,724**	**128,890**	**125,521**	**165,607**	**220,121**	**312,760**
Negro	21,496	21,394	17,437	16,994	18,291	19,456	22,174	18,202	32,127	34,445
Other	348	2,780	145	18,310	187	681	36,753[9]			
Not stated	7,561	40,806	31,539	16,932	21,249	8,898	5,275	170,401	210,382	171,645[10]
Total	3,485,761	4,324,810	5,371,315	7,206,643	8,787,949	10,376,786	11,506,655	14,009,429	18,238,247	21,568,310

Source: F.H. Leacy, *Historical Statistics of Canada, Second Edition*, Statistics Canada and Social Science Federation of Canada, pp. A110-153 - A154-184. *Notes:* A dash (-) indicates that data were not available. 1. The data for 1871 refer only to the four original provinces of Canada. The data for 1951 and later years include Newfoundland. 2. Includes Bohemian, Bukovinian and Slavic. 3. Included under Scandinavian. 4. Includes Lithuanian and Moravian. 5. Includes Bulgarian. 6. Includes Finnish and Polish. 7. Since 1921 Scandinavian has been divided into Danish, Icelandic, Norwegian and Swedish. 8. Includes Bukovinian, Galacian and Ruthenian. 9. Includes 35,416 Metis. 10. Origin 'not stated' cases in 1971 were computer assigned.

★ 995 ★

Mother Tongues of the Population in Canada, 1931 to 1976

Mother tongue	1931[1]	1941[1]	1951	1961	1971	1976
English	5,914,402	6,448,190	8,280,809	10,660,534	12,973,810	14,122,770
French	2,832,298	3,354,753	4,068,850	5,123,151	5,793,650	5,887,205
Armenian	...	...	...	...	...	10,335
Baltic languages	...	...	28,110	42,889	43,385	34,185
Estonian	...	...	8,784	13,830	14,520	11,975
Lettish	...	...	7,019	14,062	14,140	11,150
Lithuanian	5,506	6,910	12,307	14,997	14,725	11,065
Bulgarian	2,661	...	...	...	...	1,500
Celtic languages	...	...	...	...	24,360	10,060
Gaelic	...	7,533	13,974	32,708	21,200	1,620
Welsh	...	...	...	3,040	3,160	2,055
Others	...	...	...	...	-[2]	6,385
Chinese and Japanese	69,281	55,859	45,878	66,955	111,745	148,085
Chinese	...	33,500	28,289	49,099	94,855	132,560
Japanese	...	22,359	17,589	17,856	16,890	15,525
Croatian, Serbian, etc.	...	...	...	...	74,190	77,575
Croatian					{20,860	{20,390
Serbian	10,521	14,863	11,031	28,886	{5,225	{3,855
Slovenian	...	...	...	...	6,415	4,785
Yugoslav, n.e.s.[3]	...	...	...	...	41,690	48,535
Czech and Slovak	...	...	...	51,423	45,150	34,950
Czech	...	...	...	8,877	27,780	22,035
Slovak	25,099	37,604	45,516	42,546	17,370	12,915
Dutch	26,532	53,215	87,935	170,177	144,925	114,760
Finnish	39,965	37,331	31,771	44,785	36,725	28,470
Flemish	18,048	14,557	12,623	14,304	14,240	7,790
German	362,011	322,228	329,302	563,713	561,085	476,715
Greek	7,346	8,747	8,036	40,455	104,455	91,530
Native Indian and Inuit	...	130,929	144,787	166,531	179,820	133,005
Native Indian	...	...	...	...	164,525	117,105
Inuit (Eskimo)	...	...	...	...	15,295	15,900
Indo-Pakistan	...	...	1,731	4,505	32,555	58,415
Iranian	...	...	...	...	...	1,455
Italian	85,520	80,260	92,244	339,626	538,360	484,050
Magyar (Hungarian)	37,959	46,287	42,402	85,939	86,835	69,300
Polish	118,599	128,711	129,238	161,720	134,780	99,845
Portugese	...	...	150	18,213	86,925	126,535
Romanian	18,115	16,402	10,105	10,165	11,300	8,755

[Continued]

★ 995 ★

Mother Tongues of the Population in Canada, 1931 to 1976
[Continued]

Mother tongue	1931[1]	1941[1]	1951	1961	1971	1976
Russian	50,759	52,431	39,223	42,903	31,745	23,485
Scandinavian	159,854	143,917	106,848	116,714	84,335	59,410
Danish	21,453	18,776	15,714	35,035	27,395	21,315
Icelandic	16,034	15,510	11,207	8,993	7,860	5,030
Norwegian	64,125	60,084	43,831	40,054	27,405	18,070
Swedish	58,242	49,547	36,096	32,632	21,680	15,000
Semitic languages	...	...	...	...	28,550	37,100
Spanish	1,472	1,030	1,516	6,720	23,815	44,135
Syrian and Arabic	9,226	8,111	5,475	12,999	28,550	...
Turkish	...	...	...	...	...	2,595
Ukrainian	252,802	313,273	352,323	361,496	309,855	282,060
Yiddish	149,520	129,806	103,593	82,448	49,890	23,435
Other[4]	179,290	61,231	29,933	17,976	41,835	48,065
Not stated	-	-	-	-	-	445,020
Total	10,376,786	11,506,655	14,009,429	18,238,247	21,568,310	22,992,605

Source: F.H. Leacy, *Historical Statistics of Canada, Second Edition*, Statistics Canada and Social Science Federation of Canada, p. A185-237. *Notes:* A dash (-) indicates zero. Three dots (...) indicates not available. 1. Excludes Newfoundland. 2. Included with Gaelic. 3. Not elsewhere stated, includes a number of other Yugoslav languages. 4. Includes mother tongue not stated prior to 1951.

★ 996 ★

Major Indian Tribes of Canada

The Major Indian Tribes of Canada	Derivation of name	Linguistic group	Former territory	Current locations	Pre-contact numbers	Current population
Algonkian	Probably derived from Micmac term meaning "at the place of spearing fish and eels from bow of canoe".	Algonkian	Providence of Quebec	Southwestern Ottawa and the Ottawa Valley	3-4,000	4,581
Assiniboine	Meaning "the people who cook with hot stones".	Siouan	West side of Lake Winnipeg, banks of Saskatchewan Rivers	Saskatchewan and Alberta	10,000	1,342
Beaver	Given after establishment of trading posts, and commemorating the successful	Athapaskan	Valley of and Peace Rivers	Peace River area of Alberta		964

[Continued]

★ 996 ★

Major Indian Tribes of Canada
[Continued]

The Major Indian Tribes of Canada	Derivation of name	Linguistic group	Former territory	Current locations	Pre-contact numbers	Current population
	fur trade the people were engaged in.					
Bella Coola						
		Salishan	Area of the Dean and Bella Coola Rivers	Bella Coola area of British Columbia	2-3,000	716
Blackfoot						
The Blackfoot Confederacy consisted of three groups: the Blackfoot proper, the Peigan and the Blood.	From the Blackfoot name Siksika meaning "black foot".	Algonkian	Southern Alberta and Montana	Southern Alberta	15,000	9,667
Blood						
Part of the Blackfoot Confederacy which also included the Blackfoot proper and Piegan.		Algonkian	South-eastern Alberta	Near Lethbridge, Alberta		5,100
Carrier						
	From the Carrier customs where a widow was obliged to carry her deceased husband's ashes in a basket for three years.	Athapaskan	British Columbia Interior	Same		5,379
Chilcotin						
	Means "people of young man's (Chilcotin) river".	Athapaskan	Area round Chilcotin River and Anahim Lake	Chilcotin River area	2,500	1,670
Chipewyan						
	From the Cree word Chipwayanewok meaning "people of the pointed skins".	Athapaskan	Northern Private Provinces	Same	3,500	6,286

Source: Indian and Inuit Affairs Program, Membership Division, *Adoption and the Indian Child*, Indian and Northern Affairs Canada, n.p., n.d., pp. 19-22.

★ 997 ★

Post-Confederation Treaties

Treaty date and number[1]	Tribes, area ceded	Government obligation
Number 1, 1871	Chippewa, Swampy Cree 16,700 square miles	Reserves - 160 acres per family of five. To control liquor traffic. A school on each reserve. Annuity, triennial suit of clothes for the chiefs and headman.
Number 2, 1871	Chippewa, Swampy Cree 35,700 square miles	See Treaty Number 1.
Number 3, 1873	Saulteaux and others 55,000 square miles	Reserves - 1 square mile per family of five. Government right to sell or lease reserve lands with consent of the band and to appropriate reserve lands for public use with compensation. Schools. Control of liquor traffic. Government regulations over hunting and fishing in ceded area. Treaty presents of $12 per head, farm stock and equipment, flags, medals, tools, seed. Annuity, $1,500 annually for ammunition. Triennial suit of clothes for chiefs and headman.
Number 4, 1874	Cree, Saulteaux 74,600 square miles	See Treaty Number 3. Annuity, $750 annually for ammunition and twine, triennial suit of clothes for chiefs and headman. Treaty presents of $25 per chief, $15 per headman, $12 per Indian.
Number 5, 1875	Swampy Cree, Saulteaux 100,000 square miles (much larger added	See Treaty Number 3 except for reserves - 160 acres per family of five. Right to navigation and free access to shores of all

[Continued]

★ 997 ★

Post-Confederation Treaties
[Continued]

Treaty date and number[1]	Tribes, area ceded	Government obligation
	through the Adhensions of 1908-09-10)	lakes and rivers. Same annuities as Treaty Number 4 plus $500 annually for ammunition and twine, plus additional proportionate amount for Adhesions of 1908-09-10.
Number 6, 1876	Plains and Wood Cree 132,066 square miles (including the Adhesion of 1889)	See Treaty Number 3 including treaty presents and annuities. Extras included $1,500 for ammunition and twine and additional proportionate amount for Adhesion of 1889; aid in case of pestilence and famine; medicine chest for band use.
Number 7, 1876	Blackfoot, Blood, Peigan, Sarcee, Stony 42,900 square miles	See Treaty Number 3 excluding hunting and school teachers. Treaty presents and annuities similar to Treaty Number 3 except for $2,000 annually for ammunition.
Number 8, 1899	Cree, Chipewyan 324,900 square miles	See Treaty Number 3. Treaty presents - $12 per person; $32 per chief, $22 per headman agricultural implements, ammunition and twine. $1 per family head preferring hunting to farming. Annuity.
Number 9, 1905	Ojibwa and Cree with Canada and Ontario 218,320 square miles (including the Adhesions of 1929 30)	See Treaty Number 3. Compensation for expropriation included "an equivalent in land, money or other consideration". Treaty presents of $8 per person. Annuity.
Number 10, 1906	Chipewyan, Cree 85,800	See Treaty Number 3. Treaty presents - see Treaty Number

[Continued]

★ 997 ★

Post-Confederation Treaties
[Continued]

Treaty date and number[1]	Tribes, area ceded	Government obligation
	square miles	8. Annuity. Unspecified amount re twine and ammunition.
Number 11, 1921	Slave, Dogrib, Hare Loucheaux 372,000 square miles	See Treaty Number 8. Treaty presents--hunting and trapping equipment of $50 in value per band family. Annuities as Treaty Number 3. Twine and ammunition to the value of $3 per Indian hunter.
1923	Chippewa of Christian Island, Georgina Island, Rama, Mississuga of Rice Lake, Mud Lake, Scugog Lake, Alder-ville. Ceded hunting, fish-ing trapping rights over 20,100 square miles between Lake Ontario and Georgian Bay	$500,000 paid by Ontario.

Source: Indian and Inuit Affairs Program, Membership Division, *Adoption and the Indian Child*, Indian and Northern Affairs Canada, pp. 11-13. *Notes:* The "Number" listed with treaty dates corresponds to information given in column three.

Land and Water Management

★ 998 ★

Number and Acreage of Indian Reserves in Canada, 1985: Provinces and Territories

Chart shows the number of acres.

Responsibility center	Number	Acreage
Newfoundland	-	-
Prince Edward Island	4	1,667.4
Nova Scotia	38	28,322.2
New Brunswick	25	43,464.6
Quebec	33	192,030.8
Ontario	182	1,727,989.1
Manitoba	108	537,950.4
Saskatchewan	142	1,514,316.9
Alberta	91	1,631,400.1
British Columbia	1,630	842,892.2
Yukon	6	1,234.5
Northwest Territories	2	33,512.0
Total	2,261	6,554,780.2

Source: Indians and Northern Affairs Canada, *Number and Acreage of Indian Reserves, by Band,* December 31, 1985, p. 41. *Note:* A dash (-) represents zero.

★ 999 ★

Number and Acreage of Indian Reserves in Canada, 1985: Alberta Region

Responsibility center	Band	Reserves	
		Number	Acreage
Alberta Regional Office	Alexander	1	17,990.0
	Alexis	1	15,259.0
	Bigstone Cree	6	52,087.3
	Driftpile	1	15,688.0
	Duncan's	2	5,995.0
	Enoch	1	12,935.3
	Ermineskin	1	25,441.0
	Grouard	3	1,096.6
	Horse Lake	2	7,658.0
	Louis Bull	1	7,910.6
	Lubicon Lake	-	-
	Montana	1	6,980.0
	Paul	3	18,112.0
	Samson	2	34,091.7
	Sawridge	2	5,296.0
	Sturgeon Lake	3	22,399.0
	Sucker Creek	1	14,794.0
	Swan River	2	10,670.0
	Whitefish Lake	3	11,966.2
	Two or more bands	1	4,750.0
Regional Office total		37	291,119.7
Fort McMurray District	Cree	-	-
	Fort Chippewyan	8	52,398.7
	Fort McKay	3	13,465.0
	Fort McMurray	4	7,965.0
	Janvier	1	4,034.0
District total		16	77,862.7
Fort Vermilion District	Boyer River	2	17,483.0
	Little Red River	2	60,471.0
	Dene Tha'	7	74,224.0
	Tallcree	3	9,206.0
District total		14	161,384.0
Southern Alberta	Blackfoot	1	175,406.0
	Blood	2	354,667.0
	O'Chiese	2	34,280.2
	Peigan	2	112,656.0
	Sarcee	1	67,470.0
	Stoney	4	120,309.3
	Sunchild Cree	1	12,894.0
Total		13	877,682.5
St. Paul District	Beaver Lake	1	15,185.0

[Continued]

★ 999 ★

Number and Acreage of Indian Reserves in Canada, 1985:
Alberta Region
[Continued]

Responsibility center	Band	Reserves	
		Number	Acreage
	Cold Lake First Nations	3	46,264.6
	Frog Lake	2	46,604.1
	Heart Lake	1	11,110.0
	Kehewin	1	20,261.0
	Saddle Lake	2	74,914.6
District total		10	214,339.3
Alberta Regional total		90	1,622,388.2

Source: Indians and Northern Affairs Canada, *Number and Acreage of Indian Reserves, by Band,* December 31, 1985, pp. 24-26. *Notes:* A dash (-) represents zero. Pigeon Lake No. 138A, Alberta Regional Office, has been set aside for the Ermineskin, Louis Bull, Montana, and Samson Bands. During 1983, the Alberta Region was reorganized to constitute the following responsibility centres: Alberta Regional Office, Fort McMurray district, Southern Alberta, St. Paul District and Fort Vermilion District. The Cold Lake Band, St. Paul District, changed its name to Cold Lake First Nations effective March 21, 1985.

★ 1000 ★

Number and Acreage of Indian Reserves in Canada, 1985:
Atlantic Region

Responsibility center	Band	Reserves	
		Number	Acreage
Atlantic Regional Office	Abegweit	3	347.4
	Lennox Island	1	1,320.0
	Miawpukek	-	-
Regional Office total		4	1,667.4
New Brunswick District	Big Cove	1	4,120.0
	Buctouche	1	154.0
	Burnt Church	3	10,886.0
	Edmundston	1	766.0
	Eel Ground	2	2,675.6
	Eel River	3	1,414.4
	Fort Folly	1	100.4
	Indian Island	1	65.0
	Kingsclear	1	926.0
	Oromocto	1	48.2
	Pabineau	1	1,060.2
	Red Bank	3	6,201.7
	Saint Mary's	2	329.1
	Tobique	1	6,731.0
	Woodstock	1	227.0

[Continued]

★ 1000 ★

Number and Acreage of Indian Reserves in Canada, 1985:
Atlantic Region
[Continued]

Responsibility center	Band	Reserves	
		Number	Acreage
	Amalecite Tribe	1	10.0
	Two or more bands	1	7,750.0
District total		25	43,464.6
Nova Scotia District	Acadia	5	2,101.0
	Afton	1	957.9
	Annapolis Valley	2	358.1
	Bear River	3	1,703.3
	Chapel Island	1	1,464.0
	Eskasoni	2	8,730.4
	Horton	1	422.8
	Membertou	3	666.2
	Millbrook	7	1,096.5
	Pictou Landing	4	1,180.2
	Shubenacadie	4	5,168.4
	Wagmatcook	2	792.2
	Whycocomagh	1	2,047.2
	Two or more bands	1	1,634.0
District total		38	28,322.2
Atlantic Regional Total		67	73,454.2

Source: Indians and Northern Affairs Canada, *Number and Acreage of Indian Reserves, by Band,* December 31, 1985, pp. 1-3. *Notes:* A dash (-) represents zero. Malagawatch No. 4 has been set aside for the Chapel Island, Eskasoni, Membertou, Wagmatcook and Whycocomagh Bands of the Nova Scotia District. The Afton Band uses 484.8 acres and the Pictou Landing Band uses 525.2 acres of Franklin Manor No. 22, Nova Scotia District. The north and south parts of Big Hole Tract No. 8, New Brunswick District, have been set apart for the Red Bank and Eel Ground Bands, respectively. The Brothers No. 18, New Brunswick District, has been set aside for the Amalecite Tribe. The Annapolis Valley Band, Nova Scotia District, was divided into the Annapolis Valley and Horton Bands effective June 20, 1984; the new Annapolis Valley Band received the reserves Cambridge No. 32 and St. Croix No. 34; the new Horton Band received the reserve Horton No. 35.

★ 1001 ★

Number and Acreage of Indian Reserves in Canada, 1985: British
Columbia Region

Responsibility center	Band	Reserves	
		Number	Acreage
Campbell River District	Campbell River	4	430.5
	Cape Mudge	5	1,650.7
	Comox	4	704.1
	Ehattesaht	9	336.4

[Continued]

★ 1001 ★

Number and Acreage of Indian Reserves in Canada, 1985: British Columbia Region

[Continued]

Responsibility center	Band	Reserves	
		Number	Acreage
	Gwa'sala-'Nakwaxda'xw	26	1,857.2
	Kwakiutl	8	729.6
	Kwa-wa-aineuk	10	505.8
	Kwiakah	2	170.0
	Kwicksutaineuk	10	442.6
	Mamalelegala-Qwe'Qwa'Sot'Enox	3	575.4
	Nimpkish	8	957.7
	Quatsino	18	855.9
	Tanakteuk	7	785.8
	Tlatasikwala	6	8,585.0
	Tlowitsis-Mumtagila	11	464.4
	Tsawataineuk	5	538.8
Distric total		136	19,589.9
Central District	Adams Lake	7	7,130.9
	Ashcroft	4	4,988.0
	Bonaparte	6	4,553.8
	Boothroyd	19	2,774.7
	Boston Bar	12	1,504.3
	Clinton	3	1,396.7
	Coldwater	3	6,174.8
	Cloumbia Lake	1	8,405.0
	Cook's Ferry	24	10,027.7
	High Bar	3	3,722.0
	Kamloops	5	32,740.4
	Kanaka Bar	6	565.6
	Little Shuswap Lake	5	7,747.0
	Lower Kootenay	8	6,037.4
	Lower Nicola	9	17,535.6
	Lower Similkameen	9	37,748.0
	Lytton	54	14,778.4
	Neskainlith	3	6,886.3
	Nicomen	16	2,904.8
	Nooaitch	2	4,184.5
	North Thompson	5	3,760.2
	Okanagan	6	26,264.8
	Oregon Jack Creek	6	2,033.2
	Osoyoos	2	32,238.8
	Penticton	2	33,949.3
	St. Mary's	4	18,423.5
	Shackan	3	9,572.0
	Shuswap	1	2,733.1
	Siska	11	789.6
	Skeetchestn	1	19,540.1

[Continued]

★ 1001 ★

Number and Acreage of Indian Reserves in Canada, 1985: British Columbia Region

[Continued]

Responsibility center	Band	Reserves	
		Number	Acreage
	Skuppah	8	521.5
	Spallumcheen	3	9,649.7
	Spuzzum	16	1,571.9
	Tobacco Plains	1	10,569.7
	Upper Nicola	8	30,895.1
	Upper Similkameen	7	6,431.0
	Westbank	3	2,326.1
	Two or more bands	4	434.6
District total		290	393,510.1
Hazelton District	Gitanmaax	5	5,891.0
	Gitwangak	7	4,149.6
	Glen Vowell	1	1,266.0
	Hagwilget	2	417.0
	Kispiox	10	4,165.7
	Kitsegukla	4	4,728.9
	Kitwancool	3	2,131.0
	Moricetown	7	3,510.9
District total		39	26,260.1
Nanaimo District	Ahousaht	25	1,463.6
	Beecher Bay	8	731.7
	Chemainus	4	2,970.8
	Clayoquot	10	544.1
	Cowichan	9	6,160.7
	Cowichan Lake	1	97.0
	Ditidaht	17	1,796.6
	Esquimalt	1	44.0
	Halalt	2	410.0
	Hesquiaht	5	601.2
	Kyuquot	26	943.1
	Lyackson	3	1,840.0
	Malahat	1	586.0
	Mowachaht	17	650.5
	Nanaimo	6	657.4
	Nonoose	1	131.9
	Nuchatlaht	11	227.7
	Ohiaht	13	2,017.0
	Opetchesaht	5	531.4
	Pacheenaht	4	429.0
	Pauquachin	2	787.8
	Penelakut	4	1,570.7
	Qualicum	1	189.8
	Sheshaht	8	1,176.7

[Continued]

★ 1001 ★

Number and Acreage of Indian Reserves in Canada, 1985· British Columbia Region

[Continued]

Responsibility center	Band	Reserves	
		Number	Acreage
	Songhees	3	310.0
	Sooke	2	166.0
	Toquaht	7	485.3
	Tsartlip	3	802.7
	Tsawout	2	638.5
	Tseycum	1	68.4
	Uchucklesaht	2	575.0
	Ucluelet	9	492.5
	Two or more bands	4	406.0
District total		217	30,503.1
Northwest District	Canyon City	6	1,619.1
	Gitlakdamix	30	4,941.0
	Hartley Bay	14	1,285.7
	Iskut	3	200.5
	Kincolith	33	6,908.7
	Kitamaat	17	1,644.4
	Kitkatla	21	4,658.1
	Kitselas	9	2,726.6
	Kitsumkalum	3	1,380.7
	Lakalzap	3	4,536.6
	Lax Kw'alaams	71	2,593.1
	Masset	26	2,243.7
	Metlakatla	8	398.3
	Skidegate	11	1,656.5
	Tahltan	11	3,232.4
	Two or more bands	10	34,099.5
District total		276	74,124.9
Prince George District	Blueberry River	1	2,838.0
	Broman Lake	13	1,531.4
	Burns Lake	4	405.6
	Cheslatta	8	3,469.2
	Doig River	1	2,447.2
	Fort George	4	1,694.5
	Fort Nelson	4	23,618.2
	Fort Ware	3	968.3
	Fraser Lake	7	2,387.8
	Halfway River	1	9,856.6
	Ingenika	3	496.6
	Lake Babine	24	7,643.3
	McLeod Lake	5	585.9
	Necoslie	16	3,607.6
	Nee-Tahi-Buhn	10	1,746.2

[Continued]

★ 1001 ★

Number and Acreage of Indian Reserves in Canada, 1985: British Columbia Region
[Continued]

Responsibility center	Band	Reserves	
		Number	Acreage
	Prophet River	1	924.0
	Saulteau	1	7,476.9
	Stellaquo	2	2,061.6
	Stony Creek	10	7,995.4
	Stuart Trembleur Lake	19	6,132.5
	Takla Lake	17	1,994.8
	West Moberly Lake	1	5,025.0
	Two or more bands	1	883.0
District total		156	95,789.6
Vancouver District	Aitchelitz	1	52.8
	Anderson Lake	6	1,987.4
	Bella Coola	7	5,001.0
	Bridge River	2	9,737.0
	Burrard	3	267.7
	Cayoose Creek	3	1,698.4
	Cheam	2	1,240.8
	Chehalis	2	2,240.7
	Coquitlam	2	219.7
	Douglas	3	1,068.3
	Fountain	17	3,884.9
	Heiltsuk	22	3,383.4
	Homalco	11	1,541.6
	Hope	5	1,517.6
	Katzie	5	842.0
	Kitasoo	14	1,478.2
	Klahoose	10	3,354.8
	Kwaw-Kwaw-A-Pilt	1	155.0
	Lakahahmen	10	1,210.2
	Langley	6	1,364.8
	Lillooet	6	1,728.6
	Matsqui	4	1,036.3
	Mount Currie	10	7,237.5
	Musqueam	3	628.1
	New Westminster	-	-
	Ohamil	3	999.1
	Oweekeno	3	1,760.8
	Pavilion	7	5,217.6
	Peters	3	486.8
	Popkum	2	373.0
	Samahquam	5	452.0
	Scowlitz	3	585.0
	Seabird Island	1	5,290.1
	Sechelt	33	2,545.5

[Continued]

★ 1001 ★

Number and Acreage of Indian Reserves in Canada, 1985: British Columbia Region

[Continued]

Responsibility center	Band	Reserves	
		Number	Acreage
	Semiahmoo	1	319.0
	Seton Lake	6	4,450.4
	Skawahlook	2	185.1
	Skookum Chuck	10	1,670.0
	Skowkale	2	169.0
	Skwah	4	844.5
	Skway	1	538.0
	Sliammon	6	4,713.0
	Soowahlie	1	1,138.8
	Squamish	23	4,999.2
	Squiala	2	315.7
	Sumas	1	579.7
	Tsawwassen	1	673.7
	Tzeachten	1	697.0
	Union Bar	7	1,234.8
	Yakweakwioose	1	48.0
	Yale	16	556.6
	Two or more bands	3	3,443.0
District total		303	97,162.2
Williams Lake District	Alexandria	13	2,823.0
	Alexis Creek	37	9,867.4
	Alkali Lake	19	9,785.9
	Anaham	19	13,957.6
	Canim Lake	6	5,088.6
	Canoe Creek	12	13,794.0
	Kluskus	17	4,083.5
	Nazko	19	4,556.4
	Nemaiah Valley	8	3,418.0
	Quesnel	4	1,689.5
	Soda Creek	2	5,173.1
	Stone	5	5,304.0
	Toosey	4	6,381.3
	Ulkatcho	20	7,939.5
	Williams Lake	8	4,763.0
District total		193	98,624.8
	Two or more bands	1	662.0
British Columbia Regional total		1,611	836,226.7

Source: Indians and Northern Affairs Canada, *Number and Acreage of Indian Reserves, by Band,* December 31, 1985, pp. 27-37. Primary source: Original contains detailed notes on most areas. *Note:* A dash (-) represents zero.

★ 1002 ★

Number and Acreage of Indian Reserves in Canada, 1985: Manitoba Region

Responsibility center	Band	Reserves	
		Number	Acreage
Manitoba Regional Office	Berens River	2	7,145.5
	Birdtail Sioux	2	7,056.0
	Bloodvein	1	4,015.9
	Brokenhead	1	13,375.0
	Buffalo Point	2	7,442.0
	Chemahawin	2	615.5
	Crane River	1	8,704.2
	Cross Lake	4	8,537.4
	Dakota Plains	1	1,310.0
	Dakota Tipi	1	31.5
	Dauphin River	1	805.0
	Ebb and Flow	1	11,440.5
	Fairford	1	11,315.5
	Fisher River	2	15,614.0
	Fort Alexander	1	21,674.0
	Gamblers	1	1,038.0
	Garden Hill	-	-
	God's Lake	1	9,832.0
	God's River	-	-
	Grand Rapids	1	4,577.0
	Hollow Water	1	4,009.0
	Indian Birch	1	1,940.0
	Jackhead	2	3,327.0
	Keeseekoowenin	2	5,343.0
	Lake Manitoba	1	9,317.2
	Lake St. Martin	2	8,244.6
	Little Black River	1	2,147.0
	Little Grand Rapids	1	5,600.0
	Little Saskatchewan	2	3,480.0
	Long Plain	1	8,922.9
	Moose Lake	4	5,594.3
	Norway House	3	19,435.7
	Oak Lake	2	2,690.0
	Oxford House	1	12,049.0
	Pequis	3	75,151.0
	Pine Creek	1	23,848.0
	Poplar River	1	3,800.0
	Red Sucker Lake	1	255.0
	Rolling River	1	13,863.0
	Roseau River	2	6,776.0
	Sandy Bay	1	16,456.0
	Shoal River	3	3,395.0
	Sioux Valley	1	10,220.0
	St. Theresa Point	-	-
	Swan Lake	2	7,057.0

[Continued]

★ 1002 ★

Number and Acreage of Indian Reserves in Canada, 1985: Manitoba Region

[Continued]

Responsibility center	Band	Reserves	
		Number	Acreage
	The Pas	17	14,137.2
	Valley River	1	11,535.0
	Wasagamack	-	-
	Waterhen	1	4,588.0
	Waywayseecappo	1	24,855.0
	Two or more bands	3	17,903.0
Regional office total		89	460,467.9
Thompson District	Barren Lands	1	10,722.6
	Fort Churchill	1	524.0
	Fox Lake	3	4,299.7
	Mathias Colamb	2	23,265.0
	Nelson House	4	14,451.0
	Northlands	1	1,147.2
	Shamattawa	1	5,725.0
	Split Lake	3	11,333.0
	War Lake	-	-
	York Factory	-	-
District total		16	71,467.5
Manitoba Regional total		105	531,935.4

Source: Indians and Northern Affairs Canada, *Number and Acreage of Indian Reserves, by Band,* December 31, 1985, pp. 17-19. *Notes:* A dash (-) represents zero. Island Lake No. 22 and Island Lake No. 22A, Manitoba Regional Office, have been set apart for the Garden Hill, St. Theresa Point, Wasagamack and Red Sucker Lake Bands. Fishing Station No. 62A, Manitoba Regional Office, has been set apart for the Birdtail Sioux, Sioux Valley and Oak Lake Bands. The Churchill Band, Thompson District, changed its name to the Fort Churchill Band effective February 15, 1985. Fox Lake No. 2, Fox Lake Band, Thompson District, was established as a reserve effective June 20, 1985. Norway House No. 17A and Norway House No. 17B, Norway House Band, Manitoba Regional Office, were established as reserves effective October 24, 1985.

★ 1003 ★

Number and Acreage of Indian Reserves in Canada, 1985: Northwest Territories

Responsibility center	Band	Reserves	
		Number	Acreage
Northwest Territories Regional Office	Aklavik	-	-
	Arctic Red River	-	-
	Dog Rib Rae	-	-
	Fitz-Smith (ALTA-NWT) Native	-	-
	Fort Franklin	-	-
	Fort Good Hope	-	-
	Fort Liard	-	-
	Fort McPherson	-	-
	Fort Norman	-	-
	Fort Providence	-	-
	Fort Simpson	-	-
	Fort Wrigley	-	-
	Hay River	1	33,401.6
	Inuvik Dene	-	-
	Resolution	-	-
	Snowdrift	-	-
	Yellowknife "B"	-	-
	Two or more bands	1	110.4
Northwest Territories Regional total		2	33,512.0

Source: Indians and Northern Affairs Canada, *Number and Acreage of Indian Reserves, by Band,* December 31, 1985, p. 39. *Note:* A dash (-) represents zero.

★ 1004 ★

Number and Acreage of Indian Reserves in Canada, 1985: Ontario Region

Responsibility center	Band	Reserves	
		Number	Acreage
Brantford District	Mississaugas of the Credit	1	5,911.0
	Six Nations of the Grand River	2	44,910.9
District total		3	50,821.9
Bruce District	Chippewas of Nawash	2	17,750.0
	Saugeen	3	12,507.0
	Two or more bands	1	..
District total		6	30,257.0

[Continued]

★ 1004 ★

Number and Acreage of Indian Reserves in Canada, 1985.
Ontario Region
[Continued]

Responsibility center	Band	Reserves	
		Number	Acreage
Fort Frances District	Big Grassy	4	15,454.0
	Big Island	11	10,701.0
	Couchiching	1	15,870.0
	Lac La Croix	1	15,355.0
	Naicatchewenin	2	6,151.0
	Nicickousemenecaning	3	10,096.0
	Ojibways of Onegaming	4	5,084.6
	Rainy River	2	6,081.0
	Seine River	3	12,731.0
	Stangecoming	1	3,861.0
	Two or more bands	1	127.0
District total		33	101,511.6
James Bay District	Albany	1	89,810.3
	Attawapiskat	2	67,074.3
	Moose Factory	2	42,978.0
	New Post	1	5,120.0
	Weenusk	1	13,121.0
District total		7	218,103.6
Kenora District	Dalles	1	8,047.0
	Eagle Lake	1	8,875.0
	Grassy Narrows	1	10,244.0
	Islington	3	24,899.0
	Northwest Angle No. 33	2	6,390.0
	Northwest Angle No. 37	10	13,122.0
	Rat Portage	1	5,454.4
	Shoal Lake No. 39	2	9,451.0
	Shoal Lake No. 40	1	6,372.0
	Wabauskang	1	8,042.0
	Wabigoon	1	12,872.0
	Washagamis Bay	1	8,000.0
	Whitefish Bay	3	10,563.0
	Two or more bands	1	426.0
District total		29	132,757.4
Lakehead District	Fort William	1	14,409.0
	Gull Bay	1	9,735.6
	Lac des Mille Lacs	2	12,227.0
	Nipigon	-	-
	Pays Plat	1	554.8
	Pic Heron Bay	1	800.1
	Pic Mobert	2	286.0
	Red Rock	2	616.8

[Continued]

★ 1004 ★

Number and Acreage of Indian Reserves in Canada, 1985: Ontario Region
[Continued]

Responsibility center	Band	Reserves	
		Number	Acreage
	Rocky Bay	1	33.1
	Sandpoint	-	-
	Whitesand	1	0.7
District total		12	38,663.1
London District	Caldwell	-	-
	Chippewas of Sarnia	1	3,249.3
	Chippewas of Kettle and Stony Point	1	2,097.3
	Chippewas of the Thames	1	8,237.1
	Moravian of the Thames	1	3,129.3
	Munceys of the Thames	1	2,604.4
	Oneidas of the Thames	1	5,272.0
	Walpole Island	1	39,267.0
District total		7	63,856.4
Nakina District	Aroland	-	-
	Constance Lake	2	15,365.7
	Fort Hope	1	63,999.6
	Lansdowne House	-	-
	Long Lake No. 58	1	537.0
	Long Lake No. 77	1	17,242.0
	Martin Falls	1	19,199.8
	Summer Beaver	-	-
	Webequie	-	-
District total		6	116,344.1
Peterborough District	Alderville	2	3,004.9
	Beausoleil	2	13,431.5
	Chippewas of Georgina Island	2	3,343.2
	Chippewas of Rama	1	2,244.6
	Curve Lake	2	2,164.0
	Gibson	1	14,783.5
	Golden Lake	1	1,702.0
	Hiawatha	1	1,953.0
	Mohawks of Akwesasne	1	9,011.0
	Mohawks of the Bay of Quinte	1	17,974.8
	Moose Deer Point	1	619.0
	Parry Island	1	18,500.0
	Scugog	1	794.3
	Two or more bands	3	354.5
District total		20	89,880.3
Sioux Lookout District	Bearskin Lake	1	31,199.7

[Continued]

1448

★ 1004 ★

Number and Acreage of Indian Reserves in Canada, 1903.
Ontario Region
[Continued]

Responsibility center	Band	Reserves	
		Number	Acreage
	Big Trout Lake	1	73,975.7
	Caribou Lake	1	22,664.8
	Cat Lake	1	538.0
	Deer Lake	1	10,541.0
	Fort Severn	1	9,782.0
	Kasabonika Lake	1	26,703.0
	Key-Way-Win	-	-
	Kingfisher	3	17,205.9
	Lac Seul	1	66,276.0
	McDowell Lake	-	-
	Muskrat Dam Lake	1	4,793.0
	New Slate Falls	-	-
	Osnaburgh	2	46,199.0
	Pikangikum	1	4,468.0
	Poplar Hill	-	-
	Sachigo Lake	3	20,125.0
	Sandy Lake	-	-
	Saugeen Nation	-	-
	Wapekeka	2	13,915.4
	Wawakapewin	-	-
	Wunnumin	2	23,844.1
District total		22	372,230.6
Sudbury District	Abitibi Ontario	-	-
	Batchewana	3	5,496.0
	Brunswick House	2	23,015.0
	Chapleau Cree	1	267.0
	Chapleau Ojibway	4	2,520.0
	Cockburn Island	2	2,368.0
	Dokis	1	30,300.0
	Flying Post	1	14,720.0
	Garden River	1	36,821.2
	Henvey Inlet	2	30,042.0
	Magnetawan	1	11,650.0
	Matachewan	1	10,276.0
	Mattagami	1	13,000.0
	Michipicoten	2	8,970.6
	Missanabie Cree	1	216.0
	Mississauga	1	4,885.7
	Nipissing	1	51,909.0
	Serpent River	1	26,882.0
	Shawanaga	3	11,141.4
	Sheguiandah	1	5,116.2
	Sheshegwaning	1	5,000.0

[Continued]

★ 1004 ★

Number and Acreage of Indian Reserves in Canada, 1985: Ontario Region

[Continued]

Responsibility center	Band	Reserves	
		Number	Acreage
	Spanish River	1	28,000.0
	Sucker Creek	1	1,550.0
	Thessalon	1	2,327.0
	Timagami	1	725.0
	Wahnapitae	1	2,560.0
	West Bay	1	7,647.0
	Whitefish Lake	1	43,748.0
	Whitefish River	1	14,019.0
	Wikwemikong	2	115,400.0
	Two or more bands	1	19,200.0
District total		42	529,772.1
Ontario Regional total		187	1,744,198.1

Source: Indians and Northern Affairs Canada, *Number and Acreage of Indian Reserves, by Band,* December 31, 1985, pp. 8-16. Primary source: Original contains detailed notes on most areas. *Note:* A dash (-) represents zero.

★ 1005 ★

Number and Acreage of Indian Reserves in Canada, 1985: Quebec Region

Responsibility center	Band	Reserves	
		Number	Acreage
Abitibi Service Centre (Algonquins)	Abitibiwinni	1	129.0
	Grand Lac Victoria	-	-
	Kipawa	1	53.1
	Lac Simon	1	672.0
	Long Point	-	-
	Timiskaming	1	4,750.0
	Wolf Lake	-	-
Service Centre total		4	5,604.1
Abitibi Service Centre (Cree)	Chisasibi	-	-
	Eastmain	1	8.0
	Great Whale River	-	-
	Mistassini	1	5,821.1
	Nemaska	-	-
	Old Factory	-	-
	Waskaganish	-	-
	Waswanipi	1	620.0

[Continued]

★ 1005 ★

Number and Acreage of Indian Reserves in Canada, 1985: Quebec Region
[Continued]

Responsibility center	Band	Reserves	
		Number	Acreage
Service Centre total		3	6,449.1
Montreal Service Centre	Abenakis of Wolinak	1	170.8
	Barriere Lake	1	73.0
	Kahnawake	1	13,534.0
	Odanak	1	1,252.0
	Oka	-	-
	River Desert	1	42,923.0
	Two or more bands	1	18,176.0
Service Centre Total		6	76,128.8
Pointe-Bleue District	Manowan	1	1,906.0
	Montagnais of Lake St. John	1	5,786.0
	Obedjiwan	1	2,290.0
	Weymontachie	2	8,202.6
District total		5	18,184.6
Quebec Regional Office	Gaspe	-	-
	Micmacs of Maria	1	410.0
	Nation Huronne Wendat	1	280.0
	Restigouche	1	8,140.0
	Viger	2	428.4
Regional Office total		5	9,258.4
Sept-Iles District	Betsiamites	1	63,100.0
	Mingan	1	4,480.0
	Montagnais de Schefferville	2	97.3
	Montagnais de Les Escoumins	1	95.0
	Montagnais de Sept-Iles et Maliotenam	2	1,497.7
	Naskapis of Schefferville	-	-
	Natashquan	1	35.8
	Romaine	1	100.0
	St. Augustin	-	-

[Continued]

1451

★ 1005 ★

Number and Acreage of Indian Reserves in Canada, 1985: Quebec Region
[Continued]

Responsibility center	Band	Reserves	
		Number	Acreage
District total		9	69,405.8
Quebec Regional total		32	185,030.8

Source: Indians and Northern Affairs Canada, *Number and Acreage of Indian Reserves, by Band*, December 31, 1985, pp. 4-7.
Notes: A dash (-) represents zero. Abitibi No. 70, owned jointly by the Abitibiwinni and Abitibi Ontario Bands, formerly in the Abitibi District, Quebec Region is administered by the Sudbury District, Ontario Region, effective November 1, 1972. Doncaster No. 17, Montreal Service Centre, has been set apart for the Kahnawake and Oka Bands. Oka No. 16, Oka Band, Montreal Service Centre, is not a reserve within the meaning of the *Indian Act*. The Abenakis of Becancour Band, Montreal Service Centre, changed its name to the Abenakis de Wolinak Band effective July 12, 1983. The Sept-Iles Band, Sept-Iles District, changed its name to the Montagnais de Sept-Iles et Maliotenam Band effective August 9, 1983. The Rupert House Band, Abitibi Service Centre (Cree), changed its name to the Waskaganish Band effective May 11, 1984. The Hurons of Lorette Band, Quebec Regional Office, changed its name to the Nation Huronne Wendat Band effective August 22, 1985. Lorette No. 7 and Lorette No. 7A became Village de Hurons, Wendake effective the same date.

★ 1006 ★

Number and Acreage of Indian Reserves in Canada, 1985: Saskatchewan Region

Responsibility center	Band	Reserves	
		Number	Acreage
Meadow Lake District	Big C	3	23,502.5
	Buffalo River	1	20,409.8
	Canoe Lake	4	18,114.0
	English River	7	29,365.6
	Flying Dust	2	9,370.4
	Island Lake	2	16,919.0
	Joseph Bighead	1	11,614.0
	Makwa Sahgaiehcan	4	14,625.0
	Turnor Lake	3	6,656.4
	Waterhen Lake	1	19,699.4
District total		28	170,276.1
North Battleford District	Little Pine	-	-
	Lucky Man	-	-
	Moosomin	4	17,347.6
	Mosquito-Grizzly Bear's Head	2	31,565.2
	Onion Lake	2	52,320.3
	Poundmaker	1	19,169.0
	Red Pheasant	1	24,342.3
	Saulteaux	2	15,000.0
	Sweet Grass	3	42,158.0
	Thunderchild	3	16,359.1

[Continued]

★ 1006 ★

Number and Acreage of Indian Reserves in Canada, 1985
Saskatchewan Region
[Continued]

Responsibility center	Band	Reserves Number	Reserves Acreage
	Two or more bands	1	16,367.4
District total		19	234,628.9
Prince Albert District	Cumberland House	5	5,302.3
	Fond du Lac	3	60,351.0
	James Smith	2	37,311.0
	Lac La Hache	1	27,228.0
	Lac La Ronge	18	107,005.0
	Montreal Lake	2	20,435.0
	Peter Ballantyne	9	33,034.2
	Red Earth	2	5,636.0
	Shoal Lake	1	3,654.0
	Stony Rapids	3	79,614.9
	Sturgeon Lake	2	22,757.0
	Wahpeton	2	3,822.0
District total		50	406,150.4
Saskatoon District	Beardy's & Okemasis	1	28,057.0
	John Smith	1	23,936.0
	Kinistino	2	9,934.0
	Mistawasis	1	30,997.0
	Moose Woods	1	4,130.0
	Muskeg Lake	1	18,585.2
	Nut Lake	1	14,477.0
	One Arrow	1	10,210.0
District total		9	140,326.2
Shellbrook Indian Agency	Big River	2	29,565.0
	Pelican Lake	1	8,705.1
	Sandy Lake	1	42,865.0
	Witchekan Lake	1	4,224.8
Agency total		5	85,359.9
Touchwood-File Hills	Carry the Kettle	1	40,995.0
	Day Star	1	15,360.0
	Fishing Lake	2	9,653.1
	Gordon	1	35,677.0
	Little Black Bear	1	16,951.1
	Muscowpetung	1	21,865.8
	Muskowekwan	1	18,240.2
	Nikaneet	1	3,037.2
	Okanese	1	15,486.7
	Pasqua	1	22,141.0
	Peepeekisis	1	27,820.2

[Continued]

★ 1006 ★

Number and Acreage of Indian Reserves in Canada, 1985: Saskatchewan Region
[Continued]

Responsibility center	Band	Reserves	
		Number	Acreage
	Piapot	1	22,878.0
	Poorman	1	19,125.0
	Standing Buffalo	1	5,550.0
	Star Blanket	2	13,763.0
	Wood Mountain	1	5,871.6
	Two or more bands	1	1,255.8
District total		19	295,670.7
Yorkton District	Cote	1	19,986.0
	Cowessess	1	29,592.6
	Kahkewistahaw	1	20,660.0
	Keeseekoose	2	10,920.6
	Key	1	15,667.4
	Ochapowace	1	34,521.0
	Sakimay	4	26,628.0
	White Bear	1	29,747.0
District total		12	187,722.6
Saskatchewan Regional total		142	1,520,134.8

Source: Indians and Northern Affairs Canada, *Number and Acreage of Indian Reserves, by Band*, December 31, 1985, pp. 20-23. *Notes:* A dash (-) represents zero. Little Pine and Lucky Man No. 116, North Battleford District, is held in common by the Little Pine and Lucky Man Bands. Last Mountain Lake No. 80A, Touchwood-File Hills-Qu'Appelle District, has been set apart for the Muscowpetung, Pasqua, Piapot, Day Star, Gordon, Muskowekwan and Poorman Bands. Wa-Pii Moos-Toosis (White Calf) No. 83A, Star Blanket, Band, Touchwood-File Hills-Qu'Appelle District, was established as a reserve effective July 17, 1983. The Portage La Loche Band, Meadow Lake District, changed its name to the Big C Band effective July 20, 1984.

★ 1007 ★

Number and Acreage of Indian Reserves in Canada, 1985: Yukon Territory

Responsibility center	Band	Reserves	
		Number	Acreage
Yukon Regional Office	Aishihik	-	-
	Carcross-Tagish	1	160.0
	Little Salmon Carmacks	-	-
	Champagne	-	-
	Dawson	1	158.5
	Kluane	-	-
	Kwanlin Dun	1	320.3
	Liard River	9	3,541.0
	Mayo	1	320.0
	Old Crow	-	-
	Ross River	-	-
	Selkirk	-	-
	Taku River Tlingit	10	3,124.5
	Teslin	2	275.7
Yukon Regional total		25	7,900.0

Source: Indians and Northern Affairs Canada, *Number and Acreage of Indian Reserves, by Band,* December 31, 1985, p. 38. *Notes:* A dash (-) represents zero. An unnamed reserve No. 10, Atlin Band, was established in the townsite of Atlin effective February 14, 1985. The Atlin Band changed its name to the Taku River Tlingit Band effective March 5, 1985.

LISTING OF SOURCES

The following listing shows all sources used in *SRNNA* in the format in which the sources appear referenced under each table. In addition to these sources, the originators of the data frequently cited additional sources on which they based their work. Those sources are shown with each table but, because of the diversity of the citations, have not been extracted and included here.

1987 Economic Census: Survey of Minority-Owned Business Enterprises, Asian Americans, American Indians, and Other Minorities, U.S. Department of Commerce, Bureau of the Census, MB87-3, 1991.

1987 Economic Census: Survey of Minority-Owned Business Enterprises, Summary, U.S. Department of Commerce, Bureau of the Census, MB87-4, 1991.

1990 Science Report Card: NAEP's Assessment of Fourth, Eighth, and Twelfth Graders, Lee R. Jones, Ina V.S. Mullis, Senta A. Raizen, Iris R. Weiss, Elizabeth A. Weston, Prepared by Educational Testing Service under 1992 contract with the National Center for Education Statistics, Office of Educational Research and Improvement, U.S. Department of Education.

Aboriginal Peoples Output Program, 1986 Census, Statistics Canada, *A Data Book on Canada's Aboriginal Population from the 1986 Census of Canada*, March, 1989.

"Adult and Pediatric AIDS Cases, by Transmission Category, Race/Ethnic Group, and Sex, 1981-1988," *Health Status of Minorities and Low-Income Groups*, Third Edition, 1991.

Alaska Business Monthly.

American Demographics.

Anderson, D. Michael and Gregory M. Christenson, "Ethnic Breakdown of AIDS Related Knowledge and Attitudes from the National Adolescent Student Health Survey," *Journal of Health Education*, Vol. 22, No. 1, January/February 1991.

Annual Report to Congress: Indian Civil Service Retirement Act, P.L. 96-135, FY 89.

"Arrests," *Sourcebook of Criminal Justice Statistics - 1990, 1991*.

"Arrests in Cities," *Sourcebook of Criminal Justice Statistics - 1990, 1991*.

"Arrests in Rural Counties," *Sourcebook of Criminal Justice Statistics - 1990, 1991*.

"Arrests in Suburban Areas," *Sourcebook of Criminal Justice Statistics - 1990, 1991*.

"Average Number of Hours Spent per Week on Outside Reading, Homework, and Television Watching, by Selected Background Characteristics," *A Profile of the American Eighth Grader, 1990*.

"Average Salaries for Full-Time Teachers in Public Elementary and Secondary Schools, Characteristics: 1987-88," *Digest of Education Statistics 1991*, November 1991.

"Bachelor's Degrees Conferred by Institutions of Higher Education, by Racial/Ethnic Group and Sex of Student: 1976-77 to 1988-89," *Digest of Education Statistics 1991*, November 1991.

"Bachelor's Degrees Conferred by Institutions of Higher Education, by Racial/Ethnic Group, Major Field of Study, and Sex of Student: 1988-89," *Digest of Education Statistics 1991*, November 1991.

Baskerville, Dawn M., "Breaking Through the Glass Ceiling," *Black Enterprise* 22 (August 1991).

Brod, Rodney L. and John M. McQuiston, "American Indian Adult Education and Literacy: The First National Survey," *Journal of American Indian Education*, Vol. 22, No. 2, January 1983.

Bureau of Indian Affairs, *Natural Resource Information System Inventory and Production Report, 1989*, United States Department of the Interior, Report No. 55-38-X.

Bureau of Indian Affairs, U.S. Department of the Interior, Washington, D.C.

Canada's Off-Reserve Aboriginal Population: A Statistical Overview, Social Trends Analysis Directorate, Department of the Secretary of State of Canada, 1991.

Census of Population and Housing, 1990, Summary Tape File 1 on CD-ROM, U.S. Bureau of the Census, Washington, D.C., 1991.

Cigarette Tax Evasion: A Second Look, Advisory Commission on Intergovernment Relations, Washington, D.C., March 1985, Table 3-9.

Coal Data: A Reference, November 1991, Energy Information Administration, Office of Coal, Nuclear, Electric and Alternate Fuels, U.S. Department of Energy, Washington, D.C.

Code of Federal Regulations: Indians, Office of the Federal Register National Archives and Records Administration, April 1, 1991.

Code of Federal Regulations: Indians, Title 25, Revised as of April 1, 1992, Office of the Federal Register National Archives and Records Administration.

Code of Federal Regulations, Vol. 25, April 1991, Office of the Federal Register National Archives and Records Administration.

Commission for Racial Justice, United Church of Christ, *Toxic Wastes and Race in the United States: A National Report on the Racial and Socio-Economic Characteristics of Communities with Hazardous Waste Sites, 1987*.

"Comparison of Business Ownership by Minority Group: 1987 and 1982," 1987 Survey of Minority-Owned Businesses, *Minority-Owned Businesses*, Washington, D.C., U.S. Government Printing Office, 1990.

Davis, Robert L., MD, et al., "Smoking During Pregnancy Among Northwest Native Americans," Public Health Reports, January-February 1992.

Deloria, Jr., Vine, *Behind the Trail of Broken Treaties: An Indian Declaration of Independence*, University of Texas Press, Austin.

Diabetes: Status of the Disease Among American Indians, Blacks, and Hispanics, U.S. General Accounting Office, 1992.

"Doctor's Degrees Conferred by Institutions of Higher Education, by Racial/Ethnic Group and Sex of Student: 1976-77 to 1988-89," *Digest of Education Statistics 1991*, November 1991.

"Doctor's Degrees Conferred by Institutions of Higher Education, by Racial/Ethnic Group, Major Field of Study, and Sex of Student: 1988-89," *Digest of Education Statistics 1991*, November 1991.

Durning, Alan Thein, *Guardians of the Land: Indigenous Peoples and the Health of the Earth*, Worldwatch Paper 112, Worldwatch Institute, 1992.

"Eighth Graders Achievement on History, Mathematics, Reading, and Science Tests: 1988," *Digest of Education Statistics 1991*, November 1991.

"Enrollment in Public Elementary and Secondary Education, by Race/Ethnicity: 1976 and 1986," *The Condition of Education 1991*, Volume 1, Elementary and Secondary Education, 1991.

"Enrollment in Public Elementary and Secondary Schools, by Race or Ethnicity and State: Fall 1986 and Fall 1989," *Digest of Education Statistics 1991*, November 1991.

Fact Book, Albuquerque Area Office, Division of Administration, February 1980, U.S. Department of the Interior.

"Farm Operators-Tenure and Characteristics: 1982 and 1987," *Statistical Abstract of the United States*, 1991.

Federal Support for Education: Fiscal Years 1980 to 1991, National Center for Education Statistics, Survey Report, December 1991.

"Full-Time Regular Instructional Faculty in Institutions of Higher Education by Selected Characteristics and Type and Control of Institution: Fall 1987," *Digest of Education Statistics 1991*, November 1991.

"Full-Time Regular Instructional Faculty in Institutions of Higher Education, by Faculty Characteristics and by Field: 1987-88," *Digest of Education Statistics 1991*, November 1991.

F.H. Leacy, *Historical Statistics of Canada*, Second Edition, Statistics Canada and Social Science Federation of Canada.

Grobsmith, Elizabeth S. and Beth R. Ritter, "The Ponca Tribe of Nebraska: The Process of Restoration of a Federally Terminated Tribe," *Human Organization*, Vol. 51, No. 1, 1992.

Health Status of Minorities and Low-Income Groups, Third Edition, U.S. Department of Health and Human Services, Public Health Service, Health Resources and Services Administration, U.S. Government Printing Office, Washington, D.C.

Historical Statistics of the United States, Colonial Times to 1970, Part I, U.S. Department of Commerce, Bureau of the Census, Washington, D.C., 1975.

Hollmann, Frederick W., *U.S. Population Estimates, by Age, Sex, Race, and Hispanic Origin: 1989*, U.S. Department of Commerce, Bureau of the Census, Current Population Reports, Population Estimates and Projections, series P-25, No.1057, March 1990.

Hospital Inpatient Workload Summary and Comparison with Previous Year, U.S. Department of Health, Public Health Service, Indian Health Service, Rockville, MD, 1990.

Indian Country Today.

Indian Programs: BIA and Indian Tribes Are Taking Action to Address Dam Safety Concerns, United States General Accounting Office, February, 1992.

Indian Programs: Profile of the Land Ownership at 12 Reservations, United States General Accounting Office, February 1992.

Indian and Northern Affairs Canada, Indian and Inuit Affairs Program, Membership Division, *Adoption and the Indian Child*.

Indians and Northern Affairs Canada, *Number and Acreage of Indian Reserves, by Band*, December 31, 1985.

Jones, Richard, *American Indian Policy: Background, Nature, History, Current Issues, Future Trends*, Congressional Research Service Report No. 87227.

Kathleen E. Toomey, Alisa G. Oberschelp, and Joel R. Greenspan, "Sexually Transmitted Diseases and Native Americans: Trends in Reported Gonorrhea and Syphilis Morbidity, 1984-88," *Public Health Reports*, Vol. 104, No. 6, November/December 1989.

Kennedy, Richard D., M.S. and Roger E. Deapen, Ph.D., "Differences Between Oklahoma Indian Infant Mortality and Other Races," *Public Health Reports*, Vol. 106, No. 1, January-February 1991.

Lakota Times.

"Largest Metropolitan Areas—Racial and Hispanic Origin Populations: 1990," *Statistical Abstract of the United States*, 1991.

"Live Births, According to Race of Child and Selected Characteristics: United States, Selected Years 1970-88,"

Health United States 1990, 1991.

Low Income Home Energy Assistance Program: Report to Congress for FY 1989, U.S. Department of Health and Human Services (HHS), Family Support Administration, Office of Community Services, Office of Energy Assistance, October 29, 1990, 1992.

"Master's Degrees Conferred by Institutions of Higher Education, by Racial/Ethnic Group and Sex of Student: 1976-77 to 1988-89, " *Digest of Education Statistics 1991*, November 1991.

"Master's Degrees Conferred by Institutions of Higher Education, by Racial/Ethnic Group, Major Field of Study, and Sex of Student: 1988-89," *Digest of Education Statistics 1991*, November 1991.

"Metropolitan Areas With Large Numbers of Selected Racial Groups and of Hispanic Origin Population: 1990," *Statistical Abstract of the United States*, 1991.

Mineral Revenues 1990, Report on Receipts from Federal and Indian Leases, U.S. Department of the Interior, Minerals Management Service, Royalty Management Program.

"Minority-Owned Firms by Gender," 1987 Survey of Minority-Owned Businesses, *Minority-Owned Businesses*, Washington, D.C., U.S. Government Printing Office, 1990.

"Minority-Owned Firms by Industry Division: 1987," 1987 Survey of Minority-Owned Businesses, *Minority-Owned Businesses*, Washington, D.C., U.S. Government Printing Office, 1990.

National Indian Gaming Association.

National Science Board, *Science and Engineering Indicators — 1991*, Washington D.C., U.S. Government Printing Office, 1991, (NSB 91-1).

New York Times.

"Part-Time Regular Instructional Faculty in Institutions of Higher Education, by Selected Characteristics and Type and Control of Institution: Fall 1987," *Digest of Education Statistics 1991*, November 1991.

"Percent Change Within Race/Ethnicity Group, 1976 to 1986," *The Condition of Education 1991*, Volume 1, Elementary and Secondary Education, 1991.

"Percent Distribution of Drug Abuse Clients by Race/Ethnicity, by Treatment Modality in Single-Modality Drug Only and Combined Units: October 30, 1987," *Health Status of Minorities and Low-Income Groups*, Third Edition, 1991.

"Percentage of Eighth Grade Students and Percent of Eighth Grade Teachers Who Consider Problems to be Serious, by Selected Personal and School Characteristics: 1988," *The Condition of Education 1991*, Volume 1, Elementary and Secondary Education.

"Percentage of Eighth Grade Students and Percent of Eighth Grade Teachers Who Consider Student Drug and Alcohol Usage to be Serious School Problems, by Race/Ethnicity and School Type: 1988," *The Condition of Education 1991* Volume 1, Elementary and Secondary Education, 1991.

"Percentage of Eighth Grade Students Offered Drugs at School During One Semester, by Race/Ethnicity and School Type: 1988," *The Condition of Education 1991*, Volume 1, Elementary and Secondary Education, 1991.

"Percentage of Eighth Graders Aspiring to Various Education Levels, by Selected Student Characteristics," *A Profile of the American Eighth Grader*, 1990.

"Percentage of Eighth Graders Classified into Selected Quartiles Based on Self-Reported Grades From Grade Six Until Grade Eight, by Selected Background Characteristics," *A Profile of the American Eighth Grader*, 1990.

"Percentage of Eighth Graders from Different Types of Households, by Selected Background Characteristics," *A Profile of the American Eighth Grader*, 1990.

"Percentage of Eighth Graders Participating This Year in Outside-School Activities, by Selected Background

Characteristics," *A Profile of the American Eighth Grader,* 1990

"Percentage of Eighth Graders Planning to Enroll in Various High School Programs by Selected Background Characteristics," *A Profile of the American Eighth Grader,* 1990.

"Percentage of Eighth Graders Proficient at Each Mathematics Level, by Race," *A Profile of the American Eighth Grader,* 1990.

"Percentage of Eighth Graders Reporting Various Jobs Ever Worked for Pay, by Selected Background Characteristics," *A Profile of the American Eighth Grader.*

"Percentage of Eighth Graders Spending Various Numbers of Hours After School Each Day at Home With No Adult Present, by Selected Background Characteristics," *A Profile of the American Eighth Grader,* 1990.

"Percentage of Eighth Graders Who Are Enrolled in Various School Sectors, by Selected Background Characteristics," *A Profile of the American Eighth Grader,* 1990.

"Percentage of Eighth Graders Who Report Participating in Various School-Based Extracurricular Activities, by Selected Background Characteristics," *A Profile of the American Eighth Grader,* 1990.

"Percentage of Eighth Graders Who Report Repeating One or More Grades in School, by Year of Birth and Selected Background Characteristics," *A Profile of the American Eighth Grader,* 1990.

"Percentage of Eighth Graders Who Usually Have No One Home When They Return Home From School, by Selected Background Characteristics," *A Profile of the American Eighth Grader,* 1990.

"Percentage of Eighth Graders With Various Risk Factors, by Race/Ethnicity: 1988," The Condition of Education, 1991, Volume 1, Elementary and Secondary Education, 1991.

"Percentage of Undergraduates Enrolled in Fall 1986 and Average Amount Awarded in 1986-87 per Student, by Type and Source of Aid and Selected Student Characteristics," *Digest of Education Statistics 1991,* November 1991.

"Percentages of Eighth Graders Reporting Various Safety-Related Occurrences in Their School, by Selected Background Characteristics," *A Profile of the American Eighth Grader,* 1990.

"Principals in Public and Private Elementary and Secondary Schools, by Selected Characteristics: 1987-88," *Digest of Education Statistics 1991,* November 1991.

"Race/Ethnicity of Medicaid Beneficiaries, Fiscal Year 1986," *Health Status of Minorities and Low-Income Groups,* Third Edition, 1991.

"Racial/Ethnic Distribution of the U.S. Population Overall Compared With the Racial/Ethnic Distribution of AIDS Cases, 1981-1988," *Health Status of Minorities and Low-Income Groups,* Third Edition, 1991.

"Ranking of Total Combined Non-White Population of States, 1990," *Black Issues in Higher Education,* August 29, 1991.

Report on the Americas, Volume XXV, No. 3, December 1991.

"Resident Population, by Race and Hispanic Origin—States: 1990," *Statistical Abstract of the United States,* 1991.

Russel, George, *The American Indian in Question,* Phoenix: Thunderbird Enterprises, 1992.

"Selected Characteristics of Teachers and School Administrators: School Year 1987-1988," *The Condition of Education 1991,* Volume 1, Elementary and Secondary Education, 1991.

Snipp, C. Matthew, *American Indians: The First of This Land,* Russell Sage Foundation.

Sourcebook of Criminal Justice Statistics - 1990, U.S. Department of Justice, Office of Justice Programs, Bureau of Justice Statistics, U.S. Government Printing Office, Washington, D.C.

Special Supplemental Food Program for Women, Infants, and Children (WIC) Racial Participation, April 1991, Food and Nutrition Service Financial Management Program Information Division Data Base, Monitoring Branch, November 1991.

State of Native American Youth Health, February, 1992, Indian Health Service, Maternal and Child Health Bureau, and the Robert Wood Johnson Foundation.

State Resource and Services Related to Alcohol and Other Drug Abuse Problems for Fiscal Year 1990, The National Institute on Drug Abuse and The National Institute on Alcohol Abuse and Alcoholism.

"Statistics for Minority-Owned Firms by Major Industry Group: 1987," 1987 Survey of Minority-Owned Businesses, *Minority-Owned Businesses*, Washington, D.C., U.S. Government Printing Office, 1990.

"Statistics for Minority-Owned Firms by Minority and Employment Size of Firm: 1987," 1987 Survey of Minority-Owned Businesses, *Minority-Owned Businesses*, Washington, D.C., U.S. Government Printing Office, 1990.

"Statistics for Minority-Owned Firms by Minority, Industry, and Receipts Size of Firm: 1987," 1987 Survey of Minority-Owned Businesses, *Minority-Owned Businesses*, Washington, D.C., U.S. Government Printing Office, 1990.

"Statistics for Minority-Owned Firms by Minority, Industry, Division, and Legal Form of Organization: 1987," 1987 Survey of Minority-Owned Businesses, *Minority-Owned Businesses*, Washington, D.C., U.S. Government Printing Office, 1990.

"Statistics for Minority-Owned Firms by State: 1987," 1987 Survey of Minority-Owned Businesses, *Minority-Owned Businesses*, Washington, D.C., U.S. Government Printing Office, 1990.

Summary Population and Housing Characteristics, United States Summary, United States Bureau of the Census, CP H-1.

Survey of American Indian Environmental Protection Needs on Reservation Lands: 1986, September 1986, Submitted to the Environmental Protection Agency by Americans for Indian Opportunity.

"Teachers in Public and Private Elementary and Secondary Schools, by Selected Characteristics: 1987-88," *Digest of Education Statistics 1991*, November 1991.

Thornton, Russell, *American Indian Holocaust and Survival: A Population History Since 1492*, University of Oklahoma, Press, 1987.

Thornton, Russell, *We Shall Live Again: The 1870 and 1890 Ghost Dance Movements as Demographic Revitalization*, Cambridge University Press, 1986.

"Time Between High School Graduation and Award of the Baccalaureate Degree, by Race/Ethnicity, and Sex: Years of College Graduation 1977 and 1986," The Condition of Education 1991, Volume 2: Postsecondary Education, 1991.

"Total Enrollment in Institutions of Higher Education, by Control of Institution, Race/Ethnicity and Sex: Biennially, Fall 1978 Through Fall 1988," *Digest of Education Statistics 1991*, November 1991.

"Total Enrollment in Institutions of Higher Education, by Race/Ethnicity of Student and by State: Fall 1988," *Digest of Education Statistics 1991*, November 1991.

"Total Regular and Temporary Instructional Faculty in Institutions of Higher Education by Selected Characteristics and Type and Control of Institution: Fall 1987," *Digest of Education Statistics 1991*.

Toward the Year 2000: Listening to the Voice of Native America, National Advisory Council on Indian Education (NACIE), 17th Annual Report to the United States Congress, Fiscal Year 1990.

Trends in Indian Health, 1991, U.S. Department of Health and Human Services, Public Health Service, Indian Health Service.

Trends in Racial/Ethnic Enrollment in Higher Education: Fall 1980 Through Fall 1990, U.S. Department of Education, Office of Educational Research and Improvement, Postsecondary Education Statistics Division, Washington D C

Truesdell, Leon E., PhD, U.S. Department of Commerce, Bureau of the Census, *Fifteenth Census of the United States: 1930, The Indian Population of the United States and Alaska*, U.S. Government Printing Office, 1937.

Udansky, Margaret L., "Income Equality Gap Widens for Minorities," USA Today, July 24, 1992.

United States Bureau of the Census, *1980 Census of Population*, Volume 2, Subject Reports, *Characteristics of American Indians, by Tribes and Selected Areas: 1980*, PC80-2-1C, issued September 1989, U.S. Department of Commerce, U.S. Government Printing Office, Washington, D.C.

United States Bureau of the Census, *Indian Population in the United States and Alaska, 1910*, U.S. Government Printing Office, Washington, D.C., 1915.

United States Bureau of the Census, *Statistical Abstract of the United States*, 1992, Washington, D.C.

United States Bureau of the Census, *American Indians, Eskimos, and Aleuts on Identified Reservations and in the Historic Areas of Oklahoma*, U.S. Government Printing Office, Washington, D.C.

United States Congress, Senate, Hearing Before the Select Committee on Indian Affairs, *Gaming Activities on Indian Reservations and Lands*, S. Hrg. 100-341, U.S. Government Printing Office, Washington, D.C., 1988.

United States Congress, Senate, Hearing Before the Select Committee on Indian Affairs, *Implementation of the Indian Gaming Regulatory Act*, S. Hrg. 102-660, Pt. 2, U.S. Government Printing Office, Washington, D.C., 1992.

United States Congress, Senate, Hearing Before the Select Committee on Indian Affairs, *Indian Veterans*, S. HRG. 101-549, U.S. Government Printing Office, Washington, D.C.

United States Congress, Senate, Select Committee on Indian Affairs, *Federal Programs of Assistance to Native Americans*, 102d Cong., 1st sess., December 1991.

United States Department of Education, National Center for Education Statistics, *The Condition of Education 1992*, Washington, D.C., 1992.

United States Department of Justice, Office of Justice Programs, Bureau of Justice Statistics, *Correctional Populations in the United States, 1989*, NCJ-130445, October 1991.

United States Department of the Interior, Bureau of Indian Affairs, *U.S. Indian Population (1962) and Land (1963)* U.S. Government Printing Office, November 1963.

United States Equal Employment Opportunity Commission, *Job Patterns for Minorities and Women in State and Local Government, 1990*, U.S. Government Printing Office, 1990, 1991.

United States General Accounting Office, *Federal Affirmative Employment: Status of Women and Minority Representation in Federal Law Enforcement Occupations*, October 1, 1992.

USA Today.

Vilardo, Frank J., Eric L. Mitter, James A. Palmer, Henry C. Briggs, and Julie Fesenmaier, *Survey of State and Tribal Emergency Response Capabilities for Radiological Transportation Incidents*, Division of Safeguards and Transportation, Office of Nuclear Material Safety and Safeguards, U.S. Nuclear Regulatory Commission, Washington, D.C.

Walke, Roger, *Federal Programs of Assistance to Native Americans: A Report Prepared for the Senate Select Committee on Indian Affairs of the United States Senate*, S. Prt. 102-62, U.S. Government Printing Office, Washington, D.C., December 1991.

Wall Street Journal.

"Weapons Used in Homicides Among Victims 15-34 Years of Age, According to Type of Weapon and Race of

Victim: United States, 1966-88," *Health United States 1990*, 1991.

Williams, Linda F., *Congressional District Fact Book*, Second Edition, Joint Center for Political Studies, Inc., 1986.

"Youth Served by Runaway and Homeless Centers," *Sourcebook of Criminal Justice Statistics - 1990, 1991*.

KEYWORD INDEX

The *Keyword Index* holds references to more than 3,000 subjects and names, including individuals, tribes, organizations, and places. The index was generated, in part, from the descriptive tags in the tables; variant spellings of tribal names are common; an effort was made to conform spellings in all instances where documentation was available. Variant spellings, however, remain in the index to some extent. Each entry is followed by one or more page numbers marked p. or pp. After the page references, table references are provided within brackets. The phrase *p. 483 [275]* means that the item appears on page 483 in Table 275. Some abbreviations occur with some frequency: *BIA* stands for Bureau of Indian Affairs and *IHS* is the Indian Health Service.

Numbers following p. or pp. are page references. Numbers in [ ] are table references. BIA stands for Bureau of Indian Affairs; IHS stands for Indian Health Service.

1466

Numbers following p. or pp. are page references. Numbers in [ ] are table references. BIA stands for Bureau of Indian Affairs; IHS stands for Indian Health Service.

Numbers following p. or pp. are page references. Numbers in [ ] are table references. BIA stands for Bureau of Indian Affairs; IHS stands for Indian Health Service.

Numbers following p. or pp. are page references. Numbers in [ ] are table references. BIA stands for Bureau of Indian Affairs; IHS stands for Indian Health Service.

1469

Allakaket continued:
— population, pp. 293, 296 [168-169]
Allegany County
— characteristics of families, p. 471 [245]
— geographic mobility, pp. 439, 443 [234-235]
— methods of health care, p. 738 [473]
— school enrollment, pp. 534, 538 [289-290]
Allegany Reservation, NY
— acreage, tribal lands, and population, p. 1038 [658]
— characteristics of families, p. 463 [243]
— electric lighting in housing units, p. 889 [567]
— elementary school enrollment, p. 559 [302]
— exterior wall materials in housing units, p. 895 [570]
— floor materials, p. 902 [573]
— geographic mobility, pp. 422, 426 [230-231]
— heating equipment, p. 910 [576]
— high school enrollment, p. 567 [305]
— household characteristics, pp. 828, 831 [541-542]
— kitchen facilities, p. 916 [579]
— methods of health care, p. 731 [470]
— nursery and kindergarten enrollment, p. 553 [297]
— piped water, pp. 921, 924 [582-583]
— plumbing facilities, pp. 921, 924 [582-583]
— population, pp. 257, 307, 310 [152, 174-175]
— school enrollment, pp. 517, 521 [285-286]
— sewage disposal, p. 934 [588]
— source of water, p. 934 [588]
— telephones in housing units, p. 889 [567]
— traditional occupations, pp. 650, 652 [391-392]
— years of school completed, pp. 491, 497, 503 [268, 271, 274]
Allentown-Bethlehem-Easton, PA-NJ
— population, pp. 229, 246 [133, 147]
Allergies
— in adolescents, p. 720 [456]
— outpatient services, p. 758 [493]
Allotments, p. 1074 [704]
— energy assistance, p. 819 [538]
— land area, p. 87 [50]
— population, 1962, p. 87 [50]
Alpine County
— characteristics of families, p. 476 [247]
— geographic mobility, pp. 450, 455 [236-237]
— methods of health care, p. 743 [475]
— school enrollment, pp. 545, 550 [291-292]
Alsea
— population, 1910, pp. 70, 75, 77 [42, 44-45]
Altoona, PA
— population, p. 246 [147]
Alturas Rancheria, CA
— acreage, tribal land, and population, p. 1033 [657]
— characteristics of families, p. 463 [243]
— electric lighting in housing units, p. 889 [567]
— elementary school enrollment, p. 559 [302]
— exterior wall materials in housing units, p. 895 [570]
— floor materials, p. 902 [573]
— geographic mobility, pp. 422, 426 [230-231]
— heating equipment, p. 910 [576]
— high school enrollment, p. 567 [305]
— household characteristics, pp. 828, 831 [541-542]

Alturas Rancheria, CA continued:
— kitchen facilities, p. 916 [579]
— land area, p. 89 [51]
— methods of health care, p. 731 [470]
— nursery and kindergarten enrollment, p. 553 [297]
— piped water, pp. 921, 924 [582-583]
— plumbing facilities, pp. 921, 924 [582-583]
— population, pp. 258, 307, 310 [152, 174-175]
— population, 1962, p. 89 [51]
— school enrollment, pp. 517, 521 [285-286]
— sewage disposal, p. 934 [588]
— source of water, p. 934 [588]
— telephones in housing units, p. 889 [567]
— traditional occupations, pp. 650, 652 [391-392]
— years of school completed, pp. 491, 497, 503 [268, 271, 274]
Aluminum plants
— air pollution from, p. 1089 [717]
Amador County
— characteristics of families, p. 468 [244]
— geographic mobility, pp. 432, 435 [232-233]
— methods of health care, p. 735 [472]
— school enrollment, pp. 527, 530 [287-288]
Amaknak Island
— land area, p. 83 [48]
— population, 1962, p. 83 [48]
Amarillo, TX
— population, p. 247 [147]
Ambler
— household characteristics, pp. 875, 877 [561-562]
— population, pp. 293, 296 [168-169]
American Indian OIC Inc.
— adult education, p. 639 [385]
American Indian Research & Development
— education personnel recruitment, p. 638 [384]
American Indian Resource Center
— adult education, p. 640 [385]
— education personnel recruitment, p. 638 [384]
Amphetamines
— use of, p. 485 [261]
Amusement and recreation services
— minority-owned firms, p. 971 [619]
— Native-owned firms, p. 995 [628]
Anadarko Area
— bingo revenues, p. 1011 [637]
— Indian lands, p. 1054 [676]
— land area, pp. 82, 93, 96, 99-100 [47, 53, 55, 57]
— land trusteeship termination, p. 219 [125]
— population, p. 82 [47]
— population, 1962, pp. 93, 96, 99-100 [53, 55, 57]
Anaheim-Santa Ana, CA
— firm ownership, p. 1001 [631]
— population, p. 246 [146]
Anaktuvuk Pass
— household characteristics, pp. 875, 877 [561-562]
— land area, p. 85 [48]
— population, pp. 293, 296 [168-169]
— population, 1962, p. 85 [48]
Anchorage, AK
— firm ownership, p. 1001 [631]

Numbers following p. or pp. are page references. Numbers in [ ] are table references. BIA stands for Bureau of Indian Affairs; IHS stands for Indian Health Service.

Numbers following p. or pp. are page references. Numbers in [ ] are table references. BIA stands for Bureau of Indian Affairs; IHS stands for Indian Health Service.

Arapaho continued:
— Indian and White mixed-bloods in 1910, p. 135 [84]
— labor force characteristics, p. 767 [504]
— land area, p. 99 [57]
— language in 1910 and 1930, p. 193 [113]
— language spoken at home, pp. 643, 648 [387, 390]
— marital status in 1910, pp. 203, 209 [118, 120]
— marital status in 1910 and 1930, p. 202 [117]
— mixed-blood Indians in 1910, p. 115 [76]
— mixed-tribal blood Indians in 1910, p. 126 [80]
— population, pp. 234, 254, 289-290 [138, 150, 165]
— population, 1690-1890 in Texas, p. 19 [22]
— population, 1910, pp. 53, 58, 62, 68, 72, 75, 80 [36, 38, 40, 42-44, 46]
— population, 1910-1930, p. 28 [27]
— population, 1962, pp. 99, 103 [57, 59]
— population, Mountain region, p. 393 [214]
— population, North Central region, p. 346 [194]
— population, Northeast region, p. 358 [199]
— population, Pacific region, p. 395 [215]
— population, South Atlantic region, p. 369 [204]
— population, South Central region, p. 371 [205]
— school attendance in 1910, p. 142 [89]
— urban and rural population, p. 239 [142]
— veterans, p. 1105 [734]
— years of school completed, p. 509 [277]

Archaeological protection
— on reservations, p. 1091 [718]

Architecture
— baccalaureates conferred, p. 614 [359]
— doctorates conferred, p. 624 [368]
— master's degrees conferred, p. 619 [364]

Architecture and environmental design
— associate degrees conferred, p. 612 [357]
— baccalaureates conferred, p. 614 [359]
— doctorates, p. 624 [368]

Archuleta County
— characteristics of families, p. 475 [247]
— geographic mobility, pp. 447, 452 [236-237]
— methods of health care, p. 741 [474]
— school enrollment, pp. 542, 547 [291-292]

Arctic Red River Band
— reserves and acreage, p. 1446 [1003]

Arctic Slope
— household characteristics, pp. 886, 888 [565-566]
— population, pp. 291-292 [166-167]

Arctic Village
— household characteristics, pp. 875, 877 [561-562]
— land area, p. 85 [48]
— population, pp. 293, 296 [168-169]
— population, 1962, p. 85 [48]

Argentina
— native population, p. 232 [136]

Arikara
— ability to speak English in 1910, p. 185 [110]
— employment, pp. 772, 774, 779, 781 [507-508, 511-512]
— enrollment in 1930, pp. 158, 160 [95-96]
— family characteristics, p. 458 [239]
— fertility characteristics, p. 671 [406]
— full-blood Indians in 1910, pp. 116, 127 [76, 80]

Arikara continued:
— household characteristics, pp. 456, 458 [238-239]
— illiteracy in 1910, p. 162 [97]
— labor force characteristics, p. 767 [504]
— language in 1910 and 1930, p. 193 [113]
— language spoken at home, pp. 643, 648 [387, 390]
— marital status in 1910, pp. 204, 210 [118, 120]
— mixed-blood Indians in 1910, p. 116 [76]
— mixed-tribal blood Indians in 1910, p. 127 [80]
— population, p. 265 [155]
— population, 1910, pp. 58, 62-63, 66-68, 72, 75 [38, 40-44]
— population, 1910-1930, p. 33 [28]
— population, 1962, p. 97 [56]
— population, Mountain region, p. 393 [214]
— population, North Central region, p. 346 [194]
— population, Northeast region, p. 358 [199]
— population, Pacific region, p. 395 [215]
— population, South Atlantic region, p. 369 [204]
— population, South Central region, p. 371 [205]
— school attendance in 1910, p. 143 [89]
— urban and rural population, p. 239 [142]
— veterans, p. 1105 [734]
— years of school completed, p. 509 [277]

Arizona
— adult education, p. 639 [385]
— adults on probation, p. 1139 [763]
— alcohol treatment programs, p. 721 [458]
— capital punishment, p. 1136 [762]
— characteristics of families, pp. 465, 467, 470 [243-245]
— cigarettes and tax exemptions, p. 1030 [656]
— drug treatment programs, p. 726 [464]
— energy assistance, pp. 815, 819 [537-538]
— full-blood Indians in 1910, pp. 114, 116, 123, 125, 127, 134 [75-76, 78-80, 82]
— full/mixed blood population, 1910 and 1930, p. 11 [14]
— geographic mobility, pp. 424, 428, 430, 434, 438, 442 [230-235]
— household characteristics, pp. 829, 833, 835, 838, 846, 849, 866, 869 [541-544, 547-548, 555-556]
— Indian and White mixed bloods in 1910, pp. 134, 136 [83-84]
— Indian lands, pp. 1053-1055 [675-676]
— Indian population, p. 255 [151]
— Indian Trust lands, p. 1059 [681]
— inmates, p. 1140 [764]
— land area, p. 81 [47]
— languages spoken, p. 642 [386]
— literacy rates in 1900-1930, p. 171 [101]
— marital status in 1910 and 1930, p. 201 [116]
— methods of health care, pp. 732, 734, 737 [470-472]
— mineral leases, pp. 1016, 1026-1030 [645, 651, 654-655]
— mineral revenues, p. 1019 [650]
— minority-owned firms, p. 987 [624]
— mixed-blood Indians in 1910, pp. 114, 116, 123, 134 [75-76, 78, 83]
— mixed-tribal blood Indians in 1910, pp. 125, 127, 134 [79-80, 82]
— Native-owned firms, p. 996 [629]
— percentage Indian population, p. 254 [149]
— population, pp. 81, 224, 235-236, 309, 312, 314, 316, 323, 325, 339, 341 [47, 129, 139-140, 174-177, 180-181, 188-189]
— population, 1890-1910, p. 14 [18]
— population, 1890-1930, p. 17 [20]

Numbers following p. or pp. are page references. Numbers in [ ] are table references. BIA stands for Bureau of Indian Affairs; IHS stands for Indian Health Service.

Numbers following p. or pp. are page references. Numbers in [ ] are table references. BIA stands for Bureau of Indian Affairs; IHS stands for Indian Health Service.

Numbers following p. or pp. are page references. Numbers in [ ] are table references. BIA stands for Bureau of Indian Affairs; IHS stands for Indian Health Service.

Numbers following p. or pp. are page references. Numbers in [ ] are table references. BIA stands for Bureau of Indian Affairs; IHS stands for Indian Health Service.

1475

Baraga County continued:
— methods of health care, p. 736 [472]
— school enrollment, pp. 527, 531 [287-288]
Barbiturates
— use by high school seniors, pp. 592, 594 [332, 335]
Barona Rancheria, CA
— acreage, tribal land, and population, p. 1033 [657]
— characteristics of families, p. 464 [243]
— electric lighting in housing units, p. 889 [567]
— elementary school enrollment, p. 560 [302]
— energy assistance, p. 821 [538]
— exterior wall materials in housing units, p. 895 [570]
— floor materials, p. 902 [573]
— geographic mobility, pp. 422, 426 [230-231]
— heating equipment, p. 910 [576]
— high school enrollment, p. 567 [305]
— household characteristics, pp. 828, 831 [541-542]
— kitchen facilities, p. 916 [579]
— land area, p. 91 [52]
— methods of health care, p. 731 [470]
— nursery and kindergarten enrollment, p. 553 [297]
— piped water, pp. 921, 924 [582-583]
— plumbing facilities, pp. 921, 924 [582-583]
— population, pp. 307, 310 [174-175]
— population, 1962, p. 91 [52]
— school enrollment, pp. 517, 521 [285-286]
— sewage disposal, p. 934 [588]
— source of water, p. 934 [588]
— telephones in housing units, p. 889 [567]
— traditional occupations, pp. 650, 652 [391-392]
— years of school completed, pp. 491, 497, 503 [268, 271, 274]
Barrio Libre
— fertility characteristics, p. 682 [410]
— population, Mountain region, p. 414 [222]
— population, North Central region, p. 356 [198]
— population, Northeast region, p. 367 [203]
— population, Pacific region, p. 416 [223]
— population, South Atlantic region, p. 389 [212]
— population, South Central region, p. 391 [213]
Barron County
— characteristics of families, p. 473 [246]
— geographic mobility, pp. 445, 451 [236-237]
— methods of health care, p. 740 [474]
— school enrollment, pp. 540, 546 [291-292]
Barrow, AK
— hospitals, p. 752 [487]
— household characteristics, pp. 875, 877 [561-562]
— land area, p. 85 [48]
— population, pp. 293, 296 [168-169]
— population, 1962, p. 85 [48]
Barter Island
— land area, p. 85 [48]
— population, 1962, p. 85 [48]
Basket makers
— on reservations, pp. 651, 655, 659 [392, 394, 396]
Baton Rouge, LA
— population, p. 247 [147]
Battle Creek, MI
— population, p. 247 [147]

Bay Mills Chippewa
— fertility characteristics, p. 673 [407]
— land area, p. 96 [55]
— population, p. 258 [152]
— population, 1962, p. 96 [55]
— population, Mountain region, p. 397 [216]
— population, North Central region, p. 347 [195]
— population, Northeast region, p. 359 [200]
— population, Pacific region, p. 400 [217]
— population, South Atlantic region, p. 373 [206]
— population, South Central region, p. 375 [207]
Bay Mills Reservation, MI
— acreage, tribal land, and population, p. 1036 [657]
— characteristics of families, p. 464 [243]
— electric lighting in housing units, p. 889 [567]
— elementary school enrollment, p. 560 [302]
— energy assistance, p. 822 [538]
— exterior wall materials in housing units, p. 895 [570]
— floor materials, p. 902 [573]
— geographic mobility, pp. 422, 426 [230-231]
— heating equipment, p. 910 [576]
— high school enrollment, p. 567 [305]
— household characteristics, pp. 828, 831 [541-542]
— kitchen facilities, p. 916 [579]
— land area, p. 94 [53]
— methods of health care, p. 731 [470]
— nursery and kindergarten enrollment, p. 553 [297]
— piped water, pp. 922, 924 [582-583]
— plumbing facilities, pp. 922, 924 [582-583]
— population, pp. 258, 307, 310 [152, 174-175]
— population, 1962, p. 94 [53]
— school enrollment, pp. 517, 521 [285-286]
— sewage disposal, p. 934 [588]
— source of water, p. 934 [588]
— telephones in housing units, p. 889 [567]
— traditional occupations, pp. 650, 652 [391-392]
— years of school completed, pp. 491, 497, 503 [268, 271, 274]
Bayfield County
— characteristics of families, p. 472 [246]
— geographic mobility, pp. 440, 444 [234-235]
— methods of health care, p. 739 [473]
— school enrollment, pp. 535, 539 [289-290]
Bear River
— population, 1962, p. 91 [52]
Beaumont-Port Arthur, TX
— population, p. 247 [147]
Beaver
— in Canada, p. 1430 [996]
— household characteristics, pp. 875, 877 [561-562]
— land area, p. 85 [48]
— population, pp. 293, 296 [168-169]
— population, 1962, p. 85 [48]
Becker County
— characteristics of families, p. 476 [247]
— geographic mobility, pp. 449, 454 [236-237]
— methods of health care, p. 743 [475]
— school enrollment, pp. 544, 549 [291-292]
Belcourt, ND
— hospitals, p. 752 [487]

Belize
— native population, p. 232 [136]
Belkofski
— household characteristics, pp. 875, 877 [561-562]
— land area, p. 83 [48]
— population, pp. 293, 296 [168-169]
— population, 1962, p. 83 [48]
Bella Coola
— in Canada, p. 1430 [996]
— language in 1910 and 1930, p. 199 [114]
— population, 1910, p. 77 [45]
Bellingham, WA
— firm ownership, p. 1002 [631]
— population, p. 247 [147]
Beltrami County
— characteristics of families, pp. 469, 472 [245-246]
— geographic mobility, pp. 432, 436, 440, 444 [232-235]
— methods of health care, pp. 736, 739 [472-473]
— school enrollment, pp. 527, 531, 535, 539 [287-290]
Bemidji Area
— hospitals, p. 753 [487]
Benewah County
— characteristics of families, p. 465 [243]
— geographic mobility, pp. 424, 427 [230-231]
— methods of health care, p. 732 [470]
— school enrollment, pp. 519, 522 [285-286]
Benson County
— characteristics of families, p. 467 [244]
— geographic mobility, pp. 430, 434 [232-233]
— methods of health care, p. 734 [471]
— school enrollment, pp. 525, 529 [287-288]
Benton Harbor, MI
— population, p. 247 [147]
Benton Paiute Reservation, CA
— acreage, tribal land, and population, p. 1033 [657]
— characteristics of families, p. 464 [243]
— electric lighting in housing units, p. 889 [567]
— elementary school enrollment, p. 560 [302]
— energy assistance, p. 821 [538]
— exterior wall materials in housing units, p. 895 [570]
— floor materials, p. 902 [573]
— geographic mobility, pp. 422, 426 [230-231]
— heating equipment, p. 910 [576]
— high school enrollment, p. 567 [305]
— household characteristics, pp. 828, 831 [541-542]
— kitchen facilities, p. 916 [579]
— methods of health care, p. 731 [470]
— nursery and kindergarten enrollment, p. 553 [297]
— piped water, pp. 922, 924 [582-583]
— plumbing facilities, pp. 922, 924 [582-583]
— population, pp. 258, 307, 310 [152, 174-175]
— school enrollment, pp. 517, 521 [285-286]
— sewage disposal, p. 934 [588]
— source of water, p. 934 [588]
— telephones in housing units, p. 889 [567]
— traditional occupations, pp. 650, 652 [391-392]
— years of school completed, pp. 491, 497, 503 [268, 271, 274]
Bering Straits Native Corp.
— household characteristics, pp. 886, 888 [565-566]

Bering Straits Native Corp. continued:
— population, pp. 291-292 [166-167]
Bernalillo County
— characteristics of families, pp. 464, 468-469, 473 [243-246]
— geographic mobility, pp. 423, 427, 431-432, 435-436, 446, 451 [230-233, 236-237]
— methods of health care, pp. 731, 735-736, 740 [470, 472, 474]
— school enrollment, pp. 518, 522, 526-527, 530-531, 541, 546 [285-288, 291-292]
Berry Creek Rancheria, CA
— acreage, tribal land, and population, p. 1034 [657]
— characteristics of families, p. 464 [243]
— electric lighting in housing units, p. 889 [567]
— elementary school enrollment, p. 560 [302]
— energy assistance, pp. 816, 820 [537-538]
— exterior wall materials in housing units, p. 895 [570]
— floor materials, p. 902 [573]
— geographic mobility, pp. 422, 426 [230-231]
— heating equipment, p. 910 [576]
— high school enrollment, p. 567 [305]
— household characteristics, pp. 828, 831 [541-542]
— kitchen facilities, p. 916 [579]
— land area, p. 89 [51]
— methods of health care, p. 731 [470]
— nursery and kindergarten enrollment, p. 553 [297]
— piped water, pp. 922, 924 [582-583]
— plumbing facilities, pp. 922, 924 [582-583]
— population, pp. 258, 307, 310 [152, 174-175]
— population, 1962, p. 89 [51]
— school enrollment, pp. 517, 521 [285-286]
— sewage disposal, p. 934 [588]
— source of water, p. 934 [588]
— telephones in housing units, p. 889 [567]
— traditional occupations, pp. 650, 652 [391-392]
— years of school completed, pp. 491, 497, 503 [268, 271, 274]
Bethel Area Field Office
— household characteristics, pp. 875, 877 [561-562]
— land area, p. 84 [48]
— population, pp. 293, 296 [168-169]
— population, 1962, p. 84 [48]
BIA
See also: Bureau of Indian Affairs
— dam safety, p. 1079 [709]
— employment, p. 215 [122]
— land management, pp. 1052 [673-674]
— and land tract ownership, pp. 1043, 1046-1051 [660, 665-672]
— and land tract ownership records, pp. 1044-1045 [662-663]
— land tract records on selected reservations, p. 1045 [664]
— schools, minimum staffing, p. 601 [346]
— staffing of dormitories, p. 600 [345]
Bidui
— population, 1690-1890 in Texas, p. 18 [22]
Big Bend Rancheria, CA
— acreage, tribal land, and population, p. 1034 [657]
— characteristics of families, p. 464 [243]
— electric lighting in housing units, p. 889 [567]
— elementary school enrollment, p. 560 [302]
— exterior wall materials in housing units, p. 895 [570]
— floor materials, p. 902 [573]

Numbers following p. or pp. are page references. Numbers in [ ] are table references. BIA stands for Bureau of Indian Affairs; IHS stands for Indian Health Service.

1477

Big Bend Rancheria, CA continued:
— geographic mobility, pp. 422, 426 [230-231]
— heating equipment, p. 910 [576]
— high school enrollment, p. 567 [305]
— household characteristics, pp. 828, 831 [541-542]
— kitchen facilities, p. 916 [579]
— land area, p. 89 [51]
— methods of health care, p. 731 [470]
— nursery and kindergarten enrollment, p. 553 [297]
— piped water, pp. 922, 924 [582-583]
— plumbing facilities, pp. 922, 924 [582-583]
— population, pp. 258, 307, 310 [152, 174-175]
— population, 1962, p. 89 [51]
— school enrollment, pp. 517, 521 [285-286]
— sewage disposal, p. 934 [588]
— source of water, p. 934 [588]
— telephones in housing units, p. 889 [567]
— traditional occupations, pp. 650, 652 [391-392]
— years of school completed, pp. 491, 497, 503 [268, 271, 274]

Big Cypress Reservation, FL
— acreage, tribal land, and population, p. 1036 [657]
— characteristics of families, p. 464 [243]
— electric lighting in housing units, p. 890 [567]
— elementary school enrollment, p. 560 [302]
— exterior wall materials in housing units, p. 895 [570]
— floor materials, p. 902 [573]
— geographic mobility, pp. 422, 426 [230-231]
— heating equipment, p. 910 [576]
— high school enrollment, p. 567 [305]
— household characteristics, pp. 828, 831 [541-542]
— kitchen facilities, p. 916 [579]
— land area, p. 93 [53]
— methods of health care, p. 731 [470]
— nursery and kindergarten enrollment, p. 553 [297]
— piped water, pp. 922, 924 [582-583]
— plumbing facilities, pp. 922, 924 [582-583]
— population, pp. 258, 307, 310 [152, 174-175]
— population, 1962, p. 93 [53]
— school enrollment, pp. 517, 521 [285-286]
— sewage disposal, p. 934 [588]
— source of water, p. 934 [588]
— telephones in housing units, p. 890 [567]
— traditional occupations, pp. 650, 652 [391-392]
— years of school completed, pp. 491, 497, 503 [268, 271, 274]

Big Horn County
— characteristics of families, pp. 465, 471, 477 [243, 245, 247]
— geographic mobility, pp. 424, 428, 438, 442, 450, 455 [230-231, 234-237]
— methods of health care, pp. 732, 738, 744 [470, 473, 475]
— school enrollment, pp. 519, 523, 533, 537, 545, 550 [285-286, 289-292]

Big Lagoon Rancheria, CA
— acreage, tribal land, and population, p. 1034 [657]
— characteristics of families, p. 464 [243]
— electric lighting in housing units, p. 890 [567]
— elementary school enrollment, p. 560 [302]
— energy assistance, p. 820 [538]
— exterior wall materials in housing units, p. 896 [570]
— floor materials, p. 902 [573]

Big Lagoon Rancheria, CA continued:
— geographic mobility, pp. 422, 426 [230-231]
— heating equipment, p. 911 [576]
— high school enrollment, p. 568 [305]
— household characteristics, pp. 828, 831 [541-542]
— kitchen facilities, p. 916 [579]
— land area, p. 91 [52]
— methods of health care, p. 731 [470]
— nursery and kindergarten enrollment, p. 553 [297]
— piped water, pp. 922, 924 [582-583]
— plumbing facilities, pp. 922, 924 [582-583]
— population, pp. 258, 307, 310 [152, 174-175]
— population, 1962, p. 91 [52]
— school enrollment, pp. 517, 521 [285-286]
— sewage disposal, p. 934 [588]
— source of water, p. 934 [588]
— telephones in housing units, p. 890 [567]
— traditional occupations, pp. 650, 652 [391-392]
— years of school completed, pp. 491, 497, 503 [268, 271, 274]

Big Pine Rancheria, CA
— acreage, tribal land, and population, p. 1034 [657]
— characteristics of families, p. 464 [243]
— electric lighting in housing units, p. 890 [567]
— elementary school enrollment, p. 560 [302]
— energy assistance, p. 820 [538]
— exterior wall materials in housing units, p. 896 [570]
— floor materials, p. 902 [573]
— geographic mobility, pp. 422, 426 [230-231]
— heating equipment, p. 911 [576]
— high school enrollment, p. 568 [305]
— household characteristics, pp. 828, 831 [541-542]
— kitchen facilities, p. 917 [579]
— land area, p. 89 [51]
— methods of health care, p. 731 [470]
— nursery and kindergarten enrollment, p. 553 [297]
— piped water, pp. 922, 924 [582-583]
— plumbing facilities, pp. 922, 924 [582-583]
— population, pp. 258, 307, 310 [152, 174-175]
— population, 1962, p. 89 [51]
— school enrollment, pp. 517, 521 [285-286]
— sewage disposal, p. 934 [588]
— source of water, p. 934 [588]
— telephones in housing units, p. 890 [567]
— traditional occupations, pp. 650, 652 [391-392]
— years of school completed, pp. 491, 497, 503 [268, 271, 274]

Big Sandy Rancheria, CA
— acreage, tribal land, and population, p. 1034 [657]
— energy assistance, p. 820 [538]
— household characteristics, pp. 828, 831 [541-542]
— land area, pp. 88-89 [50-51]
— land trusteeship termination, p. 220 [126]
— population, pp. 307, 310 [174-175]
— population, 1962, pp. 88-89 [50-51]

Big Valley Rancheria, CA
— acreage, tribal land, and population, p. 1034 [657]
— energy assistance, p. 820 [538]
— household characteristics, pp. 828, 831 [541-542]
— land area, p. 89 [51]
— land trusteeship termination, p. 220 [126]

Numbers following p. or pp. are page references. Numbers in [ ] are table references. BIA stands for Bureau of Indian Affairs; IHS stands for Indian Health Service.

Numbers following p. or pp. are page references. Numbers in [ ] are table references. BIA stands for Bureau of Indian Affairs; IHS stands for Indian Health Service.

Numbers following p. or pp. are page references. Numbers in [ ] are table references. BIA stands for Bureau of Indian Affairs; IHS stands for Indian Health Service.

Numbers following p. or pp. are page references. Numbers in [ ] are table references. BIA stands for Bureau of Indian Affairs; IHS stands for Indian Health Service.

Numbers following p. or pp. are page references. Numbers in [ ] are table references. BIA stands for Bureau of Indian Affairs; IHS stands for Indian Health Service.

Cahto
— fertility characteristics, p. 672 [406]
— population, p. 270 [157]
— population, Mountain region, p. 393 [214]
— population, North Central region, p. 346 [194]
— population, Northeast region, p. 358 [199]
— population, Pacific region, p. 396 [215]
— population, South Atlantic region, p. 369 [204]
— population, South Central region, p. 371 [205]

Cahuilla
— employment, pp. 772, 774, 779, 781 [507-508, 511-512]
— energy assistance, p. 821 [538]
— family characteristics, p. 458 [239]
— household characteristics, pp. 456, 458 [238-239]
— labor force characteristics, p. 767 [504]
— language spoken at home, pp. 643, 648 [387, 390]
— population, pp. 273, 276, 284 [158-159, 163]
— population from pre-history to 1980, p. 104 [60]
— population, Mountain region, p. 393 [214]
— population, North Central region, p. 346 [194]
— population, Northeast region, p. 358 [199]
— population, Pacific region, pp. 395-396 [215]
— population, South Atlantic region, p. 369 [204]
— population, South Central region, p. 371 [205]
— urban and rural population, p. 240 [142]
— veterans, p. 1105 [734]
— years of school completed, p. 509 [277]

Cahuilla Reservation, CA
— acreage, tribal land, and population, p. 1034 [657]
— characteristics of families, p. 464 [243]
— electric lighting in housing units, p. 890 [567]
— elementary school enrollment, p. 560 [302]
— exterior wall materials in housing units, p. 896 [570]
— floor materials, p. 903 [573]
— geographic mobility, pp. 423, 427 [230-231]
— heating equipment, p. 911 [576]
— high school enrollment, p. 568 [305]
— household characteristics, pp. 829, 832 [541-542]
— kitchen facilities, p. 917 [579]
— methods of health care, p. 731 [470]
— nursery and kindergarten enrollment, p. 553 [297]
— piped water, pp. 922, 924 [582-583]
— plumbing facilities, pp. 922, 924 [582-583]
— population, pp. 260, 308, 311 [153, 174-175]
— school enrollment, pp. 518, 522 [285-286]
— sewage disposal, p. 934 [588]
— source of water, p. 934 [588]
— telephones in housing units, p. 890 [567]
— traditional occupations, pp. 650, 652 [391-392]
— years of school completed, pp. 491, 497, 503 [268, 271, 274]

Calaveras County
— geographic mobility, pp. 447, 452 [236-237]
— methods of health care, p. 740 [474]
— school enrollment, pp. 542, 547 [291-292]

Calculus
— in high school, p. 573 [308]

Calhoun County
— characteristics of families, p. 472 [246]
— geographic mobility, pp. 439, 443 [234-235]

Calhoun County continued:
— methods of health care, p. 738 [473]
— school enrollment, pp. 534, 538 [289-290]

California
— adults on probation, p. 1139 [763]
— alcohol treatment programs, p. 721 [458]
— capital punishment, p. 1136 [762]
— characteristics of families, pp. 465, 467 [243-244]
— cigarettes and tax exemptions, p. 1031 [656]
— drug treatment programs, p. 726 [464]
— education personnel recruitment, p. 638 [384]
— energy assistance, pp. 816, 820 [537-538]
— European contact and population, p. 4 [7]
— full-blood Indians in 1910, pp. 114, 119-120, 122-123, 125, 131, 133-134 [75, 77-79, 81-82]
— full/mixed blood population, 1910 and 1930, p. 11 [14]
— geographic mobility, pp. 424, 428, 430, 434 [230-233]
— higher education enrollment, p. 604 [349]
— household characteristics, pp. 829, 833, 835, 838 [541-544]
— Indian and White mixed bloods in 1910, pp. 134, 138 [83, 85]
— Indian lands, pp. 1053, 1056 [675-676]
— Indian population, p. 255 [151]
— Indian population from pre-European to 1980, p. 105 [61]
— Indian Trust Lands, p. 1060 [682]
— inmates, p. 1140 [764]
— land area, pp. 81, 89-91 [47, 51-52]
— land trusteeship termination, pp. 217, 220 [125-126]
— languages spoken, p. 642 [386]
— literacy rates in 1900-1930, p. 171 [101]
— marital status in 1910 and 1930, p. 201 [116]
— methods of health care, pp. 732, 734 [470-471]
— mineral leases, pp. 1028, 1030 [651, 655]
— mineral revenues, p. 1019 [650]
— minority-owned firms, p. 987 [624]
— mixed-blood Indians in 1910, pp. 114, 119-120, 122-123, 134 [75, 77-78, 83]
— mixed-tribal blood Indians in 1910, pp. 125, 131, 133-134 [79, 81-82]
— Native-owned firms, p. 996 [629]
— population, pp. 4, 81, 225, 235, 237, 309, 312, 314, 316 [6, 47, 129, 139-140, 174-177]
— population, 1890-1910, p. 14 [18]
— population, 1890-1930, p. 17 [20]
— population, 1900-1980, p. 417 [224]
— population, 1910, pp. 53-54 [36-37]
— population, 1910-1930, pp. 28-30, 32-44, 46-48, 50-51 [27-35]
— population, 1910, per 100 square miles, p. 15 [19]
— population, 1962, pp. 89-91 [51-52]
— population distribution in 1910 and 1930, p. 10 [13]
— population, prehistory to 1900, p. 18 [21]
— public school enrollment, pp. 558-559 [300-301]
— rancherias' restoration of federal recognition, p. 215 [123]
— school attendance in 1910, pp. 143, 146, 149, 152-153, 157 [89-94]
— school enrollment, pp. 519, 523, 525, 529 [285-288]
— toxic waste sites, p. 1092 [720]
— urban and rural population, 1930, p. 239 [141]
— urban population, p. 244 [144]
— use of VA hospitals, p. 762 [500]

Numbers following p. or pp. are page references. Numbers in [ ] are table references. BIA stands for Bureau of Indian Affairs; IHS stands for Indian Health Service.

Numbers following p. or pp. are page references. Numbers in [ ] are table references. BIA stands for Bureau of Indian Affairs; IHS stands for Indian Health Service.

Numbers following p. or pp. are page references. Numbers in [ ] are table references. BIA stands for Bureau of Indian Affairs; IHS stands for Indian Health Service.

Numbers following p. or pp. are page references. Numbers in [ ] are table references. BIA stands for Bureau of Indian Affairs; IHS stands for Indian Health Service.

1488

Numbers following p. or pp. are page references. Numbers in [ ] are table references. BIA stands for Bureau of Indian Affairs; IHS stands for Indian Health Service.

1489

Numbers following p. or pp. are page references. Numbers in [ ] are table references. BIA stands for Bureau of Indian Affairs; IHS stands for Indian Health Service.

Numbers following p. or pp. are page references. Numbers in [ ] are table references. BIA stands for Bureau of Indian Affairs; IHS stands for Indian Health Service.

Numbers following p. or pp. are page references. Numbers in [ ] are table references. BIA stands for Bureau of Indian Affairs; IHS stands for Indian Health Service.

Numbers following p. or pp. are page references. Numbers in [ ] are table references. BIA stands for Bureau of Indian Affairs; IHS stands for Indian Health Service.

Numbers following p. or pp. are page references. Numbers in [ ] are table references. BIA stands for Bureau of Indian Affairs; IHS stands for Indian Health Service.

1496

Numbers following p. or pp. are page references. Numbers in [ ] are table references. BIA stands for Bureau of Indian Affairs; IHS stands for Indian Health Service.

1497

Colorado continued:
— household characteristics, pp. 862, 865 [553-554]
— Indian and White mixed bloods in 1910, p. 134 [83]
— Indian lands, pp. 1053-1054 [675-676]
— Indian population, p. 255 [151]
— Indian Trust Lands, p. 1060 [683]
— inmates, p. 1140 [764]
— land area, pp. 81, 93 [47, 53]
— methods of health care, p. 742 [475]
— mineral leases, pp. 1026-1027, 1029 [651, 654]
— mineral revenues, p. 1019 [650]
— minority-owned firms, p. 987 [624]
— mixed-blood Indians in 1910, pp. 114, 120, 134 [75, 77, 83]
— mixed-tribal blood Indians in 1910, pp. 125, 131 [79, 81]
— Native-owned firms, p. 996 [629]
— population, pp. 81, 224, 236, 336, 338 [47, 129, 140, 186-187]
— population, 1890-1910, p. 14 [18]
— population, 1890-1930, p. 17 [20]
— population, 1900-1980, p. 417 [224]
— population, 1910, p. 55 [37]
— population, 1910-1930, pp. 28-32, 34-35, 37, 42, 44-45, 49, 51 [27-32, 34-35]
— population, 1910, per 100 square miles, p. 15 [19]
— population, 1962, p. 93 [53]
— school attendance in 1910, pp. 150, 157 [91, 94]
— school enrollment, pp. 544, 549 [291-292]
— urban and rural population, 1930, p. 239 [141]
— urban population, p. 244 [144]
Colorado River
— characteristics of families, p. 465 [243]
— employment, pp. 772, 774, 780, 782 [507-508, 511-512]
— energy assistance, pp. 815, 819 [537-538]
— family characteristics, p. 458 [239]
— fertility characteristics, p. 674 [407]
— household characteristics, pp. 456, 458 [238-239]
— labor force characteristics, p. 768 [504]
— land area, pp. 88-89, 96 [50-51, 55]
— language spoken at home, pp. 643, 648 [387, 390]
— population, p. 261 [153]
— population, 1962, pp. 88-89, 96 [50-51, 55]
— population, Mountain region, p. 398 [216]
— population, North Central region, p. 348 [195]
— population, Northeast region, p. 360 [200]
— population, Pacific region, p. 400 [217]
— population, South Atlantic region, p. 373 [206]
— population, South Central region, p. 376 [207]
— urban and rural population, p. 240 [142]
— veterans, p. 1105 [734]
— years of school completed, p. 509 [277]
Colorado River Off Reservation Lands
— land area, p. 88 [50]
— population, 1962, p. 88 [50]
Colorado River Reservation, AZ-CA
— acreage, tribal land, and population, p. 1033 [657]
— electric lighting in housing units, p. 890 [567]
— elementary school enrollment, p. 560 [302]
— exterior wall materials in housing units, p. 896 [570]
— floor materials, p. 903 [573]
— geographic mobility, pp. 424, 427 [230-231]

Colorado River Reservation, AZ-CA continued:
— heating equipment, p. 911 [576]
— high school enrollment, p. 568 [305]
— household characteristics, pp. 829, 833 [541-542]
— kitchen facilities, p. 917 [579]
— land area, pp. 88-89 [50-51]
— methods of health care, p. 732 [470]
— nursery and kindergarten enrollment, p. 553 [297]
— piped water, pp. 922, 924 [582-583]
— plumbing facilities, pp. 922, 924 [582-583]
— population, pp. 261, 309, 312 [153, 174-175]
— population, 1962, pp. 88-89 [50-51]
— school enrollment, pp. 519, 522 [285-286]
— sewage disposal, p. 934 [588]
— source of water, p. 934 [588]
— telephones in housing units, p. 890 [567]
— traditional occupations, pp. 650, 652 [391-392]
— years of school completed, pp. 491, 497, 503 [268, 271, 274]
Colorado Springs, CO
— population, p. 248 [147]
Columbia, pp. 1334, 1337 [943-944]
— ability to speak English in 1910, p. 187 [111]
— full-blood Indians in 1910, pp. 119, 130 [77, 81]
— illiteracy in 1910, p. 165 [98]
— language in 1910 and 1930, p. 196 [114]
— marital status in 1910, pp. 206, 211 [118, 120]
— mixed-blood Indians in 1910, p. 119 [77]
— mixed-tribal blood Indians in 1910, p. 130 [81]
— population, 1910, pp. 70, 77 [42, 45]
— school attendance in 1910, p. 147 [91]
Columbia, MO
— population, p. 248 [147]
Columbia, SC
— population, p. 248 [147]
Columbia Region
— European contact and population, p. 4 [7]
— population, p. 4 [6]
Columbia River Chinook
— fertility characteristics, p. 673 [406]
— population, Mountain region, p. 394 [214]
— population, North Central region, p. 347 [194]
— population, Northeast region, p. 359 [199]
— population, Pacific region, p. 397 [215]
— population, South Atlantic region, p. 370 [204]
— population, South Central region, p. 372 [205]
Columbia Wenatchee
— fertility characteristics, p. 677 [408]
— population, by region, p. 406 [219]
— population, Mountain region, p. 403 [218]
— population, North Central region, p. 351 [196]
— population, Northeast region, p. 363 [201]
— population, South Atlantic region, p. 379 [208]
— population, South Central region, p. 382 [209]
Columbus, GA-AL
— population, p. 248 [147]
Columbus, OH
— firm ownership, p. 1002 [631]
— population, pp. 228, 248 [133, 147]

Numbers following p. or pp. are page references. Numbers in [ ] are table references. BIA stands for Bureau of Indian Affairs; IHS stands for Indian Health Service.

1498

Numbers following p. or pp. are page references. Numbers in [ ] are table references. BIA stands for Bureau of Indian Affairs; IHS stands for Indian Health Service.

Numbers following p. or pp. are page references. Numbers in [ ] are table references. BIA stands for Bureau of Indian Affairs; IHS stands for Indian Health Service.

Numbers following p. or pp. are page references. Numbers in [ ] are table references. BIA stands for Bureau of Indian Affairs; IHS stands for Indian Health Service.

Cowlitz continued:
— population, Northeast region, p. 360 [200]
— population, Pacific region, p. 401 [217]
— population, South Atlantic region, p. 374 [206]
— population, South Central region, p. 376 [207]
— school attendance in 1910, p. 147 [91]
— urban and rural population, p. 240 [142]
— veterans, p. 1106 [734]
— years of school completed, p. 510 [277]

Coyote Valley Rancheria, CA
— acreage, tribal land, and population, p. 1034 [657]
— characteristics of families, p. 465 [243]
— electric lighting in housing units, p. 890 [567]
— elementary school enrollment, p. 560 [302]
— energy assistance, pp. 816, 820 [537-538]
— exterior wall materials in housing units, p. 896 [570]
— floor materials, p. 903 [573]
— geographic mobility, pp. 424, 428 [230-231]
— heating equipment, p. 911 [576]
— high school enrollment, p. 568 [305]
— household characteristics, pp. 834, 836 [543-544]
— kitchen facilities, p. 917 [579]
— land trusteeship termination, p. 217 [125]
— methods of health care, p. 732 [470]
— nursery and kindergarten enrollment, p. 553 [297]
— piped water, pp. 922, 924 [582-583]
— plumbing facilities, pp. 922, 924 [582-583]
— population, pp. 262, 312, 315 [154, 176-177]
— restoration of federal recognition, p. 215 [123]
— school enrollment, pp. 519, 523 [285-286]
— sewage disposal, p. 934 [588]
— source of water, p. 934 [588]
— telephones in housing units, p. 890 [567]
— traditional occupations, pp. 650, 652 [391-392]
— years of school completed, pp. 491, 497, 503 [268, 271, 274]

Coyotero Apache
— language in 1910 and 1930, p. 193 [113]
— population, 1910, p. 52 [36]

Crack cocaine
— use of, p. 486 [261]

Crafts and equipment operating
— in Alberta, pp. 1330, 1332 [941-942]
— in British Columbia, pp. 1334, 1337 [943-944]
— in Canada, pp. 1325, 1327 [939-940]
— in Manitoba, pp. 1339, 1341 [945-946]
— in New Brunswick, pp. 1344, 1346 [947-948]
— in Newfoundland, pp. 1348, 1351 [949-950]
— in Northwest Territories, pp. 1353, 1355 [951-952]
— in Nova Scotia, pp. 1358, 1360 [953-954]
— in Ontario, pp. 1362, 1365 [955-956]
— in Prince Edward Island, pp. 1367, 1369 [957-958]
— in Quebec, pp. 1372, 1374 [959-960]
— in Saskatchewan, pp. 1376, 1379 [961-962]
— in Yukon, pp. 1381, 1383 [963-964]

Craig
— household characteristics, pp. 876, 878 [561-562]
— land area, p. 83 [48]
— population, pp. 294, 297 [168-169]
— population, 1962, p. 83 [48]

Credit agencies
— minority-owned firms, p. 969 [618]
— Native-owned firms, p. 995 [628]

Cree
— ability to speak English in 1910, p. 184 [110]
— and Canadian treaties, p. 1432 [997]
— employment, pp. 772, 774, 780, 782 [507-508, 511-512]
— family characteristics, p. 458 [239]
— fertility characteristics, p. 674 [407]
— full-blood Indians in 1910, pp. 115, 126 [76, 80]
— household characteristics, pp. 456, 458 [238-239]
— illiteracy in 1910, p. 161 [97]
— Indian and White mixed bloods in 1910, p. 135 [84]
— Indian reserves, p. 1450 [1005]
— labor force characteristics, p. 768 [504]
— language, pp. 1265 [880-881]
— language in 1910 and 1930, p. 199 [114]
— language spoken at home, pp. 643, 648 [387, 390]
— marital status in 1910, pp. 203, 209 [118, 120]
— mixed-blood Indians in 1910, p. 115 [76]
— mixed-tribal blood Indians in 1910, p. 126 [80]
— population, pp. 259, 264-265, 279 [152, 154-155, 161]
— population, 1910, pp. 57-58, 61-62, 67, 70, 78 [38-42, 45]
— population, 1962, p. 94 [54]
— population, 1990, p. 234 [138]
— population, Mountain region, p. 398 [216]
— population, North Central region, p. 348 [195]
— population, Northeast region, p. 360 [200]
— population, Pacific region, p. 401 [217]
— population, South Atlantic region, p. 374 [206]
— population, South Central region, p. 376 [207]
— school attendance in 1910, p. 142 [89]
— urban and rural population, p. 240 [142]
— veterans, p. 1106 [734]
— years of school completed, p. 510 [277]

Creek
— ability to speak English in 1910, p. 187 [111]
— employment, pp. 772, 774, 780, 782 [507-508, 511-512]
— enrollment in 1930, pp. 158, 160 [95-96]
— family characteristics, p. 458 [239]
— fertility characteristics, p. 674 [407]
— full-blood Indians in 1910, pp. 118, 129 [77, 81]
— hospitals, p. 762 [499]
— household characteristics, pp. 457-458, 873-874 [238-239, 559-560]
— illiteracy in 1910, p. 164 [98]
— Indian and White mixed bloods in 1910, p. 137 [84]
— labor force characteristics, p. 768 [504]
— land area, p. 100 [57]
— language in 1910 and 1930, pp. 193, 195 [113]
— language spoken at home, pp. 643, 648 [387, 390]
— marital status in 1910, pp. 205, 211 [118, 120]
— marital status in 1910 and 1930, p. 202 [117]
— mixed-blood Indians in 1910, p. 118 [77]
— mixed-tribal blood Indians in 1910, p. 129 [81]
— population, pp. 273, 275, 344-345 [158-159, 192-193]
— population, 1910, pp. 52-53, 56, 58, 61-64, 66-68, 70, 75-76 [36-42, 44]
— population, 1910-1930, p. 38 [30]
— population, 1962, pp. 99-100 [57]

Numbers following p. or pp. are page references. Numbers in [ ] are table references. BIA stands for Bureau of Indian Affairs; IHS stands for Indian Health Service.

1502

Numbers following p. or pp. are page references. Numbers in [ ] are table references. BIA stands for Bureau of Indian Affairs; IHS stands for Indian Health Service.

Numbers following p. or pp. are page references. Numbers in [ ] are table references. BIA stands for Bureau of Indian Affairs; IHS stands for Indian Health Service.

1505

Numbers following p. or pp. are page references. Numbers in [ ] are table references. BIA stands for Bureau of Indian Affairs; IHS stands for Indian Health Service.

1506

Numbers following p. or pp. are page references. Numbers in [ ] are table references. BIA stands for Bureau of Indian Affairs; IHS stands for Indian Health Service.

Numbers following p. or pp. are page references. Numbers in [ ] are table references. BIA stands for Bureau of Indian Affairs; IHS stands for Indian Health Service.

Numbers following p. or pp. are page references. Numbers in [ ] are table references. BIA stands for Bureau of Indian Affairs; IHS stands for Indian Health Service.

Numbers following p. or pp. are page references. Numbers in [ ] are table references. BIA stands for Bureau of Indian Affairs; IHS stands for Indian Health Service.

Numbers following p. or pp. are page references. Numbers in [ ] are table references. BIA stands for Bureau of Indian Affairs; IHS stands for Indian Health Service.

1512

Numbers following p. or pp. are page references. Numbers in [ ] are table references. BIA stands for Bureau of Indian Affairs; IHS stands for Indian Health Service.

1513

Numbers following p. or pp. are page references. Numbers in [ ] are table references. BIA stands for Bureau of Indian Affairs; IHS stands for Indian Health Service.

Numbers following p. or pp. are page references. Numbers in [ ] are table references. BIA stands for Bureau of Indian Affairs; IHS stands for Indian Health Service.

Numbers following p. or pp. are page references. Numbers in [ ] are table references. BIA stands for Bureau of Indian Affairs; IHS stands for Indian Health Service.

Fort McDermitt Reservation, NV-OR continued:
— nursery and kindergarten enrollment, p. 554 [297]
— piped water, pp. 923, 925 [582-583]
— plumbing facilities, pp. 923, 925 [582-583]
— population, pp. 265, 313, 316 [155, 176-177]
— population, 1962, pp. 96, 101 [55, 57]
— school enrollment, pp. 525, 529 [287-288]
— sewage disposal, p. 935 [588]
— source of water, p. 935 [588]
— telephones in housing units, p. 890 [567]
— traditional occupations, pp. 651, 653 [391-392]
— years of school completed, pp. 492, 498, 504 [268, 271, 274]
Fort McDowell Reservation, AZ
— acreage, tribal land, and population, p. 1033 [657]
— characteristics of families, p. 467 [244]
— electric lighting in housing units, p. 890 [567]
— elementary school enrollment, p. 561 [302]
— exterior wall materials in housing units, p. 897 [570]
— floor materials, p. 904 [573]
— geographic mobility, pp. 430, 434 [232-233]
— heating equipment, p. 912 [576]
— high school enrollment, p. 569 [305]
— household characteristics, pp. 835, 838 [543-544]
— kitchen facilities, p. 917 [579]
— land area, p. 88 [50]
— methods of health care, p. 734 [471]
— nursery and kindergarten enrollment, p. 554 [297]
— piped water, pp. 923, 925 [582-583]
— plumbing facilities, pp. 923, 925 [582-583]
— population, pp. 265, 313, 316 [155, 176-177]
— population, 1962, p. 88 [50]
— school enrollment, pp. 525, 529 [287-288]
— sewage disposal, p. 935 [588]
— source of water, p. 935 [588]
— telephones in housing units, p. 890 [567]
— traditional occupations, pp. 651, 653 [391-392]
— years of school completed, pp. 492, 498, 504 [268, 271, 274]
Fort McMurray District
— Indian reserves, p. 1436 [999]
Fort McPherson Band
— reserves and acreage, p. 1446 [1003]
Fort Mohave Reservation, AZ-CA-NV
— land area, pp. 88-89, 96 [50-51, 55]
— population, 1962, pp. 88-89, 96 [50-51, 55]
Fort Mojave
— characteristics of families, p. 467 [244]
— energy assistance, p. 820 [538]
Fort Mojave Reservation, AZ-CA-NV
— acreage, tribal land, and population, p. 1033 [657]
— electric lighting in housing units, p. 891 [567]
— elementary school enrollment, p. 561 [302]
— exterior wall materials in housing units, p. 897 [570]
— floor materials, p. 904 [573]
— geographic mobility, pp. 430, 434 [232-233]
— heating equipment, p. 912 [576]
— high school enrollment, p. 569 [305]
— household characteristics, pp. 835, 838 [543-544]
— kitchen facilities, p. 917 [579]
— methods of health care, p. 734 [471]

Fort Mojave Reservation, AZ-CA-NV continued:
— nursery and kindergarten enrollment, p. 554 [297]
— piped water, pp. 923, 925 [582-583]
— plumbing facilities, pp. 923, 925 [582-583]
— population, pp. 314, 316 [176-177]
— school enrollment, pp. 525, 529 [287-288]
— sewage disposal, p. 935 [588]
— source of water, p. 935 [588]
— telephones in housing units, p. 891 [567]
— traditional occupations, pp. 651, 653 [391-392]
— years of school completed, pp. 492, 498, 504 [268, 271, 274]
Fort Myers-Cape Coral, FL
— population, p. 249 [147]
Fort Norman Band
— reserves and acreage, p. 1446 [1003]
Fort Peck
— fertility characteristics, p. 681 [409]
— land area, pp. 95, 99 [54, 56]
— Northern Cheyenne Agencies, land area, p. 99 [56]
— Northern Cheyenne Agencies, population, 1962, p. 99 [56]
— population, pp. 254, 265 [150, 155]
— population, 1962, pp. 95, 99 [54, 56]
— population, Mountain region, p. 410 [220]
— population, North Central region, p. 354 [197]
— population, Northeast region, p. 366 [202]
— population, Pacific region, p. 413 [221]
— population, South Atlantic region, p. 385 [210]
— population, South Central region, p. 388 [211]
— tribal affiliation, p. 254 [150]
Fort Peck Reservation, MT
— acreage, tribal lands, and population, p. 1037 [658]
— characteristics of families, p. 467 [244]
— electric lighting in housing units, p. 891 [567]
— elementary school enrollment, p. 561 [302]
— energy assistance, pp. 817, 822 [537-538]
— exterior wall materials in housing units, p. 897 [570]
— floor materials, p. 904 [573]
— geographic mobility, pp. 430, 434 [232-233]
— heating equipment, p. 912 [576]
— high school enrollment, p. 569 [305]
— household characteristics, pp. 835, 838 [543-544]
— kitchen facilities, p. 917 [579]
— land tract ownership, p. 1043 [661]
— land tract ownership under BIA jurisdiction, p. 1043 [660]
— land tract records on selected reservations, p. 1045 [664]
— land tracts under BIA jurisdiction, pp. 1044-1052 [662-663, 665-674]
— methods of health care, p. 734 [471]
— nursery and kindergarten enrollment, p. 554 [297]
— piped water, pp. 923, 925 [582-583]
— plumbing facilities, pp. 923, 925 [582-583]
— population, pp. 265, 314, 316 [155, 176-177]
— school enrollment, pp. 525, 529 [287-288]
— sewage disposal, p. 935 [588]
— source of water, p. 935 [588]
— telephones in housing units, p. 891 [567]
— traditional occupations, pp. 651, 653 [391-392]
— years of school completed, pp. 492, 498, 504 [268, 271, 274]

Numbers following p. or pp. are page references. Numbers in [ ] are table references. BIA stands for Bureau of Indian Affairs; IHS stands for Indian Health Service.

1519

Numbers following p. or pp. are page references. Numbers in [ ] are table references. BIA stands for Bureau of Indian Affairs; IHS stands for Indian Health Service.

Numbers following p. or pp. are page references. Numbers in [ ] are table references. BIA stands for Bureau of Indian Affairs; IHS stands for Indian Health Service.

1521

Numbers following p. or pp. are page references. Numbers in [ ] are table references. BIA stands for Bureau of Indian Affairs; IHS stands for Indian Health Service.

1523

Grand Portage Reservation, MN continued:
— population, pp. 266, 314, 316 [155, 176-177]
— population, 1962, p. 94 [54]
— school enrollment, pp. 526, 530 [287-288]
— sewage disposal, p. 935 [588]
— source of water, p. 935 [588]
— telephones in housing units, p. 891 [567]
— traditional occupations, pp. 651, 653 [391-392]
— years of school completed, pp. 492, 498, 504 [268, 271, 274]

Grand Rapids, MI
— population, pp. 229, 249 [133, 147]

Grand Rhonde
— fertility characteristics, p. 683 [410]
— land trusteeship termination, p. 218 [125]
— population, Mountain region, p. 415 [222]
— population, North Central region, p. 356 [198]
— population, Northeast region, p. 368 [203]
— population, Pacific region, p. 417 [223]
— population, South Atlantic region, p. 390 [212]
— population, South Central region, p. 391 [213]

Grand River Ute
— population, 1910, p. 77 [45]

Grand Ronde Reservation, OR
— acreage, tribal lands, and population, p. 1038 [658]
— household characteristics, pp. 835, 839 [543-544]
— population, pp. 314, 316 [176-177]

Grand Traverse Reservation, MI
— acreage, tribal land, and population, p. 1036 [657]
— adult education, p. 639 [385]
— energy assistance, pp. 816, 822 [537-538]
— household characteristics, pp. 835, 839 [543-544]
— population, pp. 314, 316 [176-177]

Grant County
— characteristics of families, p. 474 [246]
— geographic mobility, pp. 447, 452 [236-237]
— methods of health care, p. 741 [474]
— school enrollment, pp. 542, 547 [291-292]

Grants
— adult education, p. 639 [385]
— higher education, pp. 633-634 [379-380]

Grapes
— on Indian Trust Lands, pp. 1077-1078 [705-706]

Graton
— land area, p. 90 [51]
— land trusteeship termination, p. 220 [126]
— population, 1962, p. 90 [51]

Gravel
— mineral leases, p. 1026 [651]

Grayling
— household characteristics, pp. 879, 882 [563-564]
— population, pp. 294, 297 [168-169]

Grays Harbor County
— characteristics of families, pp. 465, 472 [243, 246]
— geographic mobility, pp. 423, 427, 440, 444 [230-231, 234-235]
— methods of health care, pp. 732, 739 [470, 473]
— school enrollment, pp. 518, 522, 535, 539 [285-286, 289-290]

Grazing
— on Indian Trust Lands, pp. 1058, 1077-1078 [678-679, 705-706]

Great Falls, MT
— population, p. 249 [147]

Great Lakes Agency
— land area, pp. 94, 104 [53-54, 59]
— population, 1962, pp. 94, 104 [53-54, 59]

Greeley, CO
— population, p. 249 [147]

Green Bay, WI
— population, p. 249 [147]

Greensboro-Winston-Salem-High Point, NC
— firm ownership, p. 1003 [631]
— population, pp. 229, 249 [133, 147]

Greenville Rancheria, CA
— acreage, tribal land, and population, p. 1034 [657]
— household characteristics, pp. 836, 839 [543-544]
— land area, p. 90 [51]
— land trusteeship termination, p. 220 [126]
— population, pp. 314, 317 [176-177]
— population, 1962, p. 90 [51]

Greenville-Spartanburg, SC
— population, pp. 229, 249 [133, 147]

Grindstone Creek
— land area, p. 90 [51]
— population, 1962, p. 90 [51]

Grindstone Creek Rancheria, CA
— acreage, tribal land, and population, p. 1034 [657]
— characteristics of families, p. 467 [244]
— electric lighting in housing units, p. 891 [567]
— elementary school enrollment, p. 561 [302]
— exterior wall materials in housing units, p. 897 [570]
— floor materials, p. 904 [573]
— geographic mobility, pp. 431, 435 [232-233]
— heating equipment, p. 912 [576]
— high school enrollment, p. 569 [305]
— household characteristics, pp. 836, 839 [543-544]
— kitchen facilities, p. 917 [579]
— methods of health care, p. 734 [471]
— nursery and kindergarten enrollment, p. 554 [297]
— piped water, pp. 923, 925 [582-583]
— plumbing facilities, pp. 923, 925 [582-583]
— population, pp. 267, 314, 317 [156, 176-177]
— school enrollment, pp. 526, 530 [287-288]
— sewage disposal, p. 935 [588]
— source of water, p. 935 [588]
— telephones in housing units, p. 891 [567]
— traditional occupations, pp. 651, 653 [391-392]
— years of school completed, pp. 492, 498, 504 [268, 271, 274]

Gros Ventres
— ability to speak English in 1910, p. 184 [110]
— employment, pp. 772, 775, 780, 782 [507-508, 511-512]
— enrollment in 1930, pp. 157, 159 [95-96]
— family characteristics, p. 459 [239]
— fertility characteristics, p. 675 [407]
— full-blood Indians in 1910, pp. 115, 126 [76, 80]
— household characteristics, pp. 457, 459 [238-239]
— illiteracy in 1910, p. 162 [97]
— Indian and White mixed bloods in 1910, p. 135 [84]
— labor force characteristics, p. 768 [504]
— language in 1910 and 1930, p. 193 [113]

Numbers following p. or pp. are page references. Numbers in [ ] are table references. BIA stands for Bureau of Indian Affairs; IHS stands for Indian Health Service.

1524

Numbers following p. or pp. are page references. Numbers in [ ] are table references. BIA stands for Bureau of Indian Affairs; IHS stands for Indian Health Service.

1525

Numbers following p. or pp. are page references. Numbers in [ ] are table references. BIA stands for Bureau of Indian Affairs; IHS stands for Indian Health Service.

Numbers following p. or pp. are page references. Numbers in [ ] are table references. BIA stands for Bureau of Indian Affairs; IHS stands for Indian Health Service.

Numbers following p. or pp. are page references. Numbers in [ ] are table references. BIA stands for Bureau of Indian Affairs; IHS stands for Indian Health Service.

Numbers following p. or pp. are page references. Numbers in [ ] are table references. BIA stands for Bureau of Indian Affairs; IHS stands for Indian Health Service.

Numbers following p. or pp. are page references. Numbers in [ ] are table references. BIA stands for Bureau of Indian Affairs; IHS stands for Indian Health Service.

Numbers following p. or pp. are page references. Numbers in [ ] are table references. BIA stands for Bureau of Indian Affairs; IHS stands for Indian Health Service.

1531

Numbers following p. or pp. are page references. Numbers in [ ] are table references. BIA stands for Bureau of Indian Affairs; IHS stands for Indian Health Service.

1532

Statistical Record of Native North Americans

Income

Index

Idaho continued:
— population, 1910, p. 57 [38]
— population, 1910-1930, pp. 28-29, 35, 37, 39-41, 45, 49-51 [27, 29-32, 34-35]
— population, 1910, per 100 square miles, p. 15 [19]
— population, 1962, p. 93 [55]
— population distribution in 1910 and 1930, p. 11 [13]
— school attendance in 1910, pp. 146-149, 156 [90-91, 94]
— school enrollment, pp. 519, 523, 533, 537 [285-286, 289-290]
— urban and rural population, 1930, p. 239 [141]
— urban population, p. 245 [144]

Igiugig
— household characteristics, pp. 879, 882 [563-564]
— population, pp. 295, 298 [168-169]

IHS (Indian Health Service)
See also: Indian Health Service
— accreditation of labs, pp. 750-751 [483-484]
— dental services, p. 707 [440]
— hospitalization causes, pp. 746 [477-478]
— hospitals, pp. 730, 751-752, 754 [469, 485-488]
— outpatient services, pp. 755, 757-759 [489, 492-494]
— public health nursing, p. 756 [491]
— service population, p. 747 [479]

Ikogmiut
— ability to speak English in 1910, p. 191 [112]
— Alaskan population, 1910, p. 21 [24]
— full-blood Indians in 1910, p. 123 [78]
— illiteracy in 1910, p. 169 [99]
— mixed-blood Indians in 1910, p. 123 [78]
— school attendance in 1910, p. 154 [93]

Iliamna
— household characteristics, pp. 879, 882 [563-564]
— population, pp. 295, 298 [168-169]

Illinois
— adults on probation, p. 1138 [763]
— alcohol treatment programs, p. 721 [458]
— capital punishment, p. 1137 [762]
— cigarettes and tax exemptions, p. 1031 [656]
— drug treatment programs, p. 726 [464]
— higher education enrollment, p. 604 [349]
— Indian population, p. 256 [151]
— inmates, p. 1140 [764]
— minority-owned firms, p. 974 [621]
— Native-owned firms, p. 997 [629]
— population, pp. 224, 236 [129, 140]
— population, 1890-1930, p. 16 [20]
— population, 1900-1980, p. 417 [224]
— population, 1910, p. 57 [38]
— population, 1910-1930, pp. 29-32, 34-35, 44-46, 49-51 [27-29, 32-35]
— public school enrollment, pp. 558-559 [300-301]
— school attendance in 1910, p. 156 [94]
— urban and rural population, 1930, p. 238 [141]
— urban population, p. 244 [144]

Illinois Indians
— population, 1670-1980, p. 108 [65]

Illiteracy
— 1900-1930, p. 172 [102]
— in 1910, pp. 161, 164, 167, 170, 184, 187, 190 [97-100, 110-112]
— in 1910-1930, p. 171 [101]

Imaklimiut
— Alaskan population, 1910, p. 21 [24]

Imperial County
— characteristics of families, pp. 467, 475 [244, 247]
— geographic mobility, pp. 430, 434, 448, 453 [232-233, 236-237]
— methods of health care, pp. 734, 742 [471, 475]
— school enrollment, pp. 525, 529, 543, 548 [287-288, 291-292]

Inaja & Cosmit
— population, 1962, p. 92 [52]

Inaja Band of Mission Indians
— energy assistance, p. 821 [538]

Inaja-Cosmit Reservation, CA
— acreage, tribal land, and population, p. 1034 [657]
— characteristics of families, p. 468 [244]
— electric lighting in housing units, p. 891 [567]
— elementary school enrollment, p. 561 [302]
— exterior wall materials in housing units, p. 897 [570]
— floor materials, p. 904 [573]
— geographic mobility, pp. 431, 435 [232-233]
— heating equipment, p. 912 [576]
— high school enrollment, p. 569 [305]
— household characteristics, pp. 840, 843 [545-546]
— kitchen facilities, p. 918 [579]
— land area, p. 92 [52]
— methods of health care, p. 735 [471]
— nursery and kindergarten enrollment, p. 554 [297]
— piped water, pp. 923, 925 [582-583]
— plumbing facilities, pp. 923, 925 [582-583]
— population, pp. 268, 318, 320 [156, 178-179]
— school enrollment, pp. 526, 530 [287-288]
— sewage disposal, p. 935 [588]
— source of water, p. 935 [588]
— telephones in housing units, p. 891 [567]
— traditional occupations, pp. 651, 653 [391-392]
— years of school completed, pp. 492, 498, 504 [268, 271, 274]

Inalik
— household characteristics, pp. 879, 882 [563-564]
— population, pp. 295, 298 [168-169]

Incineration
— on reservations, p. 1091 [719]

Income
— Alberta, pp. 1392-1393 [970-971]
— bingo revenues, pp. 1011, 1014 [637, 642]
— blackjack revenues, p. 1014 [641]
— British Columbia, pp. 1395-1396 [972-973]
— Canada, pp. 1386, 1388, 1390 [965, 968-969]
— and educational progress, p. 516 [284]
— employment and income, p. 1098 [727]
— gaming revenues, pp. 1014 [641-642]
— government employees, pp. 1095-1097, 1101 [723-726, 731]
— individuals in Canada, p. 1387 [966]
— local government, pp. 811, 1100-1102 [532, 729-730, 732]
— Manitoba, pp. 1398-1399 [974-975]
— and mortgage approval, p. 939 [591]
— New Brunswick, pp. 1401-1402 [976-977]
— Newfoundland, pp. 1404-1405 [978-979]
— Northwest Territories, pp. 1407-1408 [980-981]
— Nova Scotia, pp. 1410-1411 [982-983]
— Ontario, pp. 1413-1414 [984-985]

Numbers following p. or pp. are page references. Numbers in [ ] are table references. BIA stands for Bureau of Indian Affairs; IHS stands for Indian Health Service.

1533

Numbers following p. or pp. are page references. Numbers in [ ] are table references. BIA stands for Bureau of Indian Affairs; IHS stands for Indian Health Service.

Numbers following p. or pp. are page references. Numbers in [ ] are table references. BIA stands for Bureau of Indian Affairs; IHS stands for Indian Health Service.

Numbers following p. or pp. are page references. Numbers in [ ] are table references. BIA stands for Bureau of Indian Affairs; IHS stands for Indian Health Service.

Numbers following p. or pp. are page references. Numbers in [ ] are table references. BIA stands for Bureau of Indian Affairs; IHS stands for Indian Health Service.

Numbers following p. or pp. are page references. Numbers in [ ] are table references. BIA stands for Bureau of Indian Affairs; IHS stands for Indian Health Service.

Numbers following p. or pp. are page references. Numbers in [ ] are table references. BIA stands for Bureau of Indian Affairs; IHS stands for Indian Health Service.

Numbers following p. or pp. are page references. Numbers in [ ] are table references. BIA stands for Bureau of Indian Affairs; IHS stands for Indian Health Service.

Numbers following p. or pp. are page references. Numbers in [ ] are table references. BIA stands for Bureau of Indian Affairs; IHS stands for Indian Health Service.

Numbers following p. or pp. are page references. Numbers in [ ] are table references. BIA stands for Bureau of Indian Affairs; IHS stands for Indian Health Service.

Klikitat
— ability to speak English in 1910, p. 188 [111]
— characteristics of families, p. 476 [247]
— full-blood Indians in 1910, pp. 119, 130 [77, 81]
— geographic mobility, pp. 450, 455 [236-237]
— illiteracy in 1910, p. 165 [98]
— language in 1910 and 1930, p. 197 [114]
— marital status in 1910, pp. 206, 212 [119, 121]
— methods of health care, p. 743 [475]
— mixed-blood Indians in 1910, p. 119 [77]
— mixed-tribal blood Indians in 1910, p. 130 [81]
— population, 1910, pp. 70, 78 [42, 45]
— school attendance in 1910, p. 148 [91]
— school enrollment, pp. 545, 550 [291-292]
Kluane Band
— reserves and acreage, p. 1455 [1007]
Klukwan
— land area, p. 83 [48]
— population, 1962, p. 83 [48]
Knajakhotana
— ability to speak English in 1910, p. 191 [112]
— Alaskan population, 1910, p. 20 [24]
— full-blood Indians in 1910, p. 123 [78]
— illiteracy in 1910, p. 168 [99]
— mixed-blood Indians in 1910, p. 123 [78]
— school attendance in 1910, p. 154 [93]
Knik
— household characteristics, pp. 879, 882 [563-564]
— population, pp. 298, 302 [170-171]
Knox County
— characteristics of families, p. 473 [246]
— geographic mobility, pp. 446, 451 [236-237]
— methods of health care, p. 740 [474]
— school enrollment, pp. 541, 546 [291-292]
Knoxville, TN
— population, pp. 229, 250 [133, 147]
Koasati
— language in 1910 and 1930, p. 195 [113]
— population, 1910, pp. 60, 63, 76 [39-40, 44]
Kobuk
— household characteristics, pp. 879, 882 [563-564]
— population, pp. 299, 302 [170-171]
Kokhanok
— household characteristics, pp. 879, 882 [563-564]
— population, pp. 299, 302 [170-171]
Kokomo, IN
— population, p. 250 [147]
Kokrines
— land area, p. 86 [49]
— population, 1962, p. 86 [49]
Koliganek
— household characteristics, pp. 879, 883 [563-564]
— land area, p. 84 [48]
— population, pp. 299, 302 [170-171]
— population, 1962, p. 84 [48]
Kongiganak
— household characteristics, pp. 879, 883 [563-564]
— population, pp. 299, 302 [170-171]

Koniag
— household characteristics, pp. 886, 888 [565-566]
— population, pp. 292 [166-167]
Konkow
— employment, pp. 773, 775, 780, 783 [507-508, 511-512]
— family characteristics, p. 459 [239]
— fertility characteristics, p. 676 [408]
— household characteristics, pp. 457, 459 [238-239]
— labor force characteristics, p. 768 [504]
— language spoken at home, pp. 644, 649 [387, 390]
— population, p. 280 [161]
— population, by region, p. 405 [219]
— population, Mountain region, p. 403 [218]
— population, North Central region, p. 350 [196]
— population, Northeast region, p. 362 [201]
— population, South Atlantic region, p. 378 [208]
— population, South Central region, p. 381 [209]
— urban and rural population, p. 241 [142]
— veterans, p. 1106 [734]
— years of school completed, p. 510 [277]
Koochiching County
— characteristics of families, pp. 464, 472 [243, 246]
— geographic mobility, pp. 423, 426, 440, 444 [230-231, 234-235]
— methods of health care, pp. 731, 739 [470, 473]
— school enrollment, pp. 518, 521, 535, 539 [285-286, 289-290]
Koosharem
— land trusteeship termination, p. 219 [125]
Kootenai
— acreage, tribal land, and population, p. 1036 [657]
— employment, pp. 773, 775, 780, 783 [507-508, 511-512]
— energy assistance, pp. 816, 822 [537-538]
— family characteristics, p. 459 [239]
— fertility characteristics, p. 676 [408]
— household characteristics, pp. 457, 459 [238-239]
— labor force characteristics, p. 768 [504]
— land area, p. 93 [53]
— language spoken at home, pp. 644, 649 [387, 390]
— population, p. 264 [154]
— population, 1962, pp. 93-94 [53-54]
— population, by region, p. 405 [219]
— population, Mountain region, p. 403 [218]
— population, North Central region, p. 350 [196]
— population, Northeast region, p. 362 [201]
— population, South Atlantic region, p. 378 [208]
— population, South Central region, p. 381 [209]
— urban and rural population, p. 241 [142]
— veterans, p. 1106 [734]
— years of school completed, p. 510 [277]
Kootenai Reservation, ID
— characteristics of families, p. 468 [244]
— electric lighting in housing units, p. 891 [567]
— elementary school enrollment, p. 562 [303]
— exterior wall materials in housing units, p. 897 [570]
— floor materials, p. 905 [573]
— geographic mobility, pp. 432, 436 [232-233]
— heating equipment, p. 912 [576]
— high school enrollment, p. 570 [306]
— household characteristics, pp. 841, 844 [545-546]
— kitchen facilities, p. 918 [579]

Numbers following p. or pp. are page references. Numbers in [ ] are table references. BIA stands for Bureau of Indian Affairs; IHS stands for Indian Health Service.

1544

Numbers following p. or pp. are page references. Numbers in [ ] are table references. BIA stands for Bureau of Indian Affairs; IHS stands for Indian Health Service.

Numbers following p. or pp. are page references. Numbers in [ ] are table references. BIA stands for Bureau of Indian Affairs; IHS stands for Indian Health Service.

Numbers following p. or pp. are page references. Numbers in [ ] are table references. BIA stands for Bureau of Indian Affairs; IHS stands for Indian Health Service.

Numbers following p. or pp. are page references. Numbers in [ ] are table references. BIA stands for Bureau of Indian Affairs; IHS stands for Indian Health Service.

Law officers
— Native American representation, p. 1134 [759]
Lawrence, KS
— population, p. 250 [148]
Lawton, OK
— hospitals, p. 753 [487]
— Native-owned firms, p. 1004 [632]
— population, p. 250 [148]
Laytonville Rancheria, CA
— acreage, tribal land, and population, p. 1034 [657]
— characteristics of families, p. 469 [245]
— electric lighting in housing units, p. 892 [568]
— elementary school enrollment, p. 562 [303]
— exterior wall materials in housing units, p. 898 [571]
— floor materials, p. 905 [574]
— geographic mobility, pp. 432, 436 [232-233]
— high school enrollment, p. 570 [306]
— household characteristics, pp. 841, 844 [545-546]
— kitchen facilities, p. 918 [580]
— land area, p. 90 [51]
— methods of health care, p. 736 [472]
— nursery and kindergarten enrollment, p. 555 [298]
— piped water, pp. 926, 928 [584-585]
— plumbing facilities, pp. 926, 928 [584-585]
— population, pp. 270, 319, 321 [157, 178-179]
— population, 1962, p. 90 [51]
— school enrollment, pp. 527, 531 [287-288]
— sewage disposal, pp. 913, 936 [577, 589]
— source of water, pp. 913, 936 [577, 589]
— telephones in housing units, p. 892 [568]
— traditional occupations, pp. 654, 656 [393-394]
— years of school completed, pp. 493, 499, 505 [269, 272, 275]
Lead
— mineral leases, pp. 1016, 1019 [646, 649]
Leake County
— characteristics of families, p. 470 [245]
— geographic mobility, pp. 438, 442 [234-235]
— methods of health care, p. 737 [472]
— school enrollment, pp. 533, 537 [289-290]
Learning disabilities
— in adolescents, p. 720 [456]
Leather and leather products
— minority-owned firms, p. 960 [614]
— Native-owned firms, p. 994 [628]
Leech Lake Reservation, MN
— acreage, tribal lands, and population, p. 1037 [658]
— characteristics of families, p. 469 [245]
— electric lighting in housing units, p. 892 [568]
— elementary school enrollment, p. 562 [303]
— exterior wall materials in housing units, p. 898 [571]
— fertility characteristics, p. 673 [407]
— floor materials, p. 905 [574]
— geographic mobility, pp. 432, 436 [232-233]
— high school enrollment, p. 570 [306]
— household characteristics, pp. 841, 845 [545-546]
— kitchen facilities, p. 918 [580]
— land area, p. 94 [54]
— methods of health care, p. 736 [472]
— nursery and kindergarten enrollment, p. 555 [298]

Leech Lake Reservation, MN continued:
— piped water, pp. 926, 928 [584-585]
— plumbing facilities, pp. 926, 928 [584-585]
— population, pp. 270, 319, 321 [157, 178-179]
— population, 1962, p. 94 [54]
— school enrollment, pp. 527, 531 [287-288]
— sewage disposal, pp. 913, 936 [577, 589]
— source of water, pp. 913, 936 [577, 589]
— telephones in housing units, p. 892 [568]
— traditional occupations, pp. 654, 656 [393-394]
— years of school completed, pp. 493, 499, 505 [269, 272, 275]
Leelanau
— population, Mountain region, p. 397 [216]
— population, North Central region, p. 347 [195]
— population, Northeast region, p. 359 [200]
— population, Pacific region, p. 400 [217]
— population, South Atlantic region, p. 373 [206]
— population, South Central region, p. 375 [207]
Leelanau Reservation
— fertility characteristics, p. 673 [407]
Legal aid
— federal assistance, p. 1136 [761]
Legal services, p. 1136 [761]
— minority-owned firms, p. 971 [619]
— Native-owned firms, p. 995 [628]
Legal Services Corporation
— federal assistance, p. 1136 [761]
Legislators
— on reservations, pp. 650, 654, 658 [391, 393, 395]
Letters
— associate degrees conferred, p. 612 [357]
— baccalaureates conferred, p. 614 [359]
— doctorates, p. 625 [368]
Leveling
— Indian Trust Lands, p. 1057 [677]
Levelock
— household characteristics, pp. 880, 883 [563-564]
— land area, p. 84 [48]
— population, pp. 299, 302 [170-171]
— population, 1962, p. 84 [48]
Lewis County
— characteristics of families, p. 470 [245]
— geographic mobility, pp. 438, 442 [234-235]
— methods of health care, p. 737 [473]
— school enrollment, pp. 533, 537 [289-290]
Lewiston-Auburn, ME
— population, p. 250 [148]
Lexington-Fayette, KY
— population, p. 250 [148]
Liberal arts
— baccalaureates conferred, p. 614 [359]
— doctorates, p. 625 [368]
— faculty, p. 628 [372]
— full-time faculty, p. 630 [374]
— part-time faculty, p. 632 [378]
Library science
— associate degrees conferred, p. 612 [357]
— baccalaureates conferred, p. 614 [359]
— doctorates, p. 625 [368]

Numbers following p. or pp. are page references. Numbers in [ ] are table references. BIA stands for Bureau of Indian Affairs; IHS stands for Indian Health Service.

Numbers following p. or pp. are page references. Numbers in [ ] are table references. BIA stands for Bureau of Indian Affairs; IHS stands for Indian Health Service.

1550

Numbers following p. or pp. are page references. Numbers in [ ] are table references. BIA stands for Bureau of Indian Affairs; IHS stands for Indian Health Service.

Numbers following p. or pp. are page references. Numbers in [ ] are table references. BIA stands for Bureau of Indian Affairs; IHS stands for Indian Health Service.

Numbers following p. or pp. are page references. Numbers in [ ] are table references. BIA stands for Bureau of Indian Affairs; IHS stands for Indian Health Service.

1553

Lummi Reservation, WA continued:
— nursery and kindergarten enrollment, p. 555 [298]
— piped water, pp. 926, 928 [584-585]
— plumbing facilities, pp. 926, 928 [584-585]
— population, pp. 271, 319, 322 [158, 178-179]
— school enrollment, pp. 528, 532 [287-288]
— sewage disposal, pp. 913, 936 [577, 589]
— source of water, pp. 913, 936 [577, 589]
— telephones in housing units, p. 892 [568]
— traditional occupations, pp. 654, 656 [393-394]
— years of school completed, pp. 493, 499, 505 [269, 272, 275]

Lung disease
— deaths from, pp. 685-687, 689-690, 700 [413, 415-416, 418, 420, 432]
— tuberculosis, p. 705 [438]

Lutuamis
— ability to speak English in 1910, p. 187 [111]
— full-blood Indians in 1910, pp. 117, 129 [76, 81]
— illiteracy in 1910, p. 164 [98]
— Indian and White mixed-bloods in 1910, p. 137 [84]
— language in 1910 and 1930, p. 196 [114]
— marital status in 1910, pp. 205, 211 [118, 120]
— mixed-blood Indians in 1910, p. 117 [76]
— mixed-tribal blood Indians in 1910, p. 129 [81]
— school attendance in 1910, p. 146 [90]

Lyman County
— characteristics of families, p. 469 [245]
— geographic mobility, pp. 433, 436 [232-233]
— methods of health care, p. 736 [472]
— school enrollment, pp. 528, 531 [287-288]

Lynchburg, VA
— population, p. 250 [148]

Lyon County
— characteristics of families, pp. 472, 476-477 [246-247]
— geographic mobility, pp. 440, 444, 449-450, 454-455 [234-237]
— methods of health care, pp. 739, 743 [473, 475]
— school enrollment, pp. 535, 539, 544-545, 549-550 [289-292]

Lytton
— land trusteeship termination, p. 217 [125]

L'Anse Reservation, MI
— acreage, tribal lands, and population, p. 1037 [658]
— characteristics of families, p. 469 [245]
— electric lighting in housing units, p. 892 [568]
— elementary school enrollment, p. 562 [303]
— exterior wall materials in housing units, p. 898 [571]
— floor materials, p. 905 [574]
— geographic mobility, pp. 432, 436 [232-233]
— high school enrollment, p. 570 [306]
— household characteristics, pp. 841, 844 [545-546]
— kitchen facilities, p. 918 [580]
— methods of health care, p. 736 [472]
— nursery and kindergarten enrollment, p. 555 [298]
— piped water, pp. 926, 928 [584-585]
— plumbing facilities, pp. 926, 928 [584-585]

L'Anse Reservation, MI
— population, pp. 270, 318-319, 321 [157, 178-179]
— school enrollment, pp. 527, 531 [287-288]
— sewage disposal, pp. 913, 936 [577, 589]
— source of water, pp. 913, 936 [577, 589]
— telephones in housing units, p. 892 [568]

L'Anse Reservation, MI continued:
— traditional occupations, pp. 654, 656 [393-394]
— years of school completed, pp. 493, 499, 505 [269, 272, 275]

Maapa River Reservation, NV
— household characteristics, pp. 846, 848 [547-548]
— population, pp. 323, 325 [180-181]

Machine assemblers
— employment, pp. 779, 784-785 [511, 513-514]

Machine inspectors
— employment, pp. 779, 784-785 [511, 513-514]

Machine operators
— employment, pp. 779, 784-785 [511, 513-514]
— on reservations, pp. 794-795, 797 [522-524]

Machinery
— minority-owned firms, p. 960 [614]
— Native-owned firms, p. 994 [628]

Machining occupations
— in Alberta, pp. 1330, 1332 [941-942]
— in British Columbia, pp. 1334, 1337 [943-944]
— in Canada, pp. 1323, 1325, 1327 [939-940]
— in Manitoba, pp. 1339, 1341 [945-946]
— in New Brunswick, pp. 1344, 1346 [947-948]
— in Newfoundland, pp. 1348, 1351 [949-950]
— in Northwest Territories, pp. 1353, 1355 [951-952]
— in Nova Scotia, pp. 1358, 1360 [953-954]
— in Ontario, pp. 1362, 1365 [955-956]
— in Prince Edward Island, pp. 1367, 1369 [957-958]
— in Quebec, pp. 1372, 1374 [959-960]
— in Saskatchewan, pp. 1376, 1379 [961-962]
— in Yukon, pp. 1381, 1383 [963-964]

Macon-Warner Robins, GA
— population, p. 250 [148]

Madison, WI
— population, p. 250 [148]

Magdalena Dormitory
— land area, p. 98 [56]
— population, 1962, p. 98 [56]

Magemiut
— ability to speak English in 1910, p. 191 [112]
— Alaskan population, 1910, p. 23 [25]
— full-blood Indians in 1910, p. 124 [78]
— illiteracy in 1910, p. 169 [99]
— mixed-blood Indians in 1910, p. 124 [78]
— school attendance in 1910, p. 154 [93]

Mahnomen County
— characteristics of families, p. 476 [247]
— geographic mobility, pp. 449, 454 [236-237]
— methods of health care, p. 743 [475]
— school enrollment, pp. 544, 549 [291-292]

Maidu
— ability to speak English in 1910, p. 187 [111]
— employment, pp. 773, 775, 780, 783 [507-508, 511-512]
— family characteristics, p. 459 [239]
— fertility characteristics, p. 676 [408]
— full-blood Indians in 1910, pp. 117, 129 [76, 81]
— household characteristics, pp. 457, 459 [238-239]
— illiteracy in 1910, p. 164 [98]
— Indian and White mixed-bloods in 1910, p. 137 [84]
— labor force characteristics, p. 769 [504]

Numbers following p. or pp. are page references. Numbers in [ ] are table references. BIA stands for Bureau of Indian Affairs; IHS stands for Indian Health Service.

1554

Numbers following p. or pp. are page references. Numbers in [ ] are table references. BIA stands for Bureau of Indian Affairs; IHS stands for Indian Health Service.

Numbers following p. or pp. are page references. Numbers in [ ] are table references. BIA stands for Bureau of Indian Affairs; IHS stands for Indian Health Service.

1556

Numbers following p. or pp. are page references. Numbers in [ ] are table references. BIA stands for Bureau of Indian Affairs; IHS stands for Indian Health Service.

Numbers following p. or pp. are page references. Numbers in [ ] are table references. BIA stands for Bureau of Indian Affairs; IHS stands for Indian Health Service.

Numbers following p. or pp. are page references. Numbers in [ ] are table references. BIA stands for Bureau of Indian Affairs; IHS stands for Indian Health Service.

Numbers following p. or pp. are page references. Numbers in [ ] are table references. BIA stands for Bureau of Indian Affairs; IHS stands for Indian Health Service.

1560

Numbers following p. or pp. are page references. Numbers in [ ] are table references. BIA stands for Bureau of Indian Affairs; IHS stands for Indian Health Service.

1561

Numbers following p. or pp. are page references. Numbers in [ ] are table references. BIA stands for Bureau of Indian Affairs; IHS stands for Indian Health Service.

Numbers following p. or pp. are page references. Numbers in [ ] are table references. BIA stands for Bureau of Indian Affairs; IHS stands for Indian Health Service.

Numbers following p. or pp. are page references. Numbers in [ ] are table references. BIA stands for Bureau of Indian Affairs; IHS stands for Indian Health Service.

Numbers following p. or pp. are page references. Numbers in [ ] are table references. BIA stands for Bureau of Indian Affairs; IHS stands for Indian Health Service.

Numbers following p. or pp. are page references. Numbers in [ ] are table references. BIA stands for Bureau of Indian Affairs; IHS stands for Indian Health Service.

Numbers following p. or pp. are page references. Numbers in [ ] are table references. BIA stands for Bureau of Indian Affairs; IHS stands for Indian Health Service.

1568

Numbers following p. or pp. are page references. Numbers in [ ] are table references. BIA stands for Bureau of Indian Affairs; IHS stands for Indian Health Service.

Numbers following p. or pp. are page references. Numbers in [ ] are table references. BIA stands for Bureau of Indian Affairs; IHS stands for Indian Health Service.

Numbers following p. or pp. are page references. Numbers in [ ] are table references. BIA stands for Bureau of Indian Affairs; IHS stands for Indian Health Service.

Numbers following p. or pp. are page references. Numbers in [ ] are table references. BIA stands for Bureau of Indian Affairs; IHS stands for Indian Health Service.

1573

Numbers following p. or pp. are page references. Numbers in [ ] are table references. BIA stands for Bureau of Indian Affairs; IHS stands for Indian Health Service.

Numbers following p. or pp. are page references. Numbers in [ ] are table references. BIA stands for Bureau of Indian Affairs; IHS stands for Indian Health Service.

1576

Numbers following p. or pp. are page references. Numbers in [ ] are table references. BIA stands for Bureau of Indian Affairs; IHS stands for Indian Health Service.

Numbers following p. or pp. are page references. Numbers in [ ] are table references. BIA stands for Bureau of Indian Affairs; IHS stands for Indian Health Service.

Numbers following p. or pp. are page references. Numbers in [ ] are table references. BIA stands for Bureau of Indian Affairs; IHS stands for Indian Health Service.

Numbers following p. or pp. are page references. Numbers in [ ] are table references. BIA stands for Bureau of Indian Affairs; IHS stands for Indian Health Service.

Numbers following p. or pp. are page references. Numbers in [ ] are table references. BIA stands for Bureau of Indian Affairs; IHS stands for Indian Health Service.

Numbers following p. or pp. are page references. Numbers in [ ] are table references. BIA stands for Bureau of Indian Affairs; IHS stands for Indian Health Service.

Numbers following p. or pp. are page references. Numbers in [ ] are table references. BIA stands for Bureau of Indian Affairs; IHS stands for Indian Health Service.

Numbers following p. or pp. are page references. Numbers in [ ] are table references. BIA stands for Bureau of Indian Affairs; IHS stands for Indian Health Service.

1587

Numbers following p. or pp. are page references. Numbers in [ ] are table references. BIA stands for Bureau of Indian Affairs; IHS stands for Indian Health Service.

1589

Numbers following p. or pp. are page references. Numbers in [ ] are table references. BIA stands for Bureau of Indian Affairs; IHS stands for Indian Health Service.

1590

Numbers following p. or pp. are page references. Numbers in [ ] are table references. BIA stands for Bureau of Indian Affairs; IHS stands for Indian Health Service.

Numbers following p. or pp. are page references. Numbers in [ ] are table references. BIA stands for Bureau of Indian Affairs; IHS stands for Indian Health Service.

Port Gamble Clallam continued:
— population, South Atlantic region, p. 373 [206]
— population, South Central region, p. 376 [207]
Port Gamble Reservation, WA
— acreage, tribal lands, and population, p. 1039 [658]
— characteristics of families, p. 472 [246]
— electric lighting in housing units, p. 892 [568]
— elementary school enrollment, p. 564 [303]
— energy assistance, pp. 818, 824 [587, 538]
— exterior wall materials in housing units, p. 899 [571]
— floor materials, p. 907 [574]
— geographic mobility, pp. 440, 444 [234-235]
— high school enrollment, p. 571 [306]
— household characteristics, pp. 851, 854 [549-550]
— kitchen facilities, p. 919 [580]
— land area, p. 103 [59]
— methods of health care, p. 738 [473]
— nursery and kindergarten enrollment, p. 556 [298]
— piped water, pp. 927, 929 [584-585]
— plumbing facilities, pp. 927, 929 [584-585]
— population, pp. 277, 327, 329 [160, 182-183]
— school enrollment, pp. 535, 539 [289-290]
— sewage disposal, pp. 914, 936 [577, 589]
— source of water, pp. 914, 936 [577, 589]
— telephones in housing units, p. 892 [568]
— traditional occupations, pp. 655, 657 [393-394]
— years of school completed, pp. 494, 500, 506 [269, 272, 275]
Port Graham
— household characteristics, pp. 881, 884 [563-564]
— land area, p. 84 [48]
— population, pp. 300, 303 [170-171]
— population, 1962, p. 84 [48]
Port Heiden
— household characteristics, pp. 881, 884 [563-564]
— population, pp. 300, 303 [170-171]
Port Lions
— household characteristics, pp. 885, 887 [565-566]
— population, pp. 300, 303 [170-171]
Port Madison Reservation, WA
— acreage, tribal lands, and population, p. 1039 [658]
— characteristics of families, p. 472 [246]
— electric lighting in housing units, p. 893 [568]
— elementary school enrollment, p. 564 [303]
— exterior wall materials in housing units, p. 899 [571]
— floor materials, p. 907 [574]
— geographic mobility, pp. 440, 444 [234-235]
— high school enrollment, p. 571 [306]
— household characteristics, pp. 851, 854 [549-550]
— kitchen facilities, p. 919 [580]
— land area, p. 103 [59]
— methods of health care, p. 738 [473]
— nursery and kindergarten enrollment, p. 556 [298]
— piped water, pp. 927, 929 [584-585]
— plumbing facilities, pp. 927, 929 [584-585]
— population, pp. 277, 327, 329 [160, 182-183]
— population, 1962, p. 103 [59]
— school enrollment, pp. 535, 539 [289-290]
— sewage disposal, pp. 914, 937 [577, 589]
— source of water, pp. 914, 937 [577, 589]

Port Madison Reservation, WA continued:
— telephones in housing units, p. 893 [568]
— traditional occupations, pp. 655, 657 [393-394]
— years of school completed, pp. 494, 500, 506 [269, 272, 275]
Portage Creek
— household characteristics, pp. 881, 884 [563-564]
— population, pp. 300, 303 [170-171]
Portland
— bingo revenues, p. 1011 [637]
— Indian lands, p. 1056 [676]
— land area, pp. 82, 93, 101, 103 [47, 53, 57-59]
— land trusteeship termination, p. 218 [125]
— Native-owned firms, p. 1006 [633]
— population, p. 82 [47]
— population, 1962, pp. 93, 101, 103 [53, 57-59]
Portland, ME
— population, p. 251 [148]
Portland-Vancouver, OR-WA
— population, pp. 228, 251 [133, 148]
Portsmouth-Dover-Rochester, NH-ME
— population, p. 251 [148]
Postal Inspectors
— assaults on officers, p. 1134 [758]
Postneonates, p. 717 [452]
Postsecondary education, pp. 602, 605-606, 609 [347-348, 351-353, 355]
— as a goal, p. 513 [279]
— baccalaureates conferred, p. 613 [358]
— doctorates conferred, pp. 623-624 [367-368]
— enrollment, p. 607 [354]
— enrollment in 1900-1930, pp. 141 [87-88]
— expenditures, pp. 636-637 [382]
— financial aid for, p. 634 [380]
— master's degrees conferred, pp. 618-619 [363-364]
— time intervals, p. 515 [282]
— years completed, pp. 509, 512 [277-278]
Potash
— mineral leases, p. 1016 [646]
Potawatomi
— ability to speak English in 1910, p. 184 [110]
— acreage, tribal lands, and population, p. 1040 [658]
— employment, pp. 776, 778, 784-785 [509-510, 513-514]
— enrollment in 1930, pp. 157, 159 [95-96]
— family characteristics, p. 461 [241]
— fertility characteristics, pp. 678-679 [409]
— full-blood Indians in 1910, pp. 115, 126 [76, 80]
— household characteristics, pp. 460-461 [240-241]
— illiteracy in 1910, p. 162 [97]
— Indian and White mixed-bloods in 1910, p. 136 [84]
— labor force characteristics, p. 770 [505]
— land area, pp. 93, 100, 104 [53, 57, 59]
— language in 1910 and 1930, p. 193 [113]
— language spoken at home, pp. 645-646 [388-389]
— marital status in 1910, pp. 203, 209 [118, 120]
— marital status in 1910 and 1930, p. 202 [117]
— mixed-blood Indians in 1910, p. 115 [76]
— mixed-tribal blood Indians in 1910, p. 126 [80]
— population, pp. 267-269, 275, 277 [156-157, 159-160]
— population, 1910, pp. 52, 55, 57, 59, 61, 63-64, 69, 71, 73, 75, 78, 80-

Numbers following p. or pp. are page references. Numbers in [ ] are table references. BIA stands for Bureau of Indian Affairs; IHS stands for Indian Health Service.

1594

Numbers following p. or pp. are page references. Numbers in [ ] are table references. BIA stands for Bureau of Indian Affairs; IHS stands for Indian Health Service.

Numbers following p. or pp. are page references. Numbers in [ ] are table references. BIA stands for Bureau of Indian Affairs; IHS stands for Indian Health Service.

Numbers following p. or pp. are page references. Numbers in [ ] are table references. BIA stands for Bureau of Indian Affairs; IHS stands for Indian Health Service.

Numbers following p. or pp. are page references. Numbers in [ ] are table references. BIA stands for Bureau of Indian Affairs; IHS stands for Indian Health Service.

1599

Numbers following p. or pp. are page references. Numbers in [ ] are table references. BIA stands for Bureau of Indian Affairs; IHS stands for Indian Health Service.

Numbers following p. or pp. are page references. Numbers in [ ] are table references. BIA stands for Bureau of Indian Affairs; IHS stands for Indian Health Service.

1603

Index

Numbers following p. or pp. are page references. Numbers in [ ] are table references. BIA stands for Bureau of Indian Affairs; IHS stands for Indian Health Service.

1604

Numbers following p. or pp. are page references. Numbers in [ ] are table references. BIA stands for Bureau of Indian Affairs; IHS stands for Indian Health Service.

Numbers following p. or pp. are page references. Numbers in [ ] are table references. BIA stands for Bureau of Indian Affairs; IHS stands for Indian Health Service.

Numbers following p. or pp. are page references. Numbers in [ ] are table references. BIA stands for Bureau of Indian Affairs; IHS stands for Indian Health Service.

San Juan continued:
— population, 1910, pp. 65, 73, 78 [41, 43, 45]
— population, 1962, p. 98 [56]
— population, Mountain region, p. 408 [220]
— population, North Central region, p. 353 [197]
— population, Northeast region, p. 365 [202]
— population, Pacific region, p. 411 [221]
— population, South Atlantic region, p. 384 [210]
— population, South Central region, p. 387 [211]
— school attendance in 1910, p. 152 [92]
San Juan County
— characteristics of families, p. 470 [245]
— geographic mobility, pp. 438, 442, 449, 454 [234-237]
— methods of health care, pp. 737, 743 [472, 475]
— school enrollment, pp. 533, 537, 544, 549 [289-292]
San Juan Pueblo, NM
— acreage, tribal lands, and population, p. 1038 [658]
— characteristics of families, p. 473 [246]
— electric lighting in housing units, p. 893 [568]
— elementary school enrollment, p. 564 [303]
— exterior wall materials in housing units, p. 899 [571]
— floor materials, p. 907 [574]
— geographic mobility, pp. 446, 451 [236-237]
— high school enrollment, p. 571 [306]
— household characteristics, pp. 856, 859 [551-552]
— housing, pp. 856, 859 [551-552]
— kitchen facilities, p. 919 [580]
— methods of health care, p. 740 [474]
— nursery and kindergarten enrollment, p. 556 [298]
— piped water, pp. 927, 929 [584-585]
— plumbing facilities, pp. 927, 929 [584-585]
— population, pp. 281, 331, 333 [162, 184-185]
— school enrollment, pp. 541, 546 [291-292]
— sewage disposal, pp. 914, 937 [577, 589]
— source of water, pp. 914, 937 [577, 589]
— telephones in housing units, p. 893 [568]
— traditional occupations, pp. 655, 657 [393-394]
— years of school completed, pp. 494, 500, 506 [269, 272, 275]
San Juan Southern Paiute
— acreage, tribal land, and population, p. 1033 [657]
San Lorenzo de la Santa Cruz Mission
— epidemics from 1528-1892, p. 173 [103]
San Luis Obispo
— language in 1910 and 1930, p. 194 [113]
— population, 1910, p. 55 [37]
San Luiseno
— ability to speak English in 1910, p. 188 [111]
— full-blood Indians in 1910, pp. 120, 131 [77, 81]
— illiteracy in 1910, p. 166 [98]
— Indian and White mixed-bloods in 1910, p. 138 [85]
— marital status in 1910, pp. 207, 213 [119, 121]
— mixed-bloods in 1910, p. 120 [77]
— mixed-tribal bloods in 1910, p. 131 [81]
— population, 1910, p. 55 [37]
— school attendance in 1910, p. 149 [91]
San Manuel Band of Serrano Mission Indians
— energy assistance, p. 821 [538]
San Manuel Reservation, CA
— acreage, tribal land, and population, p. 1035 [657]

San Manuel Reservation, CA continued:
— characteristics of families, p. 473 [246]
— electric lighting in housing units, p. 893 [568]
— elementary school enrollment, p. 564 [303]
— exterior wall materials in housing units, p. 899 [571]
— floor materials, p. 907 [574]
— geographic mobility, pp. 446, 451 [236-237]
— high school enrollment, p. 571 [306]
— household characteristics, pp. 856, 859 [551-552]
— housing, pp. 856, 859 [551-552]
— kitchen facilities, p. 919 [580]
— land area, p. 92 [52]
— methods of health care, p. 740 [474]
— nursery and kindergarten enrollment, p. 556 [298]
— piped water, pp. 927, 929 [584-585]
— plumbing facilities, pp. 927, 929 [584-585]
— population, pp. 282, 331, 333 [162, 184-185]
— population, 1962, p. 92 [52]
— school enrollment, pp. 541, 546 [291-292]
— sewage disposal, pp. 914, 937 [577, 589]
— source of water, pp. 914, 937 [577, 589]
— telephones in housing units, p. 893 [568]
— traditional occupations, pp. 655, 657 [393-394]
— years of school completed, pp. 494, 500, 506 [269, 272, 275]
San Pascual
— fertility characteristics, p. 675 [407]
— population, Mountain region, p. 399 [216]
— population, North Central region, p. 349 [195]
— population, Northeast region, p. 361 [200]
— population, Pacific region, p. 401 [217]
— population, South Atlantic region, p. 374 [206]
— population, South Central region, p. 377 [207]
San Pasqual Reservation, CA
— acreage, tribal land, and population, p. 1035 [657]
— characteristics of families, p. 473 [246]
— electric lighting in housing units, p. 893 [568]
— elementary school enrollment, p. 564 [303]
— exterior wall materials in housing units, p. 899 [571]
— floor materials, p. 907 [574]
— geographic mobility, pp. 446, 451 [236-237]
— high school enrollment, p. 571 [306]
— household characteristics, pp. 856, 859 [551-552]
— housing, pp. 856, 859 [551-552]
— kitchen facilities, p. 919 [580]
— land area, p. 92 [52]
— methods of health care, p. 740 [474]
— nursery and kindergarten enrollment, p. 556 [298]
— piped water, pp. 927, 929 [584-585]
— plumbing facilities, pp. 927, 929 [584-585]
— population, pp. 282, 331, 333 [162, 184-185]
— population, 1962, p. 92 [52]
— school enrollment, pp. 541, 546 [291-292]
— sewage disposal, pp. 914, 937 [577, 589]
— source of water, pp. 914, 937 [577, 589]
— telephones in housing units, p. 893 [568]
— traditional occupations, pp. 655, 657 [393-394]
— years of school completed, pp. 494, 500, 506 [269, 272, 275]
San Xavier Missions
— epidemics from 1528-1892, p. 173 [103]

Numbers following p. or pp. are page references. Numbers in [ ] are table references. BIA stands for Bureau of Indian Affairs; IHS stands for Indian Health Service.

1610

Numbers following p. or pp. are page references. Numbers in [ ] are table references. BIA stands for Bureau of Indian Affairs; IHS stands for Indian Health Service.

Numbers following p. or pp. are page references. Numbers in [ ] are table references. BIA stands for Bureau of Indian Affairs; IHS stands for Indian Health Service.

Numbers following p. or pp. are page references. Numbers in [ ] are table references. BIA stands for Bureau of Indian Affairs; IHS stands for Indian Health Service.

1613

Santee Reservation, NE continued:
— land area, p. 96 [55]
— methods of health care, p. 740 [474]
— nursery and kindergarten enrollment, p. 557 [299]
— piped water, pp. 927, 929 [584-585]
— plumbing facilities, pp. 927, 929 [584-585]
— population, pp. 282, 332, 334 [162, 184-185]
— pulation in 1962, p. 96 [55]
— school enrollment, pp. 541, 546 [291-292]
— sewage disposal, pp. 914, 937 [577, 589]
— source of water, pp. 914, 937 [577, 589]
— telephones in housing units, p. 893 [568]
— traditional occupations, pp. 658-659 [395-396]
— years of school completed, pp. 495, 501, 507 [270, 273, 276]
Santee Sioux
— ability to speak English in 1910, p. 189 [111]
— acreage, tribal lands, and population, p. 1037 [658]
— fertility characteristics, p. 681 [409]
— full-blood Indians in 1910, pp. 120, 132 [77, 82]
— illiteracy in 1910, p. 166 [98]
— Indian and White mixed-bloods in 1910, p. 139 [85]
— language in 1910 and 1930, p. 197 [114]
— marital status in 1910, pp. 207, 213 [119, 121]
— mixed-bloods in 1910, p. 120 [77]
— mixed-tribal bloods in 1910, p. 132 [82]
— population, p. 282 [162]
— population, 1910, pp. 61, 63-64, 67, 71, 75, 80 [39-41, 43-44, 46]
— population, 1962, pp. 94, 96, 101 [54-55, 58]
— population, Mountain region, p. 410 [220]
— population, North Central region, p. 355 [197]
— population, Northeast region, p. 366 [202]
— population, Pacific region, p. 413 [221]
— population, South Atlantic region, p. 386 [210]
— population, South Central region, p. 388 [211]
— school attendance in 1910, p. 151 [92]
Santiam
— language in 1910 and 1930, p. 194 [113]
— population, 1910, p. 71 [43]
Santo Domingo
— ability to speak English in 1910, p. 186 [110]
— fertility characteristics, p. 679 [409]
— full-blood Indians in 1910, pp. 117, 128 [76, 80]
— illiteracy in 1910, p. 163 [97]
— land area, p. 98 [56]
— language in 1910 and 1930, p. 194 [113]
— marital status in 1910, pp. 205, 211 [118, 120]
— mixed-bloods in 1910, p. 117 [76]
— mixed-tribal bloods in 1910, p. 128 [80]
— population, pp. 282-283, 291 [162, 165]
— population, 1910, p. 66 [41]
— population, 1962, p. 98 [56]
— population, Mountain region, p. 408 [220]
— population, North Central region, p. 353 [197]
— population, Northeast region, p. 365 [202]
— population, Pacific region, p. 411 [221]
— population, South Atlantic region, p. 384 [210]
— population, South Central region, p. 387 [211]
Santo Domingo Pueblo, NM
— acreage, tribal lands, and population, p. 1038 [658]

Santo Domingo Pueblo, NM continued:
— characteristics of families, p. 473 [246]
— electric lighting in housing units, p. 893 [568]
— elementary school enrollment, p. 565 [304]
— exterior wall materials in housing units, p. 900 [571]
— floor materials, p. 908 [574]
— geographic mobility, pp. 446, 451 [236-237]
— high school enrollment, p. 572 [307]
— household characteristics, pp. 857, 859 [551-552]
— housing, pp. 857, 859 [551-552]
— kitchen facilities, p. 920 [580]
— methods of health care, p. 740 [474]
— nursery and kindergarten enrollment, p. 557 [299]
— piped water, pp. 928, 930 [584-585]
— plumbing facilities, pp. 928, 930 [584-585]
— population, pp. 282, 332, 334 [162, 184-185]
— school attendance in 1910, p. 145 [90]
— school enrollment, pp. 541, 546 [291-292]
— sewage disposal, pp. 914, 937 [577, 589]
— source of water, pp. 914, 937 [577, 589]
— telephones in housing units, p. 893 [568]
— traditional occupations, pp. 658-659 [395-396]
— years of school completed, pp. 495, 501, 507 [270, 273, 276]
Sapper
— population estimates before 1492, p. 1-2 [1-2]
Sarasota, FL
— population, p. 252 [148]
Sargent County
— characteristics of families, p. 474 [246]
— geographic mobility, pp. 447, 452 [236-237]
— methods of health care, p. 741 [474]
— school enrollment, pp. 542, 547 [291-292]
Saskatchewan
— education levels, p. 1227 [850]
— employment, pp. 1293-1296, 1319-1320, 1376, 1379 [908-911, 934-935, 961-962]
— family income, p. 1386 [965]
— geographic mobility, pp. 1172, 1196-1197 [796, 819-820]
— highest level of schooling in, pp. 1257, 1259 [873-874]
— income, pp. 1422-1423 [990-991]
— Indian reserves, p. 1435 [998]
— individual income, p. 1387 [966]
— languages spoken in, pp. 1265-1266, 1288-1289 [880-881, 904-905]
— marital status, pp. 1222-1223 [845-846]
— population, pp. 1142-1144, 1168-1169 [766-768, 792-793]
— unemployment, pp. 1319-1320 [934-935]
Saskatoon District
— Indian reserves, p. 1453 [1006]
SAT
  See also: Scholastic Aptitude Test
— average mathematics score, p. 580 [317]
— average verbal score, p. 581 [318]
— distribution of test takers, p. 579 [315]
— scores, p. 580 [316]
Sauk and Fox
— ability to speak English in 1910, p. 185 [110]
— enrollment in 1930, pp. 157, 160 [95-96]
— full-blood Indians in 1910, pp. 115, 126 [76, 80]
— illiteracy in 1910, p. 162 [97]

Numbers following p. or pp. are page references. Numbers in [ ] are table references. BIA stands for Bureau of Indian Affairs; IHS stands for Indian Health Service.

1614

Numbers following p. or pp. are page references. Numbers in [ ] are table references. BIA stands for Bureau of Indian Affairs; IHS stands for Indian Health Service.

Numbers following p. or pp. are page references. Numbers in [ ] are table references. BIA stands for Bureau of Indian Affairs; IHS stands for Indian Health Service.

Seatbelt use
— by adolescents, p. 480 [252]
Seattle, WA
— languages spoken, p. 642 [386]
— Native-owned firms, p. 1008 [633]
Seattle-Everett, WA
— population, p. 246 [146]
Seattle Indian Center
— Seattle, adult education, p. 640 [385]
Seattle-Tacoma, WA
— Native American population, p. 245 [145]
— population, pp. 228, 252 [133, 148]
Secondary education, p. 601 [346]
— as a goal, pp. 513, 515 [279, 281]
— and college graduation, p. 515 [282]
— completion, p. 514 [280]
— completion by parents, p. 516 [284]
— enrollment, pp. 558, 567, 569, 572 [300, 305-307]
— enrollment in 1900-1930, pp. 141 [87-88]
— mathematics, p. 573 [308]
— public school enrollment, pp. 551-552 [294-295]
— science courses, p. 582 [319]
— science proficiency, p. 577 [313]
— teachers and administrators, p. 598 [341]
— years completed, pp. 497, 499, 501, 503, 505, 507, 509, 512 [271-278]
Securities brokers
— minority-owned firms, p. 969 [618]
— Native-owned firms, p. 995 [628]
Security in schools, p. 596 [338]
Sedatives
— use by high school seniors, pp. 592, 594 [332, 335]
— use of, p. 485 [261]
Sediment run-off
— water pollution from, p. 1093 [721]
Seizures
— adolescents, p. 720 [456]
Selawigmiut
— ability to speak English in 1910, p. 191 [112]
— Alaskan population, 1910, p. 24 [25]
— full-blood Indians in 1910, p. 124 [78]
— illiteracy in 1910, p. 169 [99]
— mixed-bloods in 1910, p. 124 [78]
— school attendance in 1910, p. 154 [93]
Selawik
— household characteristics, pp. 885, 887 [565-566]
— housing, pp. 885, 887 [565-566]
— land area, p. 86 [49]
— population, pp. 301, 304 [170-171]
— population, 1962, p. 86 [49]
Seldovia
— household characteristics, pp. 885, 887 [565-566]
— housing, pp. 885, 887 [565-566]
— population, pp. 301, 304 [170-171]
Selkirk Band
— reserves and acreage, p. 1455 [1007]
Sells, AZ
— hospitals, p. 753 [487]

Seminole
— ability to speak English in 1910, p. 187 [111]
— employment, pp. 776, 778, 784-785 [509-510, 513-514]
— energy assistance, pp. 816, 818, 824 [537-538]
— enrollment in 1930, pp. 158, 160 [95-96]
— family characteristics, p. 462 [241]
— fertility characteristics, p. 680 [409]
— full-blood Indians in 1910, pp. 118, 129 [77, 81]
— household characteristics, pp. 460, 462, 873-874 [240-241, 559-560]
— housing, pp. 873-874 [559-560]
— illiteracy in 1910, p. 164 [98]
— Indian and White mixed-bloods in 1910, p. 137 [84]
— labor force characteristics, p. 770 [505]
— land area, pp. 93, 101 [53, 57]
— language in 1910 and 1930, p. 195 [113]
— language spoken at home, pp. 645-646 [388-389]
— marital status in 1910, pp. 205, 211 [118, 120]
— marital status in 1910 and 1930, p. 202 [117]
— mixed-bloods in 1910, p. 118 [77]
— mixed-tribal bloods in 1910, p. 129 [81]
— population, pp. 258-259, 267, 272, 344-345 [152, 156, 158, 192-193]
— population, 1910, pp. 55-56, 59, 69, 74, 76 [37-38, 42-44]
— population, 1910-1930, p. 38 [30]
— population, 1962, pp. 93, 99, 101 [53, 57]
— population, 1990, p. 233 [138]
— population, Mountain region, p. 409 [220]
— population, North Central region, p. 354 [197]
— population, Northeast region, p. 365 [202]
— population, Pacific region, p. 412 [221]
— population, South Atlantic region, p. 385 [210]
— population, South Central region, p. 387 [211]
— school attendance in 1910, p. 146 [90]
— urban and rural population, p. 243 [143]
— veterans, p. 1108 [735]
— years of school completed, p. 512 [278]
Seminole Tribe of Florida
— energy assistance, p. 821 [538]
— fertility characteristics, p. 680 [409]
— population, p. 267 [156]
— population, Mountain region, p. 409 [220]
— population, North Central region, p. 354 [197]
— population, Northeast region, p. 366 [202]
— population, Pacific region, p. 412 [221]
— population, South Atlantic region, p. 385 [210]
— population, South Central region, p. 387 [211]
Seneca
— ability to speak English in 1910, p. 186 [110]
— energy assistance, p. 817 [537]
— fertility characteristics, p. 676 [408]
— full-blood Indians in 1910, pp. 117, 128 [76, 80]
— illiteracy in 1910, p. 163 [97]
— Indian and White mixed-bloods in 1910, p. 136 [84]
— language in 1910 and 1930, p. 194 [113]
— marital status in 1910, pp. 204, 210 [118, 120]
— mixed-bloods in 1910, p. 117 [76]
— mixed-tribal bloods in 1910, p. 128 [80]
— population, pp. 258, 260, 275, 287 [152-153, 159, 164]
— population, 1910, pp. 52, 55, 59, 63, 66, 69, 71, 74-75, 80 [36-38, 40-44, 46]

Numbers following p. or pp. are page references. Numbers in [ ] are table references. BIA stands for Bureau of Indian Affairs; IHS stands for Indian Health Service.

1617

Numbers following p. or pp. are page references. Numbers in [ ] are table references. BIA stands for Bureau of Indian Affairs; IHS stands for Indian Health Service.

1618

Numbers following p. or pp. are page references. Numbers in [ ] are table references. BIA stands for Bureau of Indian Affairs; IHS stands for Indian Health Service.

1619

Numbers following p. or pp. are page references. Numbers in [ ] are table references. BIA stands for Bureau of Indian Affairs; IHS stands for Indian Health Service.

Numbers following p. or pp. are page references. Numbers in [ ] are table references. BIA stands for Bureau of Indian Affairs; IHS stands for Indian Health Service.

1621

Numbers following p. or pp. are page references. Numbers in [ ] are table references. BIA stands for Bureau of Indian Affairs; IHS stands for Indian Health Service.

Numbers following p. or pp. are page references. Numbers in [ ] are table references. BIA stands for Bureau of Indian Affairs; IHS stands for Indian Health Service.

Numbers following p. or pp. are page references. Numbers in [ ] are table references. BIA stands for Bureau of Indian Affairs; IHS stands for Indian Health Service.

Numbers following p. or pp. are page references. Numbers in [ ] are table references. BIA stands for Bureau of Indian Affairs; IHS stands for Indian Health Service.

1625

Numbers following p. or pp. are page references. Numbers in [ ] are table references. BIA stands for Bureau of Indian Affairs; IHS stands for Indian Health Service.

Squaxin Island Reservation, WA continued:
— piped water, pp. 930, 932 [586-587]
— plumbing facilities, pp. 930, 932 [586-587]
— population, p. 285 [163]
— school enrollment, pp. 542, 547 [291-292]
— sewage disposal, pp. 915, 938 [578, 590]
— source of water, pp. 915, 938 [578, 590]
— telephones in housing units, p. 894 [569]
— traditional occupations, pp. 658-659 [395-396]
— years of school completed, pp. 495, 501, 507 [270, 273, 276]
Standing Rock
— acreage, tribal lands, and population, p. 1039 [658]
— dam safety, p. 1080 [709]
— land tract ownership, p. 1043 [661]
— land tract ownership under BIA jurisdiction, p. 1043 [660]
— land tract records on selected reservations, p. 1045 [664]
— land tracts under BIA jurisdiction, pp. 1044-1052 [662-663, 665-674]
— population, p. 254 [150]
— tribal affiliation, p. 254 [150]
Standing Rock, ND-SD
— characteristics of families, p. 475 [247]
— electric lighting in housing units, p. 894 [569]
— elementary school enrollment, p. 566 [304]
— exterior wall materials in housing units, p. 900 [572]
— floor materials, p. 908 [575]
— geographic mobility, pp. 447, 453 [236-237]
— high school enrollment, p. 572 [307]
— household characteristics, pp. 861, 863 [553-554]
— housing, pp. 861, 863 [553-554]
— kitchen facilities, p. 920 [581]
— land area, pp. 99, 102 [56, 58]
— methods of health care, p. 741 [474]
— nursery and kindergarten enrollment, p. 557 [299]
— piped water, pp. 930, 932 [586-587]
— plumbing facilities, pp. 930, 932 [586-587]
— population, pp. 285, 335, 337 [163, 186-187]
— population, 1962, pp. 99, 102 [56, 58]
— school enrollment, pp. 542, 548 [291-292]
— sewage disposal, pp. 915, 938 [578, 590]
— source of water, pp. 915, 938 [578, 590]
— telephones in housing units, p. 894 [569]
— traditional occupations, pp. 658-659 [395-396]
— years of school completed, pp. 495, 501, 507 [270, 273, 276]
Standing Rock Sioux
— energy assistance, p. 817 [537]
— fertility characteristics, p. 681 [409]
— land area, p. 1040 [659]
— population, pp. 261-262, 266, 280, 285 [153-155, 161, 163]
— population, Mountain region, p. 410 [220]
— population, North Central region, p. 355 [197]
— population, Northeast region, p. 366 [202]
— population, Pacific region, p. 413 [221]
— population, South Atlantic region, p. 386 [210]
— population, South Central region, p. 388 [211]
Stanley County
— characteristics of families, p. 469 [245]
— geographic mobility, pp. 433, 436 [232-233]
— methods of health care, p. 736 [472]

Stanley County continued:
— school enrollment, pp. 528, 531 [287-288]
State College, PA
— population, p. 253 [148]
State government
— employment and income, p. 1098 [727]
— median income of full-time employees, p. 810 [531]
— part-time workers, p. 1099 [728]
Stebbins
— household characteristics, pp. 885, 887 [565-566]
— housing, pp. 885, 887 [565-566]
— land area, p. 86 [49]
— population, pp. 301, 304 [170-171]
— population, 1962, p. 86 [49]
Steel mills
— air pollution from, p. 1089 [717]
Steilacoom
— fertility characteristics, p. 680 [409]
— population, Mountain region, p. 409 [220]
— population, North Central region, p. 353 [197]
— population, Northeast region, p. 365 [202]
— population, Pacific region, p. 412 [221]
— population, South Atlantic region, p. 384 [210]
— population, South Central region, p. 387 [211]
Steubenville-Weirton, OH-WV
— population, p. 253 [148]
Stevens County
— characteristics of families, p. 475 [247]
— geographic mobility, pp. 447, 452 [236-237]
— methods of health care, p. 741 [474]
— school enrollment, pp. 542, 547 [291-292]
Stevens Village
— household characteristics, pp. 885, 887 [565-566]
— housing, pp. 885, 887 [565-566]
— land area, p. 86 [49]
— population, pp. 301, 304 [170-171]
— population, 1962, p. 86 [49]
Steward
— population estimates before 1492, p. 1-2 [1-2]
Stewart School
— land area, p. 97 [55]
— population, 1962, p. 97 [55]
Stewart's Point Rancheria, CA
— acreage, tribal land, and population, p. 1035 [657]
— characteristics of families, p. 475 [247]
— electric lighting in housing units, p. 894 [569]
— elementary school enrollment, p. 566 [304]
— exterior wall materials in housing units, p. 900 [572]
— floor materials, p. 909 [575]
— geographic mobility, pp. 447, 453 [236-237]
— high school enrollment, p. 572 [307]
— household characteristics, pp. 861, 863 [553-554]
— housing, pp. 861, 863 [553-554]
— kitchen facilities, p. 920 [581]
— land area, p. 91 [52]
— methods of health care, p. 741 [474]
— nursery and kindergarten enrollment, p. 557 [299]
— piped water, pp. 930, 932 [586-587]
— plumbing facilities, pp. 930, 932 [586-587]

Numbers following p. or pp. are page references. Numbers in [ ] are table references. BIA stands for Bureau of Indian Affairs; IHS stands for Indian Health Service.

Numbers following p. or pp. are page references. Numbers in [ ] are table references. BIA stands for Bureau of Indian Affairs; IHS stands for Indian Health Service.

1630

Numbers following p. or pp. are page references. Numbers in [ ] are table references. BIA stands for Bureau of Indian Affairs; IHS stands for Indian Health Service.

Numbers following p. or pp. are page references. Numbers in [ ] are table references. BIA stands for Bureau of Indian Affairs; IHS stands for Indian Health Service.

1632

Numbers following p. or pp. are page references. Numbers in [ ] are table references. BIA stands for Bureau of Indian Affairs; IHS stands for Indian Health Service.

Numbers following p. or pp. are page references. Numbers in [ ] are table references. BIA stands for Bureau of Indian Affairs; IHS stands for Indian Health Service.

1634

Numbers following p. or pp. are page references. Numbers in [ ] are table references. BIA stands for Bureau of Indian Affairs; IHS stands for Indian Health Service.

Numbers following p. or pp. are page references. Numbers in [ ] are table references. BIA stands for Bureau of Indian Affairs; IHS stands for Indian Health Service.

Numbers following p. or pp. are page references. Numbers in [ ] are table references. BIA stands for Bureau of Indian Affairs; IHS stands for Indian Health Service.

1637

Index

Numbers following p. or pp. are page references. Numbers in [ ] are table references. BIA stands for Bureau of Indian Affairs; IHS stands for Indian Health Service.

1638

Numbers following p. or pp. are page references. Numbers in [ ] are table references. BIA stands for Bureau of Indian Affairs; IHS stands for Indian Health Service.

1639

Numbers following p. or pp. are page references. Numbers in [ ] are table references. BIA stands for Bureau of Indian Affairs; IHS stands for Indian Health Service.

Numbers following p. or pp. are page references. Numbers in [ ] are table references. BIA stands for Bureau of Indian Affairs; IHS stands for Indian Health Service.

1641

Numbers following p. or pp. are page references. Numbers in [ ] are table references. BIA stands for Bureau of Indian Affairs; IHS stands for Indian Health Service.

Numbers following p. or pp. are page references. Numbers in [ ] are table references. BIA stands for Bureau of Indian Affairs; IHS stands for Indian Health Service.

Numbers following p. or pp. are page references. Numbers in [ ] are table references. BIA stands for Bureau of Indian Affairs; IHS stands for Indian Health Service.

1644

Statistical Record of Native North Americans　　　　　　　　　**Ventricular septal defect**

Index

Numbers following p. or pp. are page references. Numbers in [ ] are table references. BIA stands for Bureau of Indian Affairs; IHS stands for Indian Health Service.

Numbers following p. or pp. are page references. Numbers in [ ] are table references. BIA stands for Bureau of Indian Affairs; IHS stands for Indian Health Service.

Numbers following p. or pp. are page references. Numbers in [ ] are table references. BIA stands for Bureau of Indian Affairs; IHS stands for Indian Health Service.

1647

Numbers following p. or pp. are page references. Numbers in [ ] are table references. BIA stands for Bureau of Indian Affairs; IHS stands for Indian Health Service.

1648

Numbers following p. or pp. are page references. Numbers in [ ] are table references. BIA stands for Bureau of Indian Affairs; IHS stands for Indian Health Service.

Numbers following p. or pp. are page references. Numbers in [ ] are table references. BIA stands for Bureau of Indian Affairs; IHS stands for Indian Health Service.

Numbers following p. or pp. are page references. Numbers in [ ] are table references. BIA stands for Bureau of Indian Affairs; IHS stands for Indian Health Service.

Numbers following p. or pp. are page references. Numbers in [ ] are table references. BIA stands for Bureau of Indian Affairs; IHS stands for Indian Health Service.

Numbers following p. or pp. are page references. Numbers in [ ] are table references. BIA stands for Bureau of Indian Affairs; IHS stands for Indian Health Service.

Numbers following p. or pp. are page references. Numbers in [ ] are table references. BIA stands for Bureau of Indian Affairs; IHS stands for Indian Health Service.

Numbers following p. or pp. are page references. Numbers in [ ] are table references. BIA stands for Bureau of Indian Affairs; IHS stands for Indian Health Service.

1656

Numbers following p. or pp. are page references. Numbers in [ ] are table references. BIA stands for Bureau of Indian Affairs; IHS stands for Indian Health Service.

Numbers following p. or pp. are page references. Numbers in [ ] are table references. BIA stands for Bureau of Indian Affairs; IHS stands for Indian Health Service.

Numbers following p. or pp. are page references. Numbers in [ ] are table references. BIA stands for Bureau of Indian Affairs; IHS stands for Indian Health Service.

1659

Numbers following p. or pp. are page references. Numbers in [ ] are table references. BIA stands for Bureau of Indian Affairs; IHS stands for Indian Health Service.

Numbers following p. or pp. are page references. Numbers in [ ] are table references. BIA stands for Bureau of Indian Affairs; IHS stands for Indian Health Service.